It is hard to exaggerate the value of Nancy Dawson's *Al* volume is much more than a list of genealogies and di history and interpretation of the hundreds of biblical pers when they lived, and in which Scripture passages they students and veteran scholars countless hours. Highly r

Craig A. Evans, John Bisagno Distinguished Professor of
Christian Origins, Houston Christian University

How I wish I'd had this resource in Sunday school, throughout my biblical survey courses in seminary, and during my PhD! Teachers, students, and Bible lovers everywhere will find this book invaluable. Nancy Dawson is to be congratulated on this substantial achievement.

Jill Firth, lecturer in Hebrew and Old Testament,
Ridley College Melbourne Australia

What an amazing reference tool this is! I am excited to see such a careful examination of all the genealogies in the Hebrew Old Testament and in the Greek New Testament. It represents a splendid achievement and will provide a useful guide for research in the biblical understanding of chronology, lineage, history, and culture.

Richard S. Hess, distinguished professor of Old Testament
and Semitic languages, Denver Seminary

This book is a treasure chest packed deep with a delightful miscellany of biblical names and notes. Each page promises insights into the intergenerational, intermillennial networks that populated the world of the text. Accessible to the common reader, this is also a handbook for academics. It can be both a leisurely read and a reliable go-to when in a hurry.

Havilah Dharamraj, faculty in Old Testament, South Asia
Institute of Advanced Christian Studies, Bangalore, India

Researched and presented with fastidiousness born of faith, *All the Genealogies of the Bible* offers an unparalleled resource to go deeper in biblical study. Seemingly no familial connection is left unaddressed, and the results appear in both charts and explanatory commentary. Dawson has dedicated herself to this hard work so that other scholars can benefit from her gift as they join her in taking the project of exegesis into solid and insightful territory.

Amy Peeler, Kenneth T. Wessner Chair of
Biblical Studies, Wheaton College

Readers today tend to skim the plentiful genealogies in Scripture or ignore them entirely. This book, a culmination of Dawson's long years of extraordinary research into these records, offers a treasure trove of information that should kindle the reader's appreciation for their historical and theological significance. They should not be ignored or discounted since they show the importance of family to God. The surprising connections also reveal the remarkable diversity yet continuity of God's people and unveil how God's promises have been kept and God's purposes achieved through flawed individuals in history.

David E. Garland, professor of Christian Scriptures,
Truett Seminary, Baylor University

A remarkable and exhaustive achievement treating an often-overlooked genre within the Scriptures. Dawson deserves rich commendation for unraveling one of the most complicated questions we have in biblical studies.

Gary M. Burge, emeritus professor of New Testament, Wheaton College;
adjunct professor of New Testament, Calvin Seminary

This is the first of its kind: a book of genealogies that is both easy to use and comprehensive in its details and explanations. The theological significance accompanying each genealogy often gives an unexpected insight, and the diagrams bring clarity to the Bible passages. The charts and expositions remind us that these family trees consist of real people getting on with God's work and hoping to be remembered. The notes in smaller print shouldn't be ignored. They address many of the underlying genealogical complexities that have put off readers and scholars alike and offer plausible solutions. This volume will be the first one off the shelf when I'm exploring Bible genealogies, because all the information is there, and it is presented clearly.

Rev. Dr. David Instone-Brewer, honorary research fellow, Tyndale House, Cambridge

Biblical genealogies are more than simply lists of ancestors or descendants. They often indicate the historical setting of a narrative, connect one narrative to another, and identify a person by connection to his ancestors. Moreover, when they lead to Jesus, they emphasize God's enduring commitment to his promise to redeem humankind from sin and death. Nancy S. Dawson's comprehensive work on genealogies goes beyond simple genealogical lists and charts. Each genealogy is thoroughly annotated with notes that connect the reader to the scriptural text, discuss textual anomalies and difficulties, and aid in understanding the import of the persons and event to which they are connected. For any person interested in the details of the Bible's genealogies, this work will prove invaluable.

Andrew E Steinmann, distinguished professor emeritus of theology and Hebrew, Concordia University, Chicago

Genealogical context is often ignored by students of the Bible and yet it is key to identity in the ancient world as well as the message of Scripture. This volume provides a treasure trove of data enabling readers of Scripture to now engage with the many lists found throughout the Bible to discover their riches. It also will enable interpreters to locate the countless figures in the Bible within the sociological framework of the Bible's communities. This is the new starting point for those interested in biblical genealogy and lists.

Mark J. Boda, professor of Old Testament, McMaster Divinity College, Hamilton, Ontario, Canada

Genealogies. We've all skipped them. This volume tells us why we shouldn't and equips us not to do so again in the future. Readers of the Bible are indebted to Dr. Dawson for providing us with an exhaustive guide to what are probably the least accessible passages in Scripture—including the regulations for distinguishing between clean and unclean in Leviticus—and meticulously unpacking the information each contains *and* the significance of the family connections that the authors of Scripture thought so important as to include.

David A. deSilva, Trustees' Distinguished Professor of New Testament and Greek, Ashland Theological Seminary

For many, reading the genealogies of Scripture is like having devotions in a telephone book. Scholars generally commend research projects that begin with exhaustive collection of the data from the primary sources. In that respect Dawson has magnificently achieved the goal she set out to accomplish. . . . Her encyclopedic assembly of the genealogical data found in the Scriptures has yielded a trove of new and creative insights and intriguing solutions to many genealogical riddles, including the relationship between the genealogies of Jesus found in Matthew's and Luke's gospels. Given the detail with which the author has assembled the data, this volume should stimulate many biblical students' curiosity about the nature and function of genealogies in the Scriptures. However, this work should also spawn a new series of scholarly projects that build on Dawson's work and unlock the genealogical riddles that remain.

Daniel I. Block, PhD, Gunther H. Knoedler Professor Emeritus of Old Testament, Wheaton College

ALL *the* GENEALOGIES *of the* BIBLE

ALL *the* GENEALOGIES *of the* BIBLE

Visual Charts and Exegetical Commentary

NANCY S. DAWSON

EUGENE H. MERRILL
Old Testament Contributing Author

ANDREAS J. KÖSTENBERGER
New Testament Contributing Editor

ZONDERVAN ACADEMIC

All the Genealogies of the Bible

Requests for information should be addressed to:
Zondervan, *3900 Sparks Dr. SE, Grand Rapids, Michigan 49546*

Zondervan titles may be purchased in bulk for educational, business, fundraising, or sales promotional use. For information, please email SpecialMarkets@Zondervan.com.

Library of Congress Cataloging-in-Publication Data

Names: Dawson, Nancy S., author. | Merrill, Eugene H., author. | Köstenberger, Andreas J., 1957– author.
Title: All the genealogies of the Bible : visual charts and exegetical commentary / Nancy S. Dawson, Eugene H. Merrill, Andreas J. Köstenberger.
Description: Grand Rapids : Zondervan, 2023. | Includes bibliographical references and index.
Identifiers: LCCN 2023014117 (print) | LCCN 2023014118 (ebook) | ISBN 9780310536222 (hardcover) | ISBN 9780310536598 (ebook)
Subjects: LCSH: Bible—Handbooks, manuals, etc. | Genealogy in the Bible. | BISAC: RELIGION / Biblical Studies / History & Culture | RELIGION / Biblical Studies / History & Culture
Classification: LCC BS569 .D39 2023 (print) | LCC BS569 (ebook) | DDC 220.9—dc23/eng/20230512
LC record available at https://lccn.loc.gov/2023014117
LC ebook record available at https://lccn.loc.gov/2023014118

Cover design: Thinkpen Design
Cover art: © Sylverarts Vectors, Sybille Yates, Perlphoto, Jorisvo / Shutterstock; Public Domain
Interior design: Kait Lamphere

Printed in the United States of America

---

23 24 25 26 27 28 29 30 31 32 33 34 35 /TRM/ 18 17 16 15 14 13 12 11 10 9 8 7 6 5 4 3 2 1

To my husband, Dr. William D. Dawson,

for his perennial love and support

CONTENTS

Old Testament Genealogies

New Testament Genealogies

Supplementary Genealogies

PREFACE

In a rather serendipitous way, I met Nancy Dawson in my study several years ago, and I was immediately aware that I was engaged with a woman on a mission. She cut to the quick with a sack full of manuscripts she had composed, and when I saw they consisted of "endless lists of genealogies," I was immediately transfixed because I saw, like the first scholars who saw the Dead Sea Scrolls, that she had done something that, to my knowledge, had never been done before, namely, produced a work containing every genealogy of the Bible from the longest to the shortest. Those of us engaged in biblical studies have time and again come across genealogical texts, especially in the Old Testament, that we knew to be important simply because they were in the canon, but we either struggled with them endlessly and fruitlessly to see how they worked, we gave them short shrift as a nod at least to completeness of investigation, or we ignored them completely, none of which is a good option. Having now done two commentaries on 1 and 2 Chronicles (including one for Zondervan in 1988[1]), I have come to see how important this genre is to this summary and climactic conclusion to the Masoretic canon. And it is not just informative to the historical record but deeply and profoundly theological, for the working out of the saving purposes of God was through persons who lived and died and left progeny to carry on the mission. Who they were, how they were related both vertically and laterally, and what role they played—all this is an ingredient in the matrix of the *Heilsgeschichtliche* kind of theology found in the Old Testament.

I feel honored to have worked alongside Professor Dawson on this project for many years, driven by my increasing appreciation for the prodigious expenditure of time and effort invested in it. To my knowledge, it is *sui generis*, without a peer in its comprehensively studious attention to detail. Besides this are the abundant and thorough notations throughout on all matter of aspects of the various lists. These alone make up a commentary on some of the biblical books, notably 1 Chronicles 1–9. The Zondervan editorial team is to be complimented for seeing the value of a technical work like this and for carrying it to a brilliant conclusion.

Eugene H. Merrill, PhD, contributing author of the Old Testament Genealogies

1. *1, 2 Chronicles*, Bible Study Commentary, Lamplighter Books (Grand Rapids: Zondervan, 1988), 19–41.

ABBREVIATIONS

BA	*Biblical Archaeologist*
BAR	*Biblical Archaeology Review*
BASOR	*Bulletin of the American Schools of Oriental Research*
BDB	Brown, Francis, S. R. Driver, and Charles A. Briggs. *A Hebrew and English Lexicon of the Old Testament*
EBTC	Evangelical Biblical Theology Commentary
HALOT	*The Hebrew and Aramaic Lexicon of the Old Testament*
IEJ	*Israel Exploration Journal*
JBL	*Journal of Biblical Literature*
JETS	*Journal of the Evangelical Theological Society*
JNES	*Journal of Near Eastern Studies*
LXX	The Septuagint
MS	Manuscript(s)
MT	Masoretic Text
NEASB	*Near East Archaeological Society Bulletin*
NIDOTTE	*New International Dictionary of Old Testament Theology and Exegesis*
NIV	New International Version
NKJV	New King James Version
TDOT	*Theological Dictionary of the Old Testament.*
WBC	Word Biblical Commentary

PRIMARY DICTIONARIES

Anchor Yale Bible Dictionary. Yale University as assignee, New York: Doubleday, a division of Random House, 1992, accessed through Accordance Bible Software.

Easton Bible Dictionary. M.G. Easton, Third Edition, Thomas Nelson, 1897, accessed through Accordance Bible Software. Contents: Vol. 1, A–C; Vol. 2, D–G; Vol. 3, H–J; Vol. 4, K–N; Vol. 5, O–Sh; Vol. 6, Si–Z.

Eerdmans Dictionary of the Bible. David Noel Freedman, ed. Grand Rapids: Wm. B. Eerdmans Publishing, 2000, accessed through Accordance Bible Software.

Holman's Bible Dictionary. Chad Brand, Charles Draper, Archie England, eds. Nashville: Holman Bible Publishers, 2003, accessed through Accordance Bible Software.

International Standard Bible Encyclopedia (ISBE). James Orr, John L. Nuelsen, Edgar Young Mullins, Morris O. Evans, eds. (Chicago: Howard-Severance Company, 1915), Vol. 1, A–D; Vol. 2, E–J; Vol. 3, K–P; Vol. 4 Q–Z; accessed through Accordance Bible Software.

New International Dictionary of Old Testament Theology and Exegesis. Willem A. VanGemeren, ed., Grand Rapids: Zondervan, 2012.

SCRIPTURE QUOTATIONS AND BIBLES

Scripture quotations were primarily taken from *The Holy Bible, New International Version®*, NIV® Copyright 2011 by Biblica, Inc.® Used by permission. All rights reserved worldwide.

Also consulted were the following Bible translations:

English Standard Version (ESV) *Holy Bible.* Wheaton: Crossway Bibles, a division of Good News Publishers, 2016.

New American Standard Bible (NASB). La Habra, CA: The Lockman Foundation, 1977.

The NIV Study Bible (Fully Revised Edition). General Editor: Kenneth L. Barker; Associate Editors: Craig L. Blomberg, Jeannine K. Brown, Mark L. Strauss, Michael J. Williams. Grand Rapids: Zondervan, 2020.

NIV Cultural Backgrounds Study Bible. Grand Rapids: Zondervan, 2016.

New King James Version (NKJV) *Holy Bible.* Nashville: Thomas Nelson, 1982.

BIBLIOGRAPHY

The bibliography is restricted to primary sources and treatments of biblical genealogies that were helpful in this work. For additional books and journal articles on specific topics, see the references cited in the book.

Brown, Francis, with S. R. Driver and Charles A. Briggs. *The Hebrew and Aramaic Lexicon of the Old Testament* (*HALOT*) based on the Lexicon of H. F. William Gesenius. Oxford: Oxford University Press, 1952.

Brown, Francis, S. R. Driver, and Charles A. Briggs. *The Brown-Driver-Briggs Hebrew and English Lexicon* (*BDB*) based on the lexicon of William Gesenius. Peabody, MA: Hendrickson, 2015.

Curtis, Edward L., and Albert A. Madsen. *A Critical and Exegetical Commentary on the Books of Chronicles.* Edinburgh: T&T Clark, 1910.

Dorsey, David A. *The Literary Structure of the Old Testament: A Commentary on Genesis–Malachi.* Grand Rapids: Baker Academic, 1999.

Edersheim, Alfred. *The Temple–Its Ministry and Services.* Updated ed. Peabody, MA: Hendrickson, 1994.

Eusebius' Ecclesiastical (Church) History. New updated ed. Translated by C. F. Cruse. Peabody, MA: Hendrickson, 2004.

Finegan, Jack. *Handbook of Biblical Chronology.* Peabody, MA: Hendrickson, 1998.

Koehler, Ludwig, and Walter Baumgartner. *The Hebrew and Aramaic Lexicon of the Old Testament* (*HALOT*) Study Edition. Vol.1: א – ע (1-906) and Vol. 2: פ – ת Aramaic (907–2010); Translated and edited under M. E. J. Richardson. Leiden: Brill, 2001.

Jeremias, Joachim. *Jerusalem in the Time of Jesus.* Philadelphia: Fortress, 1969, 1975.

Johnson, Marshall D. *The Purpose of the Biblical Genealogies.* London: Cambridge University Press, 1969.

Josephus, Flavius. *The New Complete Works of Josephus* including *The Life of Flavius Josephus*, *Jewish Antiquities*, *Jewish Wars*, and *Against Apion.* Translated by William Whiston, Commentary by Paul L. Maier. Grand Rapids: Kregel, 1999.

Merrill, Eugene H. *Kingdom of Priests: A History of Old Testament Israel.* Grand Rapids: Baker, 1996 (1st edition) and 2008 (2nd edition).

———. *A Commentary on 1 & 2 Chronicles.* Grand Rapids: Kregel, 2015.

Rainey, Anson F., and R. Steven Notley. *The Sacred Bridge–Carta's Atlas of the Biblical World.* Jerusalem: Carta, 2014.

Steinmann, Andrew E. *From Abraham to Paul: A Biblical Chronology*. St. Louis: Concordia, 2011.

The Cambridge Ancient History Vol. 1, Part 2 (3rd edition), 1971, edited by I. E. S. Edwards, C. J. Gadd, N.G. L. Hammond; Vol. 2, Part 1 (3rd edition), 1973, edited by I. E. S. Edwards, C. J. Gadd, N. G. L. Hammond, E. Solleberger; Vol. 3, Part 1 (2nd edition), 1982, edited by John Boardman, I. E. L. Edwards, N. G. L. Hammond, E. Solleberger; and Vol. 3, Part 2 (2nd edition), 1992, edited by John Boardman, I. E. L. Edwards, N. G. L. Hammond, E. Solleberger. Cambridge: Cambridge University Press.

Shaw, Ian, ed. *The Oxford History of Ancient Egypt*. Oxford: Oxford University Press, 2000.

Thiele, Edwin R. *The Mysterious Numbers of the Hebrew Kings*. New revised ed. Grand Rapids: Kregel, 1994, from the 1983 Zondervan edition.

VanderKam, James C. *From Joshua to Caiaphas (High Priests after the Exile)*. Minneapolis: Fortress and, Assen, the Netherlands: Royal Van Gorcum, 2004.

Wilson, Robert R. *Genealogy and History in the Biblical World*. New Haven: Yale University Press, 1977.

OTHER WORKS ON THE SUBJECT OF BIBLICAL GENEALOGIES CONSULTED IN THIS WORK

Levin, Yigal. "Understanding Biblical Genealogies" in *Currents in Research: Biblical Studies* 9 (2001): 11–46.

Sparks, James T. *The Chronicler's Genealogies: Towards an Understanding of 1 Chronicles 1–9*. Atlanta: Society of Biblical Literature, 2008.

Wilson, Robert R. "The Old Testament Genealogies in Recent Research." *JBL* 94 (1975): 169–89. https://www.jstor.org/stable/3265728?origin=crossref&seq=1.

INTRODUCTION

Scripture contains extensive genealogical records that were precisely documented and preserved through countless generations. Collectively, they form a highly valued written record that was safeguarded in family archives, public registries, and royal annals. The biblical genealogies form a major literary genre of the Bible and a means to interpret biblical narratives more accurately. The genealogies are much more than a nexus of names or a list of who's who in the Bible because they address an overarching question: "Who are the people of God?" To understand the genealogies is to reveal the *big picture* of how God worked through his covenant family to bring about the line of the Messiah and salvation for his people.

In 1975, Robert R. Wilson wrote in his article, "The Old Testament Genealogies in Recent Research," that "although the general public tends to regard the Old Testament genealogies as unnecessary parentheses in the biblical text, biblical scholars have always been intrigued by them. This scholarly interest is not a modern phenomenon but one that has its roots in the biblical period."[1] While scholars debate the reliability of various extrabiblical genealogies, Christian scholars are in general agreement that the biblical genealogies are authentic, historically accurate, and reliable. Operating on that premise, this work explores and delineates the lineages of individuals, families, clans, and tribes everywhere they are documented in Scripture, including the patriarchs, judges, kings, priests, Levites, and—most importantly—Jesus the Messiah. This work allows the reader to discover God's Word anew through the unique lens of biblical genealogies and offers modern Christians a new way to appreciate their *spiritual* heritage.

Need and Intended Audience

Although they have been accepted as an important facet of Scripture, biblical genealogies have not been studied because they can present challenges and practical difficulties; readers are often confounded by them and struggle to see their significance. Sadly, there is a tendency to skip over them entirely. While taking coursework at the Duke Divinity School, I looked for a comprehensive book on biblical genealogies, but at the time, no such resource was available. Thus, a great need seemed to exist to *simplify* the genealogical data, *outline* complicated lineages, *disentangle* branches of large family trees, and *portray* familial relationships in a clear, concise manner. In 2000, responding to the prompting of the Holy Spirit, I began a critical read of Scripture to elucidate all the genealogies and to assemble them into a single complete collection. The well-researched biblical monograph that follows, which was developed over the course of two decades, now provides succinct, visual genealogical charts that will allow clergy, laity, theologians, and scholars to prepare insightful lectures and sermons, write accurate commentaries, and improve biblical lexicography. The charts serve as valuable information for personal study and aid in many fields of biblical inquiry, such as onomastics, historiography, and archaeology (e.g., toward understanding epigraphic inscriptions, ostraca, seals, bullae, and the like).

Methods

A critical reading of Scripture with a focus toward understanding the biblical genealogies was the key to analyzing and systematically documenting them. Genealogies were directly deduced from the biblical text. The myriad of filiations (lineages / branches / kinship groups) are condensed into genealogical charts that are arranged canonically according to the book of the Bible where the main character of the chart is first introduced (see Table of Contents). Naming conventions follow the New International Version (NIV) 2011 translation; any departures from the NIV are clearly noted. The use of *extrabiblical* genealogical information was confined to several New Testament charts about Jesus' immediate and extended family (see Genealogy of Jesus section below) in which attestations about his ancestry from church tradition and the apocryphal literature were evaluated for relevance and possible validity. Genealogical information deemed spurious, legendary, or in direct opposition to the scriptural account was rejected; information that appeared to be consistent and/or at least complementary to well-understood genealogies and patterns in the biblical text were evaluated and considered for inclusion in the final charts as appropriate.

This work addresses individuals across the span of biblical history (i.e., creation, antediluvian and patriarchal eras, Israelite sojourn in Egypt, exodus and wilderness years, conquest of Canaan, time of the judges, united and divided monarchy, exile, post-exile, the intertestamental era, time of Jesus and his followers in the Gospels, Pauline missionary journeys, and the church leaders of the first century).

Each chart title introduces the main character(s) to be traced. Two chart subtitles are used to indicate, first, the general timeframe for when the person(s) lived, and second, the main scriptural references used in the genealogical compilation. *Horizontal lines* in the genealogies indicate the offspring of a given parent or descendant(s) of an eponymous ancestor. *Single vertical lines* in the genealogies indicate direct father-to-son/heir relationships, and *double vertical lines* indicate where two or more generations are omitted (i.e., either generations selectively omitted by the biblical author or omitted by the author of this work to conserve space when full genealogies are given elsewhere). The exegetical commentary that follows the chart was written by the author and the contributing author-editors to address the biblical and theological significance of the genealogy. Notes below the commentary discuss additional aspects, such as textual variants; personal, hypocoristic, and place names; Hebrew notations; lifespans; chronological considerations; and the like. The notes section also points the reader to other charts in the work to consult for pertinent information. Exhaustive subject and Scripture indices at the end of the book allow the reader to readily locate the files of interest and to quickly ascertain basic familial relationships (e.g., Moses, son of Amram and Jochebed and husband of Zipporah). It should be stated up front that certain enigmatic genealogies are shrouded in complexity and cannot always be resolved with certainty; thus, scholars may approach the problems differently. The genealogical filiations and accompanying dating system used in the charts should be viewed as the author's own *best attempt* to make sense of the data in the broad context of scripture, but other conclusions are also possible. Some of the difficult issues of interpretation are often discussed within the notes section of the charts and the reader is directed to "the fine print."

Author, Contributing Author, Contributing Editor, and Proofreader

Analysis of the biblical genealogies requires an unusual combination of skills—those of a scribe, recorder, translator, historian, chronologist, draftsperson, enigmatologist (puzzle maker), curator, and archivist. My formal education in the sciences—in the areas of cell biology, taxonomy, and botany—and post-graduate coursework in theology at the Duke University Divinity School were oddly advantageous in undertaking this kind of systematic biblical research. The ability to meticulously analyze vast amounts of data, carefully organize it in a verifiable manner, and utilize visual tools to clearly convey complex concepts was fortuitous in the compilation. For this ability I owe a debt of gratitude to my science mentors, Dr. R. Dale Thomas and Dr. Patricia Walne, who helped me learn the skill of solving complicated problems. This kind of scientific rigor was needed to push forward during this course of theological inquiry. A high regard for the inspired text turned the lengthy process into a spiritual journey of work and worship, quest and query, prayer and praise.

The book has greatly benefited from the outstanding contributions of two longtime scholars in the field of theology. Dr. Eugene H. Merrill, professor emeritus of Old Testament at Dallas Theological Seminary, brought his extensive knowledge of Scripture to bear in writing insightful commentary for the large number of Old Testament charts; ours has been a multi-year, enjoyable intellectual collaboration in which the author has been the beneficiary of his exceptional insights, zeal, and gracious spirit. The New Testament charts were overseen by the astute New Testament scholar Andreas J. Köstenberger, the founder of Biblical Foundations, www.biblicalfoundations.org, and theologian in residence at Fellowship Raleigh. Together, their scholarly expertise and insights have greatly enriched the content, and in this regard, the completed work is a shared triumph.

I would also like to thank my assistant Shelli Castor for cite-checking the numerous scriptural references and proofreading the document with an eye toward clarity, style, and grammar. Her gifts of editorial excellence and friendship have been a steadfast and invaluable asset throughout the undertaking.

My deep appreciation goes to the acquisition editors-publishers, Ryan Pazdur and Madison Trammel (now at B&H Academic), for recognizing the merit of the work and to Zondervan Academic for being a willing publication partner. The author is very grateful to the editorial team, especially Kim Tanner and Amie Vaughan, for their keen oversight and expertise.

What is realized in retrospect is that the joy of what you hope to achieve in the end carries you through the process of doing the daily work, but it is the contribution of many others who make the final product possible. "Always give yourselves fully to the work of the Lord, because you know that your labor in the Lord is not in vain" (**1 Corinthians 15:58**). I thank each person who has graciously come alongside in the tedious steps of transforming an *idea* into a published *book*.

Structure and Function of Biblical Genealogies

Most genealogies in this work were "constructed" from various places in Scripture. For example, to trace the entire lineage of a given individual, a *completed* genealogical chart (family tree) may show the ancestors from **Genesis**, the nuclear family as described in **1** or **2 Samuel,** and then conclude with descendants named in **1** or **2 Chronicles**. Mastery of the genealogical content is a rather methodical process—not one that can be easily or accurately gleaned from ancestry-like software programs that merely ask for the input of a name and then generate a father-and-son relationship, and so on.

General Characteristics

The genealogies presented in this book trace at least two or more generations, with the latter type predominating in the biblical text. The Bible often presents genealogies for individuals, families, clans, and tribes to provide a context for the biblical narratives (e.g., individuals such as the patriarchs, Moses, Zerubbabel, and Nehemiah; families such as the Rechabites, Kenizzites, and Kenites; clans such as Abiezrites and Hezronites; and tribes such as Levi, Benjamin, and Judah). The family, which is the central social unit, is usually elaborated upon to describe the network of interrelationships for the larger kinship group.

Biblical genealogies are almost exclusively *patrilineal*, whereby an individual is identified by his/her father, male ancestors, and/or male descendants. Matrilineal genealogies that do occur are rare and contain no more than simple, two-generation descriptions (i.e., **2 Chronicles 24:26**). Individuals are identified within a genealogical *context* in a socio-cultural-geographic-historical milieu. The familial associations for the larger group are normally clearly given, although exceptions do occur (e.g., genealogy of Ehud the judge in **Judges 3**; Shimei in **2 Samuel 16**; Nathan, the prophet to King David in **2 Samuel 7, 12; 1 Kings 1**; and Daniel and his comrades in **Daniel 1**). Primogeniture status (establishing the rights of the firstborn son) is often noted. Occasionally, additional remarks within the biblical genealogies interject subtle comments about the marks of distinction or shame of a particular person (cf. **Judges 6:15; 1 Samuel 9:21; 1 Chronicles 4:9–10**) or why the inheritance of a person is diminished or forfeited (i.e., **Genesis 35:22–23; 1 Chronicles 5:1–2**). Typically, elaborate genealogies are given for the patriarchs, their sons/heirs, and their wives; eponymous ancestors; founders of cities; judges; kings; notable scribes; and officiants within the religious sphere (high priests, attending priests, Levites, and musicians; **1 Chronicles 6; 9; 24**). The line of the Messiah is consistently authenticated—albeit more subtly in the Old Testament narratives, and then more directly in the New Testament accounts (i.e., **Matthew 1** and **Luke 3**).

Genealogies are heterogenous, therefore understanding certain key elements reduces the likelihood of making errors in biblical interpretation. To determine who-is-who, it is important to know and understand (1) general chronology, (2) naming conventions, and (3) the lineages themselves. Having a command of these factors can distinguish whether two people with the *same* name, are in fact, the *same* person or not. To illustrate: (1) Caleb the Kenizzite is not Caleb the Hezronite, although they also were contemporaries and both were members of the tribe of Judah; (2) Phinehas, the son of Eleazar, the son of Aaron is not Phinehas, the son of Eli, the son of Ithamar, the son of Aaron, although they were near contemporaries; likewise (3) Eleazar, the son of Aaron, who lived during the wilderness years is clearly not Eleazar the Ahohite, one of David's mighty warriors who lived almost four hundred years later. To distinguish similarly or even identically named people, Scripture often adds terms of disambiguation, such as a person's hometown, ethnicity, an honorary title, an epithet, or a kinship clue (e.g., King David; Shallum the chief gatekeeper; Shammoth the Harorite; Obed-Edom the Gittite; Mary Magdalene; Mary the wife of Clopas; Mary the mother of James and Joseph; and John the Baptist).

The lineages are especially critical in determining whether a person has more than one name (e.g., Tohu, the son of Zuph in **1 Samuel 1:1** is Nahath, the son of Zophai in **1 Chronicles 6:26** and Toah, the son of Zuph in **1 Chronicles 6:34**; or the musician Ethan, the son of Kishi in **1 Chronicles 6:44** is the same person as Ethan, the son of Kushaiah in **1 Chronicles 15:17**, and also the same person as Jeduthun in **1 Chronicles 16:38, 41–42; 25:1, 3, 6; 2 Chronicles 5:12**). Variations of this type (even within the same chapter) suggest that different sources were used by the biblical author/compiler of the genealogy. Also, having an understanding of the *functions* of certain religious personnel can assist in distinguishing members of the high priesthood, the Kohathite attending priesthood, and their brethren the Levites. Certain office holders, especially the kings and priests of Israel, were eligible to serve only if they could *prove* their credentials to hold a particular hereditary office.

Other variations in genealogies that must be considered include: (1) papponymy—the ancient tradition of naming the son after the grandfather (e.g., Nahor, the son of Terah, was named after his grandfather Nahor, the son of Serug; **Genesis 11:22–26**); (2) literary telescoping—the deliberate omission of known generations (e.g., Matthew's account of Jesus ancestry in **Matthew 1:1–17** which conforms the genealogy into a 14-14-14 generational substructure); and (3) occurrence of hypocoristic names, the diminutive form of personal names (e.g., the names Joram/J(eh)oram are essentially the same, the former being a hypocoristic form of the latter).

In general, biblical genealogies consistently reveal (1) the offspring acquired by normal biological succession; (2) legal sons/heirs gained by adoption or levirate marriages; (3) son(s)-in-law or brother(s)-in-law gained by marriage; or (4) foreigners who join the larger entity by marriage or assimilation.

Genealogical Insights

Collectively, the genealogies show the *family of God*, which is composed of Jews and Gentiles who came to hold the "faith of Abraham. . . . the father of us all" (**Romans 4:16**). Examples include the Israelite patriarchs and matriarchs as well as non-Israelites who are brought into the family, such as: Caleb the Kenizzite, the spy of Canaan who married into the tribe of Judah (**Joshua 14:6–15; 1 Chronicles 2**); Rahab the Canaanite harlot of Jericho and Ruth the Moabite, both of whom married into the tribe of Judah (**Joshua 2; Ruth 1–4**, respectively); and Jael the Kenite (**Judges 4**). Many passages reassuringly affirm that the LORD is the "God of [our] ancestors" (**Deuteronomy 1:11, 21; 4:1; 6:3; 12:1; 27:3; Joshua 18:3; 2 Chronicles 13:12; 14:4; 15:12; 20:6; 28:9; 29:5; Ezra 8:28; 10:11; Daniel 2:23; Acts 5:30; 22:14; 24:14**) and that we are God's sons and daughters (**2 Corinthians 6:18**; cf. **Hosea 1:10; Romans 9:26**).

Two metaphors are especially relevant for how to envision biblical genealogies as they are presented in Scripture: a "house" and a "living tree of life."

A House Being Built Up. In the old covenant, Yahweh met Israel at the tabernacle or temple, a *physical* house (*bayit*). In the new covenant, the physical house is supplanted by a *spiritual* house (*naos*) where God comes to dwell in the hearts of believers. Several scriptural passages explain this progressive truth:

- "May the LORD make the woman [Ruth] who is coming into your home like Rachel and Leah, who together built up the family of Israel" (**Ruth 4:11**; cf. **Joshua 24:15**);
- "The stone the builders rejected [Jesus] has become the cornerstone" (**Psalm 118:22**; cf. **Matthew 21:42; Mark 12:10; Luke 20:17; Acts 4:11; Ephesians 2:20; 1 Peter 2:7**);
- "Don't you know that you yourselves are God's temple and that God's Spirit dwells in your midst" (**1 Corinthians 3:16**);
- "We are the temple of the living God. . . . I will live with them . . . I will be their God, and they will be my people" (**2 Corinthians 6:16**);
- "Christ is faithful as the Son over God's house. And we are his house" (**Hebrews 3:6**);
- "Like living stones, [believers] are being built into a spiritual house to be a holy priesthood, offering spiritual sacrifices acceptable to God through Jesus Christ" (**1 Peter 2:5**);
- "God's dwelling place is now among the people, and he will dwell with them" (**Revelation 21:3**).

A Tree of Life Growing in Height and Breadth. The final inheritors of God's promises are believers who constitute an organic, living, dynamic *family of faith* (**Romans 11:17–24**):

- "In your unfailing love [Lord] you will lead the people you have redeemed. . . . You will bring them in and plant them on the mountain of your inheritance—the place, Lord, you made for your dwelling" (**Exodus 15:13–17**); the people "will possess the land forever. They are the shoot I have planted, the work of my hands, for the display of my splendor" (**Isaiah 60:21**).
- The psalmist proclaims, "The righteous . . . grow like a cedar of Lebanon; planted in the house of the Lord, they will flourish in the courts of our God. They will still bear fruit in old age, they will stay fresh and green" (**Psalm 92:12–14**).
- Jeremiah the prophet proclaims, "You [Lord] have planted them, and they have taken root; they grow and bear fruit" (**Jeremiah 12:2**); "Blessed is the one who trusts in the Lord. . . . They will be like a tree planted by the water that sends out its roots by the stream. It does not fear when heat comes; its leaves are always green. . . . and never fails to bear fruit" (**17:7–8**). A nation can either be "uprooted, torn down and destroyed" or "built up and planted" (**18:7–10**).
- Believing Jews and Gentiles are *grafted* into the "root of Jesse" by faith (**Romans 11:17–24** cf. **Isaiah 11:1, 10; Romans 15:12**) and become "members together of one body, and sharers together in the promise in Christ Jesus" (**Ephesians 3:6**).
- "He is not the God of the dead, but of the living, for to him all are alive" (**Luke 20:38**).

Thus, the ultimate covenant family of God transcends bloodline, ethnicity, gender, and national, religious, and cultural backgrounds. *Faith in Christ* becomes the final arbiter for identity, inclusion, and security in the kingdom of God: "There is neither Jew nor Gentile, neither slave nor free, nor is there male and female, for you are all one in Christ Jesus. If you belong to Christ, then you are Abraham's seed, and heirs according to the promise" (**Galatians 3:28–29**) and "For those who are led by the Spirit of God are the children of God. The Spirit you received does not make you slaves, . . . the Spirit you received brought about your adoption to sonship. . . . The Spirit himself testifies with our spirit that we are God's children. Now if we are children, then we are heirs—heirs of God and co-heirs with Christ" (**Romans 8:14–17**).

Form

Biblical genealogies are expressed in two basic structural forms—the *linear form,* which shows straightforward father-son/heir succession and is characterized by depth, and the *segmented form*, which shows the multiple offspring of a parent or eponymous ancestor with the lineages (branches) forming a family tree and exhibiting both depth and breadth. Most genealogies in Scripture are of the segmented type. Maximal branched genealogies are characteristic for the tribe of Judah (the monarchic and messianic tribe; **1 Chronicles 4**), the tribe of Levi (the religious cult; **chs. 6, 23, 24**) and, to some degree, the tribe of Benjamin (**chs. 8–9**).

Function

As a major literary genre, biblical genealogies provide an underlying framework for Scripture and fulfill a variety of functions in the domestic, social, political, and religious spheres:

1. Ensure that names in lineages with great depth are not forgotten and that obscure, "unimportant" persons are remembered;
2. Register (record) the citizenry of the nation, as explained by this verse: "All Israel was listed in the genealogies" (**1 Chronicles 9:1**); recording the census data for families, clans, and tribes (**Numbers 1; 26**); and listing the citizenry at certain important historical junctures (e.g., leaders and groups of people who returned to post-exilic Jerusalem—see **Ezra 1–2; Nehemiah 11**);
3. Convey the exact kinship relationships for the members of a defined group over a given span of time;
4. Signify the status of a person within the hierarchical society of ancient Israel (e.g., Joel, the chief officer over post-exilic Jerusalem; **1 Chronicles 8**);
5. Provide nuanced details about individuals that can offer profound biblical and theological insights (e.g., the descendants of Jael the Kenite of **Judges 4** who integrated with the Jabez-Rechabite scribal community near Jerusalem and became keepers of the scrolls; cf. **1 Chronicles 2:55**);
6. Portray the orderly continuity of generations and often describe where descendants end up (e.g., descendants of Moses who were reckoned to the tribe of Levi and eventually officiated in Levitical capacities in Solomon's temple in **Exodus 18** and **1 Chronicles 23:13–14**; the descendants of King Solomon in **1 Chronicles 3:10–24**; the descendants of King Saul in **1 Chronicles 8–9**);
7. Determine who a person can marry (e.g., the daughters of Zelophehad in **Numbers 27:1–11; 36:1–12**; cf. **Joshua 17:3–6**);
8. Serve as a kind of *status symbol* for an individual by tracing his/her ancestry back to a famous ancestor (e.g., Jesus as the "son of David" in **Matthew 1:1**; Elishama the scribe as a famous Jerahmeelite of Judah in **1 Chronicles 2:25–41**; Haman the Agagite as a descendant of King Agag in **Esther 3:1, 10; 8:5; 9:24**);
9. Identify instances of levirate marriage (e.g., Boaz and Ruth in **Ruth 4:1–13**);
10. Document the lineages of some fringe groups (e.g., Anakites/Rephaites in **Deuteronomy 2:10**; Nabal the Calebite-Kenizzite in **1 Samuel 25**; Rechabites in **Jeremiah 35**);
11. Link together the people and periods of biblical history (e.g., the genealogy in **Ruth 4:18–22** that transitions the time of the judges to the time of the kings);
12. Explain why seemingly contradictory genealogies, like those particularly found in the tribe of Benjamin, can still be valid since the genealogies function in different ways (e.g., to establish the major genealogical associations; convey the specific regions they occupied;

stress the ancestry and descendants of person like King Saul; identify the military complement of the tribe; cf. **1 Chronicles 7–9; 12:1–7**);

13. Identify persons involved in the construction of the tabernacle (e.g., **Exodus 31**), the First Temple (e.g., **1 Kings 7**), and the Second Temple (e.g., **Ezra 3**) and the personnel who had oversight of the ark of the covenant and the temple treasuries (e.g., **2 Samuel 6; 1 Chronicles 15, 16, 26**);
14. Record the military leaders (e.g., **1 Samuel 14** for Saul, David, and Solomon) and the administrative officials under certain kings (e.g., **2 Samuel 8:15–18; 20:23–25** for David and **1 Kings 4** for Solomon);
15. Document the bloodline and the legitimacy of persons to hold a particular hereditary office, such as the members of the Eli priesthood (summarized in the chart at **1 Samuel 1**), the Aaronic priesthood (summarized in the chart at **1 Chronicles 6**), and the kings of the united and divided monarchy (summarized in the chart at **1 & 2 Kings**);
16. Arbitrate civil disputes (e.g., narrative details about Boaz and a close guardian-redeemer in **Ruth 4**);
17. Show the origin of many place names (e.g., Bethlehem-Ephrathath in **Micah 5:2**) and the founders of cities (e.g., Ziph, Hebron, and Ge Harashim, etc. in **1 Chronicles 2, 4**);
18. Reflect the territorial allotments, property lines, and cities of a given tribe (e.g., the tribe of Judah in **Joshua 15**) and controll the transfer of property from one person or group to another (e.g., the daughters of Zelophehad from the tribe of Manasseh in **Numbers 27**); and
19. Regulate behavior and certain types of conduct, especially with regards to the priesthood (e.g., priestly and Levitical duties in **Exodus 28-30; Numbers 3-4**).

More indirectly, the genealogies indicate how Gentiles (such as some Kenites, Kenizzites, and Rechabites) are brought into the family of faith (e.g., Moses' in-laws in **Exodus 2**; Caleb and Kenaz the Kenizzites in **1 Chronicles 2**; and the Rechabites in **Jeremiah 35**). Also, the genealogies of certain people explain obscure details in the narratives (e.g., why Sheba, the son of Bikri, escaped specifically to Abel Beth Maakah, **2 Samuel 20:1–22**, or why, after Absalom murdered Amnon, Absalom fled to the king of Geshur, **2 Samuel 13:37–38**). The terminus of the genealogy in a particular passage often hints at the time period when the genealogy was recorded, indicating the "live-edge" of the family (e.g., Elishama in **1 Chronicles 2:25–41** is a likely author-compiler of the dense genealogical records found in **1 Chronicles 1–9**).

Genealogy of Jesus

Given that Jesus' birth and life was the ultimate turning point of history, a major objective of this biblical inquiry was to provide a greater understanding of the genealogy of Jesus, especially as it is presented in **Matthew 1:1–17** and **Luke 3:23–38**. The *scarlet thread* of the messianic line is interwoven throughout the Old Testament narratives and genealogies.

Jesus' genealogy is specifically addressed in several charts:

1. The chart in **1 Chronicles 3** (Zerubbabel and Shealtiel) shows the *double line of the Messiah* that passes through two of David and Bathsheba's sons, Solomon (the kingly line) and Nathan (the non-kingly line) and yields a noticeable *chiastic* literary substructure. The details covered in *Excursus A* are especially enlightening because they document a pattern of multiple instances of *second marriages* in Jesus' ancestry in which *two men, in succession, marry the same woman. Excursus B* shows how the appellation "the Alpha and the Omega" for Jesus, found in the book of Revelation (**Revelation 1:8; 21:6; 22:13**), is inherent in the genealogical text and that the Son of God, even in his humanity, inhabits eternity.
2. The chart in **Matthew 1** (the Matthean account of Jesus' genealogy) explains the literary substructure of the composition and describes the (biological and legal) patrilineal descent of Jesus from Abraham, David, and his earthly father Joseph. The chart also discusses the *lineage shift* that occurs at the time of the exile and the significant inclusion of five disgraced women who would have normally been excluded from patrilineal records.
3. The chart in **Matthew 1** (the ancestry of Mary and Joseph) examines several extrabiblical sources, such as attestations from the apocryphal literature and church tradition, to discern if the alleged genealogical connections were consistent with and/or complementary to those found in the canonical text. Depending on the authenticity of the information, the maternal and paternal ancestry of Jesus' parents suggests that Mary and Joseph were part of the same extended family and possibly related to one another as second cousins once removed. Other filial associations, such as the ancestry of Joseph of Arimathea, are also discussed.
4. The chart in **Matthew 1** (the genealogy of Jesus' immediate family) analyzes and explains the various kinship groups among the *desposyni* (Jesus' relatives).
5. The chart in **Luke 3** (the Lukan account of Jesus' genealogy) analyzes the longest linear genealogy found in Scripture (a list of seventy-seven names) where Jesus' ancestry is traced in father-to-son succession back to Adam. The literary composition is explicated in detail.

Harmonization is possible between the **Matthew** and **Luke** accounts of Jesus' genealogy if the biblical genealogical patterns and the literary structure of the compositions are understood and if selective, plausible extrabiblical information is included.

Summary

The widespread importance of genealogies is evidenced in this quote: "It was not only the priests who without exception had to produce their genealogy before being allowed to take office; even the simple Israelite knew his immediate ancestors and could point to which of the twelve tribes he belonged."[2] Because biblical genealogies were meticulously documented and are preserved in God's inspired Word, they can be studied in great depth.

This work analyzes all the biblical genealogies, summarizing the data in approximately 300 family tree charts—250 from the Old Testament, 25 from the New Testament, and an additional 13 supplement charts on Israel's high priests and rulers in the biblical world (Assyrians, Babylonians, Persians, Ptolemies, Seleucids, Roman Emperors, Herodians, etc.). The ancestors and descendants of individuals are traced and the kinship relationships among the various members of families, clans, and tribes are made clear; the accompanying commentary and notes discuss the biblical and theological significance of the relationships. In its entirety, the book analyzes the large and complex family of God across the panorama of biblical history.

Contrary to the fanciful genealogical constructs alluded to in the New Testament (**1 Timothy 1:4**), biblical genealogies are anchored in *realia*, not fiction, myth, or legend. The storied layers and legacies of the biblical characters are condensed in these extravagant genealogies. To understand them is to attain a kind of wholeness, where you can see a *living* God inhabiting eternity and bringing about salvation and redemption for his covenant people through Jesus his Son. The genealogies are a repository of wisdom and a poignant testimony of God's love: "For the Lord's portion is his people" (**Deuteronomy 32:9**). Collectively, they unveil a great mystery of how a spiritual house is built by God, generation by generation, and that a believer's spiritual inheritance is secured by faith in Jesus: "Yet to all who did receive him, to those who believed in his name, he gave the right to become children of God—children born not of natural descent, nor of human decision or a husband's will, but born of God" (**John 1:12–13**).

This book serves to stabilize and conserve this sacred body of genealogical knowledge and hopefully will also serve to reinsert the understanding of genealogies back into the canon with acumen and purpose. As you sojourn through the pages of Scripture, may this collective memory and witness of the past be a useful, evergreen resource for personal study, teaching, and writing. The live-edges of genealogies and our spiritual inheritance continue—as was said over two thousand years ago: "Your bodies are mortal, and subject to fate; but they receive a sort of immortality, by the remembrance of what actions they have done" (Mattathias Maccabeus, the instigator of the Maccabean revolt, 167–160 B.C.).[3]

Nancy S. Dawson, PhD
June 2023

Notes

1. Robert R. Wilson, "The Old Testament Genealogies in Recent Research." *JBL* 94 (1975): 169.
2. Joachim Jeremias, *Jerusalem in the Time of Jesus* (Philadelphia: Fortress, 1969, 1975), 275.
3. Josephus, *Jewish Antiquities*, 12.6.3.

OLD TESTAMENT

GENESIS 2: ADAM AND EVE

Approximate Dating: primeval history ***Relevant Scriptures:*** **Genesis 2:21–25; 3:20; 4:1–2, 25; 5:1–4**

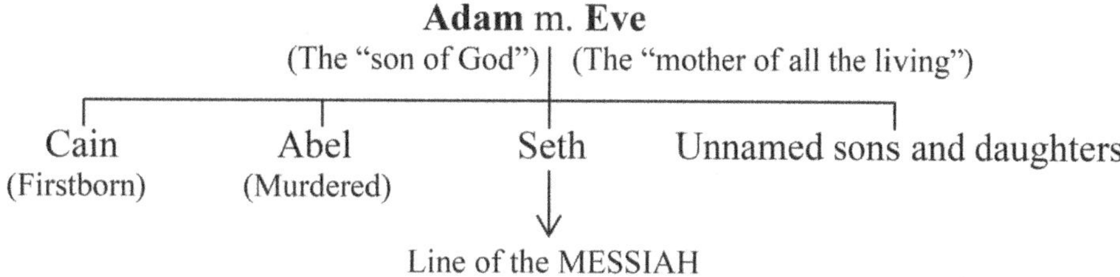

Biblical and Theological Significance

This genealogy follows the panoramic creation account described in **Genesis 1** and shows the kinship relationships of the original family. The inclusion of the Cain, Abel, and Seth names, but not the names of other sons and daughters of Adam and Eve, implies conscious choice on the part of the author—perhaps the names of all of Adam and Eve's children were unknown, or they were known but the compiler specifically chose to exclude them. This is an example of *selective inclusion*, observed in many genealogies throughout Scripture. As a general rule, names that are retained in genealogies are those mentioned in accompanying biblical narratives, as in the case of Cain, Abel, and Seth (above), or those that serve as an important intermediary lineage link whereby the name(s) ties together important figures found in the narratives.

The genealogy shown here may reflect a well-preserved oral tradition handed down to Moses, or more likely, a reliable, written source (pre-dating Moses) that Moses later used to compile the written record of the Genesis genealogies. The chart shows one of the generational accounts described as "histories" or "generations" (Heb. תּוֹלְדוֹת, *toledoth*, from the root verb ילד, *yld*, 'to beget') that form the structural order of Genesis. The *toledoth* appear in **Genesis 2:4** (the heavens and the earth); **5:1** (Adam's family); **6:9** (Noah's family); **10:1** (the families of Noah's sons); **11:10** (Shem's family); **11:27** (Terah & Abraham's family); **25:12** (Ishmael's family); **25:19** (Isaac's family); **36:1, 9** (Esau's family); and **37:2** (Jacob's family).

The account of the origin of humanity in **Genesis 1** and **2** is anchored within a historical framework and a geographical location. The genealogies indicate that the biblical accounts are about historical persons, not mythic or legendary figures. The complementary relationship of Adam and Eve reflects the relational nature of the Godhead—"Let us make mankind [humanity] in our image, in our likeness" (**Genesis 1:26**). Together, as God's representatives in the world, Adam and Eve were charged with the mandate to propagate, maintain, and rule the earth and to live in faithful covenant relationship with God (**Genesis 1:26–28**). Eve became the "mother of all the living" (**Genesis 3:20**), a point reiterated in **Acts 17:26**: "From one man [human being] he [God] made all the nations."

Adam (*'adam*) was "the son of God" (**Luke 3:38**). Eve was made from Adam (**Genesis 2:22; 1 Timothy 2:13**). The first child was Cain (**Genesis 4:1**), and the second was Abel (**v. 2**). Adam first called his wife אִשָּׁה (*'ishah*, "woman"; **Genesis 2:23**) showing their inherent *male-female* correspondence and the companionship role she would have with him. Later Adam called his wife חַוָּה (*havva*, Eve; **Genesis 3:20**). Abel was the first person to die, murdered by his brother Cain. Seth was God's gracious "substitute" (thus שֵׁת, *seth*) for Abel and through him the chosen line continued (**Genesis 4:25**).

GENESIS 4: CAIN AND LAMECH

Approximate Dating: primeval–antediluvian history ***Relevant Scriptures:*** **Genesis 4:1, 17–24**

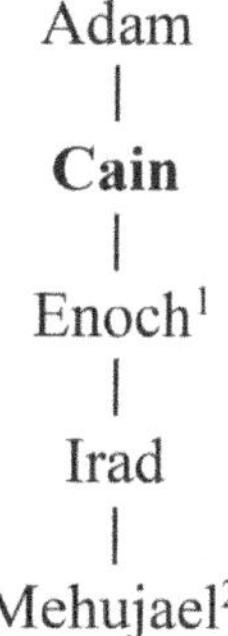

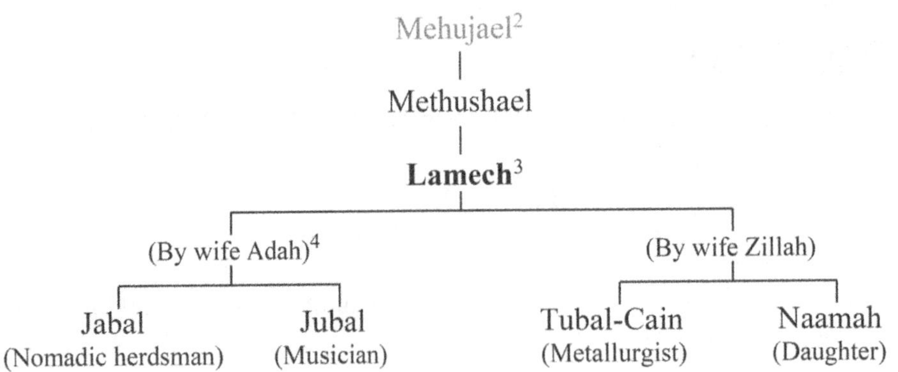

Biblical and Theological Significance

The Cainite genealogy is primarily a linear genealogy ending in a brief segmented genealogy showing the descendants of Lamech. It represents either a well-preserved oral tradition that was then written down by Moses or an ancient written record that Moses used to compile the Genesis genealogies (as suggested in **Genesis 5:1**). The genealogy for the family of Cain is embedded within the biblical narrative of **Genesis 4** and functions to tie together the key figures of Cain and Lamech.

Cain was the primogenitor of an ungodly line of descendants (**Genesis 4:19–24**). Similar to the Sethite line given in **Genesis 5:1–32** and the Shemite line given in **Genesis 11:10–26**, the Cainite–Lamech lineage ends with three sons (**Genesis 4:8**).

After Cain murdered Abel, he was banished by God to live as a fugitive-vagabond. Instead of submitting to this lifestyle, Cain settled down, built a city, and named it for his son Enoch (**Genesis 4:17–18**)—an action that is comparable to Nimrod building the city of Babel and the Tower of Babel (**Genesis 10:8–10; 11:1–9**) but contrasted with Abraham the patriarch who waited for a heavenly city built by God (**Hebrews 11:9–10**).

In only seven generations removed from the original family, the ideal of marriage was perverted into bigamy. The three sons born to Lamech became the founders of a civilized society, showing evidence of multiple occupations of music, metallurgy, and animal husbandry. According to secular historians, civilization began ca. 3500–3000 B.C. in the ancient Near East, in the Mesopotamian-Fertile Crescent region, called the "cradle of civilization." The professions presented here are well in line with that era, the so-called Early Bronze era (ca. 3200–2200 B.C.). The Cainite descendants were an urban people who occupied permanent settlements as compared to the patriarchs of Genesis, who lived a primarily nomadic life in tents.

The ungodly Cainite line is noticeably contrasted in Scripture with the chosen Sethite line[5] whereby Seth became the replacement for Abel (due to fratricide), and he established the godly line of descendants leading to Noah (**Genesis 5**). Comparison of the *non-chosen* line of Cain to the *chosen* line of Seth demonstrates the theological doctrine of separation that runs throughout Scripture, whereby ungodly descendants are separated from godly descendants (who remain in the presence of God). In the case above, the flood destroyed all the descendants of Cain.

Notes

1. Enoch the son of Cain should not be confused with Enoch the son of Jared, in the Sethite line (**Genesis 5:18–24**).
2. It is instructive to note that at least two of the names in this genealogy are theophoric; that is, they contain elements of a divine name or epithet. These are the *'el* names Mehuya-*'el* and Methusha-*'el*. El is the most ancient Semitic way of speaking of the greatest, earliest god of the various pantheons. For example, the Akkadian generic term is Ilu, the Canaanite, El, and the much later Arabic, Allah. El remains in the Hebrew Bible as a short form of the later theologically laden Eloah and its plural Elohim (e.g., **Genesis 14:20, 22; 17:1; 35:11; 48:3**).
3. Lamech, the son of Methushael, in the Cainite line (**Genesis 4:18–19**) should not be confused with Lamech, the son of Methuselah, in the Sethite line (**Genesis 5:25–30; 1 Chronicles 1:3; Luke 3:36**); for the latter, see chart "**Genesis 4**: Seth."
4. Adah, the wife of Lamech, should not be confused with Adah, the wife of Esau (**Genesis 36:2, 4, 10, 12, 16**).
5. See chart "**Genesis 4**: Seth."

GENESIS 4: SETH

Approximate Dating: primeval-antediluvian era[1, 2] ***Relevant Scriptures:*** **Genesis 4:25–26; 5:1–32;** also **1 Chronicles 1:1–4; Luke 3:36–38**

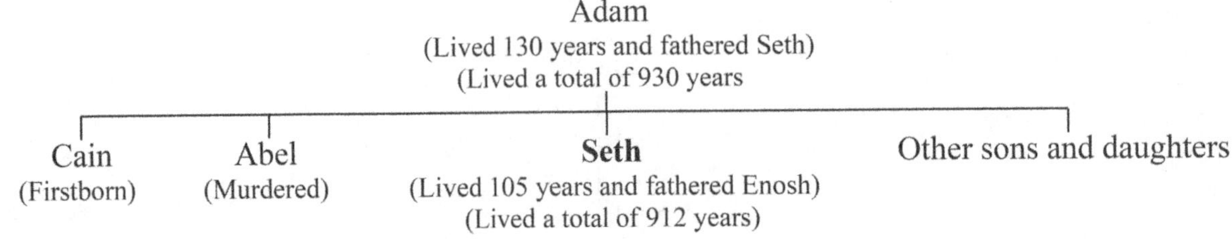

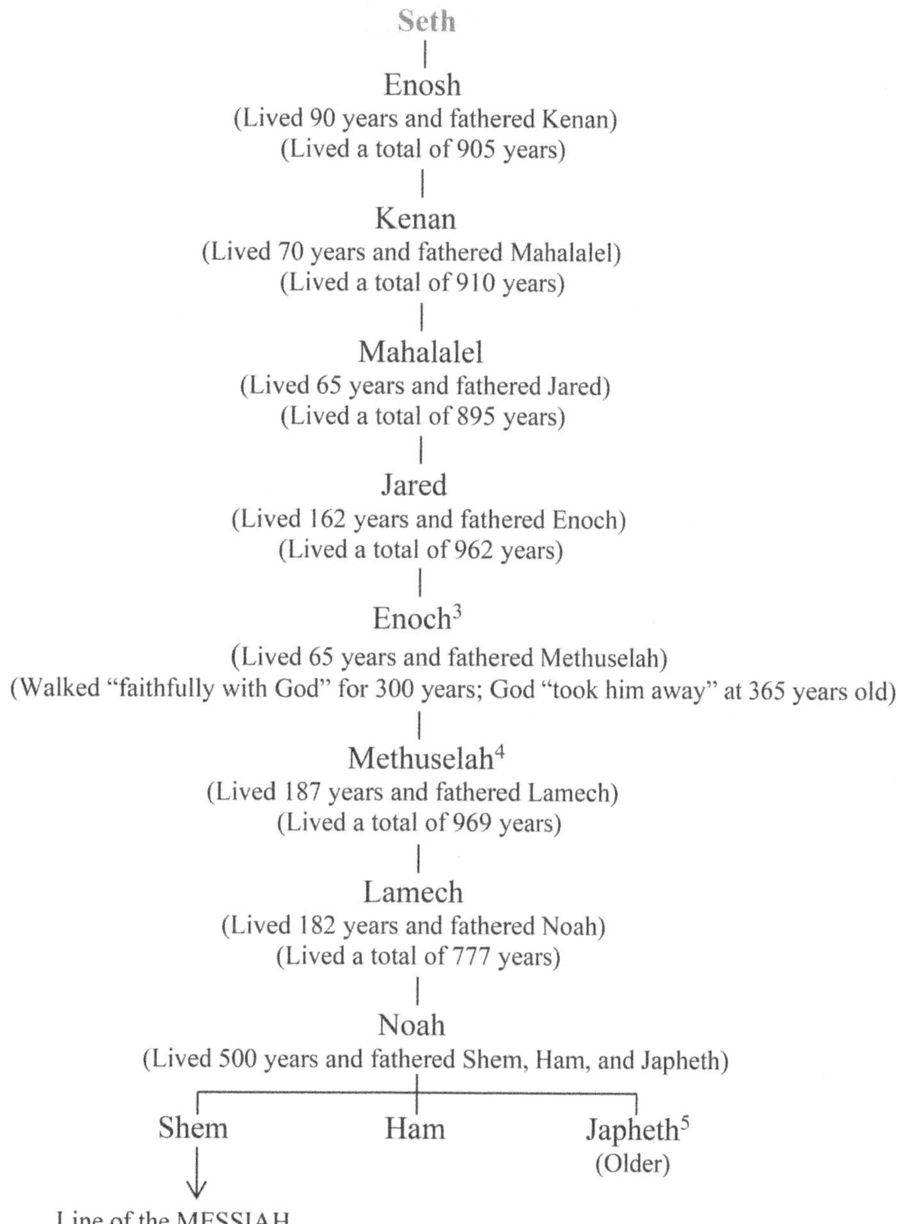

Biblical and Theological Significance

Cain's murder of his brother Abel created a crisis in the first human family. A divine mandate had been given to multiply and fill and dominate the earth, but with only one son—and a murderer at that—the prospects looked dim. But God is not frustrated and thus enabled Eve to bear yet another son, Seth. Cain and Seth are the only sons sired by Adam for whom genealogies occur in the Bible. That of Seth is, of course, of greatest interest and importance since the "Seed" of the woman (**Genesis 3:15 NKJV**) passed through his lineage.[6] The genealogy here is, by form, nonsegmented, consisting only of a list of Seth's patriarchal descendants leading to Noah, where segmentation first occurs. As is true of all the named individuals, anonymous "sons and daughters" also are mentioned (**Genesis 5:4, 7, 10, 13, 16, 19, 22, 26, 30**).

Seth (שֵׁת, *seth*, "replacement" or "substitute") was appointed by Yahweh to replace his slain brother Abel (**Genesis 4:25**). His was the godly line as opposed to the wicked line of Cain[7] (**Genesis 4:16–24**). Old Testament revelation relates Yahweh's plan of salvation as a winnowing process in which individuals are called out from time to time to be channels of redemptive grace, beginning with Eve and passing through Seth and his offspring as presented in this genealogy, at least as far as Jacob, the father of Israel.

At some point in the lifetime of Enosh son of Seth, the name "Yahweh" first began to be known (**Genesis 4:26**; cf. **Genesis 2:4**), though he certainly appears in the Mosaic narrative by that name from the very beginning (thirty-nine times in **Genesis 2–4**). Later revelation makes clear that this is God's covenant name, one used only by or on behalf of his own called-out ones (**Exodus 3:13–16; 19:3–6; 34:27–28**).

Another important character is Enoch, who "walked faithfully with God." Rather than letting Enoch die a natural death, "God took him away" (**Genesis 5:22–24**). The Hebrew verb stem used with "walk" in both instances conveys the idea of striding along on the earth with a sense of ownership or lordship (see **Job 1:7; 2:2**). God "snatched him away" (so the verb here) and he literally "was no more," a radical way of saying that he totally disappeared (**Genesis 5:24,** translation by Eugene H. Merrill). Where he went or where he is now is not disclosed in Scripture. The only other accounts of a similar phenomenon are the assumption of the prophet Elijah by a whirlwind in a "chariot of fire" into heaven (**2 Kings 2:11**) and the ascension of Jesus, who was "taken up into heaven" (**Mark 16:19; Luke 24:51**). The disappearance of Enoch may provide a glimpse ahead of time as to what it means for believers also to be "caught up . . . in the clouds to meet the Lord in the air," as the Greek ἁρπαγησόμεθα suggests (**1 Thessalonians 4:17**). An apocryphal prophecy by Enoch, the son of Jared, was used in the New Testament book of Jude to draw an analogy between Enoch's sudden departure into heaven and the sudden appearance of Jesus Christ when he returns to earth (**Jude 14–15**).[8] The main point in both texts is suddenness and the need for believers to be prepared.

Notes

1. For chronological consideration, see note 2 (below) and note 1 in chart "**Genesis 11**: Shem."
2. This genealogy—like that of Shem in chart "**Genesis 11**: Shem"—is unique in that the lifespans and paternity of the ancients are considered *an integral part* of the biblical genealogical record.
3. Enoch, the son of Jared in the Sethite line should not be confused with Enoch, the son of Cain in the Cainite line (**Genesis 4:17–18**).
4. Methuselah lived 969 years, which is the longest lifespan recorded in Scripture (**Genesis 5:25–27**).
5. Japheth was the elder brother (**Genesis 10:21**).
6. See charts "**1 Chronicles 1**: Adam's Descendants: Nations Descended from Noah's Sons and the Line of Abraham Leading to the Messiah" and "**Luke 1**: Jesus: The Lukan Account."
7. The account in **Genesis 6:1–4** shows that when the godly sons of Seth (the Sethites) intermarried with the godless "daughters of humans" from the line of Cain (the Cainites), God limited the human lifespan to 120 years.
8. "See, the Lord is coming with thousands upon thousands of his holy ones to judge everyone, and to convict all of them of all the ungodly acts they have committed in their ungodliness, and of all the defiant words ungodly sinners have spoken against him." It seems Jude uses this quotation from the pseudepigraphical Book of Enoch to highlight the second coming of Jesus Christ, a reversal of his ascension to heaven from the Mount of Olives (**Jude 14–15**; cf. **Luke 24:51; Acts 1:9–12**).

GENESIS 10: NOAH'S DESCENDANTS: THE TABLE OF SEVENTY NATIONS[1]

Approximate Dating: flood/post-flood era[2] ***Relevant Scriptures:*** **Genesis 10:1–32;** also **Genesis 9:18; 1 Chronicles 1:3–25**

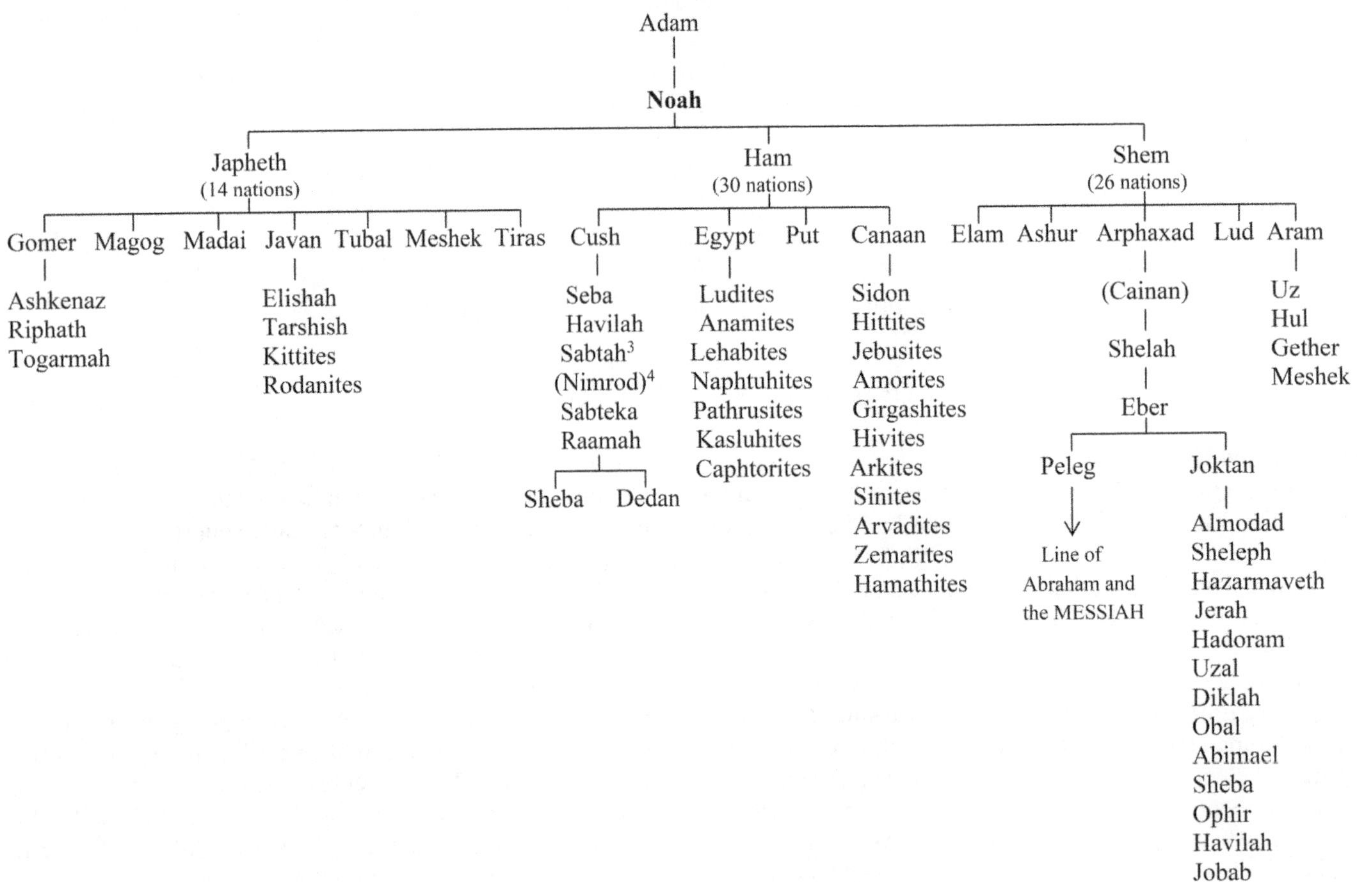

Biblical and Theological Significance

Noah became a second Adam in that he, following the worldwide destruction by the great flood, was presented, almost *verbatim*, with the divine creation mandate given to Adam. Noah and his family were to "be fruitful and increase in number and fill the earth," and to once more, bear "the image of God" which gave mankind dominion over all things (**Genesis 9:1–7**; cf. **Genesis 1:26–28; 5:1**).

Noah's three sons—Shem, Ham, and Japheth—became the eponymous originators of seventy peoples and nations. Shem was "the ancestor of all the sons of Eber" (עֵבֶר<עִבְרִי, *'ibri*, "Hebrew" **Genesis 10:21**), a statement made obviously to draw attention immediately to the Hebrew people of Mosaic times. The name Eber may also be related to the root word עָבַר (*'abar*), meaning "to pass through or over," "beyond," or "on the other side," and is often associated with passing over a body of water (such as a river; see **Genesis 31:21; Joshua 3:14**).

In contrast to the kinship relationship for the Shem–Arphaxad–Shelah generations given in **Genesis 10:24; 11:12** and **1 Chronicles 1:18**, Luke's genealogy of Jesus states that Arphaxad had a son named Cainan who, in turn, fathered Shelah (**Luke 3:36**), suggesting that the kinship relationship was Shem–Arphaxad–Cainan–Shelah (i.e., father–son).[5] The name of a later descendant, Peleg, means "division" and is associated with a historical event, for "in his time the earth [civilization] was divided" (**Genesis 10:25; 1 Chronicles 1:19**). Traditionally this has been interpreted to refer to the scattering or dispersion of people from Babel (**Genesis 11:8–9**) and/or the separation of the family of Peleg from the family of his brother, Joktan. Peleg (the elder) is recognized as the ancestor of the Semitic peoples of Mesopotamia, while Joktan (the younger) is recognized as the ancestor of the Arabian Semites, thereby accounting for the dispersion of two races of people that emerged from Eber (the father)—one migrating toward Mesopotamia and Syria, and the other migrating southward into Arabia.

Ham's son was Canaan, whose descendants occupied the promised land before the arrival of the Israelites (cf. **Genesis 12:6; 50:11; Exodus 3:8, 17; 13:5, 11; 23:23, 28; 33:2; 34:11; Deuteronomy 7:1; 20:17; Joshua 3:10; 9:1; 11:3; 12:8; 24:11; Judges 3:5; Nehemiah 9:8**). Nimrod, the son of Cush and a descendant of Ham, was "a mighty warrior on the earth" and "a mighty hunter before the LORD" (**Genesis 10:8–9**; cf. **1 Chronicles 1:10**). He built various cities / city-states: Babylon, Uruk, Akkad, and Kalneh in Shinar; and Nineveh, Rehoboth Ir (the suburbs of Nineveh), Calah, and Resen in Assyria (**Genesis 10:9–12**). The Old Testament occasionally refers to Assyria as "the land of Nimrod" (**Micah 5:6**). The Kasluhites and Caphtorites are the ancestors of the notorious Philistines (**Genesis 10:14**) and the Cretans; thus, these peoples were Hamites.

Biblical history emphasizes salvation as its recurring theme. A redemption of the fallen race came through a people (the Hebrews) and eventually through the person Jesus, the son of David, the son of Abraham. The genealogy of Noah's family adds to this unfolding pattern by establishing his son Shem as the progenitor of the messianic line. Shem (Heb. *shem*) means "name," as though anticipating "the name that is above every name" (**Philippians 2:9**). All descendants of Shem are therefore "Shemites" or "Semites." Practically speaking, in modern times, this includes and is limited to Jews and Arabs, the offspring of Isaac and Ishmael, respectively. The table of Noah's descendants (shown above) does not include all the generations until Abraham, but it makes the links necessary to establish a link between Abraham and Noah.[6]

Notes

1. The traditional designation here—"Table of Nations"—does not show the comprehensive genealogical descent of individuals but rather indicates the general dispersion, geographic organization, and territorial groupings of the people in their lands (nations).
2. In the New Testament, Jesus discusses the flood as an actual event (**Matthew 24:37–39; Luke 17:26–27**).
3. Sabtah in **Genesis 10:7** is called Sabta in **1 Chronicles 1:9**.
4. **Genesis 10:8** and **1 Chronicles 1:10** say, "Cush was the father of Nimrod," but this may mean that that Cush was Nimrod's ancestor or the founder of the Nimrod kingdom (cf. **Genesis 10:13, 15**), not his *father*.
5. The inclusion of Cainan in Luke's Gospel has been questioned and examined in-depth by Andrew E. Steinmann; for a discussion of the issues involved, see his article "Challenging the Authenticity of Cainan, Son of Arpachshad," *JETS* 60/4 (2017): 697–711. For an alternative view that Cainan (Kainan) is a valid inclusion in the Shem–Arphaxad line, see the article by Henry B. Smith Jr. and Kris J. Udd, "On the Authenticity of Kainan, Son of Arpachshad," *Detroit Baptist Seminary Journal* 24 (2019): 119–54.
6. See chart "**Genesis 11**: Abraham."

GENESIS 11: SHEM

Approximate Dating: from the time of Shem, ca. 2556–1956 B.C. to the time of Abraham, ca. 2166–1991 B.C.; the paternity and lifespans of Noah's descendants suggest that the flood occurred in ca. 2456 B.C.[1] ***Relevant Scriptures:*** **Genesis 11:10–32**; also **Genesis 9:28–29; 1 Chronicles 1:4, 17–19, 24–27; Luke 3:34–36**

**Asterisks by Noah and Terah indicate beginning and ending chronological markers for the genealogy*

*Noah
(Born ca. 3056 B.C.)
("After Noah was 500 years old, he became the father of Shem, Ham and Japheth" – **Genesis 5:32**)[2]
("After the flood Noah lived 350 years" – **Genesis 9:28**[3])
Proposed: The flood occurred in ca. 2456 B.C.[4]
(Lived a total of 950 yrs.) (Died 2106 B.C.)
|
Shem[5]
(Born ca. 2556/2555 B.C.)
(Lived 100 yrs. and then fathered Arphaxad)
(Lived a total of 600 yrs.) (Died ca. 1956 B.C.)

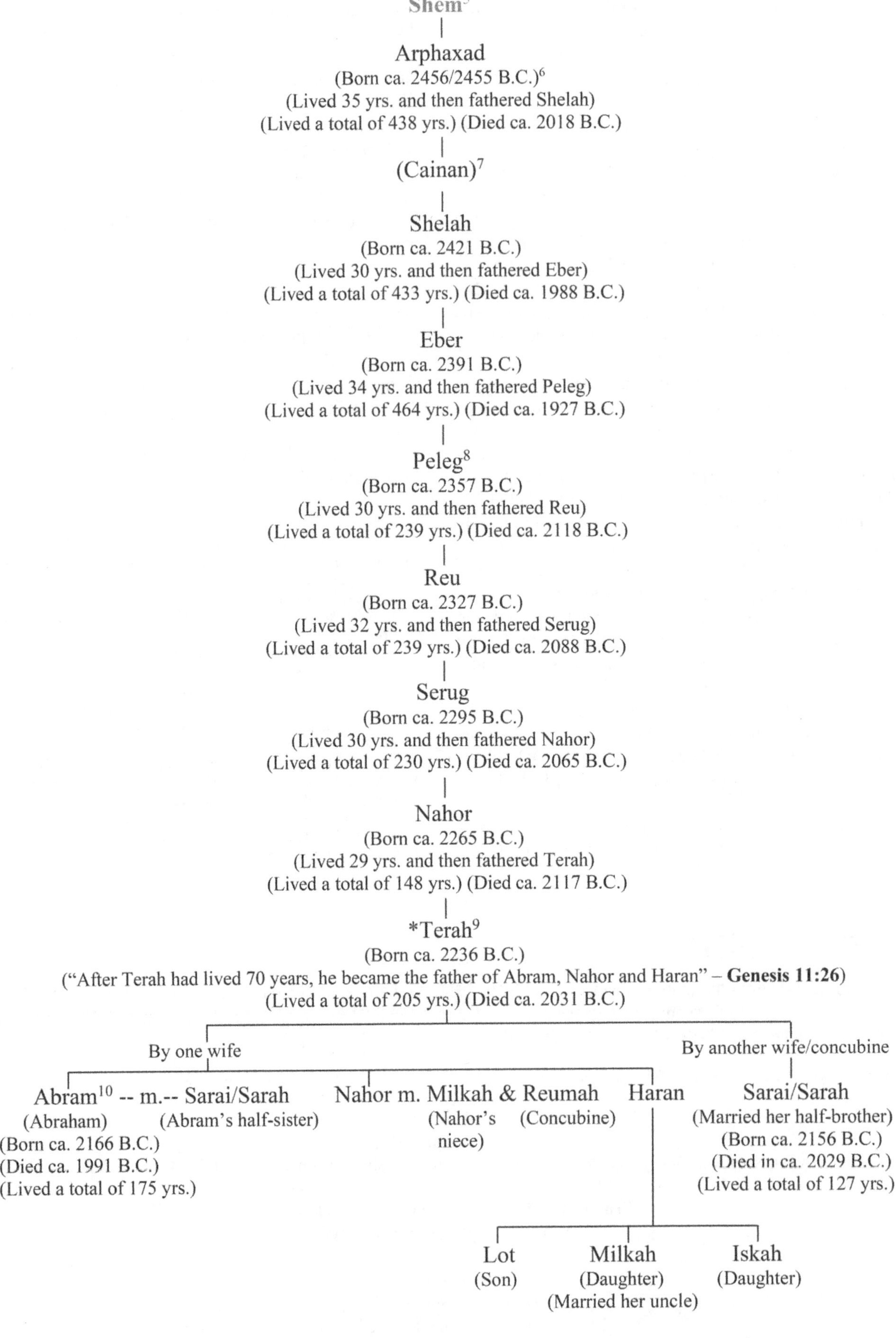
Shem[5]
Arphaxad
(Born ca. 2456/2455 B.C.)[6]
(Lived 35 yrs. and then fathered Shelah)
(Lived a total of 438 yrs.) (Died ca. 2018 B.C.)
(Cainan)[7]
Shelah
(Born ca. 2421 B.C.)
(Lived 30 yrs. and then fathered Eber)
(Lived a total of 433 yrs.) (Died ca. 1988 B.C.)
Eber
(Born ca. 2391 B.C.)
(Lived 34 yrs. and then fathered Peleg)
(Lived a total of 464 yrs.) (Died ca. 1927 B.C.)
Peleg[8]
(Born ca. 2357 B.C.)
(Lived 30 yrs. and then fathered Reu)
(Lived a total of 239 yrs.) (Died ca. 2118 B.C.)
Reu
(Born ca. 2327 B.C.)
(Lived 32 yrs. and then fathered Serug)
(Lived a total of 239 yrs.) (Died ca. 2088 B.C.)
Serug
(Born ca. 2295 B.C.)
(Lived 30 yrs. and then fathered Nahor)
(Lived a total of 230 yrs.) (Died ca. 2065 B.C.)
Nahor
(Born ca. 2265 B.C.)
(Lived 29 yrs. and then fathered Terah)
(Lived a total of 148 yrs.) (Died ca. 2117 B.C.)
*Terah[9]
(Born ca. 2236 B.C.)
("After Terah had lived 70 years, he became the father of Abram, Nahor and Haran" – **Genesis 11:26**)
(Lived a total of 205 yrs.) (Died ca. 2031 B.C.)
By one wife
By another wife/concubine
Abram[10] -- m.-- Sarai/Sarah
(Abraham)
(Abram's half-sister)
(Born ca. 2166 B.C.)
(Died ca. 1991 B.C.)
(Lived a total of 175 yrs.)
Nahor m. Milkah & Reumah
(Nahor's niece)
(Concubine)
Haran
Sarai/Sarah
(Married her half-brother)
(Born ca. 2156 B.C.)
(Died in ca. 2029 B.C.)
(Lived a total of 127 yrs.)
Lot
(Son)
Milkah
(Daughter)
(Married her uncle)
Iskah
(Daughter)

Biblical and Theological Significance

The name "Shem" (שֵׁם) means *name*, which is most appropriate since the term *the Name* is commonly applied to Yahweh. This supports the idea that the descendants of Shem would play a major role in the great plan of God's universal redemption of creation. The name also gave rise to the term *Semites*, a designation with broad application. It includes the dominant population of Mesopotamia as early as 2800 B.C., as well as the later peoples of the Fertile Crescent from Mesopotamia to Egypt, such as the Amorites, Aramaeans, Phoenicians, and, of course, the Hebrews. All Arabs of present times are also Semites. Eber is the patronymic ancestor of the Hebrews, עִבְרִים, *ʿibrim* (the descendants of Eber; **Genesis 10:21**), the name used in the Old Testament of the people who would become known as "Israel" at first and then Jews in the post-exilic period (after ca. 550 B.C.). Peleg (פֶּלֶג Heb. "division") may be a reference to the scattering of the nations as a result of the debacle at the Tower of Babel (**Genesis 11:1–9**). Terah's name is probably a by-form of the noun יָרֵחַ, "moon," a name that suggests that Abraham's ancestors worshiped Sin (or Nannar), the moon god, who was the principal deity of the pantheon of gods associated with Ur of the Chaldeans. Abraham's name (אַבְרָהָם *Abraham*, "father of a multitude") was changed from Abram ("exalted father") once he entered into covenant fellowship with Yahweh[11] (**Genesis 17:1–5**).

Notes

1. The chart is based on the Shem family line and the specific information for when the Shem ancestors fathered their sons (i.e., **Genesis 11:10–26**) and a proposed 175-year lifespan of Abraham from ca. 2166–1991 B.C., based on the reading of **Genesis 11:26** (see note 2). By working backwards, one can determine a more exact time period when each Shemite ancestor lived. However, it should be noted that some scholars and chronologists have pointed out that Abram/Abraham may *not* have been the firstborn son of Terah and that the reading of **Acts 7:4** even suggests that Terah was 130 years (not 70 years old) when Abram/Abraham was born. Therefore, the sixty-year variance would alter Abraham's lifespan from 2166–1991 B.C. to ca. 2106–1931 B.C. and affect the proposed lifespan of each Shemite ancestor as well as the proposed date of the flood in the chart. For a more complete discussion of the chronological issues, see notes 1 and 12 in chart "**Genesis 11**: Terah and Nahor."

This genealogy (like that of **Genesis 5:3–32,** which is summarized in chart "**Genesis 4**: Seth") is unique in that the lifespans and paternity of the ancients are included as *an integral part* of the biblical genealogical record.

2. The chronological *beginning marker* in **Genesis 5:32**—"After Noah was 500 years old, he became the father of Shem, Ham and Japheth"—appears to be paired with a chronological (summary) *ending marker* in **Genesis 11:26**—"After Terah had lived 70 years, he became the father of Abram, Nahor and Haran." For more information on the birth and lifespan of Abram/Abraham, see chart "**Genesis 11**: Terah and Nahor" (notes 1 and 12).

3. Noah was born in 3056 B.C., lived 950 years total (**Genesis 9:29**), and therefore died in 2106 B.C. Since he lived 350 years *after* the flood (**Genesis 9:28**; i.e., 2106 + 350=2456), this appears to establish the flood date in ca. 2456 B.C. Note that the flood is presented as an authentic historical event in **Matthew 24:37–39** and **Luke 17:26–27**. **Genesis 8:13–14** states that Noah was in his 601st year when his family disembarked from the ark, which would correspond to ca. 2455 B.C. (see note 4).

4. Details about the duration of the flood are given in **Genesis 7:24** and **8:1–17**. **Genesis 8:13–16** says that, "By the first day of the first month of Noah's six hundred and first year [2455 B.C.], the water had dried up from the earth. . . . By the twenty-seventh day of the second month [2455 B.C.] the earth was completely dry. Then God said to Noah, 'Come out of the ark, you and your wife and your sons and their wives.'" This shows that Noah's family left the ark in ca. 2455 B.C. (see notes 3 and 6).

5. Shem was the ancestor of "all the sons of Eber" (the Hebrews; **Genesis 10:21**). **Genesis 5:32** says, "After Noah was 500 years old, he became the father of Shem, Ham and Japheth." If Shem was born when Noah was 500 years old, Shem was born in ca. 2556 B.C.; if Noah was closer to 501 years old at Shem's birth, then Shem was born in ca. 2555 B.C. (the latter birthdate is more consistent with the details discussed in note 6).

6. The details about Noah's lifespan (see notes 3, 4, 5) reveal that the flood occurred in ca. 2456 B.C. **Genesis 7:7, 13** and **Genesis 8:16** confirm that only *eight* people entered the ark and (after the flood) eight people disembarked (i.e., Noah, Noah's wife, three sons—Shem, Ham and Japheth—and their three wives). This strongly indicates that Arphaxad was born to Shem and his wife just *after* the flood came to an end (i.e., sometime in 2455 B.C.).

7. Cainan is mentioned as the son of Arphaxad and the father of Shelah in **Luke 3:36** and in the Septuagint (LXX)—upon which Luke is based—but Cainan is omitted in the list of names in **Genesis 10:24; 11:12–13**; and **1 Chronicles 1:18**. The LXX clearly created a 10-name genealogy to match that connecting Adam to Noah in **Genesis 5:1–32**; see chart "**Genesis 4**: Seth." The origin of the name is unknown, though it is possible that the LXX was based on a Hebrew text tradition no longer extant. For a discussion that challenges the inclusion of Cainan (**Luke 3:36**) in Jesus' genealogy, see Andrew E. Steinmann, "Challenging the Authenticity of Cainan, Son of Arpachshad," *JETS* 60/4 (2017): 697–711 and Henry B. Smith Jr. and Kris J. Udd, "On the Authenticity of Kainan, Son of Arpachshad," *Detroit Baptist Seminary Journal* 24 (2019): 119–54.

8. The brother of Peleg was Joktan (**Genesis 10:25; 1 Chronicles 1:19**).

9. For the descendants of Terah and Nahor, see chart "**Genesis 11**: Terah and Nahor."

10. Abraham lived ca. 2166–1991 B.C. and died when he was 175 years old (**Genesis 25:7**). Isaac was born to Abraham and Sarah in 2066 B.C. when Abraham was 100 and Sarah was 90 (**Genesis 17:17; 21:5**). See chart "**Genesis 11**: Abraham."

11. In ca. 2067 B.C. when Abraham was 99 years old, God appeared to him and promised, "I will make my covenant between me and you and will greatly increase your numbers" (cf. **Genesis 17:1–2**).

GENESIS 11: TERAH AND NAHOR

Approximate Dating: from the time of Terah, ca. 2236–2031 B.C. to the time of Abram/Abraham, ca. 2166–1991 B.C.;[1] Isaac, ca. 2066–1886 B.C. and Jacob, ca. 2006 to 1859 B.C. ***Relevant Scriptures:*** **Genesis 11:10–32**; also **Genesis 20:12; 22:20–24; 24:15, 24, 29, 47, 67; 25:20; 1 Chronicles 1:17–19, 24–28, 34; Luke 3:34–36**

Line of Shem[2]

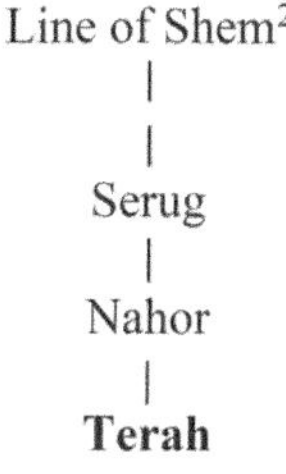

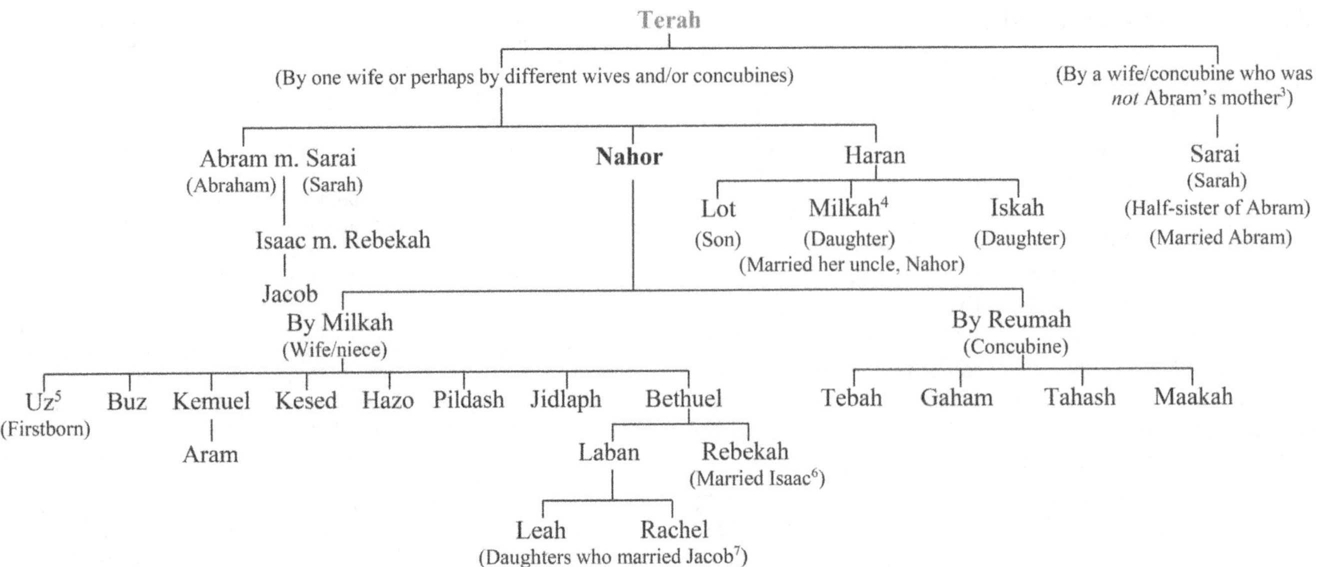

Biblical and Theological Significance

Terah (ca. 2236–2031 B.C.) lived in the ancient Sumerian city-state of Ur, in what is now southwest Iraq or Kuwait, near the Persian Gulf.[8] By that time, the Sumerians had been overthrown by Akkad, a city-state ruled by the famous Sargon the Great (2340–2284 B.C.), who established the so-called Akkadian Empire.[9] The Akkadians, contrary to the Sumerians, were a Semitic people with origins in northwest Mesopotamia and Syria. Abram was born in 2166 B.C., and his brothers Haran and Nahor must have also been born about that time (**Genesis 11:26**). By then Lower Mesopotamia had fallen again, this time into the hands of marauders from the Zagros Mountains to the east, perhaps prompting Terah's migration from Ur to Harran, located on the upper Euphrates River. Terah and his family worshiped Sin (or Nannar), the moon god and also the chief god of Harran, so that likely accounts for the migration there.[10] It is unknown whether or not Abram knew of Yahweh at that time as God, but his father Terah clearly did not. Terah was the father of Abram (Abraham), Nahor, and Haran, presumably by one wife (see note 12). Terah was also the father of Sarai (Sarah) by another wife or concubine (**Genesis 11:26, 29**), thereby making her the half-sister of Abram (Abraham) (cf. **Genesis 20:12**).[11] Haran died in Ur before Terah moved the family from Ur to Harran (**Genesis 11:26, 28**), and Terah died in Harran at the age of 205 (**Genesis 11:32**; cf. **Acts 7:4**).[12]

The ancestral line of the Messiah follows from the Terah–Abraham–Isaac–Jacob line but, nevertheless, includes some of the Terah–Nahor descendants (i.e., the matriarchs Rebekah, Leah, and Rachel) who married the patriarchs (cf. **Genesis 24:67; 29:16, 23, 28; Luke 3:34**).

Nahor was the son of Terah and the brother of Abram (Abraham), Haran, and a half-sister, Sarai (Sarah) (**Genesis 11:26–27; 20:12**). He was named after his grandfather Nahor, the son of Serug, according to the tradition of papponymy in which sons were named after grandfathers (**11:23–26**). After the death of his brother Haran, Nahor married his niece, Haran's daughter Milkah (**11:27–29**) and had eight sons by her (**22:20–23**). Nahor also had four sons by his wife/concubine Reumah (**22:24**). The text of **Genesis 31:53** suggests that Nahor eventually converted to Yahwism.[13] Nahor's grandson, Laban, seems, with some ambiguity, to have embraced Yahwistic faith (**24:31, 50; 31:53**); however, he still retained household gods and practiced divination (cf. **30:27; 31:19, 30, 34**).

A theological principle to be drawn from this genealogy is that time, place, and circumstances neither determine the saving plans of the sovereign God of the Bible nor are they impediments to his working them out. The genealogy commences following the Great flood in spite of the covenant of salvation which continued through Noah and then Shem. In the course of time, the episode of the Tower of Babel occurred—an act of hubris and humanism that shook its fist in the face of God and regarded itself as equal, if not superior, to him. Yet, the promise moved forward until God resorted to an "arbitrary" choice of a man, Terah—pagan though he was—to sire a son, Abraham, who would himself become the father of the messianic line.

Notes

1. The dating of Abram/Abraham's lifespan is difficult to establish unequivocally (see note 12)–an offset of 60 years could be in place, which would place Abram/Abraham's birth in 2106 B.C. instead of 2166 B.C. For the purposes here, the dating in the subtitle follows the wording of **Genesis 11:26** that Terah was 70 years old when Abram/Abraham was born.

2. For this lineage, see chart "**Genesis 11**: Shem."

3. In **Genesis 20:12**, Abraham explains that Sarai/Sarah was his half-sister: "Besides, she [Sarai] really is my sister, the daughter of my father [Terah] though not of my mother; and she became my wife."

4. Milkah (**Genesis 11:29; 22:20, 23; 24:15, 24, 27**), the daughter of Haran, married her uncle, Nahor. She is called "Milcah" in some translations.

5. For the possibility that Uz was an ancestor of Job, see chart "**Job 1**: Possible Ancestry of Job the Patriarch."

6. Rebekah married Isaac (son of Abraham); Isaac and Bethuel (Rebekah's father) were first cousins. As the daughter of Bethuel, Rebekah was Isaac's first cousin once removed.

7. Jacob was the son of Isaac and the grandson of Abraham (Nahor's brother). Nahor was the great-grandfather of Leah and Rachel. Jacob and Laban shared the same great-grandparent (Terah), making them second cousins; therefore Leah and Rachel (the daughters of Laban) married Jacob (their second cousin once removed).

8. The origins of the Sumerians are shrouded in mystery. What is known is that they were not Semitic, but on the other hand, they were a highly cultured

people who greatly impacted their Semitic neighbors who infiltrated into NW Mesopotamia as early as 2800 B.C.

9. The Akkadian writings were based on the cuneiform script of the Sumerians, though the languages were not at all cognate.

10. The name Terah (תֶּרַח) derives from the word for "moon" (יָרֵחַ) *yareakh*. The wording of two passages shows that, at least initially, Terah was a pagan worshiper. God had told Abram to separate from his relatives and his father's (Terah's) house in Harran (where the head of the pantheon of gods was Sin) and move to "the land that I will show you [Canaan] (**Genesis 12:1–5**)." **Joshua 24:2** recounts that, "This is what the Lord, the God of Israel, says . . . Terah the father of Abraham and Nahor lived beyond the Euphrates River and worshiped other gods." However, Laban's appeal to Jacob in **Genesis 31:53**, which specifically speaks of "the God of Abraham and the God of Nahor, [and] the God of their father [Terah]," suggests that, at some point, both Terah and Nahor converted and followed Yahweh.

11. Abraham (Abram) identifies his wife, Sarah (Sarai), as "my sister, the daughter of my father though not of my mother" (**Genesis 20:12**); therefore, she was his half-sister.

12. **Genesis 11:26** says that "After Terah had lived 70 years, he became the father of Abram, Nahor and Haran." This verse does not state which son was the firstborn and does not give the name(s) of the mother(s). (Notice a similar type of wording for Noah's offspring in **Genesis 5:32**: "After Noah was 500 years old, he became the father of Shem, Ham and Japheth"). Henry Morris and John Whitcomb paraphrase **Genesis 11:26** as follows: "And Terah lived seventy years and begat the first of his three sons, the most important of whom (not because of age but because of the Messianic line) was Abram" (John C. Whitcomb and Henry M. Morris, *The Genesis Flood*, (Grand Rapids: Baker, 1961), 480. It follows that the genealogical emphasis in **Genesis 5:32** is on the Noah-Shem line, and the emphasis in **Genesis 11:26** is on the Terah–Abram/Abraham line (i.e., the sons who carried on the messianic line—**Matthew 1:1–2; Luke 3:34, 36**—and from whom the biblical narratives continue).

Unless Terah had three different wives and/or concubines, **Genesis 11:26** does not mean that all three sons were born in the same year when Terah was 70 years old. In Stephen's address before the Sanhedrin in **Acts 7:4**, he says that "After the death of his father [Terah, who lived to be 205 years and died in Harran], God sent him [Abram] to this land [Canaan] where you are now living" (cf. **Genesis 11:32**); furthermore, **Genesis 12:4** adds, "So Abram went, as the Lord had told him; and Lot went with him. Abram was seventy-five years old when he set out from Harran." Chronologists have used these passages to establish that Abram was 75 years old when his father Terah died in Harran at age 205, thereby establishing that Abram/Abraham was born to Terah when Terah was 130 years old, not when Terah was 70 years old (as in **Genesis 11:26**). As the commentary for **Acts 7:4** in *The NIV Study Bible* explains, "It may be that Haran was Terah's firstborn and that Abraham was born 60 years later. Thus, the death of Terah at 205 years of age could have occurred just before Abraham, at 75, left Haran"; *The NIV Study Bible* (Grand Rapids: Zondervan, 2020), 1907). Taken together, Abraham may have been born in 2106 B.C. instead of 2166 B.C. (see note 1), and thus all charts where Abraham's lifespan is given should be evaluated with this in mind.

13. See note 10.

GENESIS 11: ABRAHAM

Approximate Dating: Abraham lived for 175 years, ca. 2166–1991 B.C.[1] ***Relevant Scriptures:*** **Genesis 11:10–32;** also **Genesis 3:20; 4:25; 5:1–32; 21:5; 22:20–24; 24:15; 25:6–7, 24–26; 27:42–43; 1 Chronicles 1:1–4; Luke 3:34–38**

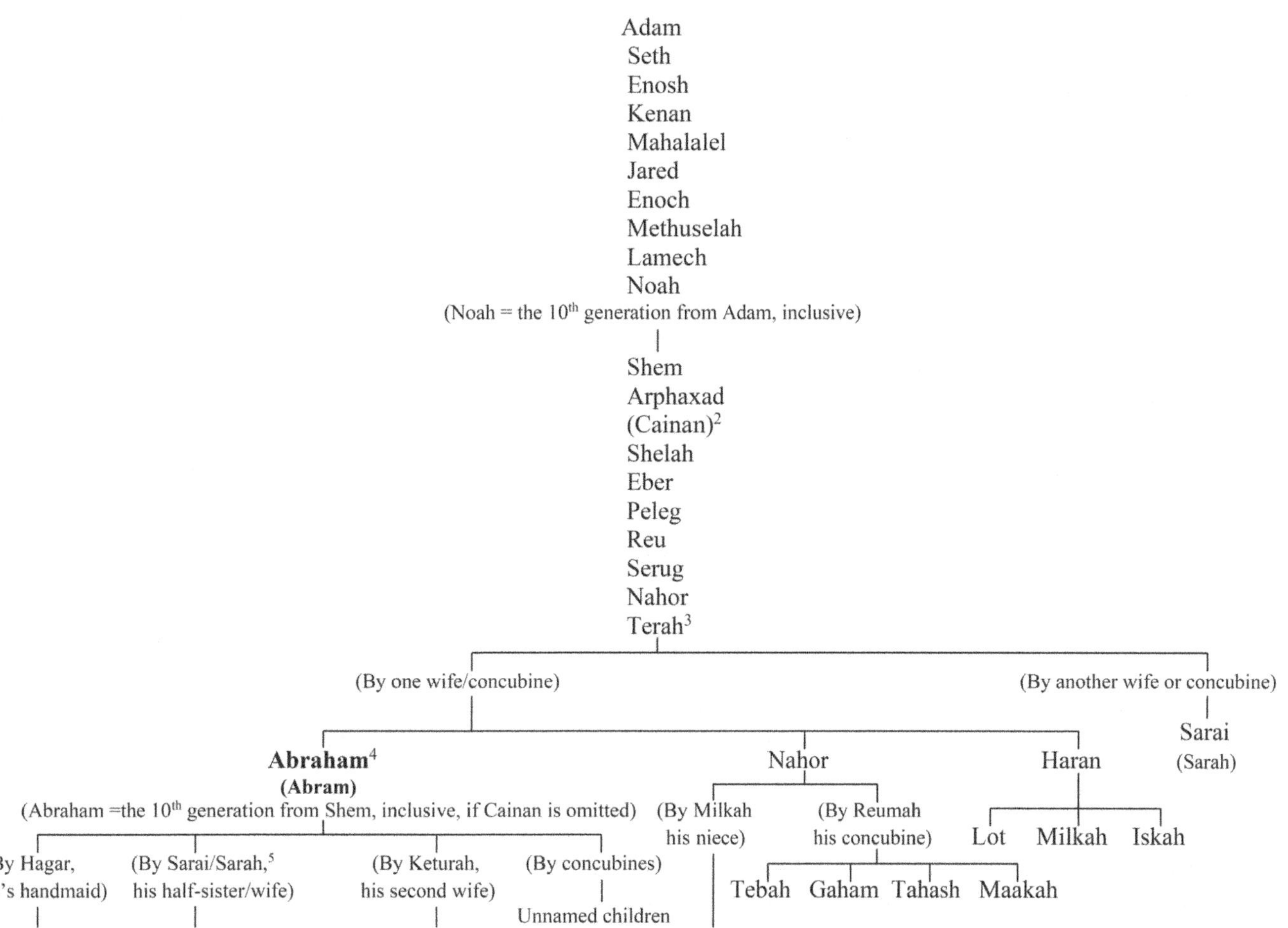

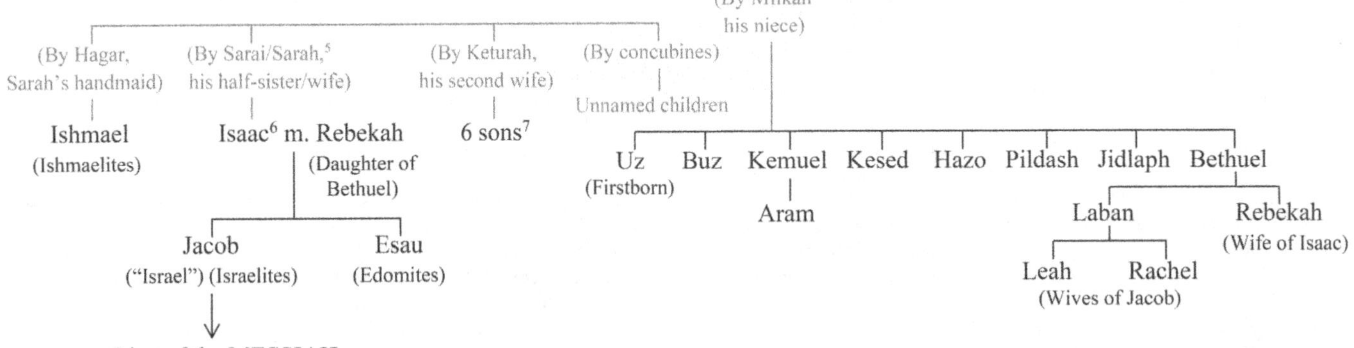

Biblical and Theological Significance

The importance of this genealogy lies chiefly in the connection between Adam, the father of the human race, and Abraham, the father of the chosen nation of Israel. What had been lost in Adam's fall would be retrieved through Abraham's "seed."[8] Ten generations link Adam with Noah, and ten generations after the flood link Shem with Abraham.[9] Symmetry or stylizing of lists was a common mnemonic device, but the 10+10 scheme may also draw attention to the working of God in history, with perfection and structures that speak of historical design with movement from judgment (as in the flood) to salvation (as in the promise to Abraham that through him all people on the earth would be blessed; **Genesis 12:1–3**).

Abraham (first, Abram) was a wealthy and prominent citizen of Ur, one of the great centers of Sumero-Akkadian civilization in the later third millennium B.C. He had no knowledge of Yahweh as God until Yahweh called him[10] and revealed to him his great plan of human redemption and universal re-creation. Abram's people worshiped Sin (Nannar in Sumerian), the moon god of Ur, but by means of a great intervention of grace, God revealed to Abram who he was and what he had in view for him. Very simply, the call consisted of four privileges and responsibilities:

1. Abram and his family must forsake the prestige, wealth, and comforts of Ur and move to an undisclosed destination. In line with the culture of the place and times, Abram, though the one called, was subject to his father Terah, who, although a pagan worshiper, was at least persuaded by his son to accompany him to Harran, another center of the Sin cult. There, Terah died and Yahweh led Abram, the new head of the family, onward to Canaan.[11] In Canaan, Abram built an altar to Yahweh at Shechem (**Genesis 12:6–7**), thus claiming the land as Yahweh's.
2. Yahweh had revealed to Abram that he would become the father of a great people by whom he would bless all peoples of the earth (**Genesis 12:2–3**).
3. This would be accomplished through an irrevocable and unconditional covenant[12] between Yahweh and Abram and his descendants forever (**Genesis 12:1–3**). This covenant was elaborated to Abraham in three other places in Genesis: **15:5, 7, 13–16, 18–21**; **17:1–21**; **22:16–18.** It was repeated to Isaac (**Genesis 26:3–5**) and finally to Jacob (**Genesis 28:13–15; 46:2–4; 48:3–4; 49:10–12; 1 Chronicles 16:16–18**).
4. The changing of Jacob's name to Israel portended a major development of the Abrahamic covenant, for it both enlarged and narrowed its functional scope:
   - It would no longer be conveyed through an individual, but through a nation—that of Israel (**Genesis 32:28–30; Exodus 19:4–6**)
   - Of that nation, one tribe would be the channel of redemption—that of Judah (**Genesis 49:8**)
   - From that tribe would come one man who would be a king—David, son of Jesse the Bethlehemite (**Genesis 49:10; Ruth 4:12, 17, 18–22; 1 Samuel 13:14; 16:12–13**)
   - A descendant of David would be the Anointed One who would, in life and death, establish righteousness, redemption, and a new creation in which the original purposes of God would find everlasting fulfillment (**Micah 5:2, 4; Matthew 2:1–6; Romans 1:3; Revelation 5:5; 22:16**)

Abraham's Family

Sarai/Sarah[13] was the wife and half-sister of Abram/Abraham; Abram clarifies the biological relationship in **Genesis 20:12** by saying that Sarai was "the daughter of my father though not of my mother." Abram asked her to lie about this to both the Egyptians (**Genesis 12:10–20**) and to the king of Gerar (**Genesis 20:1–18**) by saying that she was only his *sister* rather than his *wife*. Abraham and Sarah were childless for most of their marriage (**Genesis 11:30**). Sarah gave her Egyptian slave Hagar to Abraham, hoping that Hagar would become pregnant (**Genesis 16:1–2**). Hagar conceived Ishmael, but he was not the son of promise (**Genesis 16:4, 15; 17:20–21**). Isaac was not born until 2066 B.C. when Abraham was one hundred and Sarah was ninety (**Genesis 21:5**; cf. **17:17**).

God later tested Abraham, telling him to take "your son, your only son, whom you love" to Moriah to sacrifice him (**Genesis 22:2**). Abraham obediently took Isaac and prepared an altar for a burnt offering. Isaac asked where the lamb was for the burnt offering; Abraham answered that "God himself will provide the lamb" (**Genesis 22:7–8**). An angel stopped Abraham from completing the task, telling him that it was clear that Abraham feared God because he had not withheld his only son (**Genesis 22:10–12**). Thousands of years later, another *only Son* was sacrificed, the perfect "Lamb of God, who takes away the sin of the world" (**John 1:29**).

After Sarah died at the age of 127, Abraham married Keturah (**Genesis 25:1**; cf. **1 Chronicles 1:32**). The six sons of Keturah and Abraham are listed in **Genesis 25:1–4** and **1 Chronicles 1:32–33**.[14]

Abraham purchased the cave of Machpelah near Mamre[15]—belonging to "Ephron son of Zohar the Hittite" (**Genesis 25:9**)—on the eastern slope of Hebron as a family burial place. When Abraham died at the age of 175, he was buried in the cave of Machpelah with Sarah (**Genesis 23:19; 25:7, 9–10; 49:31**); later, this also became the burial site of Isaac and Rebekah, and Jacob and Leah (**Genesis 49:31; 50:13**). As "the man of faith," Abraham is considered the father of all believers; by faith in Jesus, both Jews and Gentiles become the "children of Abraham" (**Galatians 3:6–9**; cf. **Romans 3:22; 4:13, 16, 18**). Because of Abraham's great faith, he was counted among those in the faith hall of fame (**Hebrews 11:8–10, 12**).

Notes

1. For a discussion of the birth and lifespan of Abram/Abraham, see chart "**Genesis 11**: Terah and Nahor" (especially notes 1 and 12).
2. For a discussion of the inclusion or exclusion of Cainan in **Luke 3:36**, see Andrew E. Steinmann, "Challenging the Authenticity of Cainan, Son of Arpachshad," *JETS* 60/4 (2017): 440.
3. The name "Terah" reflects his pagan roots; it derives from *yareakh*, "moon."
4. The name is thoroughly Northwest Semitic, not East Semitic as in Mesopotamia; obviously, it took its present form with Abram's settlement in Canaan ca. 2091 B.C. "Abram" means "exalted father" and "Abraham" means "father of a multitude."
5. Sarah was born in ca. 2156 B.C.; she gave birth to Isaac in ca. 2066 B.C., and died at the age of 127 in ca. 2029 B.C.
6. Isaac was born when Abraham was 100 and Sarah was 90 years old (**Genesis 17:17; 21:2**). Isaac was 60 years old when Rebekah gave birth to Jacob and Esau (**Genesis 25:26**). Isaac lived from ca. 2066–1886 B.C., dying at 180 (**Genesis 35:28**).
7. See chart "**Genesis 25**: Abraham's Descendants through Keturah."
8. The Hebrew term "seed" (זֶרַע), when used of human sperm, is always grammatically singular; thus, as here, it can refer to Israel as a people and to a promised Messiah as an individual (**Galatians 3:16**).
9. If Cainan is omitted, the ten generations of Adam through Noah (**Genesis 5:1–29**) are matched by the ten generations of Shem through Abraham (**Genesis 11:10–26**), although the name Cainan occurs in the Septuagint and in **Luke 3:36** (see note 2).
10. In ca. 2067 B.C., "When Abram was ninety-nine years old, the Lord appeared to him and said, 'I am God Almighty, walk before me faithfully and be blameless. Then I will make my covenant between me and you and will greatly increase your numbers'" (**Genesis 17:1–2**).
11. God's call to Abram to leave Harran came when he was 75 years old (ca. 2091 B.C.): "He [Abram] took his wife Sarai, his nephew Lot, all the possessions they had accumulated and the people they had acquired in Harran, and they set out for the land of Canaan" (**Genesis 12:4–5**).
12. In the ancient Near East (ANE), two basic covenant forms and types were made between individuals and between nations—sovereign/vassal and parity treaties. The former was initiated by a superior person or power in domination over the subservient one, whereas the latter was between those of approximately equal status (cf. **Joshua 9:3–15; 1 Kings 4:1–12**); see Sandra Richter, *The Epic of Eden: A Christian Entry into the Old Testament* (Downers Grove, IL: IVP Academic), 70–75 and "Treaty Formats and Biblical Covenants" in the *NIV Cultural Backgrounds Study Bible* (Grand Rapids: Zondervan, 2016), 303. Of necessity, covenants made by God were of the former kind. Ordinarily, either kind could be broken, but violation by a vassal would obviously bring great judgment. Violation of a parity covenant might result in war. When God made a covenant, however, he could and would not ever break it because he swore to it by his own reputation (**Deuteronomy 7:12; Judges 2:1; 1 Chronicles 16:15–18; Psalm 105:8–11; Isaiah 55:3; 61:8; Jeremiah 31:1–3, 31–33; Ezekiel 16:60**).
13. Scripture and ANE custom hold that Terah was 70 when Abram was born in 2166 B.C. (**Genesis 11:26**). Abram/Abraham was 75 and his wife Sarai/Sarah was 65 years old when they left Haran in 2091 B.C. en route to Canaan (**Genesis 12:4–5**). [Given that Abram was ten years older than Sarai and that a maiden would usually be married by her mid-teen years, Abram was perhaps married to Sarai by the time he was 25.] When Isaac was born in 2066 B.C., Abraham was 100 years old and Sarah was 90 (**Genesis 17:17**; cf. **21:2**). Sarai/Sarah was born in 2156 B.C. and died in 2029 B.C., at the age of 127 (**Genesis 23:1–2**).
14. See chart "**Genesis 25**: Abraham's Descendants through Keturah."
15. Mamre was an area around Hebron, apparently named for Mamre the Amorite (a brother of Eshkol and Aner), who was an ally of Abram who helped Abram in defeating Kedorlaomer (**Genesis 14:13, 17, 24**).

GENESIS 11: LOT AND HIS DESCENDANTS, THE MOABITES AND AMMONITES

Approximate Dating: early patriarchal period, ca. 2060–2006 B.C. ***Relevant Scriptures:*** **Genesis 11:26–31; 12:13; 19:36–38; 20:12; 22:20–24; 24:15, 24, 29, 47, 67;** also **Luke 3:34; 2 Peter 2:6–7**

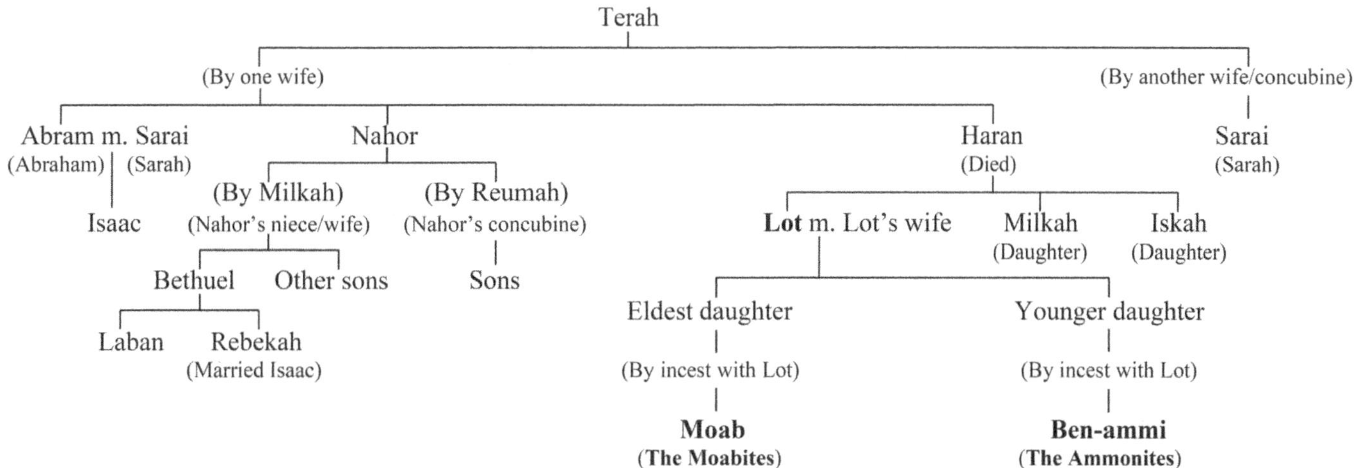

Biblical and Theological Significance

Lot was both a descendant of Terah and the head of a line that separated from Abram's family both physically and historically. He was the son of Haran, who was a brother of Abram, and thus was the latter's nephew. Lot migrated with Abram and Sarai to Canaan, and also accompanied them into Egypt (cf. **Genesis 11:31–32; 12:4–5; 13:1, 5**). Upon returning to Canaan, Abram and Lot settled in the vicinity of Bethel and Ai. They were so wealthy that Abram's and Lot's herders began to quarrel over pasture lands (**Genesis 13:6–7**). To settle the conflict, Lot chose the cities of the fertile plain of the Jordan Valley (just beyond the border of the promised land), where Sodom was located—even though he knew "the people of Sodom were wicked and were sinning greatly against the LORD" (**Genesis 13:8–13**).

Before he destroyed Sodom, the Lord sent two angels to Lot, and Lot offered them hospitality (**Genesis 19:1–3**). However, wicked townsmen pressed Lot to offer up his guests so they could "have sex with them" (**Genesis 19:5**). Lot protected the two men—even offering his virgin daughters instead! The angels, in turn, protected Lot, and urged him to take his family into the nearby hills to safety. Because Lot feared the mountains, he pleaded instead to flee to another city of the plain, one called Zoar (**Genesis 19:15, 19–20, 22**; cf. **Deuteronomy 34:3**). Despite the Lord's provision to escape the imminent destruction of Sodom, Lot's wife "looked back," desiring the possessions she left behind (cf. **Luke 17:31**), and "became a pillar of salt" (**Genesis 19:26**).

Later, Lot moved with his two daughters to a hillside cave. The virgin daughters regretted that they would never have offspring. In a scheming act of desperation and concealment, they got their father drunk on successive nights and slept with him—"To preserve our family line through our father" (**Genesis 19:32**)—and each conceived a son by him. The son of the older daughter was called Moab, who was the eponymous ancestor of the Moabites. The son of the younger was named Ben-Ammi, who was the eponymous ancestor of the Ammonites (**Genesis 19:30–38**). Lot's descendants (the Moabites and Ammonites) represent a remnant of Abraham's family that settled the southern bank of the Arnon River (cf. **Numbers 21:13, 28; Deuteronomy 2:9**). Despite these depictions of Lot's troubled life, the New Testament strikingly affirms that Lot was "a righteous man" who was distressed by the depraved conduct of the lawless (**2 Peter 2:6–8**).

Moab, the half-brother of Ben-Ammi, became the progenitor of the Moabite nation. The Moabites were pagan worshipers of Chemosh and the fire-god Molek. At various times in history, the Moabites were at war with the Israelites (cf. **Judges 3:12–30**). Remarkably however, at the same time, Ruth the Moabite married Boaz the Judahite and became an ancestress of King David and the Messiah (**Ruth 1:3–4, 22; 4:18–22; Matthew 1:5**). The Ammonites were the descendants of Ben-Ammi, the half-brother of Moab. They too warred against Israel for possession of the fertile land of Gilead. Like the Moabites, they were pagan idolaters who also worshiped the gods of Moab. The Ammonites are most often found in conjunction with the Moabites (cf. **Deuteronomy 2:16–19; Judges 10:6; 2 Chronicles 20:1; Zephaniah 2:8**). The Moabites and the Ammonites hired Balaam to curse Israel (**Deuteronomy 23:4**). Saul and David both defeated the Ammonites (**1 Samuel 11:11; 2 Samuel 10:6–14; 12:26–31**). Noteworthy is that Solomon's wife Naamah, the mother of Rehoboam, was an Ammonite (**1 Kings 14:31; 2 Chronicles 12:13**).

In reflection, it is unclear why Lot traveled to Canaan with Abram; perhaps he recognized that Abram was the chosen vehicle of covenant redemption. However, upon their later return from Egypt, Lot revealed his innate selfishness by claiming the best of the land of Canaan for himself, leaving the great patriarch—to whom the land had initially been promised—the leftovers. By this display of their respective characters, one can foresee the manifestation of divine grace in the nations that issued from the uncle and his acquisitive nephew. Abraham became the father of the chosen nation, Israel, whose kings would culminate in the Messianic One who would save his people from their sins (**Matthew 1:21**). In order to secure children, each of Lot's daughters had sex with their father (**Genesis 19:30-38**), resulting in offspring that became two of the most idolatrously corrupt and incessantly antagonistic nations that Israel contended with throughout its long history.

GENESIS 16: ISHMAEL AND HIS DESCENDANTS, THE ISHMAELITES

Approximate Dating: patriarchal era; Ishmael was born in ca. 2080 B.C., lived 137 yrs., and died in ca. 1943 B.C.[1] ***Relevant Scriptures:*** **Genesis 16:1–16**; also **Genesis 17:23–26; 21:9–21; 25:9, 12–18; 28:9; 36:2–4, 13; 37:25–28; 39:1; Judges 8:24; 1 Chronicles 1:28–31; 2:17; 27:30**

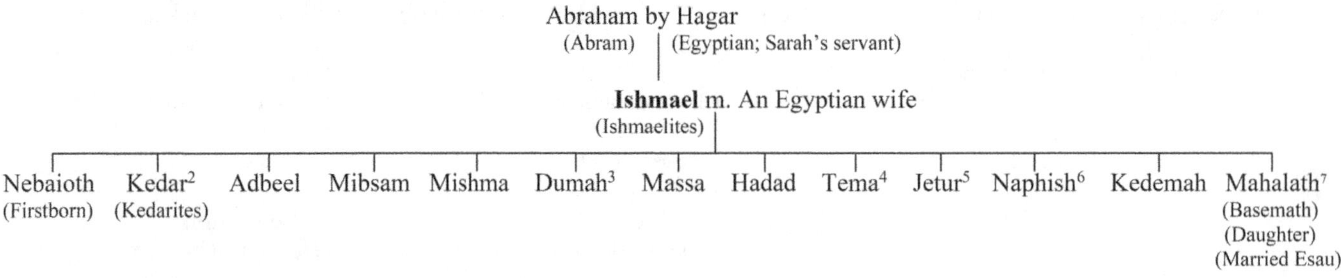

Biblical and Theological Significance

Hagar was the Egyptian maidservant-slave of Sarah, procured perhaps by Abram when he had visited Egypt in a time of famine in Canaan (**Genesis 12:10–13:1**). Since Sarah was infertile (**Genesis 11:30**), Hagar served as a surrogate wife or concubine to Abram, as was the custom in that world and time (**Genesis 16:2**). Children by such an arrangement would be counted as children of the barren wife (cf. **Genesis 16:2**). Both Abram and Sarah believed that by this means God would fulfill the covenant promise to Abram that "a son who is your own flesh and blood will be your heir" (cf. **Genesis 15:4**; cf. **vv. 1–21**). After Abram slept with Hagar and she became pregnant, in her newly elevated position she despised her mistress (thus the root of the Hebrew verb קלל). This led in turn, to Sarah oppressing her, so Hagar fled homeward toward Egypt. In a theophany appearance, the angel of Yahweh came to Hagar and told her that she would give birth to a son and should name him *Ishmael* and that she should go back to her mistress and "submit to her" (**Genesis 16:9**; cf. **vv. 7–11**).

The angel of Yahweh foretold that Ishmael would be "a wild [rebellious] . . . man; his hand will be against everyone and everyone's hand against him, and he will live in hostility toward all his brothers" (**Genesis 16:12**), but that the Lord would still increase Hagar's descendants "so much that they will be too numerous to count" (**Genesis 16:10**). Ishmael, the son of Hagar the Egyptian and Abram the Hebrew, became the progenitor of the Ishmaelites. The descendants of Hagar appear as the Hagrites (הַגְרִאִים), who are mentioned occasionally in Scripture (cf. **1 Chronicles 5:10, 19; 27:31; Psalm 83:6**), suggesting that at some point later on, Hagar married and had other children.[8]

When Abraham[9] died at the age of 175 (ca. 1991 B.C.; **Genesis 25:7**), Ishmael and Isaac buried him in the cave of Machpelah (**Genesis 25:9**), but it was Isaac, not Ishmael, who dwelt at Beer Lahai Roi (between Kadesh and Bered) where Hagar had had the original theophany with the angel of Yahweh (**Genesis 16:14; 25:11**). The twelve sons of Ishmael generally lived separately from the twelve sons of Isaac (**Genesis 25:5–6**), but Mahalath (also called Basemath), daughter of Ishmael and sister of Nebaioth, married Isaac's son Esau (**28:9; 36:3, 10**). Ishmael's sons became "twelve tribal rulers according to their settlements and camps" (**Genesis 25:16**). They and their descendants "settled in the area from Havilah to Shur, near the eastern border of Egypt, as you go toward Ashur. . . . and they lived in hostility toward all the tribes related to them" (**Genesis 25:18**). Ishmael died at the age of 137 and "was gathered to his people" (**Genesis 25:17**).

The apostle Paul uses Hagar, Ishmael, Sarah, and Isaac as an allegory to compare the old and new covenants. Ishmael, the son "by the slave woman" (Hagar), was born "according to the flesh," whereas Isaac, "his son by the free woman" (Sarah), was born "as the result of a divine promise" (**Galatians 4:23**). Paul extends the argument further: Hagar represents the former Mosaic covenant made at Mount Sinai, which "bears children who are to be slaves" (corresponding to "the present city of Jerusalem"; **Galatians 4:24–25**), whereas Sarah bears "children of promise" whose inheritance, secured by faith in God's promises, is found in "the Jerusalem that is above" (**Galatians 4:26, 28, 31**).

To this day, Arabs name Ishmael as their forebearer and thus as recipients also, with Israel, of covenantal blessings first enunciated to their common father, Abraham. One should remember that the covenantal choice of Israel, not Esau (or Ishmael), was functional (cf. **Isaiah 49:1–7**) and does not nullify God's offer of salvific grace to all mankind, including the descendants of Ishmael.

Notes

1. Abraham was born in 2166 B.C. and died in 1991 B.C. at the age of 175 (**Genesis 25:7**)–see notes 1 and 12 in chart "**Genesis 11**: Terah and Nahor." **Genesis 16:16** says that Abram/Abraham was eighty-six years old when Hagar bore Ishmael, so Ishmael was born in 2080 B.C. In 2067 B.C., when Ishmael was thirteen (**Genesis 17:25**), Abraham was 99 years of age (**Genesis 17:1**). By the time Ishmael buried Abraham in 1991 B.C., he was 89 years old (**Genesis 25:8–9**). Ishmael then lived 48 years longer and died at the age of 137 in 1943 B.C. (**Genesis 25:17**).

2. For references to Kedar, the eponymous ancestor of the Kedarites, see **Genesis 25:13; 1 Chronicles 1:29; Psalm 120:5; Song of Songs 1:5; Isaiah 21:16–17; 42:11; Jeremiah 2:10; 49:28; Ezekiel 27:21**.

3. For the prophecy against Dumah, see **Isaiah 21:11–12**.

4. For references to the personal name Tema, see **Genesis 25:15; 1 Chronicles 1:30**; for references to Tema the place name, see **Job 6:19; Isaiah 21:14; Jeremiah 25:23**.

5. For references to the personal name Jetur, see **Genesis 25:15; 1 Chronicles 1:31; 5:19**. Iturea is the place name (cf. **Luke 3:1**) meaning "related to Jetur," and the Itureans were of Ishmaelite stock.

6. For references to Naphish, see **Genesis 25:15; 1 Chronicles 1:31; 5:19**. The Naphish descendants dwelt in the Transjordan before being displaced by Reuben, Gad, and the half-tribe of Manasseh (**1 Chronicles 5:19–20**).

7. Esau's wife, Mahalath (**Genesis 28:9**) is also called Basemath (**Genesis 36:3, 10**). She should not be confused with Esau's wife, Adah (**Genesis 36:2, 4, 10, 12, 16**), who is also called Basemath (**Genesis 26:34**). See charts "**Genesis 36**: Esau, the Ancestor of the Edomites" and "**Genesis 36**: Esau's Wives."

8. According to the *ISBE* (Edward Mack, "Hagrites"), "the term *Hagrite* is a generic term roughly synonymous with Ishmaelite."

9. See chart "**Genesis 11**: Abraham."

GENESIS 25: ABRAHAM'S DESCENDANTS THROUGH KETURAH

Approximate Dating: era of the patriarchs, ca. 2029–1900 B.C. ***Relevant Scriptures:*** **Genesis 25:1–4**; also **1 Chronicles 1:32–33**

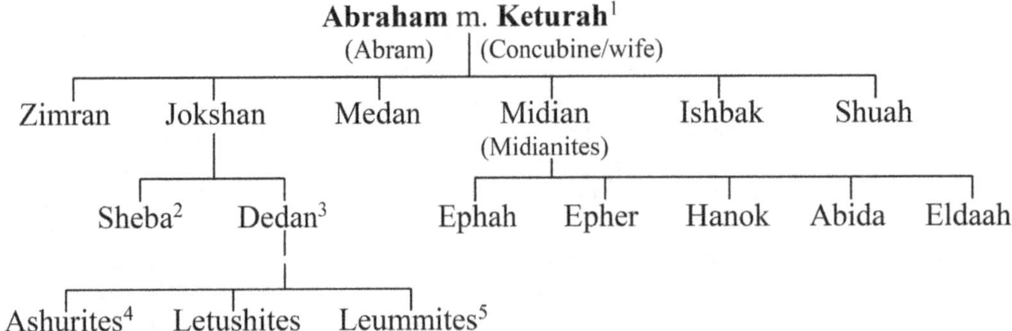

Biblical and Theological Significance

Following Sarah's death in ca. 2029 B.C., Abraham took a second "wife" (**Genesis 25:1**) from among his concubines (**1 Chronicles 1:32**; cf. **Genesis 25:6**) whose name was Keturah. Her ethnicity, origins, and previous connections to the chosen line, if any, are not disclosed. Keturah bore Abraham six sons, but, as **Genesis 25:5–6** makes clear, Abraham "left everything he owned to Isaac. But while he [Abraham] was still living, he gave gifts to the sons of his concubines and sent them away from his son Isaac [the child of promise; **Hebrews 11:11**] to the land of the east."[6] The sons of Keturah became the progenitors of small, desert-dwelling tribes in the Transjordan, Sinai, and Arabia. Of these, only Midian can presently be located in northwestern Saudi Arabia. Sheba (Saba) by consensus is what is now Yemen; Dedan was an oasis in Arabia, ca. 100 miles east of the Red Sea; and Ephah was near the modern border with Jordan in northern Saudi Arabia.

Midian was the eponymous ancestor of the dominant Midianites who were, at times, fierce antagonists to the Israelites. Joseph was sold to Midianites/Ishmaelites who took him to Egypt (**Genesis 37:27–28, 36**; cf. **37:25; 39:1**). In their travels to the promised land, the children of Israel were permitted to enter the land of Midian. However, the Midianites joined with Balak king of Moab, and together they conspired against Israel (**Numbers 22:4–7**). The Midianites treated Israel as "enemies" (**Numbers 25:18**) by deliberately seducing them into immorality and pagan worship of Baal Peor. Israel "consecrated" themselves to this "shameful idol" in immoral worship (**Hosea 9:10**; cf. **Numbers 25:3, 5**), and in response, the Lord sent a plague against Israel. At the zenith of the incident, an Israelite man named Zimri (the son of Salu, a Simeonite) brought a Midianite woman named Kozbi, (the daughter of Zur, a Midianite tribal chief) to the very entrance of the tent of meeting to *worship* Baal of Peor (cf. **Numbers 25:6–8, 14–18**). A zealous priest named Phinehas, son of Eleazar, son of Aaron, killed the Israelite man and the Midianite woman, thereby stopping the plague that had killed 24,000 Israelites (**Numbers 25:6–9**). Phinehas' honorable actions resulted in the Lord's covenant promise of a "lasting priesthood" for Phinehas and his descendants[7] (**Numbers 25:10–13**). Later during the time of the judges, the Midianites became an instrument of Yahweh to punish his people Israel for their sinful ways: "The Israelites did evil in the eyes of the Lord, and for seven years he gave them into the hands of the Midianites" (**Judges 6:1**; see **vv. 1–6**). When the Israelites called on God, he sent Gideon the judge to deliver them from Midianite oppression (**Judges 8:28**; see **Judges 6–8**).

Sheba (modern-day Yemen) is most closely connected in Scripture with the famous unnamed queen of Sheba[8] who ruled a land bereft of agriculture but rich in spices, precious metals, and gemstones. When she heard of Solomon's fame and wisdom, she traveled to Jerusalem "to test him with hard questions" (**1 Kings 10:1**) and gave him 120 talents of gold, spices in great quantity, and precious stones (**1 Kings 10:1–10; 2 Chronicles 9:1–9**).

Notes

1. Keturah, a concubine of Abraham (**1 Chronicles 1:32**), became his legitimate wife upon Sarah's death (**Genesis 25:1**). The term "concubine" (Heb.; פִּילֶגֶשׁ *pilegesh*) typically describes a woman in a king's harem who served the royal family in some way but who was also subject to being a sex partner to the king at his pleasure. Abraham's social status was such that he could have had at least a modest harem (cf. **Genesis 24:35**). The fact that Keturah is called "wife" (Heb. אִשָּׁה; *ishah*) in **Genesis 25:1** suggests that even women of such low estate could become wives and even queens. The name "Keturah" derives from Hebrew קְטֹרֶת (*qetoreth*), "fragrance, incense," redolent of the famous spice trade.

2. The more recent name Saba reflects the ancient name Sheba and establishes the location. Sheba, son of Jokshan, son of Keturah (**Genesis 25:3; 1 Chronicles 1:32**), is not (1) Sheba, the son of Raamah (a Ham descendant) in **Genesis 10:7**, where Sheba also had a brother named Dedan, nor (2) Sheba, son of Joktan, son of Eber (a Shem descendant) in **Genesis 10:22–28**; see chart "**Genesis 10**: Noah's Descendants: The Table of Seventy Nations."

3. Jeremiah's connection of Dedan with Tema (**Jeremiah 25:23**) and Isaiah's reference to "Dedanites" and their caravans (**Isaiah 21:13–14**) portrays them as a nomadic, desert people who were merchants (cf. **Ezekiel 25:13; 27:15–20; 38:13**). Dedan, the son of Jokshan in the Abraham–Keturah line (**Genesis 25:3; 1 Chronicles 1:32**), is not the Dedan in the Ham–Cush–Raamah–Dedan line of descendants listed in the Table of Nations in **Genesis 10:7** (where Dedan also had a brother named Sheba); see chart "**Genesis 10**: Noah's Descendants: The Table of Seventy Nations."

4. Of the Dedan descendants—"Ashurites, the Letushites and the Leummites" (**Genesis 25:3**)—only the Ashurites are mentioned elsewhere (**2 Samuel 2:9; Ezekiel 27:23**). The Ashurites should by no means be equated with the Assyrians because of both geographical and chronological considerations (cf. **Genesis 10:11, 22**).

5. Leummites is a place or ethnic name that means "people" in general or perhaps "tribe" (thus "לְאֹם," *HALOT* 1:513). Appearing last in the chart above, it might be intended as a nonspecific *etcetera*.

6. The inhabitants of the land to the east of Canaan are loosely associated with Abraham: the Amalekites of Amalek, the grandson of Esau (**Judges 6:3**); the Moabites and Ammonites, of Moab and Ammon, respectively, the sons of Lot (**Ezekiel 25:10**); and the Kedarites of Kedar, the son of Ishmael (**Jeremiah 49:28**); see the respective charts "**Genesis 36**: Amalek, the Ancestor of the Amalekites," "**Genesis 11**: Lot and His Descendants, the Moabites and Ammonites," and "**Genesis 16**: Ishmael and His Descendants, the Ishmaelites."

7. See chart "**1 Chronicles 6**: Levi: High Priests, Priests, Levites, and Musicians in Solomon's Temple."

8. The queen of Sheba is remembered and highly praised by these words of Jesus: "The Queen of the South will rise at the judgment with this generation and condemn it; for she came from the ends of the earth to listen to Solomon's wisdom, and now something greater than Solomon is here" (**Matthew 12:42; Luke 11:31**).

GENESIS 35: THE TWELVE SONS OF JACOB, THE EPONYMOUS ORIGINATORS OF THE TWELVE TRIBES OF ISRAEL[1]

Approximate Dating: Jacob lived from ca. 2006 to 1859 B.C.; all his sons, except Benjamin, were born during his twenty-year sojourn in Paddan Aram, ca. 1929–1909 B.C.[2, 3, 4] ***Relevant Scriptures:*** **Genesis 35:22–26;** also **1 Chronicles 2:1–2**

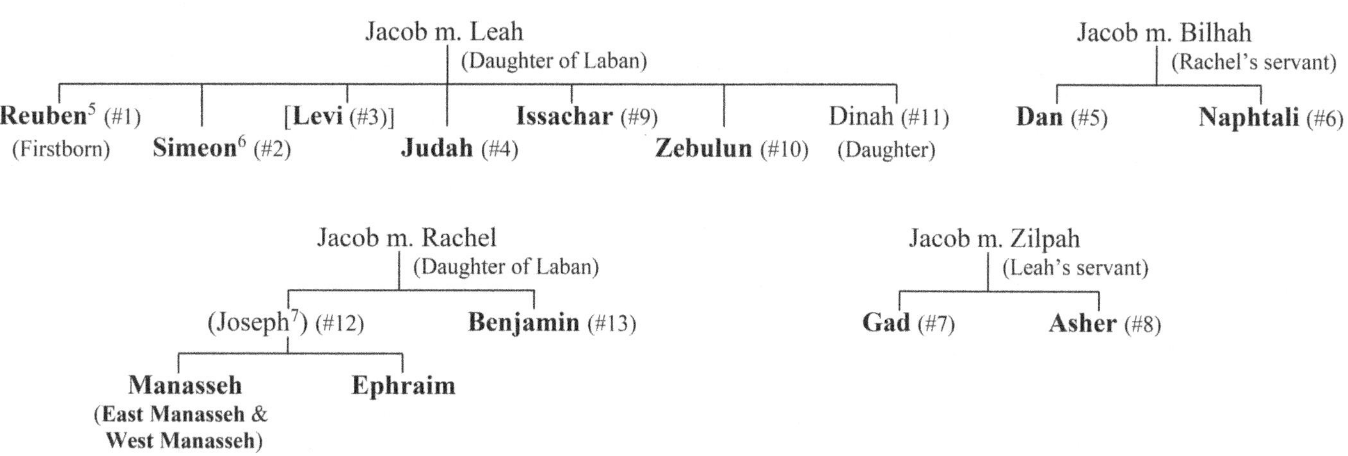

The Blessings on the Sons and Tribes of Israel by Jacob and Moses According to Birth Order

Order of Birth & Meaning of the Son's Name[8] (Genesis 29–30, 35)		Jacob's Blessing (Genesis 49:1–27; ca. 1859 B.C.)		Moses' Blessing (Deuteronomy 33:1–29; ca. 1406 B.C.)	
Reuben	"Look! A Son!"	Reuben	Loss of pre-eminence	Reuben	"May he live again"
Simeon	"He (God) has heard"	Simeon	Cursed for evil temper	Judah	"Contender for his people"
Levi	"Joined to me"/"Attached"	Levi	To be scattered	Levi	"High priest and teacher"
Judah	"Praise"	Judah	Coming ruler	Benjamin	"Will live in safety with God"
Dan	"Judging"	Zebulun	Safe harbor	Joseph (Ephraim)	"The fruitful one"
Naphtali	"Wrestling"	Issachar	Lowly servant	Joseph (Manasseh)	"Forget (the times of trouble)"
Gad	"Good fortune"	Dan	snakelike judge	Zebulun	"Rejoicing in life" with his brother; "capable seaman"
Asher	"Happy one"	Gad	An overcomer	Issachar	"Who will prosper in industry"
Issachar	"(My) reward"	Asher	Prosperous	Gad	"Executer of righteousness"
Zebulun	"Dwelling (with me)"	Naphtali	Speaker of good	Dan	"A young stalking lion"
Joseph	"May He add (more)"	Joseph	"(God) will increase (him)"	Naphtali	"In favor with the Lord"; inheritance to the Sea of Galilee
Benjamin	"(My) right hand"	Benjamin	"Divider of spoil"	Asher	"Wealthy and blessed"

Some Thoughts on the Table

To understand the table, it is important to take note of the timeline. One of the primary principles of biblical interpretation is progressive revelation. The comparative list can be derived, for example, by observing the positioning of the sons/tribes with the passing of time. Much had happened in the 450 plus years between the blessing of Jacob (1859 B.C.) and the blessing of Moses (1406 B.C.). Reuben had failed but will be re-energized; Simeon the listener will be a speaker; Levi will be scattered in his priestly duties; Judah the king will stand firm for his people; Dan the lowly snake will become a mighty lion; Naphtali, prophet-like, will bear his message afar; Gad, the overcomer, will use his gift for righteousness; Asher will be happy with prosperity and wealth; Issachar, the servant, will someday make his mark in business; Zebulun, who dwells with Yahweh, will find joy in doing so; Joseph, through his two sons, will forget his troubles and become fruitful; and Benjamin, at God's right hand, will live with him forever.

Biblical and Theological Significance

Jacob, a twin son of Isaac and Rebekah, was born ca. 2006 B.C.; he lived for the last seventeen years of his life (i.e., age 130–147) in Egypt, during Dynasty 12 (ca. 1991–1773 B.C.),[9] and died at the age of 147 in ca. 1859 B.C. (**Genesis 47:28**). Through a series of circumstances brought about largely by Jacob's sins and those of his sons (**Genesis 37:4–11, 25–28; 38:1–30**), and in fulfillment of a prophecy to Abraham centuries earlier (**Genesis 15:12–16**), Jacob's family found their resources in Canaan to be inadequate for survival, and thus Jacob moved his family *en masse* to Egypt, the breadbasket of the ancient world. The migration of the seventy-member family[10] was undertaken ca. 1876 B.C. (**1 Kings 6:1**; cf. **Exodus 12:40**).

Joseph was already there, having been sold into slavery by his own brothers about 1898 B.C. (cf. **Genesis 37:23-31, 36, 39:1-6**), but through the providence of God he was elevated to a position in the government of Egypt as a sort of Minister of Agriculture.[11] The following centuries were at first advantageous to Israel, but then a Pharaoh ascended the throne "to whom Joseph meant nothing," and Joseph's people were no longer treated fairly and favorably (**Exodus 1:8; Acts 7:18**). In fact, during the regime of Dynasty 18 (ca. 1570–1295 B.C.),[12] the Israelites were reduced to slavery. Then, "at the end of the 430 years, to the very day" (**Exodus 12:41**), under the leadership of Moses, Israel left Egypt in a miraculous exodus (1446 B.C.) and, after the wilderness sojourn, returned to Canaan forty years later (1406 B.C.).

This genealogy is important in that it lists all twelve sons of Jacob who, in due time, lent their names to the twelve tribes that descended from them. In turn, the names marked the geographical nomenclatures of the land of Israel following the conquest and subsequent distribution of the land amongst them. The tribe of Levi had been selected to be the custodians of the priesthood in the tabernacle (and later in the temple) and the Levitical divisions who assisted the priesthood (cf. **Exodus 28–30; Numbers 25:7–13; Deuteronomy 18:1-2** and charts "**1 Chronicles 6**: Levi – High Priest, Priests, Levites, and Musicians in Solomon's Temple" and "**1 Chronicles 24**: Genealogical Registry of the 24 Divisions of Kohathite Attending Priests who Rotated Service in Solomon's Temple"). They were left with no property except for the forty-eight cities throughout the land where sanctuaries were available for sacrifice and other aspects of worship (**Numbers 35:1–8; Joshua 21:1–42**), thereby fulfilling Jacob's curse on Levi's (and Simeon's) intemperate behavior regarding the people of Shechem (**Genesis 34:1–31; Numbers 18:20–24; Deuteronomy 10:9; Joshua 13:14**). As for Simeon, the tribe was so small and impotent that it was given an inheritance of land within the tribe of Judah (**Joshua 19:1–9**).

To compensate for the loss of Levi's territory and Simeon's absorption into Judah, the tribes of Ephraim and Manasseh (the sons of Joseph) were substituted to make up the twelve-tribe ideal. Ephraim was designated an allotment in the central hill country, and because of the richness of its soils and abundance of its forests and other assets, it grew to be chief of the western tribes, so much so that the whole area west of the Jordan became known as *Ephraim* (as well as *Israel*), mainly in the prophets (**Isaiah 7:2–17; 11:13; Jeremiah 31:6–20; Hosea 4:17; 5:3–14**; and so on). Manasseh was split into two geographic locations, with half the tribe east of the Jordan River and the other half west of the river (i.e., East and West Manasseh).

Judah also is of special interest in light of Jacob's blessing[13] of the tribe and prediction of its royal and messianic future, including King David and the Greater David, Jesus Christ the Lord (**Genesis 49:10; Matthew 21:9; Romans 1:3**). The tribe of Judah was given the largest allotment of the twelve. David was, of course, Judah's most celebrated native son until another was born a millennium later in Bethlehem of Judah, one who surpassed him. When the nation of Israel was divided into two following Solomon's death in 931 B.C., *Judah* came to mean the entire Southern Kingdom in the same manner that *Ephraim* came to mean the entire Northern Kingdom (**1 Kings 12:20; 14:21; 2 Chronicles 11:12–17; Psalm 78:68; 108:8; Isaiah 7:17; 11:13; Jeremiah 33:7, 14; Zechariah 11:14**).

Notes

1. The numbers next to the names indicate the birth order of Jacob's children.

2. To understand the timeframe of the birth of Jacob's 12 sons, the following details are offered:

Dating of the patriarchs. Abraham was born in 2166 B.C. and died in 1991 B.C. at the age of 175 (**Genesis 25:7**); Sarah, 10 years younger than Abraham, was born in 2156 B.C. and died in 2029 B.C. at the age of 127 (cf. **Genesis 17:17; 23:1**). Isaac was born to Abraham and Sarah in 2066 B.C. when Abraham was 100 and Sarah was 90 (**Genesis 17:17; 21:5**). Isaac was 40 when he married Rebekah in ca. 2026 B.C. (**Genesis 25:20**). Isaac was 60 when his wife Rebekah gave birth to twin boys (Esau and Jacob) in 2006 B.C. (**Genesis 25:26**). When Isaac died in 1886 B.C. at the age of 180 (**Genesis 35:28**), he was buried by both of his sons who, at that time, were 120 years old. Jacob lived from 2006 to 1859 B.C. and died at the age of 147 (**Genesis 47:28**). He spent the last 17 years of his life—from age 130 to 147—in Egypt, corresponding to the years 1876–1859 B.C. (**Genesis 47:9**).

Dating of Jacob's sojourn in Paddan Aram and the birth of Ishmael. Looking back, it seems quite clear that Jacob spent 20 years in all at Paddan Aram with his father-in-law Laban (**Genesis 31:38, 41**), where he took four wives in marriage (Leah, Rachel, Bilhah and Zilpah) and sired eleven of his twelve sons (cf. Genesis 30:25; 31:38, 41) the last son, Benjamin, was not born until Jacob returned to Canaan from Paddan Aram (cf. **Genesis 35:9–18**). **Genesis 28:6–9** shows that Jacob's journey from Canaan to Paddan Aram to find a wife was *after* his brother Esau's marriage to Judith and Adah/Basemath in 1966 B.C. **Genesis 26:34** clarifies that, at the time of his marriage, Esau (born in 2006 B.C.) was 40 years old—so it can be deduced that Jacob left for Paddan Aram no earlier than 1966 B.C. Furthermore, the narrative details show that Jacob's journey to Paddan Aram was *before* Esau married Mahalath/Basemath (the daughter of Ishmael)—"He [Esau] went to Ishmael and married Mahalath, the sister of Nebaioth and daughter of Ishmael son of Abraham, in addition to the wives he already had" (**Genesis 28:9**). Ishmael was born to Hagar in 2080 B.C. when Abraham was 86 years old. Ishmael died at the age of 137 in 1943 B.C. (**Genesis 16:16; 25:17**). The text indicates that Jacob was in Paddan Aram for a total of 20 years—"I [Jacob] have been with you [Laban] for twenty years now . . . for the twenty years I was in your household. I worked for you fourteen years for your two daughters [Leah and Rachel] and six years for your flocks" (**Genesis 31:38, 41**). To determine the exact twenty years that Jacob lived in Paddan Aram, one must work backwards and consider Joseph's story and his chronology as well.

Dating of Joseph. Joseph was born in Paddan Aram (**Genesis 30:24**). At age 17 he was sold into slavery by his brothers (**Genesis 37:2, 19–28**) and rose to power in Egypt. Eventually, at age 30, he was installed as a kind of minister of agriculture in charge of the whole land of Egypt and second-in-command to the pharaoh (**Genesis 41:43, 46**), all *before* the "seven years of abundance" (**Genesis 41:29, 34, 47–48, 53**). The time interval of the "years of abundance" is established to be ca. 1884–1878 B.C. See Biblical and Theological Significance, paragraph 1 in chart "**Genesis 37**: Joseph and His Sons Manasseh and Ephraim." This means that Joseph was born ca. 1915 B.C. (1885 + 30 = 1915). Jacob declared that he loved Joseph more than any of his other sons "because he had been born to him in his old age" (**Genesis 37:3**); at Joseph's birth, Jacob (who was born in 2006 B.C.) would have been 91 years old.

At age 17, Joseph was sold into slavery to Potiphar in 1898 B.C. (**Genesis 37:2**). For about a decade, from 1898–1888 B.C., he served Potiphar (**Genesis 37:36; 39:1–6**). Later, after the false accusation of Potiphar's wife (**Genesis 39:7–20**), Joseph was imprisoned for two years, ca. 1887–1886 B.C. (**Genesis 41:1**). After interpreting Pharaoh's dreams, Joseph was appointed by the Pharaoh as second-in-command in the Egyptian court and placed over the whole land of Egypt (**Genesis 41:41, 43**), all before the "seven years of abundance" began in 1884 B.C. Joseph died at the age of 110 years in 1805 B.C. (**Genesis 50:22**).

Conclusions regarding dating. Viewing now all the foregoing data, it is clear that if Jacob spent only 20 years in Paddan Aram, he was there from ca. 1929–1909 B.C.—seven years in service to Laban to marry Leah (1929–1923 B.C.) and seven more years to marry Rachel (1922–1916 B.C.; **Genesis 29:26–30**)—although Laban gave both wives to Jacob after Leah's bridal week (**Genesis 29:27**). Then, after the birth of Joseph in 1915 B.C. (**Genesis 30:25**) and convinced by Laban to stay longer (**Genesis 30:25–36**), Jacob worked an additional six years for the flocks (1915–1909; **Genesis 31:41**)—for a total of 20 years. Jacob then returned to Canaan in ca. 1909 B.C. Given the 20-year timeframe argued here, Esau could not have met with Ishmael to arrange the marriage to Mahalath/Basemath (**Genesis 28:9**), for Ishmael had died in 1943 B.C. (see discussion above, in "Dating of Jacob's Sojourn"). It seems best to propose that **Genesis 28:9** records that Esau met with Ishmael's eldest son, Nebaioth, to arrange his marriage to Nebaioth's sister, Mahalath/Basemath. (Other scholars have noted the chronological difficulties of **Genesis 28:9** and have tried to reconcile the issues by proposing that, instead of Jacob being in Paddan Aram for twenty years, that he was there for forty years. However, we hold to the twenty-year sojourn with the aforementioned caveat about Nebaioth.) For an additional discussion on Jacob's twenty-year sojourn in Paddan Aram, see Andrew E. Steinmann, *From Abraham to Paul: A Biblical Chronology* (St. Louis: Concordia, 2011), 74–75.

3. At the age of 130, Jacob moved his family from Canaan to Egypt in 1876 B.C. (**Genesis 47:9**); see chart "**Genesis 46**: The Extended Family of Jacob (Seventy Descendants) Who Migrated to Egypt."

4. Eleven of Jacob's sons and his daughter Dinah were all born in Paddan Aram, whereas Benjamin, the youngest, was born after Jacob returned to Canaan, when the family was "on the way to Ephrath [Bethlehem]" (**Genesis 35:18–19**). These are the approximate dates and birth order: Reuben #1 in 1928 B.C. (**Genesis 29:32**); Simeon #2 in 1927 B.C. (**Genesis 29:33**); Levi #3 in 1926 B.C. (**Genesis 29:34**); Judah #4 in 1925 B.C. (**Genesis 29:35**); Dan #5 in 1924 B.C. (**Genesis 30:1–6**); Naphtali #6 in 1923 B.C. (**Genesis 30:7–8**); Gad #7 in 1922 B.C. (**Genesis 30:9–11**); Asher #8 in 1921 B.C. (**Genesis 30:12–13**); Issachar #9 in 1920 B.C. (**Genesis 30:14–18**); Zebulun #10 in 1919 B.C. (**Genesis 30:19–20**); Dinah #11 in 1918 B.C. (**Genesis 30:21**); Joseph #12 in 1915 B.C. (**Genesis 30:22–24**); Benjamin #13 in 1908 B.C. (**Genesis 35:18**).

For a comparative discussion of the birthdates of Jacob's children, see Steinmann, *From Abraham to Paul*, 76–78.

5. For his moral violation in having sexual relations with his father's concubine Bilhah (**Genesis 35:22**), Reuben lost all the primogeniture benefits of a firstborn son and the patriarchy in due time. In fact, his motive in having sexual contact with Bilhah may well be seen as a grab for primacy even before Jacob died. Of particular importance was the transfer of the firstborn's legacy to "the sons of Joseph" (**1 Chronicles 5:1**). As the Chronicler explains, "though Judah was the strongest of his brothers and a ruler came from him, the rights of the firstborn [the double share that had been Reuben's] belonged to Joseph [and his sons, Ephraim and Manasseh]" (**1 Chronicles 5:2**; cf. **Deuteronomy 21:17**).

6. Jacob's "hated" wife—the *less loved* Leah—saw that God was making up for her less-than-exalted status in the family by giving her not only Reuben, the first of Jacob's children, but now a second (**Genesis 29:33**). Simeon's very name שִׁמְעוֹן (*shimon*), "having made things right" ("שִׁמְעוֹן," *HALOT* 2:1576), attests to this. However, his secondary position seems somewhat accentuated again. By the time of the second tribal census, Simeon's tribe was the smallest of all, barely half that of his elder brother Reuben (i.e., first census: 59,300 men in Simeon's tribe and 46,500 men in Reuben's tribe, **Numbers 1:21, 23** compared to the second census: 22,200 men in Simeon's tribe and 43,730 men in Reuben's tribe, **Numbers 26:7, 14**). The narrative gives no hint as to the radical changes that took place. Perhaps the explanation is to be found in dying Jacob's prophetic blessing of his sons. There, Simeon (along with Levi) is scolded for his barbaric revenge against Shechem, son of Hamor the Hivite, who had raped their sister Dinah (**Genesis 34:1–4, 25–31**). Jacob prophesied that God would "scatter them in Jacob and disperse them in Israel" (**Genesis 49:7**). This came to pass in the Levites and priests having no land inheritance (**Numbers 18:23-24; 26:26; 62; 35:2; Deuteronomy 10:2; 12:12; 14:27, 29; Joshua 18:7; 21:1-44**), and the Simeonites being absorbed into Judah because of the paucity of their population (**Joshua 19:1, 9; 1 Chronicles 4:27).**

7. Joseph was born in Paddan Aram in 1915 B.C. See paragraph 2 under Biblical and Theological Significance and note 2, "Dating of Joseph." before Jacob's family moved to Canaan in ca. 1909 B.C. (**Genesis 30:25**). Joseph was Jacob's favorite son "because he had been born to him in his old age" (**Genesis 37:3**; cf. **44:20**)—given that Jacob was born ca. 2006 B.C., he would have been 91 years old at the time of Joseph's birth. While in Egypt "Pharaoh gave Joseph the name Zaphenath-Paneah and gave him Asenath daughter of Potiphera, priest of On, to be his wife" (**Genesis 41:45**). Asenath bore Joseph two sons, Manasseh and Ephraim, "before the years of famine came" (**Genesis 41:50–52; 46:20, 27**). Joseph lived to see "the third generation of Ephraim's children . . . [and] the children of Makir son of Manasseh" (**Genesis 50:22–23**). Joseph died in ca. 1805 B.C. at the age of 110 and was "embalmed . . . [and] . . . placed in a coffin in Egypt" (**Genesis 50:26**). Joseph had made the Israelites swear an oath that when they left Egypt, they would carry his bones with them; his bones were carried out of Egypt with Moses and those of the exodus generation in 1446 B.C. (**Genesis 50:25; Exodus 13:19; Hebrews 11:22**). See chart "Genesis 37: Joseph and His Sons Manasseh and Ephraim."

8. Translations by E. H. Merrill.

9. See chart "**Supplement 1**: The Pharaohs of the Twelfth and Eighteenth Dynasties of Egypt."

10. See chart "**Genesis 46**: The Extended Family of Jacob (Seventy Descendants) Who Migrated to Egypt."

11. All this took place during the Twelfth Dynasty of Egypt (1991–1786 B.C./1985–1773 B.C.); depending on Egyptian chronology, this took place in the reigns of Sesostris II (ca. 1897–1878 B.C./1877–1870 B.C.) and Sesostris III (ca. 1878–1843 B.C./1870–1831 B.C.). The dates here and elsewhere in the chart are based on **1 Kings 6:1,** which states that the foundation of Solomon's great temple was laid 480 years after the exodus. Since all dates of events that late in Israel's history have been established, 480 years earlier than 966 B.C. yields 1446 B.C. for the exodus. The biblical text prior to and following these dates is adequate to provide a credible chronology as early as Abraham, if not earlier. See Eugene H. Merrill, *Kingdom of Priests: A History of Old Testament Israel* (Grand Rapids: Baker, 1996), 50.

12. See chart "**Supplement 1**: The Pharaohs of the Twelfth and Eighteenth Dynasties of Egypt."

13. Jacob's blessing on his twelve sons is found in **Genesis 49:2–27**. Moses' blessing on the Israelite tribes before they entered the promised land is found in **Deuteronomy 33:6–29**.

GENESIS 36: ESAU, THE ANCESTOR OF THE EDOMITES

Approximate Dating: time of the patriarchs; Abraham, ca. 2166–1991 B.C.; Isaac, ca. 2066–1886 B.C.; Esau, ca. 2006–1840 B.C.;[1] and Esau's twin brother, Jacob, ca. 2006–1859 B.C.[2] ***Relevant Scriptures:*** **Genesis 36:1–19, 40–43**; also **1 Chronicles 1:34–37, 51b–54**

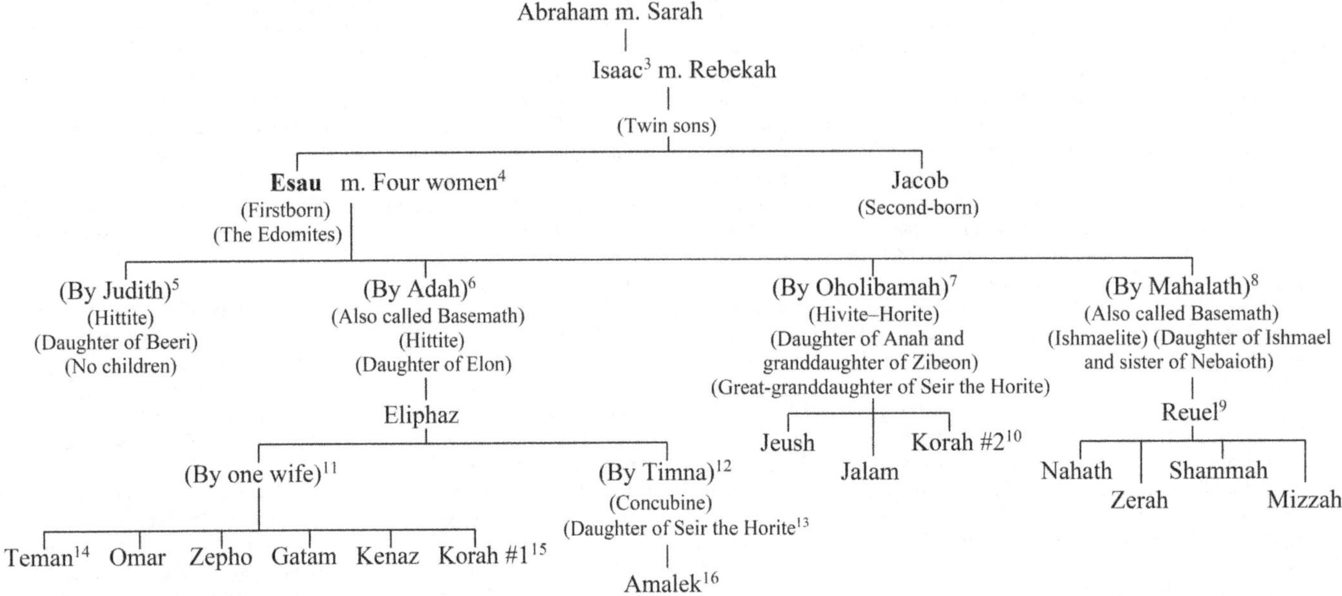

Alvah, Jetheth, Elah, Pinon, Mibzar, Magdiel and Iram have no known genealogy.

Biblical and Theological Significance

Esau, the elder twin brother of Jacob, was the primogenitor of the Edomites (Esauites; **Genesis 25:25; 36:1, 9**), a seminomadic people who occupied Edom[17] (also called Seir[18]), a wilderness area southeast and south of the Dead Sea along the Arabah depression of the Great Rift Valley (**Genesis 36:6–8**). Given their common descent from Isaac, the Edomites and Israelites were close relatives, but the lands they occupied were separate. They each had so many possessions that their lands could not sustain them both, so Esau took his family, servants, livestock, and everything else he had accumulated in Canaan and moved far away from his brother Jacob. The indigenous peoples of Seir, known as "Horites,"[19] were driven out and slaughtered by Esau who then settled in their place (**Deuteronomy 2:12, 22**). In the same way, Jacob ("Israel") later drove out the inhabitants of Canaan, the land Yahweh had given them as a possession (**Deuteronomy 2:12, 22**). At some point, the toponym "Seir" was replaced by "Edom" (**Genesis 32:3; 36:8; Deuteronomy 2:22; Joshua 24:4; Judges 5:4**). Ancient Bozrah served as Edom's capital and the location of the royal palace (cf. **Isaiah 34:6; 63:1; Jeremiah 49:13, 22; Amos 1:12**). More than a thousand years later, the land of Edom was inhabited by the Nabataeans (occupying the region of Nabatea southeast of the Dead Sea and in Petra) and the Idumaeans (occupying the region of Idumea located west of the Arabah), from whom sprang Herod the Great.[20]

The sociological development of the Edomite peoples as narrated in **Genesis 36** is as follows: (1) patriarchal, with Esau as the tribal patriarch (**vv. 1–8**); (2) Esau's genealogy for three generations (**vv. 9–14**); and (3) Esau's later descendants, called "chieftains,"[21] who were city-state rulers (*alluphim* in Hebrew; **vv. 15–19**). It appears that **Genesis 36:20–30** is retrospective to a time *prior* to Esau when city-states were in vogue with the indigenous Horites (**vv. 20, 29, 30**) and the nation was ruled by a succession of kings (see the dynastic king-list in **vv. 31–39**).[22] Then, almost as an after-thought, a few more of Esau's progeny are listed as *alluphim*-rulers (**vv. 40–42**), none of whom is otherwise mentioned. Amalek, Esau's grandson (**v. 12**), was the ancestor of the Amalekites, a nation constantly at war with Israel (cf. **Numbers 14:45; Judges 6:3, 33; 10:12; 1 Samuel 30:1, 18; 1 Chronicles 4:43**).

The message to be appropriated here is the tragic but predictable long-term results of self-centered greediness on the one hand and vengeance of brother against brother on the other. The story of Jacob and Esau—and later the Israelites and Edomites—is a story of greed and vengeance. Jacob ("Israel"), though indeed God's chosen one, took stealthy measures to secure the patriarchal blessing for himself rather than wait on God (**Genesis 25:23, 31–34**). Esau, on the other hand, sought to retrieve his estate by killing his deceitful brother (**Genesis 27:41–45**). The nations of Israel and Edom went on to engage in incessant warfare till both were at last judged by God and carried off into captivity (**Numbers 20:14–21; 1 Samuel 14:47–48; 1 Kings 11:14–16; 2 Kings 8:20–24; Jeremiah 49:7–22; Ezekiel 25:12–14**). Clearly, Esau's intermarriage with the surrounding nonchosen, pagan nations was doomed to miscarry.

Notes

1. Based on life expectancy in those times. There is no scriptural record of Esau's death.

2. For these dates and how they are determined, see Eugene H. Merrill, *Kingdom of Priests: A History of Old Testament Israel* 2nd ed. (Grand Rapids: Baker Academic, 2008), 34–35, 64–66, 96. Also, see chart "**Genesis 35**: The Twelve Sons of Jacob, the Eponymous Originators of the Twelve Tribes of Israel."

3. Isaac was 60 years old when Jacob and Esau were born in ca. 2006 B.C. (**Genesis 25:26**).

4. See chart "**Genesis 36**: Esau's Wives."

5. Presumably, Esau's wife Judith bore him no children.

6. "Adah daughter of Elon the Hittite" (**Genesis 36:2**) is also called "Basemath daughter of Elon the Hittite" (**26:34**). Adah/Basemath is not Basemath the Ishmaelite, another wife of Esau; see note 8.

7. "Oholibamah, daughter of Anah and granddaughter of Zibeon the Hivite" (**Genesis 36:2**), is called "Oholibamah, daughter of Anah and granddaughter of Zibeon [the Horite]" (**Genesis 36:14**); her father, Anah, was the son of Zibeon and the grandson of Seir the Horite (**Genesis 36:20–21, 24–25**).

8. Mahalath (**Genesis 28:9**) and Basemath (**Genesis 36:3–4, 10, 13, 17**) are the same person. She was an Ishmaelite (**Genesis 28:9; 36:3**)—the daughter of Ishmael, the son of Abraham and Hagar (**Genesis 16:15–16; 25:12; 1 Chronicles 1:28**), and the sister of Nebaioth, the firstborn son of Ishmael (**Genesis 28:9; 36:3; 1 Chronicles 1:29**). Esau married Mahalath "in addition to the wives he already had" (**Genesis 28:9**). See chart "**Genesis 16**: Ishmael and His Descendants, the Ishmaelites." Mahalath/Basemath should not be confused with another wife of Esau named Adah/Basemath; see note 6.

9. Reuel (**Genesis 36:4, 10, 13, 17; 1 Chronicles1:36–37**), the son of Esau and Mahalath/Basemath the Ishmaelite, who lived ca. 1950 BC, should not be confused with Reuel/Jethro the Kenite, the father-in-law of Moses who lived much earlier, in ca. 1550–1460 B.C. (**Exodus 2:16–21; 3:1; 4:18; 18:1–27; Numbers 10:29; Judges 4:11**); for the lineage of Jerhro/Reuel the Kenite, see chart "**Judges 4**: Heber and Jael (Kenites) and Their Descendants Who Comingled with the Pious Jabez–Rekabite Scribal Community near Jerusalem."

10. Two chiefs of Edom are named Korah: Korah (#1) was the *son* of Eliphaz and *grandson* of Adah (**Genesis 36:16**), whereas another Korah (#2) was the *son* of Oholibamah and Esau (**Genesis 36:5, 14, 18**). Korah #1 is not listed among the sons of Eliphaz in **Genesis 36:11**. It is possible that there is only *one* Korah figure whose ancestry results from the confusion of *Adah* (Esau's wife) with *Anah* (the father of Oholibamah).

11. Five sons/Edomite rulers—Teman, Omar, Zepho, Gatam, and Kenaz—are listed as the sons of Eliphaz and the grandsons of Adah/Basemath in **Genesis 36:11**. In **Genesis 36:15–16** *seven* sons/Edomite rulers—Teman, Omar, Zepho, Kenaz, Korah, Gatam, and Amalek—are listed as the grandsons of Adah. In the latter case, Amalek—the (illegitimate) son of Eliphaz's concubine (Timna; **Genesis 36:12**)—may have been considered the son of Eliphaz's primary wife. For Korah, see note 10.

12. Timna was the daughter of Seir the Horite and the sister of Lotan (**Genesis 36:20, 22; 1 Chronicles 1:38–39**).

13. For the family of Seir the Horite and the chiefs of Edom, see **Genesis 36:20–30** and **1 Chronicles 1:38–42**. For the dynasty of the Edomite kings, see **Genesis 36:31–39; 1 Chronicles 1:43–51;** and the chart "**1 Chronicles 1**: Genealogical Record of the Succession of the Kings of Edom."

14. Teman is a personal (**Genesis 36:11; 1 Chronicles 1:36**) and place name (**Ezekiel 25:13; Amos 1:12**). Teman/the Temanite clan of Edom was noted for wisdom (**Jeremiah 49:7; Obadiah 1:8–9**). Job's friend, "Eliphaz the Temanite," was from Teman (**Job 15:1; 22:1; 42:7, 9**); see chart "**Job 2**: Job's Friends–Zophar, Bildad, Eliphaz and Elihu"). In his vision, Habakkuk saw "the Holy One" coming from the east, from Teman (**Habakkuk 3:3**).

15. Regarding Korah, see note 10.

16. See chart "**Genesis 36**: Amalek, the Ancestor of the Amalekites."

17. The Semitic root of *Edom* (אֱדֹם) (*edom*) means "red," so called because of the reddish sandstone of the terrain.

18. The name Seir (שֵׂעִיר) is probably cognate to sair (שָׂעִיר), "hairy," as in **Genesis 27:11** where Esau is said to be hairy. Thus, the name of his land is a play on his own name. Moreover, a second play on words in naming comes about with Esau's ruddiness (אַדְמוֹנִי, *admoni*) at birth (**Genesis 25:25**). One can easily see the connection to the red land of Edom (אֱדֹם) here.

19. The name "Horite" (**Genesis 36:20–21, 29–30; Deuteronomy 2:12, 22**) is the Hebrew rendition of a people called "Hurrians" who were widely spread throughout the Middle East as early as 2000 B.C.

20. The Herods were of noble Idumean/Edomite ancestry (cf. **Mark 3:8**). Herod the Great's father, Antipater, was an Idumean noble, and his mother, Cypros, was Nabatean; see chart "**Matthew 2**: Herod the Great and the Herodian Dynasty."

21. A "chieftain" is a chief or military leader who unites families or a clan within a specific territory. "Chieftain" may be a better term than the common rendering, "chief." It is derived from אֶלֶף, *eleph*, "thousand," often used to describe populations or troop numbers, etc. In time, the leader or commander of such a contingent became known as אַלּוּף, *alluph*. When applied to a tribe leader (as here), the rendering "chieftain" fits well. See chart "**Genesis 36**: The Chiefs of Edom."

22. See charts "**1 Chronicles 1**: Seir the Horite" and "**1 Chronicles 1**: Genealogical Record of the Succession of Edomite Kings."

GENESIS 36: ESAU'S WIVES

Approximate Dating: ca. 2000–1900/1850 B.C.[1] ***Relevant Scriptures:*** **Genesis 36:1–21, 24–25, 29;** also **Genesis 5:32; 6:10; 9:18; 10:1–31; 11:26–29; 16:1, 3, 15–16; 19:33–38; 24:15, 24; 25:12–13; 26:34; 28:9; 1 Chronicles 1:28–29, 34–37, 40; Luke 3:34–38**

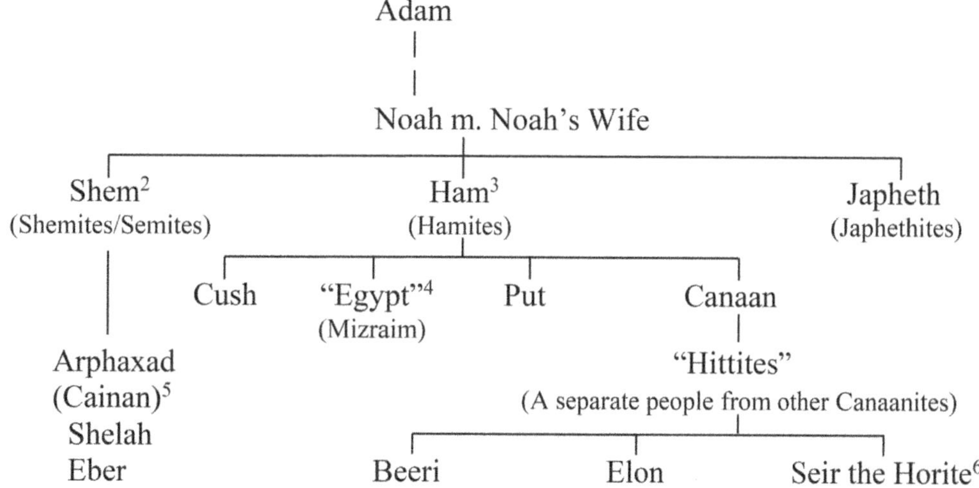

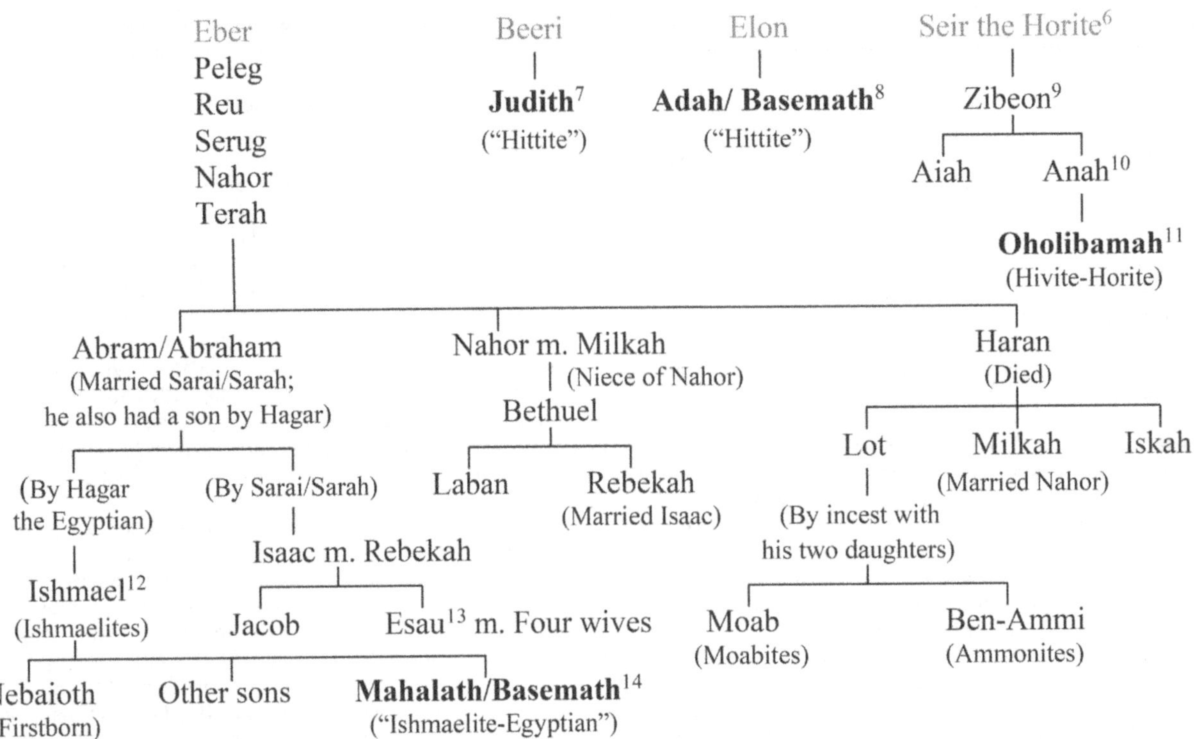

Biblical and Theological Significance

Initially, Esau married three Canaanite women—Judith, the daughter of Beeri; Adah/Basemath, the daughter of Elon the Hittite; and Oholibamah, the daughter of Anah and the granddaughter of Zibeon the Hivite/Horite (**Genesis 26:34; 36:2**). Esau was forty when he married Judith and Adah/Basemath. Isaac and Rebekah were disturbed by Esau's choice of these wives because they were from an idol-worshiping, indigenous Canaanite tribe, the Hittites, descended from Canaan's son Heth.[15] Rebekah was greatly disgusted by this and said that if Jacob did the same thing, she would rather die than live (**27:46**). After Esau learned that his father Isaac had blessed Jacob and commanded him not to marry Canaanite women but to go to Paddan Aram to get a wife, Esau realized how displeasing his Canaanite wives were to his father. He therefore took a fourth wife (a distant relative), named Mahalath (also called Basemath), the daughter of Ishmael and the granddaughter of Abraham (**Genesis 28:8–9**).

Esau's base character was revealed early on when he sold his birthright to Jacob, so his choice of such women as wives is not surprising. He was rebellious, not trusting his parents to arrange a marriage for him from among their monotheistic family. He preferred to make his own choices and perhaps thought it didn't matter since he was clearly his father's favorite son (**Genesis 25:28**).

Migrating eastward to be near his Ishmaelite relatives, Esau became a wealthy and powerful chieftain, settling in Seir, later named Edom ("Red") because of the reddish soil and stone and perhaps recalling the red lentil stew, the kind for which he sold his birthright (**Genesis 25:29–34**). Given that Edom was a land of rugged mountains, cold upper elevations, and inadequate rainfall that supported no more than subsistence agriculture, Esau's wives must have been rugged, fiercely independent women.

When they were older, Jacob and Esau met at the border of Canaan and reconciled (**Genesis 32:1–33:17**). Jacob presented a gift (**Genesis 32:8–11, 13–16**) to Esau who extended hospitality, in turn, to Jacob. Because of the size of each brother's herds and flocks and the sparseness of pasture, they went their separate ways—Esau returning to Edom (**Genesis 33:16**) and Jacob moving eventually to Shechem (**Genesis 33:18**), where his grandfather Abraham had first built an altar in Canaan (**Genesis 12:6–7**). Later, Esau and Jacob met again to bury their father, Isaac, in the family sepulcher[16] (**Genesis 35:29**). In spite of their truce, the descendants of Esau and his wives remained hostile toward Israel. This was particularly true of Adah/Basemath's son Eliphaz, the father of Amalek/the Amalekites,[17] a war-loving tribe who was always harassing Israel.

Other prominently hostile descendants included the Edomites, who refused to help Israel as they came into Canaan in 1406 B.C. (**Numbers 20:14–21**); Haman the Agagite, of a much later time (ca. 480–474 B.C.), who sought to eliminate the exilic Jews (**Esther 3:6, 8–9; 7:4–6**); and the Ishmaelites (**Psalm 83:2–6**). In the New Testament era, Idumea (the later name for Edom), ruled by the immoral and cruel Herods, persecuted and vilified the Jews (see chart "**Matthew 2**: Herod the Great and the Herodian Dynasty." When Jesus was born, Herod the Great was in power and ordered the slaughter of all the baby boys in Bethlehem to try to kill Jesus, the "king of the Jews" (**Matthew 2:2, 16**). All these attempts at genocide fulfilled Noah's curse/prophecy about the descendants of Ham's son Canaan (**Genesis 9:25–27**).

Many prophecies concerning Edom (**Isaiah 34:5–6; Jeremiah 49:7–18; Ezekiel 25:13; 35:1–15; Joel 3:19; Amos 1:11–12; Obadiah 1:1–21; Malachi 1:1–5**) were fulfilled within the span of Old and the New Testaments.

God's choice regarding the destinies of Esau and Jacob was made before they were born and was not dependent upon their actions. The differences in their characters proved God's wisdom in choosing Jacob as his covenant partner and messianic ancestor.

Excursus on the Terms "Heth/Hethites" and "Hitti/Hittites"

Some versions of the Bible incorrectly conflate "Hittites" with "Heth/Hethites" (e.g., **Genesis 10:15; 27:46**) and consider "Heth," the second son of Canaan and great-grandson of Noah (**Genesis 10:15**, NKJV), to be the forefather of the Hittites. In any case, both appear among the original occupants of the land of Canaan. Heth/Hethites are attested to in the Hebrew in **Genesis 10:15; 23:3, 5, 7, 10, 16, 18, 20; 25:10; 27:46; 49:32** and **1 Chronicles 1:13**; whereas Hittites are attested to in **Genesis 15:20; Exodus 3:8, 17; 13:5; 23:23; 34:11;** and **Deuteronomy 7:1; 20:17. Joshua 3:10** and **24:11** identify the "Canaanites" and the "Hittites" as *separate* people, though they are both descendants of Canaan, the son of Ham. It is not uncommon, of course, for peoples to be of one stock and yet be separate as families within the clan. **Numbers 13:29** speaks of the geographical location of various peoples and makes clear that the "Hittites" occupied an area different from that of the Canaanites (cf. **Joshua 9:1; 11:3; 12:8**).

The best resolution of the issues raised here is, first of all, to recognize that the so-called Hittites in Canaan must not be confused with the mighty Anatolian Empire of Hittites of ca. 1800–1200 B.C., nor were they "Hethites," a descriptor from a distinctly different root than "Hittites" and from a different language. Confusion abounds about connections among the Hethites, Hittites, Hivites, and Horites. The Hebrew spellings of each, in order, are חֵתִי, חִתִּי, חִוִּי, and חוֹרִי. It is obviously possible that ancient scribes working with poorly inscribed master texts and relatively crude writing instruments could have misread or miswrote names of these kinds. On the other hand, careful reading of the passages and contexts where these appear should lead to clear distinctions amongst them. Still, to guard against oversimplification in the matter, it is a fact that the issue of the identity of the Hittites in various parts and times of the Old Testament record has never been totally resolved because of the similarity of certain toponyms and varying chronological settings. What is known is that the Hittite predecessors (the Hatti) lived in Anatolia (now central Turkey) as early as 2000 B.C. It was 200 or more years after a Hittite overthrow of the Hatti that the Old Hittite Empire emerged (ca. 1800–1500 B.C.). The New Hittite Empire succeeded the Old Empire in 1500 B.C. and ended after 1200 B.C. Very likely, the Hittites of this period scattered throughout the northwest Aramean/Syrian region, including Canaan. This could explain references to them in Genesis as early as Abraham's latter years (he died in 1991 B.C.; cf. **Genesis 15:20; 23:1–20**). These imperial Hittites do not appear again in the Old Testament, having been forced to become an Egyptian vassal state and then to disappear after 1200 B.C.

The most important passage that poses difficulties of identification must be briefly addressed as follows:

A patriarchal burial place (Genesis 23:1–20; ca. 2029 B.C.):

When Abraham's wife Sarah died at Hebron in 2029 B.C., he asked of the sheik of the region, a certain "'Ephron the Hittite" (**Genesis 23:10**) or "Ephron son of Zohar" (**Genesis 23:8**), for a plot of ground in which to bury her. The general population of the area was the "people of the land," otherwise, "the citizens of Heth" (**Genesis 23:3, 5, 7, 10, 12, 13, 16, 18**). Briefly, the following points will perhaps clarify the conundrum under discussion:

- Not once is Heth identified as a person or group of people, only as a place (cf. **Genesis 23:3, 5, 7, 10, 16, 18, 20**).
- Ephron is never known as a "Hethite" but only as a "Hittite" (**Genesis 23:10**; see also **Genesis 49:29, 30; 50:13**).

חֵתִי and חִתִּי, *khethi* and *khitti,* are clearly different, even to the untrained eye. *Khethi* is likely derived from a root having to do with terror ("חַת," *HALOT* 1:363); the root of *khitti* is unknown, and its occurrence is as a gentilic only.

Notes

1. Esau and Jacob were born in 2006 B.C., but Esau's age at death is not recorded.

2. See chart "**Genesis 11**: Shem."

3. Noah pronounced a "curse" on his youngest son, Ham, the father of Canaan, because Ham told his brothers (Shem and Japheth) about Noah's drunkenness and nakedness, but he did nothing to cover his father's nakedness (**Genesis 9:20–25**). Ham's attitudes passed on to Canaan and then to Heth. The fulfillment of Noah's prediction—"Cursed be Canaan" in **Genesis 9:25**—is seen in the Canaanites, including the Hittites, whom God commanded the Israelites to eliminate in the time of the Conquest of Canaan (**Deuteronomy 20:17**).

4. In some translations, Egypt is called Mizraim.

5. For more information abou Cainan, see note 7 in chart "**Genesis 11**: Shem."

6. The sons of Seir the Horite—Lotan, Shobal, Zibeon, Anah, Dishon, Ezer, and Dishan—were Horite chiefs (**Genesis 36:20–21, 29–30; 1 Chronicles 1:38**; see **Genesis 36:20–30; 1 Chronicles 1:38–42**). See chart "**1 Chronicles 1**: Seir the Horite."

7. Judith is in the Adam–Noah–Ham (Hamite)–Canaan (Canaanite)–(Hittite)–Beeri line of descendants (cf. **Genesis 10:1, 6, 15; 1 Chronicles 1:1–16**). She is identified as "Judith daughter of Beeri the Hittite" (**Genesis 26:34**). If she bore children to Esau, they are not identified.

8. The daughter of Elon the Hittite is called Basemath in **Genesis 26:34** and Adah in **Genesis 36:2, 4, 10, 12, 16**.

Adah (also called Basemath) is in the Adam–Noah–Ham (Hamite)–Canaan (Canaanite)–(Hittite)–Elon line of descendants (cf. **Genesis 10:1, 6, 15; 26:34; 36:2; 1 Chronicles 1:1–15**). Adah/Basemath is a different person than Basemath/Mahalath (**Genesis 28:9; 36:3**), the Ishmaelite wife of Esau; see note 14. The grandsons of Adah/Basemath and Esau—Korah, Gatam, and Amalek—became chiefs of Edom (**Genesis 36:15–16; 1 Chronicles 1:36**).

9. Zibeon, a son of Seir the Horite, is identified as a "Horite" chief (**Genesis 36:20–21, 29**) and called Zibeon the "Hivite" (**Genesis 36:2**). See chart "**1 Chronicles 1**: Seir the Horite."

10. Anah was famous for discovering the hot springs in the desert (**Genesis 36:24**).

11. Oholibamah bore three sons to Esau—Jeush, Jalam, and Korah (**Genesis 36:5, 14, 18**). Oholibamah is in the Adam–Noah–Ham (Hamite)–Canaan (Canaanite)–(Hivite)–Zibeon (descendant of Seir the Horite)–Anah (descendant of Seir the Horite) line of descendants (cf. **Genesis 10:1, 6, 15–17; 36:2, 14, 20–25; 1 Chronicles 1:38, 40–41**). Oholibamah was the daughter of Anah, who discovered the hot springs in the desert, making her also the granddaughter of Zibeon, son of Seir the Horite (**Genesis 36:20–25**). The three sons of Oholibamah and Esau became chiefs in Edom (**Genesis 36:18**). Oholibamah means "my [God's] tent is in her" (**Genesis 36:40–41; 1 Chronicles 1:51–52**).

12. See chart "**Genesis 16**: Ishmael and His Descendants, the Ishmaelites."

13. See chart "**Genesis 36**: Esau, the Ancestor of the Edomites."

14. Mahalath in **Genesis 28:9** is the same person called Basemath in **Genesis 36:3–4, 10, 13, 17**; see note 8. The grandsons of Mahalath/Basemath—Nahath, Zerah, Shammah, and Mizzah—were chiefs of Edom (**Genesis 36:13, 17; 1 Chronicles 1:37**). After his twin brother, Jacob, had gone to Paddan Aram, Esau "realized how displeasing the Canaanite women [Judith, Adah/Basemath, and Oholibamah] were to his father Isaac" so he took the Ishmaelite Mahalath/Basemath in marriage "in addition to the wives he already had" (**Genesis 28:6–9**).

15. For a discussion of Hethites and the Hittites, see the excursus under "Biblical and Theological Significance."

16. The burial place of Abraham, Sarah, Isaac, Rebekah, Jacob, and Leah was in "the cave in the field of Machpelah, near Mamre in Canaan, which Abraham bought along with the field as a burial place from Ephron the Hittite" (**Genesis 49:30**).

17. See chart "**Genesis 36**: Amalek, the Ancestor of the Amalekites."

GENESIS 36: AMALEK, THE ANCESTOR OF THE AMALEKITES

Approximate Dating: exodus through the death of Haman, ca. 1446–474 B.C. ***Relevant Scriptures:*** **Genesis 36:1–30** also **26:34; 27:46; 28:8–9; 1 Chronicles 1:34–36; 38–39**

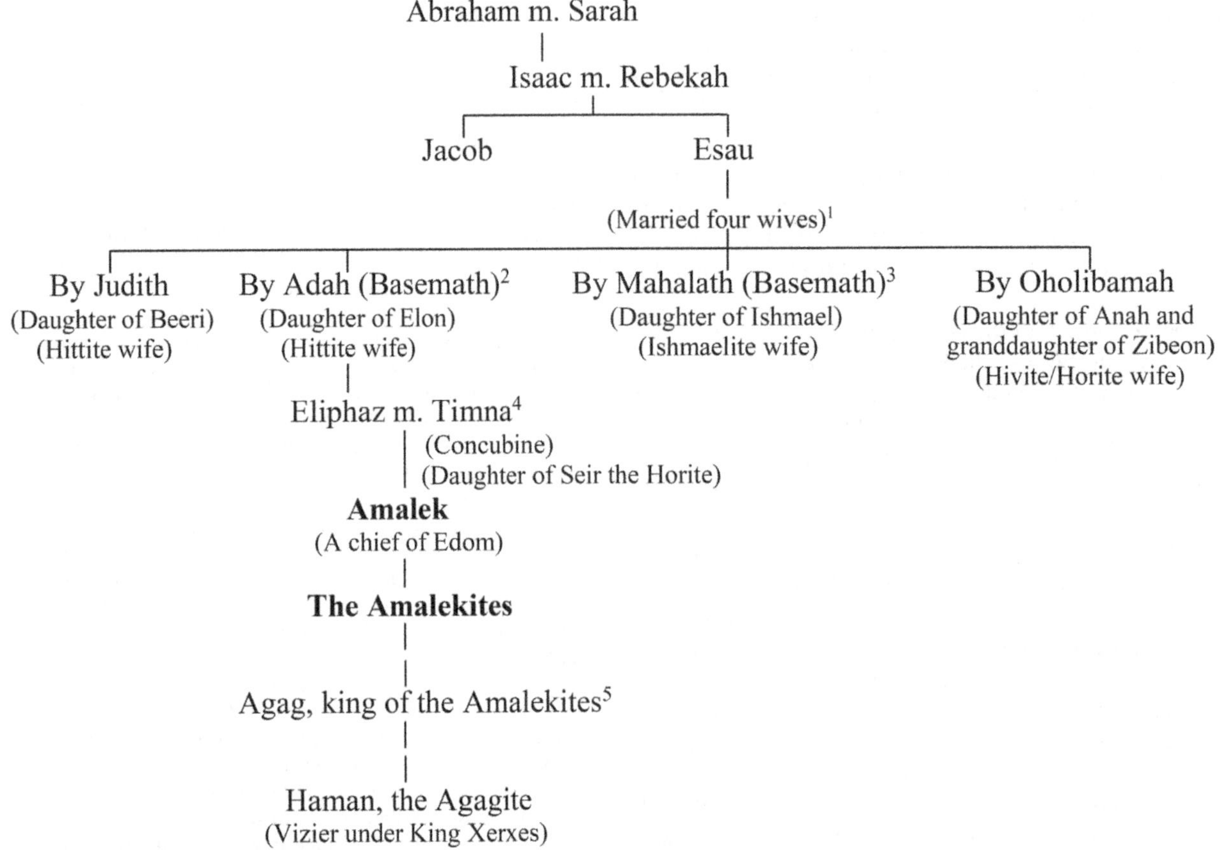

Biblical and Theological Significance

Amalek, the grandson of Esau and an *alluph* chief in Edom (**Genesis 36:16**), was the progenitor of the Amalekites, a fierce semi-nomadic group who was constantly at enmity with Israel. They inhabited the Negev region, "extending from Shur and Egypt" (**1 Samuel 27:8;** see also **Numbers 13:29**). During the exodus from Egypt, the Amalekites attacked the Israelites at Rephidim—"When you [Israel] were weary and worn out, they met you on your journey and attacked all who were lagging behind" (**Deuteronomy 25:18**; cf. **Exodus 17:8; Numbers 14:45**). They were such a powerful people that Moses and the Israelites had to wage war against them to be able to continue their trek to Canaan (**Exodus 17:8–16**). The Amalekites are described as a wicked people who "had no fear of God" (**Deuteronomy 25:18**) and were therefore placed under *herem,* God's ban on those whom he knew to be hopelessly unrepentant: "Because hands were lifted up against the throne of the LORD, the LORD will be at war against the Amalekites from generation to generation" (**Exodus 17:16; Deuteronomy 25:19**).

In the early days of the occupation of Canaan (1406–1350 B.C.) and the time of the judges (1350–1086 B.C.), the Amalekites again threatened Israel (cf. **Judges 3:13; 6:3–6, 33; 7:12; 10:12**). In the days of Saul (1051–1011 B.C.), God commanded him to "go and completely destroy those wicked people, the Amalekites; wage [holy] war against them until you have wiped them out" (**1 Samuel 15:18**; cf. **Deuteronomy 25:18–19; 1 Samuel 14:48**). Because Saul disobeyed God's command, his actions ultimately cost him the kingship (**1 Samuel 15**). David also fought against the

Amalekites (**2 Samuel 1:1**). The Amalekites raided the town of Ziklag and took "young and old" captive, including two of David's wives—"Ahinoam of Jezreel and Abigail, the widow of Nabal of Carmel"[6] (**1 Samuel 30:1–5**)—but David successfully rescued them (**vv. 3–20**). Much later in Israel's history (ca. 480–474 B.C.), Haman the Agagite (a descendant of King Agag and a high-ranking nobleman–vizier under King Xerxes) was responsible for initiating the pogrom against the Israelites who were in exile in Persia during the time of Queen Esther (cf. **Esther 3:1; 5:10, 14; 6:13; 9:7–10**).[7]

Thus, Esau, having sold his right of primogeniture status to Jacob, spurned the legacy of his father Isaac and produced through his lineage such wicked and bloody characters and peoples as the Amalekites, who incessantly engaged in strife with God's chosen people Israel and upon whom God declared holy war (**Exodus 17:16; 1 Samuel 15:1–33**). These inveterate enemies of Israel were the product of the ancient rivalry and subsequent hostility of brother against brother. Therefore, the covenant blessing of Abraham turned into cursing, the negative side of that promise.[8]

The principal theological rationale for tracing the descent of Esau, ending with the Amalekites, is twofold: (1) to demonstrate the consequences of disobeying God by rejecting his goodness and turning to worldly pursuits and self-satisfaction; and (2) to underscore how deleterious compromising with wickedness can be. It was through descent from Abraham that messianic salvation would transpire, but only as that descent maintained its covenant fidelity. Abraham himself failed to some degree, notably by taking Hagar as his wife. His intermarriage outside the covenant community, and his lack of complete faith in Yahweh, were reflected most egregiously in his grandson Esau, a man guilty on both counts. The lessons here should remind the church and those who profess faith in the Messiah of Abraham to guard against ungodly interrelationships and to maintain a bold faith in God lest they too follow in the dangerous path and tragic destiny of Esau and his descendants.

Notes

1. See chart "**Genesis 36**: Esau's Wives."
2. Adah (**Genesis 36:2, 12, 16**) is elsewhere called Basemath (**Genesis 26:34**).
3. Mahalath (**Genesis 28:9**) is elsewhere called Basemath (**Genesis 36:4, 10, 13, 17**).
4. Timna was a Horite; see chart "**1 Chronicles 1**: Seir the Horite."
5. See chart "**1 Samuel 15**: Agag, King of the Amalekites."
6. See chart "**1 Samuel 25**: Nabal and Abigail."
7. See chart "**Esther 3**: Haman the Agagite."
8. In response to the violent, vengeful, sanguinary character of Esau's descendants, the Lord pronounced vengeance on them (**Ezekiel 25:12–14; Obadiah 1:10**).

GENESIS 36: THE CHIEFS OF EDOM

Approximate Dating: patriarchal period encompassing Esau's descendants, ca. 1966–1051 B.C.[1] ***Relevant Scriptures:*** **Genesis 36:15–19, 40–43;** also **Genesis 36:1–14; 1 Chronicles 1:51b–54**

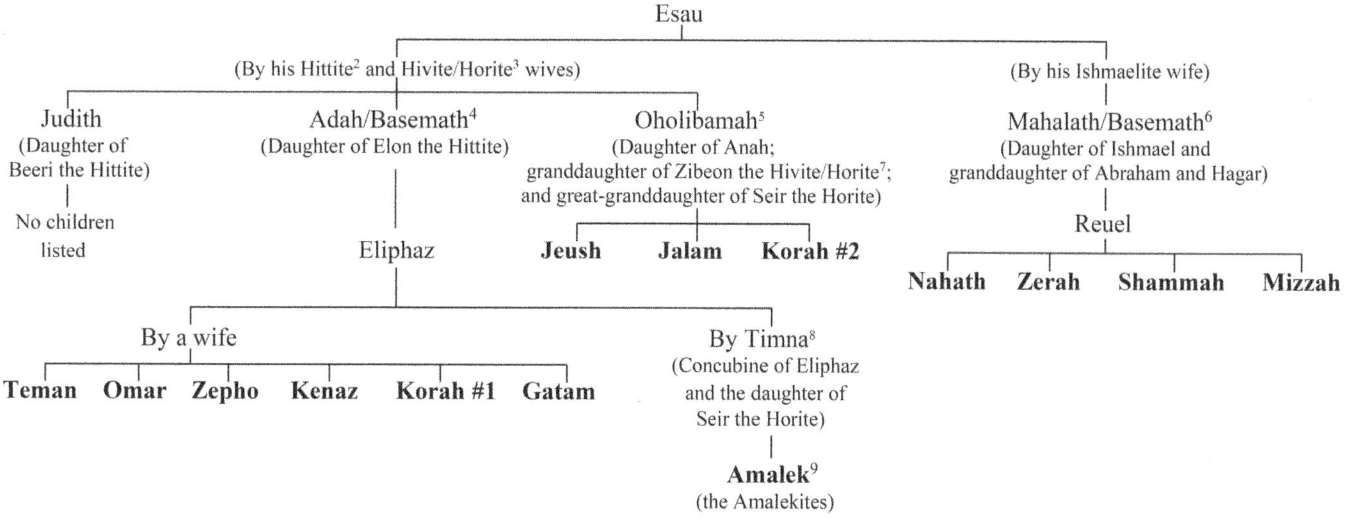

Table 1. Comparative Lists of Those Described as "Edomite Chiefs"[10]

References	Names
(1) **Genesis 36:15–19**	Teman, Omar, Zepho, Kenaz, Korah (#1), Gatam, Amalek, Nahath, Zerah, Shammah, Mizzah, Jeush, Jalam, Korah (#2)
(2) **Genesis 36:40–43**	Timna, Alvah, Jetheth, Oholibamah, Elah, Pinon, Kenaz, Teman, Mibzar, Magdiel, Iram
(3) **1 Chronicles 1:51–54**	Timna, Aliah, Jetheth, Oholibamah, Elah, Pinon, Kenaz, Teman, Mibzar, Magdiel, Iram

Notes on table 1: The Chronicler is obviously in possession of and is using the MS containing **Genesis 36:40–43**. The only names common to all three lists are Kenaz and Teman. List 1 is introduced by בְּנֵי־עֵשָׂו, "sons of Esau." Lists 2 and 3 are introduced by the construct-genitive אַלּוּפֵי עֵשָׂו, "chieftains of Esau," (i.e., founded or initiated by, or the like, with no clear statement of personal relationship).

Biblical and Theological Significance

The Chiefs of Edom

The chart records the various sons and grandsons of Esau who were "chiefs" (*alluphim*) "according to their clans and regions [settlements]" that they occupied in Edom, a region formerly occupied by Seir and his descendants[11] (**Genesis 36:40–43**; cf. **Genesis 36:15–19**; **1 Chronicles 1:35–37**). The term *alluph* (plural אַלּוּפִים, *alluphim*), never used elsewhere in the Old Testament, is likely a loanword from Hurrian or Ugaritic employed as a technical term for leadership.[12] It suggests (1) a nomadic or semi-nomadic lifestyle, rather than sedentary; and (2) a shift from mere genealogical listings to one that expresses lifestyles. The sons and grandsons named previously will now take possession of the cities and properties formerly held by the Seirites and will give birth to new settlements and the development of a type of primitive urban governance. The Esauite list of *alluphim* commences with his grandson Teman, son of Eliphaz, and continues with Omar, Zepho, Kenaz, Korah, Gatam, and Amalek, all sons of Eliphaz (**Genesis 36:15–16**). Esau's son Reuel heads another sub-line: Nahath, Zerah, Shammah, and Mizzah (**Genesis 35:17**). Finally, Esau himself, through his wife Oholibamah, generates the *alluphim* Jeush, Jalam, and Korah (**Genesis 35:18**). The locales of their officiation cannot be determined based on placenames, though from a larger, general perspective they were in the lower Arabah, the Negev, and Northern Arabia.[13]

Connections between the lineages of Esau and Seir are complicated, but they do exist. Esau himself had laid the foundation for Israel's intermarriage amongst the surrounding peoples by taking wives from among them, including Hittites, Hivites/Horites (see note 7), and Ishmaelites (**Genesis 36:2–3**). After migrating to the Transjordan, Esau's sons and grandsons undertook similar liaisons, most pertinently with the descendants of Seir (**Genesis 36:20–28**; cf. **1 Chronicles 1:35–54**). The origins of the Seirites (known in this period as Horites) are not spelled out in detail in the Bible. The first reference to them simply says they were "Horites [living] in the hill country of Seir," apparently in the Transjordan (**Genesis 14:6**). Eventually the epithet came to be known as Edom: "Horites used to live in Seir, but the descendants of Esau drove them out. They destroyed the Horites from before them and settled in their place, just as Israel [Jacob] did in the land the LORD gave them as their possession" (**Deuteronomy 2:12**; cf. **Genesis 36:43**; **Deuteronomy 2:22**).

The key theological idea is that the intermarriage of the chosen seed of Abraham with the surrounding non-elect and pagan nations was doomed to miscarry. In this case, Esau separated from Jacob and joined himself by marriage to the descendants of Seir. Esau and his descendants followed the "primitive" form of decentralized government of provincial chiefs, mimicking that of the previous indigenous people who occupied the land (i.e., the Seirites, descendants of Seir the Horite). Throughout the Middle and Late Bronze Ages of the chiefs (2000–1200 B.C.) and the Iron Age monarchy of Israel (1051–931 B.C.), Esau and those identified with him were inveterate enemies of Israel, the product of the ancient rivalry and subsequent hostility of two brothers (see **Numbers 20:14–21; 1 Samuel 14:47; 1 Kings 11:14–25; Jeremiah 49:7–22; Obadiah**).

Notes

1. These dates are tentative given the lack of strong and clear points of reference. What is generally known and accepted is that Abraham was born in 2166 B.C. and died in 1991 B.C. at the age of 175 (**Genesis 25:7**); Isaac was born to Abraham and Sarah in 2066 B.C. when Abraham was 100 and Sarah was 90 (**Genesis 17:17; 21:5**). Isaac was 60 when his wife Rebekah gave birth to twin boys (Esau and Jacob) in 2006 B.C. (**Genesis 25:26**). Esau was 40 in 1966 B.C. when he married two Canaanite women, Judith and Basemath/Adah (**Genesis 26:34; 27:46**). When Isaac died in 1886 B.C. at the age of 180 (**Genesis 35:28**), he was buried by both his sons (Jacob and Esau) who, at that time, were 120 years old. Ishmael was born to Hagar in 2080 B.C. when Abraham was 86 years old, and Ishmael died at the age of 137 in 1943 B.C. (**Genesis 16:16; 25:17**). Esau settled in Edom ca. 1966 B.C. when he was 40 years old (**Genesis 26:34**). It is unclear when Esau married Oholibamah and Mahalath/Basemath (cf. **Genesis 28:8–9; 36:2**). The narrative details of **Genesis 28:1–9** show that Esau's twin, Jacob, journeyed to Paddan Aram *before* Esau "married Mahalath, the sister of Nebaioth and daughter of Ishmael son of Abraham, in addition to the wives he already had" (**Genesis 28:9**). It appears that Jacob left for Paddan Aram in ca. 1929—and stayed there for 20 years, from ca. 1929–1909 B.C.; the text implies that Esau married Mahalath/Basemath (**Genesis 36:3**) *after* Jacob left for Paddan Aram in ca. 1929 B.C. (**Genesis 28:5–9**). Given Jacob's 20-year sojourn in Paddan Aram, Esau could not have met with *Ishmael* to arrange the marriage to Mahalath/Basemath (**Genesis 28:9**), for Ishmael had died in 1943 B.C. It seems best to propose that **Genesis 28:9** records that Esau met with *Nebaioth*, Ishmael's eldest son, to arrange the marriage. For further explanation and justification of these dates, see note 2 in chart "**Genesis 35**–Genealogy of the Twelve Sons of Jacob, the Eponymous Originators of the Twelve Tribes of Israel" and Eugene H. Merrill, *Kingdom of Priests: A History of Old Testament Israel*, 2nd ed. (Grand Rapids: Baker, 2008), 47, 61. The date 1051 B.C. marks the beginning of the monarchy under Saul, mentioned here because of his engagement with the Amalekites, the descendants of Esau.

2. These are not the Hittites known from the Late Bronze Age (1550–1200 B.C.) whose origin was in north-central Anatolia. This is ruled out by the fact that (1) the Esau/Edom genealogies demand a much earlier date; (2) the names of these Hittites in the Old Testament are Semitic; and (3) the Hittites (חִתִּי) of Anatolia are never attested to as far south as Canaan. Rather, they should be associated with the "Hethites" (חִתִּי; **Genesis 10:15, NKJV**), an indigenous Canaanite tribe (cf. **Genesis 23:3, 5, 7, 10, 16, 18, 20; 25:10; 27:46; 49:32; 1 Chronicles 1:13**; note that the NIV uses "Hittites" in all these verses whereas the NKJV uses "sons of Heth"). See Harry A. Hoffner, Jr., "Hittites," *Peoples of the Old Testament World*, eds. Alfred J. Hoerth, Gerald L. Mattingly, and Edwin M. Yamauchi (Grand Rapids: Baker, 1994), 127–155.

3. The name "Horites" (**Genesis 36:20–21, 29–30; Deuteronomy 2:12, 22**) is almost certainly the Hebrew rendition of a people called "Hurrians," who were widely spread throughout the Middle East as early as 2000 B.C.

4. Adah in **Genesis 36:2, 4, 10, 12, 16** is Basemath in **Genesis 26:34**.

5. Oholibamah, meaning "my [God's] tent is in her," is lexically bi-gender and can therefore apply to males or females. For whether she is a "chief," see note 12.

6. Basemath (**Genesis 36:3, 10, 17**) is the Mahalath of **Genesis 28:9**; here Syriac and Targum Jonathan read "Basemath."

7. The otherwise unknown Hivites may, in fact, be a rendition of Horites (as the text suggests) or possibly Hurites (Hurrians); note the differences: Hivite (without vowel markings) הווי, Horite הורי, and Hurrite הוררי. See the excursus in chart "**Genesis 36**: Esau's Wives."

8. Chief Timna is possibly the same person as Timna, the concubine of Eliphaz; however, the name "Timna" (Heb. תִּמְנָע), the etymology of which is unclear, is lexically bi-gender and therefore can apply to either male or female persons ("תִּמְנָע," *HALOT* 2:1755). Also see note 12.

9. See chart "**Genesis 36**: Amalek, the Ancestor of the Amalekites."

10. Compare the lists of Edomite "chiefs" in table 1 in this chart with the list of Horite "chiefs" who were sons of Seir: Lotan, Shobal, Zibeon, Anah, Dishon, Ezer, Dishan (**Genesis 36:20–21, 29–30**).

11. See chart "**1 Chronicles 1**: Seir the Horite."

12. *HALOT* 1:54. As for the list of names in **1 Chronicles 1:43–54**, only those named in **1 Chronicles 1:51–54**—Timna, Alvah, Jetheth, Oholibamah, Elah, Pinon, Kenaz, Teman, Mibzar, Magdiel, and Iram—are relevant to the *alluph* issue. The key is in **1 Chronicles 1:51**: "The chiefs [*alluphim*] of Edom were: [the *alluph* of] Timna, [the *alluph* of] Alvah, [the *alluph* of] Jetheth, [the *alluph* of] Oholibamah," etc. (**Genesis 36:15–19**).

13. For a helpful overview of ancient Edom, see Yohanan Aharoni, *The Land of the Bible: A Historical Geography* (Philadelphia: Westminster, 1979), 40–42.

GENESIS 37: JOSEPH AND HIS SONS MANASSEH AND EPHRAIM

Approximate Dating: time of Joseph, ca. 1915–1805 B.C. to the time of Joshua, ca. 1485–1375 B.C. ***Relevant Scriptures:*** **Genesis 37; 39–45;** also **Genesis 29:9, 28; 30:22–24; 35:24; 41:45, 50–52; 46:19–20; 48:5–6; Numbers 13:8, 16; 26:28–37; 27:1; Joshua 17:2–3; Judges 11:1; 1 Chronicles 7:14–27**

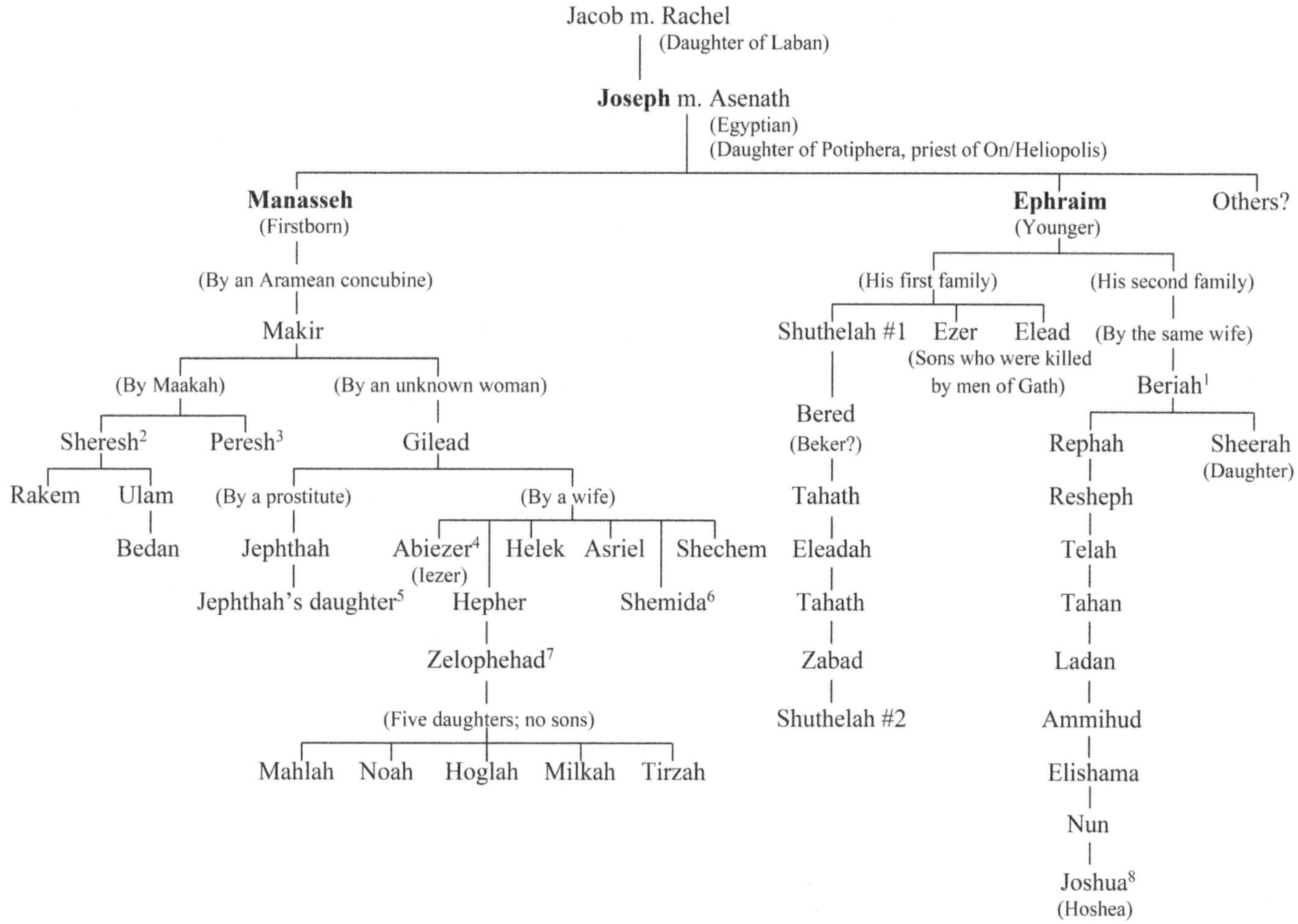

Biblical and Theological Significance

Joseph was the son of Jacob and Rachel (**Genesis 30:25; 35:24; 46:19**) and his father's favorite son (**Genesis 37:3**; cf. **Genesis 30:35; 44:20**). Joseph was born in Paddan Aram in 1915 B.C. when Jacob (born in 2006 B.C.) was ninety-one years old. Joseph's brothers hated him all the more when Jacob made Joseph an "ornate robe" and when Joseph had dreams in which his brothers bowed down to him (**Genesis 37:3–11**). When he was seventeen years old (ca. 1898 B.C.), Joseph's jealous brothers sold him to Midianite–Ishmaelite merchants (**Genesis 37:2-4, 23–31**), who in turn sold him to Potiphar, an officer of Pharaoh and the captain of the guard in Egypt (**Genesis 37:36**). For about a decade, from 1898–1888 B.C., Joseph served Potiphar (**Genesis 39:1–6**) and later (after Potiphar's wife trumped-up sexual charges against him; **Genesis 39:7–20**), Joseph was imprisoned for two years, ca. 1887–1886 B.C. (**Genesis 41:1**). After interpreting the Pharaoh's dreams (**Genesis 41:15–32**) and *before* the seven years of abundance began (i.e., 1884–1878 B.C., inclusive), the Pharaoh appointed Joseph, then age thirty, as the governor / minister of agriculture over the land of Egypt to oversee the collection and distribution of grain (**Genesis 41:46–47; 42:6**). The Pharaoh changed his name to Zaphenath-Paneah (**Genesis 41:45**) and gave him Asenath, the daughter of Potiphera, the priest of On, to be his wife. Joseph rose to power in Dynasty 12[9] (1991–1786 or 1985–1773 B.C.) of Middle Kingdom Egypt, second in authority only to the Pharaoh[10] (**Genesis 41:41-49**). His sons, Manasseh and Ephraim, were born in Egypt "before the years of famine came" (i.e., sometime before 1877 B.C. because the years of famine lasted ca. 1877–1871 B.C., inclusive) (**Genesis 41:50; 46:20, 27**). Joseph lived to see "the third generation of Ephraim's children. . . . [and] the children of Makir son of Manasseh" (**Genesis 50:22–23**). Joseph died in ca. 1805 B.C. at the age of 110 and was "embalmed . . . [and] . . . placed in a coffin in Egypt" (**Genesis 50:26**). Before his death, Joseph had made the Israelites swear an oath that, when they left Egypt, they would carry his bones with them.[11] His bones were carried with Moses and those of the exodus generation in 1446 B.C., brought to Canaan, and buried in Shechem (**Genesis 50:25; Exodus 13:19**).

Before his death in 1859 B.C., Jacob blessed Joseph's two sons, Manasseh and Ephraim, whose eponymous tribes became numbered among the twelve tribes of Jacob/Israel (**Genesis 48:5, 19–22**). In essence, the "Joseph tribe" was divided into two—the tribe of Manasseh and the tribe of Ephraim—and these two received an inheritance just as the other tribes (**Numbers 26:28–37**). Because Levi was not allotted territory in the land, but rather given the priesthood, this brought the total number of tribes to twelve, the number of Jacob's sons from the beginning.[12]

Ephraim's son Shuthelah is to be identified as the originator of the Shuthelahite clan (**Numbers 26:35**); Bered (on the basis of readings from the Peshitta [Syriac], supported by the Arabic) may better be read Beker, the originator of the Bekerite clan (**Numbers 26:35**). Tahan appears to be the eponymous ancestor of the Tahanite clan (**Numbers 26: 35**). Sheerah, the granddaughter of Ephraim, is noted for building Uzzen Sheerah and the important cities of Lower and Upper Beth Horon in the Aijalon Valley, which controlled an important pass between the hill country and the Shephelah and plain to the west (**1 Chronicles 7:24**).

The theological importance of the genealogy lies in its explanation of the origin of two major tribal areas—the tribe of Ephraim in the Northern Kingdom and the tribes of East and West Manasseh on both sides of the Jordan River. On many occasions, Israel in the north is referred to as *Ephraim*, suggesting its (and Joseph's) prominence, especially in the writings of the prophets. The name of the tribe or area derives from *peri*, meaning "fruit" or "fruitfulness," which is reminiscent of the "fruitful vine" in Jacob's blessing to Joseph in **Genesis 49:22**. This is attested to in a number of passages, as in **Genesis 41:52; 48:20; Judges 8:2**; and **Hosea 13:15**. Ironically, and sadly, a nation so blessed by its forefather, Jacob, became known as *Israel* and by that glorious name was, at its very worst, an idol-worshiping people whose destiny was to fall into the cruel hands of the Assyrians in 722 B.C. and to disappear from history.

Notes

1. Beriah was named for a tragedy that happened to Ephraim's first family—men of Gath murdered two sons of Ephraim (Ezer and Elead) "when they went down to seize their livestock" (**1 Chronicles 7:21**). Beriah's name refers not to the compound of *bara* and *yah* (meaning "Yahweh created"), but to *b* and *raah* ("with evil"). Beriah, the "substitute" offspring, was an ancestor of Joshua, the son of Nun.

2. Sheresh is possibly the twin brother of Peresh, but the text is unclear.

3. Peresh was possibly the twin brother of Sheresh, but the text is unclear.

4. Abiezer, son of Gilead, in **Joshua 17:2** is called Iezer in **Numbers 26:30**.

5. For more information about Jephthah the judge of Israel and Jephthah's daughter, see chart "**Judges 6**: Gideon (Fifth Judge) and His Son, Abimelek the False Judge, Jair (Seventh Judge), and Jephthah (Eighth Judge)–Judges of Israel from the Tribe of Manasseh."

6. The sons of Shemida were Ahian, Shechem, Likhi, and Aniam (**1 Chronicles 7:19**).

7. For more information about Zelophehad's daughters, see chart "**Judges 6**: Gideon (Fifth Judge) and His Son, Abimelek the False Judge, Jair (Seventh Judge), and Jephthah (Eighth Judge)–Judges of Israel from the Tribe of Manasseh."

8. Joshua (also called Hoshea, son of Nun; **Numbers 13:8, 16**) was of the twelfth generation from Joseph. He was born in Egypt in ca. 1485 B.C.; assisted Moses during the wilderness wanderings, ca. 1446–1406 B.C.; led the military campaigns into Canaan begun in 1406 B.C.; and died at the age of 110 in 1375 B.C. (**Joshua 24:29; Judges 2:8**). For more information on Joshua, see chart "**Joshua 1**: Joshua, the Successor of Moses and Leader of the Nation of Israel."

9. The chronology and rulers of Dynasty 12 of Egypt adopted here follows the chronological table in I. E. S. Edwards, et al., *The Cambridge Ancient History*, vol. 1, Part 2, 3rd ed. (Cambridge: Cambridge University Press, 1971), 996. as follows (B.C. dates): Ammenemes I (1991–1962); Sesostris I (1971–1928); Ammenemes II (1929–1895); Sesostris II (1897–1878); Sesostris II (1878–1843); Ammenemes III (1842–1797); Ammenemes IV (1798–1790); Sobkneferu (1789–1786); for a discussion of Joseph in Egypt and the Pharaohs of Dynasty 12, see Eugene H. Merrill, *Kingdom of Priests: A History of Old Testament Israel* (Grand Rapids: Baker, 1987), 49–55. See also the discussion of the dating in chart "**Supplement 1**: The Twelfth and Eighteenth Dynasties of Egypt."

10. The Pharaoh during the "seven years of abundance" (**Genesis 41:29, 34, 47-48, 53**; ca. 1884–1878, inclusive) was likely Sesostris II, and the Pharaoh during the "seven years of famine" (**Genesis 41:54**; ca. 1877–1871, inclusive) was likely his son-successor, Sesostris III.

11. The author of Hebrews commends Joseph for "longing for a better country"—believing that his people would be freed from Egypt and enter the land of promise—"By faith Joseph, when his end was near, spoke about the exodus of the Israelites from Egypt and gave instructions concerning the burial of his bones" (**Hebrews 11:16, 22**).

12. See chart "**Genesis 35**: The Twelve Sons of Jacob, the Eponymous Originators of the Twelve Tribes of Israel."

GENESIS 46: THE EXTENDED FAMILY OF JACOB[1] (SEVENTY DESCENDANTS) WHO MIGRATED TO EGYPT

Approximate Dating: Jacob's descent to Egypt occurred ca. 1876 B.C., seventeen years before his death in 1859 B.C.[2], [3] ***Relevant Scriptures:*** **Genesis 46:8–27**; also **Exodus 1:1–5; 6:14–16; Numbers 26:5–50; 1 Chronicles 2:1–4; 4:1, 24; 5:3; 6:1, 16; 7:1, 6, 13, 30–31; 8:1**

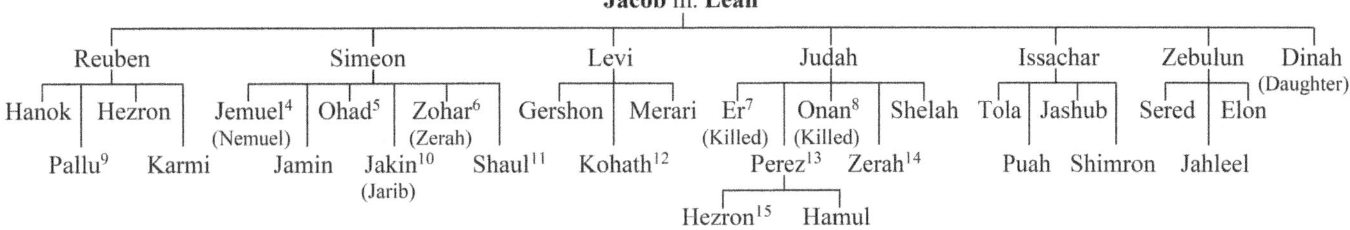

Descendants: "33 in all" (Genesis 46:15)

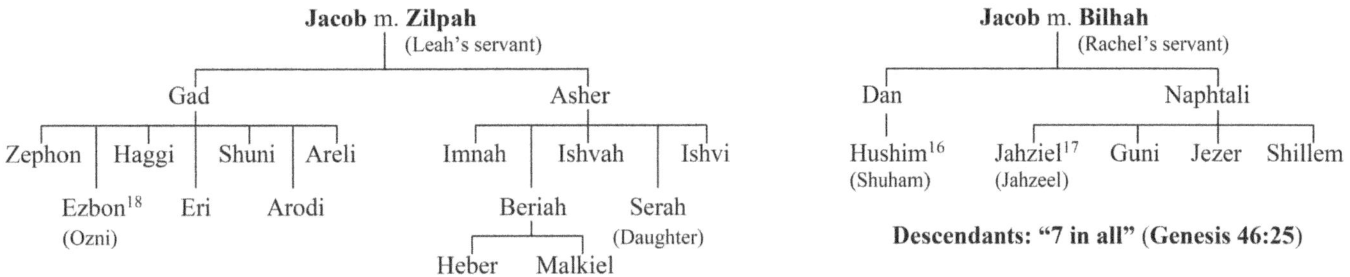

Descendants: "16 in all" (Genesis 46:18)

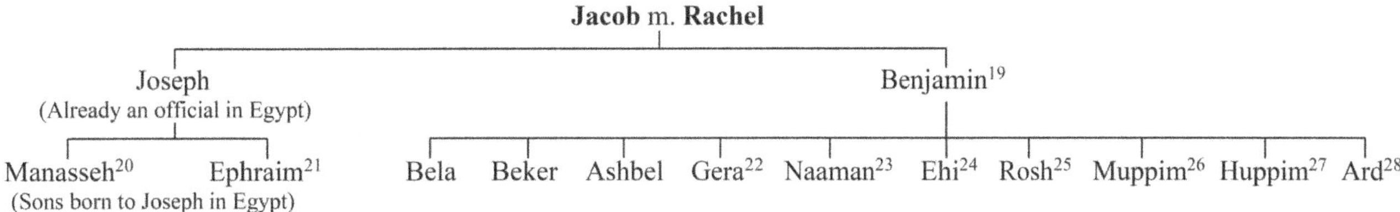

Descendants: "14 in all" (Genesis 46:22)

Biblical and Theological Significance

There is no attempt here to trace direct ancestry or descent. The interest is to name the persons who took part in the migration from Canaan to Egyptand to establish their familial relationships. Thus, the chart shows a succinct outline of the interrelationships of Jacob's (or Israel's) family, a family crucial to the continuation of the messianic hope, culminating in Jesus Christ.

The 430-year sojourn of the nation of Israel in Egypt began when Jacob, at the age of 130 years, and his family migrated to Egypt (**Genesis 47:9; Exodus 12:40–41**). **Genesis 46:26–27** notes that "All those who went to Egypt with Jacob—those who were his direct descendants, not counting his sons' wives—numbered sixty-six persons. With the two sons [Ephraim and Manasseh] who had been born to Joseph in Egypt, the members of Jacob's family, which went to Egypt, were seventy in all."[29] **Exodus 1:5** reads seventy: "The descendants of Jacob numbered seventy in all [33+16+7+14]; Joseph was already in Egypt." Luke writes in **Acts 7:14**, "After this [after Joseph's family was made known to the Pharaoh of Egypt], Joseph sent for his father Jacob and his whole family, seventy-five in all"—here, the number seventy-five appears to include Jacob, his three living wives, and some unnamed offspring, since his wife Rachel and his sons Er and Onan had died earlier in Canaan (**Genesis 35:19; Numbers 26:19**, respectively; see note 29). Later, Yahweh declared "Your ancestors who went down into Egypt were seventy in all, and now the LORD your God has made you as numerous as the stars in the sky" (**Deuteronomy 10:22**). The large extended family of Jacob was, then, a fulfillment of the promises of the Abrahamic covenant (**Genesis 22:17**). Innumerable offspring is hyperbole, a common literary device (still used) to speak of someone or something that is so grand or glorious that only exaggeration can do it justice.

To explain the apparent difficulty of seventy-five becoming an estimated two million or more who were liberated in the exodus (**Numbers 1:44–46**), one must take account of the following factors: (1) The Hebrews were in Egypt for

430 years[30] (**Exodus 12:40–41**); (2) Since a generation at this time was around twenty-five years, it is likely that as many as twenty generations must be assumed; (3) Given the promise of unusual fecundity and Yahweh's blessing in Egypt, families of ten children each would not be unusual (**Genesis 46:2–3; 47:27; Exodus 1:7**); (4) Twelve families entered Egypt, but each family (or clan) must have grown to considerable size in Canaan before the descent to Egypt, given that all the sons of Jacob were born by 1900 B.C.; and (5) The exponential growth of the Israelites, which began with seventy (or seventy-five) persons is illustrated by the use of emphatic adverbs in **Exodus 1:7**—"The Israelites were exceedingly fruitful; they multiplied greatly, increased in numbers and became so numerous that the land was filled with them." As for the seventy who went to Egypt, the narrative, though quite explicit, must be read with great care: (1) The writer is content to anonymously mention only "his [Jacob's] sons and grandsons and his daughters and granddaughters"[31] (**Genesis 46:7**); (2) He describes the ones named as "direct descendants"[32] (**Genesis 46:26**), that is, sons and daughters, grandsons, and granddaughters (**Genesis 46:8–25**), four great-grandsons, Hezron and Hamul (**Genesis 46:12c**) and Heber and Malkiel (**Genesis 46:17c**); (3) He names only male descendants except for his daughter, Dinah (**Genesis 46:15**) and his granddaughter, Serah (**Genesis 46:17**); his wives, Leah (**Genesis 46:15**), Rachel (**Genesis 46:19**), Zilpah (**Genesis 46:18**) and Bilhah (**Genesis 46:25**); the mother of one of Simeon's sons, a Canaanite woman (**Genesis 46:10**); and Joseph's wife, Asenath the Egyptian (**Genesis 46:20**).

From a theological perspective, two major themes seem quite apparent. First, God cares for those whom he has chosen to represent and serve him. The paganism and cultural and social dissolution of the Canaanite environment threatened to do irreparable damage to Israel. Thus, God graciously opened the door to Egypt so they could live there in their own enclave in the rich soils of the Delta, "in the best part of the land" [Goshen] in "the district of Rameses" (**Genesis 47:6, 11**). However, the friendliness of the Egyptian royal hosts turned to animosity against their guests, and Israel became enslaved to the pharaohs[33] and suffered greatly at their hands, even to the point of killing their infants (cf. **Exodus 1:22**). Yahweh again moved, this time to deliver Israel not *to* but *from* Egypt. He was there to provide and then to save.

Notes

1. Jacob was born ca. 2006 B.C.; beginning at age 130, he lived in Egypt for seventeen years, before his death in ca. 1859 B.C. at the age of 147 (**Genesis 47:28**). He was buried in the cave of Machpelah near Mamre in Canaan, along with his ancestors, Abraham, Sarah, Isaac, Rebekah, and his wife Leah (**Genesis 49:29–32**). See chart "**Genesis 35**: The Twelve Sons of Jacob, the Eponymous Originators of the Twelve Tribes of Israel."

2. The narrative details of **Genesis 41, 44–45** give subtle but important chronological information. (1) After two years in prison, Joseph was released and interpreted Pharaoh's dreams by saying there would be "seven years of great abundance" in Egypt followed by "seven years of famine" (**Genesis 41:1, 29–30;** see **17–30, 53–54**). (2) At age 30, Joseph was appointed by Pharaoh as second-in-command over the whole land of Egypt and in charge of the collection of grain (**Genesis 41:39–49; 44:18**). (3) Joseph's two sons (Manasseh and Ephraim) were born "before the years of famine came" (**Genesis 41:50**). (4) When Joseph revealed himself to his brothers, it was *after* the second year of the seven-year famine (**Genesis 45:6, 11**). (5) Soon thereafter, Jacob and his family migrated from Canaan to Egypt (**Genesis 45:8–9, 11, 13**). Given the chronology of those events and the known dates of Jacob's birth (2006 B.C.) and his age of 130 upon arrival in Egypt (**Genesis 47:9**), it can be deduced that Jacob's family migrated to Egypt in 1876 B.C. and that he lived the last seventeen years of his life (1876–1859 B.C.) in Egypt, dying at the age of 147 in 1859 B.C. Thus, the seven years of abundance in Egypt spanned 1884–1878 B.C., and the seven years of famine spanned 1877–1871 B.C. Also, Manasseh and Ephraim were born before 1877 B.C. (cf. **Genesis 41:50**).

3. The known dates for the seven years of abundance and the seven years of famine (note 2) also confirm the dating for Joseph's life. Joseph became a kind of minister of agriculture *before* the seven years of abundance began (i.e., before 1884 B.C.). Thus, Joseph was 30 years in ca. 1885 B.C.; working backwards, it shows that he was born in 1915 B.C., was sold at age 17 to Midianite merchants in 1898 B.C. (**Genesis 37:28**), and died at age 110 in 1805 B.C. (**Genesis 50:26**).

4. Jemuel (**Genesis 46:10; Exodus 6:15**) is called Nemuel in **Numbers 26:12** and **1 Chronicles 4:24**.

5. Ohad is mentioned in **Genesis 46:10** and **Exodus 6:15**, but his name is omitted in **Numbers 26:12** and **1 Chronicles 4:24**.

6. Zohar **Genesis 46:10; Exodus 6:15**) is called Zerah in **Numbers 26:13** and **1 Chronicles 4:24**.

7. Er, the firstborn son of Judah and an unnamed Canaanite woman (the daughter of Shua), was the first husband of Tamar (**Genesis 38:1–6**). But Er was wicked, so God killed him (**Genesis 38:7; 1 Chronicles 2:3**). Er (and his brother Onan) died in Canaan before the rest of Jacob's family migrated to Egypt (**Genesis 46:12; Numbers 26:19**).

8. Onan was the son of Judah and an unnamed Canaanite woman (the daughter of Shua) and the brother of the deceased Er (**Genesis 38:2–4; 1 Chronicles 2:3**). Onan refused to fulfill the levirate marriage obligations for his deceased brother's widow Tamar, by "[spilling] his semen on the ground to keep from providing offspring for his brother [Er]" (**Genesis 38:8–9**). For this wickedness, the Lord killed Onan while he was still in the land of Canaan (**Genesis 46:12; Numbers 26:19**).

9. Pallu is possibly the Peleth of **Numbers 16:1**.

10. Jakin in **Numbers 26:12** is Jarib in **1 Chronicles 4:24**.

11. Shaul was the son of a Canaanite woman (**Genesis 46:10; Exodus 6:15**).

12. Kohath was the eponymous ancestor of the Kohathite clan of high priests and Kohathite attending priests who served in the tabernacle and later in the temple (**Numbers 3:28; 4:4, 15; 26:57**).

13. Perez, an ancestor in the line of the Messiah (**Ruth 4:18–22; Matthew 1:1–6; Luke 3:33**), was the twin brother of Zerah.

14. Zerah, the second-born twin son of Judah and Tamar (Judah's daughter-in-law), was the twin brother of Perez (**Genesis 38:27–30**).

15. The Judah–Perez–Hezron lineage continues the line of the Messiah (**Ruth 4:18–22; Matthew 1:3; Luke 3:33**).

16. Hushim in **Genesis 46:23** is Shuham in **Numbers 26:42**.

17. Jahziel in **Genesis 46:24** and **1 Chronicles 7:13** is called Jahzeel in **Numbers 26:48**.

18. Ezbon in **Genesis 46:16** is Ozni in **Numbers 26:16**.

19. Benjamin, the youngest son, was "born to him [Jacob] in his old age" (**Genesis 44:20**), and Jacob's "life [was] closely bound up with the boy's life" (**Genesis 44:30**). Benjamin's mother, Rachel, gave birth to him in about 1901 B.C. after the family left Paddan Aram and returned to Canaan, and she died in childbirth (**Genesis 35:16–18**). As she lay dying, Rachel named her son Ben-Oni, meaning "son of my sorrow," but Jacob named him Benjamin, meaning "son of (my) right hand" or "son of the south" because all of Jacob's other sons had been born in Paddan Aram, northeast of Canaan (**Genesis 35:18**).

20. For the descendants of Manasseh, see **Numbers 26:29–33** and **1 Chronicles 7:14–19**.

21. For the descendants of Ephraim, see **Numbers 26:35–36** and **1 Chronicles 7:20–27**.

22. Gera was most likely the son of Bela and the grandson of Benjamin (**1 Chronicles 8:3**).

23. Naaman was probably the son of Bela. **Numbers 26:40** says that the descendants of Bela were through Ard and Naaman. The Chronicler lists Naaman as a son of Bela (**1 Chronicles 8:3–5**).

24. Ehi (meaning "brother") is mentioned as a son of Benjamin only in **Genesis 46:21**. Scholars have suggested that "Ehi, Rosh, Muppim, and Huppim" in **Genesis 46:21** is a mechanical corruption of "Ahiram, Shephupham [Shupham/Muppim] and Huppim [Hupham/Huram]" in **Numbers 26:38–39** (Siegfried S. Johnson, "Ehi," *Anchor Yale Bible Dictionary*, 414). The lexeme

ehki (אֵחִי) is no doubt (with most scholars) a prefix syllable with names such as Ahiram (אֲחִירָם). Therefore, together, Ehi and Rosh may refer to Ahiram (**Numbers 26:38**) or Aharah (**1 Chronicles 8:1**); see note 25 for Rosh.

25. Rosh is mentioned as a son of Benjamin only in **Genesis 46:21**. Rosh means "head" or "chief." Rosh, together with Ehi, may be a corruption of Aharah/Ahiram (see note 24 for Ehi).

26. Muppim (**Genesis 46:21**) is probably also rendered Shupham (**Numbers 26:39**) and Shephuphan (**1 Chronicles 8:5**). He was the head of the Shuppite/Shuphamite clan: "The Shuppites [Shuphamites] and Huppites [Huphamites] were the descendants of Ir [probably Iri, the son of Bela, son of Benjamin]" (**1 Chronicles 7:12**; cf. **Numbers 26:39; 1 Chronicles 7:6–7, 15**). Also "Makir [the son of Manasseh] took a wife [Maakah] from among the Huppites and Shuppites [presumably referring to Hupppim/Hupham/Huram and Muppim/Shupham/Shupham, respectively, who were the heads of the Huppite and Shuppite clans]" (**1 Chronicles 7:15**).

27. Huppim (**Genesis 46:21**), with slight scribal variation, is also Hupham (**Numbers 26:39**) and Huram (**1 Chronicles 8:5**). The Chronicler adds: "The Shuppites and Huppites were the descendants of Ir [likely Iri, the son of Bela, the son of Benjamin in **1 Chronicles 7:6–7**], and the Hushites the descendants of Aher" (**1 Chronicles 7:12**). See also the comments in note 26.

28. **Numbers 26:40** suggests that Ard was considered a descendant (son?) of Bela: "The descendants of Bela through Ard and Naaman were: through Ard, the Ardite clan; through Naaman, the Naamite clan." It is unclear, but Ard may be an alternate spelling of Aher and/or Aharah (cf. **1 Chronicles 7:12; 8:1**).

29. The reference to sixty-six persons in **Genesis 46:26** seems to refer to the descendants of Jacob who *accompanied* him to Egypt, but does not include (1) Jacob's four wives (Leah, Rachel, Zilpah, Bilhah; 4 persons); (2) Judah's deceased sons, Er and Onan (2 persons; cf. **Genesis 46:12**); nor (3) Joseph and his two sons, Manasseh and Ephraim (3 persons), who were already living in Egypt (**Genesis 46:20**). The number 70 includes the 66 persons, as explained, with the presumed addition of Jacob's four wives (Leah, Rachel, Zilpah, Bilhah), although in truth, Rachel had died in childbirth with Benjamin some 25 years earlier (**Genesis 35:19; 48:7**). The reference to the number 75 in **Acts 7:14** seems to include *all* of Jacob's (nuclear) family (including unnamed "daughters" and "granddaughters"; **Genesis 46:7**).

30. The Israelites lived in Egypt for "430 years" (**Exodus 12:40**)—the text should be understood to begin when Jacob, at the age of 130 (**Genesis 47:9**), migrated with his family to Egypt in 1876 B.C. Then, "at the end of the 430 years, to the very day, all the LORD's divisions left Egypt" (**Exodus 12:41**). Therefore, the sojourn in Egypt lasted from 1876 B.C. to 1446 B.C. For such large numbers in the Bible and elsewhere, see David M. Fouts, "Another Look at Large Numbers in Assyrian Royal Inscriptions," *JNES* 3 (1994): 205–11.

31. Of the granddaughters (plural), only one Serah is named (**Genesis 46:17**). This is "author's privilege," a principle that allows an author to include or omit whatever he or she pleases without offering justification.

32. The phrase יְרֵכוֹ מִלְּבַד, *yereko millebad* (lit. "his loins, from him only"; cf. **Exodus 1:5**) clearly separates his immediate children from his derivative offspring.

33. See chart "**Supplement 1**: The Pharaohs of the Twelfth and Eighteenth Dynasties of Egypt."

EXODUS 2: MOSES AND ZIPPORAH

Approximate Dating: Moses was born in 1526 B.C. and died at age 120 in 1406 B.C.[1] ***Relevant Scriptures:*** **Exodus 2:16, 18–22; 4:24–25; 6:18–20; 18:1–5, 27;** also **Numbers 3:19; 10:29; 26:58–59; 1 Chronicles 6:2, 18; 23:12–17; 24:20–21; 26:24–28**

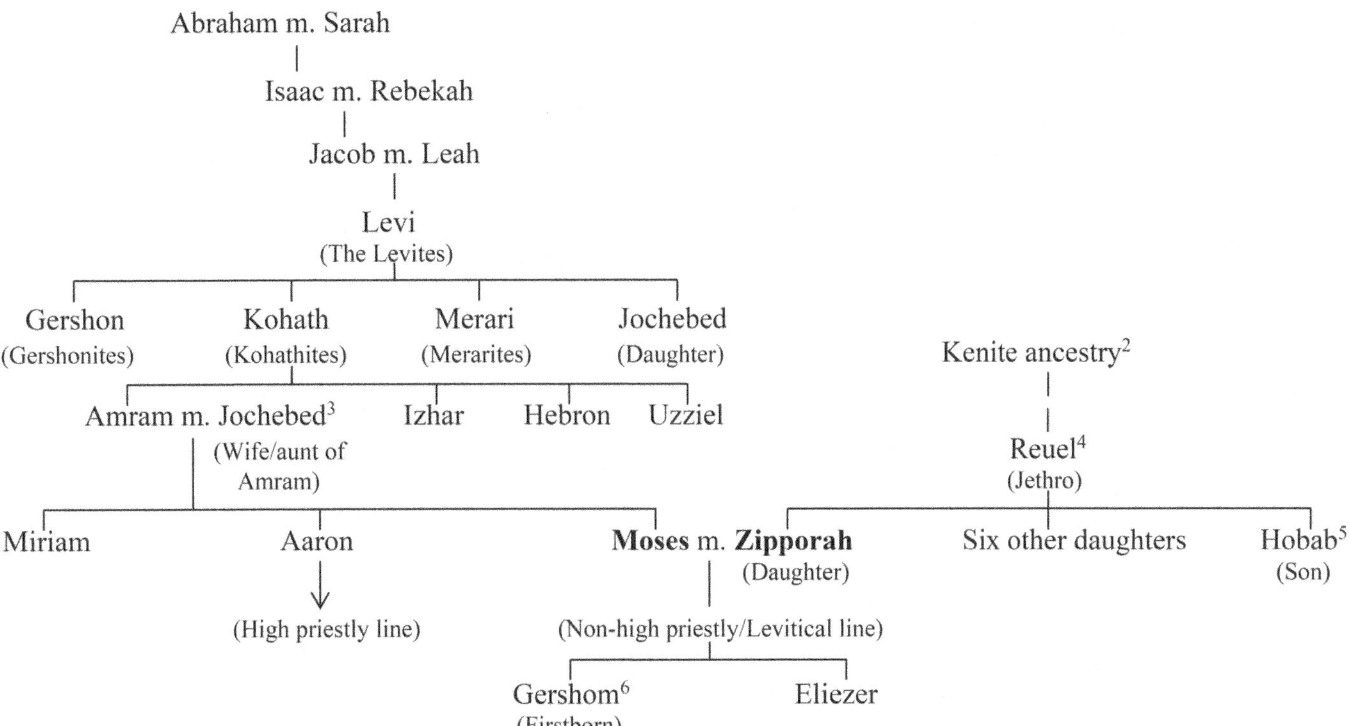

Biblical and Theological Significance

The long lifespans of Moses' father, grandfather, and great-grandfather (Amram, Kohath and Levi, respectively) accounts for a period of over four hundred years.[7] That Moses was a Levitical Kohathite accounts for the instances in which he functioned as such (**Exodus 17:15; 24:4–6**).

Moses married outside the Levitical line, taking as his wife Zipporah, the daughter of Reuel (or Jethro), a Kenite priest of Midian (**Exodus 2:16–21; 3:1; 4:18; 18:1–2, 27; Judges 1:16**). Midian is an eponym—identified in **Genesis 25:2** as (the personal name) Midian, the son of Abraham by his wife Keturah (cf. **1 Chronicles 1:32**), and also the place where

Moses lived for 40 years after he left Egypt (**Exodus 2:15; 4:19; Acts 7:23–34**). The intercultural marriage between Moses and Zipporah the Kenite was frowned upon by his brother Aaron and sister Miriam, as is clear from **Numbers 12:1–15** where Zipporah is described by them as a "Cushite"[8] (**Numbers 12:1**), an obvious slur, perhaps implying that she was as dark-skinned as the Cushan natives of the Arabian Peninsula where Midian was geographically located (cf. **Habakkuk 3:7**).[9]

When Moses died at the age of 120, he was buried in Moab "in the valley opposite Beth Peor."[10] Despite his advanced age, Moses remained mentally and physically fit: "his eyes were not weak nor his strength gone." Then, "the Israelites grieved for Moses in the plains of Moab thirty days, until the time of weeping and mourning was over" (**Deuteronomy 34:6–8**).

Moses named his firstborn son Gershom, meaning, "I have become a foreigner [stranger/sojourner] in a foreign land," probably referring to Moses living in Midian at the time with his father-in-law Jethro/Reuel (**Exodus 2:22; 18:3**). Apparently Moses had disobeyed God's command to circumcise his son(s) (see Genesis 17:13–14) and for this "the LORD met Moses and was about to kill him [Moses]" (Exodus 4:24). Sensing that her husband's life was in danger, Zipporah responded on Moses' behalf. Presumably it was Gershom the firstborn—not Eliezer—who was properly circumcised[11] by Zipporah the foreigner instead of by his father Moses, the Israelite priest (cf. **Exodus 4:24–26**)! Moses named his second-born son Eliezer in remembrance of how he had escaped Egypt: "My father's God was my helper; he saved me from the sword of Pharaoh" (**Exodus 18:4**). The sons of Moses (Gershom and Eliezer) "were counted as part of the tribe of Levi" (**1 Chronicles 23:14**)—meaning they were considered Levites (but not in the Aaronic line of Kohathite high priests). Later, the descendants of Moses served as Kohathite attending priests in Solomon's Temple, along with the descendants of Kohath (cf. **1 Chronicles 23:14–17; 26:24–28**); see chart "**Exodus 18**: Moses' Sons, Gershom and Eliezer, and Their Descendants Who Served in Solomon's Temple."

Notes

1. Principal dates in the life of Moses are: Moses' birth in ca. 1526 B.C. during Israelite bondage; Moses growing up and living in Egypt for 40 years, ca. 1526–1486 B.C. (**Exodus 2:11–15; Acts 7:23**); Moses' 40-year sojourn in Midian, ca. 1486–1446 B.C.; the burning bush incident (**Exodus 3:2; Acts 7:30**), ca. 1447 B.C.; Moses leading the Israelites out of bondage in Egypt (the exodus) in 1446 B.C.; leading the nation during the 40 years of the wilderness wanderings from 1446–1406 B.C.; and Moses' death in 1406 B.C. at the age of 120. Also, see notes about Moses in chart "**Supplement 1**: The Pharaohs of the Twelfth and Eighteenth Dynasties of Egypt."

2. The Kenite ancestry of Jethro is more apparent in the narratives about Heber and Jael, who are identified as Kenite descendants of Hobab, the son of Reuel/Jethro (**Judges 4:11**); see also the charts "**Judges 4**: Heber and Jael (Kenites) and Their Descendants Who Co-Mingled with the Pious Jabez–Rekabite Scribal Community near Jerusalem" and "**Jeremiah 35**: The Rekabites (Kenite Descendants)."

3. Jochebed was born in Egypt (**Numbers 26:59**). **Exodus 6:20** explains that "Amram married his father's [Kohath's] sister Jochebed" (i.e., Jochebed was Amram's aunt); therefore, Jochebed was the sister (or possibly half-sister) of Kohath, Gershon, and Merari. Of the three children that Jochebed bore to Amram, Miriam appears to be the oldest (cf. **Exodus 2:1–4, 7–8**), with Aaron three years older than Moses (**Exodus 7:7**) and Moses the youngest.

4. Reuel in **Exodus 2:18, 20** and **Numbers 10:29** is called Jethro in **Exodus 3:1; 4:18; 18:1–2, 5–6, 9, 12, 27**. Reuel may be a clan name or title, but *Jethro* is clearly a variant of Reuel (**Exodus 3:1; Numbers 10:29**). The clan of Reuel is the same group of people referred to as "the descendants of Moses' father-in-law, the Kenite" (**Judges 1:16**). Moses met Reuel and his family when they were *residing* in Midian—perhaps as nomadic Kenite "smiths" who migrated between Egypt and Midian. Reuel's family should be understood to be ethnic Kenites, not Midianites.

Reuel the Kenite should not be confused with Reuel son of Esau and Mahalath/Basemath, who was of mixed Edomite–Ishmaelite heritage (**Genesis 36:3–4, 10, 13, 17; 1 Chronicles 1:35, 37**; see charts "**Genesis 36**: Esau, the Ancestor of the Edomites" and "**1 Chronicles 1**: Abraham's Descendants through Esau"). Also, Reuel the Kenite should not be confused with Reuel the Benjamite (**1 Chronicles 9:8**).

5. Some translations have caused confusion as to the identity of Hobab (cf. **Numbers 10:29, Judges 4:11**). The NIV translation correctly identifies Hobab as the brother of Zipporah, the brother-in-law of Moses, and the son of Reuel. Just prior to the exodus in 1446 B.C., Moses met with Hobab and invited his family to accompany the Israelites to Canaan (**Numbers 10:29**). At first Hobab refused, but Moses persuaded him by saying, "Please do not leave us. You know where we should camp in the wilderness, and you can be our eyes. If you come with us, we will share with you whatever good things the LORD gives us" (**Numbers 10:31–32**).

6. Gershom the son of Moses (**Exodus 2:22; 18:3; Judges 18:30; 1 Chronicles 23:15–16; 26:24**) should not be confused with Gershon the son of Levi (cf. **Genesis 46:11; Exodus 6:16; Numbers 3:17; 1 Chronicles 6:1, 16**). Also, Gershom the son of Moses is not the same person as Gershom the Kohathite, a descendant of Phinehas (in the Levi–Kohath–Amram–Aaron–Eleazar–Phinehas line), mentioned in **Ezra 8:2**.

7. Levi was born ca. 1926 B.C. and lived 137 years (**Exodus 6:16**); Kohath lived 133 years (**Exodus 6:18**); Amram lived 137 years (**Exodus 6:20**). Moses, who was born ca. 1526 B.C., lived 120 years (**Deuteronomy 34:7**).

8. Kevin Burrell offers helpful insights into the ethnic Cushites: "The vast majority of the 54 references to Cushites in the Hebrew Bible concern the African nation of Cush on the southern border of ancient Egypt. Known to the ancient Egyptians mainly as Kush, the territory of the ancient Cushites covered the northern and southern regions of present-day Sudan and Egypt, respectively, and is therefore to be distinguished from the modern nation of Ethiopia, which lies much further south in the Horn of Africa. . . . That ancient Egypt and Cush shared the Nile River and a common border allowed for thousands of years of interaction between the two rival nations. Cushites and Egyptians engaged in trade, diplomacy, and incessant conflicts resulting in a dynamic landscape of social and political interconnections and millennia of bidirectional migration. Consequently, people of Cushite origin could be found at every tier of Egyptian society—including the office of the pharaoh. . . . In the New Kingdom (c. 1550–1070 B.C.E), Egypt subdued Cush and annexed the south into its empire (which also included the Levant). . . . Cushites are characterized largely as a militaristic people in the Hebrew Bible. Most references to Cush occur in the context of military engagement (i.e., **2 Chronicles 14:9–15; Isaiah 20:3–4; Jeremiah 46:9; Ezekiel 30:4–5; 38:5; Nahum 3:9**). **Isaiah 18:2**, for instance, characterizes the Cushites as a people 'feared near and far,' and a 'nation mighty and conquering.' This is consistent with Cushite military reputation in ancient Egypt and the ancient Near East in general. In terms of physical representation, Egyptian iconographic evidence consistently depicts Cushites with dark skin pigmentation, and the Greeks refer to the southerners as *Aithiops*, or Ethiopians, meaning 'burnt of face.' But far from exhibiting the kind of antipathy toward blackness we find in the modern context, the physical characteristics of the Cushite evoked no negative responses: ancient peoples like Egyptians, Assyrians, and Greeks did not develop a racialized view of identity. The biblical texts also indicate that Cushites, as a general rule, had dark pigmentation. **Jeremiah 13:23** is notable for its explicit reference to the conspicuous character of the Cushite skin. And **Isaiah 18:2** describes the Cushites as 'tall and smooth'—the latter adjective believed to describe the aesthetic appeal of their shiny black skin. Notwithstanding such references, in terms of ethnic identity, the biblical text is not primarily concerned with physical characteristics. Rather, religious concerns governed collective identity for both Israelites and non-Israelites alike. Israelite collective identity was defined by its relationship to Yahweh, the God of Israel . . . it is religious concerns that are in view here—not ethnicity, skin color, or even geography." Kevin Burrell, "The Cushites: Race and Representation in the Hebrew Bible," *ANET* 8 (2020), https://www.asor.org/anetoday/2020/12/cushites-hebrew-bible.

Given Burrell's explanation, Aaron and Miriam's disdain for Zipporah the "Cushite" in **Numbers 12:1** is probably a statement more about her questionable religious orientation (cf. **Exodus 4:25–26**) than about her Kenite ancestry and Cushite-like dark skin color.

9. Zipporah was one of the seven daughters of Jethro (Reuel), a priest who lived in Midian (**Exodus 2:16, 21; 3:1; Numbers 10:29** cf. **Judges 1:16; 4:11**); see note 4. They were Kenites, a remnant of the original occupants of Canaan

(cf. **Genesis 15:19**). At 40 years old, Moses fled Egypt because he had killed an Egyptian (**Acts 7:23–29**). He traveled to Midian and there he was married to Zipporah. Moses stayed with Jethro's family in Midian for 40 years (cf. **Exodus 2:15–21; 7:7; Acts 7:23–34**).

10. Beth Peor was near the upper east shore of the Dead Sea, just north of Mount Nebo.

11. After Moses had been in Midian for 40 years, the Lord spoke to him and said, "Go back to Egypt, for all those who wanted to kill you are dead," confront the Pharaoh, and persuade him to "let my people go" (**Exodus 4:19; 5:1**). Moses, Zipporah, and their two sons started back to Egypt (cf. **Exodus 4:19–20**). However, Moses (God's chosen leader) had failed to circumcise Gershom, his firstborn son (a glaring violation of the Abrahamic covenant; **Genesis 17:10–14**), so when the family arrived "at a lodging place" (**Exodus 4:24**) on the way to Egypt, Yahweh intended to kill Moses! Zipporah, by word and deed, intervened on Moses' behalf and circumcised the lad (cf. **Exodus 13:15**). Using a flint knife, she "cut off her son's foreskin and touched Moses' feet with it" and retorted, "'Surely you are a bridegroom of blood to me'" (referring to circumcision; **Exodus 4:25–26**). The incident caused estrangement between them, and at this point, Moses sent Zipporah and their two sons back to Midian to live with Zipporah's father, Jethro (cf. **Exodus 18:1–6**). They remained there until after the events of the exodus (**Exodus 18:5–17**). Eventually, Zipporah and her sons were reunited with Moses in the wilderness at Mount Sinai (**Exodus 18:1–6**).

EXODUS 6: MOSES, AARON, AND MIRIAM, THE LEADERS OF ISRAEL

Approximate Dating: Miriam was born ca. 1533 B.C. and died at age 126 in ca. 1407 B.C.; Aaron was born in ca. 1529 B.C. and died at age 123 in 1406 B.C.;[1] Moses was born ca. 1526 B.C. and died at age 120 in 1406 B.C.; 430 years of Israelite bondage in Egypt, ca. 1876–1446 B.C.; Exodus / wilderness wanderings, ca. 1446–1406 B.C. [2], [3] ***Relevant Scriptures:*** **Exodus 6:16–25;** also **Exodus 2:22; 15:20–21; 18:2–4; 28:1; Leviticus 10:1–2; Numbers 3:18–20, 27; 16:1; 25:7, 11; 26:58–60; Judges 20:28; 1 Chronicles 6:1–4, 16–23, 29, 49–50; 23:6–24; 24:1–3; 26:23**

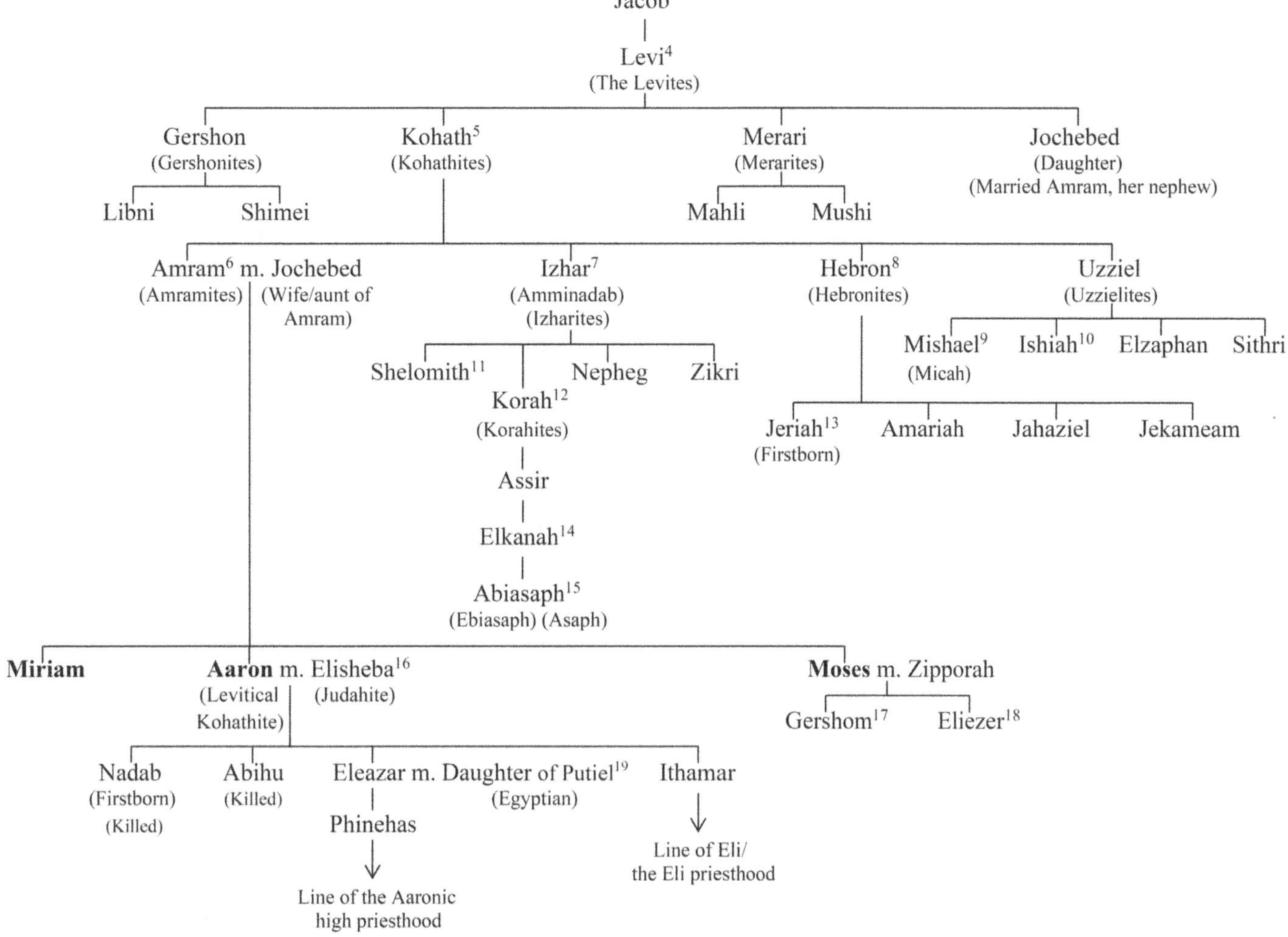

Biblical and Theological Significance

Levi, the eponymous ancestor of the high priests, the attending priests, and the Levites, sired three sons—Gershon, Kohath, and Merari (**Exodus 6:16**). The one of special interest here is Kohath, whose sister Jochebed married her own nephew, Amram (**Exodus 2:1; 6:20**), by whom she bore Miriam, Aaron, and Moses, all, in time, leaders of the nascent Israelite nation.

Miriam was the eldest of the children; no record exists to suggest that she ever married. Miriam observed her baby brother Moses being rescued from the Nile by Pharaoh's daughter, and she suggested to her that she employ a Hebrew nurse for the baby (**Exodus 2:1–4, 7–8**). Miriam is called a "prophet"[20] (**Exodus 15:20**) for she composed and sang a victory song[21] when Israel triumphed over the Egyptians at the Red Sea (**Exodus 14**). During the forty years in the desert, she led the women in praise of the Lord. When Miriam (and Aaron) reproved Moses for marrying the "Cushite"[22] woman, Zipporah (**Numbers 12:1**), God cursed Miriam with leprosy (**vv. 1–16**). She died in Kadesh Barnea about 1407 B.C. before entering the promised land (**Numbers 20:1**).

Aaron, born about 1529 B.C., was three years older than Moses (**Exodus 7:7; Numbers 33:39**; cf. **Deuteronomy 34:7**). Aaron was designated by Yahweh to be founder of the high priesthood (**Exodus 28:1; 40:12–15; Numbers 18:1, 7; 1 Chronicles 23:13**) and the "mouth" (spokesperson) for Moses (**Exodus 4:16**). Aaron's mixed marriage as a Levite to Elisheba the Judahite, who was the sister of Nahshon (**Exodus 6:23**; cf. **1 Chronicles 2:10**), inevitably resulted in an apparent quandary in that the priestly offspring of Aaron could never claim to be of a *pure* Levitical bloodline in the strictest sense. However, the Divine omnipotence overruled so that their marriage did join "kingly and priestly" lines of descendants, thus anticipating the time when the royal and priestly offices could and would find messianic fulfillment in one Man (**Psalm 110:1–4; Zechariah 6:9–15; Hebrews 7:11–28**). Aaron's sons, Nadab and Abihu, died because they made an unauthorized fire before the Lord; since they had no sons, their brothers, Eleazar and Ithamar, served as priests during the lifetime of their father, Aaron (**Numbers 3:2,4; 26:60–61** cf. **Leviticus 10:1–2; 16:1; 1 Chronicles 24:1–2**). Aaron died on Mount Hor at the age of 123 in 1406 B.C. (**Numbers 33:38–39**).

Moses was the leader of Israel during the exodus from Egypt and the forty years of the wilderness sojourn (1446–1406 B.C.). At the time of Moses' birth (1526 B.C.), the Pharaoh[23] had declared that all Hebrew boys must be slain, though the girls could live (**Exodus 1:22**). His mother, Jochebed, hid him in a papyrus basket and placed him in the Nile where his older sister Miriam could stand watch. Pharaoh's daughter[24] found Moses in the basket, and Miriam, standing by, offered to find a wet nurse—and quickly and astutely procured the services of Jochebed, their mother! After Moses was weaned, he was adopted by Pharaoh's daughter and she named him Moses, saying, "I *drew him* out of the water"[25] (**Exodus 2:10**). Moses was raised as a prince in the Egyptian royal house, but in about 1486 B.C., when he was forty years old, he killed an Egyptian for beating a fellow Hebrew and fled from Egypt in fear (**Exodus 2:11–15; Acts 7:23–29**). He came to live with Reuel (or Jethro), a Kenite priest in Midian (cf. **Exodus 2:16; 3:1; 18:1; Numbers 10:29; Judges 1:16**). Moses married Zipporah, one of Jethro's seven daughters (**Exodus 2:11–22**), who bore him two sons, Gershom and Eliezer[26] (**Acts 7:29**). When Moses was eighty, an angel of the Lord called to him from a burning bush and told him to inform Pharaoh that he was going to lead his people the Israelites out of Egypt (**Exodus 3:10; Acts 7:30**). Because of his transgression at Meribah, however, the Lord did not allow Moses to enter Canaan (**Numbers 20:7–12**), but only permitted him to view it from the top of Mount Nebo (**Deuteronomy 34:1**). Moses died at age 120 (1406 B.C.) and was buried in Moab in the valley across from Beth Peor (**Deuteronomy 34:6–7**). The Bible consistently accredits Moses as the author-compiler of the Torah (also called the Pentateuch or the "Law of Moses") (**Joshua 8:31; 23:6; 1 Kings 2:3; 2 Kings 14:6; 23:25; 2 Chronicles 23:18; 30:16; Ezra 3:2; 7:6; Nehemiah 8:1; Daniel 9:11, 13; Luke 2:22; 24:44; Acts 28:23; 1 Corinthians 9:9**).

The principal point to be made here is that the role of Israel to be a "kingdom of priests and a holy nation" (**Exodus 19:6**) necessitated within itself an apparatus whereby a sinful nation could have access to a holy God. That would be achieved by the mediation of a clergy, a body of men especially qualified to intercede between God and his people. Though Moses was the "Great Emancipator" and temporary political leader, he would not be that mediator. Rather, that awesome privilege and responsibility would be Aaron's. Furthermore, all subsequent priests and Levites were required to be from Aaron's tribe, Levi, and the office of chief priest, which began with Aaron, passed from father to firstborn son. Four hundred years later the unbroken line of high priests would run parallel to an unbroken line of kings, of whom David was the first. Thereafter, the priestly and royal character of Israel would be manifest to the world in these two unalterable successions of priest and king. In the eschatological age the two would merge in one Man, Jesus, Son of David and priest after the order of Melchizedek. The former office, of course, was occupied by only Judeans and the latter by Levitical Kohathites descended from Aaron, at least in historical times. However, Jesus, though not "qualified" as an Aaronic priestly descendant, was priest of a new order—that of "an indestructible life" (**Hebrews 7:16**; cf. **Psalm 110:4; Hebrews 1:1–8; 3:1; 7:5–6; 9:11**).

Notes

1. Jewish tradition holds that Miriam was four years older than Aaron and seven years older than Moses. Scripture says, "In the first month the whole Israelite community arrived at the Desert of Zin, and they stayed at Kadesh. There Miriam died and was buried" (**Numbers 20:1**). Aaron died in ca. 1406 B.C.—"He died on the first day of the fifth month of the fortieth year after the Israelites came out of Egypt. Aaron was a hundred and twenty-three years old when he died on Mount Hor" (**Numbers 33:38–39**).

2. The reference to 430 years (**Exodus 12:40–41**)—as compared to the rounded off number of "four hundred years" in **Genesis 15:13; Acts 7:6**—should be understood to begin when Jacob, who at the age of 130 (**Genesis 47:9**), moved his family to Egypt in ca. 1876 B.C. The sojourn and bondage in Egypt lasted from 1876 B.C. to 1446 B.C., until the exodus occurred "to the very day" in 1446 B.C. See chart "**Genesis 46**: The Extended Family of Jacob (Seventy Descendants) Who Migrated to Egypt."

3. The Hebrew nation settled in Goshen and multiplied (**Genesis 47:27**), living in bondage in Egypt for a total of 430 years, 1876–1446 B.C. (**Exodus 12:40–41**); Moses was born ca. 1526 B.C., 80 years before the exodus (**Exodus 7:7; Deuteronomy 34:7**); for forty years, Moses was raised in the royal palace as the adopted son of Pharaoh's daughter, ca. 1526–1486 B.C. (**Exodus 2:10–11; Acts 7:21**); Moses left Egypt at age 40, ca. 1486 B.C. and lived in Midian for the next 40 years, ca. 1486–1446 B.C. (**Acts 7:23–30**); Moses led the Israelites out of Egypt in the exodus, which occurred on Passover, on 14 Nissan 1446 B.C. (**Exodus 12:17, 41, 51**; cf. **1 Kings 6:1**); the giving of the Law at Mount Sinai, which occurred 50 days after the exodus, in 1446 B.C. (**Exodus 19:1–3**); the 40-year period of wilderness wanderings, from 1446–1406 B.C. (**Numbers 14:33–34; 32:13; Deuteronomy 2:7; 8:2**); the death of Moses at 120 years old on Mount Nebo, in 1406 B.C. (**Deuteronomy 34:7**); and the nation of Israel

crossing the Jordan and entering the promised land under Joshua and the initial conquest of Canaanite cities, in 1406 B.C. (**Joshua 4:19**).

4. Levi was the eponymous ancestor of the Levitical priesthood (high priests, Kohathite attending priests and Levites). Levi, born ca. 1926 B.C., lived to be 137 years old (**Exodus 6:16**), dying ca. 1789 B.C.

5. The Kohathites included the Aaronic line of high priests (Levi–Kohath–Amram–Aaron–Eleazar–Phinehas, etc.) and other priestly relatives as well. Kohath lived to be 133 years old (**Exodus 6:18**).

6. Like his grandfather (Levi), Amram lived to be 137 years old (**Exodus 6:20**).

7. Izhar (**Exodus 6:18, 21; Numbers 3:19; 16:1; 1 Chronicles 6:2, 18, 38; 23:12, 18**) is otherwise known as Amminadab (**1 Chronicles 6:22**).

8. The birth order of the sons of Hebron is given in **1 Chronicles 23:19; 24:23**.

9. Mishael in **Exodus 6:22**; **Leviticus 10:4** is called Micah by the Chronicler (**1 Chronicles 23:20; 24:24–25**). Mishael/Micah was the firstborn son of Uzziel (**1 Chronicles 23:20**). After God killed Nadab and Abihu for offering "unauthorized fire" (**Leviticus 10:1–5**), Mishael and his brother Elzaphan removed the dead bodies from the tabernacle.

10. Ishiah, the second-born son of Uzziel, is not listed in **Exodus 6:22** but he is referred to in **1 Chronicles 23:20; 24:25**.

11. **Exodus 6:21** does not mention Shelomith as a son of Izhar, but the Chronicler identifies him as Izhar's firstborn (**1 Chronicles 23:18**).

12. Korah (a Levitical Kohathite) and three Reubenites (Dathan, Abiram, and On) led 250 Israelites in the Korah rebellion to challenge Moses' authority, but ultimately it led to their deaths: "the earth opened its mouth and swallowed them" (**Numbers 16:32**; cf. **Numbers 16; 26:10; Deuteronomy 11:6; Psalm 106:16–18**); nevertheless, the line of Korah "did not die out" (**Numbers 26:11**). See chart "**Numbers 16**: Korah and Descendants of Reuben Who Died in the Korah-Reubenite Rebellion."

13. Jeriah, the chief of the Hebronites in the days of the Davidic monarchy, had 2700 followers ("relatives") who were "able men and heads of families" whom David put in charge of the Reubenites, the Gadites, and the half-tribe of East Manasseh for every religious and political matter (**1 Chronicles 26:32**).

14. Elkanah is listed among the *sons* of Korah in **Exodus 6:24**, but **1 Chronicles 6:22–23** clarifies that Elkanah was the great-great-grandson of Kohath.

15. Abiasaph (**Exodus 6:24**) is also read Ebiasaph (**1 Chronicles 6:23, 37; 9:19**) and Asaph (**1 Chronicles 26:1**). The *sons* of Korah (Assir, Elkanah, and Abiasaph) in **Exodus 6:24** were actually "sons of sons," as explained in **1 Chronicles 6:22–23**—"The descendants of Kohath: Amminadab his son, Korah his son, Assir his son, Elkanah his son, Ebiasaph his son, Assir his son . . ." This clarifies that the text of **1 Chronicles 9:19** should read, "Shallum son of Kore, the son of Ebiasaph, the *descendant* [not the son] of Korah, and his fellow gatekeepers from his family (the Korahites) were responsible for guarding the thresholds of the tent just as their ancestors had been responsible for guarding the entrance to the dwelling of the Lord."

16. Elisheba was the daughter of Amminadab and the sister of Nahshon, of the tribe of Judah (**Exodus 6:23; 1 Chronicles 2:10**). All offspring of Aaron and Elisheba (the Levitical priesthood) were of mixed Levitical–Judahite heritage.

17. Gershom, the firstborn son of Moses and Zipporah, was born in Midian. Moses named him Gershom, meaning, "I have become a stranger [sojourner] in a foreign land" (**Exodus 2:22**), probably referring to Moses (a Hebrew) living in Midian (a foreign county) with Jethro, Moses' father-in-law (**Exodus 3:1; 4:18; 18:1-2, 5, 12; 18:27**). Presumably it was Gershom (not Eliezer) who was circumcised by his mother (Zipporah) instead of Moses (**Exodus 4:24–26**); see chart "**Exodus 18**: Moses' Sons, Gershom and Eliezer, and Their Descendants Who Served in Solomon's Temple." This Gershom should not be confused with (1) Gershom (in the Levi–Kohath–Amram–Aaron–Eleazar–Phinehas line) in **Ezra 8:2**, or (2) Gershon, one of the three sons of Levi (cf. **Genesis 46:11; Exodus 6:16; Numbers 3:17–18; 1 Chronicles 6:1, 16–17**).

18. Moses named his second-born son Eliezer, meaning, "My father's [Amram] God was my helper" because God had saved Moses from the sword of Pharaoh (**Exodus 18:4**). Eliezer son of Moses is not Eliezer of Damascus, Abram's trusted servant (**Genesis 15:2**).

19. Eleazar (the Aaronic high priest) married an Egyptian woman, who bore him a son named Phinehas. Most scholars suggest that Phinehas is an Egyptian name from the root (*pꜣ-nḥśy*), meaning "black people" ("פִּינְחָס," *HALOT* 2:926). As for Putiel, the name very likely derives from Egyptian *pꜣ-dy* ("פּוּטִיאֵל," *HALOT* 2:917–18).

20. The term *prophet* usually conjures up ideas of prediction, foretelling, and the like (cf. **Exodus 4:12; Deuteronomy 13:2–3; Jeremiah 1:9; 2 Peter 1:20–21**). However, it can also convey the idea (as in this case) of giftedness in teaching, preaching, singing, and instrumental music (see **Exodus 15:20; 1 Samuel 10:5**).

21. Miriam's paean of praise proclaimed, "Sing to the Lord, for he is highly exalted. Both horse and driver he has hurled into the sea" (**Exodus 15:21**), similar to the first line of the victory hymn of Moses (**Exodus 15:1**).

22. For the Cushites, see note 8 in chart "**Exodus 2**: Moses and Zipporah."

23. The names of the pharaohs are not specifically mentioned in the Bible, and Egyptian chronology, prior to the New Kingdom period in particular, has not achieved a scholarly consensus. Nevertheless, the differences amongst the most respected models are not so significant as to preclude the chronological choice made here. This work follows the identity of the pharaohs and dates of their rule given in I. E. S. Edwards, et al., *The Cambridge Ancient History*, vol. 1, part 2, 3rd ed. (Cambridge: Cambridge University Press, 1971), 996; I. E. S. Edwards et al., *The Cambridge Ancient History*, vol. 2, part 1, 3rd ed. (Cambridge: Cambridge University Press, 1973), 819; and Ian Shaw, ed., *The Oxford History of Ancient Egypt*. (Oxford: Oxford University Press, 2000), https://archive.org/details/TheOxfordHistoryOfAncient/page/n5/mode/2up.

For the pharaonic chronology, see chart "**Supplement 1**: The Pharaohs of the Twelfth and Eighteenth Dynasties of Egypt." In addition, for further discussion of the historical setting of the exodus, see Eugene H. Merrill, *Kingdom of Priests: A History of Old Testament Israel*. (Grand Rapids: Baker, 1996), 58–64. Given that Aaron was born in 1529 B.C. and Moses in 1526 B.C., they were likely born at the end of the reign of Ahmose (1570–1546 B.C./*1550–1525 B.C.*) or the beginning of the reign of Amenhotep I (1546–1526 B.C./*1525–1504 B.C.*). The exodus occurred in 1446 B.C. in the reign of Thutmose III (1504–1450 B.C./*1479–1425 B.C.*) or Amenhotep II (1450–1425 B.C./*1425–1400 B.C.*).

24. The "Pharaoh's daughter" who rescued Moses and became his adoptive mother (**Exodus 2:5–9**) is typically identified by scholars as Hatshepsut, the daughter of Thutmose I (1526–1512 B.C./*1504–1492 B.C.*)—"Only she of all known women of the period possessed the presumption and independence to violate an ordinance of the king and under his very nose at that"; see Merrill, *Kingdom of Priests*, 60.

25. Moses' name derives from the verb מָשָׁה, *mashah*, "draw forth." His flight from Egypt in 1486 B.C. likely occurred during the reign of Thutmose III (1504–1450 B.C./*1479–1425 B.C.*). Thutmose III may have married his own half-sister, Nefrura, the daughter of Hatshepsut and Thutmose II. Thutmose III resented Hatshepsut, who was a dominant presence during his reign. She herself ruled from 1503–1483 B.C./*1473–1458 B.C.* However, upon her death, Thutmose III (and his son-successor, Amenhotep II) systematically removed the evidence of her kinship and kingship by erasure of her image and all inscriptional and monumental references to her, perhaps to discount that a powerful female had ruled over Egypt in a dynastic line of "powerful" male successors (see notes 23 and 24 above). For notes about Moses' interactions in Egypt, see chart "**Supplement 1**: The Pharaohs of the Twelfth and Eighteenth Dynasties of Egypt."

26. See charts "**Exodus 2**: Moses and Zipporah" and "**Exodus 18**: Moses' Sons, Gershom and Eliezer, and Their Descendants Who Served in Solomon's Temple."

EXODUS 18: MOSES' SONS, GERSHOM AND ELIEZER, AND THEIR DESCENDANTS WHO SERVED IN SOLOMON'S TEMPLE

Approximate Dating: from the exodus in 1446 B.C., through the period of the united monarchy, 931 B.C. ***Relevant Scriptures:*** **Exodus 18:1–6**; also **Exodus 2:21–22; Judges 18:30; 1 Chronicles 23:15–17; 24:20–21; 25:20; 26:23–28**

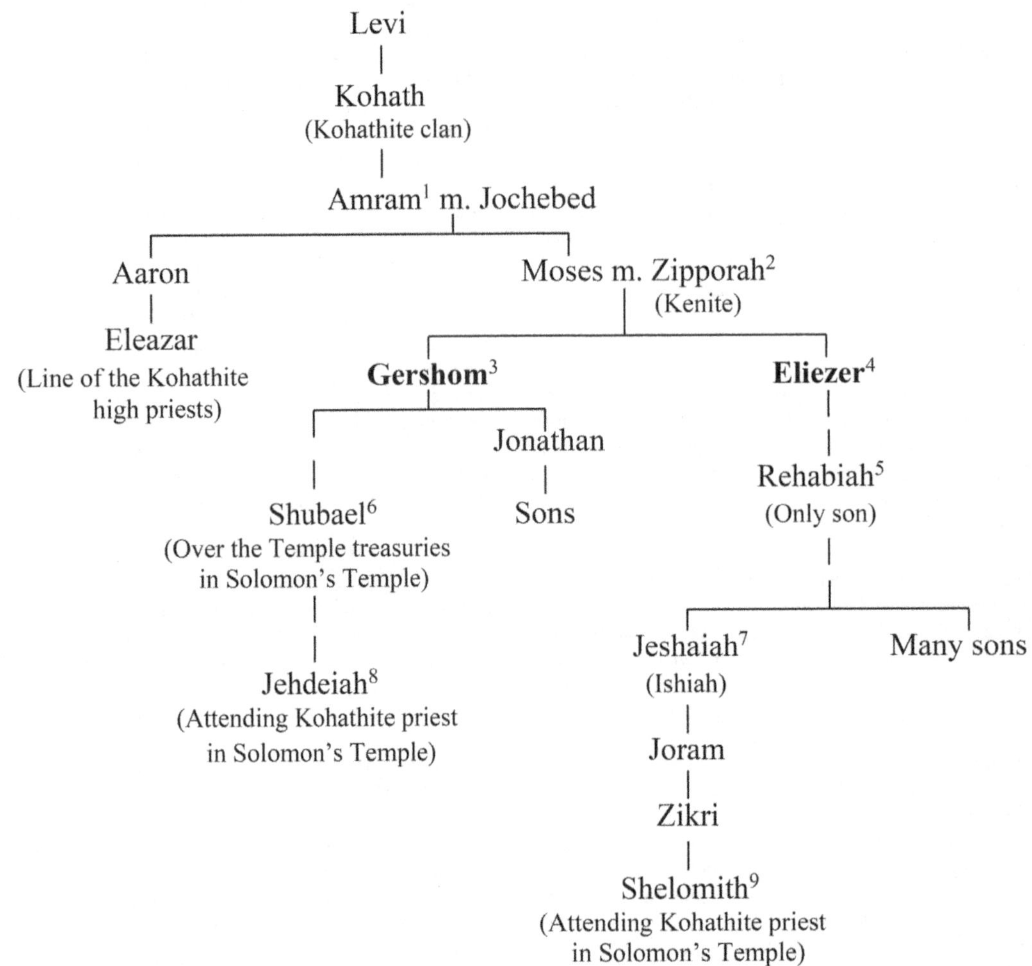

Biblical and Theological Significance

Moses, a son of Amram and Jochebed, was a descendant of Kohath, one of three sons of Levi, son of Jacob (**Genesis 29:34**). From the first, Levi was denied land in Canaan; indeed, his tribe would be "scattered" throughout (**Genesis 49:5–7**). This came to mean later that Levi was to serve as the tribe of priests and their assistants, denoted as *Levites*. This required members of the tribe to settle in some forty-eight Levitical cities in Canaan (**Joshua 21; Numbers 1:47–53**) so that every village and town would have access to community worship. In due time, Moses, in obedience to the Lord, divided the tribe into three parts—Kohathites, Gershonites, and Merarites—one for each son of Levi (**Numbers 3:14–20**). The text then goes on to specify that Kohath was the patronym of the "Amramites," the clan and family associated with Moses' father Amram (**Numbers 3:27**; cf. **Exodus 2:1–2; 6:16–20**). Moses' older brother, Aaron, was later designated to be the first in a line of high priests under whom all other attending priests and Levites would serve (**Exodus 28:1**). This included Moses, since as a Levitical Kohathite, he too could have access to the altar (**Exodus 17:15; 24:6, 8; Leviticus 8:15–19**).

The sons of Moses—Gershom and Eliezer—"were counted as part of the tribe of Levi," meaning they were considered Levitical Kohathites, and their descendants were eligible to serve in Solomon's Temple along with other Kohathite priests (**1 Chronicles 23:14–17**). Typically, according to the hereditary laws of Levitical succession, Moses' descendants would have been *ineligible* to serve in the Levitical priesthood[10] (cf. **1 Chronicles 6:1–53**) since that was reserved only for Aaron's descendants. However, God, in his sovereignty, could and did appear to alter his own programs, at least to human perception.

In one astounding instance, the initial faithfulness of the descendants of Gershom, Moses' firstborn son, soon deteriorated into gross disloyalty. In the early days of the judges, the tribe of Dan, who was dissatisfied with its lack of territorial assignment, sent men north in search of adequate land (**Judges 18:1–31**). Along the way they encountered a young self-appointed "priest" of an idolatrous Israelite named Micah. The Danite leaders, recognizing their need to be "religious," persuaded the young man to go with them to their new community in Laish in the far north. The remarkable thing here is that this priest, named Jonathan, was the son of Gershom and the grandson of Moses[11] (**Judges 18:30**).

Nonetheless, in the boundless grace of God, the descendants of Moses and Zipporah, through Gershom and Eliezer, became prominent Kohathite attending priests in Solomon's Temple. For example, Shubael—specifically identified as "a descendant of Gershom son of Moses"—became the official in charge of the treasuries in Solomon's Temple in about 971–931 B.C. (**1 Chronicles 26:24**). Additionally, Shelomith, a descendant of Eliezer, son of Moses, became the chief overseer of the treasuries that housed the dedicated offerings in Solomon's Temple (**1 Chronicles 26:26–28**). However, there is no subsequent record in Scripture that indicates that Moses' descendants served in the Second Temple in post-exilic Jerusalem (ca. 516 B.C.).

Thus, two unlikely groups of people—the descendants of Moses the Israelite and Zipporah the Kenite—became the loyal servants of Yahweh. Their high places of honor in the temple foreshadow the body of believers who are universal and inclusive, not defined by ethnicity but by their faith in the God of Abraham (cf. **Romans 4:16–18; Galatians 3:7–9, 14–16**).

Notes

1. Amram married Jochebed, "his father's sister" (i.e., his aunt; **Exodus 6:20**; cf. **Numbers 26:59**). The descendants of Amram—the Amramites (**Numbers 3:27; 1 Chronicles 26:23**)—included the descendants of Aaron and Moses.

2. For Zipporah and her heritage, see chart "**Exodus 2**: Moses and Zipporah."

3. Gershom was the firstborn son of Moses and Zipporah. His name means, "I have become a foreigner [sojourner] in a foreign land" (referring to Moses dwelling in Midian for forty years with Jethro, his father-in-law; **Exodus 18:1–3**). Gershom, the firstborn, was circumcised by Zipporah, his mother, and not by Moses, his father (which was the covenantal custom, especially for those of Levitical heritage; **Genesis 17:9–14; Exodus 4:24–26**).

Gershom the son of Moses should not be confused with (1) Gershon, one of the three sons of Levi, who was the progenitor of the Levitical Gershonites (**Genesis 46:11; Exodus 6:16; Numbers 3:17; 1 Chronicles 6:1, 16; 23:6**), nor with (2) Gershom (a descendant of Phinehas, the son of Eleazar, the son of Aaron) who returned from Babylon to Jerusalem in the post-exile in 458 B.C. (**Ezra 8:2**).

4. Eliezer was the second-born son of Moses and Zipporah (**Exodus 2:21–22, 4:20**). His name means "my God is help" referring to God saving Moses' life—"My father's God [the God of Amram] was my helper; he [God] saved me [Moses] from the sword of Pharaoh" (**Exodus 18:4**). Eliezer and Gershom were "counted as part of the tribe of Levi" (**1 Chronicles 23:14**), and their descendants were allowed to serve alongside other descendants of Kohath in Solomon's Temple (**1 Chronicles 23:14–17**). Eliezer's descendants were given specific responsibilities for the temple treasuries, including the dedicated things and the plunder from war (**1 Chronicles 26:24–28**).

5. Rehabiah, a son or descendant of Eliezer (**1 Chronicles 23:17; 26:25**), was the only male child, but "the sons of Rehabiah were very many" (**1 Chronicles 23:17**).

6. For Shubael, see **1 Chronicles 23:16; 24:20; 25:20; 26:24**. He was "from the sons of Amram" and "a descendant of Gershom son of Moses" (of the Kohathite clan of Levi–Kohath–Amram–Moses–Gershom descendants) and the head of a clan of Levites who did the work in Solomon's Temple in the days of David and Solomon (**1 Chronicles 23:16, 24**). Specifically, Shubael "was the official in charge of the [temple] treasuries" (**1 Chronicles 26:24**).

7. Jeshaiah (**1 Chronicles 26:25**) is otherwise Ishiah (**1 Chronicles 24:21**). Jeshaiah/Ishiah was the son (or more likely a descendant) of Rehabiah. Jeshaiah/Ishiah (in the Levi–Kohath–Amram–Moses–Eliezer–Rehabiah line) was a Levite from the Kohathite clan who served in Solomon's Temple (**1 Chronicles 24:20–21; 26:25**). Jeshaiah/Ishiah, the descendant of Moses, is a different person than:

(1) Ishiah the Kohathite, the brother of Micah and a descendant of the "sons of Uzziel" (Uzziel was Moses' uncle), who served in Solomon's Temple (cf. **1 Chronicles 23:12, 20; 24:24–25**);
(2) Jeshaiah, the descendant of Hananiah the Judahite (**1 Chronicles 3:21**);
(3) Jeshaiah the Merarite, the son of Jeduthun/Ethan (**1 Chronicles 25:3**);
(4) Jeshaiah the descendant of Elam, who returned to Jerusalem with Ezra in the post-exile (**Ezra 8:7**); and
(5) Jeshaiah the Merarite (Levite), who returned to Jerusalem with Ezra in the post-exile (**Ezra 8:19**).

8. Jehdeiah (Heb. יֶחְדְּיָהוּ) in **1 Chronicles 24:20** should not be confused with the name Jedaiah (Heb. יְדָיָה), as in: (1) Jedaiah the priest who was head over the second division of Kohathite attending priests in the days of David (cf. **v. 7**); (2) Jedaiah the priest "through the family of Jeshua [the high priest]" (**Ezra 2:36; Nehemiah 7:39**) whose descendants returned to Jerusalem in 538 B.C.

9. Shelomith and his brethren were overseers in Solomon's Temple over the treasuries of the dedicated things given by David, army commanders, Samuel, Saul, Abner, and Joab, as well as other dedicated things (**1 Chronicles 26:24–28**).

10. See charts "**1 Chronicles 6**: Levi: High Priests, Priests, Levites, and Musicians in Solomon's Temple" and "**Supplement 2**: The High Priests of Israel."

11. One of the most celebrated examples of obvious scribal textual manipulation is the "suspended *nun*" in **Judges 18:30**. "Jonathan son of Gershom, the son of Moses," is no doubt the original reading and is attested as such by important versions, such as the Greek Septuagint and Latin Vulgate. "Jonathan, the son of Gershom, the son of Manasseh" is clearly a reading created by post-biblical rabbinical scholars. The most likely reading on the basis of a standard text critical principle (*lectio difficilior;* the more difficult reading) is "Moses." Working on this principle, early scribes inserted the letter *nun* (or "n") between *mem* and *shin* (m and sh), thus creating the reading Manasseh (Heb. מנשה [Manasseh] for משה [Moses]). This was done to salvage the reputation of Moses, who was in fact the grandfather of Jonathan. The Danites worshiped a carved image made by Micah instead of worshiping in the house of God at Shiloh (**Judges 18:30–31**). Micah the idolater consecrated Jonathan to be his priestly assistant in idol worship among the Danites (cf. **Judges 17:1–3; 18:27–31**). **Judges 17:7** describes Jonathan as "a young Levite from Bethlehem in Judah, who had been living within the clan of Judah," and in **Judges 17:9**, Jonathan describes himself as, "I am a Levite from Bethlehem in Judah." Jonathan's sons "were priests for the tribe of Dan until the time of the captivity of the land. They continued to use the idol Micah had made, all the time the house of God was in Shiloh" (**Judges 18:30–31**).

EXODUS 31: BEZALEL, THE CHIEF ARTISAN OF THE TABERNACLE AND ITS FURNISHINGS, AND HIS ASSISTANT OHOLIAB

Approximate Dating: the tabernacle was completed by 1445 B.C.[1] and served as the place of worship for the Israelites during the wilderness wanderings, ca. 1445–1406 B.C.[2] ***Relevant Scriptures:*** **Exodus 31:2, 6; 35:30, 34–35; 36:1–2; 37:1; 38:22–23;** also **1 Chronicles 2:3–5, 9, 18–20, 24, 50; 4:4; 2 Chronicles 1:5**

Genealogy of Bezalel:

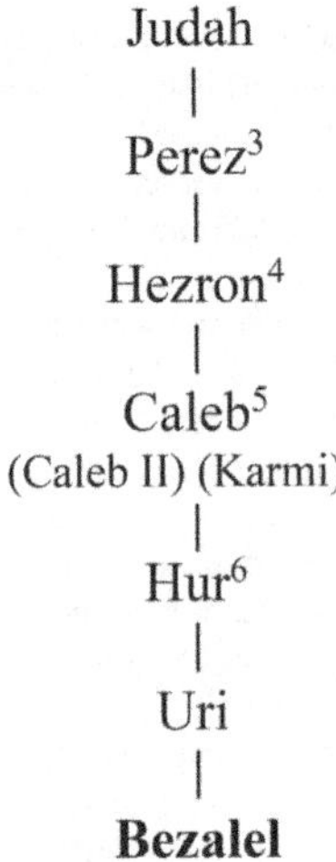

Genealogy of Oholiab:

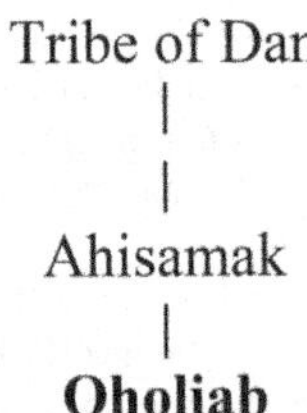

Biblical and Theological Significance

Bezalel the artisan was filled "with the Spirit of God, with wisdom, with understanding, with knowledge and with all kinds of skills—to make artistic designs for work in gold, silver and bronze, to cut and set stones, to work in wood, and to engage in all kinds of crafts" (**Exodus 31:3–5; Exodus 35:31–33**). Bezalel and his assistant, Oholiab, oversaw all the workmanship of the construction of the tabernacle (**Exodus 31:6–11; 35:10–19; 35:34–36:5; 38:22–23**). Bezalel made the ark of the testimony, the cherubim and the mercy seat, the altar of incense, the golden lampstand, the table of showbread, the laver, the bronze altar for burnt offerings, and other furnishings in the tabernacle (cf. **Exodus 37–39; 2 Chronicles 1:5**).

Bezalel and Oholiab worked alongside other gifted artisans: they were "skill[ed] to do all kinds of work as engravers, designers, embroiderers in blue, purple and scarlet yarn and fine linen, and weavers—all of them skilled workers and designers" (**Exodus 35:34–35**). Oholiab in particular was "an engraver and designer, and an embroiderer in blue, purple and scarlet yarn and fine linen" (**Exodus 38:23**). He appears to be the key weaver-designer of the fine linen and cherubim designs of the curtains in the tabernacle, the veil between the holy place and the holy of holies, the woven screen of the entrance of the tabernacle, the woven screen of the entrance of the court, and the ephod, robe and hem embellishments, breastplate, and sash of the high priest (cf. **Exodus 26:1–6, 31–33, 36; 27:16; 28:5–8, 15, 31–34; 35:35; 36:35, 37; 38:14–18; 39:1–5, 8, 22–29**).

Of special interest is the fact that Bezalel, like David, was of the tribe of Judah (**Exodus 31:2**) and a descendant of Perez and Hezron, although Bezalel was from the Perez–Hezron–Caleb (II)/Karmi line, whereas David was from the Perez–Hezron–Ram–Amminadab line[7] (cf. **1 Chronicles 2:5–15, 18–20**). Bezalel was privileged to decorate the tabernacle, and David planned for the great temple that his son Solomon completed. In one's seeking more conclusive theological interlocking, the blessing of Judah in **Genesis 49** comes to mind. There, a dying Jacob blessed his sons and said of Judah, "The scepter will not depart from Judah, nor the ruler's staff from between his feet, until he to whom it belongs shall come and the obedience of the nations shall be his" (**Genesis 49:10**). David was immediately in mind, but of course, David's descendant, Jesus Christ, the Son of David, was in the mind and plan of God.

As in most great achievements in world history, their creators and leaders receive all the recognition, attention, and praise while those who execute the plans by their skills and hard labor often receive little recognition, if any. The Hebrew Bible is refreshingly different in its presentation. The project may be the "tabernacle of Moses" or the "Temple of David (or Solomon)," but God gives note to the "little people" here and elsewhere. God sees no "big" or "little" people. To him, the weaving of linen cloth is as much kingdom work as is sitting on a golden throne.

Notes

1. The tabernacle was completed and set up on "the first day of the first month in the second year" (**Exodus 40:17**).

2. Judah was born in 1445 B.C. (see notes 2 and 4 in chart "**Genesis 35**: The Twelve Sons of Jacob, the Eponymous Originators of the Twelve Tribes of Israel"). If each of the ancestors of Bezalel lived approximately 75 years, Bezalel was born in 1475 B.C. and was approximately age 30 when the tabernacle was completed in 1445 B.C. (i.e., the year after the exodus in 1446 B.C.).

3. Perez was the twin brother of Zerah. Perez's mother was Tamar, the daughter-in-law of Judah (cf. **Genesis 38:6, 29–30; 1 Chronicles 2:4**).

4. See chart "**1 Chronicles 2**: Hezron."

5. Caleb in **1 Chronicles 2:18–19** is called Karmi in **1 Chronicles 4:1**. In this genealogy, Caleb son of Hezron (designated Caleb II in this and other charts) is not Caleb the Kenizzite, son of Jephunneh (designated Caleb I elsewhere), who was a contemporary of Moses and Joshua; see charts "**1 Chronicles 2**: Hezron" and "**1 Chronicles 2**: Caleb and Kenaz, the sons of Jephunneh the Kenizzite."

6. Hur was the firstborn of Caleb (son of Hezron) and his wife Ephrath (also called Ephrathah or Caleb Ephrathah)—a personal name and a place name for ancient Bethlehem/Bethlehem Ephrathah, whose inhabitants were the Ephrathites of Bethlehem (cf. **Genesis 35:19; 48:7; Ruth 1:2; 4:11; 1 Chronicles 2:19, 24, 50; 4:4; Micah 5:2**).

7. See charts "**1 Chronicles 2**: King David" and "**1 Samuel 16**: Jesse and the Judahites Who Lived in Bethlehem and Nearby Cities."

NUMBERS 1: GENEALOGICAL RECORD OF THE FIRST CENSUS OF THE TRIBES OF ISRAEL[1]

Approximate Dating: ca. 1445 B.C., in second year after the exodus from Egypt ***Relevant Scriptures:*** **Numbers 1:1–47**

Tribe	Number of Men	Leader of the Tribe
Reuben	46,500	Elizur, the son of Shedeur
Simeon	59,300	Shelumiel, the son of Zurishaddai
Gad	45,650	Eliasaph, the son of Deuel
Judah	74,600	Nahshon, the son of Amminadab[2]
Issachar	54,400	Nethanel, the son of Zuar
Zebulun	57,400	Eliab, the son of Helon
Ephraim (of Joseph)	40,500	Elishama, the son of Ammihud
Manasseh (of Joseph)	32,200	Gamaliel, the son of Pedahzur
Benjamin	35,400	Abidan, the son of Gideoni
Dan	62,700	Ahiezer, the son of Ammishaddai
Asher	41,500	Pagiel, the son of Okran
Naphtali	53,400	Ahira, the son of Enan

Biblical and Theological Significance

In the design and perfect plan of God, more fully explained in Deuteronomy, his chosen people were assigned to occupy and settle the land of Canaan, first promised to Abraham hundreds of years earlier. But the occupation would not come as a peaceful transition; indeed, it could happen only by a violent expulsion of the wicked residents of the land. Hints of this had already been revealed to Moses, but now the time had come to solidify the plan by preparing military forces to carry it out. The census here is clearly of a military nature as the phrase "able to serve in the army" (*letsibotam*; **Numbers 1:3**) makes plain.

The first census was a military registration conducted in the wilderness of Sinai—"on the first day of the second month of the second year after the Israelites came out of Egypt" (**Numbers 1:1–4**). Moses, Aaron, and representatives from each of the twelve tribes conducted the census: "[listing] every man by name, one by one. . . . [counting] according to their divisions all the men in Israel who are twenty years old or more and able to serve in the army. . . . [registering] their ancestry by their clans and families" (**Numbers 1:2–3, 18**). The twelve representatives of the tribes also served as the leaders of the army of Israel (**Numbers 2:3–32; 10:14–28**). The Lord said that Levi must not be counted or be included "in the census of the other Israelites" because they were appointed for service over the tabernacle (**Numbers 1:49–50**). The census revealed that the total number of men who could go to war in Israel was 603,550 (**Numbers 1:46**).

Notes

1. Compare this chart of the first census of the tribes with the chart "**Numbers 26**: The Tribes of Israel at the Time of the Second Census."
2. Nahshon is in the line of the Messiah (**Matthew 1:4; Luke 3:32**).

NUMBERS 2: GENEALOGICAL REGISTRY AND ORGANIZATION OF THE TRIBAL ENCAMPMENT IN THE WILDERNESS AND THE NUMBER OF MEN IN THE ARMY

Approximate Dating: post-exodus and time of the wilderness wanderings, ca. 1446–1406 B.C. ***Relevant Scriptures:*** **Numbers 2:1–34**

**Numbers indicate the birth order of the sons by the four wives of Jacob.[1]*

To the east of the Tabernacle (1st to break camp):

Tribe of Judah (#4) by Leah	74,600
Tribe of Issachar (#9) by Leah	54,400
Tribe of Zebulun (#10) by Leah	57,400
	186,400

To the south of the Tabernacle (2nd to break camp):

Tribe of Reuben (#1) by Leah	46,500
Tribe of Simeon (#2) by Leah	59,300
Tribe of Gad (#7) by Zilpah	45,650
	151,450

To the west of the Tabernacle (3rd to break camp):

Tribe of Ephraim, of Joseph (#12) by Rachel	40,500
Tribe of Manasseh, of Joseph (#12) by Rachel	32,200
Tribe of Benjamin (#13) by Rachel	35,400
	108,100

To the north of the Tabernacle (4th to break camp):

Tribe of Dan (#5) by Bilhah	62,700
Tribe of Asher (#8) by Zilpah	41,500
Tribe of Naphtali (#6) by Bilhah	53,400
	157,600

Biblical and Theological Significance

The organization of the tribes had a military function. The tribes of Israel "set up their tents by divisions, each of them in their own camp . . . around the tent of meeting some distance from it, each of them under their standard and holding the banners of their family" (**Numbers 1:52; 2:1**). The tribe of Levi encamped directly around the tabernacle—Moses, Aaron, and Aaron's sons on the east, the Kohathites on the south, the Merarites on the north, and the Gershonites on the west (**Numbers 3:23, 29, 35, 38**). The Levites broke camp in a protected position, "in the middle of the [other] camps," (**Numbers 2:17**) meaning *after* the tribes on the south (Reuben–Simeon–Gad), who broke camp second, and *before* the tribes on the west (Ephraim–Manasseh–Benjamin). The total number of Israelites "counted according to their families . . . by their divisions" who were able to go to war was 603,550 (**Numbers 2:32**).

Everything that God commands has purpose, including the arrangement of the camp. The political and religious leadership of the tribe of Judah is represented by that tribe's location in the east and in first place in the procession toward the promised land (**Numbers 10:14**). The word for east is קֶדֶם *gedem*, which also means "in front of." That is, since the sun rises in the east, announcing a new and fresh day of hope and anticipation, it is fitting that the tribe from which the "scepter . . . [and] ruler's staff" will come should assume leadership among the tribes (**Genesis 49:10**). David sprang from Judah, as did Jesus the Messiah of whom Isaiah obliquely speaks as coming from the east (**Isaiah 41:2**). More distantly relevant is Malachi's proclamation that "the sun of righteousness will rise with healing in its rays" (**Malachi 4:2**).

Also of importance is the centrality of the tabernacle in both location and symbolism. It must be in the midst of all the tribes, with the Levites as the protectors of holy things and religious officiants, encamped around it (**Numbers 2:17**). The tabernacle "housed" the Living God, who was ritualistically perceived to be enthroned over the ark of the covenant as the King of all creation (**Exodus 25:8; Numbers 5:3; 35:34**). The Levitical priests offered sacrifices in his name and led the congregation of Israel in hymns of praise (**Numbers 8:14–19; 1 Chronicles 15:16–24**). The tabernacle was also oriented toward the east, as was Solomon's Temple later on. Moses and Aaron were stationed at the front of the tabernacle to maintain its sanctity (**Numbers 3:38**).

Notes

1. There were twelve tribes of Israel, but the tribe of Levi (#3 by Leah) set up their tents immediately next to the tabernacle so that the "[the Lord's] wrath [would] not fall on the Israelite community" (**Numbers 1:53**). The daughter of Leah was Dinah (#11), and she is therefore omitted. The two sons of Joseph—Ephraim and Manasseh—were "reckoned as mine [Jacob/Israel]" and completed the twelve-tribe ideal (cf. **Genesis 48:5**). See chart "**Genesis 35**: The Twelve Sons of Jacob, the Eponymous Originators of the Twelve Tribes of Israel."

NUMBERS 3: AARON, THE HIGH PRIEST OF ISRAEL

Approximate Dating: Aaron was born in ca. 1529 B.C. and died at age 123 in 1406 B.C.; he served at the tabernacle, which was completed 1445 B.C., and was active during the years of the wilderness wanderings; ca. 1446–1406 B.C. ***Relevant Scriptures:*** **Numbers 3:1–4;** also **Genesis 46:11; Exodus 6:16, 18, 20, 23; Numbers 26:59–60; 1 Chronicles 6; 23:13; 24:1–2**

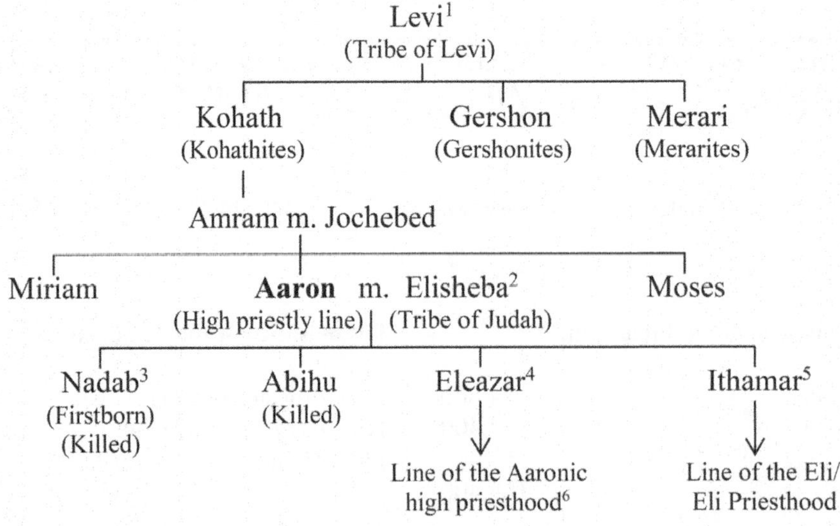

Biblical and Theological Significance

Aaron, Moses' older brother (**Exodus 7:7**), was a Levite of the Kohath clan and the first of a long line of high priests who maintained the worship apparatus of ancient Israel. When Moses resisted being the spokesperson for God because he felt he could not speak well, Aaron became the prophetic "mouth" of Moses (**Exodus 4:13–16; 7:1–2**) and spoke to the Israelites on Moses' behalf (cf. **Exodus 16:9**). In addition, Aaron assumed leadership in other situations as well:

- Aaron accompanied Moses to confront the Pharaoh (**Exodus 5:1; 6:13, 27**); Aaron's staff was the instrument that brought forth many of the plagues (**Exodus 7:10–12, 19–21; 8:6–7, 16–17**).
- Aaron accompanied Moses to Mount Sinai (**Exodus 19:23–24**) and worshiped "at a distance" (**Exodus 24:1–11**). When Moses delayed in coming down from the mountain, the Israelites encouraged Aaron to "make us gods who will go before us" (**Exodus 32:1, 23; Acts 7:40**); in compliance, Aaron fashioned an idolatrous golden calf, built an altar, and proclaimed a festival "to the Lord" (**Exodus 32:5–6, 35**). Moses held Aaron responsible for this great apostasy and for refusing to restrain the people (**Exodus 32:21, 25**).
- Aaron was considered the head of the family of Levi. Aaron and his sons were chosen by God to attend at the tabernacle (**Exodus 28:1, 41; 29–31**). The holy garments made for Aaron the high priest included the breastpiece, ephod, linen robe, woven linen tunic, turban of gold, a linen sash (**Exodus 28:4; 39:1–5**), and the names of the sons of Israel engraved on the memorial stones on the shoulders of the ephod and on the breastpiece, which represented the people before the Lord (**Exodus 28:11–12, 15–21; 29–30**). On the breastpiece of decision, Aaron wore the Urim and Thummim to "bear the means of making decisions for the Israelites over his heart before the Lord" (**Exodus 28:29–30**). He and his sons were given consecrated portions of the tabernacle offerings as food (cf. **Leviticus 10:12–15**), the "sanctuary shekel" (redemption money) for their service (**Numbers 3:46–51**), and the tithes of the Israelites for the work they performed in the tabernacle (**Numbers 18:21**). In his high priestly capacity, Aaron offered sacrifices for the people on the yearly Day of Atonement (**Exodus 30:10; Leviticus 16**) and pronounced the priestly blessing over the people (**Numbers 6:22–26**).
- When Israel moved its encampment in the desert, Aaron and his sons attended to the "most holy things," such as the veil and the ark of the testimony, as well as the coverings and furnishings of the sanctuary (**Numbers 4**).
- When twelve staffs were taken from each of the tribes, Aaron's staff "sprouted . . . budded, blossomed and produced almonds" (**Numbers 17:8**), thus confirming Aaron's priestly privilege and appointment from God. Aaron's staff, a pot of manna, and the stone tablets of the law were placed in the ark of the covenant (cf. **Numbers 17:10; Hebrews 9:4**).
- When Israel came into the promised land, Aaron and his sons were not given an inheritance of land, because the Lord said, "I am your share [portion] and your inheritance among the Israelites" (**Numbers 18:20**). Instead, the Levites were given forty-eight Levitical cities in the land (**Joshua 21:41**). The descendants of Aaron were allotted thirteen towns: Hebron, Libnah, Jattir, Eshtemoa, Holon, Debir, Ain, Juttah, and Beth Shemesh (from the tribe of Judah) and Gibeon, Geba, Anathoth, and Almon (from the tribe of Benjamin) (**Joshua 21:4–5, 11–19**).
- Because Aaron (and Moses) did not respect the Lord when water came from the rock at Meribah Kadesh in the Desert of Zin, Aaron was not permitted to come into the promised land (**Numbers 20:12, 24**). He died at the age of 123 at Mount Hor, "near the border of Edom," in 1406 B.C., the fortieth year after the Israelites came out of Egypt (**Numbers 20:23, 27–28; 33:38–39; Deuteronomy 32:50**). He "was gathered to his people" and buried at Moserah (**Numbers 20:24; Deuteronomy 10:6**). Aaron's son Eleazar succeeded him as high priest (**Deuteronomy 10:6**).

Aaron's priesthood is summarized thus: "Aaron was set apart, he and his descendants forever, to consecrate the most holy things, to offer sacrifices before the Lord, to minister before him and to pronounce blessings in his name forever" (**1 Chronicles 23:13**).

Whereas the Abrahamic genealogical descent focused ultimately on the choice of Israel as a covenant and missional people, and the Davidic descent identified the royal nature of that nation, culminating in the person of Jesus the Messiah, the Aaronic lineage traced the religious dimension of Israel as "a kingdom of priests and a holy nation" (**Exodus 19:6**). The theological significance of Israel's priesthood lies in its nature as a mediating agency between an ineffable and utterly transcendent God and mere mortals. Placating gifts and overtures such as burnt offerings or other kinds of sacrifices, while commanded by the God of Israel, were only stopgap measures that could not earn favor in and of themselves (cf. **Hebrews 9:1–10; 10:1–4**), but rather looked inward and forward to the final solution whereby God himself would interpose in the person of his sinless Son to make forgiveness and reconciliation possible. With the coming of Jesus, the perfect Son of God—a priest "in the order of Melchizedek" (**Psalm 110:4; Hebrews 5:6, 10; 6:20; 7:11, 17**)—sacrifice, tabernacle, temple, and the priesthood itself became obsolete. Jesus the high priest, who with his own blood made us perfect before the Father, ascended into heaven where he "always lives to intercede" (**Hebrews 7:25**) for those who acknowledge him as savior and Lord (**Psalm 110:4; Hebrews 3:1; 4:14–5:10; 6:19–7:28; 9:11–15; 10:11–14, 19–21**). The continuity of the priesthood, sustained as it was, was surely a token of God's faithfulness despite all odds. It made clear that there is only one community after all: the community of faith spanning both testaments and testifying to Jesus, the Great High Priest, who lives forever to make intercession between the redeemed and the Father in Heaven who made such fellowship possible through Him (**Hebrews 7:25**).

Notes

1. For a more expansive genealogy of the tribe of Levi, see chart "**1 Chronicles 6**: Levi: High Priests, Priests, Levites, and Musicians in Solomon's Temple."

2. Elisheba was a Judahite, the daughter of Amminadab (cf. **Ruth 4:19; Matthew 1:4; Luke 3:33**) and the sister of Nahshon (the leader of the tribe of Judah during the forty-year desert wanderings; **Numbers 1:7; 2:3; 7:12; 10:14**). Also, see chart "**1 Chronicles 4**: Judah."

3. Nadab, the firstborn son of Aaron (**Numbers 3:2**), was an attending priest at the tabernacle. He and his brother Abihu died because they disobeyed by offering "unauthorized fire" in the wilderness and dishonored the Lord (**Leveticus 10:1; 16:1; Numbers 3:4; 26:61**). Aaron "remained silent" because he knew his two sons had sinned (**Leviticus 10:3**). Nadab and Abihu died without sons (**Numbers 3:4; 1 Chronicles 24:2**).

4. After the deaths of Nadab and Abihu, "his [Aaron's] remaining sons" Eleazar and Ithamar became the attending priests to their father (**Exodus 28:1; Leviticus 10:6–7, 12; Numbers 3:4**). Just before Aaron's death, Moses appointed Eleazar to be Aaron's successor and the chief priest of Israel (**Numbers 20:28**). Eleazar served as the chief leader over his brethren, the Levites, who attended in the tabernacle (**Numbers 3:32**), and he also served at the time of the Israelite invasion and early occupation of the land (**Numbers 27:22**).

5. Ithamar, the son of Aaron, was the originator of the Eli priesthood (i.e., the Aaron–Ithamar–Eli line of priestly descendants), but this lineage is not as clearly delineated in Scripture as the Aaronic priesthood (cf. **1 Chronicles 6:1–15**). The Aaronic-Zadok high priesthood was centered in Jerusalem, whereas the Eli–Abiathar priesthood was centered in Shiloh; both priesthoods co-existed through the reign of King David (cf. **1 Samuel 14:3; 2 Samuel 8:17**). The line of Eli included Ahimelek, the son of Ahitub, who is explicitly called a descendant of "Ithamar" the son of Aaron (**1 Chronicles 24:3**; see **1 Samuel 14:3; 22:9, 11**). After God killed Nadab and Abihu, Ithamar and his brother Eleazar assumed a more prominent role in priestly service, although Eleazar held the more high-ranking position. Ithamar oversaw a written inventory account of the materials used for the tabernacle (**Exodus 38:21**). The Eli priesthood ended in the days of King Solomon when Solomon exiled the Elide priest, Abiathar, to Anathoth (**1 Kings 2:26–27**), thus fulfilling the Lord's prophecy and judgment against Eli (**1 Samuel 2:27–36; 22:16–19**). For the Eli priesthood, see chart "**1 Samuel 1**: Eli and the Eli Priesthood."

6. The Aaronic high priesthood is called "a priesthood that will continue throughout their generations" (**Exodus 40:15**) and "a covenant of a lasting priesthood" (**Numbers 25:13**). The succession of high priests continued through Eleazar's son Phinehas (**Exodus 40:13–15; Numbers 25:11–13**; cf. **1 Chronicles 6:1–15**) and even beyond the Old Testament period. For the line of the high priests, see charts "**1 Chronicles 6**: Levi: High Priests, Priests, Levites, and Musicians in Solomon's Temple" and "**Supplement 2**: The High Priests of Israel."

NUMBERS 3: LEVI AND THE LEVITICAL CLANS AT THE TIME OF THE FIRST CENSUS

Approximate Dating: 1445 B.C. ***Relevant Scriptures:*** **Numbers 3:16–39**

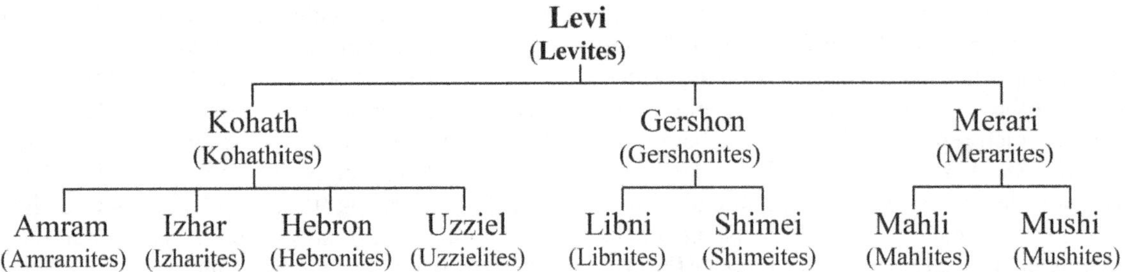

Biblical and Theological Significance

The first census, conducted by Moses and Aaron in the Wilderness of Sinai in 1445 B.C., was "on the first day of the second month of the second year after the Israelites came out of Egypt" (**Numbers 1:1–4**). Whereas the census for the other (eleven) tribes was to determine the number of men "twenty years old or more" (**Numbers 1:3**) who could go to war, the census for the tribe of Levi was conducted to number "every male a month old or more" who was eligible to be a priest or Levite[1] (**Numbers 3:15, 39**). The Kohathites, led by Elizaphan, the son of Uzziel (cf. **Numbers 3:27–31**), numbered 8,600. The Gershonites, led by Eliasaph, the son of Lael, totaled 7,500 (cf. **Numbers 3:21–26**). Finally, the Merarites, led by Zuriel, the son of Abihail (cf. **Numbers 3:33–37**), numbered 6,200. The three clans together totaled 22,000 (**Numbers 3:39**). The chief leader over all the Levites was Eleazar, the son of Aaron, the son of Amram (**Numbers 3:32**).[2]

The only way one could claim the privilege of ministering at the tabernacle (and later the temple) was by proving his descent from Levi and proving his lineage through one of the three clans. This was also important in determining the particular Levitical function expected of him. The Kohathites were charged with attending the high priest and maintaining the ark, the bread table, the golden lampstand, the altars, and the tools and instruments required for offering sacrifices (**Numbers 3:31**). The Gershonites took care of all aspects of the tent-tabernacle—its coverings, its curtains, its ropes, and all other materials essential to its construction (**Numbers 3:25–26**). Finally, the Merarites cared for the outer and inner posts of the tent, its framework, tent pegs, and courtyard pegs and ropes (**Numbers 3:36–37**). The clan organization of Kohathites–Gershonites–Merarites continued in the era of the First Temple and throughout the centuries until the Second Temple was destroyed. Obviously, the replacement of a portable shrine such as the tent-tabernacle by a solid, immovable temple necessitated changes in function, all of which are found in passages such as **1 Chronicles 6:31–49; 23:28–32**.

As was noted in the chart for Aaron, the high priest,[3] the priestly office carried heavy theological meaning in terms of worship and other ways of establishing and maintaining fellowship between Almighty God and the people. Since the high priest could never bear the load alone, the Levitical institution was established to assist in all things pertaining to priestly responsibility. Yet, an indelible line was drawn between the high priests and Levites and the privileges reserved to each. These are articulated in **Leviticus 8:1–36**, where the duties of the high priests are laid out in great detail, and in **Numbers 3–4**, where Levitical limitations are underscored.

Notes

1. The Kohathite attending priests and the Gershonite and Merarite Levites were not eligible to serve until they were 25 years old and had to retire at age 50 (**Numbers 8:24–25**).
2. See charts "**Exodus 6**: Moses, Aaron, and Miriam, the Leaders of Israel" and "**1 Chronicles 6**: Levi: High Priests, Priests, Levites, and Musicians in Solomon's Temple."
3. See chart "**Numbers 3**: Aaron, the High Priest of Israel."

NUMBERS 7 AND 10: GENEALOGICAL RECORD OF THE LEADERS OF THE TWELVE TRIBES[1] AT THE DEDICATION OF THE TABERNACLE AND THE ORDER OF THE TRIBAL DEPARTURE FROM MOUNT SINAI[2]

Approximate Dating: Second year after the exodus at the time of the departure from Mount Sinai in 1445 B.C.[3] ***Relevant Scriptures:*** **Numbers 7:10–83; 10:14–28**

**Numbers next to the names indicate birth-order.[4]*

Tribe of Judah — **Nahshon**, the son of Amminadab
Tribe of Issachar — **Nethanel**, the son of Zuar
Tribe of Zebulun — **Eliab**, the son of Helon

— Judah (4), Issachar (9) and Zebulun (10) were the sons of Leah —
— The tribes of Judah, Issachar and Zebulun encamped on the east side of the Tabernacle —

Tribe of Reuben — **Elizur**, the son of Shedeur
Tribe of Simeon — **Shelumiel**, the son of Zurishaddai
Tribe of Gad — **Eliasaph**, the son of Deuel

— Reuben (1) and Simeon (2) were the sons of Leah, and Gad (7) was the son of Zilpah (Leah's servant) —
— The tribes of Reuben, Simeon and Gad encamped on the south side of the Tabernacle —

Tribe of Ephraim — **Elishama**, the son of Ammihud
Tribe of Manasseh — **Gamaliel**, the son of Pedahzur
Tribe of Benjamin — **Abidan**, the son of Gideoni

— Ephraim and Manasseh were the sons of Joseph (12), the son of Rachel, and Benjamin (13) was the son of Rachel —
—The tribes of Ephraim, Manasseh and Benjamin encamped on the west side of the Tabernacle —

Tribe of Dan — **Ahiezer**, the son of Ammishaddai
Tribe of Asher — **Pagiel**, the son of Okran
Tribe of Naphtali — **Ahira**, the son of Enan

— Dan (5) and Naphtali (6) were the sons of Bilhah (Rachel's servant) and Asher (8) was the son of Zilpah (Leah's servant) —
— The tribes of Dan, Asher, and Naphtali encamped on the north side of the Tabernacle —

Biblical and Theological Significance

Once the tabernacle was completed, Moses "anointed and consecrated it and all its furnishings" as well as "the altar and all its utensils" (**Numbers 7:1**). Preparation for continued worship in the barren desert called for the giving of sacrificial materials such as animals, grains, oil, and the like, all of which could not be found in the desert, and therefore, must be transported on carts for that purpose. The twelve leaders of the tribes (the "heads of families") provided six covered carts and twelve oxen[5] and presented offerings on twelve successive days[6] for the dedication of the altar (**Numbers 7**).

Each leader presented the same offering: one silver platter and one silver bowl full of flour mixed with oil as a grain offering; one gold pan of incense; one bull, one ram, and one lamb as a burnt offering; one kid goat as a sin offering; and two oxen, five rams, five goats, and five lambs as a fellowship (peace) offering. The leaders were in charge of all the operations of loading the carts, instructing the priests as to the order of the tribes in leading in worship, and the lineup of the tribes in proper sequence. Importantly, Judah, the messianic tribe, was listed first in the presentation of oblations to Yahweh (**Numbers 7:12–17**): Judah's headship was first hinted at in the blessing of Jacob in **Genesis 49:10** where the appurtenances to royalty are clearly in view for that tribe and its descendants. The divine choice of the preeminence of the tribe of Judah is put beyond doubt in the procession of the tribes to Canaan in which Judah also took the lead in the departure from Sinai (**Numbers 10:14**).[7]

With the worship apparatus and personnel in place, it was time for Israel to move forward toward the destination in Canaan. The departure from Sinai took place "on the twentieth day of the second month of the second year" [referring to 1445 B.C., the second year after the exodus in 1446 B.C.] (**Numbers 10:11**). The marching order of the tribes (**Numbers 10:14–28**) followed the same order as that of the presentation of tribal offerings (**Numbers 7:12–83**): Judah, Issachar, Zebulun, Reuben, Simeon, Gad, Ephraim, Manasseh, Benjamin, Dan, Asher, and Naphtali.

Notes

1. The exclusion of Levi from the list of tribal leaders required that a "new" tribe be created to bring the descendants of Jacob up to the idealistic number of twelve. This was done by the division of the Joseph tribe into two tribes named for *his* sons—Ephraim and Manasseh (see **Genesis 46:20; 48:1–20**).

2. Compare the order of the tribes in this chart with the chart "**Numbers 2**: Genealogical Registry and Organization of the Tribal Encampment in the Wilderness and the Number of Men in the Army."

3. The tabernacle was set up "on the first day of the first month in the second year" (**Exodus 40:17**).

4. For the birth order of the sons of Jacob, see chart "**Genesis 35**: The Twelve Sons of Jacob, the Eponymous Originators of the Twelve Tribes of Israel." Issachar, like Judah, was a son of Leah, Jacob's first wife (**Genesis 29:35; 30:18**) and, in fact, was the next son born to Leah after Judah. Issachar's position in the offerings and pilgrimage reflect this birth order. Leah's sixth and last son, Zebulun, was born next (**Genesis 30:20**) and was third in both oblations and in the order of marching. Dan was the first "son" of Rachel, but he, in fact, was born to Bilhah, Rachel's servant and surrogate (**Genesis 30:4–6**). In the oblations list he is tenth in order (**Numbers 7:66**) and, again, in that position in the trek toward Canaan (**Numbers 10:25**). Naphtali was Bilhah's second son of two, following which was Leah's resort to her servant Zilpah, who produced Gad and then Asher. Rachel at last gave birth, first to Joseph (**Genesis 30:22–24**) and finally, much later, Benjamin (**Genesis 35:18**). Prior to Judah, however, Leah had borne three sons—Reuben, Simeon, and Levi. The oblation sequence, listed in the chart above, presents Reuben just after Zebulun, Simeon after Reuben, and then Gad, not Levi, as might be expected. The reason, of course, is that Levi was the priestly and Levitical tribe and therefore maintained the ark, the tabernacle, and all the furnishings therein (**Numbers 7:1–11**). The same was true of the order of transit from Sinai to Canaan, when the tribe of Levi processed between Zebulun and Reuben (**Numbers 10:16–18**). Ephraim followed Gad in the matter of the oblations (**Numbers 7:48–53**), followed by his brother Manasseh (**Numbers 7:54–59**).

5. Moses gave the carts and oxen to the Levites for their required work: two carts and four oxen to the Gershonites and four carts and eight oxen to the Merarites. However, the Kohathites carried the holy things on their shoulders, rather than on ox-driven carts (**Numbers 7:6–9**).

6. The offerings of the tribes are enumerated in **Numbers 7** in the following order: Judah in **vv. 12–17**; Issachar in **vv. 18–23**; Zebulun in **vv. 24–29**; Reuben in **vv. 30–35**; Simeon in **vv. 36–41**; Gad in **vv. 42–47**; Ephraim in **vv. 48–53**; Manasseh in **vv. 54–59**; Benjamin in **vv. 60–65**; Dan in **vv. 66–71**; Asher in **vv. 72–77**; Dan in **vv. 73–77**; and Naphtali in **vv. 78–83**.

7. The other tribes seem to have recognized and accepted the preeminence of the tribe of Judah since the word of a patriarchal blessing was considered non-negotiable (cf. **Genesis 27:33–40**).

NUMBERS 13: GENEALOGICAL RECORD OF THE TWELVE SPIES OF THE PROMISED LAND

Approximate Dating: beginning of the wilderness wanderings, in 1445 B.C.[1] ***Relevant Scriptures:*** **Numbers 13:3–16**

Tribe of Reuben	**Shammua**, the son of Zakkur
Tribe of Simeon	**Shaphat**, the son of Hori
Tribe of Judah	**Caleb**, the son of Jephunneh (Kenizzite)
Tribe of Issachar	**Igal**, the son of Joseph
Tribe of Ephraim	**Hoshea (Joshua)**, the son of Nun
Tribe of Benjamin	**Palti**, the son of Raphu
Tribe of Zebulun	**Gaddiel**, the son of Sodi
Tribe of Manasseh	**Gaddi**, the son of Susi
Tribe of Dan	**Ammiel**, the son of Gemalli
Tribe of Asher	**Sethur**, the son of Michael
Tribe of Naphtali	**Nahbi**, the son of Vophsi
Tribe of Gad	**Geuel**, the son of Maki

Biblical and Theological Significance

When the Israelites reached the Desert of Paran at Kadesh, twelve men, one from each tribe, were sent by Moses to spy out the land of Canaan. After forty days the spies returned and brought back a report. All recognized that the land was fruitful and flowed "with milk and honey" (**Numbers 13:27**),[2] but ten of the twelve gave a negative report, saying they were intimidated by large, fortified cities; the giant Anakites;[3] the Amalekites who lived in the Negev; the Hittites, Jebusites, and Amorites in the mountains; and the Canaanites along the Mediterranean and the banks of the Jordan River (cf. **Numbers 13:27–29**). Only two brought back an encouraging report—Caleb the Kenizzite,[4] who represented the tribe of Judah, and Hoshea (Joshua) from the tribe of Ephraim. They told the Israelite assembly that the land was "exceedingly good" and that "if the Lord is pleased with us" that he would lead them into that land and would give it to them (**Numbers 14:7–8**). They must not rebel against Yahweh nor fear the people of the land (**Numbers 14:9**). Nevertheless, the Israelites remained so fearful they wanted to return to Egypt (**Numbers 14:2–4**).

For their lack of faith and rejection of God's promises, the Lord pronounced a death sentence on the exodus generation for those older than twenty.[5], [6] The ten spies who brought back a bad report "died of a plague" (**Numbers 14:36–37**); only Caleb and the younger men survived to enter Canaan (**Numbers 14:30, 38**). From his youth, Joshua had been Moses' assistant (**Exodus 24:13; Joshua 1:1; 11:15**), but after Moses' death, he became Moses' successor and the new leader of Israel (**Deuteronomy 1:38; 3:28; 31:3, 7, 14, 23; 34:9; Joshua 1:1; 4:14; 11:15**). The two spies who trusted God were not overwhelmed by what they could see in the land of Canaan but trusted in what they could not see with mortal eyes—the redemptive and saving power of their God. Caleb, whose name means "dog," was dogged in carrying out the will of God, not only as a spy but as a mighty warrior. At the age of eighty-five, he came into the possession and inheritance of the promised land[7] (**Joshua 14:6–15; 15:13–19**). The renaming of Hoshea (הוֹשֵׁעַ), "salvation," to Yehoshuah (יְהוֹשֻׁעַ), "Yah(weh) saves," was to make clear that all Joshua[8] could do and did was in the name and the power of Yahweh. The Greek transliteration is Ἰήσους (*Iesous*), that is, "Yahweh saves," as in the Hebrew. One is reminded of the angelic instruction to Joseph, "You are to give him the name Jesus, because he will save his people from their sins" (**Matthew 1:21**).

Notes

1. The spies were sent to Canaan in 1445 B.C., sometime after the twenty-third day of the third month of the second year after the exodus, which had occurred in 1446 B.C. (cf. **Numbers 10:11, 33; 13:1–3**).

2. "Milk and honey" is a figure of speech or *pars pro toto* (a part for the whole) standing for food and drink of every kind. In the land there were, of course, foods and beverages besides these named here. For the combination elsewhere in the Pentateuch alone, see **Exodus 3:8, 17; 13:5; 33:3; Leviticus 20:24; Numbers 13:27; 14:8; 16:13–14; Deuteronomy 6:3; 11:9; 26:9, 15; 27:3; 31:20**.

3. See chart "**Deuteronomy 1**: The Giant Anakites, including Goliath and His Descendants."

4. See charts "**Joshua 14**: The Clan of Jephunneh the Kenizzite" and "**1 Chronicles 2**: Caleb and Kenaz, the Sons of Jephunneh the Kenizzite."

5. The reason for this age is that no one under age twenty was to participate in war in any form, including gathering intelligence as the spies were doing (**Numbers 1:2–3**). Therefore, these young men were absolved of all the sins of the unfaithful older men of war and thus, with Caleb and Joshua, were eligible to enter the promised land (**Numbers 14:30, 38**).

6. The judgment of forty years of wilderness wanderings was correlated with the forty days that the spies explored the land (**Numbers 14:34; 32:13**; cf. **Joshua 5:6**).

7. Caleb received as his inheritance the important city of Hebron (also called Kiriath Arba and formerly occupied by the descendants of Anak; see note 3), located at about 3,000 ft. in the hill country of Judah. Hebron had been the home of Abraham and Isaac and the place where Sarah died. It was captured by Joshua in the southern military campaign. After the Israelites came to possess the land, Hebron was designated as a Levitical city and a city of refuge (**Genesis 13:18; 23:2; 35:27; Numbers 13:22; Joshua 11:21; 14:15; 15:13, 54; 20:7; 21:11; Judges 1:10; Nehemiah 11:25**). Eventually, Hebron became the first capital of King David (**2 Samuel 2:1–3, 11**) before he moved his capital to Jerusalem.

8. See chart "**Joshua 1**: Joshua, the Successor of Moses and Leader of the Nation of Israel."

NUMBERS 16: KORAH AND THE DESCENDANTS OF REUBEN WHO DIED IN THE KORAH-REUBENITE REBELLION

Approximate Dating: early period of the wilderness wanderings, ca. 1444 B.C. ***Relevant Scriptures:*** **Numbers 16:1–34, 26:5–11**; also **Genesis 46:9; Exodus 6:14, 18, 20–21, 24; 1 Chronicles 5:3; 6:2, 22–24, 37; 23:12**

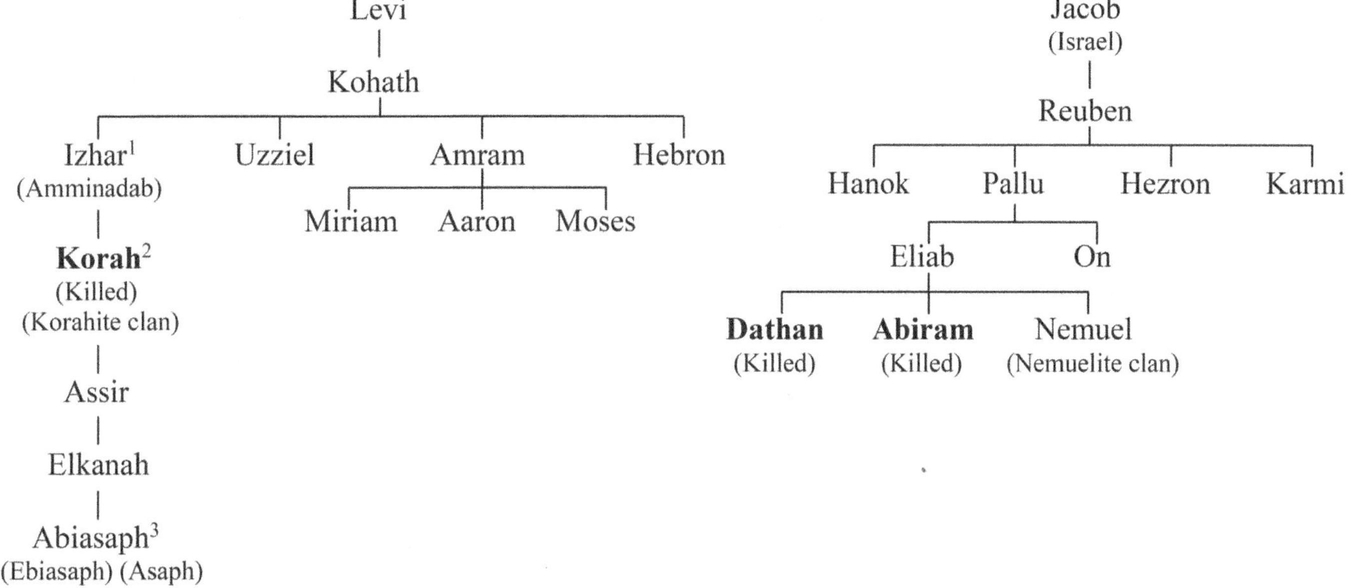

Biblical and Theological Significance

Within only two years after the exodus, two dissatisfied groups of men became envious of the leadership of Moses and Aaron and questioned their authority over the Israelites. One group, from the tribe of Reuben, was led by Dathan, Abiram, and On, and another group of Levitical Kohathites was led by Korah, leader of the Korahite clan. By rejecting God's appointed leadership, these men were in essence rejecting God (**Numbers 16:30**). Such egregious rebellion against the Lord God called for the death penalty under Mosaic Law (**Exodus 22:28; 32:10, 27–28**). In light of these precedents, it is not surprising that Yahweh slew Korah, Dathan, and Abiram, and the men in their company: "the ground under them split apart and the earth opened its mouth and swallowed them and their households, and all those associated with Korah, together with their possessions. They went down alive into the realm of the dead, with everything they owned; the earth closed over them, and they perished and were gone from the community" (**Numbers 16:31–33**). The Lord consumed 250 men on that day (**Numbers 16:35**; cf. **Psalm 106:16–18**).[4] **Numbers 26:11** makes clear that, despite the rebellion, "the line of Korah did not die out"; for example, Samuel the prophet was a remnant of the Levi–Kohath–Izhar–Korah–Assir–Elkanah line of descendants (see the chart "**1 Samuel 1**: Samuel, the Prophet–Priest–Judge of Israel").

At least three practical theological principles may be deduced from this genealogy and episode:

1. Rebellion against the duly authorized representatives or spokespeople of Almighty God is tantamount to rebellion against God himself, a principle also embedded in the New Testament (**Romans 13:1–7; Titus 3:1; 1 Peter 2:13–15**).
2. No one is so important that he or she is exempt from the judgment of God for evildoing.
3. God's program moves forward despite failure on the part of those called to serve him.

Notes

1. Izhar in **Exodus 6:18; Numbers 3:19; 16:1;** and **1 Chronicles 6:2, 18, 38; 23:12** is called Amminadab in **1 Chronicles 6:22**.

2. Korah was the eponymous ancestor of the Korahite clans (**Exodus 6:24; Numbers 26:58; 1 Chronicles 26:1; 2 Chronicles 20:19**). **Exodus 6:24** says, "the sons of Korah were Assir, Elkanah and Abiasaph. These were the Korahite clans"; however, the Chronicler clarifies that Assir, Elkanah and Abiasaph were sons-of-sons: "The descendants of Kohath: Amminadab his son, Korah his son, Assir his son, Elkanah his son, Ebiasaph his son" (**1 Chronicles 6:22–23**).

3. Abiasaph in **Exodus 6:24** is called Ebiasaph in **1 Chronicles 6:23, 37; 9:19** and Asaph in **1 Chronicles 26:1**.

4. In the conspiracy story in Numbers 16:1–40, "The conspiracy of Korah is a strictly levitical concern directed against the exclusive claims of [Moses and Aaron] . . . that of Dathan and Abiram is a more directly political conspiracy against the exclusive governing authority of Moses, who would be "prince" ["lord . . . over us"; **Numbers 16:13**] . . . The story of Abiram is often understood as a reflection of the loss of prestige by the tribe of Reuben following the period of settlement." Rodney R. Hutton, "Dathan," *Anchor Yale Bible Dictionary* Vol. 2:40.

NUMBERS 25: PHINEHAS, THE FAITHFUL HIGH PRIEST IN THE AARONIC PRIESTHOOD

Approximate Dating: during the years of the wilderness wanderings, ca. 1446–1406 B.C. ***Relevant Scriptures:*** **Numbers 25:11;** also **Exodus 6:18, 20, 23, 25; 28:1; Numbers 3:2; 26:58–60; 1 Chronicles 6:1–4; 23:12; 24:1–2; Psalm 106:28–31**

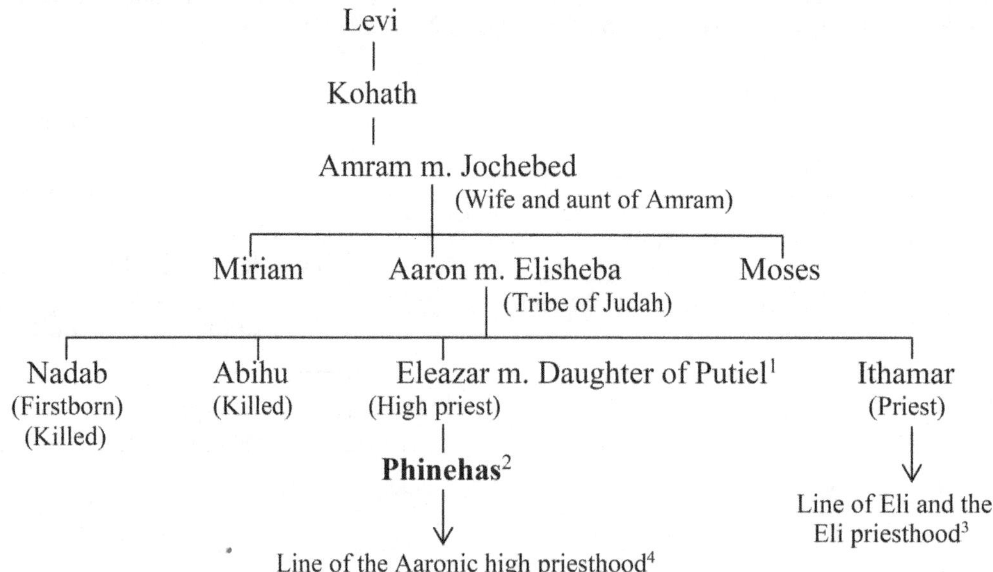

Biblical and Theological Significance

While Israel was encamped at Shittim, across the Jordan River from Jericho (cf. **Joshua 2:1**), and before they crossed into Canaan in 1406 B.C., Moabite women seduced the Israelite men and invited them to attend the pagan sacrifices to their gods, yoke themselves to Baal of Peor, and engage in sexual immorality (**Numbers 25**).[5] In an overt display of ritual prostitution, an Israelite leader from the tribe of Simeon named Zimri, son of Salu, took a Midianite woman named Kozbi, daughter of Zur (a tribal chief of a Midianite family) and slept with her at the entrance to the tent of meeting, thereby eliciting the Lord's wrath in the form of a plague

(**Numbers 25:6**). Those who "yoked themselves to the Baal of Peor" were to be put to death by Israel's judges (**Numbers 25:1–5, 14–15**). When Phinehas, the high priest, the son of Eleazar, saw this, he killed them: "he left the assembly, took a spear in his hand and followed the Israelite into the tent. He drove the spear into both of them, right through the Israelite man [Zimri] and into the woman's [Kozbi's] stomach. Then the plague against the Israelites was stopped" (**Numbers 25:7–8**). Phinehas' priestly intercession turned back God's wrath, for God ended the plague.[6] The righteous deeds of Phinehas the son of Eleazar are commended in **Psalm 106:28–31**.

Phinehas' righteous act exemplified God's zeal and his desire for purity among his people. For his faithfulness, the Lord promised Phinehas "my covenant of peace" and "a covenant of a lasting priesthood" (**Numbers 25:10–13**) for "endless generations to come" (**Psalm 106:31**; cf. the "covenant with Levi" in **Malachi 2:4, 8**). The high priesthood continued through the Aaron–Eleazar–Phinehas–Zadok line (cf. **1 Chronicles 6:1–15**).

Notes

1. Some scholars suggest that Putiel is from an Egyptian root (*p'-nḥšy*), meaning "black people" ("פִּינְחָס," *HALOT* 2:926) and may refer to an Egyptian place name (*p'-dy*, "Libya"? "פּוּטִיאֵל," *HALOT* 2:917–18). If true, this indicates that Eleazar the Aaronic high priest married an Egyptian woman and may explain why they named their son Phinehas, meaning "the black man" or "the man of dark complexion."

2. Nadab, Abihu, Eleazar, and Ithamar were consecrated as priests to serve under their father, Aaron (**Exodus 28:1**). However, after Nadab and Abihu were killed by God for offering "unauthorized fire" (**Leviticus 10:1–2**), and because they had no sons, the brothers Eleazar and Ithamar served as the primary priests during the lifetime of their father Aaron (**Numbers 3:4; 1 Chronicles 24:2**). In the promised land, Phinehas was allotted Gibeah in the hill country of Ephraim, and this was the burial site of his father, Eleazar (**Joshua 24:33**). The high priest Phinehas, son of Eleazar, is not the same person as Phinehas, son of Eli, the high priest at Shiloh (of the Elide priesthood), who was a wicked priest whom the Lord killed (cf. **1 Samuel 2:12, 34; 4:4, 11**), nor is he Phinehas, the Kohathite attending priest who is mentioned in **Ezra 8:2, 33**.

3. See chart "**1 Samuel 1**: Eli and the Eli Priesthood."

4. See charts "**1 Chronicles 6**: Levi: High Priests, Priests, Levites, and Musicians in Solomon's Temple" and "**Supplement 2**: The High Priests of Israel."

5. Canaanite mythology perceived Baal as a local deity capable of residing in many places simultaneously; thus, this Baal was situated at Peor, eight miles northeast of the Dead Sea.

6. The plague killed 24,000 unholy Israelites—the number found in the Hebrew and Greek (Septuagint) texts of **Numbers 25:9**—which corresponds to the 23,000 Israelites of **1 Corinthians 10:8**. The difference in the numbers may be accounted for by Paul's addition to the Old Testament narrative: "in one day."

NUMBERS 26: THE TRIBES OF ISRAEL AT THE TIME OF THE SECOND CENSUS

Approximate Dating: in 1406 B.C., just before entry into of the promised land of Canaan ***Relevant Scriptures:*** **Numbers 26:1–65**

Comparisons between Census #1 (*Numbers 1:1–47***) and Census #2 (***Numbers 26:1–65***) are shown in table 1.*

Biblical and Theological Significance

In preparation for entering Canaan, the Lord commanded Moses and Eleazar, the high priest, to conduct a second census of the tribes of Israel. It was taken when Israel was encamped "on the plains of Moab by the Jordan across from Jericho" (**Numbers 26:63**). It excluded all who had lived at the time of the first census (**Numbers 1:1–47**), since all the people of that generation who were twenty years and older died during the forty-year period of wandering in the desert (with the exception of Caleb the Kenizzite and Joshua; **Numbers 14:30, 38; 26:65; 32:12**).

The second census was organized according to the genealogy of the persons in the various tribes (i.e., the numbers shown in parentheses below), corresponding to "the whole Israelite community by families—all those [males] twenty years old or more who are able to serve in the army of Israel" (**Numbers 26:2**). The total number of fighting men was 601,730 (**Numbers 26:51**).

The census of the Levites (tribe of Levi), which included "all the male Levites a month old or more," numbered 23,000. "They were not counted along with the other Israelites because they received no inheritance among them" (meaning they did not go to war or receive an allotment of land; **Numbers 26:62**).

Note: The summation of the persons in the tribes of Israel listed below, omitting the Levites, adds up to 606,730, revealing an unaccounted-for discrepancy of 5,000 persons (i.e., 606,730 vs. 601,730)—perhaps they died or were exempt from military service for some reason (cf. **Deuteronomy 24:5**).

To fully comprehend the makeup of the various tribes, it is helpful to understand something of ancient Israelite (and ancient Near Eastern) sociology. The following construct may make it clear:

- The largest unit: the Nation (עַם [*am*] or גּוֹי [*goy*])
  - The Tribe (שֵׁבֶט [*shebet*])
    - The Clan (מִשְׁפָּחָה [*mishpahah*])
      - The Family (אָב בֵּית [*bet ab*] (lit. "house of the father")

Genealogy of Reuben (43,730) (Numbers 26:5–10)

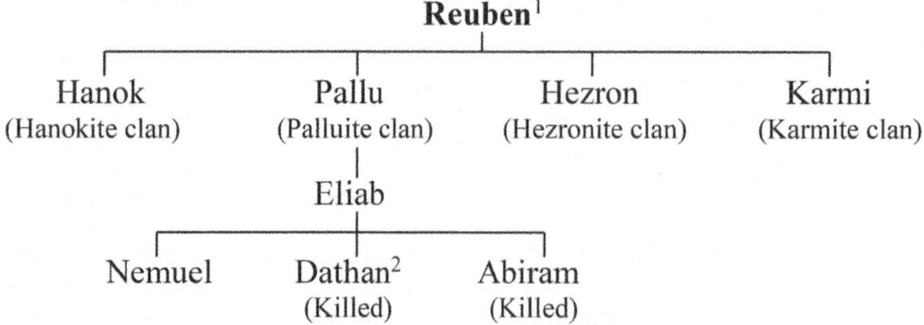

Notes

1. Reuben, the firstborn son of Jacob and Leah (**Genesis 29:32**), derived his name from the verb רָאָה (*raah*), "to see," and the noun בֵּן (*ben*), here rendered, "See! A son!" Reuben should have received Jacob's blessing of the firstborn son, but this was denied him because of his sexual encounter with Bilhah, Jacob's concubine (**Genesis 35:22; 49:3–4**). In fact, Reuben's motive may well have been seen as a grab for primacy even before Jacob died. Of particular importance is the transfer of the first son's legacy from Reuben "to the sons of Joseph" (**1 Chronicles 5:1–2**), Ephraim and Manasseh (**Genesis 48:5, 12–20**; cf. **Deuteronomy 21:17**). The tribe of Reuben had numbered 46,500 at the time of the first census, in 1445 B.C. (**Numbers 1:21**).

2. Dathan and Abiram (the great-grandsons of Reuben) died with Korah in the Korah–Reubenite rebellion against Moses and Aaron (cf. **Numbers 16:27–33; 26:8–11**). See chart "**Numbers 16**: Korah and the Descendants of Reuben who Died in the Korah-Reubenite Rebellion."

Genealogy of Simeon (22,200) (Numbers 26:12–14)

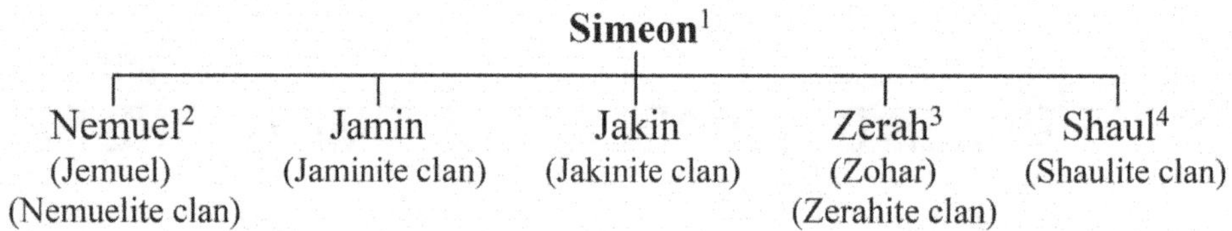

Notes

1. Simeon was the second son of Jacob and Leah. His name, שִׁמְעוֹן (*shimon*), means "He (God) has heard," alluding to Leah the "hated" wife who exclaimed, "Because the LORD heard that I am not loved, he gave me this one [Simeon] too" (**Genesis 29:33**). Another son of Simeon (Ohad) is mentioned in **Genesis 46:10** but not in the second census, likely because he died during the wilderness years. The tribe of Simeon had numbered 59,300 at the time of the first census, in 1445 B.C. (**Numbers 1:23**).

2. Nemuel (**Numbers 26:12**) is read Jemuel in **Genesis 46:10** and the Peshitta.

3. Zerah (**Numbers 26:13**) reads Zohar in **Genesis 46:10** and **Exodus 6:15**, as well as the Samaritan Pentateuch.

4. Shaul was the son of a Canaanite woman (**Genesis 46:10**).

Genealogy of Gad (40,500) (Numbers 26:15–18)

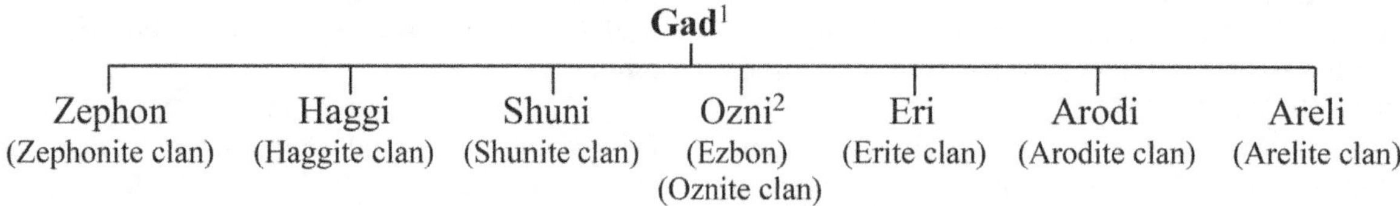

Notes

1. Gad was the son of Jacob by a concubine named Zilpah, Leah's servant (**Genesis 30:9–11**). His name means "fortune." Jacob's blessing over Gad, though first describing oppression by enemies, assures him that he would have the resources necessary for retaliation (**Genesis 49:19**). This was confirmed in Moses' blessing that Gad would be enlarged and become militarily ferocious, a leader who would uphold the righteousness of Yahweh (**Deuteronomy 33:20–21**). The tribe of Gad had numbered 45,650 at the time of the first census, in 1445 B.C. (**Numbers 1:25**).

2. Ozni in **Numbers 26:16** is Ezbon in **Genesis 46:16**.

Genealogy of Judah (76,500) (Numbers 26:19–22)

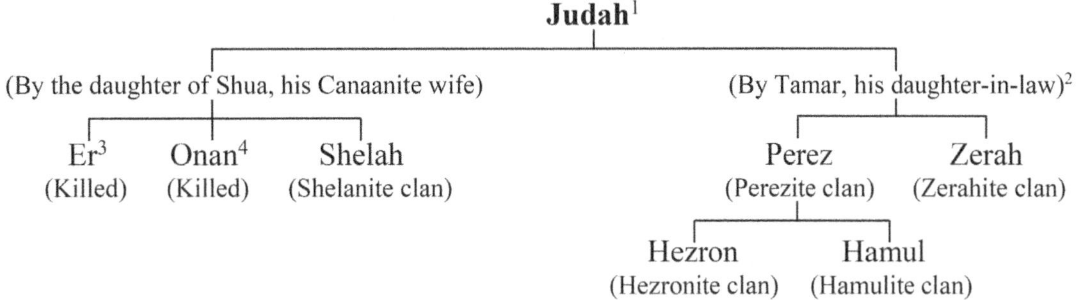

Notes

1. Judah was the fourth son of Jacob and Leah (**Genesis 29:35**). His name sounds like the Hebrew word for *praise*. The brief summary of Judah in **Numbers 26:19–22** belies the ultimate glorious and triumphant meaning and outcome of his progeny, one ending with God himself incarnate. Nothing in his personal life would seem to be auspicious of this ultimate result. He counseled his brothers to sell their younger sibling Joseph into slavery (**Genesis 37:26–27**); he married a Canaanite woman, the daughter of Shua (**Genesis 38:1–2, 12**). His sons (Er and Onan) were successively married to Tamar, but God killed them because they were wicked; after their deaths, Judah refused to give his remaining son, Shelah, as *levir* to his twice-widowed daughter-in-law, Tamar (**Genesis 38:6–11, 14**). (The *levir* was the husband's brother, the brother-in law; in this case, Shelah was the brother of Er and Onan, both of whom had been Tamar's husband.) By his own admittance, Judah said that Tamar was "more righteous than I, since I wouldn't give her to my son Shelah" (**Genesis 38:26**). In spite of all this, God, who sees the heart and who graciously forgives sin, gave the magnificent promise that "The scepter will not depart from Judah, nor the ruler's staff from between his feet, until he to whom it belongs shall come and the obedience of the nations shall be his" (**Genesis 49:10**). David knew himself to be that ruler (**1 Samuel 16:1, 12–13; 1 Kings 8:16**) but only imperfectly, for he too looked for such a descendant (**Psalm 18:50; 89:3–4, 35–37; 110:1–2**). The tribe of Judah had numbered 74,600 at the time of the first census, in 1445 B.C. (**Numbers 1:27**).

2. Tamar gave birth to twin sons, Perez and Zerah (**Genesis 38:27–30**).

3. Er, the firstborn son of Judah and the husband of Tamar (**Genesis 38:6; 1 Chronicles 2:3**), "was wicked in the LORD's sight; so the LORD put him to death [in Canaan]" (**Genesis 38:6–7; Numbers 26:19**).

4. Onan, having refused to serve as the kinsman redeemer for Er's wife, Tamar, was censured by the LORD: "what he did was wicked in the LORD's sight; so the LORD put him to death also [in Canaan]" (**Genesis 38:8–10; Numbers 26:19; 1 Chronicles 2:3**).

Genealogy of Issachar (64,300) (Numbers 26:23–25; also Judges 10:1)

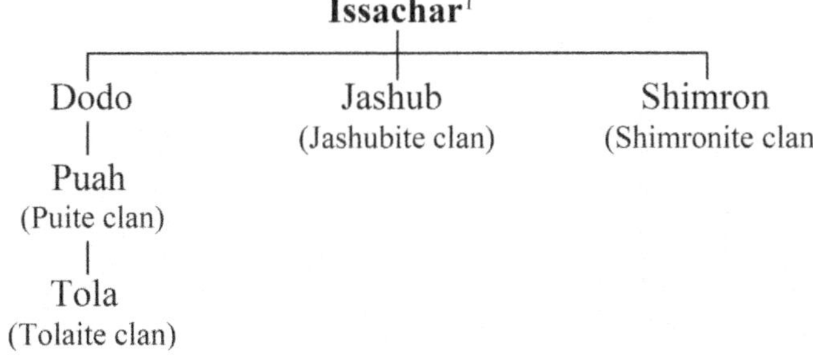

Notes

1. Issachar was the fifth son of Jacob and Leah (**Genesis 30:17–18**). The Hebrew name יִשָּׂשכָר (*yissacar*) means "hireling," "laborer." The tribe of Issachar had numbered 54,400 at the time of the first census, in 1445 B.C. (**Numbers 1:29**).

Genealogy of Zebulun (60,500) (Numbers 26:26–27)

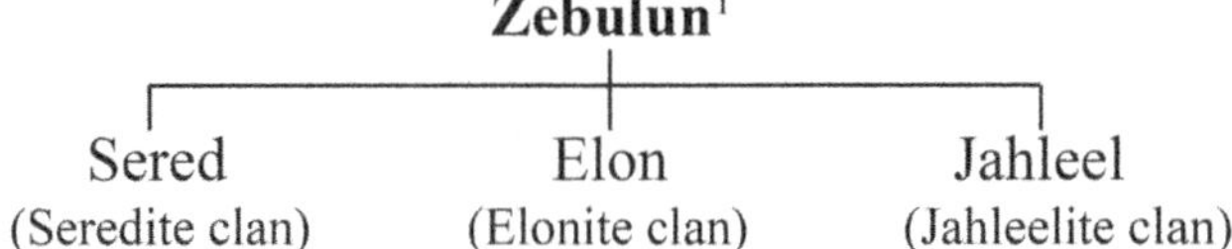

Notes

1. Zebulun was Leah's sixth and final son (**Genesis 30:19–20**). The name זְבוּלֻן (*zebulun*) means perhaps "lofty place," "honor" or "exalt," or the like. Jacob's blessing stated that Zebulun would enjoy a place by the sea and become "a haven for ships" (**Genesis 49:13**). Moses sees for Zebulun only the cryptic note, "Rejoice, Zebulun, in your going out. . . . [and] feast on the abundance of the seas" (**Deuteronomy 33:18**). The verb יָצָא (*yatsa*), "set out," "go forth," is a fitting nautical term in the context of a port city. The tribe of Zebulun had numbered 57,400 at the time of the first census, in 1445 B.C. (**Numbers 1:31**).

Genealogy of Manasseh (52,700) (Numbers 26:28–34)

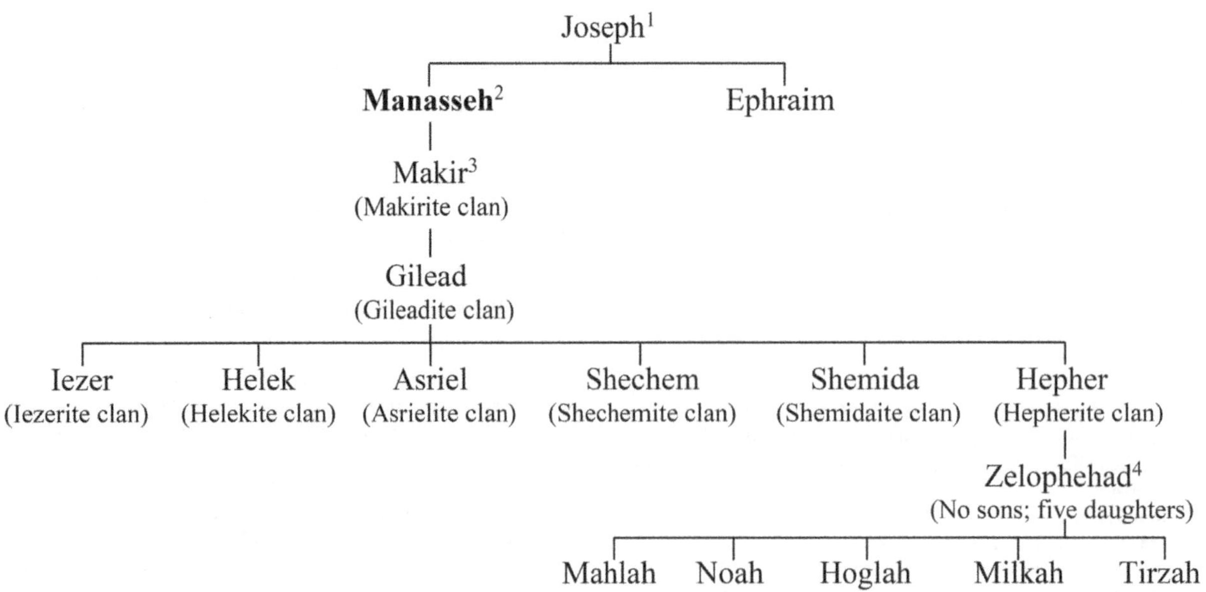

Notes

1. The Joseph tribe was divided between Manasseh and Ephraim (**Joshua 14:4**). Manasseh, in turn, was divided into two, the tribe of East Manasseh in the Transjordan and the tribe of West Manasseh in the cis-Jordan (in Canaan). In effect this kept the number of tribal allotments to twelve, since the tribe of Levi, the "priestly tribe," was not given an allotment of land (see Genealogy of Levi below). The tribe of Manasseh had numbered 32,200 at the time of the first census, in 1445 B.C. (**Numbers 1:35**).

2. Manasseh, the older son of Joseph and Asenath the Egyptian, was born in Egypt (**Genesis 41:50–51; 46:20**).

3. The phrase "Makir was the father of Gilead" (**Numbers 26:29**) means simply that the Makirites took over the area known as Gilead.

4. Zelophehad died during the years of the wilderness wanderings, leaving no male heir. His five daughters petitioned Moses and the leaders to receive the land inheritance due their father; they were given "an inheritance among their father's relatives [Zelophehad's brothers]" (**Numbers 27:6**) so that the land would remain within the tribe of Manasseh (see **Numbers 27:1–11**; cf. **Joshua 17:3–6**).

Genealogy of Ephraim (32,500) (Numbers 26:35–37; also 1 Chronicles 7:20)

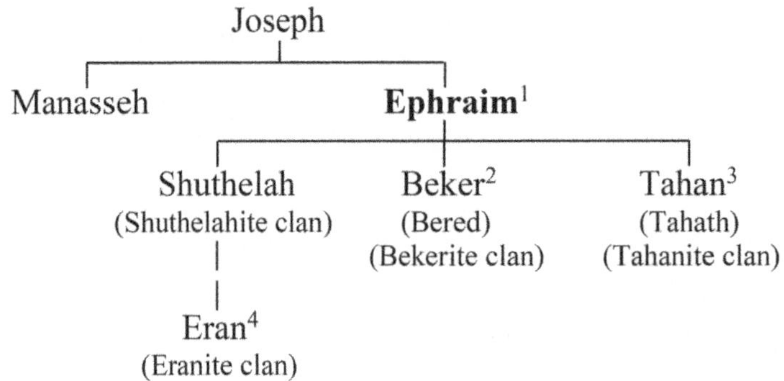

Notes

1. Ephraim, the younger son of Joseph and Asenath (Egyptian), was born in Egypt (**Genesis 41:52; 46:20**). Upon his deathbed, Jacob declared that "Ephraim and Manasseh will be mine," meaning they would be considered his own sons. In unorthodox fashion, Ephraim the second-born was given the blessing of Jacob over his older brother, Manasseh (**Genesis 48:5, 8–20**). The tribe of Ephraim had numbered 40,500 at the time of the first census, in 1445 B.C. (**Numbers 1:33**).

2. Beker in **Numbers 26:35** is the same as Bered in **1 Chronicles 7:20**, where Beker appears to be the son of Shutheleh (cf. **1 Chronicles 7:20**) and the father of Tahan (called Tahath in **1 Chronicles 7:20**). Many scholars read this part of the genealogy as vertical, not horizontal, thus rejecting the Numbers reading. See the chart "**1 Chronicles** 7: Ephraim."

3. This son of Ephraim, called Tahan in **Numbers 26:35**, is called Tahath (son of Beker/Bered) in **1 Chronicles 7:20**.

4. Eran appears to be the terminal figure of the Ephraim–Shuthelah line (cf. **1 Chronicles 7:20–27**).

Genealogy of Benjamin (45,600) (Numbers 26:38–41)

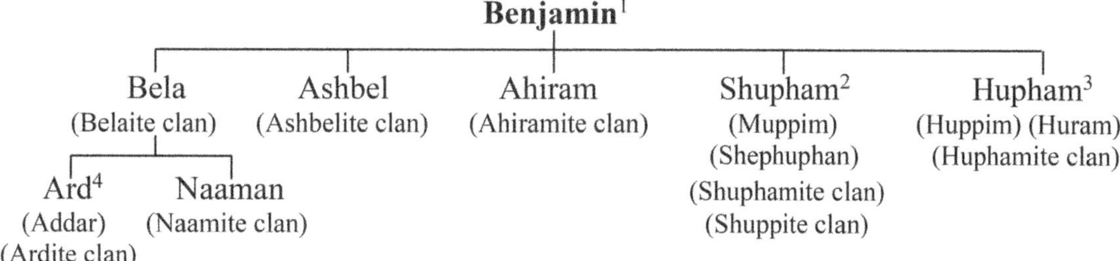

Notes

1. Benjamin was the second son of Jacob and his beloved wife, Rachel, who died in childbirth (**Genesis 35:18**). Benjamin's name means "son of the right hand." The tribe of Benjamin had numbered 35,400 at the time of the first census, in 1445 B.C. (**Numbers 1:37**).

2. This son of Benjamin, called Shupham in **Numbers 26:39**, is the same person as Muppim in **Genesis 46:21** and Shephuphan in **1 Chronicles 8:5**. The clan of the Shuphamites in **Numbers 26:39** is the same as the Shuppites in **1 Chronicles 7:12, 15**. Shupham and Hupham were possibly twins. The issue is of a graphic nature, that is, the formation of letters in the archaic script of the time. The *m* (מ) could easily be read for *sh* (ש) in archaic script.

3. This son of Benjamin, called Hupham in **Numbers 26:39**, is the same person as Huppim in **Genesis 46:21** and Huram in **1 Chronicles 8:5**. The Huphamites in **Numbers 26:39** appear to be the same as the Huppites in **Chronicles 7:12, 15**. Hupham (חופם) and Huppim (חופפם) differ in the doubling of the one letter פ (*p*) in Huppim. Later Hebrew shows the doubling by inserting a dot in פ, becoming even closer to Hupham (פּ).

4. This son of Bela is called Ard in **Genesis 46:21** and **Numbers 26:40** and Addar in **1 Chronicles 8:3**. This is a matter similar to the previous example. The name אָרד here is difficult, because Hebrew does not tolerate consonant clusters (*rd*). The Vulgate, one major Greek version, and the Samaritan Pentateuch (all late) agree with MT (our modern text); the Samaritan Pentateuch reads ארוד, and the most important and authoritative Septuagint (Greek) version/translation of the third century B.C. attests αδαρ, Adar.

Genealogy of Dan (64,400) (Numbers 26:42–43)

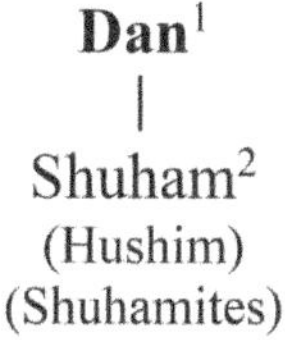

Notes

1. Dan was the first son of Jacob and Bilhah, Rachel's servant (**Genesis 30:6**). Dan's name means "judge." The tribe of Dan had numbered 62,700 at the time of the first census, in 1445 B.C. (**Numbers 1:39**).

2. This son of Dan is called Shuham in **Numbers 26:42** and Hushim in **Genesis 46:23**. Shuham/Hushim (the Shuhamites) in the tribe of Dan are different from the Hushites in the tribe of Benjamin (cf. **1 Chronicles 7:12**). See note 3 above in the Genealogy of Benjamin.

Genealogy of Asher (53,400) (Numbers 26:44–47)

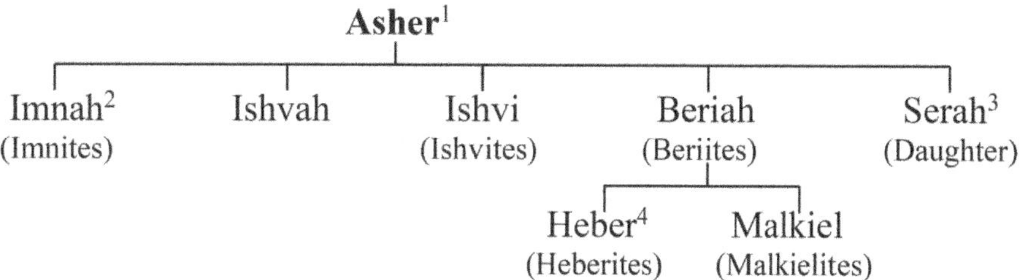

Notes

1. Asher was the second-born son of Jacob and Zilpah, Leah's servant (**Genesis 30:13**). Asher's name means "happy." The tribe of Asher had numbered 41,500 at the time of the first census, in 1445 B.C. (**Numbers 1:41**).

2. The sons of Asher in **Genesis 46:17** and **1 Chronicles 7:30** are listed as "Imnah, Ishvah, Ishvi and Beriah" but only the Imnite clan (of Imnah), the Ishvite clan (of Ishvi), and the Berite clan (of Beriah) are noted in **Numbers 26:44**.

3. Serah is mentioned in **Genesis 46:17; Numbers 26:46;** and **1 Chronicles 7:30**. The only women mentioned in the second census are Serah, the five daughters of Zelophehad, and Jochebed (mother of Moses).

4. The sons of Beriah in **Genesis 46:17** and **1 Chronicles 7:31** are "Heber and Malkiel," corresponding to the Heberite and Malkielite clans, respectively (**Numbers 26:45**).

Genealogy of Naphtali (45,400) (Numbers 26:48–50)

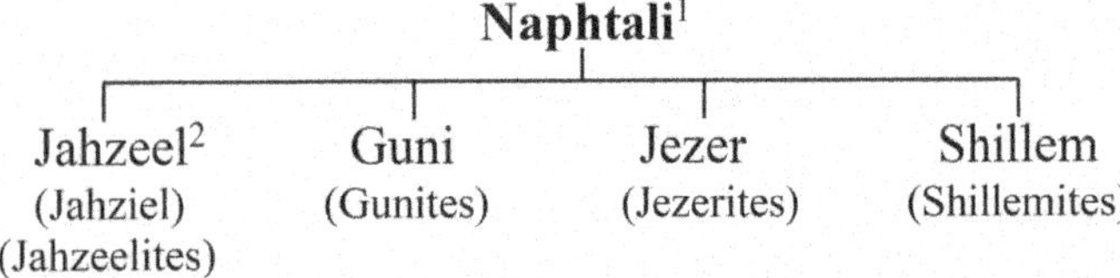

Notes

1. Naphtali was the second son born to Jacob and Bilhah, Rachel's servant. His name means "wrestling," alluding to Rachel winning the right of supremacy, "I have had a great struggle [for children] with my sister [Leah], and I have won" (**Genesis 30:8**). In what respect did she win? The answer is to be found in **Genesis 30:1–7** against the background of ancient Near Eastern nomadic culture. Filled with irrational envy of her sister, whose name did not even deserve to be uttered, Rachel lashed out at her husband Jacob for his impotence rather than herself for her barrenness: Using the imperative of the demanding verb הַב (*hab*), she screamed, "You give me a baby or else I will die!" Jacob's almost humorous response is, "Only God grants children. Do you think I am he?" Knowing full well he was not God, Rachel said in effect, "If God won't do it and you can't, then I will" (paraphrasing **Genesis 30:1–3**), and thus she resorted to the custom of surrogacy, whereby one's slave could bear a child on her mistress' behalf. The maid's name was Bilhah, but as soon as Bilhah succeeded in bearing a son, Rachel exclaimed, God has "given *me* a son," having determined that God had judged (Heb. דָּן, *dan*) her worthy of such benevolence. The child was thus named Dan (**Genesis 30:6**). A second son of Bilhah was named נַפְתָּלִי (*naphtali*), from the verb פָּתַל (*pathal*), "to struggle, strive, wrestle" (**Genesis 30:7–8**). Triumphantly, Rachel proclaimed, "I have had a great struggle with my sister [Leah], and I have won" (**Genesis 30:8**). Rachel's self-promotion, while not condemned overtly in the text, was, it seems, somewhat cut down to size in **Genesis 30:9–14** by the celebration of Leah, whose surrogate Zilpah gave birth to two more sons in addition to two others she had already delivered, making four in all, plus the four Leah herself had birthed. If numbers count, Rachel lost 8–4. However, it is important to remember that God keeps the score, and his tallies often have nothing to do with numbers. The tribe of Naphtali had numbered 53,400 at the time of the first census, in 1445 B.C. (**Numbers 1:43**).

2. This son of Naphtali is called Jahzeel in **Numbers 26:48** and Jahziel in **Genesis 46:24; 1 Chronicles 7:13**.

Genealogy of Levi (23,000) (Numbers 26:57–62)

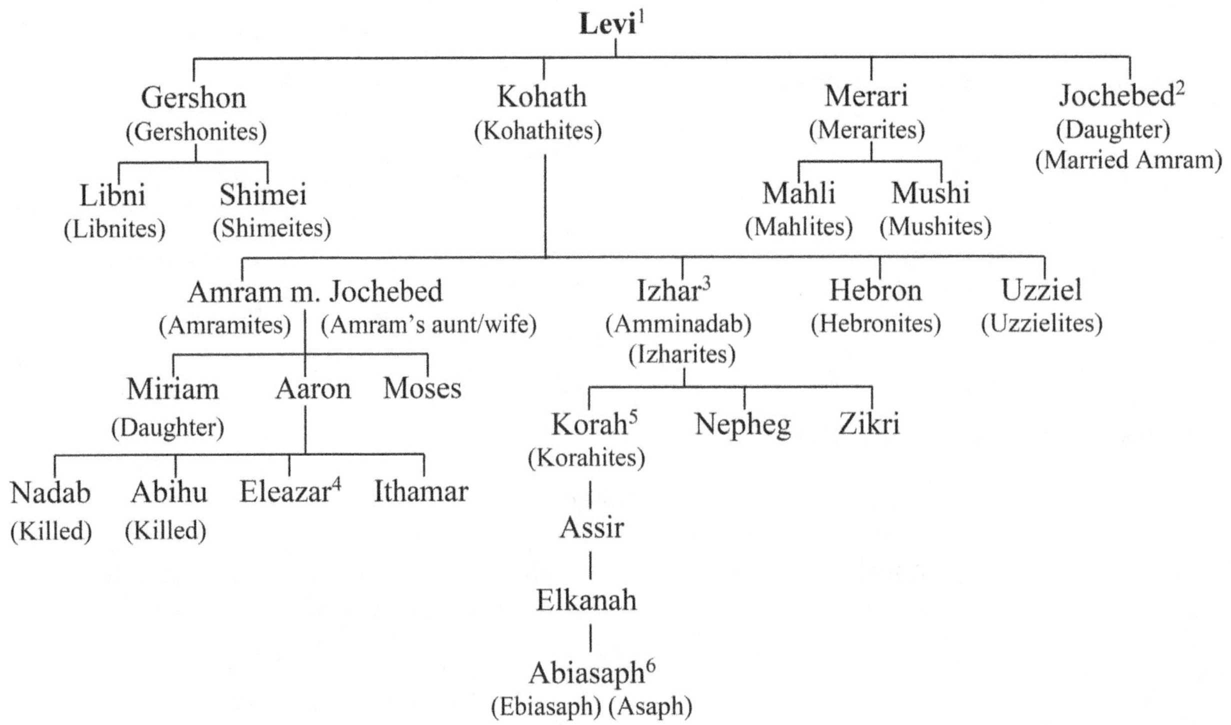

Notes

1. Levi was the third son of Jacob and Leah (**Genesis 29:34**). In the matter of land allocation, the Levites were not numbered among the other tribes because they were given no inheritance of land (**Numbers 18:20; 26:62**). The Lord told them: "I am your share and your inheritance among the Israelites" (**Numbers 18:20–24**; cf. **Deuteronomy 10:9; Joshua 13:14**). Therefore, the tribe of Levi, the priestly tribe, was scattered throughout the land into forty-eight Levitical cities in order to provide local worship—thirteen given to the descendants of Aaron, ten to the descendants of Kohath, thirteen to the descendants of Gershon, and twelve to the descendants of Merari (**Numbers 35:1–8; Joshua 21:1–41**). Six of the forty-eight towns were designated as cities of refuge (**Numbers 35:1–29**).

2. Jochebed was the daughter of Levi. She was born in Egypt and married her nephew Amram (the son of Kohath; **Exodus 6:20; Numbers 26:59**).

3. This son of Kohath is called Izhar in **Exodus 6:18, 21; Numbers 16:1; 1 Chronicles 6:2, 18, 38; 23:12** and Amminadab in **1 Chronicles 6:22**.

4. Eleazar, the son of Aaron, was the high priest during the second census (**Numbers 26:1**).

5. Korah died in the Korah–Reubenite rebellion as recounted in **Numbers 16**, but the descendants of Korah were spared (**Numbers 26:11**). In **Exodus 6:24**, the sons of Korah are "Assir, Elkanah and Abiasaph [Ebiasaph or Asaph]" but **1 Chronicles 6:22–23** clarifies that they were sons of sons: "The descendants of Kohath: Amminadab [Izhar] his son, Korah his son, Assir his son, Elkanah his son, Ebiasaph [Abiasaph or Asaph] his son" (cf. **1 Chronicles 6:37**).

6. Abiasaph (**Exodus 6:24**) is the same person as Ebiasaph (**1 Chronicles 6:23, 37; 9:19**) and Asaph (**1 Chronicles 26:1**).

Table I. Comparative Records of Census #1 (taken ca. 1445 B.C.; Numbers 1:1–46) and Census #2 (taken ca. 1406 B.C.; Numbers 26:1–51) for the Twelve Tribes of Israel (omitting the tribe of Levi[1]).

	Census #1	Census #2	Gain	Loss	Interpretation
Totals:	603,550	601,730		1,820	Insignificant difference
Reuben	46,500	43,730		2,770	Part of a rebellion against Moses (**Numbers 26:5–11**)
Simeon	59,300	22,200		37,100	Unknown, but see **Joshua 19:1–9**[2]
Gad	45,650	40,500		5,150	Death after murmuring or war? (**Numbers 16:47–49; 21:1–3, 25–26**)
Judah	74,600	76,500	1,900		Natural growth? (cf. **Genesis 49:10–12; Deuteronomy 33:7**)
Issachar	54,400	64,300	9,900		Natural growth? (cf. **Deuteronomy 33:18–19**)
Zebulun	57,400	60,500	3,100		Natural growth? (cf. **Genesis 49:13**)
Ephraim	40,500	32,500		8,000	Death after murmuring or war? (**Numbers 16:47–49; 21:1–3, 25–26**)
Manasseh	32,200	52,700	20,500		Perhaps assimilation of indigenous people
Benjamin	35,400	45,600	10,200		Unknown, but see **Deuteronomy 33:12**
Dan	62,700	64,400	1,700		Natural growth?
Asher	41,500	53,400	11,900		Unknown, but see **Genesis 49:20**; **Deuteronomy 33:24–25**
Naphtali	53,400	45,400		8,000	Death after murmuring or war? (**Numbers 16:47–49; 21:1–3, 25–26**)

Notes

1. The tribe of Levi (the Levites) was not counted along with the others, because they were responsible for the care of the tabernacle and they did not serve in the army (**Numbers 1:45–53**).

2. Judah's tribal allotment of land was more than they needed, so Simeon's inheritance "was taken from the share of Judah" (**Joshua 19:9**). The assumption is that Simeon's population was so low, it could be accommodated in just a part of Judah. Exactly how and why is not disclosed.

NUMBERS 34: GENEALOGICAL RECORD OF THE LEADERS APPOINTED TO DIVIDE THE PROMISED LAND

Approximate Dating: early occupation of Canaan, ca. 1400 B.C. ***Relevant Scriptures:*** **Numbers 34:16–28**

Key Leaders:

Eleazar the high priest (tribe of Levi)
Joshua, son of Nun, the commander of the army (tribe of Ephraim)[1]

Leaders of the Tribes:

Tribe of Judah	**Caleb**, the son of Jephunneh (Kenizzite)[2]
Tribe of Simeon	**Shemuel**, the son of Ammihud
Tribe of Benjamin	**Elidad**, the son of Kislon
Tribe of Dan	**Bukki**, the son of Jogli
Tribe of Manasseh	**Hanniel**, the son of Ephod
Tribe of Ephraim	**Kemuel**, the son of Shiphtan
Tribe of Zebulun	**Elizaphan**, the son of Parnak
Tribe of Issachar	**Paltiel**, the son of Azzan
Tribe of Asher	**Ahihud**, the son of Shelomi
Tribe of Naphtali	**Pedahel**, the son of Ammihud

Biblical and Theological Significance

After the conquest of Canaan, the Lord told Moses to "assign the inheritance to the Israelites in the land of Canaan" (**Numbers 34:29**). Moses therefore designated ten men from each tribe to assist Eleazar the high priest, the son of Aaron (**Numbers 20:25–28**), and Joshua the son of Nun, the army commander and Israel's new leader (**Numbers 27:15–23**), in the apportionment. The tribe of Levi received no allotment because, as priests, they were responsible for the spiritual and religious needs of all the other tribes and therefore must be spread throughout the land, thus having no distinctive geographical inheritance. The Lord said that he himself would be the inheritance of Levi: "I am your share and your inheritance among the Israelites," an incalculable honor and privilege (**Numbers 18:20;** cf. **Joshua 18:7**). Beyond that, they would support themselves by the tithes of the other tribes, their wages, as it were, as pastors of the people (**Numbers 18:20–24**). Moreover, and for practical reasons, the Levites received forty-eight cities taken from within the land of the other tribes (**Numbers 35:1–5; Joshua 21:l–41**).

A brief note about tribal settlement allocations might also be helpful. Judah was granted the largest territory, the tribal area from which King David sprang and that eventually made up the Southern Kingdom following the division of the monarchy in 931 B.C. Issachar settled in the Upper Arabah valley, bordering on the Sea of Kinnereth (Sea of Galilee). Zebulun ended up in the Upper Galilee, wedged between Asher to the west and Naphtali to the east. Reuben was assigned to a district in the Transjordan, north of the Arnon River to the northeast curve of the Dead Sea. Simeon was absorbed into Judah and lost any territorial distinction. Gad lay just north of Reuben and extended northward just past the Jabbok River. East Manasseh occupied regions east of the Jordan River in Gilead and Bashan (i.e., regions not occupied by the tribes of Reuben and Gad). Ephraim populated a vast area between the Mediterranean Sea and the Jordan River and between Benjamin and Judah to the south and its "brother tribe," Manasseh, to the north. West Manasseh extended from Ephraim to the Jezreel Valley on the north, and, like Ephraim, spread from the Mediterranean to the Jordan. Benjamin was bordered by Judah to the south, Ephraim to the north, the Jordan to the east, and Dan to the west. Dan thus lay west of Benjamin but also northwest of Judah and west of Ephraim. It also had a short coastline on the Mediterranean. Asher settled along the Mediterranean from Mount Carmel to the boundary with Lebanon. Its neighbor was Naphtali to the east and Zebulun to the south. Finally, Naphtali lay along the west side of the Sea of Kinnereth and north all the way to Lebanon. Zebulun was to its southwest and Issachar to the south.

Notes

1. Joshua (alias Hoshea; **Numbers 13:8, 16**) was the Ephraimite who spied out the land of Canaan and brought back a good report (**Numbers 13:8; 14:6, 30, 38**). He was Moses' successor as leader of the nation of Israel (**Numbers 27:15–23**) and the commander of the Israelite army in the conquest and early occupation of the land (**Deuteronomy 3:28; 31:1–8; 34:9; Joshua 1–12**). He was integrally involved in the allotment of land to the tribes and the appointment of the Levitical cities and cities of refuge (**Joshua 13–21**). Joshua died at the age of 110 and was buried in Timnath Serah (Timnath Heres)—"The town he asked for" in the tribe of Ephraim (**Joshua 24:29–30;** cf. **Judges 2:7–9).** See chart "**Joshua 1**: Joshua, the Successor of Moses and Leader of the Nation of Israel."

2. Caleb the Kenizzite represented the tribe of Judah as one of the twelve spies of Canaan. He and Joshua were the only persons who lived through the forty years of the wilderness wanderings, 1446–1406 B.C., because "they followed the LORD wholeheartedly" (**Numbers 32:12;** see also **Numbers 13:6; 14:6–9, 24, 30, 38, 26:65**). See charts "**Joshua 14**: The Clan of Jephunneh the Kenizzite" and "**1 Chronicles 2**: Caleb and Kenaz, the Sons of Jephunneh the Kenizzite."

DEUTERONOMY 1: THE GIANT ANAKITES,[1] INCLUDING GOLIATH AND HIS DESCENDANTS

Approximate Dating: pre-dating the early occupation of the promised land by the Israelites and continuing through the monarchic period, ca. 1880–1020 B.C. ***Relevant Scriptures:*** **Deuteronomy 1:26–28; 2:10–11, 19–21, 23;** also **Genesis 6:4; 14:5–6; 15:20; Numbers 13:22, 28, 31–33; Deuteronomy 3:11; Joshua 11:22; 14:12–15; 15:13–14; 17:15; Judges 1:10; 1 Samuel 17:4, 8, 23, 50–51; 2 Samuel 21:15–22; 1 Chronicles 20:4–8**

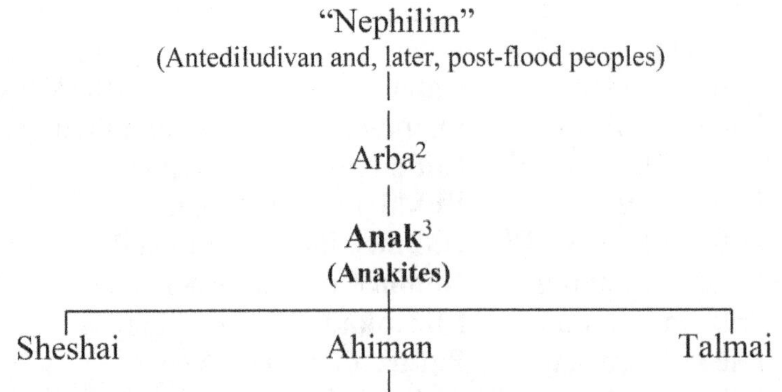
"Nephilim"
(Antediludivan and, later, post-flood peoples)
Arba[2]
Anak[3]
(Anakites)
Sheshai
Ahiman
Talmai
(The descendants of the three sons of Anak, called the **Anakites**, were identified by various names according to the geographic region they inhabited.)

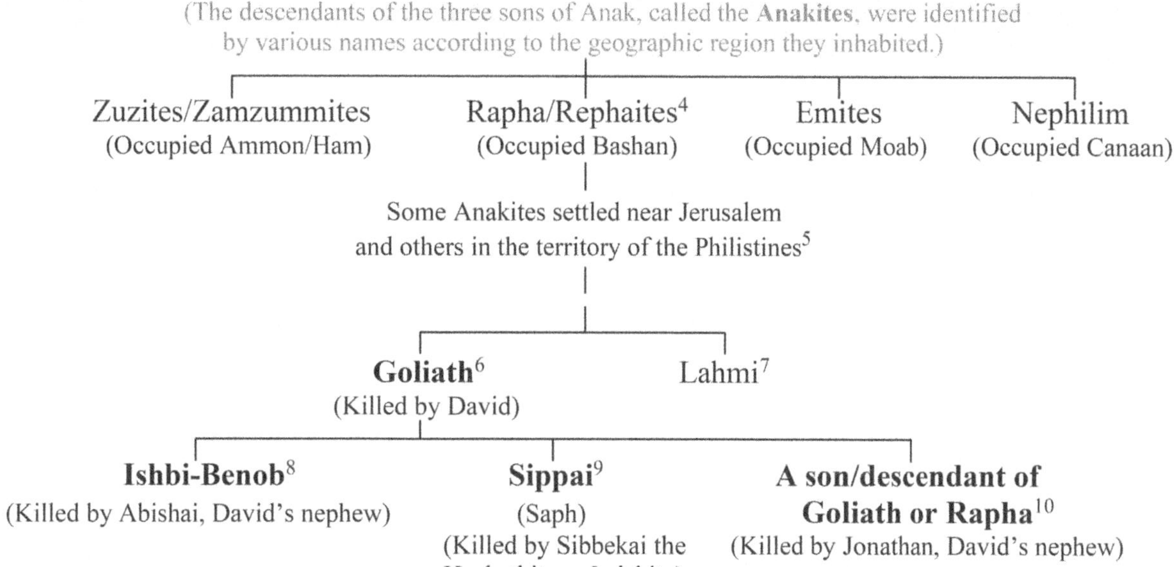

Biblical and Theological Significance

The human experience has been entertained or terrified by lingering myths and tales about giants and other formidable foes and how they were overcome by heroic champions. Though giants are common in fables or mythical stories and thus dismissed correctly as having any historical basis, their historicity cannot be tossed aside so easily, in particular by those who view the Bible as trustworthy, divine revelation. In the Hebrew narratives, people of this kind inhabited the pre-diluvian world where they are called נפלם, Nephilim, perhaps derived from the verb נפל, "to fall." All humankind had fallen, and as they increased in number, the "sons of God" saw the "daughters of humans [men] were beautiful"[11] and "married any of them they chose" (**Genesis 6:2**), and "they [the offspring] were the heroes of old, men of renown" (**Genesis 6:4**). Whatever else this might mean, God's judgment was that this greatly contributed to the wickedness of the human race and was evil[12] (**Genesis 6:3, 5–6**).

The first encounter with the Anakites/Anakim occurred when the Israelite spies observed the descendants of Anak who dwelled in the Negev in patriarchal times, specifically in Hebron (**Numbers 13:22**). Hundreds of years later, Moses sent out twelve spies from Israel to go into the land of Canaan to assess its strength of resistance to invasion (**Numbers 13:3–16**). Upon their return forty days later, the majority brought back a "bad report," for they had seen giants there. They asserted, "We saw the Nephilim[13] there (the descendants of Anak come from the Nephilim). We seemed like grasshoppers in our own eyes, and we looked the same to them" (**Numbers 13:32–33**; cf. **Numbers 13:22, 28**). The Israelites of that generation, with the exceptions of Joshua and Caleb, concluded that they would be unable to conquer Canaan because of the great size of their adversaries.

When Joshua undertook the conquest of Canaan, he "destroyed the Anakites from the hill country: from Hebron, Debir and Anab, from all the hill country of Judah, and from all the hill country of Israel. Joshua totally destroyed them and their towns. No Anakites were left in Israelite territory; only in Gaza, Gath and Ashdod did any survive" (**Joshua 11:21–22**). Hebron, formerly called Kiriath Arba (see note 2), became the inheritance of Caleb the Kenizzite, the faithful spy of the promised land who represented the tribe of Judah (cf. **Numbers 13:6; Joshua 14:6, 12–15; 15:13–14**).

Other descendants of the Nephilim are also attested, such as King Og of Bashan, one of "the last of the Rephaites" (**Deuteronomy 3:11; Joshua 12:4; 13:12**).[14] His bed (or, alternatively, "sarcophagus") is said to have been iron (or decorated with iron) and "was more than nine cubits [13.5 feet] long and four cubits [6 feet] wide" (**Deuteronomy 3:11**). The first references to the Rephaites are in **Genesis 14:5**, where they appear as defeated enemies of the kings of the east of Abraham's time (2166–1991 B.C.), and in **Genesis 15:18–20**, where they are listed as one of several peoples who originally inhabited the land that God gave to the Israelites.

Perhaps the most well-known giants were the Philistines—Aegeans who landed on Canaan's Mediterranean shores as early as 1250 B.C. and occupied the region for one thousand years. A still earlier Philistine settlement apparently had been founded along the southern seacoast and a few miles inland as early as the times of Abraham (**Genesis 21:22–34; 26:1–11, 18–22**), but it seems to have disappeared by the time of the great wave of Philistines seven hundred years later. They formed a "pentocracy" of three city-states on the southern coast (Gaza, Ashdod, and Ashkelon), and two more inland (Ekron and Gath). Gath was the home of the most famous Philistine of all, Goliath, who fought young David. This fight was disastrous for Goliath, as David cried out, "You come against me with sword and spear and javelin, but I come against you in the name of the Lord Almighty, the God of the armies of Israel, whom you have defied" (**1 Samuel 17:45**). The end of the contest was quick and final: David's God had slain the giant. This is the theology of the genealogy in a nutshell.

Notes

1. The gentilic *-ites* obscures the Hebrew plural *-im*, thus "Anakim."

2. Arba was the indigenous occupant and founder of Hebron, formerly called קִרְיַת אַרְבַּע (Kiriath Arba), "city of the four," perhaps a city of four parts (**Genesis 23:2; 35:27; Joshua 14:15; 15:13, 54; 20:7; Judges 1:10; Nehemiah 11:25**).

3. The gentilic *Anak* (better rendered *Anaq*) is usually related to the common Hebrew root ענק, "neck." The verb form means "adorn the neck" or "place around the neck." The original main idea is that of ego or haughtiness ("ענק," *HALOT* 1:858–59). A number of other terms appear to describe the same or affiliated people, the earliest being the generic term רְפָאִים (Rapha/Rephaim), or Zamzummites (**Deuteronomy 2:20**), meaning either (1) "healers" or (2) "weak," "dead spirits." Related to, or derived from them, are the likes of peoples named Anakites (or Anakim in some translations; **Deuteronomy 1:28; 9:2**; cf. **Numbers 13:22**), Nephilim (**Numbers 13:33**), and Emites (or Emim in some translations; **Deuteronomy 2:10–11**). The descendants of Anak that issued from his three sons (**Joshua 15:14**) seem to be identified in the biblical text by their various names according to the geographic region they inhabited (cf. **Deuteronomy 2:10–11, 20; 3:11**).

4. The Rephaites (or Rephaim in some translations) were considered among the indigenous people who occupied the land promised to Abraham "from the Wadi of Egypt to the great river, the Euphrates" (**Genesis 15:18**) formerly inhabited by "the Kenites, Kenizzites, Kadmonites, Hittites, Perizzites, Rephaites, Amorites, Canaanites, Girgashites and Jebusites" (**Genesis 15:19–20**). The first reference to the Rephaites is **Genesis 14:5**, where they appear as defeated enemies of the of the kings of the east (e.g., Kedorlaomer and the kings allied with him) of Abraham's time (2166–1991 B.C.).

5. Most of the Anakites (or Anakim) were driven out in the Israelite conquest of Canaan; however, many Rephaim settled near Jerusalem in the "Valley of Rephaim" (**2 Samuel 5:18**). Another remnant group of Anakites intermingled with the Philistines of Gaza, Gath, and Ashdod (cf. **Joshua 11:21–22**); Goliath of Gath belonged to this latter group.

6. Goliath—"The Gittite" of Gath (**2 Samuel 21:19; 1 Chronicles 20:5**)—was killed by David (**1 Samuel 17:50–51**).

7. Lahmi, the brother of Goliath, was killed by Elhanan, the son of Jair the Bethlehemite, from the tribe of Judah (**2 Samuel 21:19**; **1 Chronicles 20:5**).

8. Ishbi-Benob was killed by Abishai the son of Zeruiah, David's half-sister (**2 Samuel 21:16–17**).

9. Sippai (**1 Chronicles 20:4**), alias Saph (**2 Samuel 21:18**), was killed by Sibbekai the Hushathite from the tribe of Judah (see **1 Chronicles 11:29**).

10. This son of Goliath is described in **2 Samuel 21:20** and **1 Chronicles 20:6** as being "a huge man with six fingers on each hand and six toes on each foot—twenty-four in all . . . descended from Rapha." He was killed by Jonathan (David's nephew), the son of Shammah (**1 Samuel 16:9; 17:13**), who is also called Shimea (**1 Chronicles 2:13; 20:7**) or Shimeah (**2 Samuel 21:21**).

11. The notion that the "sons of God" were angels has no support elsewhere in Scripture. To the contrary, the phrase occurs scores of times to refer to the righteous or to believers, who can nonetheless commit such sins as to marry unbelievers and thereby produce more sinful offspring (**Genesis 28:1, 6; Numbers 36:3, 6, 8, 11-12; Deuteronomy 25:5–6; 1 Kings 16:31; Ezra 10:2; Nehemiah 13:27; Malachi 2:11; 2 Corinthians 6:14–18**). The righteousness of the "sons of God" is contrary to the "daughters of men" (or of an "evil place"). The Hebrew phrase בְּנוֹת הָאָדָם may be rendered as "daughters of the man," which hardly makes sense, or "daughters of mankind," "of the land," or "of the dirt, soil" ("אָדָם," *HALOT* 1:14). In any case, these women were no more evil or degraded than the men were sinless sons of God himself. The idea is that the time came when those whom God set apart as his chosen ones began to ally themselves with the evil ones of the world (**Psalm 137:8; Isaiah 23:12; 47:1–5; Jeremiah 46:24; 48:18; 50:42; Zechariah 2:7**).

12. The characterization is that mankind was *basar*, that is, "flesh" and mortal, not divine. The resulting offspring were the *nephilim*, "heroes of old, men [not angelic offspring] of renown" (**Genesis 6:4**).

13. The eponym, Nephilim, likely refers to gigantism or some other kind of birth deformity.

14. The Rephaim ("shades, spirits of the dead") are identified in the Bible and/or elsewhere as (1) physical descendants of the giant Anakites, as here, or as (2) fearsome and powerful entities of the netherworld, usually former royalty. The Canaanite Ugaritic texts speak of the latter: "You have summoned the Rephaim of the netherworld" [a canonical liturgy upon the accession of a new king; W. W. Hallo and K. Lawsom Younger, eds. *The Context of Scripture*, vol. 1 (Leiden: Brill, 2000), 357.].

JOSHUA 1: JOSHUA, THE SUCCESSOR OF MOSES AND LEADER OF THE NATION OF ISRAEL

Approximate Dating: born in Egypt ca. 1485 B.C.; assistant to Moses during the wilderness wanderings, 1446–1406 B.C.; led the military campaigns into Canaan, ca. 1406–1400 B.C.; and died at the age of 110 in 1375 B.C. ***Relevant Scriptures:*** **Joshua 1:1; 2:1, 23; 17:4; 24:29**; also **Genesis 30:22–24; 41:45, 50–52; 46:20; 48:1, 5; Exodus 33:11; Numbers 11:28; 13:8, 16; 14:6, 30, 38; 26:35–37, 65; 32:12, 28; 34:17; Deuteronomy 1:38; 31:23; Judges 2:8; 1 Chronicles 7:20–27; Nehemiah 8:17**

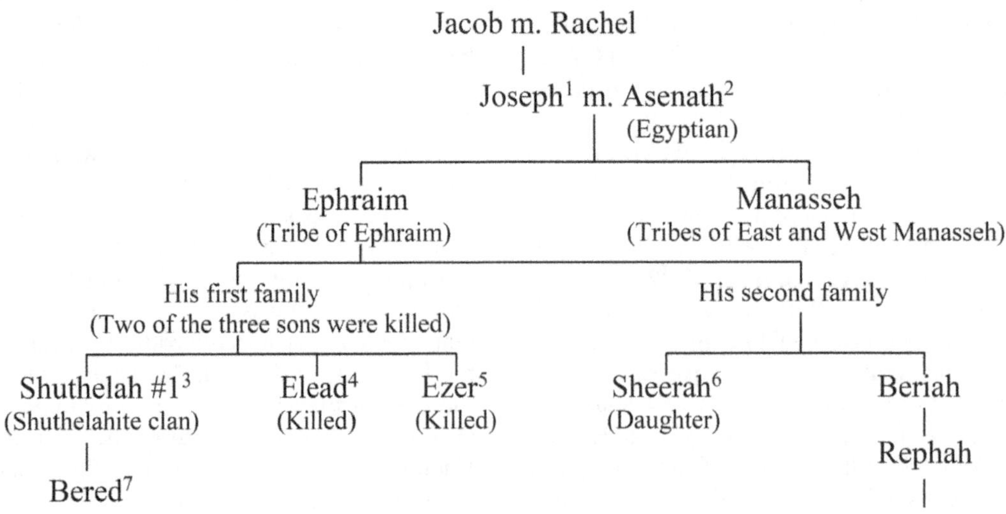

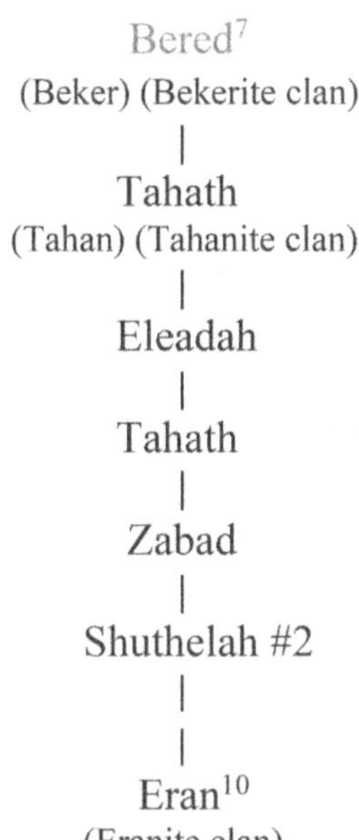

Rephah

Resheph

Telah

Tahan[8]

Ladan

Ammihud

Elishama[9]

Nun

Joshua[11]
(Hoshea)

Biblical and Theological Significance

Joshua was born during the period of Israelite bondage in Egypt. He was a descendant of Ephraim's second family after tragedy had struck the first with the death of two of Ephraim's sons. Joshua's given name was Hoshea ("salvation" or "deliverance") but Moses called him *Joshua*, "Yahweh delivers" or "Yahweh is salvation" (**Numbers 13:8, 16; Deuteronomy 32:44**). He served as an aide to Moses from his youth and had the honor of accompanying Moses (the first time) up Mount Sinai to receive the stone tablets of the Law of God (**Exodus 24:13; 32:17; 33:11; Numbers 11:28**). Joshua[12] and Caleb the Kenizzite (representing the tribes of Ephraim and Judah, respectively) were the two spies of Canaan who brought back an encouraging report to Moses (**Numbers 14:6–8**). For their belief in the Lord's promises, Joshua and Caleb were the only men of the exodus generation over twenty years old who lived through the forty years in the wilderness (1446–1406 B.C.) and who were allowed to come in and possess the promised land (**Numbers 14:28–32, 36–38; 26:63–65; 32:11–13**; cf. **Joshua 5:6**).

During the desert travels, Joshua battled the Amalekites at Rephidim (**Exodus 17:8–13**) and later, in the Transjordan, he fought against the Amorite kings Sihon and Og (**Deuteronomy 31:3–4**). Moses had led the nation of Israel through the exodus and days in the wilderness, but Joshua was God's choice to lead the nation during the subsequent invasion, conquest, and occupation of Canaan (**Numbers 27:18–23; Deuteronomy 1:38; 3:28; 31:14–23**). Joshua was also involved in the allotment of the land for each of the twelve tribes. Before his death, Moses charged Joshua with these encouraging words from the Lord: "Be strong and courageous, for you will bring the Israelites into the land I promised them on oath, and I myself will be with you" (**Deuteronomy 31:23**). Joshua, "filled with the spirit of wisdom," commanded Israel's respect so they did what the Lord commanded throughout his life (**Deuteronomy 34:9; Joshua 1:16–18; 4:14**).

Joshua the Ephraimite was involved in key events in the life of the Israelites when they came into the promised land. His predominance as a military and spiritual figure can be seen in the following list of achievements:

- He led the people in the miraculous crossing of the Jordan River (**Joshua 3–4**).
- At Gibeath Haaraloth, he circumcised all the men of military age who had been born during the wilderness journey from Egypt so they would be prepared for the conquest of Canaan (**Joshua 5:2–9**).
- In a theophany experience at Jericho, he witnessed an angelic being called the "commander of the Lord's army" (**Joshua 5:13–15**).
- In the central campaign, he led the successful invasion and destruction of Jericho (**Joshua 6**) and the fall and destruction of Ai (**Joshua 7–8**).
- He led the people in a covenant-making ceremony at Mount Ebal and Mount Gerizim and wrote a copy of the law of Moses on stones (**Joshua 8:30–35**).
- He made an (ill-conceived) peace covenant with the deceptive Gibeonites (Hivites; **Joshua 9; 11:19**).
- In the southern campaign described in **Joshua 10**, he led Israel in the defeat of a coalition of hostile Amorite kings (**Joshua 10:5–28**) by asking the Lord for an additional day of battle. The request was granted—"The sun stood still, and the moon stopped, till the nation avenged itself on its enemies" (**vv. 12–14**). The defeated city-states and their rulers in the south were (1) Makkedah (**v. 28**); (2) Libnah (**vv. 29–30**); (3) Lachish (**vv. 31–33**); (4) Eglon of Moab (**vv. 34–35**); (5) Hebron (**vv. 36–37**); and (6) Debir (**vv. 38–39**). Joshua subdued Israel's enemies "from Kadesh Barnea to Gaza and from the whole region of Goshen to Gibeon" (**vv. 40–41**).
- In the northern campaign, he led Israel to victory over a coalition of kings led by the king of Hazor, and Joshua burned Hazor (**Joshua 11:1–20**).

- He defeated the giant Anakites[13] in the land, except for those in Gaza, Gath, and Ashdod (**Joshua 11:21–22**).
- He led the defeat of the kings on the western side of the Jordan River (**Joshua 12:7–24**) and divided the land amongst the remaining nine-and-a-half tribes (**Joshua 13:7**; cf. **Joshua 15–19**).
- He appointed the cities of refuge (**Joshua 20**) and assigned Levitical cities within the tribes (**Joshua 21**).
- Before his death, he led the people in a covenant renewal ceremony at Shechem (**Joshua 23–24**).

Joshua died at the age of 110 and was buried at Timnath Serah (also called Timnath Heres), the place he had built up and requested for his inheritance, located in the hill country of Ephraim, north of Mount Gaash (**Joshua 24:29–30; Judges 2:8–9**; cf. **Joshua 19:49–50**).

Notes

1. The sons of Joseph, Manasseh and Ephraim, were born in Egypt (**Genesis 46:20**). For more information about Joseph and his family, see chart "**Genesis 37**: Joseph and His Sons (Manasseh and Ephraim)."

2. Asenath was an Egyptian, the daughter of Potiphera, the priest of On (**Genesis 41:45, 50; 46:20**).

3. The descendants of Shuthelah #1, son of Ephraim, formed the Shuthelahite clan; see also Shuthelah #2, the son of Zabad, in this same lineage (**Numbers 26:35–36**).

4. Elead and his brother Ezer (sons of Ephraim) were probably born in Egypt in the land of Goshen (cf. **Genesis 41:50–52; 46:20; 47:27**). It appears they were "killed by the native-born men of Gath, when they [Elead and Ezer] went down to seize their livestock" (**1 Chronicles 7:21**). Ephraim mourned for them for a long time despite the attempts of his relatives to comfort him. His wife, however, bore him another son whom Ephraim named Beriah, because he had suffered such misfortune (**1 Chronicles 7:22–23**).

5. For Ezer, see note 4.

6. Sheerah was either the daughter of Ephraim (as shown in the chart) or the daughter of Beriah and the granddaughter of Ephraim. This woman, Sheerah, was the notable patron-builder of Uzzen Sheerah and Upper and Lower Beth Horon, a strategic pass that led to the Aijalon Valley of Judea, which ran east-west through the region of the Shephelah (**1 Chronicles 7:24**; cf. **Joshua 10:12**; **1 Kings 9:17**).

7. Bered (**1 Chronicles 7:20**), probably the same as Beker (**Numbers 26:35**), was the head of the Bekerite clan of Ephraimites. Beker the Ephraimite should not be confused with Beker the son of Benjamin (**Genesis 46:21; 1 Chronicles 7:6, 8**).

8. The Tahanite clan is mentioned in **Numbers 26:35**.

9. As the head of the tribe of Ephraim, Elishama helped Moses conduct the first census of the children of Israel in the wilderness of Sinai in 1445 B.C. (**Numbers 1:10, 16**); see chart "**Numbers 1**: Genealogical Record of the First Census of the Tribes of Israel."

10. For the Eranite clan, see **Numbers 26:36**.

11. The differences in his names are minor, deriving from the same root, ישע, "save." "Joshua" (יְהוֹשֻׁעַ) means "Yahweh saves," whereas "Hoshea" is the nominal form הוֹשֵׁעַ, "salvation." In the New Testament, the Greek form for the Lord's name, Jesus, is Ἰησοῦς (Yēsous), a transliteration of the Hebrew root.

12. Joshua was forty years old when he spied out the land of Canaan, in 1445 B.C. (**Joshua 14:7**); see chart "**Numbers 13**: Genealogical Record of the Twelve Spies of the Promised Land." This date establishes that he was born in Egypt in ca. 1485 B.C. and died in the land of Canaan in 1375 B.C. at the age of 110 (**Joshua 24:29; Judges 2:8**), the same age as his ancestor Joseph (**Genesis 50:26**).

13. See chart "**Deuteronomy 1**: The Giant Anakites, including Goliath and His Descendants."

JOSHUA 2: RAHAB, THE PROSTITUTE OF JERICHO

Approximate Dating: early conquest of the promised land; ca. 1406 B.C. ***Relevant Scriptures:*** **Joshua 2:1, 3; 6:17, 23, 25**; also **Exodus 6:23; Ruth 4:18–22; 1 Chronicles 2:9–15; Matthew 1:5; Hebrews 11:31; James 2:25**

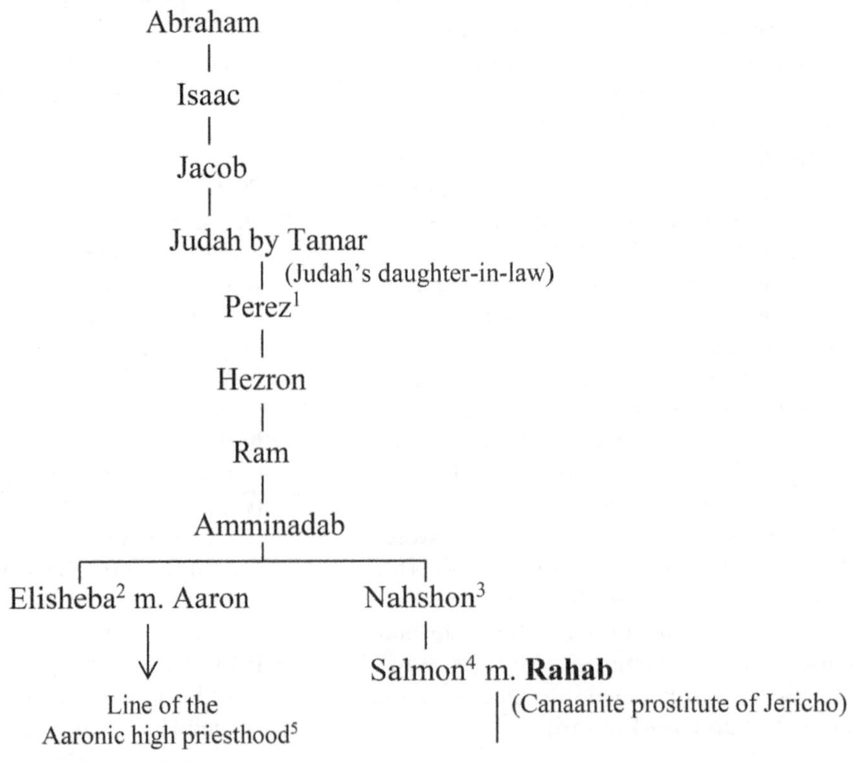

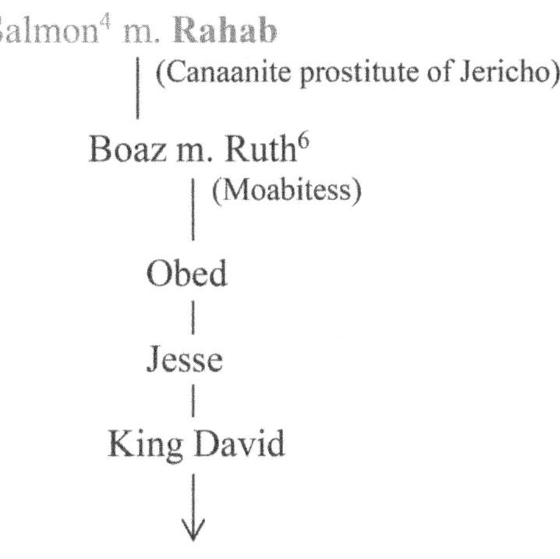

Biblical and Theological Significance

Moses died in 1406 B.C. and, that same year, the Israelites encamped on the east side of the Jordan River. The military men awaited instructions from Joshua before they crossed into the promised land to possess it. Joshua secretly sent two Israelite spies from Shittim to reconnoiter the city of Jericho (**Joshua 2:1**). There, the two spies stayed in the house of a prostitute[7] named Rahab (a Canaanite).[8] When the king of Jericho was apprised of the situation, he sent men to demand that Rahab hand the Israelites over to them. She chose instead to protect the Israelite spies by hiding them under drying stalks of flax on the roof of her house, which was located in the wall of the city of Jericho. She sent the king's men away, saying, "I don't know which way they went. Go after them quickly. You may catch up with them" (**Joshua 2:5**). Her righteous actions were confirmed with a declaration of faith in the God of Israel: "the LORD your God is God in heaven above and on the earth below" (**Joshua 2:11**). Rahab then requested that when the Israelites came into the land, they would, in turn, show kindness to her household and protect them from the coming destruction of Jericho (**Joshua 2:12–14**). When the Israelites destroyed Jericho, she and her household were spared (cf. **Joshua 6:17–25**).

The theological import of this brief genealogy can hardly be overstated. The genealogy of David shown in the chart prominently includes two women—Rahab and Ruth—who furthered the Abrahamic promise and its fulfillment in Jesus, born in Bethlehem. At the same time, two women of such mutually exclusive character and repute can be found nowhere else in sacred Scripture. Rahab was a common woman of the streets who earned her living in that odious manner; Ruth was a childless widow, humble and pure in every respect. Both found their common identity again, however, in their unwavering faith in the God of Israel. Rahab's son, Boaz, married Ruth the Moabitess; their descendants included David (**Ruth 4:18–22**) and Jesus (**Matthew 1:1–16**). Rahab's name is enshrined in Jesus' genealogy in the Gospel of Matthew (**Matthew 1:5**), and her actions are praised in the books of Hebrews and James—"By faith the prostitute Rahab, because she welcomed the spies, was not killed with those who were disobedient" (**Hebrews 11:31**) and "was not even Rahab the prostitute considered righteous for what she did when she gave lodging to the spies and sent them off in a different direction?" (**James 2:25**).

All the prevenient grace and love of God elaborated in the New Testament is found in striking brilliance here in this Old Testament genealogy.

Notes

1. Perez was the twin of Zerah (**Genesis 38:27–30**), and like the twins Esau and Jacob (**Genesis 25:23–26**), the chosen messianic line continued through the second-born twin.

2. Elisheba the sister of Nahshon (Judahite) married Aaron, the high priest (Levite; **Exodus 6:23**), and from them issued the high priesthood of Israel. See charts "**1 Chronicles 6**: Levi: High Priests, Priests, Levites, and Musicians in Solomon's Temple" and "**Supplement 2**: The High Priests of Israel."

3. Nahshon was the leader of the tribe of Judah during the forty-year period of the wilderness wanderings (cf. **Numbers 1:7; 2:3; 10:14**). Presumably Nahshon's son, Salmon, was one of the two (unnamed) spies that Joshua sent out from Shittim before the invasion of Jericho (**Joshua 2:1**); at some point, Salmon married Rahab (cf. **Ruth 4:20; 1 Chronicles 2:10–11; Matthew 1:4–5; Luke 3:32**).

4. The lineage of Salmon is given in **Ruth 4:20–21; 1 Chronicles 2:10–12; Matthew 1:4–5; Luke 3:32–34**.

5. See charts "**1 Chronicles 6**: Levi: High Priests, Priests, Levites, and Musicians in Solomon's Temple" and "**Supplement 2**: The High Priests of Israel."

6. See chart "**Ruth 1**: Boaz, Elimelek, and Naomi and the Descendants of Boaz the Judahite and Ruth the Moabitess."

7. She is described as an *ishah zona*, a "secular" harlot, as opposed to a so-called sacred prostitute (*qedesha*), a central figure (female) in the licentiously sexual cult of neighboring nations (**Deuteronomy 23:18; 1 Kings 15:12; Hosea 4:14**).

8. The exact genealogy of Rahab is unknown. The Canaanites were the descendants of Canaan, the son of Ham, the son of Noah; see chart "**Genesis 10**: Noah's Descendants: The Table of Seventy Nations."

JOSHUA 14: THE CLAN OF JEPHUNNEH THE KENIZZITE

Approximate Dating: during the wilderness wanderings, 1446–1406 B.C. and the early occupation of the promised land ***Relevant Scriptures:*** **Joshua 14:6–14; 15:13–19;** also **Judges 3:9–11; 1 Chronicles 4:13–20**

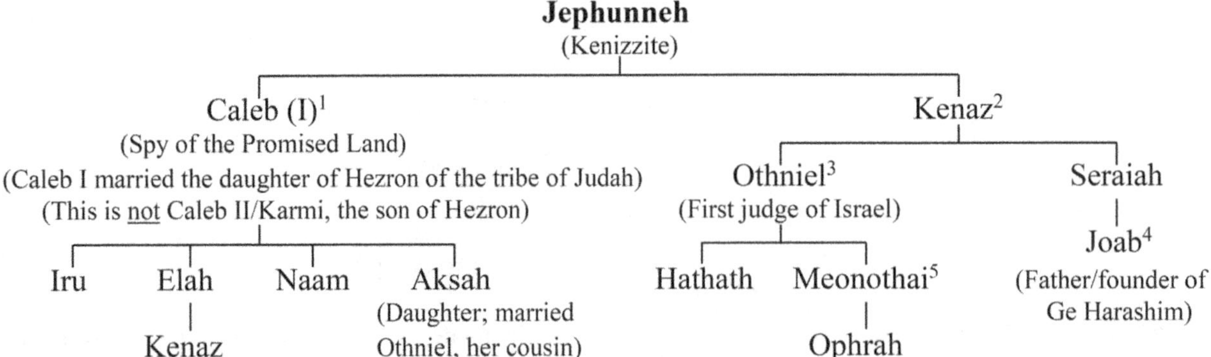

Biblical and Theological Significance

The gentilic *Kenizzite* found here should be clearly distinguished at the very beginning from the name "Kenaz," the son and grandson of Esau in **Genesis 36:11, 15, 42.**[6] The Kenizzites were a tribal people first mentioned in the early days of Abraham (ca. 2166–1991 B.C.) along with others such as Kenites, Kadmonites, Hittites, Perizzites, Rephaites, Amorites, Canaanites, Girgashites, and Jebusites (**Genesis 15:19–21**). Caleb was descended from the ancient indigenous Kenizzite people. One must presume that at some unmentioned time, Kenizzites became followers of Abraham's God Yahweh and thus were grafted into the tree of the chosen people and eventually became connected to the tribe of Judah by marriage.

Caleb the Kenizzite had become affiliated with the tribe of Judah by marriage to a daughter of Hezron (the sister of Jerahmeel, Hezron's eldest son; **1 Chronicles 2:25, 42**). Inasmuch as the spies were sent forth two years after the exodus (**Numbers 9:1**), the date of this narrative is no later than about 1445 B.C. Caleb therefore was qualified to represent the tribe of Judah as one of the twelve who spied out Canaan (**Numbers 13:6; 14:6; 34:19**) and brought back a report that the Israelites could certainly take the land (**Numbers 13:26–14:9**). Of those men who were "twenty years old or more" at the first census of Israel, only Caleb (Kenizzite) and Joshua, the son of Nun (Ephraimite), survived the forty years in the wilderness (**Numbers 14:38**; cf. **Numbers 1:1–2**). Moreover, Caleb was selected by Yahweh to be the leader of Judah in assigning the inheritance of land in Canaan amongst the families (**Numbers 34:19, 29**).

One should note the interweaving of peoples (in this case, the Kenizzites and the Judahites) designed to create a mosaic reflecting God's inscrutable ways in history and redemption. What appears to most as coincidence or accident in everyday life is nothing of the sort. The only theologically and experientially appropriate term to use is providence, whose very root, "provide," suggests, at least to the believer, that "(God) provides." The complication of the genealogy, when unraveled, makes this point crystal clear.

Notes

1. Caleb the Kenizzite, the son of Jephunneh (**1 Chronicles 2:42–49; 4:13–20**) is designated in this and other charts as Caleb (I) and should not be confused with Caleb, the son of Hezron, from the tribe of Judah (cf. **1 Chronicles 2:9, 18–20; 50–54**) designated elsewhere as Caleb (II) or Karmi. Given the scriptural references, narrative details, and the genealogical data, the text at **1 Chronicles 2:42** should read "Caleb [Caleb the Kenizzite or Caleb I] the *brother-in-law* of Jerahmeel" (not "Caleb the *brother* of Jerahmeel"). For more information about the Kenizzite clan, see "**Judges 3**: Othniel (Kenizzite), the First Judge of Israel" and "**1 Chronicles 2**: Caleb and Kenaz, the Sons of Jephunneh the Kenizzite."

2. Kenaz the Kenizzite (**1 Chronicles 4:13–20**) is a different person than Kenaz the Edomite, a descendant of Esau (**Genesis 36:11, 15, 42; 1 Chronicles 1:36, 53**).

3. More details about the marriage of Othniel to his first cousin Aksah may be found in **Judges 1:12–15**. Othniel's judgeship is summarized in **Judges 3:7–11** and discussed in chart "**Judges 3**: Othniel (Kenizzite), the First Judge of Israel." Also, see chart "**1 Chronicles 2**: Caleb and Kenaz, the Sons of Jephunneh the Kenizzite."

4. Joab was the father/founder of the Ge Harashim, a valley of skilled workers/craftsmen (**1 Chronicles 4:14**), which was inhabited by the descendants of Benjamites from Geba in the post-exile (**Nehemiah 11:31, 35**).

5. Meonothai the Kenizzite appears to be the founder of the town of Ophrah in Benjamin, which was named for his son (**Joshua 18:23; 1 Chronicles 4:14**), and he was also the founder of a city (Ophrah) in West Manasseh, called Ophrah of the Abiezrites, the home of Joash and his son Gideon, the judge of Israel (**Judges 6:11, 24; 8:27, 32; 9:5**).

6. The gentilic "Kenizzite" appears in Hebrew as קְנִזִּי (*qenizzi*) and "Kenazzite" (which is not attested) would be קְנַזִּי (*qenazzi*). Note the vowels after the "n." The gentilic "Kenite" (קֵינִי, *keni*) is clearly not cognate to the other names here.

JUDGES 1: SUMMARY LIST OF THE LEADERS AND JUDGES OF ISRAEL[1]

Approximate Dating: 1446–1050 B.C.[2] ***Relevant Scriptures:*** **book of Judges**

❖ Leaders of Israel During the Wilderness Years and the Early Conquest of Canaan

Moses—Tribe of Levi (Kohathite–Amramite clan); leader of Israel for 40 years (**Exodus 7:7; Numbers 14:33; 32:13; Deuteronomy 2:7; 8:4; 29:5; 34:7; Acts 7:23, 30**)

Joshua—Tribe of Ephraim (**Exodus 33:11; Numbers 11:28; 13:8, 16; 14:6, 30; 26:65; 33:12; 34:17; Deuteronomy 1:38; 3:28; 31:3; 34:9; Joshua 4:4, 8, 14; 8:32-35; 11:15, 23; Judges 2:6, 8**). From his youth, Joshua was the aide of Moses; later, he became Moses' successor and led Israel's invasion and conquest of Canaan

Caleb the Kenizzite (the same as Caleb I, the son of Jephunneh)—non-Israelite who married into the tribe of Judah (**Numbers 13:6, 30; 14:6, 24, 30; 26:65; 32:12; 34:19; Joshua 14:13–14; 15:13–14**). Caleb represented the tribe of Judah as a spy of the land and assisted Joshua in the conquest and tribal allotment of Canaan

❖ Terms of the Judges of Israel and the Intervening Periods of Foreign Oppression

Oppression by Cushan-Rishathaim, king of Aram Naharaim, for 8 years (**Judges 3:7–8**)

1st - **Othniel** of Judah (Kenizzite clan)—40 years (**Judges 3:9–11**)

Oppression by the Moabites for 18 years (**Judges 3:12–14**)

2nd - **Ehud** of Benjamin—80 years (**Judges 3:12–30**)

Oppression by the Philistines for an unknown number of years (**Judges 3:31**)

3rd - **Shamgar**, it seems, was an "outsider" (an ethnic foreigner) whose judgeship consisted of delivering Israel on only one occasion and probably briefly, ca. 1220 B.C. (**Judges 3:31**).[3]

Oppression by the Canaanites for 20 years (**Judges 4:1–3**)

4th - **Deborah** of Ephraim, along with Barak, the army commander from Naphtali—40 years (**Judges 4:4–5:31**)

Oppression by the Midianites for 7 years (**Judges 6:1–6**)

5th - **Gideon** of West Manasseh (Abiezrite clan)—40 years (**Judges 6:11–8:33**), and his son **Abimelek** of Manasseh (Abiezrite clan)—3 years (**Judges 9:1–57**)

Unknown oppressor(s) and period of oppression

6th - **Tola** of Issachar—23 years (**Judges 10:1–2**)

Unknown oppressor(s) and period of oppression

7th - **Jair** of East Manasseh (Gileadite clan)—22 years (**Judges 10:3–5**)

Oppression by the Ammonites and the Philistines for 18 years (**Judges 10:6–10**)

8th - **Jephthah** of East Manasseh (Gileadite clan)—6 years (**Judges 11:1–12:7**; cf. **Judges 11:26**)

Unknown oppressor(s) and period of oppression

9th - **Ibzan** of Bethlehem (probably in Zebulun)—7 years (**Judges 12:8–10**)

Unknown oppressor(s) and period of oppression

10th - **Elon** of Zebulun—10 years (**Judges 12:11–12**)

Unknown oppressor(s) and period of oppression

11th - **Abdon** of Ephraim (Pirathon area near Shechem)—8 years (**Judges 12:13–15**)

Oppression by the Philistines for 40 years (**Judges 13:1**)

12th - **Samson** of Dan (Zorah area)—20 years (**Judges 13:2–16:31**)

❖ **Transitional Figure from the Time of the Judges to the Time of the Kings**

Samuel—of the tribe of Levi (Kohathite–Izharite–Korathite clan)—lived from ca. 1110–1015 B.C. Samuel initially apprenticed as a priest under Eli, the high priest at Shiloh, who judged Israel for 40 years, ca. 1144–1104 B.C. (cf. **1 Samuel 4:18**). Samuel later became a circuit judge-prophet-Levitical priest[4] himself (**1 Samuel 7:15-17**), serving throughout most of the forty-year monarchy of King Saul (ca. 1051–1011 B.C.), until his death in ca. 1015 B.C., near the end of Saul's reign (**1 Samuel 25:1**). Samuel served as "Israel's leader all the days of his life" (**1 Samuel 7:15**; cf. **1 Samuel 1:20-22; 2:18, 35; 3:19-20; 4:18; 8:1; 10:1; 25:1; Acts 13:20**).

In sum, the era of the Judges lasted from 1350–1086 B.C., bridging the chasm between the conquest of Canaan (1406–1400 B.C.) and the establishment of the united monarchy under Saul (1051–1011 B.C.). Andrew Steinmann has proposed a structure of six cycles of judges, in groups of three (1–3) and (4–6).[5]

Biblical and Theological Significance

Moses had served as a judge of Israel during the forty years of the wilderness wanderings, deciding cases between individuals and teaching the Law of God, ca. 1446–1406 B.C. (**Exodus 18:15–16**). However, Moses is not to be included among the judges of the book by that name. Between the conquest of the promised land (under the military command of Joshua) and the time of the united monarchy (begun by Saul, the first king), Israel was ruled by judges (Heb. שׁוֹפְטִים, *shophetim*). This system of jurisprudence was unique to ancient Israel at the time when a tribal society and political "looseness" morphed into a unified but pre-monarchical national state from 1406–1050 B.C. These judges were not primarily "courtroom" judges in the legal sense but rather charismatic men—and notably one woman—all chosen by God for a special mission. The judges heard cases, administered justice, and served in a military deliverer capacity—or in a co-deliverer capacity, as in the case of Deborah—leading Israel against foreign adversaries. After defeating Israel's oppressors, each judge served in a spiritual-political capacity for the nation. Twelve of these governor/military judges—Othniel through Samson—oversaw the tribal federation of Israel; the judgeship of Gideon and his son Abimelek was considered a single term.

The exact time period of the judges continues to be debated among scholars, but in general it corresponds to the time *after* the conquest of Canaan and *before* the time of Samuel (the key transitional figure between the judges and the kings), as explained in **Acts 13:17–20**: "The God of the people of Israel chose our ancestors; he made the people prosper during their stay in Egypt; with mighty power he led them out of that country; for about forty years he endured their conduct in the wilderness; and he overthrew seven nations in Canaan, giving their land to his people as their inheritance. All this took about 450 years. After this, God gave them judges until the time of Samuel the prophet."[6, 7]

Othniel, the first judge, began his judgeship ca. 1350 B.C. The last judge, Samson, ended his term in ca. 1086 B.C., thereby yielding a total of 264 years—rounded off to 250 years—which determines the general time period of the judges.

Table 1 (below) shows that some of the years of oppression overlapped and that some of the terms of office overlapped. Therefore, it can be concluded that Israel's twelve judges did not serve *sequential* chronological terms, but rather, some served *partially concurrent* judgeships (e.g., Samson overlapped with Jephthah; see below).

The theological interpretation of this period and its structures can be summarized as follows:

- God himself "raised up" the judges (**Judges 2:16, 18; 3:9**).
- The challenges of Israel's constant warfare with neighbors and internal squabbles were part of the honing process of disciplining God's people, which shaped them to become "a kingdom of priests and a holy nation" (**Exodus 19:5–6**) and a light to the nations, as the Lord had intended (**Isaiah 49:6**).
- The ideal governance ordained from creation was a theocracy, but, when the Israelites insisted, "Appoint a king to lead us, such as all the other nations have" (**1 Samuel 8:5**), God condescended to monarchic

governance (**1 Samuel 8**). Gideon's refusal to accept the role of ruler[8] (Heb. מָשַׁל) after his many conquests may have been his sense that the right ruler had not yet come. That anticipation did come to pass but in a flawed form in Saul; in David, however, its truly messianic prototype emerged. In the interim, Gideon insisted that God was to be judge and ruler: "I will not rule over you, nor will my son rule over you. The LORD will rule over you" (**Judges 8:22–23**; cf. **Genesis 18:25; Job 9:15; Psalm 7:11; 94:2; 96:10; 2 Timothy 4:1**).

Table of the Judges of Israel[9]

Name	References	Oppressors	Years of Oppression	Years of Peace
Othniel of Judah	**Judges 3:7–11**	Aram Naharaim	(8) ca. 1358–1350	(40) ca. 1350–1310
Ehud of Benjamin	**Judges 3:12–30**	Moabites	(18) ca. 1310–1290	(80) ca. 1290–1210
Shamgar[10]	**Judges 3:31; 5:6**	Philistines	(?)	(?)
Deborah of Ephraim	**Judges 4:1–5:31**	Canaanites	(20) ca. 1210–1170[11]	(40) ca. 1170–1130
Gideon of Manasseh	**Judges 6:1–8:35**	Midianites	(7) ca. 1130–1123	(40) ca. 1123–1083
(Abimelek)[12] of Manasseh	**Judges 9:1–57**			(3) ca. 1083–1081
Tola of Issachar	**Judges 10:1–2**		(?)	(23)
Jair of Ephraim	**Judges 10:3–5**		(?)	(22)
Jephthah[13] of East Manasseh	**Judges 10:6–12:7**	Ammonites & Philistines	(18) ca. 1124–1106	(6) ca. 1106–1100
Ibzan of Judah	**Judges 12:8–10**		(?)	(7)
Elon of Zebulun	**Judges 12:11–12**		(?)	(10)
Abdon of Ephraim	**Judges 12:13–15**		(?)	(8)
Samson[14] of Dan	**Judges 13:1–16:31**	Philistines	(40) ca. 1146–1106	(20) ca. 1106–1086

*Total *known* years of oppression (8 + 18 + 20 + 7 + 18 + 40) = 111 years. (However, this number is overinflated since some years of oppression overlapped, as in the years before Jephthah and before Samson).

*Total *known* years of peace: (40 + 80 + 40 + 40 + 3 + 23 + 22 + 6 + 7 + 10 + 8 + 20) = 299 years (however, because the terms of some judges overlapped, as in the case of Jephthah and Samson's judgeships, this number is overinflated). The total known period of governance by the judges was from ca. 1350–1086 B.C. or 264 years (corresponding to a rounded-off number of 250 years).

Notes

1. The major judges are: Othniel, Ehud, Deborah, Gideon, Jephthah and Samson. The minor judges of whom limited or no military exploits are recorded are: Shamgar, Tola, Jair, Ibzan, Elon, and Abdon. For further information, see the individual chart for each leader and judge.

2. Following the 430-year period of Israelite bondage in Egypt (1876–1446 B.C.), the exodus from Egypt (1446 B.C.), the 40-year period of the wilderness wanderings (1446–1406 B.C.), and the conquest and early occupation of the promised land of Canaan (ca. 1406–1350 B.C.), the 12-tribe nation of Israel was governed by judges for approximately 250 years (ca. 1350–1100/1086 B.C.), from Othniel through Samson.

3. The genealogy of Shamgar, the son of Anath, is limited. Shamgar, the third judge of Israel, delivered the people from Philistine oppression sometime after Ehud's judgeship by striking down "six hundred Philistines with an oxgoad" (**Judges 3:31**). Before Shamgar "saved Israel" (**Judges 3:31**), there existed a great sense of fear among the Israelites—"In the days of Shamgar son of Anath, . . . the highways were abandoned; travelers took to winding paths. Villagers . . . would not fight back" (**Judges 5:6**). The name of his father, Anath (עֲנָת), is clearly non-Israelite; in fact, it is a pagan theophoric name embodying Anat, a principal goddess of the Canaanites and other peoples of the Mediterranean littoral. Moreover, Shamgar's name is not even NW Semitic like Hebrew, Aramaic, Ugaritic, or the like. Rather, the consensus of scholars is that the language is Hurrian, a non-Semitic language. (Some scholars suggest that it is an adaptation of the name Sargon, the mighty Akkadian ruler of Mesopotamia, ca. 2360–2305 B.C.) For another example, a city named Beth Anath was in the tribal area of Naphtali (cf. **Joshua 19:38; Judges 1:33**). It is possible that Shamgar was a hired mercenary who found common cause with Israel in destroying the hated Philistines.

4. The judgeship of Samuel resembled that of the "minor" judges of whom no military exploits are recorded. In his early childhood, he apprenticed under Eli at Shiloh (**1 Samuel 1:23–24**). When Eli died in 1104 B.C., Samuel continued to grow and be recognized as a prophet of the Lord (**1 Samuel 3:19–21**). Samuel lived long enough to anoint David king when David was about fifteen years of age (ca. 1025 B.C.) and died around 1015 B.C.; see charts "**1 Samuel 1**: Eli and the Eli Priesthood" and "**1 Samuel 1**: Samuel, the Prophet–Priest–Judge of Israel."

5. Andrew E. Steinmann, *From Abraham to Paul: A Biblical Chronology* (Saint Louis: Concordia, 2011), 91–102, proposes:

- *Cycle 1*: **Judges 3:7–11–Othniel**
- *Cycle 2*: **Judges 3:12–31** (Eglon the oppressor)–**Ehud** and **Shamgar** (may have been active during the 80 years of Ehud's peace, but after Ehud died; cf. **Judges 3:31**)
- *Cycle 3*: **Judges 4:1–5:31** (Jabin the oppressor)–**Deborah**
- *Cycle 4*: **Judges 6:1–10:6** (Midianite oppressors)–**Gideon–Tola–Jair**
- *Cycle 5*: **Judges 10:7–12:15** (Ammonites and Philistine oppression, which may have occurred concurrently—**Jephthah–Ibzan–Elon–Abdon** (notes that Jephthah's judgeship began at the beginning of Ammonite oppression, but his death did not bring Ammonite oppression to an end; **Judges 12:77**)
- *Cycle 6*: **Judges 13:1–16:31** (Philistine oppression)—**Samson** (judged Israel for twenty years "in the days of the Philistines" (**Judges 15:20; 16:31**) and "will take the lead in delivering Israel from the hands of the Philistines" (**Judges 13:5**).

6. See Eugene H. Merrill's article, "Paul's Use of 'About 450 Years' in **Acts 13:20**" in *Bibliotheca Sacra* 138 (1981): 246–257.

7. Another witness to the chronology of the period is useful in that it provides a secondary chronology that runs partly concurrently with the 450-year one. This is Paul's reference to a period of 430 years between the confirmation of one covenant to the inauguration of another (**Galatians 3:17**). The first was the Abrahamic, the last was the recorded bestowal of Jacob's blessings of his sons in the year 1876 B.C., when Jacob's family entered Egypt (**Genesis 47:28**). The period between 1876 B.C. and the revelation of the Sinai Covenant in 1446 B.C. was, of course, exactly 430 years!

8. This is not the term to indicate kingship but a lower level of authority. The verb "to reign" is מָלַךְ, cognate to the noun מֶלֶךְ, "king."

9. The table is based on personal communication with Eugene H. Merrill and source material in his book, *Kingdom of Priests–A History of Old Testament Israel* (Grand Rapids: Baker, 1996), 141–88. For a comparative discussion of the chronology of the judges, see Steinmann, *From Abraham to Paul*, 92–107.

10. The so-called minor judges (Shamgar, Tola, Jair, Ibzan, Elon, and Abdon) pose certain problems regarding function and chronological placement. It is likely that their judgeship was more of a normal judicial nature in which they heard cases and administered justice and therefore were not warriors of the kind seen in the major judges. Their chronological data are therefore not to be factored into the time span of the period.

11. Canaanite oppression may have occurred earlier, perhaps 1240–1220 B.C., making Deborah's judgeship earlier also (see Merrill, *Kingdom of Priests*, 164–66).

12. Following Gideon's death, his son Abimelek founded a rump judgeship for three years (**Judges 9:22**). No oppressors are mentioned in his narrative, so Abimelek is included here only to account for all the years reckoned in the book of Judges.

13. On the six-year judgeship of Jephthah, see note 14.

14. The judgeships of Jephthah and Samson seem to have coincided, as **Judges 10:7–8a** makes clear: "He [Yahweh] became angry with them. He sold them into the hands of the Philistines and the Ammonites, who *that year* shattered and crushed them." Specifically, an unassailable and important intra-biblical point of chronology that serves to ameliorate the chronological complexity in the book of **Judges** is the statement by the judge Jephthah to the king of Ammon that the latter had no reason to attack Israel in his day since they had never done so in the 300 years Israel had been in Canaan (**Judges 11:26**). Since the conquest had begun in 1406 B.C., the Ammonite and Philistine hostilities, as well as Jephthah's six-year judgeship, must be dated ca. 1106–1100 B.C. (**Judges 12:7**). Coincidentally (or providentially), the Ammonite invasion from the east had commenced the same time as the Philistine attacks from the west (**Judges 10:7**), this time calling forth the labors of the last of the judge Samson (**Judges 13**). Inasmuch as Samson's leadership began the same year as Jephthah's (i.e., in 1106 B.C.) and lasted for 20 years (**Judges 16:31**), Samson died in 1086 B.C.

JUDGES 3: OTHNIEL (KENIZZITE), THE FIRST JUDGE OF ISRAEL

Approximate Dating: ca. 1350–1310 B.C., at the beginning of the period of the judges, ca. 1350–1100/1086 B.C. ***Relevant Scriptures:*** **Judges 3:7–11;** also **Joshua 15:17; Judges 1:1–15; 1 Chronicles 2:42–50; 4:13–20**

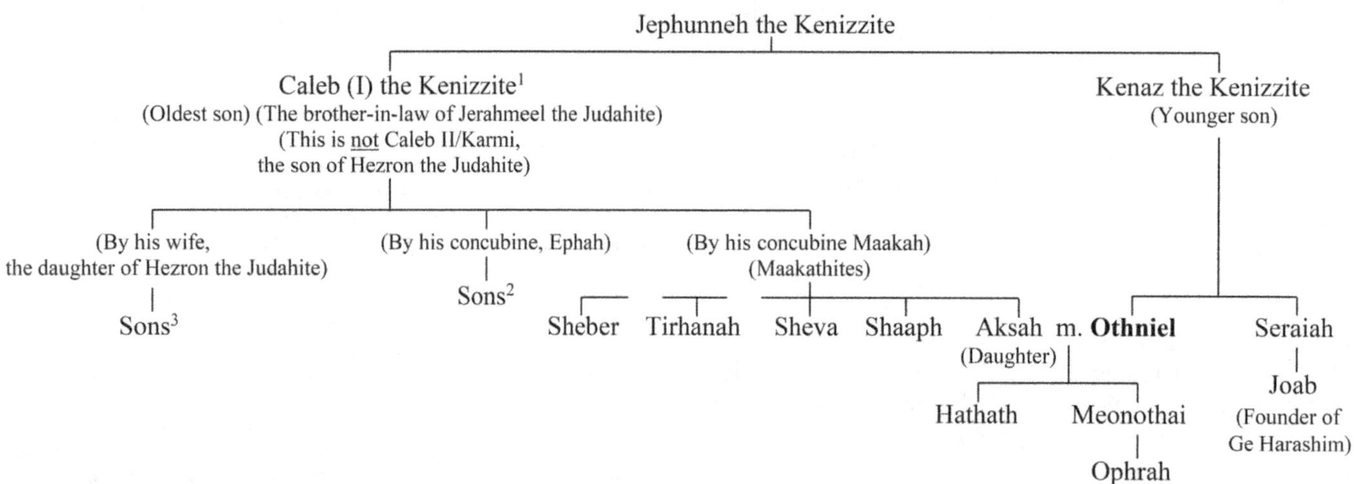

Biblical and Theological Significance

Othniel's Family

Othniel was the son of Kenaz, the youngest son of Jephunneh. Othniel's uncle, Caleb (I) the Kenizzite, is best known as the representative of the tribe of Judah who, along with other spies, reconnoitered Canaan (**Numbers 13:6**). Caleb (I) married into the tribe of Judah by taking as his wife the daughter of Hezron, the son of Perez, the son of Judah; therefore, Caleb (I) was the *brother-in-law* of Jerahmeel, the firstborn son of Hezron, of the tribe of Judah. Caleb (I) successfully conquered the city of Hebron, where some of the city and its pasturelands were given to the sons of Aaron the high priest, but "the fields and villages around the city they [gave] to Caleb [I] son of Jephunneh as his possession" (**Joshua 21:11–12**; cf. **15:13; Judges 1:20; 1 Chronicles 6:56**). Hebron was also one of the forty-eight Levitical cities and one of the six cities of refuge (**Joshua 20:7; 1 Chronicles 6:57**).

Othniel as the Judge of Israel

One of the most illustrious offspring of the Jephunneh family was Othniel the Kenizzite, the first judge of Israel. Like Caleb (I), his uncle, Othniel assimilated into the tribe of Judah and became a well-respected loyal leader, known for his military prowess. Caleb (I) promised that he would give his daughter (Aksah) in marriage to the man who could (re)-capture Debir (Kiriath Sepher or Kiriath Sannah), a city that had been initially defeated by Joshua (**Joshua 10:38–39; 15:16–17, 48–49; Judges 1:11–12**). Othniel retook the city and so won Aksah's hand. Following the example of her father (Caleb I)—who had asked Joshua for an added blessing (cf. **Joshua 14:6–15**)—Aksah asked her father for an added blessing also—"'Do me a special favor. Since you have given me land in the Negev, give me also springs of water.' So Caleb gave her the upper and lower springs [referring to a renewable flowing water source]" (**Joshua 15:19; Judges 1:15**), ensuring that Aksah and Othniel's family could have a settled (non-nomadic) existence in the harsh landscape of their inheritance. As the first judge of the nation, Othniel delivered Israel from an eight-year oppression by Cushan-Rishathaim, king of Aram Naharaim,[4] and then he ruled over Israel for forty years, ca. 1350–1310 B.C. (**Judges 3:7–11**).

Notes

1. For charts on the extended family of Caleb (I) the Kenizzite, see "**Joshua 14**: The Clan of Jephunneh the Kenizzite" and "**1 Chronicles 2**: Caleb and Kenaz, the Sons of Jephunneh the Kenizzite." Caleb the Kenizzite (designated Caleb I) is not Caleb/Karmi (designated Caleb II), the son of Hezron, who was the *brother* of Jerahmeel and Ram (cf. **1 Chronicles 2:9, 18–20**); for the distinction, see chart "**1 Chronicles 2**: Hezron"). A descendant of Othniel (not shown in the chart) named Heled/Heldai, the son of Baanah, was a soldier in David's army (see note 18 in chart "**1 Chronicles 11**: Genealogical Registry of the Mighty Warriors in King David's Army").

2. "Caleb's concubine Ephah was the mother of Haran, Moza and Gazez. Haran was the father of Gazez" (**1 Chronicles 2:46**).

3. The Caleb–Kenizzite descendants specifically associated with the families and clans in the tribe of Judah are given in **1 Chronicles 4:13–15**; the Caleb–Kenizzite descendants specifically associated with the family of Jerahmeel (the eldest son of Hezron, son of Perez, son of Judah) are given in **1 Chronicles 2:42–50**.

4. The eight years of oppression by Cushan-Rishathaim of Aram Naharaim were from ca. 1358–1350 B.C.

JUDGES 3: EHUD, THE SECOND JUDGE OF ISRAEL

Approximate Dating: ca. 1290–1210 B.C., in the period of the judges, ca. 1350–1100/1086 B.C. ***Relevant Scriptures:*** **Judges 3:15**; also **Genesis 46:21; Numbers 26:38–40; 1 Chronicles 7:6–7; 8:1–7**

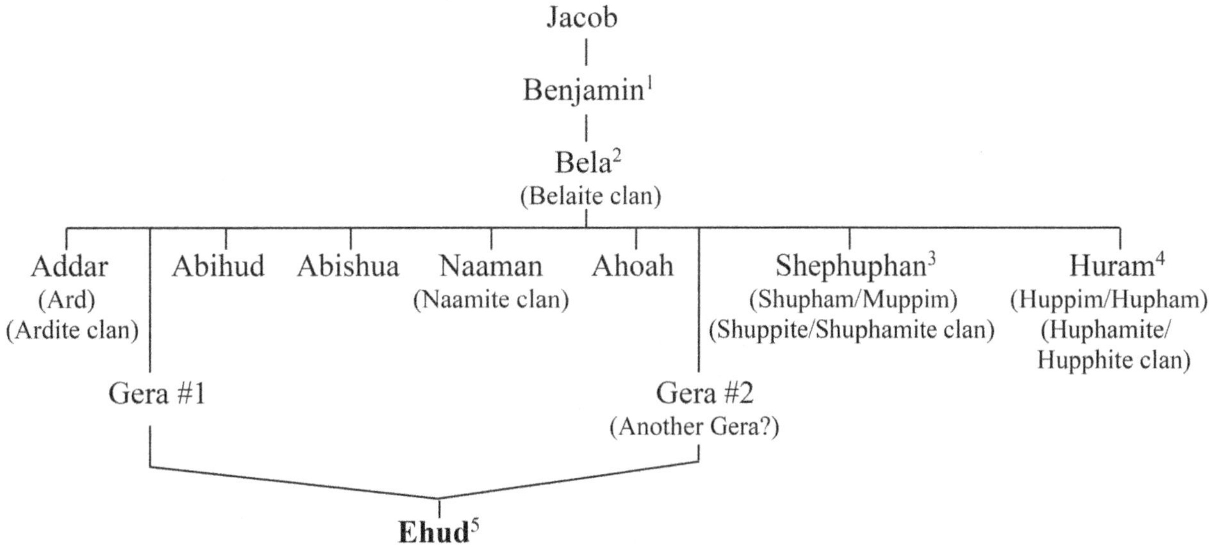

Biblical and Theological Significance

The second judge of Israel was Ehud, son of Gera, who was a Benjamite descended from the Bela/Belaite clan (**Genesis 46:21; Numbers 26:38, 40; 1 Chronicles 7:6–7; 8:1**), but **1 Chronicles 8:3, 5** suggests that there were *two* sons of Bela named Gera.[6] The exact familial relationships in the Belaite clan are insufficiently clear as to determine which "Gera" is actually Ehud's father (see note 5).

Late in the fourteenth century B.C., Israel was attacked by a coalition of Moabites, Ammonites, and Amalekites whom Yahweh had raised up to be an instrument of disciplinary punishment of his wayward people (**Judges 3:12–30**). After their plea for deliverance, Yahweh sent Ehud to Jericho to liberate them from oppression. Jericho had been taken by the Moabite king Eglon, allegedly to deliver its tribute to the king—thus hoping, perhaps, to soften his oppression. Ehud was left-handed[7] and used a specially fashioned double-edged sword "about a cubit long," hidden on his right thigh, to mislead the obese king who was "sitting alone in the upper room of his palace" (**Judges 3:16, 20**). When Eglon's attendants had left him alone, he welcomed in the Israelite envoy who, rather than offering a tribute, drew his sword and offered Eglon a bloody death. The narrative graphically recounts that when Ehud stabbed the king "[even] the handle sank in after the blade, and his bowels discharged. Ehud did not pull the sword out, and the fat closed in over it" (**Judges 3:22**). Ehud then led the Israelites in a successful military campaign that cut off the "fords of the Jordan that led to Moab" and subdued ten thousand Moabites (**Judges 3:28–29**). Ehud, the only judge from Benjamin, judged Israel for eighty years, the longest of any of the twelve judges (**Judges 3:30**). During his judgeship there was rest from oppression (ca. 1290–1210 B.C.).

Notes

1. The line of Benjamin is rather irregular and complicated. Often, the genealogies for this tribe have variant spellings for the name of the same individual; generations of descendants (sons and grandsons) are sometimes conflated; and different lineages are offered to stress, for example, (1) the military complement of the tribe, (2) the ancestry of a specific person, such as King Saul, or (3) in the case of this chart, a particular clan (the Belaites) that gave rise to an important judge—all of which may reflect the authors' literary choices or sources they used in the compilation.

2. Bela was the firstborn son of Benjamin (and the head of the Belaite clan; **Numbers 26:38**). Compare the sons of Bela listed in **1 Chronicles 7:7** (i.e., the genealogical record of the fighting men who were eligible for conscription into military service) with those who are listed in **1 Chronicles 8:3–7** (i.e., the genealogical record of the family of King Saul).

3. For the variant spellings of this person—Muppim/Shupham/Shephuphan—the head of the Shuphamite/Shuppite clan, see **Genesis 46:21; Numbers 26:39; 1 Chronicles 7:12, 15; 8:5**.

4. For the variant spellings of this person—Huppim/Hupham/Huram—the head of the Huphamite/Huppite clan, see **Genesis 46:21; Numbers 26:39; 1 Chronicles 7:12, 15; 8:5**.

5. Although they share the same name and both are Benjaminites, Ehud (the son of Gera, the son of Bela), who was the second judge of Israel (**Judges 3:12–30**), should not be confused with Ehud, the son of Bilhan, the son of Jedaiel, the son of Benjamin (**1 Chronicles 7:10**). For a comparison of these Ehud figures, see chart "**2 Samuel 16**: Possible Genealogy of Shimei, the Benjamite who Cursed King David."

6. The Syriac Peshitta omits the Gera of **1 Chronicles 8:5**; otherwise, the text evidence is strong for two sons with the same name (Gera). Explanations to account for this may be: (1) the possibility that Gera #1 died and a later, second son took the name; or (2) given the common practices of bigamy and/or concubinage in the ancient Near Eastern world, the two sons named Gera were born to different wives of Bela, each of whom had a hand in naming her children.

7. Left-handedness was common among the Benjamites (cf. **Judges 20:16; 1 Chronicles 12:2**). This is ironic in that the name Benjamin (בִּנְיָמִין) means "son of (the) right hand" or "a right-handed son," that is, the father's "right-hand son."

JUDGES 4: DEBORAH, THE FOURTH JUDGE OF ISRAEL

Approximate Dating: ca. 1170–1130 B.C.[1], in the period of the judges, ca. 1350–1100/1086 B.C. ***Relevant Scriptures:*** **Judges 4:4–5:31**

Tribe of Ephraim
|
|
Deborah m. Lappidoth

Biblical and Theological Significance

The Lord appointed judges to lead and deliver Israel from oppressors (**Judges 2:16**). Deborah was the fourth judge; she is also called a "prophet" (or "prophetess" in some translations) similar to Moses and Samuel, who also served in a judge–prophet dual capacity (**Judges 4:4**; cf. **Deuteronomy 34:10; 1 Samuel 3:20; Acts 3:22; 13:20**). Deborah presided from an open-air *courtroom* beneath a landmark palm, called the "Palm of Deborah" (**Judges 4:5**), located between Bethel and Ramah in the hill country of Ephraim, meting out justice according to the Law of Moses. After Jabin of Hazor and the Canaanites had oppressed Israel for twenty years, ca. 1210–1170 B.C., she arose as a "mother in Israel" (**Judges 5:7**) and invoked the help of Israel's military commander, Barak of Kedesh of Naphtali, to mobilize the tribes of Naphtali and Zebulun to fight against them (**Judges 4:6–7**). Barak reluctantly agreed but refused to go without Deborah (**Judges 4:8**).[2] She wholeheartedly agreed to accompany him in battle but clarified that the honor of victory would go to a *woman* rather than him (**Judges 4:8–9, 21**). When the Canaanites were defeated in battle, Sisera (the commander of the Canaanite army) fled to the tent of Heber the Kenite "because there was an alliance between Jabin king of Hazor and the family of Heber" (**Judges 4:17**). When Sisera arrived, Heber's wife Jael went out to meet him. After covering Sisera with a blanket and giving him milk, he fell asleep. Jael then killed Sisera with a single decisive blow, driving "the peg through his temple into the ground" (**Judges 4:21**), and thus, Jael the Kenite became the true military deliverer of Israel, just as Deborah had prophesied. The song that commemorates Israel's victory over the Canaanites and the death of Sisera at the hand of Jael the Kenite[3] is found in **Judges 5:1–31**.[4] Following the years of Deborah's strong leadership, peace ensued in Israel for the next forty years, ca. 1170–1130 B.C. (**Judges 5:31**).

Notes

1. See note 11 in chart "**Judges 1**: Summary List of the Leaders and Judges of Israel."

2. This by no means should indict Barak as a coward or weakling. His reluctance was founded not on the presence of Deborah but on the presence of God that Deborah represented as a woman of God. Basically, if God was not in it, he wanted no part of it!

3. For the ancestry of Jael the Kenite, see chart "**Judges 4**: Heber and Jael (Kenites) and Their Descendants Who Co-Mingled with the Pious Jabez–Rekabite Scribal Community near Jerusalem."

4. The last verses of the Song (**Judges 5:28–31**) recount the love and concern of a mother "behind the lattice" of the windows looking for her son (Sisera) who had not returned from battle. The song telling of Sisera's death at the hand of Jael ends in an imprecatory plea: "So may all your enemies perish, LORD! But may all who love you be like the sun when it rises in its strength" (**Judges 5:31**). Other recurrent biblical motifs of "looking through a window" are evident in **Genesis 26:8; 1 Samuel 19:12; 2 Samuel 6:16; 2 Kings 9:30; 1 Chronicles 15:29; Proverbs 7:6; Ecclesiastes 12:3;** and **Song of Solomon 2:9**.

JUDGES 4: HEBER AND JAEL (KENITES) AND THEIR DESCENDANTS WHO COMINGLED WITH THE PIOUS JABEZ–REKABITE SCRIBAL COMMUNITY NEAR JERUSALEM

Approximate Dating: time of the judges through the post-exilic era; ca. 1350–400 B.C.[1] ***Relevant Scriptures:*** **Judges 4:11–22**; also **Genesis 15:19; Exodus 2:1–4, 10, 16–22; 3:1; 4:18–19; 6:18, 20; 18:1–5; Numbers 10:29; 26:58–59; Judges 1:16; 5:24; 2 Kings 10:15–17, 23; 1 Chronicles 2:55; 23:14–17; 24:20–21; 26:24–26; Nehemiah 3:14; Jeremiah 35:1–19**

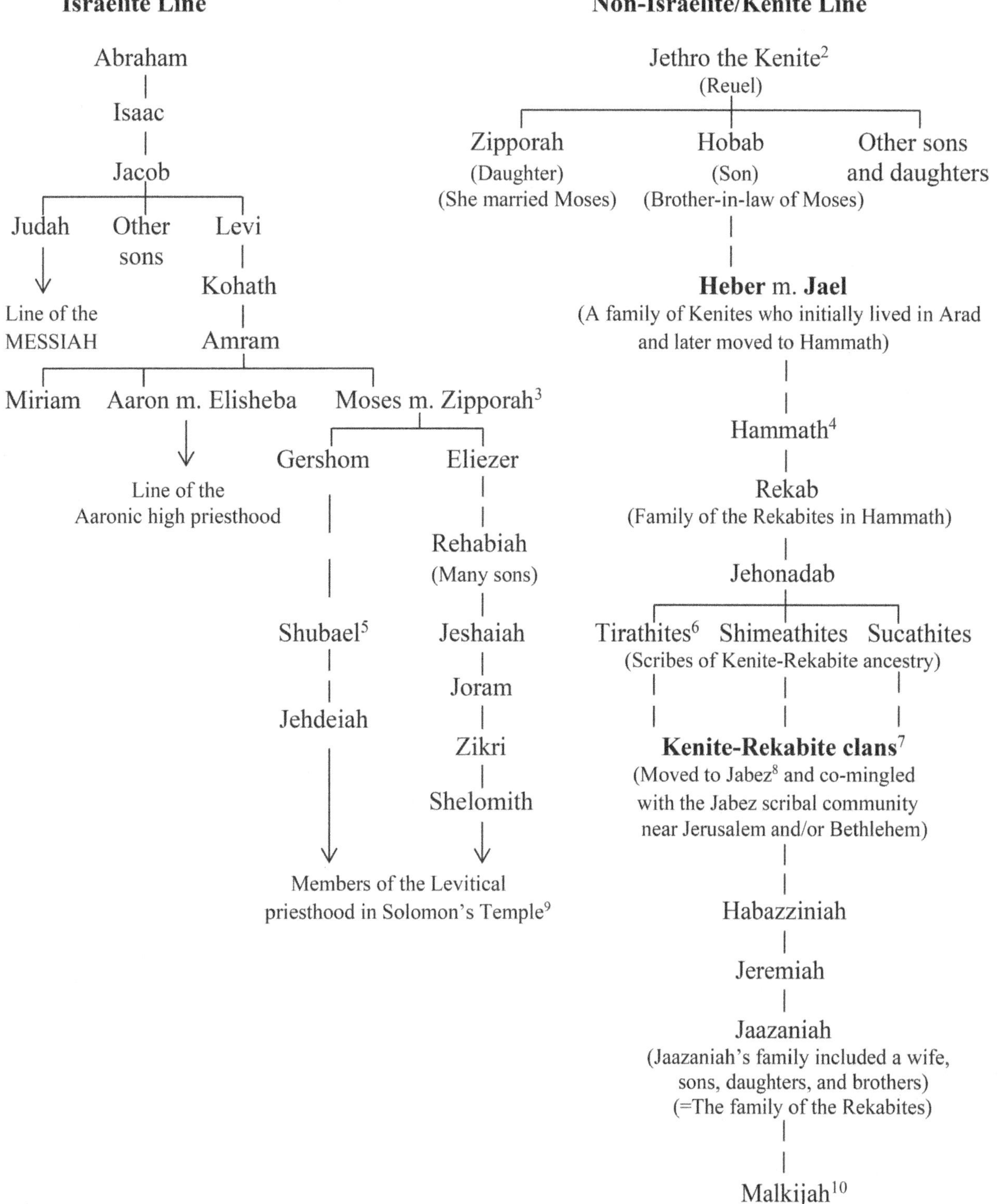

Biblical and Theological Significance

In the strictest sense, from the beginning of Israel's status as a nation, Yahweh had designated it as "a kingdom of priests and a holy nation" (**Exodus 19:4–6**). Its holiness marked it as a people separated unto Yahweh, but its "priesthood" described its role as a mediating people between Yahweh and the other nations of the earth, designed to bring them into his fellowship as well (**Genesis 12:1–3**; cf. **Isaiah 49:1–7**). The chart shows partially parallel genealogies of the Abrahamic–Levitical and Kenite lines and their divinely integrated status, which enabled the previously "outside" Kenite people to become not only "insiders," but also the keepers of the scrolls along with the Aaronic line of priests and Levites.

The Kenites and Rekabites

Traditionally desert tent-dwellers and nomads, the Kenites were an indigenous East Sinai people who had resided in the land prior to the arrival of Israel in 1406 B.C. (**Genesis 15:19**). One group of Kenites (including Jethro) lived in the geographic region occupied by the Midianites[11] (**Exodus 2:15–16**). Jethro is identified as a "priest of Midian" (**Exodus 2:16; 3:1; 18:1**) and a "Kenite" (cf. **Judges 1:16; 4:11**). When Moses fled from Egypt to Midian (**Exodus 2:11–15**), and there he married a daughter of Jethro named Zipporah (**Exodus 2:21**). Thus, Jethro (also known as Reuel) became Moses' father-in-law and counselor; Jethro was a faithful priest of Yahweh (**Exodus 2:16–22; 18:1–12**). At the time of the exodus from Egypt, Moses asked his brother-in-law Hobab, the son of Jethro, to accompany the Israelites and guide them during the wilderness years because Hobab was familiar with the nomadic ways in the desert (**Numbers 10:29–32**).

After coming into the promised land, Hobab's descendants went up from the City of Palms (Jericho) and settled in the Negev near Arad (**Judges 1:16**). Then at some point, Heber the Kenite separated his family from the clan of Kenites living in the south and moved north to Zaanannim, a town on the southern border of Naphtali's inheritance near Kedesh of Galilee (**Judges 4:11**; cf. **Joshua 19:33; 20:7; 21:32**); the reason for the migration is not given, but it may be related to their occupation.[12] There, Heber the Kenite allied himself with Jabin, the king of Hazor (**Judges 4:17**). In the war between the Israelites and the Canaanites,[13] the Israelites defeated King Jabin (Canaanite). Knowing of their defeat, Sisera, commander of the Canaanite army, fled on foot to the tent of Heber (whom he considered an ally); however, Heber's wife Jael showed her continued fidelity to Yahweh and dispatched Sisera by driving a tent peg through his temple (**Judges 4:17–23**). The poet of the *Song of Deborah* praises Jael the Kenite—not Deborah or Barak—as the true deliverer of Israel (**Judges 5:24–27**)!

The descendants of Jael included Rekab, the eponymous ancestor of the Rekabites, and his son Jehonadab. The Rekabites were noted for their piety and passion for Yahweh and adhering to an ascetic Nazirite-like lifestyle that included abstinence from wine. They maintained a nomadic way of life by living in tents, instead of farming or vineyard keeping. This enabled them to more faithfully follow the abstemious nature of their forebears (cf. **Jeremiah 35:3–10**). Upon the Babylonian invasion of northern Galilee in 605 B.C. under King Nebuchadnezzar, the Rekabites fled to Jerusalem for safety (**Jeremiah 35:11**). There they integrated (and possibly intermarried) with the pious Jabez community, which had been founded by Jabez the Asshurite of the tribe of Judah. Together, they formed a Jabez–Rekabite scribal community near Jerusalem that was dedicated to writing and preserving the ancient scrolls of God's word (**1 Chronicles 2:55**).

A number of Rekabites distinguished themselves in biblical history. For example, Jehonadab, a contemporary of King Jehu of Israel (ca. 841–814 B.C.), assisted Jehu in ridding the kingdom of remnants of the house of Ahab who worshiped Baal (**2 Kings 10:15–27**). Jaazaniah (a descendant of Jehonadab) was the head of the family of Rekabites in the pre-exile days of King Jehoiakim of Judah (ca. 609–598 B.C.) and a contemporary of Jeremiah the prophet (**Jeremiah 35:3**). Jaazaniah received through Jeremiah's prophecy an extraordinary promise from God: "'You have obeyed the command of your forefather Jehonadab and have followed all his instructions and have done everything he ordered.' Therefore this is what the LORD Almighty, the God of Israel, says: 'Jehonadab son of Rekab will never fail to have a descendant to serve me'" (**Jeremiah 35:18–19**).[14] The particular Rekabite descendants who were the inheritors of this remarkable promise and the exact role they may have had in salvation history are unknown, but the promise may be related to the vital role the Rekabites played as *keepers of the scrolls* in the Jabez–Rekabite scribal community near Jerusalem (**1 Chronicles 2:55**).

Notes

1. Jael and Heber were contemporaries of Deborah, the judge of Israel, whose judgeship lasted from ca. 1170–1130 B.C.

2. Jethro is a variant name of Reuel (cf. **Exodus 3:1; Numbers 10:29**).

3. See charts "**Exodus 2**: Moses and Zipporah" and "**Exodus 18**: Moses' Sons, Gershom and Eliezer, and Their Descendants Who Served in Solomon's Temple."

4. Hammath is a place name and a personal name. According to **1 Chronicles 2:55**, Hammath was the *father* of Rekab and the founder of the clan of the Rekabites. Hammath (the person) lived at "Hammath"—probably the same place as the Levitical city of Hammon/Hammoth Dor in the tribe of Naphtali that had been allotted to the Levitical Gershonites—located near Tiberias, on the shore of the Sea of Galilee, and known for its natural hot springs (**Joshua 21:32; 1 Chronicles 6:76**).

5. For Shubael, a descendant of Gershom son of Moses, see **1 Chronicles 23:16; 24:20; 25:20; 26:24**. Another son/descendant of Shubael named Jehdeiah is mentioned in **1 Chronicles 24:20**. Shubael—in the Levi–Kohath–Amram–Moses–Gershom line (in this chart)—is not Shubael the son of Heman (**Chronicles 25:4**) in the Levi–Kohath–Izhar–Elkanah–Samuel–Joel–Heman line; for the latter, see chart "**1 Chronicles 25**: The Twenty-Four Musician Leaders in Solomon's Temple."

6. Tirathites, Shimeathites, and Sucathites were scribes who moved from the vicinities of Hammath and Zaanannim in the north to the Jabez community near Jerusalem and/or Bethlehem (**1 Chronicles 2:55**).

7. During the Babylonian invasion under Nebuchadnezzar, the Kenite–Rekabite descendants fled to Jerusalem to escape "the Babylonian and Aramean armies" and integrated with the priestly scribal figures in the Jabez (Judahite) community near Jerusalem (**1 Chronicles 2:55; Jeremiah 35:10–11**). Also see chart "**Jeremiah 35**: The Rekabites (Kenite Descendants)."

8. Jabez is a personal name and a place name. Jabez was a *Judahite* in the following lineage: Judah–Perez–Ashhur–Koz (Hakkoz)–Harum–Aharhel–Jabez. Etymologically, Koz (Heb. קוֹץ) means "thorn," "thorn-bush," or "clippings." By itself Koz is a personal name (PN), and so is Hakkoz. The *ha-* element at the beginning of the name Koz is the definite article, thus הַקּוֹץ (Hakkoz) serves as both the personal name and the gentilic "priestly line" or "the Kozzites." For references to Hakkoz in the tribe of Levi, who was a Kohathite priest, see **1 Chronicles 24:10; Ezra 2:61–62; Nehemiah 3:4, 21; 7:63–64** and Hakkoz in chart "**1 Chronicles 24**: Genealogical Registry of the Twenty-Four Divisions of Kohathite Attending Priests Who Rotated Service in Solomon's Temple."

Despised by his brethren, Jabez pleaded with God to bless him by enlarging his territory in the tribe of Judah and to keep him from harm and pain. And, says the historian, God granted his request (**1 Chronicles 4:10**). Jabez went on then to establish a major scribal community near Jerusalem (**1 Chronicles 2:55**). For the genealogy of Jabez, see chart "**1 Chronicles 4**: Judah."

9. **First Chronicles 23:14** clarifies that Moses' descendants were considered part of the Levitical priesthood. The descendants in the Gershom–Shubael line became overseers of the temple treasuries. Also, descendants in the Eliezer–Rehabiah–Jeshaiah–Joram–Zikri–Shelomith line became overseers of the dedicated things in the Solomon's Temple (cf. **1 Chronicles 26:24–26**). For more information, see charts "**Exodus 2**: Moses and Zipporah" and "**Exodus 18**: Moses' Sons, Gershom and Eliezer, and Their Descendants Who Served in Solomon's Temple."

10. Malkijah, the descendant of Rekab, was the leader of the district of Beth Hakkerem (meaning "house of the vineyard") in post-exilic Jerusalem, which was a strategic place for signaling the approach of enemies (**Jeremiah 6:1**). Malkijah repaired the Dung (or Refuse) Gate in the city wall around Jerusalem in the post-exile (**Nehemiah 3:14**). In Nehemiah's time, the Dung Gate was located in the southern/southwestern corner of the wall of Jerusalem, leading to a trash heap (the city dump) outside the city where refuse was continually burned. Where Malkijah is called the "son of Rekab" in **Nehemiah 3:14**, the text should probably read "Malkijah a *descendant* of Rekab," since Rekab was a near-contemporary of Jehu, the king of Israel (ca. 841–814 B.C.; cf. **2 Kings 10:15–23**) and "Malkijah son of Rekab" appears as a figure some 400 years later in post-exilic Jerusalem (ca. 445 B.C.; **Nehemiah 3:14**).

It is unclear what association there may be (if any) between Malkijah the descendant of Rekab (**Nehemiah 3:4**) and other (priestly) figures named Malkijah:

- Malkijah who was the head of a division of Kohathite priests in Solomon's Temple (presumably ca. 960–586 B.C.; **1 Chronicles 24:9**);
- Malkijah the son of Harim who returned from Babylonian exile with Zerubbabel ca. 538 B.C. (see Harim in **Ezra 2:32; Nehemiah 7:42**);
- Malkijah a descendant of Harim who had taken a foreign wife in Babylon (**Ezra 10:31**);
- Malkijah who stood with Ezra the priest as Ezra read the Book of the Law to the people (**Nehemiah 8:4**);
- Malkijah the priest in the Malkijah–Pashhur–Zechariah–Amzi–Pelaliah–Jeroham–Adaiah lineage who lived in post-exilic Jerusalem (**1 Chronicles 9:12; Nehemiah 11:12; Jeremiah 21:1; 38:1**);
- Malkijah the goldsmith who made repairs in the wall around Jerusalem (**Nehemiah 3:31**); or
- Malkijah the priest who was a contemporary of Nehemiah and Ezra, 458 B.C. and 445 B.C. respectively (**Nehemiah 12:42**).

Malkijah the descendant of Rekab is not: Malkijah the Levitical Gershonite in Solomon's Temple (**1 Chronicles 6:40**), nor Malkijah "the king's son [King Zedekiah's son?]" (**Jeremiah 38:6**). The theophoric name means "Yahweh is my King," and therefore it was a very common name. In fact, there were at least thirteen persons by that name. See Paul Garner, ed. *The Complete Who's Who in the Bible* (London: Marshall Pickering, 1995) 436–437.

11. Jethro/Reuel should be understood to be an ethnic Kenite who was living in Midian and *not* an ethnic Midianite proper. Midian was the area occupied by the descendants of Midian (the Midianites), a son of Abraham and Keturah (**Genesis 25:1–2, 4**).

12. The Kenite name reflects a Hebrew root meaning "smith," which suggests they pursued a metalsmithing occupation that entailed traveling from job to job.

13. This occurred when Deborah was the judge of Israel and Barak was the commander of Israel's army; see chart "**Judges 4**: Deborah, the Fourth Judge of Israel."

14. יָצַב (*yatzab*) denotes an *official* office in which a person "stands" before God, as in priests and Levites (cf. **Numbers 11:16**).

JUDGES 6–8; 10–11: GIDEON (FIFTH JUDGE) AND HIS SON, ABIMELEK THE FALSE JUDGE, JAIR (SEVENTH JUDGE), AND JEPHTHAH (EIGHTH JUDGE): JUDGES OF ISRAEL FROM THE TRIBE OF MANASSEH

Approximate Dating: Gideon, ca. 1123–1083 B.C.; Abimelek, ca. 1083–1081 B.C.; Jephthah, ca. 1106–1100 B.C.; unknown time for Jair's judgeship; in the period of the judges, ca. 1350–1100/1086 B.C. ***Relevant Scriptures:*** **Judges 6:11, 29; 7:14; 8:13, 20, 22, 29–32; 9:1, 5, 18; 10:3–5; 11:1–2, 34;** also **Genesis 50:23; Numbers 26:28–33; 32:40; 36:1; Joshua 17:1–2; 1 Chronicles 2:21–22; 7:16–19**

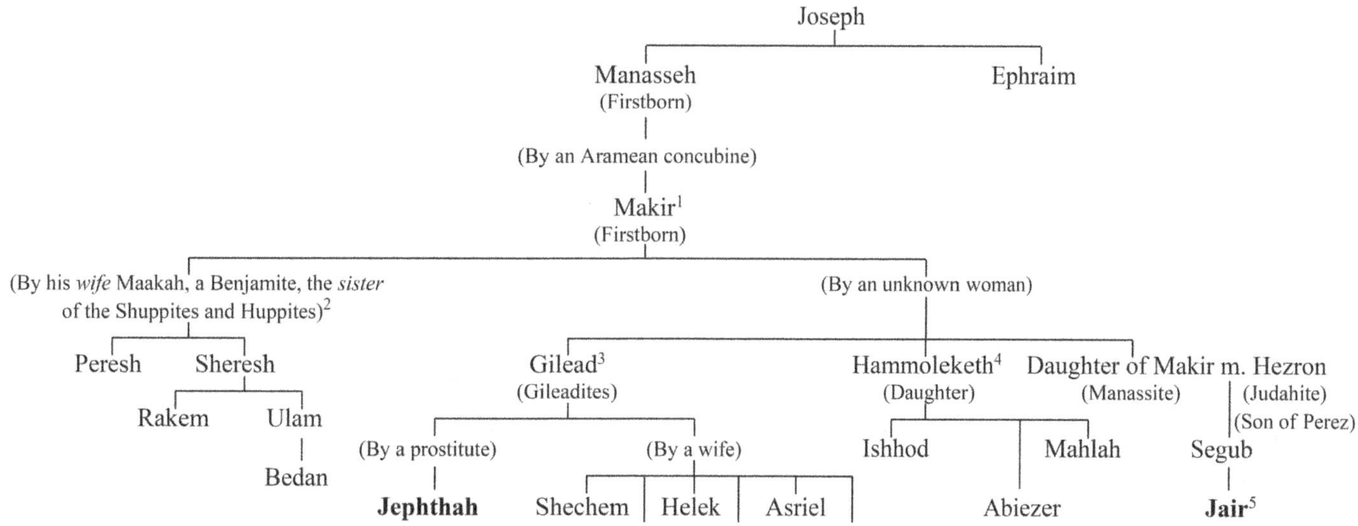

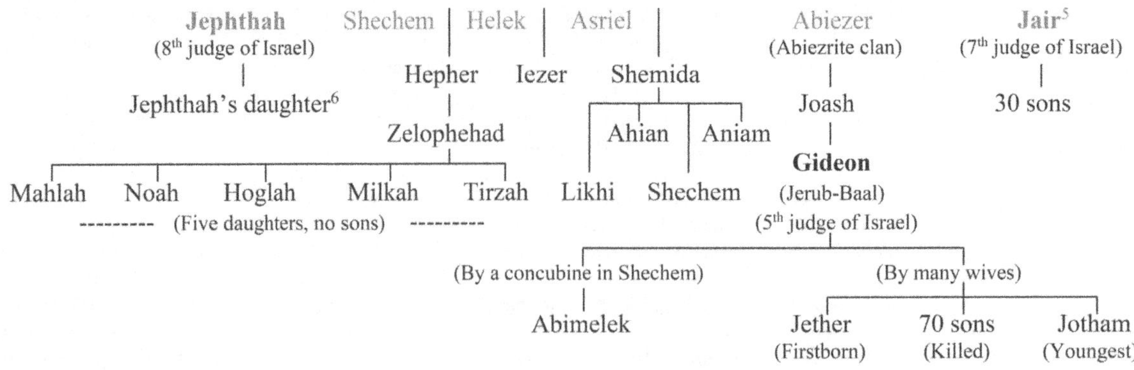

Biblical and Theological Significance

Manasseh was the older of Joseph's two sons; the younger was Ephraim. Manasseh derives from a root meaning "to forget," referring to the hard days Joseph experienced in his younger years. Ephraim connotes "fruitfulness"; thus, he should have expected plenty, but as he was the younger, he was due the second best. When Jacob blessed the two sons of Joseph, he crossed his hands and laid his right hand, the instrument of blessing, on Ephraim rather than Manasseh, the firstborn and the traditional rightful heir of the better promise (cf. **Genesis 41:51–52; 48:8–22**). Subsequently, the tribe of Ephraim settled in the central hill country of Canaan where it became by far the most powerful of the tribes. Moses, in his blessing of the tribes says, "Such are the ten thousands of Ephraim; such are the thousands of Manasseh" (**Deuteronomy 33:17**). What Manasseh appeared to have lost in the switch of Jacob's hands was made up, at least partially, in the times of the judges when three of Israel's judges hailed from the tribe of Manasseh.[7]

Jair, the Seventh Judge of Israel

Jair's grandfather was Hezron, the son of Perez, the son of Judah, and therefore, Jair's *paternal* ancestry was Judahite. At sixty years old, Hezron had married the daughter of Makir, who was from the tribe of Manasseh (Makir was the son of Manasseh and the father of Gilead; **1 Chronicles 2:21**); therefore, Jair's *maternal* ancestry was Manassite. Hezron and the daughter of Makir had a son named Segub (**1 Chronicles 2:21–22**), and Segub was the father of Jair. Often, he is described as "Jair, a descendant (or *son*) of Manasseh" (**Numbers 32:41; Deuteronomy 3:14; 1 Kings 4:13**), thereby stressing his matrilineal (rather than patrilineal) descent, which is most unusual in biblical genealogies. During Jair's term, no threats against Manasseh were recorded (**Judges 10:3–5**). He took small towns and cities in the region of Gilead and Bashan and renamed them "Havvoth Jair" (**Numbers 32:40–41; Deuteronomy 3:14; Joshua 13:30; Judges 10:4**). His military prowess is celebrated by the fact that he "had thirty sons, who rode thirty donkeys" and they controlled thirty towns in Gilead, which in the author's day, were still called Havvoth Jair (**Judges 10:4**; cf. **1 Chronicles 2:23**). Jair judged Israel for twenty-two years; at his death, he was buried in Kamon (**Judges 10:3, 5**).

Jephthah, the Eighth Judge of Israel

Manasseh's great-grandson, Jephthah, was a Gileadite from East Manasseh. He was the son of a prostitute, whose half-brothers drove him away saying, "You are not going to get any inheritance in our family . . . because you are the son of another woman" (**Judges 11:1–2**). Jephthah was considered a mighty warrior who delivered Israel from the Ammonite oppression, which lasted from ca. 1124–1106 B.C. He ruled for six years, ca. 1106–1100 B.C. (**Judges 12:1, 7**; cf. **Judges 11**). Jephthah is mentioned in Hebrews as one of the judges "who became powerful in battle and routed foreign armies" (**Hebrews 11:34**). The tragic story of Jephthah's daughter is recorded in **Judges 11:30–40**. Her father's rash vow for success in battle threatened her life: "whatever comes out of the door of my house to meet me when I return in triumph from the Ammonites will be the LORD's, and I will sacrifice it as a burnt offering" (**Judges 11:31**). Since burnt offerings were to be "an animal from either the herd or the flock . . . a male without defect" (**Leviticus 1:2–3**; see also **Leviticus 1:1–17; 22:19**), and because child sacrifice was abhorrent to Yahweh and forbidden in the Torah (cf. **Deuteronomy 12:31; 18:10–12; Joshua 6:26; 1 Kings 16:34; 2 Kings 3:27; 21:6; Jeremiah 7:31; Micah 6:7**), Jephthah probably offered his daughter as a "devoted offering" to the Lord (see **Leviticus 27:28**) whereby she remained a virgin for the rest of her life. This best explains the summary statements in **Judges 11:38–39**: "'You may go,' he said. And he let her go for two months. She and her friends went into the hills and wept because *she would never marry*. After the two months, she returned to her father, and he did to her as he had vowed. *And she was a virgin*" (italics added). At his death, Jephthah was buried in a town in Gilead (**Judges 12:7**).

Gideon, the Fifth Judge of Israel

Gideon was a fifth-generation descendant of Manasseh. The narrative of the famous judge Gideon is recounted in **Judges 6:1–8:35**. He was from Ophrah[8] of the Abiezrite clan in the tribal area of West Manasseh (**Judges 6:11, 15, 24; 8:27, 32**). Gideon describes himself, "My clan is the weakest in Manasseh, and I am the least in my family" (**Judges 6:15**). Because his father Joash was a Baal worshiper (**Judges 5:25**), the Lord instructed Gideon to tear down the altar that his father had built to Baal and to cut down the Asherah pole beside it; for his obedience, Gideon was given the nickname Jerub-Baal[9] (**Judges 6:32; 7:1; 8:29, 35; 9:1, 5, 16, 19, 57;**

1 Samuel 12:11). One of Gideon's first recorded deeds was the destruction of the altar of Baal; he then built his own altar to the Lord at Ophrah and called it "The Lord Is Peace" (**Judges 6:24**). Regrettably, Gideon dishonored himself by making an ephod of gold and placing it in Ophrah, resulting in a shrine where "all Israel prostituted themselves by worshiping it [the ephod] there, and it became a snare to Gideon and his family" (**Judges 8:27**). Gideon went on to serve as judge of Israel for forty years, ca. 1123–1083 B.C., and was a mighty deliverer of his people from the Midianites who had oppressed Israel from ca. 1130–1123 B.C. (**Judges 8:28**). Gideon "died at a good old age and was buried in the tomb of his father Joash in Ophrah of the Abiezrites" (**Judges 8:32**).

Abimelek, the False Judge

Following the death of his father (Gideon), Abimelek[10] became a self-proclaimed judge over Israel and ruled the nation illegitimately for three years, ca. 1083–1081 B.C. (**Judges 9:22**). Abimelek hired mercenaries to kill his brothers, the seventy sons of Gideon, whom he sacrificed "on one stone" to Baal (**Judges 9:1–5, 18**). Jotham, the youngest of Gideon's sons, escaped the massacre and predicted the downfall of Abimelek in a parable that he told to Abimelek's followers (**Judges 9:7–15**). Jotham also pronounced a curse on the people of Shechem for supporting Abimelek's rise to power (cf. **Judges 9:16–21**). Eventually, Abimelek was fatally wounded by a woman of Thebez who dropped a millstone on his head (**Judges 9:50–53**).[11]

The Daughters of Zelophehad

Other well-known individuals from the tribe of Manasseh include the daughters of Zelophehad. Since Zelophehad had no sons, his daughters petitioned Moses and Eleazar the priest to challenge the conventional interpretation of the laws that governed family inheritance when they arrived in the promised land[12] (**Numbers 27:1–11**): "Our father died in the wilderness. He was not among Korah's followers, who banded together against the Lord, but he died for his own sin and left no sons. Why should our father's name disappear from his clan because he had no son? Give us property among our father's relatives" (**Numbers 27:3–4**). Moses brought the case before the Lord, who said that their request was "right" and that they should "certainly" be given property as an inheritance (**Numbers 27:7**). They were given their father's property with the stipulation that they must marry within the tribe of Manasseh.[13] This decision clarified the case law that would be followed going forward, not just for the five sisters, but for fellow Israelite women and female descendants in all the tribes as well. Women could now become legal heirs and beneficiaries of the family estate[14] (cf. **Numbers 36:1–13; Joshua 17:3–6**).

Notes

1. Makir, son of Manasseh, was the eponymous ancestor of the Makirites (**Numbers 32:40**) and the father of Gilead. The clan of the Gileadites "had received the land of Gilead and Bashan because the Makirites were great soldiers" (**Joshua 17:1**).

2. Maakah, the wife of Makir, was from the tribe of Benjamin. She was the sister of Shuppim/Shupham (the Shuppites/Shuphamite clan) and Huppim/Hupham (the Huppites/Huphamite clan) (cf. **Genesis 46:21; Numbers 26:39**), who were the (twin?) sons of Benjamin (**1 Chronicles 7:12, 15–16**). Maakah had two (twin?) sons, Peresh and Sheresh (**1 Chronicles 7:16**). The translation of the NIV in **1 Chronicles 7:15–17** is confusing because Makir does not have both a "wife" and a "sister" named Maakah; the verses are better rendered as "Makir took as his wife the sister of Huppim and Shuppim, whose name was Maakah. The name of Gilead's grandson was Zelophehad, but Zelophehad begot only daughters. Maakah the wife of Makir bore a son, and she called his name Peresh. The name of his brother was Sheresh, and his sons were Ulam and Rakem. The son of Ulam was Bedan. These were the descendants of Gilead son of Makir, the son of Manasseh." (See the more accurate translation that appears in the NKJV *contra* NIV.)

3. Gilead was the founder of the Gileadite clan. The place name Gilead refers to a geographical area to the east of the Jordan River and between the Dead Sea to the south and the Sea of Galilee to the north. This region was later called *East Manasseh*, as opposed to its counterpart, *West Manasseh*, which was located to the west of the Jordan River. The first mention of Gilead is in **Genesis 31:21**, referring to Jacob's trek to Gilead in flight from his father-in-law, Laban. Since this occurred ca. 1909 B.C., 500 years before the conquest of Canaan and the settlement of the tribes (ca. 1406 B.C.), this appears to be a classic instance of renaming from the standpoint of a later time. The indigenous population was therefore anachronistically called Gileadites (**Numbers 26:29**).

4. The personal name Hammoleketh means "queen." Quite uncharacteristic for genealogies, Hammoleketh's husband is not identified. See note 7 in chart "**1 Chronicles** 7: Manasseh (the Half-Tribe of West Manasseh)."

5. Jair the judge from the tribe of Manasseh is a different person than Jair the Bethlehemite, the father of Elhanan (**2 Samuel 21:19; 1 Chronicles 20:5**).

6. For the biblical narrative about Jephthah's daughter, see **Judges 11:30–40**.

7. The fact that three judges come from the tribe of Manasseh alone dispels any notion that the twelve judges of Israel were from each of the twelve tribes.

8. Ophrah of the Abiezrites (**Judges 6:11, 24**) appears to be unrelated to Ophrah (**1 Chronicles 4:14**) the son of Meonothai, the son of Othniel the Kenizzite (the first judge of Israel). Modern scholars have suggested that the town of Ophrah that is associated with the Abiezer clan of West Manasseh was possibly near Shechem or Michmash, whereas the town of Ophrah in the tribal allotment of the Benjamites was probably near Bethel (cf. **Joshua 18:23**; *Holman's Bible Dictionary* "Ophrah").

9. This name appears to come from a root meaning, "to show oneself great" or the like ("יְרֻבַּעַל," *HALOT* 1:434). It is a mockery of the pagan deity Baal, "let him prove himself to be powerful."

10. Abimelek (אֲבִימֶלֶךְ) means "my father is king," an exaggerated title never claimed by Gideon (his father) but employed to give him standing to be such a leader.

11. The dying Abimelek "called to his armor-bearer, 'Draw your sword and kill me, so that they can't say, 'A woman killed him.' So his servant ran him through, and he died" (**Judges 9:54**).

12. The fact that three of their ancestors were judges from the tribe of Manasseh (i.e., Gideon, Jair, and Jephthah) may have influenced Zelophehad's daughters to seek a formal and *legally binding* decision to secure their father's estate.

13. The daughters of Zelophehad "married their cousins on their father's side . . . within the clans of the descendants of Manasseh son of Joseph, [so that] their inheritance remained in their father's tribe and clan" (**Numbers 36:11**).

14. The new hierarchy of inheritance is explained in **Numbers 27:8–11**: "If a man dies and leaves no son, give his inheritance to his daughter. If he has no daughter, give his inheritance to his brothers. If he has no brothers, give his inheritance to his father's brothers. If his father had no brothers, give his inheritance to the nearest relative in his clan, that he may possess it."

JUDGES 10: TOLA, THE SIXTH JUDGE OF ISRAEL

Approximate Dating: unknown term in the mid-period of the rule by judges, ca. 1350–1100/1086 B.C. ***Relevant Scriptures:*** **Judges 10:1–2**; also **Genesis 46:13; Numbers 26:23–24; 1 Chronicles 7:1–3**

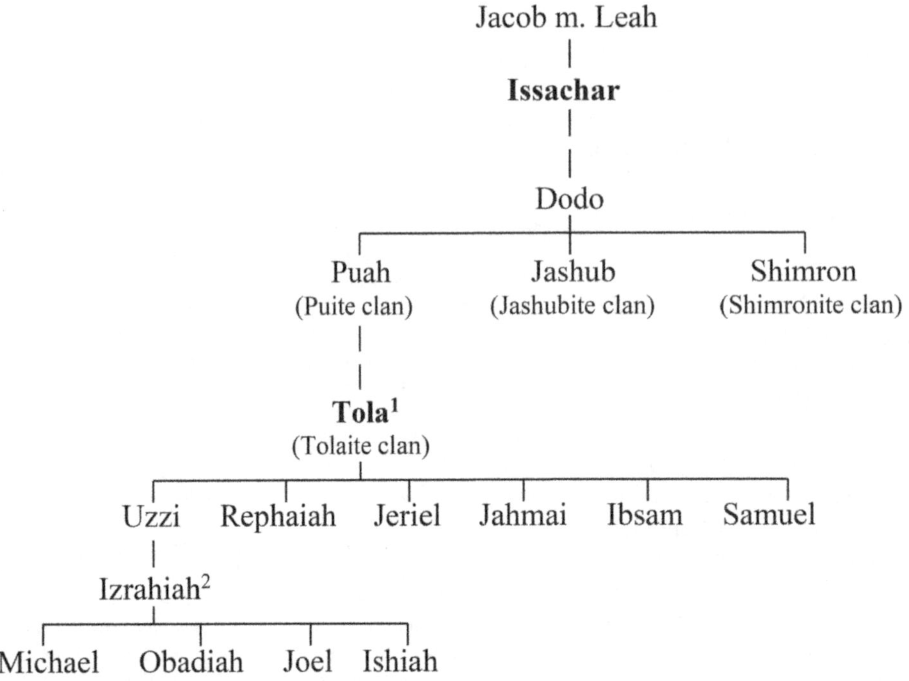

Biblical and Theological Significance

Tola, a "minor" judge over a local area in the hill country of Ephraim, served for twenty-three years (**Judges 10:1–2**) between the tenure of Gideon (and his son Abimelek; **Judges 9:56–57**) and the tenure of Jair (**Judges 10:3**). Tola hailed from the village of Shamir[3] (possibly ancient Samaria) in the hill country of Ephraim, and there he was buried (**Judges 10:1–2**). The Chronicler follows the convention of the author of Genesis, by conflating the generations of Issachar saying, "the sons of Issachar: Tola, Puah, Jashub and Shimron—four in all" (**1 Chronicles 7:1**; cf. **Genesis 46:13**). However, the author of Judges clarifies that Tola was the "son of Puah, the son of Dodo," and a *descendant* of Issachar. Tola's descendants (the Tolaites) had many wives and children, and many were called "heads of their families" and "fighting men" in their generations (**1 Chronicles 7:2–4**). In the days of King David, the fighting men of Issachar numbered 22,600 men, out of a total of 87,000 fighting men for the entire Issachar tribe (**1 Chronicles 7:2, 5**).

Notes

1. The date of Tola's judgeship is more than 700 years after the death of the tribal eponym Issachar, therefore the only way to justify the chronology of this brief genealogy is to posit the well-known and reasonable invocation of "genealogy gap," in which the names of only the most important persons are mentioned in a given line of descent (i.e., not all generations are listed).

2. Izrahiah and his four sons were called "chiefs." His sons had many wives and children, so by the time of David, the Izrahites had 36,000 fighting men (**1 Chronicles 7:4**). Shamhuth the Izrahite (**1 Chronicles 27:8**) was an official in David and Solomon's army who was the head over the fifth month; see Shamhuth in the charts "**1 Chronicles 27**: Genealogical Registry of the Officials Over the Twelve Army Divisions who Served the King Monthly in Jerusalem" and "**1 Chronicles 11**: Genealogical Registry of the Mighty Warriors in King David's Army."

3. This Shamir, a place name, should not to be confused with the Shamir of Judah (**Joshua 15:48**).

JUDGES 12: IBZAN (NINTH JUDGE) AND ELON (TENTH JUDGE): TWO JUDGES FROM THE TRIBE OF ZEBULUN

Approximate Dating: unknown terms in the latter part of the rule by judges, ca. 1350–1100/1086 B.C. ***Relevant Scriptures:*** **Judges 12:8–11**

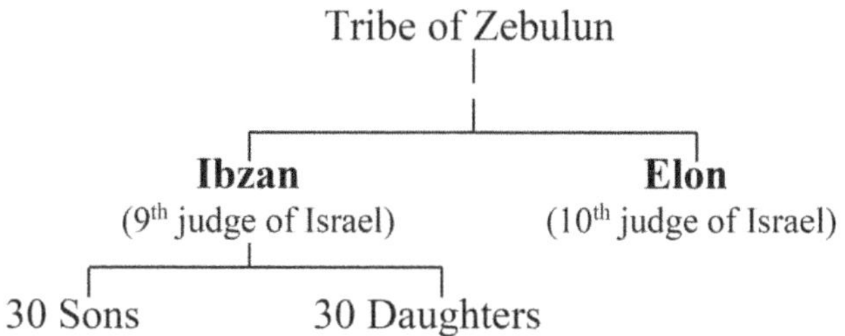

Biblical and Theological Significance

Two judges of Israel, Ibzan and Elon, were Zebulunites. Both were minor judges. Ibzan, the successor to Jephthah (**Judges 11:1–12:7**), was from Bethlehem in Galilee, in the tribe of Zebulun (**Joshua 19:15**). Little information is given about his judgeship except that he arranged marriages for his sons and daughters to those "outside his clan"—presumably to Israelite men and women outside the clan of Zebulun—in order to cement clan alliances and extend his political influence. Ibzan judged Israel for seven years. When he died, he was buried in Bethlehem of Zebulun (**Judges 12:8–10**).

Elon succeeded Ibzan as Israel's next judge and led the nation of Israel for the next ten years (**Judges 12:11**). When he died, he was buried in Aijalon "in the land of Zebulun."[1]

Notes

1. Aijalon in the tribe of Zebulun is a different place than Aijalon in the tribe of Dan (cf. **Joshua 19:42; 21:24**) and Aijalon in the hill country of Ephraim (**1 Chronicles 6:69**).

JUDGES 12: ABDON, THE ELEVENTH JUDGE OF ISRAEL

Approximate Dating: unknown term in the latter part of the rule by judges, ca. 1350–1100/1086 B.C. ***Relevant Scriptures:*** **Judges 12:13–15**

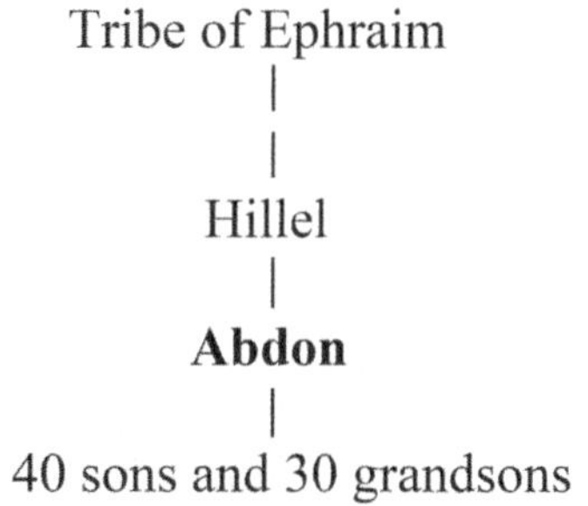

Biblical and Theological Significance

Abdon, a minor judge, succeeded Elon as the judge of Israel and led Israel for eight years (**Judges 12:14**). He appears to have been an Ephraimite from Pirathon,[1] about eight miles southwest of Shechem (**Judges 12:13**). Abdon "had forty sons and thirty grandsons,[2] who rode on seventy donkeys"[3] (**Judges 12:14**). When he died, Abdon was buried in Pirathon in Ephraim "in the hill country of the Amalekites" (**Judges 12:15**).[4]

Notes

1. Pirathon is identified with modern *Far'atā*.

2. Large numbers of children are noted for other judges as well, such as Gideon (70/71), Jair (30), and Ibzan (60) (**Judges 9:24, 56; 10:4; 12:9**, respectively). Very likely, these numbers are to be taken as representations of power and influence, greatly exaggerated and stylized, as seen in the exact numbers such as 30, 60, 70, etc.

3. Contrary to expectations, the donkey (עַיִר) was an animal of royalty (**2 Samuel 16:1–2**). One recalls that Jesus rode into Jerusalem in kingly splendor on a donkey (**Matthew 21:1–10; Mark 11:1–11; Luke 19:28–44**).

4. The only area described in this manner is the strip of territory in the northern part of the Sinai Peninsula including Kadesh Barnea. The major problem here, however, is the description of Abdon's burial place was in "Pirathon in Ephraim, in the hill country of the Amalekites" (**Judges 12:15**). Perhaps the best resolution of this conundrum is to suppose that at one time Amalekites who had settled in the central part of the country, were expelled or moved out for other reasons from that region, and were then replaced by Ephraim/Ephraimites (**Judges 3:13; 5:14; 6:3–4, 33; 7:12; 10:12**).

JUDGES 13: SAMSON, THE TWELFTH JUDGE OF ISRAEL

Approximate Dating: his judgeship lasted 40 years, from ca. 1106–1086 B.C., marking the end of the period of the judges, ca. 1350–1100/1086 B.C. ***Relevant Scriptures:*** **Judges 13:1–16:31;** also **Genesis 46:23–25; Numbers 26:42**

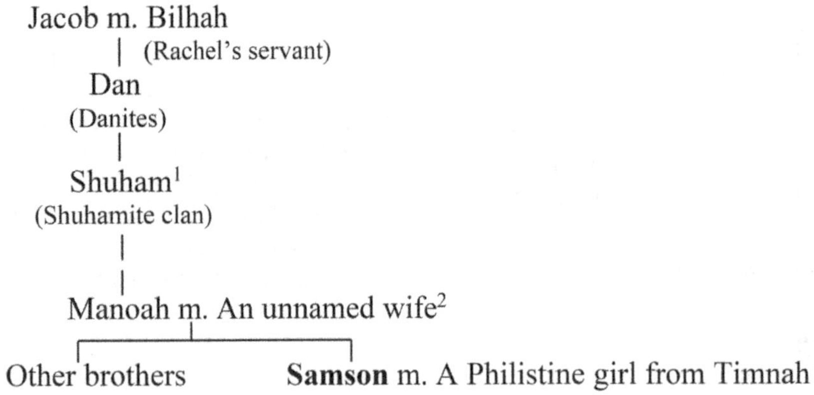

Biblical and Theological Significance

Samson was the last of the twelve judges of pre-monarchic Israel; he became the legendary heroic figure who delivered Israel from the Philistines.[3] He was born in Zorah, a small village in the hilly tribal area of Dan (**Judges 13:2**). Little is known of his ancestry—a remarkable omission that is in line with the curious omission of the tribe of Dan in all extant biblical genealogies (e.g., **1 Chronicles 4–7; Revelation 7:4–8**). The patronym for the tribe is Dan, the son born to Jacob by his concubine Bilhah, ca. 1924 B.C.[4] (**Genesis 30:6**). **Joshua 19:40–48** locates the tribe's allotment near Philistine territory just west of the tribal allotment of Benjamin and Ephraim and extending to the Mediterranean. However, because the Amorites "confined the Danites to the hill country, not allowing them to come down into the plain" (**Judges 1:34**), Dan was forced to move north to Leshem (named "Dan" and also known as Laish in **Judges 18:7, 14, 27, 29**), which was north of the Sea of Kinnereth (Galilee).

However, not all the Danites migrated north; consequently, Samson's immediate family lived amongst the pentapolis of Philistines, who were anything but friendly to the Israelites. Samson's mission was to deliver Israel from the hated Philistines and from their constant harassment. Ironically, he initially married (or was betrothed) to a Philistine woman from Timnah (a Timnite; **Judges 15:6**); however, believing that Samson did not really love her, her father gave her in marriage to Samson's companion (**Judges 14:20; 15:2**). In retaliation, Samson burned the fields of the Philistines (**Judges 15:4–5**); in turn, the Philistines took revenge on Samson by burning the Philistine girl and her father to death (**Judges 16:6**)!

Sometime later, Samson became involved with a prostitute from Gaza[5] (**Judges 16:1–3**). Then he fell in love with another Philistine woman named Delilah, a schemer from the Valley of Sorek (**Judges 16:4**). It seems that she was infatuated with Samson, but they did not marry. **Judges 16:4–20** describes how Delilah tricked Samson four successive times in exchange for money from the Philistines. She pressed him "with such nagging . . . day after day until he was sick to death of it" (v. **16**) Finally, Samson told her the true source of his strength—"The seven braids of my head" (v. **13**)—and told her that if his hair was shaved, his strength would be gone and he would become "as weak as any other man" (**v. 17**).

The men of Gaza then captured, blinded, and shackled Samson and made him grind grain in the prison. In a special dedication ceremony to honor their pagan god Dagon, the lords of the Philistines called for Samson to entertain them at the temple in Ashdod. There, his hair regrown and his strength regained, Samson pulled the pagan temple down upon the heads of more than three thousand Philistine men and women and died along with them. "Thus he killed many more when he died than while he lived" (**Judges 16:30**; see **Judges 16:21–30**). Samson's brothers and those in his father's household took Samson's body and buried him in the tomb of his father Manoah between Zorah and Eshtaol. Samson had judged Israel for twenty years, ca. 1106–1086 B.C., "in the days of the Philistines" (**Judges 15:20**), although Philistine oppression continued into the time of the kings (see note 3), thus explaining **Judges 13:1**: "Again the Israelites did evil in the eyes of the Lord, so the Lord delivered them into the hands of the Philistines for forty years." Samson's death in 1086 B.C. marked the end of the period of the judges (**Judges 16:31**).

Notes

1. Shuham in **Numbers 26:42–43** is probably the same person as Hushim in **Genesis 46:23**. Shuham/Hushim is the only son of Dan who is listed in Scripture, so it appears that Manoah and Samson were from the Shuhamite clan.

2. Manoah's wife was barren. In two theophany appearances (**Judges 13:2–5; 8–10**), an angel of the Lord appeared to her and promised that she and Manoah would have a son but warned, "Now see to it that you drink no wine or other fermented drink and that you do not eat anything unclean. You will become pregnant and have a son whose head is never to be touched by a razor because the boy is to be a Nazirite, dedicated to God from the womb" (**Judges 13:4–5**). This consecration also applied to the mother until the child was born (**Judges 13:7, 13–14**). Only three *perpetual Nazirites* are noted in Scripture—Samson (**Judges 13:5, 7; 16:17**), Samuel (**1 Samuel 1:11**), and John the Baptist (**Luke 1:15**). The name of Manoah's wife is not recorded, but it was she who named the child *Samson* (**Judges 13:24**). At some point after Samson's birth, she and Manoah had other sons (cf. **Judges 16:31**).

3. Prior to Samson's judgeship, Philistines oppressed Israel for forty years, from ca. 1146–1106 B.C. (**Judges 13:1**). Samson took "the lead in delivering Israel from the hands of the Philistines" (**Judges 13:5**), but he was not successful in permanently ousting them because the Philistines continued to oppress Israel through the reigns of Saul and David (cf. **1 Samuel 4–7; 9:16; 13:3–8; 14:52; 28:5; 2 Samuel 3:18; 5:17–19; 8:1**).

4. The Bible's assessment of Dan is not positive. Jacob's "blessing" on Dan as "a snake by the roadside, a viper along the path" (**Genesis 49:17**) is hardly an endorsement, nor is Moses' blessing in **Deuteronomy 33:22**: "Dan is a lion's cub, springing out of Bashan." For the birth of Dan, see note 4 in chart "**Genesis 35**: The Twelve Sons of Jacob, the Eponymous Originators of the Twelve Tribes of Israel."

5. The term describing this woman (זוֹנָה, *zonah*) is always used in a non-liturgical sense, that is, as a professional.

RUTH 1: BOAZ, ELIMELEK, AND NAOMI AND THE DESCENDANTS OF BOAZ THE JUDAHITE AND RUTH THE MOABITESS

Approximate Dating: latter years during the time of the judges of Israel, ca. 1250–1100 B.C.[1] ***Relevant Scriptures:*** **Ruth 1:1–5; 2:1–3; 4:10, 13–22;** also **Genesis 46:12; 1 Samuel 17:12; 1 Chronicles 2:3–15, 18–19, 24, 50–54; 4:4; Matthew 1:1–6; Luke 3:32–34**

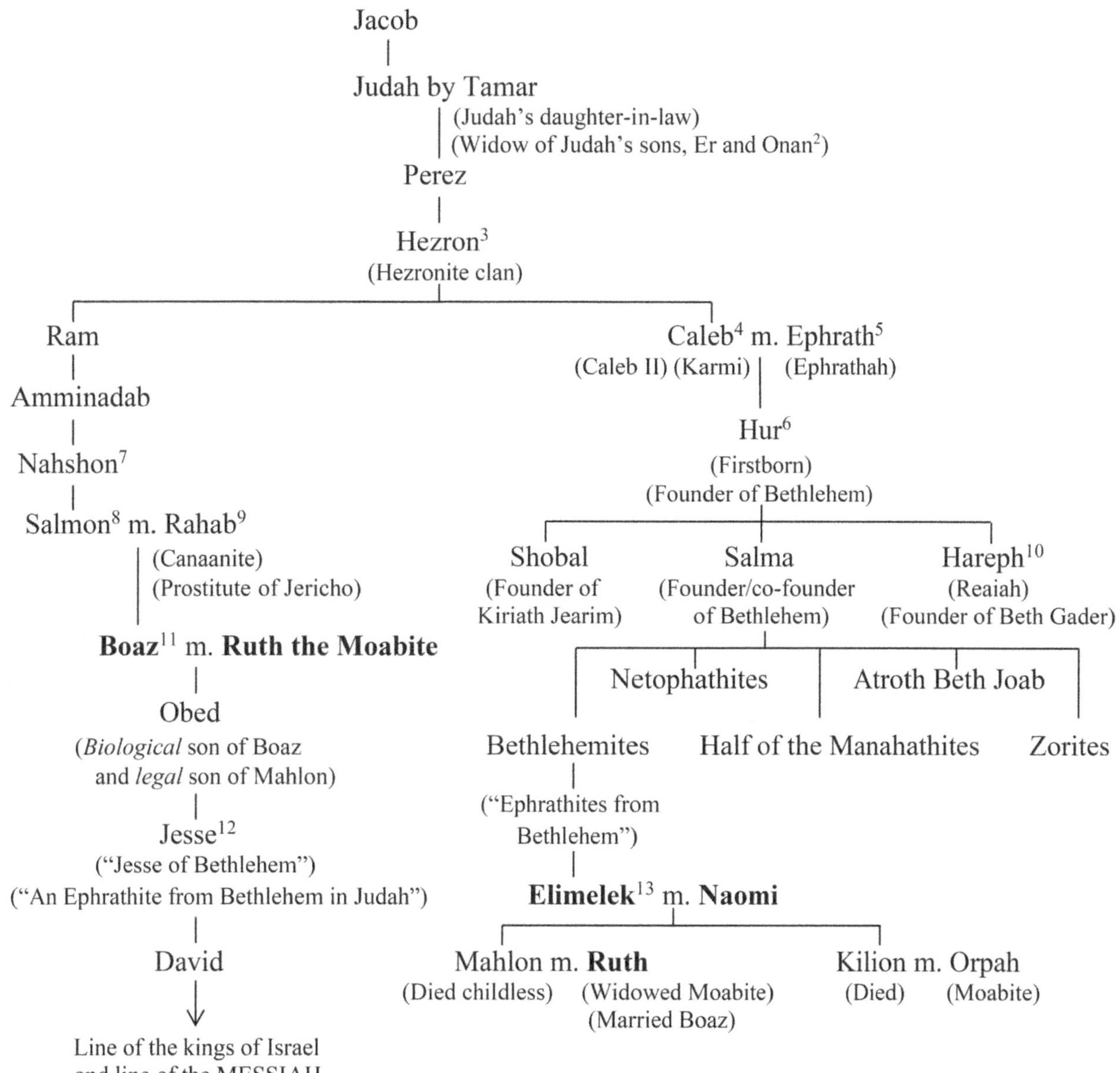

Biblical and Theological Significance

In many respects, the book of Ruth bridges the eras of the judges and the united monarchy, shifting the focus from *all* the tribes of Israel to the tribe of Judah alone, from which would come David the king, his human successors, and ultimately the promised Messiah, the "Son of David" (**Matthew 9:27; 12:23; 15:22; 20:30–31; 21:9, 15; 22:42–45; Mark 10:47–48; 12:35, 37; Luke 18:38–39; 20:41; Romans 1:3**).

The genealogy of the family of Perez and his son Hezron (**Ruth 4:18–22**) serves as a summation of the historical narrative of the book of Ruth.

The chart focuses on two branches of a large, segmented genealogy for the family of Hezron[14] (**1 Chronicles 2:1, 4–5, 9–41**). The Hezron–Caleb line of descendants (shown on the right in the chart), including Elimelek and Naomi, are referenced in **1 Chronicles 2:18–24** and **50–54**. The Hezron–Ram line of descendants (shown on the left in the chart), including Boaz, are referenced in **1 Chronicles 2:9–15** and **Ruth 4:18–21**. At a time when "everyone [in Israel] did as they saw fit"[15] (**Judges 21:25**), Boaz and Ruth are shown to be a faithful remnant (Jew and Gentile) through which the chosen line of the Messiah would arise.

The two lineages emphasize the marriage of David's great-grandfather, Boaz, to his great-grandmother, Ruth. Boaz—a Ram descendant of mixed Jewish–Canaanite/Gentile parentage himself (i.e., because of Rahab)—acted as the kinsman-redeemer (cf. **Deuteronomy 25:5–10**) for his deceased near relatives, Elimelek, Mahlon, and Kilion, who were of Hezron–Caleb/Karmi ancestry. Boaz redeemed Elimelek's land in Bethlehem that had been sold due to Naomi's poverty (**Ruth 4:2–4, 9-10**; cf. **Leviticus 25:23–38**). Ruth was a descendant of Moab, a people excluded from assembling with the worshiping community for ten generations **(Deuteronomy 23:3–4**). The book of Ruth reveals the exemplary, God-like qualities of Boaz and the loving devotion of Ruth, Naomi's daughter-in-law, who was "better to [Naomi] than seven sons" (**Ruth 4:15**). The genealogy reveals that "God turned the curse [on the Moabites] into a blessing" (**Nehemiah 13:2**). Through divine grace, a foreign Moabite-Gentile was *grafted* into the chosen tribe of Judah and the line of the Messiah. Ruth and Boaz were ancestors of the Messiah, and their hometown, Bethlehem, was the birthplace of Jesus (**Ruth 4:11; Luke 2:4–7**).

Notes

1. The book of Ruth traces David's ancestry back to Perez, the son of Judah (**Ruth 4:18**); moreover, the blessing of Boaz by the people of Bethlehem explicitly joins Bethlehem (and hence David) to Perez and Judah (**Ruth 4:11b–12**). "The ancient Jewish canonical tradition of considering [the book of] Ruth to be a part of the book of Judges rests on good historical and literary considerations. Its author places it squarely in the times 'when the judges ruled' (**Ruth 1:1**), the setting also of the last two narratives of the book of Judges. . . . Ruth must be toward the end [of the Judges era] since its heroine is only three generations before David. Moreover, the indictment which runs as a refrain throughout Judges—"In those days Israel had no king; everyone did as they saw fit" (**Judges 17:6; 18:1; 19:1; 21:25**)—and which casts the entire age as one of moral anarchy and covenant defection, is surely echoed in the opening words of Ruth—"'In the days when the judges ruled,' that is, when there was no king." Eugene H. Merrill, *Kingdom of Priests–A History of Old Testament Israel* (Grand Rapids: Baker, 1996), 182, n. 97.

2. Er, Tamar's first husband, was wicked so God killed him (**Genesis 38:6–7**). Next, Tamar was given in marriage to Er's brother, Onan, but he "spilled his semen on the ground to keep from providing offspring for his brother [Er]," so God killed Onan also (**Genesis 38:8–10**).

3. Hezron, the son of Perez, was the eponymous ancestor of the Hezronite clan (**Numbers 26:6, 21**). Hezron had four sons—Jerahmeel (firstborn), Ram, and Caleb (**1 Chronicles 2:9, 25**) and, later in his old age, Segub (the father of Jair the judge of Israel; **1 Chronicles 2:21**). For the Hezron–Ram–Boaz–Obed–Jesse–David lineage, see **Ruth 4:18–22**, and for that of the Hezron–Caleb/Karmi–Hur–Salma–Bethlehem lineage, see **1 Chronicles 2:9, 50–51, 54**. Also see charts "**1 Chronicles 2**: Hezron" and "**1 Chronicles 4**: Judah."

4. Caleb in **1 Chronicles 2:9, 18–19** is Karmi in **1 Chronicles 4:1**. Caleb/Karmi had children by three wives—Azubah, Jerioth, and Ephrath (**1 Chronicles 2:18–19**). Caleb the son of Hezron (Judahite) in **1 Chronicles 2:9, 50–54** is designated Caleb II elsewhere; he is not the same person as Caleb (I) the Kenizzite, the son of Jephunneh (cf. **1 Chronicles 2:42–49**), who married into the tribe of Judah (i.e., by marrying Hezron's daughter, the sister of Jerahmeel, Ram, and Caleb). Thus Caleb (I) the Kenizzite was the "brother-in-law"—not the *brother*—of Jerahmeel (as it reads in **1 Chronicles 2:42**, NIV). For clarification, see charts "**1 Chronicles 2**: Caleb and Kenaz, the Sons of Jephunneh the Kenizzite" and "**1 Chronicles 4**: Judah." Also, Caleb the Judahite should not be confused with Karmi, the son of Reuben (cf. **Genesis 46:9; Exodus 6:14; Numbers 26:5–6; 1 Chronicles 5:3**) nor the Zerahite descendant, Karmi, the father of Achan/Achar (**Joshua 7:1, 18; 1 Chronicles 2:7**).

5. Ephrath (**1 Chronicles 2:19**), also called Ephrathah (**1 Chronicles 2:50; 4:4**), was the third wife of Caleb (II) the Judahite (see note 4). Ephrath/Ephrathah is the ancient name for Bethlehem: called "Ephrath," near the burial place of Rachel (**Genesis 35:19; 48:7**); "Caleb Ephrathah," the place where Hezron died (**1 Chronicles 2:24**); and "Bethlehem Ephrathah," the prophesied birthplace of the Messiah (**Micah 5:2**). Bethlehem Ephrathah was the hometown of Boaz and Ruth (**Ruth 4:11**).

6. Hur was the firstborn son of Ephrath/Ephrathah (**1 Chronicles 2:50; 4:4**). Both Hur and his son Salma were considered the co-founders ("fathers") of Bethlehem (cf. **1 Chronicles 2:51; 4:4**). Hur also had another son, Uri (not shown in the chart), who was the father of Bezalel (see chart "**Exodus 31**: Bezalel, the Chief Artisan of the Tabernacle and Its Furnishings, and His Assistant Oholiab").

7. Nahshon was the leader of the tribe of Judah during the period of the wilderness wanderings (**Numbers 1:7; 2:3; 7:12, 17; 10:14; 1 Chronicles 2:10**). Nahshon's sister, Elisheba the Judahite, married Aaron the high priest (Kohathite clan of the tribe of Levi), thus linking the kingly tribe of Judah and to the priestly tribe of Levi by marriage (**Exodus 6:23**).

8. The lineage of Salmon is given in **Ruth 4:20–21; 1 Chronicles 2:10–12; Matthew 1:4–5;** and **Luke 3:32–34**.

9. Rahab the prostitute of Jericho protected the Israelite spies from harm when they spied out the promised land (cf. **Joshua 2:1–24; 6:17–25**). Rahab's marriage to Salmon is not specifically addressed in the biblical narrative in the book of Joshua, but she is clearly identified by Matthew as the mother of Boaz, an ancestress of the Messiah (**Matthew 1:5**), and one who was righteous and faithful (**Hebrews 11:31; James 2:25**). See chart "**Joshua 2**: Rahab, the Prostitute of Jericho."

10. Hareph is one of the "sons of Hur" in **1 Chronicles 2:50–51**. Hareph appears to be the same person called Reaiah the "son of Shobal" in **1 Chronicles 4:2**; thus, Hareph/Reaiah may be the *grandson* of Hur (not his son).

11. Boaz was "from the clan of Elimelek" (**Ruth 2:3**), presumably meaning that he and Elimelek were distant relatives in the Hezronite clan. Naomi identifies Boaz as a relative on her husband's side (**Ruth 2:1**; cf. **3:2**).

12. Jesse, the father of David, is called "Jesse of Bethlehem" (**1 Samuel 16:1, 18; 17:58**) and "an Ephrathite . . . who was from Bethlehem in Judah. . . . Jesse had eight sons, and in Saul's time he was very old" (**1 Samuel 17:12**).

13. Elimelek and Naomi were Judahites—"Ephrathites"—presumably from the Hezron–Caleb–Ephrath/Ephrathah clan who lived in Bethlehem during the time of the judges (**Ruth 1:1–2**). When a famine struck the region of Bethlehem in Judah, Elimelek moved his family east to the land of Moab, but there, he and his two sons, Mahlon (the husband of Ruth) and Kilion (the husband of Orpah) died, leaving Naomi, Ruth, and Orpah widows.

14. See charts "**1 Chronicles 2**: Hezron" and "**1 Chronicles 4**: Judah."

15. The book is like water in the desert for one who studies in depth the account of the judges, the catch line of which reads in four places, "In those times Israel had no king; everyone did whatever he felt like doing" (EHM translation). Such political, moral, and spiritual disintegration cried out for a healing balm, a remedy procured in great measure by the purity of the story of Ruth. It is striking to note in the "appendix" of Judges (**Judges 17–21**) that the village of Bethlehem is associated with the most sordid religious corruption (**Judges 17:7, 9; 19:1–2, 18**), whereas in Ruth, it is the home of Naomi, then Ruth, then David, and finally Jesus the Christ (**Ruth 1:1–2, 19, 22; 2:4; 4:11; Matthew 2:1, 5–6, 8**). See Eugene H. Merrill, "The Book of Ruth: Narration and Shared Themes" *Bibliotheca Sacra* 142 (1985):130–141.

1 SAMUEL 1: ELI AND THE ELI PRIESTHOOD

Approximate Dating: Eli was born ca. 1202 B.C. and died at age 98 in ca. 1104 B.C.;[1] Eli judged Israel for 40 years, ca. 1144–1104 B.C.; the Eli priesthood was active during the era of the judges and the early united monarchy period. ***Relevant Scriptures:*** **1 Samuel 1:3; 2:12–17, 34; 4:4, 11, 17, 21; 14:3; 21:1–2, 8; 22:9–20; 23:6, 9; 30:7; 2 Samuel 8:17; 15:27, 29, 35–36; 20:25;** also **Genesis 46:11; Exodus 6:16, 18, 23, 25; 28:1; Numbers 3:2–4; 25:7; 26:59–60; 1 Kings 1:42; 2:26–27, 35; 4:4; 1 Chronicles 6:1–4, 16, 18, 20; 18:16; 23:12; 24:1–3, 6; Ezra 7:1–5**

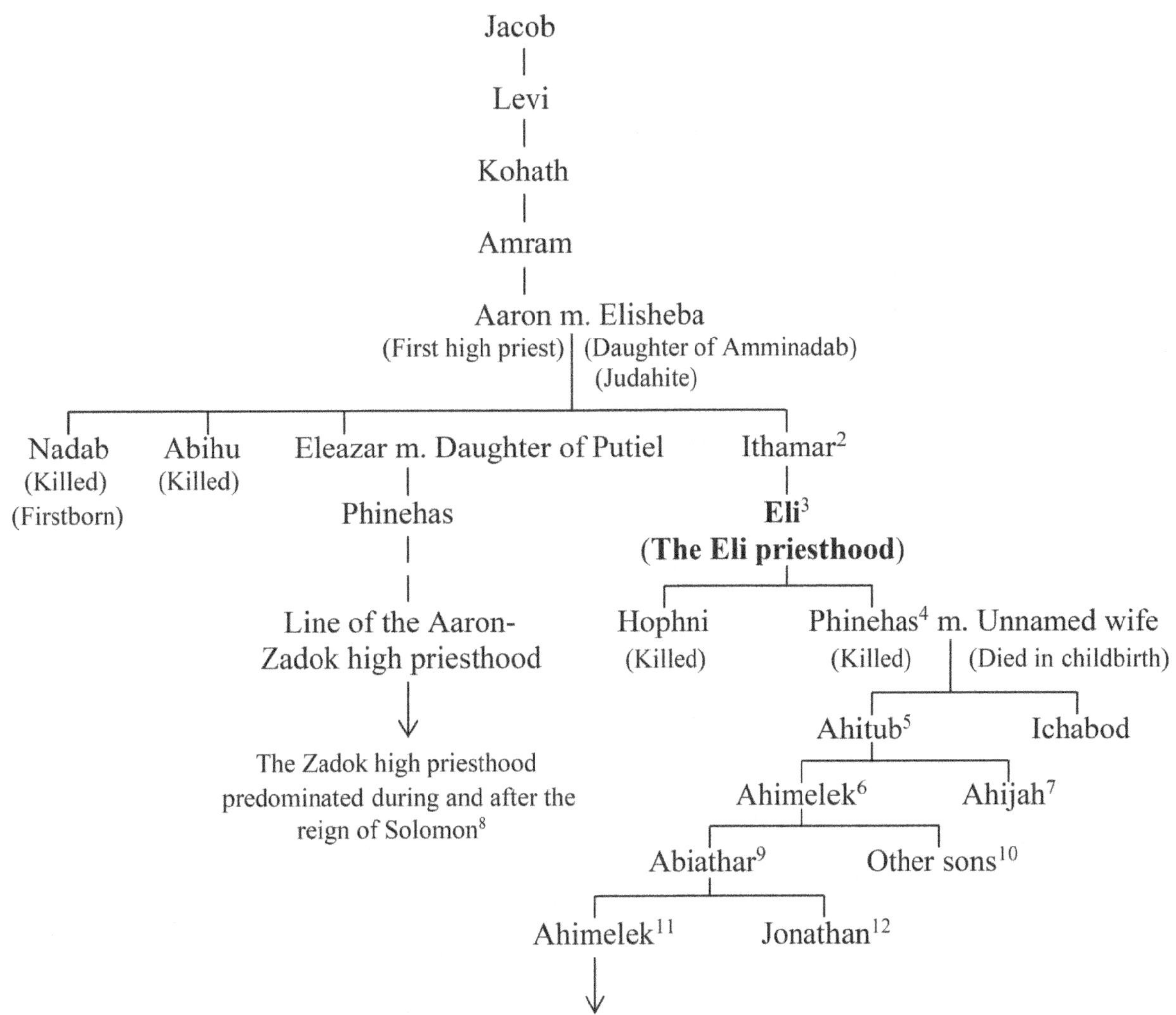

Biblical and Theological Significance

The high priesthood from the time of Aaron through the post-exile is summarized in **1 Chronicles 6:1–15** and **Ezra 7:1–5**. Because they abused their office, two of Aaron's sons, Nadab and Abihu, were slain by the Lord; subsequently, their two brothers, Eleazar and Ithamar, ministered in their place (**Numbers 3:4; 1 Chronicles 24:2**). The Eli priesthood, traced from Ahimelek back to Ithamar (**1 Chronicles 24:3**), refers to the Aaron–Ithamar–Eli line of high priestly descendants, as opposed to the Aaron–Eleazar–Phinehas–Zadok line of high priests (=the Zadok or Zadokite priesthood) (cf. **Exodus 6:25; Numbers 25:7, 11; Judges 20:28; 1 Chronicles 6:4, 50; Ezra 7:5**).

Eli served as the high priest at Shiloh along with his two sons, Hophni and Phinehas; however, as **1 Samuel 2** explains, the sons were unfit for the position (**v. 12**) for they mishandled the meat offerings (**vv. 12–17**) and fornicated with female sanctuary personnel (**v. 22**). For these sins, the Lord confronted Eli (**v. 29**) and pronounced a "curse"[14] of premature death on his sons and their descendants (**vv. 29–36**). In response, the Lord then promised to raise up a faithful priest (Samuel) and to establish a priestly house that would "minister before my anointed one always" (**v. 35**; cf. **1 Samuel 3:21**). Soon thereafter, Hophni and Phinehas died in Israel's battle with the Philistines (cf. **1 Samuel 4:1–11**).

As **1 Samuel 4** explains, Eli's life was troubled, especially in his old age. His daughter-in-law (the wife of Phinehas) went into premature labor when news arrived that the Philistines had seized the ark of the covenant (**vv. 19–21**). Its theft was a sacrilege so profound that the ninety-eight-year-old Eli fell back, broke his neck, and died, thus ending his forty-year priestly judgeship over Israel (**v. 18**). Eli's daughter-in-law died in childbirth, but before she expired, she requested that the child be named Ichabod[15]—Hebrew אִי־כָבוֹד, *i kabod,* "Where is the glory [now]?"—to signify Yahweh's departure from Israel (**vv. 21–22**).

Eli's great-grandson Ahijah was the priest who officiated at Shiloh in Saul's time (**1 Samuel 14:3**; cf. **Joshua 18:1**). Later, the Eli priesthood established a site at Nob just north of Jerusalem (**1 Samuel 22:19**), and there, Ahitub's son Ahimelek officiated (**1 Samuel 21:1–2; 22:9–11**; see also **1 Samuel 21:1–10; 23:6**). After Saul ordered the massacre of eighty-five priests at Nob (**1 Samuel 22:6–21**), Ahimelek's son Abiathar escaped and followed David (**1 Samuel 22:20–23**). Eventually Abiathar served as a high priest in Jerusalem (**1 Samuel 23:6; 30:7; 2 Samuel 15:24, 29, 35–36; 19:11; 20:25; 1 Chronicles 15:11–12**). Ahimelek (Abiathar's son) also served as a priestly official, presumably under his father's oversight (cf. **2 Samuel 8:17; 1 Chronicles 18:16; 24:3, 6, 31**). An unusual *dual* high priesthood continued throughout David's reign (1011–971 B.C.), with Abiathar (from the Eli priesthood) and Zadok (from the Aaron–Eleazar priesthood), serving as co–high priests (**2 Samuel 8:17; 15:24; 20:25; 1 Chronicles 15:11–12; 18:16; 24:3, 6, 31**).

The rupture between the Elide (Eli–Abiathar) and Zadokite (Aaron–Eleazar–Zadok) priesthoods occurred due to the succession crisis following David's death. David's fourth son, Adonijah, who had vied for the throne, was backed by Abiathar, whereas Solomon, the heir apparent, was backed by Zadok (**1 Kings 1:5–8, 32–48**). Thus, after David's death, the dual high priesthood ceased (**1 Kings 1:7–8, 19, 32, 38–40; 2:22, 27, 35**) and only the Zadok high priesthood continued to serve at Solomon's Temple[16] (**1 Chronicles 29:22**).

The Eli priesthood officially ended early in Solomon's reign when he deposed Abiathar (**1 Kings 2:26–27**), thereby fulfilling God's judgment on Eli and his descendants (cf. **1 Samuel 2:22–25, 30–36; 3:14; 1 Kings 2:27**). Thereafter, *high* priests were from the Aaron–Zadok line exclusively. *Attending* priests were from two faithful Kohathite priestly lines: sixteen heads of families of the Zadokites (Aaron–Eleazar–Zadok descendants) and eight heads of families of the Ithamarites (Aaron–Ithamar descendants), excluding any "cursed" Elide descendants (cf. **1 Chronicles 24:1–18; Ezra 8:2**).

In Scripture, the *unfaithful* Eli priesthood is contrasted with the *faithful* Aaronic "lasting priesthood" (**Exodus 40:15; Numbers 25:13; 1 Chronicles 6:49–53**). Nevertheless, it was not through either the Aaronic or Elide priesthoods that atonement under the law was ultimately achieved, but rather through the holy, perfect, sacrificial atonement of Jesus the High Priest of the "permanent [everlasting] priesthood" (**Hebrews 7:24**)—a perfection not attainable through the Levitical priesthood but in "the priest to come" (**Hebrews 7:11**)—"One [Jesus] in the order of Melchizedek, not in the order of Aaron" (**Hebrews 7:11**; cf. **Psalm 110:4; Hebrews 5:6, 10; 6:20; 9:11, 25; 1 Peter 1:19; 2:5**).

Notes

1. Eli died when he fell over backward and broke his neck upon hearing of the Philistine capture of the ark of the covenant as a result of the battle of Aphek, dated securely at 1104 B.C. Therefore, Eli died ca. 1104 B.C. at the age of 98 (**1 Samuel 4:15, 18**) and therefore must have been born in 1202 B.C.

2. A single reference in Scripture (**1 Chronicles 24:3**) clearly identifies the origin of the Eli priesthood—Ahimelek the son of Ahitub is explicitly called "a descendant of Ithamar" the son of Aaron (cf. **1 Samuel 14:3; 22:9, 11**). Thus, the Eli priesthood was derived from the Aaron–Ithamar–Eli line of descendants.

3. Scripture does not explicitly state whether Eli was the *son* or a *descendant* of Ithamar, but *son* is the favored interpretation, as indicated in the chart.

4. This Phinehas of the Eli priesthood should not be confused with Phinehas the son of Eleazar in the Aaronic priesthood (**Exodus 6:25; Numbers 25:7, 11; Judges 20:28; 1 Chronicles 6:4, 50; Ezra 7:5; 8:2**).

5. Ahitub the son of Phinehas and the father of Ahimelek (in the Eli priesthood) should not be confused with Ahitub the son of Amariah and the father of Zadok (in the Aaron–Eleazar–Zadokite priesthood).

6. When Saul was king, Ahimelek the son of Ahitub was the priest at Nob. Because Ahimelek gave David the consecrated bread (the holy bread of the presence in the holy place) and the sword of Goliath (**1 Samuel 21:1–8**; cf. **Exodus 25:30; Mark 2:26**), Saul ordered Ahimelek's death and that of "all the men of his family. . . . eighty-five men who wore the linen ephod" (**1 Samuel 22:11, 18**; cf. **1 Samuel 22:9–19**). Ahimelek was a "descendant of Ithamar" (**1 Chronicles 24:3**).

7. Ahijah officiated primarily at Shiloh, the central sanctuary and religious center during the time of the judges (**Joshua 18:1**; **1 Samuel 14:3**). After King David moved his capital from Hebron to Jerusalem, Shiloh lost its importance. Nevertheless, Shiloh continued as a semi-active worship site during the united monarchy period, during the reigns of Saul (ca. 1051–1011 B.C.), David (ca. 1011–971 B.C.), and into the time of Solomon (ca. 971–931 B.C.). Ahijah of Shiloh (of the Eli priesthood) appears to be the same person as the prophet "Ahijah the Shilonite" (**1 Kings 12:15; 15:29; 2 Chronicles 9:29; 10:15**) and "Ahijah the prophet of Shiloh" (**1 Kings 11:29**) who: (1) foretold the splitting of the united kingdom into two parts (Israel and Judah) (cf. **1 Kings 11:29–39; 2 Chronicles 10:15**); (2) recorded the acts of Solomon in a book called the "prophecy of Ahijah the Shilonite" (**2 Chronicles 9:29**); and (3) was the priest of whom King Jeroboam's wife inquired about her sick son (**1 Kings 14:1–18**). If they are the same person, this means Ahijah lived a long life, from sometime during the time of Saul (ca. 1051–1011 B.C.) until the (early) days of Jeroboam I, the first king of Israel (ca. 931–910 B.C.); thus, at his death, Ahijah would have been between 100 and 120 years old. This finding would be consistent with Ahijah being a faithful *remnant* of the Eli priesthood who was subsequently appointed as an *honorary* priest over the temple treasuries and dedicated things in Solomon's Temple; see chart "**1 Chronicles 26**–Probable Genealogy of Ahijah, the Priestly Overseer of the Temple Treasuries and Dedicated Things in Solomon's Temple." If they are different persons, then Ahijah son of Ahitub (in the Eli priesthood) and the prophet "Ahijah the Shilonite" were near contemporaries.

8. See charts "**1 Chronicles 6**: Levi: High Priests, Priests, Levites, and Musicians in Solomon's Temple" and "**Supplement 2**: The High Priests of Israel."

9. Abiathar the son of Ahimelek escaped the massacre at Nob and became a follower of David and a priest during David's reign (**1 Samuel 22:20, 23:6; 30:7; 2 Samuel 15:29; 1 Kings 2:26**). Abiathar was faithful to David during Absalom's rebellion (**2 Samuel 15**) and became one of David's counselors after the king's former counselor, Ahithophel, committed suicide (cf. **2 Samuel 11:3; 15:12; 17:23; 23:34; 1 Chronicles 27:33–34**). Later, for unclear reasons, Abiathar supported Adonijah's quest to be David's successor instead of Solomon. Therefore, when Solomon came to the throne, he removed Abiathar and exiled him to his hometown of Anathoth (**1 Kings 1:7; 2:26–35**). Abiathar and his son Ahimelek are the last recorded priests in the cursed line of the Eli priesthood to serve in *official* high priestly capacities (see Jonathan in note 12).

10. That Ahimelek had other sons besides Abiathar is suggested in the reading of **1 Samuel 22:20**.

11. Ahimelek son of Abiathar appears to have been named after his grandfather, Ahimelek son of Ahitub—an example of papponymy. Ahimelek son of Abiathar also served as a priestly official. Abiathar son of Ahimelek is mentioned in **1 Samuel 22:20; 23:6;** and **30:7**; Ahimelek son of Ahitub is mentioned in **1 Samuel 23:6**; and Ahimelek son of Abiathar is mentioned in **2 Samuel 8:17** and **1 Chronicles 18:16; 24:3, 6**.

12. Jonathan the son of Abiathar is referenced in **2 Samuel 15:27, 36** and **1 Kings 1:42**. Jonathan was a contemporary of King David.

13. For the Aaron–Ithamar descendants who ministered in Solomon's Temple as Kohathite *attending* priests, see chart "**1 Chronicles 24**: Genealogical Registry of the 24 Divisions of Kohathite Priests Who Rotated Service in Solomon's Temple." Much later, a priest named Daniel—who is specifically identified as an Aaron–Ithamar descendant and who had been an exile in Babylon—returned to Jerusalem with Ezra in 458 B.C. and attended at the Second Temple (**Ezra 8:2**).

14. The curse specifically involved the imminent death of Eli's sons (Hophni and Phineahas) and a decreased lifespan for members of the Elide clan—"No one in your family line will ever reach old age"—they will die "in the prime of life." Those remaining were plagued with hunger. They would "come and bow down before him [Samuel] for a piece of silver and a loaf of bread and plead, 'Appoint me to some priestly office so I can have food to eat'" (**1 Samuel 2:32, 33, 36**). The Eli priesthood also witnessed the "distress" at Shiloh, which was remembered as a place of ruin (**1 Samuel 2:32;** cf. **1 Samuel 22:16–18; Psalm 78:60; Jeremiah 7:12–14; 26:6, 9**).

15. Ichabod is a personal name meaning "Where is the glory [now]?" (Holman Bible Dictionary, "Ichabod").

16. See charts "**1 Kings 4**: The Chief Officials in King Solomon's Administration" and "**Supplement 2**: The High Priests of Israel."

1 SAMUEL 1: SAMUEL, THE PROPHET–PRIEST–JUDGE OF ISRAEL

Approximate Dating: Samuel lived from ca. 1110–1015 B.C.; a figure who transitioned from the time of the judges to the time of the kings ***Relevant Scriptures:*** **1 Samuel 1–2; 8:1–3;** also **Genesis 46:11; Exodus 6:24; Numbers 3:27; 1 Chronicles 6:1–3, 16, 18, 22–28, 33–38; 15:17; 26:23**

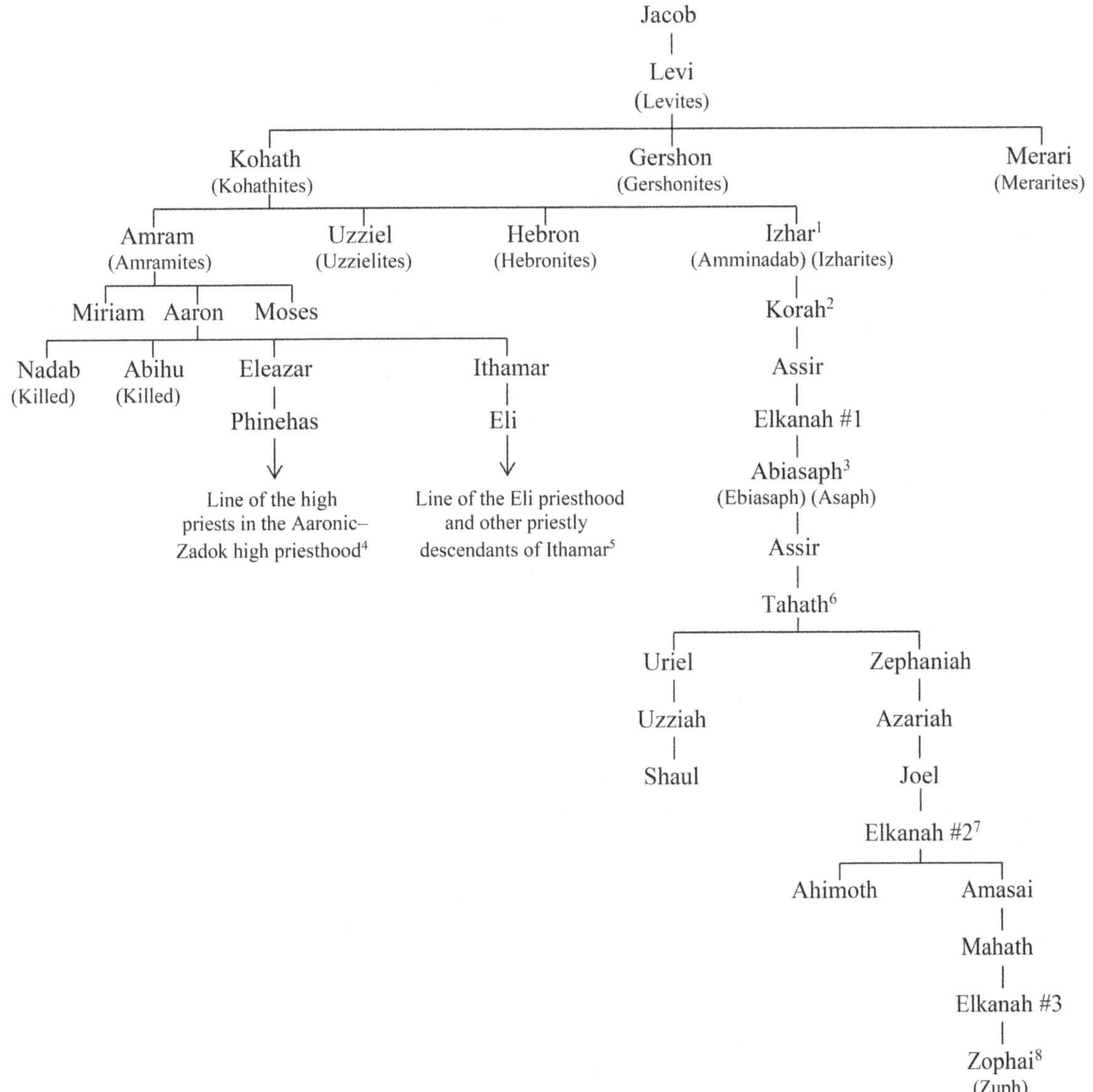

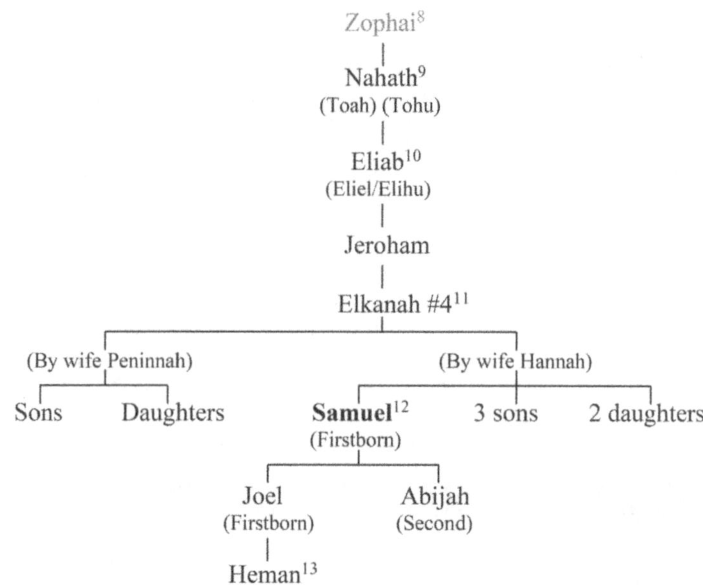

Biblical and Theological Significance

Samuel, one of the pivotal characters of Old Testament history, was the link between the period of the judges and the monarchy. Samuel was also one of a very few persons who were both prophet and priest. The prophetic office was *charismatic*—that is, an office to which one was called and gifted by God—whereas the priestly office was *hereditary*. All true priests must certify their Levitical tribal heritage and, more precisely, their descent from Kohath (son of Levi) and his progeny. High priests came strictly from the Aaronic line, from either the prominent Eleazar–Phinehas line or the secondary Ithamar–Eli line. Other *attending* priests were also Kohathites and near *relatives* of the high priests. Non-Kohathites (such as Gershonites and Merarites) served in subsidiary roles as Levites who assisted both the high priests and the Kohathite attending priests. As a priest descended from a Kohathite–Korahite clan, Samuel served a kind of apprenticeship with Eli (the Ithamarite/Elide priest) at Shiloh. Since Eli's priesthood was of a subsidiary kind, similarly, Samuel's priesthood was subsidiary as well (i.e., he was in the Kohathite–Izharite–Korahite clan but *not* in the Kohathite–Amramite–Aaronic line). The special function of the Korahites at the tabernacle and temple was to be gatekeepers, as seen in **1 Chronicles 9:19**: "Shallum son of Kore, the son of Ebiasaph, the son of Korah, and his fellow gatekeepers from his family (the Korahites) were responsible for guarding the thresholds of the tent just as their ancestors had been responsible for guarding the entrance to the dwelling of the LORD" (cf. **Numbers 16:8–9**). Samuel acted in this role himself when he was under the tutelage of Eli for a few years (**1 Samuel 2:18–22; 3:3, 15**) and later as a priest and prophet to the nation (**1 Samuel 7:15–17**).

Samuel's father Elkanah (#4) is identified as "a Zuphite [of the line of Zophai/Zuph] from the hill country of Ephraim" (**1 Samuel 1:1**), and Elkanah appears in the interesting narrative of **1 Samuel 1:1–28**. Elkanah had two wives, Hannah and Peninnah, but Hannah was barren. Nevertheless, the family was faithful to make the yearly trek to Shiloh, the site of the tabernacle of Moses that had been set up in the days of Joshua (**Joshua 18:1**); there, Hannah fervently prayed for a son, whom she committed to the Lord as a Nazirite even before he was born. Her prayers were fulfilled with Samuel's birth. After Samuel was weaned, his parents took him to Eli, the high priest at Shiloh, to serve as an apprentice (cf. **Leviticus 27:28; 1 Samuel 1:10–11, 21–28**). Soon Samuel was called by the Lord to be a prophet to the nation, and thus throughout his life he served as both priest and prophet (**1 Samuel 3:2–21; 7:15–17**; cf. **Acts 3:24; 13:20**), traveling to Bethel, Gilgal, Mizpah, and Ramah during most of Saul's forty-year reign as Israel's king.

The pious character of Samuel is contrasted with (1) Hophni and Phinehas, the wicked sons of Eli (Eli was an Aaron–Ithamar descendant;[14] **1 Samuel 1:3; 2:12**) and (2) Samuel's own sons, Joel and Abijah. When Samuel was old, he appointed his sons as judges in Beersheba, but they "did not follow his [Samuel's] ways. They turned aside after dishonest gain and accepted bribes and perverted justice" (**1 Samuel 8:3**). The crooked acts of Samuel's sons, among other factors, led the people of Israel to demand a king (**1 Samuel 8:2–5**; see **8:1–22**).

Samuel's greatest acts were no doubt his negotiation of the people's premature demand for a king and his selection and anointing of David in ca. 1026 B.C. to be king and the successor to Saul (cf. **1 Samuel 4–6; 10:1; 16:12–13**). Samuel died toward the latter part of Saul's reign (**1 Samuel 25:1**; cf. **28:3**), around 1015 B.C. The historian notes that Samuel was the leader of the nation "all the days of his life" (**1 Samuel 7:15**; cf. **1 Samuel 1:11**).

Notes

1. Izhar in **Exodus 6:18, 21; Numbers 16:1**; and **1 Chronicles 6:2, 18, 38; 23:12** is called Amminadab in **1 Chronicles 6:22**.

2. **Exodus 6:24** states that "the sons of Korah were Assir, Elkanah [#1] and Abiasaph [Ebiasaph] [Asaph]. These were the Korahite clans"; however, **1 Chronicles 6:22–24** clarifies that the *sons* of Korah (listed in **Exodus 6:24**) were actually sons-of-sons: "The descendants of Kohath: Amminadab [Izhar] his son, Korah his son, Assir his son, Elkanah [#1] his son, Ebiasaph [Abiasaph] [Asaph] his son, Assir his son, Tahath his son, Uriel his son, Uzziah his son, and Shaul his son." In recounting the lineage of Heman (a chief musician in Solomon's Temple) in **1 Chronicles 6:33–38**, again, Korah's son and grandson

(i.e., Assir and Elkanah #1, respectively) were omitted in **1 Chronicles 6:37**: "the son of Tahath, the son of Assir, the son of Ebiasaph [#1], the son of Korah." The lineage of Samuel shown in the chart records the sons of Korah as given in **1 Chronicles 6:22–24**.

3. Ebiasaph in **1 Chronicles 6:23, 37** and **9:19** is Abiasaph in **Exodus 6:24** and (the shortened form) Asaph in **1 Chronicles 26:1**.

4. See charts "**1 Chronicles 6**: Levi: High Priests, Priests, Levites, and Musicians in Solomon's Temple" and "**Supplement 2**: The High Priests of Israel."

5. See chart "**1 Samuel 1**: Eli and the Eli Priesthood."

6. Tahath the Levticial Korahite is not the same person as Tahath the Ephraimite (**1 Chronicles 7:20**).

7. The lineage of Elkanah #2 given in **1 Chronicles 6:25–26** is somewhat confusing and omits Mahath (Elkanah #2's grandson); the lineage of Elkanah #2 is clarified in **1 Chronicles 6:35–36**.

8. Zophai in **1 Chronicles 6:26** is called Zuph in **1 Chronicles 6:35**. In **1 Samuel 1:1**, Elkanah #4, the father of Samuel is identified as "a Zuphite from the hill country of Ephraim" after this ancestor (Zuph/Zophai).

9. Nahath (**1 Chronicles 6:26**), Toah (**1 Chronicles 6:34**), and Tohu (**1 Samuel 1:1**) are one and the same.

10. Eliab (**1 Chronicles 6:27**), Eliel (**1 Chronicles 6:34**), and Elihu (**1 Samuel 1:1**) are one and the same.

11. Note the repetition of the name Elkanah (אֶלְקָנָה) in the Korahite lineage. The name occurs as the father of Abiasaph/Ebiasaph/Asaph (i.e., Elkanah #1), the father of Amasai (i.e., Elkanah #2), the father of Zophai/Zuph (i.e., Elkanah #3), and most famously, the father of Samuel (i.e., Elkanah #4). The name Elkanah means "God acquired" or "God created." In the case of Elkanah #4 and Hannah, they had prayed for a son and at last they "acquired" one from the Lord. Samuel's father is identified as "a certain man from Ramathaim [the town of Ramathaim zuphim/zophim], a Zuphite [a descendant of Zuph] from [living in] the hill country of Ephraim, whose name was Elkanah son of Jeroham the son of Elihu, the son of Tohu, the son of Zuph, an Ephraimite [living within the tribal allotment of Ephraim]" (**1 Samuel 1:1**; cf. **1 Samuel 8:2; 1 Chronicles 6:25–28; 33–38**). Samuel's father, Elkanah, was *not* a descendant of Ephraim, the son of Joseph. For more information, see "Ramathaim," in *The Sacred Bridge–Carta's Atlas of the Biblical World*, Rainey and Notley, eds. (Jerusalem: Carta, 2014), 143.

12. Samuel's heritage shows that his ancestors were a faithful remnant of the Kohathite–Izhar–Korathite clan (cf. **Numbers 16**)—but not from the Kohathite line of high priests (e.g., the Aaron–Eleazar–Phinehas lineage; **Exodus 6:25**); for comparison, see chart "**1 Chronicles 6**: Levi: High Priests, Priests, Levites, and Musicians in Solomon's Temple."

13. Heman, a key musician in Solomon's Temple (**1 Chronicles 6:33**), was a descendant of Samuel the prophet (**1 Chronicles 15:17**). See chart "**1 Chronicles 6**: Levi: High Priests, Priests, Levites, and Musicians in Solomon's Temple."

14. See chart "**1 Samuel 1**: Eli and the Eli Priesthood."

1 SAMUEL 7: THE FAMILY OF ABINADAB WHO OVERSAW THE ARK OF THE COVENANT

Approximate Dating: ca. 1024–1004 B.C.[1] ***Relevant Scriptures:*** **1 Samuel 7:1–2; 2 Samuel 6:3–8; 1 Chronicles 13:5–13**

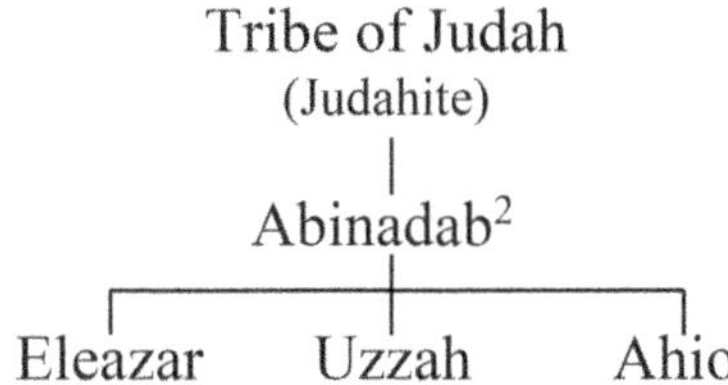

Biblical and Theological Significance

After the days of Joshua and the conquest of Canaan, the ark of the covenant—the major symbol of the presence of Yahweh among his people—had found no permanent resting place. After the Israelites overcame the inhabitants of the land, the tabernacle was erected at Bethel and then at Shiloh, in the tribal area of Ephraim, where the Eli priesthood later undertook its ministry (**Joshua 18:1; 1 Samuel 1:3; 2:11**).[3] The settlement there was established ca. 1406 B.C. The ark remained there until the days of Eli the high priest, his sons,[4] and his young apprentice-priest, Samuel son of Elkanah (**1 Samuel 4:1–11**).[5]

The Philistines went to war against Israel and wanted to capture the ark because they believed that the Israelites' God lived inside it (**1 Samuel 4:7**). The Philistines succeeded in taking the ark; they also killed Eli's sons (Hophni and Phinehas) and slew thirty thousand Israelite soldiers, a turn of events so egregious that Eli fell backward off his chair and broke his neck upon hearing the news (**1 Samuel 4:10–18**). The Philistines took the ark to Ashdod and placed it before their god Dagon; however, in the ark's presence, the idol fell (twice), breaking the head and hands from the statue's body, and a vicious plague took the lives of many people (**1 Samuel 5:1–7**). Similar incidents took place at Gath and Ekron, and so, the terrified Philistines sent the ark back to Israel on a cart drawn by two cows (whose calves had been taken from them) who, ironically, knew exactly where to go (cf. **1 Samuel 5:6–6:12**). On the way back to Shiloh, the cart arrived at Beth Shemesh,[6] where it was broken up for firewood and the animals were sacrificed (**1 Samuel 6:14**). However, seventy people looked inside the ark, and for this gross disregard of his "presence," God struck down fifty thousand people[7] (**1 Samuel 6:19**). The event prompted the leaders of the community to appeal to the people of Kiriath Jearim[8] to come and take the ark off their hands.

The ark was carried to the house of Abinadab,[9] which was located "on the hill"[10] (cf. **2 Samuel 6:3**), and the men of Kiriath Jearim consecrated Abinadab's son Eleazar to guard it (**1 Samuel 7:1**). At first glance, the heritage of Abinadab is unclear. Given that his family was charged with the oversight of the ark of the covenant, one might argue that he was a Levite. However, the fact that he lived in Kiriath Jearim (Baalah) in the hill country of Judah (**Joshua 15:1, 9, 48, 60**), and that this city was not a Levitical city (**Joshua 18:14; Judges 18:12**; cf. **Joshua 21; 1 Chronicles 2:50, 52; 6:54–81**), overrules this option and strongly suggests that Abinadab was a Judahite, not a Levite. Because of the sacral character of the ark, it had to be handled by priests and Levites only, except in highly exceptional circumstances such as those addressed here. Though Abinadab was not a Levite, some men of Kiriath Jearim *consecrated*[11] his son Eleazar to serve as the priest to attend before the ark (cf. **1 Samuel 7:1–2**). Abinadab need not be an Aaronic descendant to do this, nor did Eleazar have to be one to have custody of the ark.

The ark remained at Abinadab's house for twenty long years, ca. 1024–1004 B.C. (**1 Samuel 7:2**), until David had become king of all Israel in 1004 B.C. and prepared a place for the ark in the City of David in Jerusalem (**2 Samuel 6:12**). Sadly, the move to Jerusalem was hindered because Uzzah and Ahio, the sons of Abinadab, mishandled the ark, resulting in Uzzah's death (**2 Samuel 6:3–7**). After this incident, David was afraid to move the ark further, so he took it to the house of Obed-Edom the Levitical Merarite[12] for three months, after which it was successfully moved to the City of David (**2 Samuel 6:11–15**).

Notes

1. Important dates that conveniently provide context for the chart are:
   - Eli was born in 1202 B.C. and died at age 98 (**1 Samuel 4:15**); his death and the fall of Shiloh occurred in 1104 B.C. (**1 Samuel 4:1–4**).
   - Samuel effectively subdued the Philistines from invading Israel's territory—"throughout Samuel's lifetime [1110–1015 B.C.], the hand of the LORD was against the Philistines" (**1 Samuel 7:13**).
   - Samuel died ca. 1015 B.C., just before Saul's death in 1011 B.C. (**1 Samuel 25:1**).
   - The ark was in Kiriath Jearim for 20 years, ca. 1024–1004 B.C. (**1 Samuel 7:2**).

2. Abinadab of Kiriath Jearim is not: (1) Abinadab the son of Saul (also called Ishvi; **1 Samuel 14:49; 31:2; 1 Chronicles 8:33; 9:39; 10:2**); (2) Abinadab the brother of David (**1 Samuel 16:8; 17:13; 1 Chronicles 2:13**); nor (3) Ben-Abinadab, one of the district governors during Solomon's reign (**1 Kings 4:11**).

3. See chart "**1 Samuel 1**: Eli and the Eli Priesthood."

4. Hophni and Phinehas, the sons of Eli, were "scoundrels" who had no respect for the Lord—mishandling the meat offerings and sleeping with the women who served at the entrance to the tent of meeting (**1 Samuel 2:12–16, 22**). Furthermore, Eli honored his sons more than the Lord, failed to restrain them in their wickedness, and fattened himself on the "choice parts of every offering made" (**1 Samuel 2:29**). These actions ultimately led to the Lord's curse on Eli and the entire Eli priesthood (**1 Samuel 2:17, 22–36; 3:11–14; 4:11**); see chart "**1 Samuel 1**: Eli and the Eli Priesthood."

5. For Samuel, see chart "**1 Samuel 1**: Samuel, the Prophet–Priest–Judge of Israel."

6. Beth Shemesh was located about 18 miles west-southwest of Jerusalem and ca. 10 miles southwest of Kiriath Jearim.

7. In **1 Samuel 6:19**, the NIV says "seventy of them [were put] to death because they looked into the ark of the LORD," whereas most Hebrew manuscripts and the Septuagint say that 50,070 persons were killed.

8. Kiriath Jearim was also called Baalah, Kiriath Baal, or Baalah of Judah (**Joshua 15:9, 60; 1 Chronicles 13:6**). For the distance between Beth Shemesh and Kiriath Jearim, see note 6.

9. Abinadab's name is hypocoristic, with "God" or "Lord" only hinted at. The Hebrew elements אָבִי (*abi*) and נָדַב (*nadab*) mean, respectively, "my father" is a "voluntary giver" or the like. "Father" could be taken as referring to God or to a human father. Such a name would be very common.

10. The *Easton Bible Dictionary* (M. G. Easton "Obed-Edom"), suggests that Abinadab's house was in Gibeah—on a hill or eminence near Kirjath Jearim—which was among the group of ten cities in the hill country of Judah (**Joshua 15:55–57**). Abinadab's house may be related to the settlement of Gibea that was founded by Sheva, a descendant of Caleb the Kenizzite (**1 Chronicles 2:49**); for the latter, see chart "**1 Chronicles 2**: Caleb and Kenaz, the Sons of Jephunneh the Kenizzite."

11. To "consecrate" (Heb. Piel verb stem קִדֵּשׁ [*qaddesh*]) means to "declare holy" ("קדשׁ," *HALOT* 2:1072–73). The anointing of a layman to serve in such a manner was not to "ordain" him to the priesthood, but to sanctify him to handle or make use of an object which was normally reserved for priests and for a specified time (**1 Samuel 16:5; 1 Kings 19:16**). Abinadab, though not Levitical, was "declared to be set apart" (קִדְּשׁוּ) as a priest, at least as a custodian of the ark, which he must have handled from time to time. The verb here is the one always used for the ordination of priests ("קדשׁ," *HALOT* 2:1072–74).

12. For the ancestry of Obed-Edom, see chart "**2 Samuel 6**: Obed-Edom, the Levitical Gatekeeper and Keeper of the Ark."

1 SAMUEL 9: KING SAUL

Approximate Dating: Saul was born in ca. 1081 B.C.; in ca. 1051 B.C., at age 30, he became king and reigned 40 years, ca. 1051–1011 B.C.; he was the first king of the united monarchy ***Relevant Scriptures:*** **1 Samuel 9:1–2; 13:1; 14:49–51; 2 Samuel 3:17; 4:4; 9:6, 10, 12; 21:8;** also **Genesis 46:21; Numbers 26:38–40; 1 Samuel 18:17–19; 31:2; 1 Chronicles 8:29–40; 9:35–44; 10:2; 27:21; Acts 13:21**

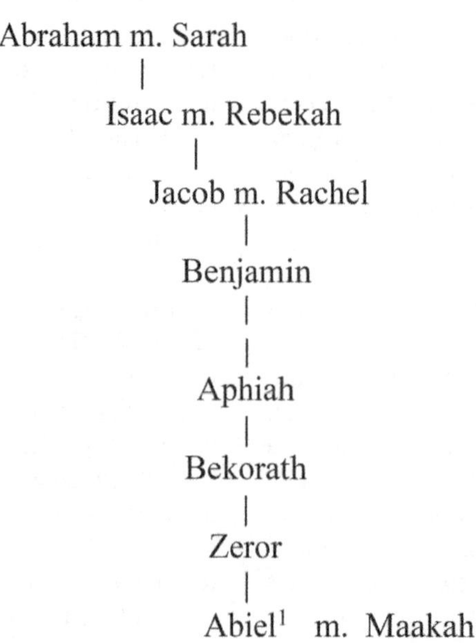

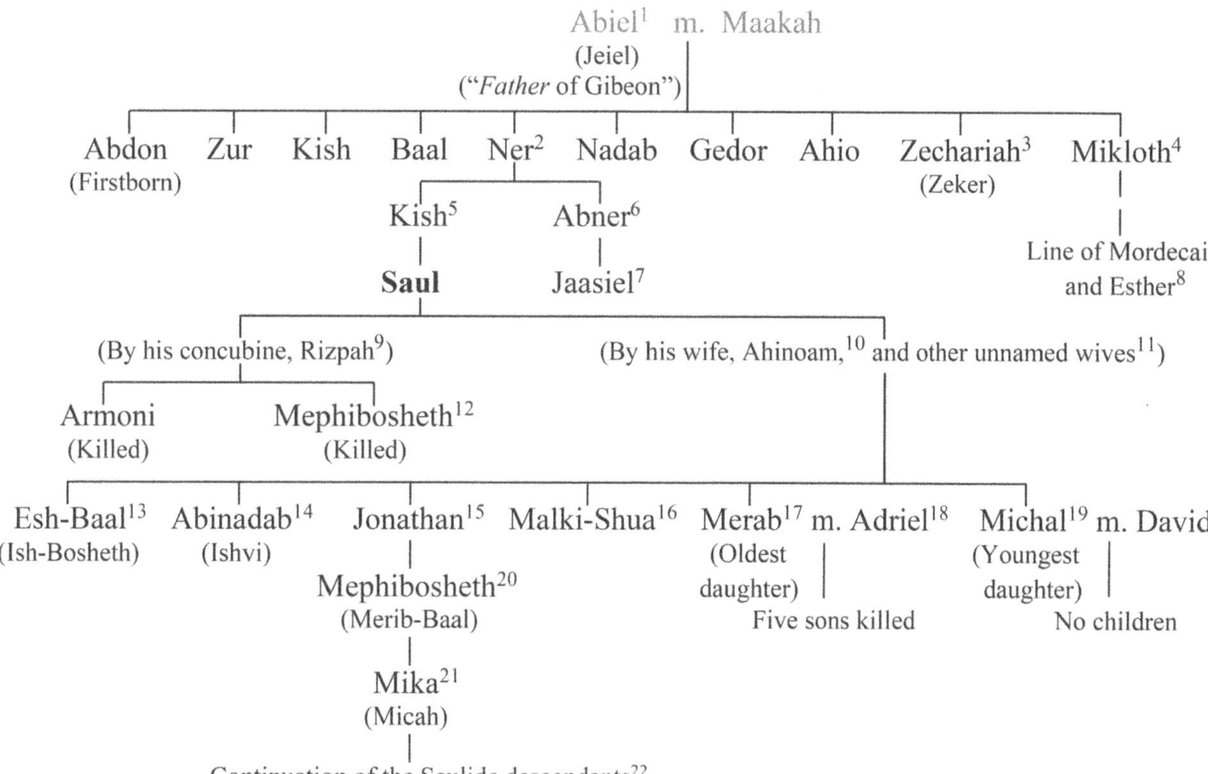

Biblical and Theological Significance

Saul's Ancestry and Rise to Power

Saul's genealogy finds its roots in Abraham through Jacob and Jacob's youngest and favorite son, Benjamin, who was born in Canaan in ca. 1908 B.C. Benjamin's descent continued under Abiel/Jeiel the Gibeonite and his wife Maakah (**1 Chronicles 8:29, 9:35**). Abiel/Jeiel—"the father of Gibeon"—was not the biological father of a man named Gibeon but rather a man of standing there.[23] Saul's grandfather, Ner, was the *son* of Abiel/Jeiel (**1 Samuel 14:51**) and the *father* of Kish (**1 Chronicles 8:33; 9:39**), thus making Abiel/Jeiel the great-grandfather of Saul.

When confronted by the people demanding a king, the prophet Samuel relented and, with divine permission, promised Israel a king. Saul was the choice of the people because he was handsome and tall (**1 Samuel 9:2**). His age at his inauguration and the length of his reign have historically been problematic, given the textual difficulties of the passage involved (**1 Samuel 13:1**).[24]

Saul's Immediate Family

With Saul and his son Ish-Bosheth/Esh–Baal,[25] the first Israelite dynasty began and ended, although Saul left a number of sons, including Jonathan, Malki-Shua, and Abinadab/Ishvi (**1 Samuel 14:49**; **1 Chronicles 8:33**). These sons were slain at Gilboa in 1011 B.C. by the Philistines and died the same day as Saul (**1 Samuel 31:2–6; 1 Chronicles 10:2–6**); Ish-Bosheth was assassinated shortly after, in ca. 1004 B.C. (**2 Samuel 4:2–8**). Jonathan left a long line of descendants who were famous archers like himself (**1 Chronicles 8:34–40**). The rest of Saul's posterity apparently died out. Saul also had two natural sons by his concubine Rizpah; both were put to death by David, along with the five sons of Saul's daughter Merab (**2 Samuel 21:8**). Saul's other daughter Michal apparently had no children with David. Saul, it seems, had other wives who were taken into the harem of David in accordance with the practice of the times (**2 Samuel 12:8**), but of them and their descendants nothing is known.

Saul's Monarchy: Life, Shortcomings, and Death

The city of Gibeon, allotted to the tribe of Benjamin (**Joshua 18:25**), was the tribal ancestral home, but "Gibeah of Saul" was Saul's hometown[26] (**1 Samuel 10:26; 11:4; 15:34; 2 Samuel 21:6; Isaiah 10:29**). Shortly after becoming king in 1051 B.C., Saul chose a group to fight the Philistines, but because Israel was greatly outnumbered, they hid themselves. Impatiently, Saul offered a burnt offering to elicit Yahweh's intervention instead of waiting for Samuel, the priest, to arrive. Samuel reprimanded Saul for his disregard of Yahweh's commands and declared that God would eventually remove the kingdom from him (**1 Samuel 13:1–14**). At another time, Yahweh told Saul to destroy the Amalekites because they had ambushed the Israelites on their return from Egypt (**1 Samuel 15:2–3;** cf. **Exodus 17:8–16**). Instead of killing them all as instructed, Saul spared King Agag and the best of the Amalekites' animals. Samuel informed Saul that "Because you have rejected the word of the LORD, he has rejected you as king" and declared that the kingdom would be taken from him (**1 Samuel 15:23**; see **15:8–24**). At this critical moment, Samuel anointed David as Israel's future king in Saul's place, although David did not immediately assume the throne (**1 Samuel 16:1–13**). After God rejected Saul as king, God's Spirit left him, and he was filled with a demonic spirit. As a result of David's defeat of Goliath (cf. **1 Samuel 17**), Saul became increasingly resentful of David's popularity among the people and pursued him with the intention of killing him. Ironically, David and Saul's son Jonathan became so close that they made a covenant to protect one another (**1 Samuel 18:1, 3**). With Jonathan's help, David escaped Saul's wrath, though that wrath was never returned by David.

On another occasion when Israel engaged the Philistines (**1 Samuel 28**), Saul called on Yahweh, but in vain (**1 Samuel 28:6**). Saul therefore resorted to a necromancer in Endor and requested that she call up Samuel from the dead. The prophet appeared, reprimanded Saul, and reminded him why he had been deposed. Samuel then declared that Yahweh would allow the Philistines to prevail and would allow them to slay Saul and his sons (**1 Samuel 28:7–19**). In the battle on Mount Gilboa, the Philistines fulfilled the prophet's message: Many Israelites (including three of Saul's sons) died, and Saul, fatally wounded, committed suicide (**1 Samuel 31:3–4**). The Philistines then dismembered Saul, but the people of Jabesh Gilead, whom Saul had saved years earlier, took the bodies of Saul and his sons and gave them a proper burial (**1 Samuel 31:8–13**). David eventually took the corpses and interred Saul and his son Jonathan in the tomb of Saul's father, Kish, at Zelah/Zela in Benjamin (**2 Samuel 21:14**).

Saul's Legacy and Successor

The transfer of power from the house of Saul to the house of David was in line with Yahweh's ancient promise that the messianic king would arise out of Judah, thus disqualifying Saul the Benjamite (**Genesis 49:10**). Moreover, Saul was unrepentantly unfaithful to Yahweh and his word (**1 Chronicles 10:13–14**). Before Saul's death in 1011 B.C., Samuel anointed David as king over Judah (**1 Samuel 16:1–13**). For unspecified reasons, Abner (Saul's army commander) maintained control over Israel in the north for about five years, ca. 1011–1006 B.C. (cf. **2 Samuel 2:8–11**). Then, in ca. 1005 B.C., Abner, seeking to establish a rump kingdom in the Transjordan, made Saul's son Ish-Bosheth king of Israel. Ish-Bosheth reigned for a brief two years from Manahaim, ca. 1005–1004 B.C. (**2 Samuel 2:8–10**). However, sometime during that term Ish-Bosheth accused Abner of sleeping with Saul's concubine Rizpah, whereupon Abner transferred his loyalty to David (**2 Samuel 3:6–21**) and promised to help David "bring all Israel" over to his side (**2 Samuel 3:12**). Following Ish-Bosheth's assassination ca. 1004 B.C. (**2 Samuel 4:1–3, 4–8**), David assumed kingship over the United Kingdom of Israel and Judah. He reigned for forty and one-half years—seven and one-half years over Judah from his capital in Hebron, and thirty-three years over all Israel from his capital in Jerusalem. When David died in 971 B.C., his son Solomon succeeded him (**2 Samuel 5:4; 1 Kings 2:11–12**; see also **1 Kings 1–2**).

Notes

1. Several references clarify Saul's ancestry. **First Samuel 9:1** (NIV) identifies Kish as "[the] son of Abiel, the son of Zeror, the son of Bekorath, the son of Aphiah of Benjamin." **First Chronicles 9:35–37** adds: "Jeiel [=Abiel] the father of Gibeon lived in Gibeon. . . . [His sons were] Abdon, followed by Zur, Kish, Baal, Ner, Nadab, Gedor, Ahio, Zechariah and Mikloth," and **1 Samuel 14:51** declares: "Saul's father Kish and Abner's father Ner were sons of Abiel." Abiel in **1 Samuel** is read Jeiel by the Chronicler. The two names are so different orthographically that they cannot be harmonized: Abiel (אֲבִיאֵל), "God is my father," hardly resembles the unpronounceable and meaningless Jeiel (יְעוּאֵל). The Qere of **1 Chronicles 9:35**, supported by consensus in the Septuagint, Targum, and Vulgate, reads יְעִיאֵל (*yeiel*), Jeiel. Abiel had some close relationship to Gibeon, perhaps as a civic or military leader, but he certainly was not its founder since, according to the archaeological evidence, that event was long before his time. See James B. Pritchard, *Gibeon: Where the Sun Stood Still* (Princeton: Princeton University Press, 1962), 148: "Gibeon first became a city at the beginning of the Early Bronze Age, about 5,000 years ago." Furthermore, Gibeon existed as a powerful city-state in the time of Joshua when some of its citizens made a peace treaty with Israel (**Joshua 9:3, 15–20**). Its ruins (Arabic *al-Jib*) are eight miles NW of Jerusalem. After Saul's time, Gibeon was the site of a confrontation between Abner (commander of Saul's army) and Joab (commander of David's army), where Abner was defeated (**2 Samuel 2:12–17**). Thus began a long war between "the house of Saul and the house of David," in which David "grew stronger and stronger, while the house of Saul grew weaker and weaker" (**2 Samuel 3:1**).

2. Ner is identified as the son of Abiel (**1 Samuel 14:51**) and the father of Kish (**1 Chronicles 8:33; 9:39**); therefore, Abiel was the *grandfather* of Kish and the *great-grandfather* of Saul. For this reason, **1 Samuel 14:50** should probably read, "The name of the commander of Saul's army was Abner son of Ner, and *Abner* was Saul's uncle"; likewise, Abner is the person referred to as "Saul's uncle" in **1 Samuel 10:14–16**.

3. "Zeker" (**1 Chronicles 8:31**) is hypocoristic for Zechariah (**1 Chronicles 9:37**).

4. Mikloth was the father of Shimeah (**1 Chronicles 8:31**). For Shimeah, see note 2 in chart "**Esther 2**: Mordecai and Esther, Jews Living in Persia."

5. Kish is the name of both Saul's father and his great-uncle (Kish the brother of Ner). Kish, Saul's father, hailed from Zelah/Zela in Benjamin (**Joshua 18:28; 2 Samuel 21:14**). Saul identifies himself to Samuel the prophet as: "Am I not a Benjamite, from the smallest tribe of Israel, and is not my clan [Kish] the least of all the clans of the tribe of Benjamin?" (**1 Samuel 9:21**).

6. Abner was Saul's uncle and the commander of his army (**1 Samuel 14:50; 26:5; 1 Kings 2:32**). After Saul's death in 1011 B.C., Abner retained power and then fought for Ish-Bosheth (Saul's son) to inherit the throne of Israel. However, when Ish-Bosheth accused Abner of adultery with his "father's concubine" (Rizpah), Abner turned against Ish-Bosheth and joined forces with David, who gladly welcomed him (**2 Samuel 3:7–13, 19–21**); it is unclear if the allegation was, in fact, true. In any event, Joab, then commander of David's army, was incensed that David would welcome his former rival (Abner). Eventually, Joab murdered Abner, ostensibly to avenge the death of Joab's brother, Asahel, whom Abner had murdered (**2 Samuel 3:27**; cf. **2:18–23**).

7. Jaasiel, the son of Abner, was the leader of the Benjamite tribe when David took a census of the people (**1 Chronicles 27:21**).

8. See charts "**1 Chronicles 8** & **9**: The Descendants of King Saul Living in Gibeon and Jerusalem (Post-Exile)" and "**Esther 2**: Mordecai and Esther, Jews Living in Persia."

9. In an attempt to strengthen "his own position in the house of Saul," Ish-Bosheth accused Abner of adultery with Saul's concubine Rizpah, the daughter of Aiah (cf. **2 Samuel 21:10–14**). See note 6 (above) and the chart "**2 Samuel 21**: Rizpah, the Concubine of King Saul."

10. Saul's wife Ahinoam was the *daughter* of Ahimaaz (**1 Samuel 14:50**); however, for chronological reasons, her father (Ahimaaz) cannot refer to the high priest, Ahimaaz the son of Zadok, who was a friend of David (**2 Samuel 15:27, 36; 17:17, 20; 18:19–30; 1 Chronicles 6:8–9, 53**; i.e., Ahimaaz #12 in the Aaron–Eleazar–Phinehas–Amariah–Ahitub–Zadok–Ahimaaz–Azariah lineage of high priests in chart "**Supplement 2**: The High Priests of Israel"). Despite the wording of **2 Samuel 12:8**, Ahinoam the wife of Saul should not be confused with Ahinoam the wife of David, who was from Jezreel of Judah (cf. **Joshua 15:56; 1 Samuel 25:43; 27:3; 30:5; 2 Samuel 2:2; 3:2; 1 Chronicles 3:1**).

11. For the reference to the unnamed wives of Saul, see **2 Samuel 12:8**.

12. The two sons of Rizpah, Armoni and Mephibosheth, along with five sons of Merab, Saul's eldest daughter, were hanged by David to avenge the Gibeonites whom Saul had wrongfully killed (**Joshua 9:3–4, 15–21; 2 Samuel 21:1, 8–9**); see chart "**2 Samuel 21**: Rizpah, the Concubine of King Saul."

13. Ish-Bosheth in **2 Samuel 2:8, 10, 12, 15; 3:7–8, 11, 14–15; 4:1, 5, 8, 12** is Esh-Baal in **1 Chronicles 8:33; 9:39**. After Saul's death in 1011 B.C.,

and for unspecified reasons, Ish-Bosheth did not immediately come to the throne; rather, there was an apparent interregnum (ca. 1011–1006 B.C.) during which time Abner (Saul's commander-in-chief) maintained control (**2 Samuel 2:8–11**). In ca. 1005 B.C., Ish-Bosheth became king of Israel at 40 years old and established a short-lived kingdom from his capital at Mahanaim in the Transjordan (rather than from Saul's capital in Gibeah). For two years (ca. 1005–1004 B.C.), he ruled over "Gilead, Ashuri [Ashurite?] and Jezreel, and also over Ephraim, Benjamin and all Israel" (**2 Samuel 2:8–11**). [Gilead was a Transjordan district loosely defined as all the country between the Arnon River to the south and the Yarmuk to the north, a distance of approximately 120 miles. Within it was a sub-district of Geshur (גְּשׁוּרִי, the *Geshshurites*; thus, the more likely Peshitta, followed by the Vulgate, rather than the MT הָאֲשׁוּרִי, the *Ashshurites*) in the north part of Gilead and the Valley of Jezreel, south and southwest of the Sea of Galilee. Mahanaim was on the River Jabbok, approximately 15 miles west of the Arabah (Jordan) Valley.] Ish-Bosheth was murdered by Rekab and Baanah (the sons of Rimmon the Beerothite), who had been troop leaders under Saul (**2 Samuel 4:2, 5–7**). Rekab and Baanah brought Ish-Bosheth's head to David, thinking that he would be pleased they had killed the rival to the Davidic throne, but instead, David was angry at the men's presumption and had them executed (**2 Samuel 4:8–12**). Ish-Bosheth's head was subsequently buried in Abner's tomb at Hebron (**2 Samuel 4:12**).

14. Abinadab (**1 Samuel 31:2; 1 Chronicles 8:33; 9:39; 10:2**) is also called Ishvi (**1 Samuel 14:49**). He and his brothers, Jonathan and Malki-Shua, were among those killed at Mount Gilboa (**1 Samuel 31:1–6**). Abinadab son of Saul should not be confused with Abinadab the father of Eleazar, Uzzah, and Ahio who resided in Kiriath Jearim (cf. **1 Samuel 7:1–2; 2 Samuel 6:1–8**); for the latter Abinadab, see chart "**1 Samuel** 7: The Family of Abinadab Who Oversaw the Ark of the Covenant."

15. Jonathan, the eldest son of Saul, became a close friend of David and supported him in his rise to become his father Saul's successor. Jonathan and David formed a covenant (**1 Samuel 18:1–4; 20:8, 16–17, 41–42; 23:16–18**) in which Jonathan promised that his covenant kindness to David would extend "between you and me, and between your descendants and my descendants forever" (**1 Samuel 20:42**). Tragically, Jonathan died in battle with his father Saul and his two brothers, Abinadab/Ishvi and Malki-Shua, when Israel fought against the Philistines at Mount Gilboa (**1 Samuel 31:2, 6**). Initially, their bodies were hung on the wall of Beth Shan, but they were later retrieved and brought to Jabesh Gilead (**1 Samuel 31:11–13**). After being convicted by the actions of Rizpah (cf. **2 Samuel 21:8–11**), David buried the bones of Jonathan and Saul at Zela/Zelah of Benjamin in the tomb of Kish, Jonathan's grandfather (**Joshua 18:28; 2 Samuel 21:12–14**). When David came to the throne of Israel, he wished to honor the covenant he had made with Jonathan by showing kindness to Jonathan's descendants (**2 Samuel 9:1**). David brought Jonathan's son Mephibosheth, who was a disabled young man (cf. **2 Samuel 4:4**), to the palace and had him eat regularly at the king's table and restored to him the land of Saul (cf. **2 Samuel 9:4–13**). The expanded genealogy of Jonathan's descendants shows that David honored his covenant with Jonathan. The descendants of Jonathan appear to be among the Benjamites of **1 Chronicles 9:3** who returned from exile and lived in the newly restored Jerusalem; see chart "**1 Chronicles 8 & 9**: The Descendants of King Saul Living in Gibeon and Jerusalem (Post-Exile)."

16. Malki-Shua and his brothers, Abinadab and Jonathan, were killed by the Philistines in the battle at Mount Gilboa (**1 Samuel 31:1–6; 1 Chronicles 10:2**).

17. Merab was the eldest daughter of Saul (**1 Samuel 14:49, 18:17**). She was initially promised in marriage to David, but at the last moment, Saul changed his mind and gave Merab to Adriel the "Meholathite" (an inhabitant of Abel Meholah in Gilead; **1 Samuel 18:18–19**). Unfortunately, five sons of Merab and Adriel, along with two sons of Saul's concubine Rizpah, were put to death by King David to avenge the wrongful death of the Gibeonites (a remnant Amorite people) whom "Saul and his blood-stained house" (**2 Samuel 21:1**) had tried to annihilate and dispossess from the land—an action which violated the covenantal peace treaty between the Israelites and the Gibeonites that had been in place since the days of Joshua (cf. **Joshua 9:3–4, 15–21; 2 Samuel 21:8–9**).

18. Adriel, meaning "God is my help," was the son of a man named Barzillai the Meholathite (**2 Samuel 21:8**); the latter appears to be a different person than Barzillai the Gileadite from Rogelim (see chart "**2 Samuel 17**: Barzillai the Gileadite"). Adriel was an inhabitant of the town of Abel Meholah, which was the hometown of Elisha the prophet (**1 Kings 19:16**). Abel Meholah was near Tabbath (**Judges 7:22**) and located on the west bank of the Jordan River and the southernmost point in the Beth Shan Valley; Anson F. Rainey and R. Steven Notley, *The Carta Bible Atlas*, 5th ed. (Jerusalem: Carta, 2011), 769.

19. Michal the younger daughter of Saul (**1 Samuel 14:49**) loved David, and Saul promised her in marriage to him for the price of 100 dead Philistines (**1 Samuel 18:20–29**). Nevertheless, as Saul became more afraid of David, he sought to arrange David's death; on one such occasion, Michal helped David escape (**1 Samuel 19:11–17**). As David took more wives for himself, Saul gave Michal (then David's wife) to a Benjamite named Palti, the son of Laish from Gallim (**1 Samuel 25:44**). At Saul's death, and as part of a covenant between Abner (Saul's general) and David, Michal was returned to David, much to Palti's regret (**2 Samuel 3:14–16**). Their marriage was unstable; when David brought the ark of the covenant to Jerusalem and danced in the streets, "she [Michal] despised him in her heart" for being an undignified king (**2 Samuel 6:16; 20–21**). For her sarcasm and disrespect of David, and perhaps also her lack of humility before Yahweh, she never bore children to David (**2 Samuel 6:23**).

20. Mephibosheth in **2 Samuel 4:4; 9:6, 8, 10–13; 16:1, 4; 19:24–25, 30; 21:7–8** is called Merib-Baal in **1 Chronicles 8:34; 9:40**. Mephibosheth the son of Jonathan appears to be named after Mephibosheth the son of Rizpah, one of the seven Saulide descendants put to death to atone for the wrongful deaths of the Gibeonites (see **2 Samuel 21:1–14**). Mephibosheth the son of Jonathan was lame in both his feet—"He [Mephibosheth] was five years old when the news about [the deaths of] Saul and Jonathan came from Jezreel. His nurse picked him up and fled, but as she hurried to leave, he fell and became disabled [lame in both feet]" (**2 Samuel 4:4**). After Jonathan's death, King David wanted to fulfill his promise to show kindness to Jonathan's descendants (**1 Samuel 20:12–15; 2 Samuel 9:1, 3, 7**). David sought out a *remnant* of Jonathan's family and found the lame Mephibosheth in the house of Makir son of Ammiel in Lo Debar, one of the men who had shown kindness to David when David fled from Absalom (**2 Samuel 9:4; 17:27**; cf. **19:24–28**). David invited Mephibosheth and his son Mika to live at the king's palace and to eat "at David's table like one of the king's sons" (**2 Samuel 9:11**). David also restored Saul's land to Mephibosheth, provided servants to work the land, and provided for Mephibosheth for the rest of his life (**2 Samuel 9:1–13**).

21. Mika in **2 Samuel 9:12** is Micah in **1 Chronicles 8:34–35** and **9:40–41**.

22. For a discussion of later generations in Saul's family, see chart "**1 Chronicles 8 & 9**: The Descendants of King Saul Living in Gibeon and Jerusalem (Post-Exile)."

23. Abiel/Jeiel—"the father of Gibeon" (**1 Chronicles 8:29; 9:35**)—likely means that he was a civic leader or military leader who lived in Gibeon.

24. The Hebrew text of **1 Samuel 13:1** reads literally, "Saul was a year at the beginning of his reign and he ruled for two years." Most likely, Saul was thirty years old at his inauguration and his tenure lasted forty years, as **Acts 13:21** proposes, and the *two years* at the end of the text probably refers to the two-year reign of Saul's son Ish-Bosheth (**2 Samuel 2:10**). Thus, the *Saulide dynasty* consisted of Saul's forty years (ca. 1051–1011 B.C.) and Ish-Bosheth's two years (1005–1004 B.C.), for a total of forty-two years as in **1 Samuel 13:1** (NIV). Ish-Bosheth reigned from Mahanaim, east of the Jordan, while David was king over Judah from his capital in Hebron (**2 Samuel 2:8–11**). In this way, the two-year reign of Ish-Bosheth was *concurrent* with the last two of the seven and one-half years that David reigned from Hebron (cf. **2 Samuel 2:10–11**). David was 30 when he became king, and he reigned for a total of 40 ½ years (ca. 1011–971 B.C.): 7 ½ years from his capital at Hebron (ca. 1011–1004 B.C.) and 33 years over Israel and Judah from his capital at Jerusalem (ca. 1004–971 B.C.) (**2 Samuel 5:4–5**).

25. The very names of Saul's sons are indicative of his proclivity toward Baalism, which had been a problem of Israel's for centuries. As for Ish-bosheth, it means "shameful man," likely a nickname for Ish-Baal, meaning "man of Baal." The Chronicler calls him Esh-Baal, "fire of Baal," still another attempt to disguise him—the fire being an oblique reference to Baal's role as the deity of lightning and storm.

26. A cluster of sites with similar names adds confusion to the Benjamite genealogy and narratives. The towns of Geba, Gibeah, and Gibeon are all located within ten miles of Jerusalem. They share in common the root גבע, meaning "hill," "height," and the like. Geba means simply "hill," in this case, approximately 677 meters above sea level and 5.5 miles north of Jerusalem; Gibeah was a famous place of worship just three miles north; and Gibeon was about seven miles northwest. Geba was well known as a Philistine outpost that King Asa of Judah refortified against the northern kingdom of Israel (**1 Samuel 13:3; 1 Kings 15:22**).

1 SAMUEL 14: THE MILITARY LEADERS UNDER SAUL, DAVID, ABSALOM, AND SOLOMON

Approximate Dating: united monarchy, ca. 1051–931 B.C. ***Relevant Scriptures:*** **1 Samuel 14:50–51**; also **1 Samuel 9:1; 26:5–6, 14; 2 Samuel 2:8–32; 3:3, 25–30; 8:16, 18; 10:9–10, 14; 14:1; 16:9; 17:25; 19:13, 21; 20:7–10, 23; 21:17; 23:18, 20–24, 37; 24:2; 1 Kings 1:7–8, 19, 26, 32, 36, 38; 2:5, 25, 32, 34; 4:4; 1 Chronicles 2:16–17; 3:2; 11:20, 22, 26; 18:15, 17; 19:10–11, 15; 26:28; 27:5, 24, 34**

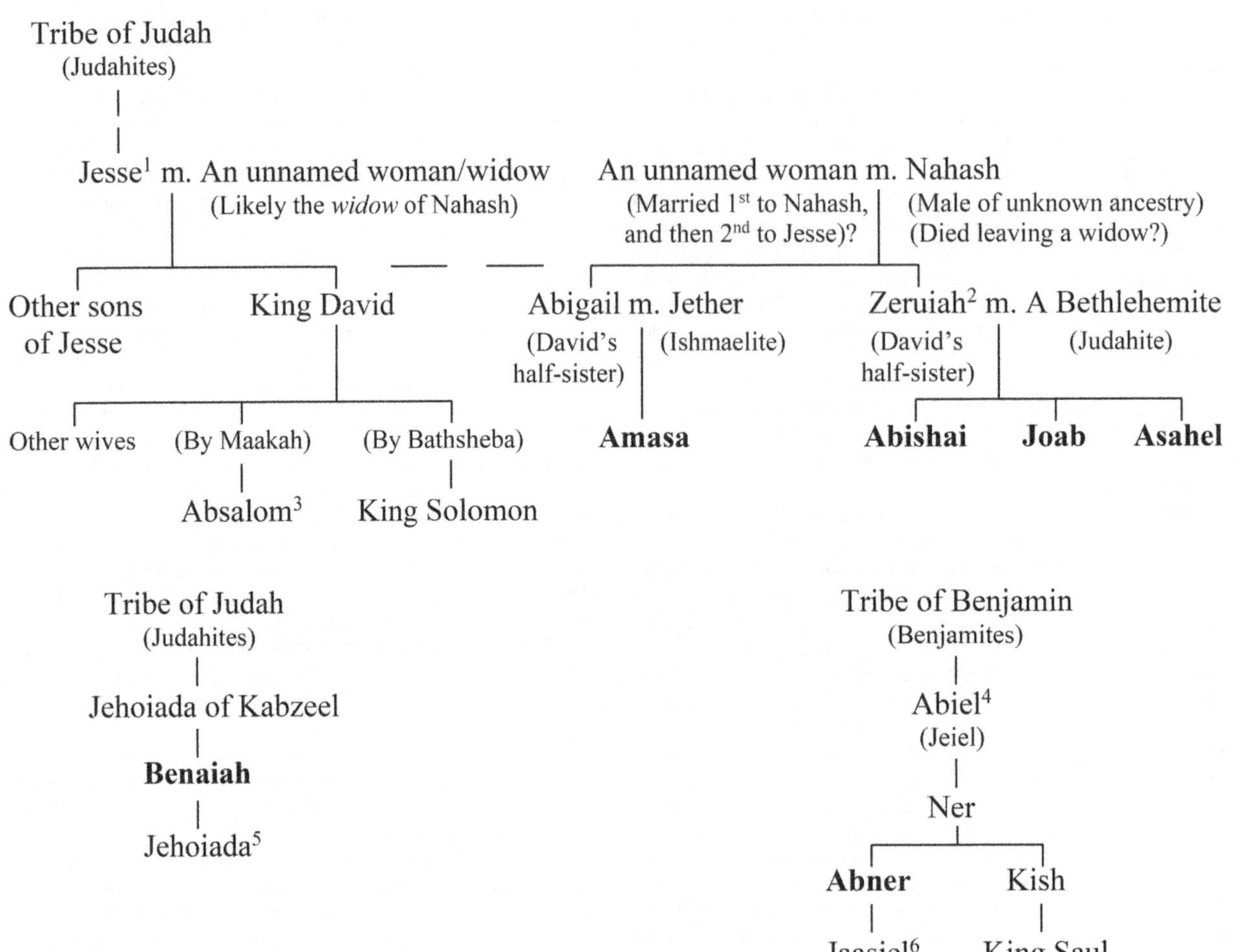

Biblical and Theological Significance

The military leaders during the reigns of Saul, David, and Solomon—with one exception—were drawn from the families of these kings. With the exception of Benaiah the Judahite, who was unconnected to any of the kings, nepotism seemed to have influenced the appointment of Israel's military leaders in the united monarchy era.

David's Family—His Nephews: Joab, Amasa, Abishai, and Asahel

One would not be surprised if some of David's own offspring held military offices of high rank, but the surprise is that virtually none did as far as the record is concerned.[7] David's principal military assets were from the families of David's half-sisters, Abigail and Zeruiah. Abigail was the daughter of Nahash and an unnamed mother who was also the mother of David, and thus, Abigail was the maternal half-sister of David and his brothers (**2 Samuel 17:25**). Zeruiah was either a full- or half-sister to Abigail (**2 Samuel 17:25; 1 Chronicles 2:16**).[8] During his reign, David described his military nephews—"These sons of Zeruiah"—as "too strong [harsh] for me" and "evildoer[s]" (**2 Samuel 3:39**), meaning they were violent, impulsive, uncontrollable, and therefore could not fully be trusted by David.

Joab led the attack on the fortress of Jebus (Jerusalem; **1 Chronicles 11:4–8**) and became the "commander of the royal army" during most of David's reign (**2 Samuel 8:16; 20:23; 1 Chronicles 27:34**). However, many times, Joab's military prowess was untempered by his ruthless zeal. After Saul died, David began to negotiate with Abner (Saul's military commander), but because Joab's brother (Asahel) had been killed by Abner, Joab deceived Abner and then slew him. During war with the Ammonites, Joab carried out David's plot to kill Uriah, the husband of Bathsheba (**2 Samuel 11:6–26**). Joab also helped reconcile Absalom and David (**2 Samuel 14:1–33**), but later, against David's explicit orders, "took three javelins in his hand and plunged them into Absalom's heart while Absalom was still alive in the oak tree" (**2 Samuel 18:4–14**). Joab subdued the revolt of Sheba son of Bikri against David (**2 Samuel 20:1–22**) and assassinated Abner and Amasa, while pretending to be their confidantes (**2 Samuel 3:26–30; 20:9–10**). Because Joab shed "blood in peacetime as if in battle" and "stained the belt around his waist and the sandals on his feet" (**1 Kings 2:5**), David pronounced a curse on Joab and his descendants (**1 Kings 2:6**). When David was on his deathbed, Joab supported Adonijah's claim to the throne over Solomon's (**1 Kings 1:7, 9, 18–19, 25**). Before he died, David instructed Solomon to avenge the murders of Amasa and Abner by killing Joab (**1 Kings 2:5–6**). Even though Joab fled to the tabernacle to claim sanctuary, Solomon ordered Benaiah son of Jehoiada of Kabzeel to kill him (**1 Kings 2:28–34**). Joab was buried at his home out in the country. Solomon then appointed Benaiah as Joab's replacement and the new commander of his army (**1 Kings 2:34–35**).

Amasa, son of David's half-sister Abigail and Jether the Ishmaelite, was the commander of Absalom's rebel army after Absalom rebelled against his father David (**2 Samuel 17:25; 1 Kings 2:5; 1 Chronicles 2:17**). After Absalom's defeat and death at the hand of Joab, David appointed Amasa (his "own flesh and blood") as the commander over his new army "for life" in place of Joab (**2 Samuel 19:13**). Eventually, Joab murdered Amasa his cousin by stabbing him to death (**2 Samuel 20:9–10**).

Abishai, David's nephew, was with David when David spared Saul (**1 Samuel 26:7–11**) and became a chief captain in David's military (**2 Samuel 23:18**). Abishai was with Joab when Joab pursued Saul's commander Abner (**2 Samuel 2:24**); together, Abishai and Joab were responsible for killing Abner (**2 Samuel 3:27–30**). Abishai commanded troops against Ammon (**2 Samuel 10**). He sought to kill Shimei for cursing David, although the king restrained him (**2 Samuel 16:5–13; 19:21**). Abishai led a third of David's troops against Absalom and his rebellion (**2 Samuel 18**). Abishai was famous for killing Ishbi-Benob, the Philistine giant who threatened David (**2 Samuel 21:15–17**).[9] Abishai was a mighty captain, famed for killing eighteen thousand Edomites (**1 Chronicles 18:12**). He was the "chief of the Three" and "held in greater honor than the Three" in David's army (**2 Samuel 23:18–19**).[10] Abishai does not appear in the struggle of Adonijah against Solomon, in which Joab was the leader (cf. **1 Kings 1:7**), so Abishai may have died before that time.[11]

Asahel, David's nephew, fought in David's army and was known as a swift runner who ran "as fleet-footed as a wild gazelle" (**2 Samuel 2:18; 23:24**). Asahel was killed at the hands of Abner (Saul's commander) in the battle at Gibeon (**2 Samuel 2:23**); in turn, Asahel's brothers, Joab and Abishai, murdered Abner because of his foul deed (**2 Samuel 3:27–30**).

Saul's Family—Abner

Abner, Saul's uncle, was the commander-in-chief of Saul's army (**1 Samuel 14:50; 17:55; 20:25; 26:5**). After Saul's death, Abner supported the accession of Saul's son Ish-Bosheth to the kingship of Israel instead of David (**2 Samuel 2:8**). However, when Ish-Bosheth accused Abner of treason for taking Saul's concubine Rizpah in sexual relations (**2 Samuel 3:7–8**), Abner denied the claim (though the accusation may have been a well-founded suspicion; see **2 Samuel 3:6**). In response, Abner transferred his loyalty to David. Joab (David's nephew and military general) strongly disapproved of Abner's presence because Abner had killed his (Joab's) brother Asahel (**2 Samuel 2:20–23**). In retaliation, Joab ruthlessly murdered Abner (**2 Samuel 3:22–30**).

Benaiah the Judahite

Benaiah, the son of Jehoiada,[12] first served in David's army and later became Solomon's chief military officer. Benaiah was from Kabzeel, a Judean town in the Negev (**Joshua 15:21; 2 Samuel 23:20**; cf. **1 Chronicles 11:22, 24**). He was among David's mighty warriors, "held in greater honor than any of the Thirty," although he was not included among the chief "Three" elite leaders (**2 Samuel 23:20–23; 1 Chronicles 11:22–25**). Benaiah had "performed great exploits" (**2 Samuel 23:20–21; 1 Chronicles 11:22–23**) and became the head of King David's bodyguards, known as the Kerethites—probably the same as the *Carites* in **2 Kings 11:4, 19**—and the Pelethites (**2 Samuel 8:18; 20:23; 1 Kings 1:38, 44; 1 Chronicles 18:17**). Benaiah wisely supported Solomon's accession to the Davidic throne instead of Adonijah (**1 Kings 1:36–38**). When Solomon came to the throne, he ordered Benaiah to: (1) execute Joab (David's army commander) for killing Abner and Amasa (**2:29–34**); (2) kill Shimei the Benjamite who had cursed David (**1 Kings 2:8–9, 46**); and (3) kill Adonijah who had vied for the throne (**1 Kings 2:25**). Benaiah became the commander-in-chief of Solomon's army (**1 Kings 2:35; 4:4**).

Notes

1. For a discussion of the parentage of David, see charts "**1 Chronicles 2**: King David" and Excursus A that analyzes the David–Shealitel–Zerubbabel–Joseph–Jesus lineage in chart "**1 Chronicles 3**: Zerubbabel and Shealtiel and the Double Line of the Messiah through King David's Sons, Nathan and Solomon."

2. Zeruiah appears to be the *full sister* of Abigail the daughter of Nahash and the *half-sister* of David (**2 Samuel 17:25; 1 Chronicles 2:16**). Zeruiah married an unnamed man from Bethlehem as shown by the verse in **2 Samuel 2:32** where Zeruiah's son Asahel, upon his death, was buried "in his father's tomb at Bethlehem." For more information on Nahash and David's (unnamed) mother, see chart "**1 Chronicles 2**: King David" and Excursus A in chart "**1 Chronicles 3**: Zerubbabel and Shealtiel and the Double Line of the Messiah through King David's Sons, Nathan and Solomon."

3. Absalom's mother was Maakah, the daughter of Talmai king of Geshur, whom David had subjugated in an early battle (**2 Samuel 3:3**).

4. Abiel (**1 Samuel 9:1; 14:51**) is Jeiel. Abiel/Jeiel was the "father [founder] of Gibeon" (**1 Chronicles 8:29, 9:35**). For Saul's ancestry, see chart "**1 Samuel 9**: King Saul."

5. Jehoiada the son of Benaiah became King David's personal counselor after David's former counselor, Ahithophel the Gilonite, committed suicide (**1 Chronicles 27:33–34**; cf. **2 Samuel 15:12; 17:23**). Jehoiada son of Benaiah appears to be named after his grandfather, Jehoiada, a case of papponymy.

6. Jaasiel the son of Abner was the leader of the tribe of Benjamin in charge of the census of his tribe (Benjamin) when David attempted to number the people (**1 Chronicles 27:21**).

7. David's sons served in a priestly–personal advisor role (see chart "**2 Samuel 8 and 20**: The Chief Officials in King David's Administration").

8. For the significance of Nahash and David's half-sister(s) in the line of the Messiah, see Excursus A in chart "**1 Chronicles 3**: Zerubbabel and

Shealtiel and the Double Line of the Messiah through King David's Sons, Nathan and Solomon."

9. See chart "**Deuteronomy 1**: The Giant Anakites, including Goliath and His Descendants."

10. See chart "**1 Chronicles 11**: Genealogical Registry of the Mighty Warriors in King David's Army."

11. Edward Mack, "Abishai," *ISBE*.

12. Benaiah the son of Jehoiada (**2 Samuel 8:18; 20:23; 23:20–22; 1 Kings 1:8, 10, 26, 32, 36, 38, 44; 2:29–31, 34–35, 46; 4:4; 1 Chronicles 11:22–25; 18:17; 27:5–6**) was a key military leader under King David. The reference to Benaiah as the "son of Jehoiada *the priest*" in **1 Chronicles 27:5** is probably a gloss for the following reasons: (1) Benaiah was a Judahite and was *not* of priestly/Levitical lineage; (2) the Levitical Kohathite named Jehoiada (in the Levi–Kohathite–Korahite–Elkanah–Berekiah–Jehoiada–Zechariah lineage) was the priest who led the coup against Queen Athaliah (see chart "**2 Chronicles 22**: Probable Genealogy for Jehoiada the Priest, who Masterminded the Overthrow of Queen Athaliah of Judah"); (3) Benaiah was from Kabzeel—and Kabzeel was *not* a Levitical city (**2 Samuel 23:20; 1 Chronicles 11:22;** cf. **Joshua 15:21; 21:1–42**); and (4) chronologically, Benaiah was a contemporary of Saul, David, Absalom, and Solomon (i.e., ca. 1051–931 B.C.) and therefore *not* connected with Jehoiada the Kohathite priest of 841–835 B.C. A gloss at **1 Chronicles 27:5** has been suggested by other scholars as well. See Edward L. Curtis and Albert A. Madsen, eds. *A Critical and Exegetical Commentary on the Books of Chronicles* (Edinburgh: T&T Clark, 1910, 1952), notes on 1 Chronicles 27:5, p. 290.

1 SAMUEL 15: AGAG, KING OF THE AMALEKITES

Approximate Dating: from the time of Abraham, ca. 2166–1991 B.C. to 1015 B.C.[1] ***Relevant Scriptures:*** **1 Samuel 15:8–9, 20, 32–33;** also **Genesis 26:34; 36:1–14; 1 Chronicles 1:34–37**

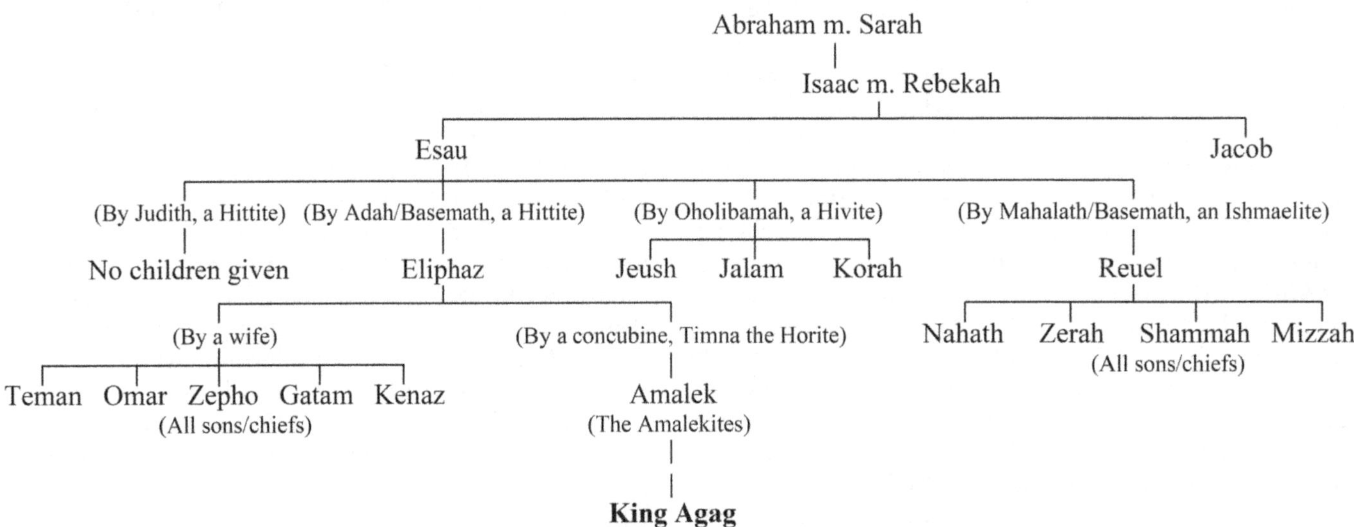

Biblical and Theological Significance

The Lord swore holy war[2] on the Amalekites—"I [the Lord] will completely blot out the name of Amalek from under heaven. . . . the Lord will be at war against the Amalekites from generation to generation" (**Exodus 17:14, 16**). Before the Israelites entered Canaan, Moses had instructed them: "Remember what the Amalekites did to you along the way when you came out of Egypt. When you were weary and worn out, they met you on your journey and attacked all who were lagging behind; they had no fear of God. When the Lord your God gives you rest from all the enemies around you in the land he is giving you to possess as an inheritance, you shall blot out the name of Amalek from under heaven. Do not forget!" (**Deuteronomy 25:17–19**). Through Samuel, the Lord told King Saul to "attack the Amalekites and totally destroy all that belongs to them. Do not spare them; put to death men and women, children and infants, cattle and sheep, camels and donkeys" (**1 Samuel 15:3**). However, contrary to the Lord's command, King Saul spared King Agag and the best of the livestock (**1 Samuel 15:9**). For Saul's overt disobedience, the Lord rejected him as the king of Israel and the kingdom was given to David (**1 Samuel 15:26; 16:1, 11–13; 28:17–18**).

Notes

1. This is a "loose" or "open" genealogy whose purpose was not to include all generations but only those that show linkage between one important personage or event of one period with a later one. This is clear from the fact that Abraham died in ca. 1991 B.C. and Agag was slain by Samuel before his death in ca. 1015 B.C., a span of about 976 years.

2. The technical term for so-called holy war is חֵרֶם (*herem*), roughly equivalent in base meaning as the Arabic *jihad*. In the Bible it refers to conflict originated by God, led by God, and successfully completed by God. The verb form *heharim* means to set something apart (for God), whether (1) living (such as a living animal that is sacrificed); (2) physical or material, such as a building for destruction or precious metals for decoration; or (3) dead, the annihilation of a person or persons who have irremediably sinned against God (as here with the Amalekites).

1 SAMUEL 16: JESSE AND THE JUDAHITES WHO LIVED IN BETHLEHEM AND NEARBY CITIES[1]

Approximate Dating: late period of the judges[2] through the united monarchy under David. ***Relevant Scriptures:*** **1 Samuel 16:1–22; 17:12–14, 25;** also **2 Samuel 2:18; 17:25; Ruth 1:1–5; 2:1–3, 19, 22; 3:16; 4:10, 13–22; 1 Chronicles 2:4–5, 9–19, 50–54; 4:1–4; Matthew 1:3–6; Luke 3:31–33**

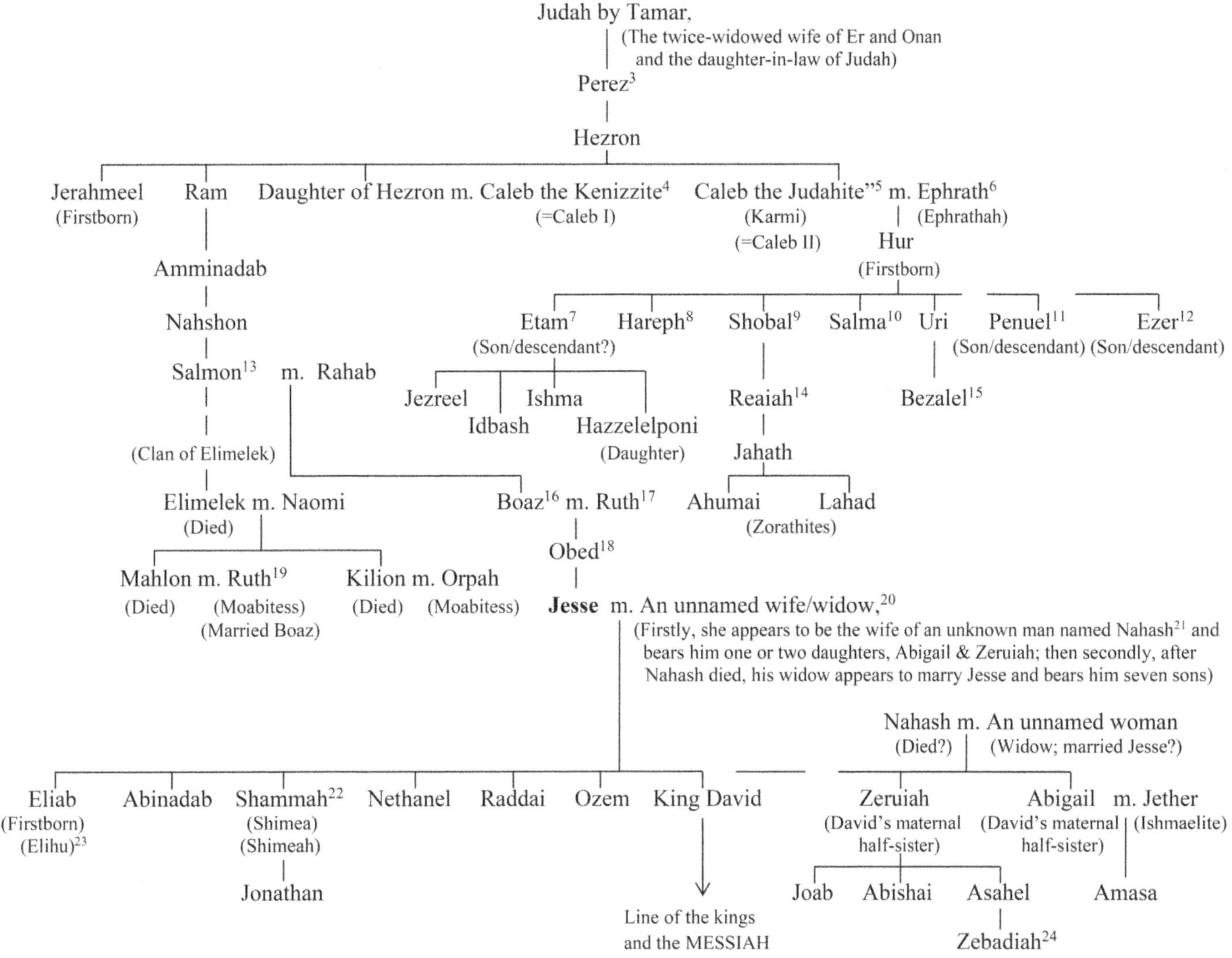

Biblical and Theological Significance

The lineage of Jesse and David is a testament to the grace and providence of God. Two Gentile women were folded into the tribe of Judah because of their faith in God and their eventual marriages to Judahites. The first was Rahab, a secular prostitute of Jericho, who believed in Israel's God and demonstrated her faith by hiding two Israelite spies on her roof when they came to reconnoiter Canaan (**Joshua 2:1–7, 11**). Because she tied a "scarlet cord in the window" (**Joshua 2:18**), she and her household were spared when the Israelite invasion forces attacked Jericho (**Joshua 2:1–21; 6:17, 23–25; Hebrews 11:31; James 2:25**). Sometime thereafter, Rahab married Salmon (probably one of the two spies) of the tribe of Judah, who in time become David's great-great-grandfather (**Ruth 4:21**), and Rahab became an ancestress of the Messiah (**Matthew 1:5**). The second woman was Ruth the Moabitess. Boaz, the son of Salmon and Rahab, was "a man of standing from the clan of Elimelek [Naomi's husband]" (**Ruth 2:1**; cf. **Ruth 1:3; 2:3**). Boaz lived in Bethlehem at the time of Naomi and Ruth's return from Moab (**Ruth 1:22**). By then, Ruth was the widowed wife of Mahlon, the son of Elimelek and Naomi (**Ruth 1:2, 5; 4:10**). Ruth married Boaz and they became David's great-grandparents. Their son Obed was Jesse's father, and Jesse sired David, "the youngest" of Jesse's sons (**1 Samuel 16:11**). The Lord was with David, and he became God's choice to replace King Saul (**1 Samuel 16:13**).

Zeruiah and Abigail are called the "sisters" of Jesse's seven sons (**1 Chronicles 2:16**). However, Abigail (and probably Zeruiah also; cf. **2 Samuel 17:25**) appear to be *half-sisters* to them because their father was a certain Nahash whose further identity is nowhere disclosed. Abigail was the mother of Amasa, and Zeruiah was the mother of Joab, Abishai, and Asahel, all of whom were military men under David.[25]

This genealogy makes the vital connection between Judah and David, between the Abrahamic covenant and the Davidic, between the patriarchal era and the monarchic, and between a messianic people and a messianic kingdom under a messianic prototype, King David. The ancient promise of the "offspring" (seed) of Eve that would crush the head of the serpent (**Genesis 3:15**)—later promised to Abraham and Sarah (**Genesis 12:1–3; 15:1–16; 17:1–16**) and then to Jacob (**Genesis 27:27–29; 28:2–5**)—was "tribalized" in the blessings of both Jacob and Moses, pinpointing the transmission of the seed through one tribe, namely, Judah (**Genesis 49:8–12; Deuteronomy 33:7**). From that tribe came the long-awaited king who would prefigure his greater *son*, Jesus Christ, Son of God, and Lord of lords. This king was the young David, whom Samuel anointed after hearing these words from heaven: "Rise and anoint him [David]; this is the one" (**1 Samuel 16:12**). Even earlier, when Saul had disobeyed the prophetic injunction and offered an unlawful sacrifice, Yahweh told the rejected king, "But now your kingdom will not endure; the Lord has sought out a man after his own heart [David][26] and appointed him ruler of his people" (**1 Samuel 13:14**).

This genealogy, with all its complexities and secondary threads, is most concerned with connecting the ancestors in the line of Judah to King David—a line that points forward for a millennium more to Bethlehem of Judea, where a *second David*, called Jesus, redeemed the world from its sin and thus laid the foundation of the final monarchy, the kingdom of God.[27]

Notes

1. Compare the genealogy in this chart to the larger segmented genealogy in "**1 Chronicles 4**: Judah."

2. As to the dating, see Eugene H. Merrill, *Kingdom of Priests: A History of Old Testament Israel* (Grand Rapids: Baker, 1996), 182, n. 97; also see note 1 in chart "**Ruth 4**: Boaz, Elimelek, and Naomi and the Descendants of Boaz the Judahite and Ruth the Moabitess."

3. Perez was the twin of Zerah (**1 Chronicles 2:4, 6**).

4. Caleb the Kenizzite, the son of Jephunneh, married into the tribe of Judah by taking as his wife an unnamed daughter of Hezron, the son of Perez, the son of Judah. The text in **1 Chronicles 2:42** can be confusing because Jerahmeel had both a *brother* named Caleb (also called Karmi) who was Judahite (designated Caleb II in some charts) and a *brother-in-law* named Caleb who was a Kenizzite (designated Caleb I in some charts). The descendants of Caleb the Kenizzite are specifically addressed in **1 Chronicles 2:42–49** because one of his descendants is his daughter named Aksah (**1 Chronicles 2:49**), and she is clearly identified elsewhere as the daughter of Caleb the Kenizzite (cf. **Joshua 15:13–19; Judges 1:12–15**). See chart "**1 Chronicles 2**: Caleb and Kenaz, the Sons of Jephunneh the Kenizzite."

5. "Caleb the Judahite" is called Caleb in **1 Chronicles 2:9, 18, 50** and Karmi in **1 Chronicles 4:1**; for clarification he is designated "Caleb II" in some charts. Caleb/Karmi (the son of Hezron, the son of Perez) from the tribe of Judah is a different person than: (1) Karmi the son of Zimri, the son of Zerah, from the tribe of Judah (**Joshua 7:1, 17–18; 1 Chronicles 2:7**); (2) Karmi from the tribe of Reuben (**Genesis 46:9; Exodus 6:14; Numbers 26:6; 1 Chronicles 2:7; 5:3**); and (3) Caleb the Kenizzite, the son of Jephunneh—designated Caleb I in some charts (**Numbers 13:6; 14:6, 30, 38; 26:65; 34:19; Deuteronomy 1:36; Joshua 14:6–14; 15:13; 21:12; 1 Chronicles 6:56**). See chart "**1 Chronicles 4**: Judah."

6. The wife of Caleb the Judahite is named Ephrath (**1 Chronicles 2:19**) and Ephrathah (**1 Chronicles 2:50**). Ephrath/Ephrathah is the matronymic ancestress of the "Ephrathites from Bethlehem"—including Jesse and David (**1 Samuel 17:12**) and Naomi and Elimelek (**Ruth 1:2**). Ephrath/Ephrathah is also the eponym for the ancient name for Bethlehem—variously termed "Ephrath," "Ephrathah," "Caleb Ephrathah," and "Bethlehem Ephrathah" (**Genesis 35:16, 19; 48:7; Ruth 4:11; 1 Chronicles 2:24; Psalm 132:6; Micah 5:2**).

7. The exact lineage of Etam is unclear, but his sons are listed within this clan in **1 Chronicles 4:3**. Etam is also a place name referring to a town in Judah (**2 Chronicles 11:6**).

8. Hareph was the founder of Beth Gader (**1 Chronicles 2:51**).

9. Shobal was the founder of Kiriath Jearim (**1 Chronicles 2:50, 52**), which is also called Baalah/Baalah of Judah (**Joshua 15:9; 1 Chronicles 13:6**) and Kiriath Baal (**Joshua 15:60; 18:14**). The descendants of Shobal are listed in **1 Chronicles 2:52–53**. For more information on Shobal, see chart "**1 Chronicles 4**: Judah."

10. Salma and his father, Hur, were the co-founders of Bethlehem (cf. **1 Chronicles 2:51, 54; 4:4**). The descendants of Salma are given in **1 Chronicles 2:54–55**. Salma the son of Hur should not be confused with his relative, Salmon the son of Nahshon (see note 13).

11. The exact lineage of Penuel is unclear. Penuel was the founder/father of Gedor (**1 Chronicles 4:4**). Jered is also mentioned as a founder/father of Gedor (**1 Chronicles 4:18**). Gedor was a town in the tribe of Judah (**Joshua 15:58**).

12. The exact lineage of Ezer is unclear. Ezer was the founder/father of Hushah (**1 Chronicles 4:4**). Sibbekai "the Hushathite," a soldier in David's army, was probably from Hushah and was renowned for killing Saph, a descendant of Rapha the giant (**2 Samuel 21:18; 23:27; 1 Chronicles 11:29**).

13. He is called Salmon (NIV) in **Ruth 4:20–21; 1 Chronicles 2:11; Matthew 1:4–5;** and **Luke 3:32**, although some translations refer to him as "Salma."

14. Reaiah (Heb. רְאָיָה) in **1 Chronicles 4:2** is possibly Haroeh (Heb. הָרֹאֶה) in **1 Chronicles 2:52**.

15. Bezalel was the chief artisan of the tabernacle of Moses (**Exodus 35:30–35; 36:1–2; 37:1; 38:22; 2 Chronicles 1:5**); see chart "**Exodus 31**: Bezalel, the Chief Artisan of the Tabernacle and Its Furnishings, and His Assistant, Oholiab."

16. See chart "**Ruth 1**: Boaz, Elimelek, and Naomi and the Descendants of Boaz the Judahite and Ruth the Moabitess."

17. Ruth the Moabitess was the widow of Mahlon, the son of Elimelek (**Ruth 1:2, 5; 4:10**). Ruth became the great-grandmother of King David (**Ruth 4:13–16**).

18. Obed appears to have at least two sons, Jesse and Jonathan—the latter is called "David's uncle" and is described as "a counselor, a man of insight and a scribe" (**1 Chronicles 27:32**).

19. See chart "**Ruth 1**: Boaz, Elimelek, and Naomi and the Descendants of Boaz the Judahite and Ruth the Moabitess."

20. The wife of Jesse who bore him seven (or eight?) sons (i.e., David and his brothers)—see note 23—is nowhere named in the Bible. Given that this is the heritage of Israel's most *famous* king (David), the omission is highly irregular and must be considered deliberate, perhaps suppressing David's "shameful" parentage and why David wrote these specific words in **Psalm 51:5**: "Surely I was sinful at birth, sinful from the time my mother conceived me." For an explanation of multiple instances of second marriages in the line of the Messiah, see Excursus A in chart "**1 Chronicles 3**: Zerubbabel and Shealtiel and the Double Line of the Messiah through King David's Sons, Nathan and Solomon."

21. Given the absence of more unambiguous, explicit wording, the indisputable identity of Nahash remains a matter complicated by the existence of four individuals bearing this name: (1) the father of Abigail and presumably Zeruiah as well (**2 Samuel 17:25**), as shown in the chart above; (2) the king of Ammon (**1 Samuel 11:1**, etc.); (3) the king of Ammon whose son was Hanun (**2 Samuel 10:1–5**, etc.); and (4) the father of Shobi (from Rabbah of the Ammonites), the latter having showed kindness to David when he was in need at Mahanaim (**2 Samuel 17:27**). Whether they are four separate persons is unclear.

22. He is variously called Shammah in **1 Samuel 16:9; 17:13**, Shimea in **1 Chronicles 2:13; 20:7** and Shimeah in **2 Samuel 13:3, 32; 21:21**. Shammah/Shimea/Shimeah was one of Jesse's sons and thus a brother of David. His son Jonathan fought with David against the Philistines and was renowned for killing a "huge man with six fingers on each hand and six toes on each foot—twenty-four in all. He also was descended from Rapha [the giant; ancestors of Goliath]" (**2 Samuel 21:20–21; 1 Chronicles 20:6–8**).

23. Eliab, the firstborn of Jesse (**1 Samuel 16:6; 17:13, 28; 1 Chronicles**

2:13; 2 Chronicles 11:18**), is identified as "Elihu, a brother of David" in **1 Chronicles 27:18**. The Chronicler calls him "Eliab his [Jesse's] firstborn" (**1 Chronicles 2:13**); Eliab and Elihu are clearly the same—one meaning "My God is a Father" and the other "He is my God." The issue is perhaps best resolved as a matter of text transmission, *'ab'* reading אב and *'hu'* reading הו. (Modern printed square script can hardly reveal the similarity compared to ancient, more flowing script.) **First Chronicles 2:13–15** identifies *seven* sons of Jesse, but for unknown reasons, the book of 1 Samuel declares that Jesse had "eight sons" (**1 Samuel 17:12**), only identifying the firstborn as "Eliab; the second, Abinadab; and the third, Shammah. David was the youngest" (**1 Samuel 17:13–14**). Abihail (Eliab's daughter) married her first cousin, Jerimoth (David's son), and together they had a daughter named Mahalath (**2 Chronicles 11:18–19**); see chart "**1 Kings 12**: Rehoboam, King of Judah." Eliab/Elihu is called "Eliah" in some translations (e.g., **2 Chronicles 11:18**, NKJV).

24. After his father Asahel was killed in the extended war between David and Saul (cf. **2 Samuel 2:18–32**), Zebadiah succeeded his father as the fourth of twelve commanders in David's army over 24,000 men (**1 Chronicles 27:7**). The name of the unit, "Asahel," was obviously assigned before Asahel's death. The writer has perhaps simply provided the information late in his discourse for reasons that the modern reader has no way of knowing. The *ISBE* notes that Asahel is mentioned "as the fourth of David's month-by-month captains (**1 Chronicles 27:7**). Superficial criticism describes this position as that of 'commander of a division of David's army,' and regards the statement, 'and Zebadiah his son after him,' as a note added to explain the otherwise incredible assertion of the text. This criticism is correct in its implication that the fourth captain was, as the text stands, the dead Asahel, in the person of his son Zebadiah. . . . The 24,000 men each month were not a fighting army mobilized for war. The position of general for a month, whatever else it may have involved, was an honor held by a distinguished veteran. There is no absurdity in the idea that the honor may in some cases have been posthumous, the deceased being represented by his father or his son or by someone else" (Willis J. Beecher, "Asahel," *ISBE*).

25. See chart "**1 Samuel 14**: The Military Leaders under King Saul, King David, Absalom, and King Solomon."

26. "A man according to my own heart" (i.e., "my own desire or wish"), the Hebrew expression כִּלְבָבוֹ אִישׁ (*ish kil'babo*), refers not to David's heart as being somehow worthy of God's choice but to the heart of God, that is, his capacity and exercise of making choices, in this case, choosing David.

27. See chart "**1 Chronicles 3**: Zerubbabel and Shealtiel and the Double Line of the Messiah through King David's Sons, Nathan and Solomon."

1 SAMUEL 25: NABAL AND ABIGAIL

Approximate Dating: early in the time of the judges into the time of the Davidic monarchy ***Relevant Scriptures:*** **1 Samuel 25:2–42**; also **Judges 1:12–14; 3:9, 11; 1 Samuel 27:3; 30:5; 2 Samuel 2:2; 3:3; 1 Chronicles 2:42–49; 3:1; 4:13–15, 19–20**

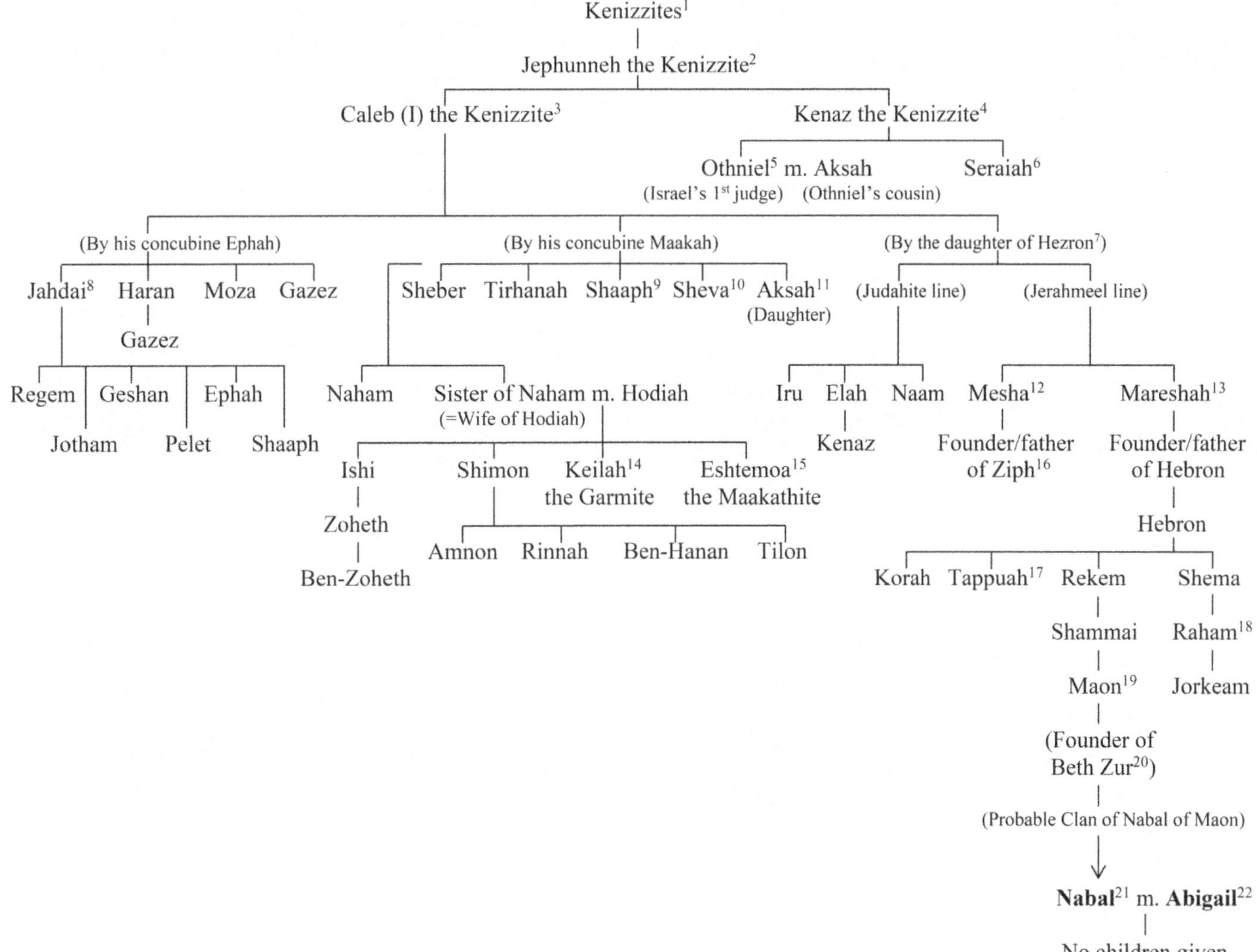

After Nabal's death, Abigail married David:

David m. **Abigail**
(Nabal's widow)

Kileab[23]
(Daniel)
(2nd son of King David)

Biblical and Theological Significance

Nabal and Abigail are important biblical characters in how their lives intertwined with that of King David. Nabal, truly a fool as his name suggests,[24] was not a worthy steward of the blessings the Lord had given him or a worthy husband of his beautiful wife, Abigail (**1 Samuel 25:3**). The backgrounds of Nabal and Abigail are important, not so much in themselves, as in the way they trace back to Caleb the Kenizzite—the honorable and great hero of the conquest (**Numbers 13:6; 14:30; Deuteronomy 1:36; Joshua 14:13**)—and why Nabal is called a "Calebite" (**1 Samuel 25:2–3**). More to the point, perhaps, are the adventures of David and Abigail (cf. **1 Samuel 27** and **30**).

Among the ways David procured his various wives, this one ranks nearly as high on the scale of under-handedness as his later and more notorious attainment of Bathsheba. The Abigail narrative is tempered somewhat, perhaps, by the fact that David, then not yet king but a fugitive from his arch-enemy Saul, had himself suffered a humiliating separation from his first wife, Michal, Saul's daughter. With Saul's madness driving him to kill David, David found himself separated from Michal and wandering about the Judean hill country with a large band of men. Quite accidentally, he happened upon Nabal, a fool wise enough to have married a beautiful and intelligent woman, Abigail. The shepherds of Nabal and David had interacted peacefully in the past (**1 Samuel 25:7**), so David requested sustenance for his beleaguered band from Nabal, a successful businessman and very wealthy landowner. When his delegation was met with Nabal's stubborn refusal, David threatened to plunder and kill his household. At a critical moment, Abigail intervened, successfully pleaded for her husband's life, and provided a feast for David and his six hundred men (**1 Samuel 25:13, 18–31**)! Acting as a quick responder, peacemaker, and a servant (*amah*), she averted a crisis. Abigail covered for her foolish husband, saved her entire household, and kept David from unwise bloodshed. As David explained to Abigail: "Praise be to the LORD, the God of Israel, who has sent you today to meet me. May you be blessed for your good judgment and for keeping me from bloodshed this day and from avenging myself with my own hands. . . . if you had not come quickly to meet me, not one male belonging to Nabal would have been left alive by daybreak" (**1 Samuel 25:32–34**). When she reported to Nabal how close a call he had brought upon his family, "his heart failed him and he became like a stone. About ten days later, the LORD struck Nabal and he died" (**1 Samuel 25:37–38**). The way was then clear for David's pursuit of Abigail as his own wife, and she married him (**1 Samuel 25:9–43**).

Because of Abigail's wise words and determined spirit, she liberated the heart of a man enflamed by thoughts of revenge and kept him from bloodguilt (cf. **1 Samuel 25:26, 31, 33**). Hers was the voice that advocated for choosing the divine qualities of mercy and grace when other, less noble options were convenient. This wealthy woman of Maon willingly exchanged her life of ease to become the humble maidservant/wife of David the fugitive trying to escape a jealous king (Saul). Her countenance, foresight, discretion, and legacy of peacemaking surely served her husband well during his reign as Israel's greatest king. She bore David one son, Kileab/Daniel.[25]

Notes

1. The Kenizzites were among the original occupants of the promised land (cf. **Genesis 15:19**).

2. See charts "**Joshua 14**: The Clan of Jephunneh the Kenizzite" and "**1 Chronicles 2**: Caleb and Kenaz, the Sons of Jephunneh the Kenizzite."

3. Caleb the son of Jephunneh the Kenizzite (non-Israelite) is mentioned in close association with the tribe of Judah (**1 Chronicles 2**) because Caleb the Kenizzite married the daughter of Hezron, thereby becoming the brother-in-law of Jerahmeel, Ram, and Caleb, the three sons of Hezron (**1 Chronicles 2:9**). Caleb the Kenizzite is not the same person as Caleb the Judahite, the son of Hezron, but they were relatives by marriage (as brothers-in-law, they shared the same name, Caleb.) The lineage of Caleb the Kenizzite is given in **1 Chronicles 2:42–49**, ending in his well-known daughter Aksah (**1 Chronicles 2:49**; cf. **Joshua 15:13–19; Judged 1:12–15**); this is opposed to the lineage of Caleb the son of Hezron, which is confined to **1 Chronicles 2:9, 18–20**. Noteworthy is that Caleb the Kenizzite represented the tribe of Judah as a spy in the promised land (**Numbers 13:6**) and was only one of two men who brought back a favorable report (**Numbers 14:6–8**). As a result, Caleb the Kenizzite and Joshua were the only persons of the exodus generation who lived through the forty years of the wilderness wanderings and entered Canaan (**Numbers 14:24, 30, 38; 26:65; Deuteronomy 1:35–38**). According to **Joshua 14:6–15**, Caleb the Kenizzite received as an inheritance the city of Hebron, formerly called Kiriath Arba (cf. **Genesis 23:2; 35:27; Joshua 11:21; 14:15; 15:13, 54; 20:7; 21:11; Judges 1:10**), located 19 miles south of Jerusalem, 15 miles west of the Dead Sea, and situated at the highest elevation of any town in Palestine. Hebron was one of the most important cities in biblical history, in part because it became the burial site of the patriarchs and matriarchs—Abraham, Sarah, Isaac, Rebekah, Jacob, and Leah (**Genesis 23:9, 17–19; 25:9; 49:30–31; 50:13**). See charts "**1 Chronicles 2**: Caleb and Kenaz, the Sons of Jephunneh the Kenizzite" and "**1 Chronicles 4**: Judah."

4. Kenaz the Kenizzite (**Joshua 15:17; Judges 1:13; 3:9, 11; 1 Chronicles 4:13**) is a different person than Kenaz the descendant of Esau (**Genesis 36:11, 15; 42; 1 Chronicles 1:36, 53**). See charts "**1 Chronicles 1**: Abraham's Descendants through Esau" and "**1 Chronicles 2**: Caleb and Kenaz, the Sons of Jephunneh the Kenizzite."

5. Othniel was the father of Hathath and Meonothai (the father and/or founder of Ophrah; **1 Chronicles 4:13–14**). See chart "**Judges 3**: Othniel (Kenizzite), the First Judge of Israel."

6. Seraiah was the father of Joab, the father/founder of Ge Harashim (**1 Chronicles 4:13–14**).

7. The "daughter of Hezron" (Judahite) was the sister of Jerahmeel, the firstborn son of Hezron; her name is never given (**1 Chronicles 2:9, 25, 42**). The existence of the "daughter of Hezron" is known because "Caleb [the Kenizzite] [was the], brother [the brother-in-law] of Jerahmeel" (**1 Chronicles 2:42**) and Jerahmeel was the son of Hezron (**1 Chronicles 2:9, 25**). For more information, see chart "**1 Chronicles 2**: Caleb and Kenaz, the Sons of Jephunneh the Kenizzite."

8. The text is unclear, but Jahdai is probably the son of Caleb and Ephah because the name of one of Jahdai's sons is Ephah, who was probably named after his grandmother (cf. **1 Chronicles 2:46–47**).

9. Caleb's son Shaaph was the founder/father of Madmannah, a city in the tribe of Judah (**Joshua 15:31; 1 Chronicles 2:49**).

10. Caleb's son Sheva was the founder/father of Gibea and Makbenah (**1 Chronicles 2:49**).

11. Caleb's daughter Aksah married her cousin Othniel, the first judge of Israel (**Judges 1:12–13; 3:7–11**).

12. Mesha was the firstborn son of Caleb I (**1 Chronicles 2:42**).

13. Mareshah was the father and/or founder of Hebron (**1 Chronicles 2:42**). Mareshah is also a place name for a town in the western foothills of the tribe of Judah, 25 miles southwest of Jerusalem (**Joshua 15:44**).

14. Naham's sister's son "the Garmite" was probably the founder/father of Keilah, a town in the western foothills of the tribe of Judah (**Joshua 15:44; 1 Chronicles 4:19**).

15. Naham's sister's son "the Maakathite" may have been the founder/father of Eshtemoa (**1 Chronicles 4:19**), probably the same place as Eshtemoh in the hill country of Judah, 10 miles south of Hebron (**Joshua 15:50**). Eshtemoa was one of the thirteen Levitical cities given to the descendants of Aaron the high priest (**Joshua 21:14; 1 Chronicles 6:57**). In **1 Chronicles 4:17**, Eshtemoa is associated with the descendants of the clan of Caleb the Kenizzite. See chart "**1 Chronicles 2**: Caleb and Kenaz, the Sons of Jephunneh the Kenizzite."

16. Ziph appears to be both a personal name and a place name, the latter corresponding to a town 60 miles due south of Jerusalem, mentioned as one of "the southernmost towns of the tribe of Judah in the Negev toward the boundary of Edom" (**Joshua 15:21, 24**). Another town named Ziph, 22 miles south of Jerusalem, is said to be one of the ten towns in the hill country of Judah (near Maon, Carmel, Juttah, Jezreel, Jokdeam, and Zanoah; **Joshua 15:55–56**). The latter Ziph appears to be most closely associated with the clan of Caleb the Kenizzzite. The text of **1 Chronicles 4:16,** "the sons of Jehallelel: Ziph, Ziphah, Tiria and Asarel" names the sons that were associated with the clan of Caleb the Kenizzite.

17. Tappuah was a town in the western foothills of the tribe of Judah (**Joshua 15:34**).

18. Shema's son Raham was the founder/father of Jorkeam (**1 Chronicles 2:44**); here, Jorkeam appears to be the same as Jokdeam, a town in the hill country of Judah (**Joshua 15:56**).

19. Maon was the son of Shammai and the great-grandson of Hebron (**1 Chronicles 2:42–45**). Maon was also a place name—referring to a city seven miles south of Hebron that was associated with the Wilderness of Maon (**1 Samuel 23:24–25**). Maon was the hometown of Nabal and Abigail (**1 Samuel 25:2–3**).

20. Beth Zur was a town in the hill country of the tribe of Judah (**Joshua 15:58**), about four miles north of Hebron.

21. Nabal of Maon is described as "surly and mean in his dealings—he was a Calebite [meaning of Kenizzite ancestry and a descendant of Caleb, the son of Jephunneh]" (**1 Samuel 25:2–3**).

22. Abigail was first married to Nabal, but after his death, she became the second wife of David (David's first wife was Ahinoam). Abigail is referred to as "the widow of Nabal of Carmel" (**1 Samuel 30:5**, **2 Samuel 2:2; 3:3**). Her marriage to David connected the honorable family of Caleb the Kenizzite to the family of King David of the tribe of Judah (**1 Samuel 25:39, 42**).

23. The son of David and Abigail is called Kileab in **2 Samuel 3:3** and Daniel in **1 Chronicles 3:1**. Kileab/Daniel was born in Hebron (cf. **2 Samuel 3:2–5; 1 Chronicles 3:1–4**).

24. The Hebrew נָבָל (*nabal*) means "worthless," "good for nothing," or even "godless" ("נָבָל," *HALOT* 1:663).

25. See chart "**1 Chronicles 3**: David's Children Born in Hebron and Jerusalem."

2 SAMUEL 5: BATHSHEBA

Approximate Dating: united monarchy under David and Solomon, ca. 1011–931 B.C.[1] ***Relevant Scriptures:*** **2 Samuel 5:13–16; 11:1–12:25; 15:12; 16:15–17:23; 23:34, 39; 1 Chronicles 3:5; 11:41; 14:4; 27:33; Matthew 1:6–16; Luke 3:23–38**

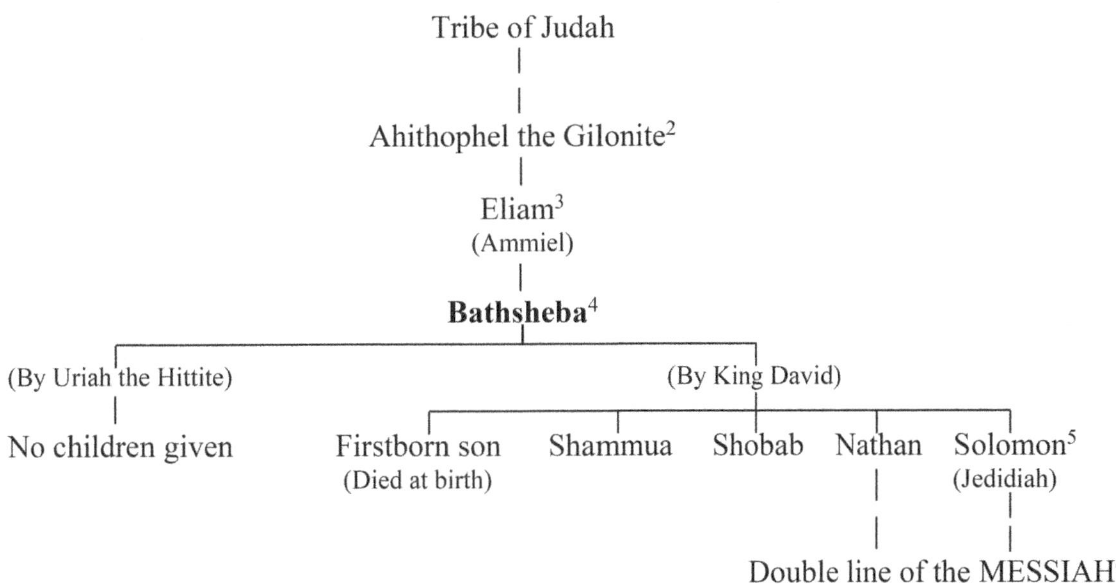

Biblical and Theological Significance

Bathsheba was a Judahite—the daughter of Eliam/Ammiel (**2 Samuel 11:3; 1 Chronicles 3:5**), one of David's mighty men (**2 Samuel 23:34**), and the granddaughter of Ahithophel the Gilonite (**2 Samuel 23:34**), who was David's court counselor-advisor (**15:12; 1 Chronicles 27:33**). Bathsheba was first married to Uriah the Hittite[7] (**2 Samuel 11:3**), one of David's military officers (**23:39; 1 Chronicles 11:41**), but no children of theirs are mentioned in Scripture.

Bathsheba is introduced in the narrative about King David under most inauspicious circumstances. She was bathing[8] in a serene sense of privacy, although the house she shared with her husband Uriah was not only adjacent to the royal palace but obviously on a lower level.[9] Bathsheba's husband, a Hittite mercenary off on a military campaign against Ammon to the east, which David had ordered, was absent. One look at the beautiful shadowy woman bathing[10] convinced David that he must get to "know" her better.

Possibly feigning ignorance, David asked one of his servants who the woman was (**2 Samuel 11:2–3**), and, very much aware of where her husband was, summoned her to come to him. He was the king . . . could she refuse?[11] David's lustful actions led to sexual transgression, which in due time resulted in a visible pregnancy and the birth of an illegitimate son who died within seven days (**2 Samuel 12:1–23**).[12] To make matters worse, David strategized for Uriah to be killed in battle, leaving the path open to take Bathsheba as his wife.

The irony of this is inescapable. David, who had arranged for the gallant warrior Uriah to be murdered so he could take his widow in marriage, seems hardly the one to chastise his son Absalom for acting in such a manner (**2 Samuel 16:22**). Ahithophel, David's counselor, had displayed his wisdom—and maybe his resentment against David for taking his granddaughter Bathsheba—in a rather cunning way, by persuading Absalom to do the same with David's concubines, an example of *lex talionis* (**2 Samuel 16:21–22**). David's words in **Psalm 41:9** may refer to Ahithophel: "Even my close friend, someone I trusted, one who shared my bread, has turned against me." When his advice to David was not heeded and Absalom's plot to assume the throne did not work, Ahithophel returned to his home and hanged himself (**2 Samuel 17:23**). After Ahithophel's suicide, the position of royal court counselor was filled by the military leader Jehoiada son of Benaiah and the Elide priest Abiathar (**1 Chronicles 27:33–34**).

Matthew 1:6 identifies Bathsheba, the mother of Solomon, as she who "had been Uriah's wife," a poignant reference to David "after he had gone in to Bathsheba" (**Psalm 51:0**, NKJV; *contra* NIV) while she was married to Uriah the Hittite (**2 Samuel 11**). The firstborn child of the union died (a son). Next, Bathsheba gave birth to another son whom they named Solomon, but the Lord "sent word through Nathan the prophet to name him Jedidiah," meaning "beloved of the Lord" (**2 Samuel 12:24–25**). In addition to Solomon, Bathsheba bore David three more sons, all born in Jerusalem (**2 Samuel 5:13–14; 1 Chronicles 3:5**), but David promised Bathsheba—her name meaning "daughter of an oath"—that the royal line would pass through *her* son Solomon (**1 Kings 1:13, 17, 30**).

When David died at age seventy, the rule of the kingdom transferred to Solomon (**1 Kings 3:7; 1 Chronicles 22:5; 23:1; 29:1–2, 20, 23, 28**). Bathsheba is last seen as the revered queen mother who "sat down at his [Solomon's] right hand" on a throne that King Solomon had prepared for her (**1 Kings 2:19**), a foreshadowing of Jesus, who would sit at the right hand of God.[13]

Bathsheba's life shows that, in God's grace and providence, an unknown soldier's wife could become a titled queen. Her attitude and choices allowed her to rise above many unfortunate circumstances in her life—living through sexual provocation and indignity, the premeditated murder of a spouse (by the man who became her second husband), the innocent death of a firstborn child, the suicide of a grandparent, and personal manipulation in the political power struggles of a royal family.[14] By embracing an outlook free of bitterness and regret, she became the noble wife of Israel's most famous king. By holding David to his promise (see note 4), she determined the royal successor to the Davidic throne and became the graceful, influential queen mother in Solomon's kingdom, imparting wise counselling skills learned from her grandfather to her sons, one of whom became the *wisest man on earth* (**1 Kings 3:12; 5:7**). Bathsheba received the *double blessing* of God and grew into his chosen role for her—as the key ancestress in the *double line* of the Messiah.[15]

Notes

1. David had become king of Judah when he was thirty years old (**2 Samuel 5:4**) and reigned for 40 years (ca. 1011–971 B.C.)—7 ½ years from Hebron and 33 years from Jerusalem (**2 Samuel 5:4–5; 1 Kings 2:11; 1 Chronicles 29:27**). Solomon ruled for 40 years, from ca. 971–931 B.C. (**2 Chronicles 9:30**).

2. Ahithophel was a "Gilonite," meaning a native of Giloh, a city in the hill country of Judah (**Joshua 15:51**). Ahithophel served as King David's personal counselor (**2 Samuel 15:12; 1 Chronicles 27:33; see also 2 Samuel 23:34**), and his advice was considered "like that of one who inquires of God" (**2 Samuel 16:23**). [This does not mean that Ahithophel was a prophet but only that he was considered so wise that he might as well have been speaking as God would have.] Unfortunately, Ahithophel betrayed David by joining Absalom's conspiracy to usurp the throne from his father (**2 Samuel 15**) and advised Absalom to sleep with his father's concubines so that "all Israel will hear that you have made yourself obnoxious to your father, and the hands of everyone with you will be more resolute" (**2 Samuel 16:21–23**). The irony is obvious. Ahithophel proposed to Absalom that he (Ahithophel) take 12,000 men and "pursue David" and kill him (**2 Samuel 17:1–2**); but Absalom also sought the advice of David's confidante, Hushai the Arkite (**2 Samuel 17:5–6**). When Ahithophel's advice was ignored over that of Hushai by Absalom and the men of Israel, Ahithophel felt publicly shamed and committed suicide by hanging himself (**2 Samuel 17:23**). This was all part of the providential plan in which "the Lord had determined to frustrate the good advice of Ahithophel in order to bring disaster on Absalom" (cf. **2 Samuel 17:14**; cf. **2 Samuel 16–17**). The vacancy in Ahithophel's office was then filled by Jehoiada son of Benaiah and by Abiathar the high priest (**1 Chronicles 27:34**).

3. Eliam (**2 Samuel 11:3; 23:34**) is also called Ammiel (**1 Chronicles 3:5**).

4. As her very name attests, Bathsheba was a daughter of Israel; Hebrew בַּת־שֶׁבַע, *bath-sheba*, meaning "daughter of the oath," that is, "of the covenant," refers to her initiative in holding David to his oath to her that *her* son (Solomon) would be David's successor (**1 Kings 1:11–35**). Matthew refers to Bathsheba in the genealogy of Jesus as the mother of Solomon, who "had been Uriah's wife" (**Matthew 1:6**). In most Hebrew manuscripts the Chronicler refers to her as בַּת־שׁוּעַ, Bathshua (e.g., **1 Chronicles 3:5**, NKJV), perhaps meaning "daughter of wealth/nobility."

5. After David and Bathsheba's first baby (a son) died shortly after birth, Bathsheba conceived again and gave birth to another son, whom they named Solomon. However, "because the Lord loved him, he sent word through Nathan the prophet to name him Jedidiah" (**2 Samuel 12:25**). Jedidiah (יְדִידְיָה) is an epithet of Solomon meaning "beloved of Yah," an expression of praise for Solomon's birth.

6. In a most profound way, the double line of Jesus' ancestry passes through David and Bathsheba, specifically through two of their four sons—Solomon (**Matthew 1:6–7**) and Nathan (**Luke 3:31**). The complete lineages of Jesus are found in Matthew's and Luke's Gospels (**Matthew 1:1–16** and **Luke 3:23–38**, respectively). Only Matthew alludes to Bathsheba, and that in a hesitating manner, calculated to show a high degree of embarrassment as to how it all came about: "David was the father of Solomon, whose mother had been Uriah's wife" (**Matthew 1:6**).

7. Uriah's name means "Yah(weh) is my light" (Heb. אוּרִיָּה, *uriiyah*). Quite possibly, then, he was a convert to the faith of Abraham.

8. Contrary to the understanding of many scholars, her bathing in **2 Samuel 11:2** was not necessarily ritualistic as required of an Israelite woman in menstruation or some similar cause of emission of blood (**Leviticus 15:19–30**). The verb for "bathing" here (רָחַץ, *rakhats*) in **2 Samuel 11:2** is the common one for ordinary cleanliness. As *The Complete Word Study Dictionary (Old Testament)* explains, רָחַץ *rakhats* is "a verb meaning to wash off, to wash away,

to bathe . . . [and] carries the connotation of washing with water in order to make clean, . . . the action involved in washing the hands or feet (**Exodus 30:19**); the face (**Genesis 43:31**); the body (**2 Samuel 11:2**); clothes (**Leviticus14:9**); or the parts of a sacrificial offering (**Leviticus 1:9**). Symbolically, such a washing was declarative of innocence (**Deuteronomy 21:6**); and was figurative of cleansing from sin (**Proverbs 30:12; Isaiah 4:4**)." 7364. רָחַץ *rāḥaṣ*, Warren Baker and Eugene Carpenter (Chattanooga, TN: AMG, 2003), accessed through Accordance 13 Bible Software.

However, the verb for ritual cleanliness (מִתְקַדְּשִׁם, *mithqaddshim*) in **2 Samuel 11:4**—"she [Bathsheba] was purifying herself from her monthly uncleanness"—does suggest she was making herself pure or "holy" after the seven days of impurity following her menstrual cycle (cf. **Leviticus 15:19–24**). (This has nothing directly to do with mikveh—the ritual bath for purification—except one supposes she had been in the mikveh prior to this episode.)

9. The narrative indicates that Bathsheba and Uriah's house—possibly special quarters for David's "mighty warriors" (**2 Samuel 23:8; 1 Chronicles 11:10**) at or near the Millo terraces (cf. **2 Samuel 5:9, 11; 23:39; 1 Chronicles 11:41**)—was among the dwellings *below* the palace, since multiple times Uriah is said to leave the king's palace and "go down" to his house (cf. **2 Samuel 11:8–10, 13**).

10. The text is not absolutely clear on the "public" vs. "private" nature of her bathing, although the time of day is clearly stated—"One evening David got up from his bed and walked around on the roof of the palace" (**2 Samuel 11:2**). Here, the text clarifies that it was early-to-mid evening (i.e., after people had retired or normally gone to bed) when David could have only made out the dusky figure of a beautiful woman, bathing in her own house or courtyard in the early twilight of nightfall.

11. Scholars differ in their opinion about the complicity of Bathsheba in the encounter, but several textual elements suggest she was on the *receiving end* of the king's shameful request: (1) the rapid sequence of events in **2 Samuel 11:2–4** where David is the initiator of the actions; (2) David's elaborate, premeditated plan for Uriah's murder and rationale for his heinous conduct (**2 Samuel 11:6–25**); (3) Nathan the prophet's portrayal of Bathsheba as an innocent victim (the sole "ewe lamb" in **2 Samuel 12:4**) who was taken by David the rich and powerful man—and Nathan's pronouncement, "You [David] are the man!" (**2 Samuel 12:7**); (4) David's acknowledgment of his sin (**2 Samuel 12:13**); and (5) David's plea for God's mercy in **Psalm 51** where, "after David had committed adultery with Bathsheba" (**Psalm 51:0**, NIV; the better translation is probably "after he [David] had gone in to Bathsheba"; NKJV) he entreated the Lord, "Have mercy on me, O God, according to your unfailing love; according to your great compassion blot out my transgressions. Wash away all my iniquity and cleanse me from my sin [cf. **2 Samuel 11:2** and compare note 8 on Bathsheba's bathing]. For I know my transgressions, and my sin is always before me. Against you, you only, have I sinned and done what is evil in your sight; so you are right in your verdict and justified when you judge. Hide your face from my sins and blot out all my iniquity. . . . Deliver me from the guilt of bloodshed" (**Psalm 51:1–4, 14**).

12. The death of the infant son was punishment from the Lord because of David's sin with Bathsheba (cf. **2 Samuel 12:13–23**).

13. See **Acts 5:31; 7:55–56; Romans 8:34; Ephesians 1:20; Colossians 3:1; Hebrews 1:3, 13; 8:1; 10:12; 12:2; 1 Peter 3:22**.

14. For Bathsheba's imprudent intermediary role in Adonijah's request for David's concubine Abishag to be given to him (Adonijah) as his wife, see **1 Kings 2:13–25**.

15. Refer to these charts for more information: "**1 Chronicles 3**: Zerubbabel and Shealtiel and the Double Line of the Messiah through King David's Sons, Nathan and Solomon," "**Matthew 1**: Jesus the Messiah–the Matthean Account," and "**Luke 3**: Jesus: The Lukan Account."

2 SAMUEL 6: OBED-EDOM, THE LEVITICAL GATEKEEPER AND KEEPER OF THE ARK

Approximate Dating: united monarchy era under King David and King Solomon; ca. 1011–931 B.C. ***Relevant Scriptures:*** **2 Samuel 6:10–12**; also **Genesis 46:11; Exodus 6:16, 19; Numbers 3:17–20; 26:57; 1 Chronicles 1:34; 2:1; 6:1, 16, 19, 44–47; 9:14, 16; 13:12–14; 15:17–24; 16:38; 23:23; 24:30; 25:3; 26:4–8, 15, 19; 2 Chronicles 25:24; Nehemiah 11:17**

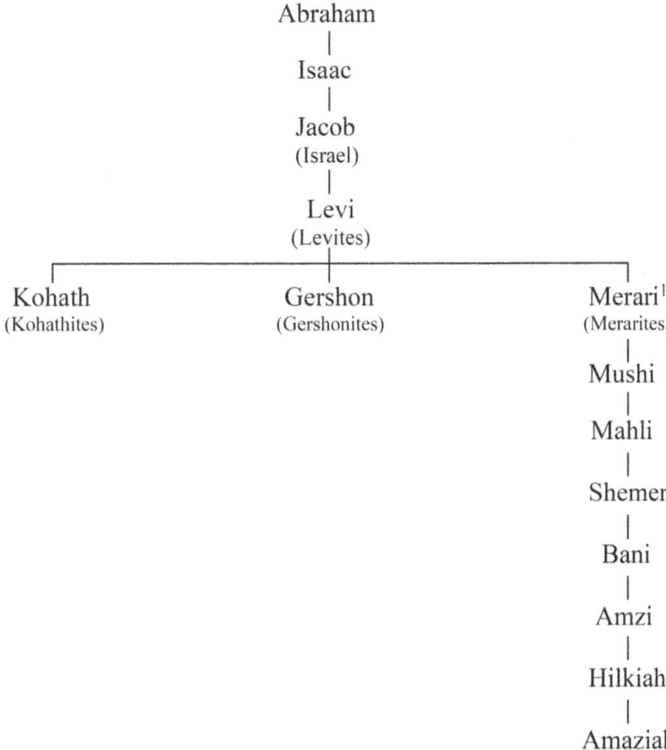

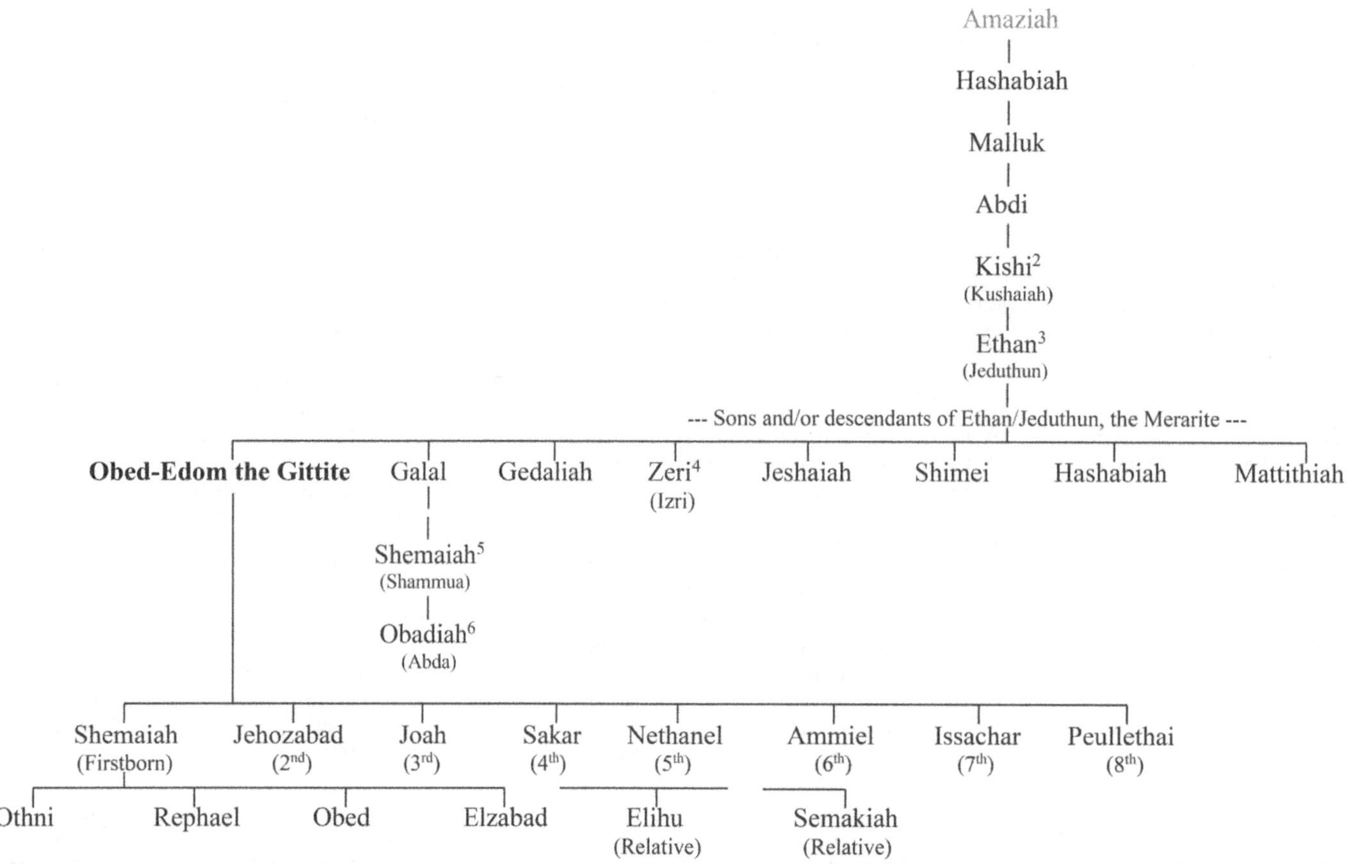

Biblical and Theological Significance

The genealogy for Obed-Edom shown in the chart is based, in large part, on the text from **1 Chronicles 16:38** which says that he was (1) the "son of Jeduthun," and Jeduthun/Ethan was one of the three key musicians in Solomon's Temple,[7] and (2) his general connection to Levitical Merarites who served there.

The Merarites' responsibilities[8] are amply described in **Numbers 3:33–37**. In the days of the wilderness wanderings, they were in charge of all the wooden parts of the tabernacle—the apparatuses necessary to its erection as the dwelling place of Yahweh. Later, they became doorkeepers of the temple, that is, ensuring its security and proper accessibility.

Several biblical passages describe him as:

1. **Obed-Edom "the Gittite"**[9] (**2 Samuel 6:10–12; 1 Chronicles 13:12–14; 15:25**). In the book of 2 Samuel, Obed-Edom is described as a contemporary of King David. After David's mishandling of the ark and the death of Uzzah (**2 Samuel 6:6–7**), the ark was taken to the house of Obed-Edom, where it resided for three months. Because of this, "the Lord blessed him [Obed-Edom] and his entire household" (**2 Samuel 6:11**); afterward, David took the ark from the house of Obed-Edom to the City of David. The texts of **1 Chronicles 13:12–14** and **15:25** basically recount the same historical event, so Obed-Edom "the Gittite" is the same person as Obed-Edom (without the epithet).
2. **Obed-Edom as a musician** (**1 Chronicles 15:21**). The movement of the ark of the covenant to the City of David was done with great rejoicing with musical instruments and singing (**1 Chronicles 15:16–22**). Like his brother Mattithiah, Obed-Edom played the harp "directing according to *sheminith*" (**1 Chronicles 15:21**) and played the lyre and harp regularly before the ark with his brethren (**1 Chronicles 16:5–6**).
3. **Obed-Edom as the patriarch of a large family** (**1 Chronicles 26:4–5**). This passage shows that Obed-Edom had eight sons (i.e., those listed by name in the chart); the passage ends with "for God had blessed Obed-Edom" (cf. **2 Samuel 6:11**).
4. **Obed-Edom as a doorkeeper for the ark** (**1 Chronicles 15:24**). Obed-Edom and another Levite named Jehiah were doorkeepers[10] for the ark of the covenant.
5. **Obed-Edom as the gatekeeper for the South Gate** (**1 Chronicles 26:15**). The lot for the prestigious South Gate fell to Obed-Edom, and the lot for the storehouse fell to his sons. The South Gate was nearest the king's palace and this gate was used most often by the king to enter the temple courts.
6. **Obed-Edom as the caretaker of Temple treasures** (**2 Chronicles 25:24**). This reference refers to a later time period when King Jehoash of Israel, 798–782 B.C., "took all the gold and silver and all the articles found in the temple of God that had been in the care of Obed-Edom, together with the palace treasures and the hostages, and returned to Samaria." This passage suggests that the family of Obed-Edom continued to be active in Solomon's Temple and were overseers of the valuable gold and silver.

Given the historical context and overlapping message of these passages, one can conclude that there is only one Obed-Edom figure. His name derives from עֶבֶד (*ebed*), "servant," plus אֱדוֹם (*edom*), "red (land, soil)."[11]

The large clan of Obed-Edom included sixty-eight Merarites who served as gatekeepers for Solomon's Temple (**1 Chronicles 16:38**). Obed-Edom's sons were in charge of the temple storehouse (**1 Chronicles 26:15**), and his sons, grandsons, and other kinsmen—sixty-two in number—are characterized as "capable men with the strength to do the work" (**1 Chronicles 26:8**).

Notes

1. For a more expansive genealogy of the Merarite descendants, see chart "**1 Chronicles 6**: Levi: High Priests, Priests, Levites, and Musicians in Solomon's Temple."

2. Kishi (**1 Chronicles 6:44**) is otherwise Kushaiah (**1 Chronicles 15:17**); another descendant in this Merarite lineage, named "Kish son of Abdi," was a contemporary of King Hezekiah, 715–686 B.C. (**2 Chronicles 29:12**).

3. Ethan (**1 Chronicles 6:44; 15:17, 19**) is also called Jeduthun (**1 Chronicles 9:16; 16:38, 41–42; 25:3, 6; 2 Chronicles 5:12; 29:14; 35:15; Nehemiah 11:17; Psalm 39:0; 62:0; 77:0**). Ethan/Jeduthun was one of the three chief musicians in Solomon's Temple; his sons and descendants were Levitical Merarites who were gatekeepers at the temple, controlling the access to the sacred complex (**1 Chronicles 16:42**; cf. **2 Chronicles 23:19**) and guarding the temple treasuries, the treasuries of the dedicated things, and the storerooms at the gates (**1 Chronicles 9:26; Nehemiah 12:25**); see chart "**1 Chronicles 26**: The Kohathite–Korahite and Merarite Gatekeepers in Solomon's Temple." Ethan the Merarite musician is not Ethan the Ezrahite, the son or descendant of Zerah, who was a Judahite (**1 Kings 4:31; 1 Chronicles 2:6; Psalm 89:0**).

4. Zeri (**1 Chronicles 25:3**) is Izri (**1 Chronicles 25:11**).

5. Shemaiah the Merarite (**1 Chronicles 9:16**) is Shammua the Merarite (**Nehemiah 11:17**). Another Shemaiah figure (a descendant of Jeduthun, a Merarite in this same lineage) was a contemporary of Hezekiah of Judah, 715–686 B.C. (**2 Chronicles 29:14**). Shemaiah/Shammua is not Shemaiah the Levite, the son of Hasshub (**1 Chronicles 9:14**).

6. The post-exilic figure named Obadiah in **1 Chronicles 9:16** is called Abda in **Nehemiah 11:17**. Obadiah and his clan "lived in the villages of the Netophathites" (**1 Chronicles 9:16**). He is likely the same person as Obadiah the gatekeeper who guarded the storerooms at the gates in the Second Temple in Jerusalem in the days of Ezra (ca. 458–444 B.C; **Nehemiah 12:25–26**), Joiakim the high priest (ca. 490–450/444 B.C.), and Nehemiah (ca. 444–432 B.C.).

7. For the Merarite heritage of Obed-Edom and his father Jeduthan (also known as Ethan, see note 3), see charts "**1 Chronicles 6**: Levi: High Priests, Preiests, and Musicians in Solomon's Temple"; "**1 Chronicles 15**: Genealogical Registry of Musicians and Doorkeepers who Led the Procession when the Ark of the Covenant was Brought to the City of David"; "**1 Chronicles 16**: Genealogical Registry of Kohathite Priests and Levites Appointed by King David to Care for the Ark of the Covenant in the City of David"; and "**1 Chronicles 25**: The Twenty-Four Musician Leaders in Solomon's Temple."

8. These instructions to the Levites were promulgated first by Moses a short time after the exodus, at Sinai, the holy mountain of covenant-making (**Exodus 19:1–6**). Each of the three clans—Kohathites, Gershonites, and Merarites—was assigned towns in Canaan after the conquest to carry out various religious functions; in particular, the Merarites were given twelve specific towns. However, early in the twelfth century B.C., the Philistines invaded Israel, so the Israelites called for the ark of the covenant to be brought from Shiloh, supposing it would ensure victory (**1 Samuel 4:1–4**). However, the Philistines captured the ark for a time until it challenged their gods in the temple of their god, Dagon (**1 Samuel 4:11; 5:1–5**). After the image of Dagon fell and broke, the Philistines sent the ark away on a driverless ox-drawn cart that headed to Beth Shemesh (**1 Samuel 6:1–20**). Later the citizens of Beth Shemesh asked the citizens of Kiriath Jearim to take the ark to their town (**1 Samuel 6:21**), which they did. The ark was taken to the home of Abinadab on the hill, where he and his son Eleazar guarded it for twenty years (**1 Samuel 7:1–5**). After David's first and unsuccessful attempt to move the ark of the covenant from Kiriath Jearim to the City of David (cf. **2 Samuel 6:1–9**; cf. **1 Chronicles 15:11–15**), David took the ark to the house of the Levitical Merarite, Obed-Edom, where it resided for three months. Then after David heard that "the Lord has blessed the household of Obed-Edom and everything he has, because of the ark of God" (**2 Samuel 6:11–12**), David moved the ark of the covenant from the house of Obed-Edom to Jerusalem, in accordance with the Mosaic restrictions (**1 Chronicles 15:15**). There it resided in a tent-tabernacle that David had prepared for it in the City of David (**2 Samuel 6:12–17; 1 Chronicles 15:1**).

9. The epithet "Gittite" raises a number of questions. Both the historian of **2 Samuel** (i.e., **2 Samuel 6:10–11**) and the Chronicler (i.e., **1 Chronicles 13:13**) clearly identify Obed-Edom as a "Gittite." To understand this descriptor, the following explanations are offered:

(1) "Gittite" typically refers to a citizen of Gath, one of the five principal Philistine city-states (**1 Samuel 6:17**; cf. **Joshua 11:22; 13:3; 1 Samuel 5:8; 7:14; 17:4, 23, 52; 21:10, 12; 22:1; 27:2–4, 11; 2 Samuel 1:20; 21:20, 22**). Known Gittites include: (a) Ittai the Gittite who was in David's army (**2 Samuel 15:19, 22; 18:2**); (b) the giant, Goliath the Gittite (**2 Samuel 21:19; 1 Chronicles 20:5**); and (c) the 600 Gittites who accompanied David when he made the desperate trek to the Transjordan (**2 Samuel 15:18**). However, given his known ancestry, as shown in the chart, Obed-Edom was clearly a Levitical Merarite—meaning a descendant of Levi's son, Merari. This fact alone precludes the notion that Obed-Edom was a "Philistine of Gath" or a "Philistine Gittite" by birth. It may suggest that David first met Obed-Edom during his forays to Gath of the Philistines when David was in Ziklag (see **1 Samuel 27**) and "lived in Philistine territory a year and four months" (**1 Samuel 27:7**). Why Obed-Edom would have been living among the Gittites (citizens) of Gath is not known.

(2) "Gittite" may be an oblique reference to the Merarite town of Dimnah (perhaps equivalent to Rimmon/Rimmono and/or confused with Gath Rimmon?). The Levitical Merarites were assigned twelve towns within Israel: Jokneam, Kartah, Dimnah, and Nahalal (from the tribe of Zebulun); Bezer, Jahaz, Kedemoth, and Mephaath (from the tribe of Reuben); and Ramoth in Gilead, Mahanaim, Heshbon, and Jazer (from the tribe of Gad) (**Joshua 21:7, 34–40; 1 Chronicles 6:77–81**). The Merarite town of Dimnah has been noted as a possible scribal error for the town of Rimmon (cf. **Joshua 19:10, 13**) or Rimmono (cf. **1 Chronicles 6:77**; (see *ISBE* entry for "Dimnah" by Paul H. Wright; *Eerdmans Dictionary* entry for "Dimnah" by Friedbert Ninow; and *Holman's Bible Dictionary* entry for "Dimnah" by Paul H. Wright). [Note that there was also a town named Rimmon that was allotted to the tribe of Judah (**Joshua 15:32**) but then given to the tribe of Simeon (**Joshua 19:7; 1 Chronicles 4:32**)]. Gath Rimmon, meaning "winepress of Rimmon," (see ISBE, entry for "Gath Rimmon," by E. Ewing) may be the source of the confusion that Obed-Edom was from "Gath/a Gittite" from Gath Rimmon.

(3) Scribes may have mistakenly thought that, because Obed-Edom had semi-priestly oversight for the ark for three months, that he was a "Gittite" from Gath-Rimmon, one of the two towns by that name given to the Kohathite attending priests (i.e., Gath Rimmon in the tribe of Dan, **Joshua 21:23–24**, or Gath Rimmon from the half tribe of Manasseh, **Joshua 21:25**). Gath Rimmon may be the source of the confusion that Obed-Edom was from "Gath/a Gittite" from there. [Note that there was also a town named Gath Hepher in the tribe of Zebulun in Lower Galilee (**Joshua 19:13**) and a town named Rimmon that was allotted to the tribe of Judah (**Joshua 15:32**), which was later given to the tribe of Simeon (**Joshua 19:7; 1 Chronicles 4:32**), but neither one was associated with high priests, Kohathite attending priests, or Levitical servants.]

10. The "doorkeeper" was not a doorman as in a hotel, but one who kept the door, guarding it against unauthorized persons. A temple doorkeeper must himself be holy and must permit entry only to authorized temple personnel involved in ritual and spiritual leadership.

11. The grammatical form is a participle that conveys the idea of continuous or ongoing action (i.e., "one who serves the (red) soil"), likely meaning that Obed-Edom was a farmer when not attending at the temple.

2 SAMUEL 7: VARIOUS NATHAN FIGURES IN THE OLD TESTAMENT

Approximate Dating: various, as noted. ***Relevant Scriptures:*** **2 Samuel 7:2–17; 12:1–15; 1 Kings 1:8–48; 1 Chronicles 2:25–41; 29:29; 2 Chronicles 9:29**

Nathan #1, a Judahite-Jerahmeelite descendant (lived ca. 1200 B.C.)

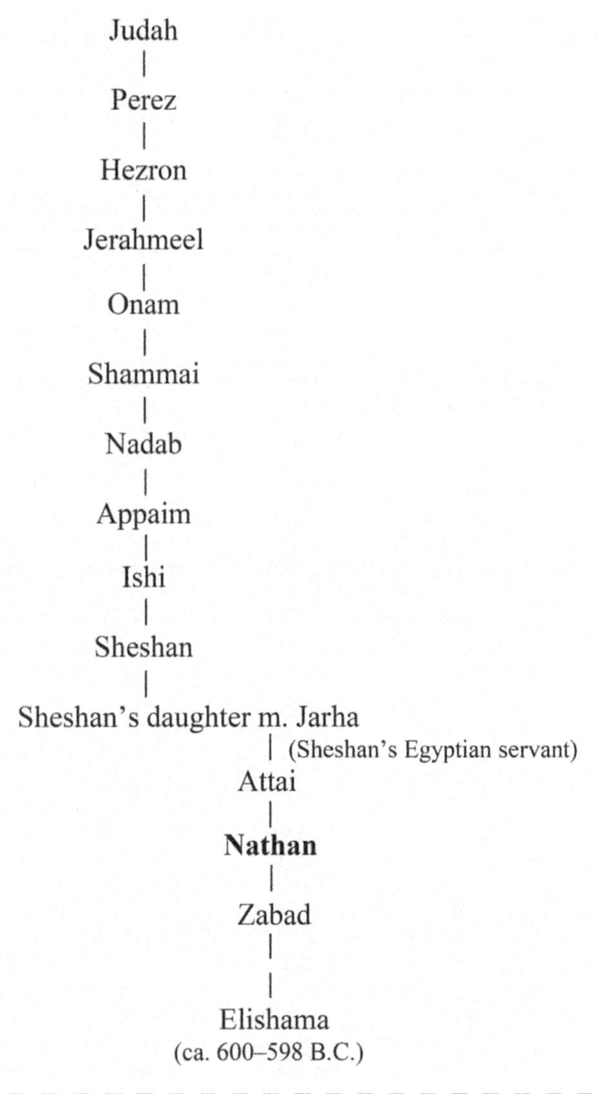

Nathan #2, the son of David (lived ca. 1010–960 B.C.)

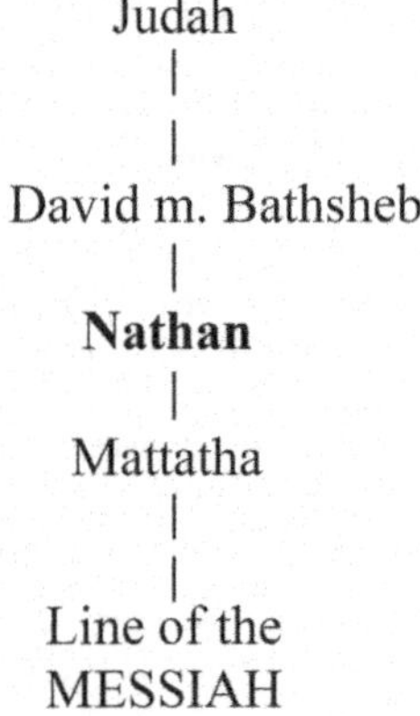

Nathan #3, the father of an official in King Solomon's administration (lived ca. 1000–970 B.C.)

Nathan
|
Azariah
(Official in charge of
the district governors in
Solomon's administration)

Nathan #4, the father of a priestly official in King Solomon's administration (lived ca. 1000–970 B.C.)

Nathan
|
Zabud
(Priest and advisor to
King Solomon)

Nathan #5, the *father* or the *brother* of Joel (Igal?) from Zobah, one of David's mighty warriors (lived ca. 1040–971 B.C.)

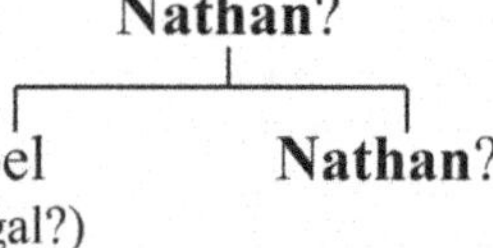

Nathan #6, a returning exile with Ezra (lived ca. 458 B.C.)

Nathan m. A pagan wife

Nathan #7, the prophet of God (lived ca. 1011–960 B.C.)

Nathan the prophet
(Unknown genealogy)

Biblical and Theological Significance

Nathan #1 is in the Judah–Hezron–Jerahmeel lineage (**1 Chronicles 2:25–41**); for this entire lineage, see the chart "**1 Chronicles 2**: Jerahmeel and His Descendant, Elishama, Who Appears to Be a Compiler of Historical and Genealogical Records in 1 & 2 Chronicles." The Nathan #1 figure in **1 Chronicles 2:36** may be the same person as Nathan #3, the father of Azariah, an official in King Solomon's administration (**1 Kings 4:5**), but Nathan #1 is not Nathan #4 (father of Zabud), who is in a priestly lineage. Given that Nathan #1 is twelve generations removed from

Judah, and that King David, in the Hezron–Ram line (a contemporary of Nathan #7, the prophet of God), is ten generations removed from Judah—it is possible that Nathan #1 the Jerahmeelite is the same person as Nathan #7 (the prophet of God; see below) or, more likely, his contemporary.

Nathan #2, the son of David, is mentioned in **2 Samuel 5:14; 1 Chronicles 3:5; 14:4;** and **Luke 3:31**. Also, the reference to the "clan of the house of Nathan" in **Zechariah 12:12** most likely refers to David's son Nathan. The double line of the Messiah passes through Solomon and Nathan, the sons of David and Bathsheba (see charts "**1 Chronicles 3**: Zerubbabel and Shealtiel and the Double Line of the Messiah through King David's Sons, Nathan and Solomon" and "**Luke 3**: Jesus: The Lukan Account").

Nathan #3 is mentioned in **1 Kings 4:5**. He was a contemporary of Nathan #4.

Nathan #4 is mentioned in **1 Kings 4:5**. He was a contemporary of Nathan #3.

Nathan #5 was the *father* or the *brother* of a mighty warrior of David named Joel (alias Igal?), who was from Zobah, an Aramean (Syrian) kingdom between Hamath and Damascus (cf. **2 Samuel 23:36; 1 Chronicles 11:38**); see the chart "**1 Chronicles 11**: Genealogical Registry of the Mighty Warriors in King David's Army."

Nathan #6, an influential man in Babylon, was sent by Ezra to persuade more Levites to return with him to Jerusalem (cf. **Ezra 8:15–17**). This Nathan figure may be the same layperson "from the descendants of Binnui" who put away his pagan wife (**Ezra 10:39**). This Nathan figure lived in the post-exile (ca. 458 B.C.).

Nathan #7, the prophet of God, is referenced in the narratives in **2 Samuel 7:2–17; 12:1–15, 25; 1 Kings 1:8–48; 1 Chronicles 2:25–41(?); 29:29;** and **2 Chronicles 9:29**. The genealogy of Nathan the prophet of God is not given in Scripture. Nathan the prophet served from ca. 1000–960 B.C. during the forty-year reign of King David (ca. 1011–971 B.C.) and the early part of King Solomon's forty-year reign (ca. 971–931 B.C.). Nathan the prophet: (1) revealed to King David that the Lord would establish his house as an enduring kingdom (**2 Samuel 7; 1 Chronicles 17**); (2) confronted David about his sinful sexual transgression with Uriah's wife Bathsheba and declared "You are the man!" (**2 Samuel 12:1–24; Psalm 51:0**); (3) told David (after his marriage to Bathsheba) that he was to name their son "Jedidiah" (=Solomon) (**2 Samuel 12:25**); (4) mediated the appointment of Solomon (rather than Adonijah) as David's successor (**1 Kings 1:11–31**) and accompanied Zadok the priest in the anointing and public announcement of Solomon as king (**1 Kings 1:32–40**); and (5) wrote an account of the events of King David's reign in a book entitled "the records of Nathan the prophet" (**1 Chronicles 29:29; 2 Chronicles 9:29**).

2 SAMUEL 8 & 20: THE CHIEF OFFICIALS IN KING DAVID'S ADMINISTRATION

Approximate Dating: united monarchy under King David, 1011–971 B.C. ***Relevant Scriptures:*** **2 Samuel 8:15–18; 20:23–26;** also **1 Chronicles 18:14–17**

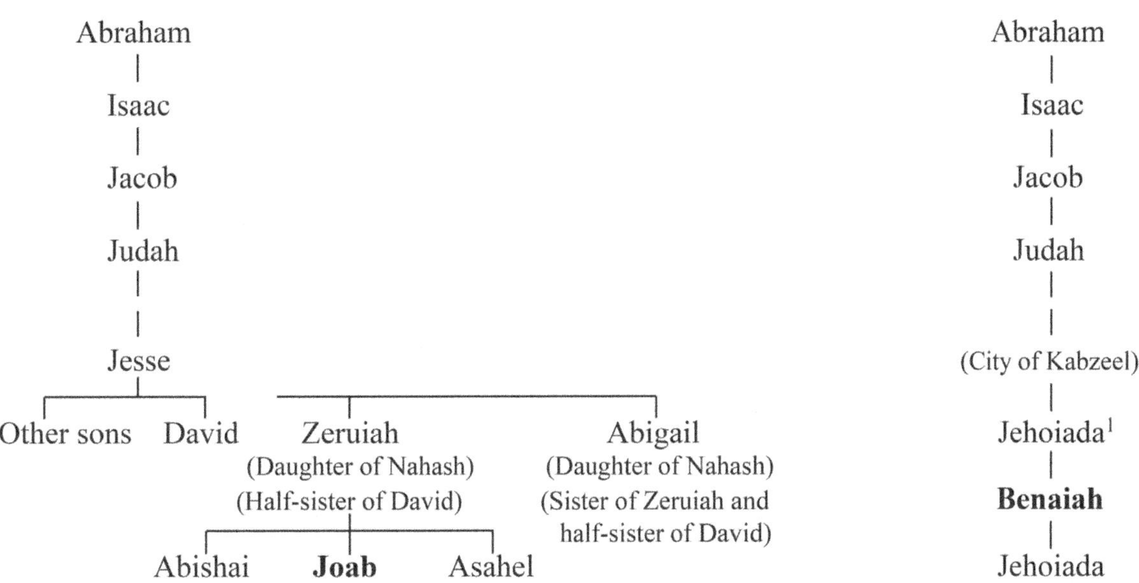

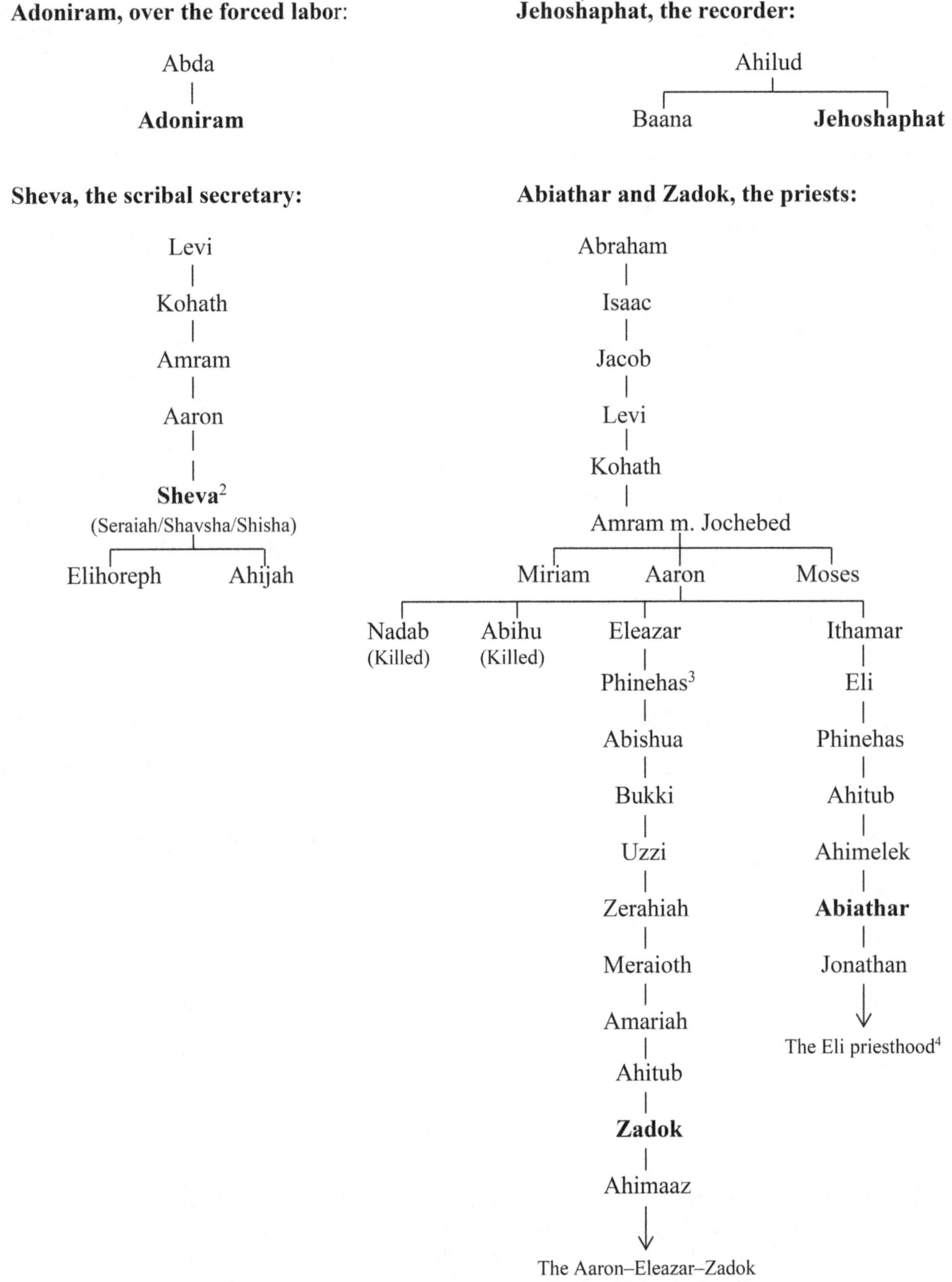

Adoniram, over the forced labor:
Abda
Adoniram
Jehoshaphat, the recorder:
Ahilud
Baana
Jehoshaphat
Sheva, the scribal secretary:
Levi
Kohath
Amram
Aaron
Sheva[2]
(Seraiah/Shavsha/Shisha)
Elihoreph
Ahijah
Abiathar and Zadok, the priests:
Abraham
Isaac
Jacob
Levi
Kohath
Amram m. Jochebed
Miriam
Aaron
Moses
Nadab
(Killed)
Abihu
(Killed)
Eleazar
Ithamar
Phinehas[3]
Abishua
Bukki
Uzzi
Zerahiah
Meraioth
Amariah
Ahitub
Zadok
Ahimaaz
The Aaron–Eleazar–Zadok
"lasting high priesthood"
Eli
Phinehas
Ahitub
Ahimelek
Abiathar
Jonathan
The Eli priesthood[4]

Ira, David's personal (non-Levitical) *priestly* advisor:

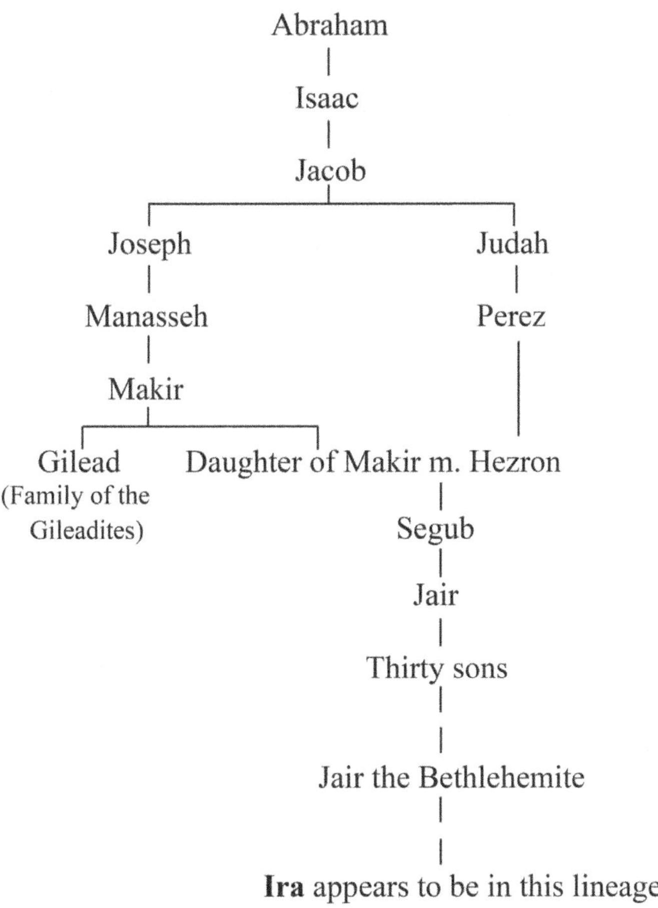

David's sons, who served as *priests* (i.e., chief officials) and personal advisors (which could have included two or more of the following sons): Amnon, Kileab (also called Daniel), Absalom, Adonijah, Shephatiah, Ithream, Shammua, Shobab, Nathan, Solomon, Ibhar, Elishua, Eliphelet (#1) (also called Elpelet), Nogah, Jerimoth,[5] Nepheg, Japhia, Elishama, Eliada (also called Beeliada) and Eliphelet (#2).[6]

Biblical and Theological Significance

Two main lists record the officials in David's administration, the first was likely composed early during his reign when he ruled "over all Israel" (**2 Samuel 8:15–18;** cf. **1 Chronicles 18:14–17**) and the second after the incident of his flight from Absalom and then return to Jerusalem to resume kingship (**2 Samuel 20:23–26**). The two lists differ slightly. David's sons served as the king's personal advisors, "priests," during the early part of his reign (**2 Samuel 8:18**). Later, Ira the Jairite assumed this title (**2 Samuel 20:26**). Notably, neither the sons of David nor Ira are of priestly Aaronic descent in the true "priestly" sense.[7]

Joab, commander-in-chief over the army. The three sons of Zeruiah (David's half-sister)[8]—Abishai, Joab, and Asahel[9]—were David's nephews. All of them served as military leaders under King David, with Joab holding the highest ranked position as the commander-in-chief of the army. David thought of Joab as an exceptional warrior but, at times, a fierce and bloodthirsty man. David comments that, at times, "these sons of Zeruiah are too strong for me. May the Lord repay the evildoer according to his evil deeds" (**2 Samuel 3:39**). Joab, in particular, was responsible, directly or indirectly, for the deaths of Abner, Absalom, and Amasa (**2 Samuel 3:26–27; 18:14–15; 20:9–10**, respectively). Eventually, David pronounced a curse on Joab because he shed the blood of the innocent "in peacetime as if in battle" and "stained the belt around his waist and the sandals on his feet" (**1 Kings 2:5**; cf. **2 Samuel 3:28–29**). In the course of determining kingly succession to the Davidic throne, Joab unwisely supported Adonijah instead of Solomon. When Solomon assumed the throne, Joab "fled to the tent of the Lord and took hold of the horns of the altar" (**1 Kings 2:28**) and refused to leave. Solomon commanded Benaiah "strike him down and bury him, and so clear me and my whole family of the guilt of the innocent blood that Joab shed" (**1 Kings 2:31**, see **vv. 28–34**). Joab was buried in his own house out in the country (**1 Kings 2:34**). King Solomon then appointed Benaiah the son of Jehoiada as the commander of his army (**1 Kings 2:35**).

Benaiah, the son of Jehoiada, over David's bodyguards, the Kerethites and Pelethites. This is a probable lineage for Benaiah based on the fact that his family was from the town of Kabzeel in the tribe of Judah (**Joshua 15:21**). Both Benaiah's father and son were named Jehoiada (a case of papponymy). Benaiah was a "valiant fighter" who "performed great exploits" (**2 Samuel 23:20–23**) and was "as famous as the three mighty warriors [of David]" (**1 Chronicles 11:24**). Benaiah was "held in greater honor than any of the Thirty [mighty warriors of David], but he was not included among the Three [chief military leaders]" (**2 Samuel 23:22–23; 1 Chronicles 11:22–25**). David appointed Benaiah over the "bodyguards"—the Kerethites and Pelethites. He was faithful to King David and to Solomon during Adonijah's attempt to secure the Davidic throne (**1 Kings 1:8**). At King Solomon's orders, Benaiah executed David's son Adonijah (**1 Kings 2:23–25**); Shimei the Benjamite who had cursed David (cf. **1 Kings 2:8–9; 36–46**); and Joab (David's army commander; **1 Kings 2:5–6, 28–35**). Benaiah then became commander-in-chief of Solomon's army (**1 Kings 4:4**). Benaiah's son, Jehoiada, succeeded Ahithophel (the former counselor to King David who hanged himself after the Absalom conspiracy to take the throne; cf. **2 Samuel 15; 17:23; 1 Chronicles 27:33–34**). The younger Jehoiada (the son of Benaiah) and Abiathar served as the counselors to King Solomon during his reign (**1 Chronicles 27:34**)

Adoniram, official over the forced labor. He is mentioned in only the later record of David's administrative officials (**2 Samuel 20:24**). Forced laborers were typically conscripted laborers (corvée labor) from among the Israelites or men from defeated nations (i.e., war captives / non-Israelite resident foreigners / Canaanite survivors). Adoniram was the taskmaster who oversaw the thousands of laborers sent to Lebanon to cut wood for Solomon's Temple (**1 Kings 5:14**). Adoniram served under three kings: David (**2 Samuel 20:24**), Solomon (**1 Kings 4:6**), and Rehoboam (**1 Kings 12:18; 2 Chronicles 10:18**). Eventually, the people of the northern tribes of Israel stoned Adoniram to death in the days of King Rehoboam (**1 Kings 12:18; 2 Chronicles 10:18**).

Jehoshaphat, the recorder. The responsibilities of the recorder are somewhat unclear. Jehoshaphat appears to serve in several capacities: as a secretary of state (who brought important matters to the notice of the king), as the court historian (who had oversight of the government archives), and as the royal herald (who handled communications between the king and the country and oversaw ceremonial tasks at the king's royal appearances). Jehoshaphat continued in this capacity during Solomon's reign (**2 Samuel 8:16; 20:24; 1 Kings 4:1–3; 1 Chronicles 18:15**). Jehoshaphat is probably the brother of Baana, the son of Ahilud, one of the twelve governors over Israel (cf. **1 Kings 4:12**).

Sheva, the scribal secretary. He is variously called Seraiah, Sheva, Shisha, and Shavsha (see note 2). He probably wrote official documents, state records, and perhaps "the book of the annals of King David" (**1 Chronicles 27:24**). His sons, Elihoreph and Ahijah, served as scribal secretaries in Solomon's administration (**1 Kings 4:3**).

Zadok and Abiathar, the co-officiating priests. Zadok (the son of Ahitub) and Abiathar (the son of Ahimelek, as well as Abiathar's son Ahimelek) served as high priests before the ark of God during David's reign (**2 Samuel 8:17; 20:25; 1 Chronicles 18:16**) and continued through the early part of Solomon's reign. However, Abiathar (from the Eli priesthood) supported Adonijah's schemes to succeed to the throne. When Solomon became king, he deposed Abiathar and sent him home to Anathoth, thus "fulfilling the word the LORD had spoken at Shiloh about the house of Eli" (**1 Kings 2:26–27**; cf. **1 Samuel 2:22–36**). Afterward, the priests who continued in Temple service were descendants in the Aaron–Eleazar–Zadok and the Aaron–Ithamar lines, excluding the line of the Ithamar–Eli–Abiathar descendants who were cursed (**1 Samuel 2:30–36; 1 Chronicles 24:1–19**).[10]

Ira, David's priest. This is the probable lineage for Ira. Since he is called a "Jairite" (**2 Samuel 20:26**), in all likelihood, Ira was a descendant of the clan of Jair, the seventh judge of Israel, from the tribe of East Manasseh (cf. **Numbers 32:41; Deuteronomy 3:14; Joshua 13:30; Judges 10:3–5; 1 Kings 4:13**). Alternatively, he may be the same person as Ira the "Ithrite," one of the military officers in David's army from Tekoa in the tribe of Judah.[11] In neither case is Ira a true "priest" in the traditional strict sense (i.e., from the line of priests in the tribe of Levi, through either the Aaron–Eleazar line or the Aaron–Ithamar line). Ira should be understood to serve as a close *personal advisor* to King David.

David's sons are called "priests" (2 Samuel 8:18). They are clearly from the tribe of Judah, not from the tribe of Levi. The sons of David served as "chief officials at the king's side" as explained in **1 Chronicles 18:17**. For their genealogy, see **2 Samuel 3:2–5; 5:13–16; 1 Chronicles 3:1–9; 14:4–7**, and the charts "**1 Chronicles 2**: King David" and "**1 Chronicles 3**: David's Children Born in Hebron and Jerusalem."

Notes

1. Jehoiada the father of Benaiah (**2 Samuel 8:18; 20:23; 23:20, 22; 1 Kings 1:8, 26, 32, 38, 44; 2:25, 28, 34–35, 46; 4:4; 1 Chronicles 11:22, 24; 18:17; 27:5**) is not to be confused with Jehoiada the priest (of the tribe of Levi), the husband of Jehosheba who protected young Joash during Queen Athaliah's reign (**2 Kings 11:4–12:9**); for the latter Jehoiada, see chart "**2 Chronicles 22**: Probable Genealogy for Jehoiada the Priest who Masterminded the Overthrow of Queen Athaliah of Judah."

2. Sheva in **2 Samuel 20:25** is the same person as Seraiah in **2 Samuel 8:17**, Shavsha in **1 Chronicles 18:16**, and Shisha in **1 Kings 4:3**. Sheva/Seraiah/Shavsha/Shisha is in a Kohathite priestly lineage, parallel to that of the line of the high priests (cf. **1 Chronicles 6:1–14**).

3. Phinehas the son of Eleazar in the Aaron–Eleazar–Zadok line (**Exodus 6:25; Numbers 25:7, 11; 31:6; Joshua 22:13, 30, 32; 24:33; Judges 20:28; 1 Chronicles 6:4, 50; 9:20; Ezra 7:5; 8:2; Psalm 106:30**) is a different person than Phinehas the son of Eli, the son of Ithamar, in the Eli priesthood (**1 Samuel 2:34; 4:4, 11, 19; 14:3**).

4. See chart "**1 Samuel 1**: Eli and the Eli priesthood."

5. Jerimoth is not mentioned by name in the lists of David's sons in **2 Samuel 5:13–16, 1 Chronicles 3:1–9** or **1 Chronicles 14:3–7**. In **2 Chronicles 11:18**, Jerimoth is called "David's son," but the context suggests that he might have been a *relative* or a *descendant* of David or perhaps a son of a concubine. Mahalath, the daughter of Jerimoth and Abihail (David's niece), married David's grandson, King Rehoboam (**2 Chronicles 11:18**).

6. See charts "**1 Chronicles 2**: King David" and "**1 Chronicles 3**: David's Children Born in Hebron and Jerusalem."

7. The term "priest" (Heb. כּוֹהֵן, *cohen*), though primarily descriptive of

a religious official, can also refer to a more secular function, as in the case of David's sons; see explanation in Willem Van Gemeren, *New International Dictionary of Old Testament Theology and Exegesis* (Grand Rapids: Zondervan, 2012), 2:600–603.

8. Zeruiah, and probably Abigail, were the half-sisters of David (**2 Samuel 17:25; 1 Chronicles 2:16**). See chart "**1 Chronicles 2**: King David."

9. These military men are identified in **1 Samuel 26:6; 2 Samuel 2:13, 18; 3:39; 14:1; 16:9–10; 17:25; 18:2; 19:21–22; 21:17; 23:18, 37; 1 Kings 2:5, 22; 1 Chronicles 2:16; 11:6, 39; 18:12, 15; 26:28; 27:24**.

10. See charts "**1 Samuel 1**: Eli and the Eli priesthood" and "**1 Chronicles 24**: Genealogical Registry of the 24 Divisions of Kohathite Attending Priests Who Rotated Service in Solomon's Temple."

11. For Ira the military man, see note 13 in chart "**1 Chronicles 11**: Genealogical Registry of the Mighty Warriors in King David's Army."

2 SAMUEL 16: POSSIBLE GENEALOGY OF SHIMEI, THE BENJAMITE WHO CURSED KING DAVID

Approximate Dating: when King David's fled from Absalom and the early part of King Solomon's reign, ca. 976–960 B.C. ***Relevant Scriptures:*** **2 Samuel 16:5–14; 19:14–23; 1 Kings 2:8–9, 36–46;** also **Genesis 46:21; Numbers 26:38–41; 1 Chronicles 7:6–12; 8:1–7**

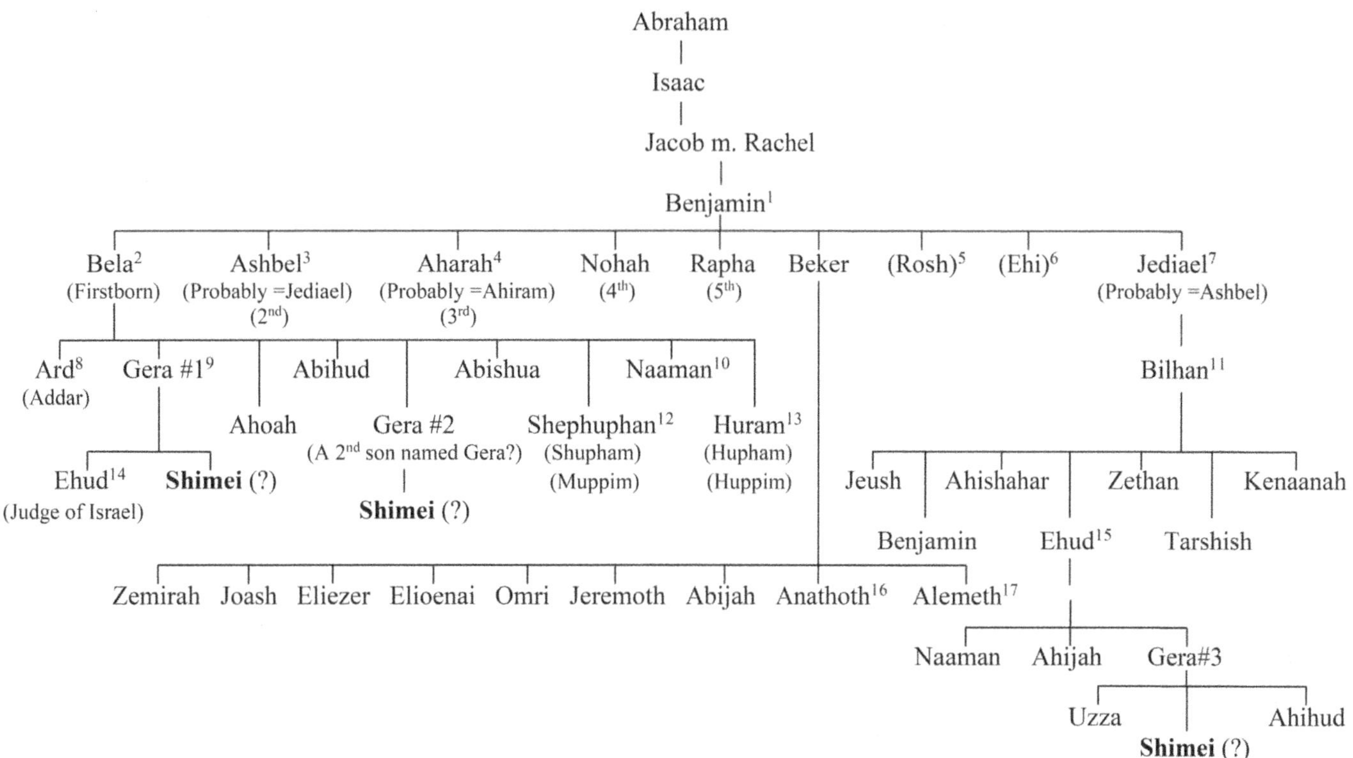

Biblical and Theological Significance

Second Samuel 16:5–14 recounts the story of Shimei the Benjaminite, who cursed David as he fled from Absalom and departed Jerusalem to go to Gilead. Shimei "pelted David and all the king's officials with stones, though all the troops and the special guard were on David's right and left. As he cursed, Shimei said, 'Get out, get out, you murderer, you scoundrel! The LORD has repaid you for all the blood you shed in the household of Saul, in whose place you have reigned. The LORD has given the kingdom into the hands of your son Absalom. You have come to ruin because you are a murderer'" (**2 Samuel 16:6–8**). Because David believed that Shimei's cursing was from the Lord—"Leave him alone; let him curse, for the LORD has told him to" (**2 Samuel 16:11**)—he did not retaliate.[18] After Absalom's death and David's return to Jerusalem and he retook the throne, Shimei had a change of heart and asked for David's mercy and forgiveness (**2 Samuel 19:16–20**). Though David forgave Shimei and vowed, "You shall not die" (**2 Samuel 19:23**),[19] he did not forget the incident. By "blaspheming" David, God's chosen messianic ruler (**Genesis 49:10**), Shimei, in essence, had blasphemed God (**2 Samuel 19:21**). After this David did not fully trust Shimei, so before his death, David advised Solomon not to "consider him [Shimei] innocent. You [Solomon] are a man of wisdom; you will know what to do to him [Shimei]. Bring his gray head down to the grave in blood" (**1 Kings 2:9**). When Solomon assumed the throne, he instructed Shimei, "Build yourself a house in Jerusalem and live there, but do not go anywhere else. The day you leave and cross the Kidron Valley, you can be sure you will die; your blood will be on your own head" (**1 Kings 2:36–37**). However, just three years later, Shimei, in his own folly, left Jerusalem to find his runaway slaves who had fled to Gath. Because he did not keep his "oath to the LORD" (**1 Kings 2:43**), Solomon ordered Shimei's death at the hand of Benaiah the son of Jehoiada (see **1 Kings 2:36–46**).

The Shimei who cursed David is identified as the son of Gera, a Benjamite from Bahurim "from the same clan as Saul's family" (**2 Samuel 16:5**; cf. **19:16, 18; 1 Kings 2:8**). Bahurim was a Benjamite village outside Jerusalem on a road north of the Mount of Olives leading to Mahanaim (cf. **2 Samuel 3:16; 17:18; 19:16–7; 1 Kings 2:8**). There are three Gera figures mentioned in the lists of the descendants of Benjamin: two who were the "sons of Bela"[20] (**1 Chronicles 8:3, 5**)—both approximately four generations removed from Benjamin (born in 1908 B.C.)—and one listed from among the "descendants of Ehud" (**1 Chronicles 8:6–7**), who was at least five generations removed from Benjamin. Thus, it is unclear which of the three Gera figures was the father of Shimei, the man who cursed David in ca. 976 B.C. (or slightly later), but chronology seems to favor the last Shimei (i.e., Shimei, son of Gera, son of Ehud, son of Bilhan, son of Jedaiel). Shimei's name is derivative of the verb שָׁמַע, *shema*, "listen" or "hear," no doubt hypocoristic for "listening to or hearing God." The names Samuel, Simeon, and Shemaiah share the same root.

Notes

1. There is considerable fluidity among the various biblical sources concerning the family of Benjamin. The sons of Benjamin listed in **Genesis 46:21** are "Bela, Beker, Ashbel, Gera, Naaman, Ehi, Rosh, Muppim, Huppim, and Ard." The descendants of Benjamin listed in **Numbers 26:38–41** are Bela, Ashbel, Ahiram, Shupham, Hupham, and the descendants (sons) through Bela, Ard, and Naaman. **First Chronicles 7:6** notes three sons of Benjamin: "Bela, Beker and Jediael." **First Chronicles 8:1–7** provides further details about the Benjaminite clan: "Benjamin was the father of Bela his firstborn, Ashbel the second son, Aharah the third, Nohah the fourth and Rapha the fifth. The sons of Bela were: Addar, Gera, Abihud, Abishua, Naaman, Ahoah, Gera, Shephuphan and Huram. These were the descendants of Ehud who were heads of families of those living in Geba and were deported to Manahath: Naaman, Ahijah, and Gera, who deported them and who was the father of Uzza and Ahihud." Since genealogies can have different functions, this may account for the particular sons or descendants who are mentioned and emphasized in a given list. The chart above is a constructed, segmented genealogy based on the persons mentioned as "sons of Benjamin" in the four references above.

2. Bela was the head of the Belaite clan (**Numbers 26:38**). Other sons of Bela listed in **1 Chronicles 7:7** are: "Ezbon, Uzzi, Uzziel, Jerimoth and Iri."

3. Ashbel was the head of the Ashbelite clan (**Numbers 26:38**). He may be the same person as Jediael; see note 7.

4. Aharah in **1 Chronicles 8:1** is probably the same person as Ahiram, the head of the Ahiramite clan (**Numbers 26:38**).

5. Rosh is mentioned as a son of Benjamin only in **Genesis 46:21**. For additional information, see note 25 in chart "**Genesis 46**: The Extended Family of Jacob (Seventy Descendants) who Migrated to Egypt."

6. Ehi (meaning "brother") is mentioned as a son of Benjamin only in **Genesis 46:21**. Ehi may be the same person as Ahiram (**Numbers 26:38**), Aharah (**1 Chronicles 8:1**), or Ahoah (**1 Chronicles 8:4**). The lexeme *ekhi* (אֵחִי) is no doubt (with most scholars) a prefix syllable with names such as Ahiram (אֲחִירָם). For additional information, see note 24 in chart "**Genesis 46**: The Extended Family of Jacob (Seventy Descendants) who Migrated to Egypt."

7. The Chronicler describes Jediael's descendants, not in genealogical terms (cf. **Genesis 46:21; 1 Chronicles 7:6; 8:1–5**) or clans (cf. **Numbers 26:38–41**), but in military terms, possibly from a census taken of Saul's army: "All these sons of Jediael were heads of families. There were 17,200 fighting men ready to go out to war" (**1 Chronicles 7:11**), as compared to 22,034 sons/descendants of Bela who were fighting men (**1 Chronicles 7:7**) and 20,200 sons/descendants of Beker who were fighting men (**1 Chronicles 7:8–9**). Jediael may be the same person called Ashbel (the Ashbelite clan) in **Genesis 46:21** and **Numbers 26:38**. For the possibility that Jediael is equivalent to Ashbel, see the discussion by Siegfried S. Johnson, "Ashbel," *Anchor Yale Bible Dictionary*.

8. Ard in **Genesis 46:21** and **Numbers 26:40**—the head of the family of Ardites—appears to be the same person as Addar (**1 Chronicles 8:3**).

9. **1 Chronicles 8:3–5** lists the sons of Bela as "Addar, Gera, Abihud, Abishua, Naaman, Ahoah, Gera, Shephuphan and Huram," implying that there are two sons by that name of "Gera." The name Gera derives from *ger* (גֵּר), "stranger, sojourner," plus the additive /a/ (א), representing, perhaps, a code for a divine name. Four different persons bore the name Gera, so it was somewhat common. Ehud the judge of Israel was the "son of Gera" (**Judges 3:15**)—probably referring to one of the (two) Gera figures who were the sons of Bela (**1 Chronicles 8:3**; cf. **Genesis 46:21**), rather than Gera the son of Ehud, the descendant of Jediael (**1 Chronicles 7:10; 8:6–7**).

10. Bela's son Naaman was the head of the Naamite clan (**Numbers 26:40**), not to be confused with Naaman the commander of the army of the king of Aram, who lived 200 years later (**2 Kings 5:1–27**).

11. Ehud was the son of Bilhan and the grandson of Jediael (**1 Chronicles 7:10; 8:6–7**). For unknown reasons—possibly due to intra-tribal jealousy, voluntary emigration, and/or religious persecution—the descendants of this Ehud moved from Geba (in the tribe of Benjamin) to Manahath (cf. the Manahathites of **1 Chronicles 2:52, 54**); for a discussion, see chart "**1 Chronicles 8**: Benjamin and His Descendants Who Settled in Geba and Manahath (Post-Exile)."

12. Shephuphan (**1 Chronicles 8:5**) is the same person as Shupham (**Numbers 26:39**) and Muppim (**Genesis 46:21**), who was the head of the Shuphamite/Shuppite clan (cf. **Numbers 26:39; 1 Chronicles 7:2, 15**).

13. Huram (**1 Chronicles 8:5**) is the same person as Huppim (**Genesis 46:21**) and Hupham (**Numbers 26:39**), who was the head of the Huphamite/Huppite clan (**Numbers 26:39; 1 Chronicles 7:12, 15**).

14. Ehud, the son/descendant of Gera #1 or Gera #2, was the judge of Israel who lived in ca. 1290–1210 B.C. and delivered the Israelites from Moabite oppression (**Judges 3:15–30**); see chart "**Judges 3**: Ehud, the Second Judge of Israel."

15. Ehud the son of Bilhan, the son of Jediael in **1 Chronicles 7:10** appears to be a different person than Ehud the judge of Israel, called "the son of Gera" (**Judges 3:15**). Ehud the son of Bilhan may have been named for Ehud the famous judge from the tribe of Benjamin who delivered the Israelites from Moabite oppression. See chart "**Judges 3**: Ehud, the Second Judge of Israel."

16. Anathoth, one of the nine sons of Beker, is also a place name for a town in the tribe of Benjamin about 3 miles northeast of Jerusalem. Importantly, Anathoth was a Levitical city given to the descendants of Aaron (**Joshua 21:18; 1 Chronicles 6:60**). When King Solomon removed Abiathar from being the high priest in Solomon's Temple, Abiathar returned to his hometown of Anathoth (**1 Kings 2:26–27**). The prophet Jeremiah also hailed from Anathoth (**Jeremiah 1:1; 32:7**).

17. Alemeth, one of the sons of Beker (**1 Chronicles 7:8**), is also a place name. Alemeth (also known as Almon) was a Levitical city given to the descendants of Aaron (cf. **Joshua 21:18; 1 Chronicles 6:60**).

18. As the *Anchor Yale Bible Dictionary* explains: "Shimei's curse highlights a major *Tendenz* of the Davidic narratives: David's burden of guilt for his hand in the death of Saul and the extermination of Saul's line, and the writer's efforts to exonerate David in the matter. . . . Abishai seeks David's permission to kill Shimei on the spot. David again refuses, rebuking Abishai and implying that Shimei has a right to curse him. Furthermore, David appeals to the Lord to look upon him in his affliction, and to repay him with good for this cursing. The impression thus created is that the sons of Zeruiah (who are addressed collectively here, though it is only Abishai who acts) are ruthless men of blood. Conversely, David righteously rejects even that claim upon his enemy's life and person which normally would have been granted him. Seen in this light, David emerges as the Wisdom tradition's paradigm of the righteous man who leaves vengeance in the hands of the Lord and does not put forth his hand in violence. Joab and Abishai are, conversely, the paradigmatic violent men—men of blood, ruthless and unrestrained in their wickedness. While Abishai fulfills this archetype in several instances, the final curse falls upon Joab, who is said to have avenged 'in time of peace blood which had been shed in war,' and to have put 'the blood of war upon the girdle about his loins and upon the sandals on his feet' . . . It is precisely the juxtaposition of these two archetypes—the righteous man who will not put forth his hand to shed blood versus the wicked who is only too quick to draw his sword—that allows the author (or authors) of the Davidic narratives to place the blame for the blood . . . shed under David (especially that of Saul's house) upon his nephews and loyal retainers, the sons of Zeruiah." D. G. Schley, "Abishai," *Anchor Yale Bible Dictionary*, 26.

19. Despite Shimei's request for David's mercy and forgiveness, there is no record of his having sought the forgiveness of Yahweh.

20. The Peshitta lacks "Gera" in **1 Chronicles 8:5**.

2 SAMUEL 17: BARZILLAI THE GILEADITE

Approximate Dating: time of the united monarchy under Saul and David, ca. 1051–971 B.C. ***Relevant Scriptures:*** **2 Samuel 17:27; 19:31–40; 21:8; 1 Kings 2:7; Ezra 2:61–62; Nehemiah 7:63–65; Jeremiah 41:17**

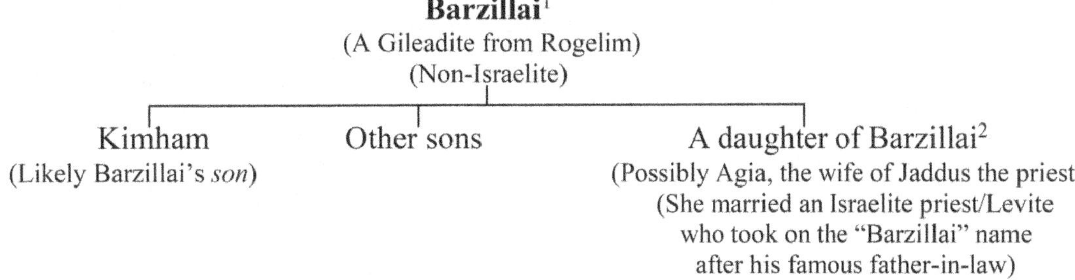

Biblical and Theological Significance

When David fled from Absalom, the wealthy, aged man named Barzillai from Rogelim, from the rugged hill country of Gilead, offered much-needed supplies to David and his band of hungry men in Mahanaim (**2 Samuel 17:27–29; 19:31–39**). For his kindness, David invited Barzillai to accompany him back to Jerusalem and live there; however, Barzillai was already eighty years old and nearing death, so he wanted to return home to Gilead and be buried among his own people. Strikingly, some of Barzillai's daughter(s) and sons,[3] including Kimham,[4] did accompany David back to Jerusalem. Thereafter, the Barzillai family was held in high esteem in Judah. On his deathbed, King David spoke a specific blessing on the Barzillai descendants, instructing his son Solomon to show them continued kindness and to seat them at the highest place of hospitality, at the king's table (**1 Kings 2:7**). Much later, the Barzillai descendants were among those who were carried into Babylonian exile, but some returned to Jerusalem in the post-exile (**Ezra 2:61; Nehemiah 7:63**).

Extremely noteworthy is that a priest, named Barzillai, was among the Kohathite attending priests who claimed eligibility to serve in the Second Temple in post-exilic Jerusalem (cf. **Ezra 2:61; Nehemiah 7:63**). The priest is identified as "Barzillai (a man who had married a daughter of Barzillai the Gileadite and was called by that name)." Considering chronology, this post-exilic priest named Barzillai was most likely a *descendant* of the Kohathite priest who had married Barzillai's daughter in the days of King David. Apparently, in a highly unusual precedent, the ancestral Kohathite priest had taken the *Barzillai* name in honor of his distinguished *father-in-law* (the aged Barzillai the Gileadite who had showed kindness to David; cf. **2 Samuel 17:27; 19:31–40**), instead of retaining his own identity and status as a member of the prestigious Aaronic–Kohathite priesthood. By post-exilic times, the eligibility status of the Barzillai priest was unclear, so a search was conducted for family records, but none were found. Thus, Barzillai and two other Kohathite attending priests, Hobaiah and Hakkoz, "were excluded from the priesthood as unclean . . . until there was a priest ministering with the Urim and Thummim [who could make a final determination]" (**Ezra 2:62–63; Nehemiah 7:64–65**). The conclusion of this matter for Barzillai is not known.[5]

Interestingly, Barzillai's *son*, Kimham,[6] eventually owned a private home called Geruth Kimham (meaning "habitation of Kimham") near Bethlehem (**Jeremiah 41:17**). This lodging place was probably built on land that was part of a royal land grant from King David to the wealthy heirs of Barzillai or bequeathed to the Barzillai-Kimham heirs from David's personal patrimony near Bethlehem in perpetuity for the favor Barzillai had shown David (cf. **2 Samuel 17:27–29; 19:31–39; 1 Kings 2:7**). It is obvious from **Jeremiah 41:11–17** that Geruth Kimham could accommodate a great number of travelers; it may have corresponded in style to a multi-storied home or a caravanserai-type inn (known for providing accommodations for traveling pilgrims in the ancient world). It is interesting to postulate that Jesus was born in the stable-storeroom quarters of this privately owned "inn" (Gr. *kataluma*) of the Kimham's descendants, because there was no "guest room" available to Mary and Joseph (**Luke 2:7**).[7]

Notes

1. The Aramaicized form of the gentilic (בַּרְזִלַּי) yields the translation "iron man," that is, a man of strength and resolve.

2. The daughter of Barzillai is identified as Agia the wife of Jaddus (1 Esdras 5:38). "The name Agia is absent in the parallel lists of Ezra 2:61–Nehemiah 7:63. Although the sons of Jaddus were excluded from priestly service, their ancestral lineage through Agia to Barzillai gave them venerable connection to Israel since the family of Barzillai had been especially favored by King David," Mark J. Fretz, "Agia" in the *Anchor Yale Bible Dictionary*, vol. 1, 92.

3. Some have discussed the possibility that "Adriel son of Barzillai the Meholathite" (**2 Samuel 21:8**)—also called "Adriel of Meholah" (**1 Samuel 18:19**)—was another of the sons of "Barzillai the Gileadite of Rogelim" (**2 Samuel 17:27**; cf. **2 Samuel 19:31–34, 39; 1 Kings 2:7**), the subject of this chart. In support of this supposition is that "Meholathite," the Aramaicized form of the gentilic (יַלִּזְרַבּ), yields the translation "iron man," that is, a man of strength and resolve. Furthermore, Meholathites were inhabitants of the town of Abel Meholah (in Gilead, approximately 14 miles southeast of Beth Shan). Given the location of Abel Meholah in Gilead and that Rogelim was also a town in the nearby hills of the Transjordan, could Adriel the Meholathite be the *son* of "Barzillari the Gileadite of Rogelim" and the *brother* of Kimham?

Geographic considerations: Henry O. Thompson explains in the *Anchor Yale Bible Dictionary* ("Rogelim," 788) that Gilead had a variety of geographical meanings—Bashan, north of the Yarmuk River, the Transjordan south of the Yarmuk River, the area south of the Jabbok River, and/or the area between the Yarmuk and Jabbok rivers. The *Holman Bible Dictionary* ("Rogelim") places Rogelim as a city on the Jabbok River in Gilead (**2 Samuel 17:27–29; 19:31**).

Possibility 1: Adriel of Meholah refers to a son of Barzillai of Rogelim.

This scenario would mean that Adriel, son of the wealthy Barzillai of Rogelim, became the son-in-law of King Saul by the marriage of Adriel to Saul's elder daughter Merab (**1 Samuel 18:19**), who had earlier been promised to David—the *Anchor Yale Bible Dictionary* explains that although the MT and LXX Codex Vaticanus of 2 Samuel 21:8 report that Adriel married the *younger* daughter, Michal, yet other manuscripts (LXX^{LN} and two Heb. manuscripts) read Merab in agreement with **1 Samuel 18:19** (instead of Michal). Therefore, "most scholars favor Merab as the true spouse, although a minority favor Michal, in spite of conflicting traditions, believing the MT testimony in 2 Sam 21:8 to be the more difficult reading and the tradition to be an older and more reliable source than 1 Sam 19:19" (Diane V. Edelman, *Anchor Yale Bible Dictionary*, "Adriel," 81).

Possibility 2: (shown in the chart above): Adriel of Meholah/Adriel son of Barzillai the Meholathite is not one of the sons of Barzillai the Gileadite from Rogelim. In this scenario, there are two different Barzillai figures, although they (and their sons) were near-contemporaries and lived in the same general vicinity. Here, Adriel of Meholah was an inhabitant of the town of Abel Meholah (cf. **Judges 7:22; 1 Kings 4:12; 19:16**), a city in Gilead about 14 miles southeast of Beth-shean (*Holman Bible Dictionary,* "Adriel" and "Meholah"). *The Sacred Bridge* atlas (Anson R. Rainey and R. Steven Notley, 176) places Abel-Meholah at the southernmost point in the Beth-Shean Valley (the latter constituted part of the "fifth" of the Solomonic administrative districts [**1 Kings 4:12**; cf. **4:8–19**]). The marriage of Merab (not Michal), the older daughter of Saul, to a man named Adriel—not the son of Barzillai the Gileadite from Rogelim—is shown in chart "**2 Samuel 21**: Rizpah, the Concubine of King Saul."

4. Kimham is called Chimham in some translations. Kimham was probably the *son* of Barzillai, as supported by the reading of **1 Kings 2:7**: "[David speaking to Solomon] show kindness to the sons of Barzillai of Gilead and let them be among those who eat at your table. They stood by me when I fled from your brother Absalom." Barzillai refers to himself (and to his son Kimham) as a "servant" of David (**2 Samuel 19:37**).

5. Nothing more is said about the Barzillai descendants, including Barzillai the priest, although the Hakkoz descendants/priests—among the descendants of Hobiah, Hakkoz, and Barzillai—were eventually permitted to serve in the temple (see note 16 in chart "**1 Chronicles 24**: Genealogical Registry of the Twenty-Four Divisions of Kohathite Attending Priests Who Rotated Service in Solomon's Temple" and note 14 in chart "**Nehemiah 12**: Genealogical Record of the Heads of Priests, Levites, and Gatekeepers Who Served in the Second Temple in the Days of Joiakim the High Priest, Ezra the Priestly Scribe, and Nehemiah the Governor").

6. Barzillai's *son* Kimham is called Barzillai's "servant" in **2 Samuel 19:37**; but the passage in **1 Kings 2:7** strongly implies that Kimham was among the *sons* of Barzillai who accompanied David back to Jerusalem: [King David speaking to Solomon] "Show kindness to the sons of Barzillai of Gilead and let them be among those who eat at your table. They stood by me when I fled from your brother Absalom."

7. This interpretation is consistent with other commentary interpretations that equate the "inn" with a "caravanserai"—"Luke 2:7," *Elliott's Commentary for English Readers*, "Luke 2:7," *Pulpit Commentary* and "Luke 2:7," *Cambridge Bible for Schools and Colleges* (all three accessed through https://biblehub.com/commentaries/luke/2-7.htm; also see M. G. Easton, "Chimham," *Easton Bible Dictionary*).

2 SAMUEL 20: POSSIBLE GENEALOGY OF SHEBA THE REBEL

Approximate Dating: ca. 971 B.C. ***Relevant Scriptures:*** **2 Samuel 20:1–22;** also **1 Chronicles 8:1–13**

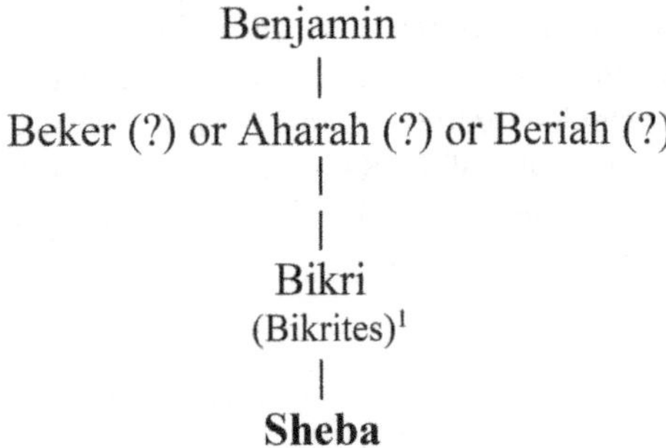

Biblical and Theological Significance

Sheba is characterized as "the troublemaker" from the hill country of Ephraim. The biblical narrative is clearly related to the declaration in **2 Samuel 3:1** that "the war between the house of Saul and the house of David lasted a long time. David grew stronger and stronger, while the house of Saul grew weaker and weaker"—a transfer of power that did not go unopposed, especially among the northern tribes. Sheba led a rebellion among the ten northern tribes to remove support from King David: "all the men of Israel deserted David to follow Sheba son of Bikri. But the men of Judah stayed by their king all the way from the Jordan to Jerusalem" (**2 Samuel 20:2**). David believed that "Sheba son of Bikri will do us more harm than Absalom did. . . . he will find fortified cities and escape from us [David, Joab, and the army of Judah]" (**2 Samuel 20:6**). The Judahites pursued him and found Sheba holed up behind the outer wall at Abel Beth Maakah.[2] As the Israelites prepared to batter down the wall, a wise woman bargained with them not to destroy a "mother city" of Israel[3] (**2 Samuel 20:15–21**). And if they would refrain, she would convince the people to throw Sheba's head over the wall as a ransom. The citizens of Abel Beth Maakah followed her wise advice, killed Sheba, and threw his head over the wall to Joab, David's army commander (**2 Samuel 20:22**), who then withdrew David's army.

With regard to Sheba's heritage, his exact ancestry is unknown. He was a Benjamite and the son of Bikri (the Bikrite clan), who may have been descendants of Beker, the son of Benjamin (**Genesis 46:21**; cf. **1 Chronicles 7:6, 8**) or Aharah, another son of Benjamin (**1 Chronicles 8:1**). Alternatively, the Bikrites may have been related to the descendants of Beriah,[4] son of Elpaal, son of Shaharaim, who were also Benjamites (cf. **1 Chronicles 8:1, 11–27**).[5]

The following theological points should be considered:

- When a divine edict and word of judgment has been declared—in this case, the replacement of Saul by David, the one God himself had chosen (**1 Samuel 13:14**)—it is foolhardy to attempt a circumvention to achieve a different result.
- The term describing Sheba as אִישׁ בְּלִיַּעַל, *ish beliyaal*, "useless," "good for nothing"[6]—of uncertain etymology but invariably a negative term and an insult—suggests a level of Benjamite leadership that had deteriorated so badly as to be in the hands of an ambitious simpleton of no standing. How the mighty have fallen! The truth is that every sword turned against the Lord and his people has a tendency to turn backward and render its owner an ultimately fatal wound.

Notes

1. The "entire region of the Bikrites" (**2 Samuel 20:14**) is not clearly delineated but appears to be in close proximity to the town of Abel Beth Maakah, located in the north, about 12 miles north of Lake Huleh and four miles west of Dan. Maakah, a word which by form is feminine, is used grammatically for both genders in that it can have either feminine or masculine referents. Thus, David's wife by that name—Maakah, the mother of Absalom—was obviously female, but the region of Maakah (cf. **Joshua 12:5; 13:11, 13; 2 Samuel 10:6, 8; 20:14–15; 1 Chronicles 19:6–7**; etc.) is genderless. The same name (Maakah) also applies to (1) a son of Nahor, the brother of Abraham (**Genesis 22:24**); (2) the father of Achish, a Philistine and the king of Gath (**1 Kings 2:39**); (3) the *granddaughter* of Absalom/Abishalom and the wife of Rehoboam (**1 Kings 15:2; 2 Chronicles 11:21–22; 15:16**); (4) the wife of Makir (**1 Chronicles 7:16**); (5) the wife of Jeiel (**1 Chronicles 8:29; 9:35**); (6) the father of Hanan (**1 Chronicles 11:43**); and (7) a concubine of Caleb the Kenizzite (**1 Chronicles 2:48**).

2. For Abel Beth Maakah, see note 1.

3. "Mother" is a metaphor to speak of a larger city or town, the citizens of which may leave to create and settle in villages ("daughters") around it.

4. See chart "**1 Chronicles 8**: The Benjamites who Settled in and around Jerusalem and in Moab (Post-Exile)."

5. The MT of **2 Samuel 20:14** (supported by Syriac and Targum *secundum*) reads "and the Berim," however, this seems doubtful, in light of **2 Samuel 20:1**, which describes Sheba as "son of Bikri, a Benjamite."

6. "בְּלִיַּעַל," *HALOT* 1:133–134.

2 SAMUEL 21: RIZPAH, THE CONCUBINE OF KING SAUL

Approximate Dating: united monarchy under Saul and David, ca. 1051–971 B.C. ***Relevant Scriptures:*** **2 Samuel 21:1–14**; also **Genesis 35:18; 1 Samuel 9:1; 14:49–51; 31:2; 2 Samuel 2:8; 3:7–11; 4:1–8, 12; 1 Chronicles 8:29–40; 9:35–44; 10:2; Esther 2:5–7, 15; 9:29**

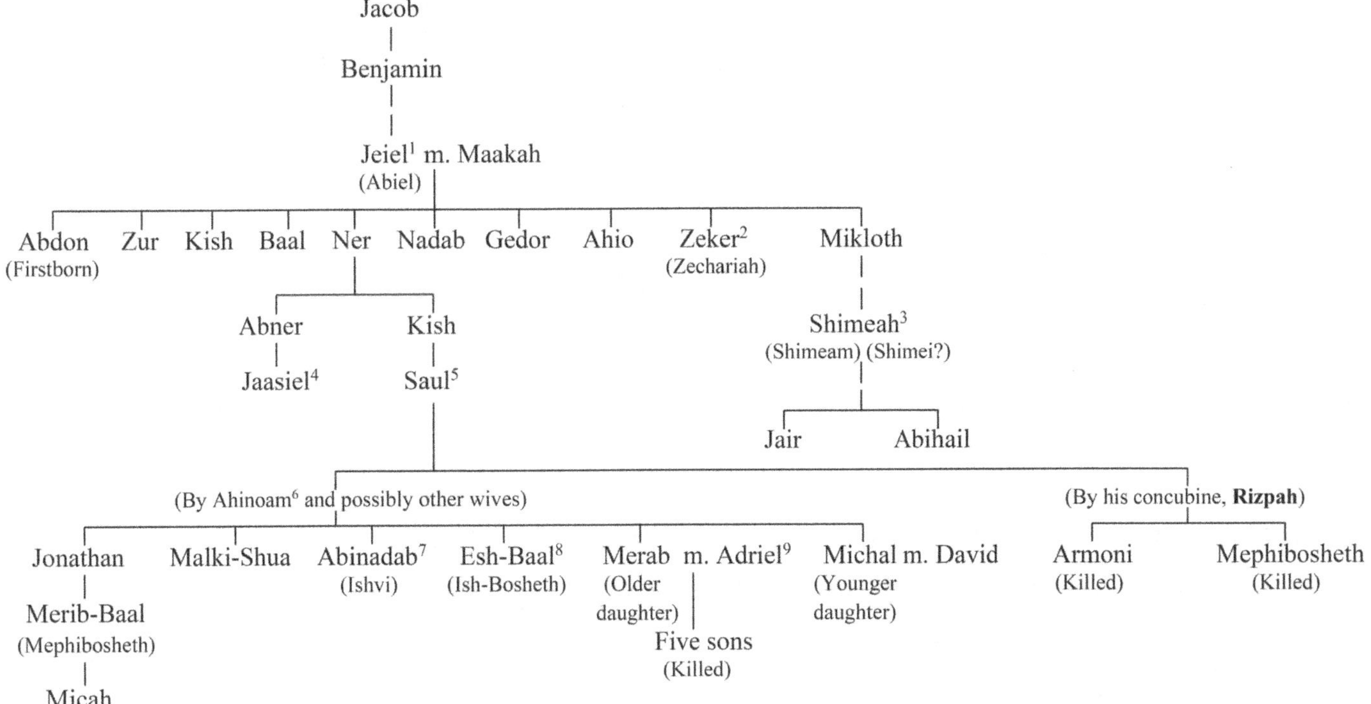

Biblical Significance

This chart shows the familial relationships of the five sons of Merab and the two sons of Rizpah who were killed by the Gibeonites for Saul's breach of the treaty with the Gibeonites (cf. **Joshua 9; 2 Samuel 21**). Rizpah was the daughter of Aiah (**2 Samuel 3:7**) and the concubine of Saul. After King Saul died, Rizpah may have been raped by Abner (the text is not clear). However, **2 Samuel 3:6** does confirm that during the war between the houses of David and Saul, "Abner had been strengthening his own position in the house of Saul." When Saul's son Ish-Bosheth rose to the throne, he accused Abner of having sexual relations with Rizpah. Abner became outraged and shifted his allegiance to David[10] (**2 Samuel 3:7–12**).

This story has roots in the early invasion of Canaan (ca. 1406 B.C.). The Gibeonites (a remnant Hivite/Amorite people) feared the Israelites, and through deceitful means they secured a peace covenant with Israel (**Joshua 9:3–27**), which was honored for many years (cf. **Joshua 10:1–27**). However, during the reign of Saul (ca. 1051–1011 B.C.), the Lord sent a three-year famine because Saul tried to annihilate the Gibeonites, perhaps because of his nationalistic "zeal for Israel and Judah" (**2 Samuel 21:1–2**). When David understood the need to appease the Lord and atone for the guilt of Saul, he handed over seven male descendants of Saul (two sons through Rizpah and five grandsons through Merab) to the Gibeonites, who "killed them and exposed their bodies on a hill before the LORD" (**2 Samuel 21:9**). Rizpah began a six-month-long vigil over the slain young men, corresponding roughly to the beginning of the barley harvest in April/May until the season of early rains in October, during which time she shooed the birds and animals away from their decomposing bodies. Her steadfast devotion and selfless actions shamed King David. In response, David gathered the bones of the dead young men; he also *re-membered* the bodies of Saul and Jonathan (which were in Jabesh Gilead) and brought their bones back to Jerusalem (**2 Samuel 21:10–13**) where they were buried in "the tomb of Saul's father Kish, at Zela in Benjamin" (**2 Samuel 21:14**; cf. Zelah in **Joshua 18:28**). "After that, God answered prayer in behalf of the [famine-plagued] land" (**2 Samuel 21:14**). Thus, a lowly concubine of uncertain heritage inspired the great King David to act, which he might not have done otherwise. Paul later observed that God "chose the foolish things of the world to shame the wise; . . . the weak things of the world to shame the strong" (**1 Corinthians 1:27**). The righteous actions of Rizpah, who kept the birds of prey from gorging on her innocent children, symbolize certain aspects of **Revelation 19:17–21**, whereupon the return of the conquering Christ and the army of the Lamb will survive, but the army of the beast will not. God will allow the birds of the air to have a supper and gorge on the corpses of those who opposed Christ, while the bride will enjoy the glorious wedding supper of the Lamb.

Notes

1. The Chronicler does not go into the early ancestry of Saul the Benjamite beyond noting that he was a descendant of Jeiel; for further information see chart "**1 Samuel 9**: King Saul."

2. Zeker (**1 Chronicles 8:31**) is hypocoristic for Zechariah (**1 Chronicles 9:37**).

3. Shimeah (שמה [*shmh*] in **1 Chronicles 8:32** and Shimeam (שמם [*shmm*] in **1 Chronicles 9:38** are likely variants of Shimei (שמע [*shm'*]), the latter referring to the ancestor(s) of the Benjamite clan called "the clan of Shimei" (**Zechariah 12:13**), who returned to Jerusalem in the post-exile and "lived near their [Benjamite] relatives in Jerusalem" (**1 Chronicles 8:32**; cf. **9:7–9, 38**). Especially noteworthy is that Shimeah/Shimeam/Shimei appears to be an ancestor of Mordecai and Esther (**Esther 2:5–7, 15**), inasmuch as some Benjamites living in Jerusalem were captured at the same time as the Judahites and were deported to Babylon along with King Jeconiah/Jehoiachin (cf. **2 Kings 24:10–12**). See chart "**Esther 2**: Mordecai and Esther, Jews Living in Persia."

4. Jaasiel son of Abner was Saul's cousin. Jaasiel's father, Abner, had served as the army commander for Saul and Ish-Bosheth (cf. **1 Samuel 14:50; 17:55; 20:25; 26:5; 2 Samuel 2:8; 4:1**). During David's reign, Jaasiel led the tribe of Benjamin and may have been involved in conducting the census for the tribe of Benjamin, although the census was never completed (**1 Chronicles 27:21**; see **vv. 16–24**).

5. The ancestry of Saul is summarized in **1 Samuel 9:1; 14:50–51**. For the genealogy of others in Saul's family, see charts "**1 Samuel 9**: King Saul" and "**1 Chronicles 8 & 9**: The Descendants of King Saul Living in Gibeon and Jerusalem (Post-Exile)."

6. Ahinoam, one of the wives of King Saul, was the daughter of Ahimaaz (not Ahimaaz the high priest; **1 Samuel 14:50; 1 Chronicles 6:8–9**). Ahinoam the wife of King Saul is a different person than Ahinoam of Jezreel, one of the wives of King David (**1 Samuel 25:43; 27:3; 30:5**). Even though **2 Samuel 12:8** says that the Lord gave to David "your master's [Saul's] house . . . and your master's [Saul's] wives into your arms," the two women named Ahinoam are most likely two different people.

7. Abinadab in **1 Samuel 31:2** and **1 Chronicles 8:33; 9:39; 10:2** appears to be the same person as Ishvi in **1 Samuel 14:49**.

8. Ish-Bosheth (**2 Samuel 2:8, 10, 12, 15; 3:7–8, 14–15; 4:1, 5, 8, 12**) is the same person as Esh-Baal (**1 Chronicles 8:33; 9:39**).

9. Adriel was the son of a man named Barzillai—probably not the same person as Barzillai the Gileadite of Rogelim (**2 Samuel 17:27; 19:31; 1 Kings 2:7**) who is discussed in the chart "**2 Samuel 17**: Barzillai the Gileadite" (cf. **2 Samuel 17:27-29**). Adriel is called "Adriel the Meholathite" which probably suggests that he was a citizen of Abel Meholah/Meholah, a town near Tabbath (**Judges 7:22**) and Jokmeam (**1 Kings 4:12**), near the Jordan River, about ten miles south of Beth Shan. Abel Meholah was also the hometown of the prophet Elisha (**1 Kings 19:16**).

10. David welcomed Abner, which infuriated David's long-standing army commander Joab, so Joab killed Abner (**2 Samuel 3:12–30**).

1 AND 2 KINGS: SUMMARY OF THE GENEALOGICAL RECORD OF THE KINGS OF THE UNITED AND DIVIDED KINGDOMS

Relevant Scriptures: **1 & 2 Kings; 1 & 2 Chronicles**

Kings of the United Kingdom

Saul (reigned 40 years) (ca. 1051–1011 B.C.)

▼

David (reigned 40 yrs.) (ca. 1011–971 B.C.)

|

Solomon (reigned 40 yrs.) (ca. 971–931 B.C.)

Legend:

| : Indicates succession of father to son (e.g., Abijah was the son of Rehoboam of Judah; Nadab was the son of Jeroboam I of Israel).

ㄣ : Successor was related to the previous king, but not directly (e.g., Queen Athaliah of Judah was the mother of Ahaziah; Joram of Israel was the brother of Ahaziah of Israel).

▼ : Successor was unrelated to the previous king; typically, the successor usurped the throne by killing the previous king.

Kings of the Divided Kingdoms

In general, the dating system for the reigns of the kings of Judah and Israel follows the chronology of Edwin R. Thiele's *The Mysterious Numbers of the Hebrew Kings* or that given in Eugene H. Merrill's *Kingdom of Priests, A History of Old Testament Israel.*

Thiele distinguishes two different dating systems: *accession year dating* whereby a ruler's reign is determined by the first year, called the accession year, that the ruler comes to the throne, and *non-accession-year dating*, in which the year the ruler comes to the throne is termed the first year, and the second official year begins with the New Year's Day following his accession. (To clarify: in "accession year dating," if King (A) died in the middle of the year, the period of time to the end of that year was called the "accession year" of the

Kings of Judah

Rehoboam[1] (17 yrs.) (931–913 B.C.) (E)

Abijah[3] (3 yrs.) (913–911 B.C.) (E)

Asa[5] (41 yrs.) (911–869 B.C.) (R)

Jehoshaphat[7] (25 yrs.) (Co-regent with Asa 872–869 B.C.)
(Official reign 872–848 B.C.) (R; later lapsed)

Jehoram[10] (8 yrs.) (Co-regent with Jehoshaphat 853–848 B.C.)
(Sole reign & official reign 848–841 B.C.) (E)

Ahaziah[12] (1 yr.) (841 B.C.) (E)

[**Queen Athaliah**[13] (6 yrs.) (841–835 B.C.) (E)]

Joash[15] (40 yrs.) (835–796 B.C.) (R)

Amaziah[17] (29 yrs.) (796–767 B.C.) (R)

Azariah (Uzziah)[19] (52 yrs.) (Co-regent with Amaziah 792–767 B.C.)
(Sole reign 767–740 B.C.) (Official reign 792–740 B.C.) (R)

Jotham[22] (16 yrs.) (Co-regent and dominant regent with Azariah
from 752–740 B.C.) (Official reign 750–735 B.C.) (R)

Ahaz[24] (16 yrs.) (Co-regent and dominant regent with Jotham
from 735–731 B.C.) (Official reign 731–715 B.C.) (E)

Hezekiah[26] (29 yrs.) (Co-regent with Ahaz 729–715 B.C.)
(Official reign 715–686 B.C.) (R)

Manasseh[29] (55 yrs.) (Co-regent with Hezekiah 697–686 B.C.)
(Official reign 697–642 B.C.) (E)

Amon[31] (2 yrs.) (642–640 B.C.) (E)

Josiah[33] (31 yrs.) (640–609 B.C.) (R)

Jehoahaz (Shallum)[35] (3 months) (609 B.C.) (E)

Eliakim (Jehoiakim)[36] (11 yrs.) (609–598 B.C.) (E)

Jehoiachin (Jeconiah)[38] (3 months) (598–597 B.C.) (E)

Zedekiah (Mattaniah)[39] (11 yrs.) (597–586 B.C.) (E)

↓

Nebuchadnezzar besieged Jerusalem 1½ years
(From the ninth year, tenth month, tenth day
of Zedekiah's reign to the eleventh year, fourth
month, ninth day of Zedekiah's reign)

↓

Fall of Jerusalem in the eleventh year, fifth month,
seventh day of King Zedekiah's reign
(Corresponding to the nineteenth year of King
Nebuchadnezzar of Babylon)

↓

Destruction of Solomon's Temple and exile of the
people of Judah to Babylon.
End of the southern kingdom of Judah (586 B.C.)

Kings of Israel

Jeroboam I[2] (22 yrs.) (931–910 B.C.) (E)

Nadab[4] (2 yrs.) (910–909 B.C.) (E)

▼

Baasha[6] (24 yrs.) (909–886 B.C.) (E)

Elah[8] (2 yrs.) (886–885 B.C.) (E)

▼

Zimri[9] (7 days) (885 B.C.) (E)

▼

Tibni & Omri[11] (Rival co-regents 5 yrs.) (885–880 B.C.)
Tibni (5 yrs.) (885–880 B.C.) (E) and
Omri (12 yrs.) (885–874 B.C.) (E)

Ahab[14] (22 yrs.) (874–853 B.C.) (E)

Ahaziah[16] (2 yrs.) (853–852 B.C.) (E)

Joram[18] (12 yrs.) (852–841 B.C.) (E)

▼

Jehu[20] (28 yrs.) (841–814 B.C.) (E)

Jehoahaz[21] (17 yrs.) (814–798 B.C.) (E)

Jehoash[23] (16 yrs.) (798–782 B.C.) (E)

Jeroboam II[25] (41 yrs.) (Co-regent with Jehoash
793–782 B.C.) (Official reign 793–753 B.C.) (E)

Zechariah[27] (6 months) (753 B.C.) (E)

▼

Shallum[28] (1 month) (752 B.C.) (E)

▼

Menahem[30] (10 yrs.) (752–742 B.C.) (E)

Pekahiah[32] (2 yrs.) (742–740 B.C.) (E)

▼

Pekah[34] (20 yrs.)
(Co-regent during the full terms of
Menahem, 752–742 B.C., and Pekahiah, 742–740 B.C.)
(Sole reign 740–732 B.C.) (Official reign 752–732 B.C.)

▼

Hoshea[37] (9 yrs.) (732–722 B.C.) (E)

↓

Three-year siege of Samaria by the Assyrians
(725–722 B.C.)

↓

Assyrians take Israel/Samaria
in the ninth year of Hoshea's reign
(Corresponding to the sixth year of the
twenty-nine-year reign of King Hezekiah of Judah)

↓

End of the northern kingdom of Israel
(722 B.C.)

new King (B) who came to rule, and King B would begin his official Year 1 in the next new year. On the other hand, in "non-accession year dating," if King (A) died in the middle of the year, the period of time to the end of the year was considered Year 1 of the new King (B) and his Year 2 began at the start of the next new year.) The kingdom of Judah used accession-year reckoning from Rehoboam to Jehoshaphat, non-accession-year reckoning from Jehoram to Joash, and accession-year reckoning once again from Amaziah to Zedekiah. The kingdom of Israel used non-accession-year reckoning from Jeroboam I to Jehoahaz and accession-year reckoning from Jehoash to Hoshea. The regnal years in Judah began with the month of Tishri in the fall, and those in Israel with the month of Nisan in the spring. (Thiele discusses in detail the chronological problems, dual dating, synchronism, co-regency/overlapping reigns, and shifts in system reckoning.)

Regnal years given below are approximations. In the chart, (E) indicates an evil king and (R) indicates a righteous king.

Biblical and Theological Significance

Monarchy lies at the very heart of biblical theology, having been introduced and emphatically emphasized at the very beginning of the book of Genesis. The first recorded words of God as to the purpose of the creation of mankind make this proposition crystal clear: "Be fruitful and increase in number; fill the earth and subdue it. Rule over the fish in the sea and the birds in the sky and over every living creature that moves on the ground" (**Genesis 1:28**). Laterally and vertically, mankind was to be sovereign over all, but under God. That mandate was never rescinded; rather, it was exemplified, particularly in the descendants of Abraham (**Genesis 12:2–3; 15:18–21; 17:4–6**) and in the covenant made with Moses on Israel's behalf: "Now if you obey me fully and keep my covenant, then out of all nations you will be my treasured possession. Although the whole earth is mine, you will be for me a kingdom of priests and a holy nation" (**Exodus 19:5–6**). Some five hundred years later, David was chosen to be the king of Israel, a prototype of this holy, priestly kingdom, albeit a flawed ruler over the flawed people, the descendants of Abraham. The chart clearly shows the catastrophic effect of attempts at human monarchy. Nonetheless, the God of inexhaustible grace promised through prophetic voices that there would be a Davidic descendant—a perfect Ruler, the Son of God himself, the long-awaited Messiah, and the eternal King—who would sit on the throne of majesty and glory, manifesting his works, even on earth. What the original Adamic kingdom could have been was finally realized in Jesus, the King of kings and Lord of lords, who ruled over an everlasting kingdom (cf. **Psalm 47:2–9; 145:13; Daniel 7:27; Zechariah 14:9; Matthew 28:18; 1 Timothy 6:15; Hebrews 1:8; Revelation 1:5; 3:14; 11:15; 17:14; 19:16**).

Notes

1. **Rehoboam**, the son of Solomon, was forty-one when he commenced his reign as the first king of the southern kingdom of Judah and reigned for seventeen years. He was haughty and promised a heavy yoke of oppression for the people (cf. **1 Kings 11:43–12:24; 14:21–31; 2 Chronicles 9:30–12:16**). See chart "**1 Kings 12**: Rehoboam, King of Judah."

2. **Jeroboam I**, the son of Nebat and the former head over Solomon's labor force, became the first king over the northern kingdom of Israel and reigned for twenty-two years. His reign is summarized as: "Jeroboam son of Nebat . . . caused Israel to sin" (**1 Kings 22:52; 2 Kings 23:15**). Thereafter, all the kings of the Northern Kingdom followed the evil, idolatrous example of Jeroboam (cf. **1 Kings 11:26–40; 12:12–20, 25–33; 13:1–14:31; 2 Chronicles 10:1–4, 12–15**). See chart "**1 Kings 11**: Jeroboam 1, King of Israel."

3. **Abijah** (or Abijam in some translations), the son of Rehoboam, became king of Judah in the eighteenth year of the twenty-two-year reign of Jeroboam I of Israel and reigned for three years. Abijah was the son of Rehoboam and Maakah (Maakah was the daughter Tamar and the granddaughter of Absalom; cf. **2 Samuel 14:27; 1 Kings 15:2, 10; 2 Chronicles 13:2**). His rule was marred by constant conflict with Israel; in the end, he followed the evil footsteps of his father, Rehoboam (cf. **1 Kings 15:1–8; 2 Chronicles 13:1–14:1**). See chart "**1 Kings 15**: Abijah, King of Judah."

4. **Nadab**, the son of Jeroboam I, became king of Israel in the second year of the forty-one-year reign of King Asa of Judah and reigned for two years. Nadab was slain by Baasha of the tribe of Issachar in the third year of Asa's reign (cf. **1 Kings 15:25–31**). See chart "**1 Kings 15**: Nadab, King of Israel."

5. **Asa**, the son of Abijah, became king of Judah in the twentieth year of the twenty-two-year reign of Jeroboam I of Israel and reigned for forty-two years. Overall, Asa was loyal to the Lord, as seen by his removal of pagan idols, male shrine prostitutes, and idolaters (including even his grandmother, Maakah, who worshiped Asherah), although some pagan high places remained in the land. Later, however, Asa used temple treasuries to make a treaty with Syria to keep King Baasha of Israel from invading Judah. Asa built up Geba and Mizpah and led the people of Judah in covenant renewal (cf. **1 Kings 15:8–24; 2 Chronicles 14:1–16:14**). See chart "**1 Kings 15**: Asa, King of Judah."

6. **Baasha** from the tribe of Issachar became king of Israel in the third year of the forty-one-year reign of Asa of Judah and reigned for twenty-four years. Baasha killed all the members of the house (household) of Jeroboam I and killed Nadab, the previous king of Israel (cf. **1 Kings 15:27–30, 33–16:13**). See chart "**1 Kings 15**: Baasha, King of Israel."

7. **Jehoshaphat**, the son of Asa, became king of Judah in the fourth year of the twenty-two-year reign of Ahab of Israel and reigned for twenty-five years. Jehoshaphat was "at peace with the king of Israel" (**1 Kings 22:44**), but unfortunately, he "allied himself" (**2 Chronicles 18:1**) with Ahab by permitting the marriage of his son Jehoram to Athaliah, the daughter of Ahab and Jezebel (see **1 Kings 22:41–50; 2 Chronicles 17:1–21:3**). See chart "**1 Kings 15**: Jehoshaphat, King of Judah."

8. **Elah** the son of Baasah became king of Israel in the twenty-sixth year of the forty-one-year reign of Asa of Judah and reigned for two years. Zimri, the commander of half the chariots of Israel's army, assassinated Elah, and he also killed all the members of Baasha's household (cf. **1 Kings 16:8–14**). See chart "**1 Kings 16**: Elah, King of Israel."

9. **Zimri** (of unknown ancestry) reigned over Israel from Tirzah for a brief seven days, corresponding to the twenty-seventh year of Asa of Judah. Before becoming king, Zimri had been the commander of half the Israelite chariots; however, Zimri conspired against Elah of Israel, killed him, and became king in his place. Zimri then destroyed the whole family of Baasha. When the people of Israel proclaimed Omri king, they besieged Tirzah, and Zimri committed suicide by burning the palace down around himself (cf. **1 Kings 16:9–10, 15–20**). See chart "**1 Kings 16**: Zimri, King of Israel."

10. **Jehoram** (or Joram in some translations) the son of Jehoshaphat became king of Judah in the fifth year of the twelve-year reign of Joram of Israel and reigned for eight years. Jehoram married Athaliah, the daughter of Ahab and the granddaughter of Omri of Israel. Because of the strong influence of his wife Athaliah, Jehoram was an evil king who eventually followed the pagan ways of Israel (cf. **2 Kings 8:16–24; 2 Chronicles 18:1, 21:1–20**). See chart "**2 Kings 8**: Jehoram, King of Judah."

11. **Tibni** and **Omri** were rival co-regents of Israel for five years, from ca. 885–880 B.C. Initially, half of the people of Israel followed Tibni the son of Ginath (otherwise unknown), and the other half followed Omri (the former commander of Israel's army), but as the two sides continued to fight, Omri's supporters won. Israel's civil war continued until Tibni's death in 880 B.C., at which time Omri assumed the sole rulership of Israel, a date corresponding to the thirty-first year of the forty-one-year reign of Asa of Judah. Omri reigned for a total of twelve years (885–874 B.C.), the first six from the capital city

of Tirzah. Then, around 880 B.C., Omri bought the hill of Shemer, renamed it Samaria, and established it as the new capital of the Northern Kingdom (**1 Kings 16:21–28**). See chart "**1 Kings 16**: Omri, King of Israel."

12. **Ahaziah**, the son of Jehoram of Judah and Athaliah (the daughter of Ahab and Jezebel of Israel) and the nephew of Joram of Israel, became king of Judah at the age of twenty-two, in the last year of the twelve-year reign of Joram of Israel, but Ahaziah reigned for only one year. Ahaziah and his forty-two brothers were killed by Jehu, the commander of the Israelite army. After Ahaziah's death, his mother, Athaliah, seized power and killed all the potential heirs to the throne of Judah, except the one-year-old infant Joash, who was rescued by Jehosheba and Jehoiada the priest (**2 Kings 8:25–9:29; 10:12–14; 11:1–3; 2 Chronicles 22:1–12**). See chart "**2 Kings 8**: Ahaziah, King of Judah."

13. **Queen Athaliah**, the daughter of Ahab of Israel and the granddaughter of Omri, was the wife of Jehoram of Judah. After her son Ahaziah of Judah was killed by Jehu, Athaliah assumed power herself and slaughtered all the legitimate heirs in the royal family who could contend for the throne, except for Joash (the one-year-old infant son of the deceased Ahaziah). Joash was rescued and hidden in Solomon's Temple for six years by Jehosheba (Ahaziah's half-sister and Joash's half-aunt) and Jehosheba's husband, Jehoiada the priest, during Athaliah's illegitimate rule over Judah. In a plan conceived by Jehoiada, Athaliah was deposed and killed by the army captains of Judah. Joash was then enthroned as the rightful ruler (**2 Kings 11:1–20; 2 Chronicles 22:10–12; 23:1–21**). See chart "**2 Kings 11**: Queen Athaliah, Illegitimate Ruler of Judah."

14. **Ahab** the son of Omri became king of Israel in the thirty-eighth year of the forty-one-year reign of Asa of Judah and reigned from Samaria for twenty-two years. Ahab married Jezebel, the daughter of Ethbaal of Sidon, who was a staunch Baal worshiper. During his reign, Ahab made a temple to Baal at Samaria and carved a wooden pole of the goddess Asherah for worship. Ahab is remembered for doing "more evil in the eyes of the LORD than any of those before him" (**1 Kings 16:30**; see **1 Kings 16:29–34; 21:1–22:40; 2 Chronicles 18:28–34**). See chart "**1 Kings 16**: Ahab, King of Israel."

15. **Joash** (or Jehoash in some translations), the son of Ahaziah, became king of Judah at the age of seven in the seventh year of the twenty-eight-year reign of Jehu of Israel and reigned for forty years. Following the death of her son Ahaziah, Queen Athaliah killed her grandchildren and all potential heirs to the throne, except Joash, the infant son of King Ahaziah. Joash was hidden away in Solomon's Temple from Queen Athaliah for six years by Jehosheba and her husband, Jehoiada, the Kohathite attending priest. Then, after a coup that deposed Athaliah, the seven-year-old Joash was crowned the rightful king to the throne of Judah (**2 Kings 11:4–21; 2 Chronicles 23:1–21**). Jehoiada became a father figure to the young king. Joash was a good king while Jehoiada was living, even calling for the restoration of Solomon's Temple. However, Joash was eventually killed by two of his servants for his complicity in allowing bad leaders of Judah to stone to death Jehoiada's son, Zechariah the prophet-priest, whom he (Joash) had grown up with (**2 Kings 11:1–12:21; 2 Chronicles 22:10–24:27**). See chart "**2 Kings 11**: Joash, King of Judah."

16. **Ahaziah** the son of Ahab became king of Israel in the seventeenth year of the twenty-five-year reign of Jehoshaphat of Judah and reigned for two years. Ahaziah was a contemporary of Elijah the prophet. Ahaziah died from a fatal fall. And because he had no sons/heirs to assume the throne, Ahaziah's brother Joram became king in his place (cf. **1 Kings 22:51–53; 2 Kings 1:1–18; 2 Chronicles 20:35–36**). See chart "**1 Kings 22**: Ahaziah, King of Israel."

17. **Amaziah** the son of Joash became king of Judah at the age of twenty-five, in the second year of the sixteen-year reign of Jehoash of Israel, and reigned for twenty-nine years. Amaziah did what was right in the Lord's sight, but the high places of pagan worship continued to be used. Amaziah executed the servants who had killed his father, Joash; he also killed 10,000 Edomites and captured Petra (the stronghold/capital of Edom). His accomplishments encouraged self-pride, leading Amaziah to initiate an ill-advised war with King Jehoash of Israel. Amaziah lost the war and was taken to Samaria by Jehoash, but Amaziah ended up surviving Israel's king by fifteen years. Amaziah was eventually killed by conspirators in Jerusalem (cf. **2 Kings 14:1–22; 2 Chronicles 24:27–25:28**). See chart "**2 Kings 12**: Amaziah, King of Judah."

18. **Joram** (or Jehoram in some translations) the son of Ahab and Jezebel became king of Israel upon the early death of his brother Ahaziah, who had no sons/heirs to assume the throne. Joram became king of Israel in the eighteenth year of the twenty-five-year reign of Jehoshaphat of Judah and reigned for twelve years. When Joram was fatally wounded in battle by Jehu, his body was thrown onto the field of Naboth, thereby fulfilling the Lord's judgment against Ahab and his wicked ways (cf. **1 Kings 21:29; 2 Kings 1:17; 3:1–8:15; 9:25**). See chart "**2 Kings 3**: Joram, King of Israel."

19. **Azariah** (or **Uzziah**) the son of Amaziah became king of Judah at age sixteen, in the twenty-seventh year of Jeroboam II's forty-one-year reign, and reigned for 52 years. While his father (Amaziah) was taken to Samaria as a captive of King Jehoash of Israel (**2 Kings 14:13**), Azariah/Uzziah held a 24-year co-regency with Amaziah before Azariah began his sole rulership. Unlike his father, Azariah/Uzziah was a good king, although the pagan high places were still in use. Azariah/Uzziah was a strong king who (1) went to war with the Philistines and the Ammonites; (2) rebuilt the destroyed walls of Jerusalem, especially the Corner Gate and the Gate of Ephraim; (3) rebuilt towers that had been destroyed in war with Joash of Israel; and (4) built up a very large army. His long list of accomplishments caused him to swell with pride. When he presumptuously burned incense in the temple—a task to be performed only by the Lord's anointed priests—the Lord punished him, inflicting him with leprosy for the rest of his life. During Azariah/Uzziah's illness, his son Jotham ruled over the people (cf. **Kings 15:1–7; 2 Chronicles 26:1–23**). See chart "**2 Kings 15**: Azariah (Uzziah), King of Judah."

20. **Jehu** the son of Jehoshaphat the son of Nimshi, was the commander of the Israelite army before he took the throne. Jehu became king of Israel after killing Jehoram in battle and then reigned over Israel for twenty-eight years. Jehu purged Israel of Baal worship, killed Ahab and all his family, and ordered that Ahab's wife Jezebel also be killed. He also killed all the family of Ahaziah of Israel. Sadly, Jehu never converted to the ways of God; nevertheless, four generations of his descendants were kings because of their right doings in God's sight (**2 Kings 9:1–10:36; 2 Chronicles 22:7**). See chart "**2 Kings 9**: Jehu, King of Israel."

21. **Jehoahaz** the son of Jehu became king of Israel in the twenty-third year of the forty-year reign of Joash of Judah and reigned for seventeen years (**2 Kings 13:1–9**). See chart "**2 Kings 13**: Jehoahaz, King of Israel."

22. **Jotham** the son of Azariah/Uzziah became king of Judah at age twenty-five in the second year of the twenty-year reign of Pekah of Israel and reigned for sixteen years. Jotham acted as co-ruler, regent, and judge after his father was afflicted with leprosy. Jotham built the Upper Gate (the High Gate of Benjamin) on the north side of the temple. Genealogical records for all the tribes were recorded during Jotham's reign (**1 Chronicles 5:17**; see **2 Kings 15:32–38; 2 Chronicles 27:1–9**). See chart "**2 Kings 15**: Jotham, King of Judah."

23. **Jehoash** the son of Jehoahaz became king of Israel in the thirty-seventh year of the forty-year reign of Joash of Judah and reigned for sixteen years. He was a contemporary of Elisha and wept when the prophet died (**2 Kings 13:9–25; 2 Chronicles 25:17–25**). See chart "**2 Kings 13**: Jehoash, King of Israel."

24. **Ahaz** the son of Jotham was co-regent (and the dominant regent) with his father. Ahaz became the sole ruler of Judah at age twenty, in the seventeenth year of the twenty-year reign of Pekah of Israel, and reigned for sixteen years. Ahaz was so evil that he sacrificed his own son to pagan gods and set up miniature altars in the land. When he went to war with Pekah of Israel, Ahaz prevailed. Ahaz then took silver and gold from Solomon's Temple to use as tribute to pay Assyria to keep Syria and the northern kingdom of Israel away. Ahaz rearranged the altar in Solomon's Temple by moving a bronze altar used for divination to the north side of the temple; he also removed the bronze "Sea" from the oxen and the bronze panels from the carts, presumably to pay tribute to the Assyrian king Tiglath-Pileser (Pul) (**2 Kings 16:1–20; 2 Chronicles 28:1–27**). See chart "**2 Kings 15**: Ahaz, King of Judah."

25. **Jeroboam II** the son of Jehoash was co-regent with his father for eleven years. Jeroboam II became king of Israel in the fifteenth year of the twenty-nine-year reign of Amaziah of Judah and ruled for forty-one years (including the years of co-regency with his father). Genealogical records for all the tribes were recorded during the reign of Jeroboam II (**2 Kings 13:10, 13; 14:16, 23–29; 15:8; 1 Chronicles 5:17**). See chart "**2 Kings 14**: Jeroboam II, King of Israel."

26. **Hezekiah** the son of Ahaz became king of Judah at age twenty-six, in the third year of the nine-year reign of Hoshea of Israel, and reigned for twenty-seven years. Hezekiah held a co-regency with his father for fourteen years; **2 Kings 18:9** notes a correlation between the fourth year of Hezekiah of Judah (725 B.C.), when Hezekiah was a co-regent with his father Ahaz, and the seventh year of Hoshea of Israel (725 B.C.). Despite his father being a poor role model, Hezekiah was a good king and was remembered as one of Judah's greatest. He purified Solomon's Temple, removed the high places of pagan worship, and broke down the bronze snake (the Nehushtan) which had survived since the days of Moses, "for up to that time the Israelites had been burning incense to it" (**2 Kings 18:4**). Beginning in the fourth year of

Hezekiah, Shalmaneser king of Assyria besieged Samaria (the capital of the Northern Kingdom), and at the end of three years, Samaria was taken. In the sixth year of Hezekiah, the Northern Kingdom fell to the Assyrians, and the people of Israel were taken captive to Assyria. In Hezekiah's fourteenth year, Sennacherib king of Assyria attacked Judah. To pacify him, Hezekiah of Judah gave Sennacherib all the silver from the temple and the palace, as well as the gold from the gold coverings of the doors and doorposts of the temple. Hezekiah then prayed for deliverance; the Lord heard his prayer and sent the angel of the Lord to the Assyrian camp, where the angel killed 185,000 men; when Sennacherib withdrew to Nineveh, he was killed by his sons. In his latter days, when Hezekiah became ill, he prayed to the Lord and the Lord added fifteen years to his life (**2 Kings 18:1–20:21; 2 Chronicles 29:1–32:33; Isaiah 38:5**). See chart "**2 Kings 16**: Hezekiah, King of Judah."

27. **Zechariah** the son of Jeroboam II became king of Israel in the thirty-eighth year of the fifty-two-year reign of Azariah/Uzziah of Judah and reigned for a brief six months. He was killed by Shallum son of Jabesh, ending four generations of rule by Jehu's descendants (the Jehu dynasty; **2 Kings 15:8–12**). See chart "**2 Kings 15**: Zechariah, King of Israel."

28. **Shallum**, the son of Jabesh, led a conspiracy and assassinated Zechariah of Israel (**2 Kings 15:10**). Shallum was king of Israel for only one month, corresponding to the thirty-ninth year of the fifty-two-year reign of Azariah/Uzziah. Soon thereafter, he was assassinated by Menahem the son of Gadi (cf. **2 Kings 15:13–14**). See chart "**2 Kings 15**: Shallum, King of Israel."

29. **Manasseh** the son of Hezekiah became king of Judah at the age of twelve, but he held a co-regency with his father Hezekiah for the first eleven years. He reigned for a total of fifty-five years (including the co-regency). Manasseh was a very evil king—for the "sins of Manasseh" made all of Judah sin, in like manner to Jeroboam I, the first king of the divided monarchy who had caused Israel (the Northern Kingdom) to sin. Manasseh rebuilt the high places of pagan worship, built altars to Baal, worshiped the cosmos in the temple courts, and defiled worship by installing an Asherah image in Solomon's Temple. His reign over Judah was analogous to the evil reigns of Ahab of Israel and Ahaz of Judah. In addition to shedding much innocent blood in Jerusalem, Manasseh practiced child sacrifice by sacrificing one of his own sons. Nevertheless, **2 Chronicles 33:10–20** relates that, after he was taken captive to Babylon, Manasseh repented; upon his return to Jerusalem, he built an enclosure around the city wall, making it higher, and removed altars throughout the land. Despite his repentance, Manasseh was buried in the palace garden and not in the City of David with other former kings (**2 Kings 21:1–18; 2 Chronicles 33:1–20**). See chart "**2 Kings 20**: Manasseh, King of Judah."

30. **Menahem** the son of Gadi murdered Israel's previous king, Shallum. Menahem became king of Israel in the thirty-ninth year of the fifty-two-year reign of Azariah/Uzziah of Judah and reigned for ten years. He was ruthless in war—known for such atrocities as ripping open pregnant women (**2 Kings 15:16**). He became subservient to Assyria and exacted monies from the population to pay the tribute (**2 Kings 15:17–22**). See chart "**2 Kings 15**: Menahem, King of Israel."

31. **Amon** the son of Manasseh was twenty-two when he became king of Judah and reigned for two years. Unlike his father Manasseh, Amon did not repent of his evil ways and his servants murdered hm; in response, the people of Judah executed the servants who had killed him (**2 Kings 21:19–26; 2 Chronicles 33:20–25**). See chart "**2 Kings 21**: Amon, King of Judah."

32. **Pekahiah** the son of Menahem became king of Israel in the fiftieth year of the fifty-two-year reign of Azariah/Uzziah of Judah. An officer named Pekah in Pekahiah's own administration killed him (**2 Kings 15:22–26**). See chart "**2 Kings 15**: Pekahiah, King of Israel."

33. **Josiah**, the son of Amon, became king of Judah at age eight and reigned for thirty-one years. When Hilkiah, the high priest, found a copy of the Book of the Law and read it to the king, Josiah wept and mourned for Judah because he realized how unfaithful and disobedient the nation of Judah had been. Josiah gave a royal speech and initiated a covenant renewal ceremony between the people and the Lord. He then proceeded to remove all pagan idols, altars, and shrines and had the pagan priests executed. Josiah's actions instigated a complete religious reform in Judah, culminating with a Passover celebration in the eighteenth year of his reign. At about the age of thirty-nine, Josiah died in battle with the Egyptians and was buried in Jerusalem. His early death meant that Josiah would be spared from seeing the exile of Judah and the destruction of Jerusalem (**2 Kings 22:1–23:30; 2 Chronicles 34:1–35:27**). See chart "**2 Kings 21**: Josiah, King of Judah."

34. **Pekah** the son of Remaliah was an officer under Pekahiah of Israel. Pekah and fifty men of Gilead assassinated Pekahiah and then Pekah assumed the throne. He reigned for a total of twenty years—initially as co-regent during the full terms of Pekahiah (two years) and Menahem (twelve years) and then, beginning in 740 B.C., corresponding to the fifty-second year of Azariah/Uzziah of Judah—Pekah became the sole ruler of Israel, and he reigned for the next eight years. During Pekah's reign, the Assyrians under Tiglath-Pilesar invaded and captured some cities of the Northern Kingdom. Pekah was killed by Hoshea of Israel (**2 Kings 15:25–32, 37; 16:5–6**). See chart "**2 Kings 15**: Pekah, King of Israel."

35. **Jehoahaz** (or **Shallum**), the fourth and youngest son of Josiah, became king of Judah at age twenty-three and reigned for a brief three months. The Pharaoh of Egypt imprisoned Jehoahaz/Shallum and then appointed Jehoahaz's brother, Jehoiakim, as the new king of Judah. Jehoahaz/Shallum died in Egypt (**2 Kings 23:31–34; 2 Chronicles 36:1–4**). See chart "**2 Kings 23**: Jehoahaz (Shallum), King of Judah."

36. **Jehoiakim** (or **Eliakim**), the second-born son of Josiah and the older half-brother of his predecessor Jehoahaz/Shallum, reigned over Judah for eleven years. **Jeremiah 25:1** correlates the fourth year of Jehoiakim's eleven-year reign in Judah to the first year of Nebuchadnezzar's reign in Babylon (605 B.C.). Jehoiakim enacted high taxes on Judah over a period of eight years to pay silver and gold tribute to Pharaoh Necho of Egypt. For three years, Jehoiakim was a vassal under the Babylonians who were ruled by King Nebuchadnezzar, but then Jehoiakim rebelled. When Babylon overthrew Egypt and became the dominant ruling power in the region, Jehoiakim was taken into Babylonian exile and died there (**2 Kings 23:34–24:7; 2 Chronicles 36:5–8**). See chart "**2 Kings 23**: Eliakim (Jehoiakim), King of Judah."

37. **Hoshea** the son of Elah killed Pekah and became king of Israel in the twelfth year of the sixteen-year reign of Ahaz of Judah and reigned for nine years. As indicated in **2 Kings 18:9**, the seventh year of Hoshea's reign corresponded to the fourth year of the reign of Hezekiah of Judah (during the time when Hezekiah was a co-regent with his father, Ahaz). Initially, Hoshea was a vassal of the Assyrians but then switched his allegiance to Egypt. When the Assyrian king discovered Hoshea's defection, he put Hoshea in prison. In the ninth year of Hoshea's reign, Israel and the capital city of Samaria were overtaken by Assyria. Hoshea was the last king of the northern kingdom of Israel (**2 Kings 15:30; 17:1–6**). See chart "**2 Kings 15**: Hoshea, King of Israel."

38. **Jehoiachin** (or **Jeconiah**) the son of Jehoiakim/Eliakim became king of Judah at age eighteen and reigned for a brief three months in Jerusalem. When Nebuchadnezzar of Babylon besieged Jerusalem, he took Jehoiachin/Jeconiah, the king's wives, the king's servants, the king's brothers, and the military officers to Babylon and imprisoned them. Remarkably, in the thirty-seventh year of his captivity in Babylon, when he was approximately fifty-five years old, Jehoiachin/Jeconiah was released from prison by Evil-Merodach (who had assumed the throne from his father Nebuchadnezzar), was allowed to eat in the Babylonian's palace, and was given a "regular allowance as long as he lived" (**2 Kings 25:30**). Jehoiachin/Jeconiah died in Babylon. Despite the pronouncement of **Jeremiah 22:24–30**, "Record this man as if childless," Jehoiachin/Jeconiah secured a (legal, if not biological) heir while in captivity; see chart "**1 Chronicles 3**: Zerubbabel and Shealtiel and the Double Line of the Messiah through King David's Sons, Nathan and Solomon"; the survival of the kingly line through Jehoiachin/Jeconiah is linked to other figures at the time of the exile, namely, Neri, Shealtiel, and Zerubbabel (as outlined in **Matthew 1:12–16; Luke 3:27**; see **2 Kings 24:8–17; 25:27–30; 2 Chronicles 36:9–10; Jeremiah 22:26; 52:31–34**). See chart "**2 Kings 24**: Jehoiachin (Jeconiah), King of Judah."

39. **Zedekiah** (or **Mattaniah**), the third son of Josiah, the half-brother of Jehoiakim/Eliakim, and the full brother of Jehoahaz/Shallum, became king of Judah at age twenty-one and reigned for eleven years. Nebuchadnezzar changed Mattaniah's name to Zedekiah, probably to signify that Judah would now be a vassal under Babylon. Zedekiah attempted to rebel against Nebuchadnezzar. Ultimately, Nebuchadnezzar besieged Jerusalem from the ninth year to the eleventh year of Zedekiah's reign; the city finally fell in the eleventh year, in the fifth month, and on the seventh day of Zedekiah's/Mattaniah's reign—corresponding to the nineteenth year of Nebuchadnezzar of Babylon—thus marking the end of the southern kingdom of Judah. Zedekiah was taken to Nebuchadnezzar's military headquarters at Riblah, where he witnessed the execution of his sons before his own eyes were put out. Zedekiah died in Babylon as a prisoner (**Jeremiah 52:10–11**; see also **2 Kings 24:17–25:26; 2 Chronicles 36:10–14; Jeremiah 37–39; 52:1–12**). See chart "**2 Kings 24**: Zedekiah (Mattaniah), King of Judah."

1 KINGS 4: THE CHIEF OFFICIALS IN KING SOLOMON'S ADMINISTRATION[1]

Approximate Dating: united monarchy, ca. 971–931 B.C. ***Relevant Scriptures:*** **1 Kings 4:1–6**[2]

Azariah, the high priest
(during most of Solomon's reign):

Abraham
|
Isaac
|
Jacob
|
Levi
|
Kohath
|
Amram
Miriam — Aaron — Moses
(Aaron)
|
Eleazar
|
Phinehas
|
Abishua
|
Bukki
|
Uzzi
|
Zerahiah
|
Meraioth
|
Amariah
|
Ahitub
|
Zadok
(High priest under David and Solomon)
|
Ahimaaz
|
Azariah
|
Johanan
|
Azariah
|
Amariah
↓
Line of the high priests

Elihoreph and Ahijah, the scribal secretaries:

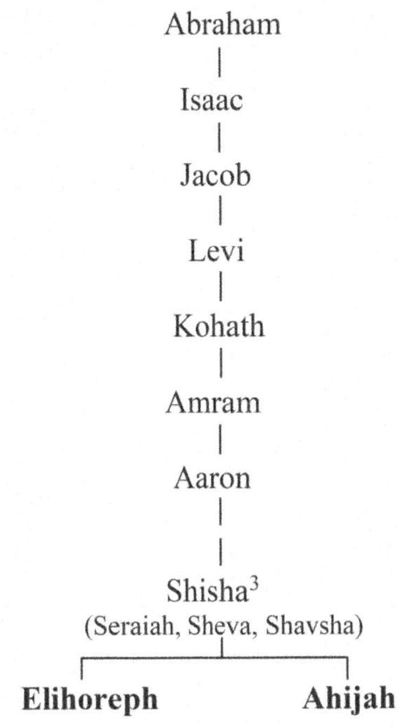

Jehoshaphat, the recorder:

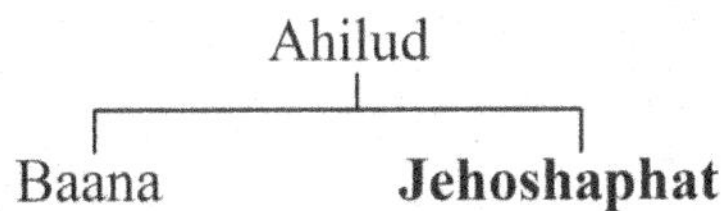

Benaiah, commander over the army:

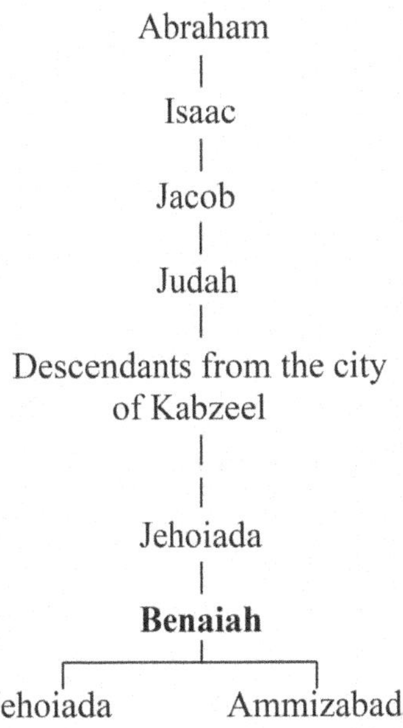

Zadok and Abiathar, the co-officiating high priests (during early part of Solomon's reign):

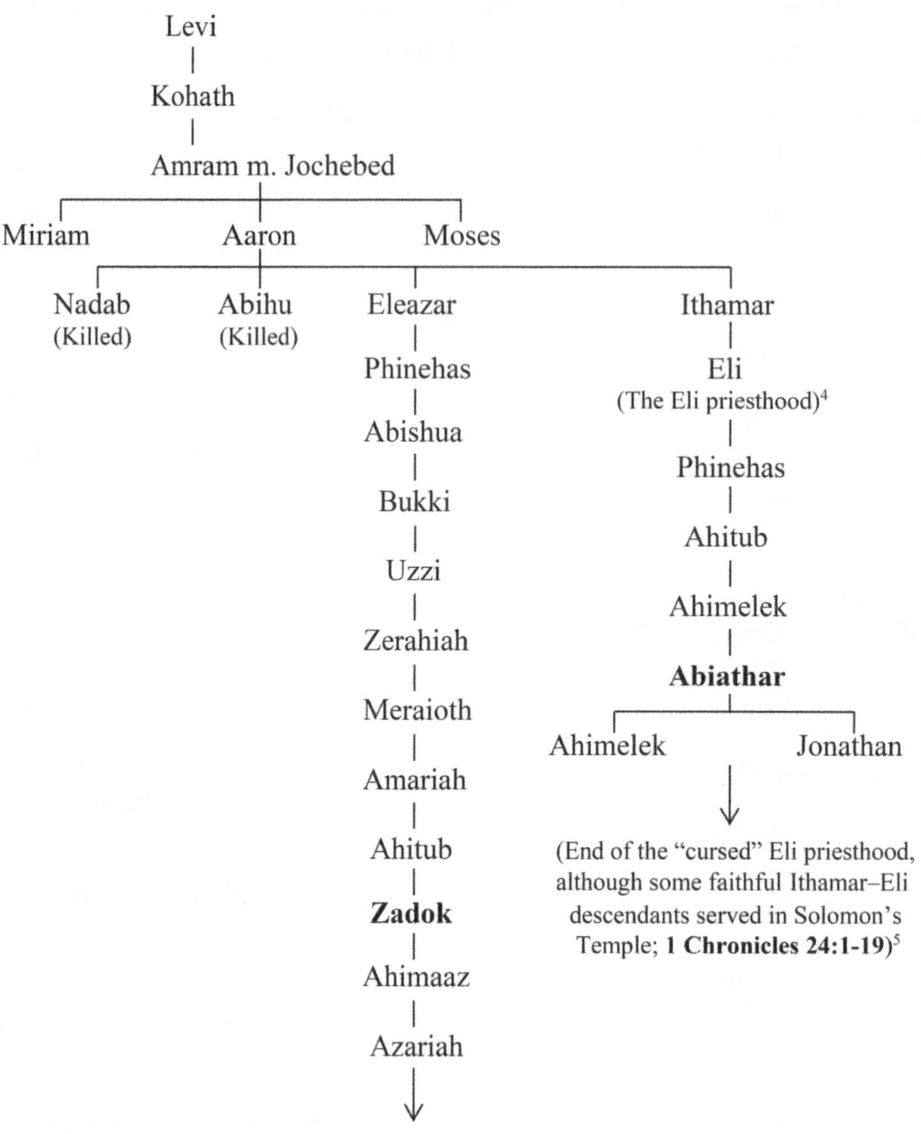

Azariah, overseer of the district governors, and Zabud, David's *priestly* advisor:

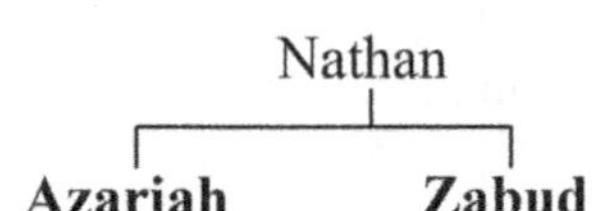

Adoniram, over the forced labor:

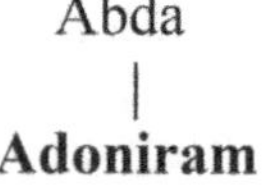

Ahishar, the palace administrator:

No known genealogy

Biblical and Theological Significance

Azariah (the high priest). The list of high priests comes primarily from **1 Chronicles 6:1–15** and is fully explained in the summary chart "**Supplement 2**: The High Priests of Israel." Although three priests in the Aaronic high priesthood are named "Azariah," the Azariah who served under King Solomon is the one mentioned in **1 Chronicles 6:9**—"Zadok [high priest under King David; **2 Samuel 8:17**] the father of Ahimaaz, Ahimaaz the father of Azariah, Azariah the father of Johanan" (cf. **1 Chronicles 6:8–9**). **First Kings 4:2** should be understood to mean that Azariah was the *grandson* of Zadok (not Zadok's *son*).

Elihoreph and Ahijah (scribal secretaries). These officials were the "sons of Shisha" (**1 Kings 4:3**). Shisha had served as the scribal secretary under King David. The lineage shows that scribal secretaries were Levitical Kohathites and relatives of the high priests (e.g., "**2 Kings 22**: Shaphan, Scribal Secretary under King Josiah and King Jehoiakim of Judah").

Jehoshaphat (recorder). He served as the keeper of the official records. Jehoshaphat had also served in the same position under King David (see **2 Samuel 8:16, 20:24; 1 Chronicles 18:15**). Jehoshaphat's brother, Baana, was one of Solomon's twelve district governors (**1 Kings 4:12**).

Benaiah (commander in chief). Benaiah, son of Jehoiada, was a native of Kabzeel, a town in the Negev of southern Judah (**Joshua 15:21; 1 Chronicles 11:22**), possibly the same place called "Jekabzeel" when the town was resettled after the exile (cf. **Nehemiah 11:25**). Benaiah had also served under King David (see **2 Samuel 8:18; 20:23; 23:20–23; 1 Kings 1:32–38; 1 Chronicles 11:22–25; 18:17**). When Solomon came to the throne, Benaiah became commander-in-chief over Solomon's army (**1 Chronicles 27:5–6**; cf. **1 Kings 2:25, 29–35**). In addition, Benaiah was the commander "for the third month" in the rotation of military men who served the king, and Benaiah's son Ammizabad was in charge of the twenty-four thousand men in Benaiah's division (**1 Chronicles 27:5–6**). Benaiah's son Jehoiada[7] (**1 Chronicles 27:34**) was named after his grandfather (a case of papponymy), and Jehoiada became King Solomon's counselor and the successor to Ahithophel, who had been the king's advisor-counselor in the days of King David (**1 Chronicles 27:33–34**; cf. **2 Samuel 15; 17:23**).

Zadok and Abiathar (co-officiating high priests). Zadok (the son of Ahitub) and Abiathar—the son of Ahimelek and also Abiathar's son Ahimelek—had served as co–high priests before the ark of the covenant under King David (**2 Samuel 8:17; 20:25; 1 Chronicles 18:16**) and continued in that capacity during the early part of Solomon's reign. Solomon was aware that Abiathar (the Elide priest) had unwisely supported Adonijah (Solomon's brother) in his schemes to take the throne after David's death. Therefore, soon after coming to the throne, Solomon dismissed Abiathar from his duties and sent him home to the Levitical city of Anathoth (in the tribe of Benjamin), thus "fulfilling the word the LORD had spoken at Shiloh about the house of Eli" (**1 Kings 2:13–27**; cf. **1 Samuel 2:22–36**). Zadok's grandson Azariah[8] then served as the main high priest in Solomon's Temple (**1 Chronicles 6:10**).

Azariah (official in charge of the twelve district governors)[9] and Zabud (personal priest and advisor to Solomon). Azariah and Zabud appear to be brothers, the sons of Nathan (but it is unclear if this refers to Nathan, the brother of Solomon, or to another Nathan figure).[10] Azariah was the officer in charge of the twelve district governors of the land, who provided the provisions for the king and the royal household during the twelve months of the year (cf. **1 Kings 4:7–19**). Zabud served as the personal "priest" or priestlike advisor to King Solomon.

Ahishar (palace administrator). He oversaw the king's palace and properties. His genealogy is unknown.

Adoniram (official over the forced labor). Forced laborers were typically conscripted laborers (corvée labor) from Israel or men from other defeated nations who did work for the king. Adoniram was the taskmaster who oversaw the thousands of laborers sent to Lebanon to cut wood for Solomon's Temple (**1 Kings 5:14**). Adoniram served under David (**2 Samuel 20:24**), Solomon (**1 Kings 4:6**), and Rehoboam. Adoniram was eventually stoned to death in the days of King Rehoboam (**1 Kings 12:18; 2 Chronicles 10:18**).

Notes

1. Compare the complement of officials in King David's administration with those in King Solomon's; see chart "**2 Samuel 8 and 20**: The Chief Officials in King David's Administration."

2. For the references supporting the ancestry of the various officials in Solomon's administration, refer to the following: (1) Azariah (**Genesis 35:23; Exodus 6:18, 20; Numbers 26:59; 1 Chronicles 6:1–16; Matthew 1:2**); (2) Elihoreph and Ahijah (note: scribal secretaries were near relatives of the high priests); see the scribal lineages and scriptural references in the following charts: (a) "**2 Samuel 8 & 20**: The Chief Officials in King David's Administration"; (b) "**2 Kings 22**: Shaphan, Scribal Scretary under King Josiah and King Jehoiakim of Judah"; (c) "**1 Chronicles 6**: Levi: High Priests, Priests, Levites, and Musicians in Solomon's Temple" and "**Ezra 8**: Ezra, the Priestly Scribe and Teacher of the Law (Post-Exile)"; (5) Adoniram (**1 Kings 4:6**); (6) Ahishar (no genealogical information); (7) Benaiah (**Joshua 15:21; 2 Samuel 8:18; 20:23; 23:20, 22; Matthew 1:2–3**); (8) Zadok and Abiathar (see the complete lineages and references in the following charts: "**1 Samuel 1**: Eli and the Eli Priesthood" and "**1 Chronicles 6**: Levi: High Priest, Priests, Levites, and Musicians in Solomon's Temple" and "**Supplement 2**: The High Priests of Israel."

3. He is variously called Seraiah (**2 Samuel 8:17**), Sheva (**2 Samuel 20:25**), Shisha (**1 Kings 4:3**), and Shavsha (**1 Chronicles 18:16**).

4. See chart "**1 Samuel 1**: Eli and the Eli Priesthood."

5. See chart "**1 Chronicles 24**: Genealogical Registry of the 24 Divisions of Kohathite Attending Priests Who Rotated Service in Solomon's Temple (Sixteen from the Aaron–Eleazar–Zadok Line and Eight from the Aaron–Ithamar Line)."

6. See chart "**Supplement 2**: The High Priests of Israel."

7. Benaiah's son Jehoiada is not the same person as Jehoiada the priest, who was the husband of Jehosheba; for the latter, see chart "**2 Chronicles 22**: Probable Genealogy for Jehoiada the Priest who Masterminded the Overthrow of Queen Athaliah of Judah."

8. This Azariah corresponds to Azariah #13 in chart "**Supplement 2**: The High Priests of Israel."

9. The twelve governors over the land, as given in **1 Kings 4:7–19** were:

(1) Ben-Hur—in the hill country of Ephraim;
(2) Ben-Deker—in Makaz, Shaalbim, Beth Shemesh, and Elon Bethhanan;
(3) Ben-Hesed—in Arubboth (including Sokoh and all the land of Hepher);
(4) Ben-Abinadab (who married Taphath the daughter of Solomon)—in Naphoth Dor;
(5) Baana son of Ahilud—in Taanach and Megiddo, and in all of Beth Shan next to Zarethan below Jezreel, from Beth Shan to Abel Meholah across to Jokmeam;

(6) Ben-Geber—in Ramoth Gilead (the settlements of Jair son of Manasseh in Gilead, as well as the region of Argob in Bashan and its sixty large walled cities);
(7) Ahinadab son of Iddo—in Mahanaim;
(8) Ahimaaz (who married Basemath the daughter of Solomon)—in Naphtali;
(9) Baana son of Hushai—in Asher and in Aloth;
(10) Jehoshaphat son of Paruah—in Issachar;
(11) Shimei son of Ela—in Benjamin; and
(12) Geber son of Uri—in Gilead (the country of Sihon king of the Amorites and the country of Og king of Bashan).

10. See chart "**2 Samuel** 7: Various Nathan Figures in the Old Testament."

1 KINGS 7: HURAM, THE MASTER CRAFTSMAN OF SOLOMON'S TEMPLE

Approximate Dating: ca. 966–960 B.C. during the construction of Solomon's Temple ***Relevant Scriptures:*** **1 Kings 7:13–14; 2 Chronicles 2:13–14; 3:1–4:22; 4:16**

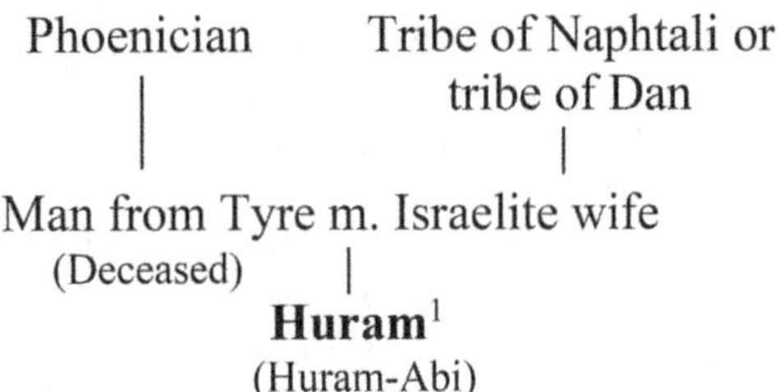

Biblical and Theological Significance

Huram (or Huram-Abi) was the son of a mixed marriage—his father had been a noted bronze craftsman from Tyre, and his mother was an Israelite from northern Galilee, either from the tribe of Naphtali or, according to the Chronicler, from the adjacent tribal region of Dan[2] (**1 Kings 7:13–14; 2 Chronicles 2:14**; cf. **Joshua 19:47; Judges 18:1–2, 7**). Both regions were renowned for idol worship during the days of the judges and the kings (**Judges 18:27–31; 1 Kings 12:26–30; 2 Kings 10:29**).

Both David and Solomon had strong connections with Tyre. David had employed Tyrian stonemasons and carpenters to cut cedars of Lebanon for the construction of his palace (**2 Samuel 5:11**). Solomon made a treaty with Hiram king of Tyre (**1 Kings 5:12**) to arrange for woodcutters from Tyre to work alongside his own laborers to construct the Temple (**1 Kings 5**). Among them was Huram (**1 Kings 7:13**), a man "filled with wisdom, with understanding and with knowledge to do all kinds of bronze work" (**1 Kings 7:13–14**) and a skilled artisan to work in gold, silver, iron, stone, wood, fabrics, and engravings (**2 Chronicles 2:14**).

Among the items that Huram oversaw were the two bronze pillars with bowl-shaped capitals decorated with pomegranates for the front of the sanctuary (**1 Kings 7:15–22, 41–42; 2 Chronicles 3:15–17; 4:12–13**); the bronze Sea with twelve bulls underneath it (**1 Kings 7:23–26, 39; 2 Chronicles 4:2–5, 15**); moveable stands and basins (**1 Kings 7:27–39, 43; 2 Chronicles 4:14**); pots, shovels, sprinkling bowls, and forks for temple worship (**1 Kings 7:40, 45; 2 Chronicles 4:16**); the bronze altar (**2 Chronicles 4:1**); the pure gold lampstands (**1 Kings 7:49; 2 Chronicles 4:7**), ten tables (**2 Chronicles 4:8**); gold basins; wick trimmers; gold sprinkling bowls, dishes, and golden censers (**1 Kings 7:50; 2 Chronicles 4:8, 22**); the golden altar of incense (**1 Kings 7:48; 2 Chronicles 4:19**); the golden table for the bread of the Presence (**1 Kings 7:48; 2 Chronicles 4:19**); and sockets of gold for all the doors in the Temple, the inner doors of gold to the most holy place, and the doors of the main hall (**1 Kings 7:50; 2 Chronicles 4:22**).

From a theological perspective, we see that God sometimes used mixed-race foreigners like Huram to advance his own kingdom plans. This suggests that even fallen humanity was not totally degraded, though frequently they have expressed themselves in immorality and violence. The works of artists, musicians, and writers show the creative hand of God. Moreover, God demands the best of human effort as an expression of worship. The perfect God of all the earth deserves and demands consecrated labor and precious materials as elements of praise and glorification. Paul reminded the Corinthians that "whatever you do, do it all for the glory of God" (**1 Corinthians 10:31**).

Notes

1. Huram in **1 Kings 7:13–14, 40, 45; 2 Chronicles 4:11** is Huram-Abi in **2 Chronicles 2:13; 4:16**.

2. Scholars have suggested that the Chronicler is making a deliberate association between the craftsman of Solomon's Temple (i.e., Huram from the tribe of Dan; **2 Chronicles 2:13–14**) and a craftsman of the Mosaic Tabernacle (i.e., Oholiab from the tribe of Dan; **Exodus 36:1–2**; see chart "**Exodus 31**: Genealogy of Bezalel, the Chief Artisan of the Tabernacle and Its Furnishings, and His Assistant Oholiab"). Also, see *The Anchor Yale Bible Dictionary*, 1992, Yale University, an assignee of Doubleday, a division of Random House, p. 12, accessed by Accordance 13 Bible Software, entry on "Dan/Danite" by Keith J. Whitelam remarks, "A Danite, Oholiab, was involved in the construction of the tabernacle with Bezelel (**Exodus 31:6; 35:34; 38:23**). They were both skilled metal workers, designers, and craftsmen. A further interesting comparison comes in **2 Chronicles 2:13** where Huramabi (see HURAM), the son of a Danite woman, is said to be a skilled craftsman from Tyre (**2 Chronicles 2:13**). This is a significant variation from **1 Kings 7:13–14**, where Huramabi is reported as the son of a woman from Naphtali. Dillard ("2 Chronicles," *World Bible Commentary*, 20) believes that the alteration was deliberate in order to draw a parallel with Oholiab. In fact, rabbinic exegesis made the connection even more apparent by declaring Huramabi to [vol. 2, p. 12] be a descendant of Oholiab. He points out that the Chronicler parallels the construction of the tabernacle with that of the temple. In so doing, Solomon is compared with Bezalel and Huramabi with Oholiab.

1 KINGS 11: KING SOLOMON

Approximate Dating: ca. 971–931 B.C. ***Relevant Scriptures:*** **1 Kings 11:1**; also **2 Samuel 5:14–16; 11:3; 12:24–25; 15:12; 23:34; 1 Kings 1:11, 30, 33; 2:1, 12–13; 3:1; 4:11, 15; 7:7–8; 9:16; 11:43; 12:21, 23; 14:21; 1 Chronicles 2:1–15; 3:5, 10–16; 14:3–4; 22:6, 9, 17; 27:33; Matthew 1:1–16; Luke 3:23–31**

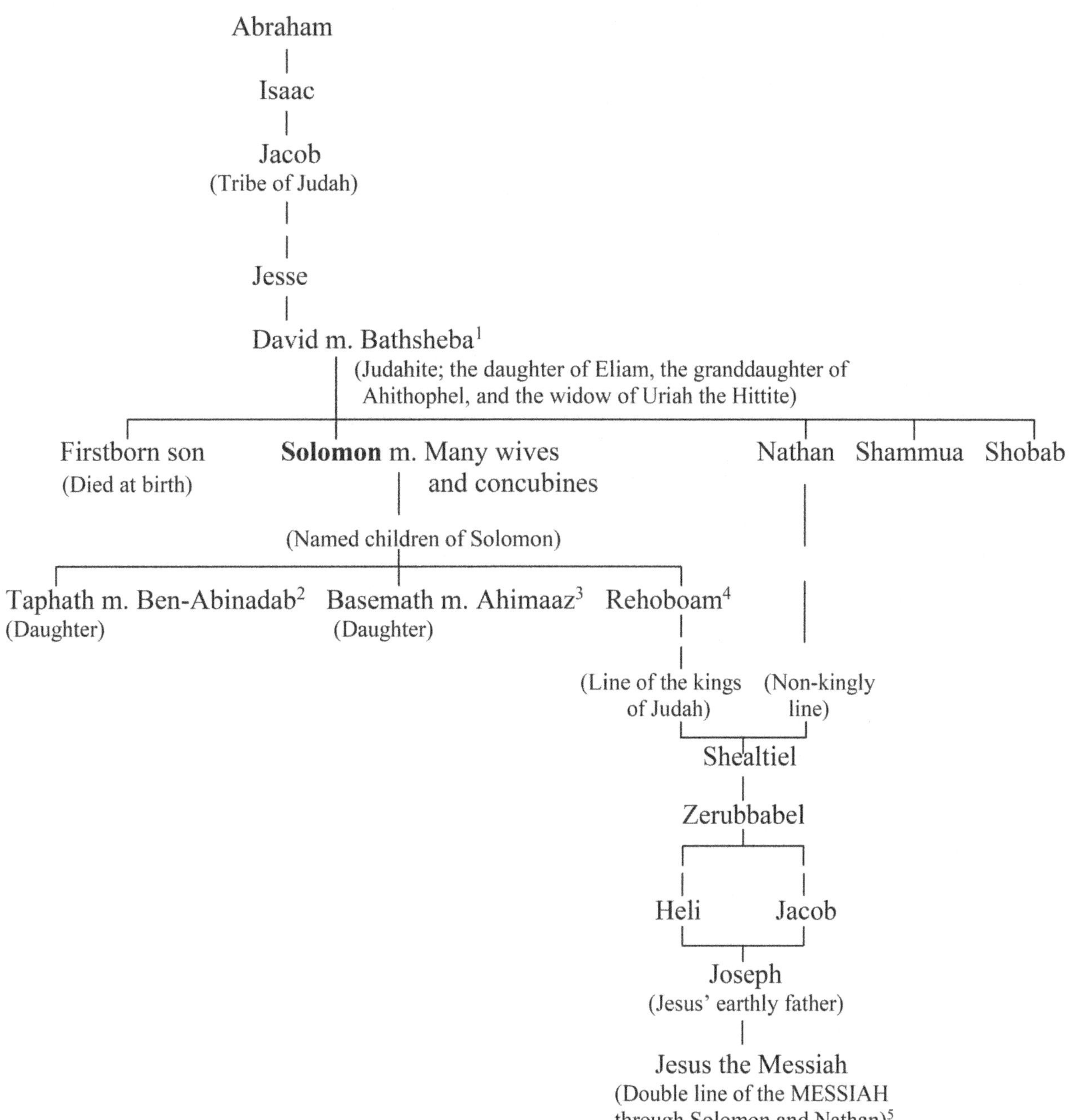

Biblical and Theological Significance

Solomon's Family

Solomon's mother, Bathsheba, had first been married to Uriah (**2 Samuel 11:3**; cf. **23:39; 1 Chronicles 11:41**), but the marriage appears to have been childless. After David "had gone in to Bathsheba" (**Psalm 51:0**, NKJV *contra* NIV[6]); **2 Samuel 11**; cf. **Matthew 1:6**), she bore a son but the child died (**2 Samuel 12:1–23**). Then "David comforted his wife Bathsheba" and she bore Solomon (**2 Samuel 21:24**), and later bore him three more sons (**1 Chronicles 3:5**; cf. **2 Samuel 5:14**).

The Lord sent word through Nathan the prophet to name the child Jedidiah, meaning "beloved of Yah(weh)," showing that God would still continue to show mercy to the heirs of the Davidic throne (**2 Samuel 12:25**). However, his birth name, Solomon, from the root שָׁלוֹם (*shalom*, "peace"), was the name by which he came to be known. In David's final days, Solomon's older half-brother Adonijah[7] prematurely declared king by David's wife before David had formally specified his successor. At Nathan's prompting, Bathsheba asked David to keep his promise that her son Solomon would become king. David confirmed this and publicly declared Solomon as his successor (**1 Kings 1:11–21;** cf. **28–35**). Solomon was a young man at the time, perhaps in his early twenties (**1 Kings 3:7; 1 Chronicles 22:5; 29:1–2**). Solomon was then anointed king in two public coronations (**1 Kings 1:32–40; 1 Chronicles 29:21–22**).

Solomon made many political/diplomatic marriages to foreign women: seven hundred to women of royal birth (**1 Kings 11:1, 3**), including a pharaoh's daughter (**1 Kings 3:1; 7:8; 9:16, 24; 11:1; 2 Chronicles 8:11**), and three hundred to concubines, including women from Moab, Ammon, Edom, Sidon, and Hatti (Hittites) (**1 Kings 11:1–3**). Only three specific children of Solomon are mentioned in Scripture, although there were surely many others.

Solomon as King over All Israel

Early in his reign, Solomon began building the temple, a dwelling place for the Lord on Mount Moriah (**1 Kings 3:2; 5:5; 2 Chronicles 3:1**; cf. **1 Chronicles 22:7–10; 28:2–3**). The site was chosen by the Lord and corresponded to the same place where Abraham had taken Isaac to be sacrificed, but where God in his mercy had provided an animal sacrifice instead (**Genesis 22:1–19**). And following the aftermath of David's prideful military census of Judah and Israel and the ensuing plague (**2 Samuel 24:1–17**), the same place where the Lord had appeared to David on the threshing floor of Araunah and showed him mercy was the same place where David had built an altar to the Lord (**2 Samuel 24:18–25**). In his later years, David made preparations for his son, Solomon, so he would have all that was needed for the temple construction (**1 Chronicles 22:5**). The work began in the 480th year after the exodus[8] (**1 Kings 6:1**), in the fourth year of Solomon's reign (the month of Ziv of 968 B.C.) and was completed seven years later (in the month of Bul of 961 B.C.); cf. **1 Kings 6:1, 38.**[9]

Solomon built other magnificent structures, including his palace (**1 Kings 9:10**); the Palace of the Forest of Lebanon with a colonnaded entrance and portico; the Hall of Justice; and a palace for his wife, the pharaoh's daughter[10] (**1 Kings 7:1–8**). He also built stepped-stone terraces (*millo*) that connected the older (Jebusite) city to Mount Moriah (**1 Kings 9:15, 24; 11:27;** cf. **2 Samuel 5:9**); built walls around Jerusalem; fortified many cities (**2 Chronicles 8:3–6;** cf. **1 Kings 9:15–24**), and built a fleet of ships that sailed from Ezion Geber (near modern Eilat) to distant ports to bring precious metals (gold and silver), ivory, and exotic animals back to Israel (**1 Kings 9:26–28; 10:22; 2 Chronicles 8:17–18**) and to transport horses imported from Egypt and Kue (Turkey) (cf. **1 Kings 4:26; 10:28–29**).

Whereas Solomon initially walked according to the instructions given him by David (**1 Kings 3:3**), he later took many foreign wives (**1 Kings 11:1**) who lured him into worshiping other gods. Thus, Solomon weakened in his devotion to the Lord (**1 Kings 11:4, 9**) by endorsing syncretic worship of both God and pagan gods in Israel and building sanctuaries for his wives' gods (**1 Kings 11:4–8, 33**). In response, the Lord announced that his kingdom would be given to one of his subordinates, Jeroboam (I) son of Nebat (**1 Kings 11:11, 26**), which was fulfilled in the days of Solomon's son Rehoboam. Furthermore, the Lord raised up two other adversaries against Solomon: Hadad the Edomite (**1 Kings 11:14–22**) and Rezon the Aramean (**1 Kings 11:23–25**).[11]

The united monarchy of Israel reached its zenith under King Solomon, who became so widely hailed for his riches and wisdom that kings from all over the known world sought to hear his teaching (**2 Chronicles 9:22–23**). Solomon was also an imperialistic ruler, dominating the lands from the Euphrates to Philistia, as far as the border of Egypt (**2 Chronicles 9:26**). After reigning for forty years, Solomon died and was buried in Jerusalem with his father. Solomon's successor was his son Rehoboam (**1 Kings 11:42–43; 14:21; 2 Chronicles 9:30–31**).

Notes

1. See chart "**2 Samuel 5**: Bathsheba."

2. Ben-Abinadab, a son-in-law of Solomon, was one of the twelve district governors in Solomon's administration; he was headquartered at Naphoth Dor—probably referring to Mount Carmel (**1 Kings 4:11**).

3. Ahimaaz, a son-in-law of Solomon, was one of the twelve governors in Solomon's administration, headquartered in Naphtali (**1 Kings 4:15**).

4. The united monarchy had existed for 120 years under the reigns of Saul (1051–1011 B.C.), David (1011–971 B.C.), and Solomon (971–931 B.C.), but when the northern tribes rejected Rehoboam as Solomon's successor, the united monarchy split apart. Jeroboam I, the son of Nebat, became the king over the ten tribes in the north (i.e., the northern kingdom of Israel), and Rehoboam became king over the southern tribes of Judah and Benjamin (i.e., the southern kingdom of Judah; **1 Kings 12:1–24**). See chart "**1 Kings 11**: Tribes of the Northern and Southern Kingdoms."

5. See charts "**1 Chronicles 3**: Zerubbabel and Shealtiel and the Double Line of the Messiah through King David's Sons, Nathan and Solomon" and "**Matthew 1**: Ancestry of Mary and Joseph (Based on Scripture and Church Tradition) and How Mary and Joseph May Have Been Related."

6. The NKJV is preferred; the NIV of **Psalm 51:0** says "after David had committed adultery with Bathsheba," but the details of the narrative account elsewhere (**2 Samuel 12:3**) suggest that she was probably the innocent party (for a discussion, see note 11 in chart "**2 Samuel 5**: Bathsheba").

7. For the fate of Adonijah, see **1 Kings 2:13–25**.

8. The exodus occurred in 1446 B.C.

9. This was considered seven years total according to inclusive reckoning of dates; for an explanation of regnal dating, see the introduction to the chart "**1 & 2 Kings**: Summary of the Genealogical Record of the Kings of the United and Divided Kingdoms."

10. The pharaoh in question was probably Siamun (ca. 986–968 B.C.) of Dynasty 21 who conquered Gezer, a city of great military importance, located in the foothills of Judah (**1 Kings 9:16;** see **Joshua 10:33; 16:3; 2 Samuel 5:25; 1 Kings 9:17**). The pharaoh gave Gezer to Solomon as a dowry for his daughter (cf. **1 Kings 3:1; 9:16**).

11. See chart "**1 Kings 11**: Genealogical List of the Adversaries of King Solomon."

1 KINGS 11: GENEALOGICAL LIST OF THE ADVERSARIES OF KING SOLOMON

Approximate Dating: ca. 971–931 B.C. ***Relevant Scriptures:*** **1 Kings 11:14–40**

Biblical and Theological Significance

Adversary from the South: Hadad the Edomite

Four distinct Hadad[1] figures are mentioned in the Bible. The first Hadad, the son of Ishmael, lived ca. 2000–1920 B.C. and settled in the territory "from Havilah to Shur, near the eastern border of Egypt, as you go toward Ashur" (**Genesis 25:15, 18; 1 Chronicles 1:30**). A second Hadad, of Avith, the son of Bedad, was the fourth in a line of eight Edomite kings who reigned "before any Israelite king reigned" (**Genesis 36:31; 1 Chronicles 1:43**; see also **Genesis 35:31–39; 36:35; 1 Chronicles 1:44–51**). A third Hadad, of Pau, the husband of Mehetabel, was the last of eight Edomite kings who reigned "before any Israelite king reigned" (**Genesis 36:31, 39; 1 Chronicles 1:43, 50–51**; see **Genesis 36:31–39; 1 Chronicles 1:43–51**).

The fourth Hadad (ca. 990 B.C.), mentioned in **1 Kings 11:14, 17, 19, 21–22, 25**, was a child when David conquered the Edomites (**2 Samuel 8:13–14; 1 Kings 11:15–17;** see **1 Chronicles 18:12–13; Psalm 60:0**). He was a descendant "from the royal line of Edom" (**1 Kings 11:14**)—presumably a descendant of Hadad son of Bedad, or Hadad of Pau (above). In the days of King Solomon, Hadad and officials of the king of Edom escaped to Egypt where they found refuge with the pharaoh in power,[2] who in turn hoped to curtail David's power. There, Hadad advanced in favor, even marrying a sister of the pharaoh's wife (Queen Tahpenes), who bore him a son, Genubath, who was raised among the pharaoh's own children (**1 Kings 11:20**). After David died, Hadad returned to Edom to cause trouble during Solomon's reign (**1 Kings 11:21–22**).

Adversary from the North: Rezon the Son of Eliada

Rezon had been a servant of Hadadezer,[3] the son of Rehob (**2 Samuel 8:3, 12**), the king of Zobah, who formed the Aram–Zobah state of Syria in Saul's time and was later defeated by David (**1 Samuel 14:47; 2 Samuel 8:9–10; 10:16–19**). Rezon became captain over raiders who led a successful revolt against Solomon. Rezon then ruled over Aram, where he remained hostile toward Israel (**1 Kings 11:23–25**).

Adversary from Within: Jeroboam the Son of Nebat

Jeroboam, an Ephraimite from Zeredah,[4] found employment with King Solomon as a builder who helped construct the Millo[5]—a terraced reinforcement on the north-northeast ridge between the Old City of David and the new temple-palace complex—and also repaired damage to the City of David.[6] The historian notes that "Jeroboam was a man of standing, and when Solomon saw how well the young man did his work, he put him in charge of the whole labor force of the tribes of Joseph" (**1 Kings 11:28**). Apparently, Jeroboam considered himself a military man and either resisted or resented his appointment as the overseer of the heavy labor borne by his fellow Ephraimites, so he rebelled against Solomon.

Ultimately, Jeroboam fled Jerusalem. He met Ahijah, the prophet of Shiloh,[7] (**1 Kings 11:29–39**) who then foretold that Solomon's kingdom would ultimately be divided. In a symbolic act, Ahijah tore the new cloak he was wearing into twelve pieces, prophesying that two tribes would split and form the southern kingdom of Judah and that the other ten tribes would be given to Jeroboam to form the northern kingdom of Israel. When Solomon tried to kill King Jeroboam, he fled to King Shishak (Shoshenq I) of Egypt (**1 Kings 11:40**). After Solomon's death, Jeroboam returned home and was made the first king of the Northern Kingdom (**1 Kings 11:26–40; 12:20**).[8]

Notes

1. Hadad is theophoric name—a northwest Semitic version of the Mesopotamian divine name "Adad," the god of rain, storm, lightning, and fertility. This suggests that the pre-Israel indigenous peoples were worshipers of Hadad and that the name would have been common, especially among royalty. Moreover, the Canaanite name for the same deity was Baal, a name featured in the Edomite king list along with Hadad (**Genesis 36:38–39; 1 Chronicles 1:49–50**).

2. This pharaoh was likely Shoshenq I (also called Shishak) of Dynasty 22 (945–924 B.C.).

3. Another example of the deity (H)adad in a theophoric name is "Hadadezer," which means "Hadad is (my) helper."

4. Zeredah was about five miles east of Shiloh.

5. From the verb *male*, "to fill." This refers to stone and/or earth used as fill to extend the dimensions of a hilltop.

6. This refers to the original location of David's palace and his seat of government on the southern/southeastern slopes of Mount Moriah between the temple area and the southern defensive wall. Recent archaeological excavations in the area have uncovered the foundations of the palace.

7. This probably is Ahijah, the son of Ahitub, in the Eli priesthood; see charts "**1 Samuel 1**: Eli and the Eli Priesthood" and "**1 Chronicles 26**: Probable Genealogy of Ahijah, the Priestly Overseer of the Temple Treasuries and Dedicated Things in Solomon's Temple."

8. See chart "**1 Kings 11**: Jeroboam I, King of Israel."

1 KINGS 11: JEROBOAM I, KING OF ISRAEL

Approximate Dating: divided monarchy, ca. 931–910 B.C. ***Relevant Scriptures:*** **1 Kings 11:26–14:20; 15:25–28; 2 Chronicles 10:3–15; 11:14; 12:15; 13:1–2, 6, 13–20**

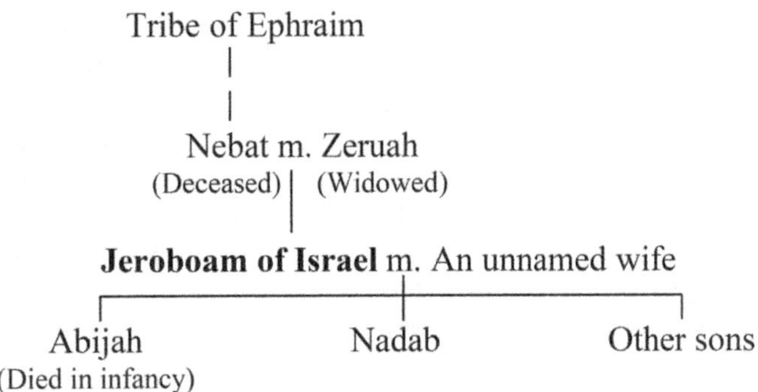

Biblical and Theological Significance

Jeroboam's Rise to Power

Jeroboam son of Nebat, known as Jeroboam I, was an Ephraimite from Zeredah (**1 Kings 11:26**) and "a man of standing" (**1 Kings 11:28**). Because of his leadership potential, Solomon appointed Jeroboam as the overseer of the forced laborers from the tribes of Joseph (Ephraim and Manasseh)[1] (**1 Kings 11:28**; cf. **5:13–14**).

The Lord used Jeroboam as an instrument of judgment against Solomon for violating covenant obligations and promoting worship of foreign deities[2] (**1 Kings 11:33**). The Lord spoke to Jeroboam through Ahijah the Shilonite[3] (cf. **1 Samuel 14:3; 12:15; 2 Chronicles 9:29; 10:15**), who symbolically tore his new garment into twelve pieces and prophesied that two tribes (Judah and Benjamin) would split away and form the southern kingdom of Judah (**1 Kings 11:29–32**), and that the other ten tribes would be given to him (Jeroboam) to form the northern kingdom of Israel (**1 Kings 11:31, 35, 37–38**).

When Solomon tried to kill Jeroboam, Jeroboam fled to Shishak in Egypt,[4] where he stayed until Solomon's death in 931 B.C. (**1 Kings 11:40**). When he learned about the accession of Solomon's son Rehoboam, Jeroboam returned from Egypt (**1 Kings 12:2; 2 Chronicles 10:3**). At Rehoboam's coronation, the people requested that he lighten the burdens Solomon had placed on them (**1 Kings 12:4**). When Rehoboam refused, the northern tribes withdrew and made Jeroboam I the king of Israel (**1 Kings 12:20**). Jeroboam located his capital at Shechem in the hill country of Ephraim and lived there (**1 Kings 12:25**).

Jeroboam's Changes to Israel's Worship

Jeroboam instigated major changes that altered worship: (1) installing golden calves of worship in Dan in the north and in Bethel in the south (**1 Kings 12:28–29; 2 Chronicles 13:8**); (2) reorganizing the Aaronic high priesthood (**2 Chronicles 11:14–15; 13:9**) in favor of non-Levitical priests (**1 Kings 12:31; 13:33; 2 Chronicles 13:9**); and (3) instigating rival feasts (**1 Kings 12:33**). These changes are repeatedly referred to as "the sin of the house of Jeroboam" (**1 Kings 12:13:34**; cf. **14:16; 15:26, 30; 16:2; 2 Kings 3:3; 10:29; 13:2; 17:22**). As a result, God's prophet pronounced judgment on Jeroboam (**1 Kings 13:1–3**), a prophecy that was fulfilled in the days of King Josiah of Judah (**2 Kings 23:15–20**).

The Curse on the House of Jeroboam

When Jeroboam's son Abijah fell sick, Jeroboam asked his wife to disguise herself and inquire of Ahijah, the prophet of Shiloh. Ahijah spoke judgment on Jeroboam, declaring that Israel's idolatry would shorten the reigns of his successors, and that, as a foretaste, Jeroboam's son would die (**1 Kings 14:9–13**). The curse continued when Baasha of Israel killed all of Jeroboam's descendants (**1 Kings 15:29–30**), including Jeroboam's successor, Nadab, who ruled for only two years (**1 Kings 15:25–28**). More devastating were the successive invasions of the Assyrians (**2 Kings 15:29; 17:6; 18:9–12; Isaiah 20:1**), which ultimately led to the exile of the northern kingdom of Israel to Assyria in 722 B.C. (**2 Kings 18:11–12**).

In a war between Israel and Judah recounted in **2 Chronicles 13:1–20**, the northern kingdom of Israel was decisively defeated, and Jeroboam was wounded. Jeroboam never recovered his strength, and he died in 910 B.C.

Final Words

Jeroboam was king over Israel for twenty-two years (ca. 931–910 B.C.), but his reign is summarized thus: "Jeroboam [I] son of Nebat . . . caused Israel to sin" (**1 Kings 22:52; 2 Kings 23:15**). Every king thereafter in the Northern Kingdom followed Jeroboam's evil, idolatrous example, and all rulers were compared to him: "[X] followed the ways of Jeroboam and committed the same sin Jeroboam had caused Israel to commit."[5] The acts of Jeroboam were recorded in the book of the annals of kings of Israel (**1 Kings 14:19**). Nadab his son succeeded him (**1 Kings 14:19; 15:25**).

Notes

1. Perhaps in accepting this "privilege," Jeroboam resented that he was now taskmaster over his own fellow Ephraimites.
2. These included deities such as Ashtoreth the goddess of the Sidonians, Chemosh the god of the Moabites, and Molek the god of the Ammonites.
3. For Ahijah of Shiloh, see charts "**1 Samuel 1**: Eli and the Eli Priesthood" and "**1 Chronicles 26**: Probable Genealogy of Ahijah, who was Over the Temple Treasuries and Dedicated Things in Solomon's Temple."
4. Known as Sheshonq/Shoshenq I of Egypt, he was a powerful ruler of Dynasty 22 from 943–924 B.C. Since Solomon died in 931 B.C., Jeroboam's escape to Egypt was obviously sometime between 943 and 931 B.C., and his return was in Sheshonq's twelfth year as pharaoh. [Shoshenq was succeeded by his son Osorkon I (924–889 B.C.)].
5. This characterization is said of all eighteen subsequent kings of Israel, except Shallum and Hoshea.

1 KINGS 11: TRIBES OF THE NORTHERN KINGDOM OF ISRAEL AND THE SOUTHERN KINGDOM OF JUDAH

Approximate Dating: ca. 931–586 B.C. ***Relevant Scriptures:*** **1 Kings 11:30–39; 12:21**

Tribes of the Northern Kingdom of Israel

1. **Reuben**
2. **Gad**
3. **Dan**
4. **Ephraim**
5. **East Manasseh** (occupied the trans-Jordan side)
6. **West Manasseh** (occupied the cis-Jordan side)
7. **Issachar**
8. **Zebulun**
9. **Naphtali**
10. **Asher**

Tribes of the Southern Kingdom of Judah

1. **Judah**[2] (and **Simeon**[3])
2. **Benjamin**[4]

Biblical and Theological Significance

Several matters are of interest in this listing, notably:

- The tribes of the Northern and Southern Kingdoms are grouped according to the rift that followed Solomon's death in 931 B.C. (**1 Kings 11:26–40**).
- For David's sake,[5] the prophet Ahijah of Shiloh decreed that the southern tribes were preserved for Solomon's son Rehoboam (**1 Kings 11:32, 34, 36**).
- Solomon tried to kill Jeroboam (**1 Kings 11:40**); nevertheless, the remaining ten tribes were ceded to Jeroboam because those tribes had sinned so grievously against Yahweh (**1 Kings 11:28, 33**).
- The division of the tribes has nothing to do with the birth order of the sons of Jacob, the "founder" of the nation (**Genesis 29:31–30:24; 35:16–18**).[6]
- The "ten tribes. . . . one tribe" separation mentioned in **1 Kings 11:31–32, 35** refers to the division of the united monarchy of all "Israel" into the ten-tribal unit that formed the Northern Kingdom of "Israel"—considering that the tribe of Levi received no territorial inheritance and that the tribe of Manasseh was split into two separate entities, comprised of the tribes of Eastern and Western Manasseh—and the one tribal unit (predominated by the tribe of Judah; see note 1) that formed the Southern Kingdom of "Judah."

The final Old Testament reference to tribal divisions and arrangements is in the apocalyptic vision of **Ezekiel 48:1–29**, where Ezekiel sees the ideal land of God in the eschatological kingdom arranged in parallel fashion from north to south as follows:[7]

Dan	Reuben	Benjamin
Asher	Judah	Simeon
Naphtali	Holy Ground:	Issachar
Manasseh	Jerusalem	Zebulun
Ephraim	and Temple	Gad

The implications of Solomon's sins were grave, indeed, in their consequences. He had contracted marriages and harem arrangements with foreign women who turned his affections away from Yahweh and into brazen idolatry (**1 Kings 11:1–4**).[8] Solomon was then largely responsible for the miserable internecine strife between the tribes, the ultimate breakup of the kingdom, and the exiles of Israel to Assyria and Judah to Babylon.

The theological point is evident—those in divinely allocated positions, whether in church or state, possess great privilege and bear awesome responsibility. Godly character and behavior almost always result in blessing at the hand of the Sovereign of Heaven; those who do otherwise—as in the case of the great and wise Solomon—can expect divine displeasure and, short of repentance, utter ruin and a legacy of nefarious influence on generations of their descendants to come.

Notes

1. The text actually says that David's descendants would be given "one tribe" (**1 Kings 11:13, 32**), which probably refers to Judah or Judah/Simeon, but if Judah is already understood without being mentioned, then the other tribe of Benjamin is meant (cf. **1 Kings 12:20–21**); see note 4.

2. David and Solomon were from the tribe of Judah.

3. The tribe of Simeon had its inheritance (land allotment) within the tribe of Judah, so it was considered part of Judah and the southern kingdom of Judah (cf. **Joshua 19:1–9**).

4. The city of Jerusalem was within the tribal territory of Benjamin (**Joshua 18:28**), but under King Rehoboam of Judah, the tribe of Benjamin was, for all practical purposes, assimilated into the house of Judah (**1 Kings 12:21**).

5. God's covenant with David was irrefragable and unconditional, so his tribe (Judah) and royal city (Jerusalem) were also guaranteed historical and eschatological blessing (**Isaiah 44:26; Jeremiah 31:23–40; Joel 3:20; Zechariah 8:13; 10:4–6**).

6. For the birth order, see chart "**Genesis 35**: The Twelve Sons of Jacob, the Eponymous Originators of the Twelve Tribes of Israel."

7. The gates of the city, called "The Lord is There," will be named after the tribes of Israel: three gates on the north (Reuben, Judah, and Levi), three on the east (Joseph, Benjamin, and Dan), three on the south (Simeon, Issachar, and Zebulun), and three on the west (Gad, Asher, and Naphtali) (**Ezekiel 48:30–35**).

8. As **1 Kings 11:5–8** explains: "He [Solomon] followed Ashtoreth the goddess of the Sidonians, and Molek the detestable god of the Ammonites. . . . On a hill east of Jerusalem, Solomon built a high place for Chemosh the detestable god of Moab, and for Molek the detestable god of the Ammonites. He did the same for all his foreign wives, who burned incense and offered sacrifices to their gods."

1 KINGS 12: REHOBOAM, KING OF JUDAH

Approximate Dating: ca. 931–913 B.C. ***Relevant Scriptures:*** **1 Kings 12:1–24; 14:21–31; 15:1–2, 9–10; 1 Chronicles 3:1–10; 2 Chronicles 11:18–12:16; 13:1–2;** also **1 Samuel 17:13, 28; 2 Samuel 13:1, 4; 14:27; 1 Kings 11:43; Matthew 1:7**

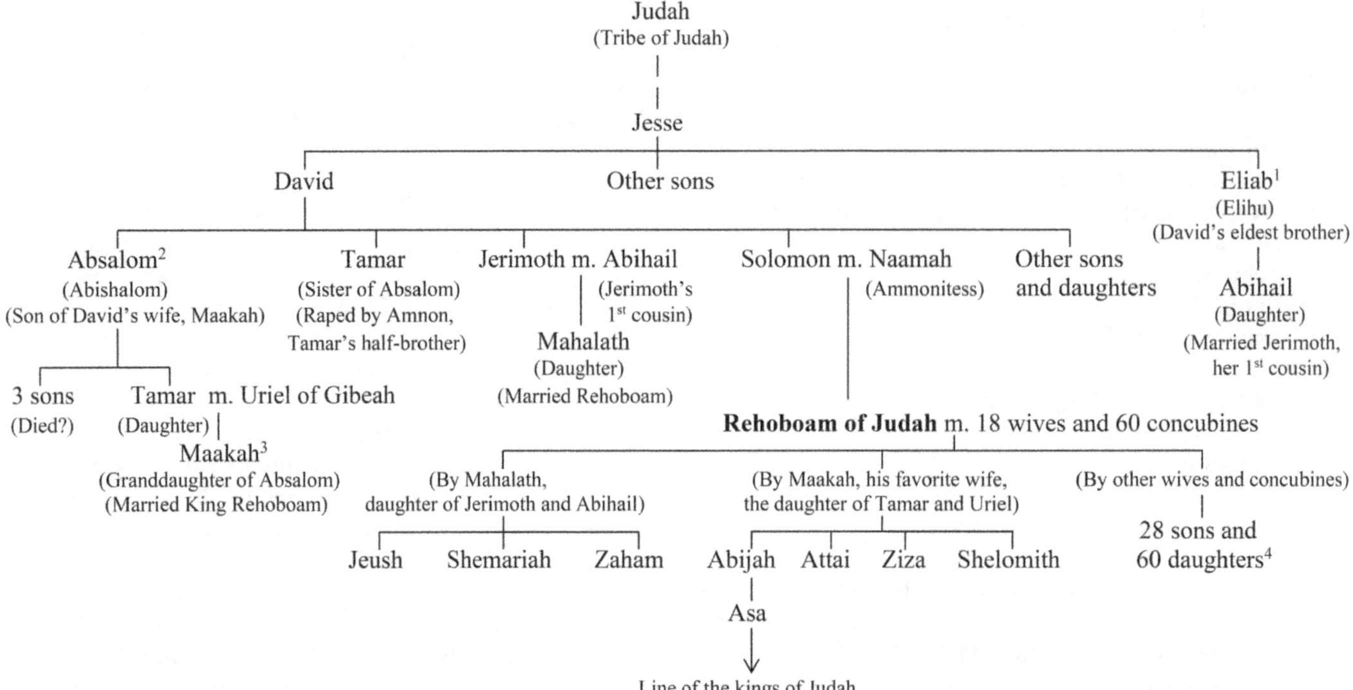

Biblical and Theological Significance

Rehoboam's Family

Rehoboam was one of Solomon's sons (**1 Kings 11:1–3**). His mother was Naamah, an Ammonite (**1 Kings 14:21, 31**), which helps explain the verdict that "he did evil" (**2 Chronicles 12:14**). Rehoboam and his wife Mahalath were half-first cousins, because they shared the same grandfather (David) and their fathers (Solomon and Jerimoth, respectively) were half-brothers. According to **1 Kings 15:2, 10**, Maakah was the *daughter* of Absalom/Abishalom, but **2 Samuel 14:27** clearly states that Absalom had three sons and a daughter named Tamar (not Maakah). Tamar married Uriel of Gibeah (**2 Chronicles 13:2**) and bore him a daughter, Maakah, who was presumably named after Absalom's mother (**2 Samuel 3:3**). Thus, Maakah was the *granddaughter*[5] of Absalom/Abishalom and the great-granddaughter of King David. Maakah was Rehoboam's favorite wife (**2 Chronicles 11:20–21**), which explains her baleful influence in the royal court throughout the reigns of Rehoboam (her husband), Abijah (her son), and Asa (her grandson). However, when Asa became king, he deposed his grandmother, Maakah, because she worshiped Asherah (**1 Kings 15:13; 2 Chronicles 15:16**). Rehoboam sent many of his twenty-eight sons and sixty daughters into the cities of Judah and Benjamin and sought spouses for them (**2 Chronicles 11:21, 23**).

Rehoboam as Judah's King

Rehoboam became king at the age of forty-one (**1 Kings 14:21; 2 Chronicles 12:13**) but was clearly unprepared for kingship (**2 Chronicles 13:7**). He was the first king of the divided monarchy, reigning over Judah for seventeen years, ca. 931–913 B.C. (**1 Kings 14:21; 2 Chronicles 12:13**). Rehoboam was a haughty ruler and promised a heavy yoke of oppression for the people of Judah (cf. **1 Kings 12:1–24; 2 Chronicles 10:1–19**). His reign was marked by continual warfare with his counterpart, Jeroboam I of Israel (**1 Kings 14:30; 2 Chronicles 12:15**). Under the influence of Rehoboam and his mother, Naamah the Ammonite, high places were built and *masseboth* (a sacred pillar devoted to Baal) and Asherah poles were erected, and the southern kingdom of Judah moved quickly into idolatry (**1 Kings 14:23; 15:13**). The Lord pronounced judgment on Rehoboam for his unfaithfulness; in his fifth year (ca. 925 B.C.), Shishak,[6] king of Egypt, invaded Jerusalem and removed all the treasures from Solomon's Temple and from Rehoboam's palace (**2 Chronicles 12:2–10**). The acts of Rehoboam were recorded in the annals of the kings of Judah (**1 Kings 14:29**). When Rehoboam died he was buried in the city of David, and his son Abijah became king of Judah (**1 Kings 14:31; 2 Chronicles 12:16**).

Notes

1. Eliab the firstborn of Jesse (**1 Samuel 16:6; 17:13, 28; 1 Chronicles 2:13; 2 Chronicles 11:18**) is the same person named Elihu, who is identified as "a brother of David" (**1 Chronicles 27:18**). See "Eliab/Elihu" in chart "**1 Chronicles 2**: King David." In some translations, Eliab/Elihu is also called "Eliah" (e.g., **2 Chronicles 11:18**; NKJV).

2. David's son Absalom (**2 Samuel 3:3; 13:1, 20; 14:27; 18:33; 19:4; 1 Chronicles 3:2; 2 Chronicles 11:20–21**) is called Abishalom (**1 Kings 15:2, 10**).

3. Maakah appears to be named after her great-grandmother (Maakah, the wife of David, who was the mother of Absalom and Tamar; **2 Samuel 13:1, 4, 20; 1 Kings 15:2, 10**).

4. The text of **2 Chronicles 11:21** says, "In all, he [Rehoboam] had eighteen wives and sixty concubines, twenty-eight sons and sixty daughters," so the number of sons may include the three sons of Mahalath and the four sons of Maakah.

5. To be consistent with the text of **2 Samuel 14:27** and **2 Chronicles 13:2**, **1 Kings 15:2, 10** should probably read "Maakah the *granddaughter* [not *daughter*] of Abishalom."

6. His Egyptian name was Pharaoh Shoshenq I (or Sheshonq I), founder of the powerful Dynasty 22, who reigned from 945–924 B.C.

1 KINGS 15: ABIJAH, KING OF JUDAH

Approximate Dating: ca. 913–911 B.C. ***Relevant Scriptures:*** **1 Kings 15:1–8; 1 Chronicles 3:2, 10; 2 Chronicles 11:20–22; 12:13–14:1; Matthew 1:7**; also **2 Samuel 14:27**

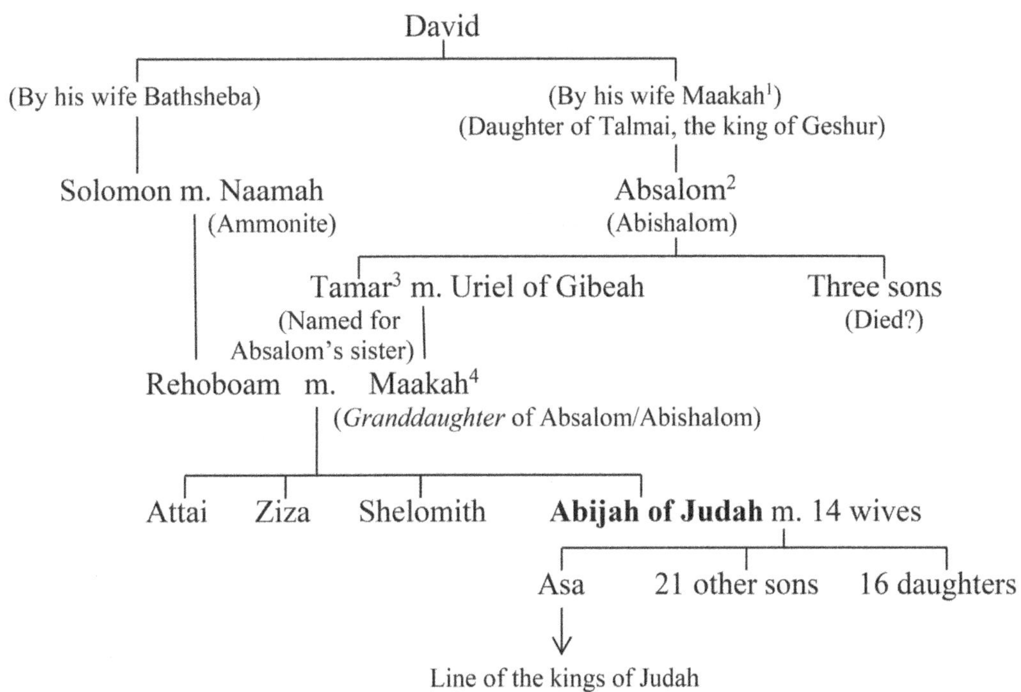

Biblical and Theological Significance

Abijah (also called Abijam in some translations) was the son of Rehoboam of Judah and Maakah, the daughter of Uriel of Gibeah and Tamar,[5] the daughter of Absalom (cf. **2 Samuel 14:27; 1 Kings 15:2, 10; 2 Chronicles 13:2**). Besides his daughter, Tamar, Absalom had three sons[6] (**2 Samuel 14:27**). Abijah had many wives, and by them many sons and daughters (**2 Chronicles 13:21**). Abijah became king in 913 B.C., corresponding to the eighteenth year of the twenty-two-year reign of King Jeroboam I of Israel, and he reigned for three years (913–911 B.C.; **1 Kings 15:1–2; 2 Chronicles 13:1–2**), having been groomed for the appointment as the favorite son of the favorite wife of his father (**2 Chronicles 11:21–22**). His tenure was marred by constant war with Israel (**1 Kings 15:6; 2 Chronicles 13:2**). In one encounter at Mount Zemaraim, Judah's host of four hundred thousand was far outnumbered by the eight hundred thousand troops from Israel; nevertheless, Abijah trusted God for victory. In the battle, King Jeroboam of Israel was fatally wounded by an act of God, Israel was subdued, and Judah won the victory through reliance on the Lord (**2 Chronicles 13:4–20**).

Sadly, in the end, Abijah was remembered as a ruler who followed in the evil footsteps of his father, Rehoboam (**1 Kings 15:3**). The events of his reign were written in the book of the annals of the kings of Judah (**1 Kings 15:7**) and in the annotations of the prophet Iddo (**2 Chronicles 13:22**). Upon his death, he was buried in the City of David and his son Asa succeeded him (**1 Kings 15:8**).

Notes

1. Maakah's father was Talmai, the king of Geshur. Geshur was located in Aram, and the territory of the Geshurites bordered the Maakathites (see **Deuteronomy 3:14; Joshua 12:5; 13:11; 2 Samuel 15:8**). Maakah was the wife of King David and the *mother* of Absalom (**2 Samuel 3:3; 1 Chronicles 3:2**). She should not be confused with Maakah the *granddaughter* of Absalom (see note 3), who was the wife of Rehoboam and the mother of Abijah (**2 Chronicles 11:20–22**).

2. Abishalom (**1 Kings 15:2, 10**) is Absalom elsewhere (such as **2 Samuel 3:3; 13:1, 20; 14:27; 18:33; 19:4; 1 Chronicles 3:2; 2 Chronicles 11:20–21**).

3. Only one woman is mentioned as a *daughter* of Absalom, and her name was Tamar (**2 Samuel 14:27**). Tamar was named after Absalom's sister, Tamar, who had been raped by Amnon (**2 Samuel 13:7–14**). Presumably Tamar married Uriel of Gibeah (cf. **2 Chronicles 13:2**) and bore Maakah. Maakah, in turn, married King Rehoboam and bore Abijah, who became king of Judah. The texts of **1 Kings 15:2, 10** and **2 Chronicles 11:21** (NIV), which describe Maakah as the *daughter* of Absalom/Abishalom, appear to

be incorrect. The correct familial relationship for Maakah is that she was the *granddaughter* of Absalom/Abishalom, as it appears in the NKJV in **1 Kings 15:2, 10** and **2 Chronicles 11:21**—for example, the latter reads "Now Rehoboam loved Maachah [Maakah] the *granddaughter* of Absalom more than all his wives and his concubines. . . . And Rehoboam appointed Abijah the son of Maachah [Maakah] as chief . . . [and] intended to make him king" (**2 Chronicles 11:21–22**, NKJV, emphasis added).

Tamar (Absalom's daughter) should not be confused with Tamar (Absalom's sister), who was raped by Amnon (**2 Samuel 13:1–20**) and subsequently lived as a deflowered, disgraced woman in Absalom's house (**2 Samuel 13:20–21**).

4. Maakah the wife of Rehoboam should be understood to be the *granddaughter* of Absalom (Abishalom); see note 3. Maakah was influential during the reigns of Rehoboam (her husband), Abijah (her son), and Asa (her grandson); Asa finally deposed his grandmother Maakah from her position as "the queen mother" because she was a devout worshiper of Asherah (**1 Kings 15:13**; cf. **2 Chronicles 13:1–14:1; 15:16**).

5. Tamar (Absalom's daughter) was a beautiful woman. Most likely, she was named after Tamar Absalom's sister, who had been raped by her half-brother Amnon (**2 Samuel 13:14**).

6. The three sons of Absalom may have all died because Absalom laments the lack of an heir (**2 Samuel 18:18**).

1 KINGS 15: ASA, KING OF JUDAH

Approximate Dating: ca. 911–869 B.C.[1] ***Relevant Scriptures:*** **1 Kings 15:8–24; 22:41–42; 1 Chronicles 3:10; 2 Chronicles 13:21; 14:1–16:14; 20:31; Matthew 1:6–8**

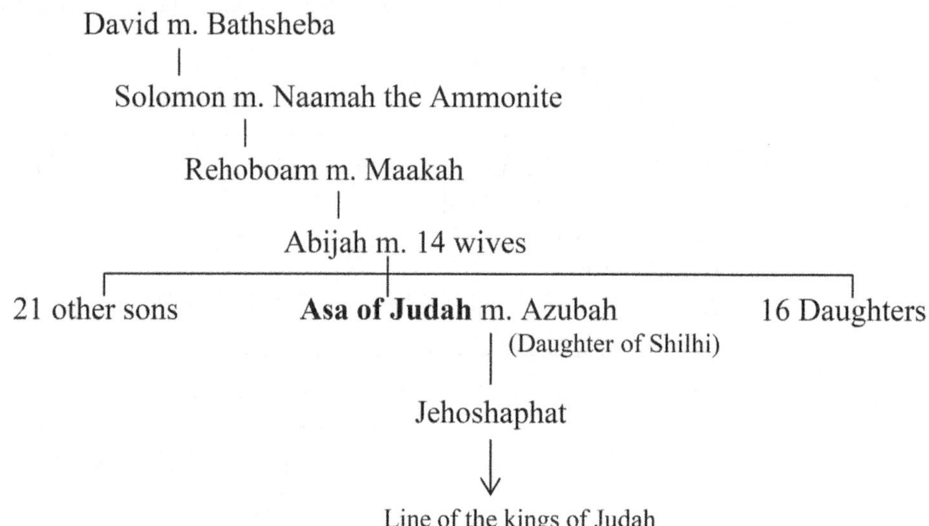

Biblical and Theological Significance

Asa's Family

Asa was the son of Abijah and an unnamed mother. His grandmother Maakah, the *granddaughter* of David's son Absalom (cf. **1 Kings 15:2, 10; 2 Chronicles 11:20–21; 13:2**), had considerable influence in the reigns of her husband (Rehoboam) and her son (Abijah); however, when Asa succeeded his father to the throne, he deposed his grandmother from the court for being an Asherah worshiper (**1 Kings 15:13; 2 Chronicles 15:16**).

Asa as Judah's King

After the death of Abijah, Judah enjoyed a period of rest from warfare for ten years (**2 Chronicles 14:1, 6**). Asa became king of Judah in ca. 911 B.C., corresponding to the twentieth year of the twenty-two-year reign of Jeroboam of Israel (**1 Kings 14:20; 15:9**), and reigned for forty-one years (911–869 B.C.; **1 Kings 15:10**). His reforms and military successes included: (1) removal of the sacred stones, Asherah poles, and altars to foreign gods, as well as pagan high places of worship (**1 Kings 15:13–14; 2 Chronicles 14:3, 5; 15:1–8, 16–17**); (2) fortification of walls, towers, and gates in Judah (**2 Chronicles 14:6–7**); (3) building an army in Judah and Benjamin (**2 Chronicles 14:8**); (4) defeating Zerah the Cushite and the cities around Gerar (**2 Chronicles 14:9–15**); (5) recommencing worship at the temple (**2 Chronicles 15:8–15**); (6) dedicating the silver, gold, and utensils that he and his father acquired to replace those taken earlier by Shishak king of Egypt (cf. **1 Kings 14:25–26; 15:14–15**); and (7) leading the people in covenant renewal (**2 Chronicles 15:8–15**).

After a period of peace, Baasha of Israel invaded Judah (cf. **1 Kings 15:16–17, 33; 2 Chronicles 16:1**).[2] On the way he built up Ramah on the border to prevent his people from worshiping in Jerusalem. Asa then took silver and gold from the temple to bribe Ben-Hadad of Aram to break his treaty with Baasha. The result halted Baasha's effort to fortify Ramah. Asa then conscripted laborers to tear down the newly built portions of Ramah and used the stone and timber to fortify Geba and Mizpah to discourage future Israelite campaigns against Judah (**1 Kings 15:17–22; 2 Chronicles 16:1–6**).

Notwithstanding these reforms, the Lord condemned Asa for relying on Ben-Hadad, and Hanani the seer foretold that Asa's latter years would be war-filled. Two years before his death, Asa contracted a disease. Even then, he did not seek help from the Lord, but only from physicians (**2 Chronicles 16:12**); during this time, Jehoshaphat his son was co-regent with his father (i.e., in the thirty-ninth through the forty-first years of Asa's forty-one-year reign; ca. 872–869 B.C.). When Asa died, he was buried in a tomb that he had built for himself in the City of David (**2 Chronicles 16:14**). In the final assessment, Asa was considered a good king who pleased the Lord his God (**1 Kings 15:11, 14; 2 Chronicles 14:2; 15:17**). Asa's son Jehoshaphat succeeded him (**1 Kings 15:24**; **2 Chronicles 17:1**).

Notes

1. For a discussion of the chronological considerations of Asa's reign, see Eugene H. Merrill, *Kingdom of Priests: A History of Old Testament Israel* (Grand Rapids: Baker, 1996), 332–34.

2. "In the thirty-sixth year of Asa's reign Baasha king of Israel went up against Judah" (**2 Chronicles 16:1**). For a more complete explanation of the dates, see Merrill, *Kingdom of Priests*, 348–50, where the thirty-sixth year is a reference to the fixed date, 931 B.C., the date of the division of the kingdom. Thus, the reference to the thirty-sixth year of Asa's reign would then be the sum of Abijah's three-year and Rehoboam's seventeen-year reigns, plus fifteen years of Asa's reign, at which time Baasha invaded, totaling 35/36 years, which harmonizes exactly with **2 Chronicles 16:1**.

1 KINGS 15: NADAB, KING OF ISRAEL

Approximate Dating: ca. 910–909 B.C. ***Relevant Scriptures:*** **1 Kings 15:25–31**; also **1 Kings 14:1–18; 2 Chronicles 11:14**

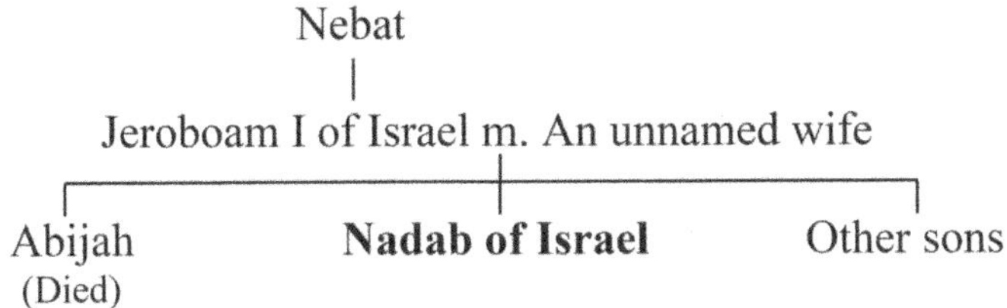

Biblical and Theological Significance

After the death of King Jeroboam I, Nadab succeeded his father as king (**1 Kings 14:20**). He came to the throne of Israel in the second year of the forty-one-year reign of Asa, king of Judah (ca. 911–869 B.C.), and reigned over Israel for two years (910–909 B.C.; **1 Kings 15:25**). Before this, Jeroboam's son Abijah became sick, and Jeroboam asked his wife to disguise herself and to ask Ahijah,[1] the prophet at Shiloh, about their son's welfare (**1 Kings 14:1–18**). Ahijah told her that her son would die;[2] the death of the child fulfilled Ahijah's prophecy that God would "cut off from Jeroboam every last male in Israel—slave or free" (**1 Kings 14:10**.

Nadab followed the evil example of his father Jeroboam by "committing the same sin his father had caused Israel to commit" (**1 Kings 15:26**). After only two years as king, Nadab was killed by Baasha son of Ahijah at Gibbethon, a town that was controlled by the Philistines. Baasha also killed "Jeroboam's whole family" (**1 Kings 15:27–29**), thereby fulfilling the curse that had been pronounced on Jeroboam's house (cf. **1 Kings 14:10–13; 15:30**). After Nadab's death, Baasha, who was unrelated to Nadab, assumed the throne of Israel (**1 Kings 15:28, 33**). The acts of Nadab were recorded in the book of the annals of the kings of Israel (**1 Kings 15:31**).

Notes

1. See charts "**1 Samuel 1**: Eli and the Eli Priesthood" and "**1 Chronicles 26**: Probable Genealogy of Ahijah, the Priestly Overseer of the Temple Treasuries and Dedicated Things in Solomon's Temple."

2. In Ahijah's prophecy, he told Jeroboam's wife, "Go back home. When you set foot in your city, the boy [Abijah] will die. All Israel will mourn for him and bury him. He is the only one belonging to Jeroboam who will be buried, because he is the only one in the house of Jeroboam in whom the Lord, the God of Israel, has found anything good" (**1 Kings 14:12**).

1 KINGS 15: BAASHA, KING OF ISRAEL

Approximate Dating: ca. 909–886 B.C. during the divided monarchy ***Relevant Scriptures:*** **1 Kings 15:16–22; 15:33–16:8, 11–13; 2 Chronicles 16:1–6**

Biblical and Theological Significance

A military officer named Baasha assassinated his own king, Nadab, and succeeded him, though he was not related to Nadab. Baasha came to the throne in the third year of the forty-one-year reign of Asa, king of Judah (ca. 911–869 B.C.) and reigned over Israel for twenty-four years, ca. 909–886 B.C. (**1 Kings 15:33**). War raged between Asa and Baasha throughout their reigns (**1 Kings 15:16, 32**), with Baasha seeking to control access to Jerusalem and Judah by building up the border city of Ramah. In response, Asa bribed Ben-Hadad of Syria to break his treaty with Baasha and collaborate in an attack on several northern cities of Israel.

The military agreement between Asa and Ben-Hadad was successful—Baasha retreated to Israel and ceased work at Ramah (**1 Kings 15:16–22**; **2 Chronicles 16:1–6**).

Baasha ruled from Tirzah, an enclave hidden by steep cliff-sides and therefore thought to be secure. Because "he did evil in the eyes of the LORD, following the ways of Jeroboam" (**1 Kings 15:34**; cf. **16:2**), the Lord sent Jehu the prophet to pronounce judgment on him: "I am about to wipe out Baasha and his house. . . . Dogs will eat those belonging to [the house of] Baasha who die in the city, and birds will feed on those who die in the country" (**1 Kings 16:3–4;** cf. the similar wording in **1 Kings 14:11**; **21:24**).

The acts of Baasha were recorded in the book of the annals of the kings of Israel (**1 Kings 16:5**). When he died, Baasha was buried in Tirzah and his son Elah succeeded him. However, as soon as Elah had seized power, he and his entire family were massacred by Zimri, one of his own military officers, thus fulfilling the words of the prophet Jehu against Baasha's household (**1 Kings 16:3–4**; cf. **16:8–13**).

1 KINGS 15: JEHOSHAPHAT, KING OF JUDAH

Approximate Dating: ca. 872–848 B.C., including a co-regency with his father, Asa, 872–869 B.C. ***Relevant Scriptures:*** **1 Kings 15:24; 22:41–50; 2 Kings 8:16; 1 Chronicles 3:10–16; 2 Chronicles 17:1–21:3; Matthew 1:8**

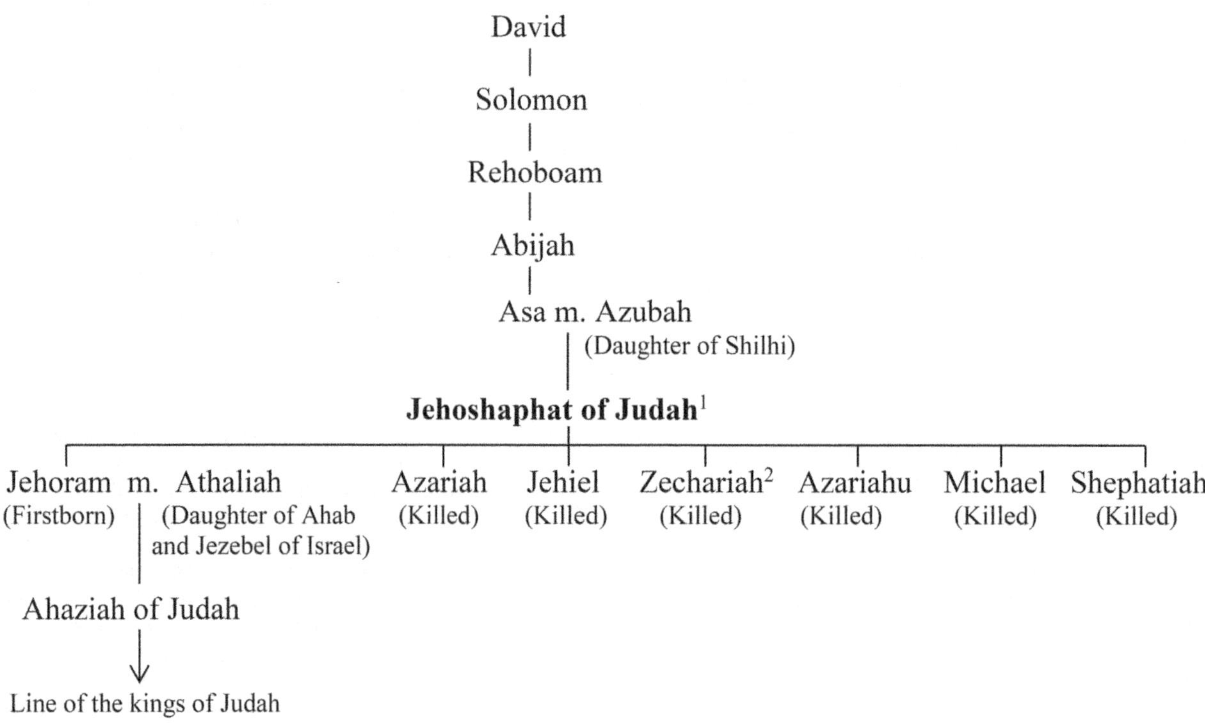

Biblical and Theological Significance

Because of Asa's illness, Jehoshaphat co-reigned[3] with his father from ca. 872–869 B.C. (**2 Chronicles 16:12**) and reigned for twenty-five official years from 872–848 B.C. (**1 Kings 22:42; 2 Chronicles 20:31**).[4] He removed (some) places of pagan worship (**1 Kings 22:43**; **2 Chronicles 17:6; 20:32–33**). Gifts and tribute came to him from all directions (**2 Chronicles 17:5**), making him wealthy and highly honored. Philistines and Arabs brought him tribute (**2 Chronicles 17:10–11**), signifying his imperialism (**2 Chronicles 17:12**). He built up the military (**2 Chronicles 17:12–19**) and instigated reforms throughout Judah, including the dispatch of teachers to instruct in the Torah and judges to enforce it (**2 Chronicles 17:7–9; 19:5–7**); he also appointed priests, Levites, and heads of families living in Jerusalem to hear disputes (**2 Chronicles 19:8–11**). Thus, Jehoshaphat turned the people of Judah back to the Lord; as a result, the Lord blessed him **(2 Chronicles 19:3–4)**.

Contrary to his early years of devotion to the Lord, Jehoshaphat later achieved political *detente* with Ahab (**1 Kings 22:44**), an arrangement solidified by the marriage of Jehoshephat's son Jehoram to Athaliah, the daughter of Ahab and Jezebel (**2 Kings 8:18, 26; 11:1–3; 2 Chronicles 18:1; 21:6; 22:2**). From this time forward, Israel and Judah were closely linked. When Jehoshaphat's son Jehoram came to the throne of Judah, he emulated the evil ways of Israel's kings, rather than the good example of his father.

In Jehoshaphat's seventeenth year, Ahaziah became king of Israel, and Jehoshaphat formed an alliance with him to build a fleet of trading ships; however, they were destroyed before they could set sail (**1 Kings 22:48–49**; **2 Chronicles 20:35–37**).

When Jehoshaphat died, he was buried in Jerusalem and his son Jehoram assumed the throne in 848 B.C. (**2 Chronicles 21:1**). The events of Jehoshaphat's reign were recorded in the annals of the kings of Judah (**1 Kings 22:45**) and in the annals of Jehu son of Hanani, which are recorded in the book of the kings of Israel (**2 Chronicles 20:34**).

Notes

1. The wife (or wives) of Jehoshaphat is not recorded. Jehoshaphat gave his sons "many gifts of silver and gold and articles of value, as well as fortified cities in Judah, but he [gave] the kingdom to Jehoram because he was his firstborn son" (**2 Chronicles 21:2–3**). Tragically, when Jehoram came to the throne, he "put all his brothers to the sword along with some of the officials of Israel" (**2 Chronicles 21:4**).

2. Zechariah was among the "officials" (princes), Levites, and priests who were sent by King Jehoshaphat to teach the Book of the Law to the people of Judah (**2 Chronicles 17:7–9**); see chart "**2 Chronicles 17**: Genealogical Record of the Teachers of the Law During the Reign of King Jehoshaphat of Judah."

3. For Jehoshaphat's co-regency with this father, Asa, see Edwin R. Thiele's *The Mysterious Numbers of the Hebrew Kings* (New rev. ed.) Grand Rapids: Kregel (repr.) 1994, from the 1983 Zondervan edition, 10–13, 63, 83, 86, 97.

4. Jehoshaphat's official reign of "twenty-five years," from 872–848 B.C. (**1 Kings 22:42; 2 Chronicles 20:31**), included the three-year co-regency with Asa (872–869 B.C.). Likewise, his son Jehoram co-reigned with him for the last six years of Jehoshaphat's reign (ca. 853–848 B.C.).

1 KINGS 16: JEHU, THE PROPHET-SEER

Approximate Dating: ca. 909–848 B.C. ***Relevant Scriptures:*** **1 Kings 16:1–4, 7; 2 Chronicles 19:2–3; 20:34**

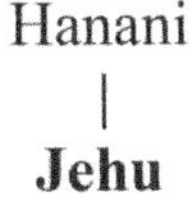

Biblical and Theological Significance

Jehu was a prophet-seer[1] in the days of both Baasha king of Israel, ca. 909–886 B.C. (**1 Kings 16:1–4, 7**), and Jehoshaphat king of Judah, ca. 872–848 B.C. (**2 Chronicles 19:2–3**) during the time when his father, Hanani, acted as seer-prophet to King Asa of Judah, ca. 911–869 B.C. (**2 Chronicles 16:7–9**).

Jehu proclaimed God's judgment on King Baasha of Israel (**1 Kings 16:1–13**). He also rebuked Jehoshaphat of Judah for his sins and warned him not to "help the wicked and love those who hate the LORD" (**2 Chronicles 19:2**). Jehu wrote a record of the acts of King Jehoshaphat of Judah, which were recorded in the "book of the kings of Israel"[2] (**2 Chronicles 20:34**).

Notes

1. The name Jehu is shared by the prophet and a king, Jehu of Israel (**1 Kings 19:16**). The name Jehu means "Yah(weh) is He," indicating a strong monotheistic confession: "Who is God?" "Yahweh is He (i.e., God)." The Hebrew technical terms for the two apparently different offices of prophet and seer are essentially synonymous. They differ only in emphasis. The term "prophet" in Hebrew, נָבִיא, *nabi* means at its root "announce," "proclaim," etc. "Seer," רֹאֶה, *roeh* or חֹזֶה, *khozeh*, focuses on reception of revelation, not proclamation. Obviously, a prophet could not proclaim what he had not seen, nor should a seer refrain from uttering the thing he had seen. The terms are used interchangeably in the Scriptures (cf. **1 Samuel 9:9**).

2. Undoubtedly this is one of the sources referred to by the Chronicler in the composition of his own work ("the book of the kings of Judah and Israel," **2 Chronicles 16:11; 25:26**; etc.).

1 KINGS 16: ELAH, KING OF ISRAEL

Approximate Dating: ca. 886–885 B.C. ***Relevant Scriptures:*** **1 Kings 16:6, 8–14**

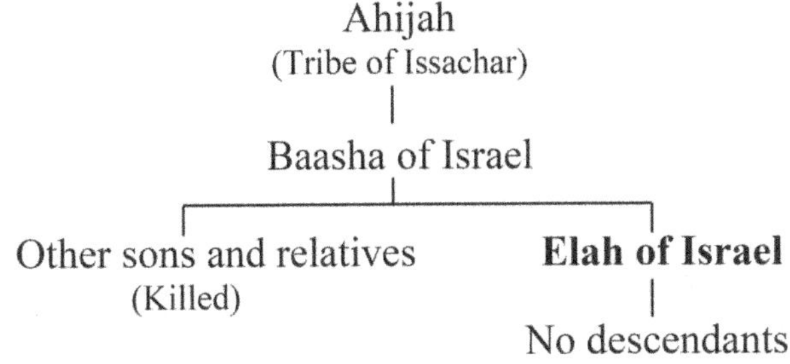

Biblical and Theological Significance

Elah became king of Israel in the twenty-sixth year of the forty-one-year reign of Asa, king of Judah (ca. 911–869 B.C.). Elah reigned for a brief two years from the city of Tirzah, the first capital of the northern kingdom of Israel (**1 Kings 16:8**). Elah was assassinated by Zimri, who was a trusted military officer over half of Elah's chariots (**1 Kings 16:9–10, 13**). This brutal act, though at the hand of a man, was part of a divine plan to destroy Baasha and Elah because both kings had caused Israel to commit idolatry so grievous that the anger of the LORD was stoked like a raging fire against them (**1 Kings 16:11–13**).

A notation is made that the events in Elah's reign were written in the book of the annals of the kings of Israel (**1 Kings 16:14**).

1 KINGS 16: ZIMRI, KING OF ISRAEL

Approximate Dating: ca. 885 B.C. ***Relevant Scriptures:*** **1 Kings 16:9–13, 15–20**

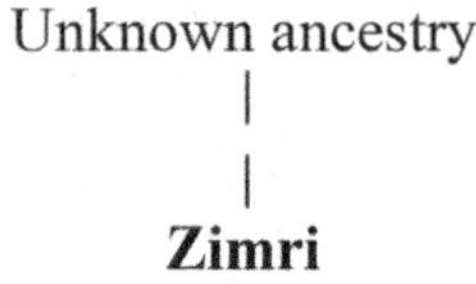

Biblical and Theological Significance

Zimri's genealogy is unknown. He assumed the throne of Israel at a time of political upheaval in the Northern Kingdom. Zimri was formerly the military officer in charge of half of King Elah's chariots. Zimri planned a coup to assume the throne from Elah (ca. 886–885 B.C.) by waiting until the king was drunk in the house of the palace administrator Arza, and then Zimri killed Elah (**1 Kings 16:9–19**). Zimri assumed the throne in ca. 885 B.C., in the twenty-seventh year of the forty-one-year reign of Asa, king of Judah (ca. 911–869 B.C.), but he only ruled for seven days (**1 Kings 16:15**). The text notes that "As soon as he [Zimri] began to reign and was seated on the throne, he killed off Baasha's [Elah's father's] whole family. He [Zimri] did not spare a single male, whether relative or friend [of Baasha]" (**1 Kings 15:11**). Zimri's actions were similar to those of Baasha, who had killed King Nadab and then destroyed all the house of Nadab's father, Jeroboam I (cf. **1 Kings 15:29**).

Zimri timed his coup to assume the throne in Tirzah when the army was out engaging in war with the Philistines at Gibbethon, a city twenty-five miles west of Jerusalem and five miles north of Ekron. When the Israelite soldiers heard that Zimri had killed King Elah and had succeeded to the throne, they refused to acknowledge his kingship and declared Omri, the commander of the Israelite army, as the king instead. Omri's army left the skirmish in Gibbethon and besieged the capital at Tirzah. When Zimri realized his defeat, he fled to the citadel of the royal palace and set the palace on fire and killed himself in the blaze (**1 Kings 16:15–19**). The acts of Zimri were recorded in the book of the annals of the kings of Israel (**1 Kings 16:20**).

1 KINGS 16: OMRI, KING OF ISRAEL

Approximate Dating: ca. 885–874 B.C. ***Relevant Scriptures:*** **1 Kings 16:16–17, 21–30**; also **1 Kings 22:40, 49, 51; 2 Kings 3:1; 8:16, 18, 25-26; 28-29; 2 Chronicles 22:2**

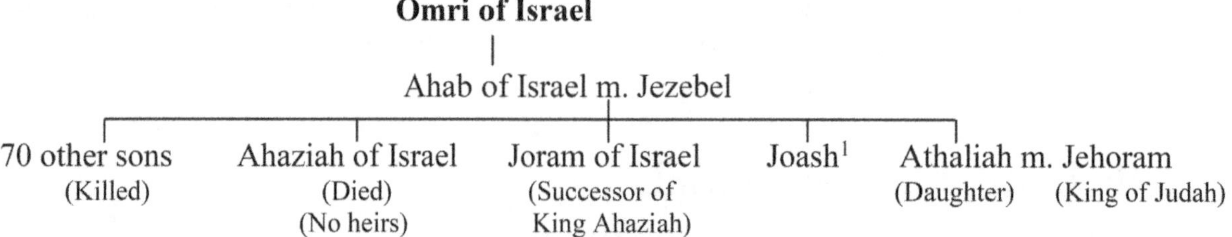

Biblical and Theological Significance

Omri, the commander of Israel's army, became king by assassinating the upstart officer Zimri, who himself had slain King Elah of Israel. Zimri had reigned in Tirzah for only seven days. A civil war ensued in Israel (ca. 885–880 B.C.) during the forty-one-year reign of Asa of Judah, ca. 911–869 B.C. (cf. **1 Kings 16:15, 21**)—with half the people following Tibni, son of Ginath (otherwise unknown), and the other half following Omri. When Tibni died in ca. 880 B.C., Omri seized power (corresponding to the thirty-first year of the forty-one-year reign of Asa of Judah; **1 Kings 16:22–23**).[2] The marriage of Athaliah (Omri's granddaughter) to Jehoram of Judah, had a profoundly negative influence on Judah (**2 Kings 8:18, 26; 2 Chronicles 18:1; 21:6**).

Omri reigned for a total of twelve years over Israel (ca. 885–874 B.C.). Initially, he reigned six years from Tirzah (the original capital of the Northern Kingdom). Then, after purchasing the hill of Samaria and fortifying and establishing Samaria[3] as the new capital, he reigned there for the next six years (**1 Kings 16:23–24**). From that point onward, Samaria became the permanent capital of the Northern Kingdom. Omri was one of the best-known monarchs in Israel. He established the so-called Omride dynasty, referring to the consecutive reigns of Omri–Ahab–Ahaziah–Joram. Although the Omride dynasty lasted for only forty-four years (ca. 885–841 B.C.), Omri attained international notoriety during that time. His status outside Israel was highly celebrated; for example, the great Assyrian kings of that era, then and later, went so far as to call Israel *mat Ḫumrî* ("land of *Ḫumrî*") or just "*Ḫumrî*" (Omri).[4]

The historian says that Omri "followed completely the ways of Jeroboam [I] son of Nebat, committing the same sin Jeroboam had caused Israel to commit, so that they aroused the anger of the LORD, the God of Israel, by their worthless idols" (**1 Kings 16:26**). When Omri died in 874 B.C., he was buried in Samaria and was succeeded by his son Ahab (**1 Kings 16:28**).

Notes

1. Joash, called "the king's son" in **1 Kings 22:26** and **2 Chronicles 18:25**, presumably refers to Ahab's son. Joash the son of Ahab is a different person than King Joash of Judah; for the latter person, see chart "**2 Kings 11**: Joash, King of Judah."

2. As Thiele explains, "The synchronism given for Omri's accession is the thirty-first year of Asa, and the length of his reign was twelve years (**1 Kings 16:23**). Omri died in the thirty-eighth year of Asa and was succeeded by Ahab (**1 Kings 16:29**). The synchronism for Omri's accession, the thirty-first year of Asa, marks the end of the rival rule of Tibni and the beginning of Omri's sole reign. But the datum for the length of Omri's reign [12 years] includes both the years of his overlap with Tibni and those of his sole reign"; Edwin R. Thiele. *The Mysterious Numbers of the Hebrew Kings* (Grand Rapids: Zondervan, 1983; repr. Grand Rapids: Kregel , 1994), 62.

3. Omri named his capital Samaria (שֹׁמְרוֹן; *shomron*) after Shemer, the owner of the hill (שֶׁמֶר; *shemer*) (**1 Kings 16:24**). Samaria was 12 miles west of Tirzah. Much later, Herod the Great rebuilt Samaria and renamed it Sebaste (after his patron Augustus Caesar; *Sebastos* is the Greek word for "Augustus"); see Eugene H. Merrill. *Kingdom of Priests: A History of Old Testament Israel*, 2nd ed. (Grand Rapids: Baker Academic, 2008), 339.

4. Shalmaneser III: Calah Bull Inscription, line 27; Marble Slab, line iv. 15a; Black Obelisk, Epigraph 2: "I received tribute from Jehu of the House of Omri." These all refer to Shalmaneser III, whose regnal dates (ca. 858–824 B.C.) are roughly contemporary with those of Ahab, Ahaziah, Joram, and Jehu. Also see *Eerdmans Dictionary* "Humri," entry by Stewart Lasine, p. 658, for "house of Omri" (*mat Ḫ-um-ri*) and footnote 54 in Eugene H. Merrill's *Kingdom of Priests* (Grand Rapids: Baker, 1987, 1996), 340.

1 KINGS 16: AHAB, KING OF ISRAEL

Approximate Dating: ca. 874–853 B.C. ***Relevant Scriptures:*** **1 Kings 16:28–34; 21:5; 22:26;** also **1 Kings 18–22; 2 Kings 1:17; 2 Chronicles 18; 21:5–6; 22:3–8; 28:7**

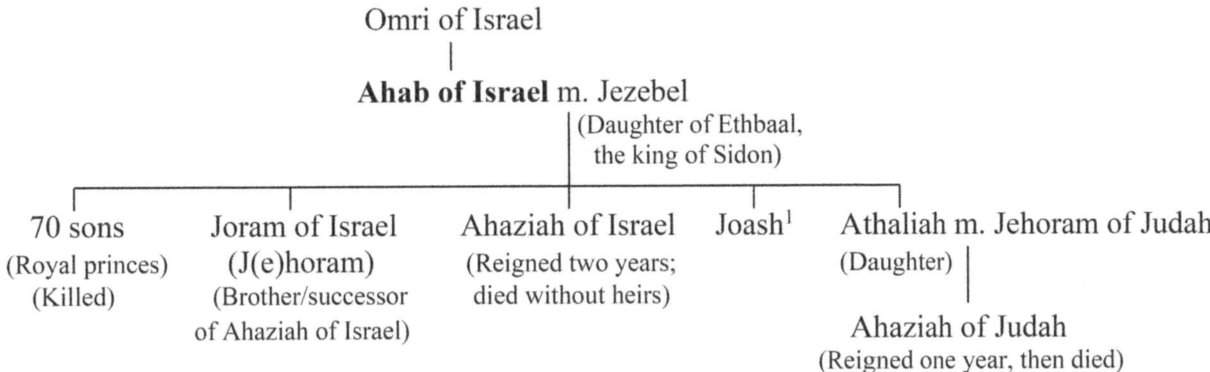

Biblical and Theological Significance

Ahab's Wife and Children

Ahab of Israel married Jezebel, the daughter of Ethbaal,[2] king of Sidon (887–856 B.C.), a well-known devout Baal worshiper (**1 Kings 16:31**). The offspring that resulted from the marriage union (and/or perhaps from Ahab's unnamed wives or concubines) included seventy sons[3] of the house of Ahab in Samaria (**2 Kings 10:1**). Later, Jehu (son of Jehoshaphat, the son of Nimshi) ordered these royal princes to be killed by the "leading men of the city" who had reared them (**2 Kings 10:6–8**). Another offspring, Ahab's infamous daughter Athaliah, married King Jehoram of Judah, thereby forming an ill-fated alliance between Israel and Judah (**2 Kings 8:18, 26; 2 Chronicles 18:1; 21:6**).

Ahab as Israel's King

Ahab became king of Israel in ca. 874 B.C., corresponding to the thirty-eighth year of the forty-one-year reign of Asa king of Judah (ca. 911–869 B.C.), and reigned for twenty-two years (ca. 874–853 B.C.) (**1 Kings 16:29**). During his reign, his wife Jezebel provided official state support for the prophets of Baal and Asherah (see **1 Kings 18:19**) and actively sought to "[kill] off the LORD's prophets" (**1 Kings 4, 13**), especially Elijah the prophet (see **1 Kings 18–19**). Jezebel and Ahab lived in Samaria (**1 Kings 16:23–24**), the capital city built by Ahab's father Omri, but also in a "country palace" in Jezreel (**1 Kings 21:1**). When Elijah confronted Ahab for contriving the murder of his (Ahab's) neighbor Naboth (**1 Kings 21:17–19**), Elijah promised that seventy sons of Ahab would die (**1 Kings 21:21**; cf. **2 Kings 10:1, 6, 10–11**) and dogs would devour Jezebel for her blatant wickedness (**1 Kings 21:23**). Humbled before God, Ahab was palliated by a promise from the LORD that he would spare him but would still bring calamity "in the days of his son [Ahaziah and/or Joram]" (**1 Kings 21:29**). Upon Ahab's death, his son Ahaziah succeeded him and reigned only one year, ca. 853–852 B.C. (**1 Kings 22:51**). In turn, when King Ahaziah of Israel died unexpectedly and without sons, his brother Joram[4] (another son of Ahab) assumed Israel's throne (**2 Kings 1:17**).

Notes

1. Joash is called "the king's [Ahab's] son" in **1 Kings 22:26** and **2 Chronicles 18:25**.

2. Jezebel, with the attenuated "Bel" for "Baal" at the end of her name, advertises the religious milieu of her father Ethbaal.

3. Very likely, these numbers are to be taken as representations of power and influence, greatly exaggerated and stylized (see note 2 in chart "**Judges 12**: Abdon, the Eleventh Judge of Israel."

4. See chart "**2 Kings 3**: Joram, King of Israel."

1 KINGS 16: HIEL OF BETHEL, THE REBUILDER OF JERICHO

Approximate Dating: during the reign of Ahab king of Israel, ca. 874–853 B.C. ***Relevant Scriptures:*** **1 Kings 16:34**

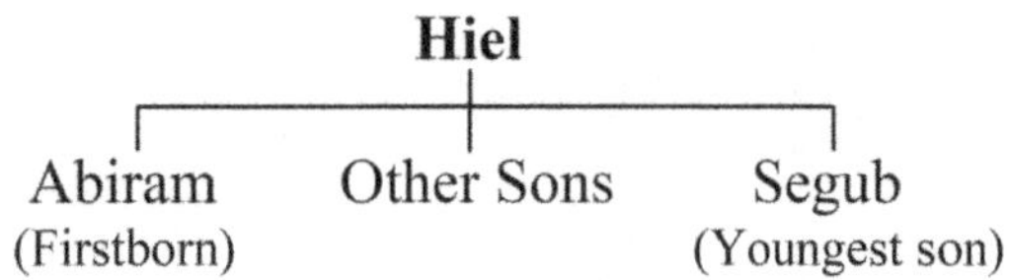

Biblical and Theological Significance

Hiel was from Bethel, a prominent town in Ephraim just north of the border with Benjamin. In a sense, Bethel lay between the Northern and Southern Kingdoms, located on the main road from Jericho to the coastal plain. During the twenty-two-year reign of Ahab, king of Israel (ca. 874–853 B.C.), Hiel rebuilt Jericho, a city in the tribe of Benjamin that had been destroyed during the conquest of Canaan in ca. 1406 B.C. (**Joshua 5:13–6:27**; cf. **18:21**). Until the days of King David, Jericho was occupied by only a few inhabitants (**2 Samuel 10:5**). Hiel desired to develop it into a full-fledged city, probably to encourage domestic and international trade. Persuaded that it would advance the cause, he sacrificed his eldest son, Abiram, to lay the foundation of the city and sacrificed his youngest son, Segub, to set up the city gates.[1] Hiel's actions fulfilled the curse that God pronounced on the city: "Cursed before the Lord is the one who undertakes to rebuild this city, Jericho: 'At the cost of his firstborn son he will lay its foundations; at the cost of his youngest he will set up its gates' " (**Joshua 6:26**). Elisha the prophet reversed the curse on Jericho by healing the bad waters and the unproductive land in a salt covenant ceremony[2] (cf. **2 Kings 2:19–22**).

Notes

1. The reference to both sons and their fate suggests that the ancient practice of infant burials in large *pithoi* (large storage jars) as sacrificial offerings to the gods who, moved by such piety, would bless the (re)construction until its successful completion.

2. Salt was a purifying agent and a preservative that symbolized life and the enduring nature of the covenant between God and Israel. For other instances of covenants of salt and the function of salt in covenant meals, see **Leviticus 2:13** (grain offerings), **Numbers 18:19** (heave offerings), **2 Chronicles 13:5** (the kingship given to David and the Davidic descendants); and **Ezekiel 43:24** (burnt offerings).

1 KINGS 17: ELIJAH THE PROPHET

Approximate Dating: ca. 874–852 B.C. ***Relevant Scriptures:*** **1 Kings 17–19; 21:17–29; 2 Kings 1–2**

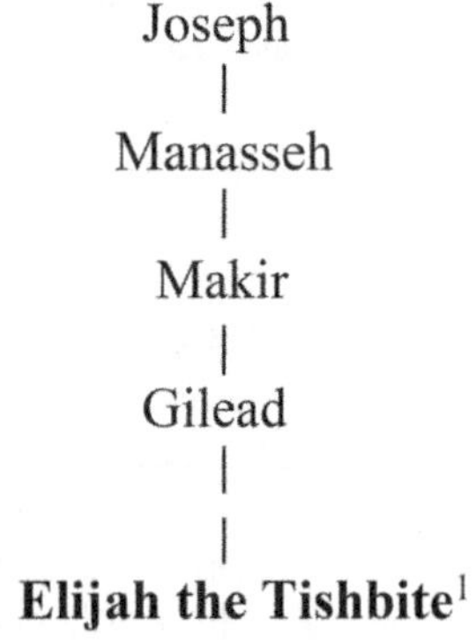

Biblical and Theological Significance

Elijah prophesied to Israel during the reigns of King Ahab (ca. 874–853 B.C.) and King Ahaziah (ca. 853–852 B.C.). After Elijah proclaimed a three-year drought to Ahab, he hid at the Kerith Ravine, east of the Jordan, where he was fed by ravens and drank from a brook (**1 Kings 17:2–7**). After the brook dried up, Elijah went to Zarephath to live with a poor Gentile widow and her son (**1 Kings 17:8–14**). The woman was so poor that she only had "a handful of flour . . . and a little olive oil" (**1 Kings 17:12**), enough for one last meal, after which she expected herself and her son to die of starvation. Elijah asked her to make a small loaf for him and then something for herself and her son, reassuring her that "the jar of flour will not be used up and the jug of oil will not run dry" until the rains returned (**1 Kings 17:14**). While at Zarephath, the widow's son died, but through Elijah's prayer and ministry, the child was brought back to life (**1 Kings 17:19–23**).

Elijah is perhaps best known for confronting the four hundred and fifty prophets of Baal and the four hundred prophets of Asherah at Mount Carmel (**1 Kings 18:19**; see **1 Kings 18:19–40**). When the Baal prophets failed to invoke a response from their god, Elijah prayed, and the Lord answered by burning up their sacrifice (**1 Kings 18:38**). The people of Israel repented from their apostasy and the Baal prophets were put to death (**1 Kings 18:39–40**). Elijah then prayed for rain and heavy rains came. Then Ahab[2] went to Jezreel to tell Jezebel what had happened at Mount Carmel, and Elijah went also. Jezebel vowed that she would kill Elijah "by this time tomorrow" (**1 Kings 19:2**). The fearful Elijah fled from Samaria to Beersheba where an angel of the Lord fed him bread and water (**1 Kings 19:3–6**). Afterward he journeyed to Mount Horeb where the Lord revealed his glory—not in a powerful wind, earthquake, or fire, but in a "gentle whisper" (**1 Kings 19:11–12**). Then, Elijah traveled to the Desert of Damascus where he anointed three people: Hazael as king of Aram, Jehu as king of Israel, and Elisha as his successor (**1 Kings 19:15–17**).

Elijah also confronted Ahab for plotting the murder of Naboth (**1 Kings 21:6–7, 17–19**), predicted that all of Ahab's descendants would die (**1 Kings 21:21**; cf. **2 Kings 10:1, 6**), and predicted that dogs would devour Jezebel at her death (**1 Kings 21:23**). When Ahab died, his son Ahaziah assumed the throne, but after only two years in office, Ahaziah fell through the lattice of an upper room. Elijah prophesied that Ahaziah would not recover (**2 Kings 1:2–16**).

Elijah wore a characteristic garment of hair, a leather belt (**2 Kings 1:8**), a cloak (**2 Kings 2:8, 13**), and a prophet's mantle that he bestowed upon Elisha, along with a *double portion* of his own prophetic spirit (**2 Kings 2:9–11**). Elijah did not see a natural death—rather, he was taken up into heaven by "a chariot of fire and horses of fire" (**2 Kings 2:11**).

Elijah's ministry foreshadowed that of John the Baptist (cf. **Matthew 17:12–13; Mark 9:13**). John possessed the "spirit and power of Elijah" (**Luke 1:17**), although he denied that he was the literal reincarnation of Elijah (**John 1:21**). Also, some thought Jesus to be Elijah incarnate (**Matthew 16:14; Mark 6:15**), but this notion was dispelled with the appearance of Elijah and Moses in "glorious splendor" at Jesus' transfiguration (**Luke 9:30–33;** see also **Matthew 17:3–4; Mark 9:4–5**).

Notes

1. Elijah was from the town of "Tishbe in Gilead," referring to the general region of the Transjordan, and for this reason he was often identified as "Elijah the Tishbite" (**1 Kings 17:1; 21:17, 28; 2 Kings 1:3, 8; 9:36**). Alternatively, Tishbite may be a corruption of Jabeshite, meaning a resident of the town of Jabesh (or Jabesh Gilead) in the northwest part of Gilead. Either way, and assuming that Tishbe (or Jabesh) was Elijah's hometown, Elijah was likely from the Manasseh–Makir–Gilead line of descendants who settled the Gilead region east of the Jordan River; see chart "**1 Chronicles** 7: Manasseh (The Half-Tribe of West Manasseh)."

2. Ahab considered Elijah the "troubler of Israel" (**1 Kings 18:17**) and his "enemy" (**1 Kings 21:20**).

1 KINGS 19: ELISHA THE PROPHET

Approximate Dating: ca. 850–790 to as late as 782 B.C. ***Relevant Scriptures:*** **1 Kings 19:16, 19; 2 Kings 3:11, 6:31**; also **1 Kings 19; 2 Kings 2–9, 13**

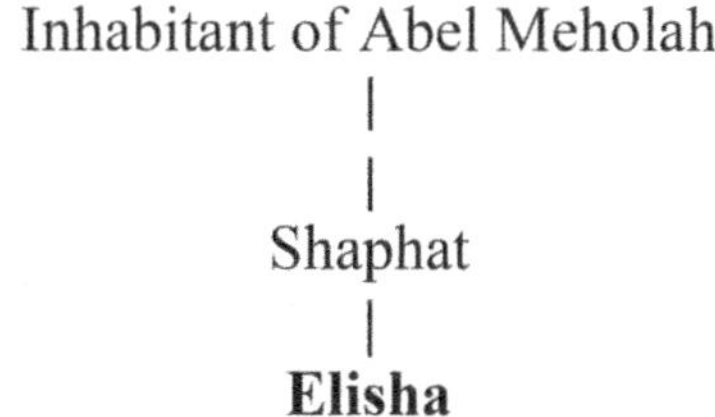

Biblical and Theological Significance

His Calling and Apprenticeship

Elisha's name means "God saves" or "my God is salvation," which characterizes the prophetic role he played as the Lord's spokesman. Elisha was a farmer from Abel Meholah;[1] his hometown was likely situated in the tribe of West Manasseh. The riverbank town was also the home of Adriel "the Meholathite" the son of Barzillai (**2 Samuel 21:8**), who married Merab, Saul's eldest daughter (**1 Samuel 18:19**).

When Elijah anointed Elisha as his successor (**1 Kings 19:16, 19**), Elisha celebrated his divine calling with a feast by slaughtering his twelve oxen, burning the plowing equipment to cook the meat, and then feeding the people. He became a disciple of Elijah, initially as his servant (**1 Kings 19:21; 2 Kings 3:11**) and then as his apprentice. He succeeded Elijah as the prophet to Israel, ministering in all some sixty-plus years (ca. 850–790/782 B.C.) throughout the reigns of Ahab, Ahaziah, Joram, Jehu, and Jehoahaz and part of the reign of Jehoash.

Gifted with the Spirit of Elijah

Elisha was given insight as to when Elijah would be taken up into heaven by God (**2 Kings 2:3, 5**). The two traveled from Gilgal to Bethel, to Jericho, and then to the Jordan River; at each step, Elijah encouraged Elisha to stay behind, but he vowed his allegiance to him (**2 Kings 2:2, 4, 6**). Elisha considered Elijah his "father" (**2 Kings 2:12**) and requested that Elijah given him an *inheritance* like that due a firstborn son (**2 Kings 2:9**). Elisha received a *double portion* of Elijah's spirit and then watched Elijah be taken up into heaven by a whirlwind (**2 Kings 2:11**).

His Prophecies and Miracles

Elisha soon became the head over a guild of prophets called "the company of the prophets," made many prophecies, and performed many miracles (**2 Kings 2:19–24; 3:1–26; 4:1–44; 5:1–27; 6:1–23; 8:7–15; 13:14–21**). Elisha died from a fatal illness in the days of King Jehoash of Israel (ca. 798–782 B.C.) (**2 Kings 13:14–20**). However, even in death, the power of God resided in Elisha's bones, enough to revive a Moabite man from the dead (**2 Kings 13:20–21**)!

Notes

1. Based on the narrative details of the flight of the Midianites from the Jezreel Valley in **Judges 7:22–8:5**, the *Anchor Yale Bible Dictionary* (Diana V. Edelman,"Abel–Meholah," p. 11) places the location for Abel Meholah "in the western ghor near the Jordan River, north of Beth-barah and near or opposite Tabbath, and north of the latitude of Succoth on the eastern bank of the Jordan, which was the first settlement Gideon reached after crossing the river. Eusebius places Abel-Meholah in the western ghor, identifying it with the Roman settlement known as Bethmaela ten Roman miles south of Scythopolis (Beth She'an)." Abel Meholah was part of Solomon's 5th district that included Taanach, Megiddo, and Beth-shean and lay opposite Jokmeam, a Levitical city given to Kohathite priests (**1 Kings 4:12; 1 Chronicles 6:68**).

1 KINGS 22: MICAIAH THE PROPHET

Approximate Dating: ca. 853 B.C. ***Relevant Scriptures:*** **1 Kings 22:8–9; 2 Chronicles 18:7–8**

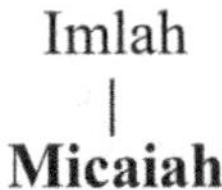

Biblical and Theological Significance

King Jehoshaphat of Judah (ca. 872–848 B.C.)—whose name means 'Yahweh judges'—lived in the period of evil kings of Israel who embraced and engaged in polytheism of the worst kind. In short, they were opposed to all the virtues and godliness that Jehoshaphat had learned from his father, Asa (**1 Kings 15:11; 2 Chronicles 14:2**). However, Jehoshaphat seemed fascinated by and even attracted to many of these kings, especially Ahab of Israel (ca. 874–853 B.C.; **1 Kings 22:2**), a connection that led to the caveat in the encomium summarizing his life and legacy: "Jehoshaphat was also at peace[1] with the king of Israel" (**1 Kings 22:44; 2 Chronicles 18:1–3**).

The prime example of this ungodly linkage is seen in Jehoshaphat's alliance with King Ahab of Israel and their campaign (at Ahab's request) against the Arameans to retake Ramoth Gilead from the king of Aram. Before going into battle, Jehoshaphat sought the counsel of a prophet of the Lord about the outcome, whereas Ahab wanted to inquire of the prophets of Baal. Ahab knew of Micaiah son of Imlah, who was a prophet of God; however, Ahab did not trust Micaiah because in the past, Micaiah had prophesied misfortune for Ahab and did not say what Ahab wanted to hear (**1 Kings 22:8; 2 Chronicles 18:7**). The Baal prophets, under Zedekiah son of Kenaanah, assured King Ahab of a successful outcome (**1 Kings 22:11–12; 2 Chronicles 18:10–11**). Micaiah, the Lord's prophet, said, "As surely as the LORD lives, I can tell him [Ahab] only what the LORD tells me" (**1 Kings 22:14**; cf. **2 Chronicles 18:13**; see **1 Kings 22:1–28; 2 Chronicles 18:1–27**). Micaiah prophesied that all Israel would be "scattered on the hills like sheep without a shepherd" and that Ahab would die in battle (**1 Kings 22:17–20, 23, 28**; **2 Chronicles 18:16–19, 22, 27**; cf. **1 Kings 22:29–38; 2 Chronicles 18:28–34**).

Micaiah's prophecy came to pass when Ahab died in battle at the hand of an archer who "drew his bow at random"[2] (**1 Kings 22:34; 2 Chronicles 18:33**), suggesting that the arrow was directed not by a bowman, but by Yahweh himself. Jehoshaphat must surely have disregarded the common biblical injunction forbidding fellowship by the righteous with the wicked (**2 Chronicles 20:35–37; 2 Corinthians 6:14**).

Notes

1. The verb וַיַּשְׁלֵם, related to the noun *shalom*, is a Hiphil *preterite* verb form with the meaning, in this context, of an intensity or eagerness in making alliances with these evil men.

2. The bowman drew his bow לְתֻמּוֹ, lit., "innocently" or "purposelessly." He had no idea where the arrow would go so its path must have been an act of God.

1 KINGS 22: AHAZIAH, KING OF ISRAEL

Approximate Dating: ca. 853–852 B.C. ***Relevant Scriptures:*** **1 Kings 22:51–53; 2 Kings 1:1–18**; also **1 Chronicles 3:11; 2 Chronicles 20:35**

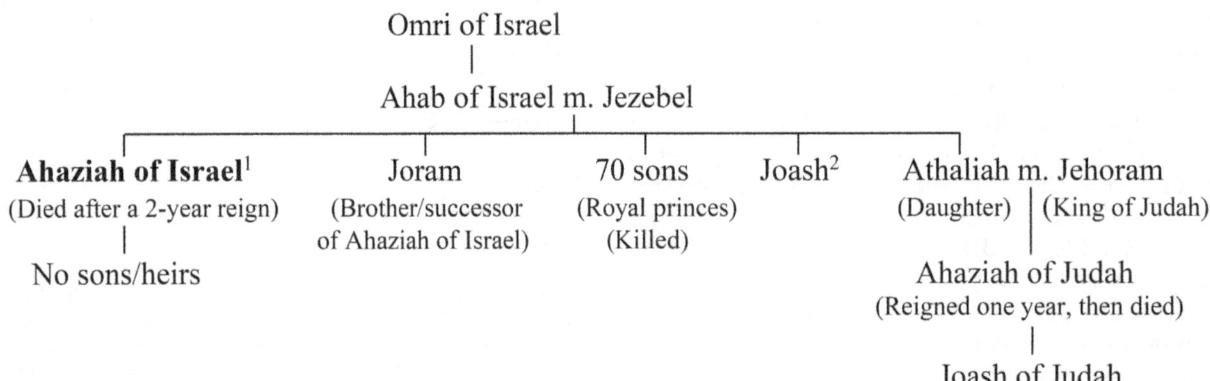

Biblical and Theological Significance

Ahaziah's sister, Athaliah, married Jehoram of Judah (**2 Kings 8:16–18, 26; 2 Chronicles 21:4–6; 22:2**), thereby joining the kingdoms of Israel and Judah through a marriage alliance. At the death of his father, Ahab, Ahaziah succeeded to the throne of Israel in the seventeenth year of the twenty-five-year reign of Jehoshaphat of Judah (872–848 B.C.; **1 Kings 22:42**) and reigned for two years (ca. 853–852 B.C.; **1 Kings 22:51**). Like his parents, Ahaziah was a Baal worshiper, thus meriting the Chronicler description that his "ways were wicked" (**2 Chronicles 20:35**). Ahaziah of Israel formed an alliance with Jehoshaphat of Judah to build merchant ships to go to Tarshish; however, the Lord cursed their efforts and the ships wrecked (**2 Chronicles 20:35–37**). Ahaziah's reign was shortened by an ill-fated fall through the lattice of an upper room in the Samarian palace. Instead of seeking Yahweh to see if he would recover, Ahaziah consulted Baal-Zebub, the Philistine deity of Ekron (**2 Kings 1:2–3, 6, 16**). The Lord sent word by Elijah the prophet that Ahaziah would "certainly die" (**2 Kings 1:4, 6, 16**). Since Ahaziah had no male heirs, his brother Joram assumed the throne of Israel.

Notes

1. Ahaziah of Israel (the son of Ahab and Jezebel), who reigned from ca. 853–852 B.C., should not be confused with Ahaziah of Judah (the son of Athaliah and Jehoram), who reigned for one year over Judah (ca. 841 B.C.; **2 Kings 8:25–26, 29; 9:16, 29; 2 Chronicles 22:1–10**).

2. Joash is called "the king's son," presumably meaning Ahab's son (**1 Kings 22:26; 2 Chronicles 18:25**). Joash son of Ahab is a different person than King Joash of Judah, the son of Ahaziah, who reigned from ca. 835–796 B.C.

2 KINGS 3: JORAM, KING OF ISRAEL

Approximate Dating: ca. 852–841 B.C. ***Relevant Scriptures:*** **2 Kings 3:1; 8:16–18, 25–26, 28–29; 2 Chronicles 22:5–6**[1]

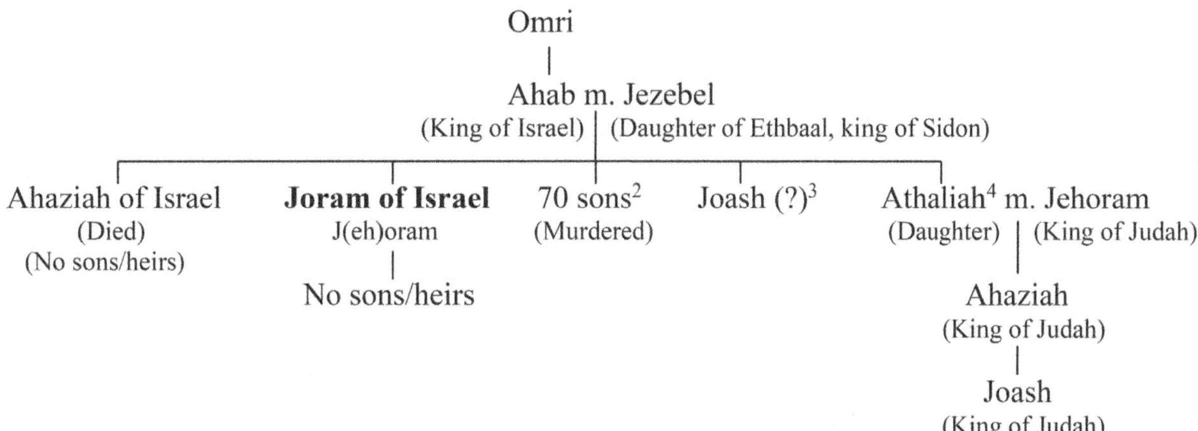

Biblical and Theological Significance

Joram's brother, Ahaziah, had succeeded to the throne when Ahab died but reigned for only two years, ca. 853–852 B.C. (**1 Kings 22:51**). When Ahaziah died of a fatal fall through a latticed opening at his palace (**2 Kings 1:2**), he left no sons to succeed him, so his brother Joram/J(eh)oram[5] assumed the throne (**2 Kings 1:17**).

Joram came to the throne of Israel in ca. 852 B.C., corresponding to the second year of King Jehoram of Judah who, at the time, was serving as co-regent with his father Jehoshaphat, 853–848 B.C. (**2 Kings 1:17**). Joram reigned for twelve years, ca. 852–841 B.C. (**3:1**). He was a contemporary of Elisha the prophet. During Joram's reign, Moabites rebelled against Israel, but a coalition of kings, composed of Joram of Israel, Jehoshaphat of Judah, and the king of Edom, defeated them (**2 Kings 3**).

The Lord used the ruthless military prowess of Jehu, the Israelite army commander, to "cut off from Ahab every last male in Israel—slave or free" and to kill Joram (**2 Kings 9:7–8, 23–26**). Joram's body was thrown "on the field that belonged to Naboth the Jezreelite" (**2 Kings 9:25**) to avenge the innocent deaths of Naboth and his sons and the deaths of the Lord's prophets at the hands of Ahab and Jezebel (**1 Kings 18:4, 13, 19:1**; cf. **1 Kings 21**). This fulfilled God's promise to Ahab (through Elijah) that he would not "bring this disaster in his [Ahab's] day, but I will bring it on his house in the days of his son [meaning in the days of Joram and/or Ahaziah]" (**1 Kings 21:29**).

Joram left no male heirs. The throne of Israel passed to Jehu, son of Jehoshaphat, son of Nimshi, who had been the military commander under both Ahab and Joram (**2 Kings 9:2–7**).

Notes

1. For additional references, see those in the relevant Scripture for chart "**1 Kings 16**: Ahab, King of Israel."

2. On the order of Jehu, the army commander, seventy sons of Ahab—possibly a symbolic number meaning "a great many"—were murdered in Samaria by the "leading men of the city" who had reared them (**2 Kings 10:1, 6–8**).

3. Joash is called "the king's [Ahab's] son" in **1 Kings 22:26**; **2 Chronicles 18:25**.

4. Athaliah (Joram's sister) married Jehoram the king of Judah, thus linking the kingdoms of Israel and Judah (**2 Kings 8:16–18**).

5. The names Joram/J(eh)oram are essentially the same, the former being a hypocoristic form of the latter and both meaning "Yahweh is lofty (or makes one lofty)." The names occasionally appear interchangeably in various translations, but the NIV uses "Joram" to refer to the king of Israel, and "Jehoram" to refer to the king of Judah.

2 KINGS 8: JEHORAM, KING OF JUDAH

Approximate Dating: co-regent with Jehoshaphat ca. 853–848 B.C.; sole monarchy ca. 848–841 B.C. ***Relevant Scriptures:*** **2 Kings 8:16–24; 1 Chronicles 3:10–12; 2 Chronicles 21:1–22:1; Matthew 1:8;** also **1 Kings 16:31; 2 Kings 11; 2 Chronicles 22-23**

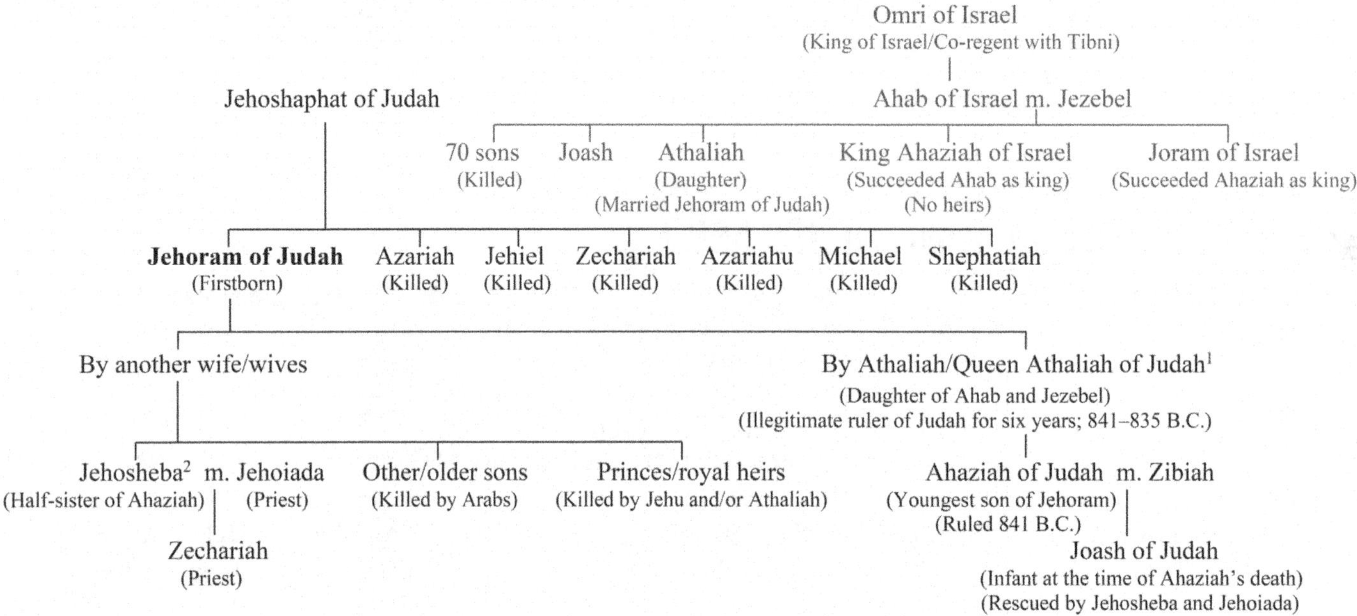

Biblical and Theological Significance

Jehoshaphat gave gifts to all of his sons, but he gave Jehoram the kingdom of Judah because he was the firstborn (**2 Chronicles 21:2–3**). The marriage of Jehoram to Athaliah of Israel (**2 Kings 8:18, 26; 2 Chronicles 21:6; 22:2**) formed an ill-fated royal alliance between the kingdoms of Judah and Israel.

Jehoram co-ruled[3] with his father Jehoshaphat from ca. 853–848 B.C. and then in 848 B.C., at the age of thirty-two, became the sole monarch, corresponding to the fifth year of the twelve-year reign of Joram of Israel, ca. 852–841 B.C. (**2 Kings 8:16–17**). Jehoram was strongly influenced by his idolatrous wife Athaliah. Immediately upon his succession, he killed all his brothers who were possible heirs to the throne (**2 Chronicles 21:1–4**). He followed the evil ways of the household of Ahab by promoting Baal worship in Judah during his eight-year official reign as Judah's king, ca. 848–841 B.C. (**2 Chronicles 21:5–6**).

Jehoram's death at age forty is described as follows: "the Lord afflicted Jehoram with an incurable disease of the bowels. In the course of time . . . he died in great pain. His people made no funeral fire in his honor, as they had for his predecessors. . . . He passed away, to no one's regret, and was buried in the City of David, but not in the tombs of the kings" (**2 Chronicles 21:18–20**). The events of Jehoram's reign were recorded in the book of the annals of the kings of Judah (**2 Kings 8:23**). His youngest son, Ahaziah, succeeded him as king of Judah (**2 Kings 8:24; 2 Chronicles 22:1**).

Notes

1. See chart "**2 Kings 11**: Queen Athaliah, the Illegitimate Ruler of Judah."
2. See chart "**2 Kings 11**: Jehosheba, the Wife of Jehoiada the Priest."
3. For Jehoram's co-regency with this father, Jehoshaphat, see Edwin R. Thiele's *The Mysterious Numbers of the Hebrew Kings* (New revised ed.) Grand Rapids: Kregel (repr.) 1994, from the 1983 Zondervan edition, 10–13, 55, 63, 98, 100.

2 KINGS 8: AHAZIAH, KING OF JUDAH

Approximate Dating: ca. 841 B.C. ***Relevant Scriptures:*** **2 Kings 8:24–29; 9:21–29; 10:1–14; 11:1–3, 12; 12:1; 2 Chronicles 21:17; 22:1–12; 24:1**

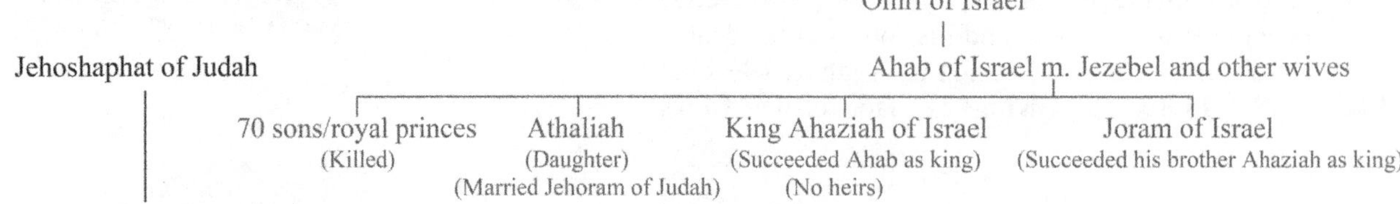

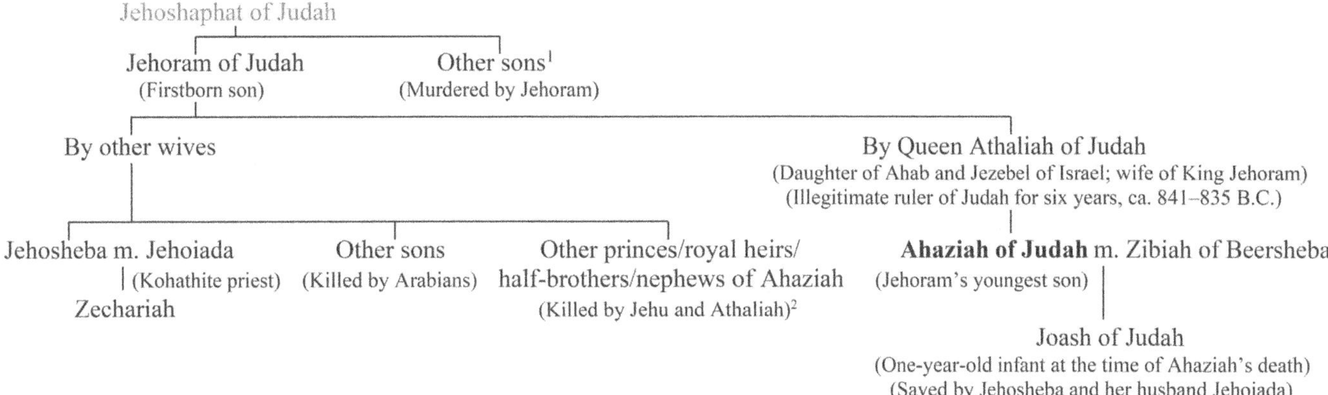

Biblical and Theological Significance

Ahaziah[3] became king of Judah in the last year of the twelve-year reign of Joram of Israel (ca. 852–841 B.C.; cf. **2 Kings 8:25; 9:29**) and reigned for only one year (ca. 841 B.C.). The NIV preserves the correct figure, that he became king at the age of twenty-two[4] (**2 Kings 8:26; 2 Chronicles 22:2**) and then "followed the ways of the house of Ahab, for his mother [Athaliah] encouraged him to act wickedly" (**2 Chronicles 22:3**; cf. **2 Kings 8:27**). After his father's (Jehoram's) death, Ahaziah followed the advice of the counselors of the house of Ahab and joined with Joram of Israel in war against the Arameans (**2 Kings 8:28–29; 9:14–16, 27; 2 Chronicles 22:4–6**), at which time Joram was wounded (**2 Kings 8:28–29**). The visit of Ahaziah of Judah to see the ailing Joram of Israel provided an opportunity for Jehu, the son of Jehoshaphat, the son of Nimshi, to kill Ahaziah (**2 Kings 9:14–27; 2 Chronicles 22:7–9**)—the Chronicler notes that Ahaziah's death was brought about by God (**2 Chronicles 22:7**). After Ahaziah's death, his mother, Athaliah, seized power and killed the remaining heirs to the throne of Judah, except for Joash, the one-year-old infant and sole surviving heir of Ahaziah. During Athaliah's illegitimate reign (ca. 841–835 B.C.), Ahaziah's son (Joash) was hidden in the temple by his half-aunt Jehosheba (who was Ahaziah's half-sister) and her husband Jehoiada, the Kohathite attending priest (**2 Kings 11:1–3; 2 Chronicles 22:10–12**). When Joash reached the age of seven, Jehoiada staged a *coup d'état* to depose Athaliah and restore the rightful heir, Joash, to the throne (**2 Kings 11:4–12; 2 Chronicles 23:1–11**). At Jehoiada's command, Athaliah was killed outside the temple near the royal palace (**2 Kings 11:13–16; 2 Chronicles 23:12–15**).

Notes

1. Upon his succession to the throne of Judah, Jehoram killed his brothers: Azariah, Jehiel, Zechariah, Azariahu, Michael, and Shephatiah (**2 Chronicles 21:2–4**). See chart "**2 Kings 8**: Jehoram, King of Judah."

2. At least forty-two relatives of Ahaziah were either killed by Jehu, the son of Jehophaphat, the son of Nimshi (**2 Kings 10:12–14; 2 Chronicles 22:8**), or murdered by Athaliah (**2 Kings 11:1**).

3. Ahaziah king of Judah, who ruled in 841 B.C., should not be confused with Ahaziah son of Ahab, who was king of Israel during the same general time period (853–852 B.C.; cf. **1 Kings 22:51**).

4. In **2 Chronicles 22:2**, some Septuagint and Syriac manuscripts read Heb. *forty-two* instead of twenty-two, which has caused confusion in various translations; for example, **2 Kings 8:26** (NKJV) says "Ahaziah was twenty-two years old when he became king," whereas **2 Chronicles 22:2** (NKJV) says "Ahaziah was forty-two years old when he became king." Given the fact that Jehoram, Ahaziah's father, was thirty-two years old when he assumed the sole rulership of Judah in 848 B.C. and that Jehoram was forty years old when he died in 841 B.C. (**2 Kings 8:17; 2 Chronicles 21:5, 20**), Jehoram's son (Ahaziah) could not have been forty-two years old (older than his father!) when he became king. The textual discrepancy in Ahaziah's age when he assumed the throne is generally considered by scholars to be a copyist error in **2 Chronicles 22:22** (i.e., where 42, "two and forty" was written instead of 22, "two and twenty").

2 KINGS 9: JEHU, KING OF ISRAEL

Approximate Dating: 841–814 B.C. ***Relevant Scriptures:*** **2 Kings 9:1–10:36; 2 Chronicles 22:7; 25:17**

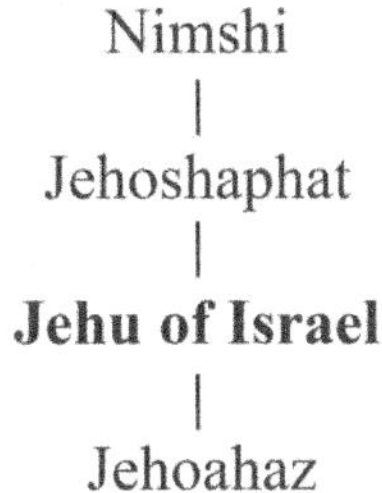

Biblical and Theological Significance

Jehu is called "the son of Nimshi" (**1 Kings 19:16; 2 Kings 9:20; 2 Chronicles 22:7**) and "the son of Jehoshaphat, the son of Nimshi" (**2 Kings 9:2, 14**). Jehu served as the military commander under Ahab and Ahab's son, Joram. The Lord's prophet Elisha sent a man from among the company of the prophets to Ramoth Gilead to anoint Jehu as the king of Israel (**2 Kings 9:1–10**). Jehu reigned over Israel for twenty-eight years, ca. 841–814 B.C. (**2 Kings 10:35–36**). The Lord used him "to destroy the house of Ahab" and the house of Omri (**2 Kings 9:1–10:31; 2 Chronicles 22:7**). Through a violent course of events, Jehu became responsible for the deaths of Joram, king of Israel; Ahaziah, king of Judah, and his relatives; Jezebel the queen of Israel; and seventy surviving members of the household of Ahab of Israel.

Thus, God's providential plan to destroy Baal worship in Israel was fulfilled at the hands of Jehu (**2 Kings 10:18–28**). Jehoahaz, the son of Jehu, succeeded his father as the next king of Israel (**2 Kings 10:35; 13:1**).

2 KINGS 11: QUEEN ATHALIAH, THE ILLEGITIMATE RULER OF JUDAH

Approximate Dating: ca. 841–835 B.C. ***Relevant Scriptures:*** **2 Kings 11:1–20; 2 Chronicles 22:2, 10–11; 23:1–15**

Omri of Israel
(King of Israel/Co-regent with Tibni)
|
Ahab of Israel m. Jezebel

- 70 sons (Killed)
- **Athaliah/Queen Athaliah of Judah** m. King Jehoram of Judah (Son of Jehoshaphat)
  (Daughter of Ahab and Jezebel)
  (Illegitimate ruler of Judah for six years)
  - Ahaziah of Judah m. Zibiah
    (Youngest and surviving son of Jehoram)
    - Joash of Judah
      (A one-year old infant at the time of Ahaziah's death in 841 B.C.)
      (Protected by Jehosheba and Jehoiada during Athaliah's rule over Judah)
- King Ahaziah of Israel (Succeeded Ahab as king) (No sons/heirs)
- King Joram of Israel (Succeeded Ahaziah as king) (No sons/heirs)

Biblical and Theological Significance

Athaliah is one of a few female villains in Scripture. Her mother was the evil Jezebel, daughter of King Ethbaal[1] of Sidon (**1 Kings 16:31**). To cement a strong alliance between Israel and Judah, an arrangement was made for Ahab's daughter, Athaliah, to marry Jehoram, the king of Judah (**2 Kings 8:16–19, 26; 2 Chronicles 21:5–6**). Their youngest son, Ahaziah, later became king of Judah. However, in 841 B.C., after the untimely deaths of both her husband, Jehoram, at age forty (**2 Kings 8:17; 2 Chronicles 21:5**) and her son Ahaziah at age twenty-three (**2 Kings 8:26; 9:27–29; 2 Chronicles 22:7–9**), Athaliah usurped Judah's throne and immediately killed all remaining royal heirs to retain the power for herself. The exception to her murders was Ahaziah's infant son, Joash, who was safely hidden in Solomon's Temple: "He remained hidden with his nurse at the temple of the LORD for six years while Athaliah ruled the land" (**2 Kings 11:3**). The young Joash was nurtured by his half-aunt Jehosheba[2] and her husband, the godly priest Jehoiada[3] (**2 Kings 11:1–2; 2 Chronicles 22:10–11**). Athaliah reigned for six years, ca. 841–835 B.C. (**2 Kings 11:3; 2 Chronicles 22:12**). Eventually, in a military coup planned by Jehoiada, Athaliah was deposed and killed, and the seven-year-old Joash was enthroned as the rightful king to the throne of Judah (**2 Kings 11:4–21; 2 Chronicles 23:1–15; 24:1**).

Notes

1. Ethbaal's name clearly betrays his religious devotion as a worshiper of Baal, the Phoenician god of fertility, as does his daughter's name.
2. Jehosheba was the daughter of King Jehoram of Judah and an unnamed wife (i.e., not Athaliah) as well as the half-aunt of Joash; see charts "**2 Kings 8**: Jehoram, King of Judah" and "**2 Kings 11**: Jehosheba, the Wife of Jehoiada the Priest."
3. Jehoiada was a Kohathite priest, but not a high priest; see charts "**2 Chronicles 22**: Probable Genealogy for Jehoiada the Priest who Masterminded the Overthrow of Queen Athaliah of Judah" and "**Supplement 2**: The High Priests of Israel."

2 KINGS 11: JEHOSHEBA, THE WIFE OF JEHOIADA THE PRIEST

Approximate Dating: ca. 850–800 B.C.; protected the infant Joash from ca. 841–835 B.C. until he was crowned king of Judah ***Relevant Scriptures:*** **2 Kings 11:2; 2 Chronicles 22:11;** also **1 Kings 16:31; 2 Kings 11; 2 Chronicles 22–23**

Lineage of Queen Athaliah (Wife of Jehoram and mother of Ahaziah):

Omri of Israel
|
Ahab of Israel m. Jezebel
(Daughter of Ethbaal of Sidon)

- 70 sons (Killed)
- Joash
- Athaliah (Daughter) (Married Jehoram of Judah)
- Ahaziah (King of Israel) (No sons)
- Joram (King of Israel)

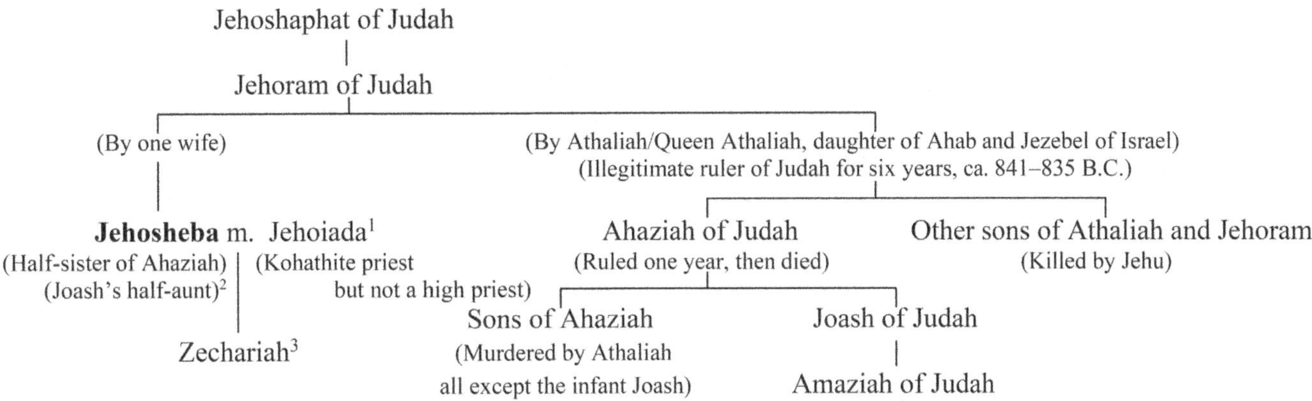

Biblical and Theological Significance

Jehosheba was the daughter of Jehoram (but not the daughter of Athaliah) and the half-sister of Ahaziah, both kings of Judah (**2 Kings 11:2; 2 Chronicles 22:11**). When Jehosheba's father, Jehoram, became king (848 B.C.), he killed all his brothers, who were potential rivals to the throne (**2 Chronicles 21:4**).[4] After his marriage to Athaliah, Jehoram mimicked the household of Ahab of Israel by promoting Baal worship in Judah; later, after a two-year illness, Jehoram died (**2 Chronicles 21:18–20; cf. 2 Kings 8:24**). Ahaziah—Jehoram's son by Queen Athaliah and Jehosheba's half-brother—then succeeded to the throne, but Ahaziah ruled for only one year (841 B.C.) and was killed by Jehu, the son of Jehoshaphat, the son of Nimshi (**2 Kings 8:25–29; 9:27–29; 2 Chronicles 22:1–9**).[5]

Athaliah saw the early deaths of her husband (Jehoram) and her son (Ahaziah) in 841 B.C. as a means of bringing Judah under *Israelite* control. When Ahaziah died, Athaliah immediately seized the throne of Judah and began murdering the royal princes/heirs to the throne (**2 Kings 11:1; 2 Chronicles 22:10**). Jehosheba successfully protected the legitimate child-king Joash, by hiding him and his nurse in the temple throughout the six years that Athaliah ruled Judah (ca. 841–835 B.C.).

Jehosheba's name, יְהוֹשֶׁבַע, is theophoric, meaning "Yahweh is [the essence of] joy or fullness." Her character was defined by compassion, ingenuity, devotion to Yahweh, and matchless courage. She understood something of Davidic succession and its messianic significance, for she was determined that, at all costs, it would not be snuffed out. Her priestly husband, Jehoiada, shared many of her same traits, and together—a wedding of palace and temple—they made a formidable pair, able to use their privilege, power, and positions to do what like-minded patriots could not do.

When Joash reached the age of seven, Jehoiada led a detailed military coup to dethrone Athaliah and enthrone Joash, thus restoring the rightful Davidic heir to the throne of Judah (**2 Kings 11:4–16; 2 Chronicles 23:1–15**). Upon his ascension, Joash undertook a major renovation of the temple and ruled as a good king until Jehoiada, the positive father figure in his life, died (**2 Chronicles 24:15**). Thereafter, Joash fell into Baal worship, listened to bad counselors in Judah, and ordered the death of Jehoiada's son, Zechariah the priest (**2 Chronicles 24:20–22**)!

Notes

1. Jehoiada appears to be the leading Kohathite–Korahite attending priest in Solomon's Temple in the days of Meraioth the high priest—and/or during the priesthood of Meraioth's predecessor(s). Jehoiada was the chief overseer of the Levitical doorkeepers who collected monies for the renovation of Solomon's Temple in the days of King Joash, 835–796 B.C. The text of **2 Chronicles 24:6** should be understood to mean that Jehoiada was a "chief [leading] priest" but *not* the high priest (for all the high priests of the period, see chart "**Supplement 2**: The High Priests of Israel"). For the lineage of Jehoiada, see chart "**2 Chronicles 22**: Probable Genealogy for Jehoiada the Priest who Masterminded the Overthrow of Queen Athaliah of Judah."

2. A half-aunt is the half-sister of one's parent (in this case Jehosheba is the half-sister of Ahaziah, the father of Joash).

3. "Zechariah son of Jehoiada the priest" (**2 Chronicles 24:20**) is doubtless "Zechariah son [descendant] of Berekiah," described as the last martyr of the Old Testament (**Matthew 23:35**; see also **Luke 11:51**). In this scenario, Zechariah (the son of Jehoiada) was a Kohathite priest (but not a high priest) and a *descendant* of Berekiah; for the probable lineage of Zechariah, see chart "**1 Chronicles 6**: Levi: High Priests, Priests, Levites, and Musicians in Solomon's Temple."

4. See chart "**2 Kings 8**: Jehoram, King of Judah."

5. See chart "**2 Kings 8**: Ahaziah, King of Judah."

2 KINGS 11: JOASH, KING OF JUDAH

Approximate Dating: 835–796 B.C. ***Relevant Scriptures:*** **2 Kings 11:2–13, 21; 12:1–21; 2 Chronicles 22:11–23:12; 24:1–27; 25:1**

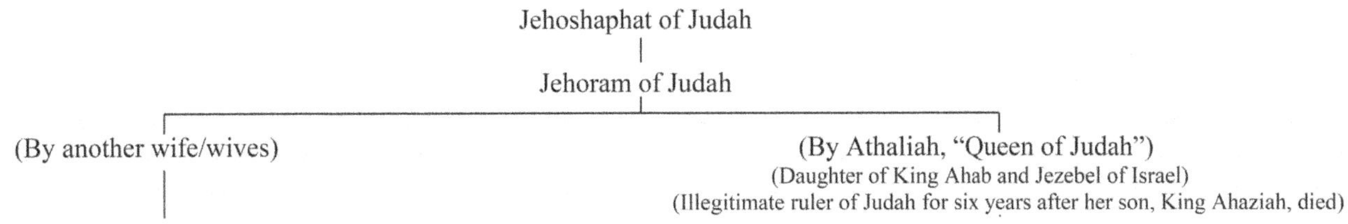

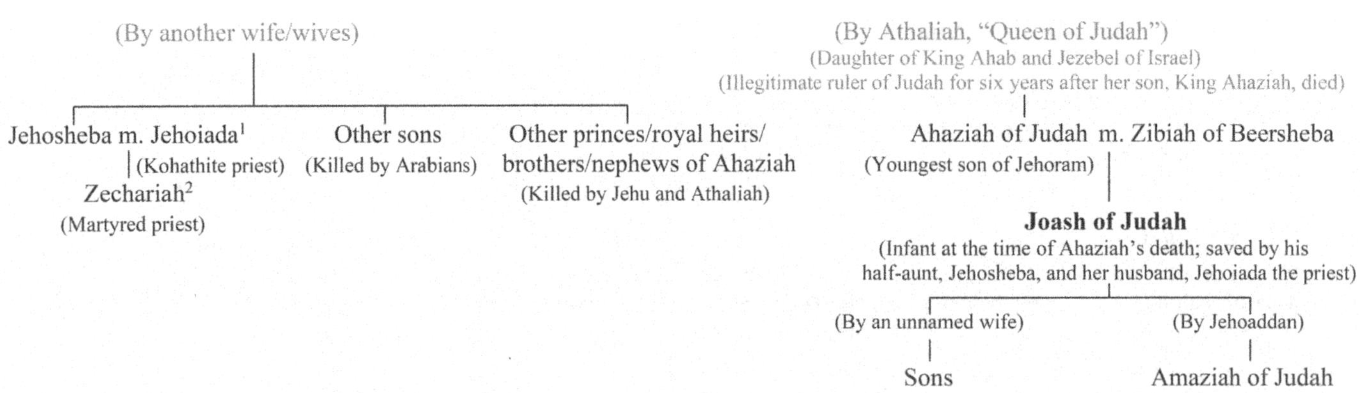

Biblical and Theological Significance

King Joash's Family

When Joash's father, Ahaziah, was killed in 841 B.C. after only one year on the throne (**2 Kings 8:26; 2 Chronicles 22:2**), Ahaziah's mother, Athaliah, attempted to end Judah's monarchy by killing the remaining heirs and ruling over Judah herself[3] (**2 Kings 11:1; 2 Chronicles 22:10**). Without Athaliah's knowledge, Jehosheba quickly rescued Joash (the one-year-old son of Ahaziah)—she "stole him away from among the royal princes, who were about to be murdered. She put him and his nurse in a bedroom [in the temple] to hide him from Athaliah; so he was not killed" (**2 Kings 11:2–3**; see **2 Chronicles 22:11**). Joash remained under the watchful eye of Jehosheba and the protection of her husband, Jehoiada, a prominent Kohathite attending priest in the temple. Eventually, Athaliah was deposed and slain in a coup led by Jehoiada, and the seven-year-old legitimate heir to the Davidic throne, Joash, was then enthroned (**2 Kings 11; 2 Chronicles 23**).

Reign of King Joash

Joash (Jehoash)[4] reigned for forty years (ca. 835–796 B.C.; **2 Kings 12:1; 2 Chronicles 24:1**). He began a temple renovation in his twenty-third year (ca. 812 B.C.), funded by the temple tax and monetary vows and offerings (**2 Kings 12:4–16; 2 Chronicles 24:4–14**). Jehoiada the priest was the constant father figure in his life and Jehoiada chose two wives for Joash (**2 Chronicles 24:3**). **Second Kings 12:2** notes that Joash was a faithful king "all the years Jehoiada the priest instructed him"[5] (cf. **2 Chronicles 24:2**). However, upon Jehoiada's death in 796 B.C., Joash abandoned temple worship, embraced the Canaanite goddess Asherah, and fostered widespread apostasy in Judah (**2 Chronicles 24:17–19**). When Jehoiada's son Zechariah chastised him, Joash ordered Zechariah to be stoned (**2 Chronicles 24:20–22**); as Zechariah lay dying, he pronounced a curse upon Joash (**2 Chronicles 24:22**). Joash was eventually severely wounded in a war with the Arameans, but his end came later in 796 B.C. when court officials[6] assassinated him for murdering the innocent Zechariah (**2 Kings 12:20–21; 2 Chronicles 24:25–26**). Joash was buried in the City of David, but he was dishonored by *not* being buried in the tombs of the kings (**2 Chronicles 24:25**), as Jehoiada had been (**2 Chronicles 24:15-16**). Joash's son Amaziah succeeded him to the throne (**2 Kings 12:21; 2 Chronicles 24:27**).

Notes

1. Jehoiada was a Kohathite priest but not a high priest; see charts "**1 Chronicles 6**: Levi: High Priests, Priests, Levites, and Musicians in Solomon's Temple"; "**2 Chronicles 22**: Probable Genealogy for Jehoiada the Priest who Masterminded the Overthrow of Queen Athaliah of Judah"; and "**Supplement 2**: The High Priests of Israel."

2. At the order of King Joash, the priestly Zechariah was "stoned . . . to death in the courtyard of the LORD's temple" (**2 Chronicles 24:21**). The Kohathite–Korahite priest, Zechariah son of Jehoiada, appears to be the last martyr of the Old Testament and the same person as the priest described by Jesus as "Zechariah son [of Jehoiada, the son/descendant] of Berekiah . . . murdered between the temple and the altar" (**Matthew 23:35**; cf. **Luke 11:51**). The Lukan account places the responsibility on all those who have shed the blood of the righteous "since the beginning of the world"—from the "blood of Abel to the blood of Zechariah"—thus (in English) from A to Z, a figure of speech called *merism*, meaning using the beginning and ending points to suggest entirety (**Luke 11:50–51**). For the probable lineage of Zechariah the martyr, see chart "**1 Chronicles 6**: Levi: High Priests, Priests, Levites, and Musicians in Solomon's Temple."

3. See chart "**2 Kings 11**: Queen Athaliah, the Illegitimate Ruler of Judah."

4. The name is spelled either as Joash or J(eh)oash, meaning "Yahweh exists." The first is called "hypocoristic" because of its apocopation of the letter //h// and the other is "theophoric" because of the retention of the //h//. Both abbreviate the divine name יְהוָה (*Yeh(o)vah*).

5. See chart "**2 Chronicles 22**: Probable Genealogy for Jehoiada the Priest who Masterminded the Overthrow of Queen Athaliah of Judah."

6. To avenge the innocent murder of Zechariah, two officials of King Joash—(1) Jozabad (Zabad) the son of Shimeath, an Ammonite woman, and (2) Jehozabad the son of Shomer (Shimrith), a Moabite woman—killed Joash (cf. **2 Kings 12:20–21**; **2 Chronicles 24:25–26**). The **2 Kings** passage says they "assassinated him at Beth Millo, on the road down to Silla," whereas the **2 Chronicles** passage says that they killed Joash "in his bed." For the genealogies of the murderers, see chart "**2 Chronicles 24**: The Servants who Murdered King Joash of Judah."

2 KINGS 12: AMAZIAH, KING OF JUDAH

Approximate Dating: ca. 796–767 B.C. ***Relevant Scriptures:*** **2 Kings 12:21; 14:1–23; 1 Chronicles 3:10–12;** also **1 Kings 22:42; 2 Kings 8:26; 12:1; 15:1–6; 2 Chronicles 20:31; 24:1, 27; 25:1, 20–28; 26:3–4; Matthew 1:8–9**

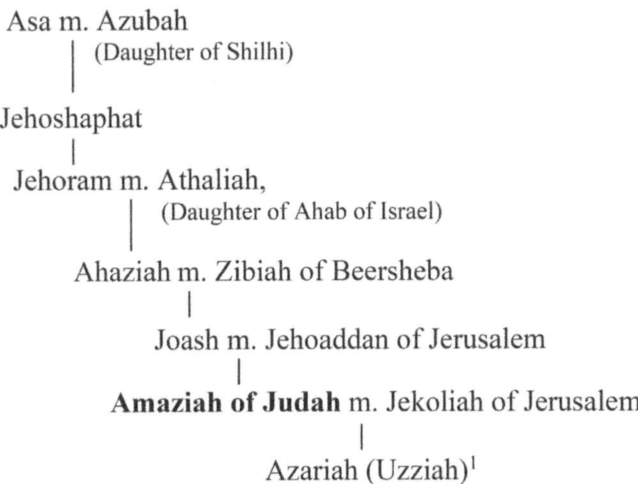

Biblical and Theological Significance

Amaziah became king of Judah at the age of twenty-five in the second year of the sixteen-year reign of Jehoash of Israel and reigned for twenty-nine years in Jerusalem (ca. 796–767 B.C.; **2 Kings 12:21; 14:1–2; 2 Chronicles 24:27; 25:1**). In general, Amaziah was considered a good king; however, he "did what was right in the eyes of the Lord, but not wholeheartedly" because he tolerated high places for pagan sacrifice and burnt offerings in Judah (**2 Chronicles 25:2**; cf. **2 Kings 14:3–4**). He executed Zabad (Jozabad) and Jehozabad, the officials who had murdered his father Joash (**2 Kings 12:21; 14:5; 2 Chronicles 24:26; 25:3**).

During his reign, Amaziah took a military census of the tribes of Judah and Benjamin and found three hundred thousand men aged twenty years and above who could go to war (**2 Chronicles 25:5**). Amaziah went to war against ten thousand men of Seir (Edomites) and killed them (**2 Chronicles 25:11**). Also, Judah's army also captured ten thousand Edomites alive and took them "to the top of a cliff and threw them down so that all were dashed to pieces" (**2 Chronicles 25:12**). Following this war, Amaziah "brought back the gods of the people of Seir [Edom]. He set them up as his own gods, bowed down to them and burned sacrifices to them" (**2 Chronicles 25:14**). Because Judah "sought the gods of Edom" (**2 Chronicles 25:20**), God allowed Judah to be defeated by Jehoash of Israel (**2 Chronicles 25:17–24; 2 Kings 14:8–14**), although Amaziah ended up surviving Israel's king by fifteen years[2] (**2 Kings 17; 2 Chronicles 25:25**; cf. **2 Kings 13:10**).

Because Amaziah had encouraged apostasy in Judah, a conspiracy in Jerusalem developed against him; he fled to Lachish but was killed there. Amaziah was buried in the "City of Judah" (**2 Chronicles 25:28**) (corresponding to the City of David in Jerusalem; cf. **2 Kings 14:20**) and his son Uzziah/Azariah was crowned king (**2 Kings 14:21; 2 Chronicles 26:1**). Uzziah/Azariah, held a co-regency[3] with his father for twenty-five years, from ca. 792–767 B.C., presumably prompted by the events in **2 Kings 14:8–21**.

Notes

1. Azariah in **2 Kings 14:21; 15:1, 6–8, 17, 23, 27;** and **1 Chronicles 3:12** is called Uzziah in **2 Kings 15:13, 30, 32, 34; 2 Chronicles 26:1, 3, 8–9, 11, 14, 16, 18–19, 21–23; 27:2; Isaiah 1:1; 6:1; 7:1; Hosea 1:1; Amos 1:1; Zechariah 14:5; Matthew 1:8–9**.

2. Jehoash reigned in Israel for sixteen years, from ca. 798–782 B.C.

3. For Uzziah/Azariah's co-regency with his father Amaziah, see Edwin R. Thiele's *The Mysterious Numbers of the Hebrew Kings* (New revised ed.) Grand Rapids: Kregel, (repr.) 1994, from the 1983 Zondervan edition, 10-13, 55, 63-64, 113.

2 KINGS 13: JEHOAHAZ, KING OF ISRAEL

Approximate Dating: ca. 814–798 B.C. ***Relevant Scriptures:*** **2 Kings 13:1–10;** also **2 Kings 9:14; 10:35; 14:1, 8, 17**

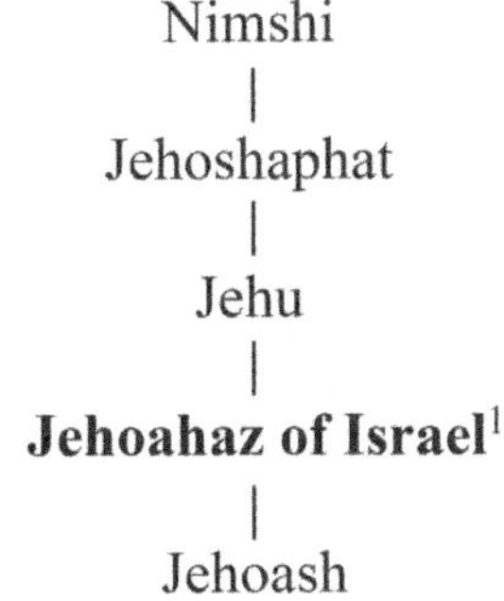

Biblical and Theological Significance

Jehoahaz became king of Israel in the twenty-third year of the forty-year reign of King Joash of Judah (835–796 B.C.) and reigned from Samaria for seventeen years (ca. 814–798 B.C.; **2 Kings 13:1**). He "did evil in the eyes of the Lord by following the sins of Jeroboam [I] son of Nebat, which he had caused Israel to commit, and he did not turn away from them" (**2 Kings 13:2**). During Jehoahaz's reign, the Arameans under Hazael oppressed Israel. When Jehoahaz appealed to the Lord for help, the Lord sent an unnamed deliverer to Israel, but Jehoahaz did not turn from his evil ways (**2 Kings 13:3–6**). Jehoahaz continued in the worship of the Asherah pole that Ahab had set up in Samaria (cf. **1 Kings 16:33**). The Lord allowed the army of Jehoahaz to be reduced to "nothing"—fifty horsemen, ten chariots, and ten thousand foot soldiers—"like the dust at threshing time" (**2 Kings 13:7**). The acts of Jehoahaz were written in the annals of the kings of Israel (**2 Kings 13:8**). When he died, Jehoahaz was buried in Samaria and his son Jehoash reigned in his place (**2 Kings 13:9–10**).

Notes

1. Jehoahaz of Israel, the son of Jehu, who reigned from ca. 814–798 B.C., should not be confused with Jehoahaz of Judah, the son of Josiah, who reigned for three months in 609 B.C. (**2 Kings 23:30–31; 2 Chronicles 36:1–2**).

2 KINGS 13: JEHOASH, KING OF ISRAEL

Approximate Dating: official reign, ca. 798–782 B.C.; his son Jeroboam II was co-regent with Jehoash from 793–782 B.C. ***Relevant Scriptures:*** **2 Kings 13:9–14:23; 2 Chronicles 25:17–25;** also **2 Kings 9:2, 14; 13:1; Hosea 1:1; Amos 1:1**

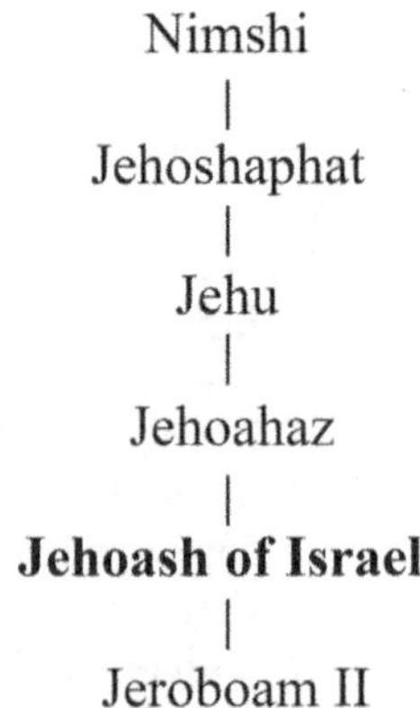

Biblical and Theological Significance

Jehoash became king of Israel in the thirty-seventh year of the forty-year reign of Joash of Judah (835–796 B.C.) and reigned from Samaria for sixteen years (ca. 798–782 B.C.; **2 Kings 13:10**). He inherited a throne that had been severely weakened by the war that his father, Jehoahaz, had fought with Aram, Israel's arch enemy (**2 Kings 13:7**). When Amaziah became king of Judah in Jehoash's second year (**2 Kings 14:1**), the Judahite king was anxious to go to war against Israel. Jehoash (the "cedar of Lebanon" in Israel) confronted Amaziah (the "thistle" in Judah) (**2 Kings 14:9–10**). King Jehoash of Israel advised King Amaziah of Judah not to go to war, but Amaziah disregarded the warning. When the two kings faced each other at Beth Shemesh in Judah, "Judah was routed by Israel, and every man fled to his home" (**2 Kings 14:12**) and King Jehoash captured King Amaziah of Judah (**2 Kings 14:11–13; 2 Chronicles 25:21–23**). Jehoash then invaded Jerusalem and broke down portions of the city walls; removed gold, silver, and precious articles from Solomon's Temple and the king's palace; and took hostages back to Samaria. It is unclear whether Amaziah was permitted to remain in Jerusalem or whether Jehoash took Amaziah back to Samaria (see **2 Kings 14:13–14; 2 Chronicles 25:23–28**). Jehoash died in 782 B.C.; Amaziah of Judah outlived Jehoash by fifteen years; Amaziah died in 767 B.C. (**2 Kings 14:17; 2 Chronicles 25:25**).

The prophets Elisha, Hosea, and Amos were contemporaries of Jehoash (**2 Kings 13:14–20; Hosea 1:1; Amos 1:1**, respectively). Jehoash held a deep respect for Elisha the prophet, calling him "my father" (**2 Kings 13:14**). On his deathbed, Elisha prophesied that the Lord would deliver Israel from Aramean oppression by the efforts of Jehoash (Jehoash symbolically enacted Elisha's prophecy by striking the ground with arrows to symbolize the number of times he would defeat the king of Aram; **2 Kings 13:15–19**). Elisha died during Jehoash's reign (**2 Kings 13:20**).

Over the course of his sixteen-year tenure, Jehoash fulfilled Elisha's prophecy by stopping Aramean expansion into Israel; three times he was able to recapture the land and the cities that the Arameans had taken during the reign of his father Jehoahaz (**2 Kings 13:22–25**).

The acts of Jehoash were recorded in the "annals of the kings of Israel." When he died, he was buried in Samaria among the kings of Israel, and his son Jeroboam II succeeded him (**2 Kings 14:15–16**).

2 KINGS 14: JEROBOAM II, KING OF ISRAEL

Approximate Dating: ca. 793–753 B.C., including a co-regency with his father, Jehoash, from ca. 793–782 B.C.[1] ***Relevant Scriptures:*** **2 Kings 14:16, 23–29; 15:8;** also **2 Kings 13:10, 13; 1 Chronicles 5:17; 2 Chronicles 25:17; Hosea 1:1; Amos 1:1; 7:10–11**

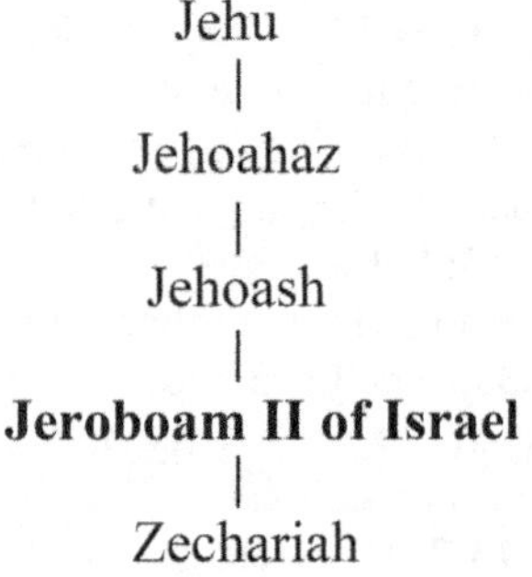

Biblical and Theological Significance

Jeroboam II became king of Israel in the fifteenth year of the twenty-nine-year reign of Amaziah, king of Judah (ca. 796–767 B.C.; **2 Kings 14:23**). Jeroboam was co-regent with his father, Jehoash, from ca. 793–782 B.C. and reigned from the capital city of Samaria for a total of forty-one years, ca. 793–753 B.C. (**2 Kings 14:16, 23**).

Jeroboam II was one of the most successful monarchs of the Northern Kingdom. He was a strong military leader who was used by the Lord to save Israel (**2 Kings 14:26–27**).

He restored the northern and southern boundaries of the kingdom to those in the former days of David and Solomon (**2 Kings 14:25**; cf. **2 Samuel 8:6; 1 Kings 8:65; 2 Chronicles 8:3–4**). The prophets Hosea and Amos were contemporaries of Jeroboam II (**Hosea 1:1; Amos 1:1**). Amos predicted that Jeroboam would "die by the sword" (**Amos 7:11**) and that a major earthquake would occur during his reign (cf. **Amos 1:1**).

The Chronicler states that the genealogical records for the tribes of Israel (presumably some of those found in **1 Chronicles 1–8**) were recorded in the divided monarchy period "during the reigns of Jotham king of Judah [750–735 B.C.] and Jeroboam king of Israel [793–753 B.C.]" (**1 Chronicles 5:17**). Such genealogical records were also recorded in the book of the kings of Israel and Judah (**1 Chronicles 9:1**).

In contrast to the burial information characteristically given for the kings of the Northern Kingdom, none is given for Jeroboam II or the kings of Israel thereafter. Overall, Jeroboam II is remembered as a wicked king who followed the sins of Jeroboam I, the son of Nebat (**2 Kings 14:24**). The acts of Jeroboam II were recorded in the annals of the kings of Israel (**2 Kings 14:28**). Zechariah, the son of Jeroboam II, succeeded his father to the throne of Israel (**2 Kings 14:29; 15:8**).

Notes

1. For a discussion of the chronology of the period, see Eugene H. Merrill, *Kingdom of Priests: A History of Old Testament Israel*, 2nd ed. (Grand Rapids: Baker Academic, 2008), 373–74.

2 KINGS 15: AZARIAH (UZZIAH), KING OF JUDAH

Approximate Dating: official 52-year reign from ca. 792–740 B.C. which included a 25-year co-regency with his father Amaziah from 792–767 B.C. and a sole regency from 767–740 B.C.; his son Jotham acted as the dominant co-regent during the time that Azariah/Uzziah had leprosy, ca. 752–740 B.C. ***Relevant Scriptures:*** **2 Kings 15:1–7; 1 Chronicles 3:10–12; 2 Chronicles 26:1–23; 27:1; Isaiah 1:1; 6:1; 7:1; Hosea 1:1; Amos 1:1; Matthew 1:8–9**

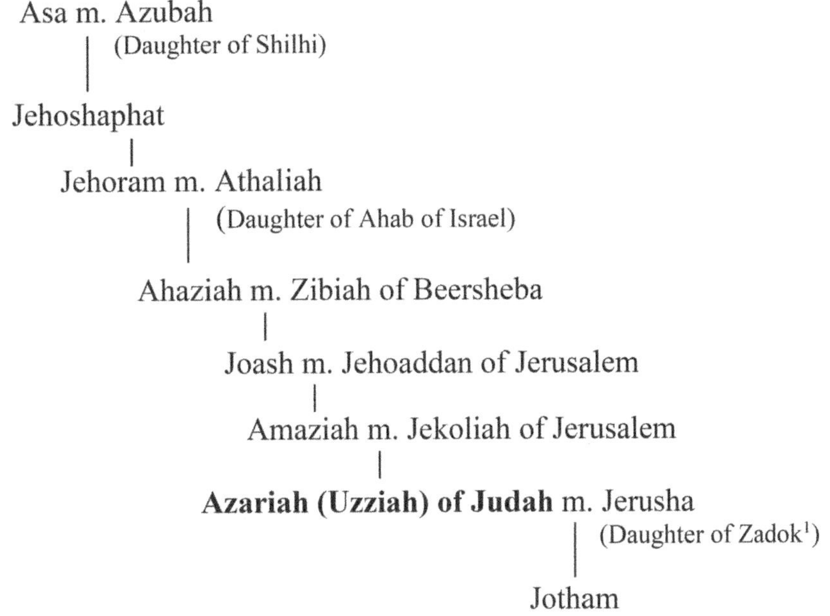

Biblical and Theological Significance

Azariah (also called Uzziah in the NIV)[2] became king when he was sixteen years old[3] (**2 Kings 14:21; 15:2; 2 Chronicles 26:1, 3**), in the twenty-seventh year of the forty-one-year reign of Jeroboam II, king of Israel, ca. 793–753 (**2 Kings 15:1**). He reigned for fifty-two official years, ca. 792–740 B.C. (**2 Kings 15:2; 2 Chronicles 26:3**), initially as coregent with his father, Amaziah, ca. 792–767 B.C. (cf. **2 Kings 14:11–21; 2 Chronicles 25:17–28**). Isaiah, Hosea, and Amos prophesied in the days of Azariah/Uzziah (**Isaiah 1:1; 6:1; Hosea 1:1; Amos 1:1**, respectively); Amos notes that there was an earthquake in the days of King Uzziah (**Amos 1:1**; cf. **Zechariah 14:5**).

Amaziah's defeat of the Edomites allowed his son Uzziah/Azariah to build up Elath as a strong Judean port as it had been in the days of Solomon (**2 Chronicles 8:17; 26:2**). Azariah/Uzziah "did what was right in the eyes of the LORD," except the high places were not removed (**2 Kings 15:3–4**). He defeated the Philistines, Arabians, and the Meunites[4]; built towers at the Corner and Valley Gates and fortified the wall around Jerusalem, built towers in the desert, dug many cisterns for his livestock, and hired farmers and vinedressers to keep the land (**2 Chronicles 26:6–10**), "for he loved the soil" (**2 Chronicles 26:10**). He also equipped an army of 307,500 men of valor (**2 Chronicles 26:13**). "His fame spread far and wide" (**2 Chronicles 26:15**), but regrettably, his international and domestic successes became a source of pride. In a moment of great hubris, Azariah/Uzziah entered the temple to burn incense on the altar of incense, a rite reserved only for the Aaronic priesthood (**2 Chronicles 26:16–18**; cf. **Exodus 30:7; Leviticus 2:2; 4:7; 6:15; 1 Samuel 2:28; 1 Chronicles 6:49**). For this presumptuous act, the Lord struck Azariah/Uzziah with leprosy. He "had leprosy until the day he died" and "lived in a separate house . . . and [was] banned from the temple" (**2 Chronicles 26:19–21**). During his days of separation, his son Jotham "had charge of the palace and governed the people of the land" on his behalf (**2 Kings 15:5; 2 Chronicles 26:21**); in this sense, Jotham was the dominant regent[5] from 752–740 B.C., until Azariah/Uzziah's death in 740 B.C. Because Azariah/Uzziah was a leper, he was buried away from the royal family tomb in a cemetery that belonged to the kings (**2 Chronicles 26:23**). His son Jotham then became the sole monarch (**2 Kings 15:7; 2 Chronicles 26:23**).

Notes

1. Jerusha's father was Zadok (**2 Kings 15:33; 2 Chronicles 27:1**); for chronological reasons, it is unlikely that her father (Zadok) corresponds directly to either of the two Zadok figures who were high priests (i.e., Zadok #11, who served under David and Solomon, 1011–931 B.C.; or Zadok #20 who served under Hezekiah, 715–686 B.C.); see chart "**Supplement 2**: The High Priests of Israel."

2. Azariah in **2 Kings 14:21; 15:1, 7–8, 17, 23, 27; 1 Chronicles 3:12** is called Uzziah in **2 Kings 15:13, 30, 32, 34; 2 Chronicles 26:1, 3, 8–9, 11, 14, 16, 18–19, 21, 23; 27:2; Isaiah 1:1; 6:1; 7:1; Hosea 1:1; Amos 1:1; Zechariah 14:5; Matthew 1:8–9**.

3. For a discussion of the chronological considerations that are needed to determine if Zechariah the son of Jehoiada (**2 Chronicles 24:20, 22**) was the same person as the Zechariah figure mentioned in **2 Chronicles 26:5**, see note 6 in chart "**2 Chronicles 22**: Probable Genealogy for Jehoiada the Priest who Masterminded the Overthrow of Queen Athaliah of Judah."

4. For a discussion of the Meunim (the Meunites), see the article by Ernst Axel Knauf on "Meunim (Meunites)" in the *Anchor Yale Bible Dictionary*, vol. 4, 802.

5. For the dominant co-regency of Jotham with his father Azariah/Uzziah, see Edwin R. Thiele's *The Mysterious Numbers of the Hebrew Kings* (New revised ed.) Grand Rapids: Kregel, (repr.) 1994, from the 1983 Zondervan edition, 10-13, 55, 64, 106–107, 120, 132, 136.

2 KINGS 15: JOTHAM, KING OF JUDAH

Approximate Dating: dominant co-regent with his father Azariah/Uzziah from ca. 752–740 B.C.; official reign ca. 750–735 B.C. ***Relevant Scriptures:*** **2 Kings 15:32–38; 1 Chronicles 3:10–13; 2 Chronicles 27:1–9; Isaiah 1:1; Hosea 1:1; Micah 1:1; Matthew 1:9**

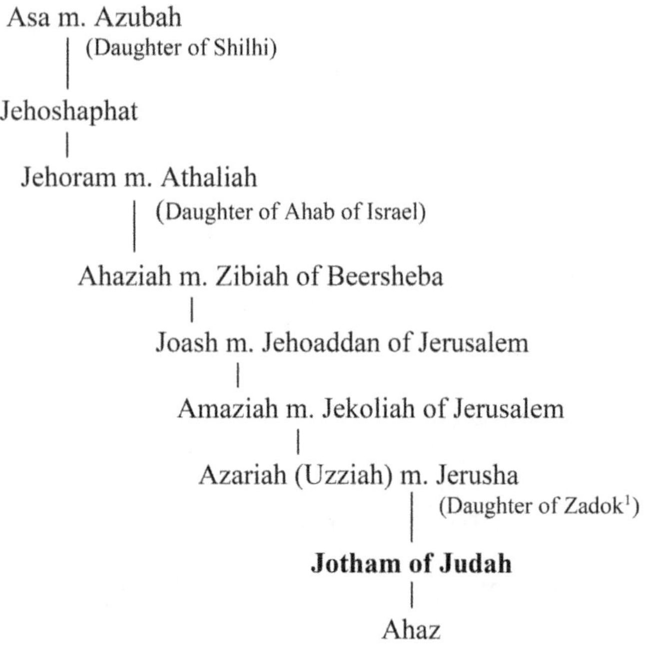

Biblical and Theological Significance

Jotham became king at the age of twenty-five in the second year of the twenty-year reign of Pekah of Israel (**2 Kings 15:32–33; 2 Chronicles 27:1, 8**). He reigned in Jerusalem—first, as the (dominant) co-regent with his father Azariah/Uzziah, who had leprosy, from ca. 752–740 B.C. (cf. **2 Kings 15:5; 2 Chronicles 26:21–23**)—and continued as the dominant regent for a total of sixteen official years, from ca. 750–735 B.C.[2]

Jotham was unable to remove the high places of worship. However, he was successful in building the Upper Gate of Benjamin on the north side of Solomon's Temple (cf. **2 Kings 15:35; 2 Chronicles 27:3; Jeremiah 20:2; 37:13; 38:7**), reinforcing the wall at the hill of Ophel in Jerusalem, building towns in the hill country, and building forts and towers in the wooded areas. These construction projects greatly fortified Judah against foreign invasion (**2 Chronicles 27:3–4**).

Jotham was successful in a war against the Ammonites, who paid him tribute for three successive years (**2 Chronicles 27:5**). He was considered a good king who "grew powerful because he walked steadfastly before the Lord his God" (**2 Chronicles 27:6**). The events of his reign were recorded in "the book of the annals of the kings of Judah" (**2 Kings 15:36**) and "the book of the kings of Israel and Judah" (**2 Chronicles 27:7**). The prophets Isaiah, Hosea, and Micah were his contemporaries (**Isaiah 1:1; Hosea 1:1; Micah 1:1**). The Chronicler notes that genealogical records[3] were recorded "during the reigns of Jotham king of Judah [ca. 750–735 B.C.] and Jeroboam [II] king of Israel [ca. 793–753 B.C.]"—dates roughly one hundred and fifty to two hundred years *before* the Babylonian invasion of 586 B.C. (**1 Chronicles 5:17**; cf. **1 Chronicles 9:1**). When Jotham died, he was buried in the City of David and his son Ahaz[4] succeeded him (**2 Kings 15:38; 2 Chronicles 27:9**).

Notes

1. For Jerusha, daughter of Zadok, see note 1 in chart "**2 Kings 15**: Azariah (Uzziah), King of Judah."

2. For a discussion of the dating of Jotham's reign, see Eugene H. Merrill, *Kingdom of Priests: A History of Old Testament Israel* (Grand Rapids: Baker, 1996), 402–404.

3. It is unknown whether the genealogies were recorded for specific tribes or for all the tribes.

4. Ahaz was the (dominant) co-regent with his father Jotham from 735–731 B.C.; see chart "**2 Kings 15**: Ahaz, King of Judah." See also Edwin R. Thiele's *The Mysterious Numbers of the Hebrew Kings*, New revised ed., (Grand Rapids: Kregel , repr., 1994, from the 1983 Zondervan edition), 10-13, 64, 132–133, 136.

2 KINGS 15: ZECHARIAH, KING OF ISRAEL

Approximate Dating: 6 months, in 753 B.C. ***Relevant Scriptures:*** **2 Kings 15:8–12**; also **2 Kings 10:35; 13:1, 9-10, 13, 25; 14:1, 8, 16–17, 23, 27; 2 Chronicles 25:17, 25; Hosea 1:1; Amos 1:1**

Biblical and Theological Significance

Zechariah became king of Israel in the thirty-eighth year of the fifty-two-year reign of Azariah (Uzziah) of Judah (ca. 792–740 B.C.). Zechariah ruled from Samaria for only six months in 753 B.C. (**2 Kings 15:8**). Like all former kings of the Northern Kingdom, Zechariah followed the sinful ways of Jeroboam I, the son of Nebat (**2 Kings 15:9**). Shallum, the son of Jabesh, assassinated Zechariah and then succeeded him to the throne (**2 Kings 15:10**). Zechariah's death marked the end of the Jehu dynasty, fulfilling the prophecies of **2 Kings 10:30** (see also **2 Kings 15:12**): "The LORD said to Jehu, 'Because you have done well in accomplishing what is right in my eyes and have done to the house of Ahab all I had in mind to do, your descendants will sit on the throne of Israel to the fourth generation [Jehoahaz–Joash–Jeroboam II–Zechariah].' " Zechariah's death precipitated a series of revolts and counter-revolts in Israel that resulted in the rapid succession of four kings in a thirteen-year period (i.e., Zechariah–Shallum–Menahem–Pekahiah). These events indicated the imminent demise of the Northern Kingdom. The prophet Hosea thus described Israel's apostasy at this time: "They set up kings without my consent; they choose princes without my approval" (**Hosea 8:4**). The events of Zechariah's reign were written in the book of the annals of the kings of Israel (**2 Kings 15:11**).

2 KINGS 15: SHALLUM, KING OF ISRAEL

Approximate Dating: one month, ca. 752 B.C. ***Relevant Scriptures:*** **2 Kings 15:10, 13–15**

Jabesh[1]
(From Jabesh Gilead)
|
Shallum of Israel

Biblical and Theological Significance

Shallum rose to power in Israel by murdering King Zechariah (the last king of the Jehu dynasty), who had ruled for six months, in 753 B.C. (**2 Kings 15:10**). Shallum became king in the thirty-ninth year of the fifty-two-year reign of Azariah (Uzziah) of Judah (ca. 792–740 B.C.) and reigned from Samaria for only one month (ca. 752 B.C.; **2 Kings 15:13**). Shortly thereafter, Menahem, the son of Gadi, assassinated Shallum and succeeded him as king of Israel (**2 Kings 15:14**). The acts of Shallum were recorded in the book of the annals of the kings of Israel (**2 Kings 15:15**).

Notes

1. As the *Anchor Yale Bible Dictionary* explains, Jabesh (the person), Heb. *yaabēesh* יָבֵשׁ, was the father of Shallum, king of Israel (**2 Kings 15:10, 13–14**). "Jabesh, however, may be a place name rather than a personal name. If such is the case, the phrase 'son of Jabesh' would refer to Shallum's place of origin, 'a person from Jabesh,' and not patronymic. This would suggest that opposition to Jehu's dynasty came from the region of Jabesh-Gilead. In Assyrian records Shallum is referred to as a 'son of a nobody' " (Pauline A. Viviano, "Jabesh," *Anchor Yale Bible Dictionary*).

2 KINGS 15: MENAHEM, KING OF ISRAEL

Approximate Dating: ca. 752–742 B.C. ***Relevant Scriptures:*** **2 Kings 15:14–23**

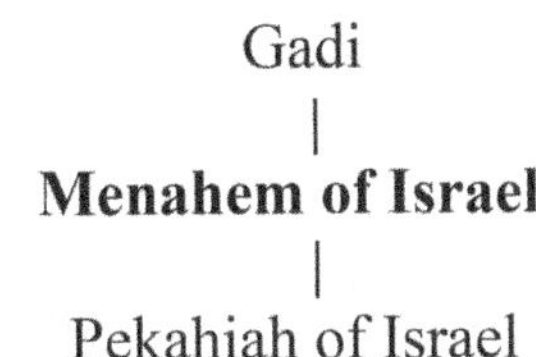

Biblical and Theological Significance

Menahem appears to be from Tirzah, the first capital of the Northern Kingdom. He led a conspiracy against King Shallum of Israel (**2 Kings 15:14**). Initially, Menahem attacked the territory of "Tiphsah" (probably a border region between the tribes of Manasseh and Ephraim) "because they refused to open their gates. He sacked Tiphsah and ripped open all the pregnant women"[1] (**2 Kings 15:16**).

Menahem became king of Israel in the thirty-ninth year of the fifty-two-year reign of King Uzziah/Azariah (792–740 B.C.) and reigned for ten years from ca. 752–742 B.C. (**2 Kings 15:17**). Menahem followed the evil ways of King Jeroboam I, the son of Nebat, who had made Israel sin (**2 Kings 15:18**). During Menahem's reign, King Pul (Tiglath Pileser III) of Assyria invaded the Northern Kingdom. To maintain some level of independence from the Assyrians, Menahem willingly accepted vassal status and paid the Assyrians one thousand talents (approximately three million shekels) of silver in tribute money by exacting fifty shekels of silver from every wealthy citizen of Israel (**2 Kings 15:19–20**). This attitude of willing subservience of Israel's king to foreign nations was decried by Hosea the prophet: "When Ephraim [the northern kingdom of Israel] saw his sickness [their weakened status before other nations], and Judah [the Southern Kingdom] his sores, then Ephraim turned to Assyria, and sent to the great king for help. But he is not able to cure you, not able to heal your sores. For I [God] will be like a lion to Ephraim, like a great lion to Judah. I will tear them to pieces and go away; I will carry them off [into exile in Assyria], with no one to rescue them" (**Hosea 5:13–14**). The deferential vassal status of Israel to Assyria during Menahem's reign foreshadowed the complete fall of the Northern Kingdom to the Assyrians in 722 B.C. The acts of Menahem were recorded in the book of the annals of the kings of Israel (**2 Kings 15:21**). When Menahem died, his son Pekahiah assumed the throne (**2 Kings 15:22–23**).

Notes

1. This was a gross atrocity of war practiced by the Arameans (cf. **2 Kings 8:12**).

2 KINGS 15: PEKAHIAH, KING OF ISRAEL

Approximate Dating: ca. 742–740 B.C. ***Relevant Scriptures:*** **2 Kings 15:22–26**

Biblical and Theological Significance

Pekahiah, the son of Menahem, became king of Israel in the fiftieth year of the fifty-two-year reign (792–740 B.C.) of Azariah/Uzziah king of Judah (**2 Kings 15:23**). Pekahiah reigned for two years from Samaria (742–740 B.C.). Pekahiah "did not turn away from the sins of Jeroboam [I] son of Nebat, which he had caused Israel to commit" (**2 Kings 15:24**). An anti-Assyrian faction in the Northern Kingdom formed a conspiracy to overthrow Pekahiah. He was assassinated in Samaria by Pekah, the son of Remaliah, who then succeeded him as Israel's next king (**2 Kings 15:25**).[1] The acts of Pekahiah were recorded in the annals of the kings of Israel (**2 Kings 15:26**).

Notes

1. Pekah reigned for twenty official years (752–732 B.C.), initially as co-regent for twelve years during the full terms of Menahem (752–742 B.C.) and Pekahiah (742–740 B.C.) and then, beginning in 740 B.C., as the sole ruler of Israel for the next eight years (740–732 B.C.). See chart "**2 Kings 15**: Pekah, King of Israel."

2 KINGS 15: PEKAH, KING OF ISRAEL

Approximate Dating: ca. 752–732 B.C. ***Relevant Scriptures:*** **2 Kings 15:25–32; 16:5–6; 2 Chronicles 28:5–15**

Remaliah
|
Pekah of Israel

Biblical and Theological Significance

Pekah, a military officer under King Pekahiah, led a revolt that ended in Pekahiah's assassination (**2 Kings 15:25**). Pekah's reign lasted for twenty official years, ca. 752–732 B.C. (**2 Kings 15:27**).[1] Like other Israelite monarchs before him, he followed the sinful ways of Jeroboam I, the son of Nebat (**2 Kings 15:28**).

Pekah, in league with Rezin of Aram, besieged Jerusalem during the reign of Ahaz of Judah (731–715 B.C.; **2 Kings 16:5–6**). Pekah and Rezin succeeded in killing one hundred and twenty thousand soldiers "in one day . . . because Judah had forsaken the LORD, the God of their ancestors" (**2 Chronicles 28:6**), but Israel was not successful in taking Jerusalem (**2 Kings 16:5**). However, thousands of captives from Judah and a great deal of plunder were seized and carried back to Samaria, with the intention of enslaving fellow Israelites (**2 Chronicles 28:6–8**). However, upon the wise counsel of the prophet Oded, these prisoners of war were returned to Judah (**2 Chronicles 28:9–15**).

At this time, Tiglath-Pileser III (Pul) of Assyria invaded Israel and took several northern cities (Ijon, Abel Beth Maakah, Janoah, Kedesh, and Hazor), as well as the regions of Gilead, Galilee, and all the land of Naphtali (**2 Kings 15:29**). Pul carried the people from these conquered territories to

Assyria (cf. **1 Chronicles 5:25–26**). Hoshea, the son of Elah, assassinated Pekah in 732 B.C. and became Israel's next king (**2 Kings 15:30**). The acts of Pekah were recorded in the annals of the kings of Israel (**2 Kings 15:31**).

Notes

1. As Merrill explains, the dating of Pekah's reign is notoriously complex, dependent largely upon the dates for the reigns of Menahem (752–742 B.C.) and Pekahiah (742–740 B.C.), which fortunately are firm. Pekah, a Gileadite, intervened in the chaotic affairs that marked the declining years of Israel. He led a coup that would place him in the seat of monarchic power. In any case, as an officer under Pekahiah, Pekah had access to him and took advantage of his position to assassinate Pekahiah in 740 B.C. If Pekah's reign began then and he reigned for twenty years, Pekah would have continued to reign two years after the 722 B.C. exile, a manifest impossibility. The text is silent regarding a co-reign of Pekah with Menahem for ten years (752–742 B.C.). The best solution is to propose that Pekah already saw himself (and was viewed by others) as somewhat of a king in Gilead, where he did indeed have a position of authority as a שָׁלִישׁ (*shalish*), the "third man" or a man of almost regal status; M. G. Easton, "Captain," *Easton's Bible Dictionary* and Eugene H. Merrill, *Kingdom of Priests: A History of Old Testament Israel* (Grand Rapids: Baker, 1996), 397 and n. 19–21. The historical record thus counts his twenty years from 752–732 B.C. Pekah would therefore have co-reigned for the full terms of both Pekahiah and Menahem (twelve years, 752–740 B.C.), and then, beginning in 740 B.C. (i.e., the fifty-second year of Azariah of Judah; **2 Kings 15:27**), he became the sole ruler of Israel for eight years (i.e., 740–732 B.C.), until Hoshea's accession in 732 B.C. For a further discussion of Pekah's reign, see Eugene H. Merrill, *Kingdom of Priests: A History of Old Testament Israel* (Grand Rapids: Baker, 1996), 397–98.

2 KINGS 15: HOSHEA, KING OF ISRAEL

Approximate Dating: ca. 732–722 B.C. ***Relevant Scriptures:*** **2 Kings 15:30; 17:1–6**

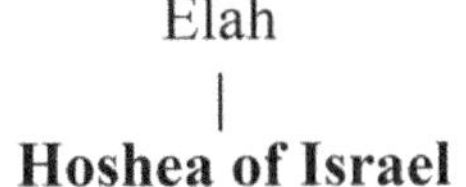

Biblical and Theological Significance

Hoshea came to power in Israel by leading a rebellion and assassinating King Pekah. Hoshea took the throne of Israel in the twelfth year of the sixteen-year reign of Ahaz, king of Judah (**2 Kings 15:30; 17:1**).[1] Scripture harmonizes the seventh year of Hoshea's reign to the fourth year of King Hezekiah of Judah (**2 Kings 18:9–12**). Hoshea reigned for nine years from Samaria, from 732–722 B.C., and "did evil in the eyes of the Lord, but not like the kings of Israel who preceded him" (**2 Kings 17:2**). Hoshea became a vassal of King Shalmaneser V of Assyria (727–722 B.C.) and paid tribute money to the Assyrians "year by year" (**2 Kings 17:4**). Late in his reign, Hoshea shifted his allegiance from the Assyrians to So,[2] the pharaoh of Egypt, hoping that the Egyptians would protect him against the Assyrians. When Shalmaneser V learned of Hoshea's pretension, he put Hoshea into prison (ca. 724/723 B.C.). A three-year siege of Samaria ensued by the Assyrians; during this time, Shalmaneser V of Assyria died and his successor, Sargon II (722/721–705 B.C.), was successful in taking Samaria. The remaining inhabitants of the northern kingdom of Israel were taken into Assyrian captivity (**2 Kings 17:4–6**). The fall of Samaria in 722 B.C. marked the end of the Northern Kingdom.

Hoshea is noted as the captive king of the Assyrian exile: "In the ninth year of Hoshea, the king of Assyria captured Samaria and deported the Israelites to Assyria. He settled them in Halah, in Gozan on the Habor River and in the towns of the Medes" (**2 Kings 17:6**; see also **2 Kings 18:11**). Presumably, Hoshea died in exile.

Notes

1. The official sixteen-year reign of Ahaz was from 731–715 B.C.; however, Ahaz had been a co-regent with his father, Jotham, from 735–731 B.C., and during that time, Ahaz was the dominant regent, not his father.
2. His full Egyptian name was Osorkon IV (ca. 730–715 B.C.).

2 KINGS 15: AHAZ, KING OF JUDAH

Approximate Dating: co-regent and dominant regent with his father Jotham, 735–731 B.C. and official reign, ca. 731–715 B.C.[1] ***Relevant Scriptures:*** **2 Kings 15:38; 16:1–20; 18:1–2; 23:12; 1 Chronicles 3:12–13; 2 Chronicles 27:9; 28:1–27; 29:1; Isaiah 7:1; Matthew 1:9–10**

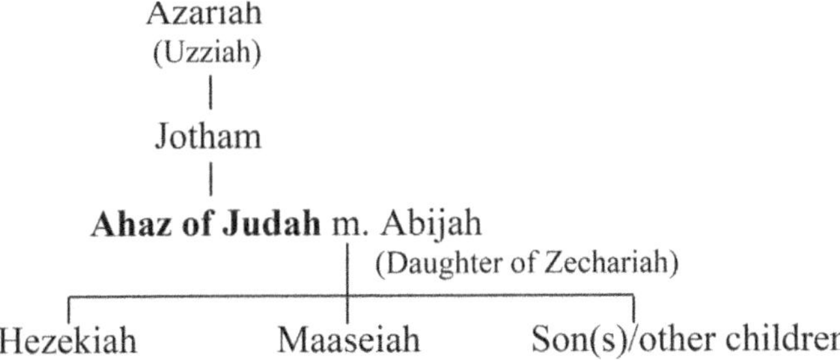

Biblical and Theological Significance

Reign of Ahaz

At age twenty, Ahaz became a co-regent (and the dominant regent) with his father, Jotham[2]; the co-regency lasted from 735–731 B.C. (cf. **2 Kings 15:32–37; 16:5–9**). Ahaz's first year as co-regent (735 B.C.) corresponded to the seventeenth year of the twenty-year official reign of Pekah king of Israel (752–732 B.C.). Ahaz's official sixteen-year reign lasted from 731–715 B.C. (**2 Kings 16:2; 2 Chronicles**

28:1). Ahaz avidly followed the paganism of foreign nations (**2 Kings 16:3–4;** cf. **2 Kings 3:26–27; 21:6**), even to the point of sacrificing his own children: "he [Ahaz] burned sacrifices in the Valley of Ben Hinnom and sacrificed his children [more than one!] in the fire" (**2 Chronicles 28:3**; cf. **Deuteronomy 12:31; 2 Kings 16:3; Jeremiah 7:31**).

As a result of his blatant apostasy, several significant events occurred during Ahaz's reign:

- He was defeated by a joint coalition of Aram (Syria) and Israel: "The LORD his God delivered him [Ahaz] into the hands of the king of Aram [Rezin]" (**2 Chronicles 28:5**, cf. **2 Kings 15:37**). As a result, many Judahites were taken prisoner to Damascus, the capital of Aram.
- In a single day, Pekah of Israel killed one hundred and twenty thousand soldiers in Judah "because Judah had forsaken the Lord, the God of their ancestors" (**2 Chronicles 28:6**). During this encounter, several important people were killed: (1) Maaseiah (Ahaz's son) was killed by Zikri, an Ephraimite warrior; (2) Azrikam, the officer in charge of the Judean palace; and (3) Elkanah, who was second in command to King Ahaz (**2 Chronicles 28:7**). The Israelites also took two hundred thousand Judahite wives, sons, and daughters as prisoners to Israel, although they were eventually returned (**2 Chronicles 28:8–15**). Twice, Ahaz appealed to Tiglath-Pileser III (Pul) of Assyria for help, using temple treasures as tribute money to bribe him. The first time, the Assyrians helped Ahaz, but the second time, they did not (**2 Kings 16:7–9; 2 Chronicles 28:16, 20–21**).
- Arameans drove Ahaz out of the seaport town of Elath, thereby allowing the Edomites to control the southern trade routes (**2 Kings 16:6**).
- Philistines took possession of several Judahite cities (**2 Chronicles 28:18**).
- Ahaz became increasingly "unfaithful to the LORD" (**2 Chronicles 28:22**), setting up pagan shrines in Jerusalem and Judah and converting the worship of the Lord at Solomon's Temple to the worship of the gods of Damascus (**2 Kings 16:10–18; 2 Chronicles 28:24–25; 29:3–11; Jeremiah 7:30**), a situation that was not reversed until the days of Hezekiah, his son and successor.[3]

Ahaz was a contemporary of the prophets Isaiah, Hosea, and Micah (**Isaiah 1:1; Hosea 1:1; Micah 1:1**). The acts of Ahaz were recorded in "the book of the kings of Judah and Israel" (**2 Chronicles 28:26**). When he died, he was buried in the City of David, but not in the tombs of the kings, and his son Hezekiah succeeded him (**2 Chronicles 28:27**; cf. **2 Kings 16:20**).

Notes

1. For a discussion of the chronology and co-regency of Ahaz and Jotham, see Eugene H. Merrill, *Kingdom of Priests: A History of Old Testament Israel*, 2nd ed. (Grand Rapids: Baker Academic, 2008), 402–404.

2. For the co-regency of Ahaz and his father, also see Edwin R. Thiele's *The Mysterious Numbers of the Hebrew Kings* (New rev. ed.), (Grand Rapids: Kregel, 1983 and Grand Rapids: Zondervan Publishing, 1994) 10–13, 64, 132–33, 136.

3. Hezekiah was co-regent with his father, Ahaz, from 729–715 B.C. See chart "**2 Kings 16**: Hezekiah, King of Judah."

2 KINGS 16: HEZEKIAH, KING OF JUDAH

Approximate Dating: official 29-year reign from 715–686 B.C.; co-regent with his father Ahaz from 729–715 B.C.; co-regent with his son Manasseh from 697–686 B.C. ***Relevant Scriptures:*** **2 Kings 16:20; 18:1–20:21; 21:1; 1 Chronicles 3:12–13; 2 Chronicles 28:27; 29:1–32:33; Isaiah 1:1; 62:4; Hosea 1:1; Matthew 1:9–10**

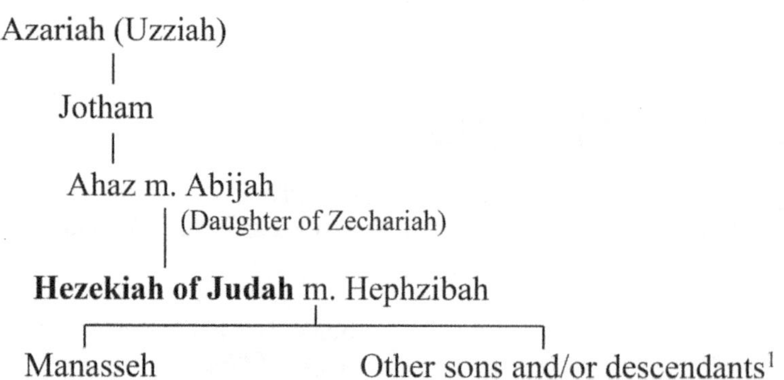

Biblical and Theological Significance

Hezekiah co-reigned with his father Ahaz for fourteen years from 729–715 B.C.[2] When Ahaz died, Hezekiah assumed the throne and reigned for twenty-nine official years, from 715–686 B.C. (**2 Kings 18:2**). To reunite Israel and Judah at Jerusalem, Hezekiah instigated reforms including (1) removal of pagan places in the land; (2) renovation and purification of Solomon's Temple; (3) re-consecration of the priesthood;[3] (4) restoration of daily worship and the collection of tithes; (5) renewed observance of Passover; and (6) repair of broken sections of the city wall, adding towers on it, building an additional defensive wall,[4] and reinforcing the terraces (millo) of the City of David (**2 Kings 18:4; 2 Chronicles 32:5**; see **2 Chronicles 29–30**).

The Assyrians took Samaria "in Hezekiah's sixth year, which was the ninth year of Hoshea king of Israel [722 B.C.]" and deported Israel to Assyria (**2 Kings 18:9–11**). In the fourteenth year of Hezekiah's reign, King Sennacherib of Assyria (705–681 B.C.) captured the fortified cities of Judah (**2 Kings 18:13**) and required tribute from Hezekiah. Hezekiah offered them an enormous tribute that temporarily stayed Sennacherib's advance (**2 Kings 18:14–16**). Later, when Sennacherib invaded again, Hezekiah prayed and the Lord sent an angel that killed 185,500 Assyrians in their own camp and decimated the Assyrian army, forcing Sennacherib to return to Nineveh, where he was then killed by two of his sons (**2 Kings 19:7, 14–37**; cf. **2 Chronicles 32:20–23**; **Isaiah 37:14–38**).

In 701 B.C., when Hezekiah became ill to the point of death (**2 Kings 20:1; 2 Chronicles 32:24; Isaiah 38:1**), he prayed for healing. The Lord promised him renewed health by the sign of a lengthened day that signified the addition of fifteen years[5] to his life (**2 Kings 20:6, 9, 11; Isaiah 38:5, 7–8**). When Marduk-Baladan[6] of Babylon heard of Hezekiah's recovery, he sent letters and gifts to Hezekiah via envoys (**2 Kings 20:12; Isaiah 39:1**). To impress him, Hezekiah flaunted the nation's wealth. The prophet Isaiah rebuked Hezekiah's ostentatious behavior and prophesied that his actions would bring the eventual invasion and deportation of Israel to Babylon (**2 Kings 20:17–18; Isaiah 39:6–7**); this prophesy came to pass in three successive deportations of Judah in 605, 597, and 586 B.C.

One of the major accomplishments of Hezekiah was the completion of a rock-hewn tunnel[7] connecting the Gihon Spring, located outside the city, to the Pool of Siloam inside (**2 Chronicles 32:30**), thereby securing Jerusalem's water supply (**2 Kings 20:20**). The events of Hezekiah's reign were recorded in "the annals of the kings of Judah and Israel" and in the "vision of the prophet Isaiah" (**2 Kings 20:20; 2 Chronicles 32:32**). Hezekiah was commended because he "trusted in the Lord, the God of Israel. There was no one like him among all the kings of Judah, either before him or after him" (**2 Kings 18:5**; cf. **2 Kings 18:5–7; 2 Chronicles 31:20–21**). When he died, Hezekiah was buried in the tombs of the kings and was succeeded by his son Manasseh (**2 Kings 20:21; 2 Chronicles 32:33**).

Notes

1. According to Isaiah's prophecy, some of Hezekiah's descendants became eunuchs in the palace of the king of Babylon (**Isaiah 39:7**; see also **2 Kings 20:18**). This prophecy appears to be fulfilled in the days of King Jehoiachin/Jeconiah (598–597 B.C.); see charts "**1 Chronicles 3**: Zerubbabel and Shealtiel and the Double Line of the Messiah through King David's Sons, Nathan and Solomon" and "**Daniel 1**: Daniel and His Comrades."
2. For a discussion of the co-regencies of Azariah (Uzziah), Jotham, Ahaz, and Hezekiah, see Eugene H. Merrill, *Kingdom of Priests: A History of Old Testament Israel* (Grand Rapids: Baker, 1996), 403–404 and note 41.
3. For the genealogy of the priests and Levites who did the work of repairing the temple, see chart "**2 Chronicles 29**: The Kohathite Priests, Levites, and Singers Who Cleansed the Temple During the Reign of King Hezekiah of Judah."
4. The construction of the seven-meter-thick defensive wall—called the Broad Wall of the Old City of Jerusalem—is dated to the reign of Hezekiah (cf. the Broad Wall in **Nehemiah 3:8; 12:38**).
5. The fifteen years that were added to Hezekiah's life correspond to the years 701–686 B.C.
6. Marduk-Baladan, the son of Baladan, was king of Babylon from 722–710 and 703–702 B.C.; he is mentioned in **2 Kings 20:12** and **Isaiah 39:1**.
7. The construction of a water channel, called Hezekiah's Tunnel, required cutting through 1750 ft. of bedrock, allowing water from the Gihon Springs outside the city wall to be diverted directly to the Pool of Siloam inside the city.

2 KINGS 18: ELIAKIM, THE PALACE ADMINISTRATOR WHO REPLACED SHEBNA THE SCRIBAL SECRETARY DURING THE REIGN OF KING HEZEKIAH OF JUDAH

Approximate Dating: 715–686 B.C. ***Relevant Scriptures:*** **2 Kings 18:18, 26, 37; 19:2; Isaiah 22:20; 36:3, 11, 22; 37:2**

(Likely of Kohathite priestly heritage)[1]

|

Hilkiah[2]

(Palace administrator)

|

Eliakim[3]

(Replaced Shebna the unfaithful steward)

Biblical and Theological Significance

Hilkiah was עַל הַבַּיִת, *al habbayit*, "over the house," or the *major domo* in the administration of King Hezekiah of Judah.[4] Nothing in the royal palace went on without his knowledge and nothing could take place without his derivative permission. Such a position was obviously granted by the king to only the most competent and trustworthy individuals. Should the individual prove worthy through a lifetime of service, it is likely that his son, if equally qualified, would succeed him as, in this case, Eliakim (Hilkiah's son) replaced Shebna and therefore succeeded his father Hilkiah as the palace administrator.

Another office of crucial importance to the regent was the position held by Shebna, of unknown pedigree (**2 Kings 18:18, 26, 37; 19:2; Isaiah 36:3, 22; 37:2**). Shebna was technically a scribe (סֹפֵר, *sopher*), which may have included the role of secretary of state as well as general administrator (סֹכֵן, *soken*) of palace affairs. The scribal office must have been occupied by scholars who were not only literate in their own tongue, but also proficient in languages of neighboring and even distant nations. Such scholars would have been educated in a scribal school such as that implied by the "clans of scribes" who lived at Jabez (**1 Chronicles 2:55**). This is why Shebna was part of the delegation with Eliakim and Joah (the son of Asaph) the stenographer (מַזְכִּיר, *mazkir*),[5] who had been summoned by an ambassador of King Sennacherib of Assyria (705–681 B.C.) to meet and discuss terms of surrender (**2 Kings 18:17–37**). Shebna no doubt was needed to translate the Assyrian and/or Aramaic language of Sennacherib into Hebrew. Usually designated as "scribal-secretary" under Hezekiah, Shebna is elevated by the prophet Isaiah to be עַל הַבָּיִת, *al habbayit*, precisely the title accorded to Hilkiah (and later his son, Eliakim) the palace administrator, which seems to grant to him the same level of authority (**Isaiah 22:15**).

Hezekiah rejected the overtures of Sennacherib, notified the prophet Isaiah of the peril of the nation of Israel, urged the prophet to pray, and then rejoiced in God's benevolent deliverance that cost Assyria one hundred and eighty-five thousand troops. Hezekiah then said that Eliakim would be called a servant of Yahweh and would be clothed with the tunic and the sash of the former royal steward Shebna, who had arrogantly taken upon himself to carve out a burial spot with engravings of his name (**Isaiah 22:16**; see **Isaiah 22:15–19**). As a result, Shebna was divested of his prestigious position, thus making way for Eliakim to succeed him and be granted authority as such: The Lord said, "I will summon my servant, Eliakim son of Hilkiah. I will clothe him with your [Shebna's] robe and fasten your [Shebna's] sash around him [Eliakim] and hand your [Shebna's] authority over to him" (**Isaiah 22:20–21**). Moreover, Eliakim would be like a *father* to the people (**Isaiah 22:21**), with keys to the "house of David" on his shoulder (**Isaiah 22:22**). This key provided access to the coming messianic kingdom, as foretold in Judah's blessing by his dying father, Jacob, as well as in David's writings (**Genesis 49:10**; cf. **Psalm 2, 21, 61, 103, 110, 122**). The phrase "on his shoulder" also occurs in **Isaiah 9:6,** referring to the Messiah: "the government will be on his shoulders." In the immediate context, Eliakim possessed the right to admit access to the royal presence or to refuse admittance (i.e., in this sense, he served as a royal gatekeeper as well). Additionally, Eliakim would go on to embody the irrefragable promises of the glory to come, as a *peg* driven into a wall so secure as to bear all the privileges and responsibilities inherent in a ruler in the line of David (cf. **Isaiah 22:20–23; Zechariah 10:4**).

Concepts such as "servant of Yahweh," "garments of authority," the "key to the house of David," "bearing the weight of his people," a "seat of honor," and "being cut off" surely conjure up messianic imagery in both the Old and New Testaments (see **Isaiah 53:8; Daniel 9:26; Matthew 11:30; Acts 3:26; 4:27; Romans 15:8; Revelation 3:7**). Likewise, specific New Testament texts like **Matthew 16:19** and **Revelation 1:18** come to mind. In the former text, Jesus gives to Peter, as a representative of the Church universal, "the keys of the kingdom of heaven," a reference to the Gospel message,[6] the truth of which became the foundation of the church (**Matthew 16:19**). Jesus also told Peter that "whatever you bind on earth will be bound in heaven, and whatever you loose on earth will be loosed in heaven" (**Matthew 16:19**), reminiscent of the LORD saying of Eliakim "what he opens no one can shut, and what he shuts no one can open" (**Isaiah 22:22**). In **Revelation 1:18** Jesus says of Himself, "I am the Living One; I was dead, and now look, I am alive for ever and ever! And I hold the keys of death and Hades." In short, he is the Lord of life and death.

Eschatological Significance

The larger Isaiah corpus is replete with messianic imagery, which is echoed to a great extent in **Isaiah 22:1–25**, as table 1 shows:

Table 1. Eliakim, Shebna, and Messianic Promises in the Book of Isaiah

Eschatological Terms	Number of references in all of Isaiah	Isaiah 22:1–25, by Verse	NT Fulfillment and Allusions
(In that) Day	Approximately 62	**5, 8, 12, 20, 25**	**Luke 17:24, 30–31; John 14:20; 16:23, 26; Romans 2:16; 1 Corinthians 1:8; 3:13; 2 Corinthians 1:14; 2 Thessalonians 2:2–3; 2 Peter 3:10**
David, city of David, house of David	10	**9, 22**	**Luke 1:69; 2:4; Acts 13:34–36**
Yahweh of Hosts/ Almighty	63	**5, 12, 14, 15, 25**	**Romans 9:29; 2 Corinthians 6:18; James 5:4; Revelation 1:8; 4:8; 11:17; 15:3; 16:7, 14; 19:6, 15; 21:22**
(My) servant	20	**20**	**Luke 1:54, 69; Acts 3:13, 26; 4:27, 30; Romans 15:8**
(My, the) shoulder	2	**22**	
House of Jacob, Son of David, Root and Offspring of David, Key of David, Lion of Judah	19	**22**	**Matthew 1:1; 12:23; 15:22; 20:30–31; 21:9, 15; 22:42, 45; Mark 12:35, 37; Luke 3:31; Romans 1:3; 2 Timothy 2:8; Revelation 3:7; 5:5; 22:16**

Eschatological Terms	Number of references in all of Isaiah	Isaiah 22:1–25, by Verse	NT Fulfillment and Allusions
Glory/Honor	16	**23–24**	**Matthew 25:31; Luke 2:9; 24:26; John 1:14; 2:11; 12:41; Acts 7:55; Romans 8:17; 1 Corinthians 2:7–8; 11:7; 15:43; Ephesians 1:14; Colossians 1:27; 2 Thessalonians 2:14; 2 Timothy 2:10; Hebrews 1:3; 2:7, 9, 10; 1 Peter 5:10; 2 Peter 1:17; Jude 25; Revelation 1:6; 4:11; 5:12, 13**

Notes

1. Eliakim's functional duties and presence in every location of Solomon's Temple strongly suggests that he was a Kohathite priest; for the lineage of the Kohathite priests (distinct from the high priestly line), see chart "**1 Chronicles 6**: Levi: High Priests, Priests, Levites, and Musicians in Solomon's Temple." The "palace administrator" in the Solomonic Temple era may correspond to the "temple overseer "(*ammarkal*) in New Testament times, the one who "held the keys and the power of supervision over the Temple" [see Joachim Jeremias, *Jerusalem in the Time of Jesus* (Philadelphia: Fortress, 1969), 160, 165–166].

2. Hilkiah was "the palace administrator" under King Hezekiah, 715–686 B.C. (**2 Kings 18:18, 37; Isaiah 36:3, 22**). He is not (1) Hilkiah the high priest who served under Josiah (640–609 B.C.) in **2 Kings 22:4, 8, 10, 12, 14; 23:4, 24; 1 Chronicles 6:13; 9:11; 2 Chronicles 34:9; 14–15, 18, 20, 22; 35:8; Ezra 7:1; Nehemiah 11:11**; (2) Hilkiah the son of Amzi, a Merarite (**1 Chronicles 6:45–46**); (3) Hilkiah son of Hosah, a Merarite (**1 Chronicles 26:10–11**); (4) Hilkiah, one of the leaders of the Kohathite priests who returned to Jerusalem with Zerubbabel in 538 B.C. (**Nehemiah 12:7**); (5) Hilkiah, who stood on the platform with Ezra in 458 B.C. (**Nehemiah 8:4**), possibly the same as Hilkiah #2 (**Nehemiah 12:7**); (6) Hilkiah the father of Jeremiah the prophet (**Jeremiah 1:1**); nor (7) Hilkiah the father of Gemariah (**Jeremiah 29:3**), who may be the same as Hilkiah #6.

3. Eliakim the palace administrator should not be confused with Eliakim (Jehoiakim) the son of Josiah, who was king over Judah from 608–598 B.C. (**2 Kings 23:34; 2 Chronicles 36:4**) or with the Eliakim figures in the line of the Messiah (**Matthew 1:13; Luke 3:30**).

4. Hezekiah was co-regent with his father, Ahaz, from 729–715 B.C.; the sole regent over Judah for 29 years, from 715–686 B.C. (**2 Chronicles 29:1**); and Manasseh was co-regent with his father, Hezekiah, from 697–686 B.C. See chart "**2 Kings 16**: Hezekiah, King of Judah."

5. The verbal root *zakar* means "to remember"; the noun is a de-verbal participle meaning "one who causes remembrance," that is, a note-taker or stenographer ("זְכַרְיָהוּ," *HALOT* 1:271). Treaties came under his oversight, and he kept national archives or records.

6. Jesus asked Peter, "Who do you say I am?" and Peter answered, "You are the Messiah, the Son of the living God." And Jesus replied, "Blessed are you, Simon [Peter] son of Jonah, for this was not revealed to you by flesh and blood, but by my Father in heaven. And I tell you that you are Peter [*petros*, "rock" or "stone"], and on this rock [*petra*, "rock" or "bedrock"/Peter's confession of faith in Jesus as the Messiah] I will build my church, and the gates of Hades will not overcome it" (**Matthew 16:15–18;** cf. **Ephesians 2:20).**

2 KINGS 20: MANASSEH, KING OF JUDAH

Approximate Dating: ca. 697–642 B.C., including a co-regency with his father, Hezekiah, 697–686 B.C. ***Relevant Scriptures:*** **2 Kings 20:21–21:19; 1 Chronicles 3:12–14; 2 Chronicles 32:33–33:23; Matthew 1:10**

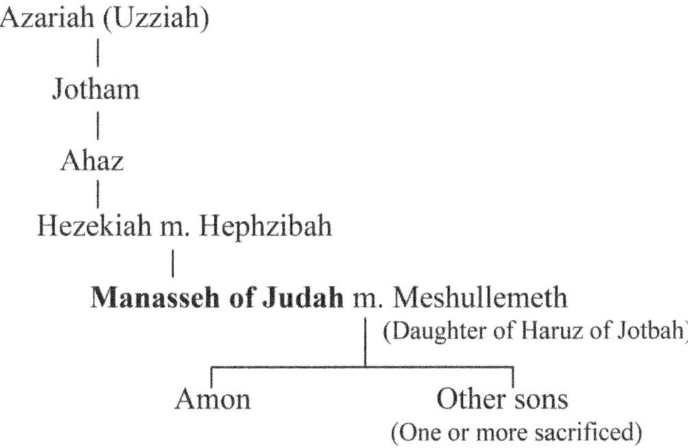

Biblical and Theological Significance

Beginning when he was twelve years old, Manasseh was co-regent[1] with his father, Hezekiah, for ten years (697–686 B.C.) and then the sole regent for another forty-five years, for a total of fifty-five years (697–642 B.C.), the longest reign of any Judean king (**2 Kings 21:1; 2 Chronicles 33:1**).

He reversed many reforms instigated by his father, Hezekiah, reintroduced idolatry to the nation, and in sum "did evil in the eyes of the Lord" (**2 Kings 21:2; 2 Chronicles 33:2**). He rebuilt the pagan high places and desecrated the temple by placing idols and altars to foreign gods there, as well as installing altars for star worship in the temple courts (**2 Kings 21:4–5; 2 Chronicles 33:4–5**). He practiced divination and witchcraft, sought omens, consulted mediums and spiritists, and even sacrificed his own children in the Valley of Ben Hinnom (**2 Kings 21:6; 2 Chronicles 33:6**; cf. **Jeremiah 32:35**)! Scripture says he "filled Jerusalem from end to end" with innocent blood (**2 Kings 21:16**) and was so corrupt that the evil of Judah exceeded that of all other nations (**2 Chronicles 33:9; 2 Kings 21:9, 11**; cf. **Jeremiah 15:4**). God held Manasseh personally responsible for the downfall of Jerusalem and the exile of the people to Babylon (**2 Kings 21:14**; cf. **2 Kings 21:10–15; 24:1–4**) and refused to pardon his wickedness (**2 Kings 24:3–4**).

As was common practice, the Assyrians treated Manasseh with the severest indignity and humiliation and took him to Babylon (**2 Chronicles 33:11**). There, Manasseh repented of his evil and entreated God to allow him to return to Jerusalem. Once back in his homeland, Manasseh rebuilt the outer wall of the City of David to encircle the hill of Ophel;

stationed troops in fortified cities; removed idols from the temple, the temple hill, and throughout Jerusalem; restored the altar of sacrifice; and instructed the people to serve the Lord (**2 Chronicles 33:12–17**).

The events of Manasseh's reign were recorded in the book of the annals of the kings of Judah (**2 Kings 21:17**) and in the annals of the kings of Israel (**2 Chronicles 33:18–19**). He was not buried in the tombs of the kings but in the garden of Uzza on the grounds of the king's palace. His son Amon then succeeded him (**2 Kings 21:18; 2 Chronicles 33:20**).

Notes

1. For the coregency of Manasseh with his father Hezekiah, see Edwin R. Thiele's *The Mysterious Numbers of the Hebrew Kings* (New revised ed.), (Grand Rapids: Kregel, 1983 and Grand Rapids: Zondervan Publishing, 1994), 10–13, 64, 174, 176–177.

2 KINGS 21: AMON, KING OF JUDAH

Approximate Dating: ca. 642–640 B.C. ***Relevant Scriptures:*** **2 Kings 21:18–26; 22:1; 1 Chronicles 3:12–14; 2 Chronicles 33:20–25; Jeremiah 1:2; 25:3; Matthew 1:10**

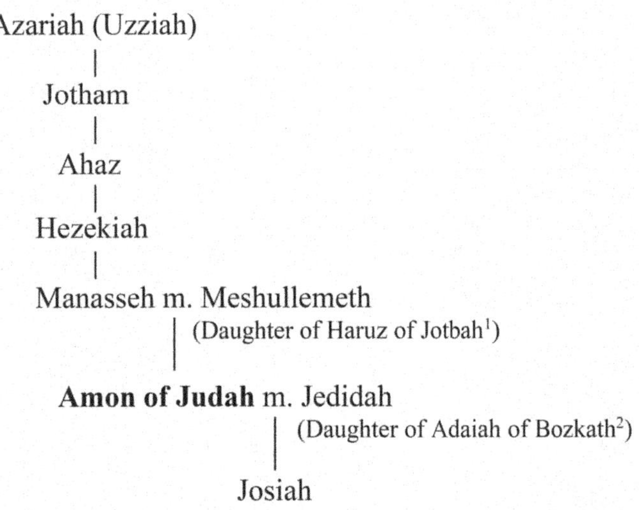

Biblical and Theological Significance

Amon became king of Judah when he was twenty-two and reigned in Jerusalem for two years (ca. 642–640 B.C.; **2 Kings 21:19; 2 Chronicles 33:21**). He followed in the ways of his father, Manasseh, and "did evil in the eyes of the Lord" (**2 Kings 21:20; 2 Chronicles 33:22**). Unlike his father, who repented from his evil ways, Amon "did not humble himself before the Lord; he increased his guilt" (**2 Chronicles 33:23**). Amon was killed in the palace by officials who conspired against him. The people of Judah executed the conspirators and made Josiah, Amon's son, king in his place (**2 Kings 21:23–24; 2 Chronicles 33:24–25**). Amon was buried in the tomb of his father (Manasseh) in the garden of Uzza on the grounds of the king's palace (**2 Kings 21:26**).

Notes

1. The location of Jotbah is unclear; it may be (1) the same place as Jotbathah, a campsite during the post-exodus sojourn (**Numbers 33:33–34**); (2) Jotapata, the fortress where Josephus was besieged by Vespasian, located in the valley of Zebulun, west of the Sea of Galilee (Josephus, *Jewish Wars* 3.7.3–36); or (3) the town of Jotbah near Hannathon (**Joshua 19:14**) or Hinnatuna, captured by Tiglath-Pileser III of Assyria during his 733 B.C. invasion, mentioned in EA 8 and EA 245 of the Amarna Letters (the clay cuneiform tablets found in the city of el-Amarna, the modern name for the ancient capital of Akhetaten, founded by pharaoh Akhenaten in the Eighteenth Dynasty of Egypt).

2. Jedidah, the daughter of Adaiah, was Amon's wife (**2 Kings 22:1**) and she was from Bozkath, a town in the western foothills of Judah (**Joshua 15:39**).

2 KINGS 21: JOSIAH, KING OF JUDAH

Approximate Dating: ca. 640–609 B.C. ***Relevant Scriptures:*** **2 Kings 21:24–23:30–31, 34, 36; 2 Kings 22:1;** also **1 Chronicles 3:12–16; 2 Chronicles 33:25–36:1; Jeremiah 1:1–2; 3:6; 22:11, 18; 25:1, 3; 26:1; 27:1; 35:1; 36:1, 9; 37:1; 45:1; 46:2; Zephaniah 1:1; Matthew 1:10–11**

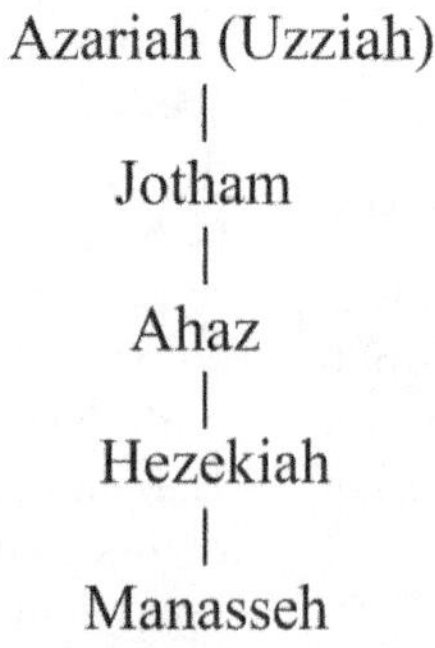

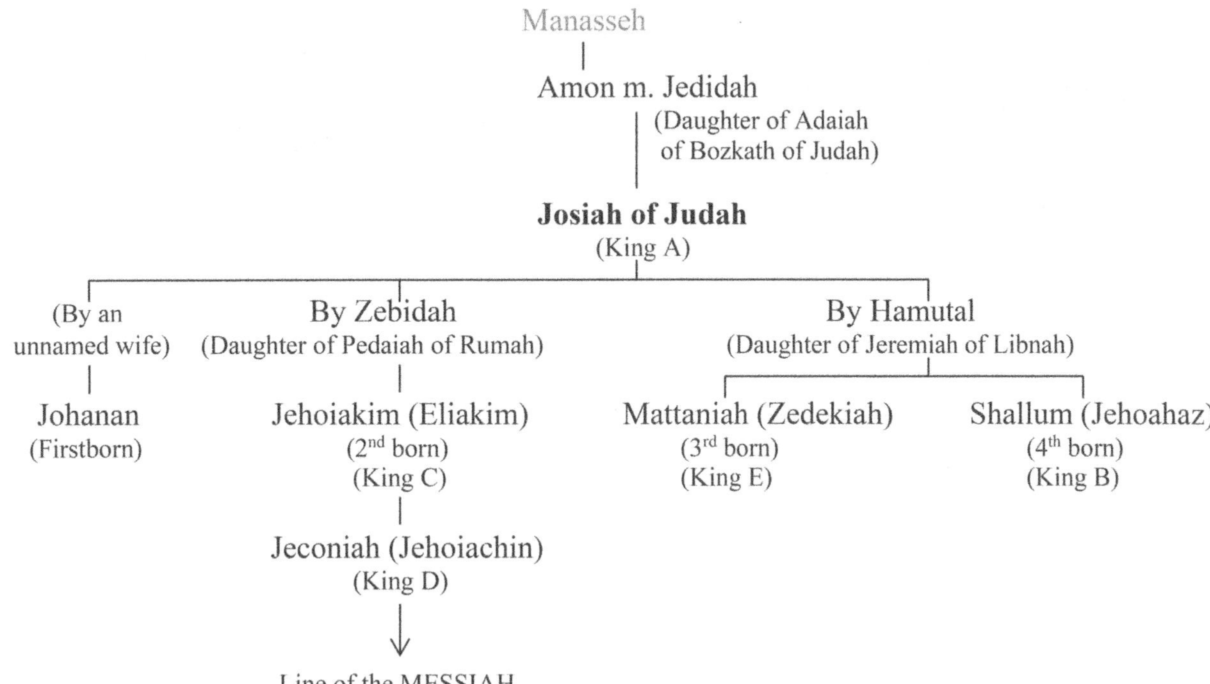

Biblical and Theological Significance

After conspirators killed King Amon, the people of Judah crowned his eight-year-old son Josiah, and he ruled for the next thirty-one years, ca. 640–609 B.C. (**2 Kings 21:24; 22:1; 2 Chronicles 33:25; 34:1**). Josiah was commended as a wise king (**2 Kings 22:2; 2 Chronicles 34:2**). By the age of twenty, he had reversed many of the idolatrous practices and pagan influences instigated by his grandfather Manasseh and his father, Amon (see **2 Kings 21; 2 Chronicles 33**). Josiah purged the land of the high places, Asherah poles, and idols; burned the bones of idolatrous priests who had attended at the Baal altars; desecrated Topheth in the Valley of Ben Himmon to prevent child sacrifice; cleansed the temple of the rooms of the male shrine prostitutes and rooms where women did weaving for Asherah; cleansed the temple court of pagan altars; removed the horses in the court, near the room of Nathan-Melek, his official; and removed the chariots that had been dedicated to the sun (**2 Kings 23:1–20; 2 Chronicles 34:3–7**).

Josiah's greatest contribution to his people was the restoration of the glory of Solomon's Temple[1] that had fallen into disrepair under his predecessors. Providentially, a previously hidden scroll was brought to light (**2 Kings 22:8–11; 2 Chronicles 34:14–18**). During the renovations, Hilkiah, the high priest (**2 Kings 22:4; 2 Chronicles 34:14–15**) found the book of the Law of Moses—probably a copy of the book of Deuteronomy—near the entrance to the temple, i.e., where much earlier in 835 B.C., the young king Joash of Judah had been given "a copy of the covenant" and was crowned "standing by the pillar, as the custom was" (**2 Kings 11:12, 14**; cf. **1 Kings 7:15, 21; 2 Kings 11:12–14; 12:9-16; 22:8; 23:3; 2 Chronicles 34:14-15**). After hearing the reading of the scroll, Josiah called for Huldah,[2] the female prophet of Jerusalem, who then authenticated the scroll and confirmed that the destruction of Jerusalem and Judah would occur, but not during Josiah's lifetime (**2 Kings 22:14–20; 2 Chronicles 34:22–28**). Josiah responded humbly by leading the people in a covenant renewal ceremony (**2 Kings 23:1–3; 2 Chronicles 34:29–32**) and initiating the reforms detailed above (**2 Kings 23:4–20; 2 Chronicles 34:33**). In 622 B.C., the people of the land observed Passover: "Neither in the days of the judges who led Israel nor in the days of the kings of Israel and the kings of Judah had any such Passover been observed" (**2 Kings 23:21–23**; see also **2 Chronicles 35:1–19**).[3] Josiah was a contemporary of the prophets Zephaniah (**Zephaniah 1:1**), Jeremiah (**2 Chronicles 35:25; Jeremiah 1:1–2**), and perhaps Habakkuk.[4]

In an ill-advised battle between Judah and Egypt, Josiah was fatally wounded at Megiddo. His servants brought him to Jerusalem, where he died. He was "buried in the tombs of his ancestors and all Judah and Jerusalem mourned for him" (**2 Chronicles 35:20–25**; cf. **2 Kings 23:29–30**). The acts of Josiah were recorded in the book of the kings of Israel and Judah (**2 Kings 23:28; 2 Chronicles 35:26–27**). His youngest son, Shallum (Jehoahaz), succeeded him to the throne of Judah (**2 Kings 23:30; 2 Chronicles 36:1**).

Notes

1. Originally constructed between 966–960 B.C., Solomon's Temple was 338 years old in the days of Josiah and had not been renovated since 812 B.C., during the reign of King Joash (**2 Kings 12:4–16; 2 Chronicles 24:4–14**).

2. See chart "**2 Kings 22**: Huldah the Prophet."

3. "The Passover had not been observed like this in Israel since the days of the prophet Samuel [ca. 1110–1015 B.C.]; and none of the kings of Israel had ever celebrated such a Passover as did Josiah, with the priests, the Levites and all Judah and Israel who were there with the people of Jerusalem" (**2 Chronicles 35:18**).

4. Habakkuk ministered in Judah from ca. 612–588 (see the Introduction to the book of Habakkuk in the *NIV Study Bible*, Fully Revised Edition (Grand Rapids: Zondervan, 2020), 1567–68.

2 KINGS 22: SHAPHAN, SCRIBAL SECRETARY UNDER KING JOSIAH AND KING JEHOIAKIM OF JUDAH

Approximate Dating: in the days of Josiah, 640–609 B.C. and Jehoiakim/Eliakim, 609–598 B.C. ***Relevant Scriptures:*** **2 Kings 22:3–14; 25:22–25; 1 Chronicles 6:1–15; 9:11; 2 Chronicles 34:14–22; Ezra 7:1–6; Nehemiah 11:11; Jeremiah 26:24; 29:3; 36:10–12; 39:14; 40:5—41:18; 43:6; Ezekiel 8:11**

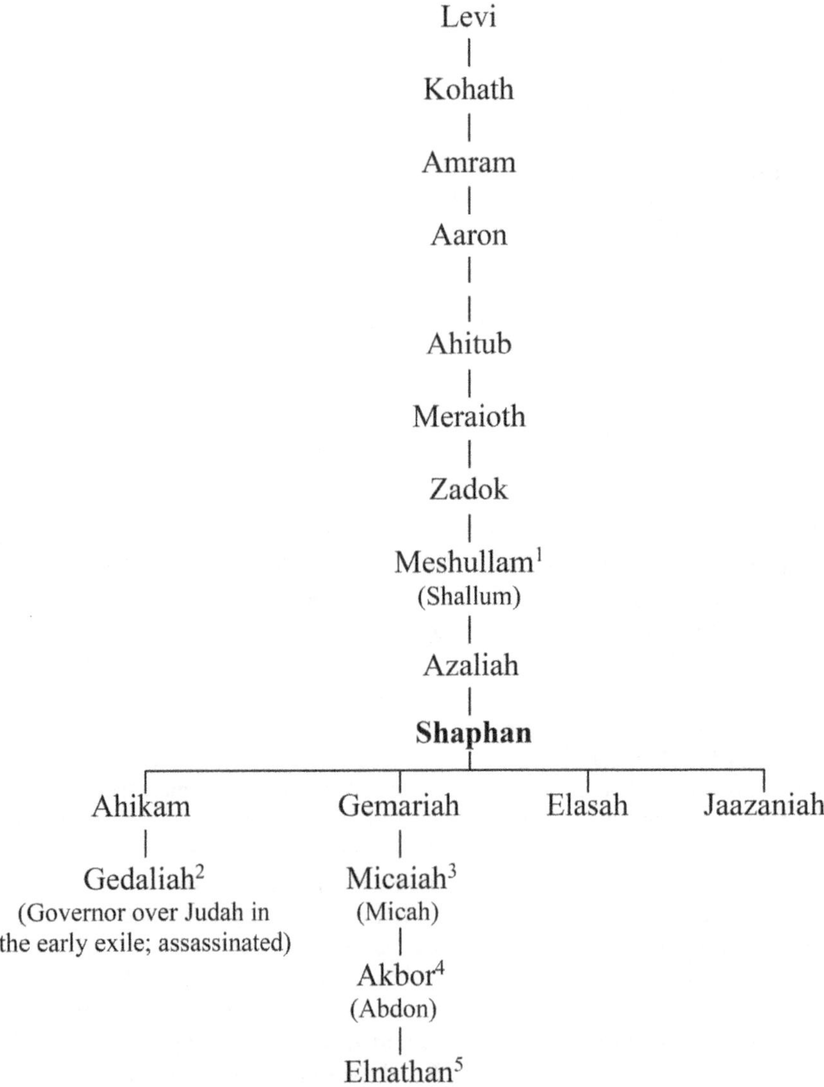

Biblical and Theological Significance

Shaphan was a Kohathite priest in a scribal lineage that paralleled that of the high priests.[6] He served as the scribal secretary under King Josiah (640–609 B.C.; **2 Kings 22:8–14; 2 Chronicles 34:8–22**). As part of the reform efforts, King Josiah sent Shaphan, Maaseiah (the ruler–mayor of Jerusalem), and Joah the recorder to repair and purify the temple (**2 Chronicles 34:8**). After Hilkiah discovered the Book of the Law during renovations of Solomon's Temple, Shaphan read the scroll to King Josiah who said: "Go and inquire of the LORD for me" (**2 Kings 22:13**). Shaphan and the other leaders—Hilkiah the priest, Ahikam (son of Shaphan), Akbor (or Abdon, son of Micah), and Asaiah (the king's attendant)—went to Huldah the prophet of Jerusalem to evaluate its genuineness (**2 Kings 22:8–14; 2 Chronicles 34:14–22**). Huldah was convinced of the scroll's authenticity and sent a message to King Josiah that the Lord would not bring the disaster during Josiah's lifetime (**2 Kings 22:18–20**). Josiah realized that "those who have gone before us have not kept the word of the LORD; they have not acted in accordance with all that is written in this book" (**2 Chronicles 34:21;** cf. **2 Kings 22:13**).

Shaphan's son, Ahikam, was a supporter of Jeremiah the prophet and saved his life (**Jeremiah 26:24**). Two scribes—Gemariah (Shaphan's son) and Elishama—served as scribal-secretaries during the reign of King Jehoiakim/Eliakim, 609–598 B.C. (cf. **Jeremiah 36:1, 10–12, 20–21; 41:1**).[7] Shaphan's son Elasah and Hilkiah's son Gemariah[8] carried a letter from Jeremiah to the captives in Babylon (**Jeremiah 29:1–3**). Regrettably, Shaphan's son Jaazaniah acted as a wicked priest to seventy elders of Israel who had turned the priestly chambers that were adjacent to the holy place into a *mock holy place* for worship of detestable crawling things, unclean animals, and idols (**Ezekiel 8:9–12**).[9] During Judah's exile to Babylon, King Nebuchadnezzar appointed Shaphan's grandson Gedaliah[10] as governor over the remnant of people in Judah (**2 Kings 25:22–25; Jeremiah 40:11**).

Notes

1. Shallum in **1 Chronicles 6:12–13** and **Ezra 7:2** is called Meshullam in **1 Chronicles 9:11** and **Nehemiah 11:11** (and possibly **Nehemiah 12:33**). See chart "**Supplement 2**: The High Priests of Israel."

2. See chart "**2 Kings 25**: Gedaliah, Governor over the Remnant People of Judah During the Early Days of the Exile."

3. Micaiah, the son of Gemariah (**2 Kings 22:12**; **Jeremiah 36:11**), is the same person as Micah the father of Abdon (**2 Chronicles 34:20**). However, he should not be confused with (1) the prophet Micah of Moresheth (**Micah 1:1**); (2) the prophet Micaiah son of Imlah, who prophesied in the days of King Jehoshaphat (cf. **1 Kings 22:8–9, 13–15, 17, 19, 24–26, 28; 2 Chronicles 17:7(?); 18:7–27**); nor (3) Micaiah the Levitical priest, the grandson of Asaph (**Nehemiah 12:35, 41**).

4. Akbor son of Micaiah (**2 Kings 22:12, 14; Jeremiah 26:22; 36:12**) is the same person as Abdon son of Micah (**2 Chronicles 34:20**).

5. Elnathan was the son of Akbor/Abdon (see note 4) and the grandson of Micaiah/Micah (see note 3) (**Jeremiah 26:22; 36:12**).

6. For an example of a scribal lineage that parallels that of the high priestly lineage, see chart "**2 Kings 22**: The Royal Advisors Sent by King Josiah to Huldah the Prophet" or "**Ezra 7**: Ezra, the Priestly Scribe and Teacher of the Law (Post-Exile."

7. The scribal chamber of Gemariah the secretary—called "the room of Gemariah son of Shaphan"—was "in the upper courtyard at the entrance of the New Gate of the temple" (**Jeremiah 36:10**). However, another scribal-secretary, Elishama, was "of royal blood" (possibly meaning a descendant/relative of King David), so his scribal chamber—called "the room of Elishama"—was in the royal palace rather than in the temple (**Jeremiah 36:12, 20–21**). For Elishama, see chart "**1 Chronicles 2**: Jerahmeel and His Descendant, Elishama, Who Appears to Be a Compiler of Historical and Genealogical Records in 1 & 2 Chronicles."

8. Gemariah is called the "son of Hilkiah" in **Jeremiah 29:3**, but the text is unclear if Gemariah is: (1) the son of Hilkiah the high priest, or possibly (2) the son of Hilkiah the palace administrator under King Hezekiah, who served from 715–686 B.C.; see chart "**2 Kings 18**: Eliakim, the Palace Administrator who Replaced Shebna the Scribal Secretary During the Reign of King Hezekiah of Judah."

9. See chart "**Ezekiel 8**: Jaazaniah the Scribe Who Served as a Priest to Idol Worshipers in Solomon's Temple in the Days of Ezekiel the Prophet (Pre-Exile)."

10. See chart "**2 Kings 25**: Gedaliah, the Governor over the Remnant People of Judah During the Early Days of the Exile."

2 KINGS 22: HULDAH THE PROPHET

Approximate Dating: ca. 622 B.C. ***Relevant Scriptures:*** **2 Kings 22:8–20; 2 Chronicles 34:14–28**

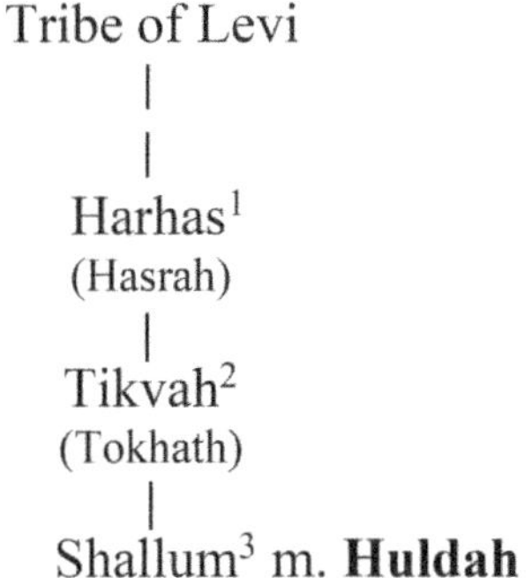

Biblical and Theological Significance

Huldah lived in the New (or Second) Quarter of Jerusalem (**2 Kings 22:14; 2 Chronicles 34:22**), so called because King Hezekiah had added defensive walls that extended beyond the original walls, thus creating a new section of the city. She was married to Shallum and may have been of Levitical descent herself since her husband's grandfather (Harhas/Hasrah) was the Levitical keeper of the royal wardrobe. When a copy of the book of the Law of Moses was found during renovations of Solomon's Temple in 622 B.C., Josiah turned to Huldah[4] for prophetic wisdom and divine interpretation—not to the high priest (Hilkiah[5]), her husband (Shallum the Levite), Gemariah[6] the scribe, or the respected male prophets of the day (such as Jeremiah[7] or Zephaniah[8]). Huldah authenticated the scroll and foretold God's impending destruction of Jerusalem because of Judah's idolatrous practices. Her prophetic utterance inspired Josiah to initiate widespread reforms in the Southern Kingdom, which deferred God's judgment and awakened the people to their covenant responsibilities. Her spiritual authority, even in an unofficial capacity, foreshadowed the one who would unite the offices of prophet, priest, and king in the *new* messianic kingdom.

The double and triple gates of Herod's Temple have traditionally been referred to as the *Huldah Gates,* after Huldah the prophet, although this terminology is not technically correct (see below). The Double and Triple Gates are situated on the broad southern extension of the enlarged platform of Herod's Temple—an extension of the former square Temple Mount. The double and triple gates served as the two main entrances for pilgrims and priests to enter the temple complex. In his book, *The Quest: Revealing the Temple Mount in Jerusalem,* Leen Ritmeyer discusses several sources that describe the circulation of two-way traffic through the gates and concludes that the name Huldah relates to a *pre-Herodian (double) gate* and "cannot refer to the two gates in the Southern Wall of Herod's Temple" near the colonnaded Royal Stoa (Royal Portico).[9] Huldah's name in Hebrew means *mole.*[10] Perhaps, like other pilgrims, she entered long, tunnel-like passageways that led, in turn, to staircases, until finally emerging from these "burrows" to the open surface of the Temple Mount.[11]

Notes

1. Harhas in **2 Kings 22:14** is Hasrah in **2 Chronicles 34:22**.

2. Huldah's father-in-law is called Tikvah in **2 Kings 22:14** and Tokhath in **2 Chronicles 34:22**.

3. Huldah's husband does not appear to be: (1) Shallum/Meshullam the high priest (**1 Chronicles 6:12–13; 9:11; Ezra 7:2; Nehemiah 11:11**); (2) Shallum the Kohathite–Korahite who was a gatekeeper (**1 Chronicles 9:17, 19, 31; Ezra 2:42; 10:24; Nehemiah 7:45**); nor (3) Shallum/Jehoahaz the son of Josiah (**1 Chronicles 3:15**).

4. Huldah is one of several women described as a *prophet* in the Old Testament, the others being Miriam (**Exodus 15:20**); Deborah (**Judges 4:4**); Noadiah (**Nehemiah 6:14**); and Isaiah's wife, called "the prophetess" (**Isaiah 8:3**). The term for prophet (masc.) is *nabi* and for prophet (fem.) is *nebi'ah*, "a proclaimer, spokesman." The difference is only in the spelling, a variation in Hebrew grammatical gender forms.

5. Hilkiah was the high priest under King Josiah, from 640–609 B.C. (cf. **2 Kings 22:1–4, 8, 10, 12**). See Hilkiah in the charts "**1 Chronicles 6**: Levi: High Priests, Priests, Levites, and Musicians in Solomon's Temple" and "**Supplement 2**: The High Priests of Israel."

6. Gemariah was a scribe and contemporary of Jeremiah the prophet, 627–586 B.C. See chart "**Jeremiah 36**: Gemariah the Scribe, a Contemporary of Jeremiah the Prophet (Pre-Exile)."

7. Jeremiah ministered from ca. 627–586 B.C. See chart "**Jeremiah 1**: Jeremiah, the Prophet-Priest of God to the Southern Kingdom of Judah (Pre-Exile)."

8. Zephaniah ministered from ca. 640–609 B.C. See chart "**Zephaniah 1**: Zephaniah, the Prophet of God to the Southern Kingdom of Judah (Pre-Exile)."

9. Leen Ritmeyer, *The Quest: Revealing the Temple Mount in Jerusalem* (Jerusalem: Carta Jerusalem, 2015), 85–89. Ritmeyer quotes two mishnaic tractates: (1) Middot (1.3) which says—the "two Hulda[h] Gates on the south . . . served for coming in and for going out" and (2) Midoot (2.2) which says—"whosoever it was that entered the Temple Mount came in on the right and went round and came out on the left, save any whom aught befell [those who were sick], for he went round to the left" (ibid., 85, 87). However, as Leen Ritmeyer explains, the Mishnah was concerned with the *earlier* square Temple Mount, as it existed at the end of the First Temple period (i.e., the square "mountain of the house"), and not with the Herodian extension toward the southern end of the mount made by Herod. Ritmeyer explains that the Hulda(h) Gates stood at the entrance of the 500-cubit square *pre-Herodian Temple Mount*, and should not be confused with the Double Gate or Triple Gate of the larger Herodian Temple Mount: "it is reasonable to suggest the Double Gate entrance [of Herod's Temple] and passageway were built to correspond with it [the original Hulda(h) Gates of pre-Herodian times]. The pilgrims . . . would normally have entered through the right or east opening and come back through the left or west opening of the Double Gate. . . . The Triple Gate, however, had a narrow approach and would appear to have been used less by pilgrims and more by those members of the priestly order who needed access to the underground storerooms. From there . . . they could also reach the Temple platform" (ibid., 87). For diagrams showing the Hasmonean and Herodian extensions of the original square Temple Mount, the location of the original Hulda(h) Gates of the First Temple period, and the tunnels that led from the Double Gate and Triple Gate of Herod's Temple to the original Huldah Gates, see ibid., 217, 336–338.

10. Some scholars derive her name from a root חֵלֶד (*kheled*) [uncertain], or חֶלֶד (*kheled*), meaning "lifespan," rather than חֹלֶד (*khōled*), meaning "mole."

11. The position of the Royal Stoa relative to the Huldah Gates can be seen in reconstructions done by Kathleen and Leen Ritmeyer in their article "Reconstructing Herod's Temple Mount in Jerusalem," *BAR* 15.6 (1989): 23–24, 26–27, 29, 32, 35–37, 40, 42, https://www.baslibrary.org/biblical-archaeology-review/15/6/1. A general discussion of the Royal Portico is given in Orit Peleg-Barkat's article, "Reimagining Herod's Royal Portico," *Peleg-Barkat, Orit. "Reimagining Herod's Royal Portico,"* *BAR* 45.4 (2019): 34–40, 86, https://www.baslibrary.org/biblical-archaeology-review/45/4/4.

2 KINGS 22: THE ROYAL ADVISORS SENT BY KING JOSIAH TO HULDAH THE PROPHET

Approximate Dating: ca. 622 B.C. ***Relevant Scriptures:*** **2 Kings 22:3–14; 2 Chronicles 34:14–20**[1]

1. **Hilkiah**
2. **Ahikam**
3. **Akbor**
4. **Shaphan**
5. **Asaiah** (the king's attendant) (unknown genealogy)[2]

Genealogy of Hilkiah, Ahikam, Akbor, and Shaphan

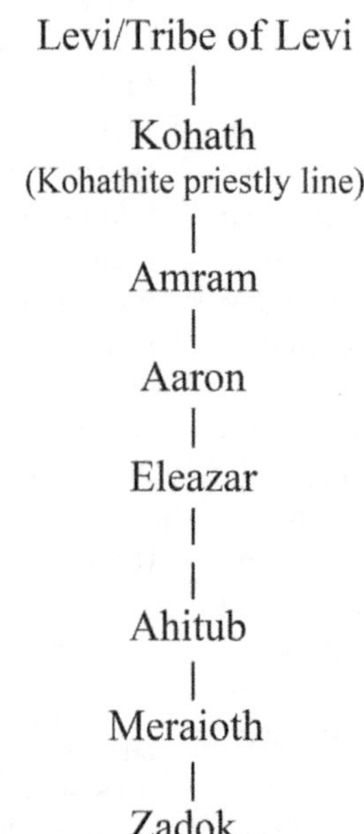

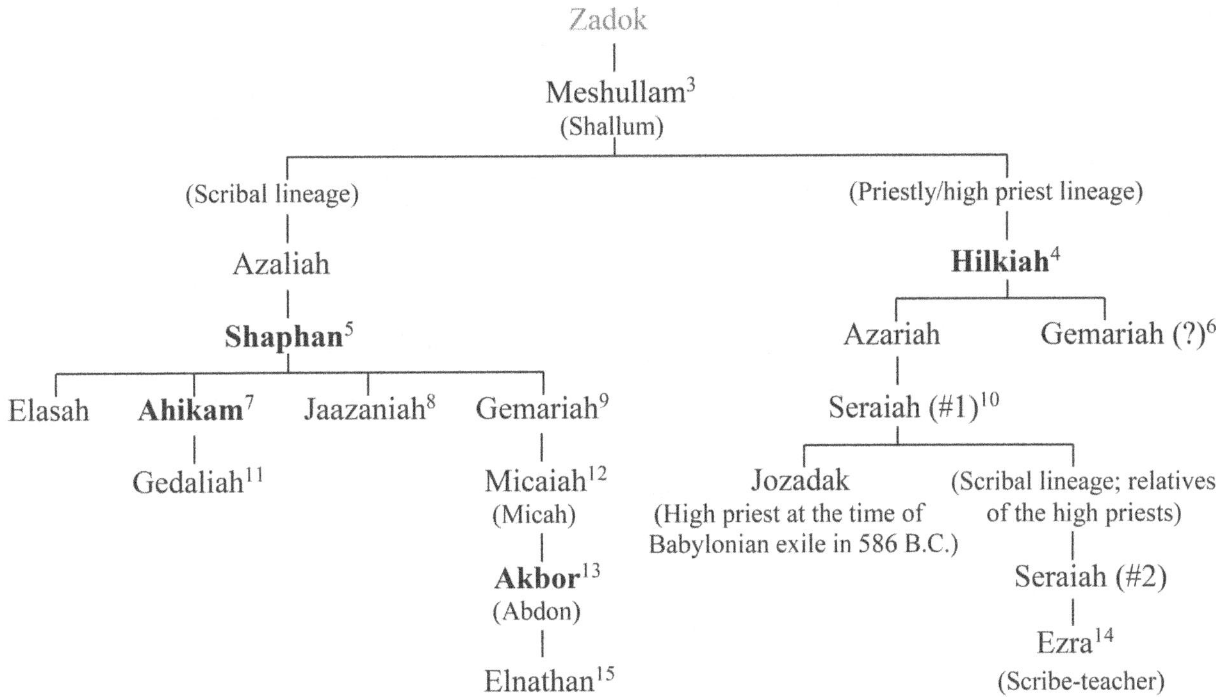

Biblical and Theological Significance

Without doubt, one of the most historically and theologically important events in biblical history was the discovery of a sacred scroll in the temple while the structure was undergoing refurbishment after the idolatrous pollution it had suffered under King Manasseh and his son Amon (**2 Kings 21:2–9, 16–17, 19–22; 2 Chronicles 33:2–9, 22**). After careful examination and validation by Huldah[16] the prophet, Hilkiah the high priest and Shaphan the scribe knew that it was the סֵפֶר הַתּוֹרָה (*sepher hattorah*), "Book [scroll] of the Law" (**2 Kings 22:8–11; 2 Chronicles 34:15–18**). More precisely, it was a copy of the book of Deuteronomy—elsewhere known as the "Book of the Law" (**Deuteronomy 28:58, 61; 29:21; 30:10; 31:26**). Furthermore, each king was to make a copy of it for himself.[17] Deuteronomy was the distillation of all the covenant requirements revealed to Moses at Sinai and then at the Plains of Moab (**Exodus 19:3–20:21; Deuteronomy 5:1–21**). Further evidence of its identification was King Josiah's reaction to its reading—he tore his garments, lamented his nation's sins, and led the people in the greatest reformation in the history of the nation. Clearly, he took to heart **Deuteronomy 17**, the "Handbook of Royal Behavior."

Notes

1. For additional references for the lineages shown, see the relevant Scriptures in the following charts: "**2 Kings 22**: Shaphan, Scribal Secretary under King Josiah and King Jehoiakim of Judah," "**1 Chronicles 6**: Levi: High Priests, Priests, Levites, and Musicians in Solomon's Temple," and "**Ezra 7**: Ezra, the Priestly Scribe and Teacher of the Law (Post-Exile)."

2. The genealogy of Asaiah is unknown. Asaiah, the attendant of King Josiah, is not (1) the same person as Asaiah the Levitical Merarite who was active in the days of King David (cf. **1 Chronicles 15:6, 11**); (2) Asaiah the Shelanite (of the descendants of Shelah, the son of Judah) who resettled in Jerusalem post-exile (**1 Chronicles 9:5**; cf. **Numbers 26:20**); nor (3) Asaiah a clan leader from among the Simeonites (**1 Chronicles 4:36**).

3. Shallum in **1 Chronicles 6:12–13** and **Ezra 7:2** is called Meshullam in **1 Chronicles 9:11** and **Nehemiah 11:11** (and possibly **Nehemiah 12:33**). Shallum/Meshullam appears to be the same person called Sallumus by Josephus (*Jewish Antiquities* 10.8.6). See Shallum (#21) in chart "**Supplement 2**: The High Priests of Israel."

4. Hilkiah was the high priest during the reign of King Josiah of Judah, ca. 640–609 B.C. (**2 Kings 22:4**; **2 Chronicles 34:9, 14**). See the lineage of the high priests given in **1 Chronicles 6:1–15; 9:11**; and **Ezra 7:1–5** as well as the chart "**Supplement 2**: The High Priests of Israel."

5. Shaphan is in a scribal lineage and in the same larger kinship group as the high priests (cf. **1 Chronicles 6:1–15**). Hilkiah the high priest appears to be Shaphan's uncle.

6. Gemariah is called the "son of Hilkiah" in **Jeremiah 29:3,** but it is unclear if Gemariah is: (1) the son of Hilkiah the high priest (as shown in the chart) or possibly (2) the son of Hilkiah the palace administrator under King Hezekiah, who served from 715–686 B.C. (see chart "**2 Kings 18**: Eliakim the Palace Administrator who Replaced Shebna the Scribal Secretary During the Reign of King Hezekiah of Judah").

7. Ahikam was an official in the days of Josiah (**2 Kings 22:12, 14; 2 Chronicles 34:20**) and Jehoiakim of Judah (the son of Josiah; **Jeremiah 26:24**). Anikam supported Jeremiah the prophet of the Lord and persuaded the priests and false prophets not to kill him (**Jeremiah 26:1–24**).

8. Jaazaniah is mentioned in **Ezekiel 8:11**.

9. Gemariah the son of Shaphan is mentioned in **Jeremiah 36:10–12, 25**.

10. For clarification of the Seraiah figures (#1 and #2) in the priestly-scribal lineage, see chart "**Ezra 7**: Ezra, the Priestly Scribe and Teacher of the Law (Post-Exile)."

11. Gedaliah was appointed by Nebuchadnezzar to be governor over the remnant of people who remained in the land of Judah during the Babylonian exile (**2 Kings 25:22**). When Jeremiah the prophet was set free at Riblah, he chose to live at Mizpah with Gedaliah rather than go to Babylon (**Jeremiah 40:6**; see also **Jeremiah 39:14; 40:9, 11, 16; 41:1; 43:6**). For more information, see chart "**2 Kings 25**: Gedaliah, Governor over the Remnant People of Judah During the Early Days of the Exile."

12. Micaiah son of Gemariah (**2 Kings 22:12**; **Jeremiah 36:11**) is the same person as Micah the father of Abdon (**2 Chronicles 34:20**).

13. Akbor son of Micaiah (**2 Kings 22:12, 14; see also Jeremiah 26:22; 36:12**) is the same person as Abdon son of Micah (**2 Chronicles 34:20**). An error in copying could easily have taken place between עכבור (Akbor) and עבדון (Abdon).

14. For the genealogy of Ezra, see chart "**Ezra 7**: Ezra, the Priestly Scribe and Teacher of the Law (Post-Exile)."

15. Elnathan is mentioned in **Jeremiah 26:22** as the attendant to King

Jehoiakim, whom the king had sent to Egypt to bring the prophet Uriah back for punishment; upon their return to Jerusalem, Uriah was killed. Elnathan tried to prevent King Jehoiakim from burning Baruch's scroll of Jeremiah's preaching (**Jeremiah 36:12–26**). This Elnathan is probably one of the three "Elnathans" mentioned in **Ezra 8:16**.

16. See chart "**2 Kings 22**: Huldah the Prophet."

17. The guideline for each king was as follows: "When he takes the throne of his kingdom, he is to write for himself on a scroll a copy of this law, taken from that of the Levitical priests [the authorized scroll]. It is to be with him, and he is to read it all the days of his life so that he may learn to revere the Lord his God and follow carefully all the words of this law and these decrees and not consider himself better than his fellow Israelites and turn from the law to the right or to the left" (**Deuteronomy 17:18–20**). The scroll found in the days of King Josiah was probably the same type of *personal copy* of the scroll—called a "copy of the covenant [the *Testimony* in **Exodus 30:6; Numbers 7:89, 2 Kings 11:12; 2 Chronicles 23:11;** NKJV]" —that was given to each king (e.g., as in the case of King Joash, when, at age seven, he was crowned king of Judah; **2 Kings 11:12; 2 Chronicles 23:11**).

2 KINGS 23: JEHOAHAZ (SHALLUM), KING OF JUDAH

Approximate Dating: ca. 609 B.C. ***Relevant Scriptures:*** **2 Kings 23:30–34; 24:8; 1 Chronicles 3:15; 2 Chronicles 36:1–4; Jeremiah 13:18**

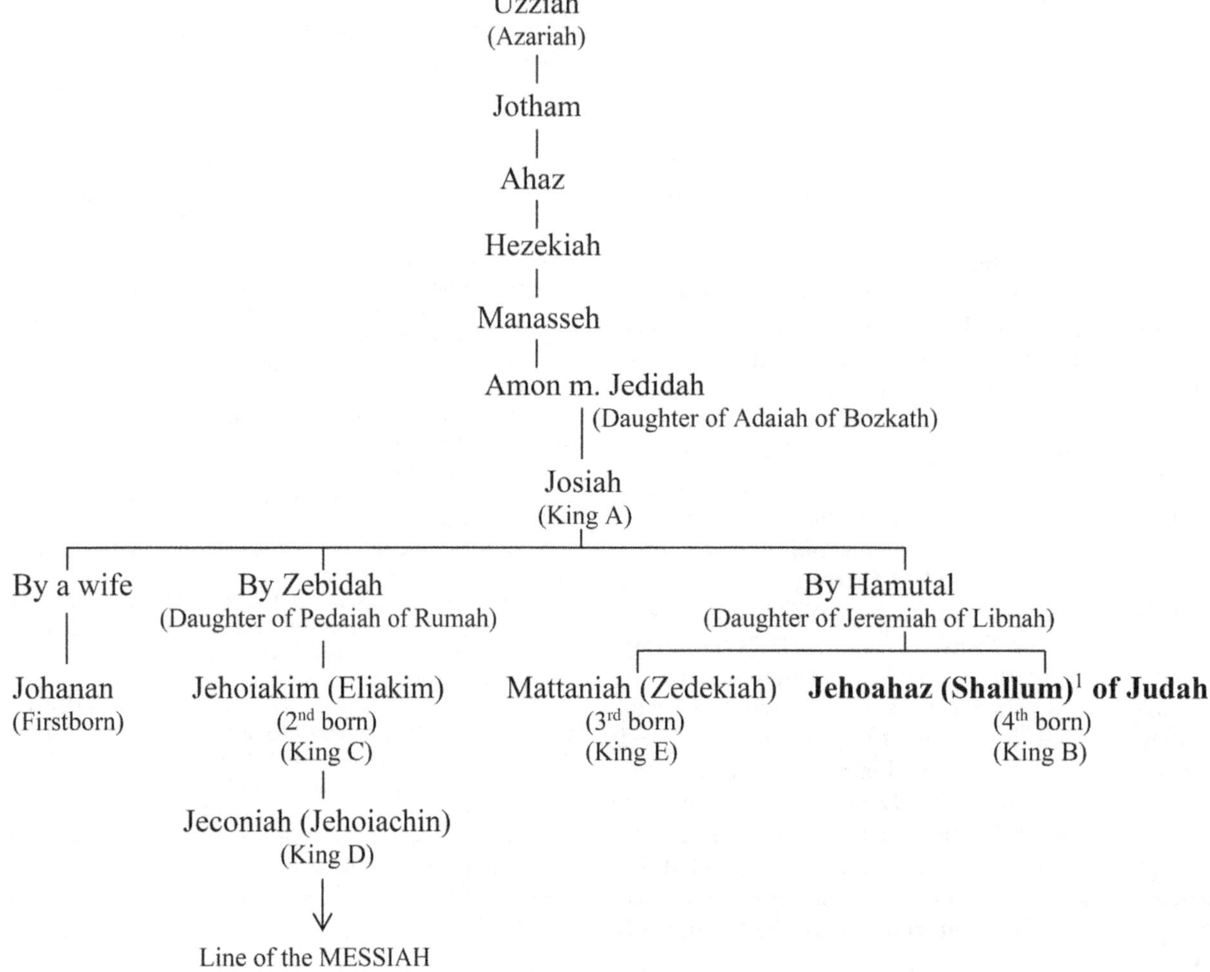

Biblical and Theological Significance

After the tragic death of Josiah in 609 B.C., the people of Judah chose Jehoahaz, Josiah's youngest son, as the successor to the throne of Judah (Jehoahaz was his throne name and Shallum was his personal name). He was twenty-three years old when he became king and retained the crown for a brief three months in 609 B.C. (**2 Kings 23:31; 2 Chronicles 36:2**).

Jeremiah notes the profligacy of Jehoahaz, who took his kingship as an opportunity to display his wealth—embellishing the king's palace "by unrighteousness," making his upper rooms "by injustice [and] making his own people work for nothing, not paying them for their labor" (**Jeremiah 22:13-14**), and enclosing himself with elaborate cedar paneling and vermillion paint. The prophet Jeremiah upbraided him by declaring, "Your eyes and your heart are set only on dishonest gain, on shedding innocent blood and on oppression and extortion" (**Jeremiah 22:17**). Jeremiah prophesied that "Shallum [Jehoahaz] son of Josiah, who succeeded his father as king of Judah . . . has gone from this place: 'He will never return. He will die in the place where they have led him captive [Egypt]; he will not see this land [Judah] again'" (**Jeremiah 22:11–12**).

Jehoahaz was captured and deposed by Pharaoh Necho II of Egypt, initially being imprisoned at Riblah (the military headquarters for the Egyptians in central Syria, between Damascus and Hamath), and then exiled to Egypt, where he died (**2 Kings 23:33–34**). When Judah became a vassal under the Egyptians, the Pharaoh imposed a tribute tax of one hundred talents of silver and one talent of gold on Judah and appointed Jehoahaz's older (half-) brother, Eliakim/Jehoiakim, king in his place (**2 Kings 23:34–35; 2 Chronicles 36:3–4**).

Notes

1. He is called Jehoahaz in **2 Kings 23:30–31, 34;** and **2 Chronicles 36:1–2, 4** and called Shallum in **1 Chronicles 3:15** and **Jeremiah 22:11**.

2 KINGS 23: ELIAKIM (JEHOIAKIM), KING OF JUDAH

Approximate Dating: ca. 609–598 B.C. ***Relevant Scriptures:*** **2 Kings 23:34–37; 24:8, 18; 1 Chronicles 3:12–16; 2 Chronicles 36:4–8; Jeremiah 1:3; 12:18, 24; 24:1; 25:1; 26:1; 27:1,[1] 20; 28:4; 35:1; 36:1, 9, 26; 37:1; 45:1; 46:2; 52:1**

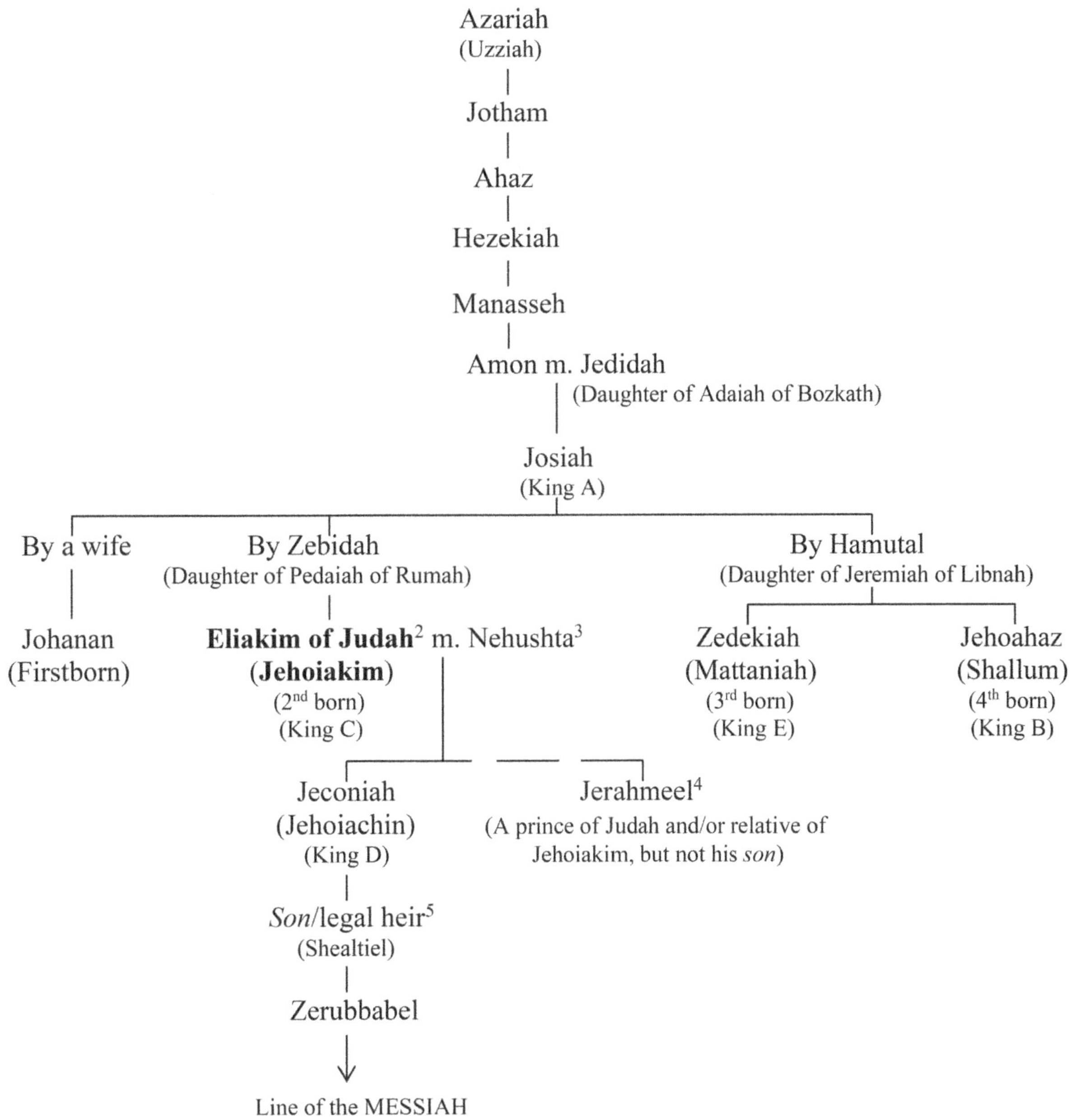

Biblical and Theological Significance

After Jehoahaz's banishment to Egypt, Pharaoh Necho II appointed Jehoahaz's half-brother Eliakim as king of Judah and changed his name to Jehoiakim.[6] He was twenty-five years old when he came to the throne and reigned for eleven years (ca. 609–598 B.C.). Eliakim/Jehoiakim is described as one who "did evil" and "detestable things" (**2 Chronicles 36:5, 8;** see also **2 Kings 23:36–37**). During the first three years, Judah was a vassal of the Egyptians, and Jehoiakim heavily taxed the people to raise the demanded tribute. Following the Babylonian defeat of the Egyptians at Carchemish in 605 B.C., Judah became a vassal of Babylon.[7, 8] After three years of vassalship, 605–602 B.C. (**2 Kings 24:1**), Jehoiakim rebelled, eliciting the Lord's punishment (**2 Kings 24:2**). Among his evil deeds, Jehoiakim was responsible for the death of the innocent prophet Uriah, the son of Shemaiah (**Jeremiah 26:20–23**). Finally, when Jeremiah spoke of the Lord's impending judgment and exile of Judah, Jehoiakim burned the first scroll of Jeremiah, and during his rulership, the prophet's life was in danger, although the Lord protected Jeremiah (**Jeremiah 36**; cf. **26:11, 15–16, 24**).

Nebuchadnezzar eventually deposed Jehoiakim, "bound him with bronze shackles" as a trophy of war, and carried him to Babylon, where he died (**2 Chronicles 36:6**; cf. **Jeremiah 22:18–27**). Jeremiah foretold that Eliakim/Jehoiakim would "have no one to sit on the throne of David" (**Jeremiah 36:29–31; 22:30**). The events in Jehoiakim's reign were recorded in the book of the annals of the kings of Judah and the book of the kings of Judah and Israel (**2 Kings 24:5; 2 Chronicles 36:8**). Upon his death, his son Jeconiah (Jehoiachin) came to the throne for a brief three months (**2 Kings 24:6, 8; 2 Chronicles 36:8–9**).

Notes

1. **Jeremiah 27:1** (NIV) says "Early in the reign of Zedekiah son of Josiah king of Judah, this word came to Jeremiah from the LORD"—while a few Hebrew manuscripts have *Zedekiah*, most of the Hebrew manuscripts say *Jehoiakim*. The NASB and the ESV both say *Zedekiah*, while the NKJV says *Jehoiakim*.

2. Eliakim in **2 Kings 23:34** and **2 Chronicles 36:4** is called Jehoiakim in **2 Kings 23:34–36; 24:1–6, 19; 1 Chronicles 3:15–16; 2 Chronicles 36:4–5; Jeremiah 1:3; 22:18, 24; 24:1; 25:1; 26:1, 21–23; 27:20; 28:4; 35:1; 36:1, 9, 28–30, 32; 37:1; 45:1; 46:2; 52:2;** and **Daniel 1:1**. Eliakim means "My God establishes" or "will establish"; Jehoiakim means "Yahweh establishes." The latter name is precisely that of the covenant God, whereas the former speaks of God more generically.

3. Nehushta, the queen mother, was taken into Babylonian captivity and died there (**2 Kings 24:15**; **Jeremiah 22:26**).

4. In **Jeremiah 36:26** (cf. **36:1**), Jerahmeel is called a "son of the king," but more likely he was a royal *relative*; for an explanation, see chart "**Jeremiah 36**: Men Sent by King Jehoiakim (Eliakim) to Seize Baruch and Jeremiah (Pre-Exile)."

5. For the son/legal heir Shealtiel, See chart "**1 Chronicles 3**: Zerubbabel and Shealtiel and the Double Line of the Messiah through King David's Sons, Nathan and Solomon."

6. Nebuchadnezzar changed the name of Mattaniah (the half-brother of Jehoiakim) to Zedekiah (**2 Kings 24:17**), another Yahwistic name. The reading of **2 Kings 23:34a** is confusing—"Pharaoh Necho made Eliakim son of Josiah king *in place of his father Josiah*"; although, the parallel in **2 Chronicles 36:4a** clearly states, "The king of Egypt made Eliakim, a [half-] brother of Jehoahaz, king over Judah and Jerusalem and changed Eliakim's name to Jehoiakim." It should be understood that Eliakim/Jehoiakim succeeded *his half-brother* Jehoahaz/Shallum as king (not his father Josiah; cf. **2 Kings 23:30, 36; 2 Chronicles 36:1, 4**). The succession of kings is as follows: Josiah–Jehoahaz (Shallum)–Eliakim (Jehoiakim)–Jeconiah (Jehoiachin)–Zedekiah (Mattaniah).

7. Jeremiah equates "the fourth year of Jehoiakim . . . [with] the first year of Nebuchadnezzar king of Babylon" (i.e., 605 B.C.; **Jeremiah 25:1; 46:2**; cf. **Daniel 1:1**).

8. For the details of the three successive invasions and deportations of Judah to Babylon (605, 597, 586 B.C.), see the section on Nebuchadnezzar in chart "**Supplement 4**: The Kings of Babylon."

2 KINGS 24: JEHOIACHIN (JECONIAH), KING OF JUDAH[1]

Approximate Dating: ca. 598–597 B.C. ***Relevant Scriptures:*** **2 Kings 24:6, 8–17; 1 Chronicles 3:16–24; 2 Chronicles 36:8–10; Esther 2:6; Jeremiah 13:18; 22:24–30; 24:1; 27:20; 28:4; 29:2; 52:31–34; Ezekiel 1:2; Matthew 1:11–12**

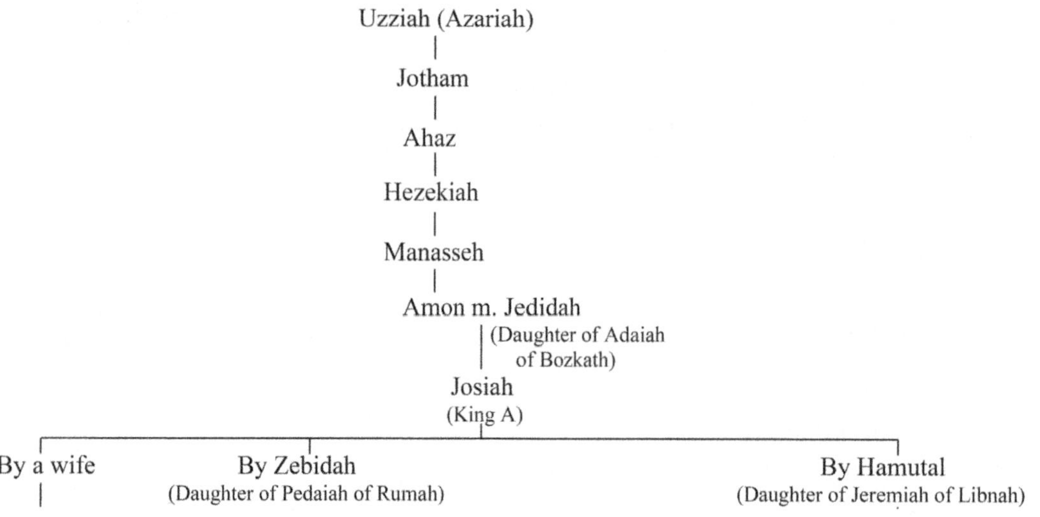

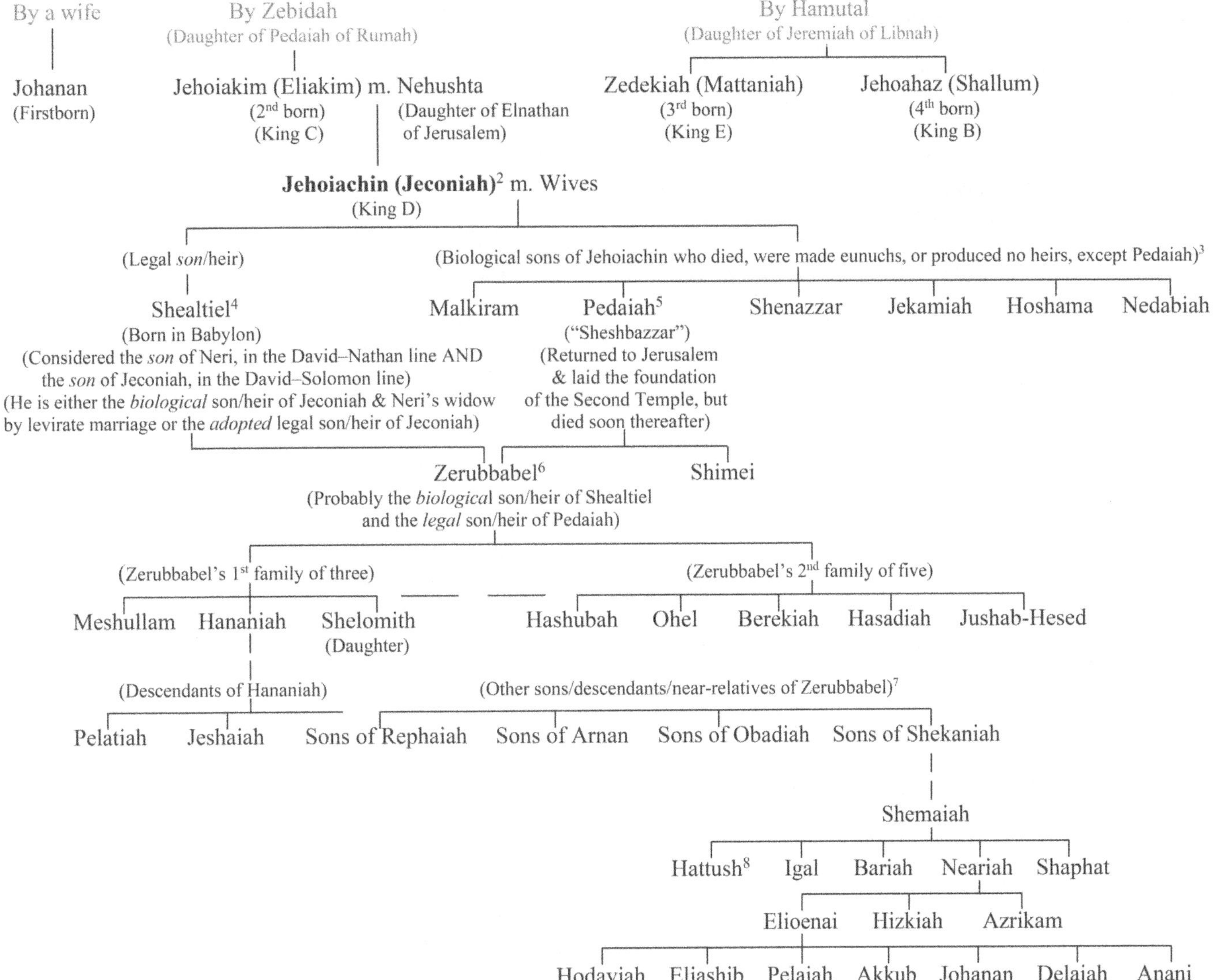

Biblical and Theological Significance

Jehoiachin (or Jeconiah) became king at age eighteen and reigned for only three months (ca. December 598 B.C.–March 597 B.C.; **2 Kings 24:8; 2 Chronicles 36:9**). Jeconiah followed his father, Jehoiakim (Eliakim), in doing evil (**2 Kings 24:9; 2 Chronicles 36:9**). In Nebuchadnezzar's first invasion of Jerusalem in 605 B.C., some of the royal family and youth of noble descent were deported,[9] thus fulfilling Isaiah's prophecy against the nation (**2 Kings 20:16–18, Isaiah 39:5–7**; cf. **Jeremiah 15:1–9**). Nebuchadnezzar's second invasion (598/597 B.C.) occurred during Jehoiachin's reign (**2 Kings 24:10–14**); a third in 587 B.C. took place during Zedekiah's tenure (**2 Kings 25:1–24**), resulting in Jerusalem's final destruction in 586 B.C. (**2 Kings 25:8–11**). In Nebuchadnezzar's second invasion, both Judeans (and Benjamites[10]) were taken captive and deported to Babylon, including King Jeconiah/Jehoiachin, the queen mother Nehushta, his wives, attendants, and nobles (presumably princes/sons of Jehoiachin), officials, warriors, skilled workers, artisans, and prominent people of the land (**2 Kings 24:10–16; Jeremiah 24:1; 29:2**). Only the peasantry remained in the homeland (**2 Kings 24:13–14; 25:12**).

However, in the thirty-seventh year of his captivity (ca. 561 B.C.), when he was about fifty-five, Jehoiachin was released from prison by Nebuchadnezzar's son/successor, Awel-Marduk.[11] Jehoiachin was placed in a seat of honor more prominent than other captive kings, and for the rest of his life, he dined with the king of Babylon and received a regular allowance (**2 Kings 25:27–30; Jeremiah 52:31–34**). King Jehoiachin and Nehushta died in exile (**Jeremiah 22:26–27**).

To address the "childless" state of King Jehoiachin, Jeremiah prophesied that none of his immediate sons/descendants would prosper and that none would ever sit on the throne of David in Jerusalem (**Jeremiah 22:24–30**). Careful analysis of the genealogy shows that Jehoiachin had six sons/princes, who either died during Jerusalem's destruction, died in captivity, were made eunuchs, or left no heirs (**1 Chronicles 3:16–18; Matthew 1:12; Luke 3:27**; cf. **2 Kings 20:16–18**), with the possible exception of Pedaiah.[12] Notwithstanding the "childless" state of King Jeconiah, the genealogy of Jesus Christ given by the gospel writers Matthew and Luke (**Matthew 1:1–16**; **Luke 3:23–38**) clearly show that King Jehoiachin did have a (biological or legal) *heir* in the person of Shealtiel. Shealtiel, who was born in

Babylonian exile, is identified as Jehoiachin's immediate *son/heir* in the David–Solomon line (**Matthew 1:12**) and also as the *son/heir* of Neri in the David–Nathan line (**Luke 3:27**).

To explain Shealtiel's presence in both the kingly line of Solomon (Matthew) and the non-kingly line of Nathan (Luke), two explanations are offered:

- One, Neri (in the Solomon–Nathan line) died during the destruction of Jerusalem or in captivity, and while in captivity, Jehoiachin (his distant near relative) entered into levirate marriage with Neri's widow and raised up a biological son, Shealtiel (cf. **Luke 3:27–31**). Thus, Shealtiel was the *biological* son of King Jehoiachin but still considered the *legal* son of Neri; OR
- Two, Neri died during the destruction of Jerusalem or in captivity, and Jehoiachin, having no living sons/heirs, adopted Shealtiel in order to secure a legal heir for himself. In this scenario Shealtiel was the *biological* son of Neri but the legally adopted *son/heir* of Jehoiachin.

In either scenario, Jehoiachin secured an heir in Shealtiel, and Shealtiel, in turn, secured a son/heir in Zerubbabel (**Ezra 3:2; 5:2; Nehemiah 12:1; Haggai 1:1, 12, 14; 2:2, 23; Matthew 1:12**). Together, Shealtiel and Zerubbabel became the key exilic and immediate post-exilic ancestors of the Messiah, carrying on both the David–Solomon and David–Nathan lines.[13] In essence, the former monarchy of Judah ended at the time of the exile, after the reigns of the "childless king" Jehoiachin/Jeconiah (**Jeremiah 23:30**) and his successor, Zedekiah/Mattaniah.[14] From that point onward, it was the biological and legal descendants of Zerubbabel who continued the Davidic line, ultimately leading to the birth of the Messiah/the messianic king (**Isaiah 11:1–2; 42:1; Haggai 2:23 Zechariah 9:9**).

Notes

1. Compare this chart with the more expanded version of King Jehoiachin's heirs in chart "**1 Chronicles 3**: Zerubbabel and Shealtiel and the Double Line of the Messiah through King David's Sons, Nathan and Solomon."

2. The lineage of King Jeconiah/Jehoiachin as a *son* of Jehoiakim is based on **1 Chronicles 3:16**; **Jeremiah 22:24, 28**; and **37:1**. Thus, **Matthew 1:11**, which reads "Josiah the *father* of Jeconiah" should read "Josiah the *grandfather* of Jeconiah."

3. Cuneiform tablets unearthed from the royal archives of Nebuchadnezzar in Babylon, found by the German archaeologist Robert Koldewey in 1899–1917, record the disbursal of rations from the royal storehouses. Among them is the "Jehoiachin Ration Tablet," which mentions rations of oil that were given to the captive King Jehoiachin of Judah—Ya'u-kīnu, king of the land of Yahudu—and five of his (unnamed) sons; "Babylonian Ration List: King Jehoiakhin in Exile, 592–1 B.C.E" in the *Center for Online Judaic Studies* (COJS), http://cojs.org/babylonian_ration_list-_king_jehoiakhin_in_exile-_592-1_bce/. Also see the article by Rachael Grellet, "A Tablet, a King and His Rations: How a Tablet of an Enslaved King's Rations Sheds Light on Biblical Accuracy," the Armstrong Institute of Biblical Archaeology, September 20, 2018, https://armstronginstitute.org/117-a-tablet-a-king-and-his-rations, which describes the amount of the rations.

4. See note 16 in chart "**1 Chronicles 3**: Zerubbabel and Shealtiel and the Double Line of the Messiah through King David's Sons, Nathan and Solomon."

5. See note 18 in chart "**1 Chronicles 3**: Zerubbabel and Shealtiel and the Double Line of the Messiah through King David's Sons, Nathan and Solomon."

6. The Chronicler emphasizes that Zerubbabel had two families–one set of offspring was Meshullam, Hananiah, and Shelomith (a daughter), and the other set (probably by another wife/concubine or by levirate marriage) was Hashubah, Ohel, Berekiah, Hasadiah, and Jushab-Hesed. For more information about Zerubbabel, see note 20 in chart "**1 Chronicles 3**: Zerubbabel and Shealtiel and the Double Line of the Messiah through King David's Sons, Nathan and Solomon."

7. See notes 27–30 in chart "**1 Chronicles 3**: Zerubbabel and Shealtiel and the Double Line of the Messiah through King David's Sons, Nathan and Solomon."

8. This is probably the same Hattush "of the descendants of David" who was the head of his father's house and returned to Jerusalem with Ezra in ca. 458 B.C. (**Ezra 8:2**).

9. Daniel and his friends were among those deported (**Daniel 1:1–7**); see chart "**Daniel 1**: Daniel and His Comrades."

10. Among these were the ancestor(s) of Mordecai and Esther (**Esther 2:6**); see chart "**Esther 2**: Mordecai and Esther, Jews Living in Persia."

11. Awel-Marduk is known as Evil-Merodach in some translations; for his lineage, see chart "**Supplement 4**: The Kings of Babylon."

12. Jeremiah prophesied that Jehoiachin/Jeconiah would be recorded "as if childless" because none of his offspring would prosper, nor would they retain the Davidic throne— " 'As surely as I live,' declares the Lord, 'even if you, Jehoiachin son of Jehoiakim king of Judah, were a signet ring on my right hand, I would still pull you off. I will deliver you into the hands of those who want to kill you, those you fear—Nebuchadnezzar king of Babylon and the Babylonians. I will hurl you and the mother who gave you birth [Nehushta] into another country, where neither of you was born, and there you both will die. You will never come back to the land you long to return to. . . . Record this man as if childless . . . for none of his offspring will prosper, none will sit on the throne of David or rule anymore in Judah' " (**Jeremiah 22:24–30**). As Albert Barnes explains, "God does not say by Jeremiah, that Jeconiah [Jehoiachin] should have no children, but that he should in his lifetime be childless, as it is said of those married to the uncle's or brother's widow (**Leviticus 20:20–21**), "they shall die childless." Jeremiah rather implies that he should have children, but that they should die untimely before him" (Albert Barnes, *Albert Barnes' Notes on the Old Testament* for **Haggai 1:1**, accessed through Accordance 13 Bible Software). Of the six sons of King Jeconiah—see notes 14 and 15 in chart "**1 Chronicles 3**: Zerubbabel and Shealtiel and the Double Line of the Messiah through King David's Sons, Nathan and Solomon"—only his son Pedaiah seems to have lived through the exile. Pedaiah is very likely the same person as Sheshbazzar, who is called "the prince of Judah" in **Ezra 1:8**. In 538 B.C., when King Cyrus of Persia made a decree allowing the Jews of the Babylonian exile to return to their homeland, he gave Sheshbazzar 5,400 precious gold and silver objects (**Ezra 1:11**), which were originally taken from Solomon's Temple by Nebuchadnezzar of Babylon, so that worship could be resumed when the temple was completed in Jerusalem (**Ezra 5:13–15**). Sheshbazzar returned to post-exilic Jerusalem, perhaps in early 538 B.C.; notice that Sheshbazzar is *not* listed among those who returned with Zerubbabel and Joshua in **Ezra 2**. Apparently, Sheshbazzar returned to Jerusalem *before* the first group of exiles returned with Zerubbabel and Joshua in (late?) 538 B.C. Cyrus appointed Sheshbazzar to be the first governor of Yehud and commissioned him to supervise the rebuilding of the Second Temple on the Solomonic foundations that had been leveled a half-century earlier by the Babylonians. Sheshbazzar was successful in laying the foundations of the house of God (**Ezra 5:16**), but sometime before 536 B.C., Sheshbazzar (Pedaiah) died: "From that day [538–536 B.C.] to the present [520 B.C.] it [the foundation] has been under construction but is not yet finished" (**Ezra 5:16**). Due to opposition from "enemies of Judah and Benjamin" (**Ezra 4:1**), work on the temple ceased for sixteen years, from 536–520 B.C. (i.e., work that had begun during Cyrus's reign was not renewed until the reign of Darius; see the succession of Persian rulers in chart "**Supplement 5**: The Kings of Persia"). In 520 B.C., Zerubbabel (Sheshbazzar's/Pedaiah's *son/heir*; **1 Chronicles 3:19**) and Joshua the high priest resumed the building of the temple (**Haggai 2:2, 21**; cf. **Ezra 3:2, 9, 4:3; 5:2; Nehemiah 12:1; Haggai 1:1, 12; Zechariah 4:9**). For more information of the identity of Sheshbazzar, see chart "**Ezra 1**: Sheshbazzar and Zerubbabel, the Governors over the Restored Community in Jerusalem (Post-Exile)."

13. For more details, see charts "**1 Chronicles 3**: Zerubbabel and Shealtiel and the Double Line of the Messiah through King David's Sons, Nathan and Solomon" and "**Matthew 1**: Ancestry of Mary and Joseph (Based on Scripture and Church Tradition) and How Mary and Joseph May Have Been Related."

14. Zedekiah/Mattaniah, Jehoiachin's half-uncle and successor, was the last king to sit on the Davidic throne. Zedekiah ruled for eleven years, ca. 597–586 B.C. See chart "**2 Kings 24**: Zedekiah (Mattaniah), King of Judah."

2 KINGS 24: ZEDEKIAH (MATTANIAH), KING OF JUDAH

Approximate Dating: ca. 597–586 B.C. ***Relevant Scriptures:*** **2 Kings 24:17–25:7; 1 Chronicles 3:15–16; 2 Chronicles 36:10–13; Jeremiah 1:3; 21:1, 3, 7; 24:8; 27:3, 12; 28:1; 29:3; 32:1; 32:1, 3–4; 34:2, 4, 6, 8, 21; 37:1, 3, 17–18, 21; 38:5, 14–17, 19, 24; 39:1–2, 4–7; 41:10; 44:30; 49:34; 51:59; 52:1, 3, 5, 8–11; Ezekiel 12:12–13; 17:12, 21**

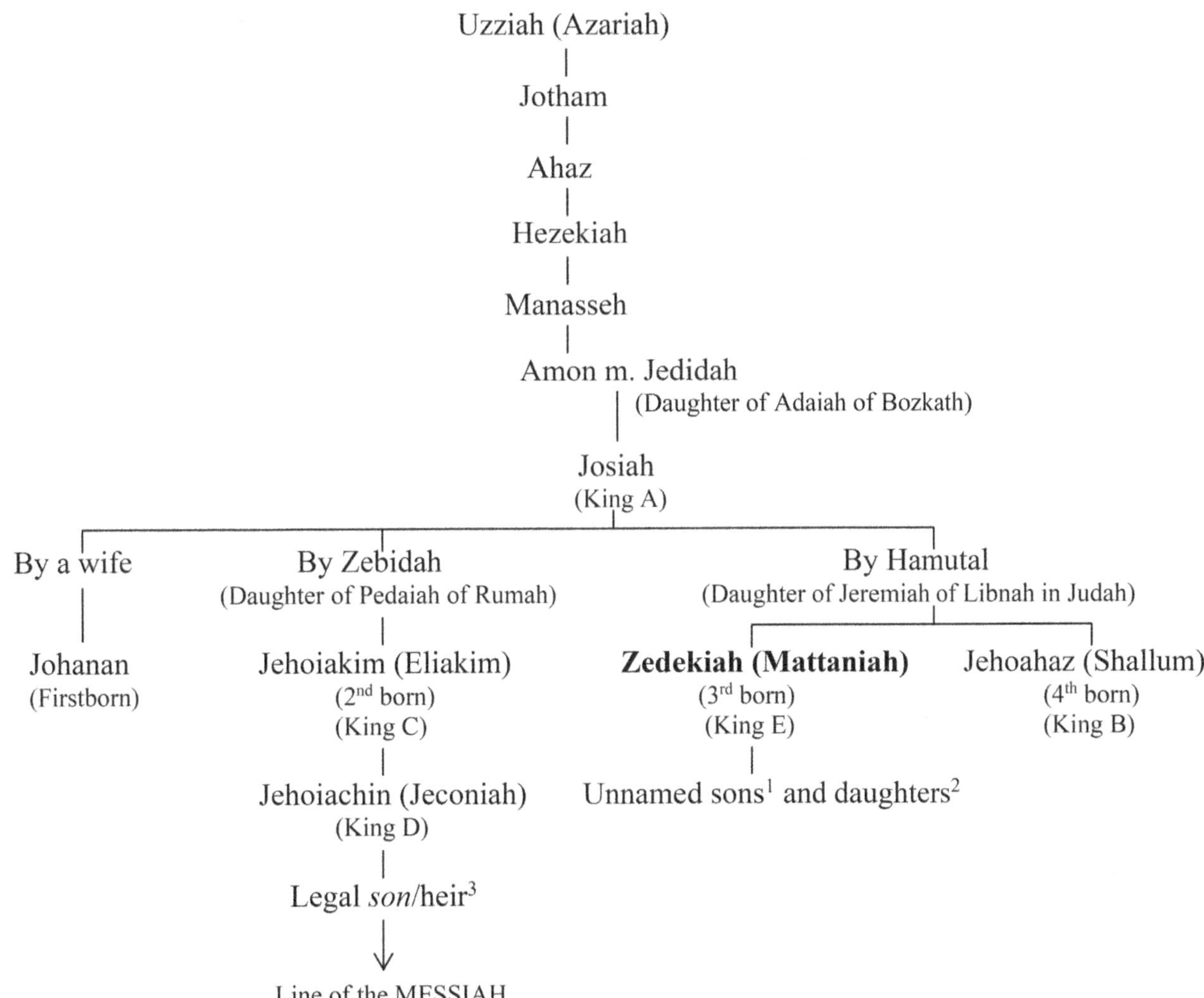

Biblical and Theological Significance

In 598–597 B.C., King Nebuchadnezzar took Jerusalem from Jehoiachin/Jeconiah and made Judah a vassal of Babylon. In March 597 B.C., Nebuchadnezzar dethroned King Jehoiachin/Jeconiah and put Mattaniah (Jehoiachin's half-uncle) on the throne in his place. Nebuchadnezzar then changed Mattaniah's name to Zedekiah and forced him and his offspring to swear an oath of allegiance to Babylon (**2 Kings 24:17; 2 Chronicles 36:13; Ezekiel 17:13**). Zedekiah was twenty-one when he became king and he reigned for eleven years in Jerusalem (ca. 597–586 B.C.); like the previous kings of Judah, he "did evil in the eyes of the Lord" (**2 Kings 24:18–19; 2 Chronicles 36:11–12**). Zedekiah's wickedness, along with the wickedness of the other kings of Judah (especially Manasseh, cf. **2 Kings 21:10–15**) was responsible for God's judgment on Jerusalem, the final downfall of Judah, and the resulting seventy years in Babylonian captivity (**2 Chronicles 36:12–14; Jeremiah 38:17–23; Ezekiel 12:1–2, 8–28; 17:11–21**).

At one point, Zedekiah rebelled against Babylonian suzerainty by asking Egypt for help. Pharaoh's army came to Judah's assistance but then returned (unsuccessfully?) to Egypt (cf. **2 Kings 24:20; 2 Chronicles 36:13; Jeremiah 37:3–7; Ezekiel 17:11–15**). In the ninth year of Zedekiah's reign[4] (588 B.C.), Nebuchadnezzar made a third and final invasion of Judah and besieged Jerusalem for the next one-and-a-half years (cf. **2 Kings 24:1, 10; 25:1–3; Jeremiah 39:1; 52:5**). In July 586 B.C., the city walls were penetrated (**2 Kings 25:1–4; Jeremiah 39:2**). Around August 586 B.C., the city of Jerusalem was destroyed completely, including Solomon's Temple, the king's palace, and the houses of the city leaders (**2 Kings 25:8–10**). The Babylonians "carried into exile the people who remained in the city, along with the rest of the populace and those who had deserted to the king of Babylon"; only a few poor people were allowed to remain in Judah as vinedressers and farmers (**2 Kings 25:11–12; Jeremiah 52:15–16**).

As prophesied by Ezekiel, Zedekiah fled Jerusalem, but the Babylonians pursued and captured him (**Ezekiel 12:10–13**). After a brief hearing at Nebuchadnezzar's military headquarters in Riblah, Zedekiah was pronounced guilty. Zedekiah was then forced to witness the execution of his sons before he himself was blinded, bound with bronze shackles, and taken to Babylon (**2 Kings 25:5–7; Jeremiah 39:5–7; 52:8–11**; cf. **Lamentations 2:9; Ezekiel 12:12-13**). He died peacefully in prison in Babylonian captivity; the people made a funeral fire and lamented his death (**Jeremiah 34:4–7; 52:11**). Zedekiah was the last Davidic king of Judah and with his death, the monarchy of Judah came to an end.

Notes

1. King Zedekiah had several wives (cf. **Jeremiah 38:23**). Some of Zedekiah's sons were killed at Riblah (**2 Kings 25:6–7; Jeremiah 39:6; 52:10**; cf. **Ezekiel 12:12–13**) and some were exiled (**Lamentations 2:9**). The identity of "Malkijah, the king's son" (**Jeremiah 38:6**) may refer to another son of Zedekiah or perhaps to a son of Jehoiakim. Given that **Jeremiah 38:6** reads—"So they took Jeremiah and put him into the cistern of Malkijah, the king's son, which was in the courtyard of the guard. They lowered Jeremiah by ropes into the cistern; it had no water in it, only mud, and Jeremiah sank down into the mud"—the cistern refers to: (1) a pit called "The Dungeon of Prince Malkijah," a strange name indeed, or (2) "The Dungeon of the Son of Hammelech." Melech means "king" and Hammelech "the king."

2. The daughters of King Zedekiah are mentioned in **Jeremiah 41:10**.

3. For more information about Jehoiachin's descendants, see chart "**1 Chronicles 3**: Zerubbabel and Shealtiel and the Double Line of the Messiah through King David's Sons, Nathan and Solomon."

4. **Jeremiah 39:1–2** gives the exact dates when the events took place: "in the ninth year of Zedekiah king of Judah [588 B.C.], in the tenth month, Nebuchadnezzar king of Babylon marched against Jerusalem with his whole army and laid siege to it. And on the ninth day of the fourth month of Zedekiah's eleventh year [586 B.C.], the city wall was broken through."

2 KINGS 25: GENEALOGICAL RECORD OF ADVISORS TO KING ZEDEKIAH AND LEADERS OF JUDAH WHO WERE EXECUTED BY THE BABYLONIANS AT RIBLAH

Approximate Dating: ca. 586 B.C. ***Relevant Scriptures:*** **2 Kings 25:18–21; Jeremiah 52:24–27**

1. **Seraiah,** the chief priest (=Seraiah #1)[1]
2. **Zephaniah,** the Kohathite attending priest, next in rank to the chief priest[2]
3. **Three doorkeepers** (presumably Levitical Merarites[3])
4. **The officer in charge of the fighting men**
5. **Five royal advisors**[4]
6. **The chief officer who was in charge of conscripting the people of the land**[5]
7. **Sixty remaining conscripts in the city**

Biblical and Theological Significance

When the final phase of the Babylonian conquest of Judah and Jerusalem concluded in July 586 B.C., certain leading figures of the government and temple were singled out a month later for execution by Nebuzaradan, an officer under King Nebuchadnezzar (**2 Kings 25:18–21**). These government officials included the sons[6] of King Zedekiah (**2 Kings 25:7**); Seraiah the chief priest along with his associate priest, Zephaniah (**2 Kings 25:18**); and members of the king's cabinet ("seven royal advisors"), commanders of Judah's military, and people of the land who were found in the city (**2 Kings 25:19–21; Jeremiah 52:24–25**). The policies were standard procedures under both the Assyrian and Babylonian regimes.[7] The main reasons were (1) to eliminate the possibility of these leaders regaining power, thus enabling Babylon to become freed of foreign control, and (2) to instill in the vanquished an indelible sense that rebellion would be a costly mistake.

Notes

1. Seraiah, called the "chief priest" (or high priest) (**2 Kings 25:18; Jeremiah 52:24**)—designated Seraiah #1 elsewhere—was the son of Azariah, the son of Hilkiah, the son of Shallum, the son of Zadok (cf. **1 Chronicles 6:12–14; 9:11; Ezra 7:1–5**). He was the father of Jozadak, the high priest who "was deported when the LORD sent Judah and Jerusalem into exile by the hand of Nebuchadnezzar" in 586 B.C. (**1 Chronicles 6:14–15**). Seraiah son of Azariah, was an *ancestor* of Ezra the scribe—possibly Ezra's *grandfather* or his *uncle* (**Ezra 7:1–5**). Ezra led a group of returning exiles back to Jerusalem in 458 B.C. (**Ezra 7:11–8:36**). For the ancestry and descendants of Seraiah/Seraiah #1, see chart "**Ezra 7**: Ezra, the Priestly Scribe and Teacher of the Law (Post-Exile)." Seraiah/Seraiah #1 corresponds to the high priest Seraiah #24 in chart "**Supplement 2**: The High Priests of Israel."

2. Zephaniah's exact ancestry is not given, but he was probably an Kohathite attending priest (i.e., a descendant of Kohath) but not a scribe. For the lineage of Kohathite attending priests, see chart "**1 Chronicles 6**: Levi: High Priests, Priests, Levites, and Musicians in Solomon's Temple."

3. Doorkeepers were Levites in the Levi–Merarite line (e.g., "**2 Samuel 6**: Obed-Edom, the Levitical Gatekeeper and Keeper of the Ark").

4. **Jeremiah 52:25** reads "seven" royal advisors. Textual evidence is inadequate to resolve the discrepancy.

5. The sixty came from among "the people of the land" (עַם הָאָרֶץ, *am haarets*), a term found throughout the Bible to speak of the ordinary citizenry. They were the draftees as opposed to the standing army, whose degree of eligibility and other matters must be noted by the scribe.

6. This action was taken to ensure that the royal family could no longer compete with Babylon for leadership of the nation.

7. For examples, see Bill T. Arnold and Bryan E. Beyer, *Readings from the Ancient Near East* (Grand Rapids: Baker Academic, 2005), 140–41.

2 KINGS 25: GEDALIAH, GOVERNOR OVER THE REMNANT PEOPLE OF JUDAH DURING THE EARLY DAYS OF THE EXILE

Approximate Dating: ca. 586 B.C. ***Relevant Scriptures:*** **2 Kings 25:22–25;** also **2 Kings 22:3, 12; 1 Chronicles 6:1–15; 9:11; 2 Chronicles 34:8, 20; Nehemiah 11:11; Jeremiah 29:3; 36:10–13; 40:5–41:18; 43:6; Ezekiel 8:11**

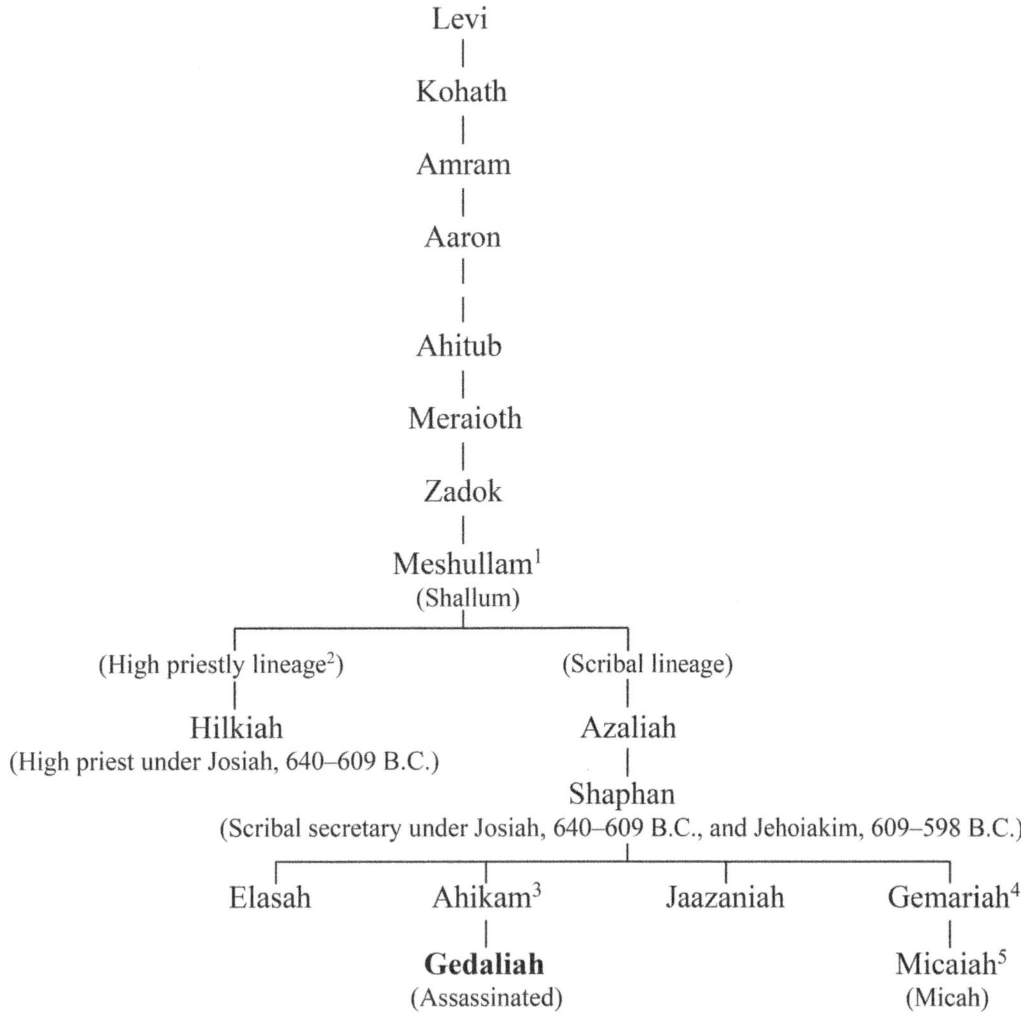

Biblical and Theological Significance

Gedaliah's Ancestry and Relatives

Gedaliah was the grandson of Shaphan[6]—the illustrious scribal secretary under Josiah (640–609 B.C.; cf. **2 Kings 22:10; 2 Chronicles 34:15, 18, 20**)—and the son of Ahikam,[7] the scribe who was a contemporary of King Jehoiakim/Eliakim (609–598 B.C.; **Jeremiah 26**). Thus, Gedaliah is in a scribal lineage that parallels that of the high priests' lineage.

Gedaliah was an avid supporter of the prophet Jeremiah, protecting him from being executed and providing him lodging after his release from prison (**Jeremiah 39:11–14; 40:1–6; 43:6**). Gedaliah's uncles, Elasah and Gemariah,[8] were commissioned to convey Jeremiah's letter to the exiled community in Babylon (**Jeremiah 29:1–3**). Gemariah had scribal chambers in the upper courtyard at the New Gate where Baruch read the scroll of Jeremiah to King Jehoiakim (**Jeremiah 36:10–12**). A wicked uncle of Gedaliah named Jaazaniah presided over the blasphemous elders who paganized the temple in the late pre-exilic period, thereby arousing the Lord's anger and contributing to the final destruction of Jerusalem and the Temple by the Babylonians (**Ezekiel 8:6–13**).[9]

Gedaliah as Governor over Jerusalem

After the fall of Jerusalem in 586 B.C., most citizens were taken into captivity, but Nebuchadnezzar appointed Gedaliah as governor over the poor in the land who remained (**2 Kings 25:22**). Gedaliah oversaw the region from a temporary "capital city," Mizpah, located just north of Jerusalem. However, Gedaliah was viewed by an anti-Babylonian rebellious faction of Jews as being sympathetic to Babylon and not committed to re-establishing Judah's independence. After only two months in office, this faction formed a coup, and Ishmael,[10] the son of Nethaniah, the son of Elishama, assassinated Gedaliah, causing the people "from the least to the greatest" to flee to Egypt for fear of the Babylonians (**2 Kings 25:25–26; Jeremiah 41:1–3, 10**). Other insurrectionists were Johanan and Jonathan, the sons of Kareah; Seraiah, the son of Tanhumeth the Netophathite; the sons of Ephai the Netophathite; and Jaazaniah the son of a Maakathite[11] (**2 Kings 25:23; Jeremiah 40:8; 42:1**).

Notes

1. Shallum in **1 Chronicles 6:12–13** and **Ezra 7:2** is Meshullam in **1 Chronicles 9:11** and **Nehemiah 11:11**. Shallum/Meshullam appears to be the same person named Sallumus, who is mentioned by Josephus (*Jewish Antiquities* 10.8.6). For Shallum/Meshullam, see chart "**Supplement 2**: The High Priests of Israel."

2. For the lineage of the high priests, see charts "**1 Chronicles 6**: Levi: High Priests, Priests, Levites, and Musicians in Solomon's Temple" and "**Supplement 2**: The High Priests of Israel."

3. See chart "**Jeremiah 26**: Ahikam, the Scribe Who Befriended Jeremiah the Prophet in the Days of King Jehoiakim of Judah."

4. The scribal chamber—called "the room of Gemariah son of Shaphan the secretary" . . . "was in the upper courtyard at the entrance of the New Gate of the temple" (**Jeremiah 36:10**).

5. Micaiah son of Gemariah in **2 Kings 22:12** and **Jeremiah 36:11–13** is called Micah in **2 Chronicles 34:20**. For his lineage, see chart "**Jeremiah 36**: The Officials and Scribes in the Palace of King Jehoiakim Who Heard the Reading of the Scroll of Jeremiah (Pre-Exile)."

6. See chart "**2 Kings 22**: Shaphan, Scribal Secretary under King Josiah and King Jehoiakim of Judah."

7. Ahikam was a supporter of Jeremiah (**Jeremiah 26:24**; see **2 Kings 22:12, 25:22** for other mentions of Ahikam).

8. This Gemariah appears to be the son of Shaphan the scribe and the great nephew of Hilkiah the high priest. Possibly another "Gemariah" (?) is called the "son of Hilkiah" in **Jeremiah 29:3**, but the meaning may be that Gemariah was the *relative* of Hilkiah the high priest through Shaphan (for the possible lineage of two Gemariah figures, see notes 4 and 6 in chart "**Jeremiah 26**: Ahikam, the Scribe Who Befriended Jeremiah the Prophet in the Days of King Jehoiakim of Judah."

9. For Jaazaniah son of Shaphan, see chart "**Ezekiel 8**: Jaazaniah the Scribe Who Served as a Priest to Idol Worshipers in Solomon's Temple in the Days of Ezekiel the Prophet (Pre-Exile)."

10. Ishmael had been one of the king's officers; he was "of royal blood" (**2 Kings 25:25; Jeremiah 41:1**), perhaps a descendant of David's son Elishama (cf. **2 Samuel 5:16; 1 Chronicles 3:8; 14:7**; see chart "**1 Chronicles 3**: David's Children Born in Hebron and Jerusalem") or a descendant of Elishama the prominent Jerahmeelite (see chart "**1 Chronicles 2**: Jerahmeel and His Descendant, Elishama, Who Appears to Be a Compiler of Historical and Genealogical Records in 1 & 2 Chronicles").

11. The insurrectionist Jaazaniah the Maakathite (**2 Kings 25:23; Jeremiah 40:8**) is not Jaazaniah the son of Shaphan (**Ezekiel 8:11**; see note 9), but he may be the same person as "Jezaniah son of Hoshaiah" (**Jeremiah 42:1**; cf. **43:2**).

1 CHRONICLES 1: ADAM'S DESCENDANTS: NATIONS DESCENDED FROM NOAH'S SONS AND THE LINE OF ABRAHAM AND HIS DESCENDANTS

Approximate Dating: primeval history, through the flood/post-flood era to the time of the patriarchs: ca. Abraham, 2166–1991 B.C.;[1] Isaac, ca. 2066–1886 B.C.; Jacob, ca. 2006–1859 B.C.[2] ***Relevant Scriptures:*** **1 Chronicles 1:1–28;** also **Genesis 5:3–32; 10:1–32; Luke 3:34–38**

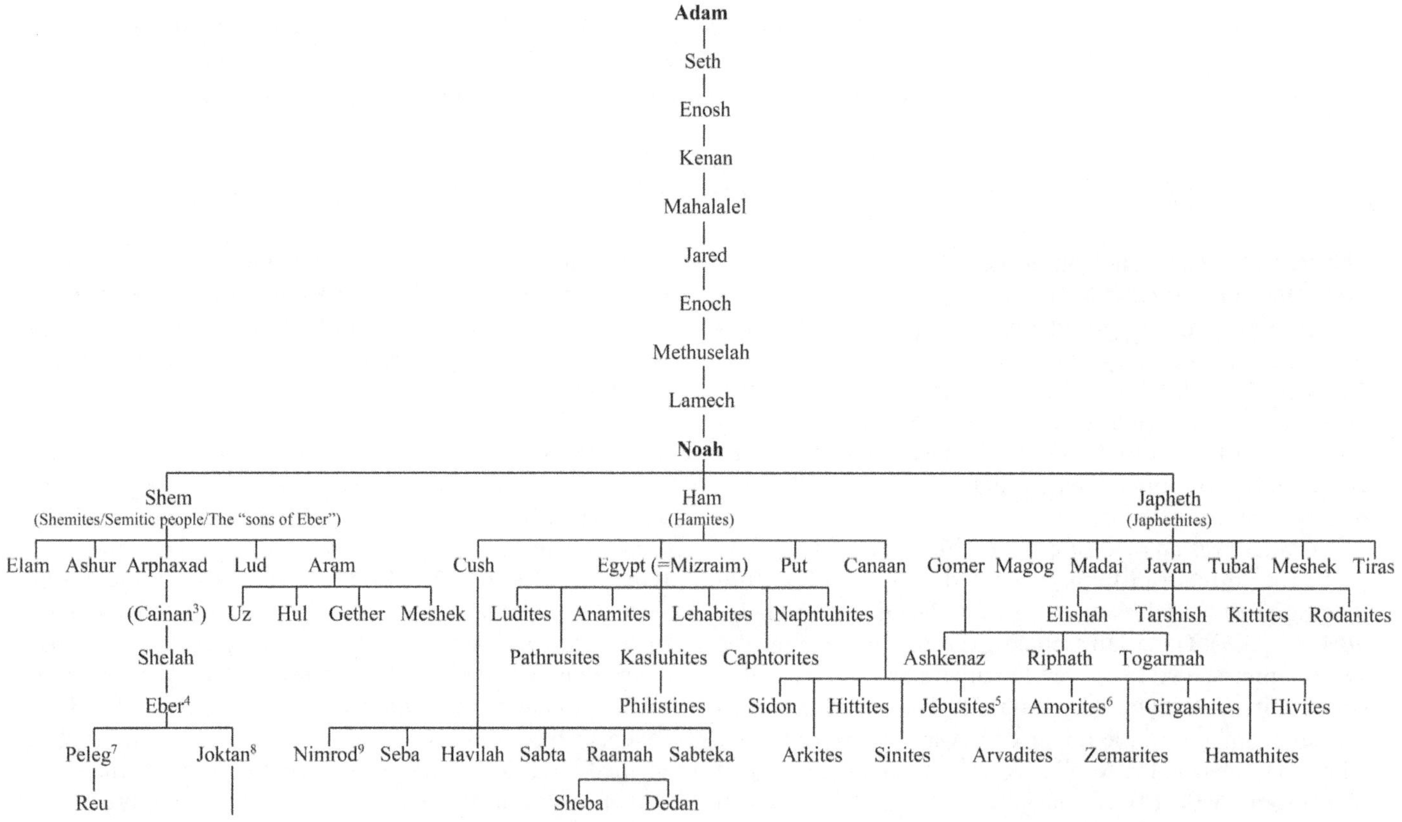

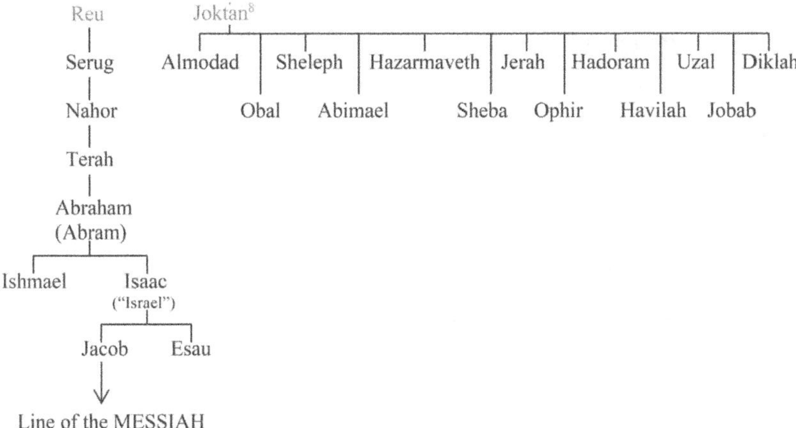

Biblical and Theological Significance

The genealogies of the Old Testament revolve around a number of critical junctures which demarcate great epochs or persons in the history of salvation. Examples thus far, as shown in the chart, are (1) Adam to Noah (in linear form) and (2) Noah to Abraham–Isaac–Jacob (in segmented form). The genealogy commencing with Noah traces his progeny through the lines of his three sons, with special attention to Shem, from which other segmentations will come into play. The Bible's scheme is clearly educational in that history increasingly shows how God was preparing for the climactic salvific event in his own Son who, as the "last Adam" (**1 Corinthians 15:45**; cf. **Romans 5:14**), would bring to pass in his being and work all that was needed to inaugurate a new heaven and a new earth (**Isaiah 65:17; 66:22; 2 Peter 3:13; Revelation 21:1**). Humanity that began with the one man, Adam, will end in one man, Jesus Christ. Adam's offspring oscillated between individuals and multitudes until the Christ: Adam, the multitudes to be destroyed; Noah, the multitudes at Babel; Abraham, the multitudes of his descendants; Jacob, the creation of a new nation; David, the rise of a kingdom; Jesus, the church, his everlasting body.

As for geographic and topographic matters, by general consensus, two locations of Cush emerged in the wake of the Noachic deluge: one south of Egypt and west of the Red Sea, corresponding roughly to Ethiopia and the upper Nile valley, and the other between the Dead Sea and the Gulf of Aqaba, an area extending to Arabia and the east coast of the Red Sea. Whether or not they were originally the same people cannot be determined. Some of the same Cushites may even earlier have settled as far east as Iran and Babylonia (cf. **Genesis 2:13; Esther 1:1; Isaiah 11:11; 18:1**). Zipporah, the wife of Moses, was called a "Cushite"[10] (**Numbers 12:1**), and Nimrod of Mesopotamia was a great Cushite chief of a much earlier time (**Genesis 10:8; 1 Chronicles 1:10**). Mizraim, the Hebrew name for Egypt, is a noun with a dual-form ending that alludes to the two parts of Egypt: Upper Egypt (south) and Lower Egypt (north). The reason for the apparent confusion of direction is resolved by the fact that the Nile River, contrary to most of the great rivers of the world, flows from south to north—from south-central Africa to the Mediterranean Sea.

Other names of geographic interest are the S(h)emitic lands of Ashur (Assyria), Aram (Aramaea or Syria), and Eber (i.e., *Hebrew*, later Israel). Hamite places include Canaan, Caphtor (Crete?), Philistia (Palestine), Sheba (Yemen?), Sidon (Lebanon), Hatti (north-central Turkey Hittites), and the "-ites" that settled in and about Canaan in various times. Significant Japhethite names and place names are Javan (Ionia, Greece), Elishah (Cyprus), and Kittim (Crete).

Notes

1. For Abraham's lifespan, see notes 1 and 12 in chart "**Genesis 11**: Terah and Nahor."

2. Adam is understood here to be a historical figure, but questions concerning other issues—such as the exact date of creation, the age of the earth, and the like—lie outside the parameters of genealogy.

3. Cainan, the son of Arphaxad and father of Shelah (**Luke 3:36**), is never mentioned in the Hebrew Old Testament (cf. **Genesis 10:24; 11:12–13; 1 Chronicles 1:18, 24**). The Septuagint (Greek Old Testament) includes Cainan at **Genesis 11:12–13**, and this appears to be Luke's source. The inclusion of Cainan in Luke's ancestry of Jesus achieves an overall balance of 77 names in the list and arrives at a "divine" number. For a discussion of the valid inclusion or exclusion of Cainan as the son of Arphaxad and the father of Shelah in **Luke 3:36** but not in **Genesis 10**, **Genesis 11**, or **1 Chronicles 1**, see Andrew E. Steinmann, "Challenging the Authenticity of Cainan, Son of Arpachshad," *JETS* 60 (2017)," 697–711, and an opposing viewpoint by Henry B. Smith Jr. and Kris J. Udd, "On the Authenticity of Kainan, Son of Arphachshad," *Detroit Baptist Seminary Journal* 24 (2019): 119–54.

4. Eber is considered the eponymous ancestor of the Hebrews. עִבְרִי, *ibri* (a Hebrew) is the gentilic of the personal name Eber עֵבֶר, *eber*.

5. The Jebusites inhabited ancient Jerusalem, also called Jebus (cf. **Joshua 15:63; 18:28; Judges 19:10; 1 Chronicles 11:4**).

6. Most of the names of Canaan's sons—collectively, the "Canaanites"—are patronyms for the ancient inhabitants of the land of Canaan (cf. **Genesis 10:15–18; 1 Chronicles 1:13–16**).

7. In Peleg's generation, "the earth was divided" (**1 Chronicles 1:19**). Hebrew פָּלַג (*palag*), "to split, divide," is likely a reference to the confusion of languages at Babel and the resulting *separation* of people (cf. **Genesis 11:1–9**).

8. Joktan is another ancient name for Yemen.

9. Nimrod was "a mighty warrior on the earth" and "a mighty hunter before the Lord" (**Genesis 10:8–9**). He was a builder of Babel and was attributed with building or dominating Babel, Uruk, Akkad, and Kalneh in lower and central Mesopotamia. He also went to the north (Assyria), where he built Nineveh, Rehoboth Ir, Calah, and Resen (**Genesis 10:10–12**). Micah the prophet called Assyria "the land of Nimrod" (**Micah 5:6**).

10. See the commentary and note 8 in chart "**Exodus 2**: Moses and Zipporah."

1 CHRONICLES 1: ABRAHAM'S DESCENDANTS THROUGH HAGAR (HAGRITES) AND ISHMAEL (ISHMAELITES)

Approximate Dating: the birth of Ishmael to Hagar in 2080 B.C.; Ishmael lived 137 yrs. and died in ca. 1943 B.C.[1] ***Relevant Scriptures:*** **1 Chronicles 1:29–30; 5:19;** also **Genesis 25:12–18; 36:2–4, 13**[2]

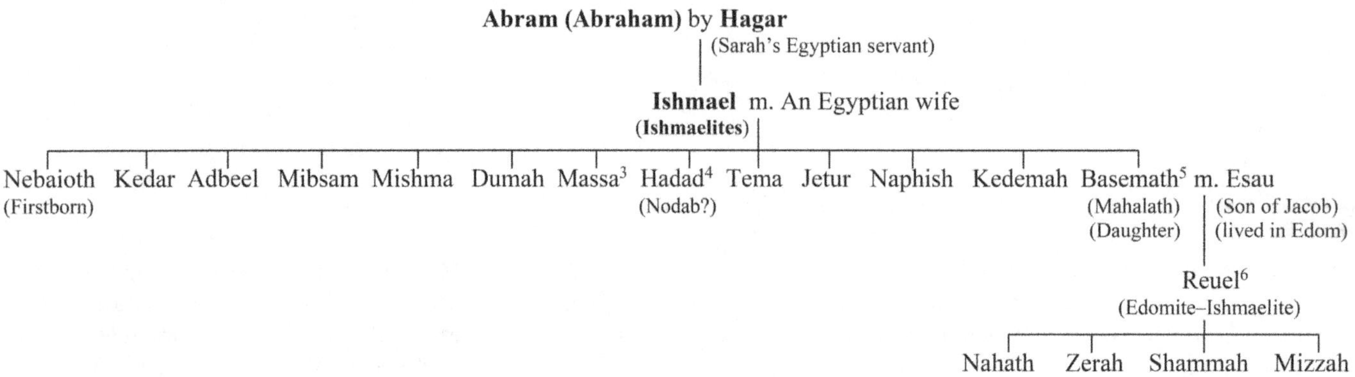

Biblical and Theological Significance

From the darkness of Mesopotamian paganism, God graciously condescended to select Abram, worshiper of the moon god Sin, to be founder of a nation whose mission would be to shed abroad through all places and all times the awesomely glorious message of redemptive grace sufficient to save all who would accept it by faith. Abram (later Abraham) eventually reached the age when he and his wife Sarai (later Sarah) were past childbearing years. In a moment of despair and doubt of ever having a son as God had promised, Sarai offered her Egyptian slave (Heb. שִׁפְחָה, *shiphkhah*) to Abram (**Genesis 16:1–3**). Ishmael, born when Abram was eighty-six years old (**Genesis 16:16**), was thus half-Hebrew and half-Egyptian. Not surprisingly, Hagar chose an Egyptian wife for Ishmael, thus perpetuating the curse that attended that line (**Genesis 21:21**). Ishmael became an archer, living in the Desert of Paran, south of Judah, west of Edom, and north of Sinai. His sons formed the twelve tribes of the Ishmaelites that became a nation of people (**Genesis 21:12–13, 20–21**). The Hagrites (**1 Chronicles 5:10; 19–21**) and the Ishmaelites (**Genesis 37:25, 27–28; 39:1; Judges 8:24; Psalm 83:6**) became the inveterate enemies of God and his people during biblical history.

In the New Testament, Sarah and Hagar represent two different covenants. Hagar is symbolic of the "bondwoman"—the "One covenant is from Mount Sinai and bears children who are to be slaves: This is Hagar. Now Hagar stands for Mount Sinai in Arabia and corresponds to the present city of Jerusalem, because she is in slavery with her children [meaning salvation by way of the Law brings bondage to sin and the curse of the Law]" (**Galatians 4:24–25**).[7]

Notes

1. Abraham was born in 2166 B.C. and died in 1991 B.C. at the age of 175 (**Genesis 25:7**); for a discussion of the birth and lifespan of Abram/Abraham, see notes 1 and 12 in chart "**Genesis 11**: Terah and Nahor." **Genesis 16:16** says that Abram/Abraham was eighty-six years old when Hagar bore Ishmael, so Ishmael was born in 2080 B.C. In 2067 B.C., when Ishmael was thirteen (**Genesis 17:25**), Abraham was 99 years of age (**Genesis 17:1**). By the time that Ishmael buried Abraham in 1991 B.C., Ishmael was 89 years old (**Genesis 25:8–9**). Ishmael lived 48 years longer than his father and died in 1943 B.C. at the age of 137 (**Genesis 25:17**).

2. The biblical narrative about Abraham and Hagar is relayed in **Genesis 16:1–16; 21:9–21**; also see chart "**Genesis 16**: Ishmael and His Descendants, the Ishmaelites."

3. Massa the sixth son of Ishmael was, of course, a grandson of Abraham (**Genesis 25:14**). Some scholars like Alfred Edersheim have proposed that **Proverbs 30:1** should read "The words of Agur, the son of her whom Massa obeys . . . " and that "Proverbs 31 embodies the words of Augur's royal brother, even 'the words of Lemuel, king of Massa, with which his mother taught him [**Proverbs 31:1**]' " (see Alfred Edersheim's *Sketches of Jewish Social Life*, ch. 7 on "The Upbringing of Jewish Children," available online at https://ccel.org/ccel/edersheim/sketches/sketches.ix.html?highlight=Proverbs%2030&queryID=22632072&resultID=126444#fna_ix-p10.2). But this conclusion, in our opinion, is very tenuous for the following reasons: (1) No other king (or other individual) in the Bible bears the name Massa; and (2) The Masoretic text tradition places a strong disjunctive accent (*athnach*) after "king," reading "The words of Lemuel the king; a massa which . . ."—rather than "The words of Lemuel, the king of Massa." Here *massa* has its common meaning of "sayings," "oracle," or "proverb."

4. Nodab (Heb. נוֹדָב) the Ishmaelite is mentioned with Jetur and Naphish only in **1 Chronicles 5:19**. Otherwise, Jetur and Naphish, with Kedemah, are identified as sons of Ishmael with no reference to Nodab (**1 Chronicles 1:31**). Obviously, Nodab cannot be Kedemah, so the supposition that a trio of sons is in view anywhere is dubious. It seems best to disconnect Nodab from the two brothers, Jetur and Naphish, since the record speaks of him only as a Hagrite warrior. These texts do not shed light on Nodab, who was therefore associated with others only as an otherwise unattested descendant of Ishmael. Moreover, any contrived confusion of Nodab with Hadad or Hadar is without logical or exegetical grounding.

5. She is called Mahalath in **Genesis 28:9**, Basemath in **Genesis 36:3, 13**, and the "sister of Nebaioth" (the firstborn of Ishmael) in **Genesis 28:9; 36:3**.

6. This Reuel of Edomite—of Ishmaelite ancestry through his mother, Basemath/Mahalath the Ishmaelitess, and his Edomite father Esau, the son of Jacob—is not the same person as Reuel/Jethro, the Kenite priest living in Midian, who was Moses' father-in-law (for Reuel, see note 4 in chart "**Exodus 2**: Moses and Zipporah").

7. The passage goes on to say that Sarah is "the Jerusalem that is above [who] is free, and she is our mother" (**Galatians 4:26**).

1 CHRONICLES 1: ABRAHAM'S DESCENDANTS THROUGH KETURAH

Approximate Dating: ca. 2066–1990 B.C.[1] ***Relevant Scriptures:*** **1 Chronicles 1:32–33**; also **Genesis 25:1–6**

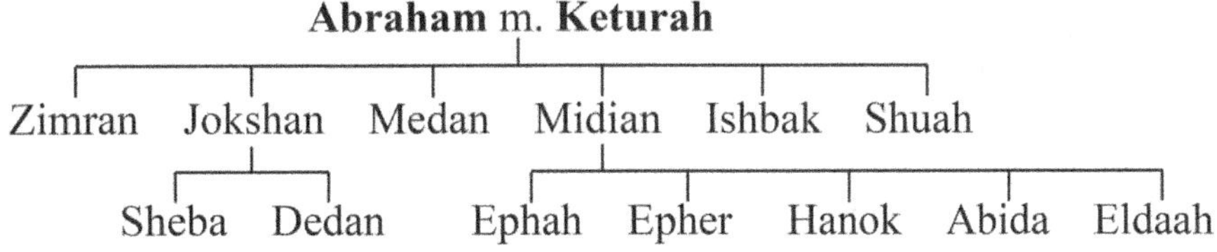

Biblical and Theological Significance

According to **Genesis 25:1**, Keturah[2] was Abraham's second "wife" (or "concubine," **1 Chronicles 1:32**), whom he married after Sarah died (cf. **Genesis 23:2**; **25:1**). Since it was rare for a concubine to be elevated to the position of wife, one is left to speculate why this was the case with Keturah. Perhaps Abraham saw in her some giftedness and potentiality worthy of such an anomalous position. Or, with more earthy feelings, he simply loved her. **Genesis 25:5–6** says that, while he was still living, Abraham gave gifts to his concubines' sons, including Keturah's, and sent them away to the east. There they established small tribes or states in the Transjordan, Sinai, and Arabia. Of these, only Midian, east of the Gulf of Aqaba, can presently be located. As for later settlements, the near consensus is that Sheba (now modern Yemen) was in the southwestern corner of the Arabian Peninsula; Dedan occupied the west coastal area of Arabia, just east of the Gulf of Aqaba; and Ephah may have been near what is now the border between Jordan and Saudi Arabia (cf. **Genesis 10:7; 25:3-4; 1 Kings 10:1; 1 Chronicles 1:9, 32; Job 6:19; Isaiah 60:6; Ezekiel 38:13**). The descendants of Dedan (**Genesis 25:3**) are not mentioned by the Chronicler nor can they all be identified with places in the modern Middle East. Keturah and her descendants are a part of the fulfillment of the Abrahamic covenant that encompassed all the nations of the earth, ancient and modern (cf. **Genesis 12:3; 18:18; 22:18; Galatians 3:8**).

The juxtaposition in **Genesis 25** of the family narratives of Keturah and Hagar[3] is significant. Hagar the Egyptian and Keturah of Arabia had much in common: (1) both from the Ancient Near East; (2) both "wives" of Abraham, the father of Israel and of the messianic hope; and (3) both matriarchs of what became the Arab[4] people of biblical interest and beyond. Strangely enough, the terms *Arab/Arabs*, *Arabia*, and *Arabians* are comparatively rare in the Bible (nineteen times in all), occurring most commonly in the post-exilic literature (eleven times) and thus suggesting that, in earliest times, they neither posed much of a threat to Israel nor interacted with the nation to any extent in commerce, trade, and the like.

A thousand years after Abraham, his descendant Solomon interacted in extensive and profitable trade arrangements. Among the merchants and traders with Solomon were "all the kings of Arabia and the governors of the territories [who] brought gold and silver" (**2 Chronicles 9:14**). Solomon's social, cultural, and commercial engagements with the Queen of Sheba are well known (**1 Kings 10:1–13; 2 Chronicles 9:1–12**). Nevertheless, the friendly interactions between Israel and the tribal states of the Arabian Peninsula in Solomonic times (971–931 B.C.) turned sour in the sixth century with the return of the Jews from Babylonia. Along with many other challenges faced by the Jews was the harassment that attended their attempts to rebuild the temple that the Babylonians had burned in 586 B.C. and to rebuild the walls of Jerusalem. Chief among those who mocked and threatened armed interference against Nehemiah and his co-laborers in 444 B.C. were Arabs led by a certain "Geshem the Arab"[5] (**Nehemiah 2:19; 4:7; 6:1–14**). Nevertheless, enemy efforts failed, for the temple rose again from Moriah (**Ezra 6:14**; cf. **Zechariah 8:9**) and the walls were completed around the city (**Nehemiah 6:15**).

Notes

1. Sarah, born ca. 2156 B.C., gave birth to Isaac ca. 2066 B.C. and died at age 127 in ca. 2029 B.C. Abraham, ten years older, died at age 175. Abraham was born in 2166 B.C. and died in 1991 B.C., thus out-living Sarah by forty-eight years. Abraham then married Keturah in ca. 2029 B.C., right after Sarah's death. (For further considerations of Abraham's lifespan, see notes 1 and 12 in chart "**Genesis 11**: Terah and Nahor").

2. The name "Keturah" derives from the Hebrew קְטֹרֶת (*qetoreth*), meaning "fragrance, incense," redolent of the famous spice trade and also of the visit of the queen of Sheba (a "Spiceland"), who brought King Solomon "large quantities of spices" (**1 Kings 10:10**).

3. For Hagar and Ishmael, see charts "**Genesis 16**: Ishmael and His Descendants, the Ishmaelites" and "**1 Chronicles 1**: Abraham's Descendants through Hagar (Hagrites) and Ishmael (Ishmaelites)."

4. "Arab" (עֲרָב) is related to the noun עֲרָבָה, "Arabah desert," as well as the Jordan River valley.

5. See chart "**Nehemiah 2**: The Enemies of Nehemiah Who Ruled in the Provinces Surrounding Judah."

1 CHRONICLES 1: ABRAHAM'S DESCENDANTS THROUGH ESAU

Approximate Dating: ca. 2006–1840 B.C.[1] ***Relevant Scriptures:*** **1 Chronicles 1:34–37;** also **Genesis 26:34; 28:9; 36:1–14**

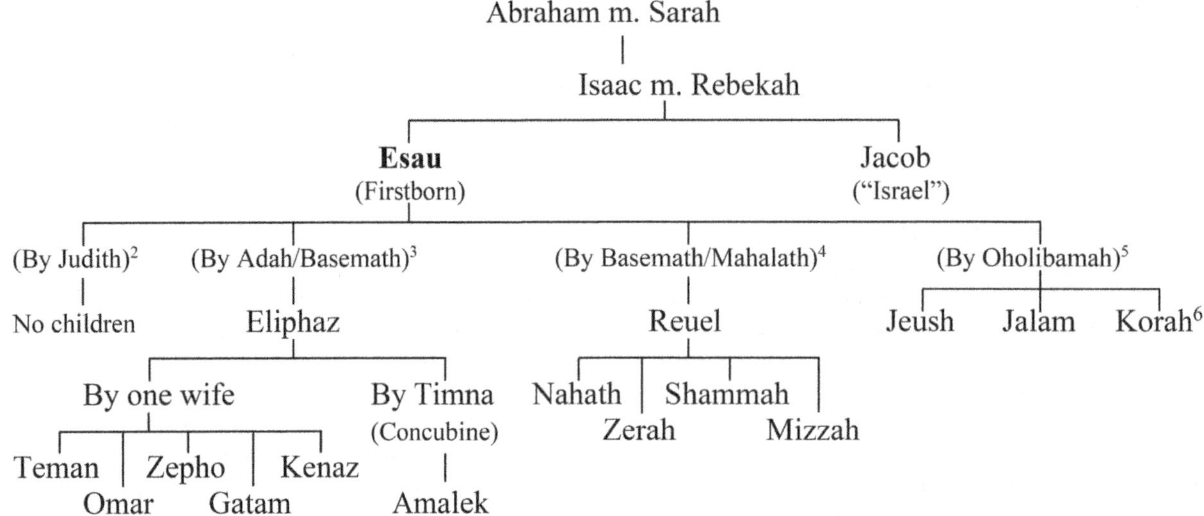

Biblical and Theological Significance

Esau, the firstborn son of Isaac and Rebekah and the twin of Jacob, was the eponymous ancestor of the Edomites.[7] According to Genesis, he took four wives[8]—Judith, Adah/Basemath, Basemath/Mahalath, and Oholibamah—and had five (named) children by them (**Genesis 36:1–19**); however, the Chronicler in **1 Chronicles 1:34–37** mentions only the male children and grandchildren of Esau by three of his wives (i.e., Adah/Basemath, Basemath/Mahalath, and Oholibamah). Presumably, Esau's wife Judith bore him no children. Esau was the ancestor of the Amalekites[9] (**Genesis 36:12; 1 Chronicles 1:36**), upon whom God had declared holy war from "generation to generation" because they attacked the rear flanks of the Israelites on their journey from Egypt to Canaan (**Exodus 17:16**).

In **Genesis 36:15–19; 36:40–43**, Esau's grandsons/descendants are called "chiefs" or the like (Heb. אֱלוּפִים, *alluphim*),[10] suggesting they had a nomadic or semi-nomadic rather than a sedentary lifestyle. Few if any of their locations can be specifically determined based on their names, though their larger habitations were the lower Arabah, the Negev, and North Arabia.[11] By the time of the exodus in 1446 B.C., the Edomites had become such a powerful people that Moses and the Israelites had to bypass them en route to Canaan by hugging the south end of the Dead Sea and then turning northward along what later was called the "King's Highway" (**Numbers 20:17**), a major trade route that connected Mesopotamia to Egypt via the Gulf of Aqaba (or eastern arm of the Red Sea; **Numbers 20:14–21**).[12]

Notes

1. Isaac was sixty years old when the twins, Jacob and Esau, were born in ca. 2006 B.C. (**Genesis 25:26**). Esau's age at death is not recorded, but his lifespan is based on the general life expectancy in those days. Esau was living at his father's (Isaac's) death in 1859 B.C. (**Genesis 35:29**).

2. Judith was the daughter of Beeri the Hittite (**Genesis 26:34**).

3. Adah, the daughter of Elon the Hittite (**Genesis 36:2**), is also called Basemath (**Genesis 26:34**). Adah/Basemath should not be confused with Basemath/Mahalath the Ishmaelite, another wife of Esau (see note 4).

4. Basemath—the daughter of Ishmael, the sister of Nebaioth, and the granddaughter of Abraham and Hagar (**Genesis 36:3–4, 10, 13, 17**)—is also called Mahalath (**Genesis 28:9**).

5. "Oholibamah daughter of Anah and granddaughter of Zibeon the Hivite" in **Genesis 36:2** is called "Oholibamah daughter of Anah and granddaughter of Zibeon [the Horite]" in **Genesis 36:14**. Oholibamah's father, Anah, was the son of Zibeon and the grandson of Seir the Horite (**Genesis 36:20–21, 24–25**); for Anah, see note 2 in chart "**1 Chronicles 1**: Seir the Horite."

6. Korah, the son of Oholibamah and Esau, should not be confused with the Levitical rebel named Korah, the son of Izhar, who was one of the main instigators of the Korah–Reubenite rebellion (**Numbers 16:1–35**).

7. Esau's other name, "Edom" (meaning red or ruddy), came about because of his complexion at birth (**Genesis 25:25**) and his craving for the red stew of his brother Jacob (**Genesis 25:30**). Also refer to the chart "**Genesis 36**: Esau, the Ancestor of the Edomites."

8. See chart "**Genesis 36**: Esau's Wives."

9. See chart "**Genesis 36**: Amalek, the Ancestor of the Amalekites."

10. The translations of the Hebrew term used here (אַלּוּף, *alluph*) attest to its ambiguity at best. It is cognate to אֶלֶף, "thousand," a military term describing a unit of such size. The commander of such a unit was an אַלּוּף; in socio-political terms, perhaps a governor or some such more local leader.

11. Yoharan Aharoni, *The Land of the Bible: A Historical Geograph.* (Philadelphia: Westminster, 1979), 40–42.

12. For the route in question, see Yohanan Aharoni and Michael Avi-Yonah, *The Macmillan Bible Atlas* (Jerusalem: Carta, 1993), 16.

1 CHRONICLES 1: SEIR THE HORITE

Approximate Dating: ca. 2150–2000 B.C.[1] ***Relevant Scriptures:*** **1 Chronicles 1:38–42;** also **Genesis 36:2, 5, 12, 14, 18, 20–30**

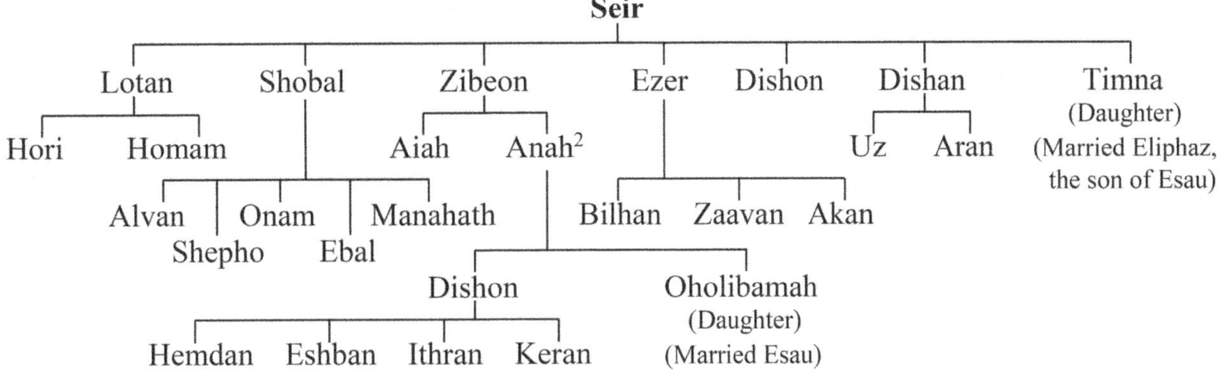

Biblical and Theological Significance

Seir is called "Seir the Horite"[3] (**Genesis 36:20**). He and his descendants were the pre-Israelite inhabitants of Seir/Mount Seir, the region that later became the kingdom of Esau and his descendants (the Edomites) who occupied the hill country of Seir or "Edom" (**Genesis 32:3; 36:9**; cf. **36:21; Deuteronomy 2:4, 8; Ezekiel 35:15**). As **Deuteronomy 2:12** explains, "Horites used to live in Seir, but the descendants of Esau drove them out. They [Esau's descendants] destroyed the Horites from before them and settled in their place."

The Family of Seir

The list of the Seir family members in **Genesis 36:20–30** identifies only those in **Genesis 36:29–30** as *alluphim* or tribal chieftains (i.e., specifically, Lotan, Shobal, Zibeon, Anah, Dishon, Ezer, and Dishan). All others were members of their families, but this does not make them *alluphim* as well. As for the list of names in **1 Chronicles 1:43–54**, only those named in **1 Chronicles 1:51–54** are relevant to the *alluph* issue. The key is in **verse 51**: "The chiefs [*alluphim*] of Edom were: [the *alluph* of] Timna, [the *alluph* of] Alvah, [the *alluph* of] Jetheth, [the *alluph* of] Oholibamah," etc.[4] Seir's daughter Timna, the sister of Lotan, became the concubine of Eliphaz (son of Esau) and the mother of Amalek (**Genesis 36:12, 22; 1 Chronicles 1:36, 39**). Seir's great-granddaughter, Oholibamah, married Esau and became the mother of Jeush, Jalam, and Korah (**Genesis 36:5; 18**). It is unclear if Seir's grandson Uz was an ancestor of Job.[5] Seir's grandson Anah is noted as the one "who discovered the hot springs in the desert while he was grazing the donkeys of his father Zibeon" (**Genesis 36:24**).

Notes

1. Esau was born in 2006 B.C. The events of **Genesis 14:1–16** also link Abraham (2166–1991 B.C.) to the land of Seir (שֵׂעִיר) and "hair production," perhaps a reference to desert livestock. It is possible that Seir was its founder, that he was named after the land of Seir, or that there is no necessary etymological connection.
2. Anah is identified as a *son* of Seir the Horite (**Genesis 36:20**), the *son* of Zibeon (**Genesis 36:24**), and the *father* of Oholibamah (**Genesis 36:25**). **Genesis 36:2** seems to clarify the exact kinship relationship by saying that "Oholibamah [was] daughter of Anah and granddaughter of Zibeon the Hivite"—therefore, Anah was presumably the *son* of Zibeon and the *grandson* of Seir (not Seir's *son*); this is the interpretation followed in the chart.
3. Hebrew חֹרִי is identified by most scholars as its way of referring to the Hurrians, whose kingdom was Mitanni, located in the very north of what is now Iraq. See Amélie Kuhrt, *The Ancient Near East c. 3000–330 B.C.*, vol. I (London: Routledge, 1995), 289–300.
4. The Hebrew grammatical construction requires this reading because the nouns (*alluph*) are all in the construct genitive pattern, in which noun 1 is followed by an explicit or implicit "of" noun 2. So, X is the *alluph* of Y.
5. See chart "**Job 1**: Possible Ancestry of Job the Patriarch."

1 CHRONICLES 1: GENEALOGICAL RECORD OF THE SUCCESSION OF EDOMITE KINGS

Approximate Dating: ca. 3000–2000 B.C. before the Edomite descendants/chiefs of Esau[1] settled there, and before Israel's monarchy began in 1051 B.C.[2] ***Relevant Scriptures:*** **1 Chronicles 1:43–51;** also **Genesis 36:31–39**

Bela[3]
(Son of Beor)
(Ruled from Dinhabah)
▼
Jobab
(Son of Zerah)
(Ruled from Bozrah)

Jobab

▼

Husham

(Ruled from the land of Teman/the Temanites)

▼

Hadad[4]

(Son of Bedad)

(Ruled from Avith)

▼

Samlah

(Ruled from Masrekah)

▼

Shaul

(Ruled from Rehoboth on the river)

▼

Baal-Hanan

(Son of Akbor)

▼

Hadad m. Mehetabel[5]

(Ruled from Pau) (Daughter of Matred)

Biblical and Theological Significance

The rulers of Edom inhabited the land of Edom, an area that was later overtaken and settled by Esau and his descendants (the Edomites; **Genesis 32:3; 36:1, 8, 19, 43**). The Edomite nation exhibited a primitive type of monarchy and occupied the general historical Early Bronze Age of the chiefs (3000–2000 B.C.) before the Iron Age monarchy of Israel (1051–931 B.C.).

It is important to bear in mind that this area of Edom (the land of Seir) was settled long before the time of Abraham, to say nothing of Isaac's sons, Jacob and Esau.[6] This is attested to by both archaeological evidence[7] and genealogical records like those in **Genesis 36:31–39**. The account above from **1 Chronicles 1:43–51** lists eight successive generations of Edomite kings who lived up to two or three hundred years prior to Esau.[8] They are identified as Horites,[9] Emites, and Rephaites in several early texts, as though they were prehistoric (**Genesis 14:5–6; 36:20–30; Deuteronomy 2:10–11**). Their tenures were non-hereditary, in contrast to the kings of Israel, who followed father-to-son succession.[10] Also, the royal cities (capitals) of the Edomite kings shifted from place to place. As for these cities, only Bozrah,[11] Teman,[12] and Rehoboth[13] are mentioned elsewhere. In sum, all that exists is the lists of the kings and their tiny states. Nothing much can be said of the inclusion of the material in the biblical narrative except (1) it provides a historical and geographical setting for the account of Esau's inheritance and allotment of territory (**Genesis 27:39–40; 36:1–8**); and (2) it illustrates the terrible error Esau made when he exchanged his birthright for a bowl of stew. From Jacob came the Messiah; from Esau came Edom, Israel's inveterate enemy, consigned to the howling desert, impassable hills, and the dust-bin of history.

Notes

1. See charts "**Genesis 36**: Esau, the Ancestor of the Edomites" and "**Genesis 36**: The Chiefs of Edom."

2. Both Genesis and Chronicles refer to the kings of Edom as those who reigned "before any Israelite king reigned" (**Genesis 36:31; 1 Chronicles 1:43**), meaning before Israel's monarchy commenced with Saul in 1051 B.C. Kings of Edom are also mentioned in **Numbers 20:14** and **Judges 11:17**.

3. The name Bela first occurs as the place name *Zoar* in the time of Abraham (cf. **Genesis 14:2, 8**), a district or region south of Sodom and Gomorrah that shared with them an agriculturally rich soil "like the garden of the LORD," an obvious reference to Eden (**Genesis 13:10**). Its prosperity can be explained also by the fact that Zoar was located on the isthmus of Wadi Zered, one of the freshwater streams that feed the Dead Sea from the eastern hills, marking the end of the Israelites' wilderness wandering and the entrance into Canaan (**Numbers 21:12; Deuteronomy 2:13–14**). This was the land claimed by Lot while Abraham was left with the hill country of Canaan (**Genesis 13:11–12**). When Yahweh's fiery judgment fell upon the "cities of the [South Dead Sea] plain" (**Genesis 19:29**), Zoar was spared for a while, thus providing a place of refuge for Lot and his daughters from which they later fled to caves overlooking the Dead Sea (**Genesis 19:18–30**). The Zoar region is mentioned in the account of the death of Moses as one of the landmarks seen by him from Pisgah (**Deuteronomy 34:1–3**). Zoar was known as late as the time of both Isaiah (**Isaiah 15:5**) and Jeremiah (**Jeremiah 48:34**).

4. Hadad the Edomite defeated Midian (the Midianites) in the country of Moab (**Genesis 36:35; 1 Chronicles 1:46**).

5. Mehetabel is the only wife-queen mentioned in the Edomite kings' list. Mehetabel was the daughter of Matred, the daughter of Me-Zahab (**Genesis 36:39; 1 Chronicles 1:50**); this is an exceptional case of tracing matrilineal descent in the Bible. To skirt the "problem" of female monarchic succession, LXX and Peshitta read בֵּן (*ben*) for בַּת (*bath*) to designate Matred as male (i.e., as the *son* of Me-Zahab, instead of a daughter). In the absence of corroborative evidence one way or the other, the rule in general is to adhere to the MT, no matter the problem with gender.

6. Abraham was born in 2166 B.C. and died in 1991 B.C. at the age of 175 (**Genesis 25:7**). Isaac was born to Abraham and Sarah in 2066 B.C. and died in 1886 B.C. at the age of 180 (**Genesis 35:28**). The twins Jacob and Esau were born in 2006 B.C. (**Genesis 25:26**). Esau was 40 in 1966 B.C. when he married two heathen Canaanite women, Judith and Adah/Basemath (**Genesis 26:34; 27:46**). Jacob lived from 2006 to 1859 B.C. and died at the age of 147 (**Genesis 47:28**), having lived in Egypt for the last 17 years of his life, from age 130 to age 147, corresponding to the years 1876–1859 B.C. (**Genesis 47:9**).

7. R. Thomas Schaub and Walter E. Rast, "Preliminary Report of the 1981 Expedition to the Dead Sea Plain, Jordan." *BASOR* 254 (1984): 35–60. Steven Collins, "Sodom: The Discovery of a lost City." *Bible and Spade* 20 (2007): 70–77. Walter E. Rast,"Sodom and Its Environs: Can Recent Archaeology Offer a Perspective?" *NEASB* 51 (2006): 19–26. Bryant G. Wood, "Locating Sodom: A Critique of the Northern Proposal." *Bible and Spade* 20 (2007): 78–84. Hershel Shanks, "Have Sodom and Gomorrah Been Found?" *BAR* 6 (1980): 26–36. W.C. Van Hatten, "Once Again: Sodom and Gomorrah" *BA* 44 (1981): 87–92.

8. Esau was born in 2006 B.C., but the date of his death is not recorded. A reasonable lifespan for Esau was ca. 2006–1900 B.C.

9. Scholarship is virtually of one mind in identifying these "Horites" as Hurrians, a people well attested to in ancient Near Eastern literature. James B. Pritchard, ed. *Ancient Near Eastern Texts Relating to the Old Testament*, 2nd ed. (Princeton: Princeton University Press, 1955), 205–206, 235, 258, 261.

As explained by Rainey and Notley, "The Horites are the autochthonous [indigenous] dwellers of Mount Seir who were displaced by the descendants of Esau, . . . [but the Horites] have no association with the Hurrians of northern Mesopotamia or Syria. . . . The resemblance in names is strictly accidental." Anson F. Rainey and R. Steven Notley, *The Sacred Bridge* (Jerusalem: Carta, 2014), 114. Thus, the settlement of indigenous Hurrians who occupied Seir were called Horites.

10. Refer to the summary chart "**1 & 2 Kings**: Summary of the Genealogical Record of the Kings of the United and Divided Kingdoms."

11. Bozrah (Arab. Buseirah) is east of the Arabah, 120 miles south of Amman, 120 miles north of the Gulf of Aqaba.

12. Most scholars now view Teman as another name for (southern) Edom. The Temanites (residents of Teman) were descendants of Teman, the son of Eliphaz, the son of Esau (**Genesis 36:10–11, 15; 1 Chronicles 1:36**). Job's friend Eliphaz was a "Temanite" (**Job 2:11**).

13. The only "Rehoboth on the river" that suits the situation of the narrative is in the central Negev, some 60 miles west of Edom, where the river may refer to the Wadi of Egypt (**Joshua 15:4**). Alternatively, it may refer to the Brook or Valley of Zered (**Numbers 21:12; Deuteronomy 2:13–14**), the place that marked the end of the wilderness wanderings and the entrance into Canaan.

1 CHRONICLES 2: JACOB (ISRAEL) AND HIS TWELVE SONS[1]

Approximate Dating: Jacob lived for 147 years, ca. 2006–1859 B.C.; Jacob lived in Egypt the last seventeen years of his life, from the age of 130 to 147, ca. 1876–1859 B.C., and died there ***Relevant Scriptures:*** **1 Chronicles 2:1–2**; also **Genesis 29:32–35; 30:6, 8, 11, 13, 18, 20, 24; 35:18, 23–26; 47:28; 49:1–28**

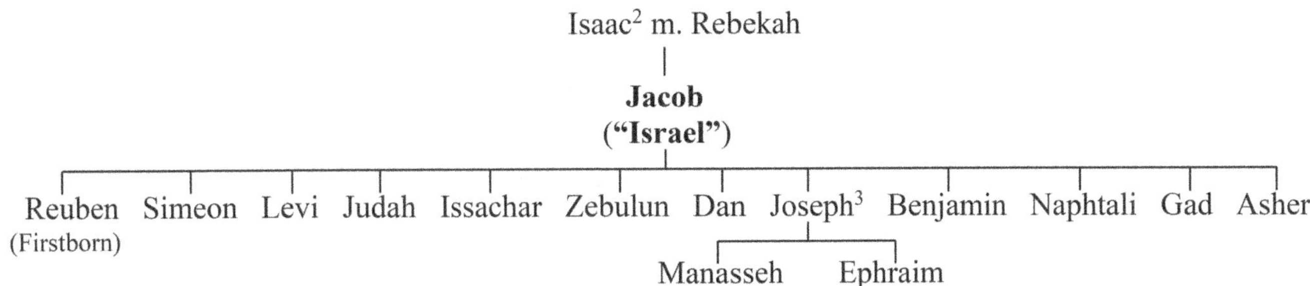

Biblical and Theological Significance

Jacob, the son of Isaac and Rebekah, was born ca. 2006 B.C. and sired twelve sons by four wives (Leah and Rachel and their two servants, Zilpah and Bilhah). Jacob deceived his twin brother (twice) to secure Esau's birthright and blessing, earning him (Jacob) the name "supplanter" or "deceiver" (**Genesis 25:26; 27:35–36**). However, in a theophany experience, Jacob *wrestled* with a man (God)—"He wept and begged for his favor" (**Hosea 12:4**)—and his name was changed to Israel "because you have struggled with God and with humans and have overcome" (**Genesis 32:22–32**). The twelve sons of Jacob became eponyms of the twelve tribes of the nation of Israel through the normal processes of generational and chronological population growth; in the New Testament these sons were known as the "twelve patriarchs" (**Acts 7:8**)

Jacob's blessing to his sons is given in **Genesis 49**. Reuben's egregious sexual relations with Bilhah, Jacob's wife-concubine (**Genesis 35:22**), turned his *blessing* (i.e., the right of primogeniture status) into a *curse*; instead of Reuben, Joseph received the *double portion*, which was realized in the land given to his sons, Manasseh and Ephraim, who became separate tribes. After the conquest of the promised land, "Israel" referred to the region occupied by the twelve tribes, which included the land east of the Jordan River that was allotted to Reuben, Gad, and the half-tribe of (East) Manasseh as well as the land to the west of the Jordan River that was occupied by the other nine-and-a-half tribes. The fact that Jacob had only one *named* daughter, Dinah (**Genesis 30:21**), does not suggest that she was the only one.[4] Jacob lived in Egypt for the last seventeen years of his life (1876–1859 B.C.)[5] and died there at the age of 147 (**Genesis 47:28; Acts 7:15**). His bones were carried to Canaan by his sons and buried "in the cave in the field of Ephron the Hittite" (i.e., the cave in the field of Machpelah near Mamre) where his grandparents (Abraham and Sarah), parents (Isaac and Rebekah), and wife (Leah) had all been buried (**Genesis 49:29–50:14**).

Notes

1. Also see charts "**Genesis 35**: The Twelve Sons of Jacob, the Eponymous Originators of the Twelve Tribes of Israel" and "**Genesis 46**: The Extended Family of Jacob (Seventy Descendants) Who Migrated to Egypt."

2. Isaac was born in ca. 2066 B.C., when Abraham was 100 years of age and his wife Sarah was 90 (**Genesis 17:17; 21:5**). Isaac was 40 when he married Rebekah in ca. 2026 B.C. (**Genesis 25:20**). In 2006 B.C., when her husband was sixty years old, Rebekah gave birth to twin sons, Jacob and Esau (**Genesis 25:26**). Isaac lived to be 180 (**Genesis 35:28**) and died in ca. 1886 B.C.; Isaac was buried by his sons, Esau and Jacob, in the cave in the field of Machpelah alongside his father (Abraham) and mother (Sarah) (**Genesis 35:29**; see also **Genesis 23:17–20; 25:8; 49:30–31**).

3. Ephraim and Manasseh were the sons of Joseph and his Egyptian wife, Asenath (**Genesis 41:45, 50–52; 46:20**). The sons were "reckoned" to Jacob (**Genesis 48:5**), and they became the eponymous ancestors of the tribe of Ephraim and the half-tribes of East and West Manasseh, respectively.

4. Ordinary rates of birth by gender surely lead to the conclusion that Jacob had at least as many daughters as sons. Dinah is probably included in Jacob's genealogy because of the narrative about Dinah, her brothers, and Shechem, the son of Hamor, in **Genesis 34**.

5. Dates are discussed in other charts; see those listed in note 1.

1 CHRONICLES 2: JUDAH SHOWING THE LINE OF THE MESSIAH

Approximate Dating: from the birth of Judah in ca. 1925 B.C. to the birth of David in ca. 1041 B.C. ***Relevant Scriptures:*** **1 Chronicles 2:1–17**; also **Genesis 38:2–15, 26–30; Exodus 6:23; Numbers 2:3; 10:14; 26:20–21; Joshua 7:1; Ruth 4:17–22; 1 Samuel 16:6–9; 17:13; 2 Samuel 2:18; 13:3, 32; 17:25; 21:21; 1 Kings 2:5; 1 Chronicles 20:7; 27:7, 32; Matthew 1:1–16; Luke 3:23–34**

Abraham m. Sarah

|

Isaac m. Rebekah

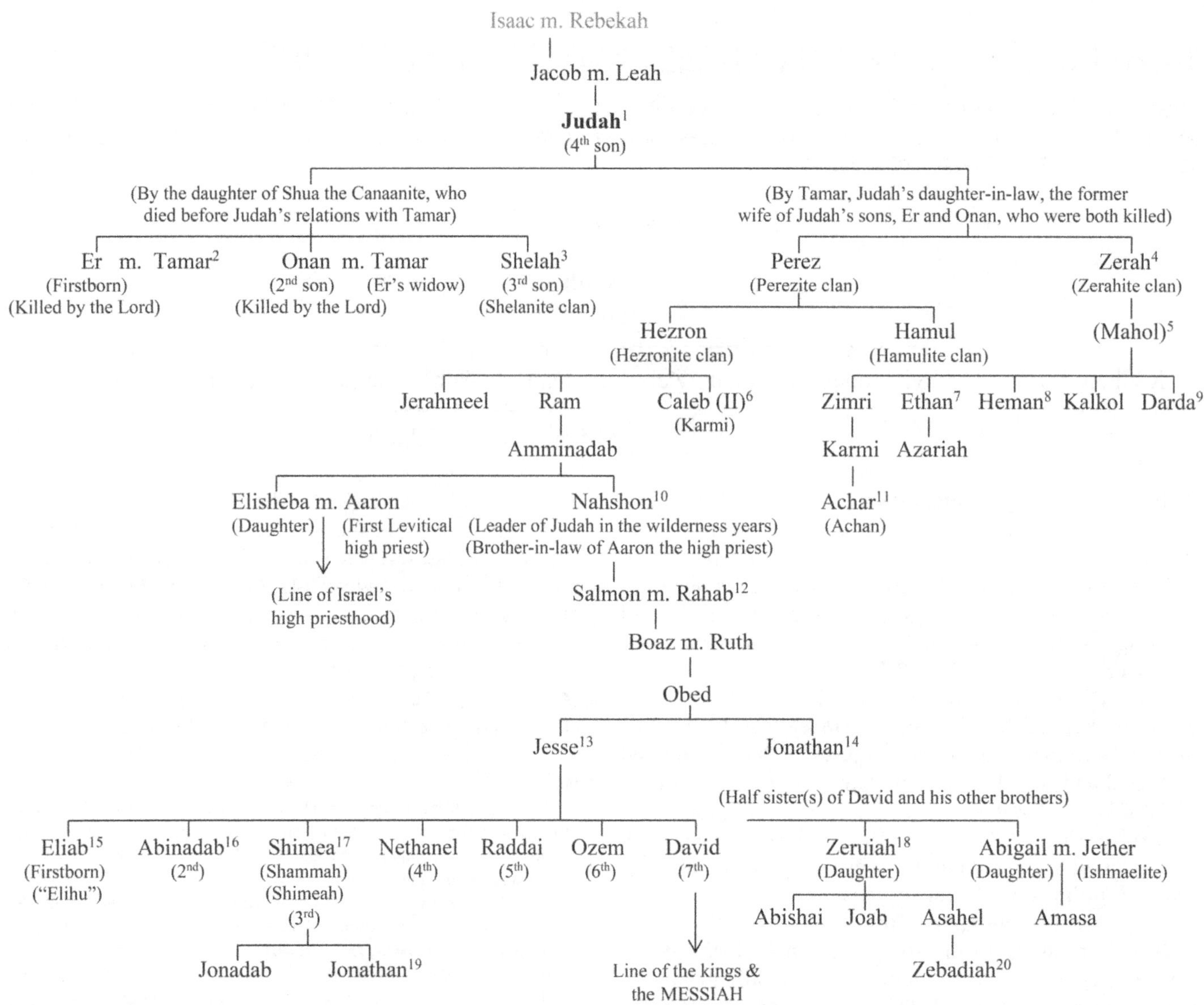

Biblical and Theological Significance

The chart emphasizes the messianic tribe of Judah that, in a sense, began with Abraham (**Genesis 15:18–21; 17:1–16**), passed through Isaac, and then Jacob, who was the father of Judah by his wife Leah, the one "not loved [unloved or loved less]" (**Genesis 29:31**). On his deathbed Jacob blessed his twelve sons, and here the prophetic blessing of the messianic significance of Judah comes into view:

> Judah, your brothers will praise you;
> your hand will be on the neck of your enemies;
> your father's sons will bow down to you.
> You are a lion's cub, Judah;
> you return from the prey, my son.
> Like a lion he crouches and lies down,
> like a lioness—who dares to rouse him?
> The scepter will not depart from Judah,
> nor the ruler's staff from between his feet,
> until he to whom it belongs shall come
> and the obedience of the nations shall be his.
> (**Genesis 49:8–10**)

This is the first clear indication in Scripture that the messianic figure to come would be a king.

Judah selected a wife named Tamar for his firstborn son, Er, whom God slew because he was wicked (**Genesis 38:6–7**). Following the levirate custom, Tamar was then given to Er's brother Onan, but Onan[21] refused to perform the duties of levirate marriage (conception of a child) with Tamar, so God also killed Onan (**Genesis 38:8–10**). At the time, the third son, Shelah, was too young for marriage, so Tamar was not given to him as a wife. However, as time passed and Tamar saw that Shelah was grown but that Judah refused to give Shelah to her as a levir (**Genesis 38:11, 14**), she disguised herself as a prostitute and waited at the entrance to a town on the road to Timnah.[22] Not realizing that it was his daughter-in-law (cf. **Leviticus 18:15**), Judah the patriarch slept with Tamar, promising to send her a young goat as payment; she agreed to the terms but requested a pledge of his seal, cord, and staff until his promise was fulfilled. When she became pregnant, Judah thought that his daughter-in-law was guilty of prostitution and declared that she should be burned to death (**Genesis 38:24**). When Tamar was brought before

Judah and she presented the pledge (seal, cord, and staff), the patriarch realized his guilt and declared, "'She is more righteous than I, since I wouldn't give her to my son Shelah.' And he did not sleep with her again" (**Genesis 38: 26**). Twin sons—Perez and Zerah—resulted from the one-time liaison (**Genesis 38:11–30**). Perez's patrimony was far more significant as he headed the favored line of offspring, beginning with his son Hezron and Hezron's sons—Jerahmeel, Ram, and Caleb/Karmi. Ram's great-grandson Salmon married the famous prostitute of Jericho named Rahab. The fruit of that marriage was their son Boaz, famous as the husband of the Moabite Ruth. Ruth in turn became the great-grandmother of King David through the Obed–Jesse line[23] (**Ruth 4:18–22**).

The messianic promise draws much closer with the birth of David. His father, Jesse, produced seven sons by an unnamed wife (or wives), but Nahash (not Jesse) was the father of Zeruiah and Abigail, the half-sister(s) of David and his brothers (**2 Samuel 17:25**). The sons of Zeruiah (Abishai, Joab, and Asahel) and the son of Abigail (Amasa) served their half-uncle King David in great military capacities[24] (**2 Samuel 2:18–32; 8:16; 10:6–14; 11:1; 17:24–25; 18:1–5; 19:13; 20:4–13; 23:18–19, 24; 1 Chronicles 11:6, 20, 26; 18:15**). Thus, the line of the coming Messiah was not as pure and sin-free as one might have expected. Every name in it is included.[25] The line includes all the kings of the southern kingdom of Judah—as wicked as many of them were, all were descendants of David and therefore ancestors of Jesus Christ. Their inclusion might be explained theologically on the following grounds: (1) to demonstrate that Jesus was a man among men with a family tree that "decent" people often want to hide; and (2) it was unthinkable that there could be a severing of the covenant line of promise, because one of David's descendants was ordained to rule forever as Savior and Lord (**2 Samuel 7:12–13; 1 Chronicles 17:10–14**). The genetics of Judah, the tribe of the Sovereign portrayed in **Genesis 49:8–12**, could not be eradicated from them, a tribute to God's grace and glory.

Notes

1. For the birth dates and birth order of the sons of Jacob, see chart "**Genesis 35**: The Twelve Sons of Jacob, the Eponymous Originators of the Twelve Tribes of Israel." The narrative suggests that Judah, a widower, was in advanced age when he impregnated his daughter-in-law, Tamar (**Genesis 38:1–30**). Given the figures of longevity recorded in Scripture for the period, an age of 75 for Judah, born ca. 1925—see note 4 in chart "**Genesis 35**: The Twelve Sons of Jacob, the Eponymous Originators of the Twelve Tribes of Israel"—at the birth of Perez and Zerah is not unrealistic. The personal name Judah became a place name as well—the toponym for the *Kingdom of Judah*, referring to the land allotted to the tribe of Judah (including Simeon and Benjamin); for the towns allotted specifically to the tribe of Judah, see **Joshua 15:20–63**.

2. Tamar's name, meaning *date palm*, provides no clue to her ethnicity. The name "Tamar" is also a toponym (cf. **Ezekiel 47:19; 48:28**) but probably does not refer to "Tadmor in the desert," classical Palmyra in Mesopotamia in **1 Kings 9:18** and **2 Chronicles 8:4**, nor to "Hazezon Tamar," referring to ancient En Gedi in **2 Chronicles 20:2** (cf. **Genesis 14:7**). The town of Tamar in Judah was southwest of the Dead Sea, northeast of Kadesh Barnea, and west of the Arabah. That her name had no pagan overtones is clear from the fact that both David and his son Absalom had daughters by that name (**1 Chronicles 3:9** and **2 Samuel 14:27**, respectively).

3. Shelah's descendants are given in **1 Chronicles 4:21–23**.

4. Prior to the wise King Solomon, the sons/descendants of Zerah were considered the wisest men of Judah (cf. **1 Kings 4:29–31, 34; 1 Chronicles 2:6**); see note 11 in chart "**1 Chronicles 4**: Judah."

5. Mahol is mentioned in **1 Kings 4:31**. It is unclear whether Mahol was the son, grandson, or descendant of Zerah, or whether Mahol is possibly another name for Zerah (cf. **1 Chronicles 2:6**).

6. Caleb the son of Hezron in **1 Chronicles 2:9** is called Karmi in **Numbers 26:6** and **1 Chronicles 4:1**. Caleb the Judahite (Hezron's son; designated Caleb II in some charts) is not Caleb the Kenizzite, the son of Jephunneh (designated Caleb I in some charts), although they were brothers-in-law. For their kinship relationship, see chart "**1 Chronicles 2**: Caleb and Kenaz, the Sons of Jephunneh the Kenizzite."

7. The distinguished and wise man "Ethan the Ezrahite" (**1 Kings 4:31**) may have been the original composer of the "*maskil* of Ethan the Ezrahite" (**Psalm 89:0**).

8. Heman the son of Mahol (**1 Kings 4:31**) may have been the original composer of the "*maskil* of Heman the Ezrahite" (**Psalm 88:0**).

9. Darda in **1 Chronicles 2:6** (cf. Darda in **1 Kings 4:31**) is called "Dara" in many Heb. manuscripts.

10. Nahshon was the representative leader from the tribe of Judah during the wilderness years (**Numbers 1:7; 2:3; 7:12, 17; 10:14**). Nahshon's sister Elisheba (**Exodus 6:23**) married Aaron the high priest, thus permanently linking the kingly tribe of Judah with the priestly tribe of Levi.

11. Achar (**1 Chronicles 2:7**), also called Achan (**Joshua 7:1, 18, 24; 22:20**), was a descendant of Zerah. In ca. 1406 B.C., after the conquest of Jericho but before the conquest of Ai, Achar/Achan brought trouble on Israel by taking devoted (accursed) things in war that belonged to God alone; his sin brought guilt on the entire congregation (**Joshua 7:1–26; 22:20**). He was stoned to death in the "Valley of Achor," which was named for him (cf. **Joshua 7:24, 26**).

12. Rahab the Canaanite, a prostitute of Jericho, protected the Israelite spies from harm (cf. **Joshua 2:1–21; 6:22–25; Hebrews 11:31; James 2:25**), and they, in turn, spared her entire family in the razing of Jericho (**Joshua 6:23–25**). Rahab married Salmon the Judahite and became the great-great-grandmother of King David and an extraordinary ancestress of the Messiah (**Matthew 1:5**); see chart "**Matthew 1**: Jesus the Messiah–the Matthean Account."

13. See chart "**1 Samuel 16**: Jesse and the Judahites Who Lived in Bethlehem and Nearby Cities."

14. Jonathan, called "David's uncle" (presumably Jesse's brother or brother-in-law), was "a counselor, a man of insight and a scribe" (**1 Chronicles 27:32**).

15. Elihu (Heb. אֱלִיהוּא) is identified as "a brother of David" in **1 Chronicles 27:18**; he is most likely the same person as Jesse's firstborn son, named "Eliab" (Heb. אֱלִיאָב) in **1 Samuel 16:6; 17:13, 28; 1 Chronicles 2:13; 2 Chronicles 11:18**. Abihail, the daughter of Elihu/Eliab, married David's son Jerimoth (**2 Chronicles 11:18**). For further discussion about Elihu=Eliab, see notes 7 and 11 in chart "**1 Chronicles 2**: King David."

16. Abinadab, the second-born son of Jesse (**1 Samuel 16:8; 17:13; 1 Chronicles 2:13**), is certainly not: (1) Abinadab who kept the ark of the covenant for twenty years (ca. 1024–1004 B.C.) before it was moved to the City of David (cf. **2 Samuel 6:3–4; 1 Chronicles 13:7**; see chart "**1 Samuel 7**: The Family of Abinadab Who Oversaw the Ark of the Covenant") or (2) Abinadab the son of Saul (**1 Samuel 31:2; 1 Chronicles 8:33; 9:39; 10:2**).

17. He is variously called Shimea (**1 Chronicles 2:13; 20:7**); Shammah (**1 Samuel 16:9, 17:13**); and Shimeah (**2 Samuel 13:3, 32; 21:21**).

18. At times, David considered the sons of Zeruiah to be "too strong" for him—too forceful, unpredictable, and vengeful in their actions (cf. **2 Samuel 3:38–39**). Joab, in particular, was responsible for the innocent deaths of Absalom (David's son) and Amasa (**2 Samuel 18:14–15** and **2 Samuel 20:8–10**, respectively); therefore, David characterized Joab as a man who needlessly shed innocent blood "in peacetime as if in battle" and who killed without the king's knowledge or approval (**1 Kings 2:5, 31–33**). On his deathbed, David cautioned Solomon to "deal with him [Joab] according to your wisdom, but do not let his gray head go down to the grave in peace" (**1 Kings 2:6**). For the fate of Joab, see chart "**1 Samuel 14**: The Military Leaders under King Saul, King David, Absalom, and King Solomon."

19. Shimea's son Jonathan killed one of the *giants* (a Rapha descendant; **2 Samuel 21:20–21; 1 Chronicles 20:6–7**). See chart "**Deuteronomy 1**: The Giant Anakites, including Goliath and His Descendants."

20. After his father, Asahel, was killed in the extended war between David and Saul (cf. **2 Samuel 2:18–32**), Zebadiah succeeded him as the fourth of twelve commanders in David's army and was over 24,000 men (**1 Chronicles 27:7**). The apparent chronological conundrum that arises here can be resolved by the supposition that this was a posthumous designation in which Asahel, already dead, was given the honorary position as the fourth of David's twelve army captains. There is no absurdity in the idea that the honor may in some cases have been posthumous, the deceased being represented by his father or his son.

21. Onan knew that, according to the terms of levirate marriage, the child conceived with Tamar would not be his, so he "spilled his semen on the ground to keep from providing offspring for his brother [Er]." This is the etymology of *onanism* (also termed "coitus interruptus").

22. Timnah was a town in the hill country of the tribe of Judah (**Joshua 15:57**). Upon the death of his first wife (the daughter of Shua the Canaanite), Judah the widower went to Timnah to shear his sheep (**Genesis 38:12–13**). Rainey and Notley clarify the geographic location of the event: "the story of Judah and Tamar . . . takes place in the northern Shephelah near the junction of the Valley of Elah with the geographical 'trough' separating the Shephelah from the hill country of Judah (Gen 38). Jacob established a partnership with a Canaanite named Hirah who was from Adullam (Gen 38:1; Khirbet esh-Sheikh Madhkûr = Ḥorbat ʿAdullam). They pastured their flocks during shearing time in the vicinity of a certain Timnah (Gen 38:12). The other toponyms in the story prove that this Timnah must be Khirbet et-Tabbâneh (Hebrew Ḥorbat Tivna) east of the Valley of Elah in the foothills. It cannot be the Timnah in the Sorek Valley (Josh 15:10; Judg 14:1)." Anson F. Rainey and R. Steven Notley, *The Sacred Bridge* (Jerusalem: Carta, 2014), 115).

23. See chart "**Ruth 1**: Boaz, Elimelek, and Naomi and the Descendants of Boaz the Judahite and Ruth the Moabitess."

24. See chart "**1 Samuel 14**: The Military Leaders under Saul, David, Absalom, and Solomon."

25. See charts "**1 Chronicles 3**: Zerubbabel and Shealtiel and the Double Line of the Messiah through King David's Sons, Nathan and Solomon"; "**Matthew 1**: Jesus the Messiah–the Matthean Account"; and "**Luke 3**: Jesus: The Lukan Account."

1 CHRONICLES 2: KING DAVID

Approximate Dating: David was born in 1041 B.C. and died in 971 B.C., having reigned over Israel from ca. 1011–971 B.C. ***Relevant Scriptures:*** **1 Chronicles 2:3–17; also Genesis 24:67; 34:1; 38:27–30; Exodus 6:23; 1 Samuel 25:42-43; 2 Samuel 2:2, 32; 3:2–5; 5:13–16; 13:1, 4; 17:25; 1 Chronicles 3:1–9; 14:3–7; 27:18; 2 Chronicles 11:18; 13:2; Matthew 1:1–16; Luke 3:23–34**

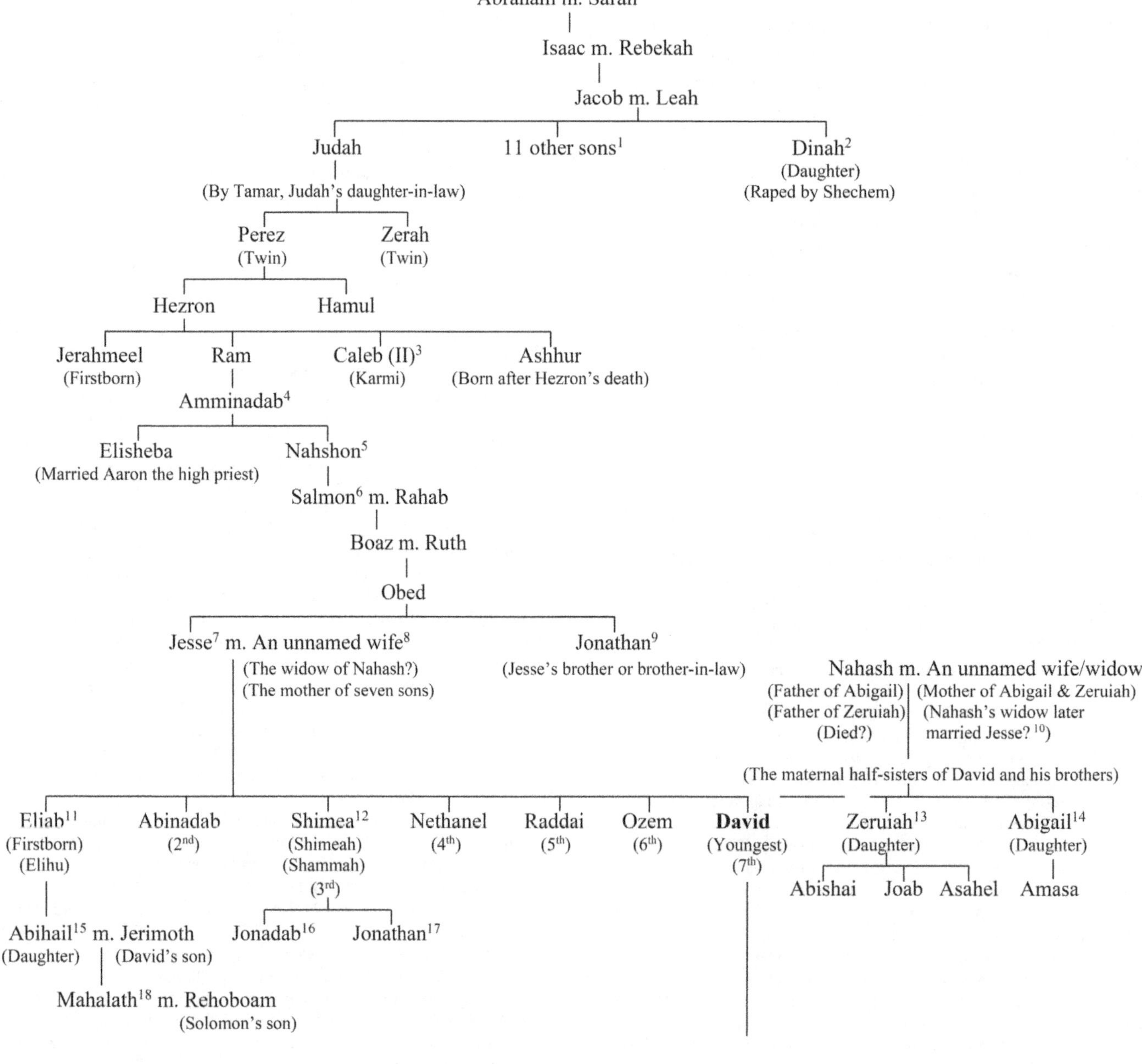

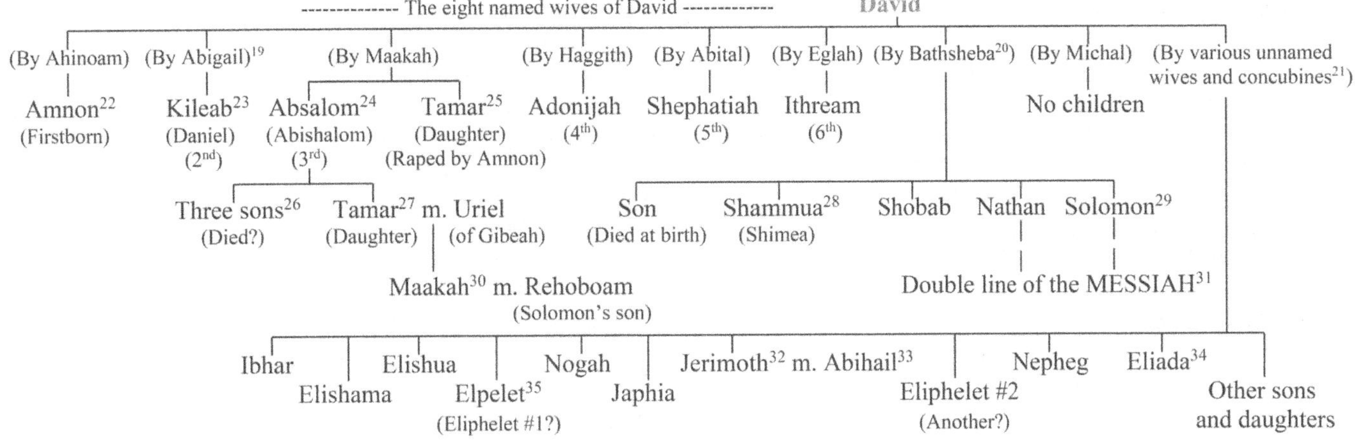

Biblical and Theological Significance

David's Biography

David was the youngest son of Jesse the Bethlehemite and a member of the tribe of Judah (**1 Samuel 16:10–11**). He was born in ca. 1041 B.C., some ten years after Saul began to reign. David become king of Judah when he was thirty years old (**2 Samuel 5:4**) and reigned for forty and one-half years (ca. 1011–971 B.C.)—seven and one-half years from Hebron (ca. 1011–1004 B.C.) and thirty-three years from Jerusalem (ca. 1004–971 B.C.; **2 Samuel 5:4–5; 1 Kings 2:11**). Upon David's death, the rule of the kingdom transferred to Bathsheba's son Solomon (**1 Kings 3:7; 1 Chronicles 22:5; 29:1–2**).

Several major turning points are evident in David's life.

David and Goliath

Soon after the prophet Samuel anointed David at about the age of fifteen, ca. 1026 B.C. (**1 Samuel 16:1, 10–13**), the Philistines went to war with Israel, and Saul and his army went out to meet them. Since David's brothers were there, their father, Jesse, sent David to take them supplies. David then volunteered to fight the Philistines' champion, Goliath. Armed solely with a slingshot and his skill as a marksman (cf. **1 Samuel 17:34–36**), David went to meet Goliath,[36] declaring that he came "in the name of the LORD Almighty" and that he would cut off Goliath's head (**1 Samuel 17:45–47**). With the first shot, a stone sunk into the giant's forehead, killing him. David took Goliath's sword and cut off the giant's head. Saul asked who this young victor was, and thus began David's friendship with Saul's son Jonathan, who "loved him [David] as himself" (**1 Samuel 18:1, 3**).

David and Saul

The accolades now given David after his defeat of Goliath —"Saul has slain his thousands, and David his tens of thousands" (**1 Samuel 18:7**)—began a series of events in which the jealous King Saul tried to kill David (**1 Samuel 18:10–11**). "Saul was afraid of David, because the LORD was with David but had departed from Saul. . . . In everything he [David] did he had great success, because the LORD was with him. When Saul saw how successful he was, he was afraid of him. But all Israel and Judah loved David because he led them in their campaigns" (**1 Samuel 18:12–16**). On Jonathan's urging, Saul swore not to put David to death (**1 Samuel 19:1–7**); however, Saul's malevolent and jealous schemes continued. When Saul's younger daughter, Michal, fell in love with David, Saul gave her in marriage to David for the bride price of "a hundred Philistine foreskins. . . . [but Saul's true intention] was to have David fall by the hands of the Philistines" (**1 Samuel 18:25**; see **vv. 17–29**). At one point, Michal helped David escape from her father who still intended him harm (**1 Samuel 19:11–24**). Then Saul went back on his betrothal of marriage and gave Michal to Paltiel (**1 Samuel 25:44**).[37] Eventually, David demanded that she be returned to him, but she bore him no children because she "despised him in her heart" when he danced joyously before the Lord as he brought the ark of God to the City of David (**2 Samuel 6:16**; cf. **3:13–16; 6:20–23**).

David Anointed King

After God removed the kingship from Saul, God chose the shepherd boy David to be Israel's next king, certifying it by him being anointed by Samuel the prophet, who was in his mideighties (**1 Samuel 16:1–13**). Later, after the Philistines defeated him, Saul committed suicide and David became king of Judah (**1 Samuel 31:1–4; 2 Samuel 2:3–4**). David reigned initially from his capital at Hebron (**2 Samuel 2:10–11**). He did not become king of all Israel until after the murder of Saul's son Ish-Bosheth, who had been placed on the throne of Israel for a brief two years (ca. 1005–1004 B.C.) by Abner, the son of Ner, the commander of Saul's army (**2 Samuel 2:8–10; 4:5–12**).[38] David killed the men who murdered Ish-Bosheth, and the tribes of Israel anointed David king (**2 Samuel 5:1–5**).

David and Nabal

Abigail was the "intelligent and beautiful" wife of Nabal,[39] the wealthy Calebite from Maon, known for being surly and mean in his dealings with others (**1 Samuel 25:2–3, 25**). While in the desert, David had helped Nabal's shepherds, so in a time of need, David asked Nabal[40] to furnish provisions for him and his hungry men, but Nabal vehemently refused. When Nabal's wife Abigail was informed, she gathered provisions and set out to intercede for her husband and to give much-needed rations to David. She praised God, extolled David's accomplishments, and took the blame for her husband's incompetence. Impressed, David informed her that had she not quickly interceded for her husband, "not one male belonging to Nabal would have been left alive" (**1 Samuel 25:34**). David thanked her and sent her back to her house, where Nabal had been feasting and getting drunk. When Abigail told Nabal what had transpired, "his heart failed him" and he died (**1 Samuel 25:37**). David then sent for Abigail, asking her to become his wife, and she accepted (**1 Samuel 25:39–42**).

The Davidic Covenant

Through the prophet Nathan, God made a covenant with David and told him that he would not take his mercy away from him as he had done with Saul, and that his kingdom of dynastic successors would last "forever" (**2 Samuel 7:15–16**). However, he also warned that covenant disobedience would result in severe consequences (**2 Samuel 7:14**).

David and Bathsheba, and the Death of Uriah

Although David is described as a man after God's own heart (**1 Samuel 13:14**), he was still fallible; his most egregious (and infamous) sin was the string of events in **2 Samuel 11:2–12:15** involving Bathsheba and her husband, Uriah. Bathsheba was the daughter of Eliam (or Ammiel)[41] (**2 Samuel 11:3; 1 Chronicles 3:5**) and the granddaughter of Ahithophel of Gilon of Judah, who was David's court counselor (**2 Samuel 15:12; 23:34; 1 Chronicles 27:33**). Bathsheba was the "very beautiful" wife of Uriah the Hittite (**2 Samuel 11:2–3**), who was one of David's military officers (**2 Samuel 23:39; 1 Chronicles 11:41**); apparently, Bathsheba and Uriah had no children. When David requested a private audience with Bathsheba at the palace (**2 Samuel 11**), "he took the ewe lamb [Bathsheba] that belonged to the poor man [Uriah]" (**2 Samuel 12:4**) and "he slept with her. . . . then she went back home. The woman conceived and sent word to David, saying, 'I am pregnant'" (**2 Samuel 11:4**). This episode, which began with David's lust, culminated in David's eventual premeditated murder of Uriah and the death of the first child (a son) born to David and Bathsheba (**2 Samuel 11; 12:9–10, 18–19**). The Lord then sent Nathan the prophet to remind David that God had given him the kingdoms of Israel and Judah and had saved him from the hand of Saul. God swore that David would face judgment "because you [David] despised me and took the wife of Uriah the Hittite to be your own" (**2 Samuel 12:10**; cf. **vv. 11–12; 16:21–22**). In response to his grief over his sin, David wrote **Psalm 51**, and in God's mercy, David was forgiven. David then took the widowed Bathsheba in marriage, and she gave birth to four sons (**1 Chronicles 3:5**), all of whom were born in Jerusalem (**2 Samuel 5:14; 11**). Her first son was Solomon (meaning "peace" or "replacement," **2 Samuel 12:24**). Matthew refers to Bathsheba in the genealogy of Christ as the mother of Solomon and the woman who "had been Uriah's wife" (**Matthew 1:6**).[42]

The "Sword Will Never Depart from Your House."

True to Nathan's prophecy (**2 Samuel 12:10**), David's family was beset by internal strife for the last years of his reign. David's son Amnon raped his half-sister Tamar, and, in retribution, Absalom (Tamar's full brother) murdered Amnon (**2 Samuel 13**). Absalom fled to Geshur near his mother's (Maakah's) family (cf. **2 Samuel 3:3**). Absalom returned three years later and was eventually forgiven by his father (**2 Samuel 13:34–39; 14:23–33**). However, within a short time, Absalom raised a rebellion against his father David (**2 Samuel 15**). Soon thereafter Absalom met his death—while riding through the forest of Ephraim,[43] he caught his head in low-lying boughs of a great oak tree and, while suspended there, David's military commander, Joab, killed him, much to David's lament (**2 Samuel 18:5–15, 29–33**).

The Restoration of Formal Temple Worship

After David's coronation, he set about to undertake a great many projects in Jerusalem suitable for a political and religious capital. Of interest here was his desire to erect a permanent place where Yahweh, Israel's God, might be worshiped according to Torah specifications. The ark of the covenant was in nearby Kiriath Jearim (**1 Chronicles 13:6**; cf. **Joshua 15:9, 60**), so David ordered that it be brought on a new cart to Jerusalem and placed in a temporary tent that he had prepared for it in the City of David (**2 Samuel 6:17; 1 Chronicles 15:1**). On the way, however, the cart tipped; to prevent the ark from falling to the ground, Uzzah[44] reached out to steady it, thereby rendering the holy ark unclean, and the Lord killed him (**2 Samuel 6:6–7**). Shaken by all this, David decided to leave the ark with the Levitical Merarite named Obed-Edom[45] until he could return again to retrieve it in the proper manner with the proper Levitical attendants. After three months, David successfully secured the ark of the covenant and brought it triumphantly into the City of David (**2 Samuel 6:12, 17; 1 Chronicles 6:31–32; 15:1–16:1; 23:32**). "Because of the wars waged against . . . David from all sides, he could not build a temple for the Name of the LORD" (**1 Kings 5:3–5**); rather, David's son Solomon completed the magnificent temple on Mount Moriah (north of the City of David) and the ark and the temporary tent were taken there. The ark of the covenant was placed in the inner sanctuary, which was the "Most Holy Place" (**1 Kings 7:51–8:13**; **2 Chronicles 5:1–6**) and "the cloud [the Divine Presence] filled the temple of the LORD" (**1 Kings 8:10**).

David's Death and Burial

As King David neared death, his son Adonijah[46] put himself forward to be Israel's next king (**1 Kings 1**). But before David died, he kept his oath to Bathsheba that their son Solomon would reign, and David formally declared Solomon as his successor (**1 Kings 1:28–30**). After the high priest Zadok anointed Solomon (**1 Kings 1:39**) and David instructed Solomon to keep the laws and commandments of the Lord, David died at age seventy and was buried in the City of David[47] (**1 Kings 2:1–10**).

Notes

1. For the names of the sons, see chart "**1 Chronicles 2**: Jacob (Israel) and His Twelve Sons."

2. The biblical narrative about the rape of Dinah by Shechem the son of Hamor the Hivite and the ensuing *honor killing* of Shechem, his father, and

all the circumcised males of the city by Simeon and Levi (the sons of Jacob), is recounted in **Genesis 34**.

3. Caleb, the son of Hezron in **1 Chronicles 2:9**—designated Caleb II elsewhere—is called Karmi in **Numbers 26:6; 1 Chronicles 4:1**. (In some translations, Caleb the Judahite is called *Chelubai* or *Kelubai*). Caleb II should not be confused with the Kenizzite named Caleb—designated Caleb I elsewhere—the son of Jephunneh; for the latter, see chart "**1 Chronicles 2**: Caleb and Kenaz, the Sons of Jephunneh the Kenizzite."

4. Amminadab the son of Ram (**Exodus 6:23; Ruth 4:19–20; 1 Chronicles 2:10; Matthew 1:4; Luke 3:33**) should not be confused with Amminadab the Levite (also called Izhar), the son of Kohath (**Exodus 6:18; 1 Chronicles 6:22**).

5. Nahshon was the leader from the tribe of Judah during the wilderness years (**Numbers 1:7; 2:3; 7:12, 17; 10:14**). Nahshon's sister Elisheba married Aaron, the first high priest of Israel (**Exodus 6:23**), and she became the *mother* of the Aaronic priesthood. In this way, the Aaronic priesthood originated as the union of a Levitical priest (Aaron) with a Judahite (Elisheba).

6. Salmon son of Nahshon (**Ruth 4:20–21; 1 Chronicles 2:11; Matthew 1:4; Luke 3:32**) should not be confused with Salma son of Hur, the father/founder/co-founder of Bethlehem (cf. **1 Chronicles 2:51, 54; 4:4**).

7. Jesse of Bethlehem of Judah (**1 Samuel 16:1, 18; 17:12**) was very old in the days of King Saul (**1 Samuel 17:12**). As the time neared for God to make known his choice for Israel's next king, Samuel was sent to Bethlehem to the household of Jesse "[because] I have chosen one of his sons to be king" (**1 Samuel 16:1**). The names of Jesse's sons appear in the record in two places—**1 Samuel 16:6–10** (a partial list of three) and **1 Chronicles 2:13–15** (a list of seven sons, including David)—but the number is unclear (i.e., **1 Samuel 16:10** refers to *seven* sons whereas **1 Samuel 17:12** suggests that there were *eight* sons). In **1 Samuel 16:5–13**, the sons passed by Samuel to be examined as he sought God's choice, but only three are named—Eliab, Abinadab, and Shammah; however, none of them was acceptable to Samuel the prophet. There was another, of course, young David, who was keeping the sheep, and with him there would be *eight* sons of Jesse. The Chronicler names only *seven* sons: Eliab, Abinadab, Shimeah, Nethanel, Raddai, Ozem, and David (and this is the list that is followed in the chart above). The confusion in the number of Jesse's sons may be related to Jesse's firstborn, "Elihu/Eliab" (see note 11).

8. There is a reference to David's (unnamed) mother and father (Jesse) living in Moab for a time (cf. **1 Samuel 22:3–4**). As a standard practice, the names of the mothers of Judah's kings are supplied, with four exceptions: David, Asa, Jehoram, and Ahaz (i.e., in contrast to the northern kingdom of Israel, where the names of the mothers of the kings are typically *not* given). The glaring omission of the name of David's mother seems to signal something unusual about her background or reputation that the narrator felt would bring reproach or shame to the righteous king of Israel. In this case, it was the reference to "Nahash" (the father of Abigail and Zeruiah, who were David's "sisters [half-sisters]," **2 Samuel 17:25; 1 Chronicles 2:16**) whose exact identity is uncertain (see below and notes 10, 13 and 14). For a discussion of David's mother—the widow of Nahash?—see Excursus A in chart "**1 Chronicles 3**: Zerubbabel and Shealtiel and the Double Line of the Messiah through King David's Sons, Nathan and Solomon."

The narrative accounts in **2 Samuel 17:27–29** and **1 Chronicles 19:1–5** may be relevant if David was distantly related to Nahash the king of Ammon, via David's half-sisters (Abigail and Zeruiah). When Nahash of Ammon died, David wished to show kindness to his son Hanun because Nahash had been kind to David (**2 Samuel 10:2; 1 Chronicles 19:1–2**). This seems not to be the ordinary protocol between monarchs on such occasions, but rather a common ancient Near East tradition stemming from covenant or familial connections resulting from intermarriage between royal houses. (Solomon's marriage to a daughter of Pharaoh Siamun of Egypt is a classic example; **1 Kings 3:1**). David kindly sent emissaries to the sons of Nahash, Hanun and Shobi, but certain Ammonite princes convinced Hanun, the heir apparent, that David intended them harm. Because of this, Hanun shamefully mistreated David's servants by shaving off half their beards and cutting their clothes so that their buttocks were uncovered—an action intended to humiliate an enemy (**2 Samuel 10:4–5; 1 Chronicles 19:3–4**). Shobi the prince of Ammon was part of the royal family and lived in "Rabbah of the Ammonites"; unlike his brother Hanun, Shobi continued to show kindness to David as his father Nahash had done (**2 Samuel 17:27–29**).

9. Jonathan (Jehonathan in some translations), "David's uncle"; served as David's counselor and a scribe in the royal court (**1 Chronicles 27:32**); he is shown in the chart as the "brother" of Jesse.

10. The biblical narrative in **1 Chronicles 19**, describing David's kindness to Nahash *the king of Ammon* and his attempt to show kindness to Hunan son of Nahash as well, would be consistent with the close family association between David and this particular Nahash. It is unclear, but Nahash the Ammonite (not just another man named Nahash) may have been the father of Abigail and Zeruiah, and they, in turn, were the maternal half-sisters of King David and his brothers—sharing the same (unnamed) mother but not the same father (cf. **2 Samuel 10:2; 17:25–27; 1 Chronicles 2:16–17; 19:1–2**). The genealogical presence of half-sisters for David and his brothers strongly implies that David's mother was married twice (see note 14). For a discussion of the possibility that David's mother was the *widow* of Nahash, see Excursus A in chart "**1 Chronicles 3**: Zerubbabel and Shealtiel and the Double Line of the Messiah through King David's Sons, Nathan and Solomon."

11. Eliab, the firstborn of Jesse (**1 Samuel 16:6; 17:13, 28; 1 Chronicles 2:13; 2 Chronicles 11:18**), is the same person named "Elihu" who is identified as "a brother of David" (**1 Chronicles 27:18**). Elihu (Heb. אֱלִיהוּא) the brother of David in **1 Chronicles 27:18** is the same person as Eliab (Heb. אֱלִיאָב) in **1 Samuel 16:6; 17:13** (see note 7), one meaning "My God is a Father" and the other "He is my God." The issue is perhaps best resolved as a matter of text transmission, *"ab"* reading אב and *"hu"* reading הו. (Modern printed square script can hardly reveal the similarity compared to ancient, more flowing script.) Eliab was jealous of David's anointing and of David's boast that he (the youngest) could kill Goliath the Philistine giant (**1 Samuel 17:28–37**). Abihail (the daughter of Eliab/Elihu) married her first cousin Jerimoth (David's son), and together they had a daughter named Mahalath who, in turn, married King Rehoboam (**2 Chronicles 11:18, 20–21**); see chart "**1 Kings 12**: Rehoboam, King of Judah." In some translations, Eliab/Elihu is also called "Eliah" (e.g., **2 Chronicles 11:18**, NKJV).

12. This brother of David is variously called Shimea (**1 Chronicles 2:13; 20:7**), Shimeah (**2 Samuel 13:3, 32**), and Shammah (**1 Samuel 16:9; 17:13**). Shimea/Shimeah/Shammah the Judahite should not be confused with Shimeah/Shimeam the Benjamite (cf. **1 Chronicles 8:32; 9:38**) nor with Shammah (Shammoth/Shamhuth?) son of Agee, who was a member of David's army (cf. **2 Samuel 23:11–12, 25, 33; 1 Chronicles 11:27**). All such names derive from the verb *shamach*, "hear, listen."

13. Zeruiah was the sister of Abigail (**2 Samuel 17:25**; cf. **1 Chronicles 2:15–16**). Both Zeruiah and Abigail were the daughters of a man named Nahash (rather than Jesse, David's father), thereby making them the maternal *half-sisters* of David and his brothers (i.e., sharing the same mother but not the same father). Zeruiah apparently married a man from Bethlehem (i.e., the father of Asahel; **2 Samuel 2:32**). The three sons of Zeruiah, listed in **1 Chronicles 2:16**, held prominent military posts in David's army; see chart "**1 Samuel 14**: The Military Leaders under Saul, David, Absalom, and Solomon."

14. Abigail is identified as the "daughter of Nahash" (**2 Samuel 17:25**). Nahash—a masculine name—is identified as the *father* of Abigail and Zeruiah (i.e., Jesse was not their father). Abigail married Jether the Ishmaelite and bore a son named Amasa (cf. **2 Samuel 17:25; 1 Chronicles 2:17**). Later, when Absalom revolted against David, Amasa was appointed as the commander of Absalom's army (**2 Samuel 17:25**). Eventually, Amasa was killed by his cousin Joab, the commander of David's army (**1 Kings 2:5, 32**).

It seems that David's mother (who is strikingly unnamed in Scripture) married twice, but the sequence of the marriages is unknown—one possibility is that she first married Nahash and gave birth to Abigail and Zeruiah and then Nahash died. Next, as the widow of Nahash, she married Jesse and gave birth to David and his brothers. In this way, Abigail and Zeruiah were the maternal half-sisters of King David and Jesse's other sons. This would be consistent with the second or levirate marriages are evident in multiples places in the ancestry of Jesus; for a discussion of these occurrences, refer to Excursus A in chart "**1 Chronicles 3**: Zerubbabel and Shealtiel and the Double Line of the Messiah through King David's Sons, Nathan and Solomon."

15. Abihail, the daughter of David's older brother Eliab, married "David's son Jerimoth" (Jerimoth was perhaps a son of one of David's concubines, and apparently a near-relative of Abihail (cf. **2 Chronicles 11:18**); see note 32.

16. Jonadab David's nephew is described as a "very shrewd man" (**2 Samuel 13:3**). When David's son Amnon became infatuated with his half-sister, Tamar—the daughter of Maakah and the "beautiful [full-] sister of Absalom"—Jonadab thought of a scheme to bring them together. Jonadab advised Amnon to feign sickness so that Tamar would come and fix food for him (**2 Samuel 13:3–5**). Tragically, Amnon used the opportunity to rape and disgrace her (**2 Samuel 13:7–20**), which subsequently led to the revenge-murder of Amnon by Absalom (see notes 24 and 25).

17. David's nephew Jonathan was famous for killing one of the Raphites

(giants) of Gath (**2 Samuel 21:20–21; 1 Chronicles 20:6–7**); see chart "**Deuteronomy 1**: The Giant Anakites, including Goliath and His Descendants."

18. Mahalath bore Rehoboam three sons: Jeush, Shemariah, and Zaham (**2 Chronicles 11:19**).

19. Abigail was the widow of Nabal of Carmel, who was of Calebite–Kenizzite ancestry (**1 Samuel 25:3, 39–42; 27:3; 30:5; 2 Samuel 2:2; 3:3; 1 Chronicles 3:1**); see chart "**1 Samuel 25**: Nabal and Abigail." Carmel (**Joshua 15:55**) in the Judean wilderness is identified as "Khirbet el-Kirmil, also about 8 miles (13 km) southeast of Hebron, not far from Maon" [Anson F. Rainey and R. Steven Notley, *The Sacred Bridge: Carta's Atlas of the Biblical World* (Jerusalem: Carta, 2014), 148].

20. Bathsheba (or the textual variant Bathshua, which is found in some translations) was the daughter of Eliam (or Ammiel; cf. **2 Samuel 11:3; 1 Chronicles 3:5**) and the granddaughter of Ahithophel the Gilonite, from Giloh of Judah (**2 Samuel 15:12; 23:34**), who was King David's court counselor (**2 Samuel 15:12; 1 Chronicles 27:33**). Bathsheba's father, Eliam/Ammiel, was also one of David's mighty men (**2 Samuel 23:34**). She was first married to Uriah the Hittite (**2 Samuel 11:3**), one of David's important military officers (**2 Samuel 23:39; 1 Chronicles 11:41**), but apparently, they had no children. After David illicitly took Uriah's wife Bathsheba and slept with her (**2 Samuel 11**), she conceived and bore David a son, but at the hand of the Lord, the child died (**2 Samuel 12:1–23**). After David's murder of Uriah, he took Bathsheba as his own wife (**2 Samuel 11:26–27**) and she bore four sons: Shimea, Shobab, Nathan, and Solomon (**1 Chronicles 3:5**), all born in Jerusalem (**2 Samuel 5:13–14**). Matthew refers to Bathsheba in the genealogy of Christ as the mother of Solomon and poignantly adds that she "had been Uriah's wife" (**Matthew 1:6**). For the messianic line that goes through two of the four sons of David and Bathsheba, see chart "**1 Chronicles 3**: Zerubbabel and Shealtiel and the Double Line of the Messiah through King David's Sons, Nathan and Solomon."

21. References to David's concubines include **2 Samuel 5:13; 15:16; 16:21–22; 19:5; 20:3**.

22. These first six sons of David—Amnon, Kileab, Absalom, Adonijah, Shephatiah, and Ithream—are listed in **2 Samuel 3:2–5** and **1 Chronicles 3:1–3**; see chart "**1 Chronicles 3**: David's Children Born in Hebron and Jerusalem."

23. Kileab (**2 Samuel 3:3**) is also called Daniel (**1 Chronicles 3:1**).

24. Absalom is also known as Abishalom (**1 Kings 15:2, 10**). To avenge Amnon's rape of Tamar (Absalom's full sister), Absalom murdered Amnon (his half-brother) in ca. 985 B.C. (**2 Samuel 13**). After the incident, Absalom went into exile for three years, ca. 985–982 B.C. (**2 Samuel 13:38**). When he finally returned to Jerusalem, he remained alienated from his father for the next two years (**2 Samuel 14:28**). Eventually, Absalom won the confidence of the people and led a rebellion against his father, in which David fled Jerusalem (**2 Samuel 15:13–30**; cf. **Psalm 3**). Absalom had three sons, all of whom apparently died, and one beautiful daughter, Tamar (**2 Samuel 14:27**), who was named after Absalom's sister (Tamar), who had been raped (**2 Samuel 13:1**).

25. Tamar the daughter of David (**2 Samuel 13:1**) was the full sister of Absalom, as pointed out in **2 Samuel 13:4; 20, 22, 32**, although she is never specifically said to be the daughter of Maakah, Absalom's mother. One of the tragedies of polygamy was the competitive relationships that inevitably followed. Tamar was raped by her half-brother, Amnon (**2 Samuel 13:14**). To avenge the act, Absalom ordered his men to murder Amnon (**2 Samuel 13:28–29**); for the narrative details about the rape of Tamar by Amnon, see **2 Samuel 13**. The tragedies became part of the fulfillment of Nathan's prophecy (after David's transgression with Bathsheba) that the sword would never depart from David's house (**2 Samuel 12:10**).

26. Presumably, Absalom's three sons died, since Absalom built a monument for himself and lamented that he had no one to carry on his name (**2 Samuel 14:27; 18:18**).

27. Tamar, the only daughter of Absalom, was "a beautiful woman" (**2 Samuel 14:27**). She was obviously named for Tamar, "the beautiful sister of Absalom" (her aunt) who had been raped by Amnon, David's son (**2 Samuel 13**); see note 25. It seems that Tamar the daughter of Absalom married Uriel of Gibeah and had a daughter Maakah, who married Solomon's son Rehoboam (cf. **2 Chronicles 11:21–22; 13:2**); see chart "**1 Kings 12**: Rehoboam, King of Judah."

28. Shimea in **2 Samuel 5:14** is called Shammua in **1 Chronicles 14:4**; he was probably named after his uncle Shimea/Shimeah/Shammah, the older brother of David (see note 12).

29. Upon David's death in 971 B.C., Solomon succeeded his father to the throne of Israel (**1 Kings 2:12**).

30. Maakah was the "daughter of Uriel of Gibeah" (**2 Chronicles 13:2**) and the *granddaughter* (not the daughter) of Absalom. The text of **2 Samuel 14:27** clarifies that Absalom had only one daughter—"three sons and a daughter were born to Absalom. His daughter's name was Tamar." Thus, Tamar married Uriel of Gibeah and they, in turn, had a daughter named Maakah. For that reason, the text of **1 Kings 15:2** and **15:10** should read, "Maakah *granddaughter* [not daughter] of Abishalom." Maakah became the favored wife of King Rehoboam (Solomon's son) and she bore him four sons—Abijah, Attai, Ziza, and Shelomith (**2 Chronicles 11:20–22**); see chart "**1 Kings 12**: Rehoboam, King of Judah."

31. See charts "**1 Chronicles 3**: Zerubbabel and Shealtiel and the Double Line of the Messiah through King David's Sons, Nathan and Solomon" and "**Matthew 1**: Ancestry of Mary and Joseph (Based on Scripture and Church Tradition) and How Mary and Joseph May Have Been Related."

32. Jerimoth is not mentioned by name in the lists of David's sons in **2 Samuel 5:13–16, 1 Chronicles 3:1–9** or **1 Chronicles 14:3–7**. In **2 Chronicles 11:18**, Jerimoth is called "David's son," but the context suggests that he might have been a *relative* or a *descendant* of David, or perhaps a son of a concubine, as suggested by Edward Lewis Curtis in *A Critical Exegetical Commentary on the Books of Chronicles* (Edinburgh: Clark, 1952), 369. Mahalath the daughter of Jerimoth and Abihail (David's niece) married King Rehoboam (David's grandson) (**2 Chronicles 11:18**).

33. For Abihail, see note 15.

34. Eliada in **1 Chronicles 3:8** is known by the variant name Beeliada in **1 Chronicles 14:7**.

35. The names of the nine sons of David who were born in Jerusalem are given in **1 Chronicles 3:5–8**. Seemingly, *two* sons of David are named "Eliphelet" in **1 Chronicles 3:6, 8**; one is called "Elpelet" in **1 Chronicles 14:5** and the other "Eliphelet" in **1 Chronicles 14:7**. For these reasons, the chart refers to them as Eliphelet #1 and Eliphelet #2. Also, refer to the chart "**1 Chronicles 3**: David's Children Born in Hebron and Jerusalem."

36. For the ancestry of Goliath, see chart "**Deuteronomy 1**: The Giant Anakites, including Goliath and His Descendants."

37. Paltiel the son of Laish was from Gallim in the tribal territory of Benjamin (**1 Samuel 25:44; 2 Samuel 3:15**).

38. Saul's son Ish-Bosheth (**2 Samuel 2:8, 10, 12, 15; 3:7–8, 11, 14–15; 4:1, 5, 8, 12**)—also called Esh-Baal (**1 Chronicles 8:33; 9:39; 10:2**)—did not immediately come to the throne after his father's death in 1011 B.C.; rather, there was an apparent interregnum (ca. 1011–1006 B.C.) during which time Abner (Saul's commander-in-chief) maintained control (**2 Samuel 2:8–11**). Ish-Bosheth did not assume the throne of Israel until 1005 B.C. His short-lived kingship lasted from ca. 1005–1004 B.C., where he ruled from his capital at Mahanaim in the Transjordan, ruling over "Gilead, Ashuri [otherwise unknown, possibly Asher; **Joshua 17:7**] and Jezreel, and also over Ephraim, Benjamin and all Israel" (**2 Samuel 2:8–11**; cf. **1 Chronicles 8:33; 9:39**).

39. See chart "**1 Samuel 25**: Nabal and Abigail."

40. The basis for David's request could be twofold: (1) David (Judahite) and Nabal (Calebite–Kenizzite) were distantly related through the marriage of the "daughter of Hezron" (David's ancestor) to Caleb the Kenizzite (Nabal's ancestor); see charts "**1 Samuel 25**: Nabal and Abigail" and "**1 Chronicles 4**: Judah"; and/or (2) David states in **1 Samuel 25:21** that he had been "watching over this fellow's [Nabal's] property in the wilderness so that nothing of his was missing." Furthermore, David's shepherds are described as "a wall around [Nabal's men and property]" the whole time they had been herding their sheep near them (**1 Samuel 25:16**). So in a time of need, David reasonably expected kindness from the wealthy Nabal (i.e., owner of 1000 goats and 3,000 sheep, who had just slaughtered sheep for his own sheep shearers), and also because David's request was not a specific demand; he only says, "Please give your servants and your son David whatever you can find for them" (**1 Samuel 25:8**).

41. Eliam in **2 Samuel 11:3** and **23:34** is Ammiel in **1 Chronicles 3:5**. A textual corruption is clearly in view between the readings. Eliam/Ammiel was one of David's mighty warriors (**2 Samuel 23:34**).

42. For the significance of Bathsheba's marriage to David, see Excursus A in chart "**1 Chronicles 3**: Zerubbabel and Shealtiel and the Double Line of the Messiah through King David's Sons, Nathan and Solomon."

43. The "forest of Ephraim," though not in the tribal area of Ephraim, was a densely forested region that, 3,000 years ago, was located in Transjordan Gilead, north of the Jabbok River (**2 Samuel 18:6**; cf. **Joshua 17:15, 18**).

44. See chart "**1 Samuel 7**: The Family of Abinadab Who Oversaw the Ark of the Covenant."

45. See chart "**2 Samuel 6**: Obed-Edom, the Levitical Gatekeeper and Keeper of the Ark."

46. Even after Solomon's accession to the throne, Adonijah continued his regal aspirations by asking for Abishag—the beautiful young woman who had attended to the elderly, ailing King David—to be given to him as his wife. Solomon understood this ruse and had Adonijah put to death (**1 Kings 2:13–25**).

47. "City of David" is not another name for Jerusalem as a whole, but for David's original settlement on the "fortress of Zion," a hillock in the southern area of the Iron II period-city, between the Kidron Valley on the east and the Tyropoeon Valley on the west (**2 Samuel 5:7–9; 6:16–19; 1 Kings 8:1; 1 Chronicles 11:5; 2 Chronicles 5:2**). With the geographic expansion of the city over the ages, the name "Zion" came to be associated with the temple/Temple Mount (**2 Chronicles 2:6; 9:11; 74:2; 78:67–68**) and, by the time of the prophets, denoted the presence of God with his restored people (cf. **Isaiah 12:6; 51:16; Ezekiel 28:14; 36:35; Zechariah 2:10–12**). Modern day "Zion" is geographically associated with the elevated Upper City, in the southwestern part of Jerusalem overlooking the junction of the Kidron and Hinnom valleys.

1 CHRONICLES 2: HEZRON

Approximate Dating: from the time of Jacob, ca. 2006 to 1859 B.C. to the time of the post-exilic descendants of Hezron in 538/400 B.C.; Judah was born ca. 1925 B.C.; Perez and Hezron were living in 1876 B.C. when the 40-member family of Jacob migrated to Egypt[1]
Relevant Scriptures: **1 Chronicles 2:18–24, 50–55;** also **Genesis 29:35; 38:12–30; 46:12; Exodus 35:30; 38:22; Numbers 26:21; Ruth 4:18–19; 1 Chronicles 2:3–5, 9; 2 Chronicles 1:5**

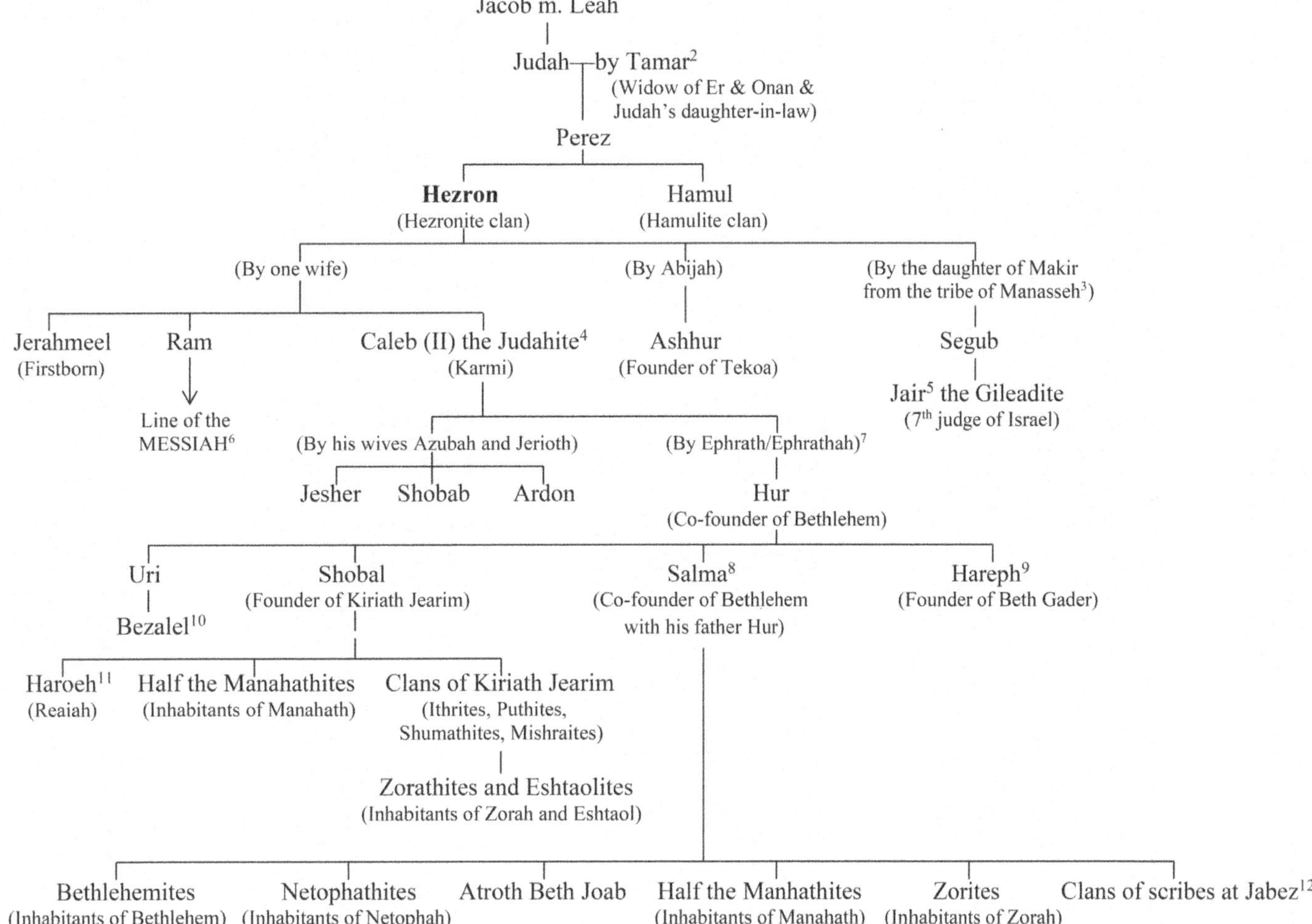

Biblical and Theological Significance

Hezron's Family

Hezron had children by three wives. When he was sixty years old, he married the (unnamed) daughter of Makir, the son of Manasseh (**1 Chronicles 2:21**; cf. **Genesis 50:23**) and became the ancestor of Jair the judge.[13] Hezron's posthumous son, Ashhur, was the founder of Tekoa, also known as the birthplace of the prophet Amos (**1 Chronicles 2:24; 4:5; Amos 1:1**). Hezron's son, Caleb/Karmi, married Ephrath/Ephrathah, who is the matronymic namesake of Bethlehem. This famous town is variously identified as "Caleb Ephrathah" (**1 Chronicles 2:24**), "Ephrath" (**Genesis 35:19; 48:7**), "Ephrathah" (**Ruth 4:11; Psalm 132:6**) and "Bethlehem Ephrathah" (**Micah 5:2**); it was the birthplace of both David and Jesus (**1 Samuel 16:1; Luke 2:4–7**, respectively; cf. **Matthew 2:1, 6, 8; Luke 2:15; John 7:42**), and ironically, was the deathplace of Hezron (**1 Chronicles 2:24**).

Hezron's Descendants

Hur and Salma were co-founders of Bethlehem (**1 Chronicles 2:51; 4:4**). Later in Israel's history after the captivity, former inhabitants of Kiriath Jearim (**Ezra 2:25; Nehemiah 7:29**), Bethlehem and Netophah (**Ezra 2:21–22; Nehemiah 7:26**), and Zorah (**Nehemiah 11:29**) returned from Babylon and re-occupied those cities in the post-exile.

Notes

1. See chart "**Genesis 46**: The Extended Family of Jacob (Seventy Descendants) Who Migrated to Egypt."

2. First, Tamar was the wife of Er (Judah's firstborn) and then second, of Er's brother Onan, but Er and Onan both died at God's hand for their offensiveness to him (**Genesis 38:6–10**). Judah then promised Tamar that she would marry his third son, Shelah, when Shelah grew up. When Judah refused to honor his word (**Genesis 38:11, 14**), Tamar, in desperation, disguised herself as a prostitute, and Judah unknowingly slept with her. She became pregnant and gave birth to twin sons, Perez and Zerah, thus explaining how Judah came to have children by his daughter-in-law (cf. **Genesis 38:12–30**).

3. This wife of Hezron is identified in **1 Chronicles 2:21–22**: "Hezron, when he was sixty years old, married the daughter of Makir the father of Gilead. He made love to her, and she bore him Segub [the father of Jair]." See chart "**1 Chronicles 7**: Manasseh (The Half-Tribe of West Manasseh)."

4. Caleb in **1 Chronicles 2:9** (designated "Caleb II the Judahite" in the chart above and elsewhere) is the same as Karmi in **1 Chronicles 4:1**. Caleb/Karmi had children by three wives—Azubah, Jerioth, and Ephrath/Ephrathah (cf. **1 Chronicles 2:18–19**). The descendants of Caleb/Karmi formed the "Karmite clan" (cf. **Numbers 26:21**). Caleb (II) the Judahite (son of Hezron, son of Perez, son of Judah) is not Caleb (I) the Kenizzite, the son of Jephunneh (although they were brothers-in-law; for clarification, see charts "**1 Chronicles 2**: Caleb and Kenaz, the Sons of Jephunneh the Kenizzite" and "**1 Chronicles 2**: Jerahmeel and His Descendant, Elishama, Who Appears to Be a Compiler of Historical and Genealogical Records in 1 & 2 Chronicles").

5. Hezron's grandson Jair was the seventh judge of Israel (**Judges 10:3**); see chart "**Judges 6**: Gideon (Fifth Judge) and His Son, Abimelek the False Judge, Jair (Seventh Judge), and Jephthah (Eighth Judge)–Judges of Israel from the Tribe of Manasseh."

6. The line of the Messiah passed through Judah–Perez–Hezron–Ram (cf. **Matthew 1:2–4**; **Luke 3:33–34**). See charts "**Matthew 1**: Jesus Christ–the Matthean Account" and "**Luke 3**: Jesus: The Lukan Account."

7. She is called Ephrath in **1 Chronicles 2:19** and Ephrathah in **1 Chronicles 2:50; 4:4**. See chart "**1 Chronicles 4**: Hur and Salma, the Co-Founders of Bethlehem."

8. Salma son of Hur in **1 Chronicles 2:51, 54** should not be confused with a fellow Judahite, Salmon son of Nahshon and father of Boaz (**Ruth 4:20–21; 1 Chronicles 2:11; Matthew 1:4–5; Luke 3:32**).

9. Hareph was the son of Hur (**1 Chronicles 2:50–51**), and therefore, he is not Haroeh/Reaiah (see note 10), the son/descendant of Shobal (**1 Chronicles 2:51**).

10. Bezalel was the artisan of the tabernacle in the wilderness and the supervisor of its construction in the days of Moses (**Exodus 31:1–5; 35:30–36:7**). See chart "**Exodus 31**: Bezalel, the Chief Artisan of the Tabernacle and Its Furnishings, and His Assistant, Oholiab."

11. Haroeh the son/descendant of Shobal in **1 Chronicles 2:52** is called Reaiah the son of Shobal in **1 Chronicles 4:2**. The son of Haroeh/Reaiah was Jahath, and Jahath's sons/descendants included Ahumai and Lahad (clans of Zorathites); see chart "**1 Chronicles 4**: Judah."

12. Jabez was the eponymous ancestor of the Jabez–Rekabite scribal community near Jerusalem, which was known for writing and preserving the ancient scrolls of God's word (**1 Chronicles 2:55**). For the lineage of Jabez, see charts "**1 Chronicles 4**: Judah" and "**Judges 4**: Heber and Jael (Kenites) and Their Descendants Who Co-Mingled with the Pious Jabez–Rekabite Scribal Community in Jerusalem."

13. See chart "**Judges 6**: Gideon (Fifth Judge) and His Son, Abimelek the False Judge, Jair (Seventh Judge), and Jephthah (Eighth Judge)–Judges of Israel from the Tribe of Manasseh."

1 CHRONICLES 2: JERAHMEEL AND HIS DESCENDANT, ELISHAMA, WHO APPEARS TO BE A COMPILER OF HISTORICAL AND GENEALOGICAL RECORDS IN 1 & 2 CHRONICLES

Approximate Dating: Jacob, 2006–1859 B.C.; Jerahmeel, ca. 1850 B.C. to the time of Elishama the scribe, ca. 609–598 B.C. ***Relevant Scriptures:*** **1 Chronicles 2:25–41**; also **Numbers 26:21; 2 Kings 25:25; 1 Chronicles 2:9–10; Jeremiah 36:12, 20–21; 41:1 Matthew 1:3–4; Luke 3:33–34**

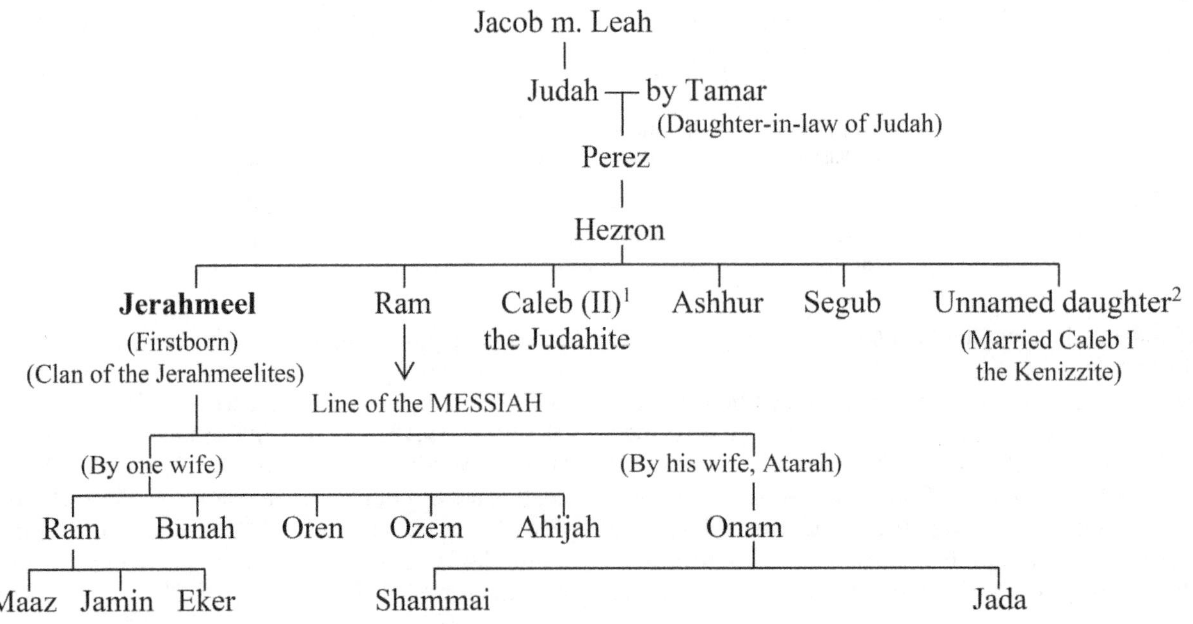

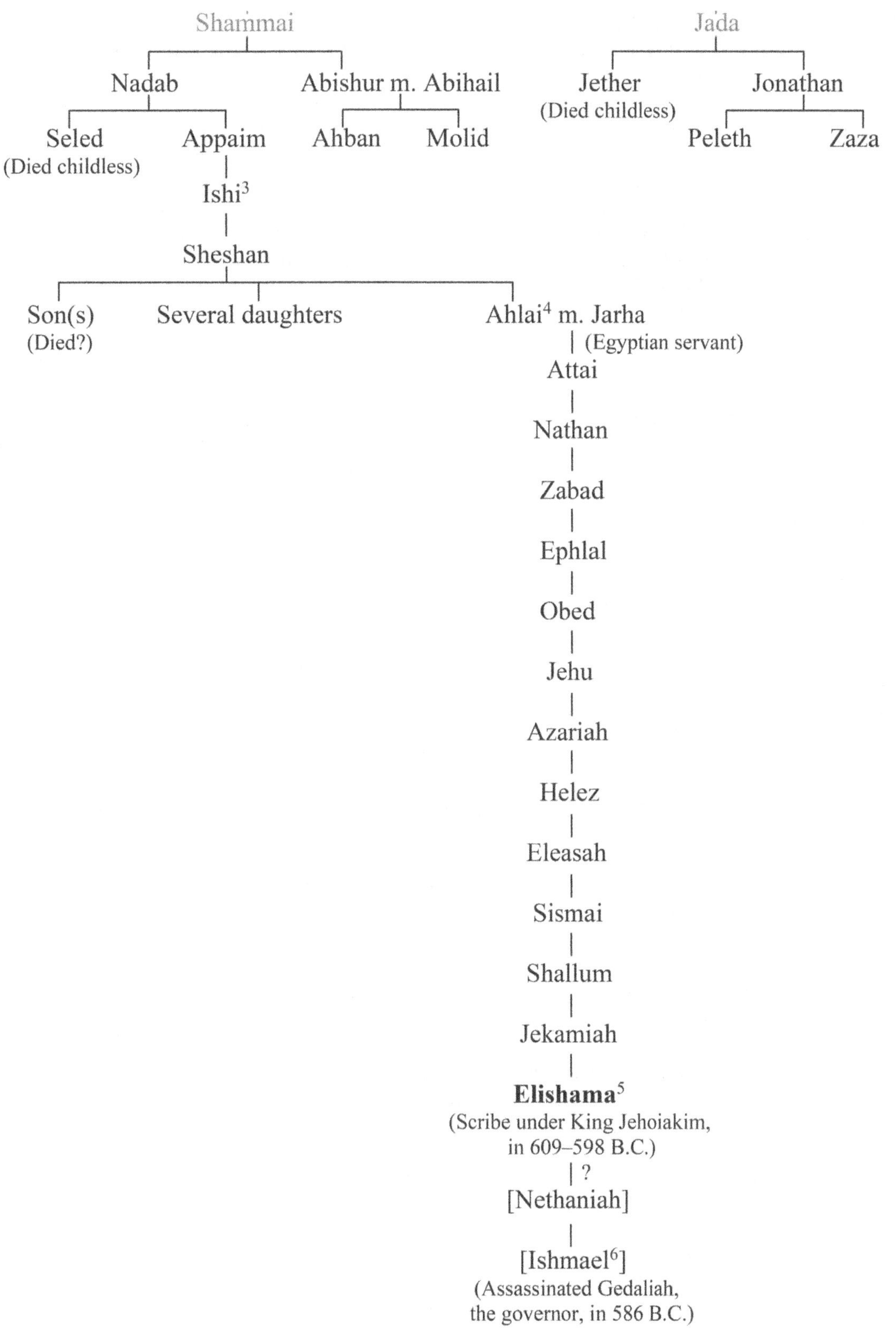

Biblical and Theological Significance

The Family of Jerahmeel

The descendants of Jerahmeel (the Jerahmeelite clan) occupied certain cities in Judah (cf. **1 Samuel 27:10; 30:29**). Jerhameel's sister married Caleb (I) the Kenizzite, son of Jephunneh; thus Caleb (II) the Judahite (also called Karmi) and Caleb I the Kenizzite were *brothers-in law.*[7] Intermarriage appears to have contributed to the close association among certain Jerahmeelites, Kenizzites, and Kenites (cf. **Joshua 14:13–15; 15:54; 1 Samuel 27:10; 30:27–31; 1 Chronicles 2:42–49, 55; 4:13–18**).

Elishama the Jerahmeelite as a Candidate to Be the Compiler of Historical and Genealogical Records

The elaborate *linear* genealogy of the Jerahmeel clan terminating with Elishama clearly shows that he served an important *functional* role in the composition of **Chronicles**. There are several men by that name in Scripture;[8] but of them, the concluding figure in the Jerahmeel clan—who is twenty-four (inclusive) generations removed from Judah—fits most closely chronologically with Elishama, the scribal secretary under King Jehoiakim/Eliakim (ca. 609–598 B.C.). Elishama occupied formal scribal chambers (called the *room of Elishama*) in the royal palace, consistent with his literacy, administrative role, and high social status in the royal court (**Jeremiah 36:12, 20–21**).

The Role of Elishama in the Overall Composition of Chronicles

Elishama appears to be an early compiler–organizer of the many historical and genealogical records found in **Chronicles** for several reasons: (1) As a scribal secretary in the royal court (i.e., an official in the court of King Jehoiakim/Eliakim), he would have had access to Israel and Judah's trove of written sources, royal annals, and past genealogies.[9] (2) Summarizing the nation's history and the genealogical heritage of the people in the pre-exile—in what could be called the "Elishama scribal records"—informed the successive wave of post-exilic returnees from Babylon (i.e., those who returned with Zerubbabel in 538 B.C., with Ezra in 458 B.C., and with Nehemiah in 444 B.C.) as to "who" they were (from an genealogical perspective) and "how" and "where" they should live in their homeland and in Jerusalem. Also, these records informed the priestly and Levitical servants at the Second Temple (completed in 516 B.C.) of their eligibility and responsibilities in their respective offices. (3) It is very possible that Elishama went into exile during one of the later deportations of Judah—in 597 B.C. (cf. **2 Kings 24:10–14**) or in 587 B.C. (cf. **2 Kings 25:1–24**)—and become a compiler-editor of information there as well.

Concerning the Dating and Authorship of Chronicles

The majority of interpreters have dated **Chronicles** to the latter half of the fifth century or the early decades of the fourth century B.C.[10] It is reasonable to date the book in the period from the time of Zerubbabel to soon after the ministries of Ezra and Nehemiah (between 538 and 400 B.C.).[11] The major themes of the book fit well with these boundaries. The Chronicler's extensive use of historical documents and devotion to numerical and chronological details indicate that he was giving his readers an accurate historical record. Here the Chronicler may have drawn heavily upon the "Elishama scribal records" written during the pre-exile (609–598 B.C.) to address the needs of the community who had recently returned from Babylonian exile and to encourage and guide them as they sought the full restoration of the kingdom.

Given that there are many elements in Chronicles that demand knowledge of persons and events long after 600 B.C.,[12] Elishama is an unlikely candidate to be the *final* compiler-editor of **1 & 2 Chronicles** (i.e., the *Chronicler*). Rather, the best solution may be to suppose there were several "chroniclers" who used the body of pre-exilic materials, such as those compiled by Elishama the Jerahmeelite scribe, which were then carried forward by other scribes (in exile or in the post-exile), and then brought to a conclusion by the final Chronicler of ca. 400 B.C. The involvement of Elishama and other scribes is strong evidence that **1 & 2 Chronicles** was an organic "living document" that developed over time and only took final form around 400/375 B.C.

Notes

1. Caleb in **1 Chronicles 2:9** (called "Caleb II the Judahite" in the chart above) is the same person as Karmi in **1 Chronicles 4:1**. The descendants of Caleb (II) the Judahite, the son of Hezron, are given in **1 Chronicles 2:18–20, 50–55**.

2. For the children of Caleb (I) the Kenizzite and the daughter of Hezron, see **1 Chronicles 2:42–45** and the charts "**1 Chronicles 2**: Caleb and Kenaz, the Sons of Jephunneh the Kenizzite" and "**1 Chronicles 4**: Judah."

3. Ishi the son of Appaim, a descendant of Jerahmeel (**1 Chronicles 2:31**) is not Ishi the father of Zoheth and the grandfather of Ben-Zoheth in **1 Chronicles 4:20**, who was a Kenizzite; see charts "**1 Chronicles 2**: Caleb and Kenaz, the Sons of Jephunneh the Kenizzite" and "**1 Chronicles 4**: Judah."

4. The son(s) of Sheshan died, leaving him no heirs (cf. **1 Chronicles 2:31, 34**), so his daughter Ahlai married Jarha.

5. The maximal depth of this lineage segment is unique among Old Testament non-kingly genealogies and clearly emphasizes a singular and influential role for Elishama. Most likely he was one of the author(s)-compiler(s)-historian(s) of **1 & 2 Chronicles** and/or *specifically* the recorder of the genealogies in **1 Chronicles 1–9**. Furthermore, given that he is the terminal figure in the Jerahmeel line, this Elishama is probably the same person identified as Elishama "the secretary," who was a court official under King Jehoiakim/Eliakim of Judah in 609–598 B.C. (**Jeremiah 36:12, 20**). It is unclear whether Elishama is related to "Ishmael son of Nethaniah, the son of Elishama" (see note 6).

6. Ishmael is identified as "Ishmael son of Nethaniah, the son of Elishama, who was of royal blood" (**2 Kings 25:25**; **Jeremiah 41:1**), but there is no unequivocable evidence that he was the grandson of Elishama the Jerahmeelite who is highlighted in the chart. (Presumably "royal blood" here indicates that Ishmael was a *distant relative* of the kings of Judah.) Ishmael son of Nethaniah assassinated Gedaliah, who was appointed the governor of the people who remained in Judah during the exilic period (**Jeremiah 41:1–3**); see charts "**2 Kings 25**: Gedaliah, Governor over the Remnant People of Judah During the Early Days of the Exile" and "**Jeremiah 36**: The Officials and Scribes in the Palace of King Jehoiakim Who Heard the Reading of the Scroll of Jeremiah (Pre-Exile)."

7. For clarity, **1 Chronicles 2:42** should read, "Caleb the *brother-in-law* of Jerahmeel" (i.e., not "Caleb the *brother* of Jerahmeel").

8. The various figures named Elishama are: (1) the grandfather of Joshua, who lived ca. 1500–1445/1400 B.C. (**Numbers 1:10; 2:18; 7:48, 53; 10:22; 1 Chronicles 7:26**); (2) the son of David, who lived ca. 1020–950 B.C. (**2 Samuel 5:16; 1 Chronicles 3:5, 8; 14:7**); (3) the priest under Jehoshaphat (ca. 872–848 B.C.; **2 Chronicles 17:8**); (4) the secretary under Jehoiakim/Eliakim (ca. 609–598 B.C.); and (5) the last individual of the Jerahmeel lineage (**1 Chronicles 2:41**), who is probably the same person as #4.

9. Elishama could have been instrumental in compiling (in whole, or in part) several written kingly sources, including:

- "Book of the annals of King David" (**1 Chronicles 27:24**),
- "Annals of Jehu" (**2 Chronicles 20:34**),
- "The book of the kings of Israel" (**2 Chronicles 20:34**),
- "The book of the kings of Israel and Judah" (**1 Chronicles 9:1; 2 Chronicles 27:7; 35:27; 36:8**),
- "The book of the kings of Judah and Israel" (**2 Chronicles 16:11; 25:26; 28:26; 32:32**),
- "The annals of the kings of Judah" (**1 Kings 14:29; 15:23; 22:45; 2 Kings 8:23; 12:19; 14:18; 15:6, 36; 20:20; 21:25; 23:28; 24:5**),
- "The annals of the kings of Israel" (**1 Kings 14:19; 15:31; 16:5, 14, 20, 27; 22:39; 2 Kings 1:18; 10:34; 13:8, 12; 14:15, 28; 15:11, 15, 21, 26, 31; 2 Chronicles 33:18**),

- "The book of the annals of Solomon" (**1 Kings 11:41**), and
- "Annotations on the book of the kings [of Judah]" (**2 Chronicles 24:27**).

Written sources from past prophets and seers that Elishama may have consulted include:

- "Records of Samuel the seer, the records of Nathan the prophet and the records of Gad the seer" (**1 Chronicles 29:29**),
- "Records of Nathan the prophet, in the prophecy of Ahijah the Shilonite and in the visions of Iddo the seer" (**2 Chronicles 9:29**),
- "Records of Shemaiah the prophet and of Iddo the seer that deal with genealogies" (**2 Chronicles 12:15**),
- "Annotations of the prophet Iddo" (**2 Chronicles 13:22**),
- "Recorded [records] by the prophet Isaiah son of Amoz" (**2 Chronicles 26:22**),
- "The vision of the prophet Isaiah son of Amoz in the book of the kings of Judah and Israel" (**2 Chronicles 32:32**),
- "The records of the seers" (**2 Chronicles 33:19**), and
- "The Laments" (**2 Chronicles 35:25**).

Additional census, genealogical, or military records that Elishama may have compiled or consulted include:

- David's census of the people recorded in **2 Samuel 24:1–2**; **1 Chronicles 21:1–2**, and Solomon's census mentioned in **2 Chronicles 2:17**,
- Genealogies that were recorded *before* the Babylonian captivity, during the reigns of Jeroboam II of Israel (ca. 793–753 B.C.) and Jotham of Judah (ca. 750–735 B.C.; **1 Chronicles 5:17**),
- Indirect reference to names that were recorded in the days of Hezekiah king of Judah (715–686 B.C.; **1 Chronicles 4:41**),
- Genealogical records for the Levitical descendants who were eligible to serve, or who did serve in the Second Temple (**1 Chronicles 9:22, 34; 23:24; 24:6; 2 Chronicles 31:16, 19**), and
- Official military records (**1 Chronicles 7:2, 4–5, 7, 9, 11, 40; 8:28**).

10. For the conventional dating of Chronicles, see the Introduction to the books of 1 & 2 Chronicles in the *NIV Study Bible*, fully revised edition, Kenneth L. Barker, ed. (Grand Rapids: Zondervan, 2011), 649, 700; also, see Eugene H. Merrill, *A Commentary on 1 & 2 Chronicles* (Grand Rapids: Kregel Publications, 2015), 22-23.

11. The first exiles returned to Jerusalem with Zerubbabel in ca. 538 B.C., the temple was completed in 516 B.C., Ezra brought returning exiles to Jerusalem in 458 B.C., and Nehemiah returned to Jerusalem in 444 B.C.

12. A clear example of post-exilic writing is evident in the specific texts of **Chronicles** that use the vassal names of Judah's kings (e.g., Jehoiakim, Zedekiah, Shallum, Jeconiah) rather than their birth names (Eliakim, Mattaniah, Jehoahaz, Jehoiachin, respectively). Also, post-exilic records for the people who returned and dwelled in Jerusalem ("from Judah, from Benjamin, and from Ephraim and Manasseh") are clearly in view in passages such as Zerubbabel's descendants in **1 Chronicles 3:19–24**; descendants of Saul and other Benjamites in **1 Chronicles 8:1–40**; and provincial leaders and priests and Levites in **1 Chronicles 9:1–34**.

1 CHRONICLES 2: CALEB AND KENAZ, THE SONS OF JEPHUNNEH THE KENIZZITE

Approximate Dating: Caleb was born ca. 1485 B.C.; in ca. 1400 B.C. at 85 years of age, he was given an inheritance of land in Canaan by Joshua; Nabal the Calebite, a descendant of Caleb the Kenizzite, interacted with David in ca. 1012 B.C.[1] ***Relevant Scriptures:*** **1 Chronicles 2:42–49; 4:13–20;** also **Joshua 14:6–14; 15:13–19; Judges 1:12–14; 3:9–11**

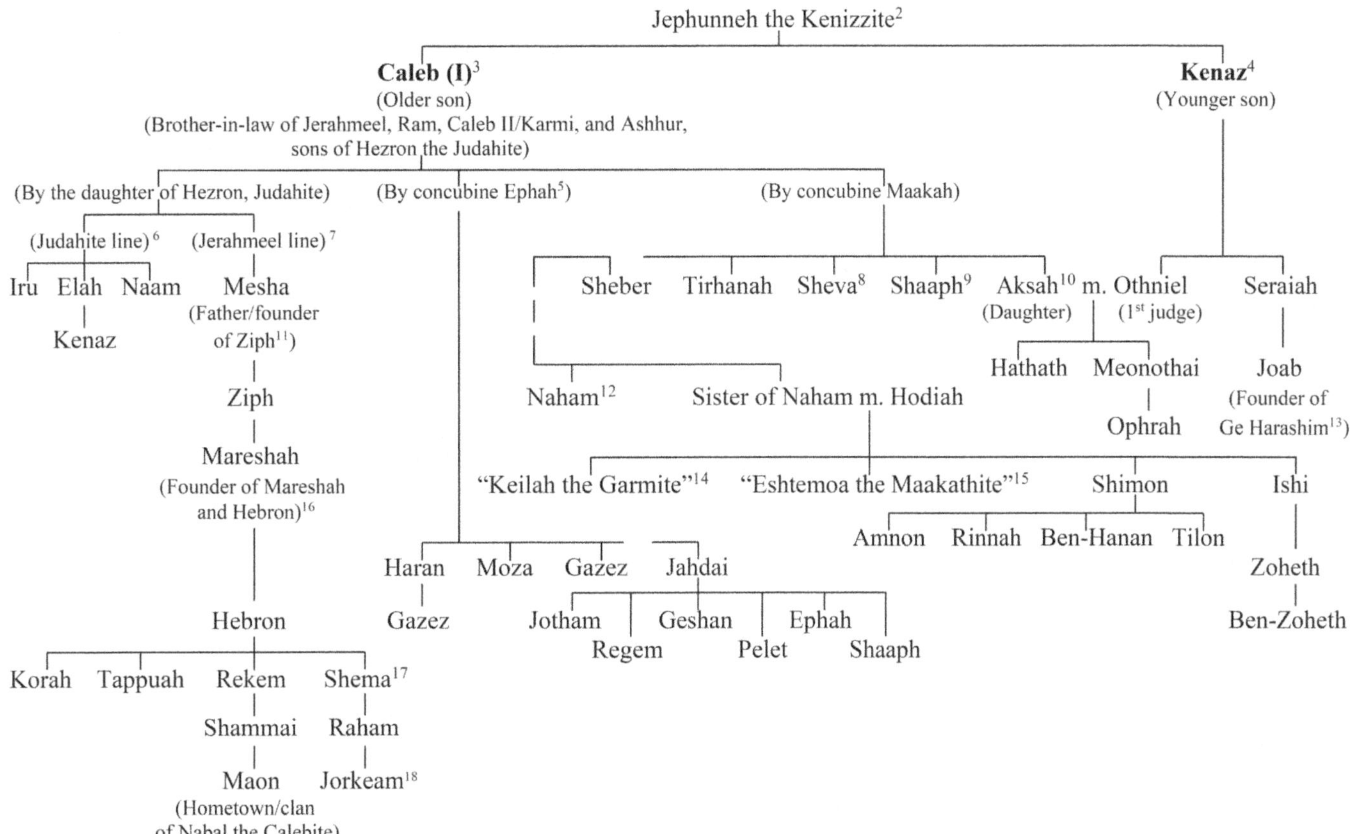

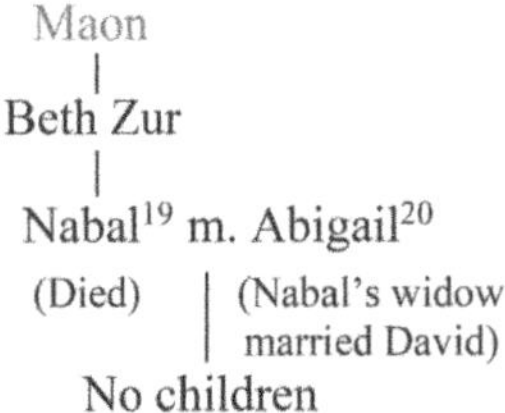

Other sons/sons-in-laws or relatives of Caleb the Kenizzite (Caleb I):[21]

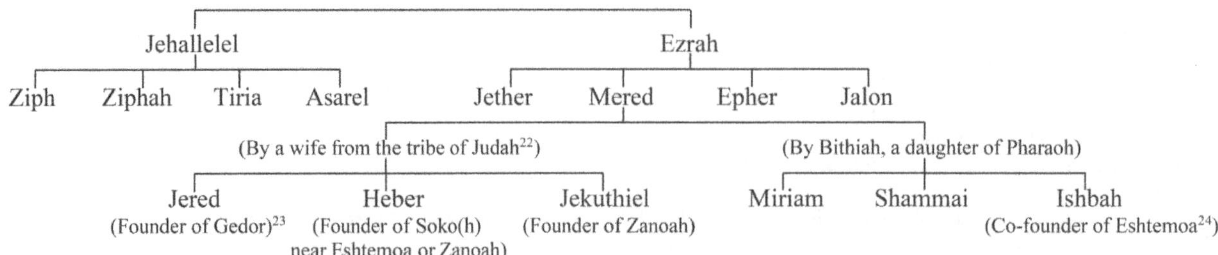

Biblical and Theological Significance

The first reference to a Caleb (designated Caleb I) is **Numbers 13:6**, where he is identified as the son of Jephunneh and a leader among the Judahites. **Joshua 14:6** adds the information that he was of Kenizzite ancestry, descended from aboriginal inhabitants of Canaan before the arrival of the Israelites (**Genesis 15:19**). Despite his foreign heritage, Caleb became an important member of the tribe of Judah, representing it as one of twelve spies sent into Canaan[29] (**Numbers 13:6**). Because of his heroic faithfulness, Joshua granted him an inheritance of land within the tribe of Judah, specifically, the important city of Hebron (formerly Kiriath Arba, that had been occupied by Arba the giant and his descendants, the Anakites[30]) (**Joshua 14:13, 15**; cf. **15:13**). Caleb went on to attack Debir (formerly Kiriath Sepher/Kiriath Sannah) in a military campaign brought to fruition by his nephew Othniel (**Joshua 15:16–17**; cf. **Judges 1:11–13**). Caleb rewarded Othniel with the hand of his own daughter, Aksah (Othniel's distant cousin), and, upon her request, they were given the upper and lower springs[31] (**Joshua 15:18–19; Judges 1:14–15**). Later, Othniel the Kenizzite became Israel's first judge[32] (**Judges 3:7–11**).

Caleb I the Kenizzite had three wives/concubines. One wife was the unnamed daughter of Hezron, the son of Perez, the son of Judah. In this way, Caleb the Kenizzite (Caleb I) became the *brother-in-law* of Jerahmeel (Hezron's firstborn), Caleb (II)/Karmi, and Ram (**1 Chronicles 2:3–9**). For this reason, the text of **1 Chronicles 2:42** should be understood to mean, "the descendants of Caleb the *brother-in-law* of Jerahmeel" not "the descendants of Caleb the *brother* of Jerahmeel."

Twenty towns within the tribe of Judah appear to be founded by the descendants of Caleb the Kenizzite, including the following:

1. Kirjath Arba/Hebron (**Joshua 14:14; 15:13–14, 54; 20:7; 21:10–12; 1 Chronicles 2:42-43**),
2. Shema (**Joshua 15:26; 1 Chronicles 2:43-44**);
3. Beth Pelet (**Joshua 15:27; 1 Chronicles 2:47?**);
4. Madmannah (**Joshua 15:31; 1 Chronicles 2:49**);
5. Zanoah (**Joshua 15:34 or 15:56; 1 Chronicles 4:18**);
6. Tappuah (**Joshua 15:34; 1 Chronicles 2:43**);
7. Soko(h) (either **Joshua 15:35** or **15:48; 1 Chronicles 4:18**);
8. Keilah (**Joshua 15:44; 1 Chronicles 4:19**);
9. Mareshah (**Joshua 15:44; 1 Chronicles 2:42**);
10. Debir/Kiraith Sannah/Kiriath Sepher (**Joshua 14:6–14; 15:15; 49; 21:12; Judges 1:11–5**);
11. Eshtemoh/Eshtemoa (**Joshua 15:50; 21:14; 1 Chronicles 4:17, 19**);
12. Maon (**Joshua 15:55; 1 Chronicles 2:45**);
13. Ziph (**Joshua 15:55; 1 Chronicles 2:42**);
14. Carmel (**Joshua 15:55; 1 Samuel 25:2–3; 27:3; 30:5; 2 Samuel 2:2; 3:3; 1 Chronicles 3:1**);
15. Jokdeam/Jorkeam (**Joshua 15:56; 1 Chronicles 2:44**);
16. Zanoah (**Joshua 15:56; 1 Chronicles 4:18**);
17. Gibea(h) of Judah—a different town than Gibeah of Benjamin—(**Joshua 15:57**; cf. **1 Chronicles 2:49**);
18. Beth Zur (**Joshua 15:58; 1 Chronicles 2:45**); and
19. Gedor (**Joshua 15:58; 1 Chronicles 4:4?, 18**);
20. Makbenah (**1 Chronicles 2:49**).

The cave of Machpelah near Mamre (=Hebron) was the burial place of the patriarchs/matriarchs (Abraham–Sarah, Isaac–Rebekah, Jacob–Leah; cf. **Genesis 23:19; 25:9; 35:29; 49:31; 50:13**). Of the towns associated with the Kenizzites, (portions of) Hebron, Debir, and Eshtemoa were also given to the descendants of Aaron, the high priest (**Joshua 14:13; 21:10–12; 1 Chronicles 6:54–58**), forming a close association between the Kenizzites and the Kohathite priesthood.

Notes

1. **Joshua 14:7** says that Caleb was 40 years when the twelve spies were initially sent out from Kadesh Barnea to spy out the land of Canaan in ca. 1445 B.C., so Caleb must have been born in 1485 B.C. Also, Caleb the Kenizzite was 85 years old when Joshua gave him the city of Hebron as his inheritance in the promised land, ca. 1400 B.C.—"So here I am today [entering Canaan], eighty-five years old! I am still as strong today as the day Moses sent me out

[as a spy of Canaan]; I'm just as vigorous to go out to battle now as I was then" (**Joshua 14:10–11, 13**).

2. The Kenizzites were among the original occupants of the promised land before the Israelites came: "Kenites, Kenizzites, Kadmonites, Hittites, Perizzites, Rephaites, Amorites, Canaanites, Girgashites and Jebusites" (**Genesis 15:19**). Descendants of Jephunneh (Kenizzite clan) intermarried with the Judahites, as evidenced by the many places they founded in the tribe of Judah.

3. At the outset, one must reckon with the fact that there are two important individuals with the name Caleb: (1) Caleb I the Kenizzite, the son of Jephunneh, and (2) Caleb II the Judahite, the son of Hezron. This is strange in a sense, since the name means "dog," hardly flattering in the ancient Middle Eastern world. On the other hand, the dog has long been recognized as the epitome of reliability, loyalty, and companionship. Caleb (I) the Kenizzite married the daughter of Hezron and thereby became the *brother-in-law* of Caleb (II) the Judahite—see chart "**1 Chronicles 2**: Jerahmeel and His Descendant, Elishama, Who Appears to Be a Compiler of Historical and Genealogical Records in 1 & 2 Chronicles."

4. Kenaz the Kenizzite, the son of Jephunneh and the younger brother of Caleb, should not be confused with Kenaz the Edomite, the son of Eliphaz (**Genesis 36:11**); for the latter Edomite clan, see chart "**Genesis 36**: Esau, the Ancestor of the Edomites."

5. Ephah the concubine of Caleb (I) in **1 Chronicles 2:46** should not be confused with Ephrath/Ephrathah, the wife of Caleb (II), the son of Hezron in **1 Chronicles 2:19, 50**.

6. The Caleb I descendants associated with the tribe of Judah are listed in **1 Chronicles 4:15**.

7. The Caleb I descendants associated with the family of Jerahmeel—via Caleb I's marriage to Hezron's daughter—are identified in **1 Chronicles 2:42–49**.

8. Sheva was the father/founder of Makbenah and Gibea (**1 Chronicles 2:49**); this Gibea in the tribe of Judah probably refers to "Gibeah" in **Joshua 15:57** but should not be confused with the town of Gibeah in the tribe of Benjamin (e.g., **Joshua 18:28; Judges 19:14; 20:4, 10; 1 Samuel 13:2, 15-16; 14:16**).

9. Shaaph was the father/founder of Madmannah (**1 Chronicles 2:49**), one of the southernmost towns in the tribe of Judah in the Negev toward Edom (**Joshua 15:31**).

10. Aksah was the daughter of Caleb's concubine; Caleb promised her in marriage to the victor who could take Debir (ancient Kiriath Sepher/Kiriath Sannah), a town held by the giant Anakim before the Israelite invasion (**Joshua 15:15, 49; Judges 1:11–15**). Othniel the son of Kenaz was successful in the military overthrow of Debir, and Aksah thus became the prize wife of her distant first cousin. Debir was located in the arid region of the Negev, so Aksah, knowing that a future, non-nomadic lifestyle would be impossible in that locale, following the bold example of her father Caleb (who had asked Joshua for an inheritance of land and received the fields and villages around Hebron; **Joshua 14:6–14; 21:12**) and petitioned her father for a *blessing*—one normally reserved for the *firstborn son*: "'Since you have given me land in the Negev, give me also springs of water.' So Caleb gave her the upper and lower springs" (**Joshua 15:19; Judges 1:15**). In this way, Othniel and Aksah, and their Kenizzite descendants in general, received some of the choicest land and "live water" within the tribe of Judah and lived alongside the Kohathite descendants of the Aaronic priesthood (**Joshua 14:13; 15:13; 21:9–13**).

11. Ziph is a personal name and a place name; Ziph was a town in the hill country of Judah (**Joshua 15:55**).

12. The line of Naham is not clear but is placed here in the chart because one of his descendants is called "Eshtemoa the Maakathite," meaning a descendant of Maakah, a concubine of Caleb (I) the Kenizzite (cf. **1 Chronicles 2:48; 4:19**).

13. Ge Harashim was a valley of skilled workers/craftsmen (**1 Chronicles 4:14**). In the post-exile, descendants of the Benjamites from Geba settled there (**Nehemiah 11:35**).

14. "Keilah the Garmite" was the founder of Keilah, a town in the western foothills of Judah (**Joshua 15:44**).

15. "Eshtemoa the Maakathite" appears to be the founder/co-founder of Eshtemoa, a town in the tribe of Judah, which was given as one of the Levitical cities to the Kohathite descendants of Aaron the high priest (**Joshua 21:14**). Eshtemoa was also founded by Ishbah, the son of Mered and Bithiah (**1 Chronicles 4:17**).

16. The ancient name for Hebron was Kiriath Arba (after the giants, the descendants of Arba, who occupied the region; **Joshua 15:13, 54; 20:7; 21:11**). Caleb the Kenizzite was successful in taking Hebron from the Anakites (**Joshua 15:14**), and Hebron was given to him as his inheritance in the promised land "because he [Caleb] followed the Lord, the God of Israel, wholeheartedly" (**Joshua 14:14**). [The historian of Joshua goes on to clarify that Hebron and its surrounding pastureland were given to the descendants of Aaron (the Kohathites), but "the fields and villages around the city they had given to Caleb son of Jephunneh as his possession" (**Joshua 21:10–12**)]. Hebron was also designated as a city of refuge (**Joshua 21:13**). Mareshah was a town in the western foothills of the tribe of Judah (**Joshua 15:44**).

17. Tappuah is a personal name (**1 Chronicles 2:43**) and a place name (**Joshua 15:34**).

18. Shema is a personal name and a place name; Shema was one of the southernmost towns in the tribe of Judah in the Negev, toward Edom (**Joshua 15:26**).

19. Maon is a personal name (**1 Chronicles 2:45**) and a place name; Maon was the father/founder of Beth Zur (**Joshua 15:58; 1 Chronicles 2:45; 2 Chronicles 11:7**).

20. Jorkeam (**1 Chronicles 2:44**) was likely the founder of *Jokdeam*, a town in the hill country of Judah (**Joshua 15:56**).

21. Nabal the fool was a wealthy man from Maon (an area near Carmel) in the hill country of Judah (**Joshua 15:55; 1 Samuel 30:5; 2 Samuel 3:3**). Nabal is identified as "a Calebite," meaning a descendant of Caleb (I) the Kenizzite (**1 Samuel 25:2–3**). For more information on Nabal, one of the terminal figures in the chart, see chart "**1 Samuel 25**: Nabal and Abigail."

22. David's rendezvous with Abigail was ca. 1012 B.C. After Nabal's death, his widow (Abigail) married David (**1 Samuel 25:42**), and she bore him one son named Kileab (Daniel; **2 Samuel 3:3; 1 Chronicles 3:1**). See chart "**1 Chronicles 2**: David's Children Born in Hebron and Jerusalem."

23. These descendants of Caleb the Kenizzite are given in **1 Chronicles 4:16–18**.

24. The NKJV identifies this wife of Mered as "Jehudijah" (**1 Chronicles 4:18**).

25. Jered the Kenizzite and Penuel from the tribe of Judah were probably co-founders of Gedor (**1 Chronicles 4:4, 18**, respectively).

26. This Soko(h) probably refers to Sokoh in the hill country of Judah (**Joshua 15:48**), near Debir (**Joshua 15:49**) and Eshtemoh (**Joshua 15:50**)—a variant spelling of Eshtemoa— or to Sokoh in the western foothills of Judah (**Joshua 15:35**).

27. Eshtemoa was co-founded by Ishbah (Kenizzite) and by "Eshtemoa the Maakathite" (see note 15).

28. Zanoah refers to the town in the western foothills of Judah (**Joshua 15:34**) or the town of Zanoah in the hill country of Judah (**Joshua 15:56**).

29. The spies were sent to Canaan in 1445 B.C. See chart "**Numbers 13**: Genealogical Record of the Twelve Spies of the Promised Land."

30. The Anakim/ites are also mentioned early in the biblical texts (**Numbers 13:22**) but nowhere else in the ancient Near Eastern literature; see chart "**Deuteronomy 1**: The Giant Anakites, including Goliath and His Descendants."

31. The springs are possibly the Gullath-illith and Gullath-tahtith of Seil el-Dilbeh located in a watered valley of southern Palestine. See George F. Moore, *A Critical and Exegetical Commentary on Judges* (Edinburgh: T&T Clark, 1908), 28–29.

32. See chart "**Judges 3**: Othniel (Kenizzite), the First Judge of Israel."

1 CHRONICLES 3: DAVID'S CHILDREN BORN IN HEBRON AND JERUSALEM

Approximate Dating: time in Hebron, ca. 1011–early 1003 B.C; time in Jerusalem, late 1003–971 B.C. ***Relevant Scriptures:*** **1 Chronicles 3:1–9**; also **2 Samuel 3:2–5; 5:13–16; 1 Chronicles 14:3–7**

Children Born in Hebron

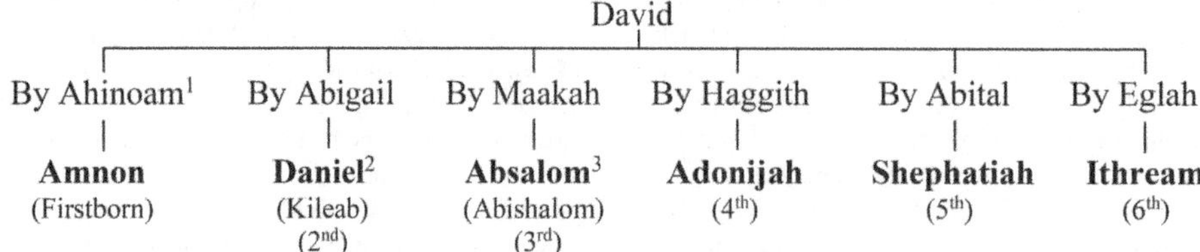

Children Born in Jerusalem

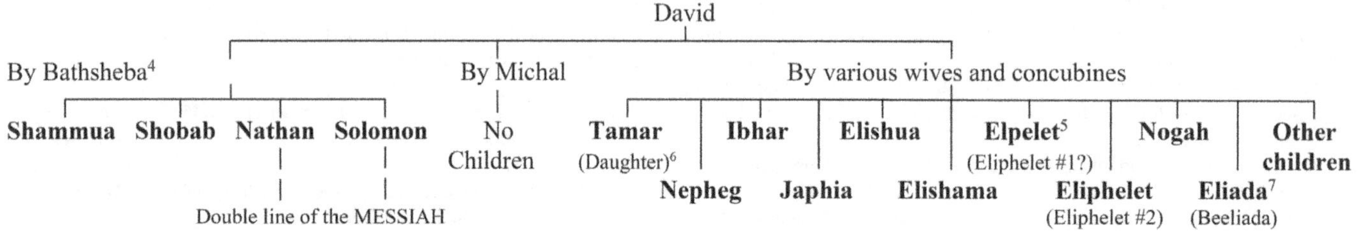

Biblical and Theological Significance

David reigned over Judah from his first capital at Hebron for seven and a half years (**2 Samuel 5:5; 1 Chronicles 3:4**). When he became king over Judah and Israel, he moved his capital from Hebron to Jerusalem (formerly Jebus) and ruled there for thirty-three years (**2 Samuel 5:5; 1 Chronicles 3:4; 11:4**). **First Chronicles 3:5–9** and **14:4–7** list thirteen sons of David, whereas **2 Samuel 5:13–16** only lists eleven of his sons.

David's Wives and Children

Ahinoam appears to be David's first wife (**1 Samuel 27:3**). She was from Jezreel, a city in Judah (**Joshua 15:56; 1 Samuel 25:43; 27:3; 30:5; 2 Samuel 2:2; 3:2; 1 Chronicles 3:1**). Note that Saul also had a wife named Ahinoam, the daughter of Ahimaaz, the son of Zadok the high priest (**1 Samuel 14:50, 2 Samuel 15:27, 35–36**). However, David's wife Ahinoam and Saul's wife Ahinoam appear to be different women.

Abigail, the Carmelitess, was the former wife of Nabal.[8] After Nabal's death, she married David (**1 Samuel 25:3, 14; 27:3; 30:5; 2 Samuel 2:2**; cf. **1 Samuel 25:39–40; 1 Chronicles 3:1**).

Maakah was the daughter of Talmai, the king of Geshur (**2 Samuel 3:3; 1 Chronicles 3:2**). After Absalom murdered Amnon, Absalom fled to the king of Geshur near his mother's family (**2 Samuel 13:37–38**). Eventually, Absalom had a granddaughter named Maakah, who appears to be named after her great-grandmother (**1 Kings 15:2, 10**; see chart "**1 Kings 12**: Rehoboam, King of Judah").

Bathsheba was the wife of Uriah, but while they were married, David "sent messengers to get her. She came to him, and he slept with her. . . . [and] the woman conceived" (**2 Samuel 11:4**). David then murdered Uriah (cf. **2 Samuel 11:6–25**). After the period of mourning was over, Bathsheba became David's wife, but the child of the union between them died (**2 Samuel 12:18**). Later, Bathsheba bore David four children; two of these children—Solomon and Nathan—form the (double) line of the Messiah[9] (cf. **Matthew 1:6; Luke 3:31**). Bathsheba was the daughter of Ammiel (**1 Chronicles 3:5**; also called Eliam, **2 Samuel 11:3; 23:34**) and the granddaughter of Ahithophel the Gilonite, who was David's court counselor (**2 Samuel 15:12; 23:34; 1 Chronicles 27:33**).

Michal, the younger daughter of King Saul, became one of David's wives (**1 Samuel 18:20–21, 27–28**); however, at one point, Saul gave Michal, David's wife, to Paltiel the son of Laish of Gallim (**1 Samuel 25:44**). Later, Michal was returned to David as his legitimate wife (**2 Samuel 3:15**), but she bore him no children; her childlessness was related to the events of **2 Samuel 6:16–23** where she "despised him [David] in her heart" for dancing before the ark of the covenant when it was brought to Jerusalem.

Another *son* of David named Jerimoth is mentioned in **2 Chronicles 11:18**, but where he was born or the name of his mother is not given.[10] Jerimoth married Abihail, the daughter of Jesse's son, Eliab. Jerimoth and Abihail had one daughter named Mahalath who married Solomon's son Rehoboam.[11]

Notes

1. After David's illicit sexual transgression with Bathsheba and heinous murder of Uriah (**2 Samuel 12:7–14**), the Lord indicted David with these words (spoken through Nathan the prophet): "I anointed you [David] king over Israel, and I delivered you from the hand of Saul. I gave your master's [Saul's] house to you, and your master's [Saul's] wives into your arms. I gave you all Israel and Judah. And if all this had been too little, I would have given you even more" (**2 Samuel 12:7–8**). It should be noted that most scholars do not accept that David's wife (Ahinoam; **1 Samuel 25:43**) was the *former* wife

(Ahinoam) of King Saul (**1 Samuel 14:50**), which could be the (mistaken) interpretation of **2 Samuel 12:8**.

2. He is called Daniel in **1 Chronicles 3:1** and Kileab in **2 Samuel 3:3**.

3. Absalom (**2 Samuel 3:3; 13:1**, etc.) is called Abishalom in **1 Kings 15:2, 10**.

4. See chart "**2 Samuel 5**: Bathsheba."

5. Two sons of David are named Eliphelet in **1 Chronicles 3:6, 8**. One of them is called "Elpelet" in **1 Chronicles 14:5** and the other "Eliphelet" in **1 Chronicles 14:7**, so the chart refers to them as Eliphelet #1 and Eliphelet #2.

6. Tamar was the full sister of Absalom (**2 Samuel 13:1**); see **2 Samuel 13** for the narrative details about the rape of Tamar by her half-brother Amnon.

7. Eliada (**1 Chronicles 3:8**) appears to be the same person as Beeliada (**1 Chronicles 14:7**).

8. See chart "**1 Samuel 25**: Nabal and Abigail."

9. See chart "**1 Chronicles 3**: Zerubbabel and Shealtiel and the Double Line of the Messiah through King David's Sons, Nathan and Solomon."

10. The context of **2 Chronicles 11:18** suggests that Jerimoth might have been a *relative* or a *descendant* of David or the son of a concubine.

11. See chart "**1 Chronicles 2**: King David."

1 CHRONICLES 3: KING SOLOMON AND HIS DESCENDANTS UNTIL THE TIME OF THE EXILE

Approximate Dating: ca. 1011–586 B.C.; Solomon's reign, ca. 971–931 B.C. ***Relevant Scriptures:*** **1 Chronicles 3:10–16**; also **1 Kings 4:11, 15; 11:1, 3; Matthew 1:6–11**

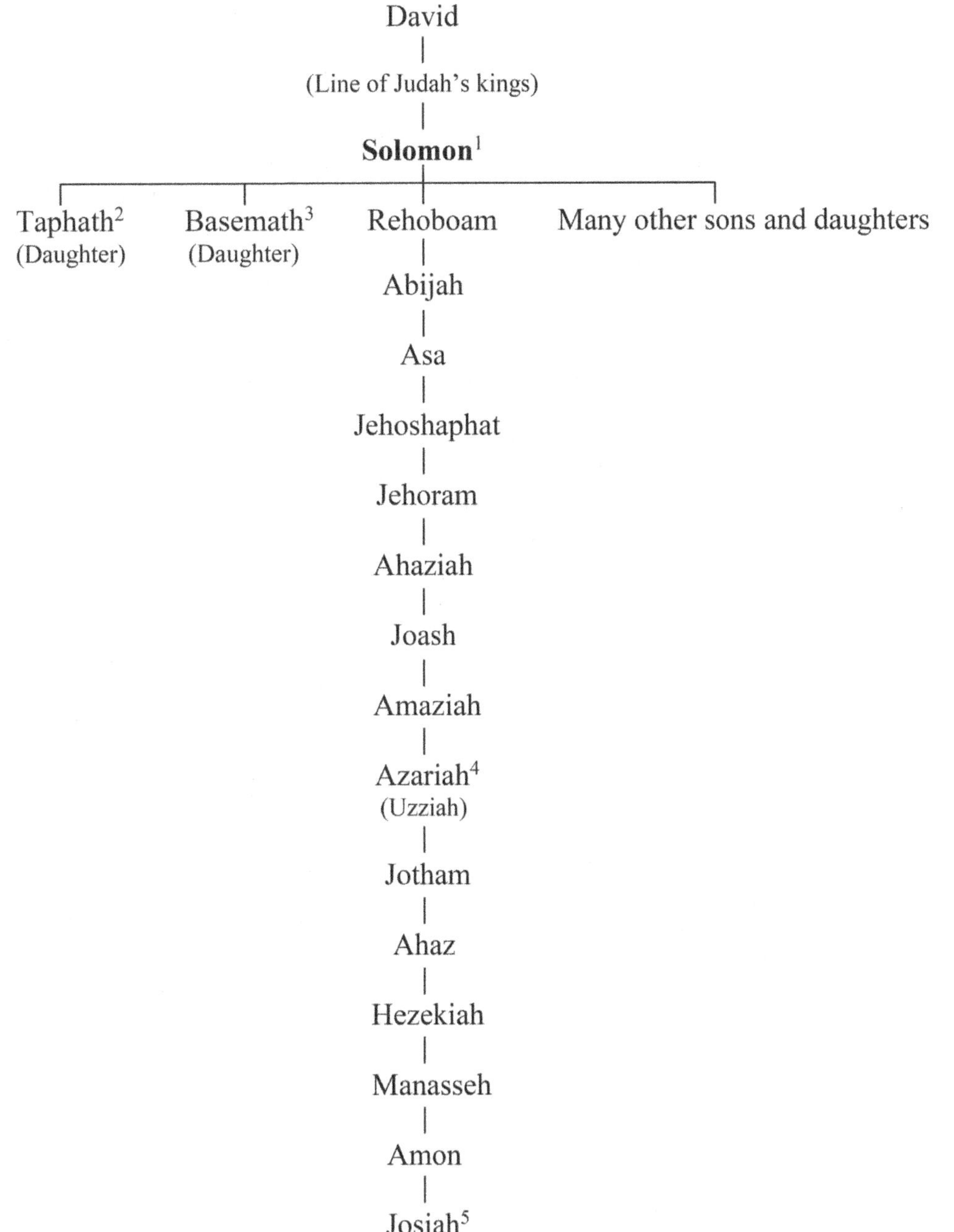

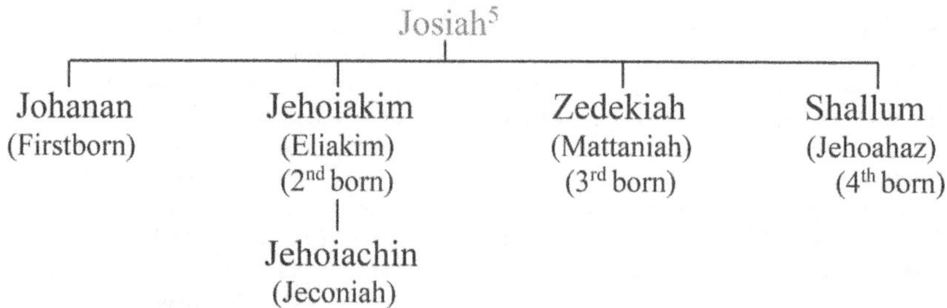

Biblical and Theological Significance

Solomon's Family

Solomon's mother, Bathsheba, the daughter of Eliam[6] (or Ammiel; **2 Samuel 11:3; 1 Chronicles 3:5**), was first married to Uriah the Hittite (**2 Samuel 11:3**). The events in **2 Samuel 11** describe David's just and shameful abuse of his royal power in taking Bathsheba (another man's wife) and then arranging for her righteous husband (Uriah) to be killed in battle, so he could marry her.[7] The child of the sinful union died shortly after birth (**2 Samuel 12:1–23**). After Bathsheba married David, she bore him four sons, including Solomon (**1 Chronicles 3:5**). The Lord called him *Jedidiah*, meaning "beloved of Yah(weh)" (**2 Samuel 12:25**). In David's final earthly days, Solomon's half-brother, Adonijah (son of Haggith), declared himself king, but Bathsheba asked David to remember his promise that *her* son Solomon would reign. David agreed and Solomon was anointed as David's successor (**1 Kings 1:15–18; 28–40; 3:7; 1 Chronicles 29:1–2, 21–22**; cf. **1 Kings 2:13–25**).

Solomon undertook many political/diplomatic marriages to foreign women: seven hundred wives of royal birth and three hundred concubines (**1 Kings 11:1, 3**), including the daughter of a pharaoh[8] (**1 Kings 3:1; 7:8; 9:16, 24; 11:1; 2 Chronicles 8:11**) and women from Moab, Ammon (including Naamah the Ammonite, Rehoboam's mother; **1 Kings 14:21, 31; 2 Chronicles 12:13**), Edom, Sidon, and Hatti (Hittites). In later years, these wives "turned his heart after other gods" (**1 Kings 11:1–11**). Only three specific children of Solomon are mentioned in Scripture, although there were surely innumerable others.

Solomon the King

After his father's death, Solomon soon began construction of the temple on Mount Moriah, where the Lord had appeared to David and showed him mercy (**2 Samuel 24:14–25**). The work began 480 years after the exodus, in Solomon's fourth year (ca. 967/966 B.C.; **1 Kings 6:1**) and was completed seven and a half years later, in the eleventh year of his reign (ca. 960/959 B.C.; **1 Kings 6:38**).

Solomon also built his palace (**1 Kings 9:10**), the Palace of the Forest of Lebanon (**2 Chronicles 9:13–16**), the Hall of Justice containing the throne room, and a palace for the pharaoh's daughter (**1 Kings 7:1–8**). He built up the Millo[9] and walls around Jerusalem and fortified cities in the land (cf. **1 Kings 9:15–24**). With the help of Hiram, the king of Tyre, Solomon built ships that sailed from Ezion Geber to far-distant ports, importing precious metals and horses and exotic animals into Israel (**1 Kings 9:26–28; 2 Chronicles 8:17–18; 1 Kings 4:26; 10:48**).

Israel reached its zenith during Solomon's forty-year reign (971–931 B.C.; **1 Kings 11:42; 2 Chronicles 9:30**). As **2 Chronicles 9** explains, Solomon "was greater in riches and wisdom than all the other kings of the earth" (**vv. 22–23**) and "ruled over all the kings from the Euphrates River to the land of the Philistines, as far as the border of Egypt" (**v. 26**). Solomon's accomplishments were recorded in the books of Nathan the prophet, the prophecies of Ahijah the Shilonite priest, and the visions of Iddo the seer (**v. 29**). When he died, Solomon was buried with his father in the City of David (**1 Kings 11:43; 2 Chronicles 9:31**), and he was succeeded by his son Rehoboam (**1 Kings 14:21**).

Notes

1. For additional information about the reign of Solomon, see chart "**1 Kings 11**: King Solomon."

2. Taphath married Ben-Ahinadab, one of the twelve district governors in Solomon's administration, who was stationed at Naphoth Dor ("heights of Dor," probably Mount Carmel; **1 Kings 4:11**); for the other district governors, see note 9 in chart "**1 Kings 4**: The Chief Officials in King Solomon's Administration."

3. Basemath married Ahimaaz, one of the twelve governors in Solomon's administration, who was stationed in Naphtali (**1 Kings 4:15**); see note 9 in the chart "**1 Kings 4**: The Chief Officials in King Solomon's Administration."

4. For more information, see chart "**2 Kings 15**: Azariah (Uzziah), King of Judah."

5. The order of the succession of the pre-exilic kings of Judah was Josiah–Shallum (Jehoahaz)–Jehoiakim (Eliakim)–Jehoiachin (Jeconiah)–Zedekiah (Mattaniah); see chart "**2 Kings 21**: Josiah, King of Judah."

6. Eliam was the son of the revered Ahithophel the Gilonite, who was King David's counselor (**2 Samuel 15:12; 16:23; 1 Chronicles 27:33**). When Ahithophel offered advice to Absalom in his rebellion against his father (David) but his advice was not heeded, Ahithophel committed suicide by hanging himself (**2 Samuel 16:15–17:23**). Ahithophel's position as the royal counselor was then filled by Jehoiada the son of Benaiah and by Abiathar the high priest (**1 Chronicles 27:34**).

7. In these actions, David broke the sixth, seventh, and tenth commandments (**Exodus 20:13–14, 17**).

8. Probably referring to Pharaoh Siamun of Dynasty 21 (978–959 B.C.).

9. The Millo is associated with the City of David (the "fortress of Zion" which David captured from the Jebusites; cf. **2 Samuel 5:7–8; 1 Chronicles 11:5**). "The word *millô'* is frequently analyzed as a noun associated . . . with the Heb. verb *mālē'* "to be full," . . . interpreted as referring to the filling of a breach in a wall, the filling of a space in the Tyropoeon Valley between the western and eastern ridges, the filling of a gap between the City of David and the temple mound, a filled stone tower, or the rebuilding of (damaged) supporting terraces. The archaeological evidence uncovered at the City of David points to the meaning "repair of supporting terraces" along the precipitous steep eastern ridge of the City of David" (W. Harold Mare, "Millo," *Anchor Yale Bible Dictionary*).

1 CHRONICLES 3: ZERUBBABEL AND SHEALTIEL AND THE DOUBLE LINE OF THE MESSIAH THROUGH KING DAVID'S SONS, NATHAN AND SOLOMON[1]

Approximate Dating: from King David, 1011–971 B.C. to the birth of Jesus, ca. late 3 or early 2 B.C.; Shealtiel and Zerubbabel were born in Babylon captivity, sometime after 586 B.C. and Shealtiel died in Babylon; Zerubbabel came to Jerusalem in ca. 538 B.C. and, with Joshua the high priest, led the people in the building of the Second Temple which was completed in 516 B.C. ***Relevant Scriptures:*** **1 Chronicles 3:10-24; Matthew 1:6-17; Luke 3:23-31;** also **2 Samuel 5:14; 1 Chronicles 3:5; 14:4; Ezra 3:2, 8; 5:2; Nehemiah 12:1; Haggai 1:12, 14; 2:2, 23; Zechariah 12:12**

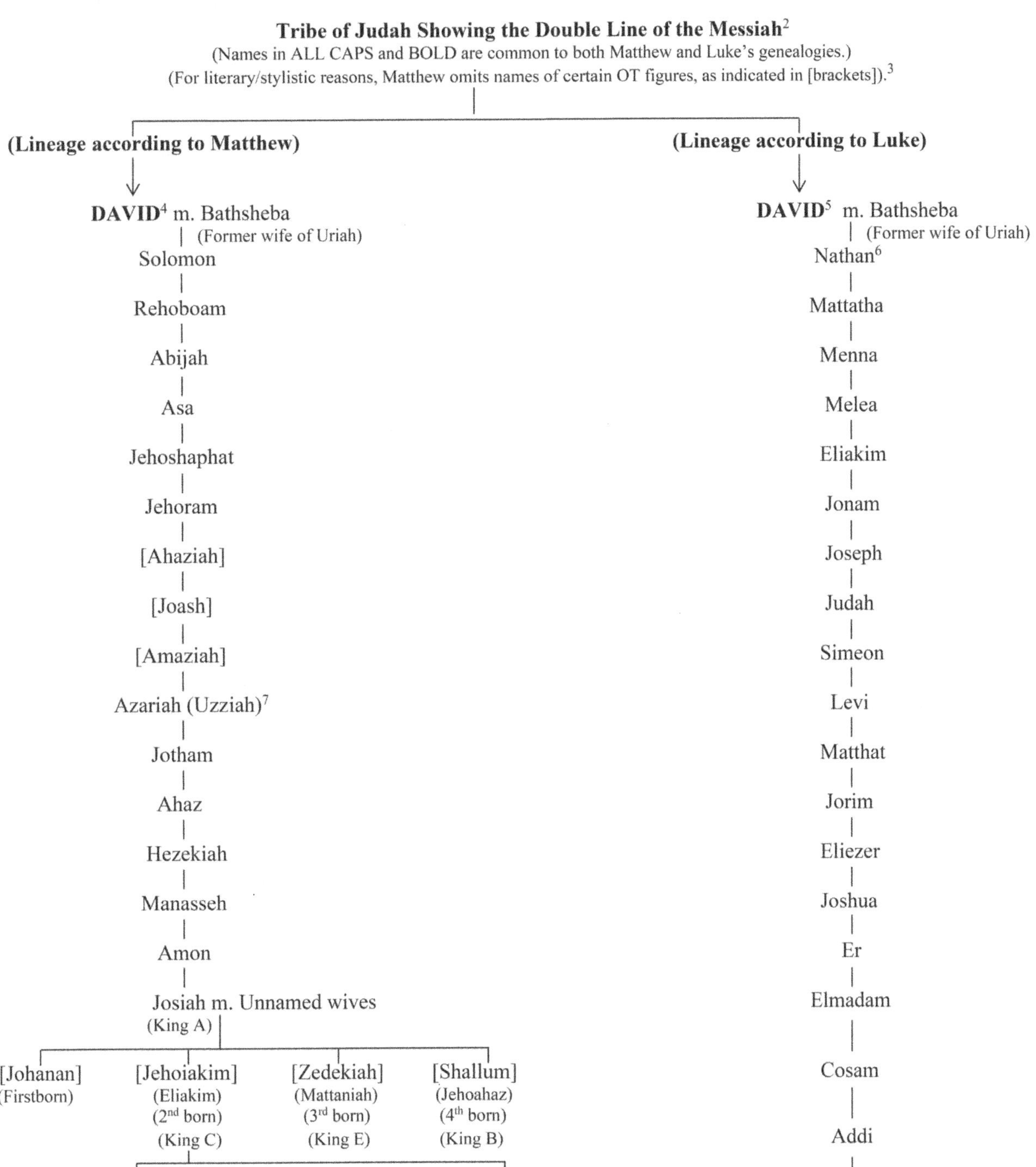

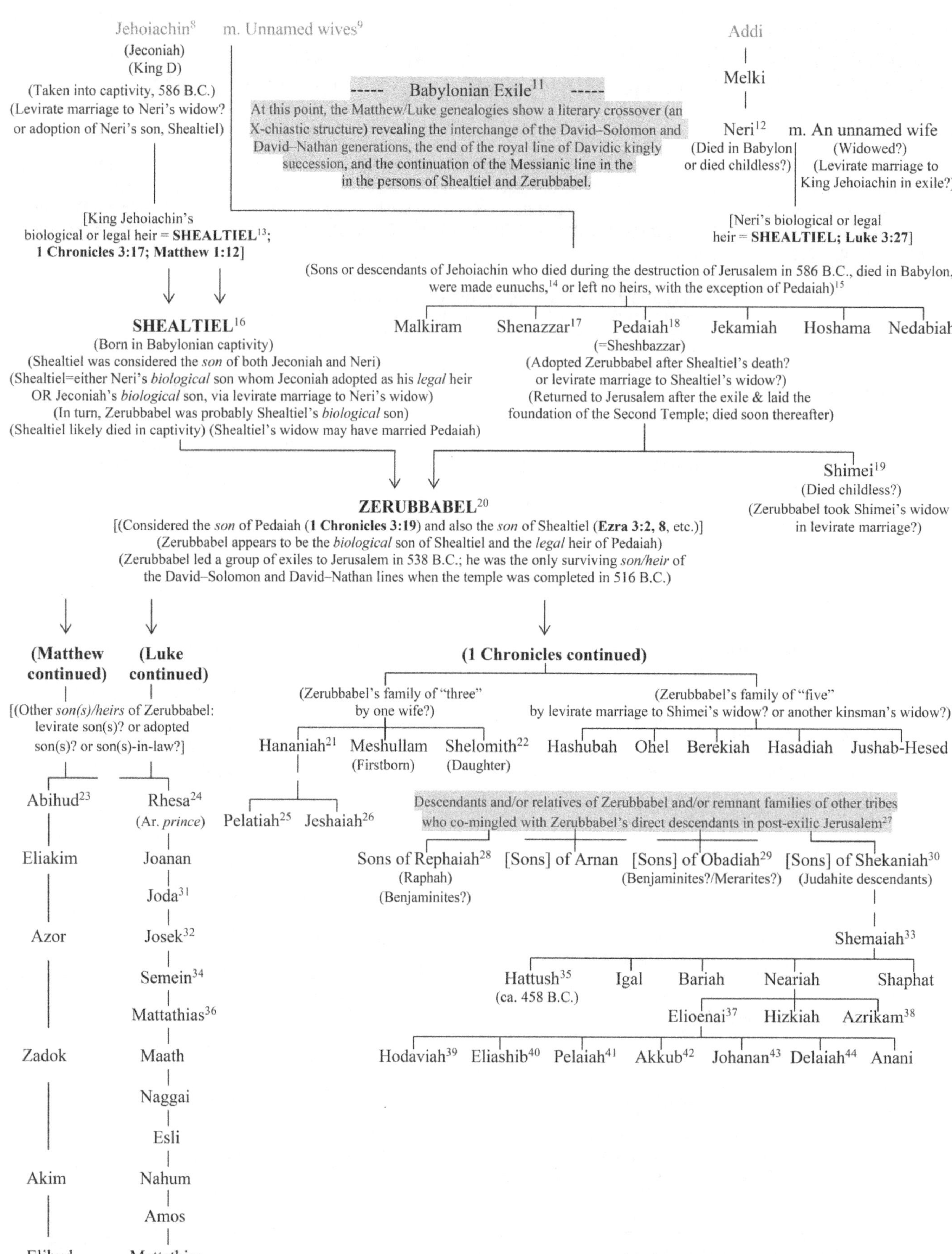
Jehoiachin[8] m. Unnamed wives[9]
(Jeconiah)
(King D)
(Taken into captivity, 586 B.C.)
(Levirate marriage to Neri's widow? or adoption of Neri's son, Shealtiel)
Addi
Melki
Neri[12] m. An unnamed wife
(Died in Babylon or died childless?)
(Widowed?) (Levirate marriage to King Jehoiachin in exile?)
----- Babylonian Exile[11] -----
At this point, the Matthew/Luke genealogies show a literary crossover (an X-chiastic structure) revealing the interchange of the David–Solomon and David–Nathan generations, the end of the royal line of Davidic kingly succession, and the continuation of the Messianic line in the in the persons of Shealtiel and Zerubbabel.
[King Jehoiachin's biological or legal heir = SHEALTIEL[13]; 1 Chronicles 3:17; Matthew 1:12]
[Neri's biological or legal heir = SHEALTIEL; Luke 3:27]
(Sons or descendants of Jehoiachin who died during the destruction of Jerusalem in 586 B.C., died in Babylon, were made eunuchs,[14] or left no heirs, with the exception of Pedaiah)[15]
SHEALTIEL[16]
(Born in Babylonian captivity)
(Shealtiel was considered the son of both Jeconiah and Neri)
(Shealtiel=either Neri's biological son whom Jeconiah adopted as his legal heir OR Jeconiah's biological son, via levirate marriage to Neri's widow)
(In turn, Zerubbabel was probably Shealtiel's biological son)
(Shealtiel likely died in captivity) (Shealtiel's widow may have married Pedaiah)
Malkiram
Shenazzar[17]
Pedaiah[18]
(=Sheshbazzar)
(Adopted Zerubbabel after Shealtiel's death? or levirate marriage to Shealtiel's widow?)
(Returned to Jerusalem after the exile & laid the foundation of the Second Temple; died soon thereafter)
Jekamiah
Hoshama
Nedabiah
Shimei[19]
(Died childless?)
(Zerubbabel took Shimei's widow in levirate marriage?)
ZERUBBABEL[20]
[(Considered the son of Pedaiah (1 Chronicles 3:19) and also the son of Shealtiel (Ezra 3:2, 8, etc.)]
(Zerubbabel appears to be the biological son of Shealtiel and the legal heir of Pedaiah)
(Zerubbabel led a group of exiles to Jerusalem in 538 B.C.; he was the only surviving son/heir of the David–Solomon and David–Nathan lines when the temple was completed in 516 B.C.)
(Matthew continued)
(Luke continued)
[(Other son(s)/heirs of Zerubbabel: levirate son(s)? or adopted son(s)? or son(s)-in-law?]
Abihud[23]
Eliakim
Azor
Zadok
Akim
Elihud
Rhesa[24]
(Ar. prince)
Joanan
Joda[31]
Josek[32]
Semein[34]
Mattathias[36]
Maath
Naggai
Esli
Nahum
Amos
Mattathias
(1 Chronicles continued)
(Zerubbabel's family of "three" by one wife?)
Hananiah[21]
Meshullam
(Firstborn)
Shelomith[22]
(Daughter)
Pelatiah[25]
Jeshaiah[26]
(Zerubbabel's family of "five" by levirate marriage to Shimei's widow? or another kinsman's widow?)
Hashubah
Ohel
Berekiah
Hasadiah
Jushab-Hesed
Descendants and/or relatives of Zerubbabel and/or remnant families of other tribes who co-mingled with Zerubbabel's direct descendants in post-exilic Jerusalem[27]
Sons of Rephaiah[28]
(Raphah)
(Benjaminites?)
[Sons] of Arnan
[Sons] of Obadiah[29]
(Benjaminites?/Merarites?)
[Sons] of Shekaniah[30]
(Judahite descendants)
Shemaiah[33]
Hattush[35]
(ca. 458 B.C.)
Igal
Bariah
Neariah
Shaphat
Elioenai[37]
Hizkiah
Azrikam[38]
Hodaviah[39]
Eliashib[40]
Pelaiah[41]
Akkub[42]
Johanan[43]
Delaiah[44]
Anani

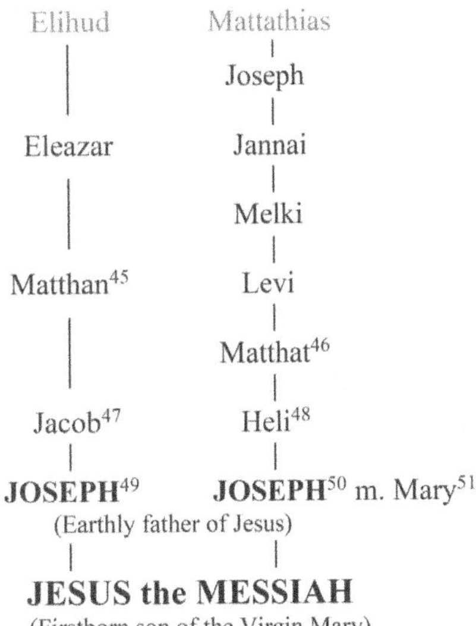

Biblical and Theological Significance

Historical Context for the Genealogy

This chart is perhaps the centerpiece and the most theologically significant of all genealogies in this work because it incorporates three key genealogical passages to explain the ancestry of Jesus the Messiah—**1 Chronicles 3:10–24**; **Matthew 1:6–17**; and **Luke 3:23–31**. Collectively, the Scriptures show that the genealogy of Jesus is traced through his earthly *father* (Joseph) and reveal that there was a *double line* leading to the Messiah—the "David–Solomon kingly line" and the "David–Nathan non-royal line," which was established by the descendants of two of the four sons[52] born to David and Bathsheba. The chart emphasizes the biblical truth that Jesus was the "son of David" (**Matthew 1:1; 9:27; 12:23; 20:30–31; 21:9, 15; 22:42; Mark 10:47–48; 12:35; Luke 18:38–39; 20:41**). The chart also accentuates the threatened state of the messianic line during the tumultuous period of the exile and discusses the crucial role that two pivotal figures—Shealtiel and Zerubbabel—played in messianic concatenation. Through the normal process of biological procreation ("nature") and legal processes, such as levirate marriage and/or adoption ("law"), the genealogical line brought forth Jesus Christ—the Son of God—into the world.

The historical background of the chart is clearly demarcated:

- David was king of Israel from ca. 1011–971 B.C. He was the key forefather of Jesus the Messiah, known as the "son of David."
- The David–Solomon and David–Nathan lines run parallel for about four hundred years (ca. 1011–586 B.C.), from the time of King David to the time of King Jehoiachin/Jeconiah (a Solomonic descendant) and Neri (a Nathan descendant).
- During the devastating destruction of Jerusalem in 586 B.C. and the ensuing seventy-year exile in Babylon (586–516 B.C.), both lines of the Messiah were in peril and at risk of dying out.
- When the exiles were permitted to return to Jerusalem, the continuance of the messianic line was insured by the genealogically mysterious and complex persons, Shealtiel and Zerubbabel.
- In the post-exile, the descendants from the line of Shealtiel–Zerubbabel separated once again into David–Solomon heirs and David–Nathan heirs and continued in parallel fashion through the Second Temple period.
- Ultimately, the double lines of the Davidic descendants merged once again in the person of Joseph (Jesus' earthly father), who represented the *biological* heir of one line and the *legal* heir of the other.
- The climax of history comes with the birth of Jesus the Messiah in approximately late 3 or early 2 B.C. (see note 56).

Explanation for the Great Threat of Messianic Extinction During the Destruction of Jerusalem and Babylonian Captivity

In the Babylonian overthrow of Jerusalem in 586 B.C., countless people were killed. Jeremiah prophesied that so many would be "winnow[ed]" that childless mothers and widows would be "more numerous than the sand of the sea" (**Jeremiah 15:7–8**). One of the casualties of war seems to have been Neri (in the David–Nathan line). On the other hand, King Jeconiah/Jehoiachin (from the David–Solomon line) was captured by King Nebuchadnezzar and taken to Babylon as a prisoner of war, as were Jeconiah's mother (Nehushta, the "queen mother"; **2 Kings 24:8; Jeremiah 13:18**), Jeconiah's wives, court officials, and "prominent people of the land" (**2 Kings 24:10–15**; cf. **Jeremiah 29:2**). **First Chronicles 3:17–18** lists the descendants of King Jeconiah as "Shealtiel . . . , Malkiram, Pedaiah [likely the same person as "Sheshbazzar"; see note 18], Shenazzar, Jekamiah, Hoshama, and Nedabiah," but it is probable that, with the exception of Pedaiah/Sheshbazzar, these sons/descendants of Jeconiah were killed during the destruction of Jerusalem, taken into captivity and made eunuchs, or left no heirs (thus fulfilling Isaiah's prophecy to King Hezekiah in **2 Kings 20:18; Isaiah 39:7**; cf. **Daniel 1:3–7**). In effect, this left the captive king, Jeconiah/Jehoiachin, with no heirs to carry on his name. Since Neri seems to have been killed in the Babylonian invasion, both messianic lines of descent (via David–Solomon and David–Nathan) faced extinction.

Insights into the Continuation of the Messianic Line

Given the great pressures of war—"sword, famine and plague" (**Jeremiah 14:12; 21:7, 9; 24:10**; etc.)—and the extended seventy-year period (i.e., 586–516 B.C. that the captives were in Babylonian exile, the messianic line was in jeopardy. However, as the Gospels of Matthew and Luke reveal, the David–Solomon line and the David–Nathan line not only continued, but were reunited in a *single* person named Shealtiel, a *remnant* figure who was born in captivity (**Matthew 1:12**). The question becomes "how" or "by what means" was the messianic line perpetuated?

A. The Identity and Importance of Shealtiel

In Luke's account of Jesus' ancestry, *Neri* is identified as the father of Shealtiel (**Luke 3:27**); in contrast, in Matthew's ancestry, *King Jeconiah* is identified as the father of Shealtiel (**Matthew 1:12**; cf. **1 Chronicles 3:17**). To explain the seeming discrepancy, two possible scenarios and explanations are discussed:

1. *Levirate marriage*: In scenario #1, after the death of his near relative/kinsman Neri (in the David–Nathan line), the captive King Jeconiah/Jehoiachin (in the David–Solomon line) entered into a legal levirate marriage (**Deuteronomy 25:5–6**) with Neri's widow—acting as the kinsman redeemer (*goel*), meaning "to act as kinsman, do the part of next of kin"—and raised up a child (Shealtiel) for the deceased Neri.[53] In this scenario, Shealtiel was the *biological* son of Jeconiah/Jehoiachin (from the David–Solomon line) and the *legal* son/heir of Neri (from the David–Nathan line).

   OR
2. *Adoption*: In scenario #2, after the death of his near relative/kinsman Neri (in the David–Nathan line), the captive King Jeconiah/Jehoiachin (in the David–Solomon line) *adopted* Neri's son, Shealtiel, to secure a future *legal* heir for himself (since Jeconiah's own biological sons—called "his children" or "his nobles [princes]"—were killed, made eunuchs, or were cursed, **Jeremiah 22:28–30**). Even though he would never return to Jerusalem, Jeconiah desired a legal heir who would be given his inheritance (although this heir would not receive the right of royal succession) once the exiles returned to their homeland. In this scenario, Shealtiel was the *biological* son of Neri (from the David–Nathan line) and the *legal* son/heir of Jeconiah (from the David–Solomon line).

In both scenarios, Shealtiel continued both the David–Nathan and the David–Solomon lines, consistent with other biblical texts such as **Matthew 1:12, Luke 3:27,** and **Jeremiah 22:24–28, 30**.

B. The Identity and Importance of Zerubbabel

Zerubbabel is called the *son of Pedaiah* (the brother of Shealtiel) in **1 Chronicles 3:19** and the *son of Shealtiel* in **Ezra 3:2, 8; 5:2; Nehemiah 12:1; Haggai 1:1, 12, 14; 2:2** and **Matthew 1:12**; Zerubbabel is also implied to be the *grandson of Neri* (**Luke 3:27**). Taken together, these verses call into question the biological vs. the legal ancestry of Zerubbabel. Again, either levirate marriage (as explained in scenario #1 above) or adoption (as explained in scenario #2 above) seems to come into play to explain the text, just as it did with Neri and Jeconiah/Jehoiachin, but which exact scenario occurred is unknown. Two scenarios are offered to explain the seeming inconsistency parentage of Zerubbabel:

1. *Levirate marriage*: In scenario #1, Shealtiel died in captivity, so Pedaiah/Sheshbazzar (Shealtiel's brother; see note 18) entered into levirate marriage with Shealtiel's widow and raised up a legal heir for the deceased Shealtiel. In this case, Zerubbabel was the *biological* son of Pedaiah/Sheshbazzar and the *legal* son/heir of Shealtiel.

   OR
2. *Adoption*: In scenario #2, Zerubbabel was born in captivity to Shealtiel, but Shealtiel died in captivity, so Pedaiah/Sheshbazzar (Shealtiel's brother) *adopted* Zerubbabel. In this case, Zerubbabel was the *biological* son of Shealtiel and the *legal* son/heir of Pedaiah/Sheshbazzar.

Genealogical Insights into the Leaders Who Returned to Jerusalem in the Post-Exile

Zerubbabel's father, Pedaiah/Sheshbazzar—who is called the "prince of Judah"—was appointed by King Cyrus as the first "governor" over Yehud (**Ezra 1:8, 11; 5:13–14**). Pedaiah/Sheshbazzar returned to Jerusalem in approximately 537 B.C. and began laying the foundation of the Second Temple (**Ezra 5:16**), but apparently died soon thereafter in ca. 536 B.C., before the foundation was fully completed. Zerubbabel had brought the first group of exiles to Jerusalem in 538 B.C.; after Pedaiah/Sheshbazzar's death, the governorship of the post-exilic (Yehud) community passed to him (i.e., his *son/heir* Zerubbabel; **Haggai 1:1, 14; 2:2, 21**). Together, under the united leadership of Zerubbabel the governor and Joshua (Jeshua) the high priest, the foundation of the temple was completed (**Ezra 3:10–12**) and the Second Temple (also called Zerubbabel's Temple)—four years in construction (520–516 B.C.)—was finally completed in 516 B.C. (**Ezra 5:2; 6:13–22**; cf. **Haggai** and **Zechariah**).

During the Second Temple period (516–ca. 3/2 B.C.), the generations of Zerubbabel's descendants constituted the two biological and legal lines of the Messiah, thereby providing continuity for the David–Solomon and the David–Nathan lines. The lines progress in parallel fashion until merging once again in the person of Joseph, Jesus' earthly father (see details below). Jesus Christ, the Son of God and Son of David, with his birth in ca. 3 or 2 B.C., was the culminating figure (terminus) of both the David–Solomon and the David–Nathan genealogical lines.

Summarizing the Historical Events

The genealogies support the conclusion that the messianic line "hung by a thread" at the time of the exile/immediate post-exile. *Shealtiel* became the key figure who brought together the two parallel David–Solomon and David–Nathan lines between 1011 and 586 B.C. After the seventy-year Babylonian captivity (586–516 B.C.), the genealogy shifts toward Zerubbabel, where the functional mandate to produce heir(s) for both the David–Solomon and the David–Nathan lines fell to him. Since the Chronicler clearly emphasizes that Zerubbabel had two families—three children in one (two sons and one daughter) and five children in another (**1 Chronicles 3:19–20**)—the *prima facie* impression is that one set of Zerubbabel's children represented the Solomonic heirs and the other set the Nathanite heirs, but which family belonged to which (i.e., to the David–Solomon line or to the David–Nathan line) is not clear.

Also, the genealogies of Jesus in **Matthew 1** and **Luke 3** emphasize that Abihud and Rhesa were Zerubbabel's direct offspring/heirs (**Matthew 1:13** and **Luke 3:27**, respectively). It is possible that Abihud (or Rhesa) may have been the husband of Shelomith, Zerubbabel's daughter; if the latter is true, then one of the lines that continued in the post-exile was through a *son-in-law* of Zerubbabel rather than through a *son*. Alternatively, Abihud (and/or Rhesa) may have been an *adopted* or *levirate* sons of Zerubbabel.

Chiastic Literary Structure

The chiastic ("X" or crossover) structural composition of the genealogy stresses the importance of Shealtiel and Zerubbabel and reveals three distinct periods of Israel's history:

1. The *monarchic period*: the kingly line of David–Solomon–Jeconiah descendants (top left), and the non-kingly line of David–Nathan–Neri descendants (top right), from ca. 1011–586 B.C.;
2. The *seventy-year period of Babylonian captivity* (ca. 586–516 B.C.) and the subsequent post-exile period (ca. 538–400 B.C.), showing the key figures, Shealtiel and Zerubbabel (middle), and individuals who lived in Yehud/Jerusalem (cf. **1 Chronicles 3:19–24**) who are identified as Zerubbabel descendants (Judahites). Seemingly *remnant* families "from Benjamin, and from Ephraim and Manasseh" also lived in post-exilic Jerusalem (**1 Chronicles 9:3**) (middle right); and
3. The *Second Temple period to the birth of Jesus* (ca. 516–3 or 2 B.C.), showing the parallel lines of descent of the David–Solomon and David–Nathan ancestors of Jesus, from Zerubbabel to Joseph (bottom left).

Major Findings

The chart affirms the following rich theological messages:

- Genealogies in the ancient world identified individuals by the father's lineage (i.e., according to *patrilineal descent*), not the mother's lineage. For this reason, both Matthew and Luke should be understood to trace the ancestry of Jesus through the biological and legal ancestors of Joseph, not those of Jesus' mother, Mary (**Matthew 1:1–16; Luke 3:23–38**).
- The narrowed structural composition of the genealogy at the time of the exile reflects the pressures of war—the Babylonia destruction of Jerusalem, the death of the citizenry "by the sword, famine and plague," widespread widowhood, and the exile of most of Judah's nobles and commoners. All these factors threatened the continuation of the messianic line (**Jeremiah 24:10; 27:8, 13; 32:36–38**; cf. **2 Kings 24:14–16; 25:8–11; Jeremiah 27:20–22**).
- During the exile, the David–Solomon–Jeconiah/Jehoiachin line and the David–Nathan–Neri line of Jesus' ancestors were at great risk of becoming extinct. The exilic period—shown in the chart as the "crossover" (chiasm or "X") point in the genealogy—shows how the two separate lines of descent were united in the persons of Shealtiel and Zerubbabel. In the Second Temple period, the concatenation of the messianic line was through two distinct, parallel lines of descent through Zerubbabel's legal and biological descendants (cf. **Matthew 1:13–16; Luke 3:23–27**), until once again, they were united in the person of Joseph (Jesus' earthly father).
- Biological succession (from father-to-son) was the primary means by which successive generations continued. However, there are also striking places where *legal* succession clearly occurred by some combination of *sons* brought forth by levirate marriage(s), adoption(s), by marriage, via sons-in-law, and/or by second marriages. This is especially discernable in the parentage of David and in the case of the heirs of Jehoiachin, Neri, Shealtiel, Zerubbabel, Abihud, Rhesa, Matthan, Matthat, Jacob, and Heli. Plausible scenarios of what happened in these instances are discussed in Excursus A below and addressed in the charts: "**1 Chronicles 2**: King David," "**2 Kings 24**: Jehoiachin (Jeconiah), King of Judah," and "**Matthew 1**: Ancestry of Mary and Joseph (Based on Scripture and Church Tradition) and How Mary and Joseph May Have Been Related."
- Of profound Christological and theological importance is the fact that Jesus' ancestry in the Lukan genealogy is derived from Adam, called "the son of God" (**Luke 3:38**). The "seed" (sperm)—which was passed by the male through all successive generations—was, biblically speaking, the repository of the human tendency to sin. As prophesied in **Isaiah 7:14**, the Messiah was born of a virgin. God the Holy Spirit planted the "seed" in the virgin's womb (**Genesis 3:15**), and therefore, Jesus did not inherit the ability to sin. Rather, the Messiah was the holy offspring of God—"God with us" (אֵל עִמָּנוּ), "Immanuel"—free from sin, though still susceptible to temptation as a man (cf. **Hebrews 4:15**). From a genealogical perspective, Joseph was considered the (non-biological) earthly father and legal guardian of Jesus (**Luke 2:4–5, 22–24; 3:23; 4:22; John 1:45; 6:42; Romans 1:3**). Thus, Jesus' ancestry is exclusively traced through Joseph's biological and legal heritage.

One of the great truths of the Christian confession is that Jesus, son of Mary, was also the Christ, the Son of God. The apostle Paul declares, "God was reconciling the world to himself in Christ" (**2 Corinthians 5:19**). Jesus, our kinsman-redeemer, offers redemption and salvation through his own sacrifice to those who believe and follow him. Through him, believers obtain "adoption to sonship" of a spiritual, not a physical, nature (**Romans 8:15; Ephesians 1:5**; cf. **Mark 16:16**). At the same time, Jesus was fully man, possessing all the faculties of humanity and experiencing all that is common to man, including temptation to do evil, a temptation to which he never yielded. Jesus the Christ was the son of Abraham and the son of David, the Sufferer and Sovereign, "born of a woman, born under the law, to redeem those under the law, that we might receive adoption to sonship" (**Galatians 4:4–5**).

Excursus A. Analysis of the David–Shealtiel–Zerubbabel–Joseph–Jesus Lineage

The following is a *condensed form* of the elaborate genealogical chart shown above for the purpose of highlighting a *repeated pattern* that is unmistakably apparent in Jesus' ancestry:

> **"Two men, in succession, married the same woman"** (i.e., in the first union, a man and woman marry, but when the first husband died—either with or without biological children—his widow married again; she then became the wife of a second man and bore him a child or children).

These instances of "second marriages" are indicated with an asterisk (*) below:

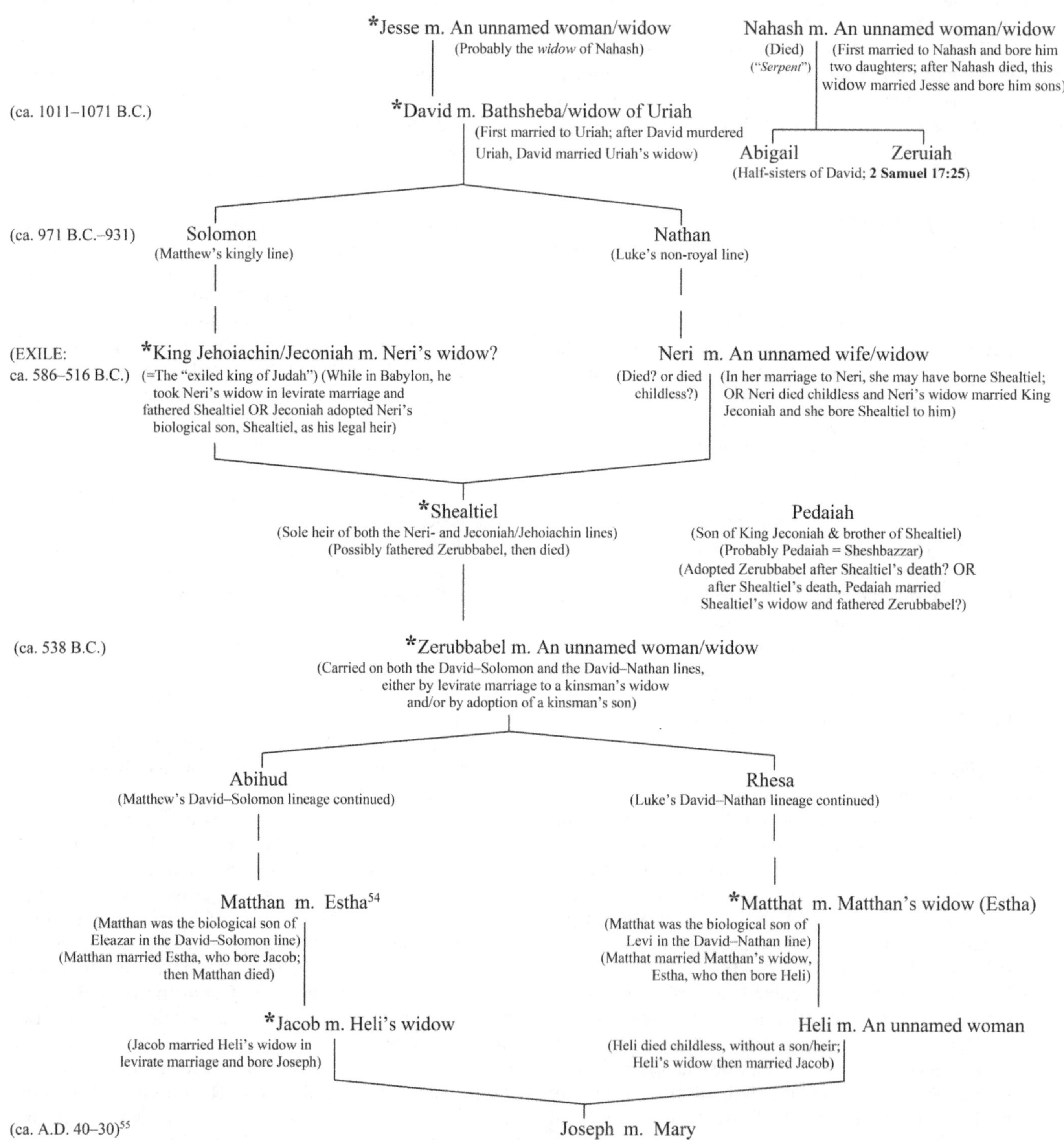

(ca. A.D. 40–30)[55] Joseph m. Mary

(Earthly father of Jesus)
(Joseph was probably the biological son of Jacob and the *legal* heir of Heli)

Jesus the MESSIAH

(ca. 5 or 3/2 B.C.)[56] (*Son of God* and *Son of Man*)
(Conceived by Mary the virgin and the Holy Spirit)

Significance of Excursus A

The condensed form of the genealogy highlights a reoccurring theme in the ancestry of Jesus: **two men, separately and in succession, married the same woman.**[57] First, the woman in each case was the wife of Husband #1 and she may or may not have had a son/heir by him. After her first husband died (or died childless without a son/heir), she (a widow) married Husband #2 and had a child (or children). There are at least seven instances of this in Jesus' ancestry between Jesse (David's father) and Joseph (Jesus' earthly father), as indicated in the excursus by an **asterisk** (*) beside the name of Husband #2.

1. **Jesse** married an unnamed woman (the former wife/widow of a man named Nahash; possibly King Nahash of Ammon?) and she bore David and his brothers. This explains why King David had two uterine half-sisters, Abigail and Zeruiah, the daughters of Nahash (cf. **2 Samuel 17:25**).
2. **King David** married Bathsheba (the former wife/widow of Uriah) who bore Solomon and Nathan, as well as two other living sons.
3. **King Jeconiah/Jehoiachin** (who is the *terminal* figure of the David–Solomon line at the time of the exile) married an unnamed woman (the former wife/widow of Neri?) while in Babylonian captivity. Neri was the *terminal* figure of the non-royal, David–Nathan line (at or near the exile). Neri is Jeconiah/Jehoiachin's distant kinsman.
4. **Shealtiel** (the figure who united the *kingly* David–Solomon line and the *non-kingly* David–Nathan line) married an unnamed woman (probably the former wife/widow of Pedaiah, Shealtiel's uterine brother) and fathered Zerubbabel.
5. **Zerubbabel** (the governor of the post-exile Yehud community) married an unnamed woman (the former wife/widow of an unnamed kinsman of Zerubbabel).
6. **Matthat** married "Estha" (the former wife/widow of Matthan, Matthat's distant relative) and bore Jacob.
7. **Jacob** married an unnamed woman (the former wife/widow of Heli, Jacob's uterine brother) and bore Joseph, the earthly father of Jesus.

In addition to these seven probable instances of second marriages in the generations between David and Jesus, there are three others (not shown in the chart) which are known from earlier generations of Jesus' ancestors.

8. **Judah** fathered twin sons by his daughter-in-law, Tamar (the former wife/widow of Er and Onan) while she was in disguise; see the chart "**1 Chronicles 2**: Judah Showing the Line of the Messiah."
9. **Salmon** the Judahite married Rahab the prostitute of Jericho; see the chart "**Joshua 2**: Rahab, the Prostitute of Jericho."
10. **Boaz** the Judahite married Ruth the Moabitess, the former wife/widow of Mahlon; see the chart "**Ruth 1**: Boaz, Elimelek, and Naomi and the Descendants of Boaz the Judahite and Ruth the Moabitess."

Thus, in all, a total of at least TEN "anomalous" marriages in the ancestry of the Messiah are discernable. Contrary to what might be expected for Jesus' heritage—such as *exclusive* father–son succession of offspring in a single, uninterrupted line, Excursus A confirms that *multiple* second marriages did occur and account for a combination of both *biological* and *legal* ancestors of the Messiah. What can this mean? Of all the infinite possible combinations of people and generations that *could* have occurred, this must have been the divine thought and the means of fulfillment.

The marriage unions shown in Excursus A recall the *dual nature* of the Messiah, as both the divine Son of God and the Son of Man, who took on human form (**John 1:14**) and yet did not sin (**Hebrews 4:15**). Jesus brought salvation by offering himself as the perfect sacrifice, dying on the cross for the sins of man. The cross—an anti-type of the *Nehushtan*[58] (cf. **Numbers 21:8–9; Isaiah 51:6–8; Luke 1:69: John 3:14-15; 8:28; Acts 2:29–32; Philippians 2:9–11**)—brought not judgment, but salvation to those who looked and believed (**Isaiah 57:15; Hebrews 9:26–28**). Whereas the serpent in Eden was the means whereby death and judgment came upon Adam and Eve (**Genesis 3**), the bronze serpent, Nehushtan, in the wilderness was raised up for the people to see and, by it, to believe in the God of healing and life (**Numbers 21:6–9**; cf. **2 Corinthians 5:21**).

Excursus B. Visual Illuminations into Jesus' Lineage Based on Matthew's and Luke's Genealogies

*"I am the Alpha [α] and the Omega [Ω/ ω/ ∞ = 8], the First and the Last, the Beginning and the End" (***Revelation 22:13***).*

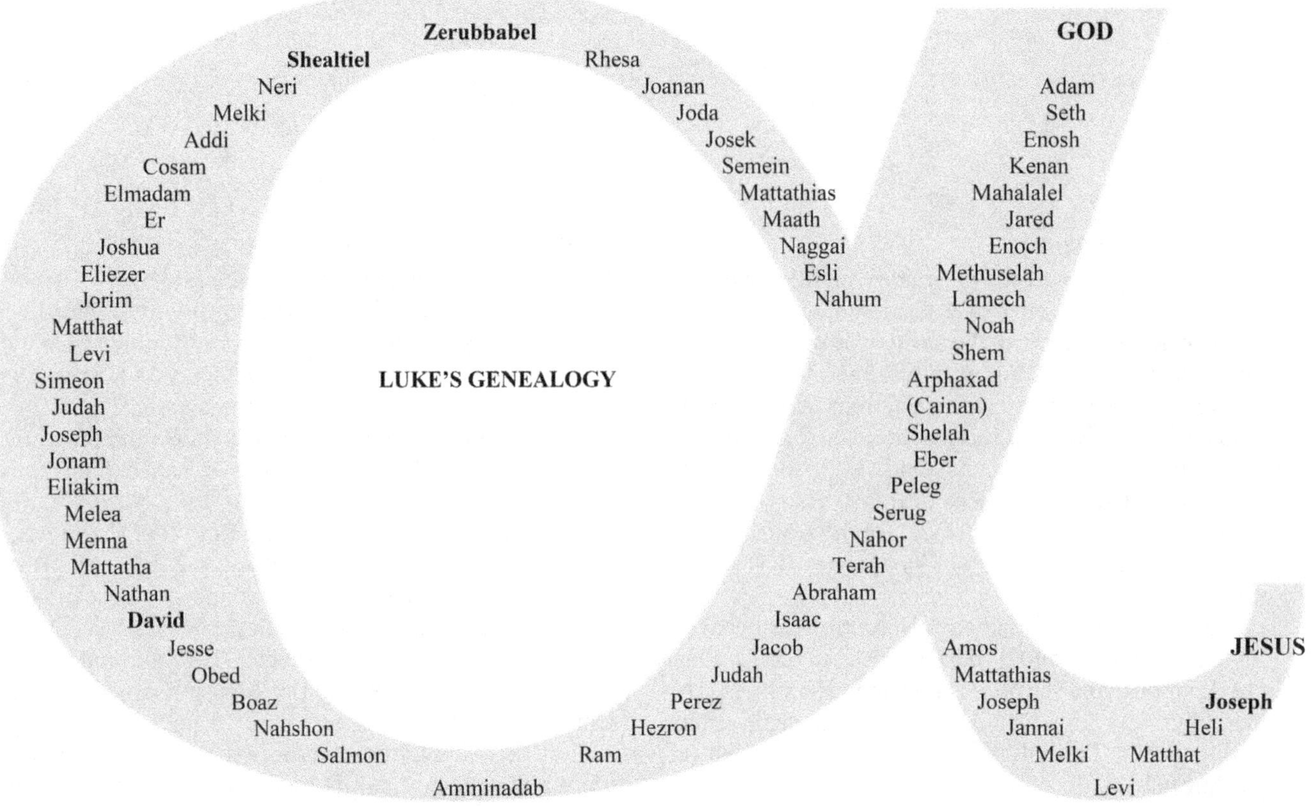

Significance of Excursus B

Excursus B ties the **1 Chronicles 3**, **Matthew 1**, and **Luke 3** genealogical lineages of Zerubbabel and Shealtiel to the glorious apex realized in **Revelation 22:13**—that Jesus was the ***Alpha*** and the ***Omega*** of all creation. The Matthew and Luke genealogies reveal a grand mystery and elegant beauty—an "alpha sign" and an "infinity sign" (shown edgewise/in the vertical aspect), a variant of the Greek letter ω (Omega; **Revelation 1:8; 21:6; 22:13**). Thus, Jesus fills eternity—the "Son of the Most High [God]" (**Mark 5:7; Luke 1:32; 8:28**) who possessed the throne of his *father* David: "the living God, the eternal King" (**Jeremiah 10:10**) . . . "he will reign over Jacob's descendants forever; his kingdom will never end" (**Luke 1:33**; cf. **2 Samuel 22:51; 2 Kings 8:19; 2 Chronicles 13:5; 21:7; Isaiah 9:6–7; Mark 11:10; Luke 1:55; John 7:42; 1 Timothy 1:17**). In this way, Christ is simultaneously the One "who is, and who was, and who is to come" (**Revelation 1:8**).

If the lineages of the key ancestors leading to the Messiah are evaluated individually, they occur as 120 (56 + 43 + 21) generations (cf. **Genesis 6:3**) as follows:

- Abraham to Jesus (56 generations, inclusive),
- King David to Jesus (43 generations, inclusive),
- Zerubbabel to Jesus (21 generations, inclusive).

Biblical and Theological Significance

In certain points in biblical history, it is clear that the continuance of the messianic line hinged on *single* individuals (Shealtiel and Zerubbabel) who lived at the time of the exile (i.e., the literary chiastic point in the chart). God, in faithful covenant with his espoused people, restored the rightful and exalted *King* to the Davidic throne. The genealogy of Jesus the Messiah shows the means by which God "establish(ed) the throne of his kingdom forever" (**2 Samuel 7:13**; cf. **2 Samuel 7:12–16; 1 Kings 2:45; 8:20–26; 9:5; 1 Chronicles 16:15; 17:7–14; 22:10; 2 Chronicles 21:7; Psalm 9:7; 29:10; 33:11**) and "remember[ed] his covenant forever, the promise he made, for a thousand generations" (**Psalm 105:8**).

In the larger theological perspective, Excursus A unveils a great mystery, showing that in God's plan, God the Father–Creator–Maker (*Husband #1*) *married* his people (Israel) in a kind of "first marriage"; but she, playing the harlot with other gods, was put away, but not forever. In the coming of the Son of Man (*Husband #2*)—the heir of all the promises—the first woman/widow was redeemed through Jesus' blood to become the chaste "bride" of Christ in the "second marriage," bringing salvation, perfection, restoration, and an ultimate inheritance. Many references reflect this dual union: **Genesis 3:15; Isaiah 54:5; 61:10; 62:5; Jeremiah 3:14, 20–25; 31:31–34; Ezekiel 16; Hosea 2:2–3:5; Matthew 9:15; Mark 2:19–20; Luke 5:34–35; John 3:29; Romans 4:13–16; 9:4–9; 2 Corinthians 11:2; Ephesians 5:25–32; Hebrews 9:15; 1 Peter 1:3–5; Revelation 19:7–8; 21:2–3**.

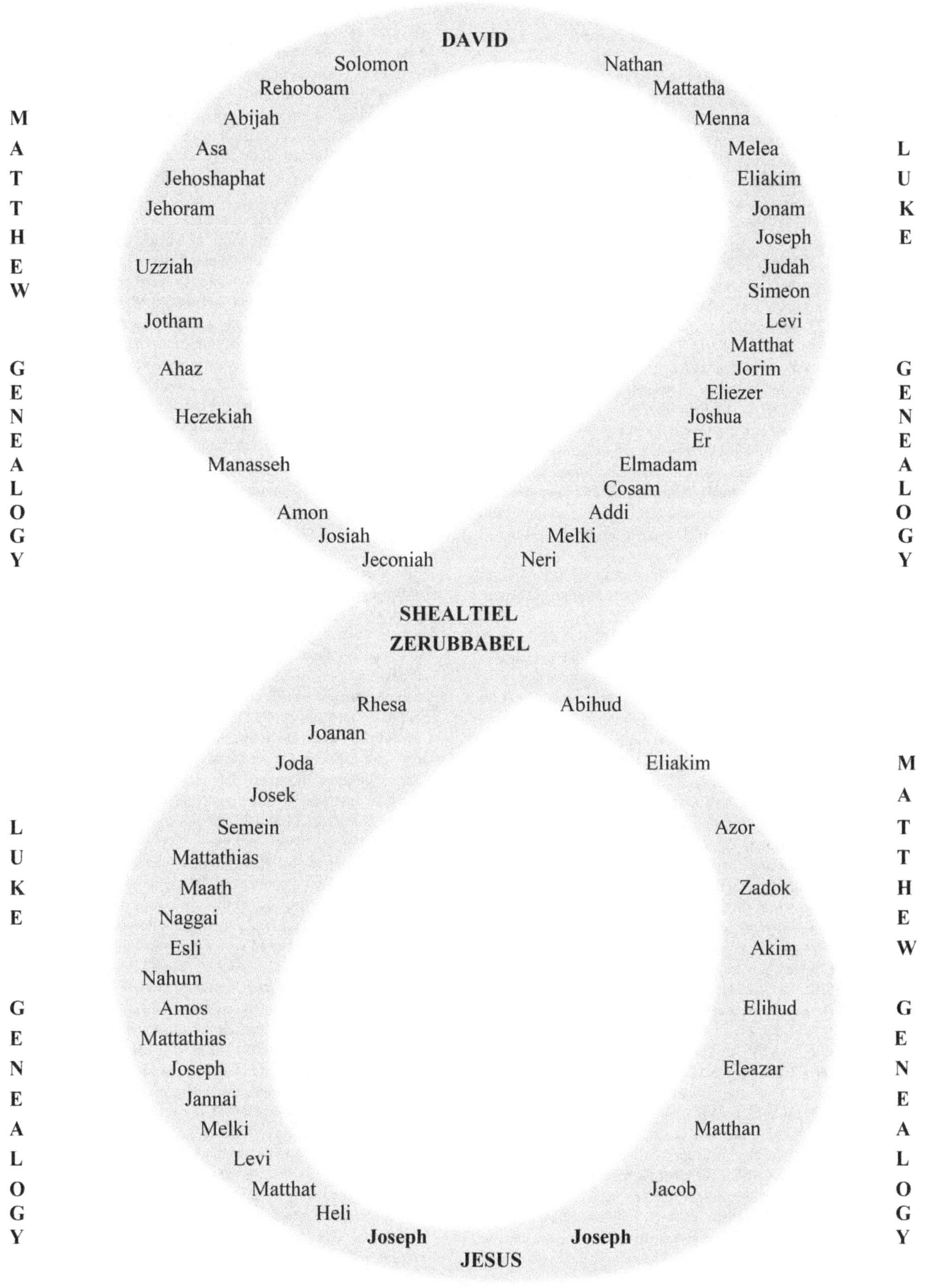

DAVID

Solomon
Rehoboam
Abijah
Asa
Jehoshaphat
Jehoram
Uzziah
Jotham
Ahaz
Hezekiah
Manasseh
Amon
Josiah
Jeconiah

Nathan
Mattatha
Menna
Melea
Eliakim
Jonam
Joseph
Judah
Simeon
Levi
Matthat
Jorim
Eliezer
Joshua
Er
Elmadam
Cosam
Addi
Melki
Neri

MATTHEW GENEALOGY

LUKE GENEALOGY

SHEALTIEL
ZERUBBABEL

Rhesa
Joanan
Joda
Josek
Semein
Mattathias
Maath
Naggai
Esli
Nahum
Amos
Mattathias
Joseph
Jannai
Melki
Levi
Matthat
Heli
Joseph

Abihud
Eliakim
Azor
Zadok
Akim
Elihud
Eleazar
Matthan
Jacob
Joseph

LUKE GENEALOGY

MATTHEW GENEALOGY

JESUS

Notes

1. See charts "**Matthew 1**: Jesus Christ–the Matthean Account" and "**Luke 3**: Jesus: the Lukan Account."

2. After misusing his kingly power—taking sexual advantage of Bathsheba and then murdering her husband to cover up his transgression—David took Bathsheba as his lawful wife, but the child conceived illegitimately died (**2 Samuel 11:26–27; 12:15–18**). However, God blessed the couple with another son, Solomon, destined to succeed David as king (**2 Samuel 12:24; 1 Kings 1:13**; cf. **1 Chronicles 22:9**). In addition, Bathsheba bore David three other sons, Shammua, Shobab, and Nathan (**1 Chronicles 3:5**), the last of whom became the progenitor of a non-royal (Nathan) line that parallels the royal (Solomon) line. The Old Testament has nothing to say of members of the non-kingly line of Nathan, but Luke, with unknown literary sources at his disposal, fills in the line, naming some 40 forefathers of Joseph, the earthly father of Jesus (**Luke 3:23–31**). Together, persons in the David–Solomon (**Matthew 1:1–16**) and the David–Nathan (**Luke 3:23–38**) lineages form the basis for the complex "dual ancestry" of Jesus the Messiah.

3. Old Testament names shown in brackets (i.e., Ahaziah–Joash–Amaziah; and the sons of Josiah) are omitted in Matthew's genealogy, but they are known biblical figures in Jesus' ancestry (cf. **1 Chronicles 3:11–12, 15**).

4. See chart "**1 Chronicles 2**: King David." David's father was Jesse, but uncharacteristic of most of Judah's kings—especially considering that David was Israel's most famous king!—*David's mother is unnamed.* David had two half-sisters (Zeruiah and Abigail; **2 Samuel 17:25**), who were the daughters of Nahash rather than Jesse, suggesting that David's mother probably married twice (see Excursus A). The line of Judah's kings proceeds through the David–Solomon line.

5. Whereas the kingly line of the Messiah passes through the David–Solomon line, the non-kingly line of the Messiah proceeds through the David–Nathan line.

6. Writing in ca. 520–518 B.C., the prophet Zechariah says that the members of the "clan of the house of Nathan" (**Zechariah 12:12**)—meaning descendants in the David–Nathan–Neri line—returned from Babylon to Jerusalem in the post-exile, along with "the clan of the house of David . . . the clan of the house of Levi . . . [and] the clan of Shimei [possibly referring to Levites or Benjamites]." In the latter case, the clan of Shimei (also called Shimeah or Shimeam) may refer to relatives of Mordecai and Esther, "who lived near their relatives in Jerusalem" (**1 Chronicles 8:32**; see also **1 Chronicles 8:21, 28; 9:3, 7–9, 38; Nehemiah 11:3–4, 7–9; Esther 2:5**). See notes 19 and 27; for Shimei/Shimeah/Shimeam the Benjamite, see note 3 in chart "**Esther 2**: Mordecai and Esther, Jews Living in Persia."

7. In the list of the succession of the kings of Judah, **Matthew 1:8–9** states that Uzziah (Azariah) reigned between Jehoram and Jotham; however, **1 Chronicles 3:11–12** notes that three additional kings reigned between Jehoram and Jotham: Ahaziah, Joash, and Amaziah. Matthew chose to omit these three kings to conform his genealogy to a 14–14–14 arrangement, a literary tool called "telescoping" (**Matthew 1:17**).

Uzziah (**2 Kings 15:13, 30, 32, 34; 2 Chronicles 26:1–23; 27:2; Isaiah 1:1; 6:1; 7:1; Hosea 1:1; Amos 1:1; Zechariah 14:5**) is otherwise Azariah (**2 Kings 14:21; 15:1, 7–8, 17, 23, 27; 1 Chronicles 3:12**).

8. Some translations (e.g., NKJV) suggest that Assir was a *son* of Jehoiachin (Jeconiah; cf. **1 Chronicles 3:17**), but the NIV translation clarifies that *Assir* is a term meaning "captive." Thus, the NIV of **1 Chronicles 3:17–18** reads: "The descendants of Jehoiachin *the captive*." Matthew writes: "*After* the exile to Babylon: Jehoiachin was the father of Shealtiel, Shealtiel the father of Zerubbabel." (**Matthew 1:12**). Jehoiachin/Jeconiah died in Babylon, but while in exile, he secured a *son*/legal heir (Shealtiel), thereby *uniting* the parallel lines of messianic descent through David and Bathsheba's sons (i.e., the royal line of Solomon and non-royal line of Nathan). Thus, by both biological and legal means, the descendants of Shealtiel and Zerubbabel carried on the messianic line.

9. The wives and mother (Nehushta) of King Jeconiah/Jehoiachin were exiled to Babylon (**2 Kings 24:15**).

10. Jehoiachin/Jeconiah and his brothers were alive at the time of the exile to Babylon (cf. **Matthew 1:11**). Jehoiachin's brothers were probably among "all the nobles of Judah and Jerusalem" (**Jeremiah 27:20**) and "the Israelites from the royal family and the nobility" (**Daniel 1:3**) who were carried away by Nebuchadnezzar to Babylon (see **Isaiah 39:7; Daniel 1:1–7**).

11. In God's judgment for their persistent unfaithfulness, many were killed during the destruction of Jerusalem and during the seventy-year Babylonian exile, 586–516 B.C. (**Jeremiah 11:22; 14:12, 16, 18; 16:4; 21:7; Ezekiel 6:11–12; 7:15; 14**). Jeremiah the prophet notes that during the tumultuous time of the destruction of Jerusalem, "widows [became] more numerous than the sand of the sea" (**Jeremiah 15:8**). Ezekiel says that only a *remnant*— "a few of them"—survived to acknowledge and witness to the Gentile nations that Israel had been unfaithful to the Lord (**Ezekiel 12:16**).

12. Neri is the shortened form of Neriah, meaning the "Lord is my light."

13. For the "childless" state of Jehoiachin, see **Jeremiah 22:28–30**; the Lord told Jeremiah to record Jehoiachin *as if* childless, but not that he actually had no children/sons. Apparently, he was judged "as good as childless" because none of his children prospered and none became king; see chart "**2 Kings 24**: Jehoiachin (Jeconiah), King of Judah."

14. According to the prophecy of Isaiah, "some of his [King Hezekiah's] descendants, your own flesh and blood who will be born to you, will be taken away, and they will become eunuchs in the palace of the king of Babylon," but the exact descendants are unknown (**2 Kings 20:18, Isaiah 39:7; Jeremiah 15:1–9**; cf. **Daniel 1:3–7**). Isaiah's prophecy seems to apply to Jehoiachin/Jeconiah and his immediate family/heirs at the time of the exile, except Pedaiah (see note 18).

15. Cuneiform tablets unearthed from the royal archives of Nebuchadnezzar in Babylon, found by Robert Koldewey between 1899 and 1917, record the disbursal of rations from the royal storehouses; among them was the "Jehoiachin Ration Tablet," which mentions rations of oil given to the captive King Jehoiachin of Judah—Ya'u-kīnu, king of the land of Yahudu—and five of his sons; "Babylonian Ration List: King Jehoiakhin in Exile, 592–1 B.C.E." in the COJS, http://cojs.org/babylonian_ration_list-_king_jehoiakhin_in_exile-_592-1_bce/. Unfortunately, the names of the royal princes who lived in Babylon with their father, Jeconiah/Jehoiachin, are not specifically given, and their fate is unknown (see note 14).

16. Shealtiel is one of only four persons—David, Shealtiel, Zerubbabel, and Joseph—common to both the Matthew and Luke accounts of Jesus' ancestry (i.e., the names shown in ALL CAPS in the chart). Matthew notes that Shealtiel was born during the Babylonian exile (**Matthew 1:12**). Luke's account of Jesus' ancestry identifies *Neri* as the father of Shealtiel (**Luke 3:27**), although Matthew's account of Jesus' ancestry identifies *King Jeconiah* as the father of Shealtiel (**Matthew 1:12**; cf. **1 Chronicles 3:17**). This chart delves into two possible scenarios to explain the apparent discrepancy regarding the identity of Shealtiel's father, since Shealtiel represents the single "scarlet thread" of the messianic line in the precarious days of the exile.

17. Shenazzar, the son of Jehoiachin/Jeconiah (**1 Chronicles 3:18**), died in the destruction of Jerusalem, in exile, or was made a eunuch in Babylonian captivity (see notes 14 and 15). Shenazzar and Sheshbazzar (Pedaiah) were brothers. They are clearly not the same person as Zerubbabel, who brought exiles to Jerusalem in 538 B.C. and served as "governor of Judah" over the newly restored Yehud community (**Haggai 1:1, 14; 2:2, 21**).

18. Pedaiah, King Jeconiah's son, appears to be the same person as "Sheshbazzar," who returned to post-exilic Jerusalem in ca. 537 B.C. (i.e., after the group of exiles returned with Zerubbabel in 538 B.C.). On the identity of Pedaiah as Sheshbazzar, also see chart "**Ezra 1**: Sheshbazzar and Zerubbabel, the Governors over the Restored Community in Jerusalem (Post-Exile)." Pedaiah/Sheshbazzar was likely an elderly man when commissioned by King Cyrus of Persia to bring some 5,400 articles of silver and gold to Jerusalem (**Ezra 1:11**) and when he was appointed as the first governor over the Yehud community (**Ezra 5:14**). In "the second month of the second year [537 B.C.?] after their arrival" (**Ezra 3:8**), Pedaiah/Sheshbazzar "came and laid the foundations of the house of God in Jerusalem" (**Ezra 5:16**; cf. **3:8–11**), but he must not have finished; as Ezra explains: "From that day to the present it [the foundation] has been under construction but is not yet finished" (**Ezra 5:16**). It is inferred that sometime around 536 B.C., Sheshbazzar/Pedaiah died in Jerusalem and therefore his *son/heir*, the younger Zerubbabel—who had returned to Jerusalem in 538 B.C.—then assumed the full governorship over Yehud (**Haggai 1:1, 14; 2:2, 21**).

Note that "Sheshbazzar" (Pedaiah) is not the same person as "Shenazzar," who was another son/descendant of Jehoiachin/Jeconiah (see note 17). As Andrew Steinmann points out, "Most scholars have abandoned the identification of Sheshbazzar with Shenazzar since Berger [first] argued that the name Sheshbazzar could not be the same as Shenazzar, because Shesh-bazzar was probably derived from *šaššu-aba-usur* ("May Šaššu [the sun god] protect the father"). Therefore, for linguistic reasons, the name Shenazzar cannot be related to the name Sheshbazzar"; see Andrew E. Steinmann, "A Chronological Note: The Return of the Exiles Under Sheshbazzar and Zerubbabel (Ezra 1–2)," *JETS* 51 (2008): 513–22, footnote 16, quoting Paul Richard Berger, "Zu den Namen ששבצר und שנאצר" ZAW 83 (1971) 98–100; Cf. Fensham, The Books of Ezra and Nehemiah 46; Coggins, The Books of Ezra and Nehemiah 13; H. G. M. Williamson, Ezra, Nehemiah, WBC 16 (Waco, TX: Word, 1985), 5.

19. No descendants of Shimei are given, so it is probable that he died in exile or near that time. Zerubbabel (Shimei's brother) may have assumed the role of the levirate and married Shimei's widow, raising up an heir (or children) for the deceased Shimei. If this is the case, it may explain why Zerubbabel is described as having two sets of children (**1 Chronicles 3:19–20**), but it is unclear as to which set of children might represent the *legal* or *biological* heirs of Zerubbabel vs. Shimei—the set of three children consisting of Meshullam, Hananiah, and Shelomith (daughter), or the set of five children consisting of Hashubah, Ohel, Berekiah, Hasadiah, and Jushab-Hesed.

For clarity, the "clan of Shimei" in **Zechariah 12:13** may refer not to returning Levites (cf. **Exodus 6:17; Numbers 3:18**) or to descendants of Shimei (the brother of Zerubbabel) but to returning Benjamites (**1 Chronicles 9:3**), specifically the clan of Esther and Mordecai (i.e., the family of Shimeah/Shimeam in **1 Chronicles 8:32** and **1 Chronicles 9:38** who returned from exile and integrated into the restored community of Judahites in Jerusalem; see notes 6 and 27; also see note 3 in chart "**Esther 2**: Mordecai and Esther, Jews Living in Persia").

20. Zerubbabel's name suggests that he was born in Babylon (*Babel*). After King Cyrus the Great of Persia conquered Babylon in October, 539 B.C. (**Daniel 5:31;** for a discussion of "Darius the Mede" as an alternative name for Cyrus the Persian, see the commentary notes for **Daniel 5:31** in the *NIV Cultural Backgrounds Study Bible* (Grand Rapids: Zondervan, 2016), 1431–32 and those in the *NIV Study Bible* (Fully Revised edition), Kenneth L. Barker, ed. (Grand Rapids: Zondervan, 2011), 1472–73), Cyrus issued a decree—"In the first year [March 538 B.C.]"—allowing the Jews in captivity to "go up to Jerusalem in Judah and build the temple of the LORD" (**Ezra 1:1–3**; see **2 Chronicles 36:22–23; Ezra 1:1–7**). The Lord removed the "signet ring" that had been King Jehoiachin's (i.e., the honor and right to rule; **Jeremiah 22:24**) and gave it to Zerubbabel, declaring "I will make you like my signet ring, for I have chosen you" (**Haggai 2:23**). In this sense, Zerubbabel became the divinely appointed legal successor and inheritor of Jehoiachin/Jeconiah's royal estate. Yet, Zerubbabel did not become *king* upon his return to Jerusalem either, but rather represented the *ideal* royal figure and the messianic hope of the returning captives.

Zerubbabel led the first group of exiles back to Jerusalem in 538 B.C. and (after Pedaiah/Sheshbazzar's death; note 18) was appointed by the Persians as the governor of the newly restored post-exilic community known as Yehud (**Haggai 1:1, 14; 2:2, 21**); see chart "**Ezra 1**: Sheshbazzar and Zerubbabel, the Governors over the Restored Community in Jerusalem (Post-Exile)." In effect, Zerubbabel became the key transition figure between the pre-exile (when Judah was ruled by Davidic kings) and the post-exile (when governors ruled over the restored community). Together, Zerubbabel and the high priest, Joshua (the son of Jozadak), led the people in Jerusalem in rebuilding the temple, called the Second Temple (**Ezra 3:1–13; 4:3; Haggai 1:1–2:5; Zechariah 4:9**). Together, these leaders were the "anointed" ones who united the royal and priestly offices (**Zechariah 4:14; 6:9–13**; cf. **Jeremiah 33:14–22**).

21. In the days of the post-exile, a certain Hananiah was appointed the commander of the citadel because "he was a man of integrity and feared God more than most people do" (**Nehemiah 7:2**); it is possible that the prophet Nehemiah is referring to Hananiah, the son of Zerubbabel (**1 Chronicles 3:19**).

22. Shelomith was the daughter of Zerubbabel (**1 Chronicles 3:19**). The root of the name Shelomith (*Shlmth*) can be vocalized as both masculine and feminine: Shelomoth the masculine and Shelomith the feminine. Also, each spelling can be either gender. Shelomith (male) in **Ezra 8:10** should not be confused with the Levites, Shelomith/Shelomoth (males), in **1 Chronicles 23:18** and **1 Chronicles 26:25–28**.

23. Abihud, Zerubbabel's *son/heir*, is named in Matthew's genealogy but not in Luke's. Since Zerubbabel returned to Jerusalem ca. 538 B.C., Abihud would have lived in the immediate post-exile period, around 525–450 B.C. Abihud's name means "my father (is) praised, honored" or "father of (Ye) hud" (אֲבִי יְהוּד), the name of Judah in Persian. It is possible that Abihud (or Rhesa) may have been the husband of Shelomith, the daughter of Zerubbabel.

24. Rhesa continues the list of Zerubbabel sons/descendants in Luke's genealogy (**Luke 3:27**). As an early post-exilic figure, Rhesa could have been the husband of Shelomith, the daughter of Zerubbabel, but no firm kinship link reveals whether Rhesa, in fact, was Zerubbabel's *son-in-law*. Some scholars have proposed that Rhesa is not a personal name at all, but rather a transliteration of the Aramaic word for "prince," implying that Rhesa may have been the head, רֵאשׁ גָּלוּתָא (*resh geluta*), over the entire Yehud community after Zerubbabel's death, or that "Rhesa" is part of a title referring to "prince Joanan."

25. **First Chronicles 3:21** reads "The descendants of Hananiah: Pelatiah and Jeshaiah, and the sons of Rephaiah, of Arnan, of Obadiah and of Shekaniah." The Pelatiah figure in this verse may be the same person as Pelatiah who was one of the leaders of the people who signed the covenant with Nehemiah in 444 B.C. (**Nehemiah 10:22**).

26. Jeshaiah is the variant English transliteration of the Hebrew name Isaiah.

27. These additional families appear to *co-mingle with* Zerubbabel's clan (Judahites) in post-exilic Jerusalem, but it is unclear if they are Zerubbabel's direct descendants or just part of a larger extended family. They may represent the remnant "tithe" (one-tenth) of families referred to in **Nehemiah 11:1–2, 4**, who were chosen to live in the holy city—"Those from Judah, from Benjamin, and from Ephraim and Manasseh who lived in Jerusalem" and "people from both Judah and Benjamin [who] lived in Jerusalem" (**1 Chronicles 9:3; Nehemiah 11:4**, respectively).

28. The Masoretic text of **1 Chronicles 3:21** contains problematic punctuation and thus given rise to various interpretations. The NIV translates this verse as "The descendants of Hananiah: Pelatiah and Jeshaiah, and the sons of Rephaiah, of Arnan, of Obadiah and of Shekaniah." The "sons of Rephaiah" in **1 Chronicles 3:21** may, in fact, refer to descendants of Saul (Benjamites) who appear to assimilate with the Judahites in post-exilic Jerusalem. [The person called *Rephaiah*, a descendant in the King Saul–Jonathan line (**1 Chronicles 9:43**), is the same person called *Raphah* in the Saulide family tree (**1 Chronicles 8:37**); see chart "**1 Chronicles 8 & 9**: The Descendants of King Saul Living in Gibeon and Jerusalem (Post-Exile)."]

29. The "[sons] of Obadiah" in **1 Chronicles 3:21** may refer to remnant Benjamites or Levitical Merarites. If they are Benjamites—which would be consistent with the reading of **Nehemiah 11:4** that "people from both Judah and Benjamin [Saulide descendants?] lived in Jerusalem"—then the "sons of Obadiah" may be the descendants of Obadiah, a descendant of Jonathan, the son of Saul (cf. **1 Chronicles 8:34–38; 9:40–44**), thus fulfilling the covenant promise between David and Jonathan (**1 Samuel 20:42**). It is less likely that "[sons] of Obadiah" refers to (1) the descendants of Obadiah son of Shemaiah, son of Galal, son of Ethan/Jeduthun (Levitical Merarites) who lived near Jerusalem in the post-exile (**1 Chronicles 9:16**) or (2) the sons of Obadiah the prophet of ca. 550 B.C.

30. There are several people named Shekaniah who lived in the post-exile. In ca. 458 B.C., when various heads of families returned to Jerusalem with Ezra, one such head was Hattush, "of the descendants of David, Hattush of the descendants of Shekaniah" (**Ezra 8:2–3**). **First Chronicles 3:22** informs that "the descendants of Shekaniah: Shemaiah and his sons: Hattush, Igal, Bariah, Neariah and Shaphat—[were] six in all," and this is the Shekaniah that is traced in the chart. Other figures named Shekaniah appear to be contemporaries or near-contemporaries of Shekaniah the Judahite who is shown in the chart: (1) Shekaniah the son of Jahaziel (of the descendants of Zattu), an Israelite who returned to Jerusalem with Ezra (**Ezra 8:5**); (2) Shekaniah the son of Jehiel (of the descendants of Elam), who proposed a plan to put away foreign wives (**Ezra 10:2–4**); (3) Shekaniah the Kohathite priest (the father of Shemaiah), who returned with Zerubbabel in 538 B.C. (**Nehemiah 12:3**; cf. **3:29**), called Shebaniah in **Nehemiah 10:4**); (4) Shekaniah son of Arah (**Nehemiah 6:18**); and (5) the priest named "Shekaniah" in **Nehemiah 12:14** who appears as "Shebaniah" (Heb. שְׁבַנְיָה, *Shebanyah*) in most Hebrew manuscripts, the Lucianic Septuagint, and Syriac Peshitta.

31. Joda (NIV) is translated as *Judah* or *Juda* in some translations. It is a *hapax legomenon*, mentioned only here.

32. Josek, the son of Joda (**Luke 3:26**), a post-exilic figure, has been erroneously identified in some translations with Joseph (e.g., Joseph, the son of Judah in **Luke 3:26** in the KJV/NKJV). Also, Josek should not be confused with Josiphiah, the father of one of the returnees with Ezra in 458 B.C. (**Ezra 8:10**).

33. This is the Shemaiah of **1 Chronicles 3:22**. He is not the same person as Shemaiah the Levitical Kohathite of **Nehemiah 3:29,** who was the keeper of the East Gate in the post-exilic Jerusalem, and who also helped Nehemiah rebuild the walls around Jerusalem (ca. 444 B.C.).

34. Semein (or Semei; **Luke 3:26**) is the Greek form of the Hebrew personal name Shimei.

35. Hattush in **1 Chronicles 3:22** is Hattush in **Ezra 8:2**, who is identified as a descendant of David through Shekaniah (**Ezra 8:2–3**) and the head of a family of exiles who returned to Jerusalem with Ezra in ca. 458 B.C. Hattush the Judahite is not (1) Hattush the priest who sealed the covenant with Nehemiah in ca. 444 B.C. (**Nehemiah 10:4**) nor (2) Hattush the son of Hashabneiah, the Levite (**Nehemiah 3:10; 9:5**).

36. Mattathias—who was the son of Semein in **Luke 3:26** and the son of Amos in **Luke 3:25**—is the Greek form of the Hebrew Mattithiah (e.g., **Ezra 10:43**).

37. Elioenai, the Hebrew spelling, is a variant of Eliehoenai. Elioenai son of Neariah (**1 Chronicles 3:23**) should not be confused with (1) Elioenai the grandson of Benjamin (**1 Chronicles 7:8**); (2) Elioenai the priest who agreed to divorce his wife (**Ezra 10:27**); (3) Elioenai the priest who led in the dedication of the wall at Jerusalem (**Nehemiah 12:41**), nor (4) Eliehoenai the son of Zerahiah, who was the head of a family of the descendants of Pahath-Moab and returned with Ezra in ca. 458 B.C. (**Ezra 8:4**).

38. Azrikam (**1 Chronicles 3:23**) is not (1) Azrikam a descendant of Saul (**1 Chronicles 8:38; 9:44**) nor (2) Azrikam the Levite (**1 Chronicles 9:14; Nehemiah 11:15**).

39. Hodaviah is short for Hodaviahu (**1 Chronicles 3:24**); compare him with (1) Hodaviah of the tribe of Manasseh (**1 Chronicles 5:24**); (2) Hodaviah of the tribe of Benjamin (**1 Chronicles 9:7**); and (3) Hodaviah the Levite/tribe of Levi (**Ezra 2:40; 3:9; Nehemiah 7:43**).

40. Eliashib the son of Elioenai (**1 Chronicles 3:24**) is not Eliashib the high priest (the son of Joiakim and the father of Joiada), who led in rebuilding the Sheep Gate (**Nehemiah 3:1; 12:10**) and whose grandson married the daughter of Sanballat the Horonite (**Nehemiah 13:28**).

41. Pelaiah (**1 Chronicles 3:24**) is not the Levite who assisted Ezra in the reading of the Law (**Nehemiah 8:7**) nor Pelaiah who sealed the covenant (**Nehemiah 10:10**).

42. Akkub the son of Elioenai (**1 Chronicles 3:24**) is not Akkub the Levitical gatekeeper in post-exilic Jerusalem (**1 Chronicles 9:17**; **Ezra 2:42; Nehemiah 7:45; 8:7; 11:19; 12:25**).

43. Johanan the son of Elioenai (**1 Chronicles 3:24**) is short for Jehohanan (and perhaps Jonathan). This Johanan is not the Levite Jehohanan (**Ezra 10:6; Nehemiah 6:18**), nor is he the high priest Jonathan, the father of Jaddua (**Nehemiah 12:11, 22**).

44. Delaiah (**1 Chronicles 3:24**) is not Delaiah son of Shemaiah (**Jeremiah 36:12**); also, he is probably not among those descendants of Delaiah who could not prove their Israelite ancestry (**Ezra 2:60; Nehemiah 7:62**).

45. Matthan the son of Eleazar is not Matthat the son of Levi. Both names are derived from the Hebrew verb *nathan*, "to give," as nouns meaning "gift." By a phonetic principle called assimilation, Matthan becomes Matthat. Under certain circumstances, Matthan would be *Matthant* and the *n* would then assimilate into the *t*. The names are hypocoristic for "gift of God." Refer to the chart "**Matthew 1**: Ancestry of Mary and Joseph (Based on Scripture and Church Tradition) and How Mary and Joseph May Have Been Related," which addresses, among other things, the ancestry of Matthan and Matthat.

46. Matthat the son of Levi is not Matthan the son of Eleazar (see note 45).

47. According to the chiastic literary structure of this chart, Jacob was most likely the uterine *brother* of Heli. Jacob and Heli shared the same mother (who is named Estha in the non-canonical literature). The kinship link is analogous to Solomon and Nathan, the uterine *brothers* who shared the same mother (Bathsheba). For more information about the heritage of Jacob and Heli, see chart "**Matthew 1**: Ancestry of Mary and Joseph (Based on Scripture and Church Tradition) and How Mary and Joseph May Have Been Related."

48. Heli is the Greek form of the Hebrew personal name Eli.

49. Joseph, the earthly father of Jesus, is called "Joseph son of David" and "Joseph, a descendant of David" (**Matthew 1:20; Luke 1:27**). Also, **Luke 2:4** states that "he [Joseph] belonged to the house and line of David." The genealogy of Jesus through the descendants of David's son Solomon represents the kingly line of father–son succession of Joseph's ancestors up to the time of the exile. During and after the exile, both biological and legal succession of heirs (through levirate marriage and/or legal adoptions and/or lineages traced through a son/heir or a son-in-law) come into play. Thus, the genealogy of Jesus the Messiah, as presented in **Matthew 1:1–16**, presents both the biological and legal ancestry of Joseph, the earthly father of Jesus.

50. The genealogy of Jesus through the descendants of David's son Nathan represents the biological (non-kingly) line of father–son succession of Joseph's ancestors up to the time of the exile. During and after the exile, both biological and legal succession of heirs (through levirate marriage and/or legal adoptions and/or lineages traced through a son/heir or a son-in-law) becomes apparent. Thus, the genealogy of Jesus the Messiah presented in **Luke 3:23–38** traces both the biological and legal lineage of Joseph, the earthly father of Jesus.

51. Matthew's and Luke's genealogies of Jesus trace the *patrilineal descent* of Jesus through his earthly father, Joseph, not through his mother, Mary (which would be *matrilineal descent*, a rare occurrence in Scripture). Mary's ancestry is more veiled in Scripture, but several references help clarify her lineage. Mary was the *relative* (or *kinswoman*) of Elizabeth (**Luke 1:36**). Since both Zechariah and Elizabeth were descendants of Aaron the high priest and therefore Levitical Kohathites (**Luke 1:5**), it can be deduced that at least one of Mary's parents was from the priestly line of the tribe of Levi—likely this was Mary's mother who, according to church tradition, is named Anne. The other parent—likely Mary's father, who according to church tradition is named Joachim—was from the tribe of Judah (cf. **Luke 1:32**; **Hebrews 7:14**). Given that Mary's paternal heritage was Judahite, this is the reason why she goes *with Joseph* to be registered in Bethlehem (**Luke 2:5**), since in a Roman census—a governmental mandate (not a Jewish religious or ritual matter)—women, as well as men, were counted.

This type of "mixed tribal marriage" of Mary's parents has precedence in the notable marriage of Aaron the high priest (a Levitical Kohathite) to Elisheba the daughter of Amminadab (a Judahite; **Exodus 6:23**; i.e., Elisheba the Judahite was the "mother" of the revered high priesthood of Israel). If church tradition is correct, an analogous but converse situation is true for Mary's parents: Joachim (Mary's father and a Davidic descendant from the tribe of Judah) married Anne (Mary's mother from the Kohathite priestly clan of the tribe of Levi). In this manner, Jesus derives his *biological* and *legal* patrilineal ancestry from his earthly father (Joseph); but from a human perspective, Jesus also derives a priestly heritage from his maternal side (i.e., through his mother Mary and grandmother Anne). See more information in chart "**Matthew 1**: Ancestry of Mary and Joseph (Based on Scripture and Church Tradition) and How Mary and Joseph May Have Been Related." For the line of the high priests of Israel, see chart "**Supplement 2**: The High Priests of Israel."

52. See charts "**2 Samuel 5**: Bathsheba" and "**1 Chronicles 2**: King David."

53. The precedence for a near relative acting as a kinsman redeemer is found in **Ruth 2:1** and **Ruth 3:9–13,** where Boaz (in the Judah–Perez–Hezron–Ram line) married Ruth, the wife of a *distant relative*, Mahlon, (in the Judah–Perez–Hezron–Caleb/Karmi–Elimelek line). In essence, Boaz and Mahlon were descendants of two brothers (Ram and Caleb), similar to Jeconiah/Jehoiachin and Neri, who were also the descendants of two brothers (Solomon and Nathan, respectively). See chart "**Ruth 4**: Boaz, Elimelek, and Naomi and the Descendants of Boaz the Judahite and Ruth the Moabitess." A later instance of levirate marriage in the Second Temple period seems to occur in ca. 100 B.C. with the marriage of Alexander Jannaeus the high priest (103–76 B.C.) to his brother's widow (Salome Alexandra); see chart "**Supplement 2**: The High Priests of Israel." For levirate marriage, see **Luke 20:28** (cf. **Deuteronomy 25:5–6**).

54. The name Estha is provided by the Christian chronographer–historian Sextus Julius Africanus (ca. A.D. 160–240), who wrote the "Epistle to Aristides" to address the apparent discrepancy between Matthew's and Luke's accounts of Christ's genealogy. Africanus comments that the names in the genealogical lists of the Israelites were "reckoned . . . according to nature or according to law" in which "nature" refers to legitimate biological offspring, whereas "law" refers to the practice of levirate marriage. According to Africanus, neither Matthew nor Luke's Gospels were in error, because "one reckons by nature, the other by law." Africanus uses the *seemingly conflicting* identities of Joseph's father in the Gospel accounts as an example: Matthew identifies Joseph's father as Jacob (**Matthew 1:16**), while Luke identifies Heli (Eli) as Joseph's father (**Luke 3:23**). Africanus proposes that Jacob and Heli/Eli were brothers and that they were both listed as Joseph's fathers because *their* fathers—Matthan and Melchi (Melki), respectively—"Married in succession the same women [and] begot children who were uterine [biological] brothers, for the law did not prohibit a widow, whether such by divorce or by the death of her husband, from marrying another. Here the reader should be aware that Africanus appears to skip two known generations that are clearly listed in Luke's account of Jesus' genealogy: "Heli [Eli] [was] the son of Matthat, the son of Levi, the son of Melki" (Luke 3:23–24); nevertheless, Africanus' assessment—invoking the principle of levirate marriage and the ensuing crossover between the Solomonic and Nathan lines—is still applicable. By Estha then (for this was the woman's name according to tradition) Matthan, a descendant of Solomon, first begot Jacob. And when Matthan was dead, Melchi [Melki] Here Africanus should have used the name Matthat, not Melchi/Melki, who traced his descent back to Nathan . . . married her [Estha] as before said and begot a son Eli [Heli]." Further, when Eli (Heli) died childless, Jacob married his brother's wife and had Joseph. According to nature, then, Joseph was Jacob's son, but according to law, Joseph was the son of Eli (Heli), "for Jacob, being the brother of the latter [Eli/Heli], raised up seed to him." Africanus concludes: "This interpretation

is neither incapable of proof nor is it an idle conjecture." This scenario is highly probable, given the practice of levirate marriage and the multiple instances of levirate marriage in the line of the Messiah (see Excursus A), but it cannot be indubitably proven due to the lack of complete information. See Eusebius of Caesarea, *Ecclesiastical History* (Book 1, Chapter 7), "The Alleged Discrepancy in the Gospels in regard to the Genealogy of Christ," and Eusebius' quotation of Sextus Julius Africanus' lengthy discussion of this topic; http://www.newadvent.org/fathers/250101.htm.

55. Scripture does not record when Joseph lived and died, but he may have been older when he and Mary were married. Joseph appears to have died sometime during Jesus' ministry but before Jesus' crucifixion (cf. **Matthew 13:55; Luke 2:42–43; John 6:42; 19:25–27**).

56. The consensus view in modern scholarship has been that Jesus was born in approximately 5 B.C., *before* Herod's death in 4 B.C. More recently, however, Andrew Steinmann has re-evaluated the reign of King Herod and offers substantive evidence that Herod died in the first quarter of 1 B.C. (not 4 B.C.) and that "Jesus' birth [was] no earlier than late summer of 3 B.C. and no later than the first months of 2 B.C." (Andrew E. Steinmann, *From Abraham to Paul: A Biblical Chronology* (St. Louis: Concordia, 2011), 252). For the larger context of the arguments, see ibid., ch. 11.

57. An ancient view that defended the perpetual virginity of Mary—propagated by Origen, Eusebius, Gregory of Nyssa, Ambrose, and Epiphanius—held that Joseph was married twice: First, he was supposedly married to an unnamed woman or a levirate wife and had children by her (i.e., which produced Jesus' siblings: James, Joseph, Simon, etc.) Second, after his first wife died, Joseph married the Virgin Mary (who bore Jesus, her *firstborn* and only son). However, such a scenario (i.e., Joseph having two wives) does *not* conform to the genealogical and historical pattern that is well-documented in Excursus A in which "*two* men married the *same* woman." Moreover, the natural inference from the scriptural text (such as **Matthew 1:20, 25**) is that, *after* Jesus was born, Mary and Joseph took up normal marital sexual relations and had sons and daughters of their own; for details, see chart "**Matthew 1**: Jesus and His Immediate Family."

58. This is a Greek rendition of the Hebrew נְחֹשֶׁת, *nekhosheth*, "a bronze or copper thing." As used in **Numbers 21:8–9**, it is a play on words for נָחָשׁ, *nakhash*, "snake." As the bronze snake was raised up in the desert as a healing symbol, so Jesus was lifted up as the Healer *par excellence*.

1 CHRONICLES 4: JUDAH[1] (ALL CLANS, INCLUDING LINEAGES OF KINGS, BETHLEHEMITES, JUDGES, FOUNDERS OF CITIES, PRIESTS, WISE MEN, AND SCRIBES)

Approximate Dating: from Judah's birth, ca. 1925 B.C. to as late as 400 B.C.[2] ***Relevant Scriptures:*** **1 Chronicles 4:1–23;** also **Genesis 38:1–12, 18, 27–30; 46:12; Exodus 31:2; 35:30; 38:22; Numbers 26:19–21; Joshua 7:1, 17–18; 15:13–60; Judges 1:12–13; 3:9; Ruth 4:18–22; 1 Samuel 16:6, 8–9; 17:12–14, 28; 2 Samuel 13:3, 32; 17:25; 1 Kings 2:5; 4:31; 1 Chronicles 2:3–55; 27:18; 2 Chronicles 11:6, 18; Psalm 89:0; Jeremiah 36:12, 20–21; 41:1; Matthew 1:1–6; Luke 3:31–33**

**Double lines in the chart indicate the line of the MESSIAH*

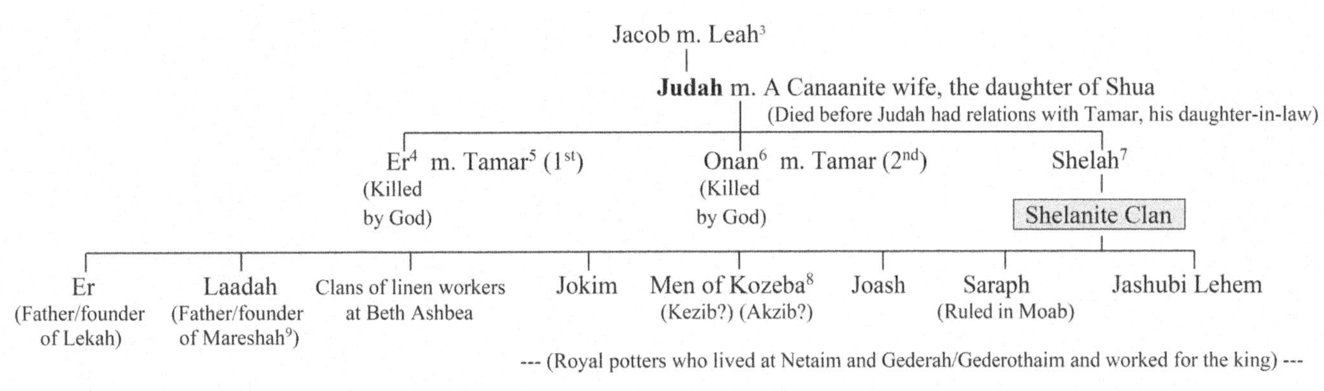

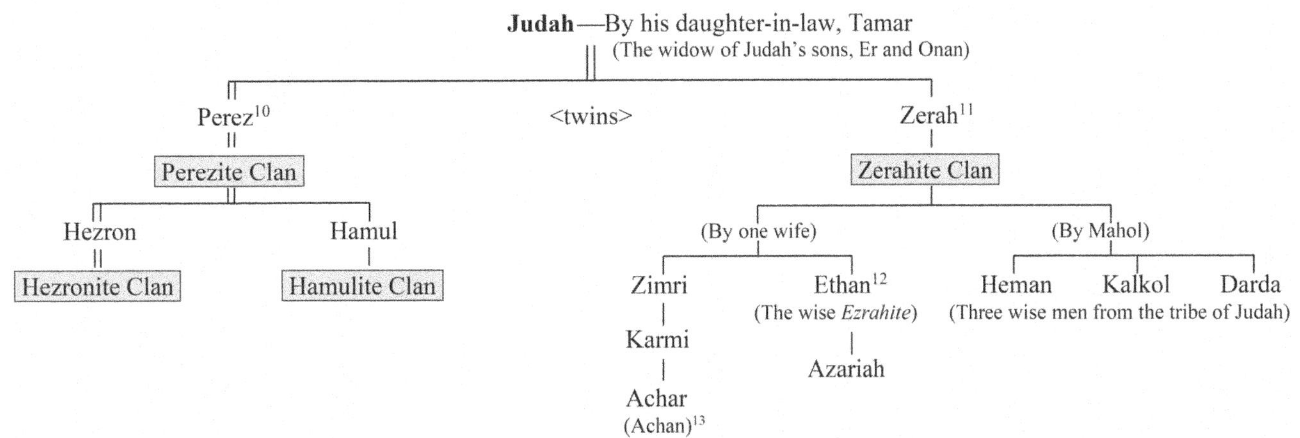

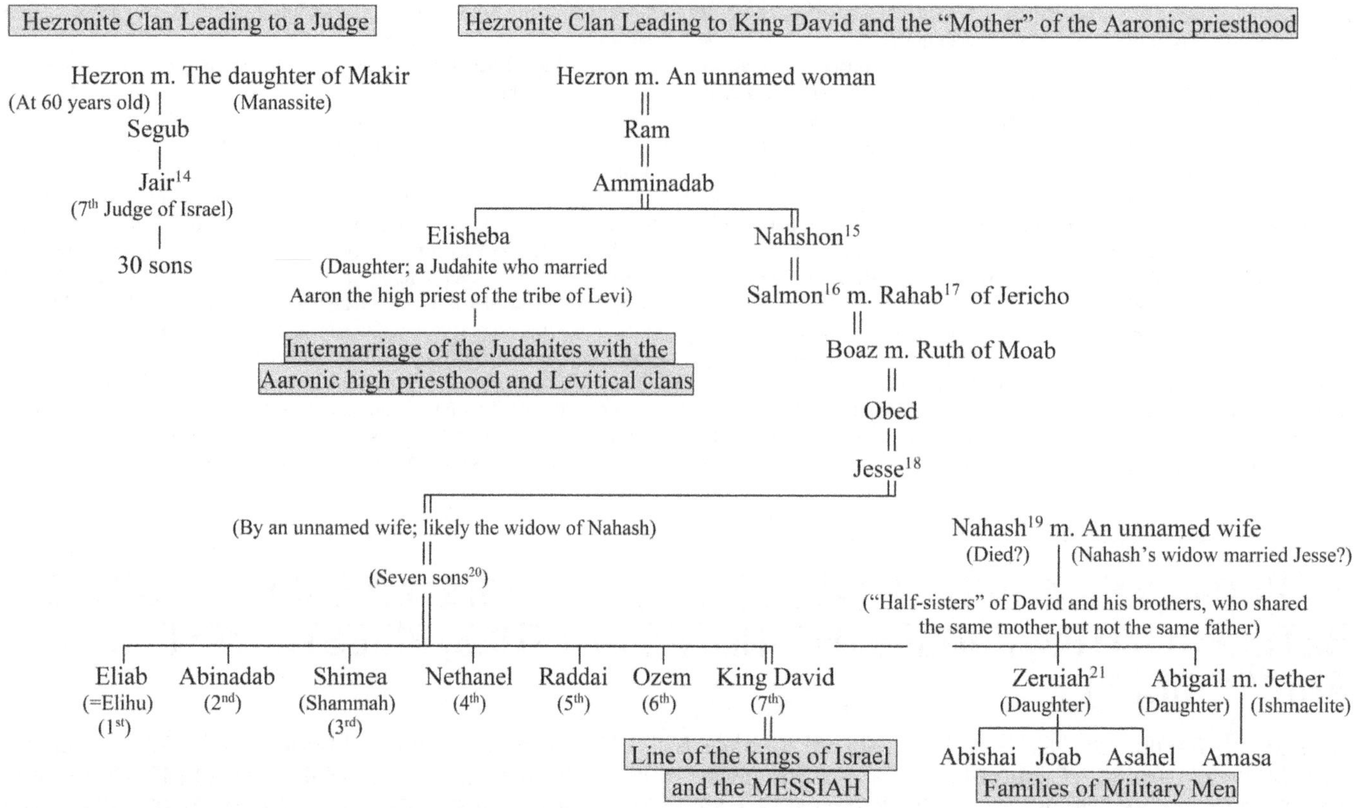

Hezronite Clan Leading to a Judge

Hezron m. The daughter of Makir
(At 60 years old) | (Manassite)
Segub
|
Jair[14]
(7th Judge of Israel)
|
30 sons

Hezronite Clan Leading to King David and the "Mother" of the Aaronic priesthood

Hezron m. An unnamed woman
||
Ram
||
Amminadab

Elisheba
(Daughter; a Judahite who married Aaron the high priest of the tribe of Levi)
|
Intermarriage of the Judahites with the Aaronic high priesthood and Levitical clans

Nahshon[15]
||
Salmon[16] m. Rahab[17] of Jericho
||
Boaz m. Ruth of Moab
||
Obed
||
Jesse[18]

(By an unnamed wife; likely the widow of Nahash)
||
(Seven sons[20])

Eliab (=Elihu) (1st) | Abinadab (2nd) | Shimea (Shammah) (3rd) | Nethanel (4th) | Raddai (5th) | Ozem (6th) | King David (7th)

King David
||
Line of the kings of Israel and the MESSIAH

Nahash[19] m. An unnamed wife
(Died?) | (Nahash's widow married Jesse?)
("Half-sisters" of David and his brothers, who shared the same mother, but not the same father)

Zeruiah[21] (Daughter) — Abishai, Joab, Asahel
Abigail (Daughter) m. Jether (Ishmaelite) — Amasa

Families of Military Men

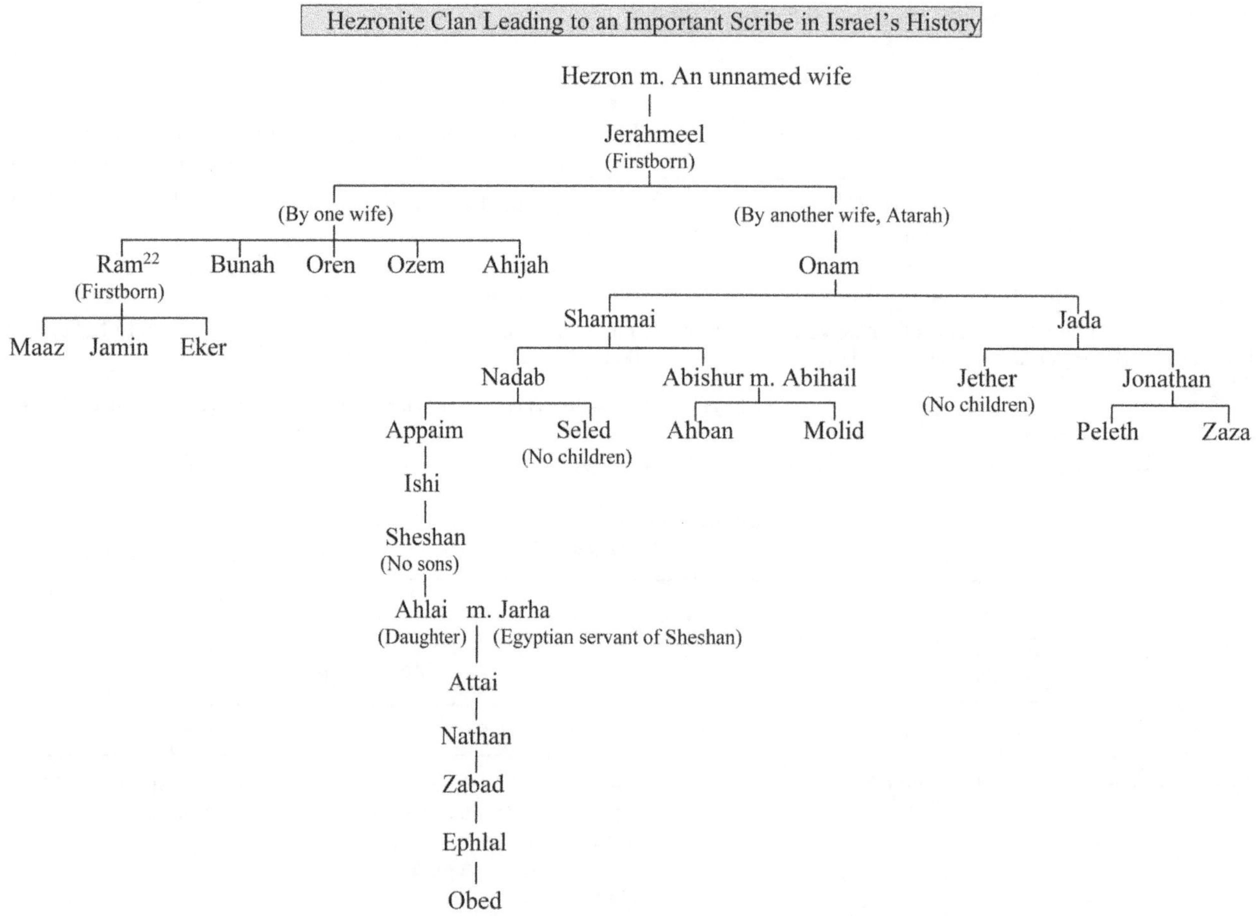

Hezronite Clan Leading to an Important Scribe in Israel's History

Hezron m. An unnamed wife
|
Jerahmeel
(Firstborn)

(By one wife)
Ram[22] (Firstborn) | Bunah | Oren | Ozem | Ahijah

Ram — Maaz | Jamin | Eker

(By another wife, Atarah)
|
Onam

Shammai | Jada

Shammai — Nadab | Abishur m. Abihail

Nadab — Appaim | Seled (No children)

Abishur m. Abihail — Ahban | Molid

Jada — Jether (No children) | Jonathan

Jonathan — Peleth | Zaza

Appaim
|
Ishi
|
Sheshan
(No sons)
|
Ahlai m. Jarha
(Daughter) | (Egyptian servant of Sheshan)
Attai
|
Nathan
|
Zabad
|
Ephlal
|
Obed

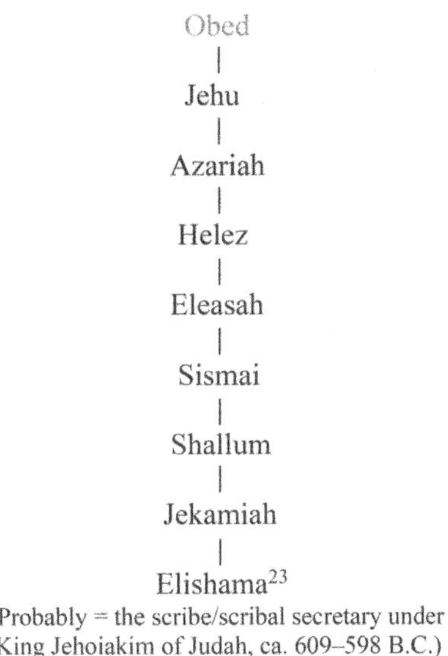

Obed
Jehu
Azariah
Helez
Eleasah
Sismai
Shallum
Jekamiah
Elishama23
(Probably = the scribe/scribal secretary under King Jehoiakim of Judah, ca. 609–598 B.C.)

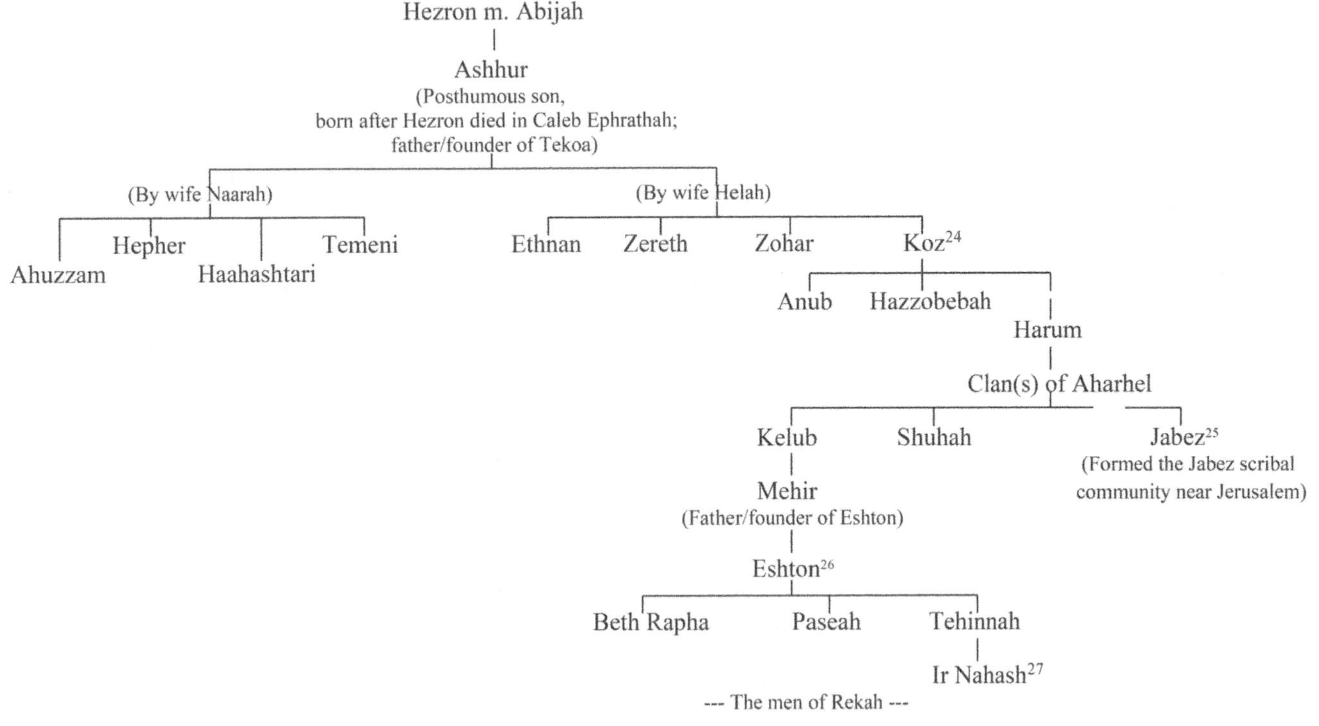

Hezronite Clan Members Who Established the Scribal Community at Jabez
Hezron m. Abijah
Ashhur
(Posthumous son, born after Hezron died in Caleb Ephrathah; father/founder of Tekoa)
(By wife Naarah)
Ahuzzam
Hepher
Haahashtari
Temeni
(By wife Helah)
Ethnan
Zereth
Zohar
Koz24
Anub
Hazzobebah
Harum
Clan(s) of Aharhel
Kelub
Shuhah
Jabez25
(Formed the Jabez scribal community near Jerusalem)
Mehir
(Father/founder of Eshton)
Eshton26
Beth Rapha
Paseah
Tehinnah
Ir Nahash27
--- The men of Rekah ---

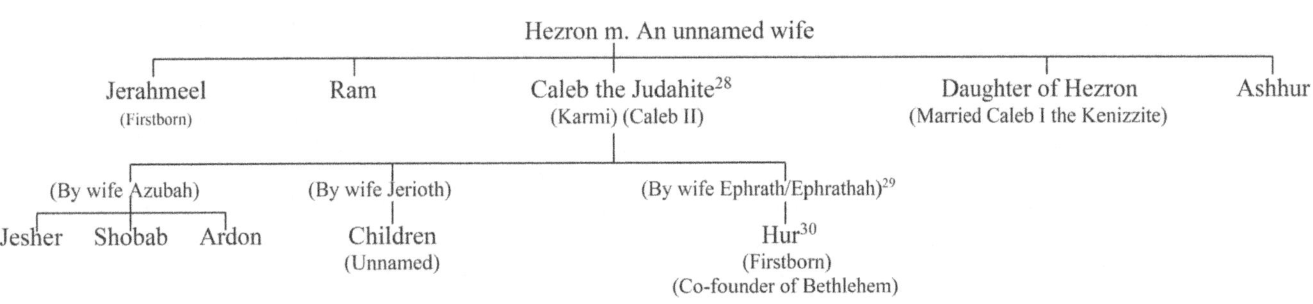

Hezronite Clan Leading to the Bethlehemites
Hezron m. An unnamed wife
Jerahmeel
(Firstborn)
Ram
Caleb the Judahite28
(Karmi) (Caleb II)
Daughter of Hezron
(Married Caleb I the Kenizzite)
Ashhur
(By wife Azubah)
Jesher
Shobab
Ardon
(By wife Jerioth)
Children
(Unnamed)
(By wife Ephrath/Ephrathah)29
Hur30
(Firstborn)
(Co-founder of Bethlehem)

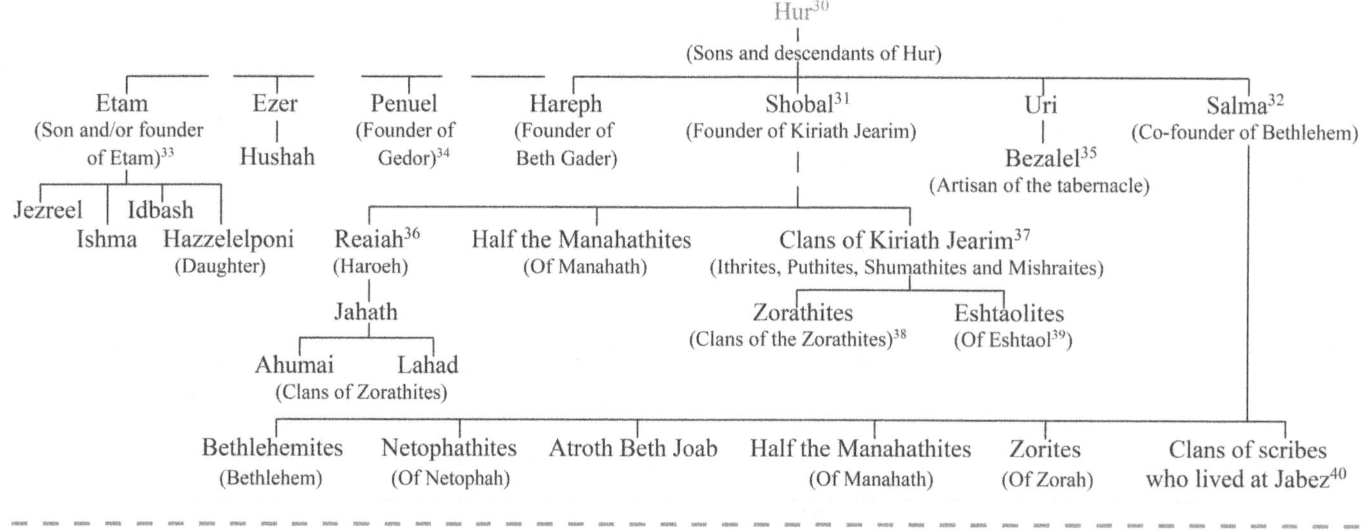

Intermarriage of the Hezronite Clan with the Kenizzites

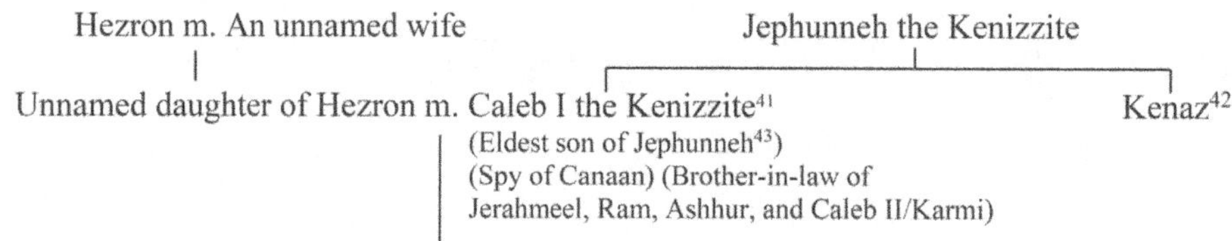

(For this lineage, see the chart "**1 Chronicles 2** - Genealogy of Caleb and Kenaz, the Sons of Jephunneh the Kenizzite")

Biblical and Theological Significance

The brief summary of Judah in the earliest of the genealogies, **Numbers 26:19–22**, belies the ultimate glorious and triumphant meaning and outcome of his progeny, one ending with God himself incarnate. Nothing in Judah's personal life would seem to indicate this ultimate outcome. He counseled his brothers to deliver their younger sibling Joseph to the Midianites to be sold into slavery (**Genesis 37:26–27**); he married a Canaanite (**Genesis 38:1–2**); and he had sex with his own daughter-in-law (believing she was a prostitute), leaving her pregnant (**Genesis 38:18–26**). In spite of all this, God, who sees the heart and who graciously forgives sin, made through Judah's father, Jacob, the magnificent promise that "The scepter will not depart from Judah, nor the ruler's staff from between his feet, until he to whom it belongs shall come and the obedience of the nations shall be his" (**Genesis 49:10**). David knew himself to be that ruler (**1 Samuel 16:1, 12; 1 Kings 8:16**) but only imperfectly, for he too looked for such a descendant (**Psalm 18:50; 89:3–4, 35–37; 110:1**). The New Testament corroborates the Old Testament importance of Judah and his dynasty. Eleven times the name appears, almost as many as all the other tribes combined. Even more striking is the epithet of Jesus as "the Son of David," linking David the messianic prototype with the Anti-type himself.[44]

The elaborate genealogy of the tribe of Judah presented in **1 Chronicles 4**—the largest segmented genealogy in Scripture—emphasizes the royal descent of the Messiah from David's descendants (shown in double parallel lines in the chart). Branch segments trace the lineages of all clans and kinship groups and identify the founders of cities and eponymous ancestors, particularly those from Bethlehem and surrounding areas in the tribe of Judah. The genealogy functions as the basis for the social organization/reorganization of the returning exiles that was necessary for the redistribution of their ancestral property; the expansive depth and breadth of the genealogy hint at social stability and reunification in the post-exile. Of much greater significance is the inescapable theological truth that Jesus of Nazareth, though proclaimed to be the Son of God (**Matthew 14:33; 16:16; Luke 8:28; Romans 1:4; 2 Corinthians 1:19; Ephesians 4:13**; *et passim*), was also fully the Son of Man (**Matthew 8:20; 10:23; Mark 2:28; John 6:62; Acts 7:56**). Only as such could he make atonement for humanity, a perfect God/Man dying for sinners.

Intermarriage accounts for close associations between the tribe of Judah and the Levitical priesthood (e.g., Elisheba the Judahite to Aaron the first high priest of the tribe of Levi), as does marriage to foreigners (e.g., Salmon the Judahite to Rahab the Canaanite of Jericho and Boaz the Judahite to Ruth the Moabite). Strikingly evident is the strong association between the line of Caleb (I) the Kenizzite and the line of Judah—resulting from intermarriage and as co-founders of cities within the tribe of Judah. For example, Caleb (I) the Kenizzite (non-Israelite) and his descendants were given Hebron, also known as "Kiriath Arba" (**Joshua 14:13–15; 15:13; Judges 1:20; 1 Chronicles 2:42**), a city associated with the patriarchs (cf. **Genesis 23:2, 19; 35:27; 49:31; 50:12-13**). Such arrangements in the past pointed to the time in the future when Israel and the nations will be united as one people of God (**Isaiah 66:19–21; Romans 9:25–26**). Also noteworthy in the tribe of Judah are the lineages of four wise men (Zerahite descendants); two of Israel's judges

(Othniel the Kenizzite and Jair the Judahite); the enigmatic scribe named Jabez who established a Judahite–Kenite scribal community near Jerusalem; and gifted artisans and craftsmen (of the Shelanite clan and Bezalel of the Hezron–Hur clan). Moreover, the elaborate linear structure of the Jerahmeel lineage (**1 Chronicles 2:25–41**), terminating with the scribal figure Elishama (a contemporary of King Jehoiakim of Judah, 609–598 B.C.), shows that he held an important office. Given that Elishama, a Judahite–Jerahmeelite descendant, had access to the exhaustive collection of administrative and national documents in the court of Jehoiakim (Eliakim), Elishama is a reasonable candidate to be one of the compilers of the historical and genealogical content in **Chronicles.**[45]

The cities of Judah (**Joshua 15:1–63; 19:1–9**)—including those originally allotted to the tribe of Simeon or given to Caleb I the Kenizzite, who married into the tribe of Judah—that were re-occupied in the post-exilic era included these towns (listed alphabetically): Adullam (**Nehemiah 11:30**); Ai/Aija (**Ezra 2:28; Nehemiah 7:32; 11:31**); Azekah (**Nehemiah 11:30**); Beersheba of Simeon (**Nehemiah 11:27, 30**); Bethlehem (**Ezra 2:21; Nehemiah 7:26**); Beth Pelet (**Nehemiah 11:26**); Beth Zur (**Nehemiah 3:16**); (presumably) Dibon of Judah (**Nehemiah 11:25**); Elam (**Ezra 2:7** or **31; Nehemiah 7:12** or **34**); Ge Harashim (**Nehemiah 11:35**); Gilgal/Beth Gilgal (**Nehemiah 12:29**); Harim of Judah (**Ezra 2:32; Nehemiah 7:35**); Hazar Shual of Simeon (**Nehemiah 11:27**); Hazor in the Negev (Kerioth Hezron? in **Joshua 15:25**) (**Nehemiah 11:33**); Jarmuth (**Nehemiah 11:29**); Jekabzeel/Kabzeel (**Nehemiah 11:25**); Jeshua (**Nehemiah 11:26**); Keilah (**Nehemiah 3:17–18**); Kiriath Arba/Hebron of Caleb I the Kenizzite (**Nehemiah 11:25**); Kiriath Jearim/Baalah/Kiriath Baal (**Ezra 2:25; Nehemiah 7:29**; cf. **Joshua 15:60**); Lachish (**Nehemiah 11:30**); Mekonah (**Nehemiah 11:28**); Moladah (**Nehemiah 11:26**), Nebo (**Ezra 2:29; Nehemiah 7:33**); Netophah (**Ezra 2:22; Nehemiah 7:26**); Rimmon/En Rimmon of Simeon (**Nehemiah 11:29**); Tekoa (**Nehemiah 3:5, 27**); Zanoah (**Nehemiah 11:30**); Ziklag of Simeon (**Nehemiah 11:28**); and Zorah (**Nehemiah 11:29**).

Notes

1. Throughout the genealogies, the term *son* occurs regularly, sometimes meaning biological sons, but often meaning anything from first generation to extended families, clans, or even tribes. For example, Judah's descendants (sons) in **1 Chronicles 4:1** were clans that ultimately sprang from him. See G. Johannes Botterweck and Helmer Ringgren, eds. *Theological Dictionary of the Old Testament*, vol. II (Grand Rapids: Eerdmans, 1975), 149–153.

2. For the approximate birth dates of each of the sons of Jacob (including Judah), see note 4 in chart "**Genesis 35**: The Twelve Sons of Jacob, the Eponymous Originators of the Twelve Tribes of Israel."

3. Jacob's "hated" wife Leah initially found some compensation in her rival Rachel's barrenness by being able to bear sons, whereas Rachel could not (**Genesis 29:21–35**). After giving birth to three sons, Leah was overjoyed at having a fourth and thus named him יְהוּדָה (Yehudah, or by syncopation Yudah), by popular etymology "Praise Yahweh" (**Genesis 29:35**). Little could the family know that this child would be the ancestor of the Messiah.

4. Er was Tamar's first husband, but he was wicked, and the Lord put him to death (**Genesis 38:6–7**). Er died in the land of Canaan before Jacob's family moved to Egypt in 1876 B.C. (**Genesis 29:46:12; Numbers 26:19**); see chart "**Genesis 46**: The Extended Family of Jacob (Seventy Descendants) who Migrated to Egypt."

5. Tamar's ancestry is not given in the Old Testament. Tradition in the Jewish literature asserts that she was a gentile proselyte. Philo (Virt. 220–22) presents Tamar as from Palestinian Syria and a convert to Judaism. See Patrick Schreiner, *Matthew, Disciple and Scribe: The First Gospel and Its Portrait of Jesus* (Grand Rapids: Baker Academic, 2019), 178; also see Richard Bauckham, "Tamar's Ancestry and Rahab's Marriage: Two Problems in the Matthean Genealogy," *NovT* 37 (1995): 319–320.

6. Onan married Tamar (his brother's widow) by levirate marriage. However, "Onan knew that the child would not be his; so whenever he slept with his brother's wife, he spilled his semen on the ground to keep from providing offspring for his brother" (**Genesis 38:9**). The Lord put Onan to death for violating the duty of the *levir*, the levirate husband (**Genesis 38:8–10**). Onan died in the land of Canaan before Jacob's family moved to Egypt in 1876 B.C. (**Genesis46:12; Numbers 26:19**); see chart "**Genesis 46**: The Extended Family of Jacob (Seventy Descendants) who Migrated to Egypt."

7. Shelah was the eponymous ancestor of the Shelanite clan (**Numbers 26:20**). The Shelanites were noted craftsmen, both weavers of fine linen at Beth Ashbea and a guild of royal potters at Netaim and Gederah who worked permanently for the king (**1 Chronicles 4:21–23**). For a descendant of Shelah who lived in the post-exile, see the lineage of Maaseiah in **Nehemiah 11:5**.

8. Kozeba may be the same place as Kezib, the birthplace of Shelah (**Genesis 38:5**), a variation of Akzib, a town in the western foothills of Judah (**Joshua 15:44**).

9. Mareshah, originally associated with the Shelahite clan, was a town in the western foothills of Judah (**Joshua 15:44**). Mareshah also had connections to the Kenizzites (who were relatives by marriage to the Judahites)—Mareshah was the father/founder of Hebron, a descendant of Caleb I the Kenizzite and the daughter of Hezron (cf. **1 Chronicles 2:42**); see chart "**1 Chronicles 2**: Caleb and Kenaz, the Sons of Jephunneh the Kenizzite." The city of Mareshah was one of fifteen towns fortified by King Rehoboam (**2 Chronicles 11:5–10**).

10. For a descendant of Perez who lived in the post-exile, see Athaiah in **Nehemiah 11:4**.

11. Four of the five sons of Zerah were considered famous wise men in Judah—Ethan, Heman, Kalkol, and Darda—who were only surpassed in wisdom by King Solomon (**1 Kings 4:31**; cf. **1 Chronicles 2:6**). A descendant of Zerah named Pethahiah, who lived in post-exilic Jerusalem, was the kings' agent in all affairs relating to the people of Judah (**Nehemiah 11:24**).

12. He is called *Ethan the Ezrahite* in **1 Kings 4:31** and may be the same person as "Ethan the Ezrahite" who composed **Psalm 89:0**. For chronological reasons, he is not the same person as Ethan (Jeduthun), a chief musician in Solomon's Temple whose lineage is shown in chart "**1 Chronicles 6**: Levi: High Priests, Priests, Levites, and Musicians in Solomon's Temple."

13. Achar in **1 Chronicles 2:7** is called Achan in **Joshua 7:1, 18–26**. Achar/Achan "brought trouble on Israel by violating the ban on taking devoted things" (i.e., the banned spoils of war that belonged to God alone; **1 Chronicles 2:7**). The Lord's wrath resulted in the defeat of the Israelites at Ai. Achar/Achan and his sons and daughters were stoned to death in the "Valley of Achor"—meaning the *valley of trouble* (**Joshua 7:24–26**). The Hebrew names look somewhat the same in this play-on-words and would have even more so in the archaic script—עָכָן<עָכֹר.

14. Jair "controlled twenty-three towns in Gilead. (But Geshur and Aram captured Havvoth Jair, as well as Kenath with its surrounding settlements—sixty towns)" (**1 Chronicles 2:22–23**); the towns were considered the inheritance of Makir the Manassite, the father of Gilead. For the lineage of Jair, see chart "**Judges 6**: Gideon (Fifth Judge) and His Son, Abimelek the False Judge, Jair (Seventh Judge), and Jephthah (Eighth Judge)–Judges of Israel from the Tribe of Manasseh."

15. Nahshon was the leader of the people of Judah during the early period of the wilderness wanderings (**1 Chronicles 2:10**; **Numbers 1:7; 2:3; 7:12; 10:14;** see also **Ruth 4:20**).

16. Salmon the son of Nahshon in **Ruth 4:20–21; 1 Chronicles 2:11; Matthew 1:4–5;** and **Luke 3:32** should not be confused with Salma the son of Hur in **1 Chronicles 2:51, 54**.

17. Rahab, the Canaanite prostitute of Jericho, hid two of the Israelite spies and kept them from harm; for her faithfulness, she and her household were spared during the destruction of Jericho (**Joshua 2:1–21; 6:22–25**). Remarkably, she is an ancestress of the Messiah (**Matthew 1:5**), an exemplar of faith (**Hebrews 11:31**), and one "justified by [her] works" (**James 2:25**).

18. Since the mothers of most kings of Israel and Judah are identified, it is highly unusual and noteworthy that David's mother's name is unknown or withheld; for possible explanations, see charts "**1 Chronicles 2**: King David" and

"**1 Chronicles 3**: Zerubbabel and Shealtiel and the Double Line of the Messiah through King David's Sons, Nathan and Solomon," especially Excursus A.

19. Nahash is a Hebrew masculine name meaning "snake." His exact identity is unknown. Nahash (rather than Jesse) appears to be the father of Abigail and Zeruiah, thus making these women the half-sisters of David and his brothers (cf. **2 Samuel 17:25**). It is unclear whether Nahash is related to the place name Ir Nahash, associated with the men of Rekah (**1 Chronicles 4:12**), Nahash the Ammonite king (**1 Samuel 11:1–2; 12:12; 2 Samuel 17:27; 1 Chronicles 19:1–2**), or neither. For more information on Nahash, see chart "**1 Chronicles 2**: King David" and Excursus A in chart "**1 Chronicles 3**: Zerubbabel and Shealtiel and the Double Line of the Messiah through King David's Sons, Nathan and Solomon."

20. Jesse had "eight sons" (**1 Samuel 17:12**), but only seven sons are noted in **1 Chronicles 2:13–15**. Very possibly the source text was in poetic form and read: "He had seven sons, even eight," stressing that David was the climax (**Micah 5:5**; cf. **Job 5:19**). "Normally, such number patterns are not to be taken literally but are a poetic way of saying 'many'"; commentary on Job 5:19 in *NIV Study Bible*, 833. Elihu, called "a brother of David" in **1 Chronicles 27:18**, is probably the same person as Eliab Jesse's "firstborn," who is identified as "David's oldest brother" (cf. **1 Samuel 16:6; 17:13, 28; 1 Chronicles 2:13; 2 Chronicles 11:18**).

21. The text of **2 Samuel 2:32** shows that Zeruiah (the mother of Asahel) married an unnamed man from Bethlehem of Judah.

22. Ram the son of Jerahmeel (**1 Chronicles 2:25, 27**) should not be confused with Ram the son of Hezron (**1 Chronicles 2:9–10, Matthew 1:3–4; Luke 3:33**).

23. The terminal figure in the Judah–Perez–Hezron–Jerahmeel line is Elishama (**1 Chronicles 2:41**), who represents the *live-edge* figure of the tribe of Judah—in fact, Elishama is likely the compiler of the genealogy! He appears to be the same person as Elishama the scribe in the court of King Jehoiakim of Judah (**Jeremiah 36:12, 20**), who is said to be "of royal blood" (**2 Kings 25:25; Jeremiah 41:1**). The first scroll of Jeremiah was stored in the scribal chamber of Elishama, although the scroll was burned by Jehoiakim and had to be rewritten (**Jeremiah 36:20–23, 26–28**). This Elishama may be the same person as Elishama who had a son named Nethaniah and a grandson named Ishmael (**Jeremiah 41:1**), in which Ishmael was known for killing Gedaliah, the governor over the inhabitants who remained in Judah during the exile period (**Jeremiah 40:1–41:10**). Given the elaborate structural composition of this genealogy, Elishama is a likely candidate to be one of the *Chroniclers*; see chart "**1 Chronicles 2**: Jerahmeel, and His Descendant, Elishama, Who Appears to Be a Compiler of Historical and Genealogical Records in 1 & 2 Chronicles."

24. Koz may be a relative of the priestly figure Barzillai (from the tribe of Levi) who married a daughter of Barzillai the Gileadite [but, quite uncharacteristically, retained the prestigious name of his father-in-law, Barzillai the Gileadite! (**Ezra 2:61**; cf. **2 Samuel 17:21–29; 19:31–40; 1 Kings 2:7; 1 Chronicles 24:10** (Hakkoz); **Ezra 2:61** (Hakkoz and *Barzillai*); **Nehemiah 7:63** (Hakkoz and *Barzillai*)]. Koz (קוֹץ), a nickname, means "thorn-bush." Hakkoz/Haqqoz (הַקּוֹץ) is the articular form, "the thorn-bush." Koz always refers to the individual and Hakkoz/Haqqoz to the order, "the Kozzite(s)."

25. Jabez is both a personal name and a place name. Jabez was from the clan of Aharhel and a descendant of Hezron, the grandson of Judah. Having been rejected by his fellow Aharhel brethren, Jabez pleaded with God for a blessing of a greater territory and deliverance from harm, and "God granted his request" (**1 Chronicles 4:10**). Jabez, along with his relatives (Beth Rapha, Paseah, and Tehinna; **1 Chronicles 4:11–12**) and the austere Rekabites of Kenite ancestry—see chart "**Jeremiah 35**: The Rekabites (Kenite Descendants)"—established a prominent scribal community at Jabez near Jerusalem (**1 Chronicles 2:55**). As for the location of Jabez, Rainey and Notley indicate that Jabez (the place name) was among the towns associated with the sons/descendants of Hur (notes 30 and 32, below) located "in the vicinity of Bethlehem and the northeastern Shephelah around the Valley of Elah." Anson F. Rainey and R. Steven Notley, *The Sacred Bridge: Carta's Atlas of the Biblical World*, 2nd ed. (Jerusalem: Carta, 2014), 154.

26. Eshton's descendants, called "the men of Rekah," formed a mixed Judahite–Kenite scribal community near Bethlehem, along with Jabez (a distant relative) and the families of the Rebakite scribes—"Tirathites, the Shimeathites, and Suchathites . . . [who were] Kenites" (cf. **1 Chronicles 2:55; 4:11–12**); see note 25. Also see chart "**Jeremiah 35**: The Rekabites (Kenite Descendants)."

27. Ir Nahash is probably a place name as well. *The Sacred Bridge* makes this association: "The Kenite "house of Rechab [the sons of Jephunneh]" (**1 Chronicles 2:55**) is associated with the clans of Caleb and Kenaz on the one hand and with the Edomite Ir-nahash ("Serpent City" [probably modified from "City of Copper"] and Ge-harashim ("Valley of Craftsmen") on the other (**1 Chronicles 4:12–14**)" (Rainey and Notley, *The Sacred Bridge*, 152).

28. Karmi in **1 Chronicles 4:1** is Caleb in **1 Chronicles 2:9; 18–19**. Karmi/Caleb the Judahite (Caleb II) is not Caleb I the Kenizzite, the son of Jephunneh. However, they were brothers-in-law, because a daughter of Hezron (i.e., the sister of Jerahmeel, Ram, Karmi/Caleb II, and Ashhur) married Caleb (I) the Kenizzite (see chart "**1 Chronicles 2**: Caleb and Kenaz, the Sons of Jephunneh the Kenizzite").

29. Ephrath in **1 Chronicles 2:19** is the same person as Ephrathah in **1 Chronicles 2:50**. Both forms of the same name derive from פְּרִי, "fruit." Ephrath, אֶפְרָת, is a nickname for the longer Ephrathah, אֶפְרָתָה. She is the eponymous ancestor of several people: David's father, who is called "an Ephrathite named Jesse, who was from Bethlehem in Judah" (**1 Samuel 17:12**), and Elimelek (husband of Naomi), Mahlon, and Kilion (the sons of Elimelek and Naomi), who were called the "Ephrathites from Bethlehem, Judah" (**Ruth 1:2**). Ephrath/Ephrathah is also a place name. When Jacob's family came to the land of Canaan, Rachel died in childbirth just before they reached Ephrath, and she was buried near there (**Genesis 35:16–19; 48:7**). Hezron, Caleb/Karmi's father, died in "Caleb Ephrathah" (**1 Chronicles 2:24**). Ephrath/Ephrathah is typically known as the ancient name for Bethlehem, called *Bethlehem Ephrathah* (**Micah 5:2**), which was prophesied by Micah to be the birthplace of the Messiah (cf. **Genesis 35:19; 48:7; Ruth 4:11**). "Bethlehem" reflects this same idea of fruitfulness: בֵּתְלֶחֶם, "bread (or food) place."

30. Hur and his son Salma were considered co-founders of Bethlehem (cf. **1 Chronicles 2:51; 4:4**). Etam, Penuel, and Ezer were descendants of Hur (cf. **1 Chronicles 4:3–4**).

31. Shobal founded the city of Kiriath Jearim in Judah (also called Baalah, or Kiriath Baal, the "town of Baal"; **Joshua 15:9, 60; 1 Chronicles 13:6**). Shobal was the father of Haroeh (Reaiah) and the ancestor of half the Manahathites (inhabitants of Manahath) and the clans of the Ithrites, Puthites, Shumathites, and Mishraites, from whom descended the Zorathites and Eshtaolites (**1 Chronicles 2:52–54**).

32. Salma and his father Hur were the co-founders of Bethlehem (cf. **1 Chronicles 2:51, 54; 4:4**). Salma the son of Hur should not be confused with Salmon the son of Nahshon (**Ruth 4:20–21; 1 Chronicles 2:11; Matthew 1:4–5; Luke 3:32**).

33. Etam appears to be near Bethlehem and Tekoa (**2 Chronicles 11:5–6**; cf. **1 Chronicles 4:32**).

34. Penuel the Judahite and Jered the Kenizzite appear to be co-founders of Gedor, a town in the hill country of Judah (cf. **Joshua 15:58; 1 Chronicles 4:4, 18**).

35. Bezalel was the "skilled person to whom the LORD has given skill and ability to know how to carry out all the work of constructing the sanctuary [the tabernacle]" during the early wilderness period (**Exodus 36:1**; cf. **31:2; 35:30**); see chart "**Exodus 31**: Bezalel, the Chief Artisan of the Tabernacle and Its Furnishings, and His Assistant, Oholiab."

36. Reaiah (רְאָיָה) in **1 Chronicles 4:2** is called Haroeh (הָרֹאֶה) in the MT of **1 Chronicles 2:52**. Many scholars, however, read with **1 Chronicles 4:2**, "Reaiah," רְאָיָה, but on no manuscript or version grounds. Both names derive from the verb "to see," the first meaning "Yah(weh) has seen" and the second "the seer," that is, as a prophet.

37. The Judahite clans who occupied Kiriath Jearim (also called Baalah, Kiriath Baal, or Mahaneh Dan) in Judah included the Ithrites (of Jether), Puthites, Shumathites, and Mishraites (**1 Chronicles 2:53**); Shobal was the founder of Kiriath Jearim (see note 31). See also **Joshua 15:9, 60; 18:14; Judges 18:12; 2 Samuel 23:38; 1 Chronicles 11:40**.

38. The Zorathites were inhabitants of Zorah, a town in the western foothills of the tribe of Judah near Eshtaol (**Joshua 15:33**) and/or Zorah, near Eshtaol in the tribal allotment of Dan (**Joshua 19:40–41**)—the latter Zorah was Samson's hometown (**Judges 13:2, 24–25**). After the captivity, some of the people of Judah reinhabited Zorah (**Nehemiah 11:29**).

39. Eshtaol, located in the western foothills of the tribe of Judah (**Joshua 15:33**), was also associated with the tribe of Dan and close to the burial place of Samson and his father, Manoah (**Joshua 19:41; Judges 16:31**). The Eshtaolites were also associated with the families of Shobal (**1 Chronicles 2:52–53**).

40. For Jabez, see note 25. As **1 Chronicles 2:55** explains, the descendants of Salma included "clans of scribes who lived at Jabez: the Tirathites, Shimeathites and Sucathites. These are the Kenites who came from Hammath, the father of the Rekabites"; see charts "**Judges 4**: Heber and Jael (Kenites) and

Their Descendants Who Co-Mingled with the Pious Jabez-Rekabite Community near Jerusalem" and "**Jeremiah 35**: The Rekabites (Kenite Descendants)."

41. Caleb (I) the son of Jephunneh was of foreign Kenizzite ancestry. The Kenizzites were among the original occupants of the promised land (**Genesis 15:19**). Caleb the Kenizzite represented the tribe of Judah as one of the twelve spies of Canaan (**Numbers 13:6**). Caleb and Joshua were the only two people who lived through the forty years of wilderness wanderings (**Numbers 14:30, 38**). Caleb married the daughter of Hezron from the tribe of Judah and became the brother-in-law of Jerahmeel the firstborn son of Hezron (cf. **1 Chronicles 2:25**). Caleb the Kenizzite, the son of Jephunneh (designated Caleb I) should not be confused with his brother-in-law of the same name, Caleb/Karmi the son of Hezron (designated Caleb II). **First Chronicles 2:42** should be understood to mean "Caleb [the Kenizzite] the *brother-in-law* [not brother] of Jerahmeel." See chart "**1 Chronicles 2**: Caleb and Kenaz, the Sons of Jephunneh the Kenizzite."

42. Kenaz the Kenizzite (the son of Jephunneh and the younger brother of Caleb I) should not be confused with Kenaz the Edomite, the son of Eliphaz (**Genesis 36:11**); for the Edomite clan, see chart "**Genesis 36**: Esau, the Ancestor of the Edomites."

43. See chart "**Joshua 14**: The Clan of Jephunneh the Kenizzite."

44. "Type" and "anti-type," in line with its etymology (Greek τυπος, "pattern, model, standard"), has to do with literary and ideological correspondence. It is a printing term describing the impression of a lead character upon parchment in such a way that the surface of the character could be read in reverse on the parchment (see **Acts 23:25; Romans 5:14**). In this case, David is the human image of which his descendant Jesus Christ will be the divine image (cf. **Matthew 1:1; 9:27; 12:23; 15:22; 20:30–31; 21:9, 15; 22:42; Mark 10:47–48; 12:35; Luke 3:31; 18:38–39; 20:41; Revelation 22:16**).

45. See chart "**1 Chronicles 2**: Jerahmeel and His Descendant, Elishama, Who Appears to Be a Compiler of Historical and Genealogical Records in 1 & 2 Chronicles."

1 CHRONICLES 4: HUR AND SALMA, THE CO-FOUNDERS OF BETHLEHEM

Approximate Dating: from the birth of Judah, ca. 1925 B.C., to the exile in 586 B.C.[1] ***Relevant Scriptures:*** **1 Chronicles 4:1–4;** also **Genesis 46:12; Exodus 31:2; 35:30; 38:22; 1 Chronicles 2:4, 18–20, 50–54; 2 Chronicles 1:5; Matthew 1:3; Luke 3:33**

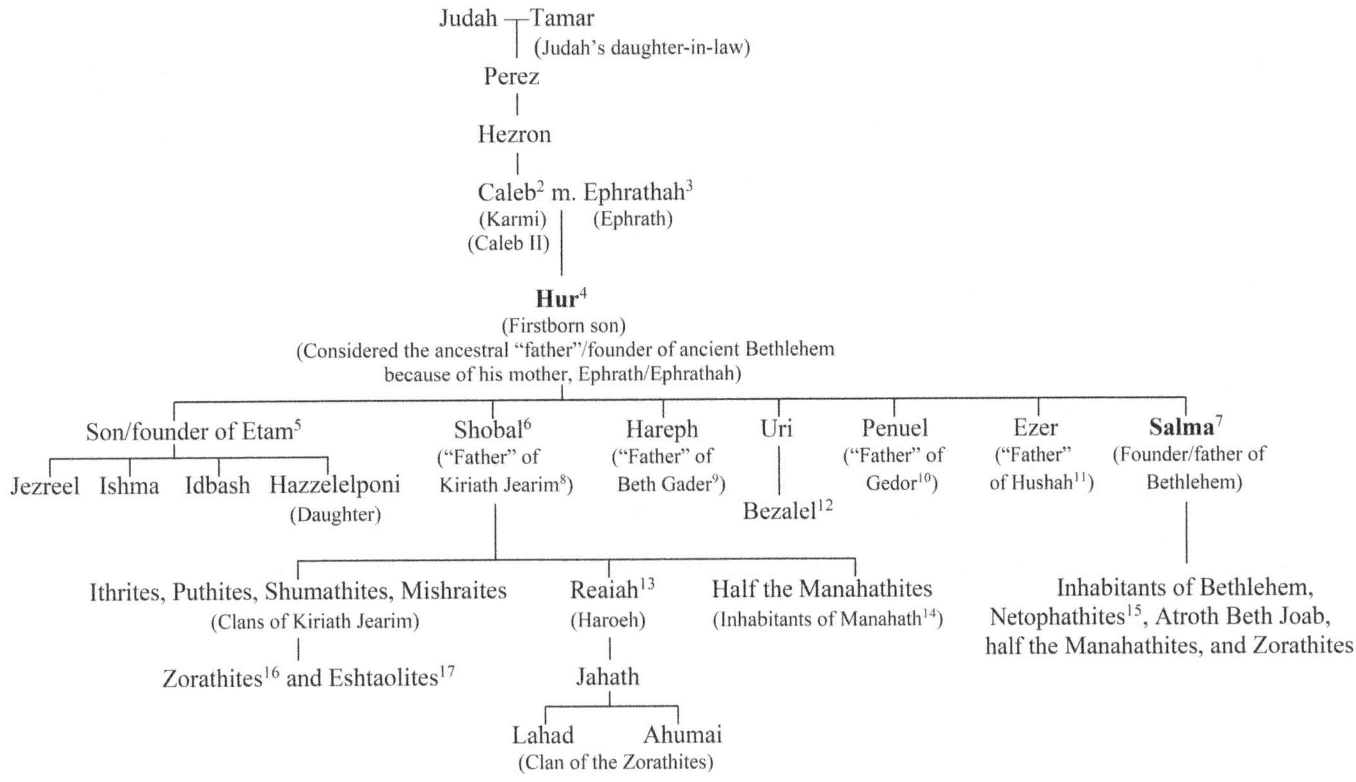

Biblical and Theological Significance

This genealogy of Hur and Salma provides a good opportunity to see the mingling of place names / geographic names (**GN**) and personal names (**PN**), in which the original settlers or founders of a place often lent their names to the place. Unless one recognizes that fact, the lineages can be extremely confusing or even meaningless. Their genealogies shows that names may be of both places and persons.[18]

Bethlehem of Judah—not to be confused with Bethlehem of Zebulun[19]—was located about five miles south of Jerusalem, off the main road to Hebron. Bethlehem, meaning "house of bread," was also known by the ancient name "Ephrath" or "Ephrathah," referring to Hur's mother (the wife of Caleb/Caleb II/Karmi). Bethlehem was most famously called the "town of David" (**Luke 2:4**) and recognized as an important place within the tribe of Judah as it was:

1. Near the place where Rachel (Jacob's wife) died and was buried (**Genesis 35:19; 48:7**);
2. Home of Micah's young Levite (**Judges 17–18**);
3. Home of the concubine who was tragically raped, murdered, and dismembered (**Judges 19–20**);
4. Family home of Elimelek and Naomi (**Ruth 1:1–2, 19**) and Boaz (**Ruth 2:4**);

5. Home of Jesse's family and the ancestral home of King David (**1 Samuel 16:1, 18; 17:15, 58; 20:6**; cf. **2 Samuel 23:14–16; 1 Chronicles 11:16–18**);
6. Family home of Asahel, Joab, and Abishai (the sons of Zeruiah and David's nephews), who were leaders in David's army (cf. **2 Samuel 2:32**);
7. Hometown of Elhanan, one of the military leaders in David's army (**2 Samuel 23:24; 1 Chronicles 11:26**);
8. One of the towns of Judah that was fortified by King Rehoboam (**2 Chronicles 11:5–6**);
9. The town where the prophet Micah prophesied that the Messiah would be born (**Micah 5:2**; cf. **Matthew 2:5–6; John 7:42**);
10. The birthplace of Jesus (**Matthew 2:1**; cf. **2:8, 16; Luke 2:15**).

Notice that the place names of Kiriath Jearim, Netophah, and Zorah indicate that Hur and Salma's descendants returned to their homeland in the post-exile (i.e., names found in **Ezra** and **Nehemiah**[20]), ca. 538/400 B.C.

Notes

1. In this chart some of the "sons" may actually be "descendants."

2. Karmi in **1 Chronicles 4:1** is called Caleb in **1 Chronicles 2:9**; Karmi/Caleb—designated Caleb II in this and other charts—had children by three wives: Azubah, Jerioth, and Ephrath/Ephrathah (cf. **1 Chronicles 2:8–19**). See chart "**1 Chronicles 2**: Hezron" for the descendants of Karmi/Caleb II by Azubah.

3. Ephrath in **1 Chronicles 2:19** is Ephrathah in **1 Chronicles 2:50; 4:4**; she is the toponymic namesake for the town of Caleb Ephrathah, Ephrathah, and Bethlehem Ephrathah, all of which are ancient names for the immediate vicinity of Bethlehem, the birthplace of Jesus (**Ruth 4:11; 1 Chronicles 2:24; Psalm 132:6; Micah 5:2**; see also **Genesis 35:16, 19; 48:7**). For Ephrath/Ephrathah, see note 29 in chart "**1 Chronicles 4**: Judah." For other offspring of Karmi/Caleb (II) the Judahite and Ephrath/Ephrathah, see chart "**1 Chronicles 2**: Hezron."

4. Hur's name (חוּר) probably means "pale" or "white." Hur (the firstborn) and, in turn, his son Salma carried on the ancestral title of "founders/fathers" of ancient Bethlehem, because their mother/grandmother (respectively) had been the toponymic namesake of the town. Hur was a contemporary of Moses who lived ca. 1526–1406 B.C. Hur is known especially for his help during a battle between the Israelites and the Amalekites that occurred at Rephidim in the wilderness, where Hur and Aaron held up Moses' hands, "one on one side, one on the other" (**Exodus 17:12**)—"As long as Moses held up his hands, the Israelites were winning, but whenever he lowered his hands, the Amalekites were winning" (**Exodus 17:11**); because of this, the Israelites were able to defeat the Amalekite army (cf. **Exodus 17:8–13**).

5. Etam is mentioned in **1 Chronicles 4:32**; it was a town fortified by King Rehoboam (**2 Chronicles 11:6**).

6. Shobal the Judahite (**1 Chronicles 2:50, 52; 4:1–2**) is unrelated to Shobal the son of Seir the Horite (cf. **Genesis 36:20, 23, 29; 1 Chronicles 1:38, 40**).

7. Salma and his father, Hur, were both considered the "founders" of Bethlehem (**1 Chronicles 2:51; 4:4**). Salma the son of Hur should not be confused with Salmon the son of Nahshon, who was also a Judahite (**Ruth 4:20; 1 Chronicles 2:11; Matthew 1:4; Luke 3:32**).

8. Kiriath Jearim—also known as Baalah (**Joshua 15:9**) or Kiriath Baal (**Joshua 15:60; 18:14**)—was a city of Judah (**Judges 18:12**). When the Philistines returned the ark of the covenant, it was kept at Kiriath Jearim for 20 years (**1 Samuel 6:21–7:2**). **First Chronicles 2:53** says, "the clans of Kiriath Jearim: the Ithrites, Puthites, Shumathites, and Mishraites. From these descended the Zorathites [inhabitants of Zorah] and the Eshtaolites [inhabitants of Eshtaol]." Zorah and Eshtaol were towns in the western foothills in the tribal allotment of Judah (**Joshua 15:33**).

9. Beth Gader, mentioned in **1 Chronicles 2:51**, was probably a border city near Bethlehem and Kiriath Jearim. See Susan E. McGarry, "Beth Gader," *Anchor Yale Bible Dictionary*, vol 1.

10. Gedor (**Joshua 15:58; 1 Chronicles 4:4, 18, 39; 8:31; 9:37; 12:7**) was approximately five miles southwest of Bethlehem.

11. Hushah (**1 Chronicles 4:4**) was approximately five miles west of Bethlehem.

12. Bezalel was the chief artisan of the tabernacle (**Exodus 31:1–5; 35:30–33; 38:22; 2 Chronicles 1:5**; see also **1 Chronicles 2:20**). See chart "**Exodus 31**: Bezalel, the Chief Artisan of the Tabernacle and Its Furnishings, and His Assistant, Oholiab."

13. Reaiah in **1 Chronicles 4:2** is Haroeh in **1 Chronicles 2:52**. He is unrelated to the temple servant named Reaiah in **Ezra 2:47** and **Nehemiah 7:50**.

14. The town of Manahath (**1 Chronicles 1:40; 2:52, 54; 8:6**) was near Jerusalem and Bethlehem.

15. Netophathites were citizens of Netophah, a town approximately three miles southeast of Bethlehem (see **2 Samuel 23:28, 29; 2 Kings 25:23; 1 Chronicles 2:54; 9:16; 11:30 (2x); 27:13, 15; Ezra 2:22; Nehemiah 7:26; 12:28; Jeremiah 40:8**).

16. Zorathites were citizens of Zorah (**Joshua 15:33; 19:41; Judges 13:2, 25; 16:31; 18:2, 8, 11; 1 Chronicles 2:53, 54; 4:2; 2 Chronicles 11:10; Nehemiah 11:29**), located approximately 12 miles southwest of Jerusalem.

17. Eshtaol (**Joshua 15:33; 19:41; Judges 13:25; 16:31; 18:2, 8, 11**) was a town approximately 20 miles northwest of Jerusalem.

18. For the connection of personal (patronymic) and place (toponymic) names in the Bible, see Richard S. Hess, "Names," *Dictionary of Daily Life in Biblical & Post-Biblical Antiquity*, vol. III. ed. Edwin M. Yamauchi and Marvin R. Wilson. (Peabody, MA: Hendrickson, 2016), 429–436.

19. Ibzan, the judge of Israel, was from Bethlehem of Zebulun; see chart "**Judges 12**: Ibzan (Ninth Judge) and Elon (Tenth Judge)–Two Judges from the Tribe of Zebulun."

20. For the post-exilic occupation of Kiriath Jearim, see **Ezra 2:25** and **Nehemiah 7:29**; for Netophah, see **Ezra 2:22** and **Nehemiah 7:26**; for Zorah, see **Nehemiah 11:29**.

1 CHRONICLES 4: SIMEON

Approximate Dating: from Simeon's birth in ca. 1927 B.C. to 538/400 B.C. ***Relevant Scriptures:*** **1 Chronicles 4:24–43**; also **Genesis 29:33; 35:23; 46:10; Exodus 6:15; Numbers 26:12–13; Joshua 19:1–9**

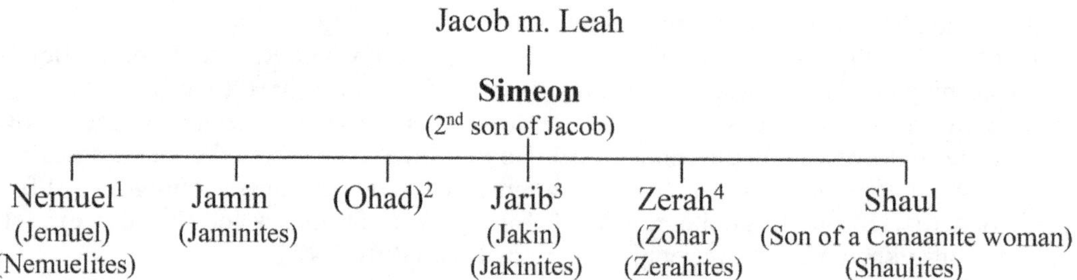

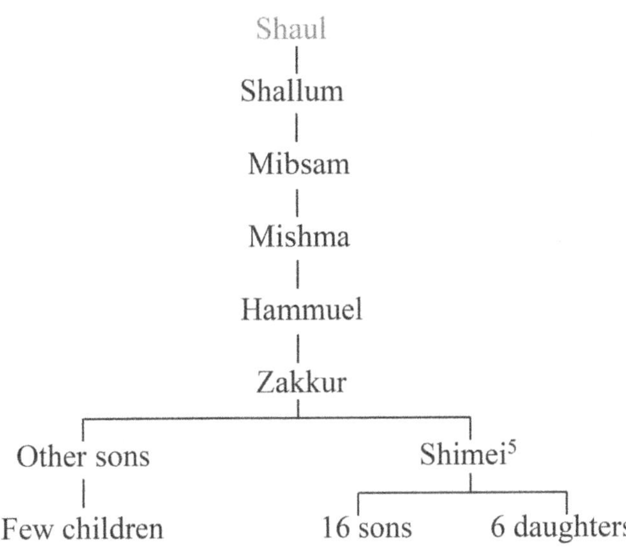

Cities and villages occupied by the families of Simeon descendants "until the reign of David" (1 Chronicles 4:31; ca. 1011 B.C.), according to **1 Chronicles 4:28–33**:

Cities: Beersheba (cf. **Joshua 15:28; Nehemiah 11:27**; also called "Sheba" in **Joshua 19:2**); Moladah (cf. **Joshua 15:26; Nehemiah 11:26**); Hazar Shual (cf. **Joshua 15:28; Nehemiah 11:27**); Bilhah (Balah in **Joshua 19:3**); Ezem (cf. **Joshua 15:29**); Tolad (Eltolad in **Joshua 15:30; 19:4**); Bethuel (Bethul in **Joshua 19:4**); Hormah (cf. **Joshua 15:30; 19:4**); Ziklag[6] (cf. **Joshua 15:31; 19:5; Nehemiah 11:28**); Beth Markaboth (cf. **Joshua 19:5**); Hazar Susim (Hazar Susah in **Joshua 19:5**); Beth Biri (Beth Lebaoth in **Joshua 19:6**); and Shaaraim[7] (Shaaraim in **Joshua 15:36**; Sharuhen in **Joshua 19:6**).

Villages: Etam (cf. **2 Chronicles 11:6**); Ain (cf. **Joshua 15:32; Joshua 19:7**; also, Ain was a Levitical city given to the descendants of Aaron the high priest; **Joshua 21:16**); Rimmon (cf. **Joshua 19:7** and "En Rimmon" in **Nehemiah 11:29**); Token (Ether?) and Ashan (cf. **Joshua 15:42; 19:7**); and the villages surrounding these as far as Baalath (cf. Baalath Beer or "Ramah in the Negev" in **Joshua 19:8, 44**; cf. **2 Chronicles 8:6**).

——Proposed chronological gap[8]——

Clan leaders of the Simeonites (according to **1 Chronicles 4:34–37**):

- Meshobab
- Jamlech
- Joshah, son of Amaziah
- Joel
- Jehu, the son of Joshibiah, the son of Seraiah, the son of Asiel
- Elioenai
- Jaakobah
- Jeshohaiah
- Asaiah
- Adiel
- Jesimiel
- Benaiah
- Ziza son of Shiphi, the son of Allon, the son of Jedaiah, the son of Shimri, the son of Shemaiah

Leaders from among five hundred descendants of Simeon who led an invasion of the hill country of Seir (Edom) and defeated the Amalekites in the days of Hezekiah of Judah, 715–686 B.C. (according to **1 Chronicles 4:42–43**):

All were the sons of Ishi:

- Pelatiah
- Neariah
- Rephaiah
- Uzziel

Biblical and Theological Significance

In the birth of Simeon, Jacob's second-born, Leah—the "unloved" wife (**Genesis 29:31**)—saw convincing evidence that God was making up for her less-than-exalted status in the family by having given her not only Reuben, Jacob's firstborn, but now a second son (**Genesis 29:33**). His very name שִׁמְעוֹן (*shimon*), "having made things right,"[9] attests to this. Simeon (by Leah) was the full brother of Reuben, Levi, Judah, Issachar, Zebulun, and Dinah[10] (cf. **Genesis 30:21; 35:23**). The tribe of Simeon received an inheritance of land and cities within the southern limits of the tribe of Judah, in effect becoming a *clan* within Judah. The reasons for this seem multifold: (1) Judah's tribal allotment of land was "more than they needed," so Simeon's inheritance "was taken from the share of Judah" (**Joshua 19:9**); (2) an unexplained lack of propagation (cf. **1 Chronicles 4:27**); (3) by the time of the second census, Simeon's tribe was the least of all and had suffered the greatest losses;[11] (4) related to the barbaric revenge of Simeon (and Levi) against Hamor the Hivite, who had defiled their sister Dinah, in which they slaughtered the entire city of Shechem, "killing every male" (**Genesis 34:25**; see **Genesis 34**); and (5) the judgment of Yahweh upon the Israelites who were seduced into sexual immorality and the worship of Baal of Peor by Moabite women (**Numbers 25:5**); specifically, an Israelite man named Zimri, the son of

Salu (the leader of a Simeonite family) brought a Midianite woman named Kozbi, the daughter of Zur, into the camp where they engaged in sexual immorality[12] "right before the eyes of Moses and the whole assembly of Israel . . . at the tent of meeting" (**Numbers 25:6–9, 14–15**), resulting in the immediate deaths of Zimri and Kozbi and a plague that killed twenty-four thousand Israelites (**Numbers 25:9**). Perhaps the explanation for the decline of the tribe of Simeon is to be found in Jacob's prophetic blessing on his sons (**Genesis 49**) where Simeon received no blessing at all.[13]

During the post-exile period, the Simeonite tribe expanded its territory greatly to the agriculturally rich land on the outskirts of Gedor, an area formerly occupied by Hamites and Meunites (**1 Chronicles 4:39–41**). Simeonite cities (subsumed into Judah's territory) that were reoccupied in the post-exilic era are identified in **Nehemiah 11**: Beersheba/Sheba (**Nehemiah 11:27, 30**); Moladah (**v. 26**); Hazar Shual (**v. 27**); Ziklag (**v. 28**) and Rimmon/En Rimmon (**v. 29**).

Notes

1. Nemuel in **Numbers 26:12** and **1 Chronicles 4:24** is otherwise called Jemuel in **Genesis 46:10** and **Exodus 6:15**.

2. Ohad the son of Simeon in **Genesis 46:10** and **Exodus 6:15** is not mentioned in **1 Chronicles 4:24**; perhaps he died in the wilderness years.

3. Jarib in **1 Chronicles 4:24** is Jakin in **Genesis 46:10; Exodus 6:15;** and **Numbers 26:12**. Jarib the Simeonite is not the Jarib figure of **Ezra 8:16; 10:18**.

4. Zerah in **Numbers 26:13** and **1 Chronicles 4:24** is Zohar in **Genesis 46:10** and **Exodus 6:15**. Simeon's son Zerah is not Zerah the Judahite, the son of Judah and Tamar (see **Genesis 38:30; 46:12; Numbers 26:20; Joshua 7:1, 18; 1 Chronicles 2:4, 6; Matthew 1:3**).

5. Shimei was the father of "sixteen sons and six daughters, but his brothers did not have many children; so their entire clan did not become as numerous as the people of Judah" (**1 Chronicles 4:27**).

6. **First Samuel 27:6–7** says that King Achish of Gath gave the town of Ziklag to David, and it was part of David's fiefdom for the year and four months that he lived in Philistine territory; "it [Ziklag] has belonged to the kings of Judah ever since."

7. An article by Garfinkel and Ganor identifies biblical Sha'arayim (meaning "two gates") as Khirbet Qeiyafa (a city that existed in ca. 1000–969 B.C.), located in the western part of the high Shephelah on a hill that borders the Elah Valley on the north, near Azekah to the west and Socoh (Sokoh) to the southeast; Yosef Garfinkel and Saar Ganor, "Khirbet Qeiyafa: Sha 'Arayim" in *The Journal of Hebrew Scriptures* 8 (2008), https://doi.org/10.5508/jhs.2008.v8.a22.

8. It is important to note that the Chronicler divided the genealogical list into two parts: (1) from Simeon to Shimei and his descendants (**1 Chronicles 4:24–33**) and (2) from Meshobab through the "sons of Ishi" (**1 Chronicles 4:34–43**). Furthermore, there is an indeterminable passage of time between them. The only clear chronological reference is in the second part, which records persons and events in the period of King Hezekiah (715–686 B.C.).

9. "שִׁמְעוֹן," *HALOT* 2:1576.

10. For the birth order, see note 4 in chart "**Genesis 35**: The Twelve Sons of Jacob, the Eponymous Originators of the Twelve Tribes of Israel."

11. See table 1 in chart "**Numbers 26**: The Tribes of Israel at the Time of the Second Census," which compares the numbers from Census #1 (**Numbers 1:1–47**) and Census #2 (**Numbers 26:1–65**) for each of the twelve tribes.

12. The Moabite women invited the Israelite men to the engage in the sexually immoral fertility rites of Baal worship (**Numbers 25:1–3**).

13. "Simeon and Levi are brothers—their swords are weapons of violence. Let me not enter their council, let me not join their assembly, for they have killed men in their anger and hamstrung oxen as they pleased. Cursed be their anger, so fierce, and their fury, so cruel! I will scatter them in Jacob and disperse them in Israel" (**Genesis 49:5–7**). In effect, the Levites and priests obtained no inheritance of land, and Simeon was absorbed into Judah.

1 CHRONICLES 5: REUBEN

Approximate Dating: from Reuben's birth in ca. 1928 B.C. to 722 B.C. ***Relevant Scriptures:*** **1 Chronicles 5:1–10;** also **Genesis 29:32; 46:8–9; 49:3–4; Exodus 6:14; Numbers 16:1; 26:5–10; Deuteronomy 11:6; Joshua 15:6**

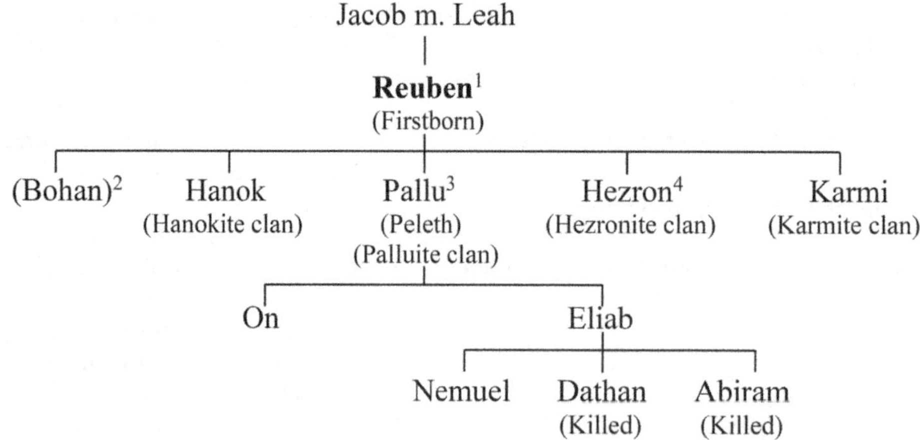

Leaders of the Clans of the Tribe of Reuben

- **Jeiel** (chief) (no recorded genealogy)
- **Beerah**:

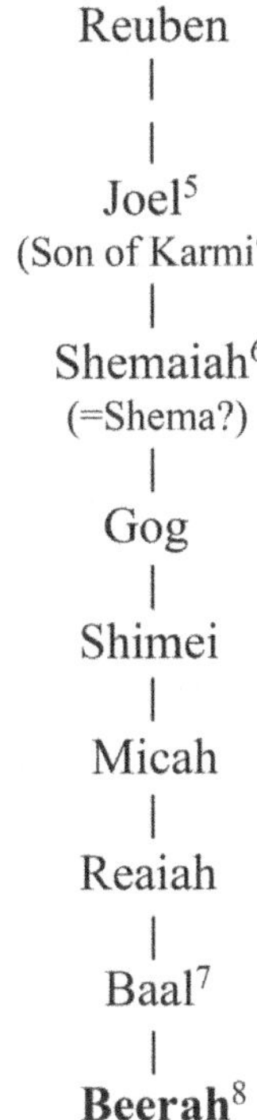

- **Zechariah** (no recorded genealogy)
- **Bela**:

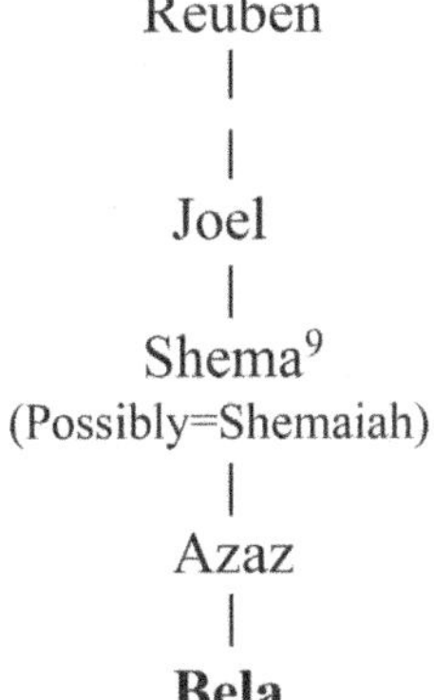

Biblical and Theological Significance

Reuben[10] was the firstborn son of Jacob and Leah (**Genesis 29:32**). Because he slept with Bilhah, his father's concubine, Reuben forfeited his primogeniture status to be Jacob's successor as head of the family and the recipient of the double portion of the inheritance (**Genesis 48:5, 21–22; 49:3–4; Deuteronomy 21:15–17; 1 Chronicles 5:1–2**). Reuben's motive in having sexual contact with Bilhah may well be seen as a grab for primacy even before Jacob died in 1859 B.C.[11] The sin of incest[12] disqualified Reuben, and additionally, the barbaric actions of Simeon and Levi regarding the Shechemites seem to have disqualified them (cf. **Genesis 49:5–7**). Precisely at this point, another sovereign choice was made: the sons of Joseph (Manasseh and Ephraim) received the birthright[13] while Judah retained the privilege of messianic hope and blessing (**Genesis 49:8–10; 1 Chronicles 5:1–2**). The Chronicler carries the Reuben line forward by several generations, but obviously very selectively. Reuben's diminishing status as a tribe may be seen in three important examples:

1. Some Reubenites—Dathan and Abiram (the sons of Eliab who were community leaders) and On, the son of Peleth—were followers of Korah, the son of Izhar (from the tribe of Levi). They were joined by 250 Israelite community leaders who led an opposition against the authority of Moses and Aaron (**Numbers 16:1–50**) in what is called the Korah-Reubenite rebellion. The incident took place in 1444 B.C., only two years after the exodus. As punishment for questioning his chosen priesthood, the Lord separated the Korah rebels from among the other Israelites and opened a great chasm in the earth that swallowed them and all their possessions (**Deuteronomy 11:6; Numbers 16:25–33; 26:8–11**).
2. The encampments of the tribes in the desert were laid out carefully around the tabernacle (**Numbers 2:1–34**). The place of honor was the eastern side because the tabernacle faced that direction (**Exodus 27:13**). Instead of occupying that esteemed estate, Reuben, with Simeon and Gad, were assigned to the south (**Numbers 2:10–16**). Judah, Issachar, and Zebulun received the honor of camping on the eastern side (**Numbers 2:3–9**); Ephraim, Manasseh, and Benjamin were stationed on the west (**Numbers 2:18–24**); and Dan, Asher, and Naphtali to the north (**Numbers 2:25–31**).[14]
3. The conquest of Canaan and subsequent parceling out of the tribal territories is also instructive. The first encounter was against the Midianites in the plains of Moab, directly across the Jordan River from Jericho. Though warned earlier by Moses not to embrace the Midianite gods (**Numbers 34:15**), the Israelites did precisely this (**Numbers 25:1–5**). Next, Reuben, Gad, and East Manasseh begged Moses to let them live in the Transjordan because of the fertility of the soils and the vast pasturelands. Sensing that perhaps they wanted to get out of fighting alongside their brothers across the river (i.e., on the cis-Jordan side), Moses reluctantly gave his permission (**Numbers 32:1–6, 28–42**). Moses then went so far as to explicitly designate how they were to share the land amongst themselves. Reuben received the central area, later rebuilding such well-known cities as Heshbon,[15] King Sihon's capital; Kiriathaim; and Nebo.[16] Some clans settled "from Aroer[17] to Nebo and Baal Meon."[18] To the east "they occupied the land up to the edge of the desert that extends to the Euphrates River, because their livestock had increased in Gilead" (**1 Chronicles 5:9**). The region was known as "Reuben" until the end of Old Testament times. No cities in Reuben are mentioned in Ezra and Nehemiah as being occupied in the post-exile era (538/400 B.C.).

Notes

1. Reuben mentions two of his sons (although unnamed) in **Genesis 42:37**.

2. Bohan is the personal name of a son (or descendant) of Reuben and is also a place name, called Stone of Bohan (**Joshua 15:6**; **18:17**). The Chronicler does not mention Bohan.

3. Pallu in **Genesis 46:9; Exodus 6:14; Numbers 26:5;** and **1 Chronicles 5:3** is Peleth in **Numbers 16:1**.

4. Hezron the son of Reuben (**Genesis 46:9; Exodus 6:14; Numbers 26:6; 1 Chronicles 5:3**) should not be confused with Hezron the son of Perez (**Genesis 46:12; Numbers 26:21; Ruth 4:18; Matthew 1:3**).

5. In the Septuagint, the problematic "Joel" reads "Joel his son." The Syriac Urmiensis reads "son of Karmi," suggesting a missing generation.

6. For Shemaiah (שְׁמְעִי) the son of Joel (**1 Chronicles 5:4**), see note 9.

7. "Baal" is, of course, the name of the chief god of the Canaanite pantheon. For an Israelite to give a son this name is an indication of how idolatry had crept into Israel at this period (late eighth century B.C.; cf. **2 Kings 17:1–17**).

8. Beerah, a leader of the Reubenites, was taken into exile by Tiglath-Pileser, king of Assyria, in 722 B.C. (**1 Chronicles 5:6**).

9. Shema (שֶׁמַע) the son of Joel (**1 Chronicles 5:8**) may be the same person named Shemaiah (שְׁמְעִי) the son of Joel (**1 Chronicles 5:4**).

10. The Hebrew term רְאוּבֵן (*reuben*) means "Look! A son."

11. On his deathbed, Jacob gave this blessing: "Reuben, you are my firstborn, my might, the first sign of my strength, excelling in honor, excelling in power. Turbulent as the waters, you will no longer excel, for you went up onto your father's bed, onto my couch and defiled it [by having sexual relations with Bilhah, Jacob's concubine/wife]" (**Genesis 49:3–4**; see **35:22**).

12. The term is entirely appropriate in light of the later Mosaic Torah, which forbid sexual relationships within families at all levels (**Leviticus 18:6–18**). The penalty for incest was ostracism from the community (**Leviticus 18:29**).

13. This birthright naturally belonged to the *firstborn* son, which typically included receiving a double share of the father's property, headship of the family, and general authority over other family members (**Genesis 27:29**). The privileges of the firstborn or right of primogeniture status could be diverted either by the son's own consent (e.g., Esau in **Genesis 25:29–34**) or by the decision of the father, as here with Reuben (for another example, see Shimri in **1 Chronicles 26:10**). However, the law prevented the father from giving the right of the firstborn to the son of the wife he loved the most instead of his actual firstborn son, born to the wife he loved less (cf. **Deuteronomy 21:15–17**), as in the children of Leah, the less-loved wife of Jacob (**Genesis 29:30**).

14. See chart "**Numbers 2**: Genealogical Registry and Organization of the Tribal Encampment in the Wilderness and the Number of Men in the Army."

15. Tell Hesban, a thoroughly excavated site, is ca. 20 miles southeast of Amman in Jordan.

16. Famous as the place from which Moses could see almost all the promised land, Nebo is only eight miles west of Heshbon (cf. **Deuteronomy 32:49–52; 34:1**).

17. Aroer was up the Arnon River about 15 miles east of the Dead Sea on the border between Moab and Edom (**Deuteronomy 2:36; Joshua 13:16; 2 Kings 10:33**).

18. Baal Meon is the ancient site on which the second city of Jordan, Ma'in, is located. It is approximately 10 miles from the northeast coast of the Dead Sea. Its historicity and importance are enhanced by its being (along with Aroer) listed on the famous Mesha Inscription of ca. 850 B.C. (**Numbers 32:38**; **Ezekiel 25:9**).

1 CHRONICLES 5: GAD[1]

Approximate Dating: from the birth of Gad in ca. 1922 B.C. to the exile in 586 B.C. ***Relevant Scriptures:*** **1 Chronicles 5:11–22;** also **Genesis 30:10–11; 46:16; Numbers 26:15–18**

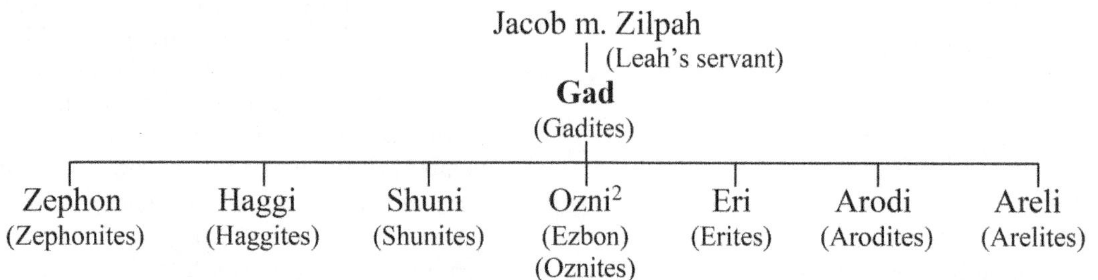

Leaders of the Tribe of Gad (According to 1 Chronicles 5:12–15)

Chief Men

- Joel (chief)
- Shapham
- Janai (in Bashan)
- Shaphat (in Bashan)

Family Relatives

- Michael
- Meshullam
- Sheba
- Jorai
- Jakan
- Zia
- Eber

Family Leaders

1. Genealogy of Abihail:

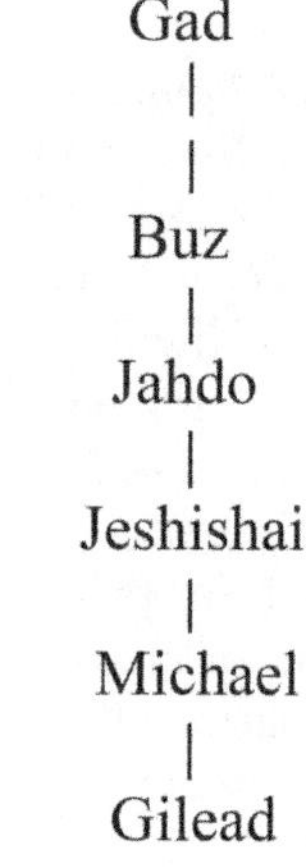

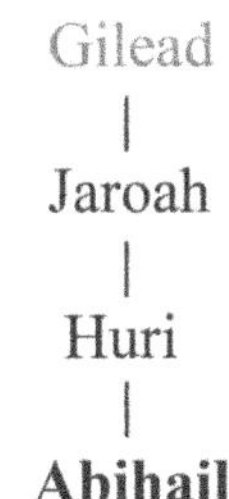

2. Genealogy of Ahi:

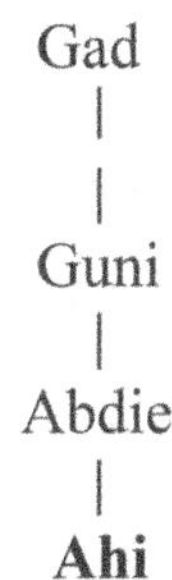

Biblical and Theological Significance

Gad was the son of Jacob and Zilpah, Leah's servant (Heb. שִׁפְחָה, *shiphkhah*; **Genesis 30:9–11**). Gad's name, meaning "fortune," was suggestive that Leah, the "not loved"[3] wife of Jacob, was now blessed by Yahweh. This was confirmed in Moses' blessing that Gad would be enlarged and become militarily ferocious and that he would be a leader who upheld the righteousness of Yahweh (**Deuteronomy 33:20–21**; cf. **Genesis 49:19**).

After the exodus and with the coming occupation of Canaan in view, the first census was taken, showing that the tribe of Gad had 45,650 men who could serve in the army (**Numbers 1:24–25**). Following the conquest of Canaan, Gad was assigned a territory in the Transjordan inhabited by Amorites in the region of Gilead (**Joshua 13:24–28**). Taken from Og and the Ammonites, the land of Gilead lay south of Bashan, extending as far south as the River Jabbok and the boundary with Reuben. Its western border was the Jordan River and it, like Bashan, petered out into the vast deserts to the east. It was heavily forested and provided havens for various groups to do mischief. At the same time, the pastures there were adequate for the famous herds of the tribes of Reuben and Gad (**Numbers 32:1–5**). However, Reuben, Gad, and the half tribe of East Manasseh were given the lush lands of the Transjordan on the condition that they assist their brotherly tribes in the cis-Jordan to win their battles and successfully settle there (**Numbers 32:1–27**).

As a tribe, the Gadites were neighbors of Reuben, dwelling in the villages and common lands and outlying villages in Bashan as far as Salekah (**Deuteronomy 3:10; Joshua 12:5; 1 Chronicles 5:11, 16**), and in all the pasturelands of Sharon,[4] good places for raising flocks (**1 Chronicles 27:29**). The genealogy for the tribe of Gad was registered periodically throughout history, including in the days of King Jeroboam II of Israel (793–753 B.C.) and King Jotham of Judah (750–735 B.C.) (**1 Chronicles 5:17**). All three Transjordan tribes—Reuben, Gad, and East Manasseh—were faithful to God. In war, they successfully defeated the Hagrites[5] (Jetur, Naphish, and Nodab, the descendants of Ishmael and Hagar), took their livestock, and "occupied the land until the exile" in 586 B.C. (**1 Chronicles 5:18–22**; cf. **vv. 10–11, 16**).

No cities that had been allotted to the tribe of Gad are mentioned as being occupied/re-occupied in the post-exile.

Notes

1. See also the Gad genealogy in "**Numbers 26**: The Tribes of Israel at the Time of the Second Census." The Chronicler(s) note that the "Reubenites, the Gadites and the half-tribe of Manasseh had 44,760 men ready for military service . . . and they occupied the land until the exile [586 B.C.]" (**1 Chronicles 5:18, 22**).

2. Ezbon in **Genesis 46:16** is called Ozni in **Numbers 26:16**.

3. "Hate" is a word in Hebrew with many fine nuances beyond the commonly understood meanings of "revulsion, distaste," and the like. In covenant contexts especially, it often means "non-chosen" as opposed to "chosen" (as in this case with Rachel).

4. Not to be confused with the "plains of Sharon" near the Mediterranean in the cis-Jordan.

5. See chart "**1 Chronicles 1**: Abraham's Descendants through Hagar (Hagrites) and Ishmael (Ishmaelites)."

1 CHRONICLES 5: MANASSEH: THE HALF-TRIBE OF EAST MANASSEH

Approximate Dating: from Manasseh's birth in Egypt before 1877 B.C. to ca. 734/722 B.C.[1] ***Relevant Scriptures:*** **1 Chronicles 5:23–26**; also **Numbers 26:28–34; 1 Chronicles 7:14–19**

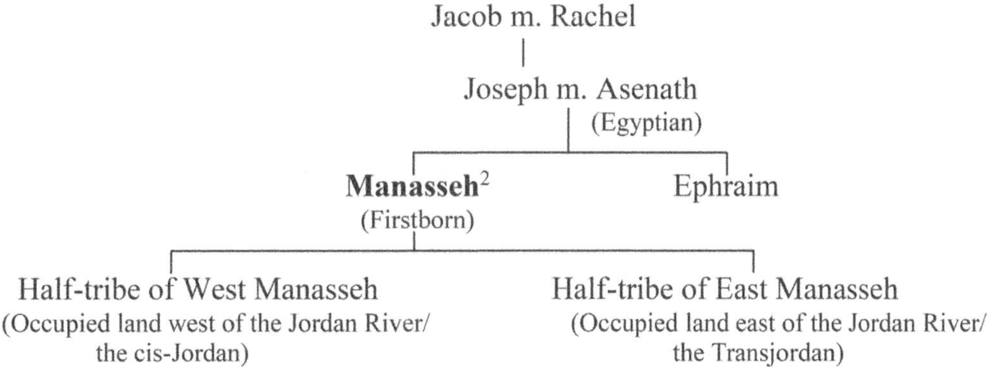

Prominent Heads of East Manassite Families[2]

- Epher
- Ishi
- Eliel
- Azriel
- Jeremiah
- Hodaviah
- Jahdiel

Biblical and Theological Significance

The more expansive genealogy for the half-tribes of East and West Manasseh is found in the chart "**1 Chronicles 7**: Manasseh (The Half-Tribe of West Manasseh)."

History of East Manasseh

The origin of the tribes of Ephraim and Manasseh differs greatly from that of the other tribes. Joseph sired two sons, Manasseh and Ephraim, both of whom were born in Egypt (**Genesis 41:50–52; 46:20**). Years later, as Jacob neared death, he told Joseph that Manasseh and Ephraim would be "reckoned as mine," thus elevating the two sons to the status of the other sons of Jacob (**Genesis 48:5**; cf. **vv. 1–5**).[3] By this blessing, Manasseh and Ephraim received the rights of the firstborn and the double portion that normally would have been given to Reuben,[4] the actual firstborn (**1 Chronicles 5:1**), Hence, they became eponymous ancestors of the tribes of Manasseh and Ephraim. Despite Manasseh's firstborn status, Ephraim was given preference; Jacob prophesied that the "younger brother [Ephraim] will be greater than he [Manasseh] and his [Ephraim's] descendants will become a group of nations" (**Genesis 48:12–20**). The more elaborate genealogies of the two sons of Joseph are recorded in **Numbers 26:28–37** and **1 Chronicles 7:14–29**.

Nothing is known of a divided Manasseh until the time just before the conquest when Moses gave instructions for the distribution of tribal lands in Canaan and the Transjordan (**Numbers 32:1–42**). "The half-tribe of Manasseh" is included along with Reuben and Gad as settling in the east (**Numbers 32:1–5, 20–27, 33, 39–42**). For the tribal allotment for the half-tribe of East Manasseh, see **Numbers 32:39–41; 36:1–12; Deuteronomy 3:12–15; Joshua 13:1–7, 29–32; 17:1–18; 18:7; 20:8; 21:25–27; 22:7–9** and **Judges 1:27**; for the half-tribe of West Manasseh, see **Joshua 17:7–13** and **Judges 1:27–28**.

A summary statement in **1 Chronicles 5:25–26** (which includes the three Transjordan tribes of East Manassites, Reubenites, and Gadites) indicts them for being unfaithful to the God of their ancestors and prostituting themselves to the gods of the peoples of the land, who, with their worshipers, were to have been totally destroyed in the conquest under Joshua and the judges (cf. **Exodus 23:31–33; Deuteronomy 7:1–5**). Therefore, centuries later God "stirred up" the spirit of King Tiglath-Pileser III (Pul) of Assyria to come against Israel and carry them off into exile (**2 Kings 16:7–9; 1 Chronicles 5:26**). The resulting diaspora took place most likely in a campaign by the Assyrian king in 734 B.C.[5] How many were taken captive cannot be known, but the Chronicler identified their destinations as Halah, Habor, Hara, and the vicinity of Gozan (a tributary of the Euphrates River). As part of the "ten lost tribes," the whereabouts of these three Transjordan tribes were known at least to the Chronicler, who said they were in those places "to this day" (**1 Chronicles 5:26**).

The Chronicler records only the names of seven heads of families for the half-tribe of East Manasseh, all of whom were praised for their valor—"brave warriors, famous men" (**1 Chronicles 5:24**)—which contributed to the tribe's ability to conquer and inhabit all the territory north of Bashan to Baal Hermon (Mount Hermon). Trans-Jordan (East) Manasseh had been assigned by Moses to a territory consisting of two regions, Bashan[6] and Gilead.[7]

No specific cities within the tribe of East Manasseh are mentioned in the post-exilic era (i.e., in **Ezra** or **Nehemiah**), although **1 Chronicles 9:3** notes that some exiles "from Judah, from Benjamin, and from Ephraim and Manasseh" returned and lived in the Yehud community of Jerusalem.

Notes

1. Manasseh and Ephraim were born in Egypt "before the years of famine came" (**Genesis 41:50**; meaning sometime before 1877 B.C., which began the first of seven years of famine, 1877–1871 B.C., inclusive). See chart "**Genesis 37**: Joseph and His Sons (Manasseh and Ephraim)."

2. Manasseh was the firstborn son of Joseph and Asenath, the daughter of Potipherah the priest of On (**Genesis 41:51**; cf. **Numbers 26:28–34**). The Chronicler does not provide genealogical information for the half-tribe of East Manasseh but rather discusses it along with the other Transjordan tribes, the Reubenites (**1 Chronicles 5:1–10**) and the Gadites (**1 Chronicles 5:11–17**). For the genealogy of the tribe of West Manasseh, see chart "**1 Chronicles 7**: Manasseh (The Half-Tribe of West Manasseh)."

3. This was not in formal adoption but through an arrangement "on paper" whereby Jacob, as the patriarch of the family, could pass on the patriarchal blessings to them. The blessing on Joseph (**Genesis 49:22–26**) included a special apportionment of land: "to you [Joseph] I give one more ridge of land [Shechem] than to your brothers, the ridge I took from the Amorites with my sword and my bow" (**Genesis 48:22**). Shechem was built primarily on the slope or shoulder of Mount Ebal and was an important city because it was located at the convergence of main highways and ancient trade routes. Shechem became the first capital of the northern kingdom of Israel.

4. Reuben forfeited his right of the firstborn by sleeping with Jacob's concubine Bilhah (**Genesis 35:22; 49:4**).

5. For the Assyrian record, see K. Lawson Younger, Jr., "Tiglath-Pileser III" in William W. Hallo and K. Lawson Younger, Jr. eds., *The Context of Scripture*, vol. 2 (Leiden: Brill, 1997–2002), 284–88.

6. Bashan, captured by the Israelites following a battle with its King Og ("the last of the Repahites"; **Joshua 13:12**), extended from the Yarmuk River in the south to Mount Hermon and east of it to the north, and from the Arabah or "Great Rift" on the west to the Arabian deserts to the east. It was celebrated for its fertile farmlands and famous "fat cows."

7. Gilead, the north-central section of the Transjordan highlands, lay east of the Jordan River and south of Bashan and was bisected by the River Jabbok. The name Gilead, together with Bashan, indicates the land east of the Jordan River, as distinguished from the Moab plateau (cf. **Deuteronomy 3:10; Joshua 13:11; 2 Kings 10:33**).

1 CHRONICLES 6: LEVI: HIGH PRIESTS, PRIESTS, LEVITES, AND MUSICIANS IN SOLOMON'S TEMPLE[1]

Approximate Dating: from Levi's birth in ca. 1926 B.C. to the exile in 586 B.C. ***Relevant Scriptures:*** **1 Chronicles 6:1–53; 9:11, 16; 15:16–24; 23:6–23; 24:1–30; 26:31–32;** also **Genesis 29:34; 46:11; Exodus 6:16–25; Numbers 3:17–21, 27, 33; 26:57–61; 2 Chronicles 29:12–14; Nehemiah 11:11**

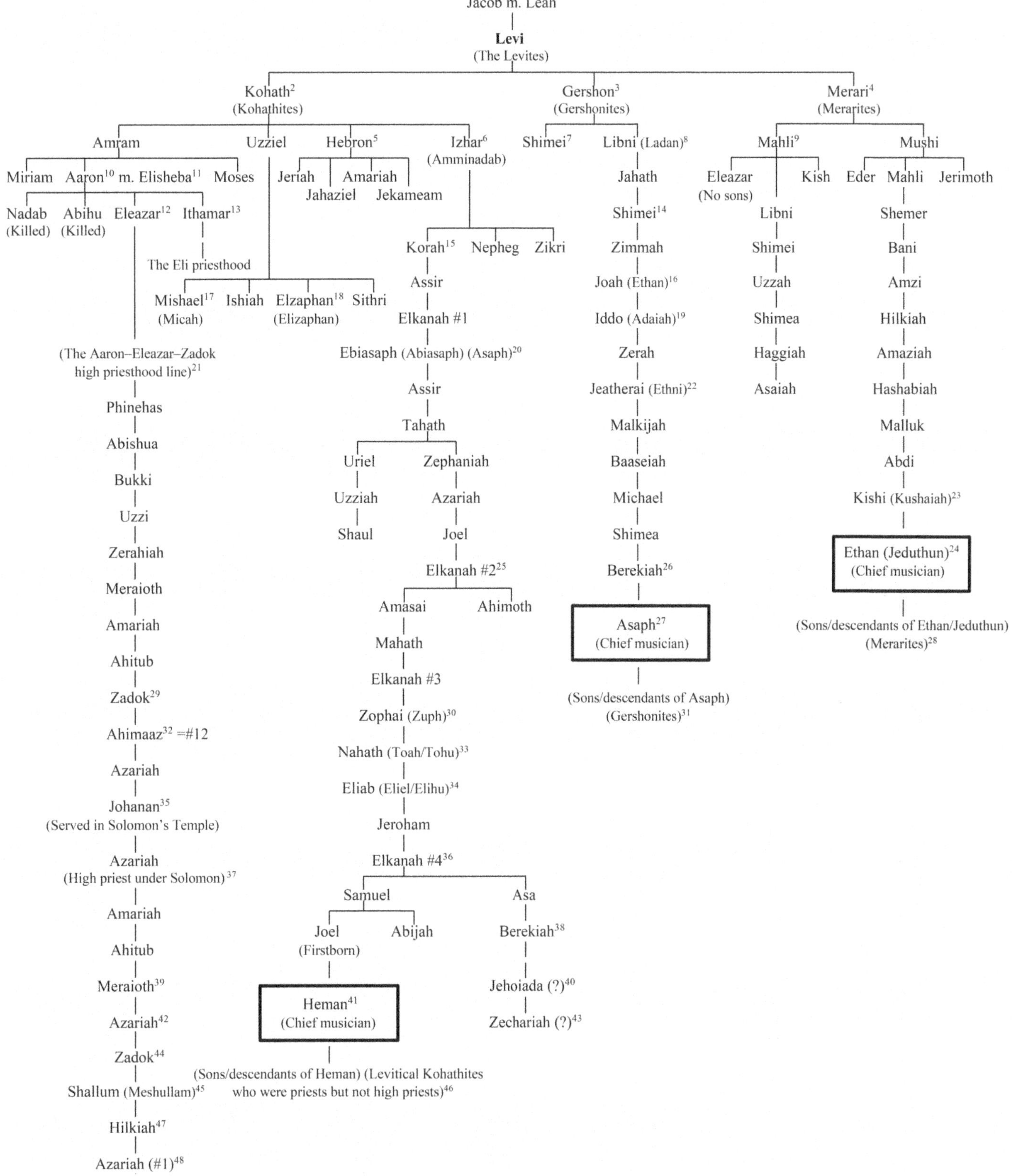

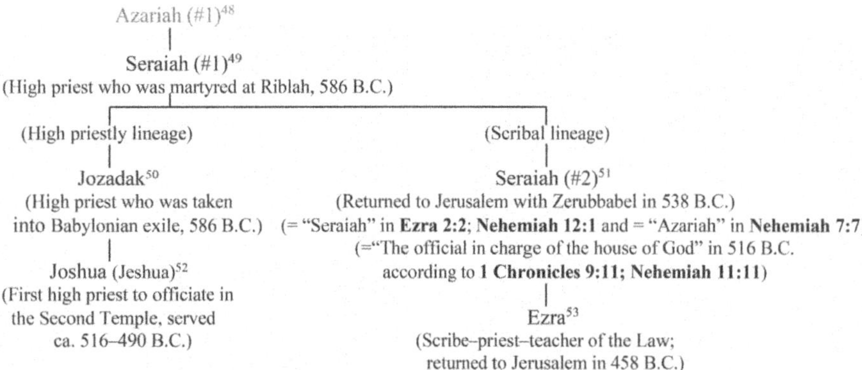

Biblical and Theological Significance

Next to the monarchy, the priesthood of Israel was its most important institution. The former modeled on earth the sovereignty of God—especially under David and his dynasty—while the latter functioned as the medium by which Israel could be in contact with her God as a community in worship, prayer, repentance, sacrifice, and festivals. The priests and Levites were descendants of Jacob's son Levi. In turn, Levi's sons, Kohath, Gershon, and Merari, became heads of three different clans of priests and Levites (**1 Chronicles 6:16**; cf. **Numbers 26:57**). All high priests and *attending* priests were descendants of Kohath (the Kohathite clan); the Levites, who attended their priestly brethren, were descendants of Gershon (the Gershonite clan) and Merari (the Merarite clan).

The earliest "priesthood" was that of Adam who, with Eve, had unfettered access to the Lord in their sinless state. Their sons, it seems, understood their fallen state and thus offered sacrifices as a means to approach the Holy One (**Genesis 4:2–6**). Individuals thereafter maintained such worship. Fathers of families also began to officiate as priests of the families (**Genesis 8:20; 22:2, 13; 31:54; 46:1**). As a Kohathite, Moses presented himself as a priest in his many requests to Pharaoh that Israel be permitted to leave Egypt to worship (**Exodus 3:18; 5:3, 8, 17; 8:25**; etc.). After the exodus and sojourn in the desert, Moses and Aaron continued that practice (**Exodus 24:5**). Following the departure from Sinai, there is not one mention of Moses or any other individual who sacrificed offerings for the community since by then the priestly institution had been organized under the headship of Aaron, Moses' brother. God had instructed Moses to select Aaron as a priest along with his sons Nadab, Abihu, Eleazar, and Ithamar (**Exodus 28:1; Leviticus 9:7**). However, Nadab and Abihu died for using "unauthorized fire" in the sacrificial offering (**Exodus 10:1; Numbers 26:61**), so afterward, the priesthood continued through Aaron's sons Eleazar and Ithamar.

After the conquest of Canaan under Joshua, the land was divided into tribal allotments, with the exception of the tribe of Levi (cf. **Numbers 18:20–21**), who was set apart from the other tribes to devote themselves to the spiritual life of the nation: "The LORD said to Aaron, 'You will have no inheritance in their land, nor will you have any share [portion] among them; I am your share and your inheritance among the Israelites" (**Numbers 18:20**; cf. **Deuteronomy 10:9**). So that no person would be more than several miles from the services of the Levitical priesthood, forty-eight cities—called Levitical cities—were designated throughout the land.[54] The following list summarizes the Levitical cities that were assigned to the Kohathite, Gershonite, and Merarite clans, according to **Joshua 21:1–42** and **1 Chronicles 6:54–81**.

- **Kohathite high priests**: Hebron (Kiriath Arba), Libnah, Jattir, Eshtemoa, Hilen (or Holon), Debir, Ashan (Ain), Juttah, Beth Shemesh, Gibeon, Geba, Anathoth, Alemeth (Almon)–13 cities
- **Kohathite priests (who were not high priests)**: Shechem, Gezer, Jokmeam, Beth Horon, Aijalon, Gath Rimmon, Kibzaim, Eltekeh, Aner (Taanach?), Bileam (the same as Ibleam?[55])–10 cities
- **Gershonites**: Golan, Ashtaroth (Be Eshterah), Kedesh (Kishion), Daberath, Ramoth (Jarmuth), Anem (En Gannim), Mashal (Mishal), Abdon, Hukok (Helkath), Rehob, Kedesh in Galilee, Hammon (Hammoth Dor), Kirathaim (Kartan)–13 cities
- **Merarites**: Jokneam, Kartah, Rimmono (Dimnah), Tabor (Nahalal), Bezer, Jahaz (Jahzah), Kedemoth, Mephaath, Ramoth in Gilead, Mahanaim, Heshbon, Jazer–12 cities

From the beginning, Aaron (the son of Amram, the son of Kohath, the son of Levi) was the chosen high priest for the nation, and his sons alone (in father-son succession) were to serve as high priests before the Lord in worship and sacrifice (**Exodus 28:1; 40:12–15; Numbers 18:1, 7; 1 Chronicles 23:13**). Other Kohathite priests who *attended* the high priests were selected by casting lots[56] from the descendants of either the Aaron–Eleazar line or the Aaron–Ithamar line—excluding the cursed (unfaithful) priests from the Eli priesthood. The *Kohathite attending* priests were organized into twenty-four divisions[57] (**1 Chronicles 24:1–19**). The descendants of Gershon and Merari served as Levitical servants alongside their Kohathite brethren (i.e., the high priest(s) and the attending priests). During the wilderness years at the tabernacle, the priests began service at age thirty and ended at age fifty (**Numbers 4:3, 23, 30, 35, 39, 43, 47**) and the Levites began service at age twenty-five and retired at age fifty[58] (**Numbers 8:24–25**). By the time of Solomon's Temple, when "the Levites no longer need to carry the tabernacle or any of the articles used in its service," the beginning age of Levitical service was adjusted down to twenty years (**1 Chronicles 23:24–27**).

The establishment of the monarchy under King David in 1011 B.C., four hundred years after Moses, called for the vast undertaking of (1) providing a central place of worship as Yahweh had commanded (**Deuteronomy 12:4–7, 13–14**); (2) creating a ritual and liturgical system fit for hundreds of thousands of worshipers; and (3) organizing a complementary clerical system. David prepared the way for the eventual construction of the temple and installation of its worship personnel by building an altar (**2 Samuel 5:7; 24:25**) and a temporary tent for the ark of the covenant in the City of David (**1 Chronicles 15:1**; cf. **6:32**). David then gave instructions to Solomon as to temple construction and worship (**1 Chronicles 15:1–16:43**). The chart focuses on the priestly and Levitical situation of the tenth century with its roots in the twentieth century B.C.

King David, along with the Aaronic priesthood, assumed authority over all religious and secular matters. David established the role and rank of the priests, Levites, and musicians in Solomon's Temple (cf. **1 Chronicles 6:31–32; 15:11–28; 23–26**). The duties of the Kohathite priests and Levites in Solomon's Temple remained the same: assisting the *high* priests (or "chief priests") in their duties, including tending the altars of burnt offering and incense; ministering in the holy place; and making atonement in the most holy place, which was accessible to the high priest alone, and then only on Yom Kippur, the Day of Atonement. The *Kohathite attending* priests and Levites rotated service at the temple throughout the year according to their priestly assignments; during the interim periods they dwelt with their families in the forty-eight Levitical cities (**Numbers 35:1–28; Joshua 21:1–42; 1 Chronicles 6:54–81**) and had small patches of land they could use for agriculture and pasturage (**Numbers 35:1–8**). They also functioned as village pastors engaged in local services in the same manner as at the central sanctuary, minus ritual activities such as those pertaining to the ark of the covenant, which remained in Jerusalem. The major festivals—פֶּסַח (*pesach*; Passover), מַצּוֹת (*matsot*; Unleavened Bread); קָצִיר (*qatsir*; First Fruits); שָׁבֻעוֹת (*shabuoth*; Weeks); רֹאשׁ הַשָּׁנָה (*rosh hashannah*; New Years); יוֹם כִּפֻּרִים (*yom kippurim*; Atonement), and סֻכּוֹת (*sukkoth*; Booths)—demanded attendance of all Levitical personnel at the great temple.

Historically, music and worship were closely connected (cf. **Exodus 15:1–18, 21; Numbers 21:17–18; Judges 5:1–31; 2 Samuel 6:5; 1 Chronicles 13:7–8; 15:16; 16:4–7**).[59] David, himself an accomplished musician, dictated the functions and terms of service of the Levitical singers and instrumentalists (**1 Chronicles 25:1–31**). The musicians were divided into groups by the casting of lots. Three chief musicians were prominent in Solomon's Temple: Heman (a Kohathite), Asaph (a Gershonite), and Ethan/Jeduthun (a Merarite); others were attending instrumentalists (**1 Chronicles 6:31–47; 15:16–22; 25:1, 6; 2 Chronicles 5:12**). The three chief musicians were under the supervision of the king, and the sons/descendants of Heman, Asaph, and Ethan/Jeduthun were under the supervision of their father (**1 Chronicles 25:6**). The chief musicians and the heads of Levitical families lived permanently in Jerusalem rather than in the outlying Levitical cities. They "stayed in the rooms of the temple and were exempt from other duties because they were responsible for the work day and night" (**1 Chronicles 9:33**). There were 288 musicians in all, with twenty-four division leaders (**1 Chronicles 25:7–31**). The vital importance of music in temple worship cannot be overstated, as is seen in the book of Psalms with its many instructions on how the individual psalms were to be set to vocal and instrumental music.[60]

The Assyrian exile of 722 B.C., and the later Babylonian exile in 586 B.C., did not spare the priests and Levites (**2 Kings 17:27–28**). Of the forty-eight Levitical cities given to the Kohathites, Gershonites, and Merarites, only five towns are noted as being re-occupied by the post-exilic returnees: Anathoth (**Ezra 2:23; Nehemiah 7:27; 11:32**), Geba (**Ezra 2:26; Nehemiah 7:30; 11:31; 12:29**), and Gibeon (**Nehemiah 7:25**; called Gibbar in **Ezra 2:20**) from the tribe of Benjamin; Jarmuth (**Nehemiah 11:29**) from the tribe of Issachar; and Kiriath Arba (Hebron) from the tribe of Judah (**Nehemiah 11:25**).[61]

Notes

1. Also, refer to the chart "**2 Chronicles 29**: The Kohathite Priests, Levites, and Singers Who Cleansed the Temple During the Reign of King Hezekiah of Judah."

2. The descendants of Kohath (the Kohathites) were the clans of Amram (the Amramites), Izhar (the Izharites), Hebron (the Hebronites), and Uzziel (the Uzzielites; **Numbers 3:27**).

3. The descendants of Gershon (the Gershonites) were the clans of Libni (the Libnites) and Shimei (the Shimeites; **Numbers 3:21**). Libni (**1 Chronicles 6:20**) is also called Ladan (**1 Chronicles 23:7**). In the chart, the line of Libni/Ladan follows the lineage given in **1 Chronicles 6:20–21**, although **1 Chronicles 23:8–9** gives the *descendants* of Ladan as "Jehiel the first, Zetham and Joel—three in all" and **1 Chronicles 26:22** clarifies that "the sons of Jehieli, [were] Zetham and his brother Joel. They were in charge of the treasuries of the temple of the Lord."

4. The descendants of Merari (the Merarites) were the clans of Mahli (the Mahlites) and Mushi (the Mushites; **Numbers 3:33**).

5. A descendant of Hebron named Eliel lived at the time of King David (**1 Chronicles 15:9**).

6. Izhar (**Exodus 6:18, 21; Numbers 16:1; 1 Chronicles 6:2, 18, 38; 23:12**) is otherwise Amminadab (**1 Chronicles 6:22**). Izhar/Amminadab the Koahathite is not Amminadab, a descendant of Uzziel (a Levitical Kohathite; **1 Chronicles 15:10**), nor Amminadab the son of Ram in the tribe of Judah (cf. **Ruth 4:19; 1 Chronicles 2:10; Matthew 1:4; Luke 3:33**).

7. The sons/descendants of Shimei, the son of Gershon, are likely those given in **1 Chronicles 23:10**: Jahath, Ziza, Jeush, and Beriah. The sons/descendants of Shimei the Gersonite given in **1 Chronicles 23:9**: "Shelomoth, Haziel, and Haran—three in all" may refer to the sons/descendants of Shimei (the son of Jahath, the son of Libni/Ladan, the son of Gershon) thereby explaining the ensuing phrase "these were the heads of the families of Ladan."

8. Libni (**Exodus 6:17; Numbers 3:18; 1 Chronicles 6:17, 20**) is otherwise Ladan (**1 Chronicles 23:7–9; 26:21**). For the "sons [descendants] of Ladan," see note 3 and the chart "**1 Chronicles 23**: The Twenty-Four Levitical Leaders (Gershonites, Kohathites, and Merarites) Who Oversaw the Religious Personnel in Solomon's Temple."

9. The Mahli–Libni–Shimei–Uzzah–Shimea–Haggiah–Asaiah lineage is given in **1 Chronicles 6:29–30**. Other sons of Mahli are Eleazar and Kish (**1 Chronicles 23:21**). However, Eleazar "died without having sons: he had only daughters. [So] Their cousins, the sons of Kish, married them" (**1 Chronicles 23:21–22**; cf. **24:28**).

10. Aaron's lineage, which is carefully documented by the Chronicler in the late fifth century, originates with Aaron the first high priest (who was born ca. 1529 B.C.) and continues to Jozadak, the high priest who was taken into exile by Nebuchadnezzer in 586 B.C. (**1 Chronicles 6:3–15**), a span of nearly 1000 years. See the discussion of the high priests in the charts "**Ezra 7**: Ezra, Priestly Scribe and Teacher of the Law (Post-Exile)" and "**Supplement 2**: The High Priests of Israel."

11. Elisheba was a Judahite, the daughter of Amminadab and the sister of Nahshon (**Exodus 6:23**). Elisheba's marriage to Aaron shows that the entire Aaronic priesthood derives its ancestry from both the tribe of Levi and the tribe of Judah.

12. Eleazar married one of the daughters of Putiel (**Exodus 6:25**), perhaps an Egyptian name from an Egyptian root (*p'-nḥśy*), meaning "black people"

("פִּינְחָס," *HALOT* 2:926), and "Putiel" may be an Egyptian place name (*p*ʾ*-dy*, "Libya"? "פּוּטִיאֵל," *HALOT* 2:917–18). If true, this indicates that the marriage of Eleazar the Aaronic high priest was indeed married to an Egyptian woman and may explain why they named their son Phinehas, meaning "Ethopian, black man."

13. The Eli priesthood descended from the Aaron–Ithamar–Eli line (**1 Samuel 1:3; 2:12–17, 34; 4:4, 11, 17, 21; 14:3; 21:1; 22:9, 11, 20; 23:6, 9; 30:7; 2 Samuel 8:17; 15:27; 1 Kings 2:26–27; 1 Chronicles 18:16; 24:3, 6**). See chart "**1 Samuel 1**: Eli and the Eli Priesthood."

14. This Shimei (the son of Jahath and the father of Zimmah) is known from the lineage in **1 Chronicles 6:42**; for unknown reasons, Shimei is not listed in the lineage of Gershon in **1 Chronicles 6:20**.

15. Korah was one of the main instigators of the Korah–Reubenite rebellion (**Numbers 16**); although Korah died, "the line of Korah [Korah's descendants] . . . did not die out" (**Numbers 26:11**). The sons of Korah wrote **Psalms 42, 44–49, 84–85,** and **87–88. Exodus 6:24** says "the sons of Korah were Assir, Elkanah, and Abiasaph [Ebiasaph]," but **1 Chronicles 6:22–24** clarifies that the *sons* listed in **Exodus 6:24** were actually sons-of-sons: "the descendants of Kohath: Amminadab [Izhar] his son, Korah his son, Assir his son, Elkanah his son, Ebiasaph [Abiasaph] his son, Assir his son, Tahath his son, Uriel his son, Uzziah his son, and Shaul his son." Likewise, in recounting the lineage of the chief musician Heman (**1 Chronicles 6:33–38**) and the lineage of Shallum the gatekeeper (**1 Chronicles 9:19**), Korah's son and grandson (i.e., Assir and Elkanah) are omitted. The chart above records the sons of Korah as given in **1 Chronicles 6:22–23**.

The descendants of Korah were known as the "Korahites" (**Exodus 6:24; 1 Chronicles 9:19**); however, because they were also descendants of Kohath, the descendants of Korah may be referred to as "Kohathite–Korahite" priests in some charts (e.g., see chart "**1 Chronicles 26**: The Kohathite–Korahite and Merarite Gatekeepers in Solomon's Temple").

16. Joah (**1 Chronicles 6:21**) is otherwise Ethan (**1 Chronicles 6:42**). **Second Chronicles 29:12** notes that Joah the Gershonite had a son named Eden.

17. Mishael (**Exodus 6:22; Leviticus 10:4**) is Micah (**1 Chronicles 23:20; 24:24**); his son/descendant was Shamir (**1 Chronicles 24:24**).

18. Elzaphan (**Exodus 6:22; Leviticus 10:4**)—also called Elizaphan (**Numbers 3:30; 1 Chronicles 15:8; 2 Chronicles 29:13**)—was a contemporary of Moses. Elzaphan's descendant Shemaiah lived at the time of King David, 1011–971 B.C. (**1 Chronicles 15:8**), and his other descendants, Shimri and Jeiel, were contemporaries of King Hezekiah, 715–686 B.C. (cf. **2 Chronicles 29:13**).

19. Iddo (**1 Chronicles 6:21**) is alias Adaiah (**1 Chronicles 6:41**). Iddo is perhaps short for Adaiah (עִדּוֹ or עֲדָיָה).

20. Ebiasaph (**1 Chronicles 6:23, 37; 9:19**) is Abiasaph (**Exodus 6:24**) and Asaph (**1 Chronicles 26:1**). He was a *descendant* of Korah, not a *son* of Korah as it reads in **Exodus 6:24** and **1 Chronicles 6:37** (NIV; cf. **1 Chronicles 6:22–23**). For descendants in the Korah–Ebiasaph/Abiasaph/Asaph–Kore line who served as gatekeepers, see charts "**1 Chronicles 9**: Registry and Genealogy of the Levitical Gatekeepers and the Priestly Overseer of the Grain Offerings in the Second Temple (Post-Exile)" and "**1 Chronicles 26**: The Kohathite–Korahite and Merarite Gatekeepers in Solomon's Temple."

21. The "lasting" Aaronic priesthood through Phinehas the son of Eleazar, the son of Aaron, is explained in **Exodus 29:9; Numbers 25:13;** and **1 Chronicles 6:49–53**. For more information on the succession of all the high priests, see chart "**Supplement 2**: The High Priests of Israel."

22. Jeatherai (**1 Chronicles 6:21**) is otherwise Ethni (**1 Chronicles 6:41**).

23. Kishi (**1 Chronicles 6:44**) is otherwise Kushaiah (**1 Chronicles 15:17**); another descendant in this Merarite lineage, named "Kish son of Abdi," was a contemporary of King Hezekiah, 715–686 B.C. (**2 Chronicles 29:12**).

24. Ethan (**1 Chronicles 6:44; 15:17, 19**) is alias Jeduthun (**1 Chronicles 9:16; 16:38, 41–42; 25:1, 3, 6; 2 Chronicles 5:12; 29:14; 35:15**). Ethan/Jeduthun was one of the three chief musicians in Solomon's Temple who made "a joyful sound with musical instruments: lyres, harps and cymbals" (**1 Chronicles 15:16**). He was also "the king's seer" (**2 Chronicles 35:15**). For the lineage of Ethan (Jeduthun), see **1 Chronicles 6:44–47** and **Nehemiah 11:17**. Jeduthun is identified as the "director of music" in the titles of **Psalms 39, 62,** and **77. Psalm 89**, titled "a *maskil* of Ethan the Ezrahite," may refer to Ethan/Jeduthun the Levitical Merarite or, more likely, to Ethan the Ezrahite, a Judahite descendant of Zerah, who was "a wise man" (cf. **1 Kings 4:31; 1 Chronicles 2:6, 8**). An Ethan/Jeduthun descendant named Abda/Obadiah who lived in post-exilic Jerusalem was among the key Levitical leaders (**Nehemiah 11:17**; cf. **1 Chronicles 9:16**).

25. Elkanah #2 (the son of Joel) is the same as the Elkanah figure in **1 Chronicles 6:25**.

26. Berekiah, the father of Asaph and the son of Shimea, was a Gershonite (**1 Chronicles 6:39; 15:17**) and therefore cannot be Berekiah the son of Asa, the son of Elkanah, a Kohathite (**1 Chronicles 9:16**).

27. For the lineage of Asaph, see **1 Chronicles 6:39–43**. He was one of the three chief musicians in Solomon's Temple and the composer of **Psalms 50** and **73–83**. For other sons of Asaph, see chart "**1 Chronicles 25**: The Twenty-Four Musician Leaders in Solomon's Temple." An Asaph descendant named Mattaniah lived in post-exilic Jerusalem and served as the director of the Levites who led in thanksgiving and prayer (**Nehemiah 11:17**); also, another Asaph descendant named Uzzi in post-exilic Jerusalem served as the chief officer over the Levites (**Nehemiah 11:22**).

28. The sons of Ethan/Jeduthun are described as Levitical gatekeepers (**1 Chronicles 16:42**) and as musicians who accompanied their father in prophesying with the harp, cymbal, and the lyre (**1 Chronicles 25:3; 2 Chronicles 5:12**). The sons of Jeduthun included Gedaliah, Zeri (Izri), Jeshaiah, Shimei, Hashabiah, and Mattithiah (**1 Chronicles 25:9, 11, 15, 17, 19, 21**). Two descendants of Ethan/Jeduthun's, named Shemaiah and Uzziel, lived in the days of King Hezekiah (715–686 B.C.) and helped in the (re)consecration of Solomon's Temple (**2 Chronicles 29:14**). Obed-Edom, one of the famous gatekeepers, was the son of Ethan/Jeduthun (**1 Chronicles 16:38**; see chart "**2 Samuel 6**: Obed-Edom, the Levitical Gatekeeper and Keeper of the Ark").

29. Zadok was the high priest under David and Solomon, ca. 1011–931 B.C. (**2 Samuel 8:17; 1 Chronicles 18:16**) and the originator of the Zadokite priesthood. He corresponds to Zadok #11 in chart "**Supplement 2**: The High Priests of Israel." Zadok was a *faithful* high priest in Solomon's Temple. The Zadokite priests are contrasted with the *unfaithful* priests of the Eli priesthood (from the Aaron–Ithamar–Eli–Abiathar line). During the reign of King David (1011–971 B.C.), Zadok and Abiathar held an unusual co–high priest position; however, the Eli priesthood (under Abiathar) ended during the early part of Solomon's reign when Solomon dismissed Abiathar and sent him home to Anathoth (**1 Kings 2:26–27, 35**); see charts "**1 Samuel 1**: Eli and the Eli Priesthood" and "**1 Chronicles 24**: Genealogical Registry of the Twenty-Four Divisions of Kohathite Attending Priests Who Rotated Service in Solomon's Temple (Sixteen from the Aaron–Eleazar–Zadok Line and Eight from the Aaron–Ithamar Line)."

30. Zophai (**1 Chronicles 6:26**) is also Zuph (**1 Chronicles 6:35**). He was the eponymous ancestor of the Zuphites (cf. **1 Samuel 1:1**).

31. The sons/descendants of Asaph ministered by "prophesying accompanied by harps, lyres and cymbals" and were under their father's (Asaph's) supervision (**1 Chronicles 25:1–2**). Asaph's descendants included Zakkur/Zabdi/Zikri, Joseph, Nethaniah, Asarelah/Jesharelah (**1 Chronicles 9:15; 25:2, 9–10, 12, 14; Nehemiah 11:17; 12:35**); Jahaziel, Zechariah, Benaiah (**2 Chronicles 20:14**), though this is not referring to the warrior, Benaiah the son of Jehoiada (**2 Samuel 8:18; 20:23; 23:20–22; 1 Kings 1:8, 26, 32, 36, 38, 44,** etc.) nor to Benaiah the Pirathonite (**2 Samuel 23:30; 1 Chronicles 11:31; 27:14**). Jeiel, Mattaniah (**2 Chronicles 20:14; 29:13**); Mika/Micaiah, Mattaniah, Hashabiah, Bani, Uzzi (**Nehemiah 11:17, 22**); Shemaiah, Jonathan, Zechariah (**Nehemiah 12:35**); Hanan (**Nehemiah 13:13**); and probably Shemaiah, Azarel, Milalai, Gilalai, Maai, Nethanel, Judah, and Hanani as well (**Nehemiah 12:36**).

32. Ahimaaz the high priest was the father of Ahinoam, the wife of Saul (cf. **1 Samuel 14:50; 2 Samuel 15:27**). Ahinoam's father corresponds to Ahimaaz #12 in chart "**Supplement 2**: The High Priests of Israel."

33. Nahath (**1 Chronicles 6:26**) is called Toah (**1 Chronicles 6:34**) and Tohu (**1 Samuel 1:1**).

34. Eliab (**1 Chronicles 6:27**) is also Eliel (**1 Chronicles 6:34**) or Elihu (**1 Samuel 1:1**).

35. Johanan, the father of Azariah, is characterized as "he who served as priest in the temple Solomon built in Jerusalem" (**1 Chronicles 6:10**).

36. Of the four men named Elkanah in the Kohathite-Izhar–Korahite line (Elkanah #1–4), Elkanah #4 "from Ramathaim, a Zuphite from the hill country of Ephraim," was the husband of Hannah and father of Samuel, the last prophet-judge of Israel (**1 Samuel 1:1**). Elkanah #4 was in a line of Kohathite attending priests but not in the line of the Kohathite high priests. Elkanah #4 was possibly an ancestor of Zechariah, the Levitical priest/musician who lived in the villages of the Netophathites (**1 Chronicles 9:16; Nehemiah 12:28**) and Zechariah is described as the last martyr of the Old Testament (**Matthew 23:35**); see note 43. For chronological reasons, Elkanah #4 (Samuel's father) is not the same person as Elkanah the Korahite who served in David's army at Ziklag, ca. 1012–1011 B.C. (cf. **1 Chronicles 12:6**).

37. Azariah served as the high priest under King Solomon, 971–931 B.C. (**1 Kings 4:2**).

38. Berekiah (the son of Asa, the son of Elkanah) lived in the villages of the Netophathites, which included the town of Netophah in the hill country of Judah near Bethlehem where musicians dwelled (**1 Chronicles 9:16; Nehemiah 12:28**; cf. **7:26**).

39. Meraioth is not mentioned in the major list of high priests in **1 Chronicles 6:1–15,** but he is noted in the lineage of "Azariah son of Hilkiah, the son of Meshullam, the son of Zadok, the son of Meraioth, the son of Ahitub, the official in charge of the house of God [Second Temple]" (**1 Chronicles 9:11**) and in the lineage of "Seraiah son of Hilkiah, the son of Meshullam, the son of Zadok, the son of Meraioth, the son of Ahitub, the official in charge of the house of God [Second Temple]" (**Nehemiah 11:11**). See Meraioth #18 in chart "**Supplement 2**: The High Priests of Israel."

40. See chart "**2 Chronicles 22**: Probable Genealogy for Jehoiada the Priest who Masterminded the Overthrow of Queen Athaliah of Judah."

41. For Heman's lineage, see **1 Chronicles 6:33–38**. Heman was one of the three chief musicians in Solomon's Temple and served as "the king's seer" (**1 Chronicles 25:5–6;** see also **1 Chronicles 15:17, 19; 16:42; 2 Chronicles 5:12**). The title of **Psalm 88**—"A song. . . . A *maskil* of Heman the Ezrahite"—probably refers to Heman the Levitical Kohathite, alluding to his wisdom and ability to prophesy in song.

42. For this enigmatic priest, see Azariah #19 in chart "**Supplement 2**: The High Priests of Israel."

43. Jesus spoke of a priest named "Zechariah son [descendant?] of Berekiah" who was "murdered between the temple and the altar" (**Matthew 23:35**; cf. **Luke 11:51**). He was most likely the priest called "Zechariah son of Jehoiada [presumably a *descendant* of Berekiah] the priest" (**2 Chronicles 24:17–22, 25**) who was murdered on the orders of King Joash, ca. 835–796 B.C. (**2 Chronicles 24:21**). Interestingly, the martyred Zechariah was from the Kohathite–Korahite line of priests and appears to be a distant relative of Elkanah #4 (Samuel's father). The other "priest" to whom Jesus alluded was Abel in **Genesis 4:8** (cf. **Matthew 23:35; Luke 11:51**). Thus, all the prophets "from A to Z" had been persecuted by those who refused to hear them. A significant association between Berekiah and Elkanah (Kohathite–Korahite line) is noted in **1 Chronicles 15:23** where these Levitical priests are identified as doorkeepers for the ark of the covenant; see note 15 in chart "**1 Chronicles 9**: Seven Levitical Leaders in the Second Temple (Post-Exile)." [Alternatively, Zechariah son of Berekiah in the Gospels *could be* a Gershonite, the brother of Asaph the musician and the son of Berekiah (see notes 26 and 27), although the Gershonites, in general, served in more of a Levitical supportive role than that suggested by the context of the New Testament passages. Thus, a Kohathite–Korathite lineage for the martyred Zechariah is favored over that of a Gershonite lineage.] For chronological reasons, Zechariah the martyred priest in the days of King Joash (ca. 835–796 B.C.) is not the prophet Zechariah (the son of Berekiah, the son of Iddo) who ministered in post-exilic Jerusalem, ca. 520–516 B.C.; for the latter, see chart "**Zechariah 1**: Zechariah, the Prophet of God to the Restored Community in Jerusalem (Post-Exile)."

44. Zadok was the high priest during the reign of King Hezekiah (715 –686 B.C.).

45. Shallum (**1 Chronicles 6:12–13**; **Ezra 7:2**), also called Meshullam (**1 Chronicles 9:11; Nehemiah 11:11**), served as the high priest between his father Zadok (who ministered in the days of King Hezekiah, 715–686 B.C.) and his son Hilkiah (who ministered in the days of King Josiah, 640–609 B.C.); therefore, Shallum/Meshullam ministered as the high priest in Solomon's Temple ca. 690–640 B.C. For chronological reasons, Shallum/Meshullam the high priest cannot be: (1) the priest named Meshullam in **Nehemiah 8:4** who was a contemporary of Ezra the scribe, in 458 B.C.; (2) the priest named Meshullam in **Nehemiah 10:7** who signed the covenant with the people in the days of Nehemiah, because Nehemiah returned to Jerusalem in 444 B.C.; (3) the priests named Meshullam in **Nehemiah 12:13** and **16** who were contemporaries of Joiakim the high priest (ca. 490–450/444 B.C.); (4) the Levite named Shallum, the father of Mattithiah, who was of Kohathite–Korahite heritage (**1 Chronicles 9:31**); nor (5) the Levite named Meshullam in **Nehemiah 12:33** who was part of the thanksgiving choir at the dedication of the wall around Jerusalem in 444 B.C.

46. Heman had fourteen sons and three daughters: "given him through the promises of God to exalt him" namely, his sons Bukkiah, Mattaniah, Uzziel (or Azarel), Shubael, Jerimoth, Hananiah, Hanani, Eliathah, Giddalti, Romamti-Ezer, Joshbekashah, Mallothi, Hothir, and Mahazioth (**1 Chronicles 25:4–5**; see also **1 Chronicles 25:13, 16, 18, 20, 22–31**); see chart "**1 Chronicles 25**: The Twenty-Four Musician Leaders in Solomon's Temple." The Heman descendants, Jehiel and Shimei, lived in the days of King Hezekiah, 715–686 B.C. (**2 Chronicles 29:14**).

47. Hilkiah ministered in the days of King Josiah of Judah, 640–609 B.C.

48. Azariah (designated Azariah #1 in this and other charts) was the high priest in Solomon's Temple, ca. 609 B.C. to as late as 598 B.C., in the days of Jehoahaz/Shallum, 609 B.C. and/or Eliakim/Jehoiakim, 608–598 B.C. Azariah's genealogy is given in **1 Chronicles 6:13–14** and portions of **Ezra 7:1**. Azariah #1 was the *son* of Hilkiah and the *father* of the martyred high priest Seraiah #1. This Azariah figure corresponds to Azariah #23 in chart "**Supplement 2**: The High Priests of Israel."

For chronological reasons, several other Azariah figures are proposed: Azariah #1, Azariah #2, and Azariah #3; for their identity, refer to the chart "**Ezra 7**: Ezra, Priestly Scribe and Teacher of the Law (Post-Exile)."

49. Seraiah—designated Seraiah #1 in this and other charts—corresponds to the high priest Seraiah (#24) in chart "**Supplement 2**: The High Priests of Israel." Seraiah (#1) was the high priest in Solomon's Temple at the time of Babylonian exile (**2 Kings 25:18**). Seraiah was brought by Nebuzaradan, the captain of the guard, to the king of Babylon and was killed at "Riblah, in the land of Hamath" (**2 Kings 25:18–21; Jeremiah 52:24–27**).

50. Jozadak (Jehozadak) was the high priest at the time of the exile: "Jozadak was deported when the LORD sent Judah and Jerusalem into exile by the hand of Nebuchadnezzar" (**1 Chronicles 6:15**). Apparently, he died while in captivity as there is no mention of his return to Jerusalem. Jozadak was the father of Joshua (the priest who returned to Jerusalem with Zerubbabel in 538 B.C.) and the father of Maaseiah, Eliezer, Jarib, and Gedaliah (**Ezra 10:18**). Together, Joshua and Zerubbabel led the people in building the Second Temple. References to Jozadak are given in **1 Chronicles 6:14–15; Ezra 3:2, 8; 5:2; 10:18; Nehemiah 12:26; Haggai 1:1, 12, 14; 2:2, 4; Zechariah 6:11**.

51. This Seraiah figure is designated Seraiah #2 in this and other charts. The identity of Seraiah #2 is not clearly stated in Scripture and must therefore be evaluated in context. For chronological reasons and considering the lineage of Ezra given in **Ezra 7:1–5** [see chart "**Ezra 7**: Ezra, Priestly Scribe and Teacher of the Law (Post-Exile)"], one must propose *several* Seraiah figures, two of whom are shown in the chart: (1) Seraiah #1, the high priest who was killed at Riblah in 586 B.C. (note 49); and (2) Seraiah #2, who is in a *scribal* lineage (parallel to that of the lineage of the high priests). Seraiah #2 is presumably a *son*/descendant of Seraiah #1 and the ancestor/*father* of Ezra the scribe.

Seraiah #2 returned to Jerusalem with Zerubbabel in 538 B.C. (**Ezra 2:2; Nehemiah 12:1**). Seraiah #2 corresponds to the person identified as "Seraiah" and identified as "the official in charge of the house of God [Second Temple]" (**Nehemiah 11:11**), who is quite confusingly called "Azariah" (designated Azariah #2 in other charts) in **1 Chronicles 9:11**.

For chronological reasons, Seraiah #2 is not the "Seraiah" figure of **Nehemiah 10:2** (designated "Seraiah #3" in other charts) who sealed the covenant with Nehemiah in 444 B.C.; Seraiah #3 was most likely the descendant of Seraiah #2.

For the proposed lineages of all the Seraiah figures (#2, #2, #3), see chart "**Ezra 7**: Ezra, Priestly Scribe and Teacher of the Law (Post-Exile)."

52. Joshua in **Ezra 2:2; 3:2, 8, (9?); 4:3; 5:2; 10:18; Nehemiah 7:7; 12:1, 7, 10, 26; Haggai 1:1, 12, 14; 2:2, 4;** and **Zechariah 3:1, 3, 6, 8–9; 6:11** is called Jeshua in **Ezra 2:36; 8:33**. Some of the descendants of Joshua and Joshua's brothers (Maaseiah, Eliezer, Jarib, and Gedaliah) married foreign women (**Ezra 10:18–19**). Some of Joshua's descendants, through "the descendants of Jedaiah" (Immer, Pashhur, and Harim) were active priests in the Second Temple (**Ezra 2:36–39; Nehemiah 7:39–42**). Jeshua the high priest is a different person than his contemporaries—Jeshua the "Levite," the son of Kadmiel, of the Hodaviah line, and/or Jeshua the son of Azaniah (cf. **Ezra 2:40; 3:9; Nehemiah 7:43; 9:4–5; 10:9; 12:8, 24**). **Nehemiah 12:10** summarizes the line of the high priests after Joshua: "Joshua was the father of Joiakim, Joiakim the father of Eliashib, Eliashib the father of Joiada, Joiada the father of Jonathan, and Jonathan the father of Jaddua." For information on the individual high priests, see chart "**Supplement 2**: The High Priests of Israel."

53. In **Ezra 7:1**, Ezra is called the "son of Seraiah." Ezra was likely the *descendant* (probably the grandson) of Seraiah #1 and the son of another Seraiah (shown in the chart as Seraiah #2). Ezra was the scribal priest and teacher of the Law who brought a group of returning exiles back to Jerusalem in 458 B.C. and for whom the book of **Ezra** is named.

54. The dispersion of the tribe of Levi throughout Israel was, in part, due to Jacob's blessing on Levi. In his blessing upon his sons, Jacob remarked that because of Simeon and Levi's tendency toward violence and cruelty, the Lord would "scatter them in Jacob and disperse them in Israel" (**Genesis 49:5–7**). The tribe of Simeon was subsumed into the tribe of Judah.

55. Bileam (**1 Chronicles 6:70**) was a Levitical city from the territory

of the half-tribe of Manasseh; for Ibleam as a variant of Bileam, see **Joshua 17:11** and **Judges 1:27**.

56. The process of casting lots (**1 Chronicles 24:5**) is not to be thought of as a random gambling, but likely as a casting of the Urim and Thummim, the precious stones embedded in the breastplate of the high priest. By their sparkle or some other sign, decisions could be determined under the leading of God; see **Exodus 28:29–30** and **1 Samuel 28:6**.

57. See chart "**1 Chronicles 24**: Genealogical Registry of the Twenty-Four Divisions of Kohathite Attending Priests Who Rotated Service in Solomon's Temple (Sixteen from the Aaron–Eleazar–Zadok Line and Eight from the Aaron–Ithamar Line)."

58. **Numbers 8:26** clarifies that, at age 50 (the age of retirement), the Levites could "assist their brothers in performing their duties at the tent of meeting, but they themselves must not do the [regular] work" (cf. **Numbers 8:23–26**).

59. David's intense interest in music as a vehicle for worship is seen in the great number of Psalms either attributed to him or written in tribute to him: **Psalms 3–9, 11–32, 34–41, 51–65, 68–70, 86, 101, 103, 108–110, 122, 124, 131, 133, 138–145**.

60. See the excellent treatment by C. Hassel Bullock, *Encountering the Book of Psalms* (Grand Rapids: Baker Academic, 2001), 24–34.

61. Technically, the city and surrounding pastureland of Hebron was given to the high priestly descendants of Aaron, but the fields and villages around the city were given to the Caleb (I) the Kenizzite, the son of Jephunneh, as his inheritance (cf. **Joshua 14:13–15; 21:9–12; 1 Chronicles 6:54–56**).

1 CHRONICLES 7: ISSACHAR[1]

Approximate Dating: from the birth of Issachar in ca. 1920 to 722 B.C. ***Relevant Scriptures:*** **1 Chronicles 7:1–5**; also **Genesis 30:18; 35:23; 46:13; Numbers 26:23–24; Judges 10:1; 1 Chronicles 2:1**

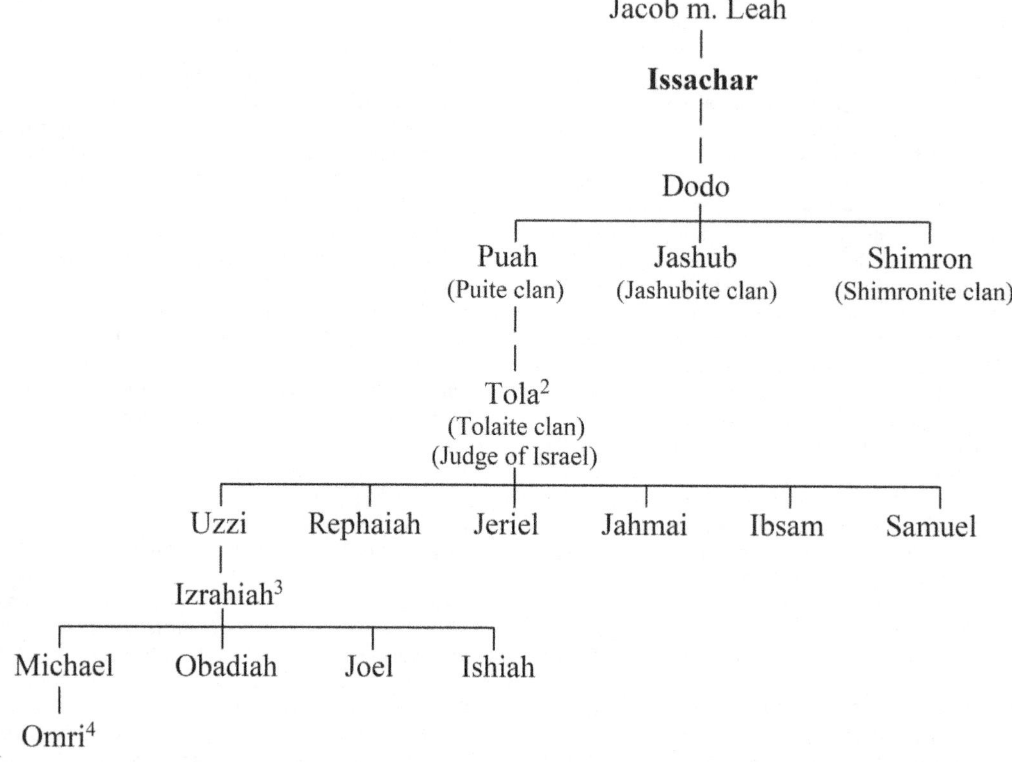

Biblical and Theological Significance

Issachar was the fifth son of Leah, whom she thought was a reward for her having given her servant Zilpah over to her husband Jacob (**Genesis 30:18**). The name Issachar, meaning "wages," recalled that Leah "hired" Jacob to sleep with her in exchange for offering to Rachel (the barren wife of Jacob) aphrodisiac mandrakes found by her (Leah's) son Reuben (**Genesis 30:1, 14–18**).

The Issachar genealogy had primarily a military function—to determine the number of fighting men from the tribe—as represented by the Tolaite, Puite, Jashubite, and Shimronite clans. Collectively, the fighting men numbered 64,300 in the second census taken before entry into the promised land (**Numbers 26:25**) and rose to 87,000 in the early monarchy period (**1 Chronicles 7:5**). At Hebron, two hundred chiefs from this tribe and their relatives, called "men who understood the times and knew what Israel should do," served in the joint ranks to make David the king over all of Israel instead of Saul (**1 Chronicles 12:32**; cf. **12:23, 32, 38**).

The Chronicler follows the convention of the author of Genesis by conflating the generations of Issachar saying, "the sons of Issachar: Tola, Puah, Jashub and Shimron—four in all" (**1 Chronicles 7:1**; cf. **Genesis 46:13**). However, the author of Judges clarifies that Tola was the "son of Puah, the son of Dodo" (**Judges 10:1**). Dodo was presumably the son/descendant of Issachar. Other persons from the tribe of Issachar were Nethanel son of Zuar (**Numbers 1:8; 2:5; 10:15**), Igal son of Joseph (**13:7**), Paltiel son of Azzan (**Numbers 34:26**), and Baasha son of Ahijah (**1 Kings 15:27**), but their specific genealogies are unknown.

In his blessing of his sons, Jacob referred to Issachar as a "rawboned donkey[5] lying down among the sheep pens" (**Genesis 49:14**). This was by no means an insult, for such an animal was highly praised as a dependable, hard-working beast easily trained and managed. Moses adds the following mysterious prophecy of Issachar (and Zebulun): "They will summon peoples to the mountain and there offer the sacrifices of the righteous; they will feast on the abundance of the seas, on the treasures hidden in the sand" (**Deuteronomy 33:18–19**). The term *seas* seems rather odd at first for a landlocked people, but Issachar's border on the Kinneret (Sea of Galilee), though minimal, was sufficient to provide for fishing in that always-rich fishing grounds. Moreover, the inclusion of Zebulun in this common blessing makes allowance for the Mediterranean, which was that tribe's western border; together, the common blessing may mean they will become wealthy by freshwater and saltwater merchantry. The mountain referred to is most likely Tabor, located on the northwest border of Issachar (**Joshua 19:22**). Its significance as a kind of "holy mountain" is attested to throughout the Scriptures (**1 Samuel 10:3; Psalm 89:12; Hosea 5:1**).

Sixteen towns and their villages were allotted to the tribe of Issachar: "Jezreel, Kesulloth, Shunem, Hapharaim, Shion, Anaharath, Rabbith, Kishion, Ebez, Remeth, En Gannim, En Haddah and Beth Pazzez. The boundary touched Tabor, Shahazumah and Beth Shemesh, and ended at the Jordan" (**Joshua 19:18–22**). The tribe of Issachar contributed four towns to be Levitical cities: Kishion, Daberath, Jarmuth, and En Gannim (**Joshua 21:28–29**).

No cities allotted to the tribe of Issachar are mentioned as being occupied in the post-exilic era (538/400 B.C.) in either **Ezra** or **Nehemiah**.

Notes

1. In this abbreviated genealogy, "genealogical gaps" are evident because only the names of important persons in this tribe are mentioned. The chart suggests where the multiple generations may have occurred (note the double vertical lines). The genealogy of Issachar primarily functions to identify fighting men in the tribe who could go to war.

2. Tola was a judge of Israel for twenty-three years. He lived in Shamir, in the hill country of Ephraim (**Judges 10:1–2**). His lineage is given as "Tola son of Puah, the son of Dodo," and Dodo was presumably the son (or descendant) of Issachar (cf. **Genesis 46:13; 1 Chronicles 7:1**). In the days of King David, the descendants of Tola numbered 22,600 fighting men (**1 Chronicles 7:2**). See chart "**Judges 10**: Tola, Sixth Judge of Israel."

3. Izrahiah and his four sons were called "chiefs." Izrahiah's sons had many wives and children. At the time of King David, the family of Izrahiah had 36,000 fighting men (**1 Chronicles 7:4**).

4. A son or descendant of Michael named Omri was head over the tribe of Issachar during the united monarchy period (**1 Chronicles 27:18**); see chart "**1 Chronicles 27**: Genealogical Record of the Leaders of the Tribes of Israel During the Davidic Monarchy."

5. חֲמֹר גָּרֶם (*khamor garem*), "bony" donkey, that is, trim and fit for work.

1 CHRONICLES 7: BENJAMIN (BENJAMITES WHO WERE FIGHTING MEN)

Approximate Dating: from the birth of Benjamin in ca. 1908 to 586 B.C. ***Relevant Scriptures:*** **1 Chronicles 7:6–12;** also **Genesis 35:18, 24; 46:19, 21; Numbers 26:38–41; 1 Chronicles 8:1–5, 11**[1]

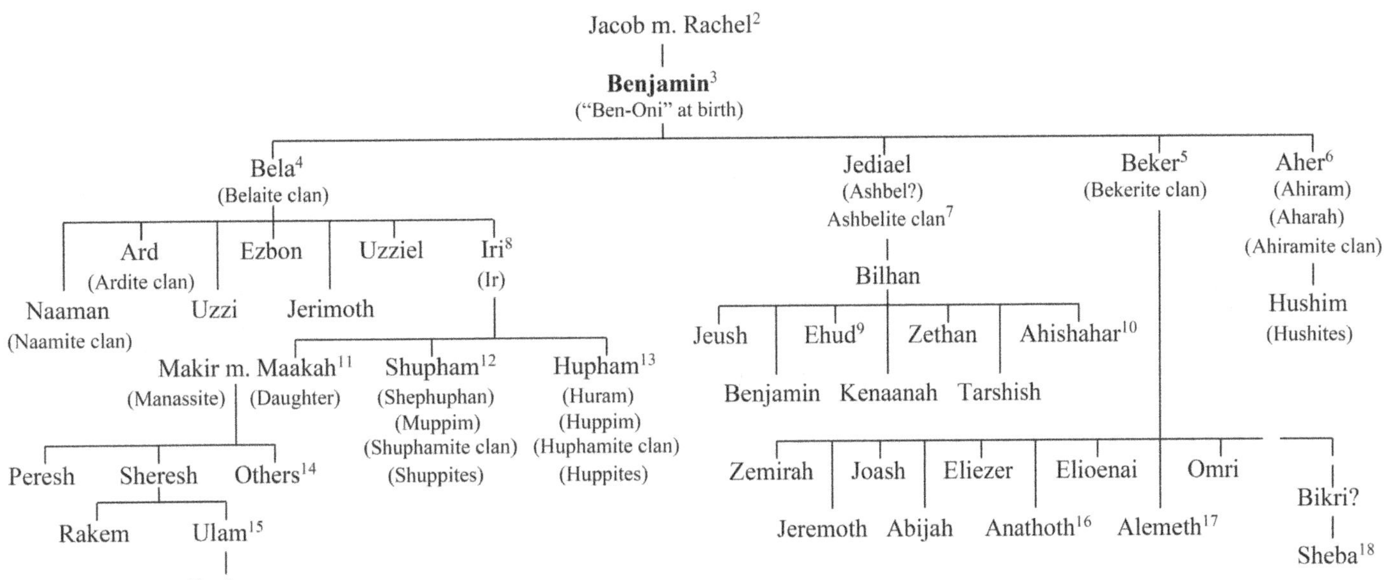

Biblical and Theological Significance

The text of **1 Chronicles 7:6–12** specifically elaborates on "fighting men" from among three of the several sons of Benjamin—specifically Bela (Belalite clan), Beker (Bekerite clan), and Jediael (possibly the same as the Ashbelite clan; **Genesis 46:21;** cf. **Numbers 26:38; 1 Chronicles 8:1**; see note 7). These fighting men numbered 22,034, 20,200, and 17,200, respectively (**1 Chronicles 7:7, 9, 11**). These numbers were clearly derived from a military census of the tribe and emphasize the militaristic aspect of the tribe[19] as a foreground to Saul,[20] who became the unifier and deliverer of the loosely federated and leaderless nation of Israel when they cried to God for relief.

The abbreviated, segmented genealogy in the chart above, which is based on **1 Chronicles 7:6–12**, should be compared to genealogical information given in more comprehensive lists of the sons/descendants of Benjamin:

- **Genesis 46:21**: "The sons of Benjamin: Bela, Beker, Ashbel, Gera, Naaman, Ehi, Rosh, Muppim, Huppim and Ard."
- **Numbers 26:38–41**: "The descendants of Benjamin by their clans were: through Bela, the Belaite clan; through Ashbel, the Ashbelite clan; through Ahiram, the Ahiramite clan; through Shupham, the Shuphamite clan; through Hupham, the Huphamite clan. The descendants of Bela through Ard and Naaman were: through Ard, the Ardite clan; through Naaman, the Naamite clan. These were the clans of Benjamin; those numbered were 45,600."
- **1 Chronicles 8:1–7**: "Benjamin was the father of Bela his firstborn, Ashbel the second son, Aharah the third, Nohah the fourth and Rapha the fifth. The sons of Bela were: Addar, Gera, Abihud, Abishua, Naaman, Ahoah, Gera, Shephuphan and Huram. These were the descendants of Ehud, who were heads of families of those living in Geba and were deported to Manahath: Naaman, Ahijah, and Gera, who deported them . . . the father of Uzza and Ahihud."

It is abundantly clear from the multiple genealogical lists for the tribe of Benjamin that the underlying purposes for their inclusion in the sacred text are varied. The dissimilar genealogical lists point to the different purpose(s) and deliberate choice(s) on the part of the compiler. Variations that may appear to be at odds or contradictory can be explained in several ways:

- Entire generations may be lacking in some lists because the omitted person (or persons) may not be relevant to the purpose/function of the list in question.
- Like other genres of literature, genealogies are constructed with certain objectives in mind: information, clarification, instruction, persuasion, points of view, and the like, and so it is with biblical literature. This does not mean that the writings are erroneous or nonfactual, but that they were composed by Spirit-filled men who were free nonetheless to take existing ideas or writings and to edit or modify them as they pleased, all without altering the intentions and objectives of the original writers.
- Is the material narrative, archival, or compendious? This and other questions of creative and/or editorial writing must be taken into consideration as well.

Notes

1. To understand the lineages of the Shuppites, Huppites, and Hushites, who are mentioned in **1 Chronicles 7:12**, selective genealogical information from **Genesis 46:21**, **Numbers 26:38–41**, and **1 Chronicles 8:1–7** is also included in the chart.

2. Benjamin, the youngest son of Jacob and Rachel, was the brother of Joseph. Rachel died giving birth to Benjamin: "As she breathed her last—for she was dying—she named her son Ben-Oni [meaning "son of my sorrow/my pain"]. But his father named him Benjamin [meaning "son of my right hand"]" (**Genesis 35:18, 24**). The land and cities allotted to the Benjamites are given in **Joshua 18:11–28**.

3. Benjamin was born in Canaan in ca. 1908 B.C. when the family was "on the way to Ephrath [Bethlehem]" (**Genesis 35:18–19**). Benjamin was "born to him [Jacob] in his old age," and Jacob's life was "closely bound up with the boy's life" (**Genesis 44:20, 30**). Given Jacob's lifespan (2006–1859 B.C.), Jacob was about 98 when Benjamin was born. For Benjamin's birth, see notes 2 & 4 in chart "**Genesis 35**: The Twelve Sons of Jacob, the Eponymous Originators of the Twelve Tribes of Israel." For post-exilic figures named Sallu and Judah from the tribe of Benjamin, see **Nehemiah 11:7, 9**.

4. Compare the restricted list of the sons of Bela in **1 Chronicles 7:7**: "The sons of Bela: Ezbon, Uzzi, Uzziel, Jerimoth, and Iri, heads of families—five in all [perhaps by one wife?]" to those listed in **1 Chronicles 8:3–5**: "The sons of Bela were Addar, Gera, Abihud, Abishua, Naaman, Ahoah, Gera, Shephuphan, and Huram." See the clans and the descendants of the Benjamites in the charts "**1 Chronicles 8**: Benjamin and His Descendants Who Settled in Geba and Manahath (Post-Exile)" and "**1 Chronicles 8**: The Benjamites Who Settled in and around Jerusalem and in Moab (Post-Exile)."

5. Beker's sons lived in Geba, approximately 7 miles north/northeast of Jerusalem.

6. Aher in **1 Chronicles 7:12** appears to be the same person as Ahiram in **Numbers 26:38** and Aharah in **1 Chronicles 8:1**.

7. Jediael, the second-born son of Benjamin (**1 Chronicles 7:6; 8:1**), may be the same person called Ashbel (of the Ashbelite clan) in **Genesis 46:21; Numbers 26:38**.

8. Iri in **1 Chronicles 7:7** appears to be the same person as Ir in **1 Chronicles 7:12**.

9. Although they share the same name, Ehud (the son of Bilhan, the son of Jedaiel, the son of Benjamin) is not the same person as Ehud the Benjamite (the son of Gera, the son of Bela) who was the second judge of Israel (cf. **Judges 3:12–30**).

10. Although some scholars have conflated Ahishahar with Shaharaim (שַׁחֲרַיִם, *shakharayim*), they appear to be distinct individuals; see the clan of Shaharaim in chart "**1 Chronicles 8**: The Benjamites Who Settled in and around Jerusalem and in Moab (Post-Exile)."

11. The NIV text of **1 Chronicles 7:15** should probably be understood to mean that Maakah was the *sister* of the Shuppites and Huppites (Benjamites) and the *wife* of Makir, the firstborn son of Manasseh (as in NKJV; *contra* NIV). The marriage of Makir the Manassite (the eponymous ancestor of the Makirite clan; **Numbers 26:29**) to Maakah the Benjaminite formed a marriage alliance between the tribe of Manasseh and the tribe of Benjamin (cf. **1 Chronicles 7:12, 15; 8:3**). See Edward Lewis Curtis and Albert Alonzo Madsen, *A Critical and Exegetical Commentary on the Books of Chronicles* (Edinburgh: T&T Clark, 1910), 152–153. See also the chart "**1 Chronicles 7**: Manasseh (The Half-Tribe of West Manasseh)."

12. Shupham was the head of the Shuphamite clan/the Shuppites (**Numbers 26:39**; see **1 Chronicles 7:12, 15**). He is also called Shephuphan (**1 Chronicles 8:5**) and Muppim (**Genesis 46:21**) and is probably the same person as *Shuppim* found in other translations. Shupham and Hupham were possibly twins.

13. Hupham, the head of the Hupahmite clan (**Numbers 26:39**), is also called Huppim (cf. **Genesis 46:21; 1 Chronicles 7:12, 15**) and Huram (**1 Chronicles 8:5**). He was the head of the Huppites. Hupham and Shupham were possibly twins.

14. See chart "**1 Chronicles 7**: Manasseh (The Half-Tribe of West Manasseh)."

15. The sons of Ulam are noted as being mighty men of valor (archers). According to **1 Chronicles 8:40**, the descendants of Ulam numbered 150 in all.

16. Anathoth is a personal name and a place name, referring to both the son of Beker and to a city within the tribe of Benjamin. Anathoth was one of the Levitical cities given to the descendants of Aaron the high priest (i.e., those in the Kohathite high priestly line; **Joshua 21:4, 18; 1 Chronicles 6:60**). Anathoth was the hometown of the Elide descendant Abiathar, who served in a co–high priest capacity with Zadok during David's reign and the early part of Solomon's reign (**Joshua 21:18; 1 Kings 2:26–27**). Anathoth was also the hometown of Jeremiah the prophet (**Jeremiah 1:1**).

17. Alemeth (called Almon in **Joshua 21:18**) is a personal name and a place name, referring to the son of Beker as well as to a city in the territory of Benjamin that was given as a Levitical city to the sons/descendants of Aaron the high priest (i.e., those in the Kohathite high priestly line; **Joshua 21:4, 18; 1 Chronicles 6:60**).

18. Sheba "the troublemaker," the son of Bikri, may have been a descendant of Beker the Benjamite (or alternatively, Sheba may have been a descendant of Aharah (?) or Beriah (?); see chart "**2 Samuel 20**: Possible Genealogy of Sheba the Rebel"). Sheba led a revolt against David when the king fled from Absalom.

Sheba found a following among the men of Israel but not the men of Judah, who remained loyal to David. At the advice of a wise woman of Abel Beth Maakah, Sheba was beheaded. The account of Sheba's revolt is found in **2 Samuel 20:1–22**.

19. Jacob's blessing in **Genesis 49:27** says, "Benjamin is a ravenous wolf; in the morning he devours the prey, in the evening he divides the plunder." The Benjamites were renowned for their military prowess and being fierce soldiers, archers, and swordsmen. Here are several examples of ruthless Benjamites: (1) the judge Ehud who brutally stabbed Eglon king of Moab (**Judges 3:12–25**); (2) King Saul, who aggressively pursed young David at various times and ordered the murder of the priests at Nob (**1 Samuel 19:10; 22:6–19**); (3) the tribe of Benjamin as a whole, who mobilized 26,000 swordsmen, including 700 select soldiers—"left-handed, each of whom could sling a stone at a hair and not miss"—to war against their fellow Israelites (**Judges 20:15–16**) (4) Abner, the military commander under Saul and David, who brutally murdered Asahel by thrusting "the butt of his spear into Asahel's stomach, and the spear came out through his back" (**2 Samuel 2:21–23**); (5) Sheba the rebel who formed an anti-David rebellion (**2 Samuel 20:1–22**); (6) Shimei the son of Gera who cursed David and his men (**2 Samuel 16:5–14**); and (7) before his conversion, Saul of Tarsus (Paul), who was known for zealously persecuting the church (**Acts 9:1–2; 22:3–5; 26:9–11; Romans 11:1; Philippians 3:5**).

20. See charts "**1 Samuel 9**: King Saul," "**1 Chronicles 8**: Benjamin and His Descendants Who Settled in Geba and Manahath (Post-Exile)," "**1 Chronicles 8**: The Benjamites Who Settled in and around Jerusalem and in Moab (Post-Exile)," "**1 Chronicles 8 & 9**: The Descendants of King Saul Living in Gibeon and Jerusalem (Post-Exile)," and "**1 Chronicles 9**: The Leaders from the Tribes of Judah and Benjamin Who Dwelled in Jerusalem (Post-Exile)."

1 CHRONICLES 7: NAPHTALI

Approximate Dating: from the birth of Naphtali in ca. 1923 to 538/400 B.C. ***Relevant Scriptures:*** **1 Chronicles 7:13**; also **Genesis 29:29; 30:3–8; 35:25; 46:24; Numbers 26:48–49**

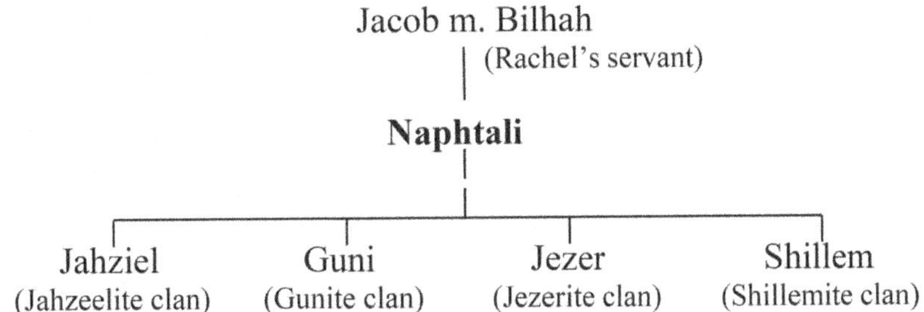

Biblical and Theological Significance

The Chronicler follows the genealogical convention of the author of Genesis by giving only the (essential) names of Naphtali's sons. Nothing further of their exact descendants or their specific locations is provided.[1] Genealogical gaps are obvious.

Jacob's wives, Rachel and Leah, competed to see who could produce the most sons; this contest left the beloved wife out of the running because Rachel was infertile. Rachel proposed that her servant Bilhah could be a surrogate mother, to which Jacob agreed (**Genesis 30:1–8**). Bilhah bore Jacob two sons, Dan and Naphtali. The latter's name derives from the root פתל, *ptl*, "winding, twisting," and with the prefix נ meaning "entangle," as in wrestling, perhaps suggestive of Rachel's struggle with her sister Leah for children. Additionally, it perhaps alludes to a long and hard labor for Bilhah that was finally rewarded with the birth of Naphtali. When Jacob blessed his twelve sons, he pronounced the enigmatic "Naphtali is a doe set free that bears beautiful fawns" (**Genesis 49:21**). Moses' farewell blessing is fuller and more intelligible—"Naphtali is abounding with the favor of the Lord and is full of his blessing; he will inherit southward to the lake [Sea of Galilee]" (**Deuteronomy 33:23**). The census report of **Numbers 1:42–43** attributed to Naphtali 53,400 men of war, the sixth largest among the tribes.

The northern border of Naphtali is not defined, but it certainly reached as far as the modern border between Lebanon and Israel. The eastern border was the Upper Jordan valley as far as Kedesh Naphtali, approximately ten miles north of Hazor. The southern boundary extended as far as the south end of Kinnereth (Sea of Galilee), with Zebulun and Asher on the west. Cities in the general allotment to Naphtali included Ziddim, Zer, Hammath, Rakkath, Kinnereth, Adamah, Ramah, Hazor, Kedesh, Edrei, En Hazor (Hazor), Iron, Migdal El, Horem, Beth Anath, and Beth Shemesh (**Joshua 19:32–38**). Additionally, the Naphtali cities of Hammoth Dor, Kartan, and Kedesh in Galilee were given as Levitical cities to the Gershonites (**Joshua 21:32–33**); also, Kedesh in Galilee was a city of refuge (**Joshua 20:7**). Naphtali was not able to completely drive out the Canaanites who lived in Beth Shemesh or Beth Anath, although Canaanites in that vicinity became forced laborers for Naphtali (**Judges 1:33**).

Otherwise, the records reveal very little else about the tribe of Naphtali and its history subsequent to the conquest and occupation of Canaan, except for the mention that Tiglath-Pileser III (Pul), king of Assyria (745–727 B.C.) "took Ijon, Abel Beth Maakah, Janoah, Kedesh and Hazor. He took Gilead and Galilee, including all the land of Naphtali, and deported the people to Assyria" (**2 Kings 15:29**).

In the post-exile era, some exiles returned from Babylon and dwelt in the Naphtali cities of Hazor (**Nehemiah 11:33**) and Ramah (**Ezra 2:26; Nehemiah 7:30; 11:33**).

Notes

1. Other descendants from the tribe of Naphtali, for which kinship links are unknown, include Ahira son of Enan (**Numbers 1:15; 2:29, 7:78, 83; 10:27**); Nahbi son of Vophsi (**Numbers 13:14**); Pedahel son of Ammihud (**Numbers 34:28**); the army commander Barak, son of Abinoam of Kedesh (**Judges 4:6**); the mother of Huram, the craftsman of Solomon's Temple (**1 Kings 7:13**); and Jerimoth son of Azriel (**1 Chronicles 27:19**).

1 CHRONICLES 7: MANASSEH (THE HALF-TRIBE OF WEST MANASSEH)

Approximate Dating: from Manasseh's birth in Egypt between 1884 and 1878 B.C. to ca. 722 B.C.[1] ***Relevant Scriptures:*** **1 Chronicles 7:14–19;** also **Genesis 41:45, 50–52; 46:19–22; Numbers 26:28–33; 27:1; 32:39–42; 36:10–12; Joshua 17:1–6, 11–13; Judges 1:27; 1 Chronicles 2:21–23; 7:12**

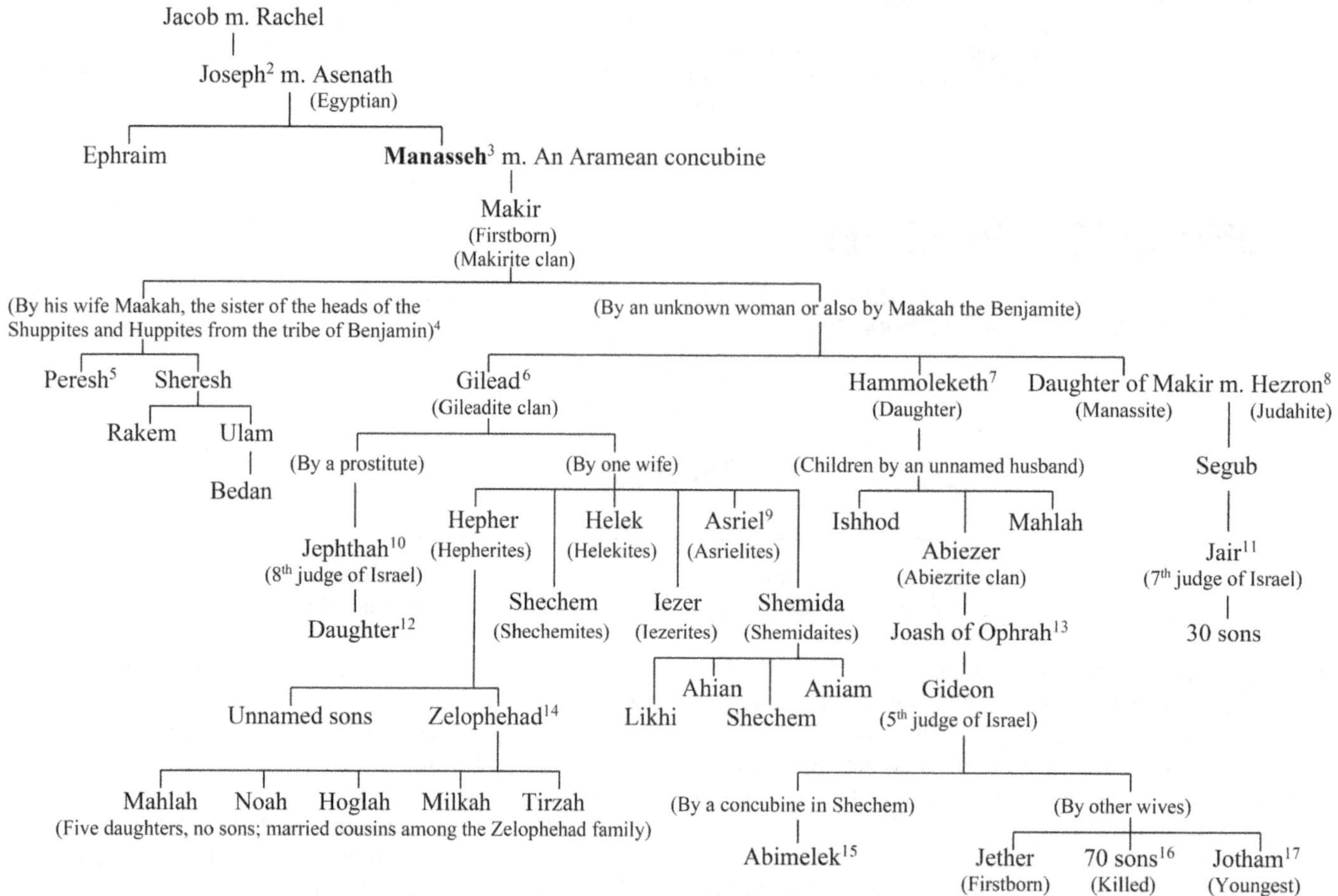

Biblical and Theological Significance

The genealogy in the chart above is for both East- and West-Manasseh. The genealogy for the Manassite tribe, containing information about both half-tribes, is complicated by the fact that the genealogy functions variously:

1. Records from a military census, stressing the complement of clans within the tribe and the number of men who could go to war (cf. **Numbers 26:2, 29–34**);
2. Records from the tribal allotment of lands and cities they occupied (even towns occupied within the tribes of Issachar and Asher) or could not overtake from the Canaanites (**Numbers 32:39–42; 36:10–12; Joshua 17:1–6, 11–13; Judges 1:27**); and
3. Similar to more traditional genealogical passages (**Genesis 41:45, 50–52; 46:19–22; 1 Chronicles 2:21–23; 7:12, 14–19**).

The territory of the half-tribe of West Manasseh extended southeast from Asher to Mikmethath, east of Shechem, and then southward to include the area of Tappuah. Then the boundary continued south to the north bank of the Kanah Ravine and from there westward to the Mediterranean. According to **Joshua 17:11–13** (cf. **Judges 1:27**), "Within Issachar and Asher, Manasseh also had Beth Shan, Ibleam and the people of Dor, Endor, Taanach and Megiddo, together with their surrounding settlements (the third in the list is Naphoth). Yet the Manassites were not able to occupy these towns, for the Canaanites were determined to live in that region. However, when the Israelites grew stronger, they subjected the Canaanites to forced labor but did not drive them out completely." The major towns in West Manasseh were Beth Shean, Dor, Endor, Ibleam, Megiddo, Shechem, Taanach, Thebez, and Tirzah.

Several noteworthy things occurred in this tribe:

1. Three judges of Israel were from the tribe of Manasseh; see the chart "**Judges 6**: Gideon (5th Judge) and His Son, Abimelek the False Judge, Jair (7th Judge), and Jephthah (8th Judge)–Judges of Israel from the Tribe of Manasseh."
2. The challenge and amendment of the Mosaic Law by the daughters of Zelophehad, which allowed women to inherit property within their father's clan (**Numbers 27:1–11; 36:1–2; Joshua 17:3–6**); and

3. Intermarriage between Manassites and other tribes:
   A. The marriage of Makir the Manassite to Maakah the Benjamite;[18] and
   B. The marriage of a Manassite woman (the daughter of Makir) to a prominent Judahite man, Hezron.[19]

First Chronicles 9:3 comments that "Those from Judah, from Benjamin, and from Ephraim and Manasseh" lived in Jerusalem in the post-exile (ca. 538/400 B.C.), but no specific towns allotted to the tribe of Manasseh are specifically mentioned in **Ezra** and **Nehemiah** as being occupied/re-occupied.

Notes

1. For Manasseh's birth, see note 2 in chart "**Genesis 46**: The Extended Family of Jacob (70 Descendants) Who Migrated to Egypt." Most of the northern tribes, including Manasseh, were destroyed in the Assyrian invasion and destruction in 722 B.C. and the people dispersed in the diaspora, although some Manssites returned and lived in Yehud in the post-exile (**1 Chronicles 9:3**).

2. Joseph was the son of Jacob and Rachel (**Genesis 30:24–25**). While in Egypt, Joseph was given in marriage to an Egyptian woman named Asenath the daughter of Potipherah, a priest of On (Heliopolis) (**Genesis 41:45–52**). Both Manasseh and Ephraim were born in Egypt (**Genesis 46:20**), "before the years of famine came" (**Genesis 41:50**) in 1877 B.C. (see note 2 in chart "**Genesis 46**: The Extended Family of Jacob (Seventy Descendants) Who Migrated to Egypt").

3. Manasseh was the firstborn son; his name means "making forgetful," as in "It is because God has made me forget all my trouble and all my father's [Jacob's] household" (**Genesis 41:51**).

4. Maakah was Makir's *wife* (**1 Chronicles 7:16**, NIV); furthermore, Maakah was the *sister* of the clan leaders of the Huppites and Shuppites of the tribe of Benjamin (**1 Chronicles 7:15**; cf. **v. 12**)—"The Shuppites and Huppites were the descendants of Ir [probably the same as Iri, the son of Bela, the son of Benjamin]" (**1 Chronicles 7:12**; cf. **vv. 6–7**). This means Maakah was the *sister* of Huppim/Hupham/Huram (the head of the Huphamite/Huppite clan) and the *sister* of Shupham/Shephuphan/Muppim (the head of the Shuphamite/Shuppite clan), who may have been twins themselves (cf. **Genesis 46:21; Numbers 26:39; 1 Chronicles 7:12; 8:3–5**).

The text of **1 Chronicles 7:15** (NIV) reads: "His [Makir's] sister's name was Maakah." This is clearly a scribal inadvertence. For MT אֲחֹתוֹ "his sister," read אִשְׁתּוֹ "his wife." The text of **1 Chronicles 7:15–17** (NKJV; *contra* NIV) is correct and clearer in its translation (and the kinship relationship that is followed in the chart above): "Machir took as his wife the sister of Huppim and Shuppim, whose name was Maachah. . . . Maachah the wife of Machir bore a son, and she called his name Peresh. The name of his brother was Sheresh, and his sons were Ulam and Rakem. The son of Ulam was Bedan. These were the sons of Gilead son of Makir, the son of Manasseh"—since those sons/descendants were considered the *sons of Gilead*, some scholars have proposed that Maakah was the wife of *Gilead* (not Makir); for an explanation, see Edward Lewis Curtis and Albert Alonzo Madsen, *A Critical and Exegetical Commentary on the Books of Chronicles* (Edinburgh: T& T Clark, 1910), 152–53, https://archive.org/details/criticalexegetic11curtuoft/page/152/mode/2up?q=1+Chronicles+7%3A18.

5. Peresh and Sheresh may have been twins.

6. Gilead is a personal name and a place name: "So Moses gave Gilead to the Makirites, the descendants of Manasseh, and they settled there" (**Numbers 32:40**; cf., **26:29**). The distinguished man Barzillai was a Gileadite (**2 Samuel 17:27; 19:31; Ezra 2:61; Nehemiah 7:63**); see chart "**2 Samuel 17**: Barzillai the Gileadite."

7. Hammoleketh means "she who reigns." She bore three sons (Ishhod, Abiezer, and Mahlah; **1 Chronicles 7:18**), but uncharacteristically, her husband is not identified. One interpretation is that she may have had the three sons by her *brother* Gilead, based, in part, on Gideon's statement that his clan was the "weakest" (דַּל, *dal*) of all the Abiezrites (see note 16) and the weakest of his people (**Judges 6:15**). However, to take those self-abasing statements as evidence of Gideon being an offspring of incest is to go beyond the evidence. Prudence would suggest that the text is simply silent as to her husband.

8. When the daughter of Makir married the sixty-year-old Hezron (the son of Perez from the tribe of Judah), this connected the tribe of Manasseh to the tribe of Judah by marriage. See chart "**1 Chronicles 2**: Hezron."

9. Asriel in **1 Chronicles 7:14** should be understood to be the son of Gilead, the grandson of Makir, and the great-grandson of Manasseh.

10. In Jephthah's six-year judgeship over Israel (ca. 1106–1100 B.C.), he delivered the Israelites from oppression by the Ammonites and the Philistines (**Judges 10:6–10; 11:4–33**). His heritage as the son of a prostitute explains the context of **Judges 11:7**: "Didn't you [elders of Gilead] hate me and drive me from my father's house? Why do you come to me now, when you're in trouble?"

11. Jair "of Gilead" was the seventh judge of Israel and led the nation for twenty-two years, although the exact years are unknown (**Judges 10:3–5**). Jair's grandfather was Hezron the Judahite (the son of Perez, the son of Judah); Jair's grandmother (Hezron's wife) was the daughter of Makir the Manassite (**1 Chronicles 2:21–22**). Strikingly, from a genealogical perspective, Jair's descent is traced *matrilineally*, for he was considered to be from the tribe of Manasseh (his *mother's* side) rather than from the tribe of Judah (his *father's* side; cf. **Numbers 32:41; Deuteronomy 3:14; Judges 10:3–5; 1 Kings 4:13; 1 Chronicles 2:21–23**). Jair and his thirty sons took small towns and cities in the region of Gilead and Bashan and renamed them "Havvoth Jair" (**Numbers 32:40–41; Deuteronomy 3:14; Judges 10:4**; cf. **Joshua 13:30; 1 Chronicles 2:23**). Jair the judge from the tribe of Manasseh is a different person than Jair the Bethlehemite, who was the father of Elhanan (**2 Samuel 21:19; 1 Chronicles 20:5**). See chart "**Judges 6**: Gideon (Fifth Judge) and His Son, Abimelek the False Judge, Jair (Seventh Judge), and Jephthah (Eighth Judge)–Judges of Israel from the Tribe of Manasseh."

12. The tragic story of Jephthah's only child, his virgin daughter, is given in **Judges 11:30–40**. Jephthah's rash vow for success in battle threatened her life: "whatever comes out of the door of my house to meet me when I return in triumph from the Ammonites will be the LORD's, and I will sacrifice it as a burnt offering" (**Judges 11:31**). Since burnt offerings were to be "an animal from either the herd or the flock . . . a male without defect from the cattle, sheep or goats" (cf. **Leviticus 1:1–17; 22:19**), and because child sacrifice was abhorrent to Yahweh and forbidden in the Torah (**Deuteronomy 12:31; 18:10–12; 2 Kings 3:27; 21:6; Psalm 40:6; Jeremiah 7:31; Hosea 6:6; Micah 6:7**), Jephthah likely offered his daughter as a "devoted offering," whereby she remained a virgin for the rest of her life, thus explaining the summary statements in **Judges 11:38–39**: "'You may go,' he said, and he let her go for two months. She and her friends went into the hills and wept because she would never marry. After the two months, she returned to her father, and he did to her as he had vowed. And she [remained] a virgin."

13. The hometown of Joash was "Ophrah of the Abiezrites" in the tribal allotment of the half-tribe of West Manasseh (**Judges 6:24; 8:32**; see also **Judges 6:11**).

14. Zelophehad had five daughters and no sons. He died during the post-exodus wilderness years, so when the family came into the promised land, his five daughters petitioned the leaders—Moses, Joshua, and Eleazar (the high priest)—to receive the allotment of land that their father would have been given (and to preserve their father's name). "So Moses brought their case before the LORD, and the LORD said to him, 'What Zelophehad's daughters are saying is right. You must certainly give them property as an inheritance among their father's relatives and give their father's inheritance to them'" (**Numbers 27:5–6**). Joshua granted them the request, and they were given "an inheritance along with the brothers of their father" (**Joshua 17:4**). This codified the legal principle that women in this situation could marry anyone of their choosing, but only within their clan (in this case, their cousins in the Hepherite clan) so that the land would continue to stay within the original allotment of "their father's tribe and clan" (**Numbers 36:6, 8, 11–12; Joshua 17:1–7**).

15. Abimelek, the son of Gideon, proclaimed himself judge over Israel and ruled the nation (illegitimately) for three years (cf. **Judges 9**).

16. Gideon (also called Jerub-Baal; **Judges 6:32; 7:1; 8:29, 35; 9:1, 5, 16, 19, 57; 1 Samuel 12:11**) was from the clan of the Abiezrites (**Judges 6:11, 24**). Gideon was a major judge who defeated and expelled the Midianites from the land (**Judges 6–8**). His son Abimelek aspired to kingship, but to no avail (cf. **Judges 8:31; 9**). The seventy sons of Gideon were murdered "on one stone" by their half-brother Abimelek in his heinous maneuver to declare himself judge over Israel (**Judges 9:1–6**). Gideon's statement in **Judges 6** may be related to his ancestry: "My clan [the Abiezrites] is the weakest in Manasseh, and I am the least in my family" (**Judges 6:15**), but the exact meaning is unclear. See chart "**Judges 6**: Gideon (Fifth Judge) and His Son, Abimelek the False Judge, Jair (Seventh Judge), and Jephthah (Eighth Judge)–Judges of Israel from the Tribe of Manasseh."

17. Jotham, the youngest of Gideon's children, escaped the massacre in

which Abimelek murdered the 70 sons of Gideon (i.e., his half-brothers; **Judges 9:5–6**). Jotham told a parable in which he predicted the eventual downfall of Abimelek and pronounced a curse on the people of Shechem for supporting Abimelek's rise to power (cf. **Judges 9:7–21**).

18. See charts "**1 Chronicles 7**: Benjamin (Benjamites Who Were Fighting Men)" and "**1 Chronicles 8**: Benjamin and His Descendants Who Settled in Geba and Manahath (Post-Exile)."

19. See chart "**1 Chronicles 2**: Hezron."

1 CHRONICLES 7: EPHRAIM

Approximate Dating: from Ephraim's birth in Egypt before 1877 B.C. to ca. 722 B.C.[1] ***Relevant Scriptures:*** **1 Chronicles 7:20–27;** also **Genesis 29:28; 30:24–25; 41:45; 46:20; Numbers 26:35–37**

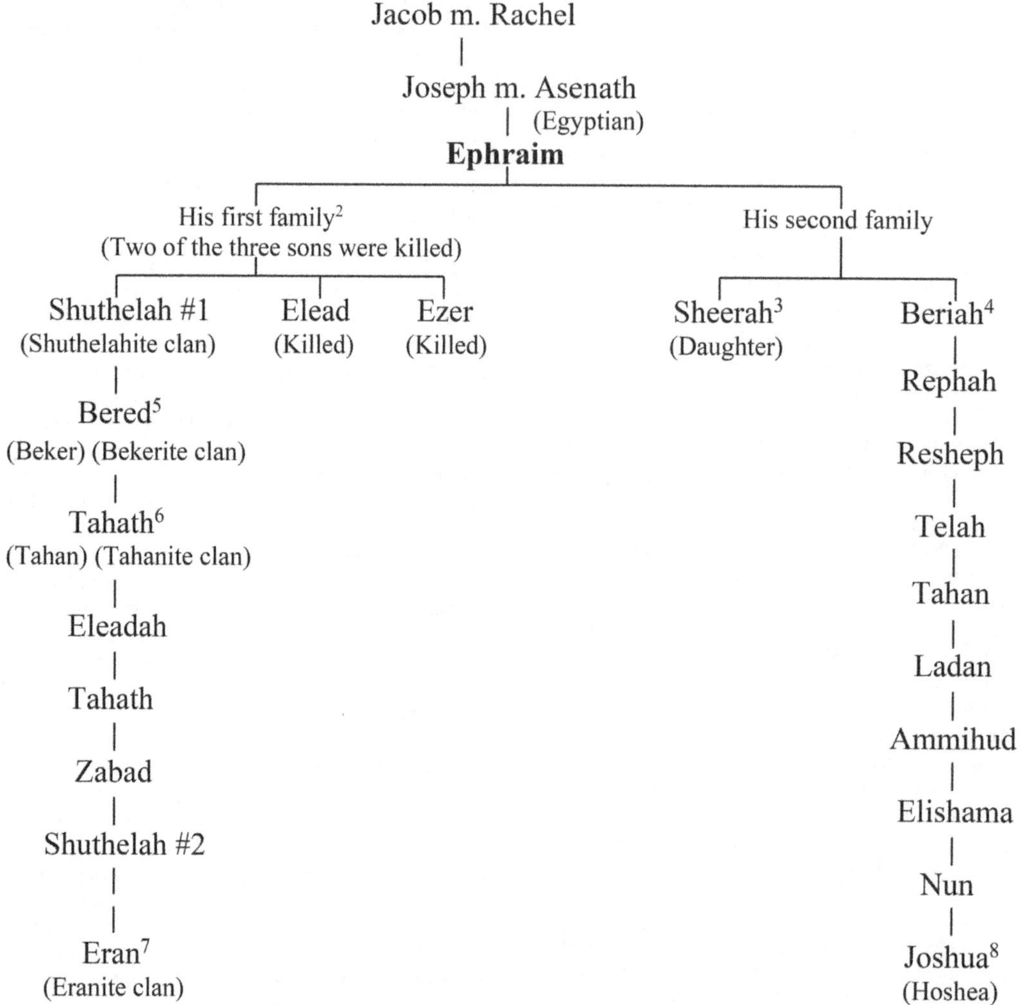

Areas Occupied by the Tribe of Ephraim

- Bethel[9]
- Naaran[10]
- Gezer[11]
- Shechem[12]
- Ayyah (var. of Aiath, Aija, or Ai?)[13]

Areas in Ephraim Along the Border with the Tribe of Manasseh[14]

- Beth Shan
- Taanach[15]
- Megiddo[16]
- Dor[17]

Biblical and Theological Significance

Ephraim was the second-born son of Joseph and his Egyptian wife Asenath (**Genesis 41:50**). Joseph named his son Ephraim, meaning "fruitfulness" or "double fruit," to signify that God had made him "fruitful in the land of my suffering [Egypt]" (**Genesis 41:52; 46:20**). The two sons of Joseph were "reckoned" (**Genesis 48:5**) as the sons of Jacob and were given an inheritance in the promised land along with the other tribes. In Jacob's patriarchal blessing, the second-born son was irregularly given preeminence over the firstborn (vv. **5–6**, **19–20**; cf. **49:22–26**). Men of Gath[18] killed two of Ephraim's sons/descendants, because Ezer and Elead tried to steal their cattle (**1 Chronicles 7:21–22**), but other children were born and, by God's grace, Ephraim became fruitful once again, giving rise to a second family that eventually included Joshua, Ephraim's most renowned descendant.

Ephraim's Settlement in Canaan

Ephraim settled in the central hill country of Canaan, where it became by far the most powerful of the tribes (cf. **Deuteronomy 33:17**). Ephraim's allotment was approximately seventy square miles. Its northern border was shared with West Manasseh, its eastern border was the Jordan, and its southern frontier was on the south bank of the Kanah Ravine and east to Jericho. Its western border was a few miles east of the Mediterranean coast between the Kanah and the unconquered territory of Philistia to the south. Important settlements in Ephraim included Jericho, Bethel (Luz), Ataroth, Gezer, Upper and Lower Beth Horon, and Shiloh (**Joshua 16:1–9**).

After 850 B.C. the entire nation north of Judah became known not only as *Israel*, but also known as *Ephraim* (e.g., **Isaiah 9:9; 11:13; Jeremiah 31:20; Hosea 4:17**). In a sense, this was a fulfillment of the meaning of the name itself—"doubly fruitful" (אֶפְרַיִם)—just as Jacob had foreseen (**Genesis 49:22–24**).

Ephraim's dignity and prowess ended in the Assyrian conquest of 722 B.C. (**2 Kings 17:1–6**). The prophets noted the carnage that comes to a people who forget their God (**Isaiah 28:1–13**).

Babylonian exiles who returned with Zerubbabel in 538 B.C. settled in the former Ephraimite towns of Bethel and nearby Ai (Ayyah?) (**Ezra 2:28; Nehemiah 7:32**). The Chronicler emphasizes that some exiles who returned to Jerusalem included "those from Judah, from Benjamin, and from Ephraim and Manasseh" (**1 Chronicles 9:3**).

Notes

1. Manasseh and Ephraim were born in Egypt "before the years of famine came" (i.e., sometime before 1877 B.C.), since the seven years of famine lasted from 1877–1871 B.C., inclusive. See chart "**Genesis 37**: Joseph and His Sons (Manasseh and Ephraim)." Many Ephraimites would have scattered in the post-Assyrian diaspora era and would not have returned to their homeland; however, **1 Chronicles 9:3** states that some of the exiles "from Judah, from Benjamin, and from Ephraim and Manasseh" returned and occupied Jerusalem in the post-exile, corresponding to a later date of 538/400 B.C.

2. The narrative suggests that Ephraim's first family consisted of three sons: Shuthelah #1, Elead, and Ezer; the descendants of these sons give rise to "clans" that comprised Ephraim's *descendants* (cf. **Numbers 26:35; 1 Chronicles 7:20**).

3. Sheerah was either *the daughter of* Ephraim (as shown in the chart) or the daughter of Beriah and the *granddaughter* of Ephraim. Sheerah was the notable builder of Uzzen Sheerah and Upper and Lower Beth Horon, which formed a strategic pass leading to the Aijalon Valley of Judea (**1 Chronicles 7:24**; cf. **1 Kings 9:17**).

4. Beriah's name means "tragedy." He was born after the elder sons (Elead and Ezer) of Ephraim were killed.

5. Bered in **1 Chronicles 7:20**—the son of Shuthelah and the father of Tahan/Tahath—is probably the same as Beker, the head of the Bekerite clan in **Numbers 26:35–36**: "These were the descendants of Ephraim by their clans: through Shuthelah, the Shuthelahite clan; through Beker, the Bekerite clan; through Tahan, the Tahanite clan. These were the descendants of Shuthelah: through Eran, the Eranite clan"—although scholars disagree on the **Numbers** reading since Beker is known as a son of *Benjamin,* not Ephraim (cf. **Genesis 46:21; 1 Chronicles 7:6**).

6. Tahath is the name of the grandfather and the grandson (**1 Chronicles 7:20**), which is probably a case of papponymy. The elder Tahath may be the same as Tahan, the head of the Tahanite clan in **Numbers 26:35** (see note 5).

7. Eran, the head of the Eranite clan, is shown in the chart as the final descendant in an eight-generation Shuthelah line, which begins with Shuthelah #1 (**1 Chronicles 7:20**) and ends with Shuthelah #2 (**1 Chronicles 7:21**). Eran is mentioned only in **Numbers 26:36**: "These were the descendants of Shuthelah: through Eran, the Eranite clan"; presumably Shuthelah here refers to Shuthelah #2.

8. Joshua the son of Nun represented the tribe of Ephraim as a spy of Canaan (**Numbers 13:8, 16**). After the death of Moses, Joshua became his successor and the new leader of the children of Israel during the courageous conquest of Canaan (**Deuteronomy 31:7–8; Joshua 1:1**). See chart "**Joshua 1**: Joshua, the Successor of Moses and Leader of the Nation of Israel."

9. Bethel was associated with the early formation of prophetism under Samuel (**1 Samuel 7:16; 10:3**) and then later under Elijah (**2 Kings 2:2**) and Elisha (**2 Kings 2:23**).

10. Naaran in **1 Chronicles 7:28** is the same as Naarah in **Joshua 16:7**.

11. Initially, Gezer was not completely subdued by the tribe of Ephraim (**Joshua 16:10**), so the Canaanite inhabitants of Gezer became forced laborers among the Ephraimites. Gezer was given as a Levitical city to the priestly descendants of Kohath the son of Levi, who were not high priests (**Joshua 21:20–21; 1 Chronicles 6:67**).

12. Shechem was important as the first site of an altar built by Abraham (**Genesis 12:6–7**); the place where Jacob bought property and built an altar (**Genesis 33:18–20**); the city where Joseph's bones were buried (**Joshua 24:32**); a city of refuge (**Joshua 20:7**); a Levitical city for the Kohathites who were not high priests (**Joshua 21:20–21**); an early capital of Israel (**1 Kings 12:1**); and the place where Jesus engaged the Samaritan woman in conversation (**John 4:5–7**).

13. Ayyah, a town in the tribe of Ephraim, may be a variant of Aiath (**Isaiah 10:28**), Aija (**Nehemiah 11:31**), which was occupied by Benjamites in the post-exile, and/or Ai, a well-known city that was taken by Joshua and the Israelites in the early conquest of Canaan (**Joshua 7:2–8:29**), located to the east of Bethel (cf. **Genesis 12:8; 13:3; Joshua 7:2; 8:9, 12:9**).

14. These cities were located northward between the Sea of Galilee and the Mediterranean Sea and were actually within the initial allotted territory of West Manasseh (cf. **Joshua 17:11**).

15. Taanach, in the southern corner of the Jezreel Valley, was one of the cities that was not completely conquered by the Israelites (**Joshua 17:11–13**).

16. Megiddo was an important city strategically located overlooking the Jezreel Valley.

17. Dor was located on the Mediterranean coast, twelve miles south of Mount Carmel.

18. Rainey and Notley assert that "here the native-born residents of Gath are not Philistines and the Gath is not Philistine Gath; it is Gath/Gittaim/Gath-rimmon (**Joshua 19:45; 2 Samuel 4:3; Nehemiah 11:33; 2 Chronciles 18:10**) [a town allotted to the tribe of Dan and given to the Levitical Kohathites who were not high priests; **Joshua 19:45; 21:20, 24**] . . . They are synonymous with the Amorites (**Judges 1:34–35**; cf. **1 Samuel 7:14**; Mazar 1954a: 227–235)"; Anson F. Rainey and R. Steven Notley, *The Sacred Bridge:Carta's Atlas of the Biblical World* (Jerusalem: Carta, 2014), 116.

1 CHRONICLES 7: ASHER

Approximate Dating: from Asher's birth in ca. 1921 B.C. to 722 B.C. ***Relevant Scriptures:*** **1 Chronicles 7:30–40**; also **Genesis 30:12–13; 35:26; 46:17, Numbers 26:44–46**

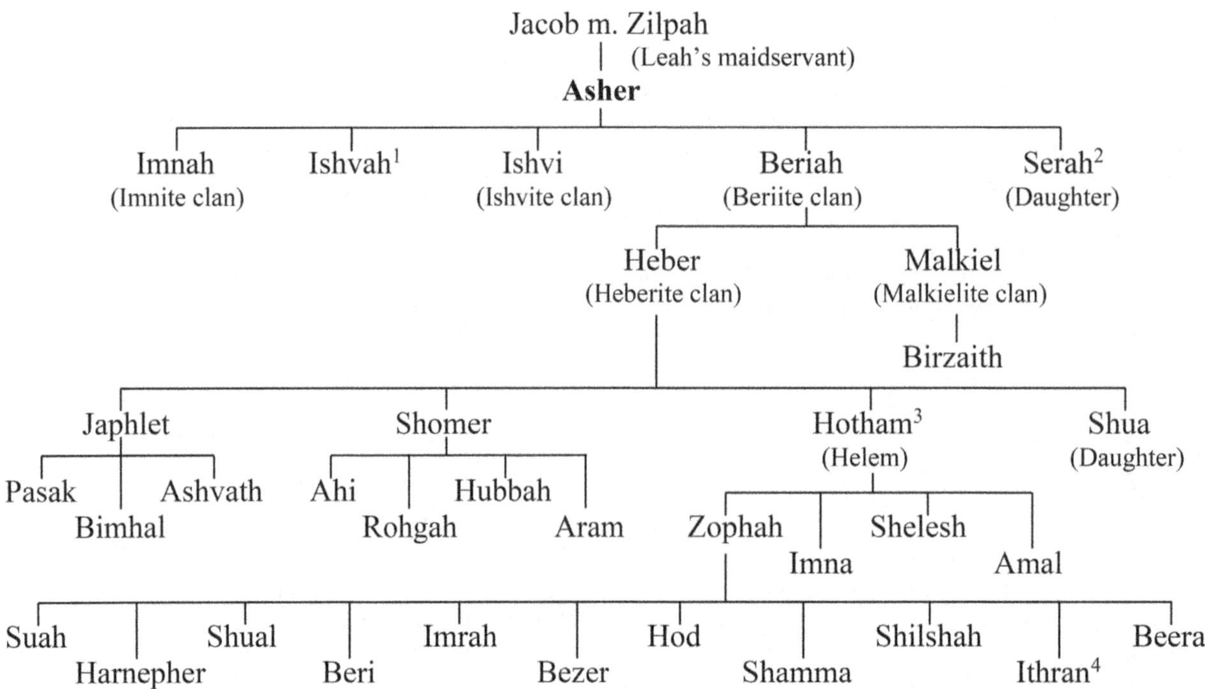

Other sons, descendants, or relatives:

Biblical and Theological Significance

Asher means "happy" or "blessed," which fits the circumstances of his birth (**Genesis 30:12–13**). Leah, thinking she was barren, bore another son through Zilpah, her servant, and exclaimed "How happy I am!" Later, his father Jacob blessed Asher with the promise that he would produce delicacies of foods "fit for a king" (**Genesis 49:20**). More specifically, Moses identified Asher's bounties as a super-abundance of oil (**Deuteronomy 33:24**). In modern times, oil explorers have sought for petroleum deposits in or offshore ancient Asher but without success; the oil of which Moses spoke was olive oil (שֶׁמֶן, *shemen*), not petroleum (שֶׁמֶן + אֲדָמָה, *shemen + adamah,* "oil *produced by* man").

In Canaan, Asher was allotted a region along the Mediterranean coast north of Mount Carmel and the Kishon wadi, south of the Phoenician city-state of Tyre, and west of the tribal territory of Zebulun.[8] However, the Asherites failed to heed God's commands (**1 Chronicles 7:1–5; 20:16–18**) and "lived among the Canaanite inhabitants of the land because they did not drive them out [completely]" (**Judges 1:32**). The major settlements of the tribe of Asher were Abdon (a Levitical city), Akko (now Acre), Akzib, Akshaph, Aphek, Rehob, and Kabul (see **Joshua 11:1; 19:24–30; 21:30–31; Judges 1:31**). The latter place is famous as a city (or a collection of cities) that King Solomon gave to King Hiram of Tyre as payment for timber and gold used in construction of the temple. When Hiram saw these cities, he turned up his nose and proclaimed the cities to be *cabul*[9] (**1 Kings 9:11–13**). None of these cities is mentioned as being in Asher or any other part of Israel in the post-exilic literature, since by 500 B.C., Phoenicia had seized and occupied the territory previously settled by Asherites. Persian occupation followed, and in the fourth century, Alexander the Great and the Macedonians took the area. Nehemiah does note that in his days (444 B.C.), "people from Tyre who lived in Jerusalem were bringing in fish and all kinds of merchandise and selling them in Jerusalem on the Sabbath to the people of Judah" (**Nehemiah 13:16**), but Nehemiah rebuked the nobles of Judah for buying from them. These merchants were very likely foreigners and not a remnant of the ancient Asherites.

Despite its small size and marginal location, Asher was not totally lost to history, nor were the people who identified themselves as "Asherites." Among the first persons to grasp the significance of the birth of Jesus was the prophet Anna, "the daughter of Penuel, of the tribe of Asher." She spoke of the newborn “to all who were looking forward to the redemption of Jerusalem” (**Luke 2:36–38**).

Notes

1. Ishvah is found in **Genesis 46:17** and **1 Chronicles 7:30** but is missing in **Numbers 26:44–46**.
2. Serah may have some connection to Timnath Serah in the hill country of Ephraim (see note 8).
3. Hotham in **1 Chronicles 7:32** is Helem in **1 Chronicles 7:35**.
4. Ithran is possibly a variant of Jether (see note 5).
5. The father of Jether is unclear. Jether of the tribe of Asher (**1 Chronicles 7:38**) is not Jether the eldest son of Gideon (**Judges 8:19–20**), Jether the Ishmaelite (**2 Samuel 17:25; 1 Chronicles 2:17**), Jether the Jerahmeelite of the tribe of Judah (**1 Chronicles 2:32**), nor Jether of the clan of Caleb the Kenizzite (**1 Chronicles 4:17**). Jether has been proposed as a variant of Ithran (of **1 Chronicles 7:37**) and therefore the same person; see Edward Lewis Curtis and Albert Alonzo Madsen, *A Critical and Exegetical Commentary on the Books of Chronicles* (Edinburgh: T&T Clark, 1910), 156.
6. The father of Ulla is unclear since his name is detached from the surrounding material. Scholars have proposed that Ulla is a textually corrupt form of a previous name in the genealogy; suggestions include Shua, Shual, Amal, and Ara (Julia M. O’Brien, “Ulla,” *Anchor Yale Bible Dictionary*).
7. Jephunneh in **1 Chronicles 7:38** is not Jephunneh the Kennizite (for the latter, see chart “**1 Chronicles 2**: Caleb and Kenaz, the Sons of Jephunneh the Kenizzite”).
8. Rainey and Notley offer these interesting insights about the tribe of Asher and their geographical settlements: “The genealogical table of Asher clearly indicates they had clan connections with southern Mount Ephraim (**Genesis 46:17–18**; **1 Chronicles 7:30–40**; cf. Edelman 1988; Demsky 1993; Aharoni 1979:244). Three Asherite clans have associations with districts along the mutual border between Benjamin and Ephraim: Japhlet (יַפְלֵט; **1 Chronicles 7:33**) with the Japhletite (הַיַּפְלֵטִי; **Joshua 16:3**); Shual (שׁוּעָל; **1 Chronicles 7:36**) and the land of Shual (אֶרֶץ שׁוּעָל; **1 Samuel 13:17**) and also the land of Shaalim (אֶרֶץ־שַׁעֲלִים; **1 Samuel 9:4**); Shelesh (שֵׁלֶשׁ; **1 Chronicles 7:35**) and Shilshah (שִׁלְשָׁה; **1 Chronicles 7:37**) and the land of Shalisha (אֶרֶץ־שָׁלִשָׁה; **1 Samuel 9:4**). Malchiel [Malkiel] was the “father of Birzaith” (Ketiv, ברזות/ Qere, בִּרְזָיִת; **1 Chronicles 7:31**), i.e. the clan had settled in Birzaith, the Qeri of which is strongly supported by the LXX form Berzaiq, which leads to an identification with the Birzhqw, Barzhqw mentioned by Josephus (Ant. XII, xi,1). The place can be identified with Khirbet Bîr Zeit north of Beitîn (Bethel). Two Asherite clans are also reckoned to the House of Joseph, Beriah in Ephraim and Benjamin (בְּרִיעָה; **1 Chronicles 7:30, 8:13**) and Shemer in Benjamin (שֶׁמֶר; **1 Chronicles 8:12** but Semmhr according to LXX). There might be some connection between Serah (שֶׂרַח; **1 Chronicles 7:30**) and Timnath Serah, the town of Joshua in Mount Ephraim (תִּמְנַת־סֶרַח; **Joshua 19:50; 24:30**; called Timnath Heres, תִּמְנַת־הֶרֶס, in **Judges 2:9**) even though different Hebrew sibilants are involved, which may be merely graphic and not phonetic (cf. **Judges 12:6**). These names seem to indicate that certain Asherite clans and families had settled very early in Mount Ephraim, where they eventually were incorporated into Benjamin and southern Ephraim.” Anson F. Rainey and R. Steven Notley. *The Sacred Bridge: Carta’s Atlas of the Biblical World* (Jerusalem: Carta, 2014), 152.
9. כָּבוּל (*cabul*), “like nothing.”

1 CHRONICLES 8: BENJAMIN AND HIS DESCENDANTS WHO SETTLED IN GEBA AND MANAHATH (POST-EXILE)[1]

Approximate Dating: from the birth of Benjamin in ca. 1908 to 538/400 B.C. ***Relevant Scriptures:*** **1 Chronicles 8:1–7; also Genesis 46:21; Numbers 26:38–41; 1 Chronicles 7:6–12**

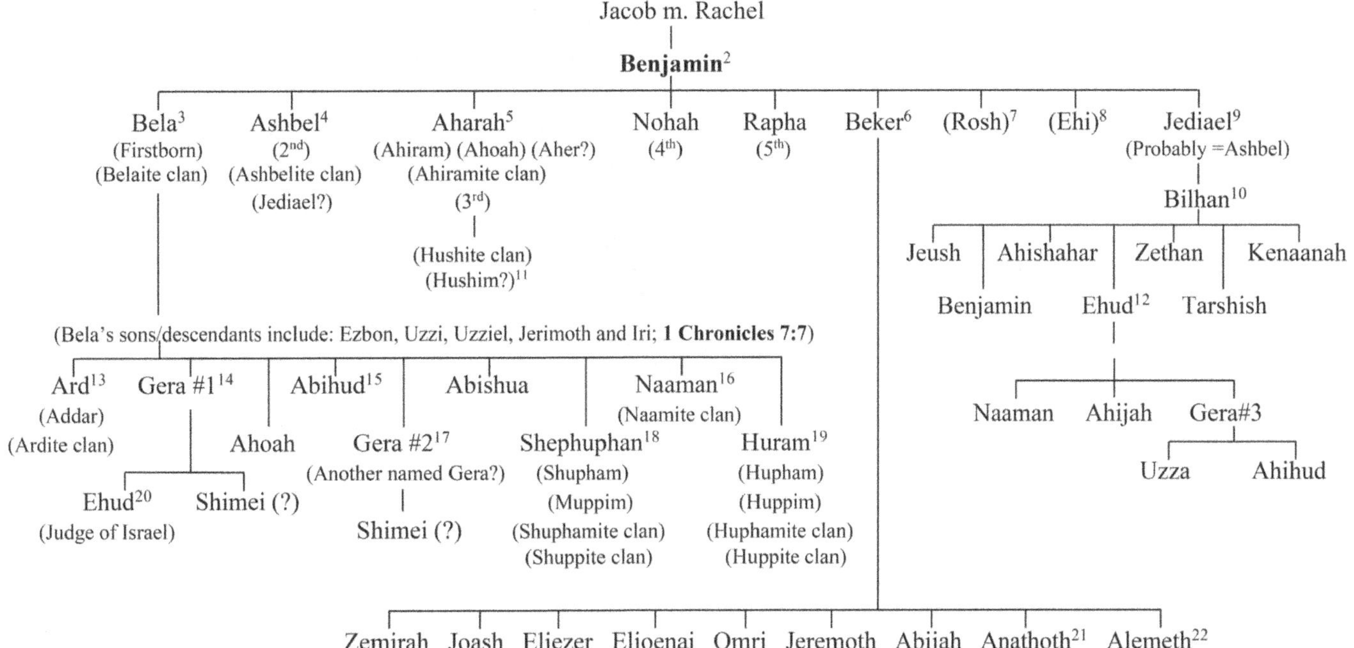

Biblical and Theological Significance

This genealogical chart is based specifically on the descendants of Benjamin given in **1 Chronicles 8:1–7**, although other descendants from this clan are known (see note 1). As close comparisons of them make clear, the genealogies of Benjamin are fraught with difficulties. The genealogical lineages in the fragmentary texts serve a variety of functions, such as lineages based on military censuses, as well as those for elucidating specific Benjamite clans and identifying those in Saul’s ancestry.[23] In the broader context,

1 Chronicles 8 discusses the ancestry and dispersion of the Benjamite clans in and around Jerusalem; for example, the emphasis in **verses 1–7** is on those who eventually came to live in Manahath, as compared to "heads of families" who eventually resided in Jerusalem (**vv. 8–28**) and Saul's ancestors who originated in Gibeon[24] (**vv. 29–40**).

Furthermore, the **1 Chronicles 8:1–7** text specifically focuses on the lineage of the descendants of Ehud (the son of Bilhan, the son of Jediael, the son of Benjamin) who were "heads of families" at Geba. According to **1 Chronicles 8:6**, "Gera" deported his brothers/brethren, Naaman and Ahijah, from the Levitical city of Geba (in the tribe of Benjamin) [25] to the city of Manahath (in the tribe of Judah),[26] which involved a distance of approximately ten miles. Scholars have offered several reasons for the "separation" or "exile"—such as intra-tribal jealousy or voluntary emigration—but perhaps the best explanation derives from a subtle religious inference that links Benjamites to Judahites in the genealogies of the tribe of Judah, because the city of Manahath was associated with Judahites and "half of the Manahathites," who were descendants of Salma (a co-founder of Bethlehem) and Shobal (the father/founder of Kiriath Jearim). Moreover, these specific Judahites were near relatives of Bethlehemites, Netophathites (Levites), and pious clans of scribes who lived and worked at Jabez (cf. **1 Chronicles 2:52, 54–55**).[27] So the explanation for the deportation to Manahath may have been for religious reasons, perhaps prompted by religious persecution.

Nothing more is known about Manahath in the post-exile. However, the city of Geba was re-inhabited (cf. **Ezra 2:26; Nehemiah 7:30; 11:31**), and Levitical singers from Geba helped Nehemiah in the dedication of the completed wall around Jerusalem in 444 B.C. (**Nehemiah 12:28–29**).

Notes

1. The chart (based on **1 Chronicles 8:1–7**) is a constructed, segmented genealogy based on the various sons and descendants of Benjamin in four genealogical references:

    (1) **Genesis 46:21** (functions as an account of Benjamin's sons at the time of the descent of Jacob's family to Egypt in 1876 B.C.)—"The sons of Benjamin: Bela, Beker, Ashbel, Gera [probably the son of Bela and a grandson of Benjamin; cf. **1 Chronicles 8:3-5**], Naaman [probably a son of Bela and a grandson of Benjamin; cf. **1 Chronicles 8:3–4**], Ehi, Rosh, Muppim, Huppim and Ard."

    (2) **Numbers 26:38–41** (functions as the second tribal census before entering Canaan)—"The descendants of Benjamin by their clans were: through Bela, the Belaite clan; through Ashbel, the Ashbelite clan; through Ahiram, the Ahiramite clan; through Shupham, the Shuphamite clan; through Hupham, the Huphamite clan. The descendants of Bela through Ard and Naaman were: through Ard, the Ardite clan; through Naaman, the Naamite clan. These were the clans of Benjamin; those numbered were 45,600."

    (3) **1 Chronicles 7:6–12** (functions as a military census at the time of David)—"Three sons of Benjamin: Bela, Beker and Jediael. The sons of Bela: Ezbon, Uzzi, Uzziel, Jerimoth and Iri, heads of families—five in all. Their genealogical record listed 22,034 fighting men. The sons of Beker: Zemirah, Joash, Eliezer, Elioenai, Omri, Jeremoth, Abijah, Anathoth and Alemeth. All these were the sons of Beker. Their genealogical record listed the heads of families and 20,200 fighting men. The son of Jediael: Bilhan. The sons of Bilhan: Jeush, Benjamin, Ehud, Kenaanah, Zethan, Tarshish and Ahishahar. All these sons of Jediael were heads of families. There were 17,200 fighting men ready to go out to war. The Shuppites and Huppites were the descendants of Ir, and the Hushites the descendants of Aher."

    (4) **1 Chronicles 8:1–7** (emphasizes birth-order and functions as an extensive genealogy of the Benjamite tribe and an introduction into Saul's ancestry)—"Benjamin was the father of Bela his firstborn, Ashbel the second son, Aharah the third, Nohah the fourth and Rapha the fifth. The sons of Bela were: Addar, Gera, Abihud, Abishua, Naaman, Ahoah, Gera, Shephuphan and Huram. These were the descendants of Ehud, who were heads of families of those living in Geba and were deported to Manahath: Naaman, Ahijah, and Gera, who deported them and who was the father of Uzza and Ahihud."

2. Benjamin, born ca. 1908 B.C., was the younger brother of Joseph. Benjamin and Joseph were the sons of Jacob and Rachel. Rachel died in childbirth with Benjamin (**Genesis 35:16–20**). The birth order of five of Benjamin's sons is given in **1 Chronicles 8:1–2**. Benjamin had other sons/descendants (who are not shown in the chart; see passages in note 1). Benjamin also had a daughter or descendant named Maakah (not shown in the chart) who married Makir the Manassite (see note 4 in chart "**1 Chronicles** 7: Manasseh (the Half-Tribe of West Manasseh)."

3. Bela was the head of the Belaite clan (**Numbers 26:38**). Other sons of Bela are listed in **1 Chronicles 7:7**: "Ezbon, Uzzi, Uzziel, Jerimoth and Iri." Some scholars have proposed that Iri in **1 Chronicles 7:7** is same person as Ir in **1 Chronicles 7:12** (see notes 18 and 19).

4. Ashbel was the head of the Ashbelite clan (**Numbers 26:38**). He appears to be the same person as Jediael; see note 9.

5. Aharah in **1 Chronicles 8:1**—and Ahoah in **1 Chronicles 8:4**—are the transcribers' variations of Ahiram, the head of the Ahiramite clan (**Numbers 26:38**); see Edward Lewis Curtis and Albert Alonzo Madsen, *A Critical and Exegetical Commentary on the Books of Chronicles* (Edinburgh: T&T Clark, 1910), 157. Also, Aher in **1 Chronicles 7:12** may be the contracted form and perhaps the same as Aharah and Ahiram (see S. K. Mosiman, "Aher," *ISBE* and "Aher," *Holman's Bible Dictionary*).

6. Beker was a son of Benjamin (**Genesis 46:21; 1 Chronicles 7:6**); the names of Beker's sons are given in **1 Chronicles 7:8**. Beker the Benjamite should not be confused with Beker the Ephraimite (**Numbers 26:35**).

7. Rosh is mentioned as a son of Benjamin only in **Genesis 46:21**. For more information on Rosh, see note 25 in chart "**Genesis 46**: The Extended Family of Jacob (Seventy Descendants) Who Migrated to Egypt."

8. Ehi (meaning "brother") is mentioned as a son of Benjamin only in **Genesis 46:21**. For more information on Ehi, see note 24 in chart "**Genesis 46**: The Extended Family of Jacob (Seventy Descendants) Who Migrated to Egypt."

9. In **1 Chronicles 7**, the Chronicler describes Jediael's descendants, not in genealogical terms (cf. **1 Chronicles 7:6**) or clans, but in military terms, possibly from a census taken of Saul's army: "All these sons of Jediael were heads of families. There were 17,200 fighting men ready to go out to war" (**v. 11**), as compared to 22,034 sons/descendants of Bela who were fighting men (**v. 7**) and 20,200 sons/descendants of Beker who were fighting men (**vv. 8–9**). Jediael (meaning "known to God") may be substituted for the heathen-sounding "Ashbel" (or "Ishbaal," meaning "man of Baal") and therefore Jediael (**vv. 6, 10–11**) is the same person as Ashbel (the Ashbelite clan) in **Genesis 46:21** and **Numbers 26:38**. For the possibility that Jediael is equivalent to Ashbel, see the discussion by Siegfried S. Johnson in the *Anchor Yale Bible Dictionary* ("Ashbel") and Edward Lewis Curtis and Albert Alonzo Madsen's *A Critical and Exegetical Commentary on the Books of Chronicles* (Edinburgh: T&T Clark, 1910), 157.

For examples of Baal-associated names in the family of Saul, see note 9 in chart "**1 Chronicles 8 & 9**: The Descendants of King Saul Living in Gibeon and Jerusalem (Post-Exile)."

10. Ehud was the son of Bilhan and the grandson of Jediael (**1 Chronicles 7:10**; cf. **8:6–7**).

11. Hushim was probably the head of the clan of Hushites (**1 Chronicles 7:12**). Hushim, a bi-gender name, is the son/descendant of Aher (**1 Chronicles 7:12**) and the wife of Shaharaim (**1 Chronicles 8:8**). For Shaharaim, see chart "**1 Chronicles 8**: The Benjamites Who Settled in and around Jerusalem and in Moab (Post-Exile)."

12. Ehud the son of Bilhan, the son of Jediael in **1 Chronicles 7:10** is a different person than Ehud the judge of Israel, called "the son of Gera" (**Judges 3:15**), although Ehud the son of Bilhan may have been named for Ehud the famous judge (see chart "**Judges 3**: Ehud, the Second Judge of Israel").

13. Addar (**1 Chronicles 8:3**) is also Ard, the originator of the Ardite clan (**Genesis 46:21; Numbers 26:40**).

14. There are three Gera figures shown in the chart—designated Gera #1,

#2, and #3. The name Gera derives from *ger* (גֵּר), "stranger, sojourner," plus the additive /a/ (א), representing, perhaps, a code for a divine name. **First Chronicles 8:3–5** lists the sons of Bela as "Addar, Gera, Abihud, Abishua, Naaman, Ahoah, Gera (?), Shephuphan and Huram"—these two "Gera" figures are shown in the chart as Gera #1 and Gera #2; a third is mentioned in **1 Chronicles 8:7** and is shown as Gera #3. Ehud the judge of Israel was the "son of Gera" (**Judges 3:15**)—probably referring to Gera #1 or Gera #2, although Gera may have been mistakenly listed *twice* in the genealogy in **1 Chronicles 8:3–5** (cf. **Genesis 46:21** and note 17 below)—rather than to Gera (#3) in **1 Chronicles 8:7**. Also, in an infamous occurrence, a Benjamite named "Shimei son of Gera [#1, #2, or #3]" cursed David (cf. **2 Samuel 16:5; 19:16, 18; 1 Kings 2:8**); for the fate of this Shimei, see **1 Kings 2:36–46** and the chart "**2 Samuel 16**: Possible Genealogy of Shimei, the Benjamite who Cursed King David."

15. Some scholars consider Abihud the ancestor of Ehud (**1 Chronicles 8:3**) in this way: "According to the MT, the first three sons of Bela were 'Addar, and Gera, and Abihud' (Heb. *ʾaddār wĕgērāʾ wăʾăbîhûd*); however, the text could easily be emended to read 'Addar, and Gera, that is, the father of Ehud' Heb. *ʾaddār wĕgērāʾ wăʾăbî ʾēhûd*). Baker (1980) argues that the two separate individuals named Gera listed as sons of Bela (**1 Chronicles 8:3, 5**) were distinguished by the *waw* explicative, which followed the first Gera, providing a detail about him being the father of Ehud. Thus, MT *wăʾăbîhûd* is divided into *wăʾăbî*, 'that is, the father of,' plus *ʾēhûd* 'Ehud,' the judge mentioned elsewhere in his own right as the son of Gera (**Judges 3:15**). Note also the EHUD who had a son named Gera (**1 Chronicles 8:6–7**). Kuhn (1923) observed that a misunderstanding of the phrase *ʾby hwdyh* produced the name *ʾăbîhûd* ('Abihud'), and the Gk *abioud* (**Matthew 1:13**) was based on the LXX rendering of this synthetic name" (Mark J. Frietz, *Anchor Yale Bible Dictionary*, "Abihud").

16. Bela's son Naaman was the head of the Naamite clan (**Numbers 26:40**), not to be confused with Naaman the commander of the army of the king of Aram, who lived some 200 years later (**2 Kings 5:1–27**).

17. Some scholars hold that Gera #2 is the son of Ehud the judge of Israel (i.e., Gera #1–Ehud–Gera #2 lineage; see the explanation by Mark J. Fretz, "Gera," *Anchor Yale Bible Dictionary*). See chart "**Judges 3**: Ehud, the Second Judge of Israel."

18. Shephuphan/Muppim/Shupham was the head of the Shuphamite/Shuppite clan (cf. **Genesis 46:21; Numbers 26:39; 1 Chronicles 7:12, 15; 8:5**). The Shuppites were "the descendants of Ir," presumably referring to *Iri*, the son of Bela, the son of Benjamin (**1 Chronicles 7:12;** see also vv. **6–7**); also see notes by G. Edwin Harmon, "Ir," *Anchor Yale Bible Dictionary* and W. Ewing, "Ir," *ISBE*.

19. Huram/Huppim/Hupham was the head of the Huphamite/Huppite clan (cf. **Genesis 46:21; Numbers 26:39; 1 Chronicles 7:12, 15; 8:5**). The Huppites were "the descendants of Ir" presumably referring to Iri, the son of Bela, the son of Benjamin (**1 Chronicles 7:12;** see also vv. **6–7**); also see the notes by G. Edwin Harmon, "Ir," *Anchor Yale Bible Dictionary* and W. Ewing, "Ir," *ISBE*.

20. Ehud, the son/descendant of Gera #1, was the judge of Israel who lived in ca. 1290–1210 B.C and delivered the Israelites from Moabite oppression (**Judges 3:15–30**); see chart "**Judges 3**: Ehud, the Second Judge of Israel."

21. Anathoth is a personal name (i.e., one of the nine sons of Beker) as well as a place name. The latter is a town in the tribe of Benjamin about three miles northeast of Jerusalem, which was a Levitical city given to the descendants of Aaron (**Joshua 21:18; 1 Chronicles 6:60**). When King Solomon removed Abiathar from being the high priest in Solomon's Temple, Abiathar returned to his hometown of Anathoth (**1 Kings 2:26–27**). The prophet Jeremiah also hailed from Anathoth (**Jereremiah 1:1; 32:7**).

22. Alemeth, the name of one of Beker's sons, is also a place name. Alemeth, also known as Almon, was a Levitical city given to the descendants of Aaron (cf. **Joshua 21:18; 1 Chronicles 6:60**).

23. For Saul's heritage, see charts "**1 Samuel 9**: King Saul" and "**1 Chronicles 8 & 9**: The Descendants of King Saul Living in Gibeon and Jerusalem (Post-Exile)."

24. The Benjamite city of Gibeon (like Geba) was given as a Levitical city to the high priestly descendants of Aaron (cf. **Joshua 18:25; 21:17; 1 Chronicles 6:57, 60**). Gibeon was re-occupied in the post-exile (cf. **Nehemiah 3:7; 7:25**).

25. The Benjamite city of Geba was located about six miles north of Jerusalem (**Joshua 18:24**). Geba and its pasturelands were given as a Levitical city to the sons (descendants) of Aaron the high priest (in the Kohathite high priestly line; **Joshua 21:4, 17; 1 Chronicles 6:60**). Geba should not be confused with the nearby "Gibeah of Saul," referring to the hometown of King Saul in the tribe of Benjamin (**1 Samuel 10:26; 11:4; 13:15–16; 14:16; 2 Samuel 21:6; 23:29; 1 Chronicles 11:31**).

26. Manahath (now el-Mâlḥah) is located about four miles southwest of Jerusalem.

27. For the Manahathites (inhabitants of Manahath) and their association with Judahites, see charts "**1 Chronicles 2**: Hezron" and "**1 Chronicles 4**: Judah."

1 CHRONICLES 8: THE BENJAMITES WHO SETTLED IN AND AROUND JERUSALEM AND IN MOAB (POST-EXILE)

Approximate Dating: ca. 460/444 B.C. ***Relevant Scriptures:*** **1 Chronicles 8:8–28**

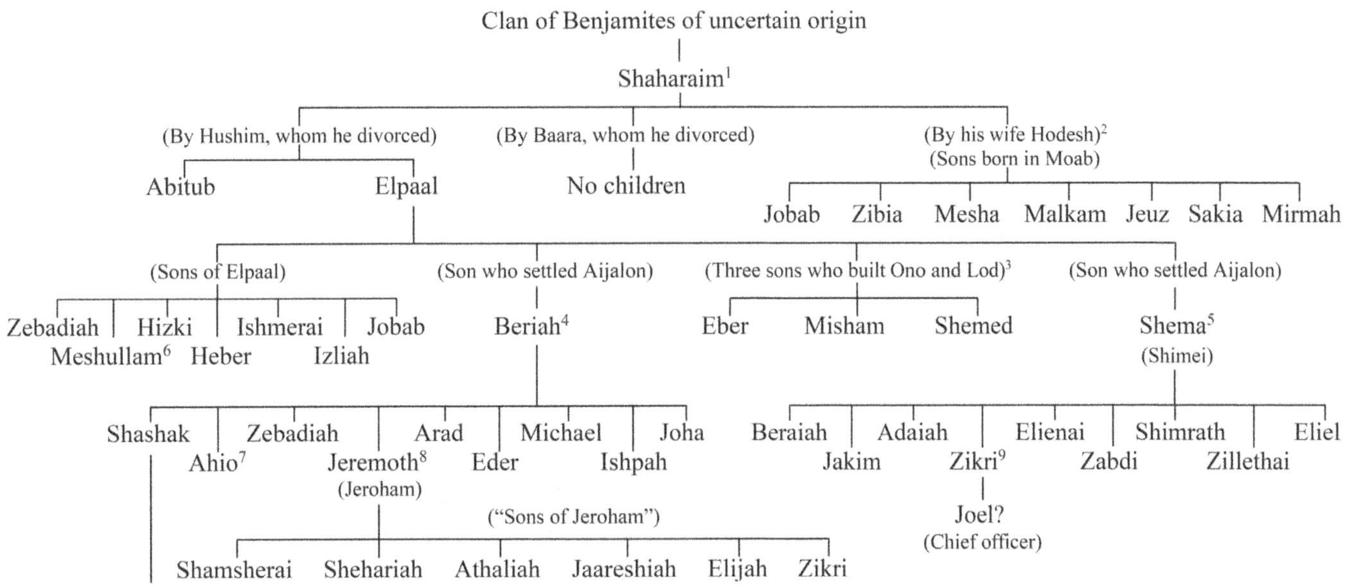

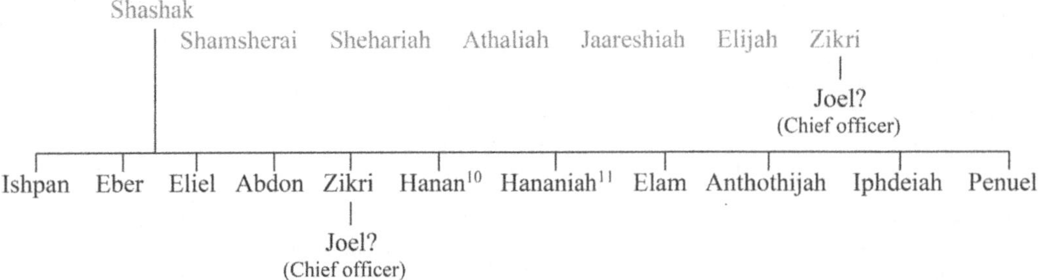

Biblical and Theological Significance

These were the heads of families and genealogies[12] who lived in post-exilic Jerusalem (**1 Chronicles 8:28**). The genealogical relationship of Shaharaim (the personal name here, שַׁחֲרַיִם *shaharayim*, means something like "black" or "dark," as opposed to שְׁעָרַיִם *shaarayim*, "two gates") to other ancestors in the tribe of Benjamin is unknown, although some scholars have mistakenly associated Shaharaim[13] with Ahishahar, the great-grandson of Benjamin[14] (cf. **1 Chronicles 7:10**).

This is a standard segmented genealogy whose greater length is obviously meant to focus first on a certain Joel, the son of Zikri. Since there are three men named Zikri in this genealogy, which one was the father of Joel is not clear. Joel was the "chief officer" over the re-inhabited population of Jerusalem in the post-exile, which was predominated by an enclave of Benjamites, as opposed to Judahites (**Nehemiah 11:9**); see the chart "**Nehemiah 11**: The "Tithe" of People Chosen to Repopulate Jerusalem in the Post-Exile." Also, five post-exilic families from the clan of Shaharaim are specifically highlighted by the Chronicler—Elpaal, Beriah, Shema (Shimei), Shashak, and Jeremoth (Jeroham); these men were "heads of families, chiefs as listed in their genealogy, and they lived in [post-exilic] Jerusalem" (**1 Chronicles 8:28**). As for other names in this passage (**1 Chronicles 8:8–28**), none except Zikri, and possibly Hanan and Hananiah (see notes), occur elsewhere.

Among the cities allotted to the Benjamites, the Chronicler stresses the occupation/re-occupation in the post-exile time of specific cities by Shaharaim's descendants—Aijalon, a Levitical city given to Kohathite priests, originally allotted to the tribe of Dan (**1 Chronicles 8:13**; cf. **Joshua 19:42; 21:20, 24**), and Ono and Lod (towns occupied by the descendants of Shaharaim; **Ezra 2:33; Nehemiah 7:37; 11:35**). Interestingly, some members of the Shaharaim clan also lived in Moab.

The settlement of Moab introduces a strange development, indeed. Shaharaim is said to have begotten offspring בִשְׂדֵה מוֹאָב "in [the fields of] Moab," meaning "in the plains of Moab" (**1 Chronicles 8:8**). The oddity lies in the fact that Benjamin nowhere is said to have had a pre-exilic Moabite connection. Its post-exilic settlement in Moab therefore seems out of place. There may be a hint, however, in the book of Nehemiah**,** in which Nehemiah excoriates "men of Judah who had married women from Ashdod, Ammon and Moab" (**13:23**). Whether or not Hodesh was a Moabite wife of Shaharaim cannot be proven; only that their sons lived in Moab is certain. Benjamin was, of course, integrated into the kingdom of Judah and therefore would have been included in this statement. When these marriages took place cannot be known, though perhaps it was in the time of the exile itself, when some Benjamites may have found refuge in these places.

Notes

1. Shaharaim was married to three women, two of whom he divorced (Baara and Hushim). Presumably, Hushim bore Abitub and Elpaal to Shaharaim before he moved to Moab. Shaharaim had six sons by his (third) wife Hodesh while living in Moab in the post-exile. Shaharaim is also a place name, see note 13. Shaharaim (שַׁחֲרַיִם) the Benjamite is not Ahishahar (אֲחִישָׁחַר) the Benjamite; see note 14.

2. Shaharaim's sons and descendants through Elpaal settled in post-exilic Jerusalem (cf. **1 Chronicles 8:12–13, 28**). After Shaharaim divorced Hushim and Baara, Shaharaim's sons by Hodesh settled in Moab (**1 Chronicles 8:8–10**).

3. Elpaal's son Shemed built (or rebuilt) Ono, located in the Shephelah, and also Lod (Lydda, the home of Dorcas, **Acts 9:32**); both towns were resettled by post-exilic returnees from Babylon (**Ezra 2:33; Nehemiah 7:37; 11:35**).

4. Beriah and his brother Shema (Shimei) inhabited Aijalon—a city in the tribe of Dan was that given as a Levitical city to the Kohathite priests—located northwest of Jerusalem between Gezer and Gibeon. Beriah and Shema/Shimei drove out the inhabitants of Gath (**1 Chronicles 8:13**; cf. **Joshua 21:24; 2 Chronicles 28:16–18**).

5. Shema (**1 Chronicles 8:13**) is Shimei (**1 Chronicles 8:21**). He and his brother Beriah inhabited Aijalon and drove out the nearby inhabitants of Gath (**1 Chronicles 8:13**). Both forms of the name (Shema/Shimei) come from the verb meaning "to hear, listen."

6. Meshullam the son of Elpaal can be compared to other men named Meshullam in the tribe of Benjamin: two mentioned in **1 Chronicles 9:7–8** (i.e., Meshullam son of Hodaviah and Meshullam son of Shephatiah) and another who settled in post-exilic Jerusalem in **Nehemiah 11:7** (i.e., Meshullam son of Joed). The name was popular; it means "given as a sacrifice."

7. Although both are Benjamites, Ahio (**1 Chronicles 8:14**) is not Ahio his relative, who was an ancestor of Saul (**1 Chronicles 8:31; 9:37**).

8. Jeremoth son of Beriah (**1 Chronicles 8:14**), by a scribal error called metathesis, is also known as Jeroham (**1 Chronicles 8:27; 9:8**); see note 5 in chart "**1 Chronicles 9**: The Leaders from the Tribes of Judah and Benjamin Who Dwelled in Jerusalem (Post-Exile)." Jeremoth/Jeroham is a different person than Jeroham son of Pashhur (**1 Chronicles 9:12**) and Jeroham son of Pelaliah (**Nehemiah 11:12**), both of whom are Kohathite priests of the tribe of Levi.

9. Three people named Zikri are identified in the chart—one the son of Shema/Shimei (**1 Chronicles 8:19–21**), one the son of Jeremoth/Jeroham (**1 Chronicles 8:27**), and one the son of Shashak (**1 Chronicles 8:23, 25**). One of these men appears to be the father of Joel the Benjamite, who was the chief officer over post-exilic Jerusalem (cf. **Nehemiah 11:9**). Zikri is a nickname for Zechariah.

10. Hanan (**1 Chronicles 8:23**) is possibly the same person as one of the two leaders of the people named Hanan who sealed the covenant with Nehemiah in 444 B.C. (cf. **Nehemiah 10:22, 26**).

11. Hananiah (**1 Chronicles 8:24**) is possibly the same person as Hananiah a leader of the people who sealed the covenant with Nehemiah in 444 B.C. (cf. **Nehemiah 10:23**).

12. The term for "genealogy" (תּוֹלְדָה), *toledah*, comes from the root יָלַד, "to beget."

13. As a place name, this site can be written as either שְׁעָרַיִם (Shaaraim in **Joshua 15:36**) or שַׁחֲרַיִם (Shaharaim in **1 Chronicles 8:8**). Though the Hebrew distinguishes the two, their pronunciations in transliteration—(*Shaarayim*) in **Joshua 15:36** and (*shakharayim*) in **1 Chronicles 4:31**—are hardly perceptible. However, since there is a difference in meaning of the two (Shaaraim, "two gates," and Shaharaim, "two dawns"), they cannot be one and the same. See note 7 on Shaaraim in chart "**1 Chronicles 4**: Simeon."

14. Since Shaharaim is in the dual number meaning "both dawns" ("שַׁחֲרַיִם," *HALOT* 2:1469) and Ahishahar appears to be from a different root meaning "my brother is righteous" ("אֲחִישָׁר," *HALOT* 1:34), the names cannot be reconciled. For Ahishahar, see chart "**1 Chronicles** 7: Benjamin (Benjamites Who Were Fighting Men)."

1 CHRONICLES 8 AND 9: THE DESCENDANTS OF KING SAUL LIVING IN GIBEON AND JERUSALEM (POST-EXILE)

Approximate Dating: from the birth of Saul in 1081 B.C. to ca. 538/400 B.C. ***Relevant Scriptures:*** **1 Chronicles 8:29–40; 9:35–44;** also **1 Samuel 9:1–2; 14:49–51; 2 Samuel 2:10; 4:4; 9:6, 10, 12; 19:24; 21:7–9; 1 Chronicles 10:2; 27:21; Esther 2:5–7, 15; 9:29**

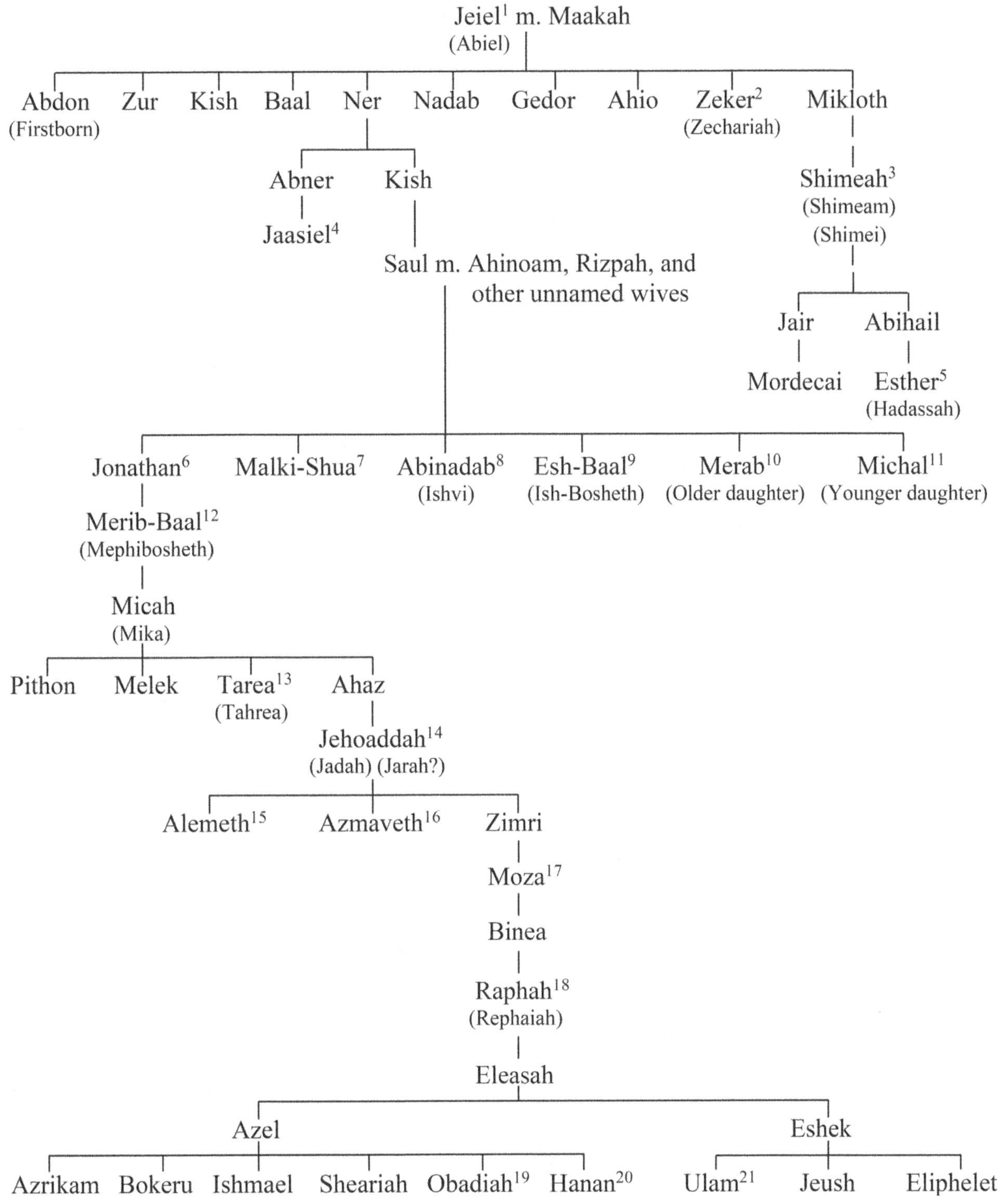

Ulam[21]
(Firstborn)
|
(Many sons, grandsons,
and great-grandsons)

Biblical and Theological Significance

This genealogy, though beginning with Saul's great-grandfather (Jeiel), focuses on Saul's descendants of the exilic and post-exilic era. For the earlier periods, see the chart "**1 Samuel 9**: King Saul."

That such attention is paid to the progeny of a king who lived and died in disgrace deserves at least brief reflection on two points:

- Saul was, after all, a king whom Yahweh assigned Samuel to anoint (**1 Samuel 10:1, 9–10, 24–25**).
- Saul illustrates the magnificent grace of God who, though never overlooking sin, is not slow to praise those who have served him despite their faults. David said it best in his funereal panegyric over Saul and Jonathan (**2 Samuel 1:17–27**):

  In life they were loved and admired,
  and in death they were not parted. . . .
  Daughters of Israel,
  weep for Saul,
  who clothed you in scarlet and finery,
  who adorned your garments with ornaments
  of gold. (**2 Samuel 1:23–24**)

The primary Saulide line that continued in post-exilic Jerusalem (the Yehud[22] community) was through the descendants of Jonathan, who, like their ancestor, became famous as archers (**1 Chronicles 8:34–39**). The prominent depth of Jonathan's genealogy is related to the covenant that Jonathan and David made with each other, for Jonathan had asked David to pledge protection for his family: "show me unfailing kindness like the LORD's kindness as long as I live . . . and do not ever cut off your kindness from my family" (**1 Samuel 20:12–15**; see **18:1–4; 20:11–16; 2 Samuel 9:1, 3, 7**). After Jonathan's death, David sought out a remnant of Jonathan's family and found his son, the lame Mephibosheth (or Merib-Baal; see note 12); David invited Mephibosheth and his son Mika to live at the king's palace and eat at the king's table (**2 Samuel 9:1–13**). Descendants of Jonathan were among the Benjamites who returned from exile and lived in the newly restored Jerusalem (**1 Chronicles 9:3**).

Also of considerable interest is the presence of other Benjamites—the Shimeah/Shimeam/Shimei descendants—who lived in the Persian city of Susa—notably Mordecai, and, by association, Esther—who played a major role in saving the lives of thousands of Jews who had not chosen to return to Yehud after the Persian conquest of Babylon in 539 B.C. So important were they that Mordecai was singled out by a brief lineage tracing him back to Kish through Jair and Shimei (**Esther 2:5**).

Other Benjamites have a strong presence in the post-exilic record. When Zerubbabel brought a group of exiles to Jerusalem in 538 B.C.; among them were ninety-five men from Gibeon (**Nehemiah 7:25**). A significant number of Benjamites (928 men) settled in Jerusalem (**11:4, 7–9, 36**); prominent among them was Joel, son of Zikri, who was their chief officer (thus Heb. פָּקִיד). Family heads of Judah and Benjamin helped to rebuild the temple in Jerusalem (**Ezra 1:5**), and in the days of Nehemiah in 444 B.C., men from Gibeon helped repair the wall around the city (**Nehemiah 3:7**).

The following towns—including those specifically allotted to the tribe of Benjamin (**Joshua 18:11–28; 21:17–28; 1 Chronicles 6:60**)—were re-settled by Benjamites who returned to their homeland in the post-exile: Anathoth (**Ezra 2:23; Nehemiah 7:27; 11:32**); Gibeon, which was also a Levitical city (**Nehemiah 3:7; 7:25**); Bethel (**Ezra 2:28; Nehemiah 7:32; 11:31**); Beth Azmaveth (Azmaveth) (**Ezra 2:24; Nehemiah 7:28; 12:29**); Geba (**Ezra 2:26; Nehemiah 7:30; 7:32; 11:31**); Beeroth (**Ezra 2:25; Nehemiah 7:29**); Ramah (**Ezra 2:26; Nehemiah 7:30; 11:33**); Hazor (**Nehemiah 11:33**); Ananiah (**Nehemiah 11:32**); Aija (Ai) (**Ezra 2:28; Nehemiah 7:32; 11:31**); Mizpah (**Nehemiah 3:7, 15, 19**); Jericho (**Ezra 2:34; Nehemiah 7:36**); Nob (**Nehemiah 11:32**); Harim (**Ezra 2:32; Nehemiah 7:35**); Mikmash (**Ezra 2:27; Nehemiah 7:31; 11:31**); Gittaim (**Nehemiah 11:33**); Hadid (**Ezra 2:33; Nehemiah 7:37; 11:34**); Zeboim; Neballat (**Nehemiah 11:34**); Kephirah (**Ezra 2:25; Nehemiah 7:29**); Jerusalem (**1 Chronicles 9:7–9 Nehemiah 11:4, 7–9; 12:29**); Ge Harashim (**Nehemiah 11:35**); Ono (**Ezra 2:33; Nehemiah 7:37; 11:35**); Lod (**Ezra 2:33; Nehemiah 7:37; 11:35**); and Kiriath/Kiriath Jearim (**Ezra 2:25; Nehemiah 7:29**).

Notes

1. The Chronicler does not go into the early ancestry of Saul beyond noting that he was a descendant of Jeiel who lived ca. 1250/1200 B.C. For further information, see chart "**1 Samuel 9**: King Saul."

2. Zeker (**1 Chronicles 8:31**) is hypocoristic for Zechariah (**1 Chronicles 9:37**).

3. Shimeah (שִׁמְאָה [*shimah*] in **1 Chronicles 8:32** is called Shimeam (שִׁמְאָם [*shim'am*]) in **1 Chronicles 9:38**. The Shimeah/Shimeam issue can be resolved best by a phonetic phenomenon in Semitic languages called "mimation," the presence of the biblical /m/ for purely phonetic reasons. Thus, the two forms can describe the same person or at least the same name. Furthermore, **1 Chronicles 8:32; 9:38** and **Esther 2:5** appear to claim three different patronyms (paternal ancestors) for Mordecai: Shimeah, Shimeam, and Shimei, respectively.

4. Jaasiel the son of Abner was Saul's first cousin. Jaasiel's father, Abner, had served as the army commander for Saul and Ish-Bosheth (cf. **1 Samuel 14:50; 17:55; 20:25; 26:5; 2 Samuel 2:8; 4:1**). Jaasiel led the tribe of Benjamin during David's reign and may have been involved in conducting the census for the tribe of Benjamin, although the census was never completed (**1 Chronicles 27:21**; cf. **vv. 16–24**).

5. Mordecai and Esther were Benjamites living in Persia (**Esther 2:5–7, 15; 9:29**). They were in the lineage of Jair, the "son of Shimei, the son of Kish" and Mikloth, "the father of Shimeah [Shimeam]" (cf. **1 Chronicles 8:32; 9:38; Esther 2:5**); see note 3. Moreover, Mordecai and Esther were "cousins" (**Esther 2:7**). See chart "**Esther 2**: Mordecai and Esther, Jews Living in Persia." Her beautiful Hebrew name, Hadassah (meaning *myrtle*), was altered in Babylonia to Esther, a Hebrew rendition of Ishtar ("star"), the chief goddess of the Babylonian pantheon.

6. Jonathan, David's best friend, died with his father Saul on Mount Gilboa (**1 Samuel 31:2, 6**); however, some of Jonathan's descendants appear to have lived through Babylonian captivity and returned to post-exilic Jerusalem (cf. **1 Chronicles 8:34–39**).

7. Malki-Shua died with his father Saul on Mount Gilboa (**1 Samuel 31:2, 6**).

8. Abinadab (**1 Samuel 31:2; 1 Chronicles 8:33; 9:39; 10:2**) is called Ishvi in **1 Samuel 14:49**.

9. Esh-Baal (**1 Chronicles 8:33; 9:39**) is otherwise Ish-Bosheth (**2 Samuel 2:8, 10, 12, 15; 3:7–8, 11, 14–15; 4:1, 5, 8, 12**). The fact that Saul named his son Esh-Baal ("Baal's fire") betrays his dalliances with Canaanite deities such as Baal. Since it was sinful for Saul to have named him this, some called him E/Ish-Bosheth, "shameful man" where "*Bosheth*," meaning shame, is a euphemism for Baal. E/Ish-bosheth, "fire of Baal," is a descriptor of Baal as the Canaanite deity of thunder and lightning.

Following Saul's death, Ish-Bosheth ruled over Israel from his capital in Manahaim ca. 1005–1004 B.C. but not over Judah, which remained loyal to David (**2 Samuel 2:10**). After only two years in office, Ish-Bosheth was assassinated; his head was buried by David in Abner's tomb at Hebron (**2 Samuel 4:12**). David then assumed kingship over all of Israel (**2 Samuel 5:1–3**). For more information on Esh-Baal/Ish-Bosheth, see chart "**1 Samuel 9**: King Saul."

10. Merab was initially betrothed to David; however, Saul changed his mind and gave her instead to Adriel of Meholah, the son of Barzillai, who was a resident of Abel Meholah (**1 Samuel 18:17–19**). See chart "**2 Samuel 17**: Barzillai the Gileadite."

11. Michal married David (**1 Samuel 18:20–28**), but she bore him no children (**2 Samuel 6:23**), probably, in part, because of the incident in **2 Samuel 6:16**.

12. Mephibosheth (**2 Samuel 4:4; 9:6, 8, 10–13; 16:1, 4; 19:24–25, 30; 21:7**) is also called Merib-Baal (**1 Chronicles 8:34; 9:40**). Jonathan may have named his son after Rizpah's son Mephibosheth, who was among those innocently killed because of Saul's grievance against the Gibeonites; see chart "**2 Samuel 21**: Rizpah, the Concubine of King Saul." Mephibosheth was five years old when his father Jonathan and his grandfather Saul were killed (**2 Samuel 4:4**). In an effort to protect the young Mephibosheth in the tumultuous days of kingly transition—from the Saulide to Davidic monarchy—when Saul's heirs were at great risk, the nurse of Mephibosheth fled in haste with the child, but accidentally dropped him and he became lame in both feet. Later, David wanted to show kindness to Saul's living descendants because of his covenant with Jonathan (**1 Samuel 18:3**). He therefore invited Mephibosheth to come and live in Jerusalem and to always eat at the king's table (**2 Samuel 4:4; 9:1–13**).

13. Tarea (**1 Chronicles 8:35**) is a vocalic variation on Tahrea (**1 Chronicles 9:41**).

14. Jehoaddah (**1 Chronicles 8:36**) is also called Jadah (or Jarah in some manuscripts; **1 Chronicles 9:42**). This is an excellent example of a double case of error in manuscript transmission, especially of names. Jadah (יָדָה), a variation of יָרָה (Jarah), is a syncopation and alteration of Jehoaddah יְהוֹעַדָּה, "Yahweh makes known," as opposed to the hypocoristic "he casts, throws."

15. Alemeth (or Almon) is a personal name as well as a place name, the latter referring to a Levitical city within the tribal area of Benjamin (cf. **Joshua 21:18; 1 Chronicles 6:60; 8:36; 9:42**). Alemeth, with Azmaveth (see note 16), was part of "greater Jerusalem" (cf. **Ezra 2:24; Nehemiah 7:28; 12:29**).

16. The personal name Azmaveth (**1 Chronicles 8:36; 9:42**) corresponds to the place name Azmaveth (**Ezra 2:24; Nehemiah 12:29**) or Beth Azmaveth (**Nehemiah 7:28**). Azmaveth appears to be one of David's mighty men (**1 Chronicles 11:33**) and the father of Jeziel and Pelet (**1 Chronicles 12:3**).

17. The personal name Moza (**1 Chronicles 8:36–37; 9:42–43**) is associated with the place name Mozah (**Joshua 18:26**), perhaps rendered as Emmaus in the New Testament.

18. Rephaiah (**1 Chronicles 9:43**) is otherwise Raphah (**1 Chronicles 8:37**). The sons of Raphah/Rephaiah (Benjamites) appear to be among the remnant families who co-intermingled with Zerubbabel's descendants (Judahites) in post-exilic Jerusalem (**1 Chronicles 3:21**; cf. **9:3; Nehemiah 11:1–4**). See chart "**1 Chronicles 3**: Zerubbabel and Shealtiel and the Double Line of the Messiah through King David's Sons, Nathan and Solomon."

19. Obadiah was a descendant of Jonathan, the son of Saul (cf. **1 Chronicles 8:34–38; 9:40–44**). The "sons of . . . Obadiah" (**1 Chronicles 3:21**) are likely among the remnant Benjamites who co-mingled with Zerubbabel's (Judahite) descendants in the post-exile. See chart "**1 Chronicles 3**: Zerubbabel and Shealtiel and the Double Line of the Messiah through King David's Sons, Nathan and Solomon." Attempts to link this Obadiah (of Jonathan and Saul) with the canonical prophet of the same name have been unsuccessful. Moreover, he cannot be the priest who signed his name to the covenant document prepared by Nehemiah in 444 B.C. (**Nehemiah 10:5**).

20. Hanan, a descendant of Jonathan (**1 Chronicles 8:38; 9:44**), is possibly one of the two leaders of the people by this name who signed the covenant with Nehemiah in 444 B.C. (cf. **Nehemiah 10:22, 26**).

21. The many descendants of Ulam, 150 in all, are called "brave warriors who could handle the bow" (**1 Chronicles 8:40**).

22. "Yehud" is abbreviated "Yehudah," a later spelling of the English "Judah." From Yehud, the gentilic "Jew" or "Jewish" emerged (Heb. יְהוּדִי, "Yehudi").

1 CHRONICLES 9: GENEALOGICAL REGISTRY OF PROVINCIAL LEADERS WHO SETTLED IN JERUSALEM (POST-EXILE)[1]

Approximate Dating: ca. 538/400 B.C. ***Relevant Scriptures:*** **1 Chronicles 9:1–34**; also **Ezra 2:1–64; Nehemiah 7:8–63; 11:1–36**

- Israelites from the tribes of Judah and Benjamin (primarily) and from the tribes of Ephraim and Manasseh (secondarily; **1 Chronicles 9:3–9**; cf. **Ezra 2:2–35; Nehemiah 7:8–38; 11:4–9, 20**)
- Priests[2] (**1 Chronicles 9:10–13**; cf. **Ezra 2:36–39, 61–63; Nehemiah 7:39–42, 63–65; 11:10–14**)
- Levites[3] (**1 Chronicles 9:14–34**; cf. **Ezra 2:40–42; Nehemiah 7:43–45; 11:15–19**)
- Nethinim or temple servants[4] (cf. **Ezra 2:43–54; Nehemiah 7:46–56, 60, 62; 11:21**)
- Descendants of the servants of Solomon[5] (cf. **Ezra 2:55–58; Nehemiah 7:57–60**)

Biblical and Theological Significance

The return of the Jews from Babylonian exile, which commenced in significant numbers in 538 B.C., was fraught with difficulties of all kinds:

- Contrary to most expectations, not all Jews were willing to return, having been treated reasonably well, especially under the Persians. In the case of the younger generations, many had been born in Babylon and had come to see themselves as its citizens.
- The remnant that had not been taken captive had settled in reasonably well in the homeland, having helped themselves to the properties and moveable assets of those who had had to abandon them.
- The political prospects were uncertain at best. Israel had become an enclave known as Yehud, part of a larger jurisdiction known by the Persian term "satrap." All 120 satraps constituted the vast and powerful Persian Empire of Cyrus the Great (559–530 B.C.). How well would local authorities govern? Would the central government in Susa come to the aid of the Jewish community in times of economic distress or threats from surrounding enemy states?

- Among a great number of other social issues to be addressed was the intermarriage of the Jews to their pagan neighbors (**Ezra 9:10–10:44; Nehemiah 10:30; 13:23–27**).
- The issue of reviving Torah faith and its institutions was not least of the challenges facing the returnees. A legitimate Levitical and Aaronic priesthood needed to be identified, one with clear and unbroken genealogical connections. Then, a proper temple must be erected, one in which the Holy One of Israel could dwell in splendor and majesty. In addition, family heirs among the returnees who had left no relatives behind made every effort to determine the location and extent of their properties with the hope of repossessing them under a benign and generous Persian regime.
- The special attention paid to the priesthood and Levitical orders set an example for the non-priestly population as to how they too must be prepared with full documentation in order to have any hope of legitimate claims to the lands of their fathers.

The Chronicler describes these concerns by recounting the process by which the authorities could be assured that *all* Israel—Ephraim (Israel) and Judah alike—had documentary evidence of their genealogical history, written in the "book of the kings of Israel and Judah" (**1 Chronicles 9:1**; cf. **2 Chronicles 27:7; 28:26; 32:32; 35:27; 36:8**). The general populace who returned from exile needed authentic documentation attesting to their citizenship and property rights, especially if they were to live in Jerusalem (**Ezra 2:3–35; 8:1–14**; cf. **2:59–60; Nehemiah 2:19–20; 7:06–38, 61–62**). Similarly, the priests, Levites, Nethinim, and descendants of Solomon's servants had to prove their ancestry as a prerequisite for service in the Second Temple (**Ezra 2:36–58; 8:1**; cf. **Ezra 2:61–63; Nehemiah 7:39–60, 63–65**).

The odd statement that "Israel" would be among the first to live in the rebuilt city is a harbinger of the promise that someday both Israel (*Ephraim*) and Judah would be reunited as the one people of God and be called Israel (**Ezekiel 37:15–23**). Nehemiah relates how this came about in his own day, in 444 B.C., when he urged the people to repopulate Jerusalem but first checked their names against the genealogical record in his possession (**Nehemiah 7:5**; cf. **vv. 7b-60**). First to gain entrance were the "men of Israel" (**vv. 7b-38**); then the priests (**vv. 39–42**); the Levites, including musicians and gatekeepers (**vv. 43–45**); the temple servants (**vv. 46–56**); and finally, the descendants of Solomon's servants (**vv. 57–59**).

Notes

1. A parallel section in **Nehemiah 11** clarifies that the people who first returned to Jerusalem were a tithe of all the returnees to their homeland: "Now the leaders of the people settled in Jerusalem. The rest of the people cast lots to bring one out of every ten of them to live in Jerusalem, the holy city, while the remaining nine were to stay in their own towns." Some resistance to living there is noted, for "the people commended all who volunteered to live in Jerusalem" (**Nehemiah 11:1–2**).
2. The priests were descendants of the Levi–Kohath priestly line, as shown in chart "**1 Chronicles 6**: Levi: High Priests, Priests, Levites, and Musicians in Solomon's Temple."
3. The Levities were descendants of the Levi–Gershon and Levi–Merari lines, as shown in chart "**1 Chronicles 6**: Levi: High Priests, Priests, Levites, and Musicians in Solomon's Temple."
4. Nethinim (from the root נתן [Nathan, "to give"]) were temple servants who may have included Gibeonites who, in ancient days, had deceived Joshua (cf. **Joshua 9**), as well as others whose ethnicity could not be determined. The Nethinim served as woodcutters, water carriers, and slaves and were given over or *dedicated* to the Levites in the general operation of the Temple, especially in the post-exilic period.
5. This group is included in a parallel section in **Nehemiah 11:3**.

1 CHRONICLES 9: THE LEADERS FROM THE TRIBES OF JUDAH AND BENJAMIN WHO DWELLED IN JERUSALEM (POST-EXILE)

Approximate Dating: ca. 538 B.C. ***Relevant Scriptures:*** **1 Chronicles 9:3–9**; also **Genesis 38:1–6, 27–30; Numbers 26:20; Ezra 1:5; Nehemiah 11:4**

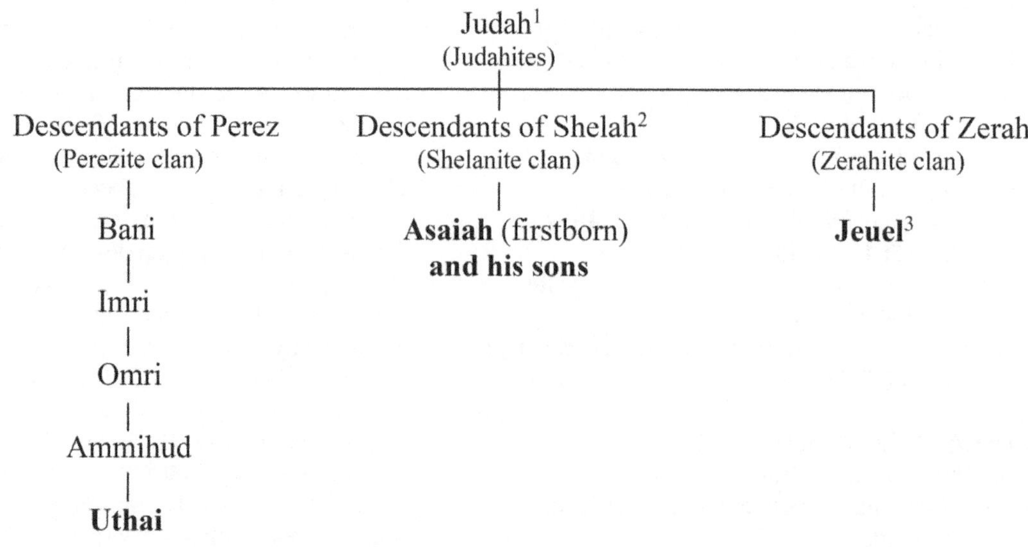

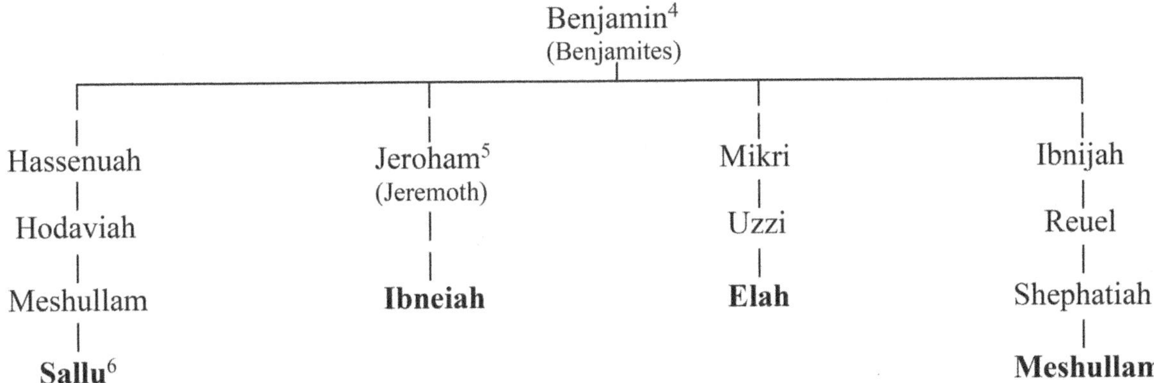

Biblical and Theological Significance

The return of the Jews from Babylonian exile commenced in significant numbers in 538 B.C. As **1 Chronicles 9:1–2** points out, "All Israel was listed in the genealogies recorded in the book of the kings of Israel and Judah. . . . [T]he first to resettle on their own property in their own towns were some Israelites, priests, Levites and temple servants." The Chronicler goes on to say that "those from Judah, from Benjamin, and from Ephraim and Manasseh" settled in Jerusalem (**1 Chronicles 9:3**). But as the chart makes clear, the Chronicler primarily focuses on the identity of the leaders of Judah and Benjamin who settled there (cf. **Ezra 1:5; 10:9; Nehemiah 11:3–4**). These two tribes had a special relationship, principally because of their geographic juxtaposition. Moreover, the first capital city of Saul had been in Gibeah of Benjamin and David's was in Jerusalem of Judah, only eight miles to the south.

Evidently, vigorous efforts were made by the governors and other leaders of Yehud to resettle people in the ancestral cities and regions from which they or their forefathers had come. However, some deportees[7] *chose* to live in Jerusalem with the Judeans, the Benjamites, and a few Ephraimites and Manassites, and they were commended for this decision (**1 Chronicles 9:1–3**; **Nehemiah 11:2–3**). The priests and Levites also had access to the city and its proximity because they had to be on hand to preside over whatever sacral ministries afforded them until another House of God could be built. Nevertheless, many other Levites felt obligated to go to their family villages and to the old Levitical cities to lead those communities in local, non-temple religious exercises.

Another observation must also be entertained and that is why Ephraimites, Manassites, and others from the north were in the land at all, considering that they had been deported under the Assyrians in 722 B.C. This, however, is to misread the narratives. First, the statement that "the people of Israel were taken from their homeland into exile in Assyria" by Shalmaneser V (727–722 B.C.; **2 Kings 17:23**)—and concluded by Sargon II (722/721–705 B.C.)—need not be taken to mean every last soul. The Chronicler more modestly says that Tiglath-Pileser III (745–727 B.C.) took away only the tribes east of the Jordan (i.e., Reuben, Gad, and Manasseh; **1 Chronicles 5:26**). Second, the famous Passover reformation of Hezekiah, which took place in his first year (715 B.C.), included multitudes from Asher, West Manasseh, Ephraim, Issachar, and Naphtali, even seven years after the Assyrian deportation (**2 Chronicles 30:11, 18**) and 136 years before the Babylonian conquest of Judah in 586 B.C. Similarly, Josiah (640–609 B.C.) entreated the people from Manasseh, Ephraim, and "from the entire remnant of Israel" to contribute to the restoration of the temple (**2 Chronicles 34:9; 35:3**). Clearly Yehud was not a vacuum to be filled by only the returnees of 538 B.C.

Notes

1. These three sons of Judah were by two women: (1) the daughter of a Canaanite man named Shua, who was the mother of Shelah (**Genesis 38:1–2, 5**) and (2) Tamar the daughter-in-law of Judah, who was the mother of the twin sons, Perez and Zerah (**Genesis 38:6, 27–30**). During Nehemiah's day, Zerah's descendants are not mentioned, only the descendants of Perez and Shelah (**Nehemiah 11:4–6**). A total of 690 people from Judah were chosen to live in Jerusalem (**1 Chronicles 9:6**), whereas a total of 956 individuals from Benjamin were chosen to live there (**1 Chronicles 9:9**), thus giving an interestingly high 4:3 ratio of Benjamites to Judahites (i.e., 956 to 690).

2. The descendants of Shelah the son of Judah are called the Shelanites/the Shelanite clan (cf. **Genesis 46:12; Numbers 26:20; 1 Chronicles 2:3; Nehemiah 11:5**).

3. Jeuel in **1 Chronicles 9:6** may be the same person named Jeuel "of the descendants of Adonikam" who returned to Jerusalem with Ezra in 458 B.C. (**Ezra 8:13**).

4. For the number of Benjamites, see note 1.

5. Jeroham (**1 Chronicles 8:27; 9:8**) is Jeremoth son of Beriah (**1 Chronicles 8:14**). The issue of two widely different renderings of the name—Jeroham יְרֹחָם meaning "he will take pity" and Jeremoth יְרֵמוֹת meaning "they rise up"—are likely due to a scribal error called metathesis in which letters are transposed. Here, the error results in and the reading of ירמת>*yrmt* forירחם >*yrhm*; a second error, reading מ (m) forח (kh); and a third, reading ת (t) for ם (final m). Other commentators such as Curtis and Madsen agree that Jeroham is Jeremoth; see Edward L. Curtis and Albert A. Madsen, *A Critical and Exegetical Commentary on the Book of Chronicles* (Edinburgh: T&T Clark, 1952), 158, 163. Jeremoth/Jeroham is a different person than Jeroham the son of Pashhur (**1 Chronicles 9:12**) and Jeroham, the son of Pelaliah (**Nehemiah 11:12**), both of whom were Kohathite priests in the tribe of Levi.

6. Sallu the son of Meshullam, the son of Hodaviah (**1 Chronicles 9:7**), who was a contemporary of Zerubbabel in 538 B.C., is not Sallu the son of Meshullam, the son of Joed (**Nehemiah 11:7**), who was a fellow Benjamite in post-exilic Jerusalem at the time of Nehemiah in 444 B.C.

7. These consisted of "Israelites" (i.e., remnants of the Assyrian deportation of 722 B.C.) and clergy (**1 Chronicles 9:2; Ezra 3:1; 6:16, 21; 7:7, 13; 8:25, 29; 9:1; 10:1, 25; Nehemiah 7:7, 61, 73; 10:39; 11:20**).

1 CHRONICLES 9: THE KOHATHITE ATTENDING PRIESTS IN THE SECOND TEMPLE (POST-EXILE)[1]

Approximate Dating: ca. 516 B.C. ***Relevant Scriptures:*** **1 Chronicles 9:10–13;** also **1 Chronicles 24:9, 14; Nehemiah 11:10–14**

Kohathite Priests (Heads of Priestly Families) Who Attended the High Priest(s)[2]

- **Jedaiah**[3] (see genealogy below)
- **Jehoiarib**[4] (syncopated as Joiarib)
- Jakin[5]

"The Official[6] in Charge of the House of God": Azariah (=Azariah #2/Seraiah #2)

Genealogy of Azariah and Jedaiah

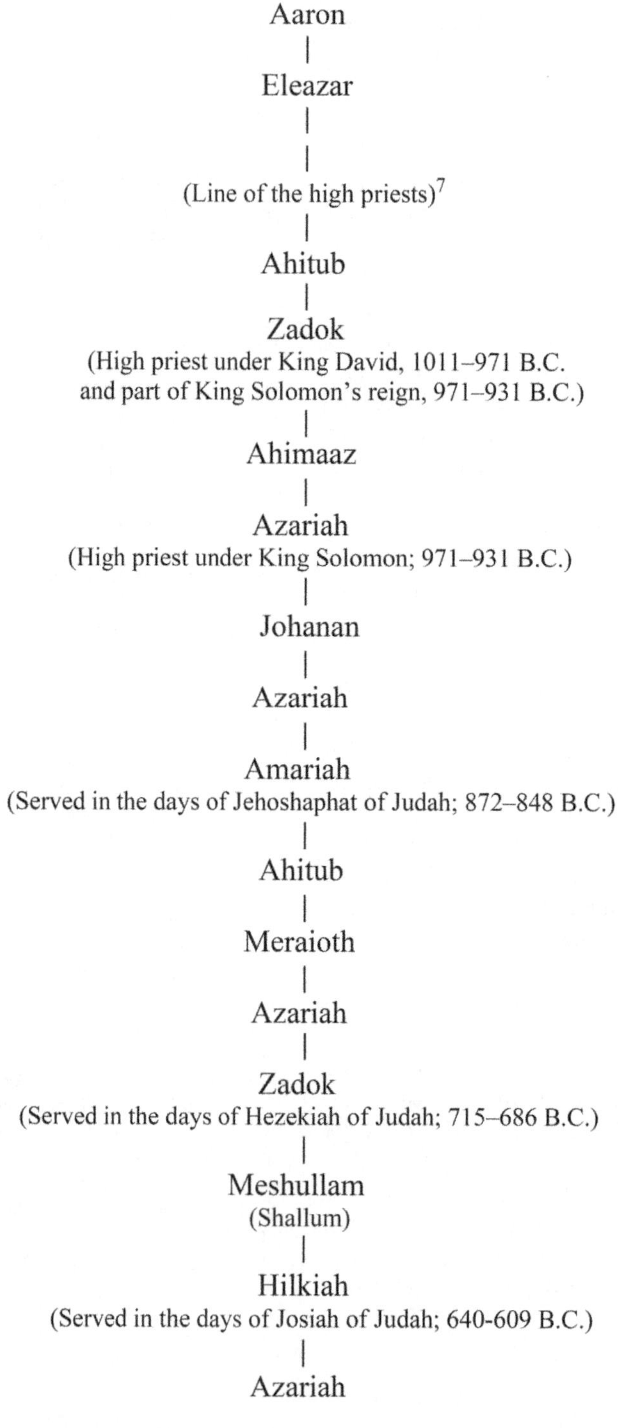

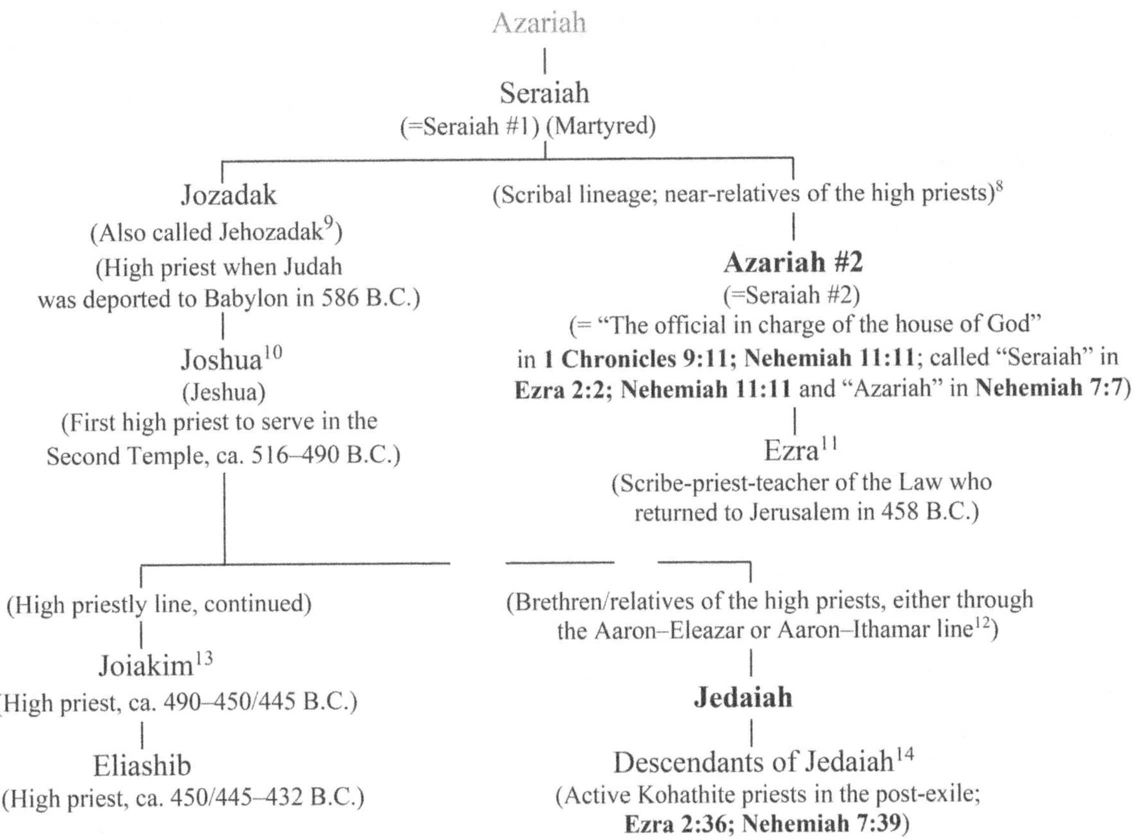

Overseers of Those Doing the Work of the House of God: Adaiah and Maasai

Genealogy of Adaiah (Levitical Kohathite) ***Genealogy of Maasai (Levitical Kohathite)***

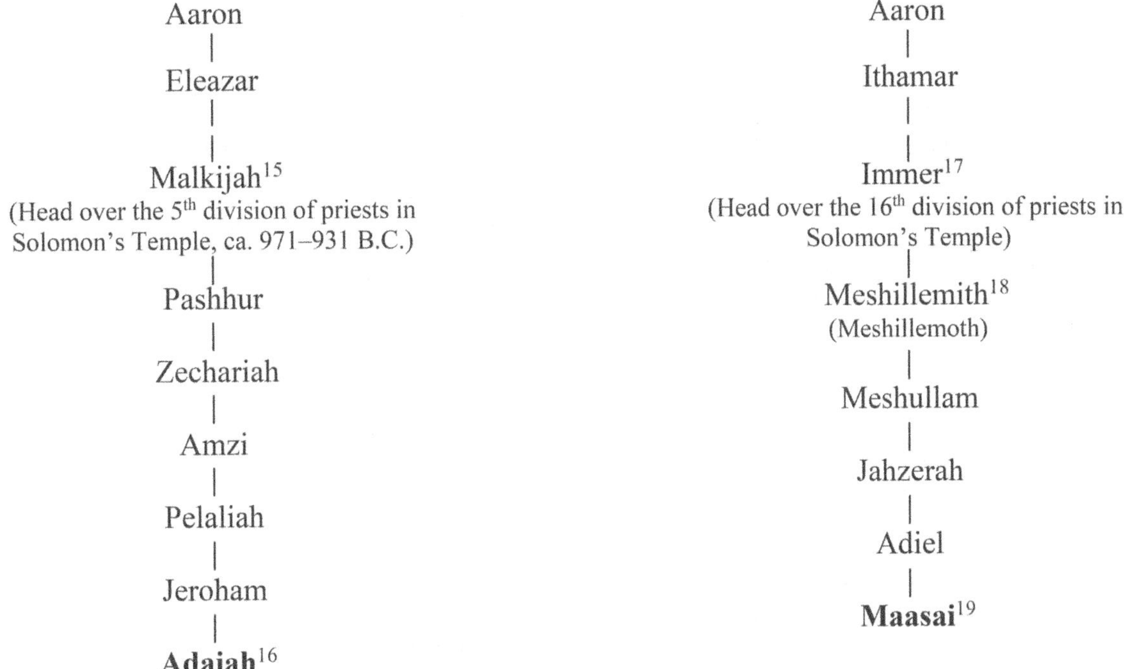

Biblical and Theological Significance

Significant numbers of Jews returned from Babylonian exile with Zerubbabel in 538 B.C.[20] The general populace had to provide documentation of their genealogical heritage (**1 Chronicles 9:1**). The importance of being able to reconstruct personal genealogies was paramount for priests who had been taken into exile, and now upon their return, had to prove their ancestry as a prerequisite to priestly ministry.

In 520 B.C., eighteen years after Zerubbabel returned

in 538 B.C., the prophets Haggai and Zechariah urged the Jerusalem community, under the leadership of Zerubbabel the governor[21] and Joshua the high priest, to begin temple construction (**Haggai 1:1–6; Zechariah 8:9–13**) and to begin the reestablishment of the priesthood (**Zechariah 3:1–5**). The most urgent project was construction of a new temple to replace the one utterly destroyed by the Babylonians in 586 B.C. (**2 Kings 25:9; 2 Chronicles 36:19**). The foundation of the new temple, begun under Sheshbazzar[22] (**Ezra 5:16**), was finally completed in the autumn of 520 B.C. and the temple itself was finished four years later in 516 B.C., to mixed reviews (**Ezra 6:15**). The older people recalled the grandeur of Solomon's Temple as compared to the modest size and inferior construction of this new edifice, and many burst out in tears of lament (**Haggai 2:3**; cf. **Ezra 3:12**). The rest of the gathered throng, however, shouted with joy (**Ezra 3:12–13**). This so-called Second Temple[23] remained in use until A.D. 70 when it was demolished by the Tenth Roman Legion under Titus.

Among the returnees to Jerusalem, "the first to resettle on their own property in their own towns were some Israelites [from Judah, Benjamin, Ephraim, and Manasseh], priests, Levites and temple servants" (**1 Chronicles 9:2–3**; cf. **Ezra 2:1–58; 8:1–14; Nehemiah 7:6–60**). The Chronicler records that "the priests, who were heads of families, numbered 1,760. They were able men, responsible for ministering in the house of God" (**1 Chronicles 9:13**). The high priests were all Kohathites and direct descendants of Aaron. Other Kohathites—either through the Aaron–Eleazar line or Aaron–Ithamar line[24]—served as *attending* priests to the high priests, and the Levitical ministers were Gershonites and Merarites, all of whom aligned along strict hereditary lines.[25]

Ezra, Nehemiah, Haggai, and Zechariah provide additional information about the returnees. The first to gain entrance to Jerusalem were the common people (thus Heb. אַנְשֵׁי עַם, *anshey am*; **Ezra 2:2–35; Nehemiah 7:7b-38**), then the priests (**Ezra 2:36–39; Nehemiah 7:39–42**), the Levites, musicians, and gatekeepers (**Ezra 2:40–42; Nehemiah 7:43–45**), the temple servants (**Ezra 2:43–54; Nehemiah 7:46–56**), and finally "the descendants of the servants of Solomon" (**Ezra 2:55–58; Nehemiah 7:57–59**).

The priestly names shared in common among **1 Chronicles 9:10–12**, **Ezra 2:36–39** and **Nehemiah 7:39–42**[26] are:

1. Jedaiah "through the family of Jeshua [the high priest]" (**Ezra 2:36; Nehemiah 7:39**) and his descendants;
2. J(eh)oiarib (or the son of Joiarib; cf. **Nehemiah 11:10**);
3. Jakin;
4. Descendants of Pashhur, the son of Malkijah (**1 Chronicles 9:12; Ezra 2:38; Nehemiah 7:41**); and
5. Descendants of Immer (**Ezra 2:37; Nehemiah 7:40**).

Ezra 8:1–14 provides the list of exiles who returned with Ezra in 458 B.C. to Jerusalem, including the priests:

1. Gershom, who was "of the descendants of Phinehas [meaning Phinehas, the son of Eleazar, the son of Aaron]" (**Ezra 8:2**), and
2. Daniel, who was "of the [faithful Elide] descendants of Ithamar [meaning Ithamar, the son of Aaron]" (**Ezra 8:2**).[27]

The prophets Haggai (**Haggai 1:1, 12, 14; 2:2, 4**) and Zechariah (**Zechariah 6:11**) refer to "Joshua son of Je(ho)zadak" as the high priest of their time (520–516 B.C.).

Notes

1. See also the chart "**Nehemiah 11**: Representative Priests Chosen to Dwell in Jerusalem in the Post-Exile."

2. The issue of the identities and interrelationships of these three—Jedaiah, Jehoiarib, and Jakin—is textually, contextually, and syntactically ambiguous at best and incomprehensible at worst. **First Chronicles 9:10** says merely "Jedaiah; Joiarib; Jakin," without reference to their relationship. **Nehemiah 12:6–7** lists "[from among the priests who returned with Zerubbabel and Joshua] Shemaiah, Joiarib, Jedaiah, Sallu, Amok, Hilkiah and Jedaiah," again with no apparent kinship. **Nehemiah 11:10** identifies the Kohathite priests as "Jedaiah; the son of Joiarib; Jakin."

It appears that the Kohathite attending priests in the Second Temple period retained the *honorary names* of the heads of the priestly divisions/courses that were set up in ca. 971 B.C. in the last days of David's reign. Moreover, the office holders in the Second Temple in 516 B.C. were likely the direct descendants of the ancestral office holders some 450 years earlier. The precedent and framework of twenty-four priestly courses continued to be a factor long after the destruction of the temple in 586 B.C. [For example, fragments of Hebrew inscriptions found in excavations at several sites in Israel commemorate the *original* priestly courses that were established in David's time; see M. Avi-Yonah, "A List of Priestly Courses from Caesarea, " *IEJ* 12 (1962): 137–139, from https://www.jstor.org/stable/27924896; and *The Priestly Class* in "Helios and the Zodiac Cycle in Ancient Palestinian Synagogues," *Symbiosis, Symbolism and the Power of the Past: Canaan, Ancient Israel, and Their Neighbors from the Late Bronze Age through Roman Palaestina: Proceedings of the Centennial Symposium*; W. F. Albright Institute of Archaeological Research and the American Schools of Oriental Research, Jerusalem, May 29–May 31, 2000, William G. Dever and Seymour Gitin, eds., (Winona Lake, IN: Eisenbrauns, 2003), 369–372.] Nevertheless, the official list(s) of Kohathite attending priests in the Old Testament ends with those in **Chronicles**, with one exception from the New Testament: Zechariah the father of John the Baptist, who served in Herod's Temple and "belonged to the priestly division of Abijah" (**Luke 1:5**; cf. **1 Chronicles 24:10**), referring to Abijah the Kohathite priest who was head over the eighth of the twenty-four priestly divisions/courses in David's time, ca. 971 B.C. In addition, a priest named Abijah (presumably a direct descendant of the ancestral Abijah in David's time) returned from exile with Zerubbabel in ca. 538 B.C. (**Nehemiah 12:4**; cf. **v. 17**). Also, a priest named Abijah was among those who sealed the covenant in the days of Nehemiah in ca. 444 B.C. (**Nehemiah 10:7**). If the method of casting lots in the original institution of the twenty-four priestly divisions (**1 Chronicles 24:7–18**) was conducted by alternating between Eleazar and Ithamar descendants, this means the Abijah line of priests—and by extension, Zechariah and John the Baptist—were Aaron–Ithamar descendants (rather than Aaron–Eleazar descendants); see chart "**1 Chronicles 24**: Genealogical Registry of the Twenty-Four Divisions of Kohathite Attending Priests Who Rotated Service in Solomon's Temple," especially note 17.

3. Jedaiah, a post-exilic priest in the Second Temple in ca. 516 B.C. (**1 Chronicles 9:10**), was likely a *descendant* of the ancestral priest named Jedaiah (presumably of the Ithamar line) who was head over the second division of priests in Solomon's Temple in ca. 971–931 B.C. (**1 Chronicles 24:7**); see chart "**1 Chronicles 24**: Genealogical Registry of the Twenty-Four Divisions of Kohathite Attending Priests Who Rotated Service in Solomon's Temple," especially note 12. It is unclear how Jedaiah (who served in the Second Temple) is related to the two priests named Jedaiah who returned to Jerusalem with Zerubbabel in 538 B.C. (i.e., Jedaiah #1 in **Nehemiah 12:6** and Jedaiah #2 in **Nehemiah 12:7**); see charts "**Nehemiah 12**: Genealogical Record of the Heads of the Kohathite Priests and Levites who Returned to Jerusalem with Zerubbabel and Joshua in the Post-Exile" and "**Nehemiah 12**: Genealogical Record of the Heads of Priests, Levites, and Gatekeepers who Served in the Second Temple in the Days of Joiakim the High Priest, Ezra the Priestly Scribe, and Nehemiah the Governor." The genealogy of Jedaiah, shown in the chart above, reflects the reading of **Ezra 2:36** and **Nehemiah 7:39**, which lists the returning priests as "the descendants of Jedaiah (through the family of Jeshua)"—presumably referring to Jeshua/Joshua the first high priest to serve in the Second Temple, from 516–490 B.C.

4. Jehoiarib, a post-exilic priest in the Second Temple in ca. 516 B.C. (**1 Chronicles 9:10**), was likely a *descendant* of the ancestral priest named Jehoiarib (presumably of the Eleazar line) who was the head of the first division of priests in Solomon's Temple in ca. 971–931 B.C. (**1 Chronicles 24:7**); see chart "**1 Chronicles 24**: Genealogical Registry of the Twenty-Four Divisions of Kohathite Attending Priests Who Rotated Service in Solomon's Temple," especially note 11. Jehoiarib/Joiarib returned to Jerusalem with Zerubbabel in ca. 538 B.C. (**Nehemiah 12:6**). Jehoiarib's descendant Mattenai was active in the days of Joiakim the high priest, ca. 490–450/444 B.C. (**Nehemiah 12:12, 19**). Later, Jehoiarib's son—called the "son of Joiarib" in **Nehemiah 11:10**—was active in the Second Temple in the days of Nehemiah, ca. 444 B.C. Jehoiarib/Joiarib the Kohathite priest is a different person than Joiarib the Levite, called a "[man] of learning," who returned with Ezra in 458 B.C. (**Ezra 8:16**).

5. Jakin, a post-exilic priest in the Second Temple in ca. 516 B.C. (**1 Chronicles 9:10**), was likely a direct *descendant* of the ancestral priest Jakin (presumably of the Eleazar line) who was the head of the twenty-first division of priests in Solomon's Temple in ca. 971–931 B.C. (**1 Chronicles 24:17**); see chart "**1 Chronicles 24**: Genealogical Registry of the Twenty-Four Divisions of Kohathite Attending Priests Who Rotated Service in Solomon's Temple." Jakin in **1 Chronicles 9:10** is likely the same person as Jakin in **Nehemiah 11:10**.

6. The term used here (נָגִיד, *nagid*) means a religious official. The "official in charge of the house of God" (cf. **1 Chronicles 9:11; 2 Chronicles 31:13; Nehemiah 11:11**) may correspond to the same individual described as "the captain of the temple" in the New Testament (**Acts 5:24**). According to Jeremias, the captain of the temple was "the highest ranking priest after the high priest," who was "selected from the nearest relations of the high priest." His duties involved assisting at the right hand of the high priest as well as overseeing the cultus and the whole body of officiating priests (such as the priests who were over the weekly and daily courses); see Joachim Jeremias, *Jerusalem in the Time of Jesus* (Philadelphia: Fortress, 1975), 160–163.

7. For the complete genealogy of the high priestly line and details about the individual high priests, see chart "**Supplement 2**: The High Priests of Israel."

8. For this scribal lineage, see chart "**Ezra 7**: Ezra, the Priestly Scribe and Teacher of the Law (Post-Exile)."

9. Jozadak (the syncopated form of Jehozadak) was the high priest who was deported (**1 Chronicles 6:15**). Apparently, he died in captivity since there is no mention of his return to Jerusalem.

10. Joshua (**Ezra 2:2; 3:2, 8; 4:3; 5:2; 10:18; Nehemiah 7:7; 12:1, 7, 10, 26; Haggai 1:1, 12, 14, 2:2, 4; Zechariah 3:1, 3–4, 6, 8–9; 6:11**), alias Jeshua (**Ezra 2:36; Nehemiah 7:39**), was the first high priest to officiate in the Second Temple. A simple syncopation of Yehoshuah>Ye(ho)shua>Yeshuah, is the same as the name "Jesus" in the (*graicized*) New Testament. Together, Zerubbabel and Joshua—"The two who are anointed to serve the Lord"—reestablished worship in post-exilic Jerusalem (**Zechariah 4:14**; cf. **Haggai 1:1, 12**); they foreshadowed the Messiah (Branch) who would unite the office of priest and king (**Zechariah 6:11–13**). Joshua/Jeshua the "son of Jozadak" the high priest, is not to be confused with the Levite, Jeshua son of Kadmiel (a descendant of Hodaviah; **Ezra 2:40; 3:9; Nehemiah 7:43; 9:4–5; 12:8, 24**) nor with Jeshua son of Azaniah (**Nehemiah 10:9**).

11. Chronological considerations suggest that Ezra was probably the *descendant* (not the *son*) of the Seraiah figure in **Ezra 7:1**. Ezra was the scribal priest and teacher of the Law who brought back a group of returning exiles to Jerusalem in ca. 458 B.C. and the one for whom the book of **Ezra** is named. For more details, see chart "**Ezra 7**: Ezra, the Priestly Scribe and Teacher of the Law (Post-Exile)."

12. For the Aaron–Eleazar and Aaron–Ithamar lines, see charts "**1 Samuel 1**: Eli and the Eli High Priesthood"; "**1 Chronicles 6**: Levi: High Priests, Priests, Levites, and Musicians in Solomon's Temple"; and "**1 Chronicles 24**: Genealogical Registry of the Twenty-Four Divisions of Kohathite Attending Priests Who Rotated Service in Solomon's Temple."

13. Joiakim the high priest was the great-great-grandfather of Jaddua, the last high priest who is named in the Old Testament (cf. **Nehemiah 12:10–12, 26**). See chart "**Supplement 2**: The High Priests of Israel."

14. Jedaiah's descendants were in the line of "the family of Jeshua [presumably referring to Jeshua/Joshua the high priest]" (**Ezra 2:36** and **Nehemiah 7:39**). Two priests named Jedaiah returned to Jerusalem with Zerubbabel in 538 B.C. and are called "leaders of the priests and their associates in the days of Joshua [the high priest, ca. 516–490 B.C.]" (cf. **Nehemiah 12:6–7**); both appear to be Kohathite attending priests, but their exact lineages are unclear. See note 3.

15. The Aaron–Eleazar ancestry of Malkijah is supported in chart "**1 Chronicles 24**: Genealogical Registry of the Twenty-Four Divisions of Kohathite Attending Priests Who Rotated Service in Solomon's Temple."

16. The abbreviated genealogy of Adaiah given in **1 Chronicles 9:12**—"Adaiah son of Jeroham, the son of Pashhur, the son of Malkijah"—omits ancestors who are identified elsewhere (cf. **Nehemiah 11:12**).

17. An Aaron–Ithamar heritage for Immer is supported in chart "**1 Chronicles 24**: Genealogical Registry of the Twenty-Four Divisions of Kohathite Attending Priests Who Rotated Service in Solomon's Temple."

18. Meshillemith in **1 Chronicles 9:12** is called Meshillemoth in **Nehemiah 11:13**.

19. The lineage of Maasai is given in **1 Chronicles 9:12**.

20. See chart "**Ezra 2**: Genealogical Record of the Captives who Returned to Jerusalem with Zerubbabel and Joshua (Post-Exile)."

21. The term for governor, פֶּחָה, *pekhah* (from Akkadian *bēl pīḫatu*), suggests that Zerubbabel did not exercise absolute power but served at the pleasure of the Persian bureaucracy, whose head was Emperor Darius I (522–486 B.C.). As governor of the state of Yehud, Zerubbabel held a relatively minor position in the Persian empire. For the spiritual leadership of Joshua/Jeshua, see note 10.

22. For the identity and role of Sheshbazzar the first governor in post-exilic Jerusalem, see chart "**Ezra 1**: Sheshbazzar and Zerubbabel, the Governors over the Restored Community in Jerusalem (Post-Exile)."

23. The original structure of the Second Temple became the framework for the great reconstruction under Herod the Great (i.e., Herod's Temple, which was completed in 19/18 B.C.).

24. See chart "**1 Chronicles 24**: Genealogical Registry of the Twenty-Four Divisions of Kohathite Priests Who Rotated Service in Solomon's Temple."

25. See chart "**1 Chronicles 6**: Levi: High Priests, Priests, Levites, and Musicians in Solomon's Temple."

26. Refer to "Table 1: Heads of Kohathite Priestly Families—NOT High Priests—from Major Scriptural Sources" in chart "**1 Chronicles 24**: Genealogical Registry of the Twenty-Four Divisions of Kohathite Attending Priests Who Rotated Service in Solomon's Temple."

27. See chart "**1 Chronicles 24**: Genealogical Registry of the Twenty-Four Divisions of Kohathite Priests Who Rotated Service in Solomon's Temple."

1 CHRONICLES 9: SEVEN LEVITICAL LEADERS IN THE SECOND TEMPLE (POST-EXILE)[1]

Approximate Dating: ca. 538/440 B.C. ***Relevant Scriptures:*** **1 Chronicles 9:14–16;** also **Genesis 46:11; Exodus 6:17, 19, 21; Numbers 3:17; 26:57; 1 Chronicles 6:1–2, 16–47; 25:1–3; 2 Chronicles 29:12–14; Ezra 8:19; Nehemiah 11:15–17, 22; 12:35**

1. **Shemaiah** (*son*/descendant of Hasshub) (Merarite)
2. **Bakbakkar**[2] (probably = Bakbukiah) (probably Gershonite)
3. **Heresh** (unknown Levitical clan)
4. **Galal** (Merarite)
5. **Mattaniah** (Gershonite)
6. **Obadiah** (Merarite)
7. **Berekiah** (Kohathite–Korahite)

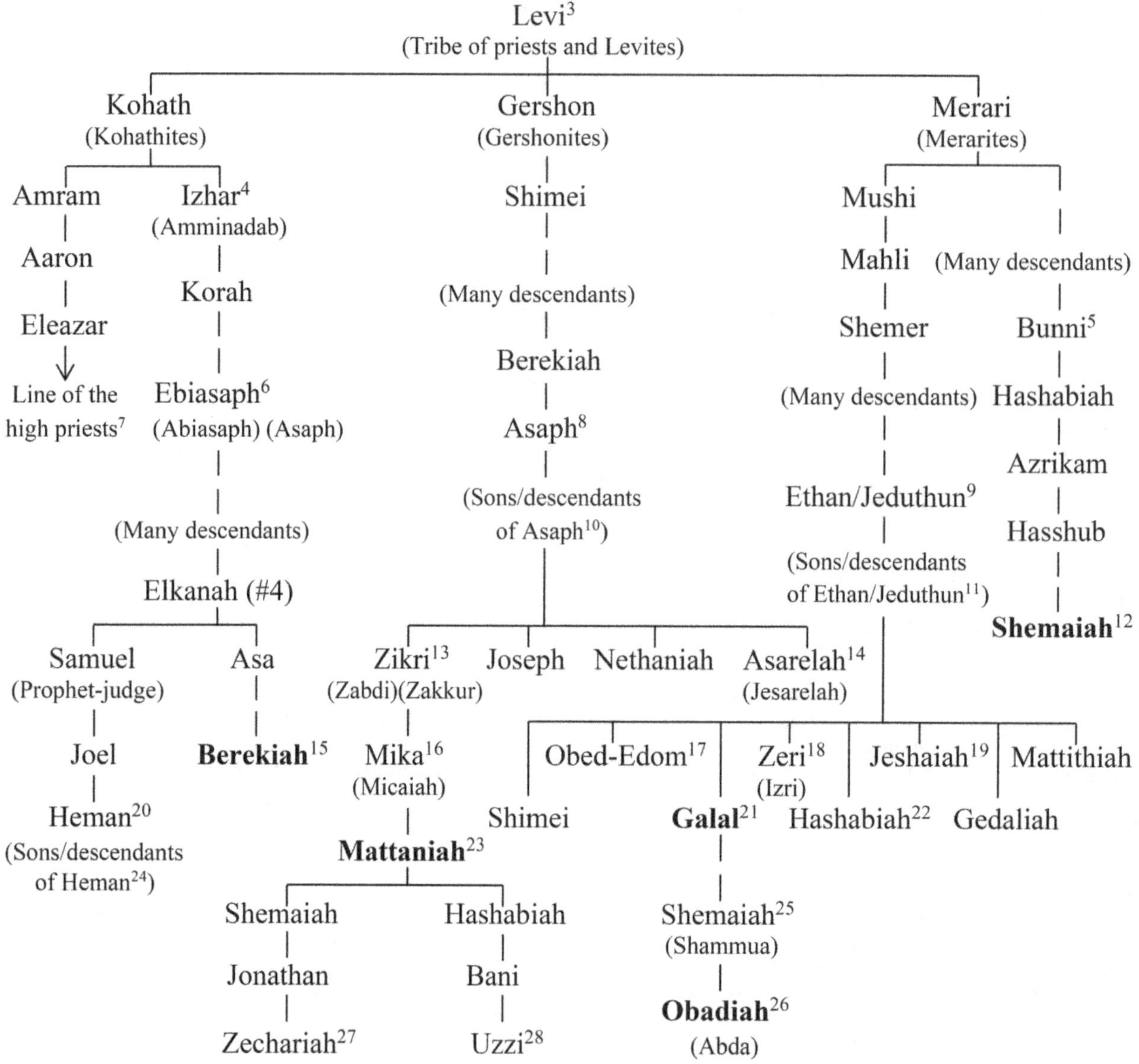

Biblical and Theological Significance

Upon their return to Israel from the Babylonian deportation, the people, most of whom had been born in Babylon during the seventy-year exile, sought to re-establish themselves in their homeland according to their ancient tribal allotments. Also, surely the plan of the leaders was to relocate the Levites back to the forty-eight scattered cities they had formerly occupied (**Nehemiah 7:73; 11:20, 36; 12:27–30**).

Of special interest in the chart is the Levitical leaders from the early Second Temple period (beginning in 516 B.C.). However, the ancestral roots of those individuals were also important in that they must be consulted to determine the legitimacy of any claims to Levitical service. The individuals here can be located securely in the post-exilic period as contemporaries of Ezra (458–444 B.C.) and/or Nehemiah (444–432 B.C.).

The Levitical leaders were part of a larger group called "priests, the Levites, the gatekeepers, the musicians and the temple servants" (**Nehemiah 7:73**; cf. **1 Chronicles 9:2; Ezra 7:24; Nehemiah 10:28; 11:3**) who promised not to intermarry with the surrounding people, but rather to follow the Law of God,[29] to bring wood for the altar, to give the first fruits of the crops—grains, as well as fruit trees, wine, and olive oil—as well as the firstborn of their sons, cattle, herds, and flocks to the temple, and to pay a third of a shekel to support the temple service (**Nehemiah 10:28–39**).[30] The Levites in particular were responsible for collecting "the tithes in all the towns" and bringing them to the temple in Jerusalem (**Nehemiah 10:37–39**). The Levites and priests[31] are listed in **Nehemiah 12:8–26,** and their assignments and responsibilities are detailed in **Nehemiah 12:27–47; 13:10–13, 30–31**.

A total of 284 Levites occupied the holy city (**Nehemiah 11:18**).

Notes

1. Compare the names of the Levites in this chart with those in "**Nehemiah 8**: Genealogical Record of the Levites who Helped the People Understand the Reading of the Law of Moses," "**Nehemiah 11**: The Levitical Leaders Chosen to Dwell in Jerusalem in the Post-Exile," "**Nehemiah 12**: Genealogical Record of the Heads of the Kohathite Priests and Levites who Returned to Jerusalem with Zerubbabel and Joshua in the Post-Exile," and "**Nehemiah 12**:

Genealogical Record of the Thanksgiving Choirs Led by Ezra and Nehemiah During the Dedication of the Wall around Jerusalem and the Celebration at the Second Temple."

2. Bakbakkar (**1 Chronicles 9:15**) is probably the same person as *Bakbukiah* the Levite (**Nehemiah 11:17; 12:9, 25**). The root of Bakbakkar is bqbq, as in (1) Baqbuq, בַּקְבּוּק "bottle," "chatterer" ("Bakbuk" in **Ezra 2:51; Nehemiah 7:53**); (2) Baqbuq בַּקְבֻּק, a "gurgling, bubbling" sound; (3) Baqbuqya בַּקְבֻּקְיָה ("Bakbukiah" the gatekeeper in **Nehemiah 11:17; 12:9, 25**); and (4) Baqbaqqar בַּקְבַּקַּר ("Bakbukiah" in **1 Chronicles 9:15** shown above), a name clearly unrelated to the others because of the ר (r). Some scholars suggest that, because of a scribal lapse, 3 and 4 are the same. Others propose that the form of 4 is a corruption of an original בַּקְבֻּק + רַב, "Baqbuq the Great" or "Baqbuq the Rich." In any event, the name as it stands in **1 Chronicles 9:15** cannot be correct, a fact also supported by the apparatus of *Biblia Hebraica Stuttgartensia*.

3. See chart "**1 Chronicles 6**: Levi: High Priests, Priests, Levites, and Musicians in Solomon's Temple."

4. Izhar in **Exodus 6:18, 21; Numbers 16:1;** and **1 Chronicles 6:2, 18, 38; 23:12** is called Amminadab in **1 Chronicles 6:22**.

5. For the lineage of Bunni, see **Nehemiah 11:15**.

6. Ebiasaph (**1 Chronicles 6:23, 37; 9:19**) is otherwise Abiasaph (**Exodus 6:24)** and, for short, Asaph (**1 Chronicles 26:1**). Ebiasaph/Abiasaph/Asaph, a Kohathite–Korahite priest (cf. **Exodus 6:24; 1 Chronicles 6:23**), should not be confused with Asaph son of Berekiah (a Gershonite), who was one of the three chief musicians in Solomon's Temple (see note 8).

7. See chart "**Supplement 2**: The High Priests of Israel."

8. Asaph son of Berekiah was one of three chief musicians in the Temple (**1 Chronicles 6:39; 15:17; 25:1**).

9. Ethan (**1 Chronicles 6:44; 15:17, 19**) is also called Jeduthun (**1 Chronicles 25:1**); he was one of three chief musicians in Solomon's Temple.

10. The sons of Asaph were chosen musicians in the temple (cf. **1 Chronicles 25:1–2, 9–10, 12, 14; 2 Chronicles 5:12; Ezra 3:10; Nehemiah 11:22; 12:35, 36?**).

11. The sons of Ethan/Jeduthun, who were Levitical Merarites, were chosen musicians in Solomon's Temple (cf. **1 Chronicles 16:42; 25:1, 3; 2 Chronicles 5:12**). They also served as gatekeepers at the temple, controlling access to the sacred complex (**1 Chronicles 16:42**; **2 Chronicles 23:19**) and guarding the temple treasuries, the treasuries of the dedicated things, and the storerooms at the gates (**1 Chronicles 9:26; 26:20–22; Nehemiah 12:25**).

12. Shemaiah son of Hasshub (a Merarite; **1 Chronicles 9:14**) is the same person as Shemaiah in **Nehemiah 11:15** who was one of the Levites among the *tithe* (tenth) of persons chosen to dwell in Jerusalem (cf. **Nehemiah 11**). He is not (1) Shemaiah the descendant of Ethan/Jeduthun (also Merarite) who was a contemporary of Hezekiah of Judah, 715–686 B.C. (**2 Chronicles 29:14**), nor (2) Shemaiah son of Mattaniah, the Gershonite (**Nehemiah 12:35**).

13. Zikri (**1 Chronicles 9:15**) is clearly Zabdi (**Nehemiah 11:17**) and Zakkur (**1 Chronicles 25:2, 10**; **Nehemiah 12:35**).

14. Asarelah (**1 Chronicles 25:2**) is alternatively Jesarelah (**1 Chronicles 25:14**).

15. Berekiah lived in Netophah of Judah, approximately three miles south of Bethlehem (**1 Chronicles 9:16**; cf. **Ezra 2:22; Nehemiah 7:26**). Berekiah the son/descendant of Asa was a Kohathite–Korahite priest (**1 Chronicles 9:16**) and therefore cannot be Berekiah the father of Asaph the Gershonite, who is also shown in this chart (cf. **1 Chronicles 6:39; 15:17**). However, one of these men named Berekiah—likely Berekiah the son/descendant of Asa—could well be the father of Zechariah, the last martyr of the Old Testament (cf. **Matthew 23:35; Luke 11:50–51**). The main reason for favoring Berekiah the Kohathite–Korahite as the father of the martyred Zechariah over Berekiah the Gershonite is the association of Berekiah and Elkanah as the doorkeepers for the ark in **1 Chronicles 15:23**. See also note 43 in chart "**1 Chronicles 6**: Levi: High Priests, Priests, Levites, and Musicians in Solomon's Temple."

16. Mika (**1 Chronicles 9:15; Nehemiah 11:17**) is otherwise Micaiah (**Nehemiah 12:35**). For other descendants in his lineage, see chart "**Nehemiah 11**: The Levitical Leaders Chosen to Dwell in Jerusalem in the Post-Exile."

17. Obed-Edom is the "son of Jeduthun" (**1 Chronicles 16:38**), but Obed-Edom may be Jeduthun's *descendant* rather than his son (see **1 Chronicles 25:3** and the chart "**2 Samuel 6**: Obed-Edom, the Levitical Gatekeeper and Keeper of the Ark").

18. Zeri (**1 Chronicles 25:3**) is otherwise Izri (**1 Chronicles 25:11**).

19. This is likely Jeshaiah the Merarite who returned to Jerusalem with Ezra in 458 B.C. (cf. **Ezra 8:19**).

20. Heman was one of three chief Levitical musicians in the temple, as well as "the king's seer" (**1 Chronicles 25:5**; see **6:33; 15:17; 25:1**).

21. Galal is mentioned in **1 Chronicles 9:15–16** and **Nehemiah 11:17**.

22. This is likely Hashabiah the Merarite who returned to Jerusalem with Ezra in 458 B.C. (cf. **Ezra 8:19, 24**).

23. For the lineage of Mattaniah son of Mika/Micaiah (a Gershonite), see **1 Chronicles 9:15** and **Nehemiah 11:17, 22; 12:35**. He is identified as "the director who led in thanksgiving and prayer" (**Nehemiah 11:17**; cf. **12:8; 13:13?**). Mattaniah the son of Mika, who served in the Second Temple, should not be confused with others of the same name: Mattaniah (a Gershonite and an Asaph descendant) who was an ancestor of Jahaziel who lived in the days of King Hezekiah of Judah, 715–686 B.C. (**2 Chronicles 20:14; 29:13**), nor the other Levites named Mattanaiah who were descendants of Heman the Kohathite (**1 Chronicles 25:4, 16**), Elam (**Ezra 10:26**), Zattu (**Ezra 10:27**), Pahath-Moab (**Ezra 10:30**), and Bani (**Ezra 10:37**).

24. Heman's sons were chosen musicians in the temple (**1 Chronicles 25:4–6**).

25. Shemaiah son of Galal (**1 Chronicles 9:16**) is also called Shammua (**Nehemiah 11:17**). He may be the son of Galal rather than his descendant. Shemaiah was a Merarite and a descendant of Ethan/Jeduthun. He is not (1) Shemaiah (also a descendant of Ethan/Jeduthun and a Merarite) who was a contemporary of Hezekiah of Judah, 715–686 B.C. (**2 Chronicles 29:14**); (2) Shemaiah son/descendant of Hasshub, also a Merarite, and his contemporary (**1 Chronicles 9:14; Nehemiah 11:15**), nor (3) Shemaiah the son of Mattaniah, a Gershonite, and his contemporary (**Nehemiah 12:35**).

26. Obadiah (**1 Chronicles 9:16**) is otherwise Abda (**Nehemiah 11:17**) and likely Obadiah the gatekeeper (**1 Chronicles 12:25**) who "lived in the villages of the Netophathites" near Jerusalem (**1 Chronicles 9:16**).

27. For the lineage of Zechariah, see **Nehemiah 12:35**.

28. For the lineage of Uzzi, the chief officer of the Levites in post-exilic Jerusalem, see **Nehemiah 11:22**.

29. For the ministries of the Levites, see **Numbers 1:47–53; 3:5–51; 8:5–26**; for their distribution throughout the land of Canaan, see **Joshua 21:1–42**.

30. As *The Bible Knowledge Commentary* (Gene A. Getz, Vol. 1, 691) for Nehemiah 10:30–39 says, "The stipulations they spelled out in the agreement include (a) avoidance of intermarriages . . . (b) keeping the Sabbath and the sabbatical year . . . and (c) supporting the temple service by giving a third of a shekel (about one-eighth of an ounce) annually (Neh. 10:32–33). According to Exodus 30:11–16 the temple gift was to be one-half a shekel annually, but here it was valued lightly. These temple offerings gave the priests and Levites money for maintaining the bread on the table of the Presence (Ex. 35:13; 39:36; Num. 4:7), for making various offerings, for celebrating monthly and annual festivals, and carrying out other duties. (See comments on Neh. 13:10–11 regarding the people's failure to keep this commitment.)." *The IVP OT Background Commentary* (John H. Walton; Victor H. Matthews, Mark W. Chavalas), p. 480 on the "Temple Tax" at Nehemiah 10:32–33 says, "Though the Persian kings Darius I and Artaxerxes I had promised to assist the building of the temple (see Ezra 6:9–10; 7:21–24), they had not endowed its operation budget (though Ezra 7:21–22 may refer to some ongoing aid). Coinage had become the economic standard during the reigns of Darius and Xerxes. The development of a cash-based economy during this period required cash support for the operations of the temple. The third of a shekel mentioned here was probably due to an adjustment made to adapt to the monetary system used in the Persian empire. At this time the basic coin of the Persian empire, the daric, weighed 8.4 grams and was equated to the Babylonian shekel. The Aramaic *zuz* was one-half of that and equivalent to the Greek drachma. The standard Israelite shekel, however, had long been 11.4 grams (as was the Assyrian shekel), but there was also a royal shekel ('heavy' shekel in Ugaritic terminology), which is represented in archaeological finds as weighing 12.5 to 12.8 grams. Therefore a *zuz*, at 4.2 grams, could be roughly equated to one-third of the traditional royal shekel."

31. For a breakdown of the priests and Levites, see chart "**Nehemiah 12**: Genealogical Record of the Heads of the Kohathite Priests and Levites Who Returned to Jerusalem with Zerubbabel and Joshua in the Post-Exile."

1 CHRONICLES 9: REGISTRY AND THE LEVITICAL GATEKEEPERS AND THE PRIESTLY OVERSEER OF THE GRAIN OFFERINGS IN THE SECOND TEMPLE (POST-EXILE)

Approximate Dating: ca. 538/400 B.C. ***Relevant Scriptures:*** **1 Chronicles 9:17–32;** also **Exodus 6:21; Numbers 16:1; 1 Chronicles 6:37; 26:1–3, 14; Ezra 2:42; Nehemiah 7:45; 11:19; 12:25**

Principal Levitical Gatekeepers[1], [2]

- **Shallum**[3] (overseer of all 212 gatekeepers)
- **Akkub**[4]
- **Talmon**[5]
- **Ahiman**
- **Their fellow Levites/brethren**

Gatekeeper at the entrance to the tent of meeting: **Zechariah**[6] (Kohathite–Korahite)
Priestly overseer of the grain offerings: **Mattithiah**[7] (Kohathite–Korahite)

Genealogy of Shallum, Zechariah, and Mattithiah (Kohathite–Korahites)

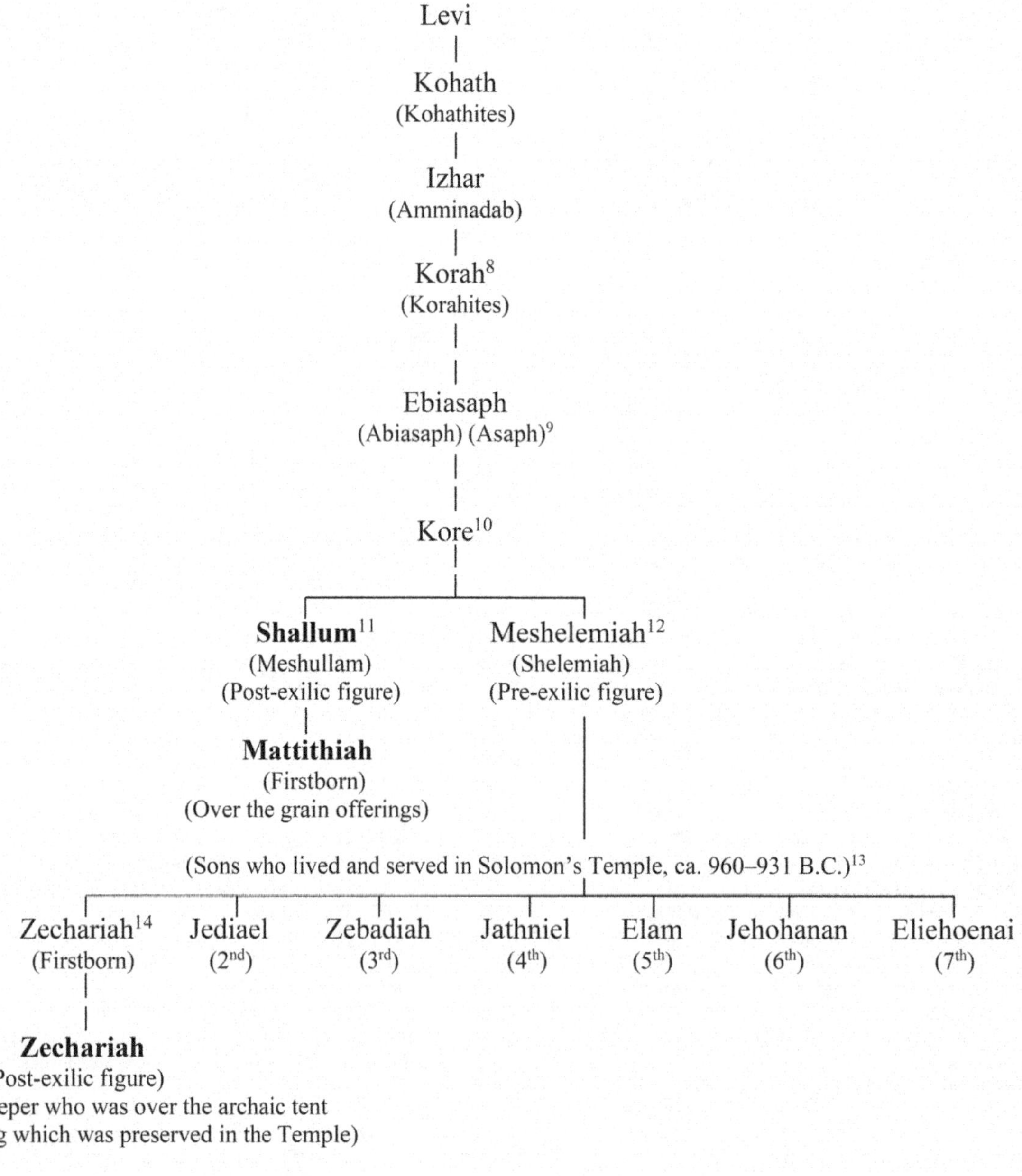

Biblical and Theological Significance

The gatekeeper office was an inherited position—passed down through specific clans within the tribe of Levi from the days of the tabernacle in the wilderness. Gatekeepers were required to be in a registered genealogy to be considered eligible for service (**1 Chronicles 9:22**). In ancient times, Levitical servants who functioned as gatekeepers were chosen from among the Kohathite–Korathite clan (or from the Merarite clan)[15] and they were appointed to guard the entrance to the tent of meeting at the tabernacle, where the high priest Phinehas, son of Eleazar, was the head over them (cf. **Exodus 6:24; 28:43; Numbers 16; 25; 1 Chronicles 9:19–20**). Later in united monarchic times, David and Samuel the seer appointed gatekeepers in Solomon's Temple (**1 Chronicles 9:22**). The Chronicler describes the organization of the Levitical gatekeepers in Solomon's Temple as the model for how the gatekeepers were to be organized when Second Temple worship was restored by the new generation of exiles who came to Jerusalem. The function of gatekeepers in the post-exilic era (**1 Chronicles 9:17–32**) can be compared to those in the time of King David (**1 Chronicles 26:1–19**).

The text of **1 Chronicles 9:18** (NKJV) suggests that, until the time of the post-exile, "*they* [the gatekeepers] *had been* gatekeepers for the camps of the children of Levi at the King's Gate on the east"—meaning at the main entrance only. However, when worship was reestablished in the Second Temple (newly completed in 516 B.C.), the gatekeepers were positioned at all entrances to the temple complex, specifically at the four cardinal directional entrances (E–W–N–S). The four principal Kohathite–Korahite gatekeepers—Shallum, Akkub, Talmon, and Ahiman—resided at the Second Temple and "were entrusted with the responsibility for [guarding] the rooms and treasuries in the house of God [and the treasuries for the dedicated things]. They would spend the night stationed around the house of God, because they had to guard it; and they had charge of the key for opening it each morning" (**1 Chronicles 26–27; 26:20; Nehemiah 12:25**). Additionally, the gatekeepers were charged with preventing anything or anyone unclean from entering the holy temple (**2 Chronicles 23:19**) and for purifying themselves and maintaining the overall purity of the sanctuary (**Nehemiah 12:30**).

Some gatekeepers from the "descendants of Shallum, Ater, Talmon, Akkub, Hatita and Shobai"—who numbered 138 (or 139)—returned to Jerusalem with Zerubbabel in 538 B.C. (**Ezra 2:42; Nehemiah 7:45**); other gatekeepers returned with Ezra in 458 B.C. (**Ezra 7:7**). Talmon and Akkub are specifically noted as being among the gatekeepers who guarded the storerooms at the gates in the days of Joiakim the high priest (ca. 490–450/444 B.C.) and in the days of Nehemiah and Ezra (458–444 B.C.; **Nehemiah 12:25–26**). The brethren of the principal gatekeepers lived in appointed Levitical villages[16] (**Ezra 2:70; Nehemiah 7:73**; cf. **Joshua 21:20–26; 34–40**) and came to serve in Jerusalem "from time to time" for "seven-day periods," lodging around the temple itself (**1 Chronicles 9:25**).

Gatekeepers were among the Temple officials, and like the priests, Levites, musicians, and temple servants, they did not have to pay taxes (**Ezra 7:24**); instead, they were provided for financially by the people "in daily portions" (**Nehemiah 12:47;** see also **10:39; 13:5**).

When Nehemiah arrived in Jerusalem in 444 B.C., he oversaw the building of the defensive walls section by section between the gates. He named the various gates according to their location, condition, or purpose (**Nehemiah 3:1–32; 8:1–16**), as follows: Sheep Gate (**v. 1**); Fish Gate (**v. 3**); Jeshanah (or "Old") Gate (**v. 6**); Valley Gate (**v. 13**); Dung Gate (**v. 14**); Fountain Gate (**v. 15**); Water Gate (**v. 26**); Horse Gate (**v. 28**); Inspection (or "Miphkad" or "Hammiphkad") Gate (v. **31**); and Ephraim Gate (**8:16**). Nehemiah stipulated that "the gates of Jerusalem are not to be opened until the sun is hot. While the gatekeepers are still on duty, have them shut the doors and bar them. Also appoint residents of Jerusalem as guards, some at their posts and some near their own houses" (**Nehemiah 7:3**).

Some of the Kohathite–Korahite brethren were also "in charge of the articles used in the temple service; they counted them when they were brought in and when they were taken out. Others were assigned to take care of the furnishings and all the other articles of the sanctuary, as well as the special flour and wine, olive oil, incense[17] and spices. But some of the [Kohathite] priests took care of mixing the spices" (**1 Chronicles 9:28–30**). For example, Mattithiah son of Shallum the Korahite was responsible for baking the offering bread (the showbread) that was placed on the table of the presence and replaced every Sabbath[18] (**1 Chronicles 9:31–32**; see also **23:29–32**).

Notes

1. The term for *gatekeeper* is simply the participial form of a reconstructed verb "to (guard a) gate:" שׁוֹעֵר (*shoer*), lit. "gater." This is the Hebrew (and English) way of deriving a functional label from the function performed; e.g. "electrician" from "electricity" or "roofer" from "roof." "Doorkeeper" is שֹׁמֵר הַסַּף (*shomer hassaph*), meaning "watcher of the (door) threshold."

2. The gatekeepers who are shown in this chart were from both the Kohathite–Korahite and the Merarite clans, but not the Gershonite clan (cf. **1 Chronicles 26:19**). Only the genealogy of Shallum the chief gatekeeper is fully known; the heritage of the others (i.e., Akkub, Talmon, Ahiman, and their brethren) was likely Kohathite–Korahite or perhaps Merarite also, but not Gershonite.

Compare the Levitical gatekeepers who served in the post-exilic Second Temple (as shown in this chart) to those who had served in Solomon's Temple ca. 960–931 B.C. (as shown in chart "**1 Chronicles 26**: The Kohathite–Korahite and Merarite Gatekeepers in Solomon's Temple") and to the gatekeepers who returned to Jerusalem in 538 B.C. with Zerubbabel, as shown in chart "**Ezra 2**: Genealogical Record of the Captives Who Returned to Jerusalem with Zerubbabel and Joshua (Post-Exile)."

3. Shallum was from the Kohathite–Korahite clan and his brethren were "responsible for guarding the thresholds of the tent just as their ancestors had been responsible for guarding the entrance to the dwelling of the Lord [in the days of Moses]" (**1 Chronicles 9:19**). As the chief gatekeeper, Shallum was over *all* 212 gatekeepers of the Second Temple (**1 Chronicles 9:17, 22**). He was also privileged to preside over the King's Gate "on the east, up to the present [post-exilic] time" (**1 Chronicles 9:18**). [The east was a significant direction in ancient times because it was the "doorway" for the sun. The tabernacle in the days of Moses, as well as Solomon's Temple and the Second Temple, were all oriented toward the east. The Hebrew word for "east" (קֶדֶם, *qedem*) also means "front" and its verbal form, "be in front of."]

Some of Shallum's descendants who had returned with Zerubbabel in 538 B.C. were gatekeepers in the Second Temple (**Ezra 2:42**; **Nehemiah 7:45**).

Shallum the Korathite (**1 Chronicles 9:17, 19**) is the same person as Meshullam (**Nehemiah 12:25**), who guarded the storerooms at the gates. Some descendants of Shallum had taken pagan wives in captivity (**Ezra 10:24**).

Shallum's son, Maaseiah the gatekeeper, was a contemporary of the prophet Jeremiah (**Jeremiah 35:4**).

Shallum the Korahite (a post-exilic figure) is not the same person as (the pre-exilic figure) Meshelemiah the Korahite (**1 Chronicles 9:21**); also, their names derive from different lexical roots—Shallum (שַׁלּוּם) derives from a term meaning "substitution," whereas (Me)shelemiah (מְשֶׁלֶמְיָה) has to do with "deliverance" or "salvation." Also, Shallum the Korahite (**1 Chronicles 9:31**), shown in the chart, should not be confused with Shallum/Meshullam the high priest, a descendant in the Levi–Kohath–Aaron–Eleazar–Zadok high priesthood line (**1 Chronicles 6:12–13; 9:11; Ezra 7:2; Nehemiah 11:11**); for Shallum/Meshullam the high priest, see chart "**Supplement 2**: The High Priests of Israel."

4. Akkub was the head of a family of gatekeepers. His descendants returned from exile with Zerubbabel in 538 B.C. and served in the Second Temple. Akkub and Talmon guarded the storerooms at the gates (cf. **Ezra 2:42**; **Nehemiah 7:45; 11:19; 12:25**).

5. Talmon was the head of a family of gatekeepers. His descendants returned from exile with Zerubbabel in 538 B.C. and served in the Second Temple. Talmon and Akkub guarded the storerooms at the gates (cf. **Ezra 2:42**; **Nehemiah 7:45; 11:19; 12:25**).

6. Zechariah the son of Meshelemiah/Shelemiah was the gatekeeper "at the entrance to the [Mosaic] tent of meeting" in the Second Temple (**1 Chronicles 9:21**), which had been preserved since ancient days.

Given the chronology, Zechariah who lived in the post-exile days (after 516 B.C.) appears to be a *descendant* of Zechariah the gatekeeper who served in Solomon's Temple (for the latter, see chart "**1 Chronicles 26**: The Kohathite–Korahite and Merarite Gatekeepers in Solomon's Temple."

7. Mattithiah the firstborn son of Shallum the Korahite "was entrusted with the responsibility for baking the offering bread" in the Second Temple (**1 Chronicles 9:31**; cf. **Leviticus 2:3; 5:13; 6:14–23; 7:9–10; 10:12; 14:20; Numbers 4:16**). He may have been involved in preparing the special flour for the grain offerings as well (cf. **1 Chronicles 23:29; Nehemiah 10:33; 13:4–5, 9**). Mattithiah the son of Shallum is not the same person as: (1) Mattithiah the musician, the son of Jeduthun, who served in Solomon's Temple (cf. **1 Chronicles 15:16–18, 21; 16:5; 25:3, 21**); (2) Mattithiah the descendant of Nebo (**Ezra 10:43**); nor (3) Mattithiah who stood with Ezra (**Nehemiah 8:4**).

8. The gatekeepers in Solomon's Temple and the Second Temple were a faithful *remnant* of the descendants of Korah, the gatekeeper who led the Korah–Reubenite rebellion in the days of Moses (**Numbers 16**). According to **Numbers 26:10–11**, "The earth opened its mouth and swallowed them [Dathan and Abiram, the Reubenite rebels] along with Korah. . . . The line of Korah, however, did not die out." A large number of the "sons [descendants] of Korah" (**Psalm 88:1**)—particularly Heman and his offspring—became musicians in Solomon's Temple (cf. "**1 Chronicles 6**: Levi: High Priests, Priests, Levites, and Musicians in Solomon's Temple").

9. Ebiasaph in **1 Chronicles 6:23, 37; 9:19** is Abiasaph in **Exodus 6:24** and the shortened form, Asaph, in **1 Chronicles 26:1**. He was a *descendant* of Korah rather than a *son* of Korah, as it reads in **Exodus 6:24**; the text should be understood to mean that Assir, Elkanah, and Abisaph were "sons of sons"—therefore, the great-grandson of Korah was Ebiasaph/Abiasaph/Asaph (cf. **1 Chronicles 6:22–24; 37–38**). Asaph the gatekeeper (Kohathite–Korahite) is not Asaph the Gershonite, who was one of the three chief Levitical musicians in Solomon's Temple (cf. **1 Chronicles 15:19; 16:5; 25:1, 6**); for the latter, see chart "**1 Chronicles 6**: Levi: High Priests, Priests, Levites, and Musicians in Solomon's Temple."

10. Kore a descendant of Ebiasaph/Abiasaph/Asaph in **1 Chronicles 26:1** is probably the same person as "Kore son of Imnah the Levite, keeper of the East Gate, [who] was in charge of the freewill offerings given to God" in the days of King Hezekiah, 715–686 B.C. (**2 Chronicles 31:14**).

11. Shallum who was the head Levitical gatekeeper in **1 Chronicles 9:17, 19** is the same person as Meshullam in **Nehemiah 12:25**.

12. Meshelemiah is a variant of "Shelemiah." Meshelemiah (the father of Zechariah; **1 Chronicles 9:21**) had been the gatekeeper for the important East Gate in Solomon's Temple (cf. **1 Chronicles 26:1–2, 9, 14**). Meshelemiah (Shelemiah) had eighteen sons and relatives, who were called "able men" to do the work in Solomon's Temple (**1 Chronicles 26:9**).

13. See "**1 Chronicles 26**: The Kohathite–Korahite and Merarite Gatekeepers in Solomon's Temple."

14. The pre-exilic figure, Zechariah son of Meshelemiah/Shelemiah, was "a wise counselor" and by the casting of lots was also chosen as the gatekeeper for the North Gate in the days of King David (**1 Chronicles 26:14**).

15. Notice that the gatekeepers in the key passage (**1 Chronicles 9:17–22**) were the descendants of Kohath through Korah (i.e., they were Kohathites–Korahites) and were also probably descendants of Kohath through Merari (i.e., they were Levitical Merarites), although this lineage is not fully elucidated. Therefore, the chart excludes the Kohathites who were Kohath–Aaron high priestly descendants and also excludes known Levitical Merarites, such as Obed-Edom and his descendants, who were also gatekeepers (**1 Chronicles 15:18, 24; 16:38; 26:15–19**). For the family of Obed-Edom, see chart "**1 Chronicles 26**: The Kohathite–Korahite and Merarite Gatekeepers in Solomon's Temple."

16. Excluding the cities allotted to the Kohathite high priests, the ten Levitical cities for the remaining attending Kohathites were Shechem (also a city of refuge), Gezer, Kibzaim, Beth Horon, Eltekeh, Gibbethon, Aijalon, Gath Rimmon of Dan, Taanach, and Gath Rimmon (**Joshua 21:20–26**). The twelve Levitical cities for the Merarites were Jokneam, Kartah, Dimnah, Nahalal, Bezer, Jahaz, Kedemoth, Mephaath, Ramoth in Gilead (also a city of refuge), Mahanaim, Heshbon, and Jazer (**Joshua 21:34–40**).

17. The Levite(s) who prepared the incense spices mixed equal amounts of gum resin, onycha, galbanum, and pure frankincense (**Exodus 30:34–38**).

18. The bread of the Presence (or *showbread* in some translations) consisted of twelve baked cakes of fine flour—two rows of six each—placed on a golden table that was in the continual presence of the "face" or presence of God (**Exodus 25:30; 35:13; 39:36; Leviticus 24:5–9**; see also **1 Samuel 21:1–6; 1 Kings 7:48; 2 Chronicles 4:19**).

1 CHRONICLES 9: GENEALOGY AND RESPONSIBILITIES OF SPECIFIC LEVITES IN THE SECOND TEMPLE

Approximate Dating: ca. 516–400 B.C. ***Relevant Scriptures:*** **1 Chronicles 9:28–33;** also **1 Chronicles 6:16, 22–23; 9:19**[1]

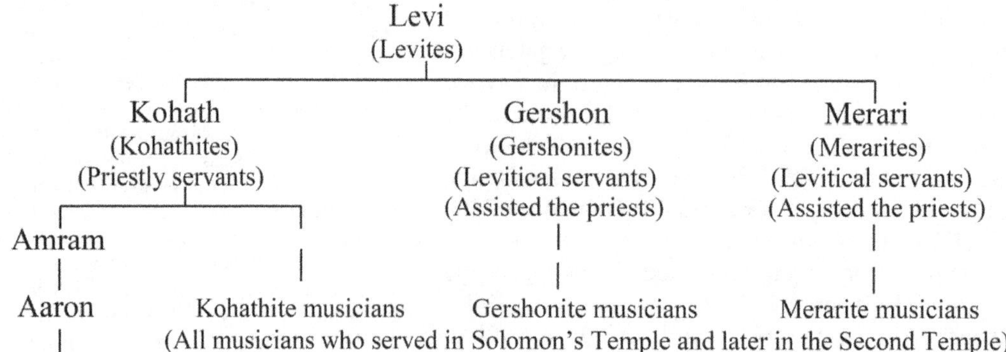

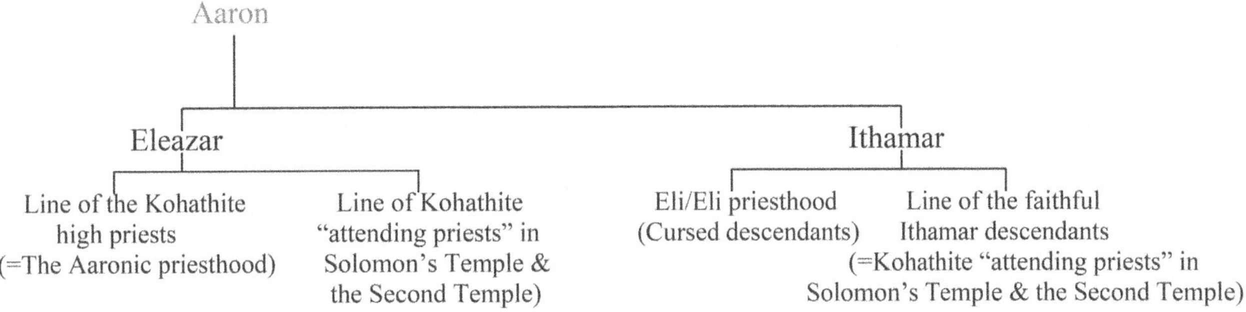

1. **Levitical responsibilities (1 Chronicles 9:28–29)**
   - Articles for temple service
   - Temple furnishings and articles of the sanctuary
   - Preparation of special flour and wine, olive oil, and incense for offerings
   - Mixing incense spices
   - Making anointing oil
2. **Preparation of the Bread of the Presence (1 Chronicles 9:31–32)**

   Unnamed Kohathites were in charge of preparing the twelve cakes that were placed on the golden table of the presence and for replacing them every Sabbath.
3. **Chief musicians (1 Chronicles 9:33–34;** cf. **1 Chronicles 6:33–47)**

   These musicians were dedicated to overseeing music in worship.[2]
   - **Descendants of Heman** (Heman had been the chief Kohathite musician in Solomon's Temple)
   - **Descendants of Asaph** (Asaph had been the chief Gershonite musician in Solomon's Temple)
   - **Descendants of Ethan/Jeduthun** (Ethan/Jeduthun had been the chief Merarite musician in Solomon's Temple)

Biblical and Theological Significance

The holiness of the temple (made with human hands but devoted to Yahweh as his dwelling place on earth) demanded that all persons and things associated with it be holy as well. By this is meant that they must be set apart from the secular and devoted exclusively to God.[3] Thus, the designated Levitical perfumers prepared the sacred anointing oil[4] for consecrating and making holy all items in the temple, such as to anoint the ark of the covenant, the table of the presence (for bread and all articles on the table), the menorah (lampstand), the altar of incense, the altar of burnt offering, and the basin and stand (**Exodus 30:22–33**). Another perfumer mixed and applied the incense formula[5] on the altar of incense just outside the most holy place (קֹדֶשׁ הַקֳּדָשִׁים), which housed the ark of the covenant, viewed as the throne of Almighty God among his people (cf. **Exodus 26:33; Leviticus 16:2-3; 16-17, 20, 23; 1 Chronicles 6:49; Hebrews 9:3**). The plume of fragrant smoke that ascended from the burning incense represented the prayers of the people to him (cf. **Revelation 5:8; 8:3–4**). The bread of the Presence (לֶחֶם הַפָּנִים)—literally, the "bread of the face," that is, where God saw it—consisted of twelve baked cakes of fine flour in two stacks of six each, placed on a golden table that was in the continual presence before the presence of God (cf. **Exodus 25:30; 35:13; 39:36; Leviticus 24:5–9; 1 Samuel 21:1–6; 1 Kings 7:48; 2 Chronicles 4:19**). The lampstand[6] signified the radiance of God and the light of understanding; the altar of burnt offerings served as a brazier that roasted animal sacrifices given to God; the offerings were totally consumed, and/or shared by the priests and individuals or shared by the whole nation as peace offerings.[7]

The temple and everything in it was made by skilled designers, masons, tailors, workers in metals and precious stones, and other artisans of all kinds, but once built, only priests and Levites were permitted to enter its holy precincts, and only into places that were permitted to their station. Laity could assemble on certain occasions in the great courtyard, the priests and Levites ministered in the holy place, and the high priest, once a year, ministered in the holy of holies before the ark of the covenant.

Notes

1. For the line of Levi and the musicians, and the line of Eleazar and Ithamar, and accompanying references, see charts "**1 Chronicles 6**: Levi: High Priests, Priests, Levites, and Musicians in Solomon's Temple" and "**1 Samuel 1**: Eli and the Eli Priesthood."

2. For the expanded genealogies of the chief musicians, see chart "**1 Chronicles 6**: Levi: High Priests, Priests, Levites, and Musicians in Solomon's Temple." The primary responsibility of the musicians was to direct the music in the temple—"to make a joyful sound with musical instruments: lyres, harps and cymbals" (**1 Chronicles 15:16**; cf. **6:31–47; 15:16–22**). Like their ancestors (the chief musicians), the descendants of Heman, Asaph, and Ethan/Jeduthun resided in the chambers around the Second Temple and lived permanently in Jerusalem, rather than in the Levitical cities, as did other Kohathite priests and Levites who rotated service throughout the year.

3. The fundamental idea of holiness in the Bible is not that of a mysterious aura or intrinsic perfection of essence (though God certainly embodies these), but separation of the profane from the sacred in identity and function. The root קדשׁ, "to cut, set apart," lies at the heart of the various technical terms such as קָדֵשׁ, "be holy," קִדֵּשׁ, "make holy," and קֹדֶשׁ, "holiness."

4. The sacred anointing oil was an exact blend of spices, and its preparation was "the work of a perfumer" who mixed liquid myrrh, fragrant cinnamon, fragrant calamus, cassia, and olive oil in specified amounts (**Exodus 30:22–24**). The anointing oil was used "to anoint the tent of meeting, the ark of the covenant law, the table and all its articles, the lampstand and its accessories, the altar of incense, the altar of burnt offering and all its utensils, and the basin with its stand. You shall consecrate them so they will be most holy, and whatever touches them will be holy" (**Exodus 30:26–31**).

5. The Lord specified how the incense mixture was to be made: "Take fragrant spices—gum resin, onycha and galbanum—and pure frankincense, all in equal amounts, and make a fragrant blend of incense, the work of a perfumer. It is to be salted and pure and sacred" (**Exodus 30:34–35**).

6. The technical term מְנוֹרָה, *menorah,* derives from the word for "lamp," *nur.*

7. The term שְׁלָמִים, *shelamim*, suggests, in this case, a number of ideas including (1) peace or unbroken fellowship between God and the worshiper; (2) salvation offering; (3) tribute to God by the offeror; or (4) reaffirmation of covenant fidelity ("שֶׁלֶם," *HALOT* 2:1536–38).

1 CHRONICLES 11: GENEALOGICAL REGISTRY OF THE MIGHTY WARRIORS IN KING DAVID'S ARMY

Approximate Dating: ca. 1011–971 B.C. ***Relevant Scriptures:*** **1 Chronicles 11:10–47;** also **2 Samuel 23:8–39; 1 Chronicles 27:1–15**

The "Three" elite leaders[1]

1. **Jashobeam**[2] (or **Josheb-Basshebeth**)
   (Hakmonite/Tahkemonite; Judahite)

   Perez of Judah
   |
   |
   Zabdiel
   |
   Jashobeam
   (Josheb-Basshebeth)

2. **Eleazar**[3] (Ahohite; Benjamite) (one of the 'Three')

   Dodai of Benjamin (Ahohite)[4]
   |
   Eleazar

3. **Abishai**[5] (Judahite) (chief of the 'Three')

   Zeruiah
   (Half-sister of David)

   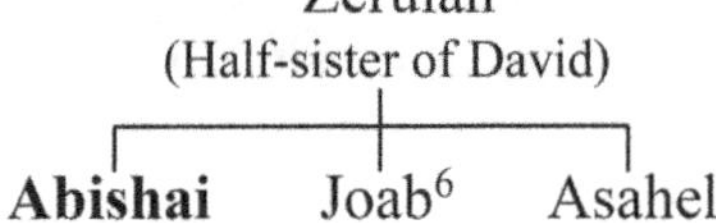

   Abishai Joab[6] Asahel

The mighty warriors – the "Thirty"

1. **Benaiah** – Leader over the "Thirty"

   Jehoiada of Judah
   |
   Benaiah[7]

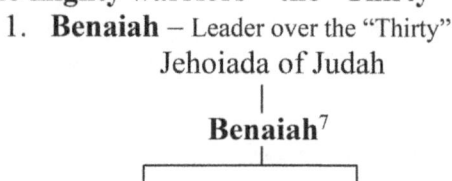

   Jehoiada Ammizabad

2. **Asahel**[8]

   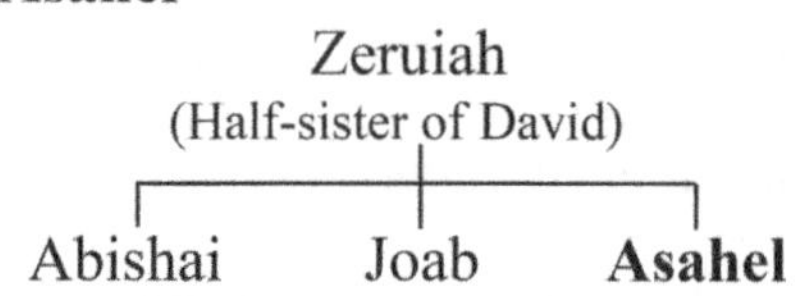

   Zeruiah
   (Half-sister of David)

   Abishai Joab **Asahel**

3. **Elhanan**[9]

   Dodo of Bethlehem
   |
   Elhanan

4. **Shammoth**[10] (Harorite) (likely the same person as Shamhuth the Izrahite and Shammah, the son of Agee/Shagee the Harodite/Hararite)

   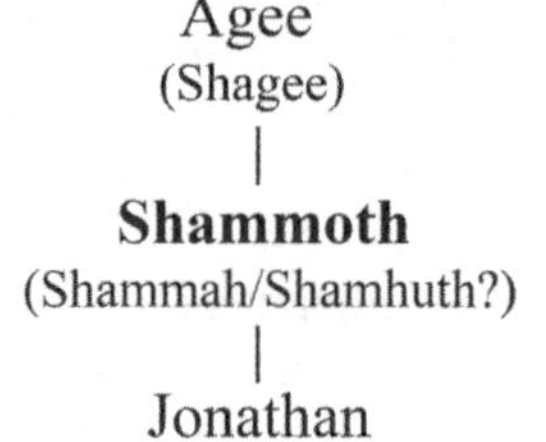

   Agee
   (Shagee)
   |
   Shammoth
   (Shammah/Shamhuth?)
   |
   Jonathan

5. **Elika** (Harodite)[11]

6. **Helez**[12] (Pelonite/Paltite; Ephraimite)

   Ephraim
   |
   |
   Helez

7. **Ira**[13] (Tekoite; Judahite)

   Ikkesh
   |
   Ira

8. **Abiezer**[14] (Anathothite; Benjamite)

9. **Sibbekai**[15] (Hushathite; Judahite/Zerahite)

10. **Ilai** (or **Zalmon**)[16] (Ahohite; Benjamite)

11. **Maharai**[17] (Netophathite; Judahite/Zerahite)

12. **Heled** (or **Heldai**)[18] (Netophathite; Kenizzite)

Othniel the Kenizzite
(First judge of Israel)
|
|
Baanah
|
Heled
(Heldai)

13. **Ithai**[19] (Benjamite from Gibeah)

Ribai
|
Ithai

14. **Benaiah**[20] (Pirathonite; Ephraimite)

15. **Hurai** (or **Hiddai**)[21] (from the ravines of Gaash; Ephraimite)

16. **Abiel** (or **Abi-Albon**)[22] (Arbathite)

17. **Azmaveth**[23] (Baharumite or Barhumite; Benjamite)

Azmaveth
├ Jeziel
└ Pelet

18. **The (unnamed) sons of Hashem** (or **Jashen**)[24] (Gizonite)

19. **Eliahba**[25] (Shaalbonite)

20. **Jonathan**[26] (Hararite)

Shagee[27]
(Agee)
|
Shammoth
(Shammah/Shamhuth?)
|
Jonathan

21. **Ahiam**[28] (Hararite)

Sakar
(Sharar)
|
Ahiam

22. **Eliphal**[29]

Ur
|
Eliphal
(Possibly = Eliphelet son of Ahasbai?)

23. **Hepher**[30] (Mekerathite; possibly meaning a Maakathite)

24. **Ahijah**[31] (Pelonite; Ephraimite)

Ephraim
|
|
Ahijah

25. **Hezro**[32] (Carmelite; probably Judahite)

26. **Naarai**[33] (or **Paarai**) (Arbite)

Ezbai
|
Naarai

27. **Joel**[34] (or **Igal**?) (Aramean)

Nathan?
├ **Joel**
└ Nathan

28. **Mibhar**[35]

Hagri
|
Mibhar

29. **Zelek** (Ammonite)

30. **Naharai**[36] (Berothite/Beerothite; Benjamite)

31. **Ira**[37] (Ithrite; Judahite)

32. **Gareb**[38] (Ithrite; Judahite)

33. **Uriah**[39] (Hittite; non-Israelite)

34. **Zabad**

Ahlai
|
Zabad

35. **Adina**[40] (Reubenite) and 30 Reubenite men

Shiza
|
Adina

36. **Hanan**[41]

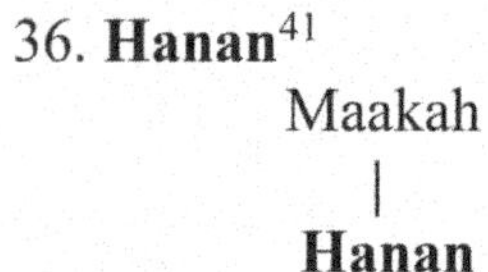

37. **Joshaphat**[42] (Mithnite)

38. **Uzzia**[43] (Ashterathite of Bashan)

39. **Shama**[44] (Aroerite; Moabite)

Hotham

Shama Jeiel

40. **Jeiel**[45] (Aroerite; Moabite)

Hotham

Shama **Jeiel**

41. **Jediael**[46] (Tizite)

Shimri

Jediael Joha

42. **Joha** (Tizite)

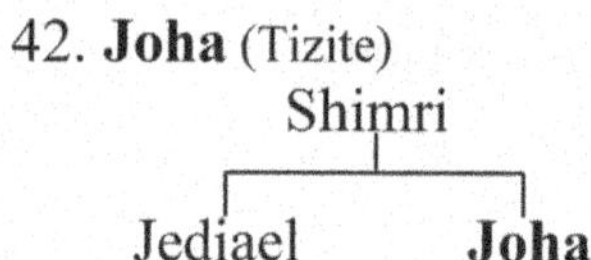

43. **Eliel**[47] (Mahavite)

44. **Jeribai**

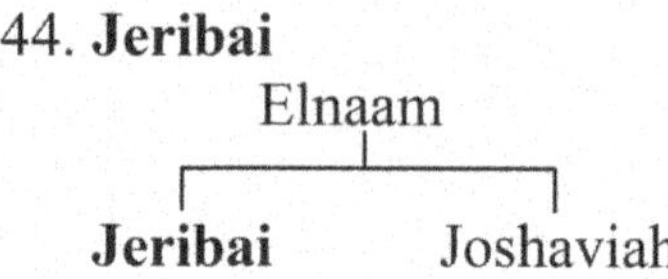

45. **Joshaviah**

Elnaam

Jeribai **Joshaviah**

46. **Ithmah** (Moabite)

47. **Eliel**

48. **Obed**

49. **Jaasiel**[48] (Mezobaite)

Biblical and Theological Significance

The comprehensive list of David's mighty warriors in **1 Chronicles 11:10–47** parallels, at least partially, the lists of individuals identified in **2 Samuel 23:8–39** and **1 Chronicles 27:1–15** (army division leaders). It gives evidence for widespread support of David from many cities throughout Judah, Benjamin, and even persons from the Transjordan region, such as Bashan (i.e., an Ashterathite of Ashtaroth in **1 Chronicles 11:44**); an Ammonite of Ammon (**1 Chronicles 11:39**); and a Moabite of Moab (**1 Chronicles 11:46**). The men who are designated "sons" may actually be "descendants." To distinguish the various individuals, the Chronicler uses familial identifiers (e.g., father, son, brother), clan names (e.g., Ahoahite), tribal associations (e.g., Reubenite) and/or geographic names and epithets (e.g., Netophathite; Carmelite; Moabite). One can observe that at least one father-son pair served (i.e., Shammoth–Jonathan) as well as five sets of brothers (i.e., Abishai and Asahel, who were under their brother Joab, the army commander; the unnamed sons of Hashem; Shama and Jeiel; Jediael and Joha; and Jeribai and Joshaviah).

The mighty warriors of David are referred to as "the thirty chief warriors" (**2 Samuel 23:13**), "the thirty chiefs" (**1 Chronicles 11:15**), or just "the Thirty" (**2 Samuel 23:23–24; 1 Chronicles 11:25; 12:4, 18; 27:6**) and must refer to a type of honorary "special forces." Excluding the three elite leaders and Joab the army commander, at least forty-eight *named* mighty warriors are given, as well as thirty *unnamed* Reubenites (#35) and at least two *unnamed* brothers ("the sons of Hashem" in #18) for a total of approximately eighty men in the Thirty. Contrary to the historian of **2 Samuel**, the Chronicler does not list "Eliam [Ammiel[49]] son of Ahithophel the Gilonite" among the members of David's army (cf. **2 Samuel 23:34**), presumably to suppress David's transgression with Eliam's daughter Bathsheba (**2 Samuel 11:3**; see **2 Samuel 11**) and/or the fact that Bathsheba's grandfather, Ahithophel, who had served as King David's counselor, later committed suicide (cf. **2 Samuel 15–16; 17:23**).

The other listing, **2 Samuel 23:8–39**, contemporaneous with David's own time (1011–971 B.C.), differs from the Chronicler's in a number of ways, chiefly in omitting sixteen names after Uriah the Hittite. Other departures by the (later) Chronicler are as follows: (1) two names in Samuel that are not in Chronicles, Eliphelet and Eliam (**2 Samuel 23:34;** Paarai in **2 Samuel 23:35** is Naarai in **1 Chronicles 11:37**); (2) eight instances of spelling variations of the men's names (**2 Samuel 23:8, 25, 28, 30, 31, 32, 35, 36**); and (3) Samuel omits several names (Eliphal, unless Eliphal=Eliphelet in **2 Samuel 23:34**; Hepher; and Ahijah). These may be accounted for by (1) authorial privilege; (2) information gleaned by the (later) Chronicler (400 B.C.) that was not available to the final editor of Samuel (ca. 560 B.C.); (3) normal variations by virtue of text sources available to each, and (4) ideological and/or theological motives. The **2 Samuel** list, which ends with the name of Uriah (**2 Samuel 23:39**; cf. **1 Chronicles 11:41**), may be intended to remind the reader, in Hertzberg's words, that "we are prohibited from making heroes of David (and his men). Even here, history was not made by men, but by the grace of God, whose help and forgiveness were needed even by David and in his time."[50]

Notes

1. The list of the "three" elite leaders in **2 Samuel** differs from the list in **1 Chronicles**: Josheb-Basshebeth (or Jashobeam), Eleazar, and Shammah (**2 Samuel 23:8–11**) compared to Jashobeam (or Josheb-Basshebeth), Eleazar, and Abishai (**1 Chronicles 11:11–20**). The chart follows the **1 Chronicles 11** reading. The Jamieson, Fausset, and Brown's Commentary: Critical and Explanatory on the Whole Bible, 1817, says for the commentary of 2 Samuel 23:19–39 that "the mighty men of champions in David's military staff were divided into three classes—the highest, Jashobeam, Eleazar, and Shammah; the second class, Abishai, Benaiah, and Asahel; and the third class, the thirty, of which Asahel was the chief."

2. "Jashobeam, a Hakmonite" (**1 Chronicles 11:11**) is "Josheb-Basshebeth, a Tahkemonite" (**2 Samuel 23:8**)—the differences in the names are partly of a scribal nature (e.g., Jashobeam, by syncopation becomes Ja(sho)sheb; the הָ of Hakmonite is much like the חָ of Tahkmonite). Jashobeam was the commander of all the officers and was held in great respect, for he had "raised his spear against three hundred men, whom he killed in one encounter" (**1 Chronicles 11:11**)—in the parallel passage in **2 Samuel 23:8**, the text says, "eight hundred men." Jashobeam the Hakmonite was one of the men who aided David, his family, and his 400 men when David fled from Saul and hid in the cave of Adullam. He was among the three mighty warriors who risked their lives to break through the Philistine camp to bring water to David from the well in Bethlehem, although David refused to drink it and poured the water on the ground as an offering to Yahweh (**2 Samuel 23:13–17**). Jashobeam was the son of Zabdiel and a descendant of Perez, the twin son of Judah and his daughter-in-law Tamar (**1 Chronicles 27:2–3**). He should not be confused with Jashobeam the Korahite (**1 Chronicles 12:6**), who was, of course, a Levitical Kohathite–Korahite.

3. Eleazar son of Dodai fought with David at Pas Dammim, also called "Ephes Dammin, between Sokoh and Azekah" (**1 Samuel 17:1**), against the Philistines. When others in the Israelite army fled, Eleazar and David "took their stand in the middle of the [barley] field . . . and struck the Philistines . . . , and the Lord brought about a great victory" (**1 Chronicles 11:14**). Eleazar was also one of the three mighty warriors who aided David when he fled from Saul and hid in the cave of Adullam (**2 Samuel 23:8–17; 1 Chronicles 11:15–19**). He is called Eleazar "the Ahohite" (a clan name), which suggests that he was a Benjamite—the descendant of Ahoah, the son of Bela, the son of Benjamin (**2 Samuel 23:9; 1 Chronicles 8:1–4; 11:12; 27:4**). Ilai/Zalmon was also an Ahohite (note 16).

4. Dodai the father of Eleazar (a Benjamite) in **1 Chronicles 11:12** is likely the same person as Dodai the Ahohite (**1 Chronicles 27:4**).

5. Abishai is called the "chief of the Three" leaders. He was David's nephew, the son of David's half-sister Zeruiah, and the brother of Asahel and Joab, David's general (**2 Samuel 2:18; 17:25; 23:18; 1 Chronicles 2:16; 27:34**). Abishai wanted to kill Shimei the Benjamite for cursing David but was restrained from doing so by the king (**2 Samuel 16:5–12; 19:21**). Abishai led a third of David's troops against Absalom when he rebelled against David (**2 Samuel 18**) and commanded David's forces against Sheba the rebel (**2 Samuel 20**). Abishai also killed the giant Ishbi-Benob, a descendant of Rapha/the Rephaites (**2 Samuel 21:15–17**). The text of **1 Chronicles 11:21** says, "He [Abishai] was doubly honored above the Three and became their commander, even though he was not included among them" (cf. **2 Samuel 23:19**).

6. Joab was David's nephew through Zeruiah, David's half-sister (**2 Samuel 17:25; 1 Chronicles 2:16**). Joab earned the right to be the commander-in-chief of David's royal army because he took the stronghold of the Jebusites in Jerusalem, which became David's capital (**1 Chronicles 11:6**; see also **2 Samuel 2:18; 8:16; 20:23; 1 Chronicles 27:34**). Joab's brothers were among David's mighty men, but because of the ruthless and blood-thirsty character of all three sons of Zeruiah (Joab, Abishai, and Asahel), David finally cursed them: "May the Lord repay the evildoer according to his evil deeds" (**2 Samuel 3:39**).

7. Benaiah, the son of Jehoiada, was a valiant fighter from Kabzeel, one of the southernmost towns in Judah near the border with Edom (**Joshua 15:21; 2 Samuel 23:20; 1 Chronicles 11:22**). Benaiah was known for killing Moab's mightiest warriors, going down into a pit to kill a lion in winter, and for killing an Egyptian giant with his own spear (**2 Samuel 23:20–23**). David appointed Benaiah over his bodyguards, the Kerethites and Pelethites (**2 Samuel 8:18; 20:23; 1 Chronicles 11:22–25; 18:17**). Benaiah was the honored leader of the Thirty, but he was not included among the Three elite leaders (**2 Samuel 23:23; 1 Chronicles 11:25; 27:6**). Benaiah refused to support Adonijah's ploy to succeed David to the throne; instead, he supported Solomon and helped anoint Solomon as king (**1 Kings 1:8–26; 32–48**). Upon Solomon's orders, Benaiah killed Adonijah and Joab and removed Abiathar as high priest (**1 Kings 2:25–46**). Benaiah eventually became the commander of Solomon's army (**1 Kings 4:4**). Also, Benaiah (the son of the elder Jehoiada) had a son named Jehoiada (a case of papponymy) who replaced Ahithophel as David's court counselor after Ahithophel committed suicide (**1 Chronicles 27:34**).

8. Asahel David's nephew was the son of Zeruiah (David's half-sister; **2 Samuel 17:25**) and the brother of Joab and Abishai (note 5; **2 Samuel 2:18; 1 Chronicles 2:16; 27:7**). Abner (Saul's army commander) slew Asahel; the incident eventually led to the revenge murder of Abner by Asahel's brother, Joab (**2 Samuel 3:27–30**).

9. "Elhanan son of Dodo from Bethlehem" (**2 Samuel 23:24; 1 Chronicles 11:26**) is not "Elhanan son of Jair the Bethlehemite" (**2 Samuel 21:19; 1 Chronicles 20:5**). Although both men were from Bethlehem, the former Elhanan was one of the Thirty but with no specific record of heroism, whereas Elhanan son of Jair was celebrated as the slayer of Lahmi the brother of Goliath (**1 Chronicles 20:5**). A third name, "Elhanan the son of Jaare-Oregim the Bethlehemite" (**2 Samuel 21:19,** NKJV) is the same person as "Elhanan son of Jair the Bethlehemite" (**2 Samuel 21:19**, NIV)—the Hebrew name Jair (יעיר) is a nickname for the longer Jaare-Oregim (יַעֲרֵי אֹרְגִים), and they are one and the same.

10. Shammoth the Harorite in **1 Chronicles 11:27** is likely the same person as (1) Shammah son of Agee (or Shagee) the Hararite in **2 Samuel 23:11, 25**, who was the father of Jonathan (cf. **2 Samuel 23:32–33; 1 Chronicles 11:34**), and (2) Shamhuth the Izrahite in **1 Chronicles 27:8**. Harodite, Hararite, and Izrahite are clan names. *Harodite* may refer to a citizen of Harod, a place associated with the spring of Harod/En Harod in the tribe of Issachar (**Judges 7:1**); alternatively, some manuscripts read *Zerahite*, meaning a descendant of Zerah, the son of Judah and his daughter-in-law Tamar (**Genesis 38:30; 46:12; Numbers 26:20; 1 Chronicles 2:4; Matthew 1:3**).

11. For Harodite, see note 10.

12. Helez was an Ephraimite (**1 Chronicles 27:10**). Helez and Ahijah (another mighty warrior of David; see note 31) were both from the Pelonite clan (**1 Chronicles 11:36**), perhaps referring to the clan of Peleth, a descendant of Jerahmeel (tribe of Judah; **1 Chronicles 2:33**). Peloni (פלני) and Peleti (פלתי) could, in an archaic script, look very much alike. No "Pelon" is attested in the Old Testament but "Pelet" is, so the latter is to be preferred here. Helez the Ephraimite is also designated as a "Paltite" (**2 Samuel 23:26**), but it is unclear if, or how, there is any association with (1) the town of Beth Pelet in the tribe of Judah in the Negev (cf. **Joshua 15:27**); (2) Pelet, the descendant of Caleb the Kenizzite (designated Caleb I elsewhere; **1 Chronicles 2:47**); (3) the Benjamite Palti the son of Raphu (**Numbers 13:9**); (4) Paltiel son of Azzan, from the tribe of Issachar (**Numbers 34:26**); or (5) Paltiel (Heb. Palti) a son of Laish, who was from Gallim (near Laishah and Anathoth; **Isaiah 10:30**)—the (second) husband of Saul's daughter Michal (**1 Samuel 25:44**), before she was given back to David.

13. Ira the Tekoite was from the town of Tekoa in the hill country of Judah, approximately six miles south of Bethlehem (cf. **2 Chronicles 11:6; Jeremiah 6:1; Amos 1:1**) that was founded by Ashhur the son of Hezron, the son of Perez, the son of Judah (**1 Chronicles 2:24**). Ira is mentioned in **2 Samuel 23:26** and **1 Chronicles 11:28; 27:9**.

14. Abiezer (**2 Samuel 23:27; 1 Chronicles 11:28; 27:12**) was from Anathoth, a Levitical city in the tribe of Benjamin given to the descendants of Aaron the high priest (**Joshua 21:18; 1 Chronicles 6:60**). Anathoth is also a personal name referring to Anathoth the son of Beker, the son of Benjamin (**1 Chronicles 7:8**). Anathoth was the hometown of Abiathar the high priest, who served in a co–high priest capacity with Zadok under King David (**1 Kings 2:26**); Jehu the Anathothite, who was a member of David's army at Ziklag (**1 Chronicles 12:3**); and Jeremiah the prophet (**Jeremiah 1:1**).

15. Sibbekai the Hushathite was a descendant of Hushah/the Hushathites, from the town of Hushah in the tribe of Judah (cf. **2 Samuel 21:18; 23:27; 1 Chronicles 4:4**). He is also known as "a Zerahite" (**1 Chronicles 27:11**; see note 10) and was renowned for killing Saph/Sippai a descendant of Rapha/the Rephaites (**2 Samuel 21:18; 1 Chronicles 20:4**).

16. Ilai the Ahohite (**1 Chronicles 11:29**) is the same person as Zalmon the Ahohite (**2 Samuel 23:28**). He was probably a Benjamite from the clan of Ahoah, the son of Bela, the son of Benjamin (cf. **1 Chronicles 8:4**). Another mighty warrior named Eleazar son of Dodai was also an Ahohite (**1 Chronicles 11:12; 27:4**); see note 3.

17. Maharai the Netophathite was from the town of Netophah in the hill

country of Judah near Bethlehem (cf. **1 Chronicles 2:54**). He is also called "a Zerahite" in **1 Chronicles 27:13**, meaning a descendant of Zerah, the twin son of Judah by Judah's daughter-in-law Tamar (cf. **Genesis 38:30; 46:12; Numbers 26:13, 20; 1 Chronicles 2:4; Matthew 1:3**).

18. Heled the son of Baanah (**2 Samuel 23:29; 1 Chronicles 11:30**), alias Heldai (**1 Chronicles 27:15**), was from the town of Netophah in the hill country of Judah (**2 Samuel 23:29; 1 Chronicles 2:54; 27:15; Ezra 2:22; Nehemiah 7:26**). Heled/Heldai was a Kenizzite, a descendant of Othniel, the first judge of Israel (**Judges 3:7–11; 1 Chronicles 27:15**); for the heritage of the Othniel, see charts "**Judges 3**: Othniel (Kenizzite), the First Judge of Israel" and "**1 Chronicles 2**: Caleb and Kenaz, the Sons of Jephunneh the Kenizzite."

19. Ithai was a Benjamite from Gibeah, the hometown of Saul (**1 Samuel 10:26; 11:4; 15:34**).

20. Benaiah the Ephraimite was from Pirathon, a town near Ophrah and Shechem (cf. **Judges 12:15; 2 Samuel 23:30; 1 Chronicles 11:31; 27:14**). He is not Benaiah the son of Jehoiada, a Judahite (see note 7).

21. Hurai (**1 Chronicles 11:32**), otherwise Hiddai (**2 Samuel 23:30**), was from the foothills of Mount Gaash in the hill country of Ephraim near Timnath Serah, the burial site of Joshua (cf. **Joshua 24:30**).

22. Abiel the Arbathite (**1 Chronicles 11:32**) is called Abi-Albon the Arbathite (**2 Samuel 23:31**). He is probably associated with Kiriath Arba (Hebron) in the hill country of Judah (**Genesis 23:2; 35:27; Joshua 14:15; 15:13, 54; 20:7; 21:11; Judges 1:10**), which was originally occupied by Arba, the forefather of the Anakites (**Joshua 14:15; 15:13**). Alternatively, Arbathite may refer to a "Beth-Arabathite." For a discussion of the meaning of Arbathite, see D.G. Schley "Arbathite" and Diane V. Edelman, "Abiel," *Anchor Yale Bible Dictionary*.

23. Azmaveth, a Benjamite (**1 Chronicles 8:36; 9:42**), came from the Baharumite (**1 Chronicles 11:33**) or Barhumite clan (**2 Samuel 23:31**)—a difference caused by syncopation of the "ha" syllable in the latter. [In an Accordance eAcademy webinar, November 19, 2020, on "The Importance of the Textual History of the Hebrew Bible," Dr. Emanuel Tov says that the correct reading is *Baharumite*, as in **1 Chronicles 11:33**.] The sons of Azmaveth, Jeziel and Pelet, are mentioned in **1 Chronicles 12:3**. The city Azmaveth/Beth Azmaveth was near Anathoth and Geba (**Ezra 2:24; Nehemiah 7:28; 12:29**).

24. Hashem (**1 Chronicles 11:34**) is otherwise Jashen (**2 Samuel 23:32**). He is called a "Gizonite," possibly referring to a citizen of Gizon or Gizah (an unknown place) or alternatively, to a citizen of Gizoh or Gimzo of Judah (**2 Chronicles 28:18**; cf. **1 Chronicles 11:34**), or Guni of Naphtali (cf. **Genesis 46:24; Numbers 26:48; 1 Chronicles 7:13**). Hashem has no familial, tribal, or clan associations given except to say that he had two or more sons who served in the army (i.e., "the [unnamed] sons of Hashem," **1 Chronicles 11:34**).

25. Eliahba was from Shaalbon/Shaalbim/Shaalbin, which—according to the near-consensus view of modern scholarship—are three renderings of the same place name. In his authoritative work, *The Land of the Bible*, Yohanan Aharoni observes that the variations "possessed locative force that could be altered or dropped without affecting the basic meaning of the name," and he presents these various renderings as a case in point. Yohanan Aharoni, *The Land of the Bible: A Historical Geography* (Philadelphia: Westminster, 1979), 120. The modern name for the place is the Arabic Selbit in ancient Ephraim, five miles NE of Gezer.

26. Jonathan "*son* of Shagee the Hararite" (**1 Chronicles 11:34**) is more likely the *son* of "Shammoth the Harorite" (**1 Chronicles 11:27**)—who is called "Shammah the Harodite" in **2 Samuel 23:25** and "Shammah the Hararite" in **2 Samuel 23:33**; therefore, Jonathan was the *grandson* of Shagee (called "Agee the Hararite" in **2 Samuel 23:11**; see note 27).

27. Shagee the Hararite (**1 Chronicles 11:34**) is Shammah the Hararite (**2 Samuel 23:33**). Another person in David's army named Ahiam is also a Hararite (**2 Samuel 23:33**). Some scholars prefer Ararite instead of Hararite. Hararite may refer to a town or mountainous region (Harar?), from the Heb. *har* meaning mountain, or possibly to the Judahite town of Haroeh (**1 Chronicles 2:52**).

28. "Ahiam son of Sakar the Hararite" in **1 Chronicles 11:35** is called "Ahiam the son of Sharar the Hararite" in **2 Samuel 23:33**.

29. Note the similar order of introduction of Eliphal the son of Ur in **1 Chronicles 11:35** to "Eliphelet son of Ahasbai the Maakathite" in **2 Samuel 23:34** (for Maakathite, see note 30).

30. Hepher the Mekerathite in **1 Chronicles 11:36** may refer to a "Maakathite," meaning a descendant of Maakah. For references to various Maakathites, see **2 Samuel 3:3; 1 Chronicles 2:48; 3:2; 7:15–16; 8:29; 9:35; 27:16**. It is unclear if Hepher the *Mekerathite* could be the same person as Eliphelet the *Maakathite* in **2 Samuel 23:34** (see note 29).

31. Since a fellow warrior, Helez, was a Pelonite (Paltite?) from Ephraim (cf. **2 Samuel 23:26; 1 Chronicles 11:27; 27:10**)—see note 12 above—presumably Ahijah "the Pelonite" (**1 Chronicles 11:36**) was from the tribe of Ephraim also.

32. Hezro was from Carmel, probably referring to the town of Carmel in the hill country of the tribe of Judah, southeast of Hebron and near Maon (**Joshua 15:55**). Carmel was the place where Nabal, Abigail's husband, sheared his sheep (**1 Samuel 25:5**) and the place where Saul had set up a monument "in his own honor" after defeating the Amalekites (**1 Samuel 15:1–12**).

33. Naarai son of Ezbai in **1 Chronicles 11:37** appears to be the same person as Paarai the Arbite in **2 Samuel 23:35**. The epithet "Arbite" may refer to the town of Arab, a village in the hill country of Judah near Hebron (cf. **Joshua 15:52**). See also Abiel the Arbathite (note 22).

34. Joel of Zobah is called the *brother* of Nathan (**1 Chronicles 11:38**), although Joel appears to be called Igal the *son* of Nathan in **2 Samuel 23:36**; the exact relationship of Joel and Nathan is unclear. Zobah was a state in southern Syria associated with the Arameans (cf. **1 Samuel 14:47; 2 Samuel 8:3, 5; 10:8**).

35. The person identified only as a "son of Hagri" in **2 Samuel 23:36** is more clearly identified as "Mibhar son of Hagri" in **1 Chronicles 11:38**.

36. Naharai the Berothite (**1 Chronicles 11:39**; or Beerothite; **2 Samuel 23:37**) was from Beeroth, in the tribe of Benjamin (**Joshua 18:25**). He was the armor-bearer for Joab, the commander-in-chief of David's royal army (**2 Samuel 23:37**).

37. Ira the Ithrite appears to be from Kiriath Jearim, a city on the northern border of Judah (**Joshua 15:9–11; 2 Samuel 23:38; 1 Chronicles 2:53**).

38. Gareb the Ithrite was from Kiriath Jearim in Judah (**2 Samuel 23:38; 1 Chronicles 2:53**).

39. Uriah the Hittite, a non-Israelite, was the husband of Bathsheba (**2 Samuel 11:3**) and a faithful warrior in David's army. To cover up his grievous sexual misconduct with Bathsheba—described by Nathan the prophet in clear, poignant words, "he [David] took the ewe lamb [Bathsheba] that belonged to the poor man [Uriah]" (**2 Samuel 12:4**)—David premeditated Uriah's murder and had Uriah deliberately killed in battle (**2 Samuel 11:6–17, 21–25**).

40. Adina was a chief of the Reubenites and commanded 30 men (**1 Chronicles 11:42**).

41. For the various possibilities for Maakah descendants, see note 30.

42. Nothing but the reference to them is known of the Mithnites.

43. Uzzia the Ashterathite was from Ashtaroth (Ashtaroth Karnaim), east of the Sea of Galilee, in the region of Bashan. Ashteroth was noted as a place formerly occupied by the giant Rephaites (**Genesis 14:5**).

44. Shama was from the city of Aroer, east of the Dead Sea, in the region of Moab.

45. Like his brother Shama (note 44), Jeiel was from the city of Aroer, east of the Dead Sea, in the region of Moab.

46. The Tizites may have come from the Transjordan region, but the location is unknown.

47. The Mahavites may refer to Mahanites or Mahanaimites, meaning inhabitants of Mahanaim east of the Jordan. See Stanley Porter, "Mahavite," in *Anchor Yale Bible Dictionary*, 473.

48. The Mezobaites may have come from the Transjordan region or perhaps from Zobah, an Aramean province.

49. Eliam in **2 Samuel 11:3; 23:34** is called Ammiel in **1 Chronicles 3:5**.

50. Hans Wilhelm Hertzberg, *I and II Samuel: A Commentary* (Philadelphia: Westminster, 1976), 408.

1 CHRONICLES 12: GENEALOGICAL REGISTRY OF THE MEN FROM THE TRIBES OF BENJAMIN, GAD, AND MANASSEH WHO JOINED DAVID'S ARMY AT ZIKLAG[1]

Approximate Dating: ca. 1012–1011 B.C. ***Relevant Scriptures:*** **1 Chronicles 12:1–22**

Benjamites Who Joined David's Army

1. **Ahiezer** the chief, the son of Shemaah the Gibeathite
2. **Joash**, the son of Shemaah the Gibeathite
3. **Jeziel**, the son of Azmaveth[2]
4. **Pelet**, the son of Azmaveth
5. **Berakah**
6. **Jehu**[3] the Anathothite
7. **Ishmaiah**[4] the Gibeonite
8. **Jeremiah**
9. **Jahaziel**
10. **Johanan**
11. **Jozabad** the Gederathite[5]
12. **Eluzai**
13. **Jerimoth**
14. **Bealiah**
15. **Shemariah**
16. **Shephatiah** the Haruphite[6]
17. **Elkanah** the Korahite[7]
18. **Ishiah** the Korahite
19. **Azarel** the Korahite
20. **Joezer** the Korahite
21. **Jashobeam** the Korahite[8]
22. **Joelah**, the son of Jeroham from Gedor[9]
23. **Zebadiah**, the son of Jeroham from Gedor[10]

Gadites[11] Who Joined David's Army

1. **Ezer**
2. **Obadiah**
3. **Eliab**
4. **Mishmannah**
5. **Jeremiah**
6. **Attai**
7. **Eliel**
8. **Johanan**
9. **Elzabad**
10. **Jeremiah**
11. **Makbannai**

Manassites[12] Who Joined David's Army

1. **Adnah**
2. **Jozabad**
3. **Jediael**
4. **Michael**
5. **Jozabad**
6. **Elihu**
7. **Zillethai**

Biblical and Theological Significance

Ever since the days of David's heroic exploits for Israel on the battlefield, Saul had become increasingly jealous and hostile to him, even to the point of trying to kill him, more than once (**1 Samuel 18:6–12; 19:9–10**). David was forced to flee for his life, taking with him a small band of loyal warriors (**1 Samuel 22:1–2; 23:1–24:22**). While he was trying to evade Saul, David made an alliance with Achish, king of the Philistine city-state of Gath (**1 Samuel 27:1–29:11**). This was the hometown of Goliath, whom David had killed more than a decade before; this alliance adds confusion as to why an Israelite king affiliated himself with an enemy of God's people. The other four kings of the Philistine pentapolis[13] mistrusted David, however, thus delivering him from the onus of having to do battle with his own Israelite peoples. Nonetheless, King Achish remained on good terms with David and went so far as to grant him the city of Ziklag[14] as a small fiefdom (**1 Samuel 27:6**).

When David was away on a campaign with Achish of Gath, Amalekite raiders set upon the defenseless town of Ziklag, burned and sacked it, and kidnapped many wives, sons, and daughters of the men in David's army, including David's wives Ahinoam and Abigail (**1 Samuel 30:1–6**). When David returned to see what had happened, he and his six hundred men crossed over the Wadi Besor, caught up with the Amalekites, and slew them. In addition to bringing back their wives and families, David and his men also brought back a great deal of plunder, which David distributed to his subjects far and wide in Israel (**1 Samuel 30:16–31**). The fighters mentioned obliquely in these narratives are the ones listed in **1 Chronicles 12:1–22**.

Saul's death in 1011 B.C. cleared the way for David to assume the throne of Judah at Hebron (**2 Samuel 2:1–4**) and then the kingship over all Israel at Jerusalem (**2 Samuel 5:1–12; 1 Chronicles 10:6–11:8**).

Notes

1. The army periodically shifted location; initially the "wilderness army" was centered at Ziklag when David was king over Judah only. Later, the army was headquartered in Hebron for seven-and-a-half years, and finally in Jerusalem and its environs when David had become king over all Israel (**2 Samuel 5:5**).

2. Azmaveth, the father of Jeziel and Pelet, is called "Azmaveth the Baharumite"; he was a Benjamite from the city of Baharum (**1 Chronicles 11:33**). Azmaveth was one of David's mighty men and a descendant of King Saul; see Azmaveth in the charts "**1 Chronicles 8 & 9**: The Descendants of King Saul Living in Gibeon and Jerusalem (Post-Exile)" and "**1 Chronicles 11**: Genealogical Registry of the Mighty Warriors in King David's Army."

3. Jehu from Anathoth (a Levitical city in the tribe of Benjamin; **Joshua 21:8; 1 Kings 2:26**) is clearly not (1) Jehu, king of Israel, who lived 100 years later than David, in 841–814 B.C. (cf. **2 Kings 9:2; 14; 2 Chronicles 22:9**), nor (2) Jehu the son of Hanani, a prophet to King Jehoshaphat of Judah and King Baashah of Israel (**1 Kings 16:1, 7; 2 Chronicles 19:2; 20:34**).

4. Ishmaiah, characterized as "a leader of the Thirty" (**1 Chronicles 12:4**), was a "Gibeonite" (i.e., a resident of Gibeon, which was a Levitical city in the tribe of Benjamin given to the descendants of Aaron the high priest; cf. **Joshua 18:25; 21:13, 17**). The "Thirty" refers to a group of heroes whose

exploits rose above the average. They were an elite unit unattached to the regular army. The term *Thirty* appears to be a technical term, not, perhaps, to be taken literally, since no list exists where exactly thirty people are found (see chart "**1 Chronicles 11**: Genealogical Registry of the Mighty Warriors in King David's Army." With the passing of time, some would die and replacements would be found. "A leader" would be one of many within the unit itself.

5. Gederah (also called Gederothaim) was a town in the western foothills of Judah (**Joshua 15:36**) where the early descendants of Shelah the son of Judah had been royal potters who worked for the king (**1 Chronicles 4:21–23**).

6. Shephatiah "the Haruphite" (**1 Chronicles 12:5**) was from a town of unknown identity and location.

7. In **1 Chronicles 12:6**, Elkanah is identified as a "Korahite"—typically meaning a Levitical descendant of Kohath and his descendant, Korah (cf. **Exodus 6:21, 24; Numbers 16:1–11; 1 Chronicles 6:22**). For chronological reasons, Elkanah the Korahite who joined David's army at Ziklag does not appear to correspond to any of the four Elkanah figures who were ancestors of Samuel the prophet; see charts "**1 Samuel 1**: Samuel, the Prophet–Priest–Judge of Israel" and "**1 Chronicles 6**: Levi: High Priests, Priests, Levites, and Musicians in Solomon's Temple."

8. In **1 Chronicles 12:6**, Jashobeam is identified as a "Korahite" as was Elkanah (note 7). Jashobeam is not to be confused with the individual "Jashobeam, a Hakmonite" in **1 Chronicles 11:11** (called "Josheb-Basshebeth, a Tahkemonite" in **2 Samuel 23:8**), the son of Zabdiel, who was a descendant of Perez (**1 Chronicles 27:2–3**) and the chief officer over the three elite leaders in David's army (see chart "**1 Chronicles 11**: Genealogical Registry of the Mighty Warriors in King David's Army").

9. Joelah, son of Jeroham of Gedor and brother of Zebadiah, was from Gedor, a town in the hill country of Judah (**Joshua 15:58**).

10. Zebadiah was the brother of Joelah and the son of Jeroham of Gedor; see note 9.

11. The Gadites were captains in David's army at Ziklag—the *least* were over 100 men, and the *greatest* were over 1,000. They had "faces of lions" and were "as swift as gazelles in the mountains"; they "put to flight everyone living in the valleys, to the east and to the west" (**1 Chronicles 12:8, 15**).

12. These men formerly supported Saul but defected to David and became captains over thousands in Manasseh. Whether this refers to the Manassites of the half-tribes of East or West Manasseh is not clear.

13. The term refers to the unique city-state formation in the Levant, a system familiar to these immigrants from the Aegean region where such entities were the norm. In the Philistine structure, the other four cites (in addition to Gath) were Ekron, Ashdod, Ashkelon, and Gaza.

14. Ziklag was in the desert ca. 25 miles south-southwest of Gath.

1 CHRONICLES 12: GENEALOGICAL REGISTRY OF THE MEN IN DAVID'S ARMY AT HEBRON

Approximate Dating: ca. 1011 B.C. ***Relevant Scriptures:*** **1 Chronicles 12:23–40**

The army that supported David at Hebron, and who declared him king over all of Israel, included a great number of men:

1. Tribe of Judah–6,800
2. Tribe of Simeon–7,100
3. Tribe of Levi–4,600
   A. Jehoiada[1]–3,700
   B. Zadok[2]–22 officers
4. Tribe of Benjamin (Saul's tribe)[3]–3,000
5. Tribe of Ephraim–20,800
6. Tribe of (West) Manasseh–18,000
7. Tribe of Issachar[4]–200 chiefs and their relatives
8. Tribe of Zebulun–50,000
9. Tribe of Naphtali–1,000 officers and 37,000 infantry
10. Tribe of Dan–28,600
11. Tribe of Asher–40,000
12. Tribes of Reuben, Gad, and the half-tribe of (East) Manasseh[5]–120,000

Biblical and Theological Significance

The Chronicler's desire to show that David's kingship was embraced enthusiastically by the whole nation is seen in his embellishment of **2 Samuel's** comparatively brief account of the delegation to Hebron. Whereas **2 Samuel** says only that all the tribes came to the king at Hebron (**2 Samuel 5:1–3**), the Chronicler lists each tribe by name and the total number of men they sent (**1 Chronicles 12:23–40**). This included three thousand Benjamites, even though they had remained loyal to Saul until the last moment. To emphasize the universal support given to David, the narrator says that the most distant tribes were not remiss in coming and that they, with the others, came laden with all kinds of provisions such as flour, fig cakes, raisin cakes, wine, olive oil, cattle, and sheep (**1 Chronicles 12:40**). For three days the coronation ceremony was accompanied by joyous festivities. Without question, David's rule over all Israel was perceived as a healing, a melding of disparate and hostile elements into the mighty people of God. The long-delayed establishment of the chosen nation under the chosen king had finally come to pass.

Notes

1. Jehoiada was a Kohathite priest (but not a high priest) and the leader of the Aaronites in 1011 B.C. He should not be confused with Jehoiada the Kohathite priest, the husband of Jehosheba, who was involved in the dethronement of Athaliah in 835 B.C.; see chart "**2 Chronicles 22**: Possible Genealogy of Jehoiada the Priest who Masterminded the Overthrow of Queen Athaliah of Judah." Jehoiada the priest (above) may have been a contemporary of Jehoiada the Judahite, the *father* of Benaiah of Kabzeel who was a mighty warrior under King David (cf. **2 Samuel 8:18; 20:23; 23:20, 22; 1 Kings 1:8, 26, 32, 36, 38, 44; 2:25, 29, 34–35, 46; 4:4; 1 Chronicles 11:22, 24; 18:17; 27:5–6**), and Jehoiada the Judahite, the *son* of Benaiah who replaced Ahithophel, David's court counselor (**1 Chronicles 27:33–34**), both of whom are shown in chart "**2 Samuel 8 & 20**: The Chief Officials in King David's Administration."

2. At this time, Zadok is described as "a brave young warrior" (**1 Chronicles 12:28**). Eventually, Zadok and Ahimelek (and later Ahimelek's son Abiathar; cf. **1 Samuel 22:20; 23:6; 30:7**) became co–high priests in David's administration (**2 Samuel 8:17; 20:25; 1 Chronicles 18:16**). For Zadok's lineage, see chart "**2 Samuel 8 & 20**: The Chief Officials in King David's Administration."

3. Until this time, most of the tribe of Benjamin had been loyal to the house of Saul (**1 Chronicles 12:29**).

4. Those from the tribe of Issachar are said to be "men who understood the times and knew what Israel should do" (**1 Chronicles 12:32**).

5. These tribes were located in the Transjordan, east of the Jordan River.

1 CHRONICLES 15: THE PRIESTS AND LEVITES WHO BROUGHT THE ARK OF THE COVENANT FROM THE HOUSE OF OBED-EDOM TO THE TENT-TABERNACLE IN THE CITY OF DAVID

Approximate Dating: ca. 1004 B.C. ***Relevant Scriptures:*** **1 Chronicles 15:1–15**; also **1 Chronicles 6:1–53; 23:6–23; 24:1–30; 26:21–22**

Heads of the Levitical Clans and Their Relatives Who Carried the Ark of the Covenant

1. Descendants of Kohath (Kohathites)–**Uriel** the leader and 120 relatives
2. Descendants of Merari (Merarites)–**Asaiah** the leader and 220 relatives
3. Descendants of Gershon (Gershonites)–**Joel** the leader and 130 relatives
4. Descendants of Elizaphan (Kohathites)–**Shemaiah** the leader and 200 relatives
5. Descendants of Hebron (Kohathites)–**Eliel** the leader and 80 relatives
6. Descendants of Uzziel (Kohathites)–**Amminadab** the leader and 112 relatives

Attending Co–High Priests

1. **Abiathar** (from the Aaron–Ithamar–Eli priesthood line)
2. **Zadok** (from the Aaron–Eleazar–Zadok priesthood line)

Genealogy of the Heads of the Levitical Clans and Zadok the High Priest (Zadokite Priesthood)

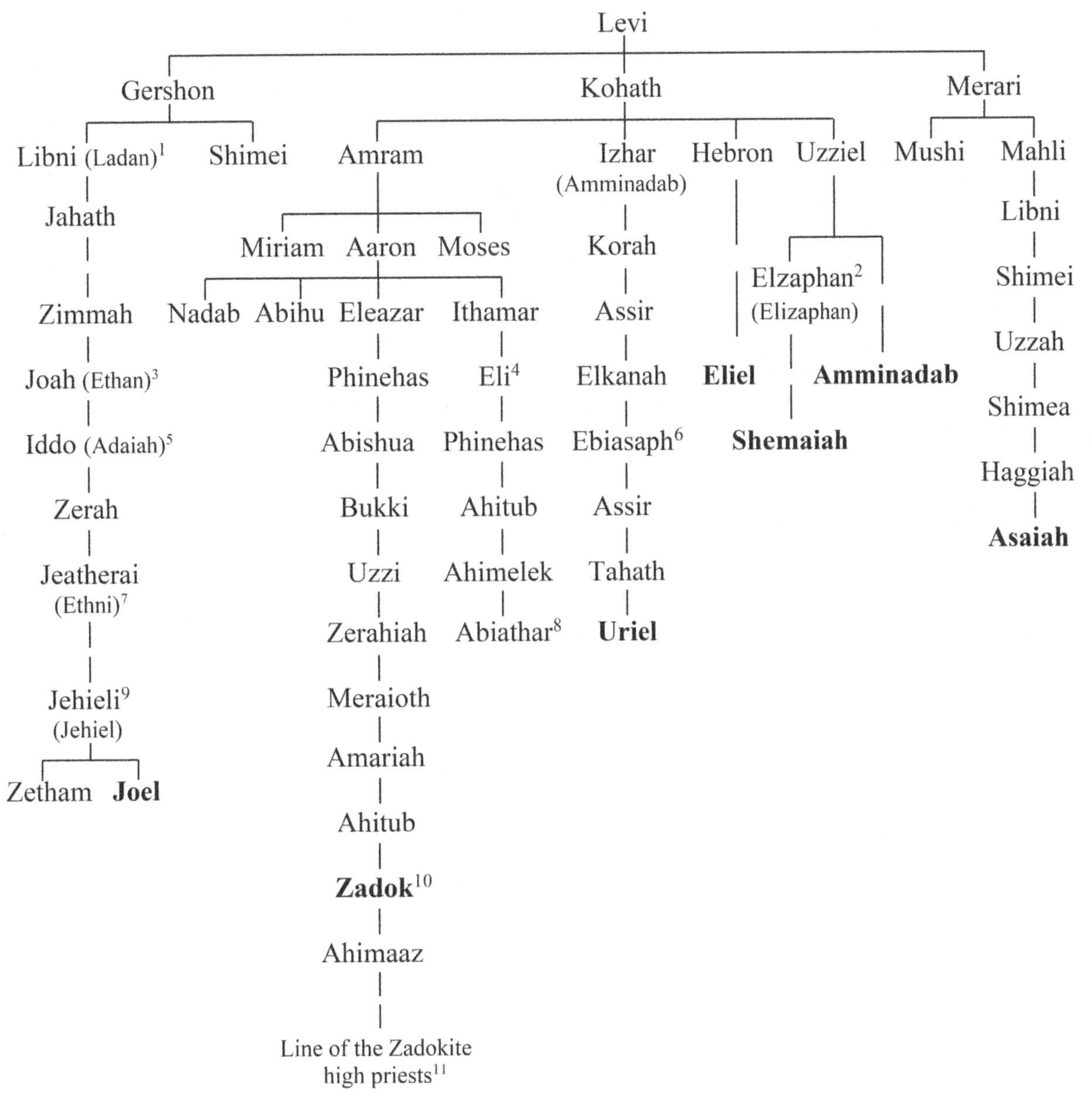

Genealogy of Abiathar the High Priest (Eli Priesthood)

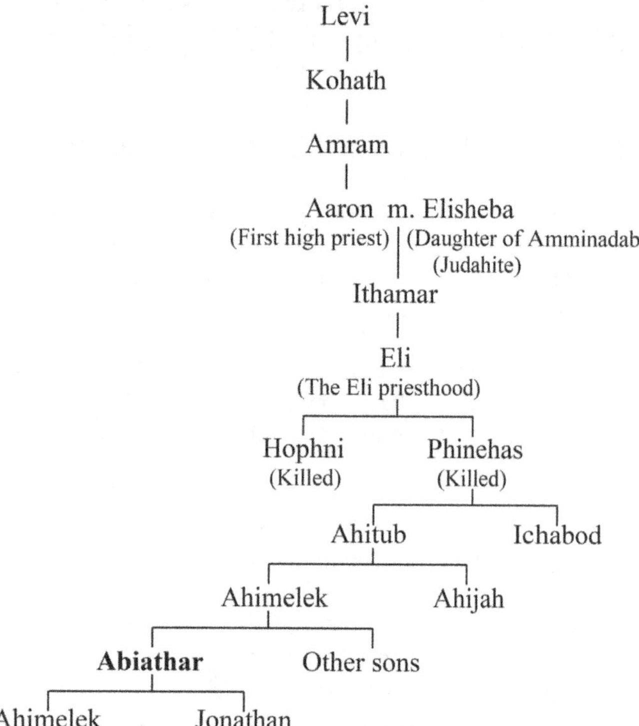

Biblical and Theological Significance

Nothing was more central to the worship of Yahweh than the ark of the covenant. The ark was constructed[12] in ca. 1445 B.C. during the early years of the Israelites' wanderings in the desert, and it resided in the most holy place of the Mosaic tent of meeting (**Exodus 25:10–22; 37:1–9**). Originally, it contained the stone tablets of the Decalogue (**Exodus 25:16**), engraved with the Ten Commandments, thus binding the Lord and Israel together in a sovereign-vassal relationship. The ark also contained a jar of manna (**Exodus 16:32–34; Hebrews 9:4**) and Aaron's priestly staff (**Numbers 17:10; Hebrews 9:4**). Aaron's staff represented priestly authority in the theocratic state; the manna symbolized God's faithful reliability toward his covenant people in all aspects. In addition, the cover of the ark—an "atonement cover of pure gold" (the *kapporeth*)—served as a royal throne for the invisible God (**Exodus 25:17–22**). Only the high priest could handle such an object—and then only with special precaution.[13] Therefore, the movement of the ark was not to be undertaken lightly. When the ark was moved, only ritually purified Levites were allowed to carry it (**Deuteronomy 10:8; 31:9, 25**); load-bearing poles, permanently inserted through golden rings at each lower corner, allowed the Levites to carry the ark of the covenant on their shoulders yet not touch it directly (**Exodus 25:12–15; 37:1–5**).

For a summary of the history and movement of the ark of the covenant during the wilderness years, after the conquest of Canaan, during the time of the judges, and the reigns of Saul, David, and Solomon, see the chart "**1 Chronicles 16**: Genealogical Registry of the Levites Who Oversaw the Ark of the Covenant in the City of David and the Tabernacle at Gibeon."

In the chart above, the Chronicler supplies details lacking in the book of Samuel, such as the names of the two high priests and the Levites privileged to bring the ark into the tent-tabernacle (**1 Chronicles 15:1–15**). These are listed above according to their clans.

Notes

1. Libni (**Exodus 6:17; Numbers 3:18; 1 Chronicles 6:17, 20**) is also called Ladan (**1 Chronicles 23:7–9; 26:21**). The name Libni/Ladan is omitted between Gershon and Jahath in **1 Chronicles 6:43**.

2. Elzaphan (**Exodus 6:22; Leviticus 10:4**) is elsewhere Elizaphan (**Numbers 3:30; 1 Chronicles 15:8; 2 Chronicles 29:13**).

3. Joah (**1 Chronicles 6:21**) is otherwise Ethan (**1 Chronicles 6:42**).

4. For the Eli/Eli priesthood, see chart "**1 Samuel 1**: Eli and the Eli Priesthood."

5. Iddo (**1 Chronicles 6:21**) is otherwise Adaiah (**1 Chronicles 6:41**), perhaps a nickname, with Iddo being short for Adaiah.

6. Ebiasaph (**1 Chronicles 6:23, 37; 9:19**) is otherwise Abiasaph (**Exodus 6:24**) and Asaph (**1 Chronicles 26:1**). He was the great-grandson of Korah, *contra* **Exodus 6:24** and **1 Chronicles 6:37** (cf. **vv. 22–23**); see chart "**1 Chronicles 6**: Levi: High Priests, Priests, Levites, and Musicians in Solomon's Temple."

7. Jeatherai (**1 Chronicles 6:21**) is otherwise Ethni (**1 Chronicles 6:41**).

8. Abiathar the priest was one of the last members of the Eli priesthood: the Aaron–Ithamar–Eli–Phinehas–Ahitub–Ahimelek–Abiathar–Ahimelek line (see **1 Samuel 2:12–36; 1 Kings 2:27**; see chart "**1 Samuel 1**: Eli and the Eli Priesthood"). The termination of the Elide high priesthood was God's judgment on Eli's wickedness and the wickedness of his sons Hophni and Phinehas (cf. **1 Samuel 2:12–17, 22, 27–36; 3:12–14**). Abiathar son of Ahimelek (of the Eli priesthood) and Zadok (of the Zadokite priesthood) were co–high priests during the reign of David, ca. 1011–971 B.C. (**2 Samuel 8:17; 15:24–29, 35–36; 17:15; 20:25; 1 Chronicles 18:16**). When Solomon came to the throne, he dismissed Abiathar, thereby fulfilling the prophecy against Eli and his household (**1 Kings 2:26–27**). Abiathar returned to his hometown of Anathoth in the tribe of Benjamin.

9. Jehieli (**1 Chronicles 26:21–22**) is also Jehiel (**1 Chronicles 23:8; 29:8**). Jehieli/Jehiel the Gershonite is not Jehiel the descendant of Heman, the Levitical Kohathite–Korahite (cf. **2 Chronicles 29:14**).

10. Initially, Zadok served as the high priest at Gibeon (**1 Chronicles 16:39**). Both he and Abiathar served as co–high priests during David's reign (**2 Samuel 8:17; 15:24–29, 35–36; 17:15; 20:25; 1 Chronicles 18:16**). Later, in the early part of Solomon's reign, Solomon removed Abiathar because he had supported Adonijah's scheme to preempt Solomon, and therefore, Zadok became the sole high priest in Solomon's Temple; this Zadok corresponds to Zadok #11 in chart "**Supplement 2**: The High Priests of Israel."

11. See charts "**1 Chronicles 6**: Levi: High Priests, Priests, Levites, and Musicians in Solomon's Temple" and "**Supplement 2**: The High Priests of Israel."

12. The ark was a box constructed of acacia wood, plated with gold inside and out with the following dimensions: "two and a half cubits long, a cubit and a half wide, and a cubit and a half high"—since a cubit was about 18 inches, the ark was approximately 3.75′ x 2.25′ x 2.25′ (L x W x H). Four gold rings fastened to its four feet, with two rings on one side and two rings on the other; poles of acacia wood overlaid with gold were inserted into the gold rings for carrying the ark (**Exodus 25:10–16**). For the genealogies of the artisans who crafted the ark and the Mosaic Tabernacle, see chart "**Exodus 31**: Bezalel, the Chief Artisan of the Tabernacle and Its Furnishings, and His Assistant, Oholiab."

13. The lid served as an altar once a year on the Day of Atonement, Yom Kippur ("Day of [sin] Covering"). The high priest, the only person who could enter the sacred precincts of the holy of holies (קְדוֹשׁ הַקֳּדָשִׁים), did so on that day and applied the blood of a sacrificed animal to the altar as an atonement for himself and the entire nation.

1 CHRONICLES 15: GENEALOGICAL REGISTRY OF MUSICIANS AND DOORKEEPERS WHO LED THE PROCESSION WHEN THE ARK OF THE COVENANT WAS BROUGHT TO THE CITY OF DAVID

Approximate Dating: ca. 1004 B.C. ***Relevant Scriptures:*** **1 Chronicles 15:16–24**

The Musicians[1]

1. **Heman**, the son of Joel (Kohathite)
2. **Asaph**, the son of Berekiah (Gershonite)
3. **Ethan** (Jeduthun), the son of Kushaiah/Kishi/Kish (Merarite)[2]

Levitical Relatives (Brethren) of the Musicians Who Played Lyres (According to Alamoth[3]*)*

1. **Zechariah**
2. **Jaaziel**
3. **Shemiramoth**
4. **Jehiel**
5. **Unni**
6. **Eliab**
7. **Maaseiah**
8. **Benaiah**

Levites Who Played Harps (According to Sheminith[4]*)*

1. **Mattithiah**
2. **Eliphelehu**
3. **Mikneiah**
4. **Obed-Edom**[5]
5. **Jeiel**
6. **Azaziah**

Head Levite in charge of the singing: **Kenaniah**

Doorkeepers for the Ark

1. **Berekiah**[6]
2. **Elkanah**[7]
3. **Obed-Edom**[8]
4. **Jehiah**

Kohathite Attending Priests Who Blew Trumpets Before the Ark

1. **Shebaniah**
2. **Joshaphat**
3. **Nethanel**
4. **Amasai**
5. **Zechariah**
6. **Benaiah**
7. **Eliezer**

Biblical and Theological Significance

The ark of the covenant was the most sacred of all the objects associated with Israel's relationship with God. It was made in the Sinai desert by skilled and Spirit-filled artisans according to the most stringent measurements and using divinely revealed materials (**Exodus 25:10–22; 37:1–9**). It served a multi-functional purpose as a repository for the original tablets of the Mosaic Covenant and as the throne of Yahweh, Israel's invisible God (**Exodus 25:16, 22**).

After the Israelites entered Canaan in 1406 B.C., the ark of the covenant resided in the tabernacle at Bethel (**Judges 20:26–27**) but was then relocated shortly after that to Shiloh (**Joshua 18:1**). The ark resided in the tabernacle at Shiloh for 350 years, ca. 1406–1050 B.C., but Shiloh ceased to be the site by the time of the Benjamite rebellion (cf. **Judges 20:18, 23, 26–28; 21:1–7**). When Shiloh was destroyed by the Philistines in 1050 B.C., they took the ark with them to Ashdod. The ark was then moved to various places in Philistine territory before being sent back to Israel, where it stayed at the house of Abinadab at Kiriath Jearim and then the house of Obed-Edom before being moved by David to the City of David.[9]

The transfer of the ark from the house of Obed-Edom to the City of David (**1 Chronicles 16:1**) was accompanied by joyful music[10] including lyres (*nebalim*), harps (*kinnorot*), cymbals (*metsiltayim*), and trumpets (*khatsotsrot*; **1 Chronicles 16:5–6**). Music was always a fundamental element in Old Testament worship[11]—especially in the temple—and the early church quickly adopted it, as the New Testament makes clear (**Acts 16:25; Romans 15:9, 11; Ephesians 5:19; Colossians 3:16; Hebrews 2:12; James 5:13; Revelation 5:9, 12; 14:3; 15:3**). The music of God's people, whether vocal or instrumental, is a vehicle of communication with him that cannot be done with mere words or sounds. As the Psalms are the words of God to those who worship him, so their singing is a glorious response from their hearts to his. Thus, it has been ever since the beginning in a great variety of melodies, tunes, lyrics, modes, and vehicles, and thus it shall be forever. As the poet said long ago, שִׁירוּ־לוֹ שִׁיר חָדָשׁ/ הֵיטִיבוּ/ נַגֵּן בִּתְרוּעָה, "Sing to him a new song; //play skillfully, and shout for joy" (**Psalm 33:3**).

Notes

1. For the genealogy of Heman, Asaph, and Ethan/Jeduthun—**1 Chronicles 6:33–38, vv. 39–43**, and **vv. 44–47**, respectively—see chart "**1 Chronicles** 6: Levi: High Priests, Priests, Levites, and Musicians in Solomon's Temple."

2. Kushaiah (**1 Chronicles 15:17**) is Kishi (**1 Chronicles 6:44**) and Kish (**2 Chronicles 29:12**).

3. *Alamoth* appears to be a musical notation indicating to play the stringed instrument at a higher octave (in the female range; **1 Chronicles 15:20**).

4. *Sheminith* (Heb. *al hashsheminit*), "on the eighth," occurs in the superscriptions of **Psalms 6** and **12** and at **1 Chronicles 15:21**. Proposed meanings are (1) "octave," (2) "on an eight-stringed instrument," or (3) "for the eighth stage of the liturgy."

5. See chart "**2 Samuel 6**: Obed-Edom, the Levitical Gatekeeper and Keeper of the Ark."

6. Given the timeframe for this chart, this is possibly Berekiah the Gershonite, the father of Asaph the musician (**1 Chronicles 6:39; 15:17**), or Berekiah son/descendant of Asa, son of Elkanah, the Korahite (**1 Chronicles 9:16**).

7. This is possibly Elkanah (Kohathite–Korahite) the father of Samuel the prophet (**1 Chronicles 6:34**). For the lineage of the Kohathite–Korahite clan,

see chart "**1 Chronicles 6**: Levi: High Priests, Priests, Levites, and Musicians in Solomon's Temple."

8. See chart "**2 Samuel 6**: Obed-Edom, the Levitical Gatekeeper and Keeper of the Ark."

9. For a detailed account of the ark's movements during this time, see chart "**1 Chronicles 16**: Genealogical Registry of the Levites Who Oversaw the Ark of the Covenant in the City of David and the Tabernacle at Gibeon."

10. The concept of music is nearly as old as the history of mankind itself. Referring to Lamech, a descendant of Cain, **Genesis 4:21** notes that one of Lamech's sons, Jubal, "was the father of all who play stringed instruments and pipes" (כִּנּוֹר and עוּגָב, *kinnor* and *ugab*). The same terms are found scores of times in the Old Testament, the former in this context in **1 Chronicles 13:8; 15:16, 21, 28; 16:5; 25:1, 3, 6**; the latter term, "pipes," is not found at all in this setting. "Stringed instruments" and/or "pipes" are mentioned in the titles of six psalms (**Psalm 4, 6, 54–55, 67, 76**).

11. For a few striking examples, see **Exodus 15:1, 21; Numbers 21:17; Deuteronomy 31:19; 2 Samuel 3:33–34; 22:50; 1 Chronicles 16:9, 23, 33; 2 Chronicles 20:21–22; 29:30; Ezra 3:11; Nehemiah 12:27; Isaiah 12:6; 23:15–16; 38:20; 42:10–11; Jeremiah 20:13; 30:19; 31:7**; and **Zephaniah 3:14**. For an excellent treatment of all aspects of Old Testament music, see C. Hassell Bullock, *Encountering the Book of Psalms* (Grand Rapids: Baker Academic, 2001), 24–34.

1 CHRONICLES 16: GENEALOGICAL REGISTRY OF KOHATHITE PRIESTS AND LEVITES APPOINTED BY KING DAVID TO CARE FOR THE ARK OF THE COVENANT IN THE CITY OF DAVID

Approximate Dating: ca. 1004–960 B.C. ***Relevant Scriptures:*** **1 Chronicles 16:4–6**; also **1 Chronicles 15:16–22**

Levitical Musicians[1]: (Gershonites and Merarites)

1. **Asaph**[2] the chief Levite
2. **Zechariah**[3]
3. **Jaaziel**[4]
4. **Shemiramoth**[5]
5. **Jehiel**[6]
6. **Mattithiah**
7. **Eliab**
8. **Benaiah**[7]
9. **Obed-Edom** (Merarite)[8]
10. **Jeiel**[9]

Priestly Musicians[10] Who Blew the Trumpets:

1. **Benaiah**[11]
2. **Jahaziel**[12]

Biblical and Theological Significance

One of the most glorious and important events in Old Testament times was the triumphant movement of the ark of the covenant to Jerusalem in 1004 B.C. The entrance into the holy city was tantamount to the entrance of Yahweh himself. Indeed, more important, perhaps, than even the ark's function as a container of such a precious cargo was its representation of the presence of Almighty God himself. When God moved, the ark moved (and *vice versa*), signifying his leadership and protection (cf. **Numbers 4:4–5**). The ark was taken to a "tent that David had pitched for it" in the City of David (**2 Samuel 6:16–17; 2 Chronicles 1:4**; cf. **1 Kings 8:1; 1 Chronicles 15:1; 16:1; 17:1**), and it remained there in the quasi-temple until Solomon's Temple was completed some forty-four years later in 960 B.C. (cf. **1 Kings 8:1–11**). The ark was then moved to its final resting place in the most holy place in Solomon's Temple "beneath the wings of the cherubim" where the "LORD, the God of Israel [was] enthroned" (**1 Kings 8:6–7; 2 Kings 19:15**; see **1 Chronicles 13:6; 2 Chronicles 5:7–8**).[13]

"Ark" (אָרוֹן, *aron*) hardly does justice as a translation in modern times because the ark was essentially a chest or trunk some 45 × 27 × 27 inches in measurement and made from the tough wood of the acacia tree that grew in the desert (**Exodus 25:10–22**). The ark was holy.[14] The ark contained the stone tablets on which were engraved the Ten Commandments (**Exodus 20:1–17**), the principles by which all other laws of Torah were but elaborations (**Exodus 21:1–23:33**; see **25:16**).

The ark had journeyed several places after the Israelites came into the promised land.[15] However, once it was settled in the City of David, David appointed the Levitical musicians and priests to minister before the ark "to extol, thank, and praise the LORD, the God of Israel" (**1 Chronicles 16:4**). David prepared a special psalm—a song of thanksgiving—for the occasion, and Asaph the chief Levitical Gershonite and his associates led the singing; when it concluded, all the people said "Amen" and "Praise the Lord" (**1 Chronicles 16:8–36**)! From that point onward, musicians ministered regularly before the ark, "according to each day's requirements" (**1 Chronicles 16:37**). Also assisting the musicians were Obed-Edom and his sixty-eight brethren; Obed-Edom and Hosah also served as gatekeepers of the ark (**v. 38**).[16]

Notes

1. **First Chronicles 16:4–5** mentions ten Levitical musicians (i.e., those named in the list above). Compare those listed above with those listed as Levitical musicians in **1 Chronicles 15:16–22** (names in bold are common to both passages): Heman (a Levitical Kohathite–Korahite, who sounded the bronze cymbals), **Asaph** (Gershonite, who sounded the bronze cymbals), Ethan/Jeduthun (Merarite, who sounded the cymbals); **Zechariah** (likely a descendant of Asaph the Gershonite, who played the lyre); **Jaaziel** (who played the lyre); **Shemiramoth** (who played the lyre); **Jehiel** (who played the lyre); Unni (who played the lyre); **Eliab** (who played the lyre); Maaseiah (who played the lyre), **Benaiah** (who played the lyre), **Mattithiah** (who played the harp), Eliphelehu (who played the harp), Mikneiah (who played the harp), **Obed-Edom** (Merarite, who played the harp), **Jeiel** (who played the harp), Azazaiah (who played the harp), and Kenaniah (over all the singing).

2. Asaph was from the clan of the Gershonites (i.e., the descendants of Gershon, the son of Levi). Asaph played the cymbals and was one of the three main musicians who served in Solomon's Temple; for his lineage, see chart "**1 Chronicles 6**: Levi—High Priests, Priests, Levites, and Musicians in Solomon's Temple."

3. Zechariah the Levite (**1 Chronicles 16:5**) is probably the same person as Zechariah the gatekeeper/musician (**1 Chronicles 15:18, 20 (24?)**. For chronological reasons, he is not: (1) Zechariah the son of Benaiah, a Levitical

descendant of Asaph, who lived in the days of King Jehoshaphat, 872–848 B.C. (**2 Chronicles 20:14; 29:13**); (2) Zechariah son of Meshelemiah, a Kohathite–Korahite gatekeeper who was stationed at the entrance to the tent of meeting in the Second Temple, ca. 516 B.C. (**1 Chronicles 9:21; 26:2**); nor (3) Zechariah son of Jonathan, who lived in the post-exilic days of Nehemiah, ca. 444 B.C. (**Nehemiah 12:35**).

4. Jaaziel (יַעֲזִיאֵל) (*yaaziel*) played the lyres and harps (**1 Chronicles 16:5**). He is the same person as Jaaziel the gatekeeper (**1 Chronicles 15:18**). For chronological reasons, he is not Jahaziel son of Zechariah, son of Benaiah, a descendant of Asaph, who lived in the days of King Jehoshaphat, 872–848 B.C. (**2 Chronicles 20:14**; cf. **29:13**). The differences in the readings of the names of Jaaziel (here in note 4), compared to Jehiel (note 6), Jeiel (note 9), and Jahaziel (note 12), are subtle and derive from the ancient manuscripts whose variations are attributable to two main factors: audible and visual. Copies were often made by transcription, wherein a scribe wrote what he heard from a skilled (or otherwise) reader; the other method was careful copying of texts that were considered accurate master copies but that were sometimes poorly crafted because of poor vision and/or impairment of the master in some way. In this way, some of the names (Jaaziel, Jehiel, Jeiel, Jahaziel) may be variants referring to the same person, but this may not apply to all.

5. Shemiramoth the Levite (**1 Chronicles 15:18, 20; 16:5**), who was a contemporary of David (1011–971 B.C.), is not the Shemiramoth the Levite who was a contemporary of Jehoshaphat, 872–848 B.C. (**2 Chronicles 17:8**), although they may share a similar ancestral line.

6. For the name Jehiel (יְחִיאֵל) (*yehiel*), see note 4. He played lyres and harps (**1 Chronicles 16:5**; cf. **15:18, 20**).

7. Benaiah the Levite (**1 Chronicles 16:5**), who played the lyres and harps, is not the same person as Benaiah the priest (Kohathite), who blew the trumpet (**1 Chronicles 16:6**; cf. **15:24**).

8. Obed-Edom (Levitical Merarite) was the son of Ethan/Jehuthun, one of the three chief musicians in Solomon's Temple. For more information about the important status of Obed-Edom, see chart "**2 Samuel 6**: Obed-Edom, the Levitical Gatekeeper and Keeper of the Ark."

9. For the name Jeiel (יְעִיאֵל) (*yeiel*), see note 4. Jeiel played the lyres and harps (**1 Chronicles 16:5**; cf. **15:18, 21**).

10. For comparison, see the priestly musicians (Kohathites) listed in **1 Chronicles 15:24**, which include Shebaniah, Joshaphat, Nethanel, Amasai, Zechariah, Benaiah, and Eliezer.

11. Benaiah the priest (**1 Chronicles 16:6**) is the same person as Benaiah the Kohathite priest who blew the trumpet before the ark (**1 Chronicles 15:24**).

12. For Jahaziel (יַחֲזִיאֵל) (*yakhaziel*), see note 4. Jahaziel was a Kohathite priest; therefore, he is not the same person as Jahaziel the Gershonite, who lived in the days of King Jehoshaphat, 872–848 B.C. (**2 Chronicles 20:14**).

13. The ark of the covenant was originally constructed under the supervision of Moses in 1445 B.C. in the deserts of Sinai, when Yahweh led his people from Egypt to the promised land of Canaan (see chart "**Exodus 31**: Bezalel, the Chief Artisan of the Tabernacle and Its Furnishings, and His Assistant, Oholiab"). When the ark was finally moved to Solomon's Temple in 960 B.C., it was 485 years old.

14. The ark was so holy that, once finished, it could never again be touched by human hands (except by the high priest on rare occasions) or looked inside and viewed, lest the offender be destroyed, as indeed some were *en route* to Jerusalem (i.e., seventy inhabitants of Beth Shemesh in **1 Samuel 6:19–20** and Uzzah, who touched the ark in **2 Samuel 6:7**). To preclude such irreverence and its consequences, the ark was carried by Levites holding the ends of long golden poles thrust through golden rings at each lower corner (**Exodus 25:12–15**). The lid of solid pure gold, called the "mercy seat "or "atonement cover" (**Exodus 25:17; Leviticus 16:13**; cf. **Hebrews 9:5**), served as an altar once a year on the Day of Atonement, Yom Kippur (the "Day of [sin] Covering"). The high priest, the only person who could enter the sacred precinct of the holy of holies, did so on that day and applied the blood of a sacrificed animal as atonement for the entire nation (**Leviticus 16:16–17; 1 Chronicles 6:49**; cf. **Hebrews 9:25; 10:19**).

15. See a summary of the "History and Movement of the Ark of the Covenant" in chart "**1 Chronicles 16**: Genealogical Registry of the Levites Who Oversaw the Ark of the Covenant in the City of David and the Tabernacle at Gibeon."

16. Even though the ark of the covenant was moved to the City of David in 1004 B.C., the original tabernacle proper (or "tent of meeting"; **2 Chronicles 1:13**), which had been constructed in 1445 B.C. in the days of the wilderness wanderings, remained at the high place in Gibeon where Zadok the high priest presided and made offerings to the Lord (**1 Chronicles 16:39**). When Solomon's Temple was finally completed in 960 B.C., the ark of the covenant—containing "nothing . . . except the two tablets"—was moved to the Most Holy Place, and the original tabernacle/tent of meeting was moved from Gibeon and stored inside the newly built temple (**2 Chronicles 5:10**; see also **4–5, 7**; cf. **1 Kings 8:4; 1 Chronicles 6:32; 9:21; 2 Chronicles 1:3–6, 13**). See the "History and Movement of the Tabernacle" in chart "**1 Chronicles 16**: Genealogical Registry of the Levites Who Oversaw the Ark of the Covenant in the City of David and the Tabernacle at Gibeon."

1 CHRONICLES 16: GENEALOGICAL REGISTRY OF THE LEVITES WHO OVERSAW THE ARK OF THE COVENANT IN THE CITY OF DAVID AND THE TABERNACLE AT GIBEON

Approximate Dating: ca. 1004–960 B.C. ***Relevant Scriptures:*** **1 Chronicles 16:37–42**

Over the Ark of the Covenant in the City of David

1. **Asaph**[1] and his associates (Gershonites)
2. **Obed-Edom**[2] and 68 brethren (Merarites)
3. **Hosah**[3] (Merarite)

Over the Mosaic Tabernacle at Gibeon, under the supervision of Zadok (Aaron–Eleazar–Zadok priesthood)

1. **Heman** (Kohathite–Korahite)
2. **Jeduthun** (Ethan) (Merarite)[4]
3. **Sons of Jeduthun (Ethan)** (Merarites)[5]

Biblical and Theological Significance

During this time in sacred history, two legitimate worship sites existed—one centered in Gibeon, where the original Mosaic tabernacle resided and sacrifices were made, and the other in the City of David, where the ark of the covenant resided in a temporary tent-tabernacle. Both places were *temporary* in the sense that David envisioned a *permanent* house for the Lord and his Name (**2 Samuel 7:1–16**)—a temple to be built on the former threshing floor of Araunah where the Lord had stopped the plague and showed David mercy after David took a prideful census of the nation (**2 Samuel 24; 1 Chronicles 21:1–22:1**).

Preparations were made for the large-scale temple in the latter years of King David's reign, 1011–971 B.C. (**22:2–19**), but actual temple construction did not begin until the fourth year (966 B.C.) of King Solomon's reign (971–931 B.C.), corresponding to the 480th year after the Israelites came out of Egypt (i.e., 1446 B.C.–966 B.C.; **1 Kings 6:1**). Solomon's Temple took seven years to build, from 966–960

B.C. (**1 Kings 5–6; 8:13**). The new temple was patterned after the former Mosaic tabernacle and was divided into three major areas: the most holy place (which housed the ark of the covenant), the holy place, and the outer courtyard.

A brief history of the ark of the covenant and the original Mosaic tabernacle are helpful for understanding the significance of the high priesthood and Levitical attendants who oversaw the cultic activities in Solomon's Temple.

History and Movement of the Tabernacle

- 1445 B.C.: Under the direction of Moses, the tabernacle was originally constructed by the artisan Bezalel in the second year (1445 B.C.) after the exodus from Egypt (1446 B.C.); it is sometimes called the Mosaic tabernacle (**Exodus 35:30–36:38; 40:17**; cf. **Numbers 7:1; 1 Chronicles 21:20; Acts 7:44**).
- 1445–1406 B.C.: The tabernacle was the central place of worship; it moved from place to place as the Israelites sojourned in the wilderness for forty years (**Exodus 40:38; Numbers 9:18–22**).
- 1406 B.C.: Following the initial conquest of Canaan, the tabernacle was set up in Bethel (**Judges 20:18–28**), where Abraham had built an altar to the Lord when he entered Canaan (**Genesis 12:28**).
- 1406 B.C.: The tabernacle was then moved and set up in a central location at Shiloh[6] and remained there for about the next 350 years (**Joshua 18:1; Judges 18:31**; cf. **Jeremiah 7:12**). The Eli priesthood[7] officiated at Shiloh (cf. **1 Samuel 1:9**); this was the place where Samuel[8] was called by God as a young boy in ca. 1100 B.C. (**1 Samuel 3**).
- Circa 1050 B.C.: Shiloh was destroyed by the Philistines; the tabernacle somehow survived and was relocated again (cf. **Psalm 78:60; Jeremiah 7:12, 14; 26:6, 9**)—apparently it was first set up at Nob[9] where the Elide priest Ahimelek presided, along with eighty-five other priests[10] (**1 Samuel 22:16–20**; cf. **21:1–9; 22:22**). Later, the tabernacle was set up in Gibeon[11] where "Zadok the priest and his fellow priests officiated" (**1 Chronicles 16:39–40**).
- 1050–960 B.C.: The tabernacle remained at Gibeon throughout David's reign and the early part of Solomon's reign (**1 Kings 3:1–4**; cf. **1 Chronicles 16:39; 21:29; 2 Chronicles 1:3–6, 13**). (The reference to a "tabernacle, the tent of meeting" in **1 Chronicles 6:32** does not refer to the original Mosaic tabernacle but to the temporary tent-tabernacle in the City of David that housed only the ark.)
- 960 B.C.: After Solomon's Temple was completed, the original Mosaic tabernacle and all the furnishings were moved to Jerusalem. The tent itself was stored within Solomon's Temple (cf. **1 Kings 8:3–4**).

History and Movement of the Ark of the Covenant

- 1445 B.C.: The ark[12] was constructed by Bezalel in 1445 B.C., in the second year after the exodus (**Exodus 37:1–9; 40:17**) and was placed in the most holy place of the tabernacle (**26:33–34**). The ark symbolized the presence of God.[13]
- 1445–1406 B.C.: The ark resided in the tabernacle and traveled as the Israelites moved from place to place during the forty-year sojourn in the wilderness[14] (**40:38; Numbers 9:18–22**). The ark (chest) contained the gold jar of manna, Aaron's staff that had budded, and the stone tablets of the covenant (**Exodus 25:16; 40:20–21; Hebrews 9:4**). The lid of the ark, called the *atonement cover*, was made of a solid slab of gold, representing the mercy seat and the throne of Israel's divine King in his earthly kingdom (cf. **Exodus 25:22**; cf. vv. **10–22; 37:1–11; 2 Samuel 6:2; Psalm 80:1; 99:1**).
- 1406–1050 B.C.: After the conquest of the land of Canaan, the ark and the Mosaic tabernacle were initially taken to Bethen and soon thereafter moved to Shiloh, which became the center of worship for approximately the next 350 years (**Joshua 18:1; Judges 18:31**; cf. **Jeremiah 7:12**). The Eli priesthood officiated at Shiloh (cf. **1 Samuel 1:9**).
- Circa 1050 B.C.: When the Philistines destroyed Shiloh, they captured the ark as a trophy of war and took it to Philistia (**1 Samuel 4:1–11**); initially it was set up in Dagon's temple in the capital city of Ashdod, but by the next day, the Philistine god Dagon had fallen to the ground before the ark. Next, the ark was moved to Gath and then to Ekron; in each place, the God of Israel afflicted the Philistines (**1 Samuel 5**). After seven months, the Philistines realized that they had taken a dangerous prize and decided to return the ark with a guilt offering to Israel (**1 Samuel 6**). A cart pulled by two cows brought the chest to the priestly town of Beth Shemesh of Judah; unfortunately, while there, seventy inhabitants of Beth Shemesh were killed because they looked inside the sacred chest (**1 Samuel 6:19–21**).
- Circa 1024–1004 B.C.: Men of Kiriath Jearim came and took the ark from Beth Shemesh to the home of Abinadab the Judahite;[15] there, Abinadab's son Eleazar was consecrated to care for the ark. The ark remained in relative obscurity in Kiriath Jearim for the next twenty years (**1 Samuel 7:1–2**).
- 1004 B.C.: After David conquered Jerusalem and became king over *all* Israel in 1004 B.C. (**2 Samuel 5**), he attempted to move the ark from Kiriath Jearim (Baalah)—located approximately ten miles southwest of Jerusalem—to the City of David. However, the ark was not transported by Levites as prescribed (**Numbers 4:5–6, 15**; cf. **Exodus 25:12–15**); rather, it was set on a new cart pulled by oxen (as the Philistines had done). Along the journey, the oxen stumbled and Uzzah (the son of Abinadab) reached out to steady the ark; for this irreverent act, God struck down Uzzah and he died. Out of fear, David had the ark taken to the house of the righteous Merarite-gatekeeper, Obed-Edom,[16] and it remained there for three months (**2 Samuel 6:1–11; 1 Chronicles 13:1–14**).
- 1004–960 B.C.: David successfully moved the ark from the house of Obed-Edom to the City of David where it was placed in a special tent (a quasi-temple) that David had erected for it (**2 Samuel 6:17**). It remained there, attended by Levites, until the construction of Solomon's Temple was completed (cf. **1 Kings 6**) on Mount Moriah (**2 Chronicles 3:1**), north of the City of David.
- 960 B.C.: Solomon moved the ark from the City of David

to the newly completed, magnificent temple of Solomon[17] on Mount Moriah and had it placed in the most holy place (**1 Kings 8:1–11; 2 Chronicles 5:1–10**; cf. **2 Chronicles 3:1**)—the Chronicler's reflection resonates with the glory of the occasion (**2 Chronicles 5:14**). At this time, however, "[there] was nothing in the ark except the two stone tablets that Moses had placed in it at Horeb, where the Lord made a covenant with the Israelites after they came out of Egypt" (**1 Kings 8:9**; **2 Chronicles 5:10**).

- 960–586 B.C.: The ark of the covenant remained in Solomon's Temple and is accounted for until the destruction of Jerusalem in 586 B.C. at the hand of King Nebuchadnezzar of Babylon (**2 Kings 25:8–9; 2 Chronicles 36:18–19**; cf. **2 Kings 24:13**). The ark may have been destroyed along with the temple or was possibly taken to Babylon as a trophy to Babylonian might and superiority. In any event, the ark disappears from the record. Only speculation remains as to its final fate. One credible explanation is that it was perhaps taken by Jeremiah, the man of God, and hidden in a cave in Israel.[18]

Notes

1. Asaph ministered daily before the ark in the tent-tabernacle in the City of David. For his genealogy, see chart "**1 Chronicles 6**: Levi: High Priests, Priests, Levites, and Musicians in Solomon's Temple."

2. Obed-Edom the Merarite, the son of Jeduthun/Ethan, was the main gatekeeper before the ark of the covenant. His large household numbered sixty-eight. For his genealogy, see chart "**2 Samuel 6**: Obed-Edom, the Levitical Gatekeeper and Keeper of the Ark."

3. Hosah, a Merarite, filled a similar role as Obed-Edom. For the family of Hosah, see chart "**1 Chronicles 26**: The Kohathite–Korahite and Merarite Gatekeepers in Solomon's Temple."

4. Ethan (**1 Chronicles 6:44; 15:17, 19**) is also named Jeduthun (**1 Chronicles 9:16; 16:38, 41–42; 25:1, 3, 6; 2 Chronicles 5:12; 29:14; 35:15; Nehemiah 11:17**; cf. the titles of **Psalm 39:0; 62:0; 77:0; 89:0**). Heman the Kohathite–Korahite and Jeduthun (Ethan) the Merarite were "responsible for the sounding of the trumpets and cymbals and for the playing of the other instruments for sacred song" (**1 Chronicles 16:42**). For the genealogy of Heman and Jeduthun/Ethan, see chart "**1 Chronicles 6**: Levi: High Priests, Priests, Levites, and Musicians in Solomon's Temple."

5. The sons of Jeduthun/Ethan (see note 4) were "stationed at the gate" as gatekeepers (**1 Chronicles 16:42**).

6. Shiloh was located in Ephraim between Bethel and Shechem (**Judges 21:19**). Shiloh was where the Lord "first made a dwelling for [his] Name" (**Jeremiah 7:12**). In ca. 1050 B.C. or shortly thereafter, Shiloh was destroyed by the Philistines when they captured the ark of the covenant. See the article "Did the Philistines Destroy the Israelite Sanctuary at Shiloh? The Archaeological Evidence," *BAR* 1 1975, http://cojs.org/did-the-philistines-destroy-the-israelite-sanctuary-at-shiloh/.

7. For Eli and his sons, see chart "**1 Samuel 1**: Eli and the Eli Priesthood."

8. For Samuel, see chart "**1 Samuel 1**: Samuel, the Prophet–Priest–Judge of Israel."

9. Nob, called "the town of the priests" (**1 Samuel 22:19**), was a town northeast of Jerusalem and southeast of Gibeah, but the ark was never taken to Nob.

10. Upon Saul's orders, Ahimelek and 85 priests at Nob—with the exception of Abiathar—were killed by Doeg the Edomite (Saul's shepherd; **1 Samuel 21:7**) because the priests had sided with David by giving David provisions, including the sword of Goliath for a weapon and the consecrated bread for food (**1 Samuel 21:1–9; 22:6–23**).

11. The city of Gibeon, located within the tribe of Benjamin (**Joshua 18:25**), was approximately 16 miles south of Shiloh, 5 miles northwest of Jerusalem, and 4 miles northeast of Kiriath Jearim; it was a city given to the Kohathite high priests (i.e., the priests who were descendants of Aaron; **Joshua 21:17**).

12. See note 13 in chart "**1 Chronicles 15**: Priests and Levites who Brought the Ark of the Covenant from the House of Obed-Edom to the Tent-Tabernacle in the City of David."

13. God spoke to Moses "between the two cherubim above the atonement cover on the ark of the covenant law" (**Numbers 7:89**; cf. **Exodus 25:22**) and the *shekhina* glory filled the tabernacle (**Exodus 40:34–35**). In the days when the Israelites sojourned in the wilderness, the ark represented the movement of the Lord himself, and *vice versa* (**Numbers 10:33, 35–36**).

14. The ark constantly led the people during their travels, accompanied by clouds by day and a pillar of fire by night (**Exodus 13:21–22; 40:38; Numbers 9:21; 10:34; 14:14; Deuteronomy 1:33**).

15. See chart "**1 Samuel 7**: The Family of Abinadab Who Oversaw the Ark of the Covenant."

16. For Uzzah, see chart "**1 Samuel 7**: The Family of Abinadab Who Oversaw the Ark of the Covenant." For Obed-Edom, see chart "**2 Samuel 6**: Obed-Edom, the Levitical Gatekeeper and Keeper of the Ark."

17. When Solomon's Temple was finished in 960 B.C., the former Mosaic tabernacle was placed in a sacred chamber within the temple, being preserved as an iconic reminder of the exodus, the giving of the Law, and the fashioning of a covenant between God and Israel that made them a "kingdom of priests and a holy nation" (**Exodus 19:6**).

18. **Second Maccabees 2:4–5** says, "Jeremiah went out to the mountain which Moses ascended [Nebo] to see the heritage promised by God. There Jeremiah found a cave chamber and brought into it the tabernacle and the ark and the incense altar and blocked up the entrance." Jonathan A. Goldstein, "A Forged Letter to the Egyptian Jews Purporting to Have Been Written in 164 B.C.E." *II Maccabees: A New Translation with Introduction and Commentary*, AB 41A (Garden City, NY: Doubleday, 1983), 156, 184.

1 CHRONICLES 23: THE TWENTY-FOUR LEVITICAL LEADERS (GERSHONITES, KOHATHITES, AND MERARITES)[1] WHO OVERSAW THE RELIGIOUS PERSONNEL IN SOLOMON'S TEMPLE[2]

Approximate Dating: Solomon's Temple was completed in 960 B.C.; these Levitical leaders served thereafter during Solomon's reign, ca. 971–931 B.C. ***Relevant Scriptures:*** **1 Chronicles 23:1–32**; also **Exodus 6:17; Numbers 3:18; 26:57; 1 Chronicles 6:1–3, 16–20, 42, 47; 24:20-30; 26:21–25**

Genealogy of the Ten Gershonite Leaders (Heads of Families)

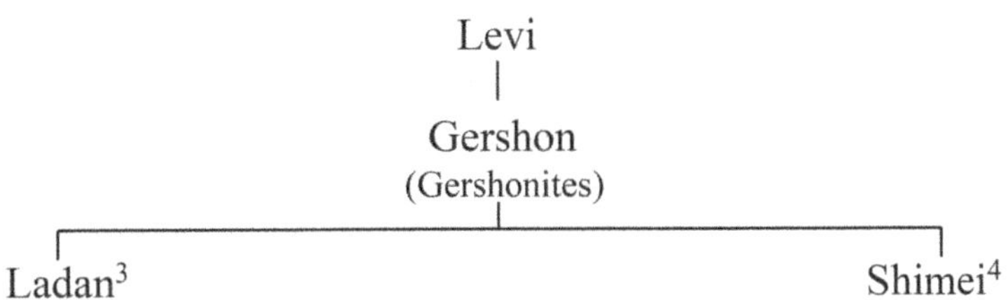

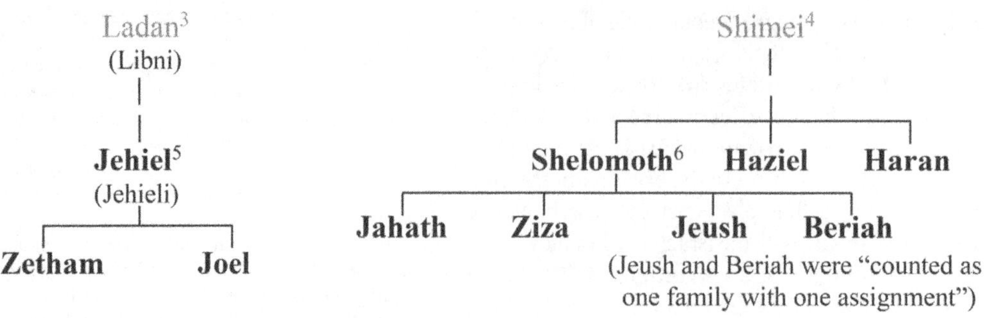

Genealogy of the Nine Kohathite Leaders (Heads of Families)

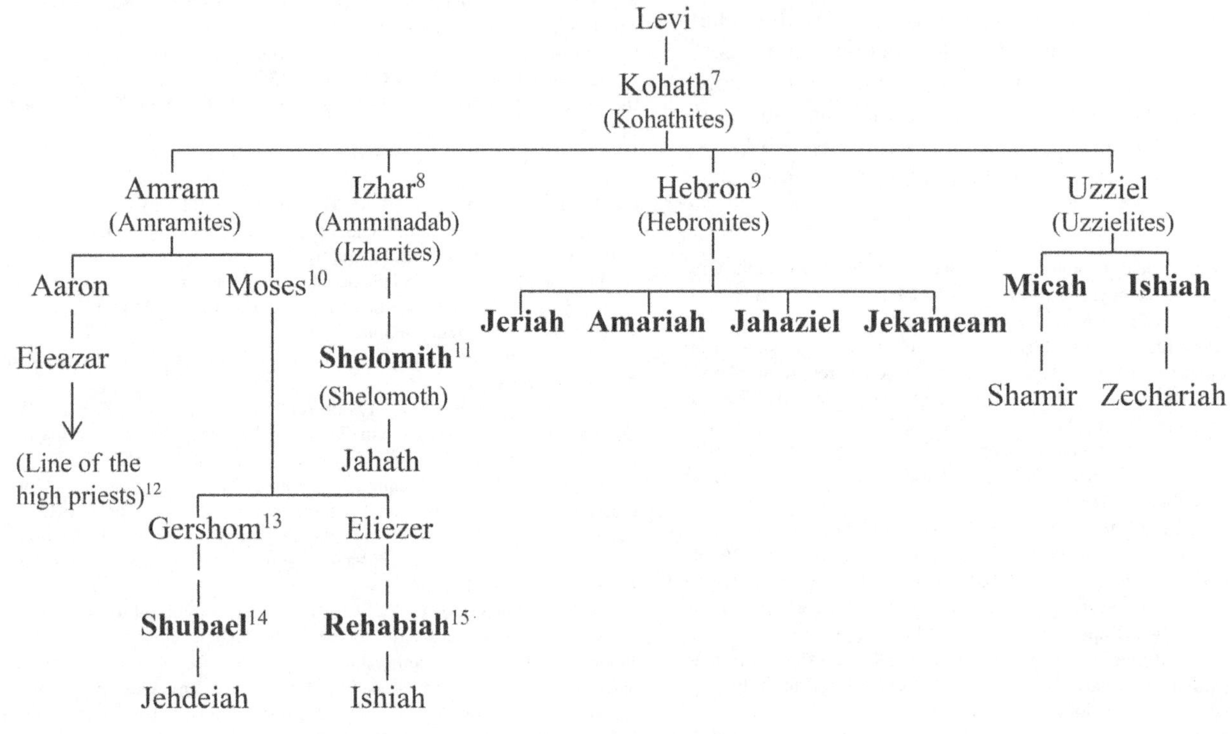

Genealogy of the Five Merarite Leaders (Heads of Families)

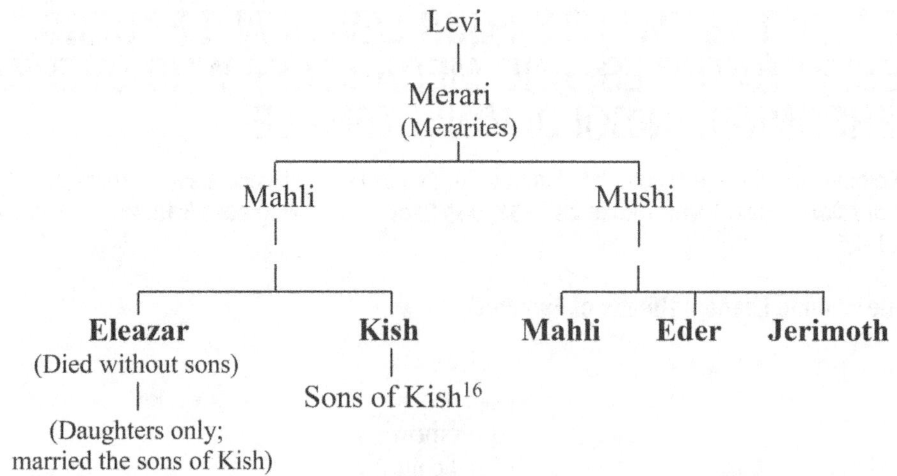

Biblical and Theological Significance

When he was "old and full of years" (**1 Chronicles 23:1**), David made preparations, not only for amassing the building materials for the future temple, but also for an organized Levitical priesthood that would serve in the permanent temple once it was built by Solomon[17] (**1 Chronicles 22**). The Levitical priesthood was overseen by twenty-four Levitical leaders from each of the three main clans (Kohathite, Gershonites, and Merarites). Originally, to be eligible for service, Levites had to be thirty years old; they apprenticed for five years (from age twenty-five to thirty) and were required to retire after age fifty (**Numbers 8:23–25**). However, David lowered the age of Levitical eligibility from thirty to twenty years old, since the temple would reside in a permanent location and no longer need transportation, as it had in the period of the wilderness wanderings. David's census of the Levitical personnel revealed a total of 38,000 Levites who were eligible for service and they were subdivided as follows: twenty-four thousand who were in charge of the temple work; six thousand who served as officials and judges; four thousand who were gatekeepers; and four thousand who praised the Lord with musical instruments, which David said he "provided for that purpose" (**1 Chronicles 23:1–5, 24–27**).

The leaders of the religious personnel were "the descendants of Levi by their families—the heads of families as they were registered under their names and counted individually" (**1 Chronicles 23:24**). Their specific duties included assisting the high priests and the Kohathite attending priests in the temple proper, the courtyard, and the side rooms, as well as in the purification of all sacred things. They also offered thanks and praise to the Lord each morning and evening, as well as assisted with burnt offerings on the Sabbath, at the monthly festival of the New Moon, and during the appointed festivals (**1 Chronicles 23:28–31**).

Notes

1. The *sons* described in **1 Chronicles 23:1–32** were primarily *descendants*.

2. Also see chart "**1 Chronicles 24**: Additional Levities (Kohathites and Merarites) who Served in Solomon's Temple."

3. Ladan (**1 Chronicles 23:7–9; 26:21**) is the same person as Libni (**Exodus 6:17; Numbers 3:18; 1 Chronicles 6:17, 20**). His descendants are given in **1 Chronicles 6:20, 39–43; 23:8–9**.

4. Shimei the Gershonite (**1 Chronicles 23:7**) is the same person as Shimei (**1 Chronicles 6:17**); for his lineage, see chart "**1 Chronicles 6**: Levi: High Priests, Priests, Levites, and Musicians in Solomon's Temple." Notice that Shimei the son of Gershon should not be confused with (1) Shimei the son of Jahath, the son of Libni/Ladan, the son of Gershon (**1 Chronicles 6:42**), nor with (2) Shimei the son of Libni, the son of Mahli, the son of Merari (**1 Chronicles 6:29**). Shimei, the son of Gershon (**1 Chronicles 6:17; 23:7**) had four sons—Jahath, Ziza, Jeush and Beriah (**1 Chronicles 23:10**). The offspring of the Shimei figure listed in 1 Chronicles 23:9—Shelomoth, Haziel, Haran—may refer to the sons/descendants of Shimei, the great-grandson of Gershon, who was in the Gershon—Libni/Ladan—Jahath—Shimei—Zimmah line (cf. **1 Chronicles 6:42–43**)—thereby explaining the phrase "These were the heads of the families of Ladan." Other scholars have proposed an alternative reading. For a possible gloss and textual error in **1 Chronicles 23:10**—reading "the sons of Shimei" instead of "the sons of Shelomoth"—see the explanation given by Edward L. Curtis and Albert A. Madsen in *A Critical and Exegetical Commentary on the Books of Chronicles* (Edinburgh: T&T Clark, 1920), 263–264. The chart shows Shelomoth (not Shimei) as the father of Jahath, Ziza, Jeush, and Beriah, but this is only one of several possible interpretations. Jeush and Beriah, the two sons of Shimei (possibly Shelomoth) "did not have many sons; so they were counted as one family with one assignment" (**1 Chronicles 23:11**).

5. Jehiel (**1 Chronicles 23:8**) is the same person as Jehieli (**1 Chronicles 26:22**). His two sons, Zetham and Joel, were over the temple treasury (**1 Chronicles 26:22**) and Jehiel/Jehieli himself received the gifts of precious stones that were given to the treasury (**1 Chronicles 29:8**).

6. Shelomoth the Gershonite in **1 Chronicles 23:9** is not Shelomith/Shelomoth the Kohathite–Izharite (see note 11).

7. The nine Kohathite leaders who served in Solomon's Temple were priests but not high priests; for the line of the high priests, see note 12.

8. Izhar in **Exodus 6:18, 21; Numbers 3:19; 16:1;** and **1 Chronicles 6:2, 18, 38; 23:12, 18** is Amminadab in **1 Chronicles 6:22**. He was the eponymous ancestor of the Izharites.

9. The names of the sons of Hebron given in **1 Chronicles 23:19** are also noted in **1 Chronicles 24:23**.

10. Remarkably, Moses' *descendants* through his sons Eliezer and Gershom (in the Levi–Kohath–Amram–Moses line) were allowed to serve as legitimate Levitical personnel alongside the descendants from the Levi–Kohath (Kohathite), Levi–Gershon (Gersonite), and Levi–Merari (Merarite) lines because "[the] sons of Moses the man of God were counted as part of the tribe of Levi" (**1 Chronicles 23:14–15**).

11. Shelomith the Kohathite–Izharite (**1 Chronicles 23:18**) is the same person as Shelomoth the Kohathite–Izharite (**1 Chronicles 24:22**).

12. The high priesthood line was restricted to those of Aaron–Eleazar–Zadok patrilineal descent. Aaron was "set apart, he and his descendants forever, to consecrate the most holy things, to offer sacrifices before the Lord, to minister before him and to pronounce blessings in his name" (**1 Chronicles 23:13**). See charts "**1 Chronicles 6**: Levi: High Priests, Priests, Levites, and Musicians in Solomon's Temple" and "**Supplement 2**: The High Priests of Israel."

13. Gershom the firstborn son of Moses and Zipporah should not be confused with Gershon the son of Levi, the progenitor of the Gershonites (**Genesis 46:11; Exodus 6:16; Numbers 3:17; 1 Chronicles 6:1, 16, 20; 15:7; 23:6**) or with Gershom a descendant of Phinehas, a priest who returned from Babylon to Jerusalem in the post-exile (**Ezra 8:2**).

14. Shubael (called Shebuel in some translations) was overseer of the temple treasuries (**1 Chronicles 26:24**). Shubael the descendant of Moses (in the Levi–Kohath–Amram–Moses–Gershom line) is a different person than Shubael a descendant of Heman, the chief musician in Solomon's Temple (in the Levi–Kohath–Izhar–Elkanah–Samuel–Joel–Heman line; **1 Chronicles 25:4, 20**); see chart "**1 Chronicles 6**: Levi: High Priests, Priests, Levites, and Musicians in Solomon's Temple."

15. Rehabiah was the only descendant/heir of Eliezer; however, Rehabiah had many sons (**1 Chronicles 23:17**). For the other sons/descendants of Rehabiah, see **1 Chronicles 24:21** and the lineage of Rehabiah given in **1 Chronicles 26:25**.

16. The sons of Kish married the daughters of Eleazar, who were their first cousins (**1 Chronicles 23:22**).

17. Solomon's Temple was begun in 966 B.C. and completed in 960 B.C. during the early years of King Solomon's reign, ca. 971–931 B.C. (**1 Kings 6:1, 37–38**).

1 CHRONICLES 24: GENEALOGICAL REGISTRY OF THE TWENTY-FOUR DIVISIONS OF KOHATHITE ATTENDING PRIESTS[1] WHO ROTATED SERVICE IN SOLOMON'S TEMPLE (SIXTEEN FROM THE AARON–ELEAZAR–ZADOK LINE AND EIGHT FROM THE AARON–ITHAMAR LINE)

Approximate Dating: the priestly divisions were established at the end of David's reign, ca. 971 B.C.; Solomon's Temple was completed in 960 B.C. and these original attending priests/office holders served from ca. 971–931 B.C. during Solomon's reign and perhaps longer. ***Relevant Scriptures:*** **1 Chronicles 24:1–19;** also **Genesis 46:11; Exodus 6:16, 18, 20, 23; Numbers 3:17, 19, 27; 1 Chronicles 6:1–3, 16, 18; 23:6, 12**

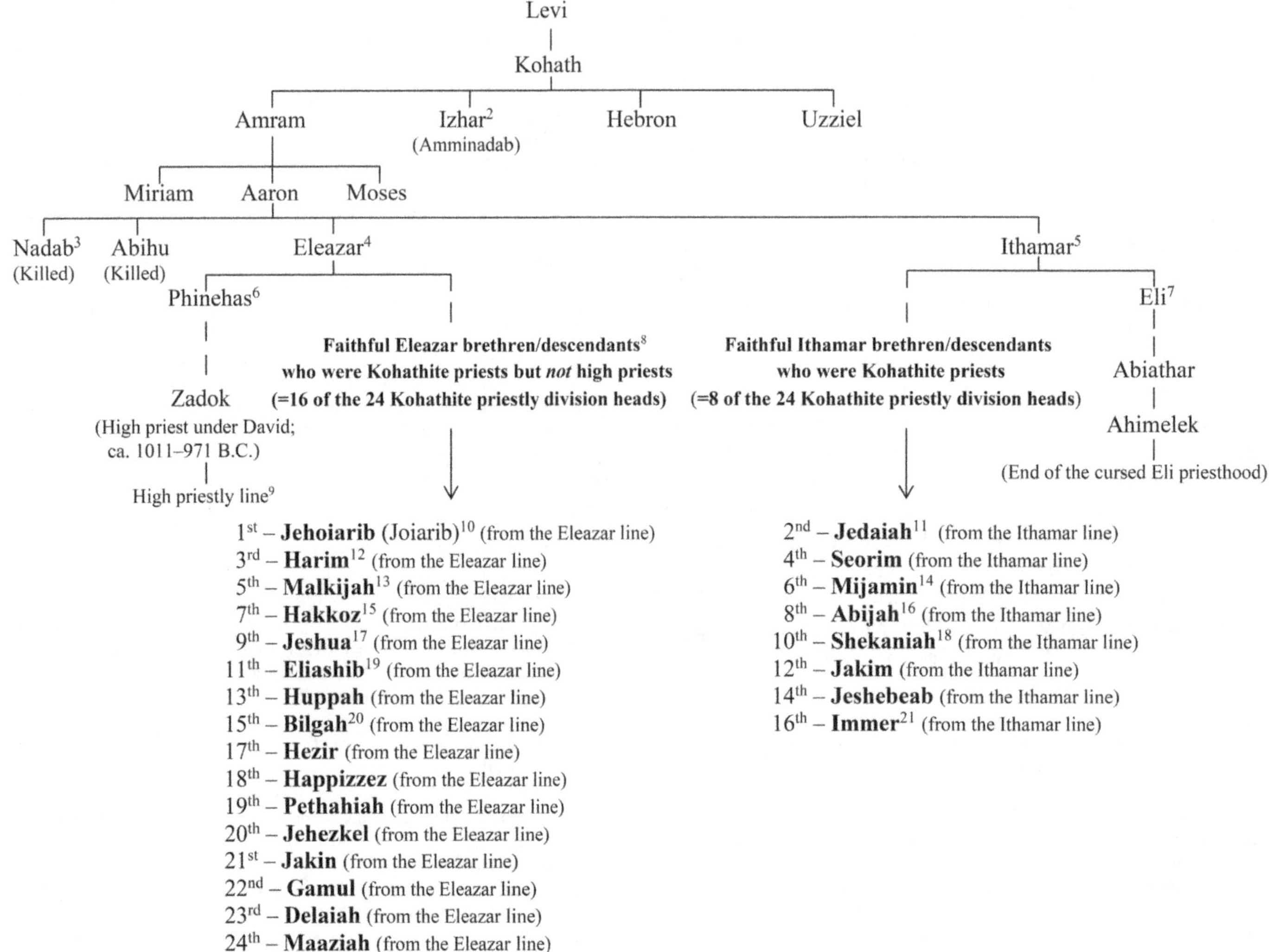

Table 1 reflects a collation of names from all the Kohathite priestly divisions recorded in the post-exilic era in order to isolate names that did, or did not, continue from the Davidic–Solomonic era. At least twelve of the twenty-four priestly divisions in the post-exile retained the original division names from the Davidic era (e.g., Jehoiarib/Joiarib, Jedaiah, Harim, etc.). Furthermore, office holders in 516–44 B.C. were most likely direct *descendants* of the family heads who held the positions in 971–931 B.C. Additional Kohathite priests (perhaps representing the heads of the twelve "missing" priestly courses) are identified by name in the table, but their affiliation with a particular priestly division is not specified in Scripture. One can only assume that the original number of twenty-four priestly divisions continued in the post-exile as well (see commentary below).

Table 1: Heads of Kohathite Attending Priestly Families—NOT High Priests—from Major Scriptural Sources

Names which are common in two or more scriptural texts are shown in **BOLD**.

	1 Chronicles 24:1–19 (Solomonic era; 971–931 B.C.)	**Ezra 2:36–39; Nehemiah 7:39–42 (Post-exile; 538 B.C.)**	**1 Chronicles 9:10–13 (Post-exile; 516 B.C.)**	**Ezra 8:2, 24; 10:20–22 (Post-exile; 458 B.C.)**	**Nehemiah 10:1–8; 11:10–14; 12:1–7, 12–21, 41–42 (Post-exile; 538–444 B.C.)**
Divisions/ courses/priestly families					
1st	**Jehoiarib**[22] (or **Joiarib**)		**Jehoiarib** (or **Joiarib**)		**Jehoiarib** (or **Joiarib** or **"the son of Joiarib"**) (Descendant = Mattenai)
2nd	**Jedaiah**[23]	**Jedaiah** ("through Jeshua"[24])	**Jedaiah**		**Jedaiah #1** & **Jedaiah #2**[25] (Descendants = Nethanel & Uzzi)
3rd	**Harim**	**Harim**		**Harim** (Descendants = Maaseiah, Elijah, Jehiel, Shemaiah, Uzziah)	**Harim**[26] (Descendant = Adna)
4th	Seorim				
5th	**Malkijah**	**Pashhur**[27] (son of **Malkijah**)	**Pashhur & Malkijah** (Descendants = Adaiah, Jeroham)	**Pashhur & Malkijah** (Descendants = Elioenai, Maaseiah, Ishmael, Nethanel, Elasah, Jozabad)	**Pashhur & Malkijah** (Descendants = Zechariah, Amzi, Pelaliah, Jeroham, Adaiah[28])
6th	**Mijamin**				**Mijamin**[29] **(or Miniamin)** (Descendant = Piltai)
7th	**Hakkoz**				(Descendants = Meremoth,[30] Uriah, Helkai)
8th	**Abijah**				**Abijah** (Descendant = Zikri)
9th	Jeshua				
10th	**Shekaniah**				**Shekaniah** (Descendant = Joseph)
11th	Eliashib				
12th	Jakim				
13th	Huppah				
14th	Jeshebeab				
15th	**Bilgah**				**Bilgai/Bilgah** (Descendant = Shammua)
16th	**Immer**	**Immer**	**Immer** (Descendant = Maasai[31])	**Immer** (Descendants = Hanani, Zebadiah)	**Immer** (Descendants = Meshillemoth, Ahzai, Azarel, Amashsai,[32] Pashhur[33])

(continued)

	1 Chronicles 24:1–19 (Solomonic era; 971–931 B.C.)	**Ezra 2:36–39; Nehemiah 7:39–42 (Post-exile; 538 B.C.)**	**1 Chronicles 9:10–13 (Post-exile; 516 B.C.)**	**Ezra 8:2, 24; 10:20–22 (Post-exile; 458 B.C.)**	**Nehemiah 10:1–8; 11:10–14; 12:1–7, 12–21, 41–42 (Post-exile; 538–444 B.C.)**
17th	Hezir				
18th	Happizzez				
19th	Pethahiah				
20th	Jehezkel				
21st	**Jakin**		**Jakin**		**Jakin**
22nd	Gamul				
23rd	Delaiah				Shemaiah?[34]
24th	**Maaziah** (**Moadiah**?[35])				Moadiah (probably = **Maaziah**)
Other priests				Gershom (of Phinehas)[36]	Zedekiah
Other priests				Daniel (of Ithamar)[37]	Azariah (possibly Azariah #3)[38]
Other priests				Sherebiah[39]	Seraiah (possibly Seraiah #2 or #3)[40] (Descendant = Meraiah)
Other priests				Hashabiah	Jeremiah[41] (Descendant = Hananiah)
Other priests					Ezra[42] (Descendant = Meshullam #1)
Other priests					Amariah[43] (Descendant = Jehohanan)
Other priests					Malluk (Descendant = Jonathan)
Other priests					Hattush[44]
Other priests					Rehum[45]
Other priests					Elioenai
Other priests					Iddo (Descendant = Zechariah)
Other priests					Ginnethon (Descendant = Meshullam #2)
Other priests					Shemaiah[46] (Descendant = Jehonathan)
Other priests					Sallu (Descendant = Kallai)
Other priests					Amok (Descendant = Eber)
Other priests					Hilkiah (Descendant = Hashabiah)
Other priests					Shebaniah

	1 Chronicles 24:1–19 (Solomonic era; 971–931 B.C.)	Ezra 2:36–39; Nehemiah 7:39–42 (Post-exile; 538 B.C.)	1 Chronicles 9:10–13 (Post-exile; 516 B.C.)	Ezra 8:2, 24; 10:20–22 (Post-exile; 458 B.C.)	Nehemiah 10:1–8; 11:10–14; 12:1–7, 12–21, 41–42 (Post-exile; 538–444 B.C.)
Other priests					Obadiah
Other priests					Daniel
Other priests					Baruch
Other priests					Eliakim
Other priests					Maaseiah
Other priests					Micaiah
Other priests					Zechariah (possibly = Zechariah, descendant of Iddo, above)
Other priests					Hananiah (probably = Hananiah, descendant of Jeremiah, above)
Other priests					Shemaiah (probably = Shemaiah above)
Other priests					Eleazar
Other priests					Jehohanan (probably = Jehohanan, descendant of Amariah, above)
Other priests					Malkijah (probably = Malkijah, above)
Other priests					Elam
Other priests					Ezer

Biblical and Theological Significance

This chart lists the twenty-four divisions of Kohathite attending priests who were appointed by King David to serve in Solomon's Temple. The priestly divisions are also called *priestly* courses (see note 48). The Kohathite priest who was the office holder was also the head of his family. **First Chronicles 24:3–4** describes the methodology used to determine the divisions: "With the help of Zadok a descendant of Eleazar [of the Aaron–Eleazar–Zadok priesthood] and Ahimelek a descendant of Ithamar [of the Ithamar–Eli priesthood], David separated them into divisions for their appointed order of ministering. A larger number of leaders were found among Eleazar's descendants than among Ithamar's, and they were divided accordingly: sixteen heads of families from Eleazar's descendants and eight heads of families from Ithamar's descendants." The division order was determined by casting lots,[47] with "one family being taken from Eleazar and then one from Ithamar" (**1 Chronicles 24:5–6**). A scribe named Shemaiah, the son of Nethanel, a Levite, "recorded their names" in front of King David, Zadok (an Eleazar descendant), Ahimelek (an Ithamar descendant), and the family heads of the priests and Levites (**1 Chronicles 24:6**). Because there were sixteen heads of families from the Eleazar descendants and only eight heads of families from the Ithamar descendants, the choice of the divisions *alternated* between descendants of Eleazar and Ithamar until the sixteenth division; then the last eight divisions were all headed by Eleazar descendants.

In the Second Temple period, Kohathite attending priests from both lines (i.e., the Aaron–Eleazar–Phineas–Zadok line and the faithful remnant of the Aaron–Ithamar–Eli line) continued to be represented; for example, in 458 B.C. the Kohathite priests, Gershom "of the descendants of Phinehas [of Eleazar]" and Daniel "of the descendants of Ithamar" are listed (**Ezra 8:2**). The composite list of priestly divisions shown in table 1 reveals that descendants from at least twelve of the original twenty-four priestly divisions from the Solomonic time served in post-exilic Jerusalem: (1) Jehoiarib/Joiarib, (2) Jedaiah, (3) Harim, (4) Malkijah–Pashhur, (5) Mijamin, (6) Hakkoz, (7) Abijah, (8) Shekaniah, (9) Bilgah, (10) Immer, (11) Jakin, (12) Maaziah (Moadiah?)—and possibly (13) Delaiah (see Shemaiah, a possible Delaiah descendant, note 35). This does not mean, however, that the other eleven or twelve original priestly divisions were not represented in the Second Temple, but only that they are not specifically identified as such in the post-exilic era in Scripture. In fact, Josephus, writing in ca. A.D. 93, comments that the "partition [of twenty-four divisions] has remained to this day".[48] Also, fragments of a Hebrew inscription found in 1962 at excavations at Caesarea corroborate that the custom of *commemorating* the names of the original priestly courses in Palestinian synagogues "dates back to the third and fourth centuries" [A.D.].[49]

Collectively, the evidence suggests that throughout Israel's history, there was genealogical and functional continuity in the ordered assemblages of Kohathite priests who assisted the high priests in their cultic duties. The priesthood organization probably existed in nascent form in the tabernacle in the days of Moses and was then codified under King David for the Kohathite attending priests who served in Solomon's Temple from 960 B.C. (when the temple was completed) to 586 B.C. (when the temple was destroyed by the Babylonians), and that arrangement continued through the Second Temple period (516 B.C.–A.D. 70). For that reason, these insights from Alfred Edersheim[50] and Joachim Jeremias[51] about the Kohathite attending priesthood in Herod's Temple seem applicable to the former Davidic era.

Alfred Edersheim provides this information:

1. According to Jewish tradition, twelve of the twenty-four priestly divisions permanently resided in Jerusalem, mainly at the Ophel,[52] whereas the rest were scattered throughout Israel. When a priestly division was serving at the temple, only a few members stayed behind to preside in their local synagogues.[53]
2. According to the Jewish Talmudic tradition, the arrangement of the Davidic twenty-four divisions could be traced back to the time of Moses, who supposedly arranged the sons of Aaron into either eight or sixteen divisions (four, or else eight, from Eleazar, and the other four or eight from Ithamar). Supposedly, David then added the other divisions for the total of twenty-four in **1 Chronicles 24**. According to Edersheim, this was one of many examples of Jewish tradition attempting to trace every institution back to the Mosaic era.[54]
3. The twenty-four divisions established under David and Solomon continued until the Babylonian captivity. The "Jedaiah" division was placed first because it was from the high priest's family—"The descendants of Jedaiah (through the family of Jeshua [the high priest])" (**Ezra 2:36; Nehemiah 7:39**).[55]
4. Each division served one week in the temple, from one Sabbath to the next and in a set rotation (cf. **2 Kings 11:9; 2 Chronicles 23:8**). Furthermore, each division served twice yearly (i.e., two weeks in the year) and during the exact same weeks of consecutive years (**Luke 1:8**).[56] In addition, all twenty-four divisions were required to officiate during the three biblical festivals—the Festival of Unleavened Bread (which included Passover), the Festival of Harvest (Firstfruits), and the Festival of Ingathering (Tabernacles or Booths; **Exodus 23:14–19**).[57] The week's service was subdivided among the various families that constituted a division (e.g., if it consisted of five 'houses of fathers,' three families each served one day and two families each served two days; if the division consisted of eight families, six each served one day and the other two in conjunction one day; if the division consisted of nine families five each served one day, and the other four took it two in conjunction for the two days). According to Edersheim, "The divisions and arrangements were determined by 'the chiefs' or 'heads of the houses of their fathers.' On Sabbaths the whole 'course' [division] was on duty; on feast days, any priest could come up and join in the ministrations of the sanctuary and during the Feast of Tabernacles, all twenty-four courses were bound to be present and officiate."[58]
5. The fundamental principle that was applied was that all Israel was to be "a kingdom of priests" (**Exodus 19:5–6**), and in that sense, "it made the priesthood only representatives of the people."[59]
6. There were no special disqualifications for the Levitical office but there were for the priestly office. The Sanhedrin first looked at the candidate's genealogy; "certain genealogies were deemed authoritative. Thus, if a candidate's father's name was inscribed in the archives of Jeshana at Zipporim [an archive of genealogical documents at Sepphoris/Zippori and/or Nazareth[60]], no further inquiry was made. If he failed to satisfy the court about his perfect legitimacy, the candidate was dressed and veiled in black, and permanently removed." If legitimacy was proven, the candidate was then examined for physical defects. Maimonides, a medieval Torah scholar, listed 140 permanent and 22 temporary physical disqualifications. Despite being disqualified to serve as a priest, men with physical disqualifications were allowed to serve elsewhere (in menial offices such as the wood-chamber) and they were entitled to Temple support. Those who passed both examinations were clothed in white raiment and their names were properly recorded in the authorized genealogical records.[61]
7. After the priests were instructed in their duties, "the formal admission" of the priests and of the high priest "was not, as of old, by anointing, but simply by investiture." The Rabbis held that the common priests were not anointed even in the first temple; the right to serve was valid simply by being a descendant of Aaron.[62]
8. Priests received a moderate income, even in the most favorable circumstances; a priest's income depended on the varying religious state of the nation, since there was no law enforcing the payment of tithes or other offerings.[63] According to the Talmud, the priests received their support from twenty-four possible sources, including the priest's part of the sin and trespass offerings; the public peace offering; some of the shewbread (also called the bread of the Presence; **Exodus 25:30; 35:13; 39:36**); portions of meat offerings; firstborn animals; portions of the thank offerings; the tithe of the tithe; heave offerings, and so forth. Some offerings were given to the special priestly division on duty for the week (e.g., redemption money for the firstborn, devoted offerings, etc.).[64]

Joachim Jeremias offers these additional points:

1. The Kohathite priests are identified as ordinary priests who formed a closed circle, a hereditary community tracing its genealogy back to Aaron and inheriting thus the dignity of office. They were divided into priestly clans by ancient tradition.[65]
2. The system of twenty-four priestly divisions prevailed during the time of Jesus. These twenty-four priestly clans included all the priests living in Judaea and Galilee. "Each priestly clan (weekly course) was divided into four to nine priestly families." These families carried out the daily courses, each serving their section during their week of duty. The twenty-four weekly courses were divided into about 156 daily courses.[66]
3. "According to M. Yom. ii.1–5, lots were cast on the morning of the days of ordinary service, in four stages: 1 + 13 + 1 + 9 = 24 services." In this way, the twenty-four priests who prepared and offered the daily morning sacrifice were chosen. Also, three additional priests were chosen (not by lot) for a total of twenty-seven priests. The morning sacrifices were repeated in the evening.[67]
4. Sabbath days and festival days required more priests than ordinary days because those special days also hosted other public sacrifices, especially on the first day of the Feast of Tabernacles. All twenty-four divisions were present in Jerusalem for the three pilgrim festivals; the twenty-three divisions of priests not on duty were called to help the one division that was.[68]
5. For the daily public sacrifices, the number of priests on duty for one daily course was estimated to be "at least fifty" and for one weekly course (composed of about six daily courses), there were about three hundred priests. "Since there were twenty-four weekly courses, the total number of priests amounts to 24 x 300 = 7,200 priests."[69]
6. Each division/course consisted, on average, of three hundred priests and four hundred Levites; each division was accompanied by lay representatives from its district. The priests that were ending their week of duty ceremonially handed over the keys of the temple as well as the ninety-three vessels to the priests that were coming on duty.[70] The priests lived at their homes for ten or eleven months, depending on the distance from their home to Jerusalem. Each division served two weeks out of the year, as well as during the three pilgrim festivals (see **Exodus 23:14–19**). Jeremias states that "only very occasionally" did priests "exercise any priestly function at home." To supplement their income from the tithes and other offerings, the priests "were obliged to follow some profession in their own district, mostly manual work."[71]
7. In conclusion, Jeremias says, "In many places, priests assisted in the local courts of justice, probably in an honorary capacity. Sometimes they were called there out of respect for their priestly status (Josephus, *Contra Apionem* 2.187), sometimes if they were trained as scribes, because of their learning, and sometimes to satisfy biblical precepts . . . to defend the interests of the Temple. There were, as Philo states, priests living in the country well versed in scriptural learning, who were entrusted during the synagogue worship with the reading and expounding of the Law."[72]

Notes

1. These are not Kohathite *high* priests, but rather Kohathite *attending* priests from the Aaron–Kohathite line, who assisted the high priests in their sacerdotal duties, including both Aaron–Eleazar–Zadok descendants and Aaron–Ithamar descendants, of which the latter *excluded* the cursed descendants of the Eli priesthood; see chart "**1 Samuel 1**: Eli and the Eli Priesthood."

2. Izhar (**Exodus 6:18, 21; Numbers 16:1; 1 Chronicles 6:2, 18, 38; 23:12**) is also called Amminadab (**1 Chronicles 6:22**).

3. Nadab and Abihu died without children (**Numbers 3:4; 1 Chronicles 24:2**).

4. Sixteen of the twenty-four division heads came from the Aaron–Eleazar–Zadok line (**1 Chronicles 24:4**); see chart "**1 Chronicles 6**: Levi: High Priests, Priests, Levites, and Musicians in Solomon's Temple."

5. Eight of the twenty-four division heads came from the Aaron–Ithamar line (remnant members of the former Eli priesthood; **1 Chronicles 24:4**; cf. **1 Samuel 1:3; 2:12–17, 34; 4:4, 11, 17, 21; 14:3; 21:1; 22:9, 11, 20; 23:6, 9; 30:7; 2 Samuel 8:17; 15:27; 1 Kings 2:26–27; 1 Chronicles 18:16; 24:3, 6**).

6. Phinehas the priest was promised a "lasting priesthood, because he was zealous for the honor of his God and made atonement for the Israelites" (**Numbers 25:13**; see **Numbers 25**).

7. See chart "**1 Samuel 1**: Eli and the Eli Priesthood."

8. The sixteen priests from the Aaron–Eleazar–Zadok line were relatives (kinsmen) of the high priests—for the distinction between the high priests in the Kohathite clan and the non-high priests in the Kohathite clan, see chart "**1 Chronicles 6**: Levi: High Priests, Priests, Levites, and Musicians in Solomon's Temple."

9. For the line of the high priests, see charts "**1 Chronicles 6**: Levi: High Priests, Priests, Levites, and Musicians in Solomon's Temple" and "**Supplement 2**: The High Priests of Israel."

10. By syncopation of vowels, the name Jehoiarib is also rendered Joiarib; both names in the NIV refer to the same person (cf. **1 Chronicles 9:10; 24:7; Nehemiah 11:10; 12:6**). Jehoiarib was the head of a priestly family that lived in the time of the united monarchy (ca. 971–931 B.C). Given the textual reading of **1 Chronicles 24:6b**, Jehoiarib was presumably from the Aaron–Eleazar line. The priestly descendants of Jehoiarib/Joiarib who lived in the post-exile are mentioned in **1 Chronicles 9:10**; and **Nehemiah 11:10; 12:6, 19**; also, a descendant of Jehoiarib/Joiarib named Mattenai served in the days of Nehemiah in 444 B.C. (**Nehemiah 12:19**). Mattathias, the leader of the famous uprising known as the Maccabean Revolt of 167–160 B.C., claimed decent from Joiarib/Jehoiarib; see chart "**Supplement 8**: The Maccabees and the Hasmonean Dynasty." It is noteworthy that Josephus claimed descent from the leader of the Jehoiarib/Joiarib division; see chart "**Supplement 9**: Flavius Josephus, the Roman-Jewish Historian."

11. Jedaiah was a relative of the high priest, Joshua/Jeshua (cf. **Ezra 2:36; Nehemiah 7:39**). A descendant of Jedaiah who served in the days of Joiakim the high priest (ca. 490–450/444 B.C.) was either Uzzi (**Nehemiah 12:19**) or Nethanel (**Nehemiah 12:21**).

12. Various descendants of Harim—presumably referring to Harim the Kohahite priest—are given as "Maaseiah, Elijah, Shemaiah, Jehiel and Uzziah" (**Ezra 10:21**). A son of Harim named Malkijah is also mentioned (**Nehemiah 3:11**). A descendant of Harim named Adna was a Kohathite priest in the Second Temple in the days of Joiakim the high priest, ca. 490–450/444 B.C. (**Nehemiah 12:15**).

13. This Malkijah (over the original fifth division) may be the *son* of Harim who was over the third division (cf. **1 Chronicles 24:8–9; Ezra 10:31; Nehemiah 3:11**). Also, Malkijah was the *father* or *ancestor* of Pashhur, a Kohathite attending priest in the Second Temple (**1 Chronicles 9:12**). Additionally, a descendant of Malkijah and Pashhur named Adaiah was a Kohathite attending priest in the Second Temple (**1 Chronicles 9:12; Nehemiah 11:12**).

14. The priest Mijamin in **1 Chronicles 24:9** who lived in the time of David was the ancestor of Mijamin the priest who returned to Jerusalem with Zerubbabel in ca. 538 B.C. (**Nehemiah 12:5**) and the priest Mijamin who sealed the covenant with Nehemiah, ca. 444 B.C. (**Nehemiah 10:7**). "Miniamin" the priest who sang in the thanksgiving choir (**Nehemiah 12:40–41**) may correspond to Mijamin; the difference between Mijamin and Miniamin is strictly *plene* spelling or transliterational (מִנְיָמִן or מִנְיָמִין).

15. After the return from exile, the priestly descendants of Hakkoz, mentioned in **Ezra 2:61–63** and **Nehemiah 7:63–65**, could not prove their Kohathite heritage—"These searched for their family records, but they could not find them and so were excluded from the priesthood as unclean. The governor, therefore, ordered them not to eat any of the most sacred food until there should be a priest ministering with the Urim and Thummim" (**Nehemiah 7:64–65**) Apparently the restrictions were removed and at least some of the Hakkoz descendants were reinstated because a descendant named Meremoth "the son of Uriah, the son of Hakkoz" helped repair the walls around Jerusalem in the days of Nehemiah, ca. 444 B.C. (cf. **Nehemiah 3:4, 21**); see note 3 in chart "**Nehemiah 8**: Genealogical Record of the Leaders and Priests Who Stood at the Left and Right Hand of Ezra During the Reading of the Law of Moses" and note 14 in chart "**Nehemiah 12**: Genealogical Record of the Heads of the Kohathite Priests and Levites Who Returned to Jerusalem with Zerubbabel and Joshua in the Post-Exile."

16. The priestly division of Abijah is particularly noteworthy because Zechariah the father of John the Baptist was a descendant of Abijah (the contemporary of King David); additionally, Zechariah's wife, Elizabeth (also a descendant of Aaron the high priest) was a *relative* of Mary the mother of Jesus (**Luke 1:5, 36**). A Kohathite attending priest named Abijah (a *descendant* of the ancestral figure Abijah) returned from exile with Zerubbabel in ca. 538 B.C. (**Nehemiah 12:4**) and was among those who sealed the covenant in the days of Nehemiah in ca. 445 B.C. (**Nehemiah 10:7**). Also, an Abijah descendant named Zikri lived in the days of Joiakim the high priest (ca. 490–450/444 B.C.)—this Zikri, like Abijah, was perhaps an *ancestor* of Zechariah and John the Baptist (**Nehemiah 12:17**). If the method of casting lots was conducted by alternating between Eleazar and Ithamar descendants, this means Abijah—and by extension, Zechariah and John the Baptist—were Aaron–Ithamar descendants (rather than Aaron–Eleazar descendants).

17. Jeshua the Kohathite priest who lived in the days of David and Solomon should not be confused with Jeshua (Joshua) the high priest, the son of Jozadak, who was the first high priest to serve in the Second Temple in 516 B.C. (see **Ezra 3:2; 5:2; 10:18; Nehemiah 7:7, 39; 12:7, 10, 26; Zechariah 6:11**).

18. A descendant of Shekaniah named Joseph was a Kohathite attending priest in the Second Temple in the days of Joiakim the high priest, ca. 490–450/444 B.C. (**Nehemiah 12:14**).

19. Eliashib was head of the eleventh division of attending priests who were active in Solomon's Temple. Eliashib the Kohathite attending priest should not be confused with Eliashib the Kohathite *high priest* who rebuilt the Sheep's Gate in post-exilic Jerusalem (cf. **Nehemiah 3:1, 20**), whose lineage is given in **Nehemiah 12:10** (see also **Nehemiah 12:22**). For the complications of these connections, see Joseph Blenkinsopp, *Ezra-Nehemiah: A Commentary*. OTL. (Philadelphia: Westminster, 1988), 339–341.

20. A descendant of Bilgah named Shammua was a Kohathite attending priest in the days of Joiakim the high priest, ca. 490–450/444 B.C. (**Nehemiah 12:18**).

21. The ancestral person named "Immer" in the following passages probably refers to the same person: **1 Chronicles 9:12** (Maasai, a descendant of Immer); **Ezra 2:37** (descendants of Immer); **Ezra 10:20** (Hanani and Zebadiah, descendants of Immer); **Nehemiah 3:29** (Zadok, a descendant of Immer, who is not Zadok the high priest); **Nehemiah 7:40** (descendants of Immer); **Nehemiah 11:13** (Amashsai, a descendant of Immer); and **Jeremiah 20:1** (Pashhur, a descendant of Immer).

22. Jeremias notes that in the list of priestly families in **1 Chronicles 24:7–18**, Jehoiarib is named first (**v. 7**) and, furthermore, that this is the priestly family to which the Maccabees belonged (*I Maccabees*, 2.1; 14.29). In **Nehemiah 10:3–9**, the name Jehoiarib is completely absent; it then appears in **Nehemiah 12:1–7** and **12–21** in a subordinate position. Jeremiah concludes that the third list(s) in **Nehemiah 12** must have been compiled during the Maccabean period (Joachim Jeremias, *Jerusalem in the Time of Jesus* (Philadelphia: Fortress, 1969), 199). For the genealogy of the Maccabees, see chart "**Supplement 8**: The Maccabees and the Hasmonean Dynasty."

23. Jedaiah is the only name that is readily apparent in all sources.

24. "Through the family of Jeshua" (**Ezra 2:36; Nehemiah 7:39**) means through the family of Joshua/Jeshua the high priest; see chart "**Ezra 2**: Joshua, the High Priest in the Second Temple, and His Descendants (Post-Exile)."

25. Two Kohathite priests are named Jedaiah (**Nehemiah 12:6, 7**); see Jedaiah #1 and #2 in chart "**Nehemiah 12**: Genealogical Record of the Heads of the Kohathite Priests and Levites Who Returned to Jerusalem with Zerubbabel and Joshua in the Post-Exile."

26. Some descendants of Harim—specifically Maaseiah, Elijah, Shemaiah, Jehiel, and Uzziah—had taken pagan wives in Babylon captivity; they returned with Ezra in 458 B.C. (**Ezra 10:21**).

27. Pashhur was the son of Malkijah (cf. **1 Chronicles 9:12; Nehemiah 11:12**). Pashhur's father, Malkijah, was the Kohathite priest over the fifth division of priests in Solomon's Temple in the days of David (cf. **1 Chronicles 24:9**). Pashhur son of Malkijah is not the same person as (1) Pashhur son of Immer, who was an immoral Kohathite priest-false prophet who died in Babylonian captivity (**Jeremiah 20:1–6**), nor (2) Pashhur the official (son of Malkijah, son of King Jehoiakim) who wanted to have Jeremiah put to death (**Jeremiah 38:1, 6**).

28. Adaiah, a post-exilic priest, was the "son of Jeroham, the son [descendant] of Pashhur, the son of Malkijah" (**1 Chronicles 9:12**). The more complete lineage for Adaiah given in **Nehemiah 11:12** is: "Adaiah son of Jeroham, the son of Pelaliah, the son of Amzi, the son of Zechariah, the son of Pashhur, the son of Malkijah." Adaiah in **1 Chronicles 9:12** is not the same person as the non-priestly figure, Adaiah in **Ezra 10:39**, an Israelite who had taken a foreign wife.

29. Mijamin the Kohathite attending priest (**1 Chronicles 24:9**), a contemporary of David, is probably the ancestor of (1) "Miniamin" the priest of **2 Chronicles 31:15**; (2) Mijamin the priest who returned to Jerusalem with Zerubbabel in 538 B.C. (**Nehemiah 12:5**); and (3) Mijamin the priest who sealed the covenant with Nehemiah, ca. 444 B.C. (**Nehemiah 10:7**). "Miniamin" the priest, who sang in the thanksgiving choir (**Nehemiah 12:40–41**), may correspond to this Mijamin the priest; the difference between Mijamin and Miniamin is strictly *plene* spelling or transliterational (מִנְיָמִן or מִנְיָמִין).

30. For Meremoth, see note 6 in chart "**Ezra 8**: Genealogical Record of Priests and Levites in Jerusalem who Weighed the Silver, Gold, and the Articles That Were Brought from Babylon."

31. Maasai was the "son of Adiel, the son of Jahzerah, the son of Meshullam, the son of Meshillemith, the son of Immer" (**1 Chronicles 9:12**).

32. Amashsai was the "son of Azarel, the son of Ahzai, the son of Meshillemoth, the son of Immer" (**Nehemiah 11:13**; cf. Maasai in **1 Chronicles 9:12**).

33. A descendant of Immer named Pashhur was the official in charge of Solomon's Temple in ca. 586 B.C., but he was an unfaithful priest (**Jeremiah 20:1**). See chart "**Jeremiah 20**: Pashhur, an Unfaithful Kohathite Priest and the Official over Solomon's Temple (Pre-Exile)."

34. Shemaiah (**Nehemiah 10:8**) could be the same person as the priestly figure Shemaiah, the descendant of Delaiah, the son of Mehetabel; see note 3 in chart "**Nehemiah 6**: Shemaiah, the Jewish Secret Informant for the Enemies of Nehemiah who Opposed the Rebuilding of the Wall around Jerusalem."

35. Note the similarity of מעזיה (Maaziah) in **1 Chronicles 24:18** and **Nehemiah 10:8** to מועדיה (Moadiah) in **Nehemiah 12:5, 17**. The high priest Caiaphas (the son-in-law of Annas), A.D. 18–36/37, may have been from the Maaziah clan of Kohathite priests (see note 4 in chart "**Matthew 26**: The Influential Family of Annas and Caiaphas, the High Priests").

36. Gershom (of Phinehas) was a Kohathite priest who returned to Jerusalem with Ezra in 458 B.C. (**Ezra 8:2**). Gershom was a descendant and/or near relative of the high priests in the Levi–Kohath–Amram–Aaron–Eleazar–Phinehas–Zadok line and a *relative* of the high priest Joiakim the high priest who served from 490–450/444 B.C.

37. Daniel was a Kohathite priest and a descendant in the Levi–Kohath–Amram–Aaron–Ithamar line of priests (**Ezra 8:2**). Daniel represents a faithful *remnant* of the cursed Ithamar–Eli line/the Eli priesthood; see chart "**1 Samuel 1**: Eli and the Eli Priesthood."

38. For the probable identity and lineage of Azariah in **Nehemiah 10:2**, see Azariah #3 in chart "**Ezra 7**: Ezra, the Priestly Scribe and Teacher of the Law (Post-Exile)."

39. Sherebiah the Kothathite priest (along with Hashabiah and ten of their brethren) was set apart by Ezra to carry silver, gold, and dedicated offerings to Jerusalem (**Ezra 8:24**).

40. Seraiah the Kohathite priest of **Ezra 2:2** and **Nehemiah 12:1** (designated Seraiah #2 in other charts), who returned with Zerubbabel to Jerusalem in 538 B.C., is not Seraiah the high priest (the *son* of Azariah and the *father* of Jozadak) who was killed at Riblah (designated Seraiah #1 elsewhere; **2 Kings 25:18–21; Jeremiah 52:24–27**); see the notes for Seraiah #1, #2 and #3 in chart "**Ezra 7**: Ezra, the Priestly Scribe and Teacher of the Law (Post-Exile)."

41. The Kohathite attending priest named Jeremiah who lived in the post-exile (cf. **Nehemiah 10:2; 12:1, 34?**) is not the same person as the prophet

Jeremiah, the son of Hilkiah, who prophesied during the reigns of Josiah, Jehoahaz, Jehoiakim, Jehoiachin, and Zedekiah, ca. 627–586 B.C. (**Jeremiah 1:1**).

42. The Ezra figure in **Nehemiah 12:1** who returned to Jerusalem with Zerubbabel in 538 B.C. does not refer to Ezra the scribe–priest and teacher of the Law who returned to Jerusalem in 458 B.C.; for the latter, see chart "**Ezra 7**: Ezra, the Priestly Scribe and Teacher of the Law (Post-Exile)."

43. The Kohathite attending priest Amariah who lived in the post-exile may be related to the priest Amariah who served in the days of King Hezekiah, 715–686 B.C. (**2 Chronicles 31:15**).

44. Hattush the Kohathite priest is not the post-exilic figure, Hattush the Judahite (**1 Chronicles 3:22; Ezra 8:2–3**) shown in chart "**1 Chronicles 3**: Zerubbabel and Shealtiel and the Double Line of the Messiah through King David's Sons, Nathan and Solomon."

45. Rehum (**Nehemiah 12:3**) may be part of the ancestral Harim family (notice the repeated pattern of priestly families in **Nehemiah 12:1–7** to those in **Nehemiah 12:12–21**).

46. The Kohathite priest Shemaiah who lived in the post-exile may be a descendant of the priest named Shemaiah who served in the days of King Hezekiah, 715–686 B.C. (**2 Chronicles 31:15**).

47. The Hebrew wording for the casting of lots (Heb. גּוֹרָלוֹת, *goraloth*) suggests the alternating method, first by an Eleazarite and then by an Ithamarite: "these with these" (**1 Chronicles 24:5**).

48. Josephus, *Jewish Antiquities* 7.14.7.

49. The partial list of priestly courses found in the Caesarea excavations included: (1) the 17th course of Hezir; (2) the 18th course of Happizzez; (3) the 19th course of Pethahiah, and (4) the 20th course of Ezekiel (Jehezkel). Of special note is that the Hapinezzez course is associated with a priestly family that settled in Nazareth. See M. Avi-Yonah, "A List of Priestly Courses from Caesarea" *IEJ* 12 (1962): 137–39.

50. Alfred Edersheim, *The Temple: Its Ministry and Services* (Peabody, MA: Hendrickson, 1993), 55–73.

51. Joachim Jeremias, *Jerusalem in the Time of Jesus* (Philadelphia: Fortress, 1969), 198–207.

52. The "ophel (Ō′ phĕl), [is a] place-name meaning 'swelling,' 'fat,' 'bulge,' or 'mound.'' It became the proper name of a portion of the hill on which the city of David was built (**2 Chronicles 27:3**). The Ophel was just south of Mount Moriah, on which the temple was constructed, joining the old city with the area of Solomon's palace and temple. The hill has been inhabited since pre-Israelite times by peoples such as the Jebusites from whom David took the site. David and later kings further fortified Ophel. It served as the living quarters for those who rebuilt the ramparts following the exile (**Nehemiah 3:26–27**). This may reflect a gradual extension of the name to an ever-larger area" (*Holman's Bible Dictionary*, "Ophel"). Josephus called the "Hill of Ophel" the "Ophlas," referring to the area south of the temple (*The Jewish Wars* 5.4.2).

53. Edersheim, *The Temple*, 56.

54. Ibid., 58–59.

55. Ibid., 59.

56. *Contra Apionem* 2.108; *Jewish Antiquities* 7.365.

57. For "The Priestly Courses and Their Geographical Settlements at Tuvia and Kahane," see Tarbiz א/ב (1978): 9–29 and Avi-Yonah, "Priestly Courses from Caesarea," 137–139.

58. Edersheim, *The Temple*, 62.

59. Ibid., 63.

60. Eusebius' comment in *Church History* 1.7.13–14 says that the *Desposyni* (the relatives of Jesus) "having obtained private [genealogical] records of their own [meaning they kept records of their own, separate from the genealogical registries archived in Jerusalem], either by remembering the names or by getting them in some other way from the registers, pride themselves on preserving the memory of their noble extraction. Among these are those already mentioned, called Desposyni, on account of their connection with the family of the Saviour. Coming from Nazara [Nazareth] and Cochaba, villages of Judea, into other parts of the world, they drew the aforesaid genealogy from memory and from the book of daily records as faithfully as possible."

In his book *The Jesus Dynasty*, Tabor elaborates on these two towns mentioned by Eusebius (above) by saying that Nazareth "comes from the Hebrew word *netzer* meaning 'branch' or 'shoot' . . . It's claim to fame was not size or economic prominence but something potentially even more significant. In the Dead Sea Scrolls, written before Jesus' lifetime, we regularly find the future Messiah or King of Israel described as the 'branch of David.' The term is taken from Isaiah 11, where the Messiah of David's lineage is called a 'Branch' [cf. **Jeremiah 23:5**]. The term stuck. The later followers of Jesus were called Nazarenes or 'Branchites.' The little village of Nazareth very likely got its name, or perhaps its nickname, because it was known as the place here members of the royal family had settled and were concentrated. It is no surprise that both Mary and Joseph lived there, as each represented different 'branches' of the 'Branch of David.' The gospels mention other 'relatives' of the family that lived there (Mark 6:4). It is entirely possible that most of the inhabitants of 'Branch Town' were members of the same extended 'Branch' family. The family's affinity for this area of Galilee continued for centuries. North of Sepphris, about twelve miles from Nazareth, was a town called Kokhaba [Cochaba] or 'Star Town.' The term 'Star' [cf. **Numbers 24:17; Revelation 22:16**], like 'Branch' is a coded term for the Messiah that is also found in the Dead Sea Scrolls. Both Nazareth and Kokhaba were noted well into the second century A.D. as towns in which families related to Jesus, and thus part of the 'royal family,' were concentrated." James D. Tabor, *The Jesus Dynasty* (New York: Simon & Schuster, 2006), 55.

61. Edersheim, *The Temple*, 66–67.

62. Ibid., 63.

63. Ibid., 72–73.

64. Jeremias, *Jerusalem*, 198.

65. Ibid., 199.

66. Ibid., 201.

67. Ibid., 202.

68. Ibid., 203–4.

69. Ibid., 203. See also Josephus, *Against Apion* 2.119. Jeremias says that according to Josephus, 200 priests "were needed each evening to close the Temple doors," contrary to the twenty in *Jewish War*, B. VII. ch. 5, sect. 3.

70. Ibid., 206. Cf. *Against Apion* 2.108.

71. Ibid., 206.

72. Ibid., 207.

1 CHRONICLES 24: ADDITIONAL LEVITES (KOHATHITES AND MERARITES) WHO SERVED IN SOLOMON'S TEMPLE

Approximate Dating: Solomon's Temple was completed in 960 B.C.; these Levites served thereafter during Solomon's reign, ca. 971–931 B.C. ***Relevant Scriptures:*** **1 Chronicles 24:20–30**; also **1 Chronicles 23:12–23**

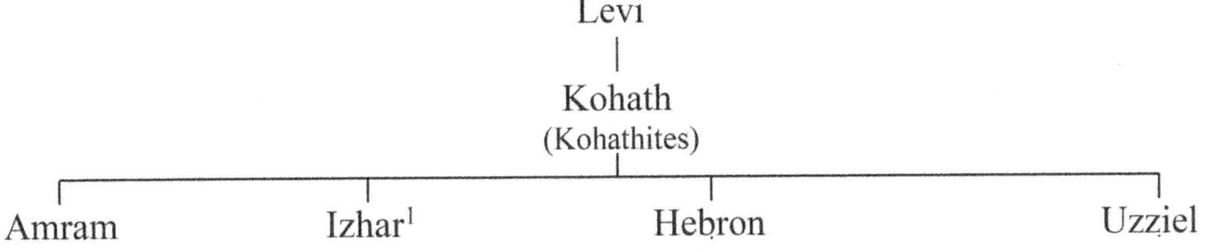

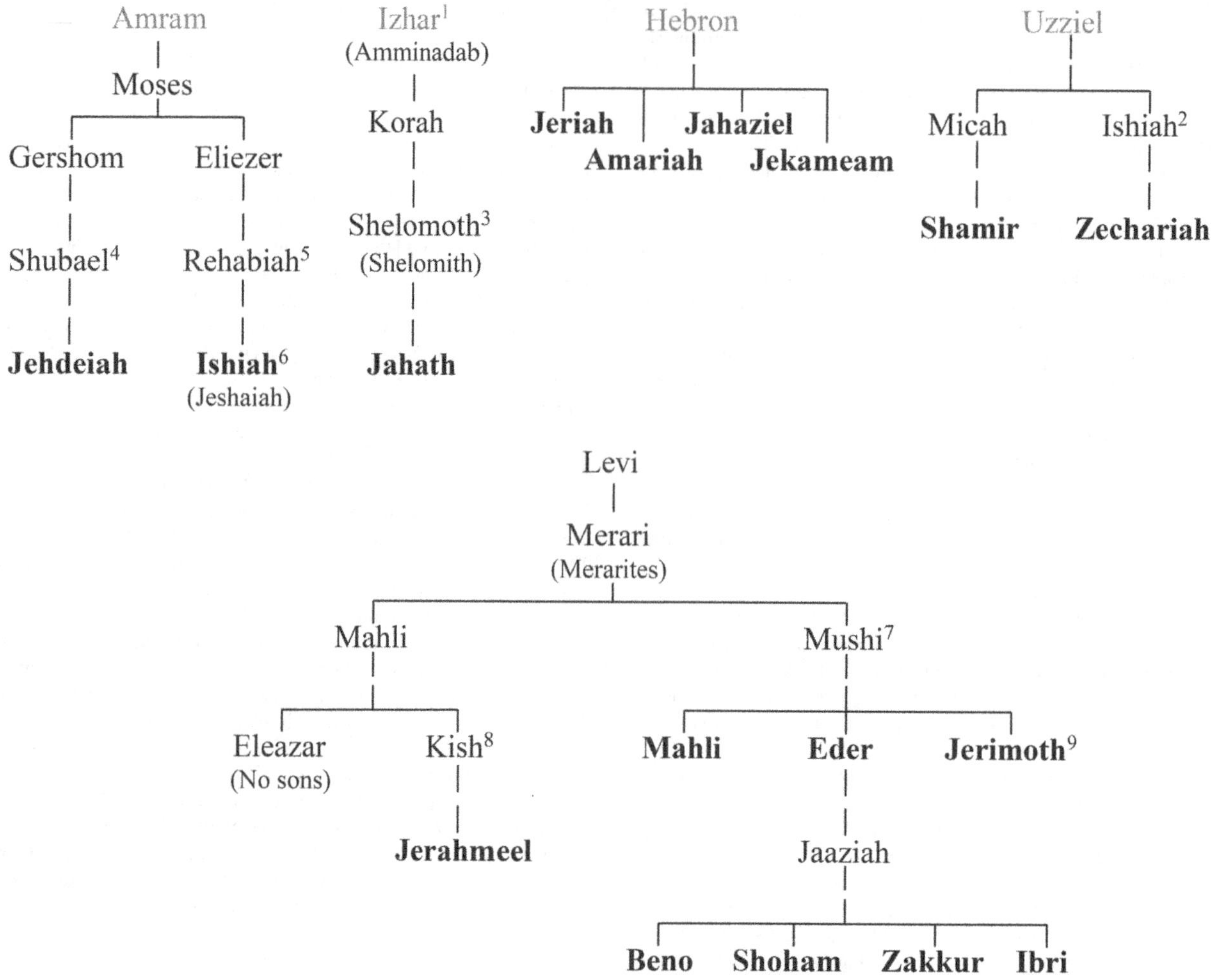

Biblical and Theological Significance

For undisclosed reasons, extra Levites were necessary to carry out the many Levitical tasks, so the ones listed here were apparently held in reserve for service as needed. Like the priests, Levites must be descendants of Levi, a son of Jacob. Moreover, here the extra Levites were divided among two of the three clans who sprang from Levi: Kohath (Kohathites) and Merari (Merarites), but not Gershon (Gershonites).[10] The Levites could not take upon themselves the role or even some single task of priests, but as assistants they nonetheless were indispensable to all that Yahweh demanded of his worshiping people and, in this instance, in the great temple of Solomon.[11] Interestingly, the descendants of Moses who lived in this time period were included among the eligible Levitical servants.[12]

Notes

1. Izhar in **Exodus 6:18, 21; Numbers 3:19; 16:1;** and **1 Chronicles 6:2, 18, 38; 23:12, 18** is Amminadab in **1 Chronicles 6:22**. He is the eponymous ancestor of the Izharites.

2. Ishiah "of the sons of Uzziel" (an Uzzielite; **1 Chronicles 24:24–25**) should not be confused with his contemporary Ishiah, "of the sons of Amram" (an Amramite), a descendant of Moses (**1 Chronicles 24:20–21**).

3. Shelomoth (**1 Chronicles 24:22**) is alias Shelomith (**1 Chronicles 23:18**).

4. Shubael the Amramite (a descendant of Amram through Moses' son Gershom) was the official in charge of the temple treasuries (cf. **1 Chronicles 23:16; 24:20; 26:24**). He is not Shubael the Kohathite–Korahite, the son of Heman (**1 Chronicles 25:4, 20**).

5. Rehabiah was the sole heir of Eliezer, but Rehabiah had many sons (**1 Chronicles 23:17**). For his descendants, see **1 Chronicles 26:25**.

6. Ishiah (**1 Chronicles 24:21**) is alternatively Jeshaiah (**1 Chronicles 26:25**). For the descendants of Ishiah/Jeshaiah, see **1 Chronicles 26:25**. Ishiah (the descendant of Amram through Moses) is not Ishiah the Uzzielite, his contemporary (**1 Chronicles 24:24–25**). See chart "**1 Chronicles 26**: The Levitical Leaders who Assisted in the Oversight of the Treasuries and Dedicated Things in Solomon's Temple and in the King's Business Throughout Israel."

7. The text of **1 Chronicles 24:30** says "the sons of Mushi: Mahli, Eder, and Jerimoth," which means they were descendants of Mushi (cf. **1 Chronicles 23:23**).

8. Kish was the brother of Eleazar. Eleazar died without sons; he only had daughters, so the sons of Kish married Eleazar's daughters (their first cousins; **1 Chronicles 23:22; 24:28**).

9. Jerimoth the Merarite is not Jerimoth the Kohathite–Korahite, the son of Heman (cf. **1 Chronicles 25:4, 22**).

10. For the sons of Levi, see **Genesis 46:11; Exodus 6:16; Numbers 3:17; 26:57; 1 Chronicles 6:1, 16; 23:6**.

11. For the ministries of the Levites in particular, see **Numbers 1:47–53; 8:15–26; 1 Chronicles 15:2–16:36; 23:28–32; 2 Chronicles 8:14; 29:12–17; 30:15–27; 35:5–14; Ezra 6:16–22; Nehemiah 9:1–6**.

12. See **1 Chronicles 23:14**: "The sons of Moses the man of God were counted as part of the tribe of Levi."

1 CHRONICLES 25: THE TWENTY-FOUR MUSICIAN LEADERS IN SOLOMON'S TEMPLE

Approximate Dating: Solomon's Temple was completed in 960 B.C.; these musicians were active during Solomon's reign, ca. 971–931 B.C. ***Relevant Scriptures:*** **1 Chronicles 25:1–31;** also **1 Chronicles 6:1–53**

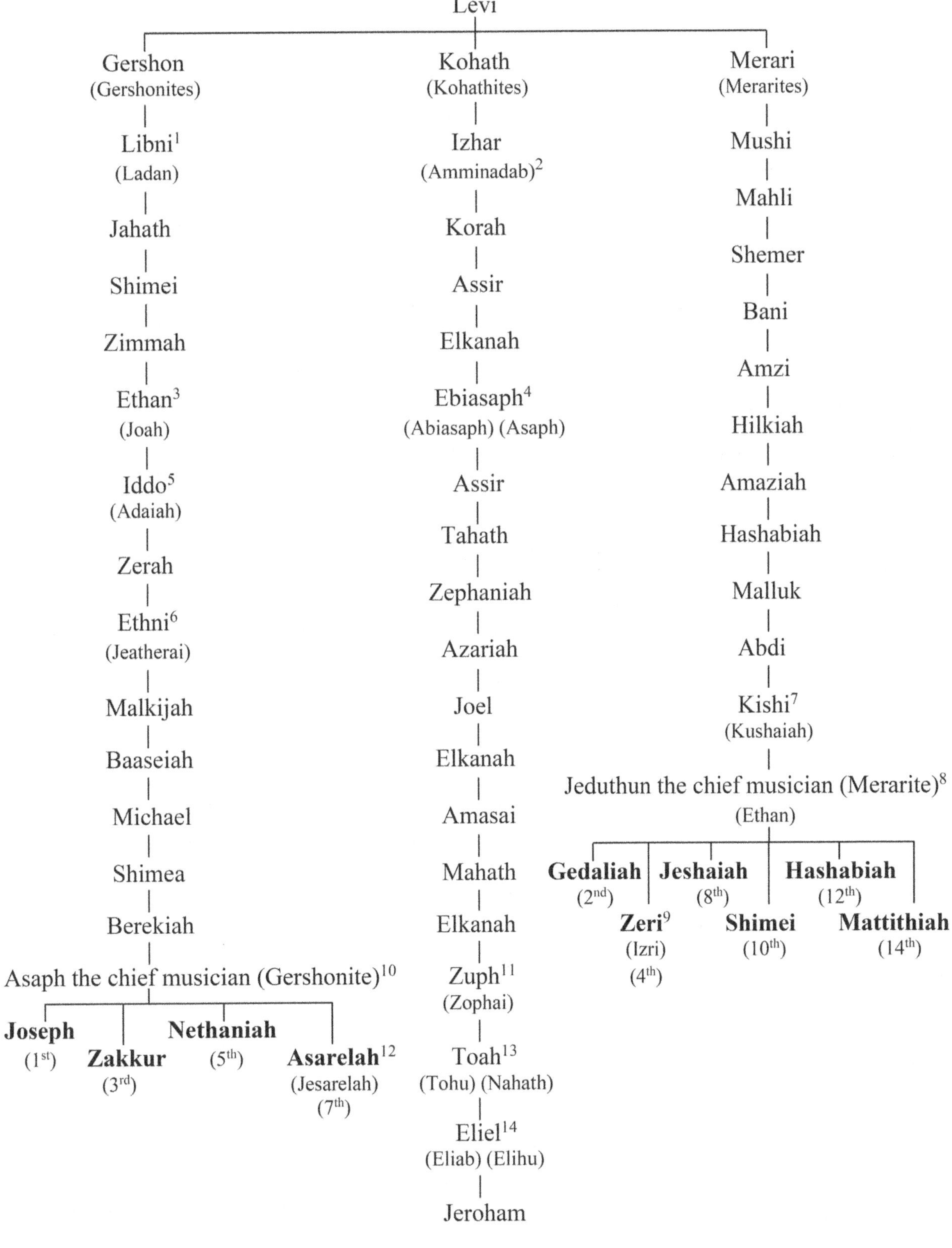

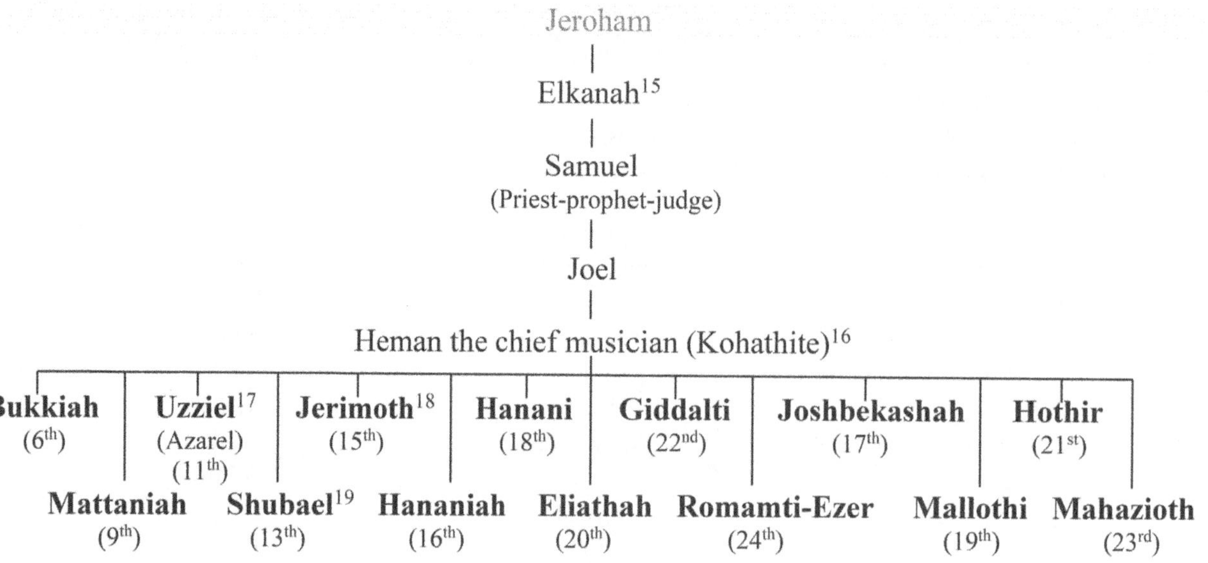

Biblical and Theological Significance

From beginning to end, the Bible underscores the importance of music as a vehicle of praise, worship, and even petition. In primeval times, Adah (the wife of Lamech) gave birth to Jubal, "the father [or progenitor] of all who play stringed instruments and pipes" (**Genesis 4:21**). The crescendo of music's importance is the collection known as the book of Psalms, which contains 150 of the greatest vocal and instrumental renditions ever composed. The fundamental theme of Psalms is expressed in its title, *tehillim*, "praises." The most common generic term for music is *shir*, "song," applicable primarily to vocal expression. The first example of a song is the one sung by Moses and the Israelites at the overthrow of Pharaoh in the Red Sea (**Exodus 15:1–18**) followed by a brief *responsa* by his sister, Miriam, described here as a prophet (**Exodus 15:20–21**). Since Miriam is never said to have predicted a message from the Lord, her role as a prophet[20] is embodied in her proclamation of praise in music.

Music, in the more limited sense of worship, is first encountered in the reign of David, a master musician himself.[21] His own passion for music in worship was abetted by the Lord's directions to him to recruit four thousand Levites for ministry in music and to organize them into three large groups (clans) according to their descent from Levi's sons Kohath, Gershon, and Merari (**1 Chronicles 23:5–23; 25:1–31**). Overseeing all was the king, to whom were accountable the three key musicians—Heman the Kohathite, who was the grandson of the great prophet Samuel; Asaph the Gershonite, and Jeduthun the Merarite (**1 Chronicles 25:6**). The supremacy of the king was not proposed just because David was king, but because of the nature of the Israelite monarchy: under Yahweh, it reflected his absolute dominion over all aspects of the life of his chosen people and, by eschatological extension, over all creation (cf. **2 Kings 22:3–7, 11–13; 23:4–9, 21–23; 1 Chronicles 15:1–16; 16:4–42**). Only in the Hasmonean era did a dyarchical form of government emerge in which the kings and/or governors shared power equally with the high priest and the priesthood, an arrangement abundantly attested to in the New Testament as well.

Notes

1. Libni in **Exodus 6:17; Numbers 3:18;** and **1 Chronicles 6:17, 20** is Ladan in **1 Chronicles 23:7–9; 26:21**. His name is omitted between Jahath and Gershon in **1 Chronicles 6:43**.

2. Izhar in **Exodus 6:18, 21; Numbers 3:19; 16:1;** and **1 Chronicles 6:2, 18, 38; 23:12, 18** is called Amminadab in **1 Chronicles 6:22**.

3. Joah in **1 Chronicles 6:21** is Ethan in **1 Chronicles 6:42**. **Second Chronicles 29:12** notes that Joah the Gershonite also had a son named Eden.

4. Ebiasaph in **1 Chronicles 6:23, 37; 9:19** is Abiasaph in **Exodus 6:24** and Asaph in **1 Chronicles 26:1**. The text of **Exodus 6:24** should be understood to mean that Assir, Elkanah, and Abiasaph were "sons of sons" (cf. **1 Chronicles 6:22–24, 37–38**). Ebiasaph/Abiasaph/Asaph was the great-grandson of Korah.

5. Iddo in **1 Chronicles 6:21** is Adaiah in **1 Chronicles 6:41**.

6. Jeatherai in **1 Chronicles 6:21** is Ethni in **1 Chronicles 6:41**.

7. Kishi in **1 Chronicles 6:44** is Kushaiah in **1 Chronicles 15:17**.

8. Ethan in **1 Chronicles 15:17, 19** is Jeduthun in **1 Chronicles 9:16; 16:38, 41–42; 25:1, 3, 6; 2 Chronicles 5:12; 29:14; 35:15; Nehemiah 11:17**. Ethan/Jeduthun was one of the three chief musicians in Solomon's Temple (**1 Chronicles 15:17, 19**). The lineage of Ethan/Jeduthun is given in **1 Chronicles 6:44–47**. The title of **Psalm 89**, called "a maskil of Ethan the Ezrahite," probably refers to him. Jeduthun is also mentioned in the titles of **Psalm 39, 62,** and **77**.

9. Zeri in **1 Chronicles 25:3** is Izri in **1 Chronicles 25:11**.

10. Asaph the Gershonite was one of the three chief musicians in Solomon's Temple. His lineage is given in **1 Chronicles 6:39–43**. Asaph and his brethren Ethan/Jeduthun and Heman sounded the bronze cymbals (**1 Chronicles 15:19**). Some of the sons of Asaph, Heman, and Ethan/Jeduthun were set apart "for the ministry of prophesying, accompanied by harps, lyres and cymbals" (**1 Chronicles 25:1**). The sons of Asaph were under the supervision of their father, "who prophesied under the king's supervision" (**1 Chronicles 25:1–2**). Asaph the Gershonite should not be confused with Asaph/Ebiasaph/Abiasaph the Kohathite–Korahite line (see note 4).

11. Zuph in **1 Chronicles 6:35** is Zophai in **1 Chronicles 6:26**.

12. Asarelah in **1 Chronicles 25:2** is Jesarelah in **1 Chronicles 25:14**.

13. Toah in **1 Chronicles 6:34** is Tohu in **1 Samuel 1:1** and Nahath in **1 Chronicles 6:26**.

14. Eliel in **1 Chronicles 6:34** is Elihu in **1 Samuel 1:1** and Eliab in **1 Chronicles 6:27**.

15. Of the four Elkanah figures in the Kohathite–Korahite line, this Elkanah was the husband of Hannah and the father of Samuel the prophet-judge of Israel (**1 Samuel 1:1**; cf. **1 Chronicles 6:27**).

16. Heman was one of the chief musicians in Solomon's Temple who prophesied with harps, stringed instruments, and cymbals (**1 Chronicles 15:16–17, 19**). The lineage of Heman is given in **1 Chronicles 6:33–38**. God blessed Heman with fourteen sons (shown in the chart) and three (unnamed) daughters (**1 Chronicles 25:5**).

17. Uzziel in **1 Chronicles 25:4** is Azarel in **1 Chronicles 25:18**.

18. Jerimoth the son of Heman, in the Kohathite–Korahite line (cf. **1 Chronicles 25:4, 22**) is a different person than Jerimoth the Merarite, the descendant of Mushi (**1 Chronicles 23:23; 24:30**).

19. Shubael the son of Heman, in the Kohathite–Korahite line (**1 Chronicles 25:4**), is a different person than his contemporary, Shubael the Levitical Kohathite–Amramite, a descendant of Gershom and Moses (cf. **1 Chronicles 23:16; 24:20; 26:24**).

20. Though prophetism is usually associated with prediction, that is by no means its principal function in the Old Testament. The term *prophet* derives from Greek *prōfēmī*, "to speak for," "to proclaim." This is akin to the Hebrew *nabi*, "speaker, spokesman." The proclamation need not be confined to speech but can be extended to any means of communicating ideas, including motion, art, and music. Miriam's prophetic gift was in composition and rendition of vocal and instrumental music.

21. David is credited with at least seventy-five psalms, one-half of all 150 of them.

1 CHRONICLES 26: THE KOHATHITE–KORAHITE AND MERARITE GATEKEEPERS IN SOLOMON'S TEMPLE[1]

Approximate Dating: Solomon's Temple was completed in 960 B.C.; gatekeepers were active during Solomon's reign, 971–931 B.C.
Relevant Scriptures: **1 Chronicles 26:1–19;** also **Exodus 6:18; Numbers 26:57–58; 1 Chronicles 6:2, 18, 22, 44–47**

Genealogy of Kohathite–Korahite Gatekeepers

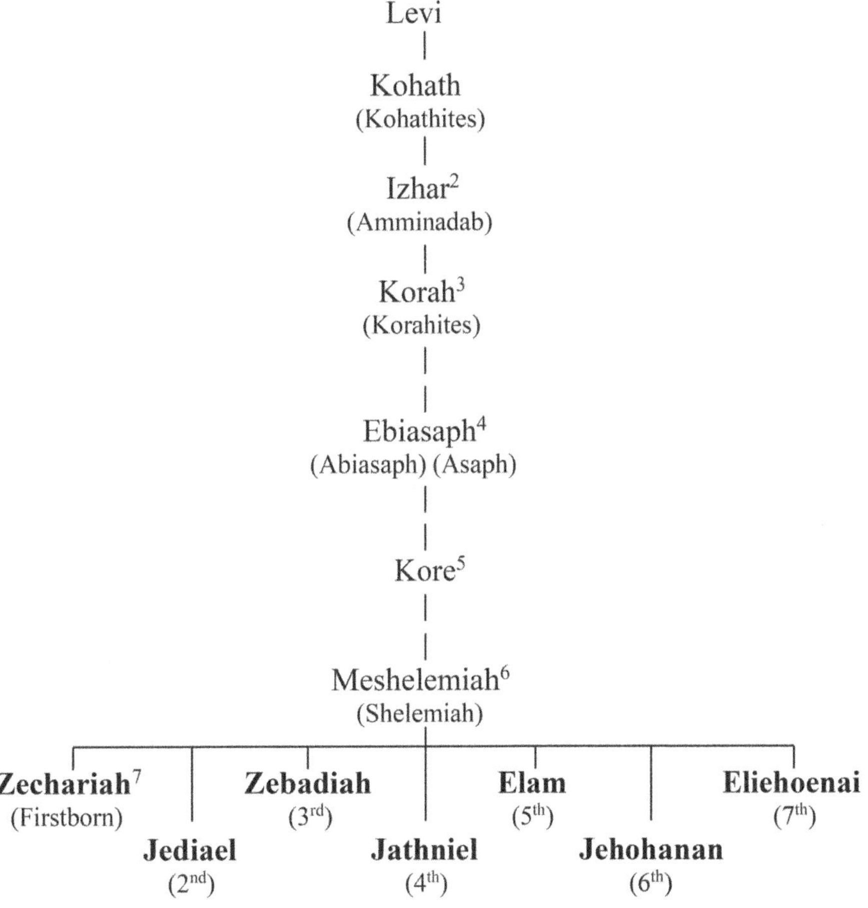

Genealogy of Merarite Gatekeepers

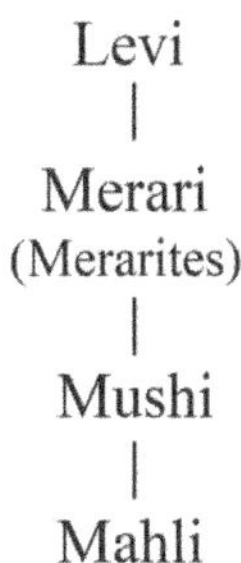

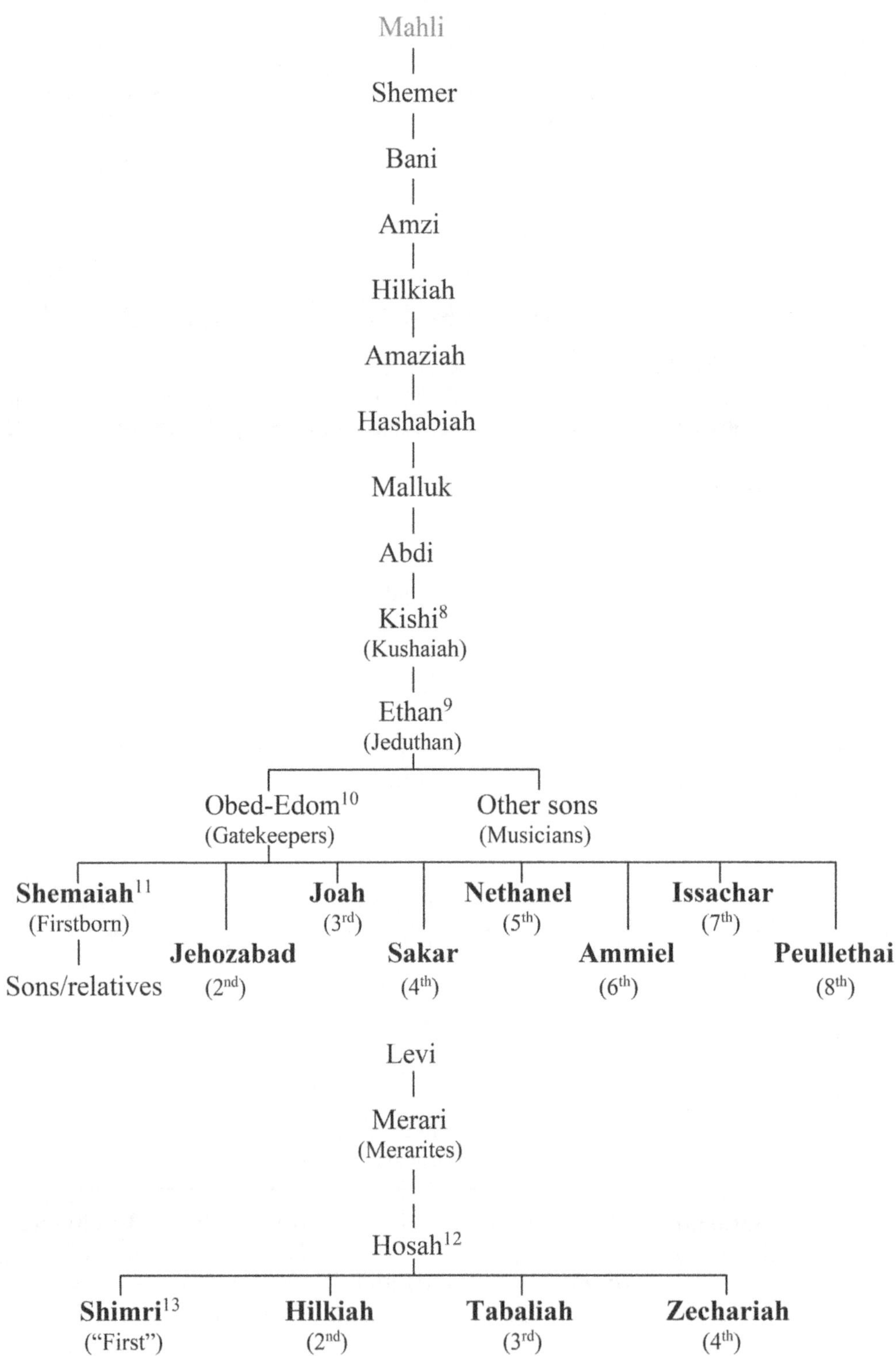

Biblical and Theological Significance

Almost all buildings have means of ingress and egress, that is, ways to enter and exit, usually through doors. However, buildings surrounded by walls or fences will feature gates as well, as will large buildings under tight security. The temple was no exception. The outer courtyard surrounding the temple complex could only be entered through gates. The same was true in the temple proper, with outer and inner doors to provide access to its various chambers (**1 Kings 6:1–36; 2 Chronicles 3:1–17; 4:9**). Given the holy character of the temple as the "House of God," vigilance and security were required to prevent illegitimate entry into the sacred places, and the Levites were charged with these duties. As the chart shows, both gatekeepers[14] and doorkeepers[15] were descendants of Levi through his sons, Kohath and Merari.

In Solomon's Temple, lots were cast for each gate "according to their families, young and old alike" (**1 Chronicles 26:13**). The East Gate was assigned to Shelemiah (also called Meshelemiah; see note 6), and his son Zechariah was chosen for the North Gate. Obed-Edom received the important South

Gate (the main one used by the king, since it was closest to the palace) and his sons guarded the storehouse. Shuppim and Hosah guarded the West Gate and the Shalleketh Gate[16] on the upper road. No unguarded space was left between: "There were six Levites a day on the east, four a day on the north, four a day on the south and two at a time at the storehouse. As for the court to the west, there were four at the road and two at the court itself" (**1 Chronicles 26:14–18**).

Notes

1. Solomon's Temple was completed in 960 B.C. For a more expansive chart of the lineages of the Korahites and Merarites, see chart "**1 Chronicles 6**: Levi: High Priests, Priests, Levites, and Musicians in Solomon's Temple." For more details about the clan of Obed-Edom, see chart "**2 Samuel 6**: Obed-Edom, the Levitical Gatekeeper and Keeper of the Ark."

2. Izhar in **Exodus 6:18, 21; Numbers 16:1; 1 Chronicles 6:2, 18, 38; 23:12** is Amminadab in **1 Chronicles 6:22**.

3. Korah died in the Korah rebellion (**Numbers 16:23–34**), but the line of Korah (the Korahites) did not die out (**Numbers 26:11, 58**); descendants in this lineage are sometimes referred to as "Kohathite-Korahites" (e.g., the designation for Zechariah, Jediael, Zebadiah, Jathniel, Elam, Jehohanan and Eliehoenai in the chart).

4. Ebiasaph in **1 Chronicles 6:23** is called Abiasaph in **Exodus 6:24** and Asaph in **1 Chronicles 26:1**. He is a different person than Asaph, one of the key musicians in Solomon's Temple (cf. **1 Chronicles 15:17, 19; 16:5; 25:1, 6**).

5. Kore is probably the same as "Kore son of Imnah the Levite" over the East Gate in the days of King Hezekiah.

6. Meshelemiah (**1 Chronicles 26:1–2, 9**), who is also called Shelemiah (**1 Chronicles 26:14**), was the head over the prestigious East Gate. Meshelemiah "had sons and relatives, who were able men—18 in all" (**1 Chronicles 26:9**). Meshelemiah/Shelemiah (a pre-exilic figure) should not be confused with the post-exilic figure named Shallum/Meshullam; see chart "**1 Chronicles 9**: Registry and Genealogy of the Levitical Gatekeepers and the Priestly Overseer of the Grain Offerings at the Second Temple (Post-Exile)."

7. Zechariah the son of Shelemiah/Meshelemiah was the key gatekeeper at the North Gate of Solomon's Temple. He is characterized as "a wise counselor" (**1 Chronicles 26:14**). According to **1 Chronicles 9:21**, his descendant (also called Zechariah) served in the Second Temple; see chart "**1 Chronicles 9**: Registry and Genealogy of the Levitical Gatekeepers and the Priestly Overseer of the Grain Offerings at the Second Temple (Post-Exile)."

8. Kishi in **1 Chronicles 6:44** is Kushaiah in **1 Chronicles 15:17**.

9. Ethan in **1 Chronicles 6:44; 15:17, 19** is Jeduthun in **1 Chronicles 25:1**. Ethan/Jeduthun the Merarite, Asaph the Gershonite, and Heman the Kohathite–Korahite were the three chief musicians in Solomon's Temple (**1 Chronicles 15:17, 19; 16:41–42; 25:1, 6; 2 Chronicles 35:15**).

10. Obed-Edom was the key gatekeeper at the South Gate between the temple and the king's palace (**1 Chronicles 26:15**). A genealogical notation says he had many sons because "God had blessed Obed-Edom" (**1 Chronicles 26:5**). The sons were over the storehouse (**1 Chronicles 26:15**); his descendants numbered 62 in all (**1 Chronicles 26:5, 8**). See chart "**2 Samuel 6**: Obed-Edom, the Levitical Gatekeeper and Keeper of the Ark."

11. The sons of Shemaiah—Othni, Rephael, Obed, and Elzabad—were leaders in their family and called "very capable men" (**1 Chronicles 26:6**). Shemaiah's relatives, Elihu and Semakiah, were also "able men" (**1 Chronicles 26:7**).

12. Hosah and Shuppim were the two gatekeepers at the West Gate and the Shalleketh Gate of the temple; only four of the 13 sons and relatives of Hosah are listed as gatekeepers (**1 Chronicles 26:10–11, 16**).

13. Shimri was designated the first of Hosah's sons: "although he was not the firstborn, his father had appointed him the first" (**1 Chronicles 26:10**).

14. The term for gatekeeper is the participial form of a reconstructed verb, "to (guard a) gate": שׁוֹעֵר (*shoer*), lit. "gater."

15. "Doorkeeper" is שֹׁמֵר הַסַּף (*shomer hassaph*), "watcher of the (door) threshold."

16. Scholars have proposed that the Shalleketh Gate (or the "gate of the chamber") was located on the causeway that led up to the western side of the temple from the Tyropeon Valley and served as the principal approach from the lower city and from the Western Hill. See Edward L. Curtis and Albert A. Madsen, *A Critical and Exegetical Commentary on the Books of Chronicles* (Edinburgh: T&T Clark, 1920), 285.

1 CHRONICLES 26: PROBABLE GENEALOGY OF AHIJAH, THE PRIESTLY OVERSEER OF THE TEMPLE TREASURIES AND DEDICATED THINGS IN SOLOMON'S TEMPLE

Approximate Dating: ca. 960 B.C. ***Relevant Scriptures:*** **1 Chronicles 26:20;**[1] also **1 Samuel 14:3; 1 Kings 11:29; 12:15; 14:2–6; 2 Chronicles 9:29; 10:15**

Probable Genealogy of Ahijah

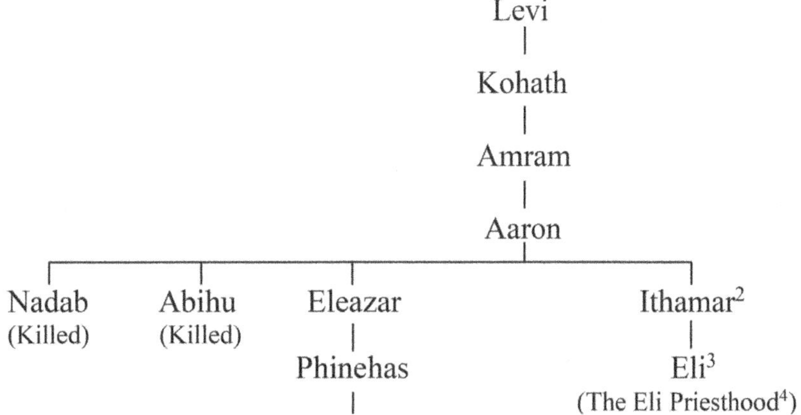

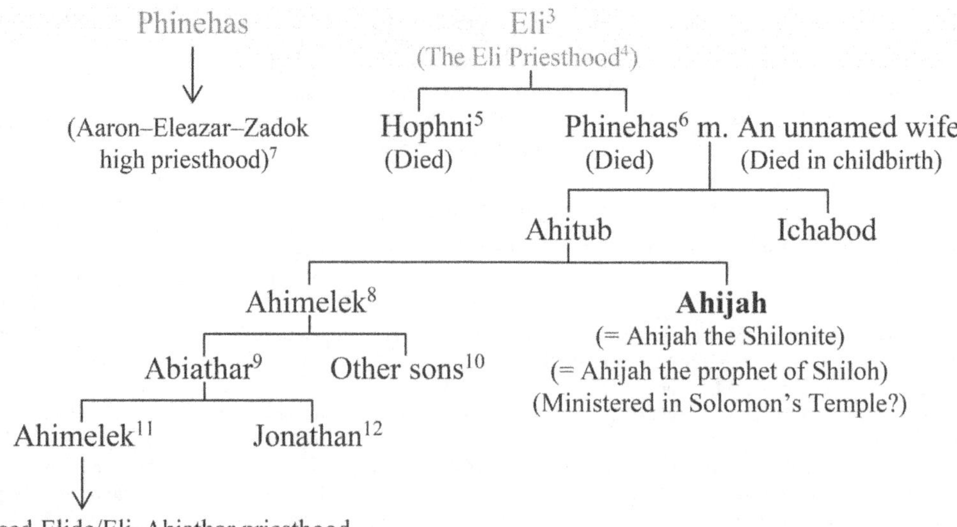

Biblical and Theological Significance

The name Ahijah (Heb. אֲחִיָּה, "Yahweh (is) my brother") is common in the Old Testament, occurring twenty-two times and referring to several different individuals. The Ahijah in the Septuagint reading of **1 Chronicles 26:20** (see note 1)—"As for the Levites, Ahijah was in charge of the treasuries of the house of God and the treasuries for the dedicated things"—suggests that Ahijah may be the same person as Ahijah the Elide high priest (the great-grandson of Eli[14]) who attended at Shiloh in the days of Saul, ca. 1051–1011 B.C. (**1 Samuel 14:3, 18**), David (ca. 1011–971 B.C.), and Solomon (971–931 B.C.),[15] and perhaps the same person as Ahijah the "prophet of Shiloh" who prophesied for a few years in the reign of Jeroboam I of Israel (931–910 B.C.; cf. **1 Kings 11:29–30; 12:15; 14:1–16, 18; 2 Chronicles 9:29; 10:15**). If, in fact, they refer to the same individual, the total time span of Ahijah's ministry, at the very least, would be approximately one hundred years, an age that is in the upper limits of mortality rates for that period.[16]

Shiloh was Ahijah's primary place of service in the early days of the united monarchy. When Shiloh was destroyed by the Philistines in ca. 1050 B.C., the tabernacle was relocated to Gibeon (where it stayed from ca. 1050–960 B.C.). Then, through a series of calamities and mishaps, David moved the ark of the covenant to the City of David in ca. 1004 B.C., where it resided in a temporary tent/quasi-temple that he had prepared for it (**2 Samuel 6:12–15; 1 Chronicles 15:1**).[17] Late in his reign, David organized the attending priests and Levites who would attend in the future temple (cf. **1 Chronicles 24, 28–29**). After Solomon came to the throne in 971 B.C. and completed the new Temple of Solomon in 960 B.C., he had the ark moved from the tent in the City of David to the most holy place of the newly constructed house of the Lord (**2 Chronicles 5:2–14**) and "brought in the things his father David had dedicated—the silver and gold and all the furnishings—and he placed them in the treasuries of God's temple" (**2 Chronicles 5:1**). The Chronicler is clear to point out that "the treasuries of the temple of God and for the treasuries for the dedicated things" and "the divisions of the priests and Levites, and for all the work of serving in the temple" were a vision "that the Spirit had put in his [David's] mind" (**1 Chronicles 28:12–13**).[18] The elderly Ahijah—seemingly a remnant priest of the former Eli priesthood—appears to be the honored Levitical servant who was in charge of the treasuries and the dedicated things in the newly constructed Solomon's Temple (**1 Chronicles 26:20**; LXX says *"As for the Levites, Ahijah was* in charge of the treasuries of the house of God and the treasuries for the dedicated things").

The same person or another (?) named Ahijah appears in the record as "the prophet of Shiloh" (**1 Kings 11:29**)—also called "Ahijah the Shilonite" (**1 Kings 12:15; 15:29; 2 Chronicles 9:29; 10:15**), showing that Shiloh was his primary place of service.[19, 20] The prophet Ahijah, among other things, foretold the splitting of the united kingdom by the symbolic tearing of a garment into twelves pieces—ten tribes would split to form Israel, and the two remaining tribes would form Judah (**1 Kings 11:29–39**). Later, when Jeroboam's son became sick, Jeroboam's wife disguised herself and went to Shiloh to inquire about the child's welfare. At that time, Ahijah was almost blind but could still hear (cf. **1 Kings 14:4, 6**); he prophesied the death of the child and the complete and utter judgment on the wicked house of Jeroboam I, the son of Nebat (**1 Kings 12:15; 14:1–18**). Ahijah was among the compilers of a written account of the acts of King Solomon, called "the prophecy of Ahijah the Shilonite" (**2 Chronicles 9:29**).

The question remains as to whether Ahijah the Elide priest was the same person as Ahijah the prophet of Shiloh in the days of Jeroboam I of Israel. The connection with Shiloh in each case is supportive of a *single* person being a priest and a prophet.[21] Also, both were obviously men of great age. For this reason, Ahijah in **1 Chronicles 26:20** (see LXX translation above) is interpreted to be the same person as the prophet of Shiloh (**1 Kings 11:29**). Ahijah is shown in the chart as a *faithful remnant* of the cursed Eli priesthood line. Having escaped the curse (**1 Samuel 2:31–36**), "his servant the prophet Ahijah" received the honor and blessing of seeing and serving in the Lord's temple in Jerusalem (**1 Kings 14:18; 15:29**).

Notes

1. The NIV of **1 Chronicles 26:20** reads, "Their fellow Levites were in charge of the treasuries of the house of God and the treasuries for the dedicated things." However, the Septuagint reads, "As for the Levites, Ahijah was in charge"; the chart follows the Septuagint reading, confirming Ahijah's involvement.

2. The lineage of Eli (the Eli priesthood) included Ahimelek the son of Ahitub (see note 8), who is explicitly called "a descendant of Ithamar" (**1 Chronicles 24:3**), the son of Aaron (cf. **Exodus 6:23; 1 Samuel 14:3; 22:9, 11; 1 Chronicles 6:3**).

3. When he was 98 years old and his eyes so dim "that he could not see" (**1 Samuel 4:15**), Eli heard that the Philistines had captured the ark of the covenant. Grief-stricken, he "fell backward off his chair by the side of the gate. His neck was broken and he died, for he was an old man, and he was heavy" (**1 Samuel 4:18**). Eli served at Shiloh as the priest-judge for Israel for 40 years (**1 Samuel 4:18**); see note 4.

4. For the details of the Elide priesthood, see chart "**1 Samuel 1**: Eli and the Eli Priesthood."

5. Hophni and Phinehas served as priests at Shiloh with their father Eli, but "Eli's sons were scoundrels; they had no regard for the Lord" (**1 Samuel 2:12**). They mishandled the meat offerings (**1 Samuel 2:12–17**) and lay with women who assembled at the door of the tabernacle of meeting (**1 Samuel 2:22**). The Lord pronounced a judgment on Eli, his sons, and their descendants: they would die in the prime of life, and the Eli priesthood would dwindle in strength and prominence. The remaining members (remnant) of Eli's family line would struggle and be forced to beg food from the new faithful priest Samuel (cf. **1 Samuel 2:31–36**). Hophni and Phinehas died in the battle between Israel and the Philistines (cf. **1 Samuel 4:1–11**).

6. Phinehas son of Eli, son of Ithamar, in the Eli priesthood (cf. **1 Samuel 1:3; 2:34; 4:4, 11**) is a different person than Phinehas son of Eleazar in the Aaron–Eleazar–Phinehas line of Kohathite priests (cf. **Exodus 6:25; Numbers 25:7, 11; Judges 20:28; 1 Chronicles 6:4, 50; Ezra 7:5; 8:2**).

7. The unfaithful line of the Eli–Abiathar priesthood is contrasted with the faithful "priesthood that will continue throughout their generations [the lasting priesthood]"—through Phinehas, the son of Eleazar, the son of Aaron (**Exodus 40:15**; cf. **Numbers 25:13; 1 Chronicles 6:49–53**).

8. In the days of King Saul, Ahimelek the son of Ahitub (cf. **1 Samuel 14:3; 22:9–11**) was a priest at Nob—called "the town of the priests"—northeast of Jerusalem and southeast of Gibeah (**1 Samuel 22:19**). David went to visit Ahimelek when he fled from Saul, and Ahimelek gave David some of the consecrated "bread of the Presence" for food (cf. **1 Samuel 21:1–10**). Saul—believing that Ahimelek had shifted his loyalty to David (although he had not)—ordered Doeg the Edomite (Saul's chief shepherd; **1 Samuel 21:7**) to murder all 85 priests "who wore the linen ephod" at Nob (**1 Samuel 22:18**). Presumably Ahimelek was killed at this time, but Ahimelek's son Abiathar escaped and fled to David. David promised Abiathar that he would be safe with him (David) because "the man who wants to kill you [Saul] is trying to kill me too" (**1 Samuel 22:23**; see **1 Samuel 21–22**).

9. When David moved the ark to the temporary tent in the City of David, and eventually to Solomon's Temple, Abiathar (Ahijah's nephew) and Zadok served in a dual, co–high priest capacity in Jerusalem (**2 Samuel 15:29; 20:25**). During Adonijah's attempt to assume the throne of his father (David), Abiathar unwisely supported Adonijah instead of Solomon. Abiathar was dismissed from his priestly duties during the early days of King Solomon's reign and returned to the Levitical city of Anathoth, his ancestral home (**1 Kings 1:7; 2:26–27**). Thus, the Eli–Abiathar priesthood ended with the term of Abiathar (and his son Jonathan; cf. **1 Kings 2:26–27**), although a faithful remnant of the Eli priesthood continued to serve as Kohathite attending priests (see note 13).

10. That Ahimelek had other sons besides Abiathar is suggested in the reading of **1 Samuel 22:20**.

11. Ahimelek the son of Abiathar appears to have been named after Ahimelek the son of Ahitub—an example of papponymy (the naming after a grandfather).

12. Jonathan the son of Abiathar is referenced in **2 Samuel 15:27, 36;** and **1 Kings 1:42**. Jonathan was a contemporary of King David. He should not be confused with Jonathan the son of Saul, a near contemporary.

13. For the Aaron–Ithamar descendants who ministered in Solomon's Temple as Kohathite *attending* priests (i.e., *not* high priests), see chart "**1 Chronicles 24**: Genealogical Registry of the Twenty-Four Divisions of Kohathite Priests Who Rotated Service in Solomon's Temple (Sixteen from the Aaron–Eleazar–Zadok Line and Eight from the Aaron–Ithamar Line)." Daniel the Kohathite attending priest, an Aaron–Ithamar descendant who had been an exile in Babylon, returned to Jerusalem with Ezra in 458 B.C. and served in the Second Temple (cf. **Ezra 8:2**).

14. See chart "**1 Samuel 1**: Eli and the Eli Priesthood."

15. For the reign of Kind David, see chart "**1 Chronicles 2**: King David"; for the reign of King Solomon, see chart "**1 Kings 11**: King Solomon."

16. This figure is calculated from the following chronological data: (1) Ahijah's grandfather Phinehas died at the same time as his (Phinehas') own father Eli did, in ca. 1104 B.C. (**1 Samuel 4:17–18**) and Ichabod the son of Phinehas, was born that same day; and (2) Ahijah's father Ahitub was brother to Ichabod and must have been about the same age, or probably a little older, if he and Ichabod had the same mother. Eli, on the other hand, died at age 98, in 1104 B.C.; see chart "**1 Samuel 1**: Eli and the Eli Priesthood," especially note 7.

17. For the movement of the ark, see chart "**1 Chronicles 16**: Genealogical Registry of the Levites Who Oversaw the Ark of the Covenant in the City of David and the Tabernacle at Gibeon."

18. David received the plans for the temple in much the same way that Moses had received the plans for the tabernacle from God (**Exodus 25–30**).

19. The qualifier—Ahijah the Shilonite—perhaps distinguishes him from his contemporary, Ahijah the son of Shisha, who was the scribal-secretary under Solomon (**1 Kings 4:3**).

20. For Shiloh as a worship center, see chart "**1 Chronicles 16**: Genealogical Registry of the Levites Who Oversaw the Ark of the Covenant in the City of David and the Tabernacle at Gibeon."

21. Although uncommon, a dual priest-prophet role is not without parallel—Jeremiah and Ezekiel are prime examples (cf. **Jeremiah 1:1**; **Ezekiel 1:3**).

1 CHRONICLES 26: THE LEVITICAL LEADERS WHO ASSISTED IN THE OVERSIGHT OF THE TREASURIES AND DEDICATED THINGS IN SOLOMON'S TEMPLE AND IN THE KING'S BUSINESS THROUGHOUT ISRAEL

Approximate Dating: Solomon's Temple was completed in 960 B.C.; these Levitical leaders were active throughout Solomon's reign, 971–931 B.C. ***Relevant Scriptures:*** **1 Chronicles 26:20–32**; also **Exodus 2:22; 6:17; 18:3; Numbers 3:19, 27; 26:57–58;1 Chronicles 6:2, 16–22, 41–43; 23:7–8; 24:20**

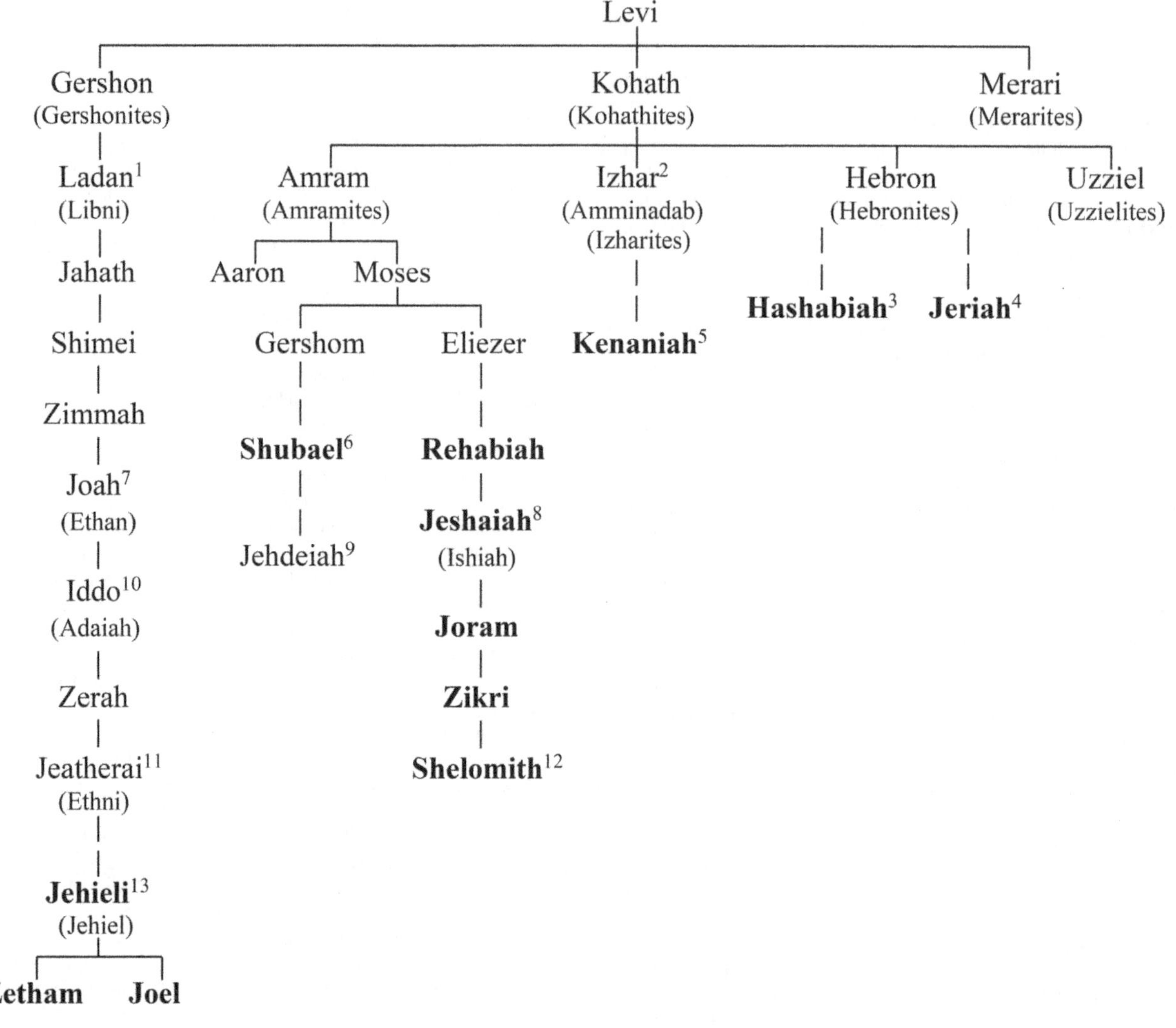

Biblical and Theological Significance

David left nothing to chance in preparing his divinely elected son Solomon for his responsibilities as heir to the throne. Most of the preparations that dominated pertained to Solomon's Temple—especially the personnel who would serve there, the priesthood, and the subservient Levites. The Chronicler is careful to designate who the Aaronic descendants were, as well as how they were to undertake their several duties. The chosen Levitical leaders were Gershonites and Kohathites (not Merarites).

From the Gershonites, Jehieli and his sons oversaw the temple treasuries (**1 Chronicles 26:22**). Because Moses' descendants were "counted as part of the tribe of Levi" (**1 Chronicles 23:14**), the descendants of Eliezer and Gershom (Kohathite–Amramites) were permitted to serve alongside their Kohathite relatives[14] (**1 Chronicles 23:14–17; 26:24–28**). Levites from the Kohath–Izharite clan did some of the necessary work outside the temple; Kenaniah and his sons served as officers and judges over Israel (**1 Chronicles 26:29**). Some 1700 Kohath–Hebronites were responsible for business west of the Jordan River. An additional 2700 Kohath–Hebronite relatives found living at Jazer in Gilead were called into service. They were responsible for overseeing business related to the tribes of Reuben, Gad, and West Manasseh in the Transjordan as well as anything else the king required (**1 Chronicles 26:30–32**).

Notes

1. Libni in **Exodus 6:17; Numbers 3:18;** and **1 Chronicles 6:17, 20** is called Ladan in **1 Chronicles 23:7–9; 26:21**.

2. Izhar in **Exodus 6:18, 21; Numbers 3:19; 16:1;** and **1 Chronicles 6:2, 18, 38; 23:12** is called Amminadab in **1 Chronicles 6:22**.

3. Hashabiah the Kohathite–Hebronite oversaw the Israelite tribes on the west side of the Jordan River (i.e., the cis-Jordan tribes) with 1700 men (**1 Chronicles 26:30**). He is a different person than:

- Hashabiah the Merarite, the son of Ethan/Jeduthun (**1 Chronicles 25:3, 19**);
- Hashabiah the son of Kemuel, the military officer over the Levites (**1 Chronicles 27:17**);
- Other Levitical Merarites named Hashabiah (**1 Chronicles 6:45; 9:14**);
- The Levitical figure named Hashabiah who lived in the days of King Josiah, 640–609 B.C. (**2 Chronicles 35:9**); and
- Levitical figures named Hashabiah also lived in the post-exile era (cf. **Ezra 8:19, 24; Nehemiah 3:17; 10:11; 11:15, 22; 12:21, 24**).

4. Jeriah, mentioned in **1 Chronicles 23:19; 24:23; 26:31–32**, was head of the Hebronites. In the fortieth year of King David's reign (ca. 971 B.C.), genealogical records for the Hebronites were found in Jazer in Gilead. Jeriah and 2700 of his relatives oversaw the Transjordan tribes of Reuben, Gad, and East Manasseh "for every matter pertaining to God and for the affairs of the king" (**1 Chronicles 26:32**). Jazer, allotted to the tribe of Gad, is mentioned in **Numbers 21:32; 32:1, 3, 35; Joshua 13:25; 21:39; 2 Samuel 24:5; 1 Chronicles 6:81; 26:31; Isaiah 16:8–9; Jeremiah 48:32**.

5. Kenaniah and his sons acted as Levitical officials and judges outside Jerusalem (**1 Chronicles 26:29**).

6. Shubael, mentioned in **1 Chronicles 23:16; 24:20; 26:24**, was overseer of the treasuries in Solomon's Temple. Shubael a descendant in the Kohath–Amram–Moses line is a different person than Shubael, the descendant of Heman the musician of Solomon's Temple, who was in the Kohath–Izhar–Korah line (cf. **1 Chronicles 25:4, 20**). For Moses' descendants, see chart "**Exodus 18**: Moses' Sons, Gershom and Eliezer, and Their Descendants Who Served in Solomon's Temple."

7. Joah (**1 Chronicles 6:21**) is also called Ethan (**1 Chronicles 6:42**).

8. Jeshaiah in **1 Chronicles 26:25** is Ishiah in **1 Chronicles 24:21**. Jeshaiah/Ishiah was the son (or perhaps the descendant) of Rehabiah. Jeshaiah/Ishiah was a contemporary of King David (cf. **1 Chronicles 24:3, 31**). Jeshaiah/Ishiah the descendant of Moses, is a different person than:

(1) Ishiah the Kohathite, of the "sons of Uzziel [Moses' uncle]" who served in Solomon's Temple (cf. **1 Chronicles 23:12, 20; 24:24–25**);
(2) Jeshaiah the descendant of Hananiah the Judahite (**1 Chronicles 3:21**);
(3) Jeshaiah the Merarite, the son of Jeduthun/Ethan the Levitical musician in Solomon's Temple (**1 Chronicles 25:3**);
(4) Jeshaiah the descendant of Elam, who returned to Jerusalem with Ezra in the post-exile (**Ezra 8:7**); and
(5) Jeshaiah the Merarite (Levite) who returned to Jerusalem with Ezra in the post-exile (**Ezra 8:19**).

9. The variations in rendering transliterations of personal names in the many modern Bible translations are illustrated here. We offer the following transliteration of the same name (Jedaiah, Jehdeiah, and Je(h)deiah; **1 Chronicles 24:7, 20; Ezra 2:36; Nehemiah 7:39; 11:10**) based squarely on the Hebrew text: יְדַעְיָה, *yedayah*.

10. Iddo (**1 Chronicles 6:21**) is called Adaiah (**1 Chronicles 6:41**).

11. Jeatherai in **1 Chronicles 6:21** is Ethni in **1 Chronicles 6:41**.

12. Shelomith was over the dedicated things (voluntary offerings and spoils of war) given to the temple by kings (such as Saul and David), heads of families, seers (such as Samuel), and military captains and officers (such as Abner and Joab; **1 Chronicles 26:25–28**).

13. Jehieli in **1 Chronicles 26:21–22** is called Jehiel in **1 Chronicles 23:8; 29:8**. "Anyone who had precious stones gave them to the treasury of the temple of the LORD in the custody of Jehiel the Gershonite" (**1 Chronicles 29:8**). Jehieli's sons were "in charge of the treasuries of the temple" (**1 Chronicles 26:22**).

14. See chart "**Exodus 18**: Moses' Sons, Gershom and Eliezer, and Their Descendants Who Served in Solomon's Temple."

1 CHRONICLES 27: GENEALOGICAL REGISTRY OF THE OFFICIALS OVER THE TWELVE ARMY DIVISIONS WHO SERVED THE KING MONTHLY IN JERUSALEM

Approximate Dating: ca. 971 B.C. ***Relevant Scriptures:*** **1 Chronicles 27:1–15**

1st Month -	**Jashobeam**[1] (the son of Zabdiel, a descendant of Perez from the tribe of Judah)
2nd Month -	**Dodai**[2] (the father of Eleazar; probably a descendant of Ahoah from the tribe of Benjamin)
3rd Month -	**Benaiah**[3] (the son of Jehoiada; from the tribe of Judah)
4th Month -	**Asahel**[4] (the son of David's half-sister, Zeruiah, and the brother of Joab)
5th Month -	**Shamhuth**[5] (the Izrahite) (probably the same as Shammah the Harodite and Shammoth the Harorite)
6th Month -	**Ira**[6] (the son of Ikkesh, from the town of Tekoa in the tribe of Judah)
7th Month -	**Helez**[7] (a Pelonite or Paltite, from the tribe of Ephraim)
8th Month -	**Sibbekai**[8] (a Hushathite, and a descendant of Zerah from the tribe of Judah)
9th Month -	**Abiezer**[9] (from Anathoth, a town in the tribe of Benjamin)
10th Month -	**Maharai**[10] (from Netophah and a descendant of Zerah from the tribe of Judah)
11th Month -	**Benaiah**[11] (from Pirathon, a town in the tribe of Ephraim)
12th Month -	**Heldai**[12] (or Heled) (from Netophah, a town in the tribe of Judah, and a descendant of Othniel the Kenizzite)

Biblical and Theological Significance

All of these men had served as key military officers in David's army.[13] Late in his reign David took measures of all kinds to prepare his son and successor Solomon for kingship (**1 Chronicles 23:1**). This included the transition of the armed forces from his control to Solomon's (**1 Chronicles 28:1-9**). The layers of their command were (1) heads over families;[14] (2) leaders over thousands[15] and hundreds; and (3) their officers,[16] all of whom served David and then Solomon in military capacities. The twelve divisions rotated month by month throughout the year, each consisting of twenty-four thousand[17] soldiers (**1 Chronicles 27:1**).

Notes

1. Jashobeam (**1 Chronicles 27:2**), also called Josheb-Basshebeth (**2 Samuel 23:8**), was a Judahite, the son of Zabdiel and a descendant of Perez the twin, the son of Judah and Tamar, Judah's daughter-in-law. He is called a Hakmonite (**1 Chronicles 11:11**) or, in a parallel passage, a Tahkemonite (**2 Samuel 23:8**). The differences in the names are partly of a scribal nature (e.g., Jashobeam, by syncopation becomes Ja(sho)sheb; the הַ of Hakmonite is much like the תַ of Tahkmonite. Jashobeam was the chief of all the officers and was held in great respect, for he had "raised his spear against three hundred men, whom he killed in one encounter" (**1 Chronicles 11:11**); in the parallel passage in **2 Samuel 23:8**, the text says, "he raised his spear against eight hundred men, whom he killed in one encounter."

2. Dodai "the Ahohite" was the father of Eleazar, who was one of the "Three" (i.e., the three elite leaders over David's mighty warriors; **1 Chronicles 11:12**). Ahohite probably refers to a descendant of Ahoah, the son of Bela, the son of Benjamin (cf. **1 Chronicles 8:4**). Mikloth was the leader of Dodai's division (**1 Chronicles 27:4**).

3. Benaiah was a native of Kabzeel, one of the southernmost towns in the tribe of Judah in the Negev (**Joshua 15:21**). He was a valiant fighter and was highly esteemed among David's mighty warriors for his great heroic deeds (**2 Samuel 23:20–23; 1 Chronicles 11:22–25**). Benaiah was in charge of the Kerethites and Pelethites, the professional troops who guarded the king (**2 Samuel 8:18; 20:23; 1 Chronicles 11:25; 18:17**). Benaiah was the honored leader of the Thirty in David's army, but still not included among the Three elite leaders (cf. **2 Samuel 23:23; 1 Chronicles 11:25; 27:6**). Benaiah's son Ammizabad was in charge of his division (**1 Chronicles 27:6**). Benaiah eventually became the commander of Solomon's army (**1 Kings 4:4**).

4. Asahel, David's nephew, was the son of David's half-sister Zeruiah (cf. **2 Samuel 2:18; 1 Chronicles 2:16; 27:7**). Asahel was the brother of Joab, the commander of David's army (**1 Chronicles 11:6**; cf. **2 Samuel 2:22**) and Abishai (who was also in David's military; **2 Samuel 23:18–19**). Asahel's son Zebadiah was his successor (**1 Chronicles 27:7**).

5. Shamhuth is called an Izrahite (**1 Chronicles 27:8**), probably referring to the family of Izrahiah the son of Uzzi, in the tribe of Issachar (**1 Chronicles 7:3**). Shamhuth is probably the same as Shammah the son of Agee/Shagee the Harodite (**2 Samuel 23:11, 25**) and Shammoth the Harorite (**1 Chronicles 11:27**), where the epithet connects him to the well (spring) of Harod on the edge of Jezreel near Mount Giboa, in the tribe of Issachar (cf. **Joshua 19:18; Judges 7:1; 1 Samuel 29:1**).

6. Ira was from Tekoa, a town in the high country of Judah, approximately six miles south of Bethlehem and twelve miles south of Jerusalem (cf. **2 Chronicles 11:6; Jeremiah 6:1; Amos 1:1**). Tekoa was founded by Ashhur, the son of Hezron, the son of Perez, the son of Judah (**1 Chronicles 2:24**). Ira is mentioned in **2 Samuel 23:26** and **1 Chronicles 11:28**; **27:9**.

7. Helez the Pelonite (**1 Chronicles 11:27**) is called Helez the Pelonite, "an Ephraimite" (**1 Chronicles 27:10**); he is probably the same as Helez the Paltite (**2 Samuel 23:26**). The Pelonite/Paltite designation may be related to scribal differences—Peloni (פלני) and Peleti (פלתי) which could, in an archaic script, look very much alike. Pelon is not attested to in the Old Testament, but Pelet is, so the latter is to be preferred here. For Helez, see note 12 in chart "**1 Chronicles 11**: Genealogical Registry of the Mighty Warriors in King David's Army."

8. Sibbekai killed Saph/Sippai, who was one of the descendants of Rapha/the Rephaites (**2 Samuel 21:18; 1 Chronicles 20:4**; see chart "**Deuteronomy 1**: The Giant Anakites, including Goliath and His Descendants"). Sibbekai was a descendant of Hushah/the Hushathites (cf. **2 Samuel 21:18; 23:27**), who were descendants of Zerah (Zerahites) the son of Judah by his daughter-in-law Tamar (**Genesis 38:30**; see **Genesis 46:12; Numbers 26:20; 1 Chronicles 2:4; 27:11; Matthew 1:3**).

9. Abiezer (**2 Samuel 23:27; 1 Chronicles 11:28; 27:12**) was from Anathoth, a Levitical city in the tribe of Benjamin given to the descendants of Aaron the high priest (**Joshua 21:18; 1 Chronicles 6:60**). Anathoth was the son of Beker, the son of Benjamin (**1 Chronicles 7:8**).

10. Maharai the Netophathite was from the town of Netophah in the hill country of Judah near Bethlehem and Anathoth (cf. **1 Chronicles 2:54; Ezra 2:21–22; Nehemiah 7:26**). He is also called "a Zerahite" in **1 Chronicles 27:13**, meaning a descendant of Zerah, the son of Judah by his daughter-in-law Tamar (cf. **Genesis 38:30; 46:12; Numbers 26:20; 1 Chronicles 2:4; Matthew 1:3**).

11. Benaiah the Pirathonite was from the town of Pirathon in the tribe of Ephraim (cf. **Judges 12:15; 2 Samuel 23:30; 1 Chronicles 11:31; 27:14**). He should not be confused with Benaiah the Judahite, the son of Jehoiada (see note 3).

12. Heldai was a resident of Netophah, a town in the hill country of Judah near Bethlehem (cf. **1 Chronicles 2:54; 27:15; Ezra 2:22; Nehemiah 7:26**). Heldai the Netophathite is probably identical to Heled the son of Baanah the Netophathite (**2 Samuel 23:29; 1 Chronicles 11:30**). Heldai/Heled was a descendant of Othniel the Kenizzite, the first judge of Israel (**Judges 1:12–13; 3:7–11; 1 Chronicles 27:15**); see charts "**Judges 3**: Othniel (Kenizzite), the First Judge of Israel" and "**1 Chronicles 2**: Caleb and Kenaz, the Sons of Jephunneh the Kenizzite."

13. See chart "**1 Chronicles 11**: Genealogical Registry of the Mighty Warriors in King David's Army."

14. "Family" here is a synecdoche, a figure of speech in which a part represents the whole. That is, "family" can mean "clan" or even "tribe."

15. "Thousands" translates אֲלָפִים, *alaphim*, which can also be rendered "unit" or "company" of indeterminate size (Francis Brown, ed., "thousands," *BDB*, 45.

16. שֹׁטְרִים, *shoterim*, were quasi-military officers, perhaps like civilian war cabinet officials.

17. This enormous number must, of necessity, be reduced, given the size of the small kingdom of David in comparison to the armies of much larger nations. As note 15 suggests, the idea may be that there were 24 units of unknown size that served each month.

1 CHRONICLES 27: GENEALOGICAL RECORD OF THE LEADERS OF THE TRIBES OF ISRAEL DURING THE DAVIDIC MONARCHY[1]

Approximate Dating: ca. 1011–971 B.C. ***Relevant Scriptures:*** **1 Chronicles 27:16–22**

Tribe of Reuben (Reubenites)	***Eliezer** (son of Zikri)
Tribe of Simeon (Simeonites)	***Shephatiah** (son of Maakah)
Tribe of Levi (Levites)	**Hashabiah**[2] (son of Kemuel)
Over the Aaronites (Kohathite priests)	**Zadok**[3] (son of Ahitub) (high priest)
Tribe of Judah	**Elihu**[4] (David's brother)

Tribe of Issachar	***Omri** (son of Michael[5])
Tribe of Zebulun	***Ishmaiah** (son of Obadiah)
Tribe of Naphtali	***Jerimoth** (son of Azriel)
Tribe of Ephraim	***Hoshea** (son of Azaziah)
Half-tribe of (West) Manasseh	***Joel** (son of Pedaiah)
Half-tribe of (East) Manasseh in Gilead	***Iddo** (son of Zechariah)
Tribe of Benjamin	**Jaasiel** (son of Abner[6])
Tribe of Dan	***Azarel** (son of Jeroham)

Biblical and Theological Significance

The function of these heads[7] of tribes in the time of the Davidic monarchy is not spelled out. The most likely proposal is that they (1) served as leaders by tribal name and definition so that the ancient linkage with Jacob and his sons would never be forgotten, and that (2) the kingdom could be broken down into provinces or "states," as it were, for ease of administration in both peaceful and wartime situations. The heads of the tribes may have been involved in counting the people for their respective tribes in the census that David initiated but did not complete (cf. **1 Chronicles 27:16–24**).

*None of the individuals who are noted with an asterisk is known elsewhere in Scripture, suggesting at least two caveats: (1) there are obviously whole generations of persons in the Bible of whom nothing or very little is said, as in this list, and (2) attempts to construct chronologies based on X numbers of generations are futile at best when one recognizes that entire generations may be missing from the genealogical records.

Notes

1. The tribes of Gad and Asher are not listed. No records from the period of the monarchy offer any insight as to reason for the omission of these two tribes.

2. The Levite Hashabiah son of Kemuel (**1 Chronicles 27:17**) who served during David's monarchy is not: (1) Hashabiah the Merarite, the father of Malluk and the son of Amaziah, who lived much earlier (**1 Chronicles 6:44–45**); (2) Hashabiah the son/descendant of Jeduthun/Ethan, the Merarite-musician who served in Solomon's Temple, 971–931 B.C. (**1 Chronicles 25:3, 19**); (3) Hashabiah, a leader of the Levites in the days of King Josiah, 640–609 B.C. (**2 Chronicles 35:9**); (4) Hashabiah, the ancestor of Shemaiah the Merarite (cf. **1 Chronicles 9:14**); nor (5) any of the post-exilic figures named Hashabiah (cf. **Ezra 8:19, 24; Nehemiah 3:17; 11:22; 12:21, 24**). Hashabiah son of Kemuel is possibly the same person as: (1) Hashabiah the ancestor of Shemaiah (**Nehemiah 11:15**); or (2) Hashabiah the Hebronite (a Levitical Kohathite) who served ca. 971–931 B.C. (**1 Chronicles 26:30**).

3. Zadok (**1 Chronicles 27:17**) and Abiathar (of the Eli priesthood) served as co–high priests during the reign of David, 1011–971 B.C. (**2 Samuel 15:27, 35–36; 17:15; 19:11; 20:25; 1 Kings 4:4; 1 Chronicles 15:11**); in some cases, the text says Zadok and Ahimelek (referring to Abiathar's son) officiated as the high priests (**2 Samuel 8:17; 1 Chronicles 18:16; 24:3, 6, 31**). Soon after coming to the throne, Solomon removed Abiathar from office; thereafter, Zadok served as the sole high priest during Solomon's reign, 971–931 B.C. (**1 Kings 1:26, 32, 34; 2:26–27; 1 Chronicles 29:22**). In the list above, Zadok was the head over the Aaronic priesthood (Kohathites).

4. Elihu (**1 Chronicles 27:18**) is probably the same as Eliab, the firstborn son of Jesse and David's eldest brother (**1 Samuel 16:6; 17:13, 28; 1 Chronicles 2:13; 2 Chronicles 11:18**). Both names are theophoric or hypocoristic: Elihu (אֱלִיהוּא) = "He (Yahweh) is my God" and Eliab (אֱלִיאָב) = "My God is (my) Father." See note 11 in chart "**1 Chronicles 2**: King David."

5. Michael the father of Omri (**1 Chronicles 27:18**) is possibly the same person as Michael the son of Izrahiah, of the tribe of Issachar (**1 Chronicles 7:3**).

6. Jaasiel son of Abner was Saul's cousin. Jaasiel's father, Abner, had served as the army commander for Saul and Saul's son Ish-Bosheth (cf. **1 Samuel 14:50; 17:55; 20:25; 26:5; 2 Samuel 2:8; 4:1**). Apparently Jaasiel was the head of the tribe of Benjamin during David's reign and may have been involved in conducting the census for the Benjamites, although the census was not completed (**1 Chronicles 27:21**; see **1 Chronicles 27:16–24**).

7. The terms נָגִיד ("in front of," or "leader of," **1 Chronicles 27:16**) and סָר ("ruler, prince," **1 Chronicles 27:22**) used here mean socio/political heads, not military ones.

1 CHRONICLES 27: GENEALOGICAL RECORD OF THE STATE OFFICIALS OVER THE KING'S PROPERTY

Approximate Dating: ca. 1004–971 B.C. ***Relevant Scriptures:*** **1 Chronicles 27:25–31**

Over the royal storehouses[1]	**Azmaveth**[2] (son of Adiel)
Over storehouses in the outlying districts, towns, and watchtowers	**Jonathan** (son of Uzziah[3])
Over workers who farmed the land	**Ezri** (son of Kelub[4])
Over the vineyards	**Shimei** (Ramathite[5])
Over vineyard produce for making wine	**Zabdi** (Shiphmite[6])
Over olive and sycamore trees in the western foothills	**Baal-Hanan** (Gederite[7])
Over stored supplies of olive oil	**Joash**[8]
Over herds grazing in Sharon[9]	**Shitrai** (Sharonite[10])
Over herds in the valleys	**Shaphat** (son of Adlai)
Over camels	**Obil** (Ishmaelite[11])
Over donkeys[12]	**Jehdeiah** (Meronothite[13])
Over flocks	**Jaziz** (Hagrite[14])

Biblical and Theological Significance

Along with many other spiritual and theological benefits, the strong reigns of David and Solomon strengthened the nation as a whole and increased the quality of life, from the peasants to the Jerusalem nobility (**2 Samuel 8:15; 2 Chronicles 1:14–17; 9:6–28**). Throughout its history, Israel was primarily an agrarian society and thus experts in agriculture of all kinds were necessary. Listed here from David's reign are bounties accrued from villages and cities, fields, vineyards, and orchards, as well as pastures filled with herds of cattle, camels, donkeys, and flocks of sheep (**1 Chronicles 27:25–31**). These were under the care of presumed experts in agriculture, viticulture, and management of fruit-bearing trees, in addition to others skilled in animal husbandry. In a land bereft of mineral resources and other natural bounties, field and forest, meadow and grazing land must be utilized to the maximum with whatever scientific tools and knowledge were available.[15]

Notes

1. The royal storehouses (אֹצָרוֹת, *otsaroth*) in this first instance refers to either such possessions as precious metals and gemstones kept at the palace or as a heading for all that follows.

2. This is possibly Azmaveth the Benjamite, a "Baharumite"—a native of Bahurim, a place on the road from Jerusalem into the Jordan Valley, and north of the Mount of Olives—who was one of the warriors in David's army (**2 Samuel 23:31; 1 Chronicles 11:33; 12:3**); see note 23 in chart "**1 Chronicles 11**: Genealogical Registry of the Mighty Warriors in King David's Army." Azamaveth's father Adiel is not Adiel of **1 Chronicles 4:36**, who was a contemporary of King Hezekiah of Judah, 715–686 B.C.

3. Uzziah the father of Jonathan does not refer to King Uzziah/Azariah of Judah, who reigned 792–740 B.C. For chronological reasons, it is unlikely that he is Uzziah a descendant of Izhar/Amminadab, the son of Kohath (**1 Chronicles 6:22, 24**). Also, he is not the post-exilic figures named Uzziah (cf. **Ezra 10:21; Nehemiah 11:4**).

4. Kelub is possibly the same person as Kelub the brother/relative of Jabez and a descendant of the Hezronite clan in the tribe of Judah (see chart "**1 Chronicles 4**: Judah").

5. Shimei was from the town of Ramah, but which town is unclear: (1) Ramah, a town in Benjamin (**Joshua 18:25**); (2) Ramah/Ramoth Negev (**Joshua 19:8; 1 Samuel 30:27**); (3) Ramah in the vicinity of Tyre (**Joshua 19:29**); and/or (4) the shortened form of Ramoth Gilead (**2 Kings 8:29; 2 Chronicles 22:6**).

6. This is the single occurrence of Shiphmite; it may refer to Siphmoth, a town in southern Judah (**1 Samuel 30:28**).

7. Baal-Hanan was probably from Geder (**Joshua 12:13**).

8. This Joash may correspond to Joash the Benjamite (son of Shemaah the Gibeathite), who had joined David's army at Ziklag (**1 Chronicles 12:3**). For chronological reasons, this does not refer to Joash the father of Gideon (ca. 1123–1083 B.C.) or King Joash of Judah (835–796 B.C.).

9. This is a reference to what is sometimes called the *shephelah*, that is, the sloping land between the coastal plain and the hill country, celebrated in Scripture for its beauty and fertility (**Song of Songs 2:1; Isaiah 33:9; 35:1–2; 65:10**).

10. Shitrai was from the agriculturally and pastorally rich region of Sharon (cf. **Isaiah 35:2**).

11. Obil the Ishmaelite was a descendant of Ishmael, the son of Abraham and Hagar (**Genesis 16:16**).

12. The animal designated commonly by the epithet "donkey" or "burro" was in fact a highly prized animal of nobility (אָתוֹנָה, *athonah*), on which kings rode (**Zechariah 9:9**).

13. Jehdeiah was from Meronoth, a town associated with Mizpah (cf. **Nehemiah 3:7**).

14. Jaziz was a descendant of Hagar, the Egyptian slave of Sarah (**Genesis 16:1**) and the mother of Ishmael, the son of Abraham (**Genesis 16:15**).

15. An example of technical expertise in fruit-tree production is Amos, the prophet who is said to have been a בּוֹלֵס שִׁקְמִים (**Amos 7:14**), "a nipper of sycamore-figs," i.e., to pierce the fruit, accelerate the ripening, and "to fit it for eating." BDB, 118, בָּלַס. Amos was from Tekoa, a region of rich fertility and benign climate where many varieties of crops could be grown (**Amos 1:1**).

1 CHRONICLES 27: GENEALOGICAL RECORD OF THE ADVISORS TO KING DAVID

Approximate Dating: ca. 1011–971 B.C. ***Relevant Scriptures:*** **1 Chronicles 27:32–34**

Counselor and secretary/scribe	**Jonathan** (David's uncle)[1]
Overseer of the king's sons	**Jehiel** (the son of Hakmoni)[2]
King's counselor	**Ahithophel**[3]
King's confidant	**Hushai** the Arkite[4]
Commander of the royal army	**Joab** (David's nephew)[5]

Biblical and Theological Significance

Every regime of size requires its chief administrators to have a bureau of subordinates who are responsible for its successful operation. David's kingship was no different. Moreover, many governments are criticized for nepotism—the placing of family members in prominent positions. However, David seems to have made this a practice; of the five posts referred to here, two were held by close relatives (Jonathan and Joab) and another by an in-law (Ahithophel, who was Bathsheba's grandfather). Nepotism, however, often bypasses more godly advisors in favor of near relatives. An example of this was David's nephews, the sons of Zeruiah (David's half-sister), who served in key positions in the army, but they were harsh, bloodthirsty men (see **2 Samuel 3:39; 19:21; 1 Kings 2:5–6**; see note 5).

This passage is part of a lengthy listing of persons responsible for all details of David's government (**1 Chronicles 23:1–27:34**). As David approached death, he appointed officials for religious and secular duties. Religious appointments included (1) designated Levites (**1 Chronicles 23:7–32**); (2) priests (**1 Chronicles 24:1–19**); (3) miscellaneous Levites (**1 Chronicles 24:20–31**); (4) musicians (**1 Chronicles 25:1–31**) and (5) gatekeepers (**1 Chronicles 26:1–19**). The non-religious officers were (1) treasurers (**1 Chronicles 26:20–28**); (2) officials and judges (**1 Chronicles 26:29**); (3) managers of various projects (**1 Chronicles 26:30–32**); (4) military leaders (**1 Chronicles 27:1–15**); (5) tribal leaders with unspecified duties (**1 Chronicles 27:16–22**); and (6) royal overseers (**1 Chronicles 27:25–32**). Within the latter category were the king's personal advisors, the subject of this register.

Notes

1. J(eh)onathan is identified as "David's uncle" and called "a counselor, a man of insight and a scribe" (**1 Chronicles 27:32**). Though literacy in Israel in the tenth century B.C. was at a relatively high level for the times, the skills essential for one being called a סֹפֵר (*sopher*), "writer," were highly prized. J(eh)onathan (David's uncle) should not be confused with David's *nephew* Jonathan (the son of Shimea/Shimeah, David's brother) who was known for killing one of the Raphites (giants) of Gath (**2 Samuel 21:20–21; 1 Chronicles 20:6–7**). For both men, see chart "**1 Chronicles 2**: King David."

2. This individual is unknown elsewhere in the record. The text says only that "he took care of the king's sons," most likely as a tutor or instructor who schooled the royal children. For the identification of the sons of King David, see charts "**1 Chronicles 2**: King David" and "**1 Chronicles 3**: David's Children Born in Hebron and Jerusalem."

3. Ahithophel's son Eliam was the father of Bathsheba (**2 Samuel 11:3; 23:34**). Perhaps Ahithophel held a grudge against David for his transgression with his granddaughter (Bathsheba), so he (Ahithophel) supported Absalom's attempt to usurp the throne from King David. When Absalom asked him for advice, Ahithophel proposed that he should take 12,000 men to pursue David and kill him. However, Absalom also sought the advice of David's friend and confidant, Hushai the Arkite (cf. **1 Chronicles 27:33**). When Ahithophel's advice was ignored by Absalom and the men of Israel in favor of that of Hushai the Arkite, Ahithophel committed suicide by hanging himself (cf. **2 Samuel 17:1–23**). After Ahithophel's death, the advisory position he had held in David's administration was given to Jehoiada the son of Benaiah and then later to Abiathar the Elide priest (**1 Chronicles 27:34**). For the genealogy of Ahithophel, see chart "**2 Samuel 5**: Bathsheba." For David's administration, see chart "**2 Samuel 8 & 20**: The Chief Officials in King David's Administration."

4. The Arkites were descendants of Canaan (cf. **Genesis 10:17; 1 Chronicles 1:15**); Hushai was possibly from the coastal Phoenician town of Irqata. Hushai the Arkite is mentioned in **2 Samuel 15:32, 37; 16:16–18; 17:5–7, 14–15; 1 Chronicles 27:33**.

5. Joab, David's half-nephew, was a brave and competent warrior, equipped in every way to take the position of שַׂר־צָבָא (*sar tsaba*), "prince of the hosts." Joab was the son of Zeruiah David's half-sister, who was the daughter of Nahash (**2 Samuel 17:25; 1 Chronicles 2:16**). However, Joab and his brothers (Abishai and Asahel) were considered "harsh" and "cruel" (קָשֶׁה *qasheh*)—"These sons of Zeruiah are too strong for me. May the LORD repay the evildoer according to his evil deeds!" (**2 Samuel 3:39**). For the genealogy of Joab, see charts "**1 Samuel 14**: The Military Leaders under King Saul, King David, Absalom, and King Solomon" and "**1 Chronicles 2**: King David."

2 CHRONICLES 17: GENEALOGICAL RECORD OF THE TEACHERS OF THE LAW DURING THE REIGN OF KING JEHOSHAPHAT OF JUDAH

Approximate Dating: ca. 872–848 B.C. ***Relevant Scriptures:*** **2 Chronicles 17:7–9**

Officials[1]

- **Ben-Hail**
- **Obadiah**
- **Zechariah**[2]
- **Nethanel**
- **Micaiah**[3]

Levites

- **Shemaiah**[4]
- **Nethaniah**
- **Zebadiah**
- **Asahel**
- **Shemiramoth**
- **Jehonathan**[5]
- **Adonijah**[6]
- **Tobijah**[7]
- **Tob-Adonijah**

Kohathite Attending Priests

- **Elishama**[8]
- **Jehoram**[9]

Biblical and Theological Significance

Jehoshaphat's evaluation in both **1 Kings 22:43** and **2 Chronicles 20:32–33** is generally favorable, especially considering the pervasively wicked period in which he lived, markedly so in the Northern Kingdom where the house of Ahab and his sons Ahaziah and Joram negatively influenced the moral and spiritual climate of the kingdom of Judah. In his personal life, Jehoshaphat was a model of fidelity to Yahweh and Torah (**2 Chronicles 17:3–6**), heightened even more by his "missioning" the kingdom by sending these men to every village to teach the "Book of the Law"—clearly referring to the book of Deuteronomy (**Deuteronomy 28:61; 29:21; 30:10; 31:26;** also called the "Book of the Law of Moses" (**Joshua 8:31; 23:6; 2 Kings 14:6; 2 Chronicles 25:4; Nehemiah 8:1**).

Notes

1. The construction here for officials is interesting in that these leaders are called "his סָרִים, *sarim*," a technical term frequently translated "prince," and almost certainly so here because of the personal pronoun. See note 2.

2. Zechariah was very likely a son of Jehoshaphat (**2 Chronicles 21:2**); see note 1. See chart "**1 Kings 15**: Jehoshaphat, King of Judah."

3. If Micaiah is possible a variant of *Michael*, then he may be a son of King Jehoshaphat; see note 1. See chart "**1 Kings 15**: Jehoshaphat, King of Judah."

4. Shemaiah was a common Levitical name, but given the time period (872–848 B.C.), Shemaiah the Levite in **2 Chronicles 17:8** is not: (1) Shemaiah the Kohathite, a contemporary of David (**1 Chronicles 15:8, 11**); (2) Shemaiah the Levitical scribe, a contemporary of David (**1 Chronicles 24:6**); (3) Shemaiah, the son of Obed-Edom (**1 Chronicles 26:4, 6–7**); (4) Shemaiah the Merarite (a descendant of Jeduthun/Ethan), a contemporary of King Hezekiah (**2 Chronicles 29:14; 31:15**); (5) Shemaiah the Levite, a contemporary of King Josiah (**2 Chronicles 35:9**); nor (6) post-exilic Merarites named Shemaiah (**1 Chronicles 9:14, 16**).

5. Jehonathan (**2 Chronicles 17:8**) is not the post-exilic priest Jehonathan (**Nehemiah 12:18**).

6. Adonijah (**2 Chronicles 17:8**) is not Adonijah, a leader of the people who signed the covenant with Nehemiah in 445 B.C. (**Nehemiah 10:16**).

7. Tobijah the Levite (**2 Chronicles 17:8**) is not the post-exilic figure Tobijah (**Zechariah 6:10, 14**).

8. Elishama was a Kohathite attending priest, not a high priest. [Rather, Amariah the son of Azariah, was the high priest during the reign of King Jehoshaphat (cf. **1 Chronicles 6:11; 2 Chronicles 19:11**); see Amariah #16 in chart "**Supplement 2**: The High Priests of Israel." Since Jehoshaphat reigned from ca. 872–848 B.C., Elishama the Kohathite priest is not Elishama the scribe/court official, a contemporary of the prophet Jeremiah (ca. 627–587 B.C.), who served under King Jehoiakim/Eliakim, 609–598 B.C. (cf. **Jeremiah 36:12, 20–21; 41:1**).

9. This is not King Jehoram the son of Jehoshaphat (cf. **1 Kings 22:50; 1 Chronicles 3:11; 2 Chronicles 21:1**).

2 CHRONICLES 17: GENEALOGICAL RECORD OF THE MILITARY LEADERS DURING THE REIGN OF KING JEHOSHAPHAT OF JUDAH

Approximate Dating: ca. 872–848 B.C. ***Relevant Scriptures:*** **2 Chronicles 17:14–19**

Commanders of Units of 1,000 Fighting Men

From the tribe of Judah:

- **Adnah**[1] (chief) with 300,000
- **Jehohanan**[2] with 280,000
- **Amasiah** the volunteer, the son of Zikri,[3] with 200,000

From the tribe of Benjamin:

- **Eliada** (a valiant soldier) with 200,000
- **Jehozabad** with 180,000

Biblical and Theological Significance

Sadly, and as an effect of the wickedness of mankind, nations have had to raise, sustain, and make use of military troops either for defense or, tragically, to engage in wars of conquest. This was clearly true in the days of Jehoshaphat, king of Judah, who was surrounded by hostile nations. These adversaries included Israel to the north, led by King Ahab. Ahab befriended Jehoshaphat to persuade him to wage war against a mutual enemy (**2 Chronicles 18:1–3**), and together they attacked the Arameans at Ramoth Gilead, in the northeast region of the Transjordan, a misguided adventure that cost Ahab's life (**2 Chronicles 18:32–34**). Later, Jehoshaphat himself was invaded by Moab and Ammon, but God graciously granted him victory (**2 Chronicles 20:1–4, 20–28**). These were among the episodes that accounted for the need for a large military presence in Judah.

The question is, how large was that presence? Taking the figures at face value, it appears that Judah could field an army of 1,160,000 men! Such enormous numbers raise the suspicion that they are inflated. However, "thousand" (אֶלֶף, *eleph*) bears the meaning not only of a literal number, but it is also a technical term for a unit such as a regiment, company, and the like, of no particular size.[4] Therefore, it is most likely that one should read the data above as "Adnah, 300 units," "Jehonan, 280 units," and so forth. The grand total by this proposal is 1,160 units. Supposing a unit to be one hundred persons, for example, the army of Judah consisted of 116,000 men, a reasonable amount for those times and circumstances.[5]

Notes

1. This is not Adnah the military man from the tribe of Manasseh, who was a contemporary of King David (**1 Chronicles 12:20**).

2. Jehohanan in **2 Chronicles 17:15** is likely the same person as Jehohanan the father of Ishmael; Ishmael participated in the military coup to remove Queen Athaliah in 835 B.C. (**2 Chronicles 23:2**). Jehohanan in **2 Chronicles 17:15** is not: (1) Jehohanan the father of Azariah the Ephraimite, who was a contemporary of King Ahaz of Judah (ca. 731–715 B.C.) (**2 Chronicles 28:12**); (2) Jehohanan the Levitical gatekeeper (**1 Chronicles 26:3**); nor (3) the Jehohanan figures of **Ezra** and **Nehemiah** (cf. **Ezra 10:6, 28; Nehemiah 6:18; 12:13, 42**), who lived in the post-exile.

3. Zikri (**2 Chronicles 17:16**) does *not* correspond to the following persons: (1) Zikri the son of Asaph (Levitical Gershonite; **1 Chronicles 9:15**); (2) Zikri the descendant of Moses' son Eliezer (**1 Chronicles 26:25**); (3) Zikri the father of Eliezer (**1 Chronicles 27:16**); (4) Zikri the father of Elishaphat, a contemporary of Jehoiada the priest, ca. 835 B.C.; **2 Chronicles 23:1**); (5) Zikri the Ephraimite warrior in the days of King Ahaz, 731–715 B.C. (**2 Chronicles 28:7**); (6) Zikri the father of Joel, a post-exilic figure (**Nehemiah 11:9**); nor (7) Zikri the Kohathite attending priest, who was head of the Abijah division in the days of Joiakim the high priest, ca. 490–450/444 B.C. (**Nehemiah 12:17**).

4. BDB, 48–49.

5. An interesting and convincing confirmation of this hypothesis is found in the Bible itself. **First Kings 20:30** notes that "the wall [of Aphek] collapsed on twenty-seven thousand [Arameans]." This obviously must be understood as 27 units, perhaps as few as 270 individuals.

2 CHRONICLES 18: GENEALOGICAL RECORD OF THE PROPHETS AND SEERS DURING THE REIGNS OF KING AHAB OF ISRAEL AND KING JEHOSHAPHAT OF JUDAH

Approximate Dating: ca. 874–848 B.C., spanning the reigns of Ahab, 874–853 B.C. and Jehoshaphat, 872–848 B.C. ***Relevant Scriptures:*** **2 Chronicles 18:6–20:19**; also **1 Chronicles 6:16, 39–43; 9:15; 25:2; Nehemiah 11:17**

1. **Zedekiah** son of Kenaanah[1]
2. **Micaiah** son of Imlah[2]
3. **Jehu** son of Hanani[3]
4. **Jahaziel** son of Zechariah (a Levite)

Lineage of Jahaziel:

Levi
|
Gershon[4]
(Gershonites)

Biblical and Theological Significance

Jahaziel, who delivered a prophetic message to King Jehoshaphat and the people of Judah (**2 Chronicles 20:14–19**), was a Levitical Gershonite and a descendant of Asaph (one of the three chief musicians in Solomon's Temple; cf. **1 Chronicles 15:16–19; 25:1, 6; 2 Chronicles 20:14**). When a vast army of Ammonites, Moabites, and Edomites came up to invade Judah, Jehoshaphat responded by proclaiming a fast throughout Judah and calling on the Lord for help. Though Jahaziel was a Levite, he also acted as a prophet[7] filled with the Spirit of the Lord. He delivered an oracle to the assembly of Judah: "Do not be afraid; do not be discouraged. Go out to face them tomorrow, and the LORD will be with you" (**2 Chronicles 20:17b**). The combined forces of Ammon, Moab, and Mount Seir were defeated by the Lord (**2 Chronicles 20:22**).

Notes

1. Zedekiah son of Kenaanah was among the prophets in Israel at this time (cf. **1 Kings 22:10–13, 24; 2 Chronicles 18:9–12, 24**). This suggests that there were guilds of prophets with certain prophets as heads. This is not Kenaanah son of Bilhan, a Benjamite (cf. **1 Chronicles 7:10**).
2. Micaiah son of Imlah was the true prophet of the Lord in Judah (cf. **1 Kings 22:8–9; 2 Chronicles 18:7–8**). See chart "**1 Kings 22**: Micaiah the Prophet."
3. Jehu son of Hanani was a prophet-seer in Jerusalem (**1 Kings 16:1, 7; 2 Chronicles 19:2; 20:34**).
4. For the complete lineage of the Gershonites, see chart "**1 Chronicles 6**: Levi: High Priests, Priests, Levites, and Musicians in Solomon's Temple."
5. Zikri (**1 Chronicles 9:15**) is also called Zabdi (**Nehemiah 11:17**) or Zakkur (**1 Chronicles 25:2; Nehemiah 12:35; 13:13**).
6. Mika (**1 Chronicles 9:15; Nehemiah 11:17, 22**) is also called Micaiah (**Nehemiah 12:35**).
7. Unlike the monarchy, which was hereditary, and the priesthood, which was both hereditary and limited to those in the tribe of Levi, prophetism was charismatic. Prophets, in essence, were called individually by God and without regard to social status or family connections. In earlier times, however, there were organizations of the prophets. Under the prophet-priest Samuel (ca. 1110–1015 B.C.), they were called "a procession of the prophets" or "a group of the prophets" (**1 Samuel 10:5–12; 19:18–24**). More than two centuries later (874 B.C.), Elijah, and then Elisha, led a school of prophets known as the "company of the prophets" (**2 Kings 2:3–15; 5:22; 6:1**). This collegial arrangement did not last long; in fact, none of the so-called canonical prophets (Hosea through Malachi) is said to have been part of a prophetic organization.

2 CHRONICLES 22: PROBABLE GENEALOGY FOR JEHOIADA THE PRIEST WHO MASTERMINDED THE OVERTHROW OF QUEEN ATHALIAH OF JUDAH[1]

Approximate Dating: overthrow of Athaliah in ca. 835 B.C.; Jehoiada lived to be 130 years old, ca. 926–796 B.C.[2] ***Relevant Scriptures:*** **2 Chronicles 22:10–24:25**; also **2 Kings 11:1–21; 1 Chronicles 6:33–39; 9:16; 15:17; 2 Chronicles 21:3; Matthew 23:35**

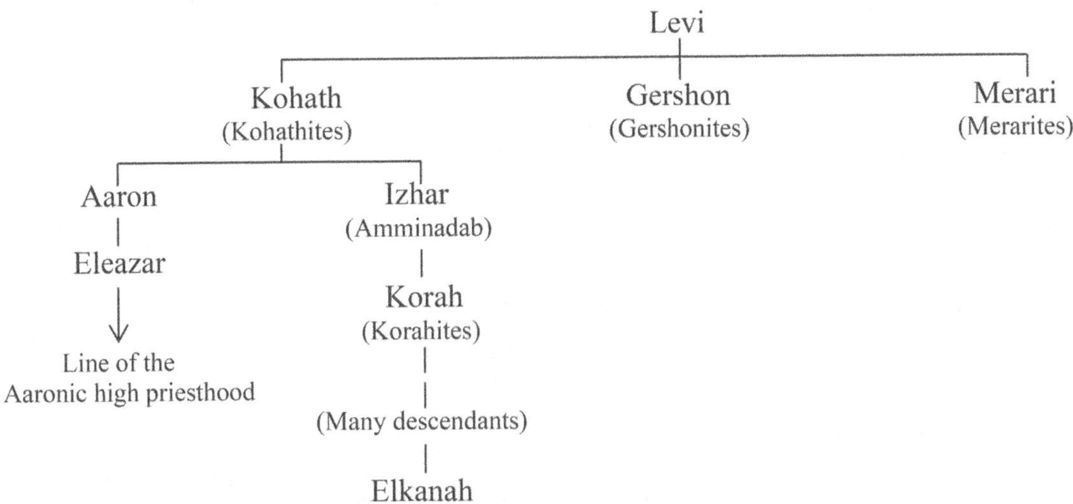

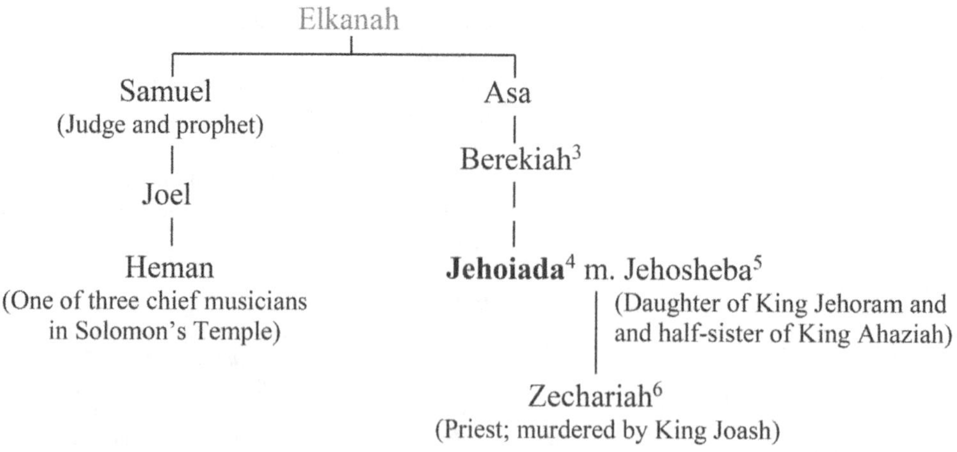

Biblical and Theological Significance

The lineage of Jehoiada is not specifically addressed in Scripture. The chart is based on the assumption that his son—"Zechariah son of Jehoiada the priest" (**2 Chronicles 24:20**)—is the *same* Zechariah who is described as the last martyr of the Old Testament: "Zechariah son [descendant] of Berekiah" (**Matthew 23:35**; cf. **Luke 11:51**). Jehoiada is typically identified as "Jehoiada the priest" (**2 Kings 11:9, 15, 18; 12:9; 1 Chronicles 27:5(?);**[7] **2 Chronicles 22:11; 23:8, 14; 24:2, 20, 25**). In **2 Chronicles 24:6**, he is atypically referred to as "Jehoiada the chief priest."[8] Jehoiada's appellation "the priest," rather than the more generic "the Levite," is consistent with the genealogy for Jehoiada shown in the chart, which identifies him as a *Kohathite* attending priest. Therefore, Jehoiada was NOT:

1. A high priest (a "chief priest"), since his name is not found in the lists of high priests, all of which have well known and clear established lineages,[9] nor is he
2. A Levitical Gershonite (i.e., in the Levi–Gershon–Shimea–Berekiah line), whose members had more of a Levitical function, rather than a priestly function (i.e., *assisting* the high priests and the Kohathite *attending* priests in their duties).

Specifically, Jehoiada was a leading Kohathite–Korahite attending priest and a descendant in the Levi–Kohath–Korah–Berekiah–Jehoiada–Zechariah line. Jehoiada was clearly the *leading* priest at the time (**2 Kings 11:4–12; 2 Chronicles 23:1–16**)—perhaps the "captain of the temple"[10]—when the high priest Meraioth #18 (or possibly Meraioth's predecessors, Azariah #15, Amariah #16 and/or Ahitub #17) seems to have been acting in a figurehead capacity only.[11] Jehoiada was married to Jehosheba, the daughter of King Jehoram of Judah.[12] Jehoiada was the leader-organizer of the temple priesthood during the reign of Queen Athaliah (841–835 B.C.) and most of the reign of King Joash (835–796 B.C.).

When her son Ahaziah died after only one year in office (ca. 841 B.C.), Queen Athaliah assumed the throne of Judah and immediately began killing *all* potential heirs, in an effort to retain the monarchy for herself. This meant that the *rightful* heir, Ahaziah's son—the one-year-old infant, Joash—was at great risk of being murdered. Jehoiada and his wife, Jehosheba, successfully protected Joash by hiding him and his nurse in the bedroom chambers of Solomon's Temple during the six-year malevolent reign of Athaliah over Judah. When Joash reached the age of seven, Jehoiada "showed his strength" (**2 Chronicles 23:1**) and masterminded an elaborate military coup to depose Athaliah by mobilizing the captains of hundreds and gathering Levites and elders from the cities of Judah. Athaliah was killed and Joash was crowned as the rightful heir to the Davidic throne (**2 Kings 11:4–16; 2 Chronicles 22:10–23:15**).

Due to Jehoiada's positive influence, Joash "did what was right in the eyes of the LORD all the years of Jehoiada the priest" (**2 Chronicles 24:2**). When Jehoiada died in 796 B.C. (see note 2), the people of Judah acknowledged his great faithfulness for being God's servant-priest at Solomon's Temple and gave him a royal burial "with the kings in the City of David" (**2 Chronicles 24:15–16**). Tragically, however, after Jehoiada's death, Joash fell into apostasy and Baal worship, refusing to listen to the Lord's prophets and following the ill-advised counsel of leaders in Judah. Joash ordered the death of Jehoiada's son, Zechariah the priest, who said as he lay dying, "May the LORD see this and call you [Joash] to account" (**2 Chronicles 24:21–22**). Jesus describes Zechariah (the son of Jehoiada, the son of Berekiah) as the last martyr of the Old Testament (cf. **Matthew 23:35; Luke 11:51**).

Court officials eventually killed King Joash for murdering Zechariah. Ironically though, when Joash died, he was "buried in the City of David, but not in the tombs of the kings" (**2 Chronicles 24:25**).

Notes

1. The larger narrative describing the overthrow of Queen Athaliah of Judah (ca. 841–835 B.C.) is recounted in parallel accounts in **2 Kings 11** and **2 Chronicles 22:10–23:21**.

2. Jehoiada died "old and full of years" at age 130 in 796 B.C. (**2 Chronicles 24:15–16**). Jehoiada and Zechariah (Jehoiada's son) died shortly before King Joash, who also died in 796 B.C. (**2 Chronicles 24:23, 25**).

3. For the lineage of Berekiah, see **1 Chronicles 9:16**. Berekiah is mentioned in **1 Chronicles 6:39; 15:17** and possibly **1 Chronicles 15:23**. See Berekiah the Kohathite in chart "**1 Chronicles 6**: Levi: High Priests, Priests, Levites, and Musicians in Solomon's Temple."

4. Jehoiada the Kohathite priest (ca. 926–796 B.C.), who was involved in the dethronement of Athaliah, should not be confused with (1) Jehoiada the Judahite, the *father* of Benaiah of Kabzeel, a mighty warrior under King David in ca. 1011 B.C. (cf. **2 Samuel 8:18; 20:23; 23:20, 22; 1 Kings 1:8, 26, 32, 36, 38, 44; 2:25, 29, 34–35, 46; 4:4; 1 Chronicles 11:22, 24; 18:17; 27:5**); (2) Jehoiada the Judahite, the *son* of Benaiah who replaced Ahithophel,

David's court counselor, after Ahithophel committed suicide (**1 Chronicles 27:34**); nor (3) Jehoiada in **Jeremiah 29:26**, a contemporary of Jeremiah the prophet (627–586 B.C.). Jehoiada #1 and #2 are shown in chart "**2 Samuel 8 & 20**: The Chief Officials in King David's Administration."

5. See chart "**2 Kings 11**: Jehosheba, the Wife of Jehoiada the Priest."

6. Several chronological considerations are necessary to determine whether Zechariah the son of Jehoiada is the same person as the Zechariah figure mentioned in **2 Chronicles 26:5**, who provided tutelage to the young king: Azariah/Uzziah "sought God during the days of Zechariah, who instructed him in the fear of God. As long as he sought the Lord, God gave him success." Since Azariah/Uzziah became king at the age of sixteen, then served as co-regent with his father Amaziah from 792–767 B.C., and later held an official 52-year reign from 792–740 B.C., this means that Azariah/Uzziah was born in 808 B.C. and that he was a young man in training from 808–792 B.C. *before* he assumed the throne in 792 B.C. The text of **2 Chronicles 24:15–25** suggests that Zechariah (Jehoiada's son) died in the window of time shortly *after* his father Jehoiada died (in 796 B.C.) and yet *before* King Joash died that same year. The chronology permits the interpretation that Zechariah the priest (the son of Jehoiada) was the same person as the Zechariah in **2 Chronicles 26:5** who provided instruction to Azariah/Uzziah *if* it is referring to the years of 808–792 B.C. (i.e., from the time Azariah/Uzziah was born to the time he was approximately age twelve), but *not* if it refers to Azariah/Uzziah as the *king*, for Zechariah (son of Jehoiada) died in 796 B.C., and Azariah/Uzziah did not come to the throne until 792 B.C. (i.e., four years *after* Zechariah died). In the latter case, the Zechariah of **2 Chronicles 26:5** would be a different person than Zechariah the son of Jehoiada (cf. **2 Chronicles 24:20, 22**). For Azariah/Uzziah, see chart "**2 Kings 15**: Azariah (Uzziah), King of Judah."

Also, Zechariah son of Jehoiada should not be confused with the prophet Zechariah, who encouraged those who rebuilt the Second Temple from 520–516 B.C.; see chart "**Zechariah 1**: Zechariah, the Prophet of God to the Restored Community in Jerusalem (Post-Exile)."

7. The passage in **1 Chronicles 27:5a** reads "The third army commander, for the third month, was Benaiah son of Jehoiada the priest" and may refer to the same person as Jehoiada in **1 Chronicles 12:26–27**, who was the leader of the family of Aaron and among the "men armed for battle" (**1 Chronicles 12:23**) who came to David at Hebron to turn Saul's kingdom over to him (David)—the chronology permits this interpretation. Some scholars have concluded that Jehoiada "the priest" in **1 Chronicles 27:5** is a probable gloss. For a discussion, see Edward L. Curtis and Albert A. Madsen, *A Critical and Exegetical Commentary on the Books of Chronicles* (Edinburgh: T&T Clark, 1920), 290.

8. Though the usual term *rosh* is used here, it can and does occasionally lose its technical meaning, "chief," to mean only "leader," "overseer," or the like.

9. See charts "**1 Chronicles 6**: Levi: High Priests, Priests, Levites, and Musicians in Solomon's Temple" and "**Supplement 2**: The High Priests of Israel."

10. For the hierarchy of the priesthood (the chief priests and chief Levites), including the captain of the temple who was "the highest ranking priest after the high priest," see Joachim Jeremias, *Jerusalem in the Time of Jesus* (Philadelphia: Fortress, 1969), 160–163.

11. See Meraioth #18 and his predecessors in chart "**Supplement 2**: The High Priests of Israel."

12. For Jehoiada, see chart "**2 Chronicles 22:** Probable Genealogy for Jehoiada the Priest who Masterminded the Overthrow of Queen Athaliah of Judah"; for Jehoram, see chart "**2 Kings 8**: Jehoram, King of Judah."

2 CHRONICLES 23: GENEALOGICAL RECORD OF THE JUDAHITE OFFICERS WHO ASSISTED JEHOIADA THE PRIEST IN THE OVERTHROW OF QUEEN ATHALIAH[1]

Approximate Dating: 835 B.C. ***Relevant Scriptures:*** **2 Chronicles 23:1–2**

1. **Azariah** son of Jeroham[2]
2. **Ishmael** son of Jehohanan[3]
3. **Azariah** son of Obed[4]
4. **Maaseiah** son of Adaiah[5]
5. **Elishaphat** son of Zikri[6]

Biblical and Theological Significance

The illicit reign of Queen Athaliah was a nadir in the history of Israel. She was a daughter of Ahab and Jezebel[7] of Israel and thus was reared in an environment of full-blown polytheistic idolatry. Ahab had formed an alliance with the good King Jehoshaphat of Judah against a number of hostile nations that threatened both Israel and Judah (**1 Kings 20:1–41; 22:1–43; 2 Chronicles 18:1–34**). Under great pressure, Ahab enticed Jehoshaphat into making a treaty with him, which led to the marriage of Athaliah to Jehoram, Jehoshaphat's son (**2 Kings 8:16–19; 2 Chronicles 21:4–7**). When Jehoram died, his son Ahaziah succeeded him, but his reign was cut short at the hands of Jehu of Israel (**2 Kings 9:23–29; 2 Chronicles 22:7–9**). Athaliah then seized power and killed the remaining heirs to the throne except Ahaziah's son, the one-year-old infant, Joash; Athaliah's actions showed that her real allegiance was to the house of her Israelite father and mother (Ahab and Jezebel). She sought to slay the infant Joash, which would have left Judah with no scion of David[8] and would have opened the door for Jehu of Israel. The young Joash was spirited away by the godly priest Jehoiada and his wife Jehosheba and hidden in the temple for six years (**2 Kings 11:1–3; 2 Chronicles 22:10–12**).

Then, "in the seventh year Jehoiada showed his strength"[9] (**2 Chronicles 23:1**). He made a covenant with the military commanders,[10] the Carites (the king's bodyguards), and the temple guards to remove Athaliah and crown the seven-year-old Joash as the rightful heir to the Davidic throne. All divisions participated—"those who were going on duty on the Sabbath and those who were going off duty"—and guards were stationed around the temple (**2 Kings 11:9–11; 2 Chronicles 23:8–10**). Jehoiada and his sons crowned Joash at the pillar to the entrance of the temple. When Athaliah heard the rejoicing "she tore her robes and shouted, 'Treason! Treason!' " (**2 Chronicles 23:13; see also 2 Kings 11:14**). Jehoiada then ordered the commanders and their men to bring Athaliah out from the temple, and she was put to death at the Horse Gate on the palace grounds (**2 Kings 11:15–16; 2 Chronicles 23:14–15**). The enthronement of Joash then commenced under the direction of Jehoiada (**2 Kings 11:17–19**; cf. **2 Chronicles 23:20–21**).

Notes

1. The larger narratives are found in **2 Kings 11:4–21** and **2 Chronicles 23:1–21**.

2. Azariah son of Jeroham, who lived in ca. 835 B.C., is not one of the three Azariah figures who were high priests (cf. **1 Chronicles 6:9–14;**

9:11); see Azariah #13, #15, and #22 in chart "**Supplement 2**: The High Priests of Israel."

3. Jehohanan (Ishmael's father) was one of the commanders during the reign of Jehoshaphat (872–848 B.C.), who led 280,000 fighting men of Judah (**2 Chronicles 17:15**).

4. Obed (Azariah's father) is conceivably the same person as Obed son of Shemaiah, son of Obed-Edom. Obed-Edom had served as the chief over the Levitical gatekeepers (Merarites) in Solomon's Temple and the overseer of the ark of the covenant in the days of King David, 1011–971 B.C. (**1 Chronicles 16:37–38; 26:6–8**).

5. For chronological reasons, this is not (1) Maaseiah the Levitical musician in the time of King David, ca. 1004 B.C. (**1 Chronicles 15:18**); (2) Maaseiah, a contemporary of King Uzziah/Azariah, 792–740 B.C. (**2 Chronicles 26:11**); (3) Maaseiah the son of King Ahab of Israel, 874–853 B.C., who was killed (**2 Chronicles 28:7**); (4) Maaseiah, the ruler of Jerusalem during the reign of King Josiah, 640–609 B.C. (**2 Chronicles 34:8**); (5) Maaseiah the brother/relative of Joshua the high priest in the Second Temple, ca. 516–490 B.C. (**Ezra 10:18**); (6) Maaseiah figures who were near-contemporaries of the prophet Jeremiah, ca. 627–586 B.C. (cf. **Jeremiah 21:1; 29:21, 25; 35:4; 37:3**); nor (7) post-exilic figures named Maaseiah (cf. **Ezra 10:21–22; Nehemiah 3:23; 8:4, 7; 10:25; 11:5, 7; 12:41–42**).

Adaiah (Maasieh's father) is not (1) Adaiah the Gershonite (**1 Chronicles 6:41**) nor (2) post-exilic figures named Adaiah (cf. **1 Chronicles 8:21; Ezra 10:29, 39; Nehemiah 11:5, 12**).

6. Elishaphat was probably the brother of Amasiah (the son of Zikri) and the commander over 200,000 soldiers in the days of King Jehoshaphat, 872–848 B.C. (cf. **2 Chronicles 17:16**).

7. See chart "**1 Kings 16**: Ahab, King of Israel."

8. Joash was historically in the direct lineage of David and proleptically in the line of Jesus the Messiah. Joash's death—without the actions of the godly priest Jehoiada who saved him—would have left no other viable linkage in the chain of redemption and would have jeopardized the ancient Abrahamic covenant promise (**2 Chronicles 23:3, 11, 16**; see also **2 Kings 11:12**).

9. The leadership of Jehoiada the Kohathite priest, in what seems to have been a secular military initiative, may strike some readers as strange, but in a theocratic society such as ancient Israel, priests could be and were involved even in military headship (see **Numbers 25:6–13; 31:6, 21, 26; 34:13–29; Joshua 19:51**). This was especially the case in so-called holy war (**Joshua 3:1–17**). Also see chart "**2 Chronicles 22**: Probable Genealogy for Jehoiada the Priest who Masterminded the Overthrow of Queen Athaliah of Judah."

10. The commanders were over units of a hundred men (**2 Kings 11:4; 2 Chronicles 23:1**).

2 CHRONICLES 24: THE SERVANTS WHO MURDERED KING JOASH OF JUDAH

Approximate Dating: ca. 796 B.C. ***Relevant Scriptures:*** **2 Chronicles 24:25–26**; also **2 Kings 12:20–21**

1. **Zabad**
2. **Jehozabad**

Genealogy of Zabad

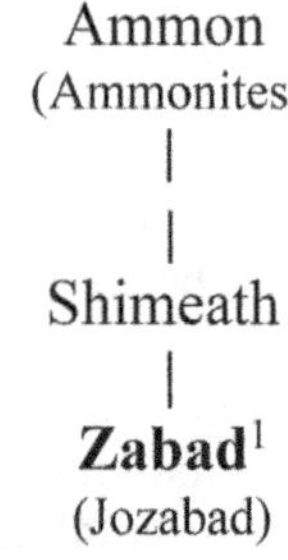

Genealogy of Jehozabad

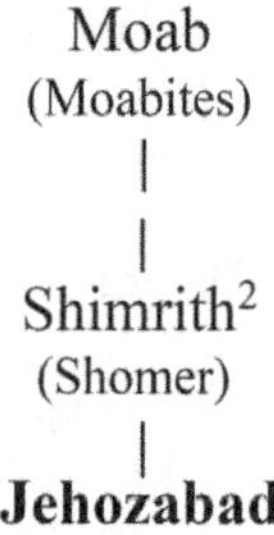

Biblical and Theological Significance

The thirty-nine-year reign of Joash (ca. 835–796 B.C.) was wracked with political oppression and spiritual apostasy. The alliance between Ahab and Jehoshaphat had introduced the evil of Israel into the Southern Kingdom with the marriage of Athaliah (the daughter of King Ahab of Israel) to King Jehoram of Judah. Upon the death of their son Ahaziah, Athaliah's partisanship for her homeland (Israel) resulted in her authorized slaughter of all potential heirs to Judah's throne, including her own children. The only surviving heir was Ahaziah's infant son, Joash, who was snatched away by Jehoiada the Kohathite priest and his wife Jehosheba, and then hidden in the temple for the next six years while Athaliah ruled the land (**2 Kings 11:2–3; 2 Chronicles 22:12**). Eventually, however, Athaliah was killed, and the seven-year-old Joash was crowned the legitimate king of Judah (**2 Kings 11:19–21; 2 Chronicles 23:20–21**). King Joash is noted as a good king in his early years—he "did what was right in the eyes of the Lord all the years Jehoiada the priest instructed him" (**2 Kings 12:2**), even accomplishing the repair of Solomon's Temple (**2 Kings 12:1–16; 2 Chronicles 24:4–14**). However, after Jehoiada's death, Joash "abandoned the temple of the Lord, the God of their ancestors, and worshiped Asherah poles and idols" (**2 Chronicles 24:18**). When Zechariah (Jehoiada's son) confronted Joash about the apostasy and his gross disobedience of the Lord's commands, Joash did not like what he heard (**2 Chronicles 24:20–22**). Soon thereafter, Arameans came against Judah and, in the battle, King Joash was severely wounded (**2 Chronicles 24:23–25**). At that point "his officials conspired against him [Joash] for murdering the son of Jehoiada the priest [Zechariah] and they killed him in his bed" (**2 Chronicles 24:25**). The two officials who assassinated King Joash of Judah were Zabad the Ammonite and Jehozabad the Moabite (**2 Kings 12:20–21; 2 Chronicles 24:25–26**)—the **2 Kings** passage says they "assassinated him [Joash] at Beth Millo, on the road down to Silla" whereas the **2 Chronicles** passage says that they killed Joash "in his bed."

Notice that the genealogies of Zabad (Jozabad) and Jehozabad are rare instances in Scripture of denoting *matrilineal* descent. In both cases, they acted as *righteous foreigners* who carried out the Lord's judgment on a wicked king.

Notes

1. Zabad (**2 Chronicles 24:26**) is otherwise and fully written Jozabad (**2 Kings 12:21**). His mother, Shimeath, was an Ammonite woman (**2 Chronicles 24:26**).
2. Jehozabad's mother, Shimrith (**2 Chronicles 24:26**), is also called Shomer (**2 Kings 12:21**).

2 CHRONICLES 28: GENEALOGICAL RECORD OF THE LEADERS OF ISRAEL WHO ADVISED THAT PRISONERS OF WAR FROM JUDAH AND JERUSALEM BE RETURNED

Approximate Dating: ca. 731–715 B.C. ***Relevant Scriptures:*** **2 Chronicles 28:12–13**

1. **Azariah** son of Jehohanan[1]
2. **Berekiah** son of Meshillemoth[2]
3. **Jehizkiah** son of Shallum[3]
4. **Amasa** son of Hadlai

Biblical and Theological Significance

During his reign over Judah (731–715 B.C.), King Ahaz[4] of Judah did not follow the Lord but rather "followed the ways of the kings of Israel" (**2 Chronicles 28:2**). He embraced Baal worship, sacrificed his own children "in the fire"[5] and "offered sacrifices and burned incense at the high places, on the hilltops and under every spreading tree"[6] (**2 Chronicles 28:1–4**). For his overt apostasy, the Lord allowed Ahaz to be defeated by King Rezin of Aram and King Pekah of Israel, resulting in the death of many Judean troops, including Ahaz's son Maaseiah (**2 Chronicles 28:5–7**). The Israelites took captive two hundred thousand[7] civilians (including wives, sons, and daughters) and spoils of war from Judah and then brought them to Samaria with the intention of making them slaves. The prophet Oded (of unknown genealogy) and four Israelite leaders (listed above) spoke up and advised the Israelite military not to keep the Judeans captive in Samaria but to return them to Judah, and the Israelites heeded their advice (cf. **2 Chronicles 28:8–15**). Oded and the leaders reasoned that if fellow descendants of Abraham and Jacob were to imprison one another, Yahweh would vent his anger against Israel (**2 Chronicles 28:12–13**). Their message was so convincing and powerfully convicting that the leaders of Israel not only released the Judean prisoners, but also returned to them what had been plundered and more (**2 Chronicles 28:14–15**), a sign of true repentance.

Notes

1. For chronological reasons, this is not: (1) Jehohanan the gatekeeper who served during Solomon's reign, 971–931 B.C. (**1 Chronicles 26:3**); (2) Jehohanan the military commander in the days of King Jehoshaphat, 872–848 B.C. (**2 Chronicles 17:15**); (3) Jehohanan the father of Ishmael, a near-contemporary of Jehoiada the priest, ca. 835 B.C. (**2 Chronicles 23:1**); (4) the high priest named Jehohanan (also known as Jonathan and Johanan), who was the grandson of Eliashib, the son of Joiakim (**Ezra 10:6**); nor (5) post-exilic figures named Jehohanan (cf. **Ezra 10:28; Nehemiah 6:18; 12:13, 42**).
2. Berekiah son of Meshillemoth is not: (1) Berekiah son of Zerubbabel (**1 Chronicles 3:20**); (2) Berekiah father of Asaph the musician (**1 Chronicles 6:39; 15:17, 23**?); (3) Berekiah son/descendant of Asa, son of Elkanah (**1 Chronicles 9:16; Matthew 23:35** (?); (4) Berekiah son of Iddo (**Zechariah 1:1, 7**); nor (5) post-exilic figures named Berekiah (cf. **Nehemiah 3:4, 30**). Meshillemoth (father of Berekiah) is possibly the same person as the Kohathite attending priest named Meshillemoth/Meshillemith son of Immer (cf. **1 Chronicles 9:12; Nehemiah 11:13**).
3. This is probably not Shallum/Meshullam son of Zadok, who served in Solomon's Temple, ca. 690–640 B.C.
4. Ahaz was co-regent, and the dominant regent, with his father Jotham, 735–731 B.C. Ahaz's official reign of sixteen years was from 731–715 B.C. In turn, Ahaz's son Hezekiah was co-regent with his father from 729–715 B.C. See chart "**2 Kings 15**: Ahaz, King of Judah."
5. This is a reference to the sacrifice of infants, an unspeakably cruel and gruesome practice especially associated with the deity Molek (Molech), the patron god of the Ammonites (**Leviticus 18:21; 20:2–5; 1 Kings 11:5, 7, 33; 2 Kings 23:10, 13; Jeremiah 32:35**).
6. These are allusions to fertility deities such as Baal and his consort Asherah who, by their copulation, were thought to be responsible for plant and animal life.
7. As suggested elsewhere (see commentary of "**2 Chronicles 17**: Genealogical Record of the Military Leaders During the Reign of King Jehoshaphat of Judah), it is best to take these figures in light of the context, with "thousands" (*elaphim*) as ciphers for something more realistic, such as "200 population groups."

2 CHRONICLES 29: THE KOHATHITE PRIESTS, LEVITES, AND SINGERS WHO CLEANSED THE TEMPLE DURING THE REIGN OF KING HEZEKIAH OF JUDAH

Approximate Dating: in 715 B.C., the first year of his 29-year reign, 715–686 B.C. ***Relevant Scriptures:*** **2 Chronicles 29:12–14;** also **Exodus 6:20–25; Leviticus 10:4; Numbers 3:19, 30; 16:1; 2 Kings 18:18, 26, 37; 19:2; 1 Chronicles 6:1–53; 9:11; 15:16–24; 23:7–23; 24:2, 20–30; 25:1–5; 2 Chronicles 31:12–15; Nehemiah 11:10–18; Isaiah 22:20; 36:3, 11, 22; 37:2**

1. **Mahath**, son of Amasai (Kohathite) (exact genealogy unknown)[1]
2. **Joel**, son of Azariah (Kohathite) (exact genealogy unknown)[2]
3. **Kish**, son of Abdi (Merarite)
4. **Azariah**, son of Jehallelel (Merarite)
5. **Joah**, son of Zimmah (Gershonite)
6. **Eden**, son of Joah (Gershonite)
7. **Shimri** and **Jeiel**, descendants of Elzaphan/Elizaphan (Kohathites)
8. **Zechariah** and **Mattaniah**, descendants of Asaph the musician (Gershonites)
9. **Jehiel** and **Shimei**, descendants of Heman the musician (Kohathites)
10. **Shemaiah** and **Uzziel**, descendants of Ethan/Jeduthun the musician (Merarites)

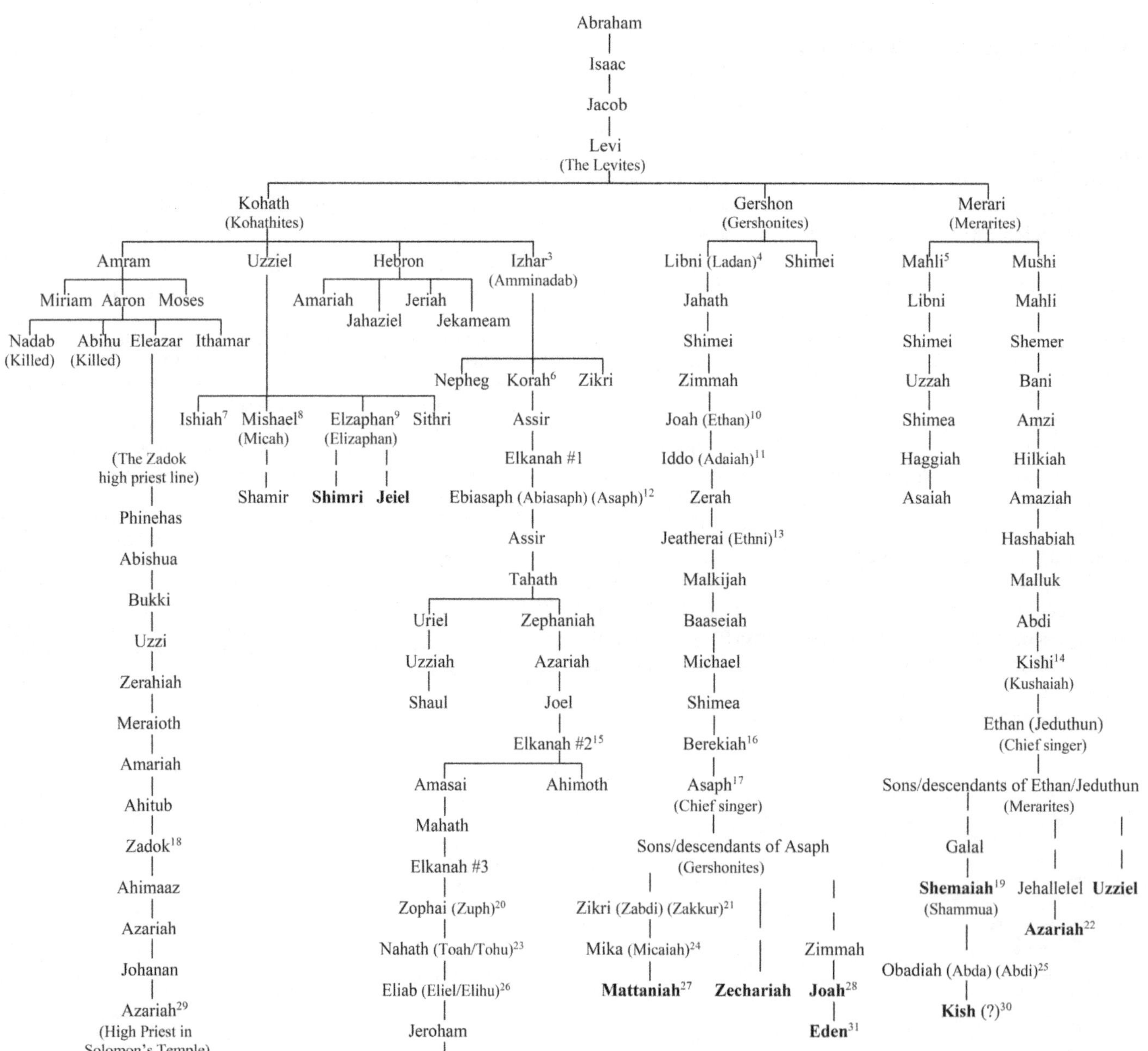

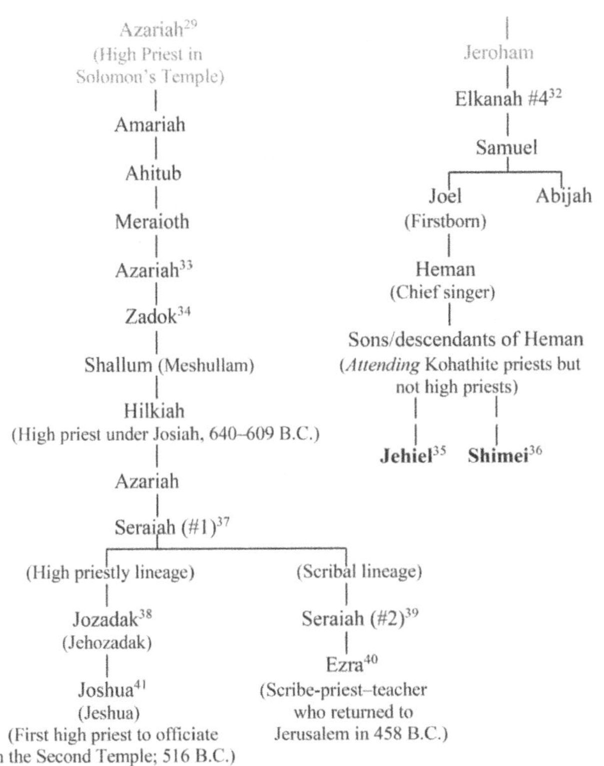

Biblical and Theological Significance

Hezekiah is reckoned as one of the most devout, powerful, and capable of all the kings of Judah—a kind of second Solomon[42]—and accountable to Yahweh, the God of Israel, for the conduct of his administration. There were secular elements even in a theocracy,[43] but the real leadership was in the hands of the king and the clergy. Upon his accession to the throne, Hezekiah directed the priests and Levites[44] to consecrate[45] themselves so that they would be spiritually qualified to re-consecrate the temple itself. Almost as a prophet, the king rehearsed the godless behavior of their fathers who had allowed the temple to become little more than a community center, totally devoid of genuine worship of the Holy One (**2 Chronicles 29:5–9**). His commission (and theirs) was to make amends by (1) renewing the covenant that had made them "a kingdom of priests and a holy nation" at Sinai almost 750 years earlier (**Exodus 19:4–6**) and (2) rehabilitating the temple and resuming its services as of old (**2 Chronicles 29:10–11**). None of this could have been accomplished without the assistance of the priesthood (priests and Levites).[46] They accomplished these tasks with alacrity and faithfulness to the satisfaction of the king, all in sixteen days (**2 Chronicles 29:17**)! Then followed a massive service of covenant reaffirmation, sacrifice, and songs of praise and worship (**2 Chronicles 29:18–36**). A few days later, Hezekiah proclaimed to the nation—Israel to the north included[47]—a celebration of Passover and a Feast of Unleavened Bread with great rejoicing, unlike any that had ever been done before (**2 Chronicles 30:1–27**). The Chronicler thus summarizes Hezekiah's accomplishments: "He did what was right in the eyes of the Lord, just as his father [ancestor] David had done" (**2 Kings 18:3; 2 Chronicles 29:2**).[48]

Notes

1. Mahath son of Amasai lived in the days of Hezekiah, 715–686 B.C.; his exact genealogy is unknown. For chronological reasons, he is not the same person as Mahath (a Kohathite–Korahite) who lived much earlier (i.e., Mahath in the Levi–Kohath–Izhar–Korah–Ebiasaph/Abiasaph/Asaph–Elkanah #2–Amasai–Mahath—Elkanah #3 line, shown in the chart), although he may be a *descendant* in this line.

2. Joel son of Azariah lived in the days of Hezekiah, 715–686 B.C.; his exact genealogy is unknown. For chronological reasons he is not the same person as Joel who lived much earlier (i.e., Joel in the Levi–Kohath–Izhar–Korah–Ebiasaph/Abiasaph/Asaph–Zephaniah–Azariah–Joel–Elkanah #2 line, shown in the chart), although he may be a *descendant* in this line.

3. Izhar in **Exodus 6:18, 21; Numbers 3:19; 16:1; 1 Chronicles 6:2, 18, 38; 23:12, 18** is Amminadab in **1 Chronicles 6:22**.

4. Libni in **Exodus 6:17; Numbers 3:18; 1 Chronicles 6:17, 20** is called Ladan in **1 Chronicles 23:7–9; 26:21**.

5. The Mahli–Libni–Shimei–Uzzah–Shimea–Haggiah–Asaiah lineage is given in **1 Chronicles 6:29–30**. Other sons of Mahli are Eleazar and Kish (**1 Chronicles 23:21**). Eleazar "died without having sons: he had only daughters. Their cousins, the sons of Kish, married them" (**1 Chronicles 23:22**; cf. **24:28**).

6. Korah led the Korah rebellion against Moses and Aaron when Israel was encamped in the wilderness. Korah was killed for his insubordination (cf. **Numbers 16**; see chart "**Numbers 16**: Korah and the Descendants of Reuben who Died in the Korah-Reubenite Rebellion." The sons of Korah are listed as Assir, Elkanah, and Abiasaph in **Exodus 6:24**, but in the list of Levitical servants in **1 Chronicles 6:22–24**, the sons and descendants of Kohath and Korah are: "the sons of Kohath: Amminadab his son [the same person as Izhar; **1 Chronicles 6:2**], Korah his son, Assir his son, Elkanah [#1] his son, Ebiasaph his son [the same person as Abiasaph in **Exodus 6:24** and Asaph in **1 Chronicles 26:1**], Assir his son, Tahath his son, Uriel his son, Uzziah his son, and Shaul his son," showing that Assir, Elkanah #2, and Abiasaph/Ebiasaph/Asaph in **Exodus 6:24** were actually "sons of sons."

7. Ishiah had a descendant named Zechariah (**1 Chronicles 24:25**).

8. Mishael in **Exodus 6:22** and **Leviticus 10:4** is called Micah in **1 Chronicles 24:24**.

9. Elzaphan in **Exodus 6:22** and **Leviticus 10:4** is called Elizaphan in **Numbers 3:30; 1 Chronicles 15:8;** and **2 Chronicles 29:13**.

10. Joah in **1 Chronicles 6:21** is called Ethan in **1 Chronicles 6:42**.

11. Iddo in **1 Chronicles 6:21** is called Adaiah in **1 Chronicles 6:41**.

12. Ebiasaph (**1 Chronicles 6:23, 37; 9:19**) is Abiasaph (**Exodus 6:24**) and Asaph (**1 Chronicles 26:1**). **First Chronicles 6:22–23** clarifies that he was a *descendant* of Korah rather than a *son* (**Exodus 6:24; 1 Chronicles 6:37**). For descendants in the Korah–Ebiasaph/Abiasaph/Asaph–Kore line who served as gatekeepers, see the charts: "**1 Chronicles 9**: Registry and Genealogy of the Levitical Gatekeepers and the Priestly Overseer of the Grain Offerings at the Second Temple (Post-Exile)" and "**1 Chronicles 26**: The Kohathite–Korahite and Merarite Gatekeepers in Solomon's Temple."

13. Jeatherai in **1 Chronicles 6:21** is called Ethni in **1 Chronicles 6:41**.

14. Kishi in **1 Chronicles 6:44** is called Kushaiah in **1 Chronicles 15:17**.

15. Elkanah #2 corresponds to the Elkanah figure in **1 Chronicles 6:25, 35**. The lineage shown in the chart for Joel–Elkanah #2–Amasai–Mahath–Elkanah#3–Zuph/Zophai is according to the father-son relationships given in **1 Chronicles 6:35–36**.

16. Berekiah is mentioned in **1 Chronicles 6:39; 9:16; 15:17**. The Berekiah figure in **Matthew 23:35**—"Zechariah son [descendant] of Berekiah"—may refer to him (i.e., Berekiah the Gershonite, who is shown in the chart); if so, this means that Jehoiada the Kohathite priest (the father of Zechariah)—who led the coup against Queen Athaliah (**2 Kings 11**)—was probably the *son* of Berekiah and the *brother* of Asaph; see chart "**2 Chronicles 22**: Probable Genealogy for Jehoiada the Priest who Masterminded the Overthrow of Queen Athaliah of Judah."

17. The lineage of Asaph is given in **1 Chronicles 6:39–43**. See references to Asaph, the chief Levitical musician in Solomon's Temple in **1 Chronicles 6:39; 15:17, 19; 16:5, 37** and to Asaph's sons in **1 Chronicles 25:1**.

18. Zadok served under King David and King Solomon; he corresponds to Zadok #11 in chart "**Supplement 2**: The High Priests of Israel." He was a descendant of the Aaron–Eleazar line, and the Zadok high priesthood is named after him.

19. Shemaiah in **1 Chronicles 9:16** is the same person as Shammua in **Nehemiah 11:17**. He may be the same person as Shemaiah in **2 Chronicles 31:15**.

20. Zophai in **1 Chronicles 6:26** is called Zuph in **1 Chronicles 6:35**.

21. Zikri in **1 Chronicles 9:15** is called Zabdi in **Nehemiah 11:17** and Zakkur in **Nehemiah 12:35**.

22. Azariah the Merarite (Levite) should not be confused with Azariah, a near contemporary (a Kohathie priest or a scribal priest?) "from the family of Zadok" (**2 Chronicles 31:10**) the high priest—who was "the official in charge of the temple of God" in the days of King Hezekiah, 715–686 B.C. (**2 Chronicles 31:11–13**).

23. Nahath in **1 Chronicles 6:26** is called Toah in **1 Chronicles 6:34** and Tohu in **1 Samuel 1:1**.

24. Mika in **1 Chronicles 9:15** and **Nehemiah 11:17, 22** is called Micaiah in **Nehemiah 12:35**.

25. Obadiah in **1 Chronicles 9:16** is called Abda in **Nehemiah 11:17** and is probably the same person as Abdi the father of Kish in **2 Chronicles 29:12**.

26. Eliab in **1 Chronicles 6:27** is called Eliel in **1 Chronicles 6:34** and Elihu in **1 Samuel 1:1**.

27. Mattaniah, a descendant of Asaph the Levitical Gershonite, is mentioned in **2 Chronicles 29:13.** The lineage of Mattaniah is given in **1 Chronicles 9:15; 2 Chronicles 20:14;** and **Nehemiah 11:17, 22; 12:35**.

28. Joah was a descendant of Asaph, who was one of the three chief musicians in Solomon's Temple. Joah was the recorder (an official spokesman) for King Hezekiah (**Isaiah 36:3, 11, 22**). Other references to Joah are **2 Kings 18:18, 26, 37** and **2 Chronicles 29:12**. This Joah should not be confused with Joah the son of Obed-Edom, who was a descendant of Ethan/Jeduthun the Merarite (**1 Chronicles 26:4;** cf. **16:38**).

29. This Azariah "served as [high] priest in the temple Solomon built in Jerusalem" (**1 Chronicles 6:10**); he corresponds to Azariah #15 in chart "**Supplement 2**: The High Priests of Israel."

30. Kish son of Abdi (a Merarite; **2 Chronicles 29:12**) is a different person than a fellow Merarite, Kishi/Kushaiah the son of Abdi (**1 Chronicles 6:44; 15:17**), who lived much earlier (see note 14).

31. Eden, the son of Joah (**2 Chronicles 29:12**), may be the same person as Eden in **2 Chronicles 31:15**.

32. Elkanah (#4) was the husband of Hannah and the father of Samuel (**1 Samuel 1:1–2, 20**); Elkanah was a common name held by at least four individuals in the Levi–Kohath–Izhar–Korah line.

33. Azariah is an enigmatic high priest; he corresponds to Azariah #19 in chart "**Supplement 2**: The High Priests of Israel."

34. This Zadok figure was the high priest in Solomon's Temple; he corresponds to Zadok #20 in chart "**Supplement 2**: The High Priests of Israel."

35. He appears to be the same person as Jehiel in **2 Chronicles 31:13**, but not (1) Jehiel one of the "descendants of Elam" (**Ezra 10:2**) or (2) Jehiel a descendant of Harim the Kohathite priest (**Ezra 10:21**), both of whom were contemporaries of Ezra in 458 B.C.

36. Shimei, a descendant of Heman (**2 Chronicles 29:14**), may be the same person as Shimei the brother of Konaniah in **2 Chronicles 31:13**.

37. Shortly after the siege of Jerusalem, Seraiah the high priest—designated Seraiah #1 in the chart—was taken by Nebuzaradan to Riblah, along with other high-ranking officials; he appears to have been killed there (**2 Kings 25:18–21; Jeremiah 52:24–27**). However, **Nehemiah 11:11** specifically states that "Seraiah son of Hilkiah, the son of Meshullam, the son of Zadok, the son of Meraioth, the son of Ahitub, [was] the official in charge of the house of God [Second Temple]" in post-exilic Jerusalem. Therefore, for chronological reasons, several Seraiah figures must be proposed: Seraiah #1 was the martyred high priest at Riblah, and his son/descendant Seraiah #2 appears to be in a scribal lineage and the *father* of Ezra the priestly scribe. For clarification of the various Seraiah figures, see chart "**Ezra 7**: Ezra, Priestly Scribe and Teacher of the Law (Post-Exile)."

38. Jozadak (more fully J(eh)ozadak) was the high priest when Nebuchadnezzar took Judah and Jerusalem into Babylonian captivity (**1 Chronicles 6:15**).

39. For details about Seraiah #2, see chart "**Ezra 7**: Ezra, the Priestly Scribe and Teacher of the Law (Post-Exile)."

40. See chart "**Ezra 7**: Ezra, the Priestly Scribe and Teacher of the Law (Post-Exile)."

41. Joshua in **Ezra 2:2; 3:2, 8; 4:3; 5:2; 10:18; Nehemiah 7:7; 12:1, 7, 10, 26; Haggai 1:1, 12, 14; 2:2, 4;** and **Zechariah 3:1, 3, 6, 8–9; 6:11** is called Jeshua in **Ezra 2:36; 8:33** and **Nehemiah 7:39**.

42. Parallels are evident between King Hezekiah and King Solomon, such as Hezekiah's attention to cleaning and restoring worship in Solomon's Temple, re-appointment and consecration of the Levitical priesthood, reinstitution of Passover, reunification of "all Israel and Judah," covenant renewal of the people with the Lord, and Hezekiah's wealth and esteem among gentiles (**2 Chronicles 29:1–32:33**). For King Solomon, see charts "**1 Kings 11**: King Solomon" and "**1 Chronicles 3**: King Solomon and His Descendants Until the Time of the Exile."

43. Israel was (at least by divine intent) a theocracy, that is, a nation over whom Yahweh was King. Human kings—even those of the line of David—were but earthly surrogates. This being said, the religious part of the monarchy was not just a department or ancillary entity, but it was in fact the *raison d'être* for the nation's very existence. Israel was, as Moses taught, "a kingdom of priests and a holy nation" (**Exodus 19:6**), a phrase that is later descriptive of the church as well (**Revelation 5:10**).

44. Records for the priesthood and/or "the genealogies of the Levites" (**2 Chronicles 31:19**)—perhaps those that had been recorded during the reign of Jotham of Judah, 750–735 B.C. and/or Jeroboam II of Israel, 793–753 B.C. (cf. **1 Chronicles 5:17**)—were followed by Hezekiah (**2 Chronicles 31:16–19**). Other priests and Levites mentioned in Hezekiah's reign in **2 Chronicles 31** are (1) Azariah (from the house of Zadok), the "chief priest," who was "the official in charge of the temple of God" (vv. **10, 13**); Azariah was probably a priestly scribe (not the high priest) because Zadok was the high priest at the time; (2) Konaniah, a chief Levite in charge of the contributions, tithes, and dedicated gifts in the storerooms of the temple (**v. 12**), and (3) Konaniah's brother Shimei, his assistant (v. **12**). Other Levitical overseers—Jehiel, Azaziah, Nahath, Asahel, Jerimoth, Jozabad, Eliel, Ismakiah, Mahath, and Benaiah—assisted Konaniah and Shimei (v. **13**). Kore the son of Imnah (a Levite) was the keeper of the East Gate and over the freewill offerings and the consecrated gifts (v. **14**). Kore's assistants—Eden, Miniamin, Jeshua, Shemaiah, Amariah, and Shekaniah—attended in the Levitical cities (**v. 15**).

45. The Hithpael verb form here (הִתְקַדְּשׁוּ) has the idea of reciprocation, that is, do something for yourself, in this case, devote yourself (to Yahweh and his call to serve). The implication of **2 Chronicles 29:33–34** is that the Kohathite priests at this time were too few in number and lax in their duties at the altar of burnt offerings because "the Levites had been more conscientious in consecrating themselves than the priests [the Kohathite attending priests] had been."

46. The priesthood was assigned to the tribe of Levi—more specifically, through Aaron the brother of Moses, and a descendant of Kohath, the son of Levi (**Exodus 6:16, 18, 20**). Aaron was the first high (or chief) priest, and all priests who held that title thereafter were his direct descendants (i.e., the Aaronic priesthood), although this eventually changed in the early Hellenistic period (for departures from father-son succession that began with high priest #34, see chart "**Supplement 2**: The High Priests of Israel"). In addition, there were heads of priests and Levites (**1 Chronicles 15:22; 24:6**) and assisting Levites

(**2 Chronicles 8:14; 13:10; Ezra 8:20**). The remaining priests and Levites, especially those not employed at the temple, ministered in the 48 Levitical towns and elsewhere as needed (**Joshua 21:1–42; 1 Chronicles 6:54–80;** see also **2 Chronicles 23:2; Nehemiah 11:3, 20–21, 36**). Another important function of the Levites was their leadership over and participation in choral and orchestral music in worship and praise of Yahweh in the temple (**1 Chronicles 6:31–32; 9:33; 15:19–22; 2 Chronicles 5:12–13; 7:6; 23:13; 34:12–13**).

47. Hezekiah's love and zeal for a united kingdom of Israel is seen in his missionary efforts to the mixed population of the north that followed the deportation of most of the Israelites by the Assyrians, who replaced them with peoples from other parts of their empire (**2 Kings 17:3–41**).

48. For others thus characterized, see **1 Kings 15:11** (Asa); **2 Kings 22:2** (Josiah); and **2 Chronicles 17:3** (Jehoshaphat). Only these three out of the thirty-nine kings of Israel and Judah measured up to this standard. For other accomplishments in Hezekiah's reign, see chart "**2 Kings 16**: Hezekiah, King of Judah."

EZRA 1: SHESHBAZZAR AND ZERUBBABEL, THE GOVERNORS OVER THE RESTORED COMMUNITY IN JERUSALEM (POST-EXILE)[1]

Approximate Dating: ca. 539–537 B.C. to 444 B.C. ***Relevant Scriptures:*** **Ezra 1:8; 2:2; 3:2, 8; 5:2, 14–16;** also **1 Chronicles 3:1–24; Nehemiah 12:1; Haggai 1:12, 14; 2:2, 23; Matthew 1:12–13; Luke 3:27**

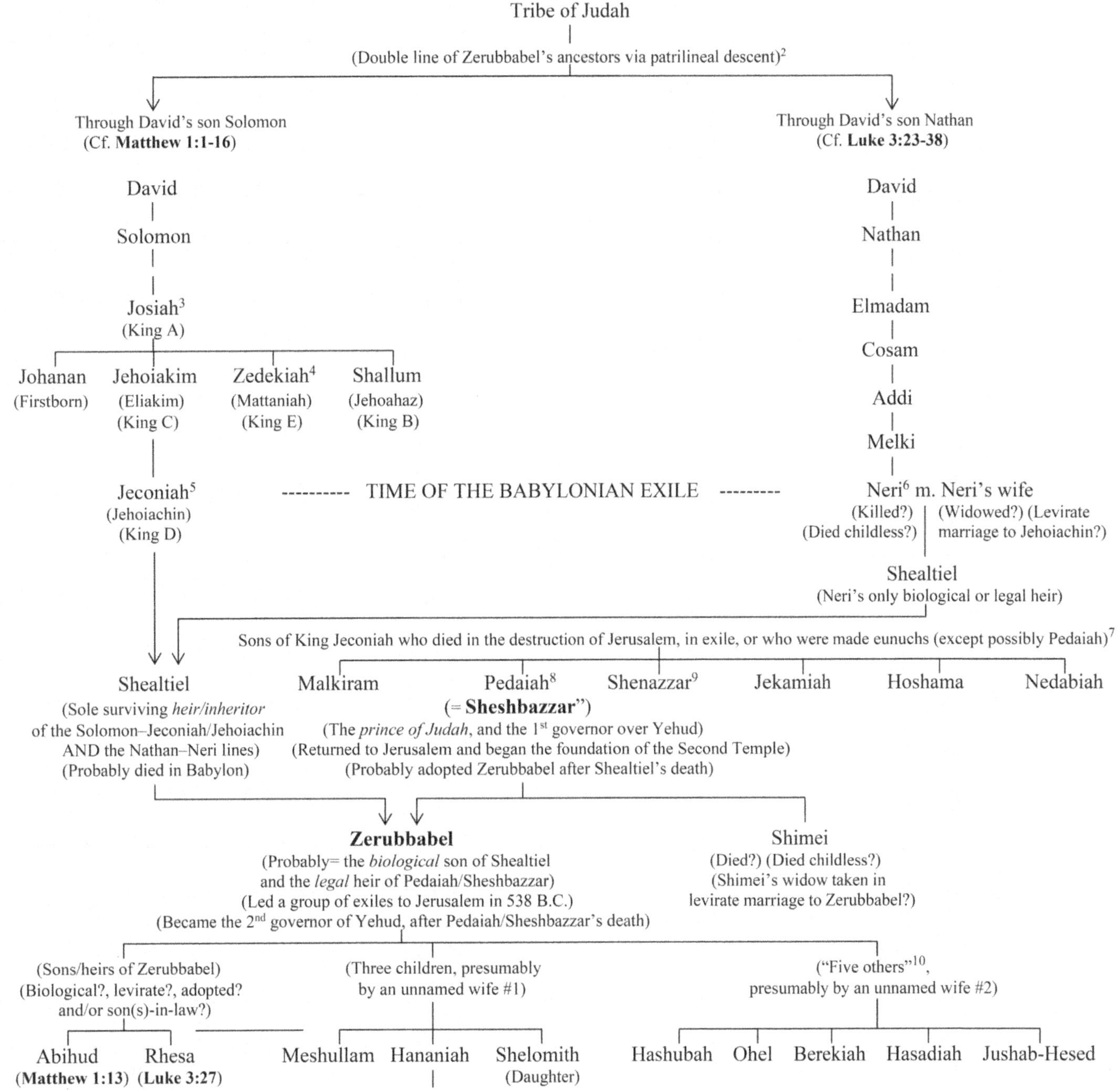

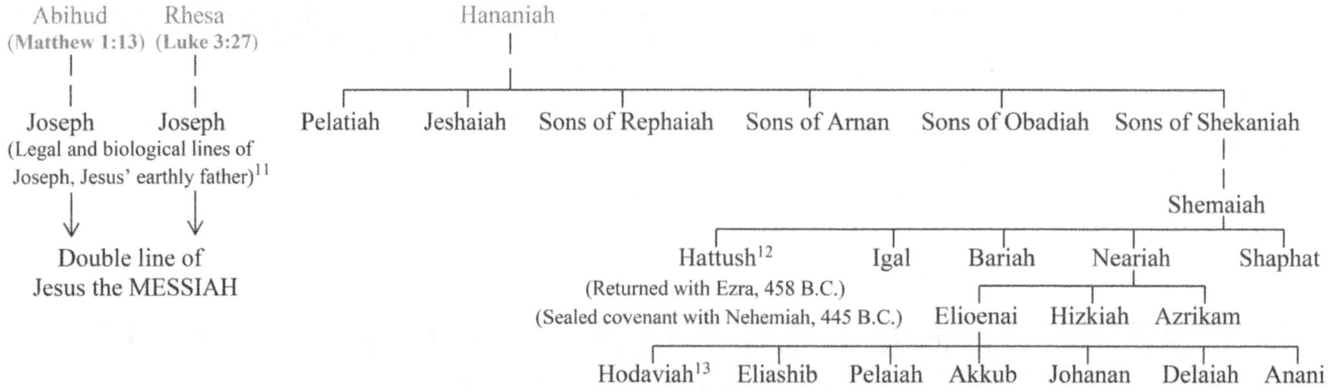

Biblical and Theological Significance

Sheshbazzar—the First Governor of Yehud

King Cyrus of Persia[14] conquered Babylon in 539 B.C. In 538 B.C., his first year (**Ezra 1:1**), Cyrus issued his famous decree that all peoples whom the Babylonians had taken into exile were now free to return to their homes, including, of course, the Jews. In the latter case, King Cyrus permitted them to take all the treasures that Nebuchadnezzar had looted from Solomon's Temple in Jerusalem and entrusted their return to "Sheshbazzar the prince of Judah" (**Ezra 1:8**), "whom he [Cyrus] had appointed governor" in Jerusalem (**Ezra 5:14**):[15] "King Cyrus brought out the articles belonging to the temple of the Lord, which Nebuchadnezzar had carried away from Jerusalem [in 586 B.C.] and. . . . counted them out to Sheshbazzar. . . . In all, there were 5,400 articles of gold and of silver. Sheshbazzar brought all these along with the exiles when they came up from Babylon to Jerusalem"[16] (**Ezra 1:7–8, 11**). Sheshbazzar's royal descent also privileged him to lay the foundations[17] of the Second Temple: "So this Sheshbazzar came and laid the foundations of the house of God in Jerusalem. From that day [538–536 B.C.] to the present [520 B.C.] it has been under construction but is not yet finished" (**Ezra 5:16**; cf. **3:6**). Sometime in 538 B.C., Zerubbabel (and Joshua the high priest) led a group of Jewish exiles back to Jerusalem, but Sheshbazzar does not appear to be among the returnees at that time (see note 16; **1 Chronicles 3:19; Ezra 2:2; 3:1–2; Nehemiah 7:7**). It can be inferred that sometime before 536 B.C., Sheshbazzar/Pedaiah (see note 8 for the dual name designation) died and leadership passed to his *son* and/or *legal heir* Zerubbabel, who then assumed the role as political leader, head of the Jewish people, and the (second) governor of the post-exilic *Yehud* community (cf. **Haggai 1:1, 14; 2:2, 21**). Zerubbabel and his associates, along with Joshua the high priest and his fellow priests, then undertook the rebuilding of the altar. However, even at that point (i.e., after the altar was finished), the foundation was not yet fully completed: "on the first day of the seventh month [537 B.C.] they began to offer burnt offerings to the Lord, though the foundation of the Lord's temple had not yet been laid [completed]" (**Ezra 3:6**). It was not until 536 B.C., "in the second month of the second year after their arrival," that Zerubbabel, Joshua, and the builders finally completed the foundation that Sheshbazzar had begun (**Ezra 3:8**), and most of the people rejoiced (**Ezra 3:10–13**).[18] Thus, the hiatus in completing the temple foundation that followed Sheshbazzar's initial efforts was brought to an end by Zerubbabel. Why Sheshbazzar did nothing to further advance the cause is best explained by his death shortly after coming to Jerusalem, although it could have resulted from some other incapacity.

Unfortunately, soon thereafter, "enemies of Judah and Benjamin" undermined the full Temple restoration effort for the next sixteen years (i.e., 536–520 B.C.; **Ezra 4:1;** see **Ezra 4**).[19] Nevertheless, by 520 B.C. in the time of Darius of Persia, with the encouragement of the prophets Haggai and Zechariah and the strong leadership of Zerubbabel and Joshua, the work on the temple resumed. With the help of the rest of the people (priests, Levites, and returnees), the Second Temple[20] was finally completed four years later in 516 B.C.—exactly seventy years after Solomon's Temple had been destroyed in 586 B.C. (**Ezra 3–6; Haggai 1:12–15**).

Zerubbabel—the Second Governor of Yehud

Zerubbabel (like Sheshbazzar) was in the kingly line of descendants from King David, but he never became a ruler/king in the traditional sense. Rather, Zerubbabel represented the royal hopes of the newly restored community and foreshadowed the future Messiah. The prophets characterize Zerubbabel as the one "anointed to serve the Lord of all the earth" (**Zechariah 4:14**) and the Lord's "signet ring, for I have chosen you" (**Haggai 2:23**). As governor of Judah (**Haggai 1:1**), Zerubbabel was the key transition figure between the former days, when the nation was ruled by Davidic kings, and the later days, when the nation was overseen by governors.

As to his complicated ancestry, Zerubbabel is called both the "son of Pedaiah" (**1 Chronicles 3:19**) and the "son of Shealtiel" (**Ezra 3:2, 8; 5:2; Nehemiah 12:1; Haggai 1:1, 12, 14; 2:2, 23**). In all likelihood, Zerubbabel's *biological* father was Shealtiel (the sole *heir* of the Jeconiah/Jehoiachin and Neri families, who represented the continuance of the Solomon and Nathan lineages). Since there is no mention of Shealtiel ever returning to Jerusalem, it can be assumed that he was born (attested in **Matthew 1:12**) *and* died in captivity. It appears that upon Shealtiel's death in captivity, his near relative Pedaiah/Sheshbazzar (note 8) *adopted* Zerubbabel in order to perpetuate the dignity and nobility of Shealtiel's generational past. In this way, it is likely that

Zerubbabel was the *biological* son of Shealtiel and then, perhaps after Shealtiel's death, the *legal* son/heir of Pedaiah/Sheshbazzar. This interpretation best explains the coming together of the descendants of Solomon (royal succession) and Nathan (non-royal succession) in the persons of Shealtiel and Zerubbabel, and it also explains why *both* Shealtiel and Zerubbabel are mentioned as ancestors of the Messiah (cf. **Matthew 1:12** and **Luke 3:27**). Additionally, it answers the question as to why Zerubbabel was the logical successor to Pedaiah/Sheshbazzar as the second ruler/governor of Yehud in Jerusalem. For an in-depth explanation of the continued Zerubbabel line, see the chart "**1 Chronicles 3**: Zerubbabel and Shealtiel and the Double Line of the Messiah through King David's Sons, Nathan and Solomon."

The two parts of Zerubbabel's name, זֶרַ + בָּבֶל, "seed of Babel," indicate his foreign birthplace, Babylon. How ironic that one who had never seen the land of his ancestors should lead the exiles back in triumphant glory to their homeland! Zerubbabel's role as the quasi-king[21] in the post-exilic community foreshadowed the long-anticipated Savior and Lord of all mankind: Jesus, Son of God and son of Mary. It is not how one begins in life that matters but how one ends. In this way, Zerubbabel paved the way for One who would be born in a lowly stable.

Notes

1. For extensive information about the David–Solomon and David–Nathan lines and Zerubbabel's ancestors and descendants, refer to the chart "**1 Chronicles 3**: Zerubbabel and Shealtiel and the Double Line of the Messiah through King David's Sons, Nathan and Solomon."

2. At the time of the exile, tremendous pressures from war and decimation, from "sword . . . or plague or famine," threatened the messianic line (**2 Chronicles 20:9;** see also **Isaiah 51:19; Jeremiah 11:22; 14:12–18; 16:4; 18:21; 21:7, 9; 27:8, 13; 29:17–18; 32:24, 36; 34:17**). The chart shows that Zerubbabel (and Shealtiel) were the only surviving common ancestors of Jesus who are recorded in both the Matthew and Luke genealogies; they represent the coming together (chiasm) of the Davidic lineages (i.e., the kingly line through Solomon and the non-kingly line through Nathan).

3. The verse "Josiah the father of Jeconiah and his brothers at the time of the exile to Babylon [586 B.C.]" in **Matthew 1:11**—translated as "Josiah begot Jeconiah and his brothers about the time they were carried away to Babylon" (NKJV, contra NIV)—should be understood to mean that Josiah had four sons (Johanan the firstborn, Jehoiakim the second son, Zedekiah the third, Shallum the fourth; **1 Chronicles 3:14–15**); also, Josiah had a grandson Jeconiah/Jehoiachin the son of Jehoiakim (cf. **2 Kings 24:6; 1 Chronicles 3:16; Jeremiah 22:24; 24:1; 27:20; 28:4**).

4. King Zedekiah of Judah was the last Davidic king of Judah (597–586 B.C.). Zedekiah rebelled against the king of Babylon in his eleventh year of his reign (586 B.C.), whereupon Nebuchadnezzar overcame him and took Zedekiah to his headquarters in Riblah in Syria. There, Zedekiah's sons were killed "before his eyes"; Zedekiah was blinded, and then he was taken captive to Babylon (**2 Kings 25:1–7; Jeremiah 39:1–7**), where he died (cf. **Jeremiah 52:8–11**), thus fulfilling the prophecy about "the prince of Jerusalem" (**Ezekiel 12:10–12**).

5. King Jehoiachin (also called Jeconiah) reigned in Jerusalem for a brief three months in 598–597 B.C. (**2 Kings 24:8–16**). Nebuchadnezzar's second invasion (598/597 B.C.) occurred during Jehoiachin's reign (**2 Kings 24:10–14**), and a third invasion in 587 B.C. took place during Zedekiah's tenure (**2 Kings 25:1–24**), resulting in the final destruction of Jerusalem in 586 B.C. (**2 Kings 25:8–11**). Nebuchadnezzar of Babylon deposed Jehoiachin in 597 B.C. and took him into captivity—"In the eighth year of the reign of the king of Babylon [Nebuchadnezzar], he took Jehoiachin prisoner" (**2 Kings 24:11–12**). Also taken into captivity were Jeconiah's mother (Nehushta; **2 Kings 24:8**), as well as "his wives," "his nobles," "his officials," (**2 Kings 24:12, 15; Jeremiah 24:1**) and "princes of Judah" (**Jeremiah 24:1** NKJV, contra NIV). The *descendants* of King Jeconiah are listed in **1 Chronicles 3:17–18** as "Shealtiel . . . Malkiram, Pedaiah, Shenazzar, Jekamiah, Hoshama, and Nedabiah." See note 7.

6. Neri is the last descendant mentioned in the David-Nathan lineage before the Babylonian exile took place in 586 B.C. (**Luke 3:27**). During Nebuchadnezzar's overthrow of Jerusalem, a great number of people were killed (see note 2), and one such person appears to have been Neri. Neri is presented as the *father* of Shealtiel in **Luke 3:27**, and yet, King Jeconiah (Jehoiachin) is also presented as the *father* of Shealtiel in **Matthew 1:12** and **1 Chronicles 3:17**, thus posing somewhat of an interpretative dilemma. To explain the apparent discrepancy, two plausible explanations are offered:

(1) Neri died during the destruction of Jerusalem or while in exile, leaving his (unnamed) wife as a widow; since King Jeconiah and Neri were his distant relatives/kinsmen (i.e., meaning in the same kinship group, being from the David–Solomon-Jeconiah line and the David–Nathan–Neri line, respectively), Jeconiah acted as a kinsman redeemer (*goel*), married Neri's widow, and raised up a child (Shealtiel) for the deceased Neri; or

(2) While in exile, Neri had a son named Shealtiel, but soon thereafter, Neri died. Because Jeconiah/Jehoiachin (a near relative and fellow captive) had no living biological *sons/heirs*—either the sons had been killed during the destruction of Jerusalem or had been made eunuchs in captivity (cf. **2 Kings 20:18**)—Jehoiachin/Jeconiah was without a *son/heir* to carry on his name. To secure a namesake in future generations, Jeconiah/Jehoiachin *adopted* Neri's son, Shealitel: in this regard, Shealtiel remained the *biological son* of Neri but the *legal son/heir* of King Jehoiachin.

Scenario #1 is favored since Pedaiah (Sheshbazzar, the prince of Judah) appears to be the only son of King Jeconiah who returned to Jerusalem (see notes 7 and 8). Both interpretations explain the double line of the Messiah at the time of the exile (the literary chiastic point in the chart) and the concatenation of the David–Solomon and David–Nathan lines in the post-exile.

7. The sons of Jeconiah/Jehoiachin appear to be killed during the Babylonian destruction of Jerusalem in 586 B.C. or were made eunuchs in Babylon, except perhaps Pedaiah (for an explanation of Pedaiah/Sheshbazzar, see note 8). According to Isaiah's prophecy, during the Babylonian destruction of Jerusalem and the subsequent exile of the citizenry, "some of your [King Hezekiah's] descendants, your own flesh and blood who will be born to you, will be taken away, and they will become eunuchs in the palace of the king of Babylon," but those exact descendants are unknown (**2 Kings 20:18**, **Isaiah 39:7**; cf. **Jeremiah 15:1–9**; **Daniel 1:3–7**). This prophecy seems to apply to King Jeconiah/Jehoiachin and his immediate family/heirs during the exile period (586–516 B.C.; **Jeremiah 22:24–30**). For a discussion of archaeological evidence suggesting that at least five of the royal princes (eunuchs?) lived with King Jeconiah/Jehoiachin in captivity, see note 15 in chart "**1 Chronicles 3**: Zerubbabel and Shealtiel and the Double Line of the Messiah through King David's Sons, Nathan and Solomon."

8. The lineage of Pedaiah, given in **1 Chronicles 3:17–19**, shows that Pedaiah was the *son/descendant* of King Jehoiachin and the *father* of Zerubbabel. We agree with other scholars, such as Curtis and Madsen, that *Sheshbazzar* was the Babylonian name for Pedaiah, and therefore they are one and the same person; see Edward L. Curtis and Albert A. Madsen, *A Critical and Exegetical Commentary on the Books of Chronicles* (Edinburgh: T&T Clark, 1920), 103.

Note that "Sheshbazzar" (Pedaiah) is not the same person as "Shenazzar," who was another son/descendant of Jehoiachin/Jeconiah (see note 9).

9. Shenazzar son of Jeconiah/Jehoiachin (**1 Chronicles 3:18**) died at the time of the exile or was likely made a eunuch in Babylon (see note 7). Shenazzar (Heb. שֶׁנְאַצַּר) is not the same person as Sheshbazzar (Heb. שֵׁשְׁבַּצַּר), "the prince of Judah" (**Ezra 1:8**). Also, Shenazzar and Sheshbazzar are clearly not the same person as Zerubbabel.

10. **First Chronicles 3:19–20** says "The sons of Zerubbabel: Meshullam and Hananiah. Shelomith was their sister. There were also five others: Hashubah, Ohel, Berekiah, Hasadiah and Jushab-Hesed." In this regard, Zerubbabel appears to have raised up *two separate families*—including levirate and/or adopted children (for Neri? Shealtiel? Jeconiah?)—to produce offspring that carried on both the David–Solomon and David–Nathan lines.

11. Joseph was considered the earthly father and legal guardian of Jesus (**Luke 2:4–5, 22–24; 4:22; John 1:45; 6:42**). He is called a "son of David" (meaning a descendant of King David; **Matthew 1:20**), who "belonged to the house and line of David" (**Luke 2:4**). The genealogy of Jesus as a descendant of *Nathan* (the son of King David and Bathsheba, as attested in **Luke 3:23–38**)

stresses that Adam was the ancestor of Jesus (the Son of God). **Luke 3:23** emphasizes that Jesus "was the son, so it was thought, of Joseph." This establishes Jesus as the legal heir of Joseph and a *Davidic* descendant himself. The genealogy of Jesus as a descendant of Solomon (who was the son of King David and Bathsheba as presented in **Matthew 1:1–16**) stresses the *kingly* ancestry of the Messiah. Together, the Matthew and Luke genealogical accounts provide the biological and legal descent of Joseph, Jesus' earthy father, a descendant from the tribe of Judah and the line of Israel's most famous king, David.

12. Hattush in **1 Chronicles 3:22** is the same person as Hattush in **Ezra 8:2**, who is identified as a descendant of David through the descendants of Shekaniah (**Ezra 8:2–3**). Hattush was the head of a family of exiles who returned to Jerusalem with Ezra in ca. 458 B.C.; he is also the same person as Hattush who sealed the covenant in the post-exilic community in Jerusalem with Nehemiah in ca. 444 B.C. (**Nehemiah 10:4**). Hattush in **1 Chronicles 3:22** and **Ezra 8:2** is not Hattush the son of Hashabneiah, the Levite (**Nehemiah 3:10; 9:5**).

13. Hodaviah the Judahite is unrelated to Hodaviah the Levite (**Ezra 2:40; 3:9; Nehemiah 7:43**).

14. For King Cyrus of Persia, see note 19; also see chart "**Supplement 5**: The Kings of Persia."

15. Sheshbazzar's paternity is unknown, but he *could have been* the offspring of any one of the last few kings of Judah (cf. **2 Kings 24:6, 12**). With this in mind, we have tentatively concluded (as indicated in the chart) that Sheshbazzar was the Babylonian name for Pedaiah, the *son* of King Jehoiachin. This interpretation is in agreement with Curtis and Madsen, who also hold that Sheshbazzar and Pedaiah were one and the same (see note 8).

16. Scripture is not clear about the timing of Sheshbazzar's journey to Jerusalem; he does not appear to return with Zerubbabel and Joshua in 538 B.C. (i.e., notice that Sheshbazzar's name is missing among the complete list of returnees in **Ezra 2:1–64**; see chart "**Ezra 2**: Genealogical Record of the Captives Who Returned to Jerusalem with Zerubbabel and Joshua (Post-Exile)"). Sheshbazzar may have returned around 539 or 537 B.C. (?) and begun laying the foundation, but when the great altar was completed "on the first day of the seventh month" of the first year, the foundation "had not yet been [completely?] laid (**Ezra 3:6**; cf. **5:16**). It was only after "the second month of the second year after their arrival" (ca. 536 B.C.) that "the builders laid [and presumably finished] the foundation of the temple of the Lord" (**Ezra 3:8–11**). Sheshbazzar appears to die shortly after 536 B.C. Work on the temple was opposed by "enemies of Judah and Benjamin" (**Ezra 4:1**) during the remaining years of Cyrus' reign, from 536–530 B.C., and continued even thereafter—"During the entire reign of Cyrus king of Persia and down to the reign of Darius king of Persia" (**Ezra 4:5**; cf. **vv. 1–4**); building on the temple did not commence again until 520 B.C., "the second year of King Darius, on the first day of the sixth month" (**Haggai 1:1**). See note 19.

17. In **Ezra 6:33**, the temple foundation is described as: "it is to be sixty cubits high and sixty cubits wide, with three courses of large stones and one of timbers."

18. It was a mixed celebration because "many of the older priests and Levites and family heads, who had seen the former [Solomon's] temple, wept aloud when they saw the [smaller-scaled] foundation of this temple being laid, while many others shouted for joy. No one could distinguish the sound of the shouts of joy from the sound of weeping, because the people made so much noise. And the sound was heard far away" (**Ezra 3:13**).

19. During this general time period, Cyrus ruled over Persia (and Babylon) from 538–530 B.C.; Cyrus was then succeeded by Cambyses II from 530–522 B.C.—possibly followed by a brief reign of Bardiya/Smerdis for a few months in 522 B.C.—and then succeeded by Darius I from 522–486 B.C. See chart "**Supplement 5**: The Kings of Persia."

20. The Second Temple that was built in post-exilic Jerusalem is sometimes called "Zerubbabel's Temple."

21. Every time leadership was called for or otherwise indicated, Zerubbabel is named (**Ezra 2:2; 3:2, 8; 4:2; 5:2; Nehemiah 7:7; 12:1**) and, in many cases, explicitly denoted as "governor" (פַּחַת, *pakhat*).

EZRA 2: JOSHUA, THE HIGH PRIEST IN THE SECOND TEMPLE, AND HIS DESCENDANTS (POST-EXILE)

Approximate Dating: ca. 516–490 B.C. ***Relevant Scriptures:*** **Ezra 2:2; 3:8; 5:2; 8:33; 10:18;** also **1 Chronicles 6:1–30; Nehemiah 12:1, 10–11, 22, 26**

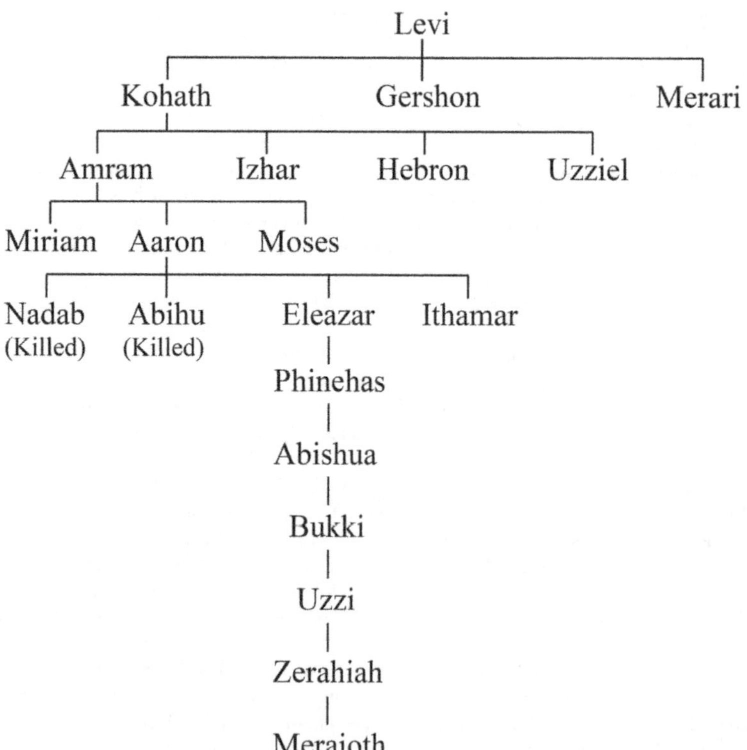

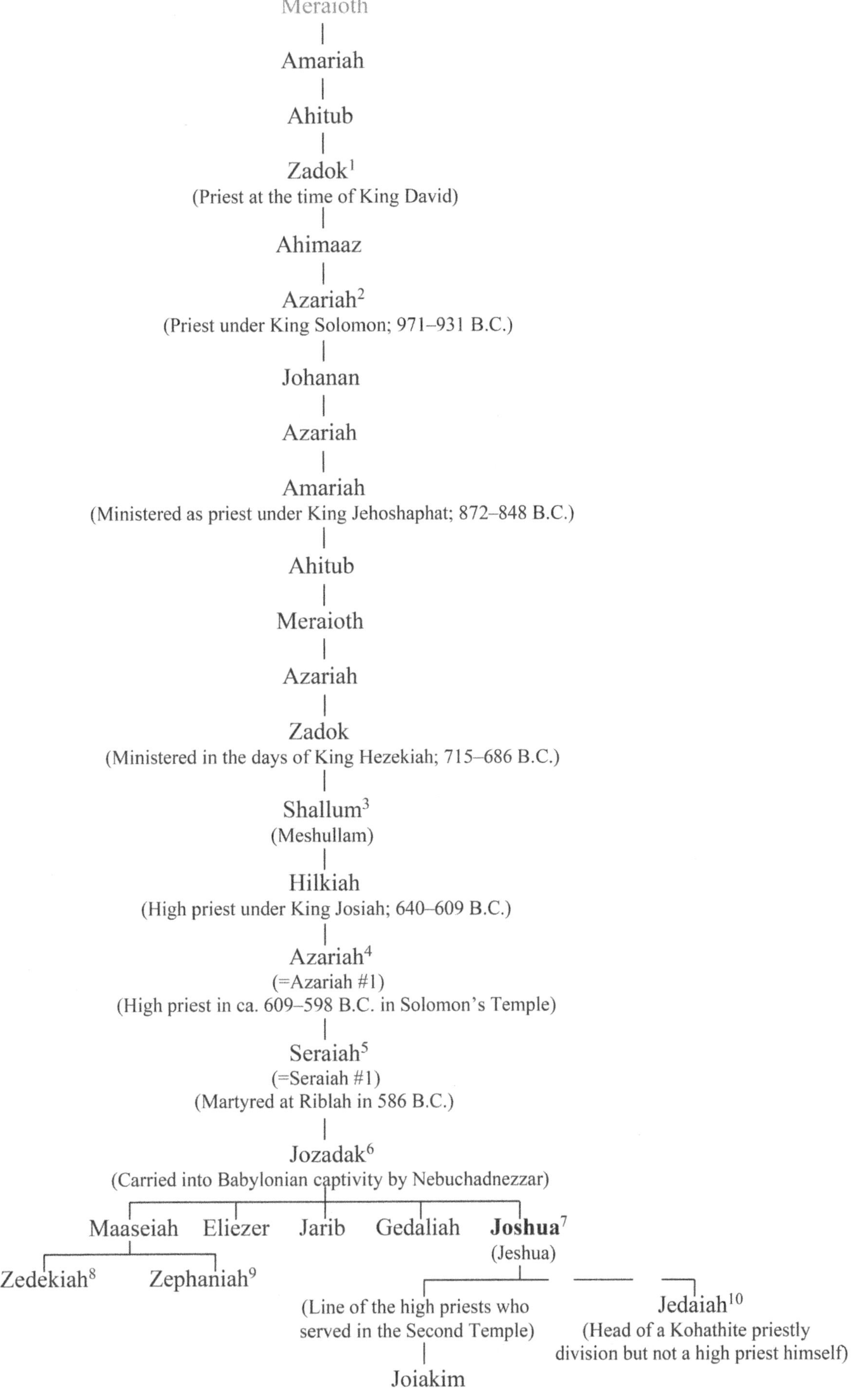
Meraioth
Amariah
Ahitub
Zadok[1]
(Priest at the time of King David)
Ahimaaz
Azariah[2]
(Priest under King Solomon; 971–931 B.C.)
Johanan
Azariah
Amariah
(Ministered as priest under King Jehoshaphat; 872–848 B.C.)
Ahitub
Meraioth
Azariah
Zadok
(Ministered in the days of King Hezekiah; 715–686 B.C.)
Shallum[3]
(Meshullam)
Hilkiah
(High priest under King Josiah; 640–609 B.C.)
Azariah[4]
(=Azariah #1)
(High priest in ca. 609–598 B.C. in Solomon's Temple)
Seraiah[5]
(=Seraiah #1)
(Martyred at Riblah in 586 B.C.)
Jozadak[6]
(Carried into Babylonian captivity by Nebuchadnezzar)
Maaseiah
Eliezer
Jarib
Gedaliah
Joshua[7]
(Jeshua)
Zedekiah[8]
Zephaniah[9]
(Line of the high priests who served in the Second Temple)
Joiakim
Jedaiah[10]
(Head of a Kohathite priestly division but not a high priest himself)

Biblical and Theological Significance

Joshua/Jeshua[14] was one of the great individuals of the post-exilic era. He was among the Babylonian exiles whose future changed when King Cyrus' great decree allowed Jews to return to their homeland. Joshua came to Jerusalem with Zerubbabel in 538 B.C. (**Ezra 2:2; Nehemiah 7:7**) and worked closely alongside Zerubbabel, the governor, and Haggai and Zechariah, the prophets, to establish the new state of Yehud, which would become a satrap under the Persian monarchy (**Ezra 2:2; 3:8; Haggai 1:1; Zechariah 3:1, 3–9; 6:11**). Upon their arrival, however, there was no great altar for sacrifice nor a rebuilt temple for resumption of worship. After a series of setbacks when work began and then halted (cf. **Ezra 3–6; Haggai 1–2**), the Second Temple was finally completed in 516 B.C., in the sixth year of the reign of Darius I (522–486 B.C.) (**Ezra 6:15**).

Joshua's ministry, which is most clearly recorded by the prophet Haggai, shows his partnership as priest with Zerubbabel, the governor, clarifying that both the secular and the sacred were essential expressions of the nature of God's kingdom (**Haggai 1:1, 12, 14; 2:2, 4**). According to the prophet Zechariah, Zerubbabel and Joshua were "the two who are anointed to serve the Lord of all the earth" (**Zechariah 4:14**), a "type" of the messianic dominion in which *the single* Messiah would embody the offices of both priest *and* king (**Psalm 110:2, 4; Zechariah 3:1–9; Hebrews 7:1–3**).

Joshua wore an ornate crown as a prototype of the Branch, a cipher for messianic royalty (**Zechariah 3:5, 8; 6:11–12**; cf. **Isaiah 11:1; Jeremiah 23:5; 33:15; Revelation 19:12**). He was a symbol of the Branch (Messiah) to come, who would "branch out," build the temple of the LORD, and rule as a "priestly king" (**Zechariah 6:11–13**). Joshua was reminiscent of David, the first in his line as both priest and king (**2 Samuel 2:11; 5:4; 6:14; 8:15; 24:24–25; Psalm 110**) and anticipatory of Jesus, the son of David—the shoot who came "from the stump of Jesse; from his roots a Branch will bear fruit" (**Isaiah 11:1**)—who is described in these very terms:

- The Son over God's house (**Hebrews 3:1–6**);
- A high priest on God's throne of grace (**Hebrews 4:14–16**);
- A high priest forever, in the order of Melchizedek, the king of Salem and priest of God Most High (**Hebrews 6:20–7:28**).

Notes

1. Both Zadok (of the Aaron–Eleazar priesthood; **1 Chronicles 6:8, 53**) and Abiathar (of the Aaron–Ithamar–Eli priesthood; cf. **2 Samuel 19:11; 20:25; 1 Chronicles 24:6**) served in a co–high priest capacity during the time of David and the early part of Solomon's reign; however, only the Zadok line of the high priests continued thereafter (cf. **1 Kings 1:7–8; 2:26–27**).

2. Azariah was the high priest in Solomon's Temple (**1 Chronicles 6:10**). He corresponds to Azariah #13 in chart "**Supplement 2**: The High Priests of Israel."

3. Shallum son of Zadok (**1 Chronicles 6:12–13; Ezra 7:2**) is otherwise called Meshullam (**1 Chronicles 9:11; Nehemiah 11:11**).

4. Azariah son of Hilkiah, whose lineage is given in **1 Chronicles 6:13–14** and **Ezra 7:1**, served in Solomon's Temple from ca. 609 B.C. (under King Jehoahaz/Shallum) to as late as 598 B.C. (under King Eliakim/Jehoiakim). In some charts he is designated Azariah #1. For chronological reasons, he is not the same person as:

(1) "Azariah the chief priest" who served in the days of King Uzziah/Azariah, 792–740 B.C., and who identified that Uzziah had leprosy in ca. 752 B.C. (**2 Chronicles 26:16–20**); or

(2) Azariah the scribal Kohathite priest—described as "the chief priest, from the family of Zadok" (**2 Chronicles 31:10**) and "Azariah the official in charge of the temple of God" (**2 Chronicles 31:13**)—who lived and served in the days of King Hezekiah, 715–686 B.C.; or

(3) the scribal priest named Azariah—designated Azariah #2/Seraiah #2 in other charts—who returned to Jerusalem with Zerubbabel in 538 B.C. and became "the official in charge of the house of God [Second Temple]" (**1 Chronicles 9:11**; cf. **Nehemiah 11:11**), who is quite confusingly called "Azariah" in **Nehemiah 7:7** and "Seraiah" in **Ezra 2:2**.

For more information about Azariah the son of Hilkiah, see Azariah #23 in chart "**Supplement 2**: The High Priests of Israel." For the various Azariah figures who were high priests vs. scribal Kohathite priests, refer to the charts "**Ezra 7**: Ezra, the Priestly Scribe and Teacher of the Law (Post-Exile)" and "**Supplement 2**: The High Priests of Israel."

5. Seraiah—identified as Seraiah #1 in other charts—was the high priest in Solomon's Temple at the time of the Babylonian conquest of Jerusalem (**2 Kings 25:18**). He was brought to the Babylonian headquarters at "Riblah, in the land of Hamath [Syria]," and there he was executed (**2 Kings 25:18–21; Jeremiah 52:24–27**). The high priestly line continued through Seraiah's son Jozadak, who became the first high priest in Solomon's Temple in 516 B.C. Apparently, the son of Seraiah #1—designated Seraiah #2 in other charts—was the *brother* of Jozadak and the *father* of Ezra; see chart "**Ezra 7**: Ezra, the Priestly Scribe and Teacher of the Law (Post-Exile)". It is this Seraiah #2 who probably served as the Kohathite "official" in charge of the Second Temple (**1 Chronicles 9:11; Nehemiah 11:11**), but he was not a high priest. The post-exilic figure Seraiah (#2) is called "Seraiah" in **Ezra 2:2** and "Azariah" in **Nehemiah 7:7**. For chronological reasons, Seraiah #2/Seraiah/Azariah should not be confused with Azariah the high priest who served as the high priest in Solomon's Temple, ca. 609–598 B.C. (who corresponds to Azariah #23 in chart "**Supplement 2**: The High Priests of Israel").

6. Jozadak (more fully Jehozadak) was the high priest when Nebuchadnezzar took Judah and Jerusalem into Babylonian captivity (**1 Chronicles 6:15**). Jozadak was the father of Joshua/Jeshua (note 7).

7. Joshua the son of Jozadak (**1 Chronicles 6:15**)—who is also called Jeshua (see note 14)—was the first high priest to officiate in the Second Temple. He is also referred to in **Ezra 2:36** and **Nehemiah 7:39** as a *relative* of Jedaiah the Kohathite attending priest: "through the family of Jeshua [Joshua]" (see Jedaiah in note 10). Joshua came to Jerusalem with Zerubbabel in 538 B.C., in the first

wave of returning exiles. The prophet Zechariah had three visions of Joshua the high priest—(1) his investiture before the angel, in which his "filthy clothes" were replaced with "fine garments" (**Zechariah 3:1–10**); (2) the anointing of Joshua and Zerubbabel, who formed the two "olive branches" on the left and right sides the lampstand of the temple (**Zechariah 4:12–14**); and (3) the royal crowning of the high priest, where Joshua symbolized the present and future "Branch" that would *branch out* and build the temple (**Zechariah 6:11–13**; cf. **3:8–9**).

The brothers of Joshua, who are mentioned in **Ezra 10:18–19**—"the descendants of Joshua son of Jozadak, and his brothers: Maaseiah, Eliezer, Jarib and Gedaliah"—were guilty of having taken pagan wives while in Babylon, but they pledged to put them away. Joshua/Jeshua is not: (1) Jeshua the Levite, the son of Kadmiel (from the line of Hodaviah; **Ezra 2:40; 3:9; Nehemiah 7:43; 12:24**); (2) Jeshua the son of Azaniah (**Nehemiah 10:9**); (3) Jeshua the Kohathite priest over the ninth division of priests in Solomon's Temple (**1 Chronicles 24:11**); (4) Jeshua a relative of Pahath-Moab (**Ezra 2:6**; **Nehemiah 7:11**); (5) Jeshua the father of Ezer (**Nehemiah 3:19**); (6) Jeshua the father of Jozabad (**Ezra 8:33**); (7) Jeshua in **2 Chronicles 31:15**; nor (8) other Levites named Jeshua (**Nehemiah 8:7; 9:4–5; 12:8**).

8. Zedekiah was a false prophet/false witness, an adulterer, and a liar who promised false hope to the Babylonian captives. Jeremiah pronounced God's judgment on Zedekiah, and in time, Zedekiah and the false prophet Ahab were "roasted in the fire" by the king of Babylon (cf. **Jeremiah 29:21–23**).

9. Zephaniah the son of Maaseiah (**Jeremiah 21:1; 29:25; 37:3**) is not Zephaniah the prophet, the son of Cushi (**Zephaniah 1:1**).

10. Jedaiah was the head of a Kohathite priestly division in the post-exile, but he was not a high priest. Furthermore, he was a *descendant* of the ancestral figure, Jedaiah, who was the head over the second of the twenty-four divisions of Kohathite attending priests who served in Solomon's Temple in the days of King David. Jedaiah was also a *relative* of Joshua/Jeshua the high priest "through the family of Jeshua" (cf. **1 Chronicles 24:7; Ezra 2:36; Nehemiah 7:39**), but the exact relationship is unknown.

11. Eliashib was the high priest in the days of Nehemiah (**Nehemiah 3:1, 20**; cf. **Nehemiah 12:10**).

12. Jonathan (**Nehemiah 12:11**) is otherwise Johanan (**Nehemiah 12:22–23**) or Jehohanan (**Ezra 10:6**).

13. Jaddua is the last high priest mentioned in the Old Testament (**Nehemiah 12:11, 22**). He served in the Second Temple, ca. 370–332 B.C. (**Nehemiah 12:11**). See Jaddua #31 in chart "**Supplement 2**: The High Priests of Israel." Jaddua the high priest should not be confused with Jaddua, a leader of the people who sealed the covenant with Nehemiah in 444 B.C. (**Nehemiah 10:21**).

14. Joshua (**Ezra 3:2, 8; 5:2; 10:18; Nehemiah 12:26; Haggai 1:1, 12, 14; 2:2, 4; Zechariah 3:1, 3-4, 6, 8–9; 6:11**) is also called Jeshua (**Ezra 2:36; Nehemiah 7:39**).

EZRA 2: GENEALOGICAL RECORD OF THE CAPTIVES WHO RETURNED TO JERUSALEM WITH ZERUBBABEL AND JOSHUA (POST-EXILE)[1]

Approximate Dating: ca. 538 B.C. ***Relevant Scriptures:*** **Ezra 2:1–65; Nehemiah 7:4–67**[2]

Chief Leaders

1. **Zerubbabel**[3] (Persian-appointed governor and king-like figure of Judahite heritage)
2. **Joshua**[4] (also called Jeshua; the high priest)

Additional Leaders (cf. Ezra 2:2; Nehemiah 7:7)[5]

1. **Nehemiah (Ezra 2:2; Nehemiah 7:7)**[6]
2. **Seraiah** [probably the same as Seraiah (designated Seraiah #2) in **Ezra 2:2**, who is called Azariah (designated Azariah #2) in **Nehemiah 7:7**][7]
3. **Reelaiah (Ezra 2:2)** (called **Raamiah** in **Nehemiah 7:7**)
4. **Mordecai**[8] **(Ezra 2:2; Nehemiah 7:7)**
5. **Bilshan (Ezra 2:2; Nehemiah 7:7)**
6. **Mispar (Ezra 2:2)** (called **Mispereth** in **Nehemiah 7:7**)
7. **Bigvai (Ezra 2:2; Nehemiah 7:7)**
8. **Rehum (Ezra 2:2)** (called **Nehum** in **Nehemiah 7:7**)
9. **Baanah (Ezra 2:2; Nehemiah 7:7**; cf. **Nehemiah 10:27)**

Heads of Israelite Families and Leaders Among the Returning Exiles

1. **Descendants of Parosh—2,172 (Ezra 2:3; 8:3; 10:25; Nehemiah 7:8; 10:14)**
2. **Descendants of Shephatiah—372 (Ezra 2:4; 8:8; Nehemiah 7:9)**
3. **Descendants of Arah—775 (Ezra 2:5)** (compared to 652 in **Nehemiah 7:10)**
4. **Descendants of Pahath-Moab**[9]**—2,812 (Ezra 2:6)** (compared to **2,818** in **Nehemiah 7:11)** (cf. **Ezra 8:4; 10:30; Nehemiah 3:11; 10:14)**
5. **Descendants of Elam—1,254** (cf. **Ezra 2:7; 8:7; 10:26; Nehemiah 7:12; 10:14)**
6. **Descendants of Zattu—945 (Ezra 2:8)** (compared to **845** in **Nehemiah 7:13)** (cf. **Ezra 8:5; Nehemiah 10:14)**
7. **Descendants of Zakkai—760 (Ezra 2:9; Nehemiah 7:14)**
8. **Descendants of Bani (Binnui?)**[10]**—642 (Ezra 2:10)** (compared to **648** in **Nehemiah 7:15)** (cf. **Ezra 8:10; 10:29, 34; Nehemiah 10:14–15)**
9. **Descendants of Bebai—623 (Ezra 2:11)** (compared to **628** in **Nehemiah 7:16)** (cf. **Nehemiah 10:15)**
10. **Descendants of Azgad—1,222 (Ezra 2:12)** (compared to **2,322** in **Nehemiah 7:17)** (cf. **Ezra 8:12; Nehemiah 10:15)**
11. **Descendants of Adonikam—666 (Ezra 2:13)** (compared to **667** in **Nehemiah 7:18)** (cf. **Ezra 8:13)**
12. **Descendants of Bigvai—2,056 (Ezra 2:14** (compared to **2,067** in **Nehemiah 7:19)** (cf. **Ezra 8:14; Nehemiah 10:16)**
13. **Descendants of Adin—454 (Ezra 2:15)** (compared to **655** in **Nehemiah 7:20)** (cf. **Ezra 8:6; Nehemiah 10:16)**
14. **Descendants of Ater** (through Hezekiah)**—98** (cf. **Ezra 2:16; Nehemiah 7:21; 10:17)**
15. **Descendants of Bezai—323 (Ezra 2:17)** (compared to **324** in **Nehemiah 7:23)** (cf. **Nehemiah 10:18)**
16. **Descendants of Jorah/Hariph**[11]**—112 (Ezra 2:18; Nehemiah 7:24)** (cf. **Nehemiah 10:19)**
17. **Descendants of Hashum—223 (Ezra 2:19)** (compared to **328** in **Nehemiah 7:22)** (cf. **Nehemiah 10:18)**
18. **Descendants of Gibbar/Gibeon**[12]**—95 (Ezra 2:20; Nehemiah 7:25)**

Men of Fifteen Towns

1. **Bethlehem of Judah—123 (Ezra 2:21; Nehemiah 7:26)**
2. **Netophah—56 (Ezra 2:22; Nehemiah 7:26)** (compared to **188** for Bethlehem and Netophah combined in **Nehemiah 7:26**)
3. **Anathoth of Benjamin** (Levitical city)—**128 (Ezra 2:23; Nehemiah 7:27)**
4. **Azmaveth—42 (Ezra 2:24)** (=Beth Azmaveth in **Nehemiah 7:28**)
5. **Kiriath Jearim, Kephirah,** and **Beeroth—743 (Ezra 2:25; Nehemiah 7:29)**
6. **Ramah** and **Geba—621 (Ezra 2:26; Nehemiah 7:30)**
7. **Mikmash—122 (Ezra 2:27; Nehemiah 7:31)**
8. **Bethel** and **Ai—223 (Ezra 2:28)** (compared to **123** in **Nehemiah 7:32**)
9. **Nebo—52 (Ezra 2:29)** (or "of the other Nebo" in **Nehemiah 7:33**)
10. **Magbish—156 (Ezra 2:30)**
11. **"Of the other Elam"—1,254 (Ezra 2:31; Nehemiah 7:34)**
12. **Harim—320 (Ezra 2:32; Nehemiah 7:35)**
13. **Lod, Hadid,** and **Ono—725 (Ezra 2:33)** (compared to **721** in **Nehemiah 7:37**)
14. **Jericho—345 (Ezra 2:34; Nehemiah 7:36)**
15. **Senaah—3,630 (Ezra 2:35)** (compared to **3,930** in **Nehemiah 7:38**)

Kohathite Attending Priests[13]

1. **Descendants of Jedaiah** (through the family of Jeshua the high priest)—**973 (Ezra 2:36; Nehemiah 7:39)**
2. **Descendants of Immer—1,052 (Ezra 2:37; Nehemiah 7:40)**
3. **Descendants of Pashhur—1,247 (Ezra 2:38; Nehemiah 7:41)**
4. **Descendants of Harim—1,017 (Ezra 2:39; Nehemiah 7:42)**

Levites

Descendants of Jeshua[14] **and his father, Kadmiel** (through the line of Hodaviah)—**74 (Ezra 2:40; Nehemiah 7:43)**

Musicians: Descendants of Asaph[15]**—128 (Ezra 2:41)** (compared to **148** in **Nehemiah 7:44**)

Gatekeepers

1. **Descendants of Shallum**
2. **Descendants of Ater**
3. **Descendants of Talmon**
4. **Descendants of Akkub**
5. **Descendants of Hatita**
6. **Descendants of Shobai**

Total gatekeepers—139 (Ezra 2:42) compared to **138 (Nehemiah 7:45)**

Temple Servants[16]

1. **Descendants of Ziha**
2. **Descendants of Hasupha**
3. **Descendants of Tabbaoth**
4. **Descendants of Keros**
5. **Descendants of Siaha** (Sia in **Nehemiah 7:47**)
6. **Descendants of Padon**
7. **Descendants of Lebanah** (Lebana in **Nehemiah 7:48**)
8. **Descendants of Hagabah** (Hagaba in **Nehemiah 7:48**)
9. **Descendants of Akkub** (in **Ezra 2:45** only)
10. **Descendants of Hagab** (in **Ezra 2:46** only)
11. **Descendants of Shalmai**
12. **Descendants of Hanan**
13. **Descendants of Giddel**
14. **Descendants of Gahar**
15. **Descendants of Reaiah**
16. **Descendants of Rezin**
17. **Descendants of Nekoda**
18. **Descendants of Gazzam**
19. **Descendants of Uzza**
20. **Descendants of Paseah**
21. **Descendants of Besai**
22. **Descendants of Asnah** (in **Ezra 2:50** only)
23. **Descendants of Meunim**
24. **Descendants of Nephusim**
25. **Descendants of Bakbuk**
26. **Descendants of Hakupha**
27. **Descendants of Harhur**
28. **Descendants of Bazluth**
29. **Descendants of Mehida**
30. **Descendants of Harsha**
31. **Descendants of Barkos**
32. **Descendants of Sisera**
33. **Descendants of Temah**
34. **Descendants of Neziah**
35. **Descendants of Hatipha**

Descendants of Solomon's Servants[17]

1. **Descendants of Sotai**
2. **Descendants of Hassophereth** (Sophereth[18] in **Nehemiah 7:57**)
3. **Descendants of Peruda** (Perida in **Nehemiah 7:57**)
4. **Descendants of Jaala**
5. **Descendants of Darkon**
6. **Descendants of Giddel**
7. **Descendants of Shephatiah**
8. **Descendants of Hattil**
9. **Descendants of Pokereth–Hazzebaim**
10. **Descendants of Ami** (Amon in **Nehemiah 7:59**)

Total of the temple servants and the descendants of Solomon's servants—392 (Ezra 2:58; Nehemiah 7:60)

Returnees—who had come from the Babylonian cities of Tel Melah, Tel Harsha, Kerub, Addon, and Immer—who could not show that their families were of Israelite descent:

Among the Laity

1. **Descendants of Delaiah**[19]
2. **Descendants of Tobiah**

3. **Descendants of Nekoda**
Total of the laity—652 (Ezra 2:60) (compared to **642** in **Nehemiah 7:62)**

Among the Kohathite Attending Priests
1. **Descendants of Hobaiah**
2. **Descendants of Hakkoz**[20]
3. **Descendants of Barzillai**[21]
Total of the priests—unspecified number

Biblical and Theological Significance

A decree of Cyrus the Great[22] of Persia granted repatriation to all peoples who had been taken captive by various Babylonian monarchs, especially the captives taken in 586 B.C. by Nebuchadnezzar II (605–562 B.C.).[23] When Cyrus brought the Babylonian Empire to an end in 539 B.C., the decree was implemented. The Jews were among those refugees who were permitted to return to Jerusalem and were also granted assistance by that beneficent ruler to do so. However, not all journeyed back at the same time as these lists attest. The first large movement was led by Zerubbabel in 538 B.C. (**Ezra 2:1–4; 3:2, 8; Nehemiah 7:7; 12:1; Haggai 1:14–15**). Ezra himself returned in 458 B.C. (**Ezra 7:1, 6**) and his later contemporary Nehemiah did so in 444 B.C. (**Nehemiah 2:9**). The lists of the families involved in these migrations appear in **Ezra 2:1–65** and **Nehemiah 7:4–67**, totaling 42,360 persons in all (**Ezra 2:64; Nehemiah 7:66**).

By the seventh month (Tishri), Jews had returned to their homeland and settled in their ancestral towns. The first item on their collective agenda was to honor and praise their God for his marvelous restoration of their community in the land of Abraham, Isaac, and Jacob. They therefore "assembled together as one in Jerusalem" (**Ezra 3:1**). Then Joshua, with Jozadak and their fellow priests, and Zerubbabel and his associates, erected an altar for burnt offerings as prescribed by what was "written in the Law of Moses the man of God" (**Ezra 32**). They did this in fulfillment of the witness of many prophetic voices (**Isaiah 40:1–11; 45:1–17; 49:8–26; Jeremiah 31:1–40; Hosea 1:2–11; Amos 9:11–15**), despite the objections and harassment of their enemies (**Ezra 4**).

The altar was indeed not a temple, but it was the down payment on a temple to be built on the foundations of Solomon's Temple, which had been demolished during the capture of Jerusalem (**Ezra 3:6, 10**). Work began with enthusiasm, but within a few years, everything ground to a halt (i.e., from 536–520 B.C.). It was not until 520 B.C., that Joshua, Zerubbabel, and the people, encouraged and supported by the prophets Haggai and Zechariah, completed the Second Temple in 516 B.C.

This record, no doubt, demonstrates the Israelites' ability and insistence on keeping ancient and cherished traditions alive and carrying forward the names of persons from one generation to the next. This is particularly the case in royal and priestly names and the names of leaders. The many differences that do exist between the written records of **Ezra 2** and **Nehemiah 7** may be accounted for by (1) the common identical or similar names of the returnees; (2) the relative lack of scribal professionalism in the wake of the exile; (3) lack of adequate protection of manuscripts in times of conflict and deportation; and (4) human laxity or carelessness, especially, again, under adverse circumstances.

According to **Ezra 2:64–65,** the number of exiles who returned to Jerusalem with Zerubbabel and Joshua was 42,360, besides 7,337 slaves and 200 singers; the account in **Nehemiah 7:66–67** also reports a total of 42,360 returning exiles, 7,337 male and female slaves, and lists 245 male and female singers. The 45 extra singers in Nehemiah's report can easily be ascribed to (1) different sources used by Nehemiah and Ezra; (2) two different original census lists of singers in the period between Ezra's return (458 B.C.) and Nehemiah's (444 B.C.), where the additional 45 singers brought Nehemiah's total to 245 when there were none previously; or (3) a source known only to Nehemiah that upped the total.[24]

Notes

1. The first exiles to return to Jerusalem numbered 42,360 (**Ezra 2:64; Nehemiah 7:66**). The total number does *not* include "their 7,337 male and female slaves; and . . . 200 [or 245] male and female singers" (**Ezra 2:65**; cf. **Nehemiah 7:66–67**).

2. In at least seventeen places in the various categories in the chart, the numbers differ between the Ezra and Nehemiah accounts (i.e., for the heads of families and leaders, the representatives from fifteen towns, some of the Levites, and some of the non-Israelite laity). As the commentary in Barker, ed., *Zondervan NIV Study Bible* (2020) for **Ezra 2:1–70** points out: "Many of these differences may be explained, however, by assuming that a cipher notation was used with vertical strokes for units and horizontal strokes for tens, which led to copying errors."

3. See charts "**1 Chronicles 3**: Zerubbabel and Shealtiel and the Double Line of the Messiah through King David's Sons, Nathan and Solomon" and "**Ezra 1**: Sheshbazzar and Zerubbabel, the Governors over the Restored Community in Jerusalem (Post-Exile)."

4. Joshua (or Jeshua) son of Jozadak (**Ezra 3:2, 8; 5:2; 10:18; Nehemiah 12:26; Haggai 1:1, 12, 14; 2:2, 4; Zechariah 6:11**) was the first high priest to serve in the Second Temple. He is also identified in **Ezra 2:36** and **Nehemiah 7:39** as a relative of Jedaiah the Kohathite priest "through the family of Jeshua [Joshua]," but the exact relationship is unknown. For the lineage of Joshua/Jeshua, see charts "**Ezra 2**: Joshua, the High Priest in the Second Temple, and His Descendants (Post-Exile)" and "**Supplement 2**: The High Priests of Israel."

5. **Ezra 2:2** mentions nine leaders and **Nehemiah 7:7** mentions ten leaders who returned with Zerubbabel and Joshua, but there are variants between the two lists. Also, Seraiah (שְׂרָיָה) of **Ezra 2:2** may have been conflated orally with Azariah (עֲזַרְיָה) in **Nehemiah 7:7**, a reading supported by LXX (see note 7).

6. The Nehemiah who returned with Zerubbabel in 538 B.C. is not (1) Nehemiah the governor who came 94 years later in 444 B.C., nor (2) Nehemiah son of Azbuk, the ruler of the half-district of Beth Zur (**Nehemiah 3:16**).

7. The identity of the leader named Seraiah who returned with Zerubbabel to Jerusalem in 538 B.C. (shown in the chart) is unclear. He is clearly not Seraiah the high priest who was martyred by the Babylonians at Riblah in 586 B.C. (designated Seraiah #1 in some charts), but he is possibly a Kohathite scribal–priest—whose lineage parallels that of the high priests, for example, see Seraiah #2 (also called Azariah #2) in the charts: "**Ezra 7**: Ezra, the Priestly Scribe and Teacher of the Law (Post-Exile)," "**1 Chronicles 9**: The Kohathite Attending Priests in the Second Temple (Post-Exile)," and "**Nehemiah 12**: Genealogical Record of the Heads of the Kohathite Priests and Levites Who Returned to Jerusalem with Zerubbabel and Joshua in the Post-Exile."

The following Seraiah and Azariah individuals are distinguished based on chronological data, although there is no specific supporting textual evidence (except as noted):

- **Azariah #1, the high priest** in Solomon's Temple ca. 609–600 B.C., was the father of the (martyred) high priest, Seraiah #1. The genealogy of Azariah #1 is given in **1 Chronicles 6:13–14; 9:11; Ezra 7:1**. Azariah #1 is the same person as Azariah #22 in chart "**Supplement 2**: The High Priests of Israel."

- **Seraiah #1, the martyred high priest**, was killed by the Babylonians at Riblah in 586 B.C. His father was Azariah #1, and his sons were, presumably, Jozadak (the high priest who was taken into Babylonian captivity in 586 B.C. and died there) and Seraiah #2 (Azariah #2) the scribe, who returned to Jerusalem and became the official in charge of the Second Temple (ca. 520–516 B.C.). Seraiah #1 the martyr could not have returned with Zerubbabel in 538 B.C., so the priest listed as "Seraiah" in **Ezra 2:2** is most likely Seraiah #2.
- **Seraiah #2, a scribe and priest**, is presumably the person named "Seraiah" in **Ezra 2:2** (listed in the chart above)—who is conflated with "Azariah" (Azariah #2) in **Nehemiah 7:7**. Therefore, Seraiah #2 (Azariah #2) returned to Jerusalem with Zerubbabel in 538 B.C. The father of Seraiah #2 (scribe) was likely Seraiah #1 the high priest; also, Seraiah #2 is likely the father of Ezra the scribe, as well as another son, Seraiah #3.
- **Seraiah #3, a scribe and priest**, is likely the "Seraiah" of **Nehemiah 10:2**, who sealed the covenant with Nehemiah in 444 B.C. (i.e., 93 years later than Seraiah #2, who was a contemporary of Zerubbabel in 538 B.C.). It is likely that Seraiah #3 was the *son* of Seraiah #2 (Azariah #2) and the *grandson* of Seraiah #1 (a case of papponymy). Also, it is likely that Seraiah #3 and his son Azariah #3 were both living in 444 B.C.
- **Azariah #3, a scribe and priest**, is presumably the "Azariah" of **Nehemiah 10:2**, who sealed the covenant with Nehemiah in 444 B.C. It is likely that Azariah #3 was the *son* of Seraiah #3 and the *grandson* of Azariah #2 (a case of papponymy). Also, it appears that Azariah #3 and his father, Seraiah #3, were both living in 444 B.C.

If the proposed identifiers listed above are true, then a repeated papponymic pattern occurs in the father-son lineage as follows: Azariah #1 the high priest—Seraiah #1 the high priest—Azariah #2/Seraiah #2 the scribe—Seraiah #3 the scribe—Azariah #3 the scribe.

8. The narrative of Mordecai and Esther is set during the reign of King Xerxes (or Ahasuerus), 486–465 B.C., which was many years after Zerubbabel's return in 538 B.C., so this figure named Mordecai is not Esther's cousin (Mordecai; **Esther 2:5, 7**).

9. Pahath-Moab was a *leader of the people* "through the line of Jeshua and Joab" (**Ezra 2:6; Nehemiah 7:11**), but he is probably unrelated to Joshua/Jeshua the high priest (see note 4), since he is not identified as a priest.

10. Bani, בָּנִי, (**Ezra 2:10**) is also rendered Binnui, בִּנּוּי (**Nehemiah 7:15**).

11. Jorah (**Ezra 2:18**) is otherwise unknown (cf. **Nehemiah 7:24; 10:19**).

12. Gibbar (**Ezra 2:20**) is otherwise unknown (cf. **Nehemiah 7:25**).

13. Compare this list of returning Kohathite priests with those in chart "**Nehemiah 12**: Genealogical Record of the Heads of the Kohathite Priests and Levites Who Returned to Jerusalem with Zerubbabel and Joshua in the Post-Exile." It is important to note that the list of Kohathite attending priests of the post-exile shown above (e.g., Jedaiah, Immer, Pashhur, and Harim; **Ezra 2:36–39** and **Nehemiah 7:39–42**) retain the same *ancestral* names of the priestly divisions that were set up by King David for service in Solomon's Temple (**1 Chronicles 24**). For example, Jedaiah was over the Davidic second division (**1 Chronicles 24:7**); Immer was over the sixteenth division (**1 Chronicles 24:14**) and Harim was over the third division (**1 Chronicles 24:8**). Pashhur son of Immer (**Jeremiah 20:1, 3**; cf. Immer in **1 Chronicles 24:14**) is a different priest than Pashhur son of Malkijah (**Nehemiah 11:12; Jeremiah 21:1**; cf. Malkijah in **1 Chronicles 24:9**). Therefore, the priestly families in **Ezra 2:36–39** and **Nehemiah 7:39–42** represent the *descendants* of the original priestly families of **1 Chronicles 24** (see chart "**1 Chronicles 24**: Genealogical Registry of the Twenty-Four Divisions of Attending Attending Priests Who Rotated Service in Solomon's Temple."

14. Jeshua the Levite appears to be the son of Kadmiel (**Nehemiah 12:24**). Jeshua the Levite is not the same person as his contemporary, Joshua/Jeshua the high priest (see note 4).

15. Asaph was one of the three chief musicians in Solomon's Temple; his descendants were Gershonites from the tribe of Levi. For the lineage of Asaph, see charts "**1 Chronicles 6**: Levi: High Priests, Priests, Levites, and Musicians in Solomon's Temple" and "**1 Chronicles 9**: Seven Levitical Leaders in the Second Temple (Post-Exile)."

16. The temple servants (called the *Nethinim* in some translations, such as the NKJV) of **Ezra 2:43–54** and **Nehemiah 7:46–56** were a body commissioned by David to assist the Levites (**Ezra 8:20**). They were of a non-Jewish background, but they were accepted by Israel (cf. **Ezra 8:20; Nehemiah 3:26, 31**). *Nethinim* (נְתִינִים) means "given, delivered over" to serve (From *ntn*, "to give," passive participle, occurring 15 times; **1 Chronicles 9:2; Ezra 2:43, 58, 70; 7:7; 8:17; Nehemiah 3:26, 31; 7:46, 60, 73; 10:28; 11:3, 21**). Many of the names of the temple servants are not Hebrew or even Semitic, implying that they were of foreign extraction; perhaps they were originally slaves or prisoners of war. The places from which they came, such as Kasiphia (**Ezra 8:17**)—clearly not in Israel or Judah—also support their identity as non-Israelites.

17. The descendants of Solomon's servants (**Ezra 2:55–58; Nehemiah 7:57–60**; cf. **2 Chronicles 9:10**) were obviously descendants of laborers [*mas*, no doubt from Akkadian (especially Alalakh) *massu, corvée* (worker), virtual slave/slavery] who were pressed into involuntary service.

18. *Sophereth* refers by extension to the office of the scribe, though its original usage was in the sphere of leather and leatherwork, as in the manufacture of writing material. Also (as here) it became a personal name, just as, for example, one who works in carpentry may belong to a family with the surname "Carpenter."

19. It is not clear if Delaiah in **Ezra 2:60** and **Nehemiah 7:62** is related to the *ancestral* Kohathite attending priest named Delaiah, who was over the twenty-third division of priests in the temple in the days of David (**1 Chronicles 24:18**).

20. Hakkoz is the name of the *ancestral* Kohathite attending priest who was over the seventh of the twenty-four priestly divisions in Solomon's Temple at the time of King David (**1 Chronicles 24:10**).

21. Barzillai was the distinguished father-in-law of these "descendants of Barzillai" (who were priests). The original Barzillai was *not* a Levitical Kohathite priest, but rather a Gileadite from Rogelim (**2 Samuel 17:27; 19:31**). During the strained and difficult days when David stayed in Mahanaim to escape Absalom, Barzillai was a very wealthy man who befriended David and offered him much-needed supplies (**2 Samuel 19:31–40**). For his kindness, David invited Barzillai to come to Jerusalem and live there, but because he was old, Barzillai chose to return home to Gilead. However, Barzillai's son Kimham and one or more of Barzillai's daughters did accompany David back to Jerusalem. The Barzillai family was highly esteemed in the royal court thereafter. On his deathbed, David spoke a specific blessing on the Barzillai descendants, instructing Solomon to show them perpetual kindness (**1 Kings 2:7**). In fact, one of the Barzillai's daughters married a Levitical priest of unknown name and heritage, and quite uncharacteristically for an Aaronic descendant, this priest took on the renowned Barzillai family name instead of retaining his Levitical agnomen! Some of the Barzillai descendants were taken into Babylonian exile but returned to Jerusalem in the post-exile (**Ezra 2:61–63; Nehemiah 7:63–65**). The biblical narrative explains why the Barzillai priests could not clearly trace their ancestry and therefore had to wait for divine judgment about ministering in the Second Temple until a high priest could inquire by the Urim and Thummim (**Ezra 2:63; Nehemiah 7:65**). See chart "**2 Samuel 17**: Barzillai the Gileadite," especially note 2.

22. For the decree of Cyrus, see **2 Chronicles 36:22–23; Ezra 1:1–4**. For the kings of Persia, see chart "**Supplement 5**: The Kings of Persia."

23. For the kings of Babylon, see chart "**Supplement 4**: The Kings of Babylon."

24. The Septuagint adds 45 to the MT total of 200 in **Ezra 2:65** in an obvious attempt to harmonize the differences. Nehemiah's 245 singers (**Nehemiah 7:67**) is attested to by Septuagint A and L. Most likely the book of Ezra reflects the original reading by virtue of the principle of *lectio difficilior*.

EZRA 3: GENEALOGICAL RECORD OF THE OVERSEERS OF THE CONSTRUCTION OF THE SECOND TEMPLE (POST-EXILE)

Approximate Dating: ca. 520–516 B.C. ***Relevant Scriptures:*** **Ezra 3:8–9**

Key Overseers

1. **Zerubbabel**, son of Shealtiel and governor of Judah[1]
2. **Joshua** (Jeshua), son of Jozadak, the high priest[2]

Levites Who Supervised the Work[3]

1. **Sons and brothers of Joshua (Jeshua)**[4]
2. **Kadmiel and his sons (descendants of Hodaviah)**[5]
3. **Sons of Henadad and their sons and brothers**[6]

Biblical and Theological Significance

"In the second month of the second year after their arrival at the house of God in Jerusalem, Zerubbabel son of Shealtiel, Joshua son of Jozadak and the rest of the people (the priests and the Levites and all who had returned from the captivity to Jerusalem) began the work [of rebuilding the house of God]" (**Ezra 3:8**). The construction took four years, from ca. 520–516 B.C.

Every major project, involving design, construction, and outfitting of a building, requires a wide variety of expertise. This was even truer of the temple, wherein the Holy One of Israel would reside. Zerubbabel and Joshua—who represented the physical and spiritual facets of the project—trained and employed a great many of the returning exiles in every detail of the endeavor. The need for a great number of competent people was similar to the needs during the construction of the great temple of Solomon (966–960 B.C.) more than four hundred forty years earlier (**1 Kings 5:13–6:10, 14–36**). In that project, God's Spirit had revealed the blueprints to David, because building to the correct specifications was of the utmost importance (**1 Chronicles 28:11–19**).[7]

Notes

1. For the lineage of Zerubbabel, see chart "**1 Chronicles 3**: Zerubbabel and Shealtiel and the Double Line of the Messiah through King David's Sons, Nathan and Solomon."

2. Joshua was the first high priest in the Second Temple, serving from ca. 516–490 B.C. Joshua in **Ezra 2:2; 3:2, 8; 4:3; 5:2; 10:18; Nehemiah 7:7; 12:1, 7, 10, 26; Haggai 1:1, 12, 14; 2:2, 4; Zechariah 3:1, 3, 6, 8–9; 6:11** is called Jeshua in **Ezra 2:36; Nehemiah 7:39**. Joshua came to Jerusalem with Zerubbabel in ca. 538 B.C. (cf. **Nehemiah 7:7; 12:1**). Together, Joshua (tribe of Levi) and Zerubbabel (tribe of Judah) were the key religious and civil leaders, respectively, who rebuilt the altar and reestablished worship in post-exilic Jerusalem. Construction of the Second Temple took approximately four years (520–516 B.C.); it was completed and dedicated in 516 B.C. (i.e., 70 years after Solomon's Temple had been destroyed by the Babylonians in 586 B.C.). See chart "**Ezra 2**: Joshua, the High Priest in the Second Temple, and His Descendants (Post-Exile)."

3. Supervising Levites had to be twenty years or older (**Ezra 3:8**).

4. Joshua the Levite (**Ezra 3:9**) is the same person as Jeshua the Levite (cf. **Ezra 2:40; 8:33; Nehemiah 7:43; 8:7; 9:4–5; 12:8, 24**), who is identified as the "son of Kadmiel" (**Nehemiah 12:24**). One of the sons of Jeshua the Levite was Jozabad (**Ezra 8:33**). Joshua/Jeshua son of Kadmiel is clearly not Joshua the high priest, the son of Jozadak (see note 2), nor is he Jeshua the Levite, the son of Azaniah who sealed the covenant with Nehemiah in 444 B.C. (**Nehemiah 10:9**).

5. Kadmiel and the sons of Kadmiel are called "descendants of Hodaviah" from the tribe of Levi (cf. **Ezra 2:40; 3:9; Nehemiah 7:43**). Their ancestor Hodaviah should not be confused with Hodaviah the *Judahite*, the son of Elioenai, a descendant of Zerubbabel (**1 Chronicles 3:24**; shown in chart "**1 Chronicles 3**: Zerubbabel and Shealtiel and the Double Line of the Messiah through King David's Sons, Nathan and Solomon" and discussed in note 39) nor with Hodaviah son of Hassenuah, the Benjaminite (**1 Chronicles 9:7**).

6. The "sons of Henadad" include Binnui (**Nehemiah 3:18, 24; 10:9**).

7. This was true of the Mosaic tabernacle as well; see **Exodus 25:1–9; 35:4–11, 25–29, 31–35; 36:1–2, 8; 38:23**.

EZRA 7: EZRA, THE PRIESTLY SCRIBE AND TEACHER OF THE LAW (POST-EXILE)

Approximate Dating: Ezra was born and lived in Babylon ca. 555–458 B.C., brought exiles to Jerusalem in 458 B.C., conducted the public reading of the Law in 444 B.C., and died soon after the celebration of the Feast of Tabernacles, Nehemiah 8:9–10:39, in 444 B.C., or possibly slightly later.[1] ***Relevant Scriptures:*** **Ezra 7:1–6; 8:33**; also **2 Kings 25:18, 21; 1 Chronicles 6:1–15, 50–53; 9:11; Nehemiah 11:11**

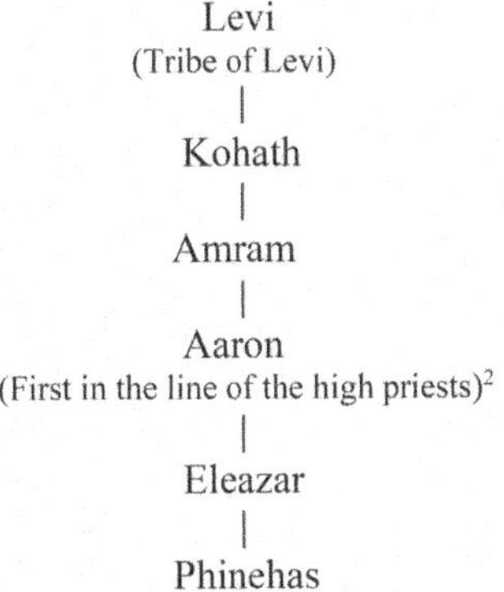

Phinehas
|
Abishua
|
Bukki
|
Uzzi
|
Zerahiah
|
Meraioth
(= Meraioth of **Ezra 7:3**)
(= Meraioth #8 in the high priest summary chart)
|
Ezra 7:1-3 omits some of the known high priests[3]
(Names of the omitted priests are shown in brackets below[4])
|
[Amariah]
(= Amariah #9 in the high priest summary chart)
|
[Ahitub]
(= Ahitub #10 in the high priest summary chart)
|
[Zadok]
(= Zadok #11 in the high priest summary chart)
(High priest under King David, 1011–971 B.C.)
|
[Ahimaaz]
(= Ahimaaz #12 in the high priest summary chart)
|
[Azariah]
(=Azariah #13 in the high priest summary chart)
|
[Johanan]
(= Johanan #14 in the high priest summary chart)
|
Azariah
(= Azariah of **Ezra 7:3**)
(= Azariah #15 in the high priest summary chart)
|
Amariah
(= Amariah of **Ezra 7:3**)
(= Amariah #16 in the high priest summary chart)
|
Ahitub
(= Ahitub of **Ezra 7:2**)
(= Ahitub #17 in the high priest summary chart)
|
[Meraioth][5]
(= Meraioth #18 in the high priest summary chart)
|
[Azariah][6]
(= Azariah #19 in the high priest summary chart)
|
Zadok
(= Zadok of **Ezra 7:2**)
(= Zadok #20 in the high priest summary chart)
(High priest in the days of Hezekiah; 715–686 B.C.)
|
Shallum[7]
(Meshullam)
(= Shallum of **Ezra 7:2**)
(= Shallum/Meshullam #21 in the high priest summary chart)
|
Hilkiah
(= Hilkiah of **Ezra 7:1**)
(= Hilkiah #22 in the high priest summary chart)
(High priest under King Josiah, ca. 640–609 B.C.)

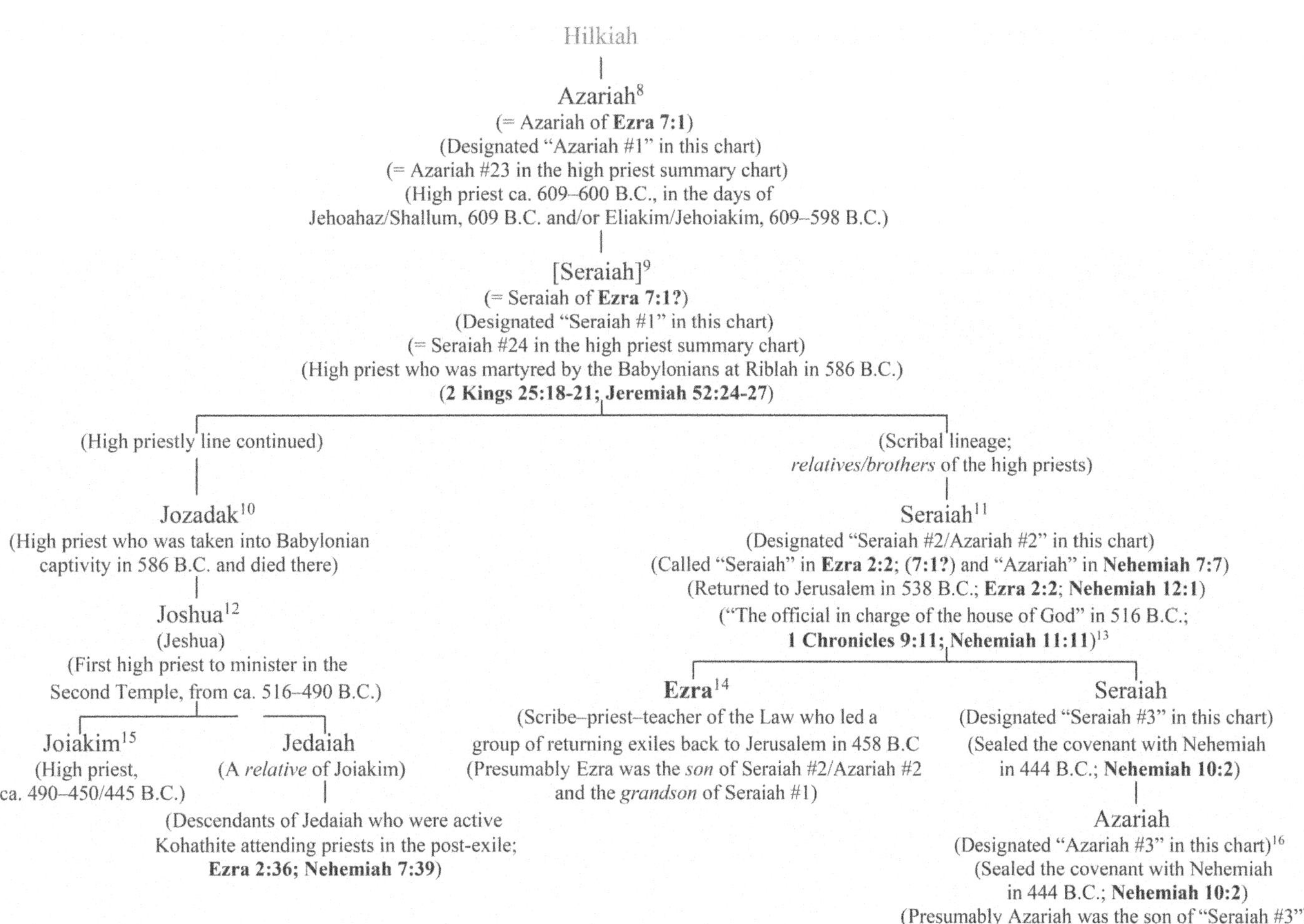

Biblical and Theological Significance

Ezra,[17] of a priestly-scribal lineage of Kohathite priests, was probably born in Babylon ca. 555 B.C. The Babylonian exile lasted for seventy years (586–516 B.C.), but thanks to an edict issued by Cyrus the Great (559–530 B.C.), an initial group of captives was able to return to Jerusalem as early as 538 B.C. This group included the high priest Joshua, the son of Jozadak, son of Seraiah (#1), and Zerubbabel the Judahite, who became governor of the new state called Yehud. Together, Joshua and Zerubbabel and the prophets Haggai and Zechariah were influential in mobilizing the people to rebuild the temple in Jerusalem, which was completed in 516 B.C. (**Ezra 2:2; 3:1–11; 5:1–2; 6:14–15; Nehemiah 12:1–7; Haggai 1:12–2:5**). However, it was not until 458 B.C.—in the seventh year of the Persian ruler, Artaxerxes I[18] (465–424 B.C.) and fifty-eight years after the Second Temple had been completed—that Ezra, the scribal priest, led a large number of exiles back to Jerusalem (**Ezra 8:1–20**). These returnees brought gold, silver, and articles for the temple (**Ezra 8:24–30**).

Ezra 7:1 identifies Ezra the priestly scribe as the "son of Seraiah, the son of Azariah, the son of Hilkiah" (i.e., in the line of the high priesthood). However, Ezra obviously was not the immediate offspring of the martyred high priest Seraiah (i.e., Seraiah #1, see notes 9 and 11), since Ezra did not return to Jerusalem until 458 B.C. and Seraiah had been killed 128 years earlier in 586 B.C. (**2 Kings 25:18–21; Jeremiah 52:24–27**). Ezra may have been called the "son" of the martyred Seraiah (i.e., Seraiah #1, Ezra's ancestor) in the sense that it established his priestly credentials. As shown in the chart, Ezra was certainly in a priestly *scribal* lineage (i.e., the Seraiah #1–Seraiah #2–Ezra line) that paralleled that of the line of the high priests (i.e., Seraiah #1–Jozadak–Joshua/Jeshua–Joiakim). In addition, Ezra was "a teacher well versed in the Law of Moses," one who had "devoted himself to the study and observance of the Law of the Lord, and to teaching its decrees and laws in Israel." He was "learned in matters concerning the commands and decrees of the Lord for Israel" and a government official who was trusted even by the Persians, who called him "Ezra the priest, the teacher of the Law of the God of heaven" (**Ezra 7:6, 10–12, 21**). King Artaxerxes I "granted him [Ezra] everything he asked, for the hand of the Lord his God was on him" (**Ezra 7:6**). Ezra stressed repentance, family purity, and separation of the covenant community of Israel from the peoples of the land (**Ezra 9–10**). Josephus comments that Ezra "died an old man, and was buried in a magnificent manner at Jerusalem"[19] about the same time that Joiakim, the high priest, died; Joiakim served from ca. 490–450/444 B.C.[20]

The final summary of the *known* high priests in the chart above—beginning with Aaron the first (who began service in the Mosaic tabernacle in 1445 B.C.) and concluding with Seraiah #1 (who died in 586 B.C.)—shows that twenty-four high priests (see note 4) held the high priestly office *before* the exile. Over this span of approximately 860 years, the tenure of each high priest was approximately thirty-six years.

Notes

1. The chronology of the book of Ezra:

Decree of Cyrus	538 B.C.
	Ezra 1:1
Completion of the foundation of the Second Temple	536 B.C.
	Ezra 3:8, 10–11
Sixteen-year delay in the rebuilding of the temple	536–520 B.C.
	Ezra 4:1–23
Resumption of temple construction under Darius I	520 B.C.
	Ezra 4:24; 6:12
First year of Xerxes I (Ahasuerus)	486 B.C.
	Ezra 4:6
First year of Artaxerxes I	465 B.C.
	Ezra 4:7
Completion of the Second Temple	516 B.C.
	Ezra 6:15
Ezra's arrival in Jerusalem under Artaxerxes I	458 B.C.
	Ezra 7:8

2. See charts "**1 Chronicles 6**: Levi: High Priests, Priests, Levites, and Musicians in Solomon's Temple" and "**Supplement 2**: The High Priests of Israel."

3. Refer to *all* the high priests of Israel and their numbered designations (#1–#77) in the summary chart "**Supplement 2**: The High Priests of Israel."

4. The lineage of Ezra given in **Ezra 7:1–5** shows literary *telescoping*: the omission of known ancestors (i.e., names shown in brackets in the chart). Specifically, six high priests between Meraioth and Azariah (**Ezra 7:3**) and two high priests between Ahitub and Zadok (**Ezra 7:2**) are omitted from Ezra's lineage. Given that the final branching shows Ezra is in a *scribal* lineage (rather than a high priestly lineage), 24 known high priests total (inclusive) held the office between the first high priest (Aaron) and Seraiah #1 (the last high priest of the exile). Since Ezra brought a group of returnees back to Jerusalem in 458 B.C. (**Ezra 7:1–8**), he cannot be the Ezra figure, a Kohathite attending priest, who returned to Jerusalem with Zerubbabel in 538 B.C. (**Nehemiah 12:1**)—for a clearer understanding of the priest named Ezra who returned with Zerubbabel, see note 43 in chart "**1 Chronicles 24**: Genealogical Registry of the Twenty-Four Divisions of Kohathite Attending Priests Who Rotated Service in Solomon's Temple." For the major references to the high priests of Israel, see **1 Chronicles 6:1–15; 9:10–11; Nehemiah 11:10–11**; also see the summary chart "**Supplement 2**: The High Priests of Israel."

5. Meraioth son of Ahitub is omitted in the list of Ezra's ancestors in **Ezra 7:1–5** but is mentioned in the lineage of the high priests at **Nehemiah 11:11**. The high priest Meraioth son of Ahitub is a different person than the high priest Meraioth son of Zerahiah (**Ezra 7:3–4**; cf. **1 Chronicles 6:6, 51–52**). Meraioth son of Ahitub corresponds to the high priest Meraioth #18 in the summary chart "**Supplement 2**: The High Priests of Israel."

6. Azariah son of Meriaoth is an enigmatic high priest. He is not listed among the high priests in Ezra's heritage in **Ezra 7:1–6**. For an explanation of Azariah's identity, see Azariah #19 in the summary chart "**Supplement 2**: The High Priests of Israel."

7. Shallum (**1 Chronicles 6:12–13; Ezra 7:2**) is otherwise Meshullam (**1 Chronicles 9:11; Nehemiah 11:11**). He corresponds to Shallum/Meshullam #21 in the summary chart "**Supplement 2**: The High Priests of Israel."

8. Azariah (designated Azariah #1 in this chart)—corresponding to Azariah #23 in "**Supplement 2**: The High Priests of Israel"—was the high priest in Solomon's Temple from ca. 609 B.C. to as late as 598 B.C., in the days of King Jehoahaz/Shallum, 609 B.C. and/or King Eliakim/Jehoiakim, 609–598 B.C. Azariah #1 was the *son* of Hilkiah and the *father* of the martyred high priest Seraiah #1; Azariah's genealogy is given in **1 Chronicles 6:13–14** and portions of **Ezra 7:1**. For chronological reasons, it is *unlikely* that the high priest Azariah #1 lived through the Babylonian exile and returned to Jerusalem with Zerubbabel in 538 B.C.; more likely, the Azariah in the days of Zerubbabel was a priestly *scribe* (designated Azariah #2, see note 11) or that he was possibly the Azariah figure who sealed the covenant with Nehemiah in 444 B.C. (**Nehemiah 10:2**; cf. 7:7; designated Azariah #3, see note 11). Azariah #1 of 609–600 B.C. should not be confused with other priests named Azariah: (1) Azariah, the "chief priest" who ministered in the days of King Uzziah/Azariah, 792–740 B.C. and discovered that the king had leprosy (**2 Chronicles 26:20**); or (2) Azariah—probably a priestly scribe—who was "the official in charge of the temple of God" in the days of King Hezekiah, 715–686 B.C. (**2 Chronicles 31:10–13**).

9. Seraiah (designated Seraiah #1 in this chart)—who corresponds to Seraiah #24 in "**Supplement 2**: The High Priests of Israel"—was the high priest in Solomon's Temple at the time of the Babylonian conquest of Jerusalem (**2 Kings 25:18**). He was brought to the king of Babylon at "Riblah, in the land of Hamath," and there at the Babylonian headquarters, he was executed in 586 B.C. (**2 Kings 25:18–21; Jeremiah 52:24–27**). The father of Seraiah #1 was Azariah #1, and Seraiah's sons were (presumably): Jozadak (the high priest who was taken into Babylonian captivity in 586 B.C.) and Seraiah #2 (Azariah #2) the scribe, who returned to Jerusalem and became the official in charge of the Second Temple (ca. 516 B.C.); see note 11. Seraiah #1 the martyr could not have returned with Zerubbabel in 538 B.C., so the priest listed as "Seraiah" in **Ezra 2:2** is most likely Seraiah #2. To distinguish Seraiah #1, #2 and #3, see explanations in note 11.

10. Jozadak/J(eh)ozadak the high priest at the time of the Babylonian captivity was deported "when the Lord sent Judah and Jerusalem into exile" (**1 Chronicles 6:15**). He probably died in captivity, for there is no further mention of him. The first high priest to serve in the Second Temple (post-exile) was Jozadak's son Joshua/Jeshua (see note 12; **Ezra 3:2, 8**; **Haggai 1:1**; **Zechariah 6:11**).

11. For chronological reasons, and considering Ezra's lineage in **Ezra 7:1–5**, one must propose at least three Seraiahs who were either high priests or priestly scribes (i.e., scribes were *relatives* of the high priests and in a *scribal lineage* that paralleled that of the high priests):

(1) **Seraiah #1** (son of Azariah #1 the high priest) was the high priest who was killed at Riblah in 586 B.C. (note 9). He was the father of Jozadak (**1 Chronicles 6:14**; see note 10) and the grandfather of Joshua/Jeshua the first high priest to serve in the newly completed Second Temple in 516 B.C. (see note 12).

(2) The application of Occam's Razor leads to the most straightforward proposition that **Seraiah #2** was a priestly scribe who was in a scribal lineage that paralleled that of the high priesthood line—presumably Seraiah #2 was the *son* of Seraiah #1, the *brother* of Jozadak the high priest, and the *father* of Ezra the scribe. Seraiah #2 was alive when his father was killed in 586 B.C., and one may suppose, since he bore his father's name as eldest of the sons, that he (Seraiah #2) was a young adult upon his father's death in 586 B.C. and was born perhaps about 600 B.C. Seraiah #2 then lived through the exile period and returned to Jerusalem with Zerubbabel in 538 B.C. (i.e., he is the "Seraiah" figure of **Ezra 2:2** and **Nehemiah 12:1** and is designated Seraiah #2, to distinguish him from Seraiah #1). Another detail to mention is that Seraiah #2 became the "the official in charge of the house of God [Second Temple]" (**Nehemiah 11:11**; cf. **1 Chronicles 9:11**; see note 13). The existence of Seraiah #2 and his exact connection to Seraiah #1 and Ezra is never clearly attested in Scripture but can be deduced by chronology alone as follows: Seraiah #1 died in 586 B.C., and if Ezra was the son of Seraiah #1 instead of Seraiah #2, Ezra would have lived from about 600–444 B.C., which is an unrealistic lifespan. Instead, the existence of Seraiah #2 as the *son* of Seraiah #1 and the *father* of Ezra offers a reasonable explanation of Ezra's birth and death within about a 100-year time frame (ca. 555–444 B.C.). Also (and confusingly), "Seraiah" (Seraiah #2, a scribe) of 538 B.C. in **Ezra 2:2** is conflated with the person called "Azariah" (Azariah #2, a scribe) of 538 B.C. in **Nehemiah 7:7**; this explains the dual identification in the chart that Seraiah #2 is Azariah #2.

(3) **Seraiah #3**, a scribe and priest, is likely the "Seraiah" of **Nehemiah 10:2**, who sealed the covenant with Nehemiah in 444 B.C. (i.e., more than 90 years later than Seraiah #2/Azariah #2, who was a contemporary of Zerubbabel in 538 B.C.). He is not Seraiah #2 since the second Seraiah was born ca. 600 B.C. It is likely that Seraiah #3 was the *son* of Seraiah #2 (Azariah #2) and the *grandson* of Seraiah #1 (a case of papponymy). Also, it is likely that Seraiah #3 and his son Azariah #3 were both living in 444 B.C. (cf. **Nehemiah 10:2**).

None of the Seraiah figures (#1, #2, or #3) should be confused with Seraiah son of Neriah (**Jeremiah 51:59**), who was a court official and a contemporary of Jeremiah the prophet in ca. 627–586 B.C.

If the proposed generations of Azariahs and Seraiahs are correct, a repeated papponymic pattern is evident: Azariah #1 (high priest)–Azariah#2/Seraiah #2 (scribal priest)–Seraiah #3 (scribal priest)–Azariah #3 (scribal priest).

12. Joshua (**Ezra 2:2; 3:2, 8; 4:3; 5:2; Nehemiah 7:7; 12:1, 7, 10, 26; Haggai 1:1, 12, 14; 2:2, 4; Zechariah 3:1, 3, 6, 8–9; 6:11**) is otherwise Jeshua (**Ezra 2:36; Nehemiah 7:39**). Joshua and Jeshua are alternative names (Heb. יְהוֹשֻׁעַ and יֵשׁוּעַ respectively) for the same person. The shorter version (Jeshua) involves the abbreviating of the longer (Joshua), an orthographic/phonetic device called *syncope* in which a "weak" syllable is passed over. The meaning of both names is the same: "Yahweh saves." Perhaps the preferences are attributable to dialectical spelling or auditory influences in post-exilic times and places. Some of Joshua's descendants included "the descendants of Jedaiah through the family of Jeshua [Joshua, the high priest]"—Immer, Pashhur, and Harim—who served as Kohathite attending priests in the Second Temple (cf. **Ezra 2:36–39; Nehemiah 7:39–42**).

13. The "official in charge of the house of God" in the Old Testament (cf. **1 Chronicles 9:11; 2 Chronicles 31:13; Nehemiah 11:11**) may correspond to the individual identified as "the captain of the Temple" in New Testament times, for according to Joachim Jeremias, this priest was "the highest ranking priest after the high priest" and "selected from the nearest relations of the high priest." Their duties involved assisting at the right hand of the high priest as well as overseeing the cultus and the whole body of officiating priests (such as the priests who were over the weekly and daily courses). See Joachim Jeremias, *Jerusalem in the Time of Jesus* (Philadelphia: Fortress, 1975), 160–163.

14. The lineage for Ezra the priestly scribe is clearly established in **Ezra 7:1–5**, where his ancestors are identified as the (pre-exilic) high priests: "Ezra son of Seraiah, the son of Azariah, the son of Hilkiah, the son of Shallum, the son of Zadok, the son of Ahitub, the son of Amariah, the son of Azariah, the son of Meraioth, the son of Zerahiah, the son of Uzzi, the son of Bukki, the son of Abishua, the son of Phinehas, the son of Eleazar, the son of Aaron the chief priest." Ezra's father appears to be Seraiah #2 (see note 11). Ezra in **Nehemiah 12:13** (a contemporary of Joiakim the high priest, ca. 490–450/444 B.C.) refers to the head of a Kohathite family of priests but not to Ezra the scribal priest and teacher of the Law.

15. Joiakim the high priest was the great-great-grandfather of Jaddua, who is the last high priest mentioned in Old Testament history (cf. **Nehemiah 12:10–12, 26**). See chart "**Supplement 2**: The High Priests of Israel."

16. Azariah #3, a scribe and priest, is presumably the "Azariah" of **Nehemiah 10:2**, who sealed the covenant with Nehemiah in 444 B.C. (see note 11). Azariah #3 was probably the *son* of Seraiah #3 and the *grandson* of Azariah #2 (a case of papponymy). Also, it appears that Azariah #3 and his father, Seraiah #3, were both living in 444 B.C.

17. "Ezra" (Aramaic עֶזְרָא) means "one who helps," probably hypocoristic for Eliezer, "God is a/my helper."

18. See chart "**Supplement 5**: The Kings of Persia."

19. Josephus, *Jewish Antiquities* 11.5.5

20. For the succession of high priests during this time, and Joiakim in particular, see the insert entitled "High Priestly Line in the Post-exilic Persian Era (**Nehemiah 12:10–11**)" in chart "**Nehemiah 12**: Genealogical Record of the Heads of the Kohathite Priests and Levites Who Returned to Jerusalem with Zerubbabel and Joshua in the Post-Exile." For all the high priests, including Joiakim, see chart "**Supplement 2**: The High Priests of Israel."

EZRA 8: GENEALOGICAL RECORD OF THE KOHATHITE PRIESTS AND THE HEADS OF ISRAELITE FAMILIES WHO RETURNED TO JERUSALEM WITH EZRA

Approximate Dating: ca. 458 B.C. ***Relevant Scriptures:*** **Ezra 8:1–14**

Kohathite Attending Priests[1]

1. **Gershom**, from the descendants of Phinehas[2]
2. **Daniel**, from the descendants of Ithamar[3]

Heads of the Israelite Families

1. **Hattush**, from the descendants of David, of the descendants of Shekaniah[4]
2. **Zechariah**, from the descendants of Parosh,[5] with 150 men
3. **Eliehoenai** son of Zerahiah[6], from the descendants of Pahath-Moab[7], with 200 men
4. **Shekaniah** son of Jahaziel, from the descendants of Zattu,[8] with 300 men
5. **Ebed** son of Jonathan, from the descendants of Adin, with 50 men
6. **Jeshaiah** son of Athaliah, from the descendants of Elam,[9] with 70 men
7. **Zebadiah**[10] son of Michael, from the descendants of Shephatiah,[11] with 80 men
8. **Obadiah** son of Jehiel, from the descendants of Joab, with 218 men
9. **Shelomith** son of Josiphiah, from the descendants of Bani,[12] with 160 men
10. **Zechariah** son of Bebai, from the descendants of Bebai,[13] with 28 men
11. **Johanan**[14] son of Hakkatan, from the descendants of Azgad,[15] with 110 men
12. **Eliphelet**, **Jeuel**, and **Shemaiah**, from the descendants of Adonikam, with 60 men
13. **Uthai** and **Zakkur**, the descendants of Bigvai,[16] with 70 men

Total number of men who returned with Ezra: 1515 (including Ezra)

Biblical and Theological Significance

The decree of Cyrus in 538 B.C. permitting all Babylonian captives, including the Jews, to return to their homelands would have had little consequence if the peoples themselves refused to comply. The Jews were particularly inclined to return and so they did in several stages, beginning in 538 B.C. with Zerubbabel and Joshua; unrecorded groups likely returned intermittently until the next large migration under the leadership of the priest/politician Ezra in 458 B.C. This enabled the community of Yehud to have the material and human resources to reorganize the populace into the theocratic state Yahweh had ordained long before to Abraham (**Genesis 15**) and Moses (**Exodus 19:4–6**). Success under Ezra was enhanced a dozen years later in 444 B.C. with the arrival of Nehemiah who, working closely with Ezra, paved the way for the Second Temple period that continued until the Christian era.

Notes

1. The identity of these two Kohathite attending priests (i.e., Gershom from the Aaron–Eleazar–Phinehas line and Daniel from the Aaron–Ithamar

line) shows that the pre-exilic system, which had been instigated by David in ca. 971 B.C., was likely still being followed in the post-exile. See table 1 in chart "**1 Chronicles 24**: Genealogical Registry of the Twenty-Four Divisions of Kohathite Attending Priests Who Rotated Service in Solomon's Temple."

2. Gershom the descendant of Phinehas is from the Levi–Kohath–Amram–Aaron–Eleazar–Phinehas–Zadok line of Kohathite high priests (the Aaronic priesthood). However, Gershom himself was not a high priest in the Second Temple (see chart "**Supplement 2**: The High Priests of Israel"), nor was he from the Eli–Phinehas–Abiathar Eli priesthood (see chart "**1 Samuel 1**: Eli and the Eli Priesthood"). Gershom appears to serve as an Kohathite attending priest in the Second Temple in much the same way that other Aaron–Eleazar–Phinehas descendants did (see chart "**1 Chronicles 24**: Genealogical Registry of the Twenty-Four Divisions of Kohathite Attending Priests Who Rotated Service in Solomon's Temple"). The Gershom who returned with Ezra in 458 B.C. (post-exile) is obviously not Gershom the son of Moses, who lived a millennium earlier (ca. 1500 B.C.).

3. Daniel is in the Levi–Kohath–Amram–Aaron–Ithamar line of priests, and he represents a faithful remnant of the Ithamar priesthood (i.e., excluding those Ithamar–Eli descendants who were cursed; cf. **1 Samuel 2:22–25, 30–36; 3:14; 1 Kings 2:26–27; 1 Chronicles 24:1–18; Ezra 8:2**; see chart "**1 Samuel 1**: Eli and the Eli Priesthood"). Daniel presumably served as an Kohathite attending priest in the Second Temple in much the same way that other Kohathite priests did (see chart "**1 Chronicles 24**: Genealogical Registry of the Twenty-Four Divisions of Kohathite Attending Priests Who Rotated Service in Solomon's Temple"). Daniel was among those who sealed the agreement with Nehemiah the governor in 444 B.C. in Jerusalem (**Nehemiah 10:6**).

4. The Hebrew formula for the genealogical descent of Hattush (**Ezra 8:2–3**) is unusual here in its brevity, but its meaning is clear. "the descendants of X, Y," etc. The preposition מִן (*min*) has a wide variety of meaning, including, in this usage, "source of, out of, away from." Here, in particular, it denotes origin or lineage; Georg Fohrer, ed., *Hebrew and Aramaic Dictionary of the Old Testament* (Berlin: Walter de Gruyter, 1973), 145. Hattush the Judahite returned to Jerusalem with Ezra in 458 B.C. (**Ezra 8:2**). Hattush was the son of Shemaiah and a descendant of Shekaniah in the David–Zerubbabel line (**1 Chronicles 3:22**); see the lineage of Hattush the Judahite in chart "**1 Chronicles 3**: Zerubbabel and Shealtiel and the Double Line of the Messiah through King David's Sons, Nathan and Solomon." Hattush the Judahite is not the same person as (1) Hattush the Kohathite priest (**Nehemiah 10:4**) who sealed the covenant with Nehemiah in 444 B.C., nor is he (2) Hattush son of Hashabneiah, a Levite who helped repair the wall around Jerusalem (**Nehemiah 3:10**; cf. **9:5**).

5. Some descendants of Parosh, numbering 2172 men, returned to Jerusalem with Zerubbabel in 538 B.C. (**Ezra 2:3; Nehemiah 7:8**), and some returned with Ezra in 458 B.C. (**Ezra 8:3**). The descendants of Parosh included Zechariah, Ramiah, Izziah, Malkijah, Mijamin, Eleazar, Malkijah, Benaiah, and Pedaiah (**Ezra 83; 10:25; Nehemiah 3:25**). Parosh himself was among the leaders of the people who sealed the covenant in Jerusalem with Nehemiah in 444 B.C. (**Nehemiah 10:14**).

6. Eliehoenai the son of Zerahiah (**Ezra 8:4**), a leader of the people, is not Eliehoenai the Korahite gatekeeper (**1 Chronicles 26:3**), and he is unrelated to "Zerahiah, the son of Uzzi, the son of Bukki" who was in a high priestly line (**Ezra 7:4;** see also **1 Chronicles 6:6, 51**).

7. Some descendants of Pahath-Moab, numbering 2812 (or 2818?) men—for number variants, see note 15—returned to Jerusalem with Zerubbabel in 538 B.C. (**Ezra 2:6; Nehemiah 7:11**), and Eliehoenai the son of Zerahiah returned with Ezra in 458 B.C. (**Ezra 8:4**; see note 6). The descendants of Pahath-Moab included Adna, Kelal, Benaiah, Maaseiah, Mattaniah, Bezalel, Binnui, Manasseh (**Ezra 10:30**), and Hasshub (**Nehemiah 3:11**). Pahath-Moab was one of the leaders of the people who sealed the covenant in Jerusalem with Nehemiah in 444 B.C. (**Nehemiah 10:14**).

8. Some descendants of Zattu, numbering 945 (or 845?) men—for number variants, see note 15—returned to Jerusalem with Zerubbabel in 538 B.C. (cf. **Ezra 2:8; Nehemiah 7:13**), and others with Ezra in 458 B.C. (**Ezra 8:5**). Additionally, some had taken pagan wives while in exile (specifically, Elioenai, Eliashib, Mattaniah, Jeremoth, Zabad, and Aziza; **Ezra 10:27**). Zattu was among the leaders of the people when Nehemiah sealed the covenant with the people of Israel in post-exilic Jerusalem in 444 B.C. (**Nehemiah 10:14**).

9. Some descendants of Elam, numbering 1254 men, returned to Jerusalem with Zerubbabel in 538 B.C. (**Ezra 2:7; Nehemiah 7:12**), and Jeshaiah the son of Athaliah returned with Ezra in 458 B.C. (**Ezra 8:7**). Elam's descendants included Mattaniah, Zechariah, Jehiel, Abdi, Jeremoth, Elijah (**Ezra 10:26**), and Shekaniah, the son of Jehiel (**Ezra 10:2**). Elam was among the leaders of the people who sealed the covenant with Nehemiah (**Nehemiah 10:14**). Elam the leader of the people was not Elam the Levitical singer (**Nehemiah 12:42**). Elam is also a place name (**Ezra 2:31; Nehemiah 7:34**).

10. Zebadiah (a Shephatiah descendant) is not Zebadiah a descendant of Immer (a priestly line), who had taken a pagan wife in captivity (**Ezra 10:20**).

11. Some descendants of Shephatiah, numbering 372 men, returned to Jerusalem with Zerubbabel in 538 B.C. (**Ezra 2:4; Nehemiah 7:9**), and Shephatiah's descendant, Zebadiah son of Michael, returned with Ezra in 458 B.C. (**Ezra 8:8**). The Shephatiah of **Ezra 8:8** does not appear to be (1) Shephatiah a descendant of Solomon's servants (**Ezra 2:57**); (2) Shephatiah a Judah-Perez descendant (**Nehemiah 11:4**); nor (3) Shephatiah son of Mattan, a contemporary of the prophet Jeremiah, ca. 627–586 B.C. (**Jeremiah 38:1**).

12. Shelomith the son of Josiphiah (a longer form of Joseph) was a descendant of Bani (possibly the same as Binnui), who was a leader among the people of Israel. Bani's descendants, numbering 642 (or 648?) men—for number variants, see note 15—returned to Jerusalem with Zerubbabel in 538 B.C. (**Ezra 2:10**; cf. **Nehemiah 7:15**). Some of the descendants of Bani took pagan wives in captivity (either those listed in **Ezra 10:29**—Meshullam, Malluk, Adaiah, Jashub, Sheal, and Jeremoth—or those listed in **Ezra 10:34–37**—Maadai, Amram, Uel, Benaiah, Bedeiah, Keluhi, Vaniah, Meremoth, Eliashib, Mattaniah, Mattenai, and Jaasu); see chart "**Ezra 10**: Priests, Levites and Israelites Who Had Taken Pagan Wives in Babylonian Captivity." Also, a person named Bani was the head of an Israelite family who sealed the covenant with Nehemiah in 444 B.C. (**Nehemiah 10:14**). Bani the Israelite does not appear to be Bani the Levite(s) (cf. **Nehemiah 3:17; 8:7; 9:4–5; 10:13**). The name Shelomith is lexically both a male and a female name. One by that name (Shelomith) was the *daughter* of Zerubbabel (**1 Chronicles 3:19**) and also a *son* of Josiphiah (**Ezra 8:10**). Shelomith son of Josiphiah is unrelated to Shelomith a descendant in the Moses–Eliezer–Rehabiah–Jeshaiah–Joram–Zikri–Shelomith line (**1 Chronicles 26:25–26, 28**) and unrelated to Shelomith the son of Izhar (**1 Chronicles 23:18**).

13. Some descendants of Bebai, numbering 623 (or 628?) men—for number variants, see note 15—returned to Jerusalem with Zerubbabel in 538 B.C. (cf. **Ezra 2:11; Nehemiah 7:16**), and Bebai's son Zechariah returned with Ezra in 458 B.C. (**Ezra 8:11**). Some of Bebai's descendants—specifically, Jehohanan, Hananiah, Zabbai, and Athlai—had taken pagan wives while in exile (**Ezra 10:28**). Bebai was among the leaders of the people when Nehemiah sealed the covenant with the people of Israel in 445 B.C. (**Nehemiah 10:15**).

14. Johanan the son of Hakkatan, who was the head of an Israelite family (**Ezra 8:12**), is not (1) Johanan/Jehohanan the Ephraimite (**2 Chronicles 28:12**); (2) Johanan/Jonathan (the high priest) (**Nehemiah 12:22–23**); nor (3) Johanan/Jonathan of the sons of Kareah (**2 Kings 25:23; Jeremiah 40:8, 13–16; 41:11, 13–16; 42:1, 8; 43:2, 4–5**).

15. Some descendants of Azgad, numbering 1222 men, returned to Jerusalem with Zerubbabel in 538 (**Ezra 2:12**) and Azgad's descendant, Johanan son of Hakkatan, returned with Ezra in 458 B.C. (**Ezra 8:12**). It is unclear whether Azgad of **Ezra 2:12** is the same as Azgad of **Nehemiah 7:17** whose descendants, numbering 2322 men, returned with Zerubbabel in 538 B.C. This total is at variance with Old Greek (Septuagint) readings and with Ezra's 1222. These number variants are almost always the result of careless or uninformed scribal practice, and they have little or no impact on the central messages of the texts. Azgad was among the leaders of the people when Nehemiah sealed the covenant with the people of Israel (**Nehemiah 10:15**).

16. There may be two Bigvai figures who were contemporaries of Zerubbabel (cf. **Ezra 2:2, 14**). Some descendants of Bigvai, numbering 2056 (or 2067?) men—for number variants, see note 15—returned to Jerusalem with Zerubbabel in 538 B.C. (cf. **Ezra 2:14; Nehemiah 7:19**), and Bigvai's descendants Uthai and Zakkur did so with Ezra in 458 B.C. (**Ezra 8:14**). Bigvai was among the leaders of the people when Nehemiah sealed the covenant in 445 B.C. (**Nehemiah 10:16**).

EZRA 8: GENEALOGICAL RECORD OF THE LEADERS AND THE LEARNED MEN COMMISSIONED BY EZRA TO SUMMON LEVITES IN BABYLON TO RETURN TO JERUSALEM AND SERVE IN THE SECOND TEMPLE

Approximate Dating: ca. 458 B.C. ***Relevant Scriptures:*** **Ezra 8:16**

The first nine are described as "leaders"[1] (רָאשִׁים), *roshim*:

1. **Eliezer**[2]
2. **Ariel**
3. **Shemaiah**[3]
4. **Elnathan #1**[4]
5. **Jarib**[5]
6. **Elnathan #2**[6]
7. **Nathan**[7]
8. **Zechariah**[8]
9. **Meshullam**[9]

These two are designated as "men of learning"[10] (מְבִינִים), *mebinim*:

1. **Joiarib**[11]
2. **Elnathan #3**[12]

Biblical and Theological Significance

Ezra understood full well that the remnant of Israelites who had escaped the exiles to Assyria and Babylon (722 and 586 B.C., respectively) would likely be of the peasantry. This poor remnant was the virtual slave labor under their overlords, left to "work the vineyards and fields," and appointed lackeys by their masters from among their own turncoat brothers (**2 Kings 25:12; Jeremiah 52:15–16;** see also **2 Kings 24:14; Lamentations 5:1–22**). Hence, if there were to be any semblance of law and order and the restoration of a national entity worthy of the name, it would have to be from among the returning exiles. Finally, with the destruction of the temple was the universal feeling that God himself had abandoned his dwelling and gone into exile, perhaps never to return.

Unable to find Levites to provide leadership among the returnees in the Ahava region, Ezra sent these reliable men (listed above) to go and summon the others to return to Jerusalem. The men named here were probably only a sample of the kinds of leaders and advisors essential to the social, economic, and spiritual wellbeing of the post-exile community.

Notes

1. The term is so generic that it is not possible to determine in what sense they were leaders. In any case, they were men of authority. Derek Kidner writes that "Ezra's careful choice of emissaries to rectify this [situation was] nine . . . for the weight they carried in the community, and an extra two [men of learning] for their diplomatic skill" (Donald J. Wiseman, ed., *Tyndale Commentary (Complete)*, 2000; "Ezra 8:15–20," 74, Accordance Bible Software.

2. Eliezer (**Ezra 8:16**) is perhaps the Eliezer of **Ezra 10:18** who was the brother of Joshua the high priest; however, he is probably not Eliezer the Levite (**Ezra 10:23**) or Eliezer the descendant of Harim (**Ezra 10:31**).

3. Shemaiah (**Ezra 8:16**) may be the same person as (1) Shemaiah the son of Hasshub, the son of Azrikam, the son of Hashabiah, a Levitical Merarite (**1 Chronicles 9:14**) or (2) Shemaiah of the descendants of Adonikam, an Israelite (**Ezra 8:13**; see also **Ezra 2:13; Nehemiah 7:18**).

4. For chronological reasons, Elnathan #1, #2, and #3 of 458 B.C. (**Ezra 8:16**) do not correspond to Elnathan son of Akbor, who heard the reading of Jeremiah's scroll in ca. 604 B.C. and then entreated King Jehoiakim not to burn it (**Jeremiah 36:12, 25**; cf. **26:22**).

5. Jarib (**Ezra 8:16**) may be Jarib the Kohathite priest, the brother of Joshua the high priest (**Ezra 10:18**).

6. For Elnathan #2, see note 4.

7. Nathan (**Ezra 8:16**) is likely the same person as Nathan a descendant of the Israelite leader Binnui (**Ezra 10:38–39**).

8. Zechariah (**Ezra 8:16**) is not the canonical prophet, but he may be (1) a descendant of the Israelite leader Parosh (**Ezra 8:3**); (2) the son or descendant of the Israelite leader Bebai (**Ezra 8:11**); (3) a descendant of the Israelite leader Elam (**Ezra 10:26**); or (4) the Zechariah figure who stood on the platform with Ezra on the occasion of the reading of the Law to the assembly of exiles who had returned to Jerusalem (**Nehemiah 8:4**).

9. Meshullam (**Ezra 8:16**) may be (1) a descendant of the Israelite leader Bani (**Ezra 10:29**) or (2) the Meshullam figure who stood with Ezra at the reading of the Law to the assembly of returning exiles (**Nehemiah 8:4**).

10. The underlying sense of the root form (*byn*) is not necessarily one of education or even intellectual prowess, but of intuitive insightfulness.

11. This Joiarib (**Ezra 8:16**) may be a *descendant* of the ancestral Joiarib/Jehoiarib (or "the son of Joiarib") (cf. **1 Chronicles 24:7**; also **9:10**). He is likely the Kohathite priest who returned to Jerusalem with Zerubbabel in 538 B.C. (cf. **Nehemiah 11:10; 12:6**), but he is not Joiarib the Judah–Shelah descendant who was the son of Zechariah (**Nehemiah 11:5**).

12. For Elnathan #3, see note 4.

EZRA 8: THE ADDITIONAL LEVITICAL MERARITES AND TEMPLE SERVANTS WHO WERE CHOSEN TO RETURN TO JERUSALEM AND SERVE IN THE SECOND TEMPLE

Approximate Dating: ca. 458 B.C. ***Relevant Scriptures:*** **Ezra 8:17–20;** also **1 Chronicles 9:14**

1. **Sherebiah**[1]
2. **Hashabiah**[2]
3. **Jeshaiah**[3]
4. **Temple servants**[4]

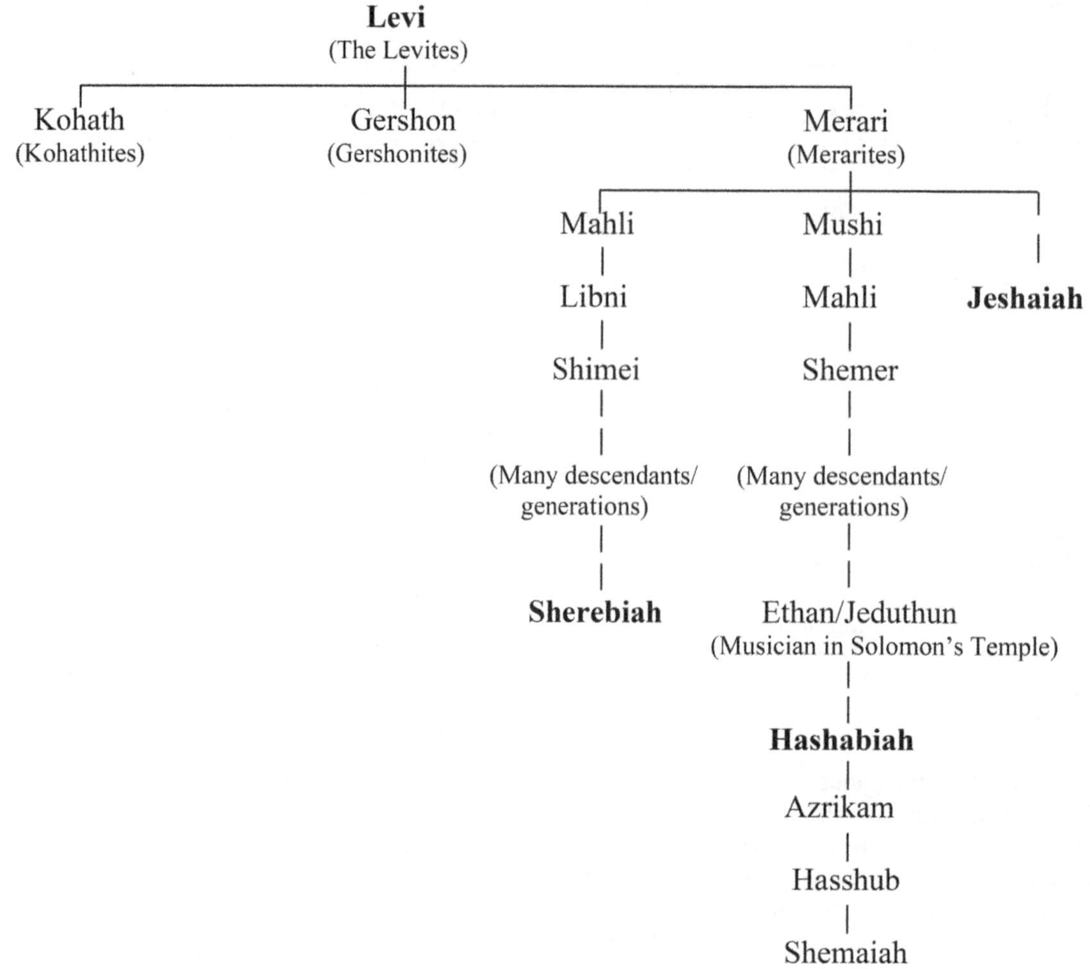

Biblical and Theological Significance

When the term *Babylonian exile* is used, the word *Babylonian* is often understood to be the place and not the Babylonians, the instruments of that disastrous series of events. The city of Babylon was not the sole destination of the deportees; indeed, they were scattered throughout both the Babylonian and Persian Empires, in some cases never to return. The relatively benign policies of the ruling regimes allowed some degree of religious tolerance, even permitting the construction of places of worship for the various communities displaced from their homelands (cf. **Nehemiah 1:1–2; Esther 3:8; 8:5, 11–12, 16–17; 9:16, 19–22; Ezekiel 1:1; 11:16**).[5] Once Ezra decided to return to Jerusalem, he assembled a large following at the Ahava Canal on the Upper Euphrates (**Ezra 8:15**), but finding no Levites among them, he sent a delegation of eleven men[6] to Kasiphia, the site of a Jewish sanctuary headed by a certain Iddo[7] (**Ezra 8:15–17**). From there, the individuals of the chart above were selected to be sent as leaders to Jerusalem. For unknown reasons, these Levitical leaders were of the clan of Merari rather than Kohathite or Gershonite clans (**Ezra 8:18–19**). The Sherebiah family numbered eighteen returnees; those from Jeshaiah and Hashabiah numbered twenty; and there were 220 temple servants whose role would be to assist them (**Ezra 8:18–20**). Twelve leading men were entrusted with the transport of gold and silver nuggets and precious vessels to be placed in a new temple (**Ezra 8:24–27**).[8] Too embarrassed to ask King Artaxerxes I for travel protection, Ezra committed himself, his people, and his journey to Yahweh, who graciously conducted them to Jerusalem in three days (**Ezra 8:31–32**).

Iddo, the chief Levite at Kasiphia—a Jewish sanctuary in Babylon in the north Euphrates Valley, but apparently not far from the Ahava River—sent these Levites to return with Ezra and serve as key attendants for the Second Temple in Jerusalem (**Ezra 8:17**). In the NIV (and other versions), "temple servants" is a "cover" translation[9] of the term נְתִינִים, perhaps from the root נתן, "to give"; thus, a given or dedicated one.[10]

Notes

1. Sherebiah a descendant of the Levi–Merari–Mahli line of Levitical Merarites is called "a capable man" (אִישׁ שֶׂכֶל; **Ezra 8:18**). His sons and brothers totaled eighteen men. He may be the same person as Sherebiah the priest (**Ezra 8:24**).

2. Hashabiah (**Ezra 8:19**) was a descendant of the sons of Merari. His brothers and nephews numbered 20 men. He is probably the same person as Hashabiah in **Ezra 8:24** and appears to be the same person as Hashabiah the priest in **1 Chronicles 9:14** who was the father of Azrikam, the grandfather of Hasshub, and the great-grandfather of Shemaiah. He is not (1) Hashabiah the Kohathite priest (of the family of Hilkiah) in **Nehemiah 12:24**, nor (2) Hashabiah the Gershonite, the son of Mattaniah (a descendant of Asaph the musician) mentioned in **Nehemiah 11:22**.

3. Jeshaiah was a descendant of the Levi–Merari clan of Levites, but it is unclear whether he is in the Mahli or Mushi line (**Ezra 8:19**).

4. The temple servants (*Nethinim* in some translations like the NKJV) were appointed by David to assist the Levites. They numbered 220 men and all were registered by name (**Ezra 8:20**). For further information, see note 4 in chart "**1 Chronicles 9**: Genealogical Registry of Provincial Leaders Who Settled in Jerusalem (Post-Exile)."

5. The glorious Babylonian Empire came to an inglorious end in 539 B.C. at the hands of the brilliant king of Persia, Cyrus II (the Great). He very soon issued a decree in 538 B.C. that all deportees scattered throughout his realm could return to their homelands with his assistance and blessing (**2 Chronicles 36:23; Ezra 1:1–4**). This, of course, included the Jews, who gratefully availed themselves of this God-sent beneficence. Upon their arrival at Jerusalem, the Jews established a satrap (province) of Persia named *Yehud* (short for Yehudah or Judah).

6. Among them were nine "leaders" (*roshim*), "heads," and two "men of learning" (*mebinim*), "instructors."

7. His title is also simply the generic *rosh*, "head."

8. See chart "**Ezra 8**: Genealogical Record of Kohathite Priests Set Apart by Ezra to Carry Silver, Gold, and the Dedicated Offerings to Jerusalem."

9. This means that the technical meaning is not known, but uses of the term seem to suggest such a meaning.

10. As explained in *Eerdmans Dictionary*, the temple servants were

> a group of temple personnel, often simply transliterated "Nethinim" (lit., "the ones given," presumably to the service of the sanctuary). These servants are distinct from the ***nĕṯûnîm*** of Num. 3:9; 8:19, taken as referring to the Levites. Except for one reference (1 Chr. 9:2), all references to the temple servants are included in Ezra and Nehemiah. Ezra 2:43–58; Neh. 7:46–60 list 392 temple servants among the exiles who returned to Jerusalem with Zerubbabel. A second group of 220 temple servants and 38 Levites returned with Ezra (Ezra 8:16–20). According to Ezra 8:20 the temple servants served the Levites. They may have been dependent upon the income of the temple, but they were not slaves (e.g., they owned property; 1 Chr. 9:2). Most likely the temple servants were a group of family guilds that served priests and Levites and worked alongside cultic personnel. Most of the personal names are Northwest Semitic, suggesting that the temple servant families originated from neighboring peoples, possibly as prisoners of war. However, these people would have long been assimilated into Israelite culture and thus not the reference of Ezekiel's condemnation of turning the temple over to foreigners (Ezek. 44:6–7). There is no other evidence of cultural distinction. (Bruce W. Gentry, "Temple Servants," David Noel Freedman, ed., *Eerdmans Dictionary* (Eerdmans, 2000), 1264, accessed through Accordance Bible Software.)

EZRA 8: GENEALOGICAL RECORD OF THE KOHATHITE PRIESTS SET APART BY EZRA TO CARRY THE SILVER, GOLD, AND THE DEDICATED OFFERINGS TO JERUSALEM

Approximate Dating: ca. 458 B.C. ***Relevant Scriptures:*** **Ezra 8:24–30**

Ezra designated twelve leading (Kohathite) priests to carry the offerings to Jerusalem:

1. **Sherebiah**[1]
2. **Hashabiah**[2]
3. **Ten of their brothers** (relatives)

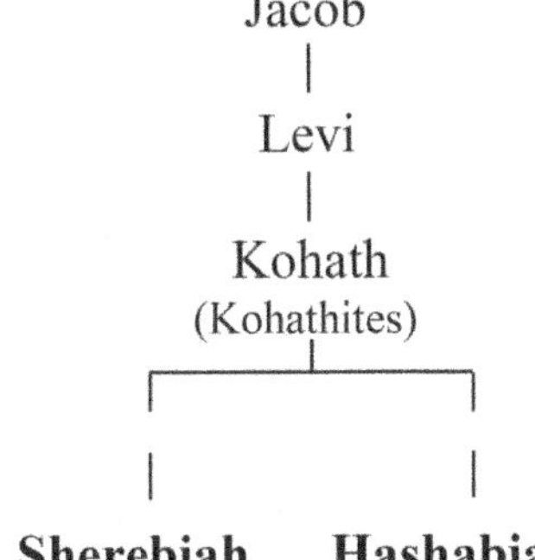

Biblical and Theological Significance

Ezra left Babylon in the seventeenth year of King Artaxerxes I of Persia[3] (r. 465–424 B.C.) "on the first day of the first month" (**Ezra 7:9**) and arrived in Jerusalem about four months later in "the fifth month"—corresponding to 458 B.C. (cf. **Ezra 7:1–9**). Twelve leading Kohathite priests were chosen by Ezra to carry a collective offering of silver, gold, and articles "that the king, his advisers, his officials and all Israel present there had donated for the house of our God" (**Ezra 8:25**; cf. **7:11–16**). The money was used, at least in part, to "buy bulls, rams and male lambs, together with their grain offerings and drink offerings" to sacrifice on the altar of the Second Temple (**Ezra 7:17**). An offering of "650 talents of silver, silver articles weighing 100 talents, 100 talents of gold, 20 bowls of gold valued at 1,000 darics,[4] and two fine articles of polished bronze, as precious as gold" (**Ezra 8:26–27**) were donated.[5] After Ezra and the exiles arrived in Jerusalem, the silver and gold were weighed in the chambers of the Second Temple before the leading priests, Levites, and family heads of Israel (**Ezra 8:29**).

Notes

1. Sherebiah appears to be a leading Kohathite attending priest in 458 B.C., so he is not Sherebiah the Levitical Merarite, a descendant of Mahli (**Ezra 8:18**) nor any of the Levites named Sherebiah (**Nehemiah 8:7; 9:4–5; 10:12; 12:8, 24**).

2. Hashabiah (**Ezra 8:24**) appears to be a leading Kohathite attending priest in 458 B.C., so he should not be confused with Hashabiah the Levitical Merarite (**Ezra 8:19**) or with Levites named Hashabiah who lived much earlier (i.e., the Hashabiah figures in **1 Chronicles 6:45; 9:14; 25:3, 19; 26:30; 27:17; 2 Chronicles 35:9**). Hashabiah (in the chart above) may be the same person as: (1) Hashabiah, the Kohathite attending priest in **Nehemiah 12:21**, who served ca. 490–450/444 B.C. and/or (2) possibly Hashabiah the ruler of half the district of Keilah, who repaired the wall in 444 B.C. in **Nehemiah 3:17**. He should not be confused with Levites named Hashabiah in **Nehemiah 10:11; 11:15, 22; 12:24**.

3. See chart "**Supplement 5**: The Kings of Persia."

4. A daric (from *dara*, a king, probably referring to Darius I), mentioned in **1 Chronicles 29:7; Ezra 2:69; 8:27;** and **Nehemiah 7:70–72**, was a gold coin, equivalent to approximately four days' wages, bearing the figure of a Persian king with his crown and armed with bow and arrow on the obverse side and an irregular incuse (stamped) square on the reverse. The daric was the standard gold coinage of the Persian realm; it was used among the Jews after their return from Babylon, while they were still under Persian domination.

5. Compare this to the building expenditures for the First Temple (**1 Chronicles 29:2–9**).

EZRA 8: GENEALOGICAL RECORD OF THE PRIESTS AND LEVITES IN JERUSALEM WHO WEIGHED THE SILVER, GOLD, AND THE ARTICLES THAT WERE BROUGHT FROM BABYLON

Approximate Dating: ca. 458 B.C. ***Relevant Scriptures:*** **Ezra 8:33–34**; cf. **Numbers 25:7, 11; 1 Chronicles 6:3–15; Ezra 2:16, 40; 3:9; Nehemiah 3:4, 18, 21, 24; 7:43; 10:9**

Priests

1. **Meremoth** son of Uriah, a Kohathite priest (Hakkoz line)
2. **Eleazar**[1] a descendant of Phinehas (of the Aaronic high priesthood)

Levites

1. **Jozabad**[2] son of Jeshua the Levite[3]
2. **Noadiah** son of Binnui[4]

Genealogy of Meremoth:

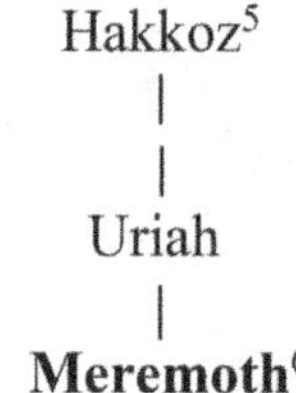

Genealogy of Eleazar:

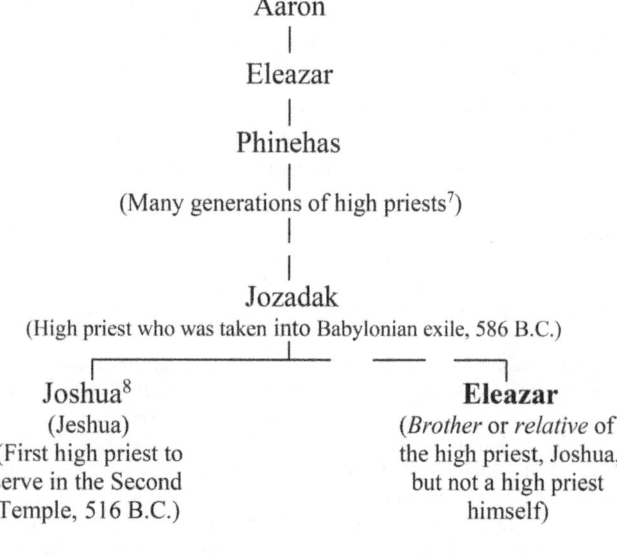

Genealogy of Jozabad:

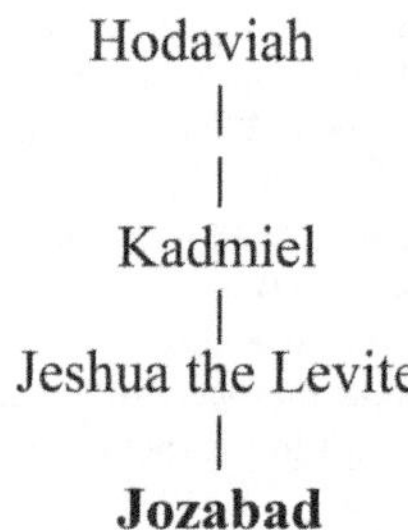

Genealogy of Noadiah:

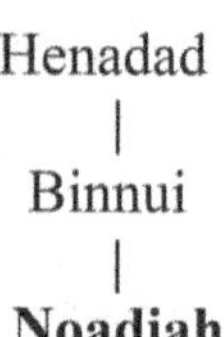

Biblical and Theological Significance

When Ezra returned to Jerusalem in 458 B.C., some of the gold and silver was used to "make a crown" for Joshua [Jeshua] the son of Jehozadak, who was the first high priest to attend in the newly completed Second Temple (**Zechariah 6:10–11**). These Kohathite priests and Levites were obviously trustworthy individuals. By weighing and registering the temple treasures of silver, gold, and articles for worship, they made sure that all of the items that Ezra had brought back from exile were accounted for, correctly inventoried, and recorded.[9]

Notes

1. Eleazar—a post-exilic Kohathite attending priest—was a descendant of Phinehas (the zealous son of Eleazar, son of Aaron the high priest; cf. **Exodus 6:23, 25; Numbers 25:6–9; 1 Chronicles 6:4, 50; Ezra 7:5**), and he should be understood to be a *relative* of the high priest(s) at this time. He should not be confused with Eleazar one of the descendants of Parosh (**Ezra 10:25**).

2. Jozabad the son of Jeshua was a head Levite. The lineage of Jozabad son of Jeshua, son of Kadmiel can be discerned from **Ezra 2:40; 3:9; 8:33; Nehemiah 7:43; 8:7; 9:4–5; 10:9; 12:8, 24**. This Jozabad should not be confused with Jozabad one of the descendants of the Kohathite priest named Pashhur (**Ezra 10:22**).

3. This is surely the Levite Jeshua, the son of Kadmiel (cf. **Ezra 2:40; Nehemiah 7:43; 8:7; 9:4–5; 12:8, 24**); he should not be confused with Joshua/Jeshua, his contemporary who was the first high priest to serve in the Second Temple.

4. Binnui son of Henadad (a Levite) returned to Jerusalem with Zerubbabel in 538 B.C. (**Nehemiah 12:8**). By 444 B.C., he helped repair the wall, served as the ruler of half of the district of Keilah, and sealed the covenant with Nehemiah (**Nehemiah 3:18, 24; 10:9**). The name Binnui [Heb. בִּנּוּי, *binnuy* is "often confused with (or substituted for) Bani [Heb. בָּנִי, *baniy*], another name popular in levitical circles during the postexilic period." D. G. Schley, "Bani," and "Binnui," *Anchor Yale Bible Dictionary* 1:580, 745.

Binnui the Levite should not be confused with (1) Binnui (Bani?) a clan leader among the Israelites, whose descendants had returned to Jerusalem with Ezra in 458 B.C. and were guilty of intermarriage with foreign women (**Ezra 8:10; 10:38**, cf. **10:29?** and **10:30?**), nor with (2) Binnui the Israelite listed in **Nehemiah 7:15**, who is associated with 648 male descendants of Parosh (i.e., the same person named *Bani* in the parallel account in **Ezra 2:10**, who is associated with 642 male descendants of Parosh).

5. Hakkoz was the head of a priestly family from among "the descendants of Hobaiah, Hakkoz and Barzillai" (**Ezra 2:61**), a group of Kohathite priests who could not (initially) prove their priestly heritage in the written genealogies when they returned to Jerusalem (cf. **Ezra 2:59–61**). In an effort to prove their ancestry, they "searched for their family records, but they could not find them and so were excluded from the priesthood as unclean. The governor ordered

them not to eat any of the most sacred food until there was a priest ministering with the Urim and Thummim" (**Ezra 2:62–63**). However, the position of authority held by Meremoth (a *descendant* of Hakkoz) in the Second Temple shows that the judgment of God (via the Urim and Thummim) was favorable toward the continued service of this Kohathite priestly family (cf. **Nehemiah 3:4, 21**). Thus, the "Hakkoz" division—the seventh of the 24 divisions of Kohathite priests in Solomon's Temple (cf. **1 Chronicles 24:10**)—clearly retained a presence in the Second Temple period; see charts "**1 Chronicles 24**: Genealogical Registry of the Twenty-Four Divisions of Kohathite Attending Priests Who Rotated Service in Solomon's Temple" and "**Nehemiah 12**: Genealogical Record of the Heads of Priests, Levites, and Gatekeepers Who Served in the Second Temple in the Days of Joiakim the High Priest, Ezra the Priestly Scribe, and Nehemiah the Governor." Hakkoz, the ancestor of Meremoth, is not the same person as Koz the son of Ashhur (tribe of Judah) in **1 Chronicles 4:8**.

6. The texts of **Nehemiah 3:4** and **21** give the lineage of Meremoth and mention that he repaired two sections of the wall around Jerusalem in 444 B.C. It is noteworthy that Meremoth was a descendant of the ancestral head of the Hakkoz division of Kohathite attending priests in Solomon's Temple (see note 5). Meremoth returned to Jerusalem with Zerubbabel in 538 B.C. (**Nehemiah 12:3**) and sealed the covenant with Nehemiah in 444 B.C. (**Nehemiah 10:5**). Meremoth the son of Uriah, the descendant of Hakkoz, is a different person than Meremoth a descendant of Bani the Israelite (**Ezra 10:36**).

7. See chart "**Supplement 2**: The High Priests of Israel."

8. See chart "**Ezra 2**: Joshua, the High Priest in the Second Temple, and His Descendants (Post-Exile)."

9. The commentary for **Ezra 8:34** in the Kenneth Barker, ed. *NIV Study Bible*, Fully Revised Edition (Grand Rapids: Zondervan, 2020), 770–71, notes that, according to Babylonian practice, almost every transaction had to be recorded in writing and furthermore, that Ezra may have had to send back to Artaxerxes I (the king of Persia, 465–424 B.C.; cf. **Ezra 7:11–28**) a signed certification that the treasures had been delivered to Jerusalem.

EZRA 10: GENEALOGICAL RECORD OF THE LEADERS WHO SUPPORTED AND WHO OPPOSED EZRA'S PLAN FOR PUTTING AWAY PAGAN WIVES

Approximate Dating: ca. 458 B.C. ***Relevant Scriptures:*** **Ezra 10:2–15**

Supported Ezra

1. **Shekaniah** son of Jehiel, of the descendants of Elam[1]
2. **Jehohanan** (Johanan) son of Eliashib[2]

Opposed Ezra

1. **Jonathan** son of Asahel[3]
2. **Jahzeiah** son of Tikvah
3. **Meshullam**[4]
4. **Shabbethai**[5] the Levite

Biblical and Theological Significance

The irregularity of the authority vested in the priesthood in post-exile Israel is attributed, in this incident, to two important considerations: (1) the six hundred years of monarchic government came to an end with the death of King Jehoiachin in Babylonian captivity, sometime after 561 B.C.; and (2) the institution of governorship with Zerubbabel in 538 B.C. was no substitute for royalty, nor did it supplant the sole authority of the priesthood in religious matters such as marriage and divorce. Therefore, the powers that hitherto had been the province of kingship devolved to Ezra for a time, as well as to the priesthood.[6] Nehemiah's arrival in 444 B.C. seemed to be a move in the direction of secular rule with his appointment as governor of the Persian satrapy of Yehud, but his contemporary, Eliashib the high priest (the son of Joiakim), had other ideas. While Nehemiah was on a leave of absence in Susa (in 432 B.C.), Eliashib, in what clearly was an attempt at a coup, made an alliance with Tobiah the Ammonite, going so far as to provide him a chamber within the precincts of the holy temple (**Nehemiah 13:1–6**).[7] Upon his return, Nehemiah evicted the pagan Tobiah[8] and sanctified the place he had polluted (**Nehemiah 13:7–9**). However, the tide of priestly power, corrupt as it was, once more overrode the governorship[9] of one generation and re-asserted itself. Never again did the priests surrender their powers to secular governance, as they did in the days of Nehemiah. What evolved throughout the Second Temple era was at most "diarchy" (double rule).[10]

The edict given by Ezra that men who had married outside the covenant community should divorce their wives in no way violated Torah proscriptions in such matters (**Deuteronomy 22:13–19; 24:1–4**). Israelites were told to never marry the heathen (**Genesis 28:1, 6; Exodus 34:16; Deuteronomy 7:1–3**), but if they did (as noted here in **Ezra 10:2**), the dissolution of the relationship could not be considered divorce (שָׁלַח), but rather, a "putting" or "sending" away (יָצָא). The verbs employed (*shalah* and *yatsa*) make the differences clear.

Shekaniah son of Jehiel, "one of the descendants of Elam" (**Ezra 10:2**; cf. **Ezra 2:7** or **2:31; 8:7; 10:26**), proposed to Ezra: "We have been unfaithful to our God by marrying foreign women from the peoples around us. But in spite of this, there is still hope for Israel. Now let us make a covenant before our God to send away all these women and their children, in accordance with the counsel of my lord [Ezra] and of those who fear the commands of our God. Let it be done according to the Law. Rise up; this matter is in your hands. We will support you, so take courage and do it" (**Ezra 10:2–4**; cf. **Ezra 9; 10:1**). Ezra formalized the plan and made a final proclamation to the unfaithful exiles (**Ezra 10:5–11**). Those assembled responded, "You are right! We must do as you say" (**Ezra 10:12**).[11] Only a few opposed the plan (specifically, Jonathan, Jahzeiah, Meshullam, and Shabbethai).

Notes

1. Shekaniah's ancestry suggests that he was from among Israel's laity (not a priest or Levite). For various Shekaniah figures, see note 30 in chart "**1 Chronicles 3**: Zerubbabel and Shealtiel and the Double Line of the Messiah through King David's Sons, Nathan and Solomon."

2. Jehohanan appears to refer to the *grandson* (not the *son*) of Eliashib the high priest—"Ezra withdrew from before the house of God and went to the room of Jehohanan son [*grandson*] of Eliashib. While he was there, he ate no food and drank no water, because he continued to mourn over the unfaithfulness of the exiles" (**Ezra 10:6**). The mention of the room of Jehohanan in **Ezra 10:6** can be understood as him "living with his parents as an adult" or as a prolepsis of what was later realized, since Jehohanan/Johanan became the high priest

in due time (**Nehemiah 12:10–11**); for a strong endorsement of this point of view, see the theories of Jacob Liver ("Yochanan" *E.M.* III 590–91) and Hayyim Tadmor ("Chronology" *E.M.* IV 307 n. 2), as explained in Benjamin E. Scolnic, *Chronology and Papponymy: A List of the Judean High Priests of the Persian Period* (Atlanta: Scholars Press, 1999), 18 and n. 50. The rendering Johanan in **Nehemiah 12:22–23** is merely a syncopated form of the longer spelling: יוֹחָנָן < יְהוֹחָנָן. For the lineage of the high priests in the Second Temple, see charts "**Ezra 2**: Joshua, the High Priest in the Second Temple, and His Descendants (Post-Exile)" and "**Supplement 2**: The High Priests of Israel."

3. This may refer to Jonathan a *descendant* of Asahel, the brother of Joab and the son of Zeruiah (cf. **2 Samuel 2:18**) or a descendant of the Levites named Asahel (cf. **2 Chronicles 17:8; 31:13**).

4. Meshullam supported Jonathan and Jahaziah's opposition to Ezra's plan (**Ezra 10:15**). This may be the Meshullam whom Ezra sent for and who returned to Jerusalem to serve as a leader/servant in the restored temple (cf. **Ezra 8:16**) and/or Meshullam/Shallum the Levitical Korathite (**1 Chronicles 9:31**).

Meshullam here does not refer to Meshullam/Shallum the high priest (the son of Zadok and father of Hilkiah) who served in ca. 690–640 B.C. (called Meshullam in **1 Chronicles 9:11; Nehemiah 11:11** and Shallum in **1 Chronicles 6:12–13; Ezra 7:2**). Compare the Meshullam who opposed Ezra to (1) Meshullam "from the descendants of Bani" (**Ezra 10:29**); (2) Meshullam the son of Berekiah (**Nehemiah 3:4, 30; 6:18**); and (3) Meshullam the son of Joed, a Benjamite (**Nehemiah 11:7**).

5. Shabbethai supported Jonathan and Jahaziah's opposition to Ezra's plan (**Ezra 10:15**). He is probably the same person named Shabbethai who was the head of the Levites who, along with Jozabad, "had charge of the outside work of the house of God" (**Nehemiah 11:16**; cf. **8:7**).

6. Ezra brought exiles back to Jerusalem in 458 B.C., and he died ca. 444 B.C. (see chart "**Ezra 7**: Ezra, the Priestly Scribe and Teacher of the Law (Post-Exile)"). The high priests who were contemporaries of Ezra were Joiakim (490–450/444 B.C.) and his son Eliashib (450/444–432 B.C.).

7. See charts "**Nehemiah 2**: The Enemies of Nehemiah Who Ruled in the Provinces Surrounding Judah" and "**Nehemiah 13**: Intermarriage of Jews and Samaritans That Compromised the Purity of the Holy Priesthood of Israel."

8. For Tobiah, see charts "**Nehemiah 2**: The Enemies of Nehemiah Who Ruled in the Provinces Surrounding Judah" and "**Nehemiah 6**: Intermarriage of Jews and the Tobiads in the Post-Exile: Meshullam's Daughter (a Jewess) and Jehohanan (a Tobiad)."

9. The term for "governor" (תִּרְשָׁתָא), *tirshatha*, is Persian, occurring only five times in the Old Testament, of which twice are in reference to Nehemiah (**Nehemiah 8:9; 10:2**). There is no record in the Bible of successors to Nehemiah in the office of governor, so one must conclude this was a one-time appointment suitable to the situation.

10. The impact of these messages of revelation emboldened Ezra and Nehemiah to assert theocratic as well as royal authority, an assertion that was embodied in the two of them—Ezra the scribal priest (**Ezra 7:21–26; 10:5–8, 16–44**) and Nehemiah the governor (**Nehemiah 8:9–12; 10:1; 12:26; 13:10–31**). The development of this shift in authority had its roots as early as the post-exilic prophets (520 B.C.). **Haggai** sets the stage for diarchy but tilted it in favor of the monarchy by always referring to the governance as "Zerubbabel the son of Shealtiel and Joshua the son of Jozadak," that is, 'political' greater than 'ecclesiastical' (**Haggai 1:1, 12, 14; 2:2, 4**). The book of Zechariah, at the same time, elevated Joshua the priest to a virtual kingship by placing on his head a silver and gold crown (**Zechariah 6:11–15**) and declaring "Here is the man whose name is the Branch, and he will branch out from his place and build the temple of the Lord. It is he who will build the temple of the Lord, and he will be clothed with majesty and will sit and rule on his throne. And he will be a priest on his throne. And there will be harmony between the two" (**Zechariah 6:12–13**). For Zerubbabel, see chart "**1 Chronicles 3**: Zerubbabel and Shealtiel and the Double Line of the Messiah through King David's Sons, Nathan and Solomon"; for Joshua, see chart "**Ezra 2**: Joshua, the High Priest in the Second Temple, and His Descendants (Post-Exile)"; for Ezra, see chart "**Ezra 7**: Ezra, the Priestly Scribe and Teacher of the Law (Post-Exile)"; and for Nehemiah, see chart "**Nehemiah 1**: Nehemiah and the Leaders who were Appointed by Nehemiah over the City of Jerusalem."

11. The author is careful to note the dates and describe the process. A proclamation went out to Judah and Benjamin that the exiles were to assemble in Jerusalem within three days, and if they refused, the dissenter would "forfeit all his property" (**Ezra 10:7–9**). The assembly gathered in Jerusalem on the twentieth day of the ninth month, but the people were "greatly distressed by the occasion and because of the rain" (**Ezra 10:7–9**). Realizing that the matter could not be settled quickly, representative officials were chosen to "act for the whole assembly" (**Ezra 10:12–14**) and then conduct the investigations on a local basis. About ten days later, the exiles (along with their respective local elders and judges) met in their own towns and their cases were decided by family heads (one from each family division) whom Ezra had chosen. By the first day of the first month, all the investigations had been completed. For the specifics of Ezra's plan, see **Ezra 10:12–17**; also see chart "**Ezra 10**: Genealogical Record of the Priests, Levites, and Israelites who Had Taken Pagan Wives in Babylonian Captivity."

EZRA 10: GENEALOGICAL RECORD OF THE PRIESTS, LEVITES, AND ISRAELITES WHO HAD TAKEN PAGAN WIVES IN BABYLONIAN CAPTIVITY

Approximate Dating: ca. 458 B.C. ***Relevant Scriptures:*** **Ezra 10:18–44**

Among the Descendants of the Kohathite Priests[1]

Descendants of Joshua (Jeshua) the high priest and Joshua's brothers:[2]

1. **Maaseiah**[3]
2. **Eliezer**
3. **Jarib**
4. **Gedaliah**

Descendants of Immer:[4]

1. **Hanani**
2. **Zebadiah**[5]

Descendants of Harim:[6]

1. **Maaseiah**
2. **Elijah**
3. **Shemaiah**[7]
4. **Jehiel**
5. **Uzziah**

Descendants of Pashhur:[8]

1. **Elioenai**[9]
2. **Maaseiah**
3. **Ishmael**
4. **Nethanel**
5. **Jozabad**
6. **Elasah**

Among the Levites[10]

1. **Jozabad**[11]
2. **Shimei**
3. **Kelaiah (Kelita)**
4. **Pethahiah**
5. **Judah**[12]
6. **Eliezer**

Among the Levitical Musicians[13]
1. **Eliashib**

Among the Levitical Gatekeepers[14]
1. **Shallum**[15]
2. **Telem**
3. **Uri**

Among the Laity of Israel[16]
Descendants of Parosh:
1. **Ramiah**
2. **Izziah**
3. **Malkijah #1**
4. **Mijamin**[17]
5. **Eleazar**[18]
6. **Malkijah #2**
7. **Benaiah**

Descendants of Elam:
1. **Mattaniah**
2. **Zechariah**
3. **Jehiel**[19]
4. **Abdi**
5. **Jeremoth**
6. **Elijah**

Descendants of Zattu:
1. **Elioenai**
2. **Eliashib**
3. **Mattaniah**
4. **Jeremoth**
5. **Zabad**
6. **Aziza**

Descendants of Bebai:
1. **Jehohanan**
2. **Hananiah**
3. **Zabbai**
4. **Athlai**

Descendants of Bani #1:
1. **Meshullam**
2. **Malluk**
3. **Adaiah**
4. **Jashub**
5. **Sheal**
6. **Jeremoth**

Descendants of Pahath-Moab:
1. **Adna**
2. **Kelal**
3. **Benaiah**
4. **Maaseiah**
5. **Mattaniah**
6. **Bezalel**
7. **Binnui**
8. **Manasseh**

Descendants of Harim:[20]
1. **Eliezer**
2. **Ishijah**
3. **Malkijah**
4. **Shemaiah**
5. **Shimeon**
6. **Benjamin**
7. **Malluk**
8. **Shemariah**

Descendants of Hashum:
1. **Mattenai**
2. **Mattattah**
3. **Zabad**
4. **Eliphelet**
5. **Jeremai**
6. **Manasseh**
7. **Shimei**

Descendants of Bani #2:
1. **Maadai**
2. **Amram**
3. **Uel**
4. **Benaiah**
5. **Bedeiah**
6. **Keluhi**
7. **Vaniah**
8. **Meremoth**
9. **Eliashib**
10. **Mattaniah**
11. **Mattenai**
12. **Jaasu**

Descendants of Binnui:
1. **Shimei**
2. **Shelemiah**
3. **Nathan**
4. **Adaiah**
5. **Maknadebai**
6. **Shashai**
7. **Sharai**
8. **Azarel**
9. **Shelemiah**
10. **Shemariah**
11. **Shallum**
12. **Amariah**
13. **Joseph**

Descendants of Nebo:
1. **Jeiel**
2. **Mattithiah**
3. **Zabad**
4. **Zebina**
5. **Jaddai**
6. **Joel**
7. **Benaiah**

A total of **111 men** from among the Kohathite priests, Levites, and Israelite families had taken pagan wives from the land of Babylon.

Biblical and Theological Significance

From the very beginning of Israel's covenant history, the Mosaic injunction was that Yahweh had called them to be a holy nation, separated from all other peoples so they could shine as a light of righteousness among them and thus draw them to him (**Leviticus 20:24–26; 1 Kings 8:53**). This was especially true in making marriages with foreign[21] women

(**Deuteronomy 7:3; Joshua 23:12**). It is striking that one of the reasons for Israel's deportation was precisely the violation of this stricture: "You must not intermarry with them, because they will surely turn your hearts after their gods" (**1 Kings 11:2**).[22] Yet, while in exile, intermarriage with the heathen continued—hence Ezra's positive response to Shekaniah's suggestion that all these wives must be "[sent] away"[23] (**Ezra 10:2–5**).

Jeremiah had addressed the issue earlier by sending a letter to the Jews in exile. Jeremiah exhorted them to make the best of their situations there and to integrate as much as possible, without violating their covenant requirements to be a separate people. They were encouraged to marry, but obviously only within the exile community (**Jeremiah 29:6**). Clearly, many of them had given little heed to the prophet, so when they returned to their homeland, they brought their heathen wives and children with them (**Ezra 9:2**). Ezra, a scholar of the Torah, was well-aware of the ancient Mosaic prohibitions, codified in covenant law, against intermarriage between Israelites and their foreign neighbors (**Exodus 34:16; Deuteronomy 7:3–4**; cf. **Joshua 23:12–13**). On those grounds, Ezra demanded that the pagan women, and the children born to them, be sent away. In the situation described here, it was not a case of typical divorce, but rather mixed marriages that were not recognized as *legitimate* unions in the first place. These pagan wives and their children were *separated*[24] from the returning exiles of Jerusalem to fend for themselves (cf. **Ezra 10:1–44**). This should have driven home to the Jewish community (and to all who claimed Yahweh as God) the doleful results that follow such flaunting of his covenantal standards.

Notes

1. The total number of priests who returned to Jerusalem is given in **Ezra 2:36–39** and **Nehemiah 7:39–42**.

2. These relatives of Joshua pledged to put away their wives, and "for their guilt they each presented a ram from the flock as a guilt offering" (**Ezra 10:19**).

3. Maaseiah the Kohathite priest in **Ezra 10:18** is probably Masseiah the priest in **Nehemiah 8:4; 12:41** or **12:42**. Others of the same name (Maaseiah) are given in **Ezra 10:21** (a descendant of Harim the priest); **Ezra 10:22** (a descendant of Pashhur the priest); **Ezra 10:30** (a descendant of Pahath-Moab the Israelite); Maaseiah the son of Ananiah and the father of Azariah (**Nehemiah 3:23**); Maaseiah the Levite who instructed the people in the Law (**Nehemiah 8:7**); and Maaseiah a leader of the people (**Nehemiah 10:25**).

4. Immer was the ancestral head over the sixteenth of the twenty-four divisions of Kohathite attending priests in Solomon's Temple, who were set up in the last days of King David. (cf. **1 Chronicles 24:14**). Immer's son/descendant Pashhur was a wicked priest and a contemporary of Jeremiah the prophet, ca. 627–586 B.C. (**Jeremiah 20:1–6**). Some priestly descendants of Immer returned to Jerusalem with Joshua the high priest and Zerubbabel the governor in 538 B.C. and were active in the post-exile (cf. **Ezra 2:1–2, 36–37; Nehemiah 7:6–7, 39–40**). Since Hanani was a Kohathite priest and Nehemiah was the governor of Yehud (444 B.C.) and likely not a priest, it is unlikely that Hanani (of Immer) is the same person named "Hanani," Nehemiah's brother (**Nehemiah 1:2**); see chart "**Nehemiah 1**: Nehemiah and the Leaders who were Appointed by Nehemiah over the City of Jerusalem."

5. Zebadiah (a Kohathite priest) is not any of the Zebadiah figures of **1 Chronicles 8:15, 17; 12:7; 26:2; 27:7; 2 Chronicles 17:8; 19:11**; and **Ezra 8:8**.

6. Harim was the ancestral head over the third of the twenty-four divisions of Kohathite attending priests in Solomon's Temple, who were set up in the last days of King David (**1 Chronicles 24:8**). Harim was the father of Malkijah the priest (**Nehemiah 3:11**; cf. **1 Chronicles 24:9**). Some descendants of Harim returned to Jerusalem and were active priests in the post-exile (cf. **Ezra 10:21; Nehemiah 3:11; 7:42; 10:5**). Harim the Kohathite priest is different from Harim the Israelite(s) in **Ezra 2:32; 10:31; Nehemiah 7:35; 10:27**.

7. Shemaiah of Harim (**Ezra 10:21**) is probably Shemaiah the priest in **Nehemiah 10:8; 12:6** but not Shemaiah the descendant of Asaph, a Levitical Gershonite (**Nehemiah 12:35, 42**).

8. Pashhur was a Kohathite priest from the tribe of Levi but not a high priest. According to **1 Chronicles 9:12; Nehemiah 11:12; Jeremiah 21:1; 38:1**, Pashhur was the *son* of Malkijah (the head over the fifth of the twenty-four divisions of Kohathite attending priests in Solomon's Temple, set up in the last days of King David; **1 Chronicles 24:9**), and Pashhur is possibly the *grandson* of Harim (**Nehemiah 3:11**, if the Harim here is referring to Harim who was the head over the third division of Kohathite priests in Solomon's Temple; cf. **1 Chronicles 24:8**). Some of the sons/descendants in the Malkijah and Harim divisions returned to Jerusalem, were active in the post-exile, and helped Nehemiah repair the wall around the city (cf. **1 Chronicles 9:2, 12; Nehemiah 3:11; 10:3, 5**). Pashhur's son was Zechariah (**Nehemiah 11:12**).

Pashhur son of Malkijah is not the cursed priest Pashhur son of Immer who died in Babylon (**Jeremiah 20:1–6**).

9. Elioenai of Pashhur (**Ezra 10:22**) is probably the same as Elioenai the priest who played the trumpet in **Nehemiah 12:41** at the dedication and completion of the wall around Jerusalem (cf. Elioenai of Zattu; **Ezra 10:27**).

10. The total number of Levites who returned to Jerusalem is given in **Ezra 2:40** and **Nehemiah 7:43**.

11. Jozabad the Levite, the son of Jeshua, returned to Jerusalem with Ezra the scribe in 458 B.C. (**Ezra 8:33; Nehemiah 11:16**). He is a different person than Jozabad "from the descendants of Pashhur" (**Ezra 10:22**).

12. Judah the Levite is also mentioned in **Nehemiah 12:8**.

13. The total number of musicians—the descendants of Asaph—who returned to Jerusalem with Zerubbabel in 538 B.C. is given in **Ezra 2:41** and **Nehemiah 7:44**.

14. The total number of gatekeepers who returned to Jerusalem is given in **Ezra 2:42** and **Nehemiah 7:45**.

15. Shallum (**Ezra 10:24**) refers to Shallum the Korahite gatekeeper (**1 Chronicles 9:17, 19, 31; Ezra 2:42; Nehemiah 7:45**), but he is not Shallum the descendant of Binnui the Israelite (**Ezra 10:42**).

16. As with nearly all names of this kind, "Israel" can be both a geographic and political name. Very frequently, "Israel" functions as an abbreviation for the more common "B'nai Yisrael," "sons of Israel," or even *'am ha-aretz*, "people of the land," meaning the ordinary and average population. The total number of people from each of these Israelite clans who returned to Jerusalem is given in **Ezra 2:2–35** and **Nehemiah 7:7–38**.

17. Mijamin (of Parosh the Israelite; **Ezra 10:25**) is not Mijamin the Kohathite priest (**1 Chronicles 24:9**); nor Mijamin the priest who returned to Jerusalem with Zerubbabel and sealed the covenant with Nehemiah (**Nehemiah 10:7; 12:5**).

18. Eleazar (of Parosh the Israelite; **Ezra 10:25**) is not Eleazar the priest who sang at the dedication of the wall around Jerusalem (**Nehemiah 12:42**).

19. Jehiel is also mentioned in **Ezra 10:2**; his son Shekaniah had made the proposal to Ezra that foreign women and their children should be sent away (**Ezra 10:2–4**).

20. Descendants of Harim (among the laity), given in **Ezra 10:31–32**, should not be confused with the descendants of Harim the Kohathite priest, given in **Ezra 10:21**.

21. The term for "foreign" (*nokri*) always has reference to nations other than Israel.

22. The situation had occurred with Solomon marrying foreign women (**1 Kings 11:1–3**). The warning in Ezra's day against "spiritual adultery" would be the same as in Solomon's day: If the returning exiles kept their foreign wives and raised up foreign children, there would be a similar consequence in the Second Temple era—a turning away from Yahweh.

23. This highly euphemistic term for divorce seems designed to avoid the much harsher term *garash*, "drive out."

24. The normal term for "divorce" is not used here. That term is שָׁלַח (*shalakh*; **Malachi 2:16**). In contrast, the verb here is יָצָא (*yatsa*), the ordinary word for sending away.

NEHEMIAH 1: NEHEMIAH AND THE LEADERS WHO WERE APPOINTED BY NEHEMIAH OVER THE CITY OF JERUSALEM

Approximate Dating: Nehemiah went to Jerusalem in 444 B.C. in the twentieth year of King Artaxerxes and served as governor of Judah for twelve years, ca. 444–433 B.C. He was briefly recalled to Persia "in the thirty-second year of Artaxerxes" (early ca. 332 B.C.) (Nehemiah 13:6). Apparently, Nehemiah returned to Jerusalem in late 432 B.C. while Eliashib[1] was still serving as the high priest. Nehemiah remained in Jerusalem the second time for an unspecified length of time.[2] ***Relevant Scriptures:*** **Nehemiah 1:1–2; 7:2**

Known Lineage for Nehemiah

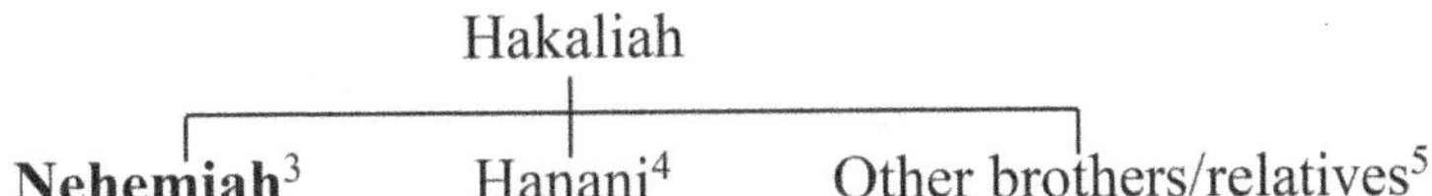

Leaders who were appointed by Nehemiah over the city of Jerusalem:

1. **Hanani** was the brother of Nehemiah (**Nehemiah 7:2**, cf. **Nehemiah 1:2; Ezra 10:20 (?)**; see lineage above.
2. **Hananiah** was the appointed leader over the citadel (the fortress within the royal palace in Jerusalem); he and Hanani appear to be over Jewish affairs in Jerusalem in general (cf. **Nehemiah 7:2**).[6] He is possibly Hananiah the Judahite, the son of Zerubbabel (**1 Chronicles 3:19**):

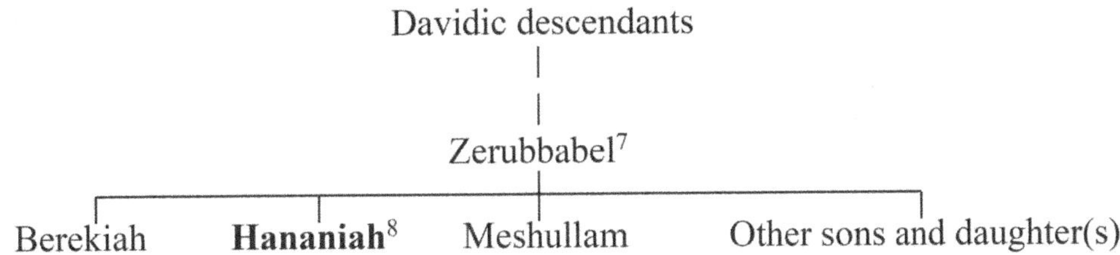

Biblical and Theological Significance

One of the most desperate times in Israel's history was its return from Babylonian exile. Only the oldest among the returnees could remember their homeland, but all knew what challenges lay ahead. Could they be restored physically and, more importantly, spiritually, as the people of Yahweh their God whom they had abysmally failed? Strong leadership was essential. God was faithful, raising up Ezra, the priestly scribe, and, soon thereafter, Nehemiah, the governor. The prophets Haggai, Zechariah, and Malachi each received instruction from God warning the returnees not to repeat the sins of their fathers.

Mighty Babylonia came to an end in 539 B.C. at the hands of Cyrus II the Great (559–530 B.C.). Once he had accrued sufficient power, he set his sights on Babylonia, governed then by the ineffectual Belshazzar. With little resistance he took the city and quickly enveloped it and the entire Babylonian Empire into the Medo-Persian Empire.

Nehemiah, a Jewish exile who served Artaxerxes I of Persia (whose reign was ca. 465–424 B.C.), was the cupbearer who tasted the king's wine and safe-guarded it from poison, a place of great honor in the royal court in Susa (**Nehemiah 1:11; 2:1**). Prior to Nehemiah's arrival in Jerusalem in 444 B.C., the first group of exiles had returned in 538 B.C. with Zerubbabel and, under his leadership, had completed the Second Temple in 516 B.C. Ezra came in the seventh year of Artaxerxes' reign (458 B.C.; **Ezra 7:8**), bringing a second group of exiles. Jerusalem still lay in ruins (**Nehemiah 2:3**), which prompted a mournful Nehemiah to seek the permission of Artaxerxes I to go to Jerusalem (**Nehemiah 2:1–6**). Nehemiah arrived in 444 B.C. with the specific aim of repairing the walls of the city that had been in a state of disrepair for almost a century (since ca. 538 B.C., when the first exiles had returned to Jerusalem with Zerubbabel). Artaxerxes I appointed Nehemiah as governor over the satrap of Judah for approximately twelve years, from the twentieth to the thirty-second year of Artaxerxes' reign (ca. 445–433 B.C.; **Nehemiah 5:14**). Nehemiah was recalled to Persia briefly in Artaxerxes' thirty-second year (432 B.C.), and he "returned to the king [of Babylon]. Some time later I asked his permission and came back to Jerusalem" (**Nehemiah 13:6–7**). Thereafter, Nehemiah stayed in Jerusalem for an unspecified period of time.

Rebuilding of the Wall around Jerusalem

During his initial days in Jerusalem in 444 B.C., Nehemiah assessed the situation and organized the workers to rebuild the wall (**Nehemiah 2:11–3:32**). A naturally gifted leader, Nehemiah was also a man of prayer who constantly waited upon the Lord for wisdom and strength (**Nehemiah 1:6, 11; 2:4–5; 4:4–5, 9; 5:19; 6:9; 9:6–38; 13:14, 22, 29–31**). Thus armed, he stood against outside enemies[9] such as Sanballat, the governor of Samaria; Tobiah the Ammonite; Geshem the Arab; and Philistines from Ashdod who opposed his plan to complete the wall (**Nehemiah 4, 6**). Nehemiah also addressed opposition from within—from among the people of Judah—who complained about famine, heavy Persian taxes, the sale of their children into slavery, and issues of usury between Jewish brethren (**Nehemiah 5:1–11**). Despite opposition, the rebuilding of the wall was completed in just fifty-two days (**Nehemiah 6:15**).[10]

Nehemiah was a contemporary of Ezra, the priestly scribe (**Nehemiah 8:9; 12:26**). Nehemiah required everyone to be registered by genealogy (**Nehemiah 7:5**); he then compared this list to a genealogical record that had been taken approximately ninety-three years earlier, when the first returnees had arrived in Jerusalem with Zerubbabel in 538 B.C. (cf. **Ezra 2:1–65**; **Nehemiah 7:4–67**).[11] The registration was used in part by Nehemiah to repopulate the small city of Jerusalem by appointing a *tithe* (ten percent) of the people to live there (as determined by casting lots; **Nehemiah 11:1**). The other 90 percent of the people would dwell elsewhere (**Nehemiah 11:25–36**).

Notes

1. For the succession of high priests at this time, see chart "**Nehemiah 12**: Genealogical Record of the Heads of the Kohathite Priests and Levites Who Returned to Jerusalem with Zerubbabel and Joshua in the Post-Exile."

2. For chronology, see **Nehemiah 2:1; 5:14; 13:6**. Eliashib was high priest from ca. 450/444–432 B.C. (cf. **Nehemiah 13**); for more information, see Eliashib #28 in chart "**Supplement 2**: The High Priests of Israel."

3. Nehemiah's exact heritage is unclear. Only his immediate family is mentioned. He is consistently called a *governor* and is unlikely to be from a priestly lineage for the following reasons: (1) he is never called a priest; (2) he never refers to himself as a priest; (3) he never undertakes priestly activity in the book that bears his name; and (4) he always defers to Ezra as the priest and teacher of the Law when they are together (**Nehemiah 8:9**).

4. Hanani is called the *brother* of Nehemiah (**Nehemiah 1:2; 7:2**), so his ancestry is also unknown (see note 3). Hanani's name derives from the root חָנַן, "be gracious." With the suffix י, the name is "grace of Y(ahweh)." Hananiah is the *plene* (full) spelling of Hanani with "*yah*" fully written out; nevertheless, Hanani and Hananiah in the chart are different people. Nehemiah's brother (Hanani) should not be confused with Hanani the son/descendant of Heman, a chief musician in Solomon's Temple, ca. 971–931 B.C. (**1 Chronicles 25:4**) nor with Hanani who played a musical instrument at the dedication of Jerusalem's wall in 444 B.C. (**Nehemiah 12:36**).

5. See references to these brothers/relatives at **Nehemiah 4:23; 5:10, 14**.

6. The Elephantine papyri mention a Hananiah who was the head of Jewish affairs in Jerusalem; see the commentary at Nehemiah 1:2 in the *NIV Study Bible*, Kenneth L. Barker, ed. (Grand Rapids: Zondervan, 2011), 778.

7. For the lineage of Zerubbabel and his offspring, see charts "**1 Chronicles 3**: Zerubbabel and Shealtiel and the Double Line of the Messiah through King David's Sons, Nathan and Solomon" and "**Ezra 1**: Sheshbazzar and Zerubbabel, Governors over the Restored Community in Jerusalem (Post-Exile)."

8. Nehemiah put Hanani (his brother) and Hananiah (likely Zerubbabel's son) in charge of Jerusalem: "Hananiah [was] the commander of the citadel, because he was a man of integrity and feared God more than most people" (**Nehemiah 7:2**).

9. See "**Nehemiah 2**: The Enemies of Nehemiah Who Ruled in the Provinces Surrounding Judah."

10. Nehemiah often prayed to the LORD: "Remember me with favor" for what he had accomplished (**Nehemiah 5:19; 13:31**; cf. **13:14, 22**).

11. See chart "**Ezra 2**: Genealogical Record of the Captives who Returned to Jerusalem with Zerubbabel and Joshua (Post-Exile)."

NEHEMIAH 2: THE ENEMIES OF NEHEMIAH[1] WHO RULED IN THE PROVINCES SURROUNDING JUDAH

Approximate Dating: during Nehemiah's time as governor in Jerusalem, 444–332 B.C. ***Relevant Scriptures:*** **Nehemiah 2:10, 19–20; 3:1, 4, 30; 6:17–19; 12:10–11; 13:28**

1. **Sanballat** the Horonite of Samaria[2]
2. **Tobiah**, the Ammonite official[3]
3. **Geshem** the Arab[4]

Genealogy of Sanballat

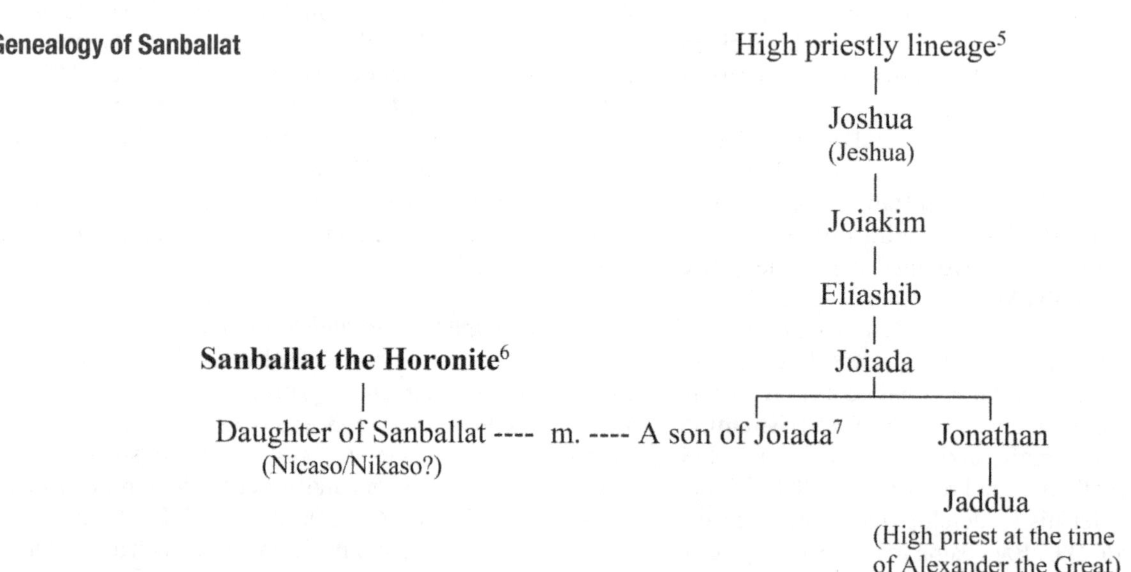

Genealogy of Tobiah

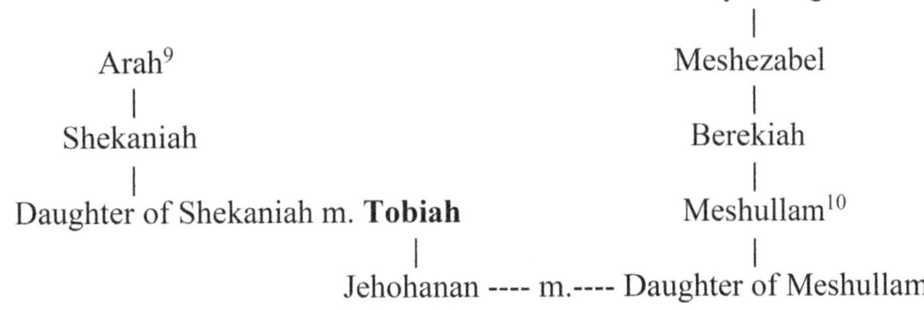

Genealogy of Geshem

Of Arab/Arabian descent

|

Geshem

(Probably Geshem, the king of Kedar, Northern Arabia)

Biblical and Theological Significance

By no means was life in post-exilic Yehud pleasant and peaceful, for the Jews did not arrive to find a vacant land. To the contrary, upon their various returns, they found a plethora of squatters[11] who had filled the vacuum left by them in the Babylonian deportation of 586 B.C.[12]

In Nehemiah's account of his arrival in Jerusalem in 444 B.C., he found Jerusalem's walls in ruins (**Nehemiah 2:13–17**). The enemies of Jewish resettlement had been tearing down Jerusalem's walls that had been completed throughout the reigns of Cyrus (538–530 B.C.), Darius I (522–486 B.C.), and Xerxes (486–465 B.C.) and into the first year of Artaxerxes I in 465 B.C. (**Ezra 4:3–16**).

Those resistant to rebuilding the wall were Sanballat of the town of Horon (see notes 2 and 6) and Tobiah (note 3) from an unnamed place in Ammon, across the Jordan River (**Nehemiah 2:10**). A third rebel was called Geshem the Arab (**Nehemiah 2:19**). These agitators first employed mockery and accusations of disloyalty toward the king to try and halt the rebuilding process (**Nehemiah 2:19**). When this failed, they plotted to take up arms (**Nehemiah 4:7–23**).

Nehemiah writes about the continued conspiracy that was targeted against him personally, saying,

> One day I went to the house of Shemaiah son of Delaiah,[13] the son of Mehetabel, who was shut in at his home. He said, "Let us meet in the house of God, inside the temple, and let us close the temple doors, because men are coming to kill you—by night they are coming to kill you." But I said, "Should a man like me run away? Or should someone like me go into the temple to save his life? I will not go!" I realized that God had not sent him, but that he had prophesied against me because Tobiah and Sanballat had hired him. He [Shemaiah] had been hired to intimidate me so that I would commit a sin by doing this, and then they would give me a bad name to discredit me (**Nehemiah 6:10–13**).

As a result of Nehemiah's strong character and leadership, the wall around Jerusalem was completed in fifty-two days, on the twenty-fifth day of Elul (**Nehemiah 6:15**). When the Israelites' enemies heard about this, they "were afraid and lost their self-confidence, because they realized that this work had been done with the help of our God" (**Nehemiah 6:16**).

Notes

1. Before coming to Jerusalem, Nehemiah had been the cupbearer to King Artaxerxes I of Persia, who reigned from 465–424 B.C. (**Nehemiah 2:1**). Nehemiah requested Artaxerxes' permission to return "to the city in Judah where my ancestors are buried" and rebuild the walls around the city of Jerusalem (**Nehemiah 2:5**). Nehemiah returned to Jerusalem in the twentieth year of Artaxerxes (444 B.C.) and, despite the conflicts with Sanballat, Tobiah, and Geshem, completed the walls of the city in 52 days (**Nehemiah 6:15**).

2. Sanballat the Horonite was probably the governor over Samaria (**Nehemiah 4:1–2**); according to the *Anchor Yale Bible Dictionary* (H. G. M. Williamson, "Sanballat," 5:973), "the Aramaic documents from Elephantine [identify Sanballat as] the 'governor of Samaria' (*paḥat šmryn*; cf. CAP, 30:29)." Sanballat's name means "Sin [in Akkadian Sin-muballit, the Babylonian moon god] gives life," suggesting that he was a foreigner or possibly a Jew born in Babylonian captivity. [Note the general shift from enemy opposition from Gentile outsiders in **Nehemiah 4** to enemy opposition from fellow Jews in **Nehemiah 5**.] The marriage of Sanballat's daughter—probably Nikaso/Nicaso—to one of the sons of the high priest, Joiada the son of Eliashib (**Nehemiah 12:10; 13:28**), reveals Sanballat's intention to maintain a strong influence over the priesthood in Jerusalem. The designation "Sanballat the Horonite" (**Nehemiah 2:10, 19; 13:38:**), suggests that he may have been a native of Beth Horon (of the tribe of Ephraim; cf. **Joshua 21:21–22**), one of the Levitical cities given to the Kohathite attending priests; alternatively, the appellation may simply convey that he wielded authority over Upper and Lower Beth Horon, located eleven miles northwest of Jerusalem, which strategically guarded the main road to Jerusalem (cf. **Joshua 10:10; 16:3, 5–6**). In this way, Sanballat regulated, or perhaps manipulated, the economy of Jerusalem. Sanballat, and his co-conspirators Tobiah and Shemaiah, ridiculed Nehemiah and strongly opposed his efforts to rebuild Jerusalem (cf. **Nehemiah 2:19–20; 4:1–23; 6:1–14**).

For further clarity on the identity of Sanballat, see note 6.

3. Tobiah was considered the enemy to the east of Judah. Tobiah appears to be a Jew, but he is called "Tobiah the Ammonite" (**Nehemiah 2:10, 19; 4:3**), possibly because his family fled to Ammon during the destruction of Jerusalem. He was appointed as an official in the region by the Persian king Artaxerxes I (**Nehemiah 2:10, 19**). Tobiah sought to thwart Nehemiah's efforts to rebuild Jerusalem because it would weaken his political authority in the area. Tobiah allied himself with Eliashib the high priest (ca. 450/444–432 B.C.), who, in turn, prepared a chamber for Tobiah in the courts of the house of God (**Nehemiah 13:7**). This action angered Nehemiah so greatly that he "threw all Tobiah's household goods out of the room" (**Nehemiah 13:8**). A partial lineage of Tobiah is given in **Nehemiah 6:17–18**: "Also, in those days the nobles of Judah were sending many letters to Tobiah and replies from Tobiah kept coming to them. For many in Judah were under oath to him, since he was son-in-law to Shekaniah son of Arah, and his son Jehohanan had married the daughter of Meshullam son of Berekiah [son of Meshezabel]" (cf. **Nehemiah 3:4, 30**).

4. Geshem, called "Geshem the Arab," was considered the enemy to the south of Judah. He joined Sanballat and Tobiah in resisting Nehemiah's effort to rebuild the temple (**Nehemiah 2:19; 6:1–7**). His genealogy is unknown. The Geshem of Nehemiah may be the same person called the king of Kedar in an inscription from North Arabia. If so, he ruled under Persian hegemony. Gashmu is the Aramaic form of Geshem; "the name in its more original form, 'Gashmu', perhaps meant 'big man,' and it is well attested in archaeological finds in North Arabia" (Paul L. Redditt, "Gashmu," *Eerdman's Dictionary*, 497).

5. The lineage of the high priests during this time is given in **Nehemiah 12:10–11**. For their tenures in the high priesthood, see chart "**Supplement 2**: The High Priests of Israel."

6. The identity and lineage of Sanballat is not well understood. Nehemiah typically refers to him as *Sanballat the Horonite*. The *ISBE* (R. Dick Wilson, "Sanballat") says that "if the appellation [Horonite] which follows his name indicates his origin, [Sanballat was] a Moabite of Horonaim, a city of Moab mentioned in **Isaiah 15:5; Jeremiah 48:2, 5, 34**; Josephus, *Ant*, XIII, xxiii; XIV, ii." ("Sanballat"). Furthermore, according to *Eerdmans Dictionary*, Sanballat is "derived from Akk. *Sin-ubal-lit*, [and] the name means 'may [the god] Sin give him life.' In view of this foreign name, scholars speculate that Sanballat may have descended from a family settled in Israel by the Assyrians in the 8th century (**2 Kings 17:24;** cf. **Ezra 4:1–3**). However, one of the Elephantine papyri [late fifth century B.C. to Bigvai the governor of Judah] gives the names of his two sons as Delaiah and Shelemiah, both compounded with the shortened name of God, *Yah*. In addition, one of the grandsons of the high priest Eliashib was his son-in-law. It seems likely, then, that Sanballat thought of himself as a loyal Yahwist" (Paul L. Redditt, "Sanballat," *Eerdmans Dictionary*, 1165). Regarding Sanballat's identity, the *Anchor Yale Bible Dictionary* explains: "we have little other information about Sanballat the Horonite except that by the year 408 B.C. he was still in office but had delegated effective power to his two sons, Delaiah and Shelemiah, presumably because of his advanced age (cf. *CAP*, 30:29). Finds of papyri and seals from the Wadi ed-Daliyeh [north of Jericho], however, have revealed more information about his descendants, who continued to hold the office of governor, and at least one who was also called Sanballat. According to Cross (1966: 204), they show that a Sanballat (II) became governor sometime early in the 4th century B.C.E., and that he was therefore probably the son of Delaiah and so the grandson of Sanballat the Horonite. They further refer to a *yš'yhw* (or *yd'yhw*; the name is damaged and therefore the precise reconstruction is hypothetical) and a Hananiah, both sons of Sanballat II and both governors after him. Because Josephus refers to a Sanballat at the start of Hellenistic rule, and because the practice of papponymy (naming a child after his paternal grandfather) was not uncommon at this period, Cross further suggests that Hananiah may have been succeeded by a Sanballat III" (H. G. M. Williamson, "Sanballat," *Anchor Yale Bible Dictionary* 5:974). This information suggests a papponymic pattern in Sanballat's descendants: Sanballat the Horonite–Delaiah–Sanballat II–(Hananiah)–Sanballat III.

7. **Nehemiah 13:28** says "One of the sons of Joiada son of Eliashib the high priest was son-in-law to Sanballat the Horonite." For notes about the marriage of Manasseh (?) and Nikaso/Nicaso (presumably the name of Sanballat's daughter), see chart "**Nehemiah 13**: Intermarriage of Jews and Samaritans That Compromised the Purity of the Holy Priesthood of Israel"; also see note 37 in chart "**Supplement 2**: The High Priests of Israel."

8. The name of Tobiah's daughter-in-law is not given in Scripture, but she appears to be from a Kohathite priestly lineage, because her father Meshullam was one of the attending priests who assisted Nehemiah in the rebuilding of the walls around Jerusalem. Also, Meshullam lived next to the temple complex (cf. **Nehemiah 3:4, 28, 30**).

9. He is possibly the same person as Arah, one of the people of the province who returned from Babylonian captivity with Zerubbabel in 538 B.C. (cf. **Ezra 2:1–2, 5**).

10. Meshullam "made repairs opposite his living quarters" (**Nehemiah 3:30**; cf. **3:4; 6:18**). This Meshullam is not the same person as Meshullam (or Shallum) the high priest of ca. 690–640 B.C. who was the great-great-grandfather of Jozadak (cf. **1 Chronicles 6:12–13; 9:11; Ezra 7:2; Nehemiah 11:11**). In all likelihood, Meshullam was an Kohathite attending priest (for this line that parallels that of the high priest lineage, see chart "**1 Chronicles 6**: Levi: High Priests, Priests, Levites, and Musicians in Solomon's Temple"; for Kohathite priests named Meshullam (#1 and #2), see chart "**1 Chronicles 24**: Genealogical Registry of the Twenty-Four Divisions of Kohathite Attending Priests Who Rotated Service in Solomon's Temple."

11. The squatters had an unmitigated hatred toward the newly arrived Jews; these foes included four main groups:

(1) Samaria to the north of Judah had been repopulated after the Assyrian deportations of 722 B.C. by ethnicities from throughout the Assyrian Empire who settled in among the remnant of Israelites that had not been taken, resulting in intermarriage and emergence of a people called "Samaritans," well known in both Old and New Testaments.

(2) The Ashdodites from the Mediterranean port of Ashdod were among the remnants of the five Philistine city-states of Gaza, Gath, Ashdod, Ekron, and Ashkelon and insinuated themselves somehow into the vicinity of Jerusalem.

(3) The Ammonites, who lived east of the Jordan near the Dead Sea, originated from Ben-Ammi, the son of Lot by one of his two daughters after the flight from Sodom and Gomorrah (**Genesis 19:30, 36, 38**). Perpetual animosity characterized the relationship between Ammon and Israel for more than a millennium.

(4) The Arabs, to the south of Judah, are mentioned sparsely in the Old Testament by that name (cf. **2 Chronicles 17:11; 21:16; 22:1; 26:7; Nehemiah 4:7**). Their name is a toponym, derived from the regions where they roamed and encamped, the Arabah (עֲרָבָה). Thus, the Arabi (עֲרָבִי) or Arabs achieved their identity. On a larger scale, the Arabs were just part of a larger people, the descendants of Ishmael, Abraham's son by the Egyptian slave (Hagar) of his wife Sarah (**Genesis 16:1–4, 7–15; 25:12–17; 28:9; 1 Chronicles 1:29–31**).

12. For more insight on this issue and its difficulties, see "**Nehemiah 6**: Intermarriage of Jews and the Tobiads in the Post-Exile: Meshullam's Daughter (a Jewess) and Jehohanan (a Tobiad)" and "**Nehemiah 13**: Intermarriage of Jews and Samaritans That Compromised the Purity of the Holy Priesthood of Israel."

13. Delaiah is possibly related to Delaiah in **Ezra 2:60**.

NEHEMIAH 6: SHEMAIAH, THE JEWISH SECRET INFORMANT FOR THE ENEMIES OF NEHEMIAH WHO OPPOSED THE REBUILDING OF THE WALL AROUND JERUSALEM

Approximate Dating: ca. 444 B.C. ***Relevant Scriptures:*** **Nehemiah 6:10**

Levi

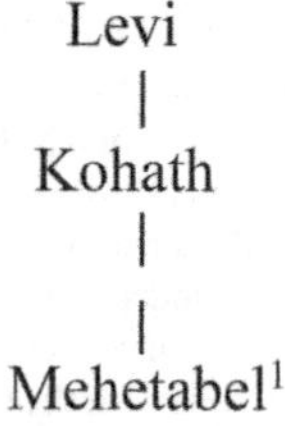

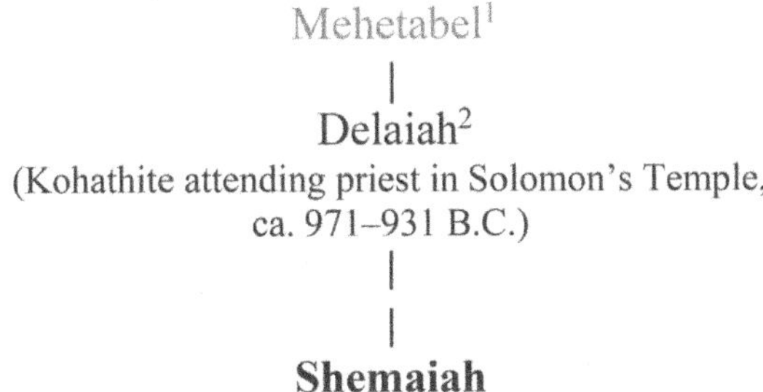

Biblical and Theological Significance

Shemaiah, a quasi-priest, was a descendant of Delaiah, very likely the ancestral head of the twenty-third of the twenty-four divisions of Kohathite attending priests who rotated service at Solomon's Temple (**1 Chronicles 24:18**).[3] Sanballat, Tobiah, and Geshem hired Shemaiah to be a Jewish secret informant regarding what was happening in and around Jerusalem and the temple (**Nehemiah 6:12**; cf. **2:19; 6:1**). He was instructed to persuade Nehemiah to find refuge in the temple and thus be unable to govern the state as the Lord had called him to do (**Nehemiah 6:12**). Artaxerxes I (465–424 B.C.), who was then the ruler of the Persian Empire (of which Yehud was a satrap or province), had given Nehemiah documents authorizing him to function as an envoy of the Persian king. Essentially, Nehemiah possessed the governorship of the small state of Yehud for at least twelve years, from 444–432 B.C. (**Nehemiah 5:14**), although he returned to Persia briefly in 432 B.C. and then returned a second time to Jerusalem, for an unspecified length of time. During the exile (586–516 B.C.), enemies of Judah from Ammon, Arabia, Samaria, and even the remnant Philistine state of Ashdod had moved in.[4] They were now determined to thwart the rise of the new Jewish polity, and disposing of Nehemiah would accomplish that goal. These political opponents hired Shemaiah the Kohathite priest (who had access to the Second Temple) to intimidate Nehemiah by saying "men are coming to kill you" and persuade him to seek refuge inside the temple (**Nehemiah 6:10**).[5] Nehemiah saw through the plot and answered Shemaiah's call for disloyalty with these words, "Should a man like me run away? Or should someone like me go into the temple to save his life? I will not go!" (**Nehemiah 6:11**). Nehemiah's words are worthy of repetition by all who would presume to lead. The work of building the wall around Jerusalem continued as planned until it was finished in fifty-two days (**Nehemiah 6:15**). Shemaiah's fate is unknown.

Notes

1. The name "Mehetabel" is one of the rare occurrences of a bi-gender nominal in Hebrew. In two (parallel) passages, it clearly refers to a female (**Genesis 36:39; 1 Chronicles 1:50**) and in one case, by contextual inference, to a male, the father of Delaiah (**Nehemiah 6:10**). See (1) in note 3.

2. The twenty-four divisions were set up in the days of King David ca. 971 B.C.; see the chart, "**1 Chronicles 24**: Genealogical Registry of the Twenty-Four Divisions of Kohathite Attending Priests Who Rotated Service in Solomon's Temple." Delaiah son of Mehetabel is not the Judahite, Delaiah, the son of Elioenai (**1 Chronicles 3:24**; cf. the Delaiah descendants who could not prove they were Israelites; **Ezra 2:60; Nehemiah 7:62**).

3. Several persons in a priestly (Kohathite) line who are named Shemaiah could conceivably be the turncoat of the chart: (1) the son of Delaiah (**Nehemiah 6:10**), which is the favored interpretation and is therefore the lineage shown in the chart; (2) the Kohathite priestly descendant of Harim (**Ezra 10:21**); (3) the Kohathite priest who signed Nehemiah's covenant (**Nehemiah 10:8**); and (4) the priest who returned from exile with Zerubbabel and Joshua in 538 B.C. (**Nehemiah 12:6**). The Levitical Kohathite heritage of Shemaiah excludes other persons named Shemaiah in **1 Chronicles 3:22; 9:14, 16; Ezra 8:13, 16; 10:31**; and **Nehemiah 3:29; 11:15; 12:34–36, 42**.

4. See note 11 in chart "**Nehemiah 2**: The Enemies of Nehemiah Who Ruled in the Provinces Surrounding Judah."

5. Shemaiah was perhaps suggesting that Nehemiah take hold of the horns of the altar of burnt offering where fugitives could seek safe asylum (cf. **Exodus 21:13–14; 27:2; 1 Kings 1:50–51; 2:28**).

NEHEMIAH 6: INTERMARRIAGE OF JEWS AND THE TOBIADS IN THE POST-EXILE: MESHULLAM'S DAUGHTER (A JEWESS) AND JEHOHANAN (A TOBIAD)

Approximate Dating: rebuilding of the walls around Jerusalem in ca. 444 B.C. ***Relevant Scriptures:*** **Nehemiah 6:17–18**

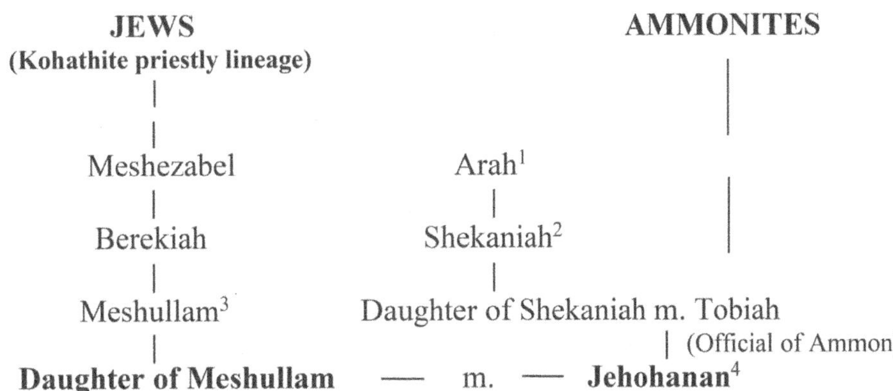

Biblical and Theological Significance

The Ammonites had a long history of hostility toward Israel and Judah[5] that continued with extra ferocity as the Jews returned to their homeland. Even before the return of the exiles to Jerusalem, Tobiah had become an influential leader in Jerusalem by inveigling his way into Jewish affairs. The leaders of the remnant of Judah had sent many letters to him, and Tobiah had been careful to reply. Many of the Jews, impressed by him, had pledged to offer him political support (**Nehemiah 6:17–19**).

When Nehemiah, the governor, arrived in 444 B.C., the erstwhile influence of three foes—Tobiah the Ammonite, Sanballat of Samaria, and Geshem the Arab—was so severely threatened that they employed every means possible to oppose the rebuilding effort in Jerusalem (**Nehemiah 2:10, 19; 4:1–3, 7–8, 11–12; 6:1–2, 5, 10–14**). Tobiah's desire to exert influence upon the noble elite and the priesthood can be seen first, in him giving his son Jehohanan in marriage to the daughter of Meshullam the Kohathite priest, and second, in Tobiah and Sanballat hiring Shemaiah, the son of Delaiah,[6] to convince Nehemiah that men were conspiring to assassinate him and that he should seek refuge in the temple (although Nehemiah saw through the ruse and refused to halt the work on the wall, which was completed in fifty-two days; **Nehemiah 6:6–15**).

After twelve years as governor over Jerusalem, Nehemiah returned to Persia in ca. 432 B.C. During this time, Tobiah took advantage of Nehemiah's absence by ingratiating himself to Eliashib the high priest (who served in the Second Temple ca. 450/444–432 B.C.). Eliashib had authority over the storerooms of the Second Temple (**Nehemiah 13:4**) and foolishly prepared a large room—formerly used to store grain offerings and temple articles—for Tobiah the Ammonite official (**Nehemiah 13:5**). When Nehemiah returned to Jerusalem late in 432 B.C., he promptly had Tobiah removed (**Nehemiah 13:4–9**).

Notes

1. The descendants of Arah were among the Israelites who returned from exile with Zerubbabel (cf. **Ezra 2:5; Nehemiah 7:10**).

2. Shekaniah appears to be in a Kohathite attending priestly lineage; however, it is unclear if he is the descendant of (1) Shekaniah the Kohathite priest, who was the head over the tenth of the 24 priestly divisions who rotated service in Solomon's Temple (cf. **1 Chronicles 24:11**); (2) Shekaniah a leader of the priests who returned to Jerusalem with Zerubbabel and with Joshua the high priest in 538 B.C. (**Nehemiah 12:1–3**); or (3) Shekaniah the father of Shemaiah the priest, the guard at the East Gate in 444 B.C. (**Nehemiah 3:29**). Alternatively, Shekaniah may not be a priest, but rather the son of a prominent leader (Arah) among the returning exiles (see note 1).

3. Meshullam son of Berekiah, son of Meshezabel, was a priest who helped Nehemiah build the walls around Jerusalem (**Nehemiah 3:4**). He appears to be the same priest named Meshullam who repaired the section "opposite his living quarters" (**Nehemiah 3:30**; cf. **v. 28**), between the section repaired by Hananiah and Hanun and the section repaired by Malkijah the goldsmith (**Nehemiah 3:30–31**; cf. **vv. 13–14**). Collectively, this suggests that Meshullam the son of Berekiah was a Kohathite attending priest. He is not the same person as (1) Meshullam son of Besodeiah (**Nehemiah 3:6**) who was his contemporary, nor (2) Meshullam/Shallum the high priest who served in Solomon's Temple, ca. 690–640 B.C. (i.e., who is called Shallum in **1 Chronicles 6:12–13; Ezra 7:2** and Meshullam in **1 Chronicles 9:11; Nehemiah 11:11**).

4. Tobiah's son Jehohanan was married into the family of Meshullam the son of Berekiah. Because of this association, Tobiah the Ammonite was kept apprised of the progress on the wall around Jerusalem (cf. **Nehemiah 3:4; 6:18**).

5. Ammonites and Moabites were among those of *mixed* descent (עֵרֶב) (cf. *foreign* descent in **Nehemiah 13:3**)—in essence, the children born to Lot and his two daughters (**Genesis 19:36–38**). Because they did not aid the children of Israel but hired Baalam to curse them, the Ammonites and Moabites were excluded from the assembly of God (**Deuteronomy 23:3–6; Nehemiah 13:1–3**; cf. **Numbers 22:1–17; 23:7**).

6. Delaiah was the son of Mehetabel. Delaiah's grandson Shemaiah is the subject of the chart "**Nehemiah 6**: Shemaiah, the Jewish Secret Informant for the Enemies of Nehemiah who Opposed the Rebuilding of the Wall around Jerusalem." Delaiah does not appear to be (1) a descendant of Delaiah the Kohathite attending priest who served in Solomon's Temple (cf. **1 Chronicles 24:18**; see chart "**1 Chronicles 24**: Genealogical Registry of the 24 Divisions of Kohathite Attending Priests Who Rotated Service in Solomon's Temple"), nor (2) the Delaiah of **Ezra 2:60** and **Nehemiah 7:62**.

NEHEMIAH 8: GENEALOGICAL RECORD OF THE LEADERS AND PRIESTS WHO STOOD AT THE LEFT AND RIGHT HAND OF EZRA DURING THE READING OF THE LAW OF MOSES

Approximate Dating: ca. 444 B.C. ***Relevant Scriptures:*** **Nehemiah 8:4**

At the **Right Hand** *of Ezra*

1. **Mattithiah**[1]
2. **Shema**
3. **Anaiah**[2]
4. **Uriah**[3]
5. **Hilkiah**[4]
6. **Maaseiah**[5]

At the **Left Hand** *of Ezra*

1. **Pedaiah**[6]
2. **Mishael**
3. **Malkijah**[7]
4. **Hashum**[8]
5. **Hashbaddanah**
6. **Zechariah**[9]
7. **Meshullam**[10]

Biblical and Theological Significance

The setting for Ezra's[11] reading of the Law was on the first day of the seventh month, that is, Tishri.[12] The scroll being read is identified as the "Book of the Law of Moses" (**Nehemiah 8:1**)—referring to the book of Deuteronomy, the last book of the Pentateuch (cf. **Deuteronomy 28:61; 29:21; 30:10; 31:26; Joshua 1:8; 8:31, 34; 23:6; 24:26; 2 Kings**

22:8, 11; 2 Chronicles 17:9; 34:14–15; Nehemiah 8:1–3; 9:3). The specific occasion was what has become known as Rosh Hashanah, New Year's Day, along with the festivals that follow, Yom Kippur and Sukkoth/Feast of Tabernacles. The purpose was to begin again as a post-exilic community of faith. Yom Kippur (the day of covering [of sin]) or the Day of Atonement), followed on the tenth of Tishri, and the Festival of Sukkoth/Tabernacles, which recounted and re-enacted the trek through the Sinai after the exodus, occurred on the fourteenth through the twenty-first. All of this was no doubt familiar to the assembly but had not been lived out in practical application. Ezra's purpose clearly was to chastise the people for their neglect of covenant compliance and to call to remembrance the nation's heritage and its calling as the people of God among the nations.

In order for the masses to hear Ezra's message, a pulpit[13] was erected for him high above them. With him, on stairs, were nine Levites whose function, it seems, was to affirm what Ezra read and to lead the congregation in appeals for repentance and proclamations of praise to Yahweh their God (**Nehemiah 9:3, 5**). Fortunately, the text of his message is preserved for the modern reader in **Nehemiah 9:5–37**. After the address, Nehemiah called for the priests, Levites, and other leaders to sign their names and affix their seals to a "binding agreement" (**Nehemiah 9:38**)[14] with Yahweh on behalf of the nation. This too is reminiscent of the role of the king in the pre-exile monarchy.[15] The king represented his people; therefore, he must first affirm his fealty to the King of kings and Lord of lords if he expected God's blessing on the nation. And so, the first name on the long list of those who signed and sealed it was that of Nehemiah, the governor (**Nehemiah 10:1**).

Notes

1. This Mattithiah is possibly Mattithiah the Levitical Korahite (**1 Chronicles 9:31**) or Mattithiah the Israelite, a descendant of Nebo (**Ezra 10:43**), but for chronological reasons he is not Mattithiah the Merarite (**1 Chronicles 25:21**).

2. This Anaiah may be the same as Anaiah the leader of the people (**Nehemiah 10:22**).

3. This Uriah appears to be a priest—the father of Meremoth the priest who handled "the silver and gold and the sacred articles" that had been brought for the Second Temple (**Ezra 8:33**) and a descendant of Hakkoz (**Nehemiah 3:4**). Hakkoz was the ancestral head over the seventh division of Kohathite attending priests in Solomon's Temple, set up in the days of King David (**1 Chronicles 24:10**). When the Hakkoz descendants returned to Jerusalem in 538 B.C., they were among the priests who could not verify their ancestry and so were temporarily excluded from the priesthood (**Ezra 2:59–63**; **Nehemiah 7:61–65**). In the days of Nehemiah, Uriah's son Meremoth repaired a section of wall next to the Fish Gate (**Nehemiah 3:4**); he also repaired a section from the entrance of the house of Eliashib the high priest to the end of the house (**Nehemiah 3:21**).

4. For chronological reasons, this Hilkiah may be the same person as the Hilkiah who was one of the leaders of the Kohathite priests who returned to Jerusalem with Zerubbabel in 538 B.C. (**Nehemiah 12:7**), but he is not: (1) Hilkiah the palace administrator under Hezekiah, 715–686 B.C. (**2 Kings 18:26; 37; Isaiah 36:3, 22**); (2) the Hilkiah figures who were Merarites (**1 Chronicles 6:45, 26:11**); (3) Hilkiah the high priest who served during the reign of King Josiah (640–609 B.C.; **2 Kings 22:4, 8–14; 23:4, 24; 1 Chronicles 6:13; 9:11; 2 Chronicles 34:9, 14–22; Ezra 7:1; Nehemiah 11:11**); (4) Hilkiah the father of the prophet Jeremiah, who prophesied ca. 627–586 B.C (**Jeremiah 1:1**); nor (5) Hilkiah the father of Gemariah (**Jeremiah 29:3**), who is possibly Hilkiah #3.

5. Maaseiah appears to be a priest, the son of Ananiah and the father of Azariah (cf. **Nehemiah 3:23**).

6. Pedaiah was probably the son of Parosh (cf. **Nehemiah 3:25**) and/or the faithful Levite whom Nehemiah appointed over the storerooms of grain, wine, and oil (cf. **Nehemiah 13:13**).

7. This Malkijah was probably the son of Harim as well as one of the Kohathite priests who sealed the covenant with Nehemiah in 444 B.C. (**Nehemiah 10:3**), the Malkijah who repaired a section of the wall and the Tower of the Ovens (**Nehemiah 3:11**), and/or Malkijah the priest who was present at the celebration of the completed wall around Jerusalem (**Nehemiah 12:42**). It is less likely that he is one of the following: the Malkijah(s) who were descendants of Parosh the Israelite (**Ezra 10:25**); Malkijah son of Rekab, who was the ruler of the district of Beth Hakkerem (**Nehemiah 3:14**); or Malkijah the goldsmith who repaired sections of the wall (**Nehemiah 3:31**). For chronological reasons, he is not Malkijah the father of Pashhur (**Nehemiah 11:12**; cf. **Jeremiah 21:1**), nor the official named Malkijah, who is presumably a Judahite (not a Levite; cf. **Jeremiah 38:1, 6**).

8. Hashum was a leader of the descendants of Hashum, who returned to Jerusalem with Zerubbabel in 538 B.C. with 223 individuals (**Ezra 2:19**). The clan had increased to 328 individuals by 444 B.C., the time of Nehemiah (**Nehemiah 7:22**).

9. The identity of this Zechariah is unclear, but the following are possible candidates for the Zechariah who stood with Ezra (although one or more of them may refer to the same person):

(1) Zechariah (a descendant of Parosh), the head of a family who returned to Jerusalem with Ezra in 458 B.C., whose clan numbered 150 men (**Ezra 8:3**);
(2) the clan leader "of the descendants of Bebai" who returned with Ezra with 28 men (**Ezra 8:11**);
(3) a leader of the people who accompanied Ezra before the departure from Babylon (**Ezra 8:16**);
(4) Zechariah "from the descendants of Elam" who had taken a pagan wife (**Ezra 10:26**);
(5) the son of Pashhur, the son of Malkijah (Kohathite priestly line); **Nehemiah 11:12; Jeremiah 21:1**);
(6) Zechariah the prophet-priest, who was the grandson of Iddo (**Ezra 5:1; 6:14; Nehemiah 12:16; Zechariah 1:1, 7**);
(7) the son of Jonathan a descendant of Asaph, the Levitical musician (**Nehemiah 12:35**);
(8) the priest who played a trumpet at the dedication of the wall (**Nehemiah 12:41**).

10. The identity of Meshullam is unclear. For chronological reasons, he is not the high priest Meshullam (Shallum), the son of Zadok and father of Hilkiah, who served in Solomon's Temple from ca. 690–640 B.C. (cf. **Nehemiah 11:10–11**). However, the following are possible candidates for the Meshullam who stood with Ezra (one or more of them may refer to the same person):

(1) the son of Zerubbabel (**1 Chronicles 3:19**);
(2) a leader who accompanied Ezra from Babylon (**Ezra 8:16**);
(3) a descendant of Bani who had taken a pagan wife (**Ezra 10:29**);
(4) the son of Berekiah (**Nehemiah 3:4, 30**);
(5) a priest who sealed the covenant with Nehemiah (**Nehemiah 10:7**);
(6) a leader of the people who sealed the covenant (**Nehemiah 10:20**);
(7) the priest who was head of the priestly family of Ezra (**Nehemiah 12:13**);
(8) the priest who was head of the priestly family of Ginnethon (**Nehemiah 12:16**);
(9) Nehemiah's helper during the dedication of the Jerusalem wall (**Nehemiah 12:33**).

11. Ezra is called סֹפֵר, *sopher*, a "reader." For his genealogy, see chart "**Ezra 7**: Ezra, the Priestly Scribe and Teacher of the Law (Post-Exile)."

12. The so-called civil calendar began in Tishri (September-October), whereas the sacred calendar commenced in Nisan in the spring (March-April). Ezra's public reading of the Law was on October 8, 444 B.C. (cf. **Nehemiah 1:1; 8:2**).

13. This was no small feat. The Hebrew term *migdal* is the common word for "tower," suggesting a very high perch.

14. The literal idiom "we are cutting a true and faithful writing" reflects the normal and technical "cutting a covenant" כָּרַת הַבְּרִית (*karath habberit*).

15. See **Deuteronomy 17:14–20; 2 Samuel 23:5; 1 Kings 11:11; 2 Kings 11:17–18; 23:1–3; 2 Chronicles 34:29–32**.

NEHEMIAH 8: GENEALOGICAL RECORD OF THE LEVITES WHO HELPED THE PEOPLE UNDERSTAND THE READING OF THE LAW OF MOSES

Approximate Dating: ca. 444 B.C. ***Relevant Scriptures:*** **Nehemiah 8:7–8**

1. **Jeshua**[1]
2. **Bani**[2]
3. **Sherebiah**[3]
4. **Jamin**
5. **Akkub**[4]
6. **Shabbethai**[5]
7. **Hodiah**[6]
8. **Maaseiah**[7]
9. **Kelita**[8]
10. **Azariah**[9]
11. **Jozabad**[10]
12. **Hanan**[11]
13. **Pelaiah**[12]

Biblical and Theological Significance

Literacy was rare in this age, except for those who were trained in scribal circles. Scribes were esteemed and highly rewarded for their services. Thus, in the situation described here, the throngs of Jerusalem gathered when Ezra, the scribal priest, stood to read the Law of Moses before the covenant community, an assembly of men and women "who were able to understand" (**Nehemiah 8:2**).[13] Levites were among the literate and knowledgeable teachers who "read from the Book of the Law of God, making it clear[14] and giving the meaning so that the people understood what was being read" (**Nehemiah 8:8**; cf. **2 Chronicles 30:22**). Therefore, the Levites were as much exegetes of Scripture as readers. In response, the people rejoiced because "they now understood the words that had been made known to them" (**Nehemiah 8:12**). The reading finished, the Levites instructed the Israelites: "Stand up and praise the LORD your God, who is from everlasting to everlasting" (**Nehemiah 9:5**).

Notes

1. Jeshua the Levite (**Nehemiah 8:7**) is either Jeshua the Levite, the son of Azaniah (**Nehemiah 10:9**) or he is Jeshua the Levite, the son of Kadmiel (**Nehemiah 7:43**; see also **Ezra 2:40; 3:8–9; Nehemiah 8:7; 9:4–5; 12:8, 24**). Jeshua the Levite is not the same person as Joshua/Jeshua the high priest (cf. **Ezra 2:36; 3:2, 8–9; 5:2; 10:18; Nehemiah 7:39; 12:10, 26; Haggai 1:1, 12, 14; 2:4; Zechariah 3:1, 3–4, 8**); for the latter, see chart "**Ezra 2**: Joshua, the High Priest in the Second Temple, and His Descendants (Post-Exile)."

2. Bani the Levite (**Nehemiah 8:7**) is the same person as the Bani the Levite in **Nehemiah 3:17; 9:4–5; 10:13**. Bani's son Uzzi was the chief officer over the Levites at the Second Temple (see lineage at **Nehemiah 11:22**).

3. Sherebiah the Levite (**Nehemiah 8:7**) is the same person as Sherebiah the Levite in **Nehemiah 9:4–5; 10:12; 12:24**.

4. Akkub the Levite (**Nehemiah 8:7**) is possibly a gatekeeper (**1 Chronicles 9:17; Ezra 2:42; Nehemiah 7:45; 8:7 (?); 11:19; 12:25**).

5. Shabbethai the Levite (**Nehemiah 8:7**) may be the same Shabbethai who opposed Ezra's plan for putting away pagan wives (**Ezra 10:15**). Shabbethai and Jozabad were two Levitical heads who oversaw the outside work of the house of God (**Nehemiah 11:16**).

6. Hodiah the Levite (**Nehemiah 8:7**) is also mentioned in **Nehemiah 9:5; 10:10** or **13**.

7. Maaseiah the Levite (**Nehemiah 8:7**) is the same person as Maaseiah the Levite (**Nehemiah 8:4**) but a different person than: (1) Masseiah the leader of the people (**Nehemiah 10:25**) and (2) several Kohathite priests named Masseiah—see (a) Maaseiah in **Ezra 10:18** who was a relative of Joshua the high priest; (b) Maaseiah the priest from the descendants of Harim in **Ezra 10:21**; (c) Maaseiah the priest from the descendants of Pashhur in **Ezra 10:22**; (d) Maaseiah the father of Azariah the priest in **Nehemiah 3:23**; and (e) Maaseiah the priest(s) who sang in the choir in **Nehemiah 12:41–42**.

Maaseiah the Levite (**Nehemiah 8:7**) is also different from (1) Maaseiah the Israelite, a descendant of Pahath-Moab (**Ezra 10:30**); (2) Maaseiah the Judahite (**Nehemiah 11:5**); (3) Maaseiah the Benjamite (**Nehemiah 11:7**); and (4) the Maaseiah figures in the book of Jeremiah (**Jeremiah 21:1; 29:21, 25; 35:4; 37:3**).

8. Kelita (**Nehemiah 8:7**) is the same person as Kelita (**Nehemiah 10:10**) and possibly the same person as Kelita (also called Kelaiah) in **Ezra 10:23** who agreed to put away a pagan wife.

9. Azariah the Levite (**Nehemiah 8:7**) does not refer to the priestly figures of **1 Chronicles 9:11; Ezra 7:1, 3; Nehemiah 10:2; 12:33** (?), but he may be the same as "Azariah son of Maaseiah" (**Nehemiah 3:23**) because of the presence of Maaseiah in both places.

10. Jozabad the Levite (**Nehemiah 8:7**)—who may be the son of Jeshua the Levite (**Ezra 8:33**; see note 1)—is probably the same Jozabad who had taken a pagan wife in captivity (**Ezra 10:23**) and who (along with Shabbethai) was head over the Levites who had charge of the outside work of the house of God (cf. **Nehemiah 11:16**). Jozabad the Levite is not the same person as Jozabad the priest "of the descendants of Pashhur [a Kohathite attending priest]" who had taken a pagan wife in exile (cf. **Ezra 10:22**).

11. Hanan the Levite (**Nehemiah 8:7**) is probably the same person as Hanan the Levite (**Nehemiah 10:10**) as well as Hanan the son of Zakkur, the son of Mattaniah, who was a faithful Levite who assisted Shelemiah the priest and Pedaiah in the oversight of the temple storerooms (**Nehemiah 13:13**). Hanan the Levite is not the same person as Hanan the temple servant (**Ezra 2:46; Nehemiah 7:49**) nor Hanan who was one of the leaders of the people (cf. **Nehemiah 10:26**).

12. Pelaiah the Levite (**Nehemiah 8:7**) is the same person as Pelaiah (**Nehemiah 10:10**), but he is not Pelaiah the Judahite (**1 Chronicles 3:24**).

13. The common verb בִּין (*bin*) used here has to do with mental acumen or innate wisdom and not necessarily formal education.

14. The cliché here (שֶׂכֶל וְשׂוֹם מְפֹרָשׁ), *me phoresh wesom sekel*, literally reads "they read . . . distinctly and with interpretation."

NEHEMIAH 9: GENEALOGICAL RECORD OF THE LEVITICAL LEADERS OF WORSHIP DURING THE FEAST OF TABERNACLES THAT WAS CELEBRATED AFTER THE COMPLETION OF THE WALL AROUND JERUSALEM

Approximate Dating: ca. 444 B.C. ***Relevant Scriptures:*** **Nehemiah 9:4–5**

Levites Who Stood on the Stairs of the Levites

1. **Jeshua**[1]
2. **Bani #1**
3. **Kadmiel**
4. **Shebaniah**
5. **Bunni**
6. **Sherebiah**
7. **Bani #2**
8. **Kenani**

Levites Who Led the Worship

1. **Jeshua**
2. **Kadmiel**
3. **Bani**
4. **Hashabneiah**[2]
5. **Sherebiah**
6. **Hodiah**
7. **Shebaniah**
8. **Pethahiah**

Biblical and Theological Significance

After the walls of Jerusalem were completed on the twenty-fifth day of Elul in 444 B.C., the people returned to their cities (**Ezra 2:70; Nehemiah 7:73**), and then a month later, returned to Jerusalem to celebrate the Feast of Tabernacles/Booths (also called the Feast of Ingathering) in the seventh month (the month of Tishri; **Exodus 23:16; 34:22**).[3] The celebration lasted from the fifteenth to the twenty-second, during which Ezra read from the Book of the Law. The last day was considered a holy day for sacred assembly (**Nehemiah 8:9**). On the twenty-fourth day of Tishri, the Israelites fasted, wore sackcloth, confessed their sins, and worshiped the Lord. It was during this time that the leaders stood on the "stairs of the Levites" and encouraged the people to "Stand up and praise the Lord your God" (**Nehemiah 9:4–5**). The leaders also offered an elaborate prayer of praise on behalf of the people, praising God for his covenant faithfulness (**Nehemiah 9:5–37**). This was followed by a covenant renewal ceremony (**Nehemiah 9:38–10:39**). Some of the Levites in **Nehemiah 9:4** are the same as those in **Nehemiah 9:5** (i.e., Jeshua, Kadmiel, Bani, Sherebiah), those in **Nehemiah 8:7** (i.e., Jeshua, Bani, Sherebiah), and those in **Nehemiah 10:9–13** (i.e., Jeshua, Binnui, Shebaniah, Bani).

Notes

1. Jeshua in **Nehemiah 9:4** is probably the same person as Jeshua in **Nehemiah 9:5**. Jeshua was probably the son of Azaniah (**Nehemiah 10:9**) or the son of Kadmiel (**Ezra 2:40; 3:9; Nehemiah 7:43; 12:8, 24**). Jeshua the Levite is not Joshua/Jeshua the high priest, who was his contemporary; for the latter, see chart "**Ezra 2**: Joshua, the High Priest in the Second Temple, and His Descendants (Post-Exile)."

2. Hashabneiah in **Nehemiah 9:5** is probably the same person as Hashabneiah the father of Hattush, in **Nehemiah 3:10**.

3. According to Torah, all national holy days must be celebrated by the entire people and at the temple. During the Babylonian exile, this had become impossible because of the uprooting of Israel's population and the destruction of Solomon's Temple. There is evidence of the Jews continuing worship in Babylon as best they could under the circumstances, but the hearts of the faithful always turned to Jerusalem (**Psalm 125–129, 133–135, 137, 147**). The festivities described in the passage illustrate the great sense of gratitude, blessing, and joy of the returnees who had been spared and could again praise God in his provisional Second Temple, which had been completed in 516 B.C.

NEHEMIAH 10: GENEALOGICAL RECORD OF THE PRIESTS, LEVITES, AND LEADERS OF THE PEOPLE WHO SEALED THE COVENANT WITH NEHEMIAH,[1] THE GOVERNOR OF JUDAH

Approximate Dating: ca. 444 B.C. ***Relevant Scriptures:*** **Nehemiah 10:1–27**

Kohathite Attending Priests[2] (Names of priests with an asterisk * have the same name as the ancestral heads who were over the priestly divisions in Solomon's Temple)

1. **Zedekiah**
2. **Seraiah** (presumably Seraiah #3)[3]
3. **Azariah** (presumably Azariah #3)[4]
4. **Jeremiah**[5]
5. ***Pashhur**[6]
6. **Amariah**
7. ***Malkijah**
8. **Hattush**[7]
9. **Shebaniah**
10. **Malluk**
11. ***Harim**[8]
12. **Meremoth**
13. **Obadiah**[9]
14. **Daniel**[10]
15. **Ginnethon**[11]
16. **Baruch**[12]
17. **Meshullam**[13]

18. ***Abijah**[14]
19. ***Mijamin**[15] (=Miniamin)
20. **Maaziah**
21. ***Bilgai**[16] (=Bilgah)
22. **Shemaiah**[17]

Levites and Their Associates

1. **Jeshua** (son of Azaniah)
2. **Binnui** (of the sons of Henadad)
3. **Kadmiel**
4. **Shebaniah**
5. **Hodiah #1**
6. **Kelita**
7. **Pelaiah**
8. **Hanan**
9. **Mika**
10. **Rehob**
11. **Hashabiah**
12. **Zakkur**
13. **Sherebiah**
14. **Shebaniah**
15. **Hodiah #2**
16. **Bani**[18]
17. **Beninu**

Leaders of the People (=Heads of Israelite families)

1. **Parosh**[19]
2. **Pahath-Moab**[20]
3. **Elam**[21]
4. **Zattu**[22]
5. **Bani**[23]
6. **Bunni**[24]
7. **Azgad**[25]
8. **Bebai**[26]
9. **Adonijah**[27]
10. **Bigvai**[28]
11. **Adin**[29]
12. **Ater**[30]
13. **Hezekiah**[31]
14. **Azzur**[32]
15. **Hodiah**[33]
16. **Hashum**[34]
17. **Bezai**[35]
18. **Hariph**[36]
19. **Anathoth**[37]
20. **Nebai**
21. **Magpiash**
22. **Meshullam**[38]
23. **Hezir**[39]
24. **Meshezabel**[40]
25. **Zadok**[41]
26. **Jaddua**[42]
27. **Pelatiah**[43]
28. **Hanan**[44]
29. **Anaiah**[45]
30. **Hoshea**
31. **Hananiah**[46]
32. **Hasshub**[47]
33. **Hallohesh**[48]
34. **Pilha**
35. **Shobek**
36. **Rehum**[49]
37. **Hashabnah**
38. **Maaseiah**[50]
39. **Ahiah**
40. **Hanan**[51]
41. **Anan**
42. **Malluk**[52]
43. **Harim**[53]
44. **Baanah**[54]

Biblical and Theological Significance

The careful student will soon discover that the various lists of pre- and post-exilic priests, Levites, leaders, and heads of families (e.g., **1 Chronicles 6:1–53; 9:10–21; 24:1–30; Ezra 2:36–39; Nehemiah 7:39–42; 10:1–27; 11:10–17; 12:1–21**), while showing certain similarities or even identity, also exhibit many differences. Ancient onomastics—especially Semitic, and most especially biblical onomastics—emphasize maintaining (oral and/or written) naming traditions through many generations. The following principles attempt to explain the enigmatic features of ancient naming conventions:

1. Names in general were carefully and prayerfully chosen, for example as (1) expressions of a particular reaction to the birth experience itself; (2) in honor of important or especially revered ancestors; (3) as a prayer for success and blessing on the child; or (4) as a prophetic word by the parent, a holy man, or the Lord himself.[55]
2. Repetition of names (like repetition in general) is a hallmark of Semitic psychology and reflection.
3. Names of persons in leadership roles, like those in the priesthood, were especially venerable, and their parents were inclined to mimic not only the names *per se* but the names in sequences,[56] such as those exhibited in the passages above.

Relatedly, how or why total numbers of persons, spellings of names, and other entities in the Hebrew Masoretic Text differ from the ancient translations—such as the Greek Septuagint, Aramaic Targums, Syriac Peshitta, Samaritan Pentateuch, and the like—are best accounted for by the various means that numbers were recorded, by visual and auditory mistakes made by scribes, and other copying inadvertences. These have no bearing on the overall integrity of the Hebrew manuscripts and the concept of biblical inerrancy as it is commonly and correctly understood.

Notes

1. See chart "**Nehemiah 1**: Nehemiah and the Leaders Appointed by Nehemiah over the City of Jerusalem."

2. The names of specific Kohathite attending priests, shown with asterisks in the list above, indicate that they are direct descendants of Kohathite attending priestly heads/divisions from the days of David and Solomon; see chart "**1 Chronicles 24**: Genealogical Registry of the Twenty-Four Divisions of Kohathite Attending Priests Who Rotated Service in the Temple," especially table 1 of the chart. Also, compare the names in the list above to the Kohathite

attending priests who returned to Jerusalem in 538 B.C., shown in chart "**Nehemiah 12**: Genealogical Record of the Heads of the Kohathite Priests and Levites Who Returned to Jerusalem with Zerubbabel and Joshua in the Post-Exile" and priests who were active in 490–450/444 B.C. in chart "**Nehemiah 12**: Genealogical Record of the Heads of Priests, Levites, and Gatekeepers Who Served in the Second Temple in the Days of Joiakim the High Priest, Ezra the Priestly Scribe, and Nehemiah the Governor."

3. Seraiah in **Nehemiah 10:2**, a contemporary of Nehemiah in 444 B.C., is tentatively designated "Seraiah #3:" The following individuals are distinguished based on chronological data, although there is no specific supporting textual evidence (except as noted):

- **Azariah #1, the high priest** in Solomon's Temple ca. 609–600 B.C., was the father of the (martyred) high priest, Seraiah #1. The genealogy of Azariah #1 is given in **1 Chronicles 6:13–14; 9:11** and **Ezra 7:1–5**. Azariah #1 is the same person as Azariah #22 in chart "**Supplement 2**: The High Priests of Israel."
- **Seraiah #1, the martyred high priest**, was killed by the Babylonians at Riblah in 586 B.C. His father was Azariah #1, and his sons were, presumably, Jozadak (the high priest who was taken into Babylonian captivity in 586 B.C. and died there) and Seraiah #2 (Azariah #2) the scribe, who returned to Jerusalem and became the official in charge of the Second Temple (ca. 516 B.C.; **1 Chronicles 9:11; Nehemiah 11:11**). Seraiah #1 the martyr could not have returned with Zerubbabel in 538 B.C., so the priest listed as "Seraiah" in **Ezra 2:2** is most likely Seraiah #2.
- **Seraiah #2, a scribe and priest**, is presumably the person named "Seraiah" in **Ezra 2:2** (listed in the chart above)—and conflated with "Azariah" (Azariah #2) in **Nehemiah 7:7**. Therefore, Seraiah #2 (Azariah #2) returned to Jerusalem with Zerubbabel in 538 B.C. The father of Seraiah #2 (scribe) was likely Seraiah #1 the high priest; also, Seraiah #2 is likely the father of Ezra the scribe and another son, Seraiah #3.
- **Seraiah #3, a scribe and priest**, is likely the "Seraiah" of **Nehemiah 10:2**, who sealed the covenant with Nehemiah in 444 B.C. (i.e., 93 years later than Seraiah #2, a contemporary of Zerubbabel in 538 B.C.). It is likely that Seraiah #3 was the *son* of Seraiah #2 (Azariah #2) and the *grandson* of Seraiah #1 (a case of papponymy). Also, it is likely that Seraiah #3 and his son Azariah #3 were both living in 444 B.C.
- **Azariah #3, a scribe and priest**, is presumably "Azariah" of **Nehemiah 10:2**, who sealed the covenant with Nehemiah in 444 B.C. It is likely that Azariah #3 was the *son* of Seraiah #3 and the *grandson* of Azariah #2 (a case of papponymy). Also, it appears that Azariah #3 and his father, Seraiah #3, were both living in 444 B.C.

If the proposed identifiers listed above are accurate, then a papponymic pattern occurs in the father-son lineage as follows: Azariah #1 the high priest—Seraiah #1 the martyred high priest—Azariah #2/Seraiah #2 the scribe—Seraiah #3 the scribe—Azariah #3 the scribe. For their tentative interrelationships, see chart "**Ezra 7**: Ezra, the Priestly Scribe and Teacher of the Law (Post-Exile)."

4. Azariah the priest (**Nehemiah 10:2**) is likely Azariah #3; see note 3.

5. Jeremiah the priest of 444 B.C. (**Nehemiah 10:2**) is not the prophet Jeremiah, ca. 627–586 B.C.

6. Pashhur of 444 B.C. (**Nehemiah 10:3**) is related to Pashhur the priest who returned to Jerusalem with Zerubbabel (**Ezra 2:38; Nehemiah 7:41**). Pashhur's descendants who took pagan wives in captivity are given in **Ezra 10:22**. Pashhur the priest (**Nehemiah 10:3**) may be related to Malkijah the priest (cf. **1 Chronicles 9:12; Nehemiah 10:3; 11:12**).

7. Hattush the priest of 444 B.C. (**Nehemiah 10:4**) should not be confused with Hattush the Judahite (**1 Chronicles 3:22**; cf. **Ezra 8:2**).

8. Harim of 444 B.C. (**Nehemiah 10:5**) is related to the Harim who returned with Zerubbabel in 538 B.C. (**Ezra 2:39**), the Harim descendants who took pagan wives in captivity (**Ezra 10:21**), and the Harim descendants who returned to Jerusalem (**Nehemiah 7:42**). Harim the Kohathite priest was probably the father of Malkijah, who helped repair the wall around post-exilic Jerusalem (**Nehemiah 3:11**).

9. This is not Obadiah the Merarite (i.e., Obadiah son of Shemaiah, the son of Galal, the son of Jeduthun) his near-contemporary (cf. **1 Chronicles 9:16**).

10. Daniel (**Nehemiah 10:6**; cf. **Ezra 8:2**) in the Levi-Kohath–Amram–Aaron–Ithamar line of priests represents a faithful remnant of the Ithamar priesthood (i.e., excluding the Ithamar–Eli's descendants who were cursed; **1 Samuel 2:22–25, 30–36; 3:14**; see **1 Kings 2:26–27; 1 Chronicles 24:1–18**; also see chart "**1 Samuel 1**: Eli and the Eli Priesthood"). Daniel was presumably an Kohathite attending priest in the Second Temple; see chart "**1 Chronicles 24**: Genealogical Registry of the Twenty-Four Divisions of Kohathite Attending Priests Who Rotated Service in Solomon's Temple."

11. Ginnethon of 444 B.C. (**Nehemiah 10:6**) is related to Ginnethon who returned to Jerusalem with Zerubbabel in 538 B.C. (**Nehemiah 12:4**). A descendant of the Ginnethon priestly family named Meshullam served in the days of Joiakim the high priest, 490–450/444 B.C. (**Nehemiah 12:16**).

12. Baruch of 444 B.C. (**Nehemiah 10:6**) is probably the same person as Baruch son of Zabbai, who repaired a section of the wall around Jerusalem in 444 B.C. (**Nehemiah 3:20**).

13. Meshullam of 444 B.C. (**Nehemiah 10:7**) may be the same as (1) Meshullam a contemporary of Ezra in 458 B.C. (**Nehemiah 8:4**); (2) Meshullam from the family "of Ezra" (**Nehemiah 12:13)**; or (3) Meshullam from the family "of Ginnethon" (**Nehemiah 12:16**). He is not Meshullam the Judahite in **1 Chronicles 3:19** or Meshullam (Shallum) the high priest (**1 Chronicles 9:11; Nehemiah 11:11**).

14. Abijah of 444 B.C. (**Nehemiah 10:7**) is related to Abijah who returned to Jerusalem with Zerubbabel in 538 B.C. (**Nehemiah 12:4**) and a descendant of the ancestral Abijah division of Kohathite priests that was established under King David and who served in Solomon's Temple (**1 Chronicles 24:10**). A descendant of the Abijah priestly family named Zikri served in the days of Joiakim the high priest, 490–450/444 B.C. (**Nehemiah 12:17**). It is likely that Abijah (and possibly Zikri) was an ancestor of Zechariah the Kohathite priest, the father of John the Baptist, who "belonged to the priestly division of Abijah" (**Luke 1:5**). See chart "**Luke 1**: Elizabeth and Zechariah and John the Baptist."

15. Mijamin of 444 B.C. (**Nehemiah 10:7**) was likely a descendant of the ancestral Mijamin, head of the Mijamin division of Kohathite priests that was established under David and served in Solomon's Temple (**1 Chronicles 24:9**). Mijamin (מִיָּמִין) is a variant of Miniamin (מִנְיָמִין), the latter resulting by the assimilation of נְ into the י.

16. Bilgai (בִּלְגַּי) is the same as Bilgah (בִּלְגָּה). There are two Bilgahs in the Old Testament (**1 Chronicles 24:14** and **Nehemiah 12:5, 18**). Bilgai (**Nehemiah 10:8**) is almost certainly the Bilgah of **Nehemiah 12:18**. The ancestral Kohathite priest named Bilgah was over the fifteenth of the twenty-four divisions of priests in Solomon's Temple (**1 Chronicles 24:14**). His descendant Shammua is mentioned in **Nehemiah 12:18**. Also, the high priest Menelaus, ca. 172–162 B.C., may be from the priestly course of Bilgah (see the notes on Menelaus #40 of the Onaid dynasty in chart "**Supplement 2**: The High Priests of Israel").

17. Shemaiah (**Nehemiah 12:6**) of 538 B.C. is probably an ancestor of Shemaiah the priest who sealed the covenant with Nehemiah in 444 B.C. (**Nehemiah 10:8**). A descendant of the Shemaiah priestly family named Jehonathan (**Nehemiah 12:18**) served in the days of Joiakim the high priest (490–450/444 B.C.).

18. For Bani, see note 23.

19. Some descendants of Parosh, numbering 2172 men, returned to Jerusalem with Zerubbabel in 538 B.C. (**Ezra 2:3; Nehemiah 7:8**) and some returned with Ezra in 458 B.C. (**Ezra 8:3**). The descendants of Parosh included Zechariah, Ramiah, Izziah, Malkijah, Mijamin, Eleazar, Malkijah, Benaiah, and Pedaiah (**Ezra 8:3; 10:25; Nehemiah 3:25**).

20. Some descendants of Pahath-Moab, numbering 2812 (or 2818?) men, returned to Jerusalem with Zerubbabel in 538 B.C. (cf. **Ezra 2:6; Nehemiah 7:11**). Eliehoenai the son of Zerahiah, a descendant of Pahath-Moab, returned with Ezra in 458 B.C. (**Ezra 8:4**). The descendants of Pahath-Moab included Adna, Kelal, Benaiah, Maaseiah, Mattaniah, Bezalel, Binnui, Manasseh and Hasshub (**Ezra 10:30; Nehemiah 3:11**).

21. Some descendants of Elam, numbering 1254 men, returned to Jerusalem with Zerubbabel in 538 B.C. (**Ezra 2:7; Nehemiah 7:12**), and Jeshaiah the son of Athaliah "of the descendants of Elam" returned with Ezra in 458 B.C. (**Ezra 8:7**). Elam's descendants included Shekaniah (son of Jehiel), Mattaniah, Zechariah, Jehiel, Abdi, Jeremoth, and Elijah (**Ezra 10:2, 26**). Elam the leader of the people is not Elam the Levitical priest (**Nehemiah 12:42**). Elam is also a place name (**Ezra 2:31; Nehemiah 7:34**).

22. Some descendants of Zattu, numbering 945 (or 845?) men returned to Jerusalem with Zerubbabel in 538 B.C. (cf. **Ezra 2:8; Nehemiah 7:13**), others with Ezra in 458 B.C. (**Ezra 8:5**), and some had taken pagan wives while in exile (specifically, Elioenai, Eliashib, Mattaniah, Jeremoth, Zabad and Aziza; **Ezra 10:27**).

23. Bani is known to Nehemiah as Binnui (cf. **Ezra 2:10; Nehemiah 7:15**). The confusion between Bani and Binnui is purely scribal in this case

(בָּנִי vs. בְּנִּי). The former was an ancestor of Shelomith, the son of Josiphiah. His descendants, numbering 642 (**Ezra 2:10**) or 648 (**Nehemiah 7:15**) returned to Jerusalem with Zerubbabel in 538 B.C. Some of the descendants of Bani had taken pagan wives in captivity (either those listed in **Ezra 10:29** or those listed in **Ezra 10:34–37**). See chart "**Ezra 10**: Genealogical Record of the Priests, Levites, and Israelites who Had Taken Pagan Wives in Babylonian Captivity." Bani the leader of the people is not Bani the Levite (cf. **Nehemiah 3:17; 8:7; 9:4–5; 10:13**).

24. Bunni, a leader of the people and a contemporary of Nehemiah in 444 B.C. (**Nehemiah 10:15**) is not Bunni the Levite in **Nehemiah 9:4** nor is he Bunni the Levitical Merarite, the father of Hashabiah (**Nehemiah 11:15**).

25. Some descendants of Azgad, numbering 1222 men, returned to Jerusalem with Zerubbabel in 538 B.C. (**Ezra 2:12**); it is unclear whether Azgad of **Ezra 2:12** is Azgad of **Nehemiah 7:17** whose descendants, numbering 2322 men, returned at the same time. Azgad's descendant Johanan son of Hakkatan returned with Ezra in 458 B.C. (**Ezra 8:12**). These totals are at variance with the Septuagint manuscripts: Vaticanus, Alexandrinus, and Codex Venetus (2802, 3622, and 1322, respectively).

26. Some descendants of Bebai, numbering 623 (or 628?) men, returned to Jerusalem with Zerubbabel in 538 B.C. (cf. **Ezra 2:11; Nehemiah 7:16**), and Bebai's son Zechariah returned with Ezra in 458 B.C. (**Ezra 8:11**). Some of Bebai's descendants—specifically, Jehohanan, Hananiah, Zabbai and Athlai—had taken pagan wives while in exile (**Ezra 10:28**).

27. This is not Adonijah the Levite who lived at the time of King Jehoshaphat, 872–848 B.C. (**2 Chronicles 17:8**).

28. There may be two Bigvai figures (cf. **Ezra 2:2, 14**). Some descendants of Bigvai, numbering 2056 (or 2067?) men returned to Jerusalem with Zerubbabel in 538 B.C. (cf. **Ezra 2:2, 14; Nehemiah 7:19**). Bigvai's descendants Uthai and Zakkur returned with Ezra in 458 B.C. (**Ezra 8:14**).

29. Adin is probably the same family whose 454 descendants (**Ezra 2:15**) or 655 descendants (**Nehemiah 7:20**) returned to Jerusalem with Zerubbabel in 538 B.C.; his descendants included Ebed, son of Jonathan, and 50 other men who returned with Ezra (**Ezra 8:6**).

30. Ater's family ("through Hezekiah") included 98 descendants who returned to Jerusalem with Zerubbabel (**Ezra 2:16; Nehemiah 7:21**). Since Ater's descendants were among the heads of Israelite families, he is not the same as Ater/ the "descendants of Ater" the gatekeeper (**Ezra 2:42; Nehemiah 7:45**) who were Levites.

31. This Hezekiah is probably the relative/ancestor of Ater (**Ezra 2:16; Nehemiah 7:21**), but he is not King Hezekiah of Judah, 715–686 B.C.

32. This Azzur is not Azzur the father of Hananiah the prophet or Azzur the father of Jaazaniah (**Jeremiah 28:1; Ezekiel 11:1**).

33. This Hodiah is not Hodiah the Levite(s) in **Nehemiah 8:7; 9:5**, who instructed the people in the Law and stood on stairs of the Levites in the days of Ezra in 444 B.C.; nor is he one of the two Levites in **Nehemiah 10:10, 13**.

34. The family of Hashum, including 223 (or 328) descendants returned to Jerusalem with Zerubbabel in 538 B.C. (cf. **Ezra 2:19; Nehemiah 7:22**). Hashum stood with Ezra during the reading of the Law in 444 B.C. (**Nehemiah 8:4**). His descendants included Mattenai, Mattattah, Zabad, Eliphelet, Jeremai, Manasseh, and Shimei (**Ezra 10:33**).

35. The family of Bezai included 323 (or 324) descendants who returned to Jerusalem with Zerubbabel (cf. **Ezra 2:17; Nehemiah 7:23**).

36. The leader Hariph had 112 descendants who returned to Jerusalem with Zerubbabel in 538 B.C. (**Nehemiah 7:24; 10:19**). **Ezra 2:18**, which also corresponds to 538 B.C. appears to identify him with "Jorah," a name found nowhere else in the Bible—note the similar sequence and similar names in **Ezra 2:15–20** (Adin–Ater–Bezai–Jorah–Hasum–Gibbar) and **Nehemiah 7:20–25** (Adin–Ater–Hashum–Bezai–Hariph–Gibeon). The fact that the very same names of returnees are associated with both men need not mean more than that they collaborated. A second possibility is that Hariph bore a nickname with the meaning "shooter" or "thrower," as in war, based on the participle of a verb *yarah*, "to cast, throw," which is the same root as the name "Jorah," which suggest that Jorah and Hariph are the same person.

37. This Anathoth was probably the leader from the town of Anathoth whose family included 128 men who returned to Jerusalem with Zerubbabel in 538 B.C. (**Ezra 2:23; Nehemiah 7:27**).

38. This Meshullam is probably the contemporary of Ezra who is mentioned in **Ezra 8:16**.

39. This Hezir is not Hezir the Kohathite priest (**1 Chronicles 24:15**).

40. This Meshezabel is possibly the same person as Meshezabel the grandfather of Meshullam (**Nehemiah 3:4**) and/or Meshezabel the father of Pethahiah (**Nehemiah 11:24**).

41. This Zadok may be the son of Baana who made repairs in the wall (**Nehemiah 3:4**) but not Zadok son of Immer, a Kokathite priest (**Nehemiah 3:29**) or Zadok the scribe (**Nehemiah 13:13**).

42. This Jaddua is not Jaddua the high priest, ca. 370–332 B.C. (**Nehemiah 12:11, 22**).

43. This is not Pelatiah the wicked counselor in ca. 592 B.C. (**Ezekiel 11:1, 13**).

44. Two leaders are named Hanan (**Nehemiah 10:22, 26**). They are not Hanan the temple servant(s) (**Ezra 2:46; Nehemiah 7:49**); Hanan the Levite(s) (**Nehemiah 8:7; 10:10; 13:13**), or Hanan the son of Igdaliah (**Jeremiah 35:4**).

45. Anaiah is probably the same person named Anaiah in **Nehemiah 8:4**.

46. It is unclear whether Hananiah is one of the descendants of Bebai (**Ezra 10:28**); the perfume-maker (**Nehemiah 3:8**); the son of Shelemiah (**Nehemiah 3:30**), and/or the commander of the citadel (**Nehemiah 7:2**). For chronological or genealogical reasons, he is not Hananiah the priest(s) (**Nehemiah 12:12, 41**); Hananiah the prophet (**Jeremiah 28:1, 5, 10, 12–13, 15, 17**); the father of Zedekiah (**Jeremiah 36:12**); the father of Shelemiah (**Jeremiah 37:13**); or Hananiah the friend of Daniel (**Daniel 1:6–7, 11, 19; 2:17**).

47. Hasshub may be the son of Pahath-Moab (**Nehemiah 3:11**) or another of the same name who also rebuilt the wall (**Nehemiah 3:23**), but he is not either of the Levites named Hasshub (**1 Chronicles 9:14; Nehemiah 11:15**).

48. Hallohesh is probably the father of Shallum, the ruler of a half-district of Jerusalem (**Nehemiah 3:12**).

49. He is not Rehum the priest, who returned to Jerusalem with Zerubbabel in 538 B.C. (cf. **Ezra 2:2; Nehemiah 12:3**); Rehum the commanding officer (**Ezra 4:8–9, 17, 23**), nor Rehum son of Bani, a Levite (**Nehemiah 3:17**).

50. Maaseiah may be a descendant of Pahath-Moab (**Ezra 10:30**). He is not (1) the priests named Maaseiah (**Ezra 10:18, 21–22; Nehemiah 3:23; 8:4; 12:41; Jeremiah 21:1; 29:25; 37:3**); (2) Maaseiah the Levite(s) (**Nehemiah 8:7; 12:42**); (3) Maaseiah the Judah-Shelah descendant (**Nehemiah 11:5**); (4) Maaseiah the Benjaminite (**Nehemiah 11:7**); (5) Maaseiah father of Zedekiah the false prophet (**Jeremiah 29:21**); or (6) Maaseiah the son of Shallum the doorkeeper (**Jeremiah 35:4**).

51. For Hanan, see note 44.

52. Malluk may be a descendant of Bani (**Ezra 10:29**) or a descendant of Harim (**Ezra 10:32**), both of which had taken pagan wives, and/or a returnee to Jerusalem with Zerubbabel (**Nehemiah 12:2**). He is not Malluk the priest (**Nehemiah 10:4**).

53. Harim (the Israelite leader) in **Nehemiah 10:27** is not Harim the Kohathite priest (**Nehemiah 10:5**; cf. **Ezra 2:39; 10:21; Nehemiah 3:11; 7:42**). Harim the Israelite leader may be associated with those Israelites from Harim who returned to Jerusalem with Zerubbabel in 538 B.C. (**Ezra 2:32; Nehemiah 7:35**). The descendants of Harim the Israelite leader are given in **Ezra 10:31**.

54. Baanah is probably the same individual as Baanah who returned to Jerusalem with Zerubbabel in 538 B.C. (**Ezra 2:2; Nehemiah 7:7**).

55. For example, see the meaning of the names of the twelve sons of Jacob in chart "**Genesis 35**: The Twelve Sons of Jacob, the Eponymous Originators of the Twelve Tribes of Israel."

56. See the recurrence of the name Elkanah in the lineage of the prophet Samuel in chart "**1 Samuel 1**: Samuel, the Prophet–Priest–Judge of Israel." For a discussion of the repeated names Seraiah and Azariah, see note 3.

NEHEMIAH 11: THE "TITHE" OF PEOPLE CHOSEN TO REPOPULATE JERUSALEM IN THE POST-EXILE

Approximate Dating: ca. 444 B.C. ***Relevant Scriptures:*** **Nehemiah 11:1–9**

Provincial Leaders from the Descendants of Judah

1. **Athaiah, a descendant of Perez:**[1]

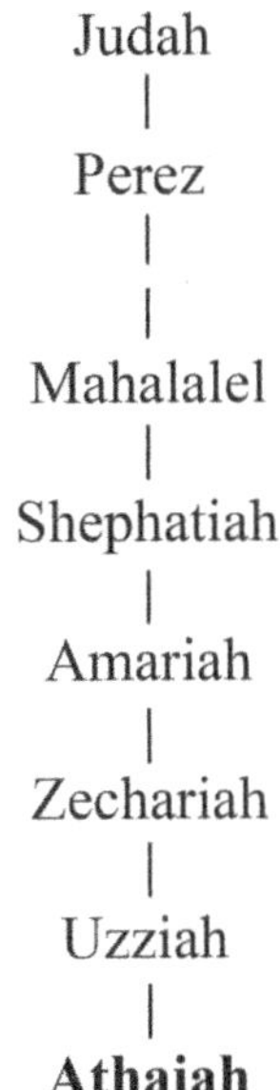

2. **Maaseiah, a descendant of Shelah:**[2]

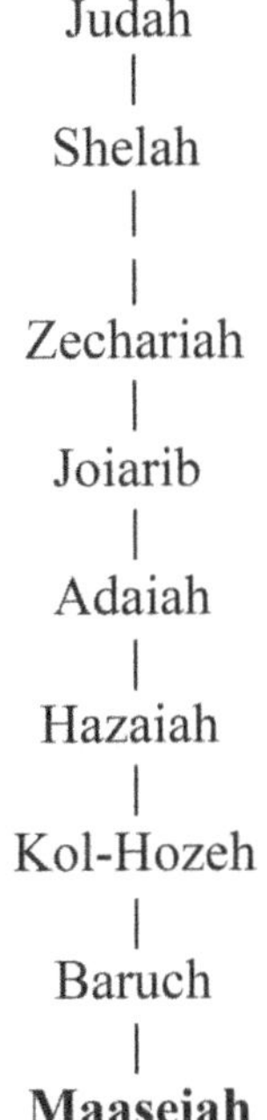

Total number of "the descendants of Perez,"[3] the son of Judah (Judahites) – 468 men

Provincial Leaders from the Descendants of Benjamin

1. **Sallu**

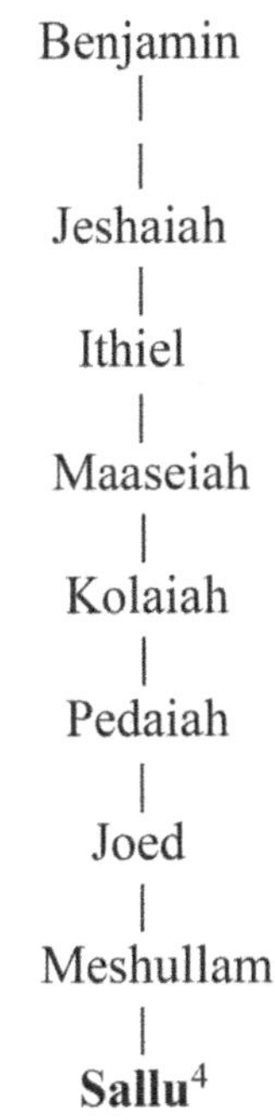

2. **Gabbai** (a follower of Sallu)
3. **Sallai** (a follower of Sallu)

Total number of the descendants of Benjamin (Benjamites) – 928 men

Chief official[5] over the city: Joel, son of Zikri (Benjamite)[6]

Official over the New Quarter[7] of the city: Judah, son of Hassenuah (Benjamite)

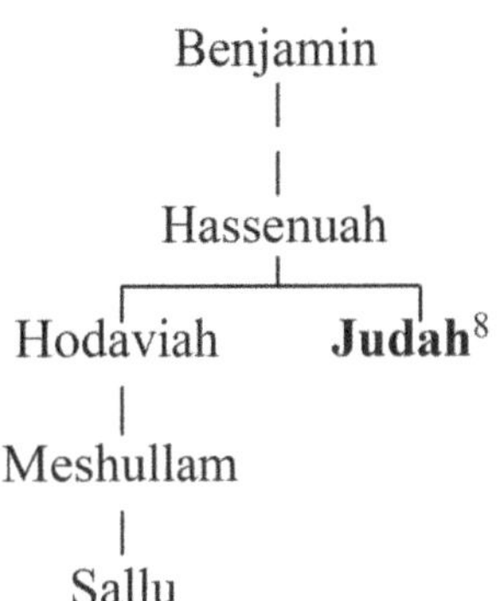

Biblical and Theological Significance

When Nehemiah returned to Jerusalem in ca. 444 B.C., he sadly found Jerusalem inadequately occupied. It had been resettled as early as the first return from Babylon in 538 B.C. when exiles returned with Zerubbabel, but it evidently lacked good political and business leaders who could make life there viable. Nehemiah's mission was to find qualified persons to live in the city, a mission that required him (so he thought) to institute a lottery system whereby the "losers" would have to become urban dwellers. **First Chronicles 9:3–21** makes clear that the Jews were certainly occupying Jerusalem in Ezra's day (post-458 B.C.; **Ezra 7:7, 15; 8:29, 32; 10:7, 9; Nehemiah 1:3; 7:3; 8:15**).

The people cast lots to determine who would live in "the holy city" of Jerusalem (**Nehemiah 11:1**); a tithe (or ten percent[9]) of people was chosen to dwell in Jerusalem from among the tribes of Judah and Benjamin, 468 and 928 respectively, for a total of 1396 people. Surprisingly, the number of the Benjamites predominated over the number of Judahites! The other 90 percent (12,564) dwelt in the lands of their inheritance.[10] Several reasons may be posited for the reluctance about settling in Jerusalem. First, the city lay in ruins, for the most part, until the work of Nehemiah was completed. Second, the city had a bad reputation for being the target of foreign enemies. And third, most of the returning Jews were people of the soil, uninterested in attempting to scratch out a living in an unprotected city in shambles. They therefore chose the countryside with its small villages and rich, abundant farmland, which suited them, and where crops and flocks were more likely to generate income. Nehemiah thus had to institute a policy of forced settlement in the city based on the outcome of casting lots, although a few "volunteered to live in Jerusalem" and were commended by the people for doing so (**Nehemiah 11:1–2**).

Notes

1. Perez and his twin brother Zerah were the sons of Judah by his daughter-in-law, Tamar (**Genesis 38:25–30**).

2. Shelah was the son of Judah and a Canaanite woman (the daughter of Shua) and was the brother of Er and Onan (**Genesis 38:1–5**).

3. The reference to "the descendants of Perez" in **Nehemiah 11:6** probably refers to the total number of *descendants of Judah*.

4. Sallu the Benjamite is obviously not Sallu the priest who returned with Zerubbabel to Jerusalem in 538 B.C. (**Nehemiah 12:7**).

5. The Hebrew term here (פָּקִיד; *paqid*), "overseer," is not as grand as mayor perhaps, but it does connote the idea that he was responsible for virtually everything there.

6. Joel the chief officer over Jerusalem was a descendant of Benjamin. His exact lineage is not clear, but he is one of the three Joel figures in chart "**1 Chronicles 8**: The Benjamites Who Settled in and around Jerusalem and in Moab (Post-Exile)": (1) Joel the son of Zikri, the son of Shema/Shimei, the son of Elpaal, the son of Shaharaim (**1 Chronicles 8:19–21**; cf. **8:11, 13**); (2) Joel the son of Zikri, the son of Jeremoth/Jeroham, the son of Beriah, the son of Elpaal, the son of Shaharaim (**1 Chronicles 8:27**; cf. **8:11, 13-14; 9:37**); or (3) Joel the son of Zikri, the son of Shashak, the son of Beriah, the son of Elpaal, the son of Shaharaim (**1 Chronicles 8:23, 25**; cf. **8:11, 13–14**).

7. The New Quarter evidently refers to an area of the city that lay outside the ancient city walls of David but had been incorporated within the new wall system. The Hebrew construction הָעִיר מִשְׁנֶה in **Nehemiah 11:9** can mean "second city" or "second over the city" (referring to Judah son of Hassenuah, perhaps as vice-overseer or the like).

8. Judah son of Hassenuah and relative of Sallu son of Meshullam was a Benjamite who lived in Jerusalem (cf. **1 Chronicles 9:7**).

9. The phrase "tithe" or "tenth of the people" is based on the Torah teaching in Mosaic times that a tenth of all that one gained and possessed must be given over to Yahweh, who made life possible with all its blessings (**Leviticus 27:30; Numbers 18:26; Deuteronomy 26:12**). Yahweh had now restored the holy city to the Jews, so it was only right that a tenth of his people—a *dedicated* portion—be given to him to live and minister there.

10. Collectively, this shows that the total number of people in Jerusalem and the surrounding area was 1396 + 12,564 = 13,960.

NEHEMIAH 11: THE REPRESENTATIVE PRIESTS[1] CHOSEN TO DWELL IN JERUSALEM IN THE POST-EXILE[2]

Approximate Dating: 444 B.C.[3] ***Relevant Scriptures:*** **Nehemiah 11:10–14**

The Main Kohathite Attending Priests[4]

1. **Jedaiah**[5] (a descendant of the ancestral Kohathite priestly family of Jedaiah in **1 Chronicles 24:7**)
2. **The son of Joiarib/J(eh)oiarib**[6] (a descendant of the ancestral Kohathite priestly family of Jehoiarib in **1 Chronicles 24:7**)
3. **Jakin**[7] (a descendant of the ancestral Kohathite priestly family of Jakin in **1 Chronicles 24:17**)

Official in charge of the house of God (the Second Temple): Seraiah #2/Azariah #2:

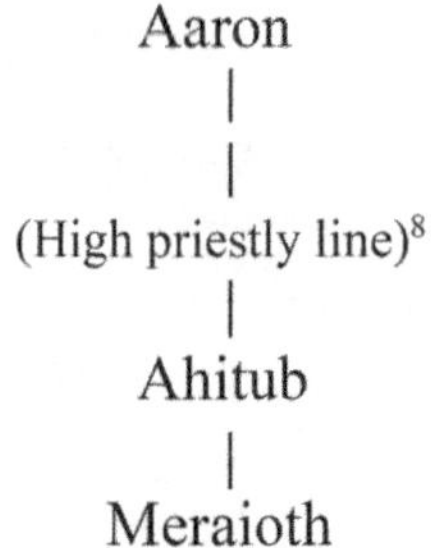

Meraioth

Zadok

Meshullam[9]
(Shallum)

Hilkiah

Azariah #1
(High priest in Solomon's Temple, ca. 609–600 B.C.)

Seraiah #1[10]
(High priest who was martyred in 586 B.C.)

(Continuation of the line of the high priests)

Jozadak[11]
(High priest when Judah was taken into Babylonian captivity in 586 B.C. and died there)

Joshua[13]
(Jeshua)
(First high priest to minister in the Second Temple from ca. 516–490 B.C.)

(Scribal lineage and/or relatives of the high priests)

Seraiah #2/Azariah #2[12]
(Came to Jerusalem in 538 B.C. with Zerubbabel)
(Called "Seraiah" in **Ezra 2:2** and "Azariah" in **Nehemiah 7:7**)
(The "official in charge of the house of God," 516 B.C.;
1 Chronicles 9:11; Nehemiah 11:11)

Ezra[14]
(Scribe–priest–teacher of the Law who led a group of returning exiles back to Jerusalem in 458 B.C.)
(Tentatively identified as the *son* of Seraiah #2 and the *grandson* of Seraiah #1)

Additional Kohathite attending priests:

1. **Adaiah**

Malkijah

Pashhur

Zechariah

Amzi

Pelaliah

Jeroham

Adaiah[15]

Adaiah and his associates who were heads of families = 242 men

2. **Amashsai**

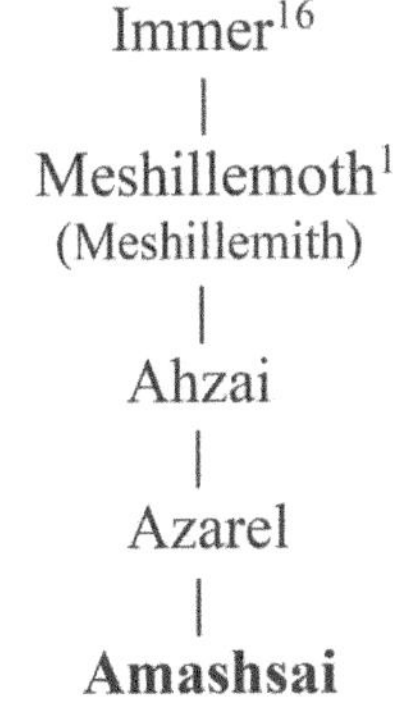

Immer[16]

Meshillemoth[17]
(Meshillemith)

Ahzai

Azarel

Amashsai

Amashai and his associates who were men of standing = 128 men

Chief officer of the Kohathite attending priests:
Zabdiel (the son of Haggedolim)[18]

Biblical and Theological Significance

When the Jews returned from Babylon beginning in 538 B.C., they found the city of Jerusalem in ruins, a scene described most eloquently by Jeremiah in his work **Lamentations** (commonly called in Judaism אֵיכָה, *ekah*, "How," the first word in the book).[19] The verse follows, "*How* deserted lies the city, once so full of people! *How* like a widow is she, who once was great among the nations!" (**Lamentations 1:1**). The full extent of devastation is captured in this verse: "The Lord has given full vent to his wrath; he has poured out his fierce anger. He kindled a fire in Zion that consumed [even] her foundations" (**Lamentations 4:11**). For many years nothing changed this awful situation, until Sheshbazzar[20] was sent to Jerusalem in ca. 539 B.C. and began laying the foundation for the temple but did not complete it (**Ezra 1:8, 11; 5:14, 16**). When Zerubbabel and Joshua arrived in 538 B.C., they built the great altar and celebrated the Festival of Tabernacles (**Ezra 3:2–6**). By the second year, the builders completed the foundation of the temple (**Ezra 3:7–13**). Nevertheless, "the peoples around them set out to discourage the people of Judah and make them afraid to go on building. They bribed officials to work against them and frustrate their plans during the entire reign of Cyrus king of Persia and down to the reign of Darius king of Persia" (**Ezra 4:4–5**). By 520 B.C., temple restoration efforts resumed. Encouraged by the two great prophets, Haggai and Zechariah, Zerubbabel the governor and Jeshua the high priest led the people, the priests, and the Levites in the reconstruction, and the Second Temple was finally completed in 516 B.C. [21] (**Ezra 6:15–16**). When Ezra and then Nehemiah finally arrived at the Holy City in 458 B.C. and 444 B.C., respectively, they were dismayed to see that the city itself still lay in ruin and disrepair (**Nehemiah 1:3–4; 2:3, 13, 17; 7:4**). However, with strong Persian royal backing, Nehemiah, now governor of the satrap Yehud, set forth with Ezra to bring to completion the walls and all other features of the temple project (**Nehemiah 6:15**).

Despite all this, both laity and priests were still reluctant to move into the city for, as far as can be determined, only the temple had been finished; the rest of the city was still uninhabitable: "the city was large and spacious, but there were few people in it, and the houses had not yet been rebuilt" (**Nehemiah 7:4**; cf. **2:17**). While the rest of the returnees were comfortably at home in their various villages, the people of Jerusalem were homeless and loath to move into the city as it was. Their leaders, with Nehemiah certainly in charge, mandated that one in ten of the people must move into the city to build it back again.[22] Special appreciation was extended to those willing to volunteer to move in. Priests and Levites were among those required to settle in Jerusalem, for some must be at hand to care for the temple, its services, and its maintenance (**Nehemiah 11:1–4a**). The chart lists those individuals, families, and clans who moved into Jerusalem in ca. 444 B.C.

Notes

1. The priests mentioned in the chart were Kohathites from the priestly families of Jedaiah, Joiarib/Jehoiarib, Jakin, Malkijah, and Immer. They were *descendants* of the original twenty-four ancestral divisions/courses that had been established in the days of David (**1 Chronicles 24:7–18**; see chart "**1 Chronicles 24**: Genealogical Registry of the Twenty-Four Divisions of Kohathite Attending Priests Who Rotated Service in Solomon's Temple"). The exception was Seraiah #2/Azariah #2, a scribal-priest identified as the "official in charge of the house of God [Second Temple]" (**1 Chronicles 9:11; Nehemiah 11:11**). Rather than being the *high/chief priest* (i.e., Seraiah #1–Jozadak–Joshua/Jeshua–Joiakim, etc.), he was in a *scribal* lineage that paralleled that of the high priests. Seraiah #2/Azariah #2 was the ancestor (possibly the *father*) of Ezra the scribe; see chart "**Ezra 7**: Ezra, the Priestly Scribe and Teacher of the Law (Post-Exile)."

2. Also see chart "**1 Chronicles 9**: The Kohathite Attending Priests in the Second Temple in (Post-Exile)."

3. The assumption is that Nehemiah, as a historian, writes first about the present (444 B.C.) and then describes the historical period to be covered (**Nehemiah 1:1–2; 7:73; 8:2, 13–14; 9:1**). The body of the work contains references to earlier times as well, as seen in **Nehemiah 1:3; 5:3, 5, 15; 7:4–5; 11:3–4, 20, 25–30; 12:1–26; 13:4–7, 10; 13:23**. Kohathite attending priests had returned from captivity as early as 538 B.C. with Zerubbabel, and more came in 458 B.C. with Ezra. For a comparison of the Kohathite priestly families represented in specific time periods, see "**Table 1**. Heads of Kohathite Priestly Families—NOT High Priests—from Eleven Major Scriptural Sources" in chart "**1 Chronicles 24**: Genealogical Registry of the Twenty-Four Divisions of Kohathite Attending Priests Who Rotated Service in Solomon's Temple."

4. See chart "**1 Chronicles 24**: Genealogical Registry of the Twenty-Four Divisions of Kohathite Attending Priests Who Rotated Service in Solomon's Temple." These priests were not high priests.

5. Jedaiah's descendants were relatives/brethren of the "family of Jeshua [Joshua]" the high priest (cf. **Ezra 2:36 Nehemiah 7:39**). His ancestor Jedaiah had been the head of the second division of Kohathite attending priests in Solomon's Temple (**1 Chronicles 24:7**).

6. Joiarib in **Nehemiah 11:10; 12:6, 19** is Jehoiarib in **1 Chronicles 9:10**. His ancestor Jehoiarib had been over the first division of Kohathite attending priests in Solomon's Temple (**1 Chronicles 24:7**). Joachim Jeremias notes that, according to **Nehemiah 11:10**, the priests of the family of Jehoiarib lived in Jerusalem, while *1 Maccabees 2:1, 18–20, 70; 13.25* says they lived partly in Modein (Joachim Jeremias, *Jerusalem in the Time of Jesus* [Philadelphia: Fortress, 1969], 200, note 178).

7. Jakin the priest is also mentioned in **1 Chronicles 9:10**.

8. For the complete father-son succession of the high priests, see charts "**1 Chronicles 6**: Levi: High Priests, Priests, Levites, and Musicians in Solomon's Temple" and "**Supplement 2**: The High Priests of Israel."

9. Shallum in **1 Chronicles 6:12–13; Ezra 7:2** is Meshullam in **1 Chronicles 9:11; Nehemiah 11:11**.

10. Shortly after the siege of Jerusalem by the Babylonians in 586 B.C., Nebuzaradan took Seraiah (#1) the chief priest/high priest and other high-ranking officials to Riblah, where Seraiah and the rest were executed (**2 Kings 25:18–21**; cf. **Jeremiah 52:24–27**). The passage in **Nehemiah 11:11** (**1 Chronicles 9:11**) gives the lineage of another Seraiah (designated Seraiah #2, to distinguish him from the high priest Seraiah #1) who was the "son of Hilkiah, the son of Meshullam, the son of Zadok, the son of Meraioth, the son of Ahitub." The scribal–priest Seraiah #2 returned to Jerusalem in 538 B.C. with Zerubbabel and became "the official in charge of the house of God [the Second Temple]" (**Nehemiah 11:11**). Quite confusingly, however, the person named "Seraiah/Seraiah #2" in **Ezra 2:2** and **Nehemiah 11:11** is called "Azariah/Azariah #2" in **1 Chronicles 9:11** and **Nehemiah 7:7**—they should be understood to be the same person; therefore, in the chart above, the scribal priest Seraiah #2 is the same as Azariah #2.

For chronological reasons, at least three Seraiah figures are proposed: (1) Seraiah #1, who was the martyred high priest in 586 B.C. (**2 Kings 25:18–21; Jeremiah 52:24–27**); (2) Seraiah #2—likely the *son* of Seraiah #1 and the *father* of Ezra (**Ezra 7:1**); Seraiah #2 returned to Jerusalem in ca. 538 B.C., with Zerubbabel (cf. **Ezra 2:2; Nehemiah 12:1**) and can be equated with Azariah #2 (cf. **1 Chronicles 9:11; Ezra 2:2**; **Nehemiah 7:7; 11:11**); and (3) Seraiah #3, who sealed the covenant with Nehemiah in 444 B.C. (**Nehemiah 10:2**). For a probable lineage for Seraiah #1, #2 and, #3, see chart "**Ezra 7**: Ezra, the Priestly Scribe and Teacher of the Law (Post-Exile)."

11. Jozadak/J(eh)ozadak was the high priest in Solomon's Temple at the time of the Babylonian captivity—"Jozadak was deported when the Lord sent Judah and Jerusalem into exile by the hand of Nebuchadnezzar" (**1 Chronicles**

6:15). Jozadak presumably died in captivity, because the first high priest to serve in the Second Temple (post-exile) was his son Joshua/Jeshua (**Ezra 3:2, 8, Haggai 1:1**; **Zechariah 6:11**). For the line of Jozadak, see chart "**Ezra 2**: Joshua, the High Priest in the Second Temple, and His Descendants (Post-Exile)."

12. For the specifics of Seraiah #2 as Azariah #2, see note 10.

13. Joshua in **Ezra 2:2; 3:2, 8; 4:3; 5:2; Nehemiah 7:7; 12:1, 7, 10, 26; Haggai 1:1, 12, 14; 2:2, 4; Zechariah 3:1, 3, 6, 8–9; 6:11** is called Jeshua in **Ezra 2:36; Nehemiah 7:39** (NIV), as well as in some other translations.

14. The lineage for Ezra the priestly scribe is established in **Ezra 7:1–5**, where his ancestors are clearly identified as the (pre-exilic) high priests—"Ezra son of Seraiah, the son of Azariah, the son of Hilkiah, the son of Shallum, the son of Zadok, the son of Ahitub, the son of Amariah, the son of Azariah, the son of Meraioth, the son of Zerahiah, the son of Uzzi, the son of Bukki, the son of Abishua, the son of Phinehas, the son of Eleazar, the son of Aaron the chief priest." Ezra's scribal lineage parallels that of the high priests. See chart "**Ezra 7**: Ezra, the Priestly Scribe and Teacher of the Law (Post-Exile)."

15. The lineage of Adaiah is complete in **Nehemiah 11:12** and compressed in **1 Chronicles 9:12**.

16. Immer was over the sixteenth of the twenty-four divisions of Kohathite attending priests who rotated service in Solomon's Temple (**1 Chronicles 24:14**).

17. Meshillemoth in **Nehemiah 11:13** is Meshillemith in **1 Chronicles 9:12**.

18. Zabdiel's heritage is unknown. He appears to be a different person than Zabdiel the father of Jashobeam (from among the descendants of Perez in the tribe of Judah, where Jashobeam had been the chief over the first of the twenty-four *military* divisions "who served the king" in the days of David and Solomon; **1 Chronicles 27:1–3**). The term "chief officer" over the priests is פָּקִיד, *paqid*, "overseer." He should not be thought of as a taskmaster, but more as an observer behalf of the king (here, governor). This nuance is based on the absence of the normal preposition עַל, *'al*, "over."

19. Jeremiah dates the beginning of his public ministry as "the thirteenth year of the reign of Josiah" and its end in the "eleventh year of Zedekiah" (**Jeremiah 1:2–3**). This is precisely 627–586 B.C.; the latter event corresponds to the fall of Jerusalem to the Babylonians and the subsequent destruction of the temple.

20. See chart "**Ezra 1**: Sheshbazzar and Zerubbabel, Governors over the Restored Community in Jerusalem (Post-Exile)."

21. After four years of work, the Second Temple was completed in 516 B.C., "on the third day of the month Adar, in the sixth year of the reign of King Darius [522–486 B.C.]" (**Ezra 6:15**).

22. See chart "**Nehemiah 11**: The "Tithe" of People Chosen to Repopulate Jerusalem in the Post-Exile."

NEHEMIAH 11: THE LEVITICAL LEADERS CHOSEN TO DWELL IN JERUSALEM IN THE POST-EXILE[1]

Approximate Dating: ca. 444 B.C.[2] ***Relevant Scriptures:*** **Nehemiah 11:15–24**

Chief person over the Levites: Shemaiah

Genealogy of Shemaiah (Levitical Merarite):

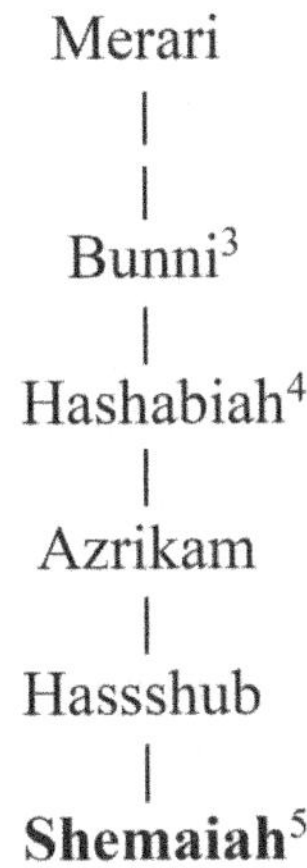

Heads[6] of the Levites

(who had "charge of the outside work of the house of God"):

1. **Shabbethai** (Levite; the same person as Shabbethai in **Ezra 10:15; Nehemiah 8:7**)
2. **Jozabad** (Levite; the same person as Jozabad in **Ezra 10:23**; **Nehemiah 8:7**)

Director who led in thanksgiving and prayer: Mattaniah

Genealogy of Mattaniah
(a musician and Levitical Gershonite):

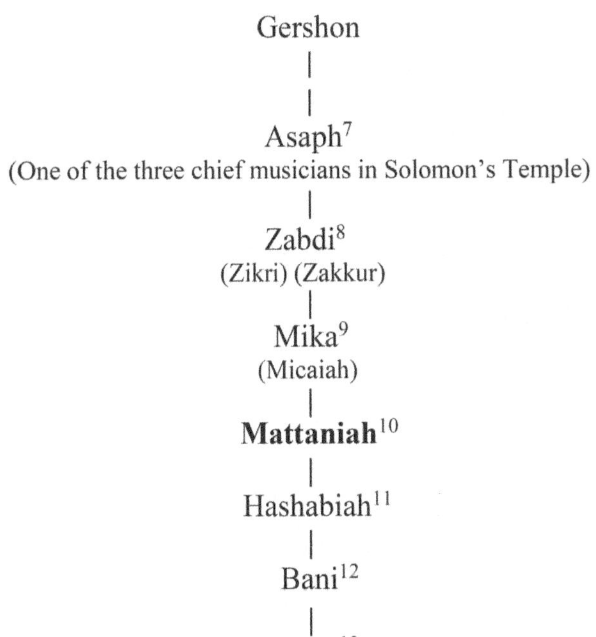

Other Levitical leaders:

1. **Bakbukiah**[14] (exact genealogy is unknown, but probably Gershonite)
2. **Abda** (or Obadiah)

Genealogy of Abda/Obadiah (Levitical Merarite):

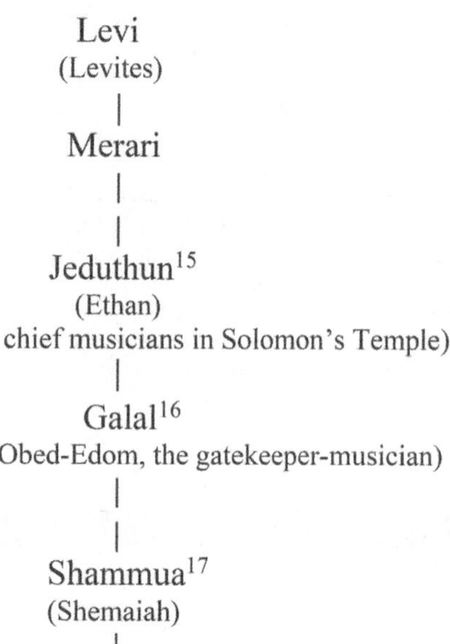

***All the Levites living in Jerusalem totaled 284.**

Key Gatekeepers:

(The 172 gatekeepers were Levites; cf. **1 Chronicles 9:17**).

1. **Akkub**[19]
2. **Talmon**[20]
3. Unnamed others

Overseers of the Temple servants (the *Nethinim*)[21] (Temple dwellers who lived at the Ophel[22]):

1. **Ziha**[23]
2. **Gishpa**[24]

Chief officer of the Levites in Jerusalem: Uzzi

Genealogy of Uzzi (Levitical Gershonite):

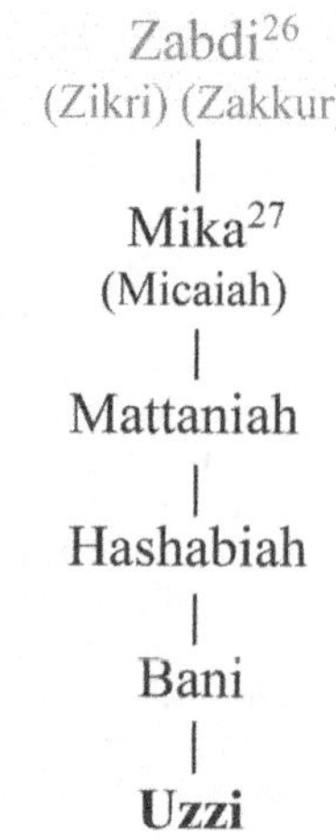

The "king's" agent in all affairs relating to the people: Pethahiah

Genealogy of Pethahiah the Zerahite (Judahite):

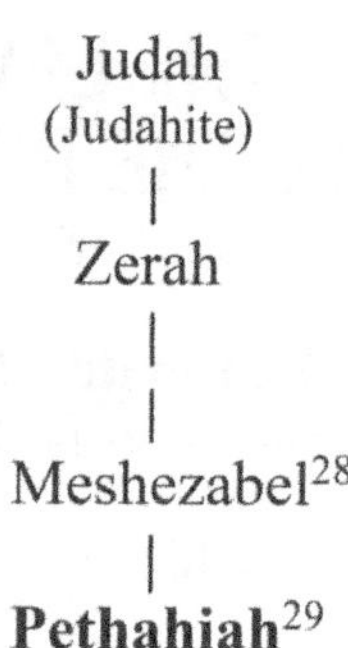

Biblical and Theological Significance

From the very beginning of religious practice in Israel, three major clerical offices were necessary for its operation—a high priest, secondary attending priests, and Levites. From the earliest days of the wilderness wanderings, Yahweh had instructed Moses to set the tribe of Levi apart to be "in charge of the tabernacle" (**Numbers 1:50–51**). The Levites were given to Aaron (the high priest) and his sons as a gift and a substitute for the firstborn (the first male offspring) that had, until then, been required as a gift to Yahweh (**Numbers 3:9, 11–13, 45; 8:14–19; 18:2–6**). The Levites received no allotment of land or an inheritance of their own (**Deuteronomy 14:29**); rather, they lived in Levitical cities carved out from the land allotted to the other tribes (cf. **Joshua 21**). Thenceforth, the descendants of the three sons of Levi—Kohath, Gershon, and Merari—functioned together with specific and unending responsibilities in the worship of their God. The duties of each of these three clans are elaborated in **Numbers 4:4–33** (i.e., Kohathites in **vv. 4–20**; Gershonites in **vv. 21–28**; and Merarites in **vv. 29–33**).

When the Second Temple was completed in 516 B.C., the organization of the Levitical personnel followed the basic divisions and duties that had been set up about 450 years earlier by King David for Solomon's Temple (cf. **1 Chronicles 23:1–26:28**). The Levites included gatekeepers and musicians, as well as "officials" and "judges"[30] who would be involved in "the work of the temple of the

Lord" (**1 Chronicles 23:4**). Apparently, when the exiles left Babylon and came to Jerusalem with either Zerubbabel (538 B.C.) or with Ezra 458 B.C., most Levites came to reside in their allotted Levitical cities (cf. **Joshua 21:4–8**). Josephus asserts that, after the wall around Jerusalem was finished in 444 B.C., "Nehemiah saw that the city was thin of people, he exhorted the priests and Levites that they would leave [their respective Levitical cities in] the country, and remove themselves to the city [Jerusalem], and there continue; and he [even] built them houses at his own expense."[31]

The chart shows the designated Levites, gatekeepers, and temple servants (non-Israelites) who were chosen to dwell permanently in Jerusalem, rather than rotate service from their respective Levitical cities, as did other temple personnel. The permanent dwellers may have served as the core personnel who organized all others who rotated service throughout the year—the Levites who lived in certain towns of Judah (**Nehemiah 11:3**) and Benjamin (**Nehemiah 11:36**).[32] In essence, the duties of the Levites were designed "to help Aaron's descendants in the service of the temple of the LORD," that is, in a sense, to be their servants (**1 Chronicles 23:28**).[33] For the sake of convenience, apartments or chambers[34] were provided in the Second Temple complex for resident priests and Levites. In general, the Levites functioned as a quasi-priesthood with limited authority and little access to all that was holy. Their tasks are described in numerous texts: **Numbers 1:50–53; 3:5–4:33; 18:1–32; 1 Chronicles 9:22–34**. Outside the precinct of the temple, non-Levitical personnel such as Pethahiah the Zerahite (a Judahite) served the king.[35]

Notes

1. Compare the Levitical personnel in this chart to those in "**1 Chronicles 23**: The Twenty-Four Levitical Leaders (Gershonites, Kohathites, and Merarites) Who Oversaw the Religious Personnel in Solomon's Temple" and "**1 Chronicles 24**: Additional Levites (Kohathites and Merarites) who Served in Solomon's Temple."

2. The assumption is that Nehemiah, as a historian, writes first about the present (444 B.C.), by describing the historical period to be covered (**Nehemiah 1:1–3**). The body of the work ensues with references to earlier times as well, as seen in **Nehemiah 5:3–5, 15; 7:4–5; 11:3–4, 20, 25–30; 12:1–26; 13:4–5, 7, 10, 23**.

3. For chronological and genealogical reasons, Bunni (the great-great-grandfather of Shemaiah the Levitical Merarite) is not the same person as Bunni in **Nehemiah 9:4**, a contemporary of Nehemiah (444 B.C.); or Bunni, a leader of the people in **Nehemiah 10:15**.

4. Hashabiah the Merarite in **Nehemiah 11:15** is probably the same person as Hashabiah in **1 Chronicles 9:14; Ezra 8:19, 24; Nehemiah 10:11**. He appears to be a descendant of Hashabiah the Merarite (the son/descendant of Jeduthun/Ethan) (**1 Chronicles 25:3, 19**); see chart "**1 Chronicles 25**: The Twenty-Four Musician Leaders in Solomon's Temple." He is not Hashabiah the Gershonite (**Nehemiah 11:22; 12:24**) or Hashabiah the Kohathite priest from the family of Hilkiah (**Nehemiah 12:21**).

5. For the lineage of Shemaiah, see **1 Chronicles 9:14** (where he is specifically called a "Merarite") and **Nehemiah 11:15**. For the lineage of Merari (the Merarites), see chart "**1 Chronicles 6**: Levi: High Priests, Priests, Levites, and Musicians in Solomon's Temple."

6. "Head" (Heb. רֹאשׁ, *rosh*).

7. The lineage of Asaph, one of the three chief musicians in Solomon's Temple, is given in **1 Chronicles 6:39–43**. For his heritage, see charts "**1 Chronicles 6**: Levi: High Priests, Priest, Levites, and Musicians in Solomon's Temple" and "**1 Chronicles 9**: Seven Levitical Leaders in the Second Temple (Post-Exile)."

8. Zabdi in **Nehemiah 11:17** is Zikri in **1 Chronicles 9:15** and Zakkur in **1 Chronicles 25:2, 10; Nehemiah 12:35**. Zakkur was one of the 24 musician leaders in Solomon's Temple (see chart "**1 Chronicles 25**: The Twenty-Four Musician Leaders in Solomon's Temple").

9. Mika in **1 Chronicles 9:15; Nehemiah 10:11; 11:17, 22** is Micaiah in **Nehemiah 12:35**.

10. Mattaniah in **Nehemiah 11:17, 22** is the same person as Mattaniah in **1 Chronicles 9:15**. He was a descendant of Asaph the Levitical Gershonite (see note 7) and presumably a descendant of Mattaniah the Levite who lived in the days of King Hezekiah, 715–686 B.C. (**2 Chronicles 29:13**). The descendants of Mattaniah are given in **2 Chronicles 20:14; and Nehemiah 11:22; 12:35**.

11. Hashabiah son of Mattaniah (a Levitical Gershonite; **Nehemiah 11:22**) is probably the same person as Hashabiah the Levite (**Nehemiah 12:24**), but he is not (1) Hashabiah son of Bunni (a Levitical Merarite; **1 Chronicles 9:14; Nehemiah 11:15**) or (2) Hashabiah the Kohathite priest, of the family of Hilkiah (**Nehemiah 12:21**).

12. Bani (**Nehemiah 11:22**) the father of Uzzi was a Levitical Gershonite who lived in 444 B.C. Therefore, he could be (1) the father of Rehum, one of the Levites who helped repair the wall around Jerusalem (**Nehemiah 3:17**); (2) Bani the Levite who helped the people understand the reading of the Law of Moses (**Nehemiah 8:7**); (3) one of the three Bani figures (all Levites) who led worship after the completion of the wall around Jerusalem (**Nehemiah 9:4–5**); and/or (4) Bani the Levite who sealed the covenant with Nehemiah (**Nehemiah 10:13**). Bani the father of Uzzi is not (1) Bani, one of the family heads among the returning exiles (cf. **Ezra 2:10; 8:10; 10:29, 34**); nor (2) Bani one of the leaders of the people (**Nehemiah 10:14**).

13. Uzzi son of Bani (a Levitical Gershonite) is the same person as Uzzi the chief officer over the Levites in Jerusalem (**Nehemiah 11:22**) and the Levite named Uzzi who was present at the dedication of the wall around Jerusalem (**Nehemiah 12:42**). He is not (1) Uzzi the high priest (**1 Chronicles 6:5–6, 51; Ezra 7:4**); (2) Uzzi the Benjamite (**1 Chronicles 9:8**); nor (3) Uzzi the Kohathite attending priest of the Jedaiah family of Jedaiah (**Nehemiah 12:19**).

14. Bakbukiah is identified as "second among his associates" (presumably a near relative) of Mattaniah the Gershonite (**Nehemiah 11:17**), so Bakbukiah is probably a Levitical Gershonite as well, but his exact lineage is unknown. Bakbukiah (**Nehemiah 11:17**) is probably the same person as Bakbukiah one of the family heads of Levites who returned to Jerusalem with Zerubbabel in 538 B.C. (**Nehemiah 12:9**) and Bakbukiah the gatekeeper in **Nehemiah 12:25**, who guarded the storerooms at the gates in the days of Ezra (ca. 458–444 B.C.), Nehemiah (444–432 B.C.), and the high priest Joiakim (490–450/444 B.C.). Also, Bakbukiah is probably the same person as Bakbakkar in **1 Chronicles 9:15**; see note 2 in chart "**1 Chronicles 9**: Seven Levitical Leaders in the Second Temple (Post-Exile)."

15. Jeduthun (**1 Chronicles 9:16; 16:38, 41–42; 25:1, 3, 6; 2 Chronicles 5:12; 29:14; 35:15**) is also called Ethan (**1 Chronicles 6:44; 15:17, 19**). For his lineage, see charts "**1 Chronicles 6**: Levi: High Priests, Priest, Levites, and Musicians in Solomon's Temple" and "**2 Chronicles 29**: The Priests, Levites, and Singers Who Cleansed the Temple During the Reign of King Hezekiah of Judah."

16. For Galal the brother of Obed-Edom, see **1 Chronicles 9:15–16; Nehemiah 11:17**; and the chart "**2 Samuel 6**: Obed-Edom, the Levitical Gatekeeper and Keeper of the Ark."

17. Shammua the Merarite (**Nehemiah 11:17**) is the same person as Shemaiah the Merarite (**1 Chronicles 9:16**). Shemaiah/Shammua is not Shemaiah the Levite, the son of Hasshub (**1 Chronicles 9:14**).

18. The post-exilic Levite named Abda in **Nehemiah 11:17** is called Obadiah in **1 Chronicles 9:16**. Obadiah/Abda and his clan "lived in the villages of the Netophathites" (**1 Chronicles 9:16**). He is likely the same person as Obadiah the gatekeeper who guarded the storerooms at the gates in the Second Temple in Jerusalem in the days of Joiakim the high priest (ca. 490–450/444 B.C.), Nehemiah (444–432 B.C.), and Ezra (458–444 B.C) (**Nehemiah 12:25–26**).

19. Akkub (**Nehemiah 11:19**) is the same person as Akkub the gatekeeper who was among those who guarded the storerooms at the gates of the Second Temple (**1 Chronicles 9:17; Nehemiah 12:25**). This family of gatekeepers returned to Jerusalem with Zerubbabel and Joshua in 538 B.C. (**Ezra 2:42; Nehemiah 7:45**). Akkub the gatekeeper is not the temple servant named Akkub (**Ezra 2:45**).

20. Talmon (**Nehemiah 11:19**) is the same person as Talmon the gatekeeper who was among those who guarded the storerooms at the gates of the Second Temple. (**1 Chronicles 9:17; Nehemiah 12:25**). This family of gatekeepers

returned to Jerusalem with Zerubbabel and Joshua in 538 B.C. (**Ezra 2:42; Nehemiah 7:45**).

21. "*Nethinim*" (נְתִינִים) is a gerundive passive participle of the common verb *nathan,* "to give," thus, "those given (over)" as servants at the temple. They were considered a low class of people with no ancestral lineage that could certify their eligibility to serve in a regular priestly capacity (**Nehemiah 7:61**). Nonetheless, they played an important part by assisting the priests and Levites with mundane chores. The body of temple servants had been established by David to assist the Levites (**Ezra 8:20**). A significant number of temple servants had returned to Jerusalem with Zerubbabel in 538 B.C. (**1 Chronicles 9:2; Ezra 2:43–54, 58, 70; Nehemiah 7:46–56, 60**), and more came to Jerusalem with Ezra in 458 B.C. (**Ezra 7:7; 8:17, 20**). Most settled in their own towns (**Nehemiah 7:73**), whereas others (those shown in the chart) were chosen to permanently dwell in Jerusalem and live in the "house of the temple servants" on the hill of Ophel (**Nehemiah 3:31**; cf. **11:3, 21**); see note 22.

22. The Ophel or "hill of Ophel" (**2 Chronicles 27:3; 33:14; Nehemiah 11:21**) refers to a rounded promontory of ancient Jerusalem, opposite the Water Gate (**Nehemiah 3:26**), located along the eastern Ophel ridge directly south of the temple—flanked on the east by the Kidron Valley and on the west by the Tyropoeon Valley. Some scholars hold that the Ophel was the former *millo* (a fill), a series of stepped stone terraces along the eastern slope between the old Jebusite City of David and the hill of Moriah (the site of the temple).

23. The descendants of Ziha were temple servants in the Second Temple (cf. **Ezra 2:43; Nehemiah 7:46; 11:21**).

24. Gishpa (Heb. *gishpa;* גִּשְׁפָּא); **Nehemiah 11:21**) may be related to Hasupha (*khasupha,* חֲשֻׂפָא; **Ezra 2:43; Nehemiah 7:46**).

25. Uzzi was among "Asaph's descendants, who were the musicians responsible for the service of the house of God" (**Nehemiah 11:22**); see note 7. Uzzi in **Nehemiah 11:22** is likely the same person as Uzzi in **Nehemiah 12:42** (but he is not Uzzi the Kohathite priest; cf. **Nehemiah 12:19**).

26. For Zabdi, see note 8.

27. For Mika, see note 9.

28. Meshezabel (**Nehemiah 11:24**) is probably the same person as Meshezabel one of the leaders of the people (**Nehemiah 10:21**) and perhaps the Meshezabel figure in **Nehemiah 3:4**.

29. Pethahiah the Zerahite served as the *king's* agent (see note 35) in all matters concerning the people (**Nehemiah 11:24**). His tribal identity as a Judean is enough alone to distinguish him from the Levites. Notably, Pethahiah's genealogy strongly suggests that the lineages of the Judahites, and the Zerahites in particular, were kept faithfully for many generations (i.e., from the time of Judah and Zerah in ca. 1925–1875 B.C. to the time of Pethahiah the Zerahite in ca. 444 B.C., almost 1,500 years later). Pethahiah the Zerahite is not Pethahiah the Kohathite priest (**1 Chronicles 24:16**) or Pethahiah the Levite (**Ezra 10:23; Nehemiah 9:5**).

30. "Judges" (שׁוֹפְטִים), *shophetim* (**1 Chronicles 23:4**; cf. **26:29**). This should be taken in a most limited sense, that is, in religious, not civil, matters. The secular judge would be the kind described in **Exodus 18** where Moses "took his seat to serve as judge for the people" (**Exodus 18:13, 16**; cf. **Joshua 23:2**).

31. Josephus, *Jewish Antiquities* 11.5.8.

32. In line with Torah injunctions, the priests and Levites in the post-exilic community served in the Jerusalem temple on a regular rotating schedule and resided in Levitical cities and towns assigned to them within the tribal territories of the other tribes (cf. **Numbers 35:1–8**). These towns included pasturelands for their livestock and field crops. The sustenance of the priests came from shares of the offerings the people gave to the Lord.

33. David said of the Levites that "the duty of the Levites was to help Aaron's descendants in the service of the temple of the Lord" (**1 Chronicles 23:28**); for specific Levitical duties, see **1 Chronicles 23:28–32**.

34. The term for "chamber" (לִשְׁכָּה, *lishkah,* connotes primarily a hall or meeting-place, but it also is found as a lexeme for "room," "apartment," or "storeroom" (**Ezra 8:29; 10:6; Nehemiah 10:37–39; Jeremiah 35:4; 36:10; Ezekiel 42:13; 44:19**). In describing the construction of Solomon's Temple, the accounts in **1 Kings 6:1–35** and **2 Chronicles 3:1–17** go into great detail, but the interest here is on the architecturally puzzling, three-story-high side chambers attached to the outer walls of the main temple structure itself: the lowest story was the same length as the temple (90 feet) and 7.5 feet wide; the next level up was the same length but 9 feet wide; and the third, and highest, was similarly long and 10.5 feet wide; each story had "offset ledges around the outside of the temple so that nothing would be inserted into the temple walls [themselves]" (cf. **1 Kings 6:6**) They were accessed by an interior stairway(s) and then through doors at each level. Each of these levels was divided into an unknown number of chambers, but in any case, they served as storage and rooms large enough for one or two people to sleep and find shelter. Though the narrative sheds no light beyond this, it is not beyond reason to suppose that priests and Levites on duty availed themselves of this convenience.

35. After the exiles returned to their homeland, Judah had no *king,* in the traditional sense; rather, the people of Yehud in post-exilic Jerusalem were led by and under the authority of *governors,* such as Sheshbazzar and Zerubbabel; see chart "**Ezra 1**: Sheshbazzar and Zerubbabel, the Governors over the Restored Community in Jerusalem (Post-Exile)". Thus, *king/king's agent* (**Nehemiah 11:24**) should be understood to be the ruling civil authority at the time.

NEHEMIAH 12: GENEALOGICAL RECORD OF THE HEADS OF THE KOHATHITE PRIESTS AND LEVITES WHO RETURNED TO JERUSALEM WITH ZERUBBABEL AND JOSHUA IN THE POST-EXILE

Approximate Dating: ca. 538 B.C. ***Relevant Scriptures:*** **Nehemiah 12:1–11**

Heads of the Kohathite Priestly Families Who Returned with Zerubbabel and Joshua[1]

1. **Seraiah** (**Nehemiah 12:1; Ezra 2:2**) of 538 B.C. is not Seraiah the high priest who was killed at Riblah (cf. **2 Kings 25:18–21; Jeremiah 52:24–27**), but he is likely Seraiah (#2), "the official in charge of the house of God [the Second Temple]" in 516 B.C. (**Nehemiah 11:11**), who is called both "Seraiah" and "Azariah" (cf. **1 Chronicles 9:11; Ezra 2:2; Nehemiah 7:7; 11:11**). For the probable lineage of the Seraiah who returned to Jerusalem in 538 B.C. (and other Seraiah and Azariah figures), see the chart "**Ezra 7**: Ezra, the Priestly Scribe and Teacher of the Law (Post-Exile)." Also, a descendant of the Seraiah priestly family named Meraiah (**Nehemiah 12:12**) served in the days of Joiakim the high priest (490–450/444 B.C.).
2. **Jeremiah** (**Nehemiah 12:1**) of 538 B.C. was likely an ancestor of the Kohathite priest named Jeremiah who sealed the covenant with Nehemiah in 444 B.C. (**Nehemiah 10:2**). A descendant of the Jeremiah priestly family named Hananiah served in the days of Joiakim the high priest, 490–450/444 B.C. (**Nehemiah 12:12**).
3. **Ezra** (**Nehemiah 12:1, 13**) of 538 B.C. does not refer to Ezra the scribal priest and teacher of the Law who led returning exiles to Jerusalem in 458 B.C. A descendant of the Ezra priestly family named Meshullam served in the days of Joiakim the high priest, 490–450/444 B.C. (**Nehemiah 12:13**).

4. **Amariah** (**Nehemiah 12:2**) of 538 B.C. was likely an ancestor of Amariah the priest who sealed the covenant with Nehemiah in 444 B.C. (**Nehemiah 10:3**). A descendant of the Amariah priestly family named Jehohanan served in the days of Joiakim the high priest, 490–450/444 B.C. (**Nehemiah 12:13**).
5. **Malluk** (**Nehemiah 12:2**) of 538 B.C. was likely an ancestor of Malluk the priest who sealed the covenant with Nehemiah in 444 B.C. (**Nehemiah 10:4**). A descendant of the Malluk priestly family named Jonathan served in the days of Joiakim the high priest, 490–450/444 B.C. (**Nehemiah 12:14**).
6. **Hattush** (**Nehemiah 12:2**) of 538 B.C. was likely an ancestor of Hattush the priest who sealed the covenant with Nehemiah in 444 B.C. (**Nehemiah 10:4**). He is not Hattush son of Shemaiah, a descendant of Shekaniah (a Judahite)—"Of the descendants of David" (**Ezra 8:2**; cf. **1 Chronicles 3:22**) who returned with Ezra in 458 B.C.
7. **Shekaniah** (**Nehemiah 12:3**) of 538 B.C. was likely a descendant of the *ancestral* Shekaniah Kohathite priestly family, established under King David, who had served in Solomon's Temple (**1 Chronicles 24:11**). Joseph (**Nehemiah 12:14**) was a descendant of this Shekaniah priestly family who lived in the days of Joiakim the high priest (490–450/444 B.C.). By common visual or auditory scribal lapses and dealing with ancient handwritten scripts, misreadings could take place on occasion. Thus שכניה (Shekaniah) could easily be confused with שבניה (Shebaniah; **Nehemiah 10:4**), who sealed the covenant with Nehemiah in 444 B.C. In a couple of Hebrew manuscripts and the Vulgate, Shekaniah in **Nehemiah 12:3** is rendered Shebaniah. Conversely, Shebaniah in **Nehemiah 12:14** appears as Shekaniah in a few Hebrew manuscripts, the Lucianic Septuagint, and Syriac Peshitta.
8. **Rehum** (**Nehemiah 12:3**; cf. **Ezra 2:2**) is Nehum (**Nehemiah 7:7**). The names Rehum (רחם) and Nehum (נחם) could easily be confused. Also, the priestly family of Rehum in **Nehemiah 12:3** seems to be equivalent or part of the priestly family Harim in **Nehemiah 12:15** (i.e., notice the direct correspondence between the order of the priests in **Nehemiah 12:1–7** [with the exception of Hattush in **12:2**] and the order of the priests in **Nehemiah 12:12–21** [where "Mijamin" in **Nehemiah 12:5** is the variant of "Miniamin" in **Nehemiah 12:17**]). Rehum/Nehum the priest of 538 B.C. is not the commanding officer named Rehum who wrote a letter to King Artaxerxes I (465–424 B.C.; **Ezra 4:8–9, 17**).
9. **Meremoth** (**Nehemiah 12:3**) of 538 B.C. was likely an ancestor of Meremoth who sealed the covenant with Nehemiah in 444 B.C. (**Nehemiah 10:5**). A descendant of the Meremoth priestly family named Helkai served in the days of Joiakim the high priest, 490–450/444 B.C. (**Nehemiah 12:15**). Meremoth is probably from the *ancestral* priestly division of Hakkoz (cf. **Nehemiah 3:4**).
10. **Iddo** (**Nehemiah 12:4**) of 538 B.C., of the priestly family of Iddo, was related to and a contemporary of Zechariah (son of Berekiah, son of Iddo), the Kohathite priest-prophet who ministered in the days of Joiakim the high priest, 490–450/444 B.C. (**Nehemiah 12:16**; cf. **Ezra 5:1; 6:14; Zechariah 1:1, 7**), and prophesied in the post-exilic days of Zerubbabel the governor and Joshua the high priest; see the chart "**Zechariah 1**: Zechariah, the Prophet of God to the Restored Community in Jerusalem (Post-Exile)."
11. **Ginnethon** (**Nehemiah 12:4**) of 538 B.C. was likely an ancestor of Ginnethon the priest who sealed the covenant with Nehemiah in 444 B.C. (**Nehemiah 10:6**). A descendant of the Ginnethon priestly family named Meshullam served in the days of Joiakim the high priest, 490–450/444 B.C. (**Nehemiah 12:16**).
12. **Abijah** (**Nehemiah 12:4**) of 538 B.C. was likely a descendant of the *ancestral* Abijah division of Kohathite priests established under King David who had served in Solomon's Temple (**1 Chronicles 24:10**) and an ancestor of Abijah the priest who sealed the covenant with Nehemiah in 444 B.C. (**Nehemiah 10:7**). A descendant of the Abijah priestly family named Zikri served in the days of Joiakim the high priest, 490–450/444 B.C. (**Nehemiah 12:17**). Also, it is likely that Abijah (and possibly Zikri) was an ancestor of Zechariah the priest, the father of John the Baptist, who "belonged to the priestly division of Abijah" (**Luke 1:5**).
13. **Mijamin** (מְיָמִין) is a variant of **Miniamin** (מִנְיָמִין), the latter resulting by the assimilation of נְ into the י. Mijamin of 538 B.C. (**Nehemiah 12:5**) was likely a descendant of the *ancestral* Mijamin, head of the Mijamin division of Kohathite priests established under King David who had served in Solomon's Temple (**1 Chronicles 24:9**). Miniamin (or Mijamin) was likely a descendant of (1) Miniamin the priest in **2 Chronicles 31:15** who was involved in the revival under Hezekiah (715–686 B.C.) and (2) an ancestor of Miniamin in **Nehemiah 12:41**, a musician who participated in the dedication of the city walls in the days of Nehemiah in 444 B.C. A descendant of the Miniamin (and the Moadiah) Kohathite priestly family named Piltai served in the days of Joiakim the high priest, 490–450/444 B.C. (**Nehemiah 12:17**). However, Mijamin (or Miniamin) is unrelated to Mijamin of the Israelite laity (a descendant of Parosh) who had married a pagan wife (**Ezra 10:25**).
14. **Moadiah** (**Nehemiah 12:5**) of 538 B.C. may be a descendant of the *ancestral* Maaziah division of Kohathite priests established under King David who had served in Solomon's Temple (**1 Chronicles 24:18**) and an ancestor of Maaziah, who sealed the covenant with Nehemiah in 444 B.C. (**Nehemiah 10:8**). Note the similarity: מועדיה (Moadiah) vs. מעזיה (Maaziah). A descendant of the Moadiah (Maaziah?) priestly family named Piltai served in the days of Joiakim the high priest, 490–450/444 B.C. (**Nehemiah 12:17**).
15. **Bilgah** (**Nehemiah 12:5**) of 538 B.C. is probably a descendant of the *ancestral* Bilgah division of Kohathite priests established under King David who had served in Solomon's Temple (**1 Chronicles 24:14**).

Bilgah (בלגה) may be an ancestor of "Bilgai" (בלגי), the priest who sealed the covenant with Nehemiah in 444 B.C. (**Nehemiah 10:8**). A descendant of the Bilgah priestly family named Shammua served in the days of Joiakim the high priest, 490–450/444 B.C. (**Nehemiah 12:18**).

16. **Shemaiah** (**Nehemiah 12:6**) of 538 B.C. is probably an ancestor of Shemaiah the priest who sealed the covenant with Nehemiah in 444 B.C. (**Nehemiah 10:8**). A descendant of the Shemaiah priestly family named Jehonathan (**Nehemiah 12:18**) served in the days of Joiakim the high priest (490–450/444 B.C.).
17. **Joiarib** (**Nehemiah 12:6**) of 538 B.C. is probably a descendant of the *ancestral* J(eh)oiarib division of Kohathite priests established under King David who had served in Solomon's Temple (**1 Chronicles 24:7**) A descendant of the Joiarib (or Jehoiarib) priestly family named Mattenai (**Nehemiah 12:19**) served in the days of Joiakim the high priest (490–450/444 B.C.).
18. **Jedaiah #1** (**Nehemiah 12:6**) of 538 B.C. may be a descendant of the *ancestral* Jedaiah division of Kohathite priests established under King David who had served in Solomon's Temple (**1 Chronicles 24:7**). A descendant of the Jedaiah #1 priestly family named Uzzi (**Nehemiah 12:19**) appears to have served in the days of Joiakim the high priest (490–450/444 B.C.); also see Jedaiah #2 below.
19. **Sallu** (**Nehemiah 12:7**). A descendant of the Sallu priestly family named Kallai (**Nehemiah 12:20**) served in the days of Joiakim the high priest (490–450/444 B.C.).
20. **Amok** (**Nehemiah 12:7**). A descendant of the Amok priestly family named Eber (**Nehemiah 12:20**) served in the days of Joiakim the high priest (490–450/444 B.C.).
21. **Hilkiah** (**Nehemiah 12:7**). A descendant of the Hilkiah priestly family named Hashabiah (**Nehemiah 12:21**) served in the days of Joiakim the high priest (490–450/444 B.C.). Hilkiah in **Nehemiah 12:7** does not refer to the high priest named Hilkiah who served 640–609 B.C. under King Josiah; see Hilkiah #22 in chart "**Supplement 2**: The High priests of Israel."
22. **Jedaiah #2** (**Nehemiah 12:7**) of 538 B.C., presumably another of the same name (see Jedaiah #1 above), may be a descendant of the *ancestral* Jedaiah division of Kohathite priests established under King David who had served in Solomon's Temple (**1 Chronicles 24:7**). A descendant of the Jedaiah #2 priestly family named Nethanel (**Nehemiah 12:21**) appears to have served in the days of Joiakim the high priest (490–450/444 B.C.).

Family Heads of Levites Who Returned with Zerubbabel and Joshua and Were in Charge of the Songs of Thanksgiving

1. **Jeshua** the Levite (**Nehemiah 12:8**) was probably the son of Kadmiel (**Nehemiah 12:24**) and the father of Jozabad (**Ezra 8:33**). Jeshua was a contemporary of Zerubbabel in 538 B.C. (**Ezra 2:40; Nehemiah 7:43**) and a contemporary of Ezra in 458 B.C. Jeshua was among the Levites who instructed the people in the Law (**Nehemiah 8:7; 9:4–5**). Another Levite named Jeshua, the son of Azaniah, was a contemporary of Nehemiah the governor (**Nehemiah 10:9**). Jeshua the Levite is not the same person as Joshua/Jeshua the high priest; see the following chart for the succession of high priests in the Second Temple. Jeshua the Levite and his descendants served in the days of Eliashib, Joiada, Johanan, and Jaddua, who held the high priesthood from ca. 450/444–332 B.C. (**Nehemiah 12:22–24**).
2. **Binnui** the Levite (**Nehemiah 12:8**) of 538 B.C. could be the same person as (1) Binnui, the father of Noadiah (a contemporary of Ezra in 458 B.C.; **Ezra 8:33**); or (2) an ancestor of Binnui, "of the sons of Henadad" who was "the ruler of the other half-district of Keilah" and a contemporary of Nehemiah (**Nehemiah 3:18, 24; 10:9**).

   It should also be considered that by the elision of the vowel ו, Binnui (בנוי) could be Bani (בני): thus, Binnui the Levite in **Nehemiah 12:8** could be (1) Bani the Levite (**Nehemiah 8:7**); (2) Bani, or Binnui, the Levite(s) (**Nehemiah 9:4** or **5**); or (3) Bani, the father of Rehum the Levite, who made repairs in the days of Nehemiah in 444 B.C. (**Nehemiah 3:17**).

   However, Binnui the Levite (**Nehemiah 12:8**) is not (1) Binnui (or Bani), one of the heads of the Israelite clans who lived in the days of Ezra in 458 B.C. and whose descendants had taken foreign wives (cf. **Ezra 10:29, 34, 38**); (2) "the descendants of Bani" the Israelite who returned to Jerusalem with Ezra in 458 B.C. (**Ezra 8:10**); (3) Binnui the Israelite who returned with Zerubbabel in 538 B.C. (**Nehemiah 7:15**); (4) Binnui the Israelite who sealed the covenant with Nehemiah in 444 B.C. (**Nehemiah 10:14**); nor (5) Bani the Israelite who sealed the covenant with Nehemiah in 444 B.C. (**Nehemiah 10:15**).
3. **Kadmiel** (**Nehemiah 12:8**) of 538 B.C. was the father of Jeshua the Levite (**Nehemiah 12:24**), and his sons/descendants were of "the line of Hodaviah" (**Ezra 2:40; 3:9; Nehemiah 7:43**). He may have been an ancestor of the Kadmiel who was a contemporary of Ezra in 458 B.C. (**Nehemiah 9:4–5**) and/or Nehemiah in 445 B.C. (**Nehemiah 10:9**). Kadmiel and his descendants served in the days of Eliashib, Joiada, Johanan, and Jaddua, who held the high priesthood from ca. 450/444–332 B.C. (**Nehemiah 12:22–24**).
4. **Sherebiah** (**Nehemiah 12:8**) of 538 B.C. is possibly the ancestor of Sherebiah the Levite who served in the days of Ezra in 458 B.C. and Nehemiah in 445 B.C. (**Nehemiah 8:7; 9:4–5; 10:12**). Sherebiah and his descendants served in the days of Eliashib, Joiada, Johanan, and Jaddua, who held the high priesthood from ca. 450/444–332 B.C. (**Nehemiah 12:22–24**). Sherebiah the Levite is not Sherebiah the priest (**Ezra 8:24**) or Sherebiah the "capable man, from the descendants of Mahli son of Levi" (a Merarite) (**Ezra 8:18**).
5. **Judah** (**Nehemiah 12:8**; cf. **Ezra 10:23**).
6. **Mattaniah** (**Nehemiah 12:8**) of 538 B.C. is the same person as Mattaniah the son of Mika/Micaiah, son of

Zikri, son of Asaph (Gershonite) who was "the director who led in thanksgiving and prayer" (**Nehemiah 11:17**; cf. **1 Chronicles 9:15; 2 Chronicles 20:14; 29:13; Nehemiah 12:35; 13:13?**). Mattaniah was also the great-grandfather of Uzzi, the chief officer over the Levites in the newly re-established city of Jerusalem (**Nehemiah 11:22**). He is possibly Mattaniah the gatekeeper (or his ancestor) who served in the days of Joiakim the high priest (490–450/444 B.C.) and in the days of Nehemiah (444 B.C.) and Ezra (458 B.C.) (**Nehemiah 12:25**). He is not Mattaniah the son of Heman (**1 Chronicles 25:4, 16**), who lived in the days of King Solomon, 971–931 B.C.

7. **Bakbukiah** (**Nehemiah 12:9**) of 538 B.C. is probably the same person as Bakbukiah the Gershonite who settled in Jerusalem (**Nehemiah 11:17**) and possibly Bakbukiah the gatekeeper (or his ancestor) who served in the days of Joiakim the high priest and in the days of Nehemiah and Ezra (**Nehemiah 12:25**).
8. **Unni** (**Nehemiah 12:9**).
9. **Their associates** (brethren/relatives) who were also Levites.

Line of the High Priests in the Post-exilic (Nehemiah 12:10-11):[1]

Jozadak
("Jehozadak")
(Carried into Babylonian captivity; 586 B.C.)
(**1 Chronicles 6:15**)
|
Joshua
(Jeshua)
(High priest who returned from exile with Zerubbabel)
(First high priest to serve in the Second Temple in 516 B.C.)
(Served ca. 516–490 B.C.)
|
Joiakim
(Served ca. 490–450/445 B.C.)
|
Eliashib
(Served ca. 450/445–432 B.C.)
(A contemporary of Nehemiah)
(Rebuilt the Sheep Gate)
|
Joiada
(Served ca. 432–410 B.C.)
|
Jonathan
(Johanan; **Nehemiah 12:23**)
(Served ca. 410–370 B.C.)
|
Jaddua[2]
(Served ca. 370–332 B.C.)
(A contemporary of Alexander the Great)

[1] **Nehemiah 12:22-23** says that "The family heads of the Levites in the days of [the high priests] Eliashib, Joiada, Johanan and Jaddua, as well as those of the [Kohathite] priests, were recorded in the reign of Darius the Persian [possibly Darius II or Darius III]. The family heads among the descendants of Levi up to the time of [the high priest] Johanan son of Eliashib [ca. 410–370 B.C.] were recorded in the book of the annals." For the succession of high priests, particularly those who served in the Second Temple, see the chart "**Supplement 2** - Genealogy of the High Priests of Israel."
[2] Jaddua is the last high priest recorded in the Old Testament.

Biblical and Theological Significance

The Decree of Cyrus not only permitted the Jews of the deportation from Israel and Judah to Babylonia the right to return to their homeland, but he generously provided them with material assets and protection to resettle the land, as well as to rebuild the temple and establish the religious exercises associated with it (cf. **Ezra 1:1–4; 5:1–6:15**). Naturally, religious personnel were also essential to the return of normalcy. These personnel occupied different ranks or levels of responsibility in pursuit of their duties. The most important position was the high priest, a man who must prove his direct descent from the first high priest, Aaron, nearly one thousand years earlier. The chart focuses on Joshua, first high priest of the Second Temple, who initiated his ministry in Jerusalem in 520 B.C. He was a son of Jozadak, the high priest in Solomon's Temple, who in 586 B.C. had seen the glorious edifice be burned to the ground by the ruthless troops of the great Nebuchadnezzar II. The chart demonstrates the legitimacy of the returning Kohathite priests and Levites who attended Joshua the high priest and those who were involved in re-establishing worship in the post-exile in the Second Temple after it was completed in 516 B.C.

Notes

1. The *ancestral* Kohathite priestly divisions/houses/courses—led by the Kohathite attending priests (such as Shekaniah, Bilgah, Abijah, Jehoiarib, Jedaiah, Mijamin, etc.)—had been established at the end of King David's reign in ca. 971 B.C. and these priests served in Solomon's Temple during King Solomon's reign, 971–931 B.C. (**1 Chronicles 24:7–18**). Surprisingly, some of the original (*ancestral*) family names are retained and appear in the post-exile period as well (538–400 B.C.). Given that this involves a period of over 500 years, the individuals who are listed in this chart were *descendants* of the *ancestral* priests/priestly houses and were the *ancestors* of Kohathite priests who served in the days of Joiakim the high priest, 490–450/444 B.C. (cf. **Nehemiah 12:12–21**). The practice of nominal repetition in ancient Israel is well attested in the Old Testament, especially when it comes to priestly officials.

After the Second Temple was completed in 516 B.C., and assuming the historical accuracy of **Nehemiah 12:10–11**, only six high priests—Joshua, Joiakim, Eliashib, Joiada, Jonathan, and Jaddua—officiated in the Second Temple between 516–332 B.C. (i.e., 184 years with an average 31-year-tenure for each priest). The long tenure of each high priest has been a point of concern for some modern scholars who have responded by expanding the number of high priests, assuming papponymy and haplography, and positing various birth dates; for a discussion of this possible occurrence, see Benjamin E. Scolnic, *Chronology and Papponymy: A List of the Judean High Priests of the Persian Period* (Atlanta: Scholars Press: Atlanta, 1999), 1–26. The chart above—as well as the chart "**Supplement 2**: The High Priests of Israel"—follows the chronology of the scholar James C. VanderKam (see *From Joshua to Caiaphas–High Priests after the Exile* (Fortress: Minneapolis and Assen, the Netherlands: Van Gorcum, 2004) who adheres to only six high priests during this period.

NEHEMIAH 12: GENEALOGICAL RECORD OF THE HEADS OF PRIESTS, LEVITES, AND GATEKEEPERS WHO SERVED IN THE SECOND TEMPLE IN THE DAYS OF JOIAKIM THE HIGH PRIEST, EZRA THE PRIESTLY SCRIBE, AND NEHEMIAH THE GOVERNOR

Approximate Dating: recorded during the high priesthood of Joiakim, ca. 490–450/444 B.C.; Ezra came to Jerusalem in 458 B.C. and Nehemiah came to Jerusalem in 444 B.C.[1] ***Relevant Scriptures:*** **Nehemiah 12:12–26**

The Heads of the Kohathite Priestly Divisions in the Second Temple

Names in **bold** (below) correspond to the names of known *ancestral* heads from among the twenty-four Kohathite priestly families who served in Solomon's Temple[2] (**1 Chronicles 24:1–19**), although only twenty heads are given in this particular genealogical record.[3]

Priestly Divisions	Priestly Heads
Family of Seraiah[4]	Meraiah
Family of Jeremiah[5]	Hananiah[6]
Family of Ezra[7]	Meshullam #1[8]
Family of Amariah[9]	Jehohanan[10]
Family of Malluk[11]	Jonathan
Family of **Shekaniah**[12]	Joseph
Family of **Harim (Rehum)**[13]	Adna
Family of Meremoth (of **Hakkoz**)[14]	Helkai
Family of Iddo	Zechariah (=Zechariah the prophet)[15]
Family of Ginnethon	Meshullam #2
Family of **Abijah**[16]	Zikri[17]
Family of **Miniamin**[18] and Moadiah (of **Mazziah**?)[19]	Piltai
Family of **Bilgah**[20]	Shammua
Family of Shemaiah[21]	Jehonathan
Family of **Joiarib (Jehoiarib)**[22]	Mattenai
Family of **Jedaiah** #1[23]	Uzzi[24]
Family of Sallu[25]	Kallai
Family of Amok[26]	Eber
Family of Hilkiah[27]	Hashabiah[28]
Family of Jedaiah #2[29]	Nethanel

Leaders of the Levites Who Officiated at the Second Temple

1. **Hashabiah**[30]
2. **Sherebiah**[31]
3. **Jeshua son of Kadmiel**[32]
4. **Their Levitical brethren/associates**

Family Heads of the Gatekeepers

1. **Mattaniah**[33]
2. **Bakbukiah**[34]
3. **Obadiah**[35]
4. **Meshullam** (Shallum)[36]
5. **Talmon**[37]
6. **Akkub**[38]

Biblical and Theological Significance

In the post-exile period, several practices concerning the priesthood and Levitical orders diverted from the Mosaic and Davidic eras. The ancient ideal was twenty-four "divisions" (מַחֲלֹקֶת; *makhaloqet*) of Kohathite attending priests: sixteen of these divisions/families were descendants of Eleazar (the son of Aaron) and eight were descendants of Ithamar (the son of Aaron; **1 Chronicles 24:4**).[39] Given the various vicissitudes created by the upheaval of the community through the cruel destruction of Jerusalem and the temple in 586 B.C. and the ensuing deportation of the Judean citizenry to Babylon, changes of all kinds were to be expected, even in religious and ecclesiastical structures. This likely explains, for example, why only twenty heads of families are listed in the post-exile, as opposed to the expected twenty-four (**Nehemiah 12:12–21**).[40] In the chart, notice that only *eight* or *nine* of the Kohathite families in the Second Temple show a direct correspondence to the known *ancestral* family names (i.e., names shown in bold). Priestly families/divisions in the Second Temple (names *not* shown in bold) cannot be accurately traced genealogically to a particular (known) *ancestral* division of Kohathite attending priests in Solomon's Temple (cf. **1 Chronicles 24:7–18**). Nevertheless, Josephus, writing in ca. A.D. 93, comments that the "partition [of twenty-four divisions of attending priests from Solomon's Temple] has remained to this day";[41] furthermore, Josephus' comment is also consistent with the Jewish tradition reported by Joachim Jeremias and Alfred Edersheim that twenty-four divisions were active.[42] Clearly, an ideal seems to have been achieved for active Kohathite priests, Levites, and gatekeepers in the Second Temple period.

Notes

1. The relevant passage, **Nehemiah 12:22–23**, reads "The family heads of the Levites in the days of [the high priests] Eliashib [450/445–432 B.C.], Joiada [432–410 B.C.], Johanan [410–370 B.C.] and Jaddua [370–332 B.C., and a contemporary of Alexander the Great], as well as those of the priests [Kohathite attending priests], were recorded in the reign of Darius the Persian. The family heads among the descendants of Levi up to the time of Johanan [the grandson] of Eliashib were recorded in the book of the annals." Thus, "Darius the Persian" in **Nehemiah 12:22** must refer to Darius III (336–330 B.C.).

Dates of the Persian Monarchs of the Period by the Name "Darius"

Darius I/Darius the Great (522–486 B.C.)
Darius II (423–404 B.C.)
Darius III (336–330 B.C.)

Also see charts "**Nehemiah 12**: Genealogical Record of the Heads of the Kohathite Priests and Levites who Returned to Jerusalem with Zerubbabel and Joshua in the Post-Exile"; "**Supplement 2**: The High Priests of Israel"; and "**Supplement 5**: The Kings of Persia."

2. For the *ancestral* Kohathite priestly divisions in Solomon's Temple, see chart "**1 Chronicles 24**: Genealogical Registry of the Twenty-Four Divisions of Kohathite Attending Priests Who Rotated Service in Solomon's Temple (Sixteen from the Aaron–Eleazar–Zadok Line and Eight from the Aaron–Ithamar Line)."

3. For additional Kohathite priestly families who served, see Jedaiah, Jehoiarib, and Jakin in chart "**1 Chronicles 9**: The Kohathite Attending Priests in the Second Temple (Post-Exile)."

4. The priestly family of Seraiah (**Nehemiah 12:12**) may refer to Seraiah #2 or Seraiah #3, who were the descendants of the high priest named Seraiah/Seraiah #1 (the son of Azariah, the son of Hilkiah). The Kohathite priest Seraiah (#2) returned to Jerusalem with Zerubbabel in 538 B.C. (**Nehemiah 12:1**), and Seraiah #3 (presumably the *son* of Seraiah #2) sealed the covenant with Nehemiah in 444 B.C. (**Nehemiah 10:2**). For the proposed lineage of Seraiah #2 and #3, see chart "**Ezra 7**: Ezra, the Priestly Scribe and Teacher of the Law (Post-Exile)."

5. The priestly family of Jeremiah (**Nehemiah 12:12**) includes the Kohathite priest Jeremiah, who returned to Jerusalem with Zerubbabel in 538 B.C. (**Nehemiah 12:1**) and Jeremiah (a descendant) who sealed the covenant with Nehemiah in 444 B.C. (**Nehemiah 10:2**). For chronological reasons, the family of Jeremiah in **Nehemiah 12:12** does not directly refer to the priest-prophet Jeremiah, who ministered from ca. 627–586 B.C., although the genealogy for the prophet Jeremiah shows he was also a Kohathite priest; see chart "**Jeremiah 1**: Jeremiah, the Prophet-Priest of God to the Southern Kingdom of Judah (Pre-Exile)."

6. Hananiah (**Nehemiah 12:12**) is probably the same priest person as Hananiah (**Nehemiah 12:41**).

7. The priestly family of Ezra (**Nehemiah 12:13**) includes the Kohathite priest Ezra, who returned to Jerusalem with Zerubbabel in 538 B.C. (**Nehemiah 12:1**). For chronological reasons, the family of Ezra in **Nehemiah 12:13** does not directly refer to the scribal priest and teacher of the Law, Ezra, who did not return to Jerusalem until 458 B.C.; for the latter, see chart "**Ezra 7**: Ezra, the Priestly Scribe and Teacher of the Law (Post-Exile)."

8. Two priests in the table are named Meshullam: Meshullam #1 was the head of the family of Ezra (**Nehemiah 12:13**) and the other, Meshullam #2, was the head of the family of Ginnethon (**Nehemiah 12:16**). One of the Meshullam figures may refer to the priest Meshullam the son of Berekiah (**Nehemiah 3:4, 30; 6:18**) or Meshullam the son of Besodeiah (**Nehemiah 3:6**), both of whom were involved in rebuilding the walls and gates around Jerusalem in the days of Nehemiah, in 444 B.C. Meshullam #1 and #2 should not be confused with the high priest named Meshullam the son of Zadok (**1 Chronicles 9:11; Nehemiah 11:11**).

9. The priestly family of Amariah (**Nehemiah 12:13**) includes the Kohathite priest Amariah, who returned to Jerusalem with Zerubbabel in 538 B.C. (**Nehemiah 12:2**) and Amariah (a descendant) who sealed the covenant with Nehemiah in 444 B.C. (**Nehemiah 10:3**).

10. Jehohanan (**Nehemiah 12:13**) is probably the same priest as Jehohanan (**Nehemiah 12:42**).

11. The priestly family of Malluk (**Nehemiah 12:14**) includes the priest Malluk who returned to Jerusalem with Zerubbabel in 538 B.C. (**Nehemiah 12:2**); this family also includes Malluk (likely a descendant) who sealed the covenant with Nehemiah in 444 B.C. (**Nehemiah 10:4**).

12. The priestly family of Shekaniah (**Nehemiah 12:14**) refers to descendants of Shekaniah the *ancestral* head over the tenth of the twenty-four divisions of Kohathite priests in Solomon's Temple (**1 Chronicles 24:11**). A Kohathite priest named Shekaniah returned to Jerusalem with Zerubbabel in 538 B.C. (**Nehemiah 12:3**) and may be the same person as, or an ancestor of, "Shebaniah" the Kohathite priest who sealed the covenant with Nehemiah in 444 B.C. (**Nehemiah 10:4**). [By common visual or auditory scribal lapses and dealing with ancient hand-written scripts, misreadings could on occasion take place—thus שכניה (Shekaniah), found in some manuscripts, could easily be confused with שבניה (Shebaniah; **Nehemiah 10:4**).] In 444 B.C., in the days of Nehemiah, "Shemaiah son of Shekaniah, the guard at the East Gate, made repairs" in the wall around Jerusalem (**Nehemiah 3:29**).

Shekaniah is not: (1) the Levite(s) named Shekaniah of **Nehemiah 9:4–5; 10:10** and/or **12**; (2) Shekaniah the Judahite (**1 Chronicles 3:21–22; Ezra 8:2–3**); (3) Shekaniah son of Jahaziel of the descendants of Zattu (**Ezra 8:5**); (4) Shekaniah son of Jehiel of the descendants of Elam (**Ezra10:2**); nor (5) Shekaniah son of Arah (**Nehemiah 6:18**).

13. The priestly family of Harim (**Nehemiah 12:15**)—which is probably a variant of Rehum (**Nehemiah 12:3**)—refers to descendants of Harim (the *ancestral* head over the third of the twenty-four divisions of Kohathite priests in Solomon's Temple; **1 Chronicles 24:8**). Harim the priest returned to Jerusalem with Zerubbabel in 538 B.C. (**Ezra 2:39; Nehemiah 7:42**). Harim (a descendant) sealed the covenant with Nehemiah in 444 B.C. (**Nehemiah 10:5**).

14. The priestly family of Meremoth (**Nehemiah 12:15**) probably refers to "Meremoth, son of Uriah, the son of Hakkoz" (**Nehemiah 3:4, 21**; see **Ezra 8:33; Nehemiah 10:5; 12:3**). The Kohathite priest named Hakkoz was the *ancestral* head over the seventh of the twenty-four divisions of Kohathite priests in Solomon's Temple (**1 Chronicles 24:10**). When the exiles returned with Zerubbabel in 538 B.C., some of the Hakkoz descendants could not locate their genealogical family records to prove their eligibility to serve in the Second Temple (cf. **Ezra 2:61–63; Nehemiah 7:63–65**). However, the inclusion of the priestly family of Meremoth in the table above shows that at least some of the Hakkoz descendants (e.g., the priest named Helkai) were favorably received and permitted to serve as part of the Kohathite attending priesthood in the Second Temple.

15. Zechariah (the son of Berekiah, the son of Iddo) was the Kohathite priest–prophet who prophesied in the post-exilic days of Zerubbabel the governor and Joshua the high priest and encouraged the people in the building

of the Second Temple (cf. **Ezra 5:1; 6:14; Nehemiah 12:4, 16; Zechariah 1:1, 7; 7:1**); for his lineage, see chart "**Zechariah 1**: Zechariah, the Prophet of God to the Restored Community in Jerusalem (Post-Exile)." This Zechariah may be the priest referred to in **Nehemiah 12:41**.

16. The priestly family of Abijah (**Nehemiah 12:17**) refers to descendants of Abijah, the *ancestral* head who was over the eighth of twenty-four divisions of Kohathite priests in Solomon's Temple (**1 Chronicles 24:10**). A Kohathite priest named Abijah (a *descendant* of the ancestral Abijah) returned from exile with Zerubbabel in ca. 538 B.C. (**Nehemiah 12:4**), and a priest named Abijah (a descendant) was among those who sealed the covenant in the days of Nehemiah in ca. 444 B.C. (**Nehemiah 10:7**).

17. Zikri is perhaps a short version of Zechariah; see note 9 in chart "**1 Chronicles 8**: The Benjamites Who Settled in and around Jerusalem and in Moab (Post-Exile)". Zikri the Kohathite priest (of the Abijah priestly division; **Nehemiah 12:17**) is likely an ancestor of Zechariah the priest, the father of John the Baptist (cf. **Luke 1:5, 8–25**).

18. The priestly family of Miniamin (**Nehemiah 12:17**) is elsewhere Mijamin in **Nehemiah 10:7; 12:5**. **Nehemiah 12:5** refers to the Mijamin figure who returned to Jerusalem with Zerubbabel in 538 B.C. and **Nehemiah 10:7** refers to Mijamin (or his descendant) who sealed the covenant with Nehemiah in 444 B.C. A priest named Miniamin is also mentioned in **Nehemiah 12:41**.

Mijamin (מְיָמִין) is a variant of Miniamin (מִנְיָמִין), the former resulting by the assimilation of נְ into the י. There is no "j" in Hebrew; the closest is "y," so Mijamin is better rendered Miyamin; unfortunately, the various English translations are inconsistent and thus the underlying Hebrew is an absolute necessity.

The family of Miniamin/Mijamin were descendants of Mijamin the *ancestral* head over the sixth of the twenty-four divisions of Kohathite priests in Solomon's Temple (**1 Chronicles 24:9**).

19. The priestly family of Moadiah (**Nehemiah 12:17**) includes the Kohathite priest named Moadiah who returned to Jerusalem with Zerubbabel in 538 B.C. (**Nehemiah 12:5**). The priestly division head Moadiah may be a descendant of the *ancestral* division head named *Maaziah* who was over the twenty-fourth of the twenty-four divisions of Kohathite priests in Solomon's Temple (**1 Chronicles 24:18**) and the same person named Maaziah who sealed the covenant with Nehemiah in 444 B.C. (**Nehemiah 10:8**). Note the similarity: מועדיה (Moadiah) vs. מעזיה (Maaziah). Given the fact that the families of Moadiah and Miniamin are combined into one unit (as shown in the table), this suggests that each family may have been significantly reduced in number during the exile period to warrant separate priestly divisions.

20. The priestly family of Bilgah (**Nehemiah 12:5**) refers to the priest named Bilgah who was the *ancestral* head of over the fifteenth of the twenty-four divisions of Kohathite priests in Solomon's Temple (**1 Chronicles 24:14**). The priestly family of Bilgah includes the priest named Bilgah who returned to Jerusalem with Zerubbabel in 538 B.C. (**Nehemiah 12:5**) and also the priest named "Bilgai" (a descendant) who sealed the covenant with Nehemiah in 444 B.C. (**Nehemiah 10:8**). The difference is easily explained orthographically: בִּלְגָּה/בִּלְגַּי.

21. The priestly family of Shemaiah (**Nehemiah 12:18**) includes the priest Shemaiah who returned with Zerubbabel in 538 B.C. (**Nehemiah 12:6**) and the priest (a descendant) named Shemaiah who signed the covenant with Nehemiah in 444 B.C. (**Nehemiah 10:8**). Shemaiah the Kohathite priest should not be confused with the Levite Shemaiah son of Hasshub (**Nehemiah 11:15**).

22. The priestly family of Joiarib (**Nehemiah 12:19**; cf. "the son of Joiarib" in **Nehemiah 11:10**)—elsewhere called "Jehoiarib" (as in **1 Chronicles 9:10**)—refers to the Kohathite priest named "Jehoiarib" who was the *ancestral* head over the first of the twenty-four Kohathite priestly divisions in Solomon's Temple (**1 Chronicles 24:7**) and includes the priest named Joiarib who returned to Jerusalem with Zerubbabel in 538 B.C. (**Nehemiah 12:6**). The difference in spelling between Joiarib and J(eh)oiarib is explained by an orthographic/phonetic device called *syncope*, in which a "weak" syllable is passed over.

23. Two priests in the table are named Jedaiah, designated Jedaiah #1 (**Nehemiah 12:19**) and Jedaiah #2 (**Nehemiah 12:21**; see other references to Jedaiah in **1 Chronicles 9:10; Ezra 2:36; Nehemiah 7:39; 11:10; 12:6–7; Zechariah 6:10,14?**). It is likely that one (or both) of the Jedaiah figures is a descendant of the Kohathite priest named Jedaiah the *ancestral* head over the second of the twenty-four Kohathite priestly divisions in Solomon's Temple (**1 Chronicles 24:7**) and that the other Jedaiah figure is a relative of Joshua/Jeshua, the first high priest to officiate in the Second Temple—whose descendants are identified as "descendants of Jedaiah (through the family of Jeshua)" in **Ezra 2:36** and **Nehemiah 7:39**. For the genealogy of Jedaiah figures, see charts "**1 Chronicles 9**: The Kohathite Attending Priests in the Second Temple (Post-Exile)" and "**Ezra 7**: Ezra, the Priestly Scribe and Teacher of the Law (Post-Exile)."

24. Uzzi (**Nehemiah 12:19**) is probably the same priest named Uzzi in **Nehemiah 12:42**.

25. The priestly family of Sallu (**Nehemiah 12:20**) includes the priest named Sallu who returned to Jerusalem with Zerubbabel in 538 B.C. (**Nehemiah 12:7**).

26. The priestly family of Amok (**Nehemiah 12:20**) includes the priest named Amok who returned to Jerusalem with Zerubbabel in 538 B.C. (**Nehemiah 12:7**).

27. The priestly family of Hilkiah (**Nehemiah 12:21**) includes the priest named Hilkiah who returned to Jerusalem with Zerubbabel in 538 B.C. (**Nehemiah 12:7**).

28. Hashabiah the Kohathite priest (**Nehemiah 12:21**) may be the same person as Hashabiah the ruler of half the district of Keilah in post-exilic Jerusalem (**Nehemiah 3:17**).

29. For Jedaiah #2, see note 23.

30. Hashabiah the Levitical leader (**Nehemiah 12:24**) is either the same person as Hashabiah the son of Mattaniah (a Levitical Gershonite from the line of Asaph; **Nehemiah 11:22**) or Hashabiah the son of Bunni (a Levitical Merarite; **1 Chronicles 9:14; Nehemiah 11:15**; for the lineages of these two Levites, see chart "**Nehemiah 11**: The Levitical Leaders Chosen to Dwell in Jerusalem in the Post-Exile." Hashabiah the Levite (**Nehemiah 12:24**) is not Hashabiah the Kohathite priest of the family of Hilkiah (**Nehemiah 12:21**), shown in the table above, nor is he Hashabiah the priest in **Ezra 8:24**.

31. Sherebiah the Levite is likely the same person as Sherebiah in **Nehemiah 9:4–5; 10:12**. Sherebiah the Levite (**Nehemiah 12:24**) should not be confused with Sherebiah the Kohathite priest (**Ezra 8:24**).

32. Jeshua the son of Kadmiel (**Nehemiah 12:24**) does not refer to Jeshua/Joshua the high priest. Kadmiel and his son Jeshua, descendants of Hodaviah, helped in the construction of the Second Temple (**Ezra 2:40; 3:9; Nehemiah 7:43**). Jeshua's son may be Jozabad (**Ezra 8:33**).

33. Mattaniah the gatekeeper was a descendant of Asaph, the main Levitical Gershonite musician in Solomon's Temple (cf. **1 Chronicles 9:15; Nehemiah 11:17, 22; 12:35**). Mattaniah was also involved in leading the thanksgiving and prayer (**Nehemiah 11:17**); for his lineage, see chart "**Nehemiah 11**: The Levitical Leaders Chosen to Dwell in Jerusalem in the Post-Exile."

34. Bakbukiah of **Nehemiah 11:17; 12:9, 25** is doubtless Bakbakkar, a descendant of Asaph the Gershonite (**1 Chronicles 9:15**) For the evidence, see note 2 in chart "**1 Chronicles 9**: Seven Levitical Leaders in the Second Temple (Post-Exile)."

35. Obadiah the gatekeeper (**Nehemiah 12:25**) is the same person as the Levitical Merarite named Abda/Obadiah (**1 Chronicles 9:16; Nehemmiah 11:17**); for his lineage, see charts "**1 Chronicles 9**: Seven Levitical Leaders in the Second Temple (Post-Exile)" and "**Nehemiah 11**: The Levitical Leaders Chosen to Dwell in Jerusalem in the Post-Exile." Obadiah the Levitical gatekeeper is not (1) Obadiah the Kohathite priest who renewed the covenant with Nehemiah (**Nehemiah 10:5**); (2) Obadiah the Israelite clan leader (**Ezra 8:9**); or (3) Obadiah the prophet (**Obadiah 1:1**).

36. Meshullam in **Nehemiah 12:25** is probably the same person as Shallum who was the head Levitical gatekeeper in **1 Chronicles 9:17, 19**; for his lineage, see chart "**1 Chronicles 9**: Registry and Genealogy of the Levitical Gatekeepers and the Priestly Overseer of the Grain Offerings in the Second Temple (Post-Exile)."

37. Talmon the Levitical gatekeeper is mentioned in **1 Chronicles 9:17; Ezra 2:42; Nehemiah 7:45; 11:19; 12:25**.

38. Akkub the Levitical gatekeeper is mentioned in **1 Chronicles 9:17; Ezra 2:42; Nehemiah 7:45; 11:19; 12:25**.

39. For the distinction between the lineages of Aaron–Eleazar versus Aaron–Ithamar, see chart "**1 Chronicles 24**: Genealogical Registry of the Twenty-Four Divisions of Kohathite Attending Priests Who Rotated Service in Solomon's Temple."

40. Whether "family" (אָבוֹת) and "division" (מַחֲלֹקֶת) are synonymous is a matter of some disagreement, but on balance, a good case can be made for it.

41. Josephus, *Jewish Antiquities* 7.14.7

42. For specific comments by Jeremias and Edersheim, see the commentary in chart "**1 Chronicles 24**: Genealogical Registry of the Twenty-Four Divisions of Kohathite Attending Priests Who Rotated Service in Solomon's Temple." For a broader discussion of the clergy (priests and the twenty-four courses), see Joachim Jeremias, *Jerusalem in the Time of Jesus* (Philadephia: Fortress Press), 148–207 and Alfred Edersheim, *The Temple: Its Ministry and Services*, Updated Edition (Peabody, MA: Hendrickson Publishers), 55–73.

NEHEMIAH 12: GENEALOGICAL RECORD OF THE THANKSGIVING CHOIRS LED BY EZRA AND NEHEMIAH DURING THE DEDICATION OF THE WALL AROUND JERUSALEM AND THE CELEBRATION AT THE SECOND TEMPLE

Approximate Dating: ca. 444 B.C. ***Relevant Scriptures:*** **Nehemiah 12:31–42**

The First Thanksgiving Choir, Led by Ezra

One was to proceed on top of the wall to the right, toward the Dung Gate . . . At the Fountain Gate they continued directly up the steps of the City of David on the ascent to the wall and passed above the site of David's palace to the Water Gate on the east. (**Nehemiah 12:31, 37**)

North Side

*Tower of Hananel → *Tower of the Hundred → *Sheep Gate → *Fish Gate → *Gate of the Guard

West Side

*Jeshanah Gate
*Gate of Ephraim
><><>< Broad Wall
*Tower of the Ovens

=TEMPLE

East Side

*Water Gate

*Dung Gate
*Steps of the City of David
*Fountain Gate

South Side

Members of the First Choir

1. **Hoshaiah**
2. **Half the leaders of Judah**
3. **Azariah**[1]
4. **Ezra**[2]
5. **Meshullam**[3]
6. **Judah**[4]
7. **Benjamin**
8. **Shemaiah**[5]
9. **Jeremiah**[6]
10. **Priests with trumpets**
11. **Zechariah** (see lineage below)

Associates of Zechariah Who Played Musical Instruments[7]

1. **Shemaiah**[8]
2. **Azarel**
3. **Milalai**
4. **Gilalai**
5. **Maai**
6. **Nethanel**[9]
7. **Judah**[10]
8. **Hanani**

Lineage of Zechariah the Gershonite (Nehemiah 12:35)

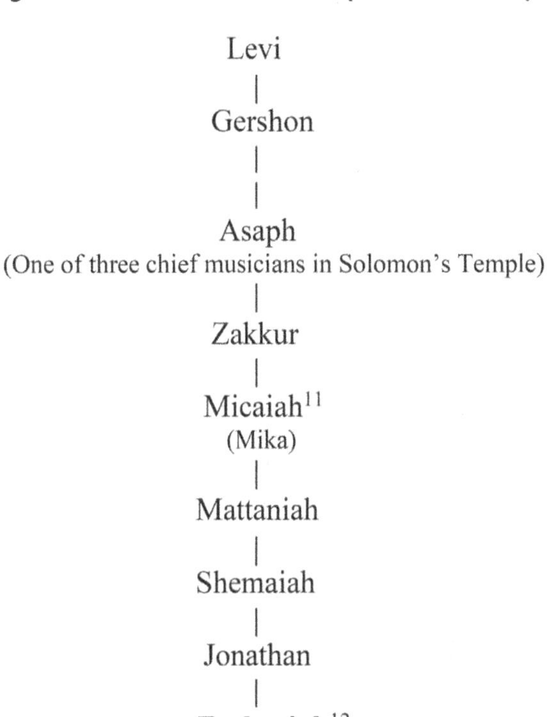

The Second Thanksgiving Choir, with Nehemiah Bringing Up the Rear

*The second choir proceeded in the opposite direction. I [Nehemiah] followed them on top of the wall, together with half the people—past the Tower of the Ovens to the Broad Wall, over the Gate of Ephraim, the Jeshanah Gate, the Fish Gate, the Tower of Hananel and the Tower of the Hundred, as far as the Sheep Gate. At the Gate of the Guard they stopped. (***Nehemiah 12:38–39***)*

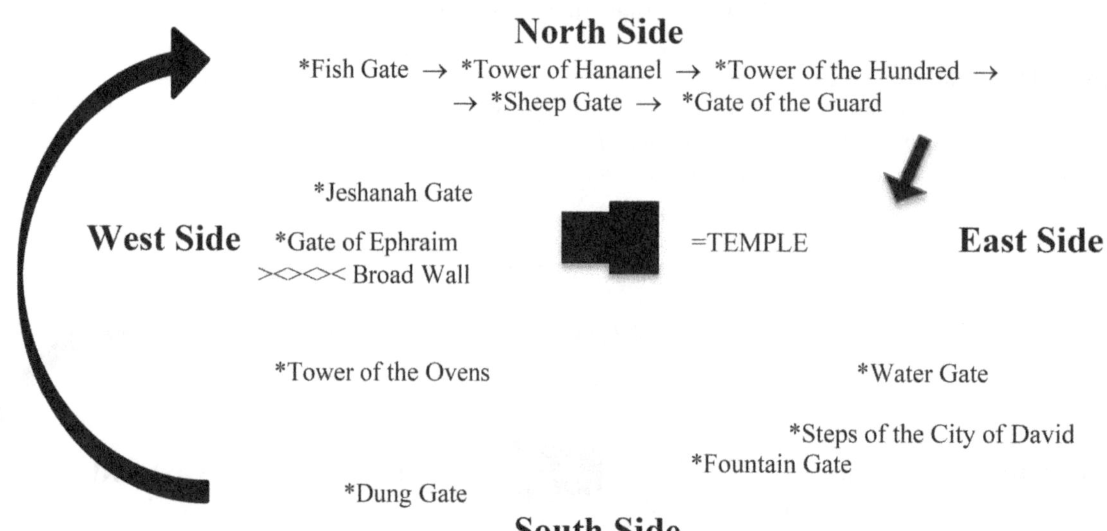

Those Present at the Celebration at the Second Temple

Kohathite Attending Priests

1. **Eliakim (Nehemiah 12:41)**
2. **Maaseiah (Nehemiah 12:41**; cf. **Ezra 10:18, 21–22; Nehemiah 3:23; 8:4)**
3. **Miniamin** (Mijamin)[13] **(Nehemiah 12:41**; cf. **1 Chronicles 24:9; Nehemiah 10:7; 12:5)**
4. **Micaiah (Nehemiah 12:41)**
5. **Elioenai (Nehemiah 12:41**; cf. **Ezra 10:22)**

Priests Who Played Trumpets

1. **Zechariah (Nehemiah 12:41**; cf. **1 Chronicles 15:24; 16:5; Nehemiah 8:4; 11:12; 12:16, 35)**
2. **Hananiah**[14] **(Nehemiah 12:41**; cf. **Nehemiah 12:12)**

Other Priests Who Were Present

1. **Maaseiah (Nehemiah 12:42**; cf. **Ezra 10:18, 21–22; Nehemiah 3:23; 8:4; 12:41)**
2. **Shemaiah (Nehemiah 12:42**; cf. **Ezra 10:21; Nehemiah 3:29; 10:8; 11:15; 12:6, 34–36)**
3. **Eleazar (Nehemiah 12:42**; cf. **Ezra 8:33)**
4. **Uzzi (Nehemiah 12:42**; cf. **Nehemiah 11:22; 12:19)**
5. **Jehohanan (Nehemiah 12:42**; cf. **Nehemiah 12:13)**
6. **Malkijah (Nehemiah 12:42**; cf. **1 Chronicles 24:9; Nehemiah 8:4; 10:3; 11:12)**
7. **Elam (Nehemiah 12:42)**
8. **Ezer (Nehemiah 12:42)**

Director of the two choirs: Jezrahiah (Nehemiah 12:42)

Biblical and Theological Significance

Music, both vocal and instrumental, has always been an integral part of all the world's known religions. In Israel's worship of Yahweh, the instrumental was never performed, it seems, apart from the vocal because the vocal could be employed by all the people, enabling the least musically gifted to have a part in the praise of their God. In formal worship, the leadership of the orchestras and choirs was the responsibility of Levites (**1 Chronicles 6:31–33; 9:33; 15:16–28; 23:5; 25:6–8; 2 Chronicles 5:12–13; 7:6; 23:13; 34:12; 35:15; Nehemiah 12:27–43**). The book of Psalms, of course, are replete with references to music and musicians.

On this special occasion, when the wall around the city of Jerusalem was finally completed in 444 B.C., a great ceremony of dedication and thanksgiving ensued, directed by Nehemiah the governor and Joshua the priest. The scene depicted in this passage must have been a stirring sight indeed. Musicians were summoned from all over the land, and when they arrived, they were ritually purified to bring them to an adequate state of holiness. Some were vocalists and others instrumentalists, all raising their praises and thanksgivings to Yahweh their God. When the two lines met, they strode over to the new temple and entered therein or gathered round about in a massive choir made up of priests, Levites, and the general population of the city.

Some sense of the great width of the wall may be seen by the files of Levites who ascended it and stood in formation in a great circle to sing and play hymns of thanksgiving (**Nehemiah 12:31–37**). One group moved in one direction, and the other in the opposite direction, meeting in the middle. All was done with instruments "prescribed by David the man of God" (**Nehemiah 12:36**), with Ezra himself leading one procession and Nehemiah the other.[15] The choirs then took their places in the Second Temple and sang together with joy under the direction of Jezrahiah—"And on that day they offered great sacrifices, rejoicing because God had given them great joy. The women and children also rejoiced. The sound of rejoicing in Jerusalem could be heard far away" (**Nehemiah 12:43**).

Notes

1. This Azariah may be "the official in charge of the house of God [Second Temple]" in the post-exile (**1 Chronicles 9:11**; cf. **Nehemiah 10:2**); for Azariah's genealogy see chart "**1 Chronicles 9**: The Kohathite Attending Priests in the Second Temple (Post-Exile)." Alternatively, he may be Azariah the Levite (**Nehemiah 8:7**).

2. This is not Ezra the scribal priest and teacher of the Law, but another priest of the same name who returned with Zerubbabel in 538 B.C. (i.e., "Ezra" the priest in **Nehemiah 12:1, 13**), who was still living in 444 B.C.

3. This may refer to Meshullam the priest (cf. **Nehemiah 3:4, 30; 6:18; 8:4; 10:7, 20; 12:13, 16**) but not to Shallum/Meshullam the high priest (cf. **1 Chronicles 6:12–13; 9:11; Ezra 7:2**; **Nehemiah 11:11**).

4. At least two Levites are named Judah (**Ezra 10:23; Nehemiah 12:8, 34, 36, 44**).

5. Shemaiah is a common Levitical name. Shemaiah in **Nehemiah 12:34** who was a member of the first choir should be compared (and perhaps distinguished from) other priestly and Levitical figures named Shemaiah who lived in the post-exile: (1) Shemaiah son of Hassub, the Levitical Merarite, who dwelled in Jerusalem (**1 Chronicles 9:14; Nehemiah 11:15**); (2) a descendant of Harim the priest who had taken a foreign wife (**Ezra 10:21**); (3) Shemaiah son of Shekaniah, who was the guard at the East Gate (**Nehemiah 3:29**); (4) Shemaiah the priest who sealed the covenant with Nehemiah (**Nehemiah 10:8**); (5) Shemaiah the priest who had returned to Jerusalem in 586 B.C. with Zerubbabel (**Nehemiah 12:6**); (6) another Shemaiah, also shown in this chart, who played a musical instrument and was an associate of Zechariah the trumpet player (**Nehemiah 12:36**); and (7) Shemaiah who was in the second choir with Nehemiah (**Nehemiah 12:42**).

6. This is not Jeremiah the prophet who prophesied from ca. 627–562 B.C.

7. As Levitical *associates* of Zechariah (the descendant of Asaph), they are likely his brethren from among the Gershonites; see chart "**1 Chronicles 6**: Levi: High Priests, Priests, Levites, and Musicians in Solomon's Temple."

8. Shemaiah the instrumentalist (**Nehemiah 12:36**) is probably a different person than Shemaiah the singer (**Nehemiah 12:34**); see note 5.

9. This may refer to Nethanel the priest a descendant of Pashhur (**Ezra 10:22**) or to Nethanel the head of the priestly family of Jedaiah (the ancestral priestly head of the Jedaiah division from the days of King David) who served in the days of Joiakim the high priest, ca. 490–450/444 B.C. (**Nehemiah 12:21**).

10. Judah is the name of an instrumentalist as well as a singer (see note 4).

11. Mika in **Nehemiah 11:22** is called Micaiah in **Nehemiah 12:35**.

12. Zechariah the Gershonite should not be confused with his contemporary, the gatekeeper Zechariah, a Kohathite-Korahite; see chart "**1 Chronicles 9**: Registry and Genealogy of the Levitical Gatekeepers and the Priestly Overseer of the Grain Offerings at the Second Temple (Post-Exile)."

13. The difference between Minjamin and Miniamin is strictly *plene* spelling or transliterational (מִנְיָמִן or מִנְיָמִין).

14. Hananiah the priest in **Nehemiah 12:41** may be the same priest named Hananiah (of Jeremiah the priest) in **Nehemiah 12:12**.

15. Alfred Edersheim suggests that services of praise were mainly sustained by the human voice of the Levites and notes that, in the Second Temple, female (as well as male) singers were represented (**Ezra 2:65; Nehemiah 7:67**). The dedication of the wall was celebrated "with songs of thanksgiving and with the music of cymbals, harps and lyres" (**Nehemiah 12:27**) such as: "Praise be to the LORD, the God of Israel from everlasting to everlasting" (**Psalm 41:13**, cf. **1 Chronicles 16:7–36**) and "Give thanks to the LORD Almighty, for the LORD is good; his love endures forever" (**Jeremiah 33:11**, cf. **Psalm 136:1**). The singing of the choirs may have been antiphonal, or in responses (**Ezra 3:10–11; Nehemiah 12:27, 40**). When the two choirs combined at the temple, they sang in unison (a practice that may have been similar in Solomon's Temple). This kind of music and responsive singing "might well serve in the Book of Revelation as imagery of heavenly realities" (cf. **Revelation 4:8, 11; 5:9, 12; 7:10–12**), where redeemed Israel will join in unison to "[sing] a new song before the throne" (**Revelation 14:1–3**; cf. **5:13; 19:6–7**). Alfred Edersheim, *The Temple: Its Ministry and Services* (Peabody, MA: Hendrickson, 1993), 53–54.

NEHEMIAH 13: GENEALOGICAL RECORD OF THE TREASURERS APPOINTED OVER THE TEMPLE STOREHOUSES

Approximate Dating: ca. 444 B.C. ***Relevant Scriptures:*** **Nehemiah 13:13**; cf. **Nehemiah 3:4, 25; 29–30; 11:17; Jeremiah 37:3**

Treasurers

1. **Shelemiah** the priest
2. **Zadok** the scribe
3. **Pedaiah** the Levite
4. **Hanan**

Possible Genealogy of Shelemiah the Kohathite Attending Priest

Shelemiah[1]
|
Hananiah

Possible Genealogy of Zadok the Scribal Priest[2]

Immer[3]
|
Zadok[4]

OR

Baana
|
Zadok[5]

Possible Genealogy of Pedaiah

Parosh[6]
|
Pedaiah[7]

Possible Genealogy of Hanan

Asaph
(Levitical Gershonite/
musician in Solomon's Temple
|
|
Mattaniah
|
Zakkur
|
Hanan[8]

Biblical and Theological Significance

Upon Nehemiah's[9] arrival in Jerusalem as governor, he had many responsibilities for reestablishing the former captives into a viable state. The organization of the temple staff, as well as the distribution of Levitical personnel throughout the land, was of first importance. Then, matters of security had to be addressed, such as the building of defensive walls and recruitment of men to serve as guards and militia. The economy of the state required strong basic principles, including fair taxation (**Nehemiah 5:4**), agricultural productivity (**Nehemiah 5:2–3, 10–11; 10:31–39**), and a disciplined and adequate labor supply (**Nehemiah 4:6, 10, 21–23; 6:9, 15**). When all this was in place and income to the treasury was beginning to multiply, Nehemiah appointed qualified persons to manage storerooms for the mandatory tithes and offerings and to manage payment to the priests, Levites, musicians, and others dependent on the largess of the government. The facilities for these had formerly been under the care of Eliashib the high priest, but his collaboration with the enemy and misappropriation of funds led to his dismissal and replacement. The storage rooms were thoroughly cleansed and renovated for proper management (**Nehemiah 13:4–9**).

Having thus reformed all the apparatuses of church and state, Nehemiah turned to persons he could trust to manage these various departments in a proper and God-honoring manner. Shelemiah the Kohathite priest, Zadok the scribe (a scribal priest), and Pedaiah the Levite, all assisted by Hanan, were commissioned to take charge because "they were considered trustworthy"[10] (**Nehemiah 13:12–13**).

Notes

1. Shelemiah the priest (**Nehemiah 13:13**) may be the same person as Shelemiah the father of Hananiah the priest, who repaired a section of the wall around Jerusalem in the days of Jeremiah (**Nehemiah 3:30**). Shelemiah the priest is not (1) a descendant of Binnui (i.e., one of the two Shelemiah figures in **Ezra 10:39, 41**); (2) the father of Hananiah the commander of the citadel, who was probably a Judahite (**Nehemiah 7:2**); or (3) other Shelemiah figures in the book of Jeremiah (cf. **Jeremiah 36:14, 26; 37:3, 13; 38:1**).

2. Scribes were typically the relatives/brethren of the (Kohathite) high priests. The high priest at the time of Nehemiah in 444 B.C. was Eliashib who served in the Second Temple from ca. 450/444–432 B.C. (cf. **Nehemiah 3:1, 20; 12:10**).

3. Immer may be the ancestor of Zadok; Immer had been the head over the sixteenth of the twenty-four divisions of Kohathite attending priests in the days of King David; therefore, Zadok the scribe in **Nehemiah 13:13** is probably a *descendant* or *relative* of Immer, but not his *son* (cf. **1 Chronicles 24:14; Ezra 2:37; Nehemiah 7:40**). For the lineage of scribes, see note 2.

4. Zadok may be the same person mentioned in **Nehemiah 3:29** "who made repairs opposite his house" during the building of the wall around Jerusalem. He is not the Zadok of **Nehemiah 10:21,** the high priest named Zadok of a much earlier time period (i.e., Zadok who served under King David, 1011–971 B.C., nor Zadok who served under King Hezekiah, 715–686 B.C.).

5. Zadok may be the same person mentioned in **Nehemiah 3:4** who repaired a section of the wall between the Fish Gate and the Jeshanah Gate (cf. **Nehemiah 3:3–6**); for other Zadok figures, see note 4.

6. Parosh the Levite (**Nehemiah 13:13**) is not Parosh, the head of an Israelite family (**Ezra 2:3; 8:3; 10:25; Nehemiah 7:8; 10:14**).

7. Pedaiah the Levite in **Nehemiah 13:13** is probably Pedaiah the son of Parosh, who was a worker on the wall around Jerusalem (**Nehemiah 3:25**); alternatively, he may be the person named Pedaiah who stood on the platform with Ezra in 458 B.C. for the reading of the Law (**Nehemiah 8:4**). For chronological reasons, Pedaiah in **Nehemiah 13:13** does not refer to Pedaiah the Judahite, the father of Zerubbabel (**1 Chronicles 3:18–19**).

8. Hanan may be a *descendant*, rather than a son, of Zakkur. Compare the genealogy of Hanan given in **Nehemiah 13:13** with other descendants of Asaph, Zakkur, and Mattaniah in **Nehemiah 11:17; 12:35**. See the lineage of Zakkur in chart "**Nehemiah 12**: Genealogical Record of the Thanksgiving Choirs Led by Ezra and Nehemiah During the Dedication of the Wall around Jerusalem and the Celebration at the Second Temple."

9. Nehemiah initially went to Jerusalem in 444 B.C., in the twentieth year of Artaxerxes I (465–424 B.C.; cf. **Nehemiah 2:1**). He held the governorship over the satrap for twelve years, from 444–433 B.C. (**Nehemiah 5:14**). Then in 432 B.C., he was recalled to Persia and upon his return to Jerusalem "learned about the evil thing Eliashib [the high priest] had done" (**Nehemiah 13:6–7**). Since Eliashib held the priesthood from 450/444–432 B.C., Nehemiah presumably stayed in Persia only briefly during 432 B.C. before returning to Jerusalem. The second time, Nehemiah remained in Jerusalem for an unspecified length of time.

10. The Hebrew term here, אָמַן (*aman*), fundamentally bears the nuance of reliability, firmness, something to lean on. These were men upon whom Nehemiah could utterly depend. Prayer is generally closed with the same word, *amen*, "may it be!"

NEHEMIAH 13: INTERMARRIAGE OF JEWS AND SAMARITANS THAT COMPROMISED THE PURITY OF THE HOLY PRIESTHOOD OF ISRAEL

Approximate Dating: ca. 450 B.C. ***Relevant Scriptures:*** **Nehemiah 13:28–29;** also Josephus' *Jewish Antiquities* 11.7.2[1]

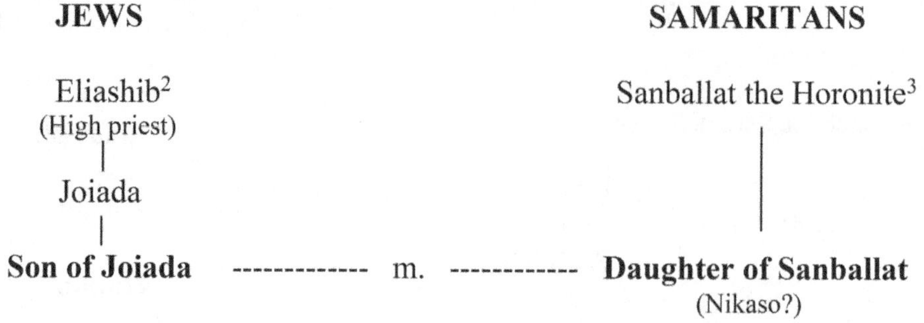

High Priestly Line in the Post-Exile (1 Chronicles 6:15; Nehemiah 12:10–12, 22, 26)

Jozadak
(High priest who was carried into Babylonian captivity in 586 B.C.)
|
Joshua
(Jeshua)
(First high priest to officiate in the Second Temple)
(ca. 516–490 B.C.)
|
Joiakim
(ca. 490–450/445 B.C.)
|
Eliashib
(ca. 450/445–432 B.C.)
|
Joiada
(ca. 432–410 B.C.)
|
Jonathan[4]
(Johanan)
(ca. 410–370 B.C.)
|
Jaddua
(ca. 370–332 B.C.)
(A contemporary of Alexander the Great)

Biblical and Theological Significance

Sanballat was the governor over Samaria. Nehemiah refers to him as Sanballat the "Horonite" (**Nehemiah 2:10, 19; 13:28**)—possibly indicating that he controlled the Samarian twin cities of Upper and Lower Beth Horon; the Horon pass led into the Aijalon Valley, the major route from the hill country to the coastal plains,[5] and, as a result, influenced the economy of Jerusalem. Beginning in 444 B.C., Sanballat and two other neighboring foes, Tobiah the Ammonite and Geshem the Arab, conspired against Nehemiah multiple times to oppose the rebuilding effort in Jerusalem (**Nehemiah 2:10, 19; 4:1–3, 7–8, 11–12; 6:1–2, 5, 10–14**).

Following the destruction of Samaria and the slaughter and deportation of most of its population by the Assyrians in 722 B.C., the king of Assyria took "people from Babylon, Kuthah, Avva, Hamath and Sepharvaim and settled them in the towns of Samaria to replace the Israelites" (**2 Kings 17:24**). Priests who had been taken captive from Samaria were sent to teach the foreigners how to worship the God of Israel; however, "each national group made its own gods in the several towns where they settled, and set them up in the shrines the people of Samaria had made at the high places" (**2 Kings 17:29**). These peoples influenced the remaining Israelites, and intermarriage occurred even though it was contrary to Mosaic Law (cf. **Deuteronomy 7:3–4; 23:2; Joshua 23:12–13; 1 Kings 11:1–2; Ezra chs, 9–10**). As the chart shows, intermarriage with the Samaritans reached as high up the social scale as the high priesthood, as exemplified by the marriage of one of the sons of Joiada,[6] the high priest, to the daughter of Sanballat (**Nehemiah 13:28**). These marriages were encouraged as a means to stay apprised of the activities in the temple and Jerusalem and to influence policies that would be favorable toward them. The Babylonian nature of his name suggests that Sanballat was either a native Babylonian sent on foreign duty or an exilic Jew who had become pro-Babylonia.

The Samaritan principality thus lost its identity and became a religious sect within Judaism by the first century A.D. However, it was never received as an authentic expression of Judaism, as the New Testament and other writings make clear (**John 4:4–28; Acts 8:4–17**). Nonetheless, certain scholars among them had generated their own version of the Pentateuch, known today as the Samaritan Pentateuch. Its quality was so superb that it is used by modern text critics as an aid in recovering the original Pentateuch of Moses.[7] However, since the rest of the Old Testament did not treat the Samaritans kindly, they rejected all writings except the Pentateuch as being canonical, especially Ezra–Nehemiah, for obvious reasons.

A small community still exists in Israel at Mount Gerizim where a small temple stands. Nearby is Jacob's Well, dug by the patriarch and protected by a stone curb, perhaps the one upon which Jesus sat as he conversed with the Samaritan woman (**John 4:6**).

Notes

1. *Jewish Antiquities* in *The Complete Works of Josephus*, trans. William Whiston, commentary by Paul L. Maier. (Grand Rapids: Kregel, 1999).

2. Eliashib the high priest in the days of Nehemiah helped rebuild the Sheep Gate in the wall around Jerusalem (**Nehemiah 3:1**). Eliashib's house was next to the city wall (**Nehemiah 3:20–21**).

3. Sanballat I (the Horonite) was the "founder of his dynasty and a contemporary of Nehemiah and Eliashib . . . [and] of Joiada and Johanan as indicated in the Bible and the Elephantine papyri." Benjamin E. Scolnic, *Chronology and Papponymy: A List of the Judean High Priests of the Persian Period* (Atlanta: Scholars Press, 1999), 13.

4. In **Nehemiah 12:11** he is called Jonathan, whereas in **Nehemiah 12:22-23**, he is identified as Johanan, and "Jehohanan son [grandson] of Eliashib" in **Ezra 10:6**. He is called John by Josephus, *Jewish Antiquities* 11.7.1-2; cf. 11.5.4.

5. For information on the strategic location of Upper and Lower Beth Horon, see John Walton et. al., IV*P Old Testament Background Commentary*, "Joshua 10:1–43," 223, accessed at Accordance Bible Software.

6. Contrary to the biblical text, Josephus writes that it was Jaddua's *brother* (Manasseh)—not Joiada's *son* (**Nehemiah 13:28**)—that married Sanballat's daughter: "when John [Jonathan/Johanan the high priest] had departed this life, his son Jaddua succeeded in the high priesthood. He [Jaddua] had a brother, whose name was Manasseh. Now there was one Sanballat, who was sent by Darius, the last king [of Persia], into Samaria. He [Sanballat] was a Cuthean by birth; of which stock were the Samaritans also . . . he [Sanballat] willingly gave his daughter, whose name was Nicaso, in marriage to Manasseh, as thinking this alliance by marriage would be a pledge and security that the nation of the Jews should continue their goodwill to him" (*Jewish Antiquities* 11.7.2; cf. 11.8.2).

7. Ellis R. Brotzman, *Old Testament Textual Criticism. A Practical Introduction* (Grand Rapids: Baker, 1994).

ESTHER 2: MORDECAI AND ESTHER, JEWS LIVING IN PERSIA

Approximate Dating: during the reign of Xerxes I in Persia, 486–465 B.C.; narrative events take place ca. 483–465 B.C.[1] ***Relevant Scriptures:*** **Esther 2:5–7, 15; 9:29;** also **1 Samuel 9:1–2; 1 Chronicles 8:29–40; 9:35–44**

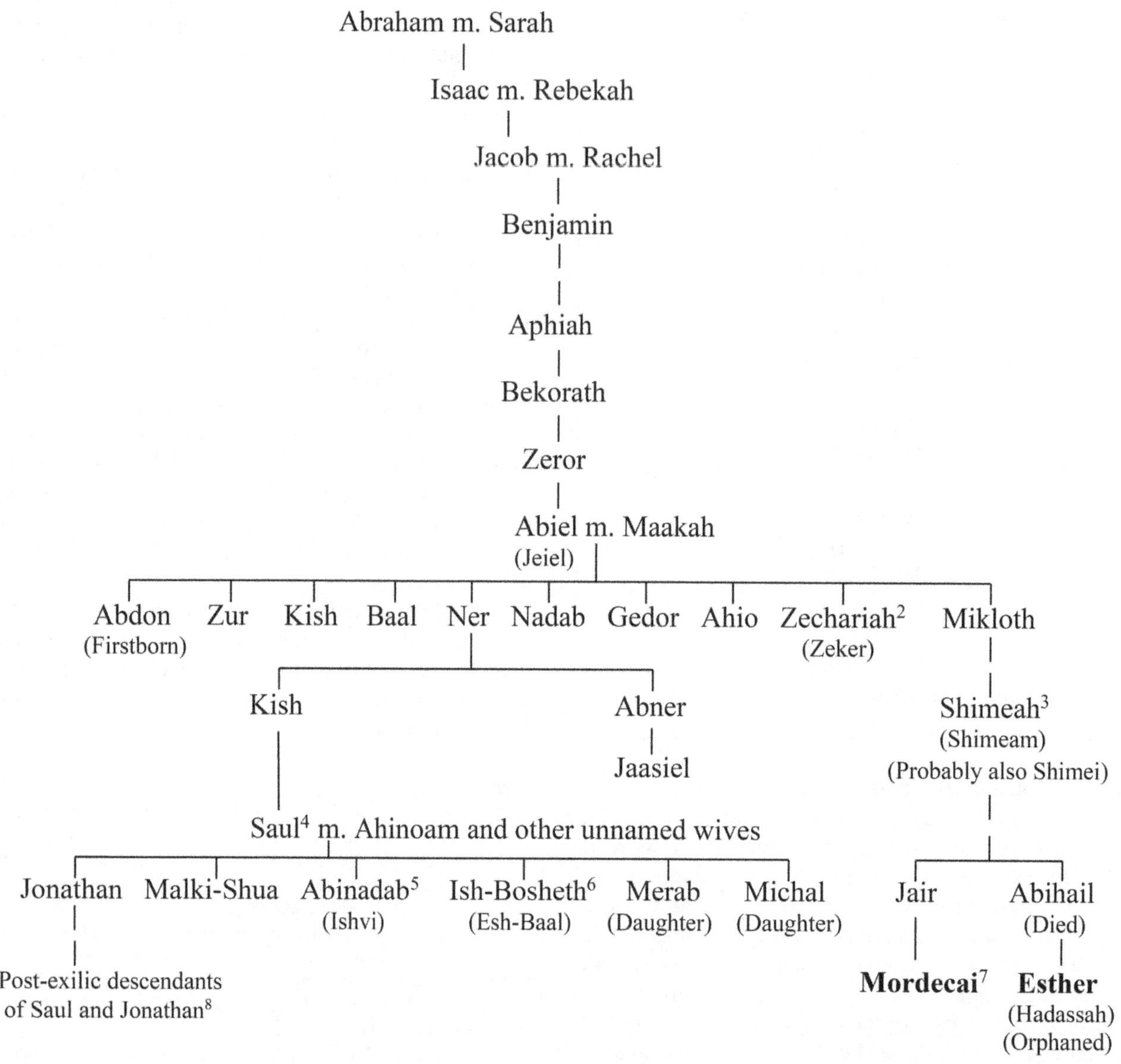

Biblical and Theological Significance

Xerxes I, or Ahasuerus (אֲחַשְׁוֵרוֹשׁ in Hebrew),[9] was a descendant of Cyrus the Great of the Achaemenid Dynasty, whose achievements had included the conquest of Babylon in 539 B.C. Cyrus, the great liberator, had benignly permitted all people who had been taken captive, including the Jews, to return to their various lands. Most Jews made their way back to Jerusalem after nearly seventy long years in captivity; however, many opted not to leave, particularly the young who had embraced Persia as their birth home. Among those who had settled comfortably in Susa (Heb. *Shushan*),[10] the winter capital of Persia, were Mordecai, the son of Jair, and his younger cousin Esther, the daughter of Mordecai's uncle Abihail (**Esther 2:7, 15; 9:29**). Mordecai's eventual prominence in the Persian court shows that Jews could rise to the highest levels of government and society. Yet Mordecai forbade Esther to disclose her Jewish identity, as well as his.[11, 12]

The book begins in the third year of Xerxes I (ca. 483 B.C.), when he was in Susa presiding over a lavish banquet in honor of his subordinates from all over the empire. After six months of exhibiting the splendor of his court, Xerxes demanded that his queen Vashti be brought before the assembly to parade her beauty before them as further evidence of his splendor (**Esther 1:10–12**). When she refused, Xerxes deposed her and sought another to take her place as queen (**Esther 2:1–4**). Thus the way was paved for the introduction of Esther, the young Jewess. After the requisite time of preparation, Esther was made queen in 479 B.C., corresponding to Xerxes' seventh year (**Esther 2:17**).[13]

Later, during the course of events, Mordecai uncovered a plan to assassinate the king (**Esther 2:19–23**; cf. **6:1–3**). When Xerxes promoted Haman to prime minister, he required all other officials to kneel in Haman's presence, although Mordecai refused to do so since such behavior was contrary to his convictions as a Jew. In retaliation, Haman the Agagite[14] devised a plan to get rid of Mordecai by initiating a pogrom against all Jews (**Esther 3:1–14**). Haman's suggestion to target Jews appealed to the king, so an edict of annihilation was issued in the twelfth year of Xerxes, 474 B.C. Disturbed by the gravity of the situation, Esther bravely revealed her Jewish identity for the first time[15] and told the king all that Haman had plotted against her people (**Esther 7:1–7**). She used her position as a means to rescue her fellow Jews from annihilation at the hands of anti-Semites (**Esther 8:11–17**). Xerxes immediately put Haman to death (impaled on the pole that Haman had built for Mordecai) and issued a countermanding decree authorizing Jews throughout the empire to protect themselves against Haman's evil purge (**Esther 7:10–8:14**). Local officials joined in the effort to put down the anti-Jewish campaign (**Esther 9:1–3**).

The Feast of Purim (from *pur*, the "lot" that was cast; cf. **Esther 3:7; 9:24**) was instituted to commemorate the miraculous deliverance of the Jews and mark the turning of sorrow into joy (**Esther 9:26–28**). Along with the Mosaic festivals, Purim has been canonized as Torah and is celebrated by every generation of Jews to commemorate God's ongoing love and care for his people Israel.

Esther was so significant that her name became attached to a book of Scripture. At the same time, the book's canonicity was challenged in early Judaism because it lacked reference to God by name. However, the hand of the God of Israel was evident, and the Spirit of God prevailed. The book offers unique insights into parts of the post-exilic experience for some Jewish people, which are otherwise undocumented. The book of Esther remains a favorite of many who see the invisible mark of God at work in redemptive history and in the personal and national affairs of his people. Thus far, the book of Esther has not been found in the Dead Sea Scrolls.

Notes

1. The 180-day display of the vast wealth of Xerxes' kingdom occurred in 483–482 B.C., followed by a seven-day grand banquet in Xerxes' third year, 483/482 B.C. (**Esther 1:3**); Esther's first appearance before Xerxes occurred in Xerxes' seventh year, December 479 or January 478 B.C. (**Esther 2:16**); Esther's tenure as queen lasted ca. 479–473 B.C.; Haman proposed a plot against the Jews in April, 474 B.C., in Xerxes' twelfth year (**Esther 3:7**); the king's mandate "to destroy, kill and annihilate all the Jews . . . . on a single day, the thirteenth day of the twelfth month, the month of Adar" corresponded to April 17, 474 B.C. (**Esther 3:12–13**); the edict of "Mordecai's orders to the Jews . . . in the name of King Xerxes" took place on June 25, 474 B.C., permitting the Jews to protect themselves from annihilation (**Esther 8:9–10**); "the day appointed for the Jews to do this" was on March 7, 473 B.C., when "the Jews struck down their enemies" (**Esther 8:12; 9:1, 5**); and the observance of "Purim, from the word *pur*" was to be observed for "two days every year" (**Esther 8:26–27**). Traditionally, modern Jews observe Purim on the 14th day of the Hebrew month of Adar (around February/March)—the day following the victory of the Jews over their enemies (the 13th day of Adar)—and observe a fast (called "the fast of Esther") on the 13th of Adar. Mordecai the Jew was "second in rank to King Xerxes," presumably until Xerxes was murdered in 465 B.C. (cf. **Esther 10:3**); see note 7 in chart "**Supplement 5**: The Kings of Persia."

2. Zeker (**1 Chronicles 8:31**) is hypocoristic for Zechariah (**1 Chronicles 9:37**).

3. Shimeah (שִׁמְאָה, *shimah*) the son/descendant of Milkoth the Benjamite in **1 Chronicles 8:32** is called Shimeam (שִׁמְאָם, *shimam*) the Benjamite in **1 Chronicles 9:38**. Shimeah/Shimeam also appears to be the same person as: (a) Shimei in **Esther 2:5** where Mordecai is identified as "Mordecai son of Jair, the son of Shimei, the son [relative] of Kish," referring to Kish the Benjamite, the father of King Saul (**1 Samuel 9:2–3; 14:51; 2 Samuel 21:14; 1 Chronicles 8:33**) and possibly (b) Shimei ("the clan of Shimei") in **Zechariah 12:13**; "the people from Benjamin numbered 956" compared to "the people from Judah [who] numbered 690" in post-exilic Jerusalem (**1 Chronicles 9:3–9**). Clans of Judahites, Levites, and Benjamites were deported to Babylon when Nebuchadnezzar made his second invasion of Jerusalem in 598/597 B.C. (cf. **2 Kings 24:10–12**), and Mordecai and Esther's ancestors appear to be among the Benjamite captives. However, some Benjamites chose to return in the post-exile and settle near their relatives in Jerusalem (**1 Chronicles 8:32; 9:38**); see chart "**1 Chronicles 8 & 9**: The Descendants of King Saul Living in Gibeon and Jerusalem (Post-Exile)."

4. For the descendants of Saul and Jonathan who lived in the post-exile, see charts "**1 Samuel 9**: King Saul" and "**1 Chronicles 8 & 9**: The Descendants of King Saul Living in Gibeon and Jerusalem (Post-Exile)."

5. Abinadab in **1 Samuel 31:2; 1 Chronicles 8:33; 9:39; 10:2** is called Ishvi in **1 Samuel 14:49**.

6. Ish-Bosheth in **2 Samuel 2:8, 10, 12, 15; 3:7–8, 11, 14–15; 4:1, 5, 8, 12** is called Esh-Baal in **1 Chronicles 8:33; 9:39**. After Saul's death in 1011 B.C., his military commander Abner held power in Israel; eventually, at age 40, Ish-Bosheth/Esh-Baal succeeded his father (Saul) as king of Israel but reigned from Mahanaim for a brief two years (ca. 1005–1004 B.C) before he was assassinated (**2 Samuel 2:8–11; 4:5–12**).

7. When Esther was orphaned, Mordecai (presumably older) raised her like she was his own daughter (**Esther 2:5–7**). Mordecai in **Ezra 2:2** and **Nehemiah 7:7** who returned to Jerusalem with Zerubbabel in ca. 538 B.C. is not the same person as Mordecai in the book of Esther.

8. For the descendants of Saul and Jonathan who lived in the post-exile, see chart "**1 Chronicles 8 & 9**: The Descendants of King Saul Living in Gibeon and Jerusalem (Post-Exile)."

9. Ahasuerus is not an alternative name but a rough attempt to transliterate Persian—an Indo-European language—into Hebrew, a Semitic language. For the genealogy and succession of the rulers of Persia, see chart "**Supplement 5**: The Kings of Persia."

10. The Hebrew name for the city, it seems, was Shushan, but nearly always the name is coupled with הַבִּירָה *habirah*, "the citadel," "the acropolis," or the like. This gives the impression of a city heavily protected and safely secured. For another well-known example, see the term applied to Jerusalem, where it is rendered "citadel" by the NIV (**Nehemiah 2:8; 7:2**). Susa was only one of the four capitals of the Persians; the others were Ecbatana, Babylon, and Persepolis. Susa was the location of Daniel's visions (**Daniel 8:2**) and where Nehemiah had served as the cupbearer to King Artaxerxes I (**Nehemiah 1:1, 11**).

11. Some of the following commentary is an excerpt from the Eugene Merrill's *Kingdom of Priests: A History of Old Testament Israel*, 2nd ed. (Grand Rapids: Baker Academic, 2008), 512–514.

12. The assimilation of Mordecai and Esther (Benjamites) into their Babylonian-Persian world is clear from their name changes. "Mordecai" is a Hebrew transliteration of the Babylonian divine name Marduk, consort of Ishtar and head of the Babylonian pantheon. Why a pious Jew should do this is not easy to answer unless it was demanded of him. His cousin's name is similarly pagan in its overtones. "Esther" is a form of Ishtar, the Babylonian goddess of love and war. Her birth name Hadassah, meaning myrtle, would have been the name she was called by the Jewish community.

13. By then Xerxes I had brought both Egypt and Babylonia under control and had launched his unsuccessful campaign against the Greek states. It will be recalled that Xerxes had returned from the west by 479 B.C., leaving Mardonius to suffer defeat in the battle of Plataea. It seems clear that Esther became queen shortly after Xerxes retired back to Persia from his Greek adventures.

14. See chart "**Esther 3**: Haman the Agagite."

15. Esther asked for two things: "grant me my life . . . and spare my people" for "I and my people have been sold to be destroyed, killed and annihilated" (**Esther 7:3–4**).

ESTHER 3: HAMAN THE AGAGITE

Approximate Dating: ca. 480 B.C. ***Relevant Scriptures:*** **Esther 3:1, 10; 5:10, 14; 6:13; 8:3, 5; 9:7–10, 12–13, 24**; also **Genesis 26:34; 36:1–14; 1 Samuel 15:8–33; 1 Chronicles 1:34–37**

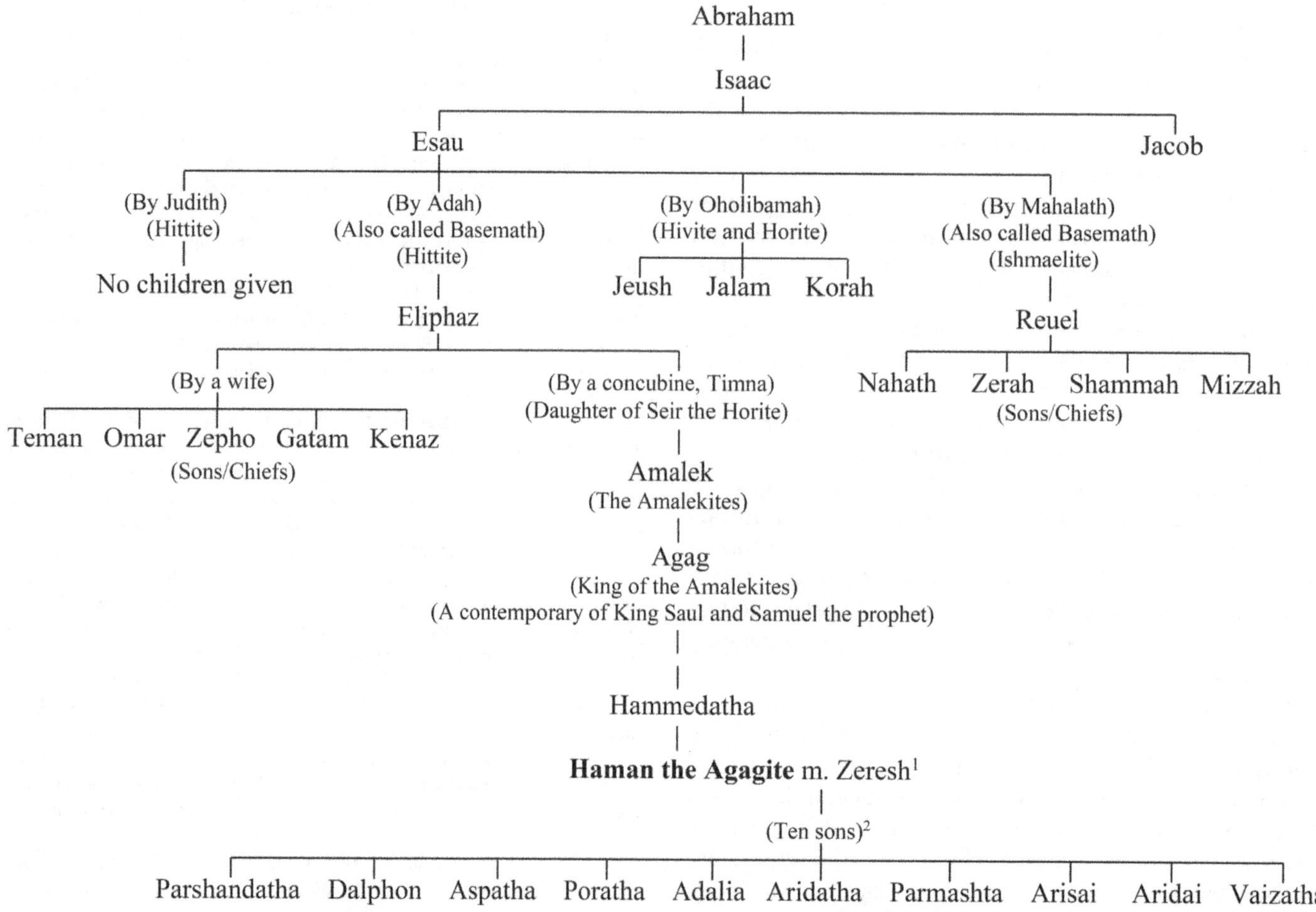

Biblical and Theological Significance

Why and how Haman's ancestors migrated to Persia may never be known. Very possibly they had been caught up in the various Assyrian and Babylonian deportations that, according to texts from the archives of these nations, encompassed other nations besides Israel and Judah (cf. **Isaiah 34:5–12; Jeremiah 49:17–19; Ezekiel 25:12–14; Obadiah 18**). On the other hand, profiteers and sycophants were willing to travel far and wide to achieve their ends. The shrewd and clever Haman the Edomite may have found himself in the land of plenty where he insinuated his way to the top of Persian bureaucracy—just under the king in rank and power.[3] There is no textual information to explain the man, his origins, and his political success, only plausible scenarios. More importantly, the story of Esther and Haman shows the perpetuation of the ancient feud between Jacob (the Israelite) and his brother Esau (the Edomite) that began before they were born (**Genesis 25:21–28; 27:1–41**) and continued to the end of the Old Testament period (**Obadiah 1–4, 10–14; Malachi 1:2–3**). After centuries of oppressing the Israelites, Edom, personified by Haman, encounters God's swift justice, and Israel is saved through the actions of Esther and Mordecai.

Notes

1. Zeresh was the wife and counselor of Haman (**Esther 5:10, 14; 6:13**). Her name is Old Persian with the less-than-flattering meaning "mop-head" ("זֶרֶשׁ," *HALOT* 1:283).

2. In Esther's request before King Xerxes, she requested that Haman's ten sons be impaled on the same pole as their father had been, and the king granted her request (**Esther 9:13–14**; cf. **7:10**).

3. Haman was the grand vizier to King Ahasuerus (Xerxes I) of Persia. He was a descendant of the Amalekites and the descendant of Agag, so he was called Haman the Agagite (**Esther 3:1, 10; 8:5**). Haman was the symbolic archenemy of the Jews, past and present (**Esther 3:10; 9:10, 24**). Esther called Haman "An adversary and enemy! This vile Haman!" (**Esther 7:6**), referring, in part, to the age-old hostility between the Jews and the Amalekites/Agagites; refer to the chart "**Genesis 36**: Amalek, the Ancestor of the Amalekites."

JOB 1: THE FAMILY OF JOB

Approximate Dating: in the general timeframe of ca. 2000–1800 B.C., as a contemporary of Abraham (2166–1991 B.C.), Isaac (2066–1886 B.C.), and/or Jacob (2006–1859 B.C.) and Esau (born 2006 B.C.) ***Relevant Scriptures:*** **Job 1:1–4, 13, 18–19; 2:9–10; 19:17; 31:10; 42:11, 13–16**

Job's Family (Known Genealogy)

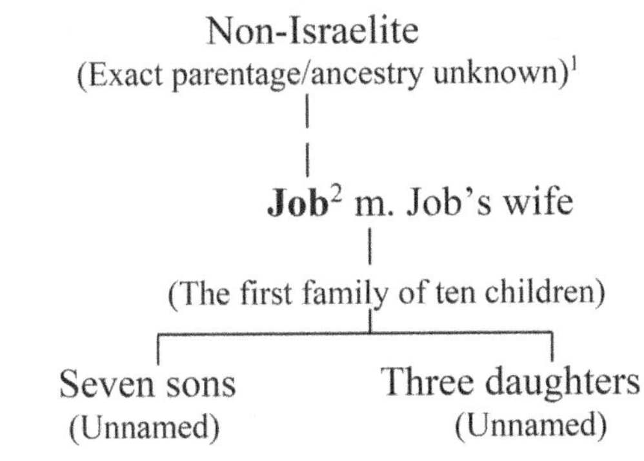

------- *Job's trials and restoration to health*[3] -------

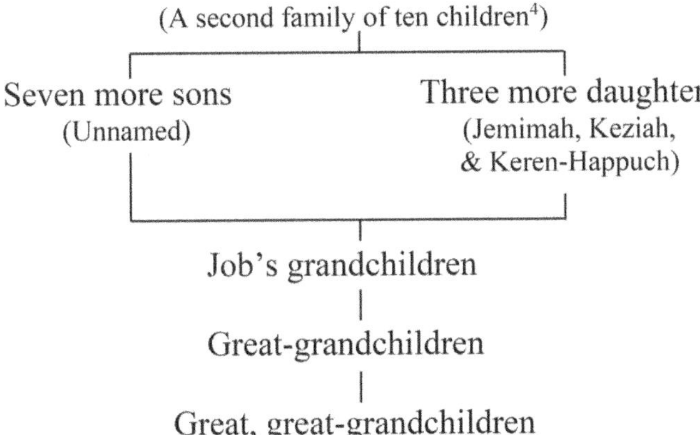

Biblical and Theological Significance

Job was a real historical person, characterized as a man who was blameless (*tam*) and upright (*yashar*). He feared God and was considered "the greatest man among all the people of the East" (**Job 1:3**). In spite of losing his first family of seven sons and three daughters and his wife trying to convince him to "Curse God and die" (**Job 2:9**),[5] Job remained faithful to God and "did not sin by charging God with wrongdoing" (**Job 1:22**). Job's second family also consisted of seven sons and three daughters. These daughters inherited properties and goods (Heb. נַחֲלָה, *nahala*) along with their brothers. The women were known for their exceptional beauty. Jemimah's name means "turtledove"; Keziah's name means "cassia," a prized variety of cinnamon; and Keren-Happuch's name means "horn of antinomy" or "horn of eye paint."[6]

After Job's trials and his prayerful intercession for his friends, the Lord restored his fortune and family (**Job 42:10–17**): "After this, Job lived a hundred and forty years;[7] he saw his children and their children to the fourth generation" (**Job 42:16**). The expression in **Job 42:17**, "full of years" (Heb. יָמִים שְׂבַע), is also used elsewhere for Abraham (**Genesis 25:8**), Isaac (**Genesis 35:29**), David (**1 Chronicles 23:1**), and Jehoiada[8] the faithful Kohathite priest (**2 Chronicles 24:15**). Job's death was the culmination of a full life and the completion of his story. The end of his life was not a failing, fading or a weakening, but a filling up to the brim—a fullness and a satiation of days.[9]

Notes

1. See chart "**Job 1**: Possible Ancestry of Job the Patriarch."

2. Job's parents are unknown; his brothers and sisters are mentioned in **Job 19:13; 42:11.**

3. **Job 42:12** reads, "The Lord blessed the latter part of Job's life more than the former part" and **Job 42:16** reads, "After this [after his trials], Job lived a hundred and forty years; he saw his children and their children to the fourth generation." Unfortunately, the "former part" of his life in years (i.e., *before* his trials) is unknown. Interestingly, **Job 42:16** in the Septuagint (LXX) reads, "And Job lived after affliction a hundred and seventy years: and all the years he lived were two hundred and forty: and Job saw his sons and his sons' sons, the fourth generation."

4. The numbers three, seven, and ten symbolized the ideal family (**Job 1:2; 42:13**; cf. **1 Samuel 1:8**).

5. Job's wife speaks only in **Job 2:9** where she says, "Are you still maintaining your integrity? Curse God and die!" Cline suggests that Job's retort to his wife in **Job 2:10**—"You are talking like a foolish woman"—should be understood to mean "You talk like a low-class, irreligious woman; such words are beneath you." David J. A. Clines, *Job 1–20*, WBC 17 (Nashville: Thomas Nelson, 2011), 50–54.

6. For a discussion of the names Jemimah, Keziah, and Keren-Happuch, see David J. A. Clines, *Job 38–42*, WBC 18B (Nashville: Thomas Nelson, 2011), 1229, notes 14a, 14 b, and 14c.

7. Compare the lifespan of Job with other patriarchal figures such as Terah, who died at 205; Abraham, who died at 175; and Isaac, who died at 180 (cf. **Genesis 11:32; 25:7; 35:28**, respectively).

8. For Jehoiada, see chart "**2 Chronicles 22**: Probably Genealogy for Jehoiada the Priest who Masterminded the Overthrow of Queen Athaliah of Judah."

9. This paraphrases David J. A. Clines, *Job 38–42*, WBC 18B (Nashville: Thomas Nelson, 2011), 1240.

JOB 1: POSSIBLE ANCESTRY OF JOB THE PATRIARCH[1]

Approximate Dating: in the general timeframe of 2000–1800 B.C., as a contemporary of Abraham (2166–1991 B.C.), Isaac (2066–1886 B.C.), and/or Jacob (2006–1859 B.C.) and Esau (born 2006 B.C.)[2]

Job's Ancestry: Two Possibilities

1. **Job as a patriarchal figure—a descendant in the Noah–Shem–Terah–Nahor line (Job 1:1,** also **Genesis 11:10–31; 22:20-23; 24:15, 24, 47; 25:19–20; 29:5; 1 Chronicles 1:24-27; Luke 3:34–36)**

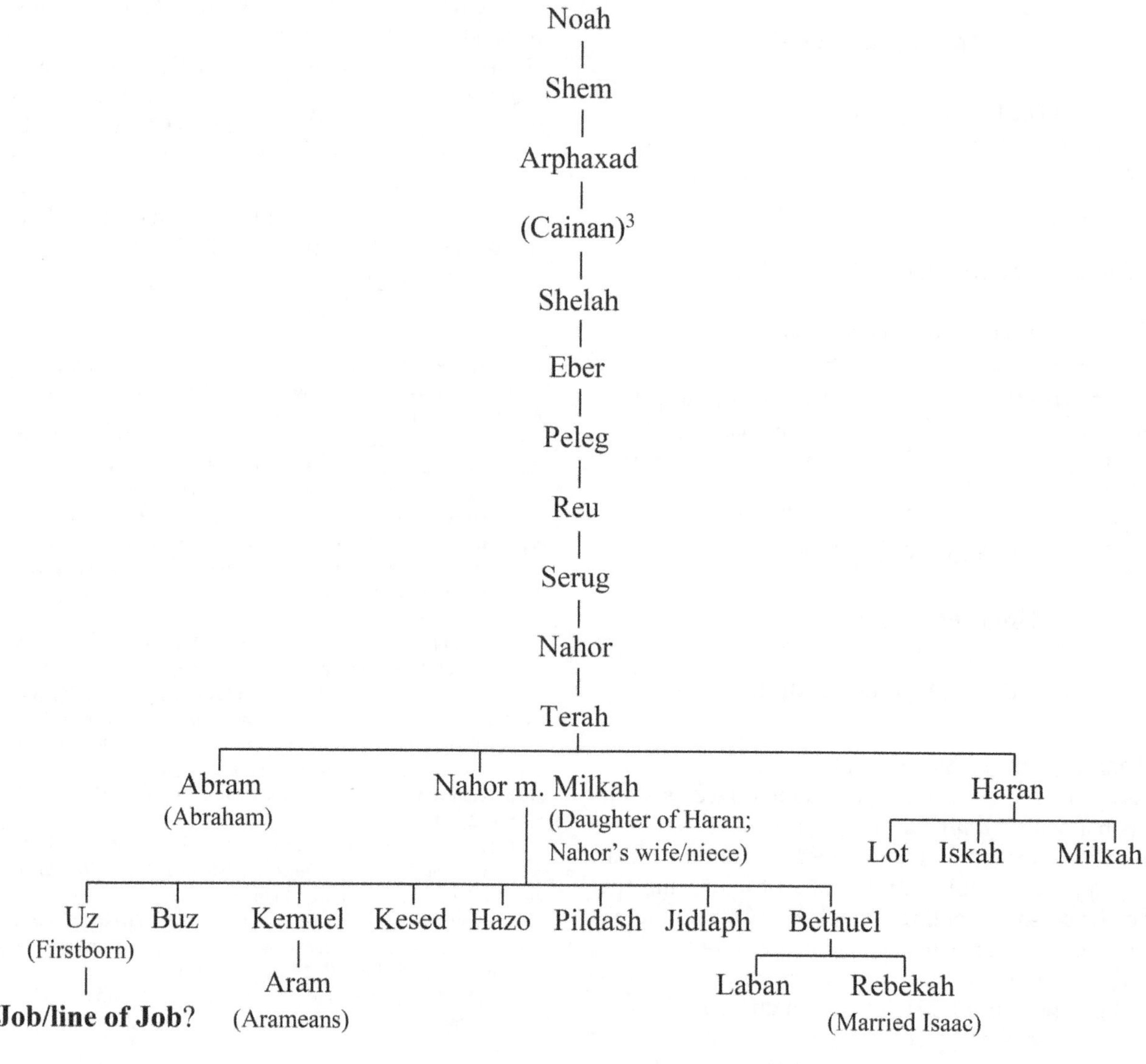

2. **Job as a patriarchal figure—a descendant of Seir the Horite, an early occupant of the land of Edom**
(Job 1:1, also **Genesis 36:2, 5, 14, 18, 20-30**; **1 Chronicles 1:38–42**)

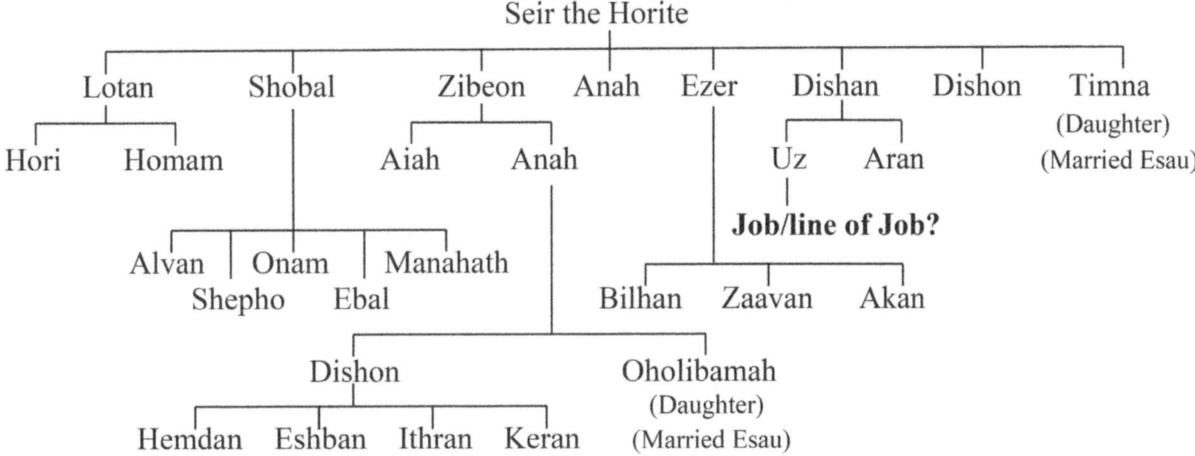

Biblical and Theological Significance

Most scholars consider the book of Job to be apocryphal, as its position in the Writings (or Wisdom) section of the Jewish canon suggests. However, the setting—geographical, cultural, and ideological or theological—is appropriate to an intentionally authentic history of a man and his family who also actually existed. The genealogy here is based, therefore, on the widely held assumption that Job was a patriarchal figure of the Abraham–Isaac–Jacob era (ca. 2000–1800 B.C.),[4] rather than a figure of the immediate post-flood period.[5] The chart presents Job as either (1) the nephew of Bethuel (Isaac's father-in-law) and therefore a distant *relative* of the patriarch Abraham, in the Noah–Shem–Terah–Nahor–Uz line, OR (2) the great-grandson of Seir the Horite, who was an early occupant of the biblical land of Edom.

A later patriarchal milieu for Job is supported by the following: (1) Job functioned as a priest who offered sacrifices for his family (**Job 1:5**); (2) he interceded for his friends (**Job 42:8**; cf. **Genesis 20:7**); and (3) he used silver currency (*kesitah*; **Job 42:11**; cf. **Genesis 33:19; Joshua 24:32**).

Job was not a direct descendant of Abraham, and he did not live in the land of Canaan. Rather, Job's homeland was the region called the "land of Uz" (**Job 1:1**). Uz is mentioned a number of times in Scripture, sometimes as the name of a person and sometimes as the name of a place. The location of Uz is unknown, although some biblical texts connect it with Edom (cf. **Genesis 36:28; 1 Chronicles 1:42; Jeremiah 25:20–21; Lamentations 4:21**). From the vantage point of an Israelite, the land of Uz formed a north-south link with Aram (Syria), Edom, and Arabia.

David Clines writes,

> The importance of the name Uz lies not in where such a place is, but in where it is not. Israelites themselves may not have known its precise location, but they will have known, as we do, that it is not in Israel. . . . The clearest pointer to the location of Uz is **Lamentations 4:21**, where "the land of Uz" stands parallel to "Edom." . . . The Septuagint appendix to the Book of Job preserves a tradition that the land of Job (Ausitis in Greek transliteration) was located "on the borders of Idumea [Edom] and Arabia (42.17b)," which indicates the same general setting.[6]

Other commentators, Walton and Vizcaino, add,

> Edom has been preferred over Aram, being based on Edom's reputation for wisdom and Eliphaz the Temanite's origin from the area of Edom. . . . Regardless of its location, this detail is significant because it indicates that Job [was] not an Israelite. His non-Israelite status explains the absence of many key theological elements in the book, including law, covenant, temple, and references to Yahweh.[7]

In the Old Testament, three characters were named Uz: (1) Uz, the son of Aram, the son of Shem, the son of Noah (**Genesis 10:22–23**); (2) Uz, the son of Nahor the Aramean, who would have been Abraham's nephew (**Genesis 22:20–21**); and (3) Uz, the son of Dishan, the son of Seir the Horite, who occupied Seir/ancient Edom (**Genesis 36:20–30**). Of these, only the latter two lived in the patriarchal age; therefore, those are the only two interpretations shown for Job's ancestry in the chart.

Since Uz is both a geographical name and a personal name, the question arises: Was the place named for a man or was the man named for the place? The name Uz occurs as a geographical name five times and as a personal name three times, too few of each to be able to answer the main question posed here. As a geographical name, the location cannot be known for Job's homeland (**Job 1:1**)—for the mingled peoples of the prophet Jeremiah, the area was the Eastern Mediterranean and the lands of the Middle East (**Jeremiah 25:15–26**); in **Lamentations 4:21**, Uz is described as the region in which Edom was located. As a personal name, Uz was a son of Aram (i.e., Syria; **Genesis 10:22–23**). Again, context leads to geographical considerations. Besides Uz, **Genesis 10:22–29** names Elam, Ashur (Assyria), Lud

(Libya), Eber (Hebrew), Sheba, Ophir, and Havilah, all well known in the biblical text as places in the East. Finally, **Genesis 36:20–28** (cf. **1 Chronicles 1:38–42**) identifies Uz as a son of Dishan and the grandson of Seir the Horite. The best resolution of all the data seems to lie in two observations. (1) The geographical onomastics outweigh those of personal names in the sense that the context in most places where *Uz* occurs is spatial or territorial in nature. (2) The misleading "son of" is well attested to as a label of origin, locale, or political and social connections typical of tribal societies.[8]

Notes

1. This genealogy is based on the general scholarly consensus that Job was a *patriarchal* figure (i.e., in either the Terah–Nahor–Uz–Job line, which places Job as a distant *relative* of Abraham, Isaac, and Jacob, or in the Seir the Horite–Dishan–Uz–Job line). Furthermore, this eliminates the supposition that Job was a post-flood figure (i.e., in the Noah–Shem–Aram–Uz lineage; **Genesis 6:10; 9:18; 10:5, 32; 10:22–23; 1 Chronicles 1:17**). Therefore, the chart presents only two possible lineages for Job the patriarch.

2. For the dating of the patriarchs, see note 2 in chart "**Genesis 35**: The Twelve Sons of Jacob, the Eponymous Originators of the Twelve Tribes of Israel."

3. For a discussion of Cainan (**Luke 3:36**), see Andrew E. Steinmann, "Challenging the Authenticity of Cainan, Son of Arpachshad," *JETS* 60 (2017): 697–711, and a counter viewpoint presented by Henry B. Smith Jr. and Kris J. Udd, "On the Authenticity of Kainan, son of Arpachshad," *Detroit Baptist Seminary Journal* 24 (2019): 119–54.

4. In archaeological terms, this is known as the Middle Bronze I-Middle Bronze IIB period. See Yohanan Aharoni, *The Land of the Bible: A Historical Geography* (Philadelphia: Westminster, 1979), 424–25. For a discussion of the lifespans of the patriarchs, Abraham, Isaac, and Jacob, see charts "**Genesis 11**: Terah and Nahor" and "**Genesis 35**: The Twelve Sons of Jacob, the Eponymous Originators of the Twelve Tribes of Israel."

5. The date of Noah's flood by those who accept its historicity ranges from as early as 10,000 B.C. to 4,000 B.C., although this work suggests it occurred as late as ca. 2456 B.C (see chart "**Genesis 11**: Shem"). Notice that Jesus discusses the flood as an actual event (**Matthew 24:37–39; Luke 17:26–27**).

6. David J. A. Clines, *Job: 1–20*, WBC 17 (Nashville: Thomas Nelson, 2011), 10.

7. John H. Walton and Kelly Lemon Vizcaino, *Job. NIV Application Commentary* (Grand Rapids: Zondervan, 2012), 56–57. Even though Job was probably not an Israelite himself, Walton and Vizcaino conclude that, "Intriguingly, however, the book frequently evidences an Israelite perspective, which suggests that the story of the non-Israelite Job has actually been given its literary shape by an Israelite author for an Israelite audience" (57).

8. Cf. "בֵּן" *HALOT* 1:138.

JOB 2: JOB'S FRIENDS: ZOPHAR, BILDAD, ELIPHAZ, AND ELIHU

Approximate Dating: the patriarchal era, ca. 2000–1800 B.C. ***Relevant Scriptures:*** **Job 2:11; 4:1; 11:1; 18:1; 20:1; 22:1; 25:1; 32:2; 42:9;** also **Genesis 25:1–2; 36:4; 10–11, 15; 1 Chronicles 1:32, 34–36, 53; 2:9, 27; Matthew 1:3–4; Luke 3:33**

Genealogy of Zophar: Unknown

Zophar of Naamath
(In Arabia)

Genealogy of Bildad the Shuhite

Abraham m. Keturah
|
Shuah
(Shuhites)
|
|
Bildad

Genealogy of Eliphaz the Temanite (Edomite)

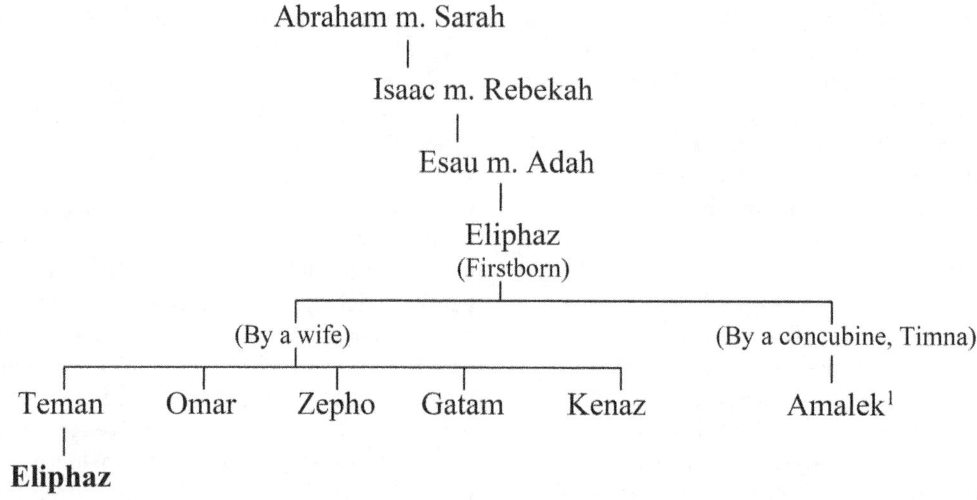

Genealogy of Elihu the Judahite

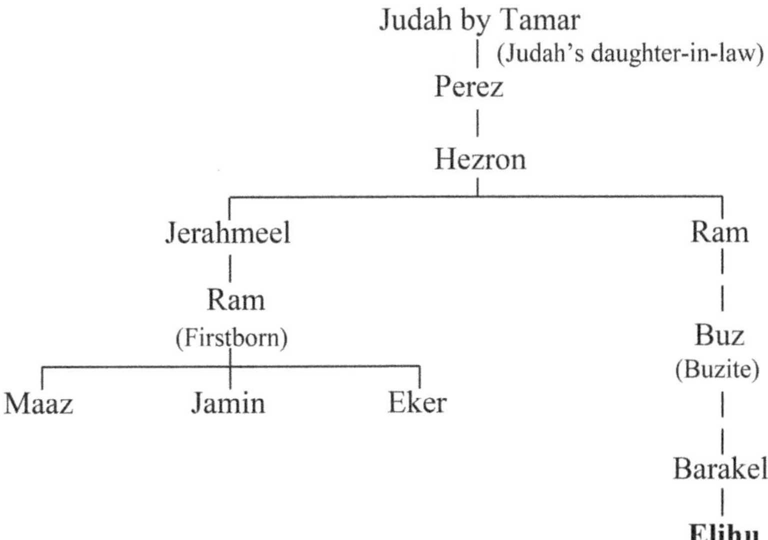

Biblical and Theological Significance

Throughout his ordeal, Job's four friends were his dialogue partners. In general, they agreed that suffering was the consequence of sin, so they believed that Job must be a sinner in need of repentance.[2] Several scholars have pointed out that the arguments of Job's friends represent the traditional views and perspectives regarding suffering in the ancient Near East.[3] For example, Zophar the *rationalist* relies on reasoning and logic; Bildad the *traditionalist* relies on what he has been told from previous generations; and Eliphaz the *mystic* relies heavily on his experience and observations.

Zophar the Naamathite

Zophar, whose name is unique in the Old Testament, acts as the voice of legalism and self-righteousness in his chidings of Job in **Job 11:1–20; 20:1–29**. His genealogy is unclear, but his place of origin is suggested by the epithet "the Naamathite" (**Job 2:11; 11:1; 20:1; 42:9**), presumably referring to inhabitants of Naamah. However, given the other geographical regions in the narrative, Naamah is probably an unknown city or region and does not correspond to the Canaanite town of Naamah that was inherited by the tribe of Judah (**Joshua 15:41**).

Bildad the Shuhite

Bildad, whose name is found only in the book of Job, speaks to Job as the voice of the past in **Job 8:1–22; 18:1–21; 25:1–6**. He appears to be from Shuah (a place name or a personal name), which is unknown otherwise in the Old Testament, except as Shuah, a son of Abraham by Keturah, and among their offspring who migrated to the East (**Genesis 25:2, 6; 1 Chronicles 1:32**).

Eliphaz the Temanite

Eliphaz's name means "My God is gold," meaning that God is of most supreme value. Eliphaz was the voice of experience who spoke to Job in **Job 4:1–5:27; 15:1–35; 22:1–30**. It is possible that he was Eliphaz, the grandson of Esau and Adah (**Genesis 36:10–11**). The personal name Teman refers to the father of Eliphaz; Teman is also a place name for a town in southern Edom (**Genesis 36:34**; **1 Chronicles 1:45**). The Temanites were renowned for their wisdom—"Is there no longer wisdom in Teman? Has counsel perished from the prudent? Has their wisdom decayed?" (**Jeremiah 49:7**).

As a geographic location, Teman was associated with several known regions:

1. Edom (the territory of Esau), and specifically with the city of Bozrah, which was, at times, the capital of Edom—is supported in **Jeremiah 49:7–8, 20**; **Amos 1:12**; **Obadiah 9**.
2. Mount Paran, located south of Judah and west of Edom, is supported in **Habakkuk 3:3**.
3. The territory of Dedan (named for a descendant of Abraham and Keturah who lived in Arabia) is supported in **Ezekiel 25:13** (cf. **Genesis 25:3**). Since Eliphaz the Edomite/Temanite (son of Teman) is the great-grandson of Esau and a contemporary of Job, this suggests the likelihood that Job lived in the late patriarchal period, shortly after Esau's generation.

Elihu the Judahite

Unlike the names of the other three friends,[4] which may be regarded as more Edomite in their connections, Elihu's name is Hebrew, meaning "My God Is He."[5] One might infer that the elaborate introduction of Elihu is to show that, although he was young, he had enough family status to entitle him to speak[6] "in God's behalf" (**Job 36:2**; cf. **32:1–37:24**). He was a descendant of Buz (Buzite), specifically from "the family of Ram" (**Job 32:2**), probably referring to Ram (the son of Hezron, the son of Perez, the son of Judah) who is in the messianic line[7] (**1 Chronicles 2:9; Matthew 1:3–4; Luke 3:33**; cf. **Matthew 1:1–16; Luke 3:23–38**). It is less likely that "the family of Ram" refers to Ram the Judahite, the eldest son of Jerahmeel, in the Judah–Perez–Hezron–Jerahmeel–Ram line[8] (**1 Chronicles 2:25, 27**). Also, there is no indication that Elihu was from the Shem–Nahor–Terah–Nahor–Buz line (cf. **Genesis 22:20–21**) or that he was related to the Buz figure of **Jeremiah 25:23** who is associated with the regions of Dedan and Tema.

Notes

1. See chart "**Genesis 36**: Amalek, the Ancestor of the Amalekites."
2. Robert L. Alden. *Job. The New American Commentary*, Vol II (Nashville: Broadman & Holman Publishers, 1993), 23.
3. John H. Walton, with Kelly Lemon Vizcaino, ed. *Job. NIV Application Commentary* (Grand Rapids: Zondervan, 2012), 106–107.
4. None of the other participants in the book bears more than his own personal name and the name of his town (e.g., Job the Uzite, Eliphaz the Temanite, Bildad the Shuhite, and Zophar the Naamathite).
5. *B.C.*D. A. Hubbard, "Elihu," *New Bible Dictionary*, 311.
6. David J. A. Clines. *Job 21–37*, WBC 18A (Nashville: Thomas Nelson, 2011), 712–713.
7. See also charts "**1 Chronicles 2**: King David" and "**1 Chronicles 4**: Judah."
8. See also chart "**1 Chronicles 2**: Jerahmeel and His Descendant, Elishama, Who Appears to Be a Compiler of Historical and Genealogical Records in 1 & 2 Chronicles."

ISAIAH 1: ISAIAH, PROPHET OF GOD TO THE SOUTHERN KINGDOM OF JUDAH (PRE-EXILE)

Approximate Dating: ministered from ca. 740–700 B.C.[1] ***Relevant Scriptures:*** **Isaiah 1:1; 7:3; 8:1, 3;** also **2 Kings 19:2**

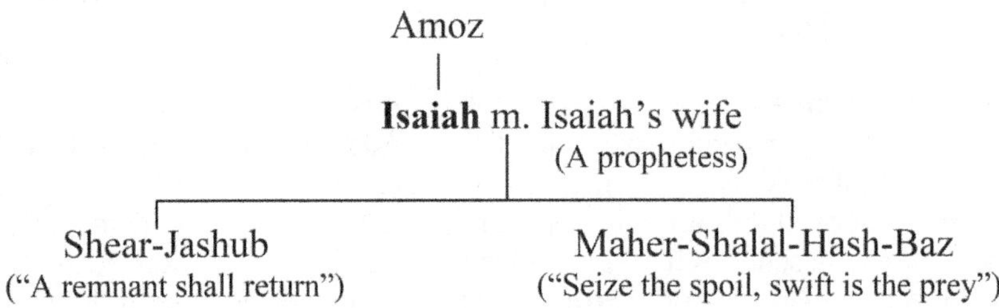

Biblical and Theological Significance

The call narrative of Isaiah (**Isaiah 6:1–13**) shows that his ministry commenced "[in] the year that King Uzziah died [740 B.C.]" (**Isaiah 6:1**). Isaiah wrote of the events that occurred in the fifty-two-year reign of King Uzziah/Azariah of Judah (792–740 B.C.; cf. **2 Kings 15:2, 6; 2 Chronicles 26:3, 22**), as well as those throughout the reigns of Jotham (750–735 B.C.), Ahaz (732–715 B.C.), and into the reign of Hezekiah (715–686 B.C.).[2] Isaiah recorded the acts of King Hezekiah "in the book of the kings of Judah and Israel" (**2 Chronicles 32:32**).

Isaiah's wife is called a "prophetess" (**Isaiah 8:3**; cf. **Judges 4:4; 2 Kings 22:14**), and their children's names were prophetic of future events. Isaiah's firstborn was Shear-Jashub, whose name—meaning "a remnant shall return" (cf. **Isaiah 10:20–22**)—confirmed that if the king of Judah would not trust the Lord, only a remnant (a tenth) of the people would return from the seventy-year Babylonian exile. From this remnant came the "holy seed," (**Isaiah 6:13**), whom Isaiah called the child/Immanuel/the Branch of the Lord/a shoot (**Isaiah 4:2; 7:14; 8:8; 9:6; 11:1–6**). Isaiah's second son was called Maher-Shalal-Hash-Baz, meaning "seize the spoil, swift is the prey"—referring to the rapid destruction of Syria/Aram ("the wealth of Damascus"), of Israel ("the plunder of Samaria") and Judah, and the impending fulfillment of God's word (**Isaiah 8:3**) when God would use the nation of Assyria to seize the spoil of Israel and Judah and overtake his rebellious people (the prey).

Isaiah's writings are cited more than any other Hebrew text in the New Testament, and he is represented more numerously among the Dead Sea Scrolls than all the other prophetic texts combined.

Notes

1. Isaiah lived from ca. 765–680 B.C. Isaiah wrote in **Isaiah 36–37** about Sennacherib's campaign against Judah in 701 B.C. Eugene H. Merrill, *Kingdom of Priests: A History of Old Testament Israel* (Grand Rapids: Baker, 1996), 423–429.
2. For details about the reigns of these kings, see charts "**2 Kings 15**: Azariah (Uzziah), King of Judah"; "**2 Kings 15**: Jotham, King of Judah"; "**2 Kings 15**: Ahaz, King of Judah"; and "**2 Kings 16**: Hezekiah, King of Judah."

JEREMIAH 1: JEREMIAH, THE PROPHET-PRIEST OF GOD TO THE SOUTHERN KINGDOM OF JUDAH (PRE-EXILE)

Approximate Dating: ministered ca. 627–586 B.C.;[1] the last datable event in Jeremiah is 562 B.C.[2] ***Relevant Scriptures:*** **Jeremiah 1:1; 29:27; 32:6–12; 37:12**; also **1 Chronicles 6:1–15; 9:11; Ezra 7:1–2; Nehemiah 11:11**

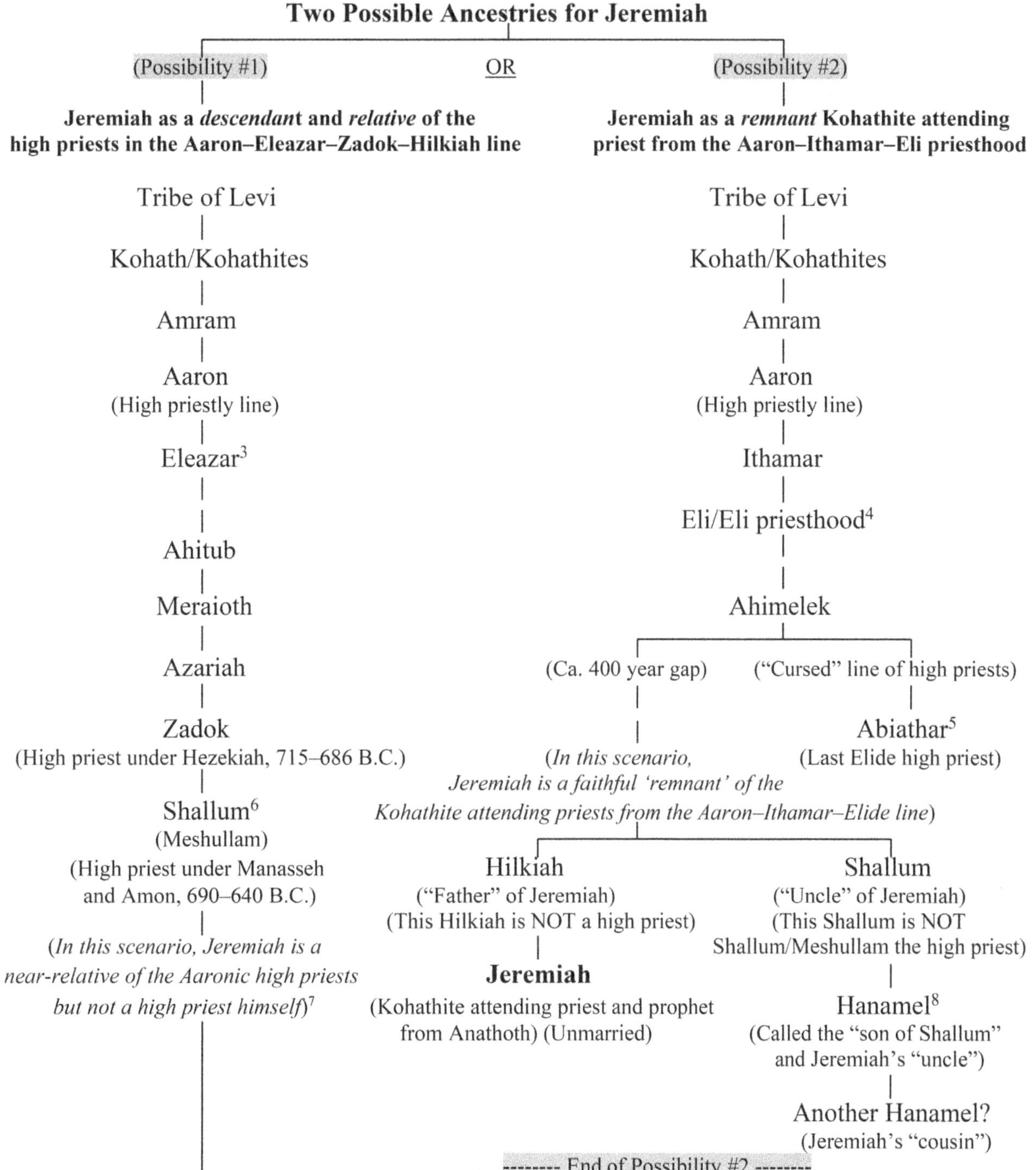

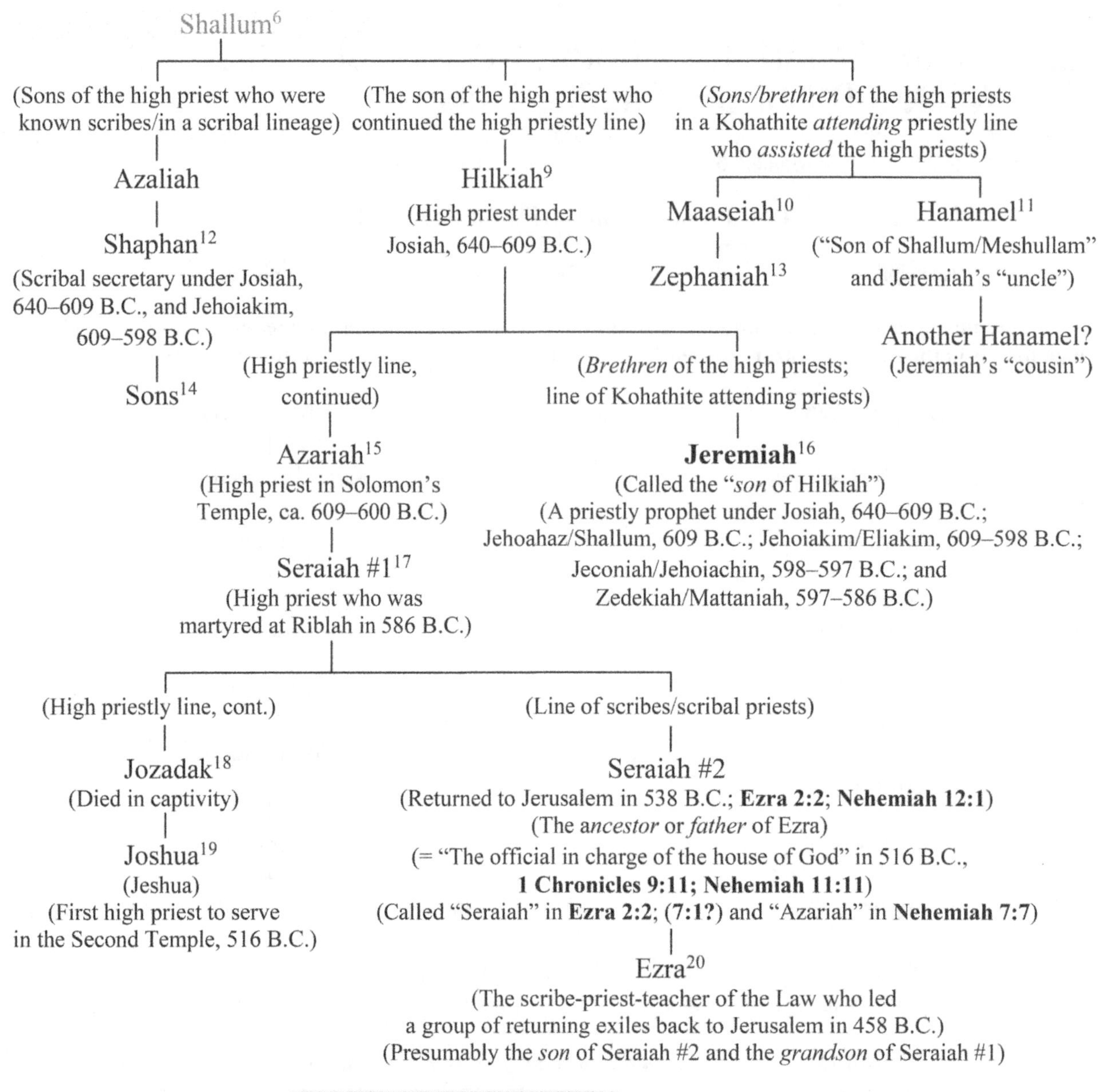

-------- End of Possibility #1 --------

Biblical and Theological Significance

His Name

The name Jeremiah refers to nine different men in the Old Testament.[21] In the full form, יִרְמְיָהוּ , it occurs 124 times in the Old Testament (110 times in the book bearing his name) and in the short (syncopated) spelling, יִרְמְיָה , seven times (**Jeremiah 27:1; 28:5, 10–12, 15; 29:1**), meaning "Yahu (has established or affirmed)".

Jeremiah's Ancestors and Family

Some scholars[22] have considered "Jeremiah son of Hilkiah, one of the priests at Anathoth" (**Jeremiah 1:1**) to be certainly from the Aaron–Ithamar Elide priesthood, based on the fact that Anathoth was the home of Abiathar, the last high priest of the Eli priesthood (who was exiled to Anathoth by King Solomon; **1 Kings 2:26**). However, the text does not preclude another interpretation that is held by other scholars. In the latter case, Jeremiah could have been from the Aaron–Eleazar–Zadok–Shallum/Meshullam line for the following reasons:

1. Anathoth, in the tribe of Benjamin, was given to the descendants in the Kohath–Aaronic high priesthood in general (**Joshua 21:13–19**), not just to the descendants of the Elide priesthood.[23]
2. Chronology supports the fact that Jeremiah's father, Hilkiah (**Jeremiah 1:1**), *could have been* the same person as Hilkiah the high priest (**1 Chronicles 6:13**) who served under King Josiah (640–609 B.C.).
3. The high priests from the Elide priesthood (i.e., Eli and Abiathar) were cursed; therefore, the only surviving members from the line of Aaron–Ithamar–Eli line were faithful Kohathite attending priests.[24] This means that even if Jeremiah was from the Elide line, he would assuredly have been among a small remnant of the

(non-cursed) *attending* priests whose genealogy paralleled that of the *cursed* Elide high priests (see note 23).

Therefore, nothing in the text explicitly establishes which one of the two options is correct; thus, both interpretations are detailed in the chart.

Jeremiah's Ministry

Jeremiah was chosen as God's prophet even before he was born (**Jeremiah 1:5**) and was divinely commanded not to marry or have children (**Jeremiah 16:2**). His call to the prophetic ministry came in 627 B.C., corresponding to the thirteenth year of the thirty-one-year reign of Josiah of Judah, 640–609 B.C. (cf. **Jeremiah 1:2–19**). His ministry continued through the successive reigns of Jehoahaz/Shallum (609 B.C.), Jehoiakim/Eliakim (609–598 B.C.), Jeconiah/Jehoiachin (598–597 B.C.) and Zedekiah/Mattaniah (597–586 B.C.). In 587 B.C.—corresponding to the tenth year of Zedekiah and the eighteenth year of Nebuchadnezzar—Jeremiah was imprisoned (**Jeremiah 32:1**) and a severe famine ensued (**2 Kings 25:3; Jeremiah 52:6**). In 586 B.C., the inhabitants of Jerusalem were carried into Babylonian captivity (**Jeremiah 1:1–3; 25:1–11; 26:1**). At one point, Jeremiah purchased a field in Anathoth[25] from Hanamel, his *cousin* (or uncle; see note 11) to symbolize God's intention to restore a remnant of people to the land after the exile (**Jeremiah 32:6–15**). Anathoth was overtaken during the Babylonian invasion, but the town was eventually resettled following the exile (**Nehemiah 7:27; 11:32**). During his Babylonian-appointed governorship over Judah, Gedaliah took Jeremiah to Mizpah, where Jeremiah "stayed with him [Gedaliah] among the people who were left behind in the land" (cf. **Jeremiah 40:6;** see also **39:11–14**).

Jeremiah's Forced Exile to Egypt

Sadly, a group of assassins slew Gedaliah in an attempt to revive the monarchy. Gedaliah's followers, led by the military officer Johanan, decided to escape to Egypt. Jeremiah urged the leaders of the movement not to resettle in Egypt, foretelling that they would die there, but if they remained in the land of Judah, they would enjoy Babylonian benevolence (**Jeremiah 42:7–22**). Contrary to the express will of God, Gedaliah's followers made their way to Egypt and forced Jeremiah and his amanuensis Baruch to accompany them[26] (**Jeremiah 43:4–7**). Jeremiah described the awful fate that would befall the escapees at the hands of Nebuchadnezzar and his armies, who would ravage Egypt[27] (**Jeremiah 43:10–44:30**). This was only the beginning of the steep decline of Egypt: first under the Babylonians (605–539 B.C.) and later under the Persians (539–358 B.C.). As for Jeremiah, any record of his final days is long lost. The last datable event in his book is his account of the release of King Jehoiachin (Jeconiah) from house arrest in Babylon in 561 B.C. (**Jeremiah 52:31–34**; cf. **2 Kings 25:27–30**).

As the so-called weeping prophet (cf. **Jeremiah 8:18; 9:1; 13:17; 22:10; 48:32**), Jeremiah experienced much sorrow in his forty or more years of ministry to Jerusalem and Judah. He wept not for himself, despite his terrible persecution, but for his sinful yet beloved nation. He suffered death threats, imprisonments,[28] physical attacks, and mocking, ridicule, and cursing at the hands of his own people (**Jeremiah 1:19; 11:18–23; 15:10; 20:7, 10; 26:8–16; 32:2–5; 37:4–38:28**). So miserable did he become, he imitated Job and wished he had never been born (**Jeremiah 20:14**; cf. **Job 3:3–19**). Jeremiah's sorrows foreshadow the sufferings of Jesus Christ (cf. **Matthew 16:21; 17:12; Mark 8:31; 9:12; Luke 9:22**). When the people of his hometown of Anathoth sought to kill him, Jeremiah compared himself to "a gentle lamb led to the slaughter" (**Jeremiah 11:19, 21–23**)—words foreshadowing Jesus Christ, the Lamb of God, who would be led to the slaughter to become the ultimate sacrifice for the sins of the people (cf. **Isaiah 53:7; John 1:29; 3:17; 1 John 4:10, 14**).

Notes

1. Jeremiah must have been fairly young at the beginning of his ministry (**Jeremiah 1:7**).

2. This date of 562 B.C. is likely an addition to what Jeremiah wrote, probably by the same writer who composed **2 Kings 25:27–30**. A ministry of 65 years for Jeremiah would be much less likely.

3. For the Aaron–Eleazar–Zadok–Hilkiah lineage, see charts "**1 Chronicles 6**: Levi: High Priests, Priests, Levites, and Musicians in Solomon's Temple" and "**Supplement 2**: The High Priests of Israel."

4. For the Eli/Eli priesthood, see chart "**1 Samuel 1**: Eli and the Eli Priesthood."

5. Abiathar the son of Ahimelek was co–high priest with Zadok (son of Ahitub) during David's reign, 1011–971 B.C. (**1 Samuel 22:20, 23:6; 30:7; 2 Samuel 15:29; 1 Kings 2:26**). Abiathar was faithful to David during Absalom's rebellion (**2 Samuel 15**) and became David's counselor after his former counselor, Ahithophel, committed suicide (**2 Samuel 17:23**; cf. **15:12; 23:34; 1 Chronicles 27:33–34**). Nevertheless, Abiathar supported Adonijah to be David's successor instead of Solomon, so once Solomon came to the throne, he removed Abiathar and exiled him to his hometown of Anathoth (**1 Kings 1:7; 2:26–35**), thus "fulfilling the word the LORD had spoken at Shiloh about the [cursed high priestly] house of Eli" (**1 Kings 2:26–27**). Abiathar and his son Ahimelek were the last recorded priests in the cursed line of the Eli priesthood to serve in an official high priestly capacity.

6. Shallum in **1 Chronicles 6:12–13** and **Ezra 7:2** is called Meshullam in **1 Chronicles 9:11** and **Nehemiah 11:11**. Shallum son of Zadok was the high priest. He is not Shallum the Levite, the husband of Huldah the prophet (see chart "**2 Kings 22**: Huldah the Prophet"). **Jeremiah 32:7** says that Shallum/Meshullam was Jeremiah's *uncle*, and Shallum/Meshullam's son Hanamel was Jeremiah's *cousin* (**Jeremiah 32:8–9**; cf. **32:12**)—"Hanamel son of Shallum *your uncle* is going to come to you and say, 'Buy my field at Anathoth, because as nearest relative it is your right and duty to buy it.'"

7. In possibility #1, the prophet Jeremiah is writing the book of Jeremiah and clearly linking himself to the noble *high priestly* line of Aaron–Eleazar–Zadak–Shallum–Hilkiah, rather than the disreputable cursed line of Elide high priests (Aaron–Ithamar–Eli–Abiathar). In **Jeremiah 1:1**, Jeremiah is likely associating himself with his revered *father* (or possibly his ancestor), Hilkiah—"the words of Jeremiah son of Hilkiah [the high priest]." Likewise, in **Jeremiah 32:7**—"Hanamel son of Shallum your [Jeremiah's] uncle"—Jeremiah associates himself with his revered *uncle* or *ancestor* Shallum/Meshullam the high priest; see notes 6 and 9.

8. For Hanamel as an uncle and a cousin (relative?) of Jeremiah, see note 11.

9. Hilkiah was the high priest during King Josiah's reign, 640–609 B.C. (**2 Kings 22:4, 8, 10, 12, 14; 2 Chronicles 34:9, 14–15, 18, 20, 22**). The only other men called Hilkiah are: (1) Hilkiah the Levite who is in a Merarite lineage (**1 Chronicles 6:45**), seven generations removed from Levi and before King David's time (i.e., not in Jeremiah's priestly heritage); (2) Hilkiah a priest or Levite who *returned* to Jerusalem with Zerubbabel in 538 B.C. (**Nehemiah 12:7**); and (3) Hilkiah the father of the Eliakim, who replaced Shebna as the palace administrator in the days of King Hezekiah of Judah, 715–686 B.C. (**Isaiah 22:20–24**; cf. **36:3, 11, 22**). Otherwise, all the Hilkiah figures in Scripture refer to the high priest Hilkiah who served from 640–609 B.C. under King Josiah.

10. Maaseiah was a Levitical doorkeeper (a guard) of the Temple (**Jeremiah 35:4**).

11. In **Jeremiah 32:7**, Hanamel is called Jeremiah's "uncle," whereas in **Jeremiah 32:8–9, 12**, Hanamel is called Jeremiah's "cousin"—for this reason they are shown as two different individuals in the chart. However, there may have been only one Hanamel figure and the correct meaning is that Hanamel was Jeremiah's *relative* in **Jeremiah 32:7–9, 12**. Hanamel sold his field in Anathoth to Jeremiah; this action foreshadowed that a remnant of people would return to Judah after the Babylonian exile was over (cf. **Jeremiah 32:36–41**).

12. For the lineage of Shaphan the scribe, see chart "**2 Kings 22**: Shaphan, Scribal Secretary under King Josiah and King Jehoiakim of Judah."

13. Zephaniah son of Maaseiah is called a priest and is mentioned in **Jeremiah 21:1; 29:25, 29; 37:3; 52:24**. He was the "priest next in rank" to Seraiah, the chief (high) priest—probably meaning Zephaniah was a close relative of Seraiah. They were both taken prisoner and executed by the commander of the guard of Nebuchadnezzar at Riblah in 586 B.C. (**2 Kings 25:18–21; Jeremiah 52:24–27**). Zephaniah the martyred priest, the son of Maaseiah, is not the same person as Zephaniah the prophet the son of Cushi (**Zephaniah 1:1**).

14. The sons of Shaphan include Ahikam, Gemariah, Elasah, and Jaazaniah; see chart "**2 Kings 22**: Shaphan, Scribal Secretary under King Josiah and King Jehoiakim of Judah."

15. This Azariah was a high priest (**1 Chronicles 6:13–14**); he corresponds to Azariah #23 in chart "**Supplement 2**: The High Priests of Israel." Albert Barnes ("Jeremiah 20:1"), in *Albert Barnes' Notes on the Old Testament* (Accordance Bible Software) asserts that this Azariah (the son of Hilkiah the high priest) could be Jeremiah's brother (cf. **1 Chronicles 6:13; Ezra 7:1**).

16. In his note to John Calvin's *Book of the Prophet Jeremiah,Chapter 1 (Jeremiah 1:1-3),* note 2 in *Calvin's Commentary* (public domain; Accordance Bible Software), the editor/translator John Owen states that "The reasons alleged against Jeremiah being the son of [Hilkiah] the high priest are by no means conclusive: indeed, all the circumstances being considered, the probability is in favor of that supposition. The family of the high priest resided no doubt at Anathoth; what is said in **1 Kings 2:26**, respecting Abiathar, is a proof of this. That the high priest [Hilkiah] resided at Jerusalem during the term of his office forms no objection; nor is the genealogy of the high priests as given in **1 Chronicles 6:1–17**, any objection; for though in **verse 13,** Azariah is said to be the son of Hilkiah, yet Jeremiah might have been one of his younger sons. Most commentators agree indeed with *Calvin, Gataker, Henry, Scott, Blayney*, etc.; but they adduce no satisfactory reasons, sufficient to invalidate the opinion of the Rabbins [archaic for Rabbis] and the intimation contained in the *Targum*: and this opinion is what the translators of the Geneva Bible have adopted. Ed."

17. Seraiah—designated here and in other charts as Seraiah #1—was the chief priest when the people of Judah were carried away into Babylonian exile. Seraiah appears to be killed at Riblah by the Babylonians (**2 Kings 25:18–21; Jeremiah 52:24–27**). Seraiah was the *father* (perhaps grandfather/ancestor?) of Ezra the scribe-prophet-teacher of the Law (**Ezra 7:1**) and the father of Jozadak the high priest (**1 Chronicles 6:14**).

18. Jozadak was the high priest when Nebuchadnezzar invaded the land and carried the people of Judah and Jerusalem into Babylonian captivity (**1 Chronicles 6:14–15**). Jozadak was the father of Joshua (Jeshua) the high priest who returned from exile with Zerubbabel in 538 B.C. (**Haggai 1:1; Zechariah 6:11**).

19. He is called Joshua in **Ezra 3:2, 8; 5:2; 10:18; Haggai 1:1; Zechariah 6:11** and Jeshua in **Ezra 2:36; Nehemiah 7:39**). For more information, see chart "**Ezra 2**: Joshua, the High Priest in the Second Temple, and His Descendants (Post-Exile)."

20. See chart "**Ezra 7**: Ezra, the Priestly Scribe and Teacher of the Law (Post-Exile)."

21. There are eight other people named Jeremiah in Scripture, in addition to Jeremiah the prophet:

(1) Jeremiah the father of Hamutal, who was the mother of King Jehoahaz and King Zedekiah (**2 Kings 23:31; 24:18; Jeremiah 52:1**);
(2) Jeremiah the son of Habazziniah and the father of Jaazaniah in **Jeremiah 35:3**;
(3) Jeremiah the warrior who was head of a family from the half-tribe of Manasseh (**1 Chronicles 5:24**);
(4) Jeremiah the Gadite who joined David's army at Ziklag (**1 Chronicles 12:10**);
(5) (Another) Jeremiah the Gadite—see note 4 above—who joined David's army at Ziklag (**1 Chronicles 12:13**);
(6) Jeremiah the Benjamite who joined David's army at Ziklag (**1 Chronicles 12:4**);
(7) Jeremiah of 538 B.C. who returned with Zerubbabel and Joshua to Jerusalem, post-exile (**Nehemiah 12:1**); and
(8) Jeremiah who sealed the covenant with Nehemiah in 444 B.C. (**Nehemiah 10:2**).

References to Jeremiah the prophet: **2 Chronicles 35:25; 36:12, 21–22; Ezra 1:1**; **Daniel 9:2; Matthew 2:17; 16:14; 27:9** and 110 places in the book of Jeremiah: **Jeremiah 1:1, 11; 7:1; 11:1; 14:1; 18:1, 18; 19:14; 20:1–3; 21:1, 3; 24:3; 25:1–2; 26:7–9, 12, 20, 24; 27:1; 28:5, 10–12, 15; 29:1, 27, 29; 30:1; 32:1–2, 6, 26; 33:1, 19, 23; 34:1, 6, 8, 12; 35:1, 12, 18; 36:1, 4–5, 8, 10, 17, 19, 26–27, 32; 37:2–4, 6, 12, 14–18, 21; 38:6–7, 9–17, 19–20, 24, 27–28; 39:11, 14–15; 40:1–2, 5–6; 40:1–2, 5–6; 42:2, 4–5, 7; 43:1–2, 6, 8; 44:1, 15, 20, 24; 45:1; 46:1, 13; 47:1; 49:34; 50:1; 51:59–60, 64.**

22. For example, Matthew Henry held that Hilkiah (Jeremiah's father) was not Hilkiah the high priest—"We are told what family the prophet was of. He was the son of Hilkiah, not that Hilkiah, it is supposed, who was high priest in Josiah's time (for then he would have been called so, and not, as here, one of the priests that were in Anathoth), but another of the same name" (Matthew Henry, **"Jeremiah 1:1–3,"** *Matthew Henry's Commentary*, Accordance Bible Software, on the book of the prophet Jeremiah.

23. According to **Joshua 21:4–26**, thirteen towns were given to the descendants of Aaron (high priestly line)—from Judah, Simeon, and Benjamin; ten towns from Ephraim, Dan, and the half-tribe of Manasseh were given to the remaining Aaronic descendants who were Kohathite attending priests. Therefore, Anathoth, from the tribe of Benjamin, was a town given to the *high priestly descendants* of Aaron (see **Joshua 21:18**), not solely a town for the Eli/Elide and Abiathar priesthood. This is why Jeremiah *could be* a descendant of the Aaron–Zadok high priestly line (i.e., possibility #1 shown in the chart).

24. See charts "**1 Samuel 1**: Eli and the Eli Priesthood" and "**1 Chronicles 24**: Genealogical Registry of the Twenty-Four Divisions of Kohathite Attending Priests Who Rotated Service in Solomon's Temple."

25. Anathoth was a city on the northern slopes of the Mount of Olives and located in the tribe of Benjamin. Anathoth was one of the thirteen cities given specifically to Aaronic descendants who were in the Kohathite *high priestly* line (**Joshua 21:1–4, 13–19; 1 Chronicles 6:54–60**). Anathoth was the hometown of Abiathar the high priest from the Elide priesthood, who served in a co–high priest capacity with Zadok during the reign of David (**2 Samuel 8:17; 20:25**); for the Elide priesthood, see note 4. Because the people of Anathoth threatened to kill Jeremiah, the Lord declared there would be no more priests from Anathoth (**Jeremiah 11:21–23; 12:6**). Anathoth is possibly modern-day Anata, northeast of Jerusalem.

26. The group settled in Tahpanhes, a fortress city on the border of Lower (northern) Egypt.

27. A token of that judgment, both on Egypt and the Jews among them, had already been made clear in the defeat of Pharaoh Necho by the Babylonians in the decisive battle of Carchemish on the Euphrates River in 605 B.C. (**Jeremiah 46:2**).

28. Jeremiah suffered imprisonment four separate times: (1) in 587 B.C., he was confined to the courtyard of the guard in the royal palace of Judah (**Jeremiah 32:1–5**; cf. **33:1**); (2) after perceiving (incorrectly) that he was deserting to the Babylonians, he was taken to the house of Jonathan the secretary, which had been made into a prison (a vaulted cell in a dungeon; **Jeremiah 37:11–20**); (3) he was returned to the courtyard of the guard, in the royal palace of Judah (**Jeremiah 37:21–38:5**; cf. **32:3**); and finally, (4) he was thrown into "the cistern of Malkijah, the king's son" in the courtyard of the guard, before he was rescued by Ebed-Melek the Cushite (**Jeremiah 38:6–13**).

JEREMIAH 20: PASHHUR, AN UNFAITHFUL KOHATHITE PRIEST AND THE OFFICIAL OVER SOLOMON'S TEMPLE (PRE-EXILE)

Approximate Dating: ca. 586 B.C. ***Relevant Scriptures:*** **Jeremiah 20:1–6**

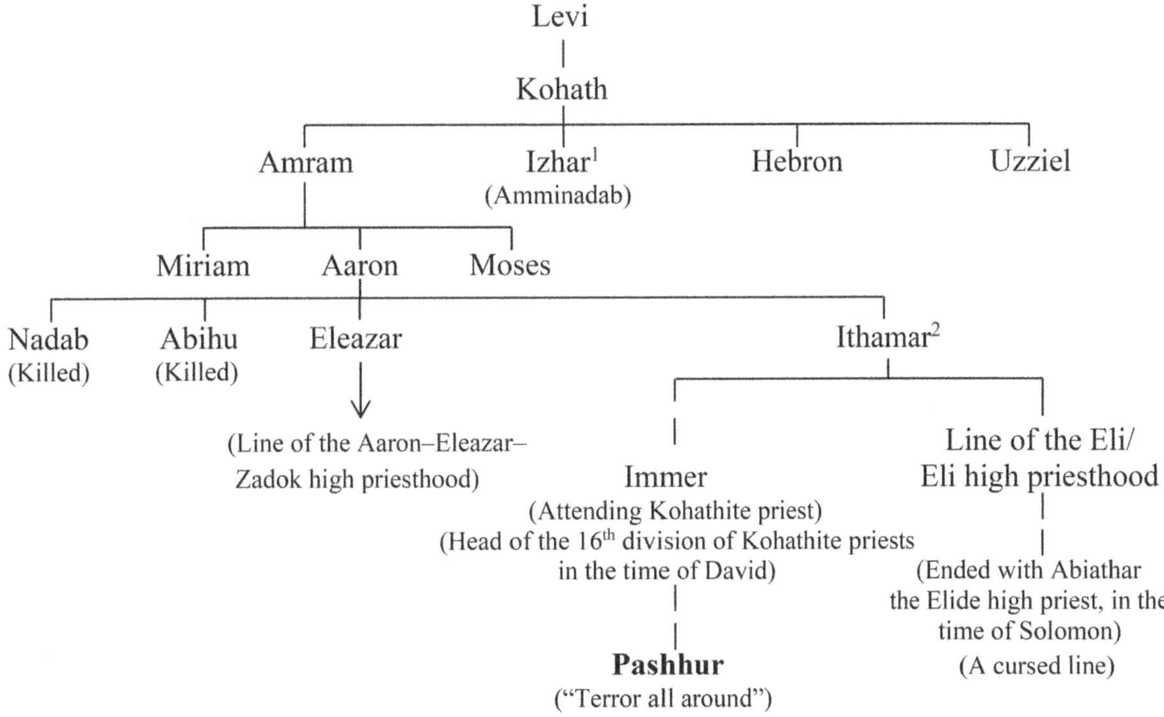

Biblical and Theological Significance

Pashhur "son [descendant] of Immer" was "the official in charge of the temple of the LORD" in the pre-exile period (**Jeremiah 20:1**). His lineage shows he was an Kohathite attending priest and a descendant of Immer, the ancestral head of the sixteenth division of attending Kohathites that had been established in the days of King David (**1 Chronicles 24:14**).[3] When Jeremiah the prophet (627–586 B.C.) stood in the court of the temple and prophesied that the Lord would "bring on this city and all the villages around it every disaster I [the LORD] pronounced against them, because they were stiff-necked and would not listen to my words" (**Jeremiah 19:15**), Pashhur silenced Jeremiah by putting him in prison stocks. Because Pashhur was an unfaithful priest, the LORD pronounced a judgment on him and his priestly household and changed his name to מָגוֹר מִסָּבִיב (*Magor-Missabib*, meaning "Terror on every side"; **Jeremiah 20:3**). Pashhur was carried into Babylonian captivity in 586 B.C., and there he died and was buried (**Jeremiah 20:6**). Pashhur, a descendant in the Immer line, is unrelated to Pashhur, the son/descendant of Malkijah, who was also a Kohathite attending priest (**1 Chronicles 9:12** and **Nehemiah 11:12**).[4]

The lesson to be learned here is that anyone who attempts to thwart the mission of God has set himself on a path of certain destruction. For example, David's great hymn on the occasion of the transfer of the ark of the covenant into his Mount Zion tent-tabernacle says, in part, "Do not touch my anointed ones; do my prophets no harm" (**1 Chronicles 16:22**).

Notes

1. Izhar (**Exodus 6:18, 21; Numbers 16:1; 1 Chronicles 6:2, 18, 38; 23:12**) is otherwise Amminadab (**1 Chronicles 6:22**).
2. See Ithamar and the Elide priestly descendants in chart "**1 Samuel 1**: Eli and the Eli Priesthood"; for other Kohathite attending priests in the Elide line, see chart "**1 Chronicles 24**: Genealogical Registry of the Twenty-Four Divisions of Kohathite Attending Priests Who Rotated Service in Solomon's Temple."
3. See chart "**1 Chronicles 24**: Genealogical Registry of the Twenty-Four Divisions of Kohathite Attending Priests Who Rotated Service in Solomon's Temple."
4. See chart "**1 Chronicles 9**: The Kohathite Attending Priests in the Second Temple (Post-Exile)."

JEREMIAH 21: PASHHUR AND ZEPHANIAH WHO WERE SENT BY KING ZEDEKIAH TO INQUIRE OF JEREMIAH ABOUT THE FATE OF JERUSALEM (PRE-EXILE)

Approximate Dating: ca. 588–586 B.C. ***Relevant Scriptures:*** **Jeremiah 21:1–2; 29:25; 37:3; Nehemiah 38:6;** also **1 Chronicles 9:12; Ezra 10:18; Nehemiah 11:12; 12:10**

Possible Genealogy of Pashhur

A. If he was a Kohathite attending priest:

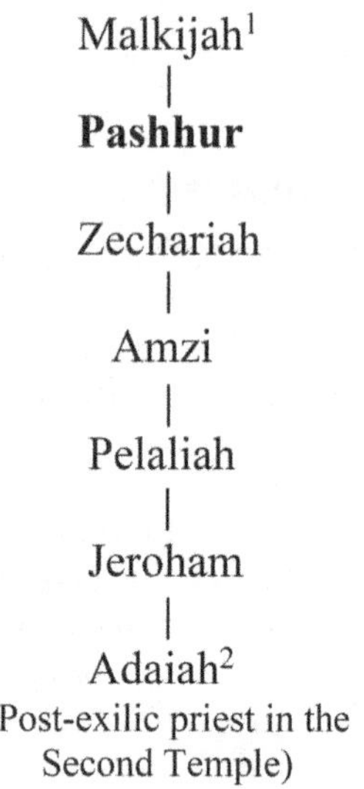

B. If he was a Judahite, the descendant of a former king:

King Josiah[3] (?) OR King Jehoiakim[4] (?)

Malkijah[5]

(Called "the king's son" in **Jeremiah 38:6**)

Pashhur

Genealogy of Zephaniah (presumably the grandson of the high priest Joshua, or Joshua's brothers)

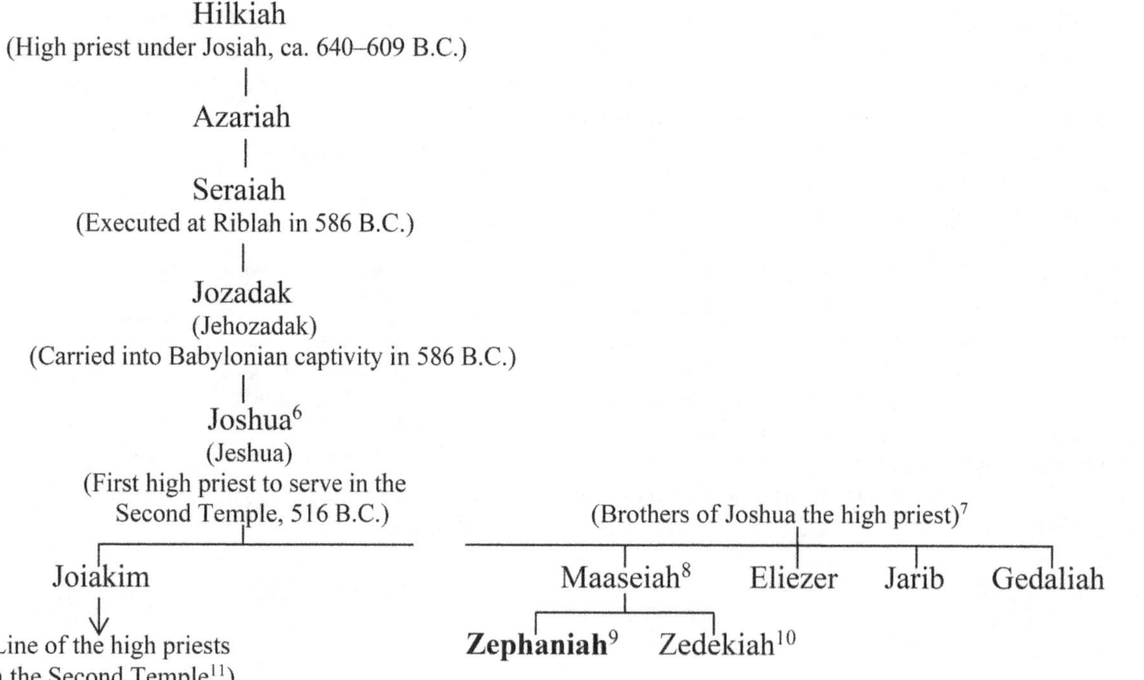

Biblical and Theological Significance

Zephaniah and Pashhur (if Pashhur was *not* Pashhur the Judahite) were both Kohathite attending priests who served in the latter days of King Zedekiah's reign (597–586 B.C.). King Nebuchadnezzar of Babylon made three campaigns against Judah: 605–604 B.C., 598–597 B.C. and 588–586 B.C. When Zedekiah rebelled against him (**2 Kings 24:20; 2 Chronicles 36:12–16; Jeremiah 52:2-3**), Nebuchadnezzar marched against Jerusalem in the ninth year of Zedekiah's reign and kept the city under siege until the eleventh year (**25:1–3**). During this time, King Zedekiah asked Pashhur and Zephaniah to inquire of the Lord, hoping that "perhaps the LORD will perform wonders for us as in times past so that he [Nebuchadnezzar] will withdraw from us" (**Jeremiah 21:2**). Through the words of the prophet Jeremiah, the LORD forewarned Zedekiah: "I myself [with the Babylonians] will fight against you with an outstretched hand. . . . I will strike down those who live in this city . . . [and] I will give Zedekiah king of Judah, his officials and the people in this city . . . into the hands of Nebuchadnezzar" (**Jeremiah 21:3–7**).

Notes

1. The ancestral Malkijah figure was the head over the fifth of the twenty-four divisions of Kohathite attending priests in Solomon's Temple (**1 Chronicles 24:9**); see chart "**1 Chronicles 24**: Genealogical Registry of the 24 Divisions of Kohathite Attending Priests Who Rotated Service in Solomon's Temple." It is unclear if Malkijah (the father of Pashhur) in **Jeremiah 21:1** was a *descendant* of the ancestral Malkijah; it is likely that Pashhur was an ancestor of Adaiah (**1 Chronicles 9:12; Nehemiah 11:12**).

2. Adaiah was a Kohathite attending priest in the Second Temple and a descendant of Pashhur son of Malkijah. Adaiah's lineage, which is given in **1 Chronicles 9:12; Nehemiah 11:12**, is the basis for the proposed genealogy for "Pashhur son of Malkijah" in **Jeremiah 21:1**, assuming that Pashhur was a Kohathite priest.

3. King Josiah reigned from 640–609 B.C. He was eight years old when he became king, so Josiah must have been born in 648 B.C. See chart "**2 Kings 21**: Josiah, King of Judah."

4. King Jehoiakim/Eliakim, the son of Josiah, reigned from 609–598 B.C. Jehoiakim was 25 years old when he became king, so Jehoiakim was born in 633 B.C. See chart "**2 Kings 23**: Eliakim (Jehoiakim), King of Judah."

5. For identity of this Malkijah, see chart "**Jeremiah 38**: The Officials to King Zedekiah Who Cast Jeremiah into the Cistern (Pre-Exile)."

6. Joshua/Jeshua was high priest in the early post-exile, ca. 516–490 B.C. See charts "**Nehemiah 12**: Genealogical Records of the Heads of the Kohathite Priests and Levites who Returned to Jerusalem with Zerubbabel and Joshua in the Post-Exile" and "**Ezra 2**: Joshua, the High Priest in the Second Temple, and His Descendants (Post-Exile)."

7. The names of the brothers of Joshua/Jeshua are given in **Ezra 10:18–19**.

8. The genealogy of Maaseiah, as shown in the chart, is based on the reading in **Ezra 10:18**; however, there are three Kohathite attending priests named Maaseiah (all of whom had taken pagan wives while in Babylonian captivity): (1) Maaseiah the brother of Joshua/Jeshua the high priest, **Ezra 10:18**; (2) Maaseiah the descendant of Harim, **Ezra 10:21**; and (3) Maaseiah the descendant of Pashhur, **Ezra 10:22**. Therefore, Maaseiah could just as well be the descendant of Harim or Pashhur rather than Jozadak (the interpretation that is shown in the chart).

9. Also see chart "**Jeremiah 37**: Jehukal the Court Official and Zephaniah the Priest in the Days of King Zedekiah of Judah (Pre-Exile)." This Zephaniah (son of Maaseiah) is not Zephaniah the prophet, who wrote the Book of Zephaniah and prophesied in the days of King Josiah, ca. 640–609.

10. The genealogy of Zedekiah is based on the assumption that Maaseiah (see note 8) is the father of both Zedekiah and Zephaniah (**Jeremiah 21:1** and **29:21**). Zedekiah was a false prophet and an unfaithful priest who committed adultery with his neighbors' wives and spoke lies in God's name. Zedekiah was taken into exile and died there, being "burned in the fire" (**Jeremiah 29:21–23**)!

11. For the line of the high priests in the Second Temple, see charts "**Nehemiah 12**: Genealogical Record of the Heads of the Kohathite Priests and Levites who Returned to Jerusalem with Zerubbabel and Joshua in the Post-Exile" and "**Supplement 2**: The High Priests of Israel."

JEREMIAH 26: URIAH THE PROPHET IN THE DAYS OF KING JEHOIAKIM OF JUDAH (PRE-EXILE)

Approximate Dating: ca. 609–598 B.C. ***Relevant Scriptures:*** **Jeremiah 26:20–23**; also **Nehemiah 6:10**

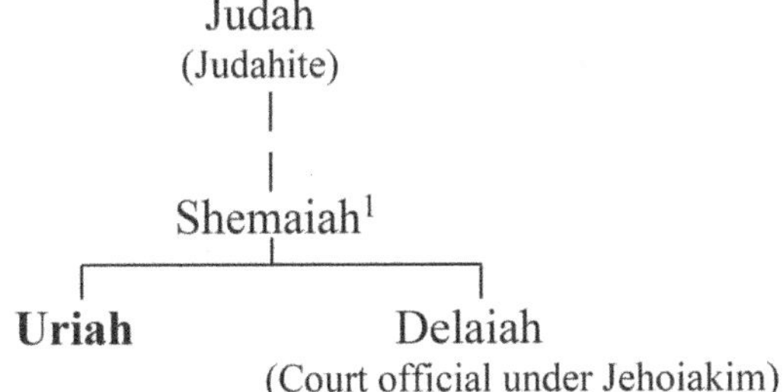

Biblical and Theological Significance

The prophet Uriah was a contemporary of Jeremiah who "prophesied the same things against this city and this land as Jeremiah did" (i.e., that the city of Jerusalem would fall to the Babylonians; **Jeremiah 26:20**). When King Jehoiakim heard Uriah's prophecy, he "was determined to put him to death" (**Jeremiah 26:21**), so Uriah fled in fear to Egypt. King Jehoiakim sent Elnathan, the son of Akbor,[2] the son of Micaiah (**Jeremiah 26:22**; cf. **2 Kings 22:12; 2 Chronicles 34:20**) and other men to bring Uriah back to Jerusalem. Upon his return, King Jehoiakim had Uriah the prophet killed. It is unclear whether the prophet Uriah was the brother of Delaiah (the son of Shemaiah),[3] a prince of Judah who was among King Jehoiakim's court officials who urged the king not to burn the scroll of Jeremiah (**Jeremiah 36:12, 25**).

Notes

1. Shemaiah was from Kiriath Jearim (also called Baalah or Kiriath Baal), a town in the hill country of Judah (**Jeremiah 26:20**; cf. **Joshua 15:9, 60**).

2. Akbor in **2 Kings 22:12, 14** and **Jeremiah 26:22; 36:12** is Abdon in **2 Chronicles 34:20**.

3. Shemaiah the Judahite is not the same person as Shemaiah the Nehelamite, the false prophet who opposed Jeremiah (**Jeremiah 29:24–32**).

JEREMIAH 26: AHIKAM, THE SCRIBE WHO BEFRIENDED JEREMIAH THE PROPHET IN THE DAYS OF KING JEHOIAKIM OF JUDAH

Approximate Dating: ca. 609–598 B.C. ***Relevant Scriptures:*** **Jeremiah 26:24**; also **2 Kings 22:12; 25:22; 2 Chronicles 34:20; Jeremiah 39:14; 40:5–7, 9, 11, 16; 43:6**

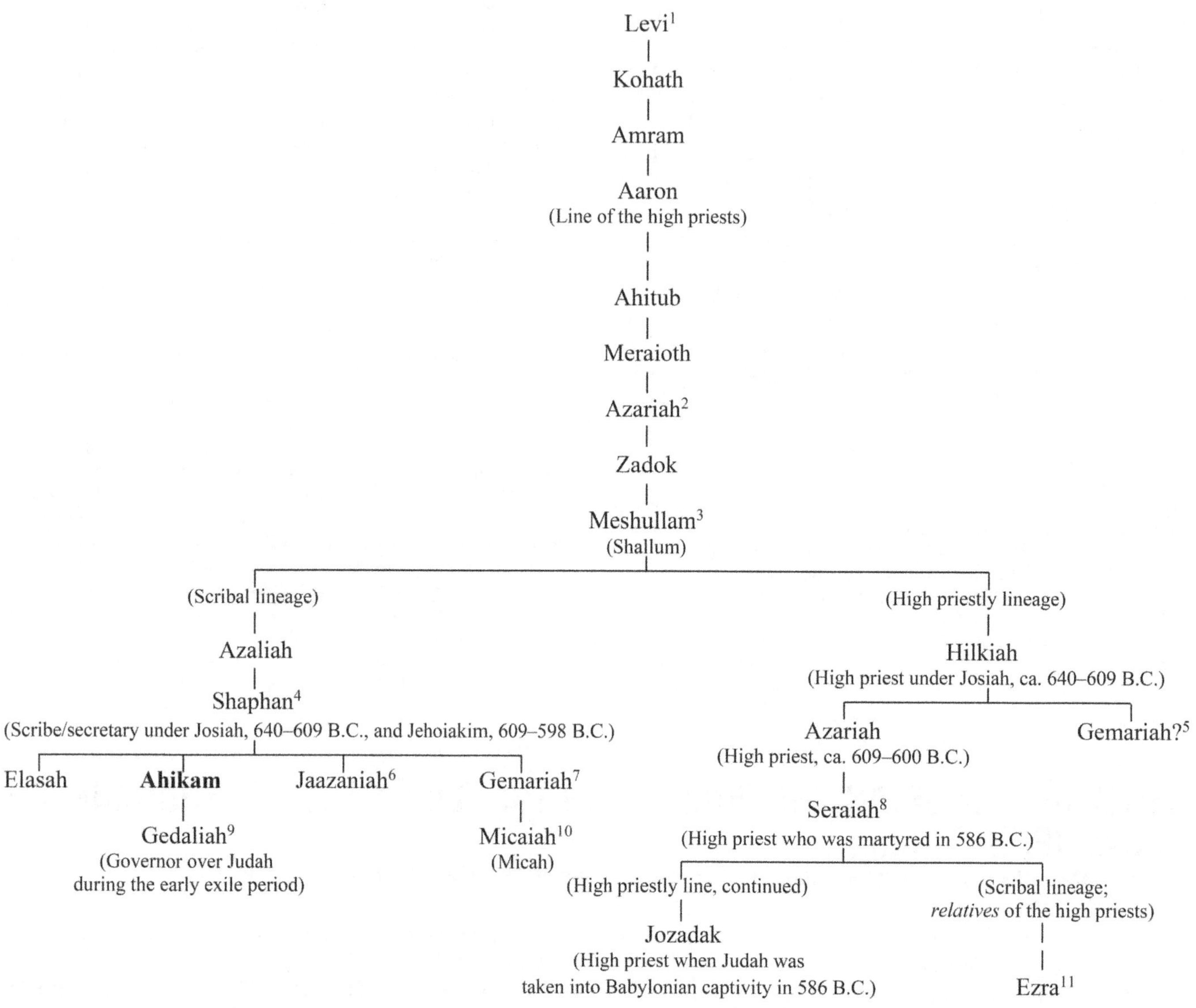

Biblical and Theological Significance

Ahikam the scribe, an official in the days of King Josiah (**2 Kings 22:12, 14**) and King Jehoiakim (**Jeremiah 26:24**) supported Jeremiah the prophet and saved his life by persuading the priests and false prophets not to kill him (**Jeremiah 26:1–24**). Ahikam's office or position is unknown, but he appears in a number of crucial moments in the kingdom of Judah's last days. First, he was present in the royal chamber as Josiah read from the scroll that was rediscovered in the archives of the refurbished Temple (**2 Kings 22:12**). Indubitably, it was the book of Deuteronomy because the title "Book of the Law" (**2 Kings 22:11**) is found only in Deuteronomy or in reference to that book (**Deuteronomy 28:61; 29:21; 30:10; Joshua 1:8; 8:31, 34; 2 Kings 14:6; 22:8, 11; Nehemiah 8:1, 3, 8; 9:3; Galatians 3:10**). The scroll spoke powerfully of the kings and their character and responsibilities (**Deuteronomy 17:14–20**), a message that the kings of Judah needed to hear. The discovery of the scroll sparked a great spiritual reformation under Josiah (**2 Kings 23:4–25; 2 Chronicles 34:19–33**). What role Ahikam may have played in all this is not clear, but Ahikam clearly supported Jeremiah in the prophet's latter years, and the support continued with Ahikam's son, Gedaliah, who was the governor of Judah under Nebuchadnezzar (**Jeremiah 26:24; 39:14; 40:5–11**). Gedaliah is almost always identified as "Gedaliah son of Ahikam" (**2 Kings 25:22; Jeremiah 39:14; 40:5–7, 9, 11, 14, 16; 41:1–2, 6, 10, 16, 18; 43:6**).

Notes

1. For the line of Levi and his descendants, including references and the branching of the scribal lineage from the high priestly line, see charts "**1 Chronicles 6:** Levi: High Priests, Priests, Levites, and Musicians in Solomon's Temple" and "**Ezra 7:** Ezra, the Priestly Scribe and Teacher of the Law (Post-Exile)."

2. For more information on Azariah, see Azariah #19 in chart "**Supplement 2**: The High Priests of Israel."

3. Shallum (**1 Chronicles 6:12–13; Ezra 7:2**) is otherwise Meshullam (**1 Chronicles 9:11; Nehemiah 11:11**; **12:33?**). See chart "**Supplement 2**: The High Priests of Israel."

4. See chart "**2 Kings 22**: Shaphan, Scribal Secretary under King Josiah and King Jehoiakim of Judah."

5. This Gemariah is proposed because he is called the "son of Hilkiah" in **Jeremiah 29:3**, although the meaning may be that Gemariah was a *relative* of Hilkiah the high priest (i.e., Gemariah, the son of Shaphan; **Jeremiah 36:10–12**) and therefore there was only one Gemariah; see note 7.

6. See chart "**Ezekiel 8**: Jaazaniah the Scribe, Who Served as a Priest to Idol Worshipers in Solomon's Temple in the Days of Ezekiel the Prophet (Pre-Exile)."

7. Gemariah (who is in a scribal lineage) was an official in the court of King Jehoiakim of Judah. The "room of Gemariah" (**Jeremiah 36:10**) was located in the upper courtyard at the New Gate, and from there, Baruch (Jeremiah's amanuensis) read the scroll of Jeremiah to the people (**Jeremiah 36:10–12, 25**).

8. This Seraiah is designated Seraiah #1 in other charts; for the differentiation of several proposed Seraiah figures, see chart "**Ezra 7**: Ezra, the Priestly Scribe and Teacher of the Law (Post-Exile)".

9. Gedaliah was appointed by Nebuchadnezzar to be the governor over the people who remained in the land of Judah during the time of the Babylonian exile (**2 Kings 25:22**). When Jeremiah was set free, he was invited by Nebuzaradan to go to Babylon, but Jeremiah refused; instead, Jeremiah chose to live with Gedaliah the governor at Mizpah (**Jeremiah 40:1–6**); also see **Jeremiah 39:14; 40:9, 11–13, 16; 41:1; 43:6**.

10. Micaiah son of Gemariah (**2 Kings 22:12; Jeremiah 36:11–13**) is the same person as Micah, the father of Abdon (**2 Chronicles 34:20**); see chart "**2 Kings 22**: Genealogy of Shaphan, Scribal Secretary under King Josiah and King Jehoiadkim of Judah."

11. For the lineage of Ezra, see chart "**Ezra 7**: Ezra, the Priestly Scribe and Teacher of the Law (Post-Exile)."

JEREMIAH 28: HANANIAH THE FALSE PROPHET (PRE-EXILE)

Approximate Dating: ca. 594 B.C. ***Relevant Scriptures:*** **Jeremiah 28:1–17**

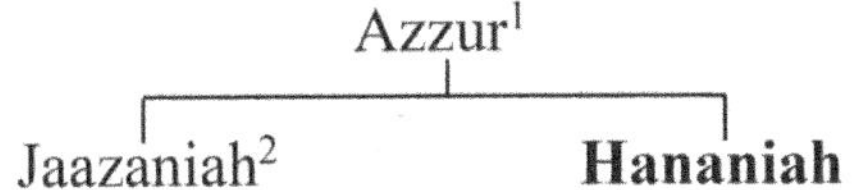

Biblical and Theological Significance

Hananiah of Gibeon was a false prophet during the reign of Zedekiah of Judah (ca. 597–586 B.C.) and the early days of the exile; he was a contemporary of Jeremiah the prophet. In ca. 594 B.C., Hananiah predicted several things: that the Babylonian bondage would be over in two years (**Jeremiah 28:3, 11**), the vessels of the temple would be restored, and King Jehoiachin and all the captives who had been taken to Babylon would return (**Jeremiah 28:3–4**). Jeremiah contended with Hananiah, accusing him of lying about being a prophet and misleading the people with his messages. Hananiah's punishment, said Jeremiah (in line with Torah)[3], would be death—an execution Yahweh himself brought to pass a few months later (**Jeremiah 28:15–17**).

Notes

1. Azzur was the father of Hananiah (**Jeremiah 28:1**) and, it seems, of Jaazaniah as well (**Ezekiel 11:1**).

2. Jaazaniah became a leader among the people of Jerusalem after most of the leadership and ruling class had been deported to Babylon. Jaazaniah, and Pelatiah the son of Benaiah, are described as "men who are plotting evil and giving wicked advice in this city [Jerusalem]" (**Ezekiel 11:1–4**). Jaazaniah the son of Azzur is not (1) Jaazaniah the son of Shaphan (**Ezekiel 8:11**) who is in a scribal lineage, nor (2) Jaazaniah the son of Jeremiah, the son of Habazziniah, a Rekabite (**Jeremiah 35:3**).

3. The book of Deuteronomy speaks of prophets who will arise from within Israel and try to lead the people into idolatry. In some cases, Yahweh will permit the prophecies that advocate the worship of other gods to come true in order to test his people to see if they really love him (**Deuteronomy 13:1–5**). False prophets could come from one's own family (**Deuteronomy 13:6–11**), but more often, they came from outside the chosen nation (**Deuteronomy 13:12–18**). In any case, such persons must be put to death because they have committed the worst of sins—rebelling against the Creator of heaven and earth, as well as worshiping the created things themselves (**Deuteronomy 13:5, 9, 15**; cf. **18:9–22**)—"Expel the wicked person from among you" (**1 Corinthians 5:13**).

JEREMIAH 29: ELASAH THE SCRIBE AND GEMARIAH THE PRIEST WHO TOOK THE LETTER OF JEREMIAH THE PROPHET TO THE CAPTIVES IN BABYLON[1]

Approximate Dating: ca. 598 B.C. ***Relevant Scriptures:*** **Jeremiah 29:3**

Genealogy of Elasah (Scribal Lineage)

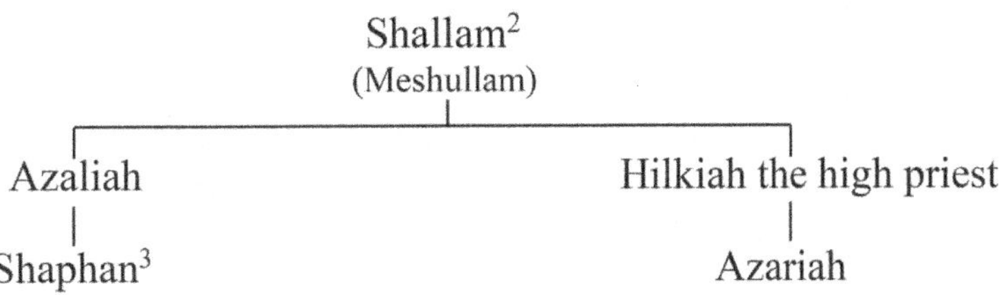

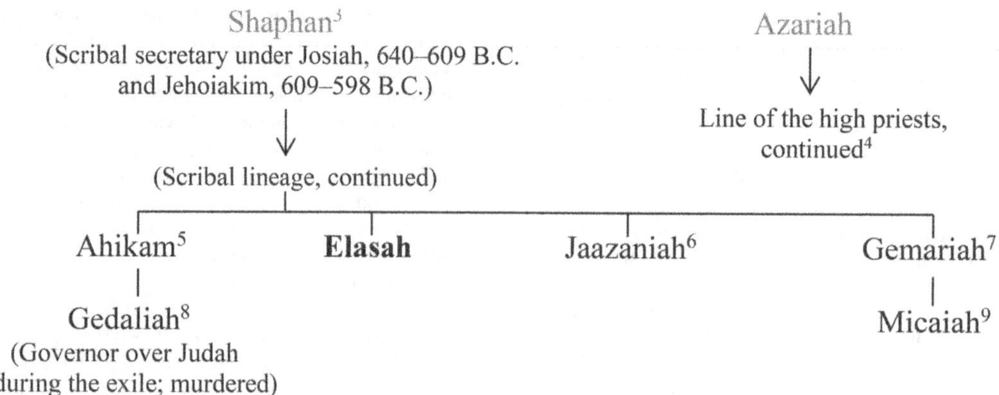

Genealogy of Gemariah (Kohathite Priestly Lineage)

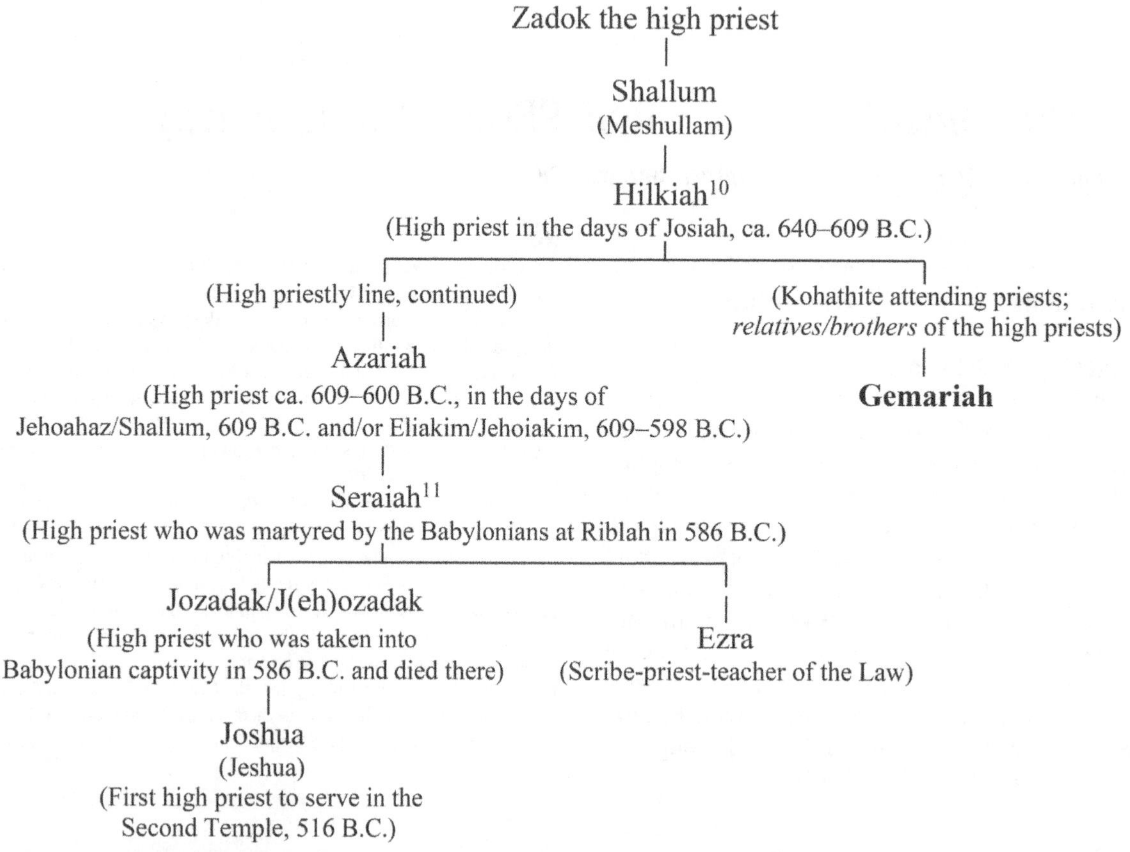

Biblical and Theological Significance

Elasah was the son of the famous scribe Shaphan, and Gemariah was the son of Hilkiah[12] the high priest. Together, Elasah and Gemariah were chosen by Jeremiah to deliver a letter Jeremiah had written to the elders, priests, prophets, and people in Babylonian captivity (**Jeremiah 29:3**). The major theme of the letter was that they would be in Babylon for seventy years, and they should remain faithful to Yahweh and at the same time be good neighbors to their captors (**Jeremiah 29:4–8**). The Babylonians—in contrast to the earlier Assyrians—were generally a welcoming imperial nation under which great freedom to settle, build, and engage in profitable business was not only tolerated, but encouraged.[13] Those not taken into exile were not to rejoice, however, said the prophet, for destruction, death, and deportation awaited those left behind, a prophecy that found fulfillment in the conquests of Nebuchadnezzar in 597 and 586 B.C. (**Jeremiah 29:15–23**).

Notes

1. The captives included King Jeconiah (also called Jehoiachin); Nehushta the queen mother (**2 Kings 24:8, 15–16**); court officials; leaders of Judah and Jerusalem; and skilled workers and artisans (**Jeremiah 29:2**).

2. Shallum (**1 Chronicles 6:12–13; Ezra 7:2**) is also Meshullam (**1 Chronicles 9:11; Nehemiah 11:11**; and possibly **12:33**). Shallum/Meshullam appears to be called Sallumus by Josephus (*Jewish Antiquities* 10.8.6). For the complete lineage of the high priests, see chart "**Supplement 2**: The High Priests of Israel."

3. Shaphan, a scribe under King Josiah of Judah (**2 Kings 22:3, 8–10, 12;**

2 Chronicles 34:8, 15–16, 18, 20**), is discussed in chart "**2 Kings 22**: Shaphan, Scribal Secretary under King Josiah and King Jehoiakim of Judah."

4. For the complete line of the high priests, see chart "**Supplement 2**: The High Priests of Israel."

5. Ahikam was sympathetic toward Jeremiah and influential in saving his life (**Jeremiah 26:24**). See chart "**Jeremiah 26**: Ahikam Who Befriended Jeremiah the Prophet in the Days of King Jehoiakim of Judah."

6. Jaazaniah son of Shaphan led seventy elders of the house of Israel in the worship of beastly idols portrayed on the walls of the Temple (**Ezekiel 8:9–11**).

7. Gemariah, the son of Shaphan the scribe, is referred to in **Jeremiah 36:10–12**. Shaphan the scribe and Hilkiah the high priest both had sons named "Gemariah," but they are different individuals.

8. Gedaliah was appointed the governor over the people who stayed in land of Judah during the period of the Babylonian captivity (**2 Kings 25:22; Jeremiah 39:14; 40:5–7, 9, 11, 14, 16; 41:1–2, 6, 10, 16, 18; 43:6**). When Jerusalem fell, the king of Babylon spared Jeremiah the prophet, and he went to live with Gedaliah "among the people" who had remained in Jerusalem (cf. **Jeremiah 39:11–14, 40:5–6**). Yet, within two months of the fall of Jerusalem in 586 B.C., Gedaliah was murdered (**2 Kings 25:8, 22–25**; cf. **Jeremiah 39:1–2; 40:7–8; 41:1–2**). Gedaliah son of Ahikam is not (1) Gedaliah the son of Jeduthun (Levites/singers; **1 Chronicles 25:3, 9**) nor (2) Gedaliah son of Pashhur (**Jeremiah 38:1**).

9. Micaiah the son of Gemariah is mentioned in **Jeremiah 36:11–13**.

10. Hilkiah was the high priest under King Josiah of Judah (**2 Kings 22:4**). See the lineage of the high priests in **Ezra 7:1–5** and the chart "**Supplement 2**: The High Priests of Israel."

11. In other charts, such as "**Ezra 7**: Ezra, the Priestly Scribe and Teacher of the Law (Post-Exile)," this high priest is designated Seraiah #1, the ancestor of Ezra. For the martyrdom of Seraiah, see **2 Kings 25:18–21; Jeremiah 52:24–27**.

12. Other figures are named Hilkiah—see note 1 in chart "**2 Kings 18**: Eliakim, the Palace Administrator who Replaced Shebna the Scribal Secretary During the Reign of King Hezekiah of Judah"—however, the context and chronology of this passage suggests that Gemariah was most likely the son of Hilkiah the high priest.

13. The "Murašû Tablets" in New Babylonian Akkadian speak of Jewish businessmen in Babylon engaged in investments, trade, and merchandising alongside their Gentile friends.

JEREMIAH 32: BARUCH, THE SCRIBE AND AMANUENSIS OF JEREMIAH THE PROPHET

Approximate Dating: ca. 605–586 B.C. ***Relevant Scriptures:*** **Jeremiah 32:12, 16; Chapter 36; 43:6; 45:1; 51:59**

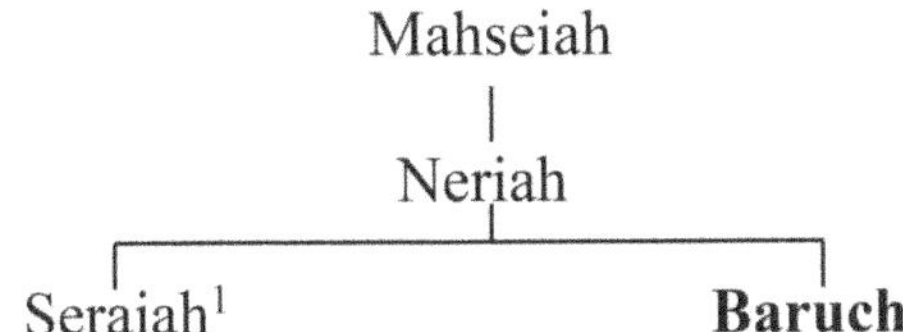

Biblical and Theological Significance

Baruch was a professional scribe and the friend and amanuensis (secretary) of Jeremiah the prophet (627–586 B.C.). In 605 B.C.,[2] when the Lord commanded Jeremiah to write down the prophecies he had received (**Jeremiah 36:1–3**), he called for Baruch to inscribe the prophecies on the parchment scroll for him—"while Jeremiah dictated[3] all the words the LORD had spoken to him, Baruch wrote them on the scroll" (**Jeremiah 36:4**; see **v. 18**). Later, on a public day of fasting[4] in the fifth year of King Jehoiakim (608–598 B.C.), Baruch read the prophecies of Jeremiah to the people (**Jeremiah 36:10**) and then read it again to a private audience of Jehoiakim's court officials (**Jeremiah 36:11–18**). When the scribes and princes heard the words of Jeremiah, they told Baruch and Jeremiah to hide. Initially, the scroll of Jeremiah was hidden in the chamber of Elishama the scribe, but eventually it was read to King Jehoiakim. Upon hearing the words, the king immediately burned the scroll and sought the lives of Baruch and Jeremiah, but "the LORD had hidden them" (**Jeremiah 36:26**). The Lord then commanded that a second scroll be written: "as Jeremiah dictated, Baruch wrote on it *all the words*[5] of the scroll that Jehoiakim king of Judah had burned in the fire" (**Jeremiah 36:32,** emphasis added). Baruch suffered anguish alongside Jeremiah (**Jeremiah 45:2–3**), but Jeremiah reassured him that despite the circumstances, the Lord would save his life (**Jeremiah 45:5**). Baruch appears to have gone to Egypt with Jeremiah (**Jeremiah 43:5–8**).

Notes

1. This Seraiah was a staff officer (quartermaster) in Zedekiah's administration (**Jeremiah 51:59**). In ca. 593 B.C., Seraiah was sent by Jeremiah to accompany King Zedekiah to Babylon. When he arrived there, Seraiah read the words of Jeremiah's prophecies against Babylon—probably those written in **Jeremiah 50–51** (**Jeremiah 51:59–64**). This Seraiah is not (1) Seraiah the scribal secretary under David (**2 Samuel 8:17**), (2) Seraiah the chief priest who was martyred at Riblah (cf. **2 Kings 25:18–21; 1 Chronicles 6:14; Ezra 7:1; Nehemiah 11:11; Jeremiah 52:24–27**), (3) Seraiah son of Tanhumeth (**2 Kings 25:23; Jeremiah 40:8**), or (4) Seraiah son of Azriel (**Jeremiah 36:26**).

2. **Jeremiah 25:1** provides a chronological marker by saying that "the fourth year of Jehoiakim son of Josiah king of Judah . . . was the first year of Nebuchadnezzar king of Babylon [605 B.C.]."

3. The verb קָרָא (*qara*) in this context means "pronounce, articulate." Jeremiah orally conveyed to Baruch all that Yahweh had "said" דָּבַר (*dabar*) to him. The difference is that Yahweh did not speak audibly, whereas Jeremiah did.

4. The fast may be related to an imminent threat to Jerusalem, since King Nebuchadnezzar had decisively defeated Pharoah Necho II of Egypt at Carchemish in 605 B.C. and almost destroyed the Philistine city of Ashkelon in 604 B.C. (cf. **Jeremiah 36:1; 47:5**).

5. The Hebrew כָּל־דִּבְרֵי הַסֵּפֶר emphatically underscores the point that "all the words" means precisely what it says: no more, no fewer, no other words (this is what Paul had in mind in his famous statement on the inspiration of Scripture in **2 Timothy 3:16**). Besides the message contained in the scroll, an important one indeed, the process of receiving divine revelation, its "incarnation" on papyrus or parchment, and its inerrant recollection, even if destroyed, testifies to the profound, fundamental theological concept that lies at the base of all others: The word of God, perfect in its origin, protected in its revelation, and preserved in its transmission, is reliable in all its essence and effects. The entire passage in **Jeremiah 36** illustrates this concept as follows:

- The message came to Jeremiah from God and contained "all the words" that God spoke on the subject of "Israel, Judah and all the other nations" (**vv. 1–2**)
- Jeremiah dictated "all the words the LORD had spoken to him" to Baruch (**v. 4**)

- Baruch read to the assembly "the words of the LORD" (**v. 8**)
- Baruch explained to the critics that "He [Jeremiah] dictated all these words to me, and I wrote them in ink on the scroll" (**v. 18**)
- The scroll was cut up and burned in the fire (**v. 23**)
- The Lord commanded Jeremiah to write on a new scroll "all the words that were on the first scroll" (**v. 28**)
- The prophet spoke and Baruch wrote "all the words of the scroll" that had been destroyed (**v. 32**)

Thus, Jeremiah and Baruch defined the truth of divine revelation of Scripture.

JEREMIAH 35: THE REKABITES (KENITE DESCENDANTS)

Approximate Dating: ca. 1050–600 B.C. ***Relevant Scriptures:*** **Jeremiah 35:1–18**; also **Genesis 15:19; Exodus 2:16–22; 3:1: 4:18; 18:1–6; Numbers 10:29; 24:21; Judges 1:16; 4:11–22; 1 Chronicles 2:55**

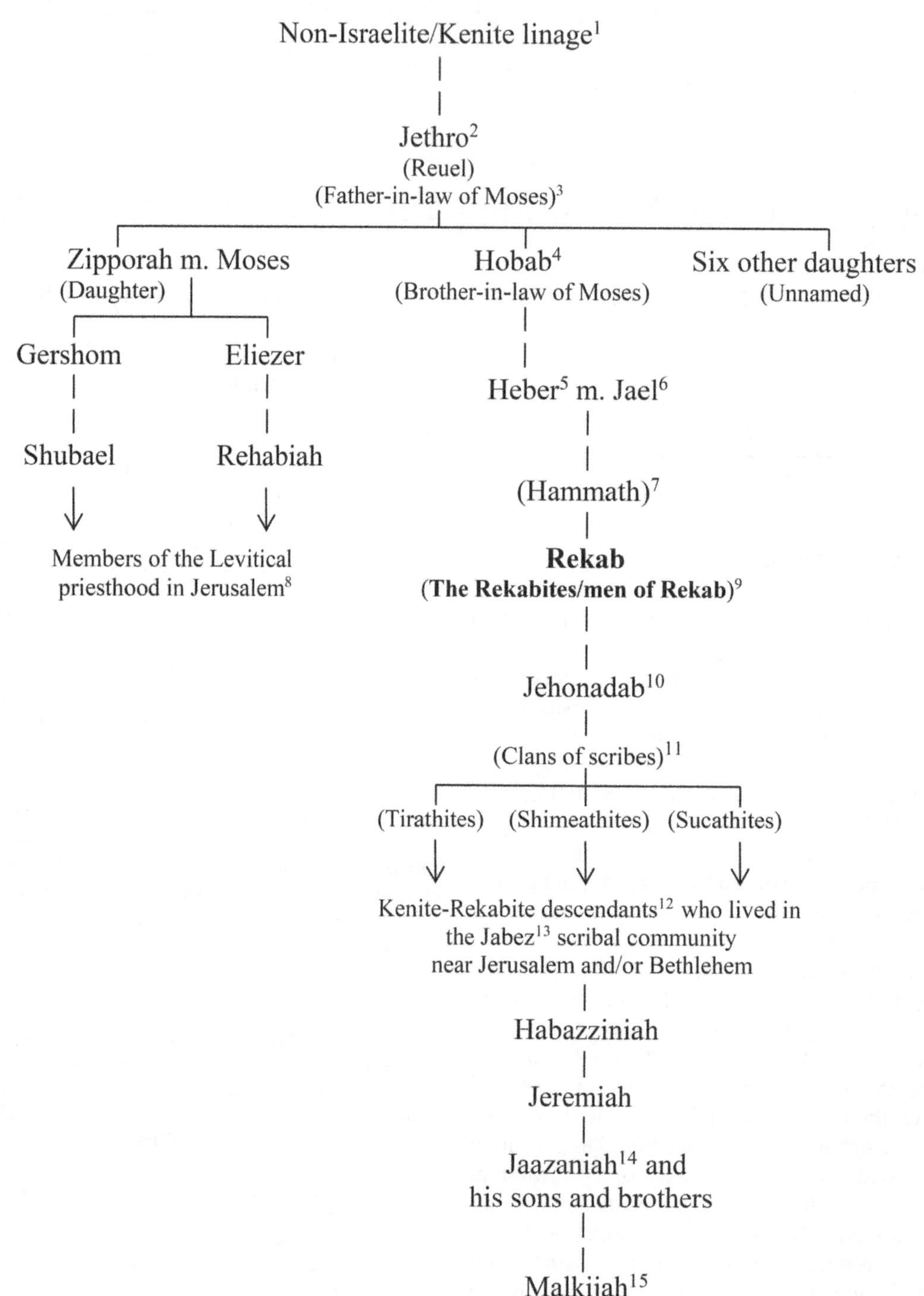

Biblical and Theological Significance

The Rekabites were a sub-family of the Kenites especially notable for their strict adherence to Torah, though they were not Israelites.[16] Because of their pious lifestyle, zealous actions, and obedience to the instructions of their godly ancestor J(eh)onadab, they became the recipients of a remarkable promise of a perpetual covenant that ensured that they would never die out as a people in service to God (**Jeremiah 35:18–19**).[17] This promise was reminiscent of the perpetual priesthood promised to Aaron's grandson, Phinehas, for his zealous actions (**Numbers 25:5–13**). The promise to the Rekabites, in essence, shamed the Israelites (cf. **Jeremiah 35:12–17**). Although the Israelites were the *chosen* nation, they had a history of covenant violation, in contrast to the integrity of these Rekabites, who were from less favorable roots. This kind of comparison in Rabbinic exegesis is called "Qal wa-Homer," "light and heavy," suggesting that if an unlikely thing such as Rekabite faithfulness could be achieved, how much easier should it be for those blessed as God's chosen people?

Notes

1. The Kenites were original occupants of Canaan (**Genesis 15:19**) who "showed kindness to all the Israelites when they came up out of Egypt" (**1 Samuel 15:6**). The Kenites lived in the Negev (**1 Samuel 27:10**) near Arad (**Judges 1:16**) and later, in the north near Hazor (**Judges 4:17**); see notes 4 and 5. The Kenite name reflects a Hebrew root meaning "smith," which suggests they pursued a metalsmithing occupation that entailed travel from job to job.

2. Jethro is also called "Reuel" (**Exodus 2:18**); he is identified as a "priest of Midian" (**Exodus 2:16; 3:1**) and "Reuel the Midianite, Moses' father-in-law" (**Numbers 10:29**). Some Kenites lived near the Midianites (the descendants of Abraham and Keturah) and are therefore described as both "Kenites" and "Midianites" (see **Numbers 10:29; Judges 4:11**).

3. Regarding the in-law connections between Moses and Zipporah's family: In technical terminology, the Hebrew for intermarriage revolves around the root חתן (*khtn*). As a verb in the hithpael stem, the meaning is (1) "marry with" or (2) "become a son-in-law." In the Qal participle *khoten*, "father-in-law" is meant. The noun חָתָן, *khatan*, conveys "son-in-law," "daughter's husband," "bridegroom."

4. Moses implored his brother-in-law, Hobab, to accompany Israel in order that his family could "be our eyes" in the wilderness (**Numbers 10:31**), which Hobab eventually agreed to do (**Numbers 10:29–33**). Initially, the Kenites settled near Jericho, but afterward, they moved to Arad (**Judges 1:16**) and assimilated with the Judahites in the semi-desert region of the Negev in the southern extreme of Judah's territory.

5. Heber is called a "Kenite" (**Judges 5:24**) and a "Kenite of the children of Hobab [Moses' brother-in-law]" (**Judges 4:11**, NKJV). Some Kenite clans assimilated into the tribe of Judah; however, at some point, Heber separated his family from the Kenites in the south near Arad and moved northward to Zaanannim, in the tribe of Naphtali, near Kedesh (the home of Barak, Israel's army commander; **Judges 4:6, 11**). Zaanannim was near Hammath—probably referring to the Levitical town of Hammoth Dor/Hammon of Naphtali (cf. **Joshua 21:32**; **1 Chronicles 6:76**). In a war with Israel in the days of Deborah the judge, Jabin, the Canaanite king of Hazor, was defeated (**Judges 4**), and the Canaanite army commander Sisera fled on foot to the tent of Heber the Kenite, whom he considered his ally. However, Heber's wife Jael—unlike her husband—had remained loyal to Israel and Yahweh. Jael killed Sisera by driving a tent peg through his temple (**Judges 4:17–22**)! Apparently, the family of Jael—either with or without Heber?—moved south once again, where they associated with a pious scribal community at Jabez that had been founded by Jabez the Asshurite, of the tribe of Judah (cf. **1 Chronicles 4:5–10**; see chart "**1 Chronicles 4**: Judah"). These Kenites and Rekabites became prominent clans of scribes—the Tirathites, Shimeathites, and Sucathites—who settled and worked at Jabez, which is thought by scholars to be near Bethlehem (**1 Chronicles 2:55**; Yoshitaka Kobayashi, "Jabez," *Anchor Yale Bible Dictionary* 3:595). For more information, see chart "**Judges 4**: Heber and Jael (Kenites) and Their Descendants Who Co-mingled with the Pious Jabez–Rekabite Scribal Community near Jerusalem."

6. The heroic deeds of Jael in the war between Israel and the Canaanites are recounted in **Judges 4:9, 17–22**. Jael is praised in the Song of Deborah as Israel's true military deliverer for having slain Sisera (**Judges 5:24**).

7. Hammath was the "father [founder] of the Rekabites" (**1 Chronicles 2:55**) and possibly the *founder* of the city of Hammath, meaning "hot spring" (cf. **Joshua 19:35**; and the variants, Hammoth Dor in **Joshua 21:32** and Hammon in **1 Chronicles 6:76**)—possibly the hot spring of Hammam Tabariyeh, two miles south of Tiberias (M.G. Easton, "Hammath," *Easton's Bible Dictionary*).

8. See chart "**Exodus 18**: Moses' Sons, Gershom and Eliezer, and Their Descendants Who Served in Solomon's Temple."

9. The Rekabites lived separated from the Israelites; they adhered to a strict, voluntary, Nazirite-like lifestyle and lived exclusively in tents (cf. **Jeremiah 35:6–10**). According to **1 Chronicles 4:8–12**, the men of Rekah (Kenites) intermarried with Judahites, specifically with the clans of Aharhel, the son of Harum, the son of Koz, the son of Ashhur, the son of Hezron, the son of Judah (see note 13). This may explain the formal position held by Malkijah the son of Rekab, who became the ruler of the district of Beth Hakkerem in Jerusalem in the post-exile (**Nehemiah 3:14**); see note 15.

10. Jehonadab (or Jonadab) the patriarchal figure of the Rekabites, lived a pious, Nazirite-like, aesthetic lifestyle and had a zeal for the Lord. He accompanied King Jehu of Israel (841–814 B.C.) to Samaria where the two of them killed the remaining members of the evil house of Ahab who were Baal worshipers (**2 Kings 10:15–17, 23–28**). He should not be confused with Jonadab, David's nephew (**2 Samuel 13:3, 5, 32, 35**).

11. For the scribal clans in **1 Chronicles 2:55**, see note 5.

12. The Kenites and Rekabites, perhaps attracted by mutual religious piety, appear to intermarry. Their descendants lived exclusive non-agrarian, tent-dwelling, nomadic lifestyles, but during the Babylonian invasion they fled to Jerusalem and became city-dwellers: "Neither you nor your descendants must ever drink wine. Also you must never build houses, sow seed or plant vineyards; you must never have any of these things, but must always live in tents. Then you will live a long time in the land where you are nomads.' We have obeyed everything our forefather Jehonadab son of Rekab commanded us. Neither we nor our wives nor our sons and daughters have ever drunk wine or built houses to live in or had vineyards, fields or crops. But when Nebuchadnezzar king of Babylon invaded this land, we said, 'Come, we must go to Jerusalem to escape the Babylonian and Aramean armies.' So we have remained in Jerusalem" (**Jeremiah 35:6–9, 11**).

13. The lineage of Jabez the Judahite is shown in chart "**1 Chronicles 4**: Judah"; see note 25. Jabez the Judahite was the eponymous ancestor of the scribal community near Jerusalem and/or Bethlehem, a mixed community of Judahites, Kenites, and Rekabites from Hammath (**1 Chronicles 2:55**).

14. Jaazaniah was a leader of the Rekabites in Jerusalem in the days of the prophet Jeremiah and King Jehoiakim/Eliakim (609–598 B.C.; cf. **Jeremiah 35:1–3**). Jeremiah summoned Jaazaniah to the house of the Lord and offered wine to him and his son and brothers, but Jaazaniah refused to drink because of his fidelity to his ancestor's instructions (**Jeremiah 35:6–9**). Jaazaniah explained that the Rekabites came to Jerusalem when Nebuchadnezzar had invaded the land (cf. **Jeremiah 35:11**). The Lord compared the piety and obedience of "the descendants of Jehonadab son of Rekab" (**Jeremiah 35:16**; see note 17) to the rebellious disobedience of Israel toward him (**Jeremiah 35:12–17**). Jaazaniah, a descendant of Jonadab the Rekabite, received an extraordinary promise from God (**Jeremiah 35:19**; see note 17).

15. Malkijah, called the "son of Rekab" (**Nehemiah 3:14**), should be understood as a *descendant* of Rekab and a member of the pious Rekabite clan. He lived in post-exilic Jerusalem around 444 B.C. and was the ruler of the district of Beth Hakkerem (**Nehemiah 3:14**)—an important district of the city whose height allowed signaling of the approach of enemies from the north (**Jeremiah 6:1**). Malkijah helped repair the Dung (or Refuse) Gate (**Nehemiah 2:13; 3:13–14; 12:31**), also called the Potsherd Gate (**Jeremiah 19:2**). In the days of Nehemiah (ca. 444–332 B.C.), the Refuse Gate was near the southern/southeastern corner of the wall, between the Valley Gate that lay to the west and the Fountain Gate that lay to the southeast. The Refuse Gate faced the Hinnom Valley, which was the city dump where refuse was continually burned.

Malkijah the Rekabite (**Nehemiah 3:14**) should not be confused with (1) Malkijah the son of Harim the Kohathite priest and the father/ancestor of Pashhur (**Nehemiah 3:11**; cf. **1 Chronicles 9:12; 24:9; Ezra 2:38–39; 10:21;**

Nehemiah 7:41–42; 10:5; 11:12), or with (2) Malkijah the goldsmith (**Nehemiah 3:31**), who lived in the same general time period (444 B.C.).

16. This is an excellent example of individuals (or peoples) who came to believe in the Yahweh of Israel as God.

17. Through the words of Jeremiah the prophet, the pious Rekabites were given a remarkable promise: "This is what the LORD Almighty, the God of Israel, says: 'You have obeyed the command of your forefather Jehonadab and have followed all his instructions and have done everything he ordered.' Therefore this is what the LORD Almighty, the God of Israel, says: 'Jehonadab son of Rekab will never fail to have a descendant to serve me'" (**Jeremiah 35:18–19**). This perhaps relates to the formal position held by Malkijah the son of Rekab, who became the ruler of the district of Beth Hakkerem in Jerusalem in the post-exile (**Nehemiah 3:14**) or to an unknown Rekabite ancestor/ancestress of the Messiah (?). The implication is that the Rekabites would be eligible leaders-servants-prophet-priests before God in the same way that the Aaronic priests and Levitical servants were chosen and set apart to stand and serve before God in the tabernacle, the temple, and before kings and the people (cf. **Numbers 16:9; Deuteronomy 10:8; 1 Kings 10:8; 1 Chronicles 23:28–31; 2 Chronicles 9:7; 29:10–19; 35:2–6; Jeremiah 17:19; 26:2; 33:18; Ezekiel 44:11, 15**). Noteworthy is that there is a tangential reference in the Second Temple period to a priest "of the sons of Rechab, the son of the Rechabites" in ca. A.D. 62 who spoke up against the stoning of James the Just (Eusebius, *Church History* 2.23.17); see note 26 in chart "**Matthew 1**: Jesus and His Immediate Family."

JEREMIAH 36: GEMARIAH THE SCRIBE, A CONTEMPORARY OF JEREMIAH THE PROPHET (PRE-EXILE)

Approximate Dating: ca. 605 B.C. ***Relevant Scriptures:*** **Jeremiah 36:10–12, 25;** also **2 Kings 22:3; 25:22; 1 Chronicles 6:12–14; 9:11; 2 Chronicles 34:8; Ezra 7:1–5; Nehemiah 11:11; Jeremiah 26:24; 29:3; 39:14; 40:5, 9, 11; 41:2; 43:6; Ezekiel 8:11**

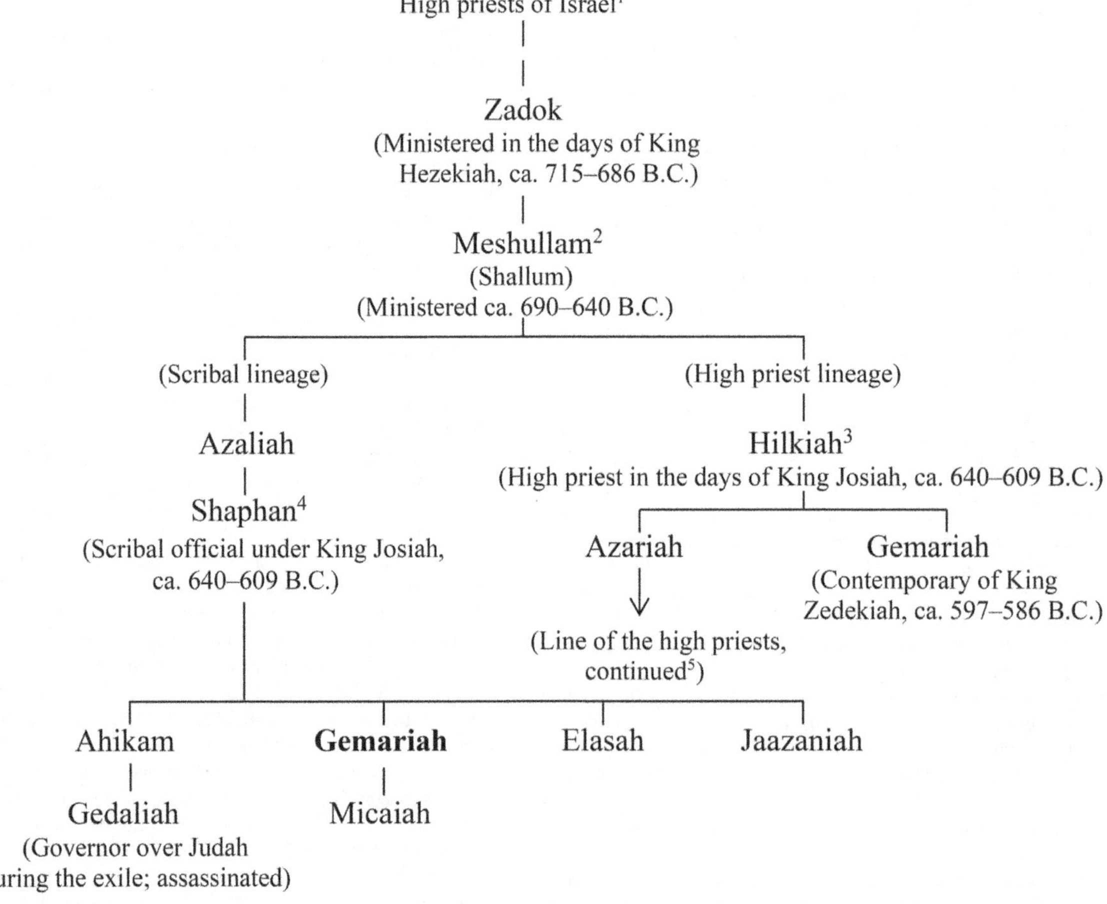

Biblical and Theological Significance

Gemariah, the son of Shaphan, was a scribal priest and a contemporary of Jeremiah the prophet (ca. 627 to as late as 562 B.C.). The prestige and importance of the scribal office is evident in that Gemariah had a chamber "in the upper courtyard at the entrance of the New Gate" (**Jeremiah 36:10**), a terrace that overlooked the great court of the temple. From that vantage point, Baruch (Jeremiah's amanuensis) read the scroll of Jeremiah to the assembly of wicked Judeans (**Jeremiah 36:10**). Gemariah sympathized with Jeremiah and pleaded with King Jehoiakim (609–598 B.C.) not to burn the prophet's scroll (**Jeremiah 36:25**). Also, a priest named Gemariah, the son of Hilkiah, carried a letter from King Zedekiah of Judah to Nebuchadnezzar of Babylon (**Jeremiah 29:3**). Although both men are named Gemariah and both are priests of the Zadok line and near contemporaries, Gemariah the son of Hilkiah is likely not the same person as Gemariah the son of Shaphan.[6]

Notes

1. See chart "**Supplement 2**: The High Priests of Israel."

2. Shallum in **1 Chronicles 6:12–13; Ezra 7:2** is Meshullam in **1 Chronicles 9:11; Nehemiah 11:11**. The various priests named Meshullam in **Nehemiah 3:4, 30; 8:4; 10:7; 12:13, 16, 33** and the Levite named Shallum in **1 Chronicles 9:31** do not refer to Shallum/Meshullam the high priest, the son of Zadok. Given the known dates that his father (Zadok) and his son (Hilkiah) served, Meshullam/Shallum probably ministered as the high priest in Solomon's Temple, ca. 690–640 B.C.

3. Hilkiah was the high priest in the days of King Josiah of Judah (640–609 B.C.). For the lineage of Hilkiah, see **1 Chronicles 9:11** and **Nehemiah 11:11**. For chronological reasons, the palace administrator named "Eliakim son of Hilkiah," who was a contemporary of King Hezekiah, 715–686 B.C., does not refer to a son of Hilkiah the high priest (**2 Kings 18:18, 26, 37; Isaiah 22:20; 36:3, 22**).

4. Shaphan was the scribal secretary in the days of Josiah (640–609 B.C.) and Jehoiakim/Eliakim (609–598 B.C.) and was a contemporary of Hilkiah the high priest (cf. **2 Kings 22:3–4**). See chart "**2 Kings 22**: Shaphan, Scribal Secretary under King Josiah and King Jehoiakim of Judah."

5. See chart "**Supplement 2**: The High Priests of Israel."

6. "Gemariah son of Hilkiah" (**Jeremiah 29:3**) appears to be a different person than the scribe "Gemariah son of Shaphan" (**Jeremiah 36:10–12**); the alternative interpretation is that Gemariah *son* of Hilkiah in **Jeremiah 29:3** means that Gemariah was a *relative* of Hilkiah (i.e., his great-nephew, the son of Shaphan).

JEREMIAH 36: THE OFFICIALS AND SCRIBES IN THE PALACE OF KING JEHOIAKIM WHO HEARD THE READING OF THE SCROLL OF JEREMIAH (PRE-EXILE)

Approximate Dating: ca. 605 B.C., in the reign of Jehoiakim, 609–598 B.C.[1] ***Relevant Scriptures:*** **Jeremiah 36:12**

1. **Elishama** the scribal secretary
2. **Delaiah** son of Shemaiah
3. **Elnathan** son of Akbor
4. **Gemariah** son of Shaphan
5. **Zedekiah** son of Hananiah
6. **Other officials**

Genealogy of Elishama (a scribal secretary, "of royal blood"):[2]

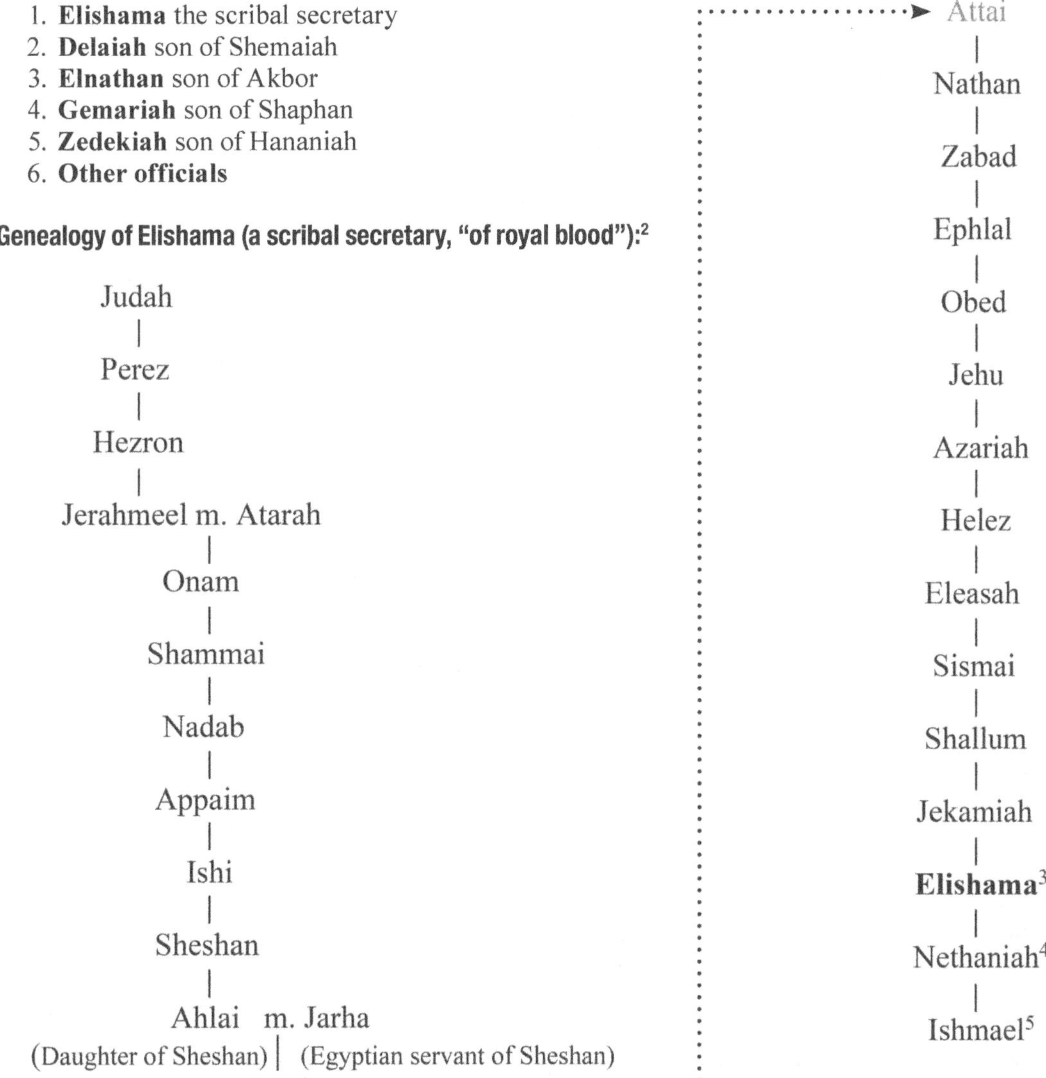

Genealogy of Delaiah (a prince-like figure):[6]

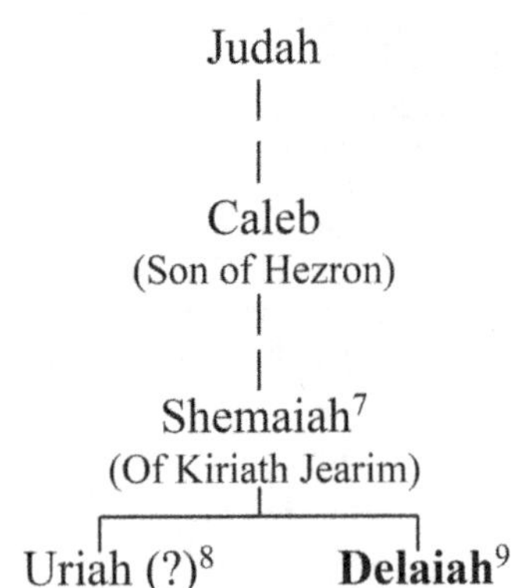

Genealogy of Elnathan and Gemariah (scribes)[10]

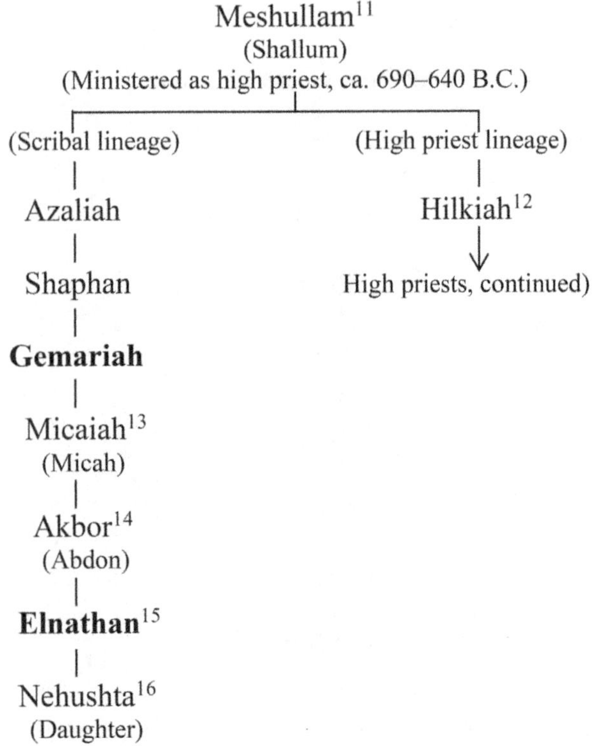

Genealogy of Zedekiah (prophet figure)

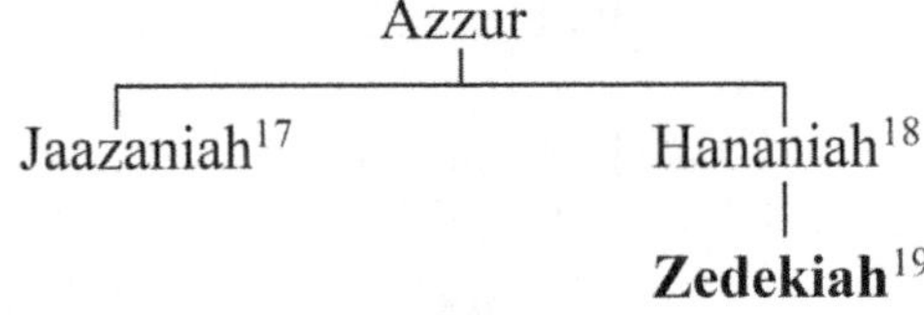

Biblical and Theological Significance

Scribes in a semi-literate world like sixth-century Israel held positions of great honor and influence. Scribal training was long and onerous and generally passed down from father to son in long lines of scribal tradition. The curriculum would include: (1) selection of proper instruments and materials such as styli, inks, leathers, or parchments and a proper bench and table; (2) mastery of the languages to be copied and written; (3) skill in the creation of readable and graphically exact and artistically eye-catching composition; and (4) in the case of dictated material (see **Jeremiah 36:1–8, 17–18, 32**), a clearly articulated orality matched by an ability and acuity to understand what is read and to reproduce it in a timely manner without error. Jeremiah's amanuensis Baruch is but one among many described as סוֹפְרִים (*sopherim*, literally, "counters"). Thanks to such efforts by later scribes, ancient manuscripts of incalculable value, such as the Dead Sea Scrolls, have enabled modern scholars to work with near perfect renditions of the Word of God, such as the Masoretic Text. "Heaven and earth will pass away, but my words will never pass away" (Jesus' words in **Matthew 24:35**).

Notes

1. According to **Jeremiah 36:1–2**, the Lord spoke to Jeremiah in the "fourth year" of King Jehoiakim/Eliakim's reign (609–598 B.C.)—corresponding to either 605 or 604 B.C.—and told him to write on a scroll "all the words I have spoken to you concerning Israel, Judah and all the other nations from the time I began speaking to you in the reign of Josiah till now." During the subsequent months, Jeremiah dictated the words to his scribe, Baruch the son of Neriah, who then wrote the scroll. Since Jeremiah was prevented from going to the temple, Baruch read the scroll of Jeremiah in the hearing of these palace officials "in the ninth month of the fifth year of Jehoiakim son of Josiah king of Judah" (**Jeremiah 36:9**), corresponding to 603 B.C.

2. For the lineage of Elishama, see chart "**1 Chronicles 2**: Jerahmeel and His Descendant, Elishama, Who Appears to be a Compiler of Historical and Genealogical Records in 1 & 2 Chronicles."

3. Elishama is said to be "of royal blood" (**2 Kings 25:25; Jeremiah 41:1**). He served as the scribal-secretary under King Jehoiakim/Eliakim and had a scribal chamber in the temple (**Jeremiah 36:20–21**) where the (first) scroll of Jeremiah had been deposited. The *royal* status of Elishama is unclear; either:

- He was a descendant of King David and perhaps named for *Elishama* David's son (**2 Samuel 5:16; 1 Chronicles 3:6, 8; 14:7**; tenth century B.C.), or
- He was an adoptee (?) into the *royal family* of Jehoiakim/Eliakim (609–598 B.C.).

Alternatively, the interpretation shown in the chart is that Elishama the son of Jekamiah (**1 Chronicles 2:41**) was the key terminal figure in the exhaustive record that is presented for the Jerahmeel clan of the tribe of Judah (**1 Chronicles 2:25–41**). The elaborate structural depth of the Jerahmeelite genealogy strongly suggests that Elishama held a prominent position in the royal court. Here, the interpretation is made that he was the key figure who assembled, organized, and formalized the various *royal* records into *authoritative* archived materials—contributing to the books of **1 & 2 Chronicles**—and was highly revered for that immense undertaking. One can assume that Elishama used all the available materials for the kings of Judah and Israel, collected historical documents, and ordered other scribes to add to them as seemed appropriate; see chart "**1 Chronicles 2**: "Genealogy of Jerahmeel and His Descendant, Elishama, Who Appears to Be a Compiler of Historical and Genealogical Records in 1 & 2 Chronicles," especially note 9.

4. The Nethaniah mentioned in **2 Kings 25:25** and **Jeremiah 40:8, 14–16; 41:1–2, 6–18** should not be confused with Nethaniah the son of Shelemiah (**Jeremiah 36:14**).

5. Ishmael (**2 Kings 25:23–25**) was part of an anti-Babylonian faction in Judah that resisted Gedaliah as the governor of Judah (**2 Kings 25:25; Jeremiah 40:8, 14; 41:1–3, 18**). Ishmael murdered Gedaliah and his Jewish supporters (**Jeremiah 41:2–3**) and killed seventy mourners from Shechem, Shiloh, and Samaria (**Jeremiah 41:4–9**). Moreover, Ishmael carried away captive all the people remaining at Mizpah, including King Zedekiah's daughters (**Jeremiah 41:10**). Ishmael's murder of Gedaliah may have been motivated by the hope of resisting the Babylonians and the hope of reestablishing the throne of Judah with himself as king.

6. For the lineage of Delaiah, see **Nehemiah 6:10** and **Jeremiah 36:12** and charts "**1 Chronicles 2**: Hezron from the Tribe of Judah" and "**Jeremiah 26**: Uriah the Prophet in the Days of King Jehoiakim of Judah (Pre-Exile)."

7. Shemaiah appears to be a descendant of Caleb the son of Hezron, from the tribe of Judah (cf. **1 Chronicles 2:18, 50–53**).

8. Uriah son of Shemaiah prophesied the same things against Jerusalem and the land as Jeremiah did (**Jeremiah 26:20**). His prophecy angered Jehoiakim so much that Uriah was afraid and fled to Egypt. However, with the assistance of Elnathan son of Akbor, King Jehoiakim brought Uriah back to Jerusalem and had him killed (**Jeremiah 26:20–23**). Uriah may have been the brother of Delaiah, or just his contemporary.

9. Delaiah sympathized with Jeremiah and tried to convince Jehoiakim not to burn Jeremiah's scroll (**Jeremiah 36:25**). He may or may not have been the brother of Uriah. This Delaiah is not the post-exilic figure Delaiah of **1 Chronicles 3:24**.

10. This is a probable genealogy for Elnathan and Gemariah; both appear to be in a scribal lineage that parallels that of the high priests.

11. Shallum (**1 Chronicles 6:12–13; Ezra 7:2**) is Meshullam (**1 Chronicles 9:11; Nehemiah 11:11**). See chart "**Jeremiah 36**: Gemariah the Scribe, a Contemporary of Jeremiah the Prophet (Pre-Exile)" to see the branching of the scribal lineage from the high priestly line.

12. Hilkiah was the high priest in the days of King Josiah of Judah (640–609 B.C.). For the lineage of Hilkiah, see **1 Chronicles 9:11** and **Nehemiah 11:11**.

13. Micaiah son of Gemariah (**2 Kings 22:12; Jeremiah 36:11, 13**) is the same person as Micah the father of Abdon/Akbor (**2 Chronicles 34:20**; see note 14). Micaiah/Micah is not (1) the prophet Micah of Moresheth (**Micah 1:1**); (2) the prophet Micaiah son of Imlah, who prophesied in the days of King Jehoshaphat (cf. **1 Kings 22:8–28; 2 Chronicles 17:7 (?); 18:7–27**); or (3) Micaiah the Levitical priest, the grandson of Asaph (**Nehemiah 12:35, 41**).

14. Akbor (**2 Kings 22:12, 14; Jeremiah 26:22; 36:12**) is Abdon (**2 Chronicles 34:20**).

15. Elnathan and Gemariah were scribes who tried to convince King Jehoiakim not to burn the scroll of Jeremiah (**Jeremiah 36:25**).

16. This Nehushta was the wife of King Jehoiakim/Eliakim (**2 Kings 24:8, 15**) and the mother of King Jehoiachin/Jeconiah (cf. **Jeremiah 13:18**). She is called the "king's mother" in **2 Kings 24:15** and the "queen mother" in **Jeremiah 13:18**. This chart shows that Nehushta's father Elnathan was from a line of scribes.

17. Jaazaniah's identity is unclear: a person by this name was the son of Shaphan the scribe (**Ezekiel 8:11**); chronology supports that he may also be the brother of the prophet Hananiah the son of Azzur (**Ezekiel 11:1**).

18. The first scroll of Jeremiah was read at the temple and at the king's palace in the fifth year of Jehoiakim/Eliakim's eleven-year reign (609–598 B.C.; **Jeremiah 36:9**). This Hananiah from Gibeon (**Jeremiah 28:1**) is the same person as Hananiah the false prophet who challenged Jeremiah's message of judgment against Zedekiah and the people of Jerusalem. Hananiah died in the seventh month of the fourth year of Zedekiah's reign (597–586 B.C.); see chart "**Jeremiah 28**: Hananiah, the False Prophet (Pre-Exile)."

19. This Zedekiah is said to be the son of Hananiah (**Jeremiah 36:12**), and Hananiah was the son of Azzur (**Jeremiah 28:1**), but it is unclear if Jaazaniah the son of "Azzur"—called a "leader of the people" and a wicked counselor—was the relative (uncle) of Zedekiah (**Ezekiel 11:1**). In any case, he is not King Zedekiah.

JEREMIAH 36: JEHUDI, THE COURT OFFICIAL IN THE DAYS OF JEREMIAH THE PROPHET (PRE-EXILE)

Approximate Dating: ca. 609 B.C. ***Relevant Scriptures:*** **Jeremiah 36:14–23**

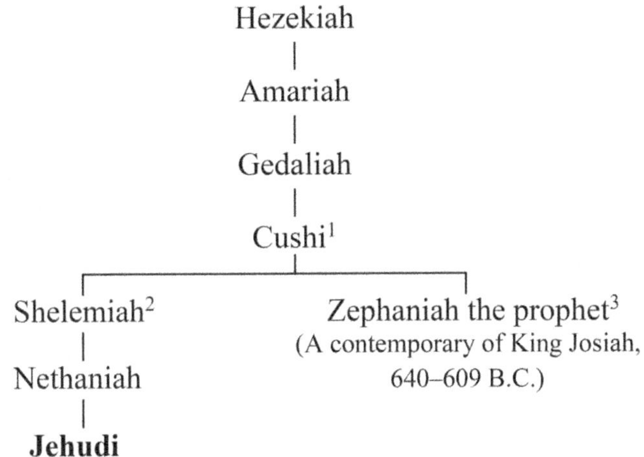

Biblical and Theological Significance

The officials[4] of Judah sent Jehudi to Baruch (Jeremiah's amanuensis) to have him bring Jeremiah's scroll so that Baruch might read it to them privately (**Jeremiah 36:10**; cf. **vv. 14–15**). Understanding the significance of the message and the scathing indictment of Judah's wicked ways (**Jeremiah 36:19**; cf. **vv. 2–3**), the officials realized they would have to inform King Jehoiakim (Eliakim). However, to protect the messengers of the Lord, the officials instructed Baruch and Jeremiah to hide first. Then, in their absence, Jehudi brought out the scroll from the chamber of Elishama the scribe and read it directly to the king with his officials standing beside him. Upon hearing the searing prophetic words condemning him and the people of Judah[5]—and even upon the official's advisement *not* to do so—Jehoiakim hastily burned the entire scroll, perhaps imagining that it would be the end of the matter (cf. **Jeremiah 36:20–27**). But, in fact, it was not the end, for the scroll that the king threw into the fire was reproduced word for word by Jeremiah as he, once again, dictated to Baruch the contents of the first scroll (**Jeremiah 36:27–28, 32**). Indeed, the words of Jeremiah's scroll exist today, preserved in Holy Scripture as the book of Jeremiah. As Isaiah said, "The grass withers and the flowers fall, but the word of our God endures forever" (**Isaiah 40:8**).

Notes

1. The lineage of Cushi, the father of Zephaniah the prophet is given in **Zephaniah 1:1**.

2. This Shelemiah is not the son of Abdeel (**Jeremiah 36:26**) or the son of Hananiah (**Jeremiah 37:13**).

3. The Lord's prophet Zephaniah prophesied in the days of King Josiah of Judah (640–609 B.C.). He appears to be the brother of Shelemiah (cf. **Zephaniah 1:1**).

4. See chart "**Jeremiah 36**: The Officials and Scribes in the Palace of King Jehoiakim Who Heard the Reading of the Scroll of Jeremiah (Pre-Exile)."

5. The words from **Jeremiah 36:30–31** show the culmination of the Lord's strong indictment against King Jehoiakim: "This is what the LORD says about Jehoiakim king of Judah: 'He will have no one to sit on the throne of David; his body will be thrown out and exposed to the heat by day and the frost by night. I will punish him and his children and his attendants for their wickedness; I will bring on them and those living in Jerusalem and the people of Judah every disaster I pronounced against them, because they have not listened.'"

JEREMIAH 36: MEN SENT BY KING JEHOIAKIM (ELIAKIM) TO SEIZE BARUCH AND JEREMIAH IN JERUSALEM (PRE-EXILE)

Approximate Dating: ca. 604 B.C. ***Relevant Scriptures:*** **Jeremiah 36:26**

1. **Jerahmeel** *"a son of the king"*
2. **Seraiah**
3. **Shelemiah**

Genealogy of Jerahmeel

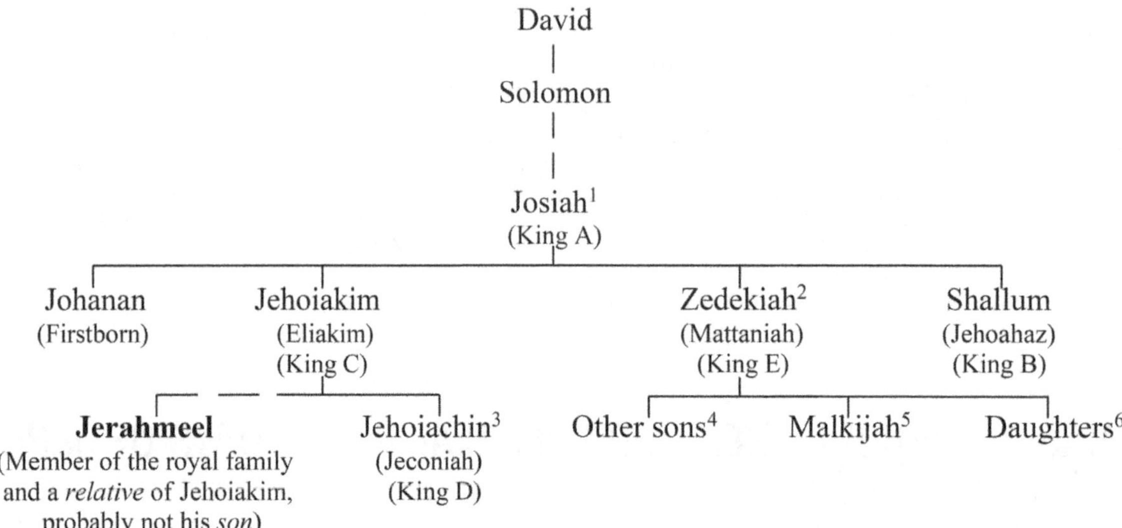

Genealogy of Seraiah

Azriel[7]

|

Seraiah[8]

Genealogy of Shelemiah

Abdeel

|

Shelemiah[9]

Biblical and Theological Significance

The prophecies of Jeremiah pronounced that the king of Babylon would come up against Judah and destroy it. As Jehudi read the scroll to King Jehoiakim, the king became so upset that he cut up the sections of columns and tossed them into the firepot "until the entire scroll was burned" (**Jeremiah 36:21–23**). Then Jehoiakim commanded these three men—Jerahmeel, Seraiah, Shelemiah—to find and arrest Baruch the scribe and Jeremiah the prophet, "but the LORD had hidden them" (**Jeremiah 36:26**).

Chronology is important to understand the identity of Jerahmeel, who is called "a son of the king" in **Jeremiah 36:26.** King Jehoiakim took office in 609 B.C. when he was twenty-five years old and reigned for eleven years (609–598 B.C.; **2 Kings 23:36; 2 Chronicles 36:5**). Jeremiah wrote the original scroll "in the fourth year of Jehoiakim," corresponding to 605 B.C. (**Jeremiah 36:1**). Baruch read the scroll to all the people in Jerusalem who had come from the towns of Judah "in the ninth month [Kislev, November-December] of the fifth year of Jehoiakim son of Josiah king of Judah," corresponding to 604 B.C. (**Jeremiah 36:9**); at this time, Jehoiakim was only twenty-nine years old. King Jehoiakim's successor—his son Jeconiah/Jehoiachin—began to reign when he was eighteen years old and reigned for a brief three months and ten days (ca. 598–597 B.C.; **2 Kings 24:8; 2 Chronicles 36:9**). Therefore, in 604 B.C. (the events of the story), Jeconiah/Jehoiachin was only twelve years old. For this reason, it is highly unlikely that "Jerahmeel, a son of the king" (**Jeremiah 36:26**) refers to a son of King Jehoiakim. Rather, Jerahmeel was more likely a member of the royal family and a *relative* of Jehoiakim, but not his son.

Notes

1. The birth order of King Josiah's sons was as follows: Johanan (firstborn), Jehoiakim (second), Zedekiah (third), Shallum (fourth; cf. **1 Chronicles 3:15–16**). The succession of the kings was: Josiah (King A; thirty-one-year reign; **2 Kings 22:1; 2 Chronicles 34:1**)—Jehoahaz (Shallum; King B; three-month reign; **2 Kings 23:31; 2 Chronicles 36:2**)—Jehoiakim (Eliakim; King C; eleven-year reign; **2 Kings 23:36; 2 Chronicles 36:5**)—Jehoiachin (Jeconiah; King D; three-month and ten-day reign; **2 Kings 24:8; 2 Chronicles 36:9**)—Zedekiah (Mattaniah; King E; eleven-year reign; **2 Kings 24:17–18; 2 Chronicles 36:11**).

2. King Zedekiah/Mattaniah was the last king of Judah. He was appointed to be king in Jerusalem by King Nebuchadnezzar of Babylon (**2 Kings 24:17**). When Zedekiah rebelled, the Babylonians came and besieged Jerusalem, destroying it. King Zedekiah and his family were taken captive to Riblah (a Syrian town located near Kadesh, on the border with Babylonia). There, Zedekiah witnessed the execution of his sons and then his own eyes were put out. Zedekiah was taken to Babylon where he was imprisoned; Zedekiah died there in exile (**2 Kings 25:5–7; Jeremiah 39:5–7; 52:9–11**).

3. King Jehoiachin/Jeconiah of Judah was the captive king of the Babylonian exile (**2 Kings 24:12, 15**). Jehoiachin was eventually released from prison by King Awel-Marduk of Babylon and given a place of honor in the palace: "So Jehoiachin put aside his prison clothes and for the rest of his life ate regularly at the king's [Awel-Marduk's] table. Day by day the king of Babylon gave Jehoiachin a regular allowance as long as he lived, till the day of his death." Jehoiachin died a natural death in Babylon (**Jeremiah 52:31–34**).

4. See **Jeremiah 39:6** where the sons of King Zedekiah were killed by the Babylonians.

5. This Malkijah appears to be a *son* of King Zedekiah (**Jeremiah 38:6**), but he is not Malkijah the father of Pashhur, a Kohathite priest (cf. **1 Chronicles 9:12; Nehemiah 11:12; Jeremiah 21:1; 38:1**).

6. The daughters of King Zedekiah are mentioned in **Jeremiah 41:10, 43:6**.

7. Azriel the father of Seraiah (**Jeremiah 36:26**) is not Azriel the father of Jerimoth (**1 Chronicles 27:19**).

8. Seraiah son of Azriel is not Seraiah #1 or #2, who were the ancestors of Ezra; for the latter, see chart "**Ezra 7**: Ezra, the Priestly Scribe and Teacher of the Law (Post-Exile)."

9. Shelemiah the son of Abdeel is a different person than his contemporaries, Shelemiah the son of Cushi (**Jeremiah 36:14**; see chart "**Jeremiah 36**: Jehudi, the Court Official in the Days of Jeremiah the Prophet (Pre-Exile)" and Shelemiah the son of Hananiah (**Jeremiah 37:13**).

JEREMIAH 37: JEHUKAL THE COURT OFFICIAL AND ZEPHANIAH THE PRIEST IN THE DAYS OF KING ZEDEKIAH OF JUDAH (PRE-EXILE)

Approximate Dating: ca. 597–586 B.C. ***Relevant Scriptures:*** **Jeremiah 37:3; 38:1–4**

Genealogy of Jehukal

Shelemiah[1]
|
Jehukal
(An official to King Zedekiah)[2]

Genealogy of Zephaniah

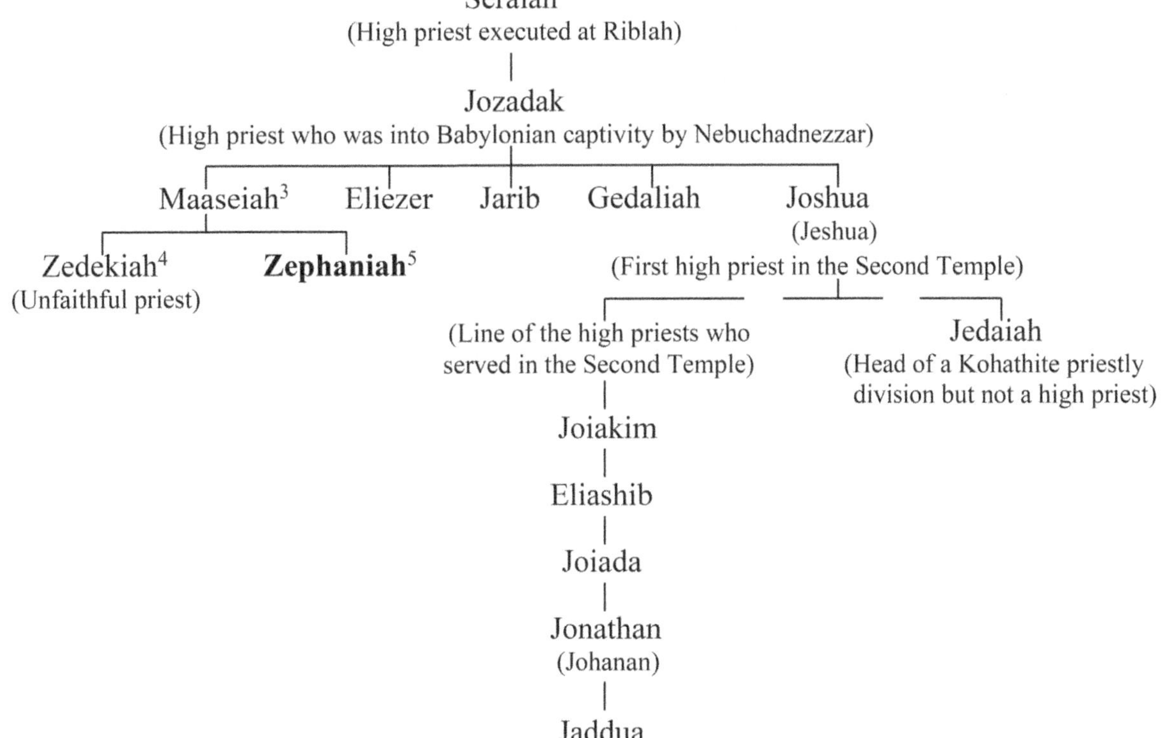

Biblical and Theological Significance

Zedekiah (Mattaniah),[6] the last ruler of Judah, asked Jehukal, an official in his court, and Zephaniah, the Kohathite attending priest, to pray to God on behalf of the nation that was in great peril (**Jeremiah 37:1–5**; cf. **2 Kings 24:1–17**). More likely, King Zedekiah's own self-interest was at the heart of his request; his sinfulness, as attested to by the Chronicler in particular, was so egregious that Yahweh withheld his grace and destroyed Zedekiah's kingship as well as Judah (**2 Chronicles 36:11–19**). There can be sin so abhorrent to the holiness and justice of God that the only remedy is for the old establishment to be overthrown in favor of a new one. Thus, the remnant of Judah was taken to a foreign land where it languished for seventy years (**Jeremiah 25:11; 29:10; Zechariah 1:12**). They returned as a chastened and repentant people, ready to rebuild the nation and to resume their mission to be a "kingdom of priests and a holy nation" (**Exodus 19:6**).

Notes

1. The name Shelemiah is common, occurring also as: (1) the priest who was over the East Gate of Solomon's Temple, who had a son named Zechariah (**1 Chronicles 26:14**); (2) two Israelites (from the descendants of Binnui) who had taken foreign wives in Babylonian exile (**Ezra 10:39, 41**); (3) the father of Hananiah, who made repairs in the wall around Jerusalem in the days of Nehemiah in 444 B.C. (**Nehemiah 3:30**); (4) the priest over the storerooms of the Second Temple (**Nehemiah 13:13**); (5) the grandfather of Jehudi, who heard Baruch reading from the scroll of Jeremiah in the days of King Jehoiakim in 609–598 B.C. (**Jeremiah 36:14**); (6) the son of Abdeel who arrested Baruch and Jeremiah (**Jeremiah 36:26**); and (7) the father of Irijah, the captain of the guard who arrested Jeremiah (**Jeremiah 37:13–14**); see chart "**Jeremiah 37**: Irijah, the Captain of the Guard in the Days of King Zedekiah of Jerusalem (Pre-Exile)."

2. Jehukal was among the king's other court officials—Shephatiah, Gedaliah, and Pashhur—who heard Jeremiah telling the people "Whoever stays in this city will die by the sword, famine or plague, but whoever goes over to the Babylonians will live" (**Jeremiah 38:2**); see chart "**Jeremiah 38**: The Officials to King Zedekiah Who Cast Jeremiah into the Cistern (Pre-Exile)." The officials advised King Zedekiah that Jeremiah should be put to death because he sought the ruin of the people rather than their good. The king allowed his officials to put Jeremiah into a cistern (**Jeremiah 38:4–6**). Jehukal may be the brother of the captain of the guard identified as "Irijah son of Shelemiah, the son of Hananiah" who arrested Jeremiah when he believed that Jeremiah was escaping to the Babylonians (**Jeremiah 37:13–14**); see chart "**Jeremiah 37**: Irijah, the Captain of the Guard in the Days of King Zedekiah of Judah (Pre-Exile)."

3. Based on the reading of **Ezra 10:18**, Maaseiah is shown in the chart as the *son* of Jozadak, the *nephew* of the high priest Joshua, and the *brother* of the wicked priest Zedekiah. However, there are others of the name "Maaseiah" in a priestly line: (1) a priest who was the descendant of the Kohathite attending priest Harim (**Ezra 10:21**); (2) a priest who was the descendant of the Kohathite attending priest Pashhur (**Ezra 10:22**); (3) Maaseiah (a priest) who stood with Ezra in 458 B.C. (**Nehemiah 8:4**); and (4) two priests (or perhaps a priest and a Levite) named Maaseiah in the days of Nehemiah in 444 B.C. (**Nehemiah 12:41–42**).

4. Zedekiah son of Maaseiah is mentioned in **Jeremiah 29:21–23** as an unfaithful priest who, along with Ahab the son of Kolaiah, prophesied lies to the exiles in Babylon in the Lord's name. The prophet Jeremiah foretold that Zedekiah son of Maaseiah and Ahab would be delivered into the hands of King Nebuchadnezzar of Babylon, who would then put them to death by burning them "in the fire" (**Jeremiah 29:22**)!

5. This Zephaniah is the same person as Zephaniah the son of Maaseiah in **Jeremiah 21:1; 29:25; 37:3**; see chart "**Jeremiah 21**: Pashhur and Zephaniah, Who Were Sent by King Zedekiah to Inquire of Jeremiah about the Fate of Jerusalem (Pre-Exile)." For chronological reasons, Zephaniah the son of Maaseiah is a different person than the prophet Zephaniah the son of Cushi, who ministered from ca. 640–609 B.C. (**Zephaniah 1:1**).

6. Zedekiah reigned from 597–586 B.C. See chart "**2 Kings 24**: Zedekiah (Mattaniah), King of Judah."

JEREMIAH 37: IRIJAH, THE CAPTAIN OF THE GUARD IN THE DAYS OF KING ZEDEKIAH OF JUDAH (PRE-EXILE)

Approximate Dating: ca. 597–586 B.C. ***Relevant Scriptures:*** **Jeremiah 37:13–14**

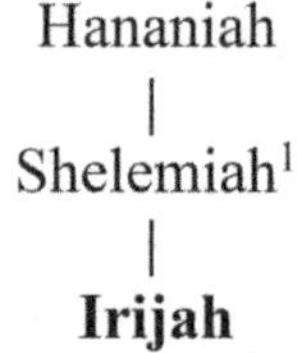

Biblical and Theological Significance

"After the Babylonian army had withdrawn from Jerusalem because of Pharaoh's army, Jeremiah started to leave the city to go to the territory of Benjamin" to obtain his share of the property in Anathoth (a Levitical town) from among the people there (**Jeremiah 37:11–12**). However, when Jeremiah reached the Benjamin Gate, the captain of the guard, whose name was Irijah, arrested him and accused him of deserting to the Babylonians. Jeremiah denied the allegation, but Irijah paid him no heed and instead took him to the officials, who were so enraged that they had Jeremiah beaten and imprisoned in the house of Jonathan the secretary, which had been made into a prison (**Jeremiah 37:13–15**)—his cell was in a vaulted dungeon, where he remained for a long time. King Zedekiah sent for him in the palace, where he asked him in hushed tones if he had heard from Yahweh. The prophet affirmed that he had but the message was not one the king had hoped for. Jeremiah would be released from prison, but Zedekiah would fall into the hands of the dreaded Babylonians (**Jeremiah 37:16–17**). This was fulfilled shortly thereafter when Nebuchadnezzar arrived at the city, breached its walls, and took the royal family to one of his outposts named Riblah, fifty miles north of Damascus and nearly two hundred miles north of Jerusalem. There, Zedekiah was forced to watch the slaughter of his family before his own eyes were gouged out (**2 Kings 25:5–7; Jeremiah 39:5–7; 52:8–11**).

An important truth to be learned here is in the poem David commissioned Asaph to sing as a temple anthem:

> Do not touch my anointed ones;
> Do my prophets no harm. (**1 Chronicles 16:22**)

The pages of Scripture are replete with examples of persecutors who violated this principle and who, like Zedekiah, met the heavy hand of Yahweh's judgment.

Notes

1. This Shelemiah was the father of Irijah, but the name Shelemiah also occurs as: (1) the priest who was over the East Gate of Solomon's Temple, who had a son named Zechariah (**1 Chronicles 26:14**); (2) two Israelites (from the descendants of Binnui) who had taken foreign wives in Babylonian exile (**Ezra 10:39, 41**); (3) the father of Hananiah, who made repairs in the wall around Jerusalem in the days of Nehemiah in 444 B.C. (**Nehemiah 3:30**); (4) the priest over the storerooms of the Second Temple (**Nehemiah 13:13**); (5) the grandfather of Jehudi, who heard Baruch reading from the scroll of Jeremiah in the days of King Jehoiakim in 609–598 B.C. (**Jeremiah 36:14**); (6) the son of Abdeel who arrested Baruch and Jeremiah (**Jeremiah 36:26**); and (7) the father of Jehukal, an official in King Zedekiah's court, whom Zedekiah asked to pray for the city (**Jeremiah 37:3; 38:1**)—if the latter identity is the case, then Irijah (in this chart) and Jehukal were brothers; see chart "**Jeremiah 37**: Jehukal the Court Official and Zephaniah the Priest in the Days of King Zedekiah of Judah (Pre-Exile)."

JEREMIAH 38: THE OFFICIALS TO KING ZEDEKIAH WHO CAST JEREMIAH INTO THE CISTERN[1] (PRE-EXILE)

Approximate Dating: 588 B.C. during the reign of Zedekiah, 597–586 B.C. ***Relevant Scriptures:*** **Jeremiah 38:1, 4, 6**

Genealogy of Shephatiah

Mattan

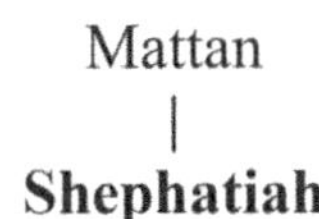

Shephatiah

Genealogy of Gedaliah

Pashhur[2]

|

Gedaliah[3]

Genealogy of Jehukal

Shelemiah[4]

|

Jehukal[5]

Possible Genealogy of Pashhur

King Josiah[6] (?) or King Jehoiakim[7] (?)

|

Malkijah[8]

(Called "the king's son" in **Jeremiah 38:6**)

|

Pashhur[9]

(Judahite, not a Kohathite priest)

Biblical and Theological Significance

Jeremiah had been called by Yahweh to proclaim judgment on his wayward people Judah lest they, like Israel a century earlier, should go into exilic bondage (**Jeremiah 1:1–3**). His was a heavy burden because Jeremiah found no joy in constantly haranguing his beloved nation (**Jeremiah 20:7–10, 14–18**). The word fell on deaf ears, however, as it often does. In fact, Jeremiah's messages were redirected against him in a series of beatings, arrests, and death threats. Chief among the prophet's persecutors was Pashhur, the son of Malkijah (**Jeremiah 21:1**), but he was not alone. Pashhur may have been among a larger anonymous conspiracy (**Jeremiah 11:9–13**). Jeremiah, the stalwart soldier for the Kingdom of God, persisted in his boldness until Jerusalem's end was just around the corner (**Jeremiah 26:1–9**). Having heard enough, the king, his officials, and the temple hierarchy committed Jeremiah to the royal prison (**Jeremiah 32:1–5**).

During his years of ministry (627–586 B.C.),[10] Jeremiah was imprisoned four separate times;[11] the fourth time, he was thrown into "the cistern of Malkijah, the king's son," in the courtyard of the guard before he was rescued by Ebed-Melek the Cushite (**Jeremiah 38:6–13**). In the latter case, the men who were responsible for the deed were "officials"[12] (**Jeremiah 38:4**) who held royal advisory positions in Zedekiah's administration (**Jeremiah 1:18; 2:26; 4:9; 21:7; 24:8; 34:21; 38:4, 25, 27; 52:10**).

Through the words of the prophet Jeremiah, the Lord forewarned Zedekiah that he would "give Zedekiah king of Judah, his officials and the people in this city . . . into the hands of Nebuchadnezzar" (**Jeremiah 21:7**). Eventually, many of the officials listed here appear to have been killed at Riblah along with King Zedekiah: "[All] the officials of Judah" along with "seven royal advisors" are listed among the people who were taken as prisoners, brought before King Nebuchadnezzar of Babylon at Riblah, and executed (**Jeremiah 52:10, 24–27**).

Notes

1. The term here (בֹּר, *bor*) is the same as the one describing the pit into which Joseph was thrown by his brothers (**Genesis 37:22–24**).

2. This Pashhur (פַּשְׁחוּר) is considered by many scholars to have an Egyptian name, which might explain the unusually large number of references to Egypt in this period (**Jeremiah 37:5; 41:17–46:26** [42 times]; cf. **2 Kings 18:21, 24; 19:9, 24; 21:15; 23:29, 34; 2 Chronicles 35:20–36:4**). Pashhur the father of Gedaliah (an official) should not be confused with Kohathite priests named Pashhur who were his near contemporaries, i.e., Pashhur the son of Immer (see chart "**Jeremiah 20**: Pashhur, an Unfaithful Kohathite Priest and the Official over Solomon's Temple (Pre-Exile)") or with Pashhur son of Malkijah, who is possibly a priest (see chart "**Jeremiah 21**: Pashhur and Zephaniah Who Were Sent by King Zedekiah to Inquire of Jeremiah about the Fate of Jerusalem (Pre-Exile).").

3. Gedaliah son of Pashhur (**Jeremiah 38:1**) should not be confused with Gedaliah son of Ahikam, son of Shaphan, who was the governor over the people who remained in Judah during the early exile (cf. **2 Kings 25:22–25; Jeremiah 39:14; 40:5–16; 41:1–3, 9–10, 16, 18; 43:6**); see chart "**2 Kings 25**: Gedaliah, Governor over the Remnant People of Judah During the Early Days of the Exile."

4. Several individuals bore this common name. In the pre-exile, the first reference is to Shelemiah the son of Cushi and the grandfather of Jehudi, the messenger who retrieved the scroll of Jeremiah so it could be read to King

Jehoiakim (**Jeremiah 36:14**). Another Shelemiah, son of Abdeel, was one of three men sent to arrest Baruch and Jeremiah after the reading of the scroll (**Jeremiah 36:26**). The third was Shelemiah, the son of Hananiah (**Jeremiah 37:13**); the fourth was the father of Jehukal (shown in the chart), who urged that Jeremiah should be killed because of what he had written (**Jeremiah 38:1**). Post-exilic men of this name included: (1) two men named Shelemiah, both descendants of Binnui (**Ezra 10:39, 41**); (2) Shelemiah the father of Hananiah, who worked on rebuilding the walls of Jerusalem (**Nehemiah 3:30**); and (3) Shelemiah the priest who assisted Nehemiah in distributing offerings among the Levites (**Nehemiah 13:13**).

5. King Zedekiah sent Jehukal the official and Zephaniah the priest to Jeremiah the prophet, asking him to pray for the nation; Jeremiah informed them that, despite their wishful thinking, the Babylonians would destroy Jerusalem (**Jeremiah 37:3–14**). For the genealogy of Jehukal and Zephaniah, see chart "**Jeremiah 37**: Jehukal the Court Official and Zephaniah the Priest in the Days of King Zedekiah of Judah (Pre-Exile)."

6. See chart "**2 Kings 21**: Josiah, King of Judah."

7. See chart "**2 Kings 23**: Eliakim (Jehoiakim), King of Judah."

8. The epithet "the king's son" applied to Malkijah (**Jeremiah 38:6**) is confusing since the king at this time was Zedekiah. The question is whether Malkijah was a biological son, perhaps a relative of Zedekiah, or just a member of the royal family. Chronological considerations (see scenarios 1–4 below) suggest that Malkijah was most likely the *son* or *relative* of one of the former kings, such as Jehoiakim (609–598 B.C.) or Josiah (640–609 B.C.). The setting of the story is the tenth year of Zedekiah's reign in ca. 587 B.C. (**Jeremiah 32:1; 39:1–2**). Since this Malkijah is part of the royal family and thus a member of the tribe of Judah, he is unrelated to the Kohathite priests named Pashhur (cf. **1 Chronicles 9:12; Nehemiah 11:12; Jeremiah 20:1**) who were from the tribe of Levi.

<u>Scenario #1: If Malkijah was the *son* of King Josiah</u>: presumably, Malkijah was 25 years old in 587 B.C. and born in 612 B.C.; his father Josiah became king in 640 B.C. at the age of 8 years old, so Josiah was born in 648 B.C. For this reason, it is possible that Malkijah was the son of King Josiah since their birth dates are 36 years apart.

<u>Scenario #2: If Malkijah was the *son* of King Jehoiakim/Eliakim</u>: presumably, Malkijah was 25 years old in 587 B.C. and born in 612 B.C.; his father Jehoiakim became king in 609 B.C. at the age of 25 years old, so Jehoiakim was born in 634 B.C. For this reason, it is possible that Malkijah was the *son* of King Jehoiakim since their birth dates are twenty-two years apart.

<u>Scenario #3: If Malkijah was the *son* of King Jehoiachin/Jeconiah</u>: presumably, Malkijah was 25 years old in 587 B.C. and born in 612 B.C.; his father Jehoiachin became king in 598 B.C. at the age of 18, so Jehoiachin was born in 616 B.C. For this reason, Malkijah could not have been the son of King Jehoiachin since their birth dates are only four years apart.

<u>Scenario #4: If Malkijah was the *son* of King Zedekiah</u>: presumably Malkijah was 25 years old in 587 B.C. and born in 612 B.C.; his father Zedekiah became king in 597 B.C. at the age of 21, so Zedekiah was born in 618 B.C. For this reason, Malkijah could not have been the son of King Zedekiah since their birth dates are only 6 years apart.

In conclusion, Malkijah "the king's son" (**Jeremiah 38:1**) was most likely the *son* of King Josiah or the *son* of King Jehoiakim/Eliakim.

9. At least three figures named Pashhur are known in the Old Testament.

(1) The first was Pashhur the unfaithful Kohathite priest (**Jeremiah 20:1**), the son/descendant of Immer—probably referring to the ancestral figure Immer, who was the head over the sixteenth of the twenty-four divisions of Kohathite attending priests in Solomon's Temple (**1 Chronicles 24:14**). Pashhur the priest is characterized as "the official in charge of the temple of the Lord" (**Jeremiah 20:1**). When Pashhur heard Jeremiah's prophesy, he had Jeremiah beaten and imprisoned (**Jeremiah 20:2**).

(2) The second Pashhur was the son of Malkijah; at King Zedekiah's request, Pashhur implored Jeremiah to pray for the nation's deliverance; when he refused, Pashhur was among those who cast Jeremiah into the cistern (**Jeremiah 38:6, 9**).

(3) The third Pashhur, a post-exilic, was a signatory to Nehemiah's covenant (**Nehemiah 10:3**).

Pashhur son of Malkijah appears to be a prince in the court of King Zedekiah (**Jeremiah 38:1**) and therefore is not Pashhur the priest (cf. **1 Chronicles 9:12; Nehemiah 10:3; 11:12; Jeremiah 21:1**).

10. The last datable event in the book of Jeremiah is 562 B.C. (cf. **Jeremiah 52:31–34**), but the ministry of Jeremiah probably ended with the destruction of Jerusalem in 586 B.C. For more about Jeremiah's long ministry, see chart "**Jeremiah 1**: Jeremiah, the Prophet-Priest of God to the Southern Kingdom of Judah During the Pre-Exile."

11. The accounts of Jeremiah's imprisonments are found in **Jeremiah 32:1–5; 33:1; 37:11–20; 37:21; 38:6–13.**

12. The generic term "officials" (שָׂרִים, *sarim*) has a broad range of meaning within the semantic field "official"; in this context it likely corresponds to the idea of "minister" in a parliamentary state or a cabinet member in a republic. The "room of the officials" was above that of "Maaseiah son of Shallum the doorkeeper" (**Jeremiah 35:4**).

JEREMIAH 38: RECORD OF OFFICERS UNDER KING NEBUCHADNEZZAR OF BABYLON WHO INVADED JERUSALEM[1]

Approximate Dating: July 18, 586 B.C. ***Relevant Scriptures:*** **Jeremiah 38:17–18, 22; 39:3, 9–13; 40:1, 5; 41:10; 43:6; 52:12, 15–16, 19, 26, 30;** also **2 Kings 25:8, 10–12, 15, 18–20; Jeremiah 50:35; 51:23, 28, 57**

1. **Nergal-Sharezer of Samgar**[2]
2. **Nebo-Sarsekim** (chief officer)
3. **Nergal-Sharezer**[3] (high official)
4. **Nebuzaradan** (commander/general of the imperial guard[4])
5. **Nebushazban** (chief officer)
6. Other unnamed officials

Biblical and Theological Significance

The tragic events of this section of Jeremiah took place right before the successful penetration of Jerusalem's walls by the battering rams of Nebuchadnezzar's army. Both the biblical account and Babylonian records recount this event; both specify the time to the very day with unerring astronomical dating (**2 Kings 25:8–10**; cf. **Jeremiah 52:4–6, 12, 28–30**). Jeremiah's advice to the foolhardy and stubborn Zedekiah, the last ruler of pre-exilic Judah, was that he should surrender in the face of the inevitable outcome of the utter destruction of the city of David and the temple. Rather than do so, Zedekiah sent Jeremiah back to the courtyard of the guard, as though he thought that removing the predictor of judgment would avert it (**Jeremiah 38:14–28**). Jeremiah was still in the guard's courtyard when Nebuchadnezzar's forces besieged Jerusalem and then breached its walls in 586 B.C. (**2 Kings 25:1–4; Jeremiah 39:1–2; 52:4–7**). The commander of the imperial guard, Nebuzaradan, took the majority of the people of Jerusalem into captivity, leaving behind some of the poor people. Jeremiah was also left, so Nebuzaradan, Nebushazban, Nergal-Sharezer, and all the other imperial officers took Jeremiah out of the courtyard of the guard. This was because King Nebuchadnezzar had told Nebuzaradan to take Jeremiah, look after him, and "don't harm him but do for him whatever he asks" (**Jeremiah 39:11–12**). These officials and officers brought Jeremiah to Gedaliah, the son of Ahikam, the son of Shaphan, who had been appointed governor over the people who remained in Judah. **Jeremiah 40:1–6** gives additional details about Jeremiah's liberation. Notably, Nebuzaradan told Jeremiah that "The LORD your God decreed this disaster for this place. And now the LORD has brought it about; he has done just as he said he would. All this happened because you people sinned against the LORD and did not obey him. But today I am freeing you from the chains on your wrists" (**Jeremiah 40:2–4**). Nebuzaradan offered to bring Jeremiah back to Babylon with him but said that he could remain in Judah if he wished. Finally, Nebuzaradan told Jeremiah to return to Gedaliah and gave Jeremiah "provisions and a present and let him go" (**Jeremiah 40:5**). As he had done in the past, God used surrounding pagan nations to humble and punish his wayward people; here, the highest military commander of a pagan nation recognized God's hand in Judah's destruction when God's own people did not.

Notes

1. For Josephus' account of the taking of Jerusalem and the burning of the Temple, see *Jewish Antiquities* 10.8.1–5. Josephus lists Nebuchadnezzar's generals as "Nergal Sharezer, Sangar Nebo, Rabsaris, Sarsechim, and Rabmag" (*Jewish Antiquities* 10.8.2).

2. It is important to note that these names are Hebrew transliterations of Neo-Babylonian names, the rendering of which is not always accurate because of phonetic differences between East Semitic (Akkadian) and Northwest Semitic such as Hebrew. Nergal-Sharezer (or Nergal-Sarezer) is an example of this since the /s/ in Sarezer occurs as /sh/ in Akkadian. Hebrew *sar* and Akkadian *shar* both mean "prince" or "of royalty." Nergal was a deity in the Babylonian pantheon, so the name of the official means "May Nergal protect the king." Nergal was a high official in the Babylonian court under Nebuchadnezzar who accompanied him in the invasion of Jerusalem and later assisted in the liberation of the prophet Jeremiah from Babylonian exile (cf. **Jeremiah 39:3, 13–14**). Some scholars have proposed that he may be Neriglissar (or Neriglissor), the son-in-law of Nebuchadnezzar who succeeded Nebuchadnezzar to the throne, but this is by no means a consensus; see chart "**Supplement 4**: The Kings of Babylon."

3. Presumably a different person than Nergal-Sharezer of Samgar (cf. **Jeremiah 39:3**).

4. Heb. *rab-tabbakhim* suggests the "chief of the bodyguards and executioners."

JEREMIAH 42: JEZANIAH/AZARIAH AND JOHANAN, THE ARMY OFFICERS WHO LED A REMNANT OF PEOPLE TO EGYPT (EARLY EXILE)

Approximate Dating: ca. October 586 B.C. ***Relevant Scriptures:*** **Jeremiah 42:1; 43:2**; also **Jeremiah 40:8**

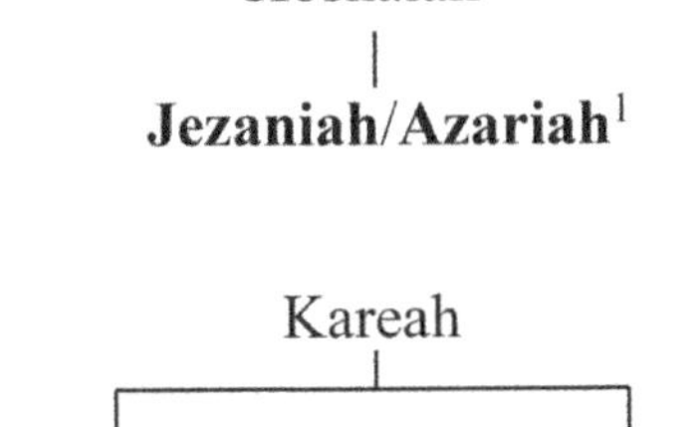

Biblical and Theological Significance

In 586 B.C., after Nebuchadnezzar destroyed Jerusalem and exiled most of the people of Judah, he established a makeshift government and appointed Gedaliah[2] as governor over those left behind in the land (**2 Kings 25:22**; cf. **Jeremiah 40:5–7, 11**). This displeased an anti-Babylonian faction of rebels, led by Ishmael,[3] the son of Nethaniah, who soon assassinated Gedaliah (**Jeremiah 41:1–9**). When Johanan[4] and other officers in King Zedekiah's army heard of Ishmael's crimes, they fought against him (**Jeremiah 41:11–15**). Despite Jeremiah's appeal to remain in Judah during the Babylonian occupation, Johanan, Azariah, and Jezaniah led a remnant to Egypt (**Jeremiah 41:16–18; 42:1–3, 7–22; 43:1–7**). The group included men, women, and children, including King Zedekiah's daughters, as well as Jeremiah the prophet[5] and Baruch (Jeremiah's scribal secretary). They traveled to the cities of Noph, Migdol, and "as far as Tahpanhes"[6] (**Jeremiah 43:6–7**; cf. **41:10, 16–17 44:1; 46:14**). For their disobedience to the Lord, the people became "destined for death" (**Jeremiah 43:11**) by the sword, famine, and plague (**Jeremiah 42:16–17, 22; 44:12–13, 27**), although some were "destined for captivity" (**Jeremiah 43:11**). Jeremiah declared that "the whole remnant of Judah who came to live in Egypt will know whose word will stand—mine or theirs" (**Jeremiah 44:28**). Only a small number escaped and returned to Judah (**Jeremiah 44:14, 28**).

Notes

1. The Hebrew text reads "Jezaniah son of Hoshaiah" in **Jeremiah 42:1**, whereas the Septuagint reads "Azariah." **Jeremiah 43:2** reads "Azariah son of Hoshaiah." It is likely that Jezaniah and Azariah are the same person. Moreover, since the Hebrew Jezaniah is a variant of Jaazaniah, this person is possibly the same as "Jaazaniah the son of the Maakathite" in **2 Kings 25:23**.

2. See charts "**2 Kings 22**: Shaphan, Scribal Secretary under King Josiah and King Jehoiakim of Judah" and "**2 Kings 25**: Gedaliah, Governor over the Remnant People of Judah During the Early Days of the Exile." For Josephus' description of Gedaliah and the events that follow, see *Jewish Antiquities* 10.9.1–5.

3. See chart "**1 Chronicles 2**: Jerahmeel and His Descendant, Elishama, Who Appears to Be a Compiler of Historical and Genealogical Records in 1 & 2 Chronicles."

4. For Josephus' description of the role of Johanan, see *Jewish Antiquities* 10.9.3–6.

5. Jeremiah went to Tahpanhes and apparently continued his ministry there until his death (**Jeremiah 43–51**).

6. Tahpanhes was the location of Pharaoh's palace in the eastern Nile Delta; Noph was the major city of Memphis; Migdol was a fortress on the border between Canaan and Egypt (**Exodus 14:2**).

EZEKIEL 1: EZEKIEL, THE PROPHET-PRIEST OF GOD (PRE-EXILE AND EXILE)

Approximate Dating: ca. 592–573 B.C. ***Relevant Scriptures:*** **Ezekiel 1:3; 24:16–18**

Priestly line of Levi
(Probably through Kohath)
|
|
Buzi
|
Ezekiel m. An unnamed wife
(Priest-prophet)

Biblical and Theological Significance

"The best insight into exilic life in Babylonia is provided by the prophet Ezekiel, who spent all his years of public ministry there. Like Jeremiah, Ezekiel was a priest, as is clear from his express testimony (**Ezekiel 1:3**) and his great interest in matters of the cult."[1] Ezekiel—whose name means "*God makes strong, hardens*"—served as God's adamant *stone* against the "obstinate and stubborn [hardened]" house of Israel (**Ezekiel 2:4**; **3:7**) in the days leading up to the fall of Jerusalem in 586 B.C. Later, Ezekiel prophesied to his fellow exiles while in Babylonian captivity (**Ezekiel 1:1**). Ezekiel ministered during a part of the eleven-year reign of King Zedekiah (597–586 B.C.). All biblical sources agree that the siege of Jerusalem began in the ninth year, in the tenth month, on the tenth day of Zedekiah's reign and ended in the eleventh year, fourth month, and ninth day, when Jerusalem's walls were breached (**2 Kings 25:1–3; Jeremiah 39:1–2; 52:4–7;** cf. **2 Chronicles 36:11**). Ezekiel relates that his vision of the cooking pot—symbolizing the siege of Jerusalem—came to him in Zedekiah's ninth year, in the tenth month, on the tenth day—the very day that the siege of Jerusalem began (**Ezekiel 24:1–2**).

The death of Ezekiel's wife (**Ezekiel 24:16–18**), which occurred shortly before the fall of Jerusalem to the Babylonians in 586 B.C., symbolized the coming destruction of Solomon's Temple, called "my sanctuary" by the Lord (**Ezekiel 24:21**). Ezekiel was not allowed to mourn for his wife in the traditional manner. God made Ezekiel temporarily mute as a sign to the people that his word of judgment on Jerusalem would be fulfilled (cf. **Ezekiel 3:26; 24:25–27**). Ezekiel's silence may have lasted for about six months. When news of Jerusalem's destruction reached him in captivity, his mouth was opened and he could preach again (**Ezekiel 33:21–22**).

Chronology of the Book of Ezekiel

Call Vision	July 31, 593 B.C. (**1:1–3**)
Temple Vision	September 17, 592 B.C. (**8:1**)
Elders Vision	August 14, 591 B.C. (**20:1**)
Babylon's Arrival	December 589–January 588 B.C. (**24:1–2**)
Tyre Vision	April 23, 587–April 13, 586 B.C. (**26:1**)
Egypt Vision	January 7, 587 B.C. **(29:1)**

The dates of Ezekiel's visions in the book correspond to the chronological records known from such texts as the Babylonian Chronicles and the Cyrus Cylinder.

Notes

1. Eugene H. Merrill, *Kingdom of Priests: A History of Old Testament Israel*, 2nd ed. (Grand Rapids: Baker Academic, 2008), 482.

EZEKIEL 8: JAAZANIAH THE SCRIBE WHO SERVED AS A PRIEST TO IDOL WORSHIPERS IN SOLOMON'S TEMPLE IN THE DAYS OF EZEKIEL THE PROPHET (PRE-EXILE)

Approximate Dating: ca. 592 B.C.[1] ***Relevant Scriptures:*** **Ezekiel 8:9–12;** also **2 Kings 22:12; 25:22–25; 2 Chronicles 34:20; Jeremiah 29:3; 39:14; 40:5–7, 9, 11, 14, 16; 41:1–2, 6, 10, 16, 18; 43:6**

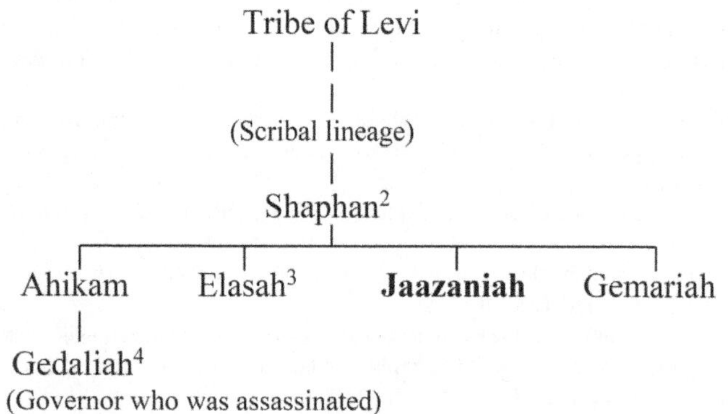

Biblical and Theological Significance

There appears to be three men named Jaazaniah in this timeframe: (1) "the Maakathite,"[5] a captain who came to Gedaliah's side when the latter was named governor by the Babylonians (**2 Kings 25:22–26; Jeremiah 40:7–9**); (2) the son of Shaphan (**Ezekiel 8:11**); and (3) the son of Azzur[6] (**Ezekiel 11:1**). This chart focuses on the second Jaazaniah, who was a priestly descendant of the famed scribe, Shaphan, who served under King Josiah (640–609 B.C.) and read **Deuteronomy** to the king in 622 B.C. (**2 Kings 22:3, 8–10; 2 Chronicles 34:15–18**). Betraying his godly heritage, Jaazaniah acted as a wicked priest to seventy elders of Israel who turned the priestly chambers adjacent to the holy place of the temple into a mock holy place for worshiping crawling things, unclean animals, and idols. God called these activities "detestable things" (**Ezekiel 8:9–12**). This abrupt and despicable *turning away* from the glorious reformation and spiritual revival under Josiah to blatant worship of pagan deities (including Tammuz[7]) under King Zedekiah occurred in the brief span of just thirty years.[8]

Notes

1. Ezekiel's vision of idolatry in the temple in Jerusalem was "in the sixth year, in the sixth month on the fifth day" (**Ezekiel 8:1**), corresponding to September 17, 592 B.C. by modern reckoning.

2. For the lineage of Shaphan (a near relative of the high priests), see chart "**2 Kings 22**: Shaphan, Scribal Secretary under King Josiah and King Jehoiakim of Judah."

3. Elasah was a scribe who helped deliver a letter from Jeremiah the prophet to captives in Babylon (**Jeremiah 29:3**).

4. Gedaliah was appointed governor over Judah by King Nebuchadnezzar (**2 Kings 25:22; Jeremiah 40:7**), but after only two months in office, he was assassinated (see chart "**2 Kings 25**: Gedaliah, Governor over the Remnant People of Judah During the Early Days of the Exile").

5. Maakathite is a reference to the citizens of a small principality south of Mount Hermon and northeast of the Sea of Galilee.

6. See Azzur in "**Ezekiel 11**: Jaazaniah and Pelatiah, the Wicked Counselors in Jerusalem (Pre-Exile)."

7. Tammuz (or Dumuzi in Sumerian) was a Babylonian fertility god, who, with his female counterpart Ishtar, was associated with fecundity and the growing season. Rituals honoring these two were often characterized by unimaginable sexual perversion undertaken to induce the gods to provide fertile land and crops.

8. The widespread reforms took place in 622 B.C., in the eighteenth year of Josiah's reign (**2 Kings 22:3–23:25**). However, by 592 B.C. (the events chronicled in **Ezekiel 8**)—during the reign of Zedekiah (597–586 B.C.)—fidelity to the Lord had disappeared and idol paganism encroached even the sanctum of the temple.

EZEKIEL 11: JAAZANIAH AND PELATIAH, THE WICKED COUNSELORS IN JERUSALEM (PRE-EXILE)

Approximate Dating: ca. 593 B.C.[1] ***Relevant Scriptures:*** **Ezekiel 11:1–13**

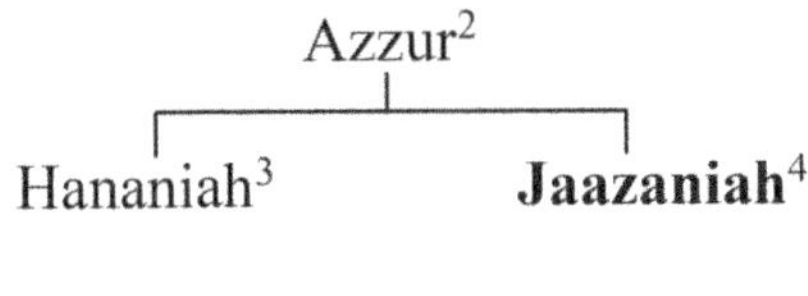

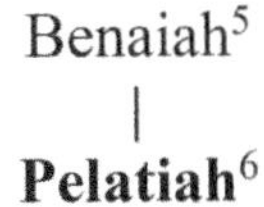

Biblical and Theological Significance

While in Babylonian captivity, Ezekiel had a vision of twenty-five men led by two key leaders, Jaazaniah and Pelatiah, who acted as wicked counselors to the citizenry in Jerusalem (**Ezekiel 11:1–4**). They are described as "men who are plotting evil and giving wicked advice" (**Ezekiel 11:2**).

These leaders thought of themselves as the choice "meat" in the cauldron "pot" of Jerusalem (**Ezekiel 11:3**). However, the Lord revealed through Ezekiel that they were actually guilty of killing many people and filling the streets with the dead (**Ezekiel 11:6**) and that they would die at the hands of foreigners when the Babylonians came up against the city in 586 B.C. (**Ezekiel 11:7–12**). The imagery here presents two options of judgment—be boiled in the cauldron or be slain by Babylonian soldiers. Choosing the cauldron would mean that these men could stay in Jerusalem even though they would be dead. Conversely, being delivered "into the hands of foreigners" (**Ezekiel 11:9**) would take them outside the holy city to be deported or killed. These choices represent the Jewish thought that it was better to die in the promised land than to live (or even die) on the outside.

Pelatiah's name, meaning "Yahweh provides escape," was a portent of the coming disaster. His abrupt death symbolized the sure fate of Jerusalem (**Ezekiel 11:13**). It is unclear whether Pelatiah was (1) a *descendant* of Benaiah, the captain over King David's professional soldiers and later the commander of Solomon's army (cf. **2 Samuel 8:18; 1 Kings 2:25–46, 4:4**); (2) a *descendant* of Benaiah, the overseer who assisted in the collection of contributions to Solomon's Temple during the reign of Hezekiah (**2 Chronicles 31:13**); or just the descendant of another man named Benaiah.

Notes

1. King Jeconiah/Jehoiachin reigned in Jerusalem for only three months and ten days (ca. December 598–March 597 B.C.; **2 Kings 24:10–14; 2 Chronicles 36:9**). When Nebuchadnezzar invaded Jerusalem in ca. 597 B.C., Jeconiah/Jehoiachin was taken captive along with much of the population of Jerusalem, including the prophet Ezekiel. The date of 593 B.C. is based on **Ezekiel 1:2**, which says that Ezekiel had visions in "the fifth year of the exile of King Jehoiachin" (cf. **Ezekiel 1:1; 4:6; 8:1; 20:1; 24:1; 26:1; 29:1, 17; 30:20; 31:1; 32:1, 17; 33:21; 40:1; 46:17**). See chart "**2 Kings 24**: Jehoiachin (Jeconiah), King of Judah."

2. Azzur is possibly the same as Azzur of Gibeon (**Jeremiah 28:1**).

3. Hananiah son of Azzur (**Jeremiah 28:1**) is likely the false prophet who challenged Jeremiah (cf. **Jeremiah 28:1–17**).

4. Jaazaniah son of Azzur (**Ezekiel 11:1**) is not the same person as (1) Jaazaniah the Maakathite, the captain who came to Gedaliah's side when Gedaliah was named governor over the people left in Jerusalem (**2 Kings 25:22–26; Jeremiah 40:7–9**) or (2) Jaazaniah son of Shaphan, the wicked priest who led idolatrous worship in the temple in the days of Ezekiel and King Zedekiah (592 B.C.; **Ezekiel 8:9–12**). For more on Jaazaniah son of Shaphan, see chart "**Ezekiel 8**: Jaazaniah the Scribe Who Served as a Priest to Idol Worshipers in Solomon's Temple in the Days of Ezekiel the Prophet (Pre-Exile)."

5. Benaiah was either the father or the *ancestor* of Pelatiah; in the latter case, it may refer to Benaiah the military commander under David and Solomon (cf. **2 Samuel 8:18; 1 Kings 2:25–46, 4:4**) or to the overseer named Benaiah who assisted in the collection of contributions to Solomon's Temple during the reign of Hezekiah (**2 Chronicles 31:13**); alternatively, it refers to another of the same name (Benaiah).

6. This Pelatiah is obviously not the leader of the people by that name in the days of Nehemiah, 444 B.C. (**Nehemiah 10:22**).

DANIEL 1: DANIEL AND HIS COMRADES

Approximate Dating: ca. 605–530 B.C. ***Relevant Scriptures:*** **Daniel 1:1–7; 1 Chronicles 3:13–18;** also **2 Kings 23:31, 34, 36; 24:8, 12, 15–18**[1]

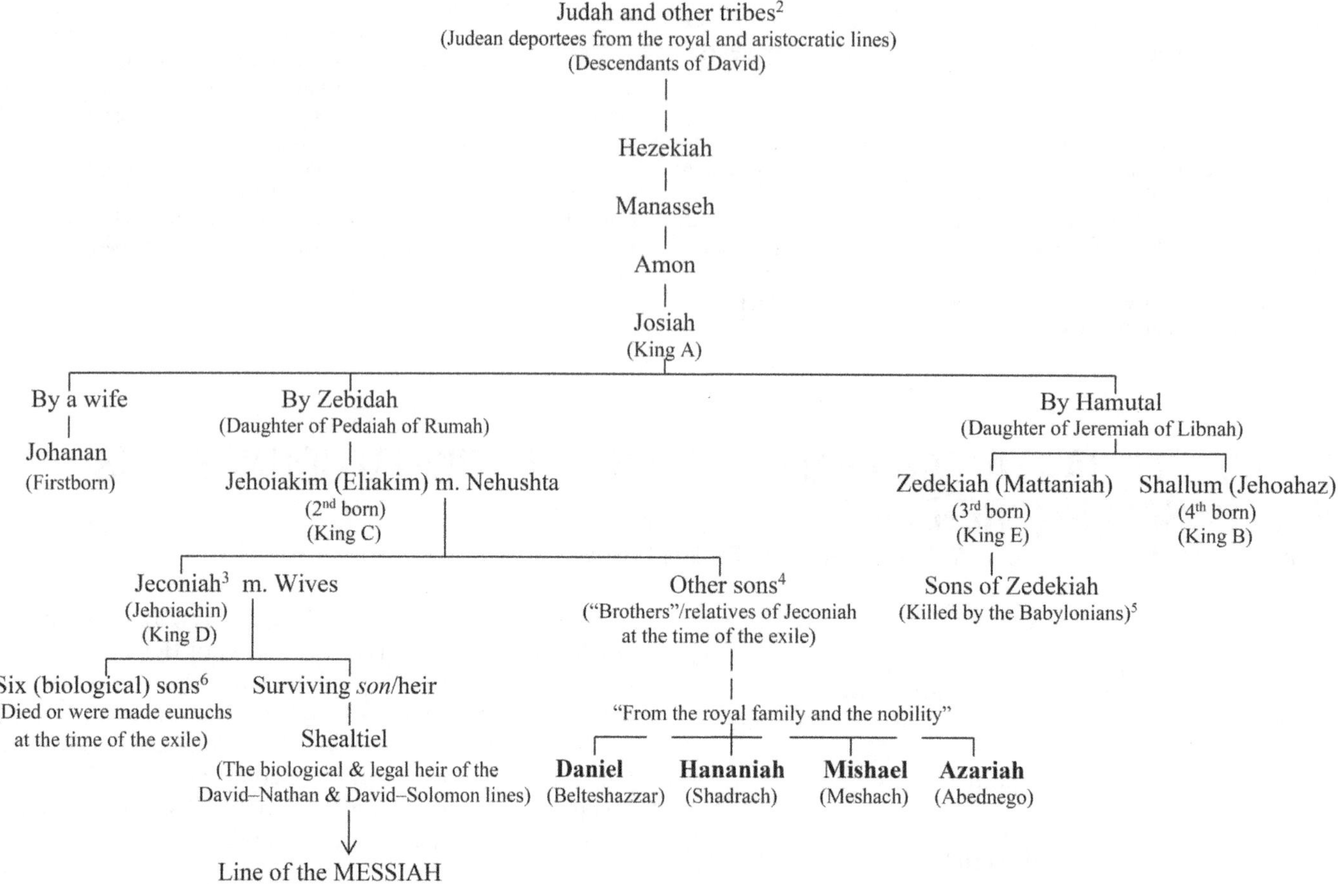

Biblical and Theological Significance

Isaiah's prophecy to King Hezekiah (715–686 B.C.)—that some of his descendants would be exiled and become eunuchs[7] in the palace of the king of Babylon (**2 Kings 20:16–18; Isaiah 39:5–7**)—seems to have been fulfilled in 605 B.C. during Nebuchadnezzar's first invasion of Judah (cf. **2 Kings 24:1; 2 Chronicles 36:5–7; Jeremiah 25:1; 46:2; Daniel 1:1**). Nebuchadnezzar took Jehoiachin/Jeconiah and certain members of the upper classes of Judah and Jerusalem to Babylon (**Jeremiah 27:20**), and Daniel and his comrades appear to have been among them[8] (cf. **2 Kings 20:18; Isaiah 39:7; Daniel 1:3–6, 10, 19**). They served in Nebuchadnezzar's palace, were given Babylonian names, and were apparently groomed to be "members of the diplomatic corps."[9] The accounts of Shadrach, Meshach, and Abednego being thrown into a blazing furnace and Daniel being thrown into a lion's den are given in **Daniel 3** and **6**, respectively.

Daniel was an exile and a public servant in Babylon for over sixty years—from ca. 605–536 B.C.—and served under five Babylonian kings (Nebuchadnezzar, Awel-Marduk, Neriglissar, Labashi-Marduk, and Nabonidus).[10] He interpreted Nebuchadnezzar's dream of the image of a large statue[11] and the writing on the wall at the feast of Belshazzar (**Daniel 2, 5**), and he had at least two visions—one of four beasts[12] (**Daniel 7**) and the other of a ram and a goat[13] (**Daniel 8**). Daniel made additional prophecies, which are listed in **Daniel 9–12**. After King Cyrus of Persia conquered Babylon in 539 B.C.[14] (cf. **Daniel 1:1–7, 21**), Daniel "prospered during the reign of Darius [the Mede] [that is] and the reign of Cyrus the Persian" (i.e., until 530 B.C.; **Daniel 6:28**).

Notes

1. For Josephus' description of Daniel ("Baltasar" or "Belteshazzar") and his friends, and the events that take place in Babylon, see *Jewish Antiquities* 10.10.1–5; 10.11.2–7; 12.7.6.
2. Two categories are in view: (1) *zera hammelukah* ("royal seed") and (2) *happartemim* ("aristocrats"). The latter term is a Persian loan word found also in **Esther 1:3** and **6:9**. Only the royal genealogical line can be traced since there is no way of knowing who the patrician or aristocratic families were.
3. See charts "**2 Kings 24**: Jehoiachin (Jeconiah), King of Judah" and "**1 Chronicles 3**: Zerubbabel and Shealtiel and the Double Line of the Messiah through King David's Sons, Nathan and Solomon."
4. Jeconiah's brothers (**Matthew 1:11**) and/or their offspring/descendants were among "all the nobles of Judah and Jerusalem" (**Jeremiah 27:20**) and "the royal family and the nobility" (**Daniel 1:3**) who were carried to Babylon (see **Isaiah 39:7; Daniel 1:1–7**).
5. The death of the sons (princes) of King Zedekiah is recorded in **2 Kings 25:7** and **Jeremiah 52:10–11**.

6. Of these sons, Pedaiah (probably Sheshbazzar) appears to have lived through the exile and returned to Jerusalem to lay the foundations of the Second Temple; see charts "**1 Chronicles 3**: Zerubbabel and Shealtiel and the Double Line of the Messiah through King David's Sons, Nathan and Solomon" and "**Ezra 1**: Genealogy Sheshbazzar and Zerubbabel, the Governors over the Restored Community in Jerusalem (Post-Exile)."

7. Neither Daniel nor his comrades are called eunuchs in the book of Daniel; however, if Isaiah's prophecy refers to them, they were, in fact, eunuchs (cf. **2 Kings 20:16–18**; **Isaiah 39:5–7**). However, the *New Bible Dictionary* states that "there is no necessity to assume, as Josephus seems to do (*Ant.* 10.186), that Daniel and his companions were 'castrates,' for they were 'without blemish' (see **Daniel 1:4**)" (R.J.A. Sheriffs "Eunuch," *New Bible Dictionary*, Third Edition, 1996, 1:347).

8. Their exact lineages are not given; they were most likely near relatives of King Jeconiah/Jehoiachin (see note 2).

9. Eugene H. Merrill, *Kingdom of Priests: A History of Old Testament Israel* (Grand Rapids: Baker, 1996), 484.

10. See chart "**Supplement 4**: The Kings of Babylon."

11. The statue of **Daniel 2** had (1) a head of gold, identified as the Neo-Babylonian Empire; (2) chest and arms of silver, identified as the Medo-Persian Empire, established in 539 B.C. with the fall of Babylon; (3) belly and thighs of bronze, identified as the Greek Empire; (4) legs of iron, identified as the Roman Empire; and (5) feet with ten toes of clay mixed with iron, identified as a future kingdom(s), "partly strong and partly brittle" (**Daniel 2:32**) before the God of heaven sets up a kingdom that will not be destroyed . . that "will crush all those kingdoms and bring them to an end, but it will itself endure forever" (**Daniel 2:44**; cf. **Revelation 11:15**: "the kingdom of the world has become the kingdom of our Lord and of his Messiah and he will reign for ever and ever").

12. The four beasts in **Daniel 7** were: (1) the "lion" (v. **4**), identified as Babylon, 626–539 B.C.; see chart "**Supplement 4**: The Kings of Babylon"; (2) the "bear" (v. **5**) identified as Medo-Persia (539–330 B.C.); see chart "**Supplement 5**: The Kings of Persia"; (3) the "leopard" (v. **6**), identified as the Greek Empire under Alexander the Great B.C.including the Ptolemaic Dynasty (323–30 B.C.), the Seleucid Dynasty (321–63 B.C.), and the Maccabees and the Hasmonean Dynasty (167–37 B.C.); see charts "**Supplement 6**: The Ptolemies and the Ptolemaic Dynasty"; "**Supplement 7**: The Seleucids and the Seleucid Dynasty"; and "**Supplement 8**: The Maccabees and the Hasmonean Dynasty" and (4) a "terrifying and frightening beast" (v. **7**), identified as Rome, 27 B.C.–A.D. 70 (the fall of Jerusalem); see chart "**Supplement 10**: The Roman Emperors."

13. The "ram" (**Daniel 8:3**) represented the Medo-Persian Empire and the "goat" (**Daniel 8:5**) represent the Greek Empire; see notes 10 and 11.

14. See charts "**Supplement 4**: The Kings of Babylon" and "**Supplement 5**: The Kings of Persia."

HOSEA 1: HOSEA, THE PROPHET OF GOD TO THE NORTHERN KINGDOM OF ISRAEL

Approximate Dating: between 793–686 B.C., most likely between 753–722 B.C.[1] ***Relevant Scriptures:*** **Hosea 1:1, 3–4, 6, 8–9, 11; 2:1, 22–23**

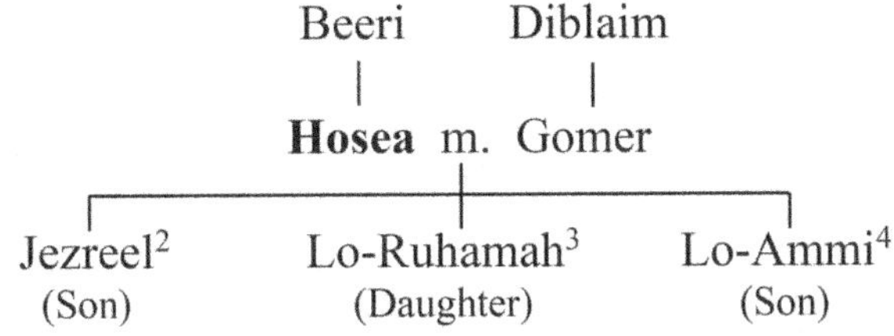

Biblical and Theological Significance

Hosea's prophetic ministry occurred approximately between 753–722 B.C. (probably just before the fall of the Northern Kingdom in 722 B.C.) during the reigns of Uzziah, Jotham, Ahaz, and Hezekiah, the kings of Judah, and in the days of Jeroboam, the king of Israel (**Hosea 1:1**).

Hosea's marriage to Gomer ("a promiscuous woman," **Hosea 1:2**) was not only a literal marriage between two people, but also symbolic of the Lord's covenant marriage to his betrothed, unfaithful people (Israel). Gomer may have been a cult or temple prostitute rather than a secular harlot. Her wayward actions symbolized the sins of the Northern Kingdom in which elements of Canaanite religious practices (e.g., worship of Baal, ritual prostitution, sexual rites, and orgies) were intermingled with the worship of Yahweh. If Israel repented wholeheartedly, she would be restored to her position as wife to her husband (**Hosea 2:2, 23**). Hosea's continued love for Gomer displayed God's covenant love and mercy for his people. The names of Hosea and Gomer's (pagan) children had prophetic and symbolic significance.

Notes

1. The first range of dates are outside (unrealistic) dates for Hosea's actual span of ministry based on the reading of **Hosea 1:1**: "The word of the LORD that came to Hosea son of Beeri during the reigns of Uzziah, Jotham, Ahaz and Hezekiah, kings of Judah, and during the reign of Jeroboam [II] son of Jehoash king of Israel." Hosea's ministry could be limited to the last year of Jeroboam II (793–753 B.C.) through the first year of Hezekiah's co-regency with his father Ahaz (i.e., 729–715 B.C.)—thus, 753–729 B.C., or a minimum of 24 years—although it could have extended further into the sole reign of Hezekiah (715–686 B.C.). Nonetheless, since there is no hint of the exile of Israel, one should assume that 722 B.C. is the latest date *ad quem*.

2. Jezreel, meaning "God sows," referred to the Jezreel Valley—a place of blessing and military victory when Israel honored God (**Judges 4:4–5:31; 6:33–7:25**), and a place of judgment and military defeat when they did not (**1 Samuel 31:1–10; 2 Kings 9:14–10:17; 15:29; 17:6; 18:10**).

3. Lo-Ruhamah, meaning "no mercy/not loved," signified God's imminent withdrawal of compassion if Israel continued to prostitute herself to Baal.

4. Lo-Ammi, meaning "not my people," signified that God would end his covenant relationship with Israel (My wife/My people) if they continued to prostitute themselves to pagan gods.

JOEL 1: JOEL, THE PROPHET OF GOD TO THE SOUTHERN KINGDOM OF JUDAH AND TO JERUSALEM

Approximate Dating: ca. 851–841 B.C. ***Relevant Scriptures:*** **Joel 1:1**

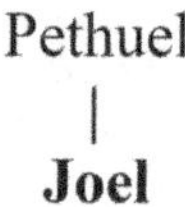

Biblical and Theological Significance

Joel[1] ministered to Israel in a critical period of its history, beginning during the reigns of Joram of Israel (852–841 B.C.) and Jehoshaphat of Judah (872–848 B.C) and ending in the reign of Jehoram of Judah (848–841 B.C.). Since Joram and Jehoram were both corrupt and idolatrous kings, Yahweh's response was to send two forms of judgment against the land: (1) a famine called "the day of the LORD"[2] (**Joel 1:15–20**) and (2) the invasion by Assyria led by Shalmaneser III (858–824 B.C.), also called "the day of the LORD" (**Joel 2:1–11; 3:14**). Joel appealed to the priests to "cry out to the LORD," declare a holy fast, and call a sacred assembly (**Joel 1:14; 2:1, 15**). He appealed to his kinsmen to return to the LORD who, by covenant, had made them his own special nation (cf. **Joel 1:5, 8, 11, 13; 2:12–13; 3:2**). Joel promised that sincere repentance would bring the LORD's forgiveness and deliverance (**Joel 2:12–14, 18–32; 3:14–21**).

Notes

1. The prophet is blessed by having a name that combines Yahweh and Elohim (*y[eh]o[wah] + el[ohim]*).
2. This common expression, which occurs some ninety times in the Bible, nearly always bespeaks Yahweh's wrath and judgment against his covenant people.

AMOS 1: AMOS, THE PROPHET OF GOD TO THE NORTHERN KINGDOM OF ISRAEL

Approximate Dating: ca. 767–753 B.C. ***Relevant Scriptures:*** **Amos 1:1**

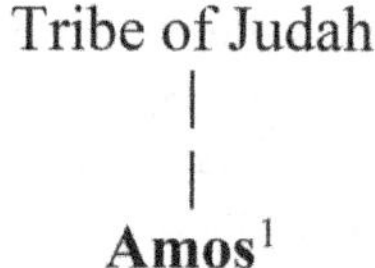

Biblical and Theological Significance

Amos was from Tekoa,[2] a city in Judah seven miles south of Bethlehem. He was a shepherd,[3] and he also took care[4] of sycamore-fig trees (**Amos 1:1; 7:14**). His ministry lasted from 767–753 B.C., during parts of the reigns of Uzziah (Azariah) of Judah (792–740 B.C.) and Jeroboam II of Israel (793–753 B.C.).[5] His ministry could have overlapped with the ministries of Jonah (775/773–730 B.C.) and Hosea (ca. 753–722 B.C. or longer). His prophecies were addressed primarily to Israel, but also to Judah, as in **Amos 6:1**: "Woe to you who are complacent in Zion." Amos clarifies that he was not a professional prophet, nor the son of a prophet (**Amos 7:14**), meaning he was not professionally trained in the school/guild of the prophets. Despite his self-perceived handicaps, Amos was a faithful man of God at a time of national spiritual and moral decay.

Notes

1. Because of chronology, Amos the prophet is not the post-exilic figure named Amos in **Luke 3:25**, a descendant who was twelve generations removed from Zerubbabel (the Davidic descendant who brought exiles to Jerusalem in 538 B.C.).
2. For other references to Tekoa, see **2 Samuel 14; 2 Chronicles 11:6; Nehemiah 3:5, 27;** and **Jeremiah 6:1**.
3. The sheep were perhaps destined for temple sacrifices. Jeremiah called for the blowing of a trumpet in Tekoa in the face of the advancing enemy (**Jeremiah 6:1**).
4. Heb. בּוֹלֵס (*boles*), or "scraper," describes the skillful process of scarring the tree bark and slitting the top of each fruit to induce a better yield and quality of sycamore figs.
5. Since only these two kings are mentioned (**Amos 1:1**; see also **7:9–10**), Amos must have served from 767–753 B.C., the only years common to the two; this is based on the fact that Uzziah/Azariah co-reigned with his father Amaziah for 25 years (792–767 B.C.) and then became sole regent in 767 B.C.; see Eugene H. Merrill. *Kingdom of Priests: A History of Old Testament Israel*, 2nd ed. (Grand Rapids: Baker Academic, 2008), 388. Another reference point is the "two years before the earthquake" (**Amos 1:1**), probably referring to a great earthquake at Hazor, 115 miles north of Jerusalem. Amos dates his call to two years before the quake (ibid., 398).

AMOS 7: AMAZIAH, THE PRIEST AT BETHEL

Approximate Dating: ca. 760 B.C.[1] ***Relevant Scriptures:*** **Amos 7:10–17**

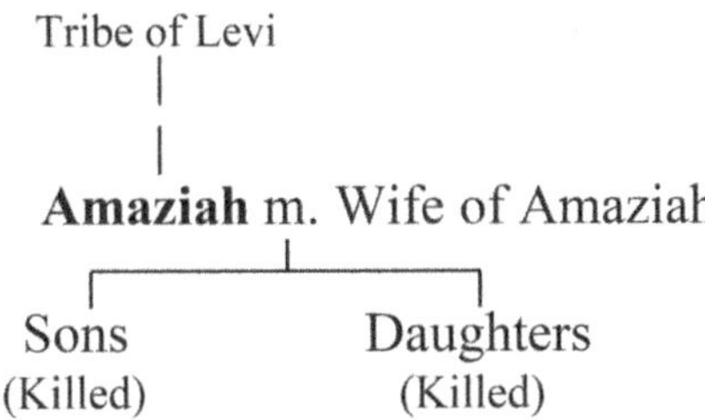

Biblical and Theological Significance

Bethel was significant for many reasons. First, Abram built an altar to Yahweh between Bethel and Ai upon entering Canaan ca. 2100 B.C. (**Genesis 12:8**). Years later, Jacob, on his way to Haran to seek a wife, arrived there and named the place Bethel, meaning "the house (or place) of God" (**Genesis 28:17–19**). Jacob later settled there for a while (**Genesis 35:1–8**; cf. **Genesis 31:13**). Centuries afterward, Bethel served as a holy place for Samuel (**1 Samuel 7:15–17**); still later, it became the location of Elijah and Elisha's "company of the prophets" (**2 Kings 2:1–14**).

During the time of Josiah's great reformation in 622 B.C., the paganized altar at Bethel was destroyed (**2 Kings 23:15–19**). During his reign, King Jeroboam I of Israel (931–910 B.C.) had converted Bethel into a shrine for idol worship after the death of Solomon and the division of the kingdom between Israel and Judah in 931 B.C. (**1 Kings 12:28–29**). Jeroboam's namesake, Jeroboam II (793–753 B.C.), continued the tradition; he employed the services of Amaziah as the chief priest at the shrine, who not only tolerated but even encouraged the worship of both Yahweh and Baal (a practice called religious syncretism). Amaziah prohibited Amos the prophet from prophesying at Bethel and instructed him to return home to Tekoa, in Judah. Amos responded to Amaziah's command by confirming his divine prophetic call (**Amos 7:15**) and predicting that Amaziah's wife would become a prostitute, that his sons and daughters would be killed (probably during the Assyrian invasion in 722 B.C.), and that Amaziah would die in Assyrian captivity as a ritually unclean priest (**Amos 7:10, 16–17**).

Notes

1. Amos's prophecy against Amaziah was near the end of the reign of Jeroboam II (793–753 B.C.), since Amos prophesied in Jeroboam's time "two years before the earthquake" of ca. 760 B.C. (**Amos 1:1**).

OBADIAH: POSSIBLE GENEALOGY OF OBADIAH, THE PROPHET OF GOD WHO PROPHESIED AGAINST THE EDOMITES (POST-EXILE)

Approximate Dating: ca. 550 B.C., after the destruction of Jerusalem in 586 B.C. ***Relevant Scriptures:*** **book of Obadiah**

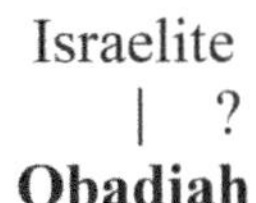

Biblical and Theological Significance

Obadiah is the author of the shortest book in the Old Testament. His genealogy, birthplace, nor his residence is given.

The theme of Obadiah expresses the ancient strife between Jacob and Esau who, after fighting about their father's bestowal of birthright and estate, became inveterate enemies (**Genesis 27:41–45**). Esau's descendants (the Edomites) settled Seir/Edom (**Genesis 32:3; 36:8; Deuteronomy 2:4–8, 12**). Jacob's descendants were later collectively called "Judah" after one of his sons (**Genesis 29:35**). The nations of Judah and Edom were constantly engaged in war, as the history of the divided monarchy and the oracles of the prophets make clear.

This chronic hostility of approximately 1400 years[1] led to Yahweh's judgment on the people of Edom, who were proud of their fortress, their accomplishments, and were especially fervent in humiliating Judah and cooperating with her enemies (**Obadiah 3–4, 10–14**). Obadiah draws attention to the violence "Jacob" (i.e., Israel; **Obadiah 10**) suffered at Edom's hands during the Babylonian conquests of 587–586 B.C. Though Edom was not the aggressor in the invasion and destruction of Jerusalem (cf. **2 Kings 24:8–25:21; 2 Chronicles 36:17–20**), it stood by as a spectator, gloated over Judah's downfall, helped itself to the valuables left behind, and stood in the way of Israel's escape (**Obadiah 10–14**). What Edom had done to Judah would be done to it in return (**Obadiah 10, 15**; cf. **Ezekiel 35:1–15**), for the "day of the LORD" that would destroy Edom was approaching (**Obadiah 15–18**). God's people would be blessed with Edom's treasures and territory (**Obadiah 17–20**), and, most importantly, "the kingdom [of Edom] will be the LORD's" (**Obadiah 21**).

Notes

1. Esau and Jacob were born in 2006 B.C. The date of the Esau-Jacob separation was ca. 1930 B.C.; Obadiah's book should be dated ca. 550 B.C.

JONAH 1: JONAH, THE PROPHET OF GOD TO THE NINEVITES OF ASSYRIA

Approximate Dating: ca. 775/773–730 B.C. ***Relevant Scriptures:*** **Jonah 1:1, 9;** also **2 Kings 14:25**

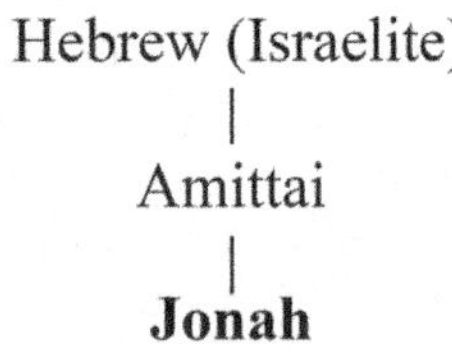

Biblical and Theological Significance

Jonah was God's missionary and prophet to the Assyrian capital of Nineveh. Jonah was from Gath Hepher in Zebulun and the only prophet from Galilee (cf. **Joshua 19:13; 2 Kings 14:25**). His ministry began during the reign of Jeroboam II of Israel (793–753 B.C.) and may have continued until ca. 730 B.C. Jonah prophesied that Jeroboam would restore "the boundaries of Israel from Lebo Hamath [northeast of Beirut, Lebanon] to the Dead Sea" (**2 Kings 14:25**). Jonah was a contemporary of Hosea (753–722 B.C. or longer), Amos (767–753 B.C.), and Isaiah (ca. 740–700 B.C.).

God called Jonah to deliver a message to the Ninevites, which vexed Jonah because the Ninevites were a notoriously violent, unscrupulous people and were Israel's staunch enemy. So, Jonah fled by setting sail on a ship from Joppa destined for Tarshish.[1] However, after a storm arose and the crew threw him overboard, Jonah was swallowed by a great fish and spent three days and nights in the fish's belly. After surviving the ordeal, Jonah reluctantly went to Nineveh (**Jonah 1:2–17; 3:2–3; 4:11**) and delivered a one-line message that conveyed God's imminent destruction: "Forty more days and Nineveh will be overthrown" (**Jonah 3:4**). Immediately the king[2] and all the people wholeheartedly repented. Although Jonah had received God's great mercy in the belly of the fish (cf. **Jonah 3–4**), he felt that God's mercy on the Ninevites "seemed very wrong" and he "became angry" (**Jonah 4:1**).

Jesus confirms the historicity of Jonah by saying that "as Jonah was a sign to the Ninevites, so also will the Son of Man be to this generation . . . The men of Nineveh will stand up at the judgment with this generation and condemn it, for they repented at the preaching of Jonah; and now something greater than Jonah is here" (**Luke 11:29–32**; cf. **Matthew 12:39–41**).

Notes

1. Anson and Rainey explain that "in the Mediterranean there were several places by that name: Tarsus in Cilicia, a Tarshish in Sardinia and, of course, Tartessos [Tartessus] in [southern] Spain." Anson F. Rainey and R. Steven Notley, *The Sacred Bridge: Carta's Atlas of the Biblical World* (Jerusalem: Carta, 2014), 165.

2. The reference to the king of Assyria as "the king of Nineveh" (**Jonah 3:6**) has led to various interpretations, but there is precedence for the capital city (in this case Nineveh) to be substituted for the country (in this case Assyria). For example, King Ahab of Israel and King Ahaziah of Israel are both called "the king of Samaria" (**1 Kings 21:1; 2 Kings 1:3**, respectively). The king of Nineveh/Assyria at this time was likely Ashur-Dan III (772–755 B.C.) or Ashur-nirari V (754–745 B.C.); see chart "**Supplement 3**: The Kings of Assyria."

MICAH 1: MICAH, THE PROPHET OF GOD TO THE NORTHERN KINGDOM OF ISRAEL AND THE SOUTHERN KINGDOM OF JUDAH

Approximate Dating: ca. 750/745–715 B.C. ***Relevant Scriptures:*** **Micah 1:1**

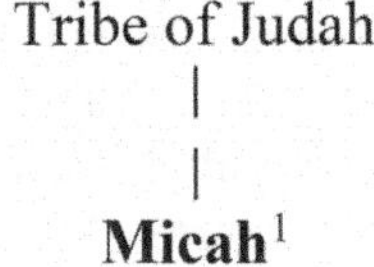

Biblical and Theological Significance

Micah's genealogy is unknown, but he appears to be a Judahite since he was from Moresheth Gath,[2] a town in the foothills of Judah (**Micah 1:1, 14**). His name means "Who is like Yahweh?" He prophesied in the days of three of Judah's kings (**Micah 1:1**; cf. **Jeremiah 26:18**): Jotham (750–735 B.C.), Ahaz (732–715 B.C.), and Hezekiah (715–686 B.C.)—most likely ministering from ca. 750/745–715 B.C.

Micah prophesied to both the Northern and Southern Kingdoms (**Micah 1:5; 2:12; 3:1, 8–9**). He predicted the fall of Samaria to the Assyrians (**Micah 1:5–7**), an event that occurred in 722 B.C., which Scripture correlates to the sixth year of the twenty-nine-year reign of King Hezekiah (**2 Kings 18:2, 10**). Micah also predicted the fall of Jerusalem and Judah and the ensuing exile to Babylon (**Micah 1:10–16; 3:12; 4:6–13**). Micah's prophecy regarding the future fall of Jerusalem (**Micah 3:12**) caused King Hezekiah to repent and seek the Lord (**Jeremiah 26:17–19**). The fall of Jerusalem was thus delayed until 586 B.C.

Micah would have been a contemporary of the prophets Isaiah (ca. 740 to after 700 B.C)[3] and Hosea (ca. 753–722 B.C. or longer). Micah foretold that the Messiah would come from Bethlehem Ephrathah, the ancient name of Bethlehem (**Micah 5:2**; cf. **Matthew 2:1, 6**).

Notes

1. Micah the prophet is not the same person as Michaiah/Micah the scribe, a contemporary of King Josiah (**2 Kings 22:12; 2 Chronicles 34:20**).

2. Possibly Tell el-Judeideh (Tel Goded); see Anson F. Rainey and R. Steven Notley, *The Sacred Bridge: Carta's Atlas of the Biblical World* (Jerusalem: Carta, 2014), 170.

3. Note the similar wording of **Isaiah 2:2–4** and **Micah 4:1–3**.

NAHUM 1: NAHUM, THE PROPHET OF GOD AGAINST THE ENEMY NATION OF ASSYRIA[1]

Approximate Dating: ca. 663–612 B.C. ***Relevant Scriptures:*** **Nahum 1:1**

Israelite
|
Nahum the Elkoshite

Biblical and Theological Significance

Nahum (meaning "consolation" or "comfort") refers to himself as "the Elkoshite" (**Nahum 1:1**), presumably meaning from Elkosh, a town of uncertain location. The name Capernaum (Heb. כפרנחום), meaning "Place/Village of Comfort," is sometimes linked to Nahum, especially as the place of his burial.

Nahum ministered ca. 663–612 B.C., *after* the Assyrian exile of Israel in 722 B.C. and shortly *after* the fall of Thebes to the Assyrians in 663 B.C., which Nahum reports as a past event (cf. **Nahum 3:8–10**), but *before* the fall of Nineveh to the Medes and Chaldeans in 612 B.C. (cf. **Nahum 3:5–7**). Nahum called Nineveh "the city of blood, full of lies, full of plunder" (**Nahum 3:1**)—a clear reference to their lust for power, ruthless trade practices, insatiable materialism, and merciless cruelty (**Nahum 3:1–7**). His prophecies foretold God's judgment on the Assyrians, who would be completely destroyed, leaving no descendants (**Nahum 1:14–15**). However, Nahum assured the oppressed people of Judah that the Lord would console and restore both Judah and Israel (**Nahum 2:2**).

Notes

1. For the Assyrians, see chart "**Supplement 3**: The Kings of Assyria."

HABAKKUK 1: HABAKKUK, THE PROPHET OF GOD TO THE SOUTHERN KINGDOM OF JUDAH (PRE-EXILE)

Approximate Dating: ca. 612–598 B.C. ***Relevant Scriptures:*** **Habakkuk 1:1**

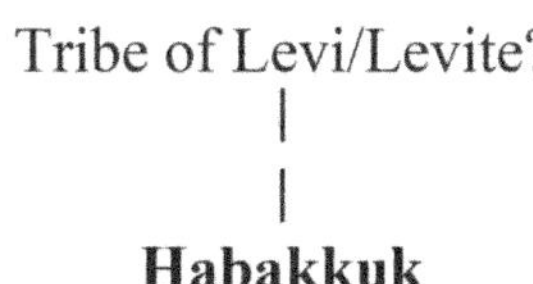

Biblical and Theological Significance

The verbal root of the name Habakkuk—חָבַק—means "to embrace." However, the reduplicated form—קוּק—is unattested elsewhere in the Hebrew Bible and thus leads most scholars to propose that the lexeme is a loanword in Hebrew, perhaps from Akkadian *ḫabbaqūqu*, "garden plant."[1]

Habakkuk was a prophet to the Southern Kingdom in the days preceding the Babylonian invasion. He appears to have prophesied in the general time frame of 612–598 B.C., just prior to the invasion of Judah by the Babylonians in 597 B.C. when King Jehoiakim was captured and taken into captivity (cf. **2 Kings 24:1–6; 2 Chronicles 36:5–8**). With a nod to the literary competence of biblical prophets, Yahweh ordered Habakkuk to write the vision that God had given him of the fall of Nineveh (the capital of the Assyrian Empire) to the Babylonians in 612 B.C. With hyperbolic elegance he was told to make the tablet large enough[2] so that all who passed by could not fail to read it (**Habakkuk 2:2–3**).

Habakkuk emphasized the heavenly temple and the holiness of God (**Habakkuk 1:12–13, 2:20**), as well as the history of God's people in the days of Moses (**Habakkuk 3:3–15**). He invoked psalm-like prayer petitions of God (**Habakkuk 1:2–3, 12–13**) and composed psalm-like poetic hymns that were played on stringed instruments such as the Shigionoth[3] (**Habakkuk 3:1, 19**). For these reasons, one can speculate that Habakkuk was of Levitical heritage, but no definitive genealogy can be offered.

Notes

1. "חֲבַקּוּק," *HALOT* 1:287.
2. The modern-day equivalent would be publishing the message on a billboard.
3. The *NIV Cultural Backgrounds Study Bible* offers this insight: "While the meaning of *shigionoth* is uncertain, it is related to *shagah* ("to go astray"), suggesting a lament or possibly a song with uneven meter (see **Psalms 7:1**). If a linguistic connection can be made with Akkadian *shegu*, then its usage, in the form *shigu*, in a prayer to Marduk indicates a sense of emotion and supplication, perhaps accompanied by a whimpering sound." *NIV Cultural Backgrounds Study Bible* (Grand Rapids: Zondervan, 2016), 1540; study note on Habakkuk 3:1.

ZEPHANIAH 1: ZEPHANIAH, THE PROPHET OF GOD TO THE SOUTHERN KINGDOM OF JUDAH (PRE-EXILE)

Approximate Dating: ca. 640–609 B.C. ***Relevant Scriptures:*** **Zephaniah 1:1**; also **Jeremiah 36:14**

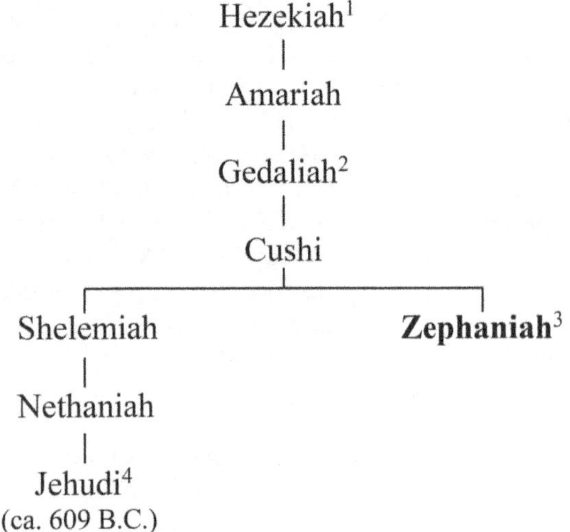

Biblical and Theological Significance

Zephaniah's lengthy genealogy recorded in **Zephaniah 1:1** is unique amongst the minor prophets, suggesting that he was an unknown man in his own time and needed a genealogical heritage to give him identity and perhaps a platform from which to proclaim his bold message of judgment to his peers (**Zephaniah 1:8, 13–14, 18; 3:1, 3, 11**). Zephaniah prophesied in the days of King Josiah of Judah, 640–609 B.C. (**Zephaniah 1:1**), and, more specifically, probably in the years preceding Josiah's reforms of 622 B.C. (cf. **2 Kings 23:1–25; 2 Chronicles 34:3–33**) or possibly in the years just before Josiah's death in 609 B.C. (cf. **2 Kings 23:29–30; 2 Chronicles 35:20–24**). Zephaniah certainly prophesied before the fall of Nineveh in 612 B.C. (**Zephaniah 2:13–15**). He was a contemporary of Jeremiah (ca. 627–586 B.C.; **Jeremiah 1:2**) and perhaps Nahum (663–612 B.C.).

Notes

1. Chronological considerations suggest that this Hezekiah is not the same person as King Hezekiah of Judah, who reigned from 715–686 B.C. (see chart "**2 Kings 16**: Hezekiah, King of Judah"). Despite this, some scholars still hold that the lengthy genealogy does indicate that Zephaniah was from royal ancestry, e.g., J. M. Smith, William H. Ward, and Julius A. Bewer, *A Critical and Exegetical Commentary on Micah, Zephaniah, Nahum, Habakkuk, Obadiah and Joel* (New York: Scribner's, 1911), 183.

2. Gedaliah the son of Amariah is not Gedaliah the son of Ahikam (**2 Kings 25:22**).

3. Zephaniah the prophet is not (1) Zephaniah the priest (second in rank to Seraiah the high priest, designated Seraiah #1 elsewhere), who was killed at Riblah in 586 B.C. (**2 Kings 25:18–21**); (2) Zephaniah son of Maaseiah, who was a Kohathite priest in the days of King Zedekiah (597–586 B.C.) and sympathetic toward the prophet Jeremiah (cf. **Jeremiah 21:1; 29:25, 29; 37:3; 52:24**); see chart "**Jeremiah 21**: Pashhur and Zephaniah, Who Were Sent by King Zedekiah to Inquire of Jeremiah about the Fate of Jerusalem (Pre-Exile)"; nor is he (3) Zephaniah the father of Josiah (**Zechariah 6:10, 14**; see vv. **9–15**); see chart "**Zechariah 6**: Genealogical Record of Men who Brought Gifts from the Israelite Captives in Babylon to the Newly Established Community in Jerusalem (Post-Exile)."

4. For the lineage of Jehudi, see **Jeremiah 36:14** and the chart "**Jeremiah 36**: Jehudi, the Court Official in the Days of Jeremiah the Prophet (Pre-Exile)."

HAGGAI 1: HAGGAI, THE PROPHET OF GOD TO THE RESTORED COMMUNITY IN JERUSALEM (POST-EXILE)

Approximate Dating: ca. 520–516 B.C. ***Relevant Scriptures:*** **Haggai 1:1**; also **Ezra 5:1**

Presumably Israelite
|
Haggai

Biblical and Theological Significance

Haggai's genealogy is unknown. He is one of the three writing prophets of the post-exilic period, the others being Zechariah and Malachi. Haggai (חַגַּי, "festival") began prophesying in Jerusalem in the second year of King Darius[1] of Persia, precisely on the first day of the sixth month (520 B.C.; **Haggai 1:1**). The exiles had returned from Babylon in 538 B.C., but they had very little to show for it.

Haggai's mission was threefold: 1) to scold Zerubbabel, the governor of Yehud, Jeshua, the high priest, and the people as a community for their indolence and self-serving spirit in building their own fine homes while the temple, God's house, had lain in ruins since it was destroyed in 586 B.C. (**Haggai 1:1–6**); 2) to urge them to look past the fact that the Second Temple would never match the glory of the first (**Haggai 1:7–15**);[2] and 3) to relay a vision in which Yahweh Tsivaoth, the Lord of Hosts, would fill a future temple with his glory, far surpassing any temple ever built by human hands (**Haggai 2:4–9**). The New Testament writers understood this promise as ultimately fulfilled in Jesus Christ (**John 1:14; 2:19–21; Hebrews 10:19–21**).

Zechariah was a contemporary of Haggai, and together they encouraged Zerubbabel and Joshua to proceed with the task of affirming the Yehud community and completing the Second Temple (also called Zerubbabel's Temple; **Ezra 5:1**).

Notes

1. Darius I ruled from 522–486 B.C., thus his second year was 520 B.C.; see chart "**Supplement 5**: The Kings of Persia." The sixth month was Elul (August-September). Adjusted to the modern Gregorian calendar, Haggai commenced his ministry on August 29, 520 B.C. Other dates are Elul 24

(**Haggai 1:15**; September 21); Tishri 21 (**Haggai 2:1**; October 17); and Kislev 24 (**Haggai 2:10**; December 18).

2. After four years of construction, the Second Temple was finally completed in 516 B.C.; however, it was damaged or defamed by various enemies in the pre-Christian era. Herod the Great built Herod's Temple on its ruins; Herod's Temple is mentioned in **Matthew 4:5; 12:5–6; 21:12–15, 23; Mark 11:15–17, 27; 12:41; 13:1–3; 14:58; Luke 19:45–20:1; 21:1–6, 37–38; John 2:14–21; Acts 21:26–30**. According to chronologist Andrew Steinmann, Herod began work on the temple in 20 B.C.; work on the temple was completed in late 19 or early 18 B.C.; and work on the temple precincts was completed in 12 B.C. (*From Abraham to Paul: A Biblical Chronology* (St. Louis: Concordia, 2011), 254.

ZECHARIAH 1: ZECHARIAH, THE PROPHET OF GOD TO THE RESTORED COMMUNITY IN JERUSALEM (POST-EXILE)

Approximate Dating: from the rebuilding of the Second Temple, 520–516 B.C. to as late as 490–450/444 B.C.[1] ***Relevant Scriptures:*** **Zechariah 1:1, 7**; also **Ezra 5:1; 6:14; Nehemiah 12:4, 16**

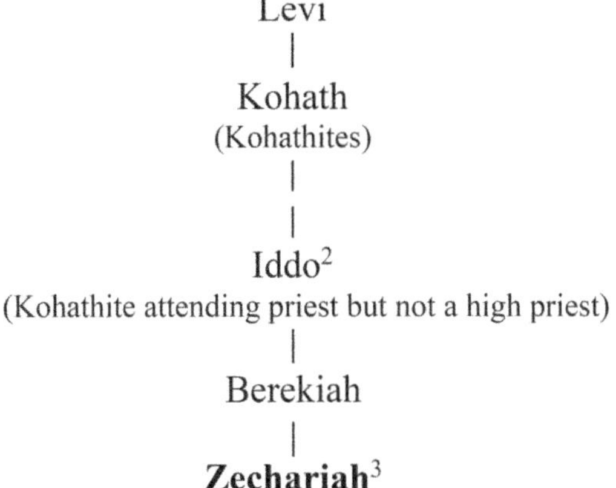

Biblical and Theological Significance

Zechariah, along with his contemporary Haggai, encouraged Zerubbabel and Joshua to begin renewing and restoring the post-exilic community and, more importantly, the temple. Zechariah's name זְכַרְיָה, "Yah(weh) remembers," is at the very heart of the prophet's message. His brief genealogy is exceptional because most of the other canonical prophets have either limited family histories or none at all.[4]

Zechariah had eight visions (**Zechariah 1:7–17; 1:18–21; 2:1–5; 3:1–10; 4:1–14; 5:1–4; 5:5–11; 6:1–8**), all of which had meaning in Zechariah's day and were related to the reestablishment of the restored community in Jerusalem and the building of the temple (see table 1 below). This series of visions ended with the purification and crowning of Joshua, who became the first high priest in the Second Temple. This event marked the transition from the first half of Zechariah (**Zechariah 1–8**) to the second half (**Zechariah 9–14**), the latter being more apocalyptic in style. Joshua, the high priest, foreshadowed the coming Messiah, "the man whose name is the Branch" (**Zechariah 6:12**). Jerusalem would become the capital of the Lord's kingdom. The Shepherd-King would arrive (**Zechariah 9:9–10**; cf. **Matthew 21:1–11; Mark 11:1–11; Luke 19:28–44; John 12:12–19**) and establish a kingdom of peace, thereby restoring the covenant between God and his people, dispelling idolatry, defeating foreign enemies, and turning Jerusalem into a place of worship of the King. In Jerusalem, the Feast of Tabernacles would be celebrated perpetually by the faithful Jewish and Gentile remnant of the nations (**Zechariah 14**).

Table 1: Zechariah's Visions

Number	Text	Main feature(s)	Interpretation	Application and Implementation
1	**1:7–17**	Man and horses	God's exercise of dominion	Jerusalem to be restored
2	**1:18–21**	Four horns	Symbols of power	Enemies to be defeated
3	**2:1–5**	Surveyor	Measuring Jerusalem's walls	City to be large and defended
4	**3:1–10**	Joshua + Satan	Satan disabled; Joshua restored	Messianic hope
5	**4:1–14**	Lamp + olive trees	The Spirit of God	God's mission will not fail
6	**5:1–4**	Flying scroll	Torah	Obedience brings victory
7	**5:5–11**	Flying basket	Evil flees	The temple replaces evil
8	**6:1–8**	Four chariots	God's providence	Israel to be secure

Notes

1. Zechariah is in a Levitical lineage—he is a Kohathite priest who served in the days of Joiakim the high priest, ca. 490–450/444 B.C. (**Nehemiah 12:16**). Zechariah is specifically identified as the priestly head of the family of Iddo division; see note 15 and the chart "**Nehemiah 12**: Genealogical Record of the Heads of Priests, Levites, and Gatekeepers who Served in the Second Temple in the Days of Joiakim the High Priest, Ezra the Priestly Scribe and Nehemiah the Governor."

2. Iddo (Heb. עִדּוֹא) the father of Berekiah and the grandfather of Zechariah (cf. **Zechariah 1:1, 7; Ezra 5:1; 6:14**) was the head of a priestly family that returned to Jerusalem with Zerubbabel in 538 B.C. (**Nehemiah 12:4**); see note 1 above. Spelling differences as well as chronological considerations preclude

his being Iddo (Heb. אדו) who was over the Levites in Kasiphia in 458 B.C. (**Ezra 8:17**).

3. For chronological reasons, Zechariah the prophet-priest is not the same person as Zechariah the priest (son of Jehoiada, son/descendant of Berekiah) who was murdered by King Joash, 835–796 B.C. (**Matthew 23:35; Luke 11:51**). For the latter, see charts "**2 Kings 11**: Joash, King of Judah" and "**1 Chronicles 6**: Levi: High Priests, Priests, Levites, and Musicians in Solomon's Temple."

4. See **Isaiah 1:1; Jeremiah 1:1; Ezekiel 1:3; Hosea 1:1; Joel 1:1; Zephaniah 1:1** and **Zechariah 1:1**. Only these seven of the sixteen prophets speak of family or heritage. See their respective charts.

ZECHARIAH 6: MEN WHO BROUGHT GIFTS FROM THE ISRAELITE CAPTIVES IN BABYLON TO THE NEWLY ESTABLISHED COMMUNITY IN JERUSALEM (POST-EXILE)

Approximate Dating: ca. 518/516 B.C. ***Relevant Scriptures:*** **Zechariah 6:9–14**

- **Heldai**[1]
- **Tobijah**
- **Jedaiah**[2] (see lineage below)

Possible Genealogy of Josiah (the Son of Zephaniah) and Jedaiah

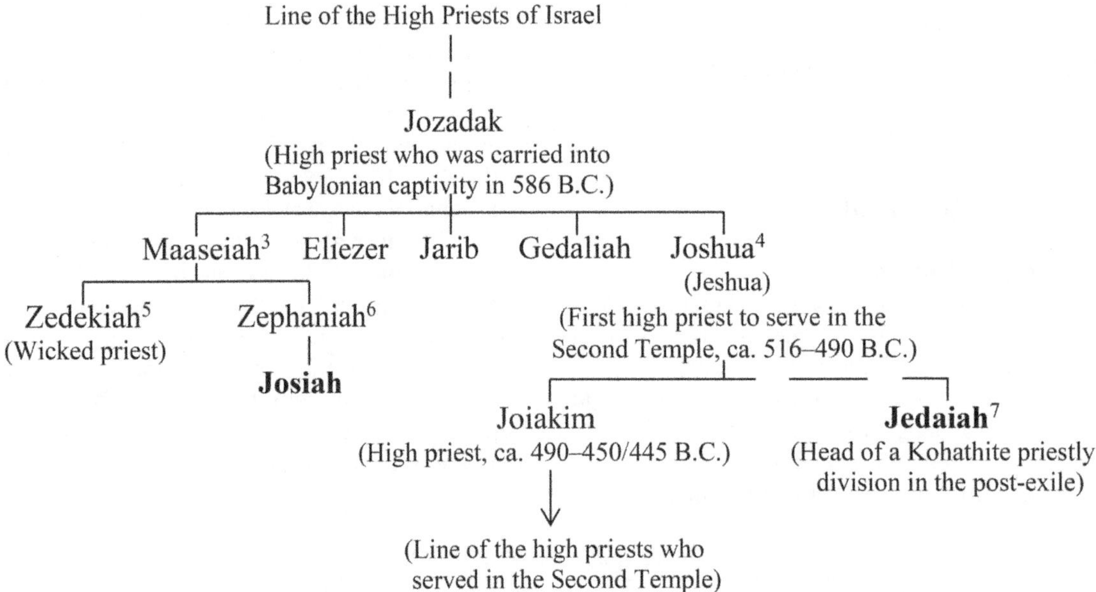

Biblical and Theological Significance

Heldai, Tobijah, and Jedaiah were exiles who had "arrived [in Jerusalem] from Babylon"; they brought gifts of gold and silver and took them to the house of Josiah the favored one,[8] the son of Zephaniah[9] (**Zechariah 6:10**). The precious metals were used to fashion an elaborate crown[10] for Joshua (Jeshua[11]), the high priest who would be the first to serve in the Second Temple when it was completed. Joshua became a "type" (foreshadowing) of the Messiah, the Branch, who would build the new temple in Jerusalem and sit and rule on his throne as *king* and *priest*, thereby combining both offices (**Isaiah 11:1; Jeremiah 33:15; Zechariah 3:8; 6:12–13;** cf. **Genesis 49:10; 1 Chronicles 17:11–12; Isaiah 9:7; Micah 5:2; Matthew 21:4–5; Mark 11:10; Luke 23:38; 1 Timothy 6:15; Hebrew 2:17; 4:14; 6:20; 7:3, 21; 8:1; 9:11; 10:21; Revelation 19:11–12, 15–16**). The men who brought the gifts appear to be of Kohathite priestly lineage, but their exact lineage is unknown. In the Septuagint, they are called "the patient ones," probably referring to the faith they maintained during the Babylonian captivity, a faith that assured them that would see the rebuilding of the temple.

Notes

1. Chronological constraints preclude this being Heldai the Netophathite from the lineage of Othniel the Kenizzite (**1 Chronicles 27:15**) or Tobijah the Levite, a contemporary of King Jehoshaphat, 872–848 B.C. (**2 Chronicles 17:8**).

2. The lineage of this Jedaiah is not clearly specified. He is probably of priestly heritage and may be the same person as the Kohathite priest named "Jedaiah"—a relative/near-brethren of Joshua the high priest—who served in the Second Temple (cf. **1 Chronicles 9:10; Ezra 2:36; Nehemiah 3:10?; 7:39; 11:10; 12:6–7**); see chart "**1 Chronicles 9**: The Kohathite Attending Priests in the Second Temple (Post-Exile)." Also see note 7 below.

3. For the identity of Maaseiah, see note 8 in chart "**Jeremiah 21**: Pashhur and Zephaniah, Who Were Sent by King Zedekiah to Inquire of Jeremiah about the Fate of Jerusalem (Pre-Exile)."

4. Joshua (**Ezra 3:2, 8; 5:2; 10:18; Nehemiah 12:26; Haggai 1:1, 12, 14; 2:2, 4; 6:11**) is also called Jeshua (**Ezra 2:36; Nehemiah 7:39**). Joshua the son of Jozadak (**1 Chronicles 6:15**) returned from Babylonian captivity with Zerubbabel in 538 B.C. and worked alongside Zerubbabel to re-establish

worship in Jerusalem (**Ezra 2:2; 3:8; Haggai 1:1; Zechariah 3:1, 3–9; 6:11**). Joshua/Jeshua served as the first high priest in the Second Temple. His brothers are mentioned in **Ezra 10:18–19**: "the descendants of Joshua son of Jozadak, and his brothers: Maaseiah, Eliezer, Jarib and Gedaliah"; they were guilty of having taken pagan wives in Babylon, but they pledged to put them away.

5. Zedekiah was a false prophet/false witness, an adulterer, and a liar who promised false hope to the Babylonian exiles; Jeremiah pronounced God's judgment on him—he and the false prophet Ahab were "roasted in the fire" by the king of Babylon (cf. **Jeremiah 29:21–23**)! See Zedekiah (note 10) in chart "**Jeremiah 21**: Pashhur and Zephaniah, Who Were Sent by King Zedekiah to Inquire of Jeremiah about the Fate of Jerusalem (Pre-Exile)."

6. Zephaniah the son of Maaseiah (**Jeremiah 21:1; 29:25; 37:3**) is not Zephaniah the prophet, the son of Cushi (**Zephaniah 1:1**).

7. Jedaiah was the head of a Kohathite priestly division in the post-exile, but he was not a high priest himself. Rather, he was a *descendant* of Jedaiah, the (ancestral) head over the second of the twenty-four divisions of Kohathite priests who served in Solomon's Temple in the days of King David (cf. **1 Chronicles 24:7**). Also, Jedaiah was a *relative* of Joshua/Jeshua the high priest (i.e., "through the family of Jeshua"; **Ezra 2:36; Nehemiah 7:39**), but the exact kinship is unknown.

8. **Zechariah 6:14** reads "The crown will be given to Heldai, Tobijah, Jedaiah and *Hen* son of Zephaniah as a memorial in the temple of the Lord," but "Hen" in this context may describe Josiah, meaning the one who is "gracious or favored" (i.e., Josiah, the son of Zephaniah in **Zechariah 6:10**).

9. This Zephaniah may be "Zephaniah, son of Maaseiah [son of Jozadak]," who was likely the *grandson* of the former high priest Jozadak (who was carried into Babylonian exile) and the *nephew* of Joshua, the first high priest to officiate in the Second Temple (**Jeremiah 21:1; 29:25; 37:3**; cf. **Ezra 10:18**). Zephaniah son of Maaseiah was sympathetic to the prophet Jeremiah (**Jeremiah 21:1–2; 29:29; 37:3**). For the probable lineage of the Zephaniah son of Maaseiah, see chart "**Ezra 2**: Joshua, the High Priest in the Second Temple, and His Descendants (Post-Exile)." It is impossible for this Zephaniah of the post-exile to be the same as Zephaniah the prophet of God, the son of Cushi (**Zephaniah 1:1**) who prophesied in the days of Josiah (640–609 B.C.) nor Zephaniah, the priest ranked second, who was executed at Riblah by the Babylonians in 586 B.C. (cf. **Jeremiah 52:24–27**).

10. The term for crown here, *atarah* (עֲטָרָה), is reserved for monarchy, thus indicating that the priest to be crowned will be a *royal priest* ruling over both a political and a spiritual realm. The messianic implications are obvious.

11. Jeshua (יֵשׁוּעַ) is an attenuated form of Jehoshua (יְהוֹשֻׁעַ), meaning "Yah(weh) saves." The Greek Iησους (Jesus) is a transliteration. For the lineage of Joshua/Jeshua, see chart "**Ezra 2**: Joshua, the High Priest in the Second Temple, and His Descendants (Post-Exile)."

MALACHI 1: MALACHI, THE PROPHET OF GOD TO THE RESTORED COMMUNITY IN JERUSALEM (POST-EXILE)

Approximate Dating: ca. 480–470 B.C.[1] ***Relevant Scriptures:*** **Malachi 1:1**

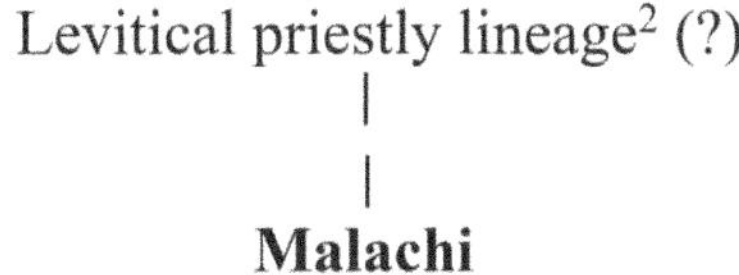

Biblical and Theological Significance

Some scholars propose that Malachi's name is a title meaning "messenger," but the fact that the word for "messenger," מַלְאָךְ, has the personal pronoun "my" (י)—thus מַלְאָכִי—makes it unlikely to be a title, but rather a personal name. Malachi likely prophesied ca. 480–470 B.C., after the Second Temple had been rebuilt in 516 B.C. (in the days of the prophets Haggai and Zechariah) but before the administrations of Ezra and Nehemiah, whom he fails to mention or indirectly refer to. When Ezra and Nehemiah arrived in Jerusalem (458 B.C. and 444 B.C., respectively), they attempted to deal with the very issues that had so troubled Malachi. Note the similarities between Malachi and Nehemiah regarding the following:

A. The defiled covenant of the priesthood and the Levites (**Malachi 1:6–2:9; Nehemiah 13:28–29**);
B. Wicked priests who had married foreign wives or divorced the wife/wives of their youth (**Malachi 2:14–16; Nehemiah 13:23–27**; cf. **Ezra 9:1–2; 10:18–24**);
C. The neglect of tithes and offerings (**Malachi 3:8–10; Nehemiah 13:10–13**); and
D. Moral decay and social sins (**Malachi 3:5; Nehemiah 5:1–11**).

Notes

1. Elsewhere we have argued, "Little is known of him—even his name, which means 'my messenger,'" but it does seem clear that his ministry preceded the governorship of Nehemiah [444–432 B.C.]. The lack of reference to Nehemiah and Ezra and the fact that Malachi inveighed against the very abuses in religious and social life that Nehemiah corrected upon his second arrival in Jerusalem suggest that Malachi uttered his oracles in precisely that period before Nehemiah's first arrival from Susa [and Ezra's as well in 458 B.C.]. A date of ca. 475 [B.C.] is therefore quite likely" (Eugene H. Merrill, *Kingdom of Priests: A History of Old Testament Israel*, 2nd ed. [Grand Rapids: Baker Academic, 2008], 514–15).

2. Malachi's genealogy is unknown. His breadth of knowledge about covenants and the priesthood suggests that he may have been in a Kohathite priestly line in the tribe of Levi, but nothing specific is known about his ancestry or hometown.

NEW TESTAMENT

MATTHEW 1: JESUS THE MESSIAH: THE MATTHEAN ACCOUNT[1]

Approximate Dating: from the birth of Abraham, ca. 2166 B.C. to the birth of Jesus in 3/2 B.C. and his death in A.D. 33 ***Relevant Scriptures:*** **Matthew 1:1–17** (Names in brackets are omitted in Matthew's genealogy but are known elsewhere from Scripture)

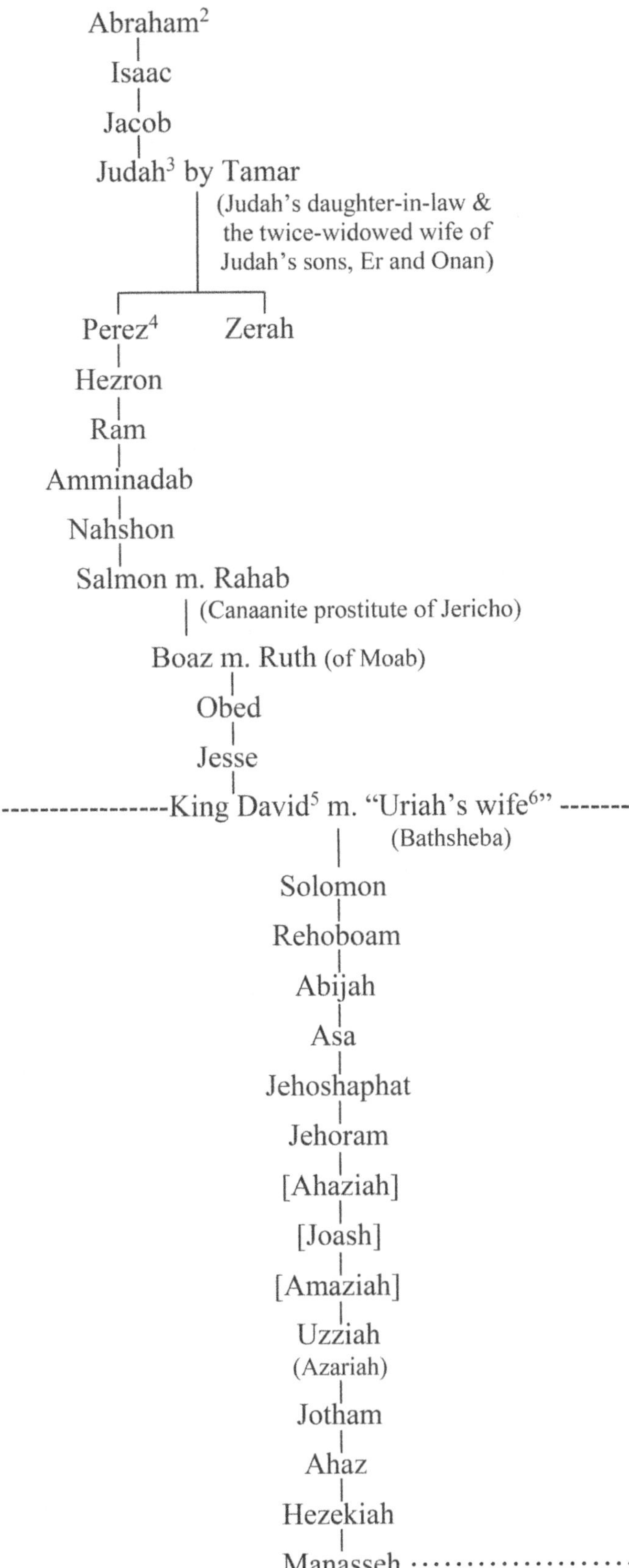

Biblical and Theological Significance

Distinctive Features of Matthew's Genealogy

The pedigree in Matthew traces the *biological* and *legal* patrilineal heritage of Jesus through Joseph, his earthly father. Matthew's genealogy is distinctive in several ways:

(1) The genealogy commences the New Testament—serving as a bridge between the Old and New Testaments (Covenants) and as an inauguration (*genesis*)[11] of a new everlasting covenant between God and man, which was prophesied in the Old Testament (**Genesis 9:16; 17:7, 13, 19; 2 Samuel 23:5; 1 Chronicles 16:15–17; Jeremiah 31:31–33; 32:40; 50:5; Ezekiel 16:60; 37:26; Malachi 3:1**) and then fulfilled in the person of Jesus the Messiah (**Matthew 16:16, 20; Mark 1:1; 14:61–62; Luke 2:11; 9:20; 23:35; John 1:41; 20:31; Acts 5:42; Romans 9:5; Galatians 3:17; Hebrews 7:22; 8:6–10; 12:24; 13:20**). Matthew's genealogy positions Jesus at the focal point of Scripture so that

all that came before pointed *to* him and all that came *after* pointed back to him. The placement of the genealogy at the beginning of Matthew's Gospel also functions to address the messianic expectations of the first-century community and to offer a preview of the narratives that follow.[12]

(2) The carefully laid-out details of the genealogy indicate that it was a major literary undertaking of a highly skilled and learned author. Matthew was a Jewish tax collector for Rome before becoming one of Jesus' disciples (**Matthew 9:9; 10:3;** cf. **Mark 3:18; 2:14**). Matthew's concise and coherent construction illustrates his competence as a compiler of a substantial amount of genealogical information. Presumably, Matthew drew upon ancient written and/or oral genealogical lists and/or scribal sources to compose the genealogy, such as those found in **Numbers 1; 1 Chronicles 1–9**, particularly **5:17; 9:1); 29:29; 2 Chronicles 9:29; 12:15; 20:34; 24:27; 26:22; 31:16–19; Ezra 2:3–65; Nehemiah 7:5–67; Luke 2:1–5**). Additionally, the church historian Eusebius (ca. A.D. 260–340) believed that Matthew may have used *private* source material from the *desposyni*, the close relatives of Jesus (see note 1), to compose the genealogy.

(3) The presentation of Jesus' ancestors follows the literary style of "*x* the father of *y*." In effect, person *x* was the father of person *y* where *y* could be a biological son / a son-in-law / an adopted son / a levirate son / or a legal heir.

(4) The list of Jesus' ancestors is organized in *ascending* order (from an earlier time to the present), directing the attention of the listener or reader to the literary *place of prominence* and the person of greatest importance: "Jesus who is called the Messiah" (**Matthew 1:16**). God's Messiah—the "Anointed One" or "Chosen One"—was the official title of the central figure of Old Testament expectation (**Isaiah 42:1; Daniel 9:25–26**; cf. **Luke 23:35; John 1:34; 20:30–31**).

(5) Matthew's genealogy presents forty ancestors of Jesus in three primary (literary) units, each having fourteen generations (a multiple of the sacred number seven), with literary "pearling"[13] between the units (where the same name occurs at the *end* of one section and the *beginning* of the next). Each unit corresponds to an era of Israel's history:

- **Unit 1**: Abraham to King David (time of the patriarchs to the time of the kings)
- **Unit 2**: King David to King Jeconiah/Jehoiachin (time of the kings to the beginning of the Babylonian captivity).
- **Unit 3**: King Jeconiah/Jehoiachin to Jesus (time of the exile, through the postexilic period, to the birth of Jesus)

Matthew imparts coherence to the literary units by using a *beginning literary marker*: "This is the genealogy of Jesus the Messiah the son of David, the son of Abraham" (**Matthew 1:1**) and a corresponding *ending literary marker*: "Thus there were fourteen generations in all from Abraham to David, fourteen from David to the exile to Babylon, and fourteen from the exile to the Messiah" (**Matthew 1:17**). The *inclusio* communicates three of Matthew's main objectives: to show that (1) Jesus was the culmination of Israel's history; (2) the long-awaited Jewish Messiah had come; and (3) Jesus was the final inheritor (*offspring, seed, heir*) of the covenant promises made to Abraham and David (**Genesis 12:1–3; 17:7; 22:18; 28:14; 2 Samuel 7:12–16; Galatians 3:16–18; Hebrews 1:2**).

To maintain the highly stylized 14–14–14 generational structure of the composition, Matthew deliberately omits the name of King Jeconiah/Jehoiachin's father (Jehoiakim/Eliakim)[14] and the names of three consecutive kings of Judah—Ahaziah,[15] Joash,[16] and Amaziah.[17] Matthew's omission of them is an example of "literary telescoping," in which he purposely shortens the entire genealogy by reducing the number of constituent elements. Since each of these kings caused apostasy in Judah, as did others, it is unclear why Matthew omits these rulers in particular.

(6) The genealogy is *linear* in structure and exhibits an overall literary construction of *a—b—c—d—a'*:

- *a* represents "Jesus the Messiah the son of David, the son of Abraham" (**Matthew 1:1**)
- *a—b* represents the generations from Abraham to King David
- *b—c* represents the generations from King David to King Jeconiah/Jehoiachin
- *c—d* represents the generations from King Jeconiah/Jehoiachin to Joseph
- *a'* represents "Jesus who is called Messiah" (**Matthew 1:16**), thereby reiterating that Jesus was the "Son of David" and the "Son of Abraham" (**Matthew 1:1**).

(7) Matthew states that the father of Joseph was Jacob (**Matthew 1:15–16**), whereas Luke states that the father of Joseph was Heli (probably the Greek form of the Hebrew name *Eli*; **Luke 3:23**). The two different names for the father of Joseph have given rise to a myriad of interpretations and possible harmonizations.[18] Two plausible scenarios are given here.

A. One scenario involves adoption. In this case, Jacob and Heli were brothers—when one brother died (Jacob or Heli), the other brother adopted his brother's son (i.e., adopted his nephew, Joseph). In this way, Joseph was considered the *biological* son of one brother and the *legal* heir of the other brother, thus accounting for the two different names for Joseph's father in the Matthew and Luke genealogies.

B. The other scenario involves levirate marriage. In this case, Jacob and Heli were brothers—when one brother died (Jacob or Heli) and left no male heirs, according to the law of levirate marriage (**Deuteronomy 25:5–6; Matthew 22:25**), the living brother (the *levir*) was to marry his deceased brother's widow and raise up an heir for him (the deceased). The son (Joseph) was then considered the *biological* son of the *levir*, and the *legal* son of the deceased brother.[19]

(8) When Matthew's genealogy (**1:1–17**) is charted alongside Luke's (**Luke 3:23–38**),[20] an unmistakable *double line* of Jesus the Messiah is evident—one *royal* lineage comprised of the David–Solomon–Jeconiah/Jechoiachin–Shealtiel–Zerubbabel–Joseph–Jesus line of descendants (i.e., those traced in Matthew's genealogy), and one *non-royal* lineage comprised of the David–Nathan–Neri–Shealtiel

–Zerubbabel–Joseph–Jesus line of descendants (i.e., those traced in Luke's genealogy), where Solomon and Nathan were biological *brothers* (i.e., the sons of David and Bathsheba).

(9) Also, when the genealogies of Matthew and Luke are charted side by side, specifically for the multiple generations from King David to Joseph, an overall *chiasmus* or "crossing" pattern (derived from the Greek letter *chi* or "*X*") becomes evident.[21] According to David Dorsey, the chiastic style of writing was a common literary device in ancient literature and was used in the Hebrew Bible as well. The chiastic pattern is unique in that it imparts an inverted parallel structure, so that the first and last elements in the text are parallel, the second and penultimate elements are parallel, and so forth.[22] By using the chiastic literary style, Matthew imparts balance and order to the overall genealogy and allows for corresponding substructural elements of the genealogy to be recognized by his audience.

This is especially valuable in understanding the literary substructure of **Units 2 and 3** (corresponding to the time of the kings, the postexile, and Second Temple period), allowing for a more definitive interpretation for the Jacob versus Heli parentage of Joseph.[23]

Sevenfold symmetrical* substructure *of Matthew's genealogy at the time of the kings through the post-exile (*Units 2 and 3*):

a—b—c—d—c′—b′—a′

Legend

a represents King David
b represents Solomon, the *biological* brother of Nathan
b—c represents the multiple generations from Solomon to King Jeconiah/Jehoiachin (i.e., from the time of the kings to the time of the exile)
d represents the "unmatched" unit (i.e., the decisive turning point or crossover point, "X", of the chiasm) corresponding to Shealtiel and Zerubbabel, who were the key figures of the exile/immediate post-exile. Shealtiel and Zerubbabel, the ancestors of Jesus, are common to the Matthew and Luke genealogies.
c′—b′ represents the multiple generations from Zerubbabel to Jacob (Joseph's father)
b′—represents Joseph's father Jacob who, by analysis, was likely the *biological* brother of Heli[24]
a′—represents Jesus (called the "son of David")

Alignment of the matching units (*b* and *b′* above) strongly suggests that Jacob (**Matthew 1:15–16**) and Heli (**Luke 3:23**) were uterine/biological brothers (i.e., the sons of the same mother) in the same way that Solomon and Nathan were uterine/biological sons of Bathsheba.

(10) Matthew's deliberate *exclusion* of certain prominent matriarchs such as Sarah, Rebekah, and Rachel and his deliberate *inclusion* of five "questionable" women in the Messiah's ancestry is noteworthy and shows selective choice on his part. The unusual narratives about these women have the *perception* of illicit, secretive activity and/or wrongdoing, but all five are vindicated:

- Tamar, possibly a Canaanite (although the text is not clear; **Genesis 38**), was the twice-widowed daughter-in-law of Judah by Judah's sons, Er and Onan, whom God put to death for their wickedness (**Genesis 38:6–10**). When Judah denied Tamar's marriage to his third son, Shelah, as stipulated in the law of levirate marriage (**Deuteronomy 25:5–6**), Tamar humbled herself by posing as a veiled prostitute and slept with Judah (who did not recognize her) to secure an heir. In the end, Judah, in his own words, declared Tamar "more righteous" than he had been to her (**Genesis 38:26**).
- Rahab, the Canaanite prostitute of Jericho (**Joshua 2**), professed that Israel's Lord was the true God. She was "considered righteous . . . when she gave lodging to the spies" (**James 2:25**; cf. **Joshua 6:17; Hebrews 11:31**). She and her household were spared in the destruction of Jericho (**Joshua 6:25**). In the end, Rahab was taken in marriage by Salmon the Judahite, the great-great-grandfather of David (**Matthew 1:5**).
- Ruth, the widow of Mahlon, was a Moabite (**Ruth 1:4; 2:10–12; 4:10**); moreover, from a religious standpoint, she was considered a total outsider (cf. **Deuteronomy 23:3**). Ruth vowed allegiance to her mother-in-law, Naomi, and claimed Israel's God as her own (**Ruth 1:16–17**). Following Naomi's instructions, Ruth spent the night with Boaz on the threshing floor (albeit in purity; **Ruth 3**). Boaz (acting as a close relative and a kinsman-redeemer) declared that the Lord—"under whose wings you have come to take refuge"—would repay Ruth for her righteous deeds to Naomi's family (**Ruth 2:11–12**). In the end, Ruth became the wife of Boaz and is said to have been "better to [Naomi] than seven sons" (**Ruth 4:15**). Ruth was the great-grandmother of David.
- "The wife of Uriah the Hittite" (elsewhere named Bathsheba; or called *Bathshua* in some translations) was a Judahite (cf. **Joshua 15:51; 2 Samuel 11:3; 15:12; 23:34**). She was sexually exploited by David, the king, which resulted in pregnancy. To cover his own sin, David premeditated the murder of Uriah in battle (**2 Samuel 11**). Eventually, Nathan the prophet rebuked David for his transgression, and the first child (a son) of David and Bathsheba's union died (**2 Samuel 12**). Eventually Uriah's widow became David's wife. Before David died, Bathsheba held him to his oath that *her* son, Solomon, would be Israel's next king (**1 Kings 1:15–17, 28–35**). Most remarkable is that, in the end, the *double line* of the Messiah is traced through Bathsheba's sons, Solomon and Nathan.[25]
- Mary, the virgin mother of Jesus, appears to be of mixed Judahite–Levitical heritage. According to church tradition, Mary was the daughter of Joachim (from the tribe of Judah) and Anne (a Kohathite from the tribe of Levi).[26] Scripture confirms that Mary was a *relative* of Elizabeth, the mother of John the Baptist; since Elizabeth was a "descendant of Aaron [the

first high priest]" (**Matthew 1:1; Luke 1:5, 36**), one of Mary's parents was also from the Levitical–Kohathite line of priests. While still betrothed but not yet married to Joseph (**Luke 1:26–35**), Mary conceived the Christ child by the Holy Spirit (**Matthew 1:18**). Despite the circumstances of Jesus' birth, in the end, Mary believed "that the Lord would fulfill his promises to her" (**Luke 1:45**) and "when the set time had fully come, God sent his Son, born of a woman" (**Galatians 4:4**).

Matthew's inclusion of these righteous women countered the allegations of impropriety that surrounded the conception and birth of Jesus and upheld the chaste character of Mary. Also, the interjection of some Gentile women (e.g., Rahab and Ruth) corrected the assumption that the Messiah's lineage would be strictly Jewish. In this way, Matthew's genealogy foreshadowed the *inclusive* nature of the messianic kingdom, where "heirs according to the promise" (**Galatians 3:29**) would be justified by their faith and belief in God's word and promises, irrespective of gender, ethnicity, past indiscretions, or social status (cf. **John 1:12–13; 11:51–52; Romans 8:16–17; Galatians 3:7–9, 26–28**): "If you belong to Christ, then you are Abraham's seed, and heirs according to the promise" (**Galatians 3:29**).

(11) Matthew characterizes Jesus as "the son of David" (**Matthew 1:1; 12:23; 22:41–46**), stressing his Davidic ancestry in "his earthly life" (**Romans 1:3**). As Jesus the Messiah, he was the rightful heir (officeholder and successor) to the throne of David. In this way, Jesus *inherited* the royal kingship and became the fulfillment of the covenant promises to David (**2 Samuel 7:12–16; Jeremiah 33:17**). Moreover, he embodied the "eternal King" (**Jeremiah 10:10**) who was over an "eternal (everlasting) kingdom," (**Daniel 4:3**) whose dominion would continue "from generation to generation" (**Lamentations 5:19**; cf. **Psalm 145:13; Daniel 7:27; 2 Peter 1:11**).

In summation, Matthew's genealogy should be understood to trace the biological line and the legal line of Jesus through his earthly father, Joseph (not through Mary, Jesus' mother).

Notes

1. The source(s) used by Matthew (and possibly Luke as well) in the compilation of Jesus' genealogy may have been based on *private* genealogical records that were kept by the *desposyni* (the blood-relatives of Jesus in the first century) for the purpose of demonstrating and legitimizing Jesus' Davidic ancestry. These private records appear to be separate from *public* genealogical records and registries that may or may not have survived. Integrating information from "The Epistle to Aristides" by Julius Africanus, Eusebius explains in his book on *Church History* that "there had been kept in the [public] archives up to that time [the time of Herod the Great] the genealogies of the Hebrews as well as of those who traced their lineage back to proselytes, such as Achior the Ammonite [*Judith* 5.5, 6, 14] and Ruth the Moabitess, and to those who were mingled with the Israelites and came out of Egypt with them, Herod, inasmuch as the lineage of the Israelites contributed nothing to his advantage, and since he was goaded with the consciousness of his own ignoble extraction [because he was an Idumean of Edomite heritage], burned all the genealogical records, thinking that he might appear of noble origin if no one else were able, from the public registers, to trace back his lineage to the patriarchs or proselytes and to those mingled with them, who were called Georae (foreigners) (**Exodus 12:19**). A few of the careful, however, having obtained private records of their own, either by remembering the names or by getting them in some other way from the registers, pride themselves on preserving the memory of their noble extraction. Among these are those already mentioned, called *Desposyni* [the term used by the early church to refer to the relatives of Jesus] on account of their connection with the family of the Saviour. Coming from Nazara [Greek for Nazareth] and Cochaba, villages of Judea, into other parts of the world, they drew the aforesaid genealogy from memory and from the book of daily records as faithfully as possible" (*Church History* 1.7.13–14).

2. To illustrate the importance of faith in the new messianic kingdom, Matthew begins his genealogy with Abraham, the first Hebrew patriarch of the Old Testament, who believed God's covenant promises (**Galatians 3:6; James 2:23**). Abraham was the forefather of Jesus Christ, and Jesus was Abraham's "seed" ("offspring"; **Galatians 3:16**; cf. **Genesis 3:15**). Abraham became the father of "descendants as numerous as the stars in the sky and as the sand on the seashore" (meaning the children of the *faith* of Abraham; **Genesis 22:17**; cf. **Genesis 15:5; 17:5–6; John 1:12–13; Romans 4:16; Galatians 3:7–9, 14, 29**).

3. Jesus "was descended from Judah," the son of Jacob (**Hebrews 7:14**). For the expanded genealogy of the tribe of Judah, see chart "**1 Chronicles 4**: Judah."

4. The casual mention of Judah and Tamar's twin sons, Perez and Zerah—in a simple segmented branch of Matthew's genealogy—is indicative of the selective nature of biblical genealogies; here, only the descendants in the Perez line are traced to the Messiah.

5. Matthew incorporates a kind of "king's list" in his genealogy (i.e., the succession of Judah's kings delineated in **Matthew 1:7–11**). Matthew traces the *royal line* of Jesus through King David and his son Solomon by following the biological, father-son succession of the kings of Judah (some of whom were faithful, and others not). By contrast, Luke's genealogy traces Jesus' lineage through Solomon's brother Nathan, in what is called the *non-kingly line* (**Luke 3:31**). In effect, the dual David–Solomon and David–Nathan lineages generate a double line of inheritance for Jesus the Messiah through two of the four (living) sons of David and Bathsheba; see chart "**1 Chronicles 3**: Zerubbabel and Shealtiel and the Double Line of the Messiah through King David's Sons, Nathan and Solomon."

6. When Matthew specifically identifies David's spouse as she who "had been Uriah's wife" (**Matthew 1:6**)—rather than by her name, Bathsheba (cf. **2 Samuel 12:24; 1 Chronicles 3:5**)—he calls direct attention to David's abuse of power in taking "Uriahs wife" and then murdering Uriah (who had been a loyal warrior in his army) so that David could marry her.

7. When the royal household of Judah was taken into Babylonian captivity, a *lineage shift* occurred in Jesus' ancestry. Matthew clarifies that King Jeconiah/Jehoiachin (of the royal line) became the father of Shealtiel *after* the king was exiled: "After they were brought to Babylon, Jeconiah begot Shealtiel, and Shealtiel begot Zerubbabel" (**Matthew 1:12**; cf. **1 Chronicles 3:17; Luke 3:27**). In Luke's genealogy, however, Luke presents Neri (of the Nathan–Neri non-royal line) as the father of Shealtiel, and Shealtiel, in turn, as the father of Zerubbabel (**Luke 3:27**). It is thought that the lineage shift occurs by either adoption and/or levirate marriage between members of the royal line and the non-royal line. These probabilities are evaluated in-depth elsewhere (see chart "**1 Chronicles 3**: Zerubbabel and Shealtiel and the Double Line of the Messiah through King David's Sons, Nathan and Solomon").

Jeremiah the prophet elaborates on the divinely rejected status of King Jeconiah/Jehoiachin in **Jeremiah 22:24–30**—by prophesying that Jeconiah would be recorded "as if childless . . . none of his offspring will prosper, none will sit on the throne of David or rule anymore in Judah [post-exile]." For more information, see chart "**2 Kings 24**: Jehoiachin (Jeconiah), King of Judah."

8. Shealtiel and Zerubbabel are two of the four common ancestors of Jesus in Matthew's and Luke's genealogies (i.e., David, Shealtiel, Zerubbabel, and Joseph; see **Matthew 1:12** and **Luke 3:27**). At the time of the exile/immediate post-exile, the continuance of the messianic line hinged on these two individuals, stressing the tenuous nature of the "scarlet thread of redemption" during this turbulent time in Israel's past. Although the importance of Shealtiel and Zerubbabel is not readily apparent in the separate linear genealogies of Matthew and Luke, their significance becomes vividly evident when Matthew's and Luke's genealogies are shown side-by-side, as they are in chart "**1 Chronicles 3**: Zerubbabel and Shealtiel and the Double Line of the Messiah through King David's Sons, Nathan and Solomon."

9. Zerubbabel was either the *legal* or *biological* son/heir of Shealtiel. When Zerubbabel arrived in Jerusalem, he became the governor (but not the king) over the post-exilic community. Perhaps most importantly, he is remembered as overseeing the rebuilding of the temple (the Second Temple or Zerubbabel's Temple). Zerubbabel and Joshua, the high priest, were responsible for the successful reestablishment of worship in Jerusalem. For more information

about Zerubbabel, see charts "**1 Chronicles 3**: Zerubbabel and Shealtiel and the Double Line of the Messiah through King David's Sons Nathan and Solomon" and "**Ezra 2**: Sheshbazzar and Zerubbabel, the Governors over the Restored Community in Jerusalem (Post-Exile)."

10. Matthew refers to Joseph (the earthly father of Jesus) as "the husband of Mary" (**Matthew 1:16**) and elsewhere calls him "Joseph son of David" (**Matthew 1:20**), emphasizing that Joseph was a direct Davidic descendant (cf. **Luke 1:27; 2:4**).

11. Brown notes that the opening Greek phrase of Matthew's Gospel, *biblo geneseōs* (**Matthew 1:1**) "most likely means 'the record of the generations (birth record) of Jesus Christ,' representing the Hebrew phrase *sēper tôlĕdôt* of **Genesis 5:1** . . . [and] constitutes the title of a genealogy of Jesus' ancestors . . . but that interpretation does not exclude a play on *genesis*, meaning "origin," so that the opening phrase in **Matthew 1:1** [could be] understood to mean "the story of the origin" . . . [where] the phrase prefaces the ancestral origin, birth, and beginnings of Jesus; but it also encompasses a view of the whole story of Jesus as a new creation, even greater than the old" (Raymond E. Brown, *An Introduction to the New Testament* [New York: Doubleday, 1997], 174).

12. The Gospel of Matthew can be divided into subsections: Jesus' genealogy and birth (**chs. 1–2**); introduction to the messianic kingdom (**chs. 3–7**); manifestations of the Messiah (**chs. 8–10**); the nature of the messianic kingdom (**chs. 11–13**); authority of the Messiah (**chs. 14–18**); kingdom blessings and judgments (**chs. 19–20**); appearances and rejection of the Messiah (**chs. 21–25**); Jesus' crucifixion, burial, and resurrection (**chs. 26–28:15**); and Jesus' commission to the disciples (**chs. 28:16–20**).

13. According to Dorsey, *pearling* (or *catchword bonding*) is a literary tool used to link topics (or words) from one unit to the next. For example, "b" develops a topic introduced in "a," and "c" then develops a topic introduced in "b," etc. See David A. Dorsey, *The Literary Structure of the Old Testament: A Commentary on Genesis–Malachi* (Grand Rapids: Baker Academic, 1999), 28.

14. King Jehoiakim (Eliakim) reigned for 11 years (ca. 609–598 B.C.). During his reign, Judah was a vassal to Babylon for three years. Jehoiakim burned the first scroll of Jeremiah and killed the innocent prophet Uriah. In general, Jehoiakim "did evil" and "detestable things" (**2 Kings 23:36–37; 2 Chronicles 36:5, 8**). See chart "**2 Kings 23**: Eliakim (Jehoiakim), King of Judah."

15. Ahaziah (the son of King Jehoram of Judah and Athaliah) reigned for one year (ca. 841 B.C.; **2 Kings 8:26; 2 Chronicles 22:2**). Ahaziah "followed the ways of the house of Ahab, for his mother [Athaliah] encouraged him to act wickedly" (**2 Chronicles 22:3**; cf. **2 Kings 8:27**). See chart "**2 Kings 8**: Ahaziah, King of Judah."

16. Joash, the infant king, began to rule Judah at age seven and reigned for 40 years (ca. 835–796 B.C.). However, after the death of Jehoiada the Kohathite priest—who had been the father figure in his life—Joash forsook the Lord, allowed widespread apostasy in Judah, and ordered the killing of Jehoiada's son Zechariah, whom he had grown up with (cf. **2 Kings 12:1; 2 Chronicles 24:17–22, 24; Matthew 23:35**; **Luke 11:51**). See chart "**2 Kings 11**: Joash, King of Judah."

17. Amaziah reigned for 29 years (ca. 796–767 B.C.; **2 Kings 14:2; 2 Chronicles 25:1**). Amaziah encouraged apostasy in Judah (cf. **2 Chronicles 25:14**). See chart "**2 Kings 12**: Amaziah, King of Judah."

18. For more information, see chart "**Matthew 1**: Ancestry of Mary and Joseph (Based on Scripture and Church Tradition) and How Mary and Joseph May Have Been Related."

19. For a discussion about the various levirate marriages that occurred in the lineage of Jesus, see Excursus A in chart "**1 Chronicles 3**: Zerubbabel and Shealtiel and the Double Line of the Messiah through King David's Sons, Nathan and Solomon."

20. See chart "**1 Chronicles 3**: Zerubbabel and Shealtiel and the Double Line of the Messiah through King David's Sons, Nathan and Solomon."

21. To visualize the chiastic pattern, see chart "**1 Chronicles 3**: Zerubbabel and Shealtiel and the Double Line of the Messiah through King David's Sons, Nathan and Solomon."

22. For an analysis of symmetric "chiastic" or "introverted" arrangements, see David A. Dorsey, *The Literary Structure of the Old Testament: A Commentary on Genesis–Malachi* (Grand Rapids: Baker Academic, 1999), 28, 30–32.

23. For more details, see charts "**1 Chronicles 3**: Zerubbabel and Shealtiel and the Double Line of the Messiah through King David's Sons, Nathan and Solomon" and "**Matthew 1**: Ancestry of Mary and Joseph (Based on Scripture and Church Tradition) and How Mary and Joseph May Have Been Related."

24. See chart "**Matthew 1**: Ancestry of Mary and Joseph (Based on Scripture and Church Tradition) and How Mary and Joseph May Have Been Related."

25. See chart "**1 Chronicles 3**: Zerubbabel and Shealtiel and the Double Line of the Messiah through King David's Sons, Nathan and Solomon."

26. See chart "**Matthew 1**: Ancestry of Mary and Joseph (Based on Scripture and Church Tradition) and How Mary and Joseph May Have Been Related."

MATTHEW 1: JESUS AND HIS IMMEDIATE FAMILY

Approximate Dating: from Jesus' birth, ca. 3–2 B.C. to his death, ca. A.D. 33. ***Relevant Scriptures:*** **Matthew 1:16, 18–21, 24–25; 2:11; 13:55–56; Mark 6:3; Luke 1:27, 35; 2:4–7, 34; 3:23; 8:19–20; John 2:12; 7:3–5, 10; Acts 1:14; Galatians 1:19**[1]

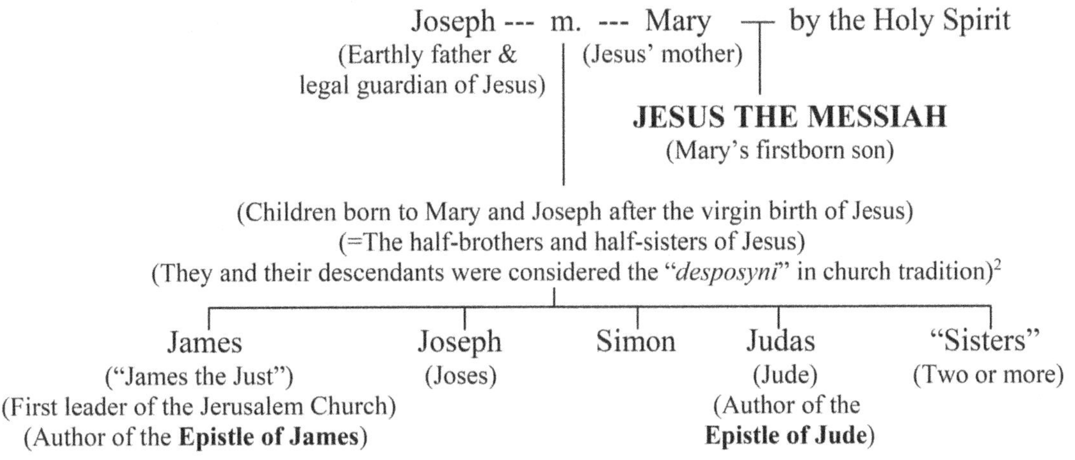

Biblical and Theological Significance

The commentary that follows focuses on specific aspects of Jesus' human and divine nature, his birth, and the members of his household. For a discussion of the ancestry of his parents, Mary and Joseph, see the chart "**Matthew 1**: Mary and Joseph (Based on Scripture and Church Tradition) and How Mary and Joseph May Have Been Related."

Jesus as Human and Divine: "Son of God–Son of David–Son of Man"

The record of Jesus' human ancestry reaches back to Adam, Abraham, Judah, and David. Jesus is called "the son of Adam" (cf. **Luke 3:23–38**), "the last Adam" (**1 Corinthians 15:45**), the "seed/son" of Abraham (**Galatians 3:16**; **Matthew 1:1**), and the "Lion of the tribe of Judah, the Root of David" (**Revelation 5:5**). A common epithet used for him is "Son of David" (i.e., a descendant of King David and a messianic title; **Matthew 1:1; 9:27; 12:23; 15:22; 20:30–31; 21:9, 15; 22:42; Mark 10:47–48; 12:35; Luke 18:38–39; 20:41**), meaning that Jesus was of Davidic descent (**John 7:42; Acts 2:29–35; Romans 1:3**) and had been given "the throne of his father David" (**Luke 1:32**).[3]

Jesus was uniquely related to God as his Son—the "Son, whom I love" (**Matthew 3:17; 17:5; Mark 1:11; 9:7; Luke 3:22; 20:13; 2 Peter 1:17**)—and as such, is referred to as "Son," "My Son," the "Son of God," the "Son of the Blessed One," "his one and only Son," "the one and only Son who is himself God," "the Son [who] is the image of the invisible God," "the Holy One of God," the "Son of the Living God," "his Son Jesus Christ/his Son, Jesus Christ our Lord," "the Father's Son," "Son of the Most High/Son of the Most High God," and "Son over God's house."[4] When Jesus speaks about God, he most often refers to him as "Father," "My Father," "My heavenly Father," or "Abba Father."[5] Typically, Jesus refers to himself as the "Son of Man."[6] In essence, Jesus was "Immanuel," meaning "God with us" (**Matthew 1:23**; cf. **Isaiah 7:14**).

Chronological Considerations Concerning Jesus' Birth in Bethlehem of Judea, the Sojourn of the Family in Egypt, and the Return of the Holy Family to Nazareth in Galilee

The consensus in modern scholarship has been that Jesus was born before the spring of 4 B.C., since Herod the Great died at that time.[7] Recently, however, the chronologist Andrew Steinmann[8] has revisited this interpretation and has offered new insights. Steinmann proposes that Jesus was born in late 3 B.C. or early 2 B.C.[9] (as shown for "approximate dating" in this chart) and offers the following:

1. The New Testament contains a number of chronological markers for the time of Jesus' birth:
   A. Jesus was born during the reigns of Augustus, 27 B.C.–A.D. 14 (**Luke 2:1**) and Herod the Great, 40–1 B.C. (**Matthew 2:1**).
   B. The first census took place while Quirinius was "governor" of Syria (**Luke 2:2**). Steinmann contends that the census conducted by Quirinius/Cyrenius was misdated by Josephus.[10] Steinmann interprets **Luke 2:2** as meaning that Quirinius was "exercising authority in a governing capacity" as *legatus juridicus*, but he was not the governor of the province (*legati pro praetore*). Steinmann quotes Eusebius [*Hist. eccl.* 1.5] who dated the census to Augustus' forty-second year (March 17, 3 B.C.–March 16, 2 B.C.); Steinmann also quotes the chronologist Jack Finegan, who said that Emperor Augustus was declared the father of his country on Feb. 5, 2 B.C. by "the whole people of Rome." In preparation for this honor, Finegan theorized that an empire-wide registration took place in 3 B.C.[11]
   C. Jesus was about thirty years old when he was baptized and began his ministry (**Luke 3:23**) during the fifteenth year of Tiberius' reign (**Luke 3:1**), corresponding to A.D. 29.[12]
2. Following Gabriel's announcement to Zechariah that he would have a son (**Luke 1:5–20**), his wife Elizabeth became pregnant and confined herself to her home for five months (**Luke 1:24**). The Annunciation came in the sixth month (**Luke 1:26–38**, especially **vv. 26, 36**). Thus, John was five-and-one half months older than Jesus. After the Annunciation, Mary spent three months in Judea with Elizabeth (**Luke 1:39–56**, especially **vv. 39, 56**). John was born to Elizabeth *after* Mary returned home to Nazareth (**Luke 1:56–79**). Sometime after this, Joseph took Mary with him to Bethlehem to be registered in the census (**Luke 2:1–5**). "If the census commenced sometime in the spring or summer of 3 B.C. [see 1B above] then Joseph may have arrived in Bethlehem in late summer or early autumn. This would place Jesus' birth no earlier than late summer of 3 B.C. and no later than the first months of 2 B.C. (**Luke 2:5–21**). In turn, John's birth took place between late spring and late autumn of 3 B.C."[13]
3. Forty days after Jesus' birth in Bethlehem came the time for Mary's purification and for Jesus to be presented at the temple in Jerusalem (**Luke 2:22–38**; cf. **Leviticus 12:1–8**). Mary and Joseph presented two doves or pigeons, the offering of the poor. The visit of the magi seems to have occurred immediately after Mary's purification rites at the temple. After the magi departed, Mary and Joseph (who were no longer poor) fled to Egypt (**Matthew 2:13–15**), and the gifts of the magi provided for their sustenance there. The holy family did not return to Nazareth until after the death of Herod in the first quarter of 1 B.C.[14]

Jesus of Nazareth

Jesus grew up in Nazareth (**Matthew 2:23; 26:71; Luke 2:39, 51; 4:16**), a small town in the hill country of lower Galilee about halfway between the Sea of Galilee and the Mediterranean Sea. Jesus was called "Jesus of Nazareth," "Jesus Christ of Nazareth," and "the prophet from Nazareth in Galilee" (**Matthew 21:11; 26:71; Mark 1:24; 10:47; Luke 4:34; 18:37; 24:19; John 1:45; 18:5, 7; Acts 2:22; 3:6; 4:10; 6:14; 10:38; 22:8; 26:9**); a "Nazarene" (**Matthew 2:23; Mark 14:67; 16:6**); and the "Branch/righteous Branch" (*netzer*; **Isaiah 4:2; 11:1; Jeremiah 23:5; 33:15; Zechariah 3:8, 6:12**). Jesus was rejected by the people of Nazareth as the Messiah of Israel (**Mark 6:1–3; Luke 4:14–30**; cf. **John 1:11**) and, for a time, he was even rejected by members of his own family (**Mark 3:21; 6:4; John 7:1–5**).

Jesus' Ministry, Crucifixion, and Resurrection

New Testament scholar Andreas Köstenberger holds that Jesus' public ministry lasted about three and a half years (ca. A.D. 29–33), placing his death in A.D. 33.[15] Chronologist Andrew Steinman specifically places the crucifixion on Friday, April 3, A.D. 33, and Jesus' resurrection on Sunday, April 5, A.D. 33.[16]

Joseph (Jesus' Father)

Joseph was considered the earthly father and legal guardian of Jesus (**Matthew 1:18–24; Luke 3:23; 4:22; John 1:45; 6:42**). Following the angel's command, Joseph named Mary's firstborn son "Jesus"—the name that the angel gave him "before he was conceived" (**Luke 2:21**; cf. **Matthew 1:21, 25**). Jesus' Hebrew name, יְהוֹשֻׁעַ, means "Yahweh saves." Jesus is specifically identified as "the carpenter's son" (**Matthew 13:55**; cf. **Mark 6:3**); "Joseph's son" (**Luke 4:22**); "Jesus of Nazareth, the son of Joseph" (**John 1:45**); and "Jesus, the son of Joseph" (**John 6:42**).

Joseph himself was a "son of David" (**Matthew 1:20**), a descendant of King David from the tribe of Judah. In accordance with the Roman census that was taken at the time of Jesus' birth, Luke stresses that Joseph "went up from the town of Nazareth in Galilee to Judea, to Bethlehem the town of David, because he [Joseph] belonged to the house and line of David" (**Luke 2:4**). In fulfillment of Micah's prophecy, Jesus was born in Bethlehem of Judea (also called Bethlehem Ephrathah or simply Ephrath or Ephrathah (cf. **Genesis 35:19; 48:7; Ruth 4:11; Psalm 132:6; Micah 5:2; Matthew 2:1–8; Luke 2:4, 15**), a village approximately six miles south of Jerusalem.

Joseph was the "husband of Mary" (**Matthew 1:16**). Scripture clearly states that "Mary was pledged to be married to Joseph, but before they came together, she was found to be pregnant through the Holy Spirit" (**Matthew 1:18**). Because Joseph was an upright man and did not want to publicly disgrace Mary, he "had in mind to divorce her quietly" (**Matthew 1:19**), but an angel of the Lord instructed him otherwise. So, Joseph "took Mary home as his wife," but they "did not consummate their marriage until she gave birth to a son" (**Matthew 1:24–25**).

Joseph does not appear in any biblical narratives after Jesus reached age twelve (i.e., after the events in **Luke 2:41–50**), with the possible exception of **John 6:42**, where people refer to Jesus as "the son of Joseph, whose father and mother we know" (though this mention of Joseph does not necessarily imply that Joseph was still alive at that time). Joseph appears to have died before or during Jesus' public ministry, but he was certainly deceased by the time of Jesus' crucifixion (cf. **Matthew 27:55; Mark 3:31; 6:3; John 2:12; 19:27; Acts 1:14**). Jesus' mother is the only parent who is mentioned at the crucifixion. On the cross Jesus handed over the care of his mother to John (son of Zebedee), who was likely Jesus' first cousin[17] (**John 19:26–27**).

The elaborate genealogies in the Gospels of Matthew and Luke (i.e., **Matthew 1:1–17** and **Luke 3:23–38**) clearly trace the line of Jesus' ancestors through *Joseph*, not through his mother Mary.

Mary (Jesus' Mother)[18]

Mary was the mother of Jesus (**Matthew 2:11–14, 20–21; 13:55; Mark 6:3; Luke 2:33–34, 48, 51; John 19:25–27**). While Mary was "pledged to be married to Joseph, but before they came together" (i.e., when she was still a virgin; **Matthew 1:18**; cf. **Isaiah 7:14; Luke 1:27, 34**), the Holy Spirit came upon her and by "the power of the Most High," she conceived (**Luke 1:35**; cf. **Matthew 1:18**). Mary gave birth to Jesus (*from the womb*; cf. **Luke 1:31; 2:21, 23**, NKJV). Jesus was "Mary's son" (**Mark 6:3**; cf. **Matthew 1:16; 13:55**) and her "firstborn"—the Greek term *prōtotokos* (**Luke 2:7**; cf. **Luke 2:21–23**). The context of **Matthew 1:16–18, 24–25; Mark 6:3;** and **Luke 1:26–27** asserts that after Jesus' birth, Mary and Joseph assumed normal marital relations and had a family of at least six children (four sons and at least two daughters).

Although the extrabiblical sources suggest a great deal of genealogical information about Mary's heritage, scriptural information about her family heritage is limited. **Romans 1:3** alludes to the fact that Mary, like Joseph, was a Davidic descendant since Jesus "as to his earthly life ['according to the flesh,' NKJV] was a descendant of David." Luke clearly establishes that Mary was a "relative" (a kinswoman/in the same kinship group) of Elizabeth, the wife of Zechariah the priest (**Luke 1:36**). Since Elizabeth and Zechariah (a Kohathite attending priest in Herod's Temple) were *both* descendants of Aaron the high priest (**Luke 1:5**), Scripture verifies that one of Mary's parents—undoubtedly her mother—was from the tribe of Levi and the clan of Kohathites also. Mary's other parent—undoubtedly her father—was from the tribe of Judah.[19] Church tradition and the apocryphal *Infancy Gospel/Protevangelium of James*, written ca. 145 A.D., hold that Mary's parents were an elderly couple named Anne and Joachim.[20]

Also, Scripture says that Jesus' mother had a "sister" (**John 19:25**). From the parallel Gospel accounts, it can be inferred that Mary's sister was *Salome*, the wife of Zebedee and the mother of James and John the apostles (cf. **Matthew 10:2; 20:20; 27:56; Mark 15:40, 16:1**). From this it can be concluded that James and John were the first cousins of Jesus.

Half-Brothers and Half-Sisters of Jesus

The earthly family of Jesus is directly or indirectly referenced in several places in Scripture (cf. **Matthew 12:46–47; 13:55–56; Mark 3:21, 31–32; 6:3–4; Luke 8:19–20; John 2:12; 6:42; 7:3, 5, 10; Acts 1:14; 12:17; 1 Corinthians 9:5**). The names of Jesus' half-brothers—James, Joseph, Simon, and Judas/Jude—are specifically mentioned in **Matthew 13:55; Mark 6:3; Acts 12:17; 1 Corinthians 15:7; Galatians 1:19; 2:9;** and **Jude 1**. The (believing) wives of Jesus' half-brothers are mentioned in **1 Corinthians 9:5**.

The genealogical chart above shows the four sons and the "sisters" of Jesus as the *biological* children of Mary and Joseph. Contrary to some church traditions, there is no reference in Scripture of a former marriage of Joseph to another woman and no hint of Mary experiencing infertility after Jesus' birth, for Jesus is spoken of as Mary's *firstborn* (**Luke 2:7**) and the *brother* of those named. However, in an effort to preserve the "perpetual virginity of Mary"[21] and the dignity of Jesus' birth, some traditions have maintained that the brothers and sisters of Jesus who are mentioned in the Gospels were either: (1) children of Joseph from an earlier marriage to another woman, or (2) children from the family of Mary's elder sister (which would make them only Jesus' cousins). For example, "Hegesippus (about 160), Clement of Alexandria (200), Jerome and Augustine (400) advocated that they were Jesus' cousins while Origin (230) and many after him in both the East and the West maintained that they were Joseph's children by an earlier marriage."[22]

James,[23] the half-brother of Jesus, is referenced in **Matthew 13:55; Mark 6:3; Acts 12:17; 15:13; 21:18; 1 Corinthians 15:7; Galatians 1:19; 2:9, 12; James 1:1**; and **Jude 1**. The name *James* is the Gentile form of the Hebrew *Jacob*, so he may have been named after his grandfather Jacob (a case of papponymy). Several details are known about James from Scripture and church tradition. Although he is called an "apostle" in **Galatians 1:19**, he was not one of the twelve apostles. James and his brothers (Joseph/Joses, Judas/Jude, and Simon) were skeptical of Jesus' earthly ministry, and, at least initially, they did not believe that Jesus was Israel's Messiah (**Mark 3:21; John 7:5**). However, after James (Jesus' half-brother) saw Jesus as the Risen Christ (**1 Corinthians 15:7**), his life was transformed. James was given the honor of presiding over the Jerusalem council in ca. A.D. 50 (**Acts 15:13–21**). Paul names James, Simon Peter/Cephas, and John (son of Zebedee) as the leading authorities—"those esteemed as pillars" in the Jerusalem church (**Galatians 2:9**). James authored the epistle that bears his name (**James 1:1**; cf. **Jude 1**).[24] In the extrabiblical literature he is referred to as *James the Just*.[25] Josephus explains that Ananus the younger assumed the high priesthood in A.D. 62. However, before the arrival of the new procurator, Albinus (A.D. 62–64), and without Albinus' knowledge, Ananus the younger unlawfully "assembled the Sanhedrin of judges, and brought before them the brother of Jesus, who was called Christ, whose name was James, and some others; and when he had formed an accusation against them as breakers of the law, he [Ananus] delivered them to be stoned".[26]

Eusebius relates that after the martyrdom of James in A.D. 62 and the subsequent conquest of Jerusalem in A.D. 70, "the apostles and disciples of the Lord that were still living came together from all directions with those that were related to the Lord according to the flesh (for the majority of them also were still alive) to take counsel as to who was worthy to succeed James. They all with one consent pronounced Symeon, the son of Clopas, of whom the Gospel also makes mention to be worthy of the episcopal throne of that parish [Jerusalem]. He [Symeon] was a cousin, as they say, of the Saviour. For Hegesippus records that Clopas[27] was a brother of Joseph [the earthly father of Jesus]."[28]

Joseph was the half-brother of Jesus (**Matthew 13:55; Mark 6:3**). In some translations, he is called *Joses* (Greek *Joses* is the variant of the Hebrew *Joseph*).

He was presumably named after his father, Joseph, but nothing specific is known about him.

Simon was the half-brother of Jesus, but nothing further is known about him. He is not the same person as Simon the Zealot, who was a disciple of Jesus (**Matthew 10:4; Mark 3:18; Acts 1:13**).

Judas—the Greek form of the Hebrew name *Judah*; English **Jude**—was the half-brother of Jesus (**Matthew 13:55; Mark 6:3**). He authored the epistle of Jude; in it he identifies himself as "Jude, a servant of Jesus Christ and a brother of James" (**Jude 1**).[29] Eusebius, quoting the early church writer Hegesippus, says that the grandchildren of Jude were brought before Emperor Domitian (r. A.D. 81–96) for questioning. After they confessed their relationship to the Lord and explained that his was not a temporal or earthly kingdom but a heavenly one, Domitian let them go and "by a decree put a stop to the persecution of the Church." After the grandchildren of Jude were released, "they ruled the churches because they were witnesses and were also relatives of the Lord. And peace being established, they lived until the time of Trajan [(r. A.D. 98–117)]."[30]

Jesus' half-sisters are mentioned (though not by name) in **Matthew 13:56**; **Mark 6:3**; and **Acts 12:17**. Presumably there were more than two, since the text of **Matthew 13:56** reads: "Aren't all his sisters with us?" rather than "Aren't both of his sisters with us?" Epiphanius of Salamis (who lived ca. 310–403) identifies two of Jesus' half-sisters as *Mary* and *Salome*.[31]

Notes

1. Extrabiblical sources consulted include Flavius Josephus, *The New Complete Works of Josephus*, trans. William Whiston, commentary by Paul L. Maier (Grand Rapids: Kregel, 1999); Eusebius, *Ecclesiastical History*, rev. ed., trans. C. F. Cruse (Peabody: Hendrickson, 2004); Jack Finegan, *Handbook of Biblical Chronology* (Peabody: Hendrickson, 1998); and Andrew E. Steinmann, *From Abraham to Paul: A Biblical Chronology* (St. Louis: Concordia, 2011).

2. The extrabiblical literature uses the term *desposyni*—meaning in Greek "belonging to the Lord"—to refer to Jesus' blood relatives and their descendants. The *desposyni* were highly respected among believers in early church history (see Eusebius' *Church History* 3.20 where he quotes the Christian writer, Hegesippus, of ca. A.D. 110–180). The "*desposyni/desposynoi* tradition" refers to the personal genealogical records that were kept by the extended family of Jesus that demonstrated and legitimized Jesus' Davidic ancestry (i.e., separate from public records and/or genealogical registries that may or may not have survived in the Second Temple period). The *desposyni* records may have been among the sources that Matthew and/or Luke used in compiling Jesus' genealogy (particularly the sections of **Matthew 1:13–17**; **Luke 3:23–30**); see note 1 in chart "**Matthew 1**: Jesus the Messiah–the Matthean Account."

The church historian Eusebius explains that "For the relatives of our Lord according to the flesh, whether with the desire of boasting or simply wishing to state the fact, in either case truly, have handed down the following account . . . But as there had been kept in the archives up to that time the genealogies of the Hebrews as well as of those who traced their lineage back to proselytes, such as Achior the Ammonite [*Judith* 5.5, 6, 14] and Ruth the Moabitess, and to those who were mingled with the Israelites and came out of Egypt with them, Herod [the Great], inasmuch as the lineage of the Israelites contributed nothing to his advantage, and since he was goaded with the consciousness of his own ignoble extraction, burned all the genealogical records, thinking that he might appear of noble origin if no one else were able, from the public registers, to trace back his lineage to the patriarchs or proselytes and to those mingled with them, who were called Georae. A few of the careful, however, having obtained private records of their own, either by remembering the names or by getting them in some other way from the registers, pride themselves on preserving the memory of their noble extraction. Among these are those already mentioned, called Desposyni, on account of their connection with the family of the Saviour. Coming from Nazara [a variant of Nazareth] and Cochaba [or Kokhaba, possibly referring to Kaukab in Galilee, northwest of Sepphoris], villages of Judea, into other parts of the world, they drew the aforesaid genealogy from memory and from the book of daily records as faithfully as possible. Whether then the case stand[s] thus or not no one could find a clearer explanation, according to my own opinion and that of every candid person. And let this suffice us, for, although we can urge no testimony in its support, we have nothing better or truer to offer. In any case the Gospel states the truth" (*Church History*, 1.7.11, 13–15).

3. For details about the Judahite–Davidic ancestry of Jesus, see charts "**1 Chronicles 3**: Zerubbabel and Shealtiel and the Double Line of the Messiah through King David's Sons, Nathan and Solomon"; "**Matthew 1**: Jesus the Messiah–the Matthean Account"; "**Matthew 1**: Ancestry of Mary and Joseph (Based on Scripture and Church Tradition) and How Mary and Joseph May Have Been Related"; and "**Luke 3**: Jesus: The Lukan Account."

4. For references to "Son of God" and variations: **Matthew 3:17; 4:3, 6; 8:29; 11:27; 14:33; 16:16; 17:5; 24:36; 26:63; 27:40, 43, 54; 28:19; Mark 1:1, 11; 3:11; 5:7; 9:7; 13:32; 14:61; 15:39; Luke 1:32, 35; 3:22; 4:3, 9, 41; 8:28; 9:35; 10:22; 22:70; John 1:14, 18, 34, 49; 3:16–18, 35–36; 5:19–23, 25–26; 6:40, 69; 8:36; 10:36; 11:4, 27; 13:32; 14:13; 17:1; 19:7; 20:31; Acts 9:20; 13:33; Romans 1:3–4, 9; 5:10; 8:3, 29, 32; 1 Corinthians 1:9; 15:28; 2 Corinthians 1:19; Galatians 1:16; 2:20; 4:4, 6; Ephesians 4:13; Colossians 1:13, 15; 1 Thessalonians 1:10; Hebrews 1:2–3, 5, 8; 3:6; 4:14; 5:5, 8; 6:6; 7:3, 28; 10:29; 2 Peter 1:17; 1 John 1:3, 7; 2:22–24; 3:8, 23; 4:9–10, 14–15; 5:5–13, 20; 2 John 3, 9; Revelation 2:18**.

5. For references to "Father" and variations: **Matthew 7:21; 10:32–33; 11:25–27; 12:50; 16:17; 18:10, 19, 35; 20:23; 24:36; 25:34; 26:39, 42, 53; Mark 14:36**; **Luke 2:49; 10:21–22; 22:29; 23:34; 24:49**; **John 5:17; 6:32, 65; 8:19, 28, 38, 49, 54; 10:17–18, 29–30, 32, 37; 12:26; 14:7, 12, 20–21, 23, 28, 31; 15:1, 8–9, 15–16, 23–24, 26; 16:3, 10, 15–17, 23, 25, 26; 17:1, 5, 11, 21, 24–25; 18:11; 20:17, 21**; **Acts 1:4, 7; Revelation 2:27; 3:5; 21**.

6. For references to "Son of Man": **Matthew 8:20; 9:6; 10:23; 11:19; 12:8, 32, 40; 13:37, 41; 16:13, 27–28; 17:9, 12, 22; 19:28; 20:18, 28; 24:27, 30, 37, 39, 44; 25:31; 26:2, 24, 45, 64; Mark 2:10, 28; 8:31, 38; 9:9, 12, 31; 10:33, 45; 13:26; 14:21, 41, 62**; **Luke 5:24; 6:5, 22; 7:34; 9:22, 26, 44, 58; 11:30; 12:8, 10, 40; 17:22, 24, 26, 30; 18:8, 31; 19:10; 21:27, 36; 22:22, 48, 69; 24:7**; **John 1:51; 3:13–14; 5:27; 6:27, 53, 62; 8:28; 9:35; 12:23, 34; 13:31**; **Acts 7:56**.

7. For more information on the dating of Herod's reign, see chart "**Matthew 2**: Herod the Great and the Herodian Dynasty." For the general consensus view on the dating of the birth of Jesus, see Andreas J. Köstenberger, L. Scott Kellum, and Charles L. Quarles, *The Cradle, The Cross, and the Crown: An Introduction to the New Testament* (Nashville: B&H, 2009), 136–39.

8. For a more complete discussion, see Steinmann, *From Abraham to Paul*, 219–54.

9. Steinmann, *From Abraham to Paul*, 249.

10. See Steinmann, *From Abraham to Paul*, 238–49, and specifically note 372 (239) where he quotes Josephus [*Ant.* 18.2.1]. Steinmann summarizes that "it is likely that Josephus misplaced the arrival of Quirinius ["the Sabine"/ Sabinus] in Judea and, therefore, misdated the census. The initiation of the census in Judea should be dated to the spring or summer of 3 B.C. . . . Once again the date of Jesus' birth must have been sometime in late 3 B.C. or early 2 B.C." (*From Abraham to Paul*, 249).

11. Steinmann, *From Abraham to Paul*, 241–242, including note 382 that quotes Jack Finegan. *Handbook of Biblical Chronology: Principles of Time Reckoning in the Ancient World and Problems of Chronology in the Bible*, Revised Edition (Peabody: Hendrickson, 1998), 305–306.

12. Steinmann, *From Abraham to Paul*, 219.

13. Ibid., 251–252.

14. Ibid., 252–253.

15. See Andreas J. Köstenberger, "Why We Believe We Can Know the Exact Date Jesus Died," First Things, April 3, 2014, https://www.firstthings.com/web-exclusives/2014/04/april-3-ad-33.

16. For a lengthy discussion, see Andrew E. Steinmann, *From Abraham to Paul: A Biblical Chronology* (St. Louis: Concordia, 2011), chs. 13–14.

17. See charts "**Matthew 1**: Ancestry of Mary and Joseph (Based on Scripture and Church Tradition) and How Mary and Joseph May Have Been Related" and "**Matthew 4**: James and John, the Apostles of Jesus."

18. To differentiate the various "Mary" figures who could be confused with Mary the mother of Jesus, see chart "**Matthew 27**: Specific People Mentioned at Jesus' Crucifixion."

19. With rare exceptions, genealogies in Scripture are exclusively *patrilineal* (i.e., tracing an individual's descent through the father/the *paternal* line). In this work, Mary is proposed to be of *mixed* heritage—in which one parent (her father) is from the tribe of Judah and the other parent (her mother) is from the tribe of Levi. This arrangement has precedence in the Old Testament (i.e., the *mixed* marriage of Aaron, the first high priest, from the tribe of Levi and the Kohathite clan, who married Elisheba from the tribe of Judah; **Exodus 6:23**). The situation is the opposite with regard to Jesus' parents. Since church tradition claims that Mary's parents were Anne and Joachim, from a genealogical perspective, Mary was a Judahite (i.e., according to patrilineal descent from her father Joachim), but Mary's mother was a Levitical Kohathite from the tribe of Levi. For a thorough discussion, see chart "**Matthew 1**: Ancestry of Mary and Joseph (Based on Scripture and Church Tradition) and How Mary and Joseph May Have Been Related."

20. For more information on Anne and Joachim, see chart "**Matthew 1**: Ancestry of Mary and Joseph (Based on Scripture and Church Tradition) and How Mary and Joseph May Have Been Related."

21. As James D. Tabor explains in detail in *The Jesus Dynasty* (New York: Simon & Schuster, 2006), 327, note 24: "In Roman Catholic teaching there are four Marian dogmas: the Immaculate Conception, the Virginal Birth (meaning Conception), Perpetual Virginity, and the bodily Assumption of Mary into heaven." Tabor explains that the Immaculate Conception "refers to the conception of Mary by her mother Anna, not the conception of Jesus. This teaching holds that Mary was born without original sin . . . This allowed her to give birth to Jesus in a special state of moral purity. The 'virgin birth' is a further teaching—that Mary, without a man, became pregnant through the agency of the Holy Spirit. It refers more to the source of the pregnancy than to the 'birth' itself. One might refer to the idea as the 'virginal conception,' since the focus is on the cause of her pregnancy. A further Catholic dogma holds that Mary remained a perpetual virgin (*semper virgine*, 'ever-virgin') her entire life. Even protestant leaders such as Luther, Calvin, Zwingli, and John Wesley shared this view, though it is less common among Protestants today. Mary was idealized over time as the divine-like holy 'Mother of God.' She was so far removed from her culture and her time that the very idea that she had sexual relations, bore additional children, and lived a normal life as a married Jewish woman seemed unthinkable for centuries. She was quite literally 'exalted to heaven,' and her actual humanity was lost, as was the importance of her forefathers" (ibid., 16–17). "Once one insists that 'the blessed Virgin Mary' was 'ever-virgin,' with no sexual experience whatsoever, then the brothers and sisters have to be explained away. . . . The conflict arises when later forms of ascetic piety and assumptions about 'holiness' are imposed on a culture for dogmatic or political reasons. What is lost is the historical reality of who Mary *truly* was as a Jewish married woman of her time. What we lose is Mary herself! The teaching of the 'perpetual virginity' is simply not found in the New Testament and it is not part of the earliest Christians creeds. The first official mention of the idea does not come until A.D. 374, from the Christian theologian Epiphanius. Most of our early Christian writings before the later 4th century A.D. took for granted that the brothers and sisters of Jesus were the natural-born children of Joseph and Mary" (ibid., 74–75).

22. John Cunningham Geikie, *The Life and Words of Christ* (New York: D. Appleton, 1877), 574–575. See also James D. Tabor's discussion of how the church, by the late 4th century A.D., began to handle what Jesus' "brothers" meant; see James D. Tabor, *The Jesus Dynasty* (Simon and Schuster, 2006), 75.

23. Given the fact that several figures in the New Testament are named "James," the half-brother of Jesus (named James) should not be confused with: (1) James the apostle, the son of Zebedee and the brother of John (**Matthew 4:21; 10:2; 17:1; Mark 1:19, 29; 3:17; 5:37; 9:2; 10:35, 41; 13:3; 14:33; Luke 5:10; 6:14; 8:51; 9:28, 54; John 21:2; Acts 1:13; 12:2**; see chart "**Matthew 4**: James and John, the Apostles of Jesus"; (2) James the apostle, the son of Alphaeus (**Matthew 10:3; Mark 3:18**; **Luke 6:15; Acts 1:13**) who was the brother (or half-brother) of Matthew; see chart "**Matthew 9**: Matthew and James, the Apostles of Jesus";; (3) "James the younger," who was the son of Mary and

the brother of Joseph (**Matthew 27:56; Mark 15:40, 47; 16:1; Luke 24:10**); see chart "**Matthew 27**: Specific People Mentioned at Jesus' Crucifixion"; or (4) James the father of the apostle Judas (not referring to Judas Iscariot) in **Luke 6:16; Acts 1:13**; see chart "**Matthew 10**: Genealogical Record of the Twelve Apostles of Jesus."

24. The **Epistle of James** was probably written between A.D. 44 and A.D. 62 (James's death).

25. For example, in his *Church History* 2.1.2-4, Eusebius writes: "Then James, whom the ancients surnamed the Just on account of the excellence of his virtue, is recorded to have been the first to be made bishop of the church of Jerusalem. This James was called the brother of the Lord because he was known as a son of Joseph, and Joseph was supposed to be the father of Christ, because the Virgin, being betrothed to him, was found with child by the Holy Ghost before they came together (**Matthew 1:18**), as the account of the holy Gospels shows."

In Church History 2:23.4-7, Eusebius discusses James's character and upbringing: "James, the brother of the Lord, succeeded to the government of the Church in conjunction with the apostles. He has been called the Just by all from the time of our Saviour to the present day; for there were many that bore the name of James. He was holy from his mother's womb; and he drank no wine nor strong drink, nor did he eat flesh. No razor came upon his head; he did not anoint himself with oil, and he did not use the bath. He alone was permitted to enter into the holy place; for he wore not woolen but linen garments [like those of the priests]. And he was in the habit of entering alone into the temple, and was frequently found upon his knees begging forgiveness for the people, so that his knees became hard like those of a camel, in consequence of his constantly bending them in his worship of God, and asking forgiveness for the people. Because of his exceeding great justice he was called the Just."

26. In his *Church History* 2.23.2–19, Eusebius elaborates on the martyrdom of James the Just saying that "leading him [James the Just] into their midst they [the Jews] demanded of him that he should renounce faith in Christ in the presence of all the people. But, contrary to the opinion of all, with a clear voice, and with greater boldness than they had anticipated, he spoke out before the whole multitude and confessed that our Saviour and Lord Jesus is the Son of God. But they were unable to bear longer the testimony of the man [James] who, on account of the excellence of ascetic virtue and of piety which he exhibited in his life, was esteemed by all as the most just of men, and consequently they slew him. Opportunity for this deed of violence was furnished by the prevailing anarchy, which was caused by the fact that Festus [Roman procurator, A.D. 60–62] had died just at this time in Judea, and that the province was thus without a governor and head. The manner of James' death has been already indicated by the above-quoted words of Clement, who records that he [James] was thrown from the pinnacle of the temple, and was beaten to death with a club. But Hegesippus, who lived immediately after the apostles, gives the most accurate account in the fifth book of his Memoirs. He [Hegesippus] writes as follows: 'James, the brother of the Lord, succeeded to the government of the Church in conjunction with the apostles. Now some of the seven sects, which existed among the people and which have been mentioned by me in the Memoirs, asked him, 'What is the gate of Jesus?' and he replied that he [Jesus] was the Saviour. On account of these words some believed that Jesus is the Christ. But the sects mentioned above did not believe either in a resurrection or in one's coming to give to every man according to his works. But as many as believed did so on account of James. Therefore when many even of the rulers believed, there was a commotion among the Jews and Scribes and Pharisees, who said that there was danger that the whole people would be looking for Jesus as the Christ. Coming therefore in a body to James they said, 'We entreat you, restrain the people; for they are gone astray in regard to Jesus, as if he were the Christ. We entreat you to persuade all that have come to the feast of the Passover concerning Jesus; for we all have confidence in you. For we bear you witness, as do all the people, that you are just, and do not respect persons (**Matthew 22:16**). Therefore, persuade the multitude not to be led astray concerning Jesus. For the whole people, and all of us also, have confidence in you. Stand therefore upon the pinnacle of the temple, that from that high position you may be clearly seen, and that your words may be readily heard by all the people. For all the tribes, with the Gentiles also, have come together on account of the Passover.' The aforesaid Scribes and Pharisees therefore placed James upon the pinnacle of the temple, and cried out to him and said: 'You just one, in whom we ought all to have confidence, forasmuch as the people are led astray after Jesus, the crucified one, declare to us, what is the gate of Jesus.' And he answered with a loud voice, 'Why do you ask me concerning Jesus, the Son of Man? He himself sits in heaven at the right hand of the great Power, and is about to come upon the clouds of heaven.' And when many were fully convinced and gloried in the testimony of James, and said, 'Hosanna to the Son of David,' these same Scribes and Pharisees said again to one another, 'We have done badly in supplying such testimony to Jesus. But let us go up and throw him down, in order that they may be afraid to believe him.' And they cried out, saying, 'Oh! Oh! The just man is also in error.' And they fulfilled the Scripture written in Isaiah, 'Let us take away the just man, because he is troublesome to us: therefore they shall eat the fruit of their doings.' So they went up and threw down the just man, and said to each other, 'Let us stone James the Just.' And they began to stone him, for he was not killed by the fall; but he turned and knelt down and said, 'I entreat you, Lord God our Father, forgive them, for they know not what they do' (**Luke 23:34**). And while they were thus stoning him one of the priests of the sons of Rechab, the son of the Rechabites, who are mentioned by Jeremiah the prophet, cried out, saying, 'Stop. What are you doing? The just one prays for you.' And one of them, who was a fuller, took the club with which he beat out clothes and struck the just man on the head. And thus he suffered martyrdom. And they buried him on the spot, by the temple, and his monument still remains by the temple. He became a true witness, both to Jews and Greeks, that Jesus is the Christ. And immediately Vespasian besieged them. These things are related at length by Hegesippus, who is in agreement with Clement. James was so admirable a man and so celebrated among all for his justice, that the more sensible even of the Jews were of the opinion that this was the cause of the [Roman] siege of Jerusalem, which happened to them immediately after his martyrdom for no other reason than their daring act against him."

In *Jewish Antiquities* 20.9.1, Josephus clearly states that he believed that the rash actions of Ananus the younger (concerning the stoning of James the Just), cost Ananus the high priesthood, for after Ananus had ruled only three months, King Agrippa took the high priesthood from him and made Jesus, the son of Damneus. For more details about Ananus the younger (#73), see in chart "**Supplement 2**: The High Priests of Israel."

27. For further details and the probable lineage of Clopas, see charts "**Matthew 1**: Mary and Joseph (Based on Scripture and Church Tradition) and How Mary and Joseph May Have Been Related" and "**Matthew 27**: Specific People Mentioned at Jesus' Crucifixion (Based on Scripture and Church Tradition)."

28. Eusebius, *Church History* 3.11; cf. 4:22.

29. Judas/Jude, the half-brother of Jesus, is obviously not the same person as Judas, the son of James, who was one of the twelve disciples (**Luke 6:16; Acts 1:13; John 14:22**) nor is he Judas Iscariot, the son of Simon Iscariot, who betrayed Jesus (**Matthew 10:4; 26:14, 25, 47, 49; 27:3, 5; Mark 3:19; 14:10, 43–45; Luke 6:16; 22:3, 47–48; John 6:71; 12:4; 13:2, 26–27, 29–30; 18:2–5; Acts 1:16, 18, 25**).

30. Eusebius, *Church History* 3:20.1–8.

31. Epiphanius (Bishop of Constantia in Cyprus, approximately A.D. 310-403), *The Panarion of Epiphanius of Salamis*, Section VII, 8.1, 9.1, 606–607, https://archive.org/details/panarionofepipha0000epip/page/n9/mode/2up.

MATTHEW 1: MARY AND JOSEPH (BASED ON SCRIPTURE AND CHURCH TRADITION) AND HOW MARY AND JOSEPH MAY HAVE BEEN RELATED[1]

Approximate Dating: from the birth of Levi, ca. 1926 B.C. and Judah, ca. 1925 B.C. to as late as A.D. 70 ***Relevant Scriptures:*** **Matthew 1:1–17; 12:46–50; 13:55–56; 27:56; Mark 3:31; 6:3; Luke 1:5–45; 3:23–33; John 7:5, 10; Acts 1:14; Romans 1:3; 1 Corinthians 9:5; Galatians 1:19** (Names in **BOLD** are known from Scripture; names that are **NOT BOLDED** are suggested by extrabiblical literature; familial relationships shown in the chart are deduced from the combined written sources)

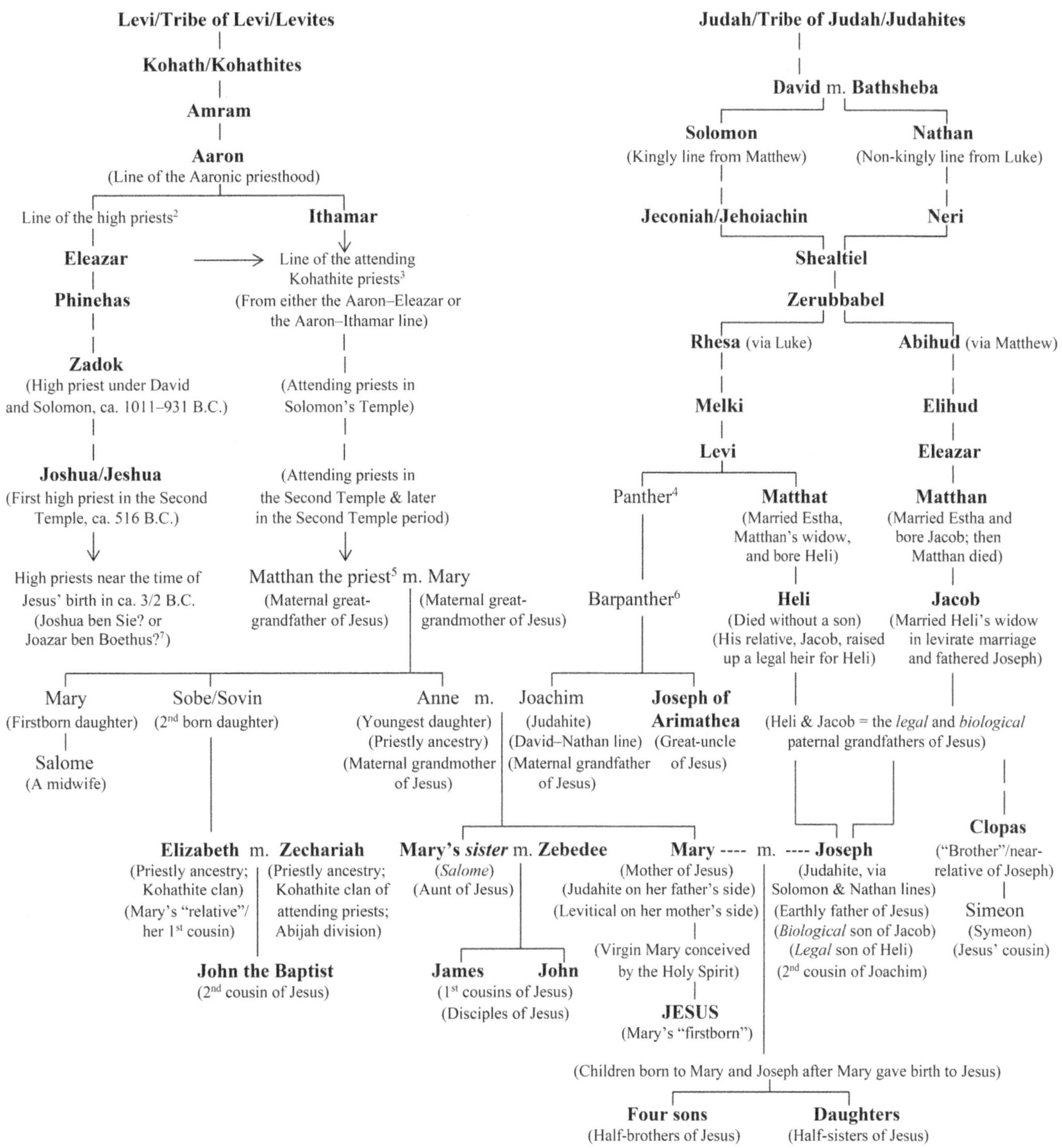

Inset below presents the specific familial relationships that are known from scripture (**names in bold**) and suggested by the extrabiblical literature.

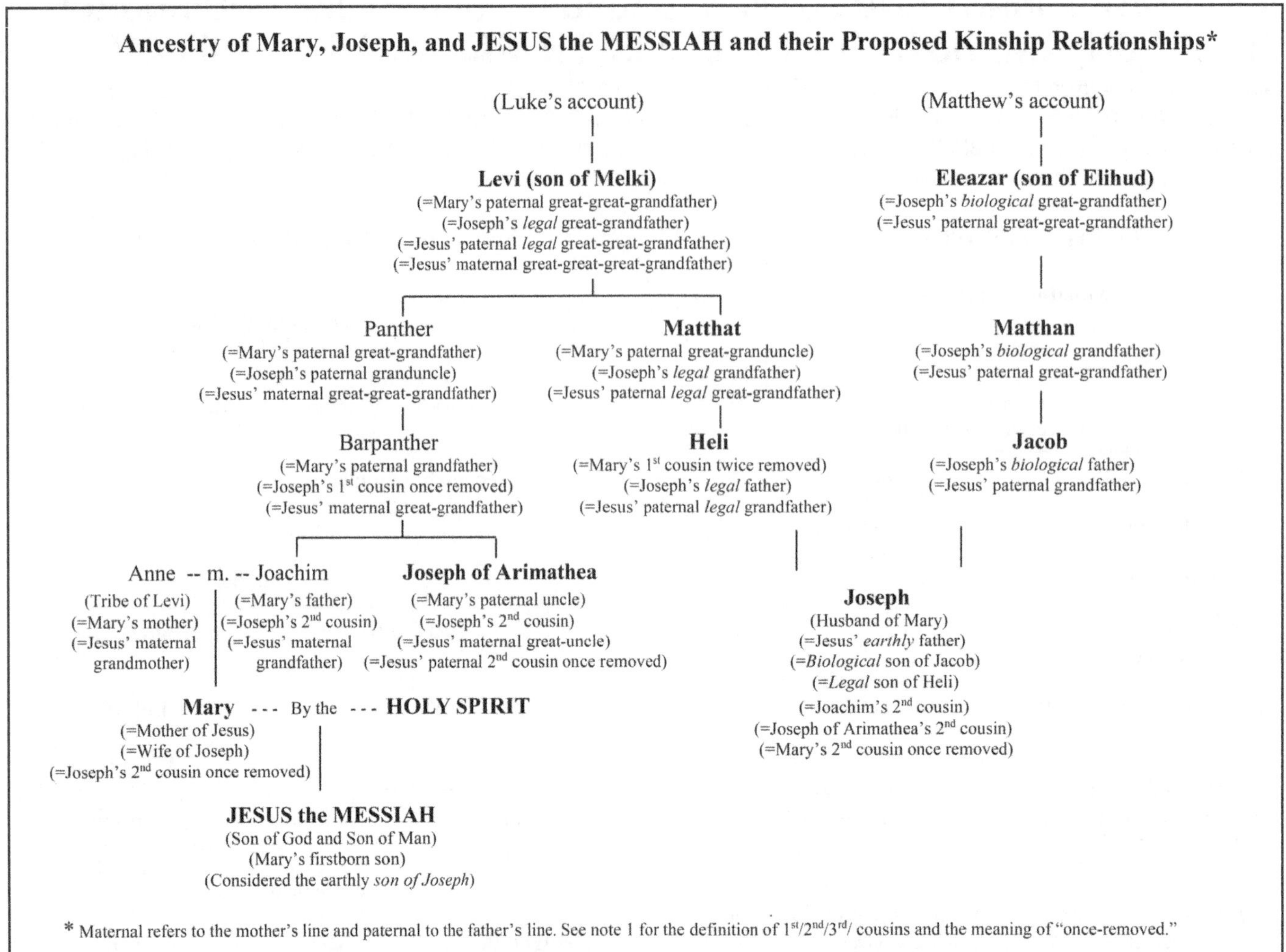

Preface

The main chart seeks to offer a comprehensive account of Mary and Joseph's ancestry using genealogical information about persons in Scripture (names that are ***bolded***) and integrating it with seemingly credible genealogical information about persons discussed in non-canonical sources, such as the writings of the Church Fathers (names ***NOT bolded***). However, the reader is advised to be cautious in drawing final conclusions since some "facts" in the extrabiblical literature may be historically accurate and reliable, but others are possibly distorted, inaccurate, or of a legendary nature.

Extrabiblical Genealogical Information from Five Sources Used to Assess Mary and Joseph's Ancestry, Presented in Historical Order

1. **Concerning Mary's Davidic ancestry:** According to the early church fathers, Mary was from the line of David. The Syrian bishop St. Ignatius of Antioch writes in the *Epistle to the Ephesians*,[8] ca. A.D. 107–110, that "For our God, Jesus Christ, was, according to the appointment of God, conceived in the womb by Mary, of the seed of David, but by the Holy Ghost." The early apologist-philosopher St. Justin Martyr wrote in ca. A.D. 165: "this Christ, Son of God, who was before the morning star and the moon . . . submitted to become incarnate, and be born of this virgin of the family of David."[9]

   Conclusion: According to patrilineal descent (i.e., deriving her ancestry from her father), Mary was from the tribe of Judah and the line of David.
2. **Concerning the parentage of Mary:** The *Protevangelium (or Infancy Gospel) of James*, attributed to James the half-brother of Jesus, is considered an apocryphal work that was probably written in the middle of the second century A.D. (although James was martyred in A.D. 62, so he is clearly not the author). It contains in "twenty-five chapters the period from this announcement [of the birth of Mary to Anne and Joachim] to the Massacre of the Innocents, including accounts of the early training of Mary in the temple, and the Lukan narrative of the birth of Christ with some legendary additions, and the death of Zacharias [Zechariah, the husband of Elizabeth] by order of Herod . . . [i]n its latest forms, the document indicates the obvious aim of the writer to promote the sanctity and veneration of the Virgin. It has been shown to contain a number of unhistorical statements. It was condemned in the

western church by Popes Damasus (382), Innocent I (405) and by the Decretum Gelasianum (496?)."[10]

Conclusion: Anne (Anna) and Joachim were likely the parents of Mary, the mother of Jesus. However, many of the narrative details (e.g., Mary at the temple, where she resided from age three to twelve, "fed by a heavenly messenger," and then given into the care and protection of the widower Joseph, who already had "sons")—are highly questionable and/or inaccurate and at odds with the scriptural account.

3. **Concerning the biological and legal ancestry of Joseph:** The Christian chronographer–historian Sextus Julius Africanus (ca. A.D. 160–240), who wrote the "Epistle to Aristides," explains the apparent discrepancy between Matthew's and Luke's accounts of Christ's genealogy: "In Israel the names of their generations were enumerated either according to nature or according to law—according to nature, indeed, by the succession of legitimate offspring, and according to law whenever another raised up children to the name of a brother dying childless . . . with the view of perpetuating the name of one deceased . . . [n]either of the evangelists (Matthew or Luke) is in error." To explain the generations, Africanus writes, "Matthan and Melchi [Melki], having taken the same woman to wife in succession, begat children who were uterine brothers, as the law did not prevent a widow, whether such by divorce or by the death of her husband, from marrying another. By Estha, then—for such is her name according to tradition—Matthan first, the descendant of Solomon, begets Jacob; and on Matthan's death, Melchi [Melki], who traces his descent back to Nathan, being of the same tribe but of another family, having married her, as has been already said, had a son Heli. Thus, then, we shall find Jacob and Heli uterine brothers, though of different families."[11]

   In a fragment of the "Epistle to Aristides," preserved by the church father and historian Eusebius of Caesarea (ca. A.D. 260–340), Eusebius follows the general reasoning of Julius Africanus by concluding that "Matthan, whose descent is traced to Solomon, begot Jacob, Matthan dying, Matthat, whose lineage is from Nathan, by marrying the widow of the former, had Heli. Hence, Heli and Jacob were brothers by the same mother . . . Heli dying childless, Jacob raised up seed to him, having Joseph, according to nature belonging to himself, but by law to Heli. Thus, Joseph was the son of both.[12]

   Conclusion: For unknown reasons, Julius Africanus omits the names of Levi and Matthat (between Melki and Heli; cf. **Luke 3:23–24**) and says that it was Matthan and Melchi/Melki who took the same woman (Estha) to wife in succession. Eusebius, in turn, follows Africanus' reasoning (i.e., invoking levirate marriage to demonstrate generational crossover between the Solomon and Nathan lines), but he corrects Africanus' error by saying that it was *Matthan* and *Matthat* (not Matthan and Melchi/Melki) who married the same woman (Estha) in succession. The chart above adheres to the textual reading of **Luke 3:23–24**: "Joseph, the son of Heli, the son of Matthat, the son of Levi, the son of Melki [Melchi]"—in essence, agreeing with Eusebius that it was Matthan (of the David-Solomon line) and Matthat (of the David-Nathan line) who married the same woman (Estha) in succession.

4. **Concerning Joseph's Davidic ancestry, the biological and legal ancestry of Joseph, and the paternal ancestry of Joachim:** The Syrian monk and priest St. John of Damascus (A.D. 675–749), in his book *An Exposition of the Orthodox Faith*, offers these insights: "But that Joseph is descended from the tribe of David is expressly demonstrated by Matthew and Luke, the most holy evangelists. But Matthew derives Joseph from David through Solomon, while Luke does so through Nathan; while over the holy Virgin's origin both pass in silence. One ought to remember that it was not the custom of the Hebrews nor of the divine Scripture to give genealogies of women; and the law was to prevent one tribe seeking wives from another. And so since Joseph was descended from the tribe of David and was a just man (for this the divine Gospel testifies), he would not have espoused the holy Virgin contrary to the law; he would not have taken her unless she had been of the same tribe. It was sufficient, therefore, to demonstrate the descent of Joseph." St. John of Damascus then references the law of levirate marriage (**Deuteronomy 25:5**), in which the offspring was the biological son of one brother but the legal son of the other brother who had died without issue. He concludes the genealogical explication as follows: "Born then of the line of Nathan, the son of David, Levi begot Melchi [Melki] and Panther: Panther begot Barpanther, so called. This Barpanther begot Joachim: Joachim begot the holy Mother of God. And of the line of Solomon, the son of David, Mathan [Matthan] had a wife of whom he begot Jacob. Now on the death of Mathan [Matthan], Melchi [Melki], of the tribe of Nathan, the son of Levi and brother of Panther, married the wife of Mathan [Matthan], Jacob's mother, of whom he begot Heli. Therefore, Jacob and Heli became [half] brothers on the mother's side, Jacob being of the tribe of Solomon and Heli of the tribe of Nathan. Then Heli of the tribe of Nathan died childless, and Jacob his brother, of the tribe of Solomon, took his wife and raised up seed to his brother and begot Joseph. Joseph, therefore, is by nature the son of Jacob, of the line of Solomon, but by law he is the son of Heli of the line of Nathan. Joachim then took to wife that revered and praiseworthy woman, Anna [Anne]."[13]

   Conclusion: In St. John of Damascus' account, he (1) omits the name Matthat, the son of Levi (clearly given in **Luke 3:24**), and (2) switches the names of Levi and Melchi/Melki by saying that "Levi begot Melchi [Melki] and Panther." Both of these are erroneous departures from the **Luke 3:23–24** reading, which clearly states that: "Joseph [was] the son of Heli, the son of Matthat, the son of Levi, the son of Melki" and so on. For that reason, the main chart above shows Melki/Melchi as the *father* of Levi (not the *son* of Levi, aka St. John) and, accordingly, interprets that it was Levi (not Melchi/Melki, aka St. John) who had two sons, Panther and Matthat. From that point onward, the chart agrees with St. John's account of the Panther–Barpanther–Joachim–Mary lineage and the levirate marriage/second marriage events that allow for the crossover between the biological and legal lines involving the Matthan–Jacob–Joseph line (via Solomon) and the Matthat–Heli–Joseph line (via Nathan).

5. **Concerning the maternal ancestry of Mary and her immediate family:** *A Rational Illustration of the Book of Common Prayer of the Church of England*, by Charles Wheatly states: "St. Ann[e] was the mother of the Blessed Virgin Mary and the wife of Joachim her father. An ancient piece of the sacred genealogy set down formerly by Hippolytus the martyr [Christian theologian and martyr, ca. 170–235, a disciple of Irenaeus, ca. 120/140–300/223, who himself was a disciple of Polycarp, ca. 69–155, a disciple of the apostle John] is preserved in Nicephorus. 'There were three sisters of Bethlehem, daughters of Matthan the priest, and Mary his wife, under the reign of Cleopatra and Casopares king of Persia, before the reign of Herod [the Great], the son of Antipater: the eldest was Mary, the second was Sobe, the youngest's name was Ann(e). The eldest being married in Bethlehem, had for daughter Salome the midwife; Sobe the second likewise married in Bethlehem, and was the mother of Elizabeth, last of all the third married in Galilee, and brought forth Mary the mother of Christ.' "[14]

   Conclusion: This text reveals the names of Mary's mother (Anne), her aunts (Mary and Sobe/Sovin), and her maternal grandparents (Matthan the priest and his wife, Mary). It substantiates the scriptural evidence that Mary (the mother of Jesus) and Elizabeth (the mother of John the Baptist) were "relatives" (**Luke 1:36**; i.e., because Mary's mother, Anne, and Elizabeth's mother, Sobe/Sovin, were sisters). On her maternal side, Mary was a descendant of Aaron (i.e., from the tribe of Levi and, more specifically, from the Kohathite clan of *attending* priests, but not the Kohathite line of high priests).

Biblical and Theological Significance

In ancient Israel, the genealogy of an individual was traced through the father's lineage (*patrilineal descent*), not through the mother (*matrilineal descent*), and this is the convention followed in Scripture as well. Characteristically, biblical genealogies trace the ancestry of a person by conveying family, clan, and tribal affiliations through the lineage of a person's father—or more precisely *of the father's house / the heads of families* (cf. **Numbers 1:2, 4, 18, 20, 22, 24, 26, 28, 30, 32, 34, 36, 38, 40, 42, 44; 3:15; 4:2, 46; Joshua 7:14; 1 Chronicles 4:33; 5:1–17; 7:4, 7, 9; 8:28; 9:1, 13; 23:24; 24:4; 26:31; 2 Chronicles 31:16–18; 35:4–5, 12; Ezra 1:5; 2:59; 8:1; Nehemiah 7:61**). Because of the disparity of most of the names in the two Gospel accounts of Jesus' genealogy, some scholars have erroneously perpetuated the idea that Matthew traced the genealogy of Joseph (**Matthew 1:1–17**) whereas Luke traced the genealogy of Mary (**Luke 3:23–38**).[15] However, as shown in the chart above, the correct interpretation is that *both* Matthew and Luke both trace the *patrilineal* descent of Jesus through Joseph, not Mary.

Introduction to Mary

Mary was chosen to become Jesus' mother because she had "found favor with God" (**Luke 1:30**). The angel Gabriel addresses her as "you who are highly favored! The Lord is with you" (**Luke 1:28**). At the time, Mary was pledged (betrothed) to Joseph and was "found to be pregnant through the Holy Spirit" before they were married (**Matthew 1:18**; cf. **Luke 1:35**). Joseph took Mary as his wife but "he did not consummate their marriage" until after she had given birth to Jesus (**Matthew 1:20, 25**; cf. **Luke 1:31**). In her song, the *Magnificat*, Mary declares "My soul glorifies the Lord and my spirit rejoices in God my Savior" (**Luke 1:46–47**), showing that she clearly saw herself as a sinner in need of salvation. This perspective is also implied in the way in which Jesus distinguished his earthly mother and siblings from his spiritual family (cf. **Mark 3:31–35; Luke 11:27–28**).[16] While on the cross, Jesus transferred the care of his mother to the "disciple whom he loved" (identified elsewhere as the apostle John, the son of Zebedee,[17] and from that time onward, John "took her into his home" (**John 19:26–27**). The scriptural account supports the conclusion that John was Mary's nephew (through Mary's sister Salome, the mother of John) and Jesus' first cousin (as shown in the chart). The church father Irenaeus and the historian Eusebius of Caesarea[18] wrote that John later went to Ephesus (cf. **Revelation 1:9**), which became the basis for some traditions purporting that Mary accompanied John and lived in Ephesus;[19] however, other traditions say she stayed in Jerusalem.[20]

Mary's Ancestry

Several passages of Scripture suggest that Mary, like Joseph, was a Davidic descendant (cf. **Luke 2:4–5** where "Joseph went there [Bethlehem] to register *with Mary*" (emphasis added) and **Romans 1:3** where Jesus "as to his earthly life" was a descendant of David, which could refer to Mary and/or Joseph). This interpretation is corroborated in the extrabiblical literature also (e.g., the early church writings of Ignatius and Justin Martyr). The chart above integrates information from the biblical text and extrabiblical sources. The combined literature shows that Mary derives her Judahite heritage from her father (Joachim), who was himself a Davidic descendant. Furthermore, Mary's paternal great-grandfather (Panther) and Joseph's paternal *legal* grandfather (Matthat) were brothers; Mary's paternal grandfather (Barpanther) was a first cousin of Heli (Joseph's *legal* father). Mary and Joseph share common ancestry with Levi, the son of Melki, from the David–Nathan line—Levi was Mary's paternal great-great-grandfather and Levi was Joseph's *legal* great-grandfather. Also, Joseph of Arimathea (the presumed brother of Joachim) appears to be Mary's paternal uncle (see below). Thus, Mary and Joseph were distantly related through their fathers. Additional aspects of these familial relationships are considered below.

Mary's Parents–Anne and Joachim

The canonical books of the New Testament never mention the parents of Mary, so all that can be ascertained comes from the extrabiblical literature. According to church tradition, her parents were Anne and Joachim. Joachim was from the tribe of Judah and a Davidic descendant who lived in the village of Nazareth in Lower Galilee.

Anne (Heb. *Hannah*), Mary's mother, was born in Bethlehem to a couple named Mary and Matthan; Anne's father was presumably a Kohathite attending priest of the Second Temple period but not a high priest (i.e., all high priests are well-documented and none of them includes a priest named Matthan).[21] Anne was the youngest of three daughters—Mary, Sobe, and Anne. Thus, Jesus' mother Mary may have been named after her maternal grandmother or her aunt (who were both named Mary). Sobe/Sovin was the mother of Elizabeth and the maternal grandmother of John the Baptizer. On her maternal side Mary (Jesus' mother) was of priestly (Kohathite) Levitical heritage through her grandfather (Matthan). Anne (a Levite) married Joachim (a Judahite), thus making Jesus' mother Mary of mixed Judahite-Levitical ancestry.[22] This is consistent with the dual office (priestly and kingly) identity of Jesus in Scripture:

- *Priest* (priestly)—but not according to the earthly order of the Aaronic priesthood;[23] rather, Jesus "was designated by God to be high priest in the order of Melchizedek" (**Hebrews 5:10**; cf. **Psalm 110:4; Hebrews 3:1; 4:14; 5:6; 6:20; 7:11, 17, 23–28; 8:1; 9:11; 10:21**)
- *King* (Davidic heir; **1 Kings 2:4, 45; 9:5; 2 Chronicles 6:16; 7:18; Isaiah 9:7; 16:5; Luke 1:32**).

Mary's Sibling–Salome

Scripture says that Jesus' mother, Mary, had a "sister" (**John 19:25**). Harmonizing the Gospel accounts (cf. **Matthew 10:2; 20:20–21; 27:56; Mark 15:40; 16:1; John 19:25**) reveals that her name was *Salome* and that she was the wife of Zebedee and the mother of James and John (two of Jesus' disciples). The genealogy shows that Salome was Jesus' aunt and may therefore explain her bold, somewhat presumptuous, request: "Grant that one of these two sons of mine may sit at your right and the other at your left in your kingdom" (**Matthew 20:21**; cf. **Mark 10:35–40**). Salome was one of the women at the cross (**Mark 15:40; John 19:25**) and among the women who came to anoint Jesus' body for burial (**Mark 16:1**). Salome (Mary's sister) may have been named after an older first cousin, Salome the midwife.

Mary's First Cousin, Elizabeth, and Her Husband, Zechariah (the Parents of John the Baptist)

A kinship link is clearly established in Scripture in **Luke 1:36** where Elizabeth is clearly identified as a Mary's *relative*: "Even Elizabeth your [Mary's] relative is going to have a child [John the Baptist] in her old age." Moreover, Elizabeth is specifically identified as "a descendant of Aaron" (**Luke 1:5**), meaning a descendant in the Levi–Kohath–Amram–Aaron priestly clan. Elizabeth's husband, Zechariah, was of priestly ancestry also—from the Abijah division of Kohathite attending priests—the eighth of twenty-four divisions (cf. **1 Chronicles 24:10; Luke 1:5**).[24] These scriptural details clearly assert that Mary and Elizabeth were in the same kinship group (i.e., the tribe of Levi–the clan of the Kohathites–the line of Aaron) and support the conclusion that Mary certainly had one parent who was of priestly ancestry—likely her mother. This interpretation is also substantiated by extrabiblical sources (e.g., Charles Wheatly's *A Rational Illustration of the Book of Common Prayer of the Church of England* in the section "Concerning the Maternal Ancestry of Mary and Her Immediate Family") which say that Elizabeth's mother (Sobe) and Mary's mother (Anne) were *sisters*. Therefore, in the chart above, Elizabeth and Mary are shown to be *first cousins*, and Jesus and John the Baptist are shown to be as *second cousins*.

Mary's Paternal Uncle, Joseph of Arimathea

The canonical Gospels convey several important details about Joseph of Arimathea.[25] Matthew identifies him as "a rich man" who had "become a disciple of Jesus" (**Matthew 27:57**). Mark says he was "a prominent member of the [Sanhedrin] Council, who was himself waiting for the kingdom of God" and "went boldly to Pilate and asked for Jesus' body" (**Mark 15:43**; cf. **Luke 23:50, 52**). Luke describes him as "a good and upright man, who had not consented to their [Sanhedrin] decision and action [regarding Jesus]" (**Luke 23:50–51**). John describes him as a secret disciple of Jesus "because he feared the Jewish leaders" (**John 19:38**). With Pilate's permission, Joseph "came and took the body away" (**John 19:38**) and "bought some linen cloth, took down the body, [and] wrapped it in the linen" (**Mark 15:46**). Joseph of Arimathea, accompanied by Nicodemus the Pharisee (see **John 3:1–15**), took Jesus' body and prepared it for burial, using about seventy-five pounds of myrrh and aloes (**John 19:39**). They placed the body in a "a new tomb . . . [where] no one had ever been laid" that was located in a garden near "the place where Jesus was crucified" (**John 19:41**; cf. **Matthew 27:60; Mark 15:46**). Matthew confirms that Joseph placed Jesus' body "in his own new tomb that he [Joseph of Arimathea] had cut out of the rock" and "rolled a big stone in front of the entrance to the tomb and went away"[26] (**Matthew 27:60**; cf. **Mark 15:46**). These events are consistent with Isaiah's messianic prophesy: "He was assigned a grave with the wicked, and with the rich in his death" (**Isaiah 53:9**).

In asking Pilate for the body of Jesus, Joseph of Arimathea publicly acknowledged that he was Jesus' disciple—if Joseph (or another relative) had not claimed the body, Jesus would have been buried that same day in a common grave for criminals (cf. **Deuteronomy 21:22–23**). Joseph's boldness before Pilate and Pilate's eventualconsent suggest that Pilate may have felt *obliged* to honor Joseph's request—initially because Joseph was a wealthy member of the Sanhedrin who had political influence but, probably more importantly, because Joseph of Arimathea was the eldest living patriarch in Mary's family and had a *legal* right to receive the body (since Jesus' father Joseph was undoubtedly deceased at the time).[27] Some traditions hold that Joseph of Arimathea was the *paternal uncle* of Mary, Jesus' mother.[28] For these reasons, Joseph is tentatively shown in the chart as Joachim's *brother* and Mary's paternal *uncle*.

Introduction to Joseph

The biblical text makes clear that Mary was "pledged [betrothed] to be married to Joseph, but before they came together, she was found to be pregnant through the Holy Spirit" (**Matthew 1:18**; cf. **Luke 1:35**). Joseph[29] took her as his wife but "did not consummate their marriage until she gave birth to a son." Following the instructions of the angel of the Lord, Joseph named him Jesus, "because he will save his people from their sins" (**Matthew 1:20–21, 25**; cf. **Luke 1:31**). Jesus was "her [Mary's] firstborn, a son" (**Luke 2:7**). In this manner, Jesus was both the biological son of Mary his mother and the Son of God by the Holy Spirit. Nevertheless, from a genealogical perspective, Joseph was still regarded the earthly father and legal guardian of Jesus (**Luke 2:22–23, 4:22; John 1:45; 6:42**), and Jesus' heritage is traced through Joseph. After the birth of Jesus, Mary's firstborn Son, Mary and Joseph had at least six children of their own (cf. **Matthew 13:55; Mark 6:3**). Details about the nuclear family are discussed in the chart "**Matthew 1**: Jesus and His Immediate Family."

Joseph's Ancestry

Joseph was from the tribe of Judah. He is called a "son [descendant] of David" (**Matthew 1:20**) and also said to have "belonged to the house and line of David" (**Luke 2:4**). Mary (Joseph's wife) was also a Davidic descendant via her father Joachim (see above). Given their dual Davidic ancestry, this explains why both Mary and Joseph went to Bethlehem to be registered in the census, for Bethlehem was "the town [the ancestral home] of David" (cf. **Luke 2:4–5**).

Scripture presents Joseph as having two different fathers—*Jacob* according to **Matthew 1:16** and *Heli* according to **Luke 3:23**. This could have occurred by (1) adoption[30] or (2) levirate marriage.[31] The extrabiblical sources—such as the writings of Julius Africanus, Eusebius, and St. John of Damascus—suggest that levirate marriage (between the Solomonic and Nathan lines) took place, accounting for Joseph's two different fathers, claiming that *Jacob* was Joseph's *biological* father and that *Heli* was Joseph's *legal* father.

Additionally, Joseph had two different paternal grandfathers—*Matthan*, according to **Matthew 1:15**, and *Matthat*, according to **Luke 3:24**. The extrabiblical literature supports the conclusion that levirate marriage also occurred in this generation, in which Matthan and Matthat married the same woman, named Estha. First, Matthan (of the David–Solomon line) married Estha and she bore a son, Jacob. Then, after Matthan's death, Matthat (of the David–Nathan line) took Estha (Matthan's widow) as his wife, and she bore Heli. In essence, Jacob and Heli had the *same* mother (Estha) but different fathers, and thus, they were biological/uterine brothers. It can be deduced that a second marriage in the Matthat and Matthan generation and a levirate marriage in the Heli and Jacob generation—involving the marriage of ONE woman in succession to TWO different men (first one from the Solomonic line and the second from the Nathan line)—accounts for the "crossover" between the David–Solomon and the David–Nathan lines in the patrilineal ancestry of Joseph.[32]

Joseph's Brother or Near Relative, Clopas

The kinship relationship between Joseph (the father of Jesus) and Clopas is not well understood. One of the best clues as to Clopas' identity comes from the early church historian Hegesippus (ca. A.D. 175–189) who wrote five books called the Hypomnemata or "Memoirs"—all of which have been lost except for a few fragments preserved by Eusebius in his *Ecclesiastical History*. Quoting Hegesippus, Eusebius states that, "after James the Just [the half-brother of Jesus] had suffered martyrdom . . . Symeon, the son of the Lord's uncle, Clopas, was appointed the next bishop. All proposed him [Symeon] as second bishop because he was a cousin of the Lord." [33] Based on this early account, Clopas is tentatively shown in the chart as the brother of Joseph and the uncle of Jesus, and Clopas' son, Symeon/Simeon, as the cousin of Jesus. Furthermore, Clopas was likely married to a woman called "Mary the wife of Clopas" (**John 19:25**) who was present at the crucifixion. Based on the account given by Hegesippus, Mary of Clopas would have been the sister-in-law of Joseph and Mary (Jesus' parents). In the scriptural accounts, this Mary (the wife of Clopas) appears to be the same person as (1) "Mary the mother of James and Joseph" (**Matthew 27:56**); (2) "Mary the mother of James the younger and of Joseph" (**Mark 15:40**); (3) "Mary the mother of James" who brought spices to anoint Jesus' body (**Mark 16:1**); (4) "the other Mary [who with Mary Magdalene] went to look at the tomb" (**Matthew 28:1**); (5) "Mary the mother of Joseph" who saw where Jesus' body was laid (**Mark 15:47**); and (6) the woman, who with Mary Magdalene and Joanna, went to tell the eleven disciples of the empty tomb (**Luke 24:9–10**). For more information about Clopas and these proposed familial relationships, see the chart "**Matthew 27**: Specific People Mentioned at Jesus' Crucifixion."

Concluding Remarks

Jesus' genealogy is traced according to *patrilineal* descent, just as other figures are in Scripture. Even though Mary conceived Jesus by divine intervention through the power of the Holy Spirit (**Luke 1:35**), the genealogies of **Matthew 1:1–17** and **Luke 3:23–38** trace the biological and legal heritage of Jesus through Joseph (i.e., Jesus' earthly father and Mary's husband). To be clear—neither one of the Gospel genealogical accounts traces the matrilineal descent of Jesus through Mary, his mother. The Judahite–Davidic ancestry of Jesus is firmly established on both his maternal and paternal side—Joseph was "of the house and line of David" and from the tribe of Judah (**Luke 2:4;** see **Matthew 1:20**), and according to the extrabiblical literature, Mary was of Judahite–Davidic ancestry on her paternal side (through Joachim) and of priestly–Levitical ancestry on her maternal side (through Anne).

Collectively, the Scripture and extrabiblical information (as summarized in the inset) strongly suggests that Joseph

(Jesus' earthly father) and Joachim (Mary's father) were *second cousins* because they shared the same paternal great-grandparent (Levi, the son of Melki). This association makes Mary and Joseph *second cousins once removed* (i.e., since Mary was one generation *removed* from Joachim her father). For these reasons, it can be reasonably concluded that Mary and Joseph were members of the same extended family.[34]

Notes

1. Familial relationships shown in the chart are based on the following known facts: ***first cousins*** share a grandparent, ***second cousins*** share a great-grandparent, ***third cousins*** share a great-great-grandparent, and so on. The term "removed" refers to the number of generations separating the cousins themselves. So, a ***first cousin once removed*** is the child (or parent) of a person's first cousin; a ***second cousin once removed*** is the child (or parent) of a person's second cousin; and a ***first cousin twice removed*** is the grandchild (or grandparent) of a person's first cousin.

2. Refer to the comprehensive list of high priests in chart "**Supplement 2**: The High Priests of Israel."

3. See chart "**1 Chronicles 24**: Genealogical Registry of the Twenty-Four Divisions of Kohathite Attending Priests Who Rotated Service in Solomon's Temple."

4. The individual named Panther (the son of Levi, the son of Melki) in Jesus' ancestry may account for some early Jewish traditions that refer to Jesus of Nazareth as "Jesus ben Pantera" or "Yeshu ben Pant(h)era" (*apud* Origen, *Contra Celsum* 1.32 and the medieval work called the *Toledot Yeshu*, the "Generations of Jesus"). It also may be a distortion of "Jesus, son of a virgin" (simply meaning "an unmarried young *parthenos*" and therefore unrelated to Pantera/Panthera). For further discussion of the ben Pant(h)era sobriquet, see Peter Schäfer, *Jesus in the Talmud* (Princeton: Princeton University Press, 2007), 15–24 and the section called "Panther, Prophet, or Problem Child: Jesus in Rabbinic, Islamic, and Popular Christian Traditions" in Craig A. Evans, *Jesus and the Manuscripts: What We Can Learn From the Oldest Texts* (Peabody, MA: Hendrickson Academic, 2020), ch. 7. In the genealogical construction that is proposed in the chart above, Panther was an ancestor of Jesus on both Jesus' maternal and paternal sides (i.e., Panther was Mary's paternal great-grandfather and Joseph's granduncle; see the inset).

5. In the chart, Matthan the priest, who was of Levitical ancestry (in the maternal line of Mary, Jesus' mother)—who is known from the extrabiblical source Charles Wheatley's, *A Rational Illustration of the Book of Common Prayer of the Church of England* (Oxford: Printed at the Theater, 1710), 67—should not be confused with Matthan the Judahite (in the line of Joseph, Jesus' earthly father), who is identified in **Matthew 1:15**.

6. Barpanther combines the Aramaic word Bar ("son") and the Latin word Pantera or Panthera ("panther"), meaning "son of Panther."

7. See chart "**Supplement 2**: The High Priests of Israel."

8. St. Ignatius of Antioch, *Epistle to the Ephesians*, chapter 18, https://www.newadvent.org/fathers/0104.htm.

9. Justin Martyr, *Dialogue with Trypho*, Chapter 45, https://www.newadvent.org/fathers/01283.htm.

10. From J. Hutchison, "Protevangelium of James," *ISBE* (Accordance Bible software). Full versions of the *Protevangelium of James* can be accessed online at https://www.newadvent.org/fathers/0847.htm, based on the text in Alexander Robers, James Donaldson, and A. Cleveland Coxe, eds. *Ante-Nicene Fathers*, vol. 8. trans. Alexander Walker (Buffalo, NY: Christian Literature, 1886) and the "Infancy Gospel of James" in Robert J. Miller, ed. *The Complete Gospels: Annotated Scholars Version* (Sonoma, CA: Polebridge, 1994), accessed through http://www.agape-biblia.org/orthodoxy/Protevangelium-of-James.pdf.

11. Quoted from "*The Epistle to Aristides,*" I–VI, in Philip Schaff, ed. "The Extant Writings of Julius Africanus," *Ante-Nicene Fathers*, vol. 6 (*Fathers of the Third Century: Gregory Thaumaturgus, Dionysius the Great, Julius Africanus, Anatolius, and Minor Writers, Methodius, Arnobius*) (New York: Christian Literature Publishing Co., 1886), 294–302, online at http://www.ccel.org/ccel/schaff/anf06.pdf.

12. From Eusebius of Caesarea, *Ecclesiastical History* 1.7, "The Alleged Discrepancy in the Gospels in regard to the Genealogy of Christ," online at http://www.newadvent.org/fathers/250101.htm.

13. John of Damascus, *An Exposition of the Orthodox Faith*, Book 4, Chapter 14, "Concerning our Lord's genealogy and concerning the holy Mother of God," https://www.newadvent.org/fathers/33044.htm (also available is St. John of Damascus, *An Exact Exposition of the Orthodox Faith*, Book 4, Chapter 14, 362–363, https://archive.org/details/AnExactExpositionOfTheOrthodoxFaith/page/n197/mode/2up).

14. Charles Wheatley, *A Rational Illustration of the Book of Common Prayer of the Church of England* (Oxford: Printed at the Theater, 1710), Sect. VII.6, 67. This book, first published in 1710 under the title *The Church of England Man's Companion; or, a Rational Illustration of the Harmony, Excellency, and Usefulness of the Book of Common Prayer*, was translated by Charles Wheatly (1686–1742) and published in 1845; internet archives of the University of Illinois at Urbana-Champaign, https://babel.hathitrust.org/cgi/pt?id=uiuo.ark:/13960/t48q0qz0v;view=1up;seq=82.

15. For the linear genealogical accounts of Jesus' ancestry, see charts "**Matthew 1**: Jesus–the Matthean Account" and "**Luke 3**: Jesus: The Lukan Account." Also, to view certain portions of the Matthew and Luke accounts of Jesus' genealogy charted side-by-side, see chart "**1 Chronicles 3**: Zerubbabel and Shealtiel and the Double Line of the Messiah through King David's Sons, Nathan and Solomon."

16. Traditionally, Catholics have adhered to the doctrine (or dogma) of the *immaculate conception* of Jesus, which states that Mary herself was conceived without original sin and that through perpetual virginity, Mary remained a virgin all her life, even after the birth of Jesus. This belief is not substantiated in Scripture, which clearly indicates that, after Jesus' birth, Mary and Joseph had at least six children of their own (i.e., the half-brothers and half-sisters of Jesus; see **Matthew 13:55; Mark 6:3**).

Catholic and Orthodox traditions also teach the *corporeal assumption* of Mary into heaven at or before her death, but there is no general agreement on the circumstances of her death. The veneration of Mary goes back at least to the second century A.D., where Mary is called the "Mother of God" (*theotokos*, a term used by the church father Origen); the "Blessed Virgin Mary," "Our Lady," "Madonna," "Mother of the Church," and "Queen of Heaven." The tradition of praying to Mary (another practice unsupported by Scripture) dates from the third century A.D. Although Catholic and Orthodox faiths honor and venerate Mary, they do not view her as divine, nor do they worship her (if they do, this goes beyond official church doctrine). She is viewed as subordinate to Christ but superior to all created beings. Especially important is that in **Luke 1:47**, Mary makes reference to "God my Savior," implying that she herself was in need of salvation like all other human beings, and therefore, she had a sinful nature.

17. See chart "**Matthew 4**: James and John, the Apostles of Jesus."

18. In his *Church History*, Eusebius writes that persecution of Christians occurred during the reign of Emperor Domitian (A.D. 81–96) and that John, the son of Zebedee, "was condemned to dwell on the island of Patmos" because of his testimony of "the divine word." Eusebius then quotes Irenaeus' *Against Heresies* 3:18, saying that if it had been necessary for the name of the Antichrist "to be proclaimed openly" at the time, then John would have declared it, because at the end of Domitian's reign, John was still alive: "the apostle and evangelist John, the one whom Jesus loved, was still living in Asia, and governing the churches of that region, having returned [after Domitian's death] from his exile on the island." Eusebius further quotes Irenaeus as stating that "John the disciple of the Lord" was among the churches in Asia until the time of Emperor Trajan (A.D. 98–117). According to Irenaeus (ca. 120/140–200/223), John went "to the neighboring territories of the Gentiles, to appoint bishops in some places, in other places to set in order whole churches, elsewhere to [appoint to ministry those who] were pointed out by the Spirit" (*Church History* 3.18.1–3; 3.23.1–6).

19. A cathedral named the Church of Mary, which dates to the early fifth century, is located in Ephesus.

20. The Church of the Sepulchre of Saint Mary (also called the Tomb of the Virgin Mary) is located in the Kidron Valley at the foot of the Mount of Olives in Jerusalem. Some Eastern Christianity traditions hold that Mary died a natural death there.

21. For the lineage of all the high priests, see chart "**Supplement 2**: The High Priests of Israel."

22. A clear precedent for mixed marriages in Israel is set with the notable marriage of Aaron, the first high priest (a Levitical Kohathite) to Elisheba, the daughter of Amminadab (a Judahite; **Exodus 6:23**). If church tradition is correct, the reverse is true in the case of Mary's parents—Mary's father, Joachim, was a David–Nathan descendant from the tribe of Judah who married Mary's mother, Anne, from the Kohathite priestly clan of the tribe of Levi.

23. See chart "**Supplement 2**: The High Priests of Israel."

24. See chart "**1 Chronicles 24**: Genealogical Registry of the Twenty-Four Divisions of Kohathite Attending Priests Who Rotated Service in Solomon's Temple."

25. Arimathea is identified as a "Judean town" (**Luke 23:51**) commonly associated with Ramathaim (the longer form of Ramah), located in the hill country of Ephraim about five miles north of Jerusalem and known as the hometown and burial site of Samuel the prophet (**1 Samuel 1:1, 19; 7:17; 25:1; 28:3**).

26. Two locations in Jerusalem have claimed to be the ancient site of Jesus' burial: (1) the Church of the Holy Sepulchre, which has the weight of tradition and history of veneration on its side (from about the fourth century) and (2) the more recently discovered nineteeth-century Garden Tomb (also called Gordon's Calvary), just north and east of the Damascus Gate (B. Spencer Haygood, "Calvary," *Holman's Bible Dictionary*, Accordance Bible Software). However, the Israeli archaeologist Gabriel Barkay has shown that the Garden Tomb was a First Temple-period tomb and could not be the correct site for the tomb of Joseph of Arimathea, where Jesus was buried. Gabriel Barkay, "Was Jesus Buried in the Garden Tomb? First-Century Jewish Burial in Jerusalem," Jerusalem Perspective 2006 Conference, Jerusalem, Israel, 19–21 June, 2006, video at https://www.jerusalemperspective.com/17471/.

27. "The Sanhedrin had declared Jesus a criminal. According to both Roman and Jewish law, unless the body of an executed criminal was immediately claimed by the next of kin, the body of the victim was cast into a common pit, where all physical record of them was completely obliterated. Certainly, the fanatical Sadducean element of the Sanhedrin who sought the total extinction of Jesus, even in death, would have allowed nothing short of a legal claim on the body of Christ." E. Raymond Capt, *Traditions of Glastonbury* (Thousand Oaks, CA: Artisan Sales, 1983), 20.

28. According to Richard W. Morgan, "Joseph of Arimathea is by Eastern [Orthodox] tradition said to have been the younger brother of the father of the Virgin Mary" (Richard W. Morgan, *St. Paul in Britain*, [London: J.H. and Jas. Parker, 1861] 139, footnote, https://archive.org/details/stpaulinbritain01morggoog/page/n4/mode/2up).

29. Joseph is not mentioned in the Gospels after the family's trip to Jerusalem when Jesus was twelve (**Luke 2:41–50**). During his ministry, Jesus is identified as "Mary's son [rather than Joseph's son] and the brother of James, Joseph, Judas and Simon" (**Mark 6:3**), suggesting that Joseph may have already been deceased. Early Christian writings suggest that Joseph died in Jesus' youth, before the beginning of Jesus' public ministry.

30. If and where adoption scenario(s) took place in Jesus' genealogy is not clearly known. If adoption did occur, typically one man (Man#1/Brother #1) has a son, but when he died unexpectedly (for example, while the child/son was still an infant or youth), his nearest male relative (Man#2/Brother #2), adopted his nephew (the son of Man #1/Brother #1) and raised the child up as his adoptive heir. Adoption is known to have occurred among the Romans; the most famous example was Emperor Augustus, who was adopted by his maternal great-uncle, Julius Caesar.

31. Levirate marriage was known to have occurred during the Second Temple period. For example, the high priest Alexander Jannaeus (103–76 B.C.) married his brother's widow, Salome Alexandra—the former wife of Aristobulus I (the brother of Alexander Jannaeus); see Alexander Jannaeus #47 in chart "**Supplement 2**: The High Priests of Israel"). Moreover, levirate marriage seems to be acceptable in New Testament times, as suggested by the passage in **Matthew 22:23–27**. According to the laws of levirate marriage (cf. **Deuteronomy 25:5–10**), when a man died without sons, the eldest brother or nearest relative (the *levir*) married the widow and had a child (i.e., this child was therefore the *biological son* of the *levir*) who would carry on the name of the man who died childless. The first son of the levirate union was considered the dead man's heir (i.e., the *legal son* of the deceased). A well-known instance of levirate marriage occurred in the Old Testament when Ruth's husband (Mahlon) died, so Boaz (a near relative of Mahlon) married Ruth (Mahlon's widow) and raised up a child (Obed) for Mahlon; see chart "**Ruth 1**: Boaz, Elimelek, and Naomi and the Descendants of Boaz the Judahite and Ruth the Moabitess."

In Jesus' genealogy, several accounts of levirate marriage (and perhaps adoption) took place (see "Excursus A" in chart "**1 Chronicles 3**: Zerubbabel and Shealtiel and the Double Line of the Messiah through King David's Sons, Nathan and Solomon"). Levirate marriage is especially noticeable in the chart above (inset) in the two generations before Joseph (the earthly father of Jesus): (1) most likely between Matthat and Matthan (Joseph's great-grandfathers), who married the same woman (Estha) in succession, and (2) for Jacob and Heli (Joseph's grandfathers), who married the same (unnamed) woman in succession.

32. See Excursus A in chart "**1 Chronicles 3**: Zerubbabel and Shealtiel and the Double Line of the Messiah through King David's Sons, Nathan and Solomon."

33. Hegesippuss, Hypomnemata ["Memoirs"], quoted in Eusebius, *Ecclesiastical History* Book 4.22.4; cf. Book 3.11.1-2, https://www.newadvent.org/fathers/2501.htm.

34. This is an example of *endogamy*, the custom of marrying only within the limits of a local community or clan.

MATTHEW 2: HEROD THE GREAT AND THE HERODIAN DYNASTY[1]

Approximate Dating: ca. 40 B.C. to A.D. 66[2] ***Relevant Scriptures:*** **Matthew 2:1–23; 14:1–12; Mark 6:14–29; 8:15; Luke 1:5; 3:1, 19–20; 9:7–9; 13:31; 23:7–16; Acts 4:27; 12:1–23; 24:24; 25:13–26:32**

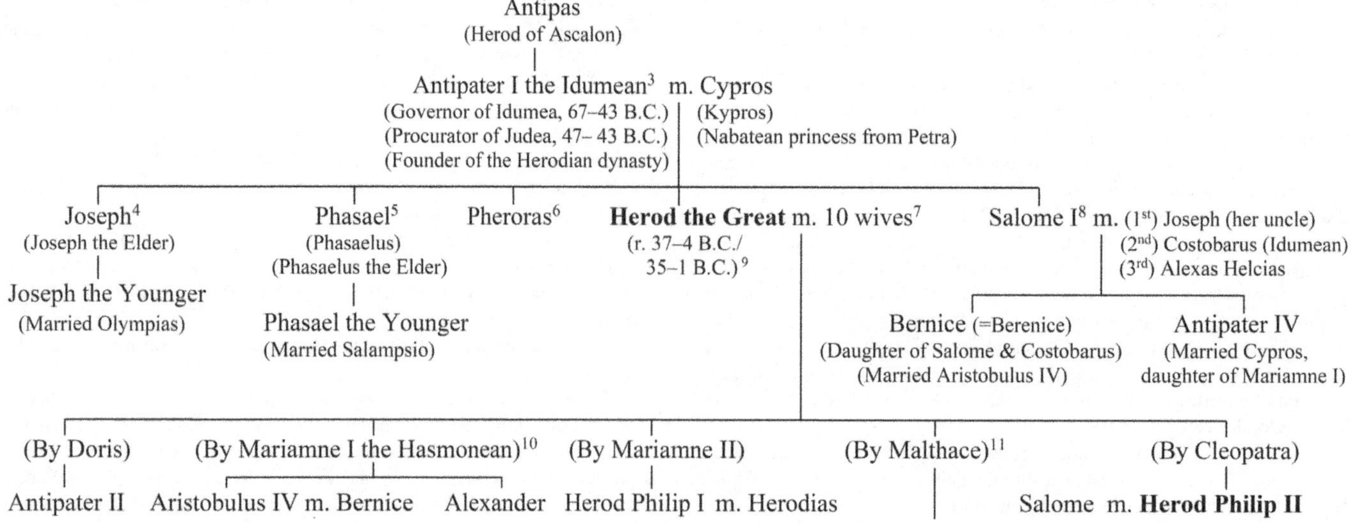

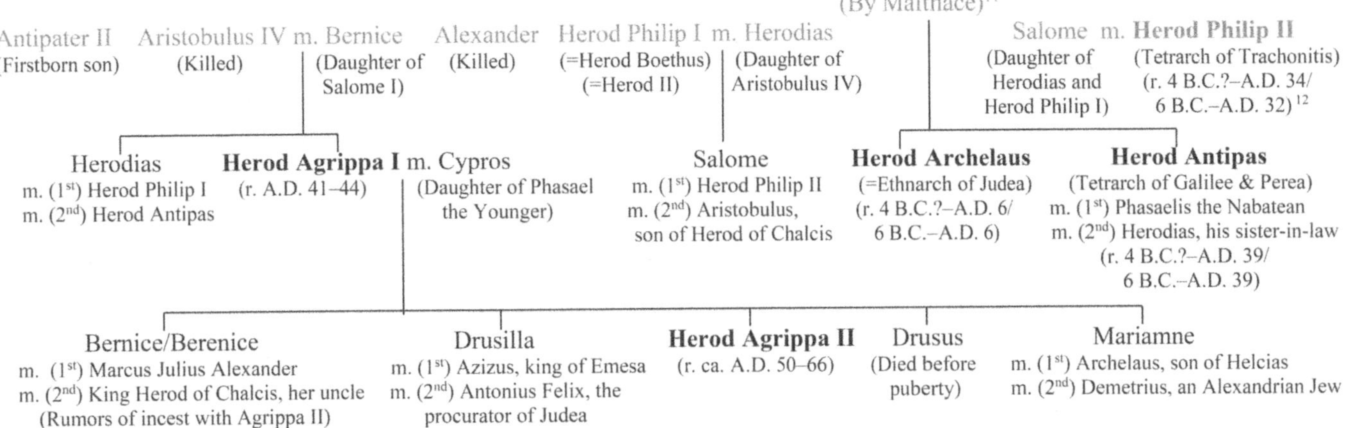

Biblical and Theological Significance

Introduction

The Herodian dynasty, named for Herod the Great, ruled Judaea from approximately 40 B.C. through A.D. 66. Herod the Great was the son of an ambitious Idumean nobleman, named Antipater I, who had been granted Roman citizenship by Julius Caesar. Herod was named king of the Jews by the Romans in 37 or 35 B.C. B.C. and ruled until 4 or 1 B.C. (see notes 12 and 16 for the dating of Herod's reign). Upon Herod's death, his sons Herod Archelaus, Herod Antipas, and Herod Philip II ruled Judaea, Galilee, and the northeastern territories, respectively. In A.D. 6, the Romans annexed Judaea. Herod Agrippa I, grandson of Herod the Great, reunited the disparate parts and ruled from A.D. 41–44. After his death, Rome reannexed Judaea, and Herod Agrippa II was left to rule the area north and east of the Sea of Galilee.

Herod's many wives and multiple children resulted in a complex dynasty featuring many familial marriages (cousin marriages, uncle-niece unions), intrigue, murder, and political machinations. The Herodian dynasty is in the background of many important events in the first five books of the New Testament: Herod the Great, hearing of the birth of Jesus, ordered the murder of all baby boys two years old or younger in Bethlehem in response to the Magi's assertion that the "king of the Jews" (**Matthew 2:2**) had been born there, often termed the *Massacre of the Innocents*[13](**Matthew 2:1–8, 12–18**); Herod Antipas imprisoned John the Baptist and later had him beheaded (**Matthew 14:1–12; Mark 6:14–29**); Herod Agrippa I ordered the death of James the son of Zebedee (**Acts 12:1–2**) and imprisoned Peter (**Acts 12:3–19**); and Herod Agrippa II listened to Paul's account of his conversion, but he did not accept Paul's message to believe and become a Christian (**Acts 25:23–26:32**).

The Herodian dynasty ultimately shows that no matter how much rulers and authorities strive against God's kingdom, that God's overarching plan—for his Son to come in the likeness of a human being, yet be without sin; to fulfill the Law and the Prophets; to establish a community of believers, the church; to show humankind how to love God and love their neighbor; to be the sacrifice for all of humanity's sins; and to rise again, conquering death—would not fail (cf. **Matthew 5:17; Ephesians 6:12**). As **Acts 12:24** concludes after Herod Agrippa I's ignominious death, "But the word of God continued to spread and flourish."

The Rule of Herod and His Sons

Herod the Great was born 73/72 B.C. to a family of Idumean[14] converts and was appointed by his father Antipater I as the governor and tetrarch of Galilee (47–37 B.C.). The consensus view has been that Herod was named king of Judea by the Romans in 40 B.C., began his reign in Jerusalem after conquering the city in 37 B.C., and then died in 4 B.C.[15] More recently, these events and dates have been questioned and revised by Andrew Steinmann.[16] Herod the Great established the Herodian dynasty. He was married to ten wives.[17] He was known for major building projects in the land, especially Herod's Temple (i.e., the rebuilding of the Second Temple).

When he died, Herod's kingdom was divided among three of his sons, in which Herod Archelaus became ethnarch of the tetrarchy of Judea; Herod Antipas became tetrarch of Galilee and Perea; and Herod Philip became tetrarch of the four territories of Bashan: Gaulanitis (western Bashan), Batanea (northeastern Bashan), Trachonitis (Argob), and Auranitis (Hauran). Herod the Great is mentioned specifically in **Matthew 2:1, 3, 7, 12–13, 15–16, 19, 22; Luke 1:5**.

Wives of Herod the Great (only five of his wives are discussed below; for the names of the others, see note 7)

Doris is described by Josephus as "a wife out of his own country [presumably an Idumean] of no ignoble blood."[18] She was the mother of Herod's eldest son, Antipater II, who was initially named Herod's successor.

Mariamne I (sometimes the *m* is doubled and spelled Mariamme I) was a Hasmonean princess. She was the daughter of Alexander II and Alexandra (the daughter of the high priest John Hyrcanus II). Thus, Mariamne I was the *granddaughter* of John Hyrcanus II.[19] Mariamne I and Herod the Great had two sons (Aristobulus IV and Alexander) and two daughters (Salampsio and Cypros). Salampsio married Phasaelus the Younger (Herod's nephew). Cypros married her first cousin, Antipater, the son of Salome I (Herod's sister) and Costobarus.[20] Mariamne I was known for her great beauty, and she was a favorite wife of Herod. However, because Herod feared the Hasmoneans, and because Salome I (Herod's sister) convinced Herod that Mariamne I had committed adultery and planned to poison him, Herod allowed Mariamne I to stand trial; she was convicted and executed in 29 B.C. Additionally, in 7 B.C., Herod the Great ordered the deaths of Alexandra (Mariamne's mother) and Aristobulus IV and Alexander (Mariamne's sons).[21]

Mariamne II (sometimes the *m* is doubled and spelled Mariamme II) was the daughter of Simon, son of Boethus, the high priest from 24/22 to 5 B.C.[22] For that reason, she is also known as Mariamne Boethus II. Mariamne II was the mother of Herod Philip I/Herod Boethus.

Malthace was a Samaritan. She was the mother of two sons (Herod Archelaus and Herod Antipas) and one daughter (Olympias, who married Joseph the Younger, the nephew of Herod the Great). Malthace died in 4 B.C. in Rome while her sons Herod Archelaus and Herod Antipas were disputing the will of their father (Herod the Great) before Emperor Augustus.

Cleopatra of Jerusalem was the mother of Herod Philip II, who became the tetrarch of Iturea and Trachonitis. She should not be confused with the renowned Cleopatra VII Philopator of Egypt.

Sons of Herod the Great

Antipater II was the firstborn son of Herod the Great and Herod's first wife, Doris. Antipater II was named after his paternal grandfather, Antipater I the Idumean (a case of papponymy). When Herod divorced Doris to marry Mariamne I, Antipater II and his mother Doris were exiled. However, after Mariamne I was executed in 29 B.C., Antipater was recalled.[23] In 13 B.C., Herod designated Antipater as his first heir/successor in his will but stipulated that if Antipater preceded him in death, then Philip I would be Herod's successor.[24] Notwithstanding, in 5 B.C. Antipater II was brought before Varus, the Roman governor of Syria,[25] charged with the intended murder of his father, and found guilty. After Emperor Augustus approved of the death sentence, Antipater II was killed in 4 B.C.[26]

Aristobulus IV was the son of Herod by his Hasmonean wife Mariamne I. Aristobulus married his cousin, Bernice/Berenice, the daughter of Costobarus, who had married Salome I (the sister of Herod the Great).[27] Aristobulus IV had five children by Bernice: (1) Herod king of Chalcis, who initially married Mariamne (the daughter of Olympias and Joseph the Younger) and they had a son, also named Aristobulus; later Herod king of Chalcis married his niece Bernice, the daughter of Herod Agrippa I; (2) Herod Agrippa I, who married Cypros; (3) Aristobulus Minor, who married Jotape (the daughter of Sampsigeramus king of Emesa) and had a (deaf) daughter, also named Jotape; (4) Herodias, who first married Herod Philip I/Herod II (the son of Mariamne II) and had a daughter named Salome; later Herodias divorced Philip I to marry Herod Antipas (her husband's half-brother); and (5) Mariamne III.[28] Of these five children of Aristobulus IV, only Herod Agrippa I and Herodias are shown in the chart.

Antipater II, Aristobulus IV's older half-brother, convinced Herod the Great that Aristobulus IV and his brother Alexander were disloyal members of the family. Herod the Great believed the accusation and had the two brothers strangled on charges of treason in 7 B.C. Herod then raised his eldest son, Antipater II, to the rank of co-regent and heir apparent.

Alexander was the son of Herod the Great by his wife Mariamne I. Alexander married Glaphyra,[29] the daughter of Archelaus, king of Cappadocia,[30] and together they had two sons—(1) Tigranes (who was appointed by Nero to be king of Armenia; Tigranes died childless) and (2) Alexander (who had a son named Tigranes; this Tigranes later had a son named Alexander who married Jotape, the daughter of Antiochus, king of Commegena; Vespasian made the younger Alexander king of an island of Cilicia.[31]

Herod Philip I—also known as Herod Philip Boethus or Herod II—was the son of Herod the Great and Mariamne II. He was the first husband of **Herodias** (daughter of Aristobulus IV), and together they had a daughter named Salome.[32] When Herod Philip I was left out of Herod the Great's will, Herodias divorced Herod Philip I to (illegally) marry her brother-in-law, Herod Antipas (Philip's half-brother). Also, Herod Antipas divorced his first wife to marry Herodias.

Herod Philip II was the son of Herod the Great and Cleopatra of Jerusalem. He was tetrarch of Iturea and Trachonitis (**Luke 3:1**) from 4 B.C.–A.D. 34 (consensus view) or 6 B.C.–A.D. 32 (according to Steinmann and Young, see note 12). Herod Philip II married Salome, the daughter of Herodias and Herod Philip I (Herodias' first husband), but they had no children.[33] He built his capital at Caesarea Philippi (Greek Panias / modern Banias). After Philip II died, his widow Salome married Aristobulus of Chalcis (the son of Herod of Chalcis) and they had three sons: Herod, Agrippa, and Aristobulus.[34] Salome's name is not given in Scripture—she is called simply the *daughter of Herodias* (**Matthew 14:6; Mark 6:22**)—but the Jewish historian Josephus identifies her as *Salome*.[35] Salome was probably named after Salome I, the sister of Herod the Great.

According to the Gospel writers, Salome (probably a mid-to-late adolescent at the time) danced before Herod Antipas (her stepfather) at his birthday, and it pleased Herod and his dinner guests (**Matthew 14:6; Mark 6:22**). In return, Herod Antipas promised her: "Ask me for anything you want, and I'll give it to you" (**Mark 6:22**). After soliciting her mother's advice, Salome declared: "I want you to give me right now the head of John the Baptist on a platter" (**Mark 6:25**). Although Antipas was "greatly distressed" (**Mark 6:25**), he agreed. At the time, John the Baptist was already imprisoned at Herod's hilltop palace, Machaerus, because John had called into question Herodias' unlawful marriage to Herod Antipas while her first husband, Herod Philip I, was still living. John the Baptist was beheaded and "his head was brought in on a platter and given to the girl, who carried it to her mother" (**Matthew 14:9, 11**; see **vv. 1–12; Mark 6:14–28**).

Herod Archelaus was the son of Herod the Great and Malthace the Samaritan. Herod Archelaus and his brother

Herod Antipas "were brought up with a certain private man at Rome."[36] After the death of his father, Archelaus was appointed by Caesar Augustus to be the ethnarch[37] (the national leader, but not the king) over Judea, which included Samaria, Judea, and Idumea (biblical Edom)—and he ruled from 4 B.C.–A.D. 6 (consensus view) or 6 B.C.–A.D. 6 (according to Steinmann and Young, see note 12). Herod Archelaus is mentioned once in Scripture, in **Matthew 2:22**. According to the narrative account in **Matthew 2:13–23**, the attempted murder of the infant Messiah was ordered by Herod the Great. However, sometime during the two years that the holy family was in Egypt, Herod the Great died: "An angel of the Lord appeared in a dream to Joseph in Egypt and said, 'Get up, take the child and his mother and go to the land of Israel, for those who were trying to take the child's life are dead [referring to Herod the Great]' " (**Matthew 2:19–20**). However, upon hearing that "Archelaus was reigning in Judea in place of his father Herod, he [Joseph] was afraid to go there. Having been warned in a dream, he [Joseph] withdrew to the district of Galilee, and he went and lived in a town called Nazareth. So was fulfilled what was said through the prophets, that he [Jesus] would be called a Nazarene" (**Matthew 2:22–23**). This is Matthew's explanation of why Jesus was born in Bethlehem of Judea but grew up in Nazareth of Galilee. Jesus' parable of the ten minas in **Luke 19:12–27** may be an indirect reference to Herod Archelaus and/or Herod Antipas (the claimants to Herod the Great's throne) when they journeyed to Rome "in order to gain the government."[38]

Archelaus' first wife was a woman named Mariamne, and his second wife was Glaphyra, the widow of Archelaus' half-brother Alexander (see note 13). Archelaus was known as an oppressive ruler and was deemed incompetent by his subjects. After reigning ten years over Judea, Samaria, and Idumea, he was deposed by the Emperor Augustus in A.D. 6.[39] The regions that Archelaus had ruled then became the Roman province of Iudaea/Judaea, which was under the rule of a Roman prefect until A.D. 41.[40] Herod Archelaus was eventually banished to Vienna in Gaul.

Herod Antipas was the son of Herod the Great and Malthace. He is the Herod most often mentioned in the New Testament. After the death of his father, Herod Antipas became the tetrarch of Galilee and Perea from 4 B.C.–A.D. 39 (consensus view) or from 6 B.C.–A.D. 39 (according to Steinmann and Young, see note 13). Herod Antipas the tetrarch is mentioned in **Matthew 14:1; Luke 3:1, 19–20; 9:7, 9; 13:31–32; 23:7–12, 15; Acts 4:27** and in *Jewish Antiquities*.[41] He built up the city of Tiberias (cf. **John 6:23**)—encompassing what had formerly been the two separate cities of Tiberias and Hammath, on the western shore of the Sea of Galilee—to replace Sepphoris as the capital of Galilee. Antipas put aside his first wife (Phasaelis, the daughter of King Aretas IV of Nabatea) to marry Herodias, the daughter of Aristobulus IV and Bernice (cf. **Mark 6:17**). John the Baptist publicly condemned Herodias' divorce of her first husband, Herod Philip I, to marry Herod Antipas (Philip's half-brother) while Philip I was still living (**Matthew 14:1–5; Mark 6:17–18; Luke 3:19**). The incident led Antipas to agree to John the Baptist's imprisonment and later, his beheading (cf. **Matthew 14:1–10; Mark 6:16–29; Luke 3:19–20**). At one point, Jesus referred to Herod Antipas as "that fox" (**Luke 13:32**), meaning he was a deceitful and shrewd ruler.

In the events leading to the trials of Jesus, **Luke 23:6–12** recounts that Jesus was arrested and first brought to trial before Pontius Pilate, the governor of Judea (A.D. 26–36), although he found no fault in Jesus. But when the people persisted and Pilate learned that Jesus was a Galilean, Pilate handed Jesus over to Herod Antipas for questioning, since Galilee was under Antipas' jurisdiction. Jesus did not respond to Antipas' questioning, so Herod Antipas and his men mocked Jesus, arrayed him in an "elegant robe," and sent him back to Pilate's court (**Luke 23:11**) where, at the people's insistence, "Pilate decided to grant their demand" (**Luke 23:24; see vv. 13–25**).

Eventually, Herod Agrippa I (Herodias' brother) accused Herod Antipas of treason against Rome. Emperor Caligula banished Herod Antipas and his wife Herodias to Gaul, where they died. It is uncertain whether Herod Antipas and Herodias had any children.

Grandsons, Great-Grandsons, and Great-Granddaughters of Herod the Great

Herod Agrippa I was the son of Aristobulus IV and Bernice/Berenice as well as the grandson of Herod the Great. He married Cypros of Judea, the daughter of Phasaelus the Younger and Salampsio, and together they had two sons (Drusus and Herod Agrippa II) and three daughters (Bernice/Berenice, Drusilla, and Mariamne).[42] In A.D. 37, Herod Agrippa I was given the lands formerly ruled by Herod Philip II and remained governor there until A.D. 41 when Emperor Claudius appointed him king of Judea. King Agrippa I ruled Palestine from A.D. 41–44. Herod Agrippa I is mentioned in **Acts 12:1**, where it states that he "arrested some who belonged to the church, intending to persecute them." Agrippa I was responsible for ordering the death of the apostle James, the son of Zebedee (**Acts 12:2**), and he was also responsible for the imprisonment of Peter (**Acts 12:3–29**). Scripture records that Herod Agrippa I died a gruesome death: "On the appointed day Herod, wearing his royal robes, sat on his throne and delivered a public address to the people. They shouted, 'This is the voice of a god, not of a man.' Immediately, because Herod did not give praise to God, an angel of the Lord struck him down, and he was eaten by worms and died" (**Acts 12:21–23**).[43]

Bernice (or **Berenice**) was the daughter of Herod Agrippa I and Cypros as well as the great-granddaughter of Herod the Great. Bernice was sixteen when her father died. Bernice is perhaps best known for her sordid love life. She had three failed marriages: first, to Marcus Julius Alexander, who died young; second, to her uncle, Herod king of Chalcis (the brother of Herodias and Herod Agrippa I) by whom she had two sons;[44] and third, in an effort to deny rumors that "she had criminal sexual intercourse with her brother [Herod Agrippa II],"[45] she convinced Polemon II of Pontus, king of Cilicia, to marry her, but she deserted him. Afterward,

Bernice spent much of her time in the court of her brother Herod Agrippa II. She is mentioned in **Acts 25:13, 23; 26:30** as being present when Herod Agrippa II heard Paul's defense. During the First Jewish-Roman War (begun in A.D. 66), Bernice initiated a love affair with the Roman military commander Titus. After Titus's defeat of the Jews, the destruction of the temple in A.D. 70, and Titus's return to Rome, Bernice lived in the palace with him as his mistress/promised wife. The Romans, however, were suspicious of her as a foreign eastern "queen" and disapproved of their relationship, so upon his accession as emperor in A.D. 79, Titus finally dismiss her A.D.[46]

Drusilla the Jewess was the youngest daughter of Herod Agrippa I and was only six years old when her father died. Drusilla was initially betrothed by her father to the king of Commagena, but the marriage did not take place.[47] After her father's death in A.D. 44, Drusilla's brother Herod Agrippa II gave her in marriage to Azizus, king of Emesa (a Syrian province),[48] but the marriage was soon dissolved. "While Felix was procurator of Judea, he saw this Drusilla, and fell in love with her; for she did indeed exceed all other women in beauty."[49] Drusilla married Antonius Felix, who was appointed procurator of Judea in A.D. 52 by Emperor Claudius, and held that position until A.D. 59/60. Drusilla and Felix had a son named Agrippa. After Paul's arrest in Jerusalem, his speech to the crowd, and the aftermath of his plea before the Sanhedrin (**Acts 21:27–23:22**), Paul was sent to Caesarea Maritima to be heard before Felix the procurator. The account of Paul's defense shows that Drusilla was present when Felix questioned Paul (**Acts 24:24**; cf. **vv. 10–26**). Paul's words about "righteousness, self-control, and the judgment to come" (**v. 25**) caused them fear, so Felix delayed hearing Paul's case, although he frequently sent for him, hoping "that Paul would offer him a bribe" (**v. 26**). Paul's imprisonment in Caesarea continued for the next two years; eventually, Emperor Nero recalled Felix to Rome, and Porcius Festus became Felix's successor (**Acts 24:27**). At the end of Felix's term as procurator of Judea, Drusilla, Felix, and their son Agrippa moved to Italy. The son Agrippa (and his wife?) "perished at the conflagration of the mountain Vesuvius" in A.D. 79.[50]

Herod Agrippa II was the son of Herod Agrippa I and Cypros and considered the last of the Herodian kings of Judea. He was brought up in the household of the Roman Emperor Claudius (r. A.D. 41–54) and was educated in Rome.[51] Because Herod Agrippa II was only seventeen when his father Herod Agrippa I died,[52] Emperor Claudius made the country a Roman province and appointed Cuspius Fadus as the procurator (A.D. 44–46), later followed by Tiberius Alexander (A.D. 46–48).[53] After the death of his uncle Herod of Chalcis, in A.D. 48, Herod Agrippa II received the kingdom of Chalcis. After ruling for three years, Herod Agrippa II gave up Chalcis to become ruler with the title of "king" over Batanaea, Trachonitis, Gaulonitis, and Lysanias in northern Palestine; however, Agrippa II was never *king* of Judea, as his father had been. When the Jewish revolt against Rome broke out in A.D. 66, Herod Agrippa II tried to convince the Jewish people not to fight against Rome. When Jerusalem was captured, Herod Agrippa II escaped to Rome. Supposedly, Herod Agrippa II never married, but rumors at the time claimed that he lived in an incestuous relationship with his older sister Bernice, who often accompanied him as his *queen* on official occasions (cf. **Acts 25:13, 23; 26:30**).

While imprisoned at Caesarea Maritima, Paul first gave his defense before Felix the procurator (**Acts 25:6–12**). Festus discussed Paul's case with Herod Agrippa II when he arrived; then Agrippa II, with Bernice present, heard Paul's case also (**Acts 25:23–26:29**). Agrippa II concluded by saying to Festus, "This man [Paul] could have been set free if he had not appealed to Caesar" (**Acts 26:32**).

Mariamne, the daughter of Herod Agrippa I, was ten when her father died.[54] Before his death, Herod Agrippa I had betrothed Mariamne to Julius Archelaus Epiphanes, the son of Antiochus, the son of Chalcias, but apparently, they never married.[55] Her brother, Herod Agrippa II, gave Mariamne in marriage to Archelaus, the son of Helcias, and they had a daughter named Bernice. Later, Mariamne put away Archelaus and married Demetrius, a "principal man among the Alexandrian Jews" who was from a wealthy family, and they had a son named Agrippinus.[56]

Notes

1. The primary extrabiblical reference consulted for the development of the genealogy of the Herodian dynasty was *Jewish Antiquities* and *Jewish Wars* by Flavius Josephus, in *The Complete Works of Josephus*, trans. William Whiston; commentary by Paul L. Maier (Grand Rapids: Kregel, 1999), especially the genealogical chart on The Herods of Judea, 568–69. Also, a useful online source was https://www.livius.org.

2. Regnal dates which are shown in the chart beneath the names of the kings follow the convention: "Consensus view of the king's reign"/ "Revised view of the king's reign" according to Steinmann and Young (see note 13) and Steinmann (see note 15).

3. Antipater I (ca. 113–43 B.C.) was of Edomite heritage and lived in Idumea, a territory southwest of the Dead Sea, from the southern portion of the Judean hill country to the northern part of the Negev. Apparently, the family converted to Judaism during the forced conversions that were required of the "Idumeans" (see note 14) by John Hyrcanus I, when Hyrcanus was ruler and high priest (134–104 B.C.). Josephus states that Antipater "was of the stock of the principal Jews who came out of Babylon into Judea; but that assertion of his was to gratify Herod [the Great], who was his son . . . This Antipater was at first called Antipas [Antipater is Greek or Gentile, and Antipas is of Hebrew or Jewish termination], and that was his father's name also" (*Jewish Antiquities* 14.1.3). Eusebius in his *Church History* offers more information about the heritage of Antipater and his son Herod by saying that Herod the Great was "the first ruler of foreign blood" and "was given the Kingdom of the Jews by the Romans. As Josephus relates, he [Herod] was an Idumean on his father's side [through Antipater I the Idumean] and an Arabian on his mother's [through Cypros the Nabatean]. But Africanus [referring to Julius Africanus' *Epistle to Aristides*] . . . says that they who were more accurately informed about him report that he was a son of Antipater, and that the latter [Antipater I] was the son of a certain Herod of Ascalon, one of the so-called servants of the temple of Apollo. This Antipater, having been taken a prisoner while a boy by Idumean robbers, lived with them, because his father, being a poor man, was unable to pay a ransom for him. Growing up in their practices he was afterward befriended by Hyrcanus, the high priest of the Jews. A son of his was that Herod [Herod the Great] who lived in the times of our Saviour" (*Church History* 1.6.1–3).

The Idumean nobleman Antipater increased his wealth and influence by marrying Cypros, the daughter of a noble from Petra in southwestern Jordan. When the Roman general Pompey invaded Palestine in 63 B.C., Antipater supported his campaign, thereby forming a long association with Rome from which both he and his son Herod benefited. Julius Caesar also favored Antipater's family, appointing him the procurator (governor) of Judea in 47 B.C. and granting him Roman citizenship, the latter eventually descending to Herod and his children (Stewart Henry Perowne, "Herod," *Encyclopedia Britannica*, https://www.britannica.com/biography/Herod-king-of-Judaea).

4. Joseph (called Joseph the Elder) was the brother of Herod the Great. Joseph the Elder had a son named Joseph the Younger who married Olympias (a daughter of Malthace and Herod the Great); together they had a daughter named Mariamne (*Jewish Antiquities* 18.5.4).

5. Phasael (called Phasaelus or Phasael the Elder) was the brother of Herod the Great. His father, Antipater I, made Phasael the governor of Jerusalem during the same time that Herod was governor of Galilee (ibid., 14.9.2; *Jewish War* 1.10.4). Phasael had a son named Phasaelus the Younger who married his first cousin, Salampsio (one of the two daughters of Mariamne I and Herod the Great). Phasael the Younger had five children by Salmapsio: three sons—Antipater, Herod, and Alexander—and two daughters, Alexandra (who married Timius of Cyprus, but they had no children) and Cypros (who married Herod Agrippa I, the son of Aristobulus IV; *Jewish Antiquities* 18.5.4).

6. Pheroras was the tetrarch of Perea for a time.

7. Herod the Great had ten wives (eight named and two unnamed). The wives of Herod the Great are discussed in *Jewish Antiquities* 17.1.3. and *Jewish War* 1.28.4. Five wives of Herod are shown and discussed in the chart (i.e., Doris, Mariamne I and II, Malthace, and Cleopatra) because from them issued the rulers of the Herodian dynasty. The other five wives were: Phedra/Phaedra (the mother of a daughter named Roxane); Pallas (the mother of a son named Phasaelus); Elpis (the mother of a daughter named Salome); and two unnamed wives who were Herod the Great's nieces (one was the unnamed daughter of Herod's sister, Salome I, and the other was the daughter of a brother of Herod the Great).

8. Salome I was the younger sister of Herod the Great. She and her mother Cypros were powerful women in Herod's court and contributed to the slanderous accusations that resulted in the deaths of Mariamne I (executed in 29 B.C.) and her sons Aristobulus IV and Alexander (killed in 7 B.C.). Salome I married three times—first, to Joseph her uncle, the brother of Antipater I; second, to Costobarus, the former governor of Idumea, and by him she had three children (Bernice/Berenice, Antipater IV, and an unnamed daughter) although Salome I divorced Costobarus (cf. *Jewish Antiquities* 15.7.10) and later, Herod had him killed on suspicions of disloyalty; and third, to Alexas Helcias. When Herod died, he bequeathed Salome a small toparchy that included the cities of Jamnia, Ashdod, and Phasaelis, as well as a large amount of coined silver. Also, Emperor Augustus allowed Salome I to live at a royal palace at Ashkelon.

9. For details about the reign of Herod the Great, see notes 13 and 15.

10. Mariamme 1 had five children—Alexander (who married Glaphyra of Cappadocia), Aristobulus IV (who married Bernice), Salampsio (who married Phasael the Younger), Cypros (who married Antipater IV), and an unnamed son. Only Alexander and Aristobulus IV are shown in the chart.

11. Malthace had three children: Herod Archelaus, Herod Antipas, and a daughter named Olympias (who married Joseph the Younger, Herod the Great's nephew). Only Herod Archelaus and Herod Antipas are shown in the chart.

12. The consensus view has been, up to now, that Herod the Great was named king of Judea by the Romans in 40 B.C., began his reign in Jerusalem after conquering the city in 37 B.C., died in 4 B.C., and that his sons did not begin their reigns until *after* their father's death. Recently, however, Andrew Steinmann and Rodger Young have argued convincingly that Herod was appointed king in late 39 B.C., began his first regnal year in Tishri 38 B.C., conquered Jerusalem on 10 Tishri 36 B.C., began his first regnal year in Jerusalem in Tishri 35 B.C., and died in early 1 B.C. (not in 4 B.C.; see note 15). Furthermore, Steinmann and Young have given what seems to be credible evidence that Herod the Great's sons—Herod Archelaus, Herod Antipas, and Herod Philip—received *royal prerogatives and titles while their father was still living* (i.e., before Herod the Great's death in 1 B.C.; cf. *Jewish War* 1.32.2; 1.32.3) and that the conveyance of authority happened sometime in the year that began in Tishri 6 B.C. Therefore, the authors conclude that the reigns of Herod's sons were antedated (backdated) to 6 B.C. However, Herod's sons did not actually assume office until Herod the Great died in the early part of 1 B.C. Steinmann and Young propose the following revised regnal dates:

- Herod Philip's reign was 6 B.C.–A.D. 32;
- Herod's Antipas' reign was 6 B.C.–A.D. 39;
- Herod Archelaus' reign was 6 B.C.–A.D. 6.

See Andrew E. Steinmann and Rodger C. Young, "Evidences that Herod the Great's Sons Antedated Their Reigns to a Time before Herod's Death" (Dallas: Dallas Theological Seminary, *Bibliotheca Sacra*, forthcoming).

13. The narrative of the massacre, which comes from Matthew's Gospel only, became the inspiration for paintings called "Massacre of the Innocents" by artists, such as Pieter Bruegel the Elder (c. 1565–67) and his son Pieter Bruehel the Younger (into the 17th century); Guido Reni (1611), and two paintings by Peter Paul Rubens (1611–1612) and (1636–1638).

14. Idumean is a Hellenistic name for the Edomites, a dominant population of the Negev that integrated into Judea once they were conquered by John Hyrcanus I and forced by Hyrcanus to be circumcised and to adopt Judaism if they wanted to live in the country of their forefathers. According to Josephus, the Idumeans (the descendants of the Edomites) were considered "half-Jews" or "half-breeds" (see *Jewish Antiquities* 13.9.1; 14.15.2). Also the ejournal article, Evie Gassner (2019). "How Jewish Was Herod?" *The Torah.com*, https://thetorah.com/article/how-jewish-was-herod. For more information on the Edomites, see chart "**Genesis 36**: Esau, the Ancestor of the Edomites."

15. Josephus, *Jewish Antiquities* 17.6.4; 17.9.3; *Jewish War* 2.1.3

16. Josephus remarks in *Jewish Antiquities* 17.6.4 that there was a lunar eclipse shortly before Herod's death, which as been traditionally ascribed to the eclipse of March 13/14, 4 B.C. However, scholar and chronologist Andrew Steinmann has suggested 1 B.C. as the more likely date of Herod's death. For further discussion of important dates in Herod's reign and a later date of 1 B.C. for his death (rather than 4 B.C.), see Steinmann, *From Abraham to Paul*, 230–38, 252–54. Steinmann proposes the following chronology:

Not long after Tishri of 39 B.C.—Herod appointed king (his investiture)
Tishri 38 B.C.—The beginning of Herod's first regnal year
10 Tishri 36 B.C.—Herod conquered Jerusalem
Tishri 35 B.C.—The beginning of Herod's first regnal year in Jerusalem
31 B.C.—Battle of Actium (September 2)
20 B.C. (Spring or Summer)—Herod began work on the temple [Herod's Temple] (cf. *Jewish Antiquities* 15.11.1)
Late 19/early 18 B.C.—Work on the temple was completed in a year and six months (cf. ibid., 15.11.1–6)
12 B.C.—Work on the temple precincts completed (cf. ibid., 15.11.5)
5 B.C.—Magi observe the star
Mid 3 B.C.—John the Baptist was born
Late 3 B.C. or early 2 B.C.—Jesus was born
40–50 days after Jesus' birth—The flight of the holy family to Egypt
1st quarter of 1 B.C.—After a thirty-four-year reign, Herod died at nearly 70 years of age, between the total lunar eclipse of January 9/10 1 B.C. and the start of Passover (April 8/Nisan 14) of that same year
Later in 1 B.C.—Mary and Joseph returned to Nazareth

17. Josephus mentions "nine wives" in *Jewish Antiquities* 17.1.3 and *Jewish War* 1.28.4, but, as other scholars have noted, there appears to be a total of ten wives (see note 7).

18. Josephus, *Jewish War* 1.12.3; cf. *Jewish Antiquities* 14.12.1.

19. See John Hyrcanus I (#45) in chart "**Supplement 2**: The High Priests of Israel."

20. Josephus, *Jewish Antiquities* 18.5.4.

21. Ibid., 15.7.8; 16.11.7.

22. Cf. ibid., 18.5.4. Also see Simon ben Boethus #54 in chart "**Supplement 2**: The High Priests of Israel."

23. Ibid., 16.3.3; 17.5.1.

24. Ibid., 17.3.2; *Jewish War* 1.29.2.

25. Josephus, *Jewish Antiquities* 17.5.2, 6.

26. Ibid., 17.5.7, *Jewish War* 1.32.5.

27. Josephus, *Jewish Antiquities* 16.1.2.

28. Ibid., 18.5.4; *Jewish War* 1.28.1.

29. Glaphyra was first married to Alexander, the son of Herod the Great; second, after Alexander's death in 7 B.C., Glaphyra married King Juba II; and third, she married Herod Archelaus, her brother-in-law (i.e., the half-brother of her deceased first husband, Alexander), while her second husband (Juda II) was still living, which violated Jewish law and caused a religious scandal in Judea (cf. Josephus, *Jewish Antiquities* 17.13.4).

30. Ibid., 16.1.2.

31. Ibid., 18.5.4; *Jewish War* 1.28.1.

32. Josephus, *Jewish Antiquities* 18.5.4.

33. Ibid.

34. Ibid.

35. Ibid., 18.5.2; 18.5.4.

36. Ibid., 17.1.3.

37. Ethnarch refers to the political governorship (the national leader/ruler)

of a particular ethnic group. In this case, Herod Archelaus held the largest rulership—the tetrarchy of Judea—and was considered the ethnarch or "chief" of the Jewish nation, more senior in rank than his brother, Herod Antipas, who held the tetrarchy of Galilee and Perea, and his half-brother, Herod Philip II, who held the tetrarchy of Trachonitis.

38. Ibid., 17.9.3–4.

39. Ibid., 17.13.2.

40. See chart "**Supplement 13**: Roman Rulers of Judea and Galilee (67 B.C.–A.D. 66)."

41. Josephus, *Jewish Antiquities,* 18.5.1, 18.7.1–2.

42. Ibid., 18.5.4.

43. For more on the death of Herod Agrippa I, see Eusebius's account in *Church History* 2.10.1–10.

44. Josephus, *Jewish Antiquities,* 19.9.1.

45. Ibid., 20.7.3.

46. Suetonius, *The Lives of the Caesars,* "The Life of Titus" 7.1–2 (https://penelope.uchicago.edu/Thayer/E/Roman/Texts/Suetonius/12Caesars/Titus*.html) and E. Badian, "Berenice: Roman aristocrat" *Encyclopedia Britannica* (https://www.britannica.com/biography/Berenice-Roman-aristocrat).

47. Josephus, *Jewish Antiquities* 19.9.1.

48. Ibid., 20.7.1.

49. Ibid., 20.7.2.

50. Ibid., 20.7.2.

51. Ibid., 19.9.2.

52. Ibid., 19.9.1.

53. Josephus, *Jewish Wars* 2.11.6; 20.5.1–2.

54. Josephus, *Jewish Antiquities* 19.9.1.

55. Ibid.

56. Ibid., 20.7.1.

MATTHEW 4: SIMON PETER AND ANDREW, THE APOSTLES OF JESUS

Approximate Dating: turn of the era to ca. 66 A.D. ***Relevant Scriptures:*** **Matthew 4:18; 10:2; 16:17; Mark 1:16; John 1:40–44; 6:8; 21:15–17; 1 Corinthians 9:5**

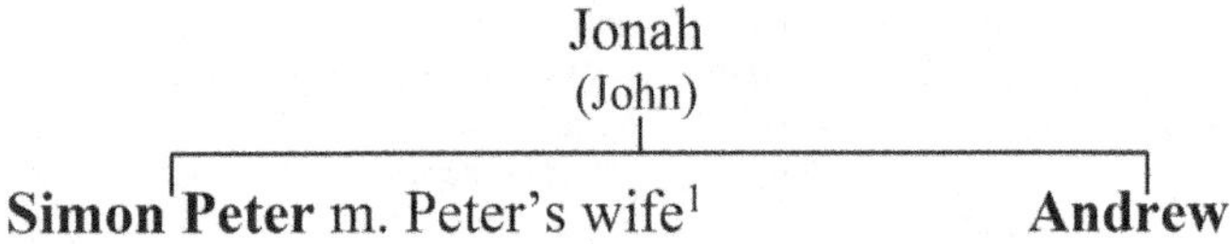

Biblical and Theological Significance

Peter was the undisputed leader of the twelve apostles. He had the unique privilege of being given the "keys of the kingdom of heaven" (**Matthew 16:19**) and of preaching the sermon on the day of Pentecost when the Holy Spirit was poured out on the newly constituted church in **Acts 2**. While Peter denied Jesus three times prior to his crucifixion, Peter was restored to ministry by the resurrected Jesus and engaged in decades of courageous, fruitful ministry, culminating in his martyrdom under Emperor Nero. Roman Catholics trace papal succession all the way back to Peter.

The Call of Peter and Andrew

The call of Simon Peter and Andrew is narrated in **Matthew 4:18–20; Mark 1:16–18; Luke 5:1–11;** and **John 1:35–42.** The hometown of these brothers was Bethsaida (**John 1:44;** cf. **12:21**). Simon Peter is variously called "Cephas," "Simon," "Peter," and "Simon son of Jonah/John" (cf. **Matthew 4:18; 10:2; 16:17–18; Mark 3:16; Luke 6:14; John 1:42, 21:15–17; Acts 10:5, 32; 11:13; 1 Corinthians 1:12; 3:22; 9:5; 15:5**). Simon was his Hebrew name and Cephas his Greek name—a transliteration of the Aramaic word for *rock* or *stone.*

Peter as a Disciple of Jesus

Peter was the most outspoken among the twelve disciples (e.g., **Matthew 16:16–19; Mark 8:29; Acts 1:15; 2:14; 4:8–12**). His strong and impulsive personality is evident in many incidents (e.g., **Matthew 16:22; 17:4; 19:27; Mark 8:32; 9:5; 10:28; Luke 5:8; 18:28; 24:12; John 13:8–9; 20:3–6; Acts 10:14**). Peter was the first to confess that Jesus was "the Messiah, the Son of the living God" (**Matthew 16:16;** cf. **Mark 8:29; Luke 9:20; John 6:69**), which anticipated Martha's confession in **John 11:27.** Jesus said he would build his church upon the "rock/chief cornerstone/living Stone" of Peter's confession (**Matthew 16:18; Ephesians 2:20; 1 Peter 2:4–8**, respectively). Peter, along with James and John (the sons of Zebedee), formed an inner circle among the disciples: they were all present at the transfiguration of Jesus (**Matthew 17:1; Mark 9:2; Luke 9:28;** cf. **2 Peter 1:16–18**), the healing of Jairus' daughter (**Mark 5:21–24, 35–43; Luke 8:51**), Jesus' Olivet discourse (**Mark 13:3**), and Jesus' arrest in Gethsemane (**Matthew 26:36–37; Mark 14:32–33, 37**). Peter was the disciple who cut off the ear of Malchus, Caiaphas' servant, in the Garden of Gethsemane (**John 18:10**). He was present in the courtyard of Caiaphas, the high priest, during Jesus' questioning before the Sanhedrin (**Matthew 26:58; Mark 14:53–54, 66–67; Luke 22:54–55; John 18:15–18**). Although Peter vowed that he would *not* deny Jesus (**Matthew 26:33–35; Mark 14:29–31; Luke 22:33; John 13:37–38**), Jesus predicted that Peter would, saying that, in fact, he would deny him three times "before the rooster crows twice" (**Mark 14:30**), and sadly, Jesus' prediction came true (**Matthew 26:69–75; Mark 14:66–72; Luke 54–62; John 18:15–18, 25–27**).

Peter's Ministry after the Death and Resurrection of Jesus

Peter delivered his first sermon on the day of Pentecost in Jerusalem (**Acts 2:14–47**). Later, he healed a lame beggar at the Beautiful Gate of the temple (**Acts 3:1–10**) and preached a second sermon at Solomon's Colonnade (**Acts 3:11–26**), boldly proclaiming that Jesus had been resurrected from the dead. For this, the Sadducees arrested Peter and John (the son of Zebedee). Peter was the spokesman before the Sanhedrin (**Acts 4:1–12**). Even though the religious leaders witnessed Peter's boldness, witness, and his ability to heal, the Sanhedrin still considered Peter and John "unschooled, ordinary men" and forbade them from teaching in the name of Jesus (**Acts 4:13, 18**). Nevertheless, Peter and John were filled with the Holy Spirit and continued to declare the gospel with even greater boldness (**Acts 4:23–31**).

Peter was the chief spokesman for the apostles at an incident involving church discipline, resulting in the deaths of Ananias and his wife, Sapphira (**Acts 5:1–11**). In the early days of the church when the apostles performed many miracles (**Acts 5:12**), people would bring the sick and demon-possessed so that "at least Peter's shadow might fall on some of them as he passed by" and be healed (**Acts 5:15**). Peter and John were imprisoned a second time along with other apostles (**Acts 5:18**) but were freed by an angel of the Lord. Peter spoke before the Sanhedrin again saying, "We must obey God rather than human beings" (**Acts 5:29**). When the Jerusalem church sent Peter and John to Samaria, they prayed for the new believers there, and believers received the Holy Spirit (**Acts 8:14–17**). While in Samaria, Peter discerned an unrepentant spirit in Simon the Sorcerer and pronounced him "full of bitterness and captive to sin" (**Acts 8:23**). Peter and John then returned to Jerusalem.

Later, Peter ministered to believers in Lydda where he healed Aeneas the paralytic (**Acts 9:32–34**). When he was summoned to Joppa, Peter brought Dorcas (Greek; Heb. *Tabitha*) back to life—this is the first recorded resurrection performed by an apostle. Peter stayed for some time in Joppa with Simon the tanner (**Acts 9:43**). Then a Gentile centurion named Cornelius summoned Peter to Caesarea, but before Peter left Joppa he was given a vision—"something like a large sheet being let down to earth by its four corners"—in which God revealed to him not to "call anything impure that God has made clean" (referring to the Gentiles; **Acts 10:9–16; 11:4–10**). When Peter went to the home of Cornelius in Caesarea and preached to his household, the Holy Spirit came upon them (**Acts 10:17–48**). Peter returned to Jerusalem but was met with strong objections from Jews because he had eaten with (unclean) Gentiles in the home of Cornelius. Peter came to understand that God does not show favoritism and that the gospel of Jesus Christ was intended for both Jews and Gentiles (**Acts 10:34–35; 15:7–9**).

After Herod Agrippa I killed James, the son of Zebedee, with the sword in A.D. 44, Herod Agrippa arrested and imprisoned Peter (**Acts 12:1–4**), probably intending to kill him as well. However, an angel of the Lord appeared, freed Peter of his chains, and led him out of the city (**Acts 12:5–10**). Peter then went to the home of Mary, the mother of John Mark, where believers had been praying for him, and from there he escaped by leaving "for another place" (**Acts 12:12–19**).

Peter as the Author of 1 and 2 Peter and His Death

Peter authored the epistles of **1** and **2 Peter**, which scholars think were written in the early to mid-A.D. 60s, respectively, shortly before his death in ca. A.D. 66 (cf. **1 Peter 1:1; 2 Peter 1:1; 3:1**). In the letters, Peter refers to himself as "an apostle of Jesus Christ" (**1 Peter 1:1**) and "a servant and apostle of Jesus Christ" (**2 Peter 1:1**). Paul, who was "the apostle to the Gentiles" (**Romans 11:13**), characterized Peter as "an apostle to the circumcised [the Jews]" (**Galatians 2:8**). Church tradition[2] holds that Peter was martyred in Rome under Emperor Nero (A.D. 54–68) by being crucified upside down (see Jesus' prediction concerning Peter's death in **John 21:18–19**).

Andrew worked alongside his brother Peter in the family fishing business in Galilee (**Matthew 4:18; Mark 1:16**). Formerly, Andrew had been a disciple of John the Baptist; when Andrew met Jesus, he recognized him as the "Messiah," and introduced his brother Peter to Jesus (**John 1:35–42**). In John's account of the feeding of the five thousand, Andrew was the disciple who identified the boy with five barley loaves and two fishes (**John 6:8–9**). Andrew was among the close circle of disciples who asked Jesus to explain his prophecy about the destruction of the temple (**Mark 13:3–4**). When certain Greeks asked to see Jesus, Philip and Andrew relayed the message to Jesus (**John 12:20–22**). Tradition holds that Andrew was martyred by crucifixion in ca. A.D. 60 on an X-shaped cross.

Notes

1. Simon Peter was married. The reference to Peter's wife in **1 Corinthians 9:5** indicates that she was a believer and that she accompanied Peter on some occasions. Moreover, the account of the healing of Peter's mother-in-law (his wife's mother) is found in **Matthew 8:14–15; Mark 1:29–31; Luke 4:38–39**.

2. Eusebius says that it was recorded that "Peter likewise [like Paul] was crucified under Nero. This account of Peter and Paul is substantiated by the fact that their names are preserved in the cemeteries of that place even to the present day. It is confirmed likewise by Caius, a member of the Church, who arose under Zephyrinus, bishop of Rome. He, in a published disputation with Proclus, the leader of the Phrygian heresy, speaks as follows concerning the places where the sacred corpses of the aforesaid apostles are laid: "'But I can show the trophies of the apostles. For if you will go to the Vatican or to the Ostian way, you will find the trophies of those who laid the foundations of this church.' And that they both suffered martyrdom at the same time is stated by Dionysius, bishop of Corinth, in his epistle to the Romans, in the following words: 'You have thus by such an admonition bound together the planting of Peter and of Paul at Rome and Corinth. For both of them planted and likewise taught us in our Corinth. And they taught together in like manner in Italy, and suffered martyrdom at the same time.' I [Eusebius] have quoted these things in order that the truth of the history might be still more confirmed." *Ecclesiastical History*, new updated ed., trans. C. F. Cruse (Peabody: Hendrickson, 2004), 2.25.5–8.

MATTHEW 4: JAMES AND JOHN, THE APOSTLES OF JESUS

Approximate Dating: ca. turn of the era to A.D. 100 ***Relevant Scriptures:*** **Matthew 4:21–22; 10:2; 17:1; 20:20–24; 26:37; 27:56; Mark 1:19–20; 3:17; 5:37; 10:35–41; 15:40; Luke 5:10–11; 6:14; John 19:25–27; 21:2; 22:2; Acts 12:2**

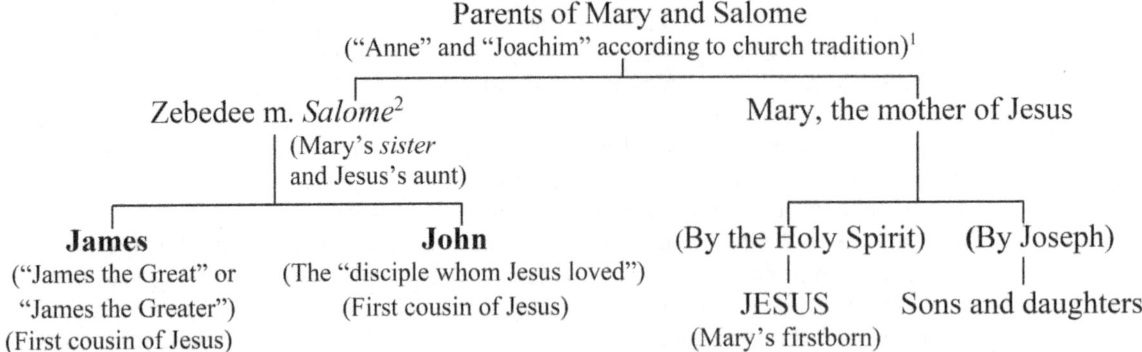

Biblical and Theological Significance

Fishermen and Eyewitnesses

Prior to becoming disciples of Jesus, James and his brother John were fishermen in Galilee who worked alongside their father, Zebedee, in a business partnership with Simon Peter and his brother Andrew (**Luke 5:10**; cf. **Matthew 4:18; Mark 1:16**). The call of James and John is recorded in **Matthew 4:21–22** and **Mark 1:19–20**. Early in his ministry, Jesus nicknamed the brothers *Boanerges*, meaning "sons of thunder" (**Mark 3:17**), which described their fiery, earnest temperament that was evident on several occasions (**Mark 9:38; 10:35–37; Luke 9:49, 54–55**). They were among Jesus' first and most faithful followers and constituted a vital part of the foundation of Jesus' apostolic community. The Gospels feature John, James, and Peter jointly at Jesus' transfiguration (**Matthew 17:1; Mark 9:2; Luke 9:28**), the healing of Jairus' daughter (**Mark 5:37–43; Luke 8:49–56**), and at the Garden of Gethsemane (**Matthew 26:37; Mark 14:33**).

Heritage of James and John

Church tradition holds that Anne and Joachim were the parents of Mary and Salome (the wife of Zebedee) and that Elizabeth (the wife of Zechariah and mother of John the Baptist) was the daughter of Sobe/Sovin (Anne's sister). If this tradition is accurate, then Anne (Mary's mother and Jesus' maternal grandmother) was the *aunt* of Elizabeth. In this way, Mary (Jesus' mother) and Salome (Mary's sister) were the *first cousins* of Elizabeth. In turn, the sons of these women—Jesus, John the Baptist, James, and John—were all *cousins*.[3]

Little is known about their father, Zebedee, other than that he owned a fishing business. The name of Zebedee's wife (Salome) can be discerned by harmonizing the Gospel accounts that mention specific women who were present at the crucifixion and who brought spices to anoint the body of Jesus at the tomb: called "the mother of Zebedee's sons" (**Matthew 27:56**); "Salome" (**Mark 15:40; 16:1**); and "his [Jesus'] mother's sister" (**John 19:25**). Taken together, it can be deduced that Salome was most likely the *sister*[4] of Mary and the mother of James and John. This kinship detail establishes that James and John were the *first cousins* of Jesus and that Salome was Jesus' *aunt*. This may explain why the "mother of Zebedee's sons" (Salome) appealed to Jesus, "Grant that one of these two sons of mine may sit at your right and the other at your left in your kingdom" (**Matthew 20:20–23**), and why James and John felt comfortable making the same bold request themselves (**Mark 10:35–41**).

James the Apostle

Since he is usually mentioned first, James was probably the eldest son of Zebedee. James was the first of the twelve apostles of Jesus to be martyred—killed "with the sword" in ca. A.D. 44 on the orders of Herod Agrippa I[5] (**Acts 12:1–2**).

In the extrabiblical literature, James the son of Zebedee is often called *James the Great* or *James the Greater* to distinguish him from: (1) James—the son of Alphaeus and the brother of Matthew/Levi—often called *James the Less* or *Lesser*, who was one of the twelve apostles[6] (cf. **Matthew 10:3; Mark 3:18; Luke 6:15; Acts 1:13**); (2) James, the half-brother of Jesus (**Matthew 13:55; Mark 6:3; Acts 12:17; Galatians 2:9; James 1:1; Jude 1**), sometimes called *James the Just*,[7] who was a key leader in the Jerusalem church and the author of the **Epistle of James** (cf. **Acts 15:13; 21:18; 1 Corinthians 15:7; Galatians 1:19**); or (3) James / "James the younger," the son of Mary (probably referring to Mary the wife of Clopas) and the brother of Joseph (**Matthew 27:56; Mark 15:40, 47; 16:1; Luke 24:10**; cf. **Matthew 27:61; 28:1; John 19:25**).

John the Apostle—Author of the Gospel of John, 1–3 John, and the Book of Revelation

Of the twelve disciples of Jesus (**Matthew 10:2; Mark 3:17; Luke 6:14–16; Acts 1:13**), John was probably the closest to Jesus. Rather than referring to himself by name in his Gospel, John identifies himself as "the disciple whom Jesus loved," "the disciple whom he [Jesus] loved," and "the one Jesus loved" (cf. **John 13:23; 19:26; 20:2; 21:7, 20**).[8] John's gospel was an eyewitness account of Jesus' earthly ministry. John is mentioned specifically at the Last Supper (**John 13:23**), Jesus' crucifixion (**John 19:26–27**), the empty tomb (**John 20:1–10**), and on the shore of the Sea of Galilee with the resurrected Christ (**John 21:7**). John is probably the other disciple who was with Peter at the high priest's courtyard (**John 18:15–16**). John helped Peter make the preparations for the Last Supper (**Luke 22:8**). He was also present when Peter healed the lame beggar at the temple (**Acts 3:1–11**), which caused them both to be jailed and later questioned by the Sanhedrin, who called them "unschooled, ordinary men" (**Acts 4:13**). Eventually, John and Peter were released and warned not to preach, although they continued to speak "the word of God boldly" (**Acts 4:31**; see **vv. 1–31**). John accompanied Peter to Samaria where they prayed for the new believers: "Peter and John placed their hands on them, and they received the Holy Spirit" (**Acts 8:17**). Peter and John also preached in many Samaritan villages (**Acts 8:25**).

Jesus' deep respect for John is evident in that, before his death on the cross, he entrusted the future care of his mother Mary—not to his half-brothers[9]—but to John, his first cousin (**John 19:26–27**).[10] After Jesus' ascension, Mary his mother, Jesus' brothers, John, and the other disciples gathered in the upper room (**John 1:12–14**). In the early portions of Acts, as noted above, John often appears alongside Peter (**Acts 3–4; 8:14–25**). Paul characterized John, Cephas (Peter), and James (the half-brother of Jesus) as "pillars" of the Jerusalem church (**Galatians 2:9**).

Since John says in **John 21:24** that he was the "disciple who testifies to these things and who wrote them down," it can be assumed that he was the author of the **Gospel of John** (cf. **13:23; 21:20–24**), which was probably written in A.D. 60s, or perhaps later in the 80s or 90s. Toward the end of his life, John wrote three epistles (**1–3 John**), two in which he refers to himself as John "the elder" (**2 John 1; 3 John 1**), probably indicating that he was an older man at the time. Finally, around A.D. 95 while exiled on the island of Patmos,[11] he wrote the book of Revelation (**1:1–2, 4, 9; 22:8**). John was the last of the twelve apostles to die and the only one to die a natural death. He died in Ephesus sometime around or shortly after A.D. 98.

Notes

1. For the extrabiblical sources that discuss Anne and Joachim as the parents of Mary and Salome, see chart "**Matthew 1**: Ancestry of Mary and Joseph (Based on Scripture and Church Tradition) and How Mary and Joseph May Have Been Related."

2. The wife of Zebedee, also called "Salome" or "Mary's sister," is *not* the same person as "Mary, the mother of James and Joseph," who is also called "Mary the mother of James the younger and of Joseph" and "Mary the mother of James" (cf. **Matthew 27:56; Mark 15:40; 16:1**; **Luke 24:10**), all of whom likely refer to "Mary the wife of Clopas" (**John 19:25**). Mary of Clopas was probably the *sister-in-law* of Mary (the mother of Jesus) and Joseph; for an explanation of this kinship relationship, see charts "**Matthew 1**: Ancestry of Mary and Joseph (Based on Scripture and Church Tradition) and How Mary and Joseph May Have Been Related" and "**Matthew 27**: Specific People Mentioned at Jesus' Crucifixion (Based on Scripture and Church Tradition)."

3. Refer to the chart "**Matthew 1**: Ancestry of Mary and Joseph (Based on Scripture and Church Tradition) and How Mary and Joseph May Have Been Related," which gives the literary sources for this church tradition attesting to the kinship relationship of these women (i.e., James and John, the sons of Salome and Zebedee, as the *first cousins* of Jesus, and John the Baptist, the son of Elizabeth, as the *second cousin* of Jesus).

4. Sources from church tradition support the claim that Salome (Zebedee's wife) was the *sister* of Mary (Jesus' mother) and not her *sister-in-law* (i.e., Zebedee was *not* Mary's *brother*, rather Zebedee was Mary's *brother-in-law*). For the extrabiblical sources and the proposed kinship relationships, see chart "**Matthew 1**: Ancestry of Mary and Joseph (Based on Scripture and Church Tradition) and How Mary and Joseph May Have Been Related."

5. Herod Agrippa I, the grandson of Herod the Great, ruled Judea from A.D. 41–44. At the Festival of Unleavened Bread in A.D. 44, Herod Agrippa I arrested Jewish Christians with the intention of persecuting them; he also had James the son of Zebedee killed and had Peter arrested and imprisoned. See information in the charts "**Matthew 2**: Herod the Great and the Herodian Dynasty" and "**Supplement 13**: Roman Rulers of Judea and Galilee."

6. See charts "**Matthew 9**: Matthew and James, the Apostles of Jesus" and "**Matthew 10**: Genealogical Record of the Twelve Apostles of Jesus."

7. See chart "**Matthew 1**: Jesus and His Immediate Family."

8. The only persons specifically called "John" in the **Gospel of John** were John the Baptist (e.g., **John 1:6**) and John the father of Simon Peter (**John 1:42; 21:15, 17**).

9. The half-brothers of Jesus (i.e., the sons of Mary and Joseph) were James, Joseph, Simon, and Judas/Jude (**Matthew 13:55; Mark 6:3**). See chart "**Matthew 1**: Jesus and His Immediate Family."

10. The rationale for Jesus' action could be: (1) the initial unbelief of Jesus' half-brothers that he was the Messiah (**John 7:5**), although later they had a change of heart and became believers (cf. **Acts 1:14; 12:17; 15:13; 21:18; 1 Corinthians 9:5; 15:7; Galatians 1:19; 2:9; James 1:1; Jude 1**); (2) a strong familial and spiritual relationship that existed between Mary and her nephew, given that both understood Jesus' deity and had invested their lives in Jesus' ministry; and/or (3) a protective intention on the part of Jesus to shield his mother and immediate family from future ongoing inspection by government officials, such as the Herods and the Roman emperors (as described by Eusebius, *Church History* 1.7; 3.20, 32).

11. The Romans used the island of Patmos as a penal settlement where political agitators and those who threatened the peace of the empire were sent (Tacitus, *Annals* 3.68; 4.30; 15.71). According to the church historian Eusebius, John was alive during the great persecution under Emperor Domitian (A.D. 81–96) and banished to the island in A.D. 95 by Emperor Domitian, "in consequence of his testimony to the divine word." After John was later released by Emperor Nerva (A.D. 96–98), he took up residence in Ephesus where he "remained until the time of Trajan [A.D. 98–117] . . . a faithful witness of the apostolic tradition" (*Church History* 3.18.1; 3.20.10–11; 3.23.3–4).

MATTHEW 9: MATTHEW AND JAMES, THE APOSTLES OF JESUS

Approximate Dating: ca. A.D. 30–65 ***Relevant Scriptures:*** **Matthew 9:9; 10:3; Mark 2:14–15; 3:18; Luke 6:15; Acts 1:13**

Alphaeus m. An unnamed woman (or women)
(Unlikely that Alphaeus=Clopas or Cleopas)[1]

Matthew
("Levi son of Alphaeus" in **Mark 2:14**[3])

James[2]
("James son of Alphaeus" in **Matthew 10:3; Mark 3:18; Luke 6:15; Acts 1:13**)
(Called "James the Less/Lesser" in church tradition[4])

Biblical and Theological Significance

Matthew, the son of Alphaeus, was one of the twelve apostles and the author of the **Gospel of Matthew**. He is usually called "Matthew" (**Matthew 9:9–10; 10:3; Mark 3:18; Luke 6:15; Acts 1:13**), although Mark and Luke also refer to him as "Levi" or "Levi son of Alphaeus" (**Mark 2:14–15; Luke 5:27–29**). Before becoming a disciple of Jesus, Matthew was a tax collector for Rome[5] (**Matthew 10:3**). Then, after becoming Jesus' disciple, Matthew held "a great banquet for Jesus at his house" that included a large crowd of tax collectors and other sinners (**Luke 5:29**; cf. **Matthew 9:10; Mark 2:15**). Narrative details suggest that Matthew was a wealthy Israelite.

Matthew is tentatively shown in the chart as the *half-brother* of the apostle "James son of Alphaeus" (**Matthew 10:3; Mark 3:18; Luke 6:15; Acts 1:13**). However, it is just as likely that Matthew/Levi and James happen to have fathers with the same name (Alphaeus), in which case, the apostles would be unrelated.[6]

Matthew's exact ancestry is unknown. In his Gospel, Matthew emphasizes Jesus' Jewish descent by tracing his ancestry through Abraham, the Davidic line of the kings of Judah and the ancestors of "Joseph, the husband of Mary" (**Matthew 1:16**) and organizes Jesus' genealogy based on Israel's history—the patriarchal, monarchic, exilic, and post-exilic generations (**Matthew 1:1–17**).[7]

James, the son of Alphaeus,[8] was one of the twelve apostles. He may have been the half-brother of Matthew/Levi. The identity of the wife of Alphaeus and mother of James the apostle is unclear. An early tradition identified Alphaeus (**Matthew 10:3; Mark 2:14; 3:18; Luke 6:15; Acts 1:13**) with the Clopas of **John 19:25**. However, scholars consider this a tenuous association.[9] A more likely interpretation is that "Mary the wife of Clopas" was the same woman called "Mary the mother of James" (**Mark 16:1; Luke 24:10**); "Mary the mother of James and Joseph" (**Matthew 27:56**); "Mary the mother of James the younger and of Joseph" (**Mark 15:40**); and "Mary the mother of Joseph" (**Mark 15:47**), but none of the familial associations mentions Matthew/Levi. For these reasons, Clopas (an Aramaic name) in **John 19:25** is *not* considered to be the same person as Alphaeus, and "Mary the wife of Clopas" is *not* considered to be the mother of James the apostle.

Notes

1. Some scholars have proposed that Alphaeus and Clopas are different variations of a common original, in which Alphaeus (Gk. *Halphaios*) is the same person as *Clopas* (Aramaic) or *Cleopas* (Greek; cf. **Luke 24:18; John 19:25**), arising from a different pronunciation of the first letter ("ch") of the Aramaic original. The interpretation shown in this and other charts is that the strictly Greek name "Alphaeus" does *not* refer to "Cleopas" (Gk. *Kleopas*), who was one of the two disciples who met Jesus on the road to Emmaus (**Luke 24:18**). Also, "Alphaeus" is *not* the Aramaic "Clopas." According to an early tradition given by Hegesippus (A.D. 110–180), Clopas (not Alphaeus) was the *brother* Joseph (Jesus' earthly father); therefore, this is the interpretation followed in this work. See note 9 below. For more information, see Clopas and "Mary the wife of Clopas" (**John 19:25**) in the charts "**Matthew 1**: Mary and Joseph (Based on Scripture and Church Tradition) and How Mary and Joseph May Have Been Related" and "**Matthew 27**: Specific People Mentioned at Jesus' Crucifixion."

2. There are three main figures named James in the New Testament: (1) James the son of Alphaeus (who is shown in the chart above); (2) James the son of Zebedee; and (3) James the half-brother of Jesus. The first two were apostles of Jesus and the third was a leader in the early church. For more information on James #2, see charts "**Matthew 4**: James and John, the Apostles of Jesus." For more information on James #3, see "**Matthew 1**: Jesus and His Immediate Family."

3. Matthew is listed in the same verses where "James son of Alphaeus" is also listed (i.e., **Matthew 10:3; Mark 3:18; Luke 6:15; Acts 1:13**), however, the fact that Matthew is never identified as "Matthew son of Alphaeus" nor as "Matthew the brother of James" suggests, at best, that Matthew was the *half-brother* (not the full brother) of James son of Alphaeus. There were two notable sets of brothers among Jesus' twelve apostles: Peter and Andrew (the sons of Jonah/John) and James and John (the sons of Zebedee); see charts "**Matthew 4**: Simon Peter and Andrew, the Apostles of Jesus" and "**Matthew 4**: James and John, the Apostles of Jesus," respectively.

4. James is called *James the Less* or *James the Lesser* by tradition, suggesting that he may have been smaller in stature than: (1) James the son of Zebedee and the brother of John, who is traditionally called *James the Great/Greater*, and/or (2) James the half-brother of Jesus, who is traditionally called *James the Just*. Also, James the son of Alphaeus is understood to be a different person than "James the younger" (**Mark 15:40**), who is described as the *brother* of Joseph and the *son* of Mary (likely referring to Mary the wife of Clopas; cf. **Matthew 27:56; Mark 15:47; 16:1; Luke 24:10**).

5. Matthew collected taxes (or tolls) for Herod Antipas, the tetrarch of Galilee and Perea. (Tax collectors are called "publicans" in some translations, such as the King James Version). Tax collectors for Rome were often contracted from among the native Jewish population, but they were a hated and despised class of people. Because they collaborated with the Roman authorities, continually interacted with Gentiles, and worked on the Sabbath, they were considered sinners, corrupt extortioners, and were deemed ceremonially unclean. Tax collectors were notorious for cheating their fellow Jews; they often became powerful and rich (e.g., Zacchaeus, "the chief tax collector" in **Luke 19:2**, who oversaw the district of Jericho and had tax collectors under him). The religious leaders accused Jesus of being a "friend of tax collectors and sinners" (**Matthew 11:19; Luke 7:34**; cf. **Mark 2:16; Luke 5:30; 15:1; 18:13**).

6. If Matthew/Levi and James had been full brothers, the text would be expected to be more unequivocal and explicit, as it is in the case of the brothers James and John (**Matthew 4:21; 10:2; 17:1; Mark 1:19; 3:17; 5:37; 10:35; Luke 5:10; Acts 12:2**) and Simon Peter and Andrew (**Matthew 4:18; 10:2; Luke 6:14; John 1:40; 6:8**).

7. See chart "**Matthew 1**: Jesus the Messiah: The Matthean Account."

8. The addition of the qualifier "son of Alphaeus" (**Matthew 10:3; Mark 3:18; Luke 6:15; Acts 1:13**) clearly distinguishes this James from: (1) the apostle James, the son of Zebedee and Salome, who is called *James the Great/Greater* in the extrabiblical literature; see chart "**Matthew 4**: James and John, the Apostles of Jesus" and (2) James, the half-brother of Jesus, who is called *James the Just* in the extrabiblical literature; see chart "**Matthew 1**: Jesus and His Immediate Family." Furthermore, a clear distinction is made between the "brothers" of Jesus and Jesus' apostles (cf. **Matthew 12:49; John 2:12; 7:3; Acts 1:12–14; 1 Corinthians 9:5; Galatians 1:19**).

9. According to *International Standard Bible Encyclopedia (ISBE)*, "The identity of Clopas and Alphaeus cannot be established resting as it does upon obscure philological resemblances of the Aramaic form of the two names [i.e., that Alphaeus and Clopas are variations of a common original, and that the variation has arisen from different pronunciations of the first letter *heth* (h) of the Aramaic original] . . . The most that such argument affords is a mere possibility" (H. E. Jacobs "Brethren [or Brothers] of the Lord," *ISBE*). Regarding the identity of Alphaeus, Clopas, and Cleopas, the *New Bible Dictionary* (R.E. Nixon, "Alphaeus") concludes: "It is improbable that Cleopas and Clopas are the same person and that Alphaeus is the same as either of them. The Aramaic of Alphaeus is *Halphai*, which could be transliterated as *Klōpas*, but even if the same individual is signified, we cannot assume from **Jn. 19:25** that this James was in any way related to our Lord and certainly not that he was James the Lord's brother." Furthermore, "the view that Clopas was the father of the apostle described in the lists of the apostles as 'James, the son of Alphaeus' rests on the assumption that Clopas and Alphaeus are renderings of the same Hebrew word—pronounced differently. In the early Latin and Syriac versions, the Cleopas of **Lk. 24:18** was confused with the Clopas of **Jn. 19:25**, but it is probable that they were two different people with two distinct names, as *eo* was usually contracted into *ou* and not into *ō*" (R.V.G. Tasker, "Clopas," *New Bible Dictionary*).

MATTHEW 10: GENEALOGICAL RECORD OF THE TWELVE APOSTLES OF JESUS

Approximate Dating: ca. 30–100 A.D. ***Relevant Scriptures:*** **Matthew 10:2–4; Mark 3:16–19; Luke 6:14–16; Acts 1:13**[1]; also **John 1:40–49**

1. **Simon Peter** (also called Peter, Simon, and Cephas), the son of Jonah and the brother of Andrew
2. **Andrew**, the son of Jonah and the brother of Simon Peter
3. **James** (also called "James the Great/Greater"), the son of Zebedee and the brother of John
4. **John** ("the disciple whom Jesus loved"), the son of Zebedee and the brother of James
5. **Philip**
6. **Bartholomew** (also called Nathanael)
7. **Thomas** (also called Didymus)
8. **Matthew** (also called Levi), the son of Alphaeus and the brother (or half-brother) of James
9. **James** (also called "James the Less/Lesser"), the son of Alphaeus and the brother (or half-brother) of Matthew
10. **Judas** (also called Thaddaeus), the son of James
11. **Simon the Zealot**
12. **Judas Iscariot**, the son of Simon Iscariot

Biblical and Theological Significance

The twelve apostles of Jesus were the founding members of the apostolic church. Jesus trained this group of close followers for three and a half years to prepare them to continue his legacy and to establish local congregations of believers after his crucifixion, burial, resurrection, and ascension. In this, the twelve fulfilled a vital function in God's plan of salvation to proclaim the message of forgiveness of sins and salvation in and through Jesus the Messiah.

Simon Peter, the son of Jonah/John (cf. **Matthew 16:17; John 1:42**), was nicknamed Cephas (a Greek transliteration of an Aramaic word meaning "rock"). Peter was the indisputable leader of the apostles (cf. **Matthew 10:2; 14:28–31; 15:15; 16:16–19; Mark 10:28; Luke 24:12; John 20:3–6; 21:7; Acts 1:15–22; 2:14–41; 3:1–4:31; 5:8–10**). Peter and his brother Andrew were fishermen from the town of Bethsaida (**Matthew 4:18; Mark 1:16; John 1:44**). Peter declared that Jesus was "the Messiah, the Son of the living God" (**Matthew 16:16**; cf. **Mark 8:29**), and Jesus said he would build his new believing community (the church) upon Peter's confession (**Matthew 16:18**).

Peter, James, and John were among an inner circle of Jesus' disciples—for example, they were present at: (1) the transfiguration in **Matthew 17:1–13; Mark 9:2–10**; and **Luke 9:28–36**; (2) the Garden of Gethsemane in **Matthew 26:36–46; Mark 14:32–42;** and **Luke 22:40–46**; (3) the raising of Jairus' daughter in **Mark 5:37–43** and **Luke 8:51–56**; and (4) Jesus' prediction of the destruction of the temple in the Olivet discourse in **Mark 13:1–37**. Before his trials, Jesus told Peter, "before the rooster crows twice, you yourself will disown me three times" (**Mark 14:30**; cf. **Matthew 26:34; Luke 22:34; John 13:38**); Peter did denounce Jesus (Luke 22:58, 60), but Jesus forgave Peter and charged him to "Feed my sheep" (**John 21:17**). Peter preached the first gospel sermon on the Day of Pentecost (**Acts 2:14–40**) and three thousand were saved (**Acts 2:41**). Also, Peter was given the vision of "a large sheet . . . contain[ing] all kinds of four-footed animals," which symbolized that the barrier between Jew ("clean") and Gentile ("unclean") had been removed (**Acts 10:9–36**). Peter wrote the New Testament epistles of **1** and **2 Peter**.[2]

Andrew, the son of Jonah/John, had been a disciple of John the Baptist (**John 1:35–40**). Andrew introduced his brother Peter to Jesus (**John 1:41–42**). His hometown was Bethsaida (**John 1:44**). The call of Andrew and Peter is found in **Matthew 4:18–20; Mark 1:16–18; Luke 5:2–11;** and **John 1:40–41**. Andrew was present when Jesus gave the Olivet discourse (**Mark 13:3**); he was also present when Greeks came to see Jesus (**John 12:20–22**). Andrew identified the boy with the five barley loaves and the two fishes in the narrative of the feeding of the five thousand (**John 6:8–13**).[3]

James was the son of Zebedee and Salome as well as the brother of John (e.g., **Matthew 10:2; 17:1; Mark 1:19–29; 5:37; 9:2; 10:35–40; 13:3; 14:33; Luke 6:14; 8:51; 9:28, 54; John 21:2; Acts 1:13**). Prior to following Jesus, James and John were partners with Peter and Andrew in a fishing business (**Luke 5:10**).[4] James and John were among the first disciples to be called by Jesus (see **Matthew 4:21–22; Mark 1:19–20; Luke 5:1–11**). According to genealogy, James and his brother John were the first cousins of Jesus.[5] Jesus nicknamed them "Boanerges," meaning "sons of thunder" (**Mark 3:17**). James was the first disciple of Jesus to be martyred—killed "with the sword" in ca. A.D. 44 on the orders of Herod Agrippa I (**Acts 12:2**).

In the extrabiblical literature, James the son of Zebedee is also called "James the Great" or "James the Greater," distinguishing him from (1) the disciple James the son of Alphaeus, sometimes called "James the Less/Lesser" (see below); and (2) James the half-brother of Jesus, sometimes called "James the Just," who was the author of the **Epistle of James** (cf. **Matthew 13:55; Mark 6:3; Acts 12:17; 15:13; 21:18; 1 Corinthians 15:7; Galatians 1:19; 2:9, 12; James 1:1; Jude 1**). Also, James, the son of Zebedee, is not "James the younger," who was the son of Mary and the brother of Joseph (cf. **Matthew 27:56; Mark 15:40, 47; 16:1; Luke 24:10**).

John, the son of Zebedee and brother of James, is best known for writing the **Gospel of John**, three epistles (**1–3 John**), and the book of Revelation. In his Gospel, John calls himself "the disciple whom Jesus loved" (**John 13:23;** cf. **19:26; 20:2; 21:7, 20**); in his letters, he calls himself "the elder" (**2 John 1; 3 John 1**). At the cross, Jesus entrusted the care of his mother to John (**John 19:26–27**). John was the last of the twelve apostles to die. Tradition holds that he was exiled to the island of Patmos where he wrote the book of

Revelation about A.D. 95 (**Revelation 1:1, 9**) and that he died in Ephesus in ca. A.D. 98 or shortly thereafter. According to genealogy, John and his brother James were the first cousins of Jesus.[6] John the disciple should not be confused with John the Baptist, the son of Zechariah and Elizabeth.

Philip, like Peter and Andrew, was from the town of Bethsaida in Galilee (**John 1:44; 12:21**). Soon after Jesus called Philip to follow him, Philip led Nathanael (Bartholomew) to Jesus (**John 1:45**). John mentions Philip at the feeding of the five thousand, where Philip declared, "It would take more than half a year's wages to buy enough bread for each one to have a bite!" (**John 6:7**, see **vv. 5–9**), and then mentions Philip again at the coming of Greeks to Jesus (**John 12:20–22**). In the upper room, Philip asked Jesus, "Lord, show us the Father and that will be enough for us" (**John 14:8**; see **vv. 9–21**).[7] Philip the apostle should not be confused with Philip the evangelist who had four virgin daughters who prophesied (cf. **Acts 21:8–9**).[8]

Bartholomew (**Matthew 10:3; Mark 3:18; Luke 6:14; Acts 1:13**)—meaning "son of Talmai"—is traditionally identified as the same person as **Nathanael**, who was from Cana of Galilee (cf. **John 1:45; 21:2**). In **John 1**, when Philip told him, "we have found the one Moses wrote about in the Law, and about whom the prophets also wrote—Jesus of Nazareth, the son of Joseph" (**1:45**), Nathanael was highly skeptical at first and exclaimed, "Nazareth! Can anything good come from there?" (**v. 46**). Jesus discerned that Nathanael was "an Israelite in whom there is no deceit" (**v. 47**). When Nathanael met Jesus, he recognized him as "the Son of God" and "the king of Israel" (**v. 49**). Nathanael was among the seven apostles who had breakfast with the risen Jesus on the shore of the Sea of Galilee (**John 21:2**).

Thomas, also called Didymus or "the Twin" (**John 11:16; 20:24; 21:2**), bears the nickname "Doubting Thomas." When Lazarus died, eleven of the disciples dissuaded Jesus from going to Bethany because Jews had tried to stone him in Judea (**John 11:8**). Perhaps in blind enthusiasm (or unknowingly foreshadowing Jesus' own death), Thomas declared "Let us also go, that we may die with him [which could refer to either Jesus or Lazarus]" (**John 11:16**). On the eve of the passion, when Jesus told the disciples that he was "going . . . to prepare a place . . . You know the way to the place where I am going" (**John 14:2–4**), Thomas asked the obvious question: "Lord, we don't know where you are going, so how can we know the way?" (**John 14:5**), which prompted Jesus' affirmation: "I am the way and the truth and the life" (**John 14:6**).

After the crucifixion, when the disciples met behind closed doors for fear of the Jewish leaders, the resurrected Christ appeared to them, but Thomas was not present (**John 20:19–24**). When the disciples told him that they had met the risen Christ, Thomas was *doubtful* and declared, "Unless I see the nail marks in his hands and put my finger where the nails were, and put my hand into his side, I will not believe" (**John 20:25**). A week later when the resurrected Christ appeared again to his followers, Thomas was present. Jesus showed him his hands and side and told him, "Stop doubting and believe" (**John 20:27**). Finally, in faith, Thomas believed and exclaimed, "My Lord and my God!" (**John 20:28**; see **vv. 24–29**). Thomas was among the group of seven disciples who went fishing at the Sea of Galilee and shared breakfast with the risen Jesus (**John 21:2**; see **vv. 1–14**).

Matthew (also called Levi) the son of Alphaeus, was a Roman tax collector (**Matthew 9:9–10; 10:3; Mark 2:14–15; Luke 5:27–29**) before he became a disciple of Jesus (**Mark 3:18; Luke 6:15**; see **Acts 1:13**). Matthew may be the brother (or half-brother) of James son of Alphaeus (cf. **Mark 2:14–15**).[9] Matthew is best known for writing the **Gospel of Matthew**, declaring the "good news of the kingdom" that begins the New Testament (**Matthew 4:23; 9:35**; see also **11:5**), and for composing the elaborate, extensive genealogy of Jesus in **Matthew 1:1–17**.[10]

James the son of Alphaeus may be the brother (or half-brother) of Matthew/Levi (**Mark 2:14**; for James as a disciple, see **Mark 3:18; Luke 6:15; Acts 1:13**).[11] In church tradition, he is sometimes called "James the Less" or "James the Lesser"—perhaps because he was smaller in stature—to distinguish him from (1) the disciple James the son of Zebedee and the brother of John, who is sometimes called "James the Great" or "James the Greater" (see above); (2) James, the half-brother of Jesus (**Matthew 13:55; Mark 6:3**), who is sometimes called "James the Just";[12] and/or (3) "James the younger," the son of Mary[13] and the brother of Joseph (**Mark 15:40**; cf. **Matthew 27:56; Mark 15:47; 16:1; Luke 24:10**).

Judas the son of James (**Luke 6:16; Acts 1:13**; cf. **John 14:22**) is also called Thaddaeus (**Matthew 10:3; Mark 3:18**); in some translations he is called "Lebbaeus" (**Matthew 10:3** NKJV). He was the disciple who asked Jesus in the upper room, "Lord, why do you intend to show yourself to us [your disciples] and not to the world?" (**John 14:22**). Judas, the son of James, should not be confused with (1) Judas Iscariot, who betrayed Jesus (see below) or (2) Judas, also called Jude, who was the half-brother of Jesus (**Matthew 13:55; Mark 6:3**) and wrote the New Testament epistle of Jude.[14]

Simon is also called "Simon the Zealot" in **Matthew 10:4, Mark 3:18**, and **Acts 1:13** to distinguish him from Simon Peter (see above) and from Simon, the half-brother of Jesus (**Matthew 13:55; Mark 6:3**; cf. **Matthew 12:46; 13:55; John 2:12; 7:5, 10; Acts 1:14**).[15] Some translations call him "Simon the Cananite" (**Matthew 10:4; Mark 3:18**; NKJV). Simon was a member of the Jewish religious faction called the Zealots, who were known for their unyielding loyalty to God and vehement opposition to Roman rule.[16]

Judas Iscariot, the son of Simon Iscariot (**John 6:71; 13:2, 26**), is infamously known as the disciple who betrayed Jesus (cf. **Matthew 10:4; 26:14, 21, 23–25, 46–49; 27:3–5; Mark 3:19; 14:10, 18, 21, 42–45; Luke 6:16; 22:3–4, 47–48; John 6:64, 71; 12:4; 13:2, 11, 21, 26–27, 29–30; 18:2–5; Acts 1:16–18, 25**). "Iscariot" is Aramaic for "man of Kerioth," probably referring to Kerioth Hezron (Hazor) in southern Judah (**Joshua 15:25**; **Jeremiah 48:24**), making Judas Iscariot the only apostle from *outside* the region of Galilee. John writes in his Gospel that Judas Iscariot was a thief: "as keeper of the money bag, he used to help himself to what was put into it" (**John 12:6**). In **John 6**, Jesus called Judas "a devil" (**John 6:70**), since Jesus "had known from the beginning which of them [the apostles] did not believe and who would betray him" (**John 6:64**). At the Last Supper, Jesus clearly pointed out to the twelve disciples that Judas Iscariot would be his betrayer (**Matthew 26:23–25**). Judas made a transaction with the Jewish chief priests to hand over Jesus to them for thirty pieces of silver (**Matthew 26:14–15; 27:3, 9; Mark 14:10–11; Luke 22:4–6**; cf. **Zechariah 11:12–13**). When Judas led a detachment of soldiers and some officials from the chief priests and the Pharisees to the Garden of Gethsemane, he identified Jesus "with a kiss" (**Luke 22:48**; cf. **Matthew 26:48–49; Mark 14:43–44; Luke 22:41–48; John 18:2–5**). However, after Jesus was condemned, Judas was "seized with remorse" (**Matthew 27:3**) because he knew he had sinned and betrayed "innocent blood" (**Matthew 27:4**). Judas returned the thirty pieces of silver to the religious authorities—"He threw the money into the temple" and "went away and hanged himself" (**Matthew 27:5**; cf. **Acts 1:18**).[17] Judas Iscariot should not be confused with (1) the disciple called Judas, the son of James (see above) or with (2) Judas/Jude, the half-brother of Jesus.[18]

Notes

1. As James Tabor points out, "A close examination of the composition of this Council of Twelve is most revealing. Each time they are listed, in Matthew, Mark, and Luke, they are consistently grouped into three tiers of four names each: (1) Simon Peter, Andrew, James, and John; (2) Philip, Bartholomew, Matthew, and Thomas; and (3) James, Jude [Judas/Thaddeus], Simon, and Judas Iscariot." James D. Tabor, *The Jesus Dynasty* (New York: Simon & Schuster, 2006), 163.

2. For more about Simon Peter, see chart "**Matthew 4**: Simon Peter and Andrew."

3. For more about Andrew, see chart "**Matthew 4**: Simon Peter and Andrew."

4. For more about James, see chart "**Matthew 4**: James and John, the Apostles of Jesus."

5. For more about James and John, the sons of Zebedee, see charts "**Matthew 1**: Mary and Joseph (Based on Scripture and Church Tradition) and How Mary and Joseph May Have Been Related" and "**Matthew 4**: James and John, the Apostles of Jesus."

6. For more about John, see charts "**Matthew 1**: Mary and Joseph (Based on Scripture and Church Tradition) and How Mary and Joseph May Have Been Related" and "**Matthew 4**: James and John, the Apostles of Jesus."

7. For more about Andrew, see chart "**Matthew 4**: Simon Peter and Andrew."

8. See Eusebius' *Church History* 3.31.2-5 which says that when Philip the apostle died, he was buried in Hierapolis and that this was also the burial place of Philip's four virgin daughters; however, her Eusebius confuses Philip the apostle with Philipi the evangelist who had the four unmarried daughters (**Acts 21:9**).

9. For more about Matthew son of Alphaeus, see chart "**Matthew 9**: Matthew and James, the Apostles of Jesus."

10. See chart "**Matthew 1**: Jesus the Messiah: The Matthean Account."

11. For more about James son of Alphaeus, see chart "**Matthew 9**: Matthew and James, the Apostles of Jesus."

12. For more about James the half-brother of Jesus, see chart "**Matthew 1**: Jesus and His Immediate Family."

13. For Mary, the mother of James the younger and Joseph, see chart "**Matthew 27**: Specific People Mentioned at Jesus' Crucifixion."

14. For Judas/Jude, the half-brother of Jesus, see chart "**Matthew 1**: Jesus and His Immediate Family."

15. For Simon, the half-brother of Jesus, see chart "**Matthew 1**: Jesus and His Immediate Family."

16. The Zealots resented Roman rule, believing that only God should rule Israel and that paying tribute to the Roman emperor was treasonous. The Zealots pressed for Jewish independence to the point of being willing to use violence against those who threatened Israel's religious integrity and national identity. See Martin Hengel, *The Zealots* (Edinburgh: T&T Clark, 1989).

17. Matthew and Luke both give accounts of Judas's suicide. Matthew reports that Judas "hanged himself" (**Matthew 27:5**) and that the chief priests used the "blood money" to buy the potter's field as a place to bury foreigners (**Matthew 27:6–7**; cf. **Zechariah 11:12–13**; also refer to the "Valley of Slaughter" in **Jeremiah 7:32; 19:6**). Luke indicates that it was Judas himself who "bought a field" (**Acts 1:18**), describing the indirect transaction involving the chief priests (as explained by Matthew). This field was where Judas hung himself. Apparently, Judas hung there for quite some time. Luke goes into more gruesome details that suggest that the body was significantly decomposed when Judas was cut down: he fell "headlong, his body burst open and all his intestines spilled out." Thus, the field became known by the people of Jerusalem as "Akeldama [Aramaic], that is, Field of Blood" (**Acts 1:18–19**). The traditional location of the field is the southeast portion of Jerusalem where the Valley of Hinnom joins the Kidron Valley.

18. For more on Judas/Jude, the half-brother of Jesus, see chart "**Matthew 1**: Jesus and His Immediate Family."

MATTHEW 26: THE INFLUENTIAL FAMILY OF ANNAS AND CAIAPHAS, THE HIGH PRIESTS[1]

Approximate Dating: first half of the first century A.D. ***Relevant Scriptures:*** **Matthew 26:3, 57; Luke 3:2; John 11:49; 18:13, 24, 28; Acts 4:6**

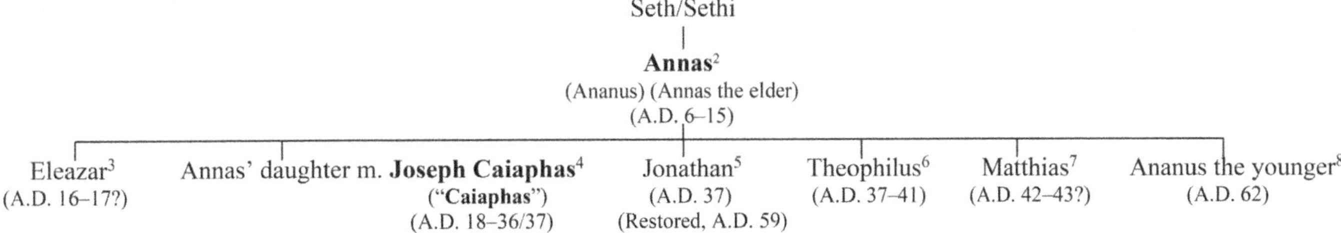

Biblical and Theological Significance

The family of Annas (also called Ananus or Annas the elder) dominated the Jewish high priesthood for over half of the first century, holding a kind of "perpetual priesthood" because Annas, all five of his sons, and his son-in-law held the high priestly office in Jerusalem between A.D. 6–62. The elder Annas, the son of Seth/Sethi, served as the Jewish high priest in A.D. 6–15 and was influential during the ministries of John the Baptist. Annas was a contemporary of several Roman prefects (governors) of Judea: Coponius (A.D. 6 or 7–9); Marcus Ambivius (A.D. 9–12); Annius Rufus (A.D. 12–15), and Valerius Gratus (A.D. 15–26).[9] Annas was also a contemporary of the Herodian rulers: Herod Antipas of Galilee and Perea (6 B.C.–A.D. 39 or 4 B.C.?–A.D. 39), Herod Philip II of Iturea and Traconitis (6 B.C.–A.D. 32 or 4 B.C.?–A.D. 34) and possibly Herod Archelaus of Judea (4 B.C.?–A.D. 6 or 6 B.C.–A.D. 6).[10] **Luke 3:2** mentions that "during the high-priesthood of Annas and Caiaphas (Annas' son-in-law), the word of God came to John [the Baptist] son of Zechariah in the wilderness." As part of Jesus' Jewish trial in ca. A.D. 33, John's Gospel records that Jesus had an *informal* hearing before Annas the elder[11] (**John 18:13–14**) before he was sent to Caiaphas, who held the high priesthood at the time (cf. **John 11:49–52**). Caiaphas formally presided over Jesus' trial and ordered his execution (**Matthew 26:57–66**), although Jesus' death sentence by crucifixion required further approval from the Roman governor Pontius Pilate (A.D. 26–36). After Jesus' crucifixion, resurrection, and ascension, Annas and Caiaphas are mentioned again, together with other members of the high priestly family—including John (perhaps referring to Jonathan, the son of Annas the elder) and Alexander—when they summoned Peter and John and challenged their preaching the gospel of the resurrected Jesus (**Acts 4:5–7**).

Notes

1. Biblical references are noted. Also refer to the chart "**Supplement 2**: The High Priests of Israel." The primary extra-biblical sources consulted for composing the genealogy were Josephus' *Jewish Antiquities* and *Jewish Wars* in *The Complete Works of Josephus*, trans. William Whiston, commentary Paul L. Maier (Grand Rapids: Kregel, 1999) and Joachim Jeremias, *Jerusalem in the Time of Jesus* (Philadelphia: Fortress, 1975). For more information about other high priests, see chart "**Supplement 2**: The High Priests of Israel."

2. **Annas** (also called **Ananus the elder**) was high priest from A.D. 6–15. Josephus describes the high priesthood of Ananus in *Jewish Antiquities* 18.2.1 by saying that Cyrenius (Quirinius) deprived Joazar of the high priesthood and "he appointed Ananus, the son of Seth, to be high priest." When Valerius Gratus became the procurator of Judea in A.D. 15, he deposed Annas: "this man [Gratus] deprived Ananus of the high priesthood, and appointed Is[h]mael, the son of Phabi [Phabi I/Fabus], to be high priest" (ibid., 18.2.2).

3. **Eleazar**, the son of Annas, was high priest from ca. A.D. 16–17(?). Josephus writes that the procurator Valerius Gratus deposed Is(h)mael "in a little time, and ordained Eleazar the son of Ananus . . . to be high priest; which office, when he had held for a year, Gratus deprived him [Eleazar] of it, and gave the high priesthood to Simon, the son of Camithus" (ibid.). Josephus describes Eleazar as "a very bold youth." As the governor of the temple, Eleazar "persuaded those that officiated in the divine service to receive no gift or sacrifice for any foreigner [non-Jews]." Josephus believed that "this was the true beginning of our war with the Romans, for they [the Jewish priests] rejected the sacrifice of Caesar on this account" (*Jewish Wars* 2.17.2).

4. **Joseph Caiaphas** (also called **Caiaphas**) married the (unnamed) daughter of Annas the elder, who had held the former high priesthood; thus, Caiaphas was Annas' son-in-law (**John 18:13**; see also **Luke 3:2**; **John 18:24; Acts 4:6**). In A.D. 18, the procurator of Judea, Valerius Gratus, removed Simon son of Camithus and "Joseph Caiaphas was made his successor" (Josephus, *Jewish Antiquities* 18.2.2). Caiaphas held the high priesthood from A.D. 18–36/37, which is the longest term of any high priest in the first century. Caiaphas' term overlapped that of Pontius Pilate, who was the governor of Judea from A.D. 26–36. John the Baptist began his ministry during the terms of Annas and Caiaphas (cf. **Luke 3:2**). Caiaphas prophesied "that Jesus would die for the Jewish nation, and not only for that nation but also for the scattered children of God, to bring them together and make them one" (**John 11:51–52**), a prophecy that sparked the beginning of the plot to kill Jesus (**John 11:53**; cf. **Matthew 26:1–4**). Although Caiaphas was the *official* high priest, Jews still considered the elder Annas to be a ruling high priest also (see notes 11). So, when Jesus was arrested, "they bound him [Jesus] and brought him first to Annas [the elder], who was the father-in-law of Caiaphas, the high priest that year" (**John 18:12–13**). Annas questioned Jesus about "his disciples and his teaching" (**John 18:19–24**). After that, Jesus was taken to the palace of the Roman governor (the Praetorium) to be questioned by Pilate (**Matthew 27:27; Mark 15:16; John 18:28, 33**). Caiaphas accused Jesus of blasphemy (i.e., claiming to be the Son of God; **Matthew 26:65**; cf. **Mark 14:63–64**).

Later when the apostles Peter and John were arrested, Annas, Caiaphas, "John"—possibly referring to Annas' son, Jonathan; see note 5—and Alexander, along with other members of the priestly family, presided over the Sanhedrin and questioned them (**Acts 4:5–7**). They asked the apostles by what power they had preached Jesus to the people (**Acts 4:1–12**). The Sanhedrin ordered Peter and John "not to speak or teach at all in the name of Jesus," to which Peter and John retorted, "Which is right in God's eyes: to listen to you, or to him? You be the judges! As for us, we cannot help speaking about what we have seen and heard" (**Acts 4:18–20**). The apostles were eventually released without punishment, and they continued to speak "the word of God boldly" (**Acts 4:31**). Lucius Vitellius (the Roman-appointed governor of Syria) deposed Caiaphas (Josephus notes that this dismissal corresponded to the same year that Pilate was removed as procurator of Judea (cf. ibid., 18.2.2). Josephus explains that Vitellius "deprived Joseph, who was also called Caiaphas, of the high priesthood, and appointed Jonathan the son of Ananus [the elder], the former high priest, to succeed him" (ibid., 18.4.3).

In June 2011, it was reported that an ossuary (a small stone chest used for the secondary burial of bones) was acquired by the Israel Antiquities Authority with an Aramaic inscription engraved in Jewish script: "Miriam Daughter of Yeshua Son of Caiaphas, Priests [of] Ma'aziah from Beth 'Imri" (see http://www.antiquities.org.il/article_eng.aspx?sec_id=25&subj_id=240&id=1849&-module_id=#as). If this inscription in fact refers to the granddaughter of Caiaphas the high priest, it suggests that Caiaphas was from the Maaziah priestly course—the last of the twenty-four Kohathite priestly divisions that served in the temple in Jerusalem (cf. **1 Chronicles 24:18** and the chart "**1 Chronicles 24**: Genealogical Registry of the Twenty-Four Divisions of Kohathite Attending Priests Who Rotated Service in Solomon's Temple").

5. **Jonathan** the son of Ananus was appointed high priest by the Roman consul Lucius Vitellius (who held three terms, ca. A.D. 34, 43, and 47). Jonathan succeeded his brother-in-law Caiaphas (*Jewish Antiquities* 18.4.3). Jonathan served two separate terms as high priest: his first in A.D. 37, which Joachim Jeremias claims was from Easter to Pentecost in A.D. 37. Jonathan appears to then be restored to the high priesthood in A.D. 59, although the exact succession of high priests during this latter time is unclear. Josephus explains that the affairs of the Jews became worse as the country became filled with robbers and impostors; also, Josephus notes that the procurator Antonius Felix, A.D. 52–59/60, "bore an ill-will" against Jonathan "because he [Jonathan] frequently gave him [Felix] admonitions about governing the Jewish affairs better than he did." In retaliation, "Felix contrived a method whereby he might get rid of him [Jonathan]" and "persuaded one of Jonathan's most faithful friends [Doras] to murder Jonathan." However, instead of carrying out the task himself, Doras devised a plan for robbers to murder Jonathan: "Certain of those robbers went up to the city, as if they were going to worship God, while they had daggers under their garments, and by thus mingling themselves among the multitude they killed Jonathan." The murder of Jonathan the high priest was never avenged. Josephus believed that this was "the reason why God, out his hatred of these men's wickedness, rejected our city; and as for the temple, he [God] no longer esteemed it sufficiently pure for him to inhabit therein, but brought the Romans upon us" (ibid. 20.8.5).

6. **Theophilus** the son of Ananus the elder was appointed by Lucius Vitellius to succeed his brother Jonathan to the high priesthood (ibid. 18.5.3). Theophilus held the high priesthood from A.D. 37–41.

7. **Matthias** was the son of Annas the elder and the brother of Jonathan and Theophilus. The appointment of Matthias came about through the recommendation of Jonathan his brother: "Now King Agrippa [I] [who ruled A.D. 41–44] took the priesthood away from Simon Cantheras [also called Simon ben Boethus; A.D. 41–42] and [desired to] put Jonathan, the son of Ananus, into it . . . [since] he was more worthy of that dignity than the other [Simon]. But this was not a thing acceptable to him [Jonathan], to recover his former dignity. So he refused it, and said, "O king! . . . If you desire that a person more worthy than myself should have this honorable employment, give me leave to name such a one. I have a brother that is pure from all sin against God, and of all offenses against yourself; I recommend him to you, as one that is fit for this dignity.' So, king [Herod Agrippa] was pleased with these words of his, and passed by Jonathan, and according to his brother's desire, bestowed the

high priesthood upon Matthias [Jonathan's brother]" (ibid. 19.6.4). Matthias held the high priesthood from A.D. 42–43(?).

8. **Ananus the younger** was the son of Annas the elder. Josephus details the account of Ananus the younger's rise to the high priesthood, stating that King Herod Agrippa II "deprived Joseph [Joseph Cabi, son of Simon, who was high priest from ca. A.D.61–62] of the high priesthood, and bestowed the succession to that dignity on the son of Ananus, who was also himself called Ananus." Josephus then mentions that Ananus the elder and his five sons "had all performed the office of a high priest to God," and distinguishes the elder Ananus from his son and namesake. Josephus describes the younger Ananus as "a bold man in his temper, and very insolent; he was also of the sect of the Sadducees, who are very rigid in judging offenders . . . therefore he [Ananus] thought he had now a proper opportunity [to exercise his authority]." Ananus then assembled the Sanhedrin and brought James the half-brother of Jesus, as well as some others, before the council. Ananus accused them and "delivered them to be stoned." Because it was unlawful for Ananus to have assembled the Sanhedrin without obtaining consent, Albinus the procurator (A.D. 62–64) angrily wrote to Ananus, threatening to punish him "for what he had done." King Herod Agrippa II then "took the high priesthood from him when he had ruled but three months" and replaced him with Jesus, the son of Damneus. (ibid. 20.9.1; also see Jeremias, *Jerusalem in the Time of Jesus* (Philadelphia: Fortress, 1969), 157, 198, 229). For more information about the death of James, the half-brother of Jesus, see chart "**Matthew 1**: Jesus and His Immediate Family."

9. For the succession and dating of the governors (prefects) of Judea, see chart "**Supplement 13**: Roman Rulers of Judea and Galilee."

10. For the tetrarchs and their dates of rule, see chart "**Matthew 2**: Herod the Great and the Herodian Dynasty."

> Joachim Jeremias writes that "Even after his removal from office, the high priest kept his title and retained his authority and . . . again and again the influence of the retired high priest is discernible. Think of the part played by Annas (in office from A.D. 6–15) in the trial of Jesus (John 18:13, 24; cf. Luke 3:2; Acts 4:6) . . . The high priest retained not only a great part of his authority, but also his cultic character, after his deposal. . . 'A high priest in office differs from the priest that is passed . . . only in [having to pay for] the bullock that is offered on the Day of Atonement and [providing] the Tenth of Ephah [of meal for the burnt offering] . . . We see that the high priest retained forever, after his deposal, the character of his office . . . He possessed a 'life-long sanctity.'" Jeremias, *Jerusalem in the Time of Jesus* (Philadelphia: Fortress, 1969, 1975), 157–58.

MATTHEW 27: SIMON OF CYRENE WHO CARRIED THE CROSS OF JESUS

Approximate Dating: ca. A.D. 33 ***Relevant Scriptures:*** **Matthew 27:32; Mark 15:21; Luke 23:26; Romans 16:13**

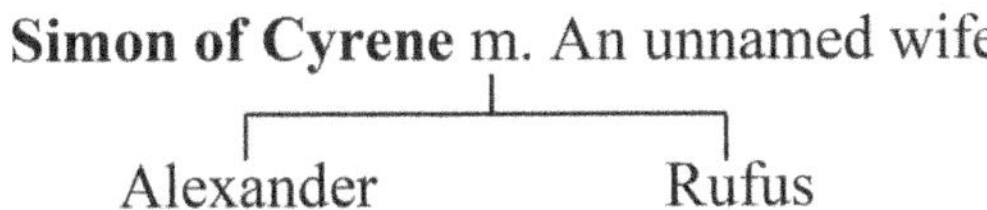

Biblical and Theological Significance

Simon was a native of Cyrene[1] (modern Libya), a town in North Africa which had a large Jewish community[2] (**Acts 2:10; 6:9; 11:19–20; 13:1**). Simon appears to have been "passing by on his way in from the country" (**Mark 15:21**) when Jesus was led to be crucified.[3] The Romans "put the cross on him [Simon] and made him carry it behind Jesus" to Golgotha (**Luke 23:26**; cf. **Matthew 27:32; Mark 15:21**). The account in **John 19:17** says that, "[Jesus] carrying his own cross" went to Golgotha and does not mention Simon, so Simon may have carried the cross for only part of the way. It is unclear if Simon the Cyrenian (**Luke 23:26**) is the same person as "Simeon called Niger" (**Acts 13:1**).[4]

Mark 15:21 clearly identifies Simon the Cyrene as the father of Alexander and Rufus. In all likelihood, Paul's reference to "Rufus, chosen in the Lord, and his mother, who has been a mother to me, too" (**Romans 16:13**) refers to Simon's family and acknowledges Paul's fondness for Simon's wife since she had been a spiritual, mother-like figure to him. Rufus and his mother appear to be living in Rome and were part of the church there when Paul wrote to the Romans (cf. **Romans 16:13**).

Notes

1. Cyrene was the capital and principal city of the Roman district of Cyrenaica during the New Testament era.

2. Apparently the Cyrenians encouraged Jewish settlement. Among those in Jerusalem at Pentecost were God-fearing Jews from the "parts of Libya near Cyrene" (**Acts 2:10**). Jews of Cyrene were also members of the Synagogue of the Freedmen in Jerusalem who argued with Stephen (**Acts 6:9**). Converts from Cyrene and Cyprus were among those who had contributed to the formation of the first Gentile church at Antioch (**Acts 11:20**). "Lucius of Cyrene" was among the prophets and teachers in that church (**Acts 13:1**).

3. The *Holman Bible Dictionary* suggests that Simon was probably a Jew, born in the Jewish diaspora outside of Palestine, and that he may have been a black man; also, Simon was probably living in Jerusalem at the time of the Passover festival (cf. **Mark 15:21**) and that he was not one of the visiting pilgrims. Trent C. Butler, ed. "Simon," *Holman Bible Dictionary* (Nashville: Holman Bible, 1991), 70.

4. Simon (Σίμων) is the Greek form of Simeon (S. Angus, "Simon," *ISBE*).

MATTHEW 27: SPECIFIC PEOPLE MENTIONED AT JESUS' CRUCIFIXION[1]

Approximate Dating: ca. A.D. 33. ***Relevant Scriptures:*** **Matthew 27:55–56; Mark 15:40; John 19:25–27;** also **Matthew 4:21; 10:2; 17:1; 26:37; Mark 1:19; 3:17; 10:35; 15:47; 16:1; Luke 1:5, 7, 13, 36; 3:2; 5:10; John 21:2; Acts 12:2**

A consolidated list of persons who were present at the cross, as recorded by the Gospel writers:

1. **Mary** the mother of Jesus (**John 19:25**);
2. **Mary Magdalene** (**Mark 15:40; John 19:25**);
3. **Salome** (**Mark 15:40**), called **his mother's [Mary's] sister** (**John 19:25**);
4. **Mary the mother of James the younger and of Joseph** (**Mark 15:40**), called **Mary the wife of Clopas** (**John 19:25**);
5. **The "disciple whom he [Jesus] loved"** (**John 19:26–27**).

Proposed genealogies for (1) Mary (Jesus' mother); (2) the mother of Zebedee's sons; (3) Mary, the wife of Clopas; and (4) John the beloved disciple:

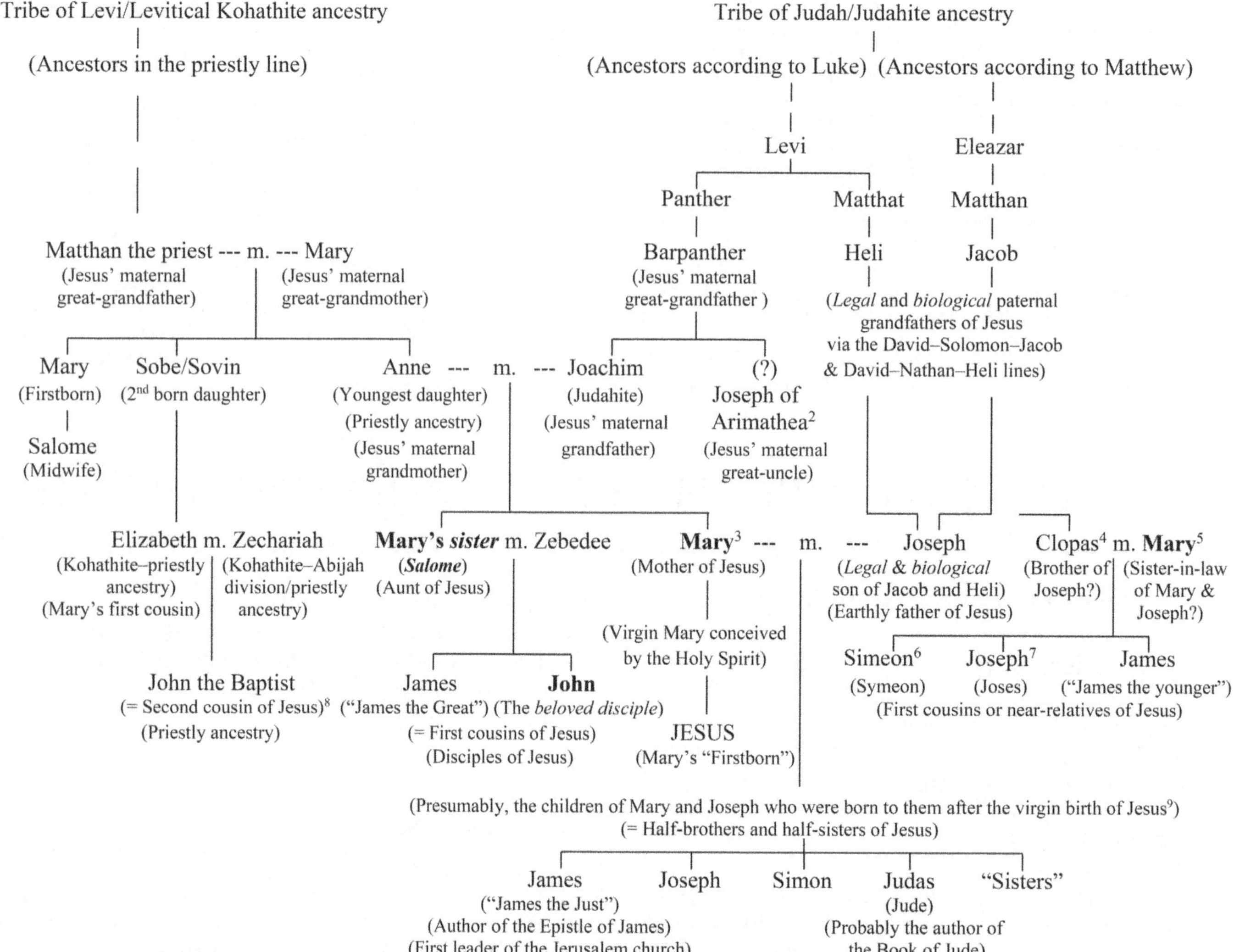

Biblical and Theological Significance

During his earthly ministry, Jesus attracted close followers. The majority of them were witnesses to or recipients of Jesus' ministry, including healing, feeding, and, in some cases, even resurrection. At certain junctures in Jesus' public ministry, when Jesus repeatedly stipulated the demands of following him, some followers left him. He predicted that he would be killed and on the third day rise again. As the time of his crucifixion drew closer, most of Jesus' closest followers and disciples left, denied, or even betrayed him. At the same time, Scripture identifies several individuals who followed Jesus all the way to the cross, epitomizing devoted followership.

The Women and the Single Disciple of Jesus at the Cross

These specific women were "watching from a distance" (**Mark 15:40**) and were likely from a larger group of Jesus' followers since Mark states that "many other women who had come up with him to Jerusalem were also there" (**Mark 15:41**). The group of women may have included Susanna and Joanna, the wife of Chuza, the manager of Herod's household (**Luke 8:2–3**). Some of these women at the cross were also present at Jesus' burial (**Matthew 27:61; Mark 15:47**) and his resurrection (**Matthew 28:1; Mark 16:1; Luke 24:1, 10; John 20:1–18**). Not every woman is identified by name, but by the process of disambiguation,[10] they can be distinguished.

Mary Magdalene[11] appears to be unmarried or possibly widowed because she is always identified by her hometown, Magdala, which was a prosperous fishing town on the western shore of the Sea of Galilee. Jesus drove out seven demons from her (**Luke 8:2**), and she became part of an inner circle of women who followed and supported Jesus. She was the first woman to declare that Jesus was "the Messiah, the Son of God, who is to come into the world" (**John 11:27**). She witnessed Jesus' crucifixion (**Matthew 27:56; Mark 15:40; John 19:25**), his burial (**Matthew 27:61; Mark 15:47**), and the empty tomb (**Matthew 28:1–10; Luke 24:10**). Remarkably, she was also the first person to witness the risen Lord after his resurrection (**Mark 16:9–11**). Jesus told her to go tell his disciples of his resurrection and impending ascension (**John 20:1–18**). Thus, Mary Magdalene was also the first person to report the "good news" that Jesus had risen from the dead.

Mary the mother of James the younger and of Joseph (Mark 15:40), called **Mary the wife of Clopas**[12] **(John 19:25)** seems to be variously called "Mary, the mother of James[13] and Joseph [Greek *Joses*]" (**Matthew 27:56**); "Mary the mother of Joseph" (**Mark 15:47**); and "Mary, the mother of James" (**Mark 16:1; Luke 24:10**).[14] She is likely the same person as "the other Mary" who, along with Mary Magdalene, saw where Jesus was buried and went to the tomb (**Matthew 27:61; 28:1**; cf. **Mark 16:1–8; Luke 23:55–24:10; Luke 24:22–24**). Since Mary the mother of James and Joseph appears to be the same person as Mary the wife of Clopas, this makes her (Mary) the *sister-in-law* of Mary (Jesus' mother) and Joseph (see the chart above and note 4 below). Mary's husband, Clopas, is probably not the same person as Cleopas who encountered the risen Christ on the road to Emmaus (**Luke 24:18**; see **Mark 16:12**), nor is he the same person as Alphaeus, the father(s) of the disciples Matthew (Levi) and James (**Mark 2:14**; cf. **Acts 1:13**).[15]

Salome (Mark 15:40; cf. **16:1)**, called **his mother's [Mary's] sister (John 19:25)**, by harmonization of the Gospel accounts, refers to **the mother of Zebedee's sons** (i.e., James and John; **Matthew 20:20; 27:56**). According to the genealogy above (which is also supported by church tradition), Salome was the *sister* (not the sister-in-law) of Mary, the mother of Jesus (cf. **John 19:25**).[16]

"The disciple whom he [Jesus] loved" is the way in which the apostle John identifies himself in his Gospel (**John 13:23–25; 19:26; 20:2; 21:7, 20, 24**). John appears to have been the only one of the twelve apostles who was present at the crucifixion, which renders the passion narrative in his Gospel particularly valuable. Because Joseph (Jesus' earthly father) was deceased at that time—and possibly for various other reasons[17] as well—Jesus entrusted his mother, Mary, into John's care (**John 19:26–27**). From the genealogies, John (the son of Zebedee) appears to be Mary's *nephew* and Jesus' *first cousin*.[18]

Notes

1. These genealogies are based primarily on Scripture (as noted). In certain places, however, extrabiblical material (from the early accounts of the church fathers) is included to offer insights into the familial relationships. The reader is advised to evaluate the genealogies with that in mind.

2. The canonical Gospels convey important details about Joseph of Arimathea. Matthew identifies him as "a rich man" who had "become a disciple of Jesus" (**Matthew 27:57**; cf. **Isaiah 53:9**). Mark says he was "a prominent member of the [Sanhedrin] Council" who was himself "waiting for the kingdom of God" and "went boldly to Pilate and asked for Jesus' body" (**Mark 15:43**). Luke describes him as "a good and upright man who had not consented to their [Council] decision and action [regarding Jesus]" (**Luke 23:50–51**). John says that Joseph was a disciple of Jesus "but secretly because he feared the Jewish leaders." With Pilate's permission, Joseph of Arimathea "came and took the body [of Jesus] away" (**John 19:38**). Joseph of Arimathea purchased a linen shroud; together, he and Nicodemus took Jesus' body, prepared it for burial, and placed it in a "a new tomb [where no one had ever been laid]" in a garden near "the place where Jesus was crucified" (**John 19:38–42**; cf. **Matthew 27:60, Mark 15:46; 16:3–4; Luke 24:2**). Matthew confirms that Joseph placed Jesus' body "in his [Joseph's] own new tomb that he had cut out of the rock" (**Matthew 27:60**).

Joseph's hometown of Arimathea, identified as a "Judean town" (**Luke 23:51**), is most commonly associated with Ramathaim/Ramathaim Zophim (the longer form of Ramah) located in the hill country of Ephraim, about five miles north of Jerusalem (which was the hometown and burial site of Samuel; cf. **1 Samuel 1:1, 19; 28:3**). By asking Pilate for Jesus' body, Joseph publicly revealed to the Sanhedrin and other religious authorities that he was a disciple of Jesus; if Joseph had not requested the body, Jesus "would have been buried *that night* in the common grave with the malefactors for it was a law of the Jews that the body of an executed man should not remain on the cross on the Sabbath [**John 19:31**]" (Albert Barnes, *Barnes' Notes on the New Testament*, on **Mark 15:43**). The *IVP New Testament Background Commentary*, 2nd ed. by Craig S. Keener on **John 19:38** notes that "Roman authorities did sometimes hand over bodies to friends or relatives who desired to bury them." Joseph's boldness in requesting the body and Pilate's permission suggest that there was irrefutable ground by which Joseph had the legal right to receive the body. (The general scholarly consensus is that Joseph, Jesus' earthly father, was deceased at this time since he is last mentioned when Jesus is twelve years old; cf. **Luke 2:41–48**.). Apocryphal legend tells us that Joseph of Arimathea was the Virgin Mary's paternal uncle (http://www.earlybritishkingdoms.com/articles/josanc.html), which is consistent with the attestation by the Eastern (Orthodox) tradition that "Joseph of Arimathea is said to have been the younger brother of the father of the Virgin Mary." Richard W. Morgan, *St. Paul in Britain*, (Oxford and J. Parker & Co., 1880), footnote to pp. 138–39, https://babel.hathitrust.org/cgi/pt?id=mdp.39015062682078&view=1up&seq=146. For these reasons, Joseph of Arimathea is (tentatively) presented in the chart as the *brother* of Joachim, Mary's father.

3. If the account regarding the family of Mary, the mother of Jesus, in Charles Wheatly's *Rational Illustration of the Book of Common Prayer of the Church of England*, Sect. VII, 6 is reliable and correct, then Mary (the youngest daughter of Anne and Joachim) could have been named after "Mary" her aunt (Anne's eldest sister) or Mary (the wife of Matthan), her maternal grandmother. For the actual quote from this source and more information on the familial relationships, see chart "**Matthew 1**: Mary and Joseph (Based on Scripture and Church Tradition) and How Mary and Joseph May Have Been Related."

4. The exact identity of Clopas is unknown. However, based on the accounts from church tradition, Clopas is shown in the chart as:

(1) the *brother* (or possibly *half-brother or near relative*) of Joseph (Jesus' earthly father);
(2) the *husband* of Mary (i.e., the woman identified as "Mary the wife of Clopas" in **John 19:25**, although some scholars say that the text allows for the interpretation that Mary could have been the *daughter or niece* of Clopas rather than his wife); and,
(3) the *father* of James, Joseph, and Simeon/Symeon (i.e., siblings who were the first cousins of Jesus on his paternal side). Eusebius quotes the early ecclesiastical writer Hegesippus (ca. A.D. 110–180) as saying that "after James the Just [the brother of Jesus] had suffered martyrdom . . . Symeon, the son of the Lord's uncle, Clopas, was appointed the next bishop [of Jerusalem]. All proposed him as second bishop because he was a cousin of the Lord" (Eusebius, *Church History* 3.11; cf. 4.21–4:22).

In this and other charts, Clopas is interpreted to be a different person than: (1) Alphaeus (**Matthew 10:3; Mark 2:14; 3:18; Luke 6:15; Acts 1:13**), the name of the father (or the two different fathers?) of the apostles Levi/Matthew and James (see chart "**Matthew 9**: Matthew and James, the Apostles of Jesus"), and (2) Cleopas (**Luke 24:18**), one of the two disciples who met the risen Christ on the road to Emmaus (**Luke 24:13–32**). Also see note 12.

5. Comparing the three major accounts of people at the cross, "Mary the mother of James [the younger] and of Joseph" (**Matthew 27:56; Mark 15:40**) is likely the same person as "Mary the wife of Clopas" (**John 19:25**); therefore, that is the interpretation shown in the chart above. For Clopas, see note 6.

6. After the death of James (the Lord's half-brother), Clopas's son, Symeon (a variant of the name Simon (see Jon B. Daniels, "Symeon," Anchor Yale Bible Dictionary) succeeded James as the next leader of the Jerusalem church. The church historian Eusebius explains that, after the martyrdom of James in A.D. 62 and the Roman conquest of Jerusalem in A.D. 70, the apostles and disciples who were still living came together with some of Jesus' relatives (see note 9) to decide who would succeed James as the next leader of the Jerusalem church: "They all with one consent pronounced Symeon, the son of Clopas, of whom the Gospel also makes mention; to be worthy of the episcopal throne of that parish. He was a cousin, as they say, of the Saviour. For Hegesippus records that Clopas was a brother of Joseph." Thus, Symeon became "the second bishop of the church of Jerusalem," but "on the ground that he was a

descendant of David and a Christian . . . he suffered martyrdom, at the age of one hundred and twenty years, while Trajan was emperor [A.D. 98–117] and Atticus governor" (Eusebius, *Church History* 3.11, 32).

The *New Bible Dictionary* explains: "The first leadership of the [Jerusalem] church was by the twelve (Galilean) apostles, especially Peter and John [the son of Zebedee], but soon gave way to that of elders in the regular Jewish manner, with James the [half-] brother of Jesus as president (Galatians 2:9; Acts 15:6ff). The latter's presidency extended through most of the life of the Jerusalem church, possibly from as early as the thirties (Galatians 1:19; cf. Acts 12:17) until his [James's] execution ca. A.D. 62. It may well have been associated with the church's Messianic conceptions. 'The throne of David' was a much more literal hope among believing Jews than we commonly realize, and James was also 'of the house and lineage of David.' Was he thought of as a legitimate Protector, or Prince Regent, pending the return of Messiah in person? Eusebius reports that a cousin of Jesus, Simeon son of Clopas, succeeded James as president, and that Vespasian, after the capture of Jerusalem in A.D. 70, is said to have ordered a search to be made for all who were of the family of David, that there might be left among the Jews no-one of the royal family." Eusebius, *Church History* 3.11–12; D. W. B. Robinson, "The church at Jerusalem".

7. Joseph (**Matthew 27:56; Mark 15:40, 47** NIV) is called Joses in some translations (e.g., NKJV, ESV, ASV, NASB).

8. John the Baptist and Jesus were likely *second cousins*—since their mothers (Elizabeth and Mary, respectively) were first cousins and because John the Baptist and Jesus shared the same maternal great-grandparents (i.e., Matthan the priest and Mary his wife).

9. The extra-biblical literature uses the term *desposyni*—which means in Greek, "belonging to the Lord"—to refer to Jesus' blood relatives and their descendants. Two of the half-brothers of Jesus—James (**Acts 15:13–21; 21:18; Galatians 2:9**) and Judas/Jude (**Jude 1**)—became leaders in the early church, and "the Lord's brothers" were involved in the missionary activities and travels at the time of Paul (**1 Corinthians 9:5**). For more information about the *desposyni*, see note 2 in chart "**Matthew 1**: Jesus and His Immediate Family."

10. Because *Mary* was the most common female name in the period (James D. Tabor, *The Jesus Dynasty* [New York: Simon & Schuster, 2006], 25), the Gospel writers use terms of disambiguation to characterize the women named Mary, using such identifiers as their hometown (e.g., "Mary of Magdalene" of Magdala), their spouse (e.g., "Mary the wife of Clopas") or their children (e.g., "Mary, the mother of James and Joseph").

11. Mary Magdalene was the most prominent of the female disciples of Jesus. With the exception of **John 19:25**, she is mentioned first in every listing of the women who came alongside Jesus and the Twelve—**Luke 8:2–3** (traveling with Jesus); **Matthew 27:55–56; Mark 15:40–41** (at the crucifixion); **Matthew 27:61; Mark 15:47** (at his burial); **Matthew 28:1; Mark 16:1** (at the tomb); and **Luke 24:10** (as an eyewitness of the resurrection). Her genealogy is unknown. She is consistently identified by her hometown of Magdala. Mary Magdalene was among the wealthy women from Galilee "who had been cured of evil spirits and diseases"; specifically, she was the woman "from whom seven demons had come out" (**Luke 8:2**). Collectively these women acted as patrons for Jesus and his male disciples, supporting them "out of their own means" (**Luke 8:3**). According to **John 20:11–18**, the risen Christ appeared *first* to Mary Magdalene and talked with her about his ascension (**John 20:17**). However, she is noticeably absent in Paul's list of witnesses to the resurrection in **1 Corinthians 15:5–8**. Regrettably, in some traditions Mary Magdalene has been erroneously confused with the unnamed sinful woman with the alabaster jar in **Luke 7:36–50**.

12. Apparently, early Latin and Syriac versions confused Cleopas of **Luke 24:18** with the Clopas of **John 19:25**. Since "Mary the wife of Clopas" was present at the crucifixion in Jerusalem (**John 19:25**), her husband (Clopas) surely knew of the recent events there, so it is improbable that the follower of Jesus named "Cleopas" (an abbreviation of Cleopatros) in **Luke 24:18** (on the road to Emmaus) was the same person as Mary's husband, Clopas. As the *New Bible Dictionary* (R.V.G. Tasker, "*Clopas*") explains, "They [Clopas and Cleopas] were two different people with two distinct names . . . as *eo* was usually contracted into *ou* and not into *ō*." Additionally, Clopas in **John 19:25** (the husband of Mary) has been confused with Alphaeus (Gk. *Halphaios;* Aramaic *Halphai,*), the father(s) of the apostles Matthew/Levi and James (cf. **Matthew 10:3; Mark 2:14; 3:18; Acts 1:13**. For discussions on Alphaeus, see chart "**Matthew 9**: Matthew, the Apostle and Author of the Gospel of Matthew, and James the Apostle." In summary, Clopas, Cleopas, and Alphaeus should be considered three distinct and different men.

13. James/James the younger, the son of Mary and Clopas, should be distinguished from: (1) James the disciple, the son of Zebedee and the brother of John; see chart "**Matthew 4**: James and John, the Apostles of Jesus"; (2) James, the son of Alphaeus, who was a disciple (**Matthew 10:3; Mark 3:18; Luke 6:15; Acts 1:13**); see chart "**Matthew 9**: Matthew and James, the Apostles of Jesus"; and (3) James, the half-brother of Jesus; see chart "**Matthew 1**: Jesus and His Immediate Family."

14. It is interesting to note that, after Jesus' death, Mary the mother of Jesus *could have also been called* "the mother of James and Joseph" since she was widowed at the time of the crucifixion and had sons by those names also (i.e., Mary's sons by Joseph were James, Joseph/Joses, Simon, and Judas/Jude' cf. **Matthew 13:55; Mark 6:3; 1 Corinthians 15:7; Galatians 1:19; 2:9; Jude 1**); see chart "**Matthew 1**: Jesus and His Immediate Family." To be clear, however, there is no basis for suggesting that Mary (the mother of Jesus and the widow of Joseph) later married Clopas and became the figure called "Mary, the wife of Clopas" (**John 19:25**), for they are clearly distinct and separate women—"Near the cross of Jesus stood *his mother*, his mother's sister, *Mary the wife of Clopas* and Mary Magdalene" (**John 19:25**, emphasis added).

15. For Clopas, Cleopas, and Alphaeus, see notes 1 and 9 in chart "**Matthew 9**: Matthew and James, the Apostles of Jesus."

16. Also see chart "**Matthew 1**: Ancestry of Mary and Joseph (Based on Scripture and Church Tradition) and How Mary and Joseph May Have Been Related."

17. It seems that Jesus' half-brothers did not believe that Jesus was the Messiah until after the crucifixion (cf. **John 7:5; Acts 1:14**). The near blood-relatives of Jesus (called the *desposyni*; see note 9) became the target of persecution by the Jewish authorities and the Romans after Jesus' death (see Eusebius' *Church History* 3.11–12). By imparting the care of Mary (a widow) to John, instead of to Jesus' half-brothers, Jesus was likely protecting his mother.

18. See chart "**Matthew 1**: Ancestry of Mary and Joseph (Based on Scripture and Church Tradition) and How Mary and Joseph May Have Been Related."

MARK 1: MARK (JOHN) THE EVANGELIST AND THE AUTHOR OF THE GOSPEL OF MARK

Approximate Dating: ca. A.D. 30–65 ***Relevant Scriptures:*** **Mark 1:1; Acts 4:36; 12:12, 25; 13:5, 13; 15:37–39; Colossians 4:10**

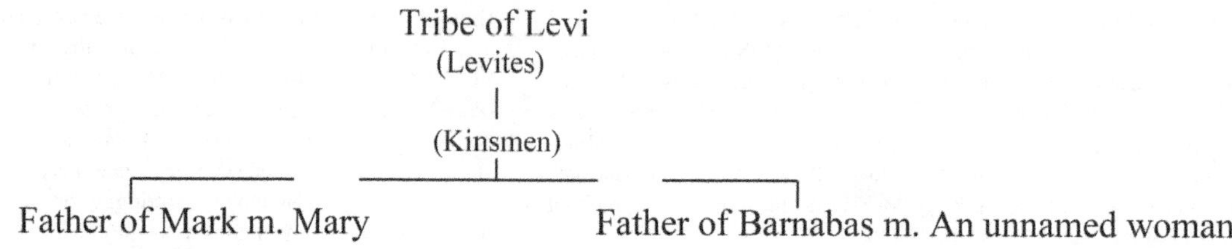

Father of Mark m. Mary
(Presumably deceased) | (Mother of Mark)

Mark/John
(John Mark)
(Cousin of Barnabas)

Father of Barnabas m. An unnamed woman

Barnabas
(Joseph)

Biblical and Theological Significance

Mark, the author of the Gospel that bears his name, was *not* one of the twelve apostles. Mark was most likely a close associate of the apostle Peter. According to tradition, Peter served as the primary eyewitness source for Mark's Gospel.[1] Also, Mark was associated with the apostle Paul at the beginning and the end of Paul's ministry. By his affiliation with both Peter and Paul, Mark provides a unique link between these two towering figures in the early Christian mission.

Mark—also called "John" or "John/Mark" (cf. **Acts 12:12, 25**)—was probably a young man from a wealthy family (i.e., a family with servants, like Rhoda; **Acts 12:12–13**), who lived near Herod's Temple. Mark's father appears to be deceased, making his mother, Mary, a widow. When Peter was imprisoned by Herod Agrippa I, people assembled near the temple and "went to the house of Mary the mother of John, also called Mark" to pray for Peter's release (**Acts 12:12**). Given that Mark was a *cousin* of Barnabas (**Colossians 4:10**) and that Barnabas (given the name "Joseph") was a Levite (**Acts 4:36**), this means that Mark was likewise of Levitical heritage also, corroborating Paul's statement that Mark was a Jew (**Colossians 4:10–11**). Luke says that Barnabas was from Cyprus (**Acts 4:36**); it is possible that Mark's family originated from Cyprus as well.

Scholars have suggested that Mark is perhaps the "young man, wearing nothing but a linen garment" who "fled naked, leaving his garment behind" after witnessing Jesus' arrest in the Garden of Gethsemane (**Mark 14:51–52**).

Mark accompanied Paul and Barnabas (his cousin) on Paul's first missionary journey to Galatia and Asia Minor in ca. A.D. 47–48. However, while in Perga in the province of Pamphylia, Mark deserted them and returned home to Jerusalem (**Acts 13:13**). Toward the end of his life, Paul forgave Mark for his defection; in writing to Timothy, Paul says "Get Mark and bring him with you, because he is helpful to me in my ministry" (**2 Timothy 4:11**). Mark's restoration to ministry serves as an example of God's gracious forgiveness toward those who struggle and fail. Mark was present as a "fellow worker" with Paul during Paul's imprisonment in Rome, serving alongside Aristarchus, Demas, and Luke (**Philemon 24**). Mark is also thought to have worked closely with Peter and derived much of the information for his Gospel directly from him. In **1 Peter 5:13**, Peter called Mark "my son [in the faith]."

Many scholars believe that Mark's Gospel was the first to be written, most likely prior to the destruction of the temple in A.D. 70 and perhaps as early as the mid-to-late 50s. In his Gospel, Mark often translates and explains Hebrew and Aramaic words for his Gentile readership (e.g., **Mark 3:17; 5:41; 7:11, 34; 10:46; 14:36**). The **Gospel of Mark** is composed in common Greek, suggesting that Mark was educated, albeit not necessarily in a formal rabbinic school like Paul (cf. **Acts 22:3**). According to tradition, Mark founded the church in Alexandria; in *Church History* Eusebius says, "When Nero was in the eighth year of his reign [ca. A.D. 62] Annianus succeeded Mark the Evangelist in the administration of the parish of Alexandria" (*Church History*, 2.24.1).

Notes

1. Eusebius writes in his *Church History* that "Mark, having become the interpreter of Peter, wrote down accurately, though not in order, whatsoever he remembered of the things said or done by Christ. For he neither heard the Lord nor followed him, but afterward, as I said, he followed Peter, who adapted his teaching to the needs of his hearers, but with no intention of giving a connected account of the Lord's discourses, so that Mark committed no error while he thus wrote some things as he remembered them. For he was careful of one thing, not to omit any of the things which he had heard, and not to state any of them falsely. These things are related by Papias concerning Mark" (*Church History* 3.39.15).

LUKE 1: LUKE, THE AUTHOR OF THE GOSPEL OF LUKE AND THE ACTS OF THE APOSTLES

Approximate Dating: ca. A.D. 25–65 ***Relevant Scriptures:*** **Luke 1:1–2**

A Gentile from Antioch of Syria

Luke

Biblical and Theological Significance

Luke wrote the two-volume work **Luke/Acts**, which, in terms of word count, comprises an entire quarter of the New Testament. He was a physician (**Colossians 4:14**) and the close friend, traveling companion, and chronicler of Paul. Luke does not appear to have been married. He was not one of the original followers or eyewitnesses of Jesus' ministry, but after "carefully investigat[ing]" and searching out original sources, he wrote an "orderly account" of the things that were handed down by those who "from the first were eyewitnesses and servants of the word" (**Luke 1:2–3**). He wrote to tell the story of Jesus, explaining how Gentiles and Jews were inheritors of the promises of salvation and affirming that Jesus was Lord of all (**Acts 10:36, 45; 11:18–24**). Luke emphasized Jesus' healing and inclusiveness, his compassion for sinners, and the role of women in his ministry. Only from Luke do we know that Elizabeth and Mary were "relatives" (**Luke 1:36**). He probably wrote both his Gospel and the sequel, Acts, prior to A.D. 70, as neither book mentions the destruction of the temple in Jerusalem that occurred in that year (cf. **Luke 21:20; Acts 1:1**).

Paul refers to Luke as a "doctor" and his friend and fellow worker in the kingdom of God (cf. **Colossians 4:14; 2 Timothy 4:11; Philemon 24**). In writing to the church at Colossae, Paul mentions that his only *Jewish* coworkers were Aristarchus, Mark (the cousin of Barnabas), and Jesus (Justus), which seems to imply that Luke was Gentile[1] and not an ethnic Jew "of the circumcision" (**Colossians 4:10–14;** cf. **Titus 1:10**). Early sources and church tradition uphold that Luke was Greek, although the circumstances of his conversion are not recounted in Scripture.

The book of Acts chronicles the progress of the Christian gospel from Jerusalem to Judea and Samaria and to the far outposts of the Roman Empire (**Acts 1:8**). The so-called we-passages in Acts most likely indicate that Luke joined Paul on several of his missionary travels:[2] from Troas to Philippi (**Acts 16:8–17**), from Philippi to Troas to Miletus (**Acts 20:5–15**), from Miletus to Jerusalem via Caesarea (**Acts 21:1–18**), and from Caesarea to Rome (**Acts 27:1–28:16**). During his second Roman imprisonment, Paul wrote: "Only Luke is with me" (**2 Timothy 4:11**). Luke was closely associated with Paul throughout his ministry and was a vital and integral part in the early Christian mission.

Notes

1. The early church fathers Jerome (ca. A.D. 347–420) and Eusebius (ca. A.D. 260–340) claimed that Luke was of "Antiochian parentage," meaning he was from Antioch in ancient Syria, as opposed to Antioch of Pisidia in Asia Minor; Alfred Plummer, *Critical and Exegetical Commentary on the Gospel According to S. Luke*, (Edinburgh: T. & T. Clark, 1922), xxi and *Eusebius' Ecclesiastical History* 3.4. Syrian Antioch was intimately connected with the history of the apostolic church; from there, Paul began his first three missionary journeys. Luke frequently refers to Antioch (**Acts 11:19–27; 13:1; 14:26; 15:22–23, 30, 35; 18:22–23**), and it was the place where believers were first called Christians (**Acts 11:26**).

2. See chart "**Acts 7**: Paul the Apostle (Also Called Saul of Tarsus)."

LUKE 1: ELIZABETH AND ZECHARIAH AND JOHN THE BAPTIST

Approximate Dating: parents lived ca. 50 B.C.–A.D. 10; John lived ca. 3 B.C.–A.D. 32 ***Relevant Scriptures:*** **Luke 1:5, 36; 3:2, 23–38;** also **Exodus 6:20; 1 Chronicles 3:1–24; 24:1–2, 7–18; Ezra 3:2, 8; 5:2; Nehemiah 12:1; Haggai 1:1, 12, 14; 2:2, 23; Matthew 1:1–16**

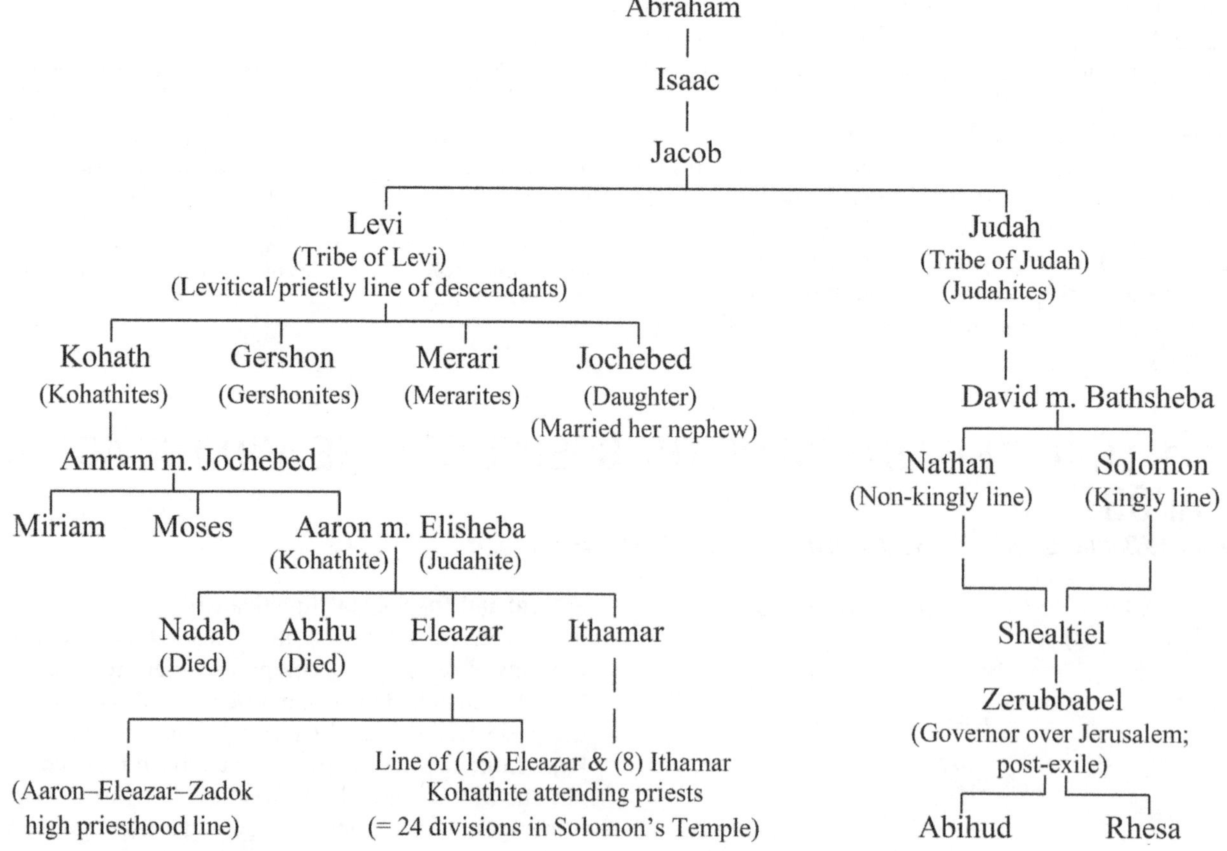

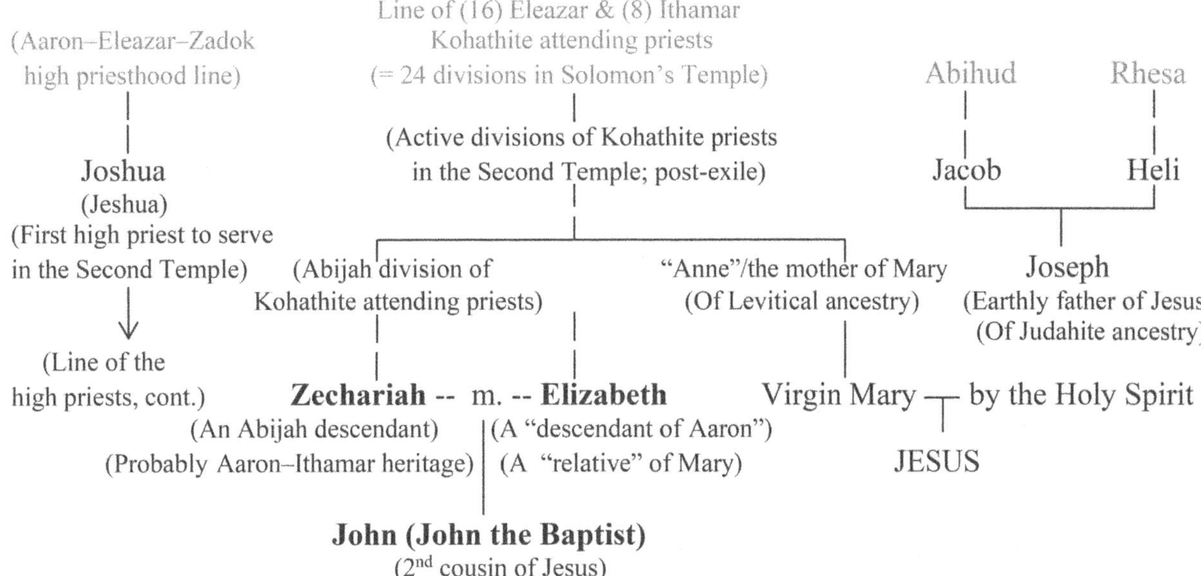

Biblical and Theological Significance

John the Baptist was the forerunner of Jesus—"a voice of one calling in the wilderness, 'Prepare the way for the Lord'" (**Matthew 3:3; Mark 1:2–3; Luke 3:4**; see **Isaiah 40:3;** cf. **Matthew 11:10; Luke 1:76; 7:27**). John's calling was utterly unique in salvation history because he alone had the privilege of heralding the coming of the Messiah to Israel and to the world. As a result, all four Gospels start their account of Jesus' life and ministry with the ministry of John the Baptist. In his humility, John serves as an example of Christian ministry that points away from the messenger to the message and person of Jesus Christ. John fulfilled his mission to call the Jewish people to repentance through baptism and to prepare for the coming of the Messiah, the Lord Jesus Christ.

John the Baptist's Ancestry

John the Baptist was a Levite (a descendant of Levi) and a Kohathite (from the Kohathite clan of priests). The Kohathite clan included both high priests and Kohathite attending priests (i.e., those who assisted the high priests). The first high priest of Israel, Aaron (the son of Amram, son of Kohath, son of Levi), married Elisheba (the daughter of Aminadab and sister of Nahshon, from the tribe of Judah; **Exodus 6:23**); consequentially, from that point onward, all high priests and attending priests were of mixed Levite-Judahite heritage. The priestly line of Aaron's descendants continued through his sons, Eleazar and Ithamar—thereafter, the exclusive high priest line passed in father–son succession from either the Aaron–Eleazar–Phinehas–Zadok–Jozadak–Joshua (Jeshua) line (called the Aaronic priesthood)[1] or from the Aaron–Ithamar–Eli–Abiathar line, and so forth (called the Eli priesthood).[2] In contrast, Kohathite *attending* priests (who were *near relatives* of the high priests) were chosen from either the Aaron–Eleazar line or the Aaron–Ithamar line.[3] John the Baptist and his ancestors were in the line of the Kohathite priests.

John's Parents–Elizabeth and Zechariah

Elizabeth and Zechariah were both of Aaronic priestly descent (**Luke 1:5**). They were "very old" when John was born (**Luke 1:7, 18**), so it is likely that they died before John began his ministry. Zechariah was an *Kohathite attending* priest in Herod's Temple "in the time of Herod [the Great] king of Judea" (37–4? B.C. or 35–1 B.C.; **Luke 1:5**).[4] In his regularly priestly rotation, Zechariah was chosen to burn incense at the altar of incense (**Luke 1:8–11**), and he was a member of the "Abijah division"[5] (**Luke 1:5**), the eighth of the twenty-four divisions (courses) of Kohathite attending priests that had been established in the days of King David (**1 Chronicles 24:10**; see **vv. 7–18**). Moreover, it can be discerned from the orderly pattern of casting of lots to choose the priestly division heads that the Abijah division constituted the Kohathite attending priests from the Aaron–Ithamar line (i.e., a faithful remnant of the Eli priesthood), rather than Kohathite priests from the Aaron–Eleazar Aaronic priesthood.[6]

Elizabeth (like her husband) "was also a descendant of Aaron" (**Luke 1:5**), either in the Kohathite high priestly line (i.e., the Aaron–Eleazar–Zadok lineage) or in the Kohathite attending priestly line.[7] Moreover, Elizabeth was a "relative" of Mary, the mother of Jesus (meaning they were in the same kinship group; **Luke 1:36**). Since both Zechariah and Elizabeth were from the tribe of Levi, the lineage of Elizabeth presents the strongest direct evidence that Mary was of priestly Aaronic ancestry also, probably through her mother (Anne)—meaning Mary was of Levitical heritage on her maternal side and of Judahite heritage on her paternal side (via Joachim); this is consistent with the familial relationships that are described and portrayed in the extra-biblical literature.[8] Furthermore, the kinship relationship of Elizabeth and Mary establishes that Jesus and John the Baptist were relatives also, probably second cousins.[9]

John's Ministry

John was "sent from God" (**John 1:6**) and was "filled with the Holy Spirit even before he [was] born" (**Luke 1:15**). His parents raised him as a Nazirite; he partook of no "wine or other fermented drink" (**Luke 1:15**; cf. **Numbers 6:2–21; Judges 13:4–5, 7, 13–14; 16:17; Amos 2:11–12**). John was about six months older than Jesus (**Luke 1:36**). According to **Luke 3:1–2**, John began his ministry in A.D. 29, "in the fifteenth year of the reign of Tiberius Caesar,"[10] when Pilate was governor over Judea,[11] Herod Philip II and Herod Antipas held tetrarchies,[12] and Annas and Caiaphas held the high priesthood[13] (spanning approximately A.D. 6–36/37). John "testified" concerning Jesus (**John 1:6–8, 15; 5:33**), characterizing him as "the Lamb of God, who takes away the sin of the world" (**John 1:29**; cf. **v. 36**). Jesus, in turn, declared: "I tell you, among those born of women there is no one greater than John" (**Luke 7:28**; cf. **Matthew 11:11**). Jesus referred to John the Baptist as "my messenger" (**Matthew 11:10**; cf. **Malachi 3:1**) and "a lamp that burned and gave light," thus shining the way to the true light of the world (**John 5:35**; cf. **1:9; 8:12; 9:5**). Jesus identified John as "the Elijah who was to come" who had been prophesied by Malachi and who would be the forerunner of the Messiah (**Matthew 11:14**; cf. **Malachi 4:5; Mark 9:13; Luke 1:17**). The religious authorities in Jerusalem thought that John might be the Messiah, but John denied being the Christ, Elijah, or the Prophet (**John 1:19–27**). John (the Baptist)[14] baptized with water and called people to repent and prepare for Jesus' coming. John publicly denounced Herod Antipas's illegitimate marriage to his brother Philip's wife[15] (**Matthew 14:3; Mark 6:17–18**). In retaliation, Herod Antipas imprisoned John (**Luke 3:19–20**) and, later, at the request of Herodias' daughter, Salome,[16] had John beheaded in ca. A.D. 32[17] (**Matthew 14:6–12; Mark 6:14–29**).

Notes

1. For more on the esteemed Aaron–Eleazar (Aaronic) high priestly line, see chart "**Supplement 2**: The High Priests of Israel."

2. For more on the Aaron–Ithamar (Elide) high priestly line, see chart "**1 Samuel 1**: Eli and the Eli Priesthood."

3. For more on the Kohathite attending priests and the distinction between the Aaron–Eleazar and Aaron–Ithamar lines, see chart "**1 Chronicles 24**: Genealogical Registry of the Twenty-Four Divisions of Kohathite Attending Priests Who Rotated Service in Solomon's Temple."

4. See chart "**Matthew 2**: Herod the Great and the Herodian Dynasty."

5. In the Old Testament, the heads of the Abijah division all carried the "Abijah" name: (1) the ancestral "Abijah" priest who was appointed in the days of King David, ca. 971 B.C. (**1 Chronicles 24:10**); (2) "Abijah" (an office holder) who returned to Jerusalem with Zerubbabel in ca. 538 B.C. (**Nehemiah 12:1, 4**); and (3) "Abijah" the priest who signed the covenant with Nehemiah in Jerusalem in ca. 444 B.C. (**Nehemiah 10:7**), who is probably the same person as Abijah #2. Also, a priestly descendant from the Abijah division named Zikri was active "in the days of Joiakim [the high priest]" in ca. 490–450/444 B.C. (**Nehemiah 12:12, 17**); therefore, Zikri may also be an ancestor of Zechariah and John the Baptist.

6. The order of the casting of lots—done by alternating between the Aaron–Eleazar line and then the Aaron–Ithamar line—to choose the twenty-four priestly division heads suggests that the Abijah division constituted Kohathite attending priests from the Aaron–Ithamar line (i.e., a faithful remnant of the Eli priesthood, rather than Kohathite priests from the Aaron–Eleazar line). For more details, see chart "**1 Chronicles 24**: Genealogical Registry of the Twenty-Four Divisions of Kohathite Attending Priests Who Rotated Service in Solomon's Temple." Also, see note 2 about Zechariah in chart "**1 Chronicles 9**: The Kohathite Attending Priests in the Second Temple (Post-Exile)."

7. Note that, remarkably, it was Elizabeth, not her husband Zechariah the priest, who pronounced the blessing on Mary, the mother of Jesus in **Luke 1:42**. For more information about Elizabeth's heritage that incorporates material from the extrabiblical literature, see chart "**Matthew 1**: Ancestry of Mary and Joseph (Based on Scripture and Church Tradition) and How Mary and Joseph May Have Been Related."

8. See chart "**Matthew 1**: Ancestry of Mary and Joseph (Based on Scripture and Church Tradition) and How Mary and Joseph May Have Been Related."

9. See chart "**Matthew 1**: Ancestry of Mary and Joseph (Based on Scripture and Church Tradition) and How Mary and Joseph May Have Been Related."

10. See chart "**Supplement 10**: The Roman Emperors."

11. See chart "**Supplement 13**: Roman Rulers of Judea and Galilee."

12. See chart "**Matthew 2**: Herod the Great and the Herodian Dynasty."

13. See chart "**Matthew 26**: The Influential Family of Annas and Caiaphas, the High Priests."

14. This appellation is given in **Matthew 3:1; 11:11–12; 14:2, 8; 16:14; 17:13; Mark 1:4; 6:14, 24–25; 8:28; Luke 7:33; 9:19**.

15. See chart "**Matthew 2**: Herod the Great and the Herodian Dynasty."

16. The daughter of Herodias is unnamed in Scripture, but Josephus identifies her as *Salome*, the stepdaughter of Herod Antipas (*Jewish Antiquities* 18.5.4). For Josephus' account of John's imprisonment and his death at the fortress of Macherus, see ibid. 18.5.2. The scheme to have John executed was initiated more by Herodias than her daughter Salome (cf. **Matthew 14:8; Mark 6:19, 24**).

17. Steinmann notes that both Matthew and Mark place the death of John the Baptist just before the Feeding of the 5000 (Nisan of A.D. 32) and concludes that John was beheaded in *Tebeth* of A.D. 32. See Andrew E. Steinmann, *From Abraham to Paul: A Biblical Chronology* (St. Louis: Concordia, 2011), 258, 267–68.

LUKE 3: JESUS: THE LUKAN ACCOUNT

Approximate Dating: Luke's writing ca. A.D. 60–62 ***Relevant Scriptures:*** **Luke 3:23–38**

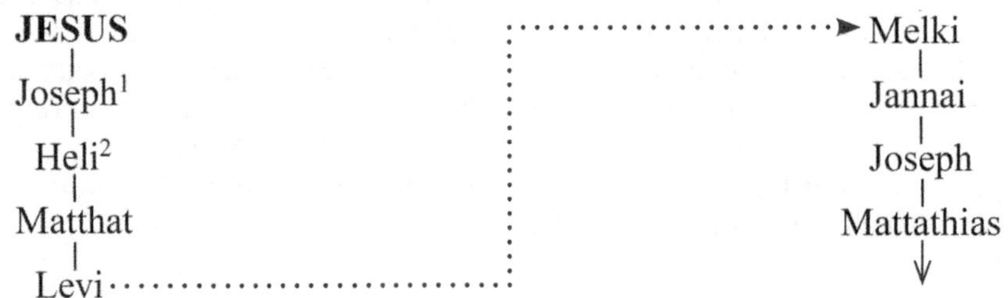

Amos[3]
Nahum
Esli
Naggai
Maath
Mattathias
Semein[4]
Josek
Joda
Joanan
Rhesa[5]
Zerubbabel
-------------- Shealtiel --------------
Neri
Melki
Addi
Cosam
Elmadam
Er
Joshua
Eliezer
Jorim
Matthat
Levi
Simeon
Judah
Joseph
Jonam
Eliakim
Melea
Menna
Mattatha
Nathan[6] .... → David

-------------- David --------------
Jesse
Obed
Boaz
Salmon[7]
Nahshon
Amminadab
Ram
Hezron
Perez
Judah
Jacob
Isaac
-------------- Abraham --------------
Terah
Nahor
Serug
Reu
Peleg
Eber
Shelah
(Cainan)[8]
Arphaxad
Shem
Noah
Lamech
Methuselah
Enoch[9]
Jared
Mahalalel
Kenan
Enosh
Seth
Adam
God

Biblical and Theological Significance

Together with Matthew's genealogy, Luke's genealogy provides an indispensable account of the ancestry of Jesus Christ. While Matthew's genealogy is found at the beginning of his Gospel, Luke's genealogy is found at the end of his introduction (**Luke 1:1–3:22**). Also, while Matthew traces Jesus' lineage back to Abraham, accentuating that Jesus was the Jewish Messiah, Luke traces Jesus' lineage back to Adam, emphasizing Jesus' mission for all of humanity. In this way, both genealogies make a vital contribution not only to our understanding of the physical descent of Jesus, but also to our grasp of the respective theological emphases of these two evangelists.

Distinctive Features of Luke's Genealogy

The genealogy of Luke traces the *patrilineal* descent of Jesus through Joseph, his earthly father (**Luke 3:23**; cf. **Matthew 13:55; Mark 6:3; John 1:45**), *not* the lineage of Jesus through his mother, Mary. Luke's genealogy displays several distinctive characteristics.

(1) The placement of the genealogy after the infancy narratives (**Luke 1:5–2:52**) and Jesus' baptism and empowering by the Holy Spirit (**Luke 3:21–22**), in effect, announces the beginning of Jesus' public ministry, which began when he was "about thirty years old" (**Luke 3:23**). This subtle detail reveals Jesus' eligibility to be a priest and king. For example, Aaron's sons could not enter the priesthood or serve in the tabernacle until they were thirty years old (**Numbers 4:3, 23, 30, 35, 39, 43, 47**); Joseph, the son of Jacob, "entered the service of Pharaoh king of Egypt" at age thirty (**Genesis 41:46**); Saul and David began to rule at age thirty (**1 Samuel 13:1; 2 Samuel 5:4**, respectively); and priests and Levites were eligible to serve in Solomon's Temple at age thirty (**1 Chronicles 23:2–3**).

(2) The list of Jesus' ancestors is arranged in *descending* order (in son-to-father succession) in a historical sequence that begins with Jesus (**Luke 3:23**) and moves back in time to Adam, the son of God (**Luke 3:38**). This contrasts with the *ascending* order of Jesus' ancestors (from father-to-son) as presented in Matthew's genealogy (**Matthew 1:1–17**).

(3) The entire genealogy can be viewed from the perspective of the first and last person named. Luke's account begins with Jesus—"He was the son, so it was thought, of Joseph" (**Luke 3:23**), immediately drawing suspicion as to Jesus' true identity. Luke's phrasing hints that some saw Jesus as illegitimate (cf. **Luke 8:41**). Luke concludes the genealogy by calling Adam "the son of God" (**Luke 3:38**), thereby establishing literary bracketing (pairing) of the two figures. The *inclusio* underscores a major theme developed in Luke's Gospel—that Jesus was both the "Son of God" (**Luke 1:35; 4:3, 9, 41; 8:28; 22:70**) and the "Son of Man" (**Luke 5:24; 6:5, 22; 7:34; 9:22, 26, 44, 58; 11:30; 12:8, 10, 40; 17:22, 24, 26, 30; 18:8, 31; 19:10; 21:27, 36; 22:22, 48, 69; 24:7**) and validates Paul's claim that Jesus was the "last Adam" (**1 Corinthians 15:45**).

(4) Luke's genealogy is the most exhaustive *linear* genealogy that occurs in Scripture. Whereas oral tradition would have preserved the names of an average of twelve generations,[10] Luke's expansive list of seventy-seven names shows that he was drawing upon historically reliable, *written* sources, such as: (1) ancient pre-Mosaic/Mosaic and/or scribal genealogies, like those found in **Genesis 5:3–32; 11:10–32;** and **1 Chronicles 1:1–4:23** or (2) possibly official, archived Second Temple records and/or private genealogies kept by certain pious families.[11] The fact that Luke had access to written documents demonstrates that Israelite society valued and preserved the genealogies and recorded them with the highest degree of accuracy.

(5) The genealogical composition is strictly *linear* in form—exhibiting maximal depth without any segmentation (branching). Genealogical links are given for every one of Jesus' ancestors, thereby establishing an uninterrupted, unambiguous sequence of Jesus' predecessors. In this way Luke offers a single, definitive account of Jesus' heritage.

(6) Kinship relationships are expressed inherently as "*x* the son of *y*" (i.e., *x* is the biological son—or possibly the son-in-law, levirate son, adopted son, or legal heir—and *y* is the father). Interestingly, Luke's account is similar in style to royal genealogies of the ancient Near East, where Luke presents a kind of "kings list" formula for assigning the kinship relationships: RN1—the son of RN2—the son of RN3, and so forth (where RN = royal name).[12]

(7) The chronicle of seventy-seven names (inclusive of God's name, **Luke 3:38**)—a multiple of the sacred number seven—has a discernible substructure. In reverse order, the genealogy delineates twenty-one names from God to Abraham (omitting Cainan), fourteen names from Abraham to David (inclusive), twenty-one names from Nathan to Shealtiel (inclusive), and twenty-one names from Shealtiel to Joseph, showing that the subsections are based on the sacred number seven also. The subsections correspond to four major eras of Israel's history:

- Creation–flood–pre-patriarchal era (Adam to Abraham)
- Patriarchal period to the time of the kings (Abraham to David; names in this section are identical to those found in **Matthew 1:2–6**.)
- Era of the Davidic–Nathan descendants and generations leading to the exile (Nathan to Shealtiel)
- Exile through the post-exile and Second Temple period (Shealtiel to Joseph)

Given the expansive historical sequence of the genealogy, Luke emphasizes, both directly and indirectly, that the birth and ministry of Jesus was foreordained from the "beginning" of creation (**Genesis 1:1**).

(8) The genealogical composition begins and ends with a parallel idea. The overall literary structure of the composition is arranged as follows: *a—b—c—d—e—f—a'*

Legend

a represents Jesus, "the son, so it was thought, of Joseph" (**Luke 3:23**), but Luke shows that Jesus was indeed the "Son of God" (**Luke 1:35; 4:3, 9, 41; 22:70**).

b—c represents the generations from Joseph to Shealtiel

c—d represents the generations from Shealtiel to David

d—e represents the generations from David to Abraham

e—f represents the generations from Abraham to Adam

a' represents Adam, who was the "son of God" (**Luke 3:38**)

(9) To begin, in **Luke 3:23** Luke uses the simple designation "Jesus" (meaning *Savior*)—the Greek New Testament equivalent of the Old Testament Hebrew name *Joshua*—to identify him. In this way, Luke emphasizes that Jesus took on human form, was given a common name found among first-century Jews (cf. **Matthew 1:21; Acts 13:6; Colossians 4:11**), and that he came "in the likeness of sinful flesh" (**Romans 8:3**; cf. **Genesis 1:26; 5:1; Philippians 2:6–8**). Therefore, Luke demonstrates that this Man (seemingly just another human being) was in fact the *Son of God* and the *last Adam*, the "life-giving spirit" who would save humanity from sin (**1 Corinthians 15:45**; see also **Matthew 1:21; John 1:29; Acts 13:39; Romans 5:18–21; 6:4–11**). The simple title used by Luke ("Jesus") can be contrasted to the more formal titles used by Matthew: "Jesus the Messiah the son of David, the son of Abraham" (**Matthew 1:1**) and "Jesus who is called the Messiah" (**Matthew 1:16**).

(10) Luke's genealogy lists no women, not even Jesus' mother Mary. Although Luke is sympathetic to women in his Gospel (cf. **Luke 7:36–50; 8:2–3, 40–56; 10:38–42; 11:27–28; 13:10–13; 18:1–8; 21:1–4; 23:27–28, 49; 24:1, 22–24**), he restricts the genealogy to enumerate only male ancestors of Jesus, thereby tracing strictly the *patrilineal* heritage of Jesus.

(11) In contrast to Matthew, who traces the *royal* line of kings between Solomon and Jeconiah/Jehoiachin (**Matthew 1:7–12**), Luke traces the lineage of Jesus through the descendants of Nathan, Solomon's brother (i.e., the *non-royal* line; **Luke 3:27–31**). When the genealogies of Matthew and Luke are viewed in parallel from the time of the Davidic monarchy to the birth of Jesus, they reveal an overall symmetrical *chiastic* pattern and a *double line* of the Messiah that passes through Solomon and Nathan, two of the four sons of David and Bathsheba.[13]

(12) Two important ancestors of Jesus who lived at the time of the exile—Shealtiel[14] and Zerubbabel[15]—are common to the genealogies of Luke and Matthew (cf. **Matthew 1:12; Luke 3:27**).

Notes

1. "Joseph" (Heb. יוֹסֵף) is a hypocoristic name meaning "(Yah) added," a predictive way of recalling the promise to Abraham that his offspring would be as numerous as "the stars in the sky" and "the sand on the seashore" (**Genesis 22:17**). Note that the name "Joseph" was the name of at least three ancestors of Jesus: (1) Joseph the son of Heli (**Luke 3:23**); (2) Joseph the son of Mattathias (**Luke 3:24–25**); (3) Joseph the son of Jonan (**Luke 3:30**), and possibly also Josek the son of Joda (**Luke 3:26**, translated "Joseph, the son of Juda(h)" in the KJV/NKJV). Jesus' earthly father is called "Joseph son of David," signifying that he was a descendant of King David (cf. **Matthew 1:20**). At the time of the Roman census that was decreed near the time of Jesus' birth (**Luke 2:1**), Luke stresses that Joseph "went up from the town of Nazareth in Galilee to Judea, to Bethlehem the [ancestral] town of David, because he [Joseph] belonged to the house and line of David" (**Luke 2:4–5**). Thus, Jesus was born, not in Nazareth, but in Bethlehem of Judea (also called "Bethlehem Ephrathah" or "Ephrath"; **Genesis 35:16, 19; 48:7;** named after Caleb's wife Ephrath; **1 Chronicles 2:19**), thus fulfilling the prophesy of Micah (**Micah 5:2**; cf. **Matthew 2:1–8; Luke 2:4, 15**).

In its basic meaning, the word "son" (Hebrew *ben*) refers to a biological son, an offspring (or a descendant) of the father or mother, but it can also be related to the Hebrew word *banah*, meaning "to build/build up/rebuild," thus conveying the process by which multiple offspring and generations *build up* a house, a family line, a family name, and a family dynasty (cf. **Ruth 4:11; 1 Peter 2:4–5**). Moreover, the term *house* often connotes the *family living in the house* rather than the actual building itself (as in **Genesis 16:2; 30:3; Deuteronomy 25:9**; cf. **Matthew 3:9; 1 Peter 2:5**). [For the association between *ben* (son) (H1121) and *banah* (to build) (H1129), see James Strong, *Hebrew Strong's Dictionary*; A.R. Hulst, *Theological Lexicon of the Old Testament (Jenni-Westermann)*, Accordance Bible Software; and Francis Brown, S. R. Driver, and Charles A. Briggs, *The Brown-Driver-Briggs Hebrew and English Lexicon* (based on the lexicon of William Gesenius) (Peabody, MA: Hendrickson, 2015), 119–122, 124–125.]

Collectively, the recurring references to "Joseph" in Luke's genealogy connotes the *progressive building up* of a literal family of believers and a spiritual house (a spiritual family of believers). By sending his Son, God restores the proper "Father–Son–children of God" relationship (cf. **Exodus 4:22; Deuteronomy 14:1; Jeremiah 3:19; Hosea 11:1**). God declared to David through the prophet Nathan: "'I declare to you that the Lord will build a house for you: When your days are over and you go to be with your ancestors, I will raise up your offspring [Solomon] to succeed you, one of your own sons, and I will establish his kingdom. He is the one who will build a house for me [a royal dynasty], and I will establish his throne forever. I will be his father, and he will be my son . . . I will set him over my house and my kingdom forever; his throne will be established forever'" (**1 Chronicles 17:10–14**). The Old and New Testament writers explain that the words about Solomon foreshadow the coming of God's Son, Jesus, and the *building up* of a family of believers, the church (cf. **1 Kings 11:38; 1 Chronicles 22:10; Jeremiah 23:5; 24:1–7; 31:3–4; 33:15–22; Zechariah 6:12; Matthew 16:18; 21:42; Luke 1:32–33; Romans 4:13–18; 8:14–17; 1 Corinthians 3:9; Galatians 3:7–9, 16, 29; Ephesians 2:21**).

2. Luke identifies the father of Joseph as Heli (the Greek form of the Hebrew name *Eli*; **Luke 3:23**), whereas Matthew identifies the father of Joseph as Jacob (**Matthew 1:15–16**). The two different names for the father of Joseph have confounded scholars and given rise to a myriad of interpretations. Yet when the genealogies of Matthew and Luke are charted side-by-side (at least for the generations from King David to Joseph), an overall symmetrical *chiastic* (the Greek letter *chi* or *X*) pattern becomes apparent, and the actual relationship of Heli and Jacob as biological (uterine) brothers can be discerned. See chart "**1 Chronicles 3**: Zerubbabel and Shealtiel and the Double Line of the Messiah through King David's Sons, Nathan and Solomon" for the side-by-side presentation of the ancestry; also, see the information given by Julius Africanus about Heli and Jacob in chart "**Matthew 1**: Ancestry of Mary and Joseph (Based on Scripture and Church Tradition) and How Mary and Joseph May Have Been Related."

3. Amos the prophet (**Amos 1:1**) could possibly be the Amos figure in **Luke 3:25**. Luke's genealogy shows Amos to be ten generations removed from Jesus (who was born ca. 3/2 B.C.). If each generation represents 70–80 years (cf. **Psalm 90:10**), then ten generations would correspond to approximately 700–800 years, roughly equivalent to the period when Amos the Old Testament prophet prophesied (ca. 767–753 B.C.).

4. Semein in **Luke 3:26** is the Greek form of the Hebrew personal name "Shimei" (cf. **Exodus 6:17; Numbers 3:18**).

5. Rhesa (ca. 500–450 B.C.) is called the *son* of Zerubbabel in Luke's genealogy (**Luke 3:27**), whereas in Matthew's genealogy, Abihud is said to be the *son* of Zerubbabel (**Matthew 1:13**). It is possible that they were biological/uterine brothers, but it is also possible that *either* Rhesa or Abihud was the husband of Shelomith (Zerubbabel's daughter), thus making him the *son-in-law* (not the *biological* son) of Zerubbabel.

6. The Nathan in Luke's genealogy (**Luke 3:31**) was the son of David and Bathsheba. He should not be confused with Nathan the prophet, who was a contemporary of David.

7. Boaz's father is called Salmon in **Ruth 4:20–21; 1 Chronicles 2:11; Matthew 1:4–5;** and **Luke 3:32** and Salma in **1 Chronicles 2:51, 54**.

8. The inclusion of Cainan in Luke's genealogy has been questioned by Andrew E. Steinmann in his article, "Challenging the Authenticity of Cainan, Son of Arpachshad," *JETS* 60 (2017): 697–711. Steinmann contends that the name Cainan is absent from the Masoretic text in the Old Testament at **Genesis 10:24; 11:12**, and **1 Chronicles 1:18** and concludes that Cainan was an accidental scribal displacement of the name from **Luke 3:37** into the text of **Luke 3:36**. Subsequently, under the influence of this later text in Luke, Christian scribes added the name to other texts, including **Genesis 10** LXX, **Genesis 11** LXX,

some manuscripts of **1 Chronicles 1** LXX, and the book of Jubilees. For a counterpoint view that Kainan (Cainan) is a *valid* inclusion in Luke's genealogy, see the article by Henry B. Smith Jr. and Kris J. Udd, "On the Authenticity of Kainan, Son of Arpachshad," *Detroit Baptist Seminary Journal* 24 (2019): 119–54, where they conclude that "instead of being spurious, Kainan's originality in LXX **Genesis 10:24** and **11:13b–14b**, the *Book of Jubilees*, and **Luke 3:36** is virtually certain" and propose that "Kainan appeared in the original Hebrew text of Genesis, but first disappeared from **Genesis 11** by a combination of scribal and mental error in a very ancient archetypal Hebrew manuscript" followed by "a complex sequence of events that occurred over the span of several centuries" (119–120). Given that Cainan is 14 generations *removed* from God, inclusive, in Luke's genealogy (i.e., a multiple of the ideal number *seven*, representing perfection and completion, as in **Genesis 2:2-3**) and that inclusion of Cainan gives a total of seventy-seven names; this work agrees with the valid inclusion of Cainan in Luke's genealogy to achieve an "ideal perfection" for Jesus' ancestry.

9. Enoch, the seventh generation from Adam, walked with God and did not see death "because God took him away" (**Genesis 5:21–24**).

10. Robert R. Wilson points out that maximal lineage genealogies that are conveyed orally seldom exceed ten to fourteen generations in depth, whereas written genealogies ensure genealogical accuracy and are not limited to a certain number of generations; see *Genealogy and History in the Biblical World* (New Haven: Yale University Press), 1977, 20–21.

11. It is thought that Matthew and/or Luke may have used genealogical information from public registries (perhaps those in the Second Temple or those from private records that were kept by Jesus' immediate family, i.e., the blood-relative of Jesus, termed the *desposyni*); see note 1 in chart "**Matthew 1**: Jesus the Messiah: The Matthean Account."

12. For a discussion of the genealogical formulas and linear structure of royal lineages, such as kings' lists and royal inscription genealogies, see Robert R. Wilson, *Genealogy and History in the Biblical World* (New Haven: Yale University Press, 1977), 59–63.

13. The *double line* of Jesus the Messiah is derived from the David–Solomon–Jeconiah–Shealtiel–Zerubbabel–Joseph–Jesus line (recorded in Matthew's genealogy) and the David–Nathan–Neri–Shealtiel–Zerubbabel–Joseph–Jesus line (recorded in Luke's genealogy). When the two lineages are charted side-by-side, the *double line* of the Messiah's ancestry is clearly evident; see chart "**1 Chronicles 3**: Zerubbabel and Shealtiel and the Double Line of the Messiah through King David's Sons, Nathan and Solomon."

14. Matthew clarifies that Shealtiel was born during the Babylonian captivity (**Matthew 1:12**). Luke shows Shealtiel as the *son of Neri* (**Luke 3:27**), whereas Matthew shows Shealtiel as the *son of King Jeconiah* (also called "Jehoiachin the captive"; **1 Chronicles 3:17; Matthew 1:12**). This seeming disparity can be resolved by either of the following scenarios:

(A) Neri (the biological father of Shealtiel) died during the destruction of Jerusalem or in Babylonian captivity. Because Jeconiah's sons died or were made eunuchs in captivity, King Jeconiah (a near relative of Neri) *adopted* Shealtiel as his legal heir. This scenario would fit the prophecy regarding Jeconiah in **Jeremiah 22:24–30** and explain the transference of the *signet ring*—meaning the 'right to rule'—from King Jeconiah/Jehoiachin to Zerubbabel (**Haggai 2:23**; cf. **Jeremiah 22:24**). When the exiles returned to their homeland in 538 B.C., Zerubbabel (the *son* of Shealtiel) became the governor (but not the king) over the post-exilic community in Jerusalem (**Haggai 1:1, 14; 2:2, 21**).

(B) Alternatively, if Neri died childless at the time of the captivity, the captive king Jeconiah/Jehoiachin (a near relative), who had royal court privileges in Babylon (cf. **2 Kings 25:27–30**), may have taken Neri's widow in levirate marriage and raised up a child (Shealtiel) for Neri. In this way, Shealtiel was the *biological* son/heir of Jeconiah/Jehoiachin but was considered the *legal* son/heir of Neri. This would be consistent with reoccurring instances of second marriages and levirate marriages in Jesus' ancestry as shown in Excursus A in chart "**1 Chronicles 3**: Zerubbabel and Shealtiel and the Double Line of the Messiah through King David's Sons, Nathan and Solomon."

15. Luke's genealogy states that Zerubbabel was the "son of Shealtiel, the son of Neri" (**Luke 3:27**); nevertheless, the Chronicler states that Zerubbabel was a *son* (*heir*) of Pedaiah (the *brother* of Shealtiel; **1 Chronicles 3:19**). Since Zerubbabel is most often presented in the Old Testament as the "son of Shealtiel" (**Ezra 3:2, 8; 5:2; Nehemiah 12:1; Haggai 1:1, 12, 14; 2:2, 23**), this presumably occurred by:

(A) Pedaiah adopting his nephew Zerubbabel (the biological son of Shealtiel) after Shealtiel's death (the favored interpretation; or

(B) Levirate marriage of Pedaiah to Shealtiel's widow, making Zerubbabel the biological son of Pedaiah but the legal heir of Shealtiel.

In either case, Zerubbabel became the *son* of Shealtiel, as shown in the genealogies of both Matthew and Luke (**Matthew 1:12–13; Luke 3:27**; cf. **1 Chronicles 3:17–19**). This detail alone confirms that Luke is *not* tracing a strictly biological line of Jesus but one that includes a legal (levirate) and/or adoptive heir as a *son*. For more information, see the discussion of Pedaiah and Shealtiel in the charts "**1 Chronicles 3**: Zerubbabel and Shealtiel and the Double Line of the Messiah through King David's Sons, Nathan and Solomon" and "**Ezra 1**: Sheshbazzar and Zerubbabel, the Governors over the Restored Community in Jerusalem (Post-Exile)."

JOHN 11: MARTHA, LAZARUS, AND MARY OF BETHANY, THE FRIENDS OF JESUS

Approximate Dating: ca. A.D. 29–33[1] ***Relevant Scriptures:*** **John 11:1–3, 5, 19, 21, 23, 28, 32, 39;** also **Luke 10:38–40**

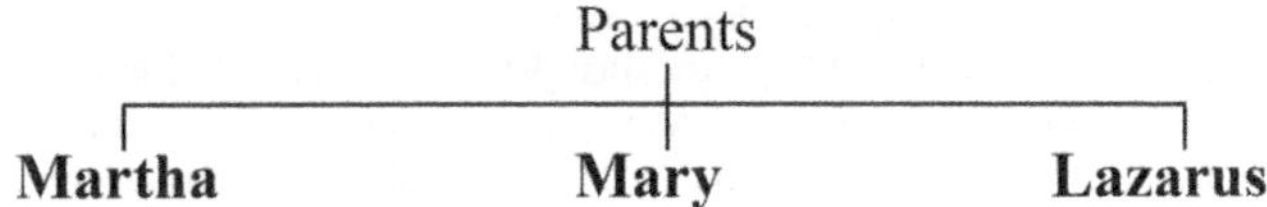

Biblical and Theological Significance

This family's home was in the village of Bethany, about two miles east of Jerusalem, on the eastern slope of the Mount of Olives near the village of Bethphage (**John 11:1, 18**; see **Mark 11:1; Luke 19:29**). Martha, Mary, and Lazarus were close friends of Jesus, and their home seems to be the preferred quiet and secluded lodging place when Jesus came to Jerusalem (**Matthew 21:17; Mark 11:11**).

Martha

Based on **Luke 10:38**, which says, "Martha opened her home to him [Jesus]," it is thought that Martha was the head of the family, implying that Lazarus and Mary were her younger siblings. Martha (like the apostle Peter) realized and declared: "I believe that you [Jesus] are the Messiah, the Son of God, who is to come into the world" (**John 11:27**; cf. **Matthew 16:16; Mark 8:29; Luke 9:20; John 6:69; Acts 8:37**). Martha is often remembered as the sister who "was distracted by all the preparations that had to be made" when Jesus came to visit, and the one whom Jesus gently rebuked: "'Martha, Martha,' the Lord answered, 'you are worried and upset about many things, but few things are needed—or indeed only one'" (**Luke 10:40–42**).

Mary of Bethany

Mary was the sister of Martha and Lazarus. Moreover, Mary is identified as "Mary, whose brother Lazarus now lay sick, was the same one who poured perfume [a pint of pure nard, "worth a year's wages"] on the Lord [six days before the Passover] and wiped his feet with her hair" (**John 11:2; 12:5**; see **12:1–8;** cf. **Matthew 26:6–13; Mark 14:3–9**). She was the more contemplative of the two sisters. When Jesus came to visit and Martha was distracted by all the preparations, Mary "sat at the Lord's feet listening to what he said." Essentially, Mary took a position normally reserved for male disciples, presumably in order to learn at the feet of the Rabbi and Jesus commended her for this: "Mary has chosen what is better, and it will not be taken away from her" (**Luke 10:42**).

Lazarus

Lazarus (the abridged form of the Hebrew name Eleazar, meaning "God helps") was loved by Jesus and was considered a close friend of the family (cf. **John 11:3, 5, 11, 36**). When Lazarus became sick, Jesus deliberately delayed going to Bethany for two days. Lazarus died and was in the grave for four days before Jesus arrived and then raised him from the dead (**John 11:1–44; 12:17**). This event became a witness to the glory of God, showed Jesus' power over death, and foreshadowed his own resurrection (**John 11:4, 25, 40**). The resurrection of Lazarus caused many Jews to transfer allegiance to Jesus, so "the chief priests made plans to kill Lazarus as well" (**John 12:10–11**; see **vv. 17–19**) and, in turn, solidified their resolve to have Jesus condemned and crucified (**John 11:45–53**).

Notes

1. Jesus was "about thirty years old when he began his [public] ministry" (**Luke 3:23**). Jesus' ministry lasted about three and a half years (ca. A.D. 29–33), placing his death at A.D. 33. See Andreas J. Köstenberger, "Why We Believe We Can Know the Exact Date Jesus Died," First Things, April 3, 2014, https://www.firstthings.com/web-exclusives/2014/04/april-3-ad-33.

ACTS 1: GENEALOGICAL RECORD OF THE PEOPLE PRESENT IN THE UPPER ROOM PRAYER MEETING AFTER JESUS' ASCENSION

Approximate Dating: ca. A.D. 33 ***Relevant Scriptures:*** **Acts 1:12–14**

1. **Peter**[1] the apostle (also called Simon, Simon Peter, or Cephas), the son of John (or Jonah) and the brother of Andrew
2. **James**[2] the apostle, the son of Zebedee
3. **John**[3] the apostle, the son of Zebedee
4. **Andrew**[4] the apostle, the brother of Peter
5. **Philip** the apostle
6. **Thomas** the apostle (also called Didymus)
7. **Bartholomew** the apostle (also called Nathanael)
8. **Matthew**[5] the apostle (also called Levi), the son of Alphaeus
9. **James**[6] the apostle, the son of Alphaeus
10. **Simon the Zealot** the apostle
11. **Judas** the apostle (also called Thaddaeus)—the son of James
12. **"Women"**
13. **Mary,** the mother of Jesus[7]
14. **Jesus' brothers**[8]

Biblical and Theological Significance

The twelve apostles, patterned after the leaders of the twelve tribes of Israel, were trained by Jesus and became the group of core leaders during his three-and-a-half-year earthly ministry. Together with the apostle Paul and others in the "Pauline circle," these men spearheaded the mission of the early church.

The list of those present in the upper room prior to Pentecost bears a close resemblance to the other New Testament apostolic lists (**Matthew 10:2–4, Mark 3:16–19, Luke 6:14–16**).[9]

The group of "women" in **Acts 1:14** may have included the wives of the apostles and wives of the Lord's brothers (cf. **1 Corinthians 9:5**); Mary Magdalene; Mary the wife of Clopas[10] (and the mother of James and Joseph); Salome (Mary's sister and the mother of Zebedee's sons); Joanna, the wife of Chuza (Herod's steward); Susanna (cf. **Matthew 27:55–56; 28:1; Mark 15:40–41; Luke 8:2–3; 23:49, 55; 24:1, 22; John 19:25**); and possibly Jesus' half-sisters (**Matthew 13:56; Mark 6:3**).

Jesus' "brothers" in **Acts 1:14** refers to his half-brothers: James, Joseph, Simon, and Judas (cf. **Matthew 13:55; Mark 6:3**). They should not be confused with any of Jesus' disciples who have similar names (i.e., James, the brother of John; James, the son of Alphaeus; Simon (Peter); Simon the Zealot; Judas/Thaddaeus, the son of James; or Judas Iscariot; cf. **Acts 1:13-14**).

Notes

1. See chart "**Matthew 4**: Simon Peter and Andrew, the Apostles of Jesus."
2. See chart "**Matthew 4**: James and John, the Apostles of Jesus."
3. See chart "**Matthew 4**: James and John, the Apostles of Jesus."
4. See chart "**Matthew 4**: Simon Peter and Andrew, the Apostles of Jesus."
5. See chart "**Matthew 9**: Matthew and James, the Apostles of Jesus."
6. See chart "**Matthew 9**: Matthew and James, the Apostles of Jesus."
7. For the proposed genealogy of Mary, the mother of Jesus, see chart "**Matthew 1**: Mary and Joseph (Based on Scripture and Church Tradition) and How Mary and Joseph May Have Been Related."
8. See chart "**Matthew 1**: Jesus and His Immediate Family."
9. For descriptions of the eleven apostles, see chart "**Matthew 10**: The Twelve Apostles of Jesus."
10. For details about Mary and Clopas, see charts "**Matthew 1**: Mary and Joseph (Based on Scripture and Church Tradition) and How Mary and Joseph May Have Been Related" and "**Matthew 27**: Specific People Mentioned at Jesus' Crucifixion."

ACTS 4: BARNABAS THE CYRENE, WHO WAS ACTIVELY INVOLVED IN THE EARLY CHURCH AND IN PAUL'S MISSIONARY JOURNEYS

Approximate Dating: ca. A.D. 33–65 ***Relevant Scriptures:*** **Acts 4:36–37; Colossians 4:10**

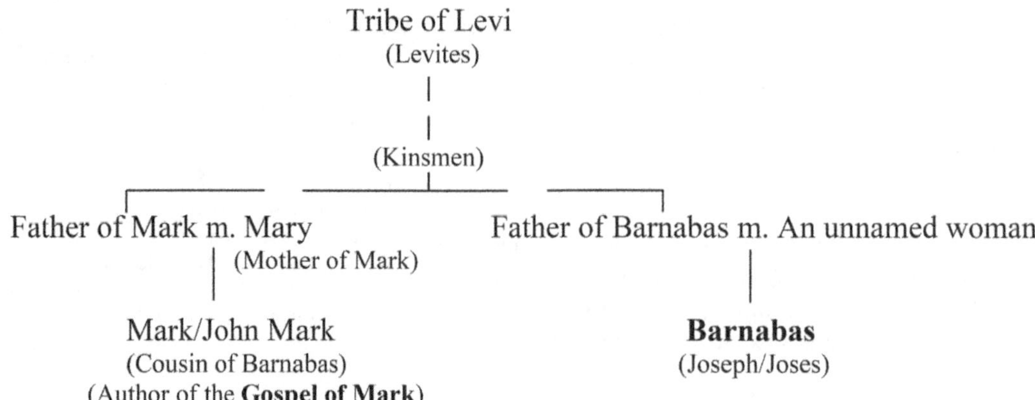

Biblical Significance

Barnabas, a Levite from the island of Cyprus, bore the name Joseph (or Joses in some translations), but the apostles called him Barnabas, meaning "son of encouragement" (**Acts 4:36**). He was involved in several specific activities among the Christian community. For example, Barnabas, of his own initiative, sold property and offered the proceeds from the sale to the nascent Jerusalem church—a gesture that was in stark contrast to the deceptive actions of Ananias and Sapphira (**Acts 4:36–511**). When the apostles were afraid to meet Saul of Tarsus after his conversion, Barnabas acted as the intermediary (**Acts 9:26–28**). Later, the Jerusalem church chose Barnabas to investigate the preaching of Hellenists in Syrian Antioch; he "encouraged them all to remain true to the Lord with all their hearts" (**Acts 11:23**). Also, Barnabas and Saul organized the collection of a monetary gift from the church in Antioch and delivered it to the believers in famine-ridden Judea (**Acts 11:19–30**).

Luke describes Barnabas as "a good man, full of the Holy Spirit and faith," through whom "a great number of people were brought to the Lord" (**Acts 11:24**), and a man who risked his life for the name of the Lord Jesus Christ (**Acts 15:25–26**). In Jerusalem, Barnabas and Paul told of the "signs and wonders God had done among the Gentiles through them" (**Acts 15:12**). Like Paul, Barnabas chose to work for a living while serving the church (**1 Corinthians 9:6**).

In A.D. 47–48, Barnabas accompanied Paul on his first missionary journey to the regions of Galatia and Asia Minor (**Acts 12:25–14:28**). They took with them Barnabas' cousin (John) Mark, but he quickly turned around and returned home to Jerusalem (**Acts 12:25; 13:13**). While in Lystra, Paul healed a man who had been lame from birth. The residents believed that the "gods [had] come down to [them] in human form" and they called Barnabas *Zeus* and called Paul *Hermes* (**Acts 14:11–12**). Barnabas and Paul both denied being gods, saying, "We too are only human, like you" (**Acts 14:15**).

After returning to Antioch, Barnabas and Paul were sent to the church in Jerusalem to settle questions about the salvation of Gentiles and to discuss whether circumcision was necessary for Gentile converts. In the aftermath, Barnabas, Paul, Silas, and Joseph (also called Barsabbas or Justus) carried a letter of decree from the Jerusalem Council to the church at Antioch in Syria. After that Barnabas, Paul, and Silas remained in Antioch for some time (**Acts 15:6–35**).

In ca. A.D. 49, Paul and Barnabas agreed to go on a second missionary journey together, but they strongly disagreed on whether to take John Mark with them since he had deserted them on the first missionary journey (**Acts 13:13; 15:36–39**; cf. **Colossians 4:10**). After a "sharp disagreement," they decided to separate—Barnabas took his cousin (Mark) and sailed to Barnabas' ancestral home in Cyprus, while Paul chose Silas and departed to minister to churches in Syria and Cilicia (**Acts 15:39–41**). Barnabas is mentioned in Paul's letters in **1 Corinthians 9:6**; **Galatians 2:1–10, 13**; and **Colossians 4:10**.

ACTS 6: RECORD OF THE SEVEN MEN CHOSEN TO BE DEACONS IN THE EARLY CHURCH

Approximate Dating: ca. A.D. 30–65 ***Relevant Scriptures:*** **Acts 6:1–6**

1. **Stephen**
2. **Philip**
3. **Procorus**
4. **Nicanor**
5. **Timon**
6. **Parmenas**
7. **Nicolas**

Biblical and Theological Significance

These seven men were chosen from among the early Christian believers to be the first deacons (cf. **Philippians 1:1**; **1 Timothy 3:8–13**). They were "full of the Spirit and wisdom" (**Acts 6:3**) and served (*diakoneō*) in an official capacity by administering food to the poor and needy (particularly Hellenistic widows), which allowed the apostles to continue to devote themselves to prayer and to proclaiming the word of God (**Acts 6:1, 4**). These seven men all have Greek names, suggesting that they were Hellenistic Jews. They were presented to the apostles, who then "prayed and laid their hands on them" (**Acts 6:6**).

Stephen is described as "a man full of faith and of the Holy Spirit" (**Acts 6:5**), who was "full of God's grace and power" and "performed great wonders and signs among the people" (**Acts 6:8**). Some men from the Greek-speaking Synagogue of the Freedmen in Jerusalem falsely accused Stephen of blaspheming against Moses. In his address before the Sanhedrin (**Acts 7**), Stephen called the Jews a "stiff-necked people" (**Acts 7:51**), who like their ancestors (cf. **Exodus 32:9; 33:3, 5; 34:9; Deuteronomy 9:6**) had uncircumcised hearts and ears, persecuted the prophets, and worst of all, had betrayed and murdered Jesus, the Righteous One (**Acts 7:51–53**). For his indictment of them, Stephen was stoned to death and became the first Christian martyr. Saul of Tarsus (later called Paul the apostle) was an eyewitness to the stoning of Stephen and "approved of their killing him" (**Acts 7:58; 8:1**). Following Stephen's martyrdom, believers were persecuted in Jerusalem, and all but the apostles fled to other parts of Judea and Samaria (**Acts 8:1**).

Philip left Jerusalem after the stoning of Stephen and became an evangelist to Samaria (**Acts 8:5**). He performed miracles, including healing the lame and those possessed with unclean spirits (**Acts 8:7**), and was influential in the conversion of many Samaritans. While in Gaza, Philip preached and explained the Scriptures to an Ethiopian eunuch, who was an important official in charge of all the treasury of the Kandake, the queen of Ethiopia. The official believed, and at his request, Philip promptly baptized him (**Acts 8:26–39**). Philip continued his ministry to other cities of the coastal region and eventually took up permanent residence in Caesarea (**Acts 8:40; 21:8**). His four virgin daughters prophesied, and they became evangelists and reliable eyewitnesses of the activities of the early church (**Acts 21:9**).

Nothing else is known about **Procorus, Nicanor, Timon,** and **Parmenas** (**Acts 6:5**), except that they were men of good reputation, like the others.

Nicolas was a proselyte (a Gentile convert to Judaism) who was from Antioch (**Acts 6:5**).

ACTS 7: PAUL THE APOSTLE (ALSO CALLED SAUL OF TARSUS)

Approximate Dating: turn of the era to ca. A.D. 66 ***Relevant Scriptures:*** **Acts 7:58; 23:6, 16; Romans 11:1; Philippians 3:5**

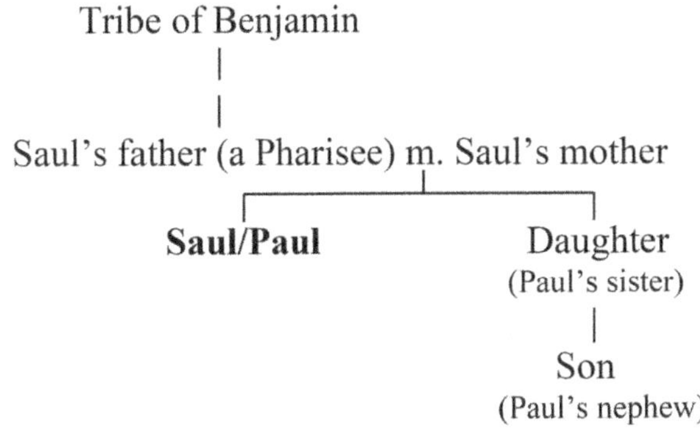

Biblical and Theological Significance

Paul (formerly Saul of Tarsus) was commissioned by the risen Christ himself and became the undisputed leader of the early church's mission to reach Gentiles (**Acts 9:1–19**). Accompanied by a close "Pauline circle" of men (such as Luke, Mark, Barnabas, and Silas), Paul planted Christian congregations across the Roman Empire. Paul maintained correspondence with many of the churches he planted and dispatched apostolic delegates, like Timothy and Titus, to follow up on the congregations.

Paul states clearly that "I am an Israelite myself, a descendant of Abraham, from the tribe of Benjamin" (**Romans 11:1**) and "a Pharisee, descended from Pharisees" (**Acts 23:6**), who served "as my ancestors did, with a clear conscience" (**2 Timothy 1:3**). In the autobiographical sections of his epistles, Paul calls himself "a Hebrew of Hebrews"—a devout, orthodox Jew, strict in following the Law (**Philippians 3:4–6**). He further relates that he advanced "in Judaism beyond many of my own age among my people" and "was extremely zealous for the traditions of my fathers" (**Galatians 1:14**).

Birth, Background, and Religious Training

Paul was a native of Tarsus (**Acts 9:11**), an influential city of Asia Minor and the capital of the Roman province of Cilicia, thus making him both a Jew and Roman citizen by birth (**Acts 16:37; 21:39; 22:3, 25–29**). The precise date of Paul's birth is unknown, but he was probably born sometime around the turn of the era (i.e., B.C. to A.D.). It is unclear whether Paul was single, married, or widowed, given his statements in **1 Corinthians 9:5**: "Don't we have the right to take a believing wife along with us [on our missionary journeys] as do the other apostles and the Lord's brothers and Cephas?" and in **1 Corinthians 7:8**, "Now to the unmarried and the widows I say: It is good for them to stay unmarried, as I do."

His Hebrew name was *Saul*, and his Greek (Roman) name was *Paul*. He may have been named after Saul, the first king of Israel, since King Saul was also a Benjamite (**1 Samuel 9:1–2, 21; Philippians 3:5**). His name change (i.e., from Saul to Paul) does not correlate with his conversion experience. In the early years of his ministry, he was typically known as *Saul* (cf. **Acts 13:2, 7, 9**), but as he ministered to Gentiles and established more congregations in the Roman provinces, he went by his Greek name, *Paul*.

Saul was highly educated. His family sent him to Jerusalem at an early age to receive religious training under the Pharisee Rabbi Gamaliel I (who was a Benjamite),[1] the most famous Jewish religious teacher of the day (**Acts 22:3**), who was known to adhere to the (more lenient) School of Hillel. Since Gamaliel was a leader of the Sanhedrin in Jerusalem, Saul's religious instruction under him probably allowed Saul to become associated with the council as well (cf. **Acts 7:54–59; 8:1; 9:1–2**).

Pre-Christian Life and Subsequent Conversion

Saul first appears in Scripture as a young man guarding the clothes of those who stoned Stephen, the church's first martyr (**Acts 7:58–8:1; 22:20**). Before his conversion, Saul zealously persecuted Christian believers in Jerusalem: "Going from house to house, he dragged off both men and women and put them in prison" (**Acts 8:3**) and "breath[ed] out murderous threats against the Lord's disciples" (**Acts 9:1**; cf. **Galatians 1:13**). He also persecuted followers of Christ in foreign cities (**Acts 26:10–11**). Prior to his conversion, Saul asked the high priest—possibly referring to Joseph Caiaphus, who held the high priesthood from A.D. 18–36/37—for papers that would authorize his travel to Damascus to arrest and imprison believers there (**Acts 9:1–2; 26:12**).

Paul's conversion took place on the road to Damascus (ca. A.D. 34/35). Luke recounts this experience in **Acts 9:1–19**; Paul himself tells his story to the Jerusalem mob in **Acts 22:6–16** and later retells it to King Agrippa I in **Acts 26:12–18**. Jesus appeared to Paul in a light shining from heaven and spoke to him: "Saul, Saul, why do you persecute me?" (**Acts 9:4–5**). Saul was blinded for three days after seeing the vision of the risen, exalted Christ (**Acts 9:9**). Saul's traveling companions took him to Damascus, where he was baptized by Ananias (**Acts 9:10–18**) and regained his sight. Through Ananias, the Lord told Saul that he would be his "chosen instrument to proclaim my name to the Gentiles and their kings and to the people of Israel" (**Acts 9:15**) and that he would serve as a "witness to all people of what you have seen and heard" (**Acts 22:15**). This revealed that the gospel message was intended for both Jews and Gentiles.

Saul's conversion radically changed his life. He went from being a zealous persecutor of Christian believers of "the Way" to becoming the foremost apostle to the Gentiles—the "uncircumcised" (**Galatians 2:7; Ephesians 2:11**), who were no longer regarded as unclean (cf. **Acts 10:28**). Paul confirms that he was "called to be an apostle of Christ Jesus" (**1 Corinthians 1:1**) and "the apostle to the Gentiles" (**Romans 11:13**), although he also preached to Jews (**Acts 9:20; Romans 1:16; 1 Corinthians 9:20**).

After his conversion, the Lord warned Paul not to return to Jerusalem because the people there would not accept his testimony (cf. **Acts 22:17–21**). Paul did not begin his missionary outreach immediately; instead, he went to Arabia for about three years (ca. A.D. 35–38) before returning to Damascus (**Galatians 1:17**; cf. **Acts 9:22–23**). He traveled to Jerusalem in ca. A.D. 38 where he conferred with Peter and James (the half-brother of Jesus), who were the leading authorities in the Jerusalem assembly (**Galatians 1:18–19**). Saul then returned to Tarsus before Barnabas brought him to Antioch (**Acts 9:30**)—the place where the disciples were first called Christians (**Acts 11:25–26**). From there, Paul and Barnabas were sent out as missionaries by the church at Antioch (**Acts 13:1–3**).

Paul's Missionary Journeys

Paul undertook three major missionary journeys throughout Asia Minor, Greece, and Macedonia.[2, 3] He planted many congregations, among them Thessalonica, Ephesus, Lystra, Derbe, Philippi, and Galatia. Fellow ministers such as Barnabas, Luke, Timothy, Silas, and John Mark accompanied Paul on various missionary journeys. He frequently revisited the congregations he had planted to further encourage them. The conversions of Lydia (**Acts 16:11–15, 40**), the Philippian jailer (**Acts 16:22–36**), Apollos (**Acts 18:24–28**), and others took place during Paul's missionary journeys, as did the calling of Timothy (**Acts 16:1–3**) and his appeal to the Athenians (**Acts 17:16–34**). Paul's three missionary journeys are described in **Acts 12:25–14:28**; **Acts 15:36–18:22**; and **Acts 18:23–21:17**.

Conspiracy and Arrest

After Paul returned from his third missionary journey, jealous Jews accused him of being a ringleader of the Nazarene sect (Jews who followed Jesus; **Acts 24:5**). Paul was arrested in the temple in Jerusalem (**Acts 21:27–30**). Paul's nephew—his sister's son—learned of a conspiracy by forty Pharisees and Sadducees to capture and kill Paul. When Paul's nephew informed him of the scheme, Paul asked a centurion to take his nephew to Jerusalem to the Roman commander, Claudius Lysias (**Acts 23:12–22**); there, Paul's nephew explained the planned ambush. Since Paul was a Roman citizen, Lysias ordered his transfer from Jerusalem to Caesarea Maritima so that his case could be heard there before Antonius Felix, the Roman procurator of Judea (A.D. 52–59/60; **Acts 23:23–35**). Felix procrastinated in giving Paul a trial. During the two-year delay in hearing Paul's case (A.D. 57–58), Felix was replaced by Porcius Festus (A.D. 60–62; **Acts 24:22–27**). Because he was a Roman citizen, Paul appealed to Festus to have his case heard by Caesar in Rome (**Acts 25:1–12**). Before Paul's transfer to Rome, King Agrippa II and Bernice came to hear him (**Acts 25:23–24**).[4] Paul recounted his early life, conversion, and his years as an apostle to the Gentiles before Herod Agrippa II (**Acts 26:1–32**). Festus finally transferred Paul to Rome to be heard before Caesar in ca. A.D. 60 (**Acts 27–28**).

Paul's Letters

Paul spoke and wrote in Greek, not Hebrew or Aramaic. He is credited with writing thirteen of the twenty-seven books of the New Testament: **Romans, 1** and **2 Corinthians, Galatians, Ephesians, Philippians, Colossians, 1** and **2 Thessalonians, 1** and **2 Timothy, Titus,** and **Philemon.**[5] Paul's epistles typically addressed specific problems or circumstances that had arisen in the congregations that he had planted (or, in the case of Colossians or Romans, that Paul did not plant).

Paul's Martyrdom

Paul's death is not recorded in Scripture, but church tradition[6] holds that he was beheaded in Rome in the 60s during the waning years of the reign of Emperor Nero (A.D. 54–68).

Notes

1. The Benjamite heritage of Rabbi Gamaliel I is discussed in Joachim Jeremias, *Jerusalem in the Time of Jesus* (Philadelphia: Fortress, 1969), 278. Gamaliel was the grandson of Hillel the Elder, who was the influential leader of the Sanhedrin from ca. 30 B.C. to A.D. 20; Hillel's followers established the pharisaical "School of Hillel" which was responsible for the formation of rabbinic Judaism.

2. **First Missionary Journey** (accompanied by Barnabas and, briefly, John Mark; **Acts 12:25–14:28**) (ca. A.D. 47–48):

- Departed from Antioch in Syria—to Seleucia (preached in Jewish synagogues)—sailed to the East coast of the island of Cyprus—preached in Salamis and Paphos—sailed to Perga in Pamphylia (John Mark returned home to Jerusalem)—Antioch in Pisidia—Iconium in Phrygia—Lystra and Derbe in the Lycaonia district of Galatia—returned to Lystra—Iconium—Antioch in Pisidia—Pamphylia—Perga—Attalia—sailed back to Antioch in Syria.

Second Missionary Journey (accompanied by Silas; **Acts 15:36–18:22**; Luke is also mentioned as accompanying them in **Acts 16:10–17**; ca. A.D. 49–51):

- Departed from Antioch in Syria—Syria—Cilicia—Derbe and Lystra (Timothy joined them)—Phrygia and the region of Galatia—Mysia—Troas—Samothrace—Neapolis—Philippi of Macedonia—throughout Amphipolis and Apollonia—Thessalonica—to Berea in Macedonia (Silas and Timothy remained there; Paul went to Athens, and then Silas and Timothy rejoined him)—to Corinth—sailed for Syria via Ephesus—Caesarea—Antioch in Syria.

Third Missionary Journey (accompanied by Luke; **Acts 18:23–21:16**; Luke is mentioned in **Acts 20:5–16** and **21:1–18**; ca. A.D. 51–54):

- Departed from Antioch in Syria—revisited Galatia and Phrygia—to Ephesus (Paul stayed there for three years)—Macedonia—Achaia—Asia—Macedonia—Greece—returned to Macedonia—sailed from Philippi—Troas—Assos—Mitylene—off Chios—Samos—Miletus—Kos—Rhodes—Patara—Phoenicia—sailed past Cyprus—Syria—Tyre—Ptolemais—Caesarea—Jerusalem.

Final Journey Recorded in Acts (Paul, who was then a Roman prisoner, was transferred from Caesarea to Rome to be heard before Caesar; Paul was accompanied by Aristarchus and Luke; **Acts 27:1–28:16**; ca. A.D. 55–58):

- Caesarea—Sidon—Cyprus—along the Syrian coast of Cilicia and Pamphylia—Myra, a city of Lycia—Cnidus—Island of Crete—Fair Havens on Crete—along the coast of Crete (where threatening winds arose)—held up on the Island of Cauda—shipwrecked on Malta, south of Sicily (stayed three months)—Syracuse—Rhegium—Puteoli—Rome (held under house arrest for two years; ca. A.D. 58–60?).

3. The dates for Paul's missionary journeys are from Andreas J. Köstenberger with T. Desmond Alexander, "*Salvation to the Ends of the Earth: A Biblical Theology of Mission*" in *New Studies in Biblical Theology* 53 (Downers Grove, IL: InterVarsity, 2020), 145.

4. For Herod Agrippa II and Bernice/Berenice, see chart "**Matthew 2**: Herod the Great and the Herodian Dynasty."

5. Pauline authorship of certain books, however, continues to be debated among scholars. Additionally, a small minority claim that Paul wrote the book of Hebrews.

6. Eusebius says that it was recorded that "Paul was beheaded in Rome itself, and that Peter likewise was crucified under Nero. This account of Peter and Paul is substantiated by the fact that their names are preserved in the cemeteries of that place even to the present day." *Ecclesiastical (Church) History*. New updated edition. Translated by C. F. Cruse. (Peabody: Hendrickson, 2004), 2.25.5.

ACTS 12: RECORD OF THE PROPHETS AND TEACHERS IN THE (SYRIAN) CHURCH AT ANTIOCH WHO COMMISSIONED BARNABAS AND SAUL ON THEIR FIRST MISSIONARY JOURNEY

Approximate Dating: ca. A.D. 47–48 ***Relevant Scriptures:*** **Acts 12:25–13:3**

1. **Barnabas**
2. **Simeon (called Niger)**
3. **Lucius of Cyrene**
4. **Manaen**
5. **Saul**

Biblical and Theological Significance

The city of Antioch became the first major mission center; it was there that the followers of the risen Jesus were first called "Christians" (**Acts 11:26**). The city served as the base from which the Christian mission originated (**Acts 13:1–3**) and the location to which the first missionaries returned after engaging in evangelistic and church-planting ministry (**Acts 14:21–28**; cf. **15:30–41**).

The above-mentioned prophets and teachers[1] from Syrian Antioch (**Acts 13:1**) laid hands on Barnabas and Saul and sent them out from the church in Antioch as they departed on their first missionary journey (**Acts 13:3**).[2]

Barnabas was a leading figure in the Jerusalem church (**Acts 9:27**). He is described as "a good man, full of the Holy Spirit and faith" by whom "a great number of people were brought to the Lord" (**Acts 11:24**). Barnabas was the apostolic delegate to the church in Antioch. He was also responsible for finding Saul in Tarsus after his conversion and for bringing him to Antioch, where for a whole year they "taught great numbers of people" (**Acts 11:25–26**). The Barnabas in **Acts 13:1–2** is the same person as Barnabas the Levite from Cyprus (**Acts 4:36**), who joined Paul on his first missionary journey.[3]

It is unclear whether this **Simeon** called **Niger** (meaning *black*) is the same person as Simon of Cyrene[4] (the father of Alexander and Rufus) who carried the cross for Jesus (cf. **Mark 15:21; Luke 23:26**).

Lucius was from Cyrene, the capital city of the Roman province of Cyrenaica (the island of Crete and the region of Cyrenaica—modern eastern Libya in North Africa). Lucius may have been among the "men from Cyprus and Cyrene [who] went to Antioch and began to speak to Greeks also, telling them the good news about the Lord Jesus . . . and a great number of people believed and turned to the Lord" (cf. **Acts 11:19–21**).

Manaen (the Greek form of the Heb. *Menahem*) had been "brought up with Herod the tetrarch," probably referring to Herod Antipas who ruled over Galilee and Perea from 4 B.C. –A.D. 39 or 6 B.C.–A.D. 39[5] (**Acts 13:1**; cf. **Matthew 14:1; Mark 6:14; Luke 3:1**).

Saul,[6] by this time, was a convert and one of the teachers in the church at Antioch. He was set apart by the Lord to be "a light for the Gentiles" so that they could hear and believe the message of the gospel (**Acts 13:47; 15:7, 12, 23; 18:6; 21:19; Romans 11:13; 15:16, 18; 16:26**, etc.).

Notes

1. Prophets and teachers were two important categories of individuals in the leadership of the early church (cf. **1 Corinthians 12:28; Ephesians 4:11**). Some scholars have inferred from the arrangement of the conjunctions in **Acts 13:1** that the first three (Barnabas, Simeon, and Lucius) were prophets, and the last two (Manaen and Saul) were teachers. Paton James Gloag, *A Critical and Exegetical Commentary on the Acts of the Apostles* (Edinburgh: T&T Clark, 1870), 3.
2. John Mark accompanied Paul and Barnabas on the journey for a short time, serving as their helper (**Acts 13:5, 13**; cf. **Acts 12:12**). For the itinerary of Paul's first missionary journey, see note 2 in chart "**Acts 7**: Paul the Apostle (Also Called Saul of Tarsus)."
3. See chart "**Acts 4**: Barnabas the Cyrene Who was Actively Involved in the Early Church and in Paul's Missionary Journeys."
4. See chart "**Matthew 27**: Simon of Cyrene who Carried the Cross of Jesus."
5. For the details about the reign of Herod Antipas, see chart "**Matthew 2**: Herod the Great and the Herodian Dynasty."
6. See chart "**Acts 7**: Paul the Apostle (Also Called Saul of Tarsus)."

TIMOTHY: TIMOTHY, COWORKER OF PAUL AND RECIPIENT OF THE PAULINE EPISTLES OF 1 & 2 TIMOTHY

Approximate Dating: ca. A.D. 45–65 ***Relevant Scriptures:*** **1 Timothy 1:2; 2 Timothy 1:2, 5;** also **Acts 16:1–3**

Lois
(Mother of Eunice)
|
Timothy's father m. Eunice
(Greek) | (Daughter of Lois; a Jewess)
|
Timothy
(Mixed Jewish-Gentile heritage)

Biblical and Theological Significance

Timothy, a native of Lystra (in modern Turkey), was of mixed Greek-Jewish parentage (**Acts 16:1–3**).[1] Timothy's mother and grandmother were Jewish Christians who had instructed him in the Old Testament Scriptures "from infancy" (**2 Timothy 3:15**). Timothy is first mentioned in Scripture during Paul's second missionary journey (ca. A.D. 49–51), although Paul may have been instrumental in Timothy's conversion during his visit to Lystra on his first missionary journey, ca. A.D. 47–48 (cf. **Acts 14:6–23**).

Paul invited Timothy to join him on his second missionary journey; but knowing that they would be evangelizing Jews and Greeks, Paul circumcised him "because of the Jews who lived in that area, for they all knew that his father was a Greek" (**Acts 16:3**).

Timothy became a prominent member of the Pauline circle and served as a young assistant and apostolic delegate of Paul. Timothy helped in the evangelizing efforts in Macedonia and Achaia (**Acts 17:13–14; 18:5; 19:22**) and in Ephesus[2] (**1 Timothy 1:3**; cf. **3:14–15**). He also traveled with Paul from Ephesus to Macedonia and on to Corinth (**Acts 20:3**). Timothy ministered to churches in Corinth, Philippi, Thessalonica, and Ephesus (**1 Corinthians 16:10–11; Philippians 2:19–23; 1 Thessalonians 3:1–3, 6; 1 Timothy 1:3**). At one point, Timothy was even imprisoned in Rome (**Hebrews 13:23**). Paul had a high regard and love for Timothy, whom he called "my true son in the faith" (**1 Timothy 1:2**) and acknowledged that Timothy had "proved himself, because as a son with his father he has served with me in the work of the gospel" (**Philippians 2:22**; cf. **1 Corinthians 4:17; 1 Timothy 1:18; 2 Timothy 1:2**).

Timothy was the recipient of two of Paul's letters (**1** and **2 Timothy**), written ca. A.D. 62 and A.D. 65, respectively.[3] He is also listed alongside Paul as co-sender or co-author at the beginning of six of Paul's letters: **2 Corinthians, Philippians, Colossians, 1** and **2 Thessalonians,** and **Philemon**.

Notes

1. As Köstenberger, et. al explain: "Due to his mixed Jewish-Gentile heritage (**Acts 16:1**), Timothy was an ideal choice for ministering in a

Hellenistic-Jewish environment and for dealing with a Jewish proto-gnostic heresy. Even at the time **1 Timothy** was written, Timothy was still fairly young (**1 Tim. 4:12**), though he had met Paul more than 10 years earlier (**Acts 16:1**; ca. A.D. 49), if not earlier. Timothy was therefore probably in his late thirties when he received **1** and **2 Timothy**" (Andreas J. Köstenberger, L. Scott Kellum, and Charles L. Quarles. *The Cradle, the Cross and the Crown: An Introduction to the New Testament* [Nashville: B&H, 2009], 643).

2. In Paul's first letter to Timothy, he told him: "train yourself to be godly" (**1 Timothy 4:7**) and instructed him to refute the false teachings, controversies, and the constant friction and quarrels among the people in the church at Ephesus (cf. **1 Timothy 1:3–7; 4:1–8; 6:3–5, 20–21**). Paul likely wrote the **Epistle of 2 Timothy** (his last letter) when he was imprisoned in Rome under Emperor Nero, shortly before Paul's death. In his letter, Paul admonished Timothy to "guard the good deposit that was entrusted to you" (**2 Timothy 1:14**), "continue in what you have learned" (**2 Timothy 3:14**), and "preach the word; be prepared, . . . rebuke and encourage" (**2 Timothy 4:2**).

3. Andreas J. Köstenberger, *1–2 Timothy and Titus*, EBTC (Bellingham, WA: Lexham, 2021), 28–30, places the date of **1 Timothy** between A.D. 62 (Paul's release from his first Roman imprisonment) and A.D. 65 and dates **2 Timothy** to A.D. 65, during Paul's second Roman imprisonment.

TITUS: TITUS, COMPANION OF PAUL THE APOSTLE AND RECIPIENT OF THE PAULINE EPISTLE OF TITUS

Approximate Dating: ca. A.D. 62–64 ***Relevant Scriptures:*** **Titus 1:4–5; Galatians 2:3**

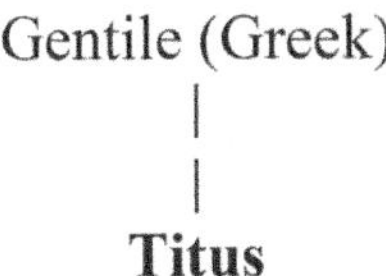

Biblical and Theological Significance

Titus was an uncircumcised Greek (Gentile) who became a Christian convert and a trusted associate of Paul the apostle.[1] Although Titus is not mentioned in the book of Acts, he appears to have accompanied Paul on his second and third missionary journeys. **Galatians 2:1–3** notes that Titus was with Paul and Barnabas when they went to Jerusalem prior to Paul's first missionary journey, ca. A.D. 47–48 (**Acts 12:25–14:28**). At the time, Paul says, "not even Titus, who was with me, was compelled to be circumcised, even though he was a Greek"[2] (**Galatians 2:3**).

Paul mentored Titus and considered him "my true son in our common faith" (**Titus 1:4**) and his "partner and co-worker" in their ministry to the church at Corinth (**2 Corinthians 8:23**). Titus likely delivered a severe letter (no longer extant) that Paul wrote to the Corinthians after Paul's "painful visit" to the church at Corinth (**2 Corinthians 2:1**; cf. **v. 13; 7:6–8, 13–15; 10:9–10**). Through his earnest care and enthusiasm for the Corinthians, Titus established a relationship with them and was instrumental in correcting issues in the Corinthian church (**2 Corinthians 7:13–15**). Titus was also involved in collecting money from the Corinthians; he accompanied Paul and Barnabas in delivering the funds to the poverty-stricken Christians in Jerusalem, who were experiencing a famine (**2 Corinthians 8; Galatians 2:1**).

After he was released from his first Roman imprisonment, Paul's letter to Titus was probably composed ca. A.D. 62–64. Paul sent Titus as his own representative to give pastoral oversight to the church on the island of Crete, including appointing elders, denouncing false teaching, and offering instruction to the Cretans in sound doctrine and good works (**Titus 1:5**).[3]

Titus is last mentioned during Paul's second Roman imprisonment when Paul wrote to Timothy saying "Titus [has gone] to Dalmatia"—referring to Dalmatia in the Roman province Illyricum, north of Greece (**2 Timothy 4:10**).

Notes

1. For the missionary journeys of Paul, see note 2 in chart "**Acts 7**: Paul the Apostle (Also Called Saul of Tarsus)."

2. Among the false believers in Jerusalem were Judaizers who believed that Gentile converts should be circumcised and follow the Mosaic law (cf. **Acts 15:5**).

3. In his letter to Titus, Paul quotes the poet Epimenides, a sixth-century B.C. native of Crete, who wrote that the Cretans were "liars, evil brutes, lazy gluttons" (**Titus 1:12**). Paul left Titus to oversee the church there and rebuke the Cretans so that they could become believers who were "sound in the faith" (**Titus 1:13**).

SUPPLEMENT 1: THE PHARAOHS OF THE TWELFTH AND EIGHTEENTH DYNASTIES OF EGYPT[1]

Approximate Dating: Twelfth Dynasty, ca. 1991–1786 or 1985–1773 B.C.; Eighteenth Dynasty, ca. 1570–1320 or 1550–1295 B.C.[2] (All dates in the chart are B.C.)

Table 1. Overall Sequence of the Egyptian Dynasties and approximate chronology[3]

Early Dynastic period	Dynasties 1–2	(ca. 3100–2686 B.C.)
Old Kingdom	Dynasties 3–8	(ca. 2686–2160 B.C.)
First Intermediate Period	Dynasties 9–11[(a)]	(ca. 2160–2055 B.C.)
Middle Kingdom	Dynasties 11[(b)]–14	(ca. 2055–1650 B.C.)
Second Intermediate Period	Dynasties 15–17	(ca. 1650–1550 B.C.)
New Kingdom Period	Dynasties 18–20	(ca. 1550–1069 B.C.)
Third Intermediate Period	Dynasties 21–25	(ca. 1069–664 B.C.)
Late Period	Dynasties 26–30	(ca. 664–342 B.C.)

[(a)] Dynasty 11 in the First Intermediate Period was over Thebes only.
[(b)] Dynasty 11 in the Middle Kingdom was over all of Egypt.

Genealogy of the 12th Dynasty of the Middle Kingdom

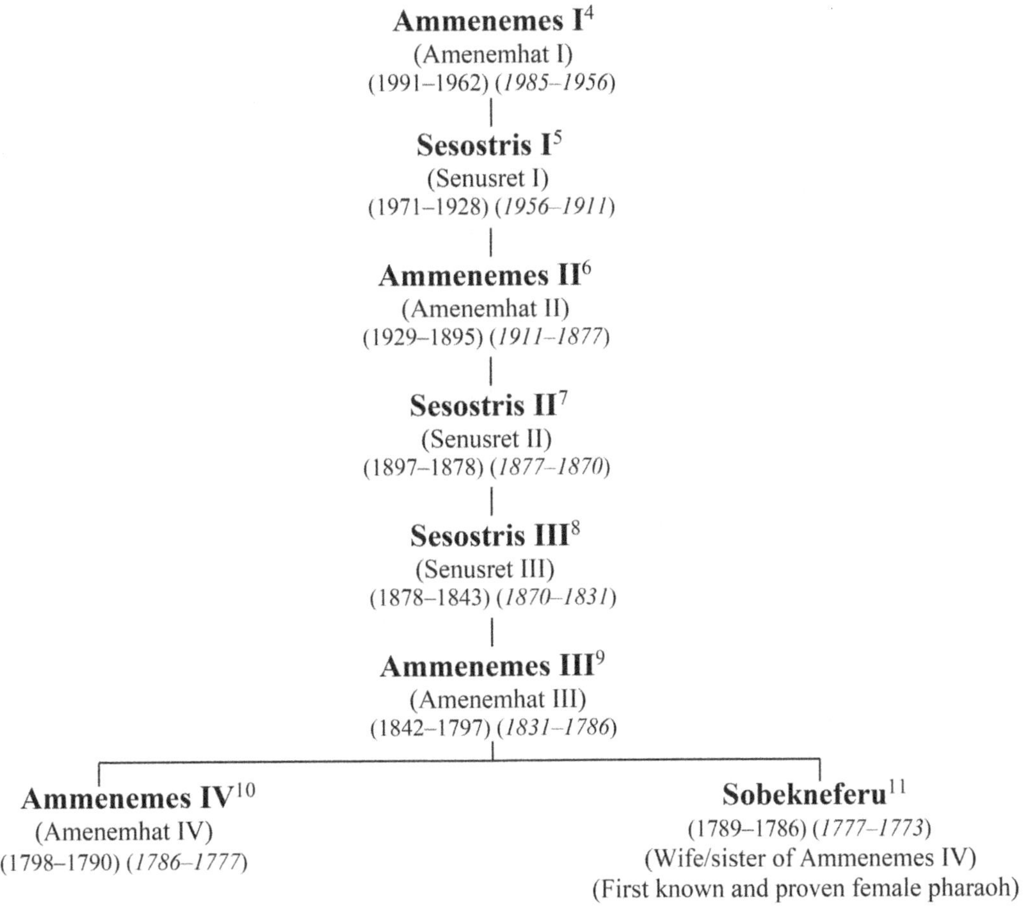

Genealogy of the 18th Dynasty of the New Kingdom

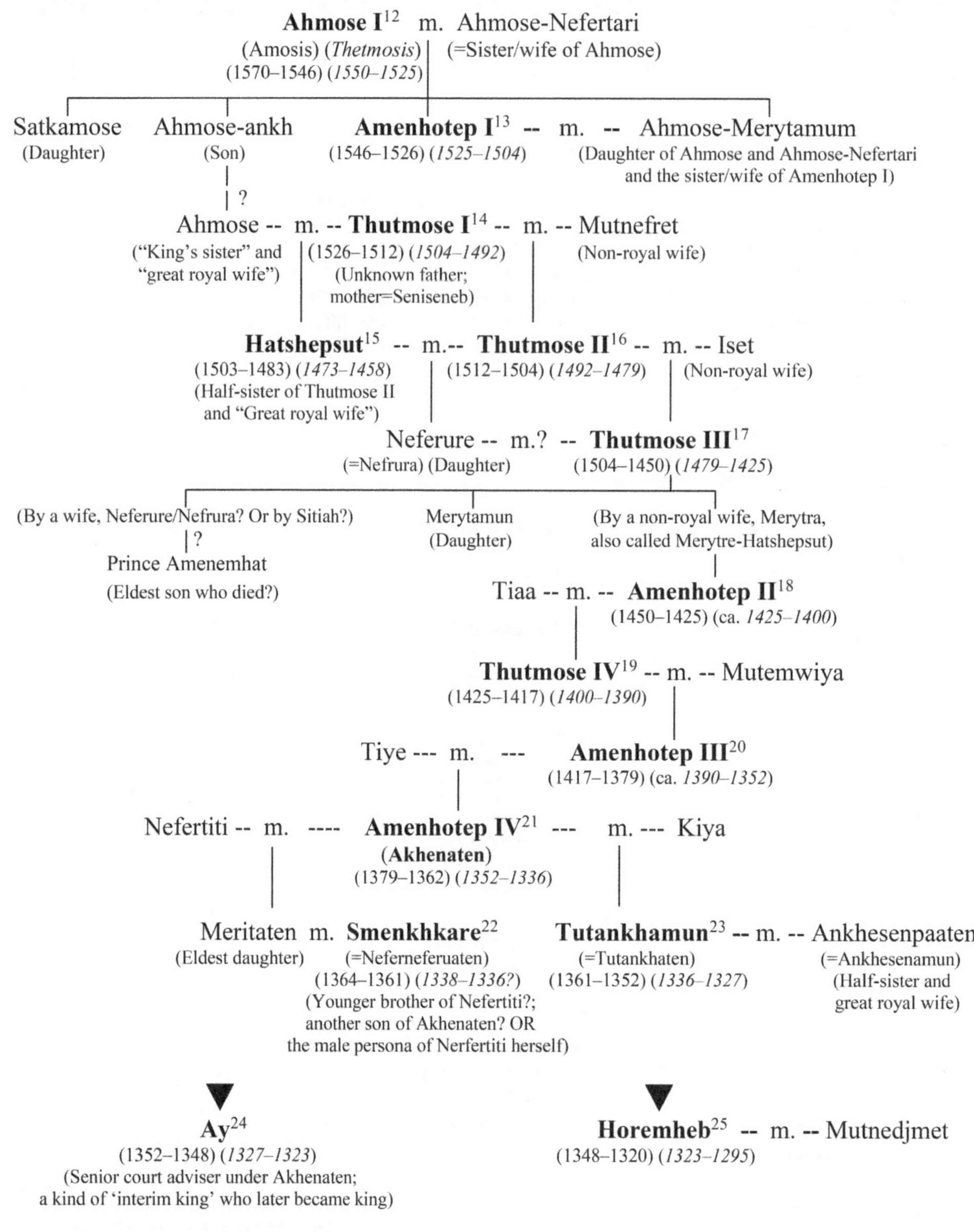

Ahmose I[12] m. Ahmose-Nefertari
(Amosis) (*Thetmosis*) (=Sister/wife of Ahmose)
(1570–1546) (*1550–1525*)
Satkamose (Daughter)
Ahmose-ankh (Son)
?
Amenhotep I[13] -- m. -- Ahmose-Merytamum
(1546–1526) (*1525–1504*)
(Daughter of Ahmose and Ahmose-Nefertari and the sister/wife of Amenhotep I)
Ahmose -- m. -- Thutmose I[14] -- m. -- Mutnefret
("King's sister" and "great royal wife")
(1526–1512) (*1504–1492*)
(Unknown father; mother=Seniseneb)
(Non-royal wife)
Hatshepsut[15] -- m.-- Thutmose II[16] -- m. -- Iset
(1503–1483) (*1473–1458*)
(Half-sister of Thutmose II and "Great royal wife")
(1512–1504) (*1492–1479*)
(Non-royal wife)
Neferure -- m.? -- Thutmose III[17]
(=Nefrura) (Daughter)
(1504–1450) (*1479–1425*)
(By a wife, Neferure/Nefrura? Or by Sitiah?)
?
Prince Amenemhat
(Eldest son who died?)
Merytamun (Daughter)
(By a non-royal wife, Merytra, also called Merytre-Hatshepsut)
Tiaa -- m. -- Amenhotep II[18]
(1450–1425) (ca. *1425–1400*)
Thutmose IV[19] -- m. -- Mutemwiya
(1425–1417) (*1400–1390*)
Tiye --- m. --- Amenhotep III[20]
(1417–1379) (ca. *1390–1352*)
Nefertiti -- m. ---- Amenhotep IV[21] --- m. --- Kiya
(Akhenaten)
(1379–1362) (*1352–1336*)
Meritaten m. Smenkhkare[22]
(Eldest daughter)
(=Neferneferuaten)
(1364–1361) (*1338–1336?*)
(Younger brother of Nefertiti?; another son of Akhenaten? OR the male persona of Nerfertiti herself)
Tutankhamun[23] -- m. -- Ankhesenpaaten
(=Tutankhaten)
(1361–1352) (*1336–1327*)
(=Ankhesenamun) (Half-sister and great royal wife)
Ay[24]
(1352–1348) (*1327–1323*)
(Senior court adviser under Akhenaten; a kind of 'interim king' who later became king)
Horemheb[25] -- m. -- Mutnedjmet
(1348–1320) (*1323–1295*)

LEGEND:

| : Line of descent from father-to-son

▼ : Successor is not related to the previous king

Biblical and Theological Significance

The Egyptian period is divided into approximately thirty successive periods called "dynasties." Since the important biblical narratives about Joseph, Moses, and the exodus take place during the reigns of certain Egyptian rulers, the chart focuses only on the genealogies of the pharaonic rulers of the Twelfth and the Eighteenth Dynasties. Discussions regarding the biblical characters are embedded within the notes below.

Notes

1. The primary works consulted to establish the history and genealogy were Ian Shaw, ed. *The Oxford History of Ancient Egypt* (Oxford: Oxford University Press, 2000) 480–485; Internet Archives, https://archive.org/details/TheOxfordHistoryOfAncient/page/n5/mode/2up and the chart of the "Egyptian Kings of the New Kingdom" in the *NIV Cultural Backgrounds Study Bible* (Grand Rapids: Zondervan, 2016), 107. Additional notes on dating and biblical events that correlate with certain Egyptian rulers are based on Eugene H. Merrill, *Kingdom of Priests: A History of Old Testament Israel* (Grand Rapids: Baker, 1996), 49–55, 57-78.

Pharaonic dating for the Twelfth Dynasty in the genealogical chart follows the chronological table in I. E. S. Edwards, et al., *The Cambridge Ancient History*, vol. 1, part 2, 3rd ed. (Cambridge: Cambridge University Press, 1971), 996. Pharaonic dating for the Eighteenth Dynasty follows the chronological table in I. E. S. Edwards, et al., *The Cambridge Ancient History*, vol. 2, part 1, 3rd ed. (Cambridge: Cambridge University Press, 1973), 819. Also taken into consideration was the dating in Jack Finegan, *Handbook of Biblical Chronology* (Peabody, MA: Hendrickson, 1998), 225.

2. Egyptian chronology is typically constructed based on ancient sources, such as (1) the history of Manetho, an Egyptian priest and chronologist of the early 3rd century B.C., who cataloged Egyptian kingship; (2) the so-called Egyptian king-lists; (3) date records from astronomical observations; (4) monument reliefs and stelae bearing biographies that refer to historical events and offer genealogical information; and (5) synchronisms with non-Egyptian sources, such as the Assyrian king-lists.

Egyptians marked years by the regnal year of the king, and dating was inclusive. However, exact dating continues to be debated and complicated by many factors, including: (1) different names for the same ruler and the fact that, by the Middle Kingdom, each king held five names, the so-called five-fold titulary; (2) lack of precise dating even from "absolute" astronomical chronologies; and (3) whether co-regencies actually took place, and if so, how long they existed.

The twofold dating system shown in the chart. For the reasons noted above, the dates shown in the genealogical charts for the Twelfth and Eighteenth Dynasties follow two sources:

(1) those in Merrill, *Kingdom of Priests*, 50, 58 [i.e., the first range of dates shown in parentheses below the pharaoh's name, which is based on the chronological tables in I. E. S. Edwards, et al., *The Cambridge Ancient History*, vol. 1, part 2, 3rd ed. (Cambridge: Cambridge University Press, 1971), 996 (12th Dynasty), and I. E. S. Edwards et al., *The Cambridge Ancient History*, vol. 2, part 1, 3rd ed. (Cambridge: Cambridge University Press, 1973), 819 (18th Dynasty)]; and

(2) the range of dates given in Ian Shaw, ed. *The Oxford History of Ancient Egypt* (Oxford: Oxford University Press, 2000), 483–485 and the chart of "Egyptian Kings of the New Kingdom" in the John Walton and Craig Keener, ed., *NIV Cultural Backgrounds Study Bible* (Grand Rapids: Zondervan, 2016), 107 (i.e., the second range of dates, which are shown in *italics*).

Depending on the source(s) used, a general variance of ±10–25 regnal years is common in pharaonic dating. For instance, slightly different regnal dates (from those shown in the chart) are given by Jack Finegan in his *Handbook of Biblical Chronology* (Peabody, MA: Hendrickson, 1998), 225 for the rulers of 18th Dynasty in his Table 116: Ahmose (1552–1526); Amenhotep I (1526–1506); Thutmose I (1506–1493); Thutmose II (1493–1479); Thutmose III (1479–1425); Hatshepsut (1478–1458); Amenhotep II (1425–1401); Thutmose IV (1401–1390); Amenhotep III (1390–1352); Amenhotep IV (1352–1348); Akhenaten (1348–1338); Smenkhkare (1338–1336); Tutankhaten/Tutankhamen (1336–1327); Ay (1327–1323); Horemheb (1323–1295).

3. The overall dynastic sequence and chronology summarized in table 1 is based on Shaw, *Oxford History*, 480–483.

4. **Ammenemes I** (1991–1962; *1985–1956*) was the son of Senusret and Nefret, who were not members of the royal family. Ammenemes I was possibly the vizier of the previous pharaoh Mentuhotep IV. Ammenemes I transferred Egypt's capital from Thebes to Amenhemhat-itj-tawy—meaning "Amenemhat [Ammenemes] the seizer of the two lands"—also known by its shortened form, Itjtawy. Ammenemes I was most likely murdered during a conspiracy that arose at the end of his reign.

5. **Sesostris I** (1971–1928; *1956–1911*) was the son of Ammenemes I. The king lists say that he reigned for 45 years. Some scholars think that his reign consisted of 35 years of sole reign and a ten-year coregency that was shared with his father, although recent scholarship has questioned this.

6. **Ammenemes II** (1929–1895; *1911–1877*) was the son of Sesostris I. His reign was generally peaceful, marked by agricultural and economic improvements. During this time, Egypt also cultivated relationships with peoples in western Asia.

Joseph in Egypt in service to Potiphar. The early events of Joseph's life appear to take place in the years of Ammenemes II's reign. Joseph was born in Paddan Aram in ca. 1915 B.C. In ca. 1898 B.C., at age 17, Joseph was sold by his brothers to Ishmaelites (**Genesis 37:25**; also called Midianites, **Genesis 37:28**), who then took Joseph to Egypt near the end of Ammenemes II's reign (cf. **Genesis 30:22–24; 37:25–28**; see chart "**Genesis 37**: Joseph and His Sons (Manasseh and Ephraim)." In Egypt, Joseph served under Potiphar, the Egyptian official and captain of the guard, from ca. 1898–1888 B.C. During that time, Ammenemes II (or perhaps Sesostris II) was the ruling pharaoh (**Genesis 37:36; 39:1–6**). After the false accusation of Potiphar's wife (**Genesis 39:7–20**), Joseph was imprisoned for two years, ca. 1887–1886 B.C. (**Genesis 41:1**).

7. **Sesostris II** (1897–1878; *1877–1870*) was the son of Ammenemes II. His first wife (possibly his sister) was Queen Nefret. The chief wife of Sesostris II was Khnumetnefer-hedjetweret, who was the mother of Sesostris III.

Joseph in service to Pharaoh Sesostris II. Through the inspiration of Yahweh, Joseph interpreted the dreams of Sesostris II (cf. **Genesis 41:1–40**), foretelling that there would be *seven years of abundance* (ca. 1884–1878 B.C., inclusive) followed by *seven years of famine* (ca. 1877–1871 B.C., inclusive; cf. **Genesis 41:25–31**). Joseph recommended to Sesostris II that he "appoint commissioners over the land to take a fifth of the harvest of Egypt during the seven years of abundance" (**Genesis 41:34**) and store it in preparation for the years of famine (**Genesis 41:35–36**). Because of Joseph's wisdom, Pharaoh Sesostris appointed him "in charge of the whole land of Egypt" and his "second-in-command" (**Genesis 41:40–43**). Sesostris II also changed Joseph's name to Zaphenath-Paneah and gave him Asenath, the daughter of Potiphera, the priest of On, to be his wife (**Genesis 41:45**). Scholar Eugene Merrill notes that Sesostris II fostered a close relationship with western Asia and that Joseph's ethnic background would have not been unwelcomed (*Kingdom of Priests*, 50).

Secular history shows that land reclamation and flood control projects were undertaken during Sesostris II's reign, including the digging of a canal to connect the Faiyum Basin with the Nile; the ruins still bear the name *Bahr Yusef*, "River of Joseph," perhaps indicating Joseph's involvement in the public works projects of Sesostris II.

8. **Sesostris III** held an unusually long reign of over thirty years (1878–1843; *1870–1831*). He is described by Manetho and Herodotus as a very visible, "composite heroic ruler." Sesostris III campaigned at least once in Palestine and claimed to have gone to Sekmem (probably referring to Shechem). The *Oxford History of Ancient Egypt* remarks that by the reign of Seostris III, "large numbers of Asiatics [existed] in Egypt" and that "some of them were prisoners taken earlier, but the biblical account of Joseph's brothers selling him as a slave . . . may suggest another way in which some of these immigrants arrived" (Shaw, *Oxford History*, 155).

Joseph's role in Egypt's famine and immigration of Jacob's family to Egypt in 1876 B.C. Either Sesostris II or Sesostris III appears to be the Egyptian ruler at the beginning of the *seven years of famine* (ca. 1878–1871 B.C.; cf. **Genesis 41:29–31, 53–54**). The famine spread to other lands as well, but Egypt was the only nation that had food (i.e., the "fifth of the harvest of Egypt" that had been collected by Joseph yearly during the *seven years of abundance* was a safeguard against the coming years of famine; cf. **Genesis 41:35–36, 54**). As a result, people from all over the region came to Egypt to buy food, including ten of Joseph's brothers (cf. **Genesis 41:57; 42:1–5**). In 1876 B.C., during Sesostris II's or Sesostris III's reign, Joseph's father, Jacob, moved his entire extended family of 70 descendants to Egypt to escape the famine in Canaan (**Genesis 45:9–47:12**; see chart "**Genesis 46**: The Extended Family of Jacob (Seventy Descendants) Who Migrated to Egypt"). Jacob died in Egypt in 1859 B.C. at the age of 147 (**Genesis 47:28**), presumably during the reign of Sesostris III. Jacob was embalmed according to Egyptian practices; his bones were eventually carried to Canaan by the post-exodus generation and buried in the cave in the field of Machpelah according to his instructions (**Genesis 49:29–50:3, 12–13**).

9. **Ammenemes III** (1842–1797; *1831–1786*) was the only known son of Sesostris III. During his reign, Egypt intensified its mining, building, and industrial activities, which in turn brought about cultural achievements in the Middle Kingdom. Originally, Ammenemes III's burial chamber at Hawara was intended to be shared with Princess Neferuptah—his sister or daughter (?) who was groomed to be his successor—but later her body was transferred to a small, separate pyramid. Joseph died in 1805 B.C. at the age of 110, during the reign of Ammenemes III (cf. **Genesis 50:22, 26**).

10. **Ammenemes IV** (1798–1790; *1786–1777*) may have been the *grandson* (rather than the son) of Ammenemes III, due to the latter's long reign; alternatively, it is also possible that this last male ruler of the 12th Dynasty was an aged *son* when he came to the throne, for he ruled for only nine years. According to Manetho, Ammenemes IV was married to his sister, Queen Sobekkara (Sobekneferu).

11. **Sobekneferu** (1789–1786; *1777–1773*) was the probably the sister-wife of Ammenemes IV. As pharaoh, she used feminine titles and wore female dress, but occasionally employed male titles as well. She also wore an unusual crown to signify iconographic elements of both male and female rulers, possibly to mollify the critics of a sole *female* ruler of Egypt. Her reign lasted less than four years.

12. **Ahmose I** (1570–1546; *1550–1525*) was the founder and first ruler of the 18th Dynasty. He built the last known royal pyramid in Egypt at Abydos; thereafter, pharaohs were often buried in royal tombs in the Valley of the Kings near the ancient Egyptian capital of Thebes. Ahmose I may not have been an adult at his accession; also, there may have been a brief co-regency of Ahmose I with his successor-son, Amenhotep I. Jack Finegan identifies Ahmose as the son of Abina (or Ibana) and the younger brother of Kamose, who was the last native pharaoh of the 17th dynasty and known for warring against the Hyksos (Semitic foreigners). After the Hyksos took Avaris (located in the Eastern Nile Delta) and made it their main base around 1730 B.C., the Hyksos ruled in Egypt for about 100 years, from ca. 1650–1542 B.C. Eventually the Hyksos were ousted by Egyptians who had retained power in Upper Egypt. The chronologist Manetho used the name *Tethmosis* for Ahmose and credited him as being "the king who drove the Hyksos out of Egypt" (Finegan, *Handbook of Biblical Chronology*, 225–226). *The Oxford History of Ancient Egypt* asserts that the reunification of Egypt took place only in the last decade of the twenty-five-year reign of Ahmose I, stating that the "[18th] dynasty may be said to have begun officially around 1530, but it was already well under way during Ahmose's reign" (Shaw, *Oxford History*, 207).

Pharaoh Ahmose's mother was Ahhotep (the daughter of a woman named Tetisheri). Genealogical documentation in *The Oxford History of Ancient Egypt* suggests that Tetisheri also bore a son (either by her full- or half-brother) whose name was Seqenenra (possibly the same person as Kamose, the last pharaoh of the 17th Dynasty) who may have been the *father* of Ahmose. Therefore, Tetisheri possibly bore *both* the mother and the father of King Ahmose. Queen Ahhotep played a key role in the reigns of Ahmose (her son) and Amenhotep I (her grandson).

Ahmose I married his sister Ahmose-Nefertari, who functioned as his "great royal wife." By her, Ahmose fathered at least two sons: Ahmose-ankh and Amenhotep I. He may also have fathered two daughters by Ahmose-Nefertari: Satkamose (the sister of Amenhotep I) and Ahmose-Merytamum (who is thought to have married her brother, Amenhotep I, although Shaw, *The Oxford History of Ancient Egypt*, 218, clarifies that no document states this explicitly).

Oppression of the Israelites in Egypt and Moses' birth in 1526 B.C. Depending on the exact regnal dates of the rulers, Ahmose I (or perhaps his son Amenhotep I) was the pharaoh referred to in the introductory story of Moses: "Then a new king [a new dynasty/the 18th dynasty?], to whom Joseph meant nothing, came to power in Egypt. . . . 'the Israelites have become far too numerous for us. Come, we must deal shrewdly with them or they will become even more numerous and, if war breaks out, will join our enemies, fight against us and leave the country.' So they [the Egyptians] put slave masters over them to oppress them with forced labor, and they built Pithom and Rameses as store cities for Pharaoh" (**Exodus 1:8–11**).

Furthermore, the pharaoh at the time commanded the Hebrew midwives, Shiphrah and Puah, to kill the Hebrew male children: "'When you are helping the Hebrew women during childbirth on the delivery stool, if you see that the baby is a boy, kill him; but if it is a girl, let her live'" (**Exodus 1:16**). However, the midwives disobeyed the royal edict and saved many Israelite children (cf. **Exodus 1:15–21**). Moses, Israel's future leader, was born in 1526 B.C., probably at the end of the reign of Ahmose I or the beginning of the reign of Amenhotep I (see chart "**Exodus 6**: Moses, Aaron, and Miriam, the Leaders of Israel").

13. **Amenhotep I** (1546–1526; *1525–1504*) was the son of Ahmose I and Ahmose-Nefertari. Like his father, he may not have been an adult at his accession, because an elder brother (Ahmose-ankh) had been designated the heir only about five years earlier. Some scholars have suggested that there may have been a brief co-regency between Ahmose I and Amenhotep I, and in that regard, Amenhotep I's reign was actually a formal *continuation* of his father's reign. *The Oxford History of Ancient Egypt* explains that restrictions were placed on royal marriages during the early 18th Dynasty: "The title held by these [royal] women, and the absence of husbands other than kings, show the limitations that were placed on females born of the king. The success of the dynastic line . . . was certainly attributable, in part, to a decision to limit access to the royal family. . . . In political and religious terms, the closed royal family apparently reached back into the Middle Kingdom . . . when princesses were frequently married to kings or associated throughout life with their reigning fathers. In order to assure the exclusivity of the line . . . [an] additional prohibition [was put in place whereby] royal daughters were to marry no one other than a king [a mandate that had existed from the days of Ahhotep, the mother of King Ahmose, and] . . . Once the custom was established at the end of the 17th Dynasty, it persisted through the 18th Dynasty" (Shaw, *Oxford History*, 217).

Quite surprisingly, however, "there were no enfeebling effects on the kinship line as a result of this practice, because it did not mean that the kings could *only* marry princesses. In fact, throughout the 18th Dynasty, kings were most commonly born to their fathers by *non-royal* secondary queens . . . Despite the restrictions on marriage for kings' daughters, several princesses who emerged as major queens (Ahhotep, Ahmose-Nefertari, Hatshepsut) were extremely active in the reigns of their husband and heirs" (Shaw, *Oxford History*, 218).

14. **Thutmose I** reigned ca. 1526–1512; *1504–1492* and was the first of the 18th Dynasty to not come to the throne by way of father-son succession. His father was unknown; his mother, Seniseneb, only held the title of "king's mother" during her son's reign. Seniseneb may have been a member of Amenhotep I's family, perhaps through Prince Ahmose-ankh. Thutmose I's principal wife was Ahmose, who held the title "king's sister, great royal wife." Some scholars have assumed that she was Thutmose's own sister (i.e., a brother-sister rulership, similar to those of the two preceding regents) or another Ahmose, a female descendant of Ahmose-ankh. Thutmose I fathered Thutmose II by a non-royal wife named Mutnefret. The mother(s) of Thutmose's two other sons, Amenmose and Wadjmose, is uncertain. Ahmose-Nefertari (the mother of Amenhotep I) died during the reign of Thutmose I. Presumably to strengthen his claim to the throne, Thutmose II (the future king) was married to Hatshepsut, his half-sister.

15. **Hatshepsut**, who reigned ca. 1503–1483; *1473–1458*, was the daughter of Thutmose I and Ahmose, his queen/principal wife. Hatshepsut held the title "the king's daughter, king's sister, wife of the god [Amun], great wife of the king." Scholars have suggested that, even before her father's death, Hatshepsut saw herself (not her half-brother, Thutmose II) as the future heir. She consistently emphasized *her* blood line and claimed the right to rule as her father's successor. Hatshepsut was married to her half-brother Thutmose II, and they had one daughter named Nefrura (or Neferure). Even before the early death of her husband, Hatshepsut is believed to have used her power to exert a strong influence on the monarchy. She gave herself the throne name "Maatkara" and publicly transformed herself into a "king"—clearly *not* trying

to legitimize her reign by claiming to rule *with* or *for* (her husband/half-brother) Thutmose II. Also, Hatshepsut acted as the primary regent for Thutmose III (the son of Thutmose II by a non-royal wife, Iset) who came to the throne in early childhood.

The infant Moses found in the Nile River in ca. 1526 B.C. and raised by Pharaoh's daughter. Based on **Exodus 2:5**, the "Pharaoh's daughter" who discovered the Hebrew baby, Moses, in the Nile, was likely Hatshepsut, the daughter of Thutmose I. Eugene Merrill concludes that "the general picture of Hatshepsut leads us to identify this bold queen [who was a princess in 1526 B.C.] as the daughter of Pharaoh [Thutmose I] who rescued Moses. Only she of all known women of the period possessed the presumption and independence to violate an ordinance of the king and under his very nose at that! Though the birth date of this daughter of Thutmose I is unknown, she was probably several years older than her husband, Thutmose II who died . . . while in his late twenties. She [Hatshepsut] may have been in her early teens by 1526 B.C., Moses' birth date, and therefore able to effect his deliverance" (Merrill, *Kingdom of Priests*, 60). **Exodus 2:10a** explains that "when the child grew older, she [Moses' mother, Jochebed] took him to Pharaoh's daughter [presumably Hatshepsut] and he became her son." Furthermore, Hatshepsut may have been grooming Moses to be *her* successor! Moses was thus raised in the Egyptian court (during the reigns of Thutmose I, Hatshepsut, Thutmose II and/or Thutmose III). In this providential way, Moses received a royal education "in all the wisdom of the Egyptians and was powerful in speech and action" (**Acts 7:22**). Moses eventually authored/compiled the Pentateuch. According to the biblical account and chronology, Moses was in Egypt for 40 years (1526–1486 B.C.).

16. **Thutmose II** was pharaoh from 1512–1504; *1492–1479*. Hatshepsut, the older half-sister of Thutmose II, became his "great royal wife" and "queen," and they had a daughter Nefrura (or Neferure). Because there are few records of his brief rule, Thutmose II's age at his accession and death are unknown. Apparently, he died relatively young and was outlived by Hatshepsut. His son/successor was Thutmose III by his non-royal wife, Iset.

Moses as an adult in Egypt and his subsequent sojourn in Midian, 1486–1446 B.C. The biblical narrative of Moses resumes during the reign of Thutmose II (or possibly Thutmose III). In 1486 B.C., when Moses was 40 years old and still living in Egypt, he visited his people (the Israelites), witnessed the hard labor that was exacted of them, and sided with their plight. When he saw an Egyptian beating an Israelite, Moses killed the Egyptian and tried to cover it up, but others knew of the murder. When the Pharaoh was told of this, he sought to kill Moses, and, in fear, Moses fled to Midian (**Exodus 2:11–15; Acts 7:23–29**). Moses stayed in Midan for 40 years (1486–1446 B.C.); he lived with a priest named Jethro and married Jethro's daughter Zipporah; see charts "**Exodus 2**: Moses and Zipporah" and "**Exodus 6**: Moses, Aaron, and Miriam, the Leaders of Israel." Moses' sojourn in Midian probably corresponds to the reign of Thutmose II and/or Thutmose III.

17. **Thutmose III** enjoyed a long fifty-four-year reign (1504–1450; *1479–1425*). He was the son of Thutmose II and a non-royal wife named Iset. Since he came to the throne while very young (a child-king), Hatshepsut (his stepmother/aunt) was the acting regent—some hold, in fact, that the dating of Thutmose III's reign may have applied to Hatshepsut's own reign as much as to his. Sometime between years 2 and 7 of Thutmose III's reign, Hatshepsut took the title "king" of Egypt. However, in the 22nd year of Thutmose III's reign, Hatshepsut's name disappears from the historical records, probably because she died. Thutmose III used his 32 years of sole rulership to make his name prominent, or more prominent, throughout Egypt and Nubia. After 17 years of military campaigns, he successfully established an Egyptian dominance in Palestine. In the last few years of his reign, Thutmose III began to dishonor the name and monuments of Hatshepsut throughout Egypt. His son, Amenhotep II, acted as his co-regent during the last two years of Thutmose's reign.

Thutmose III's wives appear to include Neferure/Nefrura (the daughter of Hatshepsut and Thutmose II) and a woman named Sitiah. Another wife, Merytra, produced several children, including the next pharaoh, Amenhotep II.

Moses' return to Egypt and the exodus of the Israelites in 1446 B.C. Depending on the accuracy of the proposed Egyptian chronology, Thutmose III (or perhaps his son, Amenhotep II) was the "Pharaoh of the Exodus." In 1446 B.C., at the age of 80, Moses returned to Egypt and spoke to the Pharaoh, telling him that the Lord had commanded him to "Let my people go" (cf. **Exodus 5:1; 7:16; 8:1**). Acting under the hand of God, Moses and his brother, Aaron, brought about the miracles of the ten plagues, with the final plague being the death of the Egyptians' firstborn sons. In 1446 B.C., Moses led the Israelites out of Egyptian bondage (**Exodus 7–14**). They sojourned in the wilderness for 40 years, and a remnant finally entered the promised land of Canaan in 1406 B.C.

18. **Amenhotep II** reigned 1450–1425; ca. *1427–1400*. He was the son of Thutmose III and Merytra. In the fifty-first year of his father's reign, Amenhotep II acted as co-regent with his father, but he shared the monarchy for a little more than two years. Amenhotep II continued the erasure and dishonoring of Hatshepsut that had begun under his father Thutmose III. The process of systematically eliminating Hatshepsut and her family line on monuments in Egypt was undertaken in several ways: in some places, it was achieved by obscuring her name with new works or by removing any evidence of her name; in other places, existing monuments were simply altered to replace Hatshepsut's name with Thutmose II (Amenhotep II's grandfather) or Thutmose III (Amenhotep II's father).

Apparently, Amenhotep II had no publicly acknowledged consort for much of his reign other than his mother, Merytra, who served as "great royal wife," although a woman named Tiaa was the mother of his son and successor, Thutmose IV. Scholars believe that the absence of wives was considered a conscious rejection of the dynastic role that queens had played from the establishment of the dynasty up through the reign of Hatshepsut; the "queen turned king" usurpation of the throne by Hatshepsut may have given Amenhotep II and his father, Thutmose III, a particular incentive to choose women from outside the main royal line as their great royal wives. Amenhotep II fathered a number of princes, but apart from Tiaa, his wives are unknown. Amenhotep II had military successes in the Levant and brought peace to Egypt.

19. **Thutmose IV** reigned from 1425–1417; *1400–1390*. He was the son of Amenhotep II. Thutmose IV designated his mother, Tiaa, as "great royal wife" during most of his reign. A non-royal wife Nefertiry, who also was designated "great royal wife," acted alongside Tiaa during the earlier years of his rule, thereby forming a kind of mother-son-wife triad. Apparently, after Nefertiry died (or was set aside), Thutmose IV married his sister (i.e., a daughter of Amenhotep II), whose name was Iaret. The mother of Amenhotep III, Mutemwiya, was never acknowledged by Thutmose IV as either a major or minor queen.

20. **Amenhotep III** had a 38-year reign (1417–1379; *ca. 1390–1352*), which was known as a period of peace and affluence. He may have been a child (age 2 to 12) at his accession to the throne, so his early reign was conducted by his mother, Mutemwiya. Amenhotep III married Queen Tiye (the daughter of Yuya and Tuya), and she became the most influential woman during his reign, although Satamun (the most elevated of Tiye's daughters) bore the title "great royal wife" simultaneously with Tiye. By pairing his wife and daughter(s) with himself and refusing to give his daughters in marriage to non-royal men, Amenhotep III enlarged his own holdings and retained the wealth in the royal family. Amenhotep III is also known to have married a Babylonian princess and two Mitannian princesses—one of whom, named Taduhepa, reached Egypt only in time to become a widow, so she was given in marriage to Amenhotep IV (the son of Amenhotep III and Tiye).

Amenhotep III was deified during his lifetime, or at least he sought to give that impression. His son, Amenhotep IV (also called Akhenaten) appears to have transformed his deified father into the disembodied solar disc Aten. Whether there was an actual co-regency between them is debated. When Amenhotep III died, he left behind a country that was wealthier and more powerful than in the past, and extraordinary luxury typified the culture.

21. **Amenhotep IV/Akhenaten** (1379–1362; *1352–1336*) was the son of Amenhotep III and Tiye. His first wife (called "king's wife") was Nefertiti, and she produced six daughters (but no son/heir); the eldest daughter, Meritaten, became the most prominent. Akhenaten took a second wife named Kiya; her title was "greatly beloved wife of the king." Sometime in Akhenaten's regnal year 12, Kiya's name disappears from monuments—possibly because she became too much of a rival to Nefertiti after Kiya bore the beloved Tutankhaten (the male heir and future king). Kiya's name was replaced on the monuments by those of Akhenaten's daughters, most frequently Meritaten. Nefertiti's influence greatly increased during the latter part of Akhenaten's reign, to the point that she became the official co-regent of her husband. Eventually, Nefertiti's role

as queen consort was taken over by her eldest daughter, Meritaten. Akhenaten died in regnal year 17.

22. **Smenkhkare** had an ephemeral reign (1364–1361; *1338–1336?*), but the actual dates are uncertain. The table of "Egyptian Kings of the New Kingdom" in the John Walton and Craig Keener, eds, *NIV Cultural Backgrounds Study Bible*, 107, refers to him as "Neferneferuaten" but "he" held virtually the same throne name as Nefertiti ("Ankh(et)kheperura"). In rare representations, he is accompanied by his queen Meritaten. The identity of Smenkhkare is uncertain. Many scholars consider him to be Nefertiti's male successor—perhaps a younger brother or even another son of Akhenaten—but others hold to the strong possibility that "he" was actually Nefertiti, who had assumed a male persona and ruled for a brief period after Akhenaten's death. Meritaten, the eldest daughter of Nefertiti, was "great royal wife" in the ceremonial sense. When Smenkhkare died, the very young Tutankhaten (the only remaining male member of the royal family) came to the throne.

23. **Tutankhamun** (1361–1352; *1336–1327*) was the son of Akhenaten by his second wife, Kiya. He came to the throne as the child-pharaoh named "Tutankhaten," but his name was eventually changed to Tutankhamun. His great royal wife was his half-sister Ankhesenpaaten (altered to Ankhesenamun). In times past, when a child had ascended the throne, a senior female member of the family presided as the regent during his early years as king. Since no such option was available to Tutankhamun, the commander-in-chief of the army (named Horemheb) gained the right to succeed Tutankhamun if he died without issue. King Tut did, in fact, die unexpectedly in his tenth regnal year.

24. **Ay**, also known as Kheperkheperura, was a senior court official under Akhenaten (and perhaps a relative of Amenhotep III's wife Tiye) and was Tutankhamun's successor. Initially, Ay served as kind of interim king for Tutankhamun's widow, Ankhesenpaaten, while she tried to secure a husband, but then Ay came to the throne in his own right. It is thought that Ay was fairly aged when he assumed the throne. He ruled for at least three years (1352–1348; *1327–1323*).

25. **Horemheb**, also known as Djeserkheperura, was a military official with no blood kinship to the royal family (a fact that he did not hide). Although Ay came to the throne before him, Horemheb was the "heir presumptive" of King Tutankhamun. His queen, Mutnedjmet, was probably his wife before his accession. Horemheb's reign (1348–1320; *1323–1295*) appears to be relatively uneventful. He was the last ruler of the 18th Dynasty.

SUPPLEMENT 2: THE HIGH PRIESTS OF ISRAEL[1]

Approximate Dating: from Aaron the first high priest, ca. 1444 B.C., to Phannias the last high priest, ca. A.D. 70[2] (numbers in the chart indicate the order of priestly succession)

High Priests from the Time of the Institution of the Aaronic Priesthood to the Babylonian Exile (Cf. 1 Chronicles 6:1–15, 50–53; 9:11; Ezra 7:1–6; Nehemiah 11:10–11)

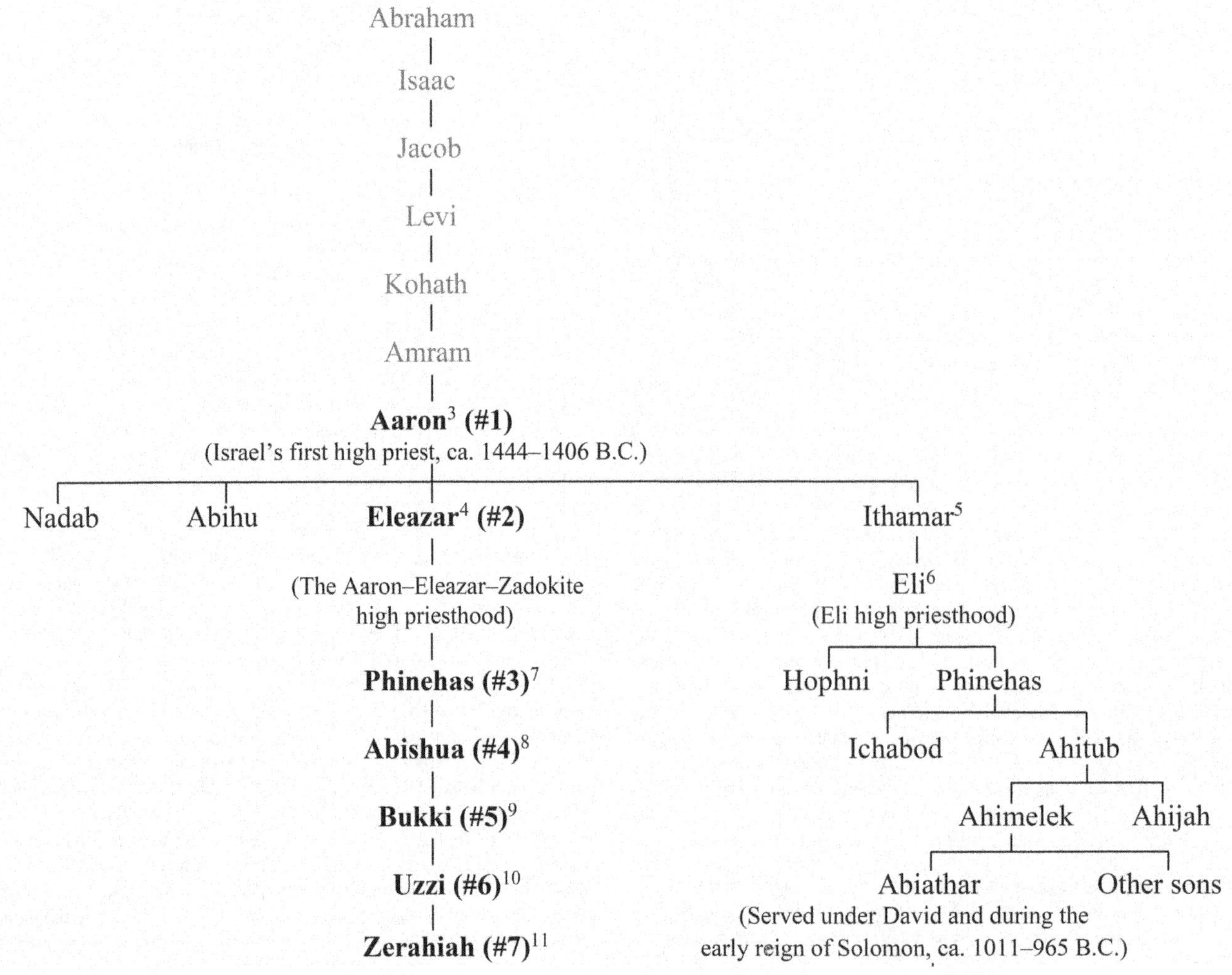

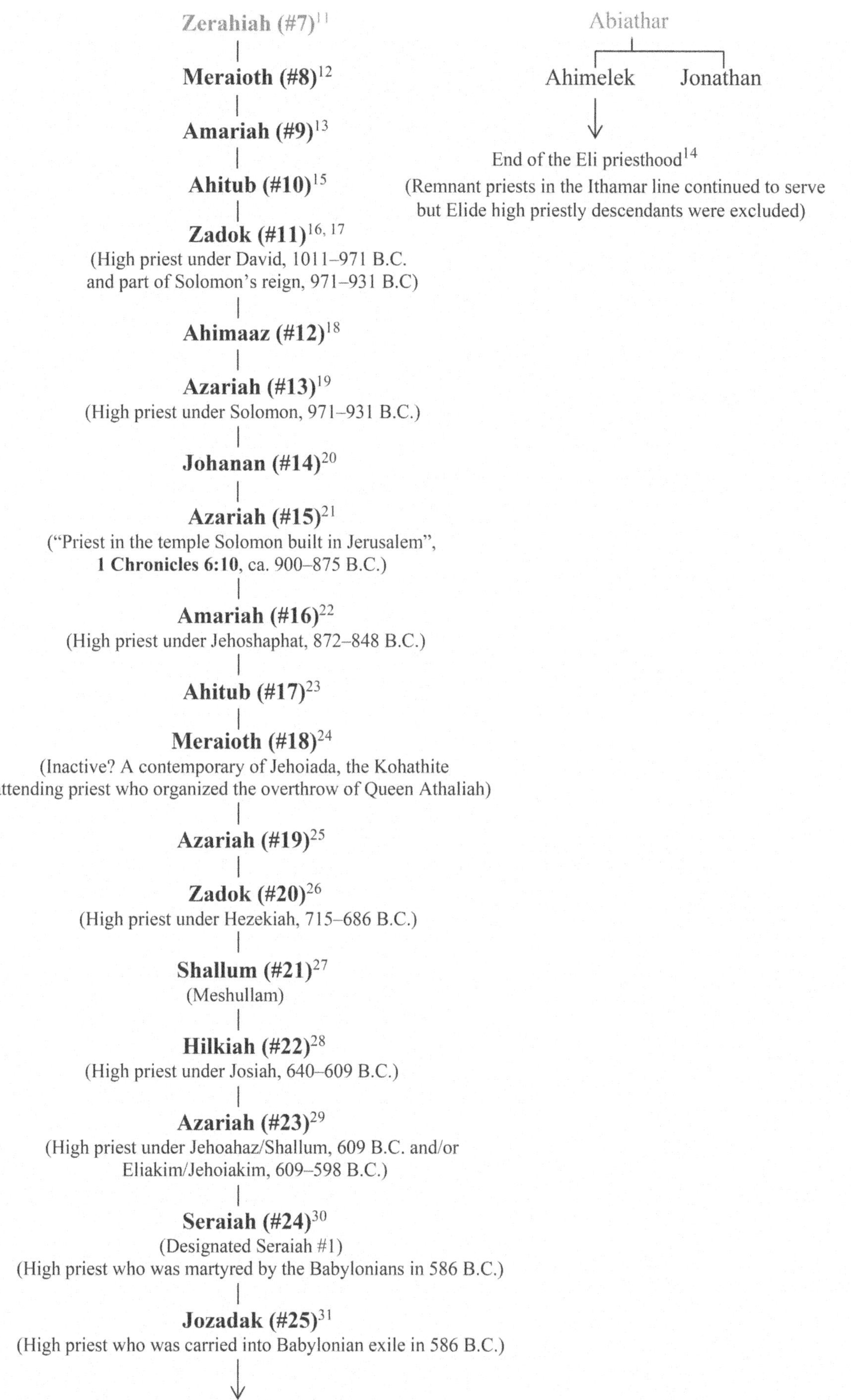

Zerahiah (#7)[11]
Meraioth (#8)[12]
Amariah (#9)[13]
Ahitub (#10)[15]
Zadok (#11)[16, 17]
(High priest under David, 1011–971 B.C.
and part of Solomon's reign, 971–931 B.C)
Ahimaaz (#12)[18]
Azariah (#13)[19]
(High priest under Solomon, 971–931 B.C.)
Johanan (#14)[20]
Azariah (#15)[21]
("Priest in the temple Solomon built in Jerusalem",
1 Chronicles 6:10, ca. 900–875 B.C.)
Amariah (#16)[22]
(High priest under Jehoshaphat, 872–848 B.C.)
Ahitub (#17)[23]
Meraioth (#18)[24]
(Inactive? A contemporary of Jehoiada, the Kohathite
attending priest who organized the overthrow of Queen Athaliah)
Azariah (#19)[25]
Zadok (#20)[26]
(High priest under Hezekiah, 715–686 B.C.)
Shallum (#21)[27]
(Meshullam)
Hilkiah (#22)[28]
(High priest under Josiah, 640–609 B.C.)
Azariah (#23)[29]
(High priest under Jehoahaz/Shallum, 609 B.C. and/or
Eliakim/Jehoiakim, 609–598 B.C.)
Seraiah (#24)[30]
(Designated Seraiah #1)
(High priest who was martyred by the Babylonians in 586 B.C.)
Jozadak (#25)[31]
(High priest who was carried into Babylonian exile in 586 B.C.)
High Priests after the Babylonian Exile
Abiathar
Ahimelek
Jonathan
End of the Eli priesthood[14]
(Remnant priests in the Ithamar line continued to serve
but Elide high priestly descendants were excluded)

High Priests after the Babylonian Exile

High Priests of the Persian Period (cf. Nehemiah 12:10–11, 22–23)

Joshua/Jeshua (#26)[32]
("Jesus")
(Arrived in Jerusalem with Zerubbabel in 538 B.C.)
(First high priest to officiate in the Second Temple, ca. 516–490 B.C.)

|

Joiakim (#27)[33]
(ca. 490–450/445 B.C.)

|

Eliashib (#28)[34]
(ca. 450/445–432 B.C.)

|

Joiada (#29)[35]
("Judas")
(ca. 432–410 B.C.)

|

Jonathan (#30)[36]
("Johanan") ("Jehohanan") ("John")
(ca. 410–370 B.C.)

|

Jaddua (#31)[37]
(ca. 370–332 B.C.)
(A contemporary of Alexander the Great)

----------------- **End of the Old Testament record of the high priests of Israel** -----------------

High Priests of the Oniad Dynasty (Early Hellenistic Period)

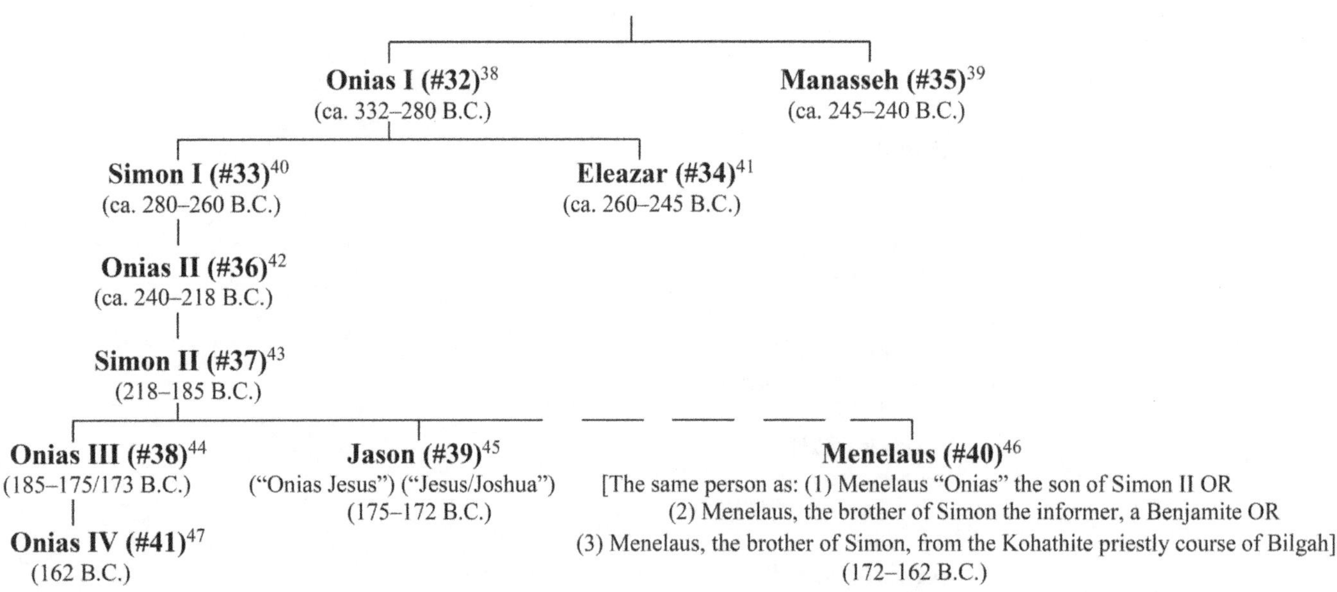

----- **End of the Oniad Dynasty and the historic, forty-fold generations of father-son and close relative priestly succession** -----------

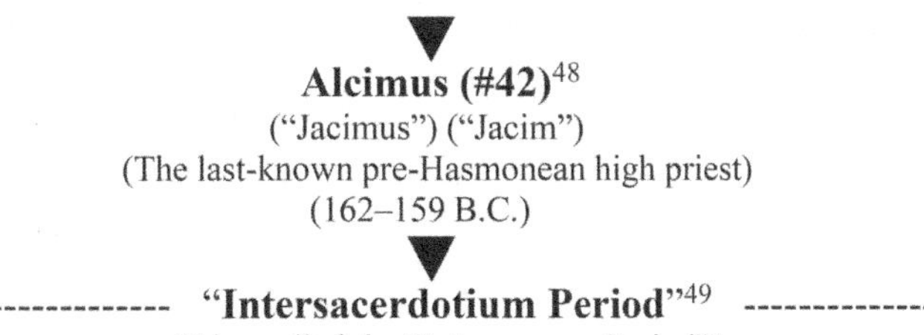

Alcimus (#42)[48]
("Jacimus") ("Jacim")
(The last-known pre-Hasmonean high priest)
(162–159 B.C.)

-------------- **"Intersacerdotium Period"**[49] --------------
(Also called the "Interregnum Period")
(Seven-year vacancy in the high priesthood from ca. 159–153/152 B.C. between the death of Alcimus and the beginning of the Hasmonean high priesthood under Jonathan Maccabeus)

High Priests of the Hasmonean Dynasty

Note: The first official high priest in the Hasmonean dynasty was Jonathan, the son of Mattathias (#43). He and all remaining high priests thereafter were *not* direct father-son descendants of the ancestral Aaronic priesthood. Rather, the Hasmonean high priests descended from the Joiarib line of Kohathite attending priests (who were *brethren/close blood relatives* of the high priests) and were in a genealogical line that paralleled that of the Aaronic high priesthood. The Kohathite attending priests assisted the Aaron/Zadokite high priests but were not high priests themselves.[50]

Joiarib
(Jehoiarib)
(Head over the 1st of the 24 divisions of attending Kohathite priests in Solomon's Temple, **1 Chronicles 24:7**)[51]
|
Asamoneus of Jerusalem
(Eponymous ancestor of the "Hasmoneans")
|
Simeon
|
John
|
Mattathias[52]
("Mattathis Maccabeus")
(Instigator of the Maccabean Revolt, which lasted from ca. 167–160 B.C.)
(Died in 166 B.C.)

Children of Mattathias:

- John ("Gaddis") ("Caddis")
- **Simon (#44)**[53] ("Simon Maccabeus" or "Matthes" or "Simon Thassi") (142–134 B.C.)
  - **John Hyrcanus I (#45)**[56] ("King"/national ruler & high priest, 134–104 B.C.)
- Judas[54] ("Judas Maccabeus") ("Judah Maccabeus") (Esteemed by the people to hold an *unofficial* 3 or 4-year high priesthood, but his exact term is unclear)
- Eleazar ("Auran")
- **Jonathan (#43)**[55] ("Jonathan Apphus") ("Jonathan Maccabeus") (152–143/142 B.C.)
  - ↓ (Ancestral line of Flavius Josephus)[57]

Children of John Hyrcanus I:

- **Aristobulus I (#46)**[58] (King & high priest, 104–103 B.C.) m. Salome Alexandra ("Alexandra") ("Co-regent" with Aristobulus I)
- **Alexander Jannaeus (#47)**[59] (King & high priest, 103–76 B.C.) m. Salome Alexandra[60] (Widow of Aristobulus I) (Queen, 103–76 B.C., and sole ruler, 76–67 B.C.)

Children of Alexander Jannaeus and Salome Alexandra:

- **John Hyrcanus II (#48)**[61] (King for 3 months in 67 B.C.) (High priest, 76–67 B.C.) (Restored high priest and ethnarch, 63–40 B.C.)
- **Aristobulus II (#49)**[62] (King & high priest, 67–63 B.C.)
  - **Antigonus II (#50)**[63] ("Antigonus") ("Antigonus Mattathias") (King & high priest, 40–37 B.C.)
  - Alexander II[64] ("Jonathan Alexander/Alexandres")
    - Aristobulus III (A high priest of the Herodian Dynasty; see below)
    - Mariamne I[65] (Hasmonean) (2nd wife of Herod the Great)

------------- **End of the Hasmonean Dynasty**[66] -------------

High Priests in the Herodian Dynasty and the Roman Period

Ananelus (#51)[68]
("Hanameel") ("Ananel")
(37–35 B.C.)

Aristobulus III (#52)[69]
(Hasmonean)
(35 B.C.)

Ananelus (restored)[70]
(35–30? B.C. or 34–30B.C.?)

Joshua ben Fabus (#53)[71]
("Jesus, son of Phabet") ("Jesus son of Phiabi/Phabus/Phabes")
(30–24/22 B.C.)

Simon ben Boethus (#54)[72]
(24/22–5 B.C.)

Matthias ben Theophilus (#55)[73]
("Mattaiah")
(5–4 B.C.)
(For one day in 5 B.C., a kinsman named
Joseph the son of Ellemus [Elam] officiated for Matthias)

Joazar ben Boethus (#56)[74]
(4 B.C)

Eleazar ben Boethus (#57)[75]
(4 B.C.)

Joshua ben Sie (#58)[76]
("Jesus, son of Sie/Seë")
(4 B.C. to ?)

Joazar ben Boethus (restored)[77]
(?–A.D. 6)

Ananus ben Seth/Sethi (#59)[78]
("Annas") ("Annas/Ananus the elder")
(A.D. 6–15)

Ishmael ben Fabus (#60)[79]
("Ishmael ben Phabi/Phiabi I") ("Ishmael ben Fabi")
(A.D. 15–16?)

Eleazar ben Ananus (#61)[80]
(A.D. 16–17?)

Simon ben Camithus (#62)[81]
("Simon/Simeon son of Kamithos")
(A.D. 17–18)

Simon ben Camithus (#62)[81]

Joseph Caiaphas (#63)[82]
("Caiaphas")
(A.D. 18–36/37)

Jonathan ben Ananus (#64)[83]
(Fifty days in A.D. 37)

Theophilus ben Ananus (#65)[84]
(A.D. 37–41)

Simon ben Boethus (#66)[85]
("Simon Cantheras") ("Simon Kantheras")
(A.D. 41–42)

Matthias ben Ananus (#67)[86]
(A.D. 42–43?)

**Elioneus ben Simon Cantheras/
Kantheras/Cimtheras (#68)**[87]
("Aljoneus") ("Elionaeus") ("Elianaius")
(A.D. 44 or 43?–45)

Joseph ben Camydus (#69)[88]
("Joseph, son of Camei/Cantos/Cainus/Kami")
(A.D. 45–48)

Ananias ben Nebedeus/Nedebaeus (#70)[89]
("Ananias, son of Nebedaius") ("Ananias")
(A.D. 48–59)

Jonathan ben Ananus (restored)[90]
(A.D. 59)

Ishmael/Ismael ben Fabus (#71)[91]
("Ishmael ben Phiabi II") ("Ishmael ben Fabi")
(A.D. 59–61)

Joseph Cabi ben Simon (#72)[92]
("Joseph Qabi")
(A.D. 61–62)

Ananus ben Ananus (#73)[93]
("Ananus the Younger")
(3 months in A.D. 62)

Joshua ben Damneus/Damnaeus/Damnai (#74)[94]
("Jesus ben Damnai") ("Jesus, son of Damnaius")
(A.D. 62–63? or 63–65)

Joshua ben Damneus/Damnaeus/Damnai (#74)[94]

Joshua ben Gamaliel (#75)[95]
("Jesus ben Gamaliel") ("Jesus ben Gamla")
(A.D. 63–64 or 63–65)

Matthias ben Theophilus (#76)[96]
(A.D. 65–67)

High Priest During the First Jewish-Roman War (A.D. 66–73)

Phannias ben Samuel (#77)[97]
("Phanas") ("Phanni") ("Pinhas of Habta")
(A.D. 67/68–70)

LEGEND:

| : Line of descent from father-to-son, or by direct hereditary priestly succession (e.g., Aaron the high priest was succeeded by his *son* Eleazar)

┌─┘ : Successor was related to the previous high priest, but not directly (e.g., Jonathan ben Ananus was the *brother-in-law* of Joseph Caiaphus, the former high priest)

 : Successor was unrelated to the previous high priest

Biblical and Theological Significance

The Bible offers no comprehensive list of high priests, only partial lists (e.g., **1 Chronicles 6:1–15; Ezra 7:1–5; Nehemiah 12:10–11**) that require reconstruction through the various time periods of Israel's history. The all-inclusive genealogy shown above substantiates that meticulous written records were kept for the highly revered high priesthood up to the time of the destruction of the temple in A.D. 70.[98] The first to hold the high priesthood was Aaron, who was divinely appointed by God and became the progenitor of the holy Aaronic priesthood (**Exodus 28:1; Hebrews 5:4**). Thereafter, Aaron's direct descendants—starting with his son Eleazar—held the office of high priest in father-to-son succession. Typically, a high priest held office for life; when he died, his eldest son (or eldest surviving son) succeeded him. The age of eligibility was at least thirty years old to serve in the tabernacle during the days in the wilderness (**Numbers 4:1–4**); however, the age of service shifted from thirty to twenty years of age by the time of the First and Second Temples (cf. **1 Chronicles 23:24, 27; 2 Chronicles 31:17**), although exceptions did occur, such as Herod the Great's appointment of Aristobulus III, who was only seventeen.

From its inception in 1444 B.C., the traditional order of Aaronic priestly succession continued throughout the monarchic and post-exilic periods, up to the time of Jaddua (ca. 370–332 B.C.), who is the last high priest mentioned in the Old Testament (cf. **Nehemiah 12:10–11, 22**).[99] Extrabiblical sources show that *father-son* succession continued during the Persian period and was normative into the early Oniad period: from Jaddua (ca. 370–332 B.C.)–Onias I (ca. 332–280 B.C.)–Simon I (ca. 280–260 B.C.). However, thereafter in the Oniad dynasty, the new office holder was either a *son* or a *near blood-relative* of his predecessor. The first major departure from this pattern came with the appointment of Alcimus in 162 B.C., who was unrelated to the former Oniad priests. In the Hasmonean dynasty that followed, the high priest was often a *brother* or *close blood relative* of the former high priest. This precedent changed dramatically in the Herodian and Roman periods when civil authorities appointed the usually unrelated high priests—although exceptions did occur, especially in certain prominent aristocratic families, such as those of Annas the Elder and Boethus, and possibly Theophilus, where several family members came to hold the high priesthood office.

By using biblical and extrabiblical sources and eliminating the tenures of high priests who served a second term (i.e., those restored to the office), the summary chart above shows that, over a 1500-year period, seventy-seven different individuals held the high priesthood.[100] The chronological order of these seventy-seven high priests is noted in parentheses after the priests' names. To evaluate the tenure of the priestly office holders, the following breakdown is offered:

- Service in the tabernacle during the wilderness years and in the temporary tent-tabernacle in the City of David (pre-Solomon's Temple), from Aaron (#1) to Zakok (#11)—eleven high priests (inclusive) from ca. 1444 B.C. to 961 B.C.—with an average tenure of forty-four years.
- Service in Solomon's Temple, from Zadok (#11) to Jozadak (#25)—fifteen high priests (inclusive) from ca. 961 B.C. to 586 B.C.—with an average tenure of twenty-five years.
- Service in the Second Temple and Herod's Temple, from Joshua (#26) to Phannias (#77)—fifty-two high priests (inclusive) from ca. 516 B.C. to A.D. 70—with an average tenure of eleven years.

In contrast to the *earthly* high priesthood of Aaron, Jesus holds the office of "high priest" in a *permanent priesthood*, according to "the order of Melchizedek" (**Hebrews 5:6, 10**; cf. **Psalm 110:4**). Eugene Merrill explains: "The Melchizedekian priesthood was superior to that of Aaron, since Aaron and Levi submitted to Melchizedek while they were yet in the loins of Abraham their father."[101] Jesus established the original "type" that no human office holder could fulfill. In theological terms, Jesus the Messiah—the "[high] priest forever" (**Psalm 110:4; Hebrews 5:6; 6:20; 7:3, 17, 21**) and the "great priest over the house of God" (**Hebrews 10:21**)—"ascended into heaven" (**Hebrews 4:14**) and "sat down at the right hand of the throne of the Majesty in heaven" (**Hebrews 1:3; 8:1**; cf. **Hebrews 2:17; 3:1; 5:5; 7:26–28; 9:11; 10:12; 12:2**). Jesus "was designated by God to be high priest in the order of Melchizedek," for Melchizedek was the "priest of God Most High" (**Hebrews 5:10; 7:1**; see **Genesis 14:18; Psalm 110:4; Hebrews 5:6; 7:11, 17**, cf. **Hebrews 7:24; 9:11, 25; 1 Peter 2:5**). Thus, it was not through the human intercessions of high priests in the Aaronic priesthood OR the Eli priesthood[102] that absolute atonement under the law was achieved, but through the perfect mediatory sacrifice of Jesus himself that the eternal priesthood was established—"because Jesus lives forever, he has a permanent priesthood" (**Hebrews 7:24**; cf. **Zechariah 6:13; Hebrews 7:23–28; 10:10**).

Notes

1. Scripture was the primary text used to determine the lineage of the high priests. Because Jaddua (#31) was the last high priest mentioned in the Old Testament, beginning with the Oniad dynasty, extrabiblical sources were consulted. The primary extrabiblical reference consulted was *Jewish Antiquities, The Jewish War, The Life of Flavius Josephus, and Against Apion* 1.7 in *The Complete Works of Josephus*, trans. by William Whiston, commentary by Paul L. Maier (Grand Rapids: Kregel, 1999).

Other important sources consulted for individual high priests and/or cited include James C. VanderKam, *From Joshua to Caiaphas (High Priests after the Exile)* (Minneapolis: Fortress and Assen, the Netherlands: Van Gorcum, 2004); Benjamin E. Scolnic, *Chronology and Papponymy: A List of the Judean High Priests of the Persian Period* (Atlanta: Scholars Press, 1999); Deborah W. Rooke, *Zadok's Heirs: The Role and Development of the High Priesthood in Ancient Israel* (Oxford: Oxford University Press, 2012); Vasile Babota, *The Institution of the Hasmonean High Priesthood* (Leiden, the Netherlands: Brill, 2014); Joachim Jeremias, *Jerusalem in the Time of Jesus* (Philadelphia: Fortress, 1975); *Holman's Bible Dictionary* and *1 and 2 Maccabees* (in the King James Version Apocrypha, accessed through Accordance Bible Software.); and the online version of the *Jewish Encyclopedia* at https://jewishencyclopedia.com.

2. The tenures for the high priests from the time of Aaron (ca. 1444 B.C.) to the time of the Babylonian exile (586 B.C.) follow the dates that can be ascertained from Scripture. The tenures of the high priests of the Persian period, in general, follow Scolnic (*Chronology and Papponymy,* 23) who quotes VanderKam; in general, the dating for the Oniad, Hasmonean, and Herodian dynasties follow the dating system of VanderKam (*From Joshua to Caiaphas,* 491–493).

3. **Aaron (#1)** was the first high priest of Israel and the progenitor of the Aaronic high priesthood. Aaron (the brother of Moses) married Elisheba from the tribe of Judah (**Exodus 6:23**), and in this regard, all members of the Aaronic priesthood thereafter were of *mixed* Levitical–Judahite ancestry, not strictly "Levitical/Kohathite priests" from the tribe of Levi. For more information, see the notes for Aaron and Elisheba in chart "**Exodus 6**: Moses, Aaron, and Miriam, the Leaders of Israel." Aaron and his four sons ministered before the Lord (**Exodus 6:23; 28:1–2; Numbers 3:2–3**). Regrettably, Nadab and Abihu were corrupt priests who "died before the LORD when they made an offering with unauthorized fire before him in the Desert of Sinai. They had no sons, so [their brothers] Eleazar and Ithamar served as priests during the lifetime of their father Aaron" (**Numbers 3:4**; cf. **1 Samuel 2:12–17; 1 Chronicles 24:1–2**). Aaron was present when his brother Moses confronted Pharaoh to release the Israelites from bondage in Egypt (**Exodus 7:6–7**). When the tabernacle was constructed in the wilderness in 1444 B.C., Aaron ministered as the first high priest before the Lord. Aaron lived to be 123 years old but did not enter the promised land (**Numbers 20:22–29**); he "died on Mount Hor" (**Deuteronomy 32:50**), and Eleazar, his third son, succeeded him as Israel's next high priest (**Numbers 20:25–28; Deuteronomy 10:6**). Together, these verses show that Aaron lived from ca. 1529–1406 B.C. and served as the Lord's anointed high priest from 1444–1406 B.C. during the forty-year sojourn of the Israelites in the wilderness.

4. **Eleazar (#2)** was the son of Aaron and father of Phinehas. Eleazar and his brother Ithamar served as "priests during the lifetime of their father Aaron" (**Numbers 3:4**). Eleazar served from ca. 1444–1360 B.C. (cf. **Exodus 6:23; Numbers 3:2–4; 20:25–28; 27:19–22; 31:6–54; Ezra 7:5**). According to **Joshua 24:33**, "Eleazar son of Aaron died and was buried at Gibeah, which had been allotted to his son Phinehas in the hill country of Ephraim."

5. A single reference in Scripture clearly identifies Ithamar, the son of Aaron, as the ancestral head of the Eli priesthood, because Ahimelek (son of Ahitub, son of Phinehas, son of Eli, son of Ithamar) is clearly identified as "a descendant of Ithamar" (**1 Chronicles 24:3**; cf. **1 Samuel 14:3; 22:9, 11**). Thus, the Eli/Elide high priesthood continued through the Aaron–Ithamar–Eli line of descendants, in contrast to the Aaronic priesthood, which continued through Ithamar's brother Eleazar, who established the Aaron–Eleazar–Phinehas–Zadok (Zadokite) line of high-priestly descendants. Josephus states that "the house of Ithamar was deprived of the sacerdotal dignity, as God had foretold to Eli, the [great-great-] grandfather of Abiathar. So it was transferred to the family of Phinehas, to Zadok" (*Jewish Antiquities* 8.1.3). Abiathar was eventually removed as the high priest (i.e., more accurately, he was removed from serving in the dual co–high priest capacity with Zadok) in the early part of Solomon's reign (**1 Kings 2:26–27**); thereafter, no Elide descendant held the high priest office. Nevertheless, a *remnant* of faithful Ithamar descendants did serve in Solomon's Temple as Kohathite *attending* priests [cf. **1 Chronicles 24:1–6**; see chart "**1 Chronicles 24**: Genealogical Registry of the Twenty-Four Divisions of Kohathite Attending Priests Who Rotated Service in Solomon's Temple (Sixteen from the Aaron-Eleazar–Zadok Line and Eight from the Aaron-Ithamar Line")].

6. Although Scripture does not explicitly say so, Eli appears to be the *son* of Ithamar, although it is possible that he may have been Ithamar's *descendant.* In addition to serving as the Lord's priest at Shiloh (**1 Samuel 1:3, 9**), Eli judged Israel for forty years (ca. 1144–1104 B.C.; **1 Samuel 4:18**). Eli was the progenitor of the Eli priesthood; for more details, see chart "**1 Samuel 1**: Eli and the Eli Priesthood."

7. **Phinehas (#3)**, the son of Eleazar and the father of Abishua, is mentioned in **Exodus 6:25; Numbers 25:7, 11; 31:6; Joshua 22:13, 30–32; Judges 20:28; 1 Chronicles 6:4, 50; 9:20;** and **Ezra 7:5**. The biblical narrative portraying the *zeal of Phinehas* and describing the "covenant of a lasting priesthood" is chronicled in **Numbers 25:1–13**. Phinehas the son of Eleazar, in the Aaronic priesthood, should not be confused with Phinehas son of Eli, in the Eli priesthood (i.e., **1 Samuel 1:3; 2:34; 4:4, 11**, etc.).

8. **Abishua (#4)** the son of Phinehas and the father of Bukki is mentioned in **1 Chronicles 6:4–5, 50** and **Ezra 7:5**. Josephus lists the priestly succession as follows: Abishua–Bukki–Jotham [referring to Uzzi #6 or Zerahiah #7?)–Meraioth–Arophaeus (presumably the same as Amariah #9)–Ahitub–Zadok (*Jewish Antiquities* 8.1.3).

9. **Bukki (#5)** the son of Abishua and the father of Uzzi is mentioned in **1 Chronicles 6:5, 51** and **Ezra 7:4**.

10. **Uzzi (#6)** the son of Bukki and the father of Zerahiah is mentioned in **1 Chronicles 6:5–6, 51** and **Ezra 7:4**.

11. **Zerahiah (#7)** the son of Uzzi and the father of Meraioth is mentioned in **1 Chronicles 6:6, 51** and **Ezra 7:4**.

12. **Meraioth (#8)** the son of Zeruahiah and the father of Amariah is mentioned in **1 Chronicles 6:6–7, 52** and **Ezra 7:3**. Two high priests are named "Meraioth:" #8 and #18. Josephus gives the lineage of Meraioth #8 as "Bukki, the son of Abishua the high priest; his son was Jotham [referring to either Uzzi #6 or Zerahiah #7?]; Jotham's son was Meraioth; Meraioth's son was Arophaeus [presumably Amariah #9]; Arophaeus's son was Ahitub; and Ahitub's son was Zakok, who was first made high priest in the reign of David" (*Jewish Antiquities* 8.1.3).

13. **Amariah (#9)** is called the son of Meraioth (#8) and the father of Ahitub (#10) in **1 Chronicles 6:7, 52**. However, in **Ezra 7:1–6**—a genealogy that exhibits literary "telescoping"—the names of six high priests between Meraioth (#8) and Azariah (#15) are omitted, specifically: Amariah (#9)–Ahitub (#10)–Zadok (#11)–Ahimaaz (#12)–Azariah (#13)–Johanan (#14; cf. **1 Chronicles 6:1–15**, especially **vs. 6–10**). Amariah (#9) appears to be known to Josephus as "Arophaeus" (*Jewish Antiquities* 8.1.3).

14. The Eli high priesthood ended with the deposition of Abiathar, who held an unusual co–high priest office with Zadok during King David's reign, ca. 1011–971 B.C. In the early part of his reign (ca. 971–931 B.C.), Solomon deposed Abiathar and sent him home to the Levitical city of Anathoth in the tribe of Benjamin (cf. **1 Kings 1:7; 2:26–27**), thereby fulfilling God's curse on Eli and his descendants (cf. **1 Samuel 2:12–17; 27–36; 1 Kings 2:27**). Notably, the *unfaithful* Eli priesthood is contrasted in Scripture with the *faithful* lasting Aaronic priesthood through Phinehas the son of Eleazar, as explained in **Exodus 40:12–15; Numbers 25:13;** and **1 Chronicles 6:49–53**. However, a *remnant* of faithful Elide descendants was chosen to serve in Solomon's Temple as Kohathite *attending* priests (i.e., priests who *assisted* the high priests), and their descendants served in the post-exilic Second Temple period as well (cf. **1 Chronicles 24:1–6; Ezra 8:2**); see chart "**1 Chronicles 24**: Genealogical Registry of the Twenty-Four Divisions of Kohathite Attending Priests Who Rotated Service in Solomon's Temple (Sixteen from the Aaron-Eleazar–Zadok Line and Eight from the Aaron-Ithamar Line)."

15. **Ahitub (#10)** the son of Amariah and the father of Zadok is mentioned in **1 Samuel 14:3; 2 Samuel 8:17;** and **1 Chronicles 6:7–8, 52**. Two high priests in the Aaronic priesthood are named Ahitub: Ahitub #10 (whom Josephus mentions in *Jewish Antiquities* 8.1.3) and Ahitub #17 (see note 23). Ahitub #10 should not be confused with Ahitub the son of Phinehas, in the Eli priesthood line.

16. **Zadok (#11)** the son of Ahitub and the father of Ahimaaz was the originator of the Zadokite priesthood. Zadok and Abiathar (from the Eli priesthood) served jointly as co–high priests during the reign of David, ca. 1011–971 B.C.

(cf. **2 Samuel 8:17; 15:27, 35–36; 20:25; 1 Chronicles 18:16**). Zadok anointed Solomon as David's successor (**1 Kings 1:45**); immediately after coming to the throne, Solomon deposed Abiathar because Abiathar had supported Adonijah's effort to be David's successor (**1 Kings 1:7; 2:26–27**). Thereafter, Zadok was the sole high priest for the duration of Solomon's reign, ca. 971–931 B.C. (**1 Kings 1:26, 32, 34; 4:4; 1 Chronicles 29:22**). It should be noted that in **1 Kings 4:2**, Azariah is called the "son of Zadok" and described as a "priest" in Solomon's administration, along with Zadok and Abiathar, but actually, Azariah was Zadok's *grandson* (see note 19). Zadok is mentioned in **2 Samuel 8:17; 15:24–36; 20:25; 1 Kings 1:8–45; 4:4; 1 Chronicles 6:8; 16:39; 18:16**. Zadok (#11) who served under David and Solomon should not be confused with Zadok (#20) who served in the days of King Hezekiah, 715–686 B.C.

17. Based on the thirteen high priests given in **1 Chronicles 6:8–15** (referring to the time period from King David to the exile)—Zadok (#11)–Ahimaaz (#12)–Azariah (#13)–Johanan(#14)–Azariah (#15)–Amariah (#16)–Ahitub (#17)–Zadok (#20)–Shallum/Meshullam (#21)–Hilkiah (#22)–Azariah (#23)–Seraiah (#24)–Jozadak (#25)—and the known terms of two others, Meraioth (#18) and Azariah (#19), the chart shows a total of *fifteen* high priests between Zadok (#11) and Jozadak (#25; inclusive). On the other hand, Josephus, using unknown sources, arrives at a succession of *eighteen* high priests (inclusive) during this time and lists them as follows: Zadok–Achimas (probably the same as Ahimaaz #12)–Az ariah–Joram–Isus–Axioramus–Phideas–Sudeas–Juelus–Jotham–Uriah–Neriah –Odeas–Sallumus (probably the same as Shallum/Meshullam #21)–Elcias–and his son [Azariah #23]–Sareas (probably the same as Seraiah #24)–Jehozadak (the same as Jozadak), the last being the high priest who was carried into Babylonian captivity (*Jewish Antiquities* 10.8.6). Obviously, Josephus inserts obscure names and at least three extra high priests who are not mentioned in the biblical record.

18. **Ahimaaz (#12)** the son of Zadok and the father of Azariah #13 is mentioned in **2 Samuel 15:27, 36; 17:17, 20; 18:19, 22–23, 27–29;** and **1 Chronicles 6:8–9, 53**. Ahimaaz was a contemporary of King David (ca. 1011–971 B.C.). Josephus refers to Ahimaaz as "Achimus" and as "Ahimaaz, the son of Zadok" (*Jewish Antiquities* 10.8.6 and 7.10.4, respectively).

19. **Azariah (#13)** the son of Ahimaaz and the father of Johanan is mentioned in **1 Chronicles 6:9**. Azariah was a priest in King Solomon's administration, ca. 971–931 B.C. (**1 Kings 4:2**). Azariah is called the "son of Zadok" in **1 Kings 4:2**, but **1 Chronicles 6:8–10** clarifies that Azariah was actually the *grandson* of Zadok, the renowned high priest under King David. Notice that four high priests in the chart are named "Azariah": (1) Azariah #13 the son of Ahimaaz and father of Johanan; (2) Azariah #15 the son of Johanan and father of Amariah; (3) Azariah #19 presumably the son of Meraioth and father of Zadok; and (4) Azariah #23 the son of Hilkiah and father of Seraiah (**1 Chronicles 6:13–14; 9:11**).

20. **Johanan (#14)** the son of Azariah #13 and the father of Azariah #15 is the high priest listed in **1 Chronicles 6:9–10**. Johanan served from ca. 930–900 B.C. He appears to be called "Joram" by Josephus (*Jewish Antiquities* 10.8.6). Johanan (#14) should not be confused with Johanan/Jonathan (#30) who was the high priest ca. 410–370 B.C. (cf. **Nehemiah 12:11, 22–23**).

21. **Azariah (#15)** the son of Johanan and father of Amariah (**1 Chronicles 6:9–11**) appears to be named after his grandfather Azariah (#13), an example of papponymy. Azariah is identified as "he who served as priest in the temple Solomon built in Jerusalem" (**1 Chronicles 6:10**), corresponding to the general time period of ca. 900–875 B.C.

22. **Amariah (#16)** the son of Azariah #15 and the father of Ahitub was the chief priest during the reign of King Jehoshaphat of Judah, ca. 872–848 B.C. (cf. **1 Chronicles 6:11; 2 Chronicles 19:11**). Amariah the son of Azariah is mentioned in the lineage of Ezra in **Ezra 7:3**.

23. **Ahitub (#17)** the son of Amariah and the father of Meraioth is mentioned in **Ezra 7:2;** and **Nehemiah 11:11** (cf. **1 Chronicles 6:11–12; 9:11**).

24. **Meraioth (#18)**, presumably the son of Ahitub and the father of Azariah #19, is not mentioned in the list of high priests in **1 Chronicles 6:1–15** nor in the lineage of Ezra (**Ezra 7:1–5**), but he is referred to in the lineages of Azariah (**1 Chronicles 9:11**) and Seraiah (**Nehemiah 11:11**). Meraioth may have been a priestly figurehead only, for during that general time, the Kohathite *attending* priest, Jehoiada (the husband of Jehosheba), took the lead role in Solomon's Temple, especially during the six-year illegitimate term of Queen Athaliah (ca. 841–835 B.C.). Also, Jehoiada—not Meraioth the high priest—took the singular lead role in deposing the usurper Athaliah and establishing the rightful heir, King Joash, on the throne of Judah.

25. **Azariah (#19)** the son of Meraioth and the father of Zadok is an enigmatic priest. He is not mentioned in the official lists of high priests, such as those found in **1 Chronicles 6:3–15**, **Ezra 7:1–5** or **Nehemiah 11:11**, where his name would be expected (note that Azariah *son/descendant* of Meraioth in **Ezra 7:3** refers to Azariah #15, not to Azariah #19). Azariah #19 and his two predecessors, Meraioth (#18) and Ahitub (#17), filled the general chronological gap between ca. 850–700 B.C. Therefore, assuming that each of the three high priests held office for approximately 50 years (which would obviously have been long terms), Azariah #19 would have served from approximately 750–700 B.C. Possibility #1: If Azariah #19 is the same person as Azariah the "priest" and "the chief priest" who was a contemporary of King Uzziah/Azariah, 792–740 B.C. (**2 Chronicles 26:17–20**), then in ca. 752 B.C., Azariah #19 and eighty other attending priests were the ones who confronted King Uzziah/Azariah for burning incense at the altar and witnessed the king breaking out in leprosy (**2 Chronicles 26:20**). Possibility #2: If, on the other hand, Azariah #19 was "the chief priest, from the family of Zadok" (**2 Chronicles 31:10**), he served in the days of King Hezekiah (715–686 B.C.). This passage goes on to say that Azariah was "the official in charge of the temple of God" (**2 Chronicles 31:13**)—this type of descriptive language often refers to a *scribal priest* rather than a *high priest* (i.e., the scribal priests were *close relatives* of the high priests, but they are in scribal lineages that parallel the high-priestly line; they are not high priests themselves). A case in point would be the post-exilic figure/scribal priest named Azariah who was "the official in charge of the house of God [the Second Temple]" (**1 Chronicles 9:11**; cf. **Nehemiah 11:11**)—for the nomenclature and genealogy of this scribal priest, see chart "**Ezra 7**: Ezra, the Priestly Scribe and Teacher of the Law (Post-Exile)."

For these reasons, Azariah #19 is tentatively assigned as the high priest in the days of King Uzziah/Azariah (i.e., Possibility #1) rather than the high priest in the days of King Hezekiah (i.e., Possibility #2).

26. **Zadok (#20)** the son of Azariah #19 and the father of Shallum/Meshullam was the high priest in the days of King Hezekiah of Judah (715–686 B.C.). Zadok is mentioned in **1 Chronicles 6:12; 9:11; 2 Chronicles 31:9–10; Ezra 7:2;** and **Nehemiah 11:11**. Note that **1 Chronicles 9:11** and **Nehemiah 11:11** show literary telescoping (i.e., Zadok was the *grandson*—not the *son*—of Meraioth; also, note that Meraioth is omitted in the list of high priests in **1 Chronicles 6:1–15**). Zadok #20, who served under Hezekiah, is a different priest than Zadok #11, who served under David and Solomon.

27. **Shallum (#21)**—the son of Zadok and the father of Hilkiah (**1 Chronicles 6:12–13; Ezra 7:2**)—is also called Meshullam (**1 Chronicles 9:11; Nehemiah 11:11**). He appears to be called "Sallumus" by Josephus (*Jewish Antiquities* 10.8.6). The various priests named Meshullam in **Nehemiah 3:4, 30; 8:4; 10:7; 12:13, 16, 33** and the Levite named Shallum in **1 Chronicles 9:31** do not refer to Shallum/Meshullam the high priest. Given the general terms of office for his father (Zadok #20) and his son (Hilkiah #22; notes 26 and 28, respectively), Shallum/Meshullam probably ministered as the high priest in Solomon's Temple ca. 690–640 B.C.

28. **Hilkiah (#22)** the son of Shallum/Meshullam and the father of Azariah #23 was the high priest during the reign of King Josiah (ca. 640–609 B.C.). Hilkiah "found the Book of the Law in the temple of the LORD" (**2 Kings 22:8; 2 Chronicles 34:14**)—an event which prompted widespread religious reforms in Judah by Josiah (cf. **2 Kings 22–23; 2 Chronicles 34–35**). Hilkiah is mentioned in **1 Chronicles 6:13; 1 Chronicles 9:11;** and **Nehemiah 11:11**. Hilkiah was an ancestor of Ezra (**Ezra 7:1**) and possibly an ancestor of the prophet Jeremiah (**Jeremiah 1:1**).

29. **Azariah (#23)** the son of Hilkiah #22 and father of Seraiah #24 was the high priest in Solomon's Temple from ca. 609 B.C. (under King Jehoahaz/Shallum) to as late as 598 B.C. (under Eliakim/Jehoiakim). Azariah's genealogy is given in **1 Chronicles 6:13–14** and **Ezra 7:1**. In chart "**Ezra 7**: Ezra, the Priestly Scribe and Teacher of the Law (Post-Exile)," the high priest Azariah #23 is designated "Azariah #1" to distinguish him from other scribal priests named Azariah who were relatives of Ezra.

For chronological reasons, Azariah #23 of 609–598 B.C. is not the same person as (1) "Azariah the chief priest" (=Azariah #19) who probably served in the days of King Uzziah/Azariah, 792–740 B.C. (**2 Chronicles 26:16–20**; see note 25); (2) the post-exilic figure named Azariah who appears to be a scribal priest—referred to as "the chief priest, from the family of Zadok" and "Azariah the official in charge of the temple of God" (**2 Chronicles 31:10, 13**)—who lived and served in the days of King Hezekiah, 715–686 B.C.; (3) the scribal priest named Azariah, who returned to Jerusalem with Zerubbabel in 538 B.C. and then became "the official in charge of the house of God [Second Temple]" (**1 Chronicles 9:11**; cf. **Nehemiah 11:11**); nor (4) the scribal priest named Azariah who sealed the covenant with Nehemiah in 444 B.C. (**Nehemiah 10:2**). To see the genealogical distinction between members of the high-priestly line (Hilkiah–Azariah–Seraiah–Jozadak–Joshua, etc.) and the parallel line of scribal priests, see chart "**Ezra 7**: Ezra, the Priestly Scribe and Teacher of the Law (Post-Exile)."

30. **Seraiah (#24)** the son of Azariah #23, the father of Jozadak #25, and the

grandfather of Joshua #26 (the first high priest to serve in the Second Temple) is mentioned in **1 Chronicles 6:14** (and possibly **Ezra 7:1**). Josephus refers to him as "Sareas" (*Jewish Antiquities* 10.8.6). Shortly after the siege of Jerusalem by the Babylonians in 586 B.C., Nebuzaradan took Seraiah #24 to the Babylonian headquarters at Riblah, where he was executed (**2 Kings 25:18–21**; cf. **Jeremiah 52:24–27**). For chronological reasons, several priestly figures named Seraiah are proposed (even though Scripture does not explicitly address their kinship relationships). First, Seraiah #24—designated "Seraiah #1" in some charts—was the martyred high priest of 586 B.C. Second, another Seraiah figure—designated "Seraiah #2" in some charts—was a scribal priest who returned to Jerusalem with Zerubbabel in 538 B.C. (**Ezra 2:2; Nehemiah 12:1**), and he is likely the *son* of "Seraiah #1" and the *father* of Ezra (**Ezra 7:1?**). [To make matters more complicated, "Seraiah #2" is called "Seraiah" in **Ezra 2:2**, but he is called "Azariah" (and designated "Azariah #2" elsewhere) in **Nehemiah 7:7**]. The genealogy of "Seraiah #2/Azariah #2" is given in **Nehemiah 11:11**: "Seraiah ["Seraiah #2/ Azariah #2"] son of Hilkiah, the son of Meshullam, the son of Zadok, the son of Meraioth, the son of Ahitub, the official in charge of the house of God [the Second Temple]." In effect, the scribal lineage of "Seraiah #2/Azariah #2" parallels that of the high-priestly line, thereby explaining the *scribal* heritage of Ezra. Third, another Seraiah individual—designated "Seraiah #3" in other charts—sealed the covenant with Nehemiah in 444 B.C. (**Nehemiah 10:2**). For the proposed genealogies and familial relationships of Seraiah figures #1, #2, and #3, see chart "**Ezra 7**: Ezra, the Priestly Scribe and Teacher of the Law (Post-Exile)."

31. **Jozadak (#25)**—the son of Seraiah and the father of Joshua/Jeshua—is known in some translations as "Jehozadak." Jozadak was the last high priest to serve in Solomon's Temple before King Nebuchadnezzar of Babylon came to Jerusalem in 586 B.C., destroyed the city and the temple, and carried Judah into exile (**1 Chronicles 6:14–15**). Since there is no mention of his return to Jerusalem, Jozadak apparently died in Babylonian captivity. Jozadak's son Joshua (#26) became the first high priest to officiate in the Second Temple in post-exilic Jerusalem (**Haggai 1:1, 12; Zechariah 6:11**). Josephus refers to him as "Jehozadak" instead of Jozadak (cf. *Jewish Antiquities* 10.8.6).

32. **Joshua (#26)** the son of Jozadak and the father of Joiakim is called Joshua in **Ezra 2:2; 3:2, 8; 4:3; 5:2; 10:18; Nehemiah 7:7; 12:1, 7, 10, 26; Haggai 1:1, 12, 14; 2:2, 4;** and **Zechariah 3:1, 3–4, 6, 8–9; 6:11** and called Jeshua in **Ezra 2:36; Nehemiah 7:39**; Josephus refers to him as "Jeshua, the son of Jehozadak" (*Jewish Antiquities* 11.3.10). Joshua/Jeshua was the first high priest to serve in the Second Temple. His term of office was from ca. 516–490 B.C. Joshua was probably born in captivity and then came to Jerusalem with Zerubbabel in ca. 538 B.C. (**Ezra 2:2; Nehemiah 7:7; 12:1**). He was a contemporary of Haggai and Zechariah, who prophesied to the restored community in Jerusalem (Yehud), ca. 520–516 B.C. Together, Joshua and Zerubbabel rebuilt the altar and reestablished worship in post-exilic Jerusalem. After the Second Temple was completed in 516 B.C., Joshua was the first high priest to officiate there. Joshua the high priest and Zerubbabel the Davidic ruler foreshadowed the messianic "Branch" (cf. **Isaiah 4:2; 11:1; Jeremiah 23:5; 33:15; Zechariah 3:8; 6:12**) who would come to "build the temple of the LORD." The Branch would be "clothed with majesty and will sit and rule on his throne. And he will be a priest on his throne. And there will be harmony between the two [the offices of priest and king]" (**Zechariah 6:13**; cf. **9–15**). Joshua/Jeshua the high priest should not be confused with the Levitical figures named Joshua or Jeshua (cf. **Ezra 2:40; 3:9; 8:33; Nehemiah 7:43; 8:7; 9:4–5; 10:9; 12:8, 24**).

33. **Joiakim (#27)** the son of Joshua/Jeshua and the father of Eliashib was the high priest from ca. 490–450/444 B.C. He is mentioned in **Nehemiah 12:10, 12, 26**. **Nehemiah 12:12–21** lists the heads of the Kohathite priestly families in the days of Joiakim. Josephus remarks that Joiakim was the high priest when, in 486 B.C., King Xerxes I succeeded his father (Darius the Great) to the throne of Persia and that Joiakim was a contemporary of Ezra the scribe-priest, who was still living in Babylon at the time (*Jewish Antiquities* 11.5.1). Josephus goes on to say that Ezra and Joiakim died at about the same time (*Jewish Antiquities* 11.5.5). Ezra brought a group of returnees back to Jerusalem in 458 B.C. and conducted the celebration of the Feast of Tabernacles (cf. **Nehemiah 8:9–10:39**); shortly thereafter, in 444 B.C. or slightly later, Ezra died, see chart "**Ezra 7**: Ezra, the Priestly Scribe and Teacher of the Law (Post-Exile)."

34. **Eliashib (#28)** the son of Joiakim and the father of Joiada was the high priest from ca. 450/444–432 B.C. The lineage of Eliashib is given in **Nehemiah 12:10**. Eliashib was a contemporary of the prophet Nehemiah; in ca. 444 B.C. Nehemiah was appointed governor over the satrap of Judah and oversaw the rebuilding of the city wall around Jerusalem. During that time, Eliashib the high priest and fellow priests were involved in rebuilding the Sheep's Gate on the north side of the temple (**Nehemiah 3:1**). The "entrance to the house of Eliashib" was located on the east side, between the House of the Heroes and the Water Gate (**Nehemiah 3:20–21**). Eliashib was specifically responsible for the storerooms of the Second Temple (**Nehemiah 13:4**). Nehemiah was recalled to the Persian court for a short time in ca. 432 B.C. in the thirty-second year of Artaxerxes' reign (**Nehemiah 13:6–7**); during his absence, Eliashib the high priest did an "evil thing" by associating with Tobiah the Ammonite, who was a strong opponent of Nehemiah in the rebuilding of Jerusalem (cf. **Nehemiah 2:10**), going so far as to provide him (Tobiah) with a large room in the temple. When Nehemiah returned to Jerusalem in late 432 B.C., he was angry with Eliashib—he "threw all Tobiah's household goods out of the [store]room" (**Nehemiah 13:8**) and replaced him with a trustworthy priest named Shelemiah, Zadok the scribe, and two Levites (**Nehemiah 13:4–13**). Additionally, a *grandson* of Eliashib married the daughter of Sanballat the Horonite; like Tobiah, Sanballat was a strong political opponent of Nehemiah and opposed the rebuilding of the walls around Jerusalem (cf. **Nehemiah 2:10, 19; 4:1, 7**). Nehemiah considered this marriage a defilement of the Levitical priesthood (**Nehemiah 13:28–29**). Eliashib the high priest who lived in the post-exile should not be confused with Eliashib the Kohathite priest who was the head over the eleventh of the twenty-four priestly divisions in the latter days of King David (**1 Chronicles 24:12**).

35. **Joiada (#29)** the son of Eliashib and the father of Jonathan/Johanan was the high priest from ca. 432–410 B.C. His lineage is given in **Nehemiah 12:10–11**. One of the sons of Joiada married into the Sanballat family and became the "son-in-law to Sanballat the Horonite" (**Nehemiah 13:28**); refer to the charts "**Nehemiah 2**: The Enemies of Nehemiah Who Ruled in the Provinces Surrounding Judah" and "**Nehemiah 13**: Intermarriage of Jews and Samaritans That Compromised the Purity of the Holy Priesthood of Israel." When Joiada died, his son Jonathan succeeded him as high priest. Josephus refers to Joiada as "Judas" (*Jewish Antiquities* 11.7.1).

36. **Jonathan (#30)** the son of Joiada and the father of Jaddua is called Johanan in **Nehemiah 12:22–23**. Jonathan is mentioned in **Nehemiah 12:11,** and he appears to be the same person as "Jehohanan, son [*grandson*] of Eliashib" in **Ezra 10:6**. Josephus refers to him as "Johanan, the son of Eliashib" (*Jewish Antiquities* 11.5.4), but then clarifies the genealogical relationship in *Jewish Antiquities* 11.7.1 by saying "when Eliashib the high priest was dead, his son Judas [Joiada] succeeded in the high priesthood, and when he was dead, his son John [Jonathan or Jehohanan] took that dignity." Jonathan/Johanan held the high priesthood from ca. 410–370 B.C. Josephus explains that Jesus (the brother of John/Jonathan/Jehohanan) "quarreled with John [the high priest] in the temple, and so provoked his brother, that in his anger his brother [John] killed him [Jesus]. . . . God did not neglect . . . punishment [of the fratricide], but the people were on that very account enslaved, and the temple was polluted by the Persians. . . . When John had departed this life, his son Jaddua succeeded in the high priesthood" (*Jewish Antiquities* 11.5.4; 11.7.1–2).

37. **Jaddua (#31)** the son of Jonathan and the father of Onias I was the high priest from ca. 370–332 B.C. He is the last high priest to be mentioned in the Old Testament (**Nehemiah 12:10–11**). Josephus writes that "when John [Jonathan/ Johanan] had departed this life, his son Jaddua succeeded in the high priesthood" (*Jewish Antiquities* 11.7.2). In *Jewish Antiquities* 11.8.4–5, Josephus explains that Jaddua was the high priest when Alexander the Great came to Jerusalem. Jaddua went out to meet Alexander and other priests and "the multitude of the citizens." The Phoenicians and Chaldeans who followed Alexander thought that they should be allowed to plunder Jerusalem, but Alexander, seeing Jaddua and the other priests dressed in their priestly finery, "saluted the high priest." According to Alexander's account, he "did not adore him [Jaddua], but that God who has honored him with his high priesthood," further commenting that he had seen Jaddua in a dream when he was considering how he would overtake Asia. From this vision, Alexander evidently believed that the God of the Jews would conduct his army and lead him to victory over the Persians. After Alexander reached the city, Josephus relates that "he offered sacrifice to God, according to the high priest's direction, and magnificently treated both the high priest [Jaddua] and the priests."

Scripture states that one of the sons *of Joiada* (*not* Jaddua) married a daughter of Sanballat the Horonite (**Nehemiah 13:28**; see chart "**Nehemiah 13**: Intermarriage of Jews and Samaritans That Compromised the Purity of the Holy Priesthood of Israel"). Josephus, however, gives a contradictory account, saying that the intermarriage took place between Manasseh (the *brother* of the high priest Jaddua) and Nicaso/Nikaso (the daughter of Sanballat), because Sanballat had hoped that the marriage alliance "would be a pledge and security that the nation of the Jews should continue their goodwill to him [Sanballat]" (*Jewish Antiquities* 11.7.2). Josephus goes on to say that the Jerusalem elders commanded Manasseh to divorce his wife and to refrain from approaching the altar, because Manasseh had been assisting his brother Jaddua the high priest. Unwilling to meet these terms, Manasseh then went to his father-in-law, Sanballat; in response, Sanballat told Manasseh that, if he agreed to not divorce his wife (Sanballat's daughter), he would "procure for him [Manasseh] the power and dignity of a high priest [in the future]," and that he would make Manasseh the governor over all of his (Sanballat's) domains and even build Manasseh a temple "like that in Jerusalem" upon Mount Gerizim (*Jewish Antiquities* 11.8.2).

38. **Onias I (#32)** the son of Jaddua and the father of Simon I and Eleazar began the Oniad dynasty of high priests and served in the priesthood from ca. 332–280 B.C. Josephus' record says that "Now when Alexander was dead [June 323 B.C.], the government was parted among his successors [called the Diadochi]. . . . About this time it was that Jaddua the high priest died, and Onias his son [Onias I] took the high priesthood" (*Jewish Antiquities* 11.8.7). *First Maccabees* 12:7, 8, 20 says that Onias I was a contemporary of Alexander the Great, the king of the Greek Empire (336–323 B.C.).

39. **Manasseh (#35)** the son of Jaddua was the brother of Onias I and the uncle of Eleazar (*Antiquities* 12.6.1). Manasseh was the high priest from ca. 245–240 B.C. Manasseh was succeeded by his great-nephew Onias II (the son of Simon I).

40. **Simon I (#33)** was the son of Onias I and the father of Onias II. Simon I is surnamed "Simon the Just" by Josephus: "He was called Simon the Just because of both his piety toward God, and his kind disposition to those of his own nation" (*Jewish Antiquities* 12.2.5; 12.4.1; cf. 12.2.1). However, many scholars today believe that *Simon the Just* actually refers to Simon II (#37; VanderKam, *From Joshua to Caiaphas,* 138). Simon I (#33) was the high priest from ca. 280–260 B.C. and was succeeded by his brother Eleazar, because Simon I's son Onias II, the rightful heir/successor, was too young to assume the priesthood (*Jewish Antiquities* 12.2.5).

41. **Eleazar (#34)** was the son of Onias I and the brother of Simon I. Simon I had a young son Onias II, who would normally have been Simon I's successor, but when Simon I died, Simon's brother Eleazar was named the high priest instead of the young boy. [Note: at this time, the age of eligibility for a high priest seems to have been a minimum of 20 (**1 Chronicles 23:24, 27; 2 Chronicles 31:17**; cf. **Numbers 4:3**; **Luke 3:23**); although later, there was a high priest who was only seventeen; see Aristobulus III (#52)]. The appointment of Eleazar (Simon I's brother) to the high priesthood is the first departure from the pattern of direct father-son succession that had been in place for almost 1200 years (i.e., since the days of the first high priest, Aaron, in 1444 B.C.). Josephus describes an important event that took place in Eleazar's term—Josephus paraphrases a *Letter of Aristeas*, describing how the librarian at the Library of Alexandria suggested to the Ptolemaic ruler, Ptolemy II Philadelphus (285–246 B.C.), that he commission a Greek translation of the Hebrew law. Ptolemy II requested that Eleazar (#34) send a copy of the Jewish laws and six skilled, intelligent men from each of the twelve tribes to translate the Jewish law from Hebrew into Greek, so that Ptolemy II might have a copy in his library (*Jewish Antiquities* 12.2.4–5; cf. VanderKam, *From Joshua to Caiaphas,* 158). Eleazar responded favorably by sending seventy-two men to Alexandria to work on this translation (*Jewish Antiquities* 12.2.6), which became known as the *Septuagint* (i.e., the Greek translation of the Old Testament); elsewhere, only 70 men are mentioned. Septuagint is Greek for "70" and is abbreviated by the Roman numeral LXX. Eleazer served as the high priest from ca. 260–245 B.C. When he died, he was succeeded by his uncle Manasseh, the brother of Onias I (*Jewish Antiquities* 12.4.1).

42. **Onias II (#36)** was the son of Simon I and the father of Simon II. Onias was too young to assume the high priesthood when his father died; furthermore, Onaias II was apparently still in his youth when his uncle Eleazar (Simon I's successor) died, so Onias II's great-uncle Manasseh (the brother of Onias I) assumed the high priesthood. Finally, after Manasseh (#35) died, Onias II came to the high priesthood and served from ca. 240–218 B.C. Josephus says that Onias II was "a great lover of money" and "sordidly covetous"; when he refused to pay the twenty talents of silver that all high priests were required to pay the king of Egypt, the high priesthood, as well as the people, were at great risk. However, Onias II's nephew Joseph (the son of Tobias and Onias II's sister) stepped in and pacified the king of Egypt (*Jewish Antiquities* 12.4.1ff); moreover, some scholars assert that Onias II may have relinquished an aspect of his high-priestly power to Joseph, who was of "great reputation among the people of Jerusalem, for gravity, wisdom, and justice" (*Jewish Antiquities* 12.4.2). Josephus says that "Onias [II] died and left the high priesthood to his son Simon [II]. And when he was dead, Onias [III] his son succeeded him in that dignity" (*Jewish Antiquities* 12.4.10).

43. **Simon II (#37)** was the son of Onias II and the father of three sons, all of whom came to the high priesthood—Onias III, Jason/Jesus, and Menelaus (see *Jewish Antiquities* 12.5.1). The tenure of Simon II is not known for sure, but it was possibly from ca. 218–185 B.C. (others suggest 219–196 B.C.). Josephus refers to Simon II in *Jewish Antiquities* 12.4.10. Some scholars believe that the appellation *Simon the Just* refers to Simon II (#37), not to Simon I (#33; VanderKam, *From Joshua to Caiaphas,*138).

44. **Onias III (#38)** was the son of Simon II, as well as his successor. The tenure of Onias III was from ca. 185–175/173 B.C. According to the apocryphal book of II *Maccabees*, Onias III was a pious man, a "zealot for the laws," and opposed the spread of Greek culture and influence (Hellenization). Also according to II *Maccabees*, a temple official named Simon who supported Hellenization persuaded the Seleucid king Seleucus IV Philopator (187–175 B.C.) to plunder the temple. The attempt was unsuccessful, but Onias III was never forgiven for what had almost happened. Upon the accession of Antiochus IV Epiphanes to the Seleucid throne in 175 B.C., a new government began, and Onias III was made to step down as high priest in favor of his brother Jason (who supported Hellenization). Onias III was eventually murdered in Antioch in 172/170 B.C. (*II Maccabees* 4:33–34); his departure "brought the rule of the Oniad high priesthood to an end" (Babota, *Hasmonean High Priesthood*, 65).

45. **Jason (#39)** the son of Simon II was the brother of Onias III. According to the *Jewish Encyclopedia*, the Hellenization of Judea reached its peak during Jason's high priesthood. Josephus explains that he was originally called "Jesus" (or Joshua) before he Hellenized his name to Jason (*Jewish Antiquities* 12.5.1). While his brother Onias III was away, Jason "obtained the high priesthood by corruption" (VanderKam, *From Joshua to Caiaphas,* 198) by *paying* Antiochus IV Epiphanes (175–164 B.C.) for the high priesthood office, offering "360 talents of silver and another 80 talents, with yet 150 more talents if he were given the right to establish by his authority a gymnasium . . . and to enroll the people of Jerusalem as citizens of Antioch" (*II Maccabees* 4:7–17). Josephus says that Jason was deposed after a short period of only three years because Antiochus became angry with him (cf. *Jewish Antiquities* 12.5.1; Jeremias, *Jerusalem in the Time of Jesus,* 184–185). According to II *Maccabees*, Jason lost his position because he sent his brother Menelaus to transact business on his behalf, and during that time, Menelaus successfully purchased the high-priestly office for himself. Jason then fled to Ammon and died there in exile (*II Maccabees* 4:26; cf. VanderKam, *From Joshua to Caiaphas,* 202–203). Jason's tenure as high priest lasted from 175–172 B.C.

46. **Menelaus (#40)** was the successor of Jason, but his heritage is debated. Menelaus is described by Josephus as the *son* of Simon II and the *brother* of Jason/Jesus and Onias III—all of whom were high priests: "Simon [II] had these three sons, to each of which the priesthood came. . . . This Jesus changed his name to Jason, but Onias was called Menelaus. Now as the former high priest, Jesus [Jason #39], raised a rebellion against Menelaus, who was ordained after him, the multitude was divided between them both" (*Jewish Antiquities* 12.5.1). However, according to II *Maccabees* (4:1, 23), Menelaus was not of Aaronite-Zadokite priestly descent; rather, he was the *brother of Simon the informer* (a traitor) who acted as "an informer against his native land, [and] slandered Onias [Onias III]" and persuaded Seleucus IV Philopator (187–175 B.C.) to plunder the temple. *Simon the informer* was of the tribe of Benjamin; thus, if the II *Maccabees'* description of Menelaus is to be believed, Menelaus was a Benjamite and therefore not of priestly heritage at all. According to the *Jewish Encyclopedia* (Isidore Singer and Isaac Broydé, "Menelaus"): "Of these two conflicting statements [whether Menelaus was the brother of Simon the Benjamite or the brother of Jason and Onias III], the evidence is in favor of the former, first because it is unlikely that two brothers would be called by the same name [*Onias*], and second, because the popular opposition to Menelaus in favor of Jason, though both belonged to the Hellenistic party, is more easily explained if the successor of Jason did *not* belong to the priestly family. It is possible that Josephus [confused] Simeon [Simon], the brother of Menelaus, with Simeon [Simon II], the father of Onias [III] and Jason" ("Menelaus"). A third description of the heritage of Menelaus is offered by Babota (*Hasmonean High Priesthood*), where she concludes that Menelaus was the brother of Simon the prostrate of the temple who acted against the high priest Onias III and that this Menelaus belonged to the (Kohathite) priestly course/division of Bilgah (cf. **1 Chronicles 24:14; Nehemiah 12:5, 18**). Joachim Jeremias also agrees with the (non-Zadokite) Bilga(h) priestly origin of Menelaus (Jeremias, *Jerusalem in the Time of Jesus,* 185–187).

Menelaus purchased the high priesthood by outbidding his *brother* Jason/Jesus by 300 talents of silver, "but he possessed no qualification for the high priesthood . . . having a hot temper of a cruel tyrant and the rage of a savage wild beast" (*II Maccabees* 4:24–25; *Jewish Antiquities* 12.9.7; VanderKam, *From Joshua to Caiaphas,* 203). Under Menelaus, the influence of the Seleucids and Hellenization increased (cf. Babota, *Hasmonean High Priesthood,* 53–54). The *Jewish Encyclopedia* (Isidore Singer and Isaac Broydé, "Menelaus") says that Menelaus took sacred vessels from the temple to pay his debts; II *Maccabees* 4:27–29 records that he failed to "pay regularly any of the money he promised to the king" and that Lysimachus, another brother of Menelaus, was appointed "as deputy in the high priesthood" (*II Maccabees* 4:29). Menelaus was the high priest from 172–162 B.C. Josephus says that "the king sent Menelaus to Berea [Aleppo], a city of Syria, and there had him put to death. . . . He had been a wicked and an impious man; and, in order to get the government to himself, had compelled his nation to transgress their own laws" (*Jewish Antiquities* 12.10.7). Menelaus' disregard for the sanctity of the high priesthood and his Hellenization of Jewish worship became key catalysts for the Jewish rebellion under the Maccabees.

47. **Onias IV (#41)** was the oldest surviving son of Onias III and the rightful heir to the high priesthood, although his brother Jason and (possibly another brother Menelaus) proceeded him. Onias IV held the priesthood for only a short time in 162 B.C. The end of his term marked the cessation of continuous Aaronic high-priestly succession that had lasted for 1282 years since its inception under Aaron. When his successor Alcimus was elected, Onias IV fled to Egypt, where he built a temple at Leontopolis (*Jewish Antiquities* 13.3; VanderKam, *From Joshua to Caiaphas,* 214–15, 218). Jeremias records that "There were in the first century A.D. two groups of high-priestly families, one legitimate, one illegitimate. The legitimate group comprised simply and solely the Zadokites serving in the Temple of Onias at Leontopolis and the families descended from this ruling line. The illegitimate were the priestly families from the midst of whom one or more members had been raised to the highest spiritual dignity by variable winds of chance and politics since 37 B. C., since the Hasmoneans who formed a group between these two and had held the high priesthood for more than a century, though descended from an ordinary priestly family [Joiarib/Jehoiarib], were finally exterminated" (Jeremias, *Jerusalem in the Time of Jesus,* 191–192). For more information on the Hasmonean high priests, refer to the chart "**Supplement 8**: The Maccabees and the Hasmonean Dynasty."

48. **Alcimus (#42**; Alcimus, Gk. or Yaqim/Yakeimos, Heb.) was a transitional figure between the high priests of the Oniad and Hasmonean Dynasties. Alcimus was the high priest from ca. 162–159 B.C. Josephus calls him both "Alcimus" and "Jacimus" and explains that he was "one that was indeed of the stock of Aaron, but not of that family of Onias [i.e., meaning he was in a Kohathite *priestly* line, but not in the Kohathite *high-priestly* line]" (*Jewish Antiquities* 12.9.7; 20.10.1; cf. *I Maccabees* 7:14). The *Jewish Encyclopedia* says that Alcimus was the leader of anti-national Hellenists in Jerusalem under the Seleucid king Demetrius I Soter (162–150 B.C.). Demetrius dispatched an army to install Alcimus as the high priest at Jerusalem. Alcimus was opposed by the Maccabees for his Hellenizing goals, but at least initially, he was favorably received by the Jews. Later, however, when Alcimus put many Jews to death, public opinion turned against him. Judas Maccabeus revolted and deposed Alcimus, but in 161/160 B.C., Judas was killed. Alcimus was then reinstated as the high priest, but then died—"Stricken suddenly by God, and fell down [from a stroke]." This occurred soon after Alcimus had called for the wall in the temple that divided the inner courtyard from the larger outer courtyard to be torn down (cf. *I Maccabees* 9:54–56). Josephus says in one place that Alcimus "had been high priest four years" (*Jewish Antiquities* 12:10.6) and in another that "when Jacimus had retained the priesthood three years, he died, and there was no one that succeeded him, but the city continued seven years without a high priest" (*Jewish Antiquities* 20.10.1); the *Jewish Encyclopedia* (Alexander Büchler, "Alcimus (also called Jakim)") agrees with the three-year term of Alcimus/Jacimus. Following the "intersacerdotium period," the Hasmoneans rose up to secure the high priesthood.

49. As Josephus explains, the "intersacerdotium period" refers to the seven-year period, ca. 159–153/152 B.C., when no *official* high priest held the priesthood in Jerusalem: "There was no one that succeeded him [Alcimus], but the city continued seven years without a high priest" (*Jewish Antiquities* 20.10.1). Some scholars hold that the vacancy period may have included the years that Judas Maccabeus held an *unofficial* high-priestly appointment, before the *official* (royal) appointment given to Judas' brother Jonathan Apphus in 152 B.C. (VanderKam, *From Joshua to Caiaphas,* 244). Exactly who officiated on the Day of Atonement during this period is unknown; some have speculated that it was an unofficial priest from the conservative circles or a priest related to the "Teacher of Righteousness" who eventually founded the Dead Sea Scrolls community at Qumran (VanderKam, *From Joshua to Caiaphas,* 246). Rooke offers an important insight by saying that the ascension of the Hasmoneans to the high priesthood "was part of a pattern whereby the duties of the high priest became one aspect of the military and civil leadership of the country; this was the pattern which then defined the high priesthood for most of the next hundred years" (Rooke, *Zadok's Heirs,* 319).

50. For notes about Joiarib/Jehoiarib and the distinction between the high-priestly line and the Kohathite attending priest line, see chart "**1 Chronicles 24**: Genealogical Registry of the Twenty-Four Divisions of Kohathite Attending Priests Who Rotated Service in Solomon's Temple (Sixteen from the Aaron-Eleazar–Zadok Line and Eight from the Aaron-Ithamar Line)."

51. For a list and a discussion of the 24 divisions (courses) of Kohathite attending priests set up in the last days of King David, see chart "**1 Chronicles 24**: Genealogical Registry of the Twenty-Four Divisions of Kohathite Attending Priests Who Rotated Service in Solomon's Temple (Sixteen from the Aaron-Eleazar–Zadok Line and Eight from the Aaron-Ithamar Line)."

52. Mattathias (also called "Mattathias Maccabeus") was the instigator of the Maccabean revolt, which lasted from 167–160 B.C. Mattathias was a Kohathite *attending* priest from the division of Joiarib (Jehoiarib)—see notes 50–51—and appears to have served as a priest in Jerusalem, although his home was in Modin. Josephus writes that "Mattathias . . . [was] the son of John, the son of Simeon, the son of Asamoneus [hence the name "Hasmonean" for the family], a priest of the order of Joiarib and a citizen of Jerusalem. He had five sons; John, who was called Gaddis, and Simon, who was called Matthes, and who was called Maccabeus, and Eleazar, who was called Auran, and Jonathan, who was called Apphus" (*Jewish Antiquities* 12.6.1). When the Seleucid ruler Antiochus IV Epiphanes (175–164 B.C.) told Mattathias to offer sacrifice to the Greek gods, Mattathias not only refused, but also killed the official bearing the message, declaring, "Whoever is zealous for the Law, and maintaineth the covenant, let him follow me" (*I Maccabees* 2:19–20, 27). His countrymen abandoned their possessions and followed Mattathias. They hid in the mountains and desert places and from there, they drove out small bands of the king's troops; punished renegade Jews; destroyed heathen temples and altars; and brought children, who through fear had not been circumcised, into the covenant of Abraham (Richard Gottheil and Samuel Krauss, "Mattathias Maccabeus," *Jewish Encyclopedia*). Before his death, Mattathias urged his sons and the Jewish people to continue steadfastly in the defense of their ancestral religion. When Mattathias died in 166 B.C., he was buried in Modin. For more information on his life, see chart "**Supplement 8**: The Maccabees and the Hasmonean Dynasty." In time, the Maccabees (the descendants of Mattathias) claimed the throne of Judea as well as the position of high priest, which is in contrast to the historical precedent for the Aaronic succession of priests from the tribe of Levi, who held only the high priesthood.

53. **Simon (#44)**—also called "Simon Maccabeus" or "Simon Thassi" or "Matthes"—was the second son of Mattathias and the older and last-surviving brother of Judas Maccabeus and Jonathan Apphus. Simon accompanied his brothers in the Jewish revolt against the Seleucids. After Jonathan Apphus was captured and later assassinated by Trypho, the people elected Simon as the high priest (*I Maccabees* 14:35). Immediately, Simon fortified Jerusalem and expelled all the Gentiles from Joppa, filling the city with Jews instead (*I Maccabees* 13:8, 10–11). Simon wrote to the Seleucid ruler, Demetrius II Nicator (whose first reign was 145–139 B.C.), requesting that Judea be exempt from taxation. Simon's request was granted; according to the *Jewish Encyclopedia* (Richard Gottheil and Samuel Krauss, "Simon Maccabeus"), this may have implied the recognition of Judea's political independence. The selection of Simon as both the high priest and the Jewish leader founded a new dynasty, called the Hasmonean Dynasty, which was formally recognized by the Roman Republic in 139 B.C. Simon served as the high priest from 142–134 B.C. However, Simon and his two oldest sons (Judas and Mattathias) were assassinated on the orders of Simon's son-in-law and rival, Ptolemy (Ptolemeus), son of Abubus (*I Maccabees* 16; *Jewish Antiquities* 13.7.4). The death of Simon marked the end of the brother-to-brother Hasmonean succession and "the high priesthood once again became a hereditary office and continued to be a family possession (with a 2-year gap from 37–35 B.C.E) [under Ananelus] until 35 B.C.E when King Herod had the last Hasmonean high priest, Aristobulus III executed" (VanderKam, *From Joshua to Caiaphas,* 285).

54. **Judas**—also called "Judas Maccabeus" or "Judah Maccabeus" and nicknamed the "Hammer"—was the son of the priest Mattathias (note 52). After his father's death in 166 B.C., Judas assumed the leadership of the Maccabean revolt against the Syrians. Josephus describes him as "a man of valor and a great warrior . . . [who] left behind him a glorious reputation and memorial, by gaining freedom for his nation, and delivering them from slavery under the Macedonians" (*Jewish Antiquities* 12.11.2). Apparently, Judas never held an *official* (royal-appointed) high-priestly position, although in relating Judas' death in 161/160 B.C., Josephus says that Judas "retained the high priesthood three years" before he died (cf. *Jewish Antiquities* 12.11.2). In *Jewish Antiquities* 12.10.6, Josephus writes that upon "the sudden death of Alcimus occurring at this

time, the people gave the office of high priest to Judas," but in the conclusion of *Jewish Antiquities* 20.10, Josephus says that there was an intermission of seven years in the office of high priest. In his commentary on *Jewish Antiquities* 12.10 (note 3, p. 416), Paul Maier clarifies that "Judas' succession to him [Alcimus] as high priest, both here, and at the conclusion of this book [20.10], directly contradicts *1 Maccabees* 9:54–57, which places his [Alcimus'] death after the death of Judas, and says not a syllable of the high priesthood of Judas." Since neither *1 Maccabees* nor the rabbinical authorities speak of Judas occupying the high priesthood, VanderKam (*From Joshua to Caiaphas,* 243) seems to rightly conclude that, after the death of Alcimus, the situation should be understood to mean that Judas Maccabeus was considered by the people and/or the Maccabean troops to be the high priest, but he actually lacked any royal confirmation.

According to *1 Maccabees* 4:36–4:59, it was Judas Maccabeus who instituted what is known today as the Jewish festival of Hanukkah. After the Seleucid king Antiochus IV Epiphanes (175–164 B.C.) invaded Judea, desecrated the Second Temple, and banned Jewish cultic practices there, the Maccabees (the sons of Mattathis Maccabeus) waged a successful three-year campaign against this tyranny. In 165 B.C., Judas Maccabeus liberated Israel from the Syrians and rededicated the temple: "Judas celebrated the festival of the restoration of the sacrifices of the temple for eight days" (*Jewish Antiquities* 12.7.7). According to the Talmud, the Seleucids had left only one intact vial of sacred oil in the Temple, just enough to light the lampstand for one day, but it burned for eight days, enough time for the Maccabees to secure more oil. The "miracle of the lights" is celebrated on the 25th day of Kislev as an eight-day "Feast of Dedication/Rededication" or "Festival of Lights" (cf. **John 10:22**), when candles are lit on each day of the festival. The revolt of the Maccabees continued until they ultimately drove the Seleucids from Judea in 160 B.C.

55. **Jonathan (#43)**—also called "Jonathan Apphus" or "Jonathan Maccabeus" or "Apphus" (*1 Maccabees* 2:5)—was the son of Mattathias and the brother of Judas. He participated in the Maccabean revolt; after the death of his brother Judas, Jonathan was officially appointed high priest in 152 B.C. by the Seleucid ruler Alexander I Balas (150–145 B.C.). Jonathan served for ten years (152–143/142 B.C.; cf. *Jewish Antiquities* 13.6.6). From that time onward, "the combination of sacerdotal and military roles (i.e., cultic and political) was to characterize much of the history of the Hasmonean high priesthood" (VanderKam, *From Joshua to Caiaphas,* 254). Jonathan's death came at the hands of Trypho, the commander of the forces of Alexander I Balas, who tricked Jonathan, took him prisoner, and killed him.

Notably, Josephus was a descendant of Jonathan's daughter; for more details on the ancestry of Josephus, see chart "**Supplement 9**: Flavius Josephus, the Roman-Jewish Historian."

56. **John Hyrcanus I (#45)** was the son of Simon Maccabeus and the nephew of Jonathan Apphus and Judas Maccabeus. He served as both the high priest and the national leader, although the *Jewish Encyclopedia* (Richard Gottheil and Meyer Kayserling, "John (Johanan) Hyrcanus I") says he "never assumed the title of king, being content with that of high priest." In the first year of Hyrcanus I, Judea's semi-independence was challenged by the new Seleucid king, Antiochus VII Sidetes (138–129 B.C.), who besieged Jerusalem. John Hyrcanus finally made a truce with the Seleucid ruler, but the terms were harsh: tear down the walls surrounding Jerusalem; pay three thousand talents of silver; participate in the Seleucids' war against the Parthians; and recognize Seleucid control of Judea (*Jewish Antiquities* 13.8; *Jewish Wars* 1.2.5). To pay the tribute money, John Hyrcanus I took valuables from King David's tomb (*Jewish Antiquities* 13.8.4). Also during his tenure, Hyrcanus: (1) destroyed the temple at Mount Gerizim (a rival worship site to Jerusalem) that had been built by the Samarian governor Sanballat some 200 years earlier (*Jewish Antiquities* 13.9.1); (2) subdued the Idumeans but permitted them to remain in their country if they agreed to be circumcised and follow the laws and customs of the Jews; and (3) began construction of a winter palace complex in Jericho, which "gives concrete witness to claims in the literature that these high priests became very rich indeed" (VanderKam, *From Joshua to Caiaphas,* 309). John Hyrcanus willed that, at his death, his wife was to rule as queen (which didn't come to pass) and that his oldest son, Aristobulus I, was to be the next high priest. Josephus concludes that John Hyrcanus I had three of the most desirable things in the world: "The government of his nation, the dignity of the high priesthood, and [the gift of] prophecy [fortelling that his two eldest sons would not continue the government of public affairs]" (*Jewish Antiquities* 13.10.7; *Jewish Wars* 1.2.8). Hyrcanus I died after he had held office for thirty years (134–104 B.C.; *Jewish Antiquities* 20.10.1).

57. See chart "**Supplement 9**: Flavius Josephus, the Roman-Jewish Historian."

58. **Aristobulus I (#46)** was the eldest son of John Hyrcanus I; he was also known by his Hebrew name, Judah or Judas (*Jewish Antiquities* 20.10.1). His tenure as high priest is discussed by Josephus in *Jewish Antiquities* 13.11.1–3 and *Jewish Wars* 1.3.1–6. His father had stipulated in his will that his wife (i.e., Aristobulus mother) was to rule over Judea as queen after his death, but Aristobulus I flouted his father's wishes. Immediately upon succeeding to the office of high priest, he threw his mother into prison, where she starved to death. Aristobulus also threw three of his brothers into prison; another brother, Antigonus, remained free but he was later murdered. Aristobulus I was the first high priest to take the title of *king* (rather than ruler, governor, or ethnarch). He "put a diadem upon his head [either 481 years and three months (*Jewish Antiquities* 13.11.1) or 471 years and three months (*Jewish Wars* 1.3.1)] after our people came down into this country, when they were set free from the Babylonian slavery." Aristobulus married Salome Alexandra; Jeremias notes that she was from a non-priestly family, which was quite remarkable at the time, since high priests typically married women from the priestly nobility (*Jerusalem in the Time of Jesus,* 155). Aristobulus gradually became completely controlled by a group headed by Queen Salome Alexandra who, by then, was regarded as his co-regent. It was during this time that they appointed Antipater I, Herod the Great's father, as the general of Idumea (*Jewish Antiquities* 14.1.3). The queen convinced her husband Aristobulus that his brother Antigonus was plotting against him; in response, Aristobulus drew Antigonus into a trap. Josephus relates that Antigonus was killed by Aristobulus' guards in Stratos Tower while coming to show his brother his new set of armor (*Jewish Antiquities* 13.11.1, 2; *Jewish Wars* 1.3.5). Josephus says that Aristobulus I "died when he had reigned no longer than a year," corresponding to 104–103 B.C. Aristobulus I and Salome Alexandra had no children. Upon her husband's death, the widowed Salome Alexandra released her remaining brothers-in-law, who were still in prison, and appointed Alexander Jannaeus (Aristobulus' oldest surviving brother) as king.

59. **Alexander Jannaeus (#47)** was the son of John Hyrcanus I and the brother of Aristobulus I. Josephus discusses his priesthood in *Jewish Antiquities* 13.12.1–5 and *Jewish Wars* 1.4.1–8. Aristobulus I had thrown his half-brother Alexander Jannaeus into prison at the beginning of his reign, but when Aristobulus died, his widow Queen Alexandra freed Alexander Jannaeus and appointed him king. In his first public act, Alexander Jannaeus—apparently following the law of levirate marriage—married his brother's widow, Salome Alexandra. During Alexander Jannaeus' reign, civil unrest from the rule of John Hyrcanus I finally ignited, pitting the Pharisees against the Hasmoneans in a clash of priorities—the Pharisees' religious concerns against the Hasmoneans' preoccupation with politics. The *Jewish Encyclopedia* (Louis Ginzberg, "Alexander Jannaeus") states that "[in] order to show his affinity with the Sadducees, he [Alexander Jannaeus], in his capacity of high priest, while offering the prescribed water libation on the Feast of Tabernacles, allowed the water to run upon his feet, thus expressing his contempt for this purely Pharisaic ceremony." The people, angered by Jannaeus' insensitive act, pelted him with citron fruits that had been used during the ceremony. In response, the incensed Jannaeus ordered his mercenaries to attack the people, resulting in 6,000 deaths. The incident ignited the Jewish Civil War, which lasted six years from 93–87 B.C. and killed at least 50,000 Jews. Before his death, Alexander Jannaeus advised his wife to put "all things into [the Pharisees'] power" because "they had great authority among the Jews" (*Jewish Antiquities* 13.15.5). Although Alexander had two sons—Hyrcanus and Aristobulus—he left the kingdom to his wife Salome Alexandra, who "was loved by the multitude . . . [and] seemed displeased at the offenses her husband had been guilty of" (*Jewish Antiquities* 13.16.1). Alexander Jannaeus died in 76 B.C., after a tenure of 27 years, and was succeeded by his wife, Salome Alexandra, who "made Hyracanus [II] high priest" (*Jewish Antiquities* 13.16.2; 20.10.1; *Jewish Wars* 1.5.1).

60. **Salome Alexandra**—called "Alexandra" by the Greeks—was first married to Aristobulus I, but they had no children. After Aristobulus I's death, she became the wife (presumably by levirate marriage) of her brother-in-law Alexander Jannaeus, who held the kingship and the high priesthood from 103–76 B.C. Then, after Alexander Jannaeus' death, she ruled as Queen Alexandra of Judea for nine years, 76–67 B.C. (*Jewish Antiquities* 20.10.1). Notably, Alexandra is only one of two women to have ever ruled over Judea; the other was Athaliah, who usurped the throne of Judah and ruled from 841–835 B.C.; see chart "**2 Kings 11**: Queen Athaliah, Illegitimate Ruler of Judah."

61. **John Hyrcanus II (#48)** was the eldest son of Alexander Jannaeus and Salome Alexandra. Hyrcanus II was the high priest from 75–66 B.C., the king for three months in 67 B.C., the governor/ethnarch from 63–40 B.C., and then restored as high priest from 63–40 B.C. After the death of his father, his mother, Queen Alexandra, appointed Hyrcanus II to the high priesthood. According

to Josephus, this was both because Hyrcanus II was the eldest and, unlike his father, "cared not to meddle with politics, and permitted the Pharisees to do [everything]" (*Jewish Antiquities* 13.16.2). Josephus characterizes him as a man "of a gentle disposition . . . while Aristobulus [his brother] was of a difficult temper, an active man, and one of a great and generous soul" (*Jewish Antiquities* 14.1.3)." When Queen Alexandra died in 67 B.C., the throne was left to John Hyrcanus II. However, barely three months into his reign as king, Hyrcanus' younger brother Aristobulus II rebelled against him and a battle ensued between them. Eventually the two brothers struck an agreement where John Hyrcanus II vacated the offices of both high priest and king but continued to receive the revenues from the high priesthood office. When an ambitious Idumean named Antipater I sought to control Judea, he realized that reaching his goal would be easier under the weaker government of John Hyrcanus II than the stronger one of Aristobulus II. Antipater convinced John Hyrcanus II that Aristobulus II sought his death, which led John Hyrcanus II to seek refuge with Aretas, king of the Nabataeans. During this period of civil unrest, the Roman general Scaurus came to Syria to take control of the region for Pompey. Both John Hyrcanus II and Aristobulus II appealed to the general to help their respective sides. In the end, Scaurus decided to support Aristobulus II; nevertheless, when Pompey came to Syria in 63 B.C., he realized (as Antipater had) that John Hyrcanus II was the better choice because he was the weaker ruler. Thus, Pompey was able to conquer Judea and it became a Roman state. In 63 B.C., Pompey "restored the high priesthood to Hyrcanus [II], and made him governor of the nation" (*Jewish Antiquities* 15.6.4). However, Julius Caesar did not give Hyrcanus II the *official* title of ethnarch. The appointment was in name only, because John Hyrcanus II left the actual rule of Judea to Antipater the Idumean, who used his authority to further his own interests. John Hyrcanus II continued to hold the high priesthood until 40 B.C., at which time his nephew Antigonus II was named king and high priest. John Hyrcanus II was then carried off to Babylon where he was treated with respect by the Jews who had remained there after the Babylonian captivity. However, fearful that John Hyrcanus' popularity would lead to a plot to restore him to the Jewish throne, Antipater's son Herod the Great called John Hyrcanus II back to Jerusalem where Herod treated him well. Eventually, however, Herod charged John Hyrcanus II of plotting with the Nabataeans and had him executed (Richard Gottheil and Isaac Broydé, "Hyrcanus II," *Jewish Encyclopedia*; cf. *Jewish Antiquities* 15.6.4).

62. **Aristobulus II (#49)** was the youngest son of Alexander Jannaeus and Salome Alexandra and the younger brother of John Hyrcanus II. Three months after John Hyrcanus II succeeded to rule the kingdom of Judea in 67 B.C., Aristobulus II revolted against him. When Aristobulus II was successfully took control of the temple, John Hyrcanus II surrendered. Aristobulus II became both the high priest and the king from 67–63 B.C., although John Hyrcanus II retained the revenues from the high priest office. Then, when the Idumean Antipater I sought control of Judea, he convinced John Hyrcanus II that his brother Aristobulus II sought his death. In response, John Hyrcanus II took refuge with Aretas, king of the Nabataeans (whom Antipater had bribed into helping the cause of John Hyrcanus). When the Romans came and took control of the region in 63 B.C., Pompey favored John Hyrcanus II because he was the weaker ruler, and Pompey restored Hyrcanus II to the high priesthood (*Jewish Antiquities* 15.3.1; 15.6.4). Meanwhile, Aristobulus II had been captured by the Romans and taken to Rome, where he was kept in chains. In ca. 50 B.C., Aristobulus was poisoned and was later buried in the royal sepulchers in Jerusalem (*Jewish Antiquities* 14.7.4; *Jewish Wars* 1.9.1; cf. *Jewish Encyclopedia*, Richard Gottheil and Louis Ginzberg "Aristobulus II" and Richard Gottheil and Isaac Broydé "Hyrcanus II").

63. **Antigonus II (#50)**—also called "Antigonus" or "Antigonus Mattathias"—was the second son of Aristobulus II. The *Jewish Encyclopedia* (Louis Ginzberg, "Antigonus Mattathias") says that Antigonus II and his father were taken prisoner to Rome by Pompey in 63 B.C. In 57 B.C., both escaped and headed back to Palestine, although Antigonus II's father (Aristobulus II) was poisoned along the way and died. Antigonus II did not want to admit defeat and therefore sought to regain the throne. In his first attempt in 42 B.C., he was defeated by Herod the Great, but in a second attempt two years later, he was successful. When Antigonus II regained the throne, the people's hatred of Rome was intense, making his transition and rule easier. The Parthians, who had captured Syria in 40 B.C. (i.e., the same year that Antigonus took the throne), also favored an anti-Roman Judean government and officially appointed Antigonus as high priest as well as king. However, the Roman government declared Herod the Great the king of Judea. Herod sought to take back the region from Antigonus and successfully took Joppa, Masada, and Galilee before he successfully besieged Jerusalem. Antigonus was put to death at Antioch in 37 B.C. "It was the first time that the Romans had ever thus put a king to death. The last king of pure Jewish blood [Antigonus II] fell before the intrigues of the first king of Judea [Herod the Great] not entirely of Jewish birth" (Louis Ginzberg, "Antigonus Mattathias," *Jewish Encyclopedia*).

64. Alexander II married his cousin Alexandra, the daughter of John Hyrcanus II (i.e., John Hyrcanus II was both Alexander II's uncle and his father-in-law).

65. For Mariamne I, the granddaughter of John Hyrcanus II, and her marriage to Herod the Great, see chart "**Matthew 2**: Herod the Great and the Herodian Dynasty."

66. In *Jewish Antiquities* 14.16.4 (cf. 17.6.3), Josephus notes that the "government of the Asamoneans [Hasmoneans] cease[d] a hundred and twenty-six years after it was set up." Josephus goes on to say that "this family was a splendid and an illustrious one, both on account of the nobility of their stock, and of the dignity of the high priesthood, [and] also for the glorious actions their ancestors had performed for our nation; but these men lost the government by their dissensions, one with another and it came to Herod [the Great], the son of Antipater, who was of no more than a vulgar family, and of no eminent extractions, but one that was subject to other kings. And this is what history tells us was the end of the Asamonean family."

67. As Babota points out, "Josephus is the most extensive source about the Jewish high priests for the Hellenistic, Hasmonean and Roman period[s]. . . . Josephus was himself a priest and a close collaborator of several pre-war high priests. This enabled him to become acquainted with oral and/or written traditions preserved in the high-priestly circles and/or archives, such as the list of the priests contained in *Antiquities* 20.224–251" (Babota, *Hasmonean High Priesthood,* 21, 33–34). An enumeration of the high priests during this time period is found in *Jewish Antiquities*, particularly 20.10.1ff.

68. **Ananelus (#51)**—also called "Hanameel" or "Ananel"—was appointed to the high priesthood by Herod the Great after the ignominious death of Antigonus II in 37 B.C. According to Josephus, Anaelus was "an obscure priest out of Babylon" (*Jewish Antiquities* 15.2.4), who was unknown in Israel: "One of those Jews that had been carried captive beyond the Euphrates . . . he was one of the stock of the high priests and had been of old a particular friend of Herod [the Great]" (*Jewish Antiquities* 15.3.1). VanderKam comments that, "although there were other Hasmonean survivors who could have been appointed high priest, Herod wanted to avoid appointing a *legitimate* member of the Hasmonean family and, in this way, downgraded the high priesthood to ensure that the incumbent would not be a rival to him [Herod]. By appointing Ananelus, Herod changed the policy, so that the high priesthood was no longer a *hereditary* office but an *appointive* one" (VanderKam, *From Joshua to Caiaphas,* 395, 398). Herod appointed Ananelus the high priest in 37 B.C. but removed him from office in 35 B.C.: "Hanameel's incumbency was of short duration. Prudence compelled Herod to remove him, and to fill his place with the Hasmonean Aristobulus [III]. . . . The youthful Hasmonean, however, was too popular with the patriotic party; though he was a brother of Mariamne [I], Herod's beloved wife, he [Aristobulus III] was treacherously drowned at Herod's instigation (35 B.C.), and Hanameel [Annanelus] was restored to the high position" (*Jewish Encyclopedia,* "Hanameel"). Josephus does not specifically record Herod's appointment of Ananelus' successor (see note 69).

69. **Aristobulus III (#52)**—whose Hebrew name was Jonathan—was the last scion of the Hasmonean royal house. He was the grandson of Aristobulus II; the son of Jonathan Alexander (Alexandres/Alexander II) and Alexandra (the daughter of Hyrcanus II and therefore Alexander's cousin); the brother of Mariamne I, the wife of Herod; and the brother-in-law of Herod the Great. Aristobulus' appointment to the high priesthood was probably at the insistence of Mariamne (Herod's wife) and Aristobulus' mother, Alexandra. Because the youthful Aristobulus III was a favorite among the people, Herod became fearful of him and instigated a system of espionage against Aristobulus III and his mother Alexandra. Josephus writes in *Jewish Antiquities* 15.3.3 that at the Hasmonean palace in Jericho, "Herod resolved to complete what he had intended against the young man [(Aristobulus III] . . . while such of Herod's acquaintance, as he had appointed to do it, dipped him [Aristobulus III] as he was swimming, and plunged him under water, in the dark of the evening, as if it had been done in sport only, [nor] did they stop until he was entirely suffocated. And thus was Aristobulus [III] murdered, having lived no more in all than eighteen years, and kept the high priesthood one year only [35 B.C.]; which high priesthood Ananelus now recovered again." After the murder of Aristobulus III, no Hasmonean thereafter held the high priesthood (VanderKam, *From Joshua to Caiaphas,* 404).

70. After Herod the Great ordered the murder of Aristobulus III, Herod

restored the former high priest Ananelus to the priesthood (*Jewish Antiquities* 15.3.3). VanderKam (*From Joshua to Caiaphas,* 398) suggests that Ananelus held a second term from ca. 35–30(?) B.C. but says it could not have been longer, since after the execution of Mariamne I in 29 B.C., Herod remarried, this time to Mariamne II (the daughter of Simon ben Boethus). Herod later appointed his father-in-law Simon ben Boethus to the high priesthood and removed Joshua ben Fabi (*Jewish Encyclopedia*, "Hanameel"). Joachim Jeremias dates Ananelus' restoration to 34 B.C., rather than 35 B.C. (*Jerusalem in the Time of Jesus,* 377).

71. **Joshua ben Fabus (#53)**—also called "Jesus, son of Phabet (or Phiabi/Phabus/Phabes)"—is mentioned by Josephus as the predecessor to Simon, the son of Boethus (*Jewish Antiquities* 15.9.3). According to VanderKam, the Phiabi family was one of four families that supplied almost all of the last 28 high priests in the Second Temple period (*From Joshua to Caiaphas,* 406).

72. **Simon ben Boethus (#54)** was the successor of Joshua ben Fabus, and he held the high priesthood from 24/22–5 B.C. Josephus writes in *Jewish Antiquities* 15.9.3 that Simon was "a citizen of Jerusalem, the son of one Boethus, a citizen of Alexandria [Egypt], and a priest of great note there." Herod the Great removed Jesus, the son of Phabet, from the high priesthood and conferred the dignity on Simon so that Herod could marry Simon's daughter, Mariamne II, who was called "the most beautiful woman of the time." Simon's daughter Mariamne II—which distinguished her from Herod's former wife of the same name (Mariamne I), who had been executed—became the third wife of Herod the Great. Mariamne II had one child by Herod, whom they named Herod II (also known as "Herod Boethus" or "Herod Philip I"). In 20 B.C., during Simon's high priesthood, Herod began rebuilding the former temple and expanding the temple complex. Simon was removed late in Herod's reign in ca. 5 B.C. (for a discussion of Herod and members of his family, see chart "**Matthew 2**: Herod the Great and the Herodian Dynasty").

73. **Matthias ben Theophilus [#55]** came to the high priesthood in this way: When Mariamne II (the third wife of Herod) was implicated in the plot of Antipater against her husband in 4 B.C., "Herod divorced her [Mariamne II] and blotted her son [Herod II/Herod Philip Boethus] out of his testament . . . and he [Herod] took the high priesthood away from his father-in-law, Simon the son of Boethus, and appointed Matthias the son of Theophilus who was born at Jerusalem to be priest in his place" (*Jewish Antiquities* 17.4.2). Jeremias refers to him as "Mattaiah" (instead of Matthias), saying that he was the brother-in-law of the next high priest, Joazar ben Boethus (#56), and that Mattaiah/Matthias served from the Day of Atonement in 5 B.C. to 12 March 4 B.C. (p. 162). Josephus says that during his priesthood "there was another person made high priest for a single day . . . Matthias the high priest had a dream in which he could not officiate himself [because of his uncleanness; cf. **Leviticus 22:4**], so Joseph, the son of Ellemus [Elam], his kinsman, assisted him in that sacred office" (*Jewish Antiquities* 17.6.4). Matthias ben Theophilus was implicated in the insurrection in which the costly golden eagle (which Herod had erected over the gate of the temple) was pulled down (Isidore Singer and Samuel Krauss, "Matthias ben Theophilus" *Jewish Encyclopedia; Jewish Antiquities* 17.6.2–4). Josephus also says that when "Herod deprived this Matthias [the son of Theophilus] of the high priesthood . . . that very night there was an eclipse of the moon" (*Jewish Antiquities* 17.6.4); in note 3 of his commentary in this section of Josephus, Maier (566) concludes that "this eclipse of the moon (which is the only eclipse of either of the luminaries mentioned by our Josephus in any of his writings) is of the greatest consequence for the determination of the time for the death of Herod and Antipater, and for the birth and entire chronology of Jesus Christ. It [the eclipse] happened March 13th, in the year of the Julian period 4710, and the 4th year before the Christian era." Response to Maier's comment: Readers should be aware that the occurrence of an eclipse in 4 B.C. is part of what is called the "consensus view" in modern scholarship that asserts that Herod died *after* a lunar eclipse in 4 B.C. However, recent scholarship has challenged the 4 B.C. date for Herod's death and suggested instead that Herod died in early 1 B.C. *after* a total lunar eclipse of January 10, 1 B.C. but *before* Passover (April 8). For more information, see Andrew E. Steinmann's comments in *From Abraham to Paul: A Biblical Chronology* (St. Louis: Concordia, 2011), 219–54.

74. **Joazar ben Boethus (#56)** was appointed by Herod and held the high priesthood in 4 B.C. When "he [Herod] deprived Matthias of the high priesthood . . . [Herod] made Joazar, who was Matthias's wife's brother, high priest in his stead"; thus Joazar was the brother-in-law of the former high priest, Matthias ben Theophilus (cf. *Jewish Antiquities* 17.6.4; 17.13.1). Also, Joazar ben Boethus appears to have been restored to the high priesthood (see note 77).

75. **Eleazar ben Boethus (#57)** was the brother of Joazar. "When Archelaus was entered on his ethnarchy, and was come into Judea, he accused Joazar, the son of Boethus, of assisting the rebel [a "spurious Alexander"] and took the high priesthood from him and put his brother [Eleazar ben Boethus] in his place . . . Eleazar [did not] abide long in the high priesthood [4 B.C. only], Jesus, the son of Sie, being put in his place while he [Eleazar] was still living" (*Jewish Antiquities* 17.13.1).

76. **Joshua ben Sie (#58)**—also called "Jesus, son of Sie/Seë"—came to the priesthood after Eleazar was deposed. Presumably, Joshua was unrelated to Eleazar his predecessor and Josephus records nothing more about him (*Jewish Antiquities* 17.13.1.). His tenure in office is unclear (4 B.C.–?). Jeremias says that Joshua/Jesus ruled until A.D. 6 (Jeremias, *Jerusalem in the Time of Jesus,* 377).

77. **Joazar ben Boethus**, the brother-in-law of Matthias ben Theophilus, appears to have been restored to the high priesthood after Joshua ben Sie was removed. Joazar's reappointment as high priest (4 B.C.–?) seems to have occurred simultaneously (or overlapped) with the first appointment of Quirinius as the governing authority over Syria. According to Steinmann, Quirinius' first term extended from ca. 4–1 B.C., and during Quirinius' term, as Luke explains "the "first census [of the entire Roman world] . . . took place while Quirinius was *governor* of Syria" (**Luke 2:1–2**)—which Steinmann holds was a type of "governing function" (i.e., a *legatus juridicus* who was coming to take account of Jewish property in the province of Syria, which included Judea), but "not necessarily denot[ing] holding the office of governor [*legati pro praetore*]" (Andrew E. Steinmann, From Abraham to Paul: A Biblical Chronology [St. Louis: Concordia, 2011], 239). Notably, this Roman census has come to be associated with the birth of Jesus; "the census in Judea should be dated to the spring or summer of 3 B.C. . . . the date of Jesus' birth must have been sometime in late 3 B.C. or early 2 B.C." (Steinmann, 249). Furthermore, Steinmann holds that Quirinius may have had two *separate* terms, because a second census, mentioned in **Acts 5:37**, appears to have been taken during Quirinius' second term. Josephus relates that Cyrenius (Quirinius) "came himself into Judea, which was now added to the province of Syria, to take an account of their substance . . . but the Jews, although at the beginning they took the report of a taxation heinously, yet did they leave off any further opposition to it, by the persuasion of Joazar, who was the son of Boethus, and high priest; so they, being persuaded by Joazar's words, gave an account of their estates, without any disputes about it" (*Jewish Antiquities* 18.1.1). Josephus states that "when Cyrenius [Quirinius] had now disposed of [Herod] Archelaus's money, and when the taxings were come to a conclusion, which were made in the thirty-seventh year of Caesar's victory over Antony at Actium, he [Cyrenius/Quirinius] deprived Joazar [ben Boethus] of the priesthood and appointed Ananus, the son of Seth, to be the high priest" (*Jewish Antiquities* 18.2.1).

78. **Ananus ben Seth/Sethi (#59)**—also called "Annas" or "Annas the elder"—held the high priesthood from A.D. 6–15. VanderKam notes that Ananus' appointment was without precedent: "This is the first recorded case of a governor of Syria [Cyrenius/Quirinius] making such an appointment" (*From Joshua to Caiaphas,* 420). Scripture clearly documents the high priesthood of Ananus in several places. **Luke 3:2** says that "during the high-priesthood of Annas and Caiaphas, the word of God came to John [the Baptist] son of Zechariah in the wilderness." Also, in A.D. 33, after Jesus was arrested in the Garden of Gethsemane, he was first taken "to Annas [the elder], who was the father-in-law of Caiaphas, the high priest that year" (**John 18:12–13**); later, Scripture says that "Annas sent him [Jesus] bound to Caiaphas the high priest" (**v. 24**). The family of Ananus/Annas was highly esteemed, for they held a kind of "perpetual high priesthood," since Caiaphas (the son-in-law of Ananus) and five of Ananus' sons—Eleazar, Jonathan, Theophilus, Matthias, and Ananus ben Ananus—all held terms of office between A.D. 18 and A.D. 63. When Valerius Gratus became the procurator of Judea in A.D. 15, he "deprived Ananus of the high priesthood, and appointed Is(h)mael, the son of Phabi, to be high priest" (*Jewish Antiquities* 18.2.2). Refer to the chart "**Matthew 26**: The Influential Family of Annas and Caiaphas, the High Priests" for more information on the priesthood of Ananus and his sons.

79. **Is(h)mael ben Fabus (#60)**—also called "Is(h)mael ben Phabi/Phiabi"—was the high priest from A.D. 15–16(?). After he had been appointed procurator of Judea, Valerius Gratus replaced Ananus with Ishmael ben Fabus who held the position briefly. Valerius Gratus "also deprived him [Ishmael] in a little time, and ordained Eleazar, the son of Ananus, who had been high priest before, to be high priest" (*Jewish Antiquities* 18.2.2).

80. **Eleazar ben Ananus (#61)** was the son of Ananus the elder. He was installed as high priest by the procurator Valerius Gratus, thereby removing Ishmael ben Fabus from the position (*Jewish Antiquities* 18.2.2). Eleazar held the position from A.D. 16–17(?). Josephus describes Eleazar as "a very bold youth." As the "governor of the temple," Eleazar persuaded those who officiated

in the divine service to receive no gift for sacrifice from any foreigner [non-Jew]. According to Josephus, "this was the beginning of the war with the Romans; for they [the Jewish priests] rejected the sacrifice of Caesar on this account" (*Jewish Wars* 17.16.2). After Eleazar had been in office "for a year," Gratus deprived him of the high priesthood and gave it to Simon the son of Camithus (*Jewish Antiquities* 18.2.2).

81. **Simon ben Camithus/Kamithos (#62)**, mentioned in *Jewish Antiquities* 18.2.2, was the high priest who succeeded Eleazar, son of Ananus. Simon was appointed by Valerius Gratus (the procurator of Judea from A.D. 15–26) and "possessed that dignity no longer than a year" corresponding to A.D. 17–18. Apparently, on the evening before the Day of Atonement, Simon was "touched by an Arab's spittle" and became ceremonially defiled, so his unnamed brother functioned as his substitute on that day (Jeremias, *Jerusalem in the Time of Jesus,* 153, 162). Jeremias proposes that because of the defilement incident, the traditional "nightly seclusion of the high priest in the week before the Day of Atonement may have been instituted about A.D. 20" (ibid., 153).

82. **Joseph Caiaphas (#63)**—or simply "Caiaphus"—married the daughter of the former high priest Ananus the elder (A.D. 6–15), and therefore he was Ananus' son-in-law. Joseph Caiaphas is mentioned in **Matthew 26:3, 57; Luke 3:2; John 11:49; 18:13–14, 24, 28; Acts 4:6**). In A.D. 18, the procurator of Judea Valerius Gratus removed Simon ben Camithus, and "Joseph Caiaphas was made his successor" (*Jewish Antiquities* 18.2.2). Caiaphas' term of office (A.D. 18–36/37) overlapped that of Pontius Pilate, who was the prefect of Judea from A.D. 26–36. John the Baptist's ministry—which began in A.D. 29, "in the fifteenth year of the reign of Tiberius Caesar" (**Luke 3:1–2**) and ended in ca. A.D. 32 with John's beheading—occurred during Caiaphas' tenure as high priest. Caiaphas prophesied "that Jesus would die for the Jewish nation, and not only for that nation but also for the scattered children of God, to bring them together and make them one" (**John 11:51–52**; cf. **Matthew 26:1–4**). Caiaphas' prophecy sparked the beginning of a plot by the religious leaders to kill Jesus (**John 11:53**; cf. **Matthew 26:1–4**). Before Jesus was taken to the Praetorium to be questioned by Pilate (**John 18:28, 33**), Caiaphas questioned Jesus about "his disciples and his teaching" (**John 18:19**) and accused Jesus of blasphemy (**Matthew 26:65; Mark 14:63–64**). When Peter and John were brought before Caiaphas and the Sanhedrin, they asked the disciples: "By what power or what name did you do this? [healing a lame man]" (**Acts 4:7;** see **vv. 1–12**). The Sanhedrin ordered Peter and John "not to speak or teach at all in the name of Jesus," to which Peter replied: "Which is right in God's eyes: to listen to you, or to him? You be the judges! As for us, we cannot help speaking about what we have seen and heard" (**Acts 4:18–20**). When Lucius Vitellius attained the governorship of Syria, he deposed Caiaphas in late A.D. 36 or early 37—at about the same time that Pilate was removed as procurator of Judea (cf. Jeremias, *Jerusalem in the Time of Jesus,* 195, 378; *Jewish Antiquities* 18.2.2)—and Vitellius then appointed Jonathan the son of Ananus (Caiaphas' brother-in-law) to the priesthood (*Jewish Antiquities* 18.4.3).

83. **Jonathan ben Ananus (#64)** was appointed by governor Vitellius to the high priesthood after Caiaphas was deposed (*Jewish Antiquities* 18.4.3). Jeremias says that Jonathan held office for only fifty days, from Easter to Pentecost in A.D. 37 (*Jerusalem in the Time of Jesus,* 195, 378). Then, on a second visit to Jerusalem, Vitellius deposed Jonathan and conferred the office on Jonathan's brother Theophilus (*Jewish Antiquities* 18.5.3; Jeremias, *Jerusalem in the Time of Jesus,* 195). Later, Jonathan ben Ananus was restored to the high priesthood (see note 90).

84. **Theophilus ben Ananus (#65)** was appointed by Vitellius in A.D. 37 to succeed his brother Jonathan to the high priesthood (*Jewish Antiquities* 18.5.3). Theophilus held the priesthood from A.D. 37–41. However, Herod Agrippa I (A.D. 41–44) "removed Theophilus, the son of Ananus, from the high priesthood and bestowed that honor of his on Simon the son of Boethus, whose name was also [Simon] Cantheras whose daughter [Mariamne II] King Herod married" (*Jewish Antiquities* 19.6.2).

85. **Simon ben Boethus (#66)**—also called "Simon Cantheras" or "Simon Kantheras"—was appointed high priest by Herod Agrippa I to replace Theophilus ben Ananus (*Jewish Antiquities* 19.6.2). Simon served as the high priest from A.D. 41–42. VanderKam says that Simon appears to be a member of the Boethus family, which included the former high priests Simon son of Boethus (24/22–5 B.C.), Joazar son of Boethus (ca. A.D. 4–6), and Eleazar son of Boethus (4 B.C.). Josephus also comments on the distinguished family connections of the Boethus family also: "Simon had two brothers and his father, Boethus [whose] daughter was married to King Herod. . . . Simon accordingly, as did his brothers and father, obtained the high priesthood" (*Jewish Antiquities* 19.6.2). As VanderKam points out, however, Josephus (in *Jewish Antiquities* 19.6.2) conflates Simon Cantheras, the son of Boethus, with his *father*, Simon the son of Boethus, whose daughter (Mariamne II) was married to King Herod. To avoid chronological error, VanderKam suggests that Josephus should have written "and his father, Simon the son [of] Boethus, whose daughter was married to King Herod," yielding a father and 3 sons, all of whom were high priests" (VanderKam, *From Joshua to Caiaphas,* 444–446). Later, Herod Agrippa took the high priesthood away from Simon ben Boethus and gave it to Matthias the son of Ananus (*Jewish Antiquities* 19.6.4).

86. **Matthias ben Ananus (#67)** was the brother of the former high priests Jonathan and Theophilus. Later in his reign over Judea (A.D. 41–44), King Agrippa "took the priesthood away from Simon [son of Boethus, surnamed Cantheras] and [desired to] put Jonathan, the son of Ananus, into it again. . . . But this was not a thing acceptable to him [Jonathan]. . . . So he refused it." Instead, Jonathan suggested to Agrippa that a more worthy candidate would be his brother Matthias. "So the king was pleased . . . and according to his brother's desire, bestowed the high priesthood upon Matthias [son of Ananus]" (*Jewish Antiquities* 19.6.4). Matthias served as the high priest from A.D. 42–43(?) but was removed by King Agrippa in favor of Elioneus, son of Cantheras (*Jewish Antiquities* 19.8.1).

87. **Elioneus ben Cantheras/Kantheras/Cimtheras (#68)**—also called "Aljoneus," "Elionaeus," and "Elianaius"—succeeded Matthias to the high priesthood. According to Jeremias, Elioneus held the position in A.D. 44 (*Jerusalem in the Time of Jesus,* 229, 378), but according to VanderKam, he was high priest from A.D. 43?–45; for those reasons, both dates are shown in the chart. After King Agrippa I moved to Tiberius in Galilee and after Agrippa's dispute with Marcus the president of Syria, Agrippa "took the high priesthood away from Matthias [son of Ananus] and made Elioneus, the son of Cantheras, high priest in his stead" (*Jewish Antiquities* 19.8.1). VanderKam (*From Joshua to Caiaphas,* 449) says that Elionaeus was a son or possibly a brother of the former high priest Simon Cantheras son of Boethus (#66). Herod king of Chalcis "removed the last high priest called Cimtheras, and bestowed that dignity on his successor Joseph, the son of Cantos" (*Jewish Antiquities* 20.1.3). Jeremias (*Jerusalem in the Time of Jesus,* 229) notes that "Elionaios, son of Kantheras" was only one of two high priests who prepared the Red Heifer (the other was Ishmael son of Phiabi).

88. **Joseph ben Camydus (#69)**—variously called "Joseph son of Camei/ Cantos/Cainus/Kami"—was appointed high priest by King Herod of Chalcis (the son of Aristobulus IV) in place of Elioneus (*Jewish Antiquities* 20.1.3). Joseph ben Camydus served from A.D. 45–48 and was then replaced by Ananias the son of Nebedeus (*Jewish Antiquities* 20.5.2).

89. **Ananias ben Nebedeus (#70)**—also called "Ananias" or "Ananias, son of Nebedaius"—was high priest from A.D. 48–59. Jeremias modifies those dates slightly by saying that Ananias held the priesthood from A.D. 47 to at least 55 (*Jerusalem in the Time of Jesus,* 378). Ananias, the final appointee of King Herod of Chalcis, replaced Joseph the son of Camydus (*Jewish Antiquities* 20.5.2). Ananias was head over the Sanhedrin and officiated when Paul pleaded his case a first time (**Acts 23:1–5**) and a second time (**24:1**). Paul was left in custody for two years before the term of Felix the procurator ended in A.D. 59/60, at which time Felix was replaced by Porcius Festus (**24:27**). Ananias ben Nebedeus was assassinated early in the war with Rome, which began in A.D. 66 and continued to A.D. 70 (*Jewish War* 2.17.9).

90. Jonathan ben Ananus appears to have been restored briefly to the high priesthood in A.D. 59, although the order of priestly succession is not exactly clear. Josephus explains that during this time, the affairs of the Jews grew worse and worse, and the country became filled with robbers and impostors. Josephus says that the procurator Felix "bore an ill-will to Jonathan . . . because he frequently gave him admonitions about governing the Jewish affairs better than he did. . . . So Felix contrived a method whereby he might get rid of him [Jonathan]. . . . Felix persuaded one of Jonathan's most faithful friends [Doras] . . . to kill him . . . promising to give him a great deal of money. Doras complied with the proposal" but, instead of killing him himself, Doras had the *Sicarii* (a splinter group of the Jewish Zealots) murder Jonathan (*Jewish Antiquities* 20.8.5; cf. *Jewish Wars* 2.13.3). Josephus attributes the innocent death of Jonathan and others as the "reason why God out of his hatred of these men's wickedness, rejected our city; and as for the temple, he no longer esteemed it sufficiently pure for him to inhabit therein, but brought the Romans upon us, and threw a fire upon the city to purge it; and brought upon us, our wives, and children, slavery, as desirous to make us wiser by our calamities" (*Jewish Antiquities* 20.8.5).

91. **Is(h)mael ben Fabus (#71)**—also called "Ishmael ben Phaibi II" or "Is(h)mael ben Fabi"—was appointed to the high priesthood by Herod Agrippa II.

He served toward the end of the tenure of Felix the procurator (A.D. 52–59/60), the beginning of Festus' rule (A.D. 59/60–62), and during the reign of Emperor Nero (A.D. 54–68). During Ishmael's term in office from A.D. 59–61, a rebellion arose "between the high priests and the principal men of the multitude of Jerusalem." The situation worsened to the point that "disorders were done after a licentious manner in the city, as if it had no government over it." Some priests were sent "into the threshing floors" and, because tithes were not given to the poorest priests, some died (*Jewish Antiquities* 20.8.8; cf. **Numbers 18:21**). When Herod Agrippa II built a large dining room in the royal palace at Jerusalem so that he "could lie down, and eat, and from there observe what was done in the temple," the Jews of Jerusalem considered this eavesdropping. In response, they erected a wall on the uppermost building "which belonged to the inner court of the temple towards the west." The high priest Ishmael was sent with a delegation to the Emperor Nero to plead that the wall of the temple be allowed to remain standing. Nero granted the request, but Ishmael was held hostage in Rome by Nero's wife Poppaea Sabina, who was a religious woman. Upon hearing this news, King Agrippa II "gave the high priesthood to Joseph, who was called Cabi, the son of Simon [Simon ben Camithus, A.D. 17–18 or Simon ben Boethus, A.D. 41–42], formerly high priest" (*Jewish Antiquities* 20.8.11). According to Jeremias (*Jerusalem in the Time of Jesus,* 229), Ishmael was only one of two high priests who prepared the Red Heifer (the other was Elionaios [Elioneus] son of Kantheras; see note 87).

92. **Joseph Cabi ben Simon (#72)**, known as "Joseph Qabi" by Jeremias (*Jerusalem in the Time of Jesus,* 94, 176), was appointed to the high priesthood by Herod Agrippa II when his predecessor Is(h)mael ben Fabus was detained in Rome by Nero and Nero's wife (*Jewish Antiquities* 20.8.11). Joseph Cabi served from A.D. 61–62. VanderKam notes that Joseph Cabi's father, Simon, could have been one of the former high priests, either Simon son of Camithus/Kamithos (A.D. 17–18) or Simon Cantheras son of Boethus (A.D. 41–42); he also notes that the removal of Joseph from the high priesthood was commensurate with the death of Festus in A.D. 62 and the civil appointment of his successor, Albinus, as the next procurator of Judea, A.D. 62–64 (VanderKam, *From Joshua to Caiaphas,* 475–476).

93. **Ananus ben Ananus (#73)**—also known as "Ananus the younger"—was appointed high priest by Herod Agrippa II in A.D. 62. He was the younger son of "Ananus the elder," who had held the high priesthood, A.D. 6–15; the four brothers of Ananus the younger had also served as high priests, "which had never happened to any other of our high priests" (*Jewish Antiquities* 20.9.1). Josephus describes the young Ananus as "a bold man in his temper, and very insolent; he was also of the sect of the Sadducees who are very rigid in judging offenders . . . and he [Ananus] thought he had now a proper opportunity [to exercise his authority]." Ananus called the Sanhedrin together and "brought before them the brother [half-brother] of Jesus, who was called Christ, whose name was James and some others . . . when he [Ananus the younger] had formed an accusation against them . . . he delivered them to be stoned" (for more information on James, the half-brother of Jesus, see chart "**Matthew 1**: Jesus and His Immediate Family"). Soon thereafter, some fair-minded citizens appealed to Herod Agrippa II and to the procurator Albinus, informing them that it had not been lawful for Ananus to assemble the Sanhedrin without consent. Herod Agrippa II agreed and deposed Ananus "when he had ruled but three months" and replaced him with Joshua ben Damneus (*Jewish Antiquities* 20.9.1). Ultimately, Ananus was executed by Idumeans who held him in contempt. Josephus states that "the death of Ananus ben Ananus was the beginning of the destruction of the city [Jerusalem]" (cf. *Jewish Wars* 4.5.2).

94. **Joshua ben Damneus/Damnaeus (#74)**—also called "Joshua ben Damnai," "Jesus ben Damnai," and "Jesus son of Damnaius"—was appointed by King Agrippa II to be the successor of Ananus son of Ananus (*Jewish Antiquities* 20.9.1). He held the priesthood from A.D. 62–63? or 63–65. The *Jewish Encyclopedia* says that Joshua ben Damneus was soon deposed by the king, and in his place Joshua (Jesus) ben Gamaliel (Gamla) received the high priesthood. However, strife broke out between the deposed priest and the new high priest, where they insulted each other in the public streets and even threw stones at each other. Nevertheless, Joshua ben Gamaliel remained the victor.

95. **Joshua ben Gamaliel (#75)**—also called "Jesus ben Gamaliel" or "Jesus ben Gamla"—was appointed by Herod Agrippa II as the successor of Joshua the son of Damneus (*Jewish Antiquities* 20.9.4). Joshua ben Gamaliel officiated as the high priest in ca. A.D. 63–64 (according to VanderKam, *From Joshua to Caiaphas*, 482–86, 492), or A.D. 63–65, according to Jeremias (*Jerusalem in the Time of Jesus,* 156, 378). The *Jewish Encyclopedia* (Richard Gottheil, Samuel Krauss; "Joshua (Jesus) ben Gamla asserts that Joshua ben Gamaliel was appointed to the priesthood because he had married the rich widow Martha of the high-priestly family of Boethus and that by bribing Agrippa II, Martha secured for him the office of high priest. [Jeremias explains that the prevailing custom in the Second Temple period was that a high priest married a virgin (and preferably a virgin from the priestly nobility or of priestly descent), while widows, divorced women, violated women, and prostitutes were forbidden (cf. **Leviticus 21:13–15**); however, apparently the marriage of the high priest Joshua son of Gamaliel to Martha the widow was accepted because she was from the prominent Boethus family (Jeremias, *Jerusalem in the Time of Jesus,* 154–155)]. Joshua did not remain in office for long. Josephus notes that the dismissal of Jesus (son of Gamaliel) in A.D. 64 corresponded to the final completion of Herod's Temple, which had begun in 20 B.C.—from these bookend dates, it seems that the temple rebuilding project took approximately 84 years to complete! At this point, however, 18,000 unemployed workmen urged Herod Agrippa II to provide newr jobs for them, so Agrippa allowed them to pave the city with white stones. Then, Herod Agrippa II "deprived Jesus, the son of Gamaliel, of the high priesthood, and gave it to Matthias, the son of Theophilus, under whom the Jews' war with the Romans took its beginning" (*Jewish Antiquities* 20.9.7).

96. **Matthias ben Theophilus (#76)** was appointed by Herod Agrippa II as the successor to Joshua ben Gamaliel (*Jewish Antiquities* 20.9.7), and he held the high priesthood from A.D. 65–67. The *Jewish Encyclopedia* (Isidore Singer, Samuel Krauss; "Matthias ben Theophilas") reasons that this Matthias was a *descendant* of the former high priest, Matthias son of Theophilus, who had held the high priesthood from 5–4 B.C. Josephus states that Matthias was in office when the war against the Romans broke out (*Jewish Antiquities* 20.9.7); moreover, Josephus clarifies that the "war began in the second year of Florus [Gessius Florus, the last procurator of Judea, A.D.64–66] and the twelfth year of the reign of Nero [A.D. 54–68]" (*Jewish Antiquities* 20.11.1). The *Jewish Encyclopedia* (ibid.) says that Matthias was killed by Simon ben Gioras, whom Matthias had invited to Jerusalem to subdue revolutionists.

97. **Phannias ben Samuel (#77)**—also called "Phanas" or "Phanni"—was from the village of Aphtha. Phannias was the last high priest of Israel. Jeremias refers to him as "Pinhas of Habta" (*Jerusalem in the Time of Jesus,* 155) because according to Rabbinic tradition, Aphtha was "Habta." Jeremias characterizes Pinhas as a stonemason and an uneducated man but acknowledges that he had the advantage of being of Zadokite priestly descent. According to Jeremias, Pinhas was chosen by lot, put into office by the Zealots in A.D. 67, and Pinhas held the high priesthood from A.D. 67–70 (ibid., 192–93; 378). On the other hand, VanderKam suggests that Phannias came to the priesthood around A.D. 68(?) after the Romans had subdued Galilee and began to enter Jerusalem in large numbers (*From Joshua to Caiaphas,* 487). Josephus describes Phannias harshly, as a buffoon dressed in the sacred vestments, "a man not only unworthy of the high priesthood, but that did not well know what the high priesthood was, such a mere rustic was he . . . they hail this man, without his own consent . . . as if they were acting a play upon the stage, and adorned him with a counterfeit face . . . and instructed him what he was to do. This horrid piece of wickedness was sport and pastime with them, but occasioned the other priests, who at a distance saw their law made a fest of, to shed tears, and sorely lament the dissolution of such a sacred dignity" (*Jewish Wars* 4.3.8).

Josephus does not confirm whether or not Phannias was actually attending at the temple when it was razed in A.D. 70. VanderKam summarizes the events as follows: "The Second Temple high priesthood came to its conclusion in A.D. 70, some 600 years after it began in 538 B.C. and . . . the ancient office, so rich in sacerdotal and political associations ended on a low note, never to be revived. Yet, though the historical form of the office ceased, the coming of an eschatological high priest had by this time, perhaps, encouraged by failings among those who held the office, became an article of hope among some Jews and Christians" (VanderKam, *From Joshua to Caiaphas,* 490).

98. Several writers corroborate that scrupulous records were kept for the office holders of the high priesthood. In his book *Jerusalem in the Time of Jesus,* Jeremias addresses "The Clergy" in Part Three (ibid., 147–221) and discusses "The Priestly Aristocracy" in particular (ibid., 181–82), claiming that "There was in the Temple at Jerusalem a kind of archive in which the genealogies of the priesthood were kept" (ibid., 214). Jeremias goes on to give two examples: (1) Josephus' statement in his biographical *Vita* that "I set down the genealogy of my family as I have found it described in the public records" and (2) Josephus' declaration in *Against Apion* 1.7 that "our forefathers did not only appoint the best of these [high] priests [but] made provision that the stock of the priests should continue unmixed and pure; for he who is partaker of the priesthood must propagate of a wife of the same nation, without having any regard to money, or any other

dignities; but he is to make a scrutiny, and take his wife's genealogy from the ancient tables and procure many witnesses to it. And this is our practice not only in Judea, but wheresoever anybody of men of our nation do live; and even there an exact catalogue of our priests' marriages is kept; I mean at Egypt and at Babylon, or in any other place of the rest of the habitable earth, wherever our priests are scattered; for they send to Jerusalem the ancient names of their parents in writing, as well as those of their remoter ancestors, and signify who are the witnesses also. But if any war falls out, such as have fallen out a great many of them already, when Antiochus Epiphanes made an invasion upon our country, as also when Pompey the Great and Quintilius Varus did so also, and mainly in the wars that have happened in our own times, those priests that survive them [the war] compose new tables of genealogy out of the old records, and examine the circumstances of the women that remain; for still they do not admit of those [wives] that have been captives, as suspecting that they had sexual intercourse with some foreigners. But what is the strongest argument of our exact management in this matter is what I am now going to say, that we have the names of our high priests from father to son set down in our records for the interval of two thousand years."

Jeremias claims that it was necessary to examine the genealogy of the priest's wife. He states that, according to Philo, "there must be examination of the purity of blood in [her] parents, grandparents and great-grandparents . . . the Mishnah says this was necessary for four generations back of both paternal and maternal ancestry if the bride was of a priestly family" (*Jerusalem in the Time of Jesus,* 216). Jeremias believed that written *lay genealogies* also existed, and he discusses the possibility that the genealogies of Jesus found in **Matthew 1:1–17** and **Luke 3:23–28** were reserved *private* genealogies. Jeremias quotes from the *Letter to Aristides* (a portion preserved in Eusebius' *Church History* 1:7.13), written by the Christian physician Julius Africanus (ca. 160–240), where Africanus asserts: "A few careful people had [private] records of their own, having either remembered the names or recovered them from copies [from registers], and took pride in preserving the memory of their aristocratic origin." Africanus further stated that the genealogical records served "as a basis for lay families wishing to establish their genealogies" (Jeremias, *Jerusalem in the Time of Jesus,* 280). In conclusion, Jeremias says that "All this, then, establishes the existence of both oral and written genealogical traditions among lay families, of both private and public character" (ibid., 283).

99. Josephus, *Jewish Antiquities* 11.8.4–5.

100. Whereas the summary of Josephus' enumeration of the high priests in *Jewish Antiquities* 20.10.1 accounts for 83 high priests between Aaron the first and Phannias the last, the author's research in this work shows that *excluding*—(1) members of the Eli priesthood, (2) the second terms of high priests who were restored to the position, and (3) the one-day appointment of Joseph the son of Ellemus/Elam during the term of Matthias ben Theophilus—there were 77 high priests who held the high priesthood in Israel. The variance of 77 high priests in this work, compared to the 83 high priests purported by Josephus, appears to arise from names of high priests from unknown source(s) that were used by Josephus (see Josephus' lists in *Jewish Antiquities* 8.1.3; 10.8.6). For example, Josephus lists *eighteen* high priests—some with very different names—between Zadok and Jehozadak (inclusive) in *Jewish Antiquities* 10.8.6, whereas Scripture clearly identifies only *fourteen* high priests who held the high priesthood during that time. Also, Josephus may have included Nadab and Abihu (the sons of Aaron, who officiated with their father) and/or member(s) of the Eli priesthood since, in *Jewish Antiquities* 20.10.1, Josephus states that "thirteen officiated as high priests in the wilderness. . . . Now these thirteen, who were the descendants of *two of the sons of Aaron* . . ." [italics added]; presumably, Josephus is referring to Eleazar and Ithamar, and from Ithamar came Eli and the members of the Eli priesthood.

101. Eugene H. Merrill. *Kingdom of Priests: A History of Old Testament Israel* (Grand Rapids: Baker, 1996), 210.

102. See charts "**1 Chronicles 6**: Levi: High Priests, Priests, Levites, and Musicians in Solomon's Temple" and "**1 Samuel 1**: Eli and the Eli Priesthood," respectively.

SUPPLEMENT 3: THE KINGS OF ASSYRIA[1]

Approximate Dating: Neo-Assyrian Empire, ca. 911–612 B.C.[2]

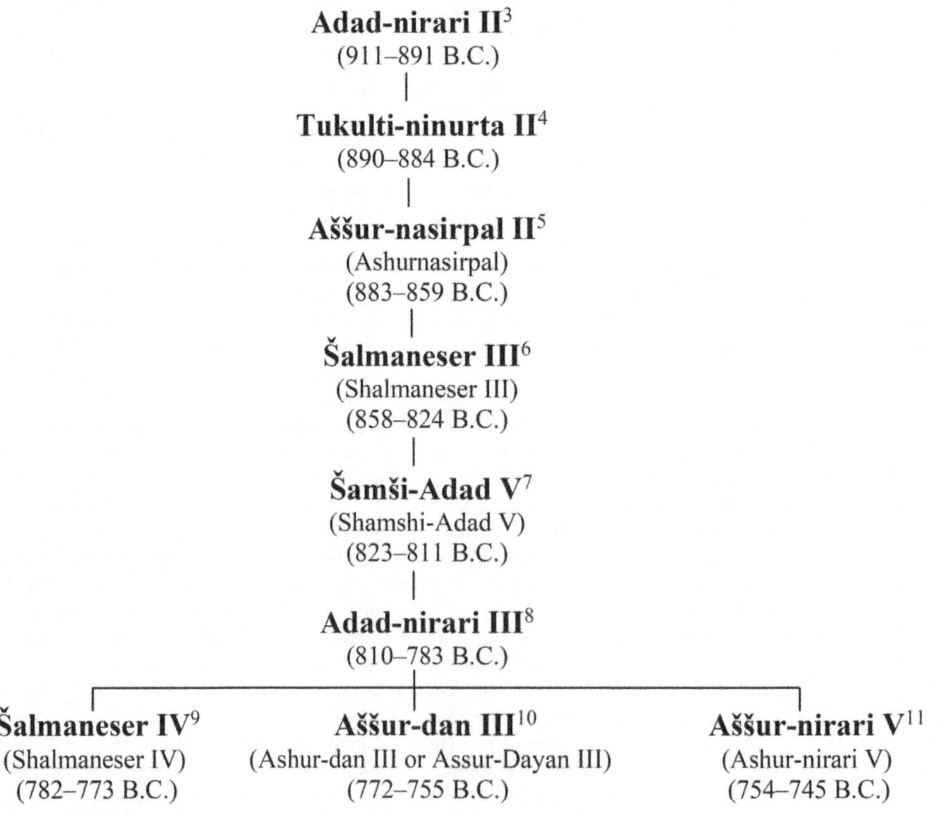

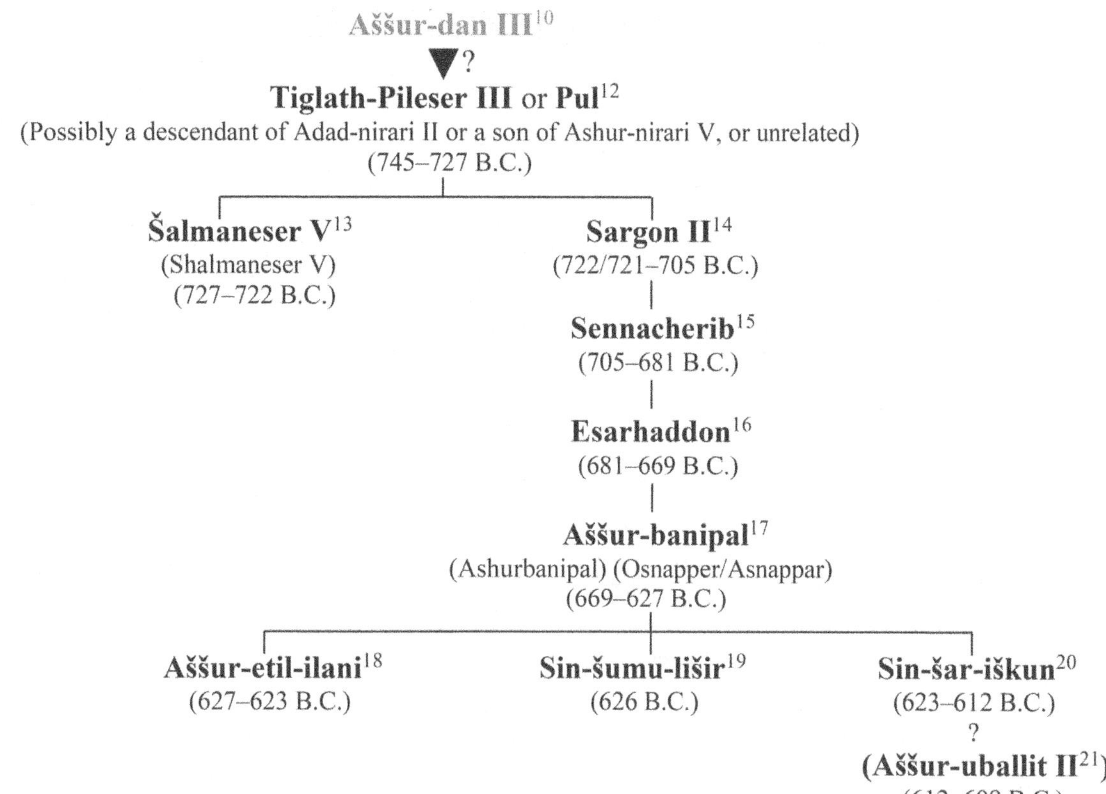

LEGEND:

| : Line of descent from father-to-son

 : Successor is not related to the previous king

Notes

1. The Neo-Assyrian Empire lasted from ca. 911–612/609 B.C. The names and dates for the various kings come primarily from the Assyrian King List (AKL), which is simply a series of sentences, most of which follow the format "X, the son of Y, reigned for Z years." (Historians have arrived at the consecutive dates through other means.) In a journal article entitled "The Assyrian King List and Chronology: A Critique" by Graham Hagens, *Orientalia*, Nova Series 74 2005: 24, Hagens proposes that there was probably some overlap between rulers and that some of them may have ruled different parts of Assyria concurrently; also "it appears likely that political interest was a more important motive in the composition of the AKL than chronological accuracy." Habens notes that other historians have discussed the problems with using king lists, especially the AKL as an accurate historical source. Hagens explains that "in times of political confusion the list tended to adhere to the theory of a single line of descent that may have ignored overlapping claimants to the throne." Genealogical information and dynastic reigns for the Assyrian rulers after Ashurbanipal are often unclear.

Extra-biblical references used in the compilation of the chart include the Hagens reference (above); also, Eugene H. Merrill, *Kingdom of Priests: A History of Old Testament Israel* (Grand Rapids: Baker, 1996); John Boardman, I. E. S. Edwards, N. G. L. Hammond and E. Sollberger, eds., B.C.*The Cambridge Ancient History,* 2nd ed., vol. 3, part 1 (Cambridge: Cambridge University Press, 1982), 891–897; John Boardman, I. E. S. Edwards, N. G. L. Hammond and E. Sollberger, eds. "Part 1—Assyria and Babylonia" in *The Cambridge Ancient History*, 2nd ed., vol. 3, part 2 (Cambridge: Cambridge University Press, 1992), 1–320; Jeffrey K. Kuan, *Neo-Assyrian Historical Inscriptions and Syria-Palestine: Israelite/Judean-Tyrian-Damascene Political and Commercial Relations in the Ninth-Eighth Centuries B.C.E.* (PhD diss., Emory University. Eugene, OR: Wipf and Stock Publishers, 1994); and online resources including *The Encyclopaedia Britannica;* bible.org; the Assyrian Eponym Chronicles (archived on livius.org); and the Assyrian King List (archived on livius.org).

2. Dates follow "Chronology of Foreign Kings" (Assyria) in Kenneth Barker, ed., *NIV Study Bible* (Grand Rapids: Zondervan, 2020), 529; the "Assyrian Kings" in John Walton and Craig Keener, eds., *Cultural Backgrounds Study Bible* (Grand Rapids: Zondervan, 2016), 1127; and Eugene H. Merrill, "The Neo-Assyrian Kings" (Table 7), *Kingdom of Priests: A History of Old Testament Israel* (Grand Rapids: Baker, 1996), 336.

3. **Adad-nirari II**, the son of Aššur-dan II, is considered the first king of the Neo-Assyrian period. He conquered areas that had been under Assyrian vassalage as well as portions of Babylon. He also secured the Kabur river region for Assyria.

4. **Tukulti-ninurta II**, the son of Adad-nirari II, consolidated the lands of the neo-Hittites, Babylonians, and the Arameans that had been conquered by his father. He also subjugated peoples in the Zagros Mountains of Iran. He sustained the westward movement and intensified the war on Assyria's enemies—a war which would later threaten Israel under his son, Ashurnasirpal (Merrill, *Kingdom of Priests,* 348).

5. **Aššur-nasirpal II** (also called "Ashurnasirpal"), the son of Tukulti-ninurta II, was a ruthless, brutal king who conquered people in Asia Minor, the Arameans (in modern Syria), and the Neo-Hittites in the region of the Khabur and Euphrates rivers. He advanced as far as the Mediterranean and exacted tributes from Phoenicia but was unsuccessful in conquering Tyre. When he returned home, he founded a new capital of the Assyrian Empire at Nimrud (ancient biblical Calah, also known as Kalhu, located in modern-day northern Iraq)—possibly named after the biblical Nimrod (cf. **Micah 5:6**)—and built a palace there.

6. **Šalmaneser III** (or Shalmaneser III), the son of Aššur-nasirpal II, expanded the frontiers of the Neo-Assyrian Empire by leading campaigns against the Babylonians, the Neo-Hittites of Carchemish, and the kingdoms of Hamath and Aram (modern Syria). He was the first Assyrian king to wage war against Israel by fighting against King Ahab in 853 B.C. This battle, termed the Battle of Qarqar, is not mentioned in the Old Testament but is known from Assyrian sources, particularly from the Kurkh Monoliths, which describe events during the reigns of Ashurnasirpal II and Shalmaneser III. The account of King Jehu of Israel (841–814 B.C.) paying tribute money to Shalmaneser III in 841 B.C. is recorded on the Black Obelisk of Shalmaneser III, which is now

in the British Museum (The Editors of Encyclopaedia, "Shalmaneser III," *Encyclopaedia Britannica*), although some scholars have argued that the king on the stela should be identified with King Joram, not king Jehu. For a discussion of this, see note 74 in Eugene H. Merrill, *Kingdom of Priests* (Grand Rapids: Baker, 1996), 349.

7. **Šamši-Adad V** (or Shamshi-Adad V), the son of Shalmaneser III, took credit for stopping a revolt brought on by his brother Assur-danin-pal against their father. He invaded Babylonia; according to the Eponym Chronicle, Shamshi-Adad spent much of his reign fending off trouble in Babylonia and in the northeast. According to Jeffrey Kuan, since the Assyrian king did not have a presence in the west, this allowed King Hazael of Aram-Damascus to defeat certain sections of Israel, such as Gad, Reuben, and Manasseh (**2 Kings 10:32–33**; Jeffrey K. Kuan, "Neo-Assyrian Historical Inscriptions and Syria-Palestine: Israelite/Judean-Tyrian-Damascene Political and Commercial Relations in the Ninth-Eighth Centuries B.C.E" (PhD diss., Emory University. Eugene, OR: Wipf and Stock Publishers, 1994), 38).

8. **Adad-nirari III**, the son of Shamsi-Adad V, was a youth when he assumed the throne and therefore his mother was influential during the early part of his reign. During his reign, Damascus was captured, which led to the eclipse of the Aramean kingdom and, in turn, allowed for the recovery of Israel under Jehoash, 798–782 B.C. (who paid tribute to the Assyrian king) and Jeroboam II, 793–753 B.C. Adad-nirari III was the father of Assyria's next three kings: Shalmaneser IV, Ashur-dan III, and Ashur-nirari V. Tiglath-Pileser III also *claimed* that he was a son of Adad-nirari, but this was likely untrue (see note 12).

9. **Šalmaneser IV** (or Shalmaneser IV) was the son of Adad-nirari III. Little is known about his reign except that he led several campaigns against Urartu in the Armenian Highlands. He was succeeded by both his brothers: first by Aššur-dan III, and second by Ashur-nirari V. His rulership was limited by the growing influence and power of high dignitaries, especially the influence of Shamshi-ilu, who was the commander-in-chief of the Assyrian army.

10. **Aššur-dan III** (also known as Assur-Dayan III) was the son of Adad-nirari III and the brother of Shalmaneser IV (his predecessor) and Ashur-nirari V (his successor). During his reign, the power of court dignitaries continued to increase. According to the Eponym Canon, two plagues struck Assyria during his reign—one in 765 B.C. and another in 759 B.C.—which contributed to internal revolts.

11. **Aššur-nirari V** (Ashur-nirari V) was the son of Adad-nirari III and the brother and successor of Aššur-dan III. During this time, few campaigns took place and the kingship continued to be severely limited by the strong influence of court dignitaries.

12. **Tiglath-Pileser III** is also known as the biblical figure **Pul**, a Babylonian name (cf. **2 Kings 15:19, 29; 16:7, 10; 1 Chronicles 5:6, 26; 2 Chronicles 28:20**). His parentage is disputed—while the AKL names him as a *son* of his predecessor (Ashur-nirari V), this is not entirely probable. A brick found in Ashur/Assur says he was the *son* of Adad-nirari III; chronologically, this is possible, but also not probable. *The Cambridge Ancient History* concludes that Tiglath-Pileser III was "most likely of non-royal parentage" (J.A. Brinkman, "Babylonia in the shadow of Assyria (747-626 B.C.)," *The Cambridge Ancient History*, vol. 3, part 2, 2nd ed., John Boardman et al., eds., (Cambridge: Cambridge University Press, 1991), 24). He likely took the throne after a revolt in the Assyrian capital city of Calah (Kalhu) and ascended the throne in April/May 745 B.C. Two isolated and contradictory accounts of Tiglath-Pileser's parentage give rise to the belief (also substantiated by the Eponym Chronicle) that he capitalized on a civil war in 745 B.C. and usurped the throne. He inaugurated the last and greatest phase of Assyrian expansion; he subjected Syria and Palestine to his rule, and later in 729 or 728 B.C., he merged the kingdoms of Assyria and Babylonia (Donald John Wiseman, "Tiglath-Pileser III," *Encyclopaedia Britannica*). When Tiglath-Pileser invaded Israel, King Menahem of Israel (752–742 B.C.) offered him a tribute of 1000 talents of silver, which Menahem raised by exacting 50 shekels of silver from every wealthy person, "so the king of Assyria withdrew and stayed in the land no longer" (**2 Kings 15:19–20**). [*The Cambridge Ancient History* uses this figure to estimate the population of Israel at the time. If a talent is judged to be 3000 shekels, that would make the men of substance number 60,000. Adding these men's families, plus the lower classes, slaves, and foreigners possibly suggests a total Israelite population of 800,000. Estimating 200,000 more for the citizenry of Judah would arrive at a population of 1,000,000 for both Israel and Judah around the time of the first exile; T. C. Mitchell, "Israel and Judah from the Coming of Assyrian Domination until the Fall of Samaria, and the Struggle for Independence in Judah (c. 750–700 B.C.)," *The Cambridge Ancient History*, vol. 3, pt. 2, 2nd ed., John Boardman et al., eds. (Cambridge: Cambridge University Press, 1991), 326. During the reign of King Pekah of Israel (ca. 752–732 B.C.), Tiglath-Pileser "took Ijon, Abel Beth Maakah, Janoah, Kedesh and Hazor. He took Gilead and Galilee, including all the land of Naphtali, and deported the people to Assyria" (**2 Kings 15:29**). Among his captives were "the Reubenites, the Gadites and the half-tribe of Manasseh" whom he took to "Halah, Habor, Hara and the river of Gozan" (**1 Chronicles 5:26**). King Ahaz of Judah (731–715 B.C.) appealed to Tiglath-Pileser for help against a Syro-Israelite attack and became his vassal (**2 Kings 16:7**). According to *The Cambridge Ancient History*, contemporary treaties between vassals and their overlords included the condition that the vassal would tacitly accept the overlord's gods (ibid., 333).This implied acceptance must have been a catalyst for the prophet Isaiah delivering a message from God to King Ahaz of Judah that warned him against involvement with Assyria (**Isaiah 7**). Upon Ahaz's request, Tiglath-Pileser waged war against Damascus, took its people captive, and killed King Rezin of Aram (740s–732 B.C.; **2 Kings 16:5–9**). When the Edomites and Philistines attacked Judah, Ahaz asked Tiglath-Pileser for help once again. To bribe the Assyrian king, Ahaz king of Israel "took some of the things from the temple of the Lord and from the royal palace and from the officials and presented them to the king of Assyria" but Tiglath-Pileser refused to help that time (**2 Chronicles 28:16–21**). In 729 B.C. Tiglath-Pileser III assumed control of Babylon and was crowned king.

13. **Šalmaneser V** (known as "Shalmaneser king of Assyria" in the Bible; **2 Kings 17:3–4; 18:9**) was the son of Tiglath-Pileser III and the elder brother of Sargon II. Shalmaneser was also the king of Babylon. King Hoshea of Israel (732–722 B.C.) became a vassal of Shalmaneser V and paid him tribute (**2 Kings 17:3**). However, Hoshea plotted against Shalmaneser and refused to pay the tribute monies, so Shalmaneser put Hoshea in prison (**2 Kings 17:4**). Then, "the king of Assyria [Shalmaneser V] invaded the entire land, marched against Samaria and laid siege to it for three years. In the ninth year of Hoshea [722 B.C.], the king of Assyria captured Samaria and deported the Israelites to Assyria. He settled them in Halah, in Gozan on the Habor River and in the towns of the Medes" (**2 Kings 17:5–8**; cf. **18:9–11**). It seems that Shalmaneser died during the Assyrian campaign just before Samaria surrendered. The Babylonian Chronicle says that the premier event of Shalmaneser V's reign was the destruction of the city of Samaria, but according to the annals of Sargon II (see note 14), Sargon appears to claim that he conquered Samaria at the beginning of his reign. It is likely that Sargon II completed the conquest that was certainly begun under Shalmaneser V.

14. **Sargon II**, a son of Tiglath-Pileser III, probably usurped the throne from his older brother Shalmaneser V. Sargon II finished what Shalmaneser V had started by completing the conquest of Samaria. During Sargon II's reign, the Assyrians completed the capture of Israel; subdued the tribes of Ephraim, Issachar, Asher, and the rest of Manasseh; and carried the Israelites away in 722/721 B.C. (**2 Kings 17:6; Isaiah 20:1**). The annals of Sargon relate that he removed 27,880 Israelites to Assyria in 722 B.C. T. C. Mitchell, "Israel and Judah from the coming of Assyrian domination until the fall of Samaria, and the struggle for independence in Judah (c. 750–700 B.C.)," *The Cambridge Ancient History*, vol. 3, pt. 2, 2nd ed., John Boardman et al., eds. (Cambridge: Cambridge University Press, 1991), 342. As **2 Kings 17:24** explains, "the king of Assyria brought people from Babylon" and other cities and "settled them in the towns of Samaria to replace the Israelites." At the same time that Sargon II had seized the Assyrian throne, a Babylonian called Marduk-apla-iddina II regained Babylonia's independence from Assyria and held on to the throne for twelve years (722–710 B.C.) until Sargon II recaptured it. In **Isaiah 20:1**, Sargon II is mentioned as having sent the "supreme [Assyrian] commander" to Ashdod to capture it. Sargon II ruled Babylonia for the remaining five years of his life (709–705 B.C.).

15. **Sennacherib**, the son of Sargon II, was probably the most famous Assyrian king and is mentioned many times in the Bible. He was a contemporary of King Hezekiah of Judah, whose official reign was from 715–686 B.C. In the fourteenth year of Hezekiah's reign, Sennacherib captured all the fortified cities of Judah (**2 Kings 18:13; 2 Chronicles 32:1; Isaiah 36:1**) and exacted tribute from Hezekiah, who gave Sennacherib 300 talents of silver and thirty talents of gold (**2 Kings 18:14–16**). Sennacherib's annals confirm that forty-six fortified Judean cities were besieged, as well as many small towns. The annals also state that Sennacherib deported 200,150 Judahites. When Hezekiah became involved in a rebellion, Sennacherib sent messengers to King Hezekiah to intimidate him into backing down, telling him to not believe that their God would save them because the gods of other nations had not prevented them from falling to the Assyrians (**2 Kings 18:19–25, 28–35; 19:10–13**; see also **2 Chronicles 32:10–15; Isaiah 36:4–10, 13–20; 37:9–13**). Hezekiah prayed for deliverance from Sennacherib (**2 Kings 19:15–19**; cf. **2 Chronicles 32:20; Isaiah 37:15–20**), and the Lord answered him by promising that Sennacherib

would not enter Jerusalem (**2 Kings 19:32–34**; cf. **Isaiah 37:33–35**). Sometime later, an angel of the Lord killed 185,000 Assyrians in their camp; seeing the destruction brought on by the Lord, Sennacherib returned to Assyria. While he was worshiping the Assyrian god Nisrok, Sennacherib was murdered by two of his sons, Adrammelek and Sharezer (**2 Kings 19:35–37**; cf. **2 Chronicles 32:20–23; Isaiah 37:36–38**). The account of Sennacherib's death is also in the Babylonian Chronicle, although the chronicle says that Sennacherib was killed "by his own son," not *sons.* "Esarhaddon his son succeeded him as king" (**2 Kings 19:37; Isaiah 37:38**).

16. **Esarhaddon**, the son of Sennacherib, is mentioned in **2 Kings 19:37; Ezra 4:2**; and **Isaiah 37:38** as succeeding his father to the throne of Assyria. Esarhaddon is the Assyrian king who brought some of the "enemies of Judah and Benjamin" to the land (**Ezra 4:1–2**; cf. **2 Kings 17:24–41**).

17. **Aššur-banipal**—called Ashurbanipal, or Osnapper/Asnappar in some translations—was the son of Esarhaddon. Ashurbanipal captured many nations and settled them "in the city of Samaria and elsewhere in Trans-Euphrates" (**Ezra 4:10**). Ashurbanipal invaded Egypt and campaigned as far as Thebes. According to the Babylonian Chronicle, his older brother Šamaš-šum-ukîn (Shamash-shum-ukin) was the king of Babylon. Having been trained as a scribe, Ashurbanipal is the only known literate Assyrian king. After his death, two of his sons (Aššur-etil-ilani and Sin-šar-iškun), an army general, and the eventual Babylonian king Nabopolassar sought control of the area. There are few written records remaining from this time, so dating is difficult to ascertain from Assurbanipal onward. Thus the dates shown in the chart are tentative.

18. **Aššur-etil-ilani** (also spelled Aššur-etel-ilani) was the son of Ashurbanipal. He vied with Nabopolassar for control of Babylonia until 623 B.C. Aššur-etil-ilani managed "to suppress at least two uprisings in his brief reign, but Babylonia, Media, Phoenicia, and Judah itself openly repudiated his authority" (Merrill, *Kingdom of Priests,* 440). Aššur-etil-ilani was possibly succeeded in 623 B.C. by his brother Sin-šar-iškun. The armies of King Nabopolassar of Babylon and King Cyaxares of the Medes conquered Nineveh, precipitating the end of the Assyrian empire in 612 B.C.

19. **Sin-šumu-lišir** was the second son of Ashurbanipal and the general under the former Assyrian king Aššur-etil-ilani. He usurped the throne and presumably reigned as king of Assyria for one year, during 626 B.C., but he may not have had control over the entire Assyrian Empire. Little is known about him due to the lack of sources covering this time.

20. **Sin-šar-iškun** was the third son of Ashurbanipal. He "commenced hostile actions against Nabopolassar with the intention of regathering Babylonia to the Assyrian fold, but Nabopolassar proved to be more than capable of resisting these efforts and undertook offensive measures of his own. Gradually the Assyrian territory was whittled away, and Sin-šar-iškun was powerless to reverse the process" (Merrill, *Kingdom of Priests,* 440).

21. After the Assyrian capital of Nineveh fell to the Medes, Babylonians, and Scythians in 612 B.C., the army officer **Aššur-uballit II** (or Ashur-uballit II) regrouped the Assyrian forces at Haran; however, he was forced to abandon the city when it came under attack by the Babylonians. He then moved west to the important city of Carchemish on the upper Euphrates. The Babylonian armies "took up the pursuit and in 605 [B.C.], under their brilliant commander and crown prince Nebuchadnezzar, crushed the Assyrian remnant once and for all . . . and so Assyria passed off the stage of world history after more than twelve hundred years of national existence" (Merrill, *Kingdom of Priests,* 441). Thus, Aššur-uballiṭ II was the last king of the Neo-Assyrian Empire. His relationship to the former king, Sin-šar-iškun, is unclear.

SUPPLEMENT 4: THE KINGS OF BABYLON[1]

Approximate Dating: Neo-Babylonian Empire, ca. 626–539 B.C.[2]

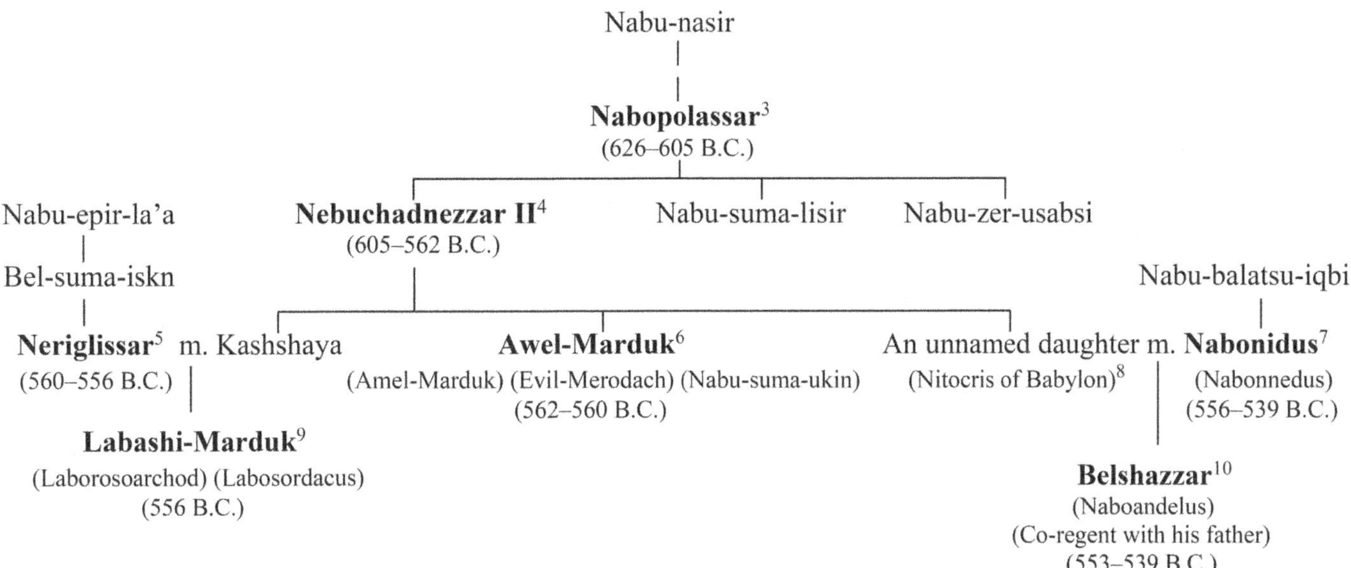

Notes

1. The Neo-Babylonian Empire, also called the Chaldean Dynasty, corresponds to the 11th dynasty of Babylon. Extrabiblical references used to compose the chart include John Boardman, I. E. S. Edwards, N. G. L. Hammond and E. Sollberger, eds., *The Cambridge Ancient History,* 2nd ed., vol. 3, part 1 (Cambridge: Cambridge University Press, 1982), 891–893; John Boardman, I. E. S. Edwards, N. G. L. Hammond and E. Sollberger, eds. "Part 1 – Assyria and Babylonia" in *The Cambridge Ancient History,* 2nd ed., vol. 3, part 2 (Cambridge: Cambridge University Press, 1992), 1–320; *Jewish Antiquities and Against Apion* in *The Complete Works of Josephus*, trans. by William Whiston, commentary by Paul L. Maier (Grand Rapids: Kregel, 1999); D. J. Wiseman, *Nebuchadrezzar and Babylon,* Schweich Lectures of the British Academy 1983 (New York: Oxford University Press, 1985); and D. J. Wiseman, *Chronicles of Chaldean Kings (626–556 B.C.) in the British Museum.* (London: The Trustees of the British Museum, 1961).

2. Regnal dates shown in the chart follow those of "The Neo-Babylonian Kings" in the *Cultural Backgrounds Study Bible* (Grand Rapids: Zondervan, 2016), 1419.

3. **Nabopolassar** claimed to be a Babylonian native but was not of a recognized royal family (D. J. Wiseman, "Nebuchadrezzar and Babylon," Schweich Lectures of the British Academy 1983 (New York: Oxford University Press, 1985), 6; https://archive.org/details/nebuchadrezzarba0000wise/mode/2up). Nabopolassar and Aššur-etil-ilani, the king of Assyria, vied for control of Babylonia until 623 B.C. Nabopolassar's armies, along with those of Cyaxares,

king of the Medes, conquered Nineveh, leading to the fall of the Assyrian Empire in 612 B.C. Nabopolassar renovated the palace, walls, and ziggurat of Babylon and transformed it into the capital. In 609 B.C, during Nabopolassar's reign, Pharaoh Necho of Egypt took Jehoahaz (Shallum) of Judah (609 B.C.) into exile; Jehoahaz died in Egypt (**2 Kings 23:31–34; 2 Chronicles 36:2–4**).

4. **Nebuchadnezzar II**—also called "Nebuchadrezzar"—was the eldest son and successor of Nabopolassar. Nebuchadnezzar reigned as king of Babylon for 43 years, from 605–562 B.C. He made three invasions of Judah—the first in 605 B.C. during the reign of King Jehoiakim/Eliakim of Judah, 609–598 B.C. (cf. **2 Kings 24:1; 2 Chronicles 36:5–7**); the second in 597 B.C. during the reign of King Jehoiachin/Jeconiah of Judah, 598–597 B.C. (cf. **2 Kings 24:10–14**); and the third in 587/586 B.C. during the reign of King Zedekiah/Mattaniah, 597–586 B.C. (cf. **2 Kings 25:1–21**).

In 605 B.C., when King Nebuchadnezzar defeated the army of Pharaoh Necho of Egypt in the battle at Carchemish—corresponding to the fourth year of the eleven-year reign of King Jehoiakim/Eliakim of Judah, 609–598 B.C. (**Jeremiah 46:2**)—Judah became a vassal of Babylon instead of Egypt. This battle is discussed in the Babylonian Chronicles, although Pharaoh Necho's name is not mentioned. According to *The Cambridge Ancient History*, the account may mean that Nebuchadnezzar fought against "garrison troops" instead of the elite army; T. C. Mitchell, "Judah until the fall of Jerusalem (c. 700–586 B.C.)," *The Cambridge Ancient History*, vol. 3, pt. 2, 2nd ed., John Boardman et al., eds., (Cambridge: Cambridge University Press, 1991), 394. King Jehoiakim/Eliakim of Judah served Nebuchadnezzar as a vassal for three years before rebelling against him (**2 Kings 24:1**). Then, Nebuchadnezzar "attacked him [Jehoiakim] and bound him with bronze shackles to take him to Babylon" (**2 Chronicles 36:6**). At that time, Nebuchadnezzar also took some of the wares from the temple and put them in his own temple in Babylon (**2 Chronicles 36:7**).

In 597 B.C., Nebuchadnezzar and his forces captured Jerusalem; took King Jehoiachin/Jeconiah of Judah as a prisoner; and placed Zedekiah/Mattaniah Jehoiakim's half-brother on the throne instead (**2 Kings 24:10–12, 15–27; 2 Chronicles 36:10**). The capture of Jerusalem and Nebuchadnezzar's appointment of Zedekiah as king is discussed in the Babylonian Chronicles—*The Cambridge Ancient History* quotes the chronicle as stating that "On the second day of Adar he [Nebuchadnezzar] captured the city [Jerusalem] and seized its king [Jehoiachin/Jeconiah]. He appointed there a ruler of his own choice [Zedekiah/Mattaniah], took heavy tribute and sent it back to Babylon," and further relates that this second day of Adar corresponded to March 15/16 597 B.C. D. J. Wiseman, "Babylonia 605–539 B.C.," *The Cambridge Ancient History*, vol. 3, part 2, 2nd ed., John Boardman et al., eds., (Cambridge University Press, 1991), 232. Nebuchadnezzar also took "the king's mother [Nehushta, the mother of Jehoiachin/Jeconiah], his wives, his officials and the prominent people of the land" as well as "the entire force of seven thousand fighting men, strong and fit for war, and a thousand skilled workers and artisans" (**2 Kings 24:15–16**; cf. **vv. 14**), leaving only the poorest people in the land. **Jeremiah 52:28** gives the number of Jewish captives taken in Nebuchadnezzar's seventh year (597 B.C.) as 3,023. During this second invasion, Nebuchadnezzar took more articles of value from the temple (**2 Chronicles 36:10**).

Nebuchadnezzar besieged Jerusalem again "in the ninth year of Zedekiah's reign, on the tenth day of the tenth month" (**2 Kings 25:1**)—corresponding to 587/586 B.C. (ibid., 234). Officers and officials who assisted Nebuchadnezzar were Nergal-Sharezer of Shamgar, Nebo-Sarsekim, Nergal-Sharezer, Nebushazban (a chief officer), and Nebuzaradan (the commander of the guard). One of the two men named Nergal-Sharezer appears to be the same person as Neriglissar, Nebuchadnezzar's son-in-law, who later became king (cf. **Jeremiah 38:17–18; 39:3, 13**). The Babylonian siege of Jerusalem lasted one-and-a-half years, until the eleventh year of King Zedekiah/Mattaniah (**2 Kings 25:1–2**; cf. **Jeremiah 21:1–10; 39:1–2; 52:4–7**). Jerusalem fell to King Nebuchadnezzar's army "on the seventh day of the fifth month, in the nineteenth year of Nebuchadnezzar king of Babylon" (**2 Kings 25:8**; **Jeremiah 52:12**), corresponding to 586 B.C. After many items of bronze, silver, and gold were removed from Solomon's Temple (**2 Kings 25:13–15**; cf. **Jeremiah 52:17–19**), Nebuchadnezzar's commanding officer, Nebuzaradan, burned the temple, the king's palace, and all the houses of Jerusalem; he also broke down the walls around Jerusalem (**2 Kings 25:9–10; Jeremiah 39:8**). He carried the people of Judah into Babylonian captivity and appointed Gedaliah as the governor of Judah, over the poorest who remained in the land (**2 Kings 25:11–12, 22; Jeremiah 39:9–10; 52:15–16**); see chart "**2 Kings 25**: Gedaliah, Governor over the Remnant People of Judah During the Early Days of the Exile." At the Babylonian headquarters at Riblah, Nebuchadnezzar killed Zedekiah/Mattaniah's sons in front of him, put out King Zedekiah's eyes, and then bound him in shackles and took him to Babylon (**2 Kings 25:5–7**; cf. **Jeremiah 39:6–7, 52:10–11**). More captives were taken in 587/586 B.C., although not to the extent of the earlier deportation that had occurred in 597 B.C. **Jeremiah 52:29** says that "in Nebuchadnezzar's eighteenth year," 832 Jewish captives were taken from Jerusalem. Then, in 582 B.C.—corresponding to Nebuchadnezzar's twenty-third year—Nebuzaradan, the commander of the Babylonian Imperial Guard, took an additional 745 Judeans captive in the final deportation (**Jeremiah 52:30**). D. J. Wiseman, "Babylonia 605–539 B.C.," *The Cambridge Ancient History*, vol. 3, pt. 2, 2nd ed., John Boardman et al., eds. (Cambridge: Cambridge University Press, 1991), 232. The Babylonian captivity of the Israelites, which had begun during Nebuchadnezzar's reign, then lasted for seventy years—from 586–516 B.C.—as predicted by Jeremiah the prophet (**Jeremiah 25:12; 29:10**).

King Nebuchadnezzar figures prominently in the Book of Daniel; during the 605 B.C. invasion, Nebuchadnezzar took noble young men of Judahite descent into Babylonian captivity to be instructed in Chaldean culture—among them were Daniel, Hananiah, Mishael, and Azariah. Nebuchadnezzar gave them the Babylonian names of Belteshazzar, Shadrach, Meshach, and Abednego, respectively; see chart "**Daniel 1**: Daniel and His Comrades." These four served King Nebuchadnezzar (cf. **2 Kings 20:18; Daniel 1:1–7, 19; 2:25**). Daniel interpreted two of Nebuchadnezzar's dreams after his magicians, sorcerers, astrologers, and wise men were unable to decipher them (**Daniel 2:24–45, 4:4–28**). Nebuchadnezzar then appointed Daniel "ruler over the entire province of Babylon and placed him in charge of all its wise men" (**Daniel 2:48**).

When Nebuchadnezzar became arrogant and hardened with pride, he made an outrageous boast—"Is not this the great Babylon I have built as the royal residence, by my mighty power and for the glory of my majesty?" (**Daniel 4:30**; cf. **5:20**)—but "even as the words were on his lips, a voice came from heaven, 'This is what is decreed for you, King Nebuchadnezzar: Your royal authority has been taken from you. You will be driven away from people and will live with the wild animals; you will eat grass like the ox. Seven times will pass by for you until you acknowledge that the Most High is sovereign over all kingdoms on earth and gives them to anyone he wishes.' Immediately what had been said about Nebuchadnezzar was fulfilled. He was driven away from people and ate grass like the ox. His body was drenched with the dew of heaven until his hair grew like the feathers of an eagle and his nails like the claws of a bird" (**Daniel 4:31–33**). Eventually, Nebuchadnezzar repented of his pride and his sanity was restored; he acknowledged that the kingdom of God was eternal and enduring "from generation to generation" (**Daniel 4:34**). The Lord restored Nebuchadnezzar's sanity as well as his kingdom, his counselors, and the nobles of Babylon (**Daniel 4:36–37**). According to tradition, Nebuchadnezzar built the Hanging Gardens of Babylon for his wife Amytis, the daughter of the Median king Cyaxares (cf. *Jewish Antiquities* 10.11.1; *Against Apion* 1.19). At one point, Nebuchadnezzar also attempted to invade Egypt but was apparently unsuccessful. After a forty-three-year reign, Nebuchadnezzar died in 562 B.C. and was succeeded by his son Awel-Marduk (*Against Apion* 1.20). Nebuchadnezzar is referenced as the king of Babylon in **2 Kings 24:1, 10–11, 13, 15; 25:1, 8, 22; 1 Chronicles 6:15; 2 Chronicles 36:6–7, 10, 13, 17; Ezra 1:7; 2:1; 5:12, 14; 6:5; Esther 2:6; Jeremiah 21:2, 7; 22:25; 24:1; 25:1, 9; 27:6, 8, 20; 28:3, 11, 14; 29:1, 3, 21; 32:1, 28; 34:1; 35:11; 37:1; 39:1, 5, 11; 43:10; 44:30; 46:2, 13, 26; 49:28, 30; 50:17; 51:34; 52:4, 12, 28–29; Ezekiel 26:7; 29:18–19; 30:10; Daniel 1:1, 18; 2:1, 28, 46; 3:1, 3, 5, 7, 9, 13–14, 16, 19, 24, 26, 28; 4:1, 4, 18, 28, 31, 33–34, 37; 5:2, 11, 18.**

5. **Neriglissar** (or Neriglissor) married Kashshaya (Nebuchadnezzar's daughter) and became Nebuchadnezzar's son-in-law. According to Josephus' quotations from Berossus (a Babylonian priest who wrote a history of Babylon), Neriglissar led the conspiracy to overthrow and kill Evil-Merodach/Awel-Marduk (*Against Apion* 1.20). Neriglissar appears to be the same person as the Babylonian official named "Nergal-Sharezer" (see note 4) who accompanied Nebuchadnezzar in the invasion of Jerusalem and later assisted in the liberation of the prophet Jeremiah from Babylonian exile (**Jeremiah 39:3, 13–14**). After Awel-Marduk's murder, Neriglissar succeeded to the throne of Babylon and ruled for four years, from 560–556 B.C.

6. **Awel-Marduk**—also called "Amel-Marduk" or "Evil-Merodach"—was the son of Nebuchadnezzar. He ruled Babylon for two years, from 562–560 B.C. (**2 Kings 25:27; Jeremiah 52:31**; *Against Apion* 1.20). Although Nebuchadnezzar had taken King Jehoiachin/Jeconiah of Judah into captivity, Awel-Marduk treated Jehoiachin with kindness while he was in prison.

Josephus relates in *Jewish Antiquities* 10.11.2 that Evil-Merodach "esteemed him [Jehoiachin/Jeconiah] among his most intimate friends. He also gave him many presents, and made him honorable above the rest of the kings that were in Babylon; for his father [Nebuchadnezzar] had not kept his faith with [Jehoiachin/Jeconiah], when he voluntarily delivered up himself to him [Nebuchadnezzar], with his wives and children, and his whole family, for the sake of his country, that it might not be taken by siege, and utterly destroyed." In the thirty-seventh year of Jehoiachin's captivity in Babylon, when Jehoiachin was about 55 years old, Awel-Marduk offered Jehoiachin/Jeconiah clemency; he released him from prison and gave him a place of honor at the king's table along with a "regular allowance" every day for the rest of his life (**2 Kings 25:27–30; Jeremiah 52:31–34**); see chart "**2 Kings 24**: Jehoiachin (Jeconiah), King of Judah." Awel-Marduk was murdered by his brother-in-law Neriglissar, who then succeeded him.

7. **Nabonidus** (also called Nabonnedus) was the last king of the Neo-Babylonian Empire. He ruled seventeen years, from 556–539 B.C. Nabonidus is somewhat of an enigmatic figure, as is his genealogy. It is unknown whether he was actually from the royal line of Chaldean kings (e.g., perhaps a son or grandson of King Nebuchadnezzar). Nabonidus married a daughter of Nebuchadnezzar (probably Nitocris, see note 8), and they had a son named Belshazzar. Note that Nebuchadnezzar is called the "father" of Belshazzar in **Daniel 5:2, 11, 18, 22** (cf. **Jeremiah 27:6–7**), but the correct meaning is probably that Nebuchadnezzar was a "predecessor" (and the grandfather) of Belshazzar. Josephus described Nabonidus as "a man of Babylon" who was involved in the conspiracy leading to the death of Labashi-Marduk (Laborosoarchod/Labosordacus; *Against Apion* 1.20). Nabonidus has also been identified as "the son of a priest of the moon-god Sin from Harran in Upper Mesopotamia" who usurped the throne (Mark W. Chavalas "Nabonidus," *Eerdman's Dictionary of the Bible*). According to *The Cambridge Ancient History*, Nabonidus referred to his father, Nabu-balatsu-iqbi, as "a learned counselor." D. J. Wiseman, "Babylonia 605–539 B.C.," *The Cambridge Ancient History*, vol. 3, part 2, 2nd ed. John Boardman et al., eds. (Cambridge: Cambridge University Press, 1991), 243. His mother, Adad-guppi, lived to be 101 years old; in her biography, she claimed to have had influence over Nabopolassar, Nebuchadnezzar, and Neriglissar, but not over Evil-Merodach or Labashi-Marduk. Nabonidus and his family were therefore closely attached to the Nabopolassar–Nebuchadnezzar–Neriglissar ruling family, which probably led to Nabonidus' marriage to Nebuchadnezzar's daughter.

Nabonidus was considered an eccentric ruler who favored the Sin moon god cult over that of Marduk, the chief god of Babylon, thus causing friction between himself and the religious establishment in Babylon. Nabonidus spent many years of his reign in the distant oasis of Tema (located on the Arabian Peninsula 250 miles southeast of Aqaba and 200 miles north-northeast of Medina), leaving the rule of Babylon to his eldest son Belshazzar. Belshazzar co-ruled with Nabonidus from 553–539 B.C. The text of **Daniel 5:7, 16, 29** makes clear that Nabonidus was considered the *primary* ruler of Babylon; Belshazzar was the *second* ruler; and, after Daniel interpreted Belshazzar's dream, Daniel was the "third highest ruler" of the kingdom. (However, Daniel may have denied the advancement; cf. **Daniel 5:16–17**.) The Nabonidus Chronicle relates that in 539 B.C., the Persian army took Babylon. Belshazzar was slain and Nabonidus surrendered soon thereafter. According to Berossus, who is quoted by Josephus in *Against Apion* 1.153, Cyrus the Great spared Nabonidus and resettled him in Carmania (corresponding to the modern-day Kerman Province of Iran), where Nabonidus lived until he died.

8. According to Herodotus, Nitocris was the wife of Nabonidus (Gr. Labynetus; *Histories* 1.185–188, http://www.perseus.tufts.edu/hopper/text?doc=Perseus:text:1999.01.0126).

9. **Labashi-Marduk**—whom Josephus calls "Laborosoarchod" (*Against Apion* 1.20) and "Labosordacus" (*Jewish Antiquities* 10.11.2)—was the son of Neriglissar and the grandson of Nebuchadnezzar. Josephus writes that, according to Berossus, "by reason of the very ill temper and ill practices he exhibited to the world, a plot was laid against him also by his friends, and he was tortured to death" (*Against Apion* 1.20). Josephus says he was child on his accession. According to *The Cambridge Ancient History*, an inscription implies that Labashi-Marduk was put in charge of "his own affairs" two years previously, so it is possible that he was a teenager or a young adult who had not reached full majority; D. J. Wiseman, "Babylonia 605–539 B.C.," *The Cambridge Ancient History*, vol. 3, part 2, 2nd ed., John Boardman et al., eds., (Cambridge: Cambridge University Press, 1991), 243. The length of Labashi-Marduk's reign is contested; the Uruk King list says that he reigned for three months, which *The Cambridge Ancient History* says agrees with the texts dated from his reign (ibid., 243). Josephus, meanwhile, quotes Berossus as saying that Labashi-Marduk's reign lasted for nine months (*Jewish Antiquities* 10.11.2; *Against Apion* 1.20). In the end, Labashi-Marduk was murdered by a band of conspirators headed by his brother-in-law Nabonidus.

10. **Belshazzar** was the son of Nabonidus and the grandson of Nebuchadnezzar; Josephus says that the Babylonians called him "Naboandelus" (*Jewish Antiquities* 10.11.2). According to the Nabonidus clay cylinder, Belshazzar was the eldest son of Nabonidus. Belshazzar was co-regent with his father from 553–539 B.C. but was left to rule Babylon while Nabonidus was in Tema, Arabia for lengthy periods. The text of **Daniel 5:7, 16, 29** makes clear that Nabonidus was considered the *primary* ruler of Babylon, Belshazzar was the *second* ruler; and after Daniel interpreted Belshazzar's dream, Daniel may have become the "third ruler" in the kingdom. **Daniel 5** describes the great feast that Belshazzar threw for a thousand of his lords during which he, his lords, his wives, and his concubines drank from the gold and silver vessels that Nebuchadnezzar had taken from Solomon's Temple (**vv. 1–2**). At the feast, a hand appeared and wrote on the wall (**v. 5**). The frightened Belshazzar called for someone to interpret the writing; when his advisors could not, the queen reminded him of Daniel's service to Nebuchadnezzar in interpreting dreams (**vv. 6–12**). When Daniel was summoned, he told Belshazzar of Nebuchadnezzar's prideful past and how God had humbled him (**vv. 18–21**) and then confronted Belshazzar about his own arrogant, sacrilegious behavior and defiance (**vv. 22–24**). Angered by Belshazzar and his court for using the vessels from the temple for their feast, God wrote on the wall in Aramaic (**v. 25**)—"MENE, MENE, TEKEL, PARSIN"—and Daniel interpreted it for the king:

> MENE: "God has numbered the days of your reign and brought it to an end."
>
> TEKEL: "You have been weighed on the scales and found wanting."
>
> PARSIN (some translations say UPHARSIN or PHARSIN): "Your kingdom is divided and given to the Medes and Persians" (**vv. 25–28**).

Belshazzar was slain "that very night" (probably October 12, 539 B.C.). "Darius the Mede" in **Daniel 5:31** is probably a reference to the Babylonian throne name of "Cyrus the Persian" (cf. **Daniel 6:28**), referring to Cyrus the Great/Cyrus II of Persia, who then took over the kingdom; see chart "**Supplement 5**: The Kings of Persia."

SUPPLEMENT 5: THE KINGS OF PERSIA[1]

Approximate Dating: First Persian Empire, ca. 559–330 B.C., also known as the Achaemenid Empire[2]

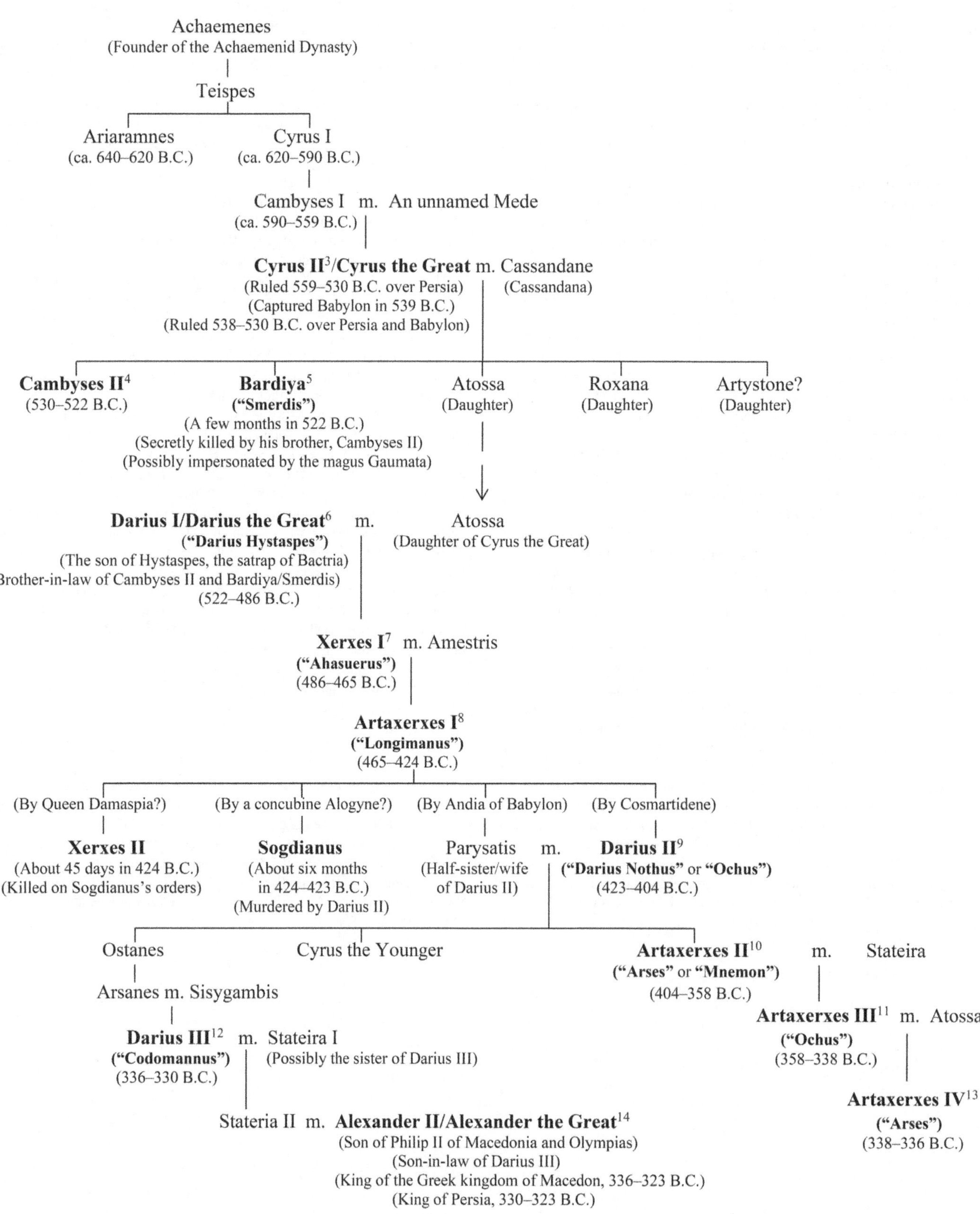

Achaemenes
(Founder of the Achaemenid Dynasty)
Teispes
Ariaramnes
(ca. 640–620 B.C.)
Cyrus I
(ca. 620–590 B.C.)
Cambyses I m. An unnamed Mede
(ca. 590–559 B.C.)
Cyrus II[3]/Cyrus the Great m. Cassandane
(Ruled 559–530 B.C. over Persia)
(Captured Babylon in 539 B.C.)
(Ruled 538–530 B.C. over Persia and Babylon)
(Cassandana)
Cambyses II[4]
(530–522 B.C.)
Bardiya[5]
("Smerdis")
(A few months in 522 B.C.)
(Secretly killed by his brother, Cambyses II)
(Possibly impersonated by the magus Gaumata)
Atossa
(Daughter)
Roxana
(Daughter)
Artystone?
(Daughter)
Darius I/Darius the Great[6] m.
("Darius Hystaspes")
(The son of Hystaspes, the satrap of Bactria)
(Brother-in-law of Cambyses II and Bardiya/Smerdis)
(522–486 B.C.)
Atossa
(Daughter of Cyrus the Great)
Xerxes I[7] m. Amestris
("Ahasuerus")
(486–465 B.C.)
Artaxerxes I[8]
("Longimanus")
(465–424 B.C.)
(By Queen Damaspia?)
(By a concubine Alogyne?)
(By Andia of Babylon)
(By Cosmartidene)
Xerxes II
(About 45 days in 424 B.C.)
(Killed on Sogdianus's orders)
Sogdianus
(About six months
in 424–423 B.C.)
(Murdered by Darius II)
Parysatis m.
(Half-sister/wife
of Darius II)
Darius II[9]
("Darius Nothus" or "Ochus")
(423–404 B.C.)
Ostanes
Cyrus the Younger
Artaxerxes II[10] m. Stateira
("Arses" or "Mnemon")
(404–358 B.C.)
Arsanes m. Sisygambis
Artaxerxes III[11] m. Atossa
("Ochus")
(358–338 B.C.)
Darius III[12] m. Stateira I
("Codomannus")
(336–330 B.C.)
(Possibly the sister of Darius III)
Artaxerxes IV[13]
("Arses")
(338–336 B.C.)
Stateria II m. Alexander II/Alexander the Great[14]
(Son of Philip II of Macedonia and Olympias)
(Son-in-law of Darius III)
(King of the Greek kingdom of Macedon, 336–323 B.C.)
(King of Persia, 330–323 B.C.)

Notes

1. Extrabiblical references consulted include John Boardman, N. G. L. Hammond, D. M. Lewis, and M. Ostwald, eds. *The Cambridge Ancient History*, 2nd ed., vol. 4 (Cambridge: Cambridge University Press, 1988); and Pierre Briant, *From Cyrus to Alexander: A History of the Persian Empire*, trans. Peter T. Daniels (Winona Lake: Eisenbraums, 2002). Online source at https://www.livius.org/articles/dynasty/achaemenids/.

2. Dating for the kings follows "The Achaemenid Dynasty" chart in the John Walton and Craig Keener, *Cultural Backgrounds Study Bible* (Grand Rapids: Zondervan, 2016), 802.

3. **Cyrus II**, also called **Cyrus the Great**, was the Persian king of the Achaemenian dynasty who ruled Persia from 559–530 B.C. Upon conquering Babylon in 539 B.C., he ruled the kingdom of Babylon and Persia until his death in 530 B.C. According to the Cyrus Cylinder, Cyrus II was the son of Cambyses and the great-grandson of Teispes, both of whom were called kings of Ansan and were "from a family [that had] always [exercised] kingship." Teispes' son was Cyrus I (ca. 620–590 B.C.), and his son was Cambyses I (ca. 590–559 B.C.), who was the father of Cyrus II (Briant, *From Cyrus to Alexander,* 17). According to a few accounts, Cyrus II married the daughter of the Median king, although the identity of this king is disputed. Since Cyrus II's mother was a Mede, this may explain why the Babylonians referred to Cyrus II/Cyrus the Great as "Darius the Mede [who] took over the kingdom [of Babylon from Belshazzar] at the age of sixty-two" (**Daniel 5:31**).This reading suggests that Cyrus may have been his throne name in Persia, whereas his throne name in Babylon was "Darius the Mede" (i.e., in the same way that the throne name of the Assyrian king Tiglath-Pileser was "Pul" in Babylon; **1 Chronicles 5:26**). Alternatively, the title "Darius the Mede" may refer to overlapping reigns of Cyrus II/Cyrus the Great and Darius the Mede (cf. **Daniel 5:28; 6:28**): in this scenario, after the fall of Babylon in 539 B.C., a brief two-year co-regency may have existed in which Cyrus II shared the throne with Darius the Mede but with Cyrus II considered to be the dominant regent. Subsequently, upon the natural death of Darius the Mede—because Darius had no male heir and because Cyrus had married Darius' daughter—Cyrus united the Medo-Persian kingdom into a single throne.

Cyrus the Great ruled over lands from Babylon all the way to the border of Egypt, first conquering the Medes, then the Lydians, and then the Babylonians. According to a translation of the Cyrus Cylinder by a curator of the British Museum (where the cylinder is located), the Cylinder says that Cyrus collected all the people who had been exiled from Judah to Babylon and "returned them to their settlements." See also T. C. Mitchell, "The Babylonian Exile and the restoration of the Jews in Palestine (586–ca. 500 B.C.)," *The Cambridge Ancient History*, vol. 3, part 2, 2nd ed. John Boardman et al., eds. (Cambridge: Cambridge University Press, 1991), 416. This interpretation agrees with the account in **Ezra 2** where the first group of Jewish exiles returned to Jerusalem with Zerubbabel in 538 B.C. (cf. **Ezra 2:2; 3:1–2; Nehemiah 7:7**). Also, in 538 B.C., Cyrus the Great decreed the rebuilding of the temple in Jerusalem (**2 Chronicles 36:21–23; Ezra 1:1–4**). According to Scripture, a scroll was found in the treasury at Ecbatana—one of the four capitals of the Persian Empire, along with Babylon, Persepolis, and Susa—during the time of Darius I (i.e., 522–486 B.C.). The scroll documented that in Cyrus the Great's first year as king of Babylon (538 B.C.), he had "issued a decree" (**Ezra 6:2–3**; cf. vv. **1–12**) that the temple should be rebuilt and that "the gold and silver articles of the house of God, which Nebuchadnezzar took from the temple in Jerusalem and brought to Babylon, [were] to be returned to their places in the temple in Jerusalem; they [were] to be deposited in the house of God" (**Ezra 6:5**). The last ten years of Cyrus' reign are not well documented. Allegedly, Cyrus died while campaigning against the Massagetae, a tribe of people living in what is now Kazakhstan and Uzbekistan. However, before leaving on the campaign, Cyrus secured the succession of his two sons, Cambyses and Bardiya/Smerdis. The eldest, Cambyses II, was named Cyrus' successor and he became king of Persia upon Cyrus' death (Briant, *From Cyrus to Alexander,* 49–50).

4. **Cambyses II** was the eldest son of Cyrus the Great by his wife Cassandane (who also bore Cyrus the Great three other children: Bardiya/Smerdis, Atossa, and Roxana). Cyrus named Cambyses II as his successor before departing on the campaign against the Massagetae. According to the Greek historian Xenophon of Athens, Cambyses' younger brother Bardiya was given extensive lands in Central Asia. According to the Greek historian Herodotus, who followed the Egyptian view of this king, Cambyses "went mad, but even before this he had been far from sound in his mind. . . . They say that from birth Cambyses suffered from a serious illness" (qtd. in Briant, *From Cyrus to Alexander,* 50). While this is possibly an exaggeration, Cambyses likely killed his younger brother (Bardiya/Smerdis), since accounts from both Herodotus and Darius I bear witness to this, although on some of the finer points the two accounts differ. The murder of Bardiya/Smerdis by his elder brother, King Cambyses II, was kept secret. After Cambyses II went to Egypt, an impostor *claiming* to be Smerdis/Bardiya appeared; in fact, he was actually a magus named "Gaumata." The Persian people rallied behind Gaumata, who then seized power shortly before Cambyses II died of a fatal fall from a horse. Gaumata's coup is dated to March 11, 522 B.C., and he officially seized power on July 1, 522 B.C. (Briant, *From Cyrus to Alexander,* 99). During Cambyses' reign, the rebuilding of Jerusalem began and work on the Second Temple commenced but was halted (**Ezra 4**); see note 6.

5. **Bardiya**—called **"Smerdis"** by the Greeks, such as Herodotus—was the son of Cyrus the Great and the younger brother of Cambyses II. Scholars are divided on whether he actually briefly ruled the Achaemenid Empire in 522 B.C. or if he was simply impersonated during that time by the magus Gaumata; see note 4.

6. **Darius I** (also called **Darius the Great** and "**Darius Hystaspes"**) was the son of Hystaspes, a satrap (provincial governor) under Cyrus the Great and Cambyses II. Darius I married several women; among them was his favorite wife, Atossa, the daughter of Cyrus the Great, thus making Darius I the brother-in-law of his predecessor, Cambyses II (and the brother-in-law of Bardiya/Smerdis, if he did in fact rule). According to Herodotus, Darius I was the leader of the group that sought to kill Gaumata, the magus who had usurped the Persian throne under the guise of being Bardiya/Smerdis (who was had been secretly slain by Cambyses II himself). Darius I killed Gaumata, but the matter of the kingship was still in question. Darius' version of events in the Behistin Inscription (ca. 490 B.C.) downplays the role of the other conspirators so that he was the central figure of the narrative. Darius I claimed the right to rule the Achaemenid Empire by claiming descent from Achaemenes, the founder of the Achaemenid (Persian) dynasty. Darius relates in the Behistin Inscription that "eight of his dynasty" had been kings before him (L.W. King and R.C. Thompson, "The Sculptures and Inscription of Darius the Great on the Rock of Behistûn in Persia" (London: British Museum Trustees, 1907), ed. Jona Lendering; https://www.livius.org/articles/place/behistun/behistun-3/). Scholars do not agree on the veracity of this statement. Darius I was one of Persia's greatest kings; he expanded the stretch of the empire from India in the east to Egypt in the west.

In 539 B.C., by the decree of Cyrus the Great, the Jews in Babylonian captivity were allowed to return to Jerusalem. The exiles returned to Jerusalem in 538 B.C. with Zerubbabel; by 537 B.C., in the second month of the second year after their arrival, the people began to rebuild the temple (**Ezra 3:8**). However, enemies of the Jews began a campaign to discourage the people and frustrate their rebuilding efforts, starting in the reign of Cyrus the Great through the reign of Darius I (**Ezra 4:5**). In effect, construction of the temple—which had begun in ca. 537 B.C. under the direction of Zerubbabel the governor and Joshua the high priest—was halted until 520 B.C., the second year of the reign of Darius I (**Ezra 4:24**). Darius I ordered that the rebuilding of the Second Temple be completed with the expenses "fully paid out of the royal treasury, from the revenues of Trans-Euphrates" and decreed that the builders should have whatever they needed to complete the temple construction (**Ezra 6:8–12**). With the encouragement of the prophets Haggai and Zechariah (**Ezra 5:1; Haggai 1:1; Zechariah 1:1**), the Second Temple was completed in 516 B.C., "On the third day of the month Adar, in the sixth year of the reign of King Darius" (**Ezra 6:15**). Darius I died in late 486 B.C. after ruling for 36 years, and his son Xerxes I assumed the throne.

7. **Xerxes I** was the son of Darius I by his wife Atossa, the daughter of Cyrus the Great. His father Darius I chose his younger son (Xerxes I) as his heir, in spite of the fact that Darius I had elder sons who had been born before he became king (J. L. Huot, "Xerxes I." *Encyclopedia Britannica*, https://www.britannica.com/biography/Xerxes-I). The name "Xerxes" is used in the NIV translation (e.g., in **Ezra 4:6** and throughout the book of Esther), although in some translations, Xerxes I is called **"Ahasuerus."** The name "Ahasuerus" is regarded more as a title by the Persians than a name (in much the same way that "Pharaoh" was a title among the Egyptians), as it signifies "possessor" (*ahaz*) and (*ve*) "head" (*rosh*). The events in the book of Esther—describing how Esther became the Persian queen and then saved the Jews from annihilation—took place from ca. 483–465 B.C., during the reign of Xerxes I. Xerxes I married Amestris and had several children by her, including Amytis, Darius, Hystaspes, and Artaxerxes I. This king is perhaps best known for his unsuccessful attempts to conquer Greece in 480–479 B.C. Xerxes I's demise transpired following a rebellion that arose when the king destroyed the golden statue of Marduk (also known as Bel), the patron saint of the ancient city of Babylon. Xerxes I was murdered by his minister Artabanus and other court officials (J. L. Huot, "Xerxes I." *Encyclopedia Britannica*, https://www.britannica.com/biography/Xerxes-I).

8. **Artaxerxes I**—sometimes referred to as **"Longimanus"** (meaning "long-handed," allegedly because his right hand was longer than his left)—was the second son of Xerxes I by his wife Amestris. His older brother Darius was accused

of killing their father, but it was court officials who had actually murdered Xerxes. Nevertheless, Artaxerxes sought revenge and killed his brother Darius. Artaxerxes then killed Artabanus, one of the officials who had murdered Xerxes I, because Artabanus had attempted to kill him also (The Editors of Encyclopaedia Britannica, "Artaxerxes I," *Encyclopedia Britannica*, https://www.britannica.com/biography/Artaxerxes-I). In 458 B.C., Ezra the scribe returned to Jerusalem with the permission of Artaxerxes I. Ezra brought with him a great number of Israelites who had been in captivity; the groups of people are listed in **Ezra 8:1–20**. Ezra and the people also brought back gold, silver, and articles for the temple (**Ezra 8:24–30**). In 444 B.C., in the twentieth year of King Artaxerxes (i.e., April 445–April 444 B.C.), the Jewish captive-exile named Nehemiah, who had served in the Persian court as the cupbearer to Artaxerxes I, returned to Jerusalem to complete the walls and to further restore the city (**Nehemiah 1–6**). The wall was completed in 52 days during 444 B.C. (**Nehemiah 6:15**). Apparently Nehemiah was recalled to the Persian court for a short time in late 432 B.C.—"In the thirty-second year of Artaxerxes [I] king of Babylon" (**Nehemiah 13:6–7**)—but then returned a second time and stayed in Jerusalem for an unknown length of time. King Artaxerxes I of Babylon died in 424 B.C.

9. **Darius II**—whose birth name appears to have been **"Darius Nothus"** or **"Ochus"**—was a son of Artaxerxes I and one of his concubines, Cosmartidene. Darius II had been the satrap of Hyrcania before he became king ("Darius II"). According to Ctesias (a Greek physician under Darius II and Artaxerxes II and also a historian of Persia), Darius II took the throne from his half-brother Sogdianus, who had usurped the throne of yet another half-brother, Xerxes II, who was said to have been the son of Artaxerxes I, possibly by his queen or a concubine. Xerxes II and Sogdianus are not mentioned in the official Babylonian documents because of their short reigns—both reigned for less than a year. According to the *Encyclopaedia Iranica*, Darius II's reign was fraught with rebellion from the various satraps who had become extremely powerful in the regions they governed (Heleen Sanchisi-Weerdenburg, "DARIUS iv. Darius II," *Encyclopaedia Iranica*, VII/1, 50–51, http://www.iranicaonline.org/articles/darius-iv). Darius II was married to his half-sister Parysatis (the daughter of Artaxerxes I and Andia of Babylon); after the death of Darius II, Parysatis promoted their younger son Cyrus's claim to the throne over that of the eldest son, Artaxerxes II.

10. **Artaxerxes II**—birth name, **"Arses"** and known by the epithet **"Mnemon"**—was the eldest son of Darius II and his wife/half-sister Parysatis. According to the *Encyclopaedia Iranica*, he was born before Darius II ascended the throne (R. Schmitt, "Artaxerxes II," *Encyclopaedia Iranica*, II/6, 656–58, https://www.iranicaonline.org/articles/artaxerxes-ii-achaemenid-king). Artaxerxes II's main wife was Stateira, the daughter of a Persian nobleman. Artaxerxes contended with various rebellions by his younger brother, Cyrus, who was favored by their mother, Parysatis, because he had been born after Darius II had become king. It seems that Persian convention, at least at one point in time, favored the succession rights of the oldest son born during his father's reign. [For example, Darius I had bypassed his elder sons, who had been born *before* their father's ascension to the throne, in favor of a younger son, Xerxes I, who had been born *after* Darius became king.] Artaxerxes II campaigned and won a war against Sparta, who had supported Cyrus; after Cyrus was killed, Artaxerxes reached a settlement—called the King's Peace—in which he took control of certain Greek cities. Artaxerxes II also had to deal with the Egyptians, who rebelled upon his accession. Attempts to retake control of Egypt were unsuccessful. Rebellions in Anatolia around 366 B.C. threatened the Achaemenid dynasty's hold on the region, but infighting between the Anatolian satraps allowed the rebellions to be quashed. The *Encyclopaedia Iranica* says that Artaxerxes II was an ineffective ruler who nevertheless surrounded himself with able men, including his son and successor, Artaxerxes III. During Artaxerxes II's reign, the power of the satraps increased, which weakened the empire, despite the Achaemenid dynasty retaining official control over most of the empire. Artaxerxes also introduced idol worship when he set up statues of the Persian goddess Anāhitā in various large cities; previously, the Persians apparently had not worshiped images of their gods (ibid.).

11. **Artaxerxes III**—also called **"Ochus"** before he ascended the throne—was the son of Artaxerxes II and Stateira. Artaxerxes III also had two legitimate older half-brothers (Ariaspes and Darius) and numerous illegitimate brothers who were born to concubines—all of whom he put to death to secure the throne. The *Encyclopaedia Britannica* calls him "a cruel but energetic ruler" (The Editors of Encyclopaedia Britannica, "Artaxerxes III," *Encyclopaedia Britannica*, https://www.britannica.com/biography/Artaxerxes-III). Artaxerxes put a final end to the satrap rebellions by ordering the satraps to dismiss their Greek mercenaries in 356 B.C. Artaxerxes attempted to conquer Egypt in 351 B.C., but when this failed, the Phoenician towns and the Cyprean princes revolted. In retaliation, Artaxerxes III defeated the city of Sidon in 345 B.C., with other Phoenician cities capitulating soon after. According to the *Encyclopaedia Iranica*, the events in the apocryphal Book of Judith may be dated to the time of "the expeditions of the generals Bagoas and Orophernes and the deportations of Jews ordered by Artaxerxes," since Bagoas is the name of the general who found the dead Holofernes (who was the Assyrian general beheaded by the Hebrew widow Judith) (R. Schmitt, "Artaxerxes III," *Encyclopaedia Iranica*, II/6, 658–59, https://www.iranicaonline.org/articles/artaxerxes-iii-throne-name-of-ochus-gk; see also Book of Judith 13:1–10; 14:14–18). Other scholars, however, find this association untenable. Artaxerxes III then attempted to conquer Egypt for a second time; this effort was successful, with Artaxerxes III defeating the Egyptian pharaoh Nectanebo II in 343 B.C. In 340 B.C., when Perinthus and Byzantium were attacked by Philip of Macedon (the father of Alexander the Great), Artaxerxes sent support to those cities. In 338 B.C., Bagoas, then the vizier of the Achaemenid Empire, is said to have murdered Artaxerxes III and his two older sons and then placed his youngest son, Arses, on the throne.

12. **Darius III**—who seems to have held the nickname **"Codomannus"**—was a distant relative of his predecessor Artaxerxes IV. The lack of Persian primary sources means that most of the information about Darius III comes from the Greeks. The Greeks viewed Darius III as an outsider who had taken the throne from Artaxerxes IV. The reign of Darius III was overshadowed by that of his contemporary, Alexander the Great. The official version of Darius III's lineage was that he was a grandson of Ostanes, who was a son of Darius II, as well as being the son of "Arsanes." What is known is that Darius III was the satrap of Armenia and was at the court of Artaxerxes IV (The Editors of Encyclopaedia Iranica, "DARIUS v. Darius III," *Encyclopaedia Iranica*, VI/1, 51-54, http://www.iranicaonline.org/articles/darius-v). Darius III was raised to the throne by Bagoas, who had murdered both Artaxerxes III and IV and their families (M. Dandamayev, "Bagoas," *Encyclopaedia Iranica*, III/4, 418-419, https://www.iranicaonline.org/articles/bagoas-the-greek-name-of-two-eunuchs-from-the-achaemenid-period). In time, Bagoas tried to murder Darius III, also by poisoning, but was forced by Darius to drink the poison instead (ibid.; The Editors of Encyclopaedia Iranica , "DARIUS v. Darius III," *Encyclopaedia Iranica*, VI/1, 51-54, http://www.iranicaonline.org/articles/darius-v). During Darius III's reign, Alexander the Great started his campaign to conquer Asia Minor. The Persians were eventually defeated by Alexander the Great and his army, and Alexander took Darius III's family captive. An attempt to strike a treaty was unsuccessful; the war waged on. Eventually, Darius III—who was said to have been taking refuge with Bessus, the satrap of Bactria—was murdered. The Greek accounts say he was murdered by Bessus himself, while other accounts differ (ibid.; Arrian of Nicomedia, Anabasis (section 3.21.6-22.2), trans. Aubrey de Sélincourt, excerpt online at https://www.livius.org/sources/content/arrian/anabasis/the-death-of-darius-iii/). Stateira II, the daughter of Darius III, married Alexander the Great. With Darius III's death, the Achaemenid Empire came to an end.

13. **Artaxerxes IV**—or **"Arses"**—was the youngest surviving son of Artaxerxes III. He was placed on the throne by Bagoas, the court eunuch who had murdered his father (Artaxerxes III) and much of his family. Bagoas, in turn, murdered Artaxerxes IV and his family after Artaxerxes IV had reigned for a brief two years)338–336 B.C.). Bagoas then raised up Darius III, a distant relative, to the throne. During the reign of Artaxerxes IV, Philip II of Macedonia (the father of Alexander the Great) began his first campaigns into Asia Minor (Jona Lendering, "Artaxerxes IV Arses," https://www.livius.org/articles/person/artaxerxes-iv-arses/; P. LeCoq, "Arses," *Encyclopaedia Iranica*, II/5, 548, https://www.iranicaonline.org/articles/arses-greek-rendering-of-an-old-persian-name-used-as-a-hypocoristic).

14. **Alexander the Great** was born in 356 B.C., the son of Philip II of Macedonia and his fourth wife Olympias. Alexander became king at the age of 20 when his father was assassinated in 336 B.C. by Pausanias (a young Macedonian noble). Alexander conquered much of the known world, starting with some of the Greek states and the Persian Empire and progressing through the Mediterranean coast, Egypt, Babylon, and Central Asia en route to India. Alexander founded the city of Alexandria in Egypt in 332 B.C.; he also founded other eponymous cities, but the Egyptian city was the longest lasting and most famous.

Alexander besieged the city of Tyre after its inhabitants would not let him (a foreigner) make a sacrifice to their god. Tyre was split between the mainland and an island about half a mile from the mainland. Enraged at the perceived slight by the people of Tyre, Alexander razed the "old city" on the mainland and built a bridge out of the rubble to gain access to the island. After a seven-month siege, both portions of the city were utterly destroyed, and many people were killed or enslaved. The remaining people fled and founded the city of Carthage in northern Africa (The Editors of Encyclopaedia Britannica, "Tyre," *Encyclopedia Britannica*, https://www.britannica.com/place/Tyre; Diodorus,

Histories, 17.41.2; 17.46.4). Alexander the Great's destruction of Tyre in 332 B.C.—which completed the process begun by Nebuchadnezzar—had been prophesied by Ezekiel some 250 years earlier (cf. **Ezekiel 26:1–14**).

Alexander died in 323 B.C. at the age of 33 while in Babylon. At his death, Alexander the Great's empire—the ancient Greek kingdom of Macedon—stretched from the Ionian Sea on the western side of Greece all the way to the Indus River in what is now Pakistan and India. After his death, Alexander's generals attempted to keep the empire intact through Alexander's infant son (Alexander IV) by Roxanne, and then by Alexander's elder half-brother (Philip Arrhidaeus, the son of Philip II of Macedon and Philinna). However, over the next few decades, the generals warred for supremacy. Eventually, the empire was divided among Alexander's rival generals, family, and friends, called the *Diadochi*: Ptolemy I (Soter) established a successful Ptolemaic kingdom in Egypt (see chart "**Supplement 6**: The Ptolemies and the Ptolemaic Dynasty"); Syria came under the control of the Seleucids, led by Seleucus I (Nicator; see chart "**Supplement 7**: The Seleucids and the Seleucid Dynasty"); Lysimachus received Asia Minor; and Cassander ruled Greece. In 323 B.C. Palestine came under the jurisdiction of the Egyptian ruler Ptolemy I (Soter).

SUPPLEMENT 6: THE PTOLEMIES AND THE PTOLEMAIC DYNASTY[1]

Approximate Dating: ca. 323–30 B.C.; the Ptolemies, centered in Alexandria, Egypt, ruled Palestine ca. 323–198 B.C.

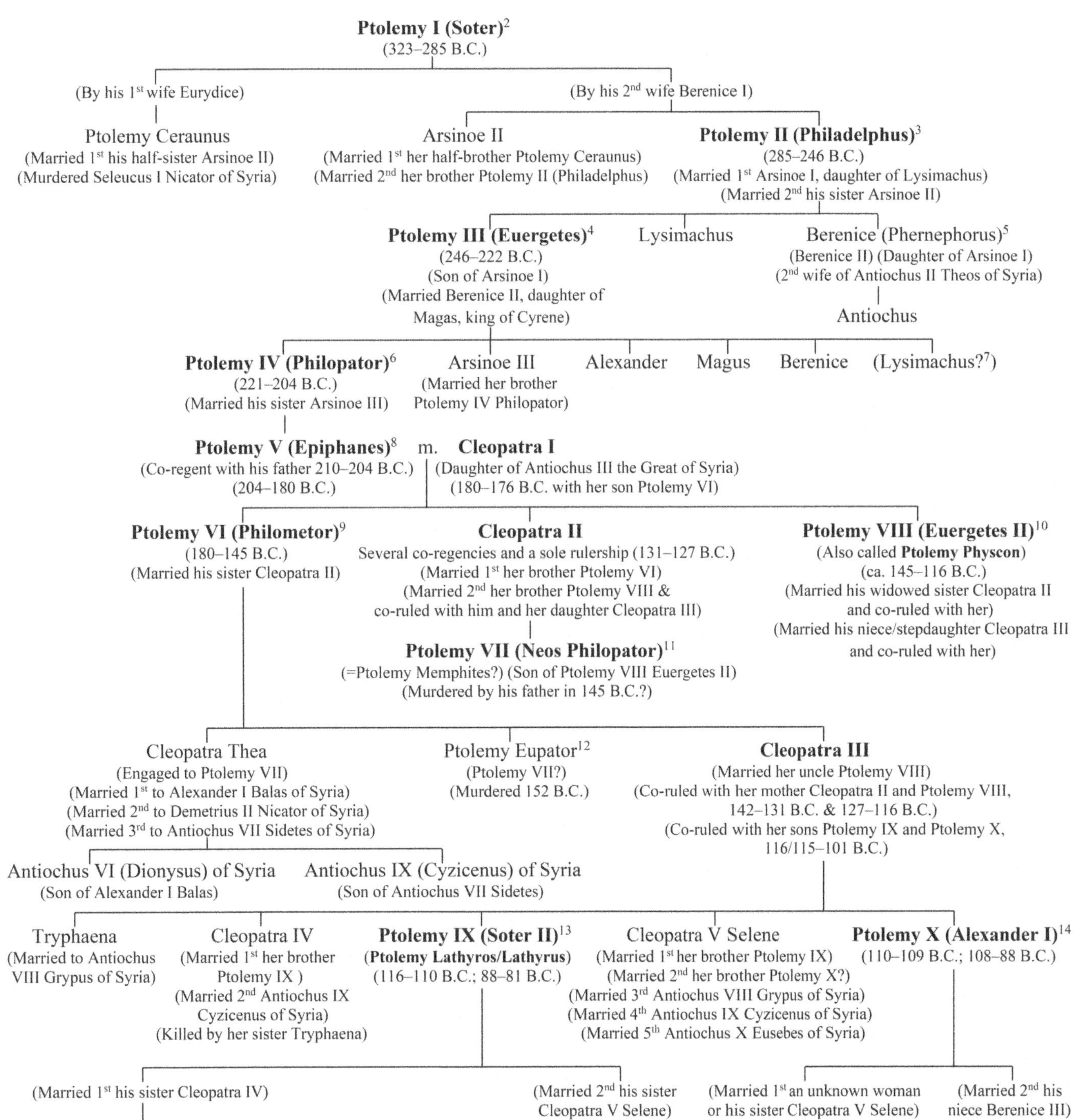

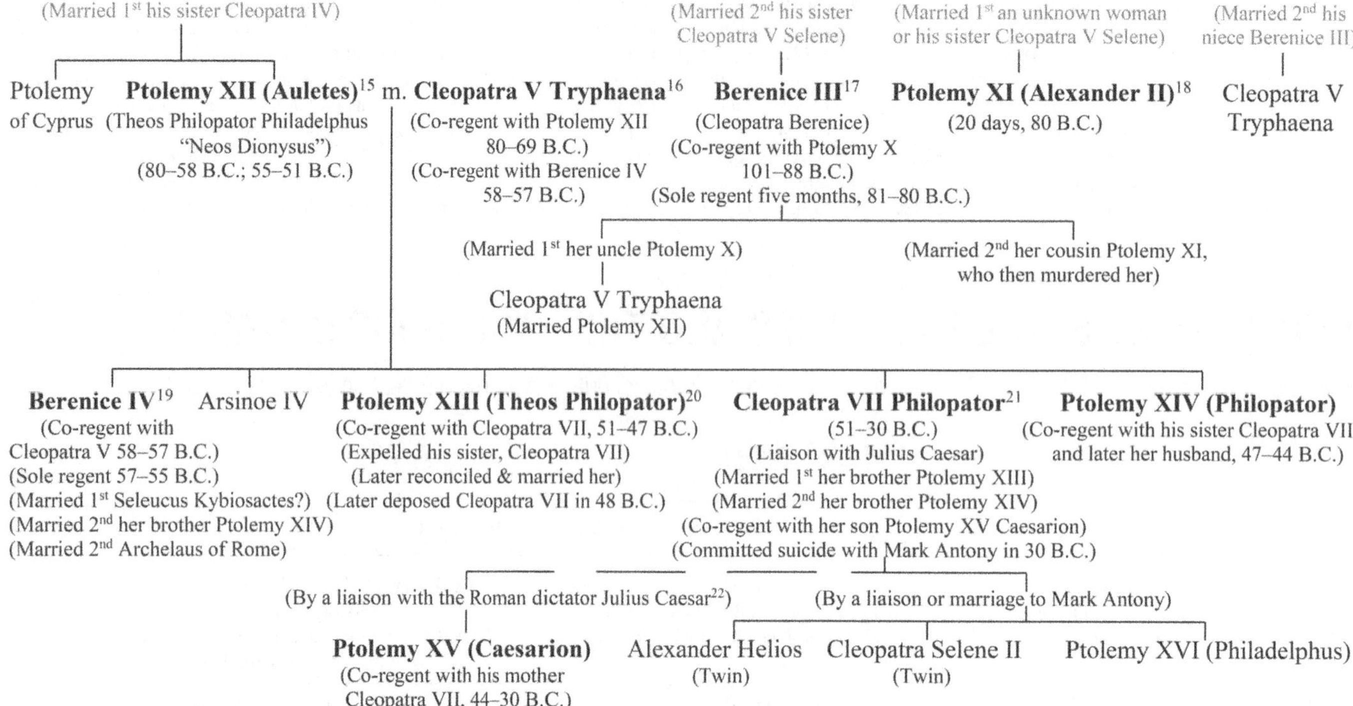

Notes

1. The following works were used in the compilation of this chart and the accompanying notes: Flavius Josephus, *Josephus: Complete Works* (including *Jewish Antiquities* and *Against Apion*), trans. William Whiston (Grand Rapids: Kregel, 1972); Polybius, *The Histories*, trans. by Robin Waterfield, Oxford World's Classics (New York: Oxford University Press, 2010); Lucian Farrar, Jr., *The Book of Daniel: The Most High Rules* (Tulsa: James Kay, 2014); A. E. Astin, ed. *The Cambridge Ancient History*, 2nd ed., vol. VIII: Rome and the Mediterranean to 133 B.C. (Cambridge: Cambridge University Press, 1989); Chris Bennett, the "Ptolemaic Dynasty" http://www.instonebrewer.com/TyndaleSites/Egypt/ptolemies/ptolemies.htm. (including Ptolemaic Chronology and Genealogy, 2001–2013, now hosted and modified by David Instone-Brewer; and online sources http://www.livius.org; and Mahlon H. Smith's Virtual Religion Index, https://virtualreligion.net.

Some variation exists for the regnal dates and co-regencies of the Ptolemies, so dates are close approximations. In general, dating follows the Kenneth Barker, ed., "Ptolemaic Kings of the Maccabean-Hasmonean Period," *NIV Study Bible* (Grand Rapids: Zondervan, 2020), 1624, based on Moisés Silva, *The Zondervan Encyclopedia of the Bible*, vol. 4 (Grand Rapids: Zondervan, 2009), 13, and the chart for the "Ptolemies and Seleucids" in the *NIV Cultural Backgrounds Study Bible* (Grand Rapids: Zondervan, 2016), 1446. For references to the Seleucid rulers of Syria, see chart "**Supplement 7**: The Seleucids and the Seleucid Dynasty."

2. **Ptolemy I (Soter)** took control of Egypt upon the death of Alexander the Great in 323 B.C. For the next three hundred years, the descendants of Ptolemy I ruled Egypt and other various lands, including Cyprus and Cyrenaica (modern Libya). Ptolemy I (Soter) was most likely the son of Lagus and Arsinoe. Chris Bennett's "Egyptian Royal Genealogy" gives a lengthy discussion of Ptolemy I's parentage. Ptolemy I was definitely the son of Arsinoe, a descendant of the Madedonian kings; some scholars say that she was the daughter of Meleager, a descendant of Alexander I of Macedon. Arsinoe was married to a man named Lagus; she was also said to be a concubine of Philip II of Macedonia (the father of Alexander the Great). Whether or not Ptolemy I's father was Lagus, Philip II, or someone else is unknown.

Ptolemy I (Soter) had served under Alexander the Great as his bodyguard. When he assumed rule over Egypt in 323 B.C., Ptolemy I proposed that the satrapies of Alexander's vast empire should be governed by Alexander's former generals. Josephus says that Ptolemy I (Soter) seized Jerusalem and entered the city on the Sabbath "as if he would offer sacrifice." The Jews evidently did not see him as an enemy, and as it was the Sabbath day, they did not defend their city when Ptolemy I attacked (*Jewish Antiquities* 12.1.1). At that time, Ptolemy I (Soter) captured many Jews—from Jerusalem and its surrounding areas, from Samaria, and from the mountains in Judea—and carried them away to Egypt. Josephus says that Ptolemy I (Soter) gave the Jews at Alexandria equal rights as citizens along with the Macedonians (*Jewish Antiquities* 12.1.1). According to the *NIV Study Bible*, the "king of the South" in **Daniel 11:5** refers to Ptolemy I (Soter), who "will become strong, but one of his commanders will become even stronger than he and will rule his own kingdom with great power." Ptolemy I (Soter) had four or five marriages/liaisons. His marriage to Eurydice produced, among others, Ptolemy Ceraunus, who murdered the Syrian ruler Seleucus I (Nicator). Ptolemy I's marriage to Berenice I produced Ptolemy II (Philadelphus) and Arsinoe II; Arsinoe II married her half-brother Ptolemy Ceraunus and later married her brother Ptolemy II (Philadelphus). Ptolemy II (Philadelphus) acted as co-regent with his father for a few years before Ptolemy I's death in 285 B.C.

3. **Ptolemy II (Philadelphus)** was the son of Ptolemy I (Soter) and Berenice I. Ptolemy II (Philadelphus) first married Arsinoe I, the daughter of Lysimachus, the king of Thrace and Nicaea of Macedon, and they had three children: Ptolemy III (Euergetes), Lysimachus, and Berenice (Phernephorus). Ptolemy II married secondly his sister Arsinoe II, but they had no children. However, after Arsinoe II's death, Ptolemy II had her posthumously adopt his children by Arsinoe I. The Seleucid king Antiochus II (Theos) married Berenice (Phernephorus), Ptolemy II's daughter, and they had one son, Antiochus. However, on the order of Seleucus II (Callinicus) and his mother Laodice, Berenice (Phernephorus) and her son (Antiochus) were murdered. Ptolemy II (Philadelphus) is the "king of the South" mentioned in **Daniel 11:5–6**. The "daughter of the king of the South" (**Daniel 11:6**) refers to Berenice (Phernephorus), Ptolemy II's daughter, who married "the king of the North" [the Seleucid ruler Antiochus II Theos, 261–246 B.C. of Syria]. Berenice's marriage to Antiochus II (Theos) of Syria ended the Ptolemies' war against the Seleucids.

During Ptolemy II's reign, the city of Alexandria blossomed into a cultural center for the arts and sciences. Ptolemy II (Philadelphus) expanded the Library of Alexandria ("Ptolemy II," Heinz Heinen, *Encyclopedia Britannica*). According to Josephus, Ptolemy II—upon the advice of his librarian—commissioned the Jewish books of the law to be translated into Greek (*Jewish Antiquities* 12.2.1). Ptolemy II wrote to the Oniad high priest Eleazar (ca. 260–245 B.C.), asking for him to send six skilled, intelligent men from each of the twelve tribes to translate the Jewish law from Hebrew into Greek so that Ptolemy II (Philadelphus) might have a copy in his library at Alexandria (*Jewish Antiquities* 12.2.4–5). Eleazar responded favorably, sending seventy-two men to Egypt to make the translation (*Jewish Antiquities*

12.2.6); this Greek translation of the Hebrew Bible came to be known as the "Septuagint" and was used, among other things, by the New Testament writers and Jesus to quote Old Testament passages. The letter from Ptolemy II to Eleazar the high priest is called the *Letter of Aristeas*, after the Egyptian officer in the royal guard who suggested that Ptolemy II free the Jews (Josephus, *Jewish Antiquities* 12.2.2–5; Achille Vander Heeren, "Septuagint Version," *The Catholic Encyclopedia*, vol. 13 (New York: Robert Appleton Company, 1912), http://www.newadvent.org/cathen/13722a.htm): Ptolemy II did order that the Jews who had been taken into captivity by his father were to be set free (Josephus, *Jewish Antiquities* 12.2.3). Scholars think that the *Letter of Aristeas* and much of the surrounding information is apocryphal and/or exaggerated. However, it is likely that this legend is based in fact—it is very likely that the Pentateuch was translated at Alexandria due to the style of the language used. It also has been calculated as having been written during the time of Ptolemy II (i.e., the middle of the third century B.C.; Achille Vander Heeren, "Septuagint Version," *The Catholic Encyclopedia*, vol. 13 (New York: Robert Appleton Company, 1912), http://www.newadvent.org/cathen/13722a.htm). Josephus writes that only the Pentateuch was translated by the seventy-two men—elsewhere only 70 men are mentioned, thus "Septuagint" is Greek for 70 and is abbreviated using the Roman numerals LXX. Later, the name Septuagint was extended to refer to the entire Greek version of the Hebrew Bible. According to the *Catholic Encyclopedia*, the later books of the Hebrew Bible that were translated into Greek differ from each other and from the Pentateuch so much in form, vocabulary, and style that "they could not be the work of the same translators" (ibid.; also see The Editors of Encyclopaedia Britannica, "Septuagint," *Encyclopedia Britannica*, https://www.britannica.com/topic/Septuagint). Ptolemy II (Philadelphus) died in 246 B.C. and was succeeded by his son Ptolemy III (Euergetes).

4. **Ptolemy III (Euergetes)** was the eldest son of Ptolemy II (Philadelphus) and his first wife, Arsinoe I. Ptolemy III (Euergetes) married Berenice II (the daughter of Magas of Cyrene and Apama II) and they had five or six children, including Ptolemy IV (Philopator) and Arsinoe III. Shortly after succeeding to the throne, Ptolemy III (Euergetes) invaded Coele Syria (modern-day Lebanon) to avenge the murder of his sister Berenice (Phernephorus)—who had been the second wife of the Seleucid king Antiochus II (Theos)—and Berenice's son, Antiochus. This invasion sparked the Third Syrian War (246–241 B.C.). Afterward, Ptolemy III focused on domestic stability, embarked on construction projects and even reformed the calendar—an extra day was now added to the calendar every four years, but this change was not popular. Polybius says that Ptolemy III died during the 139th Olympiad (224–221 B.C.) (*The Histories*, II.71). Chris Bennett's extensive research on the "Ptolemaic Dynasty" dates Ptolemy II's death to November or December 222 B.C. Ptolemy III (Euergetes) was succeeded by his son Ptolemy IV (Philopator).

5. Berenice (Phernephorus), also called Berenice II, was the daughter of Ptolemy II (Philadelphus) and the sister of Ptolemy III (Euergetes). The *NIV Cultural Backgrounds Study Bible* says that she is the "daughter of the king of the South" mentioned in **Daniel 11:6** and states that she was sent to marry the Seleucid king Antiochus II (Theos) of Syria in ca. 252 B.C. The marriage alliance ended the war between the Ptolemies and the Seleucids; John H. Walton and Craig S. Keener, eds., the *NIV Cultural Backgrounds Study Bible* (Grand Rapids: Zondervan, 2016), 1146–47. However, as **Daniel 11:6** predicts, peace was short-lived: ". . . she [Berenice] will not retain her power, and he [Antiochus II Theos] and his power will not last. In those days she [Berenice] will be betrayed." This came about when a former wife of Antiochus II (Theos), Laodice—whose sons had been removed from the line of succession—ordered the murders of Berenice (Phernephorus) and her young son Antiochus. Their deaths sparked the Third Syrian War (246–241 B.C.), led by Ptolemy III's quest to avenge the deaths of his sister and nephew.

6. **Ptolemy IV (Philopator)** was the second son of Ptolemy III (Euergetes) and Berenice II. The decline of the Ptolemaic empire began during his reign. Ptolemy IV married his sister Arsinoe III, and they had a son, Ptolemy V (Epiphanes). The Fourth Syrian War (219–217 B.C.) was fought during Ptolemy IV's reign against the Seleucid ruler Antiochus III the Great (223–187 B.C.). Polybius describes Ptolemy IV (Philopator) as ruling "as though he were on holiday," stating that he was "inaccessible" to his courtiers and administrators and disdainful toward those who managed Egyptian foreign domains. Polybius also says that Ptolemy IV was "distracted by unsuitable love affairs and stupefied by non-stop carousing" (*The Histories*, V.34). Ptolemy IV was also influenced by "disreputable associates" who, among other things, convinced Ptolemy IV to order the deaths of his mother, uncle, and brother (The Editors of Encyclopaedia Britannica, "Ptolemy IV Philopator," *Encyclopedia Britannica*, https://www.britannica.com/biography/Ptolemy-IV-Philopator). Also, during Ptolemy IV's reign, native Egyptians who had been drafted to fight in the Fourth Syrian War against Antiochus III the Great of Syria realized their power and rebelled. The Fourth Syrian War is described in detail in *The Histories*, V.58–71; 79–87. Josephus notes that during that time, the Jews "suffered greatly, and their land was sorely harassed" (*Jewish Antiquities* 12.3.3). Ptolemy IV (Philopator) is referred to in **Daniel 11:11–12** as the "king of the South" who "will march out in a rage and fight against the king of the North [referring to the Seleucid king Antiochus III the Great] who will raise a large army, but it will be defeated [referring to the defeat of the Seleucids at Raphia in 217 B.C.]. When the army is carried off, the king of the South [Ptolemy IV] will be filled with pride and will slaughter many thousands, yet he will not remain triumphant." The apocryphal book of *3 Maccabees* records that after the battle at Raphia, Ptolemy IV made a visit to Jerusalem in which he entered the temple and, impressed by its splendor, wished to enter the holy of holies, much to the consternation of the Jews, who wept and cried loudly at this intended blasphemy. The high priest Simon II (218–185 B.C.) prayed for God to deliver the Jews from such an "impious and profane man, puffed up in his audacity and power" (*3 Maccabees* 2:2). Ptolemy IV (Philopator) was then "smitten by a righteous judgment"—paralyzed in all four limbs and unable to speak (*3 Maccabees* 2:22). *Third Maccabees* pinpoints this event as the cause of Ptolemy IV's persecution of the Alexandrian Jews (cf. *3 Maccabees* 1–2). Scholars doubt the historicity of this tale, but it is possible that these events were exaggerated from actual Jewish oppression in Egypt under Ptolemaic rule (cf. Josephus' *Against Apion*, 2.5). Chris Bennett dates Ptolemy IV's death to July/August 204 B.C. ("Ptolemaic Dynasty"). His wife–sister Arsinoe III was also murdered just before or soon after, possibly by Sosibus, the head of Ptolemy IV's government.

7. See notes for "Lysimachus" in the "The Ptolemaic Dynasty" (Chris Bennett) for an explanation behind this probable son of Ptolemy III (Euergetes).

8. **Ptolemy V (Epiphanes)** was the son of Ptolemy IV (Philopator) and Arsinoe III of Egypt. Ptolemy V co-ruled Egypt with his father from 210–204 B.C. and succeeded him in 204 B.C. Ptolemy V married Cleopatra I, the daughter of the Seleucid ruler Antiochus III the Great (The Editors of Encyclopaedia Britannica, "Ptolemy V Epiphanes," Encyclopedia Britannica, https://www.britannica.com/biography/Ptolemy-V-Epiphanes; Josephus, *Jewish Antiquities* 12.4.1; Farrar, *The Book of Daniel,* 103–104). Ptolemy V and Cleopatra I were the parents of Ptolemy VI (Philometor), Ptolemy VIII (Euergetes II), and most likely, Cleopatra II ("Ptolemy V Epiphanes"). Polybius states in his *Histories* that he plans to relate "how, after Ptolemy IV's death, Antiochus III [the Great] and Philip V [of Macedon] colluded to dismember the kingdom of the boy-king who succeeded him and began to infringe on his domains" (*Histories* III.2). A fragment from Book 15 of *The Histories* does describe the actions of Antiochus III the Great and Philip V, but much of the rest of the book is now lost. See Carolyn Dewald's introduction to *The Histories*, by Herodotus, trans. Robin Waterfield (Oxford: Oxford University Press, 1998), xiv–xv. The actions of Antiochus III and Philip V are better known as the Fifth Syrian War (202–195 B.C.). Ptolemy V's involvement in the Fifth Syrian War is alluded to in **Daniel 11:14**, where Ptolemy V (Epiphanes) is identified as the "king of the South"; see Kenneth L. Barker et al., eds., *NIV Study Bible*, Fully Revised Edition (Grand Rapids: Zondervan, 2020), 1146, note on **Daniel 11:14**.

In *Jewish Antiquities* 12.4.1, Josephus describes the peace treaty between Antiochus III the Great and Ptolemy V (Epiphanes) in which Ptolemy V married Cleopatra I (Antiochus III's daughter). The peace treaty between Syria and Egypt also included the loss of all former Ptolemaic possessions outside of Egypt, except for Cyrenaica (modern Libya) and Cyprus. Ptolemy V (Epiphanes) made the declaration as an inscription on what is known as the Rosetta Stone—which famously helped archaeologists figure out how to decode hieroglyphics—which canceled debts and taxes, pardoned rebels who surrendered, released prisoners, and increased funds for the temples (The editors of *Encyclopaedia Britannica*, "Ptolemy V Epiphanes," *Encyclopedia Britannica*, https://www.britannica.com/biography/Ptolemy-V-Epiphanes). Ptolemy V (Epiphanes) dealt with rebellions by the native Egyptians and successfully stifled these insurrections. Futhermore, Ptolemy V planned to reignite war between Ptolemaic Egypt and the Syrian Seleucids, but he died (perhaps poisoned) before he could begin. C. Habicht writes in "The Seleucids and their Rivals," a chapter in *The Cambridge Ancient History* Volume VIII, "[Ptolemy V's] widow Cleopatra [I]—Antiochus' [Antiochus III's] sister—acted as regent for her son, Ptolemy VI [Philometor], and kept him from war [with the

Seleucids], but when she [Cleopatra I] died in 176 B.C., the new government, led by the king's guardians Eulaeus and Lenaeus, prepared for war against Syria. They justified it with the claim that the disputed lands [referring to southern Syria and Palestine] had been promised to Egypt as Cleopatra's dowry when she married Ptolemy V [Epiphanes]" (343).

9. **Ptolemy VI (Philometor)** was the son of Ptolemy V (Epiphanes) and Cleopatra I. Upon the death of his father, Ptolemy VI ascended the throne at about age six. He ruled jointly with his mother Cleopatra I until her death in 176 B.C. Ptolemy VI (Philometor) married his sister Cleopatra II in 173 B.C. and had four children by her, including Ptolemy Eupator, Cleopatra Thea, and Cleopatra III. Ptolemy VI (Philometor) was driven out of Alexandria in ca. 164 B.C. by his brother Ptolemy VIII (Euergetes II), who had become co-regent a few years before (cf. **Daniel 11:25–27**). Ptolemy VI (Philometor) petitioned Rome for help, and Rome responded by dividing up the Ptolemaic lands so that Ptolemy VI (Philometor) retained Egypt and Cyprus, while Ptolemy VIII (Euergetes II) received Cyrenaica (modern Libya). Not satisfied with the terms, Ptolemy VIII (Euergetes II) pushed Rome to give him Cyprus as well; Rome granted the request but was thwarted by his brother Ptolemy VI. To restore peace, Ptolemy VI (Philometor) gave his daughter in marriage, as well as control of Cyrenaica, to Ptolemy VIII (Euergetes II). The daughter in question seems to have been Cleopatra Thea; she and Ptolemy VIII (Euergetes II) seem to have been engaged but not married. After Ptolemy VI supported Alexander Balas' claim to the Seleucid throne, Ptolemy VI's daughter Cleopatra Thea was given in marriage to Alexander I (Balas). During their wedding at Ptolemais, Ptolemy VI (Philometor) honored the high priest Jonathan Maccabeus "Apphus" (*I Maccabees* 10:57–60; *Jewish Antiquities* 13.4.1–2). Josephus says that Alexander Balas gave Jonathan Maccabeus a "purple garment and made him [Jonathan Maccabeus] sit with him [Alexander Balas] on his throne" (*Jewish Antiquities* 13.4.2; for Jonathan Maccabeus, see chart "**Supplement 8**: The Maccabees and the Hasmonean Dynasty").

Ptolemy VI of Egypt offered refuge to Jews who fled Judea because of the Maccabean Revolt (167–160 B.C.). During Ptolemy VI's reign, the Jewish high priest Onias IV (162 B.C.) asked permission to build a temple in Egypt. Josephus explains that Onias wanted to build a temple in response to the prophet Isaiah, who "foretold that there certainly was to be a temple built to Almighty God in Egypt by a man that was a Jew" (*Jewish Antiquities* 13.3.1). The verse in question is **Isaiah 19:19**: "In that day there will be an altar to the LORD in the heart of Egypt, and a monument to the LORD at its border." Ptolemy VI and Cleopatra I agreed, and the temple was built at Leontopolis in the Nile Delta (*Jewish Antiquities* 13.3.2–3). According to Josephus, Alexander I Balas set a trap for Ptolemy VI; in response, Ptolemy VI changed his allegiance to Demetrius II (Nicator; *Jewish Antiquities* 13.4.6–7), dissolved the marriage of his daughter Cleopatra Thea to Alexander I Balas, and married her instead to Demetrius II (Nicator; *Jewish Antiquities* 13.4.7). Antiochus IV (Epiphanes) invaded Egypt twice during Ptolemy VI's reign but capitulated to pressure from Rome to halt his invasion. Ptolemy VI (Philometor) died of a wound received fighting against Alexander I Balas of Syria, who also died. The Seleucid king Demetrius II (Nicator) then invaded the Ptolemaic lands.

10. **Ptolemy VIII (Euergetes II)**, also known as **Ptolemy Physcon** (*Jewish Antiquities* 12.4.11), was the younger son of Ptolemy V (Epiphanes) and Cleopatra I and the younger brother of Ptolemy VI (Philometor), his predecessor. He is known as Ptolemy VIII because Ptolemy VI's son, Ptolemy Eupator, was accorded kingship, which would have made him the seventh Ptolemy. Ptolemy Eupator was struck from the kingship list, but modern scholars tend to include him for continuity. Initially, Ptolemy VIII (Euergetes II) became co-ruler alongside his brother (Ptolemy VI) and his sister (Cleopatra II, who was married at the time to Ptolemy VI). Ptolemy VIII (Euergetes II) was first engaged to his niece—probably Cleopatra Thea, but according to Chris Bennett's "Ptolemaic Dynasty," he did not marry her. After Ptolemy VI died, Ptolemy VIII (Euergetes II) married his widowed sister Cleopatra II, and they had one son. Ptolemy VIII (Euergetes II) then married his niece/stepdaughter Cleopatra III, and they had at least five children, including Ptolemy IX (Soter II), Ptolemy X (Alexander I), Cleopatra IV, Cleopatra V Selene, and Tryphaena. Ptolemy VIII (Euergetes II) drove his brother Ptolemy VI (Philometor) out of Alexandria in ca. 164 B.C. Ptolemy VI (Philometor) appealed to Rome for help. In response, Rome divided the Ptolemaic lands so that Ptolemy VIII (Euergetes II) was granted control of Cyrenaica (modern Libya), while Ptolemy VI (Philometor) regained Egypt and Cyprus. Ptolemy VIII (Euergetes II) pressed Rome to give him Cyprus as well, and Rome acquiesced. To restore peace, Ptolemy VI (Philometor) offered his daughter (Cleopatra Thea) in marriage to Ptolemy VIII (Euergetes II)—although the marriage never took place—and also gave Ptolemy VIII the control of Cyprus. Ptolemy VIII (Euergetes II) became the prime ruler after his brother's death in the summer of 145 B.C. Ptolemy VIII (Euergetes II) promptly married Ptolemy VI's widow, Cleopatra II. Eventually, civil war sprung up between Cleopatra II and Ptolemy VIII. Cleopatra II was supported by her son-in-law, Demetrius II (Nicator) of Syria, who sent troops to assist, but the mission failed. Josephus says in *Jewish Antiquities* 13.9.3 that Ptolemy VIII (Euergetes II) supported Alexander II Zabinas' quest for the Seleucid throne. John Hyrcanus I, the Jewish high priest and ruler, 134–104 B.C., asked Ptolemy VIII (Euergetes II) to send someone to take Syria from Demetrius II (Nicator), specifying that this person should be "of the family of Seleucus." Alexander II Zabinas apparently took control of Syria and allied with Hyrcanus I, but afterward he was defeated by Antiochus VIII (Grypus), the son of Demetrius II (Nicator). Josephus says in *Against Apion* that the Jewish general Onias took up arms against Ptolemy VIII (Euergetes II) "on Cleopatra's account," referring to Cleopatra II. Josephus further states that "Ptolemy [VIII] called Physcon, upon the death of his brother [Ptolemy VI] Philometor, came to Cyrene, and would have ejected Cleopatra as well as her sons out of her kingdom, that he might obtain it for himself unjustly" (*Against Apion* 2.5). Josephus then relates that Ptolemy VIII (Euergetes II) brought elephants to Alexandria to trample upon the Jews, including women and children, after Jews there had been stripped of clothing and bound. Instead of trampling the Jews, however, the elephants instead turned on the friends of Ptolemy VIII (Euergetes II). In a subsequent vision in which his concubine Ithaca/Irene was pleading with him to stop, Ptolemy VIII (Euergetes II) was convinced to indeed halt this persecution of the Jews and repent. Apparently, the Alexandrian Jews celebrated this day of deliverance. When Ptolemy VIII (Euergetes II) died in 116 B.C., he was succeeded by Cleopatra III and her son Ptolemy IX (Soter II), because Ptolemy VIII's unusual will had split his domains between them.

11. **Ptolemy VII (Neos Philopator)** is an enigmatic figure. He has been variously identified as Ptolemy Eupator (see note 12), who was the son of Ptolemy VI (Philometor) or, as shown in the chart, he was likely "Ptolemy Memphites," the son of Ptolemy VIII (Euergetes II) and Cleopatra II. The name "Ptolemy VII Neos Philopator" was first found in a list of deified pharaohs that was discovered in the nineteenth century; the name was sandwiched between the warring brother-kings—Ptolemy VI (Philometor) and Ptolemy VIII (Euergetes II)—but with no indication of the exact relationship of Neos Philopator to the two brothers. In Chris Bennett's intensive study of the "Ptolemaic Dynasty," where he conducted a detailed investigation into the identity of Neos Philopator, Bennett concluded that since Ptolemy Eupator was murdered ca. 152 B.C., Eupator could not be Ptolemy VII (Neos Philopator), as previously widely asserted. Instead, Bennett assigned Neos Philopater's identity to "Ptolemy Memphites," the son of Ptolemy VIII (Euergetes II) and Cleopatra II (who was also the mother of Ptolemy Eupator). The Roman historian Justin (or Justinus) also mentions the murder of Ptolemy Memphites, who was killed by his own father at the beginning of the civil war between Ptolemy VIII (Euergetes II) and Cleopatra II. Cleopatra II had intended to place Ptolemy Memphites on the throne, but Ptolemy VIII intercepted and murdered his son before that could happen; Justin relates that Ptolemy VIII (Euergetes II) sent the dismembered body of Memphites to Cleopatra II on her birthday (*Epitome* 38.8). Bennett posits that Ptolemy VII (Ptolemy Memphites) was included posthumously in the list of pharaohs, presumably as an act of repentance by his father Ptolemy VIII (Euergetes II). If Bennett's conjecture is correct, the discrepancy in the numbering system (i.e., why the son was numbered *before* the father) could be explained by (1) the fact that Cleopatra II had been trying to place Ptolemy Memphites on the throne and (2) the fact that the numbering system is a modern invention. Thus, the identity of Ptolemy VII (Neos Philopator) is still uncertain, although a good argument can be made for Ptolemy Memphites being posthumously awarded that title. For more information, see Chris Bennett's genealogy for the "Ptolemaic Dynasty," especially the pages for Ptolemy Memphites, Cleopatra II, and Ptolemy Eupator; also refer to Rutgers professor emeritus Mahlon H. Smith's page on Ptolemy VII (Neos Philopator) on his Virtual Religion Index site.

12. **Ptolemy Eupator** was the son of Ptolemy VI (Philometor) and Cleopatra II. He was formerly thought to have been the elusive Ptolemy VII (Neos Philopator) due to the accounts of ancient historians like Josephus and Justin, but modern scholarship has rejected this view. For instance, Chris Bennett rejects the idea that Ptolemy Eupator was Ptolemy VII (Neos Philopator) because Eupator died ca. 152 B.C. The Roman historian Justin

(not to be confused with Justin Martyr) relates that Ptolemy VIII (Euergetes II) killed his nephew Ptolemy Eupator on the very night he married Eupator's mother, Cleopatra II (*Epitome* 38.8). Chris Bennett, however, argues that Ptolemy Eupator died of an epidemic disease. Justin does not explicitly name the son of Ptolemy VI (Philometor) and Cleopatra II, but from textual clues it is apparent that he meant Ptolemy Eupator. There is a possibility that Justin was referring to another son of Ptolemy VI (Philometor) and Cleopatra II, that Justin was conflating the possible murder of Ptolemy Eupator with that of Ptolemy Memphites (see note 11), or that Justin was using poetic license to set the tone for the murder of Ptolemy Memphites. However, what is certain is that Ptolemy Eupator died before both his parents. For more information, see Chris Bennett's genealogy of the "Ptolemaic Dynasty," especially the pages for Ptolemy Eupator, Cleopatra II, and Ptolemy Memphites.

13. **Ptolemy IX (Soter II)**—also called **Ptolemy Lathyros** or **Lathyrus**—was the son of Ptolemy VIII (Euergetes II) and Cleopatra III. Ptolemy IX first married his sister Cleopatra IV, by whom he had Ptolemy XII (Auletes) and Ptolemy of Cyprus. Second, Ptolemy IX (Soter II) married his sister Cleopatra V Selene, by whom he had a daughter, Cleopatra Berenice (also known as Berenice III; see note 17). Ptolemy IX (Soter II) was expelled from Egypt in ca. 110 B.C. by his mother Cleopatra III, who replaced him with his brother Ptolemy X (Alexander I). Ptolemy IX (Soter II) then ruled Cyprus but was called back to Alexandria in ca. 88 B.C. to replace Ptolemy X (Alexander). According to Bennett's "Ptolemaic Dynasty," Ptolemy IX (Soter II) was co-regent with his daughter Berenice III for at least the last year of his reign, and possibly longer. The original research by Bennett cites Cleopatra II and Cleopatra III as examples of ruling queens who were not married to their consorts—Cleopatra II remained a queen regnant after her divorce from Ptolemy VIII (Euergetes II), and Cleopatra III ruled as queen alongside her sons Ptolemy IX and X. Ptolemy IX (Soter II) died ca. December 81 B.C. He was succeeded briefly by his daughter, Cleopatra Berenice, known as Berenice III.

14. **Ptolemy X (Alexander I)** was the son of Ptolemy VIII (Euergetes II) and Cleopatra III and the brother of Ptolemy IX (Soter II). Ptolemy X (Alexander I) married twice: first to an unknown woman, whom Chris Bennett identifies as his sister Cleopatra V Selene. Ptolemy X (Alexander I) and his first wife had a son, Ptolemy XI (Alexander II). Ptolemy X (Alexander I) married secondly his niece Berenice III; by her he had at least one child, identified by Chris Bennett as Cleopatra V Tryphaena. After the death of his father (Ptolemy VIII), Ptolemy X (Alexander I) was Cleopatra III's choice to rule, but opposition from the people of the city of Alexandria led Ptolemy X (Alexander I) to be appointed as ruler of Cyprus instead. For the next twenty to thirty years, the throne of Egypt was alternately occupied by Ptolemy IX (Soter II) "Lathyros" or Ptolemy X (Alexander I), often accompanied by their mother, Cleopatra III. Hostilities were often instigated by Cleopatra III; in 110 B.C., she deposed her son Ptolemy IX (Soter II) in favor of his brother Ptolemy X (Alexander I), but Ptolemy IX (Soter II) was recalled and restored to the throne the next year, leaving Ptolemy X (Alexander I) in charge of Cyprus again. The brothers Ptolemy IX (Soter II) and Ptolemy X (Alexander) were reconciled after their mother's death. Ptolemy IX (Soter II) even arranged the marriage of his daughter Cleopatra Berenice (Berenice III) to Ptolemy X (Alexander I). Ptolemy X (Alexander I) died in 88 B.C., and the throne reverted to Ptolemy IX (Soter II) until his death in 81 B.C.

15. **Ptolemy XII (Auletes)**—also called Ptolemy XII (Neos Dionysus)—was the son of Ptolemy IX (Soter II); Chris Bennett identifies Cleopatra IV as his mother ("Ptolemaic Dynasty"). Ptolemy XII (Auletes) was also the half-brother of Berenice III. Ptolemy XII married Cleopatra V Tryphaena—according to an extensive explanation by Chris Bennett, she was most likely the daughter of Ptolemy X (Alexander I) and Berenice III ("Ptolemaic Dynasty"). Cleopatra V Tryphaena served as co-regent with her husband from ca. 80–69/68 B.C. Ptolemy XII (Auletes) and Cleopatra V Tryphaena had five children: Berenice IV, Cleopatra VII Philopator, Arsinoe IV, Ptolemy XIII (Theos Philopator), and Ptolemy XIV (Philopator). In 59 B.C., Ptolemy XII (Auletes)—who, at the time, was facing questions about his legitimacy from Roman politicians (which in turn led to opposition from the Alexandrians and uncertainty about his status regarding Rome)—paid Julius Caesar (then a Roman consul) a total of 6,000 talents. Caesar subsequently passed a law acknowledging the kingship of Ptolemy XII (Auletes). However, in ca. 58 B.C., Ptolemy XII (Auletes) was deposed by his eldest daughter (Berenice IV) and his wife and co-regent (Cleopatra V Tryphaena). After Cleopatra V's death, Berenice IV initially reigned alone, but Ptolemy XII (Auletes) was restored to the throne in ca. 55 B.C. after promising 10,000 talents to Pompey the Great's lieutenant, Aulus Gabinius, the proconsul of Syria. Ptolemy XII (Auletes) died in ca. 51 B.C. and was succeeded by his children Ptolemy XIII (Theos Philopator) and Cleopatra VII Philopator. The extensive bribes of Ptolemy XII (Auletes) left Egypt financially unstable.

16. **Cleopatra V Tryphaena** was most likely the daughter of Ptolemy X (Alexander I) and Berenice III. Cleopatra V was married to Ptolemy XII (Auletes) and they had five children—Berenice IV, Cleopatra VII, Arsinoe IV, Ptolemy XIII Philopator, and Ptolemy XIV Philopator. (Berenice IV is the only concretely attested child, but it is generally thought that Cleopatra VII was the daughter of Cleopatra V Tryphaena as well). Cleopatra V ruled as co-regent with Ptolemy XII (Auletes) from 80–69 B.C. but was removed as co-regent sometime in 69 B.C. Some scholars think that Cleopatra V's disappearance from the ruling record in 69 B.C. perhaps points to her dying in childbirth. The supposition that she died in 69 B.C. seems to hinge on the idea that the Cleopatra Tryphaena, who was co-regent with Berenice IV, was not Cleopatra V but a purported daughter of hers, called "Cleopatra VI Tryphaena." No evidence exists for this purported daughter, however; since the numbering system of the Ptolemies is a modern invention, differentiating between people with the same name—especially when epithets are left out, or when there is more than one person with the same epithet—makes it difficult or even impossible to discern the relationship. This chart and the accompanying notes do not support the existence of a supposed daughter and namesake of Cleopatra V Tryphaena. In ca. 58 B.C., along with her eldest daughter Berenice IV, Cleopatra V Tryphaena deposed her husband Ptolemy XII (Auletes), but she died the next year.

17. **Berenice III** (also called Cleopatra Berenice) was the daughter of Ptolemy IX (Soter II) and Cleopatra V Selene. First she married her uncle, Ptolemy X (Alexander I), by whom she had Cleopatra V Tryphaena. Second, Berenice III married her cousin Ptolemy XI (Alexander II), but she was murdered by him a few months later. Berenice III ruled as co-regent with her first husband from 101–88 B.C. and was sole ruler upon her father's death for about five months, from December 81 B.C. to approximately April 80 B.C. Berenice III was apparently a popular ruler; after her death, a mob of Alexandrians killed her widower and murderer, Ptolemy XI (Alexander II), in retribution. Ptolemy XII (Auletes) then came to the throne.

18. **Ptolemy XI (Alexander II)** was the son of Ptolemy X (Alexander I), most likely by his wife-sister Cleopatra Selene. Ptolemy XI married Berenice III—the daughter of Ptolemy IX (Soter II)—who had formerly been married to his father, Ptolemy X. However, Ptolemy XI (Alexander II) murdered Berenice III after about 19 days of joint rule because she insisted on remaining the sole ruler. Soon thereafter, a mob of Alexandrians murdered Ptolemy XI (Alexander II) to avenge the murder of the popular queen, Berenice III. Ptolemy XII (Auletes) then succeeded Ptolemy XI (Alexander II) to the throne.

19. **Berenice IV** was the daughter of Ptolemy XII (Auletes) and Cleopatra V Tryphaena. According to Chris Bennett, she married first Seleucus Kybiosaktes, whom Bennett identified as the second son of the Seleucid king Antiochus X (Eusebes) and Cleopatra V Selene ("Ptolemaic Dynasty"). [This Seleucus Kybiosaktes is said by at least one ancient writer to have "claimed" to have been a Seleucid, although which Seleucid he claimed to be is unknown. One scholar has suggested that this Seleucus should be identified with Seleucus VII (Philometor).] Whoever Berenice IV's first husband actually was, their marriage did not last long because he died soon after the wedding. Berenice IV's second marriage was to Archelaus, a high priest of the Ancient Roman war goddess Bellona. This marriage was short-lived as well, ending with Archelaus' death in battle against the governor of Syria only six months after they married. Berenice IV had no known children. Along with her mother (Cleopatra V Tryphaena), Berenice IV deposed her father Ptolemy XII (Auletes) in ca. 58 B.C. After her mother's death the following year (57 B.C.), Berenice IV reigned alone, ca. 57–55 B.C., until the governor of (Roman) Syria, Aulus Gabinius, deposed her and restored her father (Ptolemy XII). Soon thereafter, Ptolemy XII (Auletes) had his daughter Berenice IV and her followers executed.

20. **Ptolemy XIII (Theos Philopator)** was the son of Ptolemy XII (Auletes) and Cleopatra V Tryphaena. Beginning in 51 B.C., he was co-regent with his sister Cleopatra VII Philopator. In 48 B.C., Ptolemy XIII expelled his sister (Cleopatra VII) from Egypt but was reconciled to her by the efforts of Julius Caesar. After the reconciliation, Ptolemy XIII (Theos Philopator) and Cleopatra VII Philopator were married. A few months later, however, Ptolemy XIII joined with his sister Arsinoe IV to depose Cleopatra VII. In 47 B.C., Ptolemy XIII (Theos Philopator) was drowned while crossing the Nile on the orders of palace insiders who sought to gain favor with Julius Caesar.

21. **Cleopatra VII Philopator**—the most famous of all the Cleopatras and the one immortalized in Shakespeare's play *Antony and Cleopatra*—was

the daughter of Ptolemy XII (Auletes) and Cleopatra V Tryphaena and the sister of Ptolemy XIII (Theos Philopator), with whom she initially co-ruled. Cleopatra VII had a liaison with Julius Caesar, resulting in one son, Ptolemy XV (Caesarion). In ca. 48 B.C., she married her brother Ptolemy XIII (Theos Philopator), but there were no children of this union. She also married her other brother, Ptolemy XIV (Philopator), but this union was childless as well. Cleopatra either married or had a liaison with Mark Antony, which resulted in three children: Alexander Helios, his twin sister Cleopatra Selene II, and Ptolemy XVI (Philadelphus). Of these children, only Cleopatra Selene left descendants. Cleopatra VII initially ruled as co-regent with her brother Ptolemy XIII (Theos Philopator) but was deposed by him and expelled ca. 48 B.C. Julius Caesar aided Cleopatra's successful attempt to regain the throne. Soon after her readmission as co-regent, she and her brother Ptolemy XIII (Theos Philopator) were married. After Ptolemy XIII's death in 47 B.C., she ruled alongside her brother Ptolemy XIV (Philopator) and then alongside her son Ptolemy XV (Caesarion), ca. 43–30 B.C. Mark Antony, the triumvir of the Roman Republic, granted Cleopatra the rule of territories in Cilicia, Phoenicia, and Syria. Their children were also gifted other lands as well—Alexander Helios received the lands of Armenia and the lands east of the Euphrates; Ptolemy XVI (Philadelphus) received the lands west of the Euphrates; and Cleopatra Selene II received Cyrene (Joyce Tyldesley, "Cleopatra," *Encyclopedia Britannica*, https://www.britannica.com/biography/Cleopatra-queen-of-Egypt). War between Octavian (Julius Caesar's successor) and Mark Antony and Cleopatra ended in victory for Octavian and with Antony and Cleopatra committing suicide in Alexandria in 30 B.C. With Cleopatra VII's death, Egypt became formally annexed to the Roman Empire.

22. For details about Julius Caesar, see chart "**Supplement 10**: The Roman Emperors."

SUPPLEMENT 7: THE SELEUCIDS AND THE SELEUCID DYNASTY[1]

Approximate Dating: Seleucid Dynasty from 321–63 B.C;[2] the Seleucids, centered in Antioch of Syria, ruled Palestine ca. 198–167 B.C.[3]

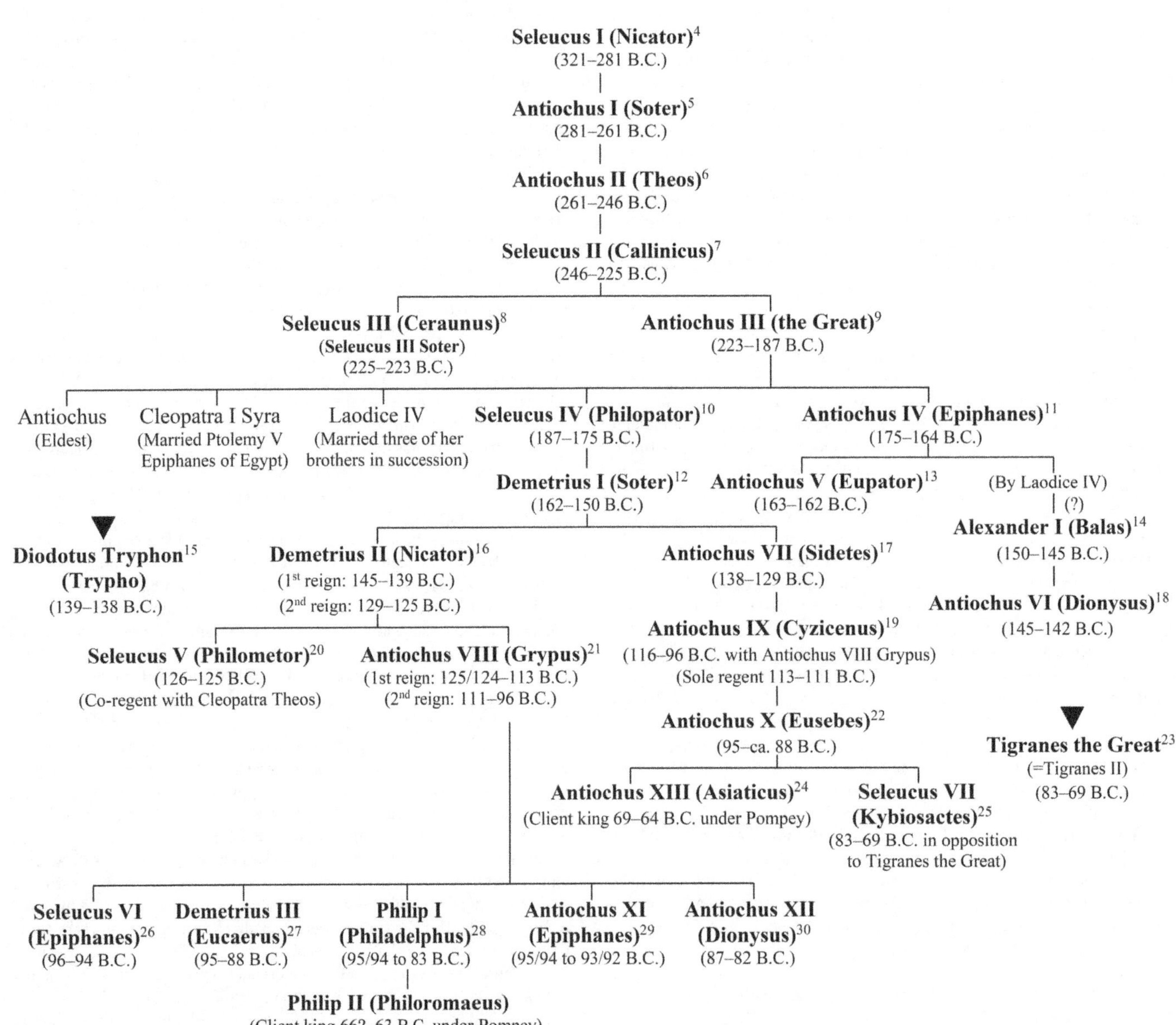

LEGEND:

 : Line of descent from father to son

▼ : Successor is not related to the previous king

Notes

1. Extra-biblical references included: *Jewish Antiquities* in *The Complete Works of Josephus*, trans William Whiston, commentary Paul L. Maier (Grand Rapids: Kregel, 1999); Appian, *The Syrian Wars*, trans. by Horace White, archived at https://www.livius.org; James R. Mueller, Katharine Doob Sakenfeld, and M. Jack Suggs, *The Oxford Study Bible: Revised English Bible with the Apocrypha* (New York: Oxford University Press, 1992); Lucian Farrar, Jr., *The Book of Daniel: The Most High Rules* (Tulsa, OK: James Kay, 2015); Austin et al., eds., *The Cambridge Ancient History: Volume VIII: Rome and the Mediterranean to 133 B.C.*, 2nd ed. (Cambridge: Cambridge University Press, 1992); Polybius, *The Histories*, trans. Robin Waterfield, intro. Brian McGing (New York: Oxford University Press, 2010); Michel Austin, *The Hellenistic World from Alexander to the Roman Conquest (A Selection of Ancient Sources in Translation)*, 2nd augmented ed. (Cambridge: Cambridge University Press, 2006); Eusebius *Chronicle/Chronicon* http://www.attalus.org/translate/eusebius.html; Diodorus Siculus, *Bibliotheca Historica, Books 1–32*, trans. Charles Henry Oldfather, C. Bradford Welles et al., LacusCurtius, https://penelope.uchicago.edu/Thayer/E/Roman/Texts/Diodorus_Siculus/home.html; Diodorus Siculus, *Bibliotheca Historica, Books 33–40*, trans. G. Booth, F. Hoefer, and Andrew Smith, http://www.attalus.org/info/diodorus.html; Justin/Justinus, *Epitome of Pompeius Trogus' Philippic Histories (Books 37-39)*, trans. Rev. J.S.Watson, http://www.attalus.org/translate/justin6.html. Online source: Chris Bennett, "Ptolemaic Dynasty," https://www.livius.org (2001–2013), hosted and modified by David Instone-Brewer through Tyndale House: http://www.instonebrewer.com/TyndaleSites/Egypt/ptolemies/ptolemies.htm (including Ptolemaic Chronology and Genealogy). For references to the high priests, see charts "**Supplement 2**: The High Priests of Israel" and/or "**Supplement 8**: The Maccabees and the Hasmonean Dynasty." For references to Ptolemaic rulers, see chart "**Supplement 6**: The Ptolemies and the Ptolemaic Dynasty."

2. After Alexander the Great's death in 323 B.C., Seleucus I (Nicator) was assigned the satrap of Babylon in 321 B.C., although the origin of the Seleucid Dynasty traditionally dates to ca. 312 B.C. (see note 4). After 114/113 B.C., the Seleucid dynasty was divided into two branches, one in the south and one in the north; the regnal dates for kings after that are approximate.

3. The Seleucid era began in October 312 B.C. (according to the Macedonian calendar) or April 311 B.C. (according to the Babylonian calendar; Austin, *The Cambridge Ancient History,* 89). The genealogy is given for the entire Seleucid Dynasty, ca. 312–63 B.C., but the notes specifically discuss in more detail the Seleucids who ruled over Palestine (198–167 B.C.). In general, the regnal dates follow the dating for the Seleucid Kings of the Maccabean-Hasmonean Period in the *NIV Study Bible* [Kenneth L. Barker, ed. *The NIV Study Bible* (Grand Rapids: Zondervan, 2020), 1624, based on Moisés Silva, *The Zondervan Encyclopedia of the Bible*, vol. 4 (Grand Rapids: Zondervan, 2009), 13]. Also consulted was the table of the "Ptolemies and Seleucids" listing the Seleucid rulers from Seleucus I (Nicator) through Demetrius I (Soter); John H. Walton and Craig S. Kenner, eds., *NIV Cultural Backgrounds Study Bible* (Grand Rapids: Zondervan, 2016), 1446.

4. **Seleucus I (Nicator)**, who ruled 321–281 B.C., was the son of Laodice and Antiochus, a Macedonian general who fought alongside Philip II of Macedonia, the father of Alexander the Great. Following Alexander the Great's death in 323 B.C., the Macedonian generals fought for dominance over Alexander's vast empire. The war between the generals, known as the War of the Diadochi, resulted in the empire being split into Greco-Macedonian kingdoms, the largest of which was the Seleucid Empire, founded by Seleucus I (Nicator). In 324 B.C., Seleucus married Apama I, the daughter of the Bactrian leader, Spitamenes, in a mass wedding ceremony ordered by Alexander, and they had three children: Antiochus I (Soter), who later inherited the Seleucid throne; Achaeus; and a daughter also called Apama. Seleucus I (Nicator) served as a general under Perdiccas (the Macedonian regent and commander of the imperial army after Alexander's death). Later, Seleucus I (Nicator) was among those who helped to assassinate Perdiccas during a campaign against Ptolemy I (Soter; 323–285 B.C.). Seleucus I (Nicator) was next given the satrapy of Babylonia in 321 B.C.—this chart dates Seleucus I's rule to this appointment. In 315 B.C., he was driven out of his satrapy by Antigonus I Monophthalmus (who controlled Asia Minor and wanted to re-unite Alexander's empire), but three years later Seleucus I returned and retook his territory; thus, the Seleucid Empire would later assign its origin to the year 312 B.C. Seleucus I embarked on a series of campaigns, ending in India, where he was given approximately 500 war elephants. In 305 B.C., Seleucus adopted the title *basileus,* or king. Seleucus I (Nicator), Ptolemy I (Soter), and two others allied together to defeat Antigonus I Monophthalmus at Ipsus in 301 B.C. Seleucus I (Nicator) was to be awarded the Levant, but Ptolemy I (Soter) took control before Seleucus I could. Seleucus did not pursue the matter, but Ptolemy's actions turned out to be the root cause of later wars between the Seleucids and the Ptolemies. Seleucus I (Nicator) was murdered in 281 B.C. by Ptolemy Ceraunus, the son of Ptolemy I (Soter), while in Greece on campaign (Rolf Strootman, "Seleucus,' *Encyclopædia Iranica*, online edition, 2015, available at http://www.iranicaonline.org/articles/seleucid-kings#SeleucusI and Rolf Strootman, "Seleucid Empire," *Encyclopædia Iranica*, online edition, 2015, available at http://www.iranicaonline.org/articles/seleucid-empire).

5. **Antiochus I (Soter)**, who ruled 281–261 B.C., was the firstborn son of Seleucus I (Nicator) and Apama I. He was born ca. 324 B.C. and is mentioned in various Babylonian Chronicles. Apparently, Antiochus I fell in love with his stepmother, Stratonice I (the daughter of Demetrius I Poliorcetes, king of Macedonia, 294–288 B.C.), who had married his father as part of an alliance with Demetrius I. His unrequited love affected his health so severely, says the *Encyclopaedia Britannica*, that Seleucus I (his father) gave Stratonice to Antiochus I Soter as his wife (Jakob Seibert, "Seleucus I Nicator," *Encyclopedia Britannica*, https://www.britannica.com/biography/Seleucus-I-Nicator; see also Appian, *The Syrian Wars*, 12.59-60). The *Encyclopaedia Iranica* dismisses the love element as folklore but does maintain that Antiochus married Stratonice before ascending the throne (D.Bing and J.Sievers, "Antiochus," *Encyclopaedia Iranica*, II/2, 125–35, https://www.iranicaonline.org/articles/antiochus-1--thirteen-kings-of-the-seleucid-dynasty#A01). In 292/291 B.C., Antiochus I (Soter) ruled jointly with his father and was entrusted with Babylonia and other Iranian lands. During the years of joint rule, Antiochus I oversaw the satrapies that were east of the Euphrates and remained in Bactria as a co-ruler. When his father, Seleucus I (Nicator), was assassinated in 281 B.C., Antiochus I (Soter) began ruling over the entire realm but was immediately confronted by revolts in Syria, independence movements in Anatolia, and a war headed by Antigonus II Gonatas, who ruled the Greek city-states and Macedonia. A peace treaty between Antiochus I (Soter) and Antigonus II Gonatas involved Antigonus marrying Antiochus' half-sister, Phila (the daughter of Seleucus I Nicator and Stratonice). Later wars with Egypt cost the Seleucid Empire the regions of Phoenicia and Asia Minor, and unrest in the far eastern parts of the empire weakened Seleucid control over that area. Antiochus I (Soter) had one of his sons, Seleucus, executed on suspicion of treason. Antiochus I (Soter) was then succeeded by his son Antiochus II (Theos) in 261 B.C.

6. **Antiochus II (Theos)**, who ruled 261–246 B.C., was the son of Antiochus I (Soter) and Stratonice I. He was born ca. 286 B.C. and died in 246 B.C. The Second Syrian War (260–253 B.C.) was fought during his reign. The peace treaty called for the marriage of Berenice (Phernephorus), the daughter Ptolemy II (Philadelphus), to Antiochus II (Theos), who repudiated his first wife, Laodice I (by whom he had two sons and three daughters). Antiochus II (Theos) and Berenice had a son named Antiochus, but after Ptolemy II (Philadelphus) died, Antiochus II (Theos) left Berenice to go back to his first wife Laodice ("Antiochus"). In *The Syrian Wars*, Appian relates that Antiochus II was poisoned by Laodice, who also killed Berenice (Phernephorus) and her son Antiochus (Appian, *The Syrian Wars* 13.65). In retaliation, Ptolemy III (Euergetes) sought revenge for the deaths of his sister and nephew, which led to the Third Syrian War (246–241 B.C.). According to the *NIV Study Bible*, Antiochus II (Theos) is "the king of the North" in **Daniel 11:6** who married "the daughter [Berenice Phernephorus] of the king of the South [Ptolemy II Philadelphus, 285–246 B.C.]." The passage goes on to say that "she [Berenice] will not retain her power, and he [Antiochus II (Theos)] and his power will not last. In those days she will be betrayed, together with the royal escort and her father and the one who supported her" (**Daniel 11:6**; cf. Farrar, *Book of Daniel,* 102).

7. **Seleucus II (Callinicus)**, who ruled 246–225 B.C., was the son of Antiochus II (Theos) and his first wife, Laodice I. Seleucus II (Callinicus)

married his niece Laodice II (who was the mother of the future kings Seleucus II Ceranunus and Antiochus III the Great). At the beginning of his reign, contention over the succession—which was directly related to the polygamy practiced by previous rulers—escalated into the Third Syrian War (246–241 B.C.). During the reign of Seleucus II (Callinicus), Ptolemy III (Euergetes) of Egypt (246–222 B.C.) invaded the heart of Seleucid territory because Antiochus II (Theos)'s second wife, Berenice (Phernephorus), and her son Antiochus were murdered. As their closest male kin, Ptolemy III (Euergetes) challenged Seleucus II (Callinicus) for control. According to the *NIV Study Bible*, Kenneth Barker, ed. (Grand Rapids: Zondervan, 2020) 1481, Seleucus II (Callinicus) is the "king of the North" in **Daniel 11:7–10**. In 243 B.C. Callinicus attempted to gain control of southern Syria and Palestine but was unsuccessful, eventually losing territory. "His sons [the future kings Seleucus III Ceraunus and Antiochus III the Great] will prepare for war and assemble a great army, which will sweep on like an irresistible flood" (**Daniel 11:10**). According to the *Encyclopaedia Iranica*, the *Third Syrian War* was "unevenly documented" (Rolf Strootman, "Seleucus," *Encyclopædia Iranica*, online edition, 2015, https://www.iranicaonline.org/articles/seleucus-kings#SeleucusII). While the Seleucid court and the army were in favor of Seleucus II's claim, the governor of Ephesus sided with Ptolemy III (Euergetes) of Egypt, giving him control of the area. Queen Laodice (the first wife of Antiochus II Theos) was executed under suspicion of having killed Berenice (Phernephorus) and her son. Ptolemy III (Euergetes) subsequently conquered much of Seleucid territory. A propaganda piece says that Ptolemy III (Euergetes) conquered Mesopotamia, Persia, Babylonia, Elam, and Media, along with other territories. The *Encyclopaedia Iranica* says that part of this claim is exaggerated, but a Babylonian Chronicle does state that an Egyptian king attacked the Seleucid capital, Seleucia (ibid.). The Third Syrian war ended in 241 B.C.; Ptolemy III (Euergetes) retained control of the territory he had conquered in Asia Minor, as well as Seleucia, but Antiochus III the Great reclaimed them for the Seleucids (cf. **Daniel 11:9**). Seleucus II (Callinicus) next fought against his brother Antiochus Hierax, who had governed Asia Minor while Seleucus II had been fighting Ptolemy III (Euergetes). Antiochus Hierax set himself up as an independent king in 242/241 B.C. In 236 B.C., after a few years of war, Seleucus II made peace with his brother. However, the battles between the two brothers encouraged unrest and quests for independence in the satrapies. The reign of Seleucus II (Callinicus) highlighted two weaknesses of the Seleucid Empire: internal familial/dynastic friction and the ambition of the outer satrapies. Seleucus II died in 225 B.C. after falling from his horse and was succeeded by his oldest son, Seleucus III (Ceraunus).

8. **Seleucus III Ceraunus**—also called **Seleucus III (Soter)**—ruled from 225–223 B.C. He was the eldest son of Seleucus II (Callinicus) and Laodice II. He sought to regain the lands in Asia Minor that had been lost during his father's reign. Appian's *The Syrian Wars* states that Seleucus III (Ceraunus) was poisoned by some members of the court because he was unpopular and sickly (14.66). He ruled for only three years and was then succeeded by his younger brother, Antiochus III the Great.

9. **Antiochus III the Great**, who ruled 223–187 B.C., was the younger son of Seleucus II (Callinicus) and Laodice II. He was born in ca. 242 B.C. and succeeded his older brother Seleucus III (Ceraunus) to the throne. The *Encyclopaedia Britannica* states that Antiochus III fought Ptolemy IV (Philopator) in Syria in 217 B.C.; Antiochus defeated one side of the army, but his infantry was defeated. Antiochus III was forced to relinquish his conquests—Lebanon, Palestine, and Phoenicia—except for Seleucia in Pieria (Hans Volkmann, "Antiochus III the Great." *Encyclopedia Britannica*, https://www.britannica.com/biography/Antiochus-III-the-Great). Josephus says that the Jews "received" Antiochus III into Jerusalem (Josephus, *Jewish Antiquities* 12.3.3; cf. **Daniel 11:15–16**) and gave him and his army—including the elephants—provisions. The Jews also helped him besiege the citadel's garrison. In thanks, Antiochus III the Great brought back those Jews who had been "scattered abroad" (ibid.). He also gave them 20,000 pieces of silver, plus large quantities of flour, wheat, and salt, and pledged to finish the temple. Furthermore, he exempted the "senate, and the priests, and the scribes of the temple, and the sacred singers" from certain taxes (ibid.). Additionally, he exempted Jerusalem's inhabitants from taxes for three years, as well as those Jews who returned within those three years. Subsequently, the inhabitants were to be exempted from a third of their taxes for an unspecified amount of time. Furthermore, Antiochus III released the Jewish slaves and their children from bondage. He also enacted strict rules regarding the temple and Jerusalem, forbidding foreigners from entering the temple grounds unless they had purified themselves. He also forbid unclean animal meat, skins, and even live animals from entering the city, authorizing only the sacrifices permitted by Jewish law. Any transgression was to result in a fine of 3000 silver drachmas to be paid to the priests. Antiochus also instructed his general Zenxis to move 2000 Jews from "Mesopotamia and Babylon" to safety, with the promise "that they shall be permitted to use their own laws" (Josephus, *Jewish Antiquities* 12.3.4). The general was instructed to give the Jews land for housing and farming. The Jews were not to pay taxes on their crops for ten years and were allotted wheat for their servants until they were able to produce crops. Antiochus' last charge to the general was for him to "take care likewise of that nation, as far as thou art able, that they may not have any disturbance given them by any one" (*Jewish Antiquities* 12.5.3–4). Antiochus III the Great was married in 222 B.C. to Laodice III (the daughter of Mithradates II of Pontus), who was his first cousin by mutual descent from Antiochus II (Theos) [i.e., Laodice's mother was sister to Seleucus II (Callinicus), who was Antiochus III's father]. The daughter of Antiochus III the Great, Cleopatra I of Syra, was married to Ptolemy V (Epiphanes) as part of an alliance with the Hellenistic Egyptian ruler. Antiochus III's daughter Laodice IV married her three brothers in succession: (1) Antiochus, the eldest, who was executed on suspicion of treason; (2) Seleucus IV (Philopator), who succeeded their father; and (3) Antiochus IV (Epiphanes). According to the *NIV Study Bible*, Kenneth Barker, ed. (Grand Rapids: Zondervan, 2020) 1482, Antiochus III the Great is "the king of the North" in **Daniel 11:11, 13**. Aside from his military exploits—which included successfully rebuilding the eastern Seleucid Empire, unsuccessfully trying to regain and retain power in Greece and Asia Minor, and effectively turning Egypt into a Seleucid protectorate—Antiochus III also made administrative reforms to the Seleucid Empire, established a "ruler cult" that viewed him and his wife as divine, and allied himself with neighboring countries by marrying his daughters to their princes. Antiochus III died on July 3/4, 187 B.C., while plundering the temple of Bel in Iran.

10. **Seleucus IV (Philopator)**, who ruled 187–175 B.C., was the son of Antiochus III the Great and Laodice III. He married his sister Laodice IV and they had three children: two sons, Antiochus and Demetrius I (Soter), and a daughter, Laodice V. According to the *Encyclopaedia Iranica*, his reign was poorly documented (Rolf Strootman, "Seleucus," *Encyclopædia Iranica*, online edition, 2015, https://www.iranicaonline.org/articles/seleucus-kings#SeleucusIV). Seleucus IV became the heir to the empire after the death of his older brother Antiochus. Seleucus IV (Philopator) attempted to regain western territories through alliances with the Achaean League in Greece and by marrying his daughter Laodice V to the Macedonian king Perseus. Seleucus IV's empire—though not so vast as his father's had been before warring with Rome—included Syria (which included Palestine and Cilicia), Babylonia, Mesopotamia, Persia, and Media. Seleucus IV (Philopator) charged his finance minister Heliodorus with collecting revenue from the temple—the event is alluded to in **Daniel 11:20:** "His successor will send out a tax collector to maintain the royal splendor. In a few years, however, he will be destroyed, yet not in anger or in battle." The full tale is related in *II Maccabees* 3:2–3, 9–40: a temple official, Simon of the tribe of Bilgah (Benjamin), told Apollonius, the governor of Greater Syria, that the temple treasury had unaccountable amounts of money, and since there was so much of it, it should be given to Seleucus IV. Apollonius told Seleucus IV, who, in turn, sent Heliodorus to retrieve the money. When Heliodorus arrived at the temple, the high priest Onias III (185–175/173 B.C.) said that Simon had lied: the treasury only had 30,000 pounds of silver and 15,000 pounds of gold, and that it was impossible for someone to be allowed to take the money. Heliodorus, however, insisted that he would be taking the money for Seleucus IV, causing the people of Jerusalem to plead for God's help and protection. Heliodorus' attempts were thwarted and he was severely injured; after some of Heliodorus' men requested that the high priest pray for Heliodorus, Onias III offered a sacrifice on Heliodorus' behalf. Heliodorus was then told to return to Seleucus IV and to tell everyone of God's immense power. Heliodorus' assignment to collect revenue is confirmed by the Heliodorus Stele (see the commentary at Daniel 11:20 in the *NIV Cultural Backgrounds Study Bible* and Farrar, *The Book of Daniel*, 104). Seleucus IV (Philopator) was assassinated by Heliodorus, who was possibly working in collusion with Seleucus IV's younger brother, the future king Antiochus IV (Epiphanes). Seleucus IV was ostensibly succeeded by his young son Antiochus, although Antiochus IV (Epiphanes) married Seleucus' widow (Laodice IV), assumed the regency, and had his nephew (Antiochus) killed five years later. Another son of Seleucus IV, Demetrius I (Soter), eventually become king in 162 B.C. after killing Antiochus IV's young successor, Antiochus V (Eupator).

11. **Antiochus IV (Epiphanes)**, who ruled 175–164 B.C., was the son of Antiochus III the Great and Laodice III (the daughter of Mithradates II of

Pontus). He was born ca. 215 B.C. *The NIV Study Bible* says that Antiochus IV was not the rightful successor to the Seleucid throne; the notes for **Daniel 8:23–25** say that Antiochus IV rose to power "by intrigue and deceit." The commentary for **Daniel 8:25** relates that Antiochus IV called himself Epiphanes, which means "God manifest." However, others referred to him as Epimanes, meaning "madman," because of his erratic behavior (see Polybius, *Histories* 26.1–14; Barker, *The NIV Study Bible,* 1478).

After Heliodorus killed Antiochus IV's brother Seleucus IV (Philopator), Antiochus IV (Epiphanes) killed Heliodorus and then usurped the throne for himself. He married Laodice IV—who was likely the widow of Seleucus IV (Philopator), as well as their sister—and also murdered his nephew, another Antiochus. Antiochus IV (Epiphanes) and Laodice IV had a son, Antiochus V (Eupator), and a daughter, Laodice VI. Antiochus IV (Epiphanes) invaded Egypt twice, but an ultimatum issued by the Romans caused him to give up Egypt.

Antiochus IV's oppression of the Jews led to the Maccabean revolt (167–160 B.C.); see chart "**Supplement 8**: The Maccabees and the Hasmonean Dynasty." *The NIV Study Bible* relates that Antiochus IV's oppression of the Jews occurred in the last few years of his reign, ca. 168–164 B.C. (Barker, *NIV Study Bible,* 1476). At the beginning, Antiochus IV (Epiphanes) issued an edict that required all his subjects to "become one people" (i.e., forcing them to reject their unique Jewish culture in favor of a Hellenistic one). Many Jewish acts of worship were changed or completely discarded, such as forbidding sacrifices and offerings in the temple. In place of Sabbath days and feast days, pagan practices were instituted. Pigs and other unclean animals were now to be offered as sacrifices, thereby completely disregarding the Mosaic Law's teachings on acceptable sacrifices. Also, baby boys were not to be circumcised; furthermore, those who performed circumcision, as well as the babies who were circumcised and their families, were killed (*I Maccabees* 1:41–48, 60–61). In short, the Jews "had to make themselves in every way abominable, unclean, and profane, and so forget the law and change all their statutes" (*I Maccabees* 1:48–49). In essence, disobeying any royal decree resulted in death (*I Maccabees* 1:50). While some Jews apparently welcomed some of these cultural changes (*I Maccabees* 1:11–15, 43, 52), many Jews resisted (*I Maccabees* 1:62–63). Antiochus IV (Epiphanes) also pillaged the temple and carried off "the gold altar, the lampstand with all its fittings, the table of the Bread of the Presence, the libation cups and bowls, the gold censers, the curtain, and the garlands . . . [He] seized the silver and gold, the precious vessels, and whatever secret treasures he found, and carried them all away when he left for his own country" (*I Maccabees* 1:21–24). In addition, all the scrolls that could be found containing the law were thrown onto the altar and burned.

The notes to *The Oxford Study Bible, Revised English Bible with the Apocrypha*, ed. M. Jack Suggs (New York: Oxford University Press, 1992) relate that Antiochus IV (Epiphanes) built a pagan altar to Zeus on the temple's altar. Anyone found possessing a copy of the law or otherwise "conforming" to the Jewish law was sentenced to death (*I Maccabees* 1:54–57). These egregious offenses against the law of the Lord infuriated Mattathias Maccabeus, who then led the Maccabean revolt against the increased Hellenization and pagan practices being forced upon the Jews. Mattathias and his sons and compatriots destroyed the pagan altars and circumcised all the uncircumcised boys they could find in Israel (*I Maccabees* 2:45–46). Antiochus IV (Epiphanes)'s mockery and ban of Jewish observances is also recounted by Josephus in *Jewish Antiquities* 12.5.4; Josephus says that Antiochus IV sacrificed pigs on the altar he had made. Josephus also describes the torture that uncompliant Jews were subjected to, such as being whipped with rods, torn to pieces, crucified, and strangled. Antiochus IV (Epiphanes) is the "little horn" described in **Daniel 8:9** "which started small but grew in power to the south and to the east and toward the Beautiful Land [Palestine]." The commentary for **Daniel 8:9–12** in the *NIV Study Bible* asserts that Antiochus IV was "a type of the even more ruthless beast of the last days (the antichrist)" (Barker, the *NIV Study Bible,* 1476). **Daniel 8:11** predicts the egotistical actions of Antiochus IV (Epiphanes): the little horn "set itself up to be as great as the commander of the army of the Lord; it took away the daily sacrifice from the Lord, and his sanctuary was thrown down." After the death of his father (Mattathias), Judas Maccabeus took over the Jewish resistance; Judas' army eventually recaptured Jerusalem and rededicated the temple in December 165 B.C. The rededication of the temple is commemorated in the Festival of Hanukkah (cf. **John 10:22**). Antiochus IV's draconian rule is also described in **Daniel 11:21–45**. This passage describes Antiochus IV as "a contemptible person" who "will do as he pleases. He will exalt and magnify himself above every god and will say unheard-of things against the God of gods" (**Daniel 11:21, 36**).

According to Polybius and Appian, Antiochus IV (Epiphanes) died of an unknown disease. The books of the Maccabees suggest that his death came after an unsuccessful attempt (or intention) to rob the temple of Diana in Elymais (Elam) Persia, although Josephus says that his death more likely came from his sacrilegious plundering of the temple at Jerusalem (*Jewish Antiquities* 12.9.1). The *Encyclopaedia Iranica* dismisses these latter accounts as legendary (D.Bing and J.Sievers, "Antiochus," *Encyclopaedia Iranica*, II/2, 125–35, https://www.iranicaonline.org/articles/antiochus-1--thirteen-kings-of-the-seleucid-dynasty#A04). But Josephus does state that Antiochus IV "fell into a distemper" because of his "anxiety" and was upset over being run out of Elymais. The distemper "lasted a great while, and as his pains increased . . . at length he perceived he should die" (*Jewish Antiquities* 12.9.1). Antiochus IV seems to have died in the latter half of 164 B.C., which Josephus correlates to "the hundred forty and ninth year" of the Seleucid Empire (*Jewish Antiquities* 12.9.2).

12. **Demetrius I (Soter)**, who ruled 162–150 B.C. (or possibly 161–150 B.C.), was the son of Seleucus IV (Philopator) and Laodice IV; he was born ca. 187 B.C. He was sent to Rome as a hostage during his father's reign. But in 175 B.C., while Demetrius was still in Rome, his father died, and Demetrius' uncle Antiochus IV (Epiphanes) usurped the throne. After Antiochus IV's death in 164 B.C., Demetrius was finally able to escape Rome in 162 B.C. with the help of the Greek historian Polybius (cf. Polybius, *Histories,* 31.IV.11–15). Demetrius I (Soter) then returned to Syria, defeated the rebel general Timarchus, and was recognized by the Roman Senate as king in place of his nephew Antiochus V (Eupator), who was murdered along with his guardian Lysias. Judas Maccabee was killed in 160 B.C. at the Battle of Elasa while fighting Demetrius' western governor-general Bacchides (cf. *I Maccabees* 9:1–22; *Jewish Antiquities* 12.10–11). Josephus recounts a letter sent from Demetrius I (Soter) to Jonathan Maccabee/"Apphus" (then the ruler, 161–143/142 B.C.) in which he released the Jews from their tax liabilities, freed the enslaved and captive Jews in the Seleucid Empire, promised that the Jews would be able to observe their laws and holidays without interference, and allowed Jewish men to enlist in his army at the same rate of pay as the Gentiles (*Jewish Antiquities* 13.2.3). Demetrius I himself died in battle in 150 B.C. while fighting Alexander I (Balas), who claimed to be a son of Antiochus IV (Epiphanes).

13. **Antiochus V (Eupator)**, who ruled 163–162 B.C., was the son of Antiochus IV (Epiphanes) and Laodice IV. He was born in ca. 172 B.C. and succeeded his father at the young age of about nine. Antiochus IV had left the general Lysias in charge of Syria, and Lysias was now tasked with the guardianship of the young king, Antiochus V (Eupator; cf. *Jewish Antiquities* 12.7.2; 12.9.2). The Romans believed it was better for Syria to be ruled by a young boy and his regent than by the rightful heir Demetrius I (Soter), the son of Seleucus IV (Philopator), so they retained Demetrius I (Soter) as a hostage (cf. Polybius, *Histories,* 31.IV.11). The Maccabean Revolt continued to foment in Judea, and Lysias advised Antiochus V (Eupator) to make peace with the Jews upon learning that the other half of the Seleucid army was returning to Syria under Antiochus IV's confidant Philip. The Jews were receptive to the proffered peace, but when Antiochus V (Eupator) saw how fortified Jerusalem was, he broke his promise and ordered his troops to tear down the walls of Jerusalem. Josephus also says that Antiochus V (Eupator) took Onias (called Menalaus) the high priest back to Syria with him (*Jewish Antiquities* 12.9.7). In 162 B.C., Demetrius I (Soter) was able to escape Rome with help from the Greek historian Polybius; he returned to Syria, where he was proclaimed king. He then murdered Antiochus V (Eupator) and Lysias.

14. **Alexander I (Balas)**—also called Alexander Epiphanes—ruled 150–145 B.C. He claimed to be the son of Antiochus IV (Epiphanes). The Greek historians Polybius and Diodorus did not believe Alexander's claim (cf. Polybius, *Histories*, 33.IX.18; Diodorus, *Bibliotheca Historica* 31.32a), but Josephus did not object to it, since he referred to Alexander I (Balas) as the son of Antiochus IV (Epiphanes) (cf. *Jewish Antiquities* 13.2.1 and Josephus, *Jewish Antiquities*, trans. William Whiston, commentary Paul L. Maier [Grand Rapids: Kregel, 1999], 13.2.1, n 1). Alexander's claim was supported by the Roman Senate due to the craftiness (or "charlatanry," according to Polybius) of his guardian Heracleides. Alexander I (Balas) was also supported by Ptolemy VI (Philometor) of Egypt and by Jonathan Maccabee; the latter committed his support after Alexander I promised Jonathan the high priesthood (cf. *Jewish Antiquities* 13.2.2). Alexander I (Balas) won the Seleucid throne by killing Demetrius I (Soter) in battle in 150 B.C. Alexander I (Balas) then married Cleopatra Thea, the daughter of Ptolemy VI (Philometor), and they had one son, Antiochus VI (Dionysus). Demetrius II (Nicator), the son of Demetrius I (Soter),

led a revolt against Alexander I (Balas); Ptolemy VI (Philometor) switched sides to support Demetrius II (Nicator). Amidst the fighting, Alexander I (Balas) fled to Arabia to join forces with an Arabian ruler named Zabdiel, but there he was killed. Josephus relates that when Zabdiel killed Alexander I, he sent Alexander's head to Ptolemy VI (Philometor; *Jewish Antiquities* 13.4.8). Diodorus, however, states that Alexander I (Balas) was killed by two of his own officers after Demetrius II (Nicator) approved of their plan (*Bibliotheca Historica* 32.9d-10.1). At any rate, Alexander Balas was killed in Arabia by presumed allies and was succeeded by Demetrius II (Nicator).

15. **Diodotus Tryphon (Trypho)**, who ruled 139–138 B.C., was not of Seleucid heritage. He had initially served as a general under the Seleucid ruler Alexander I (Balas), 150–145 B.C. (cf. *1 Maccabees* 11:39). Trypho led a revolt against Demetrius II (Nicator) from 145–139 B.C. and gained control of most of Syria and the Levant. Trypho acted as regent and tutor for Alexander I (Balas)'s young son, the boy-king Antiochus VI (Dionysus), ca. 145–142 B.C. *First Maccabees* 13:31–32 says that "Trypho dealt dishonestly with the young king Antiochus and killed him. He [Trypho] put on the crown of Asia and became king in his place. He [Trypho] brought great disaster on the land." In 143/142 B.C., Trypho killed the high priest Jonathan Apphus (the son of Mattathias Maccabeus) because Apphus supported the young king Antiochus VI (Dionysus; *Jewish Antiquities* 13.6; cf. 13.5–7 for Josephus' discussion of Trypho's rise and fall). After Antiochus VI's death in 142 B.C., Trypho declared himself king. Trypho was the sole ruler of the Seleucid Empire from 139–138 B.C., but he was eventually defeated by Antiochus VII (Sidetes), and Trypho died in 138 B.C. For more on Trypho, see Diodorus' *Bibliotheca Historica* 33.4a,28; Appian's *Syrian Wars* 14.68.

16. **Demetrius II (Nicator)** held two terms: 1st reign: 145–139 B.C. and 2nd reign: 129–125 B.C. He was the son of Demetrius I (Soter), probably by his wife Laodice V. Demetrius II went into exile when his father was killed in 150 B.C. while fighting against Alexander I (Balas), who had usurped the Seleucid throne. Demetrius married Cleopatra Thea, the daughter of Ptolemy VI (Philometor), after Ptolemy dissolved her marriage to Alexander I (Balas). In 147 B.C., Demetrius II returned to Syria, deposed Alexander I (Balas), and retook his rightful throne, earning himself the epithet "Nicator" (Victor) in the process (cf. Appian, *Syrian Wars,* 14.67). Soon after, Alexander Balas' general Diodotus Tryphon (Trypho) proclaimed Alexander's young son, Antiochus VI (Dionysus), king of the Seleucid Empire. Trypho would eventually proclaim himself king after Antiochus VI's demise. Demetrius II (Nicator) confirmed the high priesthood of Jonathan Apphus; later, after Apphus was killed by Trypho, Demetrius II allied himself with Apphus' brother, Simon Thassi (cf. *Jewish Antiquities* 13.4.9). Demetrius II (Nicator)'s recognition of Simon Thassi's high priesthood in 142 B.C. was later held by the Jews to be the *de facto* year of the independence of Judea. In 140 B.C., the Parthians (who were the inhabitants of northeastern Iran) took advantage of the conflict plaguing the Seleucid Empire and invaded. Demetrius II's initial efforts to drive them out were successful; however, he was eventually captured by the Parthians in 139 B.C. While Demetrius II (Nicator) was in captivity, his brother Antiochus VII (Sidetes) ruled the Seleucid Empire. Demetrius II was eventually released from captivity in 129 B.C. and resumed ruling, but the Seleucid Empire was greatly diminished. Furthermore, Demetrius II's earlier rule had been deeply unpopular. He had demobilized most of his army and cut their pay. He also had brutally punished the city of Antioch for supporting Alexander I (Balas), which led to the murder of many Antiochians, a subsequent revolt, and eventually to a large portion of the city burning while Jewish forces restored Demetrius II's rule (*Bibliotheca Historica,* 33.4.2–3; *Jewish Antiquities* 13.5.3). Demetrius II, who was by now married to a Parthian princess, only ruled for four years after his readeption. Ptolemy VIII (Physcon)—also called Ptolemy VIII (Euergetes II), who was the uncle of Demetrius II's first wife Cleopatra Thea—backed a new usurper, Alexander II (Zabinas). Demetrius II (Nicator) fought against Alexander II (Zabinas) but was killed near Damascus. He was then succeeded by his widow Cleopatra Thea, who served as co-regent with their sons Seleucus V (Philometor) and Antiochus VIII (Grypus).

17. **Antiochus VII (Sidetes)**, who ruled 138–129 B.C., was the son of Demetrius I (Soter) and Laodice V and was the brother of Demetrius II (Nicator). Antiochus VII (Sidetes) ruled the Seleucid Empire after defeating the usurper Diodotus Tryphon, who had attempted to seize power after Demetrius II (Nicator) was captured by the Parthians in 139 B.C. After claiming the throne, Antiochus VII (Sidetes) married Cleopatra Thea, the wife of his brother Demetrius II Nicator; they had five children. Antiochus VII then demanded that the Jews acknowledge him as overlord; when they refused, he sent an army to attack them, but the army was refuted. Not deterred, Antiochus VII besieged Jerusalem. Josephus suggests that Antiochus VII attacked Judea because he had forgotten the aid that Simon Thassi the high priest had given him while Antiochus VII (Sidetes) was fighting the usurper Trypho, and also because Antiochus VII (Sidetes) had a "covetous and wicked disposition" (*Jewish Antiquities* 13.7.2–3). Antiochus VII allowed a short truce in the fighting so that the Jews could celebrate the Feast of Tabernacles; this impressed the new high priest John Hyrcanus so much that Hyrcanus sent an embassy to Antiochus to broker peace. Antiochus VII accepted but still razed the walls of Jerusalem (*Jewish Antiquities* 13.8.2–3; cf. Diodorus, *Bibliotheca Historica,* 34/35.1). Josephus adds that Hyrcanus I "opened the sepulcher of [King] David" and gave Antiochus VII (Sidetes) 3,000 talents as part of the settlement (*Jewish Antiquities* 13.8.4). After this, Antiochus VII recognized John Hyrcanus as high priest and refrained from interfering in the Jews' religious practices. Antiochus VII then focused on the rest of his kingdom; he defeated the Parthians in 130 B.C. but was defeated by the Parthians a year later. Josephus and Diodorus, among other classical authors, relate that Antiochus VII (Sidetes) was killed fighting the Parthians, but Appian states that he committed suicide in 129 B.C. after being defeated (*Jewish Antiquities* 13.8.4; *Bibliotheca Historica* 34/35.15–17; *Syrian Wars* 14.68). Antiochus VII was succeeded by his brother Demetrius II (Nicator), who had been released from captivity. Antiochus VII's death resulted in civil war, destroying any hope for a renewed Seleucid Empire.

18. **Antiochus VI (Dionysus)**, who ruled 145–142 B.C., was the son of Alexander I (Balas) and Cleopatra Thea of Egypt (daughter of Ptolemy VI Philometor of Egypt). When his father died in battle, the throne was left to Dionysus, who was still a young child. Dionysus appears to have ruled in name only from 145–142 B.C. under the influence of his tutor and guardian, Diodotus Tryphon (Trypho), who had previously been a general under Alexander I Balas. The Jews initially supported Antiochus VI's rival, Demetrius II (Nicator), but eventually switched their allegiance to Antiochus VI (Dionysus) due to Demetrius' cruelty. Antiochus VI (Dionysus) supported the Jews and confirmed Jonathan Apphus as the high priest and ruler of Judea (Josephus *Jewish Antiquities* 13.5.4). The *Jewish Encyclopedia* states that Antiochus VI's confirmation of Jonathan Apphus and his appointment of Apphus' brother Simon Thassi as the military commander "were . . . as much in the interest of the Jews themselves as of the king, for Demetrius [II Nicator] was foe to both" (Louis Ginzberg, "Antiochus VI," *Jewish Encyclopedia*, https://jewishencyclopedia.com/articles/1591-antiochus-vi). However, the growing power of the Jews alarmed Trypho, who was successfully killed Jonathan Apphus in 143/142 B.C. Trypho then murdered the young king Antiochus VI (Dionysus), who was still under ten years of age. In his *Bibliotheca Historica*, Diodorus relates that "Diodotus, called Tryphon, killed Antiochus [VI Dionysus] son of Alexander [Balas], who was a mere child and was being raised to be king. He then put on the royal diadem, and as the throne was empty, he [Tryphon] proclaimed himself king" (*Bibliotheca Historica* 33.28).

19. **Antiochus IX (Cyzicenus)** was the ruler of the southern branch of the Seleucid kingdom [i.e., after 114/113 B.C., the Seleucid dynasty was divided into two branches; the one in the south was ruled by Antiochus IX (Cyzicenus) and the one in the north was ruled by Antiochus VIII (Grypus).] Cyzicenus, meaning "the Cyzicene," was from Cyzicus, a Greek city in Anatolia (modern-day Turkey). He was the son of Antiochus VII (Sidetes) and Cleopatra Thea, making him the half-brother of Antiochus VIII (Grypus). Antiochus IX revolted against Antiochus VIII (Grypus) in 116/115 B.C. after Grypus had forced their mother to commit suicide—the historian Justinus relates that Grypus made Cleopatra Thea drink a cup of poisoned wine that was meant for him (*Epitome* 39.2.8; cf. Appian, *Syrian Wars* 14.68). The two brothers fought off and on for twenty years despite a treaty in 116 B.C. that entitled Antiochus IX (Cyzicenus) to rule Syria (a major part of the Seleucid Empire). According to Josephus, the Jewish high priest John Hyrcanus I (134–104 B.C.) took advantage of the civil war between the brothers by declaring Judean independence and embarking on military expeditions against Samaria and Idumea, all while amassing great wealth (*Jewish Antiquities* 13.10.1). Antiochus IX (Cyzicenus) attempted to assist the Samaritans in their fight against the Jews under Hyrcanus I, but he was easily defeated. Antiochus IX (Cyzicenus) then appealed to Ptolemy IX (Soter II) of Egypt (1st reign 116–110 B.C.) for help in subduing Judea, but even the combined forces of the Seleucids and the Ptolemies could not halt Hyrcanus' invasion, so a defeated Antiochus IX (Cyzicenus) returned his attention back to the flailing Seleucid Empire and its own internal intrigues. Antiochus IX (Cyzicenus) married Cleopatra IV of Egypt (the daughter of Ptolemy VIII

Euergetes II/Ptolemy Physcon and Cleopatra III), but Cleopatra IV was killed on the orders of her own sister Tryphaena (the wife of Antiochus VIII Grypus). Second, Antiochus IX (Cyzicenus) married Cleopatra V Selene (yet another sister of Cleopatra IV and Tryphaena). Antiochus IX (Cyzicenus) later avenged his first wife (Cleopatra IV) by ordering the murder of Tryphaena. Antiochus IX's only son was Antiochus X (Eusebes), but the younger Antiochus' mother is not named in historical documents. In 96 B.C., Antiochus IX (Cyzicenus) was killed in battle by his nephew Seleucus VI (Epiphanes), the son of Antiochus VIII (Grypus).

20. **Seleucus V (Philometor)**, was the eldest son of Demetrius II (Nicator) and Cleopatra Thea and the half-brother of Antiochus IX (Cyzicenus). When his father (Demetrius II Nicator) was murdered in 125 B.C., Seleucus V claimed the throne as the eldest son and co-ruled briefly with his mother Cleopatra Thea from 126/125 B.C. According to Appian, Cleopatra Thea was involved in the murder of her husband (Demetrius II), and she feared that Seleucus V would avenge his father's murder, so Cleopatra Thea killed Seleucus V (Philometor) in favor of his younger brother Antiochus VIII (Grypus) ruling.

21. **Antiochus VIII (Grypus)** was the ruler of the northern branch of the Seleucid kingdom. His first reign was 125/124–113 B.C. and his second reign was 111–96 B.C. He was nicknamed "hook-nose." Antiochus VIII (Grypus) was the son of Demetrius II (Nicator) and Cleopatra Thea and was also the half-brother of Antiochus IX (Cyzicenus). After his father's death, Antiochus VIII (Grypus) was co-ruler with his mother; however, when Cleopatra Thea prepared a cup of poisoned wine and offered it to Grypus, he grew suspicious and forced her to drink it herself (Justin/Justinus, *Epitome* 39.2.8; Appian, *Syrian Wars* 14.68). Antiochus VIII (Grypus) was successfully defeated the usurper Alexander II (Zabinas) in 123 B.C., but this early challenge to his reign was just the beginning, as Antiochus VIII's half-brother Antiochus IX (Cyzicenus) challenged his rule in ca. 116 B.C. The two brothers fought each other intermittently for twenty years, despite a treaty granting Antiochus IX (Cyzicenus) the rule of Syria in 116 B.C. The *Jewish Encyclopedia* states that Antiochus VIII (Grypus) was on friendly terms with the Jews, while Josephus only mentions Antiochus VIII (Grypus) in the context of war with his brother (Louis Ginzberg, "Antiochus VIII Grypus," *Jewish Encyclopedia*, https://jewishencyclopedia.com/articles/1593-antiochus-viii-gryphus). The civil war between the two brothers, however, enabled John Hyrcanus I, the high priest and ruler of Israel, to assert Judean independence and to campaign against Samaria and Idumea (*Jewish Antiquities* 13.10.1; see note 19 above). In 124/123 B.C., Antiochus VIII (Grypus) was first married to Tryphaena the daughter of Ptolemy VIII (Euergetes II/Physcon) and had six children by her, including the next five Seleucid rulers: Seleucus VI (Epiphanes), Antiochus XI (Epiphanes), Demetrius III (Eucaerus), Philip I (Philadelphus), and Antiochus XII (Dionysus). Tryphaena was killed by Antiochus IX (Cyzicenus) to avenge the murder of Cyzicenus' first wife, Cleopatra IV, who had been killed upon Tryphaena's orders; the rival queens were actually both sisters-in-law and biological sisters (cf. *Epitome* 39.3). Antiochus VIII (Grypus) later married Cleopatra V Selene (also a daughter of Ptolemy VIII Euergetes II/Physcon); later, Cleopatra V Selene married Grypus' half-brother Antiochus IX Cyzicenus. Antiochus VIII (Grypus) was supported in the war against his half-brother (Cyzicenus) by Ptolemy X (Alexander I), who was both Antiochus VIII's brother-in-law and the brother of Antiochus IX's supporter Ptolemy IX (Soter II). Antiochus VIII (Grypus) died in 96 B.C.; Josephus states that he was assassinated by his minister Heracleon (*Jewish Antiquities* 13.13.4). Antiochus VIII (Grypus) was succeeded by his son Seleucus VI (Epiphanes).

22. **Antiochus X (Eusebes)**, who ruled 95/94–83 B.C., was the son of Antiochus IX (Cyzicenus); his mother is unknown. Antiochus X (Eusebes) ruled Syria after his father's death, while his cousin Seleucus VI (Epiphanes) ruled the rest of what remained of the Seleucid Empire. Antiochus X (Eusebes) married his stepmother, Cleopatra V Selene of Egypt, to advance his rule. Noting that the Syrians called Antiochus X "Antiochus Pius" because they "thought that he escaped a plot of his cousin Seleucus on account of his piety," Appian comments that he thinks the Syrians "must have given him this title by way of joke, for this Pius married [Cleopatra V] Selene, who had been the wife of his father, Cyzicenus, and of his uncle, Grypus." Appian reasons that this incestuous marriage caused "divine vengeance" to fall upon Antiochus X (Eusebes) and ultimately resulted in his ouster (*Syrian Wars* 14.69). However, before his own fall from power, Antiochus X (Eusebes) defeated his cousin Seleucus VI (Epiphanes), which, in turn, prompted Seleucus VI's brothers—Antiochus XI (Epiphanes), Philip I (Philadelphus), and Demetrius III (Eucaerus)—to war against Antiochus X (Eusebes). The end of Antiochus X's reign is shrouded in mystery; Josephus' account that Antiochus X (Eusebes) was killed during a campaign against the Parthians (cf. *Jewish Antiquities* 13.13.4) is thought to be the most reliable account by modern historians [see Marek Olbrycht, "Mithridates VI Eupator and Iran," *Mithridates VI and the Pontic Kingdom. Black Sea Studies. 9.* Ed. Jakob Munk Høtje (Aarhus, Denmark: Aarhus University Press, 2009), 163–190]. Initially, the sons of Antiochus VIII (Grypus)—Philip I (Philadelphus) and Demetrius III (Eucaerus)—were allies, but then they turned against each other. Taking advantage of the internal strife in the Seleucid Empire, Tigranes the Great of Armenia swept in and conquered the remnants of the once-mighty Seleucid empire.

23. **Tigranes the Great**—also called **Tigranes II**—was the king of Armenia from 83–69 B.C. His father, Tigranes I of Armenia, had ruled Armenia from ca. 120–95 B.C. The wife of Tigranes the Great was Cleopatra (the daughter of Mithridates VI of Pontus). In 83 B.C., the Syrians offered Tigranes II the throne of Syria. He conquered Phoenicia and Cilicia and defeated the last few remaining remnant figures of the Seleucid Empire, such as Philip I Philadelphus, although a few cities appear to have recognized the boy-king Seleucus VII as the legitimate king during Tigranes II's reign. The southern border of Tigranes II's rule extended as far as Ptolemais (modern Akko). In 69 B.C., the Roman commander Lucullus attacked Armenia, defeated Tigranes II, and appointed Antiochus XIII (Asiaticus) as the ruler of Syria. Tigranes II then surrendered to Pompey the Great (Lucullus' successor) and gave up most of his conquests. Tigranes II died in ca. 55 B.C.

24. **Antiochus XIII (Asiaticus)**, who ruled 69–64 B.C., was the son of Antiochus X (Eusebes) and Cleopatra V Selene and was the brother of Seleucus VII (Cybiosactes/Kybiosactes). Antiochus XIII (Asiaticus) was the successor of Tigranes II, who had ruled Syria. In 69 B.C., during the Third Mithridatic War—after the Roman general Lucullus attacked Armenia and defeated Tigranes—Lucullus then appointed Antiochus XIII (Asiaticus) as ruler of Syria. In 68/67, Lucullus was re-called to Rome, and the Romans gave the supreme command to Pompey the Great. In 67/66 B.C., Antiochus XIII (Asiaticus) was only supported by the population of Antioch and a local ruler from Cilicia. Antiochus XIII was expelled by his relative Philip II (Philoromaeus) from Antioch but was then restored in 66/65 B.C. When Pompey annexed Syria as a province of the Roman Empire in 64 B.C., Antiochus XIII was dethroned and murdered.

25. **Seleucus VII (Philometor)** or **"Kybiosactes**"—also called **Seleucus Cybiosactes**—was presumably the son of Antiochus X (Eusebes) and Cleopatra V Selene, the younger brother of Antiochus XIII (Asiaticus), and the presumed husband of Berenice IV of Egypt (58–55 B.C.), the daughter of Ptolemaic ruler Ptolemy XII (Auletes). He reigned 83–69 B.C. in opposition to Tigranes the Great.

26. **Seleucus VI (Epiphanes)**, who ruled 96–94 B.C., was the son of Antiochus VIII (Grypus) and Tryphaena. After the death of his father (Antiochus VIII Grypus) in 96 B.C., Grypus' second wife, Cleopatra V Selene, married her brother-in-law Antiochus IX (Cyzicenus) in an effort to put an end to the decades-long civil war between the two half-brothers. Seleucus VI (Epiphanes) continued the family branch and controlled the northern part of the Seleucid Empire; Appian says that Seleucus VI (Epiphanes) "made war on his uncle [Antiochus IX (Cyzicenus)] and took the government away from him" but the empire was not reunited. Appian further states that Seleucus VI (Epiphanes) "was violent and tyrannical" (*Syrian Wars* 14.69; cf. *Jewish Antiquities* 13.13.4). Seleucus VI minted an estimated 1200 talents to finance his war against Antiochus IX (Cyzicenus), which ended when Antiochus IX (Cyzicenus) either committed suicide or was killed by Seleucus VI (Epiphanes; accounts differ). However, Antiochus IX's son, Antiochus X (Eusebes), took control of the southern half of the empire in early 95 B.C. According to Josephus and Eusebius, Antiochus X (Eusebes) drove Seleucus VI (Epiphanes) out of Syria. Josephus, Appian, and Eusebius all agree that Seleucus VI (Epiphanes) died in Mopsuestia in Cilicia (in modern-day southern Turkey, near the border with Syria and close to the Mediterranean); modern scholarship dates his death to 94 B.C. Josephus and Appian both state that Seleucus VI (Epiphanes) burned to death in either the palace (Josephus) or the gymnasium (Appian); both imply that the inhabitants of Mopsuestia caused the fatal fire because of Seleucus VI's increased taxation (cf. *Jewish Antiquities* 13.13.4; *Syrian Wars* 14.69). Eusebius merely states that "the inhabitants intended to burn him alive" and that upon learning of this, Seleucus VI (Epiphanes) committed suicide, although Eusebius may be downplaying the violence of the late Seleucid rulers' deaths (*Chronicle/Chronicon* 260–261). Seleucus VI (Epiphanes) was succeeded by his brothers.

27. **Demetrius III (Eucaerus)** was the son of Antiochus VIII and Tryphaena. Demetrius III (Eucaerus) and his brother Philip I (Philadelphus) were made the rulers in Damascus by Ptolemy IX (Soter) "Lathyros"; they successfully waged war against Antiochus IX (Cyzicenus) and his son Antiochus X (Eusebes Philopator).

28. **Philip I (Philadelphus)** became king with his brother Antiochus XI (Epiphanes) after Seleucus VI (Epiphanes) was murdered in 94 B.C. Then, in 93 B.C., Antiochus XI (Epiphanes) took Antioch from Antiochus X (Eusebes) and became the senior king while Philip I (Philadelphus) remained in Cilicia. After his brother Antiochus XI (Epiphanes) was killed by Antiochus X (Eusebes), Philip I (Philadelphus) allied himself with his younger brother Demetrius III, who was based in Damascus. Philip later took Antioch, and the youngest brother Antiochus XII (Dionysus) took Damascus. Philip I was unsuccessful at taking Damascus for himself. He died around 83 B.C., or possibly later in 75 B.C. The Antiochenes did not accept Philip's son, Philip II, as his successor.

29. **Antiochus XI (Epiphanes)**—the son of Antiochus VIII (Grypus) and Tryphaena—was a colleague and, at times, a rival of his brother Seleucus VI (Epiphanes). When Seleucus VI (Epiphanes) was overcome by Antiochus X (Eusebes) in 94 B.C., the northern branch continued under Antiochus XI (Epiphanes) only. After a brief reign, Antiochus XI (Epiphanes) was defeated and killed in 93/92 B.C. by Antiochus X (Eusebes), who then took over the northern branch.

30. **Antiochus XII (Dionysus)** was the youngest son of Antiochus VIII (Grypus) and probably Tryphaena. When their father was assassinated in 96 B.C., Antiochus XII (Dionysus) and his brothers laid claim to the throne to eliminate Antiochus IX (Cyzicenus) and his son Antiochus X (Eusebes). His brother Philip I (Philadelphus) defeated their brother Demetris III (Eucaerus), who was centered in Damascus. Philip I remained in the Syrian capital of Antioch, which allowed Antiochus XII (Dionysus) to take control of Damascus and later expand the reach of Syria toward Judea and Nabataea; however, in those campaigns, Antiochus XII (Dionysus) was killed. The Syrian throne was then claimed by Cleopatra V Selene, the widow of Antiochus X (Eusebes), and her son Antiochus XIII (Asiaticus).

SUPPLEMENT 8: THE MACCABEES AND THE HASMONEAN DYNASTY[1] (RULERS AND HIGH PRIESTS OF ISRAEL)

Approximate Dating: Maccabean Revolt, 167–160 B.C.; Hasmonean Dynasty, ca. 167–37 B.C.

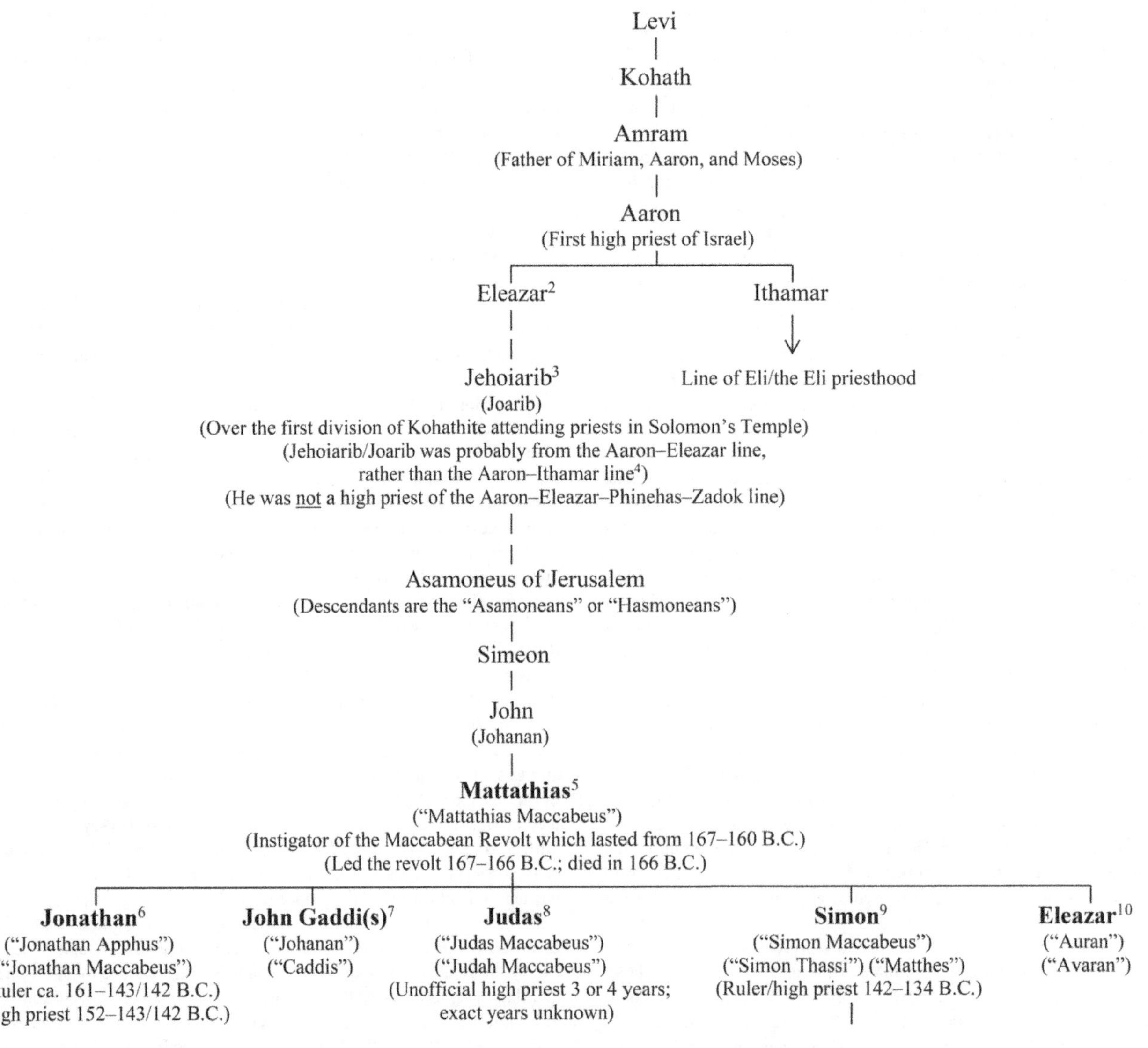

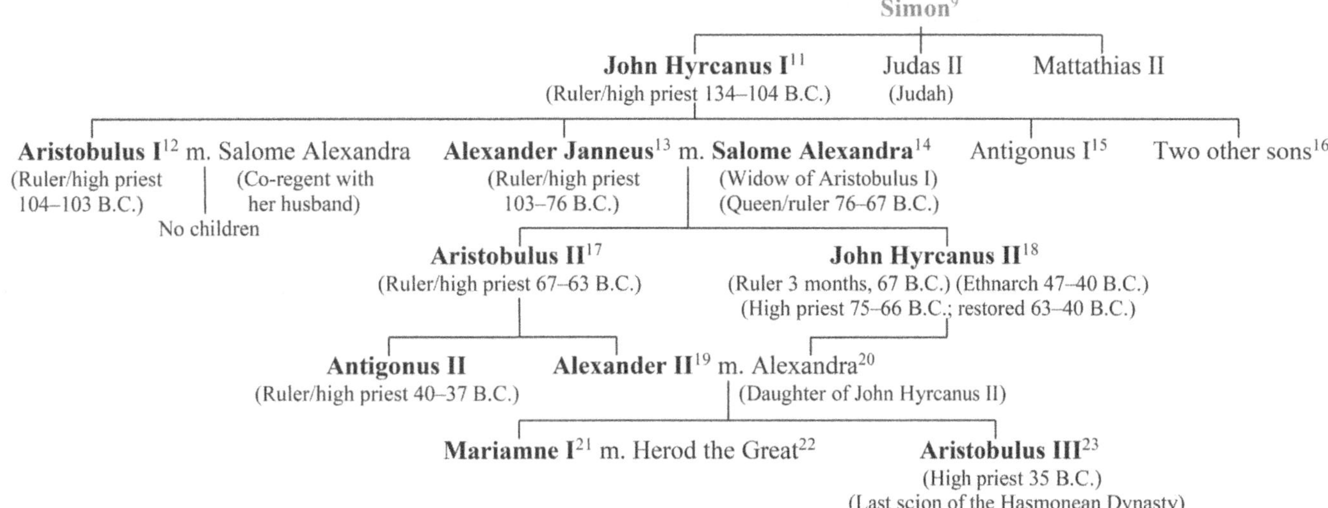

Biblical and Theological Significance

The patriarch Mattathias and his five sons led the Maccabean revolt against the Seleucid rulership of Judea and the Hellenistic (Greek) influence on the Jews. Following the desecration of the Jerusalem temple by the Seleucid ruler Antiochus Epiphanes IV, the Maccabees succeeded in their uprising against Seleucid rule, and the Jewish people celebrated the rededication of the Second Temple in 165 B.C., referred to as the "Festival of Dedication" in **John 10:22**; cf. *2 Maccabees* 10:1–8). This ushered in a century of Jewish independence from foreign rule that lasted until Pompey's Roman conquest of Palestine in 63 B.C.

Notes

1. Biblical and extra-biblical references include **1 Chronicles 24:1–7, 19**; *1 Maccabees* 2:1–5; *The Life of Flavius Josephus* and *Jewish Antiquities* in *The Complete Works of Josephus*, trans. William Whiston, commentary Paul L. Maier. (Grand Rapids: Kregel, 1999), especially *Jewish Antiquities* 12.6.1, which gives the lineage of Mattathias; Joachim Jeremias, *Jerusalem in the Time of Jesus* (Philadelphia: Fortress Press, 1975); and Claude Reignier Conder, *Judas Maccabaeus and the Jewish War of Independence*, 2nd ed. (London: Committee of the Palestine Exploration Fund, 1898). Online source consulted was the *Jewish Encyclopedia*, 1906. For notes in the chart that refer to the high priests of Israel and the Ptolemaic and Seleucid rulers, see "**Supplement 2**: The High Priests of Israel"; "**Supplement 6**: The Ptolemies and the Ptolemaic Dynasty"; and "**Supplement 7**: The Seleucids and the Seleucid Dynasty."

2. Eleazar succeeded his father, Aaron, to the high priesthood and continued the Aaronic high priesthood line (i.e., Aaron–Eleazar–Phinehas–Zadok, etc.; see chart "**Supplement 2**: The High Priests of Israel"). Eleazear's son Phinehas became his successor. Members of the Aaron–Eleazar priesthood (who were not high priests) and faithful members of the Ithamar–Elide line (who were not high priests) became Kohathite *attending* priests in the temple. Jehoiarib derives his ancestry from the line of Kohathite attending priests.

3. Jehoiarib (or Joiarib in some versions) was head over the first division (or order) of Kohathite attending priests who served in Solomon's Temple (**1 Chronicles 24:7**), but Jehoiarib was not a high priest himself. Anticipating the duties of the cultus in Solomon's Temple, King David divided the attending priestly duties between the descendants of Aaron's sons, Eleazar and Ithamar. Twenty-four divisions of Kohathite attending priests were established in all: sixteen were chosen from the Eleazar line and the remaining eight were chosen from a *faithful* remnant of the Ithamar line (excluding the *cursed* Eli descendants; cf. **1 Samuel 2**). The attending priests were chosen by casting lots. Jehoiarib/Joarib was the first priest chosen (**1 Chronicles 24:1–7, 19**); whether he was from the Eleazar or Ithamar line is not explicitly stated, but since Eleazar was named first, it is likely that Jehoiarib/Joarib came from the Aaron–Eleazar line, rather than from the Aaron–Ithamar line.

4. See chart "**1 Chronicles 24**: Genealogical Registry of the Twenty-Four Divisions of Kohathite Attending Priests Who Rotated Service in Solomon's Temple (Sixteen from the Aaron–Eleazar–Zadok Line and Eight from the Aaron–Ithamar Line)."

5. **Mattathias** was from ancient Modin (or Modein) of Judea, located about 20 miles northwest of Jerusalem. Josephus says that Mattathias was "the son [probably meaning 'descendant' since Asamoneus was Mattathias' great-grandfather] of Asamoneus, a priest of the order of Joarib [J(eh)oiarib], and a citizen of Jerusalem. He had five sons: John, who was called Gaddis, and Simon, who was called Matthes, and Judas, who was called Maccabeus, and Eleazar, who was called Auran and Jonathan, who was called Apphus" (*Jewish Antiquities* 12.6.1; cf. *1 Maccabees* 2:1–5). Mattathias and his five sons were the leaders of the Maccabean Revolt that took place from 167–160 B.C. This family revolted against the foreign rulership of Judea by the Seleucid kings of Syria. When the Seleucid ruler Antiochus IV (Epiphanes), 175–164 B.C., issued an edict that required all subjects to "become one people" and mandated that the Jews put away their distinctive cultures, Mattathias instigated a revolt against the Hellenistic and pagan practices being forced upon them. Mattathias, his sons, and their compatriots destroyed the pagan altars and circumcised all the uncircumcised boys they could find in Israel (*1 Maccabees* 2:45–46).

The family of Mattathias became known as the "Maccabees," from the Hebrew word for "hammer," because they "were said to strike hammer blows against their enemies" (AICE, "The Maccabees/Hasmoneans: History & Overview," *Jewish Virtual Library* - A Project of AICE, https://www.jewishvirtuallibrary.org/history-and-overview-of-the-maccabees; also see Joseph Jacobs and M. Seligsohn, "The Maccabees," *Jewish Encyclopedia*, https://jewishencyclopedia.com/articles/10236-maccabees, for a discussion of the etymology of "Maccabee."). Although Jews refer to them as the Maccabees, the family is also known as the Hasmoneans (after their ancestor *Asamoneus*). The Maccabees would go on to fight and claim the throne of Judea as well as the position of high priest. Before his death in 166 B.C., Mattathias charged his sons to remember the great men of old who remained faithful to God despite hardship:

> Be mindful of the desires of him who begat you, . . . preserve the customs of your country, . . . recover your ancient form of government, . . . become such sons as are worthy of me. . . . [God] will not overlook you. . . . [He] will return to you that freedom in which you shall live quietly. . . . Your bodies are mortal, and subject to fate; but they receive a sort of immortality, by the remembrance of what actions they have done. . . . pursue after glory. . . . I exhort you, especially, to agree one with another; and in what excellency anyone of you exceeds another, to yield to him so far, and by that means to reap the advantage of everyone's own virtues. . . . esteem Simon as your father, because he is a man of extraordinary wisdom, and be governed by him in what counsels he gives you. Take [Judas] Maccabeus for the general of your army, because of his courage and strength, for he will avenge your nations . . . Admit among you the righteous and religious, and augment their power. (*Jewish Antiquities* 12.6.3)

6. **Jonathan**—also called **Jonathan Maccabeus**—is given the appellation "**Apphus**" (*Jewish Antiquities* 12.6.1; *1 Maccabees* 2:4). Jonathan fought alongside his brother Judas Maccabeus in battles against the Syrians. After Judas was killed in 160 B.C., Jonathan was made the leader of the Jewish revolt. Jonathan was also appointed high priest by the Seleucid ruler Alexander I (Balas), who reigned 150–145 B.C. Jonathan remained on good terms with Alexander I (Balas), who married Cleopatra Thea (the daughter of Ptolemy VI Philometor, 180–145 B.C.). Alexander I (Balas) even invited Jonathan to join in the wedding celebration, going so far as to seat Jonathan in between himself and Ptolemy VI and to clothe Jonathan in royal robes (*Jewish Antiquities* 13.1, 4; Richard Gottheil and Samuel Krauss, "Jonathan Maccabeus," *Jewish Encyclopedia*, https://jewishencyclopedia.com/articles/8773-jonathan-maccabeus). When Alexander I (Balas) was challenged by the Seleucid ruler Demetrius II (Nicator) of Syria (1st reign 145–139 B.C.; 2nd reign 129–125 B.C.), Jonathan fought for Alexander I (Balas). However, when Ptolemy VI overthrew Alexander Balas, Jonathan initially resisted the new leadership but eventually capitulated. Demetrius II (Nicator) confirmed Jonathan as the high priest. But when Demetrius II did not keep his promise to keep Jerusalem safe, Jonathan sided with Antiochus VI (Dionysus) the son of Alexander I Balas and with Trypho (who, at the time, was the guardian of the young king Dionysus). Nevertheless, Trypho grew suspicious of Jonathan's motives, so he drew Jonathan into a trap, captured him, and killed his men. Eventually, Trypho also killed Jonathan in 143/142 B.C., instead of handing him over to his brother Simon Maccabeus ("Thassi"), who had paid for Jonathan's ransom (*Jewish Antiquities 13.4–6*; Richard Gottheil and Samuel Krauss, "Jonathan Maccabeus," *Jewish Encyclopedia*, https://jewishencyclopedia.com/articles/8773-jonathan-maccabeus). For details about Trypho, see chart "**Supplement 7**: The Seleucids and the Seleucid Dynasty."

Notably, a daughter of Jonathan Maccabeus was an ancestor of Josephus (see chart "**Supplement 9**: Flavius Josephus, the Roman-Jewish Historian").

7. **John** (or **Johanan**), surnamed **Gaddi**, was the eldest son of Mattathias. John helped his brothers wage war against the Seleucid rulers. He was killed by Nabatean Arabs in the city of Medaba (*Jewish Antiquities* 13.1.2; *1 Maccabees* 9:35–38).

8. **Judas Maccabeus**—also called **Judah Maccabee** or **Maccabeus**—was the son of Mattathias. After his father's death in 166 B.C., Judas became the general of the Maccabean army and the new leader of the Jewish revolt. Judas and his forces fought many battles against the Syrians. One battle was fought against Lysias, who was the guardian of the nine-year-old new king Antiochus V (Eupator). Some sources say that Antiochus V was eight or twelve when he assumed the Seleucid throne; cf. *Jewish Antiquities* 12.7.2–7). After the Jews won this battle, they were able to retake Jerusalem, except for the citadel. The *Jewish Encyclopedia* states that in 165 B.C., the Jews re-consecrated the Second Temple on this occasion, which led to the creation of Hanukkah (also called the Festival of Lights/Festival of Dedication; Kaufmann Kohler, "Hanukkah," *Jewish Encyclopedia*, https://jewishencyclopedia.com/articles/4236-chanukkah; cf. **John 10:22**). After two years of peace, Judas and his two brothers (Simon and Jonathan) quelled the attempts of the Idumeans, Ammonites, and Gileadites to overpower the Jewish regime. Those Jews in Gilead and Galilee were taken to safety in Jerusalem (*1 Maccabees* 5:1–53; Richard Gottheil and Samuel Krauss, "Judas Maccabeus," *Jewish Encyclopedia*, https://jewishencyclopedia.com/articles/9034-judas-maccabeus). Judas then besieged the citadel, called the Acra. In response, the Seleucid general Lysias came with 100,000 infantry, 20,000 cavalry, and even 32 elephants (*1 Maccabees* 6:30). The Syrians won the ensuing battle at Beth-zur, although *1 Maccabees* only alludes to this (6:47). The Syrians then besieged the temple. The land lacked food because it was "the seventh year," when the Jews allowed the fields to "rest" from growing crops (*1 Maccabees* 6:53; cf. **Leviticus 25:1–5**). The scarcity of food prompted Lysias to ask Antiochus V (Eupator) if they could make peace with the Jews and let them "live by their laws as they did before" (*1 Maccabees* 6:55–59). The king initially agreed, but upon seeing the fortifications on "Mount Zion," he changed his mind and issued an order for the walls to be torn down (*1 Maccabees* 6:60–63). Judas' forces then fought against those led by Alcimus, the former high priest (162–159 B.C.). After Judas defeated Alcimus, Alcimus appealed to Demetrius I (Soter), who was now king of the Syrians (Richard Gottheil and Samuel Krauss, "Judas Maccabeus," *Jewish Encyclopedia*, https://jewishencyclopedia.com/articles/9034-judas-maccabeus). Demetrius I sent forces; the ensuing battle ended with Judas fleeing to Jerusalem (ibid.). The leader of Demetrius' forces fell in battle, and Judas became ruler over Judea, though he does not appear to have received a formal royal appointment to the high priesthood. Josephus calls him *high priest* but also acknowledges the seven-year gap (called the "intersacerdotium period") between Alcimus and the royal-appointed Jonathan Apphus (for a discussion, refer to chart "**Supplement 2**: The High Priests of Israel"). During the interregnum period, Judas may have served in an unofficial high priestly capacity, but according to the *Jewish Encyclopedia*, the books of the *Maccabees*, and other secular sources, there is no mention of Judas Maccabeus having formally held the high priesthood (ibid.). Judas is described in 1 Maccabees as having made a treaty with Rome, but it was to no avail. In 160 B.C. Judas was killed at the Battle of Elasa while fighting more forces sent by Demetrius I (Soter) (*1 Maccabees* 8; Richard Gottheil and Samuel Krauss, "Judas Maccabeus," *Jewish Encyclopedia*, https://jewishencyclopedia.com/articles/9034-judas-maccabeus). Judah Maccabee's brothers continued the revolt against the Seleucids.

9. **Simon** the son of Mattathias Maccabeus—also called "**Simon Maccabeus**"—is given the appellation "**Thassi**" in *1 Maccabees* 2:3, which is related to his father's description of Simon as a "man of extraordinary wisdom." Upon his deathbed, Mattathias advised Simon's brothers to "be governed by him in what counsel he gives you" (*Jewish Antiquities* 12.6.3). Josephus calls him "Simon" (cf. *Jewish Antiquities* 12.8.2; 12.10.6;13.6.3–7; *The Jewish War* 1.2.2–3). During the Maccabean rebellion, Simon gave aid to those Jews in Galilee who were being oppressed by rival forces. He and his brother Jonathan (Apphus) avenged the death of their brother John. Due to the Jews' military successes, Antiochus VI (Dionysus), 145–142 B.C., named Simon the military commander of the region from the Ladder of Tyre to Egypt (*1 Maccabees* 11:59; Richard Gottheil and Samuel Krauss, "Simon Maccabeus," *Jewish Encyclopedia*, https://jewishencyclopedia.com/articles/13746-simon-maccabeus). After his brother Jonathan was murdered by the Seleucid ruler Trypho (139–138 B.C.), Simon became the sole leader of the Jews. *1 Maccabees* 14:4 notes that "the land of Judah enjoyed peace all the days of Simon. He sought what was good for his nation. His rule was agreeable to them, as was the honor shown him all his days." (In fact, Simon Maccabeus may be the person called "Simon the Just" in later rabbinic traditions.) In the third year of Simon's tenure as high priest, the Jews nominated him to be not only high priest, but also general and ethnarch (*1 Maccabees* 14:27, 47). Simon and his sons Mattathias II and Judas II (Judah) were killed by Simon's son-in-law Ptolemaeus (Ptolemy son of Abubus), at a banquet given by the latter (*1 Maccabees* 16:11–17; *Jewish Antiquities* 13.7.4). Simon was succeeded by his son John Hyrcanus I, who was not present when his father and brothers were murdered.

10. The heroic death of Eleazar the son of Mattathias Maccabeus is described in *1 Maccabees* 6:43–46.

11. **John Hyrcanus I** was the son of Simon Thassi. John Hyrcanus I had five sons (*Jewish Antiquities* 13.10.7), four of whom Josephus names: Aristobulus I the eldest, Antigonus I, Alexander Janneus, and Absalom (cf. *Jewish Antiquities* 13:10–12; 14.4.4). John Hyrcanus I succeeded his father as high priest after Simon's assassination. During John Hyrcanus' tenure as high priest, the Syrian king Antiochus VII (Sidetes), 138–129 B.C., besieged Jerusalem. The siege lasted for an entire summer before Antiochus VII proposed a peace treaty; John Hyrcanus asked for a cessation of hostilities for seven days, which included the Feast of Tabernacles. After the seven days were up, John Hyrcanus accepted the terms, as the people of Jerusalem lacked sufficient food. The Jews surrendered their weapons and paid tribute for Joppa and other former Syrian towns. The battlements on the walls of Jerusalem were destroyed as well. John Hyrcanus I sent hostages to Syria, including his own brother, in lieu of having Jerusalem occupied by Syrian troops. He paid 500 talents of silver—with 300 paid up front—by taking money from the treasure in David's tomb (Richard Gottheil and Meyer Kayserling, "John (Johanan) Hyrcanus I," *Jewish Encyclopedia*, https://jewishencyclopedia.com/articles/7972-hyrcanus-john-johanan-i). John Hyrcanus I was a vassal of Syria until after the deaths of the Seleucid rulers Antiochus VII (Sidetes) in 129 B.C. and his brother Demetrius II (Nicator) in 125 B.C. John Hyrcanus I took control of various Syrian towns and captured Shechem, the capital of Samaria. He then conquered the Edomites (the descendants of Esau) and forced them to convert to Judaism. John Hyrcanus I was thus able to regain Judea's independence; he also refortified the walls of Jerusalem. During his time as high priest and ruler, the three main sects of Judaism—the Pharisees, Sadducees, and Essenes—became firmly established. John Hyrcanus himself subscribed to the Pharisaic line of thought; however, he switched his affiliation to the Sadducees after stripping the Sanhedrin of all religious authority. His break with the Sadducees came about because he had asked the Pharisees if they had any matter to bring to his attention. There are two differing accounts of what was said, but both accounts imply that

Hyrcanus' ability to serve as high priest was being questioned—one account says that a Pharisee told John Hyrcanus I that he should step down as being high priest and be content to exercise political power. The other accused John Hyrcanus I of not being eligible to be high priest because of an accusation that his mother—rumored to have been a captive of war, and therefore possibly raped—made him ineligible to legally serve as high priest (ibid., *Jewish Antiquities* 13.10.5; cf. Jeremias, *Jerusalem in the Time of Jesus*, 214). The accusation against John Hyrcanus' mother was proven untrue, but the damage had been done. John Hyrcanus transferred his allegiance to the Sadducees and replaced the Pharisaical rules with the Sadducean rules as the standard method for interpreting the law. John Hyrcanus I reigned for thirty years (134–104 B.C.); after his death, the Jewish nation began to lose its independence and sovereignty. Josephus summarizes his life as follows: "And this was the fate of Hyrcanus. . . . For he was made high priest of the Jewish nation in the beginning of his mother Alexandra's reign, who held the government nine years; and when, after his mother's death, he took the kingdom himself, and held it three months, he lost it, by the means of his brother Aristobulus. He was then restored by Pompey, and received all sorts of honor from him, and enjoyed them forty years; but when he was again deprived by Antigonus, and was maimed in his body, he was made a captive by the Parthians, and thence returned home again after some time, on account of the hopes that Herod had given him; none of which came to pass according to his expectation, but he still conflicted with many misfortunes through the whole course of his life; and, what was the heaviest calamity of all, as we have related already, he came to an end which was undeserved by him. His character appeared to be that of a man of a mild and moderate disposition, and suffered the administration of affairs to be generally done by others under him. He was averse to much meddling with the public, nor had shrewdness enough to govern a kingdom. And both Antipater and Herod came to their greatness by reason of his mildness; and at last he met with such an end from them as was not agreeable either to justice or piety" (*Jewish Antiquities* 15.6.4).

12. **Aristobulus I** was the eldest son of John Hyrcanus I. According to the *Jewish Encyclopedia*, his Hebrew name was "Judah" (Richard Gottheil and Louis Ginzberg, "Aristobulus I," *Jewish Encyclopedia*, https://jewishencyclopedia.com/articles/1768-aristobulus-i). Aristobulus' father had stipulated in his will that his wife was to rule over Judea as queen upon his death. However, Aristobulus flouted his father's wishes, and immediately upon succeeding to the office of high priest, he threw his mother into prison, where she starved to death (*Jewish Antiquities* 13.11.1). Aristobulus also threw three of his brothers into prison. Aristobulus I was the first of the Hasmonean dynasty to change the government into a "kingdom" and to formally assume the title "king." Josephus, quite misleadingly, says that Aristobulus "put a diadem on his head, four hundred eighty and one years and three months after the people had been delivered from the Babylonian slavery, and were returned to their own country again" (*Jewish Antiquities* 13.11.1). [Since Aristobulus began to rule in 104 B.C., it seems that Josephus intended to refer to the year 586 B.C. (i.e., 586 - 104 = 482 years)—the year that the Jewish people were taken *into* captivity, since the exiles did not begin to *return* to their homeland until 538 B.C. with Zerubbabel.] Aristobulus I conquered Upper Galilee from the Itureans, who inhabited the lands north and east of the Sea of Galilee; the Itureans were then forcibly circumcised as part of an attempt to convert them to the Jewish faith. *The Jewish Encyclopedia* relates that Aristobulus I was feeble and that he gradually became completely controlled by a group headed by his wife, Queen Salome Alexandra, who was regarded as his co-regent (Richard Gottheil and Louis Ginzberg, "Aristobulus I," *Jewish Encyclopedia*, https://jewishencyclopedia.com/articles/1768-aristobulus-i). The queen convinced Aristobulus I that his brother Antigonus I was plotting against him, so (at the instigation of Salome Alexandra) Aristobulus drew his brother Antigonus into a trap; Josephus says that Antigonus was killed by Aristobulus' guards while coming to show Aristobulus his new set of armor at Strato's Tower (cf. *Jewish Antiquities* 13.11.2). Aristobulus I's health drastically declined after he killed his brother Antigonus, and he died shortly thereafter. His widow Salome Alexandra released her remaining brothers-in-law who were still in prison and made Alexander Janneus, the oldest surviving brother, king (Richard Gottheil and Louis Ginzberg, "Aristobulus I," *Jewish Encyclopedia*, https://jewishencyclopedia.com/articles/1768-aristobulus-i).

13. **Alexander Janneus** (also spelled Alexander Jannaeus) was the third son of John Hyrcanus I. Josephus says that "this child happened to be hated by his father as soon as he was born, and could never be permitted to come into his father's sight until he died" (*Jewish Antiquities* 13.12.1); in addition, the editor's note says that Hyrcanus ordered Alexander Janneus to be brought up in Galilee rather than Judea. His older half-brother Aristobulus I became king after their father's (Hyrcanus I) death, but he only reigned for a year. Aristobulus I had imprisoned Alexander Janneus; however, after Aristobulus' death, the widowed queen, Salome Alexandra, released Alexander Janneus. Queen Salome Alexandra and Aristobulus I had been childless; so, as the next of kin and according to the laws of levirate marriage (which seem to have been in place at the time), Alexander Janneus was obligated to marry her, even though she was thirteen years older than him. Alexander Janneus campaigned against the city of Ptolemais, now called Acre; in response, the exiled Egyptian prince Ptolemy "Lathyrus" (also called Ptolemy IX Soter II; 116–110 B.C.; 88–81/80 B.C.), son of Cleopatra III, aided the people of Ptolemais. Ptolemy Lathyrus and his army won the first battle against Alexander Janneus and his men, but Cleopatra (III), the mother of Ptolemy Lathyrus, not wanting her estranged son to be victorious, sent men to help Alexander Janneus. With these additional Egyptian forces, Alexander Janneus and his men were able to defeat Ptolemy Lathyrus. Alexander Janneus' other campaigns had mixed results.

After these various campaigns concluded, civil unrest began in Judea once again. This time, the Hasmoneans were at odds with the Pharisees. Beginning with John Hyrcanus I and continuing with his sons, the Hasmoneans favored political interests over religious concerns, in contrast to the Pharisees, who represented the popular opinion. The Pharisees did not agree with the Hasmonean pursuit of annexing lands through conquest; the Pharisees would defend their nation to the utmost from enemies but did not want to involve themselves in political machinations of the sort favored by the last few Hasmonean rulers. Alexander Janneus' distaste for the Pharisees and partisanship for the Sadducees was shown publicly when he poured the water libation over his feet during the ceremony of the Feast of Tabernacles. Enraged, the people threw citron fruits from the religious ritual at Alexander Janneus. In retaliation, he summoned groups of mercenaries and set them loose among the people, which resulted in the deaths of 6,000 Pharisees. After yet another campaign, Alexander Janneus returned to find that the Pharisees had incited the people to rebel against him; the following six years led to the deaths of at least 50,000 Jews as the common people fought against the royal army. When Alexander Janneus sought peace with the Pharisees, they replied that the only condition was his death. In response, he slew a multitude who had gathered at the Second Temple. Furthermore, 800 Pharisees were crucified upon the advice of a Sadducee. According to legend, the wives and children of the condemned men were executed before their eyes while the court watched. As a result of this horrific deed, 8,000 Pharisees emigrated to Syria and Egypt. Alexander Janneus died at the age of fifty-one. According to Josephus, Alexander entrusted the government to his wife Salome Alexandra (*Jewish Antiquities* 13; cf. Louis Ginzberg, "Alexander Jannaeus," *Jewish Encyclopedia*, https://jewishencyclopedia.com/articles/1144-alexander-jannaeus-jonathan).

14. **Salome Alexandra**, referred to by Josephus as simply "Alexandra," was first the wife of Aristobulus I; after his death she married his brother Alexander Janneus (probably by a levirate marriage arrangement). Salome Alexandra is noteworthy as the only Jewish queen regnant besides the usurper Athaliah of Judah (cf. **2 Kings 11**). According to Josephus, Salome Alexandra convinced Aristobulus I that his brother Antigonus was plotting against him, so Aristobulus drew Antigonus into a trap. Josephus records that Antigonus was killed by Aristobulus' guards while coming to show his brother his new armor (*Jewish Antiquities* 13.11.1–2). Although she and Aristobulus had been childless, Salome Alexandra bore Alexander Janneus two sons, John Hyrcanus II and Aristobulus II.

When Alexander Janneus died, he entrusted the government to his wife (Alexandra) instead of his sons. During her nine-year reign as queen, from 76–67 B.C., Salome Alexandra appointed her eldest son John Hyrcanus II as high priest because he "cared not to meddle with politics" (*Jewish Antiquities* 13.16.2). Consequently, the Pharisees regained power; in turn, they recalled their fellow Pharisees who had been banished and freed those who had been imprisoned during Alexander Janneus' reign. The Pharisees wanted Salome Alexandra to kill those who had persuaded Alexander Janneus to kill the 800 Pharisees, but they ended up taking matters into their own hands and slit the throats of some of the culprits. During her reign, the Sanhedrin was reorganized, becoming a group that oversaw both social and religious matters.

According to Josephus, Salome Alexandra "was loved by the multitude, because she seemed displeased at the offenses her husband [Alexander Janneus] had been guilty of" (*Jewish Antiquities* 13.16.1). Josephus' review of Alexandra's reign is mixed. He at once notes that she had none of the so-called "weakness of her sex" but also that because "of a desire of what does not belong to a woman," as well as her compliance with those who bore her family ill-will and her inability to surround the government with wise [male] advisors, her rule led to the deposition and destruction of the Hasmonean dynasty. For all of that, Josephus does acknowledge that, unlike her predecessors, Salome Alexandra was able to maintain peace (*Jewish Antiquities* 13.16.6). The Jewish Encyclopedia affirms that Salome Alexandra's tactful and wise ruling style enabled Judea to become respected abroad; Louis Ginzberg, "Alexandra (Salome)," *Jewish Encyclopedia*, https://jewishencyclopedia.com/articles/1167-alexandra. Upon her death in 67 B.C., Salome Alexandra was succeeded by her eldest son John Hyrcanus II, who was already serving as high priest.

15. Antigonus was killed by his brother, Aristobulus I (*Jewish Antiquities* 13.11.1–2).

16. Of these two sons of John Hyrcanus I, one appears to be named Absalom; both of them were killed by their brother Aristobulus I (*Jewish Antiquities* 13.11.1).

17. **Aristobulus II** was the youngest son of Alexander Jannaeus and his wife Salome Alexandra and was the brother of John Hyrcanus II. Three months after John Hyrcanus II succeeded to the kingship of Judea, Aristobulus II revolted against his older brother and won the ensuing battle. After Aristobulus II took control of the Second Temple, John Hyrcanus II surrendered. Aristobulus II became both high priest and king, although John Hyrcanus II retained the revenues from the high priest's office. During this time, an ambitious Idumean named Antipater I (the father of Herod the Great), sought to control Judea and realized that reaching his goal would be easier under the weaker government of John Hyrcanus II than the strong one of Aristobulus II. Antipater I convinced John Hyrcanus II that Aristobulus sought his death, thereby leading John Hyrcanus II to seek refuge with Aretas the king of the Nabataeans (whom Antipater had bribed into helping John Hyrcanus' cause). During this time of civil unrest, a Roman general named Scaurus came to Syria to take control of the region for Pompey, who was the main military leader and stateman of the Roman Republic at the time. Both John Hyrcanus II and Aristobulus II appealed to general Scaurus to help their respective sides. Scaurus decided to help Aristobulus II, but Pompey favored John Hyrcanus II, again, because he was the weaker of the two rulers. Pompey defeated the Jewish forces, took Judea's fortresses, and captured Aristobulus II, along with his sons Alexander II and Antigonus II. Aristobulus II tried to turn Jerusalem over to Pompey in exchange for an end to the hostilities. When the people would not open the gates to the city, the Roman soldiers attacked Jerusalem, severely damaging it and the temple. In ca. 63 B.C., Pompey restored John Hyrcanus II to the office of the high priest but not to the kingship. Aristobulus II escaped captivity in 57 B.C. Later, he tried to incite a revolt in Judea again but was recaptured and taken to Rome. He was released by Julius Caesar but was poisoned on his way back to Judea (See *Jewish Antiquities* 14.1–7; Richard Gottheil and Louis Ginzberg, "Aristobulus II," *Jewish Encyclopedia*, https://jewishencyclopedia.com/articles/1769-aristobulus-ii; Richard Gottheil and Isaac Broydé, "Hyrcanus II," *Jewish Encyclopedia*, https://jewishencyclopedia.com/articles/7973-hyrcanus-ii).

18. **John Hyrcanus II**, the eldest son of Alexander Janneus and his wife Salome Alexandra, ascended to the throne after the death of his mother in 67 B.C. John Hyrcanus II already held the high priesthood when he took the throne. However, barely three months into his reign, his brother Aristobulus II incited a rebellion against him. (For more detail about Aristobulus' rebellion and struggle for control of Judea, see note 17). When Pompey came to Syria in 63 B.C., he realized, as the ambitious Antipater I the Idumean had, that John Hyrcanus II was the better choice because he was the weaker ruler. Thus, Pompey was able to conquer Judea and set it up as a Roman state. John Hyrcanus II was reappointed to the high priesthood but initially held no political authority until Julius Caesar (dictator of the Roman Republic, 49–44 B.C.) gave him the title of ethnarch in 47 B.C. However, this appointment was in name only, because John Hyrcanus II left the actual rule of Judea to Antipater, who used his authority to further his own interests. John Hyrcanus II continued in the high priesthood until 40 B.C., when his nephew Antigonus II was named king and high priest. John Hyrcanus II was then carried off to Babylon; there, he was treated with respect by the Jews who had remained in Babylon after the exile. However, fearful that John Hyrcanus' popularity would lead to a plot to restore him to the Jewish throne, Herod the Great (who had defeated Antigonus II) called John Hyrcanus II back to Jerusalem. Initially, John Hyrcanus was treated well; however, in 30 B.C., Herod charged John Hyrcanus II of plotting with the Nabataeans and had him executed (Richard Gottheil and Isaac Broydé, "Hyrcanus II," *Jewish Encyclopedia*, https://jewishencyclopedia.com/articles/7973-hyrcanus-ii).

19. **Alexander II** was the eldest son of Aristobulus II. In 63 B.C., the Roman general Pompey came to Jerusalem and captured Alexander II (along with his father Aristobulus II and his brother Antigonus), but Alexander escaped. On several occasions he incited the Jews to revolt and raised an army against the Romans, but he was defeated. In 49 B.C., on the orders of Pompey, Alexander II was beheaded at Antioch (*Jewish Antiquities* 14.5–7; *The Jewish War* 1.8–9).

20. Alexandra the daughter of John Hyrcanus II married her first cousin Alexander II. She was widowed in 49 B.C. In 26 B.C. she was killed on the orders of Herod the Great (*Jewish Antiquities* 15.7.8).

21. Mariamne I was the daughter of Alexander II and his wife Alexandra and was the granddaughter of John Hyrcanus II. Mariamne I became the second wife of Herod the Great. Their marriage was encouraged by her mother Alexandra as a means to end the feud between the Hasmoneans and the Roman rulers. However, Herod, a suspicious person by nature, feared the Hasmoneans. Because of the influence of his sister Salome I, Herod the Great became increasingly convinced that Mariamne I had committed adultery with Herod's uncle Joseph and that she planned to poison him (Herod). Mariamne accused Herod of killing her grandfather (John Hyrcanus II) and her brother (Aristobulus III). Herod's violent love for his wife descended into a mixture of hatred and love. Also Mariamne was distrustful of Herod because her uncle-in-law Joseph had told her of Herod's secret plans to have her killed if Herod was found guilty of the murder of Aristobulus III (Mariamne I's brother) and then executed. Herod the Great put Mariamne I on trial for slander; she was convicted and executed in 29 B.C. when she was about 28 years old (Richard Gottheil and Samuel Krauss, "Mariamne," *Jewish Encyclopedia*, https://jewishencyclopedia.com/articles/10415-mariamne).

Herod built three fortified towers at the citadel in Jerusalem: (1) the Phasael Tower (named for his brother); (2) the Hippicus Tower (named for a friend); and (3) the Mariamne Tower (named for Mariamne I). Mariamne I bore Herod four children—two daughters (Salampsio and Cypros) and two sons, Alexander (Alexandros) and Aristobulus IV. The sons were executed by order of their father in 7 B.C. Mariamne I should not be confused with Mariamne II, the daughter of Simon ben Boethus (the high priest from 23–5 B.C.) whom Herod married after Mariamne I's execution (*Jewish Antiquities* 18.5.4). For more information, see chart "**Matthew 2**: Herod the Great and the Herodian Dynasty."

22. Herod the Great was the Rome-appointed king of Judea from 37–4 B.C. or 35–1 B.C. (for more details about Herod's reign, see chart "**Matthew 2**: Herod the Great and the Herodian Dynasty," especially note 13). Herod the Great established the Herodian Dynasty. Herod was the ruler of Judea when Jesus was born and was responsible for killing all the boys of Bethlehem who were two years old or younger (**Matthew 2:13–16**)—later known as the "Massacre of the Innocents." Herod was the son of Antipater I the "Edomite/Idumean"—meaning he was a descendant of Esau, since the Edomites were called *Idumeans* in Jesus' day—and Cypros, a Nabatean noblewoman. The Edomites had converted to Judaism in the second century B.C. Thus, although Herod was of mixed Jewish heritage, he was a practicing Jew. Julius Caesar had appointed Antipater I as procurator of Judea in 47 B.C. and granted him Roman citizenship, which he also extended to Herod's children. Herod the Great was first the governor, then the tetrarch of Galilee; in 37 B.C. (or 35 B.C.) he became the ruler of Judea after defeating Antigonus II. Herod divorced his first wife Doris to marry the Hasmonean princess Mariamne I (see note 21).

Josephus relates that Herod promised Mark Antony money if the Roman Senate would proclaim him king; Antony, Caesar, and other members of the Roman Senate gave Herod such a glowing review that the Senate proclaimed Herod the king (*Jewish Antiquities* 14.14.4). Herod is known for rebuilding the Second Temple, renaming it Herod's Temple, and expanding its grounds. He also leveled and expanded the Temple Mount so that it became a plateau instead of a mountain. In *Jewish Antiquities* 15.11.1ff, Josephus details the events surrounding Herod's revision of the temple and the components of the temple. Herod also built a royal palace and many fortresses; additionally, he built (or rebuilt) and made improvements to various cities in the region. Herod established the towns of Caesarea Maritima on the Mediterranean coast and Sebaste, which was built on the site of the ancient town of Samaria; the projects were funded by taxing the people of Judea (Joseph Jacobs and Isaac Broydé, "Herod I," *Jewish Encyclopedia*, https://jewishencyclopedia.com/articles/7598-herod-i).

Herod's family life was full of calamity and dysfunction. Josephus relates that upon the insistence of Mariamne I, Herod proclaimed her brother

Aristobulus III as high priest at the age of seventeen (*Jewish Antiquities* 13.3.1). However, just one year after his appointment, Aristobulus III drowned at the age of eighteen, and Josephus states that Herod was responsible for instigating Aristobulus III's murder (*Jewish Antiquities* 15.3.3). Herod was called by Mark Antony to stand trial for this murder. During his absence, Herod told his uncle Joseph (the brother of Antipater) to take care of Mariamne I, stipulating that if Mark Antony killed him, Joseph was to kill Mariamne. When Joseph disclosed to Mariamne Herod's secret instructions, she began to greatly distrust Herod. Also, Herod's sister Salome began to poison Herod's mind by telling him that Mariamne I had been unfaithful to him and had been intimate with Joseph. When Herod confronted Mariamne, he became convinced of her infidelity because she knew about his secret order. Even though Herod dismissed Mariamne I and her mother (Alexandra) to the fortress Alexandrium, Herod's sister Salome continued to vilify Mariamne. Mariamne I accused Herod of killing her grandfather (John Hyrcanus II) and her brother (Aristobulus III). Mariamne's distrust of her husband and Herod's extreme emotions toward her—which Josephus relates varied between love and hatred—damaged their marriage to the point where Herod, after trying multiple times to reconcile with her, had Mariamne brought to trial for slander. She was convicted and executed in 29 B.C. Josephus notes that Herod seemed to descend into madness after her death, calling for her and grieving for her greatly (*Jewish Antiquities* 15.7.4–7). Herod's sons by Mariamne I—Alexander and Aristobulus IV—also became victims of Herod's excessive jealousy because they were popular with the people. Herod became more and more convinced that they would try to overthrow him; on their father's orders, the brothers were strangled in 7 B.C.

Josephus summarizes Herod as being "a violent and bold man, and very desirous of acting tyrannically" (*Jewish Antiquities* 14.9.3). When Herod died, his kingdom was divided according to his will among three of his sons: Herod Archelaus became ethnarch of the tetrarchy of Judea, Herod Antipas became tetrarch of Galilee and Perea, and Herod Philip II became tetrarch of the territories of Iturea, Gaulantis (Golan Heights), Batanea (southern Syria), Trachonitis, and Auranitis (Hauran). For more information about the genealogy and reign of these Herodian rulers, see chart "**Matthew 2**: Herod the Great and the Herodian Dynasty."

23. For Aristobulus III, see note 69 in chart "**Supplement 2**: The High Priests of Israel."

SUPPLEMENT 9: FLAVIUS JOSEPHUS, THE ROMAN-JEWISH HISTORIAN[1]

Approximate Dating: born A.D. 37 and died ca. A.D. 100

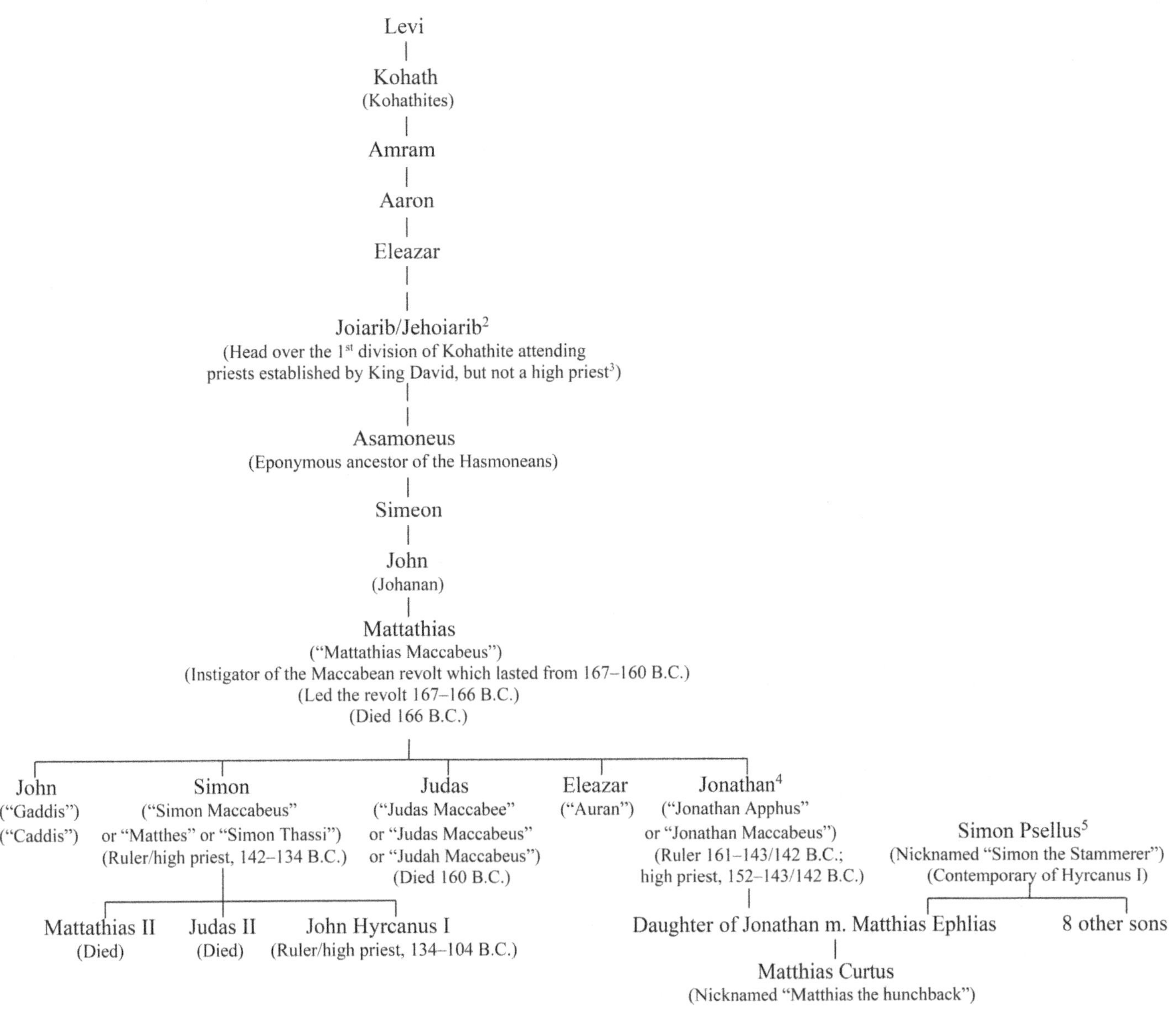

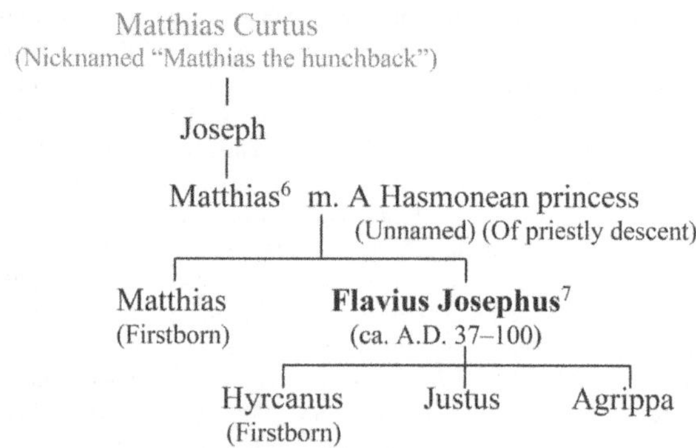

Biblical and Theological Significance

Flavius Josephus[8] (Heb. "Yosef ben Mattathias") wrote several works that provide an important reference for the political and social climates of the intertestamental period and the Roman period in Jewish history. The four-surviving works of Josephus are: (1) *The Jewish War* (composed ca. A.D. 73); (2) *Jewish Antiquities* (composed ca. A.D. 93); (3) *Life* (the autobiographical appendix to the *Jewish Antiquities*); and (4) *Against Apion* (penned shortly before his death). His accounts provide biblical scholars with critical knowledge of many biblical figures. Specifically, Josephus gives information about the stoning of James, the half-brother of Jesus in A.D. 62,[9] and he refers to Jesus in two passages.[10] In his introductory commentary to *The Complete Works of Josephus*, Paul L. Maier summarizes the great value of Josephus' writings: "aside from references to Scripture itself, the phrase 'according to Josephus' is the single most familiar refrain in biblical and intertestamental scholarship."[11] Without Josephus,

> We would have little knowledge of the intertestamental era and only a small fraction of our present information on Herod the Great, Archelaus, Herod Antipas, or the Herod Agrippas I and II. Facts about Annas, Caiaphas, and the priestly families that controlled the Jerusalem temple in Jesus' day would be blurred, as would the politics of Pontius Pilate, Felix, Festus, and the other Roman governors in Palestine. . . . We would never know about . . . the daughter of Herodias [Salome] who secured the decapitation of John the Baptist . . . and most of the details concerning the Roman destruction of Jerusalem. . . . The writings of Josephus, then, provide a vital political, topographical, economic, social, intellectual, and religious supplement to our biblical information—a crucial context for comparing, interpreting, and above all, extending our knowledge of the time.[12]

Regarding his genealogy, Josephus states that he was born in A.D. 37 in Jerusalem, the son of a priestly family on both his paternal and maternal sides. In his vita, *Josephus* claims descent from the first priestly division of Joiarib/Jehoiarib from the Aaron–Eleazar priestly line (cf. **1 Chronicles 24:7**)—the same ancestral line as the Hasmoneans, who led the Maccabean revolt and held the throne of Israel and/or the high priesthood (see chart "**Supplement 8**: The Maccabees and the Hasmonean Dynasty"). Josephus' great-great-great-grandfather, as evidenced from Josephus' own detailed account, was Jonathan Apphus, who was king of Israel from 161–143/142 B.C. and held the high priesthood from 152–143/142 B.C. Josephus had three sons—Hyrcanus (the firstborn), Justus, and Agrippa. Josephus died in ca. A.D.100 or soon thereafter.

Notes

1. The genealogy of Josephus is based on Josephus' autobiography in *The Life of Josephus*, 1ff. (see note 7) and the ancestry of Mattathias in *Jewish Antiquities* 12.6.1 in *The Complete Works of Josephus*, trans. William Whiston, commentary Paul L. Maier (Grand Rapids: Kregel, 1999). Josephus says: "I set down the genealogy of my family as I have found it described in the public records" (Flavius Josephus, *The Life of Flavius Josephus*, 1. http://penelope.uchicago.edu/josephus/autobiog.html; spelling modernized).

Also consulted was Joachim Jeremias (*Jerusalem in the Time of Jesus* (Philadelphia: Fortress, 1969). Jeremias claims that Josephus wrote his vita after A.D. 100 using the records of the birth dates of his forebears from the public registers—"a kind of archive [residing in the Temple at Jerusalem] in which the genealogies of the priesthood were kept." Joachim Jeremias, Jerusalem in the Time of Jesus, 214; cf. high priests in **1 Chronicles 6:1–15; Ezra 7:1–5; Nehemiah 12:10–11** and a summary in "**Supplement 2**: The High Priests of Israel." Jeremias also states that "Josephus asserts positively that, after such great wars as occurred under Antiochus [IV] Ephiphanes, Pompey, Quintilius Varus, Vespasian and Titus, the surviving priests established new genealogies from the ancient records (*Contra Apion* i.34f). These measures were taken partly because genealogies were lost in the confusion of war, and also because they must ensure that none of the priests' wives had been made prisoners of war. In this last case they could no longer be considered legitimate wives of priests and any offspring born to them since their capture did not qualify for priestly office" (Joachim Jeremias, *Jerusalem in the Time of Jesus*, 214).

2. Jehoiarib (also called Joiarib in Scripture and in *1 Maccabees* 2:1) was a Kohathite attending priest and the head of the first of the twenty-four divisions of Kohathite attending priests in Solomon's Temple, ca. 971–931 B.C. (**1 Chronicles 24:7**)—Joiarib (cf. **Nehemiah 11:10; 12:6**) is the shortened form of Jehoiarib (**1 Chronicles 9:10; 24:7**), meaning "Yah establishes justice." Given the textual reading of **1 Chronicles 24:6b**, Jehoiarib was presumably from the Aaron–Eleazar line of priests. The priestly descendants of Jehoiarib/Joiarib who lived in the post-exile are mentioned in **1 Chronicles 9:10**; **Nehemiah 11:10; 12:6, 19**; also, a descendant of Jehoiarib/Joiarib named Mattenai served in the days of Nehemiah in 444 B.C. (**Nehemiah 12:19**). Mattathias, the leader of the Maccabean Revolt of 167–160 B.C., claimed descent from Jehoiarib/Joiarib.

3. For information about the Kohathite attending priests, see chart "**1 Chronicles 24**: Genealogical Registry of the Twenty-Four Divisions of Kohathite Priests Who Rotated Service in Solomon's Temple (Sixteen from the Aaron–Eleazar–Zadok Line and Eight from the Aaron–Ithamar Line)." For the line of the high priests, see chart "**Supplement 2**: The High Priests of Israel."

4. In his vita, Josephus states that Jonathan was the "first of the sons of Asamoneus"—perhaps meaning that Jonathan "Apphus" was the *firstborn* of Mattathias Maccabeus, the renowned *descendant* of Asamoneus (the eponymous ancestor of the Asmonean/Hasmonean dynasty). See chart "**Supplement 8**: The Maccabees and the Hasmonean Dynasty."

5. In his vita, Josephus identifies Simon Psellus as "my grandfather's father," but as Josephus expands on his family ancestry, Simon Psellus appears

to be Josephus' great-great-great-grandfather (not his *grandfather's father*); this discrepancy has been noted by other scholars also (see Jeremias, *Jerusalem in the Time of Jesus,* 214, n. 212). Josephus says that Simon Psellus "lived at the same time as the son of Simon the high priest [presumably referring to Simon Maccabeus/Simon Thassi], who first of all the high priests was named Hyrcanus." Simon Psellus' nickname was "Simon the Stammerer"; see comments in Richard Bauckham, *The Jewish World Around the New Testament* (Grand Rapids: Baker, 2010).

6. Matthias, Josephus' father, was born ca. A.D. 4–6.

7. When Josephus summarizes his ancestral heritage in his vita, he says "I am not only sprung from a sacerdotal family in general, but from the first of the twenty-four courses [presumably referring to Jehoiarib/Joiarib, the head of the first division/course; cf. **1 Chronicles 24:7** and the chart "**1 Chronicles 24**: Genealogical Registry of the Twenty-Four Divisions of Kohathite Attending Priests Who Rotated Service in Solomon's Temple"]. . . . I am of the chief family of that first course [possibly referring to the family of the director of the weekly course] . . . also further, by my mother I am of the royal blood; for the children of Asamoneus, from whom that family was derived, had both the office of the high priesthood, and the dignity of a king. . . . my grandfather's father was named Simon, with the addition of Psellus; he lived at the same time as the son of Simon the high priest, who first of all the high priests was named Hyrcanus. This Simon Psellus had nine sons, one of whom was Matthias, called Ephlias; he married the daughter of Jonathan the high priest [Jonathan Maccabeus "Apphus"]; which Jonathan was the first of the sons [descendants?] of Asamoneus, who was high priest, and was the brother of Simon the high priest [Simon Maccabeus/Simon Thassi] also. This Matthias [Matthias Ephlias] had a son called Matthias Curtus in the first year of the government of Hyrcanus [Hyrcanus I]; his son's name was Joseph, born in the ninth year of the reign of Alexandra [Queen/ruler Salome Alexandra, who ruled 76–67 B.C.]; his son Matthias was born in the tenth year of the reign of Archelaus [Herod Archelaus]; as I was born to Matthias in the first year of the reign of Caius Caesar [referring to Emperor Caligula, byname Gaius Caesar, A.D. 37–41]. I [Josephus] have three sons: Hyrcanus, the eldest, was born in the fourth year of the reign of Vespasian [A.D. 67–79], as was Justus born in the seventh, and Agrippa in the ninth" (*The Life of Flavius Josephus*, 1). For a discussion of Herod Archelaus' reign, see chart "**Matthew 2**: Herod the Great and the Herodian Dynasty" and for references to the emperors see chart "**Supplement 10**: The Roman Emperors."

8. The namesake of Flavius Josephus was Titus Flavius Vespasianus, who lived A.D. 9–79 and reigned as Emperor Vespasian, A.D. 69–79.

9. *Jewish Antiquities* 20.9.1.

10. *Jewish Antiquities* 18.3.3; 20.9.1.

11. Flavius Josephus, *The New Complete Works of Josephus*, trans. by William Whiston, commentary by Paul L. Maier (Grand Rapids: Kregel, 1999), 7.

12. Josephus, *The New Complete Works of Josephus*, 7.

SUPPLEMENT 10: THE ROMAN EMPERORS[1]

Approximate Dating: 27 B.C.–A.D. 138

Emperors of the Julio-Claudian Dynasty (27 B.C.–A.D. 68)

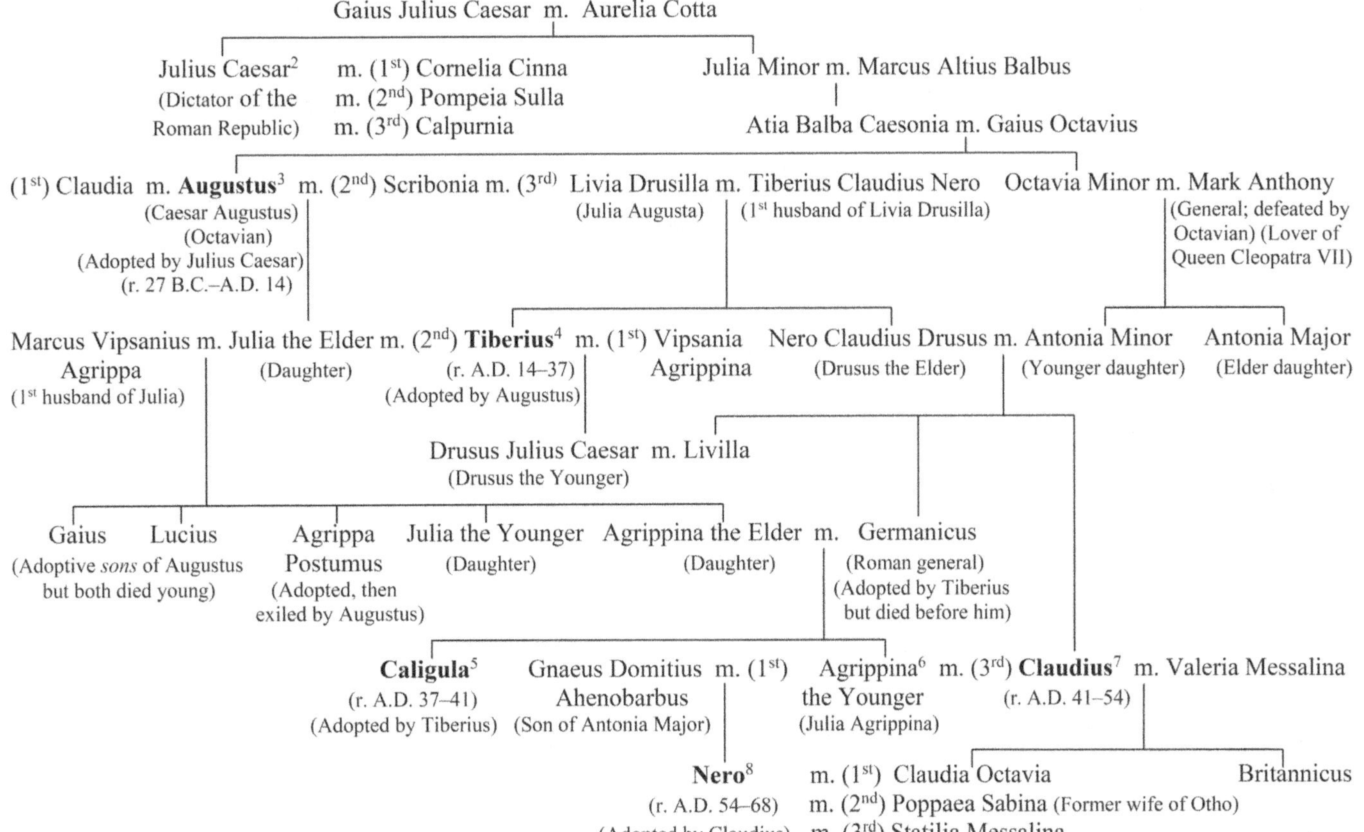

Emperors between the Julio-Claudian and Flavian Dynasties (A.D. 68–69)

Galba:

Gaius Sulpicius Galba m. Mummia Achaica

Galba[9] m. Aemilia Lepida
(r. A.D. 68–69)

Two sons
(Both died young)

Otho:

Lucius Otho m. Albia Terentia

Otho[10] m. Poppaea Sabina
(r. A.D. 69) (Mistress, then wife of Nero)

Vitellius:

Lucius Vitellius m. Sestilia
(Governor of Syria)

Petronia m. (1st) **Vitellius**[11] m. (2nd) Galena Fundana
(r. A.D. 69)

Petronianus

Vitellius Vitellia

Emperors of the Flavian Dynasty (A.D. 69–96)

Titus Flavius Sabinus m. Vespasia Polla

Titus Flavius Sabinus
(Prefect of Rome under Nero)

Vespasian[12] m. Flavia Domitilla Major
(r. A.D. 69–79)

Arrecina Tertulla m. (1st) **Titus**[13] m. (2nd) Marcia Furnilla
(r. A.D. 79–81)

Julia Flavia m. Titus Flavius Sabinus
(Widowed)
(Mistress of her uncle Domitian)

Domitian[14] m. Domitia Longina
(r. A.D. 81–96)

Son
(Died young)

Nerva-Trajan Dynasty (A.D. 96–138)

Nerva:

Marcus Cocceius Nerva m. Sergia Plautilla

Nerva[15]
(r. A.D. 96–98)

Trajan and Hadrian:

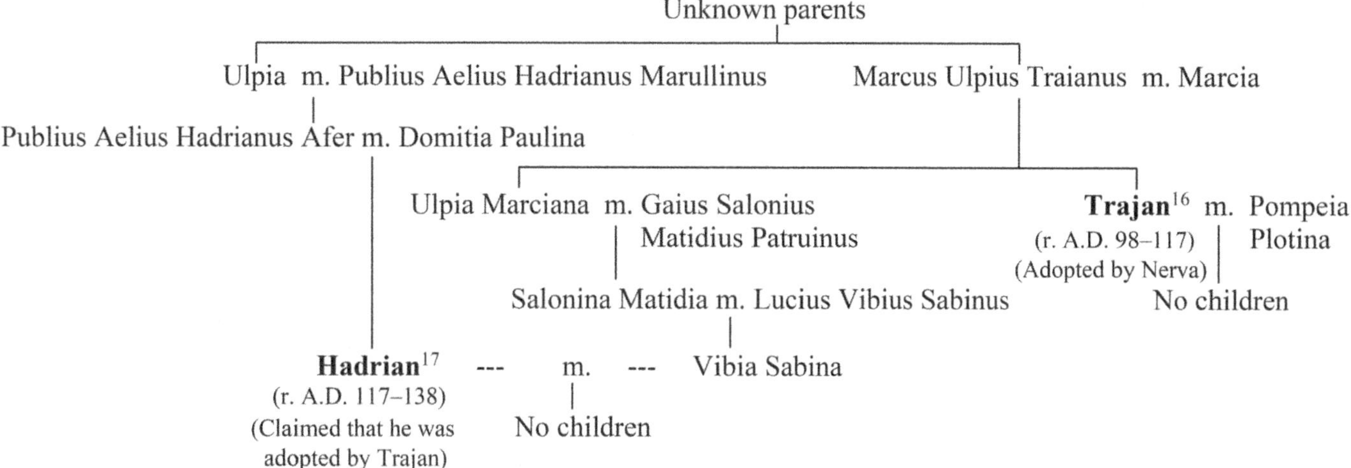

Notes

1. References for the Roman emperors include: *Jewish Antiquities* and *The Jewish War*, in *The New Complete Works of Josephus*, trans. William Whiston, (Grand Rapids: Kregel, 1999); Suetonius, *Lives of the Twelve Caesars* (Rolfe LCL), archived by Bill Thayer at http://penelope.uchicago.edu/Thayer/E/Roman/Texts/Suetonius/12Caesars/home.html; Eusebius of Caesarea, *Ecclesiastical History*, https://www.newadvent.org/fathers/2501.htm; Tacitus *Annals*, 15.44.1, at https://penelope.uchicago.edu/Thayer/E/Roman/Texts/Tacitus/Annals/15B*.html. Tacitus, *Histories* (Moore LCL), archived by Bill Thayer at https://penelope.uchicago.edu/Thayer/E/Roman/Texts/Tacitus/home.html; Cassius Dio, *Roman History* (Cary LCL), archived by Bill Thayer at https://penelope.uchicago.edu/Thayer/e/roman/texts/cassius_dio/; Chris Scarre, *Chronicle of the Roman Emperors* (London: Thames and Hudson, 1995); Philo Judaeus, *The Works of Philo Judaeus*, vol. IV, trans. C.D. Yonge, (London: Henry G. Bohn, 1855) archived at https://archive.org/details/worksofphilojuda01yonguoft/page/n1/mode/2up; E. Mary Smallwood, "Domitian's Attitude toward the Jews and Judaism," *Classical Philology* 51: 1956, 1–13, The University of Chicago Press Stable, URL: http://www.jstor.org/stable/266380; Paul Keresztes, "The Jews, the Christians, and Emperor Domitian," *Vigiliae Christianae* V27: 1973, 1–28, http://www.jstor.org/stable/1583284; Nathan T. Elkins, "Roman Emperor Nerva's Reform of the Jewish Tax," *Bible Archaeology Daily* Blog, 1 January 2019, https://www.biblicalarchaeology.org/daily/ancient-cultures/daily-life-and-practice/roman-emperor-nervas-reform-of-the-jewish-tax/; Pliny, the Younger. *The Letters of Pliny the Consul: With Occasional Remarks*, vol. 2, 5th ed., corrected (William Melmoth, Esq: London, MDCCLVII [1757]); Gavin Townend, "Some Flavian Connections," *The Journal of Roman Studies* 51: 1961, 54–62. JSTOR, www.jstor.org/stable/298836; Mark Wilson, "Alternative Facts: Domitian's Persecution of Christians," *Bible Archaeology Daily* blog, 24 July 2017, https://www.biblicalarchaeology.org/daily/biblical-topics/post-biblical-period/domitian-persecution-of-christians/; Various articles on http://www.livius.org; and Kenneth L. Barker, Mark L. Strauss, Jeannine K. Brown, Craig L. Blomberg, and Michael Williams, eds. *NIV Study Bible*, Fully Revised Edition (Grand Rapids: Zondervan, 2020).

2. Julius Caesar (born Gaius Julius Caesar) was born July 12/13, 100 B.C. He was a great Roman military general who became a powerful politician and later was the consul and dictator of the Roman Republic, 49–44 B.C. Julius Caesar was one of the three strong political leaders—including Pompey and Marcus Licinius Crassus—known as the generals of the First Triumvirate of Rome (59–53 B.C.). Julius Caesar had three wives (Cornelia Cinna, Pompeia Sulla, and Calpurnia) and three children: Julia (by Cornelia), who married the Roman general Pompey the Great; Ptolemy XV (Caesarion) by Cleopatra VII Philopator of Egypt, who was not formally acknowledged by his father; and an adoptive *son*/heir, Augustus. Julius Caesar bequeathed the Caesar name to his great-nephew, Gaius Octavius (Octavian), later known as Augustus Caesar. Julius Caesar was assassinated on the Ides of March (March 15, 44 B.C.) and was posthumously deified. His successor, Augustus Caesar, assumed the title of "son of a god" or "son of the divine" and became the first Roman emperor of the Roman Empire.

3. **Augustus Caesar** (27 B.C.–A.D. 14)—birth name Gaius Octavius and adopted name Gaius Julius Caesar Octavianus, until 27 B.C., after which he was known as Octavian—was born September 23, 63 B.C. He was the great-nephew of Julius Caesar. Augustus Caesar was a member of the Second Triumvirate along with Mark Antony and Marcus Aemilius Lepidus (43–33 B.C.). Following Julius Caesar's death in 44 B.C., Augustus, who was then 18 years old, was informed that Caesar had adopted him and named him his heir. Mark Antony, who had expected to be named the heir, seized control of Julius Caesar's possessions. Augustus, however, won over many of Mark Antony's supporters and assumed control.

Augustus was married three times—to Claudia, Scribonia, and Livia Drusilla (who by her first marriage to Tiberius Claudius Nero was the mother of the next emperor, Tiberius). Augustus' marriage to Livia Drusilla was childless but was evidently a devoted one, as she served as her husband's counselor. Augustus had one daughter, Julia the Elder, with his wife Scribonia. First, Julia the Elder married her cousin Marcus Claudius Marcellus, but he died before they had children. Julia later married Marcus Vipsanius Agrippa and bore him two sons, Lucius Caesar and Gaius Caesar. After Julia's death, her sons were adopted by their grandfather Augustus; as the emperor's adopted sons and joint heirs to the Roman Empire, Lucius and Gaius had promising political and military careers. However, Lucius died of a sudden illness on August 20, A.D. 2 in Massilia, Gaul, while traveling to meet the Roman army in Hispania. His brother Gaius Caesar also died relatively young on February 21, A.D. 4. The untimely loss of both heirs compelled Augustus to redraw the line of succession by adopting Lucius' younger brother Agrippa Postumus, as well as Augustus' stepson Tiberius on June 26, A.D. 4. However, in A.D. 7, Augustus permanently banished his adopted son Agrippa Postumus from Rome for his reckless nature and vices, thus leaving Tiberius as Augustus' sole heir and successor.

Augustus' sister Octavia Minor was married to Mark Antony; their divorce sparked war between Antony's lover—Cleopatra VII Philopator of Egypt—and Augustus. Augustus eventually defeated Mark Anthony at the Battle of Actium in 31 B.C. Augustus annexed Judea in A.D. 6 and Judea came under Roman rule; therefore, the Roman emperor "Caesar Augustus" ruled at the time of Christ's birth in ca. 3/2 B.C. (cf. **Luke 2:1**)—for a discussion of Jesus' birth date, see chart "**Matthew 1**: Jesus and His Immediate Family." Augustus transformed Roman life, enabling Roman culture to spread and impact the world. Peace ensued during and immediately after his tenure, enabling trade and communication and facilitating the spread of Christianity. Augustus died on August 19, A.D. 14.

4. **Tiberius** (A.D. 14–37)—birth name Tiberius Claudius Nero, full regnal name Tiberius Caesar Augustus—was born November 16, 42 B.C. His father, also named Tiberius Claudius Nero, was a magistrate and high priest who had formerly been a fleet captain under Julius Caesar. Tiberius' mother was Livia Drusilla, who was known as "Julia Augusta" after she became the wife of Emperor Augustus. Tiberius married Vipsania Agrippina, the daughter of Marcus Vipsanius Agrippa. By all accounts, their marriage was a true love match. However, Tiberius was forced to marry Augustus' daughter Julia the

Elder, as both her first husband (her cousin Marcus Claudius Marcellus, the son of Augustus' sister Octavia Minor) and her second husband (Marcus Vipsanius Agrippa) had died. The marriage to Julia the Elder was troubled: Julia committed adultery and Tiberius was still in love with Vipsania Agrippina.

Tiberius became Augustus' heir after Julia's two sons (Gaius Caesar and Lucius Caesar) died and after a third son, the Roman statesman Agrippa Postumus, was exiled in A.D. 7 by Augustus. Tiberius was named emperor one month after Augustus died. Suetonius relates that Tiberius forbid the Jews from practicing their religion and threatened to enslave those who did not obey. According to Josephus, Tiberius exiled the entire Jewish community from Rome and sent them to the island of Sardinia (*Jewish Antiquities* 18.3.5). Tiberius was the Roman emperor during the ministries of John the Baptist and Jesus (cf. **Luke 3:1–2**); he was also emperor when Jesus was crucified in A.D. 33 (see Tacitus' *Annals*, 15.44.1). Tiberius chose as his successor Caligula, the great-grandson of Augustus Caesar through his daughter Julia the Elder and her daughter Agrippina the Elder. Tiberius died on March 16, A.D. 37 by poison or smothering; accounts differ.

5. **Caligula** (A.D. 37–41)—birth name Gaius Julius Caesar Germanicus—was born on August 31, A.D. 12. He was the son of the Roman general Germanicus and his wife Agrippina the Elder, who was the daughter of Marcus Vipsanius Agrippa and Julia the Elder. Caligula was adopted as Tiberius' son and heir alongside another grandson of Tiberius, Tiberius Gemellus, in A.D. 35. After Tiberius' death in A.D. 37, Caligula assumed control and either ordered Gemellus to be killed or forced him to commit suicide.

Caligula had three sisters: Julia Drusilla, Julia Livilla, and Agrippina the Younger. Caligula was married four times; his wives were Junia Claudia, Livia Orestilla, Lollia Paulina, and Milonia Caesonia. He abducted his second wife and forced her to marry him; he repudiated his third wife shortly after their marriage. His fourth wife, Milonia Caesonia, was apparently much older than Caligula and already had three daughters; however, Milonia Caesonia bore Caligula's only child, Julia Drusilla. In Alexandria, the Roman governor Flaccus tried to make the Jews worship Caligula. When they refused, Flaccus persecuted them in horrific ways; Philo relates the atrocious treatment of the Jews by the Alexandrians in Volume IV of his *Works of Philo Judaeus*. In A.D. 40, the Jews sent a delegation led by Philo to meet with Caligula along with an Alexandrian delegation represented by Apion. Josephus refuted Apion's "many blasphemies against the Jews" (*Jewish Antiquities* 18.8.1) in his work *Against Apion*. The meeting was unsuccessful for the Jews. Caligula was murdered on January 24, A.D. 41 by Cassius Chaerea and other members of the Praetorian Guard (*Jewish Antiquities* 19.1.1).

6. Agrippina the Younger, also called Julia Agrippina, was the daughter of the Roman general Germanicus and Agrippina the Elder (the granddaughter of Caesar Augustus) and was the sister of Caligula. Agrippina the Younger was married first to Gnaeus Domitius Ahenobarbus (the father of Nero); second, she was married to Sallustius Passienus Crispus; and third, she was married to Emperor Claudius. Agrippina the Younger was successfully had her son Nero adopted by Claudius as his heir and successor (rather than Claudius' son Britannicus).

7. **Claudius** (A.D. 41–54)—birth name Tiberius Claudius Nero Germanicus; regnal name Tiberius Claudius Caesar Augustus Germanicus—was born August 1, A.D. 10. His father was the Roman general Nero Claudius Drusus and his mother was Antonia Minor, the younger daughter of Mark Antony and Octavia Minor (Augustus' sister). Claudius married four times—first, to Plautia Urgulanilla, second to Aelia Paetina, third to Valeria Messalina, and fourth to Julia Agrippina (Agrippina the Younger)—and had children by his first three wives. The day after Caligula's murder in A.D. 41, Claudius was made emperor by the Praetorian Guard. After Herod Agrippa I died in A.D. 44, Claudius made Judea a province. Suetonius says that Claudius expelled the Jews from Rome (ca. A.D. 49), which prompted Priscilla and Aquila to leave and go to Corinth (cf. **Acts 18:1–2**). However, Claudius also issued an edict to the Alexandrians, saying "I will therefore that the nation of the Jews be not deprived of their rights and privileges . . . which they formerly enjoyed [and should] be preserved to them, and that they may continue in their own customs" (*Jewish Antiquities* 19.5.2). Claudius issued a similar edict for Jews in the rest of the Roman Empire (*Jewish Antiquities* 19.5.3). Agrippina the Younger, Claudius' fourth wife and niece, convinced him to adopt her son Nero and name him as his heir, thereby displacing Claudius' own son Britannicus (by Valeria Messalina). Claudius was poisoned in A.D. 54; some historians hold that Agrippina was the instigator. During Claudius' reign, Paul completed his first and second missionary journeys, ca. A.D. 47–48 and A.D. 49–51, respectively (cf. **Acts 13:1–14:28; 15:36–18:22**), and the Jerusalem council was held, A.D. 50 (cf. **Acts 15:1–34**).

8. **Nero** (A.D. 54–68)—birth name Lucius Domitius Ahenobarbus, then Nero Claudius Drusus Germanicus after his adoption by Claudius; full regnal name Nero Claudius Caesar Augustus Germanicus—was born December 15, A.D. 37. Nero's mother was Agrippina the Younger, who was a great-granddaughter of Caesar Augustus. Agrippina the Younger married three times (see note 6); she persuaded her third husband (her uncle Claudius) to adopt Nero as his son and heir. After Claudius' death, which was most likely caused by Agrippina herself, Nero became the sole ruler at seventeen. Nero married first Claudia Octavia (the daughter of Claudius); second Poppaea Sabina (formerly the wife of the future emperor Otho); and third Statilia Messalina. Nero also underwent some form of marriage with two men—(1) to Sporus (who really was only a boy and whom Nero had castrated) and (2) a freedman named Doryphorus (according to Suetonius), who is probably the same person as the wealthy freedman Pythagoras (according to Tacitus and Cassius Dio).

In A.D. 64, a great fire ravaged Rome. Despite the legend, Nero did not set the fire himself since he was in his villa in a town 35 miles from Rome. However, Nero's reputation was so irreparably damaged by this time that popular opinion held him responsible. Nero blamed the Christians for the fire, which burned all but four sections of Rome. Tacitus relates: "Nero substituted as culprits, and punished with the utmost refinements of cruelty, a class of men, loathed for their vices, whom the crowd styled Christians. Christus, the founder of the name, had undergone the death penalty in the reign of Tiberius, by sentence of the procurator Pontius Pilatus." As punishment, Christians were covered with wild beasts' skins and torn to death by dogs or fastened on crosses and burned to provide light at night (Tacitus' *Histories*, Book XV, 44). According to Josephus, the war of the Jews against Rome began "in the twelfth year of the reign of Nero" (*The Jewish War* 2.14.4), which would correspond to A.D. 66. Josephus further states that Gessius Florus (A.D. 64–66), the procurator of Judea, was the spark that ignited the war because he ordered that large amounts of money be taken from the temple treasury. When some jokers passed around a basket to take up money for a supposedly destitute Florus, he had passersby arrested, brought before him, whipped, and then crucified in place of the missing troublemakers. Josephus says that 3600 people were attacked this way; some of them were men of the equestrian order, who should have never been punished in such a fashion, for although they were Jews by birth, they were also Roman citizens (*The Jewish War* 2.14.9; Whiston's commentary note says to compare this with Paul's treatment in **Acts 22:25–29**). During Nero's reign, Paul conducted his third missionary journey, A.D. 51–54 (cf. **Acts 18:23; 19:1–21:15**); he was imprisoned in Caesarea (cf. **23:23, 33–35; 24:22–27**) and then journeyed to Rome, where he was imprisoned twice—first as recorded in **Acts 25:10–12; 28:16–19, 30–31** and second as recorded in **2 Timothy 4:6–8**. Traditionally, Peter and Paul are said to have been martyred in ca. A.D. 67/68 during Nero's rule.

At the end of Nero's reign, revolts sprang up across the empire, and the legions made Galba (the leader of the revolt in Spain and the provincial governor) the new emperor. The Senate condemned Nero to die a slave's death—on a cross while being beaten by a whip. When the Praetorian Guard and his freedmen abandoned him, Nero fled. Suetonius's account of Nero's death says that he stabbed himself in the throat with a dagger. Josephus says that "after he had reigned thirteen years and eight days . . . [Nero] killed himself in the suburbs of Rome" on June 9, A.D. 68 at age 31 (*The Jewish War* 4.9.2).

9. **Galba** (A.D. 68–69)—birth name Servius Sulpicius Galba, regnal name Servius Galba Caesar Augustus—was born December 24, 3 B.C. According to Suetonius, Galba was married to a woman named Aemilia Lepida. She and their two sons died sometime before Galba became emperor. Galba never remarried, even when Nero's mother Agrippina the Younger pursued him. Initially, Galba was the governor of Nearer Spain in A.D. 60, but when Galba believed that Nero was plotting his assassination, he led a revolt in Spain against him. In his *Histories*, Tacitus relates the horrific results of disasters, battles, and "civil struggles" during the reigns of Galba through Domitian. Three civil wars occurred during a twenty-eight-year period (A.D. 68–96), and during that time, four emperors (Galba, Otho, Vitellius, and Domitian) were assassinated. Multiple surrounding peoples sought war with Rome; the area also had its share of disasters, such as the devastating eruption of Mount Vesuvius in A.D. 79. Crime and corruption predominated, and hatred permeated all classes. However, as Tacitus also relates, there were some "noble examples," such as mothers carrying their children to safety, wives following their husbands into exile, and families showing courage in the face of danger

(*Histories* 1.1–2). Tacitus' words bear a resemblance to Jesus' predictions in **Matthew 24:6–21** (cf. **Mark 13:7–19; Luke 21:10–24**). Galba—along with Otho, then the governor of Lusitania—marched on Rome after Nero's suicide and was proclaimed emperor by the Senate. When Galba chose a man called Piso as his heir instead of Otho, Otho retaliated and gained the support of the Praetorian Guard, who murdered both Galba and Piso in the Roman Forum on January 15, A.D. 69. Suetonius says that Galba died in his seventy-third year after reigning for seven months.

10. **Otho** (A.D. 69)—birth name Marcus Salvius Otho, regnal name Marcus Otho Caesar Augustus—was born about April 28, A.D. 32, according to Suetonius' account. Otho was married to Poppaea Sabina, but after she became Nero's mistress (and later his wife), Otho was sent to govern Lusitania. Otho was governor there for ten years before joining the rebellion against Nero. Otho expected to be named Galba's heir, but when Galba chose a man called Piso instead, Otho began plotting to overthrow Galba. Under Otho's direction, the Praetorian Guard murdered Galba in the Roman Forum. However, before Galba's murder, the legions in Germany had declared their support for Vitellius, who was the imperial governor of Lower Germany. Their armies clashed, and after his army was defeated, Otho committed suicide on April 16, A.D. 69, after reigning for only 95 days.

11. **Vitellius** (A.D. 69)—birth name Aulus Vitellius—was born on September 7 or 24, A.D. 15. Vitellius grew up in Tiberius' court. He was friends with Caligula and Claudius, but more so with Nero. Vitellius was first married to Petronia, by whom he had a son, Petronianus. Second, Vitellius married Galena Fundana, by whom he had a son, Vitellius, and a daughter, Vitellia. Vitellius was proconsul of Africa in ca. A.D. 61. Emperor Galba had appointed Vitellius as imperial governor of Lower Germany in A.D. 68. Later, Vitellius won over the Lower German troops, and they proclaimed him emperor on January 2, A.D. 69. The Roman Senate did not acknowledge Vitellius as the emperor until they accorded him imperial honors on April 19, A.D. 69 (soon after Otho's suicide). The legions of Upper Germany, plus the rulers of Britain, Gaul, and Spain, soon pledged their support. Vitellius marched into Italy, where he defeated Galba's successor Otho. Vitellius was recognized as emperor by the Senate and installed his German troops in place of the Praetorian Guard. Tacitus says that "the centurions who had been most active in supporting Otho were put to death, an action which more than anything else turned the forces in Illyricum against Vitellius" (*Histories* 2.60). Vespasian was proclaimed emperor on July 1, A.D. 69. On December 20, A.D. 69, Vespasian's army attacked and entered Rome, where they murdered Vitellius the same day.

12. **Vespasian** (A.D. 69–79)—birth name Titus Flavius Vespasianus, regnal name Caesar Vespasianus Augustus—was born November 17, A.D. 9. Vespasian married Flavia Domitilla Major and had three children by her—Titus, Domitian, and a daughter, Domitilla. His wife and daughter both died before he became emperor. Vespasian commanded three legions against the Jews during the Jewish revolt in Judea in February A.D. 67. He subdued almost all of Judea, except for Jerusalem. Nero sent Vespasian to Syria to gather forces to fight the Jews; Vespasian then went to Ptolemais (Akko-Ptolemais, now known as Acre or, locally, Akko/Akka), where he was joined by the people of Sepphoris of Galilee, who wanted to stay under Roman rule. Vespasian and his growing army then marched into Galilee en route to Judea (*The Jewish War* 3.1–2, 6). The Jews, frustrated with the attempts of Gessius Florus (procurator A.D. 64–66) to blame the hostilities solely on them, went to King Herod Agrippa II (r. ca. A.D. 50–66) to air their grievances against Florus. As recorded by Josephus, Herod Agrippa II spoke to the Jews, counseled them against war, and told them to pay the tribute due Caesar (as Jesus had told his followers, "give back to Caesar what is Caesar's" in **Matthew 22:21**; *The Jewish War* 2.16). Eleazar (son of Ananias the high priest), who was the governor of the temple, proclaimed that no foreigner should be allowed to offer a gift or sacrifice in the temple. The Jews thus did not accept any sacrifice made on account of Caesar; According to Josephus, "This was the true beginning of our war with the Romans" (*The Jewish War* 2.17.2).

Josephus was a Jewish general who fought against Vespasian. Josephus describes his appointment as general and his dealings with the people in *The Jewish War* 2.20.4–8. When Josephus and his men surrendered to Vespasian, he told Vespasian about a prophecy in **Numbers 24:17**: "A star will come out of Jacob; a scepter will rise out of Israel. He will crush the foreheads of Moab, the skulls of all the people of Sheth." While this was commonly held to be a messianic prophecy, Josephus attributed it to Vespasian and his imperial rule. Vespasian was impressed and merely detained Josephus instead of crucifying him (*The Jewish War* 3.8.9). Cassius Dio mentions Josephus and his claim that Vespasian would release him when he became emperor (*Roman History* 65). Vespasian eventually gained control of Galilee, the Mediterranean coast, and the Jordan Valley. Vespasian could have then attacked Jerusalem, but news of Nero's suicide and Galba's appointment reached him, halting plans for the capture of Jerusalem. Vespasian sent his son Titus to Rome to congratulate Galba, but before Titus got there, Galba was murdered (A.D. 68). Vespasian decided to postpone the war against the Jews in favor of intervening in the civil war between Vitellius and Otho for the title of emperor. By December A.D. 69, Vespasian was the sole ruler.

Because his prediction that Vespasian would become emperor had come true, Josephus (then, still called Joseph, son of Matthias; see chart "**Supplement 9**: Flavius Josephus, the Roman-Jewish Historian") received Roman citizenship and was also given the name "Flavius Josephus" (after Emperor Vespasian's birth name, Titus Flavius Vespasianus). Vespasian's son Titus resumed the Jewish War. In August A.D. 70, Jerusalem was captured, putting an end to the war. (Refer to Jesus' foretelling the destruction of Jerusalem in **Matthew 24:1–28**; also see Cassius Dio's account of the destruction of Jerusalem in his *Roman History*) After the Second Temple was destroyed, Vespasian diverted the yearly temple tax (prescribed in **Exodus 30:13**) to the reconstruction of the temple of Jupiter at Rome, which had been destroyed during the civil war. All Jews, no matter their location, were to pay two drachmas. Josephus mentions this tax, known as the *Fiscus Judaicus*, in *The Jewish War* 7.6.6. In "Domitian's Attitude toward the Jews and Judaism," Mary Smallwood implies that Vespasian could have gone further by forbidding the Jews to practice their religion, but he did not: "[Vespasian] left the Jews' privileges intact and allowed them to keep their national identity and religion, while at the same time he turned those privileges into a financial advantage for the Roman state by transforming a Jewish tax into what was virtually a price paid for the right to practice Judaism" (Smallwood, "*Domitian's Attitude*," 2). The tax continued to be collected even after the temple to Jupiter was restored and played an important role during Domitian's reign. Vespasian died on June 24, A.D. 79.

13. **Titus** (A.D. 79–81)—birth name Titus Flavius Vespasianus, regnal name Titus Vespasianus Augustus—was born December 30, A.D. 39. He was the son of Vespasian and his wife Flavia Domitilla; his younger brother Domitian would also become emperor. According to Suetonius, Titus married first Arrecina Tertulla. Second, he married Marcia Furnilla, by whom he had a daughter, Julia Flavia (or Flavia Julia), who married her cousin Titus Flavius Sabinus (who bore the same name as his paternal great-grandfather); after his death, Julia Flavia became the mistress of her uncle Emperor Domitian. Furthermore, during the First Jewish-Roman War (A.D. 66–73), Bernice/Berenice (cf. **Acts 25:13, 23; 26:30**)—the daughter of King Herod Agrippa I and a sister of King Herod Agrippa II—carried on a love affair with Titus. However, she was unpopular with the Romans, so upon Titus' accession as emperor in A.D. 79, he was forced to dismiss her. (For more about Bernice/Berenice, Herod Agrippa I, Herod Agrippa II, and the rest of the Herodian dynasty, see chart "**Matthew 2**: Herod the Great and the Herodian Dynasty")

Titus commanded a legion in Judea in A.D. 67 under his father, Vespasian. When Vespasian became emperor in A.D. 69, he immediately put Titus in charge of the war against the Jews. Titus was present when Josephus met with Vespasian and extolled his efforts (*The Jewish War* 3.8.8–9). Josephus records how Vespasian sent Titus "to destroy Jerusalem" (*The Jewish War* 4.11.5). However, Josephus also states that Vespasian and Titus were given the government by God (*The Jewish War* 5.1.1). Titus marched to Jerusalem, where the Jews contrived numerous traps for the Romans (*The Jewish War* 5.3.3ff). Josephus paints a vivid picture of Jerusalem at the time of its destruction (*The Jewish War* 5.4) and describes the temple at length (*The Jewish War* 5.5), detailing exactly what the Jews lost when their cultural and religious centers were destroyed. Cassius Dio describes the war against the Jews, saying that the Jews "were not conquered until a part of the temple was set on fire" (*Roman History* 65.6) and that Jerusalem was "destroyed on the very day of Saturn, the day which even now the Jews reverence most"—i.e., Saturday (*Roman History* 65.7.2). While the war raged, many Jews were crucified before the walls of Jerusalem (*The Jewish War* 5.11.1). Titus sent Josephus to speak to the Jews about finding peace (*The Jewish War* 5.9.3ff). According to Josephus, Titus wanted to spare the temple: "he was not in any case for burning down so vast a work as that was, because this would be a mischief to the Romans themselves, as it would be an ornament to their government while it continued" (*The Jewish War* 6.4.3). However, Cassius Dio says that Titus had to force the Romans to attack the temple (*Roman History* 66.4). A Roman soldier ended up setting fire to the temple by throwing a burning piece of wood into it. Titus ordered the fire to be stopped, but he could not be heard; he tried to go in the temple himself to quench the fire but was driven back by the flames (*The Jewish War* 6.4.5–8). Titus was proclaimed emperor by his soldiers on the steps of the sanctuary (*The Jewish War* 6.6.1; *Roman History* 66.7). After the temple was destroyed, Titus took possession of Jerusalem (*The Jewish War* 6.8.5, 7.1.1). According to Josephus, Titus credited God for the victory (*The Jewish War* 6.9.1). Titus died on September 13, A.D. 81.

14. **Domitian** (A.D. 81–96)—birth name Titus Flavius Domitianus, regnal name Caesar Domitianus Augustus—was born October 24, A.D. 51. He was the second son of Vespasian and Flavia Domitilla Major and was the younger brother of Titus. Domitian fell in love and married Domitia Longina (by convincing her first husband, Lucius Aelius Lamia Plautius Aelianus, to divorce her). Domitian had a son by her, but the child died shortly after Domitian became emperor. Suetonius and Cassius Dio detail the atrocities committed by Domitian, stating that many people were executed, most of the time for the smallest of missteps, much less large infractions. Cassius Dio says in his *Roman History* that there is no way to number those executed by Domitian because he didn't even keep records of the multitudes he had executed. in his book *Lives of the Twelve Caesars*, Suetonius mentions that the taxes on the Jews were "levied with the utmost rigour," both upon those who lived according to Jewish practices and those who concealed their heritage (12.2). The editor's note on Suetonius' chapter on Domitian states that this probably included the Christians, whom the Romans commonly lumped together with the Jews (note 48). Much has been said and written of Domitian's persecution of Christians, but the reality seems to be a little more involved than this blanket statement. Cassius Dio says in his *Roman History* that Domitian executed his cousin, the consul Flavius Clemens, and exiled Clemens' wife Flavia Domitilla. Both were charged with "atheism," which was an epithet used against both Jews and Christians because of their monotheism. To the Romans—who were a people who worshiped many gods and in Athens had an altar "to an unknown god" (cf. **Acts 17:23**)—worship of *one* god, as opposed to many, was tantamount to atheism. According to E. Mary Smallwood, before Domitian, it appears that Jewish and Christian monotheism was regarded as an "idiosyncrasy." Under Domitian, however, this "atheism" among Jews (and Christians) became a capital offense. Domitian increasingly viewed himself as a god and expected his subjects to treat him as such ("Domitian's Attitude" 5). According to Smallwood, "during the last years of his [Domitian's] principate, emperor-worship became a test of loyalty." Because the Jews and Christians did not recognize the emperor as a god, Domitian wanted "to prevent any increase" in their number ("Domitian's Attitude" 6). While Smallwood calls into question the veracity of Domitian's expulsion of Jews from Rome and/or from other parts of the empire, she does concede that a threat made by Domitian could have been magnified into the belief that Domitian was planning to exile the Jews ("Domitian's Attitude" 10)."

In Mark Wilson's review, he states that Domitian's persecution of Christians is nowhere to be found in any of the ancient writers; rather, the first appearance of Domitian persecuting Christians comes first from the church father Eusebius ("Alternative Facts" blog, https://www.biblicalarchaeology.org/daily/biblical-topics/post-biblical-period/domitian-persecution-of-christians; cf. *Ecclesiastical History* III, chapters 17–19). Eusebius' claim was furthered by Orosius, who claimed that Domitian had passed edicts endorsing cruel acts against Christians. Paul Keresztes states that the "Jewish customs" that posed problems for Domitian could also be attributed to Christians, since most Christians at the time were Jewish by birth ("The Jews, the Christians, and Emperor Domitian," 9). Keresztes further relates how dangerous Jewish proselytizing would have been to the Roman Empire, as far as the Romans were concerned: "Jewish proselytism [because of its nationalistic and separatist features] would have undermined the whole Roman system" (ibid., 12). Rome did recognize the right of the Jews to worship as their religion dictated, says Keresztes, but preferred that the Jewish religion be kept to those who were of "Jewish blood." According to Keresztes, "The denunciations of Jewish proselytes for tax-evasion became a basis for punishment for "atheism," and judging from Suetonius' and Dio Cassius' texts, we can reasonably assume that Domitian went a long way in exploiting accusations of 'Judaizing' for the benefit of his treasury (and perhaps for some political purposes)" (ibid., 13-14).

Whatever the case, the consensus is that the apostle John wrote Revelation around A.D. 95 while on the island of Patmos during Domitian's reign (**Revelation 1:9**). Domitian was assassinated on September 18, A.D. 96 in a conspiracy led by two Praetorian prefects, palace officials, and his own wife.

15. **Nerva (A.D. 96–98)**—birth name Marcus Cocceius Nerva—was born on November 8, A.D. 35. According to Cassius Dio, he became emperor at age 65. His parents were Marcus Cocceius Nerva and Sergia Plautilla. After Domitian's assassination, Nerva was recognized by the Roman Senate as emperor on September 18, A.D. 96.

Cassius Dio relates that Nerva granted amnesty to those who had been exiled during Domitian's rule, presumably including Jews who had been fortunate enough to escape Domitian's varied persecutions. Among other reforms, Nerva relaxed the Jewish tax implemented by Vespasian. As shown in an article by Nathan T. Elkins, a coin minted during Nerva's rule has on the reverse side a palm tree (symbolizing Judea) and an inscription, which translated reads "The removal of the wrongful accusation of the Fiscus Judaicus [Jewish tax]" ("Nerva's Reform") The relaxed tax seems to have applied to a solely religious definition of Judaism as opposed to an ethnic one. Defining Jews by their religion and not by their ethnicity led to clearer distinctions between Jews and Christians. As Nerva had no children and was likely never married, he adopted Trajan as his heir in October A.D. 97. Nerva died from a fever on January 28, A.D. 98.

16. **Trajan** (A.D. 98–117)—birth name Marcus Ulpius Traianus—was born on September 15/18, A.D. 53 to Marcus Ulpius Traianus, who commanded a legion during the Jewish War in A.D. 67–68, and his wife Marcia. Trajan married Pompeia Plotina, but they had no children. Trajan was a consul under Domitian and was adopted by Nerva as his heir in October, A.D. 97. Trajan enacted forms of public welfare, especially those that provided for poor children. Trajan appointed Pliny the younger as governor in Bithynia and Pontus (northern Asia Minor). Pliny consulted Trajan on many administrative matters; in one exchange he asked Trajan how to handle Christians. Pliny saw them as harmless, yet they did not adhere to Roman religious practices. Pliny ultimately said that he did not know about the nature of their crimes and did not know the appropriate punishment for them, but his writings give an insight into early Christian worship (albeit from a Roman source). According to Pliny, anonymous sources gave him names of suspected Christians and when they were interviewed, some of them said that they had previously been Christians but were no longer. Some recanted while giving Pliny information about Christian worship—specifically, that they met on a certain day to sing a hymn to Christ, went their separate ways, and then came back together for a meal. Pliny mentions that Christianity had spread to rural areas and villages. Trajan told Pliny not to hunt for Christians nor to accept unsupported, anonymous charges about them, and only those who were overly and conspicuously recalcitrant should be punished, whereas those who recanted should be pardoned.

Late in Trajan's reign, Jews in Cyrene, Egypt, and Cyprus revolted by destroying pagan temples and attacking pagan worshipers. The pagans fled to Alexandria, where they killed many Jews. According to Cassius Dio (*Roman History*), a total of 440,000 non-Jews in Cyrene and Cyprus perished; he does not give the total for Egypt. Trajan sent forces to contain the Jews; ultimately, he sent a Mauritanian commander named Lusius to rid the revolting regions of the Jews. Lusius effectively wiped them out and was rewarded with the governorship of Judea. Trajan ruled for 19 years and died in A.D. 117 after an illness while defending the Empire's borders.

17. **Hadrian** (A.D. 117–138)—birth name Publius Aelius Hadrianus—was born January 24, A.D. 76 to Publius Aelius Hadrianus Afer and his wife Domitia Paulina. Hadrian's father was a first cousin to the emperor Trajan. Hadrian married Trajan's great-niece Vibia Sabina, but they had no children. After Trajan's death, it was announced that he had chosen Hadrian as his heir. Cassius Dio, however, rejects the idea that Trajan adopted Hadrian and proposes instead that Trajan's wife, Pompeia Plotina, secured the position for him. Cassius Dio says that Hadrian built a city called Aelia Capitolina on the ruins of Jerusalem and built a temple to Jupiter on the site of the former temple. This, among other things—such as forbidding circumcision (at least of boys too young to consent) and the collapse of Solomon's tomb during Roman building operations—sparked a revolt led by Simon ben Kosiba, called the Bar Kochba (or Bar Kokhba) Revolt, ca. A.D. 132–135. The leader of the Jews, Rabbi Aqiba, viewed Simon ben Kosiba as the "Messiah." Others were skeptical, including the Jewish Christians. According to early church writers such as Justin Martyr and Eusebius, Simon ben Kosiba condemned Christians to "terrible punishment" unless they denied that Jesus was the Messiah. The Jewish governor Tineius Rufus (whom Josephus calls Terentius Rufus; cf. *The Jewish War* 7.2.1) responded harshly by killing men, women, and children. While the rebels under Simon ben Kosiba do not seem to have captured Jerusalem, they did control the countryside. Hadrian dispatched his best generals to extinguish the rebellion. The Jews hid in caves and tunnels and fought in small bands, confounding the Roman generals. According to Cassius Dio, very few Jews survived. Ultimately, according to Dio, the number

of Jews killed in battle was 580,000; those who perished from fire, famine, and disease were innumerable (*Roman History* 69.13.2–3). The last Jewish stronghold, Betar (located about 5 miles southwest of Jerusalem), fell, along with Simon ben Kosiba, most likely in late A.D. 135. Many surviving Jews were sold into slavery; those who remained were forbidden to study Mosaic Law. According to Eusebius, Hadrian barred the remaining Jews from entering Jerusalem or even the surrounding area. Judea was subsumed along with Syria under the name Syria-Palestinia. Hadrian became ill the next year, A.D. 136; according to Cassius Dio, his illness began with a "flow of blood from his nostrils" that turned into tuberculosis and then dropsy (*Roman History* 69.17.1, 20.1). Hadrian handed over the government to his successor, Antoninius Pius, and died on July 10, A.D. 138.

SUPPLEMENT 11: KEY EVENTS IN THE HISTORY OF ISRAEL (586 B.C.–A.D. 135)

Date	Event
587/586 B.C.	Fall of Jerusalem to the Babylonians; Solomon's Temple destroyed; Jews taken into Babylonian captivity; 70-year exile (586–516 B.C.)
539 B.C.	King Cyrus the Great of Persia conquered Babylon
539–330 B.C.	Persians ruled Israel
538 B.C.	First group of Jewish exiles returned to Jerusalem with Zerubbabel
516 B.C.	Second Temple was completed in Jerusalem under the leadership of Zerubbabel and Joshua; temple worship resumed
458 B.C.	Second group of Jewish exiles returned to Jerusalem with Ezra
444 B.C.	Third group of Jewish exiles returned to Jerusalem with Nehemiah; Jerusalem's walls were rebuilt in 52 days
333–330 B.C.	Alexander the Great conquered Israel
323–198 B.C.	The Ptolemies of Egypt ruled Israel
198–167 B.C.	The Seleucids of Syria ruled Israel
167–160 B.C.	The Jewish-led Maccabean revolt against the Seleucid ruler Antiochus IV (Epiphanes), ending with the rededication of the temple (Hanukkah)
142–63 B.C.	Hasmoneans ruled Palestine
63 B.C.	Roman general Pompey conquered Israel; Judea made a Roman province
37–4 B.C. or 35–1 B.C.	Herod the Great ruled as king of the Jews in Jerusalem under Roman authority
Ca. late 3 or early 2 B.C.	Birth of Jesus
4 or 6 B.C.–A.D. 6	Herod Archelaus ruled as ethnarch of Judea
4 or 6 B.C.–A.D. 39	Herod Antipas ruled as tetrarch of Galilee and Perea
4 or 6 B.C.–A.D. 32 or 34	Herod Philip II ruled as tetrarch of Iturea and Trachonitis
A.D. 33	Crucifixion of Jesus
A.D. 6–41	Roman prefects governed Judea
A.D. 41–44	Herod Agrippa I ruled as king over most of Israel
A.D. 44–66	Roman procurators ruled over most of Israel
Ca. A.D. 50–66	Herod Agrippa II ruled Batanaea, Trachonitis, Gaulonitis & Lysanias
A.D. 66	Provisional Judean government formed under Ananus ben Ananus, Joseph ben Gurion, and Joshua ben Gamla
A.D. 66–73	Destruction of the Temple & Jerusalem in A.D. 70 under Vespasian, Titus, and the Tenth Roman Legion; fall of Masada in A.D. 73
A.D. 132–135	Second Jewish revolt led by Simon bar Kokhba

SUPPLEMENT 12: RULERS OF PALESTINE IN THE INTERTESTAMENTAL PERIOD (336 B.C.–A.D. 14)

Date	Ruler/Event
336–167 B.C.	**Greek/Ptolemaic/Seleucid Rulers**[1]
336–323 B.C.	Alexander the Great
323–198 B.C.	The Ptolemies, kings of Egypt
198–167 B.C.	The Seleucids, kings of Syria
167–63 B.C.	**Jewish Rule & Independence under the Hasmonean Rulers**[2]
167–160 B.C.	Maccabean Revolt under Mattathias Maccabeus and his sons
165 B.C.	Rededication of the Second Temple (commemorated by Hanukkah)
161–143/142 B.C.	Jonathan Maccabeus "Apphus"
142–134 B.C.	Simon Maccabeus "Thassi"
134–104 B.C.	John Hyrcanus I
104–103 B.C.	Aristobulus I
103–76 B.C.	Alexander Jannaeus
76–67 B.C.	Queen Salome Alexandra
67 B.C. (3 mo.)	John Hyrcanus II
67–63 B.C.	Aristobulus II
63 B.C.–A.D. 14	**Roman Rulers**[3]
63 B.C.	Pompey annexed Judea to Roman-ruled Syria
Ethnarch 47–40 B.C.	John Hyrcanus II (Hasmonean ruler under the Romans)
48 B.C.	Pompey is overthrown by Julius Caesar
44 B.C.	Assassination of Julius Caesar
40–37 B.C.	Antigonus II (Hasmonean ruler under the Romans)
37–4 B.C. or 35–1 B.C.	Herod the Great[4] ruled the Jews under Roman authority
27 B.C.–A.D. 14	Caesar Augustus ruled the Roman Empire

Notes

1. See charts "**Supplement 6**: The Ptolemies of the Ptolemaic Dynasty" and "**Supplement 7**: The Seleucids of the Seleucid Dynasty."

2. See charts "**Supplement 8**: The Maccabees and the Hasmonean Dynasty" and "**Supplement 2**: The High Priests of Israel."

3. See chart "**Supplement 10**: The Roman Emperors." For references to the Maccabean rulers under the Romans, see chart "**Supplement 8**: The Maccabees and the Hasmonean Dynasty."

4. For details about Herod's reign, see chart "**Matthew 2**: Herod the Great and the Herodian Dynasty."

SUPPLEMENT 13: ROMAN RULERS OF JUDEA AND GALILEE (47 B.C.–CA. A.D. 66)[1]

<table>
<tr><th>Judea</th><th>Galilee
(At times including broader regions, as noted)</th></tr>
<tr><td colspan="2">Antipater I the Idumean
(Procurator of Judea 47–43 B.C.)</td></tr>
<tr><td>Phasael
(The son of Antipater I)
(Governor of Jerusalem 47–40 B.C.)</td><td>Herod
(The son of Antipater I)
(Governor 47–37 B.C.)</td></tr>
<tr><td>[Parthian Occupation][2]
(40–38 B.C.)</td><td></td></tr>
<tr><td colspan="2">Herod the Great
“King of the Jews” (37–4 B.C. or 35–1 B.C.)</td></tr>
<tr><td>Herod Archelaus
(Ethnarch/Tetrarch of Judea, Samaria & Idumea)
(4 B.C.?–A.D. 6 or 6 B.C.–A.D. 6)</td><td>Herod Antipas
(Tetrarch of Galilee & Perea)
(4 B.C.?–A.D. 39 or 6 B.C.–A.D. 39)</td></tr>
<tr><td>Coponius
(Prefect A.D. 6 or 7–9)</td><td></td></tr>
<tr><td>Marcus Ambivius/Ambibulus
(Prefect A.D. 9–12)</td><td></td></tr>
<tr><td>Annius Rufus
(Prefect ca. A.D. 12–15)</td><td></td></tr>
<tr><td>Valerius Gratus
(Prefect A.D. 15–26)</td><td></td></tr>
<tr><td>Pontius Pilate[3]
(Prefect A.D. 26–36)</td><td></td></tr>
<tr><td colspan="2">Marcellus[4]
(Prefect A.D. 36/37)</td></tr>
<tr><td colspan="2">Marullus
(Prefect A.D. 37–41)</td></tr>
<tr><td colspan="2">Herod Agrippa I
(King A.D. 41–44)</td></tr>
<tr><td colspan="2">Cuspius Fadus
(Procurator A.D. 44–ca. 46)</td></tr>
<tr><td colspan="2">Tiberius Julius Alexander
(Procurator A.D. 46–48)</td></tr>
<tr><td colspan="2">Ventidius Cumanus
(Procurator A.D. 48–52)</td></tr>
<tr><td>Antonius Felix
(Procurator A.D. 52–59/60)</td><td>Herod Agrippa II
(Over Batanaea, Trachonitis, Gaulonitis & Lysanias)
(ca. A.D. 50–66)</td></tr>
<tr><td colspan="2">Porcius Festus
(Procurator A.D. 60–62)</td></tr>
<tr><td colspan="2">Lucceius Albinius
(Procurator A.D. 62–64)</td></tr>
<tr><td colspan="2">Gessius Florus
(Procurator A.D. 64–66)</td></tr>
</table>

Biblical and Theological Significance

Several of the individuals mentioned among the Roman rulers of Judea and Galilee in the table above played significant roles in certain events recorded in the New Testament, particularly in the Gospels and in Acts. "Procurator" was the title for the official—"Governor or *praefectus (prefect)*"—appointed by Rome to rule over Judea (and later Palestine) from A.D. 6–41 and A.D. 44–66. [The title of the Roman governors changed from "prefect" (governor) to "procurator" during the reign of Emperor Claudius (r. A.D. 41–54).] As the *Jewish Encyclopedia* explains: "The procurators may be divided into two series: those preceding and those following the reign of Agrippa I. Those of the first series (6–41 C.E.) ruled over Judea alone, possessing, together with the legate, the power of supervision over the Temple, and the right to appoint and depose the high priest. Those of the second series (44–70) administered Samaria and Galilee, besides Judea."[5]

Roman citizens had the privilege of *provocatio* (i.e., the right to have a trial transferred from the provincial governor to the emperor in Rome (e.g., Paul's case; **Acts 22:25–23:11, 23–35; 25:10–12**). Jurisdiction in civil matters was usually overseen by the Sanhedrin, although prefects/procurators could exercise control in that sphere as well. Prefects/procurators typically supervised the country from their official residence at Caesarea Maritima, where they had a praetorium (a building that was formerly Herod's palace; **Acts 23:35**). On special occasions, like the Jewish high festivals, the seat of governance was temporarily transferred to Jerusalem; again, they oversaw the people from a praetorium, which was the former palace of Herod. From there, they could maintain order over the large numbers of Jewish citizens who gathered at those times. In general, procurators held short tenures and were either "openly hostile or, at best, indifferent to the needs of the Jewish population . . . (and) notorious for their rapacity (monetary extortions)."[6]

For more information on the Herodian rulers (such as **Antipater I, Phasael, Herod the Great, Herod Archelaus, Herod Antipas, Herod Agrippa I,** and **Herod Agrippa II**), see chart "**Matthew 2**: Herod the Great and the Herodian Dynasty."

Notes

1. The primary extrabiblical reference consulted was *The Complete Works of Josephus*, trans. William Whiston, commentary Paul L. Maier (Grand Rapids: Kregel, 1999); dating and titles (e.g., prefect vs. procurator) of the rulers follow the chart, "The Rulers of Judea," 664. For a discussion of the dating of the Herods, see chart "**Matthew 2**: Herod the Great and the Herodian Dynasty." Also consulted was the *Jewish Encyclopedia*, "Procurators" by Gotthard Deutsch, Samuel Krauss, https://jewishencyclopedia.com/articles/6840-governors-roman-of-judea.

2. The **Parthians**—known as the Parthian or Arsacid Empire—took Media and Mesopotamia from the Seleucids and ruled from ancient Iran from 247 B.C.–A.D. 224. They expanded westward and captured the Levant (except for the city of Tyre) in 40–39 B.C. The Parthians were eventually driven out of the Levant by military leaders under the Roman general Mark Antony in 39 and 38 B.C.

3. **Pontius Pilate** was infamous for his role in Jesus' crucifixion. Archaeological evidence confirmed by the "Pilate Stone" from Caesarea Maritima shows that Pilate was "prefect" of Roman-occupied Judea during the last half of the reign of the Roman Emperor Tiberius (r. A.D. 14–37). The Pilate figure pictured in the Gospels shows a political official who was reluctant to order Jesus' execution and who symbolically washed his hands to show his innocence in the matter (**Matthew 27:24**). Luke's account of Jesus' trial recounts that when Jesus was arrested and first brought before Pilate, Pilate "announced to the chief priests and the crowd, 'I find no basis for a charge against this man.'" However, the people persisted in their charges against Jesus. When Pilate discovered that Jesus was a Galilean, he handed him over to Herod Antipas, whose jurisdiction included Judea (**Luke 12:1–12**).

Josephus portrays Pilate as an inflexible, strong-willed, and authoritative governor. He appears to be an effective ruler since he governed for ten years at a time where most procurators ruled for only about two years. During the last year of Pilate's rule, in A.D. 36, Josephus writes that Pilate's cavalry murdered thousands of Samaritan travelers going up to Mount Gerizim (*Jewish Antiquities* 18.4.1). Because of this, Pilate was summoned to Rome and relieved of his post by Emperor Caligula (r. A.D. 41–54) and then exiled to Gaul, where Eusebius says he committed suicide (*Church History* 2.7.1).

4. **Marcellus** is described by Josephus as a friend of Vitellius who was sent by him "to take care of the affairs of Judea" (*Jewish Antiquities* 18.4.2). An article on "Procurators" in the *Jewish Encyclopedia* states, "It may be assumed, however, that Marcellus was not really a procurator of Judea, but only a subordinate official of Vitellius. Indeed, this is the only instance where Josephus, in designating the office of Marcellus, uses the expression ἐπιμελητής = 'overseer.' No official act of Marcellus is reported." Gotthard Deutsch and Samuel Krauss, "Procurators," https://jewishencyclopedia.com/articles/6840-governors-roman-of-judea.

5. Gotthard Deutsch and Samuel Krauss, "Procurators," Jewish Encyclopedia.

6. Jewish Virtual Library, "Procurator," https://www.jewishvirtuallibrary.org/procurator.

SUBJECT INDEX

SCRIPTURE INDEX

Numbers

Deuteronomy

Joshua

Judges

Ruth

1 Samuel

2 Samuel

1 Kings

2 Kings

1 Chronicles

2 Chronicles

Ezra

Nehemiah

Zechariah

Malachi

Matthew

Mark

Luke

John

Acts